2007 Product Alert

Ingenix Has You Covered!

April ICD-9-CM Updates

With semi-annual ICD-9-CM changes effective April 1 and October 1, it is more important than ever to have up-to-date ICD-9-CM coding information in order to stay in compliance with HIPAA regulations. Ingenix is committed to providing you and your staff with the ICD-9-CM code update information you need to code accurately and efficiently. We are offering several ways to make sure you are always up-to-date.

- **Updateable *Expert* ICD-9-CM code books.** The February update will have any new April 1 codes.
- **Annual *Expert* and *Professional ICD-9-CM* editions.** Just visit *Ingenix Online* and look for the ICD-9, CPT® and HCPCS Alerts link under the Quick Access Resources menu.

  No extra charges for code changes. No additional cost for updated books. No hassle for you or your staff.

Revised Coding Guidelines

Revised official ICD-9-CM guidelines have been released and became effective December 1, 2005. Significant revisions were made to chapter-specific guidelines, the V code table and the use of terminology.

Only this set of guidelines, approved by the Cooperating Parties, is official. Adherence to these guidelines when assigning ICD-9-CM diagnosis and procedure codes is required under the Health Insurance Portability and Accountability Act (HIPAA).

Medicare Code Edits Notice

Not all Medicare edits for the new 2007 ICD-9-CM codes were released in time to be published in this edition. Once these edits are released we will post them on our Web site. Please visit www.ingenixonline.com and click on the ICD-9, CPT® and HCPCS Alerts link under the Quick Access Resources menu to view these edits.

Online Quick Access Resources

Ingenix is committed to providing you with current coding information. Ingenix hopes to assist you in correct application of coding conventions and guidelines in order to support your coding practices, training processes and ongoing quality and compliance initiatives. Included in these free resources are informative articles, regulatory updates and clinical coding scenarios that you can use to keep your facility, practice and staff informed on the latest changes.

Visit *Ingenix Online,* look for the Quick Access Resources menu and click on the Code This! and Ingenix Insights: Free eAlerts links to take advantage of the following free informative resources.

Code This!: Practical clinical coding scenarios demonstrate accurate classification of codes based on interpretation of documentation in compliance with official coding guidelines and conventions. These scenarios often reflect correct application of new codes and changes or updates of official coding guidelines in a clinical format. This feature is updated monthy.

Ingenix Insights: Free eAlerts: Access coding, billing and reimbursement analysis and breaking news that matters to you. These articles include regulatory, policy and other timely topics. Visit often for late-breaking news.

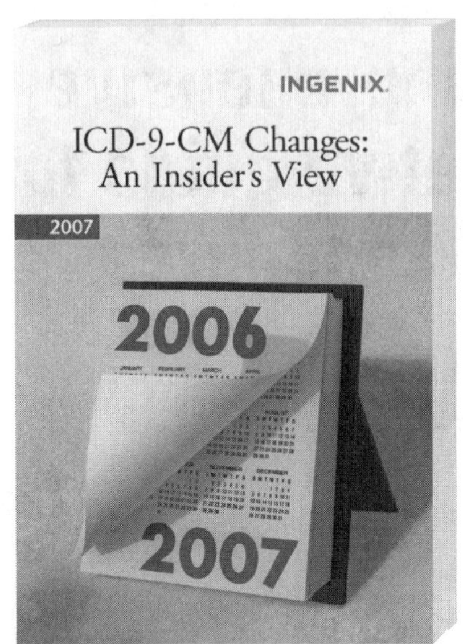

Understand and Interpret the Changes Made to the 2007 ICD-9-CM Code Set.

2007 ICD-9-CM Changes: An Insider's View

Item No.: 1077 — $59.95

Available: September 2006 — ISBN: 978-1-56337-920-8

A must-have resource for ICD-9-CM users! ***ICD-9-CM Changes: An Insider's View*** is a reference for understanding each of the code changes for 2007.

- **Ingenix Edge — Rationale for new and revised codes for 2007.** Knowing the reasons behind every new or revised code change is critical to adapting coding practices.
- **Ingenix Edge — Explanation of changes to indexes, conventions and instructional notes.** Understand what other changes will affect coding practices.
- **Ingenix Edge — Clinical presentation and treatment.** Coders must understand the clinical presentation of a condition or the intricacies of a procedure to code correctly to prevent "undercoding" or "overcoding."
- **Ingenix Edge — Clinical definitions of diagnoses and procedures.** Recognize terms in the medical records that pertain to new codes, ensuring correct application of the code changes.
- **Coding history and changes.** Understanding how the condition was coded in the past and how the change will impact coding practices.
- **Coding scenarios.** Examples of coding scenarios clarify application of the new codes.
- **Organized by chapter of ICD-9-CM.** Organizing the code changes in the context of their relationship to other codes provides insight into the rationale of the changes.
- **Detailed illustrations.** Illustrations are worth a thousand words and clarify some of the complex issues surrounding many of the code changes.
- **Annotated official addenda.** View the official addenda that contain all the changes with annotations to the three volumes of ICD-9-CM, including text deletions.

100% Money Back Guarantee

If our merchandise* ever fails to meet your expectations, please contact our Customer Service Department toll-free at 1.800.INGENIX (464.3649), option 1, for an immediate response. *Software: Credit will be granted for unopened packages only.

SAVE 5% when you order at www.ingenixonline.com (reference source code FOBW7)

or call toll-free 1.800.INGENIX(464.3649), option 1.

Also available from your medical bookstore or distributor.

FOBA7

INGENIX®

SAVE MORE and qualify for REWARDS when you order at IngenixOnline.com.

HERE ARE THE TOP THREE REASONS TO PLACE YOUR ORDER ONLINE:

1. Save an additional 5% when you order online*—use source **FOBW7**.
2. Get rewards for every $500 you spend at Ingenix Online with our eSmart program.**
3. Experience a quick, hassle-free purchase process with streamlined checkout options.

ingenix esmart
ingenix online frequent buyer program

Get rewards when you order online.

Ingenix eSmart is a program designed to reward our best Ingenix Online customers. If you are a registered online customer and qualify to participate**, all you have to do is use the returning customer checkout option for your web purchases every time you shop online. We keep track of your purchases. Once you reach $500, we send you a FREE product—it's that easy!

If you are not yet registered, go to IngenixOnline.com and register right away so we can get you started with the Ingenix eSmart program.

Are you part of our Medallion program?

Ingenix Online has enhanced options for you, for a hassle-free, streamlined purchase and account management experience!

To view your enhanced online account options, simply register with us at IngenixOnline.com. You will then be able to easily place orders from your Price List, get access to your purchase history, track shipments, change your profile, manage your address book and much more.

Could you benefit from an easy, quick way to consolidate orders for your company?

The Ingenix web-based consolidation tool is designed to streamline the purchasing process and enhance your productivity. For more information log into your account or visit www.ingenixonline.com/orderconsolidation.

(*) Additional 5% savings offer valid online, cannot be combined with any other offer and is not applicable to Partner accounts. Bookstore products, package items, eLearning products, Academy Credential Study Guides, online exams, Worker's Compensation items and conferences not included. For Medallion accounts, we compare the Price List discounts against the offer discounts and honor the better of the two.

(**) eSmart program valid for Ingenix customers who are NOT part of Medallion or Partner Accounts programs. You must be registered at Ingenix Online to have your online purchases tracked for rewards purposes. Shipping charges and taxes still apply and cannot be used for rewards. eSmart reward offers valid online only.

100% Money Back Guarantee

If our merchandise* ever fails to meet your expectations, please contact our Customer Service Department toll-free at 1.800.INGENIX (464.3649), option 1, for an immediate response. *Software and Data File: Credit will be granted for unopened packages only.

SAVE 5% when you order at www.ingenixonline.com (reference source code FOBW7)

or call toll-free 1.800.INGENIX(464.3649), option 1.

Also available from your medical bookstore or distributor.

INGENIX.

Four simple ways
to place an order.

Call

1.800.ingenix (464.3649), option 1. Mention source code FOBA7 when ordering.

Mail

PO Box 27116
Salt Lake City, UT 84127-0116
With payment and/or purchase order.

Fax

801.982.4033
With credit card information and/or purchase order.

Click

www.ingenixonline.com
Save 5% when you order online today—use source code FOBW7.

ingenix*e*smart
ingenix online frequent buyer program

GET REWARDS FOR SHOPPING ONLINE!
To find out more, visit IngenixOnline.com

eSmart program available only to Ingenix customers who are not part of Medallion, Gold Medallion or Partner Accounts programs. You must be registered at Ingenix Online to have your online purchases tracked for rewards purposes. Shipping charges and taxes still apply and cannot be used for rewards. Offer valid online only.

100% Money Back Guarantee

If our merchandise* ever fails to meet your expectations, please contact our Customer Service Department toll-free at 1.800.ingenix (464.3649), option 1 for an immediate response.

*Software: Credit will be granted for unopened packages only.

Customer Service Hours

7:00 am - 5:00 pm Mountain Time
9:00 am - 7:00 pm Eastern Time

Shipping and Handling

no. of items	fee
1	$10.95
2-4	$12.95
5-7	$14.95
8-10	$19.95
11+	Call

Order Form

Information

Customer No. ________ Contact No. ________

Source Code ________

Contact Name ________

Title ________ Specialty ________

Company ________

Street Address ________
NO PO BOXES, PLEASE

City ________ State ____ Zip ____

Telephone (   ) ________ Fax (   ) ________
IN CASE WE HAVE QUESTIONS ABOUT YOUR ORDER

E-mail ________ @ ________
REQUIRED FOR ORDER CONFIRMATION AND SELECT PRODUCT DELIVERY.

Ingenix respects your right to privacy. We will not sell or rent your e-mail address or fax number to anyone outside Ingenix and its business partners. If you would like to remove your name from Ingenix promotion, please call 1.800.ingenix (464.3649), option 1.

Product

Item No.	Qty	Description	Price	Total

Subtotal ________

UT & VA residents, please add applicable Sales tax ________

(See chart on the left) Shipping & handling charges ________
All foreign orders, please call for shipping costs

Total ________

Payment

○Please bill my credit card ○MasterCard ○VISA ○Amex ○Discover

Card No. ________ Expires ____ MONTH ____ YEAR

Signature ________

○Check enclosed, made payable to: Ingenix, Inc. ○Please bill my office

Purchase Order No. ________
ATTACH COPY OF PURCHASE ORDER

2007

INGENIX®

ICD-9-CM Professional

for Hospitals
Volumes 1, 2 & 3

International Classification of Diseases
9th Revision
Clinical Modification

Sixth Edition

Edited by:
Anita C. Hart, RHIA, CCS, CCS-P
Beth Ford, RHIT, CCS

Ingenix is committed to providing you with the ICD-9-CM code update information you need to code accurately and to be in compliance with HIPAA regulations. In the case of adoption of additional ICD-9-CM code changes effective April 1, 2007, Ingenix will provide these code changes to you at no additional cost! Just check back at http://www.IngenixOnline.com and look for the ICD-9, CPT® and HCPCS Alerts link under the Quick Access Resources menu to review the latest information concerning any new code changes.

Codes Valid October 1, 2006, through September 30, 2007

First Printing — August 2006

Made in the USA

Additional copies may be ordered from:
Your local bookstore
or
1-800-INGENIX (464-3649)

IHP ISBN 978-1-56337-913-0

PUBLISHER'S NOTICE

All the codes, indexes and other material in the ICD-9-CM are compiled from official ICD-9-CM codes and instructions as well as the Medicare regulations and manuals issued or authorized by the Centers for Medicare and Medicaid Services. The code book is designed to provide accurate and authoritative information in regard to the subject covered, and every reasonable effort has been made to ensure the accuracy of the information within these pages. However, the ultimate responsibility for correct coding lies with the provider of services.

Ingenix, its employees, agents and staff make no representation, warranty or guarantee that this compilation of codes and narratives is error-free or that the use of this code book will prevent differences of opinion or disputes with Medicare or other third-party payers as to the codes that are accepted or the amounts that will be paid to providers of services, and will bear no responsibility or liability for the results or consequences of the use of this code book.

CONTINUING EDUCATION UNITS FOR CERTIFIED MEMBERS OF THE AMERICAN ACADEMY OF PROFESSIONAL CODERS

This publication has prior approval by the American Academy of Professional Coders for continuing education units (CEUs). Granting of prior approval in no way constitutes endorsement by the Academy of the publication content nor the publisher. Instructions to submit CEUs are available within the "Preapproved CEU Vendor List" file at www.aapc.com/education/CEUs/ceus.html.

OUR COMMITMENT TO ACCURACY

Ingenix is committed to producing accurate and reliable materials. To report corrections, please visit www.ingenixonline.com/accuracy or email accuracy@ingenix.com. You can also reach customer service by calling 1.800.INGENIX (464.3649), option 1.

Preface

Since the federal government implemented diagnosis-related groups (DRGs) on October 1, 1983, medical record profes-sionals and others have had to refer to many sources for ICD-9-CM codes and coding and reimbursement principles.

ICD-9-CM for Hospitals, Volumes 1, 2 & 3, has been designed with the health information professional in mind. All three volumes of the most recent official government version of ICD-9-CM have been combined into one book.

Our technical experts have drawn upon their extensive hands-on experience to enhance the government's book with valuable features essential to correct coding and reimbursement. Without these enhancements, health information management departments would spend hours locating the information required to code each record accurately. Because of the thoroughness, accuracy, timeliness and ease of use of *ICD-9-CM for Hospitals,* health information departments nationwide have turned to them for their coding needs.

ICD-9-CM for Hospitals includes many of the enhancements described below in direct response to requests from our subscribers. As you review the content, you'll find the following:

- The complete ICD-9-CM official guidelines for coding and reporting, published by the U.S. Department of Health and Human Services and approved by the cooperating parties (American Hospital Association, American Health Information Management Association, Health Care Financing Administration and National Center for Health Statistics)
- All the official ICD-9-CM codes, indexes, notes, footnotes and symbols
- color-highlighted illustrations and clearly worded definitions integrated in the tabular, provide important clinical information
- Exclusive color coding, symbols, and footnotes that alert coders to coding and reimbursement issues, including the majority of the Medicare code edits and identification of conditions that significantly affect DRG assignment of cardiovascular and HIV cases.
- The complication and comorbidity (CC) exclusion list, integrated beneath the applicable codes makes it easier to determine complications and comorbidities excluded with a particular principal diagnosis
- The American Hospital Association (AHA's) *Coding Clinic for ICD-9-CM* references, integrated beneath the applicable codes to provide easy reference to official coding advice as designated by the four cooperating parties (AHA, AHIMA, CMS, and NCHS)
- Compliance symbol identifying diagnosis codes associated with DRGs targeted by the government for audit
- Check fourth- and fifth-digit symbols identify codes that require the addition of a fourth or fifth digit for code specificity and validity
- Symbols identify new codes and text revisions and pages are dated to indicate when the changes were made
- Synopsis of the code changes for the current year
- Color coding and symbol legend at the bottom of each page
- Exclusive QuickFlip Color Tabs for quick, easy location of terms and codes in the index and Tabular List

Please review "How to Use *ICD-9-CM for Hospitals (Volumes 1, 2 & 3)*" in this section to learn about the features that will help you assign and report correct codes, ensuring appropriate reimbursement.

USE OF OFFICIAL SOURCES

The *ICD-9-CM for Hospitals* contains the official U.S. Department of Health and Human Services, Ninth Revision, Sixth Edition ICD-9-CM codes, effective for the current year.

The color-coding, footnotes and symbols, which identify coding and reimbursement issues, are derived from official federal government sources, including the Medicare Code Edits (MCE), Version 24.0.

The American Hospital Association's (AHA) *Coding Clinic for ICD-9-CM* references are used with permission of the AHA.

IMPORTANT INFORMATION ABOUT YOUR SUBSCRIPTION SERVICE

If you have purchased the updateable *ICD-9-CM Expert for Hospitals,* your subscription includes an updating service throughout the year to keep the code book current and accurate. The February update includes new illustrations and definitions, *AHA Coding Clinic* references for third and fourth quarter, the latest MCEs, and official errata changes. In July you will receive a list of all new, revised, and invalid codes for the upcoming year.

TECHNICAL EDITORS

Anita C. Hart, RHIA, CCS, CCS-P
Product Manager, Ingenix
Ms. Hart's experience includes conducting and publishing research in clinical medicine and human genetics for Yale University, Massachusetts General Hospital, and Massachusetts Institute of Technology. In addition, Ms. Hart has supervised medical records management, health information management, coding and reimbursement, and worker's compensation issues as the office manager for a physical therapy rehabilitation clinic. Ms. Hart is an expert in physician and facility coding, reimbursement systems, and compliance issues. Ms. Hart developed *ICD-9-CM Changes: An Insider View,* and has served as technical consultant for numerous other publications for hospital and physician practices. Currrently, Ms. Hart is the Product Manager and Technical Editor for the ICD-9-CM and ICD-10-CM/PCS product lines.

Beth Ford, RHIT, CCS
Clinical/Technical Editor, Ingenix
Ms. Ford is a clinical/technical editor for Ingenix. She has extensive background in both the professional and technical components of CPT/HCPCS and ICD-9-CM coding. Ms. Ford has served as a coding supervisor and coding consultant, as well as a health information management director. She is an active member of the American Heath Information Management Association (AHIMA).

In addition to the editors, the following people have contributed to this book:

Michael E. Desposito, *Product Director and Client Relationships*
Lynn Speirs, *Senior Director, Editorial/Desktop Publishing*
Stacy Perry, *Manager, Desktop Publishing*
Tracy Betzler, *Desktop Publishing Specialist*
Irene Day, *Desktop Publishing Specialist*
Hope Dunn, *Desktop Publishing Specialist*
Kerrie Hornsby, *Desktop Publishing Specialist*
Kate Holden, *Editor*

WHAT TO DO IF YOU HAVE QUESTIONS

If you have any questions call our customer service department toll-free at 800-INGENIX (464-3649), option 1.

If you have comments on the content of this book, please email them to customerservice@ingenix.com or fax to 801-982-4033.

ADDITIONAL COPIES

Contact the customer service order department toll-free at 800-INGENIX (464-3649), option 1.

Introduction

HISTORY AND FUTURE OF ICD-9

The International Classification of Diseases, Ninth Revision, Clinical Modification (ICD-9-CM) is based on the official version of the World Health Organization's Ninth Revision, International Classification of Diseases (ICD-9). ICD-9 classifies morbidity and mortality information for statistical purposes, and for the indexing of hospital records by disease and operations, for data storage and retrieval.

This modification of ICD-9 supplants the Eighth Revision International Classification of Diseases, Adapted for Use in the United States (ICDA-8) and the Hospital Adaptation of ICDA (H-ICDA).

The concept of extending the International Classification of Diseases for use in hospital indexing was originally developed in response to a need for a more efficient basis for storage and retrieval of diagnostic data. In 1950, the U.S. Public Health Service and the Veterans Administration began independent tests of the International Classification of Diseases for hospital indexing purposes. The following year, the Columbia Presbyterian Medical Center in New York City adopted the International Classification of Diseases, Sixth Revision, with some modifications for use in its medical record department. A few years later, the Commission on Professional and Hospital Activities (CPHA) in Ann Arbor, Mich., adopted the International Classification of Diseases with similar modifications for use in hospitals participating in the Professional Activity Study.

The problem of adapting ICD for indexing hospital records was taken up by the U.S. National Committee on Vital and Health Statistics through its subcommittee on hospital statistics. The subcommittee reviewed the modifications made by the various users of ICD and proposed that uniform changes be made. This was done by a small working party.

In view of the growing interest in the use of the International Classification of Diseases for hospital indexing, a study was undertaken in 1956 by the American Hospital Association and the American Medical Record Association (then the American Association of Medical Record Librarians) of the relative efficiencies of coding systems for diagnostic indexing. This study indicated the International Classification of Diseases provided a suitable and efficient framework for indexing hospital records. The major users of the International Classification of Diseases for hospital indexing purposes then consolidated their experiences, and an adaptation was first published in December 1959. A revision was issued in 1962 and the first "Classification of Operations and Treatments" was included.

In 1966, the international conference for revising the International Classification of Diseases noted the eighth revision of ICD had been constructed with hospital indexing in mind and considered the revised classification suitable, in itself, for hospital use in some countries. However, it was recognized that the basic classification might provide inadequate detail for diagnostic indexing in other countries. A group of consultants was asked to study the eighth revision of ICD (ICD-8) for applicability to various users in the United States. This group recommended that further detail be provided for coding of hospital and morbidity data. The American Hospital Association was requested to develop the needed adaptation proposals. This was done by an advisory committee (the Advisory Committee to the Central Office on ICDA). In 1968 the United States Public Health Service published the product, Eighth Revision International Classification of Diseases, Adapted for Use in the United States. This became commonly known as ICDA-8, and beginning in 1968 it served as the basis for coding diagnostic data for both official morbidity and mortality statistics in the United States.

In 1968, the CPHA published the Hospital Adaptation of ICDA (H-ICDA) based on both the original ICD-8 and ICDA-8. In 1973, CPHA published a revision of H-ICDA, referred to as H-ICDA-2. Hospitals throughout the United States were divided in their use of these classifications until January 1979, when ICD-9-CM was made the single classification intended primarily for use in the United States, replacing these earlier related, but somewhat dissimilar, classifications.

Physicians have been required by law to submit diagnosis codes for Medicare reimbursement since the passage of the Medicare Catastrophic Coverage Act of 1988. This act requires physician offices to include the appropriate diagnosis codes when billing for services provided to Medicare beneficiaries on or after April 1, 1989. The Centers for Medicare and Medicaid Services (formerly known as Health Care Financing Administration) designated ICD-9-CM as the coding system physicians must use.

In 1993 the World Health Organization published the newest version of International Classification of Diseases, Tenth Revision, ICD-10. This version contains the greatest number of changes in the history of ICD. There are more codes (5,500 more than ICD-9) to allow more specific reporting of diseases and newly recognized conditions. ICD-10 consists of three volumes; Tabular List (volume I), instructions (volume 2) and the Alphabetic Index (volume 3). It contains 21 chapters including two supplementary ones. The codes are alphanumeric (A00–T98, V01–Y98 and Z00–Z99). Currently ICD-10 is being used in some European countries with implementation expected after the year 2009 in the United States.

ICD-9-CM BACKGROUND

In February 1977, a steering committee was convened by the National Center for Health Statistics to provide advice and counsel in developing a clinical modification of ICD-9. The organizations represented on the steering committee included the following:

- American Association of Health Data Systems
- American Hospital Association
- American Medical Record Association
- Association for Health Records
- Council on Clinical Classifications
- Centers for Medicare and Medicaid Services, Department of Health and Human Services
- WHO Center for Classification of Diseases for North America, sponsored by the National Center for Health Statistics, Department of Health and Human Services

The Council on Clinical Classifications was sponsored by the following:

- American Academy of Pediatrics
- American College of Obstetricians and Gynecologists
- American College of Physicians
- American College of Surgeons
- American Psychiatric Association
- Commission on Professional and Hospital Activities

The steering committee met periodically in 1977. Clinical guidance and technical input were provided by task forces on classification from the Council on Clinical Classification's sponsoring organizations.

ICD-9-CM is a clinical modification of the World Health Organization's ICD-9. The term "clinical" is used to emphasize the modification's intent: to serve as a useful tool to classify morbidity data for indexing medical records, medical care review, and ambulatory and other medical care programs, as well as for basic health statistics. To describe the clinical picture of the patient, the codes must be more precise than those needed only for statistical groupings and trend analysis.

CHARACTERISTICS OF ICD-9-CM

ICD-9-CM far exceeds its predecessors in the number of codes provided. The disease classification has been expanded to include health-related conditions and to provide greater specificity at the fifth-digit level of detail. These fifth digits are not optional; they are intended for use in recording the information substantiated in the clinical record.

Volume I (Tabular List) of ICD-9-CM contains four appendices:

Appendix A:	Morphology of Neoplasms
Appendix B:	Deleted Effective October 1, 2004
Appendix C:	Classification of Drugs by American Hospital Formulary Service List Number and Their ICD-9-CM Equivalents

Appendix D: Classification of Industrial Accidents According to Agency

Appendix E: List of Three-Digit Categories

These appendices are included as a reference to provide further information about the patient's clinical picture, to further define a diagnostic statement, to aid in classifying new drugs or to reference three-digit categories.

Volume 2 (Alphabetic Index) of ICD-9-CM contains many diagnostic terms that do not appear in Volume I since the index includes most diagnostic terms currently in use.

Volume 3 (Procedure Index and Procedure Tabular) of ICD-9-CM contains codes for operations and procedures. The format for the tabular is the same as Volume 1 disease tabular, except the codes consist of two digits with one or two digits following the decimal point. Conventions in the index follow Volume 2 conventions except some subterms appear immediately below the main term rather than following alphabetizing rules.

THE DISEASE CLASSIFICATION

ICD-9-CM is totally compatible with its parent system, ICD-9, thus meeting the need for comparability of morbidity and mortality statistics at the international level. A few fourth-digit codes were created in existing three-digit rubrics only when the necessary detail could not be accommodated by the use of a fifth-digit subclassification. To ensure that each rubric of ICD-9-CM collapses back to its ICD-9 counterpart the following specifications governed the ICD-9-CM disease classification:

Specifications for the Tabular List:

1. Three-digit rubrics and their contents are unchanged from ICD-9.
2. The sequence of three-digit rubrics is unchanged from ICD-9.
3. Three-digit rubrics are not added to the main body of the classification.
4. Unsubdivided three-digit rubrics are subdivided where necessary to
   - add clinical detail
   - isolate terms for clinical accuracy
5. The modification in ICD-9-CM is accomplished by adding a fifth digit to existing ICD-9 rubrics, except as noted under #7 below.
6. The optional dual classification in ICD-9 is modified.
   - Duplicate rubrics are deleted:
     - four-digit manifestation categories duplicating etiology entries
     - manifestation inclusion terms duplicating etiology entries
   - Manifestations of disease are identified, to the extent possible, by creating five-digit codes in the etiology rubrics.
   - When the manifestation of a disease cannot be included in the etiology rubrics, provision for its identification is made by retaining the ICD-9 rubrics used for classifying manifestations of disease.
7. The format of ICD-9-CM is revised from that used in ICD-9.
   - American spelling of medical terms is used.
   - Inclusion terms are indented beneath the titles of codes.
   - Codes not to be used for primary tabulation of disease are printed in italics with the notation, "code first underlying disease."

Specifications for the Alphabetic Index:

1. The format of the Alphabetic Index follows that of ICD-9.
2. When two codes are required to indicate etiology and manifestation, the manifestation code appears in brackets (e.g., diabetic cataract 250.5 *[366.41]*).

THE ICD-9-CM COORDINATION AND MAINTENANCE COMMITTEE

The four cooperating parties involved in maintaining the ICD-9-CM classification system include representatives of the American Hospital Association (AHA), the Centers for Medicare and Medicaid Services (CMS), the National Center for Health Statistics (NCHS), and the American Health Information Management Association (AHIMA).

Proposals for changes to the ICD-9-CM classification system are submitted and discussed in two open forum meetings held in April and October of each year at the Headquarters of the Centers for Medicare and Medicaid Services, Baltimore, Maryland. Comments received during and after the meetings are then discussed by the Committee. A notice of the new codes and code revisions approved by the Committee are published in the *Federal Register* as part of the proposed and final rule for the changes to the inpatient prospective payment system. The complete official document of changes to the classification system is released as the Addenda for the *International Classification of Diseases, Ninth Revision, Clinical Modification, Sixth Edition, Volumes 1, 2 and 3.*

How to Use the ICD-9-CM for Hospitals (Volumes 1, 2 & 3)

This *ICD-9-CM for Hospitals* is based on the official version of the International Classification of Diseases, Ninth Revision, Clinical Modification, Sixth Edition, issued by the U.S. Department of Health and Human Services. Annual code changes are implemented by the government and are effective Oct. 1 and valid through Sept. 30 of the following year.

The code book is totally compatible with its parent system, ICD-9, thus meeting the need for comparability of morbidity and mortality statistics at the international level.

This book is consistent with the content of the government's version of ICD-9-CM. However, to accommodate the coder's approach to coding, the Alphabetic Index has been placed before the Tabular List in both the disease and procedure classifications. This allows the user to locate the correct codes in a logical, natural manner by locating the term in the index, then confirming the accuracy of the code in the Tabular List.

STEPS TO CORRECT CODING

1. Look up the main term in the Alphabetic Index and scan the subterm entries as appropriate. Follow any cross-references such as "*see*" and "*see also*." Do not code from the Alphabetic Index without verifying the accuracy of the code in the Tabular List.
2. Locate the code in the numerically arranged Tabular List.
3. Observe the punctuation, footnotes, cross-references, color-coded prompts and other conventions described in the 'Conventions' section.
4. To determine the appropriateness of the code selection, read all instructional material:
   - "includes" and "*excludes*" notes
   - "*see*," "*see also*" and "*see category*" cross-references
   - "use additional code" and "*code first underlying disease*" instructions
   - "code also" and "*omit code*" notes
   - fourth- and fifth-digit requirements
   - CC exclusions
5. Consult definitions, relevant illustrations, CC exclusions, color coding and reimbursement prompts, the check fourth- and fifth-digit, age and sex symbols. Refer to the color/symbol legend at the bottom of each page for symbols. Refer to the list of footnotes that is included in the "Additional Conventions" section of this book for a full explanation of a footnote associated with a code.
6. Consult the official ICD-9-CM guidelines for coding and reporting, and refer to the AHA's *Coding Clinic for ICD-9-CM* for coding guidelines governing the use of specific codes.
7. Confirm and transcribe the correct code.

ORGANIZATION

Introduction

The introductory material in this book includes the history and future of ICD-9-CM as well as an overview of the classification system.

Official ICD-9-CM Conventions

This section provides a full explanation of all the official footnotes, symbols, instructional notes, and conventions found in the official government version.

Additional Conventions

Exclusive color-coding, symbols, and notations have been included in the *ICD-9-CM for Hospitals, Volumes 1, 2 & 3* to alert coders to important coding and reimbursement issues. This section provides a full explanation of the additional conventions used throughout this book.

Coding Guidelines

Included in this book are the official ICD-9-CM coding guidelines as approved by the four cooperating parties of the ICD-9-CM Coordination and Maintenance Committee. Failure to comply with the official coding guidelines may result in denied or delayed claims.

Summary of Code Changes

This section includes a complete listing of all new code changes for the current year.

Summary of AHA's Coding Clinic for ICD-9-CM Topics

This is a brief summary of the official advice concerning coding topics covered in the latest issues of AHA's *Coding Clinic for ICD-9-CM* and is found only in the *ICD-9-CM Expert for Hospitals* updateable edition.

Disease Classification: Alphabetic Index to Diseases

The Alphabetic Index to Diseases is separated by tabs labeled with the letters of the alphabet, contains diagnostic terms for illnesses, injuries and reasons for encounters with health care professionals. The Table of Drugs and Chemicals is easily located with the tab in this section.

The warning statement at the bottom of every page of the index, ▽ Subterms under main terms may continue to next column or page, is a reminder to always check for additional subterms before making final selection.

Disease Classification: Tabular List of Diseases

The Tabular List of Diseases arranges the ICD-9-CM codes and descriptors numerically. QuickFlip color tabs divide this section into chapters, identified by the code range on the tab.

The Tabular List includes two supplementary classifications:

- V Codes—Supplementary Classification of Factors Influencing Health Status and Contact with Health Services (V01–V86)
- E Codes—Supplementary Classification of External Causes of Injury and Poisoning (E800–E999)

ICD-9-CM includes four official appendixes.

- Appendix A — Morphology of Neoplasms
- Appendix B: — Deleted Effective October 1, 2004
- Appendix C — Classification of Drugs by AHFS List
- Appendix D — Classification of Industrial Accidents According to Agency
- Appendix E — List of Three-digit Categories

These appendices are included as a reference to provide further information about the patient's circumstances, help further define a diagnostic statement, maintain a tumor registry and aid in classifying new drugs.

Procedure Classification: Alphabetic Index to Procedures

The Alphabetic Index to Procedures lists common surgical and procedural terminology.

The warning statement at the bottom of every page of the index, ▽ Subterms under main terms may continue to next column or page, is a reminder to always check for additional subterms before making final selection.

Procedure Classification: Tabular List of Procedures

The Tabular List of Procedures numerically arranges the procedure codes and their descriptors.

Resources

Listed below are the exclusive resources found ONLY in the *ICD-9-CM Expert for Hospitals, Volumes 1, 2 & 3* books.

Dx/MDC/DRG List

Provides the complete list of principal diagnosis codes and the MDC and DRG to which they group, with the exception of a combination of principal and secondary diagnosis affecting DRG assignment.

CC Condition List

A complete list of all codes considered CC (Complications and Comorbidities) that will affect DRG assignment. This an essential auditing tool for assigning the most appropriate DRG.

Pharmacological Listings

The most common generic and brand names of drugs are linked with the disease processes to assist in the identification of CC, thereby improving DRG assignment practices.

Valid Three-digit Code Table

ICD-9-CM is composed of codes with either 3, 4, or 5 digits. A code is invalid if it has not been coded to the full number of digits required for that code. There are a certain number codes that are valid for reporting as three digit codes. A list of the valid three-digit code is included as a convenient reference when auditing claims.

ICD-9-CM Official Conventions

ICD-9-CM FOOTNOTES, SYMBOLS, INSTRUCTIONAL NOTES AND CONVENTIONS

This *ICD-9-CM for Hospitals* preserves all the footnotes, symbols, instructional notes and conventions found in the government's official version. Accurate coding depends upon understanding the meaning of these elements.

The following appear in the disease Tabular List, unless otherwise noted.

OFFICIAL GOVERNMENT SYMBOLS

§ The section mark preceding a code denotes a footnote on the page. This symbol is used in the Tabular List of Diseases and in the Tabular List of Procedures.

ICD-9-CM CONVENTIONS USED IN THE TABULAR LIST

In addition to the symbols and footnotes above, the ICD-9-CM disease tabular has certain abbreviations, punctuation, symbols and other conventions. Our *ICD-9-CM for Hospitals* preserves these conventions. Proper use of the conventions will lead to efficient and accurate coding.

Abbreviations

NEC Not elsewhere classifiable

This abbreviation is used when the ICD-9-CM system does not provide a code specific for the patient's condition.

NOS Not otherwise specified

This abbreviation is the equivalent of 'unspecified' and is used only when the coder lacks the information necessary to code to a more specific four-digit subcategory.

[ ] Brackets enclose synonyms, alternative terminology or explanatory phrases:

482.2 Pneumonia due to Hemophilus influenzae [H. influenzae]

Brackets that appear beneath a code indicate the fifth digits that are considered valid fifth digits for the code. This convention is applied for those instances in ICD-9-CM where not all common fifth digits are considered valid for each subcategory within a category.

715.0 Osteoarthrosis, generalized
[0,4,9]

Generalized arthrosis can only be assigned in cases for which the degenerative joint disease involves multiple joints. Therefore, this code is considered for arthrosis in the sites described as unspecified, hand (which consists of multiple joints), or multiple sites. Therefore, only fifth digits 0, 4, and 9 are valid with subcategory 715.0.

[ ] Slanted brackets that appear in the Alphabetic Indexes indicate mandatory multiple coding. Both codes must be assigned to fully describe the condition and are sequenced in the order listed.

Tachycardia
ventricular (paroxysmal)
psychogenic 316 *[427.1]*

Psychogenic paroxysmal tachycardia is reported using both 316, Psychogenic factors associated with diseases classified elsewhere, and 427.1, Paroxysmal ventricular tachydcardia.

Diversion
biliopancratic (BPD) 43.7 *[45.51] [45.91]*

Code assignment of biliopancratic diversion is reported using all three codes 43.7, Partial gastrectomy with anastomosis to jejunum, 45.51, Isolation of segment of small intestine, and 45.91, Small-to-small intestinal anastomosis.

( ) Parentheses enclose supplementary words, called nonessential modifiers, that may be present in the narrative description of a disease without affecting the code assignment:

198.4 Other parts of nervous system
Meninges (cerebral) (spinal)

: Colons are used in the Tabular List after an incomplete term that needs one or more of the modifiers that follow in order to make it assignable to a given category:

021.1 Enteric tularemia
Tularemia:
cryptogenic
intestinal
typhoidal

} Braces enclose a series of terms, each of which is modified by the statement appearing to the right of the brace:

560.2 Volvulus
Knotting
Strangulation
Torsion
Twist } of intestine, bowel, or colon

OTHER CONVENTIONS

Boldface Boldface type is used for all codes and titles in the Tabular List.

Italicized Italicized type is used for all exclusion notes and to identify codes that should not be used for describing the primary diagnosis.

INSTRUCTIONAL NOTES

These notes appear only in the Tabular List of Diseases:

Includes: An includes note further defines or clarifies the content of the chapter, subchapter, category, sub-category or subclassification. The includes note in the example below applies only to category 461.

Excludes: Terms following the word "*Excludes*" are not classified to the chapter, subchapter, category, subcategory or specific subclassification code under which it is found. The note also may provide the location of the excluded diagnosis. Excludes notes are italicized.

461 Acute sinusitis

INCLUDES abscess
empyema
infection
inflammation
suppuration } acute, of sinus (accessory) (nasal)

EXCLUDES *chronic or unspecified sinusitis (473.0-473.9)*

Use additional code:

This instruction signals the coder that an additional code should be used if the information is available to provide a more complete picture of that diagnosis.

362.13 Changes in vascular appearance
Vascular sheathing of retina
Use additional code for any associated atherosclerosis (440.8)

There are coding circumstances outside of the etiology/ manifestation convention when multiple coding for a single condition is required. The 'Use additional code' note will be found under the associated condition code in the tabular. In the index, the multiple coding requirement is indicated by the use of the slanted bracket. The two codes are to be sequenced as listed in the index. For example, retinal arterisosclerosis must be coded using two codes sequenced as listed in the index.

Arteriosclerosis, arteriosclerotic

retinal (vascular) 440.8 *[362.13]*

Code first underlying disease:

The *Code first underlying disease* instructional note found under certain codes is a sequencing rule. Most often this sequencing rule applies to the etiology/manifestation convention and is found under at the manifestation code. The manifestation code may never be used alone or as a primary diagnosis (i.e., sequenced first). The instructional note, the code and its descriptor appear in italics in the Tabular List.

590.81 Pyelitis or pyelonephritis in diseases classified elsewhere

Code first underlying disease as:
tuberculosis (016.0)

Not all codes with a 'Code first underlying disease' instructional note are part of the etiology/manifestation convention. The 'Code first' note will appear, but the title of the code and the instructional note are not in italics. These codes may be reported alone or as the secondary diagnosis. For example, disseminated chorioretinitis may be reported as a principal diagnosis. However, if the underlying condition that caused disseminated chorioretinitis is known, such as tuberculous disseminated chorioretinitis, two codes are required and sequenced as listed in the index.

363.13 Disseminated choroiditis and chorioretinitis, generalized

Code first underlying disease as:
tuberculosis (017.3)

Code, if applicable, any causal condition first:

A code with this note indicates that this code may be assigned as a principal diagnosis when the causal condition is unknown or not applicable. If a causal condition is known, then the code for that condition should be sequenced as the principal or first-listed diagnosis.

590.0 Chronic pyelonephritis

Chronic pyelitis
Chronic pyonephrosis
Code, if applicable, any causal condition first

Omit code:

"*Omit code*" is used to instruct the coder that no code is to be assigned. When this instruction is found in the Alphabetic Index to Diseases the medical term should not be coded as a diagnosis.

Metaplasia

cervix — *omit code*

When used in Volume 3, '*omit code*' is meant to indicate procedures that do not merit separate code assignments, such as minor procedures preformed in conjunction with more extensive procedures or procedures that represent an operative approach.

Arthrotomy 80.10

as operative approach — *omit code*

***See* Condition:**

The "*see* condition" note found in the Alphabetic Index to Disease instructs the coder to refer to a main term for the condition. This note will follow index terms that are nouns for anatomical sites or adjectival forms of disease term. In the example below, the index terms 'Cervix' and 'Diffuse' are followed by the — *see* condition. Coders should search the index using a condition term such as atrophy or prolapse.

Cervix — *see* condition
Diffuse — *see* condition

Morphology Codes

For each neoplastic disease listed in the index, a morphology code is provided that identifies histological type and behavior.

Example:

Myelolipoma (M8870/0) — *see* Neoplasm, by site, benign

The histology is identified by the first four digits and the behavior is identified by the digit following the slash. Appendix A of Volume 1 contains a listing of morphology codes. This appendix is helpful when the pathology report identifies the neoplasm by using an M code. The coder may refer to Appendix A to determine the nomenclature of the neoplasm that will be the main term to search in the Index. The behavior classification is as follows:

0 Benign
1 Uncertain behavior
2 Carcinoma in situ
3 Malignant, primary site
6 Malignant, secondary site.

Additional Conventions

NEW AND REVISED TEXT SYMBOLS

● A bullet at a code or line of text indicates that that the entry is new.

▲ A triangle in the Tabular List indicates that the code title is revised. In the Alphabetic Index the triangle indicates that a code has changed.

▶◀ These symbols appear at the beginning and at the end of a section of new or revised text.

When these symbols appear on a page there will be a date on the lower outside corner of the page indicating the date of the change, (e.g., October 2006).

ADDITIONAL DIGITS REQUIRED

✓3rd This symbol indicates that the code requires a third digit.

✓4th This symbol indicates that the code requires a fourth digit.

✓5th This symbol indicates that a code requires a fifth digit.

☑ This symbol found only in the Alphabetic Index sections and the Table of Drugs and Chemicals indicates that an additional digit is required. Referring to the tabular section is essential to locate the appropriate additional digit.

DEFINITIONS

DEF: This symbol indicates a definition of disease or procedure term. The definition will appear in blue type in the Disease and Procedure Tabular Lists.

AHA's *CODING CLINIC FOR ICD-9-CM* REFERENCES

The four cooperating parties have designated the AHA's *Coding Clinic for ICD-9-CM* as the official publication for coding guidelines. The references are identified by the notation **AHA:** followed by the issue, year and page number.

In the example below, AHA's *Coding Clinic for ICD-9-CM*, third quarter 1991, page 15, contains a discussion on code assignment for vitreous hemorrhage:

379.23 Vitreous hemorrhage
AHA: 3Q, '91, 15

The table below explains the abbreviations in the *Coding Clinic* references:

J-F	January/February
M-A	March/April
M-J	May/June
J-A	July/August
S-O	September/October
N-D	November/December
1Q	First quarter
2Q	Second quarter
3Q	Third quarter
4Q	Fourth quarter

MEDICARE CODE EDITS

Fiscal intermediaries use Medicare code edits (MCE) to check the coding accuracy on claims. The Medicare code edits are listed below:

1. Invalid diagnosis or procedure code
2. E-code as principal diagnosis
3. Duplicate of principal diagnosis (PDx) (as applied to a secondary diagnosis)

* 4. Age conflict
* 5. Sex conflict
* 6. Manifestation code as principal diagnosis
* 7. Nonspecific principal diagnosis
* 8. Questionable admission
*9. Unacceptable principal diagnosis
*10. Nonspecific OR procedure
*11. Noncovered procedure
12. Open biopsy check
*13. Bilateral procedure
14. Invalid age
15. Invalid sex
16. Invalid discharge status
*17. Limited coverage procedure

Starred edits are identified by colors, symbols or footnotes as described on the next page.

Age and Sex Edit Symbols

The age edits below address MCE edit 4 and are used to detect inconsistencies between the patient's age and diagnosis. They appear in the Tabular List of Diseases to the right of the code description.

Newborn Age: 0

These diagnoses are intended for newborns and neonates and the patient's age must be 0 years

Pediatric Age: 0-17

These diagnoses are intended for children and the patient's age must between 0 and 17 years

Maternity Age: 12-55

These diagnoses are intended for the patients between the age of 12 and 55 years

Adult Age: 15-124

These diagnoses are intended for the patients between the age of 15 and 124 years.

The sex symbols below address MCE edit 5 and are used to detect inconsistencies between the patient's sex and diagnosis or procedure. They appear in the Tabular Lists to the right of the code description:

♂ **Male diagnosis or procedure only**

This symbol appears to the right of the code description. This reference appears in the disease and procedure Tabular List.

♀ **Female diagnosis or procedure only**

This symbol appears to the right of the code description. This reference appears in the disease and procedure Tabular List.

Color Coding

For a quick reference to the color codes and their meaning, refer to the color/symbol legend located at the bottom of each page.

To alert the coder to important reimbursement issues affected by the code assignment, color bars have been added. The colors represent Medicare code edits as well as other reimbursement issues.

Color coding appears in both Tabular Lists. Some codes carry more than one color. Please note that the same color may appear in the disease and procedure Tabular Lists, but with different meanings.

Disease Tabular List

Manifestation Code

These codes will appear in italic type as well as with a blue color bar over the code title. A manifestation code is not allowed to be reported as a primary diagnosis because each describes a manifestation of some other underlying disease, not the disease itself. This is referred to as mandatory multiple coding of etiology and manifestation. Code the underlying disease first. A 'Code first underlying disease' instructional note will appear with underlying disease codes identified. In the Alphabetic Index these codes are listed as the secondary code in slanted bracket with the code for the underlying disease listed first. Medicare code edit (MCE) 6

Unacceptable PDx

These codes will appear with a gray color bar over the code title. These codes do not describe a current illness or injury, but a circumstance which influences a patient's health status. These are considered an unacceptable principal diagnosis for inpatient admission. Medicare code edit (MCE) 9

Questionable Admission

These codes will also appear with a gray color bar over the code title. These codes identify a condition that usually is insufficient justification for hospital admission. Since these codes are considered an unacceptable principal diagnoses for inpatient admission, they are color coded in the same manner as the "unacceptable PDx codes". Medicare code edit (MCE) 8

Nonspecific PDx

These codes will have a yellow color bar over the code title. While these codes are considered valid ICD-9-CM codes, for inpatients discharged alive, a more specific principal diagnosis should be assigned. These codes are used when the neither the diagnostic statement nor the documentation provides enough information to assign a more specified diagnosis code. These codes may be stated as "Unspecified" or "Not otherwise specified (NOS)." Medicare code edit (MCE) 7

Procedure Tabular List

Nonspecific OR Procedure

While this code is a valid unspecific or not otherwise specified (NOS) procedure code, a more precise code should be used. The code is recognized as a nonspecific operating room procedure ONLY if ALL operating room procedures performed are coded NOS. Medicare code edit (MCE 10)

Valid OR

A procedure that triggers a change in DRG assignment.

Non-OR Procedure

A non-operating room procedure that affects DRG assignment.

Adjunct Codes

These codes are not to be reported alone and are indicated by the red color bar over the code title. Adjunct codes are assigned only in addition to a primary procedure. Their purpose is to provide supplemental information about the primary procedure performed. Adjunct codes are not procedure codes, but serve to provide additional detail about the primary procedure.

Example:

PTCA balloon inflation of two vessels, with insertion of one intravascular coronary stent.

Code assignment:

00.66 Percutaneous transluminal coronary angioplasty [PTCA] or athrectomy

00.41 Procedure on two vessels

00.45 Insertion of one vascular stent

In the above example, codes 00.41 and 00.45 are adjunct codes that provide specific detail about the PTCA procedure performed.

Footnotes

All footnotes are identified by a numerical superscript that appears to the upper left of the code:

[1]**718.5 Ankylosis of joint**

The footnote 1 indicates "Nonspecific PDx = 0". This means that when code 718.50, Ankylosis of the joint, site unspecified, the diagnosis is considered a nonspecific principal diagnosis. While this code may be valid according to ICD-9-CM, a more precise diagnosis should be used for the principal diagnosis for inpatient admission.

The following list identifies the meaning of each footnote number and the classification in which the footnote appears:

Disease Tabular

1 Diagnosis code with fifth digit of 0 is considered a 'Nonspecific' diagnosis when used as a principal diagnosis.

2 Diagnosis code with fifth digit of 9 is considered a 'Nonspecific' diagnosis when used as a principal diagnosis.

3 These V codes may be used as principal diagnosis on Medicare patients.

4 This V code, with the fourth digit of 1 or 2, is unacceptable as a principal diagnosis.

5 These codes, with the fourth digit of 0, may be used as a principal diagnosis for Medicare patients.

6 Rehabilitation codes acceptable as a principal diagnosis when accompanied by a secondary diagnosis reflecting the condition treated.

7 These V codes are acceptable as principal diagnosis when accompanied by a diagnosis of personal history of malignancy. These codes group to DRG 465.

8 Diagnosis code with fifth digit of 0 is considered a 'Questionable Admission' diagnosis when used as a principal diagnosis.

9 Diagnosis qualifies as a major cardiovascular condition for DRGs 551 and 553 only when assigned as either principal or secondary diagnosis.

10 Diagnosis qualifies as a major cardiovascular condition when assigned as a secondary diagnosis only.

11 Diagnosis qualifies as a major cardiovascular condition for DRGs 547, 549, 553, 555 and 557 only when assigned as either principal or secondary diagnosis.

Procedure Tabular

12 Valid OR procedure code if accompanied by one of the following codes: 37.80, 37.81, 37.82, 37.85, 37.86, 37.87.

13 Valid OR procedure code if accompanied by one of the following codes: 37.80, 37.83.

14 Valid OR procedure code if accompanied by one of the following codes: 37.80, 37.85, 37.86, 37.87.

15 Valid OR procedure code if accompanied by any one of the following codes: 37.80, 37.81, 37.82, 37.83, 37.85, 37.86, 37.87.

16 Valid OR procedure code if accompanied by any other pacemaker procedure except 37.72, 37.76.

17 Valid OR procedure code if accompanied by any other pacemaker procedure except 37.70, 37.71, 37.73, 37.76.

18 Procedure code with fourth digit of 0 is considered a 'Nonspecific' operating room procedure.

19 Non-covered procedure only when the following diagnoses are present as either a principal or secondary diagnosis: 204.00, 205.00, 205.10, 205.11, 206.00, 207.00, 208.00.

20 Non-covered procedure only when the following diagnoses are present as either a principal or secondary diagnosis: 203.00, 203.01.

21 Non-covered procedure except when there is at least one principal or secondary diagnosis from 250.00-250.93.

Other Notations

Alphabetic Indexes

Subterms under main terms may continue to next column or page.

This warning statement is a reminder to always check for additional subterms and information that may continue onto the next page or column before making a final selection.

Disease Tabular

CC Condition

A complication or comorbidity diagnosis that may change DRG assignment. A complication is defined as a condition that arises during the hospital stay that extends the length of stay by at least one day in 75 percent of the cases. A comorbidity is a pre-existing condition that will, because of its presence with a specific principal diagnosis, that extends the length of stay by at least one day in 75 percent of the cases.

CC listed with a digit or range of digits indicates the fifth-digit assignments for that code that are considered CC conditions. Example: code 250.1 has a symbol CC 1-3 which means that only 250.11, 250.12, and 250.13 are considered CC conditions. Code 250.10 is not a CC condition.

CC Exclusion List

A exclusive feature of *ICD-9-CM for Hospitals* is the integration of the government's CC exclusion list with each affected code.

The CC exclusion list indicates secondary diagnosis codes that are excluded as CC conditions with certain principal diagnoses. This exclusion occurs because the cited conditions are inherent to the disease process of the principal diagnosis.

Listed below each code that is considered a complication or comorbidity (CC) diagnosis, are the codes or code ranges of principal diagnosis with which the CC code cannot be used.

In the example below, code 254.1 is considered a CC condition. However, the CC exclusion (CC Excl:) notation indicates that if a code from the listed code ranges is assigned as the principal diagnosis, the secondary diagnosis of 254.1 will not be recognized as a CC condition in DRG assignment.

254.1 Abscess of thymus CC

CC Excl: 254.0-254.1, 254.8-254.9, 259.8-259.9

Major Cardiovascular Complication Condition

A complication that causes the DRG to change from DRG 122 to DRG 121.

Complex Diagnosis

A diagnosis that causes the DRG assignment of a case to change from DRG 125 to DRG 124.

Medicare as Secondary Payer (MSP)

Note: The Medicare as Secondary Payer (MSP) alert identified trauma diagnoses that may be covered under automobile insurance, no-fault insurance, workmen's compensation or other types of liability insurance for which Medicare should be a secondary payer Providers must verify MSP information prior to submitting the claim to Medicare. Therefore, this edit is no longer included in the official Medicare Code Editor (MCE) for the inpatient prospective payment system (IPPS).

DRG

This symbol indicates the diagnosis is assigned to a diagnosis related group (DRG) that has been targeted for audit. The condition must be thoroughly documented in the medical record to prevent inappropriate coding or "upcoding."

HIV

This symbol indicates that the condition is considered a major HIV related diagnosis. When the condition is coded in combination with a diagnosis of human immunodeficiency virus (HIV), code 042, the case will move from DRG 490 to DRG 489.

Medicare as Secondary Payer (MSP)

Note: The Medicare as Secondary Payer (MSP) alert identified trauma diagnoses that may be covered under automobile insurance, no-fault insurance, workmen's compensation or other types of liability insurance for which Medicare should be a secondary payer Providers must verify MSP information prior to submitting the claim to Medicare. Therefore, this edit is no longer included in the official Medicare Code Editor (MCE) for the inpatient prospective payment system (IPPS).

V Code table

Note: Please note that while the official guidelines [Section 1. C.18.e.] include the V Code Table the reporting designations indicated by the Table are often in conflict with the Medicare code edits (MCE) for the inpatient prospective payment system (IPPS). Therefore, only the inpatient prospective payment system code edits are represented in this edition.

Procedure Tabular

Noncovered Procedure

A procedure not covered by Medicare. In some instances this procedure may also be identified as a valid operating room (OR) procedure that may trigger a DRG assignment. Even if a DRG assignment is made, Medicare may not reimburse for the noncovered procedure. Medicare code edit (MCE) 11.

Limited Coverage Procedure

A procedure whose medical complexity and serious nature incur associated costs that are deemed extraordinary and Medicare limits coverage to a portion of the cost. Medicare code edit (MCE) 17.

Bilateral Edit

Due to the lack of laterality in ICD-9-CM, there are certain lower extremity joint procedure codes that do not accurately reflect procedures that are performed in one admission on two or more different bilateral joints. To group to DRG 471, Bilateral or Multiple Joint Procedures of Lower Extremity, a case must be coded with a combination of two or more different major lower extremity joint procedures. The bilateral procedure symbol identifies those procedure codes that when coded twice represent the same procedure performed on both of the same bilateral joints of the lower extremity. Otherwise, a code edit will instruct the fiscal intermediary to verify that the two different procedures were performed on two different bilateral joints. Medicare code edit (MCE) 13.

Summary of Code Changes

DISEASE TABULAR LIST (VOLUME 1)

● 052.2	Postvaricella myelitis
	Includes note added
● 053.14	Herpes zoster myelitis
● 054.74	Herpes simplex myelitis
136.3	Includes term added
151	Excludes note added
152	Excludes note added
171	Includes term added
	Excludes term revised
174	Use additional code note added
175	Use additional code note added
202.1	Includes term deleted
211	Excludes note added
215.5	Includes term added
233.1	Includes term added
	Excludes term revised
235	Excludes note added
238.1	Includes term added
238.7	Includes note deleted
	Excludes terms added
	Excludes term revised
● 238.71	Essential thrombocythemia
	Includes note added
● 238.72	Low grade myelodysplastic syndrome lesions
	Includes note added
● 238.73	High grade myelodysplastic syndrome lesions
	Includes note added
● 238.74	Myelodysplastic syndrome with 5q deletion
	Includes note added
	Excludes note added
● 238.75	Myelodysplastic syndrome, unspecified
● 238.76	Myelofibrosis with myeloid metaplasia
	Includes note added
	Excludes note added
● 238.79	Other lymphatic and hematopoietic tissues
	Includes note added
▲ 255.10	~~Primary Aldosteronism~~ ▶Hyperaldosteronism, unspecified◀
	Includes term added
	Includes term deleted
277.3	Includes note deleted
● 277.30	Amyloidosis, unspecified
	Includes note added
● 277.31	Familial Mediterranean fever
	Includes note added
● 277.39	Other amyloidosis
	Includes note added
278.0	Use additional code note revised
▲ 284	Aplastic anemia and ▶other bone marrow failure syndromes◀
284.0	Includes note deleted
● 284.01	Constitutional red blood cell aplasia
	Includes note added
● 284.09	Other constitutional aplastic anemia
	Includes note added
● 284.1	Pancytopenia
	Excludes note added
● 284.2	Myelophthisis
	Includes note added
	Code first note added
	Excludes note added
284.8	Includes term deleted
	~~Excludes term deleted~~
284.9	Excludes term revised
285.0	Excludes term revised
▲ 285.2	Anemia ~~in~~ ▶of◀ other chronic ~~illness~~ ▶disease◀
	Includes note added
▲ 285.29	Anemia of other chronic ~~illness~~ ▶disease◀
	Includes note added
285.8	Includes term deleted
287	Excludes term revised
▲ 288.0	~~Agranulocytosis~~ ▶Neutropenia◀
	Includes term added
	Includes terms deleted
	Use additional code note deleted
	Use additional code note added
	Excludes term added
● 288.00	Neutropenia, unspecified
● 288.01	Congenital neutropenia
	Includes note added
● 288.02	Cyclic neutropenia
	Includes note added
● 288.03	Drug induced neutropenia
	Use additional code note added
● 288.04	Neutropenia due to infection
● 288.09	Other neutropenia
	Includes note added
● 288.4	Hemophagocytic syndromes
	Includes note added
● 288.5	Decreased white blood cell count
	Excludes note added
● 288.50	Leukocytopenia, unspecified
	Includes note added
● 288.51	Lymphocytopenia
	Includes note added
● 288.59	Other decreased white blood cell count
	Includes note added
● 288.6	Elevated white blood cell count
	Excludes note added
● 288.60	Leukocytosis, unspecified
	Includes note added
● 288.61	Lymphocytosis (symptomatic)
	Includes note added
● 288.62	Leukemoid reaction
	Includes note added
● 288.63	Monocytosis (symptomatic)
	Excludes note added
● 288.64	Plasmacytosis
● 288.65	Basophilia
● 288.69	Other elevated white blood cell count
288.8	Includes note deleted
	Excludes terms added
289.4	Excludes term revised
● 289.53	Neutropenic splenomegaly
● 289.83	Myelofibrosis
	Includes note added
	Code first note added
	Excludes note added
289.89	Includes term deleted
305.1	Excludes terms added
307.89	Code first note revised
309.81	Includes terms added
323	Includes terms revised
	Excludes terms added
▲ 323.0	Encephalitis, ▶myelitis, and encephalomyelitis◀ in viral diseases classified elsewhere
	Excludes note deleted
● 323.01	Encephalitis and encephalomyelitis in viral diseases classified elsewhere
	Excludes note added
● 323.02	Myelitis in viral diseases classified elsewhere
	Excludes note added
▲ 323.1	Encephalitis ▶, myelitis, and encephalomyelitis◀ in rickettsial diseases classified elsewhere
▲ 323.2	Encephalitis ▶, myelitis, and encephalomyelitis◀ in protozoal diseases classified elsewhere
▲ 323.4	Other encephalitis ▶, myelitis, and encephalomyelitis◀ due to infection classified elsewhere
	Excludes note deleted
● 323.41	Other encephalitis and encephalomyelitis due to infection classified elsewhere
	Excludes note added
● 323.42	Other myelitis due to infection classified elsewhere
	Excludes note added
▲ 323.5	Encephalitis ▶, myelitis, and encephalomyelitis◀ following immunization procedures
	Includes note deleted
● 323.51	Encephalitis and encephalomyelitis following immunization procedures
	Includes note added
● 323.52	Myelitis following immunization procedures
	Includes note added
▲ 323.6	Postinfectious encephalitis▶, myelitis, and encephalomyelitis◀
	Includes note deleted
	Excludes note deleted
● 323.61	Infectious acute disseminated encephalomyelitis [ADEM]
	Includes note added
	Excludes note added
● 323.62	Other postinfectious encephalitis and encephalomyelitis
	Excludes note added
● 323.63	Postinfectious myelitis
	Excludes note added
▲ 323.7	Toxic encephalitis▶, myelitis, and encephalomyelitis◀
● 323.71	Toxic encephalitis and encephalomyelitis
● 323.72	Toxic myelitis
▲ 323.8	Other causes of encephalitis ▶, myelitis, and encephalomyelitis◀
	Excludes note deleted
● 323.81	Other causes of encephalitis and encephalomyelitis
	Includes note added
● 323.82	Other causes of myelitis
	Includes note added
▲ 323.9	Unspecified causes of encephalitis ▶, myelitis, and encephalomyelitis◀
326	Instructional note revised
327	Section title added
327.5	Excludes term revised
● 331.83	Mild cognitive impairment, so stated
	Excludes note added
▲ 333.6	~~Idiopathic~~ ▶Genetic◀ torsion dystonia
▲ 333.7	~~Symptomatic~~ ▶Acquired◀torsion dystonia
	Includes note deleted
	Use additional code note deleted
● 333.71	Athetoid cerebral palsy
	Includes note added
	Excludes note added
● 333.72	Acute dystonia due to drugs
	Includes note added
	Use additional code note added
	Excludes note added
● 333.79	Other acquired torsion dystonia
333.81	Excludes note added
333.82	Includes term deleted
	Excludes note added
● 333.85	Subacute dyskinesia due to drugs
	Includes note added
	Use additional code note added
	Excludes note added
333.92	Excludes note added
● 333.94	Restless legs syndrome [RLS]
333.99	Excludes term deleted
336.9	Excludes term revised
337.1	Code first note revised
338	Section title added
● 338	Pain, not elsewhere classified
	Use additional code note added
	Excludes note added
● 338.0	Central pain syndrome
	Includes note added
● 338.1	Acute pain
● 338.11	Acute pain due to trauma
● 338.12	Acute post-thoracotomy pain
	Includes note added
● 338.18	Other acute postoperative pain
	Includes note added
● 338.19	Other acute pain
	Excludes note added
● 338.2	Chronic pain
	Excludes note added
● 338.21	Chronic pain due to trauma
● 338.22	Chronic post-thoracotomy pain
● 338.28	Other chronic postoperative pain
● 338.29	Other chronic pain
● 338.3	Neoplasm related pain (acute) (chronic)
	Includes note added

▶◀ Revised Text ● New Code ▲ Revised Code Title

● 338.4 Chronic pain syndrome
Includes note added
● 341.2 Acute (transverse) myelitis
Excludes note added
● 341.20 Acute (transverse) myelitis NOS
● 341.21 Acute (transverse) myelitis in conditions classified elsewhere
Code first note added
● 341.22 Idiopathic transverse myelitis
343 Excludes terms added
Excludes term revised
▲ 345 Epilepsy ▶and recurrent seizures◀
345.1 Excludes terms revised
▲ 345.4 ~~Partial epilepsy, with impairment of consciousness~~ ▶Localization-related (focal) (partial) epilepsy and epileptic syndromes with complex partial seizures◀
Includes terms added
▲ 345.40 ~~Partial epilepsy, with impairment of consciousness~~ ▶Localization-related (focal) (partial) epilepsy and epileptic syndromes with complex partial seizures◀, without mention of intractable epilepsy
▲ 345.41 ~~Partial epilepsy, with impairment of consciousness~~ ▶Localization-related (focal) (partial) epilepsy and epileptic syndromes with complex partial seizures◀, with intractable epilepsy
▲ 345.5 ~~Partial epilepsy, without impairment of consciousness~~ ▶Localization-related (focal) (partial) epilepsy and epileptic syndromes with simple partial seizures
Includes terms added
▲ 345.50 ~~Partial epilepsy, without impairment of consciousness~~ ▶Localization-related (focal) (partial) epilepsy and epileptic syndromes with simple partial seizures, without mention of intractable epilepsy
▲ 345.51 ~~Partial epilepsy, without impairment of consciousness~~ ▶Localization-related (focal) (partial) epilepsy and epileptic syndromes with simple partial seizures◀, with intractable epilepsy
▲ 345.8 Other forms of epilepsy ▶and recurrent seizures◀,
▲ 345.80 Other forms of epilepsy ▶and recurrent seizures◀, without mention of intractable epilepsy
▲ 345.81 Other forms of epilepsy ▶and recurrent seizures◀, with intractable epilepsy
345.9 Includes terms added
Excludes terms added
Excludes term revised
348.31 Excludes note added
349.82 Includes note added
357.4 Code first note added
Code first note revised
359.6 Code first note revised
360.0 Excludes note added
360.1 Excludes note added
● 377.43 Optic nerve hypoplasia
● 379.6 Inflammation (infection) of postprocedural bleb
Includes note added
● 379.60 Inflammation (infection) of postprocedural bleb, unspecified
● 379.61 Inflammation (infection) of postprocedural bleb, stage 1
● 379.62 Inflammation (infection) of postprocedural bleb, stage 2
● 379.63 Inflammation (infection) of postprocedural bleb, stage 3
Includes note added
▲ 389.11 Sensory hearing loss, ▶bilateral◀
▲ 389.12 Neural hearing loss, ▶bilateral◀
▲ 389.14 Central hearing loss, ▶bilateral◀
● 389.15 Sensorineural hearing loss, unilateral
● 389.16 Sensorineural hearing loss, asymmetrical
▲ 389.18 Sensorineural hearing loss of combined types, ▶bilateral◀
▲ 403 Hypertensive ▶chronic◀ kidney disease
Use additional code note deleted
▲ 403.0 Hypertensive ▶chronic◀ kidney disease, malignant
▲ 403.00 Hypertensive ▶chronic◀ kidney disease, malignant, ~~without~~ ▶with◀ chronic kidney disease ▶stage I through stage IV, or unspecified◀
Use additional code note added
▲ 403.01 Hypertensive ▶chronic◀ kidney disease, malignant, with chronic kidney disease ▶stage V or end stage renal disease◀
Use additional code note added
▲ 403.10 Hypertensive ▶chronic◀ kidney disease, benign, ~~without~~ ▶with◀ chronic kidney disease ▶stage I through stage IV, or unspecified◀
Use additional code note added
▲ 403.11 Hypertensive ▶chronic◀ kidney disease, benign, with chronic kidney disease ▶stage V or end stage renal disease◀
Use additional code note added
▲ 403.90 Hypertensive▶chronic◀ kidney disease, unspecified, ~~without~~ ▶with◀ chronic kidney disease ▶stage I through stage IV, or unspecified◀
Use additional code note added
▲ 403.91 Hypertensive ▶chronic◀ kidney disease, unspecified, with chronic kidney disease ▶stage I through stage IV, or unspecified◀
Use additional code note added
▲ 404 Hypertensive heart and ▶chronic◀ kidney disease
Use additional code note deleted
▲ 404.0 Hypertensive heart and ▶chronic◀ kidney disease, malignant
▲ 404.00 Hypertensive heart and ▶chronic◀ kidney disease, malignant, without heart failure ~~or~~ ▶and with◀ chronic kidney disease ▶stage I through stage IV, or unspecified◀
Use additional code note added
▲ 404.01 Hypertensive heart and ▶chronic◀ kidney disease, malignant, with heart failure ▶and with chronic kidney disease stage I through stage IV, or unspecified◀
Use additional code note added
▲ 404.02 Hypertensive heart and ▶chronic◀ kidney disease, malignant,▶ without heart failure and◀ with chronic kidney disease ▶stage V or end stage renal disease◀
Use additional code note added
▲ 404.03 Hypertensive heart and ▶chronic◀ kidney disease, malignant, with heart failure ~~or~~ ▶and with◀ chronic kidney disease ▶stage V or end stage renal disease◀
Use additional code note added
▲ 404.1 Hypertensive heart and ▶chronic◀ kidney disease, benign
▲ 404.10 Hypertensive heart and ▶chronic◀ kidney disease, benign, without heart failure ~~or~~ ▶and with◀ chronic kidney disease ▶stage I through stage IV, or unspecified◀
Use additional code note added
▲ 404.11 Hypertensive heart and ▶chronic◀ kidney disease, benign, with heart failure ▶and with chronic kidney disease stage I through stage IV, or unspecified◀
Use additional code note added
▲ 404.12 Hypertensive heart and ▶chronic◀ kidney disease, benign,▶ without heart failure and◀ with chronic kidney disease ▶stage V or end stage renal disease◀
Use additional code note added
▲ 404.13 Hypertensive heart and ▶chronic◀ kidney disease, benign, with heart failure ~~or~~ ▶and with◀ chronic kidney disease ▶stage V or end stage renal disease◀
Use additional code note added
▲ 404.9 Hypertensive heart and ▶chronic◀ kidney disease, unspecified
▲ 404.90 Hypertensive heart and ▶chronic◀ kidney disease, unspecified, without heart failure ~~or~~ ▶and with◀ chronic kidney disease ▶stage I through stage IV, or unspecified◀
Use additional code note added
▲ 404.91 Hypertensive heart and ▶chronic◀ kidney disease, unspecified, with heart failure ▶and with chronic kidney disease stage I through stage IV, or unspecified◀
Use additional code note added
▲ 404.92 Hypertensive heart and ▶chronic◀ kidney disease, unspecified ,▶ without heart failure and◀ with chronic kidney disease ▶stage V or end stage renal disease◀
Use additional code note added
▲ 404.93 Hypertensive heart and ▶chronic◀ kidney disease, unspecified, with heart failure ~~or~~ ▶and with◀ chronic kidney disease ▶stage V or end stage renal disease◀
Use additional code note added
420.0 Code first note revised
425.7 Code first note revised
● 429.83 Takotsubo syndrome
Includes note added
440.24 Use additional code note added
445.81 Use additional code note revised
478.1 Includes note deleted
● 478.11 Nasal mucositis (ulcerative)
Use additional code note added
● 478.19 Other disease of nasal cavity and sinuses
Includes note added
496 Excludes term added
514 Excludes term added
517.8 Code first note revised
● 518.7 Transfusion related acute lung injury [TRALI]
519.1 Includes note deleted
● 519.11 Acute bronchospasm
Includes note added
Excludes note added
● 519.19 Other diseases of trachea and bronchus
Includes note added
520.6 Includes terms added
521.06 Includes note added
521.97 Includes note added
521.08 Includes note added
521.8 Includes note deleted
● 521.81 Cracked tooth
Excludes note added
● 521.89 Other specific diseases of hard tissues of teeth
Includes note added
● 523.00 Acute gingivitis, plaque induced
Includes note added
● 523.01 Acute gingivitis, non-plaque induced
523.1 Includes terms deleted
● 523.10 Chronic gingivitis, plaque induced
Includes note added
● 523.11 Chronic gingivitis, non-plaque induced
▲ 523.3 ▶Aggressive and◀ ~~A~~acute periodontitis
Excludes terms deleted
● 523.30 Aggressive periodontitis, unspecified
● 523.31 Aggressive periodontitis, localized
Includes note added
● 523.32 Aggressive periodontitis, generalized
● 523.33 Acute periodontitis
523.4 Excludes term deleted
● 523.40 Chronic periodontitis, unspecified
● 523.41 Chronic periodontitis, localized
● 523.42 Chronic periodontitis, generalized
524.07 Includes note added
524.2 Includes note added
▲ 524.21 ▶Malocclusion,◀ Angle's class I
▲ 524.22 ▶Malocclusion,◀, Angle's class II
▲ 524.23 ▶Malocclusion,◀ Angle's class III
524.24 Includes note added
524.25 Includes note added
524.26 Includes note added
524.27 Includes term added
524.28 Includes term added
524.29 Includes note added
524.33 Includes term added
524.34 Includes term added
▲ 524.35 Rotation of ▶tooth/◀teeth
524.36 Includes note added
524.37 Includes term added
524.54 Includes note added
524.55 Includes note added
524.56 Includes note added
● 525.6 Unsatisfactory restoration of tooth
Includes note added
Excludes note added
● 525.60 Unspecified unsatisfactory restoration of tooth
Includes note added
● 525.61 Open restoration margins
Includes note added
● 525.62 Unrepairable overhanging of dental restorative materials
Includes note added
● 525.63 Fractured dental restorative material without loss of material
Excludes note added
● 525.64 Fractured dental restorative material with loss of material
Excludes note added
● 525.65 Contour of existing restoration of tooth biologically incompatible with oral health
Includes note added

▶◀ Revised Text ● New Code ▲ Revised Code Title

● 525.66 Allergy to existing dental restorative material
Use additional code note added

● 525.67 Poor aesthetics of existing restoration
Includes note added

● 525.69 Other unsatisfactory restoration of existing tooth

● 526.6 Periradicular pathology associated with previous endodontic treatment

● 526.61 Perforation of root canal space

● 526.62 Endodontic overfill

● 526.63 Endodontic underfill

● 526.69 Other periradicular pathology associated with previous endodontic treatment

▲ 528.0 Stomatitis ▶and mucositis (ulcerative)◀
Includes note deleted
Excludes terms added

● 528.00 Stomatitis and mucositis, unspecified
Includes note added

● 528.01 Mucositis (ulcerative) due to antineoplastic therapy
Use additional code note added

● 528.02 Mucositis (ulcerative) due to other drugs
Use additional code note added

● 528.09 Other stomatitis and mucositis (ulcerative)

528.3 Excludes term revised

528.71 Includes note added

528.72 Includes note added

528.79 Includes term added

530-538 Section title revised

536.8 Includes term added

● 538 Gastrointestinal mucositis (ulcerative)
Use additional code note added
Excludes note added

567 Excludes terms revised

567.23 Excludes note added

573 Excludes term revised

580-589 Section title revised

581.81 Code first note revised

582.81 Code first note revised

583.81 Code first note revised

585 Excludes note deleted
Code first note added

585.5 Excludes note added

585.6 Includes note added

599.6 Excludes term deleted

599.69 Code first note added

600 Includes note added
Use additional code note deleted

▲ 600.00 Hypertrophy (benign) of prostate without urinary obstruction ▶and other lower urinary tract symptoms [LUTS]◀

▲ 600.01 Hypertrophy (benign) of prostate with urinary obstruction ▶and other lower urinary tract symptoms [LUTS]◀
Use additional code note added

▲ 600.20 Benign localized hyperplasia of prostate without urinary obstruction ▶and other lower urinary tract symptoms [LUTS]◀

▲ 600.21 Benign localized hyperplasia of prostate with urinary obstruction ▶and other lower urinary tract symptoms [LUTS]◀
Use additional code note added

▲ 600.90 Hyperplasia of prostate, unspecified, without urinary obstruction ▶and other lower urinary tract symptoms [LUTS]◀

▲ 600.91 Hyperplasia of prostate, unspecified, with urinary obstruction ▶and other lower urinary tract symptoms [LUTS]◀
Use additional code note added

608.2 Includes note deleted

● 608.20 Torsion of testis, unspecified

● 608.21 Extravaginal torsion of spermatic cord

● 608.22 Intravaginal torsion of spermatic cord

● 608.23 Torsion of appendix testis

● 608.24 Torsion of appendix epididymis

616.8 Includes note deleted

● 616.81 Mucositis (ulcerative) of cervix, vagina, and vulva
Use additional code note added

● 616.89 Other inflammatory disease of cervix, vagina and vulva

● 618.84 Cervical stump prolapse

629.2 Includes term added

629.20 Includes term added

629.21 Includes term added

629.22 Includes term added

629.23 Includes term added

● 629.29 Other female genital mutilation status
Includes note added

● 629.81 Habitual aborter without current pregnancy
Excludes note added

● 629.89 Other specified disorders of female genital organs

629.9 Includes note deleted

640-649 Section title revised
Instructional note revised [5th digit box]

641.3 Excludes note added

642.2 Includes terms revised

646.8 Excludes term deleted

648.4 Instructional note revised

● 649 Other conditions or status of the mother complicating pregnancy, childbirth, or puerperium

● 649.0 Tobacco use disorder complicating pregnancy, childbirth, or puerperium
Includes note added

● 649.00 Tobacco use disorder complicating pregnancy, childbirth, or the puerperium, unspecified as to episode of care or not applicable

● 649.01 Tobacco use disorder complicating pregnancy, childbirth, or the puerperium, delivered, with or without mention of antepartum condition

● 649.02 Tobacco use disorder complicating pregnancy, childbirth, or the puerperium, delivered, with mention of postpartum complication

● 649.03 Tobacco use disorder complicating pregnancy, childbirth, or the puerperium, antepartum condition or complication

● 649.04 Tobacco use disorder complicating pregnancy, childbirth, or the puerperium, postpartum condition or complication

● 649.1 Obesity complicating pregnancy, childbirth, or puerperium
Use additional code note added

● 649.10 Obesity complicating pregnancy, childbirth, or the puerperium, unspecified as to episode of care or not applicable

● 649.11 Obesity complicating pregnancy, childbirth, or the puerperium, delivered, with or without mention of antepartum condition

● 649.12 Obesity complicating pregnancy, childbirth, or the puerperium, delivered, with mention of postpartum complication

● 649.13 Obesity complicating pregnancy, childbirth, or the puerperium, antepartum condition or complication

● 649.14 Obesity complicating pregnancy, childbirth, or the puerperium, postpartum condition or complication

● 649.2 Bariatric surgery status complicating pregnancy, childbirth, or puerperium
Includes note added

● 649.20 Bariatric surgery status complicating pregnancy, childbirth, or the puerperium, unspecified as to episode of care or not applicable

● 649.21 Bariatric surgery status complicating pregnancy, childbirth, or the puerperium, delivered, with or without mention of antepartum condition

● 649.22 Bariatric surgery status complicating pregnancy, childbirth, or the puerperium, delivered, with mention of postpartum complication

● 649.23 Bariatric surgery status complicating pregnancy, childbirth, or the puerperium, antepartum condition or complication

● 649.24 Bariatric surgery status complicating pregnancy, childbirth, or the puerperium, postpartum condition or complication

● 649.3 Coagulation defects complicating pregnancy, childbirth, or puerperium
Use additional code note added
Excludes note added

● 649.30 Coagulation defects complicating pregnancy, childbirth, or the puerperium, unspecified as to episode of care or not applicable

● 649.31 Coagulation defects complicating pregnancy, childbirth, or the puerperium, delivered, with or without mention of antepartum condition

● 649.32 Coagulation defects complicating pregnancy, childbirth, or the puerperium, delivered, with mention of postpartum complication

● 649.33 Coagulation defects complicating pregnancy, childbirth, or the puerperium, antepartum condition or complication

● 649.34 Coagulation defects complicating pregnancy, childbirth, or the puerperium, postpartum condition or complication

● 649.4 Epilepsy complicating pregnancy, childbirth, or puerperium
Use additional code note added
Excludes note added

● 649.40 Epilepsy complicating pregnancy, childbirth, or the puerperium, unspecified as to episode of care or not applicable

● 649.41 Epilepsy complicating pregnancy, childbirth, or the puerperium, delivered, with or without mention of antepartum condition

● 649.42 Epilepsy complicating pregnancy, childbirth, or the puerperium, delivered, with mention of postpartum complication

● 649.43 Epilepsy complicating pregnancy, childbirth, or the puerperium, antepartum condition or complication

● 649.44 Epilepsy complicating pregnancy, childbirth, or the puerperium, postpartum condition or complication

● 649.5 Spotting complicating pregnancy, childbirth, or puerperium
Excludes note added

● 649.50 Spotting complicating pregnancy, unspecified as to episode of care or not applicable

● 649.51 Spotting complicating pregnancy, delivered, with or without mention of antepartum condition

● 649.53 Spotting complicating pregnancy, antepartum condition or complication

● 649.6 Uterine size date discrepancy complicating pregnancy, childbirth, or puerperium

● 649.60 Uterine size date discrepancy, unspecified as to episode of care or not applicable

● 649.61 Uterine size date discrepancy, delivered, with or without mention of antepartum condition

● 649.62 Uterine size date discrepancy, delivered, with mention of postpartum complication

● 649.63 Uterine size date discrepancy, antepartum condition or complication

● 649.64 Uterine size date discrepancy, postpartum condition or complication

666.1 Includes term revised

692.3 Excludes term revised

693 Excludes term revised

713.7 Code first note revised

● 729.7 Nontraumatic compartment syndrome
Excludes note added

● 729.71 Nontraumatic compartment syndrome of upper extremity
Includes note added

● 729.72 Nontraumatic compartment syndrome of lower extremity
Includes note added

● 729.73 Nontraumatic compartment syndrome of abdomen

● 729.79 Nontraumatic compartment syndrome of other sites

730.0 Use additional code note added

730.1 Use additional code note added

730.2 Use additional code note added

● 731.3 Major osseous defects
Code first note added

733.0 Use additional code note added

733.4 Use additional code note added

743.8 Excludes term added

768 Excludes note added

▲ 768.3 Fetal distress first noted during labor ▶and delivery,◀ in liveborn infant
Includes term revised

768.5 Excludes note added

768.6 Excludes note added

● 768.7 Hypoxic-ischemic encephalopathy [HIE]

768.9 Excludes term deleted

770.8 Excludes note added

● 770.87 Respiratory arrest of newborn

● 770.88 Hypoxemia of newborn
Includes note added

▶◀ Revised Text ● New Code ▲ Revised Code Title

▲ 775.8 Other transitory neonatal endocrine and metabolic disturbances
Excludes term deleted
● 775.81 Other acidosis of newborn
Includes note added
● 775.89 Other neonatal endocrine and metabolic disturbances
Includes note added
776.7 Excludes term revised
779.2 Includes term added
Excludes note added
● 779.85 Cardiac arrest of newborn
▲ 780.31 Febrile convulsions ▶(simple), unspecified◀
Includes term revised
● 780.32 Complex febrile convulsions
Includes note added
Excludes note added
780.39 Excludes term added
780.58 Excludes term revised
780.6 Code first note added
▲ 780.95 Excessive crying ▶of child, adolescent, or adult◀
● 780.96 Generalized pain
Includes note added
● 780.97 Altered mental status
Includes note added
Excludes note added
780.99 Excludes term deleted
783.2 Use additional code note revised
784.3 Excludes term added
784.9 Includes note deleted
● 784.91 Postnasal drip
● 784.99 Other symptoms involving head and neck
Includes note added
785.52 Code first note deleted
788 Excludes term added
788.2 Excludes note deleted
Code first note added
788.3 Code first note added
788.4 Code first note added
788.6 Code first note added
● 788.64 Urinary hesitancy
● 788.65 Straining on urination
790 Excludes term revised
790.29 Includes term added
790.6 Includes term added
Excludes terms added
793.81 Excludes note added
793.89 Includes note added
793.9 Includes note deleted
● 793.91 Image test inconclusive due to excess body fat
Use additional code note added
● 793.99 Other nonspecific abnormal findings on radiological and other examinations of body structure
Includes note added
795.04 Includes note deleted
● 795.06 Papanicolaou smear of cervix with cytologic evidence of malignancy
795.7 Excludes terms added
● 795.8 Abnormal tumor markers
Includes note added
Excludes note added
● 795.81 Elevated carcinoembryonic antigen [CEA]
● 795.82 Elevated cancer antigen 125 [CA 125]
● 795.89 Other abnormal tumor markers
799.4 Code first note added
Excludes note deleted
▲ 873.63 Tooth (broken) ▶(fractured) (due to trauma) ◀
[Category 873.6 Internal structures of mouth, without mention of complications]
Excludes note added
▲ 873.73 Tooth (broken) ▶(fractured) (due to trauma) ◀
[Category 873.7 Internal structures of mouth, complicated]
Excludes note added
● 958.9 Traumatic compartment syndrome
Excludes note added
● 958.90 Compartment syndrome, unspecified
● 958.91 Traumatic compartment syndrome of upper extremity
Includes note added
● 958.92 Traumatic compartment syndrome of lower extremity
Includes note added
● 958.93 Traumatic compartment syndrome of abdomen
● 958.99 Traumatic compartment syndrome of other sites
960-979 Section Excludes note revised
▲ 995.2 ▶Other and◀ uUnspecified adverse effect of drug, medicinal and biological substance
● 995.20 Unspecified adverse effect of unspecified drug, medicinal and biological substance
● 995.21 Arthus phenomenon
Includes note added
● 995.22 Unspecified adverse effect of anesthesia
● 995.23 Unspecified adverse effect of insulin
● 995.27 Other drug allergy
Includes note added
● 995.29 Unspecified adverse effect of other drug, medicinal and biological substance
995.3 Excludes term added
Excludes term revised
995.4 Excludes term revised
995.9 Code first note deleted
▲ 995.91 ~~Systemic inflammatory response syndrome, unspecified~~ ▶Sepsis◀
Includes term added
Includes term deleted
Code first note added
Excludes note added
▲ 995.92 ~~Systemic inflammatory response syndrome due to infectious process without organ dysfunction~~ ▶Severe sepsis◀
Includes terms added
Includes term deleted
Code first note added
Use additional code note revised
Use additional code note added
▲ 995.93 Systemic inflammatory response syndrome due to noninfectious process without ▶acute◀ organ dysfunction
Code first note added
Excludes note added
▲ 995.94 Systemic inflammatory response syndrome due to noninfectious process with ▶acute◀ organ dysfunction
Code first note added
Use additional code note added
Use additional code note deleted
Excludes note added
996.45 Use additional code note added
996.7 Use additional code note added
997.3 Excludes terms added
998.5 Excludes terms added
999 Excludes terms revised
999.8 Excludes terms added
V01-V86 Section title revised
V07.39 Excludes terms revised
● V18.51 Colonic polyps
Excludes note added
● V18.59 Other digestive disorders
V20.2 Includes term added
V26.21 Excludes term revised
V26.3 Excludes term added
▲ V26.31 Testing ▶of female◀ for genetic disease carrier status
▲ V26.32 Other genetic testing ▶of female◀
Use additional code note added
● V26.34 Testing of male for genetic disease carrier status
● V26.35 Encounter for testing of male partner of habitual aborter
● V26.39 Other genetic testing of male
▲ V28 ▶Encounter for◀ ~~A~~antenatal screening ▶of mother◀
V45.3 Excludes note added
V45.77 Excludes term revised
● V45.86 Bariatric surgery status
Includes note added
Excludes note added
V54.1 Excludes note added
▲ V58.3 Attention to ~~surgical~~ dressings and sutures
Includes terms deleted
Includes term added
Excludes note added
● V58.30 Encounter for change or removal of nonsurgical wound dressing
Includes note added
● V58.31 Encounter for change or removal of surgical wound dressing
● V58.32 Encounter for removal of sutures
V58.41 Excludes term added
V58.49 Includes note added
V65.3 Use additional code note added
V65.4 Excludes terms revised
V70-V82 Section title revised
● V72.11 Encounter for hearing examination following failed hearing screening
● V72.19 Other examination of ears and hearing
● V82.7 Genetic screening
Excludes note added
● V82.71 Screening for genetic disease carrier status
● V82.79 Other genetic screening
V83-V84 Section title added
V85 Section title added
▲ V85 Body Mass Index ▶[BMI]◀
● V85.5 Body Mass Index, pediatric
Instructional note added
● V85.51 Body Mass Index, pediatric, less than 5th percentile for age
● V85.52 Body Mass Index, pediatric, 5th percentile to less than 85th percentile for age
● V85.53 Body Mass Index, pediatric, 85th percentile to less than 95th percentile for age
● V85.54 Body Mass Index, pediatric, greater than or equal to 95th percentile for age
V86 Section title added
● V86 Estrogen receptor status
Code first note added
● V86.0 Estrogen receptor positive status [ER+]
● V86.1 Estrogen receptor negative status [ER-]

PROCEDURE TABULAR (VOLUME 3)

● 00.44 Procedure on vessel bifurcation
Instructional note added
00.50 Instructional note added
Includes terms added
00.51 Instructional note added
Includes terms added
00.53 Instructional note added
00.54 Instructional note added
00.55 Code also note added
● 00.56 Insertion or replacement of implantable pressure sensor (lead) for intracardiac hemodynamic monitoring
Code also note added
Excludes note added
● 00.57 Implantation or replacement of subcutaneous device for intracardiac hemodynamic monitoring
Includes terms added
Code also note added
00.61 Code also note added
00.62 Code also note added
00.63 Code also note added
00.64 Code also note added
00.65 Code also note added
00.66 Code also note added
00.70 Code also note revised
00.71 Code also note revised
00.72 Code also note revised
00.73 Code also note revised
● 00.77 Hip replacement bearing surfaces, ceramic-on-polyethylene
▲ 00.8 Other knee ▶and hip◀ procedures
● 00.85 Resurfacing hip, total, acetabulum and femoral head
Includes note added
● 00.86 Resurfacing hip, partial, femoral head
Includes note added
Excludes note added
● 00.87 Resurfacing hip, partial, acetabulum
Includes note added
Excludes note added
▲ 01.26 Insertion of ▶catheter(s)◀ into cranial cavity ▶or tissue◀
Excludes note added
▲ 01.27 Removal of ▶catheter(s)◀ from cranial cavity ▶or tissue◀
● 01.28 Placement of intracranial catheter(s) via burr hole(s)
Includes note added
Code also note added
Excludes note added
02.93 Code also note revised
03.93 Code also note revised
04.92 Code also note revised
13.7 Excludes note added
● 13.90 Operations on lens, not elsewhere classified

▶◀ Revised Text ● New Code ▲ Revised Code Title

● 13.91 Implantation of intraocular telescope
Includes note added
Excludes note added
14.74 Includes note added
● 32.23 Open ablation of lung lesion or tissue
● 32.24 Percutaneous ablation of lung lesion or tissue
● 32.25 Thorascopic ablation of lung lesion or tissue
● 32.26 Other and unspecified ablation of lung lesion or tissue
32.28 Excludes terms added
32.29 Excludes terms added
● 33.7 Endoscopic insertion, replacement and removal of therapeutic device or substance in bronchus or lung
Includes note added
Excludes note added
● 33.71 Endoscopic insertion or replacement of bronchial valve(s)
Includes note added
● 33.78 Endoscopic removal of bronchial device(s) or substances
● 33.79 Endoscopic insertion of other bronchial device(s) or substances
Includes note added
34.92 Includes term added
▲ 35.53 Repair of ventricular septal defect with prosthesis, ▶open technique◀
● 35.55 Repair of ventricular septal defect with prosthesis, closed technique
36.03 Code also note added
36.06 Code also note added
36.07 Code also note added
36.09 Code also note added
36.32 Includes terms deleted
● 36.33 Endoscopic transmyocardial revascularization
Includes note added
● 36.34 Percutaneous transmyocardial revascularization
Includes note added
● 37.20 Noninvasive programmed electrical stimulation [NIPS]
Excludes note added
▲ 37.26 ~~Cardiac~~ ▶Catheter based invasive◀ electrophysiologic ~~stimulation and recording studies~~ ▶testing◀
Includes terms deleted
Excludes terms added
37.66 Instructional note added
▲ 37.7 Insertion, revision, replacement, and removal of ~~pacemaker~~ leads; insertion of temporary pacemaker system,; or revision of cardiac device pocket

37.75 Includes term revised
37.79 Includes terms added
Excludes note added
37.8 Instructional note added
● 39.74 Endovascular removal of obstruction from head and neck vessel(s)
Instructional note added
Excludes term deleted
37.96 Instructional note added
37.97 Excludes note added
37.98 Instructional note added
37.99 Includes terms deleted
Excludes terms added
38 Excludes term revised
38.0 Excludes term added
38.1 Code also note added
38.4 Includes term added
39.50 Code also note added
39.72 Excludes note added
● 39.74 Endovascular removal of obstruction from head and neck vessel(s)
Includes note added
Code also note added
Excludes note added
39.90 Code also note added
● 50.23 Open ablation of liver lesion or tissue
● 50.24 Percutaneous ablation of liver lesion or tissue
● 50.25 Laparoscopic ablation of liver lesion or tissue
● 50.26 Other and unspecified ablation of liver lesion or tissue
50.29 Excludes terms added
● 55.32 Open ablation of renal lesion or tissue
● 55.33 Percutaneous ablation of renal lesion or tissue
● 55.34 Laparoscopic ablation of renal lesion or tissue
● 55.35 Other and unspecified ablation of renal lesion or tissue
55.39 Excludes terms added
▲ 68.39 Other ▶and unspecified◀ subtotal abdominal hysterectomy
68.4 Includes note deleted
Code also note revised
Excludes note added
● 68.41 Laparoscopic total abdominal hysterectomy
Includes note added

● 68.49 Other and unspecified total abdominal hysterectomy
Includes note added
▲ 68.59 Other ▶and unspecified◀ vaginal hysterectomy
Excludes term revised
68.6 Code also note revised
Includes notes deleted
● 68.61 Laparoscopic radical abdominal hysterectomy
Includes note added
● 68.69 Other and unspecified radical abdominal hysterectomy
Includes note added
Excludes note added
68.7 Code also note revised
Excludes note revised
Includes note deleted
● 68.71 Laparoscopic radical vaginal hysterectomy [LRVH]
● 68.79 Other and unspecified radical vaginal hysterectomy
Includes note added
68.9 Excludes terms revised
80.51 Excludes term added
81.51 Code also note revised
81.52 Code also note revised
81.53 Code also note revised
84.59 Includes note added
84.73 Includes term added
86.28 Includes term added
89.45 Excludes terms revised
89.49 Excludes terms revised
89.6 Excludes terms added
93.59 Includes term added
96.05 Excludes note added
99.10 Includes terms added
99.28 Includes term added

▶◀ Revised Text ● New Code ▲ Revised Code Title

Coding Guidelines

ICD-9-CM OFFICIAL GUIDELINES FOR CODING AND REPORTING

Effective December 1, 2005
Narrative changes appear in bold text
The guidelines have been updated to include the V Code Table.

The Centers for Medicare and Medicaid Services (CMS) and the National Center for Health Statistics (NCHS), two departments within the U.S. Federal Government's Department of Health and Human Services (DHHS) provide the following guidelines for coding and reporting using the International Classification of Diseases, 9th Revision, Clinical Modification (ICD-9-CM). These guidelines should be used as a companion document to the official version of the ICD-9-CM as published on CD-ROM by the U.S. Government Printing Office (GPO).

These guidelines have been approved by the four organizations that make up the Cooperating Parties for the ICD-9-CM: the American Hospital Association (AHA), the American Health Information Management Association (AHIMA), CMS, and NCHS. These guidelines are included in the official government version of the ICD-9-CM and also appear in *Coding Clinic for ICD-9-CM*, published by the AHA.

These guidelines are a set of rules that have been developed to accompany and complement the official conventions and instructions provided within the ICD-9-CM itself. These guidelines are based on the coding and sequencing instructions in Volumes 1, 2, and 3 of ICD-9-CM, but provide additional instruction. Adherence to these guidelines when assigning ICD-9-CM diagnosis and procedure codes is required under the Health Insurance Portability and Accountability Act (HIPAA). The diagnosis codes (Volumes 1-2) have been adopted under HIPAA for all health care settings. Volume 3 procedure codes have been adopted for inpatient procedures reported by hospitals. A joint effort between the health care provider and the coder is essential to achieve complete and accurate documentation, code assignment, and reporting of diagnoses and procedures. These guidelines have been developed to assist both the health care provider and the coder in identifying those diagnoses and procedures that are to be reported. The importance of consistent, complete documentation in the medical record cannot be overemphasized. Without such documentation accurate coding cannot be achieved. The entire record should be reviewed to determine the specific reason for the encounter and the conditions treated.

The term "encounter" is used for all settings, including hospital admissions. In the context of these guidelines, the term "provider" is used throughout the guidelines to mean physician or any qualified health care practitioner who is legally accountable for establishing the patient's diagnosis. Only this set of guidelines, approved by the cooperating parties, is official.

The guidelines are organized into sections. Section I includes the structure and conventions of the classification and general guidelines that apply to the entire classification, and chapter-specific guidelines that correspond to the chapters as they are arranged in the classification. Section II includes guidelines for selection of principal diagnosis for non-outpatient settings. Section III includes guidelines for reporting additional diagnoses in non-outpatient settings. Section IV is for outpatient coding and reporting.

Section I. Conventions, general coding guidelines and chapter-specific guidelines

A. Conventions for the ICD-9-CM
- 1. Format
- 2. Abbreviations
  - a. Index abbreviations
  - b. Tabular abbreviations
- 3. Punctuation
- 4. Includes and excludes notes and inclusion terms
- 5. Other and Unspecified codes
  - a. "Other" codes
  - b. "Unspecified" codes
- 6. Etiology/manifestation convention ("code first," "use additional code," and "in diseases classified elsewhere" notes)
- 7. "And"
- 8. "With"
- 9. "See" and "see also"

B. General coding guidelines
- 1. Use of both Alphabetic Index and Tabular List
- 2. Locate each term in the Alphabetic Index
- 3. Level of detail in coding
- 4. Code or codes from 001.0 through V86.1
- 5. Selection of codes 001.0 through 999.9
- 6. Signs and symptoms
- 7. Conditions that are an integral part of a disease process
- 8. Conditions that are not an integral part of a disease process
- 9. Multiple coding for a single condition
- 10. Acute and chronic conditions
- 11. Combination code
- 12. Late effects
- 13. Impending or threatened condition

C. Chapter-specific coding guidelines
- 1. Chapter 1: Infectious and Parasitic Diseases (001–139)
  - a. Human immunodeficiency virus (HIV) infections
  - b. Septicemia, systemic inflammatory response syndrome . . . (SIRS), sepsis, severe sepsis, and septic shock
- 2. Chapter 2: Neoplasms (140–239)
  - a. Treatment directed at the malignancy
  - b. Treatment of secondary site
  - c. Coding and sequencing of complications
  - d. Primary malignancy previously excised
  - e. Admissions/encounters involving chemotherapy and radiation therapy
  - f. Admission/encounter to determine extent of malignancy
  - g. Symptoms, signs, and ill-defined conditions listed in chapter 16
  - h. Encounter for prophylactic organ removal
- 3. Chapter 3: Endocrine, Nutritional, and Metabolic Diseases and Immunity Disorders (240–279)
  - a. Diabetes mellitus
- 4. Chapter 4: Diseases of Blood and Blood-Forming Organs (280–289)
  - **a. Anemia of chronic disease**
- 5. Chapter 5: Mental Disorders (290–319)
  Reserved for future guideline expansion
- 6. Chapter 6: Diseases of Nervous System and Sense Organs (320–389)
  Reserved for future guideline expansion
- 7. Chapter 7: Diseases of Circulatory System (390–459)
  - a. Hypertension
  - b. Cerebral infarction/stroke/cerebrovascular accident (CVA)
  - c. Postoperative cerebrovascular accident
  - d. Late effects of cerebrovascular disease
  - **e. Acute myocardial infarction (AMI)**
- 8. Chapter 8: Diseases of Respiratory System (460–519)
  - a. Chronic obstructive pulmonary disease [COPD] and asthma
  - b. Chronic obstructive pulmonary disease [COPD] and bronchitis
- 9. Chapter 9: Diseases of Digestive System (520–579)
  Reserved for future guideline expansion
- 10. Chapter 10: Diseases of Genitourinary System (580–629)
  - **a. Chronic kidney disease**
- 11. Chapter 11: Complications of Pregnancy, Childbirth, and the Puerperium (630–677)
  - a. General rules for obstetric cases
  - b. Selection of OB principal or first-listed diagnosis
  - c. Fetal conditions affecting the management of the mother
  - d. HIV infection in pregnancy, childbirth and the puerperium
  - e. Current conditions complicating pregnancy
  - f. Diabetes mellitus in pregnancy
  - g. Gestational diabetes
  - h. Normal delivery, code 650
  - i. The postpartum and peripartum eriods
  - j. Code 677 Late effect of complication of pregnancy
  - k. Abortions
- 12. Chapter 12: Diseases Skin and Subcutaneous Tissue (680–709)
  Reserved for future guideline expansion
- 13. Chapter 13: Diseases of Musculoskeletal and Connective Tissue (710–739)
  Reserved for future guideline expansion

Section I. Conventions, general coding guidelines and chapter-specific guidelines

The conventions, general guidelines, and chapter-specific guidelines are applicable to all health care settings unless otherwise indicated.

A. Conventions for the ICD-9-CM

The conventions for the ICD-9-CM are the general rules for use of the classification independent of the guidelines. These conventions are incorporated within the index and tabular of the ICD-9-CM as instructional notes. The conventions are as follows:

1. Format:

The ICD-9-CM uses an indented format for ease in reference

2. Abbreviations

a. Index abbreviations

NEC "Not elsewhere classifiable"—This abbreviation in the index represents "other specified." When a specific code is not available for a condition, the index directs the coder to the "other specified" code in the tabular.

b. Tabular abbreviations

NEC "Not elsewhere classifiable"—This abbreviation in the tabular represents "other specified." When a specific code is not available for a condition, the tabular includes an NEC entry under a code to identify the code as the "other specified" code (See section I.A.5.a.,"Other" codes).

NOS "Not otherwise specified"—This abbreviation is the equivalent of unspecified. (See section I.A.5.b., "Unspecified" codes)

3. Punctuation

[ ] Brackets are used in the Tabular List to enclose synonyms, alternative wording, or explanatory phrases. Brackets are used in the index to identify manifestation codes. (See section I.A.6., Etiology/manifestations)

( ) Parentheses are used in both the index and tabular to enclose supplementary words that may be present or absent in the statement of a disease or procedure without affecting the code number to which it is assigned. The terms within the parentheses are referred to as nonessential modifiers.

: Colons are used in the Tabular List after an incomplete term needs one or more of the modifiers following the colon to make it assignable to a given category.

4. Includes and excludes notes and inclusion terms

Includes: This note appears immediately under a three-digit code title to further define, or give examples of, the content of the category.

Excludes: An excludes note under a code indicates that the terms excluded from the code are to be coded elsewhere. In some cases the codes for the excluded terms should not be used in conjunction with the code from which they are excluded. An example of this is a congenital condition excluded from an acquired form of the same condition. The congenital and acquired codes should not be used together. In other cases, the excluded terms may be used together with an excluded code. An example of this is when fractures of different bones are coded to different codes. Both codes may be used together if both types of fractures are present.

Inclusion terms: List of terms included under certain four- and five-digit codes. These terms are the conditions for which that code number is to be used. The terms may be synonyms of the code title, or, in the case of "other specified" codes, the terms are a list of the various conditions assigned to that code. The inclusion terms are not necessarily exhaustive. Additional terms found only in the index may also be assigned to a code.

5. Other and unspecified codes

a. "Other" codes—Codes titled "other" or "other specified" (usually a code with a fourth digit of 8 or fifth digit of 9 for diagnosis codes) are for use when the information in the medical record provides detail for which a specific code does not exist. Index entries with NEC in the line designate "other" codes in the tabular. These index entries represent specific disease entities for which no specific code exists so the term is included within an "other" code.

b. **"Unspecified" codes**—Codes (usually a code with a fourth digit of 9 or fifth of 0 for diagnosis codes) titled "unspecified" are for use when the information in the medical record is insufficient to assign a more specific code.

6. **Etiology/manifestation convention ("code first," "use additional code," and "in diseases classified elsewhere" notes)**—Certain conditions have both an underlying etiology and multiple body system manifestations due to the underlying etiology. For such conditions, the ICD-9-CM has a coding convention that requires the underlying condition to be sequenced first followed by the manifestation. Wherever such a combination exists, there is a "use additional code" note at the etiology code, and a "code first" note at the manifestation code. These instructional notes indicate the proper sequencing order of the codes, etiology followed by manifestation.

   In most cases the manifestation codes will have in the code title, "in diseases classified elsewhere." Codes with this title are a component of the etiology/manifestation convention. The code title indicates that it is a manifestation code. "In diseases classified elsewhere," codes are never permitted to be used as first listed or principal diagnosis codes. They must be used in conjunction with an underlying condition code, and they must be listed following the underlying condition.

   There are manifestation codes that do not have "in diseases classified elsewhere" in the title. For such codes a "use additional code" note will still be present and the rules for sequencing apply.

   In addition to the notes in the tabular, these conditions also have a specific index entry structure. In the index both conditions are listed together with the etiology code first followed by the manifestation codes in brackets. The code in brackets is always to be sequenced second.

   The most commonly used etiology/manifestation combinations are the codes for diabetes mellitus, category 250. For each code under category 250 there is a use additional code note for the manifestation that is specific for that particular diabetic manifestation. Should a patient have more than one manifestation of diabetes, more than one code from category 250 may be used with as many manifestation codes as are needed to fully describe the patient's complete diabetic condition. The category 250 diabetes codes should be sequenced first, followed by the manifestation codes.

   "Code first" and "use additional code" notes are also used as sequencing rules in the classification for certain codes that are not part of an etiology/manifestation combination. See section I.B.9., "Multiple coding for a single condition."

7. **"And"**
   The word "and" should be interpreted to mean either "and" or "or" when it appears in a title.

8. **"With"**
   The word "with" in the Alphabetic Index is sequenced immediately following the main term, not in alphabetical order.

9. **"See" and "see also"**
   The "see" instruction following a main term in the index indicates that another term should be referenced. It is necessary to go to the main term referenced with the "see" note to locate the correct code.

   A "see also" instruction following a main term in the index instructs that there is another main term that may also be referenced that may provide additional index entries that may be useful. It is not necessary to follow the "see also" note when the original main term provides the necessary code.

B. General coding guidelines

1. **Use of both Alphabetic Index and Tabular List**—Use both the Alphabetic Index and the Tabular List when locating and assigning a code. Reliance on only the Alphabetic Index or the Tabular List leads to errors in code assignments and less specificity in code selection.

2. **Locate each term in the alphabetic index**—Locate each term in the Alphabetic Index and verify the code selected in the Tabular List. Read and be guided by instructional notations that appear in both the Alphabetic Index and the Tabular List.

3. **Level of detail in coding**—Diagnosis and procedure codes are to be used at their highest number of digits available.

   ICD-9-CM diagnosis codes are composed of codes with either three, four, or five digits. Codes with three digits are included in ICD-9-CM as the heading of a category of codes that may be further subdivided by the use of four and/or fifth digits, which provide greater detail.

   A three-digit code is to be used only if it is not further subdivided. Where fourth-digit subcategories and/or fifth-digit subclassifications are provided, they must be assigned. A code is invalid if it has not been coded to the full number of digits required for that code. For example, acute myocardial infarction, code 410, has fourth digits that describe the location of the infarction (e.g., 410.2 Of inferolateral wall), and fifth digits that identify the episode of care. It would be incorrect to report a code in category 410 without a fourth and fifth digit.

   ICD-9-CM Volume 3 procedure codes are composed of codes with either three or four digits. Codes with two digits are included in ICD-9-CM as the heading of a category of codes that may be further subdivided by the use of third and/or fourth digits, which provide greater detail.

4. **Code or codes from 001.0 through V86.1**—The appropriate code or codes from 001.0 through V86.1 must be used to identify diagnoses, symptoms, conditions, problems, complaints, or other reason(s) for the encounter/visit.

5. **Selection of codes 001.0 through 999.9**—The selection of codes 001.0 through 999.9 will frequently be used to describe the reason for the admission/encounter. These codes are from the section of ICD-9-CM for the classification of diseases and injuries (e.g., infectious and parasitic diseases; neoplasms; symptoms, signs, and ill-defined conditions, etc.).

6. **Signs and symptoms**—Codes that describe symptoms and signs, as opposed to diagnoses, are acceptable for reporting purposes when a related definitive diagnosis has not been established (confirmed) by the provider. Chapter 16 of ICD-9-CM, "Symptoms, Signs, and Ill-defined Conditions" (codes 780.0-799.9) contain many, but not all, codes for symptoms.

7. **Conditions that are an integral part of a disease process**—Signs and symptoms that are integral to the disease process should not be assigned as additional codes.

8. **Conditions that are not an integral part of a disease process**—Additional signs and symptoms that may not be associated routinely with a disease process should be coded when present.

9. **Multiple coding for a single condition**—In addition to the etiology/manifestation convention that requires two codes to fully describe a single condition that affects multiple body systems, there are other single conditions that also require more than one code. "Use additional code" notes are found in the tabular at codes that are not part of an etiology/manifestation pair where a secondary code is useful to fully describe a condition. The sequencing rule is the same as the etiology/manifestation pair where a secondary code is useful to fully describe a condition. The sequencing rule is the same; "use additional code" indicates that a secondary code should be added.

   For example, for infections that are not included in chapter 1, a secondary code from category 041 Bacterial infection in conditions classified elsewhere and of unspecified site, may be required to identify the bacterial organism causing the infection. A "use additional code" note will normally be found at the infectious disease code, indicating a need for the organism code to be added as a secondary code.

   "Code first" notes are also under certain codes that are not specifically manifestation codes but may be due to an underlying cause. When a "code first" note is present and an underlying condition is present, the underlying condition should be sequenced first.

   "Code, if applicable, any causal condition first" notes indicate that this code may be assigned as a principal diagnosis when the causal condition is unknown or not applicable. If a causal condition is known, then the code for that condition should be sequenced as the principal or first-listed diagnosis.

   Multiple codes may be needed for late effects, complication codes, and obstetric codes to more fully describe a condition. See the specific guidelines for these conditions for further instruction.

10. **Acute and chronic conditions**—If the same condition is described as both acute (subacute) and chronic, and separate subentries exist in the Alphabetic Index at the same indentation level, code both and sequence the acute (subacute) code first.

11. **Combination code**—A combination code is a single code used to classify:
    - Two diagnoses
    - A diagnosis with an associated secondary process (manifestation)
    - A diagnosis with an associated complication

    Combination codes are identified by referring to subterm entries in the Alphabetic Index and by reading the inclusion and exclusion notes in the Tabular List.

    Assign only the combination code when that code fully identifies the diagnostic conditions involved or when the Alphabetic Index so directs. Multiple coding should not be used when the classification provides a combination code that clearly identifies all of the elements documented in the diagnosis. When the combination code lacks necessary specificity in describing the manifestation or complication, an additional code should be used as a secondary code.

12. **Late effects**—A late effect is the residual effect (condition produced) after the acute phase of an illness or injury has terminated. There is no time limit on when a late effect code can be used. The residual may be apparent early, such as in cerebrovascular accident cases, or it may occur months or years later, such as that due to a previous injury. Coding of late effects generally requires two codes sequenced in the following order: The condition or nature of the late effect is sequenced first... The late effect code is sequenced second.

    An exception to the above guidelines are those instances where the code for late effect is followed by a manifestation code identified in the Tabular List and title, or the late effect code has been expanded (at the fourth- and fifth-digit levels) to include the manifestation(s). The code for the acute phase of an illness or injury that led to the late effect is never used with a code for the late effect.

13. **Impending or threatened condition**—Code any condition described at the time of discharge as "impending" or "threatened" as follows:

    If it did occur, code as confirmed diagnosis. If it did not occur, reference the Alphabetic Index to determine if the condition has a subentry term for "impending" or "threatened" and also reference main term entries for "Impending" and for "Threatened." If the subterms are listed, assign the given code. If the subterms are not listed, code the existing underlying condition(s) and not the condition described as impending or threatened.

C. Chapter-specific coding guidelines

In addition to general coding guidelines, there are guidelines for specific diagnoses and/or conditions in the classification. Unless otherwise indicated, these guidelines apply to all health care settings. Please refer to section II for guidelines on the selection of principal diagnosis.

1. Chapter 1: Infectious and Parasitic Diseases (001-139)

a. Human immunodeficiency virus (HIV) infections

1) Code only confirmed cases—Code only confirmed cases of HIV infection/illness. This is an exception to the hospital inpatient guideline section II, H.

In this context, "confirmation" does not require documentation of positive serology or culture for HIV; the provider's diagnostic statement that the patient is HIV positive or has an HIV-related illness is sufficient.

2) Selection and sequencing of HIV codes

(a) Patient admitted for HIV-related condition—If a patient is admitted for an HIV-related condition, the principal diagnosis should be 042, followed by additional diagnosis codes for all reported HIV-related conditions.

(b) Patient with HIV disease admitted for unrelated condition—If a patient with HIV disease is admitted for an unrelated condition (such as a traumatic injury), the code for the unrelated condition (e.g., the nature of injury code) should be the principal diagnosis. Other diagnoses would be 042 followed by additional diagnosis codes for all reported HIV-related conditions.

(c) Whether the patient is newly diagnosed—Whether the patient is newly diagnosed or has had previous admissions/encounters for HIV conditions is irrelevant to the sequencing decision.

(d) Asymptomatic human immunodeficiency virus—V08 Asymptomatic human immunodeficiency virus [HIV] infection, is to be applied when the patient without any documentation of symptoms is listed as being "HIV positive," "known HIV," "HIV test positive," or similar terminology. Do not use this code if the term "AIDS" is used or if the patient is treated for any HIV-related illness or is described as having any condition(s) resulting from his/her HIV positive status; use 042 in these cases.

(e) Patients with inconclusive HIV serology—Patients with inconclusive HIV serology, but no definitive diagnosis or manifestations of the illness, may be assigned code 795.71 Inconclusive serologic test for human immunodeficiency virus [HIV].

(f) Previously diagnosed HIV-related illness—Patients with any known prior diagnosis of an HIV-related illness should be coded to 042. Once a patient has developed an HIV-related illness, the patient should always be assigned code 042 on every subsequent admission/encounter. Patients previously diagnosed with any HIV illness (042) should never be assigned to 795.71 or V08.

(g) HIV infection in pregnancy, childbirth and the puerperium—During pregnancy, childbirth, or the puerperium, a patient admitted (or presenting for a health care encounter) because of an HIV-related illness should receive a principal diagnosis code of 647.6x Other specified infectious and parasitic diseases in the mother classifiable elsewhere but complicating the pregnancy, childbirth or the puerperium, followed by 042 and the code(s) for the HIV-related illness(es). Codes from chapter 15 always take sequencing priority.

Patients with asymptomatic HIV infection status admitted (or presenting for a health care encounter) during pregnancy, childbirth, or the puerperium should receive codes of 647.6x and V08.

(h) Encounters for testing for HIV—If a patient is being seen to determine his/her HIV status, use code V73.89 Screening for other specified viral disease. Use code V69.8 Other problems related to lifestyle, as a secondary code if an asymptomatic patient is in a known high risk group for HIV. Should a patient with signs or symptoms or illness, or a confirmed HIV related diagnosis be tested for HIV, code the signs and symptoms or the diagnosis. An additional counseling code V65.44 may be used if counseling is provided during the encounter for the test.

When a patient returns to be informed of his/her HIV test results, use code V65.44 HIV counseling, if the results of the test are negative.

If the results are positive but the patient is asymptomatic, use code V08 Asymptomatic HIV infection. If the results are positive and the patient is symptomatic, use code 042 HIV infection, with codes for the HIV-related symptoms or diagnosis. The HIV counseling code may also be used if counseling is provided for patients with positive test results.

b. Septicemia, systemic inflammatory response syndrome (SIRS), sepsis, severe sepsis, and septic shock

1) Sepsis as principal diagnosis or secondary diagnosis

(a) Sepsis as principal diagnosis—If sepsis is present on admission and meets the definition of principal diagnosis, the underlying systemic infection code (e.g., 038.xx, 112.5, etc.) should be assigned as the principal diagnosis, followed by code 995.91 Systemic inflammatory response syndrome due to infectious process without organ dysfunction, as required by the sequencing rules in the Tabular List. Codes from subcategory 995.9 can never be assigned as a principal diagnosis.

(b) Sepsis as secondary diagnoses—When sepsis develops during the encounter (it was not present on admission), the sepsis codes may be assigned as secondary diagnoses, following the sequencing rules provided in the Tabular List.

(c) Documentation unclear as to whether sepsis present on admission—If the documentation is not clear whether the sepsis was present on admission, the provider should be queried. After provider query, if sepsis is determined at that point to have met the definition of principal diagnosis, the underlying systemic infection (038.xx, 112.5, etc.) may be used as the principal diagnosis along with code 995.91 Systemic inflammatory response syndrome due to infectious process without organ dysfunction.

2) Septicemia/sepsis—In most cases, it will be a code from category 038 Septicemia, that will be used in conjunction with a code from subcategory 995.9 such as the following:

(a) Streptococcal sepsis—If the documentation in the record states streptococcal sepsis, codes 038.0 and code 995.91 should be used, in that sequence.

(b) Streptococcal septicemia—If the documentation states streptococcal septicemia, only code 038.0 should be assigned; however, the provider should be queried whether the patient has sepsis, an infection with SIRS.

(c) Sepsis or SIRS must be documented—Either the term sepsis or SIRS must be documented to assign a code from subcategory 995.9.

3) Terms "sepsis," " severe sepsis," or "SIRS"—If the terms sepsis, severe sepsis, or SIRS are used with an underlying infection other than septicemia, such as pneumonia, cellulitis, or a nonspecified urinary tract infection, a code from category 038 should be assigned first, then code 995.91, followed by the code for the initial infection. The use of the terms sepsis or SIRS indicates that the patient's infection has advanced to the point of a systemic infection so the systemic infection should be sequenced before the localized infection. The instructional note under subcategory 995.9 instructs to assign the underlying systemic infection first.

Note: The term "urosepsis" is a nonspecific term. If that is the only term documented then only code 599.0 should be assigned based on the default for the term in the ICD-9-CM index, in addition to the code for the causal organism if known.

4) Severe sepsis—For patients with severe sepsis, the code for the systemic infection (e.g., 038.xx, 112.5, etc) or trauma should be sequenced first, followed by either code 995.92 Systemic inflammatory response syndrome due to infectious process with organ dysfunction, or code 995.94 Systemic inflammatory response syndrome due to noninfectious process with organ dysfunction. Codes for the specific organ dysfunctions should also be assigned.

5) Septic shock

(a) Sequencing of septic shock—Septic shock is a form of organ dysfunction associated with severe sepsis. A code for the initiating underlying systemic infection followed by a code for SIRS (code 995.92) must be assigned before the code for septic shock. As noted in the sequencing instructions in the Tabular List, the code for septic shock cannot be assigned as a principal diagnosis.

(b) Septic shock without documentation of severe sepsis—Septic shock cannot occur in the absence of severe sepsis. A code from subcategory 995.9 must be sequenced before the code for septic shock. The use additional code notes and the code first note provide sequencing instructions.

6) Sepsis and septic shock associated with abortion—Sepsis and septic shock associated with abortion, ectopic pregnancy, and molar pregnancy are classified to category codes in chapter 11 (630-639).

7) Negative or inconclusive blood cultures—Negative or inconclusive blood cultures do not preclude a diagnosis of septicemia or sepsis in patients with clinical evidence of the condition; however, the provider should be queried.

8) **Newborn sepsis**—See section I.C.15.j for information on the coding of newborn sepsis.

9) **Sepsis due to a postprocedural infection**—Sepsis resulting from a postprocedural infection is a complication of care. For such cases code 998.59 Other postoperative infections, should be coded first followed by the appropriate codes for the sepsis. The other guidelines for coding sepsis should then be followed for the assignment of additional codes.

10) External cause of injury codes with SIRS—An external cause code is not needed with codes 995.91 Systemic inflammatory response syndrome due to infectious process without organ dysfunction, or 995.92 Systemic inflammatory response syndrome due to infectious process with organ dysfunction.

Refer to section I.C.19.a.7 for instruction on the use of external cause of injury codes with codes for SIRS resulting from trauma.

2. Chapter 2: Neoplasms (140-239)

General guidelines

Chapter 2 of the ICD-9-CM contains the codes for most benign and all malignant neoplasms. Certain benign neoplasms, such as prostatic adenomas, may be found in the specific body system chapters. To properly code a neoplasm it is necessary to determine from the record if the neoplasm is benign, in situ, malignant, or of uncertain histologic behavior. If malignant, any secondary (metastatic) sites should also be determined.

The neoplasm table in the Alphabetic Index should be referenced first. However, if the histological term is documented, that term should be referenced first, rather than going immediately to the neoplasm table, in order to determine which column in the neoplasm table is appropriate. For example, if the documentation indicates "adenoma," refer to the term in the Alphabetic Index to review the entries under this term and the instructional note to "see also neoplasm, by site, benign." The table provides the proper code based on the type of neoplasm and the site. It is important to select the proper column in the table that corresponds to the type of neoplasm. The tabular should then be referenced to verify that the correct code has been selected from the table and that a more specific site code does not exist.

See section I. C. 18.d.4. for information regarding V codes for genetic susceptibility to cancer.

a. Treatment directed at the malignancy—If the treatment is directed at the malignancy, designate the malignancy as the principal diagnosis.

b. Treatment of secondary site—When a patient is admitted because of a primary neoplasm with metastasis and treatment is directed toward the secondary site only, the secondary neoplasm is designated as the principal diagnosis even though the primary malignancy is still present.

c. Coding and sequencing of complications—Coding and sequencing of complications associated with the malignancies or with the therapy thereof are subject to the following guidelines:

1) Anemia associated with malignancy—When admission/encounter is for management of an anemia associated with the malignancy, and the treatment is only for anemia, **the appropriate anemia code (such as code 285.22 Anemia in neoplastic disease)** is designated as the principal diagnosis and is followed by the appropriate code(s) for the malignancy.

Code 285.22 may also be used as a secondary code if the patient suffers from anemia and is being treated for the malignancy.

2) Anemia associated with chemotherapy, immunotherapy and radiation therapy—When the admission/encounter is for management of an anemia associated with chemotherapy, **immunotherapy,** or radiotherapy and the only treatment is for the anemia, the anemia is sequenced first followed by **code E933.1. The appropriate neoplasm code should be assigned as an additional code.**

3) Management of dehydration due to the malignancy—When the admission/encounter is for management of dehydration due to the malignancy or the therapy, or a combination of both, and only the dehydration is being treated (intravenous rehydration), the dehydration is sequenced first, followed by the code(s) for the malignancy.

4) Treatment of a complication resulting from a surgical procedure—When the admission/encounter is for treatment of a complication resulting from a surgical procedure, designate the complication as the principal or first-listed diagnosis if treatment is directed at resolving the complication.

d. Primary malignancy previously excised—When a primary malignancy has been previously excised or eradicated from its site and there is no further treatment directed to that site and there is no evidence of any existing primary malignancy, a code from category V10 Personal history of malignant neoplasm, should be used to indicate the former site of the malignancy. Any mention of extension, invasion, or metastasis to another site is coded as a secondary malignant neoplasm to that site. The secondary site may be the principal or first-listed with the V10 code used as a secondary code.

e. Admissions/encounters involving chemotherapy, immunotherapy, and radiation therapy

1) Episode of care involves surgical removal of neoplasm—When an episode of care involves the surgical removal of a neoplasm, primary or secondary site, followed by adjunct chemotherapy or radiation treatment **during the same episode of care,** the neoplasm code should be assigned as principal or first-listed diagnosis, using codes in the 140–198 series or where appropriate in the 200–203 series.

2) Patient admission/encounter solely for administration of chemotherapy, immunotherapy, and radiation therapy—If a patient admission/encounter is solely for the administration of chemotherapy, **immunotherapy** or radiation therapy, assign code V58.0 Encounter for radiation therapy, **V58.11 Encounter for antineoplastic chemotherapy, or V58.12 Encounter for antineoplastic immunotherapy as** the first-listed or principal diagnosis. If a patient receives **more than one of these therapies during the same admission, more than one of these codes may be assigned, in any sequence.**

3) Patient admitted for radiotherapy/chemotherapy and immunotherapy and develops complications—When a patient is admitted for the purpose of radiotherapy, **immunotherapy,** or chemotherapy and develops complications such as uncontrolled nausea and vomiting or dehydration, the principal or first-listed diagnosis is V58.0 Encounter for radiotherapy, **V58.11 Encounter for antineoplastic chemotherapy, or V58.12 Encounter for antineoplastic immunotherapy** followed by any codes for the complications.

See section I.C.18.d.8. for additional information regarding aftercare V codes.

f. Admission/encounter to determine extent of malignancy—When the reason for admission/encounter is to determine the extent of the malignancy, or for a procedure such as paracentesis or thoracentesis, the primary malignancy or appropriate metastatic site is designated as the principal or first-listed diagnosis, even though chemotherapy or radiotherapy is administered.

g. Symptoms, signs, and ill-defined conditions listed in chapter 16—Symptoms, signs, and ill-defined conditions listed in chapter 16 characteristic of, or associated with, an existing primary or secondary site malignancy cannot be used to replace the malignancy as principal or first-listed diagnosis, regardless of the number of admissions or encounters for treatment and care of the neoplasm.

h. See section I.C.18.d.14, Encounter for prophylactic organ removal

3. Chapter 3: Endocrine, Nutritional, and Metabolic Diseases and Immunity Disorders (240-279)

a. Diabetes mellitus—Codes under category 250 Diabetes mellitus, identify complications/manifestations associated with diabetes mellitus. A fifth-digit is required for all category 250 codes to identify the type of diabetes mellitus and whether the diabetes is controlled or uncontrolled.

1) Fifth digits for category 250: The following are the fifth digits for the codes under category 250:

0 type II or unspecified type, not stated as uncontrolled

1 type I, [juvenile type], not stated as uncontrolled

2 type II or unspecified type, uncontrolled

3 type I, [juvenile type], uncontrolled

The age of a patient is not the sole determining factor, though most type I diabetics develop the condition before reaching puberty. For this reason type I diabetes mellitus is also referred to as juvenile diabetes.

2) **Type of diabetes mellitus not documented**—If the type of diabetes mellitus is not documented in the medical record the default is type II.

3) **Diabetes mellitus and the use of insulin**—All type I diabetics must use insulin to replace what their bodies do not produce. However, the use of insulin does not mean that a patient is a type I diabetic. Some patients with type II diabetes mellitus are unable to control their blood sugar through diet and oral medication alone and do require insulin. If the documentation in a medical record does not indicate the type of diabetes but does indicate that the patient uses insulin, the appropriate fifth digit for type II must be used. For type II patients who routinely use insulin, code V58.67 Long-term (current) use of insulin, should also be assigned to indicate that the patient uses insulin. Code V58.67 should not be assigned if insulin is given temporarily to bring a type II patient's blood sugar under control during an encounter.

4) **Assigning and sequencing diabetes codes and associated conditions**—When assigning codes for diabetes and its associated conditions, the code(s) from category 250 must be sequenced before the codes for the associated conditions. The diabetes codes and the secondary codes that correspond to them are paired codes that follow the etiology/manifestation convention of the classification (See section I.A.6., Etiology/manifestation convention). Assign as many codes from category 250 as needed to identify all of the associated conditions that the patient has. The corresponding secondary codes are listed under each of the diabetes codes.

(a) Diabetic retinopathy/diabetic macular edema—Diabetic macular edema, code 362.07, is only present with diabetic retinopathy. Another code from subcategory 362.0 Diabetic retinopathy, must be used with code 362.07. Codes under subcategory 362.0 are diabetes manifestation codes, so they must be used following the appropriate diabetes code.

5) **Diabetes mellitus in pregnancy and gestational diabetes**

(a) For diabetes mellitus complicating pregnancy, see aection I.C.11.f., Diabetes mellitus in pregnancy.

(b) For gestational diabetes, see section I.C.11, g., Gestational diabetes.

6) **Insulin pump malfunction**

(a) Underdose of insulin due to insulin pump failure—An underdose of insulin due to an insulin pump failure should be assigned 996.57 Mechanical complication due to insulin pump, as the principal or first listed code, followed by the appropriate diabetes mellitus code based on documentation.

(b) Overdose of insulin due to insulin pump failure—The principal or first-listed code for an encounter due to an insulin pump malfunction resulting in an overdose of insulin should also be 996.57 Mechanical complication due to insulin pump, followed by code 962.3 Poisoning by insulins and antidiabetic agents, and the appropriate diabetes mellitus code based on documentation.

4. Chapter 4: Diseases of Blood and Blood Forming Organs (280-289)

a. **Anemia of chronic disease—Subcategory 285.2 Anemia in chronic illness, has codes for anemia in chronic kidney disease, code 285.21; anemia in neoplastic disease, code 285.22; and anemia in other chronic illness, code 285.29. These codes can be used as the principal/first-listed code if the reason for the encounter is to treat the anemia. They may also be used as secondary codes if treatment of the anemia is a component of an encounter but not the primary reason for the encounter. When using a code from subcategory 285 it is also necessary to use the code for the chronic condition causing the anemia.**

1) **Anemia in chronic kidney disease—When assigning code 285.21 Anemia in chronic kidney disease. It is also necessary to assign a code from category 585 Chronic kidney disease to indicate the stage of chronic kidney disease. See I.C.10.a., Chronic kidney disease (CKD).**

2) **Anemia in neoplastic disease—When assigning code 285.22 Anemia in neoplastic disease, it is also necessary to assign the neoplasm code that is responsible for the anemia. Code 285.22 is for use for anemia that is due to the malignancy, not for anemia due to antineoplastic chemotherapy drugs, which is an adverse effect.**

See I.C.2.c.1., Anemia associated with malignancy.

See I.C.2.c.2., Anemia associated with chemotherapy, immunotherapy and radiation therapy.

See I.C.17.e.1., Adverse effects.

5. Chapter 5: Mental Disorders (290-319)

Reserved for future guideline expansion

6. Chapter 6: Diseases of Nervous System and Sense Organs (320-389)

Reserved for future guideline expansion

7. Chapter 7: Diseases of Circulatory System (390-459)

a. Hypertension

Hypertension Table

The hypertension table, found under the main term, "Hypertension," in the Alphabetic Index, contains a complete listing of all conditions due to or associated with hypertension and classifies them according to malignant, benign, and unspecified.

1) **Hypertension, essential, or NOS**—Assign hypertension (arterial) (essential) (primary) (systemic) (NOS) to category code 401 with the appropriate fourth digit to indicate malignant (.0), benign (.1), or unspecified (.9). Do not use either .0 malignant or .1 benign unless medical record documentation supports such a designation.

2) **Hypertension with heart disease**—Heart conditions (425.8, 429.0–429.3, 429.8, 429.9) are assigned to a code from category 402 when a causal relationship is stated (due to hypertension) or implied (hypertensive). Use an additional code from category 428 to identify the type of heart failure in those patients with heart failure. More than one code from category 428 may be assigned if the patient has systolic or diastolic failure and congestive heart failure.

The same heart conditions (425.8, 429.0–429.3, 429.8, 429.9) with hypertension, but without a stated casual relationship, are coded separately. Sequence according to the circumstances of the admission/encounter.

3) **Hypertensive kidney disease with chronic renal failure**—Assign codes from category 403, Hypertensive **kidney** disease, when conditions classified to categories 585-587 are present. Unlike hypertension with heart disease, ICD-9-CM presumes a cause-and-effect relationship and classifies renal failure with hypertension as hypertensive renal disease.

4) **Hypertensive heart and kidney disease**—Assign codes from combination category 404, Hypertensive heart and **kidney** disease, when both hypertensive **kidney** disease and hypertensive heart disease are stated in the diagnosis. Assume a relationship between the hypertension and the **kidney** disease, whether or not the condition is so designated. Assign an additional code from category 428 to identify the type of heart failure. More than one code from category 428 may be assigned if the patient has systolic or diastolic failure and congestive heart failure.

5) **Hypertensive cerebrovascular disease**—First assign codes from 430–438 Cerebrovascular disease, then the appropriate hypertension code from categories 401–405.

6) **Hypertensive retinopathy**—Two codes are necessary to identify the condition. First assign the code from subcategory 362.11 Hypertensive retinopathy, then the appropriate code from categories 401–405 to indicate the type of hypertension.

7) **Hypertension, secondary**—Two codes are required: one to identify the underlying etiology and one from category 405 to identify the hypertension. Sequencing of codes is determined by the reason for admission/encounter.

8) **Hypertension, transient**—Assign code 796.2 Elevated blood pressure reading without diagnosis of hypertension, unless patient has an established diagnosis of hypertension. Assign code 642.3x for transient hypertension of pregnancy.

9) **Hypertension, controlled**—Assign appropriate code from categories 401–405. This diagnostic statement usually refers to an existing state of hypertension under control by therapy.

10) **Hypertension, uncontrolled**—Uncontrolled hypertension may refer to untreated hypertension or hypertension not responding to current therapeutic regimen. In either case, assign the appropriate code from categories 401-405 to designate the stage and type of hypertension. Code to the type of hypertension.

11) **Elevated blood pressure**—For a statement of elevated blood pressure without further specificity, assign code 796.2, Elevated blood pressure reading without diagnosis of hypertension, rather than a code from category 401.

b. **Cerebral infarction/stroke/cerebrovascular accident (CVA)**—The terms stroke and CVA are often used interchangeably to refer to a cerebral infarction. The terms stroke, CVA, and cerebral infarction NOS are all indexed to the default code 434.91, Cerebral artery occlusion, unspecified, with infarction. Code 436, Acute, but ill-defined, cerebrovascular disease, should not be used when the documentation states stroke or CVA.

c. **Postoperative cerebrovascular accident**—A cerebrovascular hemorrhage or infarction that occurs as a result of medical intervention is coded to 997.02, Iatrogenic cerebrovascular infarction or hemorrhage. Medical record documentation should clearly specify the cause- and-effect relationship between the medical intervention and the cerebrovascular accident in order to assign this code. A secondary code from the code range 430-432 or from a code from subcategories 433 or 434 with a fifth digit of "1" should also be used to identify the type of hemorrhage or infarct.

This guideline conforms to the use additional code note instruction at category 997. Code 436, Acute, but ill-defined, cerebrovascular disease, should not be used as a secondary code with code 997.02.

d. **Late effects of cerebrovascular disease**

1) **Category 438, late effects of cerebrovascular disease**—Category 438 is used to indicate conditions classifiable to categories 430–437 as the causes of late effects (neurologic deficits), themselves classified elsewhere. These "late effects" include neurologic deficits that persist after initial onset of conditions classifiable to 430–437. The neurologic deficits caused by cerebrovascular disease may be present from the onset or may arise at any time after the onset of the condition classifiable to 430-437.

2) **Codes from category 438 with codes from 430–437**—Codes from category 438 may be assigned on a health care record with codes from 430–437, if the patient has a current cerebrovascular accident (CVA) and deficits from an old CVA.

3) **Code V12.59**—Assign code V12.59 (and not a code from category 438) as an additional code for history of cerebrovascular disease when no neurologic deficits are present.

e. **Acute myocardial infarction (AMI)**

1) **ST elevation myocardial infarction (STEMI) and non-ST elevation myocardial infarction (NSTEMI)—The ICD-9-CM codes for acute myocardial infarction (AMI) identify the site, such as anterolateral wall or true posterior wall. Subcategories 410.0-410.6 and 410.8 are used for ST elevation myocardial infarction (STEMI). Subcategory 410.7 Subendocardial infarction, is used for non-ST elevation myocardial infarction (NSTEMI) and nontransmural MIs.**

2) **Acute myocardial infarction, unspecified—Subcategory 410.9 is the default for the unspecified term acute myocardial infarction. If only STEMI or transmural MI without the site is documented, query the provider as to the site or assign a code from subcategory 410.9.**

3) **AMI documented as nontransmural or subendocardial, but site provided—If an AMI is documented as nontransmural or subendocardial but the site is provided, it is still coded as a subendocardial AMI. If NSTEMI evolves to STEMI, assign the STEMI code. If STEMI converts to NSTEMI due to thrombolytic therapy, it is still coded as STEMI.**

8. Chapter 8: Diseases of Respiratory System (460-519)

a. **Chronic obstructive pulmonary disease [COPD] and asthma**

1) **Conditions that comprise COPD and asthma**—The conditions that comprise COPD are obstructive chronic bronchitis, subcategory 491.2, and emphysema, category 492. All asthma codes are under category 493 Asthma. Code 496 Chronic airway obstruction, not elsewhere classified, is a nonspecific code that should be used only when the documentation in a medical record does not specify the type of COPD being treated.

2) **Acute exacerbation of chronic obstructive bronchitis and asthma**—The codes for chronic obstructive bronchitis and asthma distinguish between uncomplicated cases and those in acute exacerbation. An acute exacerbation is a worsening or a decompensation of a chronic condition. An acute exacerbation is not equivalent to an infection superimposed on a chronic condition, though an exacerbation may be triggered by an infection.

3) **Overlapping nature of the conditions that comprise COPD and asthma**—Due to the overlapping nature of the conditions that make up COPD and asthma, there are many variations in the way these conditions are documented. Code selection must be based on the terms as documented. When selecting the correct code for the documented type of COPD and asthma, it is essential to first review the index and then verify the code in the Tabular List. There are many instructional notes under the different COPD subcategories and codes. It is important that all such notes be reviewed to ensure correct code assignment.

4) **Acute exacerbation of asthma and status asthmaticus**—An acute exacerbation of asthma is an increased severity of the asthma symptoms, such as wheezing and shortness of breath. Status asthmaticus refers to a patient's failure to respond to therapy administered during an asthmatic episode and is a life-threatening complication that requires emergency care. If status asthmaticus is documented by the provider with any type of COPD or with acute bronchitis, the status asthmaticus should be sequenced first. It supersedes any type of COPD, including that with acute exacerbation or acute bronchitis. It is inappropriate to assign an asthma code with fifth-digit 2, with acute exacerbation, together with an asthma code with fifth-digit 1, with status asthmaticus. Only the fifth-digit 1 should be assigned.

b. **Chronic obstructive pulmonary disease [COPD] and bronchitis**

1) **Acute bronchitis with COPD**—Acute bronchitis, code 466.0, is due to an infectious organism. When acute bronchitis is documented with COPD, code 491.22 Obstructive chronic bronchitis with acute bronchitis, should be assigned. It is not necessary to also assign code 466.0. If a medical record documents acute bronchitis with COPD with acute exacerbation, only code 491.22 should be assigned. The acute bronchitis included in code 491.22 supersedes the acute exacerbation. If a medical record documents COPD with acute exacerbation without mention of acute bronchitis, only code 491.21 should be assigned.

9. Chapter 9: Diseases of Digestive System (520-579)

Reserved for future guideline expansion

10. Chapter 10: Diseases of Genitourinary System (580-629)

a. **Chronic kidney disease**

1) **Stages of chronic kidney disease (CKD)—The ICD-9-CM classifies CKD based on severity. The severity of CKD is designated by stages I-V. Stage II, code 585.2, equates to mild CKD; stage III, code 585.3, equates to moderate CKD; and stage IV, code 585.4, equates to severe CKD. Code 585.6 End-stage renal disease (ESRD), is assigned when the provider has documented end-stage renal disease (ESRD). If both a stage of CKD and ESRD are documented, assign code 585.6 only.**

2) **Chronic kidney disease and kidney transplant status—Patients who have undergone kidney transplant may still have some form of CKD because the kidney transplant may not fully restore kidney function. Code V42.0 may be assigned with the appropriate CKD code for patients who are status post kidney transplant, based on the patient's post-transplant stage. The use additional code note under category 585 provides this instruction.**

Use of a 585 code with V42.0 does not necessarily indicate transplant rejection or failure. Patients with mild or moderate CKD following a transplant should not be coded as having transplant failure unless it is documented in the medical record. For patients with severe CKD or ESRD it is appropriate to assign code 996.81 Complications of transplanted organ, kidney transplant, when kidney transplant failure is documented. If a post kidney transplant patient has CKD and it is unclear from the documentation whether there is transplant failure or rejection, it is necessary to query the provider.

3) **Chronic kidney disease with other conditions—Patients with CKD may also suffer from other serious conditions, most commonly diabetes mellitus and hypertension. The sequencing of the CKD code in relationship to codes for other contributing conditions is based on the conventions in the tabular list. See I.C.3.a.4. for sequencing instructions for diabetes.**

See I.C.4.a.1. for anemia in CKD.

See I.C.7.a.3. for hypertensive kidney disease.

See I.C.17.f.1.b. Transplant complications, for instructions on coding of documented rejection or failure.

11. Chapter 11: Complications of Pregnancy, Childbirth, and the Puerperium (630-677)

a. General rules for obstetric cases

1) **Codes from chapter 11 and sequencing priority**—Obstetric cases require codes from chapter 11, codes in the range 630-677 Complications of pregnancy, childbirth, and the puerperium. Chapter 11 codes have sequencing priority over codes from other chapters. Additional codes from other chapters may be used in conjunction with chapter 11 codes to further specify conditions. Should the provider document that the pregnancy is incidental to the encounter, then code V22.2 should be used in place of any chapter 11 codes. It is the provider's responsibility to state that the condition being treated is not affecting the pregnancy.

2) **Chapter 11 codes used only on the maternal record**—Chapter 11 codes are to be used only on the maternal record, never on the record of the newborn.

3) **Chapter 11 fifth digits**—Categories 640-648, 651-676 have required fifth-digits, which indicate whether the encounter is antepartum, postpartum and whether a delivery has also occurred.

4) **Fifth digits, appropriate for each code**—The fifth digits, which are appropriate for each code number, are listed in brackets under each code. The fifth digits on each code should all be consistent with each other. That is, should a delivery occur all of the fifth digits should indicate the delivery.

b. Selection of OB principal or first-listed diagnosis

1) **Routine outpatient prenatal visits**—For routine outpatient prenatal visits when no complications are present, codes V22.0 Supervision of normal first pregnancy, and V22.1 Supervision of other normal pregnancy, should be used as the first-listed diagnoses. These codes should not be used in conjunction with chapter 11 codes.

2) **Prenatal outpatient visits for high-risk patients**—For prenatal outpatient visits for patients with high-risk pregnancies, a code from category V23 Supervision of high-risk pregnancy, should be used as the principal or first-listed diagnosis. Secondary chapter 11 codes may be used in conjunction with these codes if appropriate.

3) **Episodes when no delivery occurs**—In episodes when no delivery occurs, the principal diagnosis should correspond to the principal complication of the pregnancy, which necessitated the encounter. Should more than one complication exist, all of which are treated or monitored, any of the complication codes may be sequenced first.

4) **When a delivery occurs**—When a delivery occurs, the principal diagnosis should correspond to the main circumstances or complication of the delivery. In cases of cesarean delivery, the selection of the principal diagnosis should correspond to the reason the cesarean delivery was performed unless the reason for admission/encounter was unrelated to the condition resulting in the cesarean delivery.

5) **Outcome of delivery**—An outcome of delivery code, V27.0-V27.9, should be included on every maternal record when a delivery has occurred. These codes are not to be used on subsequent records or on the newborn record.

c. Fetal conditions affecting the management of the mother

1) **Fetal condition responsible for modifying the management of the mother**—Codes from category 655 Known or suspected fetal abnormality affecting management of the mother, and category 656 Other fetal and placental problems affecting the management of the mother, are assigned only when the fetal condition is actually responsible for modifying the management of the mother, i.e., by requiring diagnostic studies, additional observation, special care, or termination of pregnancy. The fact that the fetal condition exists does not justify assigning a code from this series to the mother's record.

2) **In utero surgery**—In cases when surgery is performed on the fetus, a diagnosis code from category 655 Known or suspected fetal abnormalities affecting management of the mother, should be assigned identifying the fetal condition. Procedure code 75.36 Correction of fetal defect, should be assigned on the hospital inpatient record.

No code from chapter 15, the perinatal codes, should be used on the mother's record to identify fetal conditions. Surgery performed in utero on a fetus is still to be coded as an obstetric encounter.

d. HIV infection in pregnancy, childbirth and the puerperium

During pregnancy, childbirth, or the puerperium, a patient admitted because of an HIV-related illness should receive a principal diagnosis of 647.6X Other specified infectious and parasitic diseases in the mother classifiable elsewhere, but complicating the pregnancy, childbirth, or the puerperium, followed by 042 and the code(s) for the HIV-related illness(es).

Patients with asymptomatic HIV infection status admitted during pregnancy, childbirth, or the puerperium should receive codes of 647.6X and V08.

e. Current conditions complicating pregnancy

Current conditions complicating pregnancy—Assign a code from subcategory 648.x for patients that have current conditions when the condition affects the management of the pregnancy, childbirth, or the puerperium. Use additional secondary codes from other chapters to identify the conditions, as appropriate.

f. Diabetes mellitus in pregnancy

Diabetes mellitus in pregnancy—Diabetes mellitus is a significant complicating factor in pregnancy. Pregnant women who are diabetic should be assigned code 648.0x Diabetes mellitus complicating pregnancy, and a secondary code from category 250 Diabetes mellitus, to identify the type of diabetes.

Code V58.67 Long-term (current) use of insulin, should also be assigned if the diabetes mellitus is being treated with insulin.

g. Gestational diabetes

Gestational diabetes—Gestational diabetes can occur during the second and third trimester of pregnancy in women who were not diabetic prior to pregnancy. Gestational diabetes can cause complications in the pregnancy similar to those of pre-existing diabetes mellitus. It also puts the woman at greater risk of developing diabetes after the pregnancy. Gestational diabetes is coded to 648.8x Abnormal glucose tolerance. Codes 648.0x and 648.8x should never be used together on the same record.

Code V58.67 Long-term (current) use of insulin, should also be assigned if the gestational diabetes is being treated with insulin.

h. Normal delivery, code 650

1) **Normal delivery**—Code 650 is for use in cases when a woman is admitted for a full-term normal delivery and delivers a single, healthy infant without any complications antepartum, during the delivery, or postpartum during the delivery episode. Code 650 is always a principal diagnosis. It is not to be used if any other code from chapter 11 is needed to describe a current complication of the antenatal, delivery, or perinatal period. Additional codes from other chapters may be used with code 650 if they are not related to or are in any way complicating the pregnancy.

2) **Normal delivery with resolved antepartum complication**—Code 650 may be used if the patient had a complication at some point during her pregnancy, but the complication is not present at the time of the admission for delivery.

3) **V27.0 Single liveborn, outcome of delivery**—V27.0 Single liveborn, is the only outcome of the delivery code appropriate for use with 650.

i. The postpartum and peripartum periods

1) **Postpartum and peripartum periods**—The postpartum period begins immediately after delivery and continues for six weeks following delivery. The peripartum period is defined as the last month of pregnancy to five months postpartum.

2) **Postpartum complication**—A postpartum complication is any complication occurring within the six-week period.

3) **Pregnancy-related complications after six-week period**—Chapter 11 codes may also be used to describe pregnancy-related complications after the six-week period should the provider document that a condition is pregnancy related.

4) **Postpartum complications occurring during the same admission as delivery**—Postpartum complications that occur during the same admission as the delivery are identified with a fifth digit of 2. Subsequent admissions/encounters for postpartum complications should be identified with a fifth digit of 4.

5) **Admission for routine postpartum care following delivery outside hospital**—When the mother delivers outside the hospital prior to admission and is admitted for routine postpartum care and no complications are noted, code V24.0 Postpartum care and examination immediately after delivery, should be assigned as the principal diagnosis.

6) **Admission following delivery outside hospital with postpartum conditions**—A delivery diagnosis code should not be used for a woman who has delivered prior to admission to the hospital. Any postpartum conditions and/or postpartum procedures should be coded.

j. **Code 677 Late effect of complication of pregnancy**

1) **Code 677**—Code 677 Late effect of complication of pregnancy, childbirth, and the puerperium is for use in those cases when an initial complication of a pregnancy develops a sequelae requiring care or treatment at a future date.

2) **After the initial postpartum period**—This code may be used at any time after the initial postpartum period.

3) **Sequencing of code 677**—This code, like all late effect codes, is to be sequenced following the code describing the sequelae of the complication.

k. **Abortions**

1) **Fifth digits required for abortion categories**—Fifth digits are required for abortion categories 634-637. Fifth-digit 1, incomplete, indicates that all of the products of conception have not been expelled from the uterus. Fifth-digit 2, complete, indicates that all products of conception have been expelled from the uterus prior to the episode of care.

2) **Code from categories 640-648 and 651-659**—A code from categories 640-648 and 651-659 may be used as additional codes with an abortion code to indicate the complication leading to the abortion.

Fifth-digit 3 is assigned with codes from these categories when used with an abortion code because the other fifth digits will not apply. Codes from the 660-669 series are not to be used for complications of abortion.

3) **Code 639 for complications**—Code 639 is to be used for all complications following abortion. Code 639 cannot be assigned with codes from categories 634-638.

4) **Abortion with liveborn fetus**—When an attempted termination of pregnancy results in a liveborn fetus assign code 644.21 Early onset of delivery, with an appropriate code from category V27 Outcome of delivery. The procedure code for the attempted termination of pregnancy should also be assigned.

5) **Retained products of conception following an abortion**—Subsequent admissions for retained products of conception following a spontaneous or legally induced abortion are assigned the appropriate code from category 634 Spontaneous abortion, or 635 Legally induced abortion, with a fifth digit of 1 (incomplete). This advice is appropriate even when the patient was discharged previously with a discharge diagnosis of complete abortion.

12. Chapter 12: Diseases of Skin and Subcutaneous Tissue (680-709)

Reserved for future guideline expansion

13. Chapter 13: Diseases of Musculoskeletal and Connective Tissue (710-739)

Reserved for future guideline expansion

14. Chapter 14: Congenital Anomalies (740-759)

a. **Codes in categories 740-759 Congenital anomalies**—Assign an appropriate code(s) from categories 740-759, Congenital anomalies, when an anomaly is documented. A congenital anomaly may be the principal/first-listed diagnosis on a record or a secondary diagnosis. **When a congenital anomaly does not have a unique code assignment, assign additional code(s) for any manifestations that may be present.**

When the code assignment specifically identifies the congenital anomaly, manifestations that are an inherent component of the anomaly should not be coded separately. Additional codes should be assigned for manifestations that are not an inherent component.

Codes from Chapter 14 may be used throughout the life of the patient. If a congenital anomaly has been corrected, a personal history code should be used to identify the history of the anomaly. **Although present at birth, a congenital anomaly may not be identified until later in life. Whenever the condition is diagnosed by the physician, it is appropriate to assign a code from codes 740-759.**

For the birth admission, the appropriate code from category V30 Liveborn infants, according to type of birth should be sequenced as the principal diagnosis, followed by any congenital anomaly codes, 740-759.

15. Chapter 15: Newborn (Perinatal) Guidelines (760-779)

For coding and reporting purposes the perinatal period is defined as birth through the 28th day following birth. The following guidelines are provided for reporting purposes. Hospitals may record other diagnoses as needed for internal data use.

a. **General perinatal rules**

1) **Chapter 15 codes**—They are never for use on the maternal record. Codes from chapter 11, the obstetric chapter, are never permitted on the newborn record. Chapter 15 code may be used throughout the life of the patient if the condition is still present.

2) **Sequencing of perinatal codes**—Generally, codes from chapter 15 should be sequenced as the principal/first-listed diagnosis on the newborn record, with the exception of the appropriate V30 code for the birth episode, followed by codes from any other chapter that provide additional detail. The "use additional code" note at the beginning of the chapter supports this guideline. If the index does not provide a specific code for a perinatal condition, assign code 779.89 Other specified conditions originating in the perinatal period, followed by the code from another chapter that specifies the condition. Codes for signs and symptoms may be assigned when a definitive diagnosis has not been established.

3) **Birth process or community acquired conditions**—If a newborn has a condition that may be either due to the birth process or community acquired and the documentation does not indicate which it is, the default is due to the birth process and the code from chapter 15 should be used. If the condition is community acquired, a code from chapter 15 should not be assigned.

4) **Code all clinically significant conditions**—All clinically significant conditions noted on routine newborn examination should be coded. A condition is clinically significant if it requires:

- Clinical evaluation; or
- Therapeutic treatment; or
- Diagnostic procedures; or
- Extended length of hospital stay; or
- Increased nursing care and/or monitoring; or
- Has implications for future health care needs

Note: The perinatal guidelines listed above are the same as the general coding guidelines for "additional diagnoses," except for the final point regarding implications for future health care needs. Codes should be assigned for conditions that have been specified by the provider as having implications for future health care needs. Codes from the perinatal chapter should not be assigned unless the provider has established a definitive diagnosis.

b. **Use of codes V30-V39**—When coding the birth of an infant, assign a code from categories V30-V39, according to the type of birth. A code from this series is assigned as a principal diagnosis and assigned only once to a newborn at the time of birth.

c. **Newborn transfers**—If the newborn is transferred to another institution, the V30 series is not used at the receiving hospital.

d. **Use of category V29**

1) **Assigning a code from category V29**—Assign a code from category V29 Observation and evaluation of newborns and infants for suspected conditions not found, to identify those instances when a healthy newborn is evaluated for a suspected condition that is determined after study not to be present. Do not use a code from category V29 when the patient has identified signs or symptoms of a suspected problem; in such cases, code the sign or symptom.

A code from category V29 may also be assigned as a principal diagnosis for readmissions or encounters when the V30 code no longer applies. Codes from category V29 are for use only for healthy newborns and infants for which no condition after study is found to be present.

2) **V29 code on a birth record**—A V29 code is to be used as a secondary code after the V30 Outcome of delivery, code.

e. **Use of other V codes on perinatal records**—V codes other than V30 and V29 may be assigned on a perinatal or newborn record code. The codes may be used as a principal or first-listed diagnosis for specific types of encounters or for readmissions or encounters when the V30 code no longer applies.

See section I.C.18 for information regarding the assignment of V codes.

f. **Maternal causes of perinatal morbidity**—Codes from categories 760-763 Maternal causes of perinatal morbidity and mortality, are assigned only when the maternal condition has actually affected the fetus or newborn. The fact that the mother has an associated medical condition or experiences some complication of pregnancy, labor, or delivery does not justify the routine assignment of codes from these categories to the newborn record.

g. Congenital anomalies in newborns—For the birth admission, the appropriate code from category V30 Liveborn infants according to type of birth, should be used, followed by any congenital anomaly codes, categories 740-759. Use additional secondary codes from other chapters to specify conditions associated with the anomaly, if applicable.

Also, see section I.C.14 for information on the coding of congenital anomalies.

h. Coding additional perinatal diagnoses

1) Assigning codes for conditions that require treatment—Assign codes for conditions that require treatment or further investigation, prolong the length of stay, or require resource utilization.

2) Codes for conditions specified as having implications for future health care needs—Assign codes for conditions that have been specified by the provider as having implications for future health care needs.

Note: This guideline should not be used for adult patients.

3) Codes for newborn conditions originating in the perinatal period—Assign a code for newborn conditions originating in the perinatal period (categories 760-779), as well as complications arising during the current episode of care classified in other chapters, only if the diagnoses have been documented by the responsible provider at the time of transfer or discharge as having affected the fetus or newborn.

i. Prematurity and fetal growth retardation—Providers utilize different criteria in determining prematurity. A code for prematurity should not be assigned unless it is documented. The fift-digit assignment for codes from category 764 and subcategories 765.0 and 765.1 should be based on the recorded birth weight and estimated gestational age.

A code from subcategory 765.2 Weeks of gestation, should be assigned as an additional code with category 764 and codes from 765.0 and 765.1 to specify weeks of gestation as documented by the provider in the record.

j. Newborn sepsis—Code 771.81 Septicemia [sepsis] of newborn, should be assigned with a secondary code from category 041 Bacterial infections in conditions classified elsewhere and of unspecified site, to identify the organism. It is not necessary to use a code from subcategory 995.9 Systemic inflammatory response syndrome (SIRS), on a newborn record. A code from category 038 Septicemia, should not be used on a newborn record. Code 771.81 describes the sepsis.

16. Chapter 16: Signs, Symptoms and Ill-Defined Conditions (780-799)

Reserved for future guideline expansion

17. Chapter 17: Injury and Poisoning (800-999)

a. Coding of injuries—When coding injuries, assign separate codes for each injury unless a combination code is provided, in which case the combination code is assigned. Multiple injury codes are provided in ICD-9-CM but should not be assigned unless information for a more specific code is not available. These codes are not to be used for normal, healing surgical wounds or to identify complications of surgical wounds.

The code for the most serious injury, as determined by the provider and the focus of treatment, is sequenced first.

1) Superficial injuries—Superficial injuries such as abrasions or contusions are not coded when associated with more severe injuries of the same site.

2) Primary injury with damage to nerves/blood vessels—When a primary injury results in minor damage to peripheral nerves or blood vessels, the primary injury is sequenced first with additional code(s) from categories 950-957 Injury to nerves and spinal cord, and/or 900-904 Injury to blood vessels. When the primary injury is to the blood vessels or nerves, that injury should be sequenced first.

b. Coding of fractures—The principles of multiple coding of injuries should be followed in coding fractures. Fractures of specified sites are coded individually by site in accordance with both the provisions within categories 800-829 and the level of detail furnished by medical record content. Combination categories for multiple fractures are provided for use when there is insufficient detail in the medical record (such as trauma cases transferred to another hospital), when the reporting form limits the number of codes that can be used in reporting pertinent clinical data, or when there is insufficient specificity at the fourth-digit or fifth-digit level. More specific guidelines are as follows:

1) Multiple fractures of same limb—Multiple fractures of same limb classifiable to the same three-digit or four-digit category are coded to that category.

2) Multiple unilateral or bilateral fractures of same bone—Multiple unilateral or bilateral fractures of same bone(s) but classified to different fourth-digit subdivisions (bone part) within the same three-digit category are coded individually by site.

3) Multiple fracture categories 819 and 828—Multiple fracture categories 819 and 828 classify bilateral fractures of both upper limbs (819) and both lower limbs (828), but without any detail at the fourth-digit level other than open and closed type of fractures.

4) Multiple fractures sequencing—Multiple fractures are sequenced in accordance with the severity of the fracture. The provider should be asked to list the fracture diagnoses in the order of severity.

c. Coding of burns—Current burns (940-948) are classified by depth, extent, and by agent (E code). Burns are classified by depth as first degree (erythema), second degree (blistering), and third degree (full-thickness involvement).

1) Sequencing of burn codes and related condition—Sequence first the code that reflects the highest degree of burn when more than one burn is present.

(a) When the reason for the admission or encounter is for treatment of external multiple burns, sequence first the code that reflects the burn of the highest degree.

(b) When a patient has both internal and external burns, the circumstances of admission govern the selection of the principal diagnosis or first-listed diagnosis.

(c) When a patient is admitted for burn injuries and other related conditions such as smoke inhalation and/or respiratory failure, the circumstances of admission govern the selection of the principal or first-listed diagnosis.

2) Burns of the same local site—Classify burns of the same local site (three-digit category level, 940-947) but of different degrees to the subcategory identifying the highest degree recorded in the diagnosis.

3) Non-healing burns—Non-healing burns are coded as acute burns. Necrosis of burned skin should be coded as a non-healed burn.

4) Code 958.3 Posttraumatic wound infection—Assign code 958.3 Posttraumatic wound infection, not elsewhere classified, as an additional code for any documented infected burn site.

5) Assign separate codes for each burn site—When coding burns, assign separate codes for each burn site. Category 946 Burns of multiple specified sites, should only be used if the locations of the burns are not documented. Category 949 Burn, unspecified, is extremely vague and should rarely be used.

6) Burns classified according to extent of body surface involved—Assign codes from category 948 Burns, when the site of the burn is not specified or when there is a need for additional data. It is advisable to use category 948 as additional coding when needed to provide data for evaluating burn mortality, such as that needed by burn units. It is also advisable to use category 948 as an additional code for reporting purposes when there is mention of a third-degree burn involving 20 percent or more of the body surface.

In assigning a code from category 948:

- Fourth-digit codes are used to identify the percentage of total body surface involved in a burn (all degree).
- Fifth digits are assigned to identify the percentage of body surface involved in third-degree burn.
- Fifth-digit zero (0) is assigned when less than 10 percent or when no body surface is involved in a third-degree burn.
- Category 948 is based on the classic "rule of nines" in estimating body surface involved: head and neck are assigned 9 percent, each arm 9 percent, each leg 18 percent, the anterior trunk 18 percent, posterior trunk 18 percent, and genitalia 1 percent. Providers may change these percentage assignments where necessary to accommodate infants and children who have proportionately larger heads than adults and patients who have large buttocks, thighs, or abdomen that involve burns.

7) Encounters for treatment of late effects of burns—Encounters for the treatment of the late effects of burns (i.e., scars or joint contractures) should be coded to the residual condition (sequelae) followed by the appropriate late effect code (906.5-906.9). A late effect E code may also be used, if desired.

8) Sequelae with a late effect code and current burn—When appropriate, both a sequelae with a late effect code, and a current burn code may be assigned on the same record (when both a current burn and sequelae of an old burn exist).

d. **Coding of debridement of wound, infection, or burn**—Excisional debridement involves an excisional debridement (surgical removal or cutting away), as opposed to a mechanical (brushing, scrubbing, washing) debridement.

For coding purposes, excisional debridement is assigned to code 86.22.

Nonexcisional debridement is assigned to code 86.28.

e. **Adverse effects, poisoning and toxic effects**—The properties of certain drugs, medicinal and biological substances, or combinations of such substances, may cause toxic reactions. The occurrence of drug toxicity is classified in ICD-9-CM as follows:

1) **Adverse effect**—When the drug was correctly prescribed and properly administered, code the reaction plus the appropriate code from the E930-E949 series. Codes from the E930-E949 series must be used to identify the causative substance for an adverse effect of drug, medicinal and biological substances, correctly prescribed and properly administered. The effect, such as tachycardia, delirium, gastrointestinal hemorrhaging, vomiting, hypokalemia, hepatitis, renal failure, or respiratory failure, is coded and followed by the appropriate code from the E930-E949 series.

Adverse effects of therapeutic substances correctly prescribed and properly administered (toxicity, synergistic reaction, side effect, and idiosyncratic reaction) may be due to (1) differences among patients, such as age, sex, disease, and genetic factors, and (2) drug-related factors, such as type of drug, route of administration, duration of therapy, dosage, and bioavailability.

2) **Poisoning**

(a) Error was made in drug prescription—Errors made in drug prescription or in the administration of the drug by provider, nurse, patient, or other person, use the appropriate poisoning code from the 960-979 series.

(b) Overdose of a drug intentionally taken—If an overdose of a drug was intentionally taken or administered and resulted in drug toxicity, it would be coded as a poisoning (960-979 series).

(c) Nonprescribed drug taken with correctly prescribed and properly administered drug—If a nonprescribed drug or medicinal agent was taken in combination with a correctly prescribed and properly administered drug, any drug toxicity or other reaction resulting from the interaction of the two drugs would be classified as a poisoning.

(d) Sequencing of poisoning—When coding a poisoning or reaction to the improper use of a medication (e.g., wrong dose, wrong substance, wrong route of administration) the poisoning code is sequenced first, followed by a code for the manifestation. If there is also a diagnosis of drug abuse or dependence to the substance, the abuse or dependence is coded as an additional code.

See section I.C.3.a.6.b. if poisoning is the result of insulin pump malfunctions and section I.C.19 for general use of E codes.

3) **Toxic effects**

(a) Toxic effect codes—When a harmful substance is ingested or comes in contact with a person, this is classified as a toxic effect. The toxic effect codes are in categories 980-989.

(b) Sequencing toxic effect codes—A toxic effect code should be sequenced first, followed by the codes that identify the result of the toxic effect.

(c) External cause codes for toxic effects—An external cause code from categories E860-E869 for accidental exposure, code E950.6 or E950.7 for intentional self-harm, category E962 for assault, or categories E980-E982 for undetermined, should also be assigned to indicate intent.

f. **Complications of care**

1) **Transplant complications**

(a) Transplant complications other than kidney—Codes under subcategory 996.8 Complications of transplanted organ, are for use for both complications and rejection of transplanted organs. A transplant complication code is only assigned if the complication affects the function of the transplanted organ. Two codes are required to fully describe a transplant complication, the appropriate code from subcategory 996.8 and a secondary code that identifies the complication.

Pre-existing conditions or conditions that develop after the transplant are not coded as complications unless they affect the function of the transplanted organs.

Post-transplant surgical complications that do not relate to the function of the transplanted organ are classified to the specific complication. For example, a surgical wound dehiscence would be coded as a wound dehiscence, not as a transplant complication.

Post-transplant patients who are seen for treatment unrelated to the transplanted organ should be assigned a code from category V42 Organ or tissue replaced by transplant, to identify the transplant status of the patient. A code from category V42 should never be used with a code from subcategory 996.8.

(b) Kidney transplant and chronic kidney disease—Patients with chronic kidney disease (CKD) following a transplant should not be assumed to have transplant failure or rejection unless it is documented by the provider. If documentation supports the presence of failure or rejection, then it is appropriate to assign code 996.81 Complications of transplanted organs, kidney, followed by the appropriate CKD code.

18. Classification of Factors Influencing Health Status and Contact with Health Service (Supplemental V01-V86)

Note: The chapter-specific guidelines provide additional information about the use of V codes for specified encounters.

a. **Introduction**—ICD-9-CM provides codes to deal with encounters for circumstances other than a disease or injury. The Supplementary Classification of Factors Influencing Health Status and Contact with Health Services (V01-V86) is provided to deal with occasions when circumstances other than a disease or injury (codes 001-999) are recorded as a diagnosis or problem.

There are four primary circumstances for the use of V codes:

1) A person who is not currently sick encounters the health services for some specific reason, such as to act as an organ donor, to receive prophylactic care, such as inoculations or health screenings, or to receive counseling on health related issues.

2) A person with a resolving disease or injury, or a chronic, long-term condition requiring continuous care, encounters the health care system for specific aftercare of that disease or injury (e.g., dialysis for renal disease; chemotherapy for malignancy; cast change). A diagnosis/symptom code should be used whenever a current, acute diagnosis is being treated or a sign or symptom is being studied.

3) Circumstances or problems influence a person's health status but are not in themselves a current illness or injury.

4) Newborns, to indicate birth status

b. **V codes use in any health care setting**—V codes are for use in any healthcare setting. V codes may be used as either a first-listed (principal diagnosis code in the inpatient setting) or secondary code, depending on the circumstances of the encounter. Certain V codes may only be used as first listed, others only as secondary codes. See section I.C.18.e, V code table.

c. **V codes indicate a reason for an encounter**—They are not procedure codes. A corresponding procedure code must accompany a V code to describe the procedure performed.

d. **Categories of V codes**

1) **Contact/exposure**—Category V01 indicates contact with or exposure to communicable diseases. These codes are for patients who do not show any sign or symptom of a disease but have been exposed to it by close personal contact with an infected individual or are in an area where a disease is epidemic. These codes may be used as a first-listed code to explain an encounter for testing, or, more commonly, as a secondary code to identify a potential risk.

2) **Inoculations and vaccinations**—Categories V03-V06 are for encounters for inoculations and vaccinations. They indicate that a patient is being seen to receive a prophylactic inoculation against a disease. The injection itself must be represented by the appropriate procedure code. A code from V03-V06 may be used as a secondary code if the inoculation is given as a routine part of preventive health care, such as a well-baby visit.

3) **Status**—Status codes indicate that a patient is either a carrier of a disease or has the sequelae or residual of a past disease or condition. This includes such things as the presence of prosthetic or mechanical devices resulting from past treatment.

A status code is informative, because the status may affect the course of treatment and its outcome. A status code is distinct from a history code. The history code indicates that the patient no longer has the condition.

A status code should not be used with a diagnosis code from one of the body system chapters, if the diagnosis code includes the information provided by the status code. For example, code V42.1 Heart transplant status, should not be used with code 996.83 Complications of transplanted heart. The status code does not provide additional information. The complication code indicates that the patient is a heart transplant patient.

The status V codes/categories are:

V02 Carrier or suspected carrier of infectious diseases—Carrier status indicates that a person harbors the specific organisms of a disease without manifest symptoms and is capable of transmitting the infection.

V08 Asymptomatic HIV infection status—This code indicates that a patient has tested positive for HIV but has manifested no signs or symptoms of the disease.

V09 Infection with drug-resistant microorganisms—This category indicates that a patient has an infection that is resistant to drug treatment. Sequence the infection code first.

V21 Constitutional states in development

V22.2 Pregnant state, incidental—This code is a secondary code only for use when the pregnancy is in no way complicating the reason for visit. Otherwise, a code from the obstetric chapter is required.

V26.5x Sterilization status

V42 Organ or tissue replaced by transplant

V43 Organ or tissue replaced by other means

V44 Artificial opening status

V45 Other postsurgical states

V46 Other dependence on machines

V49.6 Upper limb amputation status

V49.7 Lower limb amputation status

V49.81 Postmenopausal status

V49.82 Dental sealant status

V49.83 Awaiting organ transplant status

V58.6 Long-term (current) drug use—This subcategory indicates a patient's continuous use of a prescribed drug (including such things as aspirin therapy) for the long-term treatment of a condition or for prophylactic use. It is not for use for patients who have addictions to drugs.

Assign a code from subcategory V58.6 Long-term (current) drug use, if the patient is receiving a medication for an extended period as a prophylactic measure (such as for the prevention of deep vein thrombosis) or as treatment of a chronic condition (such as arthritis) or a disease requiring a lengthy course of treatment (such as cancer). Do not assign a code from subcategory V58.6 for medication being administered for a brief period of time to treat an acute illness or injury (such as a course of antibiotics to treat acute bronchitis).

V83 Genetic carrier status—Genetic carrier status indicates that a person carries a gene, associated with a particular disease, which may be passed to offspring who may develop that disease. The person does not have the disease and is not at risk of developing the disease.

V84 Genetic susceptibility status—Genetic susceptibility indicates that a person has a gene that increases the risk of that person developing the disease.

Codes from category V84 Genetic susceptibility to disease, should not be used as principal or first-listed codes. If the patient has the condition to which he/she is susceptible and that condition is the reason for the encounter, the code for the current condition should be sequenced first. If the patient is being seen for follow-up after completed treatment for this condition and the condition no longer exists, a follow-up code should be sequenced first, followed by the appropriate personal history and genetic susceptibility codes. If the purpose of the encounter is genetic counseling associated with procreative management, a code from subcategory V26.3 Genetic counseling and testing, should be assigned as the first-listed code, followed by a code from category V84.

Additional codes should be assigned for any applicable family or personal history. See Section I.C.18.d.14. for information on prophylactic organ removal due to a genetic susceptibility.

Note: Categories V42-V46, and subcategories V49.6, V49.7 are for use only if there are no complications or malfunctions of the organ or tissue replaced, the amputation site, or the equipment on which the patient is dependent.

4) **History (of)**—There are two types of history V codes, personal and family. Personal history codes explain a patient's past medical condition that no longer exists and is not receiving any treatment but that has the potential for recurrence, and therefore may require continued monitoring. The exceptions to this general rule are category V14 Personal history of allergy to medicinal agents, and subcategory V15.0 Allergy, other than to medicinal agents. A person who has had an allergic episode to a substance or food in the past should always be considered allergic to the substance.

Family history codes are for use when a patient has a family member(s) who has had a particular disease that causes the patient to be at higher risk of also contracting the disease.

Personal history codes may be used in conjunction with follow-up codes and family history codes may be used in conjunction with screening codes to explain the need for a test or procedure. History codes are also acceptable on any medical record regardless of the reason for visit. A history of an illness, even if no longer present, is important information that may alter the type of treatment ordered.

The history V code categories are:

V10 Personal history of malignant neoplasm

V12 Personal history of certain other diseases

V13 Personal history of other diseases
Except: V13.4 Personal history of arthritis, and V13.6 Personal history of congenital malformations. These conditions are life-long so are not true history codes.

V14 Personal history of allergy to medicinal agents

V15 Other personal history presenting hazards to health
Except: V15.7 Personal history of contraception

V16 Family history of malignant neoplasm

V17 Family history of certain chronic disabling diseases

V18 Family history of certain other specific diseases

V19 Family history of other conditions

5) **Screening**—Screening is the testing for disease or disease precursors in seemingly well individuals so that early detection and treatment can be provided for those who test positive for the disease. Screenings that are recommended for many subgroups in a population include routine mammograms for women over 40, a fecal occult blood test for everyone over 50, an amniocentesis to rule out a fetal anomaly for pregnant women over 35, because the incidence of breast cancer and colon cancer in these subgroups is higher than in the general population, as is the incidence of Down's syndrome in older mothers.

The testing of a person to rule out or confirm a suspected diagnosis because the patient has some sign or symptom is a diagnostic examination, not a screening. In these cases, the sign or symptom is used to explain the reason for the test.

A screening code may be a first-listed code if the reason for the visit is specifically the screening exam. It may also be used as an additional code if the screening is done during an office visit for other health problems. A screening code is not necessary if the screening is inherent to a routine examination, such as a Pap smear done during a routine pelvic examination.

Should a condition be discovered during the screening then the code for the condition may be assigned as an additional diagnosis.

The V code indicates that a screening exam is planned. A procedure code is required to confirm that the screening was performed.

The screening V code categories:

V28 Antenatal screening

V73-V82 Special screening examinations

6) **Observation**—There are two observation V code categories. They are for use in very limited circumstances when a person is being observed for a suspected condition that is ruled out. The observation codes are not for use if an injury or illness or any signs or symptoms related to the suspected condition are present. In such cases the diagnosis/symptom code is used with the corresponding E code to identify any external cause.

The observation codes are to be used as principal diagnosis only. The only exception to this is when the principal diagnosis is required to be a code from the V30 Live born infant, category. Then the V29 observation code is sequenced after the V30 code. Additional codes may be used in addition to the observation code but only if they are unrelated to the suspected condition being observed.

The observation V code categories:

V29 Observation and evaluation of newborns for suspected condition not found
For the birth encounter, a code from category V30 should be sequenced before the V29 code.

V71 Observation and evaluation for suspected condition not found

7) **Aftercare**—Aftercare visit codes cover situations when the initial treatment of a disease or injury has been performed and the patient requires continued care during the healing or recovery phase, or for the long-term consequences of the disease. The aftercare V code should not be used if treatment is directed at a current, acute disease or injury, the diagnosis code is to be used in these cases. Exceptions to this rule are codes V58.0 Radiotherapy, and **codes from subcategory V58.1 Encounter for chemotherapy and immunotherapy for neoplastic conditions.** These codes are to be first listed, followed by the diagnosis code when a patient's encounter is solely to receive radiation therapy or chemotherapy for the treatment of a neoplasm. Should a patient receive both chemotherapy and radiation therapy during the same encounter, codes V58.0 and V58.1 may be used together on a record with either one being sequenced first.

The aftercare codes are generally first listed to explain the specific reason for the encounter. An aftercare code may be used as an additional code when some type of aftercare is provided in addition to the reason for admission and no diagnosis code is applicable. An example of this would be the closure of a colostomy during an encounter for treatment of another condition.

Certain aftercare V code categories need a secondary diagnosis code to describe the resolving condition or sequelae, for others, the condition is inherent in the code title.

Additional V code aftercare category terms include fitting and adjustment, and attention to artificial openings.

Status V codes may be used with aftercare V codes to indicate the nature of the aftercare. For example code V45.81 Aortocoronary bypass status, may be used with code V58.73 Aftercare following surgery of the circulatory system, NEC, to indicate the surgery for which the aftercare is being performed. Also, a transplant status code may be used following code V58.44 Aftercare following organ transplant, to identify the organ transplanted. A status code should not be used when the aftercare code indicates the type of status, such as using V55.0 Attention to tracheostomy with V44.0 Tracheostomy status.

The aftercare V category/codes:

V52 Fitting and adjustment of prosthetic device and implant
V53 Fitting and adjustment of other device
V54 Other orthopedic aftercare
V55 Attention to artificial openings
V56 Encounter for dialysis and dialysis catheter care
V57 Care involving the use of rehabilitation procedures
V58.0 Radiotherapy
V58.11 Encounter for antineoplastic chemotherapy
V58.12 Encounter for antineoplastic immunotherapy
V58.3 Attention to surgical dressings and sutures
V58.41 Encounter for planned post-operative wound closure
V58.42 Aftercare, surgery, neoplasm
V58.43 Aftercare, surgery, trauma
V58.44 Aftercare involving organ transplant
V58.49 Other specified aftercare following surgery
V58.7x Aftercare following surgery
V58.81 Fitting and adjustment of vascular catheter
V58.82 Fitting and adjustment of non-vascular catheter
V58.83 Monitoring therapeutic drug
V58.89 Other specified aftercare

8) **Follow-up**—The follow-up codes are used to explain continuing surveillance following completed treatment of a disease, condition, or injury. They imply that the condition has been fully treated and no longer exists. They should not be confused with aftercare codes that explain current treatment for a healing condition or its sequelae. Follow-up codes may be used in conjunction with history codes to provide the full picture of the healed condition and its treatment. The follow-up code is sequenced first, followed by the history code.

A follow-up code may be used to explain repeated visits. Should a condition be found to have recurred on the follow-up visit, then the diagnosis code should be used in place of the follow-up code.

The follow-up V code categories:

V24 Postpartum care and evaluation
V67 Follow-up examination

9) **Donor**—Category V59 is the donor codes. They are used for living individuals who are donating blood or other body tissue. These codes are only for individuals donating for others, not for self-donations. They are not for use to identify cadaveric donations.

10) **Counseling**—Counseling V codes are used when a patient or family member receives assistance in the aftermath of an illness or injury, or when support is required in coping with family or social problems. They are not necessary for use in conjunction with a diagnosis code when the counseling component of care is considered integral to standard treatment.

The counseling V categories/codes:

V25.0 General counseling and advice for contraceptive management
V26.3 Genetic counseling
V26.4 General counseling and advice for procreative management
V61 Other family circumstances
V65.1 Person consulted on behalf of another person
V65.3 Dietary surveillance and counseling
V65.4 Other counseling, not elsewhere classified

11) **Obstetrics and related conditions**—See section I.C.11., the obstetrics guidelines for further instruction on the use of these codes.

V codes for pregnancy are for use in those circumstances when none of the problems or complications included in the codes from the obstetrics chapter exist (a routine prenatal visit or postpartum care). Codes V22.0 Supervision of normal first pregnancy, and V22.1 Supervision of other normal pregnancy, are always first listed and are not to be used with any other code from the OB chapter.

The outcome of delivery, category V27, should be included on all maternal delivery records. It is always a secondary code.

V codes for family planning (contraceptive) or procreative management and counseling should be included on an obstetric record either during the pregnancy or the postpartum stage, if applicable.

Obstetrics and related conditions V code categories:

V22 Normal pregnancy
V23 Supervision of high-risk pregnancy
Except: V23.2 Pregnancy with history of abortion. Code 646.3 Habitual aborter, from the OB chapter is required to indicate a history of abortion during a pregnancy.
V24 Postpartum care and evaluation
V25 Encounter for contraceptive management
Except V25.0x (See section I.C.18.d.11, Counseling)
V26 Procreative management
Except V26.5x Sterilization status, V26.3 and V26.4 (See section I.C.18.d.11., Counseling)
V27 Outcome of delivery
V28 Antenatal screening (See section I.C.18.d.6., Screening)

12) **Newborn, infant and child**—See section I.C.15, the newborn guidelines, for further instruction on the use of these codes.

Newborn V code categories:

V20 Health supervision of infant or child
V29 Observation and evaluation of newborns for suspected condition not found (See section I.C.18.d.7, Observation).
V30-V39 Liveborn infant according to type of birth

13) **Routine and administrative examinations**—The V codes allow for the description of encounters for routine examinations, such as a general check-up or, examinations for administrative purposes, such as a pre-employment physical. The codes are for use as first-listed codes only, and are not to be used if the examination is for diagnosis of a suspected condition or for treatment purposes. In such cases the diagnosis code is used. During a routine exam, should a diagnosis or condition be discovered, it should be coded as an additional code. Pre-existing and chronic conditions and history codes may also be included as additional codes as long as the examination is for administrative purposes and not focused on any particular condition.

Preoperative examination V codes are for use only in those situations when a patient is being cleared for surgery and no treatment is given.

The V code categories/code for routine and administrative examinations:

V20.2 Routine infant or child health check Any injections given should have a corresponding procedure code.
V70 General medical examination
V72 Special investigations and examinations
Except V72.5 and V72.6

14) **Miscellaneous V codes**—The miscellaneous V codes capture a number of other health care encounters that do not fall into one of the other categories. Certain of these codes identify the reason for the encounter, others are for use as additional codes that provide useful information on circumstances that may affect a patient's care and treatment.

Prophylactic Organ Removal

For encounters specifically for prophylactic removal of breasts, ovaries, or another organ due to a genetic susceptibility to cancer or a family history of cancer, the principal or first-listed code should be a code from subcategory V50.4 Prophylactic organ removal, followed by the appropriate genetic susceptibility code and the appropriate family history code.

If the patient has a malignancy of one site and is having prophylactic removal at another site to prevent either a new primary malignancy or metastatic disease, a code for the malignancy should also be assigned in addition to a code from subcategory V50.4. A V50.4 code should not be assigned if the patient is having organ removal for treatment of a malignancy, such as the removal of the testes for the treatment of prostate cancer.

Miscellaneous V code categories/codes:

V07 Need for isolation and other prophylactic measures
V50 Elective surgery for purposes other than remedying health states
V58.5 Orthodontics
V60 Housing, household, and economic circumstances
V62 Other psychosocial circumstances
V63 Unavailability of other medical facilities for care
V64 Persons encountering health services for specific procedures, not carried out
V66 Convalescence and palliative care
V68 Encounters for administrative purposes
V69 Problems related to lifestyle

15) **Nonspecific V codes**—Certain V codes are so nonspecific, or potentially redundant with other codes in the classification, that there can be little justification for their use in the inpatient setting. Their use in the outpatient setting should be limited to those instances when there is no further documentation to permit more precise coding. Otherwise, any sign or symptom or any other reason for a visit that is captured in another code should be used.

Nonspecific V code categories/codes:

V11 Personal history of mental disorder—A code from the mental disorders chapter, with an in remission fifth digit, should be used.
V13.4 Personal history of arthritis
V13.6 Personal history of congenital malformations
V15.7 Personal history of contraception
V23.2 Pregnancy with history of abortion
V40 Mental and behavioral problems
V41 Problems with special senses and other special functions
V47 Other problems with internal organs
V48 Problems with head, neck, and trunk
V49 Problems with limbs and other problems
Exceptions:
V49.6 Upper limb amputation status
V49.7 Lower limb amputation status
V49.81 Postmenopausal status
V49.82 Dental sealant status
V49.83 Awaiting organ transplant status
V51 Aftercare involving the use of plastic surgery
V58.2 Blood transfusion, without reported diagnosis
V58.9 Unspecified aftercare
V72.5 Radiological examination, NEC
V72.6 Laboratory examination
Codes V72.5 and V72.6 are not to be used if any sign or symptoms, or reason for a test is documented. See section IV.K. and section IV.L. of the outpatient guidelines.

V Code Table

Items in bold indicate a change from the April 2005 table. Items underlined have been moved within the table since April 2005.

FIRST LISTED: V codes/categories/subcategories which are only acceptable as principal/first listed.

Codes:

V22.0 Supervision of normal first pregnancy
V22.1 Supervision of other normal pregnancy
V46.12 Encounter for respirator dependence during power failure
V46.13 Encounter for weaning from respirator [ventilator]
V56.0 Extracorporeal dialysis
V58.0 Radiotherapy
V58.0 and **V58.1** may be used together on a record with either one being sequenced first, when a patient receives both chemotherapy and radiation therapy during the same encounter.
V58.11 Encounter for antineoplastic chemotherapy
V58.0 and V58.11 may be used together on a record, with either one being sequenced first, when a patient receives both chemotherapy and radiation therapy during the same encounter.
V58.12 Encounter for antineoplastic immunotherapy

Categories/Subcategories:

V20 Health supervision of infant or child
V24 Postpartum care and examination
V29 Observation and evaluation of newborns for suspected condition not found
Exception: A code from the V30-V39 may be sequenced before the V29 if it is the newborn record.
V30-V39 Liveborn infants according to type of birth
V57 Care involving use of rehabilitation procedures
V59 Donors
V66 Convalescence and palliative care
Exception: V66.7 Palliative care
V68 Encounters for administrative purposes
V70 General medical examination
Exception: V70.7 Examination of participant in clinical trial
V71 Observation and evaluation for suspected conditions not found
V72 Special investigations and examinations
Exceptions:
V72.4 Pregnancy examination or test
V72.5 Radiological examination, NEC
V72.6 Laboratory examination
V72.86 Encounter for blood typing

FIRST OR ADDITIONAL: V code categories/subcategories which may be either principal/first-listed, or additional codes.

Codes:

V15.88 History of fall
V43.22 Fully implantable artificial heart status
V46.14 Mechanical complication of respirator [ventilator]
V49.81 Asymptomatic postmenopausal status (age-related) (natural)
V49.84 Bed confinement status
V49.89 Other specified conditions influencing health status
V70.7 Examination of participant in clinical trial
V72.5 Radiological examination, NEC
V72.6 Laboratory examination
V72.86 Encounter for blood typing

Categories/Subcategories:

V01 Contact with or exposure to communicable diseases
V02 Carrier or suspected carrier of infectious diseases
V03-V06 Need for prophylactic vaccination and inoculations
V07 Need for isolation and other prophylactic measures
V08 Asymptomatic HIV infection status
V10 Personal history of malignant neoplasm
V12 Personal history of certain other diseases
V13 Personal history of other diseases
Exception:
V13.4 Personal history of arthritis
V13.69 Personal history of other congenital malformations

V16-V19	Family history of disease
V23	Supervision of high-risk pregnancy
V25	Encounter for contraceptive management
V26	Procreative management **Exception:** V26.5 Sterilization status
V28	Antenatal screening
V45.7	Acquired absence of organ
V49.6x	**Upper limb amputation status**
V49.7x	**Lower limb amputation status**
V50	Elective surgery for purposes other than remedying health states
V52	Fitting and adjustment of prosthetic device and implant
V53	Fitting and adjustment of other device
V54	Other orthopedic aftercare
V55	Attention to artificial openings
V56	Encounter for dialysis and dialysis catheter care **Exception: V56.0 Extracorporeal dialysis**
V58.3	Attention to surgical dressings and sutures
V58.4	Other aftercare following surgery
V58.7	Aftercare following surgery to specified body systems, not elsewhere classified
V58.8	Other specified procedures and aftercare
V61	Other family circumstances
V63	Unavailability of other medical facilities for care
V65	Other persons seeking consultation without complaint or sickness
V67	Follow-up examination
V69	Problems related to lifestyle
V72.4	**Pregnancy examination or test**
V73-V82	Special screening examinations
V83	Genetic carrier status

ADDITIONAL ONLY: V code categories/subcategories which may only be used as additional codes, not principal/first listed.

Codes:

V13.61	Personal history of hypospadias
V22.2	Pregnancy state, incidental
V46.11	**Dependence on respirator, status**
V49.82	Dental sealant status
V49.83	Awaiting organ transplant status
V66.7	Palliative care
V85	Body mass index

Categories/Subcategories:

V09	Infection with drug-resistant microorganisms
V14	Personal history of allergy to medicinal agents
V15	Other personal history presenting hazards to health **Exception:** V15.7 Personal history of contraception
V15.88	**History of fall**
V21	Constitutional states in development
V26.5	Sterilization status
V27	Outcome of delivery
V42	Organ or tissue replaced by transplant
V43	Organ or tissue replaced by other means **Exception:** V43.22 Fully implantable artificial heart status
V44	Artificial opening status
V45	Other postsurgical states Exception: Subcategory V45.7 Acquired absence of organ
V46	Other dependence on machines **Exception:** V46.12 Encounter for respirator dependence during power failure
V46.13	**Encounter for weaning from respirator [ventilator]**
~~V49.6x~~	~~Upper limb amputation status~~
~~V49.7x~~	~~Lower limb amputation status~~
V58.6	**Long-term current drug use**
V60	Housing, household, and economic circumstances
V62	Other psychosocial circumstances
V64	Persons encountering health services for specified procedure, not carried out
V84	Genetic susceptibility to disease
V85	**Body Mass Index**

NONSPECIFIC CODES AND CATEGORIES:

V11	Personal history of mental disorder
V13.4	Personal history of arthritis
V13.69	Personal history of congenital malformations
V15.7	Personal history of contraception
V40	Mental and behavioral problems
V41	Problems with special senses and other special functions
V47	Other problems with internal organs
V48	Problems with head, neck, and trunk
V49.0	**Deficiencies of limbs**
V49.1	**Mechanical problems with limbs**
V49.2	**Motor problems with limbs**
V49.3	**Sensory problems with limbs**
V49.4	**Disfigurements in limbs**
V49.5	**Other problems with limbs**
V49.9	**Unspecified condition influencing health status**
V51	Aftercare involving the use of plastic surgery
V58.2	Blood transfusion, without reported diagnosis
V58.5	Orthodontics
V58.9	Unspecified aftercare
V72.5	Radiological examination, NEC
V72.6	Laboratory examination

19. Supplemental Classification of External Causes of Injury and Poisoning (E-codes, E800-E999)

Introduction: These guidelines are provided for those who are currently collecting E codes in order that there will be standardization in the process. If your institution plans to begin collecting E codes, these guidelines are to be applied. The use of E codes is supplemental to the application of ICD-9-CM diagnosis codes. E codes are never to be recorded as principal diagnoses (first-listed in non-inpatient setting) and are not required for reporting to CMS.

External causes of injury and poisoning codes (E codes) are intended to provide data for injury research and evaluation of injury prevention strategies. E codes capture how the injury or poisoning happened (cause), the intent (unintentional or accidental; or intentional, such as suicide or assault), and the place where the event occurred.

Some major categories of E codes include:

- Transport accidents
- Poisoning and adverse effects of drugs, medicinal substances and biologicals
- Accidental falls
- Accidents caused by fire and flames
- Accidents due to natural and environmental factors
- Late effects of accidents, assaults or self injury
- Assaults or purposely inflicted injury
- Suicide or self inflicted injury

These guidelines apply to the coding and collection of E codes from records in hospitals, outpatient clinics, emergency departments, other ambulatory care settings and provider offices, and nonacute care settings, except when other specific guidelines apply.

a. General E code coding guidelines

1) **Used with any code in the range of 001-V86.1**—An E code may be used with any code in the range of 001-V86.1, which indicates an injury, poisoning, or adverse effect due to an external cause.

2) **Assign the appropriate E code for all initial treatments**—Assign the appropriate E code for the initial encounter of an injury, poisoning, or adverse effect of drugs, not for subsequent treatment.

3) **Use the full range of E codes**—Use the full range of E codes to completely describe the cause, the intent and the place of occurrence, if applicable, for all injuries, poisonings, and adverse effects of drugs.

4) **Assign as many E codes as necessary**
Assign as many E codes as necessary to fully explain each cause. If only one E code can be recorded, assign the E code most related to the principal diagnosis.

5) **The selection of the appropriate E code**—The selection of the appropriate E code is guided by the Index to External Causes, which is located after the Alphabetical Index to Diseases and by inclusion and exclusion notes in the Tabular List.

6) **E code can never be a principal diagnosis**—An E code can never be a principal (first-listed) diagnosis.

7) **External cause code(s) with systemic inflammatory response syndrome (SIRS)**—An external cause code(s) may be used with codes 995.93 Systemic inflammatory response syndrome due to noninfectious process without organ dysfunction, and 995.94 Systemic inflammatory response syndrome due to noninfectious process with organ dysfunction, if trauma was the initiating insult that precipitated the

SIRS. The external cause(s) code should correspond to the most serious injury resulting from the trauma. The external cause code(s) should only be assigned if the trauma necessitated the admission in which the patient also developed SIRS. If a patient is admitted with SIRS but the trauma has been treated previously, the external cause codes should not be used.

b. **Place of occurrence guideline**—Use an additional code from category E849 to indicate the place of occurrence for injuries and poisonings. The place of occurrence describes the place where the event occurred and not the patient's activity at the time of the event.

Do not use E849.9 if the place of occurrence is not stated.

c. **Adverse effects of drugs, medicinal and biological substances guidelines**

1) **Do not code directly from the Table of Drugs**—Do not code directly from the Table of Drugs and Chemicals. Always refer back to the Tabular List.

2) **Use as many codes as necessary to describe**—Use as many codes as necessary to describe completely all drugs, medicinal or biological substances.

3) **If the same E code would describe the causative agent**—If the same E code would describe the causative agent for more than one adverse reaction, assign the code only once.

4) **If two or more drugs, medicinal or biological substances**—If two or more drugs, medicinal or biological substances are reported, code each individually unless the combination code is listed in the Table of Drugs and Chemicals. In that case, assign the E code for the combination.

5) **When a reaction results from the interaction of a drug(s)**—When a reaction results from the interaction of a drug(s) and alcohol, use poisoning codes and E codes for both.

6) **If the reporting format limits the number of E codes**—If the reporting format limits the number of E codes that can be used in reporting clinical data, code the one most related to the principal diagnosis. Include at least one from each category (cause, intent, place) if possible.

If there are different fourth-digit codes in the same three-digit category, use the code for "other specified" of that category. If there is no "other specified" code in that category, use the appropriate "unspecified" code in that category.

If the codes are in different three-digit categories, assign the appropriate E code for other multiple drugs and medicinal substances.

7) **Codes from the E930-E949 series**—Codes from the E930-E949 series must be used to identify the causative substance for an adverse effect of drug, medicinal and biological substances, correctly prescribed and properly administered. The effect, such as tachycardia, delirium, gastrointestinal hemorrhaging, vomiting, hypokalemia, hepatitis, renal failure, or respiratory failure, is coded and followed by the appropriate code from the E930-E949 series.

d. **Multiple cause E code coding guidelines**—If two or more events cause separate injuries, an E code should be assigned for each cause. The first listed E code will be selected in the following order:

E codes for child and adult abuse take priority over all other E codes. See section I.C.19.e., Child and adult abuse guidelines.

E codes for terrorism events take priority over all other E codes except child and adult abuse.

E codes for cataclysmic events take priority over all other E codes except child and adult abuse and terrorism.

E codes for transport accidents take priority over all other E codes except cataclysmic events and child and adult abuse and terrorism.

The first-listed E code should correspond to the cause of the most serious diagnosis due to an assault, accident, or self-harm, following the order of hierarchy listed above.

e. **Child and adult abuse guideline**

1) **Intentional injury**—When the cause of an injury or neglect is intentional child or adult abuse, the first-listed E code should be assigned from categories E960-E968 Homicide and injury purposely inflicted by other persons, (except category E967). An E code from category E967 Child and adult battering and other maltreatment, should be added as an additional code to identify the perpetrator, if known.

2) **Accidental intent**—In cases of neglect when the intent is determined to be accidental E code E904.0 Abandonment or neglect of infant and helpless person, should be the first-listed E code.

f. **Unknown or suspected intent guideline**

1) **If the intent (accident, self-harm, assault) of the cause of an injury or poisoning is unknown**—If the intent (accident, self-harm, assault) of the cause of an injury or poisoning is unknown or unspecified, code the intent as undetermined, E980-E989.

2) **If the intent (accident, self-harm, assault) of the cause of an injury or poisoning is questionable**—If the intent (accident, self-harm, assault) of the cause of an injury or poisoning is questionable, probable or suspected, code the intent as undetermined, E980-E989.

g. **Undetermined cause**—When the intent of an injury or poisoning is known, but the cause is unknown, use codes E928.9 Unspecified accident, E958.9 Suicide and self-inflicted injury by unspecified means, and E968.9 Assault by unspecified means.

These E codes should rarely be used, as the documentation in the medical record, in both the inpatient outpatient and other settings, should normally provide sufficient detail to determine the cause of the injury.

h. **Late effects of external cause guidelines**

1) **Late effect E codes**—Late effect E codes exist for injuries and poisonings but not for adverse effects of drugs, misadventures, and surgical complications.

2) **Late effect E codes (E929, E959, E969, E977, E989, or E999.1)**—A late effect E code (E929, E959, E969, E977, E989, or E999.1) should be used with any report of a late effect or sequela resulting from a previous injury or poisoning (905-909).

3) **Late effect E code with a related current injury**—A late effect E code should never be used with a related current nature of injury code.

4) **Use of late effect E codes for subsequent visits**—Use a late effect E code for subsequent visits when a late effect of the initial injury or poisoning is being treated. There is no late effect E code for adverse effects of drugs. Do not use a late effect E code for subsequent visits for follow-up care (e.g., to assess healing, to receive rehabilitative therapy) of the injury or poisoning when no late effect of the injury has been documented.

i. **Misadventures and complications of care guidelines**

1) **Code range E870-E876**—Assign a code in the range of E870-E876 if misadventures are stated by the provider.

2) **Code range E878-E879**—Assign a code in the range of E878-E879 if the provider attributes an abnormal reaction or later complication to a surgical or medical procedure, but does not mention misadventure at the time of the procedure as the cause of the reaction.

j. **Terrorism guidelines**

1) **Cause of injury identified by the federal government (FBI) as terrorism**—When the cause of an injury is identified by the federal government (FBI) as terrorism, the first-listed E code should be a code from category E979 Terrorism. The definition of terrorism employed by the FBI is found at the inclusion note at E979. The terrorism E code is the only E code that should be assigned. Additional E codes from the assault categories should not be assigned.

2) **Cause of an injury is suspected to be the result of terrorism**—When the cause of an injury is suspected to be the result of terrorism a code from category E979 should not be assigned. Assign a code in the range of E codes based on the documentation of intent and mechanism.

3) **Code E979.9 Terrorism, secondary effects**—Assign code E979.9 Terrorism, secondary effects, for conditions occurring subsequent to the terrorist event. This code should not be assigned for conditions that are due to the initial terrorist act.

4) **Statistical tabulation of terrorism codes**—For statistical purposes these codes will be tabulated within the category for assault, expanding the current category from E960-E969 to include E979 and E999.1.

Section II. Selection of Principal Diagnosis

The circumstances of inpatient admission always govern the selection of principal diagnosis. The principal diagnosis is defined in the Uniform Hospital Discharge Data Set (UHDDS) as "that condition established after study to be chiefly responsible for occasioning the admission of the patient to the hospital for care."

The UHDDS definitions are used by hospitals to report inpatient data elements in a standardized manner. These data elements and their definitions can be found in the July 31, 1985, *Federal Register* (vol. 50, no. 147), pp. 31038-40.

Since that time the application of the UHDDS definitions has been expanded to include all non-outpatient settings (acute care, short-term, long-term care and psychiatric hospitals; home health agencies; rehab facilities; nursing homes, etc.).

In determining principal diagnosis the coding conventions in the ICD-9-CM, Volumes 1 and 2 take precedence over these official coding guidelines. (See section I.A., Conventions, for the ICD-9-CM).

The importance of consistent, complete documentation in the medical record cannot be overemphasized. Without such documentation the application of all coding guidelines is a difficult, if not impossible, task.

A. Codes for symptoms, signs, and ill-defined conditions
Codes for symptoms, signs, and ill-defined conditions from chapter 16 are not to be used as principal diagnosis when a related definitive diagnosis has been established.

B. Two or more interrelated conditions, each potentially meeting the definition for principal diagnosis.
When there are two or more interrelated conditions (such as diseases in the same ICD-9-CM chapter or manifestations characteristically associated with a certain disease) potentially meeting the definition of principal diagnosis, either condition may be sequenced first, unless the circumstances of the admission, the therapy provided, the Tabular List, or the Alphabetic Index indicate otherwise.

C. Two or more diagnoses that equally meet the definition for principal diagnosis
In the unusual instance when two or more diagnoses equally meet the criteria for principal diagnosis as determined by the circumstances of admission, diagnostic workup and/or therapy provided, and the Alphabetic Index, Tabular List, or another coding guidelines do not provide sequencing direction, any one of the diagnoses may be sequenced first.

D. Two or more comparative or contrasting conditions.
In those rare instances when two or more contrasting or comparative diagnoses are documented as "either/or" (or similar terminology), they are coded as if the diagnoses were confirmed and the diagnoses are sequenced according to the circumstances of the admission. If no further determination can be made as to which diagnosis should be principal, either diagnosis may be sequenced first.

E. A symptom(s) followed by contrasting/comparative diagnoses
When a symptom(s) is followed by contrasting/comparative diagnoses, the symptom code is sequenced first. All the contrasting/comparative diagnoses should be coded as additional diagnoses.

F. Original treatment plan not carried out
Sequence as the principal diagnosis the condition, which after study occasioned the admission to the hospital, even though treatment may not have been carried out due to unforeseen circumstances.

G. Complications of surgery and other medical care
When the admission is for treatment of a complication resulting from surgery or other medical care, the complication code is sequenced as the principal diagnosis. If the complication is classified to the 996-999 series and the code lacks the necessary specificity in describing the complication, an additional code for the specific complication should be assigned.

H. Uncertain diagnosis
If the diagnosis documented at the time of discharge is qualified as "probable," "suspected," "likely," "questionable," "possible," or "still to be ruled out," code the condition as if it existed or was established. The bases for these guidelines are the diagnostic workup, arrangements for further workup or observation, and initial therapeutic approach that correspond most closely with the established diagnosis.

Note: This guideline is applicable only to short-term, acute, long-term care and psychiatric hospitals.

I. Admission from observation unit

1. **Admission following medical observation—When a patient is admitted to an observation unit for a medical condition that either worsens or does not improve, and is subsequently admitted as an inpatient of the same hospital for this same medical condition, the principal diagnosis would be the medical condition that led to the hospital admission.**
2. **Admission following post-operative observation—When a patient is admitted to an observation unit to monitor a condition (or complication) that develops following outpatient surgery and then is subsequently admitted as an inpatient of the same hospital, hospitals should apply the Uniform Hospital Discharge Data Set (UHDDS) definition of principal diagnosis as "that condition established after study to be chiefly responsible for occasioning the admission of the patient to the hospital for care."**

J. Admission from outpatient surgery
When a patient receives surgery in the hospital's outpatient surgery department and is subsequently admitted for continuing inpatient care at the same hospital, the following guidelines should be followed in selecting the principal diagnosis for the inpatient admission:

- **If the reason for the inpatient admission is a complication, assign the complication as the principal diagnosis.**
- **If no complication, or other condition, is documented as the reason for the inpatient admission, assign the reason for the outpatient surgery as the principal diagnosis.**
- **If the reason for the inpatient admission is another condition unrelated to the surgery, assign the unrelated condition as the principal diagnosis.**

Section III. Reporting Additional Diagnoses

GENERAL RULES FOR OTHER (ADDITIONAL) DIAGNOSES

For reporting purposes the definition for "other diagnoses" is interpreted as additional conditions that affect patient care in terms of requiring:

- Clinical evaluation; or
- Therapeutic treatment; or
- Diagnostic procedures; or
- Extended length of hospital stay; or
- Increased nursing care and/or monitoring.

The UHDDS item #11-b defines other diagnoses as "all conditions that coexist at the time of admission, that develop subsequently, or that affect the treatment received and/or the length of stay. Diagnoses that relate to an earlier episode which have no bearing on the current hospital stay are to be excluded." UHDDS definitions apply to inpatients in acute care, short-term, long-term care and psychiatric hospital settings. The UHDDS definitions are used by acute care short-term hospitals to report inpatient data elements in a standardized manner. These data elements and their definitions can be found in the July 31, 1985, *Federal Register* (vol. 50, no. 147), pp. 31038-40.

Since that time the application of the UHDDS definitions has been expanded to include all non-outpatient settings (acute care, short-term, long-term care and psychiatric hospitals; home health agencies; rehab facilities; nursing homes, etc.).

The following guidelines are to be applied in designating other diagnoses when neither the Alphabetic Index nor the Tabular List in ICD-9-CM provides direction. The listing of the diagnoses in the patient record is the responsibility of the attending provider.

A. Previous conditions
If the provider has included a diagnosis in the final diagnostic statement, such as the discharge summary or the face sheet, it should ordinarily be coded. Some providers include in the diagnostic statement resolved conditions or diagnoses and status-post procedures from previous admission that have no bearing on the current stay. Such conditions are not to be reported and are coded only if required by hospital policy.

However, history codes (V10-V19) may be used as secondary codes if the historical condition or family history has an impact on current care or influences treatment.

B. Abnormal findings
Abnormal findings (laboratory, x-ray, pathologic, and other diagnostic results) are not coded and reported unless the provider indicates their clinical significance. If the findings are outside the normal range and the attending provider has ordered other tests to evaluate the condition or prescribed treatment, it is appropriate to ask the provider whether the abnormal finding should be added.

Please note: This differs from the coding practices in the outpatient setting for coding encounters for diagnostic tests that have been interpreted by a provider.

C. Uncertain Diagnosis
If the diagnosis documented at the time of discharge is qualified as "probable," "suspected," "likely," "questionable," "possible," or "still to be ruled out," code the condition as if it existed or was established. The bases for these guidelines are the diagnostic workup, arrangements for further workup or observation, and initial therapeutic approach that correspond most closely with the established diagnosis.

Note: This guideline is applicable only to short-term, acute, long-term care and psychiatric hospitals.

Section IV. Diagnostic Coding and Reporting Guidelines for Outpatient Services

These coding guidelines for outpatient diagnoses have been approved for use by hospitals/providers in coding and reporting hospital-based outpatient services and provider-based office visits.

Information about the use of certain abbreviations, punctuation, symbols, and other conventions used in the ICD-9-CM Tabular List (code numbers and titles), can be found in section IA of these guidelines, under "Conventions for the ICD-9-CM." Information about the correct sequence to use in finding a code is also described in section I.

The terms "encounter" and "visit" are often used interchangeably in describing outpatient service contacts and, therefore, appear together in these guidelines without distinguishing one from the other.

Though the conventions and general guidelines apply to all settings, coding guidelines for outpatient and provider reporting of diagnoses will vary in a number of instances from those for inpatient diagnoses, recognizing that:

- The Uniform Hospital Discharge Data Set (UHDDS) definition of principal diagnosis applies only to inpatients in acute, short-term, long-term care and psychiatric hospitals.
- Coding guidelines for inconclusive diagnoses (probable, suspected, rule out, etc.) were developed for inpatient reporting and do not apply to outpatients.

A. Selection of first-listed condition

In the outpatient setting, the term "first-listed diagnosis" is used in lieu of principal diagnosis.

In determining the first-listed diagnosis the coding conventions of ICD-9-CM, as well as the general and disease-specific guidelines take precedence over the outpatient guidelines.

Diagnoses often are not established at the time of the initial encounter/visit. It may take two or more visits before the diagnosis is confirmed.

The most critical rule involves beginning the search for the correct code assignment through the Alphabetic Index. Never begin searching initially in the Tabular List as this will lead to coding errors.

1. **Outpatient surgery—When a patient presents for outpatient surgery, code the reason for the surgery as the first-listed diagnosis (reason for the encounter), even if the surgery is not performed due to a contraindication.**
2. **Observation stay—When a patient is admitted for observation for a medical condition, assign a code for the medical condition as the first-listed diagnosis. When a patient presents for outpatient surgery and develops complications requiring admission to observation, code the reason for the surgery as the first reported diagnosis (reason for the encounter), followed by codes for the complications as secondary diagnoses.**

B. Codes from 001.0 through V86.1

The appropriate code or codes from 001.0 through V86.1 must be used to identify diagnoses, symptoms, conditions, problems, complaints, or other reason(s) for the encounter/visit.

C. Accurate reporting of ICD-9-CM diagnosis codes

For accurate reporting of ICD-9-CM diagnosis codes, the documentation should describe the patient's condition, using terminology which includes specific diagnoses as well as symptoms, problems, or reasons for the encounter. There are ICD-9-CM codes to describe all of these.

D. Selection of codes 001.0 through 999.9

The selection of codes 001.0 through 999.9 will frequently be used to describe the reason for the encounter. These codes are from the section of ICD-9-CM for the classification of diseases and injuries (e.g. infectious and parasitic diseases; neoplasms; symptoms, signs, and ill-defined conditions, etc.).

E. Codes that describe symptoms and signs

Codes that describe symptoms and signs, as opposed to diagnoses, are acceptable for reporting purposes when a diagnosis has not been established (confirmed) by the provider. Chapter 16 of ICD-9-CM, Symptoms, Signs, and Ill-defined Conditions (codes 780.0-799.9) contain many, but not all, codes for symptoms.

F. Encounters for circumstances other than a disease or injury

ICD-9-CM provides codes to deal with encounters for circumstances other than a disease or injury. The Supplementary Classification of Factors Influencing Health Status and Contact with Health Services (V01.0-V84.8) is provided to deal with occasions when circumstances other than a disease or injury are recorded as diagnosis or problems.

G. Level of Detail in Coding

1. **ICD-9-CM codes with three, four, or five digits**—ICD-9-CM is composed of codes with either three, four, or five digits. Codes with three digits are included in ICD-9-CM as the heading of a category of codes that may be further subdivided by the use of fourth and/or fifth digits, which provide greater specificity.
2. **Use of full number of digits required for a code**—A three-digit code is to be used only if it is not further subdivided. Where fourth-digit subcategories and/or fifth-digit subclassifications are provided, they must be assigned. A code is invalid if it has not been coded to the full number of digits required for that code. See also discussion under section I.b.3., General coding guidelines, Level of detail in coding.

H. ICD-9-CM code for the diagnosis, condition, problem, or other reason for encounter/visit

List first the ICD-9-CM code for the diagnosis, condition, problem, or other reason for encounter/visit shown in the medical record to be chiefly responsible for the services provided. List additional codes that describe any coexisting conditions. In some cases the first-listed diagnosis may be a symptom when a diagnosis has not been established (confirmed) by the physician.

I. "Probable," "suspected," "questionable," "rule out," or "working diagnosis"

Do not code diagnoses documented as "probable," "suspected," "questionable," "rule out," or "working diagnosis." Rather, code the condition(s) to the highest degree of certainty for that encounter/visit, such as symptoms, signs, abnormal test results, or other reason for the visit. **Please note:** This differs from the coding practices used by short-term, acute care, long-term care, and psychiatric hospitals.

J. Chronic diseases

Chronic diseases treated on an ongoing basis may be coded and reported as many times as the patient receives treatment and care for the condition(s).

K. Code all documented conditions that coexist

Code all documented conditions that coexist at the time of the encounter/visit, and require or affect patient care treatment or management. Do not code conditions that were previously treated and no longer exist. However, history codes (V10-V19) may be used as secondary codes if the historical condition or family history has an impact on current care or influences treatment.

L. Patients receiving diagnostic services only

For patients receiving diagnostic services only during an encounter/visit, sequence first the diagnosis, condition, problem, or other reason for encounter/visit shown in the medical record to be chiefly responsible for the outpatient services provided during the encounter/visit. Codes for other diagnoses (e.g., chronic conditions) may be sequenced as additional diagnoses.

For outpatient encounters for diagnostic tests that have been interpreted by a physician and the final report is available at the time of coding, code any confirmed or definitive diagnosis(es) documented in the interpretation. Do not code related signs and symptoms as additional diagnoses.

Please note: This differs from the coding practice in the hospital inpatient setting regarding abnormal findings on test results.

M. Patients receiving therapeutic services only

For patients receiving therapeutic services only during an encounter/visit, sequence first the diagnosis, condition, problem, or other reason for encounter/visit shown in the medical record to be chiefly responsible for the outpatient services provided during the encounter/visit. Codes for other diagnoses (e.g., chronic conditions) may be sequenced as additional diagnoses.

The only exception to this rule is that when the primary reason for the admission/encounter is chemotherapy, radiation therapy, or rehabilitation, the appropriate V code for the service is listed first, and the diagnosis or problem for which the service is being performed is listed second.

N. Patients receiving preoperative evaluations only

For patients receiving preoperative evaluations only, sequence first a code from category V72.8 Other specified examinations, to describe the pre-op consultations. Assign a code for the condition to describe the reason for the surgery as an additional diagnosis. Code also any findings related to the pre-op evaluation.

O. Ambulatory surgery

For ambulatory surgery, code the diagnosis for which the surgery was performed. If the postoperative diagnosis is known to be different from the preoperative diagnosis at the time the diagnosis is confirmed, select the postoperative diagnosis for coding, since it is the most definitive.

P. Routine outpatient prenatal visits

For routine outpatient prenatal visits when no complications are present, code V22.0 Supervision of normal first pregnancy, or V22.1 Supervision of other normal pregnancy, should be used as the principal diagnosis. These codes should not be used in conjunction with chapter 11 codes.

A

- **AAT** (alpha-1 antitrypsin) deficiency 273.4
- **AAV (disease) (illness) (infection)** — *see* Human immunodeficiency virus (disease) (illness) (infection)
- **Abactio** — *see* Abortion, induced
- **Abactus venter** — *see* Abortion, induced
- **Abarognosis** 781.99
- **Abasia** (-astasia) 307.9
  - atactica 781.3
  - choreic 781.3
  - hysterical 300.11
  - paroxysmal trepidant 781.3
  - spastic 781.3
  - trembling 781.3
  - trepidans 781.3
- **Abderhalden-Kaufmann-Lignac syndrome** (cystinosis) 270.0
- **Abdomen, abdominal** — *see also* condition
  - accordion 306.4
  - acute 789.0 ☑
  - angina 557.1
  - burst 868.00
  - convulsive equivalent (*see also* Epilepsy) 345.5 ☑
  - heart 746.87
  - muscle deficiency syndrome 756.79
  - obstipum 756.79
- **Abdominalgia** 789.0 ☑
  - periodic 277.31 ▲
- **Abduction contracture, hip or other joint** — *see* Contraction, joint
- **Abercrombie's syndrome** (amyloid degeneration) 277.39 ▲
- **Aberrant** (congenital) — *see also* Malposition, congenital
  - adrenal gland 759.1
  - blood vessel NEC 747.60
    - arteriovenous NEC 747.60
    - cerebrovascular 747.81
    - gastrointestinal 747.61
    - lower limb 747.64
    - renal 747.62
    - spinal 747.82
    - upper limb 747.63
  - breast 757.6
  - endocrine gland NEC 759.2
  - gastrointestinal vessel (peripheral) 747.61
  - hepatic duct 751.69
  - lower limb vessel (peripheral) 747.64
  - pancreas 751.7
  - parathyroid gland 759.2
  - peripheral vascular vessel NEC 747.60
  - pituitary gland (pharyngeal) 759.2
  - renal blood vessel 747.62
  - sebaceous glands, mucous membrane, mouth 750.26
  - spinal vessel 747.82
  - spleen 759.0
  - testis (descent) 752.51
  - thymus gland 759.2
  - thyroid gland 759.2
  - upper limb vessel (peripheral) 747.63
- **Aberratio**
  - lactis 757.6
  - testis 752.51
- **Aberration** — *see also* Anomaly
  - chromosome — *see* Anomaly, chromosome(s)
  - distantial 368.9
  - mental (*see also* Disorder, mental, nonpsychotic) 300.9
- **Abetalipoproteinemia** 272.5
- **Abionarce** 780.79
- **Abiotrophy** 799.89
- **Ablatio**
  - placentae — *see* Placenta, ablatio
  - retinae (*see also* Detachment, retina) 361.9
- **Ablation**
  - pituitary (gland) (with hypofunction) 253.7
- **Ablation** — *continued*
  - placenta — *see* Placenta, ablatio
  - uterus 621.8
- **Ablepharia, ablepharon, ablephary** 743.62
- **Ablepsia** — *see* Blindness
- **Ablepsy** — *see* Blindness
- **Ablutomania** 300.3
- **Abnormal, abnormality, abnormalities** — *see also* Anomaly
  - acid-base balance 276.4
    - fetus or newborn — *see* Distress, fetal
  - adaptation curve, dark 368.63
  - alveolar ridge 525.9
  - amnion 658.9 ☑
    - affecting fetus or newborn 762.9
  - anatomical relationship NEC 759.9
  - apertures, congenital, diaphragm 756.6
  - auditory perception NEC 388.40
  - autosomes NEC 758.5
    - 13 758.1
    - 18 758.2
    - 21 or 22 758.0
    - D_1 758.1
    - E_3 758.2
    - G 758.0
  - ballistocardiogram 794.39
  - basal metabolic rate (BMR) 794.7
  - biosynthesis, testicular androgen 257.2
  - blood level (of)
    - cobalt 790.6
    - copper 790.6
    - iron 790.6
    - lead 790.6 ●
    - lithium 790.6
    - magnesium 790.6
    - mineral 790.6
    - zinc 790.6
  - blood pressure
    - elevated (without diagnosis of hypertension) 796.2
    - low (*see also* Hypotension) 458.9
      - reading (incidental) (isolated) (nonspecific) 796.3
  - bowel sounds 787.5
  - breathing behavior — *see* Respiration
  - caloric test 794.19
  - cervix (acquired) NEC 622.9
    - congenital 752.40
    - in pregnancy or childbirth 654.6 ☑
      - causing obstructed labor 660.2 ☑
        - affecting fetus or newborn 763.1
  - chemistry, blood NEC 790.6
  - chest sounds 786.7
  - chorion 658.9 ☑
    - affecting fetus or newborn 762.9
  - chromosomal NEC 758.89
    - analysis, nonspecific result 795.2
    - autosomes (*see also* Abnormal, autosomes NEC) 758.5
    - fetal, (suspected) affecting management of pregnancy 655.1 ☑
    - sex 758.81
  - clinical findings NEC 796.4
  - communication — *see* Fistula
  - configuration of pupils 379.49
  - coronary
    - artery 746.85
    - vein 746.9
  - cortisol-binding globulin 255.8
  - course, Eustachian tube 744.24
  - dentofacial NEC 524.9
    - functional 524.50
    - specified type NEC 524.89
  - development, developmental NEC 759.9
    - bone 756.9
    - central nervous system 742.9
  - direction, teeth 524.30
  - Dynia (*see also* Defect, coagulation) 286.9
- **Abnormal, abnormality, abnormalities** — *see also* Anomaly — *continued*
  - Ebstein 746.2
  - echocardiogram 793.2
  - echoencephalogram 794.01
  - echogram NEC — *see* Findings, abnormal, structure
  - electrocardiogram (ECG) (EKG) 794.31
  - electroencephalogram (EEG) 794.02
  - electromyogram (EMG) 794.17
    - ocular 794.14
  - electro-oculogram (EOG) 794.12
  - electroretinogram (ERG) 794.11
  - erythrocytes 289.9
    - congenital, with perinatal jaundice 282.9 *[774.0]*
  - Eustachian valve 746.9
  - excitability under minor stress 301.9
  - fat distribution 782.9
  - feces 787.7
  - fetal heart rate — *see* Distress, fetal
  - fetus NEC
    - affecting management of pregnancy — *see* Pregnancy, management affected by, fetal
    - causing disproportion 653.7 ☑
      - affecting fetus or newborn 763.1
      - causing obstructed labor 660.1 ☑
        - affecting fetus or newborn 763.1
  - findings without manifest disease — *see* Findings, abnormal
  - fluid
    - amniotic 792.3
    - cerebrospinal 792.0
    - peritoneal 792.9
    - pleural 792.9
    - synovial 792.9
    - vaginal 792.9
  - forces of labor NEC 661.9 ☑
    - affecting fetus or newborn 763.7
  - form, teeth 520.2
  - function studies
    - auditory 794.15
    - bladder 794.9
    - brain 794.00
    - cardiovascular 794.30
    - endocrine NEC 794.6
    - kidney 794.4
    - liver 794.8
    - nervous system
      - central 794.00
      - peripheral 794.19
    - oculomotor 794.14
    - pancreas 794.9
    - placenta 794.9
    - pulmonary 794.2
    - retina 794.11
    - special senses 794.19
    - spleen 794.9
    - thyroid 794.5
    - vestibular 794.16
  - gait 781.2
    - hysterical 300.11
  - gastrin secretion 251.5
  - globulin
    - cortisol-binding 255.8
    - thyroid-binding 246.8
  - glucagon secretion 251.4
  - glucose 790.29
    - in pregnancy, childbirth, or puerperium 648.8 ☑
      - fetus or newborn 775.0
    - non-fasting 790.29
  - gravitational (G) forces or states 994.9
  - hair NEC 704.2
  - hard tissue formation in pulp 522.3
  - head movement 781.0
  - heart
    - rate
      - fetus, affecting liveborn infant
        - before the onset of labor 763.81
        - during labor 763.82
- **Abnormal, abnormality, abnormalities** — *see also* Anomaly — *continued*
  - heart — *continued*
    - rate — *continued*
      - fetus, affecting liveborn infant — *continued*
        - unspecified as to time of onset 763.83
      - intrauterine
        - before the onset of labor 763.81
        - during labor 763.82
        - unspecified as to time of onset 763.83
      - newborn
        - before the onset of labor 763.81
        - during labor 763.82
        - unspecified as to time of onset 763.83
    - shadow 793.2
    - sounds NEC 785.3
  - hemoglobin (*see also* Disease, hemoglobin) 282.7
    - trait — *see* Trait, hemoglobin, abnormal
  - hemorrhage, uterus — *see* Hemorrhage, uterus
  - histology NEC 795.4
  - increase
    - in
      - appetite 783.6
      - development 783.9
  - involuntary movement 781.0
  - jaw closure 524.51
  - karyotype 795.2
  - knee jerk 796.1
  - labor NEC 661.9 ☑
    - affecting fetus or newborn 763.7
  - laboratory findings — *see* Findings, abnormal
  - length, organ or site, congenital — *see* Distortion
  - loss of height 781.91
  - loss of weight 783.21
  - lung shadow 793.1
  - mammogram 793.80
    - calcification 793.89 ●
    - calculus 793.89 ●
    - microcalcification 793.81
  - Mantoux test 795.5
  - membranes (fetal)
    - affecting fetus or newborn 762.9
    - complicating pregnancy 658.8 ☑
  - menstruation — *see* Menstruation
  - metabolism (*see also* condition) 783.9
  - movement 781.0
    - disorder NEC 333.90
      - sleep related, unspecified 780.58
      - specified NEC 333.99
    - head 781.0
    - involuntary 781.0
    - specified type NEC 333.99
  - muscle contraction, localized 728.85
  - myoglobin (Aberdeen) (Annapolis) 289.9
  - narrowness, eyelid 743.62
  - optokinetic response 379.57
  - organs or tissues of pelvis NEC
    - in pregnancy or childbirth 654.9 ☑
      - affecting fetus or newborn 763.89
      - causing obstructed labor 660.2 ☑
        - affecting fetus or newborn 763.1
  - origin — *see* Malposition, congenital
  - palmar creases 757.2
  - Papanicolaou (smear)
    - cervix 795.00

Note — Use the following fifth-digit subclassification with categories 634–637:

0 unspecified
1 incomplete
2 complete

☑ Additional Digit Required — Refer to the Tabular List for Digit Selection

Subterms under main terms may continue to next column or page

▶◀ Revised Text ● New Line ▲ Revised Code

Abortion — *continued*
illegal — *continued*
with — *continued*
unspecified complication(s) 636.8 ☑
urinary tract infection 636.7 ☑
fetus 779.6
induced 637.9 ☑
illegal — *see* Abortion, illegal
legal indications — *see* Abortion, legal
medical indications — *see* Abortion, legal
therapeutic — *see* Abortion, legal
late — *see* Abortion, spontaneous
legal (legal indication) (medical indication) (under medical supervision) 635.9 ☑
with
damage to pelvic organ (laceration) (rupture) (tear) 635.2 ☑
embolism (air) (amniotic fluid) (blood clot) (pulmonary) (pyemic) (septic) (soap) 635.6 ☑
genital tract and pelvic infection 635.0 ☑
hemorrhage, delayed or excessive 635.1 ☑
metabolic disorder 635.4 ☑
renal failure (acute) 635.3 ☑
sepsis (genital tract) (pelvic organ) 635.0 ☑
urinary tract 635.7 ☑
shock (postoperative) (septic) 635.5 ☑
specified complication NEC 635.7 ☑
toxemia 635.3 ☑
unspecified complication(s) 635.8 ☑
urinary tract infection 635.7 ☑
fetus 779.6
medical indication — *see* Abortion, legal
mental hygiene problem — *see* Abortion, legal
missed 632
operative — *see* Abortion, legal
psychiatric indication — *see* Abortion, legal
recurrent — *see* Abortion, spontaneous
self-induced — *see* Abortion, illegal
septic — *see* Abortion, by type, with sepsis
spontaneous 634.9 ☑
with
damage to pelvic organ (laceration) (rupture) (tear) 634.2 ☑
embolism (air) (amniotic fluid) (blood clot) (pulmonary) (pyemic) (septic) (soap) 634.6 ☑
genital tract and pelvic infection 634.0 ☑
hemorrhage, delayed or excessive 634.1 ☑
metabolic disorder 634.4 ☑
renal failure 634.3 ☑
sepsis (genital tract) (pelvic organ) 634.0 ☑
urinary tract 634.7 ☑
shock (postoperative) (septic) 634.5 ☑
specified complication NEC 634.7 ☑
toxemia 634.3 ☑
unspecified complication(s) 634.8 ☑
urinary tract infection 634.7 ☑
fetus 761.8
threatened 640.0 ☑

Abortion — *continued*
spontaneous — *continued*
threatened — *continued*
affecting fetus or newborn 762.1
surgical — *see* Abortion, legal
therapeutic — *see* Abortion, legal
threatened 640.0 ☑
affecting fetus or newborn 762.1
tubal — *see* Pregnancy, tubal
voluntary — *see* Abortion, legal
Abortus fever 023.9
Aboulomania 301.6
Abrachia 755.20
Abrachiatism 755.20
Abrachiocephalia 759.89
Abrachiocephalus 759.89
Abrami's disease (acquired hemolytic jaundice) 283.9
Abramov-Fiedler myocarditis (acute isolated myocarditis) 422.91
Abrasion — *see also* Injury, superficial, by site
cornea 918.1
dental 521.20
extending into
dentine 521.22
pulp 521.23
generalized 521.25
limited to enamel 521.21
localized 521.24
teeth, tooth (dentifrice) (habitual) (hard tissues) (occupational) (ritual) (traditional) (wedge defect) (*see also* Abrasion, dental) 521.20
Abrikossov's tumor (M9580/0) — *see also* Neoplasm, connective tissue, benign
malignant (M9580/3) — *see* Neoplasm, connective tissue, malignant
Abrism 988.8
Abruption, placenta — *see* Placenta, abruptio
Abruptio placentae — *see* Placenta, abruptio
Abscess (acute) (chronic) (infectional) (lymphangitic) (metastatic) (multiple) (pyogenic) (septic) (with lymphangitis) — *see also* Cellulitis 682.9
abdomen, abdominal
cavity 567.22
wall 682.2
abdominopelvic 567.22
accessory sinus (chronic) (*see also* Sinusitis) 473.9
adrenal (capsule) (gland) 255.8
alveolar 522.5
with sinus 522.7
amebic 006.3
bladder 006.8
brain (with liver or lung abscess) 006.5
liver (without mention of brain or lung abscess) 006.3
with
brain abscess (and lung abscess) 006.5
lung abscess 006.4
lung (with liver abscess) 006.4
with brain abscess 006.5
seminal vesicle 006.8
specified site NEC 006.8
spleen 006.8
anaerobic 040.0
ankle 682.6
anorectal 566
antecubital space 682.3
antrum (chronic) (Highmore) (*see also* Sinusitis, maxillary) 473.0
anus 566
apical (tooth) 522.5
with sinus (alveolar) 522.7
appendix 540.1

Abscess — *see also* Cellulitis — *continued*
areola (acute) (chronic) (nonpuerperal) 611.0
puerperal, postpartum 675.1 ☑
arm (any part, above wrist) 682.3
artery (wall) 447.2
atheromatous 447.2
auditory canal (external) 380.10
auricle (ear) (staphylococcal) (streptococcal) 380.10
axilla, axillary (region) 682.3
lymph gland or node 683
back (any part) 682.2
Bartholin's gland 616.3
with
abortion — *see* Abortion, by type, with sepsis
ectopic pregnancy (*see also* categories 633.0–633.9) 639.0
molar pregnancy (*see also* categories 630–632) 639.0
complicating pregnancy or puerperium 646.6 ☑
following
abortion 639.0
ectopic or molar pregnancy 639.0
bartholinian 616.3
Bezold's 383.01
bile, biliary, duct or tract (*see also* Cholecystitis) 576.8
bilharziasis 120.1
bladder (wall) 595.89
amebic 006.8
bone (subperiosteal) (*see also* Osteomyelitis) 730.0 ☑
accessory sinus (chronic) (*see also* Sinusitis) 473.9
acute 730.0 ☑
chronic or old 730.1 ☑
jaw (lower) (upper) 526.4
mastoid — *see* Mastoiditis, acute
petrous (*see also* Petrositis) 383.20
spinal (tuberculous) (*see also* Tuberculosis) 015.0 ☑ *[730.88]*
nontuberculous 730.08
bowel 569.5
brain (any part) 324.0
amebic (with liver or lung abscess) 006.5
cystic 324.0
late effect — *see* category 326
otogenic 324.0
tuberculous (*see also* Tuberculosis) 013.3 ☑
breast (acute) (chronic) (nonpuerperal) 611.0
newborn 771.5
puerperal, postpartum 675.1 ☑
tuberculous (*see also* Tuberculosis) 017.9 ☑
broad ligament (chronic) (*see also* Disease, pelvis, inflammatory) 614.4
acute 614.3
Brodie's (chronic) (localized) (*see also* Osteomyelitis) 730.1 ☑
bronchus 519.19 ▲
buccal cavity 528.3
bulbourethral gland 597.0
bursa 727.89
pharyngeal 478.29
buttock 682.5
canaliculus, breast 611.0
canthus 372.20
cartilage 733.99
cecum 569.5
with appendicitis 540.1
cerebellum, cerebellar 324.0
late effect — *see* category 326
cerebral (embolic) 324.0
late effect — *see* category 326
cervical (neck region) 682.1
lymph gland or node 683

Abscess — *see also* Cellulitis — *continued*
cervical — *continued*
stump (*see also* Cervicitis) 616.0
cervix (stump) (uteri) (*see also* Cervicitis) 616.0
cheek, external 682.0
inner 528.3
chest 510.9
with fistula 510.0
wall 682.2
chin 682.0
choroid 363.00
ciliary body 364.3
circumtonsillar 475
cold (tuberculous) (*see also* Tuberculosis, abscess)
articular — *see* Tuberculosis, joint
colon (wall) 569.5
colostomy or enterostomy 569.61
conjunctiva 372.00
connective tissue NEC 682.9
cornea 370.55
with ulcer 370.00
corpus
cavernosum 607.2
luteum (*see also* Salpingo-oophoritis) 614.2
Cowper's gland 597.0
cranium 324.0
cul-de-sac (Douglas') (posterior) (*see also* Disease, pelvis, inflammatory) 614.4
acute 614.3
dental 522.5
with sinus (alveolar) 522.7
dentoalveolar 522.5
with sinus (alveolar) 522.7
diaphragm, diaphragmatic 567.22
digit NEC 681.9
Douglas' cul-de-sac or pouch (*see also* Disease, pelvis, inflammatory) 614.4
acute 614.3
Dubois' 090.5
ductless gland 259.8
ear
acute 382.00
external 380.10
inner 386.30
middle — *see* Otitis media
elbow 682.3
endamebic — *see* Abscess, amebic
entamebic — *see* Abscess, amebic
enterostomy 569.61
epididymis 604.0
epidural 324.9
brain 324.0
late effect — *see* category 326
spinal cord 324.1
epiglottis 478.79
epiploon, epiploic 567.22
erysipelatous (*see also* Erysipelas) 035
esophagostomy 530.86
esophagus 530.19
ethmoid (bone) (chronic) (sinus) (*see also* Sinusitis, ethmoidal) 473.2
external auditory canal 380.10
extradural 324.9
brain 324.0
late effect — *see* category 326
spinal cord 324.1
extraperitoneal — *see* Abscess, peritoneum
eye 360.00
eyelid 373.13
face (any part, except eye) 682.0
fallopian tube (*see also* Salpingo-oophoritis) 614.2
fascia 728.89
fauces 478.29
fecal 569.5
femoral (region) 682.6
filaria, filarial (*see also* Infestation, filarial) 125.9

☑ Additional Digit Required — Refer to the Tabular List for Digit Selection

Subterms under main terms may continue to next column or page

▶◀ Revised Text ● New Line ▲ Revised Code

Index

Abscess — Absence

☑ Additional Digit Required — Refer to the Tabular List for Digit Selection
Subterms under main terms may continue to next column or page

- **Absence** — *continued*
  - scrotum, congenital 752.89
  - seminal tract or duct (congenital) 752.89
    - acquired V45.77
  - septum (congenital) (*see also* Imperfect, closure, septum)
    - atrial 745.69
      - and ventricular 745.7
    - between aorta and pulmonary artery 745.0
    - ventricular 745.3
      - and atrial 745.7
  - sex chromosomes 758.81
  - shoulder girdle, congenital (complete) (partial) 755.59
  - skin (congenital) 757.39
  - skull bone 756.0
    - with
      - anencephalus 740.0
      - encephalocele 742.0
      - hydrocephalus 742.3
        - with spina bifida (*see also* Spina bifida) 741.0 ☑
      - microcephalus 742.1
  - spermatic cord (congenital) 752.89
  - spinal cord 742.59
  - spine, congenital 756.13
  - spleen (congenital) 759.0
    - acquired V45.79
  - sternum, congenital 756.3
  - stomach (acquired) (partial) (postoperative) V45.75
    - with postgastric surgery syndrome 564.2
    - congenital 750.7
  - submaxillary gland(s) (congenital) 750.21
  - superior vena cava (congenital) 747.49
  - tarsal(s), congenital (complete) (partial) (with absence of distal elements, incomplete) (*see also* Deformity, reduction, lower limb) 755.38
  - teeth, tooth (congenital) 520.0
    - with abnormal spacing 524.30
    - acquired 525.10
      - with malocclusion 524.30
      - due to
        - caries 525.13
        - extraction 525.10
        - periodontal disease 525.12
        - trauma 525.11
  - tendon (congenital) 756.81
  - testis (congenital) 752.89
    - acquired V45.77
  - thigh (acquired) 736.89
  - thumb (acquired) V49.61
    - congenital 755.29
  - thymus gland (congenital) 759.2
  - thyroid (gland) (surgical) 246.8
    - with hypothyroidism 244.0
    - cartilage, congenital 748.3
    - congenital 243
  - tibia, congenital (complete) (partial) (with absence of distal elements, incomplete) (*see also* Deformity, reduction, lower limb) 755.36
    - with
      - complete absence of distal elements 755.31
      - fibula 755.35
        - with
          - complete absence of distal elements 755.31
          - femur (incomplete) 755.33
            - with complete absence of distal elements 755.31
  - toe (acquired) V49.72
    - congenital (complete) (partial) 755.39
      - meaning all toes 755.31
      - transverse 755.31
    - great V49.71
  - tongue (congenital) 750.11
  - tooth, teeth (congenital) 520.0

- **Absence** — *continued*
  - tooth, teeth — *continued*
    - with abnormal spacing 524.30
    - acquired 525.10
      - with malocclusion 524.30
      - due to
        - caries 525.13
        - extraction 525.10
        - periodontal disease 525.12
        - trauma 525.11
  - trachea (cartilage) (congenital) (rings) 748.3
  - transverse aortic arch (congenital) 747.21
  - tricuspid valve 746.1
  - ulna, congenital (complete) (partial) (with absence of distal elements, incomplete) (*see also* Deformity, reduction, upper limb) 755.27
    - with
      - complete absence of distal elements 755.21
      - radius 755.25
        - with
          - complete absence of distal elements 755.21
          - humerus (incomplete) 755.23
  - umbilical artery (congenital) 747.5
  - ureter (congenital) 753.4
    - acquired V45.74
  - urethra, congenital 753.8
    - acquired V45.74
  - urinary system, part NEC, congenital 753.8
    - acquired V45.74
  - uterus (acquired) V45.77
    - congenital 752.3
  - uvula (congenital) 750.26
  - vagina, congenital 752.49
    - acquired V45.77
  - vas deferens (congenital) 752.89
    - acquired V45.77
  - vein (congenital) (peripheral) NEC (*see also* Anomaly, peripheral vascular system) 747.60
    - brain 747.81
    - great 747.49
    - portal 747.49
    - pulmonary 747.49
  - vena cava (congenital) (inferior) (superior) 747.49
  - ventral horn cell 742.59
  - ventricular septum 745.3
  - vermis of cerebellum 742.2
  - vertebra, congenital 756.13
  - vulva, congenital 752.49
- **Absentia epileptica** — *see also* Epilepsy 345.0 ☑
- **Absinthemia** — *see also* Dependence 304.6 ☑
- **Absinthism** — *see also* Dependence 304.6 ☑
- **Absorbent system disease** 459.89
- **Absorption**
  - alcohol, through placenta or breast milk 760.71
  - antibiotics, through placenta or breast milk 760.74
  - anticonvulsants, through placenta or breast milk 760.77
  - antifungals, through placenta or breast milk 760.74
  - anti-infective, through placenta or breast milk 760.74
  - antimetabolics, through placenta or breast milk 760.78
  - chemical NEC 989.9
    - specified chemical or substance — *see* Table of Drugs and Chemicals
    - through placenta or breast milk (fetus or newborn) 760.70
      - alcohol 760.71
      - anticonvulsants 760.77
      - antifungals 760.74

- **Absorption** — *continued*
  - chemical — *continued*
    - through placenta or breast milk — *continued*
      - anti-infective agents 760.74
      - antimetabolics 760.78
      - cocaine 760.75
      - "crack" 760.75
      - diethylstilbestrol [DES] 760.76
      - hallucinogenic agents 760.73
      - medicinal agents NEC 760.79
      - narcotics 760.72
      - obstetric anesthetic or analgesic drug 763.5
      - specified agent NEC 760.79
      - suspected, affecting management of pregnancy 655.5 ☑
  - cocaine, through placenta or breast milk 760.75
  - drug NEC (*see also* Reaction, drug)
    - through placenta or breast milk (fetus or newborn) 760.70
      - alcohol 760.71
      - anticonvulsants 760.77
      - antifungals 760.74
      - anti-infective agents 760.74
      - antimetabolics 760.78
      - cocaine 760.75
      - "crack" 760.75
      - diethylstilbestrol [DES] 760.76
      - hallucinogenic agents 760.73
      - medicinal agents NEC 760.79
      - narcotics 760.72
      - obstetric anesthetic or analgesic drug 763.5
      - specified agent NEC 760.79
      - suspected, affecting management of pregnancy 655.5 ☑
  - fat, disturbance 579.8
  - hallucinogenic agents, through placenta or breast milk 760.73
  - immune sera, through placenta or breast milk 760.79
  - lactose defect 271.3
  - medicinal agents NEC, through placenta or breast milk 760.79
  - narcotics, through placenta or breast milk 760.72
  - noxious substance — *see* Absorption, chemical
  - protein, disturbance 579.8
  - pus or septic, general — *see* Septicemia
  - quinine, through placenta or breast milk 760.74
  - toxic substance — *see* Absorption, chemical
  - uremic — *see* Uremia
- **Abstinence symptoms or syndrome**
  - alcohol 291.81
  - drug 292.0
- **Abt-Letterer-Siwe syndrome** (acute histiocytosis X) (M9722/3) 202.5 ☑
- **Abulia** 799.89
- **Abulomania** 301.6
- **Abuse**
  - adult 995.80
    - emotional 995.82
    - multiple forms 995.85
    - neglect (nutritional) 995.84
    - physical 995.81
    - psychological 995.82
    - sexual 995.83
  - alcohol — *see* also Alcoholism 305.0 ☑
    - dependent 303.9 ☑
    - non-dependent 305.0 ☑
  - child 995.50
    - counseling
      - perpetrator
        - non-parent V62.83
        - parent V61.22
      - victim V61.21
    - emotional 995.51

- **Abuse** — *continued*
  - child — *continued*
    - multiple forms 995.59
    - neglect (nutritional) 995.52
    - physical 995.54
      - shaken infant syndrome 995.55
    - psychological 995.51
    - sexual 995.53
  - drugs, nondependent 305.9 ☑

    Note — Use the following fifth-digit subclassification with the following codes: 305.0, 305.2–305.9:

0	*unspecified*
1	*continuous*
2	*episodic*
3	*in remission*

    - amphetamine type 305.7 ☑
    - antidepressants 305.8 ☑
    - anxiolytic 305.4 ☑
    - barbiturates 305.4 ☑
    - caffeine 305.9 ☑
    - cannabis 305.2 ☑
    - cocaine type 305.6 ☑
    - hallucinogens 305.3 ☑
    - hashish 305.2 ☑
    - hypnotic 305.4 ☑
    - inhalant 305.9 ☑
    - LSD 305.3 ☑
    - marijuana 305.2 ☑
    - mixed 305.9 ☑
    - morphine type 305.5 ☑
    - opioid type 305.5 ☑
    - phencyclidine (PCP) 305.9 ☑
    - sedative 305.4 ☑
    - specified NEC 305.9 ☑
    - tranquilizers 305.4 ☑
  - spouse 995.80
  - tobacco 305.1
- **Acalcerosis** 275.40
- **Acalcicosis** 275.40
- **Acalculia** 784.69
  - developmental 315.1
- **Acanthocheilonemiasis** 125.4
- **Acanthocytosis** 272.5
- **Acanthokeratodermia** 701.1
- **Acantholysis** 701.8
  - bullosa 757.39
- **Acanthoma** (benign) (M8070/0) — *see also* Neoplasm, by site, benign
  - malignant (M8070/3) — *see* Neoplasm, by site, malignant
- **Acanthosis** (acquired) (nigricans) 701.2
  - adult 701.2
  - benign (congenital) 757.39
  - congenital 757.39
  - glycogenic
    - esophagus 530.89
  - juvenile 701.2
  - tongue 529.8
- **Acanthrocytosis** 272.5
- **Acapnia** 276.3
- **Acarbia** 276.2
- **Acardia** 759.89
- **Acardiacus amorphus** 759.89
- **Acardiotrophia** 429.1
- **Acardius** 759.89
- **Acariasis** 133.9
  - sarcoptic 133.0
- **Acaridiasis** 133.9
- **Acarinosis** 133.9
- **Acariosis** 133.9
- **Acarodermatitis** 133.9
  - urticarioides 133.9
- **Acarophobia** 300.29
- **Acatalasemia** 277.89
- **Acatalasia** 277.89
- **Acatamathesia** 784.69
- **Acataphasia** 784.5
- **Acathisia** 781.0
  - due to drugs 333.99
- **Acceleration, accelerated**
  - atrioventricular conduction 426.7
  - idioventricular rhythm 427.89

- **Accessory** (congenital)
  - adrenal gland 759.1
  - anus 751.5
  - appendix 751.5
  - atrioventricular conduction 426.7
  - auditory ossicles 744.04
  - auricle (ear) 744.1
  - autosome(s) NEC 758.5
    - 21 or 22 758.0
  - biliary duct or passage 751.69
  - bladder 753.8
  - blood vessels (peripheral) (congenital) NEC (*see also* Anomaly, peripheral vascular system) 747.60
    - cerebral 747.81
    - coronary 746.85
  - bone NEC 756.9
    - foot 755.67
  - breast tissue, axilla 757.6
  - carpal bones 755.56
  - cecum 751.5
  - cervix 752.49
  - chromosome(s) NEC 758.5
    - 13-15 758.1
    - 16-18 758.2
    - 21 or 22 758.0
    - autosome(s) NEC 758.5
    - D_1 758.1
    - E_3 758.2
    - G 758.0
    - sex 758.81
  - coronary artery 746.85
  - cusp(s), heart valve NEC 746.89
    - pulmonary 746.09
  - cystic duct 751.69
  - digits 755.00
  - ear (auricle) (lobe) 744.1
  - endocrine gland NEC 759.2
  - external os 752.49
  - eyelid 743.62
  - eye muscle 743.69
  - face bone(s) 756.0
  - fallopian tube (fimbria) (ostium) 752.19
  - fingers 755.01
  - foreskin 605
  - frontonasal process 756.0
  - gallbladder 751.69
  - genital organ(s)
    - female 752.89
      - external 752.49
      - internal NEC 752.89
    - male NEC 752.89
      - penis 752.69
  - genitourinary organs NEC 752.89
  - heart 746.89
    - valve NEC 746.89
      - pulmonary 746.09
  - hepatic ducts 751.69
  - hymen 752.49
  - intestine (large) (small) 751.5
  - kidney 753.3
  - lacrimal canal 743.65
  - leaflet, heart valve NEC 746.89
    - pulmonary 746.09
  - ligament, broad 752.19
  - liver (duct) 751.69
  - lobule (ear) 744.1
  - lung (lobe) 748.69
  - muscle 756.82
  - navicular of carpus 755.56
  - nervous system, part NEC 742.8
  - nipple 757.6
  - nose 748.1
  - organ or site NEC — *see* Anomaly, specified type NEC
  - ovary 752.0
  - oviduct 752.19
  - pancreas 751.7
  - parathyroid gland 759.2
  - parotid gland (and duct) 750.22
  - pituitary gland 759.2
  - placental lobe — *see* Placenta, abnormal
  - preauricular appendage 744.1
  - prepuce 605
- **Accessory** — *continued*
  - renal arteries (multiple) 747.62
  - rib 756.3
    - cervical 756.2
  - roots (teeth) 520.2
  - salivary gland 750.22
  - sesamoids 755.8
  - sinus — *see* condition
  - skin tags 757.39
  - spleen 759.0
  - sternum 756.3
  - submaxillary gland 750.22
  - tarsal bones 755.67
  - teeth, tooth 520.1
    - causing crowding 524.31
  - tendon 756.89
  - thumb 755.01
  - thymus gland 759.2
  - thyroid gland 759.2
  - toes 755.02
  - tongue 750.13
  - tragus 744.1
  - ureter 753.4
  - urethra 753.8
  - urinary organ or tract NEC 753.8
  - uterus 752.2
  - vagina 752.49
  - valve, heart NEC 746.89
    - pulmonary 746.09
  - vertebra 756.19
  - vocal cords 748.3
  - vulva 752.49
- **Accident, accidental** — *see also* condition
  - birth NEC 767.9
  - cardiovascular (*see also* Disease, cardiovascular) 429.2
  - cerebral (*see also* Disease, cerebrovascular, acute) 434.91
  - cerebrovascular (current) (CVA) (*see also* Disease, cerebrovascular, acute) 434.91
    - embolic 434.11
    - healed or old V12.59
    - hemorrhagic — *see* Hemorrhage, brain
    - impending 435.9
    - ischemic 434.91
    - late effect — *see* Late effect(s) (of) cerebrovascular disease
    - postoperative 997.02
    - thrombotic 434.01
  - coronary (*see also* Infarct, myocardium) 410.9 ☑
  - craniovascular (*see also* Disease, cerebrovascular, acute) 436
  - during pregnancy, to mother, affecting fetus or newborn 760.5
  - heart, cardiac (*see also* Infarct, myocardium) 410.9 ☑
  - intrauterine 779.89
  - vascular — *see* Disease, cerebrovascular, acute
- **Accommodation**
  - disorder of 367.51
    - drug-induced 367.89
    - toxic 367.89
  - insufficiency of 367.4
  - paralysis of 367.51
    - hysterical 300.11
  - spasm of 367.53
- **Accouchement** — *see* Delivery
- **Accreta placenta** (without hemorrhage) 667.0 ☑
  - with hemorrhage 666.0 ☑
- **Accretio cordis** (nonrheumatic) 423.1
- **Accretions on teeth** 523.6
- **Accumulation secretion, prostate** 602.8
- **Acephalia, acephalism, acephaly** 740.0
- **Acephalic** 740.0
- **Acephalobrachia** 759.89
- **Acephalocardia** 759.89
- **Acephalocardius** 759.89
- **Acephalochiria** 759.89
- **Acephalochirus** 759.89
- **Acephalogaster** 759.89
- **Acephalostomus** 759.89
- **Acephalothorax** 759.89
- **Acephalus** 740.0
- **Acetonemia** 790.6
  - diabetic 250.1 ☑
- **Acetonglycosuria** 982.8
- **Acetonuria** 791.6
- **Achalasia** 530.0
  - cardia 530.0
  - digestive organs congenital NEC 751.8
  - esophagus 530.0
  - pelvirectal 751.3
  - psychogenic 306.4
  - pylorus 750.5
  - sphincteral NEC 564.89
- **Achard-Thiers syndrome** (adrenogenital) 255.2
- **Ache(s)** — *see* Pain
- **Acheilia** 750.26
- **Acheiria** 755.21
- **Achillobursitis** 726.71
- **Achillodynia** 726.71
- **Achlorhydria, achlorhydric** 536.0
  - anemia 280.9
  - diarrhea 536.0
  - neurogenic 536.0
  - postvagotomy 564.2
  - psychogenic 306.4
  - secondary to vagotomy 564.2
- **Achloroblepsia** 368.52
- **Achloropsia** 368.52
- **Acholia** 575.8
- **Acholuric jaundice** (familial) (splenomegalic) — *see also* Spherocytosis 282.0
  - acquired 283.9
- **Achondroplasia** 756.4
- **Achrestic anemia** 281.8
- **Achroacytosis, lacrimal gland** 375.00
  - tuberculous (*see also* Tuberculosis) 017.3 ☑
- **Achroma, cutis** 709.00
- **Achromate** (congenital) 368.54
- **Achromatopia** 368.54
- **Achromatopsia** (congenital) 368.54
- **Achromia**
  - congenital 270.2
  - parasitica 111.0
  - unguium 703.8
- **Achylia**
  - gastrica 536.8
    - neurogenic 536.3
    - psychogenic 306.4
  - pancreatica 577.1
- **Achylosis** 536.8
- **Acid**
  - burn (*see also* Burn, by site)
    - from swallowing acid — *see* Burn, internal organs
  - deficiency
    - amide nicotinic 265.2
    - amino 270.9
    - ascorbic 267
    - folic 266.2
    - nicotinic (amide) 265.2
    - pantothenic 266.2
  - intoxication 276.2
  - peptic disease 536.8
  - stomach 536.8
    - psychogenic 306.4
- **Acidemia** 276.2
  - arginosuccinic 270.6
  - fetal
    - affecting management of pregnancy 656.3 ☑
    - before onset of labor, in liveborn infant 768.2
    - during labor ▶and delivery◀ in liveborn infant 768.3
    - intrauterine 656.3 ☑
    - unspecified as to time of onset, in liveborn infant 768.4
  - newborn 775.81 ●
  - pipecolic 270.7
- **Acidity, gastric** (high) (low) 536.8
  - psychogenic 306.4
- **Acidocytopenia** 288.59 ▲
- **Acidocytosis** 288.3
- **Acidopenia** 288.59 ▲
- **Acidosis** 276.2
  - diabetic 250.1 ☑
  - fetal, affecting management of pregnancy 756.8 ☑
  - fetal, affecting newborn 775.81 ▲
  - kidney tubular 588.89
    - newborn 775.81 ●
  - lactic 276.2
  - metabolic NEC 276.2
    - with respiratory acidosis 276.4
      - of newborn 775.81 ●
    - late, of newborn 775.7
  - newborn 775.81 ●
  - renal
    - hyperchloremic 588.89
    - tubular (distal) (proximal) 588.89
  - respiratory 276.2
    - complicated by
      - metabolic acidosis 276.4
        - of newborn 775.81 ●
      - metabolic alkalosis 276.4
- **Aciduria** 791.9
  - arginosuccinic 270.6
  - beta-aminoisobutyric (BAIB) 277.2
  - glutaric
    - type I 270.7
    - type II (type IIA, IIB, IIC) 277.85
    - type III 277.86
  - glycolic 271.8
  - methylmalonic 270.3
    - with glycinemia 270.7
  - organic 270.9
  - orotic (congenital) (hereditary) (pyrimidine deficiency) 281.4
- **Acladiosis** 111.8
  - skin 111.8
- **Aclasis**
  - diaphyseal 756.4
  - tarsoepiphyseal 756.59
- **Acleistocardia** 745.5
- **Aclusion** 524.4
- **Acmesthesia** 782.0
- **Acne** (pustular) (vulgaris) 706.1
  - agminata (*see also* Tuberculosis) 017.0 ☑
  - artificialis 706.1
  - atrophica 706.0
  - cachecticorum (Hebra) 706.1
  - conglobata 706.1
  - conjunctiva 706.1
  - cystic 706.1
  - decalvans 704.09
  - erythematosa 695.3
  - eyelid 706.1
  - frontalis 706.0
  - indurata 706.1
  - keloid 706.1
  - lupoid 706.0
  - necrotic, necrotica 706.0
    - miliaris 704.8
  - neonatal 706.1
  - nodular 706.1
  - occupational 706.1
  - papulosa 706.1
  - rodens 706.0
  - rosacea 695.3
  - scorbutica 267
  - scrofulosorum (Bazin) (*see also* Tuberculosis) 017.0 ☑
  - summer 692.72
  - tropical 706.1
  - varioliformis 706.0
- **Acneiform drug eruptions** 692.3
- **Acnitis** (primary) — *see also* Tuberculosis 017.0 ☑
- **Acomia** 704.00
- **Acontractile bladder** 344.61
- **Aconuresis** — *see also* Incontinence 788.30
- **Acosta's disease** 993.2
- **Acousma** 780.1
- **Acoustic** — *see* condition
- **Acousticophobia** 300.29

☑ Additional Digit Required — Refer to the Tabular List for Digit Selection

Subterms under main terms may continue to next column or page

▶◀ Revised Text ● New Line ▲ Revised Code

- **Acquired** — *see* condition
- **Acquired immune deficiency syndrome** — *see* Human immunodeficiency virus (disease) (illness) (infection)
- **Acquired immunodeficiency syndrome** — *see* Human immunodeficiency virus (disease) (illness) (infection)
- **Acragnosis** 781.99
- **Acrania** 740.0
- **Acroagnosis** 781.99
- **Acroasphyxia, chronic** 443.89
- **Acrobrachycephaly** 756.0
- **Acrobystiolith** 608.89
- **Acrobystitis** 607.2
- **Acrocephalopolysyndactyly** 755.55
- **Acrocephalosyndactyly** 755.55
- **Acrocephaly** 756.0
- **Acrochondrohyperplasia** 759.82
- **Acrocyanosis** 443.89
  - newborn 770.83
    - meaning transient blue hands and feet — *omit code*
- **Acrodermatitis** 686.8
  - atrophicans (chronica) 701.8
  - continua (Hallopeau) 696.1
  - enteropathica 686.8
  - Hallopeau's 696.1
  - perstans 696.1
  - pustulosa continua 696.1
  - recalcitrant pustular 696.1
- **Acrodynia** 985.0
- **Acrodysplasia** 755.55
- **Acrohyperhidrosis** — *see also* Hyperhidrosis 780.8
- **Acrokeratosis verruciformis** 757.39
- **Acromastitis** 611.0
- **Acromegaly, acromegalia** (skin) 253.0
- **Acromelalgia** 443.82
- **Acromicria, acromikria** 756.59
- **Acronyx** 703.0
- **Acropachyderma** 757.39
- **Acropachy, thyroid** — *see also* Thyrotoxicosis 242.9 ☑
- **Acroparesthesia** 443.89
  - simple (Schultz's type) 443.89
  - vasomotor (Nothnagel's type) 443.89
- **Acropathy thyroid** — *see also* Thyrotoxicosis 242.9 ☑
- **Acrophobia** 300.29
- **Acroposthitis** 607.2
- **Acroscleriasis** — *see also* Scleroderma 710.1
- **Acroscleroderma** — *see also* Scleroderma 710.1
- **Acrosclerosis** — *see also* Scleroderma 710.1
- **Acrosphacelus** 785.4
- **Acrosphenosyndactylia** 755.55
- **Acrospiroma, eccrine** (M8402/0) — *see* Neoplasm, skin, benign
- **Acrostealgia** 732.9
- **Acrosyndactyly** — *see also* Syndactylism 755.10
- **Acrotrophodynia** 991.4
- **Actinic** — *see also* condition
  - cheilitis (due to sun) 692.72
    - chronic NEC 692.74
    - due to radiation, except from sun 692.82
  - conjunctivitis 370.24
  - dermatitis (due to sun) (*see also* Dermatitis, actinic) 692.70
    - due to
      - roentgen rays or radioactive substance 692.82
      - ultraviolet radiation, except from sun 692.82
      - sun NEC 692.70
  - elastosis solare 692.74
  - granuloma 692.73
  - keratitis 370.24
  - ophthalmia 370.24
  - reticuloid 692.73
- **Actinobacillosis, general** 027.8
- **Actinobacillus**
  - lignieresii 027.8
- **Actinobacillus** — *continued*
  - mallei 024
  - muris 026.1
- **Actinocutitis** NEC — *see also* Dermatitis, actinic 692.70
- **Actinodermatitis** NEC — *see also* Dermatitis, actinic 692.70
- **Actinomyces**
  - israelii (infection) — *see* Actinomycosis
  - muris-ratti (infection) 026.1
- **Actinomycosis, actinomycotic** 039.9
  - with
    - pneumonia 039.1
  - abdominal 039.2
  - cervicofacial 039.3
  - cutaneous 039.0
  - pulmonary 039.1
  - specified site NEC 039.8
  - thoracic 039.1
- **Actinoneuritis** 357.89
- **Action, heart**
  - disorder 427.9
    - postoperative 997.1
  - irregular 427.9
    - postoperative 997.1
    - psychogenic 306.2
- **Active** — *see* condition
- **Activity decrease, functional** 780.99
- **Acute** — *see also* condition
  - abdomen NEC 789.0 ☑
  - gallbladder (*see also* Cholecystitis, acute) 575.0
- **Acyanoblepsia** 368.53
- **Acyanopsia** 368.53
- **Acystia** 753.8
- **Acystinervia** — *see* Neurogenic, bladder
- **Acystineuria** — *see* Neurogenic, bladder
- **Adactylia, adactyly** (congenital) 755.4
  - lower limb (complete) (intercalary) (partial) (terminal) (*see also* Deformity, reduction, lower limb) 755.39
    - meaning all digits (complete) (partial) 755.31
    - transverse (complete) (partial) 755.31
  - upper limb (complete) (intercalary) (partial) (terminal) (*see also* Deformity, reduction, upper limb) 755.29
    - meaning all digits (complete) (partial) 755.21
    - transverse (complete) (partial) 755.21
- **Adair-Dighton syndrome** (brittle bones and blue sclera, deafness) 756.51
- **Adamantinoblastoma** (M9310/0) — *see* Ameloblastoma
- **Adamantinoma** (M9310/0) — *see* Ameloblastoma
- **Adamantoblastoma** (M9310/0) — *see* Ameloblastoma
- **Adams-Stokes (-Morgagni) disease or syndrome** (syncope with heart block) 426.9
- **Adaptation reaction** — *see also* Reaction, adjustment 309.9
- **Addiction** — *see also* Dependence
  - absinthe 304.6 ☑
  - alcoholic (ethyl) (methyl) (wood) 303.9 ☑
    - complicating pregnancy, childbirth, or puerperium 648.4 ☑
      - affecting fetus or newborn 760.71
    - suspected damage to fetus affecting management of pregnancy 655.4 ☑
  - drug (*see also* Dependence) 304.9 ☑
  - ethyl alcohol 303.9 ☑
  - heroin 304.0 ☑
  - hospital 301.51
  - methyl alcohol 303.9 ☑
  - methylated spirit 303.9 ☑
  - morphine (-like substances) 304.0 ☑
  - nicotine 305.1
- **Addiction** — *see also* Dependence — *continued*
  - opium 304.0 ☑
  - tobacco 305.1
  - wine 303.9 ☑
- **Addison's**
  - anemia (pernicious) 281.0
  - disease (bronze) (primary adrenal insufficiency) 255.4
    - tuberculous (*see also* Tuberculosis) 017.6 ☑
  - keloid (morphea) 701.0
  - melanoderma (adrenal cortical hypofunction) 255.4
- **Addison-Biermer anemia** (pernicious) 281.0
- **Addison-Gull disease** — *see* Xanthoma
- **Addisonian crisis or melanosis** (acute adrenocortical insufficiency) 255.4
- **Additional** — *see also* Accessory
  - chromosome(s) 758.5
    - 13-15 758.1
    - 16-18 758.2
    - 21 758.0
    - autosome(s) NEC 758.5
    - sex 758.81
- **Adduction contracture, hip or other joint** — *see* Contraction, joint
- **ADEM** (acute disseminated encephalomyelitis) (postinfectious) 136.9 *[323.61]* ▲
  - infectious 136.9 *[323.61]* ▲
  - noninfectious 323.81 ▲
- **Adenasthenia gastrica** 536.0
- **Aden fever** 061
- **Adenitis** — *see also* Lymphadenitis 289.3
  - acute, unspecified site 683
    - epidemic infectious 075
  - axillary 289.3
    - acute 683
    - chronic or subacute 289.1
  - Bartholin's gland 616.89 ▲
  - bulbourethral gland (*see also* Urethritis) 597.89
  - cervical 289.3
    - acute 683
    - chronic or subacute 289.1
  - chancroid (Ducrey's bacillus) 099.0
  - chronic (any lymph node, except mesenteric) 289.1
    - mesenteric 289.2
  - Cowper's gland (*see also* Urethritis) 597.89
  - epidemic, acute 075
  - gangrenous 683
  - gonorrheal NEC 098.89
  - groin 289.3
    - acute 683
    - chronic or subacute 289.1
  - infectious 075
  - inguinal (region) 289.3
    - acute 683
    - chronic or subacute 289.1
  - lymph gland or node, except mesenteric 289.3
    - acute 683
    - chronic or subacute 289.1
    - mesenteric (acute) (chronic) (nonspecific) (subacute) 289.2
  - mesenteric (acute) (chronic) (nonspecific) (subacute) 289.2
    - due to Pasteurella multocida (P. septica) 027.2
  - parotid gland (suppurative) 527.2
  - phlegmonous 683
  - salivary duct or gland (any) (recurring) (suppurative) 527.2
  - scrofulous (*see also* Tuberculosis) 017.2 ☑
  - septic 289.3
  - Skene's duct or gland (*see also* Urethritis) 597.89
  - strumous, tuberculous (*see also* Tuberculosis) 017.2 ☑
  - subacute, unspecified site 289.1
- **Adenitis** — *see also* Lymphadenitis — *continued*
  - sublingual gland (suppurative) 527.2
  - submandibular gland (suppurative) 527.2
  - submaxillary gland (suppurative) 527.2
  - suppurative 683
  - tuberculous — *see* Tuberculosis, lymph gland
  - urethral gland (*see also* Urethritis) 597.89
  - venereal NEC 099.8
  - Wharton's duct (suppurative) 527.2
- **Adenoacanthoma** (M8570/3) — *see* Neoplasm, by site, malignant
- **Adenoameloblastoma** (M9300/0) 213.1
  - upper jaw (bone) 213.0
- **Adenocarcinoma** (M8140/3) — *see also* Neoplasm, by site, malignant

> *Note — The list of adjectival modifiers below is not exhaustive. A description of adenocarcinoma that does not appear in this list should be coded in the same manner as carcinoma with that description. Thus, "mixed acidophil-basophil adenocarcinoma," should be coded in the same manner as "mixed acidophil-basophil carcinoma," which appears in the list under "Carcinoma."*
>
> *Except where otherwise indicated, the morphological varieties of adenocarcinoma in the list below should be coded by site as for "Neoplasm, malignant."*

  - with
    - apocrine metaplasia (M8573/3)
    - cartilaginous (and osseous) metaplasia (M8571/3)
    - osseous (and cartilaginous) metaplasia (M8571/3)
    - spindle cell metaplasia (M8572/3)
    - squamous metaplasia (M8570/3)
  - acidophil (M8280/3)
    - specified site — *see* Neoplasm, by site, malignant
    - unspecified site 194.3
  - acinar (M8550/3)
  - acinic cell (M8550/3)
  - adrenal cortical (M8370/3) 194.0
  - alveolar (M8251/3)
    - and
      - epidermoid carcinoma, mixed (M8560/3)
      - squamous cell carcinoma, mixed (M8560/3)
  - apocrine (M8401/3)
    - breast — *see* Neoplasm, breast, malignant
    - specified site NEC — *see* Neoplasm, skin, malignant
    - unspecified site 173.9
  - basophil (M8300/3)
    - specified site — *see* Neoplasm, by site, malignant
    - unspecified site 194.3
  - bile duct type (M8160/3)
    - liver 155.1
    - specified site NEC — *see* Neoplasm, by site, malignant
    - unspecified site 155.1
  - bronchiolar (M8250/3) — *see* Neoplasm, lung, malignant
  - ceruminous (M8420/3) 173.2
  - chromophobe (M8270/3)
    - specified site — *see* Neoplasm, by site, malignant
    - unspecified site 194.3
  - clear cell (mesonephroid type) (M8310/3)
  - colloid (M8480/3)
  - cylindroid type (M8200/3)
  - diffuse type (M8145/3)
    - specified site — *see* Neoplasm, by site, malignant
    - unspecified site 151.9

- **Adenoma** — *see* also Neoplasm, by site, benign — *continued*
  - sebaceous, sebaceum (gland) (senile) (M8410/0) (*see also* Neoplasm, skin, benign)
    - disseminata 759.5
  - Sertoli cell (M8640/0)
    - specified site — *see* Neoplasm, by site, benign
    - unspecified site
      - female 220
      - male 222.0
  - skin appendage (M8390/0) — *see* Neoplasm, skin, benign
  - sudoriferous gland (M8400/0) — *see* Neoplasm, skin, benign
  - sweat gland or duct (M8400/0) — *see* Neoplasm, skin, benign
  - testicular (M8640/0)
    - specified site — *see* Neoplasm, by site, benign
    - unspecified site
      - female 220
      - male 222.0
  - thyroid 226
  - trabecular (M8190/0)
  - tubular (M8211/0) (*see also* Neoplasm, by site, benign)
    - papillary (M8460/3)
    - Pick's (M8640/0)
      - specified site — *see* Neoplasm, by site, benign
      - unspecified site
        - female 220
        - male 222.0
  - tubulovillous (M8263/0)
  - villoglandular (M8263/0)
  - villous (M8261/1) — *see* Neoplasm, by site, uncertain behavior
  - water-clear cell (M8322/0) 227.1
  - wolffian duct (M9110/0)
- **Adenomyoma** (M8932/0) — *see also* Neoplasm, by site, benign
  - prostate 600.20
    - with ●
      - other lower urinary tract symptoms (LUTS) 600.21 ●
      - urinary ●
        - obstruction 600.21 ●
        - retention 600.21 ●
- **Adenomyometritis** 617.0
- **Adenomyosis** (uterus) (internal) 617.0
- **Adenopathy** (lymph gland) 785.6
  - inguinal 785.6
  - mediastinal 785.6
  - mesentery 785.6
  - syphilitic (secondary) 091.4
  - tracheobronchial 785.6
    - tuberculous (*see also* Tuberculosis) 012.1 ☑
      - primary, progressive 010.8 ☑
  - tuberculous (*see also* Tuberculosis, lymph gland) 017.2 ☑
    - tracheobronchial 012.1 ☑
      - primary, progressive 010.8 ☑
- **Adenopharyngitis** 462
- **Adenophlegmon** 683
- **Adenosalpingitis** 614.1
- **Adenosarcoma** (M8960/3) 189.0
- **Adenosclerosis** 289.3
- **Adenosis**
  - breast (sclerosing) 610.2
  - vagina, congenital 752.49
- **Adentia** (complete) (partial) — *see also* Absence, teeth 520.0
- **Adherent**
  - labium (minus) 624.4
  - pericardium (nonrheumatic) 423.1
    - rheumatic 393
  - placenta 667.0 ☑
    - with hemorrhage 666.0 ☑
  - prepuce 605
  - scar (skin) NEC 709.2
  - tendon in scar 709.2
- **Adhesion(s), adhesive** (postinfectional) (postoperative)
  - abdominal (wall) (*see also* Adhesions, peritoneum) 568.0
  - amnion to fetus 658.8 ☑
    - affecting fetus or newborn 762.8
  - appendix 543.9
  - arachnoiditis — *see* Meningitis
  - auditory tube (Eustachian) 381.89
  - bands (*see also* Adhesions, peritoneum)
    - cervix 622.3
    - uterus 621.5
  - bile duct (any) 576.8
  - bladder (sphincter) 596.8
  - bowel (*see also* Adhesions, peritoneum) 568.0
  - cardiac 423.1
    - rheumatic 398.99
  - cecum (*see also* Adhesions, peritoneum) 568.0
  - cervicovaginal 622.3
    - congenital 752.49
    - postpartal 674.8 ☑
      - old 622.3
  - cervix 622.3
  - clitoris 624.4
  - colon (*see also* Adhesions, peritoneum) 568.0
  - common duct 576.8
  - congenital (*see also* Anomaly, specified type NEC)
    - fingers (*see also* Syndactylism, fingers) 755.11
    - labium (majus) (minus) 752.49
    - omental, anomalous 751.4
    - ovary 752.0
    - peritoneal 751.4
    - toes (*see also* Syndactylism, toes) 755.13
    - tongue (to gum or roof of mouth) 750.12
  - conjunctiva (acquired) (localized) 372.62
    - congenital 743.63
    - extensive 372.63
  - cornea — *see* Opacity, cornea
  - cystic duct 575.8
  - diaphragm (*see also* Adhesions, peritoneum) 568.0
  - due to foreign body — *see* Foreign body
  - duodenum (*see also* Adhesions, peritoneum) 568.0
    - with obstruction 537.3
  - ear, middle — *see* Adhesions, middle ear
  - epididymis 608.89
  - epidural — *see* Adhesions, meninges
  - epiglottis 478.79
  - Eustachian tube 381.89
  - eyelid 374.46
    - postoperative 997.99
      - surgically created V45.69
  - gallbladder (*see also* Disease, gallbladder) 575.8
  - globe 360.89
  - heart 423.1
    - rheumatic 398.99
  - ileocecal (coil) (*see also* Adhesions, peritoneum) 568.0
  - ileum (*see also* Adhesions, peritoneum) 568.0
  - intestine (postoperative) (*see also* Adhesions, peritoneum) 568.0
    - with obstruction 560.81
      - with hernia (*see also* Hernia, by site, with obstruction)
        - gangrenous — *see* Hernia, by site, with gangrene
  - intra-abdominal (*see also* Adhesions, peritoneum) 568.0
  - iris 364.70
    - to corneal graft 996.79
  - joint (*see also* Ankylosis) 718.5 ☑
  - kidney 593.89
- **Adhesion(s), adhesive** — *continued*
  - labium (majus) (minus), congenital 752.49
  - liver 572.8
  - lung 511.0
  - mediastinum 519.3
  - meninges 349.2
    - cerebral (any) 349.2
      - congenital 742.4
    - congenital 742.8
    - spinal (any) 349.2
      - congenital 742.59
    - tuberculous (cerebral) (spinal) (*see also* Tuberculosis, meninges) 013.0 ☑
  - mesenteric (*see also* Adhesions, peritoneum) 568.0
  - middle ear (fibrous) 385.10
    - drum head 385.19
      - to
        - incus 385.11
        - promontorium 385.13
        - stapes 385.12
    - specified NEC 385.19
  - nasal (septum) (to turbinates) 478.19 ▲
  - nerve NEC 355.9
    - spinal 355.9
      - root 724.9
        - cervical NEC 723.4
        - lumbar NEC 724.4
        - lumbosacral 724.4
        - thoracic 724.4
  - ocular muscle 378.60
  - omentum (*see also* Adhesions, peritoneum) 568.0
  - organ or site, congenital NEC — *see* Anomaly, specified type NEC
  - ovary 614.6
    - congenital (to cecum, kidney, or omentum) 752.0
  - parauterine 614.6
  - parovarian 614.6
  - pelvic (peritoneal)
    - female (postoperative) (postinfection) 614.6
    - male (postoperative) (postinfection) (*see also* Adhesions, peritoneum) 568.0
    - postpartal (old) 614.6
    - tuberculous (*see also* Tuberculosis) 016.9 ☑
  - penis to scrotum (congenital) 752.69
  - periappendiceal (*see also* Adhesions, peritoneum) 568.0
  - pericardium (nonrheumatic) 423.1
    - rheumatic 393
    - tuberculous (*see also* Tuberculosis) 017.9 ☑ *[420.0]*
  - pericholecystic 575.8
  - perigastric (*see also* Adhesions, peritoneum) 568.0
  - periovarian 614.6
  - periprostatic 602.8
  - perirectal (*see also* Adhesions, peritoneum) 568.0
  - perirenal 593.89
  - peritoneum, peritoneal (fibrous) (postoperative) 568.0
    - with obstruction (intestinal) 560.81
      - with hernia (*see also* Hernia, by site, with obstruction)
        - gangrenous — *see* Hernia, by site, with gangrene
      - duodenum 537.3
    - congenital 751.4
    - female (postoperative) (postinfective) 614.6
    - pelvic, female 614.6
    - pelvic, male 568.0
    - postpartal, pelvic 614.6
    - to uterus 614.6
  - peritubal 614.6
  - periureteral 593.89
  - periuterine 621.5
  - perivesical 596.8
  - perivesicular (seminal vesicle) 608.89
  - pleura, pleuritic 511.0
    - tuberculous (*see also* Tuberculosis, pleura) 012.0 ☑
  - pleuropericardial 511.0
  - postoperative (gastrointestinal tract) (*see also* Adhesions, peritoneum) 568.0
    - eyelid 997.99
      - surgically created V45.69
    - pelvic female 614.9
    - pelvic male 568.0
    - urethra 598.2
  - postpartal, old 624.4
  - preputial, prepuce 605
  - pulmonary 511.0
  - pylorus (*see also* Adhesions, peritoneum) 568.0
  - Rosenmüller's fossa 478.29
  - sciatic nerve 355.0
  - seminal vesicle 608.89
  - shoulder (joint) 726.0
  - sigmoid flexure (*see also* Adhesions, peritoneum) 568.0
  - spermatic cord (acquired) 608.89
    - congenital 752.89
  - spinal canal 349.2
    - nerve 355.9
      - root 724.9
        - cervical NEC 723.4
        - lumbar NEC 724.4
        - lumbosacral 724.4
        - thoracic 724.4
  - stomach (*see also* Adhesions, peritoneum) 568.0
  - subscapular 726.2
  - tendonitis 726.90
    - shoulder 726.0
  - testicle 608.89
  - tongue (congenital) (to gum or roof of mouth) 750.12
    - acquired 529.8
  - trachea 519.19 ▲
  - tubo-ovarian 614.6
  - tunica vaginalis 608.89
  - ureter 593.89
  - uterus 621.5
    - to abdominal wall 614.6
      - in pregnancy or childbirth 654.4 ☑
        - affecting fetus or newborn 763.89
  - vagina (chronic) (postoperative) (postradiation) 623.2
  - vaginitis (congenital) 752.49
  - vesical 596.8
  - vitreous 379.29
- **Adie (-Holmes) syndrome** (tonic pupillary reaction) 379.46
- **Adiponecrosis neonatorum** 778.1
- **Adiposa dolorosa** 272.8
- **Adiposalgia** 272.8
- **Adiposis**
  - cerebralis 253.8
  - dolorosa 272.8
  - tuberosa simplex 272.8
- **Adiposity** 278.02
  - heart (*see also* Degeneration, myocardial) 429.1
  - localized 278.1
- **Adiposogenital dystrophy** 253.8
- **Adjustment**
  - prosthesis or other device — *see* Fitting of
  - reaction — *see* Reaction, adjustment
- **Administration, prophylactic**
  - antibiotics V07.39
  - antitoxin, any V07.2
  - antivenin V07.2
  - chemotherapeutic agent NEC V07.39
  - chemotherapy NEC V07.39
  - diphtheria antitoxin V07.2
  - fluoride V07.31
  - gamma globulin V07.2
  - immune sera (gamma globulin) V07.2

☑ Additional Digit Required — Refer to the Tabular List for Digit Selection

Subterms under main terms may continue to next column or page

- **Admission** — *continued*
  - for — *continued*
    - examination (*see also* Examination) — *continued*
      - eye V72.0
      - follow-up (routine) — *see* Examination, follow-up
      - for admission to
        - old age home V70.3
        - school V70.3
      - general V70.9
        - specified reason NEC V70.8
      - gynecological V72.31
      - health supervision (child) (infant) V20.2
      - hearing V72.19 ▲
        - following failed hearing screening V72.11 ●
      - immigration V70.3
      - infant, routine V20.2 ●
      - insurance certification V70.3
      - laboratory V72.6
      - marriage license V70.3
      - medical (general) (*see also* Examination, medical) V70.9
      - medicolegal reasons V70.4
      - naturalization V70.3
      - pelvic (annual) (periodic) V72.31
      - postpartum checkup V24.2
      - pregnancy (possible) (unconfirmed) V72.40
        - negative result V72.41
        - positive result V72.42
      - preoperative V72.84
        - cardiovascular V72.81
        - respiratory V72.82
        - specified NEC V72.83
      - preprocedural V72.84
        - cardiovascular V72.81
        - general physical V72.83
        - respiratory V72.82
        - specified NEC V72.83
      - prison V70.3
      - psychiatric (general) V70.2
        - requested by authority V70.1
      - radiological NEC V72.5
      - respiratory, preoperative V72.82
      - school V70.3
      - screening — *see* Screening
      - skin hypersensitivity V72.7
      - specified type NEC V72.85
      - sport competition V70.3
      - vision V72.0
      - well baby and child care V20.2
    - exercise therapy V57.1
    - face-lift, cosmetic reason V50.1
    - fitting (of)
      - artificial
        - arm (complete) (partial) V52.0
        - eye V52.2
        - leg (complete) (partial) V52.1
      - biliary drainage tube V58.82
      - brain neuropacemaker V53.02
      - breast V52.4
        - implant V52.4
        - prosthesis V52.4
      - cardiac pacemaker V53.31
      - catheter
        - non-vascular V58.82
        - vascular V58.81
      - cerebral ventricle (communicating) shunt V53.01
      - chest tube V58.82
      - colostomy belt V55.2
      - contact lenses V53.1
      - cystostomy device V53.6
      - dental prosthesis V52.3
      - device, unspecified type V53.90
        - abdominal V53.5
        - cerebral ventricle (communicating) shunt V53.01
        - insulin pump V53.91
        - intrauterine contraceptive V25.1
        - nervous system V53.09
        - orthodontic V53.4
        - other device V53.99
        - prosthetic V52.9
          - breast V52.4
          - dental V52.3
          - eye V52.2
        - special senses V53.09
        - substitution
          - auditory V53.09
          - nervous system V53.09
          - visual V53.09
      - diaphragm (contraceptive) V25.02
      - fistula (sinus tract) drainage tube V58.82
      - growth rod V54.02
      - hearing aid V53.2
      - ileostomy device V55.2
      - intestinal appliance or device NEC V53.5
      - intrauterine contraceptive device V25.1
      - neuropacemaker (brain) (peripheral nerve) (spinal cord) V53.02
      - orthodontic device V53.4
      - orthopedic (device) V53.7
        - brace V53.7
        - cast V53.7
        - shoes V53.7
      - pacemaker
        - brain V53.02
        - cardiac V53.31
        - carotid sinus V53.39
        - spinal cord V53.02
      - pleural drainage tube V58.82
      - prosthesis V52.9
        - arm (complete) (partial) V52.0
        - breast V52.4
        - dental V52.3
        - eye V52.2
        - leg (complete) (partial) V52.1
        - specified type NEC V52.8
      - spectacles V53.1
      - wheelchair V53.8
    - follow-up examination (routine) (following) V67.9
      - cancer chemotherapy V67.2
      - chemotherapy V67.2
      - high-risk medication NEC V67.51
      - injury NEC V67.59
      - psychiatric V67.3
      - psychotherapy V67.3
      - radiotherapy V67.1
      - specified surgery NEC V67.09
      - surgery V67.00
        - vaginal pap smear V67.01
      - treatment (for) V67.9
        - combined V67.6
        - fracture V67.4
        - involving high-risk medication NEC V67.51
        - mental disorder V67.3
        - specified NEC V67.59
    - hair transplant, for cosmetic reason V50.0
    - health advice, education, or instruction V65.4 ☑
    - hormone replacement therapy (postmenopausal) V07.4
    - hospice care V66.7
    - immunotherapy, antineoplastic V58.12
    - insertion (of)
      - subdermal implantable contraceptive V25.5
    - insulin pump titration V53.91
    - insulin pump training V65.46
    - intrauterine device
      - insertion V25.1
      - management V25.42
    - investigation to determine further disposition V63.8
    - isolation V07.0
    - issue of
      - medical certificate NEC V68.0
      - repeat prescription NEC V68.1
        - contraceptive device NEC V25.49
    - kidney dialysis V56.0
    - lengthening of growth rod V54.02
    - mental health evaluation V70.2
      - requested by authority V70.1
    - nonmedical reason NEC V68.89
    - nursing care evaluation V63.8
    - observation (without need for further medical care) (*see also* Observation) V71.9
      - accident V71.4
      - alleged rape or seduction V71.5
      - criminal assault V71.6
      - following accident V71.4
        - at work V71.3
      - foreign body ingestion V71.89
      - growth and development variations, childhood V21.0
      - inflicted injury NEC V71.6
      - ingestion of deleterious agent or foreign body V71.89
      - injury V71.6
      - malignant neoplasm V71.1
      - mental disorder V71.09
      - newborn — *see* Observation, suspected, condition, newborn
      - rape V71.5
      - specified NEC V71.89
      - suspected disorder V71.9
        - abuse V71.81
        - accident V71.4
          - at work V71.3
        - benign neoplasm V71.89
        - cardiovascular V71.7
        - exposure
          - anthrax V71.82
          - biological agent NEC V71.83
          - SARS V71.83
        - heart V71.7
        - inflicted injury NEC V71.6
        - malignant neoplasm V71.1
        - mental NEC V71.09
        - neglect V71.81
        - specified condition NEC V71.89
        - tuberculosis V71.2
      - tuberculosis V71.2
    - occupational therapy V57.21
    - organ transplant, donor — *see* Donor
    - ovary, ovarian removal, prophylactic V50.42
    - palliative care V66.7
    - Papanicolaou smear
      - cervix V76.2
        - for suspected malignant neoplasm V76.2
          - no disease found V71.1
        - routine, as part of gynecological examination V72.31
        - to confirm findings of recent normal smear following initial abnormal smear V72.32
      - vaginal V76.47
        - following hysterectomy for malignant condition V67.01
    - passage of sounds or bougie in artificial opening — *see* Attention to, artificial, opening
    - paternity testing V70.4
    - peritoneal dialysis V56.32
    - physical therapy NEC V57.1
    - plastic surgery
      - cosmetic NEC V50.1
      - following healed injury or operation V51
    - postmenopausal hormone replacement therapy V07.4
    - postpartum observation
      - immediately after delivery V24.0
      - routine follow-up V24.2
    - poststerilization (for restoration) V26.0
    - procreative management V26.9
      - specified type NEC V26.8
    - prophylactic
      - administration of
        - antibiotics V07.39
        - antitoxin, any V07.2
        - antivenin V07.2
        - chemotherapeutic agent NEC V07.39
        - chemotherapy NEC V07.39
        - diphtheria antitoxin V07.2
        - fluoride V07.31
        - gamma globulin V07.2
        - immune sera (gamma globulin) V07.2
        - RhoGAM V07.2
        - tetanus antitoxin V07.2
      - breathing exercises V57.0
      - chemotherapy NEC V07.39
        - fluoride V07.31
      - measure V07.9
        - specified type NEC V07.8
      - organ removal V50.49
        - breast V50.41
        - ovary V50.42
    - psychiatric examination (general) V70.2
      - requested by authority V70.1
    - radiation management V58.0
    - radiotherapy V58.0
    - reforming of artificial opening — *see* Attention to, artificial, opening
    - rehabilitation V57.9
      - multiple types V57.89
      - occupational V57.21
      - orthoptic V57.4
      - orthotic V57.81
      - physical NEC V57.1
      - specified type NEC V57.89
      - speech V57.3
      - vocational V57.22
    - removal of
      - cardiac pacemaker V53.31
      - cast (plaster) V54.89
      - catheter from artificial opening — *see* Attention to, artificial, opening
      - cerebral ventricle (communicating) shunt V53.01
      - cystostomy catheter V55.5
      - device
        - cerebral ventricle (communicating) shunt V53.01
        - fixation
          - external V54.89
          - internal V54.01
        - intrauterine contraceptive V25.42
        - traction, external V54.89
      - drains V58.49 ●
      - dressing
        - wound V58.30 ●
          - nonsurgical V58.30 ●
          - surgical V58.31 ●
      - fixation device
        - external V54.89
        - internal V54.01
      - intrauterine contraceptive device V25.42

☑ Additional Digit Required — Refer to the Tabular List for Digit Selection

▽ Subterms under main terms may continue to next column or page

▶◀ Revised Text ● New Line ▲ Revised Code

☑ Additional Digit Required — Refer to the Tabular List for Digit Selection
Subterms under main terms may continue to next column or page

Aneurysm — *continued*
- congenital — *continued*
  - cerebral — *see* Aneurysm, brain, congenital
  - coronary 746.85
  - gastrointestinal 747.61
  - lower limb 747.64
  - pulmonary 747.3
  - renal 747.62
  - retina 743.58
  - specified site NEC 747.89
  - spinal 747.82
  - upper limb 747.63
- conjunctiva 372.74
- conus arteriosus (*see also* Aneurysm, heart) 414.10
- coronary (arteriosclerotic) (artery) (vein) (*see also* Aneurysm, heart) 414.11
  - arteriovenous 746.85
  - congenital 746.85
  - syphilitic 093.89
- cylindrical 441.9
  - ruptured 441.5
  - syphilitic 093.9
- dissecting 442.9
  - aorta 441.00
    - abdominal 441.02
    - thoracic 441.01
    - thoracoabdominal 441.03
  - syphilitic 093.9
- ductus arteriosus 747.0
- embolic — *see* Embolism, artery
- endocardial, infective (any valve) 421.0
- femoral 442.3
- gastroduodenal 442.84
- gastroepiploic 442.84
- heart (chronic or with a stated duration of over 8 weeks) (infectional) (wall) 414.10
  - acute or with a stated duration of 8 weeks or less (*see also* Infarct, myocardium) 410.9 ☑
  - congenital 746.89
  - valve — *see* Endocarditis
- hepatic 442.84
- iliac (common) 442.2
- infective (any valve) 421.0
- innominate (nonsyphilitic) 442.89
  - syphilitic 093.89
- interauricular septum (*see also* Aneurysm, heart) 414.10
- interventricular septum (*see also* Aneurysm, heart) 414.10
- intracranial — *see* Aneurysm, brain
- intrathoracic (nonsyphilitic) 441.2
  - ruptured 441.1
  - syphilitic 093.0
- jugular vein 453.8
- lower extremity 442.3
- lung (pulmonary artery) 417.1
- malignant 093.9
- mediastinal (nonsyphilitic) 442.89
  - syphilitic 093.89
- miliary (congenital) (ruptured) (*see also* Hemorrhage, subarachnoid) 430
- mitral (heart) (valve) 424.0
- mural (arteriovenous) (heart) (*see also* Aneurysm, heart) 414.10
- mycotic, any site 421.0
  - without endocarditis — *see* Aneurysm by site ●
  - ruptured, brain (*see also* Hemorrhage, subarachnoid) 430
- myocardium (*see also* Aneurysm, heart) 414.10
- neck 442.81
- pancreaticoduodenal 442.84
- patent ductus arteriosus 747.0
- peripheral NEC 442.89
  - congenital NEC (*see also* Aneurysm, congenital) 747.60
- popliteal 442.3
- pulmonary 417.1

Aneurysm — *continued*
- pulmonary — *continued*
  - arteriovenous 747.3
    - acquired 417.0
  - syphilitic 093.89
  - valve (heart) (*see also* Endocarditis, pulmonary) 424.3
- racemose 442.9
  - congenital (peripheral) NEC 747.60
- radial 442.0
- Rasmussen's (*see also* Tuberculosis) 011.2 ☑
- renal 442.1
- retinal (acquired) 362.17
  - congenital 743.58
  - diabetic 250.5 ☑ *[362.01]*
- sinus, aortic (of Valsalva) 747.29
- specified site NEC 442.89
- spinal (cord) 442.89
  - congenital 747.82
  - syphilitic (hemorrhage) 094.89
- spleen, splenic 442.83
- subclavian 442.82
  - syphilitic 093.89
- superior mesenteric 442.84
- syphilitic 093.9
  - aorta 093.0
  - central nervous system 094.89
  - congenital 090.5
  - spine, spinal 094.89
- thoracoabdominal 441.7
  - ruptured 441.6
- thorax, thoracic (arch) (nonsyphilitic) 441.2
  - dissecting 441.01
  - ruptured 441.1
  - syphilitic 093.0
- traumatic (complication) (early) — *see* Injury, blood vessel, by site
- tricuspid (heart) (valve) — *see* Endocarditis, tricuspid
- ulnar 442.0
- upper extremity 442.0
- valve, valvular — *see* Endocarditis
- venous 456.8
  - congenital NEC (*see also* Aneurysm, congenital) 747.60
- ventricle (arteriovenous) (*see also* Aneurysm, heart) 414.10
- visceral artery NEC 442.84

Angiectasis 459.89

Angiectopia 459.9

Angiitis 447.6
- allergic granulomatous 446.4
- hypersensitivity 446.20
  - Goodpasture's syndrome 446.21
  - specified NEC 446.29
- necrotizing 446.0
- Wegener's (necrotizing respiratory granulomatosis) 446.4

Angina (attack) (cardiac) (chest) (effort) (heart) (pectoris) (syndrome) (vasomotor) 413.9
- abdominal 557.1
- accelerated 411.1
- agranulocytic 288.03 ▲
- aphthous 074.0
- catarrhal 462
- crescendo 411.1
- croupous 464.4
- cruris 443.9
  - due to atherosclerosis NEC (*see also* Arteriosclerosis, extremities) 440.20
- decubitus 413.0
- diphtheritic (membranous) 032.0
- erysipelatous 034.0
- erythematous 462
- exudative, chronic 476.0
- faucium 478.29
- gangrenous 462
  - diphtheritic 032.0
- infectious 462
- initial 411.1
- intestinal 557.1

Angina — *continued*
- ludovici 528.3
- Ludwig's 528.3
- malignant 462
  - diphtheritic 032.0
- membranous 464.4
  - diphtheritic 032.0
- mesenteric 557.1
- monocytic 075
- nocturnal 413.0
- phlegmonous 475
  - diphtheritic 032.0
- preinfarctional 411.1
- Prinzmetal's 413.1
- progressive 411.1
- pseudomembranous 101
- psychogenic 306.2
- pultaceous, diphtheritic 032.0
- scarlatinal 034.1
- septic 034.0
- simple 462
- stable NEC 413.9
- staphylococcal 462
- streptococcal 034.0
- stridulous, diphtheritic 032.3
- syphilitic 093.9
  - congenital 090.5
- tonsil 475
- trachealis 464.4
- unstable 411.1
- variant 413.1
- Vincent's 101

Angioblastoma (M9161/1) — *see* Neoplasm, connective tissue, uncertain behavior

Angiocholecystitis — *see also* Cholecystitis, acute 575.0

Angiocholitis — *see also* Cholecystitis, acute 576.1

Angiodysgensis spinalis 336.1

Angiodysplasia (intestinalis) (intestine) 569.84
- with hemorrhage 569.85
- duodenum 537.82
  - with hemorrhage 537.83
- stomach 537.82
  - with hemorrhage 537.83

Angioedema (allergic) (any site) (with urticaria) 995.1
- hereditary 277.6

Angioendothelioma (M9130/1) — *see also* Neoplasm, by site, uncertain behavior
- benign (M9130/0) (*see also* Hemangioma, by site) 228.00
- bone (M9260/3) — *see* Neoplasm, bone, malignant
- Ewing's (M9260/3) — *see* Neoplasm, bone, malignant
- nervous system (M9130/0) 228.09

Angiofibroma (M9160/0) — *see also* Neoplasm, by site, benign
- juvenile (M9160/0) 210.7
  - specified site — *see* Neoplasm, by site, benign
  - unspecified site 210.7

Angiohemophilia (A) (B) 286.4

Angioid streaks (choroid) (retina) 363.43

Angiokeratoma (M9141/0) — *see also* Neoplasm, skin, benign
- corporis diffusum 272.7

Angiokeratosis
- diffuse 272.7

Angioleiomyoma (M8894/0) — *see* Neoplasm, connective tissue, benign

Angioleucitis 683

Angiolipoma (M8861/0) — *see also* Lipoma, by site 214.9
- infiltrating (M8861/1) — *see* Neoplasm, connective tissue, uncertain behavior

Angioma (M9120/0) — *see also* Hemangioma, by site 228.00
- capillary 448.1
- hemorrhagicum hereditaria 448.0

Angioma — *see also* Hemangioma, by site — *continued*
- malignant (M9120/3) — *see* Neoplasm, connective tissue, malignant
- pigmentosum et atrophicum 757.33
- placenta — *see* Placenta, abnormal
- plexiform (M9131/0) — *see* Hemangioma, by site
- senile 448.1
- serpiginosum 709.1
- spider 448.1
- stellate 448.1

Angiomatosis 757.32
- bacillary 083.8
- corporis diffusum universale 272.7
- cutaneocerebral 759.6
- encephalocutaneous 759.6
- encephalofacial 759.6
- encephalotrigeminal 759.6
- hemorrhagic familial 448.0
- hereditary familial 448.0
- heredofamilial 448.0
- meningo-oculofacial 759.6
- multiple sites 228.09
- neuro-oculocutaneous 759.6
- retina (Hippel's disease) 759.6
- retinocerebellosa 759.6
- retinocerebral 759.6
- systemic 228.09

Angiomyolipoma (M8860/0)
- specified site — *see* Neoplasm, connective tissue, benign
- unspecified site 223.0

Angiomyoliposarcoma (M8860/3) — *see* Neoplasm, connective tissue, malignant

Angiomyoma (M8894/0) — *see* Neoplasm, connective tissue, benign

Angiomyosarcoma (M8894/3) — *see* Neoplasm, connective tissue, malignant

Angioneurosis 306.2

Angioneurotic edema (allergic) (any site) (with urticaria) 995.1
- hereditary 277.6

Angiopathia, angiopathy 459.9
- diabetic (peripheral) 250.7 ☑ *[443.81]*
- peripheral 443.9
  - diabetic 250.7 ☑ *[443.81]*
  - specified type NEC 443.89
- retinae syphilitica 093.89
- retinalis (juvenilis) 362.18
  - background 362.10
  - diabetic 250.5 ☑ *[362.01]*
  - proliferative 362.29
  - tuberculous (*see also* Tuberculosis) 017.3 ☑ *[362.18]*

Angiosarcoma (M9120/3) — *see* Neoplasm, connective tissue, malignant

Angiosclerosis — *see* Arteriosclerosis

Angioscotoma, enlarged 368.42

Angiospasm 443.9
- brachial plexus 353.0
- cerebral 435.9
- cervical plexus 353.2
- nerve
  - arm 354.9
    - axillary 353.0
    - median 354.1
    - ulnar 354.2
  - autonomic (*see also* Neuropathy, peripheral, autonomic) 337.9
  - axillary 353.0
  - leg 355.8
    - plantar 355.6
  - lower extremity — *see* Angiospasm, nerve, leg
  - median 354.1
  - peripheral NEC 355.9
  - spinal NEC 355.9
  - sympathetic (*see also* Neuropathy, peripheral, autonomic) 337.9
  - ulnar 354.2

Arteriosclerosis, arteriosclerotic — *continued*
- arteries of extremities — *see* Arteriosclerosis, extremities
- basilar (artery) (*see also* Occlusion, artery, basilar) 433.0 ☑
- brain 437.0
- bypass graft
  - coronary artery 414.05
    - autologous artery (gastroepiploic) (internal mammary) 414.04
    - autologous vein 414.02
    - nonautologous biological 414.03
    - of transplanted heart 414.07
  - extremity 440.30
    - autologous vein 440.31
    - nonautologous biological 440.32
- cardiac — *see* Arteriosclerosis, coronary
- cardiopathy — *see* Arteriosclerosis, coronary
- cardiorenal (*see also* Hypertension, cardiorenal) 404.90
- cardiovascular (*see also* Disease, cardiovascular) 429.2
- carotid (artery) (common) (internal) (*see also* Occlusion, artery, carotid) 433.1 ☑
- central nervous system 437.0
- cerebral 437.0
  - late effect — *see* Late effect(s) (of) cerebrovascular disease
- cerebrospinal 437.0
- cerebrovascular 437.0
- coronary (artery) 414.00
  - graft — *see* Arteriosclerosis, bypass graft
  - native artery 414.01
    - of transplanted heart 414.06
- extremities (native artery) NEC 440.20
  - bypass graft 440.30
    - autologous vein 440.31
    - nonautologous biological 440.32
  - claudication (intermittent) 440.21
    - and
      - gangrene 440.24
      - rest pain 440.22
        - and
          - gangrene 440.24
          - ulceration 440.23
            - and gangrene 440.24
      - ulceration 440.23
        - and gangrene 440.24
  - gangrene 440.24
  - rest pain 440.22
    - and
      - gangrene 440.24
      - ulceration 440.23
        - and gangrene 440.24
  - specified site NEC 440.29
  - ulceration 440.23
    - and gangrene 440.24
- heart (disease) (*see also* Arteriosclerosis, coronary)
  - valve 424.99
    - aortic 424.1
    - mitral 424.0
    - pulmonary 424.3
    - tricuspid 424.2
- kidney (*see also* Hypertension, kidney) 403.90
- labyrinth, labyrinthine 388.00
- medial NEC (*see also* Arteriosclerosis, extremities) 440.20
- mesentery (artery) 557.1
- Mönckeberg's (*see also* Arteriosclerosis, extremities) 440.20
- myocarditis 429.0
- nephrosclerosis (*see also* Hypertension, kidney) 403.90
- peripheral (of extremities) — *see* Arteriosclerosis, extremities
- precerebral 433.9 ☑
  - specified artery NEC 433.8 ☑

Arteriosclerosis, arteriosclerotic — *continued*
- pulmonary (idiopathic) 416.0
- renal (*see also* Hypertension, kidney) 403.90
  - arterioles (*see also* Hypertension, kidney) 403.90
  - artery 440.1
- retinal (vascular) 440.8 *[362.13]*
- specified artery NEC 440.8
  - with gangrene 440.8 *[785.4]*
- spinal (cord) 437.0
- vertebral (artery) (*see also* Occlusion, artery, vertebral) 433.2 ☑

Arteriospasm 443.9

Arteriovenous — *see* condition

Arteritis 447.6
- allergic (*see also* Angiitis, hypersensitivity) 446.20
- aorta (nonsyphilitic) 447.6
  - syphilitic 093.1
- aortic arch 446.7
- brachiocephalica 446.7
- brain 437.4
  - syphilitic 094.89
- branchial 446.7
- cerebral 437.4
  - late effect — *see* Late effect(s) (of) cerebrovascular disease
  - syphilitic 094.89
- coronary (artery) (*see also* Arteriosclerosis, coronary)
  - rheumatic 391.9
    - chronic 398.99
  - syphilitic 093.89
- cranial (left) (right) 446.5
- deformans — *see* Arteriosclerosis
- giant cell 446.5
- necrosing or necrotizing 446.0
- nodosa 446.0
- obliterans (*see also* Arteriosclerosis)
  - subclaviocarotica 446.7
- pulmonary 417.8
- retina 362.18
- rheumatic — *see* Fever, rheumatic
- senile — *see* Arteriosclerosis
- suppurative 447.2
- syphilitic (general) 093.89
  - brain 094.89
  - coronary 093.89
  - spinal 094.89
- temporal 446.5
- young female, syndrome 446.7

Artery, arterial — *see* condition

Arthralgia — *see also* Pain, joint 719.4 ☑
- allergic (*see also* Pain, joint) 719.4 ☑
- in caisson disease 993.3
- psychogenic 307.89
- rubella 056.71
- Salmonella 003.23
- temporomandibular joint 524.62

Arthritis, arthritic (acute) (chronic) (subacute) 716.9 ☑
- meaning Osteoarthritis — *see* Osteoarthrosis

> *Note — Use the following fifth-digit subclassification with categories 711–712, 715–716:*
>
> 0 *site unspecified*
> 1 *shoulder region*
> 2 *upper arm*
> 3 *forearm*
> 4 *hand*
> 5 *pelvic region and thigh*
> 6 *lower leg*
> 7 *ankle and foot*
> 8 *other specified sites*
> 9 *multiple sites*

- allergic 716.2 ☑
- ankylosing (crippling) (spine) 720.0
  - sites other than spine 716.9 ☑

Arthritis, arthritic — *continued*
- atrophic 714.0
  - spine 720.9
- back (*see also* Arthritis, spine) 721.90
- Bechterew's (ankylosing spondylitis) 720.0
- blennorrhagic 098.50
- cervical, cervicodorsal (*see also* Spondylosis, cervical) 721.0
- Charcôt's 094.0 *[713.5]*
  - diabetic 250.6 ☑ *[713.5]*
  - syringomyelic 336.0 *[713.5]*
  - tabetic 094.0 *[713.5]*
- chylous (*see also* Filariasis) 125.9 *[711.7]* ☑
- climacteric NEC 716.3 ☑
- coccyx 721.8
- cricoarytenoid 478.79
- crystal (-induced) — *see* Arthritis, due to crystals
- deformans (*see also* Osteoarthrosis) 715.9 ☑
  - spine 721.90
    - with myelopathy 721.91
- degenerative (*see also* Osteoarthrosis) 715.9 ☑
  - idiopathic 715.09
  - polyarticular 715.09
  - spine 721.90
    - with myelopathy 721.91
- dermatoarthritis, lipoid 272.8 *[713.0]*
- due to or associated with
  - acromegaly 253.0 *[713.0]*
  - actinomycosis 039.8 *[711.4]* ☑
  - amyloidosis 277.39 *[713.7]* ▲
  - bacterial disease NEC 040.89 *[711.4]* ☑
  - Behçet's syndrome 136.1 *[711.2]* ☑
  - blastomycosis 116.0 *[711.6]* ☑
  - brucellosis (*see also* Brucellosis) 023.9 *[711.4]* ☑
  - caisson disease 993.3
  - coccidioidomycosis 114.3 *[711.6]* ☑
  - coliform (Escherichia coli) 711.0 ☑
  - colitis, ulcerative (*see also* Colitis, ulcerative) 556.9 *[713.1]*
  - cowpox 051.0 *[711.5]* ☑
  - crystals (*see also* Gout)
    - dicalcium phosphate 275.49 *[712.1]* ☑
    - pyrophosphate 275.49 *[712.2]* ☑
    - specified NEC 275.49 *[712.8]* ☑
  - dermatoarthritis, lipoid 272.8 *[713.0]*
  - dermatological disorder NEC 709.9 *[713.3]*
  - diabetes 250.6 ☑ *[713.5]*
  - diphtheria 032.89 *[711.4]* ☑
  - dracontiasis 125.7 *[711.7]* ☑
  - dysentery 009.0 *[711.3]* ☑
  - endocrine disorder NEC 259.9 *[713.0]*
  - enteritis NEC 009.1 *[711.3]* ☑
    - infectious (*see also* Enteritis, infectious) 009.0 *[711.3]* ☑
      - specified organism NEC 008.8 *[711.3]* ☑
    - regional (*see also* Enteritis, regional) 555.9 *[713.1]*
    - specified organism NEC 008.8 *[711.3]* ☑
  - epiphyseal slip, nontraumatic (old) 716.8 ☑
  - erysipelas 035 *[711.4]* ☑
  - erythema
    - epidemic 026.1
    - multiforme 695.1 *[713.3]*
    - nodosum 695.2 *[713.3]*
  - Escherichia coli 711.0 ☑
  - filariasis NEC 125.9 *[711.7]* ☑
  - gastrointestinal condition NEC 569.9 *[713.1]*
  - glanders 024 *[711.4]* ☑
  - Gonococcus 098.50

Arthritis, arthritic — *continued*
- due to or associated with — *continued*
  - gout 274.0
  - helminthiasis NEC 128.9 *[711.7]* ☑
  - hematological disorder NEC 289.9 *[713.2]*
  - hemochromatosis 275.0 *[713.0]*
  - hemoglobinopathy NEC (*see also* Disease, hemoglobin) 282.7 *[713.2]*
  - hemophilia (*see also* Hemophilia) 286.0 *[713.2]*
  - Hemophilus influenzae (H. influenzae) 711.0 ☑
  - Henoch (-Schönlein) purpura 287.0 *[713.6]*
  - H. influenzae 711.0 ☑
  - histoplasmosis NEC (*see also* Histoplasmosis) 115.99 *[711.6]* ☑
  - hyperparathyroidism 252.00 *[713.0]*
  - hypersensitivity reaction NEC 995.3 *[713.6]*
  - hypogammaglobulinemia (*see also* Hypogamma-globulinemia) 279.00 *[713.0]*
  - hypothyroidism NEC 244.9 *[713.0]*
  - infection (*see also* Arthritis, infectious) 711.9 ☑
  - infectious disease NEC 136.9 *[711.8]* ☑
  - leprosy (*see also* Leprosy) 030.9 *[711.4]* ☑
  - leukemia NEC (M9800/3) 208.9 *[713.2]*
  - lipoid dermatoarthritis 272.8 *[713.0]*
  - Lyme disease 088.81 *[711.8]* ☑
  - Mediterranean fever, familial 277.31 *[713.7]* ▲
  - meningococcal infection 036.82
  - metabolic disorder NEC 277.9 *[713.0]*
  - multiple myelomatosis (M9730/3) 203.0 *[713.2]*
  - mumps 072.79 *[711.5]* ☑
  - mycobacteria 031.8 *[711.4]* ☑
  - mycosis NEC 117.9 *[711.6]* ☑
  - neurological disorder NEC 349.9 *[713.5]*
  - ochronosis 270.2 *[713.0]*
  - O'Nyong Nyong 066.3 *[711.5]* ☑
  - parasitic disease NEC 136.9 *[711.8]* ☑
  - paratyphoid fever (*see also* Fever, paratyphoid) 002.9 *[711.3]* ☑
  - Pneumococcus 711.0 ☑
  - poliomyelitis (*see also* Poliomyelitis) 045.9 ☑ *[711.5]* ☑
  - Pseudomonas 711.0 ☑
  - psoriasis 696.0
  - pyogenic organism (E. coli) (H. influenzae) (Pseudomonas) (Streptococcus) 711.0 ☑
  - rat-bite fever 026.1 *[711.4]* ☑
  - regional enteritis (*see also* Enteritis, regional) 555.9 *[713.1]*
  - Reiter's disease 099.3 *[711.1]* ☑
  - respiratory disorder NEC 519.9 *[713.4]*
  - reticulosis, malignant (M9720/3) 202.3 *[713.2]*
  - rubella 056.71
  - salmonellosis 003.23
  - sarcoidosis 135 *[713.7]*
  - serum sickness 999.5 *[713.6]*
  - Staphylococcus 711.0 ☑
  - Streptococcus 711.0 ☑
  - syphilis (*see also* Syphilis) 094.0 *[711.4]* ☑
  - syringomyelia 336.0 *[713.5]*
  - thalassemia 282.49 *[713.2]*
  - tuberculosis (*see also* Tuberculosis, arthritis) 015.9 ☑ *[711.4]* ☑

☑ Additional Digit Required — Refer to the Tabular List for Digit Selection

Subterms under main terms may continue to next column or page

- **Asphyxia, asphyxiation** — *continued*
  - bedclothes 994.7
  - birth (*see also* Asphyxia, newborn) 768.9
  - bunny bag 994.7
  - carbon monoxide 986
  - caul (*see also* Asphyxia, newborn) 768.9
  - cave-in 994.7
    - crushing — *see* Injury, internal, intrathoracic organs
  - constriction 994.7
  - crushing — *see* Injury, internal, intrathoracic organs
  - drowning 994.1
  - fetal, affecting newborn 768.9
  - food or foreign body (in larynx) 933.1
    - bronchioles 934.8
    - bronchus (main) 934.1
    - lung 934.8
    - nasopharynx 933.0
    - nose, nasal passages 932
    - pharynx 933.0
    - respiratory tract 934.9
      - specified part NEC 934.8
    - throat 933.0
    - trachea 934.0
  - gas, fumes, or vapor NEC 987.9
    - specified — *see* Table of Drugs and Chemicals
  - gravitational changes 994.7
  - hanging 994.7
  - inhalation — *see* Inhalation
  - intrauterine
    - fetal death (before onset of labor) 768.0
      - during labor 768.1
    - liveborn infant — *see* Distress, fetal, liveborn infant
  - local 443.0
  - mechanical 994.7
    - during birth (*see also* Distress, fetal) 768.9
  - mucus 933.1
    - bronchus (main) 934.1
    - larynx 933.1
    - lung 934.8
    - nasal passages 932
    - newborn 770.18
    - pharynx 933.0
    - respiratory tract 934.9
      - specified part NEC 934.8
    - throat 933.0
    - trachea 934.0
    - vaginal (fetus or newborn) 770.18
  - newborn 768.9
    - with neurologic involvement 768.5
    - blue 768.6
    - livida 768.6
    - mild or moderate 768.6
    - pallida 768.5
    - severe 768.5
    - white 768.5
  - pathological 799.01
  - plastic bag 994.7
  - postnatal (*see also* Asphyxia, newborn) 768.9
    - mechanical 994.7
  - pressure 994.7
  - reticularis 782.61
  - strangulation 994.7
  - submersion 994.1
  - traumatic NEC — *see* Injury, internal, intrathoracic organs
  - vomiting, vomitus — *see* Asphyxia, food or foreign body
- **Aspiration**
  - acid pulmonary (syndrome) 997.3
    - obstetric 668.0 ☑
  - amniotic fluid 770.13
    - with respiratory symptoms 770.14
  - bronchitis 507.0
  - clear amniotic fluid 770.13
    - with
      - pneumonia 770.14
      - pneumonitis 770.14
- **Aspiration** — *continued*
  - clear amniotic fluid — *continued*
    - with — *continued*
      - respiratory symptoms 770.14
  - contents of birth canal 770.17
    - with respiratory symptoms 770.18
  - fetal 770.10
    - blood 770.15
      - with
        - pneumonia 770.16
        - pneumonitis 770.16
    - pneumonitis 770.18
  - food, foreign body, or gasoline (with asphyxiation) — *see* Asphyxia, food or foreign body
  - meconium 770.11
    - with
      - pneumonia 770.12
      - pneumonitis 770.12
      - respiratory symptoms 770.12
    - below vocal cords 770.11
      - with respiratory symptoms 770.12
  - mucus 933.1
    - into
      - bronchus (main) 934.1
      - lung 934.8
      - respiratory tract 934.9
        - specified part NEC 934.8
      - trachea 934.0
    - newborn 770.17
    - vaginal (fetus or newborn) 770.17
  - newborn 770.10
    - with respiratory symptoms 770.18
    - blood 770.15
      - with
        - pneumonia 770.16
        - pneumonitis 770.16
        - respiratory symptoms 770.16
  - pneumonia 507.0
    - fetus or newborn 770.18
      - meconium 770.12
  - pneumonitis 507.0
    - fetus or newborn 770.18
      - meconium 770.12
    - obstetric 668.0 ☑
  - postnatal stomach contents 770.85
    - with
      - pneumonia 770.86
      - pneumonitis 770.86
      - respiratory symptoms 770.86
  - syndrome of newborn (massive) 770.18
    - meconium 770.12
  - vernix caseosa 770.12
- **Asplenia** 759.0
  - with mesocardia 746.87
- **Assam fever** 085.0
- **Assimilation, pelvis**
  - with disproportion 653.2 ☑
    - affecting fetus or newborn 763.1
    - causing obstructed labor 660.1 ☑
      - affecting fetus or newborn 763.1
- **Assmann's focus** — *see also* Tuberculosis 011.0 ☑
- **Astasia** (-abasia) 307.9
  - hysterical 300.11
- **Asteatosis** 706.8
  - cutis 706.8
- **Astereognosis** 780.99
- **Asterixis** 781.3
  - in liver disease 572.8
- **Asteroid hyalitis** 379.22
- **Asthenia, asthenic** 780.79
  - cardiac (*see also* Failure, heart) 428.9
    - psychogenic 306.2
  - cardiovascular (*see also* Failure, heart) 428.9
    - psychogenic 306.2
  - heart (*see also* Failure, heart) 428.9
    - psychogenic 306.2
  - hysterical 300.11
  - myocardial (*see also* Failure, heart) 428.9
    - psychogenic 306.2
  - nervous 300.5
- **Asthenia, asthenic** — *continued*
  - neurocirculatory 306.2
  - neurotic 300.5
  - psychogenic 300.5
  - psychoneurotic 300.5
  - psychophysiologic 300.5
  - reaction, psychoneurotic 300.5
  - senile 797
  - Stiller's 780.79
  - tropical anhidrotic 705.1
- **Asthenopia** 368.13
  - accommodative 367.4
  - hysterical (muscular) 300.11
  - psychogenic 306.7
- **Asthenospermia** 792.2
- **Asthma, asthmatic** (bronchial) (catarrh) (spasmodic) 493.9 ☑

> *Note — Use the following fifth-digit subclassification with category 493:*
>
> 0 *without mention of status asthmaticus or acute exacerbation or unspecified*
>
> 1 *with status asthmaticus*
>
> 2 *with acute exacerbation*

  - with
    - chronic obstructive pulmonary disease (COPD) 493.2 ☑
    - hay fever 493.0 ☑
    - rhinitis, allergic 493.0 ☑
  - allergic 493.9 ☑
    - stated cause (external allergen) 493.0 ☑
  - atopic 493.0 ☑
  - cardiac (*see also* Failure, ventricular, left) 428.1
  - cardiobronchial (*see also* Failure, ventricular, left) 428.1
  - cardiorenal (*see also* Hypertension, cardiorenal) 404.90
  - childhood 493.0 ☑
  - Colliers' 500
  - cough variant 493.82
  - croup 493.9 ☑
  - detergent 507.8
  - due to
    - detergent 507.8
    - inhalation of fumes 506.3
    - internal immunological process 493.0 ☑
  - endogenous (intrinsic) 493.1 ☑
  - eosinophilic 518.3
  - exercise induced bronchospasm 493.81
  - exogenous (cosmetics) (dander or dust) (drugs) (dust) (feathers) (food) (hay) (platinum) (pollen) 493.0 ☑
  - extrinsic 493.0 ☑
  - grinders' 502
  - hay 493.0 ☑
  - heart (*see also* Failure, ventricular, left) 428.1
  - IgE 493.0 ☑
  - infective 493.1 ☑
  - intrinsic 493.1 ☑
  - Kopp's 254.8
  - late-onset 493.1 ☑
  - meat-wrappers' 506.9
  - Millar's (laryngismus stridulus) 478.75
  - millstone makers' 502
  - miners' 500
  - Monday morning 504
  - New Orleans (epidemic) 493.0 ☑
  - platinum 493.0 ☑
  - pneumoconiotic (occupational) NEC 505
  - potters' 502
  - psychogenic 316 *[493.9]* ☑
  - pulmonary eosinophilic 518.3
  - red cedar 495.8
  - Rostan's (*see also* Failure, ventricular, left) 428.1
- **Asthma, asthmatic** — *continued*
  - sandblasters' 502
  - sequoiosis 495.8
  - stonemasons' 502
  - thymic 254.8
  - tuberculous (*see also* Tuberculosis, pulmonary) 011.9 ☑
  - Wichmann's (laryngismus stridulus) 478.75
  - wood 495.8
- **Astigmatism** (compound) (congenital) 367.20
  - irregular 367.22
  - regular 367.21
- **Astroblastoma** (M9430/3)
  - nose 748.1
  - specified site — *see* Neoplasm, by site, malignant
  - unspecified site 191.9
- **Astrocytoma** (cystic) (M9400/3)
  - anaplastic type (M9401/3)
    - specified site — *see* Neoplasm, by site, malignant
    - unspecified site 191.9
  - fibrillary (M9420/3)
    - specified site — *see* Neoplasm, by site, malignant
    - unspecified site 191.9
  - fibrous (M9420/3)
    - specified site — *see* Neoplasm, by site, malignant
    - unspecified site 191.9
  - gemistocytic (M9411/3)
    - specified site — *see* Neoplasm, by site, malignant
    - unspecified site 191.9
  - juvenile (M9421/3)
    - specified site — *see* Neoplasm, by site, malignant
    - unspecified site 191.9
  - nose 748.1
  - pilocytic (M9421/3)
    - specified site — *see* Neoplasm, by site, malignant
    - unspecified site 191.9
  - piloid (M9421/3)
    - specified site — *see* Neoplasm, by site, malignant
    - unspecified site 191.9
  - protoplasmic (M9410/3)
    - specified site — *see* Neoplasm, by site, malignant
    - unspecified site 191.9
  - specified site — *see* Neoplasm, by site, malignant
  - subependymal (M9383/1) 237.5
    - giant cell (M9384/1) 237.5
  - unspecified site 191.9
- **Astroglioma** (M9400/3)
  - nose 748.1
  - specified site — *see* Neoplasm, by site, malignant
  - unspecified site 191.9
- **Asymbolia** 784.60
- **Asymmetrical breathing** 786.09
- **Asymmetry** — *see also* Distortion
  - chest 786.9
  - face 754.0
  - jaw NEC 524.12
    - maxillary 524.11
  - pelvis with disproportion 653.0 ☑
    - affecting fetus or newborn 763.1
    - causing obstructed labor 660.1 ☑
      - affecting fetus or newborn 763.1
- **Asynergia** 781.3
- **Asynergy** 781.3
  - ventricular 429.89
- **Asystole** (heart) — *see also* Arrest, cardiac 427.5
- **Ataxia, ataxy, ataxic** 781.3
  - acute 781.3
  - brain 331.89
  - cerebellar 334.3
    - hereditary (Marie's) 334.2
    - in
      - alcoholism 303.9 ☑ *[334.4]*

Atrophoderma, atrophodermia — *continued*
- pigmentosum 757.33
- reticulatum symmetricum faciei 701.8
- senile 701.8
- symmetrical 701.8
- vermiculata 701.8

Atrophy, atrophic
- adrenal (autoimmune) (capsule) (cortex) (gland) 255.4
  - with hypofunction 255.4
- alveolar process or ridge (edentulous) 525.20
  - mandible 525.20
    - minimal 525.21
    - moderate 525.22
    - severe 525.23
  - maxilla 525.20
    - minimal 525.24
    - moderate 525.25
    - severe 525.26
- appendix 543.9
- Aran-Duchenne muscular 335.21
- arm 728.2
- arteriosclerotic — *see* Arteriosclerosis
- arthritis 714.0
  - spine 720.9
- bile duct (any) 576.8
- bladder 596.8
- blanche (of Milian) 701.3
- bone (senile) 733.99
  - due to
    - disuse 733.7
    - infection 733.99
    - tabes dorsalis (neurogenic) 094.0
  - posttraumatic 733.99
- brain (cortex) (progressive) 331.9
  - with dementia 290.10
  - Alzheimer's 331.0
    - with dementia — *see* Alzheimer's, dementia
  - circumscribed (Pick's) 331.11
    - with dementia
      - with behavioral disturbance 331.11 *[294.11]*
      - without behavioral disturbance 331.11 *[294.10]*
  - congenital 742.4
  - hereditary 331.9
  - senile 331.2
- breast 611.4
  - puerperal, postpartum 676.3 ☑
- buccal cavity 528.9
- cardiac (brown) (senile) (*see also* Degeneration, myocardial) 429.1
- cartilage (infectional) (joint) 733.99
- cast, plaster of Paris 728.2
- cerebellar — *see* Atrophy, brain
- cerebral — *see* Atrophy, brain
- cervix (endometrium) (mucosa) (myometrium) (senile) (uteri) 622.8
  - menopausal 627.8
- Charcôt-Marie-Tooth 356.1
- choroid 363.40
  - diffuse secondary 363.42
  - hereditary (*see also* Dystrophy, choroid) 363.50
    - gyrate
      - central 363.54
      - diffuse 363.57
      - generalized 363.57
  - senile 363.41
- ciliary body 364.57
- colloid, degenerative 701.3
- conjunctiva (senile) 372.89
- corpus cavernosum 607.89
- cortical (*see also* Atrophy, brain) 331.9
- Cruveilhier's 335.21
- cystic duct 576.8
- dacryosialadenopathy 710.2
- degenerative
  - colloid 701.3
  - senile 701.3
- Déjérine-Thomas 333.0

Atrophy, atrophic — *continued*
- diffuse idiopathic, dermatological 701.8
- disuse
  - bone 733.7
  - muscle 728.2
  - pelvic muscles and anal sphincter 618.83
- Duchenne-Aran 335.21
- ear 388.9
- edentulous alveolar ridge 525.20
  - mandible 525.20
    - minimal 525.21
    - moderate 525.22
    - severe 525.23
  - maxilla 525.20
    - minimal 525.24
    - moderate 525.25
    - severe 525.26
- emphysema, lung 492.8
- endometrium (senile) 621.8
  - cervix 622.8
- enteric 569.89
- epididymis 608.3
- eyeball, cause unknown 360.41
- eyelid (senile) 374.50
- facial (skin) 701.9
- facioscapulohumeral (Landouzy-Déjérine) 359.1
- fallopian tube (senile), acquired 620.3
- fatty, thymus (gland) 254.8
- gallbladder 575.8
- gastric 537.89
- gastritis (chronic) 535.1 ☑
- gastrointestinal 569.89
- genital organ, male 608.89
- glandular 289.3
- globe (phthisis bulbi) 360.41
- gum (*see also* Recession, gingival) 523.20
- hair 704.2
- heart (brown) (senile) (*see also* Degeneration, myocardial) 429.1
- hemifacial 754.0
  - Romberg 349.89
- hydronephrosis 591
- infantile 261
  - paralysis, acute (*see also* Poliomyelitis, with paralysis) 045.1 ☑
- intestine 569.89
- iris (generalized) (postinfectional) (sector shaped) 364.59
  - essential 364.51
  - progressive 364.51
  - sphincter 364.54
- kidney (senile) (*see also* Sclerosis, renal) 587
  - with hypertension (*see also* Hypertension, kidney) 403.90
  - congenital 753.0
  - hydronephrotic 591
  - infantile 753.0
- lacrimal apparatus (primary) 375.13
  - secondary 375.14
- Landouzy-Déjérine 359.1
- laryngitis, infection 476.0
- larynx 478.79
- Leber's optic 377.16
- lip 528.5
- liver (acute) (subacute) (*see also* Necrosis, liver) 570
  - chronic (yellow) 571.8
  - yellow (congenital) 570
    - with
      - abortion — *see* Abortion, by type, with specified complication NEC
      - ectopic pregnancy (*see also* categories 633.0–633.9) 639.8
      - molar pregnancy (*see also* categories 630–632) 639.8
    - chronic 571.8
    - complicating pregnancy 646.7 ☑

Atrophy, atrophic — *continued*
- liver (*see also* Necrosis, liver) — *continued*
  - yellow — *continued*
    - following
      - abortion 639.8
      - ectopic or molar pregnancy 639.8
    - from injection, inoculation or transfusion (onset within 8 months after administration) — *see* Hepatitis, viral
    - healed 571.5
    - obstetric 646.7 ☑
    - postabortal 639.8
    - postimmunization — *see* Hepatitis, viral
    - posttransfusion — *see* Hepatitis, viral
    - puerperal, postpartum 674.8 ☑
- lung (senile) 518.89
  - congenital 748.69
- macular (dermatological) 701.3
  - syphilitic, skin 091.3
    - striated 095.8
- muscle, muscular 728.2
  - disuse 728.2
  - Duchenne-Aran 335.21
  - extremity (lower) (upper) 728.2
  - familial spinal 335.11
  - general 728.2
  - idiopathic 728.2
  - infantile spinal 335.0
  - myelopathic (progressive) 335.10
  - myotonic 359.2
  - neuritic 356.1
  - neuropathic (peroneal) (progressive) 356.1
  - peroneal 356.1
  - primary (idiopathic) 728.2
  - progressive (familial) (hereditary) (pure) 335.21
    - adult (spinal) 335.19
    - infantile (spinal) 335.0
    - juvenile (spinal) 335.11
    - spinal 335.10
      - adult 335.19
      - hereditary or familial 335.11
      - infantile 335.0
  - pseudohypertrophic 359.1
  - spinal (progressive) 335.10
    - adult 335.19
    - Aran-Duchenne 335.21
    - familial 335.11
    - hereditary 335.11
    - infantile 335.0
    - juvenile 335.11
  - syphilitic 095.6
- myocardium (*see also* Degeneration, myocardial) 429.1
- myometrium (senile) 621.8
  - cervix 622.8
- myotatic 728.2
- myotonia 359.2
- nail 703.8
  - congenital 757.5
- nasopharynx 472.2
- nerve (*see also* Disorder, nerve)
  - abducens 378.54
  - accessory 352.4
  - acoustic or auditory 388.5
  - cranial 352.9
    - first (olfactory) 352.0
    - second (optic) (*see also* Atrophy, optic nerve) 377.10
    - third (oculomotor) (partial) 378.51
      - total 378.52
    - fourth (trochlear) 378.53
    - fifth (trigeminal) 350.8
    - sixth (abducens) 378.54
    - seventh (facial) 351.8
    - eighth (auditory) 388.5
    - ninth (glossopharyngeal) 352.2
    - tenth (pneumogastric) (vagus) 352.3

Atrophy, atrophic — *continued*
- nerve (*see also* Disorder, nerve) — *continued*
  - cranial — *continued*
    - eleventh (accessory) 352.4
    - twelfth (hypoglossal) 352.5
  - facial 351.8
  - glossopharyngeal 352.2
  - hypoglossal 352.5
  - oculomotor (partial) 378.51
    - total 378.52
  - olfactory 352.0
  - peripheral 355.9
  - pneumogastric 352.3
  - trigeminal 350.8
  - trochlear 378.53
  - vagus (pneumogastric) 352.3
- nervous system, congenital 742.8
- neuritic (*see also* Disorder, nerve) 355.9
- neurogenic NEC 355.9
  - bone
    - tabetic 094.0
- nutritional 261
- old age 797
- olivopontocerebellar 333.0
- optic nerve (ascending) (descending) (infectional) (nonfamilial) (papillomacular bundle) (postretinal) (secondary NEC) (simple) 377.10
  - associated with retinal dystrophy 377.13
  - dominant hereditary 377.16
  - glaucomatous 377.14
  - hereditary (dominant) (Leber's) 377.16
  - Leber's (hereditary) 377.16
  - partial 377.15
  - postinflammatory 377.12
  - primary 377.11
  - syphilitic 094.84
    - congenital 090.49
    - tabes dorsalis 094.0
- orbit 376.45
- ovary (senile), acquired 620.3
- oviduct (senile), acquired 620.3
- palsy, diffuse 335.20
- pancreas (duct) (senile) 577.8
- papillary muscle 429.81
- paralysis 355.9
- parotid gland 527.0
- patches skin 701.3
  - senile 701.8
- penis 607.89
- pharyngitis 472.1
- pharynx 478.29
- pluriglandular 258.8
- polyarthritis 714.0
- prostate 602.2
- pseudohypertrophic 359.1
- renal (*see also* Sclerosis, renal) 587
- reticulata 701.8
- retina (*see also* Degeneration, retina) 362.60
  - hereditary (*see also* Dystrophy, retina) 362.70
- rhinitis 472.0
- salivary duct or gland 527.0
- scar NEC 709.2
- sclerosis, lobar (of brain) 331.0
  - with dementia
    - with behavioral disturbance 331.0 *[294.11]*
    - without behavioral disturbance 331.0 *[294.10]*
- scrotum 608.89
- seminal vesicle 608.89
- senile 797
  - degenerative, of skin 701.3
- skin (patches) (senile) 701.8
- spermatic cord 608.89
- spinal (cord) 336.8
  - acute 336.8
  - muscular (chronic) 335.10
    - adult 335.19
    - familial 335.11

☑ Additional Digit Required — Refer to the Tabular List for Digit Selection

Subterms under main terms may continue to next column or page

▶◀ Revised Text ● New Line ▲ Revised Code

B

Bacteria — *continued*
  in urine (*see also* Bacteriuria) 599.0
Bacterial — *see* condition
Bactericholia — *see also* Cholecystitis, acute 575.0
Bacterid, bacteride (Andrews' pustular) 686.8
Bacteriuria, bacteruria 791.9
  with
    urinary tract infection 599.0
  asymptomatic 791.9
    in pregnancy or puerperium 646.5 ☑
      affecting fetus or newborn 760.1
Bad
  breath 784.99 ▲
  heart — *see* Disease, heart
  trip (*see also* Abuse, drugs, nondependent) 305.3 ☑
Baehr-Schiffrin disease (thrombotic thrombocytopenic purpura) 446.6
Baelz's disease (cheilitis glandularis apostematosa) 528.5
Baerensprung's disease (eczema marginatum) 110.3
Bagassosis (occupational) 495.1
Baghdad boil 085.1
Bagratuni's syndrome (temporal arteritis) 446.5
Baker's
  cyst (knee) 727.51
    tuberculous (*see also* Tuberculosis) 015.2 ☑
  itch 692.89
Bakwin-Krida syndrome (craniometaphyseal dysplasia) 756.89
Balanitis (circinata) (gangraenosa) (infectious) (vulgaris) 607.1
  amebic 006.8
  candidal 112.2
  chlamydial 099.53
  due to Ducrey's bacillus 099.0
  erosiva circinata et gangraenosa 607.1
  gangrenous 607.1
  gonococcal (acute) 098.0
    chronic or duration of 2 months or over 098.2
  nongonococcal 607.1
  phagedenic 607.1
  venereal NEC 099.8
  xerotica obliterans 607.81
Balanoposthitis 607.1
  chlamydial 099.53
  gonococcal (acute) 098.0
    chronic or duration of 2 months or over 098.2
  ulcerative NEC 099.8
Balanorrhagia — *see* Balanitis
Balantidiasis 007.0
Balantidiosis 007.0
Balbuties, balbutio 307.0
Bald
  patches on scalp 704.00
  tongue 529.4
Baldness — *see also* Alopecia 704.00
Balfour's disease (chloroma) 205.3 ☑
Balint's syndrome (psychic paralysis of visual fixation) 368.16
Balkan grippe 083.0
Ball
  food 938
  hair 938
Ballantyne (-Runge) syndrome (postmaturity) 766.22
Balloon disease — *see also* Effect, adverse, high altitude 993.2
Ballooning posterior leaflet syndrome 424.0
Baló's disease or concentric sclerosis 341.1
Bamberger's disease (hypertrophic pulmonary osteoarthropathy) 731.2
Bamberger-Marie disease (hypertrophic pulmonary osteoarthropathy) 731.2
Bamboo spine 720.0
Bancroft's filariasis 125.0
Band(s)
  adhesive (*see also* Adhesions, peritoneum) 568.0
  amniotic 658.8 ☑
    affecting fetus or newborn 762.8
  anomalous or congenital (*see also* Anomaly, specified type NEC)
    atrial 746.9
    heart 746.9
    intestine 751.4
    omentum 751.4
    ventricular 746.9
  cervix 622.3
  gallbladder (congenital) 751.69
  intestinal (adhesive) (*see also* Adhesions, peritoneum) 568.0
    congenital 751.4
  obstructive (*see also* Obstruction, intestine) 560.81
  periappendiceal (congenital) 751.4
  peritoneal (adhesive) (*see also* Adhesions, peritoneum) 568.0
    with intestinal obstruction 560.81
    congenital 751.4
  uterus 621.5
  vagina 623.2
Bandl's ring (contraction)
  complicating delivery 661.4 ☑
    affecting fetus or newborn 763.7
Bang's disease (Brucella abortus) 023.1
Bangkok hemorrhagic fever 065.4
Bannister's disease 995.1
Bantam-Albright-Martin disease (pseudohypoparathyroidism) 275.49
Banti's disease or syndrome (with cirrhosis) (with portal hypertension) — *see* Cirrhosis, liver
Bar
  calcaneocuboid 755.67
  calcaneonavicular 755.67
  cubonavicular 755.67
  prostate 600.90
    with
      other lower urinary tract symptoms (LUTS) 600.91 ●
      urinary ●
        obstruction 600.91 ●
        retention 600.91 ●
  talocalcaneal 755.67
Baragnosis 780.99
Barasheh, barashek 266.2
Barcoo disease or rot — *see also* Ulcer, skin 707.9
Bard-Pic syndrome (carcinoma, head of pancreas) 157.0
Bärensprung's disease (eczema marginatum) 110.3
Baritosis 503
Barium lung disease 503
Barlow (-Möller) disease or syndrome (meaning infantile scurvy) 267
Barlow's syndrome (meaning mitral valve prolapse) 424.0
Barodontalgia 993.2
Baron Münchausen syndrome 301.51
Barosinusitis 993.1
Barotitis 993.0
Barotrauma 993.2
  odontalgia 993.2
  otitic 993.0
  sinus 993.1
Barraquer's disease or syndrome (progressive lipodystrophy) 272.6
Barré-Guillain syndrome 357.0
Barrel chest 738.3
Barré-Liéou syndrome (posterior cervical sympathetic) 723.2
Barrett's esophagus 530.85
Barrett's syndrome or ulcer (chronic peptic ulcer of esophagus) 530.85
Bársony-Polgár syndrome (corkscrew esophagus) 530.5
Bársony-Teschendorf syndrome (corkscrew esophagus) 530.5
Bartholin's
  adenitis (*see also* Bartholinitis) 616.89 ▲
  gland — *see* condition
Bartholinitis (suppurating) 616.89 ▲
  gonococcal (acute) 098.0
    chronic or duration of 2 months or over 098.2
Barth syndrome 759.89
Bartonellosis 088.0
Bartter's syndrome (secondary hyperaldosteronism with juxtaglomerular hyperplasia) 255.13
Basal — *see* condition
Basan's (hidrotic) **ectodermal dysplasia** 757.31
Baseball finger 842.13
Basedow's disease or syndrome (exophthalmic goiter) 242.0 ☑
Basic — *see* condition
Basilar — *see* condition
Bason's (hidrotic) **ectodermal dysplasia** 757.31
Basopenia 288.59 ▲
Basophilia 288.65 ▲
Basophilism (corticoadrenal) (Cushing's) (pituitary) (thymic) 255.0
Bassen-Kornzweig syndrome (abetalipoproteinemia) 272.5
Bat ear 744.29
Bateman's
  disease 078.0
  purpura (senile) 287.2
Bathing cramp 994.1
Bathophobia 300.23
Batten's disease, retina 330.1 *[362.71]*
Batten-Mayou disease 330.1 *[362.71]*
Batten-Steinert syndrome 359.2
Battered
  adult (syndrome) 995.81
  baby or child (syndrome) 995.54
  spouse (syndrome) 995.81
Battey mycobacterium infection 031.0
Battledore placenta — *see* Placenta, abnormal
Battle exhaustion — *see also* Reaction, stress, acute 308.9
Baumgarten-Cruveilhier (cirrhosis) **disease, or syndrome** 571.5
Bauxite
  fibrosis (of lung) 503
  workers' disease 503
Bayle's disease (dementia paralytica) 094.1
Bazin's disease (primary) — *see also* Tuberculosis 017.1 ☑
Beach ear 380.12
Beaded hair (congenital) 757.4
Beals syndrome 759.82
Beard's disease (neurasthenia) 300.5
Bearn-Kunkel (-Slater) syndrome (lupoid hepatitis) 571.49
Beat
  elbow 727.2
  hand 727.2
  knee 727.2
Beats
  ectopic 427.60
  escaped, heart 427.60
    postoperative 997.1
  premature (nodal) 427.60
    atrial 427.61
    auricular 427.61
    postoperative 997.1
    specified type NEC 427.69
    supraventricular 427.61
    ventricular 427.69
Beau's
  disease or syndrome (*see also* Degeneration, myocardial) 429.1
  lines (transverse furrows on fingernails) 703.8
Bechterew's disease (ankylosing spondylitis) 720.0
Bechterew-Strümpell-Marie syndrome (ankylosing spondylitis) 720.0
Becker's
  disease (idiopathic mural endomyocardial disease) 425.2
  dystrophy 359.1
Beck's syndrome (anterior spinal artery occlusion) 433.8 ☑
Beckwith (-Wiedemann) syndrome 759.89
Bedclothes, asphyxiation or suffocation by 994.7
Bed confinement status V49.84
Bednar's aphthae 528.2
Bedsore 707.00
  with gangrene 707.00 *[785.4]*
Bedwetting — *see also* Enuresis 788.36
Beer-drinkers' heart (disease) 425.5
Bee sting (with allergic or anaphylactic shock) 989.5
Begbie's disease (exophthalmic goiter) 242.0 ☑
Behavior disorder, disturbance — *see also* Disturbance, conduct
  antisocial, without manifest psychiatric disorder
    adolescent V71.02
    adult V71.01
    child V71.02
  dyssocial, without manifest psychiatric disorder
    adolescent V71.02
    adult V71.01
    child V71.02
  high risk — *see* Problem
Behçet's syndrome 136.1
Behr's disease 362.50
Beigel's disease or morbus (white piedra) 111.2
Bejel 104.0
Bekhterev's disease (ankylosing spondylitis) 720.0
Bekhterev-Strümpell-Marie syndrome (ankylosing spondylitis) 720.0
Belching — *see also* Eructation 787.3
Bell's
  disease (*see also* Psychosis, affective) 296.0 ☑
  mania (*see also* Psychosis, affective) 296.0 ☑
  palsy, paralysis 351.0
    infant 767.5
    newborn 767.5
    syphilitic 094.89
  spasm 351.0
Bence-Jones albuminuria, albuminosuria, or proteinuria 791.0
Bends 993.3
Benedikt's syndrome (paralysis) 344.89
Benign — *see also* condition
  cellular changes, cervix 795.09
  prostate
    with
      other lower urinary tract symptoms (LUTS) 600.21 ●
      urinary ●
        obstruction 600.21 ●
        retention 600.21 ●
    hyperplasia 600.20
    neoplasm 222.2
Bennett's
  disease (leukemia) 208.9 ☑
  fracture (closed) 815.01
    open 815.11
Benson's disease 379.22
Bent
  back (hysterical) 300.11
  nose 738.0
    congenital 754.0
Bereavement V62.82
  as adjustment reaction 309.0
Bergeron's disease (hysteroepilepsy) 300.11
Berger's paresthesia (lower limb) 782.0
Beriberi (acute) (atrophic) (chronic) (dry) (subacute) (wet) 265.0
  with polyneuropathy 265.0 *[357.4]*

☑ Additional Digit Required — Refer to the Tabular List for Digit Selection

Subterms under main terms may continue to next column or page

▶◀ Revised Text ● New Line ▲ Revised Code

Beriberi — *continued*
- heart (disease) 265.0 *[425.7]*
- leprosy 030.1
- neuritis 265.0 *[357.4]*

Berlin's disease or edema (traumatic) 921.3
Berloque dermatitis 692.72
Bernard-Horner syndrome — *see also* Neuropathy, peripheral, autonomic 337.9
Bernard-Sergent syndrome (acute adrenocortical insufficiency) 255.4
Bernard-Soulier disease or thrombopathy 287.1
Bernhardt's disease or paresthesia 355.1
Bernhardt-Roth disease or syndrome (paresthesia) 355.1
Bernheim's syndrome — *see also* Failure, heart 428.0
Bertielliasis 123.8
Bertolotti's syndrome (sacralization of fifth lumbar vertebra) 756.15
Berylliosis (acute) (chronic) (lung) (occupational) 503
Besnier's
- lupus pernio 135
- prurigo (atopic dermatitis) (infantile eczema) 691.8

Besnier-Boeck disease or sarcoid 135
Besnier-Boeck-Schaumann disease (sarcoidosis) 135
Best's disease 362.76
Bestiality 302.1
Beta-adrenergic hyperdynamic circulatory state 429.82
Beta-aminoisobutyric aciduria 277.2
Beta-mercaptolactate-cysteine disulfiduria 270.0
Beta thalassemia (major) (minor) (mixed) 282.49
Beurmann's disease (sporotrichosis) 117.1
Bezoar 938
- intestine 936
- stomach 935.2

Bezold's abscess — *see also* Mastoiditis 383.01
Bianchi's syndrome (aphasia-apraxia-alexia) 784.69
Bicornuate or bicornis uterus 752.3
- in pregnancy or childbirth 654.0 ☑
  - with obstructed labor 660.2 ☑
    - affecting fetus or newborn 763.1
  - affecting fetus or newborn 763.89

Bicuspid aortic valve 746.4
Biedl-Bardet syndrome 759.89
Bielschowsky's disease 330.1
Bielschowsky-Jansky
- amaurotic familial idiocy 330.1
- disease 330.1

Biemond's syndrome (obesity, polydactyly, and mental retardation) 759.89
Biermer's anemia or disease (pernicious anemia) 281.0
Biett's disease 695.4
Bifid (congenital) — *see also* Imperfect, closure
- apex, heart 746.89
- clitoris 752.49
- epiglottis 748.3
- kidney 753.3
- nose 748.1
- patella 755.64
- scrotum 752.89
- toe 755.66
- tongue 750.13
- ureter 753.4
- uterus 752.3
- uvula 749.02
  - with cleft lip (*see also* Cleft, palate, with cleft lip) 749.20

Biforis uterus (suprasimplex) 752.3
Bifurcation (congenital) — *see also* Imperfect, closure
- gallbladder 751.69

Bifurcation — *see also* Imperfect, closure — *continued*
- kidney pelvis 753.3
- renal pelvis 753.3
- rib 756.3
- tongue 750.13
- trachea 748.3
- ureter 753.4
- urethra 753.8
- uvula 749.02
  - with cleft lip (*see also* Cleft, palate, with cleft lip) 749.20
- vertebra 756.19

Bigeminal pulse 427.89
Bigeminy 427.89
Big spleen syndrome 289.4
Bilateral — *see* condition
Bile duct — *see* condition
Bile pigments in urine 791.4
Bilharziasis — *see also* Schistosomiasis 120.9
- chyluria 120.0
- cutaneous 120.3
- galacturia 120.0
- hematochyluria 120.0
- intestinal 120.1
- lipemia 120.9
- lipuria 120.0
- Oriental 120.2
- piarhemia 120.9
- pulmonary 120.2
- tropical hematuria 120.0
- vesical 120.0

Biliary — *see* condition
Bilious (attack) — *see also* Vomiting
- fever, hemoglobinuric 084.8

Bilirubinuria 791.4
Biliuria 791.4
Billroth's disease
- meningocele (*see also* Spina bifida) 741.9 ☑

Bilobate placenta — *see* Placenta, abnormal
Bilocular
- heart 745.7
- stomach 536.8

Bing-Horton syndrome (histamine cephalgia) 346.2 ☑
Binswanger's disease or dementia 290.12
Biörck (-Thorson) syndrome (malignant carcinoid) 259.2
Biparta, bipartite — *see also* Imperfect, closure
- carpal scaphoid 755.59
- patella 755.64
- placenta — *see* Placenta, abnormal
- vagina 752.49

Bird
- face 756.0
- fanciers' lung or disease 495.2

Bird's disease (oxaluria) 271.8
Birth
- abnormal fetus or newborn 763.9
- accident, fetus or newborn — *see* Birth, injury
- complications in mother — *see* Delivery, complicated
- compression during NEC 767.9
- defect — *see* Anomaly
- delayed, fetus 763.9
- difficult NEC, affecting fetus or newborn 763.9
- dry, affecting fetus or newborn 761.1
- forced, NEC, affecting fetus or newborn 763.89
- forceps, affecting fetus or newborn 763.2
- hematoma of sternomastoid 767.8
- immature 765.1 ☑
  - extremely 765.0 ☑
- inattention, after or at 995.52
- induced, affecting fetus or newborn 763.89
- infant — *see* Newborn
- injury NEC 767.9

Birth — *continued*
- injury — *continued*
  - adrenal gland 767.8
  - basal ganglia 767.0
  - brachial plexus (paralysis) 767.6
  - brain (compression) (pressure) 767.0
  - cerebellum 767.0
  - cerebral hemorrhage 767.0
  - conjunctiva 767.8
  - eye 767.8
  - fracture
    - bone, any except clavicle or spine 767.3
    - clavicle 767.2
    - femur 767.3
    - humerus 767.3
    - long bone 767.3
    - radius and ulna 767.3
    - skeleton NEC 767.3
    - skull 767.3
    - spine 767.4
    - tibia and fibula 767.3
  - hematoma 767.8
    - liver (subcapsular) 767.8
    - mastoid 767.8
    - skull 767.19
    - sternomastoid 767.8
    - testes 767.8
    - vulva 767.8
  - intracranial (edema) 767.0
  - laceration
    - brain 767.0
    - by scalpel 767.8
    - peripheral nerve 767.7
  - liver 767.8
  - meninges
    - brain 767.0
    - spinal cord 767.4
  - nerves (cranial, peripheral) 767.7
    - brachial plexus 767.6
    - facial 767.5
  - paralysis 767.7
    - brachial plexus 767.6
    - Erb (-Duchenne) 767.6
    - facial nerve 767.5
    - Klumpke (-Déjérine) 767.6
    - radial nerve 767.6
    - spinal (cord) (hemorrhage) (laceration) (rupture) 767.4
  - rupture
    - intracranial 767.0
    - liver 767.8
    - spinal cord 767.4
    - spleen 767.8
    - viscera 767.8
  - scalp 767.19
  - scalpel wound 767.8
  - skeleton NEC 767.3
  - specified NEC 767.8
  - spinal cord 767.4
  - spleen 767.8
  - subdural hemorrhage 767.0
  - tentorial, tear 767.0
  - testes 767.8
  - vulva 767.8
- instrumental, NEC, affecting fetus or newborn 763.2
- lack of care, after or at 995.52
- multiple
  - affected by maternal complications of pregnancy 761.5
  - healthy liveborn — *see* Newborn, multiple
- neglect, after or at 995.52
- newborn — *see* Newborn
- palsy or paralysis NEC 767.7
- precipitate, fetus or newborn 763.6
- premature (infant) 765.1 ☑
- prolonged, affecting fetus or newborn 763.9
- retarded, fetus or newborn 763.9
- shock, newborn 779.89
- strangulation or suffocation
  - due to aspiration of clear amniotic fluid 770.13

Birth — *continued*
- strangulation or suffocation — *continued*
  - due to aspiration of clear amniotic fluid — *continued*
    - with respiratory symptoms 770.14
  - mechanical 767.8
- trauma NEC 767.9
- triplet
  - affected by maternal complications of pregnancy 761.5
  - healthy liveborn — *see* Newborn, multiple
- twin
  - affected by maternal complications of pregnancy 761.5
  - healthy liveborn — *see* Newborn, twin
- ventouse, affecting fetus or newborn 763.3

Birthmark 757.32
Bisalbuminemia 273.8
Biskra button 085.1
Bite(s)
- with intact skin surface — *see* Contusion
- animal — *see* Wound, open, by site
  - intact skin surface — *see* Contusion
- centipede 989.5
- chigger 133.8
- fire ant 989.5
- flea — *see* Injury, superficial, by site
- human (open wound) (*see also* Wound, open, by site)
  - intact skin surface — *see* Contusion
- insect
  - nonvenomous — *see* Injury, superficial, by site
  - venomous 989.5
- mad dog (death from) 071
- open ●
  - anterior 524.24 ●
  - posterior 524.25 ●
- poisonous 989.5
- red bug 133.8
- reptile 989.5
  - nonvenomous — *see* Wound, open, by site
- snake 989.5
  - nonvenomous — *see* Wound, open, by site
- spider (venomous) 989.5
  - nonvenomous — *see* Injury, superficial, by site
- venomous 989.5

Biting
- cheek or lip 528.9
- nail 307.9

Black
- death 020.9
- eye NEC 921.0
- hairy tongue 529.3
- heel 924.20 ●
- lung disease 500
- palm 923.20 ●

Blackfan-Diamond anemia or syndrome (congenital hypoplastic anemia) 284.01 ▲
Blackhead 706.1
Blackout 780.2
Blackwater fever 084.8
Bladder — *see* condition
Blast
- blindness 921.3
- concussion — *see* Blast, injury
- injury 869.0
  - with open wound into cavity 869.1
  - abdomen or thorax — *see* Injury, internal, by site
  - brain (*see also* Concussion, brain) 850.9
    - with skull fracture — *see* Fracture, skull

☑ Additional Digit Required — Refer to the Tabular List for Digit Selection
▽ Subterms under main terms may continue to next column or page
▶◀ Revised Text ● New Line ▲ Revised Code

Burn (acid) (cathode ray) (caustic) (chemical) (electric heating appliance) (electricity) (fire) (flame) (hot liquid or object) (irradiation) (lime) (radiation) (steam) (thermal) (x-ray) 949.0

> *Note — Use the following fifth-digit subclassification with category 948 to indicate the percent of body surface with third degree burn:*
>
> *0 Less than 10% or unspecified*
> *1 10–19%*
> *2 20–29%*
> *3 30–39%*
> *4 40–49%*
> *5 50–59%*
> *6 60–69%*
> *7 70–79%*
> *8 80–89%*
> *9 90% or more of body surface*

- with
  - blisters — *see* Burn, by site, second degree
  - erythema — *see* Burn, by site, first degree
  - skin loss (epidermal) (*see also* Burn, by site, second degree)
    - full thickness (*see also* Burn, by site, third degree)
      - with necrosis of underlying tissues — *see* Burn, by site, third degree, deep
- first degree — *see* Burn, by site, first degree
- second degree — *see* Burn, by site, second degree
- third degree — *see* Burn, by site, third degree
  - deep — *see* Burn, by site, third degree, deep
- abdomen, abdominal (muscle) (wall) 942.03
  - with
    - trunk — *see* Burn, trunk, multiple sites
  - first degree 942.13
  - second degree 942.23
  - third degree 942.33
    - deep 942.43
      - with loss of body part 942.53
- ankle 945.03
  - with
    - lower limb(s) — *see* Burn, leg, multiple sites
  - first degree 945.13
  - second degree 945.23
  - third degree 945.33
    - deep 945.43
      - with loss of body part 945.53
- anus — *see* Burn, trunk, specified site NEC
- arm(s) 943.00
  - first degree 943.10
  - second degree 943.20
  - third degree 943.30
    - deep 943.40
      - with loss of body part 943.50
  - lower — *see* Burn, forearm(s)
  - multiple sites, except hand(s) or wrist(s) 943.09
    - first degree 943.19
    - second degree 943.29
    - third degree 943.39
      - deep 943.49
        - with loss of body part 943.59
  - upper 943.03
    - first degree 943.13
    - second degree 943.23
    - third degree 943.33
      - deep 943.43

Burn — *continued*

- arm(s) — *continued*
  - upper — *continued*
    - third degree — *continued*
      - deep — *continued*
        - with loss of body part 943.53
- auditory canal (external) — *see* Burn, ear
- auricle (ear) — *see* Burn, ear
- axilla 943.04
  - with
    - upper limb(s), except hand(s) or wrist(s) — *see* Burn, arm(s), multiple sites
  - first degree 943.14
  - second degree 943.24
  - third degree 943.34
    - deep 943.44
      - with loss of body part 943.54
- back 942.04
  - with
    - trunk — *see* Burn, trunk, multiple sites
  - first degree 942.14
  - second degree 942.24
  - third degree 942.34
    - deep 942.44
      - with loss of body part 942.54
- biceps
  - brachii — *see* Burn, arm(s), upper
  - femoris — *see* Burn, thigh
- breast(s) 942.01
  - with
    - trunk — *see* Burn, trunk, multiple sites
  - first degree 942.11
  - second degree 942.21
  - third degree 942.31
    - deep 942.41
      - with loss of body part 942.51
- brow — *see* Burn, forehead
- buttock(s) — *see* Burn, back
- canthus (eye) 940.1
  - chemical 940.0
- cervix (uteri) 947.4
- cheek (cutaneous) 941.07
  - with
    - face or head — *see* Burn, head, multiple sites
  - first degree 941.17
  - second degree 941.27
  - third degree 941.37
    - deep 941.47
      - with loss of body part 941.57
- chest wall (anterior) 942.02
  - with
    - trunk — *see* Burn, trunk, multiple sites
  - first degree 942.12
  - second degree 942.22
  - third degree 942.32
    - deep 942.42
      - with loss of body part 942.52
- chin 941.04
  - with
    - face or head — *see* Burn, head, multiple sites
  - first degree 941.14
  - second degree 941.24
  - third degree 941.34
    - deep 941.44
      - with loss of body part 941.54
- clitoris — *see* Burn, genitourinary organs, external
- colon 947.3
- conjunctiva (and cornea) 940.4
  - chemical
    - acid 940.3
    - alkaline 940.2
- cornea (and conjunctiva) 940.4
  - chemical
    - acid 940.3
    - alkaline 940.2
- costal region — *see* Burn, chest wall

Burn — *continued*

- due to ingested chemical agent — *see* Burn, internal organs
- ear (auricle) (canal) (drum) (external) 941.01
  - with
    - face or head — *see* Burn, head, multiple sites
  - first degree 941.11
  - second degree 941.21
  - third degree 941.31
    - deep 941.41
      - with loss of a body part 941.51
- elbow 943.02
  - with
    - hand(s) and wrist(s) — *see* Burn, multiple specified sites
    - upper limb(s), except hand(s) or wrist(s) (*see also* Burn, arm(s), multiple sites)
  - first degree 943.12
  - second degree 943.22
  - third degree 943.32
    - deep 943.42
      - with loss of body part 943.52
- electricity, electric current — *see* Burn, by site
- entire body — *see* Burn, multiple, specified sites
- epididymis — *see* Burn, genitourinary organs, external
- epigastric region — *see* Burn, abdomen
- epiglottis 947.1
- esophagus 947.2
- extent (percent of body surface)
  - less than 10 percent 948.0 ☑
  - 10-19 percent 948.1 ☑
  - 20-29 percent 948.2 ☑
  - 30-39 percent 948.3 ☑
  - 40-49 percent 948.4 ☑
  - 50-59 percent 948.5 ☑
  - 60-69 percent 948.6 ☑
  - 70-79 percent 948.7 ☑
  - 80-89 percent 948.8 ☑
  - 90 percent or more 948.9 ☑
- extremity
  - lower — *see* Burn, leg
  - upper — *see* Burn, arm(s)
- eye(s) (and adnexa) (only) 940.9
  - with
    - face, head, or neck 941.02
      - first degree 941.12
      - second degree 941.22
      - third degree 941.32
        - deep 941.42
          - with loss of body part 941.52
    - other sites (classifiable to more than one category in 940–945) — *see* Burn, multiple, specified sites
    - resulting rupture and destruction of eyeball 940.5
  - specified part — *see* Burn, by site
- eyeball (*see also* Burn, eye)
  - with resulting rupture and destruction of eyeball 940.5
- eyelid(s) 940.1
  - chemical 940.0
- face — *see* Burn, head
- finger (nail) (subungual) 944.01
  - with
    - hand(s) — *see* Burn, hand(s), multiple sites
    - other sites — *see* Burn, multiple, specified sites
    - thumb 944.04
      - first degree 944.14
      - second degree 944.24
      - third degree 944.34
        - deep 944.44
          - with loss of body part 944.54

Burn — *continued*

- finger — *continued*
  - first degree 944.11
  - second degree 944.21
  - third degree 944.31
    - deep 944.41
      - with loss of body part 944.51
  - multiple (digits) 944.03
    - with thumb — *see* Burn, finger, with thumb
    - first degree 944.13
    - second degree 944.23
    - third degree 944.33
      - deep 944.43
        - with loss of body part 944.53
- flank — *see* Burn, abdomen
- foot 945.02
  - with
    - lower limb(s) — *see* Burn, leg, multiple sites
  - first degree 945.12
  - second degree 945.22
  - third degree 945.32
    - deep 945.42
      - with loss of body part 945.52
- forearm(s) 943.01
  - with
    - upper limb(s), except hand(s) or wrist(s) — *see* Burn, arm(s), multiple sites
  - first degree 943.11
  - second degree 943.21
  - third degree 943.31
    - deep 943.41
      - with loss of body part 943.51
- forehead 941.07
  - with
    - face or head — *see* Burn, head, multiple sites
  - first degree 941.17
  - second degree 941.27
  - third degree 941.37
    - deep 941.47
      - with loss of body part 941.57
- fourth degree — *see* Burn, by site, third degree, deep
- friction — *see* Injury, superficial, by site
- from swallowing caustic or corrosive substance NEC — *see* Burn, internal organs
- full thickness — *see* Burn, by site, third degree
- gastrointestinal tract 947.3
- genitourinary organs
  - external 942.05
    - with
      - trunk — *see* Burn, trunk, multiple sites
    - first degree 942.15
    - second degree 942.25
    - third degree 942.35
      - deep 942.45
        - with loss of body part 942.55
  - internal 947.8
- globe (eye) — *see* Burn, eyeball
- groin — *see* Burn, abdomen
- gum 947.0
- hand(s) (phalanges) (and wrist) 944.00
  - first degree 944.10
  - second degree 944.20
  - third degree 944.30
    - deep 944.40
      - with loss of body part 944.50
  - back (dorsal surface) 944.06
    - first degree 944.16
    - second degree 944.26
    - third degree 944.36
      - deep 944.46
        - with loss of body part 944.56
  - multiple sites 944.08
    - first degree 944.18
    - second degree 944.28

☑ Additional Digit Required — Refer to the Tabular List for Digit Selection

Subterms under main terms may continue to next column or page

▶◀ Revised Text ● New Line ▲ Revised Code

Note — The term "cancer" when modified by an adjective or adjectival phrase indicating a morphological type should be coded in the same manner as "carcinoma" with that adjective or phrase. Thus, "squamous-cell cancer" should be coded in the same manner as "squamous-cell carcinoma," which appears in the list under "Carcinoma."

Note — Except where otherwise indicated, the morphological varieties of carcinoma in the list below should be coded by site as for "Neoplasm, malignant."

- **Carcinoma** — *see also* Neoplasm, by site, malignant — *continued*
  - fibroepithelial type basal cell (M8093/3) — *see* Neoplasm, skin, malignant
  - follicular (M8330/3)
    - and papillary (mixed) (M8340/3) 193
    - moderately differentiated type (M8332/3) 193
    - pure follicle type (M8331/3) 193
    - specified site — *see* Neoplasm, by site, malignant
    - trabecular type (M8332/3) 193
    - unspecified site 193
    - well differentiated type (M8331/3) 193
  - gelatinous (M8480/3)
  - giant cell (M8031/3)
    - and spindle cell (M8030/3)
  - granular cell (M8320/3)
  - granulosa cell (M8620/3) 183.0
  - hepatic cell (M8170/3) 155.0
  - hepatocellular (M8170/3) 155.0
    - and bile duct, mixed (M8180/3) 155.0
  - hepatocholangiolitic (M8180/3) 155.0
  - Hürthle cell (thyroid) 193
  - hypernephroid (M8311/3)
  - in
    - adenomatous
      - polyp (M8210/3)
      - polyposis coli (M8220/3) 153.9
    - pleomorphic adenoma (M8940/3)
    - polypoid adenoma (M8210/3)
    - situ (M8010/3) — *see* Carcinoma, in situ
    - tubular adenoma (M8210/3)
    - villous adenoma (M8261/3)
  - infiltrating duct (M8500/3)
    - with Paget's disease (M8541/3) — *see* Neoplasm, breast, malignant
    - specified site — *see* Neoplasm, by site, malignant
    - unspecified site 174.9
  - inflammatory (M8530/3)
    - specified site — *see* Neoplasm, by site, malignant
    - unspecified site 174.9
  - in situ (M8010/2) (*see also* Neoplasm, by site, in situ)
    - epidermoid (M8070/2) (*see also* Neoplasm, by site, in situ)
      - with questionable stromal invasion (M8076/2)
        - specified site — *see* Neoplasm, by site, in situ
        - unspecified site 233.1
      - Bowen's type (M8081/2) — *see* Neoplasm, skin, in situ
    - intraductal (M8500/2)
      - specified site — *see* Neoplasm, by site, in situ
      - unspecified site 233.0
    - lobular (M8520/2)
      - specified site — *see* Neoplasm, by site, in situ
      - unspecified site 233.0
    - papillary (M8050/2) — *see* Neoplasm, by site, in situ
    - squamous cell (M8070/2) (*see also* Neoplasm, by site, in situ)
      - with questionable stromal invasion (M8076/2)
        - specified site — *see* Neoplasm, by site, in situ
        - unspecified site 233.1
    - transitional cell (M8120/2) — *see* Neoplasm, by site, in situ
  - intestinal type (M8144/3)
    - specified site — *see* Neoplasm, by site, malignant
    - unspecified site 151.9

- **Carcinoma** — *see also* Neoplasm, by site, malignant — *continued*
  - intraductal (noninfiltrating) (M8500/2)
    - papillary (M8503/2)
      - specified site — *see* Neoplasm, by site, in situ
      - unspecified site 233.0
    - specified site — *see* Neoplasm, by site, in situ
    - unspecified site 233.0
  - intraepidermal (M8070/2) (*see also* Neoplasm, skin, in situ)
    - squamous cell, Bowen's type (M8081/2) — *see* Neoplasm, skin, in situ
  - intraepithelial (M8010/2) (*see also* Neoplasm, by site, in situ)
    - squamous cell (M8072/2) — *see* Neoplasm, by site, in situ
  - intraosseous (M9270/3) 170.1
    - upper jaw (bone) 170.0
  - islet cell (M8150/3)
    - and exocrine, mixed (M8154/3)
      - specified site — *see* Neoplasm, by site, malignant
      - unspecified site 157.9
    - pancreas 157.4
    - specified site NEC — *see* Neoplasm, by site, malignant
    - unspecified site 157.4
  - juvenile, breast (M8502/3) — *see* Neoplasm, breast, malignant
  - Kulchitsky's cell (carcinoid tumor of intestine) 259.2
  - large cell (M8012/3)
    - squamous cell, non-keratinizing type (M8072/3)
  - Leydig cell (testis) (M8650/3)
    - specified site — *see* Neoplasm, by site, malignant
    - unspecified site 186.9
      - female 183.0
      - male 186.9
  - liver cell (M8170/3) 155.0
  - lobular (infiltrating) (M8520/3)
    - non-infiltrating (M8520/3)
      - specified site — *see* Neoplasm, by site, in situ
      - unspecified site 233.0
    - specified site — *see* Neoplasm, by site, malignant
    - unspecified site 174.9
  - lymphoepithelial (M8082/3)
  - medullary (M8510/3)
    - with
      - amyloid stroma (M8511/3)
        - specified site — *see* Neoplasm, by site, malignant
        - unspecified site 193
      - lymphoid stroma (M8512/3)
        - specified site — *see* Neoplasm, by site, malignant
        - unspecified site 174.9
  - mesometanephric (M9110/3)
  - mesonephric (M9110/3)
  - metastatic (M8010/6) — *see* Metastasis, cancer
  - metatypical (M8095/3) — *see* Neoplasm, skin, malignant
  - morphea type basal cell (M8092/3) — *see* Neoplasm, skin, malignant
  - mucinous (M8480/3)
  - mucin-producing (M8481/3)
  - mucin-secreting (M8481/3)
  - mucoepidermoid (M8430/3)
  - mucoid (M8480/3)
    - cell (M8300/3)
      - specified site — *see* Neoplasm, by site, malignant
      - unspecified site 194.3
  - mucous (M8480/3)
  - nonencapsulated sclerosing (M8350/3) 193

- **Carcinoma** — *see also* Neoplasm, by site, malignant — *continued*
  - noninfiltrating
    - intracystic (M8504/2) — *see* Neoplasm, by site, in situ
    - intraductal (M8500/2)
      - papillary (M8503/2)
        - specified site — *see* Neoplasm, by site, in situ
        - unspecified site 233.0
      - specified site — *see* Neoplasm, by site, in situ
      - unspecified site 233.0
    - lobular (M8520/2)
      - specified site — *see* Neoplasm, by site, in situ
      - unspecified site 233.0
  - oat cell (M8042/3)
    - specified site — *see* Neoplasm, by site, malignant
    - unspecified site 162.9
  - odontogenic (M9270/3) 170.1
    - upper jaw (bone) 170.0
  - onocytic (M8290/3)
  - oxyphilic (M8290/3)
  - papillary (M8050/3)
    - and follicular (mixed) (M8340/3) 193
    - epidermoid (M8052/3)
    - intraductal (noninfiltrating) (M8503/2)
      - specified site — *see* Neoplasm, by site, in situ
      - unspecified site 233.0
    - serous (M8460/3)
      - specified site — *see* Neoplasm, by site, malignant
      - surface (M8461/3)
        - specified site — *see* Neoplasm, by site, malignant
        - unspecified site 183.0
      - unspecified site 183.0
    - squamous cell (M8052/3)
    - transitional cell (M8130/3)
  - papillocystic (M8450/3)
    - specified site — *see* Neoplasm, by site, malignant
    - unspecified site 183.0
  - parafollicular cell (M8510/3)
    - specified site — *see* Neoplasm, by site, malignant
    - unspecified site 193
  - pleomorphic (M8022/3)
  - polygonal cell (M8034/3)
  - prickle cell (M8070/3)
  - pseudoglandular, squamous cell (M8075/3)
  - pseudomucinous (M8470/3)
    - specified site — *see* Neoplasm, by site, malignant
    - unspecified site 183.0
  - pseudosarcomatous (M8033/3)
  - regaud type (M8082/3) — *see* Neoplasm, nasopharynx, malignant
  - renal cell (M8312/3) 189.0
  - reserve cell (M8041/3)
  - round cell (M8041/3)
  - Schmincke (M8082/3) — *see* Neoplasm, nasopharynx, malignant
  - Schneiderian (M8121/3)
    - specified site — *see* Neoplasm, by site, malignant
    - unspecified site 160.0
  - scirrhous (M8141/3)
  - sebaceous (M8410/3) — *see* Neoplasm, skin, malignant
  - secondary (M8010/6) — *see* Neoplasm, by site, malignant, secondary
  - secretory, breast (M8502/3) — *see* Neoplasm, breast, malignant
  - serous (M8441/3)
    - papillary (M8460/3)
      - specified site — *see* Neoplasm, by site, malignant

- **Carcinoma** — *see also* Neoplasm, by site, malignant — *continued*
  - serous — *continued*
    - papillary — *continued*
      - unspecified site 183.0
    - surface, papillary (M8461/3)
      - specified site — *see* Neoplasm, by site, malignant
      - unspecified site 183.0
  - Sertoli cell (M8640/3)
    - specified site — *see* Neoplasm, by site, malignant
    - unspecified site 186.9
  - signet ring cell (M8490/3)
    - metastatic (M8490/6) — *see* Neoplasm, by site, secondary
  - simplex (M8231/3)
  - skin appendage (M8390/3) — *see* Neoplasm, skin, malignant
  - small cell (M8041/3)
    - fusiform cell type (M8043/3)
    - squamous cell, non-keratinizing type (M8073/3)
  - solid (M8230/3)
    - with amyloid stroma (M8511/3)
      - specified site — *see* Neoplasm, by site, malignant
      - unspecified site 193
  - spheroidal cell (M8035/3)
  - spindle cell (M8032/3)
    - and giant cell (M8030/3)
  - spinous cell (M8070/3)
  - squamous (cell) (M8070/3)
    - adenoid type (M8075/3)
    - and adenocarcinoma, mixed (M8560/3)
    - intraepidermal, Bowen's type — *see* Neoplasm, skin, in situ
    - keratinizing type (large cell) (M8071/3)
    - large cell, non-keratinizing type (M8072/3)
    - microinvasive (M8076/3)
      - specified site — *see* Neoplasm, by site, malignant
      - unspecified site 180.9
    - non-keratinizing type (M8072/3)
    - papillary (M8052/3)
    - pseudoglandular (M8075/3)
    - small cell, non-keratinizing type (M8073/3)
    - spindle cell type (M8074/3)
    - verrucous (M8051/3)
  - superficial spreading (M8143/3)
  - sweat gland (M8400/3) — *see* Neoplasm, skin, malignant
  - theca cell (M8600/3) 183.0
  - thymic (M8580/3) 164.0
  - trabecular (M8190/3)
  - transitional (cell) (M8120/3)
    - papillary (M8130/3)
    - spindle cell type (M8122/3)
  - tubular (M8211/3)
  - undifferentiated type (M8020/3)
  - urothelial (M8120/3)
  - ventriculi 151.9
  - verrucous (epidermoid) (squamous cell) (M8051/3)
  - villous (M8262/3)
  - water-clear cell (M8322/3) 194.1
  - wolffian duct (M9110/3)
- **Carcinosarcoma** (M8980/3) — *see also* Neoplasm, by site, malignant
  - embryonal type (M8981/3) — *see* Neoplasm, by site, malignant
- **Cardiac** — *see also* condition
  - death — *see* Disease, heart
  - device
    - defibrillator, automatic implantable V45.02
    - in situ NEC V45.00
    - pacemaker
      - cardiac
        - fitting or adjustment V53.31
        - in situ V45.01

- **Cardiac** — *see also* condition — *continued*
  - device — *continued*
    - pacemaker — *continued*
      - carotid sinus
        - fitting or adjustment V53.39
        - in situ V45.09
  - pacemaker — *see* Cardiac, device, pacemaker
  - tamponade 423.9
- **Cardia, cardial** — *see* condition
- **Cardialgia** — *see also* Pain, precordial 786.51
- **Cardiectasis** — *see* Hypertrophy, cardiac
- **Cardiochalasia** 530.81
- **Cardiomalacia** — *see also* Degeneration, myocardial 429.1
- **Cardiomegalia glycogenica diffusa** 271.0
- **Cardiomegaly** — *see also* Hypertrophy, cardiac 429.3
  - congenital 746.89
  - glycogen 271.0
  - hypertensive (*see also* Hypertension, heart) 402.90
  - idiopathic 429.3
- **Cardiomyoliposis** — *see also* Degeneration, myocardial 429.1
- **Cardiomyopathy** (congestive) (constrictive) (familial) (infiltrative) (obstructive) (restrictive) (sporadic) 425.4
  - alcoholic 425.5
  - amyloid 277.39 *[425.7]* ▲
  - beriberi 265.0 *[425.7]*
  - cobalt-beer 425.5
  - congenital 425.3
  - due to
    - amyloidosis 277.39 *[425.7]* ▲
    - beriberi 265.0 *[425.7]*
    - cardiac glycogenosis 271.0 *[425.7]*
    - Chagas' disease 086.0
    - Friedreich's ataxia 334.0 *[425.8]*
    - hypertension — *see* Hypertension, with, heart involvement
    - mucopolysaccharidosis 277.5 *[425.7]*
    - myotonia atrophica 359.2 *[425.8]*
    - progressive muscular dystrophy 359.1 *[425.8]*
    - sarcoidosis 135 *[425.8]*
  - glycogen storage 271.0 *[425.7]*
  - hypertensive — *see* Hypertension, with, heart involvement
  - hypertrophic
    - nonobstructive 425.4
    - obstructive 425.1
      - congenital 746.84
  - idiopathic (concentric) 425.4
  - in
    - Chagas' disease 086.0
    - sarcoidosis 135 *[425.8]*
  - ischemic 414.8
  - metabolic NEC 277.9 *[425.7]*
    - amyloid 277.39 *[425.7]* ▲
    - thyrotoxic (*see also* Thyrotoxicosis) 242.9 ☑ *[425.7]*
    - thyrotoxicosis (*see also* Thyrotoxicosis) 242.9 ☑ *[425.7]*
  - newborn 425.4
    - congenital 425.3
  - nutritional 269.9 *[425.7]*
    - beriberi 265.0 *[425.7]*
  - obscure of Africa 425.2
  - peripartum 674.5 ☑
  - postpartum 674.5 ☑
  - primary 425.4
  - secondary 425.9
  - stress inuced 429.83 ●
  - takotsubo 429.83 ▲
  - thyrotoxic (*see also* Thyrotoxicosis) 242.9 ☑ *[425.7]*
  - toxic NEC 425.9
  - tuberculous (*see also* Tuberculosis) 017.9 ☑ *[425.8]*
- **Cardionephritis** — *see* Hypertension, cardiorenal
- **Cardionephropathy** — *see* Hypertension, cardiorenal
- **Cardionephrosis** — *see* Hypertension, cardiorenal
- **Cardioneurosis** 306.2
- **Cardiopathia nigra** 416.0
- **Cardiopathy** — *see also* Disease, heart 429.9
  - hypertensive (*see also* Hypertension, heart) 402.90
  - idiopathic 425.4
  - mucopolysaccharidosis 277.5 *[425.7]*
- **Cardiopericarditis** — *see also* Pericarditis 423.9
- **Cardiophobia** 300.29
- **Cardioptosis** 746.87
- **Cardiorenal** — *see* condition
- **Cardiorrhexis** — *see also* Infarct, myocardium 410.9 ☑
- **Cardiosclerosis** — *see* Arteriosclerosis, coronary
- **Cardiosis** — *see* Disease, heart
- **Cardiospasm** (esophagus) (reflex) (stomach) 530.0
  - congenital 750.7
- **Cardiostenosis** — *see* Disease, heart
- **Cardiosymphysis** 423.1
- **Cardiothyrotoxicosis** — *see* Hyperthyroidism
- **Cardiovascular** — *see* condition
- **Carditis** (acute) (bacterial) (chronic) (subacute) 429.89
  - Coxsackie 074.20
  - hypertensive (*see also* Hypertension, heart) 402.90
  - meningococcal 036.40
  - rheumatic — *see* Disease, heart, rheumatic
  - rheumatoid 714.2
- **Care** (of)
  - child (routine) V20.1
  - convalescent following V66.9
    - chemotherapy V66.2
    - medical NEC V66.5
    - psychotherapy V66.3
    - radiotherapy V66.1
    - surgery V66.0
    - surgical NEC V66.0
    - treatment (for) V66.5
      - combined V66.6
      - fracture V66.4
      - mental disorder NEC V66.3
      - specified type NEC V66.5
  - end-of-life V66.7
  - family member (handicapped) (sick)
    - creating problem for family V61.49
    - provided away from home for holiday relief V60.5
    - unavailable, due to
      - absence (person rendering care) (sufferer) V60.4
      - inability (any reason) of person rendering care V60.4
  - holiday relief V60.5
  - hospice V66.7
  - lack of (at or after birth) (infant) (child) 995.52
    - adult 995.84
  - lactation of mother V24.1
  - palliative V66.7
  - postpartum
    - immediately after delivery V24.0
    - routine follow-up V24.2
  - prenatal V22.1
    - first pregnancy V22.0
    - high-risk pregnancy V23.9
      - specified problem NEC V23.89
  - terminal V66.7
  - unavailable, due to
    - absence of person rendering care V60.4
    - inability (any reason) of person rendering care V60.4
  - well baby V20.1
- **Caries** (bone) — *see also* Tuberculosis, bone 015.9 ☑ *[730.8]* ☑
  - arrested 521.04
  - cementum 521.03
  - cerebrospinal (tuberculous) 015.0 ☑ *[730.88]*
  - dental (acute) (chronic) (incipient) (infected) 521.00
    - with pulp exposure 521.03
    - extending to
      - dentine 521.02
      - pulp 521.03
    - other specified NEC 521.09
    - pit and fissure 521.06
    - primary ●
      - pit and fissure origin 521.06 ●
      - root surface 521.08 ●
      - smooth surface origin 521.07 ●
    - root surface 521.08
    - smooth surface 521.07
  - dentin (acute) (chronic) 521.02
  - enamel (acute) (chronic) (incipient) 521.01
  - external meatus 380.89
  - hip (*see also* Tuberculosis) 015.1 ☑ *[730.85]*
  - initial 521.01
  - knee 015.2 ☑ *[730.86]*
  - labyrinth 386.8
  - limb NEC 015.7 ☑ *[730.88]*
  - mastoid (chronic) (process) 383.1
  - middle ear 385.89
  - nose 015.7 ☑ *[730.88]*
  - orbit 015.7 ☑ *[730.88]*
  - ossicle 385.24
  - petrous bone 383.20
  - sacrum (tuberculous) 015.0 ☑ *[730.88]*
  - spine, spinal (column) (tuberculous) 015.0 ☑ *[730.88]*
  - syphilitic 095.5
    - congenital 090.0 *[730.8]* ☑
  - teeth (internal) 521.00
    - initial 521.01
  - vertebra (column) (tuberculous) 015.0 ☑ *[730.88]*
- **Carini's syndrome** (ichthyosis congenita) 757.1
- **Carious teeth** 521.00
- **Carneous mole** 631
- **Carnosinemia** 270.5
- **Carotid body or sinus syndrome** 337.0
- **Carotidynia** 337.0
- **Carotinemia** (dietary) 278.3
- **Carotinosis** (cutis) (skin) 278.3
- **Carpal tunnel syndrome** 354.0
- **Carpenter's syndrome** 759.89
- **Carpopedal spasm** — *see also* Tetany 781.7
- **Carpoptosis** 736.05
- **Carrier** (suspected) **of**
  - amebiasis V02.2
  - bacterial disease (meningococcal, staphylococcal) NEC V02.59
  - cholera V02.0
  - cystic fibrosis gene V83.81
  - defective gene V83.89
  - diphtheria V02.4
  - dysentery (bacillary) V02.3
    - amebic V02.2
  - Endamoeba histolytica V02.2
  - gastrointestinal pathogens NEC V02.3
  - genetic defect V83.89
  - gonorrhea V02.7
  - group B streptococcus V02.51
  - HAA (hepatitis Australian-antigen) V02.61
  - hemophilia A (asymptomatic) V83.01
    - symptomatic V83.02
  - hepatitis V02.60
    - Australian-antigen (HAA) V02.61
    - B V02.61
    - C V02.62
    - serum V02.61
    - specified type NEC V02.69
    - viral V02.60
  - infective organism NEC V02.9
  - malaria V02.9
  - paratyphoid V02.3
  - Salmonella V02.3
    - typhosa V02.1
  - serum hepatitis V02.61
  - Shigella V02.3
  - Staphylococcus NEC V02.59
  - Streptococcus NEC V02.52
    - group B V02.51
  - typhoid V02.1
  - venereal disease NEC V02.8
- **Carrión's disease** (Bartonellosis) 088.0
- **Car sickness** 994.6
- **Carter's**
  - relapsing fever (Asiatic) 087.0
- **Cartilage** — *see* condition
- **Caruncle** (inflamed)
  - abscess, lacrimal (*see also* Dacryocystitis) 375.30
  - conjunctiva 372.00
    - acute 372.00
  - eyelid 373.00
  - labium (majus) (minus) 616.89 ▲
  - lacrimal 375.30
  - urethra (benign) 599.3
  - vagina (wall) 616.89 ▲
- **Cascade stomach** 537.6
- **Caseation lymphatic gland** — *see also* Tuberculosis 017.2 ☑
- **Caseous**
  - bronchitis — *see* Tuberculosis, pulmonary
  - meningitis 013.0 ☑
  - pneumonia — *see* Tuberculosis, pulmonary
- **Cassidy (-Scholte) syndrome** (malignant carcinoid) 259.2
- **Castellani's bronchitis** 104.8
- **Castleman's tumor or lymphoma** (mediastinal lymph node hyperplasia) 785.6
- **Castration, traumatic** 878.2
  - complicated 878.3
- **Casts in urine** 791.7
- **Catalepsy** 300.11
  - catatonic (acute) (*see also* Schizophrenia) 295.2 ☑
  - hysterical 300.11
  - schizophrenic (*see also* Schizophrenia) 295.2 ☑
- **Cataphasia** 307.0
- **Cataplexy** (idiopathic) — *see* Narcolepsy
- **Cataract** (anterior cortical) (anterior polar) (black) (capsular) (central) (cortical) (hypermature) (immature) (incipient) (mature) 366.9
  - anterior
    - and posterior axial embryonal 743.33
    - pyramidal 743.31
    - subcapsular polar
      - infantile, juvenile, or presenile 366.01
      - senile 366.13
  - associated with
    - calcinosis 275.40 *[366.42]*
    - craniofacial dysostosis 756.0 *[366.44]*
    - galactosemia 271.1 *[366.44]*
    - hypoparathyroidism 252.1 *[366.42]*
    - myotonic disorders 359.2 *[366.43]*
    - neovascularization 366.33
  - blue dot 743.39
  - cerulean 743.39
  - complicated NEC 366.30
  - congenital 743.30
    - capsular or subcapsular 743.31
    - cortical 743.32
    - nuclear 743.33
    - specified type NEC 743.39
    - total or subtotal 743.34
    - zonular 743.32
  - coronary (congenital) 743.39
    - acquired 366.12

Cataract — *continued*
cupuliform 366.14
diabetic 250.5 ☑ *[366.41]*
drug-induced 366.45
due to
chalcosis 360.24 *[366.34]*
chronic choroiditis (*see also* Choroiditis) 363.20 *[366.32]*
degenerative myopia 360.21 *[366.34]*
glaucoma (*see also* Glaucoma) 365.9 *[366.31]*
infection, intraocular NEC 366.32
inflammatory ocular disorder NEC 366.32
iridocyclitis, chronic 364.10 *[366.33]*
pigmentary retinal dystrophy 362.74 *[366.34]*
radiation 366.46
electric 366.46
glassblowers' 366.46
heat ray 366.46
heterochromic 366.33
in eye disease NEC 366.30
infantile (*see also* Cataract, juvenile) 366.00
intumescent 366.12
irradiational 366.46
juvenile 366.00
anterior subcapsular polar 366.01
combined forms 366.09
cortical 366.03
lamellar 366.03
nuclear 366.04
posterior subcapsular polar 366.02
specified NEC 366.09
zonular 366.03
lamellar 743.32
infantile, juvenile, or presenile 366.03
morgagnian 366.18
myotonic 359.2 *[366.43]*
myxedema 244.9 *[366.44]*
nuclear 366.16
posterior, polar (capsular) 743.31
infantile, juvenile, or presenile 366.02
senile 366.14
presenile (*see also* Cataract, juvenile) 366.00
punctate
acquired 366.12
congenital 743.39
secondary (membrane) 366.50
obscuring vision 366.53
specified type, not obscuring vision 366.52
senile 366.10
anterior subcapsular polar 366.13
combined forms 366.19
cortical 366.15
hypermature 366.18
immature 366.12
incipient 366.12
mature 366.17
nuclear 366.16
posterior subcapsular polar 366.14
specified NEC 366.19
total or subtotal 366.17
snowflake 250.5 ☑ *[366.41]*
specified NEC 366.8
subtotal (senile) 366.17
congenital 743.34
sunflower 360.24 *[366.34]*
tetanic NEC 252.1 *[366.42]*
total (mature) (senile) 366.17
congenital 743.34
localized 366.21
traumatic 366.22
toxic 366.45
traumatic 366.20
partially resolved 366.23
total 366.22
zonular (perinuclear) 743.32

Cataract — *continued*
zonular — *continued*
infantile, juvenile, or presenile 366.03
Cataracta 366.10
brunescens 366.16
cerulea 743.39
complicata 366.30
congenita 743.30
coralliformis 743.39
coronaria (congenital) 743.39
acquired 366.12
diabetic 250.5 ☑ *[366.41]*
floriformis 360.24 *[366.34]*
membranacea
accreta 366.50
congenita 743.39
nigra 366.16
Catarrh, catarrhal (inflammation) — *see also* condition 460
acute 460
asthma, asthmatic (*see also* Asthma) 493.9 ☑
Bostock's (*see also* Fever, hay) 477.9
bowel — *see* Enteritis
bronchial 490
acute 466.0
chronic 491.0
subacute 466.0
cervix, cervical (canal) (uteri) — *see* Cervicitis
chest (*see also* Bronchitis) 490
chronic 472.0
congestion 472.0
conjunctivitis 372.03
due to syphilis 095.9
congenital 090.0
enteric — *see* Enteritis
epidemic 487.1
Eustachian 381.50
eye (acute) (vernal) 372.03
fauces (*see also* Pharyngitis) 462
febrile 460
fibrinous acute 466.0
gastroenteric — *see* Enteritis
gastrointestinal — *see* Enteritis
gingivitis 523.00 ▲
hay (*see also* Fever, hay) 477.9
infectious 460
intestinal — *see* Enteritis
larynx (*see also* Laryngitis, chronic) 476.0
liver 070.1
with hepatic coma 070.0
lung (*see also* Bronchitis) 490
acute 466.0
chronic 491.0
middle ear (chronic) — *see* Otitis media, chronic
mouth 528.00 ▲
nasal (chronic) (*see also* Rhinitis) 472.0
acute 460
nasobronchial 472.2
nasopharyngeal (chronic) 472.2
acute 460
nose — *see* Catarrh, nasal
ophthalmia 372.03
pneumococcal, acute 466.0
pulmonary (*see also* Bronchitis) 490
acute 466.0
chronic 491.0
spring (eye) 372.13
suffocating (*see also* Asthma) 493.9 ☑
summer (hay) (*see also* Fever, hay) 477.9
throat 472.1
tracheitis 464.10
with obstruction 464.11
tubotympanal 381.4
acute (*see also* Otitis media, acute, nonsuppurative) 381.00
chronic 381.10
vasomotor (*see also* Fever, hay) 477.9
vesical (bladder) — *see* Cystitis

Catarrhus aestivus — *see also* Fever, hay 477.9
Catastrophe, cerebral — *see also* Disease, cerebrovascular, acute 436
Catatonia, catatonic (acute) 781.99
with
affective psychosis — *see* Psychosis, affective
agitation 295.2 ☑
dementia (praecox) 295.2 ☑
due to or associated with physical condition 293.89
excitation 295.2 ☑
excited type 295.2 ☑
in conditions classified elsewhere 293.89
schizophrenia 295.2 ☑
stupor 295.2 ☑
Cat's ear 744.29
Cat-scratch — *see also* Injury, superficial
disease or fever 078.3
Cauda equina — *see also* condition
syndrome 344.60
Cauliflower ear 738.7
Caul over face 768.9
Causalgia 355.9
lower limb 355.71
upper limb 354.4
Cause
external, general effects NEC 994.9
not stated 799.9
unknown 799.9
Caustic burn — *see also* Burn, by site
from swallowing caustic or corrosive substance — *see* Burn, internal organs
Cavare's disease (familial periodic paralysis) 359.3
Cave-in, injury
crushing (severe) (*see also* Crush, by site) 869.1
suffocation 994.7
Cavernitis (penis) 607.2
lymph vessel — *see* Lymphangioma
Cavernositis 607.2
Cavernous — *see* condition
Cavitation of lung — *see also* Tuberculosis 011.2 ☑
nontuberculous 518.89
primary, progressive 010.8 ☑
Cavity
lung — *see* Cavitation of lung
optic papilla 743.57
pulmonary — *see* Cavitation of lung
teeth 521.00
vitreous (humor) 379.21
Cavovarus foot, congenital 754.59
Cavus foot (congenital) 754.71
acquired 736.73
Cazenave's
disease (pemphigus) NEC 694.4
lupus (erythematosus) 695.4
CDGS (carbohydrate-deficient glycoprotein syndrome) 271.8
Cecitis — *see* Appendicitis
Cecocele — *see* Hernia
Cecum — *see* condition
Celiac
artery compression syndrome 447.4
disease 579.0
infantilism 579.0
Cell, cellular — *see also* condition
anterior chamber (eye) (positive aqueous ray) 364.04
Cellulitis (diffuse) (with lymphangitis) — *see also* Abscess 682.9
abdominal wall 682.2
anaerobic (*see also* Gas gangrene) 040.0
ankle 682.6
anus 566
areola 611.0
arm (any part, above wrist) 682.3
auditory canal (external) 380.10
axilla 682.3

Cellulitis — *see also* Abscess — *continued*
back (any part) 682.2
breast 611.0
postpartum 675.1 ☑
broad ligament (*see also* Disease, pelvis, inflammatory) 614.4
acute 614.3
buttock 682.5
cervical (neck region) 682.1
cervix (uteri) (*see also* Cervicitis) 616.0
cheek, external 682.0
internal 528.3
chest wall 682.2
chronic NEC 682.9
colostomy 569.61
corpus cavernosum 607.2
digit 681.9
Douglas' cul-de-sac or pouch (chronic) (*see also* Disease, pelvis, inflammatory) 614.4
acute 614.3
drainage site (following operation) 998.59
ear, external 380.10
enterostomy 569.61
erysipelar (*see also* Erysipelas) 035
esophagostomy 530.86
eyelid 373.13
face (any part, except eye) 682.0
finger (intrathecal) (periosteal) (subcutaneous) (subcuticular) 681.00
flank 682.2
foot (except toe) 682.7
forearm 682.3
gangrenous (*see also* Gangrene) 785.4
genital organ NEC
female — *see* Abscess, genital organ, female
male 608.4
glottis 478.71
gluteal (region) 682.5
gonococcal NEC 098.0
groin 682.2
hand (except finger or thumb) 682.4
head (except face) NEC 682.8
heel 682.7
hip 682.6
jaw (region) 682.0
knee 682.6
labium (majus) (minus) (*see also* Vulvitis) 616.10
larynx 478.71
leg, except foot 682.6
lip 528.5
mammary gland 611.0
mouth (floor) 528.3
multiple sites NEC 682.9
nasopharynx 478.21
navel 682.2
newborn NEC 771.4
neck (region) 682.1
nipple 611.0
nose 478.19 ▲
external 682.0
orbit, orbital 376.01
palate (soft) 528.3
pectoral (region) 682.2
pelvis, pelvic
with
abortion — *see* Abortion, by type, with sepsis
ectopic pregnancy (*see also* categories 633.0–633.9) 639.0
molar pregnancy (*see also* categories 630–632) 639.0
female (*see also* Disease, pelvis, inflammatory) 614.4
acute 614.3
following
abortion 639.0
ectopic or molar pregnancy 639.0
male 567.21

☑ Additional Digit Required — Refer to the Tabular List for Digit Selection
Subterms under main terms may continue to next column or page

Note — for malignant change occurring in a neoplasm, use the appropriate M code with behavior digit /3 e.g., malignant change in uterine fibroid — M8890/3. For malignant change occurring in a nonneoplastic condition (e.g., gastric ulcer) use the M code M8000/3.

- **Charcôt's** — *continued*
  - syndrome (intermittent claudication) 443.9
    - due to atherosclerosis 440.21
- **Charcôt-Marie-Tooth disease, paralysis, or syndrome** 356.1
- **CHARGE association** (syndrome) 759.89
- **Charleyhorse** (quadriceps) 843.8
  - muscle, except quadriceps — *see* Sprain, by site
- **Charlouis' disease** — *see also* Yaws 102.9
- **Chauffeur's fracture** — *see* Fracture, ulna, lower end
- **Cheadle (-Möller) (-Barlow) disease or syndrome** (infantile scurvy) 267
- **Checking** (of)
  - contraceptive device (intrauterine) V25.42
  - device
    - fixation V54.89
      - external V54.89
      - internal V54.09
    - traction V54.89
  - Kirschner wire V54.89
  - plaster cast V54.89
  - splint, external V54.89
- **Checkup**
  - following treatment — *see* Examination
  - health V70.0
  - infant (not sick) V20.2
  - newborn, routine ●
    - initial V20.2 ●
    - subsequent V20.2 ●
  - pregnancy (normal) V22.1
    - first V22.0
    - high-risk pregnancy V23.9
      - specified problem NEC V23.89
- **Chédiak-Higashi (-Steinbrinck) anomaly, disease, or syndrome** (congenital gigantism of peroxidase granules) 288.2
- **Cheek** — *see also* condition
  - biting 528.9
- **Cheese itch** 133.8
- **Cheese washers' lung** 495.8
- **Cheilitis** 528.5
  - actinic (due to sun) 692.72
    - chronic NEC 692.74
      - due to radiation, except from sun 692.82
    - due to radiation, except from sun 692.82
  - acute 528.5
  - angular 528.5
  - catarrhal 528.5
  - chronic 528.5
  - exfoliative 528.5
  - gangrenous 528.5
  - glandularis apostematosa 528.5
  - granulomatosa 351.8
  - infectional 528.5
  - membranous 528.5
  - Miescher's 351.8
  - suppurative 528.5
  - ulcerative 528.5
  - vesicular 528.5
- **Cheilodynia** 528.5
- **Cheilopalatoschisis** — *see also* Cleft, palate, with cleft lip 749.20
- **Cheilophagia** 528.9
- **Cheiloschisis** — *see also* Cleft, lip 749.10
- **Cheilosis** 528.5
  - with pellagra 265.2
  - angular 528.5
  - due to
    - dietary deficiency 266.0
    - vitamin deficiency 266.0
- **Cheiromegaly** 729.89
- **Cheiropompholyx** 705.81
- **Cheloid** — *see also* Keloid 701.4
- **Chemical burn** — *see also* Burn, by site
  - from swallowing chemical — *see* Burn, internal organs
- **Chemodectoma** (M8693/1) — *see* Paraganglioma, nonchromaffin
- **Chemoprophylaxis** NEC V07.39
- **Chemosis, conjunctiva** 372.73
- **Chemotherapy**
  - convalescence V66.2
  - encounter (for) V58.11
  - maintenance V58.11
  - prophylactic NEC V07.39
    - fluoride V07.31
- **Cherubism** 526.89
- **Chest** — *see* condition
- **Cheyne-Stokes respiration** (periodic) 786.04
- **Chiari's**
  - disease or syndrome (hepatic vein thrombosis) 453.0
  - malformation
    - type I 348.4
    - type II (*see also* Spina bifida) 741.0 ☑
    - type III 742.0
    - type IV 742.2
  - network 746.89
- **Chiari-Frommel syndrome** 676.6 ☑
- **Chicago disease** (North American blastomycosis) 116.0
- **Chickenpox** — *see also* Varicella 052.9
  - exposure to V01.71
  - vaccination and inoculation (prophylactic) V05.4
- **Chiclero ulcer** 085.4
- **Chiggers** 133.8
- **Chignon** 111.2
  - fetus or newborn (from vacuum extraction) 767.19
- **Chigoe disease** 134.1
- **Chikungunya fever** 066.3
- **Chilaiditi's syndrome** (subphrenic displacement, colon) 751.4
- **Chilblains** 991.5
  - lupus 991.5
- **Child**
  - behavior causing concern V61.20
- **Childbed fever** 670.0 ☑
- **Childbirth** — *see also* Delivery
  - puerperal complications — *see* Puerperal
- **Childhood, period of rapid growth** V21.0
- **Chill(s)** 780.99
  - with fever 780.6
  - congestive 780.99
    - in malarial regions 084.6
  - septic — *see* Septicemia
  - urethral 599.84
- **Chilomastigiasis** 007.8
- **Chin** — *see* condition
- **Chinese dysentery** 004.9
- **Chiropractic dislocation** — *see also* Lesion, nonallopathic, by site 739.9
- **Chitral fever** 066.0
- **Chlamydia, chlamydial** — *see* condition
- **Chloasma** 709.09
  - cachecticorum 709.09
  - eyelid 374.52
    - congenital 757.33
    - hyperthyroid 242.0 ☑
  - gravidarum 646.8 ☑
  - idiopathic 709.09
  - skin 709.09
  - symptomatic 709.09
- **Chloroma** (M9930/3) 205.3 ☑
- **Chlorosis** 280.9
  - Egyptian (*see also* Ancylostomiasis) 126.9
  - miners' (*see also* Ancylostomiasis) 126.9
- **Chlorotic anemia** 280.9
- **Chocolate cyst** (ovary) 617.1
- **Choked**
  - disk or disc — *see* Papilledema
  - on food, phlegm, or vomitus NEC (*see also* Asphyxia, food) 933.1
  - phlegm 933.1
- **Choked** — *continued*
  - while vomiting NEC (*see also* Asphyxia, food) 933.1
- **Chokes** (resulting from bends) 993.3
- **Choking sensation** 784.99 ▲
- **Cholangiectasis** — *see also* Disease, gallbladder 575.8
- **Cholangiocarcinoma** (M8160/3)
  - and hepatocellular carcinoma, combined (M8180/3) 155.0
  - liver 155.1
  - specified site NEC — *see* Neoplasm, by site, malignant
  - unspecified site 155.1
- **Cholangiohepatitis** 575.8
  - due to fluke infestation 121.1
- **Cholangiohepatoma** (M8180/3) 155.0
- **Cholangiolitis** (acute) (chronic) (extrahepatic) (gangrenous) 576.1
  - intrahepatic 575.8
  - paratyphoidal (*see also* Fever, paratyphoid) 002.9
  - typhoidal 002.0
- **Cholangioma** (M8160/0) 211.5
  - malignant — *see* Cholangiocarcinoma
- **Cholangitis** (acute) (ascending) (catarrhal) (chronic) (infective) (malignant) (primary) (recurrent) (sclerosing) (secondary) (stenosing) (suppurative) 576.1
  - chronic nonsuppurative destructive 571.6
  - nonsuppurative destructive (chronic) 571.6
- **Cholecystdocholithiasis** — *see* Choledocholithiasis
- **Cholecystitis** 575.10
  - with
    - calculus, stones in
      - bile duct (common) (hepatic) — *see* Choledocholithiasis
      - gallbladder — *see* Cholelithiasis
  - acute 575.0
  - acute and chronic 575.12
  - chronic 575.11
  - emphysematous (acute) (*see also* Cholecystitis, acute) 575.0
  - gangrenous (*see also* Cholecystitis, acute) 575.0
  - paratyphoidal, current (*see also* Fever, paratyphoid) 002.9
  - suppurative (*see also* Cholecystitis, acute) 575.0
  - typhoidal 002.0
- **Choledochitis** (suppurative) 576.1
- **Choledocholith** — *see* Choledocholithiasis
- **Choledocholithiasis** 574.5 ☑

> *Note — Use the following fifth-digit subclassification with category 574:*
>
> 0 *without mention of obstruction*
>
> 1 *with obstruction*

  - with
    - cholecystitis 574.4 ☑
      - acute 574.3 ☑
      - chronic 574.4 ☑
    - cholelithiasis 574.9 ☑
      - with
        - cholecystitis 574.7 ☑
          - acute 574.6 ☑
            - and chronic 574.8 ☑
          - chronic 574.7 ☑
- **Cholelithiasis** (impacted) (multiple) 574.2 ☑

> *Note — Use the following fifth-digit subclassification with category 574:*
>
> 0 *without mention of obstruction*
>
> 1 *with obstruction*

  - with
    - cholecystitis 574.1 ☑
      - acute 574.0 ☑
      - chronic 574.1 ☑
- **Cholelithiasis** — *continued*
  - with — *continued*
    - choledocholithiasis 574.9 ☑
      - with
        - cholecystitis 574.7 ☑
          - acute 574.6 ☑
            - and chronic 574.8 ☑
          - chronic cholecystitis 574.7 ☑
- **Cholemia** — *see also* Jaundice 782.4
  - familial 277.4
  - Gilbert's (familial nonhemolytic) 277.4
- **Cholemic gallstone** — *see* Cholelithiasis
- **Choleperitoneum, choleperitonitis** — *see also* Disease, gallbladder 567.81
- **Cholera** (algid) (Asiatic) (asphyctic) (epidemic) (gravis) (Indian) (malignant) (morbus) (pestilential) (spasmodic) 001.9
  - antimonial 985.4
  - carrier (suspected) of V02.0
  - classical 001.0
  - contact V01.0
  - due to
    - Vibrio
      - cholerae (Inaba, Ogawa, Hikojima serotypes) 001.0
        - El Tor 001.1
  - El Tor 001.1
  - exposure to V01.0
  - vaccination, prophylactic (against) V03.0
- **Cholerine** — *see also* Cholera 001.9
- **Cholestasis** 576.8
  - due to total parenteral nutrition (TPN) 573.8 ●
- **Cholesteatoma** (ear) 385.30
  - attic (primary) 385.31
  - diffuse 385.35
  - external ear (canal) 380.21
  - marginal (middle ear) 385.32
    - with involvement of mastoid cavity 385.33
    - secondary (with middle ear involvement) 385.33
  - mastoid cavity 385.30
  - middle ear (secondary) 385.32
    - with involvement of mastoid cavity 385.33
  - postmastoidectomy cavity (recurrent) 383.32
  - primary 385.31
  - recurrent, postmastoidectomy cavity 383.32
  - secondary (middle ear) 385.32
    - with involvement of mastoid cavity 385.33
- **Cholesteatosis** (middle ear) — *see also* Cholesteatoma 385.30
  - diffuse 385.35
- **Cholesteremia** 272.0
- **Cholesterin**
  - granuloma, middle ear 385.82
  - in vitreous 379.22
- **Cholesterol**
  - deposit
    - retina 362.82
    - vitreous 379.22
  - imbibition of gallbladder (*see also* Disease, gallbladder) 575.6
- **Cholesterolemia** 272.0
  - essential 272.0
  - familial 272.0
  - hereditary 272.0
- **Cholesterosis, cholesterolosis** (gallbladder) 575.6
  - with
    - cholecystitis — *see* Cholecystitis
    - cholelithiasis — *see* Cholelithiasis
  - middle ear (*see also* Cholesteatoma) 385.30
- **Cholocolic fistula** — *see also* Fistula, gallbladder 575.5
- **Choluria** 791.4
- **Chondritis** (purulent) 733.99

☑ Additional Digit Required — Refer to the Tabular List for Digit Selection
Subterms under main terms may continue to next column or page

Complications — *continued*
- cardiorenal (*see also* Hypertension, cardiorenal) 404.90
- carotid artery bypass graft 996.1
  - atherosclerosis — *see* Arteriosclerosis, extremities
  - embolism 996.74
  - occlusion NEC 996.74
  - thrombus 996.74
- cataract fragments in eye 998.82
- catheter device NEC (*see also* Complications, due to (presence of) any device, implant, or graft classified to 996.0–996.5 NEC)
  - mechanical — *see* Complications, mechanical, catheter
- cecostomy 569.60
- cesarean section wound 674.3 ☑
- chin implant (prosthetic) NEC 996.79
  - infection or inflammation 996.69
  - mechanical 996.59
- colostomy (enterostomy) 569.60
  - specified type NEC 569.69
- contraceptive device, intrauterine NEC 996.76
  - infection 996.65
  - inflammation 996.65
  - mechanical 996.32
- cord (umbilical) — *see* Complications, umbilical cord
- cornea
  - due to
    - contact lens 371.82
- coronary (artery) bypass (graft) NEC 996.03
  - atherosclerosis — *see* Arteriosclerosis, coronary
  - embolism 996.72
  - infection or inflammation 996.61
  - mechanical 996.03
  - occlusion NEC 996.72
  - specified type NEC 996.72
  - thrombus 996.72
- cystostomy 997.5
- delivery 669.9 ☑
  - procedure (instrumental) (manual) (surgical) 669.4 ☑
  - specified type NEC 669.8 ☑
- dialysis (hemodialysis) (peritoneal) (renal) NEC 999.9
  - catheter NEC (*see also* Complications, due to (presence of) any device, implant, or graft classified to 996.0–996.5 NEC)
    - infection or inflammation 996.62
      - peritoneal 996.68
    - mechanical 996.1
      - peritoneal 996.56
- due to (presence of) any device, implant, or graft classified to 996.0–996.5 NEC 996.70
  - with infection or inflammation — *see* Complications, infection or inflammation, due to (presence of) any device, implant, or graft classified to 996.0–996.5 NEC
  - arterial NEC 996.74
    - coronary NEC 996.03
      - atherosclerosis — *see* Arteriosclerosis, coronary
      - embolism 996.72
      - occlusion NEC 996.72
      - specified type NEC 996.72
      - thrombus 996.72
    - renal dialysis 996.73
  - arteriovenous fistula or shunt NEC 996.74
  - bone growth stimulator 996.78
  - breast NEC 996.79
  - cardiac NEC 996.72
    - defibrillator 996.72
    - pacemaker 996.72
    - valve prosthesis 996.71

Complications — *continued*
- due to any device, implant, or graft classified to 996.0–996.5 — *continued*
  - catheter NEC 996.79
    - spinal 996.75
    - urinary, indwelling 996.76
    - vascular NEC 996.74
      - renal dialysis 996.73
    - ventricular shunt 996.75
  - coronary (artery) bypass (graft) NEC 996.03
    - atherosclerosis — *see* Arteriosclerosis, coronary
    - embolism 996.72
    - occlusion NEC 996.72
    - thrombus 996.72
  - electrodes
    - brain 996.75
    - heart 996.72
  - esophagostomy 530.87
  - gastrointestinal NEC 996.79
  - genitourinary NEC 996.76
  - heart valve prosthesis NEC 996.71
  - infusion pump 996.74
  - insulin pump 996.57
  - internal
    - joint prosthesis 996.77
    - orthopedic NEC 996.78
    - specified type NEC 996.79
  - intrauterine contraceptive device NEC 996.76
  - joint prosthesis, internal NEC 996.77
  - mechanical — *see* Complications, mechanical
  - nervous system NEC 996.75
  - ocular lens NEC 996.79
  - orbital NEC 996.79
  - orthopedic NEC 996.78
    - joint, internal 996.77
  - renal dialysis 996.73
  - specified type NEC 996.79
  - urinary catheter, indwelling 996.76
  - vascular NEC 996.74
  - ventricular shunt 996.75
- during dialysis NEC 999.9
- ectopic or molar pregnancy NEC 639.9
- electroshock therapy NEC 999.9
- enterostomy 569.60
  - specified type NEC 569.69
- esophagostomy 530.87
  - infection 530.86
  - mechanical 530.87
- external (fixation) device with internal component(s) NEC 996.78
  - infection or inflammation 996.67
  - mechanical 996.49
- extracorporeal circulation NEC 999.9
- eye implant (prosthetic) NEC 996.79
  - infection or inflammation 996.69
  - mechanical
    - ocular lens 996.53
    - orbital globe 996.59
- gastrointestinal, postoperative NEC (*see also* Complications, surgical procedures) 997.4
- gastrostomy 536.40
  - specified type NEC 536.49
- genitourinary device, implant or graft NEC 996.76
  - infection or inflammation 996.65
    - urinary catheter, indwelling 996.64
  - mechanical (*see also* Complications, mechanical, by type) 996.30
    - specified NEC 996.39
- graft (bypass) (patch) (*see also* Complications, due to (presence of) any device, implant, or graft classified to 996.0–996.5 NEC)
  - bone marrow 996.85
  - corneal NEC 996.79
    - infection or inflammation 996.69

Complications — *continued*
- graft (*see also* Complications, due to any device, implant, or graft classified to 996.0–996.5) — *continued*
  - corneal — *continued*
    - rejection or reaction 996.51
  - mechanical — *see* Complications, mechanical, graft
  - organ (immune or nonimmune cause) (partial) (total) 996.80
    - bone marrow 996.85
    - heart 996.83
    - intestines 996.87
    - kidney 996.81
    - liver 996.82
    - lung 996.84
    - pancreas 996.86
    - specified NEC 996.89
  - skin NEC 996.79
    - infection or inflammation 996.69
    - rejection 996.52
      - artificial 996.55
      - decellularized allodermis 996.55
- heart (*see also* Disease, heart transplant (immune or nonimmune cause)) 996.83
- hematoma (intraoperative) (postoperative) 998.12
- hemorrhage (intraoperative) (postoperative) 998.11
- hyperalimentation therapy NEC 999.9
- immunization (procedure) — *see* Complications, vaccination
- implant (*see also* Complications, due to (presence of) any device, implant, or graft classified to 996.0–996.5 NEC)
  - mechanical — *see* Complications, mechanical, implant
- infection and inflammation
  - due to (presence of) any device, implant or graft classified to 996.0–996.5 NEC 996.60
    - arterial NEC 996.62
      - coronary 996.61
      - renal dialysis 996.62
    - arteriovenous fistula or shunt 996.62
    - artificial heart 996.61
    - bone growth stimulator 996.67
    - breast 996.69
    - cardiac 996.61
    - catheter NEC 996.69
      - peritoneal 996.68
      - spinal 996.63
      - urinary, indwelling 996.64
      - vascular NEC 996.62
      - ventricular shunt 996.63
    - coronary artery bypass 996.61
    - electrodes
      - brain 996.63
      - heart 996.61
    - gastrointestinal NEC 996.69
    - genitourinary NEC 996.65
      - indwelling urinary catheter 996.64
    - heart assist device 996.61
    - heart valve 996.61
    - infusion pump 996.62
    - insulin pump 996.69
    - intrauterine contraceptive device 996.65
    - joint prosthesis, internal 996.66
    - ocular lens 996.69
    - orbital (implant) 996.69
    - orthopedic NEC 996.67
      - joint, internal 996.66
    - specified type NEC 996.69
    - urinary catheter, indwelling 996.64
    - ventricular shunt 996.63
- infusion (procedure) 999.9

Complications — *continued*
- infusion — *continued*
  - blood — *see* Complications, transfusion
  - infection NEC 999.3
  - sepsis NEC 999.3
- inhalation therapy NEC 999.9
- injection (procedure) 999.9
  - drug reaction (*see also* Reaction, drug) 995.27 ▲
  - infection NEC 999.3
  - sepsis NEC 999.3
  - serum (prophylactic) (therapeutic) — *see* Complications, vaccination
  - vaccine (any) — *see* Complications, vaccination
- inoculation (any) — *see* Complications, vaccination
- insulin pump 996.57
- internal device (catheter) (electronic) (fixation) (prosthetic) (*see also* Complications, due to (presence of) any device, implant, or graft classified to 996.0–996.5 NEC)
  - mechanical — *see* Complications, mechanical
- intestinal transplant (immune or nonimmune cause) 996.87
- intraoperative bleeding or hemorrhage 998.11
- intrauterine contraceptive device (*see also* Complications, contraceptive device) 996.76
  - with fetal damage affecting management of pregnancy 655.8 ☑
  - infection or inflammation 996.65
- jejunostomy 569.60
- kidney transplant (immune or nonimmune cause) 996.81
- labor 669.9 ☑
  - specified condition NEC 669.8 ☑
- liver transplant (immune or nonimmune cause) 996.82
- lumbar puncture 349.0
- mechanical
  - anastomosis — *see* Complications, mechanical, graft
  - artificial heart 996.09
  - bypass — *see* Complications, mechanical, graft
  - catheter NEC 996.59
    - cardiac 996.09
    - cystostomy 996.39
    - dialysis (hemodialysis) 996.1
      - peritoneal 996.56
    - during a procedure 998.2
    - urethral, indwelling 996.31
  - colostomy 569.62
  - device NEC 996.59
    - balloon (counterpulsation), intra-aortic 996.1
    - cardiac 996.00
      - automatic implantable defibrillator 996.04
      - long-term effect 429.4
      - specified NEC 996.09
    - contraceptive, intrauterine 996.32
    - counterpulsation, intra-aortic 996.1
    - fixation, external, with internal components 996.49
    - fixation, internal (nail, rod, plate) 996.40
    - genitourinary 996.30
      - specified NEC 996.39
    - insulin pump 996.57
    - nervous system 996.2
    - orthopedic, internal 996.40
      - prosthetic joint (*see also* Complications, mechanical, device, orthopedic, prosthetic, joint) 996.47
    - prosthetic NEC 996.59

☑ Additional Digit Required — Refer to the Tabular List for Digit Selection
Subterms under main terms may continue to next column or page

- **Contraction, contracture, contracted** — *continued*
  - paralytic — *continued*
    - muscle — *continued*
      - ocular (*see also* Strabismus, paralytic) 378.50
  - pelvis (acquired) (general) 738.6
    - affecting fetus or newborn 763.1
    - complicating delivery 653.1 ☑
      - causing obstructed labor 660.1 ☑
      - generally contracted 653.1 ☑
        - causing obstructed labor 660.1 ☑
      - inlet 653.2 ☑
        - causing obstructed labor 660.1 ☑
      - midpelvic 653.8 ☑
        - causing obstructed labor 660.1 ☑
      - midplane 653.8 ☑
        - causing obstructed labor 660.1 ☑
      - outlet 653.3 ☑
        - causing obstructed labor 660.1 ☑
  - plantar fascia 728.71
  - premature
    - atrial 427.61
    - auricular 427.61
    - auriculoventricular 427.61
    - heart (junctional) (nodal) 427.60
    - supraventricular 427.61
    - ventricular 427.69
  - prostate 602.8
  - pylorus (*see also* Pylorospasm) 537.81
  - rectosigmoid (*see also* Obstruction, intestine) 560.9
  - rectum, rectal (sphincter) 564.89
    - psychogenic 306.4
  - ring (Bandl's) 661.4 ☑
    - affecting fetus or newborn 763.7
  - scar — *see* Cicatrix
  - sigmoid (*see also* Obstruction, intestine) 560.9
  - socket, eye 372.64
  - spine (*see also* Curvature, spine) 737.9
  - stomach 536.8
    - hourglass 536.8
      - congenital 750.7
    - psychogenic 306.4
  - tendon (sheath) (*see also* Short, tendon) 727.81
  - toe 735.8
  - ureterovesical orifice (postinfectional) 593.3
  - urethra 599.84
  - uterus 621.8
    - abnormal 661.9 ☑
      - affecting fetus or newborn 763.7
    - clonic, hourglass or tetanic 661.4 ☑
      - affecting fetus or newborn 763.7
    - dyscoordinate 661.4 ☑
      - affecting fetus or newborn 763.7
    - hourglass 661.4 ☑
      - affecting fetus or newborn 763.7
    - hypotonic NEC 661.2 ☑
      - affecting fetus or newborn 763.7
    - incoordinate 661.4 ☑
      - affecting fetus or newborn 763.7
    - inefficient or poor 661.2 ☑
      - affecting fetus or newborn 763.7
    - irregular 661.2 ☑
      - affecting fetus or newborn 763.7
    - tetanic 661.4 ☑
      - affecting fetus or newborn 763.7
  - vagina (outlet) 623.2
  - vesical 596.8
    - neck or urethral orifice 596.0
  - visual field, generalized 368.45
  - Volkmann's (ischemic) 958.6
- **Contusion** (skin surface intact) 924.9
  - with
    - crush injury — *see* Crush
- **Contusion** — *continued*
  - with — *continued*
    - dislocation — *see* Dislocation, by site
    - fracture — *see* Fracture, by site
    - internal injury (*see also* Injury, internal, by site)
      - heart — *see* Contusion, cardiac
      - kidney — *see* Contusion, kidney
      - liver — *see* Contusion, liver
      - lung — *see* Contusion, lung
      - spleen — *see* Contusion, spleen
    - intracranial injury — *see* Injury, intracranial
    - nerve injury — *see* Injury, nerve
    - open wound — *see* Wound, open, by site
  - abdomen, abdominal (muscle) (wall) 922.2
    - organ(s) NEC 868.00
  - adnexa, eye NEC 921.9
  - ankle 924.21
    - with other parts of foot 924.20
  - arm 923.9
    - lower (with elbow) 923.10
    - upper 923.03
      - with shoulder or axillary region 923.09
  - auditory canal (external) (meatus) (and other part(s) of neck, scalp, or face, except eye) 920
  - auricle, ear (and other part(s) of neck, scalp, or face except eye) 920
  - axilla 923.02
    - with shoulder or upper arm 923.09
  - back 922.31
  - bone NEC 924.9
  - brain (cerebral) (membrane) (with hemorrhage) 851.8 ☑

> *Note — Use the following fifth-digit subclassification with categories 851–854:*
>
> 0 *unspecified state of consciousness*
>
> 1 *with no loss of consciousness*
>
> 2 *with brief [less than one hour] loss of consciousness*
>
> 3 *with moderate [1–24 hours] loss of consciousness*
>
> 4 *with prolonged [more than 24 hours] loss of consciousness and return to pre-existing conscious level*
>
> 5 *with prolonged [more than 24 hours] loss of consciousness, without return to pre-existing conscious level*
>
> *Use fifth-digit 5 to designate when a patient is unconscious and dies before regaining consciousness, regardless of the duration of the loss of consciousness*
>
> 6 *with loss of consciousness of unspecified duration*
>
> 9 *with concussion, unspecified*

- with
  - open intracranial wound 851.9 ☑
  - skull fracture — *see* Fracture, skull, by site
- cerebellum 851.4 ☑
  - with open intracranial wound 851.5 ☑
- cortex 851.0 ☑
  - with open intracranial wound 851.1 ☑
- occipital lobe 851.4 ☑
  - with open intracranial wound 851.5 ☑
- stem 851.4 ☑
  - with open intracranial wound 851.5 ☑

- **Contusion** — *continued*
  - breast 922.0
  - brow (and other part(s) of neck, scalp, or face, except eye) 920
  - buttock 922.32
  - canthus 921.1
  - cardiac 861.01
    - with open wound into thorax 861.11
  - cauda equina (spine) 952.4
  - cerebellum — *see* Contusion, brain, cerebellum
  - cerebral — *see* Contusion, brain
  - cheek(s) (and other part(s) of neck, scalp, or face, except eye) 920
  - chest (wall) 922.1
  - chin (and other part(s) of neck, scalp, or face, except eye) 920
  - clitoris 922.4
  - conjunctiva 921.1
  - conus medullaris (spine) 952.4
  - cornea 921.3
  - corpus cavernosum 922.4
  - cortex (brain) (cerebral) — *see* Contusion, brain, cortex
  - costal region 922.1
  - ear (and other part(s) of neck, scalp, or face except eye) 920
  - elbow 923.11
    - with forearm 923.10
  - epididymis 922.4
  - epigastric region 922.2
  - eye NEC 921.9
  - eyeball 921.3
  - eyelid(s) (and periocular area) 921.1
  - face (and neck, or scalp, any part, except eye) 920
  - femoral triangle 922.2
  - fetus or newborn 772.6
  - finger(s) (nail) (subungual) 923.3
  - flank 922.2
  - foot (with ankle) (excluding toe(s)) 924.20
  - forearm (and elbow) 923.10
  - forehead (and other part(s) of neck, scalp, or face, except eye) 920
  - genital organs, external 922.4
  - globe (eye) 921.3
  - groin 922.2
  - gum(s) (and other part(s) of neck, scalp, or face, except eye) 920
  - hand(s) (except fingers alone) 923.20
  - head (any part, except eye) (and face) (and neck) 920
  - heart — *see* Contusion, cardiac
  - heel 924.20
  - hip 924.01
    - with thigh 924.00
  - iliac region 922.2
  - inguinal region 922.2
  - internal organs (abdomen, chest, or pelvis) NEC — *see* Injury, internal, by site
  - interscapular region 922.33
  - iris (eye) 921.3
  - kidney 866.01
    - with open wound into cavity 866.11
  - knee 924.11
    - with lower leg 924.10
  - labium (majus) (minus) 922.4
  - lacrimal apparatus, gland, or sac 921.1
  - larynx (and other part(s) of neck, scalp, or face, except eye) 920
  - late effect — *see* Late, effects (of), contusion
  - leg 924.5
    - lower (with knee) 924.10
  - lens 921.3
  - lingual (and other part(s) of neck, scalp, or face, except eye) 920
  - lip(s) (and other part(s) of neck, scalp, or face, except eye) 920
  - liver 864.01
- **Contusion** — *continued*
  - liver — *continued*
    - with
      - laceration — *see* Laceration, liver
      - open wound into cavity 864.11
  - lower extremity 924.5
    - multiple sites 924.4
  - lumbar region 922.31
  - lung 861.21
    - with open wound into thorax 861.31
  - malar region (and other part(s) of neck, scalp, or face, except eye) 920
  - mandibular joint (and other part(s) of neck, scalp, or face, except eye) 920
  - mastoid region (and other part(s) of neck, scalp, or face, except eye) 920
  - membrane, brain — *see* Contusion, brain
  - midthoracic region 922.1
  - mouth (and other part(s) of neck, scalp, or face, except eye) 920
  - multiple sites (not classifiable to same three-digit category) 924.8
    - lower limb 924.4
    - trunk 922.8
    - upper limb 923.8
  - muscle NEC 924.9
  - myocardium — *see* Contusion, cardiac
  - nasal (septum) (and other part(s) of neck, scalp, or face, except eye) 920
  - neck (and scalp or face, any part, except eye) 920
  - nerve — *see* Injury, nerve, by site
  - nose (and other part(s) of neck, scalp, or face, except eye) 920
  - occipital region (scalp) (and neck or face, except eye) 920
    - lobe — *see* Contusion, brain, occipital lobe
  - orbit (region) (tissues) 921.2
  - palate (soft) (and other part(s) of neck, scalp, or face, except eye) 920
  - parietal region (scalp) (and neck, or face, except eye) 920
    - lobe — *see* Contusion, brain
  - penis 922.4
  - pericardium — *see* Contusion, cardiac
  - perineum 922.4
  - periocular area 921.1
  - pharynx (and other part(s) of neck, scalp, or face, except eye) 920
  - popliteal space (*see also* Contusion, knee) 924.11
  - prepuce 922.4
  - pubic region 922.4
  - pudenda 922.4
  - pulmonary — *see* Contusion, lung
  - quadriceps femoralis 924.00
  - rib cage 922.1
  - sacral region 922.32
  - salivary ducts or glands (and other part(s) of neck, scalp, or face, except eye) 920
  - scalp (and neck, or face any part, except eye) 920
  - scapular region 923.01
    - with shoulder or upper arm 923.09
  - sclera (eye) 921.3
  - scrotum 922.4
  - shoulder 923.00
    - with upper arm or axillar regions 923.09
  - skin NEC 924.9
  - skull 920
  - spermatic cord 922.4
  - spinal cord (*see also* Injury, spinal, by site)
    - cauda equina 952.4
    - conus medullaris 952.4
  - spleen 865.01

Cowpox — *continued*
- due to vaccination 999.0
- eyelid 051.0 *[373.5]*
  - postvaccination 999.0 *[373.5]*

Coxa
- plana 732.1
- valga (acquired) 736.31
  - congenital 755.61
  - late effect of rickets 268.1
- vara (acquired) 736.32
  - congenital 755.62
  - late effect of rickets 268.1

Coxae malum senilis 715.25

Coxalgia (nontuberculous) 719.45
- tuberculous (*see also* Tuberculosis) 015.1 ☑ *[730.85]*

Coxalgic pelvis 736.30

Coxitis 716.65

Coxsackie (infection) (virus) 079.2
- central nervous system NEC 048
- endocarditis 074.22
- enteritis 008.67
- meningitis (aseptic) 047.0
- myocarditis 074.23
- pericarditis 074.21
- pharyngitis 074.0
- pleurodynia 074.1
- specific disease NEC 074.8

Crabs, meaning pubic lice 132.2

Crack baby 760.75

Cracked ●
- nipple 611.2 ●
  - puerperal, postpartum 676.1 ☑ ●
- tooth 521.81 ●

Cradle cap 690.11

Craft neurosis 300.89

Craigiasis 007.8

Cramp(s) 729.82
- abdominal 789.0 ☑
- bathing 994.1
- colic 789.0 ☑
  - psychogenic 306.4
- due to immersion 994.1
- extremity (lower) (upper) NEC 729.82
- fireman 992.2
- heat 992.2
- hysterical 300.11
- immersion 994.1
- intestinal 789.0 ☑
  - psychogenic 306.4
- linotypist's 300.89
  - organic 333.84
- muscle (extremity) (general) 729.82
  - due to immersion 994.1
  - hysterical 300.11
- occupational (hand) 300.89
  - organic 333.84
- psychogenic 307.89
- salt depletion 276.1
- sleep related leg 327.52
- stoker 992.2
- stomach 789.0 ☑
- telegraphers' 300.89
  - organic 333.84
- typists' 300.89
  - organic 333.84
- uterus 625.8
  - menstrual 625.3
- writers' 333.84
  - organic 333.84
  - psychogenic 300.89

Cranial — *see* condition

Cranioclasis, fetal 763.89

Craniocleidodysostosis 755.59

Craniofenestria (skull) 756.0

Craniolacunia (skull) 756.0

Craniopagus 759.4

Craniopathy, metabolic 733.3

Craniopharyngeal — *see* condition

Craniopharyngioma (M9350/1) 237.0

Craniorachischisis (totalis) 740.1

Cranioschisis 756.0

Craniostenosis 756.0

Craniosynostosis 756.0

Craniotabes (cause unknown) 733.3
- rachitic 268.1

Craniotabes — *continued*
- syphilitic 090.5

Craniotomy, fetal 763.89

Cranium — *see* condition

Craw-craw 125.3

Creaking joint 719.60
- ankle 719.67
- elbow 719.62
- foot 719.67
- hand 719.64
- hip 719.65
- knee 719.66
- multiple sites 719.69
- pelvic region 719.65
- shoulder (region) 719.61
- specified site NEC 719.68
- wrist 719.63

Creeping
- eruption 126.9
- palsy 335.21
- paralysis 335.21

Crenated tongue 529.8

Creotoxism 005.9

Crepitus
- caput 756.0
- joint 719.60
  - ankle 719.67
  - elbow 719.62
  - foot 719.67
  - hand 719.64
  - hip 719.65
  - knee 719.66
  - multiple sites 719.69
  - pelvic region 719.65
  - shoulder (region) 719.61
  - specified site NEC 719.68
  - wrist 719.63

Crescent or conus choroid, congenital 743.57

Cretin, cretinism (athyrotic) (congenital) (endemic) (metabolic) (nongoitrous) (sporadic) 243
- goitrous (sporadic) 246.1
- pelvis (dwarf type) (male type) 243
  - with disproportion (fetopelvic) 653.1 ☑
    - affecting fetus or newborn 763.1
    - causing obstructed labor 660.1 ☑
      - affecting fetus or newborn 763.1
- pituitary 253.3

Cretinoid degeneration 243

Creutzfeldt-Jakob disease (syndrome) (new variant) 046.1
- with dementia
  - with behavioral disturbance 046.1 *[294.11]*
  - without behavioral disturbance 046.1 *[294.10]*

Crib death 798.0

Cribriform hymen 752.49

Cri-du-chat syndrome 758.31

Crigler-Najjar disease or syndrome (congenital hyperbilirubinemia) 277.4

Crimean hemorrhagic fever 065.0

Criminalism 301.7

Crisis
- abdomen 789.0 ☑
- addisonian (acute adrenocortical insufficiency) 255.4
- adrenal (cortical) 255.4
- asthmatic — *see* Asthma
- brain, cerebral (*see also* Disease, cerebrovascular, acute) 436
- celiac 579.0
- Dietl's 593.4
- emotional NEC 309.29
  - acute reaction to stress 308.0
  - adjustment reaction 309.9
  - specific to childhood or adolescence 313.9
- gastric (tabetic) 094.0
- glaucomatocyclitic 364.22
- heart (*see also* Failure, heart) 428.9

Crisis — *continued*
- hypertensive — *see* Hypertension
- nitritoid
  - correct substance properly administered 458.29
  - overdose or wrong substance given or taken 961.1
- oculogyric 378.87
  - psychogenic 306.7
- Pel's 094.0
- psychosexual identity 302.6
- rectum 094.0
- renal 593.81
- sickle cell 282.62
- stomach (tabetic) 094.0
- tabetic 094.0
- thyroid (*see also* Thyrotoxicosis) 242.9 ☑
- thyrotoxic (*see also* Thyrotoxicosis) 242.9 ☑
- vascular — *see* Disease, cerebrovascular, acute

Crocq's disease (acrocyanosis) 443.89

Crohn's disease — *see also* Enteritis, regional 555.9

Cronkhite-Canada syndrome 211.3

Crooked septum, nasal 470

Cross
- birth (of fetus) complicating delivery 652.3 ☑
  - with successful version 652.1 ☑
  - causing obstructed labor 660.0 ☑
- bite, anterior or posterior 524.27 ▲
- eye (*see also* Esotropia) 378.00

Crossed ectopia of kidney 753.3

Crossfoot 754.50

Croup, croupous (acute) (angina) (catarrhal) (infective) (inflammatory) (laryngeal) (membranous) (nondiphtheritic) (pseudomembranous) 464.4
- asthmatic (*see also* Asthma) 493.9 ☑
- bronchial 466.0
- diphtheritic (membranous) 032.3
- false 478.75
- spasmodic 478.75
  - diphtheritic 032.3
- stridulous 478.75
  - diphtheritic 032.3

Crouzon's disease (craniofacial dysostosis) 756.0

Crowding, teeth 524.31

CRST syndrome (cutaneous systemic sclerosis) 710.1

Cruchet's disease (encephalitis lethargica) 049.8

Cruelty in children — *see also* Disturbance, conduct 312.9

Crural ulcer — *see also* Ulcer, lower extremity 707.10

Crush, crushed, crushing (injury) 929.9
- with
  - fracture — *see* Fracture, by site
- abdomen 926.19
  - internal — *see* Injury, internal, abdomen
- ankle 928.21
  - with other parts of foot 928.20
- arm 927.9
  - lower (and elbow) 927.10
  - upper 927.03
    - with shoulder or axillary region 927.09
- axilla 927.02
  - with shoulder or upper arm 927.09
- back 926.11
- breast 926.19
- buttock 926.12
- cheek 925.1
- chest — *see* Injury, internal, chest
- ear 925.1
- elbow 927.11
  - with forearm 927.10
- face 925.1
- finger(s) 927.3
  - with hand(s) 927.20

Crush, crushed, crushing — *continued*
- finger(s) — *continued*
  - with hand(s) — *continued*
    - and wrist(s) 927.21
- flank 926.19
- foot, excluding toe(s) alone (with ankle) 928.20
- forearm (and elbow) 927.10
- genitalia, external (female) (male) 926.0
  - internal — *see* Injury, internal, genital organ NEC
- hand, except finger(s) alone (and wrist) 927.20
- head — *see* Fracture, skull, by site
- heel 928.20
- hip 928.01
  - with thigh 928.00
- internal organ (abdomen, chest, or pelvis) — *see* Injury, internal, by site
- knee 928.11
  - with leg, lower 928.10
- labium (majus) (minus) 926.0
- larynx 925.2
- late effect — *see* Late, effects (of), crushing
- leg 928.9
  - lower 928.10
    - and knee 928.11
  - upper 928.00
- limb
  - lower 928.9
    - multiple sites 928.8
  - upper 927.9
    - multiple sites 927.8
- multiple sites NEC 929.0
- neck 925.2
- nerve — *see* Injury, nerve, by site
- nose 802.0
  - open 802.1
- penis 926.0
- pharynx 925.2
- scalp 925.1
- scapular region 927.01
  - with shoulder or upper arm 927.09
- scrotum 926.0
- shoulder 927.00
  - with upper arm or axillary region 927.09
- skull or cranium — *see* Fracture, skull, by site
- spinal cord — *see* Injury, spinal, by site
- syndrome (complication of trauma) 958.5
- testis 926.0
- thigh (with hip) 928.00
- throat 925.2
- thumb(s) (and fingers) 927.3
- toe(s) 928.3
  - with foot 928.20
    - and ankle 928.21
- tonsil 925.2
- trunk 926.9
  - chest — *see* Injury, internal, intrathoracic organs NEC
  - internal organ — *see* Injury, internal, by site
  - multiple sites 926.8
  - specified site NEC 926.19
- vulva 926.0
- wrist 927.21
  - with hand(s), except fingers alone 927.20

Crusta lactea 690.11

Crusts 782.8

Crutch paralysis 953.4

Cruveilhier-Baumgarten cirrhosis, disease, or syndrome 571.5

Cruveilhier's disease 335.21

Cruz-Chagas disease — *see also* Trypanosomiasis 086.2

- **Crying** ●
  - constant, continuous ●
    - adolescent 780.95 ●
    - adult 780.95 ●
    - baby 780.92 ●
    - child 780.95 ●
    - infant 780.92 ●
    - newborn 780.92 ●
  - excessive ●
    - adolescent 780.95 ●
    - adult 780.95 ●
    - baby 780.92 ●
    - child 780.95 ●
    - infant 780.92 ●
    - newborn 780.92 ●
- **Cryoglobulinemia** (mixed) 273.2
- **Crypt** (anal) (rectal) 569.49
- **Cryptitis** (anal) (rectal) 569.49
- **Cryptococcosis** (European) (pulmonary) (systemic) 117.5
- **Cryptococcus** 117.5
  - epidermicus 117.5
  - neoformans, infection by 117.5
- **Cryptopapillitis** (anus) 569.49
- **Cryptophthalmos** (eyelid) 743.06
- **Cryptorchid, cryptorchism, cryptorchidism** 752.51
- **Cryptosporidiosis** 007.4
- **Cryptotia** 744.29
- **Crystallopathy**
  - calcium pyrophosphate (*see also* Arthritis) 275.49 *[712.2]* ☑
  - dicalcium phosphate (*see also* Arthritis) 275.49 *[712.1]* ☑
  - gouty 274.0
  - pyrophosphate NEC (*see also* Arthritis) 275.49 *[712.2]* ☑
  - uric acid 274.0
- **Crystalluria** 791.9
- **Csillag's disease** (lichen sclerosis et atrophicus) 701.0
- **Cuban itch** 050.1
- **Cubitus**
  - valgus (acquired) 736.01
    - congenital 755.59
    - late effect of rickets 268.1
  - varus (acquired) 736.02
    - congenital 755.59
    - late effect of rickets 268.1
- **Cultural deprivation** V62.4
- **Cupping of optic disc** 377.14
- **Curling esophagus** 530.5
- **Curling's ulcer** — *see* Ulcer, duodenum
- **Curschmann (-Batten) (-Steinert) disease or syndrome** 359.2
- **Curvature**
  - organ or site, congenital NEC — *see* Distortion
  - penis (lateral) 752.69
  - Pott's (spinal) (*see also* Tuberculosis) 015.0 ☑ *[737.43]*
  - radius, idiopathic, progressive (congenital) 755.54
  - spine (acquired) (angular) (idiopathic) (incorrect) (postural) 737.9
    - congenital 754.2
    - due to or associated with
      - Charcôt-Marie-Tooth disease 356.1 *[737.40]*
      - mucopolysaccharidosis 277.5 *[737.40]*
      - neurofibromatosis 237.71 *[737.40]*
      - osteitis
        - deformans 731.0 *[737.40]*
        - fibrosa cystica 252.01 *[737.40]*
      - osteoporosis (*see also* Osteoporosis) 733.00 *[737.40]*
      - poliomyelitis (*see also* Poliomyelitis) 138 *[737.40]*
      - tuberculosis (Pott's curvature) (*see also* Tuberculosis) 015.0 ☑ *[737.43]*
    - kyphoscoliotic (*see also* Kyphoscoliosis) 737.30
- **Curvature** — *continued*
  - spine — *continued*
    - kyphotic (*see also* Kyphosis) 737.10
    - late effect of rickets 268.1 *[737.40]*
    - Pott's 015.0 ☑ *[737.40]*
    - scoliotic (*see also* Scoliosis) 737.30
    - specified NEC 737.8
    - tuberculous 015.0 ☑ *[737.40]*
- **Cushing's**
  - basophilism, disease, or syndrome (iatrogenic) (idiopathic) (pituitary basophilism) (pituitary dependent) 255.0
  - ulcer — *see* Ulcer, peptic
- **Cushingoid due to steroid therapy**
  - correct substance properly administered 255.0
  - overdose or wrong substance given or taken 962.0
- **Cut** (external) — *see* Wound, open, by site
- **Cutaneous** — *see also* condition
  - hemorrhage 782.7
  - horn (cheek) (eyelid) (mouth) 702.8
  - larva migrans 126.9
- **Cutis** — *see also* condition
  - hyperelastic 756.83
    - acquired 701.8
  - laxa 756.83
    - senilis 701.8
  - marmorata 782.61
  - osteosis 709.3
  - pendula 756.83
    - acquired 701.8
  - rhomboidalis nuchae 701.8
  - verticis gyrata 757.39
    - acquired 701.8
- **Cyanopathy, newborn** 770.83
- **Cyanosis** 782.5
  - autotoxic 289.7
  - common atrioventricular canal 745.69
  - congenital 770.83
  - conjunctiva 372.71
  - due to
    - endocardial cushion defect 745.60
    - nonclosure, foramen botalli 745.5
    - patent foramen botalli 745.5
    - persistent foramen ovale 745.5
  - enterogenous 289.7
  - fetus or newborn 770.83
  - ostium primum defect 745.61
  - paroxysmal digital 443.0
  - retina, retinal 362.10
- **Cycle**
  - anovulatory 628.0
  - menstrual, irregular 626.4
- **Cyclencephaly** 759.89
- **Cyclical vomiting** 536.2
  - psychogenic 306.4
- **Cyclitic membrane** 364.74
- **Cyclitis** — *see also* Iridocyclitis 364.3
  - acute 364.00
    - primary 364.01
    - recurrent 364.02
  - chronic 364.10
    - in
      - sarcoidosis 135 *[364.11]*
      - tuberculosis (*see also* Tuberculosis) 017.3 ☑ *[364.11]*
  - Fuchs' heterochromic 364.21
  - granulomatous 364.10
  - lens induced 364.23
  - nongranulomatous 364.00
  - posterior 363.21
  - primary 364.01
  - recurrent 364.02
  - secondary (noninfectious) 364.04
    - infectious 364.03
  - subacute 364.00
    - primary 364.01
    - recurrent 364.02
- **Cyclokeratitis** — *see* Keratitis
- **Cyclophoria** 378.44
- **Cyclopia, cyclops** 759.89
- **Cycloplegia** 367.51
- **Cyclospasm** 367.53
- **Cyclosporiasis** 007.5
- **Cyclothymia** 301.13
- **Cyclothymic personality** 301.13
- **Cyclotropia** 378.33
- **Cyesis** — *see* Pregnancy
- **Cylindroma** (M8200/3) — *see also* Neoplasm, by site, malignant
  - eccrine dermal (M8200/0) — *see* Neoplasm, skin, benign
  - skin (M8200/0) — *see* Neoplasm, skin, benign
- **Cylindruria** 791.7
- **Cyllosoma** 759.89
- **Cynanche**
  - diphtheritic 032.3
  - tonsillaris 475
- **Cynorexia** 783.6
- **Cyphosis** — *see* Kyphosis
- **Cyprus fever** — *see also* Brucellosis 023.9
- **Cyriax's syndrome** (slipping rib) 733.99
- **Cyst** (mucus) (retention) (serous) (simple)

> *Note — In general, cysts are not neoplastic and are classified to the appropriate category for disease of the specified anatomical site. This generalization does not apply to certain types of cysts which are neoplastic in nature, for example, dermoid, nor does it apply to cysts of certain structures, for example, branchial cleft, which are classified as developmental anomalies.*
>
> *The following listing includes some of the most frequently reported sites of cysts as well as qualifiers which indicate the type of cyst. The latter qualifiers usually are not repeated under the anatomical sites. Since the code assignment for a given site may vary depending upon the type of cyst, the coder should refer to the listings under the specified type of cyst before consideration is given to the site.*

  - accessory, fallopian tube 752.11
  - adenoid (infected) 474.8
  - adrenal gland 255.8
    - congenital 759.1
  - air, lung 518.89
  - allantoic 753.7
  - alveolar process (jaw bone) 526.2
  - amnion, amniotic 658.8 ☑
  - anterior chamber (eye) 364.60
    - exudative 364.62
    - implantation (surgical) (traumatic) 364.61
    - parasitic 360.13
  - anterior nasopalatine 526.1
  - antrum 478.19 ▲
  - anus 569.49
  - apical (periodontal) (tooth) 522.8
  - appendix 543.9
  - arachnoid, brain 348.0
  - arytenoid 478.79
  - auricle 706.2
  - Baker's (knee) 727.51
    - tuberculous (*see also* Tuberculosis) 015.2 ☑
  - Bartholin's gland or duct 616.2
  - bile duct (*see also* Disease, biliary) 576.8
  - bladder (multiple) (trigone) 596.8
  - Blessig's 362.62
  - blood, endocardial (*see also* Endocarditis) 424.90
  - blue dome 610.0
  - bone (local) 733.20
    - aneurysmal 733.22
    - jaw 526.2
      - developmental (odontogenic) 526.0
      - fissural 526.1
      - latent 526.89
    - solitary 733.21
    - unicameral 733.21
- **Cyst** — *continued*
  - brain 348.0
    - congenital 742.4
    - hydatid (*see also* Echinococcus) 122.9
    - third ventricle (colloid) 742.4
  - branchial (cleft) 744.42
  - branchiogenic 744.42
  - breast (benign) (blue dome) (pedunculated) (solitary) (traumatic) 610.0
    - involution 610.4
    - sebaceous 610.8
  - broad ligament (benign) 620.8
    - embryonic 752.11
  - bronchogenic (mediastinal) (sequestration) 518.89
    - congenital 748.4
  - buccal 528.4
  - bulbourethral gland (Cowper's) 599.89
  - bursa, bursal 727.49
    - pharyngeal 478.26
  - calcifying odontogenic (M9301/0) 213.1
    - upper jaw (bone) 213.0
  - canal of Nuck (acquired) (serous) 629.1
    - congenital 752.41
  - canthus 372.75
  - carcinomatous (M8010/3) — *see* Neoplasm, by site, malignant
  - cartilage (joint) — *see* Derangement, joint
  - cauda equina 336.8
  - cavum septi pellucidi NEC 348.0
  - celomic (pericardium) 746.89
  - cerebellopontine (angle) — *see* Cyst, brain
  - cerebellum — *see* Cyst, brain
  - cerebral — *see* Cyst, brain
  - cervical lateral 744.42
  - cervix 622.8
    - embryonal 752.41
    - nabothian (gland) 616.0
  - chamber, anterior (eye) 364.60
    - exudative 364.62
    - implantation (surgical) (traumatic) 364.61
    - parasitic 360.13
  - chiasmal, optic NEC (*see also* Lesion, chiasmal) 377.54
  - chocolate (ovary) 617.1
  - choledochal (congenital) 751.69
    - acquired 576.8
  - choledochus 751.69
  - chorion 658.8 ☑
  - choroid plexus 348.0
  - chyle, mesentery 457.8
  - ciliary body 364.60
    - exudative 364.64
    - implantation 364.61
    - primary 364.63
  - clitoris 624.8
  - coccyx (*see also* Cyst, bone) 733.20
  - colloid
    - third ventricle (brain) 742.4
    - thyroid gland — *see* Goiter
  - colon 569.89
  - common (bile) duct (*see also* Disease, biliary) 576.8
  - congenital NEC 759.89
    - adrenal glands 759.1
    - epiglottis 748.3
    - esophagus 750.4
    - fallopian tube 752.11
    - kidney 753.10
      - multiple 753.19
      - single 753.11
    - larynx 748.3
    - liver 751.62
    - lung 748.4
    - mediastinum 748.8
    - ovary 752.0
    - oviduct 752.11
    - pancreas 751.7
    - periurethral (tissue) 753.8

D

- **Daae (-Finsen) disease** (epidemic pleurodynia) 074.1
- **Dabney's grip** 074.1
- **Da Costa's syndrome** (neurocirculatory asthenia) 306.2
- **Dacryoadenitis, dacryadenitis** 375.00
  - acute 375.01
  - chronic 375.02
- **Dacryocystitis** 375.30
  - acute 375.32
  - chronic 375.42
  - neonatal 771.6
  - phlegmonous 375.33
  - syphilitic 095.8
    - congenital 090.0
  - trachomatous, active 076.1
    - late effect 139.1
  - tuberculous (*see also* Tuberculosis) 017.3 ☑
- **Dacryocystoblenorrhea** 375.42
- **Dacryocystocele** 375.43
- **Dacryolith, dacryolithiasis** 375.57
- **Dacryoma** 375.43
- **Dacryopericystitis** (acute) (subacute) 375.32
  - chronic 375.42
- **Dacryops** 375.11
- **Dacryosialadenopathy, atrophic** 710.2
- **Dacryostenosis** 375.56
  - congenital 743.65
- **Dactylitis**
  - bone (*see also* Osteomyelitis) 730.2 ☑
  - sickle-cell 282.62 ▲
    - Hb-C 282.64 ●
    - Hb-SS 282.62 ●
    - specified NEC 282.69 ●
  - syphilitic 095.5
  - tuberculous (*see also* Tuberculosis) 015.5 ☑
- **Dactylolysis spontanea** 136.0
- **Dactylosymphysis** — *see also* Syndactylism 755.10
- **Damage**
  - arteriosclerotic — *see* Arteriosclerosis
  - brain 348.9
    - anoxic, hypoxic 348.1
      - during or resulting from a procedure 997.01
      - ischemic, in newborn 768.7 ●
    - child NEC 343.9
    - due to birth injury 767.0
    - minimal (child) (*see also* Hyperkinesia) 314.9
    - newborn 767.0
  - cardiac (*see also* Disease, heart)
  - cardiorenal (vascular) (*see also* Hypertension, cardiorenal) 404.90
  - central nervous system — *see* Damage, brain
  - cerebral NEC — *see* Damage, brain
  - coccyx, complicating delivery 665.6 ☑
  - coronary (*see also* Ischemia, heart) 414.9
  - eye, birth injury 767.8
  - heart (*see also* Disease, heart)
    - valve — *see* Endocarditis
  - hypothalamus NEC 348.9
  - liver 571.9
    - alcoholic 571.3
  - myocardium (*see also* Degeneration, myocardial) 429.1
  - pelvic
    - joint or ligament, during delivery 665.6 ☑
    - organ NEC
      - with
        - abortion — *see* Abortion, by type, with damage to pelvic organs
        - ectopic pregnancy (*see also* categories 633.0–633.9) 639.2

- **Damage** — *continued*
  - pelvic — *continued*
    - organ — *continued*
      - with — *continued*
        - molar pregnancy (*see also* categories 630–632) 639.2
      - during delivery 665.5 ☑
      - following
        - abortion 639.2
        - ectopic or molar pregnancy 639.2
  - renal (*see also* Disease, renal) 593.9
  - skin, solar 692.79
    - acute 692.72
    - chronic 692.74
  - subendocardium, subendocardial (*see also* Degeneration, myocardial) 429.1
  - vascular 459.9
- **Dameshek's syndrome** (erythroblastic anemia) 282.49
- **Dana-Putnam syndrome** (subacute combined sclerosis with pernicious anemia) 281.0 *[336.2]*
- **Danbolt (-Closs) syndrome** (acrodermatitis enteropathica) 686.8
- **Dandruff** 690.18
- **Dandy fever** 061
- **Dandy-Walker deformity or syndrome** (atresia, foramen of Magendie) 742.3
  - with spina bifida (*see also* Spina bifida) 741.0 ☑
- **Dangle foot** 736.79
- **Danielssen's disease** (anesthetic leprosy) 030.1
- **Danlos' syndrome** 756.83
- **Darier's disease** (congenital) (keratosis follicularis) 757.39
  - due to vitamin A deficiency 264.8
  - meaning erythema annulare centrifugum 695.0
- **Darier-Roussy sarcoid** 135
- **Darling's**
  - disease (*see also* Histoplasmosis, American) 115.00
  - histoplasmosis (*see also* Histoplasmosis, American) 115.00
- **Dartre** 054.9
- **Darwin's tubercle** 744.29
- **Davidson's anemia** (refractory) 284.9
- **Davies-Colley syndrome** (slipping rib) 733.99
- **Davies' disease** 425.0
- **Dawson's encephalitis** 046.2
- **Day blindness** — *see also* Blindness, day 368.60
- **Dead**
  - fetus
    - retained (in utero) 656.4 ☑
      - early pregnancy (death before 22 completed weeks gestation) 632
      - late (death after 22 completed weeks gestation) 656.4 ☑
    - syndrome 641.3 ☑
  - labyrinth 386.50
  - ovum, retained 631
- **Deaf and dumb** NEC 389.7
- **Deaf mutism** (acquired) (congenital) NEC 389.7
  - endemic 243
  - hysterical 300.11
  - syphilitic, congenital 090.0
- **Deafness** (acquired) (complete) (congenital) (hereditary) (middle ear) (partial) 389.9
  - with blue sclera and fragility of bone 756.51
  - auditory fatigue 389.9
  - aviation 993.0
    - nerve injury 951.5
  - boilermakers' 951.5
  - central, ▶bilateral◀ 389.14
    - with conductive hearing loss 389.2

- **Deafness** — *continued*
  - conductive (air) 389.00
    - with sensorineural hearing loss 389.2
    - combined types 389.08
    - external ear 389.01
    - inner ear 389.04
    - middle ear 389.03
    - multiple types 389.08
    - tympanic membrane 389.02
  - emotional (complete) 300.11
  - functional (complete) 300.11
  - high frequency 389.8
  - hysterical (complete) 300.11
  - injury 951.5
  - low frequency 389.8
  - mental 784.69
  - mixed conductive and sensorineural 389.2
  - nerve, ▶bilateral◀ 389.12
    - with conductive hearing loss 389.2
  - neural, ▶bilateral◀ 389.12
    - with conductive hearing loss 389.2
  - noise-induced 388.12
    - nerve injury 951.5
  - nonspeaking 389.7
  - perceptive 389.10
    - with conductive hearing loss 389.2
    - central, ▶bilateral◀ 389.14
    - combined types, ▶bilateral◀ 389.18
    - multiple types, ▶bilateral◀ 389.18
    - neural, ▶bilateral◀ 389.12
    - sensorineural 389.10 ●
      - asymmetrical 389.16 ●
      - bilateral 389.18 ●
      - unilateral 389.15 ●
    - sensory, ▶bilateral◀ 389.11
  - psychogenic (complete) 306.7
  - sensorineural (*see also* Deafness, perceptive) 389.10
    - asymmetrical 389.16 ●
    - bilateral 389.18 ●
    - unilateral 389.15 ●
  - sensory, ▶bilateral◀ 389.11
    - with conductive hearing loss 389.2
  - specified type NEC 389.8
  - sudden NEC 388.2
  - syphilitic 094.89
  - transient ischemic 388.02
  - transmission — *see* Deafness, conductive
  - traumatic 951.5
  - word (secondary to organic lesion) 784.69
    - developmental 315.31
- **Death**
  - after delivery (cause not stated) (sudden) 674.9 ☑
  - anesthetic
    - due to
      - correct substance properly administered 995.4
      - overdose or wrong substance given 968.4
        - specified anesthetic — *see* Table of Drugs and Chemicals
    - during delivery 668.9 ☑
  - brain 348.8
  - cardiac — *see* Disease, heart
  - cause unknown 798.2
  - cot (infant) 798.0
  - crib (infant) 798.0
  - fetus, fetal (cause not stated) (intrauterine) 779.9
    - early, with retention (before 22 completed weeks gestation) 632
    - from asphyxia or anoxia (before labor) 768.0
      - during labor 768.1
    - late, affecting management of pregnancy (after 22 completed weeks gestation) 656.4 ☑
  - from pregnancy NEC 646.9 ☑

- **Death** — *continued*
  - instantaneous 798.1
  - intrauterine (*see also* Death, fetus) 779.9
    - complicating pregnancy 656.4 ☑
  - maternal, affecting fetus or newborn 761.6
  - neonatal NEC 779.9
  - sudden (cause unknown) 798.1
    - during delivery 669.9 ☑
      - under anesthesia NEC 668.9 ☑
    - infant, syndrome (SIDS) 798.0
    - puerperal, during puerperium 674.9 ☑
  - unattended (cause unknown) 798.9
  - under anesthesia NEC
    - due to
      - correct substance properly administered 995.4
      - overdose or wrong substance given 968.4
        - specified anesthetic — *see* Table of Drugs and Chemicals
    - during delivery 668.9 ☑
  - violent 798.1
- **de Beurmann-Gougerot disease** (sporotrichosis) 117.1
- **Debility** (general) (infantile) (postinfectional) 799.3
  - with nutritional difficulty 269.9
  - congenital or neonatal NEC 779.9
  - nervous 300.5
  - old age 797
  - senile 797
- **Débove's disease** (splenomegaly) 789.2
- **Decalcification**
  - bone (*see also* Osteoporosis) 733.00
  - teeth 521.89 ▲
- **Decapitation** 874.9
  - fetal (to facilitate delivery) 763.89
- **Decapsulation, kidney** 593.89
- **Decay**
  - dental 521.00
  - senile 797
  - tooth, teeth 521.00
- **Decensus, uterus** — *see* Prolapse, uterus
- **Deciduitis** (acute)
  - with
    - abortion — *see* Abortion, by type, with sepsis
    - ectopic pregnancy (*see also* categories 633.0–633.9) 639.0
    - molar pregnancy (*see also* categories 630–632) 639.0
  - affecting fetus or newborn 760.8
  - following
    - abortion 639.0
    - ectopic or molar pregnancy 639.0
  - in pregnancy 646.6 ☑
  - puerperal, postpartum 670.0 ☑
- **Deciduoma malignum** (M9100/3) 181
- **Deciduous tooth** (retained) 520.6
- **Decline** (general) — *see also* Debility 799.3
- **Decompensation**
  - cardiac (acute) (chronic) (*see also* Disease, heart) 429.9
    - failure — *see* Failure, heart
  - cardiorenal (*see also* Hypertension, cardiorenal) 404.90
  - cardiovascular (*see also* Disease, cardiovascular) 429.2
  - heart (*see also* Disease, heart) 429.9
    - failure — *see* Failure, heart
  - hepatic 572.2
  - myocardial (acute) (chronic) (*see also* Disease, heart) 429.9
    - failure — *see* Failure, heart
  - respiratory 519.9
- **Decompression sickness** 993.3
- **Decrease, decreased**
  - blood
    - platelets (*see also* Thrombocytopenia) 287.5
    - pressure 796.3

☑ Additional Digit Required — Refer to the Tabular List for Digit Selection

Subterms under main terms may continue to next column or page

Degeneration, degenerative — *continued*
- nervous system 349.89
  - amyloid 277.39 *[357.4]* ▲
  - autonomic (*see also* Neuropathy, peripheral, autonomic) 337.9
  - fatty 349.89
  - peripheral autonomic NEC (*see also* Neuropathy, peripheral, autonomic) 337.9
- nipple 611.9
- nose 478.19 ▲
- oculoacousticocerebral, congenital (progressive) 743.8
- olivopontocerebellar (familial) (hereditary) 333.0
- osseous labyrinth 386.8
- ovary 620.8
  - cystic 620.2
  - microcystic 620.2
- pallidal, pigmentary (progressive) 333.0
- pancreas 577.8
  - tuberculous (*see also* Tuberculosis) 017.9 ☑
- papillary muscle 429.81
- paving stone 362.61
- penis 607.89
- peritoneum 568.89
- pigmentary (diffuse) (general)
  - localized — *see* Degeneration, by site
  - pallidal (progressive) 333.0
  - secondary 362.65
- pineal gland 259.8
- pituitary (gland) 253.8
- placenta (fatty) (fibrinoid) (fibroid) — *see* Placenta, abnormal
- popliteal fat pad 729.31
- posterolateral (spinal cord) (*see also* Degeneration, combined) 266.2 *[336.2]*
- pulmonary valve (heart) (*see also* Endocarditis, pulmonary) 424.3
- pulp (tooth) 522.2
- pupillary margin 364.54
- renal (*see also* Sclerosis, renal) 587
  - fibrocystic 753.19
  - polycystic 753.12
    - adult type (APKD) 753.13
    - autosomal dominant 753.13
    - autosomal recessive 753.14
    - childhood type (CPKD) 753.14
    - infantile type 753.14
- reticuloendothelial system 289.89
- retina (peripheral) 362.60
  - with retinal defect (*see also* Detachment, retina, with retinal defect) 361.00
  - cystic (senile) 362.50
  - cystoid 362.53
  - hereditary (*see also* Dystrophy, retina) 362.70
    - cerebroretinal 362.71
    - congenital 362.75
    - juvenile (Stargardt's) 362.75
    - macula 362.76
  - Kuhnt-Junius 362.52
  - lattice 362.63
  - macular (*see also* Degeneration, macula) 362.50
  - microcystoid 362.62
  - palisade 362.63
  - paving stone 362.61
  - pigmentary (primary) 362.74
    - secondary 362.65
  - posterior pole (*see also* Degeneration, macula) 362.50
  - secondary 362.66
  - senile 362.60
    - cystic 362.53
    - reticular 362.64
- saccule, congenital (causing impairment of hearing) 744.05
- sacculocochlear 386.8
- senile 797

Degeneration, degenerative — *continued*
- senile — *continued*
  - brain 331.2
  - cardiac, heart, or myocardium (*see also* Degeneration, myocardial) 429.1
  - motor centers 331.2
  - reticule 362.64
  - retina, cystic 362.50
  - vascular — *see* Arteriosclerosis
- silicone rubber poppet (prosthetic valve) 996.02
- sinus (cystic) (*see also* Sinusitis) 473.9
  - polypoid 471.1
- skin 709.3
  - amyloid 277.39 ▲
  - colloid 709.3
- spinal (cord) 336.8
  - amyloid 277.39 ▲
  - column 733.90
  - combined (subacute) (*see also* Degeneration, combined) 266.2 *[336.2]*
    - with anemia (pernicious) 281.0 *[336.2]*
  - dorsolateral (*see also* Degeneration, combined) 266.2 *[336.2]*
  - familial NEC 336.8
  - fatty 336.8
  - funicular (*see also* Degeneration, combined) 266.2 *[336.2]*
  - heredofamilial NEC 336.8
  - posterolateral (*see also* Degeneration, combined) 266.2 *[336.2]*
  - subacute combined — *see* Degeneration, combined
  - tuberculous (*see also* Tuberculosis) 013.8 ☑
- spine 733.90
- spleen 289.59
  - amyloid 277.39 ▲
  - lardaceous 277.39 ▲
- stomach 537.89
  - lardaceous 277.39 ▲
- strionigral 333.0
- sudoriparous (cystic) 705.89
- suprarenal (capsule) (gland) 255.8
  - with hypofunction 255.4
- sweat gland 705.89
- synovial membrane (pulpy) 727.9
- tapetoretinal 362.74
  - adult or presenile form 362.50
- testis (postinfectional) 608.89
- thymus (gland) 254.8
  - fatty 254.8
  - lardaceous 277.39 ▲
- thyroid (gland) 246.8
- tricuspid (heart) (valve) — *see* Endocarditis, tricuspid
- tuberculous NEC (*see also* Tuberculosis) 011.9 ☑
- turbinate 733.90
- uterus 621.8
  - cystic 621.8
- vascular (senile) (*see also* Arteriosclerosis)
  - hypertensive — *see* Hypertension
- vitreoretinal (primary) 362.73
  - secondary 362.66
- vitreous humor (with infiltration) 379.21
- wallerian NEC — *see* Disorder, nerve
- waxy (any site) 277.39 ▲
- Wilson's hepatolenticular 275.1

Deglutition
- paralysis 784.99 ▲
  - hysterical 300.11
- pneumonia 507.0

Degos' disease or syndrome 447.8

Degradation disorder, branched-chain amino acid 270.3

Dehiscence
- anastomosis — *see* Complications, anastomosis
- cesarean wound 674.1 ☑

Dehiscence — *continued*
- episiotomy 674.2 ☑
- operation wound 998.32
  - internal 998.31
- perineal wound (postpartum) 674.2 ☑
- postoperative 998.32
  - abdomen 998.32
    - internal 998.31
  - internal 998.31
- uterine wound 674.1 ☑

Dehydration (cachexia) 276.51
- with
  - hypernatremia 276.0
  - hyponatremia 276.1
- newborn 775.5

Deiters' nucleus syndrome 386.19

Déjérine's disease 356.0

Déjérine-Klumpke paralysis 767.6

Déjérine-Roussy syndrome 338.0 ▲

Déjérine-Sottas disease or neuropathy (hypertrophic) 356.0

Déjérine-Thomas atrophy or syndrome 333.0

de Lange's syndrome (Amsterdam dwarf, mental retardation, and brachycephaly) 759.89

Delay, delayed
- adaptation, cones or rods 368.63
- any plane in pelvis
  - affecting fetus or newborn 763.1
  - complicating delivery 660.1 ☑
- birth or delivery NEC 662.1 ☑
  - affecting fetus or newborn 763.89
  - second twin, triplet, or multiple mate 662.3 ☑
- closure (*see also* Fistula)
  - cranial suture 756.0
  - fontanel 756.0
- coagulation NEC 790.92
- conduction (cardiac) (ventricular) 426.9
- delivery NEC 662.1 ☑
  - second twin, triplet, etc. 662.3 ☑
    - affecting fetus or newborn 763.89
- development
  - in childhood 783.40
    - physiological 783.40
  - intellectual NEC 315.9
  - learning NEC 315.2
  - reading 315.00
  - sexual 259.0
  - speech 315.39
    - associated with hyperkinesis 314.1
  - spelling 315.09
- gastric emptying 536.8
- menarche 256.39
  - due to pituitary hypofunction 253.4
- menstruation (cause unknown) 626.8
- milestone in childhood 783.42
- motility — *see* Hypomotility
- passage of meconium (newborn) 777.1
- primary respiration 768.9
- puberty 259.0
- separation of umbilical cord 779.83
- sexual maturation, female 259.0

Del Castillo's syndrome (germinal aplasia) 606.0

Déleage's disease 359.89

Deletion syndrome
- 5p 758.31
- 22q11.2 758.32
- autosomal NEC 758.39
- constitutional 5q deletion 758.39 ●

Delhi (boil) (button) (sore) 085.1

Delinquency (juvenile) 312.9
- group (*see also* Disturbance, conduct) 312.2 ☑
- neurotic 312.4

Delirium, delirious 780.09
- acute (psychotic) 293.0
- alcoholic 291.0
  - acute 291.0
  - chronic 291.1

Delirium, delirious — *continued*
- alcoholicum 291.0
- chronic (*see also* Psychosis) 293.89
  - due to or associated with physical condition — *see* Psychosis, organic
- drug-induced 292.81
- due to conditions classified elsewhere 293.0
- eclamptic (*see also* Eclampsia) 780.39
- exhaustion (*see also* Reaction, stress, acute) 308.9
- hysterical 300.11
- in
  - presenile dementia 290.11
  - senile dementia 290.3
- induced by drug 292.81
- manic, maniacal (acute) (*see also* Psychosis, affective) 296.0 ☑
  - recurrent episode 296.1 ☑
  - single episode 296.0 ☑
- puerperal 293.9
- senile 290.3
- subacute (psychotic) 293.1
- thyroid (*see also* Thyrotoxicosis) 242.9 ☑
- traumatic (*see also* Injury, intracranial)
  - with
    - lesion, spinal cord — *see* Injury, spinal, by site
    - shock, spinal — *see* Injury, spinal, by site
- tremens (impending) 291.0
- uremic — *see* Uremia
- withdrawal
  - alcoholic (acute) 291.0
    - chronic 291.1
  - drug 292.0

Delivery

> *Note — Use the following fifth-digit subclassification with categories 640–648, 651–676:*
>
> 0 *unspecified as to episode of care*
>
> 1 *delivered, with or without mention of antepartum condition*
>
> 2 *delivered, with mention of postpartum complication*
>
> 3 *antepartum condition or complication*
>
> 4 *postpartum condition or complication*

- breech (assisted) (buttocks) (complete) (frank) (spontaneous) 652.2 ☑
  - affecting fetus or newborn 763.0
  - extraction NEC 669.6 ☑
- cesarean (for) 669.7 ☑
  - abnormal
    - cervix 654.6 ☑
    - pelvic organs or tissues 654.9 ☑
    - pelvis (bony) (major) NEC 653.0 ☑
    - presentation or position 652.9 ☑
      - in multiple gestation 652.6 ☑
    - size, fetus 653.5 ☑
    - soft parts (of pelvis) 654.9 ☑
    - uterus, congenital 654.0 ☑
    - vagina 654.7 ☑
    - vulva 654.8 ☑
  - abruptio placentae 641.2 ☑
  - acromion presentation 652.8 ☑
  - affecting fetus or newborn 763.4
  - anteversion, cervix or uterus 654.4 ☑
  - atony, uterus, ▶with hemorrhage◀ 666.1 ☑
  - bicornis or bicornuate uterus 654.0 ☑
  - breech presentation (buttocks) (complete) (frank) 652.2 ☑
  - brow presentation 652.4 ☑

Delivery — *continued*
- cesarean — *continued*
  - cephalopelvic disproportion (normally formed fetus) 653.4 ☑
  - chin presentation 652.4 ☑
  - cicatrix of cervix 654.6 ☑
  - contracted pelvis (general) 653.1 ☑
    - inlet 653.2 ☑
    - outlet 653.3 ☑
  - cord presentation or prolapse 663.0 ☑
  - cystocele 654.4 ☑
  - deformity (acquired) (congenital)
    - pelvic organs or tissues NEC 654.9 ☑
    - pelvis (bony) NEC 653.0 ☑
  - displacement, uterus NEC 654.4 ☑
  - disproportion NEC 653.9 ☑
  - distress
    - fetal 656.8 ☑
    - maternal 669.0 ☑
  - eclampsia 642.6 ☑
  - face presentation 652.4 ☑
  - failed
    - forceps 660.7 ☑
    - trial of labor NEC 660.6 ☑
    - vacuum extraction 660.7 ☑
    - ventouse 660.7 ☑
  - fetal deformity 653.7 ☑
  - fetal-maternal hemorrhage 656.0 ☑
  - fetus, fetal
    - distress 656.8 ☑
    - prematurity 656.8 ☑
  - fibroid (tumor) (uterus) 654.1 ☑
  - footling 652.8 ☑
    - with successful version 652.1 ☑
  - hemorrhage (antepartum) (intrapartum) NEC 641.9 ☑
  - hydrocephalic fetus 653.6 ☑
  - incarceration of uterus 654.3 ☑
  - incoordinate uterine action 661.4 ☑
  - inertia, uterus 661.2 ☑
    - primary 661.0 ☑
    - secondary 661.1 ☑
  - lateroversion, uterus or cervix 654.4 ☑
  - mal lie 652.9 ☑
  - malposition
    - fetus 652.9 ☑
      - in multiple gestation 652.6 ☑
    - pelvic organs or tissues NEC 654.9 ☑
    - uterus NEC or cervix 654.4 ☑
  - malpresentation NEC 652.9 ☑
    - in multiple gestation 652.6 ☑
  - maternal
    - diabetes mellitus 648.0 ☑
    - heart disease NEC 648.6 ☑
  - meconium in liquor 656.8 ☑
    - staining only 792.3
  - oblique presentation 652.3 ☑
  - oversize fetus 653.5 ☑
  - pelvic tumor NEC 654.9 ☑
  - placental insufficiency 656.5 ☑
  - placenta previa 641.0 ☑
    - with hemorrhage 641.1 ☑
  - poor dilation, cervix 661.0 ☑
  - pre-eclampsia 642.4 ☑
    - severe 642.5 ☑
  - previous
    - cesarean delivery, section 654.2 ☑
    - surgery (to)
      - cervix 654.6 ☑
      - gynecological NEC 654.9 ☑
      - rectum 654.8 ☑
      - uterus NEC 654.9 ☑
        - previous cesarean delivery, section 654.2 ☑
      - vagina 654.7 ☑
  - prolapse
    - arm or hand 652.7 ☑

Delivery — *continued*
- cesarean — *continued*
  - prolapse — *continued*
    - uterus 654.4 ☑
  - prolonged labor 662.1 ☑
  - rectocele 654.4 ☑
  - retroversion, uterus or cervix 654.3 ☑
  - rigid
    - cervix 654.6 ☑
    - pelvic floor 654.4 ☑
    - perineum 654.8 ☑
    - vagina 654.7 ☑
    - vulva 654.8 ☑
  - sacculation, pregnant uterus 654.4 ☑
  - scar(s)
    - cervix 654.6 ☑
    - cesarean delivery, section 654.2 ☑
    - uterus NEC 654.9 ☑
      - due to previous cesarean delivery, section 654.2 ☑
  - Shirodkar suture in situ 654.5 ☑
  - shoulder presentation 652.8 ☑
  - stenosis or stricture, cervix 654.6 ☑
  - transverse presentation or lie 652.3 ☑
  - tumor, pelvic organs or tissues NEC 654.4 ☑
  - umbilical cord presentation or prolapse 663.0 ☑
- completely normal case — *see* category 650
- complicated (by) NEC 669.9 ☑
  - abdominal tumor, fetal 653.7 ☑
    - causing obstructed labor 660.1 ☑
  - abnormal, abnormality of
    - cervix 654.6 ☑
      - causing obstructed labor 660.2 ☑
    - forces of labor 661.9 ☑
    - formation of uterus 654.0 ☑
    - pelvic organs or tissues 654.9 ☑
      - causing obstructed labor 660.2 ☑
    - pelvis (bony) (major) NEC 653.0 ☑
      - causing obstructed labor 660.1 ☑
    - presentation or position NEC 652.9 ☑
      - causing obstructed labor 660.0 ☑
    - size, fetus 653.5 ☑
      - causing obstructed labor 660.1 ☑
    - soft parts (of pelvis) 654.9 ☑
      - causing obstructed labor 660.2 ☑
    - uterine contractions NEC 661.9 ☑
    - uterus (formation) 654.0 ☑
      - causing obstructed labor 660.2 ☑
    - vagina 654.7 ☑
      - causing obstructed labor 660.2 ☑
  - abnormally formed uterus (any type) (congenital) 654.0 ☑
    - causing obstructed labor 660.2 ☑
  - acromion presentation 652.8 ☑
    - causing obstructed labor 660.0 ☑
  - adherent placenta 667.0 ☑
    - with hemorrhage 666.0 ☑
  - adhesions, uterus (to abdominal wall) 654.4 ☑
  - advanced maternal age NEC 659.6 ☑
    - multigravida 659.6 ☑
    - primigravida 659.5 ☑

Delivery — *continued*
- complicated — *continued*
  - air embolism 673.0 ☑
  - amnionitis 658.4 ☑
  - amniotic fluid embolism 673.1 ☑
  - anesthetic death 668.9 ☑
  - annular detachment, cervix 665.3 ☑
  - antepartum hemorrhage — *see* Delivery, complicated, hemorrhage
  - anteversion, cervix or uterus 654.4 ☑
    - causing obstructed labor 660.2 ☑
  - apoplexy 674.0 ☑
    - placenta 641.2 ☑
  - arrested active phase 661.1 ☑
  - asymmetrical pelvis bone 653.0 ☑
    - causing obstructed labor 660.1 ☑
  - atony, uterus ▶with hemorrhage◀ (hypotonic) (inertia) 666.1 ☑
    - hypertonic 661.4 ☑
  - Bandl's ring 661.4 ☑
  - battledore placenta — *see* Placenta, abnormal
  - bicornis or bicornuate uterus 654.0 ☑
    - causing obstructed labor 660.2 ☑
  - birth injury to mother NEC 665.9 ☑
  - bleeding (*see also* Delivery, complicated, hemorrhage) 641.9 ☑
  - breech presentation (assisted) (buttocks) (complete) (frank) (spontaneous) 652.2 ☑
    - with successful version 652.1 ☑
  - brow presentation 652.4 ☑
  - cephalopelvic disproportion (normally formed fetus) 653.4 ☑
    - causing obstructed labor 660.1 ☑
  - cerebral hemorrhage 674.0 ☑
  - cervical dystocia 661.0 ☑
  - chin presentation 652.4 ☑
    - causing obstructed labor 660.0 ☑
  - cicatrix
    - cervix 654.6 ☑
      - causing obstructed labor 660.2 ☑
    - vagina 654.7 ☑
      - causing obstructed labor 660.2 ☑
  - coagulation defect 649.3 ☑ ●
  - colporrhexis 665.4 ☑
    - with perineal laceration 664.0 ☑
  - compound presentation 652.8 ☑
    - causing obstructed labor 660.0 ☑
  - compression of cord (umbilical) 663.2 ☑
    - around neck 663.1 ☑
    - cord prolapsed 663.0 ☑
  - contraction, contracted pelvis 653.1 ☑
    - causing obstructed labor 660.1 ☑
    - general 653.1 ☑
      - causing obstructed labor 660.1 ☑
    - inlet 653.2 ☑
      - causing obstructed labor 660.1 ☑
    - midpelvic 653.8 ☑
      - causing obstructed labor 660.1 ☑
    - midplane 653.8 ☑
      - causing obstructed labor 660.1 ☑
    - outlet 653.3 ☑
      - causing obstructed labor 660.1 ☑

Delivery — *continued*
- complicated — *continued*
  - contraction ring 661.4 ☑
  - cord (umbilical) 663.9 ☑
    - around neck, tightly or with compression 663.1 ☑
      - without compression 663.3 ☑
    - bruising 663.6 ☑
    - complication NEC 663.9 ☑
      - specified type NEC 663.8 ☑
    - compression NEC 663.2 ☑
    - entanglement NEC 663.3 ☑
      - with compression 663.2 ☑
    - forelying 663.0 ☑
    - hematoma 663.6 ☑
    - marginal attachment 663.8 ☑
    - presentation 663.0 ☑
    - prolapse (complete) (occult) (partial) 663.0 ☑
    - short 663.4 ☑
    - specified complication NEC 663.8 ☑
    - thrombosis (vessels) 663.6 ☑
    - vascular lesion 663.6 ☑
    - velamentous insertion 663.8 ☑
  - Couvelaire uterus 641.2 ☑
  - cretin pelvis (dwarf type) (male type) 653.1 ☑
    - causing obstructed labor 660.1 ☑
  - crossbirth 652.3 ☑
    - with successful version 652.1 ☑
    - causing obstructed labor 660.0 ☑
  - cyst (Gartner's duct) 654.7 ☑
  - cystocele 654.4 ☑
    - causing obstructed labor 660.2 ☑
  - death of fetus (near term) 656.4 ☑
    - early (before 22 completed weeks gestation) 632
  - deformity (acquired) (congenital)
    - fetus 653.7 ☑
      - causing obstructed labor 660.1 ☑
    - pelvic organs or tissues NEC 654.9 ☑
      - causing obstructed labor 660.2 ☑
    - pelvis (bony) NEC 653.0 ☑
      - causing obstructed labor 660.1 ☑
  - delay, delayed
    - delivery in multiple pregnancy 662.3 ☑
      - due to locked mates 660.5 ☑
    - following rupture of membranes (spontaneous) 658.2 ☑
      - artificial 658.3 ☑
  - depressed fetal heart tones 659.7 ☑
  - diastasis recti 665.8 ☑
  - dilatation
    - bladder 654.4 ☑
      - causing obstructed labor 660.2 ☑
    - cervix, incomplete, poor or slow 661.0 ☑
  - diseased placenta 656.7 ☑
  - displacement uterus NEC 654.4 ☑
    - causing obstructed labor 660.2 ☑
  - disproportion NEC 653.9 ☑
    - causing obstructed labor 660.1 ☑
  - disruptio uteri — *see* Delivery, complicated, rupture, uterus
  - distress
    - fetal 656.8 ☑
    - maternal 669.0 ☑
  - double uterus (congenital) 654.0 ☑
    - causing obstructed labor 660.2 ☑
  - dropsy amnion 657.0 ☑

Note — Use the following fifth-digit subclassification with category 304:

0	*unspecified*
1	*continuous*
2	*episodic*
3	*in remission*

- **Dependence** — *continued*
  - Pernoston 304.1 ☑
  - peronine 304.0 ☑
  - pethidine (hydrochloride) 304.0 ☑
  - petrichloral 304.1 ☑
  - peyote 304.5 ☑
  - Phanodron 304.1 ☑
  - phenacetin 304.6 ☑
  - phenadoxone 304.0 ☑
  - phenaglycodol 304.1 ☑
  - phenazocine 304.0 ☑
  - phencyclidine 304.6 ☑
  - phenmetrazine 304.4 ☑
  - phenobal 304.1 ☑
  - phenobarbital 304.1 ☑
  - phenobarbitone 304.1 ☑
  - phenomorphan 304.0 ☑
  - phenonyl 304.1 ☑
  - phenoperidine 304.0 ☑
  - pholcodine 304.0 ☑
  - piminodine 304.0 ☑
  - Pipadone 304.0 ☑
  - Pitkin's solution 304.6 ☑
  - Placidyl 304.1 ☑
  - polysubstance 304.8 ☑
  - Pontocaine 304.6 ☑
  - pot 304.3 ☑
  - potassium bromide 304.1 ☑
  - Preludin 304.4 ☑
  - Prinadol 304.0 ☑
  - probarbital 304.1 ☑
  - procaine 304.6 ☑
  - propanal 304.1 ☑
  - propoxyphene 304.6 ☑
  - psilocibin 304.5 ☑
  - psilocin 304.5 ☑
  - psilocybin 304.5 ☑
  - psilocyline 304.5 ☑
  - psilocyn 304.5 ☑
  - psychedelic agents 304.5 ☑
  - psychostimulant NEC 304.4 ☑
  - psychotomimetic agents 304.5 ☑
  - pyrahexyl 304.3 ☑
  - Pyramidon 304.6 ☑
  - quinalbarbitone 304.1 ☑
  - racemoramide 304.0 ☑
  - racemorphan 304.0 ☑
  - Rela 304.6 ☑
  - scopolamine 304.6 ☑
  - secobarbital 304.1 ☑
  - Seconal 304.1 ☑
  - sedative NEC 304.1 ☑
    - nonbarbiturate with barbiturate effect 304.1 ☑
  - Sedormid 304.1 ☑
  - sernyl 304.1 ☑
  - sodium bromide 304.1 ☑
  - Soma 304.6 ☑
  - Somnal 304.1 ☑
  - Somnos 304.1 ☑
  - Soneryl 304.1 ☑
  - soporific (drug) NEC 304.1 ☑
  - specified drug NEC 304.6 ☑
  - speed 304.4 ☑
  - spinocaine 304.6 ☑
  - Stovaine 304.6 ☑
  - STP 304.5 ☑
  - stramonium 304.6 ☑
  - Sulfonal 304.1 ☑
  - sulfonethylmethane 304.1 ☑
  - sulfonmethane 304.1 ☑
  - Surital 304.1 ☑
  - synthetic drug with morphine-like effect 304.0 ☑
  - talbutal 304.1 ☑
  - tetracaine 304.6 ☑
  - tetrahydrocannabinol 304.3 ☑
  - tetronal 304.1 ☑
  - THC 304.3 ☑
  - thebacon 304.0 ☑
  - thebaine 304.0 ☑
  - thiamil 304.1 ☑
  - thiamylal 304.1 ☑
  - thiopental 304.1 ☑
- **Dependence** — *continued*
  - tobacco 305.1
  - toluene, toluol 304.6 ☑
  - tranquilizer NEC 304.1 ☑
    - nonbarbiturate with barbiturate effect 304.1 ☑
  - tribromacetaldehyde 304.6 ☑
  - tribromethanol 304.6 ☑
  - tribromomethane 304.6 ☑
  - trichloroethanol 304.6 ☑
  - trichoroethyl phosphate 304.1 ☑
  - triclofos 304.1 ☑
  - Trional 304.1 ☑
  - Tuinal 304.1 ☑
  - Turkish Green 304.3 ☑
  - urethan(e) 304.6 ☑
  - Valium 304.1 ☑
  - Valmid 304.1 ☑
  - veganin 304.0 ☑
  - veramon 304.1 ☑
  - Veronal 304.1 ☑
  - versidyne 304.6 ☑
  - vinbarbital 304.1 ☑
  - vinbarbitone 304.1 ☑
  - vinyl bitone 304.1 ☑
  - vitamin B_6 266.1
  - wine 303.9 ☑
  - Zactane 304.6 ☑
- **Dependency**
  - passive 301.6
  - reactions 301.6
- **Depersonalization** (episode, in neurotic state) (neurotic) (syndrome) 300.6
- **Depletion**
  - carbohydrates 271.9
  - complement factor 279.8
  - extracellular fluid 276.52
  - plasma 276.52
  - potassium 276.8
    - nephropathy 588.89
  - salt or sodium 276.1
    - causing heat exhaustion or prostration 992.4
    - nephropathy 593.9
  - volume 276.50
    - extracellular fluid 276.52
    - plasma 276.52
- **Deposit**
  - argentous, cornea 371.16
  - bone, in Boeck's sarcoid 135
  - calcareous, calcium — *see* Calcification
  - cholesterol
    - retina 362.82
    - skin 709.3
    - vitreous (humor) 379.22
  - conjunctival 372.56
  - cornea, corneal NEC 371.10
    - argentous 371.16
    - in
      - cystinosis 270.0 *[371.15]*
      - mucopolysaccharidosis 277.5 *[371.15]*
  - crystalline, vitreous (humor) 379.22
  - hemosiderin, in old scars of cornea 371.11
  - metallic, in lens 366.45
  - skin 709.3
  - teeth, tooth (betel) (black) (green) (materia alba) (orange) (soft) (tobacco) 523.6
  - urate, in kidney (*see also* Disease, renal) 593.9
- **Depraved appetite** 307.52
- **Depression** 311
  - acute (*see also* Psychosis, affective) 296.2 ☑
    - recurrent episode 296.3 ☑
    - single episode 296.2 ☑
  - agitated (*see also* Psychosis, affective) 296.2 ☑
    - recurrent episode 296.3 ☑
    - single episode 296.2 ☑
  - anaclitic 309.21
  - anxiety 300.4
- **Depression** — *continued*
  - arches 734
    - congenital 754.61
  - autogenous (*see also* Psychosis, affective) 296.2 ☑
    - recurrent episode 296.3 ☑
    - single episode 296.2 ☑
  - basal metabolic rate (BMR) 794.7
  - bone marrow 289.9
  - central nervous system 799.1
    - newborn 779.2
  - cerebral 331.9
    - newborn 779.2
  - cerebrovascular 437.8
    - newborn 779.2
  - chest wall 738.3
  - endogenous (*see also* Psychosis, affective) 296.2 ☑
    - recurrent episode 296.3 ☑
    - single episode 296.2 ☑
  - functional activity 780.99
  - hysterical 300.11
  - involutional, climacteric, or menopausal (*see also* Psychosis, affective) 296.2 ☑
    - recurrent episode 296.3 ☑
    - single episode 296.2 ☑
  - manic (*see also* Psychosis, affective) 296.80
  - medullary 348.8
    - newborn 779.2
  - mental 300.4
  - metatarsal heads — *see* Depression, arches
  - metatarsus — *see* Depression, arches
  - monopolar (*see also* Psychosis, affective) 296.2 ☑
    - recurrent episode 296.3 ☑
    - single episode 296.2 ☑
  - nervous 300.4
  - neurotic 300.4
  - nose 738.0
  - postpartum 648.4 ☑
  - psychogenic 300.4
    - reactive 298.0
  - psychoneurotic 300.4
  - psychotic (*see also* Psychosis, affective) 296.2 ☑
    - reactive 298.0
    - recurrent episode 296.3 ☑
    - single episode 296.2 ☑
  - reactive 300.4
    - neurotic 300.4
    - psychogenic 298.0
    - psychoneurotic 300.4
    - psychotic 298.0
  - recurrent 296.3 ☑
  - respiratory center 348.8
    - newborn 770.89
  - scapula 736.89
  - senile 290.21
  - situational (acute) (brief) 309.0
    - prolonged 309.1
  - skull 754.0
  - sternum 738.3
  - visual field 368.40
- **Depressive reaction** — *see also* Reaction, depressive
  - acute (transient) 309.0
    - with anxiety 309.28
  - prolonged 309.1
  - situational (acute) 309.0
    - prolonged 309.1
- **Deprivation**
  - cultural V62.4
  - emotional V62.89
    - affecting
      - adult 995.82
      - infant or child 995.51
  - food 994.2
    - specific substance NEC 269.8
  - protein (familial) (kwashiorkor) 260
  - sleep V69.4
  - social V62.4
    - affecting
      - adult 995.82
- **Deprivation** — *continued*
  - social — *continued*
    - affecting — *continued*
      - infant or child 995.51
  - symptoms, syndrome
    - alcohol 291.81
    - drug 292.0
  - vitamins (*see also* Deficiency, vitamin) 269.2
  - water 994.3
- **de Quervain's**
  - disease (tendon sheath) 727.04
  - thyroiditis (subacute granulomatous thyroiditis) 245.1
- **Derangement**
  - ankle (internal) 718.97
    - current injury (*see also* Dislocation, ankle) 837.0
    - recurrent 718.37
  - cartilage (articular) NEC (*see also* Disorder, cartilage, articular) 718.0 ☑
    - knee 717.9
      - recurrent 718.36
    - recurrent 718.3 ☑
  - collateral ligament (knee) (medial) (tibial) 717.82
    - current injury 844.1
      - lateral (fibular) 844.0
    - lateral (fibular) 717.81
      - current injury 844.0
  - cruciate ligament (knee) (posterior) 717.84
    - anterior 717.83
      - current injury 844.2
    - current injury 844.2
  - elbow (internal) 718.92
    - current injury (*see also* Dislocation, elbow) 832.00
    - recurrent 718.32
  - gastrointestinal 536.9
  - heart — *see* Disease, heart
  - hip (joint) (internal) (old) 718.95
    - current injury (*see also* Dislocation, hip) 835.00
    - recurrent 718.35
  - intervertebral disc — *see* Displacement, intervertebral disc
  - joint (internal) 718.90
    - ankle 718.97
    - current injury (*see also* Dislocation, by site)
      - knee, meniscus or cartilage (*see also* Tear, meniscus) 836.2
    - elbow 718.92
    - foot 718.97
    - hand 718.94
    - hip 718.95
    - knee 717.9
    - multiple sites 718.99
    - pelvic region 718.95
    - recurrent 718.30
      - ankle 718.37
      - elbow 718.32
      - foot 718.37
      - hand 718.34
      - hip 718.35
      - knee 718.36
      - multiple sites 718.39
      - pelvic region 718.35
      - shoulder (region) 718.31
      - specified site NEC 718.38
      - temporomandibular (old) 524.69
      - wrist 718.33
    - shoulder (region) 718.91
    - specified site NEC 718.98
    - spine NEC 724.9
    - temporomandibular 524.69
    - wrist 718.93
  - knee (cartilage) (internal) 717.9
    - current injury (*see also* Tear, meniscus) 836.2
    - ligament 717.89
      - capsular 717.85

Dermatitis — *continued*
- eyelid — *continued*
  - infective — *continued*
    - due to — *continued*
      - leprosy (*see also* Leprosy) 030.0 *[373.4]*
      - lupus vulgaris (tuberculous) (*see also* Tuberculosis) 017.0 ☑ *[373.4]*
      - mycotic dermatitis (*see also* Dermatomycosis) 111.9 *[373.5]*
      - vaccinia 051.0 *[373.5]*
        - postvaccination 999.0 *[373.5]*
      - yaws (*see also* Yaws) 102.9 *[373.4]*
- facta, factitia 698.4
  - psychogenic 316 *[698.4]*
- ficta 698.4
  - psychogenic 316 *[698.4]*
- flexural 691.8
- follicularis 704.8
- friction 709.8
- fungus 111.9
  - specified type NEC 111.8
- gangrenosa, gangrenous (infantum) (*see also* Gangrene) 785.4
- gestationis 646.8 ☑
- gonococcal 098.89
- gouty 274.89
- harvest mite 133.8
- heat 692.89
- herpetiformis (bullous) (erythematous) (pustular) (vesicular) 694.0
  - juvenile 694.2
  - senile 694.5
- hiemalis 692.89
- hypostatic, hypostatica 454.1
  - with ulcer 454.2
- impetiginous 684
- infantile (acute) (chronic) (intertriginous) (intrinsic) (seborrheic) 690.12
- infectiosa eczematoides 690.8
- infectious (staphylococcal) (streptococcal) 686.9
  - eczematoid 690.8
- infective eczematoid 690.8
- Jacquet's (diaper dermatitis) 691.0
- leptus 133.8
- lichenified NEC 692.9
- lichenoid, chronic 701.0
- lichenoides purpurica pigmentosa 709.1
- meadow 692.6
- medicamentosa (correct substance properly administered) (internal use) (*see also* Dermatitis, due to, drugs or medicinals) 693.0
  - due to contact with skin 692.3
- mite 133.8
- multiformis 694.0
  - juvenile 694.2
  - senile 694.5
- napkin 691.0
- neuro 698.3
- neurotica 694.0
- nummular NEC 692.9
- osteatosis, osteatotic 706.8
- papillaris capillitii 706.1
- pellagrous 265.2
- perioral 695.3
- perstans 696.1
- photosensitivity (sun) 692.72
  - other light 692.82
- pigmented purpuric lichenoid 709.1
- polymorpha dolorosa 694.0
- primary irritant 692.9
- pruriginosa 694.0
- pruritic NEC 692.9
- psoriasiform nodularis 696.2
- psychogenic 316
- purulent 686.00
- pustular contagious 051.2
- pyococcal 686.00
- pyocyaneus 686.09
- pyogenica 686.00
- radiation 692.82
- repens 696.1
- Ritter's (exfoliativa) 695.81
- Schamberg's (progressive pigmentary dermatosis) 709.09
- schistosome 120.3
- seasonal bullous 694.8
- seborrheic 690.10
  - infantile 690.12
- sensitization NEC 692.9
- septic (*see also* Septicemia) 686.00
  - gonococcal 098.89
- solar, solare NEC (*see also* Dermatitis, due to, sun) 692.70
- stasis 459.81
  - due to
    - postphlebitic syndrome 459.12
      - with ulcer 459.13
    - varicose veins — *see* Varicose
  - ulcerated or with ulcer (varicose) 454.2
- sunburn (*see also* Sunburn) 692.71
- suppurative 686.00
- traumatic NEC 709.8
- trophoneurotica 694.0
- ultraviolet, except from sun 692.82
  - due to sun NEC (*see also* Dermatitis, due to, sun) 692.82
- varicose 454.1
  - with ulcer 454.2
- vegetans 686.8
- verrucosa 117.2
- xerotic 706.8

Dermatoarthritis, lipoid 272.8 *[713.0]*

Dermatochalasia, dermatochalasis 374.87

Dermatofibroma (lenticulare) (M8832/0) — *see also* Neoplasm, skin, benign
- protuberans (M8832/1) — *see* Neoplasm, skin, uncertain behavior

Dermatofibrosarcoma (protuberans) (M8832/3) — *see* Neoplasm, skin, malignant

Dermatographia 708.3

Dermatolysis (congenital) (exfoliativa) 757.39
- acquired 701.8
- eyelids 374.34
- palpebrarum 374.34
- senile 701.8

Dermatomegaly NEC 701.8

Dermatomucomyositis 710.3

Dermatomycosis 111.9
- furfuracea 111.0
- specified type NEC 111.8

Dermatomyositis (acute) (chronic) 710.3

Dermatoneuritis of children 985.0

Dermatophiliasis 134.1

Dermatophytide — *see* Dermatophytosis

Dermatophytosis (Epidermophyton) (infection) (microsporum) (tinea) (Trichophyton) 110.9
- beard 110.0
- body 110.5
- deep seated 110.6
- fingernails 110.1
- foot 110.4
- groin 110.3
- hand 110.2
- nail 110.1
- perianal (area) 110.3
- scalp 110.0
- scrotal 110.8
- specified site NEC 110.8
- toenails 110.1
- vulva 110.8

Dermatopolyneuritis 985.0

Dermatorrhexis 756.83
- acquired 701.8

Dermatosclerosis — *see also* Scleroderma 710.1
- localized 701.0

Dermatosis 709.9
- Andrews' 686.8
- atopic 691.8
- Bowen's (M8081/2) — *see* Neoplasm, skin, in situ
- bullous 694.9
  - specified type NEC 694.8
- erythematosquamous 690.8
- exfoliativa 695.89
- factitial 698.4
- gonococcal 098.89
- herpetiformis 694.0
  - juvenile 694.2
  - senile 694.5
- hysterical 300.11
- linear IgA 694.8
- menstrual NEC 709.8
- neutrophilic, acute febrile 695.89
- occupational (*see also* Dermatitis) 692.9
- papulosa nigra 709.8
- pigmentary NEC 709.00
  - progressive 709.09
  - Schamberg's 709.09
  - Siemens-Bloch 757.33
- progressive pigmentary 709.09
- psychogenic 316
- pustular subcorneal 694.1
- Schamberg's (progressive pigmentary) 709.09
- senile NEC 709.3
- specified NEC 702.8
- Unna's (seborrheic dermatitis) 690.10

Dermographia 708.3

Dermographism 708.3

Dermoid (cyst) (M9084/0) — *see also* Neoplasm, by site, benign
- with malignant transformation (M9084/3) 183.0

Dermopathy
- infiltrative, with thyrotoxicosis 242.0 ☑
- senile NEC 709.3

Dermophytosis — *see* Dermatophytosis

Descemet's membrane — *see* condition

Descemetocele 371.72

Descending — *see* condition

Descensus uteri (complete) (incomplete) (partial) (without vaginal wall prolapse) 618.1
- with mention of vaginal wall prolapse — *see* Prolapse, uterovaginal

Desensitization to allergens V07.1

Desert
- rheumatism 114.0
- sore (*see also* Ulcer, skin) 707.9

Desertion (child) (newborn) 995.52
- adult 995.84

Desmoid (extra-abdominal) (tumor) (M8821/1) — *see also* Neoplasm, connective tissue, uncertain behavior
- abdominal (M8822/1) — *see* Neoplasm, connective tissue, uncertain behavior

Despondency 300.4

Desquamative dermatitis NEC 695.89

Destruction
- articular facet (*see also* Derangement, joint) 718.9 ☑
  - vertebra 724.9
- bone 733.90
  - syphilitic 095.5
- joint (*see also* Derangement, joint) 718.9 ☑
  - sacroiliac 724.6
- kidney 593.89
- live fetus to facilitate birth NEC 763.89
- ossicles (ear) 385.24
- rectal sphincter 569.49
- septum (nasal) 478.19 ▲
- tuberculous NEC (*see also* Tuberculosis) 011.9 ☑
- tympanic membrane 384.82
- tympanum 385.89
- vertebral disc — *see* Degeneration, intervertebral disc

Destructiveness — *see also* Disturbance, conduct 312.9
- adjustment reaction 309.3

Detachment
- cartilage (*see also* Sprain, by site)
  - knee — *see* Tear, meniscus
- cervix, annular 622.8
  - complicating delivery 665.3 ☑
- choroid (old) (postinfectional) (simple) (spontaneous) 363.70
  - hemorrhagic 363.72
  - serous 363.71
- knee, medial meniscus (old) 717.3
  - current injury 836.0
- ligament — *see* Sprain, by site
- placenta (premature) — *see* Placenta, separation
- retina (recent) 361.9
  - with retinal defect (rhegmatogenous) 361.00
    - giant tear 361.03
    - multiple 361.02
    - partial
      - with
        - giant tear 361.03
        - multiple defects 361.02
        - retinal dialysis (juvenile) 361.04
        - single defect 361.01
    - retinal dialysis (juvenile) 361.04
    - single 361.01
    - subtotal 361.05
    - total 361.05
  - delimited (old) (partial) 361.06
  - old
    - delimited 361.06
    - partial 361.06
    - total or subtotal 361.07
  - pigment epithelium (RPE) (serous) 362.42
    - exudative 362.42
    - hemorrhagic 362.43
  - rhegmatogenous (*see also* Detachment, retina, with retinal defect) 361.00
  - serous (without retinal defect) 361.2
  - specified type NEC 361.89
  - traction (with vitreoretinal organization) 361.81
- vitreous humor 379.21

Detergent asthma 507.8

Deterioration
- epileptic
  - with behavioral disturbance 345.9 ☑ *[294.11]*
  - without behavioral disturbance 345.9 ☑ *[294.10]*
- heart, cardiac (*see also* Degeneration, myocardial) 429.1
- mental (*see also* Psychosis) 298.9
- myocardium, myocardial (*see also* Degeneration, myocardial) 429.1
- senile (simple) 797
- transplanted organ — *see* Complications, transplant, organ, by site

de Toni-Fanconi syndrome (cystinosis) 270.0

Deuteranomaly 368.52

Deuteranopia (anomalous trichromat) (complete) (incomplete) 368.52

Deutschländer's disease — *see* Fracture, foot

Development
- abnormal, bone 756.9
- arrested 783.40
  - bone 733.91
  - child 783.40
  - due to malnutrition (protein-calorie) 263.2
  - fetus or newborn 764.9 ☑
  - tracheal rings (congenital) 748.3

☑ Additional Digit Required — Refer to the Tabular List for Digit Selection

Subterms under main terms may continue to next column or page

▶◀ Revised Text ● New Line ▲ Revised Code

Development — *continued*
defective, congenital (*see also* Anomaly)
cauda equina 742.59
left ventricle 746.9
with atresia or hypoplasia of aortic orifice or valve with hypoplasia of ascending aorta 746.7
in hypoplastic left heart syndrome 746.7
delayed (*see also* Delay, development) 783.40
arithmetical skills 315.1
language (skills) 315.31
expressive 315.31
mixed receptive-expressive 315.32
learning skill, specified NEC 315.2
mixed skills 315.5
motor coordination 315.4
reading 315.00
specified
learning skill NEC 315.2
type NEC, except learning 315.8
speech 315.39
associated with hyperkinesia 314.1
phonological 315.39
spelling 315.09
written expression 315.2
imperfect, congenital (*see also* Anomaly)
heart 746.9
lungs 748.60
improper (fetus or newborn) 764.9 ☑
incomplete (fetus or newborn) 764.9 ☑
affecting management of pregnancy 656.5 ☑
bronchial tree 748.3
organ or site not listed — *see* Hypoplasia
respiratory system 748.9
sexual, precocious NEC 259.1
tardy, mental (*see also* Retardation, mental) 319
Developmental — *see* condition
Devergie's disease (pityriasis rubra pilaris) 696.4
Deviation
conjugate (eye) 378.87
palsy 378.81
spasm, spastic 378.82
esophagus 530.89
eye, skew 378.87
mandible, opening and closing 524.53
midline (jaw) (teeth) 524.29
specified site NEC — *see* Malposition
occlusal plane 524.76
organ or site, congenital NEC — *see* Malposition, congenital
septum (acquired) (nasal) 470
congenital 754.0
sexual 302.9
bestiality 302.1
coprophilia 302.89
ego-dystonic
homosexuality 302.0
lesbianism 302.0
erotomania 302.89
Clérambault's 297.8
exhibitionism (sexual) 302.4
fetishism 302.81
transvestic 302.3
frotteurism 302.89
homosexuality, ego-dystonic 302.0
pedophilic 302.2
lesbianism, ego-dystonic 302.0
masochism 302.83
narcissism 302.89
necrophilia 302.89
nymphomania 302.89
pederosis 302.2
pedophilia 302.2
sadism 302.84

Deviation — *continued*
sexual — *continued*
sadomasochism 302.84
satyriasis 302.89
specified type NEC 302.89
transvestic fetishism 302.3
transvestism 302.3
voyeurism 302.82
zoophilia (erotica) 302.1
teeth, midline 524.29
trachea 519.19 ▲
ureter (congenital) 753.4
Devic's disease 341.0
Device
cerebral ventricle (communicating) in situ V45.2
contraceptive — *see* Contraceptive, device
drainage, cerebrospinal fluid V45.2
Devil's
grip 074.1
pinches (purpura simplex) 287.2
Devitalized tooth 522.9
Devonshire colic 984.9
specified type of lead — *see* Table of Drugs and Chemicals
Dextraposition, aorta 747.21
with ventricular septal defect, pulmonary stenosis or atresia, and hypertrophy of right ventricle 745.2
in tetralogy of Fallot 745.2
Dextratransposition, aorta 745.11
Dextrinosis, limit (debrancher enzyme deficiency) 271.0
Dextrocardia (corrected) (false) (isolated) (secondary) (true) 746.87
with
complete transposition of viscera 759.3
situs inversus 759.3
Dextroversion, kidney (left) 753.3
Dhobie itch 110.3
Diabetes, diabetic (brittle) (congenital) (familial) (mellitus) (poorly controlled) (severe) (slight) (without complication) 250.0 ☑

Note — Use the following fifth-digit subclassification with category 250:

0 type II or unspecified type, not stated as uncontrolled

Fifth-digit 0 is for use for type II patients, even if the patient requires insulin

1 type I [juvenile type], not stated as uncontrolled

2 type II or unspecified type, uncontrolled

Fifth-digit 2 is for use for type II patients, even if the patient requires insulin

3 type I [juvenile type], uncontrolled

with
coma (with ketoacidosis) 250.3 ☑
hyperosmolar (nonketotic) 250.2 ☑
complication NEC 250.9 ☑
specified NEC 250.8 ☑
gangrene 250.7 ☑ *[785.4]*
hyperosmolarity 250.2 ☑
ketosis, ketoacidosis 250.1 ☑
osteomyelitis 250.8 ☑ *[731.8]*
specified manisfestations NEC 250.8 ☑
acetonemia 250.1 ☑
acidosis 250.1 ☑
amyotrophy 250.6 ☑ *[358.1]*
angiopathy, peripheral 250.7 ☑ *[443.81]*
asymptomatic 790.29
autonomic neuropathy (peripheral) 250.6 ☑ *[337.1]*

Diabetes, diabetic — *continued*
bone change 250.8 ☑ *[731.8]*
bronze, bronzed 275.0
cataract 250.5 ☑ *[366.41]*
chemical 790.29
complicating pregnancy, childbirth, or puerperium 648.8 ☑
coma (with ketoacidosis) 250.3 ☑
hyperglycemic 250.3 ☑
hyperosmolar (nonketotic) 250.2 ☑
hypoglycemic 250.3 ☑
insulin 250.3 ☑
complicating pregnancy, childbirth, or puerperium (maternal) 648.0 ☑
affecting fetus or newborn 775.0
complication NEC 250.9 ☑
specified NEC 250.8 ☑
dorsal sclerosis 250.6 ☑ *[340]*
dwarfism-obesity syndrome 258.1
gangrene 250.7 ☑ *[785.4]*
gastroparesis 250.6 ☑ *[536.3]*
gestational 648.8 ☑
complicating pregnancy, childbirth, or puerperium 648.8 ☑
glaucoma 250.5 ☑ *[365.44]*
glomerulosclerosis (intercapillary) 250.4 ☑ *[581.81]*
glycogenosis, secondary 250.8 ☑ *[259.8]*
hemochromatosis 275.0
hyperosmolar coma 250.2 ☑
hyperosmolarity 250.2 ☑
hypertension-nephrosis syndrome 250.4 ☑ *[581.81]*
hypoglycemia 250.8 ☑
hypoglycemic shock 250.8 ☑
insipidus 253.5
nephrogenic 588.1
pituitary 253.5
vasopressin-resistant 588.1
intercapillary glomerulosclerosis 250.4 ☑ *[581.81]*
iritis 250.5 ☑ *[364.42]*
ketosis, ketoacidosis 250.1 ☑
Kimmelstiel (-Wilson) disease or syndrome (intercapillary glomerulosclerosis) 250.4 ☑ *[581.81]*
Lancereaux's (diabetes mellitus with marked emaciation) 250.8 ☑ *[261]*
latent (chemical) 790.29
complicating pregnancy, childbirth, or puerperium 648.8 ☑
lipoidosis 250.8 ☑ *[272.7]*
macular edema 250.5 ☑ *[362.07]*
maternal
with manifest disease in the infant 775.1
affecting fetus or newborn 775.0
microaneurysms, retinal 250.5 ☑ *[362.01]*
mononeuropathy 250.6 ☑ *[355.9]*
neonatal, transient 775.1
nephropathy 250.4 ☑ *[583.81]*
nephrosis (syndrome) 250.4 ☑ *[581.81]*
neuralgia 250.6 ☑ *[357.2]*
neuritis 250.6 ☑ *[357.2]*
neurogenic arthropathy 250.6 ☑ *[713.5]*
neuropathy 250.6 ☑ *[357.2]*
nonclinical 790.29
osteomyelitis 250.8 ☑ *[731.8]*
peripheral autonomic neuropathy 250.6 ☑ *[337.1]*
phosphate 275.3
polyneuropathy 250.6 ☑ *[357.2]*
renal (true) 271.4
retinal
edema 250.5 ☑ *[362.07]*
hemorrhage 250.5 ☑ *[362.01]*
microaneurysms 250.5 ☑ *[362.01]*
retinitis 250.5 ☑ *[362.01]*
retinopathy 250.5 ☑ *[362.01]*

Diabetes, diabetic — *continued*
retinopathy — *continued*
background 250.5 ☑ *[362.01]*
nonproliverative 250.5 ☑ *[362.03]*
mild 250.5 ☑ *[362.04]*
moderate 250.5 ☑ *[362.05]*
severe 250.5 ☑ *[362.06]*
proliferative 250.5 ☑ *[362.02]*
steroid induced
correct substance properly administered 251.8
overdose or wrong substance given or taken 962.0
stress 790.29
subclinical 790.29
subliminal 790.29
sugar 250.0 ☑
ulcer (skin) 250.8 ☑ *[707.9]*
lower extremity 250.8 ☑ *[707.10]*
ankle 250.8 ☑ *[707.13]*
calf 250.8 ☑ *[707.12]*
foot 250.8 ☑ *[707.15]*
heel 250.8 ☑ *[707.14]*
knee 250.8 ☑ *[707.19]*
specified site NEC 250.8 ☑ *[707.19]*
thigh 250.8 ☑ *[707.11]*
toes 250.8 ☑ *[707.15]*
specified site NEC 250.8 ☑ *[707.8]*
xanthoma 250.8 ☑ *[272.2]*
Diacyclothrombopathia 287.1
Diagnosis deferred 799.9
Dialysis (intermittent) (treatment)
anterior retinal (juvenile) (with detachment) 361.04
extracorporeal V56.0
hemodialysis V56.0
status only V45.1
peritoneal V56.8
status only V45.1
renal V56.0
status only V45.1
specified type NEC V56.8
Diamond-Blackfan anemia or syndrome (congenital hypoplastic anemia) 284.01 ▲
Diamond-Gardener syndrome (autoerythrocyte sensitization) 287.2
Diaper rash 691.0
Diaphoresis (excessive) NEC — *see also* Hyperhidrosis) 780.8
Diaphragm — *see* condition
Diaphragmalgia 786.52
Diaphragmitis 519.4
Diaphyseal aclasis 756.4
Diaphysitis 733.99
Diarrhea, diarrheal (acute) (autumn) (bilious) (bloody) (catarrhal) (choleraic) (chronic) (gravis) (green) (infantile) (lienteric) (noninfectious) (presumed noninfectious) (putrefactive) (secondary) (sporadic) (summer) (symptomatic) (thermic) 787.91
achlorhydric 536.0
allergic 558.3
amebic (*see also* Amebiasis) 006.9
with abscess — *see* Abscess, amebic
acute 006.0
chronic 006.1
nondysenteric 006.2
bacillary — *see* Dysentery, bacillary
bacterial NEC 008.5
balantidial 007.0
bile salt-induced 579.8
cachectic NEC 787.91
chilomastix 007.8
choleriformis 001.1
coccidial 007.2
Cochin-China 579.1
anguilluliasis 127.2
psilosis 579.1
Dientamoeba 007.8
dietetic 787.91

- **Diarrhea, diarrheal** — *continued*
  - due to
    - achylia gastrica 536.8
    - Aerobacter aerogenes 008.2
    - Bacillus coli — *see* Enteritis, E. coli
    - bacteria NEC 008.5
    - bile salts 579.8
    - Capillaria
      - hepatica 128.8
      - philippinensis 127.5
    - Clostridium perfringens (C) (F) 008.46
    - Enterobacter aerogenes 008.2
    - enterococci 008.49
    - Escherichia coli — *see* Enteritis, E. coli
    - Giardia lamblia 007.1
    - Heterophyes heterophyes 121.6
    - irritating foods 787.91
    - Metagonimus yokogawai 121.5
    - Necator americanus 126.1
    - Paracolobactrum arizonae 008.1
    - Paracolon bacillus NEC 008.47
      - Arizona 008.1
    - Proteus (bacillus) (mirabilis) (Morganii) 008.3
    - Pseudomonas aeruginosa 008.42
    - S. japonicum 120.2
    - specified organism NEC 008.8
      - bacterial 008.49
      - viral NEC 008.69
    - Staphylococcus 008.41
    - Streptococcus 008.49
      - anaerobic 008.46
    - Strongyloides stercoralis 127.2
    - Trichuris trichiuria 127.3
    - virus NEC (*see also* Enteritis, viral) 008.69
  - dysenteric 009.2
    - due to specified organism NEC 008.8
  - dyspeptic 787.91
  - endemic 009.3
    - due to specified organism NEC 008.8
  - epidemic 009.2
    - due to specified organism NEC 008.8
  - fermentative 787.91
  - flagellate 007.9
  - Flexner's (ulcerative) 004.1
  - functional 564.5
    - following gastrointestinal surgery 564.4
    - psychogenic 306.4
  - giardial 007.1
  - Giardia lamblia 007.1
  - hill 579.1
  - hyperperistalsis (nervous) 306.4
  - infectious 009.2
    - due to specified organism NEC 008.8
    - presumed 009.3
  - inflammatory 787.91
    - due to specified organism NEC 008.8
  - malarial (*see also* Malaria) 084.6
  - mite 133.8
  - mycotic 117.9
  - nervous 306.4
  - neurogenic 564.5
  - parenteral NEC 009.2
  - postgastrectomy 564.4
  - postvagotomy 564.4
  - prostaglandin induced 579.8
  - protozoal NEC 007.9
  - psychogenic 306.4
  - septic 009.2
    - due to specified organism NEC 008.8
  - specified organism NEC 008.8
    - bacterial 008.49
    - viral NEC 008.69
  - Staphylococcus 008.41
  - Streptococcus 008.49
    - anaerobic 008.46
- **Diarrhea, diarrheal** — *continued*
  - toxic 558.2
  - travelers' 009.2
    - due to specified organism NEC 008.8
  - trichomonal 007.3
  - tropical 579.1
  - tuberculous 014.8 ☑
  - ulcerative (chronic) (*see also* Colitis, ulcerative) 556.9
  - viral (*see also* Enteritis, viral) 008.8
  - zymotic NEC 009.2
- **Diastasis**
  - cranial bones 733.99
    - congenital 756.0
  - joint (traumatic) — *see* Dislocation, by site
  - muscle 728.84
    - congenital 756.89
  - recti (abdomen) 728.84
    - complicating delivery 665.8 ☑
    - congenital 756.79
- **Diastema, teeth, tooth** 524.30
- **Diastematomyelia** 742.51
- **Diataxia, cerebral, infantile** 343.0
- **Diathesis**
  - allergic V15.09
  - bleeding (familial) 287.9
  - cystine (familial) 270.0
  - gouty 274.9
  - hemorrhagic (familial) 287.9
    - newborn NEC 776.0
  - oxalic 271.8
  - scrofulous (*see also* Tuberculosis) 017.2 ☑
  - spasmophilic (*see also* Tetany) 781.7
  - ulcer 536.9
  - uric acid 274.9
- **Diaz's disease or osteochondrosis** 732.5
- **Dibothriocephaliasis** 123.4
  - larval 123.5
- **Dibothriocephalus** (infection) (infestation) (latus) 123.4
  - larval 123.5
- **Dicephalus** 759.4
- **Dichotomy, teeth** 520.2
- **Dichromat, dichromata** (congenital) 368.59
- **Dichromatopsia** (congenital) 368.59
- **Dichuchwa** 104.0
- **Dicroceliasis** 121.8
- **Didelphys, didelphic** — *see also* Double uterus 752.2
- **Didymitis** — *see also* Epididymitis 604.90
- **Died** — *see also* Death
  - without
    - medical attention (cause unknown) 798.9
    - sign of disease 798.2
- **Dientamoeba diarrhea** 007.8
- **Dietary**
  - inadequacy or deficiency 269.9
  - surveillance and counseling V65.3
- **Dietl's crisis** 593.4
- **Dieulafoy lesion** (hemorrhagic)
  - of
    - duodenum 537.84
    - esophagus 530.82 ●
    - intestine 569.86
    - stomach 537.84
- **Difficult**
  - birth, affecting fetus or newborn 763.9
  - delivery NEC 669.9 ☑
- **Difficulty**
  - feeding 783.3
    - adult 783.3
    - breast 676.8 ☑
    - child 783.3
    - elderly 783.3
    - infant 783.3
    - newborn 779.3
    - nonorganic (infant) NEC 307.59
  - mechanical, gastroduodenal stoma 537.89
- **Difficulty** — *continued*
  - reading 315.00
  - specific, spelling 315.09
  - swallowing (*see also* Dysphagia) 787.2
  - walking 719.7
- **Diffuse** — *see* condition
- **Diffused ganglion** 727.42
- **Di George's syndrome** (thymic hypoplasia) 279.11
- **Digestive** — *see* condition
- **Di Guglielmo's disease or syndrome** (M9841/3) 207.0 ☑
- **Diktyoma** (M9051/3) — *see* Neoplasm, by site, malignant
- **Dilaceration, tooth** 520.4
- **Dilatation**
  - anus 564.89
    - venule — *see* Hemorrhoids
  - aorta (focal) (general) (*see also* Aneurysm, aorta) 441.9
    - congenital 747.29
    - infectional 093.0
    - ruptured 441.5
    - syphilitic 093.0
  - appendix (cystic) 543.9
  - artery 447.8
  - bile duct (common) (cystic) (congenital) 751.69
    - acquired 576.8
  - bladder (sphincter) 596.8
    - congenital 753.8
    - in pregnancy or childbirth 654.4 ☑
      - causing obstructed labor 660.2 ☑
        - affecting fetus or newborn 763.1
  - blood vessel 459.89
  - bronchus, bronchi 494.0
    - with acute exacerbation 494.1
  - calyx (due to obstruction) 593.89
  - capillaries 448.9
  - cardiac (acute) (chronic) (*see also* Hypertrophy, cardiac) 429.3
    - congenital 746.89
      - valve NEC 746.89
        - pulmonary 746.09
    - hypertensive (*see also* Hypertension, heart) 402.90
  - cavum septi pellucidi 742.4
  - cecum 564.89
    - psychogenic 306.4
  - cervix (uteri) (*see also* Incompetency, cervix)
    - incomplete, poor, slow
      - affecting fetus or newborn 763.7
      - complicating delivery 661.0 ☑
        - affecting fetus or newborn 763.7
  - colon 564.7
    - congenital 751.3
    - due to mechanical obstruction 560.89
    - psychogenic 306.4
  - common bile duct (congenital) 751.69
    - acquired 576.8
      - with calculus, choledocholithiasis, or stones — *see* Choledocholithiasis
  - cystic duct 751.69
    - acquired (any bile duct) 575.8
  - duct, mammary 610.4
  - duodenum 564.89
  - esophagus 530.89
    - congenital 750.4
    - due to
      - achalasia 530.0
      - cardiospasm 530.0
  - Eustachian tube, congenital 744.24
  - fontanel 756.0
  - gallbladder 575.8
    - congenital 751.69
  - gastric 536.8
    - acute 536.1
    - psychogenic 306.4
  - heart (acute) (chronic) (*see also* Hypertrophy, cardiac) 429.3
- **Dilatation** — *continued*
  - heart (*see also* Hypertrophy, cardiac) — *continued*
    - congenital 746.89
    - hypertensive (*see also* Hypertension, heart) 402.90
    - valve (*see also* Endocarditis)
      - congenital 746.89
  - ileum 564.89
    - psychogenic 306.4
  - inguinal rings — *see* Hernia, inguinal
  - jejunum 564.89
    - psychogenic 306.4
  - kidney (calyx) (collecting structures) (cystic) (parenchyma) (pelvis) 593.89
  - lacrimal passages 375.69
  - lymphatic vessel 457.1
  - mammary duct 610.4
  - Meckel's diverticulum (congenital) 751.0
  - meningeal vessels, congenital 742.8
  - myocardium (acute) (chronic) (*see also* Hypertrophy, cardiac) 429.3
  - organ or site, congenital NEC — *see* Distortion
  - pancreatic duct 577.8
  - pelvis, kidney 593.89
  - pericardium — *see* Pericarditis
  - pharynx 478.29
  - prostate 602.8
  - pulmonary
    - artery (idiopathic) 417.8
      - congenital 747.3
    - valve, congenital 746.09
  - pupil 379.43
  - rectum 564.89
  - renal 593.89
  - saccule vestibularis, congenital 744.05
  - salivary gland (duct) 527.8
  - sphincter ani 564.89
  - stomach 536.8
    - acute 536.1
    - psychogenic 306.4
  - submaxillary duct 527.8
  - trachea, congenital 748.3
  - ureter (idiopathic) 593.89
    - congenital 753.20
    - due to obstruction 593.5
  - urethra (acquired) 599.84
  - vasomotor 443.9
  - vein 459.89
  - ventricular, ventricle (acute) (chronic) (*see also* Hypertrophy, cardiac) 429.3
    - cerebral, congenital 742.4
    - hypertensive (*see also* Hypertension, heart) 402.90
  - venule 459.89
    - anus — *see* Hemorrhoids
  - vesical orifice 596.8
- **Dilated, dilation** — *see* Dilatation
- **Diminished**
  - hearing (acuity) (*see also* Deafness) 389.9
  - pulse pressure 785.9
  - vision NEC 369.9
  - vital capacity 794.2
- **Diminuta taenia** 123.6
- **Diminution, sense or sensation** (cold) (heat) (tactile) (vibratory) — *see also* Disturbance, sensation 782.0
- **Dimitri-Sturge-Weber disease** (encephalocutaneous angiomatosis) 759.6
- **Dimple**
  - parasacral 685.1
    - with abscess 685.0
  - pilonidal 685.1
    - with abscess 685.0
  - postanal 685.1
    - with abscess 685.0
- **Dioctophyma renale** (infection) (infestation) 128.8
- **Dipetalonemiasis** 125.4

- **Diphallus** 752.69
- **Diphtheria, diphtheritic** (gangrenous) (hemorrhagic) 032.9
  - carrier (suspected) of V02.4
  - cutaneous 032.85
  - cystitis 032.84
  - faucial 032.0
  - infection of wound 032.85
  - inoculation (anti) (not sick) V03.5
  - laryngeal 032.3
  - myocarditis 032.82
  - nasal anterior 032.2
  - nasopharyngeal 032.1
  - neurological complication 032.89
  - peritonitis 032.83
  - specified site NEC 032.89
- **Diphyllobothriasis** (intestine) 123.4
  - larval 123.5
- **Diplacusis** 388.41
- **Diplegia** (upper limbs) 344.2
  - brain or cerebral 437.8
  - congenital 343.0
  - facial 351.0
    - congenital 352.6
  - infantile or congenital (cerebral) (spastic) (spinal) 343.0
  - lower limbs 344.1
  - syphilitic, congenital 090.49
- **Diplococcus, diplococcal** — *see* condition
- **Diplomyelia** 742.59
- **Diplopia** 368.2
  - refractive 368.15
- **Dipsomania** — *see also* Alcoholism 303.9 ☑
  - with psychosis (*see also* Psychosis, alcoholic) 291.9
- **Dipylidiasis** 123.8
  - intestine 123.8
- **Direction, teeth, abnormal** 524.30
- **Dirt-eating child** 307.52
- **Disability**
  - heart — *see* Disease, heart
  - learning NEC 315.2
  - special spelling 315.09
- **Disarticulation** — *see also* Derangement, joint 718.9 ☑
  - meaning
    - amputation
      - status — *see* Absence, by site
      - traumatic — *see* Amputation, traumatic
    - dislocation, traumatic or congenital — *see* Dislocation
- **Disaster, cerebrovascular** — *see also* Disease, cerebrovascular, acute 436
- **Discharge**
  - anal NEC 787.99
  - breast (female) (male) 611.79
  - conjunctiva 372.89
  - continued locomotor idiopathic (*see also* Epilepsy) 345.5 ☑
  - diencephalic autonomic idiopathic (*see also* Epilepsy) 345.5 ☑
  - ear 388.60
    - blood 388.69
    - cerebrospinal fluid 388.61
  - excessive urine 788.42
  - eye 379.93
  - nasal 478.19 ▲
  - nipple 611.79
  - patterned motor idiopathic (*see also* Epilepsy) 345.5 ☑
  - penile 788.7
  - postnasal — *see* Sinusitis
  - sinus, from mediastinum 510.0
  - umbilicus 789.9
  - urethral 788.7
    - bloody 599.84
  - vaginal 623.5
- **Discitis** 722.90
  - cervical, cervicothoracic 722.91
  - lumbar, lumbosacral 722.93
  - thoracic, thoracolumbar 722.92
- **Discogenic syndrome** — *see* Displacement, intervertebral disc
- **Discoid**
  - kidney 753.3
  - meniscus, congenital 717.5
  - semilunar cartilage 717.5
- **Discoloration**
  - mouth 528.9
  - nails 703.8
  - teeth 521.7
    - due to
      - drugs 521.7
      - metals (copper) (silver) 521.7
      - pulpal bleeding 521.7
    - during formation 520.8
    - extrinsic 523.6
    - intrinsic posteruptive 521.7
- **Discomfort**
  - chest 786.59
  - visual 368.13
- **Discomycosis** — *see* Actinomycosis
- **Discontinuity, ossicles, ossicular chain** 385.23
- **Discrepancy**
  - centric occlusion
    - maximum intercuspation 524.55 ●
    - of teeth 524.55 ●
  - leg length (acquired) 736.81
    - congenital 755.30
  - uterine size-date 649.6 ☑ ▲
- **Discrimination**
  - political V62.4
  - racial V62.4
  - religious V62.4
  - sex V62.4
- **Disease, diseased** — *see also* Syndrome
  - Abrami's (acquired hemolytic jaundice) 283.9
  - absorbent system 459.89
  - accumulation — *see* Thesaurismosis
  - acid-peptic 536.8
  - Acosta's 993.2
  - Adams-Stokes (-Morgagni) (syncope with heart block) 426.9
  - Addison's (bronze) (primary adrenal insufficiency) 255.4
    - anemia (pernicious) 281.0
    - tuberculous (*see also* Tuberculosis) 017.6 ☑
  - Addison-Gull — *see* Xanthoma
  - adenoids (and tonsils) (chronic) 474.9
  - adrenal (gland) (capsule) (cortex) 255.9
    - hyperfunction 255.3
    - hypofunction 255.4
    - specified type NEC 255.8
  - ainhum (dactylolysis spontanea) 136.0
  - akamushi (scrub typhus) 081.2
  - Akureyri (epidemic neuromyasthenia) 049.8
  - Albarrán's (colibacilluria) 791.9
  - Albers-Schönberg's (marble bones) 756.52
  - Albert's 726.71
  - Albright (-Martin) (-Bantam) 275.49
  - Alibert's (mycosis fungoides) (M9700/3) 202.1 ☑
  - Alibert-Bazin (M9700/3) 202.1 ☑
  - alimentary canal 569.9
  - alligator skin (ichthyosis congenita) 757.1
    - acquired 701.1
  - Almeida's (Brazilian blastomycosis) 116.1
  - Alpers' 330.8
  - alpine 993.2
  - altitude 993.2
  - alveoli, teeth 525.9
  - Alzheimer's — *see* Alzheimer's
  - amyloid (any site) 277.30 ▲
  - anarthritic rheumatoid 446.5
  - Anders' (adiposis tuberosa simplex) 272.8
  - Andersen's (glycogenosis IV) 271.0
  - Anderson's (angiokeratoma corporis diffusum) 272.7
  - Andes 993.2

Disease, diseased — *see also* Syndrome — *continued*

  - Andrews' (bacterid) 686.8
  - angiospastic, angiospasmodic 443.9
    - cerebral 435.9
      - with transient neurologic deficit 435.9
    - vein 459.89
  - anterior
    - chamber 364.9
    - horn cell 335.9
      - specified type NEC 335.8
  - antral (chronic) 473.0
    - acute 461.0
  - anus NEC 569.49
  - aorta (nonsyphilitic) 447.9
    - syphilitic NEC 093.89
  - aortic (heart) (valve) (*see also* Endocarditis, aortic) 424.1
  - apollo 077.4
  - aponeurosis 726.90
  - appendix 543.9
  - aqueous (chamber) 364.9
  - arc-welders' lung 503
  - Armenian 277.31 ▲
  - Arnold-Chiari (*see also* Spina bifida) 741.0 ☑
  - arterial 447.9
    - occlusive (*see also* Occlusion, by site) 444.22
      - with embolus or thrombus — *see* Occlusion, by site
      - due to stricture or stenosis 447.1
    - specified type NEC 447.8
  - arteriocardiorenal (*see also* Hypertension, cardiorenal) 404.90
  - arteriolar (generalized) (obliterative) 447.9
    - specified type NEC 447.8
  - arteriorenal — *see* Hypertension, kidney
  - arteriosclerotic (*see also* Arteriosclerosis)
    - cardiovascular 429.2
    - coronary — *see* Arteriosclerosis, coronary
    - heart — *see* Arteriosclerosis, coronary
    - vascular — *see* Arteriosclerosis
  - artery 447.9
    - cerebral 437.9
    - coronary — *see* Arteriosclerosis, coronary
    - specified type NEC 447.8
  - arthropod-borne NEC 088.9
    - specified type NEC 088.89
  - Asboe-Hansen's (incontinentia pigmenti) 757.33
  - atticoantral, chronic (with posterior or superior marginal perforation of ear drum) 382.2
  - auditory canal, ear 380.9
  - Aujeszky's 078.89
  - auricle, ear NEC 380.30
  - Australian X 062.4
  - autoimmune NEC 279.4
    - hemolytic (cold type) (warm type) 283.0
    - parathyroid 252.1
    - thyroid 245.2
  - aviators' (*see also* Effect, adverse, high altitude) 993.2
  - ax(e)-grinders' 502
  - Ayala's 756.89
  - Ayerza's (pulmonary artery sclerosis with pulmonary hypertension) 416.0
  - Azorean (of the nervous system) 334.8
  - Babington's (familial hemorrhagic telangiectasia) 448.0
  - back bone NEC 733.90
  - bacterial NEC 040.89
    - zoonotic NEC 027.9
      - specified type NEC 027.8

Disease, diseased — *see also* Syndrome — *continued*

  - Baehr-Schiffrin (thrombotic thrombocytopenic purpura) 446.6
  - Baelz's (cheilitis glandularis apostematosa) 528.5
  - Baerensprung's (eczema marginatum) 110.3
  - Balfour's (chloroma) 205.3 ☑
  - balloon (*see also* Effect, adverse, high altitude) 993.2
  - Baló's 341.1
  - Bamberger (-Marie) (hypertrophic pulmonary osteoarthropathy) 731.2
  - Bang's (Brucella abortus) 023.1
  - Bannister's 995.1
  - Banti's (with cirrhosis) (with portal hypertension) — *see* Cirrhosis, liver
  - Barcoo (*see also* Ulcer, skin) 707.9
  - barium lung 503
  - Barlow (-Möller) (infantile scurvy) 267
  - barometer makers' 985.0
  - Barraquer (-Simons) (progressive lipodystrophy) 272.6
  - basal ganglia 333.90
    - degenerative NEC 333.0
    - specified NEC 333.89
  - Basedow's (exophthalmic goiter) 242.0 ☑
  - basement membrane NEC 583.89
    - with
      - pulmonary hemorrhage (Goodpasture's syndrome) 446.21 *[583.81]*
  - Bateman's 078.0
    - purpura (senile) 287.2
  - Batten's 330.1 *[362.71]*
  - Batten-Mayou (retina) 330.1 *[362.71]*
  - Batten-Steinert 359.2
  - Battey 031.0
  - Baumgarten-Cruveilhier (cirrhosis of liver) 571.5
  - bauxite-workers' 503
  - Bayle's (dementia paralytica) 094.1
  - Bazin's (primary) (*see also* Tuberculosis) 017.1 ☑
  - Beard's (neurasthenia) 300.5
  - Beau's (*see also* Degeneration, myocardial) 429.1
  - Bechterew's (ankylosing spondylitis) 720.0
  - Becker's (idiopathic mural endomyocardial disease) 425.2
  - Begbie's (exophthalmic goiter) 242.0 ☑
  - Behr's 362.50
  - Beigel's (white piedra) 111.2
  - Bekhterev's (ankylosing spondylitis) 720.0
  - Bell's (*see also* Psychosis, affective) 296.0 ☑
  - Bennett's (leukemia) 208.9 ☑
  - Benson's 379.22
  - Bergeron's (hysteroepilepsy) 300.11
  - Berlin's 921.3
  - Bernard-Soulier (thrombopathy) 287.1
  - Bernhardt (-Roth) 355.1
  - beryllium 503
  - Besnier-Boeck (-Schaumann) (sarcoidosis) 135
  - Best's 362.76
  - Beurmann's (sporotrichosis) 117.1
  - Bielschowsky (-Jansky) 330.1
  - Biermer's (pernicious anemia) 281.0
  - Biett's (discoid lupus erythematosus) 695.4
  - bile duct (*see also* Disease, biliary) 576.9
  - biliary (duct) (tract) 576.9
    - with calculus, choledocholithiasis, or stones — *see* Choledocholithiasis
  - Billroth's (meningocele) (*see also* Spina bifida) 741.9 ☑
  - Binswanger's 290.12

☑ Additional Digit Required — Refer to the Tabular List for Digit Selection

Subterms under main terms may continue to next column or page

▶◀ Revised Text ● New Line ▲ Revised Code

- **Disease, diseased** — *see also* Syndrome — *continued*
  - nervous system — *continued*
    - specified NEC 349.89
    - sympathetic (*see also* Neuropathy, peripheral, autonomic) 337.9
    - vegetative (*see also* Neuropathy, peripheral, autonomic) 337.9
  - Nettleship's (urticaria pigmentosa) 757.33
  - Neumann's (pemphigus vegetans) 694.4
  - neurologic (central) NEC (*see also* Disease, nervous system) 349.9
    - peripheral NEC 355.9
  - neuromuscular system NEC 358.9
  - Newcastle 077.8
  - Nicolas (-Durand) — Favre (climatic bubo) 099.1
  - Niemann-Pick (lipid histiocytosis) 272.7
  - nipple 611.9
    - Paget's (M8540/3) 174.0
  - Nishimoto (-Takeuchi) 437.5
  - nonarthropod-borne NEC 078.89
    - central nervous system NEC 049.9
    - enterovirus NEC 078.89
  - nonautoimmune hemolytic NEC 283.10
  - Nonne-Milroy-Meige (chronic hereditary edema) 757.0
  - Norrie's (congenital progressive oculoacousticocerebral degeneration) 743.8
  - nose 478.19 ▲
  - nucleus pulposus — *see* Disease, intervertebral disc
  - nutritional 269.9
    - maternal, affecting fetus or newborn 760.4
  - oasthouse, urine 270.2
  - obliterative vascular 447.1
  - Odelberg's (juvenile osteochondrosis) 732.1
  - Oguchi's (retina) 368.61
  - Ohara's (*see also* Tularemia) 021.9
  - Ollier's (chondrodysplasia) 756.4
  - Opitz's (congestive splenomegaly) 289.51
  - Oppenheim's 358.8
  - Oppenheim-Urbach (necrobiosis lipoidica diabeticorum) 250.8 ☑ *[709.3]*
  - optic nerve NEC 377.49
  - orbit 376.9
    - specified NEC 376.89
  - Oriental liver fluke 121.1
  - Oriental lung fluke 121.2
  - Ormond's 593.4
  - Osgood-Schlatter 732.4
  - Osgood's tibia (tubercle) 732.4
  - Osler (-Vaquez) (polycythemia vera) (M9950/1) 238.4
  - Osler-Rendu (familial hemorrhagic telangiectasia) 448.0
  - osteofibrocystic 252.01
  - Otto's 715.35
  - outer ear 380.9
  - ovary (noninflammatory) NEC 620.9
    - cystic 620.2
    - polycystic 256.4
    - specified NEC 620.8
  - Owren's (congenital) (*see also* Defect, coagulation) 286.3
  - Paas' 756.59
  - Paget's (osteitis deformans) 731.0
    - with infiltrating duct carcinoma of the breast (M8541/3) — *see* Neoplasm, breast, malignant
    - bone 731.0
      - osteosarcoma in (M9184/3) — *see* Neoplasm, bone, malignant
    - breast (M8540/3) 174.0
    - extramammary (M8542/3) (*see also* Neoplasm, skin, malignant)

- **Disease, diseased** — *see also* Syndrome — *continued*
  - Paget's — *continued*
    - extramammary (*see also* Neoplasm, skin, malignant) — *continued*
      - anus 154.3
        - skin 173.5
    - malignant (M8540/3)
      - breast 174.0
      - specified site NEC (M8542/3) — *see* Neoplasm, skin, malignant
      - unspecified site 174.0
    - mammary (M8540/3) 174.0
    - nipple (M8540/3) 174.0
  - palate (soft) 528.9
  - Paltauf-Sternberg 201.9 ☑
  - pancreas 577.9
    - cystic 577.2
      - congenital 751.7
    - fibrocystic 277.00
  - Panner's 732.3
    - capitellum humeri 732.3
    - head of humerus 732.3
    - tarsal navicular (bone) (osteochondrosis) 732.5
  - panvalvular — *see* Endocarditis, mitral
  - parametrium 629.9
  - parasitic NEC 136.9
    - cerebral NEC 123.9
    - intestinal NEC 129
    - mouth 112.0
    - skin NEC 134.9
    - specified type — *see* Infestation
    - tongue 112.0
  - parathyroid (gland) 252.9
    - specified NEC 252.8
  - Parkinson's 332.0
  - parodontal 523.9
  - Parrot's (syphilitic osteochondritis) 090.0
  - Parry's (exophthalmic goiter) 242.0 ☑
  - Parson's (exophthalmic goiter) 242.0 ☑
  - Pavy's 593.6
  - Paxton's (white piedra) 111.2
  - Payr's (splenic flexure syndrome) 569.89
  - pearl-workers' (chronic osteomyelitis) (*see also* Osteomyelitis) 730.1 ☑
  - Pel-Ebstein — *see* Disease, Hodgkin's
  - Pelizaeus-Merzbacher 330.0
    - with dementia
      - with behavioral disturbance 330.0 *[294.11]*
      - without behavioral disturbance 330.0 *[294.10]*
  - Pellegrini-Stieda (calcification, knee joint) 726.62
  - pelvis, pelvic
    - female NEC 629.9
      - specified NEC 629.89 ▲
    - gonococcal (acute) 098.19
      - chronic or duration of 2 months or over 098.39
    - infection (*see also* Disease, pelvis, inflammatory) 614.9
    - inflammatory (female) (PID) 614.9
      - with
        - abortion — *see* Abortion, by type, with sepsis
        - ectopic pregnancy (*see also* categories 633.0–633.9) 639.0
        - molar pregnancy (*see also* categories 630–632) 639.0
      - acute 614.3
      - chronic 614.4
      - complicating pregnancy 646.6 ☑
        - affecting fetus or newborn 760.8

- **Disease, diseased** — *see also* Syndrome — *continued*
  - pelvis, pelvic — *continued*
    - inflammatory — *continued*
      - following
        - abortion 639.0
        - ectopic or molar pregnancy 639.0
      - peritonitis (acute) 614.5
        - chronic NEC 614.7
      - puerperal, postpartum, childbirth 670.0 ☑
      - specified NEC 614.8
    - organ, female NEC 629.9
      - specified NEC 629.89 ▲
    - peritoneum, female NEC 629.9
      - specified NEC 629.89 ▲
  - penis 607.9
    - inflammatory 607.2
  - peptic NEC 536.9
    - acid 536.8
  - periapical tissues NEC 522.9
  - pericardium 423.9
    - specified type NEC 423.8
  - perineum
    - female
      - inflammatory 616.9
        - specified NEC 616.89 ▲
      - noninflammatory 624.9
        - specified NEC 624.8
    - male (inflammatory) 682.2
  - periodic (familial) (Reimann's) NEC 277.31 ▲
    - paralysis 359.3
  - periodontal NEC 523.9
    - specified NEC 523.8
  - periosteum 733.90
  - peripheral
    - arterial 443.9
    - autonomic nervous system (*see also* Neuropathy, autonomic) 337.9
    - nerve NEC (*see also* Neuropathy) 356.9
      - multiple — *see* Polyneuropathy
    - vascular 443.9
      - specified type NEC 443.89
  - peritoneum 568.9
    - pelvic, female 629.9
      - specified NEC 629.89 ▲
  - Perrin-Ferraton (snapping hip) 719.65
  - persistent mucosal (middle ear) (with posterior or superior marginal perforation of ear drum) 382.2
  - Perthes' (capital femoral osteochondrosis) 732.1
  - Petit's (*see also* Hernia, lumbar) 553.8
  - Peutz-Jeghers 759.6
  - Peyronie's 607.85
  - Pfeiffer's (infectious mononucleosis) 075
  - pharynx 478.20
  - Phocas' 610.1
  - photochromogenic (acid-fast bacilli) (pulmonary) 031.0
    - nonpulmonary 031.9
  - Pick's
    - brain 331.11
      - with dementia
        - with behavioral disturbance 331.11 *[294.11]*
        - without behavioral disturbance 331.11 *[294.10]*
    - cerebral atrophy 331.11
      - with dementia
        - with behavioral disturbance 331.11 *[294.11]*
        - without behavioral disturbance 331.11 *[294.10]*
    - lipid histiocytosis 272.7
    - liver (pericardial pseudocirrhosis of liver) 423.2
    - pericardium (pericardial pseudocirrhosis of liver) 423.2
    - polyserositis (pericardial pseudocirrhosis of liver) 423.2

- **Disease, diseased** — *see also* Syndrome — *continued*
  - Pierson's (osteochondrosis) 732.1
  - pigeon fanciers' or breeders' 495.2
  - pineal gland 259.8
  - pink 985.0
  - Pinkus' (lichen nitidus) 697.1
  - pinworm 127.4
  - pituitary (gland) 253.9
    - hyperfunction 253.1
    - hypofunction 253.2
  - pituitary snuff-takers' 495.8
  - placenta
    - affecting fetus or newborn 762.2
    - complicating pregnancy or childbirth 656.7 ☑
  - pleura (cavity) (*see also* Pleurisy) 511.0
  - Plummer's (toxic nodular goiter) 242.3 ☑
  - pneumatic
    - drill 994.9
    - hammer 994.9
  - policeman's 729.2
  - Pollitzer's (hidradenitis suppurativa) 705.83
  - polycystic (congenital) 759.89
    - congenital 748.4
    - kidney or renal 753.12
      - adult type (APKD) 753.13
      - autosomal dominant 753.13
      - autosomal recessive 753.14
      - childhood type (CPKD) 753.14
      - infantile type 753.14
    - liver or hepatic 751.62
    - lung or pulmonary 518.89
    - ovary, ovaries 256.4
    - spleen 759.0
  - Pompe's (glycogenosis II) 271.0
  - Poncet's (tuberculous rheumatism) (*see also* Tuberculosis) 015.9 ☑
  - Posada-Wernicke 114.9
  - Potain's (pulmonary edema) 514
  - Pott's (*see also* Tuberculosis) 015.0 ☑ *[730.88]*
    - osteomyelitis 015.0 ☑ *[730.88]*
    - paraplegia 015.0 ☑ *[730.88]*
    - spinal curvature 015.0 ☑ *[737.43]*
    - spondylitis 015.0 ☑ *[720.81]*
  - Potter's 753.0
  - Poulet's 714.2
  - pregnancy NEC (*see also* Pregnancy) 646.9 ☑
  - Preiser's (osteoporosis) 733.09
  - Pringle's (tuberous sclerosis) 759.5
  - Profichet's 729.9
  - prostate 602.9
    - specified type NEC 602.8
  - protozoal NEC 136.8
    - intestine, intestinal NEC 007.9
  - pseudo-Hurler's (mucolipidosis III) 272.7
  - psychiatric (*see also* Psychosis) 298.9
  - psychotic (*see also* Psychosis) 298.9
  - Puente's (simple glandular cheilitis) 528.5
  - puerperal NEC (*see also* Puerperal) 674.9 ☑
  - pulmonary (*see also* Disease, lung)
    - amyloid 277.39 *[517.8]* ▲
    - artery 417.9
    - circulation, circulatory 417.9
      - specified NEC 417.8
    - diffuse obstructive (chronic) 496
      - with
        - acute bronchitis 491.22
        - asthma (chronic) (obstructive) 493.2 ☑
        - exacerbation NEC (acute) 491.21
    - heart (chronic) 416.9
      - specified NEC 416.8
    - hypertensive (vascular) 416.0
      - cardiovascular 416.0
    - obstructive diffuse (chronic) 496

☑ Additional Digit Required — Refer to the Tabular List for Digit Selection

Subterms under main terms may continue to next column or page

▶◀ Revised Text ● New Line ▲ Revised Code

Disease, diseased — *see also* Syndrome — *continued*
pulmonary (*see also* Disease, lung) — *continued*
obstructive diffuse — *continued*
with
acute bronchitis 491.22
asthma (chronic) (obstructive) 493.2 ☑
bronchitis (chronic) 491.20
with
exacerbation (acute) 491.21
acute 491.22
exacerbation NEC (acute) 491.21
decompensated 491.21 ●
with exacerbation 491.21 ●
valve (*see also* Endocarditis, pulmonary) 424.3
pulp (dental) NEC 522.9
pulseless 446.7
Putnam's (subacute combined sclerosis with pernicious anemia) 281.0 *[336.2]*
Pyle (-Cohn) (craniometaphyseal dysplasia) 756.89
pyramidal tract 333.90
Quervain's
tendon sheath 727.04
thyroid (subacute granulomatous thyroiditis) 245.1
Quincke's — *see* Edema, angioneurotic
Quinquaud (acne decalvans) 704.09
rag sorters' 022.1
Raynaud's (paroxysmal digital cyanosis) 443.0
reactive airway — *see* Asthma
Recklinghausen's (M9540/1) 237.71
bone (osteitis fibrosa cystica) 252.01
Recklinghausen-Applebaum (hemochromatosis) 275.0
Reclus' (cystic) 610.1
rectum NEC 569.49
Refsum's (heredopathia atactica polyneuritiformis) 356.3
Reichmann's (gastrosuccorrhea) 536.8
Reimann's (periodic) 277.31 ▲
Reiter's 099.3
renal (functional) (pelvis) (*see also* Disease, kidney) 593.9
with
edema (*see also* Nephrosis) 581.9
exudative nephritis 583.89
lesion of interstitial nephritis 583.89
stated generalized cause — *see* Nephritis
acute 593.9
basement membrane NEC 583.89
with
pulmonary hemorrhage (Goodpasture's syndrome) 446.21 *[583.81]*
chronic (*see also* Disease, kidney, chronic) 593.9
complicating pregnancy or puerperium NEC 646.2 ☑
with hypertension — *see* Toxemia, of pregnancy
affecting fetus or newborn 760.1
cystic, congenital (*see also* Cystic, disease, kidney) 753.10
diabetic 250.4 ☑ *[583.81]*
due to
amyloidosis 277.39 *[583.81]* ▲
diabetes mellitus 250.4 ☑ *[583.81]*
systemic lupus erythematosis 710.0 *[583.81]*
end-stage 585.6
exudative 583.89

Disease, diseased — *see also* Syndrome — *continued*
renal (*see also* Disease, kidney) — *continued*
fibrocystic (congenital) 753.19
gonococcal 098.19 *[583.81]*
gouty 274.10
hypertensive (*see also* Hypertension, kidney) 403.90
immune complex NEC 583.89
interstitial (diffuse) (focal) 583.89
lupus 710.0 *[583.81]*
maternal, affecting fetus or newborn 760.1
hypertensive 760.0
phosphate-losing (tubular) 588.0
polycystic (congenital) 753.12
adult type (APKD) 753.13
autosomal dominant 753.13
autosomal recessive 753.14
childhood type (CPKD) 753.14
infantile type 753.14
specified lesion or cause NEC (*see also* Glomerulonephritis) 583.89
subacute 581.9
syphilitic 095.4
tuberculous (*see also* Tuberculosis) 016.0 ☑ *[583.81]*
tubular (*see also* Nephrosis, tubular) 584.5
Rendu-Osler-Weber (familial hemorrhagic telangiectasia) 448.0
renovascular (arteriosclerotic) (*see also* Hypertension, kidney) 403.90
respiratory (tract) 519.9
acute or subacute (upper) NEC 465.9
due to fumes or vapors 506.3
multiple sites NEC 465.8
noninfectious 478.9
streptococcal 034.0
chronic 519.9
arising in the perinatal period 770.7
due to fumes or vapors 506.4
due to
aspiration of liquids or solids 508.9
external agents NEC 508.9
specified NEC 508.8
fumes or vapors 506.9
acute or subacute NEC 506.3
chronic 506.4
fetus or newborn NEC 770.9
obstructive 496
specified type NEC 519.8
upper (acute) (infectious) NEC 465.9
multiple sites NEC 465.8
noninfectious NEC 478.9
streptococcal 034.0
retina, retinal NEC 362.9
Batten's or Batten-Mayou 330.1 *[362.71]*
degeneration 362.89
vascular lesion 362.17
rheumatic (*see also* Arthritis) 716.8 ☑
heart — *see* Disease, heart, rheumatic
rheumatoid (heart) — *see* Arthritis, rheumatoid
rickettsial NEC 083.9
specified type NEC 083.8
Riedel's (ligneous thyroiditis) 245.3
Riga (-Fede) (cachectic aphthae) 529.0
Riggs' (compound periodontitis) 523.40 ▲
Ritter's 695.81
Rivalta's (cervicofacial actinomycosis) 039.3
Robles' (onchocerciasis) 125.3 *[360.13]*
Roger's (congenital interventricular septal defect) 745.4
Rokitansky's (*see also* Necrosis, liver) 570

Disease, diseased — *see also* Syndrome — *continued*
Romberg's 349.89
Rosenthal's (factor XI deficiency) 286.2
Rossbach's (hyperchlorhydria) 536.8
psychogenic 306.4
Roth (-Bernhardt) 355.1
Runeberg's (progressive pernicious anemia) 281.0
Rust's (tuberculous spondylitis) (*see also* Tuberculosis) 015.0 ☑ *[720.81]*
Rustitskii's (multiple myeloma) (M9730/3) 203.0 ☑
Ruysch's (Hirschsprung's disease) 751.3
Sachs (-Tay) 330.1
sacroiliac NEC 724.6
salivary gland or duct NEC 527.9
inclusion 078.5
streptococcal 034.0
virus 078.5
Sander's (paranoia) 297.1
Sandhoff's 330.1
sandworm 126.9
Savill's (epidemic exfoliative dermatitis) 695.89
Schamberg's (progressive pigmentary dermatosis) 709.09
Schaumann's (sarcoidosis) 135
Schenck's (sporotrichosis) 117.1
Scheuermann's (osteochondrosis) 732.0
Schilder (-Flatau) 341.1
Schimmelbusch's 610.1
Schlatter-Osgood 732.4
Schlatter's tibia (tubercle) 732.4
Schmorl's 722.30
cervical 722.39
lumbar, lumbosacral 722.32
specified region NEC 722.39
thoracic, thoracolumbar 722.31
Scholz's 330.0
Schönlein (-Henoch) (purpura rheumatica) 287.0
Schottmüller's (*see also* Fever, paratyphoid) 002.9
Schüller-Christian (chronic histiocytosis X) 277.89
Schultz's (agranulocytosis) 288.09 ▲
Schwalbe-Ziehen-Oppenheimer 333.6
Schweninger-Buzzi (macular atrophy) 701.3
sclera 379.19
scrofulous (*see also* Tuberculosis) 017.2 ☑
scrotum 608.9
sebaceous glands NEC 706.9
Secretan's (posttraumatic edema) 782.3
semilunar cartilage, cystic 717.5
seminal vesicle 608.9
Senear-Usher (pemphigus erythematosus) 694.4
serum NEC 999.5
Sever's (osteochondrosis calcaneum) 732.5
Sézary's (reticulosis) (M9701/3) 202.2 ☑
Shaver's (bauxite pneumoconiosis) 503
Sheehan's (postpartum pituitary necrosis) 253.2
shimamushi (scrub typhus) 081.2
shipyard 077.1
sickle cell 282.60
with
crisis 282.62
Hb-S disease 282.61
other abnormal hemoglobin (Hb-D) (Hb-E) (Hb-G) (Hb-J) (Hb-K) (Hb-O) (Hb-P) (high fetal gene) (without crisis) 282.68
with crisis 282.69

Disease, diseased — *see also* Syndrome — *continued*
sickle cell — *continued*
elliptocytosis 282.60
Hb-C (without crisis) 282.63
with
crisis 282.64
vaso-occlusive pain 282.64
Hb-S 282.61
with
crisis 282.62
Hb-C (without crisis) 282.63
with
crisis 282.64
vaso-occlusive pain 282.64
other abnormal hemoglobin (Hb-D) (Hb-E) (Hb-G) (Hb-J) (Hb-K) (Hb-O) (Hb-P) (high fetal gene) (without crisis) 282.68
with crisis 282.69
spherocytosis 282.60
thalassemia (without crisis) 282.41
with
crisis 282.42
vaso-occlusive pain 282.42
Siegal-Cattan-Mamou (periodic) 277.31 ▲
silo fillers' 506.9
Simian B 054.3
Simmonds' (pituitary cachexia) 253.2
Simons' (progressive lipodystrophy) 272.6
Sinding-Larsen (juvenile osteopathia patellae) 732.4
sinus (*see also* Sinusitis)
brain 437.9
specified NEC 478.19 ▲
Sirkari's 085.0
sixth 057.8
Sjögren (-Gougerot) 710.2
with lung involvement 710.2 *[517.8]*
Skevas-Zerfus 989.5
skin NEC 709.9
due to metabolic disorder 277.9
specified type NEC 709.8
sleeping (*see also* Narcolepsy) 347.00
meaning sleeping sickness (*see also* Trypanosomiasis) 086.5
small vessel 443.9
Smith-Strang (oasthouse urine) 270.2
Sneddon-Wilkinson (subcorneal pustular dermatosis) 694.1
South African creeping 133.8
Spencer's (epidemic vomiting) 078.82
Spielmeyer-Stock 330.1
Spielmeyer-Vogt 330.1
spine, spinal 733.90
combined system (*see also* Degeneration, combined) 266.2 *[336.2]*
with pernicious anemia 281.0 *[336.2]*
cord NEC 336.9
congenital 742.9
demyelinating NEC 341.8
joint (*see also* Disease, joint, spine) 724.9
tuberculous 015.0 ☑ *[730.8]* ☑
spinocerebellar 334.9
specified NEC 334.8
spleen (organic) (postinfectional) 289.50
amyloid 277.39 ▲
lardaceous 277.39 ▲
polycystic 759.0
specified NEC 289.59
sponge divers' 989.5
Stanton's (melioidosis) 025
Stargardt's 362.75
Startle 759.89
Steinert's 359.2
Sternberg's — *see* Disease, Hodgkin's

> *Note — "Closed" includes simple, complete, partial, uncomplicated, and unspecified dislocation.*
>
> *"Open" includes dislocation specified as infected or compound and dislocation with foreign body.*
>
> *"Chronic," "habitual," "old," or "recurrent" dislocations should be coded as indicated under the entry "Dislocation, recurrent," and "pathological" as indicated under the entry "Dislocation, pathological."*
>
> *For late effect of dislocation see Late, effect, dislocation.*

☑ Additional Digit Required — Refer to the Tabular List for Digit Selection

▾ Subterms under main terms may continue to next column or page

▸◂ Revised Text ● New Line ▲ Revised Code

☑ Additional Digit Required — Refer to the Tabular List for Digit Selection

Subterms under main terms may continue to next column or page

▶◀ Revised Text ● New Line ▲ Revised Code

Note — Use the following fifth-digit subclassification with categories 312.0–312.2:
0 unspecified
1 mild
2 moderate
3 severe

☑ Additional Digit Required — Refer to the Tabular List for Digit Selection
Subterms under main terms may continue to next column or page
▶◀ Revised Text ● New Line ▲ Revised Code

Division — *continued*
ligament (*see also* Sprain, by site) — *continued*
with open wound — *see* Wound, open, by site
muscle (partial or complete) (current) (*see also* Sprain, by site)
with open wound — *see* Wound, open, by site
nerve — *see* Injury, nerve, by site
penis glans 752.69
spinal cord — *see* Injury, spinal, by site
vein 459.9
traumatic — *see* Injury, vascular, by site
Divorce V61.0
Dix-Hallpike neurolabyrinthitis 386.12
Dizziness 780.4
hysterical 300.11
psychogenic 306.9
Doan-Wiseman syndrome (primary splenic neutropenia) 289.53 ▲
Dog bite — *see* Wound, open, by site
Döhle body-panmyelopathic syndrome 288.2
Döhle-Heller aortitis 093.1
Dolichocephaly, dolichocephalus 754.0
Dolichocolon 751.5
Dolichostenomelia 759.82
Donohue's syndrome (leprechaunism) 259.8
Donor
blood V59.01
other blood components V59.09
stem cells V59.02
whole blood V59.01
bone V59.2
marrow V59.3
cornea V59.5
egg (oocyte) (ovum) V59.70
over age 35 V59.73
anonymous recipient V59.73
designated recipient V59.74
under age 35 V59.71
anonymous recipient V59.71
designated recipient V59.72
heart V59.8
kidney V59.4
liver V59.6
lung V59.8
lymphocyte V59.8
organ V59.9
specified NEC V59.8
potential, examination of V70.8
skin V59.1
specified organ or tissue NEC V59.8
sperm V59.8
stem cells V59.02
tissue V59.9
specified type NEC V59.8
Donovanosis (granuloma venereum) 099.2
DOPS (diffuse obstructive pulmonary syndrome) 496
Double
albumin 273.8
aortic arch 747.21
auditory canal 744.29
auricle (heart) 746.82
bladder 753.8
external (cervical) os 752.49
kidney with double pelvis (renal) 753.3
larynx 748.3
meatus urinarius 753.8
organ or site NEC — *see* Accessory
orifice
heart valve NEC 746.89
pulmonary 746.09
outlet, right ventricle 745.11
pelvis (renal) with double ureter 753.4
penis 752.69
tongue 750.13
ureter (one or both sides) 753.4
with double pelvis (renal) 753.4
urethra 753.8

Double — *continued*
urinary meatus 753.8
uterus (any degree) 752.2
with doubling of cervix and vagina 752.2
in pregnancy or childbirth 654.0 ☑
affecting fetus or newborn 763.89
vagina 752.49
with doubling of cervix and uterus 752.2
vision 368.2
vocal cords 748.3
vulva 752.49
whammy (syndrome) 360.81
Douglas' pouch, cul-de-sac — *see* condition
Down's disease or syndrome (mongolism) 758.0
Down-growth, epithelial (anterior chamber) 364.61
Dracontiasis 125.7
Dracunculiasis 125.7
Dracunculosis 125.7
Drainage
abscess (spontaneous) — *see* Abscess
anomalous pulmonary veins to hepatic veins or right atrium 747.41
stump (amputation) (surgical) 997.62
suprapubic, bladder 596.8
Dream state, hysterical 300.13
Drepanocytic anemia — *see also* Disease, sickle cell 282.60
Dresbach's syndrome (elliptocytosis) 282.1
Dreschlera (infection) 118
hawaiiensis 117.8
Dressler's syndrome (postmyocardial infarction) 411.0
Dribbling (post-void) 788.35
Drift, ulnar 736.09
Drinking (alcohol) — *see also* Alcoholism
excessive, to excess NEC (*see also* Abuse, drugs, nondependent) 305.0 ☑
bouts, periodic 305.0 ☑
continual 303.9 ☑
episodic 305.0 ☑
habitual 303.9 ☑
periodic 305.0 ☑
Drip, postnasal (chronic) 784.91 ▲
due to ●
allergic rhinitis — *see* Rhinitis, allergic ●
common cold 460 ●
gastroesophageal reflux — *see* Reflux, gastroesophageal ●
nasopharyngitis — *see* Nasopharyngitis ●
other known condition — code to condition ●
sinusitis — *see* Sinusitis ●
Drivers' license examination V70.3
Droop
Cooper's 611.8
facial 781.94
Drop
finger 736.29
foot 736.79
hematocrit (precipitous) 790.01
toe 735.8
wrist 736.05
Dropped
dead 798.1
heart beats 426.6
Dropsy, dropsical — *see also* Edema 782.3
abdomen 789.5
amnion (*see also* Hydramnios) 657.0 ☑
brain — *see* Hydrocephalus
cardiac (*see also* Failure, heart) 428.0
cardiorenal (*see also* Hypertension, cardiorenal) 404.90
chest 511.9

Dropsy, dropsical — *see also* Edema — *continued*
fetus or newborn 778.0
due to isoimmunization 773.3
gangrenous (*see also* Gangrene) 785.4
heart (*see also* Failure, heart) 428.0
hepatic — *see* Cirrhosis, liver
infantile — *see* Hydrops, fetalis
kidney (*see also* Nephrosis) 581.9
liver — *see* Cirrhosis, liver
lung 514
malarial (*see also* Malaria) 084.9
neonatorum — *see* Hydrops, fetalis
nephritic 581.9
newborn — *see* Hydrops, fetalis
nutritional 269.9
ovary 620.8
pericardium (*see also* Pericarditis) 423.9
renal (*see also* Nephrosis) 581.9
uremic — *see* Uremia
Drowned, drowning 994.1
lung 518.5
Drowsiness 780.09
Drug — *see also* condition
addiction (*see also* listing under Dependence) 304.9 ☑
adverse effect NEC, correct substance properly administered 995.20 ▲
allergy 995.27 ●
dependence (*see also* listing under Dependence) 304.9 ☑
habit (*see also* listing under Dependence) 304.9 ☑
hypersensitivity 995.27 ●
induced
circadian rhythm sleep disorder 292.85
hypersomnia 292.85
insomnia 292.85
mental disorder 292.9
anxiety 292.89
mood 292.84
sexual 292.89
sleep 292.85
specified type 292.89
parasomnia 292.85
persisting
amnestic disorder 292.83
dementia 292.82
psychotic disorder
with
delusions 292.11
hallucinations 292.12
sleep disorder 292.85
intoxication 292.89
overdose — *see* Table of Drugs and Chemicals
poisoning — *see* Table of Drugs and Chemicals
therapy (maintenance) status NEC
chemotherapy, antineoplastic V58.11
immunotherapy, antineoplastic V58.12
long-term (current) use V58.69
antibiotics V58.62
anticoagulants V58.61
anti-inflammatories, non-steroidal (NSAID) V58.64
antiplatelets V58.63
antithrombotics V58.63
aspirin V58.66
insulin V58.67
steroids V58.65
wrong substance given or taken in error — *see* Table of Drugs and Chemicals
Drunkenness — *see also* Abuse, drugs, nondependent 305.0 ☑
acute in alcoholism (*see also* Alcoholism) 303.0 ☑
chronic (*see also* Alcoholism) 303.9 ☑
pathologic 291.4
simple (acute) 305.0 ☑

Drunkenness — *see also* Abuse, drugs, nondependent — *continued*
simple — *continued*
in alcoholism 303.0 ☑
sleep 307.47
Drusen
optic disc or papilla 377.21
retina (colloid) (hyaloid degeneration) 362.57
hereditary 362.77
Drusenfieber 075
Dry, dryness — *see also* condition
eye 375.15
syndrome 375.15
larynx 478.79
mouth 527.7
nose 478.19 ▲
skin syndrome 701.1
socket (teeth) 526.5
throat 478.29
DSAP (disseminated superficial actinic porokeratosis) 692.75
Duane's retraction syndrome 378.71
Duane-Stilling-Türk syndrome (ocular retraction syndrome) 378.71
Dubini's disease (electric chorea) 049.8
Dubin-Johnson disease or syndrome 277.4
Dubois' abscess or disease 090.5
Duchenne's
disease 094.0
locomotor ataxia 094.0
muscular dystrophy 359.1
pseudohypertrophy, muscles 359.1
paralysis 335.22
syndrome 335.22
Duchenne-Aran myelopathic, muscular atrophy (nonprogressive) (progressive) 335.21
Duchenne-Griesinger disease 359.1
Ducrey's
bacillus 099.0
chancre 099.0
disease (chancroid) 099.0
Duct, ductus — *see* condition
Duengero 061
Duhring's disease (dermatitis herpetiformis) 694.0
Dukes (-Filatov) disease 057.8
Dullness
cardiac (decreased) (increased) 785.3
Dumb ague — *see also* Malaria 084.6
Dumbness — *see also* Aphasia 784.3
Dumdum fever 085.0
Dumping syndrome (postgastrectomy) 564.2
nonsurgical 536.8
Duodenitis (nonspecific) (peptic) 535.60
with hemorrhage 535.61
due to
Strongyloides stercoralis 127.2
Duodenocholangitis 575.8
Duodenum, duodenal — *see* condition
Duplay's disease, periarthritis, or syndrome 726.2
Duplex — *see also* Accessory
kidney 753.3
placenta — *see* Placenta, abnormal
uterus 752.2
Duplication — *see also* Accessory
anus 751.5
aortic arch 747.21
appendix 751.5
biliary duct (any) 751.69
bladder 753.8
cecum 751.5
and appendix 751.5
clitoris 752.49
cystic duct 751.69
digestive organs 751.8
duodenum 751.5
esophagus 750.4
fallopian tube 752.19
frontonasal process 756.0
gallbladder 751.69
ileum 751.5

- **Dystonia**
  - acute ●
    - due to drugs 333.72 ●
    - neuroleptic-induced acute 333.72 ●
  - deformans progressiva 333.6
  - lenticularis 333.6
  - musculorum deformans 333.6
  - torsion (idiopathic) 333.6
    - acquired 333.79 ●
    - fragments (of) 333.89
    - genetic 333.6 ●
    - symptomatic 333.79 ▲
- **Dystonic**
  - movements 781.0
- **Dystopia kidney** 753.3
- **Dystrophia myotonica** 359.2
- **Dystrophy, dystrophia** 783.9
  - adiposogenital 253.8
  - asphyxiating thoracic 756.4
  - Becker's type 359.1
  - brevicollis 756.16
  - Bruch's membrane 362.77
  - cervical (sympathetic) NEC 337.0
  - chondro-osseus with punctate epiphyseal dysplasia 756.59
  - choroid (hereditary) 363.50
    - central (areolar) (partial) 363.53
      - total (gyrate) 363.54
    - circinate 363.53
    - circumpapillary (partial) 363.51
      - total 363.52
    - diffuse
      - partial 363.56
      - total 363.57
    - generalized
      - partial 363.56
      - total 363.57
    - gyrate
      - central 363.54
      - generalized 363.57
    - helicoid 363.52
    - peripapillary — *see* Dystrophy, choroid, circumpapillary
    - serpiginous 363.54
  - cornea (hereditary) 371.50
    - anterior NEC 371.52
    - Cogan's 371.52
    - combined 371.57
    - crystalline 371.56
    - endothelial (Fuchs') 371.57
    - epithelial 371.50
      - juvenile 371.51
      - microscopic cystic 371.52
    - granular 371.53
    - lattice 371.54
    - macular 371.55
    - marginal (Terrien's) 371.48
    - Meesman's 371.51
    - microscopic cystic (epithelial) 371.52
    - nodular, Salzmann's 371.46
    - polymorphous 371.58
    - posterior NEC 371.58
    - ring-like 371.52
    - Salzmann's nodular 371.46
    - stromal NEC 371.56
  - dermatochondrocorneal 371.50
  - Duchenne's 359.1
  - due to malnutrition 263.9
  - Erb's 359.1
  - familial
    - hyperplastic periosteal 756.59
    - osseous 277.5
  - foveal 362.77
  - Fuchs', cornea 371.57
  - Gowers' muscular 359.1
  - hair 704.2
  - hereditary, progressive muscular 359.1
  - hypogenital, with diabetic tendency 759.81
  - Landouzy-Déjérine 359.1
  - Leyden-Möbius 359.1
  - mesodermalis congenita 759.82
  - muscular 359.1
    - congenital (hereditary) 359.0

- **Dystrophy, dystrophia** — *continued*
  - muscular — *continued*
    - congenital — *continued*
      - myotonic 359.2
    - distal 359.1
    - Duchenne's 359.1
    - Erb's 359.1
    - fascioscapulohumeral 359.1
    - Gowers' 359.1
    - hereditary (progressive) 359.1
    - Landouzy-Déjérine 359.1
    - limb-girdle 359.1
    - myotonic 359.2
    - progressive (hereditary) 359.1
      - Charcôt-Marie-Tooth 356.1
    - pseudohypertrophic (infantile) 359.1
  - myocardium, myocardial (*see also* Degeneration, myocardial) 429.1
  - myotonic 359.2
  - myotonica 359.2
  - nail 703.8
    - congenital 757.5
  - neurovascular (traumatic) (*see also* Neuropathy, peripheral, autonomic) 337.9
  - nutritional 263.9
  - ocular 359.1
  - oculocerebrorenal 270.8
  - oculopharyngeal 359.1
  - ovarian 620.8
  - papillary (and pigmentary) 701.1
  - pelvicrural atrophic 359.1
  - pigmentary (*see also* Acanthosis) 701.2
  - pituitary (gland) 253.8
  - polyglandular 258.8
  - posttraumatic sympathetic — *see* Dystrophy, sympathetic
  - progressive ophthalmoplegic 359.1
  - retina, retinal (hereditary) 362.70
    - albipunctate 362.74
    - Bruch's membrane 362.77
    - cone, progressive 362.75
    - hyaline 362.77
    - in
      - Bassen-Kornzweig syndrome 272.5 *[362.72]*
      - cerebroretinal lipidosis 330.1 *[362.71]*
      - Refsum's disease 356.3 *[362.72]*
      - systemic lipidosis 272.7 *[362.71]*
    - juvenile (Stargardt's) 362.75
    - pigmentary 362.74
    - pigment epithelium 362.76
    - progressive cone (-rod) 362.75
    - pseudoinflammatory foveal 362.77
    - rod, progressive 362.75
    - sensory 362.75
    - vitelliform 362.76
  - Salzmann's nodular 371.46
  - scapuloperoneal 359.1
  - skin NEC 709.9
  - sympathetic (posttraumatic) (reflex) 337.20
    - lower limb 337.22
    - specified site NEC 337.29
    - upper limb 337.21
  - tapetoretinal NEC 362.74
  - thoracic asphyxiating 756.4
  - unguium 703.8
    - congenital 757.5
  - vitreoretinal (primary) 362.73
    - secondary 362.66
  - vulva 624.0
- **Dysuria** 788.1
  - psychogenic 306.53

E

- **Eagle-Barrett syndrome** 756.71
- **Eales' disease** (syndrome) 362.18
- **Ear** — *see also* condition
  - ache 388.70
    - otogenic 388.71
    - referred 388.72
  - lop 744.29

- **Ear** — *see also* condition — *continued*
  - piercing V50.3
  - swimmers' acute 380.12
  - tank 380.12
  - tropical 111.8 *[380.15]*
  - wax 380.4
- **Earache** 388.70
  - otogenic 388.71
  - referred 388.72
- **Early satiety** 780.94
- **Eaton-Lambert syndrome** — *see also* Neoplasm, by site, malignant 199.1 *[358.1]*
- **Eberth's disease** (typhoid fever) 002.0
- **Ebstein's**
  - anomaly or syndrome (downward displacement, tricuspid valve into right ventricle) 746.2
  - disease (diabetes) 250.4 ☑ *[581.81]*
- **Eccentro-osteochondrodysplasia** 277.5
- **Ecchondroma** (M9210/0) — *see* Neoplasm, bone, benign
- **Ecchondrosis** (M9210/1) 238.0
- **Ecchordosis physaliphora** 756.0
- **Ecchymosis** (multiple) 459.89
  - conjunctiva 372.72
  - eye (traumatic) 921.0
  - eyelids (traumatic) 921.1
  - newborn 772.6
  - spontaneous 782.7
  - traumatic — *see* Contusion
- **Echinococciasis** — *see* Echinococcus
- **Echinococcosis** — *see* Echinococcus
- **Echinococcus** (infection) 122.9
  - granulosus 122.4
    - liver 122.0
    - lung 122.1
    - orbit 122.3 *[376.13]*
    - specified site NEC 122.3
    - thyroid 122.2
  - liver NEC 122.8
    - granulosus 122.0
    - multilocularis 122.5
  - lung NEC 122.9
    - granulosus 122.1
    - multilocularis 122.6
  - multilocularis 122.7
    - liver 122.5
    - specified site NEC 122.6
  - orbit 122.9 *[376.13]*
    - granulosus 122.3 *[376.13]*
    - multilocularis 122.6 *[376.13]*
  - specified site NEC 122.9
    - granulosus 122.3
    - multilocularis 122.6 *[376.13]*
  - thyroid NEC 122.9
    - granulosus 122.2
    - multilocularis 122.6
- **Echinorhynchiasis** 127.7
- **Echinostomiasis** 121.8
- **Echolalia** 784.69
- **ECHO virus infection** NEC 079.1
- **Eclampsia, eclamptic** (coma) (convulsions) (delirium) 780.39
  - female, child-bearing age NEC — *see* Eclampsia, pregnancy
  - gravidarum — *see* Eclampsia, pregnancy
  - male 780.39
  - not associated with pregnancy or childbirth 780.39
  - pregnancy, childbirth, or puerperium 642.6 ☑
    - with pre-existing hypertension 642.7 ☑
      - affecting fetus or newborn 760.0
  - uremic 586
- **Eclipse blindness** (total) 363.31
- **Economic circumstance affecting care** V60.9
  - specified type NEC V60.8
- **Economo's disease** (encephalitis lethargica) 049.8
- **Ectasia, ectasis**
  - aorta (*see also* Aneurysm, aorta) 441.9
    - ruptured 441.5

- **Ectasia, ectasis** — *continued*
  - breast 610.4
  - capillary 448.9
  - cornea (marginal) (postinfectional) 371.71
  - duct (mammary) 610.4
  - kidney 593.89
  - mammary duct (gland) 610.4
  - papillary 448.9
  - renal 593.89
  - salivary gland (duct) 527.8
  - scar, cornea 371.71
  - sclera 379.11
- **Ecthyma** 686.8
  - contagiosum 051.2
  - gangrenosum 686.09
  - infectiosum 051.2
- **Ectocardia** 746.87
- **Ectodermal dysplasia, congenital** 757.31
- **Ectodermosis erosiva pluriorificialis** 695.1
- **Ectopic, ectopia** (congenital) 759.89
  - abdominal viscera 751.8
    - due to defect in anterior abdominal wall 756.79
  - ACTH syndrome 255.0
  - adrenal gland 759.1
  - anus 751.5
  - auricular beats 427.61
  - beats 427.60
  - bladder 753.5
  - bone and cartilage in lung 748.69
  - brain 742.4
  - breast tissue 757.6
  - cardiac 746.87
  - cerebral 742.4
  - cordis 746.87
  - endometrium 617.9
  - gallbladder 751.69
  - gastric mucosa 750.7
  - gestation — *see* Pregnancy, ectopic
  - heart 746.87
  - hormone secretion NEC 259.3
  - hyperparathyroidism 259.3
  - kidney (crossed) (intrathoracic) (pelvis) 753.3
    - in pregnancy or childbirth 654.4 ☑
      - causing obstructed labor 660.2 ☑
  - lens 743.37
  - lentis 743.37
  - mole — *see* Pregnancy, ectopic
  - organ or site NEC — *see* Malposition, congenital
  - ovary 752.0
  - pancreas, pancreatic tissue 751.7
  - pregnancy — *see* Pregnancy, ectopic
  - pupil 364.75
  - renal 753.3
  - sebaceous glands of mouth 750.26
  - secretion
    - ACTH 255.0
    - adrenal hormone 259.3
    - adrenalin 259.3
    - adrenocorticotropin 255.0
    - antidiuretic hormone (ADH) 259.3
    - epinephrine 259.3
    - hormone NEC 259.3
    - norepinephrine 259.3
    - pituitary (posterior) 259.3
  - spleen 759.0
  - testis 752.51
  - thyroid 759.2
  - ureter 753.4
  - ventricular beats 427.69
  - vesicae 753.5
- **Ectrodactyly** 755.4
  - finger (*see also* Absence, finger, congenital) 755.29
  - toe (*see also* Absence, toe, congenital) 755.39
- **Ectromelia** 755.4
  - lower limb 755.30
  - upper limb 755.20
- **Ectropion** 374.10

☑ Additional Digit Required — Refer to the Tabular List for Digit Selection

Subterms under main terms may continue to next column or page

▶◀ Revised Text ● New Line ▲ Revised Code

- **Embolism** — *continued*
  - air — *continued*
    - with
      - abortion — *see* Abortion, by type, with embolism
      - ectopic pregnancy (*see also* categories 633.0–633.9) 639.6
      - molar pregnancy (*see also* categories 630–632) 639.6
    - due to implanted device — *see* Complications, due to (presence of) any device, implant, or graft classified to 996.0–996.5 NEC
    - following
      - abortion 639.6
      - ectopic or molar pregnancy 639.6
      - infusion, perfusion, or transfusion 999.1
    - in pregnancy, childbirth, or puerperium 673.0 ☑
    - traumatic 958.0
  - amniotic fluid (pulmonary) 673.1 ☑
    - with
      - abortion — *see* Abortion, by type, with embolism
      - ectopic pregnancy (*see also* categories 633.0–633.9) 639.6
      - molar pregnancy (*see also* categories 630–632) 639.6
    - following
      - abortion 639.6
      - ectopic or molar pregnancy 639.6
  - aorta, aortic 444.1
    - abdominal 444.0
    - bifurcation 444.0
    - saddle 444.0
    - thoracic 444.1
  - artery 444.9
    - auditory, internal 433.8 ☑
    - basilar (*see also* Occlusion, artery, basilar) 433.0 ☑
    - bladder 444.89
    - carotid (common) (internal) (*see also* Occlusion, artery, carotid) 433.1 ☑
    - cerebellar (anterior inferior) (posterior inferior) (superior) 433.8 ☑
    - cerebral (*see also* Embolism, brain) 434.1 ☑
    - choroidal (anterior) 433.8 ☑
    - communicating posterior 433.8 ☑
    - coronary (*see also* Infarct, myocardium) 410.9 ☑
      - without myocardial infarction 411.81
    - extremity 444.22
      - lower 444.22
      - upper 444.21
    - hypophyseal 433.8 ☑
    - mesenteric (with gangrene) 557.0
    - ophthalmic (*see also* Occlusion, retina) 362.30
    - peripheral 444.22
    - pontine 433.8 ☑
    - precerebral NEC — *see* Occlusion, artery, precerebral
    - pulmonary — *see* Embolism, pulmonary
    - renal 593.81
    - retinal (*see also* Occlusion, retina) 362.30
    - specified site NEC 444.89
    - vertebral (*see also* Occlusion, artery, vertebral) 433.2 ☑
  - auditory, internal 433.8 ☑
  - basilar (artery) (*see also* Occlusion, artery, basilar) 433.0 ☑
  - birth, mother — *see* Embolism, obstetrical

- **Embolism** — *continued*
  - blood-clot
    - with
      - abortion — *see* Abortion, by type, with embolism
      - ectopic pregnancy (*see also* categories 633.0–633.9) 639.6
      - molar pregnancy (*see also* categories 630–632) 639.6
    - following
      - abortion 639.6
      - ectopic or molar pregnancy 639.6
    - in pregnancy, childbirth, or puerperium 673.2 ☑
  - brain 434.1 ☑
    - with
      - abortion — *see* Abortion, by type, with embolism
      - ectopic pregnancy (*see also* categories 633.0–633.9) 639.6
      - molar pregnancy (*see also* categories 630–632) 639.6
    - following
      - abortion 639.6
      - ectopic or molar pregnancy 639.6
    - late effect — *see* Late effect(s) (of) cerebrovascular disease
    - puerperal, postpartum, childbirth 674.0 ☑
  - capillary 448.9
  - cardiac (*see also* Infarct, myocardium) 410.9 ☑
  - carotid (artery) (common) (internal) (*see also* Occlusion, artery, carotid) 433.1 ☑
  - cavernous sinus (venous) — *see* Embolism, intracranial venous sinus
  - cerebral (*see also* Embolism, brain) 434.1 ☑
  - cholesterol — *see* Atheroembolism
  - choroidal (anterior) (artery) 433.8 ☑
  - coronary (artery or vein) (systemic) (*see also* Infarct, myocardium) 410.9 ☑
    - without myocardial infarction 411.81
  - due to (presence of) any device, implant, or graft classifiable to 996.0–996.5 — *see* Complications, due to (presence of) any device, implant, or graft classified to 996.0–996.5 NEC
  - encephalomalacia (*see also* Embolism, brain) 434.1 ☑
  - extremities 444.22
    - lower 444.22
    - upper 444.21
  - eye 362.30
  - fat (cerebral) (pulmonary) (systemic) 958.1
    - with
      - abortion — *see* Abortion, by type, with embolism
      - ectopic pregnancy (*see also* categories 633.0–633.9) 639.6
      - molar pregnancy (*see also* categories 630–632) 639.6
    - complicating delivery or puerperium 673.8 ☑
    - following
      - abortion 639.6
      - ectopic or molar pregnancy 639.6
    - in pregnancy, childbirth, or the puerperium 673.8 ☑
  - femoral (artery) 444.22
    - vein 453.8
      - deep 453.41
  - following
    - abortion 639.6

- **Embolism** — *continued*
  - following — *continued*
    - ectopic or molar pregnancy 639.6
    - infusion, perfusion, or transfusion
      - air 999.1
      - thrombus 999.2
  - heart (fatty) (*see also* Infarct, myocardium) 410.9 ☑
  - hepatic (vein) 453.0
  - iliac (artery) 444.81
  - iliofemoral 444.81
  - in pregnancy, childbirth, or puerperium (pulmonary) — *see* Embolism, obstetrical
  - intestine (artery) (vein) (with gangrene) 557.0
  - intracranial (*see also* Embolism, brain) 434.1 ☑
    - venous sinus (any) 325
      - late effect — *see* category 326
      - nonpyogenic 437.6
        - in pregnancy or puerperium 671.5 ☑
  - kidney (artery) 593.81
  - lateral sinus (venous) — *see* Embolism, intracranial venous sinus
  - longitudinal sinus (venous) — *see* Embolism, intracranial venous sinus
  - lower extremity 444.22
  - lung (massive) — *see* Embolism, pulmonary
  - meninges (*see also* Embolism, brain) 434.1 ☑
  - mesenteric (artery) (with gangrene) 557.0
  - multiple NEC 444.9
  - obstetrical (pulmonary) 673.2 ☑
    - air 673.0 ☑
    - amniotic fluid (pulmonary) 673.1 ☑
    - blood-clot 673.2 ☑
    - cardiac 674.8 ☑
    - fat 673.8 ☑
    - heart 674.8 ☑
    - pyemic 673.3 ☑
    - septic 673.3 ☑
    - specified NEC 674.8 ☑
  - ophthalmic (*see also* Occlusion, retina) 362.30
  - paradoxical NEC 444.9
  - penis 607.82
  - peripheral arteries NEC 444.22
    - lower 444.22
    - upper 444.21
  - pituitary 253.8
  - popliteal (artery) 444.22
  - portal (vein) 452
  - postoperative NEC 997.2
    - cerebral 997.02
    - mesenteric artery 997.71
    - other vessels 997.79
    - peripheral vascular 997.2
    - pulmonary 415.11
    - renal artery 997.72
  - precerebral artery (*see also* Occlusion, artery, precerebral) 433.9 ☑
  - puerperal — *see* Embolism, obstetrical
  - pulmonary (artery) (vein) 415.19
    - with
      - abortion — *see* Abortion, by type, with embolism
      - ectopic pregnancy (*see also* categories 633.0–633.9) 639.6
      - molar pregnancy (*see also* categories 630–632) 639.6
    - following
      - abortion 639.6
      - ectopic or molar pregnancy 639.6
    - iatrogenic 415.11
    - in pregnancy, childbirth, or puerperium — *see* Embolism, obstetrical
    - postoperative 415.11

- **Embolism** — *continued*
  - pyemic (multiple) 038.9
    - with
      - abortion — *see* Abortion, by type, with embolism
      - ectopic pregnancy (*see also* categories 633.0–633.9) 639.6
      - molar pregnancy (*see also* categories 630–632) 639.6
    - Aerobacter aerogenes 038.49
    - enteric gram-negative bacilli 038.40
    - Enterobacter aerogenes 038.49
    - Escherichia coli 038.42
    - following
      - abortion 639.6
      - ectopic or molar pregnancy 639.6
    - Hemophilus influenzae 038.41
    - pneumococcal 038.2
    - Proteus vulgaris 038.49
    - Pseudomonas (aeruginosa) 038.43
    - puerperal, postpartum, childbirth (any organism) 673.3 ☑
    - Serratia 038.44
    - specified organism NEC 038.8
    - staphylococcal 038.10
      - aureus 038.11
      - specified organism NEC 038.19
    - streptococcal 038.0
  - renal (artery) 593.81
    - vein 453.3
  - retina, retinal (*see also* Occlusion, retina) 362.30
  - saddle (aorta) 444.0
  - septicemic — *see* Embolism, pyemic
  - sinus — *see* Embolism, intracranial venous sinus
  - soap
    - with
      - abortion — *see* Abortion, by type, with embolism
      - ectopic pregnancy (*see also* categories 633.0–633.9) 639.6
      - molar pregnancy (*see also* categories 630–632) 639.6
    - following
      - abortion 639.6
      - ectopic or molar pregnancy 639.6
  - spinal cord (nonpyogenic) 336.1
    - in pregnancy or puerperium 671.5 ☑
    - pyogenic origin 324.1
      - late effect — *see* category 326
  - spleen, splenic (artery) 444.89
  - thrombus (thromboembolism) following infusion, perfusion, or transfusion 999.2
  - upper extremity 444.21
  - vein 453.9
    - with inflammation or phlebitis — *see* Thrombophlebitis
    - cerebral (*see also* Embolism, brain) 434.1 ☑
    - coronary (*see also* Infarct, myocardium) 410.9 ☑
      - without myocardial infarction 411.81
    - hepatic 453.0
    - lower extremity 453.8
      - deep 453.40
        - calf 453.42
        - distal (lower leg) 453.42
        - femoral 453.41
        - iliac 453.41
        - lower leg 453.42
        - peroneal 453.42
        - popliteal 453.41
        - proximal (upper leg) 453.41
        - thigh 453.41
        - tibial 453.42
    - mesenteric (with gangrene) 557.0
    - portal 452

☑ Additional Digit Required — Refer to the Tabular List for Digit Selection
Subterms under main terms may continue to next column or page

Note — use the following fifth-digit subclassification with categories 345.0, 345.1, 345.4–345.9:

0 without mention of intractable epilepsy

1 with intractable epilepsy

- **Exhibitionism** (sexual) 302.4
- **Exomphalos** 756.79
- **Exophoria** 378.42
  - convergence, insufficiency 378.83
  - divergence, excess 378.85
- **Exophthalmic**
  - cachexia 242.0 ☑
  - goiter 242.0 ☑
  - ophthalmoplegia 242.0 ☑ *[376.22]*
- **Exophthalmos** 376.30
  - congenital 743.66
  - constant 376.31
  - endocrine NEC 259.9 *[376.22]*
  - hyperthyroidism 242.0 ☑ *[376.21]*
  - intermittent NEC 376.34
  - malignant 242.0 ☑ *[376.21]*
  - pulsating 376.35
    - endocrine NEC 259.9 *[376.22]*
  - thyrotoxic 242.0 ☑ *[376.21]*
- **Exostosis** 726.91
  - cartilaginous (M9210/0) — *see* Neoplasm, bone, benign
  - congenital 756.4
  - ear canal, external 380.81
  - gonococcal 098.89
  - hip 726.5
  - intracranial 733.3
  - jaw (bone) 526.81
  - luxurians 728.11
  - multiple (cancellous) (congenital) (hereditary) 756.4
  - nasal bones 726.91
  - orbit, orbital 376.42
  - osteocartilaginous (M9210/0) — *see* Neoplasm, bone, benign
  - spine 721.8
    - with spondylosis — *see* Spondylosis
  - syphilitic 095.5
  - wrist 726.4
- **Exotropia** 378.10
  - alternating 378.15
    - with
      - A pattern 378.16
      - specified noncomitancy NEC 378.18
      - V pattern 378.17
      - X pattern 378.18
      - Y pattern 378.18
    - intermittent 378.24
  - intermittent 378.20
    - alternating 378.24
    - monocular 378.23
  - monocular 378.11
    - with
      - A pattern 378.12
      - specified noncomitancy NEC 378.14
      - V pattern 378.13
      - X pattern 378.14
      - Y pattern 378.14
    - intermittent 378.23
- **Explanation of**
  - investigation finding V65.4 ☑
  - medication V65.4 ☑
- **Exposure** 994.9
  - cold 991.9
    - specified effect NEC 991.8
  - effects of 994.9
  - exhaustion due to 994.4
  - to
    - AIDS virus V01.79
    - anthrax V01.81
    - asbestos V15.84
    - body fluids (hazardous) V15.85
    - cholera V01.0
    - communicable disease V01.9
      - specified type NEC V01.89
    - Escherichia coli (E. coli) V01.83
    - German measles V01.4
    - gonorrhea V01.6
    - hazardous body fluids V15.85
    - HIV V01.79
    - human immunodeficiency virus V01.79
    - lead V15.86
- **Exposure** — *continued*
  - to — *continued*
    - meningococcus V01.84
    - parasitic disease V01.89
    - poliomyelitis V01.2
    - potentially hazardous body fluids V15.85
    - rabies V01.5
    - rubella V01.4
    - SARS-associated coronavirus V01.82
    - smallpox V01.3
    - syphilis V01.6
    - tuberculosis V01.1
    - varicella V01.71
    - venereal disease V01.6
    - viral disease NEC V01.79
      - varicella V01.71
- **Exsanguination, fetal** 772.0
- **Exstrophy**
  - abdominal content 751.8
  - bladder (urinary) 753.5
- **Extensive** — *see* condition
- **Extra** — *see also* Accessory
  - rib 756.3
    - cervical 756.2
- **Extraction**
  - with hook 763.89
  - breech NEC 669.6 ☑
    - affecting fetus or newborn 763.0
  - cataract postsurgical V45.61
  - manual NEC 669.8 ☑
    - affecting fetus or newborn 763.89
- **Extrasystole** 427.60
  - atrial 427.61
  - postoperative 997.1
  - ventricular 427.69
- **Extrauterine gestation or pregnancy** — *see* Pregnancy, ectopic
- **Extravasation**
  - blood 459.0
    - lower extremity 459.0
  - chyle into mesentery 457.8
  - pelvicalyceal 593.4
  - pyelosinus 593.4
  - urine 788.8
    - from ureter 788.8
- **Extremity** — *see* condition
- **Extrophy** — *see* Exstrophy
- **Extroversion**
  - bladder 753.5
  - uterus 618.1
    - complicating delivery 665.2 ☑
      - affecting fetus or newborn 763.89
    - postpartal (old) 618.1
- **Extruded tooth** 524.34 ●
- **Extrusion**
  - alveolus and teeth 524.75
  - breast implant (prosthetic) 996.54
  - device, implant, or graft — *see* Complications, mechanical
  - eye implant (ball) (globe) 996.59
  - intervertebral disc — *see* Displacement, intervertebral disc
  - lacrimal gland 375.43
  - mesh (reinforcing) 996.59
  - ocular lens implant 996.53
  - prosthetic device NEC — *see* Complications, mechanical
  - vitreous 379.26
- **Exudate, pleura** — *see* Effusion, pleura
- **Exudates, retina** 362.82
- **Exudative** — *see* condition
- **Eye, eyeball, eyelid** — *see* condition
- **Eyestrain** 368.13
- **Eyeworm disease of Africa** 125.2

F

- **Faber's anemia or syndrome** (achlorhydric anemia) 280.9
- **Fabry's disease** (angiokeratoma corporis diffusum) 272.7
- **Face, facial** — *see* condition
- **Facet of cornea** 371.44
- **Faciocephalalgia, autonomic** — *see also* Neuropathy, peripheral, autonomic 337.9
- **Facioscapulohumeral myopathy** 359.1
- **Factitious disorder, illness** — *see* Illness, factitious
- **Factor**
  - deficiency — *see* Deficiency, factor
  - psychic, associated with diseases classified elsewhere 316
  - risk — *see* Problem
- **Fahr-Volhard disease** (malignant nephrosclerosis) 403.00
- **Failure, failed**
  - adenohypophyseal 253.2
  - attempted abortion (legal) (*see also* Abortion, failed) 638.9
  - bone marrow (anemia) 284.9
    - acquired (secondary) 284.8
    - congenital 284.09 ▲
    - idiopathic 284.9
  - cardiac (*see also* Failure, heart) 428.9
    - newborn 779.89
  - cardiorenal (chronic) 428.9
    - hypertensive (*see also* Hypertension, cardiorenal) 404.93
  - cardiorespiratory 799.1
    - specified during or due to a procedure 997.1
      - long-term effect of cardiac surgery 429.4
  - cardiovascular (chronic) 428.9
  - cerebrovascular 437.8
  - cervical dilatation in labor 661.0 ☑
    - affecting fetus or newborn 763.7
  - circulation, circulatory 799.89
    - fetus or newborn 779.89
    - peripheral 785.50
  - compensation — *see* Disease, heart
  - congestive (*see also* Failure, heart) 428.0
  - coronary (*see also* Insufficiency, coronary) 411.89
  - dental restoration ●
    - marginal integrity 525.61 ●
    - periodontal anatomical integrity ● 525.65 ●
  - descent of head (at term) 652.5 ☑
    - affecting fetus or newborn 763.1
    - in labor 660.0 ☑
      - affecting fetus or newborn 763.1
  - device, implant, or graft — *see* Complications, mechanical
  - engagement of head NEC 652.5 ☑
    - in labor 660.0 ☑
  - extrarenal 788.9
  - fetal head to enter pelvic brim 652.5 ☑
    - affecting fetus or newborn 763.1
    - in labor 660.0 ☑
      - affecting fetus or newborn 763.1
  - forceps NEC 660.7 ☑
    - affecting fetus or newborn 763.1
  - fusion (joint) (spinal) 996.49
  - growth in childhood 783.43
  - heart (acute) (sudden) 428.9
    - with
      - abortion — *see* Abortion, by type, with specified complication NEC
      - acute pulmonary edema (*see also* Failure, ventricular, left) 428.1
        - with congestion (*see also* Failure, heart) 428.0
      - decompensation (*see also* Failure, heart) 428.0
      - dilation — *see* Disease, heart
      - ectopic pregnancy (*see also* categories 633.0–633.9) 639.8
      - molar pregnancy (*see also* categories 630–632) 639.8
    - arteriosclerotic 440.9
    - combined left-right sided 428.0
- **Failure, failed** — *continued*
  - heart — *continued*
    - combined systolic and diastolic 428.40
      - acute 428.41
      - acute on chronic 428.43
      - chronic 428.42
    - compensated (*see also* Failure, heart) 428.0
    - complicating
      - abortion — *see* Abortion, by type, with specified complication NEC
      - delivery (cesarean) (instrumental) 669.4 ☑
      - ectopic pregnancy (*see also* categories 633.0–633.9) 639.8
      - molar pregnancy (*see also* categories 630–632) 639.8
      - obstetric anesthesia or sedation 668.1 ☑
      - surgery 997.1
    - congestive (compensated) (decompensated) (*see also* Failure, heart) 428.0
      - with rheumatic fever (conditions classifiable to 390)
        - active 391.8
        - inactive or quiescent (with chorea) 398.91
      - fetus or newborn 779.89
      - hypertensive (*see also* Hypertension, heart) 402.91
        - with renal disease (*see also* Hypertension, cardiorenal) 404.91
          - with renal failure 404.93
        - benign 402.11
        - malignant 402.01
      - rheumatic (chronic) (inactive) (with chorea) 398.91
        - active or acute 391.8
          - with chorea (Sydenham's) 392.0
    - decompensated (*see also* Failure, heart) 428.0
    - degenerative (*see also* Degeneration, myocardial) 429.1
    - diastolic 428.30
      - acute 428.31
      - acute on chronic 428.33
      - chronic 428.32
    - due to presence of (cardiac) prosthesis 429.4
    - fetus or newborn 779.89
    - following
      - abortion 639.8
      - cardiac surgery 429.4
      - ectopic or molar pregnancy 639.8
    - high output NEC 428.9
    - hypertensive (*see also* Hypertension, heart) 402.91
      - with renal disease (*see also* Hypertension, cardiorenal) 404.91
        - with renal failure 404.93
      - benign 402.11
      - malignant 402.01
    - left (ventricular) (*see also* Failure, ventricular, left) 428.1
      - with right-sided failure (see also Failure, heart) 428.0
    - low output (syndrome) NEC 428.9
    - organic — *see* Disease, heart
    - postoperative (immediate) 997.1
      - long term effect of cardiac surgery 429.4
    - rheumatic (chronic) (congestive) (inactive) 398.91
    - right (secondary to left heart failure, conditions classifiable to 428.1) (ventricular) (*see also* Failure, heart) 428.0
    - senile 797

- **Fibroma** — *see also* Neoplasm, connective tissue, benign — *continued*
  - cementifying (M9274/0) — *see* Neoplasm, bone, benign
  - chondromyxoid (M9241/0) — *see* Neoplasm, bone, benign
  - desmoplastic (M8823/1) — *see* Neoplasm, connective tissue, uncertain behavior
  - facial (M8813/0) — *see* Neoplasm, connective tissue, benign
  - invasive (M8821/1) — *see* Neoplasm, connective tissue, uncertain behavior
  - molle (M8851/0) (*see also* Lipoma, by site) 214.9
  - myxoid (M8811/0) — *see* Neoplasm, connective tissue, benign
  - nasopharynx, nasopharyngeal (juvenile) (M9160/0) 210.7
  - nonosteogenic (nonossifying) — *see* Dysplasia, fibrous
  - odontogenic (M9321/0) 213.1
    - upper jaw (bone) 213.0
  - ossifying (M9262/0) — *see* Neoplasm, bone, benign
  - periosteal (M8812/0) — *see* Neoplasm, bone, benign
  - prostate 600.20
    - with
      - other lower urinary tract symptoms (LUTS) 600.21 ●
      - urinary ●
        - obstruction 600.21 ●
        - retention 600.21 ●
  - soft (M8851/0) (*see also* Lipoma, by site) 214.9
- **Fibromatosis** 728.79 ▲
  - abdominal (M8822/1) — *see* Neoplasm, connective tissue, uncertain behavior
  - aggressive (M8821/1) — *see* Neoplasm, connective tissue, uncertain behavior
  - congenital generalized (CGF) 759.89 ●
  - Dupuytren's 728.6
  - gingival 523.8
  - plantar fascia 728.71
  - proliferative 728.79
  - pseudosarcomatous (proliferative) (subcutaneous) 728.79
  - subcutaneous pseudosarcomatous (proliferative) 728.79
- **Fibromyalgia** 729.1
- **Fibromyoma** (M8890/0) — *see also* Neoplasm, connective tissue, benign
  - uterus (corpus) (*see also* Leiomyoma, uterus) 218.9
    - in pregnancy or childbirth 654.1 ☑
      - affecting fetus or newborn 763.89
      - causing obstructed labor 660.2 ☑
        - affecting fetus or newborn 763.1
- **Fibromyositis** — *see also* Myositis 729.1
  - scapulohumeral 726.2
- **Fibromyxolipoma** (M8852/0) — *see also* Lipoma, by site 214.9
- **Fibromyxoma** (M8811/0) — *see* Neoplasm, connective tissue, benign
- **Fibromyxosarcoma** (M8811/3) — *see* Neoplasm, connective tissue, malignant
- **Fibro-odontoma, ameloblastic** (M9290/0) 213.1
  - upper jaw (bone) 213.0
- **Fibro-osteoma** (M9262/0) — *see* Neoplasm, bone, benign
- **Fibroplasia, retrolental** 362.21
- **Fibropurulent** — *see* condition
- **Fibrosarcoma** (M8810/3) — *see also* Neoplasm, connective tissue, malignant
  - ameloblastic (M9330/3) 170.1
    - upper jaw (bone) 170.0
  - congenital (M8814/3) — *see* Neoplasm, connective tissue, malignant
  - fascial (M8813/3) — *see* Neoplasm, connective tissue, malignant
  - infantile (M8814/3) — *see* Neoplasm, connective tissue, malignant
  - odontogenic (M9330/3) 170.1
    - upper jaw (bone) 170.0
  - periosteal (M8812/3) — *see* Neoplasm, bone, malignant
- **Fibrosclerosis**
  - breast 610.3
  - corpora cavernosa (penis) 607.89
  - familial multifocal NEC 710.8
  - multifocal (idiopathic) NEC 710.8
  - penis (corpora cavernosa) 607.89
- **Fibrosis, fibrotic**
  - adrenal (gland) 255.8
  - alveolar (diffuse) 516.3
  - amnion 658.8 ☑
  - anal papillae 569.49
  - anus 569.49
  - appendix, appendiceal, noninflammatory 543.9
  - arteriocapillary — *see* Arteriosclerosis
  - bauxite (of lung) 503
  - biliary 576.8
    - due to Clonorchis sinensis 121.1
  - bladder 596.8
    - interstitial 595.1
    - localized submucosal 595.1
    - panmural 595.1
  - bone, diffuse 756.59
  - breast 610.3
  - capillary (*see also* Arteriosclerosis)
    - lung (chronic) (*see also* Fibrosis, lung) 515
  - cardiac (*see also* Myocarditis) 429.0
  - cervix 622.8
  - chorion 658.8 ☑
  - corpus cavernosum 607.89
  - cystic (of pancreas) 277.00
    - with
      - manifestations
        - gastrointestinal 277.03
        - pulmonary 277.02
        - specified NEC 277.09
      - meconium ileus 277.01
      - pulmonary exacerbation 277.02
  - due to (presence of) any device, implant, or graft — *see* Complications, due to (presence of) any device, implant, or graft classified to 996.0–996.5 NEC
  - ejaculatory duct 608.89
  - endocardium (*see also* Endocarditis) 424.90
  - endomyocardial (African) 425.0
  - epididymis 608.89
  - eye muscle 378.62
  - graphite (of lung) 503
  - heart (*see also* Myocarditis) 429.0
  - hepatic (*see also* Cirrhosis, liver)
    - due to Clonorchis sinensis 121.1
  - hepatolienal — *see* Cirrhosis, liver
  - hepatosplenic — *see* Cirrhosis, liver
  - infrapatellar fat pad 729.31
  - interstitial pulmonary, newborn 770.7
  - intrascrotal 608.89
  - kidney (*see also* Sclerosis, renal) 587
  - liver — *see* Cirrhosis, liver
  - lung (atrophic) (capillary) (chronic) (confluent) (massive) (perialveolar) (peribronchial) 515
    - with
      - anthracosilicosis (occupational) 500
      - anthracosis (occupational) 500
      - asbestosis (occupational) 501
      - bagassosis (occupational) 495.1

Fibrosis, fibrotic — *continued*

- lung — *continued*
  - with — *continued*
    - bauxite 503
    - berylliosis (occupational) 503
    - byssinosis (occupational) 504
    - calcicosis (occupational) 502
    - chalicosis (occupational) 502
    - dust reticulation (occupational) 504
    - farmers' lung 495.0
    - gannister disease (occupational) 502
    - graphite 503
    - pneumonoconiosis (occupational) 505
    - pneumosiderosis (occupational) 503
    - siderosis (occupational) 503
    - silicosis (occupational) 502
    - tuberculosis (*see also* Tuberculosis) 011.4 ☑
  - diffuse (idiopathic) (interstitial) 516.3
  - due to
    - bauxite 503
    - fumes or vapors (chemical) (inhalation) 506.4
    - graphite 503
  - following radiation 508.1
  - postinflammatory 515
  - silicotic (massive) (occupational) 502
  - tuberculous (*see also* Tuberculosis) 011.4 ☑
- lymphatic gland 289.3
- median bar 600.90
  - with
    - other lower urinary tract symptoms (LUTS) 600.91 ●
    - urinary ●
      - obstruction 600.91 ●
      - retention 600.91 ●
- mediastinum (idiopathic) 519.3
- meninges 349.2
- muscle NEC 728.2
  - iatrogenic (from injection) 999.9
- myocardium, myocardial (*see also* Myocarditis) 429.0
- oral submucous 528.8
- ovary 620.8
- oviduct 620.8
- pancreas 577.8
  - cystic 277.00
    - with
      - manifestations
        - gastrointestinal 277.03
        - pulmonary 277.02
        - specified NEC 277.09
      - meconium ileus 277.01
      - pulmonary exacerbation 277.02
- penis 607.89
- periappendiceal 543.9
- periarticular (*see also* Ankylosis) 718.5 ☑
- pericardium 423.1
- perineum, in pregnancy or childbirth 654.8 ☑
  - affecting fetus or newborn 763.89
  - causing obstructed labor 660.2 ☑
    - affecting fetus or newborn 763.1
- perineural NEC 355.9
  - foot 355.6
- periureteral 593.89
- placenta — *see* Placenta, abnormal
- pleura 511.0
- popliteal fat pad 729.31
- preretinal 362.56
- prostate (chronic) 600.90
  - with
    - other lower urinary tract symptoms (LUTS) 600.91 ●

Fibrosis, fibrotic — *continued*

- prostate — *continued*
  - with — *continued*
    - urinary ●
      - obstruction 600.91 ●
      - retention 600.91 ●
- pulmonary (chronic) (*see also* Fibrosis, lung) 515
  - alveolar capillary block 516.3
  - interstitial
    - diffuse (idiopathic) 516.3
    - newborn 770.7
- radiation — *see* Effect, adverse, radiation
- rectal sphincter 569.49
- retroperitoneal, idiopathic 593.4
- sclerosing mesenteric (idiopathic) 567.82
- scrotum 608.89
- seminal vesicle 608.89
- senile 797
- skin NEC 709.2
- spermatic cord 608.89
- spleen 289.59
  - bilharzial (*see also* Schistosomiasis) 120.9
- subepidermal nodular (M8832/0) — *see* Neoplasm, skin, benign
- submucous NEC 709.2
  - oral 528.8
  - tongue 528.8
- syncytium — *see* Placenta, abnormal
- testis 608.89
  - chronic, due to syphilis 095.8
- thymus (gland) 254.8
- tunica vaginalis 608.89
- ureter 593.89
- urethra 599.84
- uterus (nonneoplastic) 621.8
  - bilharzial (*see also* Schistosomiasis) 120.9
  - neoplastic (*see also* Leiomyoma, uterus) 218.9
- vagina 623.8
- valve, heart (*see also* Endocarditis) 424.90
- vas deferens 608.89
- vein 459.89
  - lower extremities 459.89
- vesical 595.1

- **Fibrositis** (periarticular) (rheumatoid) 729.0
  - humeroscapular region 726.2
  - nodular, chronic
    - Jaccoud's 714.4
    - rheumatoid 714.4
  - ossificans 728.11
  - scapulohumeral 726.2
- **Fibrothorax** 511.0
- **Fibrotic** — *see* Fibrosis
- **Fibrous** — *see* condition
- **Fibroxanthoma** (M8831/0) — *see also* Neoplasm, connective tissue, benign
  - atypical (M8831/1) — *see* Neoplasm, connective tissue, uncertain behavior
  - malignant (M8831/3) — *see* Neoplasm, connective tissue, malignant
- **Fibroxanthosarcoma** (M8831/3) — *see* Neoplasm, connective tissue, malignant
- **Fiedler's**
  - disease (leptospiral jaundice) 100.0
  - myocarditis or syndrome (acute isolated myocarditis) 422.91
- **Fiessinger-Leroy (-Reiter) syndrome** 099.3
- **Fiessinger-Rendu syndrome** (erythema muliforme exudativum) 695.1
- **Fifth disease** (eruptive) 057.0
  - venereal 099.1
- **Filaria, filarial** — *see* Infestation, filarial
- **Filariasis** — *see also* Infestation, filarial 125.9

☑ Additional Digit Required — Refer to the Tabular List for Digit Selection

Subterms under main terms may continue to next column or page

Findings, abnormal, without diagnosis — *continued*
- structure, body — *continued*
  - genitourinary organs 793.5
  - head 793.0
    - echogram (ultrasound) 794.01
  - intrathoracic organs NEC 793.2
  - lung 793.1
  - musculoskeletal 793.7
  - placenta 793.99 ▲
  - retroperitoneum 793.6
  - skin 793.99 ▲
  - subcutaneous tissue NEC 793.99 ▲
- synovial fluid 792.9
- thermogram — *see* Findings, abnormal, structure
- throat culture, positive 795.39
- thyroid (function) 794.5
  - metabolism (rate) 794.5
  - scan 794.5
  - uptake 794.5
- total proteins 790.99
- toxicology (drugs) (heavy metals) 796.0
- transaminase (level) 790.4
- triglycerides 272.9
- tuberculin skin test (without active tuberculosis) 795.5
- tumor markers NEC 795.89 ●
- ultrasound (*see also* Findings, abnormal, structure)
  - cardiogram 793.2
- uric acid, blood 790.6
- urine, urinary constituents 791.9
  - acetone 791.6
  - albumin 791.0
  - bacteria 791.9
  - bile 791.4
  - blood 599.7
  - casts or cells 791.7
  - chyle 791.1
  - culture, positive 791.9
  - glucose 791.5
  - hemoglobin 791.2
  - ketone 791.6
  - protein 791.0
  - pus 791.9
  - sugar 791.5
- vaginal fluid 792.9
- vanillylmandelic acid, elevated 791.9
- vectorcardiogram (VCG) 794.39
- ventriculogram (cerebral) 793.0
- VMA, elevated 791.9
- Wassermann reaction
  - false positive 795.6
  - positive 097.1
    - follow-up of latent syphilis — *see* Syphilis, latent
    - only finding — *see* Syphilis, latent
- white blood cell 288.9
  - count 288.9
    - elevated 288.60 ▲
    - low 288.50 ▲
  - differential 288.9
  - morphology 288.9
- wound culture 795.39
- xerography 793.89
- zinc, blood 790.6

Finger — *see* condition

Fire, St. Anthony's — *see also* Erysipelas 035

Fish
- hook stomach 537.89
- meal workers' lung 495.8

Fisher's syndrome 357.0

Fissure, fissured
- abdominal wall (congenital) 756.79
- anus, anal 565.0
  - congenital 751.5
- buccal cavity 528.9
- clitoris (congenital) 752.49
- ear, lobule (congenital) 744.29
- epiglottis (congenital) 748.3
- larynx 478.79
  - congenital 748.3

Fissure, fissured — *continued*
- lip 528.5
  - congenital (*see also* Cleft, lip) 749.10
- nipple 611.2
  - puerperal, postpartum 676.1 ☑
- palate (congenital) (*see also* Cleft, palate) 749.00
- postanal 565.0
- rectum 565.0
- skin 709.8
  - streptococcal 686.9
- spine (congenital) (*see also* Spina bifida) 741.9 ☑
- sternum (congenital) 756.3
- tongue (acquired) 529.5
  - congenital 750.13

Fistula (sinus) 686.9
- abdomen (wall) 569.81
  - bladder 596.2
  - intestine 569.81
  - ureter 593.82
  - uterus 619.2
- abdominorectal 569.81
- abdominosigmoidal 569.81
- abdominothoracic 510.0
- abdominouterine 619.2
  - congenital 752.3
- abdominovesical 596.2
- accessory sinuses (*see also* Sinusitis) 473.9
- actinomycotic — *see* Actinomycosis
- alveolar
  - antrum (*see also* Sinusitis, maxillary) 473.0
  - process 522.7
- anorectal 565.1
- antrobuccal (*see also* Sinusitis, maxillary) 473.0
- antrum (*see also* Sinusitis, maxillary) 473.0
- anus, anal (infectional) (recurrent) 565.1
  - congenital 751.5
  - tuberculous (*see also* Tuberculosis) 014.8 ☑
- aortic sinus 747.29
- aortoduodenal 447.2
- appendix, appendicular 543.9
- arteriovenous (acquired) 447.0
  - brain 437.3
    - congenital 747.81
      - ruptured (*see also* Hemorrhage, subarachnoid) 430
    - ruptured (*see also* Hemorrhage, subarachnoid) 430
  - cerebral 437.3
    - congenital 747.81
  - congenital (peripheral) 747.60
    - brain — *see* Fistula, arteriovenous, brain, congenital
    - coronary 746.85
    - gastrointestinal 747.61
    - lower limb 747.64
    - pulmonary 747.3
    - renal 747.62
    - specified site NEC 747.69
    - upper limb 747.63
  - coronary 414.19
    - congenital 746.85
  - heart 414.19
  - pulmonary (vessels) 417.0
    - congenital 747.3
  - surgically created (for dialysis) V45.1
    - complication NEC 996.73
      - atherosclerosis — *see* Arteriosclerosis, extremities
      - embolism 996.74
      - infection or inflammation 996.62
      - mechanical 996.1
      - occlusion NEC 996.74
      - thrombus 996.74

Fistula — *continued*
- arteriovenous — *continued*
  - traumatic — *see* Injury, blood vessel, by site
- artery 447.2
- aural 383.81
  - congenital 744.49
- auricle 383.81
  - congenital 744.49
- Bartholin's gland 619.8
- bile duct (*see also* Fistula, biliary) 576.4
- biliary (duct) (tract) 576.4
  - congenital 751.69
- bladder (neck) (sphincter) 596.2
  - into seminal vesicle 596.2
- bone 733.99
- brain 348.8
  - arteriovenous — *see* Fistula, arteriovenous, brain
- branchial (cleft) 744.41
- branchiogenous 744.41
- breast 611.0
  - puerperal, postpartum 675.1 ☑
- bronchial 510.0
- bronchocutaneous, bronchomediastinal, bronchopleural, bronchopleuromediastinal (infective) 510.0
  - tuberculous (*see also* Tuberculosis) 011.3 ☑
- bronchoesophageal 530.89
  - congenital 750.3
- buccal cavity (infective) 528.3
- canal, ear 380.89
- carotid-cavernous
  - congenital 747.81
    - with hemorrhage 430
  - traumatic 900.82
    - with hemorrhage (*see also* Hemorrhage, brain, traumatic) 853.0 ☑
    - late effect 908.3
- cecosigmoidal 569.81
- cecum 569.81
- cerebrospinal (fluid) 349.81
- cervical, lateral (congenital) 744.41
- cervicoaural (congenital) 744.49
- cervicosigmoidal 619.1
- cervicovesical 619.0
- cervix 619.8
- chest (wall) 510.0
- cholecystocolic (*see also* Fistula, gallbladder) 575.5
- cholecystocolonic (*see also* Fistula, gallbladder) 575.5
- cholecystoduodenal (*see also* Fistula, gallbladder) 575.5
- cholecystoenteric (*see also* Fistula, gallbladder) 575.5
- cholecystogastric (*see also* Fistula, gallbladder) 575.5
- cholecystointestinal (*see also* Fistula, gallbladder) 575.5
- choledochoduodenal 576.4
- cholocolic (*see also* Fistula, gallbladder) 575.5
- coccyx 685.1
  - with abscess 685.0
- colon 569.81
- colostomy 569.69
- colovaginal (acquired) 619.1
- common duct (bile duct) 576.4
- congenital, NEC — *see* Anomaly, specified type NEC
- cornea, causing hypotony 360.32
- coronary, arteriovenous 414.19
  - congenital 746.85
- costal region 510.0
- cul-de-sac, Douglas' 619.8
- cutaneous 686.9
- cystic duct (*see also* Fistula, gallbladder) 575.5
  - congenital 751.69
- dental 522.7
- diaphragm 510.0

Fistula — *continued*
- diaphragm — *continued*
  - bronchovisceral 510.0
  - pleuroperitoneal 510.0
  - pulmonoperitoneal 510.0
- duodenum 537.4
- ear (canal) (external) 380.89
- enterocolic 569.81
- enterocutaneous 569.81
- enteroenteric 569.81
- entero-uterine 619.1
  - congenital 752.3
- enterovaginal 619.1
  - congenital 752.49
- enterovesical 596.1
- epididymis 608.89
  - tuberculous (*see also* Tuberculosis) 016.4 ☑
- esophagobronchial 530.89
  - congenital 750.3
- esophagocutaneous 530.89
- esophagopleurocutaneous 530.89
- esophagotracheal 530.84
  - congenital 750.3
- esophagus 530.89
  - congenital 750.4
- ethmoid (*see also* Sinusitis, ethmoidal) 473.2
- eyeball (cornea) (sclera) 360.32
- eyelid 373.11
- fallopian tube (external) 619.2
- fecal 569.81
  - congenital 751.5
- from periapical lesion 522.7
- frontal sinus (*see also* Sinusitis, frontal) 473.1
- gallbladder 575.5
  - with calculus, cholelithiasis, stones (*see also* Cholelithiasis) 574.2 ☑
  - congenital 751.69
- gastric 537.4
- gastrocolic 537.4
  - congenital 750.7
  - tuberculous (*see also* Tuberculosis) 014.8 ☑
- gastroenterocolic 537.4
- gastroesophageal 537.4
- gastrojejunal 537.4
- gastrojejunocolic 537.4
- genital
  - organs
    - female 619.9
      - specified site NEC 619.8
    - male 608.89
  - tract-skin (female) 619.2
- hepatopleural 510.0
- hepatopulmonary 510.0
- horseshoe 565.1
- ileorectal 569.81
- ileosigmoidal 569.81
- ileostomy 569.69
- ileovesical 596.1
- ileum 569.81
- in ano 565.1
  - tuberculous (*see also* Tuberculosis) 014.8 ☑
- inner ear (*see also* Fistula, labyrinth) 386.40
- intestine 569.81
- intestinocolonic (abdominal) 569.81
- intestinoureteral 593.82
- intestinouterine 619.1
- intestinovaginal 619.1
  - congenital 752.49
- intestinovesical 596.1
- involving female genital tract 619.9
  - digestive-genital 619.1
  - genital tract-skin 619.2
  - specified site NEC 619.8
  - urinary-genital 619.0
- ischiorectal (fossa) 566
- jejunostomy 569.69
- jejunum 569.81
- joint 719.80
  - ankle 719.87

Fixation — *continued*
- uterus (acquired) — *see* Malposition, uterus
- vocal cord 478.5

Flaccid — *see also* condition
- foot 736.79
- forearm 736.09
- palate, congenital 750.26

Flail
- chest 807.4
  - newborn 767.3
- joint (paralytic) 718.80
  - ankle 718.87
  - elbow 718.82
  - foot 718.87
  - hand 718.84
  - hip 718.85
  - knee 718.86
  - multiple sites 718.89
  - pelvic region 718.85
  - shoulder (region) 718.81
  - specified site NEC 718.88
  - wrist 718.83

Flajani (-Basedow) syndrome or disease (exophthalmic goiter) 242.0 ☑

Flap, liver 572.8

Flare, anterior chamber (aqueous) (eye) 364.04

Flashback phenomena (drug) (hallucinogenic) 292.89

Flat
- chamber (anterior) (eye) 360.34
- chest, congenital 754.89
- electroencephalogram (EEG) 348.8
- foot (acquired) (fixed type) (painful) (postural) (spastic) 734
  - congenital 754.61
    - rocker bottom 754.61
    - vertical talus 754.61
  - rachitic 268.1
  - rocker bottom (congenital) 754.61
  - vertical talus, congenital 754.61
- organ or site, congenital NEC — *see* Anomaly, specified type NEC
- pelvis 738.6
  - with disproportion (fetopelvic) 653.2 ☑
    - affecting fetus or newborn 763.1
    - causing obstructed labor 660.1 ☑
      - affecting fetus or newborn 763.1
    - congenital 755.69

Flatau-Schilder disease 341.1

Flattening
- head, femur 736.39
- hip 736.39
- lip (congenital) 744.89
- nose (congenital) 754.0
  - acquired 738.0

Flatulence 787.3

Flatus 787.3
- vaginalis 629.89 ▲

Flax dressers' disease 504

Flea bite — *see* Injury, superficial, by site

Fleischer (-Kayser) ring (corneal pigmentation) 275.1 *[371.14]*

Fleischner's disease 732.3

Fleshy mole 631

Flexibilitas cerea — *see also* Catalepsy 300.11

Flexion
- cervix ▶— *see* Flexion, uterus◀
- contracture, joint (*see also* Contraction, joint) 718.4 ☑
- deformity, joint (*see also* Contraction, joint) 736.9 ▲
  - hip, congenital (*see also* Subluxation, congenital, hip) 754.32
- uterus (*see also* Malposition, uterus) 621.6

Flexner's
- bacillus 004.1
- diarrhea (ulcerative) 004.1
- dysentery 004.1

Flexner-Boyd dysentery 004.2

Flexure — *see* condition

Floater, vitreous 379.24

Floating
- cartilage (joint) (*see also* Disorder, cartilage, articular) 718.0 ☑
  - knee 717.6
- gallbladder (congenital) 751.69
- kidney 593.0
  - congenital 753.3
- liver (congenital) 751.69
- rib 756.3
- spleen 289.59

Flooding 626.2

Floor — *see* condition

Floppy
- infant NEC 781.99
- valve syndrome (mitral) 424.0

Flu — *see also* Influenza
- gastric NEC 008.8

Fluctuating blood pressure 796.4

Fluid
- abdomen 789.5
- chest (*see also* Pleurisy, with effusion) 511.9
- heart (*see also* Failure, heart) 428.0
- joint (*see also* Effusion, joint) 719.0 ☑
- loss (acute) 276.50
  - with
    - hypernatremia 276.0
    - hyponatremia 276.1
- lung (*see also* Edema, lung)
  - encysted 511.8
- peritoneal cavity 789.5
- pleural cavity (*see also* Pleurisy, with effusion) 511.9
- retention 276.6

Flukes NEC — *see also* Infestation, fluke 121.9
- blood NEC (*see also* Infestation, Schistosoma) 120.9
- liver 121.3

Fluor (albus) (vaginalis) 623.5
- trichomonal (Trichomonas vaginalis) 131.00

Fluorosis (dental) (chronic) 520.3

Flushing 782.62
- menopausal 627.2

Flush syndrome 259.2

Flutter
- atrial or auricular 427.32
- heart (ventricular) 427.42
  - atrial 427.32
- impure 427.32
- postoperative 997.1
- ventricular 427.42

Flux (bloody) (serosanguineous) 009.0

Focal — *see* condition

Fochier's abscess — *see* Abscess, by site

Focus, Assmann's — *see also* Tuberculosis 011.0 ☑

Fogo selvagem 694.4

Foix-Alajouanine syndrome 336.1

Folds, anomalous — *see also* Anomaly, specified type NEC
- Bowman's membrane 371.31
- Descemet's membrane 371.32
- epicanthic 743.63
- heart 746.89
- posterior segment of eye, congenital 743.54

Folie à deux 297.3

Follicle
- cervix (nabothian) (ruptured) 616.0
- graafian, ruptured, with hemorrhage 620.0
- nabothian 616.0

Folliclis (primary) — *see also* Tuberculosis 017.0 ☑

Follicular — *see also* condition
- cyst (atretic) 620.0

Folliculitis 704.8
- abscedens et suffodiens 704.8
- decalvans 704.09
- gonorrheal (acute) 098.0

Folliculitis — *continued*
- gonorrheal — *continued*
  - chronic or duration of 2 months or more 098.2
- keloid, keloidalis 706.1
- pustular 704.8
- ulerythematosa reticulata 701.8

Folliculosis, conjunctival 372.02

Følling's disease (phenylketonuria) 270.1

Follow-up (examination) (routine) (following) V67.9
- cancer chemotherapy V67.2
- chemotherapy V67.2
- fracture V67.4
- high-risk medication V67.51
- injury NEC V67.59
- postpartum
  - immediately after delivery V24.0
  - routine V24.2
- psychiatric V67.3
- psychotherapy V67.3
- radiotherapy V67.1
- specified condition NEC V67.59
- specified surgery NEC V67.09
- surgery V67.00
  - vaginal pap smear V67.01
- treatment V67.9
  - combined NEC V67.6
  - fracture V67.4
  - involving high-risk medication NEC V67.51
  - mental disorder V67.3
  - specified NEC V67.59

Fong's syndrome (hereditary osteoonychodysplasia) 756.89

Food
- allergy 693.1
- anaphylactic shock — *see* Anaphylactic shock, due to, food
- asphyxia (from aspiration or inhalation) (*see also* Asphyxia, food) 933.1
- choked on (*see also* Asphyxia, food) 933.1
- deprivation 994.2
  - specified kind of food NEC 269.8
- intoxication (*see also* Poisoning, food) 005.9
- lack of 994.2
- poisoning (*see also* Poisoning, food) 005.9
- refusal or rejection NEC 307.59
- strangulation or suffocation (*see also* Asphyxia, food) 933.1
- toxemia (*see also* Poisoning, food) 005.9

Foot — *see also* condition
- and mouth disease 078.4
- process disease 581.3

Foramen ovale (nonclosure) (patent) (persistent) 745.5

Forbes-Albright syndrome (nonpuerperal amenorrhea and lactation associated with pituitary tumor) 253.1

Forbes'(glycogen storage) disease 271.0

Forced birth or delivery NEC 669.8 ☑
- affecting fetus or newborn NEC 763.89

Forceps
- delivery NEC 669.5 ☑
  - affecting fetus or newborn 763.2

Fordyce's disease (ectopic sebaceous glands) (mouth) 750.26

Fordyce-Fox disease (apocrine miliaria) 705.82

Forearm — *see* condition

Foreign body

> *Note — For foreign body with open wound, or other injury, see Wound, open, or the type of injury specified.*

- accidentally left during a procedure 998.4
- anterior chamber (eye) 871.6
  - magnetic 871.5

Foreign body — *continued*
- anterior chamber — *continued*
  - magnetic — *continued*
    - retained or old 360.51
  - retained or old 360.61
- ciliary body (eye) 871.6
  - magnetic 871.5
    - retained or old 360.52
  - retained or old 360.62
- entering through orifice (current) (old)
  - accessory sinus 932
  - air passage (upper) 933.0
    - lower 934.8
  - alimentary canal 938
  - alveolar process 935.0
  - antrum (Highmore) 932
  - anus 937
  - appendix 936
  - asphyxia due to (*see also* Asphyxia, food) 933.1
  - auditory canal 931
  - auricle 931
  - bladder 939.0
  - bronchioles 934.8
  - bronchus (main) 934.1
  - buccal cavity 935.0
  - canthus (inner) 930.1
  - cecum 936
  - cervix (canal) uterine 939.1
  - coil, ileocecal 936
  - colon 936
  - conjunctiva 930.1
  - conjunctival sac 930.1
  - cornea 930.0
  - digestive organ or tract NEC 938
  - duodenum 936
  - ear (external) 931
  - esophagus 935.1
  - eye (external) 930.9
    - combined sites 930.8
    - intraocular — *see* Foreign body, by site
    - specified site NEC 930.8
  - eyeball 930.8
    - intraocular — *see* Foreign body, intraocular
  - eyelid 930.1
    - retained or old 374.86
  - frontal sinus 932
  - gastrointestinal tract 938
  - genitourinary tract 939.9
  - globe 930.8
    - penetrating 871.6
      - magnetic 871.5
        - retained or old 360.50
      - retained or old 360.60
  - gum 935.0
  - Highmore's antrum 932
  - hypopharynx 933.0
  - ileocecal coil 936
  - ileum 936
  - inspiration (of) 933.1
  - intestine (large) (small) 936
  - lacrimal apparatus, duct, gland, or sac 930.2
  - larynx 933.1
  - lung 934.8
  - maxillary sinus 932
  - mouth 935.0
  - nasal sinus 932
  - nasopharynx 933.0
  - nose (passage) 932
  - nostril 932
  - oral cavity 935.0
  - palate 935.0
  - penis 939.3
  - pharynx 933.0
  - pyriform sinus 933.0
  - rectosigmoid 937
    - junction 937
  - rectum 937
  - respiratory tract 934.9
    - specified part NEC 934.8
  - sclera 930.1
  - sinus 932
    - accessory 932

Note — For fracture of any of the following sites with fracture of other bones — see Fracture, multiple.

"Closed" includes the following descriptions of fractures, with or without delayed healing, unless they are specified as open or compound:

comminuted	*linear*
depressed	*simple*
elevated	*slipped epiphysis*
fissured	*spiral*
greenstick	*unspecified*
impacted	

"Open" includes the following descriptions of fractures, with or without delayed healing:

compound	*puncture*
infected	*with foreign body*
missile	

For late effect of fracture, see Late, effect, fracture, by site.

Note — Multiple fractures of sites classifiable to the same three- or four-digit category are coded to that category, except for sites classifiable to 810–818 or 820–827 in different limbs.

Multiple fractures of sites classifiable to different fourth-digit subdivisions within the same three-digit category should be dealt with according to coding rules.

Multiple fractures of sites classifiable to different three-digit categories (identifiable from the listing under "Fracture"), and of sites classifiable to 810–818 or 820–827 in different limbs should be coded according to the following list, which should be referred to in the following priority order: skull or face bones, pelvis or vertebral column, legs, arms.

Note — Use the following fifth-digit subclassification with categories 800, 801, 803, and 804:

0 unspecified state of consciousness

1 with no loss of consciousness

2 with brief [less than one hour] loss of consciousness

3 with moderate [1–24 hours] loss of consciousness

4 with prolonged [more than 24 hours] loss of consciousness and return to pre-existing conscious level

5 with prolonged [more than 24 hours] loss of consciousness, without return to pre-existing conscious level

Use fifth-digit 5 to designate when a patient is unconscious and dies before regaining consciousness, regardless of the duration of the loss of consciousness

6 with loss of consciousness of unspecified duration

9 with concussion, unspecified

Fracture — *continued*
parry — *see* Fracture, Monteggia's
patella (closed) 822.0
open 822.1
pathologic (cause unknown) 733.10
ankle 733.16
femur (neck) 733.14
specified NEC 733.15
fibula 733.16
hip 733.14
humerus 733.11
radius (distal) 733.12
specified site NEC 733.19
tibia 733.16
ulna 733.12
vertebrae (collapse) 733.13
wrist 733.12
pedicle (of vertebral arch) — *see* Fracture, vertebra, by site
pelvis, pelvic (bone(s)) (with visceral injury) (closed) 808.8
multiple (with disruption of pelvic circle) 808.43
open 808.53
open 808.9
rim (closed) 808.49
open 808.59
peritrochanteric (closed) 820.20
open 820.30
phalanx, phalanges, of one
foot (closed) 826.0
with bone(s) of same lower limb 827.0
open 827.1
open 826.1
hand (closed) 816.00
with metacarpal bone(s) of same hand 817.0
open 817.1
distal 816.02
open 816.12
middle 816.01
open 816.11
multiple sites NEC 816.03
open 816.13
open 816.10
proximal 816.01
open 816.11
pisiform (closed) 814.04
open 814.14
pond — *see* Fracture, skull, vault
Pott's (closed) 824.4
open 824.5
prosthetic device, internal — *see* Complications, mechanical
pubis (with visceral injury) (closed) 808.2
open 808.3
Quervain's (closed) 814.01
open 814.11
radius (alone) (closed) 813.81
with ulna NEC 813.83
open 813.93
distal end — *see* Fracture, radius, lower end
epiphysis
lower — *see* Fracture, radius, lower end
upper — *see* Fracture, radius, upper end
head — *see* Fracture, radius, upper end
lower end or extremity (distal end) (lower epiphysis) 813.42
with ulna (lower end) 813.44
open 813.54
open 813.52
torus 813.45
neck — *see* Fracture, radius, upper end
open NEC 813.91
pathologic 733.12
proximal end — *see* Fracture, radius, upper end
shaft (closed) 813.21
with ulna (shaft) 813.23

Fracture — *continued*
radius — *continued*
shaft — *continued*
with ulna — *continued*
open 813.33
open 813.31
upper end 813.07
with ulna (upper end) 813.08
open 813.18
epiphysis 813.05
open 813.15
head 813.05
open 813.15
multiple sites 813.07
open 813.17
neck 813.06
open 813.16
open 813.17
specified site NEC 813.07
open 813.17
ramus
inferior or superior (with visceral injury) (closed) 808.2
open 808.3
ischium — *see* Fracture, ischium
mandible 802.24
open 802.34
rib(s) (closed) 807.0 ☑

Note — Use the following fifth-digit subclassification with categories 807.0–807.1:

0 rib(s), unspecified
1 one rib
2 two ribs
3 three ribs
4 four ribs
5 five ribs
6 six ribs
7 seven ribs
8 eight or more ribs
9 multiple ribs, unspecified

with flail chest (open) 807.4
open 807.1 ☑
root, tooth 873.63
complicated 873.73
sacrum — *see* Fracture, vertebra, sacrum
scaphoid
ankle (closed) 825.22
open 825.32
wrist (closed) 814.01
open 814.11
scapula (closed) 811.00
acromial, acromion (process) 811.01
open 811.11
body 811.09
open 811.19
coracoid process 811.02
open 811.12
glenoid (cavity) (fossa) 811.03
open 811.13
neck 811.03
open 811.13
open 811.10
semilunar
bone, wrist (closed) 814.02
open 814.12
cartilage (interior) (knee) — *see* Tear, meniscus
sesamoid bone — *see* Fracture, by site
Shepherd's (closed) 825.21
open 825.31
shoulder (*see also* Fracture, humerus, upper end)
blade — *see* Fracture, scapula
silverfork — *see* Fracture, radius, lower end
sinus (ethmoid) (frontal) (maxillary) (nasal) (sphenoidal) — *see* Fracture, skull, base

Fracture — *continued*
Skillern's — *see* Fracture, radius, shaft
skull (multiple NEC) (with face bones) (closed) 803.0 ☑

Note — Use the following fifth-digit subclassification with categories 800, 801, 803, and 804:

0 unspecified state of consciousness
1 with no loss of consciousness
2 with brief [less than one hour] loss of consciousness
3 with moderate [1-24 hours] loss of consciousness
4 with prolonged [more than 24 hours] loss of consciousness and return to pre-existing conscious level
5 with prolonged [more than 24 hours] loss of consciousness, without return to pre-existing conscious level

Use fifth-digit 5 to designate when a patient is unconscious and dies before regaining consciousness, regardless of the duration of the loss of consciousness

6 with loss of consciousness of unspecified duration
9 with concussion, unspecified

with
contusion, cerebral 803.1 ☑
epidural hemorrhage 803.2 ☑
extradural hemorrhage 803.2 ☑
hemorrhage (intracranial) NEC 803.3 ☑
intracranial injury NEC 803.4 ☑
laceration, cerebral 803.1 ☑
other bones — *see* Fracture, multiple, skull
subarachnoid hemorrhage 803.2 ☑
subdural hemorrhage 803.2 ☑
base (antrum) (ethmoid bone) (fossa) (internal ear) (nasal sinus) (occiput) (sphenoid) (temporal bone) (closed) 801.0 ☑
with
contusion, cerebral 801.1 ☑
epidural hemorrhage 801.2 ☑
extradural hemorrhage 801.2 ☑
hemorrhage (intracranial) NEC 801.3 ☑
intracranial injury NEC 801.4 ☑
laceration, cerebral 801.1 ☑
subarachnoid hemorrhage 801.2 ☑
subdural hemorrhage 801.2 ☑
open 801.5 ☑
with
contusion, cerebral 801.6 ☑
epidural hemorrhage 801.7 ☑
extradural hemorrhage 801.7 ☑
hemorrhage (intracranial) NEC 801.8 ☑

Fracture — *continued*
skull — *continued*
base — *continued*
open — *continued*
with — *continued*
intracranial injury NEC 801.9 ☑
laceration, cerebral 801.6 ☑
subarachnoid hemorrhage 801.7 ☑
subdural hemorrhage 801.7 ☑
birth injury 767.3
face bones — *see* Fracture, face bones
open 803.5 ☑
with
contusion, cerebral 803.6 ☑
epidural hemorrhage 803.7 ☑
extradural hemorrhage 803.7 ☑
hemorrhage (intracranial) NEC 803.8 ☑
intracranial injury NEC 803.9 ☑
laceration, cerebral 803.6 ☑
subarachnoid hemorrhage 803.7 ☑
subdural hemorrhage 803.7 ☑
vault (frontal bone) (parietal bone) (vertex) (closed) 800.0 ☑
with
contusion, cerebral 800.1 ☑
epidural hemorrhage 800.2 ☑
extradural hemorrhage 800.2 ☑
hemorrhage (intracranial) NEC 800.3 ☑
intracranial injury NEC 800.4 ☑
laceration, cerebral 800.1 ☑
subarachnoid hemorrhage 800.2 ☑
subdural hemorrhage 800.2 ☑
open 800.5 ☑
with
contusion, cerebral 800.6 ☑
epidural hemorrhage 800.7 ☑
extradural hemorrhage 800.7 ☑
hemorrhage (intracranial) NEC 800.8 ☑
intracranial injury NEC 800.9 ☑
laceration, cerebral 800.6 ☑
subarachnoid hemorrhage 800.7 ☑
subdural hemorrhage 800.7 ☑
Smith's 813.41
open 813.51
sphenoid (bone) (sinus) — *see* Fracture, skull, base
spine (*see also* Fracture, vertebra, by site due to birth trauma) 767.4
spinous process — *see* Fracture, vertebra, by site
spontaneous — *see* Fracture, pathologic
sprinters' — *see* Fracture, ilium
stapes — *see* Fracture, skull, base

Fracture — *continued*
  stave (*see also* Fracture, metacarpus, metacarpal bone(s))
    spine — *see* Fracture, tibia, upper end
  sternum (closed) 807.2
    with flail chest (open) 807.4
    open 807.3
  Stieda's — *see* Fracture, femur, lower end
  stress 733.95
    fibula 733.93
    metatarsals 733.94
    specified site NEC 733.95
    tibia 733.93
  styloid process
    metacarpal (closed) 815.02
      open 815.12
    radius — *see* Fracture, radius, lower end
    temporal bone — *see* Fracture, skull, base
    ulna — *see* Fracture, ulna, lower end
  supracondylar, elbow 812.41
    open 812.51
  symphysis pubis (with visceral injury) (closed) 808.2
    open 808.3
  talus (ankle bone) (closed) 825.21
    open 825.31
  tarsus, tarsal bone(s) (with metatarsus) of one foot (closed) NEC 825.29
    open 825.39
  temporal bone (styloid) — *see* Fracture, skull, base
  tendon — *see* Sprain, by site
  thigh — *see* Fracture, femur, shaft
  thumb (and finger(s)) of one hand (closed) (*see also* Fracture, phalanx, hand) 816.00
    with metacarpal bone(s) of same hand 817.0
      open 817.1
    metacarpal(s) — *see* Fracture, metacarpus
    open 816.10
  thyroid cartilage (closed) 807.5
    open 807.6
  tibia (closed) 823.80
    with fibula 823.82
      open 823.92
    condyles — *see* Fracture, tibia, upper end
    distal end 824.8
      open 824.9
    epiphysis
      lower 824.8
        open 824.9
      upper — *see* Fracture, tibia, upper end
    head (involving knee joint) — *see* Fracture, tibia, upper end
    intercondyloid eminence — *see* Fracture, tibia, upper end
    involving ankle 824.0
      open 824.9
    lower end or extremity (anterior lip) (posterior lip) 824.8
      open 824.9
    malleolus (internal) (medial) 824.0
      open 824.1
    open NEC 823.90
    pathologic 733.16
    proximal end — *see* Fracture, tibia, upper end
    shaft 823.20
      with fibula 823.22
        open 823.32
      open 823.30
    spine — *see* Fracture, tibia, upper end
    stress 733.93
    torus 823.40
      with fibula 823.42

Fracture — *continued*
  tibia — *continued*
    tuberosity — *see* Fracture, tibia, upper end
    upper end or extremity (condyle) (epiphysis) (head) (spine) (proximal end) (tuberosity) 823.00
      with fibula 823.02
        open 823.12
      open 823.10
  toe(s), of one foot (closed) 826.0
    with bone(s) of same lower limb 827.0
      open 827.1
    open 826.1
  tooth (root) 873.63
    complicated 873.73
  torus
    fibula 823.41
      with tibia 823.42
    radius 813.45
    tibia 823.40
      with fibula 823.42
  trachea (closed) 807.5
    open 807.6
  transverse process — *see* Fracture, vertebra, by site
  trapezium (closed) 814.05
    open 814.15
  trapezoid bone (closed) 814.06
    open 814.16
  trimalleolar (closed) 824.6
    open 824.7
  triquetral (bone) (closed) 814.03
    open 814.13
  trochanter (greater) (lesser) (closed) (*see also* Fracture, femur, neck, by site) 820.20
    open 820.30
  trunk (bones) (closed) 809.0
    open 809.1
  tuberosity (external) — *see* Fracture, by site
  ulna (alone) (closed) 813.82
    with radius NEC 813.83
      open 813.93
    coronoid process (closed) 813.02
      open 813.12
    distal end — *see* Fracture, ulna, lower end
    epiphysis
      lower — *see* Fracture, ulna, lower end
      upper — *see* Fracture, ulna, upper end
    head — *see* Fracture, ulna, lower end
    lower end (distal end) (head) (lower epiphysis) (styloid process) 813.43
      with radius (lower end) 813.44
        open 813.54
      open 813.53
    olecranon process (closed) 813.01
      open 813.11
    open NEC 813.92
    pathologic 733.12
    proximal end — *see* Fracture, ulna, upper end
    shaft 813.22
      with radius (shaft) 813.23
        open 813.33
      open 813.32
    styloid process — *see* Fracture, ulna, lower end
    transverse — *see* Fracture, ulna, by site
    upper end (epiphysis) 813.04
      with radius (upper end) 813.08
        open 813.18
      multiple sites 813.04
        open 813.14
      open 813.14
      specified site NEC 813.04
        open 813.14

Fracture — *continued*
  unciform (closed) 814.08
    open 814.18
  vertebra, vertebral (back) (body) (column) (neural arch) (pedicle) (spine) (spinous process) (transverse process) (closed) 805.8
    with
      hematomyelia — *see* Fracture, vertebra, by site, with spinal cord injury
      injury to
        cauda equina — *see* Fracture, vertebra, sacrum, with spinal cord injury
        nerve — *see* Fracture, vertebra, by site, with spinal cord injury
      paralysis — *see* Fracture, vertebra, by site, with spinal cord injury
      paraplegia — *see* Fracture, vertebra, by site, with spinal cord injury
      quadriplegia — *see* Fracture, vertebra, by site, with spinal cord injury
      spinal concussion — *see* Fracture, vertebra, by site, with spinal cord injury
      spinal cord injury (closed) NEC 806.8

> *Note — Use the following fifth-digit subclassification with categories 806.0–806.3:*
>
> *C_1–C_4 or unspecified level and D_1–D_6 (T_1–T_6) or unspecified level with*
>
> 0 *unspecified spinal cord injury*
> 1 *complete lesion of cord*
> 2 *anterior cord syndrome*
> 3 *central cord syndrome*
> 4 *specified injury NEC*
>
> *C_5–C_7 level and D_7–D_{12} level with:*
>
> 5 *unspecified spinal cord injury*
> 6 *complete lesion of cord*
> 7 *anterior cord syndrome*
> 8 *central cord syndrome*
> 9 *specified injury NEC*

        cervical 806.0 ☑
          open 806.1 ☑
        dorsal, dorsolumbar 806.2 ☑
          open 806.3 ☑
        open 806.9
        thoracic, thoracolumbar 806.2 ☑
          open 806.3 ☑
    atlanto-axial — *see* Fracture, vertebra, cervical
    cervical (hangman) (teardrop) (closed) 805.00
      with spinal cord injury — *see* Fracture, vertebra, with spinal cord injury, cervical
      first (atlas) 805.01
        open 805.11
      second (axis) 805.02
        open 805.12
      third 805.03
        open 805.13
      fourth 805.04
        open 805.14
      fifth 805.05
        open 805.15
      sixth 805.06
        open 805.16
      seventh 805.07
        open 805.17
      multiple sites 805.08

Fracture — *continued*
  vertebra, vertebral — *continued*
    cervical — *continued*
      multiple sites — *continued*
        open 805.18
      open 805.10
    coccyx (closed) 805.6
      with spinal cord injury (closed) 806.60
        cauda equina injury 806.62
          complete lesion 806.61
            open 806.71
          open 806.72
        open 806.70
        specified type NEC 806.69
          open 806.79
      open 805.7
    collapsed 733.13
    compression, not due to trauma 733.13
    dorsal (closed) 805.2
      with spinal cord injury — *see* Fracture, vertebra, with spinal cord injury, dorsal
      open 805.3
    dorsolumbar (closed) 805.2
      with spinal cord injury — *see* Fracture, vertebra, with spinal cord injury, dorsal
      open 805.3
    due to osteoporosis 733.13
    fetus or newborn 767.4
    lumbar (closed) 805.4
      with spinal cord injury (closed) 806.4
        open 806.5
      open 805.5
    nontraumatic 733.13
    open NEC 805.9
    pathologic (any site) 733.13
    sacrum (closed) 805.6
      with spinal cord injury 806.60
        cauda equina injury 806.62
          complete lesion 806.61
            open 806.71
          open 806.72
        open 806.70
        specified type NEC 806.69
          open 806.79
      open 805.7
    site unspecified (closed) 805.8
      with spinal cord injury (closed) 806.8
        open 806.9
      open 805.9
    stress (any site) 733.95
    thoracic (closed) 805.2
      with spinal cord injury — *see* Fracture, vertebra, with spinal cord injury, thoracic
      open 805.3
  vertex — *see* Fracture, skull, vault
  vomer (bone) 802.0
    open 802.1
  Wagstaffe's — *see* Fracture, ankle
  wrist (closed) 814.00
    open 814.10
    pathologic 733.12
  xiphoid (process) — *see* Fracture, sternum
  zygoma (zygomatic arch) (closed) 802.4
    open 802.5
Fragile X syndrome 759.83
Fragilitas
  crinium 704.2
  hair 704.2
  ossium 756.51
    with blue sclera 756.51
  unguium 703.8
    congenital 757.5
Fragility
  bone 756.51
    with deafness and blue sclera 756.51
  capillary (hereditary) 287.8

G

Note — Use the following fifth-digit subclassification for category 535:

0 without mention of hemorrhage

1 with hemorrhage

- **Glycogen**
  - infiltration (*see also* Disease, glycogen storage) 271.0
  - storage disease (*see also* Disease, glycogen storage) 271.0
- **Glycogenosis** — *see also* Disease, glycogen storage 271.0
  - cardiac 271.0 *[425.7]*
  - Cori, types I-VII 271.0
  - diabetic, secondary 250.8 ☑ *[259.8]*
  - diffuse (with hepatic cirrhosis) 271.0
  - generalized 271.0
  - glucose-6-phosphatase deficiency 271.0
  - hepatophosphorylase deficiency 271.0
  - hepatorenal 271.0
  - myophosphorylase deficiency 271.0
- **Glycopenia** 251.2
- **Glycopeptide**
  - intermediate staphylococcus aureus (GISA) V09.8 ☑
  - resistant
    - enterococcus V09.8 ☑
    - staphylococcus aureus (GRSA) V09.8 ☑
- **Glycoprolinuria** 270.8
- **Glycosuria** 791.5
  - renal 271.4
- **Gnathostoma** (spinigerum) (infection) (infestation) 128.1
  - wandering swellings from 128.1
- **Gnathostomiasis** 128.1
- **Goiter** (adolescent) (colloid) (diffuse) (dipping) (due to iodine deficiency) (endemic) (euthyroid) (heart) (hyperplastic) (internal) (intrathoracic) (juvenile) (mixed type) (nonendemic) (parenchymatous) (plunging) (sporadic) (subclavicular) (substernal) 240.9
  - with
    - hyperthyroidism (recurrent) (*see also* Goiter, toxic) 242.0 ☑
    - thyrotoxicosis (*see also* Goiter, toxic) 242.0 ☑
  - adenomatous (*see also* Goiter, nodular) 241.9
  - cancerous (M8000/3) 193
  - complicating pregnancy, childbirth, or puerperium 648.1 ☑
  - congenital 246.1
  - cystic (*see also* Goiter, nodular) 241.9
  - due to enzyme defect in synthesis of thyroid hormone (butane-insoluble iodine) (coupling) (deiodinase) (iodide trapping or organification) (iodotyrosine dehalogenase) (peroxidase) 246.1
  - dyshormonogenic 246.1
  - exophthalmic (*see also* Goiter, toxic) 242.0 ☑
  - familial (with deaf-mutism) 243
  - fibrous 245.3
  - lingual 759.2
  - lymphadenoid 245.2
  - malignant (M8000/3) 193
  - multinodular (nontoxic) 241.1
    - toxic or with hyperthyroidism (*see also* Goiter, toxic) 242.2 ☑
  - nodular (nontoxic) 241.9
    - with
      - hyperthyroidism (*see also* Goiter, toxic) 242.3 ☑
      - thyrotoxicosis (*see also* Goiter, toxic) 242.3 ☑
    - endemic 241.9
    - exophthalmic (diffuse) (*see also* Goiter, toxic) 242.0 ☑
    - multinodular (nontoxic) 241.1
    - sporadic 241.9
    - toxic (*see also* Goiter, toxic) 242.3 ☑
    - uninodular (nontoxic) 241.0
  - nontoxic (nodular) 241.9
    - multinodular 241.1
    - uninodular 241.0
- **Goiter** — *continued*
  - pulsating (*see also* Goiter, toxic) 242.0 ☑
  - simple 240.0
  - toxic 242.0 ☑

> *Note — Use the following fifth-digit subclassification with category 242:*
>
> 0 *without mention of thyrotoxic crisis or storm*
>
> 1 *with mention of thyrotoxic crisis or storm*

    - adenomatous 242.3 ☑
      - multinodular 242.2 ☑
      - uninodular 242.1 ☑
    - multinodular 242.2 ☑
    - nodular 242.3 ☑
      - multinodular 242.2 ☑
      - uninodular 242.1 ☑
    - uninodular 242.1 ☑
  - uninodular (nontoxic) 241.0
    - toxic or with hyperthyroidism (*see also* Goiter, toxic) 242.1 ☑
- **Goldberg (-Maxwell) (-Morris) syndrome** (testicular feminization) 259.5
- **Goldblatt's**
  - hypertension 440.1
  - kidney 440.1
- **Goldenhar's syndrome** (oculoauriculovertebral dysplasia) 756.0
- **Goldflam-Erb disease or syndrome** 358.00
- **Goldscheider's disease** (epidermolysis bullosa) 757.39
- **Goldstein's disease** (familial hemorrhagic telangiectasia) 448.0
- **Golfer's elbow** 726.32
- **Goltz-Gorlin syndrome** (dermal hypoplasia) 757.39
- **Gonadoblastoma** (M9073/1)
  - specified site — *see* Neoplasm, by site uncertain behavior
  - unspecified site
    - female 236.2
    - male 236.4
- **Gonecystitis** — *see also* Vesiculitis 608.0
- **Gongylonemiasis** 125.6
  - mouth 125.6
- **Goniosynechiae** 364.73
- **Gonococcemia** 098.89
- **Gonococcus, gonococcal** (disease) (infection) — *see also* condition 098.0
  - anus 098.7
  - bursa 098.52
  - chronic NEC 098.2
  - complicating pregnancy, childbirth, or puerperium 647.1 ☑
    - affecting fetus or newborn 760.2
  - conjunctiva, conjunctivitis (neonatorum) 098.40
  - dermatosis 098.89
  - endocardium 098.84
  - epididymo-orchitis 098.13
    - chronic or duration of 2 months or over 098.33
  - eye (newborn) 098.40
  - fallopian tube (chronic) 098.37
    - acute 098.17
  - genitourinary (acute) (organ) (system) (tract) (*see also* Gonorrhea) 098.0
    - lower 098.0
      - chronic 098.2
    - upper 098.10
      - chronic 098.30
  - heart NEC 098.85
  - joint 098.50
  - keratoderma 098.81
  - keratosis (blennorrhagica) 098.81
  - lymphatic (gland) (node) 098.89
  - meninges 098.82
  - orchitis (acute) 098.13
    - chronic or duration of 2 months or over 098.33
- **Gonococcus, gonococcal** — *see also* condition — *continued*
  - pelvis (acute) 098.19
    - chronic or duration of 2 months or over 098.39
  - pericarditis 098.83
  - peritonitis 098.86
  - pharyngitis 098.6
  - pharynx 098.6
  - proctitis 098.7
  - pyosalpinx (chronic) 098.37
    - acute 098.17
  - rectum 098.7
  - septicemia 098.89
  - skin 098.89
  - specified site NEC 098.89
  - synovitis 098.51
  - tendon sheath 098.51
  - throat 098.6
  - urethra (acute) 098.0
    - chronic or duration of 2 months or over 098.2
  - vulva (acute) 098.0
    - chronic or duration of 2 months or over 098.2
- **Gonocytoma** (M9073/1)
  - specified site — *see* Neoplasm, by site, uncertain behavior
  - unspecified site
    - female 236.2
    - male 236.4
- **Gonorrhea** 098.0
  - acute 098.0
  - Bartholin's gland (acute) 098.0
    - chronic or duration of 2 months or over 098.2
  - bladder (acute) 098.11
    - chronic or duration of 2 months or over 098.31
  - carrier (suspected of) V02.7
  - cervix (acute) 098.15
    - chronic or duration of 2 months or over 098.35
  - chronic 098.2
  - complicating pregnancy, childbirth, or puerperium 647.1 ☑
    - affecting fetus or newborn 760.2
  - conjunctiva, conjunctivitis (neonatorum) 098.40
  - contact V01.6
  - Cowper's gland (acute) 098.0
    - chronic or duration of 2 months or over 098.2
  - duration of two months or over 098.2
  - exposure to V01.6
  - fallopian tube (chronic) 098.37
    - acute 098.17
  - genitourinary (acute) (organ) (system) (tract) 098.0
    - chronic 098.2
    - duration of two months or over 098.2
  - kidney (acute) 098.19
    - chronic or duration of 2 months or over 098.39
  - ovary (acute) 098.19
    - chronic or duration of 2 months or over 098.39
  - pelvis (acute) 098.19
    - chronic or duration of 2 months or over 098.39
  - penis (acute) 098.0
    - chronic or duration of 2 months or over 098.2
  - prostate (acute) 098.12
    - chronic or duration of 2 months or over 098.32
  - seminal vesicle (acute) 098.14
    - chronic or duration of 2 months or over 098.34
  - specified site NEC — *see* Gonococcus
  - spermatic cord (acute) 098.14
    - chronic or duration of 2 months or over 098.34
  - urethra (acute) 098.0
- **Gonorrhea** — *continued*
  - urethra — *continued*
    - chronic or duration of 2 months or over 098.2
  - vagina (acute) 098.0
    - chronic or duration of 2 months or over 098.2
  - vas deferens (acute) 098.14
    - chronic or duration of 2 months or over 098.34
  - vulva (acute) 098.0
    - chronic or duration of 2 months or over 098.2
- **Goodpasture's syndrome** (pneumorenal) 446.21
- **Good's syndrome** 279.06
- **Gopalan's syndrome** (burning feet) 266.2
- **Gordon's disease** (exudative enteropathy) 579.8
- **Gorlin-Chaudhry-Moss syndrome** 759.89
- **Gougerot-Blum syndrome** (pigmented purpuric lichenoid dermatitis) 709.1
- **Gougerot-Carteaud disease or syndrome** (confluent reticulate papillomatosis) 701.8
- **Gougerot-Hailey-Hailey disease** (benign familial chronic pemphigus) 757.39
- **Gougerot (-Houwer) -Sjögren syndrome** (keratoconjunctivitis sicca) 710.2
- **Gougerot's syndrome** (trisymptomatic) 709.1
- **Gouley's syndrome** (constrictive pericarditis) 423.2
- **Goundou** 102.6
- **Gout, gouty** 274.9
  - with specified manifestations NEC 274.89
  - arthritis (acute) 274.0
  - arthropathy 274.0
  - degeneration, heart 274.82
  - diathesis 274.9
  - eczema 274.89
  - episcleritis 274.89 *[379.09]*
  - external ear (tophus) 274.81
  - glomerulonephritis 274.10
  - iritis 274.89 *[364.11]*
  - joint 274.0
  - kidney 274.10
  - lead 984.9
    - specified type of lead — *see* Table of Drugs and Chemicals
  - nephritis 274.10
  - neuritis 274.89 *[357.4]*
  - phlebitis 274.89 *[451.9]*
  - rheumatic 714.0
  - saturnine 984.9
    - specified type of lead — *see* Table of Drugs and Chemicals
  - spondylitis 274.0
  - synovitis 274.0
  - syphilitic 095.8
  - tophi 274.0
    - ear 274.81
    - heart 274.82
    - specified site NEC 274.82
- **Gowers'**
  - muscular dystrophy 359.1
  - syndrome (vasovagal attack) 780.2
- **Gowers-Paton-Kennedy syndrome** 377.04
- **Gradenigo's syndrome** 383.02
- **Graft-versus-host disease** (bone marrow) 996.85
  - due to organ transplant NEC — *see* Complications, transplant, organ
- **Graham Steell's murmur** (pulmonic regurgitation) — *see also* Endocarditis, pulmonary 424.3
- **Grain-handlers' disease or lung** 495.8
- **Grain mite** (itch) 133.8
- **Grand**
  - mal (idiopathic) (*see also* Epilepsy) 345.1 ☑

H

Note — Hematomas are coded according to origin and the nature and site of the hematoma or the accompanying injury. Hematomas of unspecified origin are coded as injuries of the sites involved, except:

(a) hematomas of genital organs which are coded as diseases of the organ involved unless they complicate pregnancy or delivery

(b) hematomas of the eye which are coded as diseases of the eye.

For late effect of hematoma classifiable to 920–924 see Late, effect, contusion

Note — Use the following fifth-digit subclassification with categories 851–854:

0 unspecified state of consciousness

1 with no loss of consciousness

2 with brief [less than one hour] loss of consciousness

3 with moderate [1–24 hours] loss of consciousness

4 with prolonged [more than 24 hours] loss of consciousness and return to pre-existing conscious level

5 with prolonged [more than 24 hours] loss of consciousness, without return to pre-existing conscious level

Use fifth-digit 5 to designate when a patient is unconscious and dies before regaining consciousness, regardless of the duration of the loss of consciousness

6 with loss of consciousness of unspecified duration

9 with concussion, unspecified

Hematoma — *see also* Contusion — *continued*
- ovary (corpus luteum) (nontraumatic) 620.1
  - traumatic — *see* Injury, internal, ovary
- pelvis (female) (nontraumatic) 629.89 ▲
  - complicating delivery 665.7 ☑
  - male 608.83
  - traumatic (*see also* Injury, internal, pelvis)
    - specified organ NEC (*see also* Injury, internal, pelvis) 867.6
- penis (nontraumatic) 607.82
- pericranial (and neck, or face any part, except eye) 920
  - due to injury at birth 767.19
- perineal wound (obstetrical) 674.3 ☑
  - complicating delivery 664.5 ☑
- perirenal, cystic 593.81
- pinna 380.31
- placenta — *see* Placenta, abnormal
- postoperative 998.12
- retroperitoneal (nontraumatic) 568.81
  - traumatic — *see* Injury, internal, retroperitoneum
- retropubic, male 568.81
- scalp (and neck, or face any part, except eye) 920
  - fetus or newborn 767.19
- scrotum (nontraumatic) 608.83
  - traumatic 922.4
- seminal vesicle (nontraumatic) 608.83
  - traumatic — *see* Injury, internal, seminal, vesicle
- spermatic cord (*see also* Injury, internal, spermatic cord)
  - nontraumatic 608.83
- spinal (cord) (meninges) (*see also* Injury, spinal, by site)
  - fetus or newborn 767.4
  - nontraumatic 336.1
- spleen 865.01
  - with
    - laceration — *see* Laceration, spleen
    - open wound into cavity 865.11
- sternocleidomastoid, birth injury 767.8
- sternomastoid, birth injury 767.8
- subarachnoid (*see also* Hematoma, brain, subarachnoid)
  - fetus or newborn 772.2
  - nontraumatic (*see also* Hemorrhage, subarachnoid) 430
  - newborn 772.2
- subdural (*see also* Hematoma, brain, subdural)
  - fetus or newborn (localized) 767.0
  - nontraumatic (*see also* Hemorrhage, subdural) 432.1
- subperiosteal (syndrome) 267
  - traumatic — *see* Hematoma, by site
- superficial, fetus or newborn 772.6
- syncytium — *see* Placenta, abnormal
- testis (nontraumatic) 608.83
  - birth injury 767.8
  - traumatic 922.4
- tunica vaginalis (nontraumatic) 608.83
- umbilical cord 663.6 ☑
  - affecting fetus or newborn 762.6
- uterine ligament (nontraumatic) 620.7
  - traumatic — *see* Injury, internal, pelvis
- uterus 621.4
  - traumatic — *see* Injury, internal, pelvis
- vagina (nontraumatic) (ruptured) 623.6
  - complicating delivery 665.7 ☑
  - traumatic 922.4
- vas deferens (nontraumatic) 608.83

Hematoma — *see also* Contusion — *continued*
- vas deferens — *continued*
  - traumatic — *see* Injury, internal, vas deferens
- vitreous 379.23
- vocal cord 920
- vulva (nontraumatic) 624.5
  - complicating delivery 664.5 ☑
  - fetus or newborn 767.8
  - traumatic 922.4

Hematometra 621.4

Hematomyelia 336.1
- with fracture of vertebra (*see also* Fracture, vertebra, by site, with spinal cord injury) 806.8
- fetus or newborn 767.4

Hematomyelitis 323.9
- late effect — *see* category 326

Hematoperitoneum — *see also* Hemoperitoneum 568.81

Hematopneumothorax — *see also* Hemothorax 511.8

Hematopoiesis, cyclic 288.02 ●

Hematoporphyria (acquired) (congenital) 277.1

Hematoporphyrinuria (acquired) (congenital) 277.1

Hematorachis, hematorrhachis 336.1
- fetus or newborn 767.4

Hematosalpinx 620.8
- with
  - ectopic pregnancy (*see also* categories 633.0–633.9) 639.2
  - infectional (*see also* Salpingo-oophoritis) 614.2
  - molar pregnancy (*see also* categories 630–632) 639.2

Hematospermia 608.82

Hematothorax — *see also* Hemothorax 511.8

Hematotympanum 381.03

Hematuria (benign) (essential) (idiopathic) 599.7
- due to S. hematobium 120.0
- endemic 120.0
- intermittent 599.7
- malarial 084.8
- paroxysmal 599.7
- sulfonamide
  - correct substance properly administered 599.7
  - overdose or wrong substance given or taken 961.0
- tropical (bilharziasis) 120.0
- tuberculous (*see also* Tuberculosis) 016.9 ☑

Hematuric bilious fever 084.8

Hemeralopia 368.10

Hemiabiotrophy 799.89

Hemi-akinesia 781.8

Hemianalgesia — *see also* Disturbance, sensation 782.0

Hemianencephaly 740.0

Hemianesthesia — *see also* Disturbance, sensation 782.0

Hemianopia, hemianopsia (altitudinal) (homonymous) 368.46
- binasal 368.47
- bitemporal 368.47
- heteronymous 368.47
- syphilitic 095.8

Hemiasomatognosia 307.9

Hemiathetosis 781.0

Hemiatrophy 799.89
- cerebellar 334.8
- face 349.89
  - progressive 349.89
- fascia 728.9
- leg 728.2
- tongue 529.8

Hemiballism (us) 333.5

Hemiblock (cardiac) (heart) (left) 426.2

Hemicardia 746.89

Hemicephalus, hemicephaly 740.0

Hemichorea 333.5

Hemicrania 346.9 ☑
- congenital malformation 740.0

Hemidystrophy — *see* Hemiatrophy

Hemiectromelia 755.4

Hemihypalgesia — *see also* Disturbance, sensation 782.0

Hemihypertrophy (congenital) 759.89
- cranial 756.0

Hemihypesthesia — *see also* Disturbance, sensation 782.0

Hemi-inattention 781.8

Hemimelia 755.4
- lower limb 755.30
  - paraxial (complete) (incomplete) (intercalary) (terminal) 755.32
    - fibula 755.37
    - tibia 755.36
  - transverse (complete) (partial) 755.31
- upper limb 755.20
  - paraxial (complete) (incomplete) (intercalary) (terminal) 755.22
    - radial 755.26
    - ulnar 755.27
  - transverse (complete) (partial) 755.21

Hemiparalysis — *see also* Hemiplegia 342.9 ☑

Hemiparesis — *see also* Hemiplegia 342.9 ☑

Hemiparesthesia — *see also* Disturbance, sensation 782.0

Hemiplegia 342.9 ☑
- acute (*see also* Disease, cerebrovascular, acute) 436
- alternans facialis 344.89
- apoplectic (*see also* Disease, cerebrovascular, acute) 436
  - late effect or residual
    - affecting
      - dominant side 438.21
      - nondominant side 438.22
      - unspecified side 438.20
- arteriosclerotic 437.0
  - late effect or residual
    - affecting
      - dominant side 438.21
      - nondominant side 438.22
      - unspecified side 438.20
- ascending (spinal) NEC 344.89
- attack (*see also* Disease, cerebrovascular, acute) 436
- brain, cerebral (current episode) 437.8
  - congenital 343.1
- cerebral — *see* Hemiplegia, brain
- congenital (cerebral) (spastic) (spinal) 343.1
- conversion neurosis (hysterical) 300.11
- cortical — *see* Hemiplegia, brain
- due to
  - arteriosclerosis 437.0
    - late effect or residual
      - affecting
        - dominant side 438.21
        - nondominant side 438.22
        - unspecified side 438.20
  - cerebrovascular lesion (*see also* Disease, cerebrovascular, acute) 436
    - late effect
      - affecting
        - dominant side 438.21
        - nondominant side 438.22
        - unspecified side 438.20
- embolic (current) (*see also* Embolism, brain) 434.1 ☑
  - late effect
    - affecting
      - dominant side 438.21
      - nondominant side 438.22
      - unspecified side 438.20
- flaccid 342.0 ☑
- hypertensive (current episode) 437.8

Hemiplegia — *continued*
- infantile (postnatal) 343.4
- late effect
  - birth injury, intracranial or spinal 343.4
  - cerebrovascular lesion — *see* Late effect(s) (of) cerebrovascular disease
  - viral encephalitis 139.0
- middle alternating NEC 344.89
- newborn NEC 767.0
- seizure (current episode) (*see also* Disease, cerebrovascular, acute) 436
- spastic 342.1 ☑
  - congenital or infantile 343.1
- specified NEC 342.8 ☑
- thrombotic (current) (*see also* Thrombosis, brain) 434.0 ☑
  - late effect — *see* Late effect(s) (of) cerebrovascular disease

Hemisection, spinal cord — *see* Fracture, vertebra, by site, with spinal cord injury

Hemispasm 781.0
- facial 781.0

Hemispatial neglect 781.8

Hemisporosis 117.9

Hemitremor 781.0

Hemivertebra 756.14

Hemobilia 576.8

Hemocholecyst 575.8

Hemochromatosis (acquired) (diabetic) (hereditary) (liver) (myocardium) (primary idiopathic) (secondary) 275.0
- with refractory anemia 238.72 ▲

Hemodialysis V56.0

Hemoglobin — *see also* condition
- abnormal (disease) — *see* Disease, hemoglobin
- AS genotype 282.5
- fetal, hereditary persistence 282.7
- high-oxygen-affinity 289.0
- low NEC 285.9
- S (Hb-S), heterozygous 282.5

Hemoglobinemia 283.2
- due to blood transfusion NEC 999.8
  - bone marrow 996.85
- paroxysmal 283.2

Hemoglobinopathy (mixed) — *see also* Disease, hemoglobin 282.7
- with thalassemia 282.49
- sickle-cell 282.60
  - with thalassemia (without crisis) 282.41
    - with
      - crisis 282.42
      - vaso-occlusive pain 282.42

Hemoglobinuria, hemoglobinuric 791.2
- with anemia, hemolytic, acquired (chronic) NEC 283.2
- cold (agglutinin) (paroxysmal) (with Raynaud's syndrome) 283.2
- due to
  - exertion 283.2
  - hemolysis (from external causes) NEC 283.2
- exercise 283.2
- fever (malaria) 084.8
- infantile 791.2
- intermittent 283.2
- malarial 084.8
- march 283.2
- nocturnal (paroxysmal) 283.2
- paroxysmal (cold) (nocturnal) 283.2

Hemolymphangioma (M9175/0) 228.1

Hemolysis
- fetal — *see* Jaundice, fetus or newborn
- intravascular (disseminated) NEC 286.6
  - with
    - abortion — *see* Abortion, by type, with hemorrhage, delayed or excessive

☑ Additional Digit Required — Refer to the Tabular List for Digit Selection

Subterms under main terms may continue to next column or page

Note — Use the following fifth-digit subclassification with categories 851–854:

0 *unspecified state of consciousness*
1 *with no loss of consciousness*
2 *with brief [less than one hour] loss of consciousness*
3 *with moderate [1–24 hours] loss of consciousness*
4 *with prolonged [more than 24 hours] loss of consciousness and return to pre-existing conscious level*
5 *with prolonged [more than 24 hours] loss of consciousness, without return to pre-existing conscious level*

Use fifth-digit 5 to designate when a patient is unconscious and dies before regaining consciousness, regardless of the duration of the loss of consciousness

6 *with loss of consciousness of unspecified duration*
9 *with concussion, unspecified*

History of — *continued*
- subcutaneous tissue disease V13.3
- surgery (major) to
  - great vessels V15.1
  - heart V15.1
  - major organs NEC V15.2
- syndrome, nephrotic V13.03
- thrombophlebitis V12.52
- thrombosis V12.51
- tobacco use V15.82
- trophoblastic disease V13.1
  - affecting management of pregnancy V23.1
- tuberculosis V12.01
- ulcer, peptic V12.71
- urinary system disorder V13.00
  - calculi V13.01
  - infection V13.02
  - nephrotic syndrome V13.03
  - specified NEC V13.09

His-Werner disease (trench fever) 083.1

Hives (bold) — *see also* Urticaria 708.9

HIV infection (disease) (illness) — *see* Human immunodeficiency virus (disease) (illness) (infection)

Hoarseness 784.49

Hobnail liver — *see* Cirrhosis, portal

Hobo, hoboism V60.0

Hodgkin's
- disease (M9650/3) 201.9 ☑
  - lymphocytic
    - depletion (M9653/3) 201.7 ☑
      - diffuse fibrosis (M9654/3) 201.7 ☑
      - reticular type (M9655/3) 201.7 ☑
    - predominance (M9651/3) 201.4 ☑
  - lymphocytic-histiocytic predominance (M9651/3) 201.4 ☑
  - mixed cellularity (M9652/3) 201.6 ☑
  - nodular sclerosis (M9656/3) 201.5 ☑
    - cellular phase (M9657/3) 201.5 ☑
- granuloma (M9661/3) 201.1 ☑
- lymphogranulomatosis (M9650/3) 201.9 ☑
- lymphoma (M9650/3) 201.9 ☑
- lymphosarcoma (M9650/3) 201.9 ☑
- paragranuloma (M9660/3) 201.0 ☑
- sarcoma (M9662/3) 201.2 ☑

Hodgson's disease (aneurysmal dilatation of aorta) 441.9
- ruptured 441.5

Hodi-potsy 111.0

Hoffa (-Kastert) disease or syndrome (liposynovitis prepatellaris) 272.8

Hoffmann-Bouveret syndrome (paroxysmal tachycardia) 427.2

Hoffman's syndrome 244.9 *[359.5]*

Hole
- macula 362.54
- optic disc, crater-like 377.22
- retina (macula) 362.54
  - round 361.31
    - with detachment 361.01

Holla disease — *see also* Spherocytosis 282.0

Holländer-Simons syndrome (progressive lipodystrophy) 272.6

Hollow foot (congenital) 754.71
- acquired 736.73

Holmes' syndrome (visual disorientation) 368.16

Holoprosencephaly 742.2
- due to
  - trisomy 13 758.1
  - trisomy 18 758.2

Holthouse's hernia — *see* Hernia, inguinal

Homesickness 309.89

Homocystinemia 270.4

Homocystinuria 270.4

Homologous serum jaundice (prophylactic) (therapeutic) — *see* Hepatitis, viral

Homosexuality — omit code
- ego-dystonic 302.0
- pedophilic 302.2
- problems with 302.0

Homozygous Hb-S disease 282.61

Honeycomb lung 518.89
- congenital 748.4

Hong Kong ear 117.3

HOOD (hereditary osteo-onychodysplasia) 756.89

Hooded
- clitoris 752.49
- penis 752.69

Hookworm (anemia) (disease) (infestation) — *see* Ancylostomiasis

Hoppe-Goldflam syndrome 358.00

Hordeolum (external) (eyelid) 373.11
- internal 373.12

Horn
- cutaneous 702.8
  - cheek 702.8
  - eyelid 702.8
  - penis 702.8
- iliac 756.89
- nail 703.8
  - congenital 757.5
- papillary 700

Horner's
- syndrome (*see also* Neuropathy, peripheral, autonomic) 337.9
  - traumatic 954.0
- teeth 520.4

Horseshoe kidney (congenital) 753.3

Horton's
- disease (temporal arteritis) 446.5
- headache or neuralgia 346.2 ☑

Hospice care V66.7

Hospitalism (in children) NEC 309.83

Hourglass contraction, contracture
- bladder 596.8
- gallbladder 575.2
  - congenital 751.69
- stomach 536.8
  - congenital 750.7
  - psychogenic 306.4
- uterus 661.4 ☑
  - affecting fetus or newborn 763.7

Household circumstance affecting care V60.9
- specified type NEC V60.8

Housemaid's knee 727.2

Housing circumstance affecting care V60.9
- specified type NEC V60.8

HTLV-I infection 079.51

HTLV-II infection 079.52

HTLV-III/LAV (disease) (illness) (infection) — *see* Human immunodeficiency virus (disease) (illness) (infection)

HTLV-III (disease) (illness) (infection) — *see* Human immunodeficiency virus (disease) (illness) (infection)

Huchard's disease (continued arterial hypertension) 401.9

Hudson-Stähli lines 371.11

Huguier's disease (uterine fibroma) 218.9

Human bite (open wound) — see also Wound, open, by site
- intact skin surface — *see* Contusion

Human immunodeficiency virus (disease) (illness) 042
- infection V08
  - with symptoms, symptomatic 042

Human immunodeficiency virus-2 infection 079.53

Human immunovirus (disease) (illness) (infection) — *see* Human immunodeficiency virus (disease) (illness) (infection)

Human papillomavirus 079.4

Human papillomavirus — *continued*
- cervical
  - high risk, DNA test positive 795.05
  - low risk, DNA test positive 795.09

Human T-cell lymphotrophic virus-I infection 079.51

Human T-cell lymphotrophic virus-II infection 079.52

Human T-cell lymphotrophic virus-III (disease) (illness) (infection) — *see* Human immunodeficiency virus (disease) (illness) (infection)

Humpback (acquired) 737.9
- congenital 756.19

Hum, venous — omit code

Hunchback (acquired) 737.9
- congenital 756.19

Hunger 994.2
- air, psychogenic 306.1
- disease 251.1

Hunner's ulcer — *see also* Cystitis 595.1

Hunt's
- neuralgia 053.11
- syndrome (herpetic geniculate ganglionitis) 053.11
  - dyssynergia cerebellaris myoclonica 334.2

Hunter's glossitis 529.4

Hunterian chancre 091.0

Hunter (-Hurler) syndrome (mucopolysaccharidosis II) 277.5

Huntington's
- chorea 333.4
- disease 333.4

Huppert's disease (multiple myeloma) (M9730/3) 203.0 ☑

Hurler (-Hunter) disease or syndrome (mucopolysaccharidosis II) 277.5

Hürthle cell
- adenocarcinoma (M8290/3) 193
- adenoma (M8290/0) 226
- carcinoma (M8290/3) 193
- tumor (M8290/0) 226

Hutchinson's
- disease meaning
  - angioma serpiginosum 709.1
  - cheiropompholyx 705.81
  - prurigo estivalis 692.72
  - summer eruption, or summer prurigo 692.72
- incisors 090.5
- melanotic freckle (M8742/2) (*see also* Neoplasm, skin, in situ)
  - malignant melanoma in (M8742/3) — *see* Melanoma
- teeth or incisors (congenital syphilis) 090.5

Hutchinson-Boeck disease or syndrome (sarcoidosis) 135

Hutchinson-Gilford disease or syndrome (progeria) 259.8

Hyaline
- degeneration (diffuse) (generalized) 728.9
  - localized — *see* Degeneration, by site
- membrane (disease) (lung) (newborn) 769

Hyalinosis cutis et mucosae 272.8

Hyalin plaque, sclera, senile 379.16

Hyalitis (asteroid) 379.22
- syphilitic 095.8

Hydatid
- cyst or tumor (*see also* Echinococcus)
  - fallopian tube 752.11
- mole — *see* Hydatidiform mole
- Morgagni (congenital) 752.89
  - fallopian tube 752.11

Hydatidiform mole (benign) (complicating pregnancy) (delivered) (undelivered) 630
- invasive (M9100/1) 236.1
- malignant (M9100/1) 236.1
- previous, affecting management of pregnancy V23.1

Hydatidosis — *see* Echinococcus

Hyde's disease (prurigo nodularis) 698.3

Hydradenitis 705.83

Hydradenoma (M8400/0) — *see* Hidradenoma

Hydralazine lupus or syndrome
- correct substance properly administered 695.4
- overdose or wrong substance given or taken 972.6

Hydramnios 657.0 ☑
- affecting fetus or newborn 761.3

Hydrancephaly 742.3
- with spina bifida (*see also* Spina bifida) 741.0 ☑

Hydranencephaly 742.3
- with spina bifida (*see also* Spina bifida) 741.0 ☑

Hydrargyrism NEC 985.0

Hydrarthrosis — *see also* Effusion, joint 719.0 ☑
- gonococcal 098.50
- intermittent (*see also* Rheumatism, palindromic) 719.3 ☑
- of yaws (early) (late) 102.6
- syphilitic 095.8
  - congenital 090.5

Hydremia 285.9

Hydrencephalocele (congenital) 742.0

Hydrencephalomeningocele (congenital) 742.0

Hydroa 694.0
- aestivale 692.72
- gestationis 646.8 ☑
- herpetiformis 694.0
- pruriginosa 694.0
- vacciniforme 692.72

Hydroadenitis 705.83

Hydrocalycosis — *see also* Hydronephrosis 591
- congenital 753.29

Hydrocalyx — *see also* Hydronephrosis 591

Hydrocele (calcified) (chylous) (idiopathic) (infantile) (inguinal canal) (recurrent) (senile) (spermatic cord) (testis) (tunica vaginalis) 603.9
- canal of Nuck (female) 629.1
  - male 603.9
- congenital 778.6
- encysted 603.0
  - congenital 778.6
- female NEC 629.89 ▲
- infected 603.1
- round ligament 629.89 ▲
- specified type NEC 603.8
  - congenital 778.6
- spinalis (*see also* Spina bifida) 741.9 ☑
- vulva 624.8

Hydrocephalic fetus
- affecting management or pregnancy 655.0 ☑
- causing disproportion 653.6 ☑
  - with obstructed labor 660.1 ☑
    - affecting fetus or newborn 763.1

Hydrocephalus (acquired) (external) (internal) (malignant) (noncommunicating) (obstructive) (recurrent) 331.4
- aqueduct of Sylvius stricture 742.3
  - with spina bifida (*see also* Spina bifida) 741.0 ☑
- chronic 742.3
  - with spina bifida (*see also* Spina bifida) 741.0 ☑
- communicating 331.3
- congenital (external) (internal) 742.3
  - with spina bifida (*see also* Spina bifida) 741.0 ☑
- due to
  - stricture of aqueduct of Sylvius 742.3
    - with spina bifida (*see also* Spina bifida) 741.0 ☑
  - toxoplasmosis (congenital) 771.2

Hydrocephalus — *continued*
  fetal affecting management of pregnancy 655.0 ☑
  foramen Magendie block (acquired) 331.3
    congenital 742.3
      with spina bifida (*see also* Spina bifida) 741.0 ☑
  newborn 742.3
    with spina bifida (*see also* Spina bifida) 741.0 ☑
  otitic 348.2 ▲
  syphilitic, congenital 090.49
  tuberculous (*see also* Tuberculosis) 013.8 ☑
Hydrocolpos (congenital) 623.8
Hydrocystoma (M8404/0) — *see* Neoplasm, skin, benign
Hydroencephalocele (congenital) 742.0
Hydroencephalomeningocele (congenital) 742.0
Hydrohematopneumothorax — *see also* Hemothorax 511.8
Hydromeningitis — *see* Meningitis
Hydromeningocele (spinal) — *see also* Spina bifida 741.9 ☑
  cranial 742.0
Hydrometra 621.8
Hydrometrocolpos 623.8
Hydromicrocephaly 742.1
Hydromphalus (congenital) (since birth) 757.39
Hydromyelia 742.53
Hydromyelocele — *see also* Spina bifida 741.9 ☑
Hydronephrosis 591
  atrophic 591
  congenital 753.29
  due to S. hematobium 120.0
  early 591
  functionless (infected) 591
  infected 591
  intermittent 591
  primary 591
  secondary 591
  tuberculous (*see also* Tuberculosis) 016.0 ☑
Hydropericarditis — *see also* Pericarditis 423.9
Hydropericardium — *see also* Pericarditis 423.9
Hydroperitoneum 789.5
Hydrophobia 071
Hydrophthalmos — *see also* Buphthalmia 743.20
Hydropneumohemothorax — *see also* Hemothorax 511.8
Hydropneumopericarditis — *see also* Pericarditis 423.9
Hydropneumopericardium — *see also* Pericarditis 423.9
Hydropneumothorax 511.8
  nontuberculous 511.8
    bacterial 511.1
  pneumococcal 511.1
  staphylococcal 511.1
  streptococcal 511.1
  traumatic 860.0
    with open wound into thorax 860.1
  tuberculous (*see also* Tuberculosis, pleura) 012.0 ☑
Hydrops 782.3
  abdominis 789.5
  amnii (complicating pregnancy) (*see also* Hydramnios) 657.0 ☑
  articulorum intermittens (*see also* Rheumatism, palindromic) 719.3 ☑
  cardiac (*see also* Failure, heart) 428.0
  congenital — *see* Hydrops, fetalis
  endolymphatic (*see also* Disease, Ménière's) 386.00
  fetal(is) or newborn 778.0
    due to isoimmunization 773.3
    not due to isoimmunization 778.0
  gallbladder 575.3

Hydrops — *continued*
  idiopathic (fetus or newborn) 778.0
  joint (see also Effusion, joint) 719.0 ☑
  labyrinth (*see also* Disease, Ménière's) 386.00
  meningeal NEC 331.4
  nutritional 262
  pericardium — *see* Pericarditis
  pleura (*see also* Hydrothorax) 511.8
  renal (*see also* Nephrosis) 581.9
  spermatic cord (*see also* Hydrocele) 603.9
Hydropyonephrosis — *see also* Pyelitis 590.80
  chronic 590.00
Hydrorachis 742.53
Hydrorrhea (nasal) 478.19 ▲
  gravidarum 658.1 ☑
  pregnancy 658.1 ☑
Hydrosadenitis 705.83
Hydrosalpinx (fallopian tube) (follicularis) 614.1
Hydrothorax (double) (pleural) 511.8
  chylous (nonfilarial) 457.8
    filaria (*see also* Infestation, filarial) 125.9
  nontuberculous 511.8
    bacterial 511.1
  pneumococcal 511.1
  staphylococcal 511.1
  streptococcal 511.1
  traumatic 862.29
    with open wound into thorax 862.39
  tuberculous (*see also* Tuberculosis, pleura) 012.0 ☑
Hydroureter 593.5
  congenital 753.22
Hydroureteronephrosis — *see also* Hydronephrosis 591
Hydrourethra 599.84
Hydroxykynureninuria 270.2
Hydroxyprolinemia 270.8
Hydroxyprolinuria 270.8
Hygroma (congenital) (cystic) (M9173/0) 228.1
  prepatellar 727.3
  subdural — *see* Hematoma, subdural
Hymen — *see* condition
Hymenolepiasis (diminuta) (infection) (infestation) (nana) 123.6
Hymenolepsis (diminuta) (infection) (infestation) (nana) 123.6
Hypalgesia — *see also* Disturbance, sensation 782.0
Hyperabduction syndrome 447.8
Hyperacidity, gastric 536.8
  psychogenic 306.4
Hyperactive, hyperactivity
  basal cell, uterine cervix 622.10
  bladder 596.51
  bowel (syndrome) 564.9
    sounds 787.5
  cervix epithelial (basal) 622.10
  child 314.01
  colon 564.9
  gastrointestinal 536.8
    psychogenic 306.4
  intestine 564.9
  labyrinth (unilateral) 386.51
    with loss of labyrinthine reactivity 386.58
    bilateral 386.52
  nasal mucous membrane 478.19 ▲
  stomach 536.8
  thyroid (gland) (*see also* Thyrotoxicosis) 242.9 ☑
Hyperacusis 388.42
Hyperadrenalism (cortical) 255.3
  medullary 255.6
Hyperadrenocorticism 255.3
  congenital 255.2
  iatrogenic
    correct substance properly administered 255.3

Hyperadrenocorticism — *continued*
  iatrogenic — *continued*
    overdose or wrong substance given or taken 962.0
Hyperaffectivity 301.11
Hyperaldosteronism (atypical) (hyperplastic) (normoaldosteronal) (normotensive) (primary) 255.10
  secondary 255.14
Hyperalgesia — *see also* Disturbance, sensation 782.0
Hyperalimentation 783.6
  carotene 278.3
  specified NEC 278.8
  vitamin A 278.2
  vitamin D 278.4
Hyperaminoaciduria 270.9
  arginine 270.6
  citrulline 270.6
  cystine 270.0
  glycine 270.0
  lysine 270.7
  ornithine 270.6
  renal (types I, II, III) 270.0
Hyperammonemia (congenital) 270.6
Hyperamnesia 780.99
Hyperamylasemia 790.5
Hyperaphia 782.0
Hyperazotemia 791.9
Hyperbetalipoproteinemia (acquired) (essential) (familial) (hereditary) (primary) (secondary) 272.0
  with prebetalipoproteinemia 272.2
Hyperbilirubinemia 782.4
  congenital 277.4
  constitutional 277.4
  neonatal (transient) (*see also* Jaundice, fetus or newborn) 774.6
    of prematurity 774.2
Hyperbilirubinemica encephalopathia, newborn 774.7
  due to isoimmunization 773.4
Hypercalcemia, hypercalcemic (idiopathic) 275.42
  nephropathy 588.89
Hypercalcinuria 275.40
Hypercapnia 786.09
  with mixed acid-based disorder 276.4
  fetal, affecting newborn 770.89
Hypercarotinemia 278.3
Hypercementosis 521.5
Hyperchloremia 276.9
Hyperchlorhydria 536.8
  neurotic 306.4
  psychogenic 306.4
Hypercholesterinemia — *see* Hypercholesterolemia
Hypercholesterolemia 272.0
  with hyperglyceridemia, endogenous 272.2
  essential 272.0
  familial 272.0
  hereditary 272.0
  primary 272.0
  pure 272.0
Hypercholesterolosis 272.0
Hyperchylia gastrica 536.8
  psychogenic 306.4
Hyperchylomicronemia (familial) (with hyperbetalipoproteinemia) 272.3
Hypercoagulation syndrome (primary) 289.81
  secondary 289.82
Hypercorticosteronism
  correct substance properly administered 255.3
  overdose or wrong substance given or taken 962.0
Hypercortisonism
  correct substance properly administered 255.3
  overdose or wrong substance given or taken 962.0
Hyperdynamic beta-adrenergic state or syndrome (circulatory) 429.82
Hyperekplexia 759.89

Hyperelectrolytemia 276.9
Hyperemesis 536.2
  arising during pregnancy — *see* Hyperemesis, gravidarum
  gravidarum (mild) (before 22 completed weeks gestation) 643.0 ☑
    with
      carbohydrate depletion 643.1 ☑
      dehydration 643.1 ☑
      electrolyte imbalance 643.1 ☑
      metabolic disturbance 643.1 ☑
    affecting fetus or newborn 761.8
    severe (with metabolic disturbance) 643.1 ☑
  psychogenic 306.4
Hyperemia (acute) 780.99
  anal mucosa 569.49
  bladder 596.7
  cerebral 437.8
  conjunctiva 372.71
  ear, internal, acute 386.30
  enteric 564.89
  eye 372.71
  eyelid (active) (passive) 374.82
  intestine 564.89
  iris 364.41
  kidney 593.81
  labyrinth 386.30
  liver (active) (passive) 573.8
  lung 514
  ovary 620.8
  passive 780.99
  pulmonary 514
  renal 593.81
  retina 362.89
  spleen 289.59
  stomach 537.89
Hyperesthesia (body surface) — *see also* Disturbance, sensation 782.0
  larynx (reflex) 478.79
    hysterical 300.11
  pharynx (reflex) 478.29
Hyperestrinism 256.0
Hyperestrogenism 256.0
Hyperestrogenosis 256.0
Hyperexplexia 759.89
Hyperextension, joint 718.80
  ankle 718.87
  elbow 718.82
  foot 718.87
  hand 718.84
  hip 718.85
  knee 718.86
  multiple sites 718.89
  pelvic region 718.85
  shoulder (region) 718.81
  specified site NEC 718.88
  wrist 718.83
Hyperfibrinolysis — *see* Fibrinolysis
Hyperfolliculinism 256.0
Hyperfructosemia 271.2
Hyperfunction
  adrenal (cortex) 255.3
    androgenic, acquired benign 255.3
    medulla 255.6
    virilism 255.2
  corticoadrenal NEC 255.3
  labyrinth — *see* Hyperactive, labyrinth
  medulloadrenal 255.6
  ovary 256.1
    estrogen 256.0
  pancreas 577.8
  parathyroid (gland) 252.00
  pituitary (anterior) (gland) (lobe) 253.1
  testicular 257.0
Hypergammaglobulinemia 289.89
  monoclonal, benign (BMH) 273.1
  polyclonal 273.0
  Waldenström's 273.0
Hyperglobulinemia 273.8
Hyperglycemia 790.29 ▲
  maternal
    affecting fetus or newborn 775.0
    manifest diabetes in infant 775.1
  postpancreatectomy (complete) (partial) 251.3

Index

Hydrocephalus — Hyperglycemia

☑ Additional Digit Required — Refer to the Tabular List for Digit Selection
Subterms under main terms may continue to next column or page

	Malignant	Benign	Unspecified
Hypertension, hypertensive (arterial) (arteriolar) (crisis) (degeneration) (disease) (essential) (fluctuating) (idiopathic) (intermittent) (labile) (low renin) (orthostatic) (paroxysmal) (primary) (systemic) (uncontrolled) (vascular)	401.0	401.1	401.9
with			
chronic kidney disease			
stage I through stage IV, or unspecified ●	403.00	403.10	403.90
stage V or end stage renal disese ●	403.01	403.11	403.91
heart involvement (conditions classifiable to 429.0–429.3, 429.8, 429.9 due to hypertension) (*see also* Hypertension, heart)	402.00	402.10	402.90
with kidney involvement — *see* Hypertension, cardiorenal			
renal involvement (only conditions classifiable to 585, 586, 587) (excludes conditions classifiable to 584) (*see also* Hypertension, kidney)	403.00	403.10	403.90
with heart involvement — *see* Hypertension, cardiorenal			
failure (and sclerosis) (*see also* Hypertension, kidney)	403.01	403.11	403.91
sclerosis without failure (*see also* Hypertension, kidney)	403.00	403.10	403.90
accelerated (*see also* Hypertension, by type, malignant))	401.0	—	—
antepartum — *see* Hypertension, complicating pregnancy, childbirth, or the puerperium			
cardiorenal (disease)	404.00	404.10	404.90
with			
chronic kidney disease			
stage I through stage IV, or unspecified ●	404.00	404.10	404.90
and heart failure ●	404.01	404.11	404.91
stage V or end stage renal disease ●	404.02	404.12	404.92
and heart failure ●	404.03	404.13	404.93
heart failure	404.01	404.11	404.91
and chronic kidney disease	404.02	404.12	404.92
stage I through stage IV or unspecified ●	404.02	404.12	404.92
stave V or end stage renal disease ●	404.03	404.13	404.93
cardiovascular disease (arteriosclerotic) (sclerotic)	402.00	402.10	402.90
with			
heart failure	402.01	402.11	402.91
renal involvement (conditions classifiable to 403) (*see also* Hypertension, cardiorenal)	404.00	404.10	404.90
cardiovascular renal (disease) (sclerosis) (*see also* Hypertension, cardiorenal)	404.00	404.10	404.90
cerebrovascular disease NEC	437.2	437.2	437.2
complicating pregnancy, childbirth, or the puerperium	642.2 ☑	642.0 ☑	642.9 ☑
with			
albuminuria (and edema) (mild)	—	—	642.4 ☑
severe	—	—	642.5 ☑
chronic kidney disesae ●	642.2 ☑	642.2 ☑	642.2 ☑
and heart disease ●	642.2 ☑	642.2 ☑	642.2 ☑
edema (mild)	—	—	642.4 ☑
severe	—	—	642.5 ☑
heart disease	642.2 ☑	642.2 ☑	642.2 ☑
and ▶chronic kidney◀ disease	642.2 ☑	642.2 ☑	642.2 ☑
renal disease	642.2 ☑	642.2 ☑	642.2 ☑
and heart disease	642.2 ☑	642.2 ☑	642.2 ☑
chronic	642.2 ☑	642.0 ☑	642.0 ☑
with pre-eclampsia or eclampsia	642.7 ☑	642.7 ☑	642.7 ☑
fetus or newborn	760.0	760.0	760.0
essential	—	642.0 ☑	642.0 ☑
with pre-eclampsia or eclampsia	—	642.7 ☑	642.7 ☑
fetus or newborn	760.0	760.0	760.0
fetus or newborn	760.0	760.0	760.0
gestational	—	—	642.3 ☑
pre-existing	642.2 ☑	642.0 ☑	642.0 ☑
with pre-eclampsia or eclampsia	642.7 ☑	642.7 ☑	642.7 ☑
fetus or newborn	760.0	760.0	760.0
secondary to renal disease	642.1 ☑	642.1 ☑	642.1 ☑
with pre-eclampsia or eclampsia	642.7 ☑	642.7 ☑	642.7 ☑
fetus or newborn	760.0	760.0	760.0
transient	—	—	642.3 ☑
due to			
aldosteronism, primary	405.09	405.19	405.99
brain tumor	405.09	405.19	405.99
bulbar poliomyelitis	405.09	405.19	405.99
calculus			
kidney	405.09	405.19	405.99
ureter	405.09	405.19	405.99
coarctation, aorta	405.09	405.19	405.99
Cushing's disease	405.09	405.19	405.99
glomerulosclerosis (*see also* Hypertension, kidney)	403.00	403.10	403.90
periarteritis nodosa	405.09	405.19	405.99
pheochromocytoma	405.09	405.19	405.99
polycystic kidney(s)	405.09	405.19	405.99
polycythemia	405.09	405.19	405.99
porphyria	405.09	405.19	405.99
pyelonephritis	405.09	405.19	405.99

	Malignant	Benign	Unspecified
Hypertension, hypertensive — *continued*			
due to — *continued*			
renal (artery)			
aneurysm	405.01	405.11	405.91
anomaly	405.01	405.11	405.91
embolism	405.01	405.11	405.91
fibromuscular hyperplasia	405.01	405.11	405.91
occlusion	405.01	405.11	405.91
stenosis	405.01	405.11	405.91
thrombosis	405.01	405.11	405.91
encephalopathy	437.2	437.2	437.2
gestational (transient) NEC	—	—	642.3 ☑
Goldblatt's	440.1	440.1	440.1
heart (disease) (conditions classifiable to 429.0–429.3, 429.8, 429.9 due to hypertension)	402.00	402.10	402.90
with heart failure	402.01	402.11	402.91
hypertensive kidney disease (conditions classifiable to 403) (*see also* Hypertension, cardiorenal)	404.00	404.10	404.90
renal sclerosis (*see also* Hypertension, cardiorenal)	404.00	404.10	404.90
intracranial, benign	—	348.2	—
intraocular	—	—	365.04
kidney	403.00	403.10	403.90
with			
chronic kidney disease			
stage I through stage IV, or unspecified ●	403.00	403.10	403.90
stage V or end stage renal disese ●	403.01	403.11	403.91
heart involvement (conditions classifiable to 429.0–429.3, 429.8, 429.9 due to hypertension) (*see also* Hypertension, cardiorenal)	404.00	404.10	404.90
hypertensive heart (disease) (conditions classifiable to 402) (*see also* Hypertension, cardiorenal)	404.00	404.10	404.90
lesser circulation	—	—	416.0
necrotizing	401.0	—	—
ocular	—	—	365.04
portal (due to chronic liver disease)	—	—	572.3
postoperative	—	—	997.91
psychogenic	—	—	306.2
puerperal, postpartum — *see* Hypertension, complicating pregnancy, childbirth, or the puerperium			
pulmonary (artery)	—	—	416.8
with cor pulmonale (chronic)	—	—	416.8
acute	—	—	415.0
idiopathic	—	—	416.0
primary	—	—	416.0
of newborn	—	—	747.83
secondary	—	—	416.8
renal (disease) (*see also* Hypertension, kidney)	403.00	403.10	403.90
renovascular NEC	405.01	405.11	405.91
secondary NEC	405.09	405.19	405.99
due to			
aldosteronism, primary	405.09	405.19	405.99
brain tumor	405.09	405.19	405.99
bulbar poliomyelitis	405.09	405.19	405.99
calculus			
kidney	405.09	405.19	405.99
ureter	405.09	405.19	405.99
coarctation, aorta	405.09	405.19	405.99
Cushing's disease	405.09	405.19	405.99
glomerulosclerosis (*see also* Hypertension, kidney)	403.00	403.10	403.90
periarteritis nodosa	405.09	405.19	405.99
pheochromocytoma	405.09	405.19	405.99
polycystic kidney(s)	405.09	405.19	405.99
polycythemia	405.09	405.19	405.99
porphyria	405.09	405.19	405.99
pyelonephritis	405.09	405.19	405.99
renal (artery)			
aneurysm	405.01	405.11	405.91
anomaly	405.01	405.11	405.91
embolism	405.01	405.11	405.91
fibromuscular hyperplasia	405.01	405.11	405.91
occlusion	405.01	405.11	405.91
stenosis	405.01	405.11	405.91
thrombosis	405.01	405.11	405.91
transient	—	—	796.2
of pregnancy	—	—	642.3 ☑
vascular degeneration	401.0	401.1	401.9
venous, chronic (asymptomatic) (idiopathic)	—	—	459.30
with			
complication, NEC	—	—	459.39
inflammation	—	—	459.32
with ulcer	—	—	459.33
ulcer	—	—	459.31
with inflammation	—	—	459.33
due to			
deep vein thrombosis (*see also* Syndrome, postphlebetic)	—	—	459.10

- **Hyperthecosis, ovary** 256.8
- **Hyperthermia** (of unknown origin) — *see also* Pyrexia 780.6
  - malignant (due to anesthesia) 995.86
  - newborn 778.4
- **Hyperthymergasia** — *see also* Psychosis, affective 296.0 ☑
  - reactive (from emotional stress, psychological trauma) 298.1
  - recurrent episode 296.1 ☑
  - single episode 296.0 ☑
- **Hyperthymism** 254.8
- **Hyperthyroid** (recurrent) — *see* Hyperthyroidism
- **Hyperthyroidism** (latent) (preadult) (recurrent) (without goiter) 242.9 ☑

> *Note — Use the following fifth-digit subclassification with category 242:*
>
> 0 *without mention of thyrotoxic crisis or storm*
>
> 1 *with mention of thyrotoxic crisis or storm*

  - with
    - goiter (diffuse) 242.0 ☑
      - adenomatous 242.3 ☑
        - multinodular 242.2 ☑
        - uninodular 242.1 ☑
      - nodular 242.3 ☑
        - multinodular 242.2 ☑
        - uninodular 242.1 ☑
    - thyroid nodule 242.1 ☑
  - complicating pregnancy, childbirth, or puerperium 648.1 ☑
  - neonatal (transient) 775.3
- **Hypertonia** — *see* Hypertonicity
- **Hypertonicity**
  - bladder 596.51
  - fetus or newborn 779.89
  - gastrointestinal (tract) 536.8
  - infancy 779.89
    - due to electrolyte imbalance 779.89
  - muscle 728.85
  - stomach 536.8
    - psychogenic 306.4
  - uterus, uterine (contractions) 661.4 ☑
    - affecting fetus or newborn 763.7
- **Hypertony** — *see* Hypertonicity
- **Hypertransaminemia** 790.4
- **Hypertrichosis** 704.1
  - congenital 757.4
  - eyelid 374.54
  - lanuginosa 757.4
    - acquired 704.1
- **Hypertriglyceridemia, essential** 272.1
- **Hypertrophy, hypertrophic**
  - adenoids (infectional) 474.12
    - and tonsils (faucial) (infective) (lingual) (lymphoid) 474.10
  - adrenal 255.8
  - alveolar process or ridge 525.8
  - anal papillae 569.49
  - apocrine gland 705.82
  - artery NEC 447.8
    - carotid 447.8
    - congenital (peripheral) NEC 747.60
      - gastrointestinal 747.61
      - lower limb 747.64
      - renal 747.62
      - specified NEC 747.69
      - spinal 747.82
      - upper limb 747.63
    - renal 447.3
  - arthritis (chronic) (*see also* Osteoarthrosis) 715.9 ☑
    - spine (*see also* Spondylosis) 721.90
  - arytenoid 478.79
  - asymmetrical (heart) 429.9
  - auricular — *see* Hypertrophy, cardiac
  - Bartholin's gland 624.8
  - bile duct 576.8
  - bladder (sphincter) (trigone) 596.8
  - blind spot, visual field 368.42
  - bone 733.99
  - brain 348.8

Hypertrophy, hypertrophic — *continued*

  - breast 611.1
    - cystic 610.1
    - fetus or newborn 778.7
    - fibrocystic 610.1
    - massive pubertal 611.1
    - puerperal, postpartum 676.3 ☑
    - senile (parenchymatous) 611.1
  - cardiac (chronic) (idiopathic) 429.3
    - with
      - rheumatic fever (conditions classifiable to 390)
        - active 391.8
          - with chorea 392.0
        - inactive or quiescent (with chorea) 398.99
    - congenital NEC 746.89
    - fatty (*see also* Degeneration, myocardial) 429.1
    - hypertensive (*see also* Hypertension, heart) 402.90
    - rheumatic (with chorea) 398.99
      - active or acute 391.8
        - with chorea 392.0
    - valve (*see also* Endocarditis) 424.90
      - congenital NEC 746.89
  - cartilage 733.99
  - cecum 569.89
  - cervix (uteri) 622.6
    - congenital 752.49
    - elongation 622.6
  - clitoris (cirrhotic) 624.2
    - congenital 752.49
  - colon 569.89
    - congenital 751.3
  - conjunctiva, lymphoid 372.73
  - cornea 371.89
  - corpora cavernosa 607.89
  - duodenum 537.89
  - endometrium (uterus) (*see also* Hyperplasia, endometrium) 621.30
    - cervix 622.6
  - epididymis 608.89
  - esophageal hiatus (congenital) 756.6
    - with hernia — *see* Hernia, diaphragm
  - eyelid 374.30
  - falx, skull 733.99
  - fat pad 729.30
    - infrapatellar 729.31
    - knee 729.31
    - orbital 374.34
    - popliteal 729.31
    - prepatellar 729.31
    - retropatellar 729.31
    - specified site NEC 729.39
  - foot (congenital) 755.67
  - frenum, frenulum (tongue) 529.8
    - linguae 529.8
    - lip 528.5
  - gallbladder or cystic duct 575.8
  - gastric mucosa 535.2 ☑
  - gingiva 523.8
  - gland, glandular (general) NEC 785.6
  - gum (mucous membrane) 523.8
  - heart (idiopathic) (*see also* Hypertrophy, cardiac)
    - valve (*see also* Endocarditis)
      - congenital NEC 746.89
  - hemifacial 754.0
  - hepatic — *see* Hypertrophy, liver
  - hiatus (esophageal) 756.6
  - hilus gland 785.6
  - hymen, congenital 752.49
  - ileum 569.89
  - infrapatellar fat pad 729.31
  - intestine 569.89
  - jejunum 569.89
  - kidney (compensatory) 593.1
    - congenital 753.3
  - labial frenulum 528.5
  - labium (majus) (minus) 624.3
  - lacrimal gland, chronic 375.03
  - ligament 728.9

Hypertrophy, hypertrophic — *continued*

  - ligament — *continued*
    - spinal 724.8
  - linguae frenulum 529.8
  - lingual tonsil (infectional) 474.11
  - lip (frenum) 528.5
    - congenital 744.81
  - liver 789.1
    - acute 573.8
    - cirrhotic — *see* Cirrhosis, liver
    - congenital 751.69
    - fatty — *see* Fatty, liver
  - lymph gland 785.6
    - tuberculous — *see* Tuberculosis, lymph gland
  - mammary gland — *see* Hypertrophy, breast
  - maxillary frenulum 528.5
  - Meckel's diverticulum (congenital) 751.0
  - medial meniscus, acquired 717.3
  - median bar 600.90
    - with
      - other lower urinary tract symptoms (LUTS) 600.91 ●
      - urinary ●
        - obstruction 600.91 ●
        - retention 600.91 ●
  - mediastinum 519.3
  - meibomian gland 373.2
  - meniscus, knee, congenital 755.64
  - metatarsal head 733.99
  - metatarsus 733.99
  - mouth 528.9
  - mucous membrane
    - alveolar process 523.8
    - nose 478.19 ▲
    - turbinate (nasal) 478.0
  - muscle 728.9
  - muscular coat, artery NEC 447.8
    - carotid 447.8
    - renal 447.3
  - myocardium (*see also* Hypertrophy, cardiac) 429.3
    - idiopathic 425.4
  - myometrium 621.2
  - nail 703.8
    - congenital 757.5
  - nasal 478.19 ▲
    - alae 478.19 ▲
    - bone 738.0
    - cartilage 478.19 ▲
    - mucous membrane (septum) 478.19 ▲
    - sinus (*see also* Sinusitis) 473.9
    - turbinate 478.0
  - nasopharynx, lymphoid (infectional) (tissue) (wall) 478.29
  - neck, uterus 622.6
  - nipple 611.1
  - normal aperture diaphragm (congenital) 756.6
  - nose (*see also* Hypertrophy, nasal) 478.19 ▲
  - orbit 376.46
  - organ or site, congenital NEC — *see* Anomaly, specified type NEC
  - osteoarthropathy (pulmonary) 731.2
  - ovary 620.8
  - palate (hard) 526.89
    - soft 528.9
  - pancreas (congenital) 751.7
  - papillae
    - anal 569.49
    - tongue 529.3
  - parathyroid (gland) 252.01
  - parotid gland 527.1
  - penis 607.89
  - phallus 607.89
    - female (clitoris) 624.2
  - pharyngeal tonsil 474.12
  - pharyngitis 472.1
  - pharynx 478.29

Hypertrophy, hypertrophic — *continued*

  - pharynx — *continued*
    - lymphoid (infectional) (tissue) (wall) 478.29
  - pituitary (fossa) (gland) 253.8
  - popliteal fat pad 729.31
  - preauricular (lymph) gland (Hampstead) 785.6
  - prepuce (congenital) 605
    - female 624.2
  - prostate (asymptomatic) (early) (recurrent) 600.90
    - with
      - other lower urinary tract symptlms (LUTS) 600.91 ●
      - urinary ●
        - obstruction 600.91 ●
        - retention 600.91 ●
    - adenofibromatous 600.20
      - with
        - other lower urinary tract symptoms (LUTS) 600.21 ●
        - urinary ●
          - obstruction 600.21 ●
          - retention 600.21 ●
    - benign 600.00
      - with
        - other lower urinary tract symptoms (LUTS) 600.01 ●
        - urinary ●
          - obstruction 600.01 ●
          - retention 600.01 ●
    - congenital 752.89
  - pseudoedematous hypodermal 757.0
  - pseudomuscular 359.1
  - pylorus (muscle) (sphincter) 537.0
    - congenital 750.5
    - infantile 750.5
  - rectal sphincter 569.49
  - rectum 569.49
  - renal 593.1
  - rhinitis (turbinate) 472.0
  - salivary duct or gland 527.1
    - congenital 750.26
  - scaphoid (tarsal) 733.99
  - scar 701.4
  - scrotum 608.89
  - sella turcica 253.8
  - seminal vesicle 608.89
  - sigmoid 569.89
  - skin condition NEC 701.9
  - spermatic cord 608.89
  - spinal ligament 724.8
  - spleen — *see* Splenomegaly
  - spondylitis (spine) (*see also* Spondylosis) 721.90
  - stomach 537.89
  - subaortic stenosis (idiopathic) 425.1
  - sublingual gland 527.1
    - congenital 750.26
  - submaxillary gland 527.1
  - suprarenal (gland) 255.8
  - tendon 727.9
  - testis 608.89
    - congenital 752.89
  - thymic, thymus (congenital) (gland) 254.0
  - thyroid (gland) (*see also* Goiter) 240.9
    - primary 242.0 ☑
    - secondary 242.2 ☑
  - toe (congenital) 755.65
    - acquired 735.8
  - tongue 529.8
    - congenital 750.15
    - frenum 529.8
    - papillae (foliate) 529.3
  - tonsil (faucial) (infective) (lingual) (lymphoid) 474.11
    - with
      - adenoiditis 474.01
      - tonsillitis 474.00
        - and adenoiditis 474.02
    - and adenoids 474.10

Index
Hypertrophy, hypertrophic — Hypoplasia, hypoplasis

☑ Additional Digit Required — Refer to the Tabular List for Digit Selection
▸◂ Revised Text ● New Line ▲ Revised Code
Subterms under main terms may continue to next column or page

I

- **Iatrogenic syndrome of excess cortisol** 255.0
- **Iceland disease** (epidemic neuromyasthenia) 049.8
- **Ichthyosis** (congenita) 757.1
  - acquired 701.1
  - fetalis gravior 757.1
  - follicularis 757.1
  - hystrix 757.39
  - lamellar 757.1
  - lingual 528.6
  - palmaris and plantaris 757.39
  - simplex 757.1
  - vera 757.1
  - vulgaris 757.1
- **Ichthyotoxism** 988.0
  - bacterial (*see also* Poisoning, food) 005.9
- **Icteroanemia, hemolytic** (acquired) 283.9
  - congenital (*see also* Spherocytosis) 282.0
- **Icterus** — *see also* Jaundice 782.4
  - catarrhal — *see* Icterus, infectious
  - conjunctiva 782.4
    - newborn 774.6
  - epidemic — *see* Icterus, infectious
  - febrilis — *see* Icterus, infectious
  - fetus or newborn — *see* Jaundice, fetus or newborn
  - gravis (*see also* Necrosis, liver) 570
    - complicating pregnancy 646.7 ☑
      - affecting fetus or newborn 760.8
    - fetus or newborn NEC 773.0
    - obstetrical 646.7 ☑
      - affecting fetus or newborn 760.8
  - hematogenous (acquired) 283.9
  - hemolytic (acquired) 283.9
    - congenital (*see also* Spherocytosis) 282.0
  - hemorrhagic (acute) 100.0
    - leptospiral 100.0
    - newborn 776.0
    - spirochetal 100.0
  - infectious 070.1
    - with hepatic coma 070.0
    - leptospiral 100.0
    - spirochetal 100.0
  - intermittens juvenilis 277.4
  - malignant (*see also* Necrosis, liver) 570
  - neonatorum (*see also* Jaundice, fetus or newborn) 774.6
  - pernicious (*see also* Necrosis, liver) 570
  - spirochetal 100.0
- **Ictus solaris, solis** 992.0
- **Ideation**
  - suicidal V62.84
- **Identity disorder** 313.82
  - dissociative 300.14
  - gender role (child) 302.6
    - adult 302.85
  - psychosexual (child) 302.6
    - adult 302.85
- **Idioglossia** 307.9
- **Idiopathic** — *see* condition
- **Idiosyncrasy** — *see also* Allergy 995.3
  - drug, medicinal substance, and biological — *see* Allergy, drug
- **Idiot, idiocy** (congenital) 318.2
  - amaurotic (Bielschowsky) (-Jansky) (family) (infantile (late)) (juvenile (late)) (Vogt-Spielmeyer) 330.1
  - microcephalic 742.1
  - Mongolian 758.0
  - oxycephalic 756.0
- **Id reaction** (due to bacteria) 692.89
- **IgE asthma** 493.0 ☑
- **Ileitis** (chronic) — *see also* Enteritis 558.9
  - infectious 009.0
  - noninfectious 558.9
  - regional (ulcerative) 555.0
    - with large intestine 555.2
- **Ileitis** — *see also* Enteritis — *continued*
  - segmental 555.0
    - with large intestine 555.2
  - terminal (ulcerative) 555.0
    - with large intestine 555.2
- **Ileocolitis** — *see also* Enteritis 558.9
  - infectious 009.0
  - regional 555.2
  - ulcerative 556.1
- **Ileostomy status** V44.2
  - with complication 569.60
- **Ileotyphus** 002.0
- **Ileum** — *see* condition
- **Ileus** (adynamic) (bowel) (colon) (inhibitory) (intestine) (neurogenic) (paralytic) 560.1
  - arteriomesenteric duodenal 537.2
  - due to gallstone (in intestine) 560.31
  - duodenal, chronic 537.2
  - following gastrointestinal surgery 997.4
  - gallstone 560.31
  - mechanical (*see also* Obstruction, intestine) 560.9
  - meconium 777.1
    - due to cystic fibrosis 277.01
  - myxedema 564.89
  - postoperative 997.4
  - transitory, newborn 777.4
- **Iliac** — *see* condition
- **Iliotibial band friction syndrome** 728.89
- **Illegitimacy** V61.6
- **Ill, louping** 063.1
- **Illness** — *see also* Disease
  - factitious 300.19
    - with
      - combined psychological and physical signs and symptoms 300.19
      - predominantly
        - physical signs and symptoms 300.19
        - psychological symptoms 300.16
    - chronic (with physical symptoms) 301.51
  - heart — *see* Disease, heart
  - manic-depressive (*see also* Psychosis, affective) 296.80
  - mental (*see also* Disorder, mental) 300.9
- **Imbalance** 781.2
  - autonomic (*see also* Neuropathy, peripheral, autonomic) 337.9
  - electrolyte 276.9
    - with
      - abortion — *see* Abortion, by type, with metabolic disorder
      - ectopic pregnancy (*see also* categories 633.0–633.9) 639.4
      - hyperemesis gravidarum (before 22 completed weeks gestation) 643.1 ☑
      - molar pregnancy (*see also* categories 630–632) 639.4
    - following
      - abortion 639.4
      - ectopic or molar pregnancy 639.4
    - neonatal, transitory NEC 775.5
  - endocrine 259.9
  - eye muscle NEC 378.9
    - heterophoria — *see* Heterophoria
  - glomerulotubular NEC 593.89
  - hormone 259.9
  - hysterical (*see also* Hysteria) 300.10
  - labyrinth NEC 386.50
  - posture 729.9
  - sympathetic (*see also* Neuropathy, peripheral, autonomic) 337.9
- **Imbecile, imbecility** 318.0
  - moral 301.7
- **Imbecile, imbecility** — *continued*
  - old age 290.9
  - senile 290.9
  - specified IQ — *see* IQ
  - unspecified IQ 318.0
- **Imbedding, intrauterine device** 996.32
- **Imbibition, cholesterol** (gallbladder) 575.6
- **Imerslund (-Gräsbeck) syndrome** (anemia due to familial selective vitamin B_{12} malabsorption) 281.1
- **Iminoacidopathy** 270.8
- **Iminoglycinuria, familial** 270.8
- **Immature** — *see also* Immaturity
  - personality 301.89
- **Immaturity** 765.1 ☑
  - extreme 765.0 ☑
  - fetus or infant light-for-dates — *see* Light-for-dates
  - lung, fetus or newborn 770.4
  - organ or site NEC — *see* Hypoplasia
  - pulmonary, fetus or newborn 770.4
  - reaction 301.89
  - sexual (female) (male) 259.0
- **Immersion** 994.1
  - foot 991.4
  - hand 991.4
- **Immobile, immobility**
  - intestine 564.89
  - joint — *see* Ankylosis
  - syndrome (paraplegic) 728.3
- **Immunization**
  - ABO
    - affecting management of pregnancy 656.2 ☑
      - fetus or newborn 773.1
  - complication — *see* Complications, vaccination
  - Rh factor
    - affecting management of pregnancy 656.1 ☑
      - fetus or newborn 773.0
    - from transfusion 999.7
- **Immunodeficiency** 279.3
  - with
    - adenosine-deaminase deficiency 279.2
    - defect, predominant
      - B-cell 279.00
      - T-cell 279.10
    - hyperimmunoglobulinemia 279.2
    - lymphopenia, hereditary 279.2
    - thrombocytopenia and eczema 279.12
    - thymic
      - aplasia 279.2
      - dysplasia 279.2
  - autosomal recessive, Swiss-type 279.2
  - common variable 279.06
  - severe combined (SCID) 279.2
  - to Rh factor
    - affecting management of pregnancy 656.1 ☑
      - fetus or newborn 773.0
  - X-linked, with increased IgM 279.05
- **Immunotherapy, prophylactic** V07.2
  - antineoplastic V58.12
- **Impaction, impacted**
  - bowel, colon, rectum 560.30
    - with hernia (*see also* Hernia, by site, with obstruction)
      - gangrenous — *see* Hernia, by site, with gangrene
    - by
      - calculus 560.39
      - gallstone 560.31
    - fecal 560.39
    - specified type NEC 560.39
  - calculus — *see* Calculus
  - cerumen (ear) (external) 380.4
  - cuspid 520.6
  - dental 520.6
  - fecal, feces 560.39
    - with hernia (*see also* Hernia, by site, with obstruction)
- **Impaction, impacted** — *continued*
  - fecal, feces — *continued*
    - with hernia (*see also* Hernia, by site, with obstruction) — *continued*
      - gangrenous — *see* Hernia, by site, with gangrene
  - fracture — *see* Fracture, by site
  - gallbladder — *see* Cholelithiasis
  - gallstone(s) — *see* Cholelithiasis
    - in intestine (any part) 560.31
  - intestine(s) 560.30
    - with hernia (*see also* Hernia, by site, with obstruction)
      - gangrenous — *see* Hernia, by site, with gangrene
    - by
      - calculus 560.39
      - gallstone 560.31
    - fecal 560.39
    - specified type NEC 560.39
  - intrauterine device (IUD) 996.32
  - molar 520.6
  - shoulder 660.4 ☑
    - affecting fetus or newborn 763.1
  - tooth, teeth 520.6
  - turbinate 733.99
- **Impaired, impairment** (function)
  - arm V49.1
    - movement, involving
      - musculoskeletal system V49.1
      - nervous system V49.2
  - auditory discrimination 388.43
  - back V48.3
  - body (entire) V49.89
  - cognitive, mild, so stated 331.83 ●
  - glucose
    - fasting 790.21
    - tolerance test (oral) 790.22
  - hearing (*see also* Deafness) 389.9
  - heart — *see* Disease, heart
  - kidney (*see also* Disease, renal) 593.9
    - disorder resulting from 588.9
      - specified NEC 588.89
  - leg V49.1
    - movement, involving
      - musculoskeletal system V49.1
      - nervous system V49.2
  - limb V49.1
    - movement, involving
      - musculoskeletal system V49.1
      - nervous system V49.2
  - liver 573.8
  - mastication 524.9
  - mild cognitive, so stated 331.83 ●
  - mobility
    - ear ossicles NEC 385.22
    - incostapedial joint 385.22
    - malleus 385.21
  - myocardium, myocardial (*see also* Insufficiency, myocardial) 428.0
  - neuromusculoskeletal NEC V49.89
    - back V48.3
    - head V48.2
    - limb V49.2
    - neck V48.3
    - spine V48.3
    - trunk V48.3
  - rectal sphincter 787.99
  - renal (*see also* Disease, renal) 593.9
    - disorder resulting from 588.9
      - specified NEC 588.89
  - spine V48.3
  - vision NEC 369.9
    - both eyes NEC 369.3
    - moderate 369.74
      - both eyes 369.25
        - with impairment of lesser eye (specified as)
          - blind, not further specified 369.15
          - low vision, not further specified 369.23
          - near-total 369.17
          - profound 369.18
          - severe 369.24

☑ Additional Digit Required — Refer to the Tabular List for Digit Selection

Subterms under main terms may continue to next column or page

▶◀ Revised Text ● New Line ▲ Revised Code

Index
Inanition — Infantilism

Infantilism — *continued*
  with dwarfism (hypophyseal) 253.3
  Brissaud's (infantile myxedema) 244.9
  celiac 579.0
  Herter's (nontropical sprue) 579.0
  hypophyseal 253.3
  hypothalamic (with obesity) 253.8
  idiopathic 259.9
  intestinal 579.0
  pancreatic 577.8
  pituitary 253.3
  renal 588.0
  sexual (with obesity) 259.0
Infants, healthy liveborn — *see* Newborn
Infarct, infarction
  adrenal (capsule) (gland) 255.4
  amnion 658.8 ☑
  anterior (with contiguous portion of intraventricular septum) NEC (*see also* Infarct, myocardium) 410.1 ☑
  appendices epiploicae 557.0
  bowel 557.0
  brain (stem) 434.91
    embolic (*see also* Embolism, brain) 434.11
    healed or old without residuals V12.59
    iatrogenic 997.02
    lacunar 434.91
    late effect — *see* Late effect(s) (of) cerebrovascular disease
    postoperative 997.02
    puerperal, postpartum, childbirth 674.0 ☑
    thrombotic (*see also* Thrombosis, brain) 434.01
  breast 611.8
  Brewer's (kidney) 593.81
  cardiac (*see also* Infarct, myocardium) 410.9 ☑
  cerebellar (*see also* Infarct, brain) 434.91
    embolic (*see also* Embolism, brain) 434.11
  cerebral (*see also* Infarct, brain) 434.91
    embolic (*see also* Embolism, brain) 434.11
    thrombotic (*see also* Infarct, brain) 434.01
  chorion 658.8 ☑
  colon (acute) (agnogenic) (embolic) (hemorrhagic) (nonocclusive) (nonthrombotic) (occlusive) (segmental) (thrombotic) (with gangrene) 557.0
  coronary artery (*see also* Infarct, myocardium) 410.9 ☑
  cortical 434.91
  embolic (*see also* Embolism) 444.9
  fallopian tube 620.8
  gallbladder 575.8
  heart (*see also* Infarct, myocardium) 410.9 ☑
  hepatic 573.4
  hypophysis (anterior lobe) 253.8
  impending (myocardium) 411.1
  intestine (acute) (agnogenic) (embolic) (hemorrhagic) (nonocclusive) (nonthrombotic) (occlusive) (thrombotic) (with gangrene) 557.0
  kidney 593.81
  lacunar 434.91
  liver 573.4
  lung (embolic) (thrombotic) 415.19
    with
      abortion — *see* Abortion, by type, with, embolism
      ectopic pregnancy (*see also* categories 633.0–633.9) 639.6
      molar pregnancy (*see also* categories 630–632) 639.6

Infarct, infarction — *continued*
  lung — *continued*
    following
      abortion 639.6
      ectopic or molar pregnancy 639.6
    iatrogenic 415.11
    in pregnancy, childbirth, or puerperium — *see* Embolism, obstetrical
    postoperative 415.11
  lymph node or vessel 457.8
  medullary (brain) — *see* Infarct, brain
  meibomian gland (eyelid) 374.85
  mesentery, mesenteric (embolic) (thrombotic) (with gangrene) 557.0
  midbrain — *see* Infarct, brain
  myocardium, myocardial (acute or with a stated duration of 8 weeks or less) (with hypertension) 410.9 ☑

Note — Use the following fifth-digit subclassification with category 410:

0 episode unspecified

1 initial episode

2 subsequent episode without recurrence

    with symptoms after 8 weeks from date of infarction 414.8
    anterior (wall) (with contiguous portion of intraventricular septum) NEC 410.1 ☑
    anteroapical (with contiguous portion of intraventricular septum) 410.1 ☑
    anterolateral (wall) 410.0 ☑
    anteroseptal (with contiguous portion of intraventricular septum) 410.1 ☑
    apical-lateral 410.5 ☑
    atrial 410.8 ☑
    basal-lateral 410.5 ☑
    chronic (with symptoms after 8 weeks from date of infarction) 414.8
    diagnosed on ECG, but presenting no symptoms 412
    diaphragmatic wall (with contiguous portion of intraventricular septum) 410.4 ☑
    healed or old, currently presenting no symptoms 412
    high lateral 410.5 ☑
    impending 411.1
    inferior (wall) (with contiguous portion of intraventricular septum) 410.4 ☑
    inferolateral (wall) 410.2 ☑
    inferoposterior wall 410.3 ☑
    lateral wall 410.5 ☑
    non-ST elevation (NSTEMI)
    nontransmural 410.7 ☑
    papillary muscle 410.8 ☑
    past (diagnosed on ECG or other special investigation, but currently presenting no symptoms) 412
      with symptoms NEC 414.8
    posterior (strictly) (true) (wall) 410.6 ☑
    posterobasal 410.6 ☑
    posteroinferior 410.3 ☑
    posterolateral 410.5 ☑
    previous, currently presenting no symptoms 412
    septal 410.8 ☑
    specified site NEC 410.8 ☑
    ST elevation (STEMI) 410.9 ☑
      anterior (wall) 410.1 ☑
      anterolateral (wall) 410.0 ☑
      inferior (wall) 410.4 ☑
      inferolateral (wall) 410.2 ☑

Infarct, infarction — *continued*
  myocardium, myocardial — *continued*
    ST elevation — *continued*
      inferoposterior wall 410.3 ☑
      lateral wall 410.5 ☑
      posterior (strictly) (true) (wall) 410.6 ☑
      specified site NEC 410.8 ☑
    subendocardial 410.7 ☑
    syphilitic 093.82
  non-ST elevation myocardial infarction (NSTEMI) 410.7 ☑
  nontransmural 410.7 ☑
  omentum 557.0
  ovary 620.8
  pancreas 577.8
  papillary muscle (*see also* Infarct, myocardium) 410.8 ☑
  parathyroid gland 252.8
  pituitary (gland) 253.8
  placenta (complicating pregnancy) 656.7 ☑
    affecting fetus or newborn 762.2
  pontine — *see* Infarct, brain
  posterior NEC (*see also* Infarct, myocardium) 410.6 ☑
  prostate 602.8
  pulmonary (artery) (hemorrhagic) (vein) 415.19
    with
      abortion — *see* Abortion, by type, with embolism
      ectopic pregnancy (*see also* categories 633.0–633.9) 639.6
      molar pregnancy (*see also* categories 630–632) 639.6
    following
      abortion 639.6
      ectopic or molar pregnancy 639.6
    iatrogenic 415.11
    in pregnancy, childbirth, or puerperium — *see* Embolism, obstetrical
    postoperative 415.11
  renal 593.81
    embolic or thrombotic 593.81
  retina, retinal 362.84
    with occlusion — *see* Occlusion, retina
  spinal (acute) (cord) (embolic) (nonembolic) 336.1
  spleen 289.59
    embolic or thrombotic 444.89
  subchorionic — *see* Infarct, placenta
  subendocardial (*see also* Infarct, myocardium) 410.7 ☑
  suprarenal (capsule) (gland) 255.4
  syncytium — *see* Infarct, placenta
  testis 608.83
  thrombotic (*see also* Thrombosis) 453.9
    artery, arterial — *see* Embolism
  thyroid (gland) 246.3
  ventricle (heart) (*see also* Infarct, myocardium) 410.9 ☑
Infecting — *see* condition
Infection, infected, infective (opportunistic) 136.9
  with lymphangitis — *see* Lymphangitis
  abortion — *see* Abortion, by type, with, sepsis
  abscess (skin) — *see* Abscess, by site
  Absidia 117.7
  Acanthocheilonema (perstans) 125.4
    streptocerca 125.6
  accessory sinus (chronic) (*see also* Sinusitis) 473.9
  Achorion — *see* Dermatophytosis
  Acremonium falciforme 117.4
  acromioclavicular (joint) 711.91
  actinobacillus
    lignieresii 027.8
    mallei 024

Infection, infected, infective — *continued*
  actinobacillus — *continued*
    muris 026.1
  actinomadura — *see* Actinomycosis
  Actinomyces (israelii) (*see also* Actinomycosis)
    muris-ratti 026.1
  Actinomycetales (actinomadura) (Actinomyces) (Nocardia) (Streptomyces) — *see* Actinomycosis
  actinomycotic NEC (*see also* Actinomycosis) 039.9
  adenoid (chronic) 474.01
    acute 463
    and tonsil (chronic) 474.02
      acute or subacute 463
  adenovirus NEC 079.0
    in diseases classified elsewhere — *see* category 079 ☑
    unspecified nature or site 079.0
  Aerobacter aerogenes NEC 041.85
    enteritis 008.2
  aerogenes capsulatus (*see also* Gangrene, gas) 040.0
  aertrycke (*see also* Infection, Salmonella) 003.9
  ajellomyces dermatitidis 116.0
  alimentary canal NEC (*see also* Enteritis, due to, by organism) 009.0
  Allescheria boydii 117.6
  Alternaria 118
  alveolus, alveolar (process) (pulpal origin) 522.4
  ameba, amebic (histolytica) (*see also* Amebiasis) 006.9
    acute 006.0
    chronic 006.1
    free-living 136.2
    hartmanni 007.8
    specified
      site NEC 006.8
      type NEC 007.8
  amniotic fluid or cavity 658.4 ☑
    affecting fetus or newborn 762.7
  anaerobes (cocci) (gram-negative) (gram-positive) (mixed) NEC 041.84
  anal canal 569.49
  Ancylostoma braziliense 126.2
  Angiostrongylus cantonensis 128.8
  anisakiasis 127.1
  Anisakis larva 127.1
  anthrax (*see also* Anthrax) 022.9
  antrum (chronic) (*see also* Sinusitis, maxillary) 473.0
  anus (papillae) (sphincter) 569.49
  arbor virus NEC 066.9
  arbovirus NEC 066.9
  argentophil-rod 027.0
  Ascaris lumbricoides 127.0
  ascomycetes 117.4
  Aspergillus (flavus) (fumigatus) (terreus) 117.3
  atypical
    acid-fast (bacilli) (*see also* Mycobacterium, atypical) 031.9
    mycobacteria (*see also* Mycobacterium, atypical) 031.9
  auditory meatus (circumscribed) (diffuse) (external) (*see also* Otitis, externa) 380.10
  auricle (ear) (*see also* Otitis, externa) 380.10
  axillary gland 683
  Babesiasis 088.82
  Babesiosis 088.82
  Bacillus NEC 041.89
    abortus 023.1
    anthracis (*see also* Anthrax) 022.9
    cereus (food poisoning) 005.89
    coli — *see* Infection, Escherichia coli
    coliform NEC 041.85
    Ducrey's (any location) 099.0
    Flexner's 004.1

☑ Additional Digit Required — Refer to the Tabular List for Digit Selection
Subterms under main terms may continue to next column or page

Injury — *continued*
- eyeball — *continued*
  - penetrating — *continued*
    - foreign body — *continued*
      - magnetic 871.5
  - superficial 918.9
- eyebrow 959.09
- eyelid(s) 921.1
  - laceration — *see* Laceration, eyelid
  - superficial 918.0
- face (and neck) 959.09
- fallopian tube — *see* Injury, internal, fallopian tube
- finger(s) (nail) 959.5
- flank 959.19
- foot (and ankle) (and knee) (and leg, except thigh) 959.7
- forceps NEC 767.9
  - scalp 767.19
- forearm (and elbow) (and wrist) 959.3
- forehead 959.09
- gallbladder — *see* Injury, internal, gallbladder
- gasserian ganglion 951.2
- gastrointestinal tract — *see* Injury, internal, gastrointestinal tract
- genital organ(s)
  - with
    - abortion — *see* Abortion, by type, with, damage to pelvic organs
    - ectopic pregnancy (*see also* categories 633.0–633.9) 639.2
    - molar pregnancy (*see also* categories 630–632) 639.2
  - external 959.14
    - fracture of corpus cavernosum penis 959.13
  - following
    - abortion 639.2
    - ectopic or molar pregnancy 639.2
  - internal — *see* Injury, internal, genital organs
  - obstetrical trauma NEC 665.9 ☑
    - affecting fetus or newborn 763.89
- gland
  - lacrimal 921.1
    - laceration 870.8
  - parathyroid 959.09
  - salivary 959.09
  - thyroid 959.09
- globe (eye) (*see also* Injury, eyeball) 921.3
- grease gun — *see* Wound, open, by site, complicated
- groin 959.19
- gum 959.09
- hand(s) (except fingers) 959.4
- head NEC 959.01
  - with
    - loss of consciousness 850.5
    - skull fracture — *see* Fracture, skull, by site
- heart — *see* Injury, internal, heart
- heel 959.7
- hip (and thigh) 959.6
- hymen 959.14
- hyperextension (cervical) (vertebra) 847.0
- ileum — *see* Injury, internal, ileum
- iliac region 959.19
- infrared rays NEC 990
- instrumental (during surgery) 998.2
  - birth injury — *see* Birth, injury
  - nonsurgical (*see also* Injury, by site) 959.9
  - obstetrical 665.9 ☑
    - affecting fetus or newborn 763.89
    - bladder 665.5 ☑
    - cervix 665.3 ☑
    - high vaginal 665.4 ☑
    - perineal NEC 664.9 ☑
    - urethra 665.5 ☑
    - uterus 665.5 ☑
- internal 869.0

> *Note — For injury of internal organ(s) by foreign body entering through a natural orifice (e.g., inhaled, ingested, or swallowed) — see Foreign body, entering through orifice.*
>
> *For internal injury of any of the following sites with internal injury of any other of the sites — see Injury, internal, multiple.*

  - with
    - fracture
      - pelvis — *see* Fracture, pelvis
      - specified site, except pelvis — *see* Injury, internal, by site
    - open wound into cavity 869.1
  - abdomen, abdominal (viscera) NEC 868.00
    - with
      - fracture, pelvis — *see* Fracture, pelvis
        - open wound into cavity 868.10
      - specified site NEC 868.09
        - with open wound into cavity 868.19
  - adrenal (gland) 868.01
    - with open wound into cavity 868.11
  - aorta (thoracic) 901.0
    - abdominal 902.0
  - appendix 863.85
    - with open wound into cavity 863.95
  - bile duct 868.02
    - with open wound into cavity 868.12
  - bladder (sphincter) 867.0
    - with
      - abortion — *see* Abortion, by type, with damage to pelvic organs
      - ectopic pregnancy (*see also* categories 633.0–633.9) 639.2
      - molar pregnancy (*see also* categories 630–632) 639.2
      - open wound into cavity 867.1
    - following
      - abortion 639.2
      - ectopic or molar pregnancy 639.2
    - obstetrical trauma 665.5 ☑
      - affecting fetus or newborn 763.89
  - blood vessel — *see* Injury, blood vessel, by site
  - broad ligament 867.6
    - with open wound into cavity 867.7
  - bronchus, bronchi 862.21
    - with open wound into cavity 862.31
  - cecum 863.89
    - with open wound into cavity 863.99
  - cervix (uteri) 867.4
    - with
      - abortion — *see* Abortion, by type, with damage to pelvic organs
      - ectopic pregnancy (*see also* categories 633.0–633.9) 639.2
      - molar pregnancy (*see also* categories 630–632) 639.2
      - open wound into cavity 867.5
    - following
      - abortion 639.2
      - ectopic or molar pregnancy 639.2
    - obstetrical trauma 665.3 ☑
      - affecting fetus or newborn 763.89
  - chest (*see also* Injury, internal, intrathoracic organs) 862.8
    - with open wound into cavity 862.9
  - colon 863.40
    - with
      - open wound into cavity 863.50
    - rectum 863.46
      - with open wound into cavity 863.56
    - ascending (right) 863.41
      - with open wound into cavity 863.51
    - descending (left) 863.43
      - with open wound into cavity 863.53
    - multiple sites 863.46
      - with open wound into cavity 863.56
    - sigmoid 863.44
      - with open wound into cavity 863.54
    - specified site NEC 863.49
      - with open wound into cavity 863.59
    - transverse 863.42
      - with open wound into cavity 863.52
  - common duct 868.02
    - with open wound into cavity 868.12
  - complicating delivery 665.9 ☑
    - affecting fetus or newborn 763.89
  - diaphragm 862.0
    - with open wound into cavity 862.1
  - duodenum 863.21
    - with open wound into cavity 863.31
  - esophagus (intrathoracic) 862.22
    - with open wound into cavity 862.32
    - cervical region 874.4
      - complicated 874.5
  - fallopian tube 867.6
    - with open wound into cavity 867.7
  - gallbladder 868.02
    - with open wound into cavity 868.12
  - gastrointestinal tract NEC 863.80
    - with open wound into cavity 863.90
  - genital organ NEC 867.6
    - with open wound into cavity 867.7
  - heart 861.00
    - with open wound into thorax 861.10
  - ileum 863.29
    - with open wound into cavity 863.39
  - intestine NEC 863.89
    - with open wound into cavity 863.99
    - large NEC 863.40
      - with open wound into cavity 863.50
    - small NEC 863.20
      - with open wound into cavity 863.30
  - intra-abdominal (organ) 868.00
    - with open wound into cavity 868.10
    - multiple sites 868.09
      - with open wound into cavity 868.19
    - specified site NEC 868.09
      - with open wound into cavity 868.19
  - intrathoracic organs (multiple) 862.8
    - with open wound into cavity 862.9
    - diaphragm (only) — *see* Injury, internal, diaphragm
    - heart (only) — *see* Injury, internal, heart
    - lung (only) — *see* Injury, internal, lung
    - specified site NEC 862.29
      - with open wound into cavity 862.39
  - intrauterine (*see also* Injury, internal, uterus) 867.4
    - with open wound into cavity 867.5
  - jejunum 863.29
    - with open wound into cavity 863.39
  - kidney (subcapsular) 866.00
    - with
      - disruption of parenchyma (complete) 866.03
        - with open wound into cavity 866.13
      - hematoma (without rupture of capsule) 866.01
        - with open wound into cavity 866.11
      - laceration 866.02
        - with open wound into cavity 866.12
      - open wound into cavity 866.10
  - liver 864.00
    - with
      - contusion 864.01
        - with open wound into cavity 864.11
      - hematoma 864.01
        - with open wound into cavity 864.11
      - laceration 864.05
        - with open wound into cavity 864.15
        - major (disruption of hepatic parenchyma) 864.04
          - with open wound into cavity 864.14
        - minor (capsule only) 864.02
          - with open wound into cavity 864.12
        - moderate (involving parenchyma) 864.03
          - with open wound into cavity 864.13
        - multiple 864.04
        - stellate 864.04
          - with open wound into cavity 864.14
      - open wound into cavity 864.10
  - lung 861.20
    - with open wound into thorax 861.30
    - hemopneumothorax — *see* Hemopneumothorax, traumatic
    - hemothorax — *see* Hemothorax, traumatic
    - pneumohemothorax — *see* Pneumohemothorax, traumatic

- **Injury** — *continued*
  - internal — *continued*
    - lung — *continued*
      - pneumothorax — *see* Pneumothorax, traumatic
      - transfusion related, acute (TRALI) 518.7 ●
    - mediastinum 862.29
      - with open wound into cavity 862.39
    - mesentery 863.89
      - with open wound into cavity 863.99
    - mesosalpinx 867.6
      - with open wound into cavity 867.7
    - multiple 869.0

> *Note — Multiple internal injuries of sites classifiable to the same three- or four-digit category should be classified to that category.*
>
> *Multiple injuries classifiable to different fourth-digit subdivisions of 861 (heart and lung injuries) should be dealt with according to coding rules.*

-
      - internal
        - with open wound into cavity 869.1
      - intra-abdominal organ (sites classifiable to 863–868)
        - with
          - intrathoracic organ(s) (sites classifiable to 861–862) 869.0
            - with open wound into cavity 869.1
          - other intra-abdominal organ(s) (sites classifiable to 863–868, except where classifiable to the same three-digit category) 868.09
            - with open wound into cavity 868.19
      - intrathoracic organ (sites classifiable to 861–862)
        - with
          - intra-abdominal organ(s) (sites classifiable to 863–868) 869.0
            - with open wound into cavity 869.1
          - other intrathoracic organ(s) (sites classifiable to 861–862, except where classifiable to the same three-digit category) 862.8
            - with open wound into cavity 862.9
    - myocardium — *see* Injury, internal, heart
    - ovary 867.6
      - with open wound into cavity 867.7
    - pancreas (multiple sites) 863.84
      - with open wound into cavity 863.94
      - body 863.82
        - with open wound into cavity 863.92
      - head 863.81
        - with open wound into cavity 863.91
      - tail 863.83
        - with open wound into cavity 863.93
    - pelvis, pelvic (organs) (viscera) 867.8
      - with
        - fracture, pelvis — *see* Fracture, pelvis
        - open wound into cavity 867.9

- **Injury** — *continued*
  - internal — *continued*
    - pelvis, pelvic — *continued*
      - specified site NEC 867.6
        - with open wound into cavity 867.7
    - peritoneum 868.03
      - with open wound into cavity 868.13
    - pleura 862.29
      - with open wound into cavity 862.39
    - prostate 867.6
      - with open wound into cavity 867.7
    - rectum 863.45
      - with
        - colon 863.46
          - with open wound into cavity 863.56
        - open wound into cavity 863.55
    - retroperitoneum 868.04
      - with open wound into cavity 868.14
    - round ligament 867.6
      - with open wound into cavity 867.7
    - seminal vesicle 867.6
      - with open wound into cavity 867.7
    - spermatic cord 867.6
      - with open wound into cavity 867.7
      - scrotal — *see* Wound, open, spermatic cord
    - spleen 865.00
      - with
        - disruption of parenchyma (massive) 865.04
          - with open wound into cavity 865.14
        - hematoma (without rupture of capsule) 865.01
          - with open wound into cavity 865.11
        - open wound into cavity 865.10
        - tear, capsular 865.02
          - with open wound into cavity 865.12
          - extending into parenchyma 865.03
            - with open wound into cavity 865.13
    - stomach 863.0
      - with open wound into cavity 863.1
    - suprarenal gland (multiple) 868.01
      - with open wound into cavity 868.11
    - thorax, thoracic (cavity) (organs) (multiple) (*see also* Injury, internal, intrathoracic organs) 862.8
      - with open wound into cavity 862.9
    - thymus (gland) 862.29
      - with open wound into cavity 862.39
    - trachea (intrathoracic) 862.29
      - with open wound into cavity 862.39
      - cervical region (*see also* Wound, open, trachea) 874.02
    - ureter 867.2
      - with open wound into cavity 867.3
    - urethra (sphincter) 867.0
      - with
        - abortion — *see* Abortion, by type, with damage to pelvic organs
        - ectopic pregnancy (*see also* categories 633.0–633.9) 639.2

- **Injury** — *continued*
  - internal — *continued*
    - urethra — *continued*
      - with — *continued*
        - molar pregnancy (*see also* categories 630–632) 639.2
        - open wound into cavity 867.1
      - following
        - abortion 639.2
        - ectopic or molar pregnancy 639.2
      - obstetrical trauma 665.5 ☑
        - affecting fetus or newborn 763.89
    - uterus 867.4
      - with
        - abortion — *see* Abortion, by type, with damage to pelvic organs
        - ectopic pregnancy (*see also* categories 633.0–633.9) 639.2
        - molar pregnancy (*see also* categories 630–632) 639.2
        - open wound into cavity 867.5
      - following
        - abortion 639.2
        - ectopic or molar pregnancy 639.2
      - obstetrical trauma NEC 665.5 ☑
        - affecting fetus or newborn 763.89
    - vas deferens 867.6
      - with open wound into cavity 867.7
    - vesical (sphincter) 867.0
      - with open wound into cavity 867.1
    - viscera (abdominal) (*see also* Injury, internal, multiple) 868.00
      - with
        - fracture, pelvis — *see* Fracture, pelvis
        - open wound into cavity 868.10
      - thoracic NEC (*see also* Injury, internal, intrathoracic organs) 862.8
        - with open wound into cavity 862.9
  - interscapular region 959.19
  - intervertebral disc 959.19
  - intestine — *see* Injury, internal, intestine
  - intra-abdominal (organs) NEC — *see* Injury, internal, intra-abdominal

- **Injury** — *continued*
  - intracranial 854.0 ☑

> *Note — Use the following fifth-digit subclassification with categories 851–854:*
>
> *0 unspecified state of consciousness*
>
> *1 with no loss of consciousness*
>
> *2 with brief [less than one hour] loss of consciousness*
>
> *3 with moderate [1–24 hours] loss of consciousness*
>
> *4 with prolonged [more than 24 hours] loss of consciousness and return to pre-existing conscious level*
>
> *5 with prolonged [more than 24 hours] loss of consciousness, without return to pre-existing conscious level*
>
> *Use fifth-digit 5 to designate when a patient is unconscious and dies before regaining consciousness, regardless of the duration of the loss of consciousness*
>
> *6 with loss of consciousness of unspecified duration*
>
> *9 with concussion, unspecified*

-
    - with
      - open intracranial wound 854.1 ☑
      - skull fracture — *see* Fracture, skull, by site
    - contusion 851.8 ☑
      - with open intracranial wound 851.9 ☑
      - brain stem 851.4 ☑
        - with open intracranial wound 851.5 ☑
      - cerebellum 851.4 ☑
        - with open intracranial wound 851.5 ☑
      - cortex (cerebral) 851.0 ☑
        - with open intracranial wound 851.2 ☑
    - hematoma — *see* Injury, intracranial, hemorrhage
    - hemorrhage 853.0 ☑
      - with
        - laceration — *see* Injury, intracranial, laceration
        - open intracranial wound 853.1 ☑
      - extradural 852.4 ☑
        - with open intracranial wound 852.5 ☑
      - subarachnoid 852.0 ☑
        - with open intracranial wound 852.1 ☑
      - subdural 852.2 ☑
        - with open intracranial wound 852.3 ☑
    - laceration 851.8 ☑
      - with open intracranial wound 851.9 ☑
      - brain stem 851.6 ☑
        - with open intracranial wound 851.7 ☑
      - cerebellum 851.6 ☑
        - with open intracranial wound 851.7 ☑
      - cortex (cerebral) 851.2 ☑
        - with open intracranial wound 851.3 ☑
  - intraocular — *see* Injury, eyeball, penetrating
  - intrathoracic organs (multiple) — *see* Injury, internal, intrathoracic organs
  - intrauterine — *see* Injury, internal, intrauterine

- **Injury** — *continued*
  - iris 921.3
    - penetrating — *see* Injury, eyeball, penetrating
  - jaw 959.09
  - jejunum — *see* Injury, internal, jejunum
  - joint NEC 959.9
    - old or residual 718.80
      - ankle 718.87
      - elbow 718.82
      - foot 718.87
      - hand 718.84
      - hip 718.85
      - knee 718.86
      - multiple sites 718.89
      - pelvic region 718.85
      - shoulder (region) 718.81
      - specified site NEC 718.88
      - wrist 718.83
  - kidney — *see* Injury, internal, kidney
  - knee (and ankle) (and foot) (and leg, except thigh) 959.7
  - labium (majus) (minus) 959.14
  - labyrinth, ear 959.09
  - lacrimal apparatus, gland, or sac 921.1
    - laceration 870.8
  - larynx 959.09
  - late effect — *see* Late, effects (of), injury
  - leg, except thigh (and ankle) (and foot) (and knee) 959.7
    - upper or thigh 959.6
  - lens, eye 921.3
    - penetrating — *see* Injury, eyeball, penetrating
  - lid, eye — *see* Injury, eyelid
  - lip 959.09
  - liver — *see* Injury, internal, liver
  - lobe, parietal — *see* Injury, intracranial
  - lumbar (region) 959.19
    - plexus 953.5
  - lumbosacral (region) 959.19
    - plexus 953.5
  - lung — *see* Injury, internal, lung
  - malar region 959.09
  - mastoid region 959.09
  - maternal, during pregnancy, affecting fetus or newborn 760.5
  - maxilla 959.09
  - mediastinum — *see* Injury, internal, mediastinum
  - membrane
    - brain (*see also* Injury, intracranial) 854.0 ☑
    - tympanic 959.09
  - meningeal artery — *see* Hemorrhage, brain, traumatic, subarachnoid
  - meninges (cerebral) — *see* Injury, intracranial
  - mesenteric
    - artery — *see* Injury, blood vessel, mesenteric, artery
    - plexus, inferior 954.1
    - vein — *see* Injury, blood vessel, mesenteric, vein
  - mesentery — *see* Injury, internal, mesentery
  - mesosalpinx — *see* Injury, internal, mesosalpinx
  - middle ear 959.09
  - midthoracic region 959.11
  - mouth 959.09
  - multiple (sites not classifiable to the same four-digit category in 959.0–959.7) 959.8
    - internal 869.0
      - with open wound into cavity 869.1
  - musculocutaneous nerve 955.4
  - nail
    - finger 959.5
    - toe 959.7
  - nasal (septum) (sinus) 959.09

- **Injury** — *continued*
  - nasopharynx 959.09
  - neck (and face) 959.09
  - nerve 957.9
    - abducens 951.3
    - abducent 951.3
    - accessory 951.6
    - acoustic 951.5
    - ankle and foot 956.9
    - anterior crural, femoral 956.1
    - arm (*see also* Injury, nerve, upper limb) 955.9
    - auditory 951.5
    - axillary 955.0
    - brachial plexus 953.4
    - cervical sympathetic 954.0
    - cranial 951.9
      - first or olfactory 951.8
      - second or optic 950.0
      - third or oculomotor 951.0
      - fourth or trochlear 951.1
      - fifth or trigeminal 951.2
      - sixth or abducens 951.3
      - seventh or facial 951.4
      - eighth, acoustic, or auditory 951.5
      - ninth or glossopharyngeal 951.8
      - tenth, pneumogastric, or vagus 951.8
      - eleventh or accessory 951.6
      - twelfth or hypoglossal 951.7
      - newborn 767.7
    - cutaneous sensory
      - lower limb 956.4
      - upper limb 955.5
    - digital (finger) 955.6
      - toe 956.5
    - facial 951.4
      - newborn 767.5
    - femoral 956.1
    - finger 955.9
    - foot and ankle 956.9
    - forearm 955.9
    - glossopharyngeal 951.8
    - hand and wrist 955.9
    - head and neck, superficial 957.0
    - hypoglossal 951.7
    - involving several parts of body 957.8
    - leg (*see also* Injury, nerve, lower limb) 956.9
    - lower limb 956.9
      - multiple 956.8
      - specified site NEC 956.5
    - lumbar plexus 953.5
    - lumbosacral plexus 953.5
    - median 955.1
      - forearm 955.1
      - wrist and hand 955.1
    - multiple (in several parts of body) (sites not classifiable to the same three-digit category) 957.8
    - musculocutaneous 955.4
    - musculospiral 955.3
      - upper arm 955.3
    - oculomotor 951.0
    - olfactory 951.8
    - optic 950.0
    - pelvic girdle 956.9
      - multiple sites 956.8
      - specified site NEC 956.5
    - peripheral 957.9
      - multiple (in several regions) (sites not classifiable to the same three-digit category) 957.8
      - specified site NEC 957.1
    - peroneal 956.3
      - ankle and foot 956.3
      - lower leg 956.3
    - plantar 956.5
    - plexus 957.9
      - celiac 954.1
      - mesenteric, inferior 954.1
      - spinal 953.9

- **Injury** — *continued*
  - nerve — *continued*
    - plexus — *continued*
      - spinal — *continued*
        - brachial 953.4
        - lumbosacral 953.5
        - multiple sites 953.8
      - sympathetic NEC 954.1
    - pneumogastric 951.8
    - radial 955.3
      - wrist and hand 955.3
    - sacral plexus 953.5
    - sciatic 956.0
      - thigh 956.0
    - shoulder girdle 955.9
      - multiple 955.8
      - specified site NEC 955.7
    - specified site NEC 957.1
    - spinal 953.9
      - plexus — *see* Injury, nerve, plexus, spinal
      - root 953.9
        - cervical 953.0
        - dorsal 953.1
        - lumbar 953.2
        - multiple sites 953.8
        - sacral 953.3
    - splanchnic 954.1
    - sympathetic NEC 954.1
      - cervical 954.0
    - thigh 956.9
    - tibial 956.5
      - ankle and foot 956.2
      - lower leg 956.5
      - posterior 956.2
    - toe 956.9
    - trigeminal 951.2
    - trochlear 951.1
    - trunk, excluding shoulder and pelvic girdles 954.9
      - specified site NEC 954.8
      - sympathetic NEC 954.1
    - ulnar 955.2
      - forearm 955.2
      - wrist (and hand) 955.2
    - upper limb 955.9
      - multiple 955.8
      - specified site NEC 955.7
    - vagus 951.8
    - wrist and hand 955.9
  - nervous system, diffuse 957.8
  - nose (septum) 959.09
  - obstetrical NEC 665.9 ☑
    - affecting fetus or newborn 763.89
  - occipital (region) (scalp) 959.09
    - lobe (*see also* Injury, intracranial) 854.0 ☑
  - optic 950.9
    - chiasm 950.1
    - cortex 950.3
    - nerve 950.0
    - pathways 950.2
  - orbit, orbital (region) 921.2
    - penetrating 870.3
      - with foreign body 870.4
  - ovary — *see* Injury, internal, ovary
  - paint-gun — *see* Wound, open, by site, complicated
  - palate (soft) 959.09
  - pancreas — *see* Injury, internal, pancreas
  - parathyroid (gland) 959.09
  - parietal (region) (scalp) 959.09
    - lobe — *see* Injury, intracranial
  - pelvic
    - floor 959.19
      - complicating delivery 664.1 ☑
        - affecting fetus or newborn 763.89
    - joint or ligament, complicating delivery 665.6 ☑
      - affecting fetus or newborn 763.89
    - organs (*see also* Injury, internal, pelvis)

- **Injury** — *continued*
  - pelvic — *continued*
    - organs (*see also* Injury, internal, pelvis) — *continued*
      - with
        - abortion — *see* Abortion, by type, with damage to pelvic organs
        - ectopic pregnancy (*see also* categories 633.0–633.9) 639.2
        - molar pregnancy (*see also* categories 633.0–633.9) 639.2
      - following
        - abortion 639.2
        - ectopic or molar pregnancy 639.2
      - obstetrical trauma 665.5 ☑
        - affecting fetus or newborn 763.89
  - pelvis 959.19
  - penis 959.14
    - fracture of corpus cavernosum 959.13
  - perineum 959.14
  - peritoneum — *see* Injury, internal, peritoneum
  - periurethral tissue
    - with
      - abortion — *see* Abortion, by type, with damage to pelvic organs
      - ectopic pregnancy (*see also* categories 633.0–633.9) 639.2
      - molar pregnancy (*see also* categories 630–632) 639.2
    - complicating delivery 665.5 ☑
      - affecting fetus or newborn 763.89
    - following
      - abortion 639.2
      - ectopic or molar pregnancy 639.2
  - phalanges
    - foot 959.7
    - hand 959.5
  - pharynx 959.09
  - pleura — *see* Injury, internal, pleura
  - popliteal space 959.7
  - post-cardiac surgery (syndrome) 429.4 ●
  - prepuce 959.14
  - prostate — *see* Injury, internal, prostate
  - pubic region 959.19
  - pudenda 959.14
  - radiation NEC 990
  - radioactive substance or radium NEC 990
  - rectovaginal septum 959.14
  - rectum — *see* Injury, internal, rectum
  - retina 921.3
    - penetrating — *see* Injury, eyeball, penetrating
  - retroperitoneal — *see* Injury, internal, retroperitoneum
  - roentgen rays NEC 990
  - round ligament — *see* Injury, internal, round ligament
  - sacral (region) 959.19
    - plexus 953.5
  - sacroiliac ligament NEC 959.19
  - sacrum 959.19
  - salivary ducts or glands 959.09
  - scalp 959.09
    - due to birth trauma 767.19
    - fetus or newborn 767.19
  - scapular region 959.2
  - sclera 921.3
    - penetrating — *see* Injury, eyeball, penetrating
    - superficial 918.2
  - scrotum 959.14

- **Injury** — *continued*
  - superficial — *continued*
    - tympanum, tympanic membrane (and other part(s) of face, neck, or scalp, except eye) 910 ☑
    - upper extremity NEC 913 ☑
    - uvula (and other part(s) of face, neck, or scalp, except eye) 910 ☑
    - vagina (and other part(s) of trunk) 911 ☑
    - vulva (and other part(s) of trunk) 911 ☑
    - wrist (and elbow) (and forearm) 913 ☑
  - supraclavicular fossa 959.19
  - supraorbital 959.09
  - surgical complication (external or internal site) 998.2
  - symphysis pubis 959.19
    - complicating delivery 665.6 ☑
      - affecting fetus or newborn 763.89
  - temple 959.09
  - temporal region 959.09
  - testis 959.14
  - thigh (and hip) 959.6
  - thorax, thoracic (external) 959.11
    - cavity — *see* Injury, internal, thorax
    - internal — *see* Injury, internal, intrathoracic organs
  - throat 959.09
  - thumb(s) (nail) 959.5
  - thymus — *see* Injury, internal, thymus
  - thyroid (gland) 959.09
  - toe (nail) (any) 959.7
  - tongue 959.09
  - tonsil 959.09
  - tooth NEC 873.63
    - complicated 873.73
  - trachea — *see* Injury, internal, trachea
  - trunk 959.19
  - tunica vaginalis 959.14
  - tympanum, tympanic membrane 959.09
  - ultraviolet rays NEC 990
  - ureter — *see* Injury, internal, ureter
  - urethra (sphincter) — *see* Injury, internal, urethra
  - uterus — *see* Injury, internal, uterus
  - uvula 959.09
  - vagina 959.14
  - vascular — *see* Injury, blood vessel
  - vas deferens — *see* Injury, internal, vas deferens
  - vein (*see also* Injury, blood vessel, by site) 904.9
  - vena cava
    - inferior 902.10
    - superior 901.2
  - vesical (sphincter) — *see* Injury, internal, vesical
  - viscera (abdominal) — *see* Injury, internal, viscera
    - with fracture, pelvis — *see* Fracture, pelvis
  - visual 950.9
    - cortex 950.3
  - vitreous (humor) 871.2
  - vulva 959.14
  - whiplash (cervical spine) 847.0
  - wringer — *see* Crush, by site
  - wrist (and elbow) (and forearm) 959.3
  - x-ray NEC 990
- **Inoculation** — *see also* Vaccination
  - complication or reaction — *see* Complication, vaccination
- **Insanity, insane** — *see also* Psychosis 298.9
  - adolescent (*see also* Schizophrenia) 295.9 ☑
- **Insanity, insane** — *see also* Psychosis — *continued*
  - alternating (*see also* Psychosis, affective, circular) 296.7
  - confusional 298.9
    - acute 293.0
    - subacute 293.1
  - delusional 298.9
  - paralysis, general 094.1
    - progressive 094.1
  - paresis, general 094.1
  - senile 290.20
- **Insect**
  - bite — *see* Injury, superficial, by site
  - venomous, poisoning by 989.5
- **Insemination, artificial** V26.1
- **Insensitivity**
  - androgen 259.5
    - partial 259.5
- **Insertion**
  - cord (umbilical) lateral or velamentous 663.8 ☑
    - affecting fetus or newborn 762.6
  - intrauterine contraceptive device V25.1
  - placenta, vicious — *see* Placenta, previa
  - subdermal implantable contraceptive V25.5
  - velamentous, umbilical cord 663.8 ☑
    - affecting fetus or newborn 762.6
- **Insolation** 992.0
  - meaning sunstroke 992.0
- **Insomnia, unspecified** 780.52
  - with sleep apnea, unspecified 780.51
  - adjustment 307.41
  - alcohol induced 291.82
  - behavioral, of childhood V69.5
  - drug induced 292.85
  - due to
    - medical condition classified elsewhere 327.01
    - mental disorder 327.02
  - idiopathic 307.42
  - nonorganic origin 307.41
    - persistent (primary) 307.42
    - transient 307.41
  - organic 327.00
    - other 327.09
  - paradoxical 307.42
  - primary 307.42
  - psychophysiological 307.42
  - subjective complaint 307.49
- **Inspiration**
  - food or foreign body (*see also* Asphyxia, food or foreign body) 933.1
  - mucus (*see also* Asphyxia, mucus) 933.1
- **Inspissated bile syndrome, newborn** 774.4
- **Instability**
  - detrusor 596.59
  - emotional (excessive) 301.3
  - joint (posttraumatic) 718.80
    - ankle 718.87
    - elbow 718.82
    - foot 718.87
    - hand 718.84
    - hip 718.85
    - knee 718.86
    - lumbosacral 724.6
    - multiple sites 718.89
    - pelvic region 718.85
    - sacroiliac 724.6
    - shoulder (region) 718.81
    - specified site NEC 718.88
    - wrist 718.83
  - lumbosacral 724.6
  - nervous 301.89
  - personality (emotional) 301.59
  - thyroid, paroxysmal 242.9 ☑
  - urethral 599.83
  - vasomotor 780.2
- **Insufficiency, insufficient**
  - accommodation 367.4
  - adrenal (gland) (acute) (chronic) 255.4
- **Insufficiency, insufficient** — *continued*
  - adrenal — *continued*
    - medulla 255.5
    - primary 255.4
    - specified site NEC 255.5
  - adrenocortical 255.4
  - anterior ▶(occlusal)◀ guidance 524.54
  - anus 569.49
  - aortic (valve) 424.1
    - with
      - mitral (valve) disease 396.1
        - insufficiency, incompetence, or regurgitation 396.3
        - stenosis or obstruction 396.1
      - stenosis or obstruction 424.1
        - with mitral (valve) disease 396.8
    - congenital 746.4
    - rheumatic 395.1
      - with
        - mitral (valve) disease 396.1
          - insufficiency, incompetence, or regurgitation 396.3
          - stenosis or obstruction 396.1
        - stenosis or obstruction 395.2
          - with mitral (valve) disease 396.8
    - specified cause NEC 424.1
    - syphilitic 093.22
  - arterial 447.1
    - basilar artery 435.0
    - carotid artery 435.8
    - cerebral 437.1
    - coronary (acute or subacute) 411.89
    - mesenteric 557.1
    - peripheral 443.9
    - precerebral 435.9
    - vertebral artery 435.1
    - vertebrobasilar 435.3
  - arteriovenous 459.9
  - basilar artery 435.0
  - biliary 575.8
  - cardiac (*see also* Insufficiency, myocardial) 428.0
    - complicating surgery 997.1
    - due to presence of (cardiac) prosthesis 429.4
    - postoperative 997.1
      - long-term effect of cardiac surgery 429.4
    - specified during or due to a procedure 997.1
      - long-term effect of cardiac surgery 429.4
  - cardiorenal (*see also* Hypertension, cardiorenal) 404.90
  - cardiovascular (*see also* Disease, cardiovascular) 429.2
    - renal (*see also* Hypertension, cardiorenal) 404.90
  - carotid artery 435.8
  - cerebral (vascular) 437.9
  - cerebrovascular 437.9
    - with transient focal neurological signs and symptoms 435.9
    - acute 437.1
      - with transient focal neurological signs and symptoms 435.9
  - circulatory NEC 459.9
    - fetus or newborn 779.89
  - convergence 378.83
  - coronary (acute or subacute) 411.89
    - chronic or with a stated duration of over 8 weeks 414.8
  - corticoadrenal 255.4
  - dietary 269.9
  - divergence 378.85
  - food 994.2
  - gastroesophageal 530.89
  - gonadal
    - ovary 256.39
- **Insufficiency, insufficient** — *continued*
  - gonadal — *continued*
    - testis 257.2
  - gonadotropic hormone secretion 253.4
  - heart (*see also* Insufficiency, myocardial)
    - fetus or newborn 779.89
    - valve (*see also* Endocarditis) 424.90
      - congenital NEC 746.89
  - hepatic 573.8
  - idiopathic autonomic 333.0
  - interocclusal distance of teeth (ridge) 524.36
  - kidney
    - acute 593.9
    - chronic 585.9
  - labyrinth, labyrinthine (function) 386.53
    - bilateral 386.54
    - unilateral 386.53
  - lacrimal 375.15
  - liver 573.8
  - lung (acute) (*see also* Insufficiency, pulmonary) 518.82
    - following trauma, surgery, or shock 518.5
    - newborn 770.89
  - mental (congenital) (*see also* Retardation, mental) 319
  - mesenteric 557.1
  - mitral (valve) 424.0
    - with
      - aortic (valve) disease 396.3
        - insufficiency, incompetence, or regurgitation 396.3
        - stenosis or obstruction 396.2
      - obstruction or stenosis 394.2
        - with aortic valve disease 396.8
    - congenital 746.6
    - rheumatic 394.1
      - with
        - aortic (valve) disease 396.3
          - insufficiency, incompetence, or regurgitation 396.3
          - stenosis or obstruction 396.2
        - obstruction or stenosis 394.2
          - with aortic valve disease 396.8
      - active or acute 391.1
        - with chorea, rheumatic (Sydenham's) 392.0
    - specified cause, except rheumatic 424.0
  - muscle
    - heart — *see* Insufficiency, myocardial
    - ocular (*see also* Strabismus) 378.9
  - myocardial, myocardium (with arteriosclerosis) 428.0
    - with rheumatic fever (conditions classifiable to 390)
      - active, acute, or subacute 391.2
        - with chorea 392.0
      - inactive or quiescent (with chorea) 398.0
    - congenital 746.89
    - due to presence of (cardiac) prosthesis 429.4
    - fetus or newborn 779.89
    - following cardiac surgery 429.4
    - hypertensive (*see also* Hypertension, heart) 402.91
      - benign 402.11
      - malignant 402.01
    - postoperative 997.1
      - long-term effect of cardiac surgery 429.4
    - rheumatic 398.0
      - active, acute, or subacute 391.2
        - with chorea (Sydenham's) 392.0

Insufficiency, insufficient — *continued*
- myocardial, myocardium — *continued*
  - syphilitic 093.82
- nourishment 994.2
- organic 799.89
- ovary 256.39
  - postablative 256.2
- pancreatic 577.8
- parathyroid (gland) 252.1
- peripheral vascular (arterial) 443.9
- pituitary (anterior) 253.2
  - posterior 253.5
- placental — *see* Placenta, insufficiency
- platelets 287.5
- prenatal care in current pregnancy V23.7
- progressive pluriglandular 258.9
- pseudocholinesterase 289.89
- pulmonary (acute) 518.82
  - following
    - shock 518.5
    - surgery 518.5
    - trauma 518.5
  - newborn 770.89
  - valve (*see also* Endocarditis, pulmonary) 424.3
    - congenital 746.09
- pyloric 537.0
- renal 593.9 ▲
  - acute 593.9
  - chronic 585.9
  - due to a procedure 997.5
- respiratory 786.09
  - acute 518.82
    - following shock, surgery, or trauma 518.5
  - newborn 770.89
- rotation — *see* Malrotation
- suprarenal 255.4
  - medulla 255.5
- tarso-orbital fascia, congenital 743.66
- tear film 375.15
- testis 257.2
- thyroid (gland) (acquired) (*see also* Hypothyroidism)
  - congenital 243
- tricuspid (*see also* Endocarditis, tricuspid) 397.0
  - congenital 746.89
  - syphilitic 093.23
- urethral sphincter 599.84
- valve, valvular (heart) (*see also* Endocarditis) 424.90
- vascular 459.9
  - intestine NEC 557.9
  - mesenteric 557.1
  - peripheral 443.9
  - renal (*see also* Hypertension, kidney) 403.90
- velopharyngeal
  - acquired 528.9
  - congenital 750.29
- venous (peripheral) 459.81
- ventricular — *see* Insufficiency, myocardial
- vertebral artery 435.1
- vertebrobasilar artery 435.3
- weight gain during pregnancy 646.8 ☑
- zinc 269.3

Insufflation
- fallopian
  - fertility testing V26.21
  - following sterilization reversal V26.22
- meconium 770.11
  - with respiratory symptoms 770.12

Insular — *see* condition

Insulinoma (M8151/0)
- malignant (M8151/3)
  - pancreas 157.4
  - specified site — *see* Neoplasm, by site, malignant
  - unspecified site 157.4
- pancreas 211.7

Insulinoma — *continued*
- specified site — *see* Neoplasm, by site, benign
- unspecified site 211.7

Insuloma — *see* Insulinoma

Insult
- brain 437.9
  - acute 436
- cerebral 437.9
  - acute 436
- cerebrovascular 437.9
  - acute 436
- vascular NEC 437.9
  - acute 436

Insurance examination (certification) V70.3

Intemperance — *see also* Alcoholism 303.9 ☑

Interception of pregnancy (menstrual extraction) V25.3

Interference ●
- balancing side 524.56 ●
- non-working side 524.56 ●

Intermenstrual
- bleeding 626.6
  - irregular 626.6
  - regular 626.5
- hemorrhage 626.6
  - irregular 626.6
  - regular 626.5
- pain(s) 625.2

Intermittent — *see* condition

Internal — *see* condition

Interproximal wear 521.10

Interruption
- aortic arch 747.11
- bundle of His 426.50
- fallopian tube (for sterilization) V25.2
- phase-shift, sleep cycle 307.45
- repeated REM-sleep 307.48
- sleep
  - due to perceived environmental disturbances 307.48
  - phase-shift, of 24-hour sleep-wake cycle 307.45
  - repeated REM-sleep type 307.48
- vas deferens (for sterilization) V25.2

Intersexuality 752.7

Interstitial — *see* condition

Intertrigo 695.89
- labialis 528.5

Intervertebral disc — *see* condition

Intestine, intestinal — *see also* condition
- flu 487.8

Intolerance
- carbohydrate NEC 579.8
- cardiovascular exercise, with pain (at rest) (with less than ordinary activity) (with ordinary activity) V47.2
- cold 780.99
- dissacharide (hereditary) 271.3
- drug
  - correct substance properly administered 995.27 ▲
  - wrong substance given or taken in error 977.9
    - specified drug — *see* Table of Drugs and Chemicals
- effort 306.2
- fat NEC 579.8
- foods NEC 579.8
- fructose (hereditary) 271.2
- glucose (-galactose) (congenital) 271.3
- gluten 579.0
- lactose (hereditary) (infantile) 271.3
- lysine (congenital) 270.7
- milk NEC 579.8
- protein (familial) 270.7
- starch NEC 579.8
- sucrose (-isomaltose) (congenital) 271.3

Intoxicated NEC — *see also* Alcoholism 305.0 ☑

Intoxication
- acid 276.2
- acute
  - alcoholic 305.0 ☑
    - with alcoholism 303.0 ☑
    - hangover effects 305.0 ☑
  - caffeine 305.9 ☑
  - hallucinogenic (*see also* Abuse, drugs, nondependent) 305.3 ☑
- alcohol (acute) 305.0 ☑
  - with alcoholism 303.0 ☑
  - hangover effects 305.0 ☑
  - idiosyncratic 291.4
  - pathological 291.4
- alimentary canal 558.2
- ammonia (hepatic) 572.2
- caffeine 305.9 ☑
- chemical (*see also* Table of Drugs and Chemicals)
  - via placenta or breast milk 760.70
    - alcohol 760.71
    - anticonvulsants
    - antifungals
    - anti-infective agents 760.74
    - antimetabolics
    - cocaine 760.75
    - "crack" 760.75
    - hallucinogenic agents NEC 760.73
    - medicinal agents NEC 760.79
    - narcotics 760.72
    - obstetric anesthetic or analgesic drug 763.5
    - specified agent NEC 760.79
    - suspected, affecting management of pregnancy 655.5 ☑
- cocaine, through placenta or breast milk 760.75
- delirium
  - alcohol 291.0
  - drug 292.81
- drug 292.89
  - with delirium 292.81
  - correct substance properly administered (*see also* Allergy, drug) 995.27 ▲
  - newborn 779.4
  - obstetric anesthetic or sedation 668.9 ☑
    - affecting fetus or newborn 763.5
  - overdose or wrong substance given or taken — *see* Table of Drugs and Chemicals
  - pathologic 292.2
  - specific to newborn 779.4
  - via placenta or breast milk 760.70
    - alcohol 760.71
    - anticonvulsants 760.77
    - antifungals 760.74
    - anti-infective agents 760.74
    - antimetabolics 760.78
    - cocaine 760.75
    - "crack" 760.75
    - hallucinogenic agents 760.73
    - medicinal agents NEC 760.79
    - narcotics 760.72
    - obstetric anesthetic or analgesic drug 763.5
    - specified agent NEC 760.79
    - suspected, affecting management of pregnancy 655.5 ☑
- enteric — *see* Intoxication, intestinal
- fetus or newborn, via placenta or breast milk 760.70
  - alcohol 760.71
  - anticonvulsants 760.77
  - antifungals 760.74
  - anti-infective agents 760.74
  - antimetabolics 760.78
  - cocaine 760.75
  - "crack" 760.75
  - hallucinogenic agents 760.73
  - medicinal agents NEC 760.79

Intoxication — *continued*
- fetus or newborn, via placenta or breast milk — *continued*
  - narcotics 760.72
  - obstetric anesthetic or analgesic drug 763.5
  - specified agent NEC 760.79
  - suspected, affecting management of pregnancy 655.5 ☑
- food — *see* Poisoning, food
- gastrointestinal 558.2
- hallucinogenic (acute) 305.3 ☑
- hepatocerebral 572.2
- idiosyncratic alcohol 291.4
- intestinal 569.89
  - due to putrefaction of food 005.9
- methyl alcohol (*see also* Alcoholism) 305.0 ☑
  - with alcoholism 303.0 ☑
- pathologic 291.4
  - drug 292.2
- potassium (K) 276.7
- septic
  - with
    - abortion — *see* Abortion, by type, with sepsis
    - ectopic pregnancy (*see also* categories 633.0–633.9) 639.0
    - molar pregnancy (*see also* categories 630–632) 639.0
  - during labor 659.3 ☑
  - following
    - abortion 639.0
    - ectopic or molar pregnancy 639.0
  - generalized — *see* Septicemia
  - puerperal, postpartum, childbirth 670.0 ☑
- serum (prophylactic) (therapeutic) 999.5
- uremic — *see* Uremia
- water 276.6

Intracranial — *see* condition

Intrahepatic gallbladder 751.69

Intraligamentous — *see also* condition
- pregnancy — *see* Pregnancy, cornual

Intraocular — *see also* condition
- sepsis 360.00

Intrathoracic — *see also* condition
- kidney 753.3
- stomach — *see* Hernia, diaphragm

Intrauterine contraceptive device
- checking V25.42
- insertion V25.1
- in situ V45.51
- management V25.42
- prescription V25.02
  - repeat V25.42
- reinsertion V25.42
- removal V25.42

Intraventricular — *see* condition

Intrinsic deformity — *see* Deformity

Intruded tooth 524.34 ●

Intrusion, repetitive, of sleep (due to environmental disturbances) (with atypical polysomnographic features) 307.48

Intumescent, lens (eye) NEC 366.9
- senile 366.12

Intussusception (colon) (enteric) (intestine) (rectum) 560.0
- appendix 543.9
- congenital 751.5
- fallopian tube 620.8
- ileocecal 560.0
- ileocolic 560.0
- ureter (with obstruction) 593.4

Invagination
- basilar 756.0
- colon or intestine 560.0

Invalid (since birth) 799.89

Invalidism (chronic) 799.89

Inversion
- albumin-globulin (A-G) ratio 273.8
- bladder 596.8

☑ Additional Digit Required — Refer to the Tabular List for Digit Selection

Subterms under main terms may continue to next column or page

▶◀ Revised Text ● New Line ▲ Revised Code

J

K

☑ Additional Digit Required — Refer to the Tabular List for Digit Selection

Subterms under main terms may continue to next column or page

Kussmaul's
- coma (diabetic) 250.3 ☑
- disease (polyarteritis nodosa) 446.0
- respiration (air hunger) 786.09

Kwashiorkor (marasmus type) 260

Kyasanur Forest disease 065.2

Kyphoscoliosis, kyphoscoliotic (acquired) — *see also* Scoliosis 737.30
- congenital 756.19
- due to radiation 737.33
- heart (disease) 416.1
- idiopathic 737.30
  - infantile
    - progressive 737.32
    - resolving 737.31
- late effect of rickets 268.1 *[737.43]*
- specified NEC 737.39
- thoracogenic 737.34
- tuberculous (*see also* Tuberculosis) 015.0 ☑ *[737.43]*

Kyphosis, kyphotic (acquired) (postural) 737.10
- adolescent postural 737.0
- congenital 756.19
- dorsalis juvenilis 732.0
- due to or associated with
  - Charcôt-Marie-Tooth disease 356.1 *[737.41]*
  - mucopolysaccharidosis 277.5 *[737.41]*
  - neurofibromatosis 237.71 *[737.41]*
  - osteitis
    - deformans 731.0 *[737.41]*
    - fibrosa cystica 252.01 *[737.41]*
  - osteoporosis (*see also* Osteoporosis) 733.0 ☑ *[737.41]*
  - poliomyelitis (*see also* Poliomyelitis) 138 *[737.41]*
  - radiation 737.11
  - tuberculosis (*see also* Tuberculosis) 015.0 ☑ *[737.41]*
- Kümmell's 721.7
- late effect of rickets 268.1 *[737.41]*
- Morquio-Brailsford type (spinal) 277.5 *[737.41]*
- pelvis 738.6
- postlaminectomy 737.12
- specified cause NEC 737.19
- syphilitic, congenital 090.5 *[737.41]*
- tuberculous (*see also* Tuberculosis) 015.0 ☑ *[737.41]*

Kyrle's disease (hyperkeratosis follicularis in cutem penetrans) 701.1

L

Labia, labium — *see* condition

Labiated hymen 752.49

Labile
- blood pressure 796.2
- emotions, emotionality 301.3
- vasomotor system 443.9

Labioglossal paralysis 335.22

Labium leporinum — *see also* Cleft, lip 749.10

Labor — *see also* Delivery
- with complications — *see* Delivery, complicated
- abnormal NEC 661.9 ☑
  - affecting fetus or newborn 763.7
- arrested active phase 661.1 ☑
  - affecting fetus or newborn 763.7
- desultory 661.2 ☑
  - affecting fetus or newborn 763.7
- dyscoordinate 661.4 ☑
  - affecting fetus or newborn 763.7
- early onset (22-36 weeks gestation) 644.2 ☑
- failed
  - induction 659.1 ☑
    - mechanical 659.0 ☑
    - medical 659.1 ☑
    - surgical 659.0 ☑
  - trial (vaginal delivery) 660.6 ☑
- false 644.1 ☑

Labor — *see also* Delivery — *continued*
- forced or induced, affecting fetus or newborn 763.89
- hypertonic 661.4 ☑
  - affecting fetus or newborn 763.7
- hypotonic 661.2 ☑
  - affecting fetus or newborn 763.7
  - primary 661.0 ☑
    - affecting fetus or newborn 763.7
  - secondary 661.1 ☑
    - affecting fetus or newborn 763.7
- incoordinate 661.4 ☑
  - affecting fetus or newborn 763.7
- irregular 661.2 ☑
  - affecting fetus or newborn 763.7
- long — *see* Labor, prolonged
- missed (at or near term) 656.4 ☑
- obstructed NEC 660.9 ☑
  - affecting fetus or newborn 763.1
  - due to female genital mutilation 660.8 ☑
  - specified cause NEC 660.8 ☑
    - affecting fetus or newborn 763.1
- pains, spurious 644.1 ☑
- precipitate 661.3 ☑
  - affecting fetus or newborn 763.6
- premature 644.2 ☑
  - threatened 644.0 ☑
- prolonged or protracted 662.1 ☑
  - first stage 662.0 ☑
    - affecting fetus or newborn 763.89
  - second stage 662.2 ☑
    - affecting fetus or newborn 763.89
  - affecting fetus or newborn 763.89
- threatened NEC 644.1 ☑
- undelivered 644.1 ☑

Labored breathing — *see also* Hyperventilation 786.09

Labyrinthitis (inner ear) (destructive) (latent) 386.30
- circumscribed 386.32
- diffuse 386.31
- focal 386.32
- purulent 386.33
- serous 386.31
- suppurative 386.33
- syphilitic 095.8
- toxic 386.34
- viral 386.35

Laceration — *see also* Wound, open, by site
- accidental, complicating surgery 998.2
- Achilles tendon 845.09
  - with open wound 892.2
- anus (sphincter) 879.6
  - with
    - abortion — *see* Abortion, by type, with damage to pelvic organs
    - ectopic pregnancy (*see also* categories 633.0–633.9) 639.2
    - molar pregnancy (*see also* categories 630–632) 639.2
  - complicated 879.7
  - complicating delivery 664.2 ☑
    - with laceration of anal or rectal mucosa 664.3 ☑
  - following
    - abortion 639.2
    - ectopic or molar pregnancy 639.2
  - nontraumatic, nonpuerperal 565.0
- bladder (urinary)
  - with
    - abortion — *see* Abortion, by type, with damage to pelvic organs
    - ectopic pregnancy (*see also* categories 633.0–633.9) 639.2
    - molar pregnancy (*see also* categories 630–632) 639.2

Laceration — *see also* Wound, open, by site — *continued*
- bladder — *continued*
  - following
    - abortion 639.2
    - ectopic or molar pregnancy 639.2
  - obstetrical trauma 665.5 ☑
- blood vessel — *see* Injury, blood vessel, by site
- bowel
  - with
    - abortion — *see* Abortion, by type, with damage to pelvic organs
    - ectopic pregnancy (*see also* categories 633.0–633.9) 639.2
    - molar pregnancy (*see also* categories 630–632) 639.2
  - following
    - abortion 639.2
    - ectopic or molar pregnancy 639.2
  - obstetrical trauma 665.5 ☑
- brain (cerebral) (membrane) (with hemorrhage) 851.8 ☑

> *Note — Use the following fifth-digit subclassification with categories 851–854:*
>
> 0 *unspecified state of consciousness*
>
> 1 *with no loss of consciousness*
>
> 2 *with brief [less than one hour] loss of consciousness*
>
> 3 *with moderate [1–24 hours] loss of consciousness*
>
> 4 *with prolonged [more than 24 hours] loss of consciousness and return to pre-existing conscious level*
>
> 5 *with prolonged [more than 24 hours] loss of consciousness, without return to pre-existing conscious level*
>
> *Use fifth-digit 5 to designate when a patient is unconscious and dies before regaining consciousness, regardless of the duration of the loss of consciousness*
>
> 6 *with loss of consciousness of unspecified duration*
>
> 9 *with concussion, unspecified*

  - with
    - open intracranial wound 851.9 ☑
    - skull fracture — *see* Fracture, skull, by site
  - cerebellum 851.6 ☑
    - with open intracranial wound 851.7 ☑
  - cortex 851.2 ☑
    - with open intracranial wound 851.3 ☑
  - during birth 767.0
  - stem 851.6 ☑
    - with open intracranial wound 851.7 ☑
- broad ligament
  - with
    - abortion — *see* Abortion, by type, with damage to pelvic organs
    - ectopic pregnancy (*see also* categories 633.0–633.9) 639.2
    - molar pregnancy (*see also* categories 630–632) 639.2
  - following
    - abortion 639.2
    - ectopic or molar pregnancy 639.2

Laceration — *see also* Wound, open, by site — *continued*
- broad ligament — *continued*
  - nontraumatic 620.6
  - obstetrical trauma 665.6 ☑
  - syndrome (nontraumatic) 620.6
- capsule, joint — *see* Sprain, by site
- cardiac — *see* Laceration, heart
- causing eversion of cervix uteri (old) 622.0
- central, complicating delivery 664.4 ☑
- cerebellum — *see* Laceration, brain, cerebellum
- cerebral (*see also* Laceration, brain)
  - during birth 767.0
- cervix (uteri)
  - with
    - abortion — *see* Abortion, by type, with damage to pelvic organs
    - ectopic pregnancy (*see also* categories 633.0–633.9) 639.2
    - molar pregnancy (*see also* categories 630–632) 639.2
  - following
    - abortion 639.2
    - ectopic or molar pregnancy 639.2
  - nonpuerperal, nontraumatic 622.3
  - obstetrical trauma (current) 665.3 ☑
  - old (postpartal) 622.3
  - traumatic — *see* Injury, internal, cervix
- chordae heart 429.5
- complicated 879.9
- cornea — *see* Laceration, eyeball
  - superficial 918.1
- cortex (cerebral) — *see* Laceration, brain, cortex
- esophagus 530.89
- eye(s) — *see* Laceration, ocular
- eyeball NEC 871.4
  - with prolapse or exposure of intraocular tissue 871.1
  - penetrating — *see* Penetrating wound, eyeball
  - specified as without prolapse of intraocular tissue 871.0
- eyelid NEC 870.8
  - full thickness 870.1
    - involving lacrimal passages 870.2
  - skin (and periocular area) 870.0
    - penetrating — *see* Penetrating wound, orbit
- fourchette
  - with
    - abortion — *see* Abortion, by type, with damage to pelvic organs
    - ectopic pregnancy (*see also* categories 633.0–633.9) 639.2
    - molar pregnancy (*see also* categories 630–632) 639.2
  - complicating delivery 664.0 ☑
  - following
    - abortion 639.2
    - ectopic or molar pregnancy 639.2
- heart (without penetration of heart chambers) 861.02
  - with
    - open wound into thorax 861.12
    - penetration of heart chambers 861.03
      - with open wound into thorax 861.13
- hernial sac — *see* Hernia, by site
- internal organ (abdomen) (chest) (pelvis) NEC — *see* Injury, internal, by site
  - NEC — *see* Injury, internal, by site
- kidney (parenchyma) 866.02

- **Lack of** — *continued*
  - housing — *continued*
    - adequate V60.1
  - material resources V60.2
  - medical attention 799.89
  - memory (*see also* Amnesia) 780.93
    - mild, following organic brain damage 310.1
  - ovulation 628.0
  - person able to render necessary care V60.4
  - physical exercise V69.0
  - physiologic development in childhood 783.40
  - posterior occlusal support 524.57
  - prenatal care in current pregnancy V23.7
  - shelter V60.0
  - sleep V69.4
  - water 994.3
- **Lacrimal** — *see* condition
- **Lacrimation, abnormal** — *see also* Epiphora 375.20
- **Lacrimonasal duct** — *see* condition
- **Lactation, lactating** (breast) (puerperal) (postpartum)
  - defective 676.4 ☑
  - disorder 676.9 ☑
    - specified type NEC 676.8 ☑
  - excessive 676.6 ☑
  - failed 676.4 ☑
  - mastitis NEC 675.2 ☑
  - mother (care and/or examination) V24.1
  - nonpuerperal 611.6
  - suppressed 676.5 ☑
- **Lacticemia** 271.3
  - excessive 276.2
- **Lactosuria** 271.3
- **Lacunar skull** 756.0
- **Laennec's cirrhosis** (alcoholic) 571.2
  - nonalcoholic 571.5
- **Lafora's disease** 333.2
- **Lagleyze-von Hippel disease** (retinocerebral angiomatosis) 759.6
- **Lag, lid** (nervous) 374.41
- **Lagophthalmos** (eyelid) (nervous) 374.20
  - cicatricial 374.23
  - keratitis (*see also* Keratitis) 370.34
  - mechanical 374.22
  - paralytic 374.21
- **La grippe** — *see* Influenza
- **Lahore sore** 085.1
- **Lakes, venous** (cerebral) 437.8
- **Laki-Lorand factor deficiency** — *see also* Defect, coagulation 286.3
- **Lalling** 307.9
- **Lambliasis** 007.1
- **Lame back** 724.5
- **Lancereaux's diabetes** (diabetes mellitus with marked emaciation) 250.8 ☑ *[261]*
- **Landouzy-Déjérine dystrophy** (fascioscapulohumeral atrophy) 359.1
- **Landry's disease or paralysis** 357.0
- **Landry-Guillain-Barré syndrome** 357.0
- **Lane's**
  - band 751.4
  - disease 569.89
  - kink (*see also* Obstruction, intestine) 560.9
- **Langdon Down's syndrome** (mongolism) 758.0
- **Language abolition** 784.69
- **Lanugo** (persistent) 757.4
- **Laparoscopic surgical procedure converted to open procedure** V64.41
- **Lardaceous**
  - degeneration (any site) 277.39 ▲
  - disease 277.39 ▲
  - kidney 277.39 *[583.81]* ▲
  - liver 277.39 ▲
- **Large**
  - baby (regardless of gestational age) 766.1
- **Large** — *continued*
  - baby — *continued*
    - exceptionally (weight of 4500 grams or more) 766.0
    - of diabetic mother 775.0
  - ear 744.22
  - fetus (*see also* Oversize, fetus)
    - causing disproportion 653.5 ☑
      - with obstructed labor 660.1 ☑
  - for dates
    - fetus or newborn (regardless of gestational age) 766.1
      - affecting management of pregnancy 656.6 ☑
      - exceptionally (weight of 4500 grams or more) 766.0
  - physiological cup 743.57
  - stature 783.9
  - waxy liver 277.39 ▲
  - white kidney — *see* Nephrosis
- **Larsen-Johansson disease** (juvenile osteopathia patellae) 732.4
- **Larsen's syndrome** (flattened facies and multiple congenital dislocations) 755.8
- **Larva migrans**
  - cutaneous NEC 126.9
    - ancylostoma 126.9
  - of Diptera in vitreous 128.0
  - visceral NEC 128.0
- **Laryngeal** — *see also* condition 786.2
  - syncope 786.2
- **Laryngismus** (acute) (infectious) (stridulous) 478.75
  - congenital 748.3
  - diphtheritic 032.3
- **Laryngitis** (acute) (edematous) (fibrinous) (gangrenous) (infective) (infiltrative) (malignant) (membranous) (phlegmonous) (pneumococcal) (pseudomembranous) (septic) (subglottic) (suppurative) (ulcerative) (viral) 464.00
  - with
    - influenza, flu, or grippe 487.1
    - obstruction 464.01
    - tracheitis (*see also* Laryngotracheitis) 464.20
      - with obstruction 464.21
      - acute 464.20
        - with obstruction 464.21
      - chronic 476.1
  - atrophic 476.0
  - Borrelia vincentii 101
  - catarrhal 476.0
  - chronic 476.0
    - with tracheitis (chronic) 476.1
    - due to external agent — *see* Condition, respiratory, chronic, due to
  - diphtheritic (membranous) 032.3
  - due to external agent — *see* Inflammation, respiratory, upper, due to
  - Hemophilus influenzae 464.00
    - with obstruction 464.01
  - H. influenzae 464.00
    - with obstruction 464.01
  - hypertrophic 476.0
  - influenzal 487.1
  - pachydermic 478.79
  - sicca 476.0
  - spasmodic 478.75
    - acute 464.00
      - with obstruction 464.01
  - streptococcal 034.0
  - stridulous 478.75
  - syphilitic 095.8
    - congenital 090.5
  - tuberculous (*see also* Tuberculosis, larynx) 012.3 ☑
  - Vincent's 101
- **Laryngocele** (congenital) (ventricular) 748.3
- **Laryngofissure** 478.79
  - congenital 748.3
- **Laryngomalacia** (congenital) 748.3
- **Laryngopharyngitis** (acute) 465.0
  - chronic 478.9
    - due to external agent — *see* Condition, respiratory, chronic, due to
  - due to external agent — *see* Inflammation, respiratory, upper, due to
  - septic 034.0
- **Laryngoplegia** — *see also* Paralysis, vocal cord 478.30
- **Laryngoptosis** 478.79
- **Laryngospasm** 478.75
  - due to external agent — *see* Condition, respiratory, acute, due to
- **Laryngostenosis** 478.74
  - congenital 748.3
- **Laryngotracheitis** (acute) (infectional) (viral) — *see also* Laryngitis 464.20
  - with obstruction 464.21
  - atrophic 476.1
  - Borrelia vincenti 101
  - catarrhal 476.1
  - chronic 476.1
    - due to external agent — *see* Condition, respiratory, chronic, due to
  - diphtheritic (membranous) 032.3
  - due to external agent — *see* Inflammation, respiratory, upper, due to
  - H. influenzae 464.20
    - with obstruction 464.21
  - hypertrophic 476.1
  - influenzal 487.1
  - pachydermic 478.75
  - sicca 476.1
  - spasmodic 478.75
    - acute 464.20
      - with obstruction 464.21
  - streptococcal 034.0
  - stridulous 478.75
  - syphilitic 095.8
    - congenital 090.5
  - tuberculous (*see also* Tuberculosis, larynx) 012.3 ☑
  - Vincent's 101
- **Laryngotracheobronchitis** — *see also* Bronchitis 490
  - acute 466.0
  - chronic 491.8
  - viral 466.0
- **Laryngotracheobronchopneumonitis** — *see* Pneumonia, broncho-
- **Larynx, laryngeal** — *see* condition
- **Lasègue's disease** (persecution mania) 297.9
- **Lassa fever** 078.89
- **Lassitude** — *see also* Weakness 780.79
- **Late** — *see also* condition
  - effect(s) (of) (*see also* condition)
    - abscess
      - intracranial or intraspinal (conditions classifiable to 324) — *see* category 326
    - adverse effect of drug, medicinal or biological substance 909.5
    - allergic reaction 909.9
    - amputation
      - postoperative (late) 997.60
      - traumatic (injury classifiable to 885–887 and 895–897) 905.9
    - burn (injury classifiable to 948–949) 906.9
      - extremities NEC (injury classifiable to 943 or 945) 906.7
        - hand or wrist (injury classifiable to 944) 906.6
      - eye (injury classifiable to 940) 906.5
      - face, head, and neck (injury classifiable to 941) 906.5
      - specified site NEC (injury classifiable to 942 and 946–947) 906.8
- **Late** — *see also* condition — *continued*
  - effect(s) (*see also* condition) — *continued*
    - cerebrovascular disease (conditions classifiable to 430–437) 438.9
      - with
        - alterations of sensations 438.6
        - aphasia 438.11
        - apraxia 438.81
        - ataxia 438.84
        - cognitive deficits 438.0
        - disturbances of vision 438.7
        - dysphagia 438.82
        - dysphasia 438.12
        - facial droop 438.83
        - facial weakness 438.83
        - hemiplegia/hemiparesis
          - affecting
            - dominant side 438.21
            - nondominant side 438.22
            - unspecified side 438.20
        - monoplegia of lower limb
          - affecting
            - dominant side 438.41
            - nondominant side 438.42
            - unspecified side 438.40
        - monoplegia of upper limb
          - affecting
            - dominant side 438.31
            - nondominant side 438.32
            - unspecified side 438.30
        - paralytic syndrome NEC
          - affecting
            - bilateral 438.53
            - dominant side 438.51
            - nondominant side 438.52
            - unspecified side 438.50
        - specified type NEC 438.19
        - speech and language deficit 438.10
        - vertigo 438.85
      - specified type NEC 438.89
    - childbirth complication(s) 677
    - complication(s) of
      - childbirth 677
      - delivery 677
      - pregnancy 677
      - puerperium 677
      - surgical and medical care (conditions classifiable to 996–999) 909.3
      - trauma (conditions classifiable to 958) 908.6
    - contusion (injury classifiable to 920–924) 906.3
    - crushing (injury classifiable to 925–929) 906.4
    - delivery complication(s) 677
    - dislocation (injury classifiable to 830–839) 905.6
    - encephalitis or encephalomyelitis (conditions classifiable to 323) — *see* category 326
      - in infectious diseases 139.8
        - viral (conditions classifiable to 049.8, 049.9, 062–064) 139.0
    - external cause NEC (conditions classifiable to 995) 909.9
      - certain conditions classifiable to categories 991-994 909.4
    - foreign body in orifice (injury classifiable to 930–939) 908.5

- **Late** — *see also* condition — *continued*
  - effect(s) (*see also* condition) — *continued*
    - fracture (multiple) (injury classifiable to 828–829) 905.5
      - extremity
        - lower (injury classifiable to 821–827) 905.4
          - neck of femur (injury classifiable to 820) 905.3
        - upper (injury classifiable to 810–819) 905.2
      - face and skull (injury classifiable to 800–804) 905.0
      - skull and face (injury classifiable to 800–804) 905.0
      - spine and trunk (injury classifiable to 805 and 807–809) 905.1
        - with spinal cord lesion (injury classifiable to 806) 907.2
    - infection
      - pyogenic, intracranial — *see* category 326
    - infectious diseases (conditions classifiable to 001–136) NEC 139.8
    - injury (injury classifiable to 959) 908.9
      - blood vessel 908.3
        - abdomen and pelvis (injury classifiable to 902) 908.4
        - extremity (injury classifiable to 903–904) 908.3
        - head and neck (injury classifiable to 900) 908.3
          - intracranial (injury classifiable to 850–854) 907.0
            - with skull fracture 905.0
        - thorax (injury classifiable to 901) 908.4
      - internal organ NEC (injury classifiable to 867 and 869) 908.2
        - abdomen (injury classifiable to 863–866 and 868) 908.1
        - thorax (injury classifiable to 860–862) 908.0
      - intracranial (injury classifiable to 850–854) 907.0
        - with skull fracture (injury classifiable to 800–801 and 803–804) 905.0
      - nerve NEC (injury classifiable to 957) 907.9
        - cranial (injury classifiable to 950–951) 907.1
        - peripheral NEC (injury classifiable to 957) 907.9
          - lower limb and pelvic girdle (injury classifiable to 956) 907.5
          - upper limb and shoulder girdle (injury classifiable to 955) 907.4
        - roots and plexus(es), spinal (injury classifiable to 953) 907.3
        - trunk (injury classifiable to 954) 907.3
      - spinal
        - cord (injury classifiable to 806 and 952) 907.2
        - nerve root(s) and plexus(es) (injury classifiable to 953) 907.3
      - superficial (injury classifiable to 910–919) 906.2

- **Late** — *see also* condition — *continued*
  - effect(s) (*see also* condition) — *continued*
    - injury — *continued*
      - tendon (tendon injury classifiable to 840–848, 880–884 with .2, and 890–894 with .2) 905.8
    - meningitis
      - bacterial (conditions classifiable to 320) — *see* category 326
      - unspecified cause (conditions classifiable to 322) — *see* category 326
    - myelitis (*see also* Late, effect(s) (of), encephalitis) — *see* category 326
    - parasitic diseases (conditions classifiable to 001–136 NEC) 139.8
    - phlebitis or thrombophlebitis of intracranial venous sinuses (conditions classifiable to 325) — *see* category 326
    - poisoning due to drug, medicinal or biological substance (conditions classifiable to 960–979) 909.0
    - poliomyelitis, acute (conditions classifiable to 045) 138
    - pregnancy complication(s) 677
    - puerperal complication(s) 677
    - radiation (conditions classifiable to 990) 909.2
    - rickets 268.1
    - sprain and strain without mention of tendon injury (injury classifiable to 840–848, except tendon injury) 905.7
      - tendon involvement 905.8
    - toxic effect of
      - drug, medicinal or biological substance (conditions classifiable to 960–979) 909.0
      - nonmedical substance (conditions classifiable to 980–989) 909.1
    - trachoma (conditions classifiable to 076) 139.1
    - tuberculosis 137.0
      - bones and joints (conditions classifiable to 015) 137.3
      - central nervous system (conditions classifiable to 013) 137.1
      - genitourinary (conditions classifiable to 016) 137.2
      - pulmonary (conditions classifiable to 010–012) 137.0
      - specified organs NEC (conditions classifiable to 014, 017–018) 137.4
    - viral encephalitis (conditions classifiable to 049.8, 049.9, 062–064) 139.0
    - wound, open
      - extremity (injury classifiable to 880–884 and 890–894, except .2) 906.1
        - tendon (injury classifiable to 880–884 with .2 and 890–894 with .2) 905.8
      - head, neck, and trunk (injury classifiable to 870–879) 906.0
  - infant
    - post-term (gestation period over 40 completed weeks to 42 completed weeks) 766.21
    - prolonged gestation (period over 42 completed weeks) 766.22
- **Latent** — *see* condition
- **Lateral** — *see* condition
- **Laterocession** — *see* Lateroversion
- **Lateroflexion** — *see* Lateroversion
- **Lateroversion**
  - cervix — *see* Lateroversion, uterus
  - uterus, uterine (cervix) (postinfectional) (postpartal, old) 621.6
    - congenital 752.3
    - in pregnancy or childbirth 654.4 ☑
      - affecting fetus or newborn 763.89
- **Lathyrism** 988.2
- **Launois-Bensaude's lipomatosis** 272.8
- **Launois-Cléret syndrome** (adiposogenital dystrophy) 253.8
- **Launois' syndrome** (pituitary gigantism) 253.0
- **Laurence-Moon-Biedl syndrome** (obesity, polydactyly, and mental retardation) 759.89
- **LAV** (disease) (illness) (infection) — *see* Human immunodeficiency virus (disease) (illness) (infection)
- **LAV/HTLV-III** (disease) (illness) (infection) — *see* Human immunodeficiency virus (disease) (illness) (infection)
- **Lawford's syndrome** (encephalocutaneous angiomatosis) 759.6
- **Laxative habit** — *see also* Abuse, drugs, nondependent 305.9 ☑
- **Lax, laxity** — *see also* Relaxation
  - ligament 728.4
  - skin (acquired) 701.8
    - congenital 756.83
- **Lazy leukocyte syndrome** 288.09 ▲
- **LCAD** (long chain/very long chain acyl CoA dehydrogenase deficiency, VLCAD) 277.85
- **LCHAD** (long chain 3-hydroxyacyl CoA dehydrogenase deficiency) 277.85
- **Lead** — *see also* condition
  - exposure to V15.86
  - incrustation of cornea 371.15
  - poisoning 984.9
    - specified type of lead — *see* Table of Drugs and Chemicals
- **Lead miners' lung** 503
- **Leakage**
  - amniotic fluid 658.1 ☑
    - with delayed delivery 658.2 ☑
    - affecting fetus or newborn 761.1
  - bile from drainage tube (T tube) 997.4
  - blood (microscopic), fetal, into maternal circulation 656.0 ☑
    - affecting management of pregnancy or puerperium 656.0 ☑
  - device, implant, or graft — *see* Complications, mechanical
  - spinal fluid at lumbar puncture site 997.09
  - urine, continuous 788.37
- **Leaky heart** — *see* Endocarditis
- **Learning defect, specific** NEC (strephosymbolia) 315.2
- **Leather bottle stomach** (M8142/3) 151.9
- **Leber's**
  - congenital amaurosis 362.76
  - optic atrophy (hereditary) 377.16
- **Lederer's anemia or disease** (acquired infectious hemolytic anemia) 283.19
- **Lederer-Brill syndrome** (acquired infectious hemolytic anemia) 283.19
- **Leeches** (aquatic) (land) 134.2
- **Left-sided neglect** 781.8
- **Leg** — *see* condition
- **Legal investigation** V62.5
- **Legg (-Calvé) -Perthes disease or syndrome** (osteochondrosis, femoral capital) 732.1
- **Legionnaires' disease** 482.84
- **Leigh's disease** 330.8
- **Leiner's disease** (exfoliative dermatitis) 695.89
- **Leiofibromyoma** (M8890/0) — *see also* Leiomyoma
  - uterus (cervix) (corpus) (*see also* Leiomyoma, uterus) 218.9
- **Leiomyoblastoma** (M8891/1) — *see* Neoplasm, connective tissue, uncertain behavior
- **Leiomyofibroma** (M8890/0) — *see also* Neoplasm, connective tissue, benign
  - uterus (cervix) (corpus) (*see also* Leiomyoma, uterus) 218.9
- **Leiomyoma** (M8890/0) — *see also* Neoplasm, connective tissue, benign
  - bizarre (M8893/0) — *see* Neoplasm, connective tissue, benign
  - cellular (M8892/1) — *see* Neoplasm, connective tissue, uncertain behavior
  - epithelioid (M8891/1) — *see* Neoplasm, connective tissue, uncertain behavior
  - prostate (polypoid) 600.20
    - with
      - other lower urinary tract symptoms (LUTS) 600.21 ●
      - urinary ●
        - obstruction 600.21 ●
        - retention 600.21 ●
  - uterus (cervix) (corpus) 218.9
    - interstitial 218.1
    - intramural 218.1
    - submucous 218.0
    - subperitoneal 218.2
    - subserous 218.2
  - vascular (M8894/0) — *see* Neoplasm, connective tissue, benign
- **Leiomyomatosis** (intravascular) (M8890/1) — *see* Neoplasm, connective tissue, uncertain behavior
- **Leiomyosarcoma** (M8890/3) — *see also* Neoplasm, connective tissue, malignant
  - epithelioid (M8891/3) — *see* Neoplasm, connective tissue, malignant
- **Leishmaniasis** 085.9
  - American 085.5
    - cutaneous 085.4
    - mucocutaneous 085.5
  - Asian desert 085.2
  - Brazilian 085.5
  - cutaneous 085.9
    - acute necrotizing 085.2
    - American 085.4
    - Asian desert 085.2
    - diffuse 085.3
    - dry form 085.1
    - Ethiopian 085.3
    - eyelid 085.5 *[373.6]*
    - late 085.1
    - lepromatous 085.3
    - recurrent 085.1
    - rural 085.2
    - ulcerating 085.1
    - urban 085.1
    - wet form 085.2
    - zoonotic form 085.2
  - dermal (*see also* Leishmaniasis, cutaneous)
    - post kala-azar 085.0
  - eyelid 085.5 *[373.6]*
  - infantile 085.0
  - Mediterranean 085.0
  - mucocutaneous (American) 085.5
  - naso-oral 085.5
  - nasopharyngeal 085.5
  - Old World 085.1
  - tegumentaria diffusa 085.4
  - vaccination, prophylactic (against) V05.2
  - visceral (Indian) 085.0
- **Leishmanoid, dermal** — *see also* Leishmaniasis, cutaneous
  - post kala-azar 085.0

- **Lesion▶(s)◀** — *continued*
  - spinal cord — *continued*
    - traumatic (*see also* Injury, spinal, by site) — *continued*
      - with — *continued*
        - broken — *continued*
          - neck — *see* Fracture, vertebra, cervical, with spinal cord injury
        - fracture, vertebra — *see* Fracture, vertebra, by site, with spinal cord injury
  - spleen 289.50
  - stomach 537.89
  - superior glenoid labrum (SLAP) 840.7
  - syphilitic — *see* Syphilis
  - tertiary — *see* Syphilis, tertiary
  - thoracic root (nerve) 353.3
  - tonsillar fossa 474.9
  - tooth, teeth 525.8
    - white spot 521.01
  - traumatic NEC (*see also* nature and site of injury) 959.9
  - tricuspid (valve) — *see* Endocarditis, tricuspid
  - trigeminal nerve 350.9
  - ulcerated or ulcerative — *see* Ulcer
  - uterus NEC 621.9
  - vagina 623.8
  - vagus nerve 352.3
  - valvular — *see* Endocarditis
  - vascular 459.9
    - affecting central nervous system (*see also* Lesion, cerebrovascular) 437.9
    - following trauma (*see also* Injury, blood vessel, by site) 904.9
    - retina 362.17
    - traumatic — *see* Injury, blood vessel, by site
    - umbilical cord 663.6 ☑
      - affecting fetus or newborn 762.6
  - visual
    - cortex NEC (*see also* Disorder, visual, cortex) 377.73
    - pathway NEC (*see also* Disorder, visual, pathway) 377.63
  - warty — *see* Verruca
  - white spot, on teeth 521.01
  - x-ray NEC 990
- **Lethargic** — *see* condition
- **Lethargy** 780.79
- **Letterer-Siwe disease** (acute histiocytosis X) (M9722/3) 202.5 ☑
- **Leucinosis** 270.3
- **Leucocoria** 360.44
- **Leucosarcoma** (M9850/3) 207.8 ☑
- **Leukasmus** 270.2
- **Leukemia, leukemic** (congenital) (M9800/3) 208.9 ☑

> *Note — Use the following fifth-digit subclassification for categories 203–208:*
>
> 0 *without mention of remission*
>
> 1 *with remission*

  - acute NEC (M9801/3) 208.0 ☑
  - aleukemic NEC (M9804/3) 208.8 ☑
    - granulocytic (M9864/3) 205.8 ☑
  - basophilic (M9870/3) 205.1 ☑
  - blast (cell) (M9801/3) 208.0 ☑
  - blastic (M9801/3) 208.0 ☑
    - granulocytic (M9861/3) 205.0 ☑
  - chronic NEC (M9803/3) 208.1 ☑
  - compound (M9810/3) 207.8 ☑
  - eosinophilic (M9880/3) 205.1 ☑
  - giant cell (M9910/3) 207.2 ☑
  - granulocytic (M9860/3) 205.9 ☑
    - acute (M9861/3) 205.0 ☑
    - aleukemic (M9864/3) 205.8 ☑
    - blastic (M9861/3) 205.0 ☑
    - chronic (M9863/3) 205.1 ☑
    - subacute (M9862/3) 205.2 ☑
    - subleukemic (M9864/3) 205.8 ☑

- **Leukemia, leukemic** — *continued*
  - hairy cell (M9940/3) 202.4 ☑
  - hemoblastic (M9801/3) 208.0 ☑
  - histiocytic (M9890/3) 206.9 ☑
  - lymphatic (M9820/3) 204.9 ☑
    - acute (M9821/3) 204.0 ☑
    - aleukemic (M9824/3) 204.8 ☑
    - chronic (M9823/3) 204.1 ☑
    - subacute (M9822/3) 204.2 ☑
    - subleukemic (M9824/3) 204.8 ☑
  - lymphoblastic (M9821/3) 204.0 ☑
  - lymphocytic (M9820/3) 204.9 ☑
    - acute (M9821/3) 204.0 ☑
    - aleukemic (M9824/3) 204.8 ☑
    - chronic (M9823/3) 204.1 ☑
    - subacute (M9822/3) 204.2 ☑
    - subleukemic (M9824/3) 204.8 ☑
  - lymphogenous (M9820/3) — *see* Leukemia, lymphoid
  - lymphoid (M9820/3) 204.9 ☑
    - acute (M9821/3) 204.0 ☑
    - aleukemic (M9824/3) 204.8 ☑
    - blastic (M9821/3) 204.0 ☑
    - chronic (M9823/3) 204.1 ☑
    - subacute (M9822/3) 204.2 ☑
    - subleukemic (M9824/3) 204.8 ☑
  - lymphosarcoma cell (M9850/3) 207.8 ☑
  - mast cell (M9900/3) 207.8 ☑
  - megakaryocytic (M9910/3) 207.2 ☑
  - megakaryocytoid (M9910/3) 207.2 ☑
  - mixed (cell) (M9810/3) 207.8 ☑
  - monoblastic (M9891/3) 206.0 ☑
  - monocytic (Schilling-type) (M9890/3) 206.9 ☑
    - acute (M9891/3) 206.0 ☑
    - aleukemic (M9894/3) 206.8 ☑
    - chronic (M9893/3) 206.1 ☑
    - Naegeli-type (M9863/3) 205.1 ☑
    - subacute (M9892/3) 206.2 ☑
    - subleukemic (M9894/3) 206.8 ☑
  - monocytoid (M9890/3) 206.9 ☑
    - acute (M9891/3) 206.0 ☑
    - aleukemic (M9894/3) 206.8 ☑
    - chronic (M9893/3) 206.1 ☑
    - myelogenous (M9863/3) 205.1 ☑
    - subacute (M9892/3) 206.2 ☑
    - subleukemic (M9894/3) 206.8 ☑
  - monomyelocytic (M9860/3) — *see* Leukemia, myelomonocytic
  - myeloblastic (M9861/3) 205.0 ☑
  - myelocytic (M9863/3) 205.1 ☑
    - acute (M9861/3) 205.0 ☑
  - myelogenous (M9860/3) 205.9 ☑
    - acute (M9861/3) 205.0 ☑
    - aleukemic (M9864/3) 205.8 ☑
    - chronic (M9863/3) 205.1 ☑
    - monocytoid (M9863/3) 205.1 ☑
    - subacute (M9862/3) 205.2 ☑
    - subleukemic (M9864) 205.8 ☑
  - myeloid (M9860/3) 205.9 ☑
    - acute (M9861/3) 205.0 ☑
    - aleukemic (M9864/3) 205.8 ☑
    - chronic (M9863/3) 205.1 ☑
    - subacute (M9862/3) 205.2 ☑
    - subleukemic (M9864/3) 205.8 ☑
  - myelomonocytic (M9860/3) 205.9 ☑
    - acute (M9861/3) 205.0 ☑
    - chronic (M9863/3) 205.1 ☑
  - Naegeli-type monocytic (M9863/3) 205.1 ☑
  - neutrophilic (M9865/3) 205.1 ☑
  - plasma cell (M9830/3) 203.1 ☑
  - plasmacytic (M9830/3) 203.1 ☑
  - prolymphocytic (M9825/3) — *see* Leukemia, lymphoid
  - promyelocytic, acute (M9866/3) 205.0 ☑
  - Schilling-type monocytic (M9890/3) — *see* Leukemia, monocytic
  - stem cell (M9801/3) 208.0 ☑
  - subacute NEC (M9802/3) 208.2 ☑
  - subleukemic NEC (M9804/3) 208.8 ☑
  - thrombocytic (M9910/3) 207.2 ☑
  - undifferentiated (M9801/3) 208.0 ☑
- **Leukemoid reaction** ▶(basophilic)◀ (lymphocytic) (monocytic) (myelocytic) ▶(neutrophilic)◀ 288.62 ▲
- **Leukoclastic vasculitis** 446.29
- **Leukocoria** 360.44
- **Leukocythemia** — *see* Leukemia
- **Leukocytopenia** 288.50 ●
- **Leukocytosis** 288.60 ▲
  - basophilic 288.8
  - eosinophilic 288.3
  - lymphocytic 288.8
  - monocytic 288.8
  - neutrophilic 288.8
- **Leukoderma** 709.09
  - syphilitic 091.3
    - late 095.8
- **Leukodermia** — *see also* Leukoderma 709.09
- **Leukodystrophy** (cerebral) (globoid cell) (metachromatic) (progressive) (sudanophilic) 330.0
- **Leukoedema, mouth or tongue** 528.79
- **Leukoencephalitis**
  - acute hemorrhagic (postinfectious) NEC 136.9 *[323.61]* ▲
    - postimmunization or postvaccinal 323.51 ▲
  - subacute sclerosing 046.2
    - van Bogaert's 046.2
  - van Bogaert's (sclerosing) 046.2
- **Leukoencephalopathy** — *see also* Encephalitis 323.9
  - acute necrotizing hemorrhagic (postinfectious) 136.9 *[323.61]* ▲
    - postimmunization or postvaccinal 323.51 ▲
  - metachromatic 330.0
  - multifocal (progressive) 046.3
  - progressive multifocal 046.3
- **Leukoerythroblastosis** 289.9 ▲
- **Leukoerythrosis** 289.0
- **Leukokeratosis** — *see also* Leukoplakia 702.8
  - mouth 528.6
  - nicotina palati 528.79
  - tongue 528.6
- **Leukokoria** 360.44
- **Leukokraurosis vulva, vulvae** 624.0
- **Leukolymphosarcoma** (M9850/3) 207.8 ☑
- **Leukoma** (cornea) (interfering with central vision) 371.03
  - adherent 371.04
- **Leukomalacia, periventricular** 779.7
- **Leukomelanopathy, hereditary** 288.2
- **Leukonychia** (punctata) (striata) 703.8
  - congenital 757.5
- **Leukopathia**
  - unguium 703.8
    - congenital 757.5
- **Leukopenia** 288.50 ▲
  - basophilic 288.59 ●
  - cyclic 288.02 ▲
  - eosinophilic 288.59 ●
  - familial 288.59 ▲
  - malignant ▶(*see also* Agranulocytosis)◀ 288.09 ▲
  - periodic 288.02 ▲
  - transitory neonatal 776.7
- **Leukopenic** — *see* condition
- **Leukoplakia** 702.8
  - anus 569.49
  - bladder (postinfectional) 596.8
  - buccal 528.6
  - cervix (uteri) 622.2
  - esophagus 530.83
  - gingiva 528.6
  - kidney (pelvis) 593.89
  - larynx 478.79
  - lip 528.6
  - mouth 528.6
  - oral soft tissue (including tongue) (mucosa) 528.6

- **Leukoplakia** — *continued*
  - palate 528.6
  - pelvis (kidney) 593.89
  - penis (infectional) 607.0
  - rectum 569.49
  - syphilitic 095.8
  - tongue 528.6
  - tonsil 478.29
  - ureter (postinfectional) 593.89
  - urethra (postinfectional) 599.84
  - uterus 621.8
  - vagina 623.1
  - vesical 596.8
  - vocal cords 478.5
  - vulva 624.0
- **Leukopolioencephalopathy** 330.0
- **Leukorrhea** (vagina) 623.5
  - due to trichomonas (vaginalis) 131.00
  - trichomonal (Trichomonas vaginalis) 131.00
- **Leukosarcoma** (M9850/3) 207.8 ☑
- **Leukosis** (M9800/3) — *see* Leukemia
- **Lev's disease or syndrome** (acquired complete heart block) 426.0
- **Levi's syndrome** (pituitary dwarfism) 253.3
- **Levocardia** (isolated) 746.87
  - with situs inversus 759.3
- **Levulosuria** 271.2
- **Lewandowski's disease** (primary) — *see also* Tuberculosis 017.0 ☑
- **Lewandowski-Lutz disease** (epidermodysplasia verruciformis) 078.19
- **Lewy body dementia** 331.82
- **Lewy body disease** 331.82
- **Leyden's disease** (periodic vomiting) 536.2
- **Leyden-Möbius dystrophy** 359.1
- **Leydig cell**
  - carcinoma (M8650/3)
    - specified site — *see* Neoplasm, by site, malignant
    - unspecified site
      - female 183.0
      - male 186.9
  - tumor (M8650/1)
    - benign (M8650/0)
      - specified site — *see* Neoplasm, by site, benign
      - unspecified site
        - female 220
        - male 222.0
    - malignant (M8650/3)
      - specified site — *see* Neoplasm, by site, malignant
      - unspecified site
        - female 183.0
        - male 186.9
    - specified site — *see* Neoplasm, by site, uncertain behavior
    - unspecified site
      - female 236.2
      - male 236.4
- **Leydig-Sertoli cell tumor** (M8631/0)
  - specified site — *see* Neoplasm, by site, benign
  - unspecified site
    - female 220
    - male 222.0
- **LGSIL** (low grade squamous intraepithelial lesion) 795.03
- **Liar, pathologic** 301.7
- **Libman-Sacks disease or syndrome** 710.0 *[424.91]*
- **Lice** (infestation) 132.9
  - body (pediculus corporis) 132.1
  - crab 132.2
  - head (pediculus capitis) 132.0
  - mixed (classifiable to more than one of the categories 132.0–132.2) 132.3
  - pubic (pediculus pubis) 132.2
- **Lichen** 697.9
  - albus 701.0
  - annularis 695.89
  - atrophicus 701.0

- **Lyell's disease or syndrome** (toxic epidermal necrolysis) 695.1
  - due to drug
    - correct substance properly administered 695.1
    - overdose or wrong substance given or taken 977.9
      - specified drug — *see* Table of Drugs and Chemicals
- **Lyme disease** 088.81
- **Lymph**
  - gland or node — *see* condition
  - scrotum (*see also* Infestation, filarial) 125.9
- **Lymphadenitis** 289.3
  - with
    - abortion — *see* Abortion, by type, with sepsis
    - ectopic pregnancy (*see also* categories 633.0–633.9) 639.0
    - molar pregnancy (*see also* categories 630–632) 639.0
  - acute 683
    - mesenteric 289.2
  - any site, except mesenteric 289.3
    - acute 683
    - chronic 289.1
    - mesenteric (acute) (chronic) (nonspecific) (subacute) 289.2
    - subacute 289.1
      - mesenteric 289.2
  - breast, puerperal, postpartum 675.2 ☑
  - chancroidal (congenital) 099.0
  - chronic 289.1
    - mesenteric 289.2
  - dermatopathic 695.89
  - due to
    - anthracosis (occupational) 500
    - Brugia (Wuchereria) malayi 125.1
    - diphtheria (toxin) 032.89
    - lymphogranuloma venereum 099.1
    - Wuchereria bancrofti 125.0
  - following
    - abortion 639.0
    - ectopic or molar pregnancy 639.0
  - generalized 289.3
  - gonorrheal 098.89
  - granulomatous 289.1
  - infectional 683
  - mesenteric (acute) (chronic) (nonspecific) (subacute) 289.2
    - due to Bacillus typhi 002.0
    - tuberculous (*see also* Tuberculosis) 014.8 ☑
  - mycobacterial 031.8
  - purulent 683
  - pyogenic 683
  - regional 078.3
  - septic 683
  - streptococcal 683
  - subacute, unspecified site 289.1
  - suppurative 683
  - syphilitic (early) (secondary) 091.4
    - late 095.8
  - tuberculous — *see* Tuberculosis, lymph gland
  - venereal 099.1
- **Lymphadenoid goiter** 245.2
- **Lymphadenopathy** (general) 785.6
  - due to toxoplasmosis (acquired) 130.7
    - congenital (active) 771.2
- **Lymphadenopathy-associated virus** (disease) (illness) (infection) — *see* Human immunodeficiency virus (disease) (illness) (infection)
- **Lymphadenosis** 785.6
  - acute 075
- **Lymphangiectasis** 457.1
  - conjunctiva 372.89
  - postinfectional 457.1
  - scrotum 457.1
- **Lymphangiectatic elephantiasis, nonfilarial** 457.1
- **Lymphangioendothelioma** (M9170/0) 228.1
- **Lymphangioendothelioma** — *continued*
  - malignant (M9170/3) — *see* Neoplasm, connective tissue, malignant
- **Lymphangioma** (M9170/0) 228.1
  - capillary (M9171/0) 228.1
  - cavernous (M9172/0) 228.1
  - cystic (M9173/0) 228.1
  - malignant (M9170/3) — *see* Neoplasm, connective tissue, malignant
- **Lymphangiomyoma** (M9174/0) 228.1
- **Lymphangiomyomatosis** (M9174/1) — *see* Neoplasm, connective tissue, uncertain behavior
- **Lymphangiosarcoma** (M9170/3) — *see* Neoplasm, connective tissue, malignant
- **Lymphangitis** 457.2
  - with
    - abortion — *see* Abortion, by type, with sepsis
    - abscess — *see* Abscess, by site
    - cellulitis — *see* Abscess, by site
    - ectopic pregnancy (*see also* categories 633.0–633.9) 639.0
    - molar pregnancy (*see also* categories 630–632) 639.0
  - acute (with abscess or cellulitis) 682.9
    - specified site — *see* Abscess, by site
  - breast, puerperal, postpartum 675.2 ☑
  - chancroidal 099.0
  - chronic (any site) 457.2
  - due to
    - Brugia (Wuchereria) malayi 125.1
    - Wuchereria bancrofti 125.0
  - following
    - abortion 639.0
    - ectopic or molar pregnancy 639.0
  - gangrenous 457.2
  - penis
    - acute 607.2
    - gonococcal (acute) 098.0
      - chronic or duration of 2 months or more 098.2
  - puerperal, postpartum, childbirth 670.0 ☑
  - strumous, tuberculous (*see also* Tuberculosis) 017.2 ☑
  - subacute (any site) 457.2
  - tuberculous — *see* Tuberculosis, lymph gland
- **Lymphatic** (vessel) — *see* condition
- **Lymphatism** 254.8
  - scrofulous (*see also* Tuberculosis) 017.2 ☑
- **Lymphectasia** 457.1
- **Lymphedema** — *see also* Elephantiasis 457.1
  - acquired (chronic) 457.1
  - chronic hereditary 757.0
  - congenital 757.0
  - idiopathic hereditary 757.0
  - praecox 457.1
  - secondary 457.1
  - surgical NEC 997.99
    - postmastectomy (syndrome) 457.0
- **Lymph-hemangioma** (M9120/0) — *see* Hemangioma, by site
- **Lymphoblastic** — *see* condition
- **Lymphoblastoma** (diffuse) (M9630/3) 200.1 ☑
  - giant follicular (M9690/3) 202.0 ☑
  - macrofollicular (M9690/3) 202.0 ☑
- **Lymphoblastosis, acute benign** 075
- **Lymphocele** 457.8
- **Lymphocythemia** 288.51 ▲
- **Lymphocytic** — *see also* condition
  - chorioencephalitis (acute) (serous) 049.0
  - choriomeningitis (acute) (serous) 049.0
- **Lymphocytoma** (diffuse) (malignant) (M9620/3) 200.1 ☑
- **Lymphocytomatosis** (M9620/3) 200.1 ☑
- **Lymphocytopenia** 288.51 ▲
- **Lymphocytosis** (symptomatic) 288.61 ▲
  - infectious (acute) 078.89
- **Lymphoepithelioma** (M8082/3) — *see* Neoplasm, by site, malignant
- **Lymphogranuloma** (malignant) (M9650/3) 201.9 ☑
  - inguinale 099.1
  - venereal (any site) 099.1
    - with stricture of rectum 099.1
  - venereum 099.1
- **Lymphogranulomatosis** (malignant) (M9650/3) 201.9 ☑
  - benign (Boeck's sarcoid) (Schaumann's) 135
  - Hodgkin's (M9650/3) 201.9 ☑
- **Lymphohistiocytosis, familial hemophagocytic** 288.4 ●
- **Lymphoid** — *see* condition
- **Lympholeukoblastoma** (M9850/3) 207.8 ☑
- **Lympholeukosarcoma** (M9850/3) 207.8 ☑
- **Lymphoma** (malignant) (M9590/3) 202.8 ☑

> *Note — Use the following fifth-digit subclassification with categories 200–202:*
>
> 0 *unspecified site, extranodal and solid organ sites*
>
> 1 *lymph nodes of head, face, and neck*
>
> 2 *intrathoracic lymph nodes*
>
> 3 *intra-abdominal lymph nodes*
>
> 4 *lymph nodes of axilla and upper limb*
>
> 5 *lymph nodes of inguinal region and lower limb*
>
> 6 *intrapelvic lymph nodes*
>
> 7 *spleen*
>
> 8 *lymph nodes of multiple sites*

  - benign (M9590/0) — *see* Neoplasm, by site, benign
  - Burkitt's type (lymphoblastic) (undifferentiated) (M9750/3) 200.2 ☑
  - Castleman's (mediastinal lymph node hyperplasia) 785.6
  - centroblastic-centrocytic
    - diffuse (M9614/3) 202.8 ☑
    - follicular (M9692/3) 202.0 ☑
  - centroblastic type (diffuse) (M9632/3) 202.8 ☑
    - follicular (M9697/3) 202.0 ☑
  - centrocytic (M9622/3) 202.8 ☑
  - compound (M9613/3) 200.8 ☑
  - convoluted cell type (lymphoblastic) (M9602/3) 202.8 ☑
  - diffuse NEC (M9590/3) 202.8 ☑
  - follicular (giant) (M9690/3) 202.0 ☑
    - center cell (diffuse) (M9615/3) 202.8 ☑
      - cleaved (diffuse) (M9623/3) 202.8 ☑
        - follicular (M9695/3) 202.0 ☑
      - non-cleaved (diffuse) (M9633/3) 202.8 ☑
        - follicular (M9698/3) 202.0 ☑
    - centroblastic-centrocytic (M9692/3) 202.0 ☑
    - centroblastic type (M9697/3) 202.0 ☑
    - lymphocytic
      - intermediate differentiation (M9694/3) 202.0 ☑
      - poorly differentiated (M9696/3) 202.0 ☑
- **Lymphoma** — *continued*
  - follicular — *continued*
    - mixed (cell type) (lymphocytic-histiocytic) (small cell and large cell) (M9691/3) 202.0 ☑
  - germinocytic (M9622/3) 202.8 ☑
  - giant, follicular or follicle (M9690/3) 202.0 ☑
  - histiocytic (diffuse) (M9640/3) 200.0 ☑
    - nodular (M9642/3) 200.0 ☑
    - pleomorphic cell type (M9641/3) 200.0 ☑
  - Hodgkin's (M9650/3) (*see also* Disease, Hodgkin's) 201.9 ☑
  - immunoblastic (type) (M9612/3) 200.8 ☑
  - large cell (M9640/3) 200.0 ☑
    - nodular (M9642/3) 200.0 ☑
    - pleomorphic cell type (M9641/3) 200.0 ☑
  - lymphoblastic (diffuse) (M9630/3) 200.1 ☑
    - Burkitt's type (M9750/3) 200.2 ☑
    - convoluted cell type (M9602/3) 202.8 ☑
  - lymphocytic (cell type) (diffuse) (M9620/3) 200.1 ☑
    - with plasmacytoid differentiation, diffuse (M9611/3) 200.8 ☑
    - intermediate differentiation (diffuse) (M9621/3) 200.1 ☑
      - follicular (M9694/3) 202.0 ☑
      - nodular (M9694/3) 202.0 ☑
    - nodular (M9690/3) 202.0 ☑
    - poorly differentiated (diffuse) (M9630/3) 200.1 ☑
      - follicular (M9696/3) 202.0 ☑
      - nodular (M9696/3) 202.0 ☑
    - well differentiated (diffuse) (M9620/3) 200.1 ☑
      - follicular (M9693/3) 202.0 ☑
      - nodular (M9693/3) 202.0 ☑
  - lymphocytic-histiocytic, mixed (diffuse) (M9613/3) 200.8 ☑
    - follicular (M9691/3) 202.0 ☑
    - nodular (M9691/3) 202.0 ☑
  - lymphoplasmacytoid type (M9611/3) 200.8 ☑
  - lymphosarcoma type (M9610/3) 200.1 ☑
  - macrofollicular (M9690/3) 202.0 ☑
  - mixed cell type (diffuse) (M9613/3) 200.8 ☑
    - follicular (M9691/3) 202.0 ☑
    - nodular (M9691/3) 202.0 ☑
  - nodular (M9690/3) 202.0 ☑
    - histiocytic (M9642/3) 200.0 ☑
    - lymphocytic (M9690/3) 202.0 ☑
      - intermediate differentiation (M9694/3) 202.0 ☑
      - poorly differentiated (M9696/3) 202.0 ☑
    - mixed (cell type) (lymphocytic-histiocytic) (small cell and large cell) (M9691/3) 202.0 ☑
  - non-Hodgkin's type NEC (M9591/3) 202.8 ☑
  - reticulum cell (type) (M9640/3) 200.0 ☑
  - small cell and large cell, mixed (diffuse) (M9613/3) 200.8 ☑
    - follicular (M9691/3) 202.0 ☑
    - nodular (9691/3) 202.0 ☑
  - stem cell (type) (M9601/3) 202.8 ☑
  - T-cell 202.1 ☑
  - undifferentiated (cell type) (non-Burkitt's) (M9600/3) 202.8 ☑
    - Burkitt's type (M9750/3) 200.2 ☑
- **Lymphomatosis** (M9590/3) — *see also* Lymphoma
  - granulomatous 099.1
- **Lymphopathia**
  - venereum 099.1
  - veneris 099.1

- **Lymphopenia** 288.51 ▲
  - familial 279.2
- **Lymphoreticulosis, benign** (of inoculation) 078.3
- **Lymphorrhea** 457.8
- **Lymphosarcoma** (M9610/3) 200.1 ☑
  - diffuse (M9610/3) 200.1 ☑
    - with plasmacytoid differentiation (M9611/3) 200.8 ☑
    - lymphoplasmacytic (M9611/3) 200.8 ☑
  - follicular (giant) (M9690/3) 202.0 ☑
    - lymphoblastic (M9696/3) 202.0 ☑
    - lymphocytic, intermediate differentiation (M9694/3) 202.0 ☑
    - mixed cell type (M9691/3) 202.0 ☑
  - giant follicular (M9690/3) 202.0 ☑
  - Hodgkin's (M9650/3) 201.9 ☑
  - immunoblastic (M9612/3) 200.8 ☑
  - lymphoblastic (diffuse) (M9630/3) 200.1 ☑
    - follicular (M9696/3) 202.0 ☑
    - nodular (M9696/3) 202.0 ☑
  - lymphocytic (diffuse) (M9620/3) 200.1 ☑
    - intermediate differentiation (diffuse) (M9621/3) 200.1 ☑
      - follicular (M9694/3) 202.0 ☑
      - nodular (M9694/3) 202.0 ☑
  - mixed cell type (diffuse) (M9613/3) 200.8 ☑
    - follicular (M9691/3) 202.0 ☑
    - nodular (M9691/3) 202.0 ☑
  - nodular (M9690/3) 202.0 ☑
    - lymphoblastic (M9696/3) 202.0 ☑
    - lymphocytic, intermediate differentiation (M9694/3) 202.0 ☑
    - mixed cell type (M9691/3) 202.0 ☑
  - prolymphocytic (M9631/3) 200.1 ☑
  - reticulum cell (M9640/3) 200.0 ☑
- **Lymphostasis** 457.8
- **Lypemania** — *see also* Melancholia 296.2 ☑
- **Lyssa** 071

M

- **Macacus ear** 744.29
- **Maceration**
  - fetus (cause not stated) 779.9
  - wet feet, tropical (syndrome) 991.4
- **Machado-Joseph disease** 334.8
- **Machupo virus hemorrhagic fever** 078.7
- **Macleod's syndrome** (abnormal transradiancy, one lung) 492.8
- **Macrocephalia, macrocephaly** 756.0
- **Macrocheilia** (congenital) 744.81
- **Macrochilia** (congenital) 744.81
- **Macrocolon** (congenital) 751.3
- **Macrocornea** 743.41
  - associated with buphthalmos 743.22
- **Macrocytic** — *see* condition
- **Macrocytosis** 289.89
- **Macrodactylia, macrodactylism** (fingers) (thumbs) 755.57
  - toes 755.65
- **Macrodontia** 520.2
- **Macroencephaly** 742.4
- **Macrogenia** 524.05
- **Macrogenitosomia** (female) (male) (praecox) 255.2
- **Macrogingivae** 523.8
- **Macroglobulinemia** (essential) (idiopathic) (monoclonal) (primary) (syndrome) (Waldenström's) 273.3
- **Macroglossia** (congenital) 750.15
  - acquired 529.8
- **Macrognathia, macrognathism** (congenital) 524.00
  - mandibular 524.02
    - alveolar 524.72
  - maxillary 524.01
    - alveolar 524.71
- **Macrogyria** (congenital) 742.4
- **Macrohydrocephalus** — *see also* Hydrocephalus 331.4
- **Macromastia** — *see also* Hypertrophy, breast 611.1
- **Macrophage activation syndrome** 288.4 ●
- **Macropsia** 368.14
- **Macrosigmoid** 564.7
  - congenital 751.3
- **Macrospondylitis, acromegalic** 253.0
- **Macrostomia** (congenital) 744.83
- **Macrotia** (external ear) (congenital) 744.22
- **Macula**
  - cornea, corneal
    - congenital 743.43
      - interfering with vision 743.42
    - interfering with central vision 371.03
    - not interfering with central vision 371.02
  - degeneration (*see also* Degeneration, macula) 362.50
    - hereditary (*see also* Dystrophy, retina) 362.70
  - edema, cystoid 362.53
- **Maculae ceruleae** 132.1
- **Macules and papules** 709.8
- **Maculopathy, toxic** 362.55
- **Madarosis** 374.55
- **Madelung's**
  - deformity (radius) 755.54
  - disease (lipomatosis) 272.8
  - lipomatosis 272.8
- **Madness** — *see also* Psychosis 298.9
  - myxedema (acute) 293.0
    - subacute 293.1
- **Madura**
  - disease (actinomycotic) 039.9
    - mycotic 117.4
  - foot (actinomycotic) 039.4
    - mycotic 117.4
- **Maduromycosis** (actinomycotic) 039.9
  - mycotic 117.4
- **Maffucci's syndrome** (dyschondroplasia with hemangiomas) 756.4
- **Magenblase syndrome** 306.4
- **Main en griffe** (acquired) 736.06
  - congenital 755.59
- **Maintenance**
  - chemotherapy regimen or treatment V58.11
  - dialysis regimen or treatment
    - extracorporeal (renal) V56.0
    - peritoneal V56.8
    - renal V56.0
  - drug therapy or regimen
    - chemotherapy, antineoplastic V58.11
    - immunotherapy, antineoplastic V58.12
  - external fixation NEC V54.89
  - radiotherapy V58.0
  - traction NEC V54.89
- **Majocchi's**
  - disease (purpura annularis telangiectodes) 709.1
  - granuloma 110.6
- **Major** — *see* condition
- **Mal**
  - cerebral (idiopathic) (*see also* Epilepsy) 345.9 ☑
  - comital (*see also* Epilepsy) 345.9 ☑
  - de los pintos (*see also* Pinta) 103.9
  - de Meleda 757.39
  - de mer 994.6
  - lie — *see* Presentation, fetal
  - perforant (*see also* Ulcer, lower extremity) 707.15
- **Malabar itch** 110.9
  - beard 110.0
  - foot 110.4
  - scalp 110.0
- **Malabsorption** 579.9
  - calcium 579.8
  - carbohydrate 579.8
- **Malabsorption** — *continued*
  - disaccharide 271.3
  - drug-induced 579.8
  - due to bacterial overgrowth 579.8
  - fat 579.8
  - folate, congenital 281.2
  - galactose 271.1
  - glucose-galactose (congenital) 271.3
  - intestinal 579.9
  - isomaltose 271.3
  - lactose (hereditary) 271.3
  - methionine 270.4
  - monosaccharide 271.8
  - postgastrectomy 579.3
  - postsurgical 579.3
  - protein 579.8
  - sucrose (-isomaltose) (congenital) 271.3
  - syndrome 579.9
    - postgastrectomy 579.3
    - postsurgical 579.3
- **Malacia, bone** 268.2
  - juvenile (*see also* Rickets) 268.0
  - Kienböck's (juvenile) (lunate) (wrist) 732.3
    - adult 732.8
- **Malacoplakia**
  - bladder 596.8
  - colon 569.89
  - pelvis (kidney) 593.89
  - ureter 593.89
  - urethra 599.84
- **Malacosteon** 268.2
  - juvenile (*see also* Rickets) 268.0
- **Maladaptation** — *see* Maladjustment
- **Maladie de Roger** 745.4
- **Maladjustment**
  - conjugal V61.10
    - involving divorce or estrangement V61.0
  - educational V62.3
  - family V61.9
    - specified circumstance NEC V61.8
  - marital V61.10
    - involving divorce or estrangement V61.0
  - occupational V62.2
  - simple, adult (*see also* Reaction, adjustment) 309.9
  - situational acute (*see also* Reaction, adjustment) 309.9
  - social V62.4
- **Malaise** 780.79
- **Malakoplakia** — *see* Malacoplakia
- **Malaria, malarial** (fever) 084.6
  - algid 084.9
  - any type, with
    - algid malaria 084.9
    - blackwater fever 084.8
    - fever
      - blackwater 084.8
      - hemoglobinuric (bilious) 084.8
    - hemoglobinuria, malarial 084.8
    - hepatitis 084.9 *[573.2]*
    - nephrosis 084.9 *[581.81]*
    - pernicious complication NEC 084.9
      - cardiac 084.9
      - cerebral 084.9
  - cardiac 084.9
  - carrier (suspected) of V02.9
  - cerebral 084.9
  - complicating pregnancy, childbirth, or puerperium 647.4 ☑
  - congenital 771.2
  - congestion, congestive 084.6
    - brain 084.9
  - continued 084.0
  - estivo-autumnal 084.0
  - falciparum (malignant tertian) 084.0
  - hematinuria 084.8
  - hematuria 084.8
  - hemoglobinuria 084.8
  - hemorrhagic 084.6
  - induced (therapeutically) 084.7
    - accidental — *see* Malaria, by type
  - liver 084.9 *[573.2]*
- **Malaria, malarial** — *continued*
  - malariae (quartan) 084.2
  - malignant (tertian) 084.0
  - mixed infections 084.5
  - monkey 084.4
  - ovale 084.3
  - pernicious, acute 084.0
  - Plasmodium, P.
    - falciparum 084.0
    - malariae 084.2
    - ovale 084.3
    - vivax 084.1
  - quartan 084.2
  - quotidian 084.0
  - recurrent 084.6
    - induced (therapeutically) 084.7
      - accidental — *see* Malaria, by type
  - remittent 084.6
  - specified types NEC 084.4
  - spleen 084.6
  - subtertian 084.0
  - tertian (benign) 084.1
    - malignant 084.0
  - tropical 084.0
  - typhoid 084.6
  - vivax (benign tertian) 084.1
- **Malassez's disease** (testicular cyst) 608.89
- **Malassimilation** 579.9
- **Maldescent, testis** 752.51
- **Maldevelopment** — *see also* Anomaly, by site
  - brain 742.9
  - colon 751.5
  - hip (joint) 755.63
    - congenital dislocation (*see also* Dislocation, hip, congenital) 754.30
  - mastoid process 756.0
  - middle ear, except ossicles 744.03
    - ossicles 744.04
  - newborn (not malformation) 764.9 ☑
  - ossicles, ear 744.04
  - spine 756.10
  - toe 755.66
- **Male type pelvis** 755.69
  - with disproportion (fetopelvic) 653.2 ☑
    - affecting fetus or newborn 763.1
    - causing obstructed labor 660.1 ☑
      - affecting fetus or newborn 763.1
- **Malformation** (congenital) — *see also* Anomaly
  - bone 756.9
  - bursa 756.9
  - Chiari
    - type I 348.4
    - type II (*see also* Spina bifida) 741.0 ☑
    - type III 742.0
    - type IV 742.2
  - circulatory system NEC 747.9
    - specified type NEC 747.89
  - cochlea 744.05
  - digestive system NEC 751.9
    - lower 751.5
    - specified type NEC 751.8
    - upper 750.9
  - eye 743.9
  - gum 750.9
  - heart NEC 746.9
    - specified type NEC 746.89
    - valve 746.9
  - internal ear 744.05
  - joint NEC 755.9
    - specified type NEC 755.8
  - Mondini's (congenital) (malformation, cochlea) 744.05
  - muscle 756.9
  - nervous system (central) 742.9
  - pelvic organs or tissues
    - in pregnancy or childbirth 654.9 ☑
      - affecting fetus or newborn 763.89
      - causing obstructed labor 660.2 ☑

☑ Additional Digit Required — Refer to the Tabular List for Digit Selection

▽ Subterms under main terms may continue to next column or page

Melanoma (malignant) (M8720/3) 172.9

> *Note — Except where otherwise indicated, the morphological varieties of melanoma in the list below should be coded by site as for "Melanoma (malignant)". Internal sites should be coded to malignant neoplasm of those sites.*

- abdominal wall 172.5
- ala nasi 172.3
- amelanotic (M8730/3) — *see* Melanoma, by site
- ankle 172.7
- anus, anal 154.3
  - canal 154.2
- arm 172.6
- auditory canal (external) 172.2
- auricle (ear) 172.2
- auricular canal (external) 172.2
- axilla 172.5
- axillary fold 172.5
- back 172.5
- balloon cell (M8722/3) — *see* Melanoma, by site
- benign (M8720/0) — *see* Neoplasm, skin, benign
- breast (female) (male) 172.5
- brow 172.3
- buttock 172.5
- canthus (eye) 172.1
- cheek (external) 172.3
- chest wall 172.5
- chin 172.3
- choroid 190.6
- conjunctiva 190.3
- ear (external) 172.2
- epithelioid cell (M8771/3) (*see also* Melanoma, by site)
  - and spindle cell, mixed (M8775/3) — *see* Melanoma, by site
- external meatus (ear) 172.2
- eye 190.9
- eyebrow 172.3
- eyelid (lower) (upper) 172.1
- face NEC 172.3
- female genital organ (external) NEC 184.4
- finger 172.6
- flank 172.5
- foot 172.7
- forearm 172.6
- forehead 172.3
- foreskin 187.1
- gluteal region 172.5
- groin 172.5
- hand 172.6
- heel 172.7
- helix 172.2
- hip 172.7
- in
  - giant pigmented nevus (M8761/3) — *see* Melanoma, by site
  - Hutchinson's melanotic freckle (M8742/3) — *see* Melanoma, by site
  - junctional nevus (M8740/3) — *see* Melanoma, by site
  - precancerous melanosis (M8741/3) — *see* Melanoma, by site
- interscapular region 172.5
- iris 190.0
- jaw 172.3
- juvenile (M8770/0) — *see* Neoplasm, skin, benign
- knee 172.7
- labium
  - majus 184.1
  - minus 184.2
- lacrimal gland 190.2
- leg 172.7
- lip (lower) (upper) 172.0
- liver 197.7
- lower limb NEC 172.7
- male genital organ (external) NEC 187.9
- meatus, acoustic (external) 172.2
- meibomian gland 172.1

Melanoma — *continued*

- metastatic
  - of or from specified site — *see* Melanoma, by site
  - site not of skin — *see* Neoplasm, by site, malignant, secondary
  - to specified site — *see* Neoplasm, by site, malignant, secondary
  - unspecified site 172.9
- nail 172.9
  - finger 172.6
  - toe 172.7
- neck 172.4
- nodular (M8721/3) — *see* Melanoma, by site
- nose, external 172.3
- orbit 190.1
- penis 187.4
- perianal skin 172.5
- perineum 172.5
- pinna 172.2
- popliteal (fossa) (space) 172.7
- prepuce 187.1
- pubes 172.5
- pudendum 184.4
- retina 190.5
- scalp 172.4
- scrotum 187.7
- septum nasal (skin) 172.3
- shoulder 172.6
- skin NEC 172.8
- spindle cell (M8772/3) (*see also* Melanoma, by site)
  - type A (M8773/3) 190.0
  - type B (M8774/3) 190.0
- submammary fold 172.5
- superficial spreading (M8743/3) — *see* Melanoma, by site
- temple 172.3
- thigh 172.7
- toe 172.7
- trunk NEC 172.5
- umbilicus 172.5
- upper limb NEC 172.6
- vagina vault 184.0
- vulva 184.4

Melanoplakia 528.9

Melanosarcoma (M8720/3) — *see also* Melanoma

- epithelioid cell (M8771/3) — *see* Melanoma

Melanosis 709.09

- addisonian (primary adrenal insufficiency) 255.4
  - tuberculous (*see also* Tuberculosis) 017.6 ☑
- adrenal 255.4
- colon 569.89
- conjunctiva 372.55
  - congenital 743.49
- corii degenerativa 757.33
- cornea (presenile) (senile) 371.12
  - congenital 743.43
    - interfering with vision 743.42
- eye 372.55
  - congenital 743.49
- jute spinners' 709.09
- lenticularis progressiva 757.33
- liver 573.8
- precancerous (M8741/2) (*see also* Neoplasm, skin, in situ)
  - malignant melanoma in (M8741/3) — *see* Melanoma
- prenatal 743.43
  - interfering with vision 743.42
- Riehl's 709.09
- sclera 379.19
  - congenital 743.47
- suprarenal 255.4
- tar 709.09
- toxic 709.09

Melanuria 791.9

Melasma 709.09

- adrenal (gland) 255.4
- suprarenal (gland) 255.4

MELAS syndrome (mitochondrial encephalopathy, lactic acidosis and stroke-like episodes) 277.87

Melena 578.1

- due to
  - swallowed maternal blood 777.3
  - ulcer — *see* Ulcer, by site, with hemorrhage
- newborn 772.4
  - due to swallowed maternal blood 777.3

Meleney's

- gangrene (cutaneous) 686.09
- ulcer (chronic undermining) 686.09

Melioidosis 025

Melitensis, febris 023.0

Melitococcosis 023.0

Melkersson (-Rosenthal) syndrome 351.8

Mellitus, diabetes — *see* Diabetes

Melorheostosis (bone) (leri) 733.99

Meloschisis 744.83

Melotia 744.29

Membrana

- capsularis lentis posterior 743.39
- epipapillaris 743.57

Membranacea placenta — *see* Placenta, abnormal

Membranaceous uterus 621.8

Membrane, membranous — *see also* condition

- folds, congenital — *see* Web
- Jackson's 751.4
- over face (causing asphyxia), fetus or newborn 768.9
- premature rupture — *see* Rupture, membranes, premature
- pupillary 364.74
  - persistent 743.46
- retained (complicating delivery) (with hemorrhage) 666.2 ☑
  - without hemorrhage 667.1 ☑
- secondary (eye) 366.50
- unruptured (causing asphyxia) 768.9
- vitreous humor 379.25

Membranitis, fetal 658.4 ☑

- affecting fetus or newborn 762.7

Memory disturbance, loss or lack — *see also* Amnesia 780.93

- mild, following organic brain damage 310.1

Menadione (vitamin K) **deficiency** 269.0

Menarche, precocious 259.1

Mendacity, pathologic 301.7

Mendelson's syndrome (resulting from a procedure) 997.3

- obstetric 668.0 ☑

Mende's syndrome (ptosis-epicanthus) 270.2

Ménétrier's disease or syndrome (hypertrophic gastritis) 535.2 ☑

Ménière's disease, syndrome, or vertigo 386.00

- cochlear 386.02
- cochleovestibular 386.01
- inactive 386.04
- in remission 386.04
- vestibular 386.03

Meninges, meningeal — *see* condition

Meningioma (M9530/0) — *see also* Neoplasm, meninges, benign

- angioblastic (M9535/0) — *see* Neoplasm, meninges, benign
- angiomatous (M9534/0) — *see* Neoplasm, meninges, benign
- endotheliomatous (M9531/0) — *see* Neoplasm, meninges, benign
- fibroblastic (M9532/0) — *see* Neoplasm, meninges, benign
- fibrous (M9532/0) — *see* Neoplasm, meninges, benign
- hemangioblastic (M9535/0) — *see* Neoplasm, meninges, benign
- hemangiopericytic (M9536/0) — *see* Neoplasm, meninges, benign

Meningioma — *see also* Neoplasm, meninges, benign — *continued*

- malignant (M9530/3) — *see* Neoplasm, meninges, malignant
- meningiothelial (M9531/0) — *see* Neoplasm, meninges, benign
- meningotheliomatous (M9531/0) — *see* Neoplasm, meninges, benign
- mixed (M9537/0) — *see* Neoplasm, meninges, benign
- multiple (M9530/1) 237.6
- papillary (M9538/1) 237.6
- psammomatous (M9533/0) — *see* Neoplasm, meninges, benign
- syncytial (M9531/0) — *see* Neoplasm, meninges, benign
- transitional (M9537/0) — *see* Neoplasm, meninges, benign

Meningiomatosis (diffuse) (M9530/1) 237.6

Meningism — *see also* Meningismus 781.6

Meningismus (infectional) (pneumococcal) 781.6

- due to serum or vaccine 997.09 *[321.8]*
- influenzal NEC 487.8

Meningitis (basal) (basic) (basilar) (brain) (cerebral) (cervical) (congestive) (diffuse) (hemorrhagic) (infantile) (membranous) (metastatic) (nonspecific) (pontine) (progressive) (simple) (spinal) (subacute) (sympathetica) (toxic) 322.9

- abacterial NEC (*see also* Meningitis, aseptic) 047.9
- actinomycotic 039.8 *[320.7]*
- adenoviral 049.1
- Aerobacter aerogenes 320.82
  - anaerobes (cocci) (gram-negative) (gram-positive) (mixed) (NEC) 320.81
- arbovirus NEC 066.9 *[321.2]*
  - specified type NEC 066.8 *[321.2]*
- aseptic (acute) NEC 047.9
  - adenovirus 049.1
  - Coxsackie virus 047.0
  - due to
    - adenovirus 049.1
    - Coxsackie virus 047.0
    - ECHO virus 047.1
    - enterovirus 047.9
    - mumps 072.1
    - poliovirus (*see also* Poliomyelitis) 045.2 ☑ *[321.2]*
  - ECHO virus 047.1
  - herpes (simplex) virus 054.72
    - zoster 053.0
  - leptospiral 100.81
  - lymphocytic choriomeningitis 049.0
  - noninfective 322.0
- Bacillus pyocyaneus 320.89
- bacterial NEC 320.9
  - anaerobic 320.81
  - gram-negative 320.82
    - anaerobic 320.81
- Bacteroides (fragilis) (oralis) (melaninogenicus) 320.81
- cancerous (M8000/6) 198.4
- candidal 112.83
- carcinomatous (M8010/6) 198.4
- caseous (*see also* Tuberculosis, meninges) 013.0 ☑
- cerebrospinal (acute) (chronic) (diplococcal) (endemic) (epidemic) (fulminant) (infectious) (malignant) (meningococcal) (sporadic) 036.0
  - carrier (suspected) of V02.59
- chronic NEC 322.2
- clear cerebrospinal fluid NEC 322.0
- Clostridium (haemolyticum) (novyi) NEC 320.81
- coccidioidomycosis 114.2
- Coxsackie virus 047.0
- cryptococcal 117.5 *[321.0]*

☑ Additional Digit Required — Refer to the Tabular List for Digit Selection
Subterms under main terms may continue to next column or page
▶◀ Revised Text ● New Line ▲ Revised Code

☑ Additional Digit Required — Refer to the Tabular List for Digit Selection
▽ Subterms under main terms may continue to next column or page
▶◀ Revised Text ● New Line ▲ Revised Code

☑ Additional Digit Required — Refer to the Tabular List for Digit Selection

Subterms under main terms may continue to next column or page

- **Myocarditis** — *continued*
  - meningococcal 036.43
  - nonrheumatic, active 422.90
  - parenchymatous 422.90
  - pneumococcal (acute) (subacute) 422.92
  - rheumatic (chronic) (inactive) (with chorea) 398.0
    - active or acute 391.2
      - with chorea (acute) (rheumatic) (Sydenham's) 392.0
  - septic 422.92
  - specific (giant cell) (productive) 422.91
  - staphylococcal (acute) (subacute) 422.92
  - suppurative 422.92
  - syphilitic (chronic) 093.82
  - toxic 422.93
    - rheumatic (*see also* Myocarditis, acute rheumatic) 391.2
  - tuberculous (*see also* Tuberculosis) 017.9 ☑ *[422.0]*
  - typhoid 002.0 *[422.0]*
  - valvular — *see* Endocarditis
  - viral, except Coxsackie 422.91
    - Coxsackie 074.23
    - of newborn (Coxsackie) 074.23
- **Myocardium, myocardial** — *see* condition
- **Myocardosis** — *see also* Cardiomyopathy 425.4
- **Myoclonia** (essential) 333.2
  - epileptica 333.2
  - Friedrich's 333.2
  - massive 333.2
- **Myoclonic**
  - epilepsy, familial (progressive) 333.2
  - jerks 333.2
- **Myoclonus** (familial essential) (multifocal) (simplex) 333.2
  - with epilepsy and with ragged red fibers (MERRF syndrome) 277.87
  - facial 351.8
  - massive (infantile) 333.2
  - pharyngeal 478.29
- **Myodiastasis** 728.84
- **Myoendocarditis** — *see also* Endocarditis
  - acute or subacute 421.9
- **Myoepithelioma** (M8982/0) — *see* Neoplasm, by site, benign
- **Myofascitis** (acute) 729.1
  - low back 724.2
- **Myofibroma** (M8890/0) — *see also* Neoplasm, connective tissue, benign
  - uterus (cervix) (corpus) (*see also* Leiomyoma) 218.9
- **Myofibromatosis** ●
  - infantile 759.89 ●
- **Myofibrosis** 728.2
  - heart (*see also* Myocarditis) 429.0
  - humeroscapular region 726.2
  - scapulohumeral 726.2
- **Myofibrositis** — *see also* Myositis 729.1
  - scapulohumeral 726.2
- **Myogelosis** (occupational) 728.89
- **Myoglobinuria** 791.3
- **Myoglobulinuria, primary** 791.3
- **Myokymia** — *see also* Myoclonus
  - facial 351.8
- **Myolipoma** (M8860/0)
  - specified site — *see* Neoplasm, connective tissue, benign
  - unspecified site 223.0
- **Myoma** (M8895/0) — *see also* Neoplasm, connective tissue, benign
  - cervix (stump) (uterus) (*see also* Leiomyoma) 218.9
  - malignant (M8895/3) — *see* Neoplasm, connective tissue, malignant
  - prostate 600.20
- **Myoma** — *see also* Neoplasm, connective tissue, benign — *continued*
  - prostate — *continued*
    - with
      - other lower urinary tract symptoms (LUTS) 600.21 ●
      - urinary ●
        - obstruction 600.21 ●
        - retention 600.21 ●
  - uterus (cervix) (corpus) (*see also* Leiomyoma) 218.9
    - in pregnancy or childbirth 654.1 ☑
      - affecting fetus or newborn 763.89
      - causing obstructed labor 660.2 ☑
        - affecting fetus or newborn 763.1
- **Myomalacia** 728.9
  - cordis, heart (*see also* Degeneration, myocardial) 429.1
- **Myometritis** — *see also* Endometritis 615.9
- **Myometrium** — *see* condition
- **Myonecrosis, clostridial** 040.0
- **Myopathy** 359.9
  - alcoholic 359.4
  - amyloid 277.39 *[359.6]* ▲
  - benign, congenital 359.0
  - central core 359.0
  - centronuclear 359.0
  - congenital (benign) 359.0
  - critical illness 359.81
  - distal 359.1
  - due to drugs 359.4
  - endocrine 259.9 *[359.5]*
    - specified type NEC 259.8 *[359.5]*
  - extraocular muscles 376.82
  - facioscapulohumeral 359.1
  - in
    - Addison's disease 255.4 *[359.5]*
    - amyloidosis 277.39 *[359.6]* ▲
    - cretinism 243 *[359.5]*
    - Cushing's syndrome 255.0 *[359.5]*
    - disseminated lupus erythematosus 710.0 *[359.6]*
    - giant cell arteritis 446.5 *[359.6]*
    - hyperadrenocorticism NEC 255.3 *[359.5]*
    - hyperparathyroidism 252.01 *[359.5]*
    - hypopituitarism 253.2 *[359.5]*
    - hypothyroidism (*see also* Hypothyroidism) 244.9 *[359.5]*
    - malignant neoplasm NEC (M8000/3) 199.1 *[359.6]*
    - myxedema (*see also* Myxedema) 244.9 *[359.5]*
    - polyarteritis nodosa 446.0 *[359.6]*
    - rheumatoid arthritis 714.0 *[359.6]*
    - sarcoidosis 135 *[359.6]*
    - scleroderma 710.1 *[359.6]*
    - Sjögren's disease 710.2 *[359.6]*
    - thyrotoxicosis (*see also* Thyrotoxicosis) 242.9 ☑ *[359.5]*
  - inflammatory 359.89
  - intensive care (ICU) 359.81
  - limb-girdle 359.1
  - myotubular 359.0
  - necrotizing, acute 359.81
  - nemaline 359.0
  - ocular 359.1
  - oculopharyngeal 359.1
  - of critical illness 359.81
  - primary 359.89
  - progressive NEC 359.89
  - quadriplegic, acute 359.81
  - rod body 359.0
  - scapulohumeral 359.1
  - specified type NEC 359.89
  - toxic 359.4
- **Myopericarditis** — *see also* Pericarditis 423.9
- **Myopia** (axial) (congenital) (increased curvature or refraction, nucleus of lens) 367.1
  - degenerative, malignant 360.21
  - malignant 360.21
  - progressive high (degenerative) 360.21
- **Myosarcoma** (M8895/3) — *see* Neoplasm, connective tissue, malignant
- **Myosis** (persistent) 379.42
  - stromal (endolymphatic) (M8931/1) 236.0
- **Myositis** 729.1
  - clostridial 040.0
  - due to posture 729.1
  - epidemic 074.1
  - fibrosa or fibrous (chronic) 728.2
    - Volkmann's (complicating trauma) 958.6
  - infective 728.0
  - interstitial 728.81
  - multiple — *see* Polymyositis
  - occupational 729.1
  - orbital, chronic 376.12
  - ossificans 728.12
    - circumscribed 728.12
    - progressive 728.11
    - traumatic 728.12
  - progressive fibrosing 728.11
  - purulent 728.0
  - rheumatic 729.1
  - rheumatoid 729.1
  - suppurative 728.0
  - syphilitic 095.6
  - traumatic (old) 729.1
- **Myospasia impulsiva** 307.23
- **Myotonia** (acquisita) (intermittens) 728.85
  - atrophica 359.2
  - congenita 359.2
  - dystrophica 359.2
- **Myotonic pupil** 379.46
- **Myriapodiasis** 134.1
- **Myringitis**
  - with otitis media — *see* Otitis media
  - acute 384.00
    - specified type NEC 384.09
  - bullosa hemorrhagica 384.01
  - bullous 384.01
  - chronic 384.1
- **Mysophobia** 300.29
- **Mytilotoxism** 988.0
- **Myxadenitis labialis** 528.5
- **Myxedema** (adult) (idiocy) (infantile) (juvenile) (thyroid gland) — *see also* Hypothyroidism 244.9
  - circumscribed 242.9 ☑
  - congenital 243
  - cutis 701.8
  - localized (pretibial) 242.9 ☑
  - madness (acute) 293.0
    - subacute 293.1
  - papular 701.8
  - pituitary 244.8
  - postpartum 674.8 ☑
  - pretibial 242.9 ☑
  - primary 244.9
- **Myxochondrosarcoma** (M9220/3) — *see* Neoplasm, cartilage, malignant
- **Myxofibroma** (M8811/0) — *see also* Neoplasm, connective tissue, benign
  - odontogenic (M9320/0) 213.1
    - upper jaw (bone) 213.0
- **Myxofibrosarcoma** (M8811/3) — *see* Neoplasm, connective tissue, malignant
- **Myxolipoma** (M8852/0) — *see also* Lipoma, by site 214.9
- **Myxoliposarcoma** (M8852/3) — *see* Neoplasm, connective tissue, malignant
- **Myxoma** (M8840/0) — *see also* Neoplasm, connective tissue, benign
  - odontogenic (M9320/0) 213.1
    - upper jaw (bone) 213.0
- **Myxosarcoma** (M8840/3) — *see* Neoplasm, connective tissue, malignant

N

- **Naegeli's**
  - disease (hereditary hemorrhagic thrombasthenia) 287.1
  - leukemia, monocytic (M9863/3) 205.1 ☑
  - syndrome (incontinentia pigmenti) 757.33
- **Naffziger's syndrome** 353.0
- **Naga sore** — *see also* Ulcer, skin 707.9
- **Nägele's pelvis** 738.6
  - with disproportion (fetopelvic) 653.0 ☑
    - affecting fetus or newborn 763.1
    - causing obstructed labor 660.1 ☑
      - affecting fetus or newborn 763.1
- **Nager-de Reynier syndrome** (dysostosis mandibularis) 756.0
- **Nail** — *see also* condition
  - biting 307.9
  - patella syndrome (hereditary osteoonychodysplasia) 756.89
- **Nanism, nanosomia** — *see also* Dwarfism 259.4
  - hypophyseal 253.3
  - pituitary 253.3
  - renis, renalis 588.0
- **Nanukayami** 100.89
- **Napkin rash** 691.0
- **Narcissism** 301.81
- **Narcolepsy** 347.00
  - with cataplexy 347.01
  - in conditions classified elsewhere 347.10
    - with cataplexy 347.11
- **Narcosis**
  - carbon dioxide (respiratory) 786.09
  - due to drug
    - correct substance properly administered 780.09
    - overdose or wrong substance given or taken 977.9
      - specified drug — *see* Table of Drugs and Chemicals
- **Narcotism (chronic)** — *see also* Dependence 304.9 ☑
  - acute
    - correct substance properly administered 349.82
    - overdose or wrong substance given or taken 967.8
      - specified drug — *see* Table of Drugs and Chemicals
- **NARP** (ataxia and retinitis pigmentosa) 277.87
- **Narrow**
  - anterior chamber angle 365.02
  - pelvis (inlet) (outlet) — *see* Contraction, pelvis
- **Narrowing**
  - artery NEC 447.1
    - auditory, internal 433.8 ☑
    - basilar 433.0 ☑
      - with other precerebral artery 433.3 ☑
      - bilateral 433.3 ☑
    - carotid 433.1 ☑
      - with other precerebral artery 433.3 ☑
      - bilateral 433.3 ☑
    - cerebellar 433.8 ☑
    - choroidal 433.8 ☑
    - communicating posterior 433.8 ☑
    - coronary (*see also* Arteriosclerosis, coronary)
      - congenital 746.85
        - due to syphilis 090.5
    - hypophyseal 433.8 ☑
    - pontine 433.8 ☑
    - precerebral NEC 433.9 ☑
      - multiple or bilateral 433.3 ☑
      - specified NEC 433.8 ☑

	Malignant					
	Primary	Secondary	Ca in situ	Benign	Uncertain Behavior	Unspecified
Neoplasm, neoplastic	199.1	199.1	234.9	229.9	238.9	239.9

Notes — 1. The list below gives the code numbers for neoplasms by anatomical site. For each site there are six possible code numbers according to whether the neoplasm in question is malignant, benign, in situ, of uncertain behavior, or of unspecified nature. The description of the neoplasm will often indicate which of the six columns is appropriate; e.g., malignant melanoma of skin, benign fibroadenoma of breast, carcinoma in situ of cervix uteri.

Where such descriptors are not present, the remainder of the Index should be consulted where guidance is given to the appropriate column for each morphological (histological) variety listed; e.g., Mesonephroma — see Neoplasm, malignant; Embryoma — see also Neoplasm, uncertain behavior; Disease, Bowen's — see Neoplasm, skin, in situ. However, the guidance in the Index can be overridden if one of the descriptors mentioned above is present; e.g., malignant adenoma of colon is coded to 153.9 and not to 211.3 as the adjective "malignant" overrides the Index entry "Adenoma — see also Neoplasm, benign."

*2. Sites marked with the sign * (e.g., face NEC*) should be classified to malignant neoplasm of skin of these sites if the variety of neoplasm is a squamous cell carcinoma or an epidermoid carcinoma, and to benign neoplasm of skin of these sites if the variety of neoplasm is a papilloma (any type).*

	Primary	Secondary	Ca in situ	Benign	Uncertain Behavior	Unspecified
abdomen, abdominal	195.2	198.89	234.8	229.8	238.8	239.8
cavity	195.2	198.89	234.8	229.8	238.8	239.8
organ	195.2	198.89	234.8	229.8	238.8	239.8
viscera	195.2	198.89	234.8	229.8	238.8	239.8
wall	173.5	198.2	232.5	216.5	238.2	239.2
connective tissue	171.5	198.89	—	215.5	238.1	239.2
abdominopelvic	195.8	198.89	234.8	229.8	238.8	239.8
accessory sinus — *see* Neoplasm, sinus						
acoustic nerve	192.0	198.4	—	225.1	237.9	239.7
acromion (process)	170.4	198.5	—	213.4	238.0	239.2
adenoid (pharynx) (tissue)	147.1	198.89	230.0	210.7	235.1	239.0
adipose tissue (*see also* Neoplasm, connective tissue)	171.9	198.89	—	215.9	238.1	239.2
adnexa (uterine)	183.9	198.82	233.3	221.8	236.3	239.5
adrenal (cortex) (gland) (medulla)	194.0	198.7	234.8	227.0	237.2	239.7
ala nasi (external)	173.3	198.2	232.3	216.3	238.2	239.2
alimentary canal or tract NEC	159.9	197.8	230.9	211.9	235.5	239.0
alveolar	143.9	198.89	230.0	210.4	235.1	239.0
mucosa	143.9	198.89	230.0	210.4	235.1	239.0
lower	143.1	198.89	230.0	210.4	235.1	239.0
upper	143.0	198.89	230.0	210.4	235.1	239.0
ridge or process	170.1	198.5	—	213.1	238.0	239.2
carcinoma	143.9	—	—	—	—	—
lower	143.1	—	—	—	—	—
upper	143.0	—	—	—	—	—
lower	170.1	198.5	—	213.1	238.0	239.2
mucosa	143.9	198.89	230.0	210.4	235.1	239.0
lower	143.1	198.89	230.0	210.4	235.1	239.0
upper	143.0	198.89	230.0	210.4	235.1	239.0
upper	170.0	198.5	—	213.0	238.0	239.2
sulcus	145.1	198.89	230.0	210.4	235.1	239.0
alveolus	143.9	198.89	230.0	210.4	235.1	239.0
lower	143.1	198.89	230.0	210.4	235.1	239.0
upper	143.0	198.89	230.0	210.4	235.1	239.0
ampulla of Vater	156.2	197.8	230.8	211.5	235.3	239.0
ankle NEC*	195.5	198.89	232.7	229.8	238.8	239.8
anorectum, anorectal (junction)	154.8	197.5	230.7	211.4	235.2	239.0
antecubital fossa or space*	195.4	198.89	232.6	229.8	238.8	239.8
antrum (Highmore) (maxillary)	160.2	197.3	231.8	212.0	235.9	239.1
pyloric	151.2	197.8	230.2	211.1	235.2	239.0
tympanicum	160.1	197.3	231.8	212.0	235.9	239.1
anus, anal	154.3	197.5	230.6	211.4	235.5	239.0
canal	154.2	197.5	230.5	211.4	235.5	239.0
contiguous sites with rectosigmoid junction or rectum	154.8	—	—	—	—	—
margin	173.5	198.2	232.5	216.5	238.2	239.2
skin	173.5	198.2	232.5	216.5	238.2	239.2
sphincter	154.2	197.5	230.5	211.4	235.5	239.0
aorta (thoracic)	171.4	198.89	—	215.4	238.1	239.2

	Malignant					
	Primary	Secondary	Ca in situ	Benign	Uncertain Behavior	Unspecified
Neoplasm, neoplastic — *continued*						
aorta — *continued*						
abdominal	171.5	198.89	—	215.5	238.1	239.2
aortic body	194.6	198.89	—	227.6	237.3	239.7
aponeurosis	171.9	198.89	—	215.9	238.1	239.2
palmar	171.2	198.89	—	215.2	238.1	239.2
plantar	171.3	198.89	—	215.3	238.1	239.2
appendix	153.5	197.5	230.3	211.3	235.2	239.0
arachnoid (cerebral)	192.1	198.4	—	225.2	237.6	239.7
spinal	192.3	198.4	—	225.4	237.6	239.7
areola (female)	174.0	198.81	233.0	217	238.3	239.3
male	175.0	198.81	233.0	217	238.3	239.3
arm NEC*	195.4	198.89	232.6	229.8	238.8	239.8
artery — *see* Neoplasm, connective tissue						
aryepiglottic fold	148.2	198.89	230.0	210.8	235.1	239.0
hypopharyngeal aspect	148.2	198.89	230.0	210.8	235.1	239.0
laryngeal aspect	161.1	197.3	231.0	212.1	235.6	239.1
marginal zone	148.2	198.89	230.0	210.8	235.1	239.0
arytenoid (cartilage)	161.3	197.3	231.0	212.1	235.6	239.1
fold — *see* Neoplasm, aryepiglottic						
atlas	170.2	198.5	—	213.2	238.0	239.2
atrium, cardiac	164.1	198.89	—	212.7	238.8	239.8
auditory						
canal (external) (skin)	173.2	198.2	232.2	216.2	238.2	239.2
internal	160.1	197.3	231.8	212.0	235.9	239.1
nerve	192.0	198.4	—	225.1	237.9	239.7
tube	160.1	197.3	231.8	212.0	235.9	239.1
Eustachian	160.1	197.3	231.8	212.0	235.9	239.1
opening	147.2	198.89	230.0	210.7	235.1	239.0
auricle, ear	173.2	198.2	232.2	216.2	238.2	239.2
cartilage	171.0	198.89	—	215.0	238.1	239.2
auricular canal (external)	173.2	198.2	232.2	216.2	238.2	239.2
internal	160.1	197.3	231.8	212.0	235.9	239.1
autonomic nerve or nervous system NEC	171.9	198.89	—	215.9	238.1	239.2
axilla, axillary	195.1	198.89	234.8	229.8	238.8	239.8
fold	173.5	198.2	232.5	216.5	238.2	239.2
back NEC*	195.8	198.89	232.5	229.8	238.8	239.8
Bartholin's gland	184.1	198.82	233.3	221.2	236.3	239.5
basal ganglia	191.0	198.3	—	225.0	237.5	239.6
basis pedunculi	191.7	198.3	—	225.0	237.5	239.6
bile or biliary (tract)	156.9	197.8	230.8	211.5	235.3	239.0
canaliculi (biliferi) (intrahepatic)	155.1	197.8	230.8	211.5	235.3	239.0
canals, interlobular	155.1	197.8	230.8	211.5	235.3	239.0
contiguous sites	156.8	—	—	—	—	—
duct or passage (common) (cystic) (extrahepatic)	156.1	197.8	230.8	211.5	235.3	239.0
contiguous sites with gallbladder	156.8	—	—	—	—	—
interlobular	155.1	197.8	230.8	211.5	235.3	239.0
intrahepatic	155.1	197.8	230.8	211.5	235.3	239.0
and extrahepatic	156.9	197.8	230.8	211.5	235.3	239.0
bladder (urinary)	188.9	198.1	233.7	223.3	236.7	239.4
contiguous sites	188.8	—	—	—	—	—
dome	188.1	198.1	233.7	223.3	236.7	239.4
neck	188.5	198.1	233.7	223.3	236.7	239.4
orifice	188.9	198.1	233.7	223.3	236.7	239.4
ureteric	188.6	198.1	233.7	223.3	236.7	239.4
urethral	188.5	198.1	233.7	223.3	236.7	239.4
sphincter	188.8	198.1	233.7	223.3	236.7	239.4
trigone	188.0	198.1	233.7	223.3	236.7	239.4
urachus	188.7	—	233.7	223.3	236.7	239.4
wall	188.9	198.1	233.7	223.3	236.7	239.4
anterior	188.3	198.1	233.7	223.3	236.7	239.4
lateral	188.2	198.1	233.7	223.3	236.7	239.4
posterior	188.4	198.1	233.7	223.3	236.7	239.4
blood vessel — *see* Neoplasm, connective tissue						

☑ Additional Digit Required — Refer to the Tabular List for Digit Selection

Subterms under main terms may continue to next column or page

▶◀ Revised Text ● New Line ▲ Revised Code

	Malignant					
	Primary	Secondary	Ca in situ	Benign	Uncertain Behavior	Unspecified
Neoplasm, neoplastic — *continued*						
brain — *continued*						
tapetum	191.8	198.3	—	225.0	237.5	239.6
temporal lobe	191.2	198.3	—	225.0	237.5	239.6
thalamus	191.0	198.3	—	225.0	237.5	239.6
uncus	191.2	198.3	—	225.0	237.5	239.6
ventricle (floor)	191.5	198.3	—	225.0	237.5	239.6
branchial (cleft) (vestiges)	146.8	198.89	230.0	210.6	235.1	239.0
breast (connective tissue) (female) (glandular tissue) (soft parts)	174.9	198.81	233.0	217	238.3	239.3
areola	174.0	198.81	233.0	217	238.3	239.3
male	175.0	198.81	233.0	217	238.3	239.3
axillary tail	174.6	198.81	233.0	217	238.3	239.3
central portion	174.1	198.81	233.0	217	238.3	239.3
contiguous sites	174.8	—	—	—	—	—
ectopic sites	174.8	198.81	233.0	217	238.3	239.3
inner	174.8	198.81	233.0	217	238.3	239.3
lower	174.8	198.81	233.0	217	238.3	239.3
lower-inner quadrant	174.3	198.81	233.0	217	238.3	239.3
lower-outer quadrant	174.5	198.81	233.0	217	238.3	239.3
male	175.9	198.81	233.0	217	238.3	239.3
areola	175.0	198.81	233.0	217	238.3	239.3
ectopic tissue	175.9	198.81	233.0	217	238.3	239.3
nipple	175.0	198.81	233.0	217	238.3	239.3
mastectomy site (skin)	173.5	198.2	—	—	—	—
specified as breast tissue	174.8	198.81	—	—	—	—
midline	174.8	198.81	233.0	217	238.3	239.3
nipple	174.0	198.81	233.0	217	238.3	239.3
male	175.0	198.81	233.0	217	238.3	239.3
outer	174.8	198.81	233.0	217	238.3	239.3
skin	173.5	198.2	232.5	216.5	238.2	239.2
tail (axillary)	174.6	198.81	233.0	217	238.3	239.3
upper	174.8	198.81	233.0	217	238.3	239.3
upper-inner quadrant	174.2	198.81	233.0	217	238.3	239.3
upper-outer quadrant	174.4	198.81	233.0	217	238.3	239.3
broad ligament	183.3	198.82	233.3	221.0	236.3	239.5
bronchiogenic, bronchogenic (lung)	162.9	197.0	231.2	212.3	235.7	239.1
bronchiole	162.9	197.0	231.2	212.3	235.7	239.1
bronchus	162.9	197.0	231.2	212.3	235.7	239.1
carina	162.2	197.0	231.2	212.3	235.7	239.1
contiguous sites with lung or trachea	162.8	—	—	—	—	—
lower lobe of lung	162.5	197.0	231.2	212.3	235.7	239.1
main	162.2	197.0	231.2	212.3	235.7	239.1
middle lobe of lung	162.4	197.0	231.2	212.3	235.7	239.1
upper lobe of lung	162.3	197.0	231.2	212.3	235.7	239.1
brow	173.3	198.2	232.3	216.3	238.2	239.2
buccal (cavity)	145.9	198.89	230.0	210.4	235.1	239.0
commissure	145.0	198.89	230.0	210.4	235.1	239.0
groove (lower) (upper)	145.1	198.89	230.0	210.4	235.1	239.0
mucosa	145.0	198.89	230.0	210.4	235.1	239.0
sulcus (lower) (upper)	145.1	198.89	230.0	210.4	235.1	239.0
bulbourethral gland	189.3	198.1	233.9	223.81	236.99	239.5
bursa — *see* Neoplasm, connective tissue						
buttock NEC*	195.3	198.89	232.5	229.8	238.8	239.8
calf*	195.5	198.89	232.7	229.8	238.8	239.8
calvarium	170.0	198.5	—	213.0	238.0	239.2
calyx, renal	189.1	198.0	233.9	223.1	236.91	239.5
canal						
anal	154.2	197.5	230.5	211.4	235.5	239.0
auditory (external)	173.2	198.2	232.2	216.2	238.2	239.2
auricular (external)	173.2	198.2	232.2	216.2	238.2	239.2
canaliculi, biliary (biliferi) (intrahepatic)	155.1	197.8	230.8	211.5	235.3	239.0

	Malignant					
	Primary	Secondary	Ca in situ	Benign	Uncertain Behavior	Unspecified
Neoplasm, neoplastic — *continued*						
canthus (eye) (inner) (outer)	173.1	198.2	232.1	216.1	238.2	239.2
capillary — *see* Neoplasm, connective tissue						
caput coli	153.4	197.5	230.3	211.3	235.2	239.0
cardia (gastric)	151.0	197.8	230.2	211.1	235.2	239.0
cardiac orifice (stomach)	151.0	197.8	230.2	211.1	235.2	239.0
cardio-esophageal junction	151.0	197.8	230.2	211.1	235.2	239.0
cardio-esophagus	151.0	197.8	230.2	211.1	235.2	239.0
carina (bronchus)	162.2	197.0	231.2	212.3	235.7	239.1
carotid (artery)	171.0	198.89	—	215.0	238.1	239.2
body	194.5	198.89	—	227.5	237.3	239.7
carpus (any bone)	170.5	198.5	—	213.5	238.0	239.2
cartilage (articular) (joint) NEC (*see also* Neoplasm, bone)	170.9	198.5	—	213.9	238.0	239.2
arytenoid	161.3	197.3	231.0	212.1	235.6	239.1
auricular	171.0	198.89	—	215.0	238.1	239.2
bronchi	162.2	197.3	—	212.3	235.7	239.1
connective tissue — *see* Neoplasm, connective tissue						
costal	170.3	198.5	—	213.3	238.0	239.2
cricoid	161.3	197.3	231.0	212.1	235.6	239.1
cuneiform	161.3	197.3	231.0	212.1	235.6	239.1
ear (external)	171.0	198.89	—	215.0	238.1	239.2
ensiform	170.3	198.5	—	213.3	238.0	239.2
epiglottis	161.1	197.3	231.0	212.1	235.6	239.1
anterior surface	146.4	198.89	230.0	210.6	235.1	239.0
eyelid	171.0	198.89	—	215.0	238.1	239.2
intervertebral	170.2	198.5	—	213.2	238.0	239.2
larynx, laryngeal	161.3	197.3	231.0	212.1	235.6	239.1
nose, nasal	160.0	197.3	231.8	212.0	235.9	239.1
pinna	171.0	198.89	—	215.0	238.1	239.2
rib	170.3	198.5	—	213.3	238.0	239.2
semilunar (knee)	170.7	198.5	—	213.7	238.0	239.2
thyroid	161.3	197.3	231.0	212.1	235.6	239.1
trachea	162.0	197.3	231.1	212.2	235.7	239.1
cauda equina	192.2	198.3	—	225.3	237.5	239.7
cavity						
buccal	145.9	198.89	230.0	210.4	235.1	239.0
nasal	160.0	197.3	231.8	212.0	235.9	239.1
oral	145.9	198.89	230.0	210.4	235.1	239.0
peritoneal	158.9	197.6	—	211.8	235.4	239.0
tympanic	160.1	197.3	231.8	212.0	235.9	239.1
cecum	153.4	197.5	230.3	211.3	235.2	239.0
central						
nervous system — *see* Neoplasm, nervous system						
white matter	191.0	198.3	—	225.0	237.5	239.6
cerebellopontine (angle)	191.6	198.3	—	225.0	237.5	239.6
cerebellum, cerebellar	191.6	198.3	—	225.0	237.5	239.6
cerebrum, cerebral (cortex) (hemisphere) (white matter)	191.0	198.3	—	225.0	237.5	239.6
meninges	192.1	198.4	—	225.2	237.6	239.7
peduncle	191.7	198.3	—	225.0	237.5	239.6
ventricle (any)	191.5	198.3	—	225.0	237.5	239.6
cervical region	195.0	198.89	234.8	229.8	238.8	239.8
cervix (cervical) (uteri) (uterus)	180.9	198.82	233.1	219.0	236.0	239.5
canal	180.0	198.82	233.1	219.0	236.0	239.5
contiguous sites	180.8	—	—	—	—	—
endocervix (canal) (gland)	180.0	198.82	233.1	219.0	236.0	239.5
exocervix	180.1	198.82	233.1	219.0	236.0	239.5
external os	180.1	198.82	233.1	219.0	236.0	239.5
internal os	180.0	198.82	233.1	219.0	236.0	239.5
nabothian gland	180.0	198.82	233.1	219.0	236.0	239.5
squamocolumnar junction	180.8	198.82	233.1	219.0	236.0	239.5
stump	180.8	198.82	233.1	219.0	236.0	239.5

	Malignant					
	Primary	Secondary	Ca in situ	Benign	Uncertain Behavior	Unspecified
Neoplasm, neoplastic — *continued*						
cheek	195.0	198.89	234.8	229.8	238.8	239.8
external	173.3	198.2	232.3	216.3	238.2	239.2
inner aspect	145.0	198.89	230.0	210.4	235.1	239.0
internal	145.0	198.89	230.0	210.4	235.1	239.0
mucosa	145.0	198.89	230.0	210.4	235.1	239.0
chest (wall) NEC	195.1	198.89	234.8	229.8	238.8	239.8
chiasma opticum	192.0	198.4	—	225.1	237.9	239.7
chin	173.3	198.2	232.3	216.3	238.2	239.2
choana	147.3	198.89	230.0	210.7	235.1	239.0
cholangiole	155.1	197.8	230.8	211.5	235.3	239.0
choledochal duct	156.1	197.8	230.8	211.5	235.3	239.0
choroid	190.6	198.4	234.0	224.6	238.8	239.8
plexus	191.5	198.3	—	225.0	237.5	239.6
ciliary body	190.0	198.4	234.0	224.0	238.8	239.8
clavicle	170.3	198.5	—	213.3	238.0	239.2
clitoris	184.3	198.82	233.3	221.2	236.3	239.5
clivus	170.0	198.5	—	213.0	238.0	239.2
cloacogenic zone	154.8	197.5	230.7	211.4	235.5	239.0
coccygeal						
body or glomus	194.6	198.89	—	227.6	237.3	239.7
vertebra	170.6	198.5	—	213.6	238.0	239.2
coccyx	170.6	198.5	—	213.6	238.0	239.2
colon (*see also* Neoplasm, intestine, large) and rectum	154.0	197.5	230.4	211.4	235.2	239.0
columnella	173.3	198.2	232.3	216.3	238.2	239.2
column, spinal — *see* Neoplasm, spine						
commissure						
labial, lip	140.6	198.89	230.0	210.4	235.1	239.0
laryngeal	161.0	197.3	231.0	212.1	235.6	239.1
common (bile) duct	156.1	197.8	230.8	211.5	235.3	239.0
concha	173.2	198.2	232.2	216.2	238.2	239.2
nose	160.0	197.3	231.8	212.0	235.9	239.1
conjunctiva	190.3	198.4	234.0	224.3	238.8	239.8
connective tissue NEC	171.9	198.89	—	215.9	238.1	239.2

Note — For neoplasms of connective tissue (blood vessel, bursa, fascia, ligament, muscle, peripheral nerves, sympathetic and parasympathetic nerves and ganglia, synovia, tendon, etc.) or of morphological types that indicate connective tissue, code according to the list under "Neoplasm, connective tissue"; for sites that do not appear in this list, code to neoplasm of that site; e.g.,

liposarcoma, shoulder 171.2

leiomyosarcoma, stomach 151.9

neurofibroma, chest wall 215.4

Morphological types that indicate connective tissue appear in the proper place in the alphabetic index with the instruction "see Neoplasm, connective tissue..."

	Primary	Secondary	Ca in situ	Benign	Uncertain Behavior	Unspecified
abdomen	171.5	198.89	—	215.5	238.1	239.2
abdominal wall	171.5	198.89	—	215.5	238.1	239.2
ankle	171.3	198.89	—	215.3	238.1	239.2
antecubital fossa or space	171.2	198.89	—	215.2	238.1	239.2
arm	171.2	198.89	—	215.2	238.1	239.2
auricle (ear)	171.0	198.89	—	215.0	238.1	239.2
axilla	171.4	198.89	—	215.4	238.1	239.2
back	171.7	198.89	—	215.7	238.1	239.2
breast (female) (*see also* Neoplasm, breast)	174.9	198.81	233.0	217	238.3	239.3
male	175.9	198.81	233.0	217	238.3	239.3
buttock	171.6	198.89	—	215.6	238.1	239.2
calf	171.3	198.89	—	215.3	238.1	239.2
cervical region	171.0	198.89	—	215.0	238.1	239.2
cheek	171.0	198.89	—	215.0	238.1	239.2
chest (wall)	171.4	198.89	—	215.4	238.1	239.2
chin	171.0	198.89	—	215.0	238.1	239.2
contiguous sites	171.8	—	—	—	—	—
diaphragm	171.4	198.89	—	215.4	238.1	239.2
ear (external)	171.0	198.89	—	215.0	238.1	239.2
elbow	171.2	198.89	—	215.2	238.1	239.2
extrarectal	171.6	198.89	—	215.6	238.1	239.2
extremity	171.8	198.89	—	215.8	238.1	239.2
lower	171.3	198.89	—	215.3	238.1	239.2
upper	171.2	198.89	—	215.2	238.1	239.2

	Malignant					
	Primary	Secondary	Ca in situ	Benign	Uncertain Behavior	Unspecified
Neoplasm, neoplastic — *continued*						
connective tissue — *continued*						
eyelid	171.0	198.89	—	215.0	238.1	239.2
face	171.0	198.89	—	215.0	238.1	239.2
finger	171.2	198.89	—	215.2	238.1	239.2
flank	171.7	198.89	—	215.7	238.1	239.2
foot	171.3	198.89	—	215.3	238.1	239.2
forearm	171.2	198.89	—	215.2	238.1	239.2
forehead	171.0	198.89	—	215.0	238.1	239.2
gastric	171.5	198.89	—	215.5	238.1	—
gastrointestinal	171.5	198.89	—	215.5	238.1	—
gluteal region	171.6	198.89	—	215.6	238.1	239.2
great vessels NEC	171.4	198.89	—	215.4	238.1	239.2
groin	171.6	198.89	—	215.6	238.1	239.2
hand	171.2	198.89	—	215.2	238.1	239.2
head	171.0	198.89	—	215.0	238.1	239.2
heel	171.3	198.89	—	215.3	238.1	239.2
hip	171.3	198.89	—	215.3	238.1	239.2
hypochondrium	171.5	198.89	—	215.5	238.1	239.2
iliopsoas muscle	171.6	198.89	—	215.5	238.1	239.2
infraclavicular region	171.4	198.89	—	215.4	238.1	239.2
inguinal (canal) (region)	171.6	198.89	—	215.6	238.1	239.2
intestine	171.5	198.89	—	215.5	238.1	—
intrathoracic	171.4	198.89	—	215.4	238.1	239.2
ischorectal fossa	171.6	198.89	—	215.6	238.1	239.2
jaw	143.9	198.89	230.0	210.4	235.1	239.0
knee	171.3	198.89	—	215.3	238.1	239.2
leg	171.3	198.89	—	215.3	238.1	239.2
limb NEC	171.9	198.89	—	215.8	238.1	239.2
lower	171.3	198.89	—	215.3	238.1	239.2
upper	171.2	198.89	—	215.2	238.1	239.2
nates	171.6	198.89	—	215.6	238.1	239.2
neck	171.0	198.89	—	215.0	238.1	239.2
orbit	190.1	198.4	234.0	224.1	238.8	239.8
pararectal	171.6	198.89	—	215.6	238.1	239.2
para-urethral	171.6	198.89	—	215.6	238.1	239.2
paravaginal	171.6	198.89	—	215.6	238.1	239.2
pelvis (floor)	171.6	198.89	—	215.6	238.1	239.2
pelvo-abdominal	171.8	198.89	—	215.8	238.1	239.2
perineum	171.6	198.89	—	215.6	238.1	239.2
perirectal (tissue)	171.6	198.89	—	215.6	238.1	239.2
periurethral (tissue)	171.6	198.89	—	215.6	238.1	239.2
popliteal fossa or space	171.3	198.89	—	215.3	238.1	239.2
presacral	171.6	198.89	—	215.6	238.1	239.2
psoas muscle	171.5	198.89	—	215.5	238.1	239.2
pterygoid fossa	171.0	198.89	—	215.0	238.1	239.2
rectovaginal septum or wall	171.6	198.89	—	215.6	238.1	239.2
rectovesical	171.6	198.89	—	215.6	238.1	239.2
retroperitoneum	158.0	197.6	—	211.8	235.4	239.0
sacrococcygeal region	171.6	198.89	—	215.6	238.1	239.2
scalp	171.0	198.89	—	215.0	238.1	239.2
scapular region	171.4	198.89	—	215.4	238.1	239.2
shoulder	171.2	198.89	—	215.2	238.1	239.2
skin (dermis) NEC	173.9	198.2	232.9	216.9	238.2	239.2
stomach	171.5	198.89	—	215.5	238.1	—
submental	171.0	198.89	—	215.0	238.1	239.2
supraclavicular region	171.0	198.89	—	215.0	238.1	239.2
temple	171.0	198.89	—	215.0	238.1	239.2
temporal region	171.0	198.89	—	215.0	238.1	239.2
thigh	171.3	198.89	—	215.3	238.1	239.2
thoracic (duct) (wall)	171.4	198.89	—	215.4	238.1	239.2
thorax	171.4	198.89	—	215.4	238.1	239.2
thumb	171.2	198.89	—	215.2	238.1	239.2
toe	171.3	198.89	—	215.3	238.1	239.2
trunk	171.7	198.89	—	215.7	238.1	239.2
umbilicus	171.5	198.89	—	215.5	238.1	239.2
vesicorectal	171.6	198.89	—	215.6	238.1	239.2
wrist	171.2	198.89	—	215.2	238.1	239.2
conus medullaris	192.2	198.3	—	225.3	237.5	239.7
cord (true) (vocal)	161.0	197.3	231.0	212.1	235.6	239.1

	Malignant					
	Primary	Secondary	Ca in situ	Benign	Uncertain Behavior	Unspecified
Neoplasm, neoplastic — *continued*						
cord — *continued*						
false	161.1	197.3	231.0	212.1	235.6	239.1
spermatic	187.6	198.82	233.6	222.8	236.6	239.5
spinal (cervical) (lumbar) (thoracic)	192.2	198.3	—	225.3	237.5	239.7
cornea (limbus)	190.4	198.4	234.0	224.4	238.8	239.8
corpus						
albicans	183.0	198.6	233.3	220	236.2	239.5
callosum, brain	191.8	198.3	—	225.0	237.5	239.6
cavernosum	187.3	198.82	233.5	222.1	236.6	239.5
gastric	151.4	197.8	230.2	211.1	235.2	239.0
penis	187.3	198.82	233.5	222.1	236.6	239.5
striatum, cerebrum	191.0	198.3	—	225.0	237.5	239.6
uteri	182.0	198.82	233.2	219.1	236.0	239.5
isthmus	182.1	198.82	233.2	219.1	236.0	239.5
cortex						
adrenal	194.0	198.7	234.8	227.0	237.2	239.7
cerebral	191.0	198.3	—	225.0	237.5	239.6
costal cartilage	170.3	198.5	—	213.3	238.0	239.2
costovertebral joint	170.3	198.5	—	213.3	238.0	239.2
Cowper's gland	189.3	198.1	233.9	223.81	236.99	239.5
cranial (fossa, any)	191.9	198.3	—	225.0	237.5	239.6
meninges	192.1	198.4	—	225.2	237.6	239.7
nerve (any)	192.0	198.4	—	225.1	237.9	239.7
craniobuccal pouch	194.3	198.89	234.8	227.3	237.0	239.7
craniopharyngeal (duct) (pouch)	194.3	198.89	234.8	227.3	237.0	239.7
cricoid	148.0	198.89	230.0	210.8	235.1	239.0
cartilage	161.3	197.3	231.0	212.1	235.6	239.1
cricopharynx	148.0	198.89	230.0	210.8	235.1	239.0
crypt of Morgagni	154.8	197.5	230.7	211.4	235.2	239.0
crystalline lens	190.0	198.4	234.0	224.0	238.8	239.8
cul-de-sac (Douglas')	158.8	197.6	—	211.8	235.4	239.0
cuneiform cartilage	161.3	197.3	231.0	212.1	235.6	239.1
cutaneous — *see* Neoplasm, skin						
cutis — *see* Neoplasm, skin						
cystic (bile) duct (common)	156.1	197.8	230.8	211.5	235.3	239.0
dermis — *see* Neoplasm, skin						
diaphragm	171.4	198.89	—	215.4	238.1	239.2
digestive organs, system, tube, or tract NEC	159.9	197.8	230.9	211.9	235.5	239.0
contiguous sites with peritoneum	159.8	—	—	—	—	—
disc, intervertebral	170.2	198.5	—	213.2	238.0	239.2
disease, generalized	199.0	199.0	234.9	229.9	238.9	199.0
disseminated	199.0	199.0	234.9	229.9	238.9	199.0
Douglas' cul-de-sac or pouch	158.8	197.6	—	211.8	235.4	239.0
duodenojejunal junction	152.8	197.4	230.7	211.2	235.2	239.0
duodenum	152.0	197.4	230.7	211.2	235.2	239.0
dura (cranial) (mater)	192.1	198.4	—	225.2	237.6	239.7
cerebral	192.1	198.4	—	225.2	237.6	239.7
spinal	192.3	198.4	—	225.4	237.6	239.7
ear (external)	173.2	198.2	232.2	216.2	238.2	239.2
auricle or auris	173.2	198.2	232.2	216.2	238.2	239.2
canal, external	173.2	198.2	232.2	216.2	238.2	239.2
cartilage	171.0	198.89	—	215.0	238.1	239.2
external meatus	173.2	198.2	232.2	216.2	238.2	239.2
inner	160.1	197.3	231.8	212.0	235.9	239.8
lobule	173.2	198.2	232.2	216.2	238.2	239.2
middle	160.1	197.3	231.8	212.0	235.9	239.8
contiguous sites with accessory sinuses or nasal cavities	160.8	—	—	—	—	—
skin	173.2	198.2	232.2	216.2	238.2	239.2
earlobe	173.2	198.2	232.2	216.2	238.2	239.2
ejaculatory duct	187.8	198.82	233.6	222.8	236.6	239.5
elbow NEC*	195.4	198.89	232.6	229.8	238.8	239.8
endocardium	164.1	198.89	—	212.7	238.8	239.8
Neoplasm, neoplastic — *continued*						
endocervix (canal) (gland)	180.0	198.82	233.1	219.0	236.0	239.5
endocrine gland NEC	194.9	198.89	—	227.9	237.4	239.7
pluriglandular NEC	194.8	198.89	234.8	227.8	237.4	239.7
endometrium (gland) (stroma)	182.0	198.82	233.2	219.1	236.0	239.5
ensiform cartilage	170.3	198.5	—	213.3	238.0	239.2
enteric — *see* Neoplasm, intestine						
ependyma (brain)	191.5	198.3	—	225.0	237.5	239.6
epicardium	164.1	198.89	—	212.7	238.8	239.8
epididymis	187.5	198.82	233.6	222.3	236.6	239.5
epidural	192.9	198.4	—	225.9	237.9	239.7
epiglottis	161.1	197.3	231.0	212.1	235.6	239.1
anterior aspect or surface	146.4	198.89	230.0	210.6	235.1	239.0
cartilage	161.3	197.3	231.0	212.1	235.6	239.1
free border (margin)	146.4	198.89	230.0	210.6	235.1	239.0
junctional region	146.5	198.89	230.0	210.6	235.1	239.0
posterior (laryngeal) surface	161.1	197.3	231.0	212.1	235.6	239.1
suprahyoid portion	161.1	197.3	231.0	212.1	235.6	239.1
esophagogastric junction	151.0	197.8	230.2	211.1	235.2	239.0
esophagus	150.9	197.8	230.1	211.0	235.5	239.0
abdominal	150.2	197.8	230.1	211.0	235.5	239.0
cervical	150.0	197.8	230.1	211.0	235.5	239.0
contiguous sites	150.8	—	—	—	—	—
distal (third)	150.5	197.8	230.1	211.0	235.5	239.0
lower (third)	150.5	197.8	230.1	211.0	235.5	239.0
middle (third)	150.4	197.8	230.1	211.0	235.5	239.0
proximal (third)	150.3	197.8	230.1	211.0	235.5	239.0
specified part NEC	150.8	197.8	230.1	211.0	235.5	239.0
thoracic	150.1	197.8	230.1	211.0	235.5	239.0
upper (third)	150.3	197.8	230.1	211.0	235.5	239.0
ethmoid (sinus)	160.3	197.3	231.8	212.0	235.9	239.1
bone or labyrinth	170.0	198.5	—	213.0	238.0	239.2
Eustachian tube	160.1	197.3	231.8	212.0	235.9	239.1
exocervix	180.1	198.82	233.1	219.0	236.0	239.5
external						
meatus (ear)	173.2	198.2	232.2	216.2	238.2	239.2
os, cervix uteri	180.1	198.82	233.1	219.0	236.0	239.5
extradural	192.9	198.4	—	225.9	237.9	239.7
extrahepatic (bile) duct	156.1	197.8	230.8	211.5	235.3	239.0
contiguous sites with gallbladder	156.8	—	—	—	—	—
extraocular muscle	190.1	198.4	234.0	224.1	238.8	239.8
extrarectal	195.3	198.89	234.8	229.8	238.8	239.8
extremity*	195.8	198.89	232.8	229.8	238.8	239.8
lower*	195.5	198.89	232.7	229.8	238.8	239.8
upper*	195.4	198.89	232.6	229.8	238.8	239.8
eye NEC	190.9	198.4	234.0	224.9	238.8	239.8
contiguous sites	190.8	—	—	—	—	—
specified sites NEC	190.8	198.4	234.0	224.8	238.8	239.8
eyeball	190.0	198.4	234.0	224.0	238.8	239.8
eyebrow	173.3	198.2	232.3	216.3	238.2	239.2
eyelid (lower) (skin) (upper)	173.1	198.2	232.1	216.1	238.2	239.2
cartilage	171.0	198.89	—	215.0	238.1	239.2
face NEC*	195.0	198.89	232.3	229.8	238.8	239.8
fallopian tube (accessory)	183.2	198.82	233.3	221.0	236.3	239.5
falx (cerebelli) (cerebri)	192.1	198.4	—	225.2	237.6	239.7
fascia (*see also* Neoplasm, connective tissue)						
palmar	171.2	198.89	—	215.2	238.1	239.2
plantar	171.3	198.89	—	215.3	238.1	239.2
fatty tissue — *see* Neoplasm, connective tissue						
fauces, faucial NEC	146.9	198.89	230.0	210.6	235.1	239.0
pillars	146.2	198.89	230.0	210.6	235.1	239.0
tonsil	146.0	198.89	230.0	210.5	235.1	239.0
femur (any part)	170.7	198.5	—	213.7	238.0	239.2
fetal membrane	181	198.82	233.2	219.8	236.1	239.5

	Malignant					
	Primary	Secondary	Ca in situ	Benign	Uncertain Behavior	Unspecified
Neoplasm, neoplastic — *continued*						
fibrous tissue — *see* Neoplasm, connective tissue						
fibula (any part)	170.7	198.5	—	213.7	238.0	239.2
filum terminale	192.2	198.3	—	225.3	237.5	239.7
finger NEC*	195.4	198.89	232.6	229.8	238.8	239.8
flank NEC*	195.8	198.89	232.5	229.8	238.8	239.8
follicle, nabothian	180.0	198.82	233.1	219.0	236.0	239.5
foot NEC*	195.5	198.89	232.7	229.8	238.8	239.8
forearm NEC*	195.4	198.89	232.6	229.8	238.8	239.8
forehead (skin)	173.3	198.2	232.3	216.3	238.2	239.2
foreskin	187.1	198.82	233.5	222.1	236.6	239.5
fornix						
pharyngeal	147.3	198.89	230.0	210.7	235.1	239.0
vagina	184.0	198.82	233.3	221.1	236.3	239.5
fossa (of)						
anterior (cranial)	191.9	198.3	—	225.0	237.5	239.6
cranial	191.9	198.3	—	225.0	237.5	239.6
ischiorectal	195.3	198.89	234.8	229.8	238.8	239.8
middle (cranial)	191.9	198.3	—	225.0	237.5	239.6
pituitary	194.3	198.89	234.8	227.3	237.0	239.7
posterior (cranial)	191.9	198.3	—	225.0	237.5	239.6
pterygoid	171.0	198.89	—	215.0	238.1	239.2
pyriform	148.1	198.89	230.0	210.8	235.1	239.0
Rosenmüller	147.2	198.89	230.0	210.7	235.1	239.0
tonsillar	146.1	198.89	230.0	210.6	235.1	239.0
fourchette	184.4	198.82	233.3	221.2	236.3	239.5
frenulum						
labii — *see* Neoplasm, lip, internal						
linguae	141.3	198.89	230.0	210.1	235.1	239.0
frontal						
bone	170.0	198.5	—	213.0	238.0	239.2
lobe, brain	191.1	198.3	—	225.0	237.5	239.6
meninges	192.1	198.4	—	225.2	237.6	239.7
pole	191.1	198.3	—	225.0	237.5	239.6
sinus	160.4	197.3	231.8	212.0	235.9	239.1
fundus						
stomach	151.3	197.8	230.2	211.1	235.2	239.0
uterus	182.0	198.82	233.2	219.1	236.0	239.5
gallbladder	156.0	197.8	230.8	211.5	235.3	239.0
contiguous sites with extrahepatic bile ducts	156.8	—	—	—	—	—
gall duct (extrahepatic)	156.1	197.8	230.8	211.5	235.3	239.0
intrahepatic	155.1	197.8	230.8	211.5	235.3	239.0
ganglia (*see also* Neoplasm, connective tissue)	171.9	198.89	—	215.9	238.1	239.2
basal	191.0	198.3	—	225.0	237.5	239.6
ganglion (*see also* Neoplasm, connective tissue)	171.9	198.89	—	215.9	238.1	239.2
cranial nerve	192.0	198.4	—	225.1	237.9	239.7
Gartner's duct	184.0	198.82	233.3	221.1	236.3	239.5
gastric — *see* Neoplasm, stomach						
gastrocolic	159.8	197.8	230.9	211.9	235.5	239.0
gastroesophageal junction	151.0	197.8	230.2	211.1	235.2	239.0
gastrointestinal (tract) NEC	159.9	197.8	230.9	211.9	235.5	239.0
generalized	199.0	199.0	234.9	229.9	238.9	199.0
genital organ or tract						
female NEC	184.9	198.82	233.3	221.9	236.3	239.5
contiguous sites	184.8	—	—	—	—	—
specified site NEC	184.8	198.82	233.3	221.8	236.3	239.5
male NEC	187.9	198.82	233.6	222.9	236.6	239.5
contiguous sites	187.8	—	—	—	—	—
specified site NEC	187.8	198.82	233.6	222.8	236.6	239.5
genitourinary tract						
female	184.9	198.82	233.3	221.9	236.3	239.5
male	187.9	198.82	233.6	222.9	236.6	239.5

	Malignant					
	Primary	Secondary	Ca in situ	Benign	Uncertain Behavior	Unspecified
Neoplasm, neoplastic — *continued*						
gingiva (alveolar) (marginal)	143.9	198.89	230.0	210.4	235.1	239.0
lower	143.1	198.89	230.0	210.4	235.1	239.0
mandibular	143.1	198.89	230.0	210.4	235.1	239.0
maxillary	143.0	198.89	230.0	210.4	235.1	239.0
upper	143.0	198.89	230.0	210.4	235.1	239.0
gland, glandular (lymphatic) (system) (*see also* Neoplasm, lymph gland)						
endocrine NEC	194.9	198.89	—	227.9	237.4	239.7
salivary — *see* Neoplasm, salivary, gland						
glans penis	187.2	198.82	233.5	222.1	236.6	239.5
globus pallidus	191.0	198.3	—	225.0	237.5	239.6
glomus						
coccygeal	194.6	198.89	—	227.6	237.3	239.7
jugularis	194.6	198.89	—	227.6	237.3	239.7
glosso-epiglottic fold(s)	146.4	198.89	230.0	210.6	235.1	239.0
glossopalatine fold	146.2	198.89	230.0	210.6	235.1	239.0
glossopharyngeal sulcus	146.1	198.89	230.0	210.6	235.1	239.0
glottis	161.0	197.3	231.0	212.1	235.6	239.1
gluteal region*	195.3	198.89	232.5	229.8	238.8	239.8
great vessels NEC	171.4	198.89	—	215.4	238.1	239.2
groin NEC	195.3	198.89	232.5	229.8	238.8	239.8
gum	143.9	198.89	230.0	210.4	235.1	239.0
contiguous sites	143.8	—	—	—	—	—
lower	143.1	198.89	230.0	210.4	235.1	239.0
upper	143.0	198.89	230.0	210.4	235.1	239.0
hand NEC*	195.4	198.89	232.6	229.8	238.8	239.8
head NEC*	195.0	198.89	232.4	229.8	238.8	239.8
heart	164.1	198.89	—	212.7	238.8	239.8
contiguous sites with mediastinum or thymus	164.8	—	—	—	—	—
heel NEC*	195.5	198.89	232.7	229.8	238.8	239.8
helix	173.2	198.2	232.2	216.2	238.2	239.2
hematopoietic, hemopoietic tissue NEC	202.8 ☑	198.89	—	—	—	238.79 ▲
hemisphere, cerebral	191.0	198.3	—	225.0	237.5	239.6
hemorrhoidal zone	154.2	197.5	230.5	211.4	235.5	239.0
hepatic	155.2	197.7	230.8	211.5	235.3	239.0
duct (bile)	156.1	197.8	230.8	211.5	235.3	239.0
flexure (colon)	153.0	197.5	230.3	211.3	235.2	239.0
primary	155.0	—	—	—	—	—
hilus of lung	162.2	197.0	231.2	212.3	235.7	239.1
hip NEC*	195.5	198.89	232.7	229.8	238.8	239.8
hippocampus, brain	191.2	198.3	—	225.0	237.5	239.6
humerus (any part)	170.4	198.5	—	213.4	238.0	239.2
hymen	184.0	198.82	233.3	221.1	236.3	239.5
hypopharynx, hypopharyngeal NEC	148.9	198.89	230.0	210.8	235.1	239.0
contiguous sites	148.8	—	—	—	—	—
postcricoid region	148.0	198.89	230.0	210.8	235.1	239.0
posterior wall	148.3	198.89	230.0	210.8	235.1	239.0
pyriform fossa (sinus)	148.1	198.89	230.0	210.8	235.1	239.0
specified site NEC	148.8	198.89	230.0	210.8	235.1	239.0
wall	148.9	198.89	230.0	210.8	235.1	239.0
posterior	148.3	198.89	230.0	210.8	235.1	239.0
hypophysis	194.3	198.89	234.8	227.3	237.0	239.7
hypothalamus	191.0	198.3	—	225.0	237.5	239.6
ileocecum, ileocecal (coil) (junction) (valve)	153.4	197.5	230.3	211.3	235.2	239.0
ileum	152.2	197.4	230.7	211.2	235.2	239.0
ilium	170.6	198.5	—	213.6	238.0	239.2
immunoproliferative NEC	203.8 ☑	—	—	—	—	—
infraclavicular (region)*	195.1	198.89	232.5	229.8	238.8	239.8
inguinal (region)*	195.3	198.89	232.5	229.8	238.8	239.8
insula	191.0	198.3	—	225.0	237.5	239.6

	Malignant					
	Primary	Secondary	Ca in situ	Benign	Uncertain Behavior	Unspecified
Neoplasm, neoplastic — *continued*						
insular tissue (pancreas)	157.4	197.8	230.9	211.7	235.5	239.0
brain	191.0	198.3	—	225.0	237.5	239.6
interarytenoid fold	148.2	198.89	230.0	210.8	235.1	239.0
hypopharyngeal aspect	148.2	198.89	230.0	210.8	235.1	239.0
laryngeal aspect	161.1	197.3	231.0	212.1	235.6	239.1
marginal zone	148.2	198.89	230.0	210.8	235.1	239.0
interdental papillae	143.9	198.89	230.0	210.4	235.1	239.0
lower	143.1	198.89	230.0	210.4	235.1	239.0
upper	143.0	198.89	230.0	210.4	235.1	239.0
internal						
capsule	191.0	198.3	—	225.0	237.5	239.6
os (cervix)	180.0	198.82	233.1	219.0	236.0	239.5
intervertebral cartilage or disc	170.2	198.5	—	213.2	238.0	239.2
intestine, intestinal	159.0	197.8	230.7	211.9	235.2	239.0
large	153.9	197.5	230.3	211.3	235.2	239.0
appendix	153.5	197.5	230.3	211.3	235.2	239.0
caput coli	153.4	197.5	230.3	211.3	235.2	239.0
cecum	153.4	197.5	230.3	211.3	235.2	239.0
colon	153.9	197.5	230.3	211.3	235.2	239.0
and rectum	154.0	197.5	230.4	211.4	235.2	239.0
ascending	153.6	197.5	230.3	211.3	235.2	239.0
caput	153.4	197.5	230.3	211.3	235.2	239.0
contiguous sites	153.8	—	—	—	—	—
descending	153.2	197.5	230.3	211.3	235.2	239.0
distal	153.2	197.5	230.3	211.3	235.2	239.0
left	153.2	197.5	230.3	211.3	235.2	239.0
pelvic	153.3	197.5	230.3	211.3	235.2	239.0
right	153.6	197.5	230.3	211.3	235.2	239.0
sigmoid (flexure)	153.3	197.5	230.3	211.3	235.2	239.0
transverse	153.1	197.5	230.3	211.3	235.2	239.0
contiguous sites	153.8	—	—	—	—	—
hepatic flexure	153.0	197.5	230.3	211.3	235.2	239.0
ileocecum, ileocecal (coil) (valve)	153.4	197.5	230.3	211.3	235.2	239.0
sigmoid flexure (lower) (upper)	153.3	197.5	230.3	211.3	235.2	239.0
splenic flexure	153.7	197.5	230.3	211.3	235.2	239.0
small	152.9	197.4	230.7	211.2	235.2	239.0
contiguous sites	152.8	—	—	—	—	—
duodenum	152.0	197.4	230.7	211.2	235.2	239.0
ileum	152.2	197.4	230.7	211.2	235.2	239.0
jejunum	152.1	197.4	230.7	211.2	235.2	239.0
tract NEC	159.0	197.8	230.7	211.9	235.2	239.0
intra-abdominal	195.2	198.89	234.8	229.8	238.8	239.8
intracranial NEC	191.9	198.3	—	225.0	237.5	239.6
intrahepatic (bile) duct	155.1	197.8	230.8	211.5	235.3	239.0
intraocular	190.0	198.4	234.0	224.0	238.8	239.8
intraorbital	190.1	198.4	234.0	224.1	238.8	239.8
intrasellar	194.3	198.89	234.8	227.3	237.0	239.7
intrathoracic (cavity) (organs NEC)	195.1	198.89	234.8	229.8	238.8	239.8
contiguous sites with respiratory organs	165.8	—	—	—	—	—
iris	190.0	198.4	234.0	224.0	238.8	239.8
ischiorectal (fossa)	195.3	198.89	234.8	229.8	238.8	239.8
ischium	170.6	198.5	—	213.6	238.0	239.2
island of Reil	191.0	198.3	—	225.0	237.5	239.6
islands or islets of Langerhans	157.4	197.8	230.9	211.7	235.5	239.0
isthmus uteri	182.1	198.82	233.2	219.1	236.0	239.5
jaw	195.0	198.89	234.8	229.8	238.8	239.8
bone	170.1	198.5	—	213.1	238.0	239.2
carcinoma	143.9	—	—	—	—	—
lower	143.1	—	—	—	—	—
upper	143.0	—	—	—	—	—
lower	170.1	198.5	—	213.1	238.0	239.2
upper	170.0	198.5	—	213.0	238.0	239.2
carcinoma (any type) (lower) (upper)	195.0	—	—	—	—	—
skin	173.3	198.2	232.3	216.3	238.2	239.2

	Malignant					
	Primary	Secondary	Ca in situ	Benign	Uncertain Behavior	Unspecified
Neoplasm, neoplastic — *continued*						
jaw — *continued*						
soft tissues	143.9	198.89	230.0	210.4	235.1	239.0
lower	143.1	198.89	230.0	210.4	235.1	239.0
upper	143.0	198.89	230.0	210.4	235.1	239.0
jejunum	152.1	197.4	230.7	211.2	235.2	239.0
joint NEC (*see also* Neoplasm, bone)	170.9	198.5	—	213.9	238.0	239.2
acromioclavicular	170.4	198.5	—	213.4	238.0	239.2
bursa or synovial membrane — *see* Neoplasm, connective tissue						
costovertebral	170.3	198.5	—	213.3	238.0	239.2
sternocostal	170.3	198.5	—	213.3	238.0	239.2
temporomandibular	170.1	198.5	—	213.1	238.0	239.2
junction						
anorectal	154.8	197.5	230.7	211.4	235.5	239.0
cardioesophageal	151.0	197.8	230.2	211.1	235.2	239.0
esophagogastric	151.0	197.8	230.2	211.1	235.2	239.0
gastroesophageal	151.0	197.8	230.2	211.1	235.2	239.0
hard and soft palate	145.5	198.89	230.0	210.4	235.1	239.0
ileocecal	153.4	197.5	230.3	211.3	235.2	239.0
pelvirectal	154.0	197.5	230.4	211.4	235.2	239.0
pelviureteric	189.1	198.0	233.9	223.1	236.91	239.5
rectosigmoid	154.0	197.5	230.4	211.4	235.2	239.0
squamocolumnar, of cervix	180.8	198.82	233.1	219.0	236.0	239.5
kidney (parenchyma)	189.0	198.0	233.9	223.0	236.91	239.5
calyx	189.1	198.0	233.9	223.1	236.91	239.5
hilus	189.1	198.0	233.9	223.1	236.91	239.5
pelvis	189.1	198.0	233.9	223.1	236.91	239.5
knee NEC*	195.5	198.89	232.7	229.8	238.8	239.8
labia (skin)	184.4	198.82	233.3	221.2	236.3	239.5
majora	184.1	198.82	233.3	221.2	236.3	239.5
minora	184.2	198.82	233.3	221.2	236.3	239.5
labial (*see also* Neoplasm, lip)						
sulcus (lower) (upper)	145.1	198.89	230.0	210.4	235.1	239.0
labium (skin)	184.4	198.82	233.3	221.2	236.3	239.5
majus	184.1	198.82	233.3	221.2	236.3	239.5
minus	184.2	198.82	233.3	221.2	236.3	239.5
lacrimal						
canaliculi	190.7	198.4	234.0	224.7	238.8	239.8
duct (nasal)	190.7	198.4	234.0	224.7	238.8	239.8
gland	190.2	198.4	234.0	224.2	238.8	239.8
punctum	190.7	198.4	234.0	224.7	238.8	239.8
sac	190.7	198.4	234.0	224.7	238.8	239.8
Langerhans, islands or islets	157.4	197.8	230.9	211.7	235.5	239.0
laryngopharynx	148.9	198.89	230.0	210.8	235.1	239.0
larynx, laryngeal NEC	161.9	197.3	231.0	212.1	235.6	239.1
aryepiglottic fold	161.1	197.3	231.0	212.1	235.6	239.1
cartilage (arytenoid) (cricoid) (cuneiform) (thyroid)	161.3	197.3	231.0	212.1	235.6	239.1
commissure (anterior) (posterior)	161.0	197.3	231.0	212.1	235.6	239.1
contiguous sites	161.8	—	—	—	—	—
extrinsic NEC	161.1	197.3	231.0	212.1	235.6	239.1
meaning hypopharynx	148.9	198.89	230.0	210.8	235.1	239.0
interarytenoid fold	161.1	197.3	231.0	212.1	235.6	239.1
intrinsic	161.0	197.3	231.0	212.1	235.6	239.1
ventricular band	161.1	197.3	231.0	212.1	235.6	239.1
leg NEC*	195.5	198.89	232.7	229.8	238.8	239.8
lens, crystalline	190.0	198.4	234.0	224.0	238.8	239.8
lid (lower) (upper)	173.1	198.2	232.1	216.1	238.2	239.2
ligament (*see also* Neoplasm, connective tissue)						
broad	183.3	198.82	233.3	221.0	236.3	239.5
Mackenrodt's	183.8	198.82	233.3	221.8	236.3	239.5
non-uterine — *see* Neoplasm, connective tissue						

	Malignant					
	Primary	Secondary	Ca in situ	Benign	Uncertain Behavior	Unspecified
Neoplasm, neoplastic — *continued*						
ligament (*see also* Neoplasm, connective tissue) — *continued*						
round	183.5	198.82	—	221.0	236.3	239.5
sacro-uterine	183.4	198.82	—	221.0	236.3	239.5
uterine	183.4	198.82	—	221.0	236.3	239.5
utero-ovarian	183.8	198.82	233.3	221.8	236.3	239.5
uterosacral	183.4	198.82	—	221.0	236.3	239.5
limb*	195.8	198.89	232.8	229.8	238.8	239.8
lower*	195.5	198.89	232.7	229.8	238.8	239.8
upper*	195.4	198.89	232.6	229.8	238.8	239.8
limbus of cornea	190.4	198.4	234.0	224.4	238.8	239.8
lingual NEC (*see also* Neoplasm, tongue)	141.9	198.89	230.0	210.1	235.1	239.0
lingula, lung	162.3	197.0	231.2	212.3	235.7	239.1
lip (external) (lipstick area) (vermillion border)	140.9	198.89	230.0	210.0	235.1	239.0
buccal aspect — *see* Neoplasm, lip, internal						
commissure	140.6	198.89	230.0	210.4	235.1	239.0
contiguous sites	140.8	—	—	—	—	—
with oral cavity or pharynx	149.8	—	—	—	—	—
frenulum — *see* Neoplasm, lip, internal						
inner aspect — *see* Neoplasm, lip, internal						
internal (buccal) (frenulum) (mucosa) (oral)	140.5	198.89	230.0	210.0	235.1	239.0
lower	140.4	198.89	230.0	210.0	235.1	239.0
upper	140.3	198.89	230.0	210.0	235.1	239.0
lower	140.1	198.89	230.0	210.0	235.1	239.0
internal (buccal) (frenulum) (mucosa) (oral)	140.4	198.89	230.0	210.0	235.1	239.0
mucosa — *see* Neoplasm, lip, internal						
oral aspect — *see* Neoplasm, lip, internal						
skin (commissure) (lower) (upper)	173.0	198.2	232.0	216.0	238.2	239.2
upper	140.0	198.89	230.0	210.0	235.1	239.0
internal (buccal) (frenulum) (mucosa) (oral)	140.3	198.89	230.0	210.0	235.1	239.0
liver	155.2	197.7	230.8	211.5	235.3	239.0
primary	155.0	—	—	—	—	—
lobe						
azygos	162.3	197.0	231.2	212.3	235.7	239.1
frontal	191.1	198.3	—	225.0	237.5	239.6
lower	162.5	197.0	231.2	212.3	235.7	239.1
middle	162.4	197.0	231.2	212.3	235.7	239.1
occipital	191.4	198.3	—	225.0	237.5	239.6
parietal	191.3	198.3	—	225.0	237.5	239.6
temporal	191.2	198.3	—	225.0	237.5	239.6
upper	162.3	197.0	231.2	212.3	235.7	239.1
lumbosacral plexus	171.6	198.4	—	215.6	238.1	239.2
lung	162.9	197.0	231.2	212.3	235.7	239.1
azygos lobe	162.3	197.0	231.2	212.3	235.7	239.1
carina	162.2	197.0	231.2	212.3	235.7	239.1
contiguous sites with bronchus or trachea	162.8	—	—	—	—	—
hilus	162.2	197.0	231.2	212.3	235.7	239.1
lingula	162.3	197.0	231.2	212.3	235.7	239.1
lobe NEC	162.9	197.0	231.2	212.3	235.7	239.1
lower lobe	162.5	197.0	231.2	212.3	235.7	239.1

	Malignant					
	Primary	Secondary	Ca in situ	Benign	Uncertain Behavior	Unspecified
Neoplasm, neoplastic — *continued*						
lung — *continued*						
main bronchus	162.2	197.0	231.2	212.3	235.7	239.1
middle lobe	162.4	197.0	231.2	212.3	235.7	239.1
upper lobe	162.3	197.0	231.2	212.3	235.7	239.1
lymph, lymphatic						
channel NEC (*see also* Neoplasm, connective tissue)	171.9	198.89	—	215.9	238.1	239.2
gland (secondary)	—	196.9	—	229.0	238.8	239.8
abdominal	—	196.2	—	229.0	238.8	239.8
aortic	—	196.2	—	229.0	238.8	239.8
arm	—	196.3	—	229.0	238.8	239.8
auricular (anterior) (posterior)	—	196.0	—	229.0	238.8	239.8
axilla, axillary	—	196.3	—	229.0	238.8	239.8
brachial	—	196.3	—	229.0	238.8	239.8
bronchial	—	196.1	—	229.0	238.8	239.8
bronchopulmonary	—	196.1	—	229.0	238.8	239.8
celiac	—	196.2	—	229.0	238.8	239.8
cervical	—	196.0	—	229.0	238.8	239.8
cervicofacial	—	196.0	—	229.0	238.8	239.8
Cloquet	—	196.5	—	229.0	238.8	239.8
colic	—	196.2	—	229.0	238.8	239.8
common duct	—	196.2	—	229.0	238.8	239.8
cubital	—	196.3	—	229.0	238.8	239.8
diaphragmatic	—	196.1	—	229.0	238.8	239.8
epigastric, inferior	—	196.6	—	229.0	238.8	239.8
epitrochlear	—	196.3	—	229.0	238.8	239.8
esophageal	—	196.1	—	229.0	238.8	239.8
face	—	196.0	—	229.0	238.8	239.8
femoral	—	196.5	—	229.0	238.8	239.8
gastric	—	196.2	—	229.0	238.8	239.8
groin	—	196.5	—	229.0	238.8	239.8
head	—	196.0	—	229.0	238.8	239.8
hepatic	—	196.2	—	229.0	238.8	239.8
hilar (pulmonary)	—	196.1	—	229.0	238.8	239.8
splenic	—	196.2	—	229.0	238.8	239.8
hypogastric	—	196.6	—	229.0	238.8	239.8
ileocolic	—	196.2	—	229.0	238.8	239.8
iliac	—	196.6	—	229.0	238.8	239.8
infraclavicular	—	196.3	—	229.0	238.8	239.8
inguina, inguinal	—	196.5	—	229.0	238.8	239.8
innominate	—	196.1	—	229.0	238.8	239.8
intercostal	—	196.1	—	229.0	238.8	239.8
intestinal	—	196.2	—	229.0	238.8	239.8
intra-abdominal	—	196.2	—	229.0	238.8	239.8
intrapelvic	—	196.6	—	229.0	238.8	239.8
intrathoracic	—	196.1	—	229.0	238.8	239.9
jugular	—	196.0	—	229.0	238.8	239.8
leg	—	196.5	—	229.0	238.8	239.8
limb						
lower	—	196.5	—	229.0	238.8	239.8
upper	—	196.3	—	229.0	238.8	239.8
lower limb	—	196.5	—	229.0	238.8	238.9
lumbar	—	196.2	—	229.0	238.8	239.8
mandibular	—	196.0	—	229.0	238.8	239.8
mediastinal	—	196.1	—	229.0	238.8	239.8
mesenteric (inferior) (superior)	—	196.2	—	229.0	238.8	239.8
midcolic	—	196.2	—	229.0	238.8	239.8
multiple sites in categories 196.0–196.6	—	196.8	—	229.0	238.8	239.8
neck	—	196.0	—	229.0	238.8	239.8
obturator	—	196.6	—	229.0	238.8	239.8
occipital	—	196.0	—	229.0	238.8	239.8
pancreatic	—	196.2	—	229.0	238.8	239.8
para-aortic	—	196.2	—	229.0	238.8	239.8
paracervical	—	196.6	—	229.0	238.8	239.8
parametrial	—	196.6	—	229.0	238.8	239.8
parasternal	—	196.1	—	229.0	238.8	239.8
parotid	—	196.0	—	229.0	238.8	239.8
pectoral	—	196.3	—	229.0	238.8	239.8
pelvic	—	196.6	—	229.0	238.8	239.8
peri-aortic	—	196.2	—	229.0	238.8	239.8

	Malignant					
	Primary	Secondary	Ca in situ	Benign	Uncertain Behavior	Unspecified
Neoplasm, neoplastic — *continued*						
lymph, lymphatic — *continued*						
gland — *continued*						
peripancreatic	—	196.2	—	229.0	238.8	239.8
popliteal	—	196.5	—	229.0	238.8	239.8
porta hepatis	—	196.2	—	229.0	238.8	239.8
portal	—	196.2	—	229.0	238.8	239.8
preauricular	—	196.0	—	229.0	238.8	239.8
prelaryngeal	—	196.0	—	229.0	238.8	239.8
presymphysial	—	196.6	—	229.0	238.8	239.8
pretracheal	—	196.0	—	229.0	238.8	239.8
primary (any site) NEC	202.9 ☑	—	—	—	—	—
pulmonary (hiler)	—	196.1	—	229.0	238.8	239.8
pyloric	—	196.2	—	229.0	238.8	239.8
retroperitoneal	—	196.2	—	229.0	238.8	239.8
retropharyngeal	—	196.0	—	229.0	238.8	239.8
Rosenmüller's	—	196.5	—	229.0	238.8	239.8
sacral	—	196.6	—	229.0	238.8	239.8
scalene	—	196.0	—	229.0	238.8	239.8
site NEC	—	196.9	—	229.0	238.8	239.8
splenic (hilar)	—	196.2	—	229.0	238.8	239.8
subclavicular	—	196.3	—	229.0	238.8	239.8
subinguinal	—	196.5	—	229.0	238.8	239.8
sublingual	—	196.0	—	229.0	238.8	239.8
submandibular	—	196.0	—	229.0	238.8	239.8
submaxillary	—	196.0	—	229.0	238.8	239.8
submental	—	196.0	—	229.0	238.8	239.8
subscapular	—	196.3	—	229.0	238.8	239.8
supraclavicular	—	196.0	—	229.0	238.8	239.8
thoracic	—	196.1	—	229.0	238.8	239.8
tibial	—	196.5	—	229.0	238.8	239.8
tracheal	—	196.1	—	229.0	238.8	239.8
tracheobronchial	—	196.1	—	229.0	238.8	239.8
upper limb	—	196.3	—	229.0	238.8	239.8
Virchow's	—	196.0	—	229.0	238.8	239.8
node (*see also* Neoplasm, lymph gland)						
primary NEC	202.9 ☑	—	—	—	—	—
vessel (*see also* Neoplasm, connective tissue)	171.9	198.89	—	215.9	238.1	239.2
malar	170.0	198.5	—	213.0	238.0	239.2
region — *see* Neoplasm, cheek						
mammary gland — *see* Neoplasm, breast						
mandible	170.1	198.5	—	213.1	238.0	239.2
alveolar						
mucose	143.1	198.89	230.0	210.4	235.1	239.0
ridge or process	170.1	198.5	—	213.1	238.0	239.2
carcinoma	143.1	—	—	—	—	—
carcinoma	143.1	—	—	—	—	—
marrow (bone) NEC	202.9 ☑	198.5	—	—	—	238.79 ▲
mastectomy site (skin)	173.5	198.2	—	—	—	—
specified as breast tissue	174.8	198.81	—	—	—	—
mastoid (air cells) (antrum) (cavity)	160.1	197.3	231.8	212.0	235.9	239.1
bone or process	170.0	198.5	—	213.0	238.0	239.2
maxilla, maxillary (superior)	170.0	198.5	—	213.0	238.0	239.2
alveolar						
mucosa	143.0	198.89	230.0	210.4	235.1	239.0
ridge or process	170.0	198.5	—	213.0	238.0	239.2
carcinoma	143.0	—	—	—	—	—
antrum	160.2	197.3	231.8	212.0	235.9	239.1
carcinoma	143.0	—	—	—	—	—
inferior — *see* Neoplasm, mandible						
sinus	160.2	197.3	231.8	212.0	235.9	239.1
meatus						
external (ear)	173.2	198.2	232.2	216.2	238.2	239.2
Meckel's diverticulum	152.3	197.4	230.7	211.2	235.2	239.0
Neoplasm, neoplastic — *continued*						
mediastinum, mediastinal	164.9	197.1	—	212.5	235.8	239.8
anterior	164.2	197.1	—	212.5	235.8	239.8
contiguous sites with heart and thymus	164.8	—	—	—	—	—
posterior	164.3	197.1	—	212.5	235.8	239.8
medulla						
adrenal	194.0	198.7	234.8	227.0	237.2	239.7
oblongata	191.7	198.3	—	225.0	237.5	239.6
meibomian gland	173.1	198.2	232.1	216.1	238.2	239.2
meninges (brain) (cerebral) (cranial) (intracranial)	192.1	198.4	—	225.2	237.6	239.7
spinal (cord)	192.3	198.4	—	225.4	237.6	239.7
meniscus, knee joint (lateral) (medial)	170.7	198.5	—	213.7	238.0	239.2
mesentery, mesenteric	158.8	197.6	—	211.8	235.4	239.0
mesoappendix	158.8	197.6	—	211.8	235.4	239.0
mesocolon	158.8	197.6	—	211.8	235.4	239.0
mesopharynx — *see* Neoplasm, oropharynx						
mesosalpinx	183.3	198.82	233.3	221.0	236.3	239.5
mesovarium	183.3	198.82	233.3	221.0	236.3	239.5
metacarpus (any bone)	170.5	198.5	—	213.5	238.0	239.2
metastatic NEC (*see also* Neoplasm, by site, secondary)	—	199.1	—	—	—	—
metatarsus (any bone)	170.8	198.5	—	213.8	238.0	239.2
midbrain	191.7	198.3	—	225.0	237.5	239.6
milk duct — *see* Neoplasm, breast						
mons						
pubis	184.4	198.82	233.3	221.2	236.3	239.5
veneris	184.4	198.82	233.3	221.2	236.3	239.5
motor tract	192.9	198.4	—	225.9	237.9	239.7
brain	191.9	198.3	—	225.0	237.5	239.6
spinal	192.2	198.3	—	225.3	237.5	239.7
mouth	145.9	198.89	230.0	210.4	235.1	239.0
contiguous sites	145.8	—	—	—	—	—
floor	144.9	198.89	230.0	210.3	235.1	239.0
anterior portion	144.0	198.89	230.0	210.3	235.1	239.0
contiguous sites	144.8	—	—	—	—	—
lateral portion	144.1	198.89	230.0	210.3	235.1	239.0
roof	145.5	198.89	230.0	210.4	235.1	239.0
specified part NEC	145.8	198.89	230.0	210.4	235.1	239.0
vestibule	145.1	198.89	230.0	210.4	235.1	239.0
mucosa						
alveolar (ridge or process)	143.9	198.89	230.0	210.4	235.1	239.0
lower	143.1	198.89	230.0	210.4	235.1	239.0
upper	143.0	198.89	230.0	210.4	235.1	239.0
buccal	145.0	198.89	230.0	210.4	235.1	239.0
cheek	145.0	198.89	230.0	210.4	235.1	239.0
lip — *see* Neoplasm, lip, internal						
nasal	160.0	197.3	231.8	212.0	235.9	239.1
oral	145.0	198.89	230.0	210.4	235.1	239.0
Müllerian duct						
female	184.8	198.82	233.3	221.8	236.3	239.5
male	187.8	198.82	233.6	222.8	236.6	239.5
multiple sites NEC	199.0	199.0	234.9	229.9	238.9	199.0
muscle (*see also* Neoplasm, connective tissue)						
extraocular	190.1	198.4	234.0	224.1	238.8	239.8
myocardium	164.1	198.89	—	212.7	238.8	239.8
myometrium	182.0	198.82	233.2	219.1	236.0	239.5
myopericardium	164.1	198.89	—	212.7	238.8	239.8
nabothian gland (follicle)	180.0	198.82	233.1	219.0	236.0	239.5
Nackenrodt's ligament	183.8	198.82	233.3	221.8	236.3	239.5
nail	173.9	198.2	232.9	216.9	238.2	239.2
finger	173.6	198.2	232.6	216.6	238.2	239.2
toe	173.7	198.2	232.7	216.7	238.2	239.2

	Malignant					
	Primary	Secondary	Ca in situ	Benign	Uncertain Behavior	Unspecified
Neoplasm, neoplastic — *continued*						
nares, naris (anterior) (posterior)	160.0	197.3	231.8	212.0	235.9	239.1
nasal — *see* Neoplasm, nose						
nasolabial groove	173.3	198.2	232.3	216.3	238.2	239.2
nasolacrimal duct	190.7	198.4	234.0	224.7	238.8	239.8
nasopharynx, nasopharyngeal	147.9	198.89	230.0	210.7	235.1	239.0
contiguous sites	147.8	—	—	—	—	—
floor	147.3	198.89	230.0	210.7	235.1	239.0
roof	147.0	198.89	230.0	210.7	235.1	239.0
specified site NEC	147.8	198.89	230.0	210.7	235.1	239.0
wall	147.9	198.89	230.0	210.7	235.1	239.0
anterior	147.3	198.89	230.0	210.7	235.1	239.0
lateral	147.2	198.89	230.0	210.7	235.1	239.0
posterior	147.1	198.89	230.0	210.7	235.1	239.0
superior	147.0	198.89	230.0	210.7	235.1	239.0
nates	173.5	198.2	232.5	216.5	238.2	239.2
neck NEC*	195.0	198.89	234.8	229.8	238.8	239.8
nerve (autonomic) (ganglion) (parasympathetic) (peripheral) (sympathetic) (*see also* Neoplasm, connective tissue)						
abducens	192.0	198.4	—	225.1	237.9	239.7
accessory (spinal)	192.0	198.4	—	225.1	237.9	239.7
acoustic	192.0	198.4	—	225.1	237.9	239.7
auditory	192.0	198.4	—	225.1	237.9	239.7
brachial	171.2	198.89	—	215.2	238.1	239.2
cranial (any)	192.0	198.4	—	225.1	237.9	239.7
facial	192.0	198.4	—	225.1	237.9	239.7
femoral	171.3	198.89	—	215.3	238.1	239.2
glossopharyngeal	192.0	198.4	—	225.1	237.9	239.7
hypoglossal	192.0	198.4	—	225.1	237.9	239.7
intercostal	171.4	198.89	—	215.4	238.1	239.2
lumbar	171.7	198.89	—	215.7	238.1	239.2
median	171.2	198.89	—	215.2	238.1	239.2
obturator	171.3	198.89	—	215.3	238.1	239.2
oculomotor	192.0	198.4	—	225.1	237.9	239.7
olfactory	192.0	198.4	—	225.1	237.9	239.7
optic	192.0	198.4	—	225.1	237.9	239.7
peripheral NEC	171.9	198.89	—	215.9	238.1	239.2
radial	171.2	198.89	—	215.2	238.1	239.2
sacral	171.6	198.89	—	215.6	238.1	239.2
sciatic	171.3	198.89	—	215.3	238.1	239.2
spinal NEC	171.9	198.89	—	215.9	238.1	239.2
trigeminal	192.0	198.4	—	225.1	237.9	239.7
trochlear	192.0	198.4	—	225.1	237.9	239.7
ulnar	171.2	198.89	—	215.2	238.1	239.2
vagus	192.0	198.4	—	225.1	237.9	239.7
nervous system (central) NEC	192.9	198.4	—	225.9	237.9	239.7
autonomic NEC	171.9	198.89	—	215.9	238.1	239.2
brain (*see also* Neoplasm, brain)						
membrane or meninges	192.1	198.4	—	225.2	237.6	239.7
contiguous sites	192.8	—	—	—	—	—
parasympathetic NEC	171.9	198.89	—	215.9	238.1	239.2
sympathetic NEC	171.9	198.89	—	215.9	238.1	239.2
nipple (female)	174.0	198.81	233.0	217	238.3	239.3
male	175.0	198.81	233.0	217	238.3	239.3
nose, nasal	195.0	198.89	234.8	229.8	238.8	239.8
ala (external)	173.3	198.2	232.3	216.3	238.2	239.2
bone	170.0	198.5	—	213.0	238.0	239.2
cartilage	160.0	197.3	231.8	212.0	235.9	239.1
cavity	160.0	197.3	231.8	212.0	235.9	239.1
contiguous sites with accessory sinuses or middle ear	160.8	—	—	—	—	—
choana	147.3	198.89	230.0	210.7	235.1	239.0
external (skin)	173.3	198.2	232.3	216.3	238.2	239.2
fossa	160.0	197.3	231.8	212.0	235.9	239.1
internal	160.0	197.3	231.8	212.0	235.9	239.1

	Malignant					
	Primary	Secondary	Ca in situ	Benign	Uncertain Behavior	Unspecified
Neoplasm, neoplastic — *continued*						
nose, nasal — *continued*						
mucosa	160.0	197.3	231.8	212.0	235.9	239.1
septum	160.0	197.3	231.8	212.0	235.9	239.1
posterior margin	147.3	198.89	230.0	210.7	235.1	239.0
sinus — *see* Neoplasm, sinus						
skin	173.3	198.2	232.3	216.3	238.2	239.2
turbinate (mucosa)	160.0	197.3	231.8	212.0	235.9	239.1
bone	170.0	198.5	—	213.0	238.0	239.2
vestibule	160.0	197.3	231.8	212.0	235.9	239.1
nostril	160.0	197.3	231.8	212.0	235.9	239.1
nucleus pulposus	170.2	198.5	—	213.2	238.0	239.2
occipital						
bone	170.0	198.5	—	213.0	238.0	239.2
lobe or pole, brain	191.4	198.3	—	225.0	237.5	239.6
odontogenic — *see* Neoplasm, jaw bone						
oesophagus — *see* Neoplasm, esophagus						
olfactory nerve or bulb	192.0	198.4	—	225.1	237.9	239.7
olive (brain)	191.7	198.3	—	225.0	237.5	239.6
omentum	158.8	197.6	—	211.8	235.4	239.0
operculum (brain)	191.0	198.3	—	225.0	237.5	239.6
optic nerve, chiasm, or tract	192.0	198.4	—	225.1	237.9	239.7
oral (cavity)	145.9	198.89	230.0	210.4	235.1	239.0
contiguous sites with lip or pharynx	149.8	—	—	—	—	—
ill-defined	149.9	198.89	230.0	210.4	235.1	239.0
mucosa	145.9	198.89	230.0	210.4	235.1	239.0
orbit	190.1	198.4	234.0	224.1	238.8	239.8
bone	170.0	198.5	—	213.0	238.0	239.2
eye	190.1	198.4	234.0	224.1	238.8	239.8
soft parts	190.1	198.4	234.0	224.1	238.8	239.8
organ of Zuckerkandl	194.6	198.89	—	227.6	237.3	239.7
oropharynx	146.9	198.89	230.0	210.6	235.1	239.0
branchial cleft (vestige)	146.8	198.89	230.0	210.6	235.1	239.0
contiguous sites	146.8	—	—	—	—	—
junctional region	146.5	198.89	230.0	210.6	235.1	239.0
lateral wall	146.6	198.89	230.0	210.6	235.1	239.0
pillars of fauces	146.2	198.89	230.0	210.6	235.1	239.0
posterior wall	146.7	198.89	230.0	210.6	235.1	239.0
specified part NEC	146.8	198.89	230.0	210.6	235.1	239.0
vallecula	146.3	198.89	230.0	210.6	235.1	239.0
os						
external	180.1	198.82	233.1	219.0	236.0	239.5
internal	180.0	198.82	233.1	219.0	236.0	239.5
ovary	183.0	198.6	233.3	220	236.2	239.5
oviduct	183.2	198.82	233.3	221.0	236.3	239.5
palate	145.5	198.89	230.0	210.4	235.1	239.0
hard	145.2	198.89	230.0	210.4	235.1	239.0
junction of hard and soft palate	145.5	198.89	230.0	210.4	235.1	239.0
soft	145.3	198.89	230.0	210.4	235.1	239.0
nasopharyngeal surface	147.3	198.89	230.0	210.7	235.1	239.0
posterior surface	147.3	198.89	230.0	210.7	235.1	239.0
superior surface	147.3	198.89	230.0	210.7	235.1	239.0
palatoglossal arch	146.2	198.89	230.0	210.6	235.1	239.0
palatopharyngeal arch	146.2	198.89	230.0	210.6	235.1	239.0
pallium	191.0	198.3	—	225.0	237.5	239.6
palpebra	173.1	198.2	232.1	216.1	238.2	239.2
pancreas	157.9	197.8	230.9	211.6	235.5	239.0
body	157.1	197.8	230.9	211.6	235.5	239.0
contiguous sites	157.8	—	—	—	—	—
duct (of Santorini) (of Wirsung)	157.3	197.8	230.9	211.6	235.5	239.0
ectopic tissue	157.8	197.8	230.9	211.6	235.5	239.0
head	157.0	197.8	230.9	211.6	235.5	239.0
islet cells	157.4	197.8	230.9	211.7	235.5	239.0
neck	157.8	197.8	230.9	211.6	235.5	239.0
tail	157.2	197.8	230.9	211.6	235.5	239.0
para-aortic body	194.6	198.89	—	227.6	237.3	239.7
paraganglion NEC	194.6	198.89	—	227.6	237.3	239.7

	Malignant					
	Primary	Secondary	Ca in situ	Benign	Uncertain Behavior	Unspecified
Neoplasm, neoplastic — *continued*						
parametrium	183.4	198.82	—	221.0	236.3	239.5
paranephric	158.0	197.6	—	211.8	235.4	239.0
pararectal	195.3	198.89	—	229.8	238.8	239.8
parasagittal (region)	195.0	198.89	234.8	229.8	238.8	239.8
parasellar	192.9	198.4	—	225.9	237.9	239.7
parathyroid (gland)	194.1	198.89	234.8	227.1	237.4	239.7
paraurethral	195.3	198.89	—	229.8	238.8	239.8
gland	189.4	198.1	233.9	223.89	236.99	239.5
paravaginal	195.3	198.89	—	229.8	238.8	239.8
parenchyma, kidney	189.0	198.0	233.9	223.0	236.91	239.5
parietal						
bone	170.0	198.5	—	213.0	238.0	239.2
lobe, brain	191.3	198.3	—	225.0	237.5	239.6
paroophoron	183.3	198.82	233.3	221.0	236.3	239.5
parotid (duct) (gland)	142.0	198.89	230.0	210.2	235.0	239.0
parovarium	183.3	198.82	233.3	221.0	236.3	239.5
patella	170.8	198.5	—	213.8	238.0	239.2
peduncle, cerebral	191.7	198.3	—	225.0	237.5	239.6
pelvirectal junction	154.0	197.5	230.4	211.4	235.2	239.0
pelvis, pelvic	195.3	198.89	234.8	229.8	238.8	239.8
bone	170.6	198.5	—	213.6	238.0	239.2
floor	195.3	198.89	234.8	229.8	238.8	239.8
renal	189.1	198.0	233.9	223.1	236.91	239.5
viscera	195.3	198.89	234.8	229.8	238.8	239.8
wall	195.3	198.89	234.8	229.8	238.8	239.8
pelvo-abdominal	195.8	198.89	234.8	229.8	238.8	239.8
penis	187.4	198.82	233.5	222.1	236.6	239.5
body	187.3	198.82	233.5	222.1	236.6	239.5
corpus (cavernosum)	187.3	198.82	233.5	222.1	236.6	239.5
glans	187.2	198.82	233.5	222.1	236.6	239.5
skin NEC	187.4	198.82	233.5	222.1	236.6	239.5
periadrenal (tissue)	158.0	197.6	—	211.8	235.4	239.0
perianal (skin)	173.5	198.2	232.5	216.5	238.2	239.2
pericardium	164.1	198.89	—	212.7	238.8	239.8
perinephric	158.0	197.6	—	211.8	235.4	239.0
perineum	195.3	198.89	234.8	229.8	238.8	239.8
periodontal tissue NEC	143.9	198.89	230.0	210.4	235.1	239.0
periosteum — *see* Neoplasm, bone						
peripancreatic	158.0	197.6	—	211.8	235.4	239.0
peripheral nerve NEC	171.9	198.89	—	215.9	238.1	239.2
perirectal (tissue)	195.3	198.89	—	229.8	238.8	239.8
perirenal (tissue)	158.0	197.6	—	211.8	235.4	239.0
peritoneum, peritoneal (cavity)	158.9	197.6	—	211.8	235.4	239.0
contiguous sites	158.8	—	—	—	—	—
with digestive organs	159.8	—	—	—	—	—
parietal	158.8	197.6	—	211.8	235.4	239.0
pelvic	158.8	197.6	—	211.8	235.4	239.0
specified part NEC	158.8	197.6	—	211.8	235.4	239.0
peritonsillar (tissue)	195.0	198.89	234.8	229.8	238.8	239.8
periurethral tissue	195.3	198.89	—	229.8	238.8	239.8
phalanges	170.9	198.5	—	213.9	238.0	239.2
foot	170.8	198.5	—	213.8	238.0	239.2
hand	170.5	198.5	—	213.5	238.0	239.2
pharynx, pharyngeal	149.0	198.89	230.0	210.9	235.1	239.0
bursa	147.1	198.89	230.0	210.7	235.1	239.0
fornix	147.3	198.89	230.0	210.7	235.1	239.0
recess	147.2	198.89	230.0	210.7	235.1	239.0
region	149.0	198.89	230.0	210.9	235.1	239.0
tonsil	147.1	198.89	230.0	210.7	235.1	239.0
wall (lateral) (posterior)	149.0	198.89	230.0	210.9	235.1	239.0
pia mater (cerebral) (cranial)	192.1	198.4	—	225.2	237.6	239.7
spinal	192.3	198.4	—	225.4	237.6	239.7
pillars of fauces	146.2	198.89	230.0	210.6	235.1	239.0
pineal (body) (gland)	194.4	198.89	234.8	227.4	237.1	239.7
pinna (ear) NEC	173.2	198.2	232.2	216.2	238.2	239.2
cartilage	171.0	198.89	—	215.0	238.1	239.2
piriform fossa or sinus	148.1	198.89	230.0	210.8	235.1	239.0
pituitary (body) (fossa) (gland) (lobe)	194.3	198.89	234.8	227.3	237.0	239.7

	Malignant					
	Primary	Secondary	Ca in situ	Benign	Uncertain Behavior	Unspecified
Neoplasm, neoplastic — *continued*						
placenta	181	198.82	233.2	219.8	236.1	239.5
pleura, pleural (cavity)	163.9	197.2	—	212.4	235.8	239.1
contiguous sites	163.8	—	—	—	—	—
parietal	163.0	197.2	—	212.4	235.8	239.1
visceral	163.1	197.2	—	212.4	235.8	239.1
plexus						
brachial	171.2	198.89	—	215.2	238.1	239.2
cervical	171.0	198.89	—	215.0	238.1	239.2
choroid	191.5	198.3	—	225.0	237.5	239.6
lumbosacral	171.6	198.89	—	215.6	238.1	239.2
sacral	171.6	198.89	—	215.6	238.1	239.2
pluri-endocrine	194.8	198.89	234.8	227.8	237.4	239.7
pole						
frontal	191.1	198.3	—	225.0	237.5	239.6
occipital	191.4	198.3	—	225.0	237.5	239.6
pons (varolii)	191.7	198.3	—	225.0	237.5	239.6
popliteal fossa or space*	195.5	198.89	234.8	229.8	238.8	239.8
postcricoid (region)	148.0	198.89	230.0	210.8	235.1	239.0
posterior fossa (cranial)	191.9	198.3	—	225.0	237.5	239.6
postnasal space	147.9	198.89	230.0	210.7	235.1	239.0
prepuce	187.1	198.82	233.5	222.1	236.6	239.5
prepylorus	151.1	197.8	230.2	211.1	235.2	239.0
presacral (region)	195.3	198.89	—	229.8	238.8	239.8
prostate (gland)	185	198.82	233.4	222.2	236.5	239.5
utricle	189.3	198.1	233.9	223.81	236.99	239.5
pterygoid fossa	171.0	198.89	—	215.0	238.1	239.2
pubic bone	170.6	198.5	—	213.6	238.0	239.2
pudenda, pudendum (female)	184.4	198.82	233.3	221.2	236.3	239.5
pulmonary	162.9	197.0	231.2	212.3	235.7	239.1
putamen	191.0	198.3	—	225.0	237.5	239.6
pyloric						
antrum	151.2	197.8	230.2	211.1	235.2	239.0
canal	151.1	197.8	230.2	211.1	235.2	239.0
pylorus	151.1	197.8	230.2	211.1	235.2	239.0
pyramid (brain)	191.7	198.3	—	225.0	237.5	239.6
pyriform fossa or sinus	148.1	198.89	230.0	210.8	235.1	239.0
radius (any part)	170.4	198.5	—	213.4	238.0	239.2
Rathke's pouch	194.3	198.89	234.8	227.3	237.0	239.7
rectosigmoid (colon) (junction)	154.0	197.5	230.4	211.4	235.2	239.0
contiguous sites with anus or rectum	154.8	—	—	—	—	—
rectouterine pouch	158.8	197.6	—	211.8	235.4	239.0
rectovaginal septum or wall	195.3	198.89	234.8	229.8	238.8	239.8
rectovesical septum	195.3	198.89	234.8	229.8	238.8	239.8
rectum (ampulla)	154.1	197.5	230.4	211.4	235.2	239.0
and colon	154.0	197.5	230.4	211.4	235.2	239.0
contiguous sites with anus or rectosigmoid junction	154.8	—	—	—	—	—
renal	189.0	198.0	233.9	223.0	236.91	239.5
calyx	189.1	198.0	233.9	223.1	236.91	239.5
hilus	189.1	198.0	233.9	223.1	236.91	239.5
parenchyma	189.0	198.0	233.9	223.0	236.91	239.5
pelvis	189.1	198.0	233.9	223.1	236.91	239.5
respiratory						
organs or system NEC	165.9	197.3	231.9	212.9	235.9	239.1
contiguous sites with intrathoracic organs	165.8	—	—	—	—	—
specified sites NEC	165.8	197.3	231.8	212.8	235.9	239.1
tract NEC	165.9	197.3	231.9	212.9	235.9	239.1
upper	165.0	197.3	231.9	212.9	235.9	239.1
retina	190.5	198.4	234.0	224.5	238.8	239.8
retrobulbar	190.1	198.4	—	224.1	238.8	239.8
retrocecal	158.0	197.6	—	211.8	235.4	239.0
retromolar (area) (triangle) (trigone)	145.6	198.89	230.0	210.4	235.1	239.0
retro-orbital	195.0	198.89	234.8	229.8	238.8	239.8

	Malignant					
	Primary	Secondary	Ca in situ	Benign	Uncertain Behavior	Unspecified
Neoplasm, neoplastic — *continued*						
retroperitoneal (space) (tissue)	158.0	197.6	—	211.8	235.4	239.0
contiguous sites	158.8	—	—	—	—	—
retroperitoneum	158.0	197.6	—	211.8	235.4	239.0
contiguous sites	158.8	—	—	—	—	—
retropharyngeal	149.0	198.89	230.0	210.9	235.1	239.0
retrovesical (septum)	195.3	198.89	234.8	229.8	238.8	239.8
rhinencephalon	191.0	198.3	—	225.0	237.5	239.6
rib	170.3	198.5	—	213.3	238.0	239.2
Rosenmüller's fossa	147.2	198.89	230.0	210.7	235.1	239.0
round ligament	183.5	198.82	—	221.0	236.3	239.5
sacrococcyx, sacrococcygeal	170.6	198.5	—	213.6	238.0	239.2
region	195.3	198.89	234.8	229.8	238.8	239.8
sacrouterine ligament	183.4	198.82	—	221.0	236.3	239.5
sacrum, sacral (vertebra)	170.6	198.5	—	213.6	238.0	239.2
salivary gland or duct (major)	142.9	198.89	230.0	210.2	235.0	239.0
contiguous sites	142.8	—	—	—	—	—
minor NEC	145.9	198.89	230.0	210.4	235.1	239.0
parotid	142.0	198.89	230.0	210.2	235.0	239.0
pluriglandular	142.8	198.89	—	210.2	235.0	239.0
sublingual	142.2	198.89	230.0	210.2	235.0	239.0
submandibular	142.1	198.89	230.0	210.2	235.0	239.0
submaxillary	142.1	198.89	230.0	210.2	235.0	239.0
salpinx (uterine)	183.2	198.82	233.3	221.0	236.3	239.5
Santorini's duct	157.3	197.8	230.9	211.6	235.5	239.0
scalp	173.4	198.2	232.4	216.4	238.2	239.2
scapula (any part)	170.4	198.5	—	213.4	238.0	239.2
scapular region	195.1	198.89	234.8	229.8	238.8	239.8
scar NEC (*see also* Neoplasm, skin)	173.9	198.2	232.9	216.9	238.2	239.2
sciatic nerve	171.3	198.89	—	215.3	238.1	239.2
sclera	190.0	198.4	234.0	224.0	238.8	239.8
scrotum (skin)	187.7	198.82	—	222.4	236.6	239.5
sebaceous gland — *see* Neoplasm, skin						
sella turcica	194.3	198.89	234.8	227.3	237.0	239.7
bone	170.0	198.5	—	213.0	238.0	239.2
semilunar cartilage (knee)	170.7	198.5	—	213.7	238.0	239.2
seminal vesicle	187.8	198.82	233.6	222.8	236.6	239.5
septum						
nasal	160.0	197.3	231.8	212.0	235.9	239.1
posterior margin	147.3	198.89	230.0	210.7	235.1	239.0
rectovaginal	195.3	198.89	234.8	229.8	238.8	239.8
rectovesical	195.3	198.89	234.8	229.8	238.8	239.8
urethrovaginal	184.9	198.82	233.3	221.9	236.3	239.5
vesicovaginal	184.9	198.82	233.3	221.9	236.3	239.5
shoulder NEC*	195.4	198.89	232.6	229.8	238.8	239.8
sigmoid flexure (lower) (upper)	153.3	197.5	230.3	211.3	235.2	239.0
sinus (accessory)	160.9	197.3	231.8	212.0	235.9	239.1
bone (any)	170.0	198.5	—	213.0	238.0	239.2
contiguous sites with middle ear or nasal cavities	160.8	—	—	—	—	—
ethmoidal	160.3	197.3	231.8	212.0	235.9	239.1
frontal	160.4	197.3	231.8	212.0	235.9	239.1
maxillary	160.2	197.3	231.8	212.0	235.9	239.1
nasal, paranasal NEC	160.9	197.3	231.8	212.0	235.9	239.1
pyriform	148.1	198.89	230.0	210.8	235.1	239.0
sphenoidal	160.5	197.3	231.8	212.0	235.9	239.1
skeleton, skeletal NEC	170.9	198.5	—	213.9	238.0	239.2
Skene's gland	189.4	198.1	233.9	223.89	236.99	239.5
skin NEC	173.9	198.2	232.9	216.9	238.2	239.2
abdominal wall	173.5	198.2	232.5	216.5	238.2	239.2
ala nasi	173.3	198.2	232.3	216.3	238.2	239.2
ankle	173.7	198.2	232.7	216.7	238.2	239.2
antecubital space	173.6	198.2	232.6	216.6	238.2	239.2
anus	173.5	198.2	232.5	216.5	238.2	239.2
arm	173.6	198.2	232.6	216.6	238.2	239.2
auditory canal (external)	173.2	198.2	232.2	216.2	238.2	239.2
Neoplasm, neoplastic — *continued*						
skin — *continued*						
auricle (ear)	173.2	198.2	232.2	216.2	238.2	239.2
auricular canal (external)	173.2	198.2	232.2	216.2	238.2	239.2
axilla, axillary fold	173.5	198.2	232.5	216.5	238.2	239.2
back	173.5	198.2	232.5	216.5	238.2	239.2
breast	173.5	198.2	232.5	216.5	238.2	239.2
brow	173.3	198.2	232.3	216.3	238.2	239.2
buttock	173.5	198.2	232.5	216.5	238.2	239.2
calf	173.7	198.2	232.7	216.7	238.2	239.2
canthus (eye) (inner) (outer)	173.1	198.2	232.1	216.1	238.2	239.2
cervical region	173.4	198.2	232.4	216.4	238.2	239.2
cheek (external)	173.3	198.2	232.3	216.3	238.2	239.2
chest (wall)	173.5	198.2	232.5	216.5	238.2	239.2
chin	173.3	198.2	232.3	216.3	238.2	239.2
clavicular area	173.5	198.2	232.5	216.5	238.2	239.2
clitoris	—	198.82	233.3	221.2	236.3	239.5
columnella	173.3	198.2	232.3	216.3	238.2	239.2
concha	173.2	198.2	232.2	216.2	238.2	239.2
contiguous sites	173.8	—	—	—	—	—
ear (external)	173.2	198.2	232.2	216.2	238.2	239.2
elbow	173.6	198.2	232.6	216.6	238.2	239.2
eyebrow	173.3	198.2	232.3	216.3	238.2	239.2
eyelid	173.1	198.2	232.1	—	238.2	239.2
face NEC	173.3	198.2	232.3	216.3	238.2	239.2
female genital organs (external)	184.4	198.82	233.3	221.2	236.3	239.5
clitoris	184.3	198.82	233.3	221.2	236.3	239.5
labium NEC	184.4	198.82	233.3	221.2	236.3	239.5
majus	184.1	198.82	233.3	221.2	236.3	239.5
minus	184.2	198.82	233.3	221.2	236.3	239.5
pudendum	184.4	198.82	233.3	221.2	236.3	239.5
vulva	184.4	198.82	233.3	221.2	236.3	239.5
finger	173.6	198.2	232.6	216.6	238.2	239.2
flank	173.5	198.2	232.5	216.5	238.2	239.2
foot	173.7	198.2	232.7	216.7	238.2	239.2
forearm	173.6	198.2	232.6	216.6	238.2	239.2
forehead	173.3	198.2	232.3	216.3	238.2	239.2
glabella	173.3	198.2	232.3	216.3	238.2	239.2
gluteal region	173.5	198.2	232.5	216.5	238.2	239.2
groin	173.5	198.2	232.5	216.5	238.2	239.2
hand	173.6	198.2	232.6	216.6	238.2	239.2
head NEC	173.4	198.2	232.4	216.4	238.2	239.2
heel	173.7	198.2	232.7	216.7	238.2	239.2
helix	173.2	198.2	—	216.2	238.2	239.2
hip	173.7	198.2	232.7	216.7	238.2	239.2
infraclavicular region	173.5	198.2	232.5	216.5	238.2	239.2
inguinal region	173.5	198.2	232.5	216.5	238.2	239.2
jaw	173.3	198.2	232.3	216.3	238.2	239.2
knee	173.7	198.2	232.7	216.7	238.2	239.2
labia						
majora	184.1	198.82	233.3	221.2	236.3	239.5
minora	184.2	198.82	233.3	221.2	236.3	239.5
leg	173.7	198.2	232.7	216.7	238.2	239.2
lid (lower) (upper)	—	198.2	232.1	216.1	238.2	239.2
limb NEC	173.9	198.2	232.9	216.9	238.2	239.5
lower	173.7	198.2	232.7	216.7	238.2	239.2
upper	173.6	198.2	232.6	216.6	238.2	239.2
lip (lower) (upper)	173.0	198.2	232.0	216.0	238.2	239.2
male genital organs	187.9	198.82	233.6	222.9	236.6	239.5
penis	187.4	198.82	233.5	222.1	236.6	239.5
prepuce	187.1	198.82	233.5	222.1	236.6	239.5
scrotum	187.7	198.82	233.6	222.4	236.6	239.5
mastectomy site	173.5	198.2	—	—	—	—
specified as breast tissue	174.8	198.81	—	—	—	—
meatus, acoustic (external)	173.2	198.2	232.2	216.2	238.2	239.2
nates	173.5	198.2	232.5	216.5	238.2	239.0
neck	173.4	198.2	232.4	216.4	238.2	239.2
nose (external)	173.3	198.2	232.3	216.3	238.2	239.2
palm	173.6	198.2	232.6	216.6	238.2	239.2
palpebra	173.1	198.2	232.1	216.1	238.2	239.2
penis NEC	187.4	198.82	233.5	222.1	236.6	239.5
perianal	173.5	198.2	232.5	216.5	238.2	239.2

	Malignant					
	Primary	Secondary	Ca in situ	Benign	Uncertain Behavior	Unspecified
Neoplasm, neoplastic — *continued*						
skin — *continued*						
perineum	173.5	198.2	232.5	216.5	238.2	239.2
pinna	173.2	198.2	232.2	216.2	238.2	239.2
plantar	173.7	198.2	232.7	216.7	238.2	239.2
popliteal fossa or space	173.7	198.2	232.7	216.7	238.2	239.2
prepuce	187.1	198.82	233.5	222.1	236.6	239.5
pubes	173.5	198.2	232.5	216.5	238.2	239.2
sacrococcygeal region	173.5	198.2	232.5	216.5	238.2	239.2
scalp	173.4	198.2	232.4	216.4	238.2	239.2
scapular region	173.5	198.2	232.5	216.5	238.2	239.2
scrotum	187.7	198.82	233.6	222.4	236.6	239.5
shoulder	173.6	198.2	232.6	216.6	238.2	239.2
sole (foot)	173.7	198.2	232.7	216.7	238.2	239.2
specified sites NEC	173.8	198.2	232.8	216.8	232.8	239.2
submammary fold	173.5	198.2	232.5	216.5	238.2	239.2
supraclavicular region	173.4	198.2	232.4	216.4	238.2	239.2
temple	173.3	198.2	232.3	216.3	238.2	239.2
thigh	173.7	198.2	232.7	216.7	238.2	239.2
thoracic wall	173.5	198.2	232.5	216.5	238.2	239.2
thumb	173.6	198.2	232.6	216.6	238.2	239.2
toe	173.7	198.2	232.7	216.7	238.2	239.2
tragus	173.2	198.2	232.2	216.2	238.2	239.2
trunk	173.5	198.2	232.5	216.5	238.2	239.2
umbilicus	173.5	198.2	232.5	216.5	238.2	239.2
vulva	184.4	198.82	233.3	221.2	236.3	239.5
wrist	173.6	198.2	232.6	216.6	238.2	239.2
skull	170.0	198.5	—	213.0	238.0	239.2
soft parts or tissues — *see* Neoplasm, connective tissue						
specified site NEC	195.8	198.89	234.8	229.8	238.8	239.8
specified site — *see* Neoplasm, skin						
spermatic cord	187.6	198.82	233.6	222.8	236.6	239.5
sphenoid	160.5	197.3	231.8	212.0	235.9	239.1
bone	170.0	198.5	—	213.0	238.0	239.2
sinus	160.5	197.3	231.8	212.0	235.9	239.1
sphincter						
anal	154.2	197.5	230.5	211.4	235.5	239.0
of Oddi	156.1	197.8	230.8	211.5	235.3	239.0
spine, spinal (column)	170.2	198.5	—	213.2	238.0	239.2
bulb	191.7	198.3	—	225.0	237.5	239.6
coccyx	170.6	198.5	—	213.6	238.0	239.2
cord (cervical) (lumbar) (sacral) (thoracic)	192.2	198.3	—	225.3	237.5	239.7
dura mater	192.3	198.4	—	225.4	237.6	239.7
lumbosacral	170.2	198.5	—	213.2	238.0	239.2
membrane	192.3	198.4	—	225.4	237.6	239.7
meninges	192.3	198.4	—	225.4	237.6	239.7
nerve (root)	171.9	198.89	—	215.9	238.1	239.2
pia mater	192.3	198.4	—	225.4	237.6	239.7
root	171.9	198.89	—	215.9	238.1	239.2
sacrum	170.6	198.5	—	213.6	238.0	239.2
spleen, splenic NEC	159.1	197.8	230.9	211.9	235.5	239.0
flexure (colon)	153.7	197.5	230.3	211.3	235.2	239.0
stem, brain	191.7	198.3	—	225.0	237.5	239.6
Stensen's duct	142.0	198.89	230.0	210.2	235.0	239.0
sternum	170.3	198.5	—	213.3	238.0	239.2
stomach	151.9	197.8	230.2	211.1	235.2	239.0
antrum (pyloric)	151.2	197.8	230.2	211.1	235.2	239.0
body	151.4	197.8	230.2	211.1	235.2	239.0
cardia	151.0	197.8	230.2	211.1	235.2	239.0
cardiac orifice	151.0	197.8	230.2	211.1	235.2	239.0
contiguous sites	151.8	—	—	—	—	—
corpus	151.4	197.8	230.2	211.1	235.2	239.0
fundus	151.3	197.8	230.2	211.1	235.2	239.0
greater curvature NEC	151.6	197.8	230.2	211.1	235.2	239.0
lesser curvature NEC	151.5	197.8	230.2	211.1	235.2	239.0
prepylorus	151.1	197.8	230.2	211.1	235.2	239.0
pylorus	151.1	197.8	230.2	211.1	235.2	239.0
wall NEC	151.9	197.8	230.2	211.1	235.2	239.0
Neoplasm, neoplastic — *continued*						
stomach — *continued*						
wall — *continued*						
anterior NEC	151.8	197.8	230.2	211.1	235.2	239.0
posterior NEC	151.8	197.8	230.2	211.1	235.2	239.0
stroma, endometrial	182.0	198.82	233.2	219.1	236.0	239.5
stump, cervical	180.8	198.82	233.1	219.0	236.0	239.5
subcutaneous (nodule) (tissue) NEC — *see* Neoplasm, connective tissue						
subdural	192.1	198.4	—	225.2	237.6	239.7
subglottis, subglottic	161.2	197.3	231.0	212.1	235.6	239.1
sublingual	144.9	198.89	230.0	210.3	235.1	239.0
gland or duct	142.2	198.89	230.0	210.2	235.0	239.0
submandibular gland	142.1	198.89	230.0	210.2	235.0	239.0
submaxillary gland or duct	142.1	198.89	230.0	210.2	235.0	239.0
submental	195.0	198.89	234.8	229.8	238.8	239.8
subpleural	162.9	197.0	—	212.3	235.7	239.1
substernal	164.2	197.1	—	212.5	235.8	239.8
sudoriferous, sudoriparous gland, site unspecified	173.9	198.2	232.9	216.9	238.2	239.2
specified site — *see* Neoplasm, skin						
supraclavicular region	195.0	198.89	234.8	229.8	238.8	239.8
supraglottis	161.1	197.3	231.0	212.1	235.6	239.1
suprarenal (capsule) (cortex) (gland) (medulla)	194.0	198.7	234.8	227.0	237.2	239.7
suprasellar (region)	191.9	198.3	—	225.0	237.5	239.6
sweat gland (apocrine) (eccrine), site unspecified	173.9	198.2	232.9	216.9	238.2	239.2
sympathetic nerve or nervous system NEC	171.9	198.89	—	215.9	238.1	239.2
symphysis pubis	170.6	198.5	—	213.6	238.0	239.2
synovial membrane — *see* Neoplasm, connective tissue						
tapetum, brain	191.8	198.3	—	225.0	237.5	239.6
tarsus (any bone)	170.8	198.5	—	213.8	238.0	239.2
temple (skin)	173.3	198.2	232.3	216.3	238.2	239.2
temporal						
bone	170.0	198.5	—	213.0	238.0	239.2
lobe or pole	191.2	198.3	—	225.0	237.5	239.6
region	195.0	198.89	234.8	229.8	238.8	239.8
skin	173.3	198.2	232.3	216.3	238.2	239.2
tendon (sheath) — *see* Neoplasm, connective tissue						
tentorium (cerebelli)	192.1	198.4	—	225.2	237.6	239.7
testis, testes (descended) (scrotal)	186.9	198.82	233.6	222.0	236.4	239.5
ectopic	186.0	198.82	233.6	222.0	236.4	239.5
retained	186.0	198.82	233.6	222.0	236.4	239.5
undescended	186.0	198.82	233.6	222.0	236.4	239.5
thalamus	191.0	198.3	—	225.0	237.5	239.6
thigh NEC*	195.5	198.89	234.8	229.8	238.8	239.8
thorax, thoracic (cavity) (organs NEC)	195.1	198.89	234.8	229.8	238.8	239.8
duct	171.4	198.89	—	215.4	238.1	239.2
wall NEC	195.1	198.89	234.8	229.8	238.8	239.8
throat	149.0	198.89	230.0	210.9	235.1	239.0
thumb NEC*	195.4	198.89	232.6	229.8	238.8	239.8
thymus (gland)	164.0	198.89	—	212.6	235.8	239.8
contiguous sites with heart and mediastinum	164.8	—	—	—	—	—
thyroglossal duct	193	198.89	234.8	226	237.4	239.7
thyroid (gland)	193	198.89	234.8	226	237.4	239.7
cartilage	161.3	197.3	231.0	212.1	235.6	239.1
tibia (any part)	170.7	198.5	—	213.7	238.0	239.2
toe NEC*	195.5	198.89	232.7	229.8	238.8	239.8
tongue	141.9	198.89	230.0	210.1	235.1	239.0
anterior (two-thirds) NEC	141.4	198.89	230.0	210.1	235.1	239.0

	Malignant					
	Primary	Secondary	Ca in situ	Benign	Uncertain Behavior	Unspecified
Neoplasm, neoplastic — *continued*						
tongue — *continued*						
anterior — *continued*						
dorsal surface	141.1	198.89	230.0	210.1	235.1	239.0
ventral surface	141.3	198.89	230.0	210.1	235.1	239.0
base (dorsal surface)	141.0	198.89	230.0	210.1	235.1	239.0
border (lateral)	141.2	198.89	230.0	210.1	235.1	239.0
contiguous sites	141.8	—	—	—	—	—
dorsal surface NEC	141.1	198.89	230.0	210.1	235.1	239.0
fixed part NEC	141.0	198.89	230.0	210.1	235.1	239.0
foreamen cecum	141.1	198.89	230.0	210.1	235.1	239.0
frenulum linguae	141.3	198.89	230.0	210.1	235.1	239.0
junctional zone	141.5	198.89	230.0	210.1	235.1	239.0
margin (lateral)	141.2	198.89	230.0	210.1	235.1	239.0
midline NEC	141.1	198.89	230.0	210.1	235.1	239.0
mobile part NEC	141.4	198.89	230.0	210.1	235.1	239.0
posterior (third)	141.0	198.89	230.0	210.1	235.1	239.0
root	141.0	198.89	230.0	210.1	235.1	239.0
surface (dorsal)	141.1	198.89	230.0	210.1	235.1	239.0
base	141.0	198.89	230.0	210.1	235.1	239.0
ventral	141.3	198.89	230.0	210.1	235.1	239.0
tip	141.2	198.89	230.0	210.1	235.1	239.0
tonsil	141.6	198.89	230.0	210.1	235.1	239.0
tonsil	146.0	198.89	230.0	210.5	235.1	239.0
fauces, faucial	146.0	198.89	230.0	210.5	235.1	239.0
lingual	141.6	198.89	230.0	210.1	235.1	239.0
palatine	146.0	198.89	230.0	210.5	235.1	239.0
pharyngeal	147.1	198.89	230.0	210.7	235.1	239.0
pillar (anterior) (posterior)	146.2	198.89	230.0	210.6	235.1	239.0
tonsillar fossa	146.1	198.89	230.0	210.6	235.1	239.0
tooth socket NEC	143.9	198.89	230.0	210.4	235.1	239.0
trachea (cartilage) (mucosa)	162.0	197.3	231.1	212.2	235.7	239.1
contiguous sites with bronchus or lung	162.8	—	—	—	—	—
tracheobronchial	162.8	197.3	231.1	212.2	235.7	239.1
contiguous sites with lung	162.8	—	—	—	—	—
tragus	173.2	198.2	232.2	216.2	238.2	239.2
trunk NEC*	195.8	198.89	232.5	229.8	238.8	239.8
tubo-ovarian	183.8	198.82	233.3	221.8	236.3	239.5
tunica vaginalis	187.8	198.82	233.6	222.8	236.6	239.5
turbinate (bone)	170.0	198.5	—	213.0	238.0	239.2
nasal	160.0	197.3	231.8	212.0	235.9	239.1
tympanic cavity	160.1	197.3	231.8	212.0	235.9	239.1
ulna (any part)	170.4	198.5	—	213.4	238.0	239.2
umbilicus, umbilical	173.5	198.2	232.5	216.5	238.2	239.2
uncus, brain	191.2	198.3	—	225.0	237.5	239.6
unknown site or unspecified	199.1	199.1	234.9	229.9	238.9	239.9
urachus	188.7	198.1	233.7	223.3	236.7	239.4
ureter-bladder junction)	188.6	198.1	233.7	223.3	236.7	239.4
ureter, ureteral	189.2	198.1	233.9	223.2	236.91	239.5
orifice (bladder)	188.6	198.1	233.7	223.3	236.7	239.4
urethra, urethral (gland)	189.3	198.1	233.9	223.81	236.99	239.5
orifice, internal	188.5	198.1	233.7	223.3	236.7	239.4
urethrovaginal (septum)	184.9	198.82	233.3	221.9	236.3	239.5
urinary organ or system NEC	189.9	198.1	233.9	223.9	236.99	239.5
bladder — *see* Neoplasm, bladder						
contiguous sites	189.8	—	—	—	—	—
specified sites NEC	189.8	198.1	233.9	223.89	236.99	239.5
utero-ovarian	183.8	198.82	233.3	221.8	236.3	239.5
ligament	183.3	198.82	—	221.0	236.3	239.5
uterosacral ligament	183.4	198.82	—	221.0	236.3	239.5
uterus, uteri, uterine	179	198.82	233.2	219.9	236.0	239.5
adnexa NEC	183.9	198.82	233.3	221.8	236.3	239.5
contiguous sites	183.8	—	—	—	—	—
body	182.0	198.82	233.2	219.1	236.0	239.5
contiguous sites	182.8	—	—	—	—	—
cervix	180.9	198.82	233.1	219.0	236.0	239.5

	Malignant					
	Primary	Secondary	Ca in situ	Benign	Uncertain Behavior	Unspecified
Neoplasm, neoplastic — *continued*						
uterus, uteri, uterine — *continued*						
cornu	182.0	198.82	233.2	219.1	236.0	239.5
corpus	182.0	198.82	233.2	219.1	236.0	239.5
endocervix (canal) (gland)	180.0	198.82	233.1	219.0	236.0	239.5
endometrium	182.0	198.82	233.2	219.1	236.0	239.5
exocervix	180.1	198.82	233.1	219.0	236.0	239.5
external os	180.1	198.82	233.1	219.0	236.0	239.5
fundus	182.0	198.82	233.2	219.1	236.0	239.5
internal os	180.0	198.82	233.1	219.0	236.0	239.5
isthmus	182.1	198.82	233.2	219.1	236.0	239.5
ligament	183.4	198.82	—	221.0	236.3	239.5
broad	183.3	198.82	233.3	221.0	236.3	239.5
round	183.5	198.82	—	221.0	236.3	239.5
lower segment	182.1	198.82	233.2	219.1	236.0	239.5
myometrium	182.0	198.82	233.2	219.1	236.0	239.5
squamocolumnar junction	180.8	198.82	233.1	219.0	236.0	239.5
tube	183.2	198.82	233.3	221.0	236.3	239.5
utricle, prostatic	189.3	198.1	233.9	223.81	236.99	239.5
uveal tract	190.0	198.4	234.0	224.0	238.8	239.8
uvula	145.4	198.89	230.0	210.4	235.1	239.0
vagina, vaginal (fornix) (vault) (wall)	184.0	198.82	233.3	221.1	236.3	239.5
vaginovesical	184.9	198.82	233.3	221.9	236.3	239.5
septum	194.9	198.82	233.3	221.9	236.3	239.5
vallecula (epiglottis)	146.3	198.89	230.0	210.6	235.1	239.0
vascular — *see* Neoplasm, connective tissue						
vas deferens	187.6	198.82	233.6	222.8	236.6	239.5
Vater's ampulla	156.2	197.8	230.8	211.5	235.3	239.0
vein, venous — *see* Neoplasm, connective tissue						
vena cava (abdominal) (inferior)	171.5	198.89	—	215.5	238.1	239.2
superior	171.4	198.89	—	215.4	238.1	239.2
ventricle (cerebral) (floor) (fourth) (lateral) (third)	191.5	198.3	—	225.0	237.5	239.6
cardiac (left) (right)	164.1	198.89	—	212.7	238.8	239.8
ventricular band of larynx	161.1	197.3	231.0	212.1	235.6	239.1
ventriculus — see Neoplasm, stomach						
vermillion border — *see* Neoplasm, lip						
vermis, cerebellum	191.6	198.3	—	225.0	237.5	239.6
vertebra (column)	170.2	198.5	—	213.2	238.0	239.2
coccyx	170.6	198.5	—	213.6	238.0	239.2
sacrum	170.6	198.5	—	213.6	238.0	239.2
vesical — *see* Neoplasm, bladder						
vesicle, seminal	187.8	198.82	233.6	222.8	236.6	239.5
vesicocervical tissue	184.9	198.82	233.3	221.9	236.3	239.5
vesicorectal	195.3	198.89	234.8	229.8	238.8	239.8
vesicovaginal	184.9	198.82	233.3	221.9	236.3	239.5
septum	184.9	198.82	233.3	221.9	236.3	239.5
vessel (blood) — *see* Neoplasm, connective tissue						
vestibular gland, greater	184.1	198.82	233.3	221.2	236.3	239.5
vestibule						
mouth	145.1	198.89	230.0	210.4	235.1	239.0
nose	160.0	197.3	231.8	212.0	235.9	239.1
Virchow's gland	—	196.0	—	229.0	238.8	239.8
viscera NEC	195.8	198.89	234.8	229.8	238.8	239.8
vocal cords (true)	161.0	197.3	231.0	212.1	235.6	239.1
false	161.1	197.3	231.0	212.1	235.6	239.1
vomer	170.0	198.5	—	213.0	238.0	239.2
vulva	184.4	198.82	233.3	221.2	236.3	239.5
vulvovaginal gland	184.4	198.82	233.3	221.2	236.3	239.5
Waldeyer's ring	149.1	198.89	230.0	210.9	235.1	239.0
Wharton's duct	142.1	198.89	230.0	210.2	235.0	239.0

	Malignant					
	Primary	Secondary	Ca in situ	Benign	Uncertain Behavior	Unspecified
Neoplasm, neoplastic — *continued*						
white matter (central)						
(cerebral)	191.0	198.3	—	225.0	237.5	239.6
windpipe	162.0	197.3	231.1	212.2	235.7	239.1
Wirsung's duct	157.3	197.8	230.9	211.6	235.5	239.0
wolffian (body) (duct)						
female	184.8	198.82	233.3	221.8	236.3	239.5
male	187.8	198.82	233.6	222.8	236.6	239.5
womb — *see* Neoplasm, uterus						
wrist NEC*	195.4	198.89	232.6	229.8	238.8	239.8
xiphoid process	170.3	198.5	—	213.3	238.0	239.2
Zuckerkandl's organ	194.6	198.89	—	227.6	237.3	239.7

☑ Additional Digit Required — Refer to the Tabular List for Digit Selection

Subterms under main terms may continue to next column or page

▶◀ Revised Text   ● New Line   ▲ Revised Code

Note — Use the following fifth-digit subclassification with category 715:

0	*site unspecified*
1	*shoulder region*
2	*upper arm*
3	*forearm*
4	*hand*
5	*pelvic region and thigh*
6	*lower leg*
7	*ankle and foot*
8	*other specified sites except spine*
9	*multiple sites*

P

☑ Additional Digit Required — Refer to the Tabular List for Digit Selection

Subterms under main terms may continue to next column or page

▶◀ Revised Text ● New Line ▲ Revised Code

Paralysis, paralytic — *continued*
- bulbar — *continued*
  - pseudo 335.23
  - supranuclear 344.89
- bulbospinal 358.00
- cardiac (*see also* Failure, heart) 428.9
- cerebral
  - current episode 437.8
  - spastic, infantile — *see* Palsy, cerebral
- cerebrocerebellar 437.8
  - diplegic infantile 343.0
- cervical
  - plexus 353.2
  - sympathetic NEC 337.0
- Céstan-Chenais 344.89
- Charcôt-Marie-Tooth type 356.1
- childhood — *see* Palsy, cerebral
- Clark's 343.9
- colon (*see also* Ileus) 560.1
- compressed air 993.3
- compression
  - arm NEC 354.9
  - cerebral — *see* Paralysis, brain
  - leg NEC 355.8
  - lower extremity NEC 355.8
  - upper extremity NEC 354.9
- congenital (cerebral) (spastic) (spinal) — *see* Palsy, cerebral
- conjugate movement (of eye) 378.81
  - cortical (nuclear) (supranuclear) 378.81
- convergence 378.83
- cordis (*see also* Failure, heart) 428.9
- cortical (*see also* Paralysis, brain) 437.8
- cranial or cerebral nerve (*see also* Disorder, nerve, cranial) 352.9
- creeping 335.21
- crossed leg 344.89
- crutch 953.4
- deglutition 784.99 ▲
  - hysterical 300.11
- dementia 094.1
- descending (spinal) NEC 335.9
- diaphragm (flaccid) 519.4
  - due to accidental section of phrenic nerve during procedure 998.2
- digestive organs NEC 564.89
- diplegic — *see* Diplegia
- divergence (nuclear) 378.85
- divers' 993.3
- Duchenne's 335.22
- due to intracranial or spinal birth injury — *see* Palsy, cerebral
- embolic (current episode) (*see also* Embolism, brain) 434.1 ☑
  - late effect — *see* Late effect(s) (of) cerebrovascular disease
- enteric (*see also* Ileus) 560.1
  - with hernia — *see* Hernia, by site, with obstruction
- Erb (-Duchenne) (birth) (newborn) 767.6
- Erb's syphilitic spastic spinal 094.89
- esophagus 530.89
- essential, infancy (*see also* Poliomyelitis) 045.9 ☑
- extremity
  - lower — *see* Paralysis, leg
  - spastic (hereditary) 343.3
    - noncongenital or noninfantile 344.1
  - transient (cause unknown) 781.4
  - upper — *see* Paralysis, arm
- eye muscle (extrinsic) 378.55
  - intrinsic 367.51
- facial (nerve) 351.0
  - birth injury 767.5
  - congenital 767.5
  - following operation NEC 998.2
  - newborn 767.5
- familial 359.3
  - periodic 359.3
  - spastic 334.1

Paralysis, paralytic — *continued*
- fauces 478.29
- finger NEC 354.9
- foot NEC 355.8
- gait 781.2
- gastric nerve 352.3
- gaze 378.81
- general 094.1
  - ataxic 094.1
  - insane 094.1
  - juvenile 090.40
  - progressive 094.1
  - tabetic 094.1
- glossopharyngeal (nerve) 352.2
- glottis (*see also* Paralysis, vocal cord) 478.30
- gluteal 353.4
- Gubler (-Millard) 344.89
- hand 354.9
  - hysterical 300.11
  - psychogenic 306.0
- heart (*see also* Failure, heart) 428.9
- hemifacial, progressive 349.89
- hemiplegic — *see* Hemiplegia
- hyperkalemic periodic (familial) 359.3
- hypertensive (current episode) 437.8
- hypoglossal (nerve) 352.5
- hypokalemic periodic 359.3
- Hyrtl's sphincter (rectum) 569.49
- hysterical 300.11
- ileus (*see also* Ileus) 560.1
- infantile (*see also* Poliomyelitis) 045.9 ☑
  - atrophic acute 045.1 ☑
  - bulbar 045.0 ☑
  - cerebral — *see* Palsy, cerebral
  - paralytic 045.1 ☑
  - progressive acute 045.9 ☑
  - spastic — *see* Palsy, cerebral
  - spinal 045.9 ☑
- infective (*see also* Poliomyelitis) 045.9 ☑
- inferior nuclear 344.9
- insane, general or progressive 094.1
- internuclear 378.86
- interosseous 355.9
- intestine (*see also* Ileus) 560.1
- intracranial (current episode) (*see also* Paralysis, brain) 437.8
  - due to birth injury 767.0
- iris 379.49
  - due to diphtheria (toxin) 032.81 *[379.49]*
- ischemic, Volkmann's (complicating trauma) 958.6
- isolated sleep, recurrent
- Jackson's 344.89
- jake 357.7
- Jamaica ginger (jake) 357.7
- juvenile general 090.40
- Klumpke (-Déjérine) (birth) (newborn) 767.6
- labioglossal (laryngeal) (pharyngeal) 335.22
- Landry's 357.0
- laryngeal nerve (recurrent) (superior) (*see also* Paralysis, vocal cord) 478.30
- larynx (*see also* Paralysis, vocal cord) 478.30
  - due to diphtheria (toxin) 032.3
- late effect
  - due to
    - birth injury, brain or spinal (cord) — *see* Palsy, cerebral
    - edema, brain or cerebral — *see* Paralysis, brain
    - lesion
      - late effect — *see* Late effect(s) (of) cerebrovascular disease
    - spinal (cord) — *see* Paralysis, spinal
- lateral 335.24
- lead 984.9

Paralysis, paralytic — *continued*
- lead — *continued*
  - specified type of lead — *see* Table of Drugs and Chemicals
- left side — *see* Hemiplegia
- leg 344.30
  - affecting
    - dominant side 344.31
    - nondominant side 344.32
  - both (*see also* Paraplegia) 344.1
  - crossed 344.89
  - hysterical 300.11
  - psychogenic 306.0
  - transient or transitory 781.4
    - traumatic NEC (*see also* Injury, nerve, lower limb) 956.9
- levator palpebrae superioris 374.31
- limb NEC 344.5
  - all four — *see* Quadriplegia
  - quadriplegia — *see* Quadriplegia
- lip 528.5
- Lissauer's 094.1
- local 355.9
- lower limb (*see also* Paralysis, leg)
  - both (*see also* Paraplegia) 344.1
- lung 518.89
  - newborn 770.89
- median nerve 354.1
- medullary (tegmental) 344.89
- mesencephalic NEC 344.89
  - tegmental 344.89
- middle alternating 344.89
- Millard-Gubler-Foville 344.89
- monoplegic — *see* Monoplegia
- motor NEC 344.9
  - cerebral — *see* Paralysis, brain
  - spinal — *see* Paralysis, spinal
- multiple
  - cerebral — *see* Paralysis, brain
  - spinal — *see* Paralysis, spinal
- muscle (flaccid) 359.9
  - due to nerve lesion NEC 355.9
  - eye (extrinsic) 378.55
    - intrinsic 367.51
    - oblique 378.51
  - iris sphincter 364.8
  - ischemic (complicating trauma) (Volkmann's) 958.6
  - pseudohypertrophic 359.1
- muscular (atrophic) 359.9
  - progressive 335.21
- musculocutaneous nerve 354.9
- musculospiral 354.9
- nerve (*see also* Disorder, nerve)
  - third or oculomotor (partial) 378.51
    - total 378.52
  - fourth or trochlear 378.53
  - sixth or abducens 378.54
  - seventh or facial 351.0
    - birth injury 767.5
    - due to
      - injection NEC 999.9
      - operation NEC 997.09
    - newborn 767.5
  - accessory 352.4
  - auditory 388.5
  - birth injury 767.7
  - cranial or cerebral (*see also* Disorder, nerve, cranial) 352.9
  - facial 351.0
    - birth injury 767.5
    - newborn 767.5
  - laryngeal (*see also* Paralysis, vocal cord) 478.30
  - newborn 767.7
  - phrenic 354.8
    - newborn 767.7
  - radial 354.3
    - birth injury 767.6
    - newborn 767.6
  - syphilitic 094.89
  - traumatic NEC (*see also* Injury, nerve, by site) 957.9
  - trigeminal 350.9
  - ulnar 354.2
- newborn NEC 767.0

Paralysis, paralytic — *continued*
- normokalemic periodic 359.3
- obstetrical, newborn 767.7
- ocular 378.9
- oculofacial, congenital 352.6
- oculomotor (nerve) (partial) 378.51
  - alternating 344.89
  - external bilateral 378.55
  - total 378.52
- olfactory nerve 352.0
- palate 528.9
- palatopharyngolaryngeal 352.6
- paratrigeminal 350.9
- periodic (familial) (hyperkalemic) (hypokalemic) (normokalemic) (secondary) 359.3
- peripheral
  - autonomic nervous system — *see* Neuropathy, peripheral, autonomic
  - nerve NEC 355.9
- peroneal (nerve) 355.3
- pharynx 478.29
- phrenic nerve 354.8
- plantar nerves 355.6
- pneumogastric nerve 352.3
- poliomyelitis (current) (*see also* Poliomyelitis, with paralysis) 045.1 ☑
  - bulbar 045.0 ☑
- popliteal nerve 355.3
- pressure (*see also* Neuropathy, entrapment) 355.9
- progressive 335.21
  - atrophic 335.21
  - bulbar 335.22
  - general 094.1
  - hemifacial 349.89
  - infantile, acute (*see also* Poliomyelitis) 045.9 ☑
  - multiple 335.20
- pseudobulbar 335.23
- pseudohypertrophic 359.1
  - muscle 359.1
- psychogenic 306.0
- pupil, pupillary 379.49
- quadriceps 355.8
- quadriplegic (*see also* Quadriplegia) 344.0 ☑
- radial nerve 354.3
  - birth injury 767.6
- rectum (sphincter) 569.49
- rectus muscle (eye) 378.55
- recurrent
  - isolated sleep 327.43
  - laryngeal nerve (*see also* Paralysis, vocal cord) 478.30
- respiratory (muscle) (system) (tract) 786.09
  - center NEC 344.89
    - fetus or newborn 770.87 ▲
  - congenital 768.9
  - newborn 768.9
- right side — *see* Hemiplegia
- Saturday night 354.3
- saturnine 984.9
  - specified type of lead — *see* Table of Drugs and Chemicals
- sciatic nerve 355.0
- secondary — *see* Paralysis, late effect
- seizure (cerebral) (current episode) (*see also* Disease, cerebrovascular, acute) 436
  - late effect — *see* Late effect(s) (of) cerebrovascular disease
- senile NEC 344.9
- serratus magnus 355.9
- shaking (*see also* Parkinsonism) 332.0
- shock (*see also* Disease, cerebrovascular, acute) 436
  - late effect — *see* Late effect(s) (of) cerebrovascular disease
- shoulder 354.9
- soft palate 528.9
- spasmodic — *see* Paralysis, spastic
- spastic 344.9

Index

Paralysis, paralytic — Paralysis, paralytic

☑ Additional Digit Required — Refer to the Tabular List for Digit Selection

Subterms under main terms may continue to next column or page

▶◀ Revised Text ● New Line ▲ Revised Code

- **Perforation, perforative** — *continued*
  - by — *continued*
    - instrument (any) during a procedure, accidental 998.2
  - cecum 540.0
    - with peritoneal abscess 540.1
  - cervix (uteri) (*see also* Injury, internal, cervix)
    - with
      - abortion — *see* Abortion, by type, with damage to pelvic organs
      - ectopic pregnancy (*see also* categories 633.0–633.9) 639.2
      - molar pregnancy (*see also* categories 630–632) 639.2
    - following
      - abortion 639.2
      - ectopic or molar pregnancy 639.2
    - obstetrical trauma 665.3 ☑
  - colon 569.83
  - common duct (bile) 576.3
  - cornea (*see also* Ulcer, cornea) 370.00
    - due to ulceration 370.06
  - cystic duct 575.4
  - diverticulum (*see also* Diverticula) 562.10
    - small intestine 562.00
  - duodenum, duodenal (ulcer) — *see* Ulcer, duodenum, with perforation
  - ear drum — *see* Perforation, tympanum
  - enteritis — *see* Enteritis
  - esophagus 530.4
  - ethmoidal sinus (*see also* Sinusitis, ethmoidal) 473.2
  - foreign body (external site) (*see also* Wound, open, by site, complicated)
    - internal site, by ingested object — *see* Foreign body
  - frontal sinus (*see also* Sinusitis, frontal) 473.1
  - gallbladder or duct (*see also* Disease, gallbladder) 575.4
  - gastric (ulcer) — *see* Ulcer, stomach, with perforation
  - heart valve — *see* Endocarditis
  - ileum (*see also* Perforation, intestine) 569.83
  - instrumental
    - external — *see* Wound, open, by site
    - pregnant uterus, complicating delivery 665.9 ☑
    - surgical (accidental) (blood vessel) (nerve) (organ) 998.2
  - intestine 569.83
    - with
      - abortion — *see* Abortion, by type, with damage to pelvic organs
      - ectopic pregnancy (*see also* categories 633.0–633.9) 639.2
      - molar pregnancy (*see also* categories 630–632) 639.2
    - fetus or newborn 777.6
    - obstetrical trauma 665.5 ☑
    - ulcerative NEC 569.83
  - jejunum, jejunal 569.83
    - ulcer — *see* Ulcer, gastrojejunal, with perforation
  - mastoid (antrum) (cell) 383.89
  - maxillary sinus (*see also* Sinusitis, maxillary) 473.0
  - membrana tympani — *see* Perforation, tympanum
  - nasal
    - septum 478.19 ▲
      - congenital 748.1
      - syphilitic 095.8
    - sinus (*see also* Sinusitis) 473.9

- **Perforation, perforative** — *continued*
  - nasal — *continued*
    - sinus (*see also* Sinusitis) — *continued*
      - congenital 748.1
  - palate (hard) 526.89
    - soft 528.9
      - syphilitic 095.8
        - syphilitic 095.8
  - palatine vault 526.89
    - syphilitic 095.8
      - congenital 090.5
  - pelvic
    - floor
      - with
        - abortion — *see* Abortion, by type, with damage to pelvic organs
        - ectopic pregnancy (*see also* categories 633.0–633.9) 639.2
        - molar pregnancy (*see also* categories 630–632) 639.2
      - obstetrical trauma 664.1 ☑
    - organ
      - with
        - abortion — *see* Abortion, by type, with damage to pelvic organs
        - ectopic pregnancy (*see also* categories 633.0–633.9) 639.2
        - molar pregnancy (*see also* categories 630–632) 639.2
      - following
        - abortion 639.2
        - ectopic or molar pregnancy 639.2
      - obstetrical trauma 665.5 ☑
  - perineum — *see* Laceration, perineum
  - periurethral tissue
    - with
      - abortion — *see* Abortion, by type, with damage to pelvic organs
      - ectopic pregnancy (*see also* categories 630–632) 639.2
      - molar pregnancy (*see also* categories 630–632) 639.2
  - pharynx 478.29
  - pylorus, pyloric (ulcer) — *see* Ulcer, stomach, with perforation
  - rectum 569.49
  - root canal space 526.61 ●
  - sigmoid 569.83
  - sinus (accessory) (chronic) (nasal) (*see also* Sinusitis) 473.9
  - sphenoidal sinus (*see also* Sinusitis, sphenoidal) 473.3
  - stomach (due to ulcer) — *see* Ulcer, stomach, with perforation
  - surgical (accidental) (by instrument) (blood vessel) (nerve) (organ) 998.2
  - traumatic
    - external — *see* Wound, open, by site
    - eye (*see also* Penetrating wound, ocular) 871.7
    - internal organ — *see* Injury, internal, by site
  - tympanum (membrane) (persistent posttraumatic) (postinflammatory) 384.20
    - with
      - otitis media — *see* Otitis media
    - attic 384.22
    - central 384.21
    - healed 384.81
    - marginal NEC 384.23
    - multiple 384.24
    - pars flaccida 384.22
    - total 384.25

- **Perforation, perforative** — *continued*
  - tympanum — *continued*
    - traumatic — *see* Wound, open, ear, drum
  - typhoid, gastrointestinal 002.0
  - ulcer — *see* Ulcer, by site, with perforation
  - ureter 593.89
  - urethra
    - with
      - abortion — *see* Abortion, by type, with damage to pelvic organs
      - ectopic pregnancy (*see also* categories 633.0–633.9) 639.2
      - molar pregnancy (*see also* categories 630–632) 639.2
    - following
      - abortion 639.2
      - ectopic or molar pregnancy 639.2
    - obstetrical trauma 665.5 ☑
  - uterus (*see also* Injury, internal, uterus)
    - with
      - abortion — *see* Abortion, by type, with damage to pelvic organs
      - ectopic pregnancy (*see also* categories 633.0–633.9) 639.2
      - molar pregnancy (*see also* categories 630–632) 639.2
    - by intrauterine contraceptive device 996.32
    - following
      - abortion 639.2
      - ectopic or molar pregnancy 639.2
    - obstetrical trauma — *see* Injury, internal, uterus, obstetrical trauma
  - uvula 528.9
    - syphilitic 095.8
  - vagina — *see* Laceration, vagina
  - viscus NEC 799.89
    - traumatic 868.00
      - with open wound into cavity 868.10
- **Periadenitis mucosa necrotica recurrens** 528.2
- **Periangiitis** 446.0
- **Periantritis** 535.4 ☑
- **Periappendicitis** (acute) — *see also* Appendicitis 541
- **Periarteritis** (disseminated) (infectious) (necrotizing) (nodosa) 446.0
- **Periarthritis** (joint) 726.90
  - Duplay's 726.2
  - gonococcal 098.50
  - humeroscapularis 726.2
  - scapulohumeral 726.2
  - shoulder 726.2
  - wrist 726.4
- **Periarthrosis** (angioneural) — *see* Periarthritis
- **Peribronchitis** 491.9
  - tuberculous (*see also* Tuberculosis) 011.3 ☑
- **Pericapsulitis, adhesive** (shoulder) 726.0
- **Pericarditis** (granular) (with decompensation) (with effusion) 423.9
  - with
    - rheumatic fever (conditions classifiable to 390)
      - active (*see also* Pericarditis, rheumatic) 391.0
      - inactive or quiescent 393
  - actinomycotic 039.8 *[420.0]*
  - acute (nonrheumatic) 420.90
    - with chorea (acute) (rheumatic) (Sydenham's) 392.0
    - bacterial 420.99
    - benign 420.91

- **Pericarditis** — *continued*
  - acute — *continued*
    - hemorrhagic 420.90
    - idiopathic 420.91
    - infective 420.90
    - nonspecific 420.91
    - rheumatic 391.0
      - with chorea (acute) (rheumatic) (Sydenham's) 392.0
    - sicca 420.90
    - viral 420.91
  - adhesive or adherent (external) (internal) 423.1
    - acute — *see* Pericarditis, acute
    - rheumatic (external) (internal) 393
  - amebic 006.8 *[420.0]*
  - bacterial (acute) (subacute) (with serous or seropurulent effusion) 420.99
  - calcareous 423.2
  - cholesterol (chronic) 423.8
    - acute 420.90
  - chronic (nonrheumatic) 423.8
    - rheumatic 393
  - constrictive 423.2
  - Coxsackie 074.21
  - due to
    - actinomycosis 039.8 *[420.0]*
    - amebiasis 006.8 *[420.0]*
    - Coxsackie (virus) 074.21
    - histoplasmosis (*see also* Histoplasmosis) 115.93
    - nocardiosis 039.8 *[420.0]*
    - tuberculosis (*see also* Tuberculosis) 017.9 ☑ *[420.0]*
  - fibrinocaseous (*see also* Tuberculosis) 017.9 ☑ *[420.0]*
  - fibrinopurulent 420.99
  - fibrinous — *see* Pericarditis, rheumatic
  - fibropurulent 420.99
  - fibrous 423.1
  - gonococcal 098.83
  - hemorrhagic 423.0
  - idiopathic (acute) 420.91
  - infective (acute) 420.90
  - meningococcal 036.41
  - neoplastic (chronic) 423.8
    - acute 420.90
  - nonspecific 420.91
  - obliterans, obliterating 423.1
  - plastic 423.1
  - pneumococcal (acute) 420.99
  - postinfarction 411.0
  - purulent (acute) 420.99
  - rheumatic (active) (acute) (with effusion) (with pneumonia) 391.0
    - with chorea (acute) (rheumatic) (Sydenham's) 392.0
    - chronic or inactive (with chorea) 393
  - septic (acute) 420.99
  - serofibrinous — *see* Pericarditis, rheumatic
  - staphylococcal (acute) 420.99
  - streptococcal (acute) 420.99
  - suppurative (acute) 420.99
  - syphilitic 093.81
  - tuberculous (acute) (chronic) (*see also* Tuberculosis) 017.9 ☑ *[420.0]*
  - uremic 585.9 *[420.0]*
  - viral (acute) 420.91
- **Pericardium, pericardial** — *see* condition
- **Pericellulitis** — *see also* Cellulitis 682.9
- **Pericementitis** 523.40 ▲
  - acute 523.30 ▲
  - chronic (suppurative) 523.40 ▲
- **Pericholecystitis** — *see also* Cholecystitis 575.10
- **Perichondritis**
  - auricle 380.00
    - acute 380.01
    - chronic 380.02
  - bronchus 491.9
  - ear (external) 380.00

Note — Use the following fifth-digit subclassification with category 730:

0	*site unspecified*
1	*shoulder region*
2	*upper arm*
3	*forearm*
4	*hand*
5	*pelvic region and thigh*
6	*lower leg*
7	*ankle and foot*
8	*other specified sites*
9	*multiple sites*

☑ Additional Digit Required — Refer to the Tabular List for Digit Selection

Subterms under main terms may continue to next column or page

▶◀ Revised Text ● New Line ▲ Revised Code

☑ Additional Digit Required — Refer to the Tabular List for Digit Selection

Subterms under main terms may continue to next column or page

▶◀ Revised Text ● New Line ▲ Revised Code

- **Pneumonia** — *continued*
  - intrauterine — *continued*
    - aspiration — *continued*
      - postnatal stomach contents 770.86
  - Klebsiella pneumoniae 482.0
  - Legionnaires' 482.84
  - lipid, lipoid (exogenous) (interstitial) 507.1
    - endogenous 516.8
  - lobar (diplococcal) (disseminated) (double) (interstitial) (pneumococcal, any type) 481
    - with influenza 487.0
    - bacterial 482.9
      - specified type NEC 482.89
    - chronic (*see also* Fibrosis, lung) 515
    - Escherichia coli (E. coli) 482.82
    - Friedländer's bacillus 482.0
    - Hemophilus influenzae (H. influenzae) 482.2
    - hypostatic 514
    - influenzal 487.0
    - Klebsiella 482.0
    - ornithosis 073.0
    - Proteus 482.83
    - Pseudomonas 482.1
    - psittacosis 073.0
    - specified organism NEC 483.8
      - bacterial NEC 482.89
    - staphylococcal 482.40
      - aureus 482.41
      - specified type NEC 482.49
    - streptococcal — *see* Pneumonia, streptococcal
    - viral, virus (*see also* Pneumonia, viral) 480.9
  - lobular (confluent) — *see* Pneumonia, broncho-
  - Löffler's 518.3
  - massive — *see* Pneumonia, lobar
  - meconium aspiration 770.12
  - metastatic NEC 038.8 *[484.8]*
  - Mycoplasma (pneumoniae) 483.0
  - necrotic 513.0
  - nitrogen dioxide 506.9
  - orthostatic 514
  - parainfluenza virus 480.2
  - parenchymatous (*see also* Fibrosis, lung) 515
  - passive 514
  - patchy — *see* Pneumonia, broncho-
  - Peptococcus 482.81
  - Peptostreptococcus 482.81
  - plasma cell 136.3
  - pleurolobar — see Pneumonia, lobar
  - pleuropneumonia-like organism (PPLO) 483.0
  - pneumococcal (broncho) (lobar) 481
  - Pneumocystis (carinii) ▶(jiroveci)◀ 136.3
  - postinfectional NEC 136.9 *[484.8]*
  - postmeasles 055.1
  - postoperative 997.3
  - primary atypical 486
  - Proprionibacterium 482.81
  - Proteus 482.83
  - Pseudomonas 482.1
  - psittacosis 073.0
  - radiation 508.0
  - respiratory syncytial virus 480.1
  - resulting from a procedure 997.3
  - rheumatic 390 *[517.1]*
  - Salmonella 003.22
  - SARS-associated coronavirus 480.3
  - segmented, segmental — *see* Pneumonia, broncho-
  - Serratia (marcescens) 482.83
  - specified
    - bacteria NEC 482.89
    - organism NEC 483.8
    - virus NEC 480.8
  - spirochetal 104.8 *[484.8]*
  - staphylococcal (broncho) (lobar) 482.40
- **Pneumonia** — *continued*
  - staphylococcal — *continued*
    - aureus 482.41
    - specified type NEC 482.49
  - static, stasis 514
  - streptococcal (broncho) (lobar) NEC 482.30
    - Group
      - A 482.31
      - B 482.32
      - specified NEC 482.39
    - pneumoniae 481
    - specified type NEC 482.39
  - Streptococcus pneumoniae 481
  - traumatic (complication) (early) (secondary) 958.8
  - tuberculous (any) (*see also* Tuberculosis) 011.6 ☑
  - tularemic 021.2
  - TWAR agent 483.1
  - varicella 052.1
  - Veillonella 482.81
  - viral, virus (broncho) (interstitial) (lobar) 480.9
    - with influenza, flu, or grippe 487.0
    - adenoviral 480.0
    - parainfluenza 480.2
    - respiratory syncytial 480.1
    - SARS-associated coronavirus 480.3
    - specified type NEC 480.8
  - white (congenital) 090.0
- **Pneumonic** — *see* condition
- **Pneumonitis** (acute) (primary) — *see also* Pneumonia 486
  - allergic 495.9
    - specified type NEC 495.8
  - aspiration 507.0
    - due to fumes or gases 506.0
    - fetal 770.18
      - due to
        - blood 770.16
        - clear amniotic fluid 770.14
        - meconium 770.12
        - postnatal stomach contents 770.86
    - newborn 770.18
      - due to
        - blood 770.16
        - clear amniotic fluid 770.14
        - meconium 770.12
        - postnatal stomach contents 770.86
    - obstetric 668.0 ☑
  - chemical 506.0
    - due to fumes or gases 506.0
  - cholesterol 516.8
  - chronic (*see also* Fibrosis, lung) 515
  - congenital rubella 771.0
  - crack 506.0
  - due to
    - crack (cocaine) 506.0
    - fumes or vapors 506.0
    - inhalation
      - food (regurgitated), milk, vomitus 507.0
      - oils, essences 507.1
      - saliva 507.0
      - solids, liquids NEC 507.8
    - toxoplasmosis (acquired) 130.4
      - congenital (active) 771.2 *[484.8]*
  - eosinophilic 518.3
  - fetal aspiration 770.18
    - due to
      - blood 770.16
      - clear amniotic fluid 770.14
      - meconium 770.12
      - postnatal stomach contents 770.86
  - hypersensitivity 495.9
  - interstitial (chronic) (*see also* Fibrosis, lung) 515
    - lymphoid 516.8
  - lymphoid, interstitial 516.8
  - meconium aspiration 770.12
- **Pneumonitis** — *see also* Pneumonia — *continued*
  - postanesthetic
    - correct substance properly administered 507.0
    - obstetric 668.0 ☑
    - overdose or wrong substance given 968.4
      - specified anesthetic — *see* Table of Drugs and Chemicals
  - postoperative 997.3
    - obstetric 668.0 ☑
  - radiation 508.0
  - rubella, congenital 771.0
  - "ventilation" 495.7
  - wood-dust 495.8
- **Pneumonoconiosis** — *see* Pneumoconiosis
- **Pneumoparotid** 527.8
- **Pneumopathy** NEC 518.89
  - alveolar 516.9
    - specified NEC 516.8
  - due to dust NEC 504
  - parietoalveolar 516.9
    - specified condition NEC 516.8
- **Pneumopericarditis** — *see also* Pericarditis 423.9
  - acute 420.90
- **Pneumopericardium** — *see also* Pericarditis
  - congenital 770.2
  - fetus or newborn 770.2
  - traumatic (post) (*see also* Pneumothorax, traumatic) 860.0
    - with open wound into thorax 860.1
- **Pneumoperitoneum** 568.89
  - fetus or newborn 770.2
- **Pneumophagia** (psychogenic) 306.4
- **Pneumopleurisy, pneumopleuritis** — *see also* Pneumonia 486
- **Pneumopyopericardium** 420.99
- **Pneumopyothorax** — *see also* Pyopneumothorax 510.9
  - with fistula 510.0
- **Pneumorrhagia** 786.3
  - newborn 770.3
  - tuberculous (*see also* Tuberculosis, pulmonary) 011.9 ☑
- **Pneumosiderosis** (occupational) 503
- **Pneumothorax** (acute) (chronic) 512.8
  - congenital 770.2
  - due to operative injury of chest wall or lung 512.1
    - accidental puncture or laceration 512.1
  - fetus or newborn 770.2
  - iatrogenic 512.1
  - postoperative 512.1
  - spontaneous 512.8
    - fetus or newborn 770.2
    - tension 512.0
  - sucking 512.8
    - iatrogenic 512.1
    - postoperative 512.1
  - tense valvular, infectional 512.0
  - tension 512.0
    - iatrogenic 512.1
    - postoperative 512.1
    - spontaneous 512.0
  - traumatic 860.0
    - with
      - hemothorax 860.4
        - with open wound into thorax 860.5
      - open wound into thorax 860.1
  - tuberculous (*see also* Tuberculosis) 011.7 ☑
- **Pocket(s)**
  - endocardial (*see also* Endocarditis) 424.90
  - periodontal 523.8
- **Podagra** 274.9
- **Podencephalus** 759.89
- **Poikilocytosis** 790.09
- **Poikiloderma** 709.09
  - Civatte's 709.09
- **Poikiloderma** — *continued*
  - congenital 757.33
  - vasculare atrophicans 696.2
- **Poikilodermatomyositis** 710.3
- **Pointed ear** 744.29
- **Poise imperfect** 729.9
- **Poisoned** — *see* Poisoning
- **Poisoning** (acute) — *see also* Table of Drugs and Chemicals
  - Bacillus, B.
    - aertrycke (*see also* Infection, Salmonella) 003.9
    - botulinus 005.1
    - cholerae (suis) (*see also* Infection, Salmonella) 003.9
    - paratyphosus (*see also* Infection, Salmonella) 003.9
    - suipestifer (*see also* Infection, Salmonella) 003.9
  - bacterial toxins NEC 005.9
  - berries, noxious 988.2
  - blood (general) — *see* Septicemia
  - botulism 005.1
  - bread, moldy, mouldy — *see* Poisoning, food
  - damaged meat — *see* Poisoning, food
  - death-cap (Amanita phalloides) (Amanita verna) 988.1
  - decomposed food — *see* Poisoning, food
  - diseased food — *see* Poisoning, food
  - drug — *see* Table of Drugs and Chemicals
  - epidemic, fish, meat, or other food — *see* Poisoning, food
  - fava bean 282.2
  - fish (bacterial) (*see also* Poisoning, food)
    - noxious 988.0
  - food (acute) (bacterial) (diseased) (infected) NEC 005.9
    - due to
      - bacillus
        - aertrycke (*see also* Poisoning, food, due to Salmonella) 003.9
        - botulinus 005.1
        - cereus 005.89
        - choleraesuis (*see also* Poisoning, food, due to Salmonella) 003.9
        - paratyphosus (*see also* Poisoning, food, due to Salmonella) 003.9
        - suipestifer (*see also* Poisoning, food, due to Salmonella) 003.9
      - Clostridium 005.3
        - botulinum 005.1
        - perfringens 005.2
        - welchii 005.2
      - Salmonella (aertrycke) (callinarum) (choleraesuis) (enteritidis) (paratyphi) (suipestifer) 003.9
        - with
          - gastroenteritis 003.0
          - localized infection(s) (*see also* Infection, Salmonella) 003.20
          - septicemia 003.1
          - specified manifestation NEC 003.8
      - specified bacterium NEC 005.89
      - Staphylococcus 005.0
      - Streptococcus 005.89
      - Vibrio parahaemolyticus 005.4
      - Vibrio vulnificus 005.81
    - noxious or naturally toxic 988.0
      - berries 988.2
      - fish 988.0
      - mushroom 988.1
      - plants NEC 988.2
  - ice cream — *see* Poisoning, food
  - ichthyotoxism (bacterial) 005.9
  - kreotoxism, food 005.9

Poisoning — *see also* Table of Drugs and Chemicals — *continued*
  malarial — *see* Malaria
  meat — *see* Poisoning, food
  mushroom (noxious) 988.1
  mussel (*see also* Poisoning, food)
    noxious 988.0
  noxious foodstuffs (*see also* Poisoning, food, noxious) 988.9
    specified type NEC 988.8
  plants, noxious 988.2
  pork (*see also* Poisoning, food)
    specified NEC 988.8
    Trichinosis 124
  ptomaine — *see* Poisoning, food
  putrefaction, food — *see* Poisoning, food
  radiation 508.0
  Salmonella (*see also* Infection, Salmonella) 003.9
  sausage (*see also* Poisoning, food)
    Trichinosis 124
  saxitoxin 988.0
  shellfish (*see also* Poisoning, food)
    noxious 988.0
  Staphylococcus, food 005.0
  toxic, from disease NEC 799.89
  truffles — *see* Poisoning, food
  uremic — *see* Uremia
  uric acid 274.9
Poison ivy, oak, sumac or other plant dermatitis 692.6
Poker spine 720.0
Policeman's disease 729.2
Polioencephalitis (acute) (bulbar) — *see also* Poliomyelitis, bulbar 045.0 ☑
  inferior 335.22
  influenzal 487.8
  superior hemorrhagic (acute) (Wernicke's) 265.1
  Wernicke's (superior hemorrhagic) 265.1
Polioencephalomyelitis (acute) (anterior) (bulbar) — *see also* Polioencephalitis 045.0 ☑
Polioencephalopathy, superior hemorrhagic 265.1
  with
    beriberi 265.0
    pellagra 265.2
Poliomeningoencephalitis — *see* Meningoencephalitis
Poliomyelitis (acute) (anterior) (epidemic) 045.9 ☑

Note — Use the following fifth-digit subclassification with category 045:
0 poliovirus, unspecified type
1 poliovirus, type I
2 poliovirus, type II
3 poliovirus, type III

  with
    paralysis 045.1 ☑
      bulbar 045.0 ☑
  abortive 045.2 ☑
  ascending 045.9 ☑
    progressive 045.9 ☑
  bulbar 045.0 ☑
  cerebral 045.0 ☑
  chronic 335.21
  congenital 771.2
  contact V01.2
  deformities 138
  exposure to V01.2
  late effect 138
  nonepidemic 045.9 ☑
  nonparalytic 045.2 ☑
  old with deformity 138
  posterior, acute 053.19
  residual 138
  sequelae 138
  spinal, acute 045.9 ☑
  syphilitic (chronic) 094.89
Poliomyelitis — *continued*
  vaccination, prophylactic (against) V04.0
Poliosis (eyebrow) (eyelashes) 704.3
  circumscripta (congenital) 757.4
    acquired 704.3
  congenital 757.4
Pollakiuria 788.41
  psychogenic 306.53
Pollinosis 477.0
Pollitzer's disease (hidradenitis suppurativa) 705.83
Polyadenitis — *see also* Adenitis 289.3
  malignant 020.0
Polyalgia 729.9
Polyangiitis (essential) 446.0
Polyarteritis (nodosa) (renal) 446.0
Polyarthralgia 719.49
  psychogenic 306.0
Polyarthritis, polyarthropathy NEC 716.59
  due to or associated with other specified conditions — *see* Arthritis, due to or associated with
  endemic (*see also* Disease, Kaschin-Beck) 716.0 ☑
  inflammatory 714.9
    specified type NEC 714.89
  juvenile (chronic) 714.30
    acute 714.31
  migratory — *see* Fever, rheumatic
  rheumatic 714.0
    fever (acute) — *see* Fever, rheumatic
Polycarential syndrome of infancy 260
Polychondritis (atrophic) (chronic) (relapsing) 733.99
Polycoria 743.46
Polycystic (congenital) (disease) 759.89
  degeneration, kidney — *see* Polycystic, kidney
  kidney (congenital) 753.12
    adult type (APKD) 753.13
    autosomal dominant 753.13
    autosomal recessive 753.14
    childhood type (CPKD) 753.14
    infantile type 753.14
  liver 751.62
  lung 518.89
    congenital 748.4
  ovary, ovaries 256.4
  spleen 759.0
Polycythemia (primary) (rubra) (vera) (M9950/1) 238.4
  acquired 289.0
  benign 289.0
    familial 289.6
  due to
    donor twin 776.4
    fall in plasma volume 289.0
    high altitude 289.0
    maternal-fetal transfusion 776.4
    stress 289.0
  emotional 289.0
  erythropoietin 289.0
  familial (benign) 289.6
  Gaisböck's (hypertonica) 289.0
  high altitude 289.0
  hypertonica 289.0
  hypoxemic 289.0
  neonatorum 776.4
  nephrogenous 289.0
  relative 289.0
  secondary 289.0
  spurious 289.0
  stress 289.0
Polycytosis cryptogenica 289.0
Polydactylism, polydactyly 755.00
  fingers 755.01
  toes 755.02
Polydipsia 783.5
Polydystrophic oligophrenia 277.5
Polyembryoma (M9072/3) — *see* Neoplasm, by site, malignant
Polygalactia 676.6 ☑
Polyglandular
  deficiency 258.9
  dyscrasia 258.9
  dysfunction 258.9
  syndrome 258.8
Polyhydramnios — *see also* Hydramnios 657.0 ☑
Polymastia 757.6
Polymenorrhea 626.2
Polymicrogyria 742.2
Polymyalgia 725
  arteritica 446.5
  rheumatica 725
Polymyositis (acute) (chronic) (hemorrhagic) 710.4
  with involvement of
    lung 710.4 *[517.8]*
    skin 710.3
  ossificans (generalisata) (progressiva) 728.19
  Wagner's (dermatomyositis) 710.3
Polyneuritis, polyneuritic — *see also* Polyneuropathy 356.9
  alcoholic 357.5
    with psychosis 291.1
  cranialis 352.6
  demyelinating, chronic inflammatory 357.81
  diabetic 250.6 ☑ *[357.2]*
  due to lack of vitamin NEC 269.2 *[357.4]*
  endemic 265.0 *[357.4]*
  erythredema 985.0
  febrile 357.0
  hereditary ataxic 356.3
  idiopathic, acute 357.0
  infective (acute) 357.0
  nutritional 269.9 *[357.4]*
  postinfectious 357.0
Polyneuropathy (peripheral) 356.9
  alcoholic 357.5
  amyloid 277.39 *[357.4]* ▲
  arsenical 357.7
  critical illness 357.82
  diabetic 250.6 ☑ *[357.2]*
  due to
    antitetanus serum 357.6
    arsenic 357.7
    drug or medicinal substance 357.6
      correct substance properly administered 357.6
      overdose or wrong substance given or taken 977.9
        specified drug — *see* Table of Drugs and Chemicals
    lack of vitamin NEC 269.2 *[357.4]*
    lead 357.7
    organophosphate compounds 357.7
    pellagra 265.2 *[357.4]*
    porphyria 277.1 *[357.4]*
    serum 357.6
    toxic agent NEC 357.7
  hereditary 356.0
  idiopathic 356.9
    progressive 356.4
  in
    amyloidosis 277.39 *[357.4]* ▲
    avitaminosis 269.2 *[357.4]*
      specified NEC 269.1 *[357.4]*
    beriberi 265.0 *[357.4]*
    collagen vascular disease NEC 710.9 *[357.1]*
    deficiency
      B-complex NEC 266.2 *[357.4]*
      vitamin B 266.1 *[357.4]*
      vitamin B6 266.9 *[357.4]*
    diabetes 250.6 ☑ *[357.2]*
    diphtheria (*see also* Diphtheria) 032.89 *[357.4]*
    disseminated lupus erythematosus 710.0 *[357.1]*
    herpes zoster 053.13
    hypoglycemia 251.2 *[357.4]*
Polyneuropathy — *continued*
  in — *continued*
    malignant neoplasm (M8000/3) NEC 199.1 *[357.3]*
    mumps 072.72
    pellagra 265.2 *[357.4]*
    polyarteritis nodosa 446.0 *[357.1]*
    porphyria 277.1 *[357.4]*
    rheumatoid arthritis 714.0 *[357.1]*
    sarcoidosis 135 *[357.4]*
    uremia 585.9 *[357.4]*
  lead 357.7
  nutritional 269.9 *[357.4]*
    specified NEC 269.8 *[357.4]*
  postherpetic 053.13
  progressive 356.4
  sensory (hereditary) 356.2
Polyonychia 757.5
Polyopia 368.2
  refractive 368.15
Polyorchism, polyorchidism (three testes) 752.89
Polyorrhymenitis (peritoneal) — *see also* Polyserositis 568.82
  pericardial 423.2
Polyostotic fibrous dysplasia 756.54
Polyotia 744.1
Polyphagia 783.6
Polypoid — *see* condition
Polyposis — *see also* Polyp
  coli (adenomatous) (M8220/0) 211.3
    adenocarcinoma in (M8220/3) 153.9
    carcinoma in (M8220/3) 153.9
  familial (M8220/0) 211.3
  intestinal (adenomatous) (M8220/0) 211.3
  multiple (M8221/0) — *see* Neoplasm, by site, benign
Polyp, polypus

Note — Polyps of organs or sites that do not appear in the list below should be coded to the residual category for diseases of the organ or site concerned.

  accessory sinus 471.8
  adenoid tissue 471.0
  adenomatous (M8210/0) (*see also* Neoplasm, by site, benign)
    adenocarcinoma in (M8210/3) — *see* Neoplasm, by site, malignant
    carcinoma in (M8210/3) — *see* Neoplasm, by site, malignant
    multiple (M8221/0) — *see* Neoplasm, by site, benign
  antrum 471.8
  anus, anal (canal) (nonadenomatous) 569.0
    adenomatous 211.4
  Bartholin's gland 624.6
  bladder (M8120/1) 236.7
  broad ligament 620.8
  cervix (uteri) 622.7
    adenomatous 219.0
    in pregnancy or childbirth 654.6 ☑
      affecting fetus or newborn 763.89
      causing obstructed labor 660.2 ☑
    mucous 622.7
    nonneoplastic 622.7
  choanal 471.0
  cholesterol 575.6
  clitoris 624.6
  colon (M8210/0) (*see also* Polyp, adenomatous) 211.3
  corpus uteri 621.0
  dental 522.0
  ear (middle) 385.30
  endometrium 621.0
  ethmoidal (sinus) 471.8
  fallopian tube 620.8
  female genital organs NEC 624.8
  frontal (sinus) 471.8
  gallbladder 575.6
  gingiva 523.8

- **Polyp, polypus** — *continued*
  - gum 523.8
  - labia 624.6
  - larynx (mucous) 478.4
  - malignant (M8000/3) — *see* Neoplasm, by site, malignant
  - maxillary (sinus) 471.8
  - middle ear 385.30
  - myometrium 621.0
  - nares
    - anterior 471.9
    - posterior 471.0
  - nasal (mucous) 471.9
    - cavity 471.0
    - septum 471.9
  - nasopharyngeal 471.0
  - neoplastic (M8210/0) — *see* Neoplasm, by site, benign
  - nose (mucous) 471.9
  - oviduct 620.8
  - paratubal 620.8
  - pharynx 478.29
    - congenital 750.29
  - placenta, placental 674.4 ☑
  - prostate 600.20
    - with
      - other lower urinary tract symptoms (LUTS) 600.21 ●
      - urinary ●
        - obstruction 600.21 ●
        - retention 600.21 ●
  - pudenda 624.6
  - pulp (dental) 522.0
  - rectosigmoid 211.4
  - rectum (nonadenomatous) 569.0
    - adenomatous 211.4
  - septum (nasal) 471.9
  - sinus (accessory) (ethmoidal) (frontal) (maxillary) (sphenoidal) 471.8
  - sphenoidal (sinus) 471.8
  - stomach (M8210/0) 211.1
  - tube, fallopian 620.8
  - turbinate, mucous membrane 471.8
  - ureter 593.89
  - urethra 599.3
  - uterine
    - ligament 620.8
    - tube 620.8
  - uterus (body) (corpus) (mucous) 621.0
    - in pregnancy or childbirth 654.1 ☑
      - affecting fetus or newborn 763.89
      - causing obstructed labor 660.2 ☑
  - vagina 623.7
  - vocal cord (mucous) 478.4
  - vulva 624.6
- **Polyradiculitis** (acute) 357.0
- **Polyradiculoneuropathy** (acute) (segmentally demyelinating) 357.0
- **Polysarcia** 278.00
- **Polyserositis** (peritoneal) 568.82
  - due to pericarditis 423.2
  - paroxysmal (familial) 277.31 ▲
  - pericardial 423.2
  - periodic ▶(familial)◀ 277.31 ▲
  - pleural — *see* Pleurisy
  - recurrent 277.31 ▲
  - tuberculous (*see also* Tuberculosis, polyserositis) 018.9 ☑
- **Polysialia** 527.7
- **Polysplenia syndrome** 759.0
- **Polythelia** 757.6
- **Polytrichia** — *see also* Hypertrichosis 704.1
- **Polyunguia** (congenital) 757.5
  - acquired 703.8
- **Polyuria** 788.42
- **Pompe's disease** (glycogenosis II) 271.0
- **Pompholyx** 705.81
- **Poncet's disease** (tuberculous rheumatism) — *see also* Tuberculosis 015.9 ☑
- **Pond fracture** — *see* Fracture, skull, vault
- **Ponos** 085.0
- **Pons, pontine** — *see* condition
- **Poor**
  - aesthetics of existing restoration of tooth 525.67 ●
  - contractions, labor 661.2 ☑
    - affecting fetus or newborn 763.7
  - fetal growth NEC 764.9 ☑
    - affecting management of pregnancy 656.5 ☑
  - incorporation
    - artificial skin graft 996.55
    - decellularized allodermis graft 996.55
  - obstetrical history V13.29
    - affecting management of current pregnancy V23.49
      - pre-term labor V23.41
    - pre-term labor V13.21
  - sucking reflex (newborn) 796.1
  - vision NEC 369.9
- **Poradenitis, nostras** 099.1
- **Porencephaly** (congenital) (developmental) (true) 742.4
  - acquired 348.0
  - nondevelopmental 348.0
  - traumatic (post) 310.2
- **Porocephaliasis** 134.1
- **Porokeratosis** 757.39
  - disseminated superficial actinic (DSAP) 692.75
- **Poroma, eccrine** (M8402/0) — *see* Neoplasm, skin, benign
- **Porphyria** (acute) (congenital) (constitutional) (erythropoietic) (familial) (hepatica) (idiopathic) (idiosyncratic) (intermittent) (latent) (mixed hepatic) (photosensitive) (South African genetic) (Swedish) 277.1
  - acquired 277.1
  - cutaneatarda
    - hereditaria 277.1
    - symptomatica 277.1
  - due to drugs
    - correct substance properly administered 277.1
    - overdose or wrong substance given or taken 977.9
      - specified drug — *see* Table of Drugs and Chemicals
  - secondary 277.1
  - toxic NEC 277.1
  - variegata 277.1
- **Porphyrinuria** (acquired) (congenital) (secondary) 277.1
- **Porphyruria** (acquired) (congenital) 277.1
- **Portal** — *see* condition
- **Port wine nevus or mark** 757.32
- **Posadas-Wernicke disease** 114.9
- **Position**
  - fetus, abnormal (*see also* Presentation, fetal) 652.9 ☑
  - teeth, faulty (*see also* Anomaly, position tooth) 524.30
- **Positive**
  - culture (nonspecific) 795.39
    - AIDS virus V08
    - blood 790.7
    - HIV V08
    - human immunodeficiency virus V08
    - nose 795.39
    - skin lesion NEC 795.39
    - spinal fluid 792.0
    - sputum 795.39
    - stool 792.1
    - throat 795.39
    - urine 791.9
    - wound 795.39
  - findings, anthrax 795.31
  - HIV V08
  - human immunodeficiency virus (HIV) V08
  - PPD 795.5
  - serology
    - AIDS virus V08
- **Positive** — *continued*
  - serology — *continued*
    - AIDS virus — *continued*
      - inconclusive 795.71
    - HIV V08
      - inconclusive 795.71
    - human immunodeficiency virus (HIV) V08
      - inconclusive 795.71
    - syphilis 097.1
      - with signs or symptoms — *see* Syphilis, by site and stage
      - false 795.6
  - skin test 795.7 ☑
    - tuberculin (without active tuberculosis) 795.5
  - VDRL 097.1
    - with signs or symptoms — *see* Syphilis, by site and stage
    - false 795.6
  - Wassermann reaction 097.1
    - false 795.6
- **Postcardiotomy syndrome** 429.4
- **Postcaval ureter** 753.4
- **Postcholecystectomy syndrome** 576.0
- **Postclimacteric bleeding** 627.1
- **Postcommissurotomy syndrome** 429.4
- **Postconcussional syndrome** 310.2
- **Postcontusional syndrome** 310.2
- **Postcricoid region** — *see* condition
- **Post-dates** (pregnancy) — *see* Pregnancy
- **Postencephalitic** — *see also* condition
  - syndrome 310.8
- **Posterior** — *see* condition
- **Posterolateral sclerosis** (spinal cord) — *see* Degeneration, combined
- **Postexanthematous** — *see* condition
- **Postfebrile** — *see* condition
- **Postgastrectomy dumping syndrome** 564.2
- **Posthemiplegic chorea** 344.89
- **Posthemorrhagic anemia** (chronic) 280.0
  - acute 285.1
  - newborn 776.5
- **Posthepatitis syndrome** 780.79
- **Postherpetic neuralgia** (intercostal) (syndrome) (zoster) 053.19
  - geniculate ganglion 053.11
  - ophthalmica 053.19
  - trigeminal 053.12
- **Posthitis** 607.1
- **Postimmunization complication or reaction** — *see* Complications, vaccination
- **Postinfectious** — *see* condition
- **Postinfluenzal syndrome** 780.79
- **Postlaminectomy syndrome** 722.80
  - cervical, cervicothoracic 722.81
  - kyphosis 737.12
  - lumbar, lumbosacral 722.83
  - thoracic, thoracolumbar 722.82
- **Postleukotomy syndrome** 310.0
- **Postlobectomy syndrome** 310.0
- **Postmastectomy lymphedema** (syndrome) 457.0
- **Postmaturity, postmature** (fetus or newborn) (gestation period over 42 completed weeks) 766.22
  - affecting management of pregnancy
    - post-term pregnancy 645.1 ☑
    - prolonged pregnancy 645.2 ☑
  - syndrome 766.22
- **Postmeasles** — *see also* condition
  - complication 055.8
    - specified NEC 055.79
- **Postmenopausal**
  - endometrium (atrophic) 627.8
    - suppurative (see also Endometritis) 615.9
  - hormone replacement therapy V07.4
  - status (age related) (natural) V49.81
- **Postnasal drip** 784.91 ▲
- **Postnatal** — *see* condition
- **Postoperative** — *see also* condition
  - confusion state 293.9
- **Postoperative** — *see also* condition — *continued*
  - psychosis 293.9
  - status NEC (*see also* Status (post)) V45.89
- **Postpancreatectomy hyperglycemia** 251.3
- **Postpartum** — *see also* condition
  - anemia 648.2 ☑
  - cardiomyopathy 674.5 ☑
  - observation
    - immediately after delivery V24.0
    - routine follow-up V24.2
- **Postperfusion syndrome** NEC 999.8
  - bone marrow 996.85
- **Postpoliomyelitic** — *see* condition
- **Postsurgery status** NEC — *see also* Status (post V45.89
- **Post-term** (pregnancy) 645.1 ☑
  - infant (gestation period over 40 completed weeks to 42 completed weeks) 766.21
- **Posttraumatic** — *see* condition
- **Posttraumatic brain syndrome, nonpsychotic** 310.2
- **Post-traumatic stress disorder** (PTSD) 309.81 ●
- **Post-typhoid abscess** 002.0
- **Postures, hysterical** 300.11
- **Postvaccinal reaction or complication** — *see* Complications, vaccination
- **Postvagotomy syndrome** 564.2
- **Postvalvulotomy syndrome** 429.4
- **Postvasectomy sperm count** V25.8
- **Potain's disease** (pulmonary edema) 514
- **Potain's syndrome** (gastrectasis with dyspepsia) 536.1
- **Pott's**
  - curvature (spinal) (*see also* Tuberculosis) 015.0 ☑ *[737.43]*
  - disease or paraplegia (*see also* Tuberculosis) 015.0 ☑ *[730.88]*
  - fracture (closed) 824.4
    - open 824.5
  - gangrene 440.24
  - osteomyelitis (*see also* Tuberculosis) 015.0 ☑ *[730.88]*
  - spinal curvature (*see also* Tuberculosis) 015.0 ☑ *[737.43]*
  - tumor, puffy (*see also* Osteomyelitis) 730.2 ☑
- **Potter's**
  - asthma 502
  - disease 753.0
  - facies 754.0
  - lung 502
  - syndrome (with renal agenesis) 753.0
- **Pouch**
  - bronchus 748.3
  - Douglas' — *see* condition
  - esophagus, esophageal (congenital) 750.4
    - acquired 530.6
  - gastric 537.1
  - Hartmann's (abnormal sacculation of gallbladder neck) 575.8
    - of intestine V44.3
      - attention to V55.3
  - pharynx, pharyngeal (congenital) 750.27
- **Poulet's disease** 714.2
- **Poultrymen's itch** 133.8
- **Poverty** V60.2
- **Prader-Labhart-Willi-Fanconi syndrome** (hypogenital dystrophy with diabetic tendency) 759.81
- **Prader-Willi syndrome** (hypogenital dystrophy with diabetic tendency) 759.81
- **Preachers' voice** 784.49
- **Pre-AIDS** — *see* Human immunodeficiency virus (disease) (illness) (infection)
- **Preauricular appendage** 744.1
- **Prebetalipoproteinemia** (acquired) (essential) (familial) (hereditary) (primary) (secondary) 272.1

☑ Additional Digit Required — Refer to the Tabular List for Digit Selection

Subterms under main terms may continue to next column or page

▶◀ Revised Text ● New Line ▲ Revised Code

Prebetalipoproteinemia — *continued*
- with chylomicronemia 272.3

Precipitate labor 661.3 ☑
- affecting fetus or newborn 763.6

Preclimacteric bleeding 627.0
- menorrhagia 627.0

Precocious
- adrenarche 259.1
- menarche 259.1
- menstruation 626.8
- pubarche 259.1
- puberty NEC 259.1
- sexual development NEC 259.1
- thelarche 259.1

Precocity, sexual (constitutional) (cryptogenic) (female) (idiopathic) (male) NEC 259.1
- with adrenal hyperplasia 255.2

Precordial pain 786.51
- psychogenic 307.89

Predeciduous teeth 520.2

Prediabetes, prediabetic 790.29
- complicating pregnancy, childbirth, or puerperium 648.8 ☑
  - fetus or newborn 775.89 ▲

Predislocation status of hip, at birth — *see also* Subluxation, congenital, hip 754.32

Preeclampsia (mild) 642.4 ☑
- with pre-existing hypertension 642.7 ☑
- affecting fetus or newborn 760.0
- severe 642.5 ☑
- superimposed on pre-existing hypertensive disease 642.7 ☑

Preeruptive color change, teeth, tooth 520.8

Preexcitation 426.7
- atrioventricular conduction 426.7
- ventricular 426.7

Preglaucoma 365.00

Pregnancy (single) (uterine) (without sickness) V22.2

> *Note — Use the following fifth-digit subclassification with categories 640–648, 651–676:*
>
> 0 *unspecified as to episode of care*
>
> 1 *delivered, with or without mention of antepartum condition*
>
> 2 *delivered, with mention of postpartum complication*
>
> 3 *antepartum condition or complication*
>
> 4 *postpartum condition or complication*

- abdominal (ectopic) 633.00
  - with intrauterine pregnancy 633.01
  - affecting fetus or newborn 761.4
- abnormal NEC 646.9 ☑
- ampullar — *see* Pregnancy, tubal
- broad ligament — *see* Pregnancy, cornual
- cervical — *see* Pregnancy, cornual
- combined (extrauterine and intrauterine) — *see* Pregnancy, cornual
- complicated (by)
  - abnormal, abnormality NEC 646.9 ☑
    - cervix 654.6 ☑
    - cord (umbilical) 663.9 ☑
    - glucose tolerance (conditions classifiable to 790.21–790.29) 648.8 ☑
    - pelvic organs or tissues NEC 654.9 ☑
    - pelvis (bony) 653.0 ☑
    - perineum or vulva 654.8 ☑
    - placenta, placental (vessel) 656.7 ☑
    - position
      - cervix 654.4 ☑
      - placenta 641.1 ☑

Pregnancy — *continued*
- complicated — *continued*
  - abnormal, abnormality — *continued*
    - position — *continued*
      - placenta — *continued*
        - without hemorrhage 641.0 ☑
      - uterus 654.4 ☑
    - size, fetus 653.5 ☑
    - uterus (congenital) 654.0 ☑
  - abscess or cellulitis
    - bladder 646.6 ☑
    - genitourinary tract (conditions classifiable to 590, 595, 597, 599.0, 614.0–614.5, 614.7–614.9, 615) 646.6 ☑
    - kidney 646.6 ☑
    - urinary tract NEC 646.6 ☑
  - adhesion, pelvic peritoneal 648.9 ☑
  - air embolism 673.0 ☑
  - albuminuria 646.2 ☑
    - with hypertension — *see* Toxemia, of pregnancy
  - amnionitis 658.4 ☑
  - amniotic fluid embolism 673.1 ☑
  - anemia (conditions classifiable to 280–285) 648.2 ☑
  - appendicitis 648.9 ☑ ●
  - atrophy, yellow (acute) (liver) (subacute) 646.7 ☑
  - bacilluria, asymptomatic 646.5 ☑
  - bacteriuria, asymptomatic 646.5 ☑
  - bariatric surgery status 649.2 ☑●
  - bicornis or bicornuate uterus 654.0 ☑
  - biliary problems 646.8 ☑
  - bone and joint disorders (conditions classifiable to 720–724 or conditions affecting lower limbs classifiable to 711–719, 725–738) 648.7 ☑
  - breech presentation (buttocks) (complete) (frank) 652.2 ☑
    - with successful version 652.1 ☑
  - cardiovascular disease (conditions classifiable to 390–398, 410–429) 648.6 ☑
    - congenital (conditions classifiable to 745–747) 648.5 ☑
  - cerebrovascular disorders (conditions classifiable to 430–434, 436–437) 674.0 ☑
  - cervicitis (conditions classifiable to 616.0) 646.6 ☑
  - chloasma (gravidarum) 646.8 ☑
  - cholelithiasis 646.8 ☑
  - chorea (gravidarum) — *see* Eclampsia, pregnancy
  - coagulation defect 649.3 ☑ ●
  - contraction, pelvis (general) 653.1 ☑
    - inlet 653.2 ☑
    - outlet 653.3 ☑
  - convulsions (eclamptic) (uremic) 642.6 ☑
    - with pre-existing hypertension 642.7 ☑
  - current disease or condition (nonobstetric)
    - abnormal glucose tolerance 648.8 ☑
    - anemia 648.2 ☑
    - bone and joint (lower limb) 648.7 ☑
    - cardiovascular 648.6 ☑
      - congenital 648.5 ☑
    - cerebrovascular 674.0 ☑
    - diabetic 648.0 ☑
    - drug dependence 648.3 ☑
    - female genital mutilation 648.9 ☑
    - genital organ or tract 646.6 ☑
    - gonorrheal 647.1 ☑

Pregnancy — *continued*
- complicated — *continued*
  - current disease or condition — *continued*
    - hypertensive 642.2 ☑
      - chronic kidney 642.2 ☑ ●
      - renal 642.1 ☑
    - infectious 647.9 ☑
      - specified type NEC 647.8 ☑
    - liver 646.7 ☑
    - malarial 647.4 ☑
    - nutritional deficiency 648.9 ☑
    - parasitic NEC 647.8 ☑
    - periodontal disease 648.9 ☑
    - renal 646.2 ☑
      - hypertensive 642.1 ☑
    - rubella 647.5 ☑
    - specified condition NEC 648.9 ☑
    - syphilitic 647.0 ☑
    - thyroid 648.1 ☑
    - tuberculous 647.3 ☑
    - urinary 646.6 ☑
    - venereal 647.2 ☑
    - viral NEC 647.6 ☑
  - cystitis 646.6 ☑
  - cystocele 654.4 ☑
  - death of fetus (near term) 656.4 ☑
    - early pregnancy (before 22 completed weeks gestation) 632
  - deciduitis 646.6 ☑
  - decreased fetal movements 655.7 ☑
  - diabetes (mellitus) (conditions classifiable to 250) 648.0 ☑
  - disorders of liver 646.7 ☑
  - displacement, uterus NEC 654.4 ☑
  - disproportion — *see* Disproportion
  - double uterus 654.0 ☑
  - drug dependence (conditions classifiable to 304) 648.3 ☑
  - dysplasia, cervix 654.6 ☑
  - early onset of delivery (spontaneous) 644.2 ☑
  - eclampsia, eclamptic (coma) (convulsions) (delirium) (nephritis) (uremia) 642.6 ☑
    - with pre-existing hypertension 642.7 ☑
  - edema 646.1 ☑
    - with hypertension — *see* Toxemia, of pregnancy
  - effusion, amniotic fluid 658.1 ☑
    - delayed delivery following 658.2 ☑
  - embolism
    - air 673.0 ☑
    - amniotic fluid 673.1 ☑
    - blood-clot 673.2 ☑
    - cerebral 674.0 ☑
    - pulmonary NEC 673.2 ☑
    - pyemic 673.3 ☑
    - septic 673.3 ☑
  - emesis (gravidarum) — *see* Pregnancy, complicated, vomiting
  - endometritis (conditions classifiable to 615.0–615.9) 646.6 ☑
    - decidual 646.6 ☑
  - epilepsy 649.4 ☑ ●
  - excessive weight gain NEC 646.1 ☑
  - face presentation 652.4 ☑
  - failure, fetal head to enter pelvic brim 652.5 ☑
  - false labor (pains) 644.1 ☑
  - fatigue 646.8 ☑
  - fatty metamorphosis of liver 646.7 ☑
  - female genital mutilation 648.9 ☑
  - fetal
    - death (near term) 656.4 ☑
      - early (before 22 completed weeks gestation) 632
    - deformity 653.7 ☑
    - distress 656.8 ☑

Pregnancy — *continued*
- complicated — *continued*
  - fetal — *continued*
    - reduction of multiple fetuses reduced to single fetus 651.7 ☑
  - fibroid (tumor) (uterus) 654.1 ☑
  - footling presentation 652.8 ☑
    - with successful version 652.1 ☑
  - gallbladder disease 646.8 ☑
  - gastric banding status 649.2 ☑ ●
  - gastric bypass status for obesity ●
  - goiter 648.1 ☑
  - gonococcal infection (conditions classifiable to 098) 647.1 ☑
  - gonorrhea (conditions classifiable to 098) 647.1 ☑
  - hemorrhage 641.9 ☑
    - accidental 641.2 ☑
    - before 22 completed weeks gestation NEC 640.9 ☑
    - cerebrovascular 674.0 ☑
    - due to
      - afibrinogenemia or other coagulation defect (conditions classifiable to 286.0–286.9) 641.3 ☑
      - leiomyoma, uterine 641.8 ☑
      - marginal sinus (rupture) 641.2 ☑
      - premature separation, placenta 641.2 ☑
      - trauma 641.8 ☑
    - early (before 22 completed weeks gestation) 640.9 ☑
    - threatened abortion 640.0 ☑
    - unavoidable 641.1 ☑
  - hepatitis (acute) (malignant) (subacute) 646.7 ☑
    - viral 647.6 ☑
  - herniation of uterus 654.4 ☑
  - high head at term 652.5 ☑
  - hydatidiform mole (delivered) (undelivered) 630
  - hydramnios 657.0 ☑
  - hydrocephalic fetus 653.6 ☑
  - hydrops amnii 657.0 ☑
  - hydrorrhea 658.1 ☑
  - hyperemesis (gravidarum) — *see* Hyperemesis, gravidarum
  - hypertension — *see* Hypertension, complicating pregnancy
  - hypertensive
    - chronic kidney disease 642.2 ☑ ●
    - heart and chronic kidney disease 642.2 ☑ ●
    - heart and renal disease 642.2 ☑
    - heart disease 642.2 ☑
    - renal disease 642.2 ☑
  - hypertensive heart and chronic kidney disease 642.2 ☑ ●
  - hyperthyroidism 648.1 ☑
  - hypothyroidism 648.1 ☑
  - hysteralgia 646.8 ☑
  - icterus gravis 646.7 ☑
  - incarceration, uterus 654.3 ☑
  - incompetent cervix (os) 654.5 ☑
  - infection 647.9 ☑
    - amniotic fluid 658.4 ☑
    - bladder 646.6 ☑
    - genital organ (conditions classifiable to 614.0–614.5, 614.7–614.9, 615) 646.6 ☑
    - kidney (conditions classifiable to 590.0–590.9) 646.6 ☑
    - urinary (tract) 646.6 ☑
      - asymptomatic 646.5 ☑
  - infective and parasitic diseases NEC 647.8 ☑
  - inflammation
    - bladder 646.6 ☑

- **Pregnancy** — *continued*
  - complicated — *continued*
    - inflammation — *continued*
      - genital organ (conditions classifiable to 614.0–614.5, 614.7–614.9, 615) 646.6 ☑
      - urinary tract NEC 646.6 ☑
    - insufficient weight gain 646.8 ☑
    - intrauterine fetal death (near term) NEC 656.4 ☑
      - early (before 22 completed weeks' gestation) 632
    - malaria (conditions classifiable to 084) 647.4 ☑
    - malformation, uterus (congenital) 654.0 ☑
    - malnutrition (conditions classifiable to 260–269) 648.9 ☑
    - malposition
      - fetus — *see* Pregnancy, complicated, malpresentation
      - uterus or cervix 654.4 ☑
    - malpresentation 652.9 ☑
      - with successful version 652.1 ☑
      - in multiple gestation 652.6 ☑
      - specified type NEC 652.8 ☑
    - marginal sinus hemorrhage or rupture 641.2 ☑
    - maternal obesity syndrome 646.1 ☑
    - menstruation 640.8 ☑
    - mental disorders (conditions classifiable to 290–303, ▶305.0, 305.2-305.9, 306–316,◀ 317–319) 648.4 ☑
    - mentum presentation 652.4 ☑
    - missed
      - abortion 632
      - delivery (at or near term) 656.4 ☑
      - labor (at or near term) 656.4 ☑
    - necrosis
      - genital organ or tract (conditions classifiable to 614.0–614.5, 614.7–614.9, 615) 646.6 ☑
      - liver (conditions classifiable to 570) 646.7 ☑
      - renal, cortical 646.2 ☑
    - nephritis or nephrosis (conditions classifiable to 580–589) 646.2 ☑
      - with hypertension 642.1 ☑
    - nephropathy NEC 646.2 ☑
    - neuritis (peripheral) 646.4 ☑
    - nutritional deficiency (conditions classifiable to 260–269) 648.9 ☑
    - obesity 649.1 ☑ ●
      - surgery status 649.2 ☑ ●
    - oblique lie or presentation 652.3 ☑
      - with successful version 652.1 ☑
    - obstetrical trauma NEC 665.9 ☑
    - oligohydramnios NEC 658.0 ☑
    - onset of contractions before 37 weeks 644.0 ☑
    - oversize fetus 653.5 ☑
    - papyraceous fetus 646.0 ☑
    - patent cervix 654.5 ☑
    - pelvic inflammatory disease (conditions classifiable to 614.0–614.5, 614.7–614.9, 615) 646.6 ☑
    - pelvic peritoneal adhesion 648.9 ☑
    - placenta, placental
      - abnormality 656.7 ☑
      - abruptio or ablatio 641.2 ☑
      - detachment 641.2 ☑
      - disease 656.7 ☑
      - infarct 656.7 ☑
      - low implantation 641.1 ☑
        - without hemorrhage 641.0 ☑
      - malformation 656.7 ☑

- **Pregnancy** — *continued*
  - complicated — *continued*
    - placenta, placental — *continued*
      - malposition 641.1 ☑
        - without hemorrhage 641.0 ☑
      - marginal sinus hemorrhage 641.2 ☑
      - previa 641.1 ☑
        - without hemorrhage 641.0 ☑
      - separation (premature) (undelivered) 641.2 ☑
    - placentitis 658.4 ☑
    - polyhydramnios 657.0 ☑
    - postmaturity
      - post-term 645.1 ☑
      - prolonged 645.2 ☑
    - prediabetes 648.8 ☑
    - pre-eclampsia (mild) 642.4 ☑
      - severe 642.5 ☑
      - superimposed on pre-existing hypertensive disease 642.7 ☑
    - premature rupture of membranes 658.1 ☑
      - with delayed delivery 658.2 ☑
    - previous
      - infertility V23.0
      - nonobstetric condition V23.89
      - poor obstetrical history V23.49
      - premature delivery V23.41
      - trophoblastic disease (conditions classifiable to 630) V23.1
    - prolapse, uterus 654.4 ☑
    - proteinuria (gestational) 646.2 ☑
      - with hypertension — *see* Toxemia, of pregnancy
    - pruritus (neurogenic) 646.8 ☑
    - psychosis or psychoneurosis 648.4 ☑
    - ptyalism 646.8 ☑
    - pyelitis (conditions classifiable to 590.0–590.9) 646.6 ☑
    - renal disease or failure NEC 646.2 ☑
      - with secondary hypertension 642.1 ☑
      - hypertensive 642.2 ☑
    - retention, retained dead ovum 631
    - retroversion, uterus 654.3 ☑
    - Rh immunization, incompatibility, or sensitization 656.1 ☑
    - rubella (conditions classifiable to 056) 647.5 ☑
    - rupture
      - amnion (premature) 658.1 ☑
        - with delayed delivery 658.2 ☑
      - marginal sinus (hemorrhage) 641.2 ☑
      - membranes (premature) 658.1 ☑
        - with delayed delivery 658.2 ☑
      - uterus (before onset of labor) 665.0 ☑
    - salivation (excessive) 646.8 ☑
    - salpingo-oophoritis (conditions classifiable to 614.0–614.2) 646.6 ☑
    - septicemia (conditions classifiable to 038.0–038.9) 647.8 ☑
      - postpartum 670.0 ☑
      - puerperal 670.0 ☑
    - smoking 649.0 ☑ ●
    - spasms, uterus (abnormal) 646.8 ☑
    - specified condition NEC 646.8 ☑
    - spotting 649.5 ☑ ●
    - spurious labor pains 644.1 ☑
    - status post ●
      - bariatric surgery 649.2 ☑ ●
      - gastric banding 649.2 ☑ ●
      - gastric bypass for obesity 649.2 ☑ ●

- **Pregnancy** — *continued*
  - complicated — *continued*
    - status post — *continued*
      - obesity surgery 649.2 ☑ ●
    - superfecundation 651.9 ☑
    - superfetation 651.9 ☑
    - syphilis (conditions classifiable to 090–097) 647.0 ☑
    - threatened
      - abortion 640.0 ☑
      - premature delivery 644.2 ☑
      - premature labor 644.0 ☑
    - thrombophlebitis (superficial) 671.2 ☑
      - deep 671.3 ☑
    - thrombosis 671.9 ☑
      - venous (superficial) 671.2 ☑
        - deep 671.3 ☑
    - thyroid dysfunction (conditions classifiable to 240–246) 648.1 ☑
    - thyroiditis 648.1 ☑
    - thyrotoxicosis 648.1 ☑
    - tobacco use disorder 649.0 ☑ ●
    - torsion of uterus 654.4 ☑
    - toxemia — *see* Toxemia, of pregnancy
    - transverse lie or presentation 652.3 ☑
      - with successful version 652.1 ☑
    - trauma 648.9 ☑
      - obstetrical 665.9 ☑
    - tuberculosis (conditions classifiable to 010–018) 647.3 ☑
    - tumor
      - cervix 654.6 ☑
      - ovary 654.4 ☑
      - pelvic organs or tissue NEC 654.4 ☑
      - uterus (body) 654.1 ☑
        - cervix 654.6 ☑
      - vagina 654.7 ☑
      - vulva 654.8 ☑
    - unstable lie 652.0 ☑
    - uremia — *see* Pregnancy, complicated, renal disease
    - urethritis 646.6 ☑
    - vaginitis or vulvitis (conditions classifiable to 616.1) 646.6 ☑
    - varicose
      - placental vessels 656.7 ☑
      - veins (legs) 671.0 ☑
        - perineum 671.1 ☑
        - vulva 671.1 ☑
    - varicosity, labia or vulva 671.1 ☑
    - venereal disease NEC (conditions classifiable to 099) 647.2 ☑
    - viral disease NEC (conditions classifiable to 042, 050–055, 057–079) 647.6 ☑
    - vomiting (incoercible) (pernicious) (persistent) (uncontrollable) (vicious) 643.9 ☑
      - due to organic disease or other cause 643.8 ☑
      - early — *see* Hyperemesis, gravidarum
      - late (after 22 completed weeks gestation) 643.2 ☑
    - young maternal age 659.8 ☑
  - complications NEC 646.9 ☑
  - cornual 633.80
    - with intrauterine pregnancy 633.81
    - affecting fetus or newborn 761.4
  - death, maternal NEC 646.9 ☑
  - delivered — *see* Delivery
  - ectopic (ruptured) NEC 633.90
    - with intrauterine pregnancy 633.91
    - abdominal — *see* Pregnancy, abdominal
    - affecting fetus or newborn 761.4
    - combined (extrauterine and intrauterine) — *see* Pregnancy, cornual
    - ovarian — *see* Pregnancy, ovarian

- **Pregnancy** — *continued*
  - ectopic — *continued*
    - specified type NEC 633.80
      - with intrauterine pregnancy 633.81
      - affecting fetus or newborn 761.4
    - tubal — *see* Pregnancy, tubal
  - examination, pregnancy
    - negative result V72.41
    - not confirmed V72.40
    - positive result V72.42
  - extrauterine — *see* Pregnancy, ectopic
  - fallopian — *see* Pregnancy, tubal
  - false 300.11
    - labor (pains) 644.1 ☑
  - fatigue 646.8 ☑
  - illegitimate V61.6
  - incidental finding V22.2
  - in double uterus 654.0 ☑
  - interstitial — *see* Pregnancy, cornual
  - intraligamentous — *see* Pregnancy, cornual
  - intramural — *see* Pregnancy, cornual
  - intraperitoneal — *see* Pregnancy, abdominal
  - isthmian — *see* Pregnancy, tubal
  - management affected by
    - abnormal, abnormality
      - fetus (suspected) 655.9 ☑
        - specified NEC 655.8 ☑
      - placenta 656.7 ☑
    - advanced maternal age NEC 659.6 ☑
      - multigravida 659.6 ☑
      - primigravida 659.5 ☑
    - antibodies (maternal)
      - anti-c 656.1 ☑
      - anti-d 656.1 ☑
      - anti-e 656.1 ☑
      - blood group (ABO) 656.2 ☑
        - Rh(esus) 656.1 ☑
    - appendicitis 648.9 ☑ ●
    - bariatric surgery status 649.2 ☑ ●
    - coagulation defect 649.3 ☑ ●
    - elderly multigravida 659.6 ☑
    - elderly primigravida 659.5 ☑
    - epilepsy 649.4 ☑ ●
    - fetal (suspected)
      - abnormality 655.9 ☑
        - acid-base balance 656.8 ☑
        - heart rate or rhythm 659.7 ☑
        - specified NEC 655.8 ☑
      - acidemia 656.3 ☑
      - anencephaly 655.0 ☑
      - bradycardia 659.7 ☑
      - central nervous system malformation 655.0 ☑
      - chromosomal abnormalities (conditions classifiable to 758.0–758.9) 655.1 ☑
      - damage from
        - drugs 655.5 ☑
          - obstetric, anesthetic, or sedative 655.5 ☑
        - environmental toxins 655.8 ☑
        - intrauterine contraceptive device 655.8 ☑
        - maternal
          - alcohol addiction 655.4 ☑
          - disease NEC 655.4 ☑
          - drug use 655.5 ☑
          - listeriosis 655.4 ☑
          - rubella 655.3 ☑
          - toxoplasmosis 655.4 ☑
          - viral infection 655.3 ☑
        - radiation 655.6 ☑
      - death (near term) 656.4 ☑
        - early (before 22 completed weeks' gestation) 632
      - distress 656.8 ☑
      - excessive growth 656.6 ☑
      - fetal-maternal hemorrhage 656.0 ☑
      - growth retardation 656.5 ☑

- **Pressure** — *continued*
  - increased — *continued*
    - intracranial — *continued*
      - due to — *continued*
        - hydrocephalus — *see* hydrocephalus
        - injury at birth 767.8
    - intraocular 365.00
  - lumbosacral plexus 353.1
  - mediastinum 519.3
  - necrosis (chronic) (skin) (*see also* Decubitus) 707.00
  - nerve — *see* Compression, nerve
  - paralysis (*see also* Neuropathy, entrapment) 355.9
  - sore (chronic) (*see also* Decubitus) 707.00
  - spinal cord 336.9
  - ulcer (chronic) (*see also* Decubitus) 707.00
  - umbilical cord — *see* Compression, umbilical cord
  - venous, increased 459.89
- **Pre-syncope** 780.2
- **Preterm infant NEC** 765.1 ☑
  - extreme 765.0 ☑
- **Priapism** (penis) 607.3
- **Prickling sensation** — *see also* Disturbance, sensation 782.0
- **Prickly heat** 705.1
- **Primary** — *see* condition
- **Primigravida, elderly**
  - affecting
    - fetus or newborn 763.89
    - management of pregnancy, labor, and delivery 659.5 ☑
- **Primipara, old**
  - affecting
    - fetus or newborn 763.89
    - management of pregnancy, labor, and delivery 659.5 ☑
- **Primula dermatitis** 692.6
- **Primus varus** (bilateral) (metatarsus) 754.52
- **P.R.I.N.D.** 436
- **Pringle's disease** (tuberous sclerosis) 759.5
- **Prinzmetal's angina** 413.1
- **Prinzmetal-Massumi syndrome** (anterior chest wall) 786.52
- **Prizefighter ear** 738.7
- **Problem** (with) V49.9
  - academic V62.3
  - acculturation V62.4
  - adopted child V61.29
  - aged
    - in-law V61.3
    - parent V61.3
    - person NEC V61.8
  - alcoholism in family V61.41
  - anger reaction (*see also* Disturbance, conduct) 312.0 ☑
  - behavioral V40.9
    - specified NEC V40.3
  - behavior, child 312.9
  - betting V69.3
  - cardiorespiratory NEC V47.2
  - career choice V62.2
  - care of sick or handicapped person in family or household V61.49
  - communication V40.1
  - conscience regarding medical care V62.6
  - delinquency (juvenile) 312.9
  - diet, inappropriate V69.1
  - digestive NEC V47.3
  - ear NEC V41.3
  - eating habits, inappropriate V69.1
  - economic V60.2
    - affecting care V60.9
      - specified type NEC V60.8
  - educational V62.3
  - enuresis, child 307.6
  - exercise, lack of V69.0
  - eye NEC V41.1
  - family V61.9
    - specified circumstance NEC V61.8
  - fear reaction, child 313.0
  - feeding (elderly) (infant) 783.3
    - newborn 779.3
    - nonorganic 307.59
  - fetal, affecting management of pregnancy 656.9 ☑
    - specified type NEC 656.8 ☑
  - financial V60.2
  - foster child V61.29
    - specified NEC V41.8
  - functional V41.9
    - specified type NEC V41.8
  - gambling V69.3
  - genital NEC V47.5
  - head V48.9
    - deficiency V48.0
    - disfigurement V48.6
    - mechanical V48.2
    - motor V48.2
    - movement of V48.2
    - sensory V48.4
    - specified condition NEC V48.8
  - hearing V41.2
  - high-risk sexual behavior V69.2
  - identity 313.82
  - influencing health status NEC V49.89
  - internal organ NEC V47.9
    - deficiency V47.0
    - mechanical or motor V47.1
  - interpersonal NEC V62.81
  - jealousy, child 313.3
  - learning V40.0
  - legal V62.5
  - life circumstance NEC V62.89
  - lifestyle V69.9
    - specified NEC V69.8
  - limb V49.9
    - deficiency V49.0
    - disfigurement V49.4
    - mechanical V49.1
    - motor V49.2
    - movement, involving
      - musculoskeletal system V49.1
      - nervous system V49.2
    - sensory V49.3
    - specified condition NEC V49.5
  - litigation V62.5
  - living alone V60.3
  - loneliness NEC V62.89
  - marital V61.10
    - involving
      - divorce V61.0
      - estrangement V61.0
      - psychosexual disorder 302.9
      - sexual function V41.7
    - relationship V61.10
  - mastication V41.6
  - medical care, within family V61.49
  - mental V40.9
    - specified NEC V40.2
  - mental hygiene, adult V40.9
  - multiparity V61.5
  - nail biting, child 307.9
  - neck V48.9
    - deficiency V48.1
    - disfigurement V48.7
    - mechanical V48.3
    - motor V48.3
    - movement V48.3
    - sensory V48.5
    - specified condition NEC V48.8
  - neurological NEC 781.99
  - none (feared complaint unfounded) V65.5
  - occupational V62.2
  - parent-child V61.20
    - relationship V61.20
  - partner V61.10
    - relationship V61.10
  - personal NEC V62.89
    - interpersonal conflict NEC V62.81
  - personality (*see also* Disorder, personality) 301.9
  - phase of life V62.89
  - placenta, affecting management of pregnancy 656.9 ☑
    - specified type NEC 656.8 ☑
  - poverty V60.2
  - presence of sick or handicapped person in family or household V61.49
  - psychiatric 300.9
  - psychosocial V62.9
    - specified type NEC V62.89
  - relational NEC V62.81
  - relationship, childhood 313.3
  - religious or spiritual belief
    - other than medical care V62.89
    - regarding medical care V62.6
  - self-damaging behavior V69.8
  - sexual
    - behavior, high-risk V69.2
    - function NEC V41.7
  - sibling
    - relational V61.8
    - relationship V61.8
  - sight V41.0
  - sleep disorder, child 307.40
  - sleep, lack of V69.4
  - smell V41.5
  - speech V40.1
  - spite reaction, child (*see also* Disturbance, conduct) 312.0 ☑
  - spoiled child reaction (*see also* Disturbance, conduct) 312.1 ☑
  - swallowing V41.6
  - tantrum, child (*see also* Disturbance, conduct) 312.1 ☑
  - taste V41.5
  - thumb sucking, child 307.9
  - tic (child) 307.21
  - trunk V48.9
    - deficiency V48.1
    - disfigurement V48.7
    - mechanical V48.3
    - motor V48.3
    - movement V48.3
    - sensory V48.5
    - specified condition NEC V48.8
  - unemployment V62.0
  - urinary NEC V47.4
  - voice production V41.4
- **Procedure** (surgical) **not done** NEC V64.3
  - because of
    - contraindication V64.1
    - patient's decision V64.2
      - for reasons of conscience or religion V62.6
    - specified reason NEC V64.3
- **Procidentia**
  - anus (sphincter) 569.1
  - rectum (sphincter) 569.1
  - stomach 537.89
  - uteri 618.1
- **Proctalgia** 569.42
  - fugax 564.6
  - spasmodic 564.6
    - psychogenic 307.89
- **Proctitis** 569.49
  - amebic 006.8
  - chlamydial 099.52
  - gonococcal 098.7
  - granulomatous 555.1
  - idiopathic 556.2
    - with ulcerative sigmoiditis 556.3
  - tuberculous (*see also* Tuberculosis) 014.8 ☑
  - ulcerative (chronic) (nonspecific) 556.2
    - with ulcerative sigmoiditis 556.3
- **Proctocele**
  - female (without uterine prolapse) 618.04
    - with uterine prolapse 618.4
      - complete 618.3
      - incomplete 618.2
  - male 569.49
- **Proctocolitis, idiopathic** 556.2
  - with ulcerative sigmoiditis 556.3
- **Proctoptosis** 569.1
- **Proctosigmoiditis** 569.89
  - ulcerative (chronic) 556.3
- **Proctospasm** 564.6
  - psychogenic 306.4
- **Prodromal-AIDS** — *see* Human immunodeficiency virus (disease) (illness) (infection)
- **Profichet's disease or syndrome** 729.9
- **Progeria** (adultorum) (syndrome) 259.8
- **Prognathism** (mandibular) (maxillary) 524.00
- **Progonoma** (melanotic) (M9363/0) — *see* Neoplasm, by site, benign
- **Progressive** — *see* condition
- **Prolapse, prolapsed**
  - anus, anal (canal) (sphincter) 569.1
  - arm or hand, complicating delivery 652.7 ☑
    - causing obstructed labor 660.0 ☑
      - affecting fetus or newborn 763.1
    - fetus or newborn 763.1
  - bladder (acquired) (mucosa) (sphincter)
    - congenital (female) (male) 756.71
    - female (*see also* Cystocele, female) 618.01
    - male 596.8
  - breast implant (prosthetic) 996.54
  - cecostomy 569.69
  - cecum 569.89
  - cervix, cervical (hypertrophied) 618.1
    - anterior lip, obstructing labor 660.2 ☑
      - affecting fetus or newborn 763.1
    - congenital 752.49
    - postpartal (old) 618.1
    - stump 618.84 ●
  - ciliary body 871.1
  - colon (pedunculated) 569.89
  - colostomy 569.69
  - conjunctiva 372.73
  - cord — *see* Prolapse, umbilical cord
  - disc (intervertebral) — *see* Displacement, intervertebral disc
  - duodenum 537.89
  - eye implant (orbital) 996.59
    - lens (ocular) 996.53
  - fallopian tube 620.4
  - fetal extremity, complicating delivery 652.8 ☑
    - causing obstructed labor 660.0 ☑
    - fetus or newborn 763.1
  - funis — *see* Prolapse, umbilical cord
  - gastric (mucosa) 537.89
  - genital, female 618.9
    - specified NEC 618.89
  - globe 360.81
  - ileostomy bud 569.69
  - intervertebral disc — *see* Displacement, intervertebral disc
  - intestine (small) 569.89
  - iris 364.8
    - traumatic 871.1
  - kidney (*see also* Disease, renal) 593.0
    - congenital 753.3
  - laryngeal muscles or ventricle 478.79
  - leg, complicating delivery 652.8 ☑
    - causing obstructed labor 660.0 ☑
    - fetus or newborn 763.1
  - liver 573.8
  - meatus urinarius 599.5
  - mitral valve 424.0
  - ocular lens implant 996.53
  - organ or site, congenital NEC — *see* Malposition, congenital
  - ovary 620.4
  - pelvic (floor), female 618.89
  - perineum, female 618.89
  - pregnant uterus 654.4 ☑
  - rectum (mucosa) (sphincter) 569.1
    - due to Trichuris trichiuria 127.3
  - spleen 289.59

☑ Additional Digit Required — Refer to the Tabular List for Digit Selection

Subterms under main terms may continue to next column or page

Note — Use the following fifth-digit subclassification with categories 296.0–296.6:

0 unspecified
1 mild
2 moderate
3 severe, without mention of psychotic behavior
4 severe, specified as with psychotic behavior
5 in partial or unspecified remission
6 in full remission

Note — Use the following fifth-digit subclassification with category 299:

0 current or active state
1 residual state

Psychosis — *continued*
- manic-depressive — *continued*
  - depressive 296.2 ☑
    - recurrent episode 296.3 ☑
      - with hypomania (bipolar II) 296.89
    - single episode 296.2 ☑
  - hypomanic 296.0 ☑
    - recurrent episode 296.1 ☑
    - single episode 296.0 ☑
  - manic 296.0 ☑
    - atypical 296.81
    - recurrent episode 296.1 ☑
    - single episode 296.0 ☑
  - mixed NEC 296.89
  - perplexed 296.89
  - stuporous 296.89
- menopausal (*see also* Psychosis, involutional) 298.8
- mixed schizophrenic and affective (*see also* Schizophrenia) 295.7 ☑
- multi-infarct (cerebrovascular) (*see also* Psychosis, arteriosclerotic) 290.40
- organic NEC 294.9
  - due to or associated with
    - addiction
      - alcohol (*see also* Psychosis, alcoholic) 291.9
      - drug (*see also* Psychosis, drug) 292.9
    - alcohol intoxication, acute (*see also* Psychosis, alcoholic) 291.9
    - alcoholism (*see also* Psychosis, alcoholic) 291.9
    - arteriosclerosis (cerebral) (*see also* Psychosis, arteriosclerotic) 290.40
    - cerebrovascular disease
      - acute (psychosis) 293.0
      - arteriosclerotic (*see also* Psychosis, arteriosclerotic) 290.40
    - childbirth — *see* Psychosis, puerperal
    - dependence
      - alcohol (*see also* Psychosis, alcoholic) 291.9
      - drug 292.9
    - disease
      - alcoholic liver (*see also* Psychosis, alcoholic) 291.9
      - brain
        - arteriosclerotic (*see also* Psychosis, arteriosclerotic) 290.40
      - cerebrovascular
        - acute (psychosis) 293.0
        - arteriosclerotic (*see also* Psychosis, arteriosclerotic) 290.40
      - endocrine or metabolic 293.9
        - acute (psychosis) 293.0
        - subacute (psychosis) 293.1
      - Jakob-Creutzfeldt (new variant)
        - with behavioral disturbance 046.1 *[294.11]*
        - without behavioral disturbance 046.1 *[294.10]*
      - liver, alcoholic (*see also* Psychosis, alcoholic) 291.9
    - disorder
      - cerebrovascular
        - acute (psychosis) 293.0
      - endocrine or metabolic 293.9
        - acute (psychosis) 293.0
        - subacute (psychosis) 293.1
    - epilepsy
      - with behavioral disturbance 345.9 ☑ *[294.11]*

Psychosis — *continued*
- organic — *continued*
  - due to or associated with — *continued*
    - epilepsy — *continued*
      - without behavioral disturbance 345.9 ☑ *[294.10]*
      - transient (acute) 293.0
    - Huntington's chorea
      - with behavioral disturbance 333.4 *[294.11]*
      - without behavioral disturbance 333.4 *[294.10]*
    - infection
      - brain 293.9
        - acute (psychosis) 293.0
        - chronic 294.8
        - subacute (psychosis) 293.1
      - intracranial NEC 293.9
        - acute (psychosis) 293.0
        - chronic 294.8
        - subacute (psychosis) 293.1
    - intoxication
      - alcoholic (acute) (*see also* Psychosis, alcoholic) 291.9
        - pathological 291.4
      - drug (*see also* Psychosis, drug) 292.2
    - ischemia
      - cerebrovascular (generalized) (*see also* Psychosis, arteriosclerotic) 290.40
    - Jakob-Creutzfeldt disease (syndrome) (new variant)
      - with behavioral disturbance 046.1 *[294.11]*
      - without behavioral disturbance 046.1 *[294.10]*
    - multiple sclerosis
      - with behavioral disturbance 340 *[294.11]*
      - without behavioral disturbance 340 *[294.10]*
    - physical condition NEC 293.9
      - with
        - delusions 293.81
        - hallucinations 293.82
    - presenility 290.10
    - puerperium — *see* Psychosis, puerperal
    - sclerosis, multiple
      - with behavioral disturbance 340 *[294.11]*
      - without behavioral disturbance 340 *[294.10]*
    - senility 290.20
    - status epilepticus
      - with behavioral disturbance 345.3 *[294.11]*
      - without behavioral disturbance 345.3 *[294.10]*
    - trauma
      - brain (birth) (from electrical current) (surgical) 293.9
        - acute (psychosis) 293.0
        - chronic 294.8
        - subacute (psychosis) 293.1
        - unspecified physical condition 293.9
          - with
            - delusion 293.81
            - hallucinations 293.82
  - infective 293.9
    - acute (psychosis) 293.0
    - subacute 293.1
  - posttraumatic 293.9
    - acute 293.0
    - subacute 293.1
  - specified type NEC 294.8

Psychosis — *continued*
- organic — *continued*
  - transient 293.9
    - with
      - anxiety 293.84
      - delusions 293.81
      - depression 293.83
      - hallucinations 293.82
    - depressive type 293.83
    - hallucinatory type 293.82
    - paranoid type 293.81
    - specified type NEC 293.89
- paranoic 297.1
- paranoid (chronic) 297.9
  - alcoholic 291.5
  - chronic 297.1
  - climacteric 297.2
  - involutional 297.2
  - menopausal 297.2
  - protracted reactive 298.4
  - psychogenic 298.4
    - acute 298.3
  - schizophrenic (*see also* Schizophrenia) 295.3 ☑
  - senile 290.20
- paroxysmal 298.9
  - senile 290.20
- polyneuritic, alcoholic 291.1
- postoperative 293.9
- postpartum — *see* Psychosis, puerperal
- prepsychotic (*see also* Schizophrenia) 295.5 ☑
- presbyophrenic (type) 290.8
- presenile (*see also* Dementia, presenile) 290.10
- prison 300.16
- psychogenic 298.8
  - depressive 298.0
  - paranoid 298.4
    - acute 298.3
- puerperal
  - specified type — *see* categories 295-298 ☑
  - unspecified type 293.89
    - acute 293.0
    - chronic 293.89
    - subacute 293.1
- reactive (emotional stress) (psychological trauma) 298.8
  - brief 298.8
  - confusion 298.2
  - depressive 298.0
  - excitation 298.1
- schizo-affective (depressed) (excited) (*see also* Schizophrenia) 295.7 ☑
- schizophrenia, schizophrenic (*see also* Schizophrenia) 295.9 ☑
  - borderline type 295.5 ☑
    - of childhood (*see also* Psychosis, childhood) 299.8 ☑
  - catatonic (excited) (withdrawn) 295.2 ☑
  - childhood type (*see also* Psychosis, childhood) 299.9 ☑
  - hebephrenic 295.1 ☑
  - incipient 295.5 ☑
  - latent 295.5 ☑
  - paranoid 295.3 ☑
  - prepsychotic 295.5 ☑
  - prodromal 295.5 ☑
  - pseudoneurotic 295.5 ☑
  - pseudopsychopathic 295.5 ☑
  - schizophreniform 295.4 ☑
  - simple 295.0 ☑
  - undifferentiated type 295.9 ☑
- schizophreniform 295.4 ☑
- senile NEC 290.20
  - with
    - delusional features 290.20
    - depressive features 290.21
  - depressed type 290.21
  - paranoid type 290.20
  - simple deterioration 290.20

Psychosis — *continued*
- senile — *continued*
  - specified type — *see* categories 295-298 ☑
- shared 297.3
- situational (reactive) 298.8
- symbiotic (childhood) (*see also* Psychosis, childhood) 299.1 ☑
- toxic (acute) 293.9

Psychotic — *see also* condition 298.9
- episode 298.9
  - due to or associated with physical conditions (*see also* Psychosis, organic) 293.9

Pterygium (eye) 372.40
- central 372.43
- colli 744.5
- double 372.44
- peripheral (stationary) 372.41
  - progressive 372.42
- recurrent 372.45

Ptilosis 374.55

Ptomaine (poisoning) — *see also* Poisoning, food 005.9

Ptosis (adiposa) 374.30
- breast 611.8
- cecum 569.89
- colon 569.89
- congenital (eyelid) 743.61
  - specified site NEC — *see* Anomaly, specified type NEC
- epicanthus syndrome 270.2
- eyelid 374.30
  - congenital 743.61
  - mechanical 374.33
  - myogenic 374.32
  - paralytic 374.31
- gastric 537.5
- intestine 569.89
- kidney (*see also* Disease, renal) 593.0
  - congenital 753.3
- liver 573.8
- renal (*see also* Disease, renal) 593.0
  - congenital 753.3
- splanchnic 569.89
- spleen 289.59
- stomach 537.5
- viscera 569.89

PTSD (Post-traumatic stress disorder) ● 309.81 ●

Ptyalism 527.7
- hysterical 300.11
- periodic 527.2
- pregnancy 646.8 ☑
- psychogenic 306.4

Ptyalolithiasis 527.5

Pubalgia 848.8

Pubarche, precocious 259.1

Pubertas praecox 259.1

Puberty V21.1
- abnormal 259.9
- bleeding 626.3
- delayed 259.0
- precocious (constitutional) (cryptogenic) (idiopathic) NEC 259.1
  - due to
    - adrenal
      - cortical hyperfunction 255.2
      - hyperplasia 255.2
    - cortical hyperfunction 255.2
    - ovarian hyperfunction 256.1
      - estrogen 256.0
    - pineal tumor 259.8
    - testicular hyperfunction 257.0
- premature 259.1
  - due to
    - adrenal cortical hyperfunction 255.2
    - pineal tumor 259.8
    - pituitary (anterior) hyperfunction 253.1

Puckering, macula 362.56

Pudenda, pudendum — *see* condition

Puente's disease (simple glandular cheilitis) 528.5

- **Puerperal**
  - abscess
    - areola 675.1 ☑
    - Bartholin's gland 646.6 ☑
    - breast 675.1 ☑
    - cervix (uteri) 670.0 ☑
    - fallopian tube 670.0 ☑
    - genital organ 670.0 ☑
    - kidney 646.6 ☑
    - mammary 675.1 ☑
    - mesosalpinx 670.0 ☑
    - nabothian 646.6 ☑
    - nipple 675.0 ☑
    - ovary, ovarian 670.0 ☑
    - oviduct 670.0 ☑
    - parametric 670.0 ☑
    - para-uterine 670.0 ☑
    - pelvic 670.0 ☑
    - perimetric 670.0 ☑
    - periuterine 670.0 ☑
    - retro-uterine 670.0 ☑
    - subareolar 675.1 ☑
    - suprapelvic 670.0 ☑
    - tubal (ruptured) 670.0 ☑
    - tubo-ovarian 670.0 ☑
    - urinary tract NEC 646.6 ☑
    - uterine, uterus 670.0 ☑
    - vagina (wall) 646.6 ☑
    - vaginorectal 646.6 ☑
    - vulvovaginal gland 646.6 ☑
  - accident 674.9 ☑
  - adnexitis 670.0 ☑
  - afibrinogenemia, or other coagulation defect 666.3 ☑
  - albuminuria (acute) (subacute) 646.2 ☑
    - pre-eclamptic 642.4 ☑
  - anemia (conditions classifiable to 280–285) 648.2 ☑
  - anuria 669.3 ☑
  - apoplexy 674.0 ☑
  - asymptomatic bacteriuria 646.5 ☑
  - atrophy, breast 676.3 ☑
  - blood dyscrasia 666.3 ☑
  - caked breast 676.2 ☑
  - cardiomyopathy 674.5 ☑
  - cellulitis — *see* Puerperal, abscess
  - cerebrovascular disorder (conditions classifiable to 430–434, 436–437) 674.0 ☑
  - cervicitis (conditions classifiable to 616.0) 646.6 ☑
  - coagulopathy (any) 666.3 ☑
  - complications 674.9 ☑
    - specified type NEC 674.8 ☑
  - convulsions (eclamptic) (uremic) 642.6 ☑
    - with pre-existing hypertension 642.7 ☑
  - cracked nipple 676.1 ☑
  - cystitis 646.6 ☑
  - cystopyelitis 646.6 ☑
  - deciduitis (acute) 670.0 ☑
  - delirium NEC 293.9
  - diabetes (mellitus) (conditions classifiable to 250) 648.0 ☑
  - disease 674.9 ☑
    - breast NEC 676.3 ☑
    - cerebrovascular (acute) 674.0 ☑
    - nonobstetric NEC (*see also* Pregnancy, complicated, current disease or condition) 648.9 ☑
    - pelvis inflammatory 670.0 ☑
    - renal NEC 646.2 ☑
    - tubo-ovarian 670.0 ☑
    - Valsuani's (progressive pernicious anemia) 648.2 ☑
  - disorder
    - lactation 676.9 ☑
      - specified type NEC 676.8 ☑
    - nonobstetric NEC (*see also* Pregnancy, complicated, current disease or condition) 648.9 ☑
  - disruption
    - cesarean wound 674.1 ☑
    - episiotomy wound 674.2 ☑
    - perineal laceration wound 674.2 ☑
  - drug dependence (conditions classifiable to 304) 648.3 ☑
  - eclampsia 642.6 ☑
    - with pre-existing hypertension 642.7 ☑
  - embolism (pulmonary) 673.2 ☑
    - air 673.0 ☑
    - amniotic fluid 673.1 ☑
    - blood-clot 673.2 ☑
    - brain or cerebral 674.0 ☑
    - cardiac 674.8 ☑
    - fat 673.8 ☑
    - intracranial sinus (venous) 671.5 ☑
    - pyemic 673.3 ☑
    - septic 673.3 ☑
    - spinal cord 671.5 ☑
  - endometritis (conditions classifiable to 615.0–615.9) 670.0 ☑
  - endophlebitis — *see* Puerperal, phlebitis
  - endotrachelitis 646.6 ☑
  - engorgement, breasts 676.2 ☑
  - erysipelas 670.0 ☑
  - failure
    - lactation 676.4 ☑
    - renal, acute 669.3 ☑
  - fever 670.0 ☑
    - meaning pyrexia (of unknown origin) 672.0 ☑
    - meaning sepsis 670.0 ☑
  - fissure, nipple 676.1 ☑
  - fistula
    - breast 675.1 ☑
    - mammary gland 675.1 ☑
    - nipple 675.0 ☑
  - galactophoritis 675.2 ☑
  - galactorrhea 676.6 ☑
  - gangrene
    - gas 670.0 ☑
    - uterus 670.0 ☑
  - gonorrhea (conditions classifiable to 098) 647.1 ☑
  - hematoma, subdural 674.0 ☑
  - hematosalpinx, infectional 670.0 ☑
  - hemiplegia, cerebral 674.0 ☑
  - hemorrhage 666.1 ☑
    - brain 674.0 ☑
    - bulbar 674.0 ☑
    - cerebellar 674.0 ☑
    - cerebral 674.0 ☑
    - cortical 674.0 ☑
    - delayed (after 24 hours) (uterine) 666.2 ☑
    - extradural 674.0 ☑
    - internal capsule 674.0 ☑
    - intracranial 674.0 ☑
    - intrapontine 674.0 ☑
    - meningeal 674.0 ☑
    - pontine 674.0 ☑
    - subarachnoid 674.0 ☑
    - subcortical 674.0 ☑
    - subdural 674.0 ☑
    - uterine, delayed 666.2 ☑
    - ventricular 674.0 ☑
  - hemorrhoids 671.8 ☑
  - hepatorenal syndrome 674.8 ☑
  - hypertrophy
    - breast 676.3 ☑
    - mammary gland 676.3 ☑
  - induration breast (fibrous) 676.3 ☑
  - infarction
    - lung — *see* Puerperal, embolism
    - pulmonary — *see* Puerperal, embolism
  - infection
    - Bartholin's gland 646.6 ☑
    - breast 675.2 ☑
      - with nipple 675.9 ☑
        - specified type NEC 675.8 ☑
    - cervix 646.6 ☑
    - endocervix 646.6 ☑
    - fallopian tube 670.0 ☑
    - generalized 670.0 ☑
    - genital tract (major) 670.0 ☑
      - minor or localized 646.6 ☑
    - kidney (bacillus coli) 646.6 ☑
    - mammary gland 675.2 ☑
      - with nipple 675.9 ☑
        - specified type NEC 675.8 ☑
    - nipple 675.0 ☑
      - with breast 675.9 ☑
        - specified type NEC 675.8 ☑
    - ovary 670.0 ☑
    - pelvic 670.0 ☑
    - peritoneum 670.0 ☑
    - renal 646.6 ☑
    - tubo-ovarian 670.0 ☑
    - urinary (tract) NEC 646.6 ☑
      - asymptomatic 646.5 ☑
    - uterus, uterine 670.0 ☑
    - vagina 646.6 ☑
  - inflammation (*see also* Puerperal, infection)
    - areola 675.1 ☑
    - Bartholin's gland 646.6 ☑
    - breast 675.2 ☑
    - broad ligament 670.0 ☑
    - cervix (uteri) 646.6 ☑
    - fallopian tube 670.0 ☑
    - genital organs 670.0 ☑
      - localized 646.6 ☑
    - mammary gland 675.2 ☑
    - nipple 675.0 ☑
    - ovary 670.0 ☑
    - oviduct 670.0 ☑
    - pelvis 670.0 ☑
    - periuterine 670.0 ☑
    - tubal 670.0 ☑
    - vagina 646.6 ☑
    - vein — *see* Puerperal, phlebitis
  - inversion, nipple 676.3 ☑
  - ischemia, cerebral 674.0 ☑
  - lymphangitis 670.0 ☑
    - breast 675.2 ☑
  - malaria (conditions classifiable to 084) 647.4 ☑
  - malnutrition 648.9 ☑
  - mammillitis 675.0 ☑
  - mammitis 675.2 ☑
  - mania 296.0 ☑
    - recurrent episode 296.1 ☑
    - single episode 296.0 ☑
  - mastitis 675.2 ☑
    - purulent 675.1 ☑
    - retromammary 675.1 ☑
    - submammary 675.1 ☑
  - melancholia 296.2 ☑
    - recurrent episode 296.3 ☑
    - single episode 296.2 ☑
  - mental disorder (conditions classifiable to 290–303, ▶305.0, 305.2–305.9, 306–316◀, 317–319) 648.4 ☑
  - metritis (septic) (suppurative) 670.0 ☑
  - metroperitonitis 670.0 ☑
  - metrorrhagia 666.2 ☑
  - metrosalpingitis 670.0 ☑
  - metrovaginitis 670.0 ☑
  - milk leg 671.4 ☑
  - monoplegia, cerebral 674.0 ☑
  - necrosis
    - kidney, tubular 669.3 ☑
    - liver (acute) (subacute) (conditions classifiable to 570) 674.8 ☑
    - ovary 670.0 ☑
    - renal cortex 669.3 ☑
  - nephritis or nephrosis (conditions classifiable to 580–589) 646.2 ☑
    - with hypertension 642.1 ☑
  - nutritional deficiency (conditions classifiable to 260–269) 648.9 ☑
  - occlusion, precerebral artery 674.0 ☑
  - oliguria 669.3 ☑
  - oophoritis 670.0 ☑
  - ovaritis 670.0 ☑
  - paralysis
    - bladder (sphincter) 665.5 ☑
    - cerebral 674.0 ☑
  - paralytic stroke 674.0 ☑
  - parametritis 670.0 ☑
  - paravaginitis 646.6 ☑
  - pelviperitonitis 670.0 ☑
  - perimetritis 670.0 ☑
  - perimetrosalpingitis 670.0 ☑
  - perinephritis 646.6 ☑
  - perioophoritis 670.0 ☑
  - periphlebitis — *see* Puerperal, phlebitis
  - perisalpingitis 670.0 ☑
  - peritoneal infection 670.0 ☑
  - peritonitis (pelvic) 670.0 ☑
  - perivaginitis 646.6 ☑
  - phlebitis 671.9 ☑
    - deep 671.4 ☑
    - intracranial sinus (venous) 671.5 ☑
    - pelvic 671.4 ☑
    - specified site NEC 671.5 ☑
    - superficial 671.2 ☑
  - phlegmasia alba dolens 671.4 ☑
  - placental polyp 674.4 ☑
  - pneumonia, embolic — *see* Puerperal, embolism
  - prediabetes 648.8 ☑
  - pre-eclampsia (mild) 642.4 ☑
    - with pre-existing hypertension 642.7 ☑
    - severe 642.5 ☑
  - psychosis, unspecified (*see also* Psychosis, puerperal) 293.89
  - pyelitis 646.6 ☑
  - pyelocystitis 646.6 ☑
  - pyelohydronephrosis 646.6 ☑
  - pyelonephritis 646.6 ☑
  - pyelonephrosis 646.6 ☑
  - pyemia 670.0 ☑
  - pyocystitis 646.6 ☑
  - pyohemia 670.0 ☑
  - pyometra 670.0 ☑
  - pyonephritis 646.6 ☑
  - pyonephrosis 646.6 ☑
  - pyo-oophoritis 670.0 ☑
  - pyosalpingitis 670.0 ☑
  - pyosalpinx 670.0 ☑
  - pyrexia (of unknown origin) 672.0 ☑
  - renal
    - disease NEC 646.2 ☑
    - failure, acute 669.3 ☑
  - retention
    - decidua (fragments) (with delayed hemorrhage) 666.2 ☑
      - without hemorrhage 667.1 ☑
    - placenta (fragments) (with delayed hemorrhage) 666.2 ☑
      - without hemorrhage 667.1 ☑
    - secundines (fragments) (with delayed hemorrhage) 666.2 ☑
      - without hemorrhage 667.1 ☑
  - retracted nipple 676.0 ☑
  - rubella (conditions classifiable to 056) 647.5 ☑
  - salpingitis 670.0 ☑
  - salpingo-oophoritis 670.0 ☑
  - salpingo-ovaritis 670.0 ☑
  - salpingoperitonitis 670.0 ☑
  - sapremia 670.0 ☑
  - secondary perineal tear 674.2 ☑
  - sepsis (pelvic) 670.0 ☑
  - septicemia 670.0 ☑
  - subinvolution (uterus) 674.8 ☑

☑ Additional Digit Required — Refer to the Tabular List for Digit Selection
Subterms under main terms may continue to next column or page

☑ Additional Digit Required — Refer to the Tabular List for Digit Selection

Subterms under main terms may continue to next column or page

▶◀ Revised Text ● New Line ▲ Revised Code

- **Reflex** — *see also* condition — *continued*
  - neurogenic bladder — *continued*
    - atonic — *continued*
      - with cauda equina syndrome 344.61
  - vasoconstriction 443.9
  - vasovagal 780.2
- **Reflux**
  - esophageal 530.81
    - with esophagitis 530.11
  - esophagitis 530.11
  - gastroesophageal 530.81
  - mitral — *see* Insufficiency, mitral
  - ureteral — *see* Reflux, vesicoureteral
  - vesicoureteral 593.70
    - with
      - reflux nephropathy 593.73
        - bilateral 593.72
        - unilateral 593.71
- **Reformed gallbladder** 576.0
- **Reforming, artificial openings** — *see also* Attention to, artificial, opening V55.9
- **Refractive error** — *see also* Error, refractive 367.9
- **Refsum's disease or syndrome** (heredopathia atactica polyneuritiformis) 356.3
- **Refusal of**
  - food 307.59
    - hysterical 300.11
  - treatment because of, due to
    - patient's decision NEC V64.2
    - reason of conscience or religion V62.6
- **Regaud**
  - tumor (M8082/3) — *see* Neoplasm, nasopharynx, malignant
  - type carcinoma (M8082/3) — *see* Neoplasm, nasopharynx, malignant
- **Regional** — *see* condition
- **Regulation feeding** (elderly) (infant) 783.3
  - newborn 779.3
- **Regurgitated**
  - food, choked on 933.1
  - stomach contents, choked on 933.1
- **Regurgitation**
  - aortic (valve) (*see also* Insufficiency, aortic) 424.1
    - congenital 746.4
    - syphilitic 093.22
  - food (*see also* Vomiting)
    - with reswallowing — *see* Rumination
    - newborn 779.3
  - gastric contents — *see* Vomiting
  - heart — *see* Endocarditis
  - mitral (valve) (*see also* Insufficiency, mitral)
    - congenital 746.6
  - myocardial — *see* Endocarditis
  - pulmonary (heart) (valve) (*see also* Endocarditis, pulmonary) 424.3
  - stomach — *see* Vomiting
  - tricuspid — *see* Endocarditis, tricuspid
  - valve, valvular — *see* Endocarditis
  - vesicoureteral — *see* Reflux, vesicoureteral
- **Rehabilitation** V57.9
  - multiple types V57.89
  - occupational V57.21
  - specified type NEC V57.89
  - speech V57.3
  - vocational V57.22
- **Reichmann's disease or syndrome** (gastrosuccorrhea) 536.8
- **Reifenstein's syndrome** (hereditary familial hypogonadism, male) 259.5
- **Reilly's syndrome or phenomenon** — *see also* Neuropathy, peripheral, autonomic 337.9
- **Reimann's periodic disease** 277.31 ▲
- **Reinsertion, contraceptive device** V25.42
- **Reiter's disease, syndrome, or urethritis** 099.3 *[711.1]* ☑
- **Rejection**
  - food, hysterical 300.11
  - transplant 996.80
    - bone marrow 996.85
    - corneal 996.51
    - organ (immune or nonimmune cause) 996.80
      - bone marrow 996.85
      - heart 996.83
      - intestines 996.87
      - kidney 996.81
      - liver 996.82
      - lung 996.84
      - pancreas 996.86
      - specified NEC 996.89
    - skin 996.52
      - artificial 996.55
      - decellularized allodermis 996.55
- **Relapsing fever** 087.9
  - Carter's (Asiatic) 087.0
  - Dutton's (West African) 087.1
  - Koch's 087.9
  - louse-borne (epidemic) 087.0
  - Novy's (American) 087.1
  - Obermeyer's (European) 087.0
  - Spirillum 087.9
  - tick-borne (endemic) 087.1
- **Relaxation**
  - anus (sphincter) 569.49
    - due to hysteria 300.11
  - arch (foot) 734
    - congenital 754.61
  - back ligaments 728.4
  - bladder (sphincter) 596.59
  - cardio-esophageal 530.89
  - cervix (*see also* Incompetency, cervix) 622.5
  - diaphragm 519.4
  - inguinal rings — *see* Hernia, inguinal
  - joint (capsule) (ligament) (paralytic) (*see also* Derangement, joint) 718.90
    - congenital 755.8
  - lumbosacral joint 724.6
  - pelvic floor 618.89
  - pelvis 618.89
  - perineum 618.89
  - posture 729.9
  - rectum (sphincter) 569.49
  - sacroiliac (joint) 724.6
  - scrotum 608.89
  - urethra (sphincter) 599.84
  - uterus (outlet) 618.89
  - vagina (outlet) 618.89
  - vesical 596.59
- **Remains**
  - canal of Cloquet 743.51
  - capsule (opaque) 743.51
- **Remittent fever** (malarial) 084.6
- **Remnant**
  - canal of Cloquet 743.51
  - capsule (opaque) 743.51
  - cervix, cervical stump (acquired) (postoperative) 622.8
  - cystic duct, postcholecystectomy 576.0
  - fingernail 703.8
    - congenital 757.5
  - meniscus, knee 717.5
  - thyroglossal duct 759.2
  - tonsil 474.8
    - infected 474.00
  - urachus 753.7
- **Remote effect of cancer** — *see* condition
- **Removal** (of)
  - catheter (urinary) (indwelling) V53.6
    - from artificial opening — *see* Attention to, artificial, opening
    - non-vascular V58.82
- **Removal** — *continued*
  - catheter — *continued*
    - vascular V58.81
  - cerebral ventricle (communicating) shunt V53.01
  - device (*see also* Fitting (of))
    - contraceptive V25.42
    - fixation
      - external V54.89
      - internal V54.01
    - traction V54.89
  - drains V58.49 ●
  - dressing
    - wound V58.30 ●
      - nonsurgical V58.30 ●
      - surgical V58.31 ●
  - ileostomy V55.2
  - Kirschner wire V54.89
  - nonvascular catheter V58.82
  - pin V54.01
  - plaster cast V54.89
  - plate (fracture) V54.01
  - rod V54.01
  - screw V54.01
  - splint, external V54.89
  - staples V58.32 ●
  - subdermal implantable contraceptive V25.43
  - ▶sutures◀ V58.32 ▲
  - traction device, external V54.89
  - vascular catheter V58.81
  - wound packing V58.30 ●
    - nonsurgical V58.30 ●
    - surgical V58.31 ●
- **Ren**
  - arcuatus 753.3
  - mobile, mobilis (*see also* Disease, renal) 593.0
    - congenital 753.3
  - unguliformis 753.3
- **Renal** — *see also* condition
  - glomerulohyalinosis-diabetic syndrome 250.4 ☑ *[581.81]*
- **Rendu-Osler-Weber disease or syndrome** (familial hemorrhagic telangiectasia) 448.0
- **Reninoma** (M8361/1) 236.91
- **Rénon-Delille syndrome** 253.8
- **Repair**
  - pelvic floor, previous, in pregnancy or childbirth 654.4 ☑
    - affecting fetus or newborn 763.89
  - scarred tissue V51
- **Replacement by artificial or mechanical device or prosthesis of** — *see also* Fitting (of
  - artificial skin V43.83
  - bladder V43.5
  - blood vessel V43.4
  - breast V43.82
  - eye globe V43.0
  - heart
    - with
      - assist device V43.21
      - fully implantable artificial heart V43.22
    - valve V43.3
  - intestine V43.89
  - joint V43.60
    - ankle V43.66
    - elbow V43.62
    - finger V43.69
    - hip (partial) (total) V43.64
    - knee V43.65
    - shoulder V43.61
    - specified NEC V43.69
    - wrist V43.63
  - kidney V43.89
  - larynx V43.81
  - lens V43.1
  - limb(s) V43.7
  - liver V43.89
  - lung V43.89
  - organ NEC V43.89
  - pancreas V43.89
  - skin (artificial) V43.83
- **Replacement by artificial or mechanical device or prosthesis of** — *see also* Fitting (of — *continued*
  - tissue NEC V43.89
- **Reprogramming**
  - cardiac pacemaker V53.31
- **Request for expert evidence** V68.2
- **Reserve, decreased or low**
  - cardiac — *see* Disease, heart
    - kidney (*see also* Disease, renal) 593.9
- **Residual** — *see also* condition
  - bladder 596.8
  - foreign body — *see* Retention, foreign body
  - state, schizophrenic (*see also* Schizophrenia) 295.6 ☑
  - urine 788.69
- **Resistance, resistant** (to)
  - activated protein C 289.81

> *Note — use the following subclassification for categories V09.5, V09.7, V09.8, V09.9:*
>
> 0 *without mention of resistance to multiple drugs*
>
> 1 *with resistance to multiple drugs*
>
> *V09.5 quinolones and fluoroquinolones*
>
> *V09.7 antimycobacterial agents*
>
> *V09.8 specified drugs NEC*
>
> *V09.9 unspecified drugs*

  - drugs by microorganisms V09.9 ☑
    - Amikacin V09.4
    - aminoglycosides V09.4
    - Amodiaquine V09.5 ☑
    - Amoxicillin V09.0
    - Ampicillin V09.0
    - antimycobacterial agents V09.7 ☑
    - Azithromycin V09.2
    - Azlocillin V09.0
    - Aztreonam V09.1
    - Bacampicillin V09.0
    - Bacitracin V09.8 ☑
    - Benznidazole V09.8 ☑
    - B-lactam antibiotics V09.1
    - Capreomycin V09.7 ☑
    - Carbenicillin V09.0
    - Cefaclor V09.1
    - Cefadroxil V09.1
    - Cefamandole V09.1
    - Cefatetan V09.1
    - Cefazolin V09.1
    - Cefixime V09.1
    - Cefonicid V09.1
    - Cefoperazone V09.1
    - Ceforanide V09.1
    - Cefotaxime V09.1
    - Cefoxitin V09.1
    - Ceftazidime V09.1
    - Ceftizoxime V09.1
    - Ceftriaxone V09.1
    - Cefuroxime V09.1
    - Cephalexin V09.1
    - Cephaloglycin V09.1
    - Cephaloridine V09.1
    - Cephalosporins V09.1
    - Cephalothin V09.1
    - Cephapirin V09.1
    - Cephradine V09.1
    - Chloramphenicol V09.8 ☑
    - Chloraquine V09.5 ☑
    - Chlorguanide V09.8 ☑
    - Chlorproguanil V09.8 ☑
    - Chlortetracyline V09.3
    - Cinoxacin V09.5 ☑
    - Ciprofloxacin V09.5 ☑
    - Clarithromycin V09.2
    - Clindamycin V09.8 ☑
    - Clioquinol V09.5 ☑
    - Clofazimine V09.7 ☑
    - Cloxacillin V09.0

- **Rudimentary** — *see also* Agenesis — *continued*
  - respiratory organs in thoracopagus 759.4
  - tracheal bronchus 748.3
  - uterine horn 752.3
  - uterus 752.3
    - in male 752.7
    - solid or with cavity 752.3
  - vagina 752.49
- **Rud's syndrome** (mental deficiency, epilepsy, and infantilism) 759.89
- **Ruiter-Pompen (-Wyers) syndrome** (angiokeratoma corporis diffusum) 272.7
- **Ruled out condition** — *see also* Observation, suspected V71.9
- **Rumination** — *see also* Vomiting
  - disorder 307.53
  - neurotic 300.3
  - obsessional 300.3
  - psychogenic 307.53
- **Runaway reaction** — *see also* Disturbance, conduct
  - socialized 312.2 ☑
  - undersocialized, unsocialized 312.1 ☑
- **Runeberg's disease** (progressive pernicious anemia) 281.0
- **Runge's syndrome** (postmaturity) 766.22
- **Rupia** 091.3
  - congenital 090.0
  - tertiary 095.9
- **Rupture, ruptured** 553.9
  - abdominal viscera NEC 799.89
    - obstetrical trauma 665.5 ☑
  - abscess (spontaneous) — *see* Abscess, by site
  - amnion — *see* Rupture, membranes
  - aneurysm — *see* Aneurysm
  - anus (sphincter) — *see* Laceration, anus
  - aorta, aortic 441.5
    - abdominal 441.3
    - arch 441.1
    - ascending 441.1
    - descending 441.5
      - abdominal 441.3
      - thoracic 441.1
    - syphilitic 093.0
    - thoracoabdominal 441.6
    - thorax, thoracic 441.1
    - transverse 441.1
    - traumatic (thoracic) 901.0
      - abdominal 902.0
    - valve or cusp (*see also* Endocarditis, aortic) 424.1
  - appendix (with peritonitis) 540.0
    - with peritoneal abscess 540.1
    - traumatic — *see* Injury, internal, gastrointestinal tract
  - arteriovenous fistula, brain (congenital) 430
  - artery 447.2
    - brain (*see also* Hemorrhage, brain) 431
    - coronary (*see also* Infarct, myocardium) 410.9 ☑
    - heart (*see also* Infarct, myocardium) 410.9 ☑
    - pulmonary 417.8
    - traumatic (complication) (*see also* Injury, blood vessel, by site) 904.9
  - bile duct, except cystic (*see also* Disease, biliary) 576.3
    - cystic 575.4
    - traumatic — *see* Injury, internal, intra-abdominal
  - bladder (sphincter) 596.6
    - with
      - abortion — *see* Abortion, by type, with damage to pelvic organs

Rupture, ruptured — *continued*

- bladder — *continued*
  - with — *continued*
    - ectopic pregnancy (*see also* categories 633.0–633.9) 639.2
    - molar pregnancy (*see also* categories 630–632) 639.2
  - following
    - abortion 639.2
    - ectopic or molar pregnancy 639.2
  - nontraumatic 596.6
  - obstetrical trauma 665.5 ☑
  - spontaneous 596.6
  - traumatic — *see* Injury, internal, bladder
- blood vessel (*see also* Hemorrhage) 459.0
  - brain (*see also* Hemorrhage, brain) 431
  - heart (*see also* Infarct, myocardium) 410.9 ☑
  - traumatic (complication) (*see also* Injury, blood vessel, by site) 904.9
- bone — *see* Fracture, by site
- bowel 569.89
  - traumatic — *see* Injury, internal, intestine
- Bowman's membrane 371.31
- brain
  - aneurysm (congenital) (*see also* Hemorrhage, subarachnoid) 430
    - late effect — *see* Late effect(s) (of) cerebrovascular disease
    - syphilitic 094.87
  - hemorrhagic (*see also* Hemorrhage, brain) 431
  - injury at birth 767.0
  - syphilitic 094.89
- capillaries 448.9
- cardiac (*see also* Infarct, myocardium) 410.9 ☑
- cartilage (articular) (current) (*see also* Sprain, by site)
  - knee — *see* Tear, meniscus
  - semilunar — *see* Tear, meniscus
- cecum (with peritonitis) 540.0
  - with peritoneal abscess 540.1
  - traumatic 863.89
    - with open wound into cavity 863.99
- cerebral aneurysm (congenital) (*see also* Hemorrhage, subarachnoid) 430
  - late effect — *see* Late effect(s) (of) cerebrovascular disease
- cervix (uteri)
  - with
    - abortion — *see* Abortion, by type, with damage to pelvic organs
    - ectopic pregnancy (*see also* categories 633.0–633.9) 639.2
    - molar pregnancy (*see also* categories 630–632) 639.2
  - following
    - abortion 639.2
    - ectopic or molar pregnancy 639.2
  - obstetrical trauma 665.3 ☑
  - traumatic — *see* Injury, internal, cervix
- chordae tendineae 429.5
- choroid (direct) (indirect) (traumatic) 363.63
- circle of Willis (*see also* Hemorrhage, subarachnoid) 430
  - late effect — *see* Late effect(s) (of) cerebrovascular disease
- colon 569.89

Rupture, ruptured — *continued*

- colon — *continued*
  - traumatic — *see* Injury, internal, colon
- cornea (traumatic) (*see also* Rupture, eye)
  - due to ulcer 370.00
- coronary (artery) (thrombotic) (*see also* Infarct, myocardium) 410.9 ☑
- corpus luteum (infected) (ovary) 620.1
- cyst — *see* Cyst
- cystic duct (*see also* Disease, gallbladder) 575.4
- Descemet's membrane 371.33
  - traumatic — *see* Rupture, eye
- diaphragm (*see also* Hernia, diaphragm)
  - traumatic — *see* Injury, internal, diaphragm
- diverticulum
  - bladder 596.3
  - intestine (large) (*see also* Diverticula) 562.10
    - small 562.00
- duodenal stump 537.89
- duodenum (ulcer) — *see* Ulcer, duodenum, with perforation
- ear drum (*see also* Perforation, tympanum) 384.20
  - with otitis media — *see* Otitis media
  - traumatic — *see* Wound, open, ear
- esophagus 530.4
  - traumatic 862.22
    - with open wound into cavity 862.32
    - cervical region — *see* Wound, open, esophagus
- eye (without prolapse of intraocular tissue) 871.0
  - with
    - exposure of intraocular tissue 871.1
    - partial loss of intraocular tissue 871.2
    - prolapse of intraocular tissue 871.1
  - due to burn 940.5
- fallopian tube 620.8
  - due to pregnancy — *see* Pregnancy, tubal
  - traumatic — *see* Injury, internal, fallopian tube
- fontanel 767.3
- free wall (ventricle) (*see also* Infarct, myocardium) 410.9 ☑
- gallbladder or duct (*see also* Disease, gallbladder) 575.4
  - traumatic — *see* Injury, internal, gallbladder
- gastric (*see also* Rupture, stomach) 537.89
  - vessel 459.0
- globe (eye) (traumatic) — *see* Rupture, eye
- graafian follicle (hematoma) 620.0
- heart (auricle) (ventricle) (*see also* Infarct, myocardium) 410.9 ☑
  - infectional 422.90
  - traumatic — *see* Rupture, myocardium, traumatic
- hymen 623.8
- internal
  - organ, traumatic (*see also* Injury, internal, by site)
    - heart — *see* Rupture, myocardium, traumatic
    - kidney — *see* Rupture, kidney
    - liver — *see* Rupture, liver
    - spleen — *see* Rupture, spleen, traumatic
  - semilunar cartilage — *see* Tear, meniscus
- intervertebral disc — *see* Displacement, intervertebral disc

Rupture, ruptured — *continued*

- intervertebral disc — *see* Displacement, intervertebral disc — *continued*
  - traumatic (current) — *see* Dislocation, vertebra
- intestine 569.89
  - traumatic — *see* Injury, internal, intestine
- intracranial, birth injury 767.0
- iris 364.76
  - traumatic — *see* Rupture, eye
- joint capsule — *see* Sprain, by site
- kidney (traumatic) 866.03
  - with open wound into cavity 866.13
  - due to birth injury 767.8
  - nontraumatic 593.89
- lacrimal apparatus (traumatic) 870.2
- lens (traumatic) 366.20
- ligament (*see also* Sprain, by site)
  - with open wound — *see* Wound, open, by site
  - old (*see also* Disorder, cartilage, articular) 718.0 ☑
- liver (traumatic) 864.04
  - with open wound into cavity 864.14
  - due to birth injury 767.8
  - nontraumatic 573.8
- lymphatic (node) (vessel) 457.8
- marginal sinus (placental) (with hemorrhage) 641.2 ☑
  - affecting fetus or newborn 762.1
- meaning hernia — *see* Hernia
- membrana tympani (*see also* Perforation, tympanum) 384.20
  - with otitis media — *see* Otitis media
  - traumatic — *see* Wound, open, ear
- membranes (spontaneous)
  - artificial
    - delayed delivery following 658.3 ☑
      - affecting fetus or newborn 761.1
    - fetus or newborn 761.1
  - delayed delivery following 658.2 ☑
    - affecting fetus or newborn 761.1
  - premature (less than 24 hours prior to onset of labor) 658.1 ☑
    - affecting fetus or newborn 761.1
    - delayed delivery following 658.2 ☑
      - affecting fetus or newborn 761.1
- meningeal artery (*see also* Hemorrhage, subarachnoid) 430
  - late effect — *see* Late effect(s) (of) cerebrovascular disease
- meniscus (knee) (*see also* Tear, meniscus)
  - old (*see also* Derangement, meniscus) 717.5
    - site other than knee — *see* Disorder, cartilage, articular
  - site other than knee — *see* Sprain, by site
- mesentery 568.89
  - traumatic — *see* Injury, internal, mesentery
- mitral — *see* Insufficiency, mitral
- muscle (traumatic) NEC (*see also* Sprain, by site)
  - with open wound — *see* Wound, open, by site
  - nontraumatic 728.83
- musculotendinous cuff (nontraumatic) (shoulder) 840.4
- mycotic aneurysm, causing cerebral hemorrhage (*see also* Hemorrhage, subarachnoid) 430
  - late effect — *see* Late effect(s) (of) cerebrovascular disease
- myocardium, myocardial (*see also* Infarct, myocardium) 410.9 ☑

- **Sclerosis, sclerotic** — *continued*
  - annularis fibrosi
    - aortic 424.1
    - mitral 424.0
  - aorta, aortic 440.0
    - valve (*see also* Endocarditis, aortic) 424.1
  - artery, arterial, arteriolar, arteriovascular — *see* Arteriosclerosis
  - ascending multiple 340
  - Baló's (concentric) 341.1
  - basilar — *see* Sclerosis, brain
  - bone (localized) NEC 733.99
  - brain (general) (lobular) 341.9
    - Alzheimer's — *see* Alzheimer's, dementia
    - artery, arterial 437.0
    - atrophic lobar 331.0
      - with dementia
        - with behavioral disturbance 331.0 *[294.11]*
        - without behavioral disturbance 331.0 *[294.10]*
    - diffuse 341.1
      - familial (chronic) (infantile) 330.0
      - infantile (chronic) (familial) 330.0
      - Pelizaeus-Merzbacher type 330.0
    - disseminated 340
    - hereditary 334.2
    - infantile (degenerative) (diffuse) 330.0
    - insular 340
    - Krabbe's 330.0
    - miliary 340
    - multiple 340
    - Pelizaeus-Merzbacher 330.0
    - progressive familial 330.0
    - senile 437.0
    - tuberous 759.5
  - bulbar, progressive 340
  - bundle of His 426.50
    - left 426.3
    - right 426.4
  - cardiac — *see* Arteriosclerosis, coronary
  - cardiorenal (*see also* Hypertension, cardiorenal) 404.90
  - cardiovascular (*see also* Disease, cardiovascular) 429.2
    - renal (*see also* Hypertension, cardiorenal) 404.90
  - centrolobar, familial 330.0
  - cerebellar — *see* Sclerosis, brain
  - cerebral — *see* Sclerosis, brain
  - cerebrospinal 340
    - disseminated 340
    - multiple 340
  - cerebrovascular 437.0
  - choroid 363.40
    - diffuse 363.56
  - combined (spinal cord) (*see also* Degeneration, combined)
    - multiple 340
  - concentric, Baló's 341.1
  - cornea 370.54
  - coronary (artery) — *see* Arteriosclerosis, coronary
  - corpus cavernosum
    - female 624.8
    - male 607.89
  - Dewitzky's
    - aortic 424.1
    - mitral 424.0
  - diffuse NEC 341.1
  - disease, heart — *see* Arteriosclerosis, coronary
  - disseminated 340
  - dorsal 340
  - dorsolateral (spinal cord) — *see* Degeneration, combined
  - endometrium 621.8
  - extrapyramidal 333.90
  - eye, nuclear (senile) 366.16

- **Sclerosis, sclerotic** — *continued*
  - Friedreich's (spinal cord) 334.0
  - funicular (spermatic cord) 608.89
  - gastritis 535.4 ☑
  - general (vascular) — *see* Arteriosclerosis
  - gland (lymphatic) 457.8
  - hepatic 571.9
  - hereditary
    - cerebellar 334.2
    - spinal 334.0
  - idiopathic cortical (Garré's) (*see also* Osteomyelitis) 730.1 ☑
  - ilium, piriform 733.5
  - insular 340
    - pancreas 251.8
  - Islands of Langerhans 251.8
  - kidney — *see* Sclerosis, renal
  - larynx 478.79
  - lateral 335.24
    - amyotrophic 335.20
    - descending 335.24
    - primary 335.24
    - spinal 335.24
  - liver 571.9
  - lobar, atrophic (of brain) 331.0
    - with dementia
      - with behavioral disturbance 331.0 *[294.11]*
      - without behavioral disturbance 331.0 *[294.10]*
  - lung (*see also* Fibrosis, lung) 515
  - mastoid 383.1
  - mitral — *see* Endocarditis, mitral
  - Mönckeberg's (medial) (*see also* Arteriosclerosis, extremities) 440.20
  - multiple (brain stem) (cerebral) (generalized) (spinal cord) 340
  - myocardium, myocardial — *see* Arteriosclerosis, coronary
  - nuclear (senile), eye 366.16
  - ovary 620.8
  - pancreas 577.8
  - penis 607.89
  - peripheral arteries (*see also* Arteriosclerosis, extremities) 440.20
  - plaques 340
  - pluriglandular 258.8
  - polyglandular 258.8
  - posterior (spinal cord) (syphilitic) 094.0
  - posterolateral (spinal cord) — *see* Degeneration, combined
  - prepuce 607.89
  - primary lateral 335.24
  - progressive systemic 710.1
  - pulmonary (*see also* Fibrosis, lung) 515
    - artery 416.0
    - valve (heart) (*see also* Endocarditis, pulmonary) 424.3
  - renal 587
    - with
      - cystine storage disease 270.0
      - hypertension (*see also* Hypertension, kidney) 403.90
      - hypertensive heart disease (conditions classifiable to 402) (*see also* Hypertension, cardiorenal) 404.90
    - arteriolar (hyaline) (*see also* Hypertension, kidney) 403.90
    - hyperplastic (*see also* Hypertension, kidney) 403.90
  - retina (senile) (vascular) 362.17
  - rheumatic
    - aortic valve 395.9
    - mitral valve 394.9
  - Schilder's 341.1
  - senile — *see* Arteriosclerosis
  - spinal (cord) (general) (progressive) (transverse) 336.8
    - ascending 357.0
    - combined (*see also* Degeneration, combined)
      - multiple 340

- **Sclerosis, sclerotic** — *continued*
  - spinal — *continued*
    - combined (*see also* Degeneration, combined) — *continued*
      - syphilitic 094.89
    - disseminated 340
    - dorsolateral — *see* Degeneration, combined
    - hereditary (Friedreich's) (mixed form) 334.0
    - lateral (amyotrophic) 335.24
    - multiple 340
    - posterior (syphilitic) 094.0
  - stomach 537.89
  - subendocardial, congenital 425.3
  - systemic (progressive) 710.1
    - with lung involvement 710.1 *[517.2]*
  - tricuspid (heart) (valve) — *see* Endocarditis, tricuspid
  - tuberous (brain) 759.5
  - tympanic membrane (*see also* Tympanosclerosis) 385.00
  - valve, valvular (heart) — *see* Endocarditis
  - vascular — *see* Arteriosclerosis
  - vein 459.89
- **Sclerotenonitis** 379.07
- **Sclerotitis** — *see also* Scleritis 379.00
  - syphilitic 095.0
  - tuberculous (*see also* Tuberculosis) 017.3 ☑ *[379.09]*
- **Scoliosis** (acquired) (postural) 737.30
  - congenital 754.2
  - due to or associated with
    - Charcôt-Marie-Tooth disease 356.1 *[737.43]*
    - mucopolysaccharidosis 277.5 *[737.43]*
    - neurofibromatosis 237.71 *[737.43]*
    - osteitis
      - deformans 731.0 *[737.43]*
      - fibrosa cystica 252.01 *[737.43]*
    - osteoporosis (*see also* Osteoporosis) 733.00 *[737.43]*
    - poliomyelitis 138 *[737.43]*
    - radiation 737.33
    - tuberculosis (*see also* Tuberculosis) 015.0 ☑ *[737.43]*
  - idiopathic 737.30
    - infantile
      - progressive 737.32
      - resolving 737.31
  - paralytic 737.39
  - rachitic 268.1
  - sciatic 724.3
  - specified NEC 737.39
  - thoracogenic 737.34
  - tuberculous (*see also* Tuberculosis) 015.0 ☑ *[737.43]*
- **Scoliotic pelvis** 738.6
  - with disproportion (fetopelvic) 653.0 ☑
    - affecting fetus or newborn 763.1
    - causing obstructed labor 660.1 ☑
      - affecting fetus or newborn 763.1
- **Scorbutus, scorbutic** 267
  - anemia 281.8
- **Scotoma** (ring) 368.44
  - arcuate 368.43
  - Bjerrum 368.43
  - blind spot area 368.42
  - central 368.41
  - centrocecal 368.41
  - paracecal 368.42
  - paracentral 368.41
  - scintillating 368.12
  - Seidel 368.43
- **Scratch** — *see* Injury, superficial, by site
- **Screening** (for) V82.9
  - alcoholism V79.1
  - anemia, deficiency NEC V78.1
    - iron V78.0
  - anomaly, congenital V82.89
  - antenatal, ▶of mother◀ V28.9
    - alphafetoprotein levels, raised V28.1

- **Screening** — *continued*
  - antenatal, ▶of mother◀ — *continued*
    - based on amniocentesis V28.2
      - chromosomal anomalies V28.0
      - raised alphafetoprotein levels V28.1
    - fetal growth retardation using ultrasonics V28.4
      - ultrasonics V28.4
    - isoimmunization V28.5
    - malformations using ultrasonics V28.3
    - raised alphafetoprotein levels V28.1
    - specified condition NEC V28.8
    - Streptococcus B V28.6
  - arterial hypertension V81.1
  - arthropod-borne viral disease NEC V73.5
  - asymptomatic bacteriuria V81.5
  - bacterial
    - conjunctivitis V74.4
    - disease V74.9
      - specified condition NEC V74.8
  - bacteriuria, asymptomatic V81.5
  - blood disorder NEC V78.9
    - specified type NEC V78.8
  - bronchitis, chronic V81.3
  - brucellosis V74.8
  - cancer — *see* Screening, malignant neoplasm
  - cardiovascular disease NEC V81.2
  - cataract V80.2
  - Chagas' disease V75.3
  - chemical poisoning V82.5
  - cholera V74.0
  - cholesterol level V77.91
  - chromosomal
    - anomalies
      - by amniocentesis, antenatal V28.0
      - maternal postnatal V82.4
    - athletes V70.3
  - condition
    - cardiovascular NEC V81.2
    - eye NEC V80.2
    - genitourinary NEC V81.6
    - neurological V80.0
    - respiratory NEC V81.4
    - skin V82.0
    - specified NEC V82.89
  - congenital
    - anomaly V82.89
      - eye V80.2
    - dislocation of hip V82.3
    - eye condition or disease V80.2
  - conjunctivitis, bacterial V74.4
  - contamination NEC (*see also* Poisoning) V82.5
  - coronary artery disease V81.0
  - cystic fibrosis V77.6
  - deficiency anemia NEC V78.1
    - iron V78.0
  - dengue fever V73.5
  - depression V79.0
  - developmental handicap V79.9
    - in early childhood V79.3
    - specified type NEC V79.8
  - diabetes mellitus V77.1
  - diphtheria V74.3
  - disease or disorder V82.9
    - bacterial V74.9
      - specified NEC V74.8
    - blood V78.9
      - specified type NEC V78.8
    - blood-forming organ V78.9
      - specified type NEC V78.8
    - cardiovascular NEC V81.2
      - hypertensive V81.1
      - ischemic V81.0
    - Chagas' V75.3
    - chlamydial V73.98
      - specified NEC V73.88
    - ear NEC V80.3
    - endocrine NEC V77.99
    - eye NEC V80.2

Seven-day fever — *continued*
- of — *continued*
  - Queensland 100.89

Sever's disease or osteochondrosis (calcaneum) 732.5

Sex chromosome mosaics 758.81

Sextuplet
- affected by maternal complications of pregnancy 761.5
- healthy liveborn — *see* Newborn, multiple
- pregnancy (complicating delivery) NEC 651.8 ☑
  - with fetal loss and retention of one or more fetus(es) 651.6 ☑
  - following (elective) fetal reduction 651.7 ☑

Sexual
- anesthesia 302.72
- deviation (*see also* Deviation, sexual) 302.9
- disorder (*see also* Deviation, sexual) 302.9
- frigidity (female) 302.72
- function, disorder of (psychogenic) 302.70
  - specified type NEC 302.79
- immaturity (female) (male) 259.0
- impotence 607.84
  - organic origin NEC 607.84
  - psychogenic 302.72
- precocity (constitutional) (cryptogenic) (female) (idiopathic) (male) NEC 259.1
  - with adrenal hyperplasia 255.2
- sadism 302.84

Sexuality, pathological — *see also* Deviation, sexual 302.9

Sézary's disease, reticulosis, or syndrome (M9701/3) 202.2 ☑

Shadow, lung 793.1

Shaken infant syndrome 995.55

Shaking
- head (tremor) 781.0
- palsy or paralysis (*see also* Parkinsonism) 332.0

Shallowness, acetabulum 736.39

Shaver's disease or syndrome (bauxite pneumoconiosis) 503

Shearing
- artificial skin graft 996.55
- decellularized allodermis graft 996.55

Sheath (tendon) — *see* condition

Shedding
- nail 703.8
- teeth, premature, primary (deciduous) 520.6

Sheehan's disease or syndrome (postpartum pituitary necrosis) 253.2

Shelf, rectal 569.49

Shell
- shock (current) (*see also* Reaction, stress, acute) 308.9
  - lasting state 300.16
- teeth 520.5

Shield kidney 753.3

Shifting
- pacemaker 427.89
- sleep-work schedule (affecting sleep) 327.36

Shift, mediastinal 793.2

Shiga's
- bacillus 004.0
- dysentery 004.0

Shigella (dysentery) — *see also* Dysentery, bacillary 004.9
- carrier (suspected) of V02.3

Shigellosis — *see also* Dysentery, bacillary 004.9

Shingles — *see also* Herpes, zoster 053.9
- eye NEC 053.29

Shin splints 844.9

Shipyard eye or disease 077.1

Shirodkar suture, in pregnancy 654.5 ☑

Shock 785.50

Shock — *continued*
- with
  - abortion — *see* Abortion, by type, with shock
  - ectopic pregnancy (*see also* categories 633.0–633.9) 639.5
  - molar pregnancy (*see also* categories 630–632) 639.5
- allergic — *see* Shock, anaphylactic
- anaclitic 309.21
- anaphylactic 995.0
  - chemical — *see* Table of Drugs and Chemicals
  - correct medicinal substance properly administered 995.0
  - drug or medicinal substance
    - correct substance properly administered 995.0
    - overdose or wrong substance given or taken 977.9
      - specified drug — *see* Table of Drugs and Chemicals
  - following sting(s) 989.5
  - food — *see* Anaphylactic shock, due to, food
  - immunization 999.4
  - serum 999.4
- anaphylactoid — *see* Shock, anaphylactic
- anesthetic
  - correct substance properly administered 995.4
  - overdose or wrong substance given 968.4
    - specified anesthetic — *see* Table of Drugs and Chemicals
- birth, fetus or newborn NEC 779.89
- cardiogenic 785.51
- chemical substance — *see* Table of Drugs and Chemicals
- circulatory 785.59
- complicating
  - abortion — *see* Abortion, by type, with shock
  - ectopic pregnancy (*see also* categories 633.0–633.9) 639.5
  - labor and delivery 669.1 ☑
  - molar pregnancy (*see also* categories 630–632) 639.5
- culture 309.29
- due to
  - drug 995.0
    - correct substance properly administered 995.0
    - overdose or wrong substance given or taken 977.9
      - specified drug — *see* Table of Drugs and Chemicals
  - food — *see* Anaphylactic shock, due to, food
- during labor and delivery 669.1 ☑
- electric 994.8
- endotoxic 785.52
  - due to surgical procedure 998.0
- following
  - abortion 639.5
  - ectopic or molar pregnancy 639.5
  - injury (immediate) (delayed) 958.4
  - labor and delivery 669.1 ☑
- gram-negative 785.52
- hematogenic 785.59
- hemorrhagic
  - due to
    - disease 785.59
    - surgery (intraoperative) (postoperative) 998.0
    - trauma 958.4
- hypovolemic NEC 785.59
  - surgical 998.0
  - traumatic 958.4
- insulin 251.0
  - therapeutic misadventure 962.3
- kidney 584.5

Shock — *continued*
- kidney — *continued*
  - traumatic (following crushing) 958.5
- lightning 994.0
- lung 518.5
- nervous (*see also* Reaction, stress, acute) 308.9
- obstetric 669.1 ☑
  - with
    - abortion — *see* Abortion, by type, with shock
    - ectopic pregnancy (*see also* categories 633.0–633.9) 639.5
    - molar pregnancy (*see also* categories 630–632) 639.5
  - following
    - abortion 639.5
    - ectopic or molar pregnancy 639.5
- paralysis, paralytic (*see also* Disease, cerebrovascular, acute) 436
  - late effect — *see* Late effect(s) (of) cerebrovascular disease
- pleural (surgical) 998.0
  - due to trauma 958.4
- postoperative 998.0
  - with
    - abortion — *see* Abortion, by type, with shock
    - ectopic pregnancy (*see also* categories 633.0–633.9) 639.5
    - molar pregnancy (*see also* categories 630–632) 639.5
  - following
    - abortion 639.5
    - ectopic or molar pregnancy 639.5
- psychic (*see also* Reaction, stress, acute) 308.9
  - past history (of) V15.49
- psychogenic (*see also* Reaction, stress, acute) 308.9
- septic 785.52
  - with
    - abortion — *see* Abortion, by type, with shock
    - ectopic pregnancy (*see also* categories 633.0–633.9) 639.5
    - molar pregnancy (*see also* categories 630–632) 639.5
  - due to
    - surgical procedure 998.0
    - transfusion NEC 999.8
      - bone marrow 996.85
  - following
    - abortion 639.5
    - ectopic or molar pregnancy 639.5
    - surgical procedure 998.0
    - transfusion NEC 999.8
      - bone marrow 996.85
- spinal (*see also* Injury, spinal, by site)
  - with spinal bone injury — *see* Fracture, vertebra, by site, with spinal cord injury
- surgical 998.0
- therapeutic misadventure NEC (*see also* Complications) 998.89
- thyroxin 962.7
- toxic 040.82
- transfusion — *see* Complications, transfusion
- traumatic (immediate) (delayed) 958.4

Shoemakers' chest 738.3

Short, shortening, shortness
- Achilles tendon (acquired) 727.81
- arm 736.89
  - congenital 755.20
- back 737.9
- bowel syndrome 579.3
- breath 786.05

Short, shortening, shortness — *continued*
- chain acyl CoA dehydrogenase deficiency (SCAD) 277.85
- common bile duct, congenital 751.69
- cord (umbilical) 663.4 ☑
  - affecting fetus or newborn 762.6
- cystic duct, congenital 751.69
- esophagus (congenital) 750.4
- femur (acquired) 736.81
  - congenital 755.34
- frenulum linguae 750.0
- frenum, lingual 750.0
- hamstrings 727.81
- hip (acquired) 736.39
  - congenital 755.63
- leg (acquired) 736.81
  - congenital 755.30
- metatarsus (congenital) 754.79
  - acquired 736.79
- organ or site, congenital NEC — *see* Distortion
- palate (congenital) 750.26
- P-R interval syndrome 426.81
- radius (acquired) 736.09
  - congenital 755.26
- round ligament 629.89 ▲
- sleeper 307.49
- stature, constitutional (hereditary) 783.43
- tendon 727.81
  - Achilles (acquired) 727.81
    - congenital 754.79
  - congenital 756.89
- thigh (acquired) 736.81
  - congenital 755.34
- tibialis anticus 727.81
- umbilical cord 663.4 ☑
  - affecting fetus or newborn 762.6
- urethra 599.84
- uvula (congenital) 750.26
- vagina 623.8

Shortsightedness 367.1

Shoshin (acute fulminating beriberi) 265.0

Shoulder — *see* condition

Shovel-shaped incisors 520.2

Shower, thromboembolic — *see* Embolism

Shunt (status)
- aortocoronary bypass V45.81
- arterial-venous (dialysis) V45.1
- arteriovenous, pulmonary (acquired) 417.0
  - congenital 747.3
  - traumatic (complication) 901.40
- cerebral ventricle (communicating) in situ V45.2
- coronary artery bypass V45.81
- surgical, prosthetic, with complications — *see* Complications, shunt
- vascular NEC V45.89

Shutdown
- renal 586
  - with
    - abortion — *see* Abortion, by type, with renal failure
    - ectopic pregnancy (*see also* categories 633.0–633.9) 639.3
    - molar pregnancy (*see also* categories 630–632) 639.3
  - complicating
    - abortion 639.3
    - ectopic or molar pregnancy 639.3
  - following labor and delivery 669.3 ☑

Shwachman's syndrome 288.02 ▲

Shy-Drager syndrome (orthostatic hypotension with multisystem degeneration) 333.0

Sialadenitis (any gland) (chronic) (suppurative) 527.2
- epidemic — *see* Mumps

- **Status** — *continued*
  - thymicus 254.8
  - thymolymphaticus 254.8
  - tooth extraction 525.10
  - tracheostomy V44.0
  - transplant
    - blood vessel V42.89
    - bone V42.4
      - marrow V42.81
    - cornea V42.5
    - heart V42.1
      - valve V42.2
    - intestine V42.84
    - kidney V42.0
    - liver V42.7
    - lung V42.6
    - organ V42.9
      - specified site NEC V42.89
    - pancreas V42.83
    - peripheral stem cells V42.82
    - skin V42.3
    - stem cells, peripheral V42.82
    - tissue V42.9
      - specified type NEC V42.89
    - vessel, blood V42.89
  - tubal ligation V26.51
  - ureterostomy V44.6
  - urethrostomy V44.6
  - vagina, artificial V44.7
  - vascular shunt NEC V45.89
    - aortocoronary (bypass) V45.81
  - vasectomy V26.52
  - ventilator [respirator] V46.11
    - encounter
      - during
        - mechanical failure V46.14
        - power failure V46.12
      - for weaning V46.13
  - wrist prosthesis V43.63
- **Stave fracture** — *see* Fracture, metacarpus, metacarpal bone(s)
- **Steal**
  - subclavian artery 435.2
  - vertebral artery 435.1
- **Stealing, solitary, child problem** — *see also* Disturbance, conduct 312.1 ☑
- **Steam burn** — *see* Burn, by site
- **Steatocystoma multiplex** 706.2
- **Steatoma** (infected) 706.2
  - eyelid (cystic) 374.84
    - infected 373.13
- **Steatorrhea** (chronic) 579.8
  - with lacteal obstruction 579.2
  - idiopathic 579.0
    - adult 579.0
    - infantile 579.0
  - pancreatic 579.4
  - primary 579.0
  - secondary 579.8
  - specified cause NEC 579.8
  - tropical 579.1
- **Steatosis** 272.8
  - heart (*see also* Degeneration, myocardial) 429.1
  - kidney 593.89
  - liver 571.8
- **Steele-Richardson (-Olszewski) Syndrome** 333.0
- **Steinbrocker's syndrome** — *see also* Neuropathy, peripheral, autonomic 337.9
- **Steinert's disease** 359.2
- **Stein-Leventhal syndrome** (polycystic ovary) 256.4
- **Stein's syndrome** (polycystic ovary) 256.4
- **STEMI** (ST elevation myocardial infarction — *see also* — Infarct, myocardium, ST elevation 410.9 ☑ ●
- **Stenocardia** — *see also* Angina 413.9
- **Stenocephaly** 756.0
- **Stenosis** (cicatricial) — *see also* Stricture
  - ampulla of Vater 576.2
    - with calculus, cholelithiasis, or stones — *see* Choledocholithiasis
- **Stenosis** — *see also* Stricture — *continued*
  - anus, anal (canal) (sphincter) 569.2
    - congenital 751.2
  - aorta (ascending) 747.22
    - arch 747.10
    - arteriosclerotic 440.0
    - calcified 440.0
  - aortic (valve) 424.1
    - with
      - mitral (valve)
        - insufficiency or incompetence 396.2
        - stenosis or obstruction 396.0
    - atypical 396.0
    - congenital 746.3
    - rheumatic 395.0
      - with
        - insufficiency, incompetency or regurgitation 395.2
          - with mitral (valve) disease 396.8
        - mitral (valve)
          - disease (stenosis) 396.0
          - insufficiency or incompetence 396.2
          - stenosis or obstruction 396.0
    - specified cause, except rheumatic 424.1
    - syphilitic 093.22
  - aqueduct of Sylvius (congenital) 742.3
    - with spina bifida (*see also* Spina bifida) 741.0 ☑
    - acquired 331.4
  - artery NEC 447.1
    - basilar — *see* Narrowing, artery, basilar
    - carotid (common) (internal) — *see* Narrowing, artery, carotid
    - celiac 447.4
    - cerebral 437.0
      - due to
        - embolism (*see also* Embolism, brain) 434.1 ☑
        - thrombus (*see also* Thrombosis, brain) 434.0 ☑
    - precerebral — *see* Narrowing, artery, precerebral
    - pulmonary (congenital) 747.3
      - acquired 417.8
    - renal 440.1
    - vertebral — *see* Narrowing, artery, vertebral
  - bile duct or biliary passage (*see also* Obstruction, biliary) 576.2
    - congenital 751.61
  - bladder neck (acquired) 596.0
    - congenital 753.6
  - brain 348.8
  - bronchus 519.19 ▲
    - syphilitic 095.8
  - cardia (stomach) 537.89
    - congenital 750.7
  - cardiovascular (*see also* Disease, cardiovascular) 429.2
  - carotid artery — *see* Narrowing, artery, carotid
  - cervix, cervical (canal) 622.4
    - congenital 752.49
    - in pregnancy or childbirth 654.6 ☑
      - affecting fetus or newborn 763.89
      - causing obstructed labor 660.2 ☑
        - affecting fetus or newborn 763.1
  - colon (*see also* Obstruction, intestine) 560.9
    - congenital 751.2
  - colostomy 569.62
  - common bile duct (*see also* Obstruction, biliary) 576.2
    - congenital 751.61
  - coronary (artery) — *see* Arteriosclerosis, coronary
- **Stenosis** — *see also* Stricture — *continued*
  - cystic duct (*see also* Obstruction, gallbladder) 575.2
    - congenital 751.61
  - due to (presence of) any device, implant, or graft classifiable to 996.0–996.5 — *see* Complications, due to (presence of) any device, implant, or graft classified to 996.0–996.5 NEC
  - duodenum 537.3
    - congenital 751.1
  - ejaculatory duct NEC 608.89
  - endocervical os — *see* Stenosis, cervix
  - enterostomy 569.62
  - esophagostomy 530.87
  - esophagus 530.3
    - congenital 750.3
    - syphilitic 095.8
      - congenital 090.5
  - external ear canal 380.50
    - secondary to
      - inflammation 380.53
      - surgery 380.52
      - trauma 380.51
  - gallbladder (*see also* Obstruction, gallbladder) 575.2
  - glottis 478.74
  - heart valve (acquired) (*see also* Endocarditis)
    - congenital NEC 746.89
      - aortic 746.3
      - mitral 746.5
      - pulmonary 746.02
      - tricuspid 746.1
  - hepatic duct (*see also* Obstruction, biliary) 576.2
  - hymen 623.3
  - hypertrophic subaortic (idiopathic) 425.1
  - infundibulum cardiac 746.83
  - intestine (*see also* Obstruction, intestine) 560.9
    - congenital (small) 751.1
      - large 751.2
  - lacrimal
    - canaliculi 375.53
    - duct 375.56
      - congenital 743.65
    - punctum 375.52
      - congenital 743.65
    - sac 375.54
      - congenital 743.65
  - lacrimonasal duct 375.56
    - congenital 743.65
    - neonatal 375.55
  - larynx 478.74
    - congenital 748.3
    - syphilitic 095.8
      - congenital 090.5
  - mitral (valve) (chronic) (inactive) 394.0
    - with
      - aortic (valve)
        - disease (insufficiency) 396.1
        - insufficiency or incompetence 396.1
        - stenosis or obstruction 396.0
      - incompetency, insufficiency or regurgitation 394.2
        - with aortic valve disease 396.8
    - active or acute 391.1
      - with chorea (acute) (rheumatic) (Sydenham's) 392.0
    - congenital 746.5
    - specified cause, except rheumatic 424.0
    - syphilitic 093.21
  - myocardium, myocardial (*see also* Degeneration, myocardial) 429.1
    - hypertrophic subaortic (idiopathic) 425.1
  - nares (anterior) (posterior) 478.19 ▲
    - congenital 748.0
- **Stenosis** — *see also* Stricture — *continued*
  - nasal duct 375.56
    - congenital 743.65
  - nasolacrimal duct 375.56
    - congenital 743.65
    - neonatal 375.55
  - organ or site, congenital NEC — *see* Atresia
  - papilla of Vater 576.2
    - with calculus, cholelithiasis, or stones — *see* Choledocholithiasis
  - pulmonary (artery) (congenital) 747.3
    - with ventricular septal defect, dextraposition of aorta and hypertrophy of right ventricle 745.2
    - acquired 417.8
    - infundibular 746.83
    - in tetralogy of Fallot 745.2
    - subvalvular 746.83
    - valve (*see also* Endocarditis, pulmonary) 424.3
      - congenital 746.02
    - vein 747.49
      - acquired 417.8
    - vessel NEC 417.8
  - pulmonic (congenital) 746.02
    - infundibular 746.83
    - subvalvular 746.83
  - pylorus (hypertrophic) 537.0
    - adult 537.0
    - congenital 750.5
    - infantile 750.5
  - rectum (sphincter) (*see also* Stricture, rectum) 569.2
  - renal artery 440.1
  - salivary duct (any) 527.8
  - sphincter of Oddi (*see also* Obstruction, biliary) 576.2
  - spinal 724.00
    - cervical 723.0
    - lumbar, lumbosacral 724.02
    - nerve (root) NEC 724.9
    - specified region NEC 724.09
    - thoracic, thoracolumbar 724.01
  - stomach, hourglass 537.6
  - subaortic 746.81
    - hypertrophic (idiopathic) 425.1
  - supra (valvular)-aortic 747.22
  - trachea 519.19 ▲
    - congenital 748.3
    - syphilitic 095.8
    - tuberculous (*see also* Tuberculosis) 012.8 ☑
  - tracheostomy 519.02
  - tricuspid (valve) (*see also* Endocarditis, tricuspid) 397.0
    - congenital 746.1
    - nonrheumatic 424.2
  - tubal 628.2
  - ureter (*see also* Stricture, ureter) 593.3
    - congenital 753.29
  - urethra (*see also* Stricture, urethra) 598.9
  - vagina 623.2
    - congenital 752.49
    - in pregnancy or childbirth 654.7 ☑
      - affecting fetus or newborn 763.89
      - causing obstructed labor 660.2 ☑
        - affecting fetus or newborn 763.1
  - valve (cardiac) (heart) (*see also* Endocarditis) 424.90
    - congenital NEC 746.89
      - aortic 746.3
      - mitral 746.5
      - pulmonary 746.02
      - tricuspid 746.1
      - urethra 753.6
  - valvular (*see also* Endocarditis) 424.90

☑ Additional Digit Required — Refer to the Tabular List for Digit Selection

Subterms under main terms may continue to next column or page

▶◀ Revised Text ● New Line ▲ Revised Code

Stenosis — *see also* Stricture — *continued*
- valvular (*see also* Endocarditis) — *continued*
  - congenital NEC 746.89
    - urethra 753.6
- vascular graft or shunt 996.1
  - atherosclerosis — *see* Arteriosclerosis, extremities
  - embolism 996.74
  - occlusion NEC 996.74
  - thrombus 996.74
- vena cava (inferior) (superior) 459.2
  - congenital 747.49
- ventricular shunt 996.2
- vulva 624.8

Stercolith — *see also* Fecalith 560.39
- appendix 543.9

Stercoraceous, stercoral ulcer 569.82
- anus or rectum 569.41

Stereopsis, defective
- with fusion 368.33
- without fusion 368.32

Stereotypes NEC 307.3

Sterility
- female — *see* Infertility, female
- male (*see also* Infertility, male) 606.9

Sterilization, admission for V25.2
- status
  - tubal ligation V26.51
  - vasectomy V26.52

Sternalgia — *see also* Angina 413.9

Sternopagus 759.4

Sternum bifidum 756.3

Sternutation 784.99 ▲

Steroid
- effects (adverse) (iatrogenic)
  - cushingoid
    - correct substance properly administered 255.0
    - overdose or wrong substance given or taken 962.0
  - diabetes
    - correct substance properly administered 251.8
    - overdose or wrong substance given or taken 962.0
  - due to
    - correct substance properly administered 255.8
    - overdose or wrong substance given or taken 962.0
  - fever
    - correct substance properly administered 780.6
    - overdose or wrong substance given or taken 962.0
  - withdrawal
    - correct substance properly administered 255.4
    - overdose or wrong substance given or taken 962.0
- responder 365.03

Stevens-Johnson disease or syndrome (erythema multiforme exudativum) 695.1

Stewart-Morel syndrome (hyperostosis frontalis interna) 733.3

Sticker's disease (erythema infectiosum) 057.0

Stickler syndrome 759.89

Sticky eye 372.03

Stieda's disease (calcification, knee joint) 726.62

Stiff
- back 724.8
- neck (*see also* Torticollis) 723.5

Stiff-baby 759.89

Stiff-man syndrome 333.91

Stiffness, joint NEC 719.50
- ankle 719.57
- back 724.8
- elbow 719.52
- finger 719.54
- hip 719.55
- knee 719.56

Stiffness, joint — *continued*
- multiple sites 719.59
- sacroiliac 724.6
- shoulder 719.51
- specified site NEC 719.58
- spine 724.9
- surgical fusion V45.4
- wrist 719.53

Stigmata, congenital syphilis 090.5

Stillbirth, stillborn NEC 779.9

Still's disease or syndrome 714.30

Stiller's disease (asthenia) 780.79

Still-Felty syndrome (rheumatoid arthritis with splenomegaly and leukopenia) 714.1

Stilling-Türk-Duane syndrome (ocular retraction syndrome) 378.71

Stimulation, ovary 256.1

Sting (animal) (bee) (fish) (insect) (jellyfish) (Portuguese man-o-war) (wasp) (venomous) 989.5
- anaphylactic shock or reaction 989.5
- plant 692.6

Stippled epiphyses 756.59

Stitch
- abscess 998.59
- burst (in external operation wound) 998.32
  - internal 998.31
- in back 724.5

Stojano's (subcostal) **syndrome** 098.86

Stokes-Adams syndrome (syncope with heart block) 426.9

Stokes' disease (exophthalmic goiter) 242.0 ☑

Stokvis' (-Talma) disease (enterogenous cyanosis) 289.7

Stomach — *see* condition

Stoma malfunction
- colostomy 569.62
- cystostomy 997.5
- enterostomy 569.62
- esophagostomy 530.87
- gastrostomy 536.42
- ileostomy 569.62
- nephrostomy 997.5
- tracheostomy 519.02
- ureterostomy 997.5

Stomatitis 528.00 ▲
- angular 528.5
  - due to dietary or vitamin deficiency 266.0
- aphthous 528.2
- candidal 112.0
- catarrhal 528.00 ▲
- denture 528.9
- diphtheritic (membranous) 032.0
- due to
  - dietary deficiency 266.0
  - thrush 112.0
  - vitamin deficiency 266.0
- epidemic 078.4
- epizootic 078.4
- follicular 528.00 ▲
- gangrenous 528.1
- herpetic 054.2
- herpetiformis 528.2
- malignant 528.00 ▲
- membranous acute 528.00 ▲
- monilial 112.0
- mycotic 112.0
- necrotic 528.1
  - ulcerative 101
- necrotizing ulcerative 101
- parasitic 112.0
- septic 528.00 ▲
- specified NEC 528.09 ●
- spirochetal 101
- suppurative (acute) 528.00 ▲
- ulcerative 528.00 ▲
  - necrotizing 101
- ulceromembranous 101
- vesicular 528.00 ▲
  - with exanthem 074.3
- Vincent's 101

Stomatocytosis 282.8

Stomatomycosis 112.0

Stomatorrhagia 528.9

Stone(s) — *see also* Calculus
- bladder 594.1
  - diverticulum 594.0
- cystine 270.0
- heart syndrome (*see also* Failure, ventricular, left) 428.1
- kidney 592.0
- prostate 602.0
- pulp (dental) 522.2
- renal 592.0
- salivary duct or gland (any) 527.5
- ureter 592.1
- urethra (impacted) 594.2
- urinary (duct) (impacted) (passage) 592.9
  - bladder 594.1
    - diverticulum 594.0
  - lower tract NEC 594.9
  - specified site 594.8
- xanthine 277.2

Stonecutters' lung 502
- tuberculous (*see also* Tuberculosis) 011.4 ☑

Stonemasons'
- asthma, disease, or lung 502
  - tuberculous (*see also* Tuberculosis) 011.4 ☑
- phthisis (*see also* Tuberculosis) 011.4 ☑

Stoppage
- bowel (*see also* Obstruction, intestine) 560.9
- heart (*see also* Arrest, cardiac) 427.5
- intestine (*see also* Obstruction, intestine) 560.9
- urine NEC (*see also* Retention, urine) 788.20

Storm, thyroid (apathetic) — *see also* Thyrotoxicosis 242.9 ☑

Strabismus (alternating) (congenital) (nonparalytic) 378.9
- concomitant (*see also* Heterotropia) 378.30
  - convergent (*see also* Esotropia) 378.00
  - divergent (*see also* Exotropia) 378.10
- convergent (*see also* Esotropia) 378.00
- divergent (*see also* Exotropia) 378.10
- due to adhesions, scars — *see* Strabismus, mechanical
- in neuromuscular disorder NEC 378.73
  - intermittent 378.20
    - vertical 378.31
- latent 378.40
  - convergent (esophoria) 378.41
  - divergent (exophoria) 378.42
  - vertical 378.43
- mechanical 378.60
  - due to
    - Brown's tendon sheath syndrome 378.61
    - specified musculofascial disorder NEC 378.62
- paralytic 378.50
  - third or oculomotor nerve (partial) 378.51
    - total 378.52
  - fourth or trochlear nerve 378.53
  - sixth or abducens nerve 378.54
- specified type NEC 378.73
- vertical (hypertropia) 378.31

Strain — *see also* Sprain, by site
- eye NEC 368.13
- heart — *see* Disease, heart
- meaning gonorrhea — *see* Gonorrhea
- on urination 788.65 ●
- physical NEC V62.89
- postural 729.9
- psychological NEC V62.89

Strands
- conjunctiva 372.62
- vitreous humor 379.25

Strangulation, strangulated 994.7
- appendix 543.9
- asphyxiation or suffocation by 994.7
- bladder neck 596.0
- bowel — *see* Strangulation, intestine
- colon — *see* Strangulation, intestine
- cord (umbilical) — *see* Compression, umbilical cord
- due to birth injury 767.8
- food or foreign body (*see also* Asphyxia, food) 933.1
- hemorrhoids 455.8
  - external 455.5
  - internal 455.2
- hernia (*see also* Hernia, by site, with obstruction)
  - gangrenous — *see* Hernia, by site, with gangrene
- intestine (large) (small) 560.2
  - with hernia (*see also* Hernia, by site, with obstruction)
    - gangrenous — *see* Hernia, by site, with gangrene
  - congenital (small) 751.1
    - large 751.2
- mesentery 560.2
- mucus (*see also* Asphyxia, mucus) 933.1
  - newborn 770.18
- omentum 560.2
- organ or site, congenital NEC — *see* Atresia
- ovary 620.8
  - due to hernia 620.4
- penis 607.89
  - foreign body 939.3
- rupture (*see also* Hernia, by site, with obstruction) 552.9
  - gangrenous (*see also* Hernia, by site, with gangrene) 551.9
- stomach, due to hernia (*see also* Hernia, by site, with obstruction) 552.9
  - with gangrene (*see also* Hernia, by site, with gangrene) 551.9
- umbilical cord — *see* Compression, umbilical cord
- vesicourethral orifice 596.0

Strangury 788.1

Strawberry
- gallbladder (*see also* Disease, gallbladder) 575.6
- mark 757.32
- tongue (red) (white) 529.3

Straw itch 133.8

Streak, ovarian 752.0

Strephosymbolia 315.01
- secondary to organic lesion 784.69

Streptobacillary fever 026.1

Streptobacillus moniliformis 026.1

Streptococcemia 038.0

Streptococcicosis — *see* Infection, streptococcal

Streptococcus, streptococcal — *see* condition

Streptoderma 686.00

Streptomycosis — *see* Actinomycosis

Streptothricosis — *see* Actinomycosis

Streptothrix — *see* Actinomycosis

Streptotrichosis — *see* Actinomycosis

Stress
- fracture — *see* Fracture, stress
- polycythemia 289.0
- reaction (gross) (*see also* Reaction, stress, acute) 308.9

Stretching, nerve — *see* Injury, nerve, by site

Striae (albicantes) (atrophicae) (cutis distensae) (distensae) 701.3

Striations of nails 703.8

Stricture — *see also* Stenosis 799.89
- ampulla of Vater 576.2
  - with calculus, cholelithiasis, or stones — *see* Choledocholithiasis
- anus (sphincter) 569.2

☑ Additional Digit Required — Refer to the Tabular List for Digit Selection

▼ Subterms under main terms may continue to next column or page

☑ Additional Digit Required — Refer to the Tabular List for Digit Selection

▽ Subterms under main terms may continue to next column or page

▶◀ Revised Text ● New Line ▲ Revised Code

☑ Additional Digit Required — Refer to the Tabular List for Digit Selection
Subterms under main terms may continue to next column or page
▶◀ Revised Text ● New Line ▲ Revised Code

☑ Additional Digit Required — Refer to the Tabular List for Digit Selection
Subterms under main terms may continue to next column or page
▶◀ Revised Text ● New Line ▲ Revised Code

☑ Additional Digit Required — Refer to the Tabular List for Digit Selection
Subterms under main terms may continue to next column or page

▶◀ Revised Text ● New Line ▲ Revised Code

Trichostrongylus (instabilis) infection 127.6
Trichotillomania 312.39
Trichromat, anomalous (congenital) 368.59
Trichromatopsia, anomalous (congenital) 368.59
Trichuriasis 127.3
Trichuris trichiuria (any site) (infection) (infestation) 127.3
Tricuspid (valve) — *see* condition
Trifid — *see also* Accessory
  kidney (pelvis) 753.3
  tongue 750.13
Trigeminal neuralgia — *see also* Neuralgia, trigeminal 350.1
Trigeminoencephaloangiomatosis 759.6
Trigeminy 427.89
  postoperative 997.1
Trigger finger (acquired) 727.03
  congenital 756.89
Trigonitis (bladder) (chronic) (pseudomembranous) 595.3
  tuberculous (*see also* Tuberculosis) 016.1 ☑
Trigonocephaly 756.0
Trihexosidosis 272.7
Trilobate placenta — *see* Placenta, abnormal
Trilocular heart 745.8
Trimethylaminuria 270.8 ●
Tripartita placenta — *see* Placenta, abnormal
Triple — *see also* Accessory
  kidneys 753.3
  uteri 752.2
  X female 758.81
Triplegia 344.89
  congenital or infantile 343.8
Triplet
  affected by maternal complications of pregnancy 761.5
  healthy liveborn — *see* Newborn, multiple
  pregnancy (complicating delivery) NEC 651.1 ☑
    with fetal loss and retention of one or more fetus(es) 651.4 ☑
    following (elective) fetal reduction 651.7 ☑
Triplex placenta — *see* Placenta, abnormal
Triplication — *see* Accessory
Trismus 781.0
  neonatorum 771.3
  newborn 771.3
Trisomy (syndrome) NEC 758.5
  13 (partial) 758.1
  16-18 758.2
  18 (partial) 758.2
  21 (partial) 758.0
  22 758.0
  autosomes NEC 758.5
  D_1 758.1
  E_3 758.2
  G (group) 758.0
  group D_1 758.1
  group E 758.2
  group G 758.0
Tritanomaly 368.53
Tritanopia 368.53
Troisier-Hanot-Chauffard syndrome (bronze diabetes) 275.0
Trombidiosis 133.8
Trophedema (hereditary) 757.0
  congenital 757.0
Trophoblastic disease — *see also* Hydatidiform mole 630
  previous, affecting management of pregnancy V23.1
Tropholymphedema 757.0
Trophoneurosis NEC 356.9
  arm NEC 354.9
  disseminated 710.1
  facial 349.89
Trophoneurosis — *continued*
  leg NEC 355.8
  lower extremity NEC 355.8
  upper extremity NEC 354.9
Tropical — *see also* condition
  maceration feet (syndrome) 991.4
  wet foot (syndrome) 991.4
Trouble — *see also* Disease
  bowel 569.9
  heart — *see* Disease, heart
  intestine 569.9
  kidney (*see also* Disease, renal) 593.9
  nervous 799.2
  sinus (*see also* Sinusitis) 473.9
Trousseau's syndrome (thrombophlebitis migrans) 453.1
Truancy, childhood — *see also* Disturbance, conduct
  socialized 312.2 ☑
  undersocialized, unsocialized 312.1 ☑
Truncus
  arteriosus (persistent) 745.0
  common 745.0
  communis 745.0
Trunk — *see* condition
Trychophytide — *see* Dermatophytosis
Trypanosoma infestation — *see* Trypanosomiasis
Trypanosomiasis 086.9
  with meningoencephalitis 086.9 *[323.2]*
  African 086.5
    due to Trypanosoma 086.5
      gambiense 086.3
      rhodesiense 086.4
  American 086.2
    with
      heart involvement 086.0
      other organ involvement 086.1
    without mention of organ involvement 086.2
  Brazilian — *see* Trypanosomiasis, American
  Chagas' — *see* Trypanosomiasis, American
  due to Trypanosoma
    cruzi — *see* Trypanosomiasis, American
    gambiense 086.3
    rhodesiense 086.4
  gambiensis, Gambian 086.3
  North American — *see* Trypanosomiasis, American
  rhodesiensis, Rhodesian 086.4
  South American — *see* Trypanosomiasis, American
T-shaped incisors 520.2
Tsutsugamushi fever 081.2
Tubercle — *see also* Tuberculosis
  brain, solitary 013.2 ☑
  Darwin's 744.29
  epithelioid noncaseating 135
  Ghon, primary infection 010.0 ☑
Tuberculid, tuberculide (indurating) (lichenoid) (miliary) (papulonecrotic) (primary) (skin) (subcutaneous) — *see also* Tuberculosis 017.0 ☑
Tuberculoma — *see also* Tuberculosis
  brain (any part) 013.2 ☑
  meninges (cerebral) (spinal) 013.1 ☑
  spinal cord 013.4 ☑
Tuberculosis, tubercular, tuberculous (calcification) (calcified) (caseous) (chromogenic acid-fast bacilli) (congenital) (degeneration) (disease) (fibrocaseous) (fistula) (gangrene) (interstitial) (isolated circumscribed lesions) (necrosis) (parenchymatous) (ulcerative) 011.9 ☑

> *Note — Use the following fifth-digit subclassification with categories 010–018:*
>
> 0 *unspecified*
>
> 1 *bacteriological or histological examination not done*
>
> 2 *bacteriological or histological examination unknown (at present)*
>
> 3 *tubercle bacilli found (in sputum) by microscopy*
>
> 4 *tubercle bacilli not found (in sputum) by microscopy, but found by bacterial culture*
>
> 5 *tubercle bacilli not found by bacteriological exam–ination, but tuberculosis confirmed histologically*
>
> 6 *tubercle bacilli not found by bacteriological or histological examination, but tuberculosis confirmed by other methods [inoculation of animals]*
>
> *For tuberculous conditions specified as late effects or sequelae, see category 137.*

  abdomen 014.8 ☑
    lymph gland 014.8 ☑
  abscess 011.9 ☑
    arm 017.9 ☑
    bone (*see also* Osteomyelitis, due to, tuberculosis) 015.9 ☑ *[730.8]* ☑
      hip 015.1 ☑ *[730.85]*
      knee 015.2 ☑ *[730.86]*
      sacrum 015.0 ☑ *[730.88]*
      specified site NEC 015.7 ☑ *[730.88]*
      spinal 015.0 ☑ *[730.88]*
      vertebra 015.0 ☑ *[730.88]*
    brain 013.3 ☑
    breast 017.9 ☑
    Cowper's gland 016.5 ☑
    dura (mater) 013.8 ☑
      brain 013.3 ☑
      spinal cord 013.5 ☑
    epidural 013.8 ☑
      brain 013.3 ☑
      spinal cord 013.5 ☑
    frontal sinus — *see* Tuberculosis, sinus
    genital organs NEC 016.9 ☑
      female 016.7 ☑
      male 016.5 ☑
    genitourinary NEC 016.9 ☑
    gland (lymphatic) — *see* Tuberculosis, lymph gland
    hip 015.1 ☑
    iliopsoas 015.0 ☑ *[730.88]*
    intestine 014.8 ☑
    ischiorectal 014.8 ☑
    joint 015.9 ☑
      hip 015.1 ☑
      knee 015.2 ☑
      specified joint NEC 015.8 ☑
      vertebral 015.0 ☑ *[730.88]*
    kidney 016.0 ☑ *[590.81]*
    knee 015.2 ☑
    lumbar 015.0 ☑ *[730.88]*
    lung 011.2 ☑
      primary, progressive 010.8 ☑
    meninges (cerebral) (spinal) 013.0 ☑
    pelvic 016.9 ☑
Tuberculosis, tubercular, tuberculous — *continued*
  abscess — *continued*
    pelvic — *continued*
      female 016.7 ☑
      male 016.5 ☑
    perianal 014.8 ☑
      fistula 014.8 ☑
    perinephritic 016.0 ☑ *[590.81]*
    perineum 017.9 ☑
    perirectal 014.8 ☑
    psoas 015.0 ☑ *[730.88]*
    rectum 014.8 ☑
    retropharyngeal 012.8 ☑
    sacrum 015.0 ☑ *[730.88]*
    scrofulous 017.2 ☑
    scrotum 016.5 ☑
    skin 017.0 ☑
      primary 017.0 ☑
    spinal cord 013.5 ☑
    spine or vertebra (column) 015.0 ☑ *[730.88]*
    strumous 017.2 ☑
    subdiaphragmatic 014.8 ☑
    testis 016.5 ☑
    thigh 017.9 ☑
    urinary 016.3 ☑
      kidney 016.0 ☑ *[590.81]*
    uterus 016.7 ☑
  accessory sinus — *see* Tuberculosis, sinus
  Addison's disease 017.6 ☑
  adenitis (*see also* Tuberculosis, lymph gland) 017.2 ☑
  adenoids 012.8 ☑
  adenopathy (*see also* Tuberculosis, lymph gland) 017.2 ☑
    tracheobronchial 012.1 ☑
      primary progressive 010.8 ☑
  adherent pericardium 017.9 ☑ *[420.0]*
  adnexa (uteri) 016.7 ☑
  adrenal (capsule) (gland) 017.6 ☑
  air passage NEC 012.8 ☑
  alimentary canal 014.8 ☑
  anemia 017.9 ☑
  ankle (joint) 015.8 ☑
    bone 015.5 ☑ *[730.87]*
  anus 014.8 ☑
  apex (*see also* Tuberculosis, pulmonary) 011.9 ☑
  apical (*see also* Tuberculosis, pulmonary) 011.9 ☑
  appendicitis 014.8 ☑
  appendix 014.8 ☑
  arachnoid 013.0 ☑
  artery 017.9 ☑
  arthritis (chronic) (synovial) 015.9 ☑ *[711.40]*
    ankle 015.8 ☑ *[730.87]*
    hip 015.1 ☑ *[711.45]*
    knee 015.2 ☑ *[711.46]*
    specified site NEC 015.8 ☑ *[711.48]*
    spine or vertebra (column) 015.0 ☑ *[720.81]*
    wrist 015.8 ☑ *[730.83]*
  articular — *see* Tuberculosis, joint
  ascites 014.0 ☑
  asthma (*see also* Tuberculosis, pulmonary) 011.9 ☑
  axilla, axillary 017.2 ☑
    gland 017.2 ☑
  bilateral (*see also* Tuberculosis, pulmonary) 011.9 ☑
  bladder 016.1 ☑
  bone (*see also* Osteomyelitis, due to, tuberculosis) 015.9 ☑ *[730.8]* ☑
    hip 015.1 ☑ *[730.85]*
    knee 015.2 ☑ *[730.86]*
    limb NEC 015.5 ☑ *[730.88]*
    sacrum 015.0 ☑ *[730.88]*
    specified site NEC 015.7 ☑ *[730.88]*
    spinal or vertebral column 015.0 ☑ *[730.88]*
  bowel 014.8 ☑

- Tuberculosis, tubercular, tuberculous *— continued*
  - bowel *— continued*
    - miliary 018.9 ☑
  - brain 013.2 ☑
  - breast 017.9 ☑
  - broad ligament 016.7 ☑
  - bronchi, bronchial, bronchus 011.3 ☑
    - ectasia, ectasis 011.5 ☑
    - fistula 011.3 ☑
      - primary, progressive 010.8 ☑
    - gland 012.1 ☑
      - primary, progressive 010.8 ☑
    - isolated 012.2 ☑
    - lymph gland or node 012.1 ☑
      - primary, progressive 010.8 ☑
  - bronchiectasis 011.5 ☑
  - bronchitis 011.3 ☑
  - bronchopleural 012.0 ☑
  - bronchopneumonia, bronchopneumonic 011.6 ☑
  - bronchorrhagia 011.3 ☑
  - bronchotracheal 011.3 ☑
    - isolated 012.2 ☑
  - bronchus *— see* Tuberculosis, bronchi
  - bronze disease (Addison's) 017.6 ☑
  - buccal cavity 017.9 ☑
  - bulbourethral gland 016.5 ☑
  - bursa (*see also* Tuberculosis, joint) 015.9 ☑
  - cachexia NEC (*see also* Tuberculosis, pulmonary) 011.9 ☑
  - cardiomyopathy 017.9 ☑ *[425.8]*
  - caries (*see also* Tuberculosis, bone) 015.9 ☑ *[730.8]* ☑
  - cartilage (*see also* Tuberculosis, bone) 015.9 ☑ *[730.8]* ☑
    - intervertebral 015.0 ☑ *[730.88]*
  - catarrhal (*see also* Tuberculosis, pulmonary) 011.9 ☑
  - cecum 014.8 ☑
  - cellular tissue (primary) 017.0 ☑
  - cellulitis (primary) 017.0 ☑
  - central nervous system 013.9 ☑
    - specified site NEC 013.8 ☑
  - cerebellum (current) 013.2 ☑
  - cerebral (current) 013.2 ☑
    - meninges 013.0 ☑
  - cerebrospinal 013.6 ☑
    - meninges 013.0 ☑
  - cerebrum (current) 013.2 ☑
  - cervical 017.2 ☑
    - gland 017.2 ☑
    - lymph nodes 017.2 ☑
  - cervicitis (uteri) 016.7 ☑
  - cervix 016.7 ☑
  - chest (*see also* Tuberculosis, pulmonary) 011.9 ☑
  - childhood type or first infection 010.0 ☑
  - choroid 017.3 ☑ *[363.13]*
  - choroiditis 017.3 ☑ *[363.13]*
  - ciliary body 017.3 ☑ *[364.11]*
  - colitis 014.8 ☑
  - colliers' 011.4 ☑
  - colliquativa (primary) 017.0 ☑
  - colon 014.8 ☑
    - ulceration 014.8 ☑
  - complex, primary 010.0 ☑
  - complicating pregnancy, childbirth, or puerperium 647.3 ☑
    - affecting fetus or newborn 760.2
  - congenital 771.2
  - conjunctiva 017.3 ☑ *[370.31]*
  - connective tissue 017.9 ☑
    - bone *— see* Tuberculosis, bone
  - contact V01.1
  - converter (tuberculin skin test) (without disease) 795.5
  - cornea (ulcer) 017.3 ☑ *[370.31]*
  - Cowper's gland 016.5 ☑
  - coxae 015.1 ☑ *[730.85]*
  - coxalgia 015.1 ☑ *[730.85]*
  - cul-de-sac of Douglas 014.8 ☑

- Tuberculosis, tubercular, tuberculous *— continued*
  - curvature, spine 015.0 ☑ *[737.40]*
  - cutis (colliquativa) (primary) 017.0 ☑
  - cystitis 016.1 ☑
  - cyst, ovary 016.6 ☑
  - dacryocystitis 017.3 ☑ *[375.32]*
  - dactylitis 015.5 ☑
  - diarrhea 014.8 ☑
  - diffuse (*see also* Tuberculosis, miliary) 018.9 ☑
    - lung *— see* Tuberculosis, pulmonary
    - meninges 013.0 ☑
  - digestive tract 014.8 ☑
  - disseminated (*see also* Tuberculosis, miliary) 018.9 ☑
    - meninges 013.0 ☑
  - duodenum 014.8 ☑
  - dura (mater) 013.9 ☑
    - abscess 013.8 ☑
      - cerebral 013.3 ☑
      - spinal 013.5 ☑
  - dysentery 014.8 ☑
  - ear (inner) (middle) 017.4 ☑
    - bone 015.6 ☑
    - external (primary) 017.0 ☑
    - skin (primary) 017.0 ☑
  - elbow 015.8 ☑
  - emphysema *— see* Tuberculosis, pulmonary
  - empyema 012.0 ☑
  - encephalitis 013.6 ☑
  - endarteritis 017.9 ☑
  - endocarditis (any valve) 017.9 ☑ *[424.91]*
  - endocardium (any valve) 017.9 ☑ *[424.91]*
  - endocrine glands NEC 017.9 ☑
  - endometrium 016.7 ☑
  - enteric, enterica 014.8 ☑
  - enteritis 014.8 ☑
  - enterocolitis 014.8 ☑
  - epididymis 016.4 ☑
  - epididymitis 016.4 ☑
  - epidural abscess 013.8 ☑
    - brain 013.3 ☑
    - spinal cord 013.5 ☑
  - epiglottis 012.3 ☑
  - episcleritis 017.3 ☑ *[379.00]*
  - erythema (induratum) (nodosum) (primary) 017.1 ☑
  - esophagus 017.8 ☑
  - Eustachian tube 017.4 ☑
  - exposure to V01.1
  - exudative 012.0 ☑
    - primary, progressive 010.1 ☑
  - eye 017.3 ☑
    - glaucoma 017.3 ☑ *[365.62]*
  - eyelid (primary) 017.0 ☑
    - lupus 017.0 ☑ *[373.4]*
  - fallopian tube 016.6 ☑
  - fascia 017.9 ☑
  - fauces 012.8 ☑
  - finger 017.9 ☑
  - first infection 010.0 ☑
  - fistula, perirectal 014.8 ☑
  - Florida 011.6 ☑
  - foot 017.9 ☑
  - funnel pelvis 137.3
  - gallbladder 017.9 ☑
  - galloping (*see also* Tuberculosis, pulmonary) 011.9 ☑
  - ganglionic 015.9 ☑
  - gastritis 017.9 ☑
  - gastrocolic fistula 014.8 ☑
  - gastroenteritis 014.8 ☑
  - gastrointestinal tract 014.8 ☑
  - general, generalized 018.9 ☑
    - acute 018.0 ☑
    - chronic 018.8 ☑
  - genital organs NEC 016.9 ☑
    - female 016.7 ☑
    - male 016.5 ☑

- Tuberculosis, tubercular, tuberculous *— continued*
  - genitourinary NEC 016.9 ☑
  - genu 015.2 ☑
  - glandulae suprarenalis 017.6 ☑
  - glandular, general 017.2 ☑
  - glottis 012.3 ☑
  - grinders' 011.4 ☑
  - groin 017.2 ☑
  - gum 017.9 ☑
  - hand 017.9 ☑
  - heart 017.9 ☑ *[425.8]*
  - hematogenous *— see* Tuberculosis, miliary
  - hemoptysis (*see also* Tuberculosis, pulmonary) 011.9 ☑
  - hemorrhage NEC (*see also* Tuberculosis, pulmonary) 011.9 ☑
  - hemothorax 012.0 ☑
  - hepatitis 017.9 ☑
  - hilar lymph nodes 012.1 ☑
    - primary, progressive 010.8 ☑
  - hip (disease) (joint) 015.1 ☑
    - bone 015.1 ☑ *[730.85]*
  - hydrocephalus 013.8 ☑
  - hydropneumothorax 012.0 ☑
  - hydrothorax 012.0 ☑
  - hypoadrenalism 017.6 ☑
  - hypopharynx 012.8 ☑
  - ileocecal (hyperplastic) 014.8 ☑
  - ileocolitis 014.8 ☑
  - ileum 014.8 ☑
  - iliac spine (superior) 015.0 ☑ *[730.88]*
  - incipient NEC (*see also* Tuberculosis, pulmonary) 011.9 ☑
  - indurativa (primary) 017.1 ☑
  - infantile 010.0 ☑
  - infection NEC 011.9 ☑
    - without clinical manifestation 010.0 ☑
  - infraclavicular gland 017.2 ☑
  - inguinal gland 017.2 ☑
  - inguinalis 017.2 ☑
  - intestine (any part) 014.8 ☑
  - iris 017.3 ☑ *[364.11]*
  - iritis 017.3 ☑ *[364.11]*
  - ischiorectal 014.8 ☑
  - jaw 015.7 ☑ *[730.88]*
  - jejunum 014.8 ☑
  - joint 015.9 ☑
    - hip 015.1 ☑
    - knee 015.2 ☑
    - specified site NEC 015.8 ☑
    - vertebral 015.0 ☑ *[730.88]*
  - keratitis 017.3 ☑ *[370.31]*
    - interstitial 017.3 ☑ *[370.59]*
  - keratoconjunctivitis 017.3 ☑ *[370.31]*
  - kidney 016.0 ☑
  - knee (joint) 015.2 ☑
  - kyphoscoliosis 015.0 ☑ *[737.43]*
  - kyphosis 015.0 ☑ *[737.41]*
  - lacrimal apparatus, gland 017.3 ☑
  - laryngitis 012.3 ☑
  - larynx 012.3 ☑
  - leptomeninges, leptomeningitis (cerebral) (spinal) 013.0 ☑
  - lichenoides (primary) 017.0 ☑
  - linguae 017.9 ☑
  - lip 017.9 ☑
  - liver 017.9 ☑
  - lordosis 015.0 ☑ *[737.42]*
  - lung *— see* Tuberculosis, pulmonary
  - luposa 017.0 ☑
    - eyelid 017.0 ☑ *[373.4]*
  - lymphadenitis *— see* Tuberculosis, lymph gland
  - lymphangitis *— see* Tuberculosis, lymph gland
  - lymphatic (gland) (vessel) *— see* Tuberculosis, lymph gland
  - lymph gland or node (peripheral) 017.2 ☑
    - abdomen 014.8 ☑
    - bronchial 012.1 ☑

- Tuberculosis, tubercular, tuberculous *— continued*
  - lymph gland or node *— continued*
    - bronchial *— continued*
      - primary, progressive 010.8 ☑
    - cervical 017.2 ☑
    - hilar 012.1 ☑
      - primary, progressive 010.8 ☑
    - intrathoracic 012.1 ☑
      - primary, progressive 010.8 ☑
    - mediastinal 012.1 ☑
      - primary, progressive 010.8 ☑
    - mesenteric 014.8 ☑
    - peripheral 017.2 ☑
    - retroperitoneal 014.8 ☑
    - tracheobronchial 012.1 ☑
      - primary, progressive 010.8 ☑
  - malignant NEC (*see also* Tuberculosis, pulmonary) 011.9 ☑
  - mammary gland 017.9 ☑
  - marasmus NEC (*see also* Tuberculosis, pulmonary) 011.9 ☑
  - mastoiditis 015.6 ☑
  - maternal, affecting fetus or newborn 760.2
  - mediastinal (lymph) gland or node 012.1 ☑
    - primary, progressive 010.8 ☑
  - mediastinitis 012.8 ☑
    - primary, progressive 010.8 ☑
  - mediastinopericarditis 017.9 ☑ *[420.0]*
  - mediastinum 012.8 ☑
    - primary, progressive 010.8 ☑
  - medulla 013.9 ☑
    - brain 013.2 ☑
    - spinal cord 013.4 ☑
  - melanosis, Addisonian 017.6 ☑
  - membrane, brain 013.0 ☑
  - meninges (cerebral) (spinal) 013.0 ☑
  - meningitis (basilar) (brain) (cerebral) (cerebrospinal) (spinal) 013.0 ☑
  - meningoencephalitis 013.0 ☑
  - mesentery, mesenteric 014.8 ☑
    - lymph gland or node 014.8 ☑
  - miliary (any site) 018.9 ☑
    - acute 018.0 ☑
    - chronic 018.8 ☑
    - specified type NEC 018.8 ☑
  - millstone makers' 011.4 ☑
  - miners' 011.4 ☑
  - moulders' 011.4 ☑
  - mouth 017.9 ☑
  - multiple 018.9 ☑
    - acute 018.0 ☑
    - chronic 018.8 ☑
  - muscle 017.9 ☑
  - myelitis 013.6 ☑
  - myocarditis 017.9 ☑ *[422.0]*
  - myocardium 017.9 ☑ *[422.0]*
  - nasal (passage) (sinus) 012.8 ☑
  - nasopharynx 012.8 ☑
  - neck gland 017.2 ☑
  - nephritis 016.0 ☑ *[583.81]*
  - nerve 017.9 ☑
  - nose (septum) 012.8 ☑
  - ocular 017.3 ☑
  - old NEC 137.0
    - without residuals V12.01
  - omentum 014.8 ☑
  - oophoritis (acute) (chronic) 016.6 ☑
  - optic 017.3 ☑ *[377.39]*
    - nerve trunk 017.3 ☑ *[377.39]*
    - papilla, papillae 017.3 ☑ *[377.39]*
  - orbit 017.3 ☑
  - orchitis 016.5 ☑ *[608.81]*
  - organ, specified NEC 017.9 ☑
  - orificialis (primary) 017.0 ☑
  - osseous (*see also* Tuberculosis, bone) 015.9 ☑ *[730.8]* ☑
  - osteitis (*see also* Tuberculosis, bone) 015.9 ☑ *[730.8]* ☑
  - osteomyelitis (*see also* Tuberculosis, bone) 015.9 ☑ *[730.8]* ☑
  - otitis (media) 017.4 ☑

V

☑ Additional Digit Required — Refer to the Tabular List for Digit Selection

Subterms under main terms may continue to next column or page

▶◀ Revised Text ● New Line ▲ Revised Code

W

Note — For fracture with open wound, see Fracture.

For laceration, traumatic rupture, tear or penetrating wound of internal organs, such as heart, lung, liver, kidney, pelvic organs, etc., whether or not accompanied by open wound or fracture in the same region, see Injury, internal.

For contused wound, see Contusion. For crush injury, see Crush. For abrasion, insect bite (nonvenomous), blister, or scratch, see Injury, superficial.

Complicated includes wounds with:

delayed healing

delayed treatment

foreign body

primary infection

For late effect of open wound, see Late, effect, wound, open, by site.

☑ Additional Digit Required — Refer to the Tabular List for Digit Selection

Subterms under main terms may continue to next column or page

Note — Multiple open wounds of sites classifiable to the same four-digit category should be classified to that category unless they are in different limbs.

Multiple open wounds of sites classifiable to different four-digit categories, or to different limbs, should be coded separately.

- **Wound, open** — *continued*
  - ocular — *continued*
    - muscle — *continued*
      - intraocular — *see* Wound, open, eyeball
    - penetrating (*see also* Penetrating wound, ocular) 871.7
  - orbit 870.8
    - penetrating 870.3
      - with foreign body 870.4
  - orbital region 870.9
  - ovary — *see* Injury, internal, pelvic organs
  - palate 873.65
    - complicated 873.75
  - palm 882.0
    - with tendon involvement 882.2
    - complicated 882.1
  - parathyroid (gland) 874.2
    - complicated 874.3
  - parietal region — *see* Wound, open, scalp
  - pelvic floor or region 879.6
    - complicated 879.7
  - penis 878.0
    - complicated 878.1
  - perineum 879.6
    - complicated 879.7
  - periocular area 870.8
    - laceration of skin 870.0
  - pharynx 874.4
    - complicated 874.5
  - pinna 872.01
    - complicated 872.11
  - popliteal space 891.0
    - with tendon involvement 891.2
    - complicated 891.1
  - prepuce 878.0
    - complicated 878.1
  - pubic region 879.2
    - complicated 879.3
  - pudenda 878.8
    - complicated 878.9
  - rectovaginal septum 878.8
    - complicated 878.9
  - sacral region 877.0
    - complicated 877.1
  - sacroiliac region 877.0
    - complicated 877.1
  - salivary (ducts) (glands) 873.69
    - complicated 873.79
  - scalp 873.0
    - complicated 873.1
  - scalpel, fetus or newborn 767.8
  - scapular region 880.01
    - with tendon involvement 880.21
    - complicated 880.11
    - involving other sites of upper arm 880.09
      - with tendon involvement 880.29
      - complicated 880.19
  - sclera (*see also* Wound, open, intraocular) 871.9
  - scrotum 878.2
    - complicated 878.3
  - seminal vesicle — *see* Injury, internal, pelvic organs
  - shin 891.0
    - with tendon involvement 891.2
    - complicated 891.1
  - shoulder 880.00
    - with tendon involvement 880.20
    - complicated 880.10
    - involving other sites of upper arm 880.09
      - with tendon involvement 880.29
      - complicated 880.19
  - skin NEC 879.8
    - complicated 879.9
  - skull (*see also* Injury, intracranial, with open intracranial wound)
    - with skull fracture — *see* Fracture, skull
  - spermatic cord (scrotal) 878.2
    - complicated 878.3

- **Wound, open** — *continued*
  - spermatic cord — *continued*
    - pelvic region — *see* Injury, internal, spermatic cord
  - spinal cord — *see* Injury, spinal
  - sternal region 875.0
    - complicated 875.1
  - subconjunctival — *see* Wound, open, intraocular
  - subcutaneous NEC 879.8
    - complicated 879.9
  - submaxillary region 873.44
    - complicated 873.54
  - submental region 873.44
    - complicated 873.54
  - subungual
    - finger(s) (thumb) — *see* Wound, open, finger
    - toe(s) — *see* Wound, open, toe
  - supraclavicular region 874.8
    - complicated 874.9
  - supraorbital 873.42
    - complicated 873.52
  - surgical, non-healing 998.83
  - temple 873.49
    - complicated 873.59
  - temporal region 873.49
    - complicated 873.59
  - testis 878.2
    - complicated 878.3
  - thigh 890.0
    - with tendon involvement 890.2
    - complicated 890.1
  - thorax, thoracic (external) 875.0
    - complicated 875.1
  - throat 874.8
    - complicated 874.9
  - thumb (nail) (subungual) 883.0
    - with tendon involvement 883.2
    - complicated 883.1
  - thyroid (gland) 874.2
    - complicated 874.3
  - toe(s) (nail) (subungual) 893.0
    - with tendon involvement 893.2
    - complicated 893.1
  - tongue 873.64
    - complicated 873.74
  - tonsil — *see* Wound, open, neck
  - trachea (cervical region) 874.02
    - with larynx 874.00
      - complicated 874.10
    - complicated 874.12
    - intrathoracic — *see* Injury, internal, trachea
  - trunk (multiple) NEC 879.6
    - complicated 879.7
    - specified site NEC 879.6
      - complicated 879.7
  - tunica vaginalis 878.2
    - complicated 878.3
  - tympanic membrane 872.61
    - complicated 872.71
  - tympanum 872.61
    - complicated 872.71
  - umbilical region 879.2
    - complicated 879.3
  - ureter — *see* Injury, internal, ureter
  - urethra — *see* Injury, internal, urethra
  - uterus — *see* Injury, internal, uterus
  - uvula 873.69
    - complicated 873.79
  - vagina 878.6
    - complicated 878.7
  - vas deferens — *see* Injury, internal, vas deferens
  - vitreous (humor) 871.2
  - vulva 878.4
    - complicated 878.5
  - wrist 881.02
    - with tendon involvement 881.22
    - complicated 881.12
- **Wright's syndrome** (hyperabduction) 447.8
  - pneumonia 390 *[517.1]*
- **Wringer injury** — *see* Crush injury, by site
- **Wrinkling of skin** 701.8
- **Wrist** — *see also* condition
  - drop (acquired) 736.05
- **Wrong drug** (given in error) NEC 977.9
  - specified drug or substance — *see* Table of Drugs and Chemicals
- **Wry neck** — *see also* Torticollis
  - congenital 754.1
- **Wuchereria infestation** 125.0
  - bancrofti 125.0
  - Brugia malayi 125.1
  - malayi 125.1
- **Wuchereriasis** 125.0
- **Wuchereriosis** 125.0
- **Wuchernde struma langhans** (M8332/3) 193

X

- **Xanthelasma** 272.2
  - eyelid 272.2 *[374.51]*
  - palpebrarum 272.2 *[374.51]*
- **Xanthelasmatosis** (essential) 272.2
- **Xanthelasmoidea** 757.33
- **Xanthine stones** 277.2
- **Xanthinuria** 277.2
- **Xanthofibroma** (M8831/0) — *see* Neoplasm, connective tissue, benign
- **Xanthoma(s), xanthomatosis** 272.2
  - with
    - hyperlipoproteinemia
      - type I 272.3
      - type III 272.2
      - type IV 272.1
      - type V 272.3
  - bone 272.7
  - craniohypophyseal 277.89
  - cutaneotendinous 272.7
  - diabeticorum 250.8 ☑ *[272.2]*
  - disseminatum 272.7
  - eruptive 272.2
  - eyelid 272.2 *[374.51]*
  - familial 272.7
  - hereditary 272.7
  - hypercholesterinemic 272.0
  - hypercholesterolemic 272.0
  - hyperlipemic 272.4
  - hyperlipidemic 272.4
  - infantile 272.7
  - joint 272.7
  - juvenile 272.7
  - multiple 272.7
  - multiplex 272.7
  - primary familial 272.7
  - tendon (sheath) 272.7
  - tuberosum 272.2
  - tuberous 272.2
  - tubo-eruptive 272.2
- **Xanthosis** 709.09
  - surgical 998.81
- **Xenophobia** 300.29
- **Xeroderma** (congenital) 757.39
  - acquired 701.1
    - eyelid 373.33
  - eyelid 373.33
  - pigmentosum 757.33
  - vitamin A deficiency 264.8
- **Xerophthalmia** 372.53
  - vitamin A deficiency 264.7
- **Xerosis**
  - conjunctiva 372.53
    - with Bitôt's spot 372.53
      - vitamin A deficiency 264.1
    - vitamin A deficiency 264.0
  - cornea 371.40
    - with corneal ulceration 370.00
      - vitamin A deficiency 264.3
    - vitamin A deficiency 264.2
  - cutis 706.8
  - skin 706.8
- **Xerostomia** 527.7
- **Xiphodynia** 733.90
- **Xiphoidalgia** 733.90
- **Xiphoiditis** 733.99
- **Xiphopagus** 759.4
- **XO syndrome** 758.6
- **X-ray**
  - effects, adverse, NEC 990
  - of chest
    - for suspected tuberculosis V71.2
    - routine V72.5
- **XXX syndrome** 758.81
- **XXXXY syndrome** 758.81
- **XXY syndrome** 758.7
- **Xyloketosuria** 271.8
- **Xylosuria** 271.8
- **Xylulosuria** 271.8
- **XYY syndrome** 758.81

Y

- **Yawning** 786.09
  - psychogenic 306.1
- **Yaws** 102.9
  - bone or joint lesions 102.6
  - butter 102.1
  - chancre 102.0
  - cutaneous, less than five years after infection 102.2
  - early (cutaneous) (macular) (maculopapular) (micropapular) (papular) 102.2
    - frambeside 102.2
    - skin lesions NEC 102.2
  - eyelid 102.9 *[373.4]*
  - ganglion 102.6
  - gangosis, gangosa 102.5
  - gumma, gummata 102.4
    - bone 102.6
  - gummatous
    - frambeside 102.4
    - osteitis 102.6
    - periostitis 102.6
  - hydrarthrosis 102.6
  - hyperkeratosis (early) (late) (palmar) (plantar) 102.3
  - initial lesions 102.0
  - joint lesions 102.6
  - juxta-articular nodules 102.7
  - late nodular (ulcerated) 102.4
  - latent (without clinical manifestations) (with positive serology) 102.8
  - mother 102.0
  - mucosal 102.7
  - multiple papillomata 102.1
  - nodular, late (ulcerated) 102.4
  - osteitis 102.6
  - papilloma, papillomata (palmar) (plantar) 102.1
  - periostitis (hypertrophic) 102.6
  - ulcers 102.4
  - wet crab 102.1
- **Yeast infection** — *see also* Candidiasis 112.9
- **Yellow**
  - atrophy (liver) 570
    - chronic 571.8
    - resulting from administration of blood, plasma, serum, or other biological substance (within 8 months of administration) — *see* Hepatitis, viral
  - fever — *see* Fever, yellow
  - jack (*see also* Fever, yellow) 060.9
  - jaundice (*see also* Jaundice) 782.4
  - vernix syndrome 762.2
- **Yersinia septica** 027.8

Z

- **Zagari's disease** (xerostomia) 527.7
- **Zahorsky's disease** (exanthema subitum) 057.8
  - syndrome (herpangina) 074.0
- **Zellweger syndrome** 277.86
- **Zenker's diverticulum** (esophagus) 530.6
- **Ziehen-Oppenheim disease** 333.6
- **Zieve's syndrome** (jaundice, hyperlipemia, and hemolytic anemia) 571.1
- **Zika fever** 066.3

☑ Additional Digit Required — Refer to the Tabular List for Digit Selection

▽ Subterms under main terms may continue to next column or page

SECTION 2

Alphabetic Index to Poisoning and External Causes of Adverse Effects of Drugs and Other Chemical Substances

TABLE OF DRUGS AND CHEMICALS

This table contains a classification of drugs and other chemical substances to identify poisoning states and external causes of adverse effects.

Each of the listed substances in the table is assigned a code according to the poisoning classification (960-989). These codes are used when there is a statement of poisoning, overdose, wrong substance given or taken, or intoxication.

The table also contains a listing of external causes of adverse effects. An adverse effect is a pathologic manifestation due to ingestion or exposure to drugs or other chemical substances (e.g., dermatitis, hypersensitivity reaction, aspirin gastritis). The adverse effect is to be identified by the appropriate code found in Section 1, Index to Diseases and Injuries. An external cause code can then be used to identify the circumstances involved. The table headings pertaining to external causes are defined below:

Accidental poisoning (E850-E869) — accidental overdose of drug, wrong substance given or taken, drug taken inadvertently, accidents in the usage of drugs and biologicals in medical and surgical procedures, and to show external causes of poisonings classifiable to 980-989.

Therapeutic use (E930-E949) — a correct substance properly administered in therapeutic or prophylactic dosage as the external cause of adverse effects.

Suicide attempt (E950-E952) — instances in which self-inflicted injuries or poisonings are involved.

Assault (E961-E962) — injury or poisoning inflicted by another person with the intent to injure or kill.

Undetermined (E980-E982) — to be used when the intent of the poisoning or injury cannot be determined whether it was intentional or accidental.

The American Hospital Formulary Service list numbers are included in the table to help classify new drugs not identified in the table by name. The AHFS list numbers are keyed to the continually revised American Hospital Formulary Service (AHFS).* These listings are found in the table under the main term **Drug**.

Excluded from the table are radium and other radioactive substances. The classification of adverse effects and complications pertaining to these substances will be found in Section 1, Index to Diseases and Injuries, and Section 3, Index to External Causes of Injuries.

Although certain substances are indexed with one or more subentries, the majority are listed according to one use or state. It is recognized that many substances may be used in various ways, in medicine and in industry, and may cause adverse effects whatever the state of the agent (solid, liquid, or fumes arising from a liquid). In cases in which the reported data indicates a use or state not in the table, or which is clearly different from the one listed, an attempt should be made to classify the substance in the form which most nearly expresses the reported facts.

*American Hospital Formulary Service, 2 vol. (Washington, D.C.: American Society of Hospital Pharmacists, 1959-)

Substance	Poisoning	External Cause (E-Code) Accident	Therapeutic Use	Suicide Attempt	Assault	Undetermined
1-propanol	980.3	E860.4	—	E950.9	E962.1	E980.9
2-propanol	980.2	E860.3	—	E950.9	E962.1	E980.9
2, 4-D (dichlorophenoxyacetic acid)	989.4	E863.5	—	E950.6	E962.1	E980.7
2, 4-toluene diisocyanate	983.0	E864.0	—	E950.7	E962.1	E980.6
2, 4, 5-T (trichlorophenoxyacetic acid)	989.2	E863.5	—	E950.6	E962.1	E980.7
14-hydroxydihydromorphinone	965.09	E850.2	E935.2	E950.0	E962.0	E980.0
ABOB	961.7	E857	E931.7	E950.4	E962.0	E980.4
Abrus (seed)	988.2	E865.3	—	E950.9	E962.1	E980.9
Absinthe	980.0	E860.1	—	E950.9	E962.1	E980.9
beverage	980.0	E860.0	—	E950.9	E962.1	E980.9
Acenocoumarin, acenocoumarol	964.2	E858.2	E934.2	E950.4	E962.0	E980.4
Acepromazine	969.1	E853.0	E939.1	E950.3	E962.0	E980.3
Acetal	982.8	E862.4	—	E950.9	E962.1	E980.9
Acetaldehyde (vapor)	987.8	E869.8	—	E952.8	E962.2	E982.8
liquid	989.89	E866.8	—	E950.9	E962.1	E980.9
Acetaminophen	965.4	E850.4	E935.4	E950.0	E962.0	E980.0
Acetaminosalol	965.1	E850.3	E935.3	E950.0	E962.0	E980.0
Acetanilid(e)	965.4	E850.4	E935.4	E950.0	E962.0	E980.0
Acetarsol, acetarsone	961.1	E857	E931.1	E950.4	E962.0	E980.4
Acetazolamide	974.2	E858.5	E944.2	E950.4	E962.0	E980.4
Acetic						
acid	983.1	E864.1	—	E950.7	E962.1	E980.6
with sodium acetate (ointment)	976.3	E858.7	E946.3	E950.4	E962.0	E980.4
irrigating solution	974.5	E858.5	E944.5	E950.4	E962.0	E980.4
lotion	976.2	E858.7	E946.2	E950.4	E962.0	E980.4
anhydride	983.1	E864.1	—	E950.7	E962.1	E980.6
ether (vapor)	982.8	E862.4	—	E950.9	E962.1	E980.9
Acetohexamide	962.3	E858.0	E932.3	E950.4	E962.0	E980.4
Acetomenaphthone	964.3	E858.2	E934.3	E950.4	E962.0	E980.4
Acetomorphine	965.01	E850.0	E935.0	E950.0	E962.0	E980.0
Acetone (oils) (vapor)	982.8	E862.4	—	E950.9	E962.1	E980.9
Acetophenazine (maleate)	969.1	E853.0	E939.1	E950.3	E962.0	E980.3
Acetophenetidin	965.4	E850.4	E935.4	E950.0	E962.0	E980.0
Acetophenone	982.0	E862.4	—	E950.9	E962.1	E980.9
Acetorphine	965.09	E850.2	E935.2	E950.0	E962.0	E980.0
Acetosulfone (sodium)	961.8	E857	E931.8	E950.4	E962.0	E980.4
Acetrizoate (sodium)	977.8	E858.8	E947.8	E950.4	E962.0	E980.4
Acetylcarbromal	967.3	E852.2	E937.3	E950.2	E962.0	E980.2
Acetylcholine (chloride)	971.0	E855.3	E941.0	E950.4	E962.0	E980.4
Acetylcysteine	975.5	E858.6	E945.5	E950.4	E962.0	E980.4
Acetyldigitoxin	972.1	E858.3	E942.1	E950.4	E962.0	E980.4
Acetyldihydrocodeine	965.09	E850.2	E935.2	E950.0	E962.0	E980.0
Acetyldihydrocodeinone	965.09	E850.2	E935.2	E950.0	E962.0	E980.0
Acetylene (gas) (industrial)	987.1	E868.1	—	E951.8	E962.2	E981.8
incomplete combustion of — see Carbon monoxide, fuel, utility						
tetrachloride (vapor)	982.3	E862.4	—	E950.9	E962.1	E980.9
Acetyliodosalicylic acid	965.1	E850.3	E935.3	E950.0	E962.0	E980.0
Acetylphenylhydrazine	965.8	E850.8	E935.8	E950.0	E962.0	E980.0
Acetylsalicylic acid	965.1	E850.3	E935.3	E950.0	E962.0	E980.0
Achromycin	960.4	E856	E930.4	E950.4	E962.0	E980.4
ophthalmic preparation	976.5	E858.7	E946.5	E950.4	E962.0	E980.4
topical NEC	976.0	E858.7	E946.0	E950.4	E962.0	E980.4
Acidifying agents	963.2	E858.1	E933.2	E950.4	E962.0	E980.4
Acids (corrosive) NEC	983.1	E864.1	—	E950.7	E962.1	E980.6
Aconite (wild)	988.2	E865.4	—	E950.9	E962.1	E980.9
Aconitine (liniment)	976.8	E858.7	E946.8	E950.4	E962.0	E980.4
Aconitum ferox	988.2	E865.4	—	E950.9	E962.1	E980.9
Acridine	983.0	E864.0	—	E950.7	E962.1	E980.6
vapor	987.8	E869.8	—	E952.8	E962.2	E982.8
Acriflavine	961.9	E857	E931.9	E950.4	E962.0	E980.4
Acrisorcin	976.0	E858.7	E946.0	E950.4	E962.0	E980.4
Acrolein (gas)	987.8	E869.8	—	E952.8	E962.2	E982.8
liquid	989.89	E866.8	—	E950.9	E962.1	E980.9
Actaea spicata	988.2	E865.4	—	E950.9	E962.1	E980.9
Acterol	961.5	E857	E931.5	E950.4	E962.0	E980.4
ACTH	962.4	E858.0	E932.4	E950.4	E962.0	E980.4
Acthar	962.4	E858.0	E932.4	E950.4	E962.0	E980.4
Actinomycin (C) (D)	960.7	E856	E930.7	E950.4	E962.0	E980.4
Adalin (acetyl)	967.3	E852.2	E937.3	E950.2	E962.0	E980.2
Adenosine (phosphate)	977.8	E858.8	E947.8	E950.4	E962.0	E980.4
ADH	962.5	E858.0	E932.5	E950.4	E962.0	E980.4
Adhesives	989.89	E866.6	—	E950.9	E962.1	E980.9
Adicillin	960.0	E856	E930.0	E950.4	E962.0	E980.4
Adiphenine	975.1	E855.6	E945.1	E950.4	E962.0	E980.4
Adjunct, pharmaceutical	977.4	E858.8	E947.4	E950.4	E962.0	E980.4

Substance	Poisoning	External Cause (E-Code) Accident	Therapeutic Use	Suicide Attempt	Assault	Undetermined
Adrenal (extract, cortex or medulla) (glucocorticoids) (hormones) (mineralocorticoids)	962.0	E858.0	E932.0	E950.4	E962.0	E980.4
ENT agent	976.6	E858.7	E946.6	E950.4	E962.0	E980.4
ophthalmic preparation	976.5	E858.7	E946.5	E950.4	E962.0	E980.4
topical NEC	976.0	E858.7	E946.0	E950.4	E962.0	E980.4
Adrenalin	971.2	E855.5	E941.2	E950.4	E962.0	E980.4
Adrenergic blocking agents	971.3	E855.6	E941.3	E950.4	E962.0	E980.4
Adrenergics	971.2	E855.5	E941.2	E950.4	E962.0	E980.4
Adrenochrome (derivatives)	972.8	E858.3	E942.8	E950.4	E962.0	E980.4
Adrenocorticotropic hormone	962.4	E858.0	E932.4	E950.4	E962.0	E980.4
Adrenocorticotropin	962.4	E858.0	E932.4	E950.4	E962.0	E980.4
Adriamycin	960.7	E856	E930.7	E950.4	E962.0	E980.4
Aerosol spray — see Sprays						
Aerosporin	960.8	E856	E930.8	E950.4	E962.0	E980.4
ENT agent	976.6	E858.7	E946.6	E950.4	E962.0	E980.4
ophthalmic preparation	976.5	E858.7	E946.5	E950.4	E962.0	E980.4
topical NEC	976.0	E858.7	E946.0	E950.4	E962.0	E980.4
Aethusa cynapium	988.2	E865.4	—	E950.9	E962.1	E980.9
Afghanistan black	969.6	E854.1	E939.6	E950.3	E962.0	E980.3
Aflatoxin	989.7	E865.9	—	E950.9	E962.1	E980.9
African boxwood	988.2	E865.4	—	E950.9	E962.1	E980.9
Agar (-agar)	973.3	E858.4	E943.3	E950.4	E962.0	E980.4
Agricultural agent NEC	989.89	E863.9	—	E950.6	E962.1	E980.7
Agrypnal	967.0	E851	E937.0	E950.1	E962.0	—
Air contaminant(s), source or type not specified	987.9	E869.9	—	E952.9	E962.2	E982.9
specified type — see specific substance						
Akee	988.2	E865.4	—	E950.9	E962.1	E980.9
Akrinol	976.0	E858.7	E946.0	E950.4	E962.0	E980.4
Alantolactone	961.6	E857	E931.6	E950.4	E962.0	E980.4
Albamycin	960.8	E856	E930.8	E950.4	E962.0	E980.4
Albumin (normal human serum)	964.7	E858.2	E934.7	E950.4	E962.0	E980.4
Albuterol	975.7	E858.6	E945.7	E950.4	E962.0	E980.4
Alcohol	980.9	E860.9	—	E950.9	E962.1	E980.9
absolute	980.0	E860.1	—	E950.9	E962.1	E980.9
beverage	980.0	E860.0	E947.8	E950.9	E962.1	E980.9
amyl	980.3	E860.4	—	E950.9	E962.1	E980.9
antifreeze	980.1	E860.2	—	E950.9	E962.1	E980.9
butyl	980.3	E860.4	—	E950.9	E962.1	E980.9
dehydrated	980.0	E860.1	—	E950.9	E862.1	E980.9
beverage	980.0	E860.0	E947.8	E950.9	E962.1	E980.9
denatured	980.0	E860.1	—	E950.9	E962.1	E980.9
deterrents	977.3	E858.8	E947.3	E950.4	E962.0	E980.4
diagnostic (gastric function)	977.8	E858.8	E947.8	E950.4	E962.0	E980.4
ethyl	980.0	E860.1	—	E950.9	E962.1	E980.9
beverage	980.0	E860.0	E947.8	E950.9	E962.1	E980.9
grain	980.0	E860.1	—	E950.9	E962.1	E980.9
beverage	980.0	E860.0	E947.8	E950.9	E962.1	E980.9
industrial	980.9	E860.9	—	E950.9	E962.1	E980.9
isopropyl	980.2	E860.3	—	E950.9	E962.1	E980.9
methyl	980.1	E860.2	—	E950.9	E962.1	E980.9
preparation for consumption	980.0	E860.0	E947.8	E950.9	E962.1	E980.9
propyl	980.3	E860.4	—	E950.9	E962.1	E980.9
secondary	980.2	E860.3	—	E950.9	E962.1	E980.9
radiator	980.1	E860.2	—	E950.9	E962.1	E980.9
rubbing	980.2	E860.3	—	E950.9	E962.1	E980.9
specified type NEC	980.8	E860.8	—	E950.9	E962.1	E980.9
surgical	980.9	E860.9	—	E950.9	E962.1	E980.9
vapor (from any type of alcohol)	987.8	E869.8	—	E952.8	E962.2	E982.8
wood	980.1	E860.2	—	E950.9	E962.1	E980.9
Alcuronium chloride	975.2	E858.6	E945.2	E950.4	E962.0	E980.4
Aldactone	974.4	E858.5	E944.4	E950.4	E962.0	E980.4
Aldicarb	989.3	E863.2	—	E950.6	E962.1	E980.7
Aldomet	972.6	E858.3	E942.6	E950.4	E962.0	E980.4
Aldosterone	962.0	E858.0	E932.0	E950.4	E962.0	E980.4
Aldrin (dust)	989.2	E863.0	—	E950.6	E962.1	E980.7
Algeldrate	973.0	E858.4	E943.0	E950.4	E962.0	E980.4
Alidase	963.4	E858.1	E933.4	E950.4	E962.0	E980.4
Aliphatic thiocyanates	989.0	E866.8	—	E950.9	E962.1	E980.9
Alkaline antiseptic solution (aromatic)	976.6	E858.7	E946.6	E950.4	E962.0	E980.4

☑ Additional Digit Required — Refer to the Tabular List for Digit Selection

Subterms under main terms may continue to next column or page

		External Cause (E-Code)				
	Poisoning	**Accident**	**Therapeutic Use**	**Suicide Attempt**	**Assault**	**Undetermined**
Alkalinizing agents (medicinal)	963.3	E858.1	E933.3	E950.4	E962.0	E980.4
Alkalis, caustic	983.2	E864.2	—	E950.7	E962.1	E980.6
Alkalizing agents (medicinal)	963.3	E858.1	E933.3	E950.4	E962.0	E980.4
Alka-seltzer	965.1	E850.3	E935.3	E950.0	E962.0	E980.0
Alkavervir	972.6	E858.3	E942.6	E950.4	E962.0	E980.4
Allegron	969.0	E854.0	E939.0	E950.3	E962.0	E980.3
Alleve — Naproxen						
Allobarbital, allobarbitone	967.0	E851	E937.0	E950.1	E962.0	E980.1
Allopurinol	974.7	E858.5	E944.7	E950.4	E962.0	E980.4
Allylestrenol	962.2	E858.0	E932.2	E950.4	E962.0	E980.4
Allylisopropylacetylurea	967.8	E852.8	E937.8	E950.2	E962.0	E980.2
Allylisopropylmalonylurea	967.0	E851	E937.0	E950.1	E962.0	E980.1
Allyltribromide	967.3	E852.2	E937.3	E950.2	E962.0	E980.2
Aloe, aloes, aloin	973.1	E858.4	E943.1	E950.4	E962.0	E980.4
Alosetron	973.8	E858.4	E943.8	E950.4	E962.0	E980.4
Aloxidone	966.0	E855.0	E936.0	E950.4	E962.0	E980.4
Aloxiprin	965.1	E850.3	E935.3	E950.0	E962.0	E980.0
Alpha amylase	963.4	E858.1	E933.4	E950.4	E962.0	E980.4
Alphaprodine (hydrochloride)	965.09	E850.2	E935.2	E950.0	E962.0	E980.0
Alpha tocopherol	963.5	E858.1	E933.5	E950.4	E962.0	E980.4
Alseroxylon	972.6	E858.3	E942.6	E950.4	E962.0	E980.4
Alum (ammonium) (potassium)	983.2	E864.2	—	E950.7	E962.1	E980.6
medicinal (astringent) NEC	976.2	E858.7	E946.2	E950.4	E962.0	E980.4
Aluminium, aluminum (gel) (hydroxide)	973.0	E858.4	E943.0	E950.4	E962.0	E980.4
acetate solution	976.2	E858.7	E946.2	E950.4	E962.0	E980.4
aspirin	965.1	E850.3	E935.3	E950.0	E962.0	E980.0
carbonate	973.0	E858.4	E943.0	E950.4	E962.0	E980.4
glycinate	973.0	E858.4	E943.0	E950.4	E962.0	E980.4
nicotinate	972.2	E858.3	E942.2	E950.4	E962.0	E980.4
ointment (surgical) (topical)	976.3	E858.7	E946.3	E950.4	E962.0	E980.4
phosphate	973.0	E858.4	E943.0	E950.4	E962.0	E980.4
subacetate	976.2	E858.7	E946.2	E950.4	E962.0	E980.4
topical NEC	976.3	E858.7	E946.3	E950.4	E962.0	E980.4
Alurate	967.0	E851	E937.0	E950.1	E962.0	E980.1
Alverine (citrate)	975.1	E858.6	E945.1	E950.4	E962.0	E980.4
Alvodine	965.09	E850.2	E935.2	E950.0	E962.0	E980.0
Amanita phalloides	988.1	E865.5	—	E950.9	E962.1	E980.9
Amantadine (hydrochloride)	966.4	E855.0	E936.4	E950.4	E962.0	E980.4
Ambazone	961.9	E857	E931.9	E950.4	E962.0	E980.4
Ambenonium	971.0	E855.3	E941.0	E950.4	E962.0	E980.4
Ambutonium bromide	971.1	E855.4	E941.1	E950.4	E962.0	E980.4
Ametazole	977.8	E858.8	E947.8	E950.4	E962.0	E980.4
Amethocaine (infiltration) (topical)	968.5	E855.2	E938.5	E950.4	E962.0	E980.4
nerve block (peripheral) (plexus)	968.6	E855.2	E938.6	E950.4	E962.0	E980.4
spinal	968.7	E855.2	E938.7	E950.4	E962.0	E980.4
Amethopterin	963.1	E858.1	E933.1	E950.4	E962.0	E980.4
Amfepramone	977.0	E858.8	E947.0	E950.4	E962.0	E980.4
Amidon	965.02	E850.1	E935.1	E950.0	E962.0	E980.0
Amidopyrine	965.5	E850.5	E935.5	E950.0	E962.0	E980.0
Aminacrine	976.0	E858.7	E946.0	E950.4	E962.0	E980.4
Aminitrozole	961.5	E857	E931.5	E950.4	E962.0	E980.4
Aminoacetic acid	974.5	E858.5	E944.5	E950.4	E962.0	E980.4
Amino acids	974.5	E858.5	E944.5	E950.4	E962.0	E980.4
Aminocaproic acid	964.4	E858.2	E934.4	E950.4	E962.0	E980.4
Aminoethylisothiourium	963.8	E858.1	E933.8	E950.4	E962.0	E980.4
Aminoglutethimide	966.3	E855.0	E936.3	E950.4	E962.0	E980.4
Aminometradine	974.3	E858.5	E944.3	E950.4	E962.0	E980.4
Aminopentamide	971.1	E855.4	E941.1	E950.4	E962.0	E980.4
Aminophenazone	965.5	E850.5	E935.5	E950.0	E962.0	E980.0
Aminophenol	983.0	E864.0	—	E950.7	E962.1	E980.6
Aminophenylpyridone	969.5	E853.8	E939.5	E950.3	E962.0	E980.3
Aminophyllin	975.7	E858.6	E945.7	E950.4	E962.0	E980.4
Aminopterin	963.1	E858.1	E933.1	E950.4	E962.0	E980.4
Aminopyrine	965.5	E850.5	E935.5	E950.0	E962.0	E980.0
Aminosalicylic acid	961.8	E857	E931.8	E950.4	E962.0	E980.4
Amiphenazole	970.1	E854.3	E940.1	E950.4	E962.0	E980.4
Amiquinsin	972.6	E858.3	E942.6	E950.4	E962.0	E980.4
Amisometradine	974.3	E858.5	E944.3	E950.4	E962.0	E980.4
Amitriptyline	969.0	E854.0	E939.0	E950.3	E962.0	E980.3
Ammonia (fumes) (gas) (vapor)	987.8	E869.8	—	E952.8	E962.2	E982.8
liquid (household) NEC	983.2	E861.4	—	E950.7	E962.1	E980.6
spirit, aromatic	970.8	E854.3	E940.8	E950.4	E962.0	E980.4
Ammoniated mercury	976.0	E858.7	E946.0	E950.4	E962.0	E980.4
Ammonium						
carbonate	983.2	E864.2	—	E950.7	E962.1	E980.6
chloride (acidifying agent)	963.2	E858.1	E933.2	E950.4	E962.0	E980.4
expectorant	975.5	E858.6	E945.5	E950.4	E962.0	E980.4
compounds (household) NEC	983.2	E861.4	—	E950.7	E962.1	E980.6
fumes (any usage)	987.8	E869.8	—	E952.8	E962.2	E982.8
industrial	983.2	E864.2	—	E950.7	E962.1	E980.6
ichthyosulfonate	976.4	E858.7	E946.4	E950.4	E962.0	E980.4
mandelate	961.9	E857	E931.9	E950.4	E962.0	E980.4
Amobarbital	967.0	E851	E937.0	E950.1	E962.0	E980.1
Amodiaquin(e)	961.4	E857	E931.4	E950.4	E962.0	E980.4
Amopyroquin(e)	961.4	E857	E931.4	E950.4	E962.0	E980.4
Amphenidone	969.5	E853.8	E939.5	E950.3	E962.0	E980.3
Amphetamine	969.7	E854.2	E939.7	E950.3	E962.0	E980.3
Amphomycin	960.8	E856	E930.8	E950.4	E962.0	E980.4
Amphotericin B	960.1	E856	E930.1	E950.4	E962.0	E980.4
topical	976.0	E858.7	E946.0	E950.4	E962.0	E980.4
Ampicillin	960.0	E856	E930.0	E950.4	E962.0	E980.4
Amprotropine	971.1	E855.4	E941.1	E950.4	E962.0	E980.4
Amygdalin	977.8	E858.8	E947.8	E950.4	E962.0	E980.4
Amyl						
acetate (vapor)	982.8	E862.4	—	E950.9	E962.1	E980.9
alcohol	980.3	E860.4	—	E950.9	E962.1	E980.9
nitrite (medicinal)	972.4	E858.3	E942.4	E950.4	E962.0	E980.4
Amylase (alpha)	963.4	E858.1	E933.4	E950.4	E962.0	E980.4
Amylene hydrate	980.8	E860.8	—	E950.9	E962.1	E980.9
Amylobarbitone	967.0	E851	E937.0	E950.1	E962.0	E980.1
Amylocaine	968.9	E855.2	E938.9	E950.4	E962.0	E980.4
infiltration (subcutaneous)	968.5	E855.2	E938.5	E950.4	E962.0	E980.4
nerve block (peripheral) (plexus)	968.6	E855.2	E938.6	E950.4	E962.0	E980.4
spinal	968.7	E855.2	E938.7	E950.4	E962.0	E980.4
topical (surface)	968.5	E855.2	E938.5	E950.4	E962.0	E980.4
Amytal (sodium)	967.0	E851	E937.0	E950.1	E962.0	E980.1
Analeptics	970.0	E854.3	E940.0	E950.4	E962.0	E980.4
Analgesics	965.9	E850.9	E935.9	E950.0	E962.0	E980.0
aromatic NEC	965.4	E850.4	E935.4	E950.0	E962.0	E980.0
non-narcotic NEC	965.7	E850.7	E935.7	E950.0	E962.0	E980.0
specified NEC	965.8	E850.8	E935.8	E950.0	E962.0	E980.0
Anamirta cocculus	988.2	E865.3	—	E950.9	E962.1	E980.9
Ancillin	960.0	E856	E930.0	E950.4	E962.0	E980.4
Androgens (anabolic congeners)	962.1	E858.0	E932.1	E950.4	E962.0	E980.4
Androstalone	962.1	E858.0	E932.1	E950.4	E962.0	E980.4
Androsterone	962.1	E858.0	E932.1	E950.4	E962.0	E980.4
Anemone pulsatilla	988.2	E865.4	—	E950.9	E962.1	E980.9
Anesthesia, anesthetic (general) NEC	968.4	E855.1	E938.4	E950.4	E962.0	E980.4
block (nerve) (plexus)	968.6	E855.2	E938.6	E950.4	E962.0	E980.4
gaseous NEC	968.2	E855.1	E938.2	E950.4	E962.0	E980.4
halogenated hydrocarbon derivatives NEC	968.2	E855.1	E938.2	E950.4	E962.0	E980.4
infiltration (intradermal) (subcutaneous) (submucosal)	968.5	E855.2	E938.5	E950.4	E962.0	E980.4
intravenous	968.3	E855.1	E938.3	E950.4	E962.0	E980.4
local NEC	968.9	E855.2	E938.9	E950.4	E962.0	E980.4
nerve blocking (peripheral) (plexus)	968.6	E855.2	E938.6	E950.4	E962.0	E980.4
rectal NEC	968.3	E855.1	E938.3	E950.4	E962.0	E980.4
spinal	968.7	E855.2	E938.7	E950.4	E962.0	E980.4
surface	968.5	E855.2	E938.5	E950.4	E962.0	E980.4
topical	968.5	E855.2	E938.5	E950.4	E962.0	E980.4
Aneurine	963.5	E858.1	E933.5	E950.4	E962.0	E980.4
Anginine — *see* Glyceryl trinitrate						
Angio-Conray	977.8	E858.8	E947.8	E950.4	E962.0	E980.4
Angiotensin	971.2	E855.5	E941.2	E950.4	E962.0	E980.4
Anhydrohydroxyprogesterone	962.2	E858.0	E932.2	E950.4	E962.0	E980.4
Anhydron	974.3	E858.5	E944.3	E950.4	E962.0	E980.4
Anileridine	965.09	E850.2	E935.2	E950.0	E962.0	E980.0
Aniline (dye) (liquid)	983.0	E864.0	—	E950.7	E962.1	E980.6
analgesic	965.4	E850.4	E935.4	E950.0	E962.0	E980.0
derivatives, therapeutic NEC	965.4	E850.4	E935.4	E950.0	E962.0	E980.0
vapor	987.8	E869.8	—	E952.8	E962.2	E982.8
Aniscoropine	971.1	E855.4	E941.1	E950.4	E962.0	E980.4
Anisindione	964.2	E858.2	E934.2	E950.4	E962.0	E980.4
Anorexic agents	977.0	E858.8	E947.0	E950.4	E962.0	E980.4

☑ Additional Digit Required — Refer to the Tabular List for Digit Selection

▽ Subterms under main terms may continue to next column or page

		External Cause (E-Code)				
	Poisoning	Accident	Therapeutic Use	Suicide Attempt	Assault	Undetermined
Ant (bite) (sting)	—	E905.5	—	E950.9	E962.1	E980.9
Antabuse	977.3	E858.8	E947.3	E950.4	E962.0	E980.4
Antacids	973.0	E858.4	E943.0	E950.4	E962.0	E980.4
Antazoline	963.0	E858.1	E933.0	E950.4	E962.0	E980.4
Anthralin	976.4	E858.7	E946.4	E950.4	E962.0	E980.4
Anthramycin	960.7	E856	E930.7	E950.4	E962.0	E980.4
Antiadrenergics	971.3	E855.6	E941.3	E950.4	E962.0	E980.4
Antiallergic agents	963.0	E858.1	E933.0	E950.4	E962.0	E980.4
Antianemic agents NEC	964.1	E858.2	E934.1	E950.4	E962.0	E980.4
Antiaris toxicaria	988.2	E865.4	—	E950.9	E962.1	E980.9
Antiarteriosclerotic agents	972.2	E858.3	E942.2	E950.4	E962.0	E980.4
Antiasthmatics	975.7	E858.6	E945.7	E950.4	E962.0	E980.4
Antibiotics	960.9	E856	E930.9	E950.4	E962.0	E980.4
antifungal	960.1	E856	E930.1	E950.4	E962.0	E980.4
antimycobacterial	960.6	E856	E930.6	E950.4	E962.0	E980.4
antineoplastic	960.7	E856	E930.7	E950.4	E962.0	E980.4
cephalosporin (group)	960.5	E856	E930.5	E950.4	E962.0	E980.4
chloramphenicol (group)	960.2	E856	E930.2	E950.4	E962.0	E980.4
macrolides	960.3	E856	E930.3	E950.4	E962.0	E980.4
specified NEC	960.8	E856	E930.8	E950.4	E962.0	E980.4
tetracycline (group)	960.4	E856	E930.4	E950.4	E962.0	E980.4
Anticancer agents NEC	963.1	E858.1	E933.1	E950.4	E962.0	E980.4
antibiotics	960.7	E856	E930.7	E950.4	E962.0	E980.4
Anticholinergics	971.1	E855.4	E941.1	E950.4	E962.0	E980.4
Anticholinesterase (organophosphorus) (reversible)	971.0	E855.3	E941.0	E950.4	E962.0	E980.4
Anticoagulants	964.2	E858.2	E934.2	E950.4	E962.0	E980.4
antagonists	964.5	E858.2	E934.5	E950.4	E962.0	E980.4
Anti-common cold agents NEC	975.6	E858.6	E945.6	E950.4	E962.0	E980.4
Anticonvulsants NEC	966.3	E855.0	E936.3	E950.4	E962.0	E980.4
Antidepressants	969.0	E854.0	E939.0	E950.3	E962.0	E980.3
Antidiabetic agents	962.3	E858.0	E932.3	E950.4	E962.0	E980.4
Antidiarrheal agents	973.5	E858.4	E943.5	E950.4	E962.0	E980.4
Antidiuretic hormone	962.5	E858.0	E932.5	E950.4	E962.0	E980.4
Antidotes NEC	977.2	E858.8	E947.2	E950.4	E962.0	E980.4
Antiemetic agents	963.0	E858.1	E933.0	E950.4	E962.0	E980.4
Antiepilepsy agent NEC	966.3	E855.0	E936.3	E950.4	E962.0	E980.4
Antifertility pills	962.2	E858.0	E932.2	E950.4	E962.0	E980.4
Antiflatulents	973.8	E858.4	E943.8	E950.4	E962.0	E980.4
Antifreeze	989.89	E866.8	—	E950.9	E962.1	E980.9
alcohol	980.1	E860.2	—	E950.9	E962.1	E980.9
ethylene glycol	982.8	E862.4	—	E950.9	E962.1	E980.9
Antifungals (nonmedicinal) (sprays)	989.4	E863.6	—	E950.6	E962.1	E980.7
medicinal NEC	961.9	E857	E931.9	E950.4	E962.0	E980.4
antibiotic	960.1	E856	E930.1	E950.4	E962.0	E980.4
topical	976.0	E858.7	E946.0	E950.4	E962.0	E980.4
Antigastric secretion agents	973.0	E858.4	E943.0	E950.4	E962.0	E980.4
Antihelmintics	961.6	E857	E931.6	E950.4	E962.0	E980.4
Antihemophilic factor (human)	964.7	E858.2	E934.7	E950.4	E962.0	E980.4
Antihistamine	963.0	E858.1	E933.0	E950.4	E962.0	E980.4
Antihypertensive agents NEC	972.6	E858.3	E942.6	E950.4	E962.0	E980.4
Anti-infectives NEC	961.9	E857	E931.9	E950.4	E962.0	E980.4
antibiotics	960.9	E856	E930.9	E950.4	E962.0	E980.4
specified NEC	960.8	E856	E930.8	E950.4	E962.0	E980.4
antihelmintic	961.6	E857	E931.6	E950.4	E962.0	E980.4
antimalarial	961.4	E857	E931.4	E950.4	E962.0	E980.4
antimycobacterial NEC	961.8	E857	E931.8	E950.4	E962.0	E980.4
antibiotics	960.6	E856	E930.6	E950.4	E962.0	E980.4
antiprotozoal NEC	961.5	E857	E931.5	E950.4	E962.0	—
blood	961.4	E857	E931.4	E950.4	E962.0	E980.4
antiviral	961.7	E857	E931.7	E950.4	E962.0	E980.4
arsenical	961.1	E857	E931.1	E950.4	E962.0	E980.4
ENT agents	976.6	E858.7	E946.6	E950.4	E962.0	E980.4
heavy metals NEC	961.2	E857	E931.2	E950.4	E962.0	E980.4
local	976.0	E858.7	E946.0	E950.4	E962.0	E980.4
ophthalmic preparation	976.5	E858.7	E946.5	E950.4	E962.0	E980.4
topical NEC	976.0	E858.7	E946.0	E950.4	E962.0	E980.4
Anti-inflammatory agents (topical)	976.0	E858.7	E946.0	E950.4	E962.0	E980.4
Antiknock (tetraethyl lead)	984.1	E862.1	—	E950.9	—	E980.9
Antilipemics	972.2	E858.3	E942.2	E950.4	E962.0	E980.4
Antimalarials	961.4	E857	E931.4	E950.4	E962.0	E980.4
Antimony (compounds) (vapor) NEC	985.4	E866.2	—	E950.9	E962.1	E980.9
Antimony (compounds) (vapor) — *continued*						
anti-infectives	961.2	E857	E931.2	E950.4	E962.0	E980.4
pesticides (vapor)	985.4	E863.4	—	E950.6	E962.2	E980.7
potassium tartrate	961.2	E857	E931.2	E950.4	E962.0	E980.4
tartrated	961.2	E857	E931.2	E950.4	E962.0	E980.4
Antimuscarinic agents	971.1	E855.4	E941.1	E950.4	E962.0	E980.4
Antimycobacterials NEC	961.8	E857	E931.8	E950.4	E962.0	E980.4
antibiotics	960.6	E856	E930.6	E950.4	E962.0	E980.4
Antineoplastic agents	963.1	E858.1	E933.1	E950.4	E962.0	E980.4
antibiotics	960.7	E856	E930.7	E950.4	E962.0	E980.4
Anti-Parkinsonism agents	966.4	E855.0	E936.4	E950.4	E962.0	E980.4
Antiphlogistics	965.69	E850.6	E935.6	E950.0	E962.0	E980.0
Antiprotozoals NEC	961.5	E857	E931.5	E950.4	E962.0	E980.4
blood	961.4	E857	E931.4	E950.4	E962.0	E980.4
Antipruritics (local)	976.1	E858.7	E946.1	E950.4	E962.0	E980.4
Antipsychotic agents NEC	969.3	E853.8	E939.3	E950.3	E962.0	E980.3
Antipyretics	965.9	E850.9	E935.9	E950.0	E962.0	E980.0
specified NEC	965.8	E850.8	E935.8	E950.0	E962.0	E980.0
Antipyrine	965.5	E850.5	E935.5	E950.0	E962.0	E980.0
Antirabies serum (equine)	979.9	E858.8	E949.9	E950.4	E962.0	E980.4
Antirheumatics	965.69	E850.6	E935.6	E950.0	E962.0	E980.0
Antiseborrheics	976.4	E858.7	E946.4	E950.4	E962.0	E980.4
Antiseptics (external) (medicinal)	976.0	E858.7	E946.0	E950.4	E962.0	E980.4
Antistine	963.0	E858.1	E933.0	E950.4	E962.0	E980.4
Antithyroid agents	962.8	E858.0	E932.8	E950.4	E962.0	E980.4
Antitoxin, any	979.9	E858.8	E949.9	E950.4	E962.0	E980.4
Antituberculars	961.8	E857	E931.8	E950.4	E962.0	E980.4
antibiotics	960.6	E856	E930.6	E950.4	E962.0	E980.4
Antitussives	975.4	E858.6	E945.4	E950.4	E962.0	E980.4
Antivaricose agents (sclerosing)	972.7	E858.3	E942.7	E950.4	E962.0	E980.4
Antivenin (crotaline) (spider-bite)	979.9	E858.8	E949.9	E950.4	E962.0	E980.4
Antivert	963.0	E858.1	E933.0	E950.4	E962.0	E980.4
Antivirals NEC	961.7	E857	E931.7	E950.4	E962.0	E980.4
Ant poisons — *see* Pesticides						
Antrol	989.4	E863.4	—	E950.6	E962.1	E980.7
fungicide	989.4	E863.6	—	E950.6	E962.1	E980.7
Apomorphine hydrochloride (emetic)	973.6	E858.4	E943.6	E950.4	E962.0	E980.4
Appetite depressants, central	977.0	E858.8	E947.0	E950.4	E962.0	E980.4
Apresoline	972.6	E858.3	E942.6	E950.4	E962.0	E980.4
Aprobarbital, aprobarbitone	967.0	E851	E937.0	E950.1	E962.0	E980.1
Apronalide	967.8	E852.8	E937.8	E950.2	E962.0	E980.2
Aqua fortis	983.1	E864.1	—	E950.7	E962.1	E980.6
Arachis oil (topical)	976.3	E858.7	E946.3	E950.4	E962.0	E980.4
cathartic	973.2	E858.4	E943.2	E950.4	E962.0	E980.4
Aralen	961.4	E857	E931.4	E950.4	E962.0	E980.4
Arginine salts	974.5	E858.5	E944.5	E950.4	E962.0	E980.4
Argyrol	976.0	E858.7	E946.0	E950.4	E962.0	E980.4
ENT agent	976.6	E858.7	E946.6	E950.4	E962.0	E980.4
ophthalmic preparation	976.5	E858.7	E946.5	E950.4	E962.0	E980.4
Aristocort	962.0	E858.0	E932.0	E950.4	E962.0	E980.4
ENT agent	976.6	E858.7	E946.6	E950.4	E962.0	E980.4
ophthalmic preparation	976.5	E858.7	E946.5	E950.4	E962.0	E980.4
topical NEC	976.0	E858.7	E946.0	E950.4	E962.0	E980.4
Aromatics, corrosive	983.0	E864.0	—	E950.7	E962.1	E980.6
disinfectants	983.0	E861.4	—	E950.7	E962.1	E980.6
Arsenate of lead (insecticide)	985.1	E863.4	—	E950.8	E962.1	E980.8
herbicide	985.1	E863.5	—	E950.8	E962.1	E980.8
Arsenic, arsenicals (compounds) (dust) (fumes) (vapor) NEC	985.1	E866.3	—	E950.8	E962.1	E980.8
anti-infectives	961.1	E857	E931.1	E950.4	E962.0	E980.4
pesticide (dust) (fumes)	985.1	E863.4	—	E950.8	E962.1	E980.8
Arsine (gas)	985.1	E866.3	—	E950.8	E962.1	E980.8
Arsphenamine (silver)	961.1	E857	E931.1	E950.4	E962.0	E980.4
Arsthinol	961.1	E857	E931.1	E950.4	E962.0	E980.4
Artane	971.1	E855.4	E941.1	E950.4	E962.0	E980.4
Arthropod (venomous) NEC	989.5	E905.5	—	E950.9	E962.1	E980.9
Asbestos	989.81	E866.8	—	E950.9	E962.1	E980.9
Ascaridole	961.6	E857	E931.6	E950.4	E962.0	E980.4
Ascorbic acid	963.5	E858.1	E933.5	E950.4	E962.0	E980.4
Asiaticoside	976.0	E858.7	E946.0	E950.4	E962.0	E980.4
Aspidium (oleoresin)	961.6	E857	E931.6	E950.4	E962.0	E980.4

		External Cause (E-Code)				
	Poisoning	Accident	Therapeutic Use	Suicide Attempt	Assault	Undetermined
Aspirin	965.1	E850.3	E935.3	E950.0	E962.0	E980.0
Astringents (local)	976.2	E858.7	E946.2	E950.4	E962.0	E980.4
Atabrine	961.3	E857	E931.3	E950.4	E962.0	E980.4
Ataractics	969.5	E853.8	E939.5	E950.3	E962.0	E980.3
Atonia drug, intestinal	973.3	E858.4	E943.3	E950.4	E962.0	E980.4
Atophan	974.7	E858.5	E944.7	E950.4	E962.0	E980.4
Atropine	971.1	E855.4	E941.1	E950.4	E962.0	E980.4
Attapulgite	973.5	E858.4	E943.5	E950.4	E962.0	E980.4
Attenuvax	979.4	E858.8	E949.4	E950.4	E962.0	E980.4
Aureomycin	960.4	E856	E930.4	E950.4	E962.0	E980.4
ophthalmic preparation	976.5	E858.7	E946.5	E950.4	E962.0	E980.4
topical NEC	976.0	E858.7	E946.0	E950.4	E962.0	E980.4
Aurothioglucose	965.69	E850.6	E935.6	E950.0	E962.0	E980.0
Aurothioglycanide	965.69	E850.6	E935.6	E950.0	E962.0	E980.0
Aurothiomalate	965.69	E850.6	E935.6	E950.0	E962.0	E980.0
Automobile fuel	981	E862.1	—	E950.9	E962.1	E980.9
Autonomic nervous system agents NEC	971.9	E855.9	E941.9	E950.4	E962.0	E980.4
Avlosulfon	961.8	E857	E931.8	E950.4	E962.0	E980.4
Avomine	967.8	E852.8	E937.8	E950.2	E962.0	E980.2
Azacyclonol	969.5	E853.8	E939.5	E950.3	E962.0	E980.3
Azapetine	971.3	E855.6	E941.3	E950.4	E962.0	E980.4
Azaribine	963.1	E858.1	E933.1	E950.4	E962.0	E980.4
Azaserine	960.7	E856	E930.7	E950.4	E962.0	E980.4
Azathioprine	963.1	E858.1	E933.1	E950.4	E962.0	E980.4
Azosulfamide	961.0	E857	E931.0	E950.4	E962.0	E980.4
Azulfidine	961.0	E857	E931.0	E950.4	E962.0	E980.4
Azuresin	977.8	E858.8	E947.8	E950.4	E962.0	E980.4
Bacimycin	976.0	E858.7	E946.0	E950.4	E962.0	E980.4
ophthalmic preparation	976.5	E858.7	E946.5	E950.4	E962.0	E980.4
Bacitracin	960.8	E856	E930.8	E950.4	E962.0	E980.4
ENT agent	976.6	E858.7	E946.6	E950.4	E962.0	E980.4
ophthalmic preparation	976.5	E858.7	E946.5	E950.4	E962.0	E980.4
topical NEC	976.0	E858.7	E946.0	E950.4	E962.0	E980.4
Baking soda	963.3	E858.1	E933.3	E950.4	E962.0	E980.4
BAL	963.8	E858.1	E933.8	E950.4	E962.0	E980.4
Bamethan (sulfate)	972.5	E858.3	E942.5	E950.4	E962.0	E980.4
Bamipine	963.0	E858.1	E933.0	E950.4	E962.0	E980.4
Baneberry	988.2	E865.4	—	E950.9	E962.1	E980.9
Banewort	988.2	E865.4	—	E950.9	E962.1	E980.9
Barbenyl	967.0	E851	E937.0	E950.1	E962.0	E980.1
Barbital, barbitone	967.0	E851	E937.0	E950.1	E962.0	E980.1
Barbiturates, barbituric acid	967.0	E851	E937.0	E950.1	E962.0	E980.1
anesthetic (intravenous)	968.3	E855.1	E938.3	E950.4	E962.0	E980.4
Barium (carbonate) (chloride) (sulfate)	985.8	E866.4	—	E950.9	E962.1	E980.9
diagnostic agent	977.8	E858.8	E947.8	E950.4	E962.0	E980.4
pesticide	985.8	E863.4	—	E950.6	E962.1	E980.7
rodenticide	985.8	E863.7	—	E950.6	E962.1	E980.7
Barrier cream	976.3	E858.7	E946.3	E950.4	E962.0	E980.4
Battery acid or fluid	983.1	E864.1	—	E950.7	E962.1	E980.6
Bay rum	980.8	E860.8	—	E950.9	E962.1	E980.9
BCG vaccine	978.0	E858.8	E948.0	E950.4	E962.0	E980.4
Bearsfoot	988.2	E865.4	—	E950.9	E962.1	E980.9
Beclamide	966.3	E855.0	E936.3	E950.4	E962.0	E980.4
Bee (sting) (venom)	989.5	E905.3	—	E950.9	E962.1	E980.9
Belladonna (alkaloids)	971.1	E855.4	E941.1	E950.4	E962.0	E980.4
Bemegride	970.0	E854.3	E940.0	E950.4	E962.0	E980.4
Benactyzine	969.8	E855.8	E939.8	E950.3	E962.0	E980.3
Benadryl	963.0	E858.1	E933.0	E950.4	E962.0	E980.4
Bendrofluazide	974.3	E858.5	E944.3	E950.4	E962.0	E980.4
Bendroflumethiazide	974.3	E858.5	E944.3	E950.4	E962.0	E980.4
Benemid	974.7	E858.5	E944.7	E950.4	E962.0	E980.4
Benethamine penicillin G	960.0	E856	E930.0	E950.4	E962.0	E980.4
Benisone	976.0	E858.7	E946.0	E950.4	E962.0	E980.4
Benoquin	976.8	E858.7	E946.8	E950.4	E962.0	E980.4
Benoxinate	968.5	E855.2	E938.5	E950.4	E962.0	E980.4
Bentonite	976.3	E858.7	E946.3	E950.4	E962.0	E980.4
Benzalkonium (chloride)	976.0	E858.7	E946.0	E950.4	E962.0	E980.4
ophthalmic preparation	976.5	E858.7	E946.5	E950.4	E962.0	E980.4
Benzamidosalicylate (calcium)	961.8	E857	E931.8	E950.4	E962.0	E980.4
Benzathine penicillin	960.0	E856	E930.0	E950.4	E962.0	E980.4
Benzcarbimine	963.1	E858.1	E933.1	E950.4	E962.0	E980.4
Benzedrex	971.2	E855.5	E941.2	E950.4	E962.0	E980.4
Benzedrine (amphetamine)	969.7	E854.2	E939.7	E950.3	E962.0	E980.3
Benzene (acetyl) (dimethyl) (methyl) (solvent) (vapor)	982.0	E862.4	—	E950.9	E962.1	E980.9
hexachloride (gamma) (insecticide) (vapor)	989.2	E863.0	—	E950.6	E962.1	E980.7

		External Cause (E-Code)				
	Poisoning	Accident	Therapeutic Use	Suicide Attempt	Assault	Undetermined
Benzethonium	976.0	E858.7	E946.0	E950.4	E962.0	E980.4
Benzhexol (chloride)	966.4	E855.0	E936.4	E950.4	E962.0	E980.4
Benzilonium	971.1	E855.4	E941.1	E950.4	E962.0	E980.4
Benzin(e) — *see* Ligroin						
Benziodarone	972.4	E858.3	E942.4	E950.4	E962.0	E980.4
Benzocaine	968.5	E855.2	E938.5	E950.4	E962.0	E980.4
Benzodiapin	969.4	E853.2	E939.4	E950.3	E962.0	E980.3
Benzodiazepines (tranquilizers) NEC	969.4	E853.2	E939.4	E950.3	E962.0	E980.3
Benzoic acid (with salicylic acid) (anti-infective)	976.0	E858.7	E946.0	E950.4	E962.0	E980.4
Benzoin	976.3	E858.7	E946.3	E950.4	E962.0	E980.4
Benzol (vapor)	982.0	E862.4	—	E950.9	E962.1	E980.9
Benzomorphan	965.09	E850.2	E935.2	E950.0	E962.0	E980.0
Benzonatate	975.4	E858.6	E945.4	E950.4	E962.0	E980.4
Benzothiadiazides	974.3	E858.5	E944.3	E950.4	E962.0	E980.4
Benzoylpas	961.8	E857	E931.8	E950.4	E962.0	E980.4
Benzperidol	969.5	E853.8	E939.5	E950.3	E962.0	E980.3
Benzphetamine	977.0	E858.8	E947.0	E950.4	E962.0	E980.4
Benzpyrinium	971.0	E855.3	E941.0	E950.4	E962.0	E980.4
Benzquinamide	963.0	E858.1	E933.0	E950.4	E962.0	E980.4
Benzthiazide	974.3	E858.5	E944.3	E950.4	E962.0	E980.4
Benztropine	971.1	E855.4	E941.1	E950.4	E962.0	E980.4
Benzyl						
acetate	982.8	E862.4	—	E950.9	E962.1	E980.9
benzoate (anti-infective)	976.0	E858.7	E946.0	E950.4	E962.0	E980.4
morphine	965.09	E850.2	E935.2	E950.0	E962.0	E980.0
penicillin	960.0	E856	E930.0	E950.4	E962.0	E980.4
Bephenium hydroxynapthoate	961.6	E857	E931.6	E950.4	E962.0	E980.4
Bergamot oil	989.89	E866.8	—	E950.9	E962.1	E980.9
Berries, poisonous	988.2	E865.3	—	E950.9	E962.1	E980.9
Beryllium (compounds) (fumes)	985.3	E866.4	—	E950.9	E962.1	E980.9
Beta-carotene	976.3	E858.7	E946.3	E950.4	E962.0	E980.4
Beta-Chlor	967.1	E852.0	E937.1	E950.2	E962.0	E980.2
Betamethasone	962.0	E858.0	E932.0	E950.4	E962.0	E980.4
topical	976.0	E858.7	E946.0	E950.4	E962.0	E980.4
Betazole	977.8	E858.8	E947.8	E950.4	E962.0	E980.4
Bethanechol	971.0	E855.3	E941.0	E950.4	E962.0	E980.4
Bethanidine	972.6	E858.3	E942.6	E950.4	E962.0	E980.4
Betula oil	976.3	E858.7	E946.3	E950.4	E962.0	E980.4
Bhang	969.6	E854.1	E939.6	E950.3	E962.0	E980.3
Bialamicol	961.5	E857	E931.5	E950.4	E962.0	E980.4
Bichloride of mercury — *see* Mercury, chloride						
Bichromates (calcium) (crystals) (potassium) (sodium)	983.9	E864.3	—	E950.7	E962.1	E980.6
fumes	987.8	E869.8	—	E952.8	E962.2	E982.8
Biguanide derivatives, oral	962.3	E858.0	E932.3	E950.4	E962.0	E980.4
Biligrafin	977.8	E858.8	E947.8	E950.4	E962.0	E980.4
Bilopaque	977.8	E858.8	E947.8	E950.4	E962.0	E980.4
Bioflavonoids	972.8	E858.3	E942.8	E950.4	E962.0	E980.4
Biological substance NEC	979.9	E858.8	E949.9	E950.4	E962.0	E980.4
Biperiden	966.4	E855.0	E936.4	E950.4	E962.0	E980.4
Bisacodyl	973.1	E858.4	E943.1	E950.4	E962.0	E980.4
Bishydroxycoumarin	964.2	E858.2	E934.2	E950.4	E962.0	E980.4
Bismarsen	961.1	E857	E931.1	E950.4	E962.0	E980.4
Bismuth (compounds) NEC	985.8	E866.4	—	E950.9	E962.1	E980.9
anti-infectives	961.2	E857	E931.2	E950.4	E962.0	E980.4
subcarbonate	973.5	E858.4	E943.5	E950.4	E962.0	E980.4
sulfarsphenamine	961.1	E857	E931.1	E950.4	E962.0	E980.4
Bithionol	961.6	E857	E931.6	E950.4	E962.0	E980.4
Bitter almond oil	989.0	E866.8	—	E950.9	E962.1	E980.9
Bittersweet	988.2	E865.4	—	E950.9	E962.1	E930.9
Black						
flag	989.4	E863.4	—	E950.6	E962.1	E980.7
henbane	988.2	E865.4	—	E950.9	E962.1	E980.9
leaf (40)	989.4	E863.4	—	E950.6	E962.1	E980.7
widow spider (bite)	989.5	E905.1	—	E950.9	E962.1	E980.9
antivenin	979.9	E858.8	E949.9	E950.4	E962.0	E980.4
Blast furnace gas (carbon monoxide from)	986	E868.8	—	E952.1	E962.2	E982.1
Bleach NEC	983.9	E864.3	—	E950.7	E962.1	E980.6
Bleaching solutions	983.9	E864.3	—	E950.7	E962.1	E980.6
Bleomycin (sulfate)	960.7	E856	E930.7	E950.4	E962.0	E980.4
Blockain	968.9	E855.2	E938.9	E950.4	E962.0	E980.4
infiltration (subcutaneous)	968.5	E855.2	E938.5	E950.4	E962.0	E980.4

☑ Additional Digit Required — Refer to the Tabular List for Digit Selection

▼ Subterms under main terms may continue to next column or page

▶◀ Revised Text ● New Line ▲ Revised Code

	Poisoning	External Cause (E-Code) Accident	Therapeutic Use	Suicide Attempt	Assault	Undetermined
Blockain — *continued*						
nerve block (peripheral) (plexus)	968.6	E855.2	E938.6	E950.4	E962.0	E980.4
topical (surface)	968.5	E855.2	E938.5	E950.4	E962.0	E980.4
Blood (derivatives) (natural) (plasma) (whole)	964.7	E858.2	E934.7	E950.4	E962.0	E980.4
affecting agent	964.9	E858.2	E934.9	E950.4	E962.0	E980.4
specified NEC	964.8	E858.2	E934.8	E950.4	E962.0	E980.4
substitute (macromolecular)	964.8	E858.2	E934.8	E950.4	E962.0	E980.4
Blue velvet	965.09	E850.2	E935.2	E950.0	E962.0	E980.0
Bone meal	989.89	E866.5	—	E950.9	E962.1	E980.9
Bonine	963.0	E858.1	E933.0	E950.4	E962.0	E980.4
Boracic acid	976.0	E858.7	E946.0	E950.4	E962.0	E980.4
ENT agent	976.6	E858.7	E946.6	E950.4	E962.0	E980.4
ophthalmic preparation	976.5	E858.7	E946.5	E950.4	E962.0	E980.4
Borate (cleanser) (sodium)	989.6	E861.3	—	E950.9	E962.1	E980.9
Borax (cleanser)	989.6	E861.3	—	E950.9	E962.1	E980.9
Boric acid	976.0	E858.7	E946.0	E950.4	E962.0	E980.4
ENT agent	976.6	E858.7	E946.6	E950.4	E962.0	E980.4
ophthalmic preparation	976.5	E858.7	E946.5	E950.4	E962.0	E980.4
Boron hydride NEC	989.89	E866.8	—	E950.9	E962.1	E980.9
fumes or gas	987.8	E869.8	—	E952.8	E962.2	E982.8
Botox	975.3	E858.6	E945.3	E950.4	E962.0	E980.4
Brake fluid vapor	987.8	E869.8	—	E952.8	E962.2	E982.8
Brass (compounds) (fumes)	985.8	E866.4	—	E950.9	E962.1	E980.9
Brasso	981	E861.3	—	E950.9	E962.1	E980.9
Bretylium (tosylate)	972.6	E858.3	E942.6	E950.4	E962.0	E980.4
Brevital (sodium)	968.3	E855.1	E938.3	E950.4	E962.0	E980.4
British antilewisite	963.8	E858.1	E933.8	E950.4	E962.0	E980.4
Bromal (hydrate)	967.3	E852.2	E937.3	E950.2	E962.0	E980.2
Bromelains	963.4	E858.1	E933.4	E950.4	E962.0	E980.4
Bromides NEC	967.3	E852.2	E937.3	E950.2	E962.0	E980.2
Bromine (vapor)	987.8	E869.8	—	E952.8	E962.2	E982.8
compounds (medicinal)	967.3	E852.2	E937.3	E950.2	E962.0	E980.2
Bromisovalum	967.3	E852.2	E937.3	E950.2	E962.0	E980.2
Bromobenzyl cyanide	987.5	E869.3	—	E952.8	E962.2	E982.8
Bromodiphenhydramine	963.0	E858.1	E933.0	E950.4	E962.0	E980.4
Bromoform	967.3	E852.2	E937.3	E950.2	E962.0	E980.2
Bromophenol blue reagent	977.8	E858.8	E947.8	E950.4	E962.0	E980.4
Bromosalicylhydroxamic acid	961.8	E857	E931.8	E950.4	E962.0	E980.4
Bromo-seltzer	965.4	E850.4	E935.4	E950.0	E962.0	E980.0
Brompheniramine	963.0	E858.1	E933.0	E950.4	E962.0	E980.4
Bromural	967.3	E852.2	E937.3	E950.2	E962.0	E980.2
Brown spider (bite) (venom)	989.5	E905.1	—	E950.9	E962.1	E980.9
Brucia	988.2	E865.3	—	E950.9	E962.1	E980.9
Brucine	989.1	E863.7	—	E950.6	E962.1	E980.7
Brunswick green — *see* Copper						
Bruten — *see* Ibuprofen						
Bryonia (alba) (dioica)	988.2	E865.4	—	E950.9	E962.1	E980.9
Buclizine	969.5	E853.8	E939.5	E950.3	E962.0	E980.3
Bufferin	965.1	E850.3	E935.3	E950.0	E962.0	E980.0
Bufotenine	969.6	E854.1	E939.6	E950.3	E962.0	E980.3
Buphenine	971.2	E855.5	E941.2	E950.4	E962.0	E980.4
Bupivacaine	968.9	E855.2	E938.9	E950.4	E962.0	E980.4
infiltration (subcutaneous)	968.5	E855.2	E938.5	E950.4	E962.0	E980.4
nerve block (peripheral) (plexus)	968.6	E855.2	E938.6	E950.4	E962.0	E980.4
Busulfan	963.1	E858.1	E933.1	E950.4	E962.0	E980.4
Butabarbital (sodium)	967.0	E851	E937.0	E950.1	E962.0	E980.1
Butabarbitone	967.0	E851	E937.0	E950.1	E962.0	E980.1
Butabarpal	967.0	E851	E937.0	E950.1	E962.0	E980.1
Butacaine	968.5	E855.2	E938.5	E950.4	E962.0	E980.4
Butallylonal	967.0	E851	E937.0	E950.1	E962.0	E980.1
Butane (distributed in mobile container)	987.0	E868.0	—	E951.1	E962.2	E981.1
distributed through pipes	987.0	E867	—	E951.0	E962.2	E981.0
incomplete combustion of — see Carbon monoxide, butane						
Butanol	980.3	E860.4	—	E950.9	E962.1	E980.9
Butanone	982.8	E862.4	—	E950.9	E962.1	E980.9
Butaperazine	969.1	E853.0	E939.1	E950.3	E962.0	E980.3
Butazolidin	965.5	E850.5	E935.5	E950.0	E962.0	E980.0
Butethal	967.0	E851	E937.0	E950.1	E962.0	E980.1
Butethamate	971.1	E855.4	E941.1	E950.4	E962.0	E980.4
Buthalitone (sodium)	968.3	E855.1	E938.3	E950.4	E962.0	E980.4
Butisol (sodium)	967.0	E851	E937.0	E950.1	E962.0	E980.1
Butobarbital, butobarbitone	967.0	E851	E937.0	E950.1	E962.0	E980.1

	Poisoning	External Cause (E-Code) Accident	Therapeutic Use	Suicide Attempt	Assault	Undetermined
Butriptyline	969.0	E854.0	E939.0	E950.3	E962.0	E980.3
Buttercups	988.2	E865.4	—	E950.9	E962.1	E980.9
Butter of antimony — *see* Antimony						
Butyl						
acetate (secondary)	982.8	E862.4	—	E950.9	E962.1	E980.9
alcohol	980.3	E860.4	—	E950.9	E962.1	E980.9
carbinol	980.8	E860.8	—	E950.9	E962.1	E980.9
carbitol	982.8	E862.4	—	E950.9	E962.1	E980.9
cellosolve	982.8	E862.4	—	E950.9	E962.1	E980.9
chloral (hydrate)	967.1	E852.0	E937.1	E950.2	E962.0	E980.2
formate	982.8	E862.4	—	E950.9	E962.1	E980.9
scopolammonium bromide	971.1	E855.4	E941.1	E950.4	E962.0	E980.4
Butyn	968.5	E855.2	E938.5	E950.4	E962.0	E980.4
Butyrophenone (-based tranquilizers)	969.2	E853.1	E939.2	E950.3	E962.0	E980.3
Cacodyl, cacodylic acid — *see* Arsenic						
Cactinomycin	960.7	E856	E930.7	E950.4	E962.0	E980.4
Cade oil	976.4	E858.7	E946.4	E950.4	E962.0	E980.4
Cadmium (chloride) (compounds) (dust) (fumes) (oxide)	985.5	E866.4	—	E950.9	E962.1	E980.9
sulfide (medicinal) NEC	976.4	E858.7	E946.4	E950.4	E962.0	E980.4
Caffeine	969.7	E854.2	E939.7	E950.3	E962.0	E980.3
Calabar bean	988.2	E865.4	—	E950.9	E962.1	E980.9
Caladium seguinium	988.2	E865.4	—	E950.9	E962.1	E980.9
Calamine (liniment) (lotion)	976.3	E858.7	E946.3	E950.4	E962.0	E980.4
Calciferol	963.5	E858.1	E933.5	E950.4	E962.0	E980.4
Calcium (salts) NEC	974.5	E858.5	E944.5	E950.4	E962.0	E980.4
acetylsalicylate	965.1	E850.3	E935.3	E950.0	E962.0	E980.0
benzamidosalicylate	961.8	E857	E931.8	E950.4	E962.0	E980.4
carbaspirin	965.1	E850.3	E935.3	E950.0	E962.0	E980.0
carbimide (citrated)	977.3	E858.8	E947.3	E950.4	E962.0	E980.4
carbonate (antacid)	973.0	E858.4	E943.0	E950.4	E962.0	E980.4
cyanide (citrated)	977.3	E858.8	E947.3	E950.4	E962.0	E980.4
dioctyl sulfosuccinate	973.2	E858.4	E943.2	E950.4	E962.0	E980.4
disodium edathamil	963.8	E858.1	E933.8	E950.4	E962.0	E980.4
disodium edetate	963.8	E858.1	E933.8	E950.4	E962.0	E980.4
EDTA	963.8	E858.1	E933.8	E950.4	E962.0	E980.4
hydrate, hydroxide	983.2	E864.2	—	E950.7	E962.1	E980.6
mandelate	961.9	E857	E931.9	E950.4	E962.0	E980.4
oxide	983.2	E864.2	—	E950.7	E962.1	E980.6
Calomel — see Mercury, chloride						
Caloric agents NEC	974.5	E858.5	E944.5	E950.4	E962.0	E980.4
Calusterone	963.1	E858.1	E933.1	E950.4	E962.0	E980.4
Camoquin	961.4	E857	E931.4	E950.4	E962.0	E980.4
Camphor (oil)	976.1	E858.7	E946.1	E950.4	E962.0	E980.4
Candeptin	976.0	E858.7	E946.0	E950.4	E962.0	E980.4
Candicidin	976.0	E858.7	E946.0	E950.4	E962.0	E980.4
Cannabinols	969.6	E854.1	E939.6	E950.3	E962.0	E980.3
Cannabis (derivatives) (indica) (sativa)	969.6	E854.1	E939.6	E950.3	E962.0	E980.3
Canned heat	980.1	E860.2	—	E950.9	E962.1	E980.9
Cantharides, cantharidin, cantharis	976.8	E858.7	E946.8	E950.4	E962.0	E980.4
Capillary agents	972.8	E858.3	E942.8	E950.4	E962.0	E980.4
Capreomycin	960.6	E856	E930.6	E950.4	E962.0	E980.4
Captodiame, captodiamine	969.5	E853.8	E939.5	E950.3	E962.0	E980.3
Caramiphen (hydrochloride)	971.1	E855.4	E941.1	E950.4	E962.0	E980.4
Carbachol	971.0	E855.3	E941.0	E950.4	E962.0	E980.4
Carbacrylamine resins	974.5	E858.5	E944.5	E950.4	E962.0	E980.4
Carbamate (sedative)	967.8	E852.8	E937.8	E950.2	E962.0	E980.2
herbicide	989.3	E863.5	—	E950.6	E962.1	E980.7
insecticide	989.3	E863.2	—	E950.6	E962.1	E980.7
Carbamazepine	966.3	E855.0	E936.3	E950.4	E962.0	E980.4
Carbamic esters	967.8	E852.8	E937.8	E950.2	E962.0	E980.2
Carbamide	974.4	E858.5	E944.4	E950.4	E962.0	E980.4
topical	976.8	E858.7	E946.8	E950.4	E962.0	E980.4
Carbamylcholine chloride	971.0	E855.3	E941.0	E950.4	E962.0	E980.4
Carbarsone	961.1	E857	E931.1	E950.4	E962.0	E980.4
Carbaryl	989.3	E863.2	—	E950.6	E962.1	E980.7
Carbaspirin	965.1	E850.3	E935.3	E950.0	E962.0	E980.0
Carbazochrome	972.8	E858.3	E942.8	E950.4	E962.0	E980.4
Carbenicillin	960.0	E856	E930.0	E950.4	E962.0	E980.4
Carbenoxolone	973.8	E858.4	E943.8	E950.4	E962.0	E980.4
Carbetapentane	975.4	E858.6	E945.4	E950.4	E962.0	E980.4
Carbimazole	962.8	E858.0	E932.8	E950.4	E962.0	E980.4
Carbinol	980.1	E860.2	—	E950.9	E962.1	E980.9
Carbinoxamine	963.0	E858.1	E933.0	E950.4	E962.0	E980.4
Carbitol	982.8	E862.4	—	E950.9	E962.1	E980.9

☑ Additional Digit Required — Refer to the Tabular List for Digit Selection

Subterms under main terms may continue to next column or page

▶◀ Revised Text ● New Line ▲ Revised Code

		External Cause (E-Code)				
	Poisoning	Accident	Therapeutic Use	Suicide Attempt	Assault	Undetermined
Carbocaine	968.9	E855.2	E938.9	E950.4	E962.0	E980.4
infiltration (subcutaneous)	968.5	E855.2	E938.5	E950.4	E962.0	E980.4
nerve block (peripheral) (plexus)	968.6	E855.2	E938.6	E950.4	E962.0	E980.4
topical (surface)	968.5	E855.2	E938.5	E950.4	E962.0	E980.4
Carbol-fuchsin solution	976.0	E858.7	E946.0	E950.4	E962.0	E980.4
Carbolic acid — *see also* Phenol)	983.0	E864.0	—	E950.7	E962.1	E980.6
Carbomycin	960.8	E856	E930.8	E950.4	E962.0	E980.4
Carbon						
bisulfide (liquid) (vapor)	982.2	E862.4	—	E950.9	E962.1	E980.9
dioxide (gas)	987.8	E869.8	—	E952.8	E962.2	E982.8
disulfide (liquid) (vapor)	982.2	E862.4	—	E950.9	E962.1	E980.9
monoxide (from incomplete combustion of) (in)						
NEC	986	E868.9	—	E952.1	E962.2	E982.1
blast furnace gas	986	E868.8	—	E952.1	E962.2	E982.1
butane (distributed in mobile container)	986	E868.0	—	E951.1	E962.2	E981.1
distributed through pipes	986	E867	—	E951.0	E962.2	E981.0
charcoal fumes	986	E868.3	—	E952.1	E962.2	E982.1
coal						
gas (piped)	986	E867	—	E951.0	E962.2	E981.0
solid (in domestic stoves, fireplaces)	986	E868.3	—	E952.1	E962.2	E982.1
coke (in domestic stoves, fireplaces)	986	E868.3	—	E952.1	E962.2	E982.1
exhaust gas (motor) not in transit	986	E868.2	—	E952.0	E962.2	E982.0
combustion engine, any not in watercraft	986	E868.2	—	E952.0	E962.2	E982.0
farm tractor, not in transit	986	E868.2	—	E952.0	E962.2	E982.0
gas engine	986	E868.2	—	E952.0	E962.2	E982.0
motor pump	986	E868.2	—	E952.0	E962.2	E982.0
motor vehicle, not in transit	986	E868.2	—	E952.0	E962.2	E982.0
fuel (in domestic use)	986	E868.3	—	E952.1	E962.2	E982.1
gas (piped)	986	E867	—	E951.0	E962.2	E981.0
in mobile container	986	E868.0	—	E951.1	E962.2	E981.1
utility	986	E868.1	—	E951.8	E962.2	E981.1
in mobile container	986	E868.0	—	E951.1	E962.2	E981.1
piped (natural)	986	E867	—	E951.0	E962.2	E981.0
illuminating gas	986	E868.1	—	E951.8	E962.2	E981.8
industrial fuels or gases, any	986	E868.8	—	E952.1	E962.2	E982.1
kerosene (in domestic stoves, fireplaces)	986	E868.3	—	E952.1	E962.2	E982.1
kiln gas or vapor	986	E868.8	—	E952.1	E962.2	E982.1
motor exhaust gas, not in transit	986	E868.2	—	E952.0	E962.2	E982.0
piped gas (manufactured) (natural)	986	E867	—	E951.0	E962.2	E981.0
producer gas	986	E868.8	—	E952.1	E962.2	E982.1
propane (distributed in mobile container)	986	E868.0	—	E951.1	E962.2	E981.1
distributed through pipes	986	E867	—	E951.0	E962.2	E981.0
specified source NEC	986	E868.8	—	E952.1	E962.2	E982.1
stove gas	986	E868.1	—	E951.8	E962.2	E981.8
piped	986	E867	—	E951.0	E962.2	E981.0
utility gas	986	E868.1	—	E951.8	E962.2	E981.8
piped	986	E867	—	E951.0	E962.2	E981.0
water gas	986	E868.1	—	E951.8	E962.2	E981.8
wood (in domestic stoves, fireplaces)	986	E868.3	—	E952.1	E962.2	E982.1
tetrachloride (vapor) NEC	987.8	E869.8	—	E952.8	E962.2	E982.8
liquid (cleansing agent) NEC	982.1	E861.3	—	E950.9	E962.1	E980.9
solvent	982.1	E862.4	—	E950.9	E962.1	E980.9
Carbonic acid (gas)	987.8	E869.8	—	E952.8	E962.2	E982.8
anhydrase inhibitors	974.2	E858.5	E944.2	E950.4	E962.0	E980.4
Carbowax	976.3	E858.7	E946.3	E950.4	E962.0	E980.4
Carbrital	967.0	E851	E937.0	E950.1	E962.0	E980.1
Carbromal (derivatives)	967.3	E852.2	E937.3	E950.2	E962.0	E980.2
Cardiac						
depressants	972.0	E858.3	E942.0	E950.4	E962.0	E980.4
rhythm regulators	972.0	E858.3	E942.0	E950.4	E962.0	E980.4
Cardiografin	977.8	E858.8	E947.8	E950.4	E962.0	E980.4
Cardio-green	977.8	E858.8	E947.8	E950.4	E962.0	E980.4
Cardiotonic glycosides	972.1	E858.3	E942.1	E950.4	E962.0	E980.4
Cardiovascular agents NEC	972.9	E858.3	E942.9	E950.4	E962.0	E980.4
Cardrase	974.2	E858.5	E944.2	E950.4	E962.0	E980.4
Carfusin	976.0	E858.7	E946.0	E950.4	E962.0	E980.4
Carisoprodol	968.0	E855.1	E938.0	E950.4	E962.0	E980.4
Carmustine	963.1	E858.1	E933.1	E950.4	E962.0	E980.4
Carotene	963.5	E858.1	E933.5	E950.4	E962.0	E980.4
Carphenazine (maleate)	969.1	E853.0	E939.1	E950.3	E962.0	E980.3
Carter's Little Pills	973.1	E858.4	E943.1	E950.4	E962.0	E980.4
Cascara (sagrada)	973.1	E858.4	E943.1	E950.4	E962.0	E980.4
Cassava	988.2	E865.4	—	E950.9	E962.1	E980.9
Castellani's paint	976.0	E858.7	E946.0	E950.4	E962.0	E980.4
Castor						
bean	988.2	E865.3	—	E950.9	E962.1	E980.9
oil	973.1	E858.4	E943.1	E950.4	E962.0	E980.4
Caterpillar (sting)	989.5	E905.5	—	E950.9	E962.1	E980.9
Catha (edulis)	970.8	E854.3	E940.8	E950.4	E962.0	E980.4
Cathartics NEC	973.3	E858.4	E943.3	E950.4	E962.0	E980.4
contact	973.1	E858.4	E943.1	E950.4	E962.0	E980.4
emollient	973.2	E858.4	E943.2	E950.4	E962.0	E980.4
intestinal irritants	973.1	E858.4	E943.1	E950.4	E962.0	E980.4
saline	973.3	E858.4	E943.3	E950.4	E962.0	E980.4
Cathomycin	960.8	E856	E930.8	E950.4	E962.0	E980.4
Caustic(s)	983.9	E864.4	—	E950.7	E962.1	E980.6
alkali	983.2	E864.2	—	E950.7	E962.1	E980.6
hydroxide	983.2	E864.2	—	E950.7	E962.1	E980.6
potash	983.2	E864.2	—	E950.7	E962.1	E980.6
soda	983.2	E864.2	—	E950.7	E962.1	E980.6
specified NEC	983.9	E864.3	—	E950.7	E962.1	E980.6
Ceepryn	976.0	E858.7	E946.0	E950.4	E962.0	E980.4
ENT agent	976.6	E858.7	E946.6	E950.4	E962.0	E980.4
lozenges	976.6	E858.7	E946.6	E950.4	E962.0	E980.4
Celestone	962.0	E858.0	E932.0	E950.4	E962.0	E980.4
topical	976.0	E858.7	E946.0	E950.4	E962.0	E980.4
Cellosolve	982.8	E862.4	—	E950.9	E962.1	E980.9
Cell stimulants and proliferants	976.8	E858.7	E946.8	E950.4	E962.0	E980.4
Cellulose derivatives, cathartic	973.3	E858.4	E943.3	E950.4	E962.0	E980.4
nitrates (topical)	976.3	E858.7	E946.3	E950.4	E962.0	E980.4
Centipede (bite)	989.5	E905.4	—	E950.9	E962.1	E980.9
Central nervous system						
depressants	968.4	E855.1	E938.4	E950.4	E962.0	E980.4
anesthetic (general) NEC	968.4	E855.1	E938.4	E950.4	E962.0	E980.4
gases NEC	968.2	E855.1	E938.2	E950.4	E962.0	E980.4
intravenous	968.3	E855.1	E938.3	E950.4	E962.0	E980.4
barbiturates	967.0	E851	E937.0	E950.1	E962.0	E980.1
bromides	967.3	E852.2	E937.3	E950.2	E962.0	E980.2
cannabis sativa	969.6	E854.1	E939.6	E950.3	E962.0	E980.3
chloral hydrate	967.1	E852.0	E937.1	E950.2	E962.0	E980.2
hallucinogenics	969.6	E854.1	E939.6	E950.3	E962.0	E980.3
hypnotics	967.9	E852.9	E937.9	E950.2	E962.0	E980.2
specified NEC	967.8	E852.8	E937.8	E950.2	E962.0	E980.2
muscle relaxants	968.0	E855.1	E938.0	E950.4	E962.0	E980.4
paraldehyde	967.2	E852.1	E937.2	E950.2	E962.0	E980.2
sedatives	967.9	E852.9	E937.9	E950.2	E962.0	E980.2
mixed NEC	967.6	E852.5	E937.6	E950.2	E962.0	E980.2
specified NEC	967.8	E852.8	E937.8	E950.2	E962.0	E980.2
muscle-tone depressants	—	—	—	—	—	E980.4
stimulants	970.9	E854.3	E940.9	E950.4	E962.0	E980.4
amphetamines	969.7	E854.2	E939.7	E950.3	E962.0	E980.3
analeptics	970.0	E854.3	E940.0	E950.4	E962.0	E980.4
antidepressants	969.0	E854.0	E939.0	E950.3	E962.0	E980.3
opiate antagonists	970.1	E854.3	E940.0	E950.4	E962.0	E980.4
specified NEC	970.8	E854.3	E940.8	E950.4	E962.0	E980.4
Cephalexin	960.5	E856	E930.5	E950.4	E962.0	E980.4
Cephaloglycin	960.5	E856	E930.5	E950.4	E962.0	E980.4
Cephaloridine	960.5	E856	E930.5	E950.4	E962.0	E980.4
Cephalosporins NEC	960.5	E856	E930.5	E950.4	E962.0	E980.4
N (adicillin)	960.0	E856	E930.0	E950.4	E962.0	E980.4
Cephalothin (sodium)	960.5	E856	E930.5	E950.4	E962.0	E980.4
Cerbera (odallam)	988.2	E865.4	—	E950.9	E962.1	E980.9
Cerberin	972.1	E858.3	E942.1	E950.4	E962.0	E980.4
Cerebral stimulants	970.9	E854.3	E940.9	E950.4	E962.0	E980.4
psychotherapeutic	969.7	E854.2	E939.7	E950.3	E962.0	E980.3
specified NEC	970.8	E854.3	E940.8	E950.4	E962.0	E980.4
Cetalkonium (chloride)	976.0	E858.7	E946.0	E950.4	E962.0	E980.4
Cetoxime	963.0	E858.1	E933.0	E950.4	E962.0	E980.4
Cetrimide	976.2	E858.7	E946.2	E950.4	E962.0	E980.4
Cetylpyridinium	976.0	E858.7	E946.0	E950.4	E962.0	E980.4
ENT agent	976.6	E858.7	E946.6	E950.4	E962.0	E980.4

		External Cause (E-Code)				
	Poisoning	Accident	Therapeutic Use	Suicide Attempt	Assault	Undetermined
Cetylpyridinium — *continued*						
lozenges	976.6	E858.7	E946.6	E950.4	E962.0	E980.4
Cevadilla — see Sabadilla						
Cevitamic acid	963.5	E858.1	E933.5	E950.4	E962.0	E980.4
Chalk, precipitated	973.0	E858.4	E943.0	E950.4	E962.0	E980.4
Charcoal						
fumes (carbon monoxide)	986	E868.3	—	E952.1	E962.2	E982.1
industrial	986	E868.8	—	E952.1	E962.2	E982.1
medicinal (activated)	973.0	E858.4	E943.0	E950.4	E962.0	E980.4
Chelating agents NEC	977.2	E858.8	E947.2	E950.4	E962.0	E980.4
Chelidonium majus	988.2	E865.4	—	E950.9	E962.1	E980.9
Chemical substance	989.9	E866.9	—	E950.9	E962.1	E980.9
specified NEC	989.89	E866.8	—	E950.9	E962.1	E980.9
Chemotherapy, antineoplastic	963.1	E858.1	E933.1	E950.4	E962.0	E980.4
Chenopodium (oil)	961.6	E857	E931.6	E950.4	E962.0	E980.4
Cherry laurel	988.2	E865.4	—	E950.9	E962.1	E980.9
Chiniofon	961.3	E857	E931.3	E950.4	E962.0	E980.4
Chlophedianol	975.4	E858.6	E945.4	E950.4	E962.0	E980.4
Chloral (betaine) (formamide) (hydrate)	967.1	E852.0	E937.1	E950.2	E962.0	E980.2
Chloralamide	967.1	E852.0	E937.1	E950.2	E962.0	E980.2
Chlorambucil	963.1	E858.1	E933.1	E950.4	E962.0	E980.4
Chloramphenicol	960.2	E856	E930.2	E950.4	E962.0	E980.4
ENT agent	976.6	E858.7	E946.6	E950.4	E962.0	E980.4
ophthalmic preparation	976.5	E858.7	E946.5	E950.4	E962.0	E980.4
topical NEC	976.0	E858.7	E946.0	E950.4	E962.0	E980.4
Chlorate(s) (potassium) (sodium) NEC	983.9	E864.3	—	E950.7	E962.1	E980.6
herbicides	989.4	E863.5	—	E950.6	E962.1	E980.7
Chlorcylizine	963.0	E858.1	E933.0	E950.4	E962.0	E980.4
Chlordan(e) (dust)	989.2	E863.0	—	E950.6	E962.1	E980.7
Chlordantoin	976.0	E858.7	E946.0	E950.4	E962.0	E980.4
Chlordiazepoxide	969.4	E853.2	E939.4	E950.3	E962.0	E980.3
Chloresium	976.8	E858.7	E946.8	E950.4	E962.0	E980.4
Chlorethiazol	967.1	E852.0	E937.1	E950.2	E962.0	E980.2
Chlorethyl — *see* Ethyl, chloride						
Chloretone	967.1	E852.0	E937.1	E950.2	E962.0	E980.2
Chlorex	982.3	E862.4	—	E950.9	E962.1	E980.9
Chlorhexadol	967.1	E852.0	E937.1	E950.2	E962.0	E980.2
Chlorhexidine (hydrochloride)	976.0	E858.7	E946.0	E950.4	E962.0	E980.4
Chlorhydroxyquinolin	976.0	E858.7	E946.0	E950.4	E962.0	E980.4
Chloride of lime (bleach)	983.9	E864.3	—	E950.7	E962.1	E980.6
Chlorinated						
camphene	989.2	E863.0	—	E950.6	E962.1	E980.7
diphenyl	989.89	E866.8	—	E950.9	E962.1	E980.9
hydrocarbons NEC	989.2	E863.0	—	E950.6	E962.1	E980.7
solvent	982.3	E862.4	—	E950.9	E962.1	E980.9
lime (bleach)	983.9	E864.3	—	E950.7	E962.1	E980.6
naphthalene — see Naphthalene						
pesticides NEC	989.2	E863.0	—	E950.6	E962.1	E980.7
soda — see Sodium, hypochlorite						
Chlorine (fumes) (gas)	987.6	E869.8	—	E952.8	E962.2	E982.8
bleach	983.9	E864.3	—	E950.7	E962.1	E980.6
compounds NEC	983.9	E864.3	—	E950.7	E962.1	E980.6
disinfectant	983.9	E861.4	—	E950.7	E962.1	E980.6
releasing agents NEC	983.9	E864.3	—	E950.7	E962.1	E980.6
Chlorisondamine	972.3	E858.3	E942.3	E950.4	E962.0	E980.4
Chlormadinone	962.2	E858.0	E932.2	E950.4	E962.0	E980.4
Chlormerodrin	974.0	E858.5	E944.0	E950.4	E962.0	E980.4
Chlormethiazole	967.1	E852.0	E937.1	E950.2	E962.0	E980.2
Chlormethylenecycline	960.4	E856	E930.4	E950.4	E962.0	E980.4
Chlormezanone	969.5	E853.8	E939.5	E950.3	E962.0	E980.3
Chloroacetophenone	987.5	E869.3	—	E952.8	E962.2	E982.8
Chloroaniline	983.0	E864.0	—	E950.7	E962.1	E980.6
Chlorobenzene, chlorobenzol	982.0	E862.4	—	E950.9	E962.1	E980.9
Chlorobutanol	967.1	E852.0	E937.1	E950.2	E962.0	E980.2
Chlorodinitrobenzene	983.0	E864.0	—	E950.7	E962.1	E980.6
dust or vapor	987.8	E869.8	—	E952.8	E962.2	E982.8
Chloroethane — see Ethyl, chloride						
Chloroform (fumes) (vapor)	987.8	E869.8	—	E952.8	E962.2	E982.8
anesthetic (gas)	968.2	E855.1	E938.2	E950.4	E962.0	E980.4
liquid NEC	968.4	E855.1	E938.4	E950.4	E962.0	E980.4
solvent	982.3	E862.4	—	E950.9	E962.1	E980.9
Chloroguanide	961.4	E857	E931.4	E950.4	E962.0	E980.4
Chloromycetin	960.2	E856	E930.2	E950.4	E962.0	E980.4
Chloromycetin — *continued*						
ENT agent	976.6	E858.7	E946.6	E950.4	E962.0	E980.4
ophthalmic preparation	976.5	E858.7	E946.5	E950.4	E962.0	E980.4
otic solution	976.6	E858.7	E946.6	E950.4	E962.0	E980.4
topical NEC	976.0	E858.7	E946.0	E950.4	E962.0	E980.4
Chloronitrobenzene	983.0	E864.0	—	E950.7	E962.1	E980.6
dust or vapor	987.8	E869.8	—	E952.8	E962.2	E982.8
Chlorophenol	983.0	E864.0	—	E950.7	E962.1	E980.6
Chlorophenothane	989.2	E863.0	—	E950.6	E962.1	E980.7
Chlorophyll (derivatives)	976.8	E858.7	E946.8	E950.4	E962.0	E980.4
Chloropicrin (fumes)	987.8	E869.8	—	E952.8	E962.2	E982.8
fumigant	989.4	E863.8	—	E950.6	E962.1	E980.7
fungicide	989.4	E863.6	—	E950.6	E962.1	E980.7
pesticide (fumes)	989.4	E863.4	—	E950.6	E962.1	E980.7
Chloroprocaine	968.9	E855.2	E938.9	E950.4	E962.0	E980.4
infiltration (subcutaneous)	968.5	E855.2	E938.5	E950.4	E962.0	E980.4
nerve block (peripheral) (plexus)	968.6	E855.2	E938.6	E950.4	E962.0	E980.4
Chloroptic	976.5	E858.7	E946.5	E950.4	E962.0	E980.4
Chloropurine	963.1	E858.1	E933.1	E950.4	E962.0	E980.4
Chloroquine (hydrochloride) (phosphate)	961.4	E857	E931.4	E950.4	E962.0	E980.4
Chlorothen	963.0	E858.1	E933.0	E950.4	E962.0	E980.4
Chlorothiazide	974.3	E858.5	E944.3	E950.4	E962.0	E980.4
Chlorotrianisene	962.2	E858.0	E932.2	E950.4	E962.0	E980.4
Chlorovinyldichloroarsine	985.1	E866.3	—	E950.8	E962.1	E980.8
Chloroxylenol	976.0	E858.7	E946.0	E950.4	E962.0	E980.4
Chlorphenesin (carbamate)	968.0	E855.1	E938.0	E950.4	E962.0	E980.4
topical (antifungal)	976.0	E858.7	E946.0	E950.4	E962.0	E980.4
Chlorpheniramine	963.0	E858.1	E933.0	E950.4	E962.0	E980.4
Chlorphenoxamine	966.4	E855.0	E936.4	E950.4	E962.0	E980.4
Chlorphentermine	977.0	E858.8	E947.0	E950.4	E962.0	E980.4
Chlorproguanil	961.4	E857	E931.4	E950.4	E962.0	E980.4
Chlorpromazine	969.1	E853.0	E939.1	E950.3	E962.0	E980.3
Chlorpropamide	962.3	E858.0	E932.3	E950.4	E962.0	E980.4
Chlorprothixene	969.3	E853.8	E939.3	E950.3	E962.0	E980.3
Chlorquinaldol	976.0	E858.7	E946.0	E950.4	E962.0	E980.4
Chlortetracycline	960.4	E856	E930.4	E950.4	E962.0	E980.4
Chlorthalidone	974.4	E858.5	E944.4	E950.4	E962.0	E980.4
Chlortrianisene	962.2	E858.0	E932.2	E950.4	E962.0	E980.4
Chlor-Trimeton	963.0	E858.1	E933.0	E950.4	E962.0	E980.4
Chlorzoxazone	968.0	E855.1	E938.0	E950.4	E962.0	E980.4
Choke damp	987.8	E869.8	—	E952.8	E962.2	E982.8
Cholebrine	977.8	E858.8	E947.8	E950.4	E962.0	E980.4
Cholera vaccine	978.2	E858.8	E948.2	E950.4	E962.0	E980.4
Cholesterol-lowering agents	972.2	E858.3	E942.2	E950.4	E962.0	E980.4
Cholestyramine (resin)	972.2	E858.3	E942.2	E950.4	E962.0	E980.4
Cholic acid	973.4	E858.4	E943.4	E950.4	E962.0	E980.4
Choline						
dihydrogen citrate	977.1	E858.8	E947.1	E950.4	E962.0	E980.4
salicylate	965.1	E850.3	E935.3	E950.0	E962.0	E980.0
theophyllinate	974.1	E858.5	E944.1	E950.4	E962.0	E980.4
Cholinergics	971.0	E855.3	E941.0	E950.4	E962.0	E980.4
Cholografin	977.8	E858.8	E947.8	E950.4	E962.0	E980.4
Chorionic gonadotropin	962.4	E858.0	E932.4	E950.4	E962.0	E980.4
Chromates	983.9	E864.3	—	E950.7	E962.1	E980.6
dust or mist	987.8	E869.8	—	E952.8	E962.2	E982.8
lead	984.0	E866.0	—	E950.9	E962.1	E980.9
paint	984.0	E861.5	—	E950.9	E962.1	E980.9
Chromic acid	983.9	E864.3	—	E950.7	E962.1	E980.6
dust or mist	987.8	E869.8	—	E952.8	E962.2	E982.8
Chromium	985.6	E866.4	—	E950.9	E962.1	E980.9
compounds — see Chromates						
Chromonar	972.4	E858.3	E942.4	E950.4	E962.0	E980.4
Chromyl chloride	983.9	E864.3	—	E950.7	E962.1	E980.6
Chrysarobin (ointment)	976.4	E858.7	E946.4	E950.4	E962.0	E980.4
Chrysazin	973.1	E858.4	E943.1	E950.4	E962.0	E980.4
Chymar	963.4	E858.1	E933.4	E950.4	E962.0	E980.4
ophthalmic preparation	976.5	E858.7	E946.5	E950.4	E962.0	E980.4
Chymotrypsin	963.4	E858.1	E933.4	E950.4	E962.0	E980.4
ophthalmic preparation	976.5	E858.7	E946.5	E950.4	E962.0	E980.4
Cicuta maculata or virosa	988.2	E865.4	—	E950.9	E962.1	E980.9
Cigarette lighter fluid	981	E862.1	—	E950.9	E962.1	E980.9
Cinchocaine (spinal)	968.7	E855.2	E938.7	E950.4	E962.0	E980.4
topical (surface)	968.5	E855.2	E938.5	E950.4	E962.0	E980.4
Cinchona	961.4	E857	E931.4	E950.4	E962.0	E980.4
Cinchonine alkaloids	961.4	E857	E931.4	E950.4	E962.0	E980.4
Cinchophen	974.7	E858.5	E944.7	E950.4	E962.0	E980.4
Cinnarizine	963.0	E858.1	E933.0	E950.4	E962.0	E980.4
Citanest	968.9	E855.2	E938.9	E950.4	E962.0	E980.4

	Poisoning	External Cause (E-Code) Accident	Therapeutic Use	Suicide Attempt	Assault	Undetermined
Citanest — *continued*						
infiltration (subcutaneous)	968.5	E855.2	E938.5	E950.4	E962.0	E980.4
nerve block (peripheral) (plexus)	968.6	E855.2	E938.6	E950.4	E962.0	E980.4
Citric acid	989.89	E866.8	—	E950.9	E962.1	E980.9
Citrovorum factor	964.1	E858.2	E934.1	E950.4	E962.0	E980.4
Claviceps purpurea	988.2	E865.4	—	E950.9	E962.1	E980.9
Cleaner, cleansing agent NEC	989.89	E861.3	—	E950.9	E962.1	E980.9
of paint or varnish	982.8	E862.9	—	E950.9	E962.1	E980.9
Clematis vitalba	988.2	E865.4	—	E950.9	E962.1	E980.9
Clemizole	963.0	E858.1	E933.0	E950.4	E962.0	E980.4
penicillin	960.0	E856	E930.0	E950.4	E962.0	E980.4
Clidinium	971.1	E855.4	E941.1	E950.4	E962.0	E980.4
Clindamycin	960.8	E856	E930.8	E950.4	E962.0	E980.4
Cliradon	965.09	E850.2	E935.2	E950.0	E962.0	E980.0
Clocortolone	962.0	E858.0	E932.0	E950.4	E962.0	E980.4
Clofedanol	975.4	E858.6	E945.4	E950.4	E962.0	E980.4
Clofibrate	972.2	E858.3	E942.2	E950.4	E962.0	E980.4
Clomethiazole	967.1	E852.0	E937.1	E950.2	E962.0	E980.2
Clomiphene	977.8	E858.8	E947.8	E950.4	E962.0	E980.4
Clonazepam	969.4	E853.2	E939.4	E950.3	E962.0	E980.3
Clonidine	972.6	E858.3	E942.6	E950.4	E962.0	E980.4
Clopamide	974.3	E858.5	E944.3	E950.4	E962.0	E980.4
Clorazepate	969.4	E853.2	E939.4	E950.3	E962.0	E980.3
Clorexolone	974.4	E858.5	E944.4	E950.4	E962.0	E980.4
Clorox (bleach)	983.9	E864.3	—	E950.7	E962.1	E980.6
Clortermine	977.0	E858.8	E947.0	E950.4	E962.0	E980.4
Clotrimazole	976.0	E858.7	E946.0	E950.4	E962.0	E980.4
Cloxacillin	960.0	E856	E930.0	E950.4	E962.0	E980.4
Coagulants NEC	964.5	E858.2	E934.5	E950.4	E962.0	E980.4
Coal (carbon monoxide from) — *see also* Carbon, monoxide, coal						
oil — see Kerosene						
tar NEC	983.0	E864.0	—	E950.7	E962.1	E980.6
fumes	987.8	E869.8	—	E952.8	E962.2	E982.8
medicinal (ointment)	976.4	E858.7	E946.4	E950.4	E962.0	E980.4
analgesics NEC	965.5	E850.5	E935.5	E950.0	E962.0	E980.0
naphtha (solvent)	981	E862.0	—	E950.9	E962.1	E980.9
Cobalt (fumes) (industrial)	985.8	E866.4	—	E950.9	E962.1	E980.9
Cobra (venom)	989.5	E905.0	—	E950.9	E962.1	E980.9
Coca (leaf)	970.8	E854.3	E940.8	E950.4	E962.0	E980.4
Cocaine (hydrochloride) (salt)	970.8	E854.3	E940.8	E950.4	E962.0	E980.4
topical anesthetic	968.5	E855.2	E938.5	E950.4	E962.0	E980.4
Coccidioidin	977.8	E858.8	E947.8	E950.4	E962.0	E980.4
Cocculus indicus	988.2	E865.3	—	E950.9	E962.1	E980.9
Cochineal	989.89	E866.8	—	E950.9	E962.1	E980.9
medicinal products	977.4	E858.8	E947.4	E950.4	E962.0	E980.4
Codeine	965.09	E850.2	E935.2	E950.0	E962.0	E980.0
Coffee	989.89	E866.8	—	E950.9	E962.1	E980.9
Cogentin	971.1	E855.4	E941.1	E950.4	E962.0	E980.4
Coke fumes or gas (carbon monoxide)	986	E868.3	—	E952.1	E962.2	E982.1
industrial use	986	E868.8	—	E952.1	E962.2	E982.1
Colace	973.2	E858.4	E943.2	E950.4	E962.0	E980.4
Colchicine	974.7	E858.5	E944.7	E950.4	E962.0	E980.4
Colchicum	988.2	E865.3	—	E950.9	E962.1	E980.9
Cold cream	976.3	E858.7	E946.3	E950.4	E962.0	E980.4
Colestipol	972.2	E858.3	E942.2	E950.4	E962.0	E980.4
Colistimethate	960.8	E856	E930.8	E950.4	E962.0	E980.4
Colistin	960.8	E856	E930.8	E950.4	E962.0	E980.4
Collagen	977.8	E866.8	E947.8	E950.9	E962.1	E980.9
Collagenase	976.8	E858.7	E946.8	E950.4	E962.0	E980.4
Collodion (flexible)	976.3	E858.7	E946.3	E950.4	E962.0	E980.4
Colocynth	973.1	E858.4	E943.1	E950.4	E962.0	E980.4
Coloring matter — *see* Dye(s)						
Combustion gas — see Carbon, monoxide						
Compazine	969.1	E853.0	E939.1	E950.3	E962.0	E980.3
Compound						
42 (warfarin)	989.4	E863.7	—	E950.6	E962.1	E980.7
269 (endrin)	989.2	E863.0	—	E950.6	E962.1	E980.7
497 (dieldrin)	989.2	E863.0	—	E950.6	E962.1	E980.7
1080 (sodium fluoroacetate)	989.4	E863.7	—	E950.6	E962.1	E980.7
3422 (parathion)	989.3	E863.1	—	E950.6	E962.1	E980.7
3911 (phorate)	989.3	E863.1	—	E950.6	E962.1	E980.7
3956 (toxaphene)	989.2	E863.0	—	E950.6	E962.1	E980.7
4049 (malathion)	989.3	E863.1	—	E950.6	E962.1	E980.7
Compound — *continued*						
4124 (dicapthon)	989.4	E863.4	—	E950.6	E962.1	E980.7
E (cortisone)	962.0	E858.0	E932.0	E950.4	E962.0	E980.4
F (hydrocortisone)	962.0	E858.0	E932.0	E950.4	E962.0	E980.4
Congo red	977.8	E858.8	E947.8	E950.4	E962.0	E980.4
Coniine, conine	965.7	E850.7	E935.7	E950.0	E962.0	E980.0
Conium (maculatum)	988.2	E865.4	—	E950.9	E962.1	E980.9
Conjugated estrogens (equine)	962.2	E858.0	E932.2	E950.4	E962.0	E980.4
Contac	975.6	E858.6	E945.6	E950.4	E962.0	E980.4
Contact lens solution	976.5	E858.7	E946.5	E950.4	E962.0	E980.4
Contraceptives (oral)	962.2	E858.0	E932.2	E950.4	E962.0	E980.4
vaginal	976.8	E858.7	E946.8	E950.4	E962.0	E980.4
Contrast media (roentgenographic)	977.8	E858.8	E947.8	E950.4	E962.0	E980.4
Convallaria majalis	988.2	E865.4	—	E950.9	E962.1	E980.9
Copper (dust) (fumes) (salts) NEC	985.8	E866.4	—	E950.9	E962.1	E980.9
arsenate, arsenite	985.1	E866.3	—	E950.8	E962.1	E980.8
insecticide	985.1	E863.4	—	E950.8	E962.1	E980.8
emetic	973.6	E858.4	E943.6	E950.4	E962.0	E980.4
fungicide	985.8	E863.6	—	E950.6	E962.1	E980.7
insecticide	985.8	E863.4	—	E950.6	E962.1	E980.7
oleate	976.0	E858.7	E946.0	E950.4	E962.0	E980.4
sulfate	983.9	E864.3	—	E950.7	E962.1	E980.6
cupric	973.6	E858.4	E943.6	E950.4	E962.0	E980.4
cuprous	983.9	E864.3	—	E950.7	E962.1	E980.6
fungicide	983.9	E863.6	—	E950.7	E962.1	E980.6
Copperhead snake (bite) (venom)	989.5	E905.0	—	E950.9	E962.1	E980.9
Coral (sting)	989.5	E905.6	—	E950.9	E962.1	E980.9
snake (bite) (venom)	989.5	E905.0	—	E950.9	E962.1	E980.9
Cordran	976.0	E858.7	E946.0	E950.4	E962.0	E980.4
Corn cures	976.4	E858.7	E946.4	E950.4	E962.0	E980.4
Cornhusker's lotion	976.3	E858.7	E946.3	E950.4	E962.0	E980.4
Corn starch	976.3	E858.7	E946.3	E950.4	E962.0	E980.4
Corrosive	983.9	E864.4	—	E950.7	E962.1	E980.6
acids NEC	983.1	E864.1	—	E950.7	E962.1	E980.6
aromatics	983.0	E864.0	—	E950.7	E962.1	E980.6
disinfectant	983.0	E861.4	—	E950.7	E962.1	E980.6
fumes NEC	987.9	E869.9	—	E952.9	E962.2	E982.9
specified NEC	983.9	E864.3	—	E950.7	E962.1	E980.6
sublimate — see Mercury, chloride						
Cortate	962.0	E858.0	E932.0	E950.4	E962.0	E980.4
Cort-Dome	962.0	E858.0	E932.0	E950.4	E962.0	E980.4
ENT agent	976.6	E858.7	E946.6	E950.4	E962.0	E980.4
ophthalmic preparation	976.5	E858.7	E946.5	E950.4	E962.0	E980.4
topical NEC	976.0	E858.7	E946.0	E950.4	E962.0	E980.4
Cortef	962.0	E858.0	E932.0	E950.4	E962.0	E980.4
ENT agent	976.6	E858.7	E946.6	E950.4	E962.0	E980.4
ophthalmic preparation	976.5	E858.7	E946.5	E950.4	E962.0	E980.4
topical NEC	976.0	E858.7	E946.0	E950.4	E962.0	E980.4
Corticosteroids (fluorinated)	962.0	E858.0	E932.0	E950.4	E962.0	E980.4
ENT agent	976.6	E858.7	E946.6	E950.4	E962.0	E980.4
ophthalmic preparation	976.5	E858.7	E946.5	E950.4	E962.0	E980.4
topical NEC	976.0	E858.7	E946.0	E950.4	E962.0	E980.4
Corticotropin	962.4	E858.0	E932.4	E950.4	E962.0	E980.4
Cortisol	962.0	E858.0	E932.0	E950.4	E962.0	E980.4
ENT agent	976.6	E858.7	E946.6	E950.4	E962.0	E980.4
ophthalmic preparation	976.5	E858.7	E946.5	E950.4	E962.0	E980.4
topical NEC	976.0	E858.7	E946.0	E950.4	E962.0	E980.4
Cortisone derivatives (acetate)	962.0	E858.0	E932.0	E950.4	E962.0	E980.4
ENT agent	976.6	E858.7	E946.6	E950.4	E962.0	E980.4
ophthalmic preparation	976.5	E858.7	E946.5	E950.4	E962.0	E980.4
topical NEC	976.0	E858.7	E946.0	E950.4	E962.0	E980.4
Cortogen	962.0	E858.0	E932.0	E950.4	E962.0	E980.4
ENT agent	976.6	E858.7	E946.6	E950.4	E962.0	E980.4
ophthalmic preparation	976.5	E858.7	E946.5	E950.4	E962.0	E980.4
Cortone	962.0	E858.0	E932.0	E950.4	E962.0	E980.4
ENT agent	976.6	E858.7	E946.6	E950.4	E962.0	E980.4
ophthalmic preparation	976.5	E858.7	E946.5	E950.4	E962.0	E980.4
Cortril	962.0	E858.0	E932.0	E950.4	E962.0	E980.4
ENT agent	976.6	E858.7	E946.6	E950.4	E962.0	E980.4
ophthalmic preparation	976.5	E858.7	E946.5	E950.4	E962.0	E980.4
topical NEC	976.0	E858.7	E946.0	E950.4	E962.0	E980.4
Cosmetics	989.89	E866.7	—	E950.9	E962.1	E980.9
Cosyntropin	977.8	E858.8	E947.8	E950.4	E962.0	E980.4
Cotarnine	964.5	E858.2	E934.5	E950.4	E962.0	E980.4

	Poisoning	External Cause (E-Code) Accident	Therapeutic Use	Suicide Attempt	Assault	Undetermined
Cottonseed oil	976.3	E858.7	E946.3	E950.4	E962.0	E980.4
Cough mixtures						
(antitussives)	975.4	E858.6	E945.4	E950.4	E962.0	E980.4
containing opiates	965.09	E850.2	E935.2	E950.0	E962.0	E980.0
expectorants	975.5	E858.6	E945.5	E950.4	E962.0	E980.4
Coumadin	964.2	E858.2	E934.2	E950.4	E962.0	E980.4
rodenticide	989.4	E863.7	—	E950.6	E962.1	E980.7
Coumarin	964.2	E858.2	E934.2	E950.4	E962.0	E980.4
Coumetarol	964.2	E858.2	E934.2	E950.4	E962.0	E980.4
Cowbane	988.2	E865.4	—	E950.9	E962.1	E980.9
Cozyme	963.5	E858.1	E933.5	E950.4	E962.0	E980.4
Crack	970.8	E854.3	E940.8	E950.4	E962.0	E980.4
Creolin	983.0	E864.0	—	E950.7	E962.1	E980.6
disinfectant	983.0	E861.4	—	E950.7	E962.1	E980.6
Creosol (compound)	983.0	E864.0	—	E950.7	E962.1	E980.6
Creosote (beechwood) (coal tar)	983.0	E864.0	—	E950.7	E962.1	E980.6
medicinal (expectorant)	975.5	E858.6	E945.5	E950.4	E962.0	E980.4
syrup	975.5	E858.6	E945.5	E950.4	E962.0	E980.4
Cresol	983.0	E864.0	—	E950.7	E962.1	E980.6
disinfectant	983.0	E861.4	—	E950.7	E962.1	E980.6
Cresylic acid	983.0	E864.0	—	E950.7	E962.1	E980.6
Cropropamide	965.7	E850.7	E935.7	E950.0	E962.0	E980.0
with crotethamide	970.0	E854.3	E940.0	E950.4	E962.0	E980.4
Crotamiton	976.0	E858.7	E946.0	E950.4	E962.0	E980.4
Crotethamide	965.7	E850.7	E935.7	E950.0	E962.0	E980.0
with cropropamide	970.0	E854.3	E940.0	E950.4	E962.0	E980.4
Croton (oil)	973.1	E858.4	E943.1	E950.4	E962.0	E980.4
chloral	967.1	E852.0	E937.1	E950.2	E962.0	E980.2
Crude oil	981	E862.1	—	E950.9	E962.1	E980.9
Cryogenine	965.8	E850.8	E935.8	E950.0	E962.0	E980.0
Cryolite (pesticide)	989.4	E863.4	—	E950.6	E962.1	E980.7
Cryptenamine	972.6	E858.3	E942.6	E950.4	E962.0	E980.4
Crystal violet	976.0	E858.7	E946.0	E950.4	E962.0	E980.4
Cuckoopint	988.2	E865.4	—	E950.9	E962.1	E980.9
Cumetharol	964.2	E858.2	E934.2	E950.4	E962.0	E980.4
Cupric sulfate	973.6	E858.4	E943.6	E950.4	E962.0	E980.4
Cuprous sulfate	983.9	E864.3	—	E950.7	E962.1	E980.6
Curare, curarine	975.2	E858.6	E945.2	E950.4	E962.0	E980.4
Cyanic acid — *see* Cyanide(s)						
Cyanide(s) (compounds) (hydrogen) (potassium) (sodium) NEC	989.0	E866.8	—	E950.9	E962.1	E980.9
dust or gas (inhalation) NEC	987.7	E869.8	—	E952.8	E962.2	E982.8
fumigant	989.0	E863.8	—	E950.6	E962.1	E980.7
mercuric — see Mercury						
pesticide (dust) (fumes)	989.0	E863.4	—	E950.6	E962.1	E980.7
Cyanocobalamin	964.1	E858.2	E934.1	E950.4	E962.0	E980.4
Cyanogen (chloride) (gas) NEC	987.8	E869.8	—	E952.8	E962.2	E982.8
Cyclaine	968.5	E855.2	E938.5	E950.4	E962.0	E980.4
Cyclamen europaeum	988.2	E865.4	—	E950.9	E962.1	E980.9
Cyclandelate	972.5	E858.3	E942.5	E950.4	E962.0	E980.4
Cyclazocine	965.09	E850.2	E935.2	E950.0	E962.0	E980.0
Cyclizine	963.0	E858.1	E933.0	E950.4	E962.0	E980.4
Cyclobarbital, cyclobarbitone	967.0	E851	E937.0	E950.1	E962.0	E980.1
Cycloguanil	961.4	E857	E931.4	E950.4	E962.0	E980.4
Cyclohexane	982.0	E862.4	—	E950.9	E962.1	E980.9
Cyclohexanol	980.8	E860.8	—	E950.9	E962.1	E980.9
Cyclohexanone	982.8	E862.4	—	E950.9	E962.1	E980.9
Cyclomethycaine	968.5	E855.2	E938.5	E950.4	E962.0	E980.4
Cyclopentamine	971.2	E855.5	E941.2	E950.4	E962.0	E980.4
Cyclopenthiazide	974.3	E858.5	E944.3	E950.4	E962.0	E980.4
Cyclopentolate	971.1	E855.4	E941.1	E950.4	E962.0	E980.4
Cyclophosphamide	963.1	E858.1	E933.1	E950.4	E962.0	E980.4
Cyclopropane	968.2	E855.1	E938.2	E950.4	E962.0	E980.4
Cycloserine	960.6	E856	E930.6	E950.4	E962.0	E980.4
Cyclothiazide	974.3	E858.5	E944.3	E950.4	E962.0	E980.4
Cycrimine	966.4	E855.0	E936.4	E950.4	E962.0	E980.4
Cymarin	972.1	E858.3	E942.1	E950.4	E962.0	E980.4
Cyproheptadine	963.0	E858.1	E933.0	E950.4	E962.0	E980.4
Cyprolidol	969.0	E854.0	E939.0	E950.3	E962.0	E980.3
Cytarabine	963.1	E858.1	E933.1	E950.4	E962.0	E980.4
Cytisus						
laburnum	988.2	E865.4	—	E950.9	E962.1	E980.9
scoparius	988.2	E865.4	—	E950.9	E962.1	E980.9
Cytomel	962.7	E858.0	E932.7	E950.4	E962.0	E980.4
Cytosine (antineoplastic)	963.1	E858.1	E933.1	E950.4	E962.0	E980.4
Cytoxan	963.1	E858.1	E933.1	E950.4	E962.0	E980.4

	Poisoning	External Cause (E-Code) Accident	Therapeutic Use	Suicide Attempt	Assault	Undetermined
Dacarbazine	963.1	E858.1	E933.1	E950.4	E962.0	E980.4
Dactinomycin	960.7	E856	E930.7	E950.4	E962.0	E980.4
DADPS	961.8	E857	E931.8	E950.4	E962.0	E980.4
Dakin's solution (external)	976.0	E858.7	E946.0	E950.4	E962.0	E980.4
Dalmane	969.4	E853.2	E939.4	E950.3	E962.0	E980.3
DAM	977.2	E858.8	E947.2	E950.4	E962.0	E980.4
Danilone	964.2	E858.2	E934.2	E950.4	E962.0	E980.4
Danthron	973.1	E858.4	E943.1	E950.4	E962.0	E980.4
Dantrolene	975.2	E858.6	E945.2	E950.4	E962.0	E980.4
Daphne (gnidium) (mezereum)	988.2	E865.4	—	E950.9	E962.1	E980.9
berry	988.2	E865.3	—	E950.9	E962.1	E980.9
Dapsone	961.8	E857	E931.8	E950.4	E962.0	E980.4
Daraprim	961.4	E857	E931.4	E950.4	E962.0	E980.4
Darnel	988.2	E865.3	—	E950.9	E962.1	E980.9
Darvon	965.8	E850.8	E935.8	E950.0	E962.0	E980.0
Daunorubicin	960.7	E856	E930.7	E950.4	E962.0	E980.4
DBI	962.3	E858.0	E932.3	E950.4	E962.0	E980.4
D-Con (rodenticide)	989.4	E863.7	—	E950.6	E962.1	E980.7
DDS	961.8	E857	E931.8	E950.4	E962.0	E980.4
DDT	989.2	E863.0	—	E950.6	E962.1	E980.7
Deadly nightshade	988.2	E865.4	—	E950.9	E962.1	E980.9
berry	988.2	E865.3	—	E950.9	E962.1	E980.9
Deanol	969.7	E854.2	E939.7	E950.3	E962.0	E980.3
Debrisoquine	972.6	E858.3	E942.6	E950.4	E962.0	E980.4
Decaborane	989.89	E866.8	—	E950.9	E962.1	E980.9
fumes	987.8	E869.8	—	E952.8	E962.2	E982.8
Decadron	962.0	E858.0	E932.0	E950.4	E962.0	E980.4
ENT agent	976.6	E858.7	E946.6	E950.4	E962.0	E980.4
ophthalmic preparation	976.5	E858.7	E946.5	E950.4	E962.0	E980.4
topical NEC	976.0	E858.7	E946.0	E950.4	E962.0	E980.4
Decahydronaphthalene	982.0	E862.4	—	E950.9	E962.1	E980.9
Decalin	982.0	E862.4	—	E950.9	E962.1	E980.9
Decamethonium	975.2	E858.6	E945.2	E950.4	E962.0	E980.4
Decholin	973.4	E858.4	E943.4	E950.4	E962.0	E980.4
sodium (diagnostic)	977.8	E858.8	E947.8	E950.4	E962.0	E980.4
Declomycin	960.4	E856	E930.4	E950.4	E962.0	E980.4
Deferoxamine	963.8	E858.1	E933.8	E950.4	E962.0	E980.4
Dehydrocholic acid	973.4	E858.4	E943.4	E950.4	E962.0	E980.4
DeKalin	982.0	E862.4	—	E950.9	E962.1	E980.9
Delalutin	962.2	E858.0	E932.2	E950.4	E962.0	E980.4
Delphinium	988.2	E865.3	—	E950.9	E962.1	E980.9
Deltasone	962.0	E858.0	E932.0	E950.4	E962.0	E980.4
Deltra	962.0	E858.0	E932.0	E950.4	E962.0	E980.4
Delvinal	967.0	E851	E937.0	E950.1	E962.0	E980.1
Demecarium (bromide)	971.0	E855.3	E941.0	E950.4	E962.0	E980.4
Demeclocycline	960.4	E856	E930.4	E950.4	E962.0	E980.4
Demecolcine	963.1	E858.1	E933.1	E950.4	E962.0	E980.4
Demelanizing agents	976.8	E858.7	E946.8	E950.4	E962.0	E980.4
Demerol	965.09	E850.2	E935.2	E950.0	E962.0	E980.0
Demethylchlortetracycline	960.4	E856	E930.4	E950.4	E962.0	E980.4
Demethyltetracycline	960.4	E856	E930.4	E950.4	E962.0	E980.4
Demeton	989.3	E863.1	—	E950.6	E962.1	E980.7
Demulcents	976.3	E858.7	E946.3	E950.4	E962.0	E980.4
Demulen	962.2	E858.0	E932.2	E950.4	E962.0	E980.4
Denatured alcohol	980.0	E860.1	—	E950.9	E962.1	E980.9
Dendrid	976.5	E858.7	E946.5	E950.4	E962.0	E980.4
Dental agents, topical	976.7	E858.7	E946.7	E950.4	E962.0	E980.4
Deodorant spray (feminine hygiene)	976.8	E858.7	E946.8	E950.4	E962.0	E980.4
Deoxyribonuclease	963.4	E858.1	E933.4	E950.4	E962.0	E980.4
Depressants						
appetite, central	977.0	E858.8	E947.0	E950.4	E962.0	E980.4
cardiac	972.0	E858.3	E942.0	E950.4	E962.0	E980.4
central nervous system (anesthetic)	968.4	E855.1	E938.4	E950.4	E962.0	E980.4
psychotherapeutic	969.5	E853.9	E939.5	E950.3	E962.0	E980.3
Dequalinium	976.0	E858.7	E946.0	E950.4	E962.0	E980.4
Dermolate	976.2	E858.7	E946.2	E950.4	E962.0	E980.4
DES	962.2	E858.0	E932.2	E950.4	E962.0	E980.4
Desenex	976.0	E858.7	E946.0	E950.4	E962.0	E980.4
Deserpidine	972.6	E858.3	E942.6	E950.4	E962.0	E980.4
Desipramine	969.0	E854.0	E939.0	E950.3	E962.0	E980.3
Deslanoside	972.1	E858.3	E942.1	E950.4	E962.0	E980.4
Desocodeine	965.09	E850.2	E935.2	E950.0	E962.0	E980.0
Desomorphine	965.09	E850.2	E935.2	E950.0	E962.0	E980.0
Desonide	976.0	E858.7	E946.0	E950.4	E962.0	E980.4
Desoxycorticosterone derivatives	962.0	E858.0	E932.0	E950.4	E962.0	E980.4
Desoxyephedrine	969.7	E854.2	E939.7	E950.3	E962.0	E980.3
DET	969.6	E854.1	E939.6	E950.3	E962.0	E980.3

	Poisoning	External Cause (E-Code) Accident	Therapeutic Use	Suicide Attempt	Assault	Undetermined
Detergents (ingested) (synthetic)	989.6	E861.0	—	E950.9	E962.1	E980.9
ENT agent	976.6	E858.7	E946.6	E950.4	E962.0	E980.4
external medication	976.2	E858.7	E946.2	E950.4	E962.0	E980.4
ophthalmic preparation	976.5	E858.7	E946.5	E950.4	E962.0	E980.4
topical NEC	976.0	E858.7	E946.0	E950.4	E962.0	E980.4
Deterrent, alcohol	977.3	E858.8	E947.3	E950.4	E962.0	E980.4
Detrothyronine	962.7	E858.0	E932.7	E950.4	E962.0	E980.4
Dettol (external medication)	976.0	E858.7	E946.0	E950.4	E962.0	E980.4
Dexamethasone	962.0	E858.0	E932.0	E950.4	E962.0	E980.4
Dexamphetamine	969.7	E854.2	E939.7	E950.3	E962.0	E980.3
Dexedrine	969.7	E854.2	E939.7	E950.3	E962.0	E980.3
Dexpanthenol	963.5	E858.1	E933.5	E950.4	E962.0	E980.4
Dextran	964.8	E858.2	E934.8	E950.4	E962.0	E980.4
Dextriferron	964.0	E858.2	E934.0	E950.4	E962.0	E980.4
Dextroamphetamine	969.7	E854.2	E939.7	E950.3	E962.0	E980.3
Dextro calcium pantothenate	963.5	E858.1	E933.5	E950.4	E962.0	E980.4
Dextromethorphan	975.4	E858.6	E945.4	E950.4	E962.0	E980.4
Dextromoramide	965.09	E850.2	E935.2	E950.0	E962.0	E980.0
Dextro pantothenyl alcohol	963.5	E858.1	E933.5	E950.4	E962.0	E980.4
topical	976.8	E858.7	E946.8	E950.4	E962.0	E980.4
Dextropropoxyphene (hydrochloride)	965.8	E850.8	E935.8	E950.0	E962.0	E980.0
Dextrorphan	965.09	E850.2	E935.2	E950.0	E962.0	E980.0
Dextrose NEC	974.5	E858.5	E944.5	E950.4	E962.0	E980.4
Dextrothyroxin	962.7	E858.0	E932.7	E950.4	E962.0	E980.4
DFP	971.0	E855.3	E941.0	E950.4	E962.0	E980.4
DHE-45	972.9	E858.3	E942.9	E950.4	E962.0	E980.4
Diabinese	962.3	E858.0	E932.3	E950.4	E962.0	E980.4
Diacetyl monoxime	977.2	E858.8	E947.2	E950.4	E962.0	E980.4
Diacetylmorphine	965.01	E850.0	E935.0	E950.0	E962.0	E980.0
Diagnostic agents	977.8	E858.8	E947.8	E950.4	E962.0	E980.4
Dial (soap)	976.2	E858.7	E946.2	E950.4	E962.0	E980.4
sedative	967.0	E851	E937.0	E950.1	E962.0	E980.1
Diallylbarbituric acid	967.0	E851	E937.0	E950.1	E962.0	E980.1
Diaminodiphenylsulfone	961.8	E857	E931.8	E950.4	E962.0	E980.4
Diamorphine	965.01	E850.0	E935.0	E950.0	E962.0	E980.0
Diamox	974.2	E858.5	E944.2	E950.4	E962.0	E980.4
Diamthazole	976.0	E858.7	E946.0	E950.4	E962.0	E980.4
Diaphenylsulfone	961.8	E857	E931.8	E950.4	E962.0	E980.4
Diasone (sodium)	961.8	E857	E931.8	E950.4	E962.0	E980.4
Diazepam	969.4	E853.2	E939.4	E950.3	E962.0	E980.3
Diazinon	989.3	E863.1	—	E950.6	E962.1	E980.7
Diazomethane (gas)	987.8	E869.8	—	E952.8	E962.2	E982.8
Diazoxide	972.5	E858.3	E942.5	E950.4	E962.0	E980.4
Dibenamine	971.3	E855.6	E941.3	E950.4	E962.0	E980.4
Dibenzheptropine	963.0	E858.1	E933.0	E950.4	E962.0	E980.4
Dibenzyline	971.3	E855.6	E941.3	E950.4	E962.0	E980.4
Diborane (gas)	987.8	E869.8	—	E952.8	E962.2	E982.8
Dibromomannitol	963.1	E858.1	E933.1	E950.4	E962.0	E980.4
Dibucaine (spinal)	968.7	E855.2	E938.7	E950.4	E962.0	E980.4
topical (surface)	968.5	E855.2	E938.5	E950.4	E962.0	E980.4
Dibunate sodium	975.4	E858.6	E945.4	E950.4	E962.0	E980.4
Dibutoline	971.1	E855.4	E941.1	E950.4	E962.0	E980.4
Dicapthon	989.4	E863.4	—	E950.6	E962.1	E980.7
Dichloralphenazone	967.1	E852.0	E937.1	E950.2	E962.0	E980.2
Dichlorodifluoromethane	987.4	E869.2	—	E952.8	E962.2	E982.8
Dichloroethane	982.3	E862.4	—	E950.9	E962.1	E980.9
Dichloroethylene	982.3	E862.4	—	E950.9	E962.1	E980.9
Dichloroethyl sulfide	987.8	E869.8	—	E952.8	E962.2	E982.8
Dichlorohydrin	982.3	E862.4	—	E950.9	E962.1	E980.9
Dichloromethane (solvent) (vapor)	982.3	E862.4	—	E950.9	E962.1	E980.9
Dichlorophen(e)	961.6	E857	E931.6	E950.4	E962.0	E980.4
Dichlorphenamide	974.2	E858.5	E944.2	E950.4	E962.0	E980.4
Dichlorvos	989.3	E863.1	—	E950.6	E962.1	E980.7
Diclofenac sodium	965.69	E850.6	E935.6	E950.0	E962.0	E980.0
Dicoumarin, dicumarol	964.2	E858.2	E934.2	E950.4	E962.0	E980.4
Dicyanogen (gas)	987.8	E869.8	—	E952.8	E962.2	E982.8
Dicyclomine	971.1	E855.4	E941.1	E950.4	E962.0	E980.4
Dieldrin (vapor)	989.2	E863.0	—	E950.6	E962.1	E980.7
Dienestrol	962.2	E858.0	E932.2	E950.4	E962.0	E980.4
Dietetics	977.0	E858.8	E947.0	E950.4	E962.0	E980.4
Diethazine	966.4	E855.0	E936.4	E950.4	E962.0	E980.4
Diethyl						
barbituric acid	967.0	E851	E937.0	E950.1	E962.0	E980.1
carbamazine	961.6	E857	E931.6	E950.4	E962.0	E980.4
carbinol	980.8	E860.8	—	E950.9	E962.1	E980.9
carbonate	982.8	E862.4	—	E950.9	E962.1	E980.9

	Poisoning	External Cause (E-Code) Accident	Therapeutic Use	Suicide Attempt	Assault	Undetermined
Diethyl — *continued*						
dioxide	982.8	E862.4	—	E950.9	E962.1	E980.9
ether (vapor) — see ther(s)						
glycol (monoacetate) (monoethyl ether)	982.8	E862.4	—	E950.9	E962.1	E980.9
propion	977.0	E858.8	E947.0	E950.4	E962.0	E980.4
stilbestrol	962.2	E858.0	E932.2	E950.4	E962.0	E980.4
Diethylene						
Diethylsulfone-diethylmethane	967.8	E852.8	E937.8	E950.2	E962.0	E980.2
Difencloxazine	965.09	E850.2	E935.2	E950.0	E962.0	E980.0
Diffusin	963.4	E858.1	E933.4	E950.4	E962.0	E980.4
Diflos	971.0	E855.3	E941.0	E950.4	E962.0	E980.4
Digestants	973.4	E858.4	E943.4	E950.4	E962.0	E980.4
Digitalin(e)	972.1	E858.3	E942.1	E950.4	E962.0	E980.4
Digitalis glycosides	972.1	E858.3	E942.1	E950.4	E962.0	E980.4
Digitoxin	972.1	E858.3	E942.1	E950.4	E962.0	E980.4
Digoxin	972.1	E858.3	E942.1	E950.4	E962.0	E980.4
Dihydrocodeine	965.09	E850.2	E935.2	E950.0	E962.0	E980.0
Dihydrocodeinone	965.09	E850.2	E935.2	E950.0	E962.0	E980.0
Dihydroergocristine	972.9	E858.3	E942.9	E950.4	E962.0	E980.4
Dihydroergotamine	972.9	E858.3	E942.9	E950.4	E962.0	E980.4
Dihydroergotoxine	972.9	E858.3	E942.9	E950.4	E962.0	E980.4
Dihydrohydroxycodeinone	965.09	E850.2	E935.2	E950.0	E962.0	E980.0
Dihydrohydroxymorphinone	965.09	E850.2	E935.2	E950.0	E962.0	E980.0
Dihydroisocodeine	965.09	E850.2	E935.2	E950.0	E962.0	E980.0
Dihydromorphine	965.09	E850.2	E935.2	E950.0	E962.0	E980.0
Dihydromorphinone	965.09	E850.2	E935.2	E950.0	E962.0	E980.0
Dihydrostreptomycin	960.6	E856	E930.6	E950.4	E962.0	E980.4
Dihydrotachysterol	962.6	E858.0	E932.6	E950.4	E962.0	E980.4
Dihydroxyanthraquinone	973.1	E858.4	E943.1	E950.4	E962.0	E980.4
Dihydroxycodeinone	965.09	E850.2	E935.2	E950.0	E962.0	E980.0
Diiodohydroxyquin	961.3	E857	E931.3	E950.4	E962.0	E980.4
topical	976.0	E858.7	E946.0	E950.4	E962.0	E980.4
Diiodohydroxyquinoline	961.3	E857	E931.3	E950.4	E962.0	E980.4
Dilantin	966.1	E855.0	E936.1	E950.4	E962.0	E980.4
Dilaudid	965.09	E850.2	E935.2	E950.0	E962.0	E980.0
Diloxanide	961.5	E857	E931.5	E950.4	E962.0	E980.4
Dimefline	970.0	E854.3	E940.0	E950.4	E962.0	E980.4
Dimenhydrinate	963.0	E858.1	E933.0	E950.4	E962.0	E980.4
Dimercaprol	963.8	E858.1	E933.8	E950.4	E962.0	E980.4
Dimercaptopropanol	963.8	E858.1	E933.8	E950.4	E962.0	E980.4
Dimetane	963.0	E858.1	E933.0	E950.4	E962.0	E980.4
Dimethicone	976.3	E858.7	E946.3	E950.4	E962.0	E980.4
Dimethindene	963.0	E858.1	E933.0	E950.4	E962.0	E980.4
Dimethisoquin	968.5	E855.2	E938.5	E950.4	E962.0	E980.4
Dimethisterone	962.2	E858.0	E932.2	E950.4	E962.0	E980.4
Dimethoxanate	975.4	E858.6	E945.4	E950.4	E962.0	E980.4
Dimethyl						
arsine, arsinic acid — see Arsenic						
carbinol	980.2	E860.3	—	E950.9	E962.1	E980.9
diguanide	962.3	E858.0	E932.3	E950.4	E962.0	E980.4
ketone	982.8	E862.4	—	E950.9	E962.1	E980.9
vapor	987.8	E869.8	—	E952.8	E962.2	E982.8
meperidine	965.09	E850.2	E935.2	E950.0	E962.0	E980.0
parathion	989.3	E863.1	—	E950.6	E962.1	E980.7
polysiloxane	973.8	E858.4	E943.8	E950.4	E962.0	E980.4
sulfate (fumes)	987.8	E869.8	—	E952.8	E962.2	E982.8
liquid	983.9	E864.3	—	E950.7	E962.1	E980.6
sulfoxide NEC	982.8	E862.4	—	E950.9	E962.1	E980.9
medicinal	976.4	E858.7	E946.4	E950.4	E962.0	E980.4
triptamine	969.6	E854.1	E939.6	E950.3	E962.0	E980.3
tubocurarine	975.2	E858.6	E945.2	E950.4	E962.0	E980.4
Dindevan	964.2	E858.2	E934.2	E950.4	E962.0	E980.4
Dinitrobenzene	983.0	E864.0	—	E950.7	E962.1	E980.6
vapor	987.8	E869.8	—	E952.8	E962.2	E982.8
Dinitro (-ortho-) cresol (herbicide) (spray)	989.4	E863.5	—	E950.6	E962.1	E980.7
insecticide	989.4	E863.4	—	E950.6	E962.1	E980.7
Dinitro-orthocresol (herbicide)	989.4	E863.5	—	E950.6	E962.1	E980.7
insecticide	989.4	E863.4	—	E950.6	E962.1	E980.7
Dinitrophenol (herbicide) (spray)	989.4	E863.5	—	E950.6	E962.1	E980.7
insecticide	989.4	E863.4	—	E950.6	E962.1	E980.7
Dinoprost	975.0	E858.6	E945.0	E950.4	E962.0	E980.4
Dioctyl sulfosuccinate (calcium) (sodium)	973.2	E858.4	E943.2	E950.4	E962.0	E980.4
Diodoquin	961.3	E857	E931.3	E950.4	E962.0	E980.4
Dione derivatives NEC	966.3	E855.0	E936.3	E950.4	E962.0	E980.4
Dionin	965.09	E850.2	E935.2	E950.0	E962.0	E980.0

		External Cause (E-Code)				
	Poisoning	Accident	Therapeutic Use	Suicide Attempt	Assault	Undetermined
Dioxane	982.8	E862.4	—	E950.9	E962.1	E980.9
Dioxin — *see* Herbicide						
Dioxyline	972.5	E858.3	E942.5	E950.4	E962.0	E980.4
Dipentene	982.8	E862.4	—	E950.9	E962.1	E980.9
Diphemanil	971.1	E855.4	E941.1	E950.4	E962.0	E980.4
Diphenadione	964.2	E858.2	E934.2	E950.4	E962.0	E980.4
Diphenhydramine	963.0	E858.1	E933.0	E950.4	E962.0	E980.4
Diphenidol	963.0	E858.1	E933.0	E950.4	E962.0	E980.4
Diphenoxylate	973.5	E858.4	E943.5	E950.4	E962.0	E980.4
Diphenylchloroarsine	985.1	E866.3	—	E950.8	E962.1	E980.8
Diphenylhydantoin (sodium)	966.1	E855.0	E936.1	E950.4	E962.0	E980.4
Diphenylpyraline	963.0	E858.1	E933.0	E950.4	E962.0	E980.4
Diphtheria						
antitoxin	979.9	E858.8	E949.9	E950.4	E962.0	E980.4
toxoid	978.5	E858.8	E948.5	E950.4	E962.0	E980.4
with tetanus toxoid	978.9	E858.8	E948.9	E950.4	E962.0	E980.4
with pertussis component	978.6	E858.8	E948.6	E950.4	E962.0	E980.4
vaccine	978.5	E858.8	E948.5	E950.4	E962.0	E980.4
Dipipanone	965.09	E850.2	E935.2	E950.0	E962.0	E980.0
Diplovax	979.5	E858.8	E949.5	E950.4	E962.0	E980.4
Diprophylline	975.1	E858.6	E945.1	E950.4	E962.0	E980.4
Dipyridamole	972.4	E858.3	E942.4	E950.4	E962.0	E980.4
Dipyrone	965.5	E850.5	E935.5	E950.0	E962.0	E980.0
Diquat	989.4	E863.5	—	E950.6	E962.1	E980.7
Disinfectant NEC	983.9	E861.4	—	E950.7	E962.1	E980.6
alkaline	983.2	E861.4	—	E950.7	E962.1	E980.6
aromatic	983.0	E861.4	—	E950.7	E962.1	E980.6
Disipal	966.4	E855.0	E936.4	E950.4	E962.0	E980.4
Disodium edetate	963.8	E858.1	E933.8	E950.4	E962.0	E980.4
Disulfamide	974.4	E858.5	E944.4	E950.4	E962.0	E980.4
Disulfanilamide	961.0	E857	E931.0	E950.4	E962.0	E980.4
Disulfiram	977.3	E858.8	E947.3	E950.4	E962.0	E980.4
Dithiazanine	961.6	E857	E931.6	E950.4	E962.0	E980.4
Dithioglycerol	963.8	E858.1	E933.8	E950.4	E962.0	E980.4
Dithranol	976.4	E858.7	E946.4	E950.4	E962.0	E980.4
Diucardin	974.3	E858.5	E944.3	E950.4	E962.0	E980.4
Diupres	974.3	E858.5	E944.3	E950.4	E962.0	E980.4
Diuretics NEC	974.4	E858.5	E944.4	E950.4	E962.0	E980.4
carbonic acid anhydrase inhibitors	974.2	E858.5	E944.2	E950.4	E962.0	E980.4
mercurial	974.0	E858.5	E944.0	E950.4	E962.0	E980.4
osmotic	974.4	E858.5	E944.4	E950.4	E962.0	E980.4
purine derivatives	974.1	E858.5	E944.1	E950.4	E962.0	E980.4
saluretic	974.3	E858.5	E944.3	E950.4	E962.0	E980.4
Diuril	974.3	E858.5	E944.3	E950.4	E962.0	E980.4
Divinyl ether	968.2	E855.1	E938.2	E950.4	E962.0	E980.4
D-lysergic acid diethylamide	969.6	E854.1	E939.6	E950.3	E962.0	E980.3
DMCT	960.4	E856	E930.4	E950.4	E962.0	E980.4
DMSO	982.8	E862.4	—	E950.9	E962.1	E980.9
DMT	969.6	E854.1	E939.6	E950.3	E962.0	E980.3
DNOC	989.4	E863.5	—	E950.6	E962.1	E980.7
DOCA	962.0	E858.0	E932.0	E950.4	E962.0	E980.4
Dolophine	965.02	E850.1	E935.1	E950.0	E962.0	E980.0
Doloxene	965.8	E850.8	E935.8	E950.0	E962.0	E980.0
DOM	969.6	E854.1	E939.6	E950.3	E962.0	E980.3
Domestic gas — *see* Gas, utility						
Domiphen (bromide) (lozenges)	976.6	E858.7	E946.6	E950.4	E962.0	E980.4
Dopa (levo)	966.4	E855.0	E936.4	E950.4	E962.0	E980.4
Dopamine	971.2	E855.5	E941.2	E950.4	E962.0	E980.4
Doriden	967.5	E852.4	E937.5	E950.2	E962.0	E980.2
Dormiral	967.0	E851	E937.0	E950.1	E962.0	E980.1
Dormison	967.8	E852.8	E937.8	E950.2	E962.0	E980.2
Dornase	963.4	E858.1	E933.4	E950.4	E962.0	E980.4
Dorsacaine	968.5	E855.2	E938.5	E950.4	E962.0	E980.4
Dothiepin hydrochloride	969.0	E854.0	E939.0	E950.3	E962.0	E980.3
Doxapram	970.0	E854.3	E940.0	E950.4	E962.0	E980.4
Doxepin	969.0	E854.0	E939.0	E950.3	E962.0	E980.3
Doxorubicin	960.7	E856	E930.7	E950.4	E962.0	E980.4
Doxycycline	960.4	E856	E930.4	E950.4	E962.0	E980.4
Doxylamine	963.0	E858.1	E933.0	E950.4	E962.0	E980.4
Dramamine	963.0	E858.1	E933.0	E950.4	E962.0	E980.4
Drano (drain cleaner)	983.2	E864.2	—	E950.7	E962.1	E980.6
Dromoran	965.09	E850.2	E935.2	E950.0	E962.0	E980.0
Dromostanolone	962.1	E858.0	E932.1	E950.4	E962.0	E980.4
Droperidol	969.2	E853.1	E939.2	E950.3	E962.0	E980.3
Drotrecogin alfa	964.2	E858.2	E934.2	E950.4	E962.0	E980.4
Drug	977.9	E858.9	E947.9	E950.5	E962.0	E980.5
Drug — *continued*						
AHFS List						
4:00 antihistamine drugs	963.0	E858.1	E933.0	E950.4	E962.0	E980.4
8:04 amebacides	961.5	E857	E931.5	E950.4	E962.0	E980.4
arsenical anti-infectives	961.1	E857	E931.1	E950.4	E962.0	E980.4
quinoline derivatives	961.3	E857	E931.3	E950.4	E962.0	E980.4
8:08 anthelmintics	961.6	E857	E931.6	E950.4	E962.0	E980.4
quinoline derivatives	961.3	E857	E931.3	E950.4	E962.0	E980.4
8:12.04 antifungal antibiotics	960.1	E856	E930.1	E950.4	E962.0	E980.4
8:12.06 cephalosporins	960.5	E856	E930.5	E950.4	E962.0	E980.4
8:12.08 chloramphenicol	960.2	E856	E930.2	E950.4	E962.0	E980.4
8:12.12 erythromycins	960.3	E856	E930.3	E950.4	E962.0	E980.4
8:12.16 penicillins	960.0	E856	E930.0	E950.4	E962.0	E980.4
8:12.20 streptomycins	960.6	E856	E930.6	E950.4	E962.0	E980.4
8:12.24 tetracyclines	960.4	E856	E930.4	E950.4	E962.0	E980.4
8:12.28 other antibiotics	960.8	E856	E930.8	E950.4	E962.0	E980.4
antimycobacterial	960.6	E856	E930.6	E950.4	E962.0	E980.4
macrolides	960.3	E856	E930.3	E950.4	E962.0	E980.4
8:16 antituberculars	961.8	E857	E931.8	E950.4	E962.0	E980.4
antibiotics	960.6	E856	E930.6	E950.4	E962.0	E980.4
8:18 antivirals	961.7	E857	E931.7	E950.4	E962.0	E980.4
8:20 plasmodicides (antimalarials)	961.4	E857	E931.4	E950.4	E962.0	E980.4
8:24 sulfonamides	961.0	E857	E931.0	E950.4	E962.0	E980.4
8:26 sulfones	961.8	E857	E931.8	E950.4	E962.0	E980.4
8:28 treponemicides	961.2	E857	E931.2	E950.4	E962.0	E980.4
8:32 trichomonacides	961.5	E857	E931.5	E950.4	E962.0	E980.4
nitrofuran derivatives	961.9	E857	E931.9	E950.4	E962.0	E980.4
quinoline derivatives	961.3	E857	E931.3	E950.4	E962.0	E980.4
8:36 urinary germicides	961.9	E857	E931.9	E950.4	E962.0	E980.4
quinoline derivatives	961.3	E857	E931.3	E950.4	E962.0	E980.4
8:40 other anti-infectives	961.9	E857	E931.9	E950.4	E962.0	E980.4
10:00 antineoplastic agents	963.1	E858.1	E933.1	E950.4	E962.0	E980.4
antibiotics	960.7	E856	E930.7	E950.4	E962.0	E980.4
progestogens	962.2	E858.0	E932.2	E950.4	E962.0	E980.4
12:04 parasympathomimetic (cholinergic) agents	971.0	E855.3	E941.0	E950.4	E962.0	E980.4
12:08 parasympatholytic (cholinergic-blocking) agents	971.1	E855.4	E941.1	E950.4	E962.0	E980.4
12:12 Sympathomimetic (adrenergic) agents	971.2	E855.5	E941.2	E950.4	E962.0	E980.4
12:16 sympatholytic (adrenergic-blocking) agents	971.3	E855.6	E941.3	E950.4	E962.0	E980.4
12:20 skeletal muscle relaxants						
central nervous system muscle-tone depressants	968.0	E855.1	E938.0	E950.4	E962.0	E980.4
myoneural blocking agents	975.2	E858.6	E945.2	E950.4	E962.0	E980.4
16:00 blood derivatives	964.7	E858.2	E934.7	E950.4	E962.0	E980.4
20:04.04 iron preparations	964.0	E858.2	E934.0	E950.4	E962.0	E980.4
20:04.08 liver and stomach preparations	964.1	E858.2	E934.1	E950.4	E962.0	E980.4
20:04 antianemia drugs	964.1	E858.2	E934.1	E950.4	E962.0	E980.4
20:12.04 anticoagulants	964.2	E858.2	E934.2	E950.4	E962.0	E980.4
20:12.08 antiheparin agents	964.5	E858.2	E934.5	E950.4	E962.0	E980.4
20:12.12 coagulants	964.5	E858.2	E934.5	E950.4	E962.0	E980.4
20:12.16 hemostatics NEC	964.5	E858.2	E934.5	E950.4	E962.0	E980.4
capillary active drugs	972.8	E858.3	E942.8	E950.4	E962.0	E980.4
24:04 cardiac drugs	972.9	E858.3	E942.9	E950.4	E962.0	E980.4
cardiotonic agents	972.1	E858.3	E942.1	E950.4	E962.0	E980.4
rhythm regulators	972.0	E858.3	E942.0	E950.4	E962.0	E980.4
24:06 antilipemic agents	972.2	E858.3	E942.2	E950.4	E962.0	E980.4
thyroid derivatives	962.7	E858.0	E932.7	E950.4	E962.0	E980.4
24:08 hypotensive agents	972.6	E858.3	E942.6	E950.4	E962.0	E980.4
adrenergic blocking agents	971.3	E855.6	E941.3	E950.4	E962.0	E980.4
ganglion blocking agents	972.3	E858.3	E942.3	E950.4	E962.0	E980.4
vasodilators	972.5	E858.3	E942.5	E950.4	E962.0	E980.4
24:12 vasodilating agents NEC	972.5	E858.3	E942.5	E950.4	E962.0	E980.4
coronary	972.4	E858.3	E942.4	E950.4	E962.0	E980.4
nicotinic acid derivatives	972.2	E858.3	E942.2	E950.4	E962.0	E980.4
24:16 sclerosing agents	972.7	E858.3	E942.7	E950.4	E962.0	E980.4
28:04 general anesthetics	968.4	E855.1	E938.4	E950.4	E962.0	E980.4
gaseous anesthetics	968.2	E855.1	E938.2	E950.4	E962.0	E980.4
halothane	968.1	E855.1	E938.1	E950.4	E962.0	E980.4

	Poisoning	External Cause (E-Code) Accident	Therapeutic Use	Suicide Attempt	Assault	Undetermined
Drug — *continued*						
28:04 general anesthetics — *continued*						
intravenous anesthetics	968.3	E855.1	E938.3	E950.4	E962.0	E980.4
28:08 analgesics and antipyretics	965.9	E850.9	E935.9	E950.0	E962.0	E980.0
antirheumatics	965.69	E850.6	E935.6	E950.0	E962.0	E980.0
aromatic analgesics	965.4	E850.4	E935.4	E950.0	E962.0	E980.0
non-narcotic NEC	965.7	E850.7	E935.7	E950.0	E962.0	E980.0
opium alkaloids	965.00	E850.2	E935.2	E950.0	E962.0	E980.0
heroin	965.01	E850.0	E935.0	E950.0	E962.0	E980.0
methadone	965.02	E850.1	E935.1	E950.0	E962.0	E980.0
specified type NEC	965.09	E850.2	E935.2	E950.0	E962.0	E980.0
pyrazole derivatives	965.5	E850.5	E935.5	E950.0	E962.0	E980.0
salicylates	965.1	E850.3	E935.3	E950.0	E962.0	E980.0
specified NEC	965.8	E850.8	E935.8	E950.0	E962.0	E980.0
28:10 narcotic antagonists	970.1	E854.3	E940.1	E950.4	E962.0	E980.4
28:12 anticonvulsants	966.3	E855.0	E936.3	E950.4	E962.0	E980.4
barbiturates	967.0	E851	E937.0	E950.1	E962.0	E980.1
benzodiazepine-based tranquilizers	969.4	E853.2	E939.4	E950.3	E962.0	E980.3
bromides	967.3	E852.2	E937.3	E950.2	E962.0	E980.2
hydantoin derivatives	966.1	E855.0	E936.1	E950.4	E962.0	E980.4
oxazolidine (derivatives)	966.0	E855.0	E936.0	E950.4	E962.0	E980.4
succinimides	966.2	E855.0	E936.2	E950.4	E962.0	E980.4
28:16.04 antidepressants	969.0	E854.0	E939.0	E950.3	E962.0	E980.3
28:16.08 tranquilizers	969.5	E853.9	E939.5	E950.3	E962.0	E980.3
benzodiazepine-based	969.4	E853.2	E939.4	E950.3	E962.0	E980.3
butyrophenone-based	969.2	E853.1	E939.2	E950.3	E962.0	E980.3
major NEC	969.3	E853.8	E939.3	E950.3	E962.0	E980.3
phenothiazine-based	969.1	E853.0	E939.1	E950.3	E962.0	E980.3
28:16.12 other psychotherapeutic agents	969.8	E855.8	E939.8	E950.3	E962.0	E980.3
28:20 respiratory and cerebral stimulants	970.9	E854.3	E940.9	E950.4	E962.0	E980.4
analeptics	970.0	E854.3	E940.0	E950.4	E962.0	E980.4
anorexigenic agents	977.0	E858.8	E947.0	E950.4	E962.0	E980.4
psychostimulants	969.7	E854.2	E939.7	E950.3	E962.0	E980.3
specified NEC	970.8	E854.3	E940.8	E950.4	E962.0	E980.4
28:24 sedatives and hypnotics	967.9	E852.9	E937.9	E950.2	E962.0	E980.2
barbiturates	967.0	E851	E937.0	E950.1	E962.0	E980.1
benzodiazepine-based tranquilizers	969.4	E853.2	E939.4	E950.3	E962.0	E980.3
chloral hydrate (group)	967.1	E852.0	E937.1	E950.2	E962.0	E980.2
glutethamide group	967.5	E852.4	E937.5	E950.2	E962.0	E980.2
intravenous anesthetics	968.3	E855.1	E938.3	E950.4	E962.0	E980.4
methaqualone (compounds)	967.4	E852.3	E937.4	E950.2	E962.0	E980.2
paraldehyde	967.2	E852.1	E937.2	E950.2	E962.0	E980.2
phenothiazine-based tranquilizers	969.1	E853.0	E939.1	E950.3	E962.0	E980.3
specified NEC	967.8	E852.8	E937.8	E950.2	E962.0	E980.2
thiobarbiturates	968.3	E855.1	E938.3	E950.4	E962.0	E980.4
tranquilizer NEC	969.5	E853.9	E939.5	E950.3	E962.0	E980.3
36:04 to 36:88 diagnostic agents	977.8	E858.8	E947.8	E950.4	E962.0	E980.4
40:00 electrolyte, caloric, and water balance agents NEC	974.5	E858.5	E944.5	E950.4	E962.0	E980.4
40:04 acidifying agents	963.2	E858.1	E933.2	E950.4	E962.0	E980.4
40:08 alkalinizing agents	963.3	E858.1	E933.3	E950.4	E962.0	E980.4
40:10 ammonia detoxicants	974.5	E858.5	E944.5	E950.4	E962.0	E980.4
40:12 replacement solutions	974.5	E858.5	E944.5	E950.4	E962.0	E980.4
plasma expanders	964.8	E858.2	E934.8	E950.4	E962.0	E980.4
40:16 sodium-removing resins	974.5	E858.5	E944.5	E950.4	E962.0	E980.4
40:18 potassium-removing resins	974.5	E858.5	E944.5	E950.4	E962.0	E980.4
40:20 caloric agents	974.5	E858.5	E944.5	E950.4	E962.0	E980.4
40:24 salt and sugar substitutes	974.5	E858.5	E944.5	E950.4	E962.0	E980.4
40:28 diuretics NEC	974.4	E858.5	E944.4	E950.4	E962.0	E980.4
carbonic acid anhydrase inhibitors	974.2	E858.5	E944.2	E950.4	E962.0	E980.4
mercurials	974.0	E858.5	E944.0	E950.4	E962.0	E980.4
purine derivatives	974.1	E858.5	E944.1	E950.4	E962.0	E980.4
saluretics	974.3	E858.5	E944.3	E950.4	E962.0	E980.4
thiazides	974.3	E858.5	E944.3	E950.4	E962.0	E980.4
40:36 irrigating solutions	974.5	E858.5	E944.5	E950.4	E962.0	E980.4
Drug — *continued*						
40:40 uricosuric agents	974.7	E858.5	E944.7	E950.4	E962.0	E980.4
44:00 enzymes	963.4	E858.1	E933.4	E950.4	E962.0	E980.4
fibrinolysis-affecting agents	964.4	E858.2	E934.4	E950.4	E962.0	E980.4
gastric agents	973.4	E858.4	E943.4	E950.4	E962.0	E980.4
48:00 expectorants and cough preparations						
antihistamine agents	963.0	E858.1	E933.0	E950.4	E962.0	E980.4
antitussives	975.4	E858.6	E945.4	E950.4	E962.0	E980.4
codeine derivatives	965.09	E850.2	E935.2	E950.0	E962.0	E980.0
expectorants	975.5	E858.6	E945.5	E950.4	E962.0	E980.4
narcotic agents NEC	965.09	E850.2	E935.2	E950.0	E962.0	E980.0
52:04.04 antibiotics (EENT)						
ENT agent	976.6	E858.7	E946.6	E950.4	E962.0	E980.4
ophthalmic preparation	976.5	E858.7	E946.5	E950.4	E962.0	E980.4
52:04.06 antivirals (EENT)						
ENT agent	976.6	E858.7	E946.6	E950.4	E962.0	E980.4
ophthalmic preparation	976.5	E858.7	E946.5	E950.4	E962.0	E980.4
52:04.08 sulfonamides (EENT)						
ENT agent	976.6	E858.7	E946.6	E950.4	E962.0	E980.4
ophthalmic preparation	976.5	E858.7	E946.5	E950.4	E962.0	E980.4
52:04.12 miscellaneous anti-infectives (EENT)						
ENT agent	976.6	E858.7	E946.6	E950.4	E962.0	E980.4
ophthalmic preparation	976.5	E858.7	E946.5	E950.4	E962.0	E980.4
52:04 anti-infectives (EENT)						
ENT agent	976.6	E858.7	E946.6	E950.4	E962.0	E980.4
ophthalmic preparation	976.5	E858.7	E946.5	E950.4	E962.0	E980.4
52:08 anti-inflammatory agents (EENT)						
ENT agent	976.6	E858.7	E946.6	E950.4	E962.0	E980.4
ophthalmic preparation	976.5	E858.7	E946.5	E950.4	E962.0	E980.4
52:10 carbonic anhydrase inhibitors	974.2	E858.5	E944.2	E950.4	E962.0	E980.4
52:12 contact lens solutions	976.5	E858.7	E946.5	E950.4	E962.0	E980.4
52:16 local anesthetics (EENT)	968.5	E855.2	E938.5	E950.4	E962.0	E980.4
52:20 miotics	971.0	E855.3	E941.0	E950.4	E962.0	E980.4
52:24 mydriatics						
adrenergics	971.2	E855.5	E941.2	E950.4	E962.0	E980.4
anticholinergics	971.1	E855.4	E941.1	E950.4	E962.0	E980.4
antimuscarinics	971.1	E855.4	E941.1	E950.4	E962.0	E980.4
parasympatholytics	971.1	E855.4	E941.1	E950.4	E962.0	E980.4
spasmolytics	971.1	E855.4	E941.1	E950.4	E962.0	E980.4
sympathomimetics	971.2	E855.5	E941.2	E950.4	E962.0	E980.4
52:28 mouth washes and gargles	976.6	E858.7	E946.6	E950.4	E962.0	E980.4
52:32 vasoconstrictors (EENT)	971.2	E855.5	E941.2	E950.4	E962.0	E980.4
52:36 unclassified agents (EENT)						
ENT agent	976.6	E858.7	E946.6	E950.4	E962.0	E980.4
ophthalmic preparation	976.5	E858.7	E946.5	E950.4	E962.0	E980.4
56:04 antacids and adsorbents	973.0	E858.4	E943.0	E950.4	E962.0	E980.4
56:08 antidiarrhea agents	973.5	E858.4	E943.5	E950.4	E962.0	E980.4
56:10 antiflatulents	973.8	E858.4	E943.8	E950.4	E962.0	E980.4
56:12 cathartics NEC	973.3	E858.4	E943.3	E950.4	E962.0	E980.4
emollients	973.2	E858.4	E943.2	E950.4	E962.0	E980.4
irritants	973.1	E858.4	E943.1	E950.4	E962.0	E980.4
56:16 digestants	973.4	E858.4	E943.4	E950.4	E962.0	E980.4
56:20 emetics and antiemetics						
antiemetics	963.0	E858.1	E933.0	E950.4	E962.0	E980.4
emetics	973.6	E858.4	E943.6	E950.4	E962.0	E980.4
56:24 lipotropic agents	977.1	E858.8	E947.1	E950.4	E962.0	E980.4
56:40 miscellaneous G.I. drugs	973.8	E858.4	E943.8	E950.4	E962.0	E980.4
60:00 gold compounds	965.69	E850.6	E935.6	E950.0	E962.0	E980.0
64:00 heavy metal antagonists	963.8	E858.1	E933.8	E950.4	E962.0	E980.4
68:04 adrenals	962.0	E858.0	E932.0	E950.4	E962.0	E980.4
68:08 androgens	962.1	E858.0	E932.1	E950.4	E962.0	E980.4
68:12 contraceptives, oral	962.2	E858.0	E932.2	E950.4	E962.0	E980.4
68:16 estrogens	962.2	E858.0	E932.2	E950.4	E962.0	E980.4
68:18 gonadotropins	962.4	E858.0	E932.4	E950.4	E962.0	E980.4
68:20.08 insulins	962.3	E858.0	E932.3	E950.4	E962.0	E980.4
68:20 insulins and antidiabetic agents	962.3	E858.0	E932.3	E950.4	E962.0	E980.4
68:24 parathyroid	962.6	E858.0	E932.6	E950.4	E962.0	E980.4
68:28 pituitary (posterior)	962.5	E858.0	E932.5	E950.4	E962.0	E980.4
anterior	962.4	E858.0	E932.4	E950.4	E962.0	E980.4

		External Cause (E-Code)				
	Poisoning	Accident	Therapeutic Use	Suicide Attempt	Assault	Undetermined
Drug — *continued*						
68:32 progestogens	962.2	E858.0	E932.2	E950.4	E962.0	E980.4
68:34 other corpus luteum hormones NEC	962.2	E858.0	E932.2	E950.4	E962.0	E980.4
68:36 thyroid and antithyroid						
antithyroid	962.8	E858.0	E932.8	E950.4	E962.0	E980.4
thyroid (derivatives)	962.7	E858.0	E932.7	E950.4	E962.0	E980.4
72:00 local anesthetics NEC	968.9	E855.2	E938.9	E950.4	E962.0	E980.4
infiltration (intradermal) (subcutaneous) (submucosal)	968.5	E855.2	E938.5	E950.4	E962.0	E980.4
nerve blocking (peripheral) (plexus) (regional)	968.6	E855.2	E938.6	E950.4	E962.0	E980.4
spinal	968.7	E855.2	E938.7	E950.4	E962.0	E980.4
topical (surface)	968.5	E855.2	E938.5	E950.4	E962.0	E980.4
76:00 oxytocics	975.0	E858.6	E945.0	E950.4	E962.0	E980.4
78:00 radioactive agents	990	—	—	—	—	—
80:04 serums NEC	979.9	E858.8	E949.9	E950.4	E962.0	E980.4
immune gamma globulin (human)	964.6	E858.2	E934.6	E950.4	E962.0	E980.4
80:08 toxoids NEC	978.8	E858.8	E948.8	E950.4	E962.0	E980.4
diphtheria	978.5	E858.8	E948.5	E950.4	E962.0	E980.4
and diphtheria	978.9	E858.8	E948.9	E950.4	E962.0	E980.4
with pertussis component	978.6	E858.8	E948.6	E950.4	E962.0	E980.4
and tetanus	978.9	E858.8	E948.9	E950.4	E962.0	E980.4
with pertussis component	978.6	E858.8	E948.6	E950.4	E962.0	E980.4
tetanus	978.4	E858.8	E948.4	E950.4	E962.0	E980.4
80:12 vaccines	979.9	E858.8	E949.9	E950.4	E962.0	E980.4
bacterial NEC	978.8	E858.8	E948.8	E950.4	E962.0	E980.4
with						
other bacterial components	978.9	E858.8	E948.9	E950.4	E962.0	E980.4
pertussis component	978.6	E858.8	E948.6	E950.4	E962.0	E980.4
viral and rickettsial components	979.7	E858.8	E949.7	E950.4	E962.0	E980.4
rickettsial NEC	979.6	E858.8	E949.6	E950.4	E962.0	E980.4
with						
bacterial component	979.7	E858.8	E949.7	E950.4	E962.0	E980.4
pertussis component	978.6	E858.8	E948.6	E950.4	E962.0	E980.4
viral component	979.7	E858.8	E949.7	E950.4	E962.0	E980.4
viral NEC	979.6	E858.8	E949.6	E950.4	E962.0	E980.4
with						
bacterial component	979.7	E858.8	E949.7	E950.4	E962.0	E980.4
pertussis component	978.6	E858.8	E948.6	E950.4	E962.0	E980.4
rickettsial component	979.7	E858.8	E949.7	E950.4	E962.0	E980.4
84:04.04 antibiotics (skin and mucous membrane)	976.0	E858.7	E946.0	E950.4	E962.0	E980.4
84:04.08 fungicides (skin and mucous membrane)	976.0	E858.7	E946.0	E950.4	E962.0	E980.4
84:04.12 scabicides and pediculicides (skin and mucous membrane)	976.0	E858.7	E946.0	E950.4	E962.0	E980.4
84:04.16 miscellaneous local anti-infectives (skin and mucous membrane)	976.0	E858.7	E946.0	E950.4	E962.0	E980.4
84:06 anti-inflammatory agents (skin and mucous membrane)	976.0	E858.7	E946.0	E950.4	E962.0	E980.4
84:08 antipruritics and local anesthetics						
antipruritics	976.1	E858.7	E946.1	E950.4	E962.0	E980.4
local anesthetics	968.5	E855.2	E938.5	E950.4	E962.0	E980.4
84:12 astringents	976.2	E858.7	E946.2	E950.4	E962.0	E980.4
84:16 cell stimulants and proliferants	976.8	E858.7	E946.8	E950.4	E962.0	E980.4
84:20 detergents	976.2	E858.7	E946.2	E950.4	E962.0	E980.4
84:24 emollients, demulcents, and protectants	976.3	E858.7	E946.3	E950.4	E962.0	E980.4
84:28 keratolytic agents	976.4	E858.7	E946.4	E950.4	E962.0	E980.4
84:32 keratoplastic agents	976.4	E858.7	E946.4	E950.4	E962.0	E980.4
84:36 miscellaneous agents (skin and mucous membrane)	976.8	E858.7	E946.8	E950.4	E962.0	E980.4

		External Cause (E-Code)				
	Poisoning	Accident	Therapeutic Use	Suicide Attempt	Assault	Undetermined
Drug — *continued*						
86:00 spasmolytic agents	975.1	E858.6	E945.1	E950.4	E962.0	E980.4
antiasthmatics	975.7	E858.6	E945.7	E950.4	E962.0	E980.4
papaverine	972.5	E858.3	E942.5	E950.4	E962.0	E980.4
theophylline	974.1	E858.5	E944.1	E950.4	E962.0	E980.4
88:04 vitamin A	963.5	E858.1	E933.5	E950.4	E962.0	E980.4
88:08 vitamin B complex	963.5	E858.1	E933.5	E950.4	E962.0	E980.4
hematopoietic vitamin	964.1	E858.2	E934.1	E950.4	E962.0	E980.4
nicotinic acid derivatives	972.2	E858.3	E942.2	E950.4	E962.0	E980.4
88:12 vitamin C	963.5	E858.1	E933.5	E950.4	E962.0	E980.4
88:16 vitamin D	963.5	E858.1	E933.5	E950.4	E962.0	E980.4
88:20 vitamin E	963.5	E858.1	E933.5	E950.4	E962.0	E980.4
88:24 vitamin K activity	964.3	E858.2	E934.3	E950.4	E962.0	E980.4
88:28 multivitamin preparations	963.5	E858.1	E933.5	E950.4	E962.0	E980.4
92:00 unclassified therapeutic agents	977.8	E858.8	E947.8	E950.4	E962.0	E980.4
specified NEC	977.8	E858.8	E947.8	E950.4	E962.0	E980.4
Duboisine	971.1	E855.4	E941.1	E950.4	E962.0	E980.4
Dulcolax	973.1	E858.4	E943.1	E950.4	E962.0	E980.4
Duponol (C) (EP)	976.2	E858.7	E946.2	E950.4	E962.0	E980.4
Durabolin	962.1	E858.0	E932.1	E950.4	E962.0	E980.4
Dyclone	968.5	E855.2	E938.5	E950.4	E962.0	E980.4
Dyclonine	968.5	E855.2	E938.5	E950.4	E962.0	E980.4
Dydrogesterone	962.2	E858.0	E932.2	E950.4	E962.0	E980.4
Dyes NEC	989.89	E866.8	—	E950.9	E962.1	E980.9
diagnostic agents	977.8	E858.8	E947.8	E950.4	E962.0	E980.4
pharmaceutical NEC	977.4	E858.8	E947.4	E950.4	E962.0	E980.4
Dyfols	971.0	E855.3	E941.0	E950.4	E962.0	E980.4
Dymelor	962.3	E858.0	E932.3	E950.4	E962.0	E980.4
Dynamite	989.89	E866.8	—	E950.9	E962.1	E980.9
fumes	987.8	E869.8	—	E952.8	E962.2	E982.8
Dyphylline	975.1	E858.6	E945.1	E950.4	E962.0	E980.4
Ear preparations	976.6	E858.7	E946.6	E950.4	E962.0	E980.4
Echothiopate, ecothiopate	971.0	E855.3	E941.0	E950.4	E962.0	E980.4
Ecstasy	969.7	E854.2	E939.7	E950.3	E962.0	E980.3
Ectylurea	967.8	E852.8	E937.8	E950.2	E962.0	E980.2
Edathamil disodium	963.8	E858.1	E933.8	E950.4	E962.0	E980.4
Edecrin	974.4	E858.5	E944.4	E950.4	E962.0	E980.4
Edetate, disodium (calcium)	963.8	E858.1	E933.8	E950.4	E962.0	E980.4
Edrophonium	971.0	E855.3	E941.0	E950.4	E962.0	E980.4
Elase	976.8	E858.7	E946.8	E950.4	E962.0	E980.4
Elaterium	973.1	E858.4	E943.1	E950.4	E962.0	E980.4
Elder	988.2	E865.4	—	E950.9	E962.1	E980.9
berry (unripe)	988.2	E865.3	—	E950.9	E962.1	E980.9
Electrolytes NEC	974.5	E858.5	E944.5	E950.4	E962.0	E980.4
Electrolytic agent NEC	974.5	E858.5	E944.5	E950.4	E962.0	E980.4
Embramine	963.0	E858.1	E933.0	E950.4	E962.0	E980.4
Emetics	973.6	E858.4	E943.6	E950.4	E962.0	E980.4
Emetine (hydrochloride)	961.5	E857	E931.5	E950.4	E962.0	E980.4
Emollients	976.3	E858.7	E946.3	E950.4	E962.0	E980.4
Emylcamate	969.5	E853.8	E939.5	E950.3	E962.0	E980.3
Encyprate	969.0	E854.0	E939.0	E950.3	E962.0	E980.3
Endocaine	968.5	E855.2	E938.5	E950.4	E962.0	E980.4
Endrin	989.2	E863.0	—	E950.6	E962.1	E980.7
Enflurane	968.2	E855.1	E938.2	E950.4	E962.0	E980.4
Enovid	962.2	E858.0	E932.2	E950.4	E962.0	E980.4
ENT preparations (anti-infectives)	976.6	E858.7	E946.6	E950.4	E962.0	E980.4
Enzodase	963.4	E858.1	E933.4	E950.4	E962.0	E980.4
Enzymes NEC	963.4	E858.1	E933.4	E950.4	E962.0	E980.4
Epanutin	966.1	E855.0	E936.1	E950.4	E962.0	E980.4
Ephedra (tincture)	971.2	E855.5	E941.2	E950.4	E962.0	E980.4
Ephedrine	971.2	E855.5	E941.2	E950.4	E962.0	E980.4
Epiestriol	962.2	E858.0	E932.2	E950.4	E962.0	E980.4
Epilim — see Sodium valproate						
Epinephrine	971.2	E855.5	E941.2	E950.4	E962.0	E980.4
Epsom salt	973.3	E858.4	E943.3	E950.4	E962.0	E980.4
Equanil	969.5	E853.8	E939.5	E950.3	E962.0	E980.3
Equisetum (diuretic)	974.4	E858.5	E944.4	E950.4	E962.0	E980.4
Ergometrine	975.0	E858.6	E945.0	E950.4	E962.0	E980.4
Ergonovine	975.0	E858.6	E945.0	E950.4	E962.0	E980.4
Ergot NEC	988.2	E865.4	—	E950.9	E962.1	E980.9
medicinal (alkaloids)	975.0	E858.6	E945.0	E950.4	E962.0	E980.4
Ergotamine (tartrate) (for migraine) NEC	972.9	E858.3	E942.9	E950.4	E962.0	E980.4
Ergotrate	975.0	E858.6	E945.0	E950.4	E962.0	E980.4
Erythrityl tetranitrate	972.4	E858.3	E942.4	E950.4	E962.0	E980.4
Erythrol tetranitrate	972.4	E858.3	E942.4	E950.4	E962.0	E980.4
Erythromycin	960.3	E856	E930.3	E950.4	E962.0	E980.4
ophthalmic preparation	976.5	E858.7	E946.5	E950.4	E962.0	E980.4

		External Cause (E-Code)				
	Poisoning	Accident	Therapeutic Use	Suicide Attempt	Assault	Undetermined
Erythromycin — *continued*						
topical NEC	976.0	E858.7	E946.0	E950.4	E962.0	E980.4
Eserine	971.0	E855.3	E941.0	E950.4	E962.0	E980.4
Eskabarb	967.0	E851	E937.0	E950.1	E962.0	E980.1
Eskalith	969.8	E855.8	E939.8	E950.3	E962.0	E980.3
Estradiol (cypionate) (dipropionate) (valerate)	962.2	E858.0	E932.2	E950.4	E962.0	E980.4
Estriol	962.2	E858.0	E932.2	E950.4	E962.0	E980.4
Estrogens (with progestogens)	962.2	E858.0	E932.2	E950.4	E962.0	E980.4
Estrone	962.2	E858.0	E932.2	E950.4	E962.0	E980.4
Etafedrine	971.2	E855.5	E941.2	E950.4	E962.0	E980.4
Ethacrynate sodium	974.4	E858.5	E944.4	E950.4	E962.0	E980.4
Ethacrynic acid	974.4	E858.5	E944.4	E950.4	E962.0	E980.4
Ethambutol	961.8	E857	E931.8	E950.4	E962.0	E980.4
Ethamide	974.2	E858.5	E944.2	E950.4	E962.0	E980.4
Ethamivan	970.0	E854.3	E940.0	E950.4	E962.0	E980.4
Ethamsylate	964.5	E858.2	E934.5	E950.4	E962.0	E980.4
Ethanol	980.0	E860.1	—	E950.9	E962.1	E980.9
beverage	980.0	E860.0	—	E950.9	E962.1	E980.9
Ethchlorvynol	967.8	E852.8	E937.8	E950.2	E962.0	E980.2
Ethebenecid	974.7	E858.5	E944.7	E950.4	E962.0	E980.4
Ether(s) (diethyl) (ethyl) (vapor)	987.8	E869.8	—	E952.8	E962.2	E982.8
anesthetic	968.2	E855.1	E938.2	E950.4	E962.0	E980.4
petroleum — see Ligroin						
solvent	982.8	E862.4	—	E950.9	E962.1	E980.9
Ethidine chloride (vapor)	987.8	E869.8	—	E952.8	E962.2	E982.8
liquid (solvent)	982.3	E862.4	—	E950.9	E962.1	E980.9
Ethinamate	967.8	E852.8	E937.8	E950.2	E962.0	E980.2
Ethinylestradiol	962.2	E858.0	E932.2	E950.4	E962.0	E980.4
Ethionamide	961.8	E857	E931.8	E950.4	E962.0	E980.4
Ethisterone	962.2	E858.0	E932.2	E950.4	E962.0	E980.4
Ethobral	967.0	E851	E937.0	E950.1	E962.0	E980.1
Ethocaine (infiltration) (topical)	968.5	E855.2	E938.5	E950.4	E962.0	E980.4
nerve block (peripheral) (plexus)	968.6	E855.2	E938.6	E950.4	E962.0	E980.4
spinal	968.7	E855.2	E938.7	E950.4	E962.0	E980.4
Ethoheptazine (citrate)	965.7	E850.7	E935.7	E950.0	E962.0	E980.0
Ethopropazine	966.4	E855.0	E936.4	E950.4	E962.0	E980.4
Ethosuximide	966.2	E855.0	E936.2	E950.4	E962.0	E980.4
Ethotoin	966.1	E855.0	E936.1	E950.4	E962.0	E980.4
Ethoxazene	961.9	E857	E931.9	E950.4	E962.0	E980.4
Ethoxzolamide	974.2	E858.5	E944.2	E950.4	E962.0	E980.4
Ethyl						
acetate (vapor)	982.8	E862.4	—	E950.9	E962.1	E980.9
alcohol	980.0	E860.1	—	E950.9	E962.1	E980.9
beverage	980.0	E860.0	—	E950.9	E962.1	E980.9
aldehyde (vapor)	987.8	E869.8	—	E952.8	E962.2	E982.8
liquid	989.89	E866.8	—	E950.9	E962.1	E980.9
aminobenzoate	968.5	E855.2	E938.5	E950.4	E962.0	E980.4
biscoumacetate	964.2	E858.2	E934.2	E950.4	E962.0	E980.4
bromide (anesthetic)	968.2	E855.1	E938.2	E950.4	E962.0	E980.4
carbamate (antineoplastic)	963.1	E858.1	E933.1	E950.4	E962.0	E980.4
carbinol	980.3	E860.4	—	E950.9	E962.1	E980.9
chaulmoograte	961.8	E857	E931.8	E950.4	E962.0	E980.4
chloride (vapor)	987.8	E869.8	—	E952.8	E962.2	E982.8
anesthetic (local)	968.5	E855.2	E938.5	E950.4	E962.0	E980.4
inhaled	968.2	E855.1	E938.2	E950.4	E962.0	E980.4
solvent	982.3	E862.4	—	E950.9	E962.1	E980.9
estranol	962.1	E858.0	E932.1	E950.4	E962.0	E980.4
ether — see Ether(s)						
formate (solvent) NEC	982.8	E862.4	—	E950.9	E962.1	E980.9
iodoacetate	987.5	E869.3	—	E952.8	E962.2	E982.8
lactate (solvent) NEC	982.8	E862.4	—	E950.9	E962.1	E980.9
methylcarbinol	980.8	E860.8	—	E950.9	E962.1	E980.9
morphine	965.09	E850.2	E935.2	E950.0	E962.0	E980.0
Ethylene (gas)	987.1	E869.8	—	E952.8	E962.2	E982.8
anesthetic (general)	968.2	E855.1	E938.2	E950.4	E962.0	E980.4
chlorohydrin (vapor)	982.3	E862.4	—	E950.9	E962.1	E980.9
dichloride (vapor)	982.3	E862.4	—	E950.9	E962.1	E980.9
glycol(s) (any) (vapor)	982.8	E862.4	—	E950.9	E962.1	E980.9
Ethylidene						
chloride NEC	982.3	E862.4	—	E950.9	E962.1	E980.9
diethyl ether	982.8	E862.4	—	E950.9	E962.1	E980.9
Ethynodiol	962.2	E858.0	E932.2	E950.4	E962.0	E980.4
Etidocaine	968.9	E855.2	E938.9	E950.4	E962.0	E980.4
infiltration (subcutaneous)	968.5	E855.2	E938.5	E950.4	E962.0	E980.4
nerve (peripheral) (plexus)	968.6	E855.2	E938.6	E950.4	E962.0	E980.4
Etilfen	967.0	E851	E937.0	E950.1	E962.0	E980.1
Etomide	965.7	E850.7	E935.7	E950.0	E962.0	E980.0
Etorphine	965.09	E850.2	E935.2	E950.0	E962.0	E980.0
Etoval	967.0	E851	E937.0	E950.1	E962.0	E980.1
Etryptamine	969.0	E854.0	E939.0	E950.3	E962.0	E980.3
Eucaine	968.5	E855.2	E938.5	E950.4	E962.0	E980.4
Eucalyptus (oil) NEC	975.5	E858.6	E945.5	E950.4	E962.0	E980.4
Eucatropine	971.1	E855.4	E941.1	E950.4	E962.0	E980.4
Eucodal	965.09	E850.2	E935.2	E950.0	E962.0	E980.0
Euneryl	967.0	E851	E937.0	E950.1	E962.0	E980.1
Euphthalmine	971.1	E855.4	E941.1	E950.4	E962.0	E980.4
Eurax	976.0	E858.7	E946.0	E950.4	E962.0	E980.4
Euresol	976.4	E858.7	E946.4	E950.4	E962.0	E980.4
Euthroid	962.7	E858.0	E932.7	E950.4	E962.0	E980.4
Evans blue	977.8	E858.8	E947.8	E950.4	E962.0	E980.4
Evipal	967.0	E851	E937.0	E950.1	E962.0	E980.1
sodium	968.3	E855.1	E938.3	E950.4	E962.0	E980.4
Evipan	967.0	E851	E937.0	E950.1	E962.0	E980.1
sodium	968.3	E855.1	E938.3	E950.4	E962.0	E980.4
Exalgin	965.4	E850.4	E935.4	E950.0	E962.0	E980.0
Excipients, pharmaceutical	977.4	E858.8	E947.4	E950.4	E962.0	E980.4
Exhaust gas — *see* Carbon, monoxide						
Ex-Lax (phenolphthalein)	973.1	E858.4	E943.1	E950.4	E962.0	E980.4
Expectorants	975.5	E858.6	E945.5	E950.4	E962.0	E980.4
External medications (skin) (mucous membrane)	976.9	E858.7	E946.9	E950.4	E962.0	E980.4
dental agent	976.7	E858.7	E946.7	E950.4	E962.0	E980.4
ENT agent	976.6	E858.7	E946.6	E950.4	E962.0	E980.4
ophthalmic preparation	976.5	E858.7	E946.5	E950.4	E962.0	E980.4
specified NEC	976.8	E858.7	E946.8	E950.4	E962.0	E980.4
Eye agents (anti-infective)	976.5	E858.7	E946.5	E950.4	E962.0	E980.4
Factor IX complex (human)	964.5	E858.2	E934.5	E950.4	E962.0	E980.4
Fecal softeners	973.2	E858.4	E943.2	E950.4	E962.0	E980.4
Fenbutrazate	977.0	E858.8	E947.0	E950.4	E962.0	E980.4
Fencamfamin	970.8	E854.3	E940.8	E950.4	E962.0	E980.4
Fenfluramine	977.0	E858.8	E947.0	E950.4	E962.0	E980.4
Fenoprofen	965.61	E850.6	E935.6	E950.0	E962.0	E980.0
Fentanyl	965.09	E850.2	E935.2	E950.0	E962.0	E980.0
Fentazin	969.1	E853.0	E939.1	E950.3	E962.0	E980.3
Fenticlor, fentichlor	976.0	E858.7	E946.0	E950.4	E962.0	E980.4
Fer de lance (bite) (venom)	989.5	E905.0	—	E950.9	E962.1	E980.9
Ferric — *see* Iron						
Ferrocholinate	964.0	E858.2	E934.0	E950.4	E962.0	E980.4
Ferrous fumerate, gluconate, lactate, salt NEC, sulfate (medicinal)	964.0	E858.2	E934.0	E950.4	E962.0	E980.4
Ferrum — see Iron						
Fertilizers NEC	989.89	E866.5	—	E950.9	E962.1	E980.4
with herbicide mixture	989.4	E863.5	—	E950.6	E962.1	E980.7
Fibrinogen (human)	964.7	E858.2	E934.7	E950.4	E962.0	E980.4
Fibrinolysin	964.4	E858.2	E934.4	E950.4	E962.0	E980.4
Fibrinolysis-affecting agents	964.4	E858.2	E934.4	E950.4	E962.0	E980.4
Filix mas	961.6	E857	E931.6	E950.4	E962.0	E980.4
Fiorinal	965.1	E850.3	E935.3	E950.0	E962.0	E980.0
Fire damp	987.1	E869.8	—	E952.8	E962.2	E982.8
Fish, nonbacterial or noxious	988.0	E865.2	—	E950.9	E962.1	E980.9
shell	988.0	E865.1	—	E950.9	E962.1	E980.9
Flagyl	961.5	E857	E931.5	E950.4	E962.0	E980.4
Flavoxate	975.1	E858.6	E945.1	E950.4	E962.0	E980.4
Flaxedil	975.2	E858.6	E945.2	E950.4	E962.0	E980.4
Flaxseed (medicinal)	976.3	E858.7	E946.3	E950.4	E962.0	E980.4
Florantyrone	973.4	E858.4	E943.4	E950.4	E962.0	E980.4
Floraquin	961.3	E857	E931.3	E950.4	E962.0	E980.4
Florinef	962.0	E858.0	E932.0	E950.4	E962.0	E980.4
ENT agent	976.6	E858.7	E946.6	E950.4	E962.0	E980.4
ophthalmic preparation	976.5	E858.7	E946.5	E950.4	E962.0	E980.4
topical NEC	976.0	E858.7	E946.0	E950.4	E962.0	E980.4
Flowers of sulfur	976.4	E858.7	E946.4	E950.4	E962.0	E980.4
Floxuridine	963.1	E858.1	E933.1	E950.4	E962.0	E980.4
Flucytosine	961.9	E857	E931.9	E950.4	E962.0	E980.4
Fludrocortisone	962.0	E858.0	E932.0	E950.4	E962.0	E980.4
ENT agent	976.6	E858.7	E946.6	E950.4	E962.0	E980.4
ophthalmic preparation	976.5	E858.7	E946.5	E950.4	E962.0	E980.4
topical NEC	976.0	E858.7	E946.0	E950.4	E962.0	E980.4
Flumethasone	976.0	E858.7	E946.0	E950.4	E962.0	E980.4
Flumethiazide	974.3	E858.5	E944.3	E950.4	E962.0	E980.4
Flumidin	961.7	E857	E931.7	E950.4	E962.0	E980.4
Flunitrazepam	969.4	E853.2	E939.4	E950.3	E962.0	E980.3

	Poisoning	External Cause (E-Code) Accident	Therapeutic Use	Suicide Attempt	Assault	Undetermined
Fluocinolone	976.0	E858.7	E946.0	E950.4	E962.0	E980.4
Fluocortolone	962.0	E858.0	E932.0	E950.4	E962.0	E980.4
Fluohydrocortisone	962.0	E858.0	E932.0	E950.4	E962.0	E980.4
ENT agent	976.6	E858.7	E946.6	E950.4	E962.0	E980.4
ophthalmic preparation	976.5	E858.7	E946.5	E950.4	E962.0	E980.4
topical NEC	976.0	E858.7	E946.0	E950.4	E962.0	E980.4
Fluonid	976.0	E858.7	E946.0	E950.4	E962.0	E980.4
Fluopromazine	969.1	E853.0	E939.1	E950.3	E962.0	E980.3
Fluoracetate	989.4	E863.7	—	E950.6	E962.1	E980.7
Fluorescein (sodium)	977.8	E858.8	E947.8	E950.4	E962.0	E980.4
Fluoride(s) (pesticides) (sodium) NEC	989.4	E863.4	—	E950.6	E962.1	E980.7
hydrogen — see Hydrofluoric acid						
medicinal	976.7	E858.7	E946.7	E950.4	E962.0	E980.4
not pesticide NEC	983.9	E864.4	—	E950.7	E962.1	E980.6
stannous	976.7	E858.7	E946.7	E950.4	E962.0	E980.4
Fluorinated corticosteroids	962.0	E858.0	E932.0	E950.4	E962.0	E980.4
Fluorine (compounds) (gas)	987.8	E869.8	—	E952.8	E962.2	E982.8
salt — see Fluoride(s)						
Fluoristan	976.7	E858.7	E946.7	E950.4	E962.0	E980.4
Fluoroacetate	989.4	E863.7	—	E950.6	E962.1	E980.7
Fluorodeoxyuridine	963.1	E858.1	E933.1	E950.4	E962.0	E980.4
Fluorometholone (topical) NEC	976.0	E858.7	E946.0	E950.4	E962.0	E980.4
ophthalmic preparation	976.5	E858.7	E946.5	E950.4	E962.0	E980.4
Fluorouracil	963.1	E858.1	E933.1	E950.4	E962.0	E980.4
Fluothane	968.1	E855.1	E938.1	E950.4	E962.0	E980.4
Fluoxetine hydrochloride	969.0	E854.0	E939.0	E950.3	E962.0	E980.3
Fluoxymesterone	962.1	E858.0	E932.1	E950.4	E962.0	E980.4
Fluphenazine	969.1	E853.0	E939.1	E950.3	E962.0	E980.3
Fluprednisolone	962.0	E858.0	E932.0	E950.4	E962.0	E980.4
Flurandrenolide	976.0	E858.7	E946.0	E950.4	E962.0	E980.4
Flurazepam (hydrochloride)	969.4	E853.2	E939.4	E950.3	E962.0	E980.3
Flurbiprofen	965.61	E850.6	E935.6	E950.0	E962.0	E980.0
Flurobate	976.0	E858.7	E946.0	E950.4	E962.0	E980.4
Flurothyl	969.8	E855.8	E939.8	E950.3	E962.0	E980.3
Fluroxene	968.2	E855.1	E938.2	E950.4	E962.0	E980.4
Folacin	964.1	E858.2	E934.1	E950.4	E962.0	E980.4
Folic acid	964.1	E858.2	E934.1	E950.4	E962.0	E980.4
Follicle stimulating hormone	962.4	E858.0	E932.4	E950.4	E962.0	E980.4
Food, foodstuffs, nonbacterial or noxious	988.9	E865.9	—	E950.9	E962.1	E980.9
berries, seeds	988.2	E865.3	—	E950.9	E962.1	E980.9
fish	988.0	E865.2	—	E950.9	E962.1	E980.9
mushrooms	988.1	E865.5	—	E950.9	E962.1	E980.9
plants	988.2	E865.9	—	E950.9	E962.1	E980.9
specified type NEC	988.2	E865.4	—	E950.9	E962.1	E980.9
shellfish	988.0	E865.1	—	E950.9	E962.1	E980.9
specified NEC	988.8	E865.8	—	E950.9	E962.1	E980.9
Fool's parsley	988.2	E865.4	—	E950.9	E962.1	E980.9
Formaldehyde (solution)	989.89	E861.4	—	E950.9	E962.1	E980.9
fungicide	989.4	E863.6	—	E950.6	E962.1	E980.7
gas or vapor	987.8	E869.8	—	E952.8	E962.2	E982.8
Formalin	989.89	E861.4	—	E950.9	E962.1	E980.9
fungicide	989.4	E863.6	—	E950.6	E962.1	E980.7
vapor	987.8	E869.8	—	E952.8	E962.2	E982.8
Formic acid	983.1	E864.1	—	E950.7	E962.1	E980.6
automobile	981	E862.1	—	E950.9	E962.1	E980.9
exhaust gas, not in transit	986	E868.2	—	E952.0	E962.2	E982.0
vapor NEC	987.1	E869.8	—	E952.8	E962.2	E982.8
gas (domestic use) (*see also* Carbon, monoxide, fuel)						
utility	987.1	E868.1	—	E951.8	E962.2	E981.8
incomplete combustion of — see Carbon, monoxide, fuel, utility						
in mobile container	987.0	E868.0	—	E951.1	E962.2	E981.1
piped (natural)	987.1	E867	—	E951.0	E962.2	E981.0
industrial, incomplete combustion	986	E868.3	—	E952.1	E962.2	E982.1
vapor	987.8	E869.8	—	E952.8	E962.2	E982.8
Fowler's solution	985.1	E866.3	—	E950.8	E962.1	E980.8
Foxglove	988.2	E865.4	—	E950.9	E962.1	E980.9
Fox green	977.8	E858.8	E947.8	E950.4	E962.0	E980.4
Framycetin	960.8	E856	E930.8	E950.4	E962.0	E980.4
Frangula (extract)	973.1	E858.4	E943.1	E950.4	E962.0	E980.4
Frei antigen	977.8	E858.8	E947.8	E950.4	E962.0	E980.4
Freons	987.4	E869.2	—	E952.8	E962.2	E982.8
Fructose	974.5	E858.5	E944.5	E950.4	E962.0	E980.4
Frusemide	974.4	E858.5	E944.4	E950.4	E962.0	E980.4
FSH	962.4	E858.0	E932.4	E950.4	E962.0	E980.4
Fuel						
Fugillin	960.8	E856	E930.8	E950.4	E962.0	E980.4
Fulminate of mercury	985.0	E866.1	—	E950.9	E962.1	E980.9
Fulvicin	960.1	E856	E930.1	E950.4	E962.0	E980.4
Fumadil	960.8	E856	E930.8	E950.4	E962.0	E980.4
Fumagillin	960.8	E856	E930.8	E950.4	E962.0	E980.4
Fumes (from)	987.9	E869.9	—	E952.9	E962.2	E982.9
carbon monoxide — see Carbon, monoxide						
charcoal (domestic use)	986	E868.3	—	E952.1	E962.2	E982.1
chloroform — see Chloroform						
coke (in domestic stoves, fireplaces)	986	E868.3	—	E952.1	E962.2	E982.1
corrosive NEC	987.8	E869.8	—	E952.8	E962.2	E982.8
ether — see Ether(s)						
freons	987.4	E869.2	—	E952.8	E962.2	E982.8
hydrocarbons	987.1	E869.8	—	E952.8	E962.2	E982.8
petroleum (liquefied)	987.0	E868.0	—	E951.1	E962.2	E981.1
distributed through pipes (pure or mixed with air)	987.0	E867	—	E951.0	E962.2	E981.0
lead — see Lead						
metals — see specified metal						
nitrogen dioxide	987.2	E869.0	—	E952.8	E962.2	E982.8
pesticides — see Pesticides						
petroleum (liquefied)	987.0	E868.0	—	E951.1	E962.2	E981.1
distributed through pipes (pure or mixed with air)	987.0	E867	—	E951.0	E962.2	E981.0
polyester	987.8	E869.8	—	E952.8	E962.2	E982.8
specified, source other (*see also* substance specified)	987.8	E869.8	—	E952.8	E962.2	E982.8
sulfur dioxide	987.3	E869.1	—	E952.8	E962.2	E982.8
Fumigants	989.4	E863.8	—	E950.6	E962.1	E980.7
Fungicides — *see also* Antifungals	989.4	E863.6	—	E950.6	E962.1	E980.7
Fungi, noxious, used as food	988.1	E865.5	—	E950.9	E962.1	E980.9
Fungizone	960.1	E856	E930.1	E950.4	E962.0	E980.4
topical	976.0	E858.7	E946.0	E950.4	E962.0	E980.4
Furacin	976.0	E858.7	E946.0	E950.4	E962.0	E980.4
Furadantin	961.9	E857	E931.9	E950.4	E962.0	E980.4
Furazolidone	961.9	E857	E931.9	E950.4	E962.0	E980.4
Furnace (coal burning) (domestic), gas from	986	E868.3	—	E952.1	E962.2	E982.1
industrial	986	E868.8	—	E952.1	E962.2	E982.1
Furniture polish	989.89	E861.2	—	E950.9	E962.1	E980.9
Furosemide	974.4	E858.5	E944.4	E950.4	E962.0	E980.4
Furoxone	961.9	E857	E931.9	E950.4	E962.0	E980.4
Fusel oil (amyl) (butyl) (propyl)	980.3	E860.4	—	E950.9	E962.1	E980.9
Fusidic acid	960.8	E856	E930.8	E950.4	E962.0	E980.4
Gallamine	975.2	E858.6	E945.2	E950.4	E962.0	E980.4
Gallotannic acid	976.2	E858.7	E946.2	E950.4	E962.0	E980.4
Gamboge	973.1	E858.4	E943.1	E950.4	E962.0	E980.4
Gamimune	964.6	E858.2	E934.6	E950.4	E962.0	E980.4
Gamma-benzene hexachloride (vapor)	989.2	E863.0	—	E950.6	E962.1	E980.7
Gamma globulin	964.6	E858.2	E934.6	E950.4	E962.0	E980.4
Gamma hydroxy butyrate (GHB)	968.4	E855.1	E938.4	E950.4	E962.0	E980.4
Gamulin	964.6	E858.2	E934.6	E950.4	E962.0	E980.4
Ganglionic blocking agents	972.3	E858.3	E942.3	E950.4	E962.0	E980.4
Ganja	969.6	E854.1	E939.6	E950.3	E962.0	E980.3
Garamycin	960.8	E856	E930.8	E950.4	E962.0	E980.4
ophthalmic preparation	976.5	E858.7	E946.5	E950.4	E962.0	E980.4
topical NEC	976.0	E858.7	E946.0	E950.4	E962.0	E980.4
Gardenal	967.0	E851	E937.0	E950.1	E962.0	E980.1
Gardepanyl	967.0	E851	E937.0	E950.1	E962.0	E980.1
Gas	987.9	E869.9	—	E952.9	E962.2	E982.9
acetylene	987.1	E868.1	—	E951.8	E962.2	E981.8
incomplete combustion of — see Carbon, monoxide, fuel, utility						
air contaminants, source or type not specified	987.9	E869.9	—	E952.9	E962.2	E982.9
anesthetic (general) NEC	968.2	E855.1	E938.2	E950.4	E962.0	E980.4

	Poisoning	External Cause (E-Code) Accident	Therapeutic Use	Suicide Attempt	Assault	Undetermined
Gas — *continued*						
blast furnace	986	E868.8	—	E952.1	E962.2	E982.1
butane — see Butane						
carbon monoxide — see Carbon, monoxide						
chlorine	987.6	E869.8	—	E952.8	E962.2	E982.8
coal — see Carbon, monoxide, coal						
cyanide	987.7	E869.8	—	E952.8	E962.2	E982.8
dicyanogen	987.8	E869.8	—	E952.8	E962.2	E982.8
domestic — see Gas, utility						
exhaust — see Carbon, monoxide, exhaust gas						
from wood- or coal-burning stove or fireplace	986	E868.3	—	E952.1	E962.2	E982.1
fuel (domestic use) (*see also* Carbon, monoxide, fuel)						
industrial use	986	E868.8	—	E952.1	E962.2	E982.1
utility	987.1	E868.1	—	E951.8	E962.2	E981.8
incomplete combustion of — see Carbon, monoxide, fuel, utility						
in mobile container	987.0	E868.0	—	E951.1	E962.2	E981.1
piped (natural)	987.1	E867	—	E951.0	E962.2	E981.0
garage	986	E868.2	—	E952.0	E962.2	E982.0
hydrocarbon NEC	987.1	E869.8	—	E952.8	E962.2	E982.8
incomplete combustion of — see Carbon, monoxide, fuel, utility						
liquefied (mobile container)	987.0	E868.0	—	E951.1	E962.2	E981.1
piped	987.0	E867	—	E951.0	E962.2	E981.0
hydrocyanic acid	987.7	E869.8	—	E952.8	E962.2	E982.8
illuminating — see Gas, utility						
incomplete combustion, any — see Carbon, monoxide						
kiln	986	E868.8	—	E952.1	E962.2	E982.1
lacrimogenic	987.5	E869.3	—	E952.8	E962.2	E982.8
marsh	987.1	E869.8	—	E952.8	E962.2	E982.8
motor exhaust, not in transit	986	E868.8	—	E952.1	E962.2	E982.1
mustard — see Mustard, gas						
natural	987.1	E867	—	E951.0	E962.2	E981.0
nerve (war)	987.9	E869.9	—	E952.9	E962.2	E982.9
oils	981	E862.1	—	E950.9	E962.1	E980.9
petroleum (liquefied) (distributed in mobile containers)	987.0	E868.0	—	E951.1	E962.2	E981.1
piped (pure or mixed with air)	987.0	E867	—	E951.1	E962.2	E981.1
piped (manufactured) (natural) NEC	987.1	E867	—	E951.0	E962.2	E981.0
producer	986	E868.8	—	E952.1	E962.2	E982.1
propane — see Propane						
refrigerant (freon)	987.4	E869.2	—	E952.8	E962.2	E982.8
not freon	987.9	E869.9	—	E952.9	E962.2	E982.9
sewer	987.8	E869.8	—	E952.8	E962.2	E982.8
specified source NEC (see also substance specified)	987.8	E869.8	—	E952.8	E962.2	E982.8
stove — see Gas, utility						
tear	987.5	E869.3	—	E952.8	E962.2	E982.8
utility (for cooking, heating, or lighting) (piped) NEC	987.1	E868.1	—	E951.8	E962.2	E981.8
incomplete combustion of — see Carbon, monoxide, fuel, utilty						
in mobile container	987.0	E868.0	—	E951.1	E962.2	E981.1
piped (natural)	987.1	E867	—	E951.0	E962.2	E981.0
water	987.1	E868.1	—	E951.8	E962.2	E981.8
incomplete combustion of — see Carbon, monoxide, fuel, utility						
Gaseous substance — see Gas						
Gasoline, gasolene	981	E862.1	—	E950.9	E962.1	E980.9
vapor	987.1	E869.8	—	E952.8	E962.2	E982.8
Gastric enzymes	973.4	E858.4	E943.4	E950.4	E962.0	E980.4
Gastrografin	977.8	E858.8	E947.8	E950.4	E962.0	E980.4
Gastrointestinal agents	973.9	E858.4	E943.9	E950.4	E962.0	E980.4
specified NEC	973.8	E858.4	E943.8	E950.4	E962.0	E980.4
Gaultheria procumbens	988.2	E865.4	—	E950.9	E962.1	E980.9
Gelatin (intravenous)	964.8	E858.2	E934.8	E950.4	E962.0	E980.4
absorbable (sponge)	964.5	E858.2	E934.5	E950.4	E962.0	E980.4
Gelfilm	976.8	E858.7	E946.8	E950.4	E962.0	E980.4
Gelfoam	964.5	E858.2	E934.5	E950.4	E962.0	E980.4
Gelsemine	970.8	E854.3	E940.8	E950.4	E962.0	E980.4
Gelsemium (sempervirens)	988.2	E865.4	—	E950.9	E962.1	E980.9
Gemonil	967.0	E851	E937.0	E950.1	E962.0	E980.1
Gentamicin	960.8	E856	E930.8	E950.4	E962.0	E980.4
ophthalmic preparation	976.5	E858.7	E946.5	E950.4	E962.0	E980.4
topical NEC	976.0	E858.7	E946.0	E950.4	E962.0	E980.4
Gentian violet	976.0	E858.7	E946.0	E950.4	E962.0	E980.4
Gexane	976.0	E858.7	E946.0	E950.4	E962.0	E980.4
Gila monster (venom)	989.5	E905.0	—	E950.9	E962.1	E980.9
Ginger, Jamaica	989.89	E866.8	—	E950.9	E962.1	E980.9
Gitalin	972.1	E858.3	E942.1	E950.4	E962.0	E980.4
Gitoxin	972.1	E858.3	E942.1	E950.4	E962.0	E980.4
Glandular extract (medicinal) NEC	977.9	E858.9	E947.9	E950.5	E962.0	E980.5
Glaucarubin	961.5	E857	E931.5	E950.4	E962.0	E980.4
Globin zinc insulin	962.3	E858.0	E932.3	E950.4	E962.0	E980.4
Glucagon	962.3	E858.0	E932.3	E950.4	E962.0	E980.4
Glucochloral	967.1	E852.0	E937.1	E950.2	E962.0	E980.2
Glucocorticoids	962.0	E858.0	E932.0	E950.4	E962.0	E980.4
Glucose	974.5	E858.5	E944.5	E950.4	E962.0	E980.4
oxidase reagent	977.8	E858.8	E947.8	E950.4	E962.0	E980.4
Glucosulfone sodium	961.8	E857	E931.8	E950.4	E962.0	E980.4
Glue(s)	989.89	E866.6	—	E950.9	E962.1	E980.9
Glutamic acid (hydrochloride)	973.4	E858.4	E943.4	E950.4	E962.0	E980.4
Glutaraldehyde	989.89	E861.4	—	E950.9	E962.1	E980.9
Glutathione	963.8	E858.1	E933.8	E950.4	E962.0	E980.4
Glutethimide (group)	967.5	E852.4	E937.5	E950.2	E962.0	E980.2
Glycerin (lotion)	976.3	E858.7	E946.3	E950.4	E962.0	E980.4
Glycerol (topical)	976.3	E858.7	E946.3	E950.4	E962.0	E980.4
Glyceryl						
guaiacolate	975.5	E858.6	E945.5	E950.4	E962.0	E980.4
triacetate (topical)	976.0	E858.7	E946.0	E950.4	E962.0	E980.4
trinitrate	972.4	E858.3	E942.4	E950.4	E962.0	E980.4
Glycine	974.5	E858.5	E944.5	E950.4	E962.0	E980.4
Glycobiarsol	961.1	E857	E931.1	E950.4	E962.0	E980.4
Glycols (ether)	982.8	E862.4	—	E950.9	E962.1	E980.9
Glycopyrrolate	971.1	E855.4	E941.1	E950.4	E962.0	E980.4
Glymidine	962.3	E858.0	E932.3	E950.4	E962.0	E980.4
Gold (compounds) (salts)	965.69	E850.6	E935.6	E950.0	E962.0	E980.0
Golden sulfide of antimony	985.4	E866.2	—	E950.9	E962.1	E980.9
Goldylocks	988.2	E865.4	—	E950.9	E962.1	E980.9
Gonadal tissue extract	962.9	E858.0	E932.9	E950.4	E962.0	E980.4
beverage	980.0	E860.0	—	E950.9	E962.1	E980.9
female	962.2	E858.0	E932.2	E950.4	E962.0	E980.4
male	962.1	E858.0	E932.1	E950.4	E962.0	E980.4
Gonadotropin	962.4	E858.0	E932.4	E950.4	E962.0	E980.4
Grain alcohol	980.0	E860.1	—	E950.9	E962.1	E980.9
Gramicidin	960.8	E856	E930.8	E950.4	E962.0	E980.4
Gratiola officinalis	988.2	E865.4	—	E950.9	E962.1	E980.9
Grease	989.89	E866.8	—	E950.9	E962.1	E980.9
Green hellebore	988.2	E865.4	—	E950.9	E962.1	E980.9
Green soap	976.2	E858.7	E946.2	E950.4	E962.0	E980.4
Grifulvin	960.1	E856	E930.1	E950.4	E962.0	E980.4
Griseofulvin	960.1	E856	E930.1	E950.4	E962.0	E980.4
Growth hormone	962.4	E858.0	E932.4	E950.4	E962.0	E980.4
Guaiacol	975.5	E858.6	E945.5	E950.4	E962.0	E980.4
Guaiac reagent	977.8	E858.8	E947.8	E950.4	E962.0	E980.4
Guaifenesin	975.5	E858.6	E945.5	E950.4	E962.0	E980.4
Guaiphenesin	975.5	E858.6	E945.5	E950.4	E962.0	E980.4
Guanatol	961.4	E857	E931.4	E950.4	E962.0	E980.4
Guanethidine	972.6	E858.3	E942.6	E950.4	E962.0	E980.4
Guano	989.89	E866.5	—	E950.9	E962.1	E980.9
Guanochlor	972.6	E858.3	E942.6	E950.4	E962.0	E980.4
Guanoctine	972.6	E858.3	E942.6	E950.4	E962.0	E980.4
Guanoxan	972.6	E858.3	E942.6	E950.4	E962.0	E980.4
Hair treatment agent NEC	976.4	E858.7	E946.4	E950.4	E962.0	E980.4
Halcinonide	976.0	E858.7	E946.0	E950.4	E962.0	E980.4
Halethazole	976.0	E858.7	E946.0	E950.4	E962.0	E980.4
Hallucinogens	969.6	E854.1	E939.6	E950.3	E962.0	E980.3
Haloperidol	969.2	E853.1	E939.2	E950.3	E962.0	E980.3
Haloprogin	976.0	E858.7	E946.0	E950.4	E962.0	E980.4
Halotex	976.0	E858.7	E946.0	E950.4	E962.0	E980.4
Halothane	968.1	E855.1	E938.1	E950.4	E962.0	E980.4
Halquinols	976.0	E858.7	E946.0	E950.4	E962.0	E980.4
Harmonyl	972.6	E858.3	E942.6	E950.4	E962.0	E980.4
Hartmann's solution	974.5	E858.5	E944.5	E950.4	E962.0	E980.4
Hashish	969.6	E854.1	E939.6	E950.3	E962.0	E980.3

	Poisoning	External Cause (E-Code)				
		Accident	Therapeutic Use	Suicide Attempt	Assault	Undetermined
Hawaiian wood rose seeds	969.6	E854.1	E939.6	E950.3	E962.0	E980.3
Headache cures, drugs, powders NEC	977.9	E858.9	E947.9	E950.5	E962.0	E980.9
Heavenly Blue (morning glory)	969.6	E854.1	E939.6	E950.3	E962.0	E980.3
Heavy metal antagonists	963.8	E858.1	E933.8	E950.4	E962.0	E980.4
anti-infectives	961.2	E857	E931.2	E950.4	E962.0	E980.4
Hedaquinium	976.0	E858.7	E946.0	E950.4	E962.0	E980.4
Hedge hyssop	988.2	E865.4	—	E950.9	E962.1	E980.9
Heet	976.8	E858.7	E946.8	E950.4	E962.0	E980.4
Helenin	961.6	E857	E931.6	E950.4	E962.0	E980.4
Hellebore (black) (green) (white)	988.2	E865.4	—	E950.9	E962.1	E980.9
Hemlock	988.2	E865.4	—	E950.9	E962.1	E980.9
Hemostatics	964.5	E858.2	E934.5	E950.4	E962.0	E980.4
capillary active drugs	972.8	E858.3	E942.8	E950.4	E962.0	E980.4
Henbane	988.2	E865.4	—	E950.9	E962.1	E980.9
Heparin (sodium)	964.2	E858.2	E934.2	E950.4	E962.0	E980.4
Heptabarbital, heptabarbitone	967.0	E851	E937.0	E950.1	E962.0	E980.1
Heptachlor	989.2	E863.0	—	E950.6	E962.1	E980.7
Heptalgin	965.09	E850.2	E935.2	E950.0	E962.0	E980.0
Herbicides	989.4	E863.5	—	E950.6	E962.1	E980.7
Heroin	965.01	E850.0	E935.0	E950.0	E962.0	E980.0
Herplex	976.5	E858.7	E946.5	E950.4	E962.0	E980.4
HES	964.8	E858.2	E934.8	E950.4	E962.0	E980.4
Hetastarch	964.8	E858.2	E934.8	E950.4	E962.0	E980.4
Hexachlorocyclohexane	989.2	E863.0	—	E950.6	E962.1	E980.7
Hexachlorophene	976.2	E858.7	E946.2	E950.4	E962.0	E980.4
Hexadimethrine (bromide)	964.5	E858.2	E934.5	E950.4	E962.0	E980.4
Hexafluorenium	975.2	E858.6	E945.2	E950.4	E962.0	E980.4
Hexa-germ	976.2	E858.7	E946.2	E950.4	E962.0	E980.4
Hexahydrophenol	980.8	E860.8	—	E950.9	E962.1	E980.9
Hexalin	980.8	E860.8	—	E950.9	E962.1	E980.9
Hexamethonium	972.3	E858.3	E942.3	E950.4	E962.0	E980.4
Hexamethyleneamine	961.9	E857	E931.9	E950.4	E962.0	E980.4
Hexamine	961.9	E857	E931.9	E950.4	E962.0	E980.4
Hexanone	982.8	E862.4	—	E950.9	E962.1	E980.9
Hexapropymate	967.8	E852.8	E937.8	E950.2	E962.0	E980.2
Hexestrol	962.2	E858.0	E932.2	E950.4	E962.0	E980.4
Hexethal (sodium)	967.0	E851	E937.0	E950.1	E962.0	E980.1
Hexetidine	976.0	E858.7	E946.0	E950.4	E962.0	E980.4
Hexobarbital, hexobarbitone	967.0	E851	E937.0	E950.1	E962.0	E980.1
sodium (anesthetic)	968.3	E855.1	E938.3	E950.4	E962.0	E980.4
soluble	968.3	E855.1	E938.3	E950.4	E962.0	E980.4
Hexocyclium	971.1	E855.4	E941.1	E950.4	E962.0	E980.4
Hexoestrol	962.2	E858.0	E932.2	E950.4	E962.0	E980.4
Hexone	982.8	E862.4	—	E950.9	E962.1	E980.9
Hexylcaine	968.5	E855.2	E938.5	E950.4	E962.0	E980.4
Hexylresorcinol	961.6	E857	E931.6	E950.4	E962.0	E980.4
Hinkle's pills	973.1	E858.4	E943.1	E950.4	E962.0	E980.4
Histalog	977.8	E858.8	E947.8	E950.4	E962.0	E980.4
Histamine (phosphate)	972.5	E858.3	E942.5	E950.4	E962.0	E980.4
Histoplasmin	977.8	E858.8	E947.8	E950.4	E962.0	E980.4
Holly berries	988.2	E865.3	—	E950.9	E962.1	E980.9
Homatropine	971.1	E855.4	E941.1	E950.4	E962.0	E980.4
Homo-tet	964.6	E858.2	E934.6	E950.4	E962.0	E980.4
Hormones (synthetic substitute) NEC	962.9	E858.0	E932.9	E950.4	E962.0	E980.4
adrenal cortical steroids	962.0	E858.0	E932.0	E950.4	E962.0	E980.4
antidiabetic agents	962.3	E858.0	E932.3	E950.4	E962.0	E980.4
follicle stimulating	962.4	E858.0	E932.4	E950.4	E962.0	E980.4
gonadotropic	962.4	E858.0	E932.4	E950.4	E962.0	E980.4
growth	962.4	E858.0	E932.4	E950.4	E962.0	E980.4
ovarian (substitutes)	962.2	E858.0	E932.2	E950.4	E962.0	E980.4
parathyroid (derivatives)	962.6	E858.0	E932.6	E950.4	E962.0	E980.4
pituitary (posterior)	962.5	E858.0	E932.5	E950.4	E962.0	E980.4
anterior	962.4	E858.0	E932.4	E950.4	E962.0	E980.4
thyroid (derivative)	962.7	E858.0	E932.7	E950.4	E962.0	E980.4
Hornet (sting)	989.5	E905.3	—	E950.9	E962.1	E980.9
Horticulture agent NEC	989.4	E863.9	—	E950.6	E962.1	E980.7
Hyaluronidase	963.4	E858.1	E933.4	E950.4	E962.0	E980.4
Hyazyme	963.4	E858.1	E933.4	E950.4	E962.0	E980.4
Hycodan	965.09	E850.2	E935.2	E950.0	E962.0	E980.0
Hydantoin derivatives	966.1	E855.0	E936.1	E950.4	E962.0	E980.4
Hydeltra	962.0	E858.0	E932.0	E950.4	E962.0	E980.4
Hydergine	971.3	E855.6	E941.3	E950.4	E962.0	E980.4
Hydrabamine penicillin	960.0	E856	E930.0	E950.4	E962.0	E980.4
Hydralazine, hydrallazine	972.6	E858.3	E942.6	E950.4	E962.0	E980.4
Hydrargaphen	976.0	E858.7	E946.0	E950.4	E962.0	E980.4
Hydrazine	983.9	E864.3	—	E950.7	E962.1	E980.6
Hydriodic acid	975.5	E858.6	E945.5	E950.4	E962.0	E980.4
Hydrocarbon gas	987.1	E869.8	—	E952.8	E962.2	E982.8
incomplete combustion of — see Carbon, monoxide, fuel, utility						
liquefied (mobile container)	987.0	E868.0	—	E951.1	E962.2	E981.1
piped (natural)	987.0	E867	—	E951.0	E962.2	E981.0
Hydrochloric acid (liquid)	983.1	E864.1	—	E950.7	E962.1	E980.6
medicinal	973.4	E858.4	E943.4	E950.4	E962.0	E980.4
vapor	987.8	E869.8	—	E952.8	E962.2	E982.8
Hydrochlorothiazide	974.3	E858.5	E944.3	E950.4	E962.0	E980.4
Hydrocodone	965.09	E850.2	E935.2	E950.0	E962.0	E980.0
Hydrocortisone	962.0	E858.0	E932.0	E950.4	E962.0	E980.4
ENT agent	976.6	E858.7	E946.6	E950.4	E962.0	E980.4
ophthalmic preparation	976.5	E858.7	E946.5	E950.4	E962.0	E980.4
topical NEC	976.0	E858.7	E946.0	E950.4	E962.0	E980.4
Hydrocortone	962.0	E858.0	E932.0	E950.4	E962.0	E980.4
ENT agent	976.6	E858.7	E946.6	E950.4	E962.0	E980.4
ophthalmic preparation	976.5	E858.7	E946.5	E950.4	E962.0	E980.4
topical NEC	976.0	E858.7	E946.0	E950.4	E962.0	E980.4
Hydrocyanic acid — see Cyanide(s)						
Hydroflumethiazide	974.3	E858.5	E944.3	E950.4	E962.0	E980.4
Hydrofluoric acid (liquid)	983.1	E864.1	—	E950.7	E962.1	E980.6
vapor	987.8	E869.8	—	E952.8	E962.2	E982.8
Hydrogen	987.8	E869.8	—	E952.8	E962.2	E982.8
arsenide	985.1	E866.3	—	E950.8	E962.1	E980.8
arseniureted	985.1	E866.3	—	E950.8	E962.1	E980.8
cyanide (salts)	989.0	E866.8	—	E950.9	E962.1	E980.9
gas	987.7	E869.8	—	E952.8	E962.2	E982.8
fluoride (liquid)	983.1	E864.1	—	E950.7	E962.1	E980.6
vapor	987.8	E869.8	—	E952.8	E962.2	E982.8
peroxide (solution)	976.6	E858.7	E946.6	E950.4	E962.0	E980.4
phosphureted	987.8	E869.8	—	E952.8	E962.2	E982.8
sulfide (gas)	987.8	E869.8	—	E952.8	E962.2	E982.8
arseniureted	985.1	E866.3	—	E950.8	E962.1	E980.8
sulfureted	987.8	E869.8	—	E952.8	E962.2	E982.8
Hydromorphinol	965.09	E850.2	E935.2	E950.0	E962.0	E980.0
Hydromorphinone	965.09	E850.2	E935.2	E950.0	E962.0	E980.0
Hydromorphone	965.09	E850.2	E935.2	E950.0	E962.0	E980.0
Hydromox	974.3	E858.5	E944.3	E950.4	E962.0	E980.4
Hydrophilic lotion	976.3	E858.7	E946.3	E950.4	E962.0	E980.4
Hydroquinone	983.0	E864.0	—	E950.7	E962.1	E980.6
vapor	987.8	E869.8	—	E952.8	E962.2	E982.8
Hydrosulfuric acid (gas)	987.8	E869.8	—	E952.8	E962.2	E982.8
Hydrous wool fat (lotion)	976.3	E858.7	E946.3	E950.4	E962.0	E980.4
Hydroxide, caustic	983.2	E864.2	—	E950.7	E962.1	E980.6
Hydroxocobalamin	964.1	E858.2	E934.1	E950.4	E962.0	E980.4
Hydroxyamphetamine	971.2	E855.5	E941.2	E950.4	E962.0	E980.4
Hydroxychloroquine	961.4	E857	E931.4	E950.4	E962.0	E980.4
Hydroxydihydrocodeinone	965.09	E850.2	E935.2	E950.0	E962.0	E980.0
Hydroxyethyl starch	964.8	E858.2	E934.8	E950.4	E962.0	E980.4
Hydroxyphenamate	969.5	E853.8	E939.5	E950.3	E962.0	E980.3
Hydroxyphenylbutazone	965.5	E850.5	E935.5	E950.0	E962.0	E980.0
Hydroxyprogesterone	962.2	E858.0	E932.2	E950.4	E962.0	E980.4
Hydroxyquinoline derivatives	961.3	E857	E931.3	E950.4	E962.0	E980.4
Hydroxystilbamidine	961.5	E857	E931.5	E950.4	E962.0	E980.4
Hydroxyurea	963.1	E858.1	E933.1	E950.4	E962.0	E980.4
Hydroxyzine	969.5	E853.8	E939.5	E950.3	E962.0	E980.3
Hyoscine (hydrobromide)	971.1	E855.4	E941.1	E950.4	E962.0	E980.4
Hyoscyamine	971.1	E855.4	E941.1	E950.4	E962.0	E980.4
Hyoscyamus (albus) (niger)	988.2	E865.4	—	E950.9	E962.1	E980.9
Hypaque	977.8	E858.8	E947.8	E950.4	E962.0	E980.4
Hypertussis	964.6	E858.2	E934.6	E950.4	E962.0	E980.4
Hypnotics NEC	967.9	E852.9	E937.9	E950.2	E962.0	E980.2
Hypochlorites — *see* Sodium, hypochlorite						
Hypotensive agents NEC	972.6	E858.3	E942.6	E950.4	E962.0	E980.4
Ibufenac	965.69	E850.6	E935.6	E950.0	E962.0	E980.0
Ibuprofen	965.61	E850.6	E935.6	E950.0	E962.0	E980.0
ICG	977.8	E858.8	E947.8	E950.4	E962.0	E980.4
Ichthammol	976.4	E858.7	E946.4	E950.4	E962.0	E980.4
Ichthyol	976.4	E858.7	E946.4	E950.4	E962.0	E980.4
Idoxuridine	976.5	E858.7	E946.5	E950.4	E962.0	E980.4
IDU	976.5	E858.7	E946.5	E950.4	E962.0	E980.4
Iletin	962.3	E858.0	E932.3	E950.4	E962.0	E980.4
Ilex	988.2	E865.4	—	E950.9	E962.1	E980.9

☑ Additional Digit Required — Refer to the Tabular List for Digit Selection

Subterms under main terms may continue to next column or page

▶◀ Revised Text ● New Line ▲ Revised Code

		External Cause (E-Code)				
	Poisoning	Accident	Therapeutic Use	Suicide Attempt	Assault	Undetermined
Illuminating gas — see Gas, utility						
Ilopan	963.5	E858.1	E933.5	E950.4	E962.0	E980.4
Ilotycin	960.3	E856	E930.3	E950.4	E962.0	E980.4
ophthalmic preparation	976.5	E858.7	E946.5	E950.4	E962.0	E980.4
topical NEC	976.0	E858.7	E946.0	E950.4	E962.0	E980.4
Imipramine	969.0	E854.0	E939.0	E950.3	E962.0	E980.3
Immu-G	964.6	E858.2	E934.6	E950.4	E962.0	E980.4
Immuglobin	964.6	E858.2	E934.6	E950.4	E962.0	E980.4
Immune serum globulin	964.6	E858.2	E934.6	E950.4	E962.0	E980.4
Immunosuppressive agents	963.1	E858.1	E933.1	E950.4	E962.0	E980.4
Immu-tetanus	964.6	E858.2	E934.6	E950.4	E962.0	E980.4
Indandione (derivatives)	964.2	E858.2	E934.2	E950.4	E962.0	E980.4
Inderal	972.0	E858.3	E942.0	E950.4	E962.0	E980.4
Indian						
hemp	969.6	E854.1	E939.6	E950.3	E962.0	E980.3
tobacco	988.2	E865.4	—	E950.9	E962.1	E980.9
Indigo carmine	977.8	E858.8	E947.8	E950.4	E962.0	E980.4
Indocin	965.69	E850.6	E935.6	E950.0	E962.0	E980.0
Indocyanine green	977.8	E858.8	E947.8	E950.4	E962.0	E980.4
Indomethacin	965.69	E850.6	E935.6	E950.0	E962.0	E980.0
Industrial						
alcohol	980.9	E860.9	—	E950.9	E962.1	E980.9
fumes	987.8	E869.8	—	E952.8	E962.2	E982.8
solvents (fumes) (vapors)	982.8	E862.9	—	E950.9	E962.1	E980.9
Influenza vaccine	979.6	E858.8	E949.6	E950.4	E962.0	E982.8
Ingested substances NEC	989.9	E866.9	—	E950.9	E962.1	E980.9
INH (isoniazid)	961.8	E857	E931.8	E950.4	E962.0	E980.4
Inhalation, gas (noxious) — *see* Gas						
Ink	989.89	E866.8	—	E950.9	E962.1	E980.9
Innovar	967.6	E852.5	E937.6	E950.2	E962.0	E980.2
Inositol niacinate	972.2	E858.3	E942.2	E950.4	E962.0	E980.4
Inproquone	963.1	E858.1	E933.1	E950.4	E962.0	E980.4
Insecticides — *see also* Pesticides	989.4	E863.4	—	E950.6	E962.1	E980.7
chlorinated	989.2	E863.0	—	E950.6	E962.1	E980.7
mixtures	989.4	E863.3	—	E950.6	E962.1	E980.7
organochlorine (compounds)	989.2	E863.0	—	E950.6	E962.1	E980.7
organophosphorus (compounds)	989.3	E863.1	—	E950.6	E962.1	E980.7
Insect (sting), venomous	989.5	E905.5	—	E950.9	E962.1	E980.9
Insular tissue extract	962.3	E858.0	E932.3	E950.4	E962.0	E980.4
Insulin (amorphous) (globin) (isophane) (Lente) (NPH) (protamine) (Semilente) (Ultralente) (zinc)	962.3	E858.0	E932.3	E950.4	E962.0	E980.4
Intranarcon	968.3	E855.1	E938.3	E950.4	E962.0	E980.4
Inulin	977.8	E858.8	E947.8	E950.4	E962.0	E980.4
Invert sugar	974.5	E858.5	E944.5	E950.4	E962.0	E980.4
Inza — *see* Naproxen						
Iodide NEC — *see also* Iodine	976.0	E858.7	E946.0	E950.4	E962.0	E980.4
mercury (ointment)	976.0	E858.7	E946.0	E950.4	E962.0	E980.4
methylate	976.0	E858.7	E946.0	E950.4	E962.0	E980.4
potassium (expectorant) NEC	975.5	E858.6	E945.5	E950.4	E962.0	E980.4
Iodinated glycerol	975.5	E858.6	E945.5	E950.4	E962.0	E980.4
Iodine (antiseptic, external) (tincture) NEC	976.0	E858.7	E946.0	E950.4	E962.0	E980.4
diagnostic	977.8	E858.8	E947.8	E950.4	E962.0	E980.4
for thyroid conditions (antithyroid)	962.8	E858.0	E932.8	E950.4	E962.0	E980.4
vapor	987.8	E869.8	—	E952.8	E962.2	E982.8
Iodized oil	977.8	E858.8	E947.8	E950.4	E962.0	E980.4
Iodobismitol	961.2	E857	E931.2	E950.4	E962.0	E980.4
Iodochlorhydroxyquin	961.3	E857	E931.3	E950.4	E962.0	E980.4
topical	976.0	E858.7	E946.0	E950.4	E962.0	E980.4
Iodoform	976.0	E858.7	E946.0	E950.4	E962.0	E980.4
Iodopanoic acid	977.8	E858.8	E947.8	E950.4	E962.0	E980.4
Iodophthalein	977.8	E858.8	E947.8	E950.4	E962.0	E980.4
Ion exchange resins	974.5	E858.5	E944.5	E950.4	E962.0	E980.4
Iopanoic acid	977.8	E858.8	E947.8	E950.4	E962.0	E980.4
Iophendylate	977.8	E858.8	E947.8	E950.4	E962.0	E980.4
Iothiouracil	962.8	E858.0	E932.8	E950.4	E962.0	E980.4
Ipecac	973.6	E858.4	E943.6	E950.4	E962.0	E980.4
Ipecacuanha	973.6	E858.4	E943.6	E950.4	E962.0	E980.4
Ipodate	977.8	E858.8	E947.8	E950.4	E962.0	E980.4
Ipral	967.0	E851	E937.0	E950.1	E962.0	E980.1
Ipratropium	975.1	E858.6	E945.1	E950.4	E962.0	E980.4
Iproniazid	969.0	E854.0	E939.0	E950.3	E962.0	E980.3
Iron (compounds) (medicinal) (preparations)	964.0	E858.2	E934.0	E950.4	E962.0	E980.4
dextran	964.0	E858.2	E934.0	E950.4	E962.0	E980.4
nonmedicinal (dust) (fumes) NEC	985.8	E866.4	—	E950.9	E962.1	E980.9
Irritant drug	977.9	E858.9	E947.9	E950.5	E962.0	E980.5
Ismelin	972.6	E858.3	E942.6	E950.4	E962.0	E980.4
Isoamyl nitrite	972.4	E858.3	E942.4	E950.4	E962.0	E980.4
Isobutyl acetate	982.8	E862.4	—	E950.9	E962.1	E980.9
Isocarboxazid	969.0	E854.0	E939.0	E950.3	E962.0	E980.3
Isoephedrine	971.2	E855.5	E941.2	E950.4	E962.0	E980.4
Isoetharine	971.2	E855.5	E941.2	E950.4	E962.0	E980.4
Isofluorophate	971.0	E855.3	E941.0	E950.4	E962.0	E980.4
Isoniazid (INH)	961.8	E857	E931.8	E950.4	E962.0	E980.4
Isopentaquine	961.4	E857	E931.4	E950.4	E962.0	E980.4
Isophane insulin	962.3	E858.0	E932.3	E950.4	E962.0	E980.4
Isopregnenone	962.2	E858.0	E932.2	E950.4	E962.0	E980.4
Isoprenaline	971.2	E855.5	E941.2	E950.4	E962.0	E980.4
Isopropamide	971.1	E855.4	E941.1	E950.4	E962.0	E980.4
Isopropanol	980.2	E860.3	—	E950.9	E962.1	E980.9
topical (germicide)	976.0	E858.7	E946.0	E950.4	E962.0	E980.4
Isopropyl						
acetate	982.8	E862.4	—	E950.9	E962.1	E980.9
alcohol	980.2	E860.3	—	E950.9	E962.1	E980.9
topical (germicide)	976.0	E858.7	E946.0	E950.4	E962.0	E980.4
ether	982.8	E862.4	—	E950.9	E962.1	E980.9
Isoproterenol	971.2	E855.5	E941.2	E950.4	E962.0	E980.4
Isosorbide dinitrate	972.4	E858.3	E942.4	E950.4	E962.0	E980.4
Isothipendyl	963.0	E858.1	E933.0	E950.4	E962.0	E980.4
Isoxazolyl penicillin	960.0	E856	E930.0	E950.4	E962.0	E980.4
Isoxsuprine hydrochloride	972.5	E858.3	E942.5	E950.4	E962.0	E980.4
I-thyroxine sodium	962.7	E858.0	E932.7	E950.4	E962.0	E980.4
Jaborandi (pilocarpus) (extract)	971.0	E855.3	E941.0	E950.4	E962.0	E980.4
Jalap	973.1	E858.4	E943.1	E950.4	E962.0	E980.4
Jamaica						
dogwood (bark)	965.7	E850.7	E935.7	E950.0	E962.0	E980.0
ginger	989.89	E866.8	—	E950.9	E962.1	E980.9
Jatropha	988.2	E865.4	—	E950.9	E962.1	E980.9
curcas	988.2	E865.3	—	E950.9	E962.1	E980.9
Jectofer	964.0	E858.2	E934.0	E950.4	E962.0	E980.4
Jellyfish (sting)	989.5	E905.6	—	E950.9	E962.1	E980.9
Jequirity (bean)	988.2	E865.3	—	E950.9	E962.1	E980.9
Jimson weed	988.2	E865.4	—	E950.9	E962.1	E980.9
seeds	988.2	E865.3	—	E950.9	E962.1	E980.9
Juniper tar (oil) (ointment)	976.4	E858.7	E946.4	E950.4	E962.0	E980.4
Kallikrein	972.5	E858.3	E942.5	E950.4	E962.0	E980.4
Kanamycin	960.6	E856	E930.6	E950.4	E962.0	E980.4
Kantrex	960.6	E856	E930.6	E950.4	E962.0	E980.4
Kaolin	973.5	E858.4	E943.5	E950.4	E962.0	E980.4
Karaya (gum)	973.3	E858.4	E943.3	E950.4	E962.0	E980.4
Kemithal	968.3	E855.1	E938.3	E950.4	E962.0	E980.4
Kenacort	962.0	E858.0	E932.0	E950.4	E962.0	E980.4
Keratolytics	976.4	E858.7	E946.4	E950.4	E962.0	E980.4
Keratoplastics	976.4	E858.7	E946.4	E950.4	E962.0	E980.4
Kerosene, kerosine (fuel) (solvent) NEC	981	E862.1	—	E950.9	E962.1	E980.9
insecticide	981	E863.4	—	E950.6	E962.1	E980.7
vapor	987.1	E869.8	—	E952.8	E962.2	E982.8
Ketamine	968.3	E855.1	E938.3	E950.4	E962.0	E980.4
Ketobemidone	965.09	E850.2	E935.2	E950.0	E962.0	E980.0
Ketols	982.8	E862.4	—	E950.9	E962.1	E980.9
Ketone oils	982.8	E862.4	—	E950.9	E962.1	E980.9
Ketoprofen	965.61	E850.6	E935.6	E950.0	E962.0	E980.0
Kiln gas or vapor (carbon monoxide)	986	E868.8	—	E952.1	E962.2	E982.1
Konsyl	973.3	E858.4	E943.3	E950.4	E962.0	E980.4
Kosam seed	988.2	E865.3	—	E950.9	E962.1	E980.9
Krait (venom)	989.5	E905.0	—	E950.9	E962.1	E980.9
Kwell (insecticide)	989.2	E863.0	—	E950.6	E962.1	E980.7
anti-infective (topical)	976.0	E858.7	E946.0	E950.4	E962.0	E980.4
Laburnum (flowers) (seeds)	988.2	E865.3	—	E950.9	E962.1	E980.9
leaves	988.2	E865.4	—	E950.9	E962.1	E980.9
Lacquers	989.89	E861.6	—	E950.9	E962.1	E980.9
Lacrimogenic gas	987.5	E869.3	—	E952.8	E962.2	E982.8
Lactic acid	983.1	E864.1	—	E950.7	E962.1	E980.6
Lactobacillus acidophilus	973.5	E858.4	E943.5	E950.4	E962.0	E980.4
Lactoflavin	963.5	E858.1	E933.5	E950.4	E962.0	E980.4
Lactuca (virosa) (extract)	967.8	E852.8	E937.8	E950.2	E962.0	E980.2

	Poisoning	External Cause (E-Code) Accident	Therapeutic Use	Suicide Attempt	Assault	Undetermined
Lactucarium	967.8	E852.8	E937.8	E950.2	E962.0	E980.2
Laevulose	974.5	E858.5	E944.5	E950.4	E962.0	E980.4
Lanatoside (C)	972.1	E858.3	E942.1	E950.4	E962.0	E980.4
Lanolin (lotion)	976.3	E858.7	E946.3	E950.4	E962.0	E980.4
Largactil	969.1	E853.0	E939.1	E950.3	E962.0	E980.3
Larkspur	988.2	E865.3	—	E950.9	E962.1	E980.9
Laroxyl	969.0	E854.0	E939.0	E950.3	E962.0	E980.3
Lasix	974.4	E858.5	E944.4	E950.4	E962.0	E980.4
Latex	989.82	E866.8	—	E950.9	E962.1	E980.9
Lathyrus (seed)	988.2	E865.3	—	E950.9	E962.1	E980.9
Laudanum	965.09	E850.2	E935.2	E950.0	E962.0	E980.0
Laudexium	975.2	E858.6	E945.2	E950.4	E962.0	E980.4
Laurel, black or cherry	988.2	E865.4	—	E950.9	E962.1	E980.9
Laurolinium	976.0	E858.7	E946.0	E950.4	E962.0	E980.4
Lauryl sulfoacetate	976.2	E858.7	E946.2	E950.4	E962.0	E980.4
Laxatives NEC	973.3	E858.4	E943.3	E950.4	E962.0	E980.4
emollient	973.2	E858.4	E943.2	E950.4	E962.0	E980.4
L-dopa	966.4	E855.0	E936.4	E950.4	E962.0	E980.4
Lead (dust) (fumes) (vapor) NEC	984.9	E866.0	—	E950.9	E962.1	E980.9
acetate (dust)	984.1	E866.0	—	E950.9	E962.1	E980.9
anti-infectives	961.2	E857	E931.2	E950.4	E962.0	E980.4
antiknock compound (tetraethyl)	984.1	E862.1	—	E950.9	E962.1	E980.9
arsenate, arsenite (dust) (insecticide) (vapor)	985.1	E863.4	—	E950.8	E962.1	E980.8
herbicide	985.1	E863.5	—	E950.8	E962.1	E980.8
carbonate	984.0	E866.0	—	E950.9	E962.1	E980.9
paint	984.0	E861.5	—	E950.9	E962.1	E980.9
chromate	984.0	E866.0	—	E950.9	E962.1	E980.9
paint	984.0	E861.5	—	E950.9	E962.1	E980.9
dioxide	984.0	E866.0	—	E950.9	E962.1	E980.9
inorganic (compound)	984.0	E866.0	—	E950.9	E962.1	E980.9
paint	984.0	E861.5	—	E950.9	E962.1	E980.9
iodide	984.0	E866.0	—	E950.9	E962.1	E980.9
pigment (paint)	984.0	E861.5	—	E950.9	E962.1	E980.9
monoxide (dust)	984.0	E866.0	—	E950.9	E962.1	E980.9
paint	984.0	E861.5	—	E950.9	E962.1	E980.9
organic	984.1	E866.0	—	E950.9	E962.1	E980.9
oxide	984.0	E866.0	—	E950.9	E962.1	E980.9
paint	984.0	E861.5	—	E950.9	E962.1	E980.9
paint	984.0	E861.5	—	E950.9	E962.1	E980.9
salts	984.0	E866.0	—	E950.9	E962.1	E980.9
specified compound NEC	984.8	E866.0	—	E950.9	E962.1	E980.9
tetra-ethyl	984.1	E862.1	—	E950.9	E962.1	E980.9
Lebanese red	969.6	E854.1	E939.6	E950.3	E962.0	E980.3
Lente Iletin (insulin)	962.3	E858.0	E932.3	E950.4	E962.0	E980.4
Leptazol	970.0	E854.3	E940.0	E950.4	E962.0	E980.4
Leritine	965.09	E850.2	E935.2	E950.0	E962.0	E980.0
Letter	962.7	E858.0	E932.7	E950.4	E962.0	E980.4
Lettuce opium	967.8	E852.8	E937.8	E950.2	E962.0	E980.2
Leucovorin (factor)	964.1	E858.2	E934.1	E950.4	E962.0	E980.4
Leukeran	963.1	E858.1	E933.1	E950.4	E962.0	E980.4
Levalbuterol	975.7	E858.6	E945.7	E950.4	E962.0	E980.4
Levallorphan	970.1	E854.3	E940.1	E950.4	E962.0	E980.4
Levanil	967.8	E852.8	E937.8	E950.2	E962.0	E980.2
Levarterenol	971.2	E855.5	E941.2	E950.4	E962.0	E980.4
Levodopa	966.4	E855.0	E936.4	E950.4	E962.0	E980.4
Levo-dromoran	965.09	E850.2	E935.2	E950.0	E962.0	E980.0
Levoid	962.7	E858.0	E932.7	E950.4	E962.0	E980.4
Levo-iso-methadone	965.02	E850.1	E935.1	E950.0	E962.0	E980.0
Levomepromazine	967.8	E852.8	E937.8	E950.2	E962.0	E980.2
Levoprome	967.8	E852.8	E937.8	E950.2	E962.0	E980.2
Levopropoxyphene	975.4	E858.6	E945.4	E950.4	E962.0	E980.4
Levorphan, levophanol	965.09	E850.2	E935.2	E950.0	E962.0	E980.0
Levothyroxine (sodium)	962.7	E858.0	E932.7	E950.4	E962.0	E980.4
Levsin	971.1	E855.4	E941.1	E950.4	E962.0	E980.4
Levulose	974.5	E858.5	E944.5	E950.4	E962.0	E980.4
Lewisite (gas)	985.1	E866.3	—	E950.8	E962.1	E980.8
Librium	969.4	E853.2	E939.4	E950.3	E962.0	E980.3
Lidex	976.0	E858.7	E946.0	E950.4	E962.0	E980.4
Lidocaine (infiltration) (topical)	968.5	E855.2	E938.5	E950.4	E962.0	E980.4
nerve block (peripheral) (plexus)	968.6	E855.2	E938.6	E950.4	E962.0	E980.4
spinal	968.7	E855.2	E938.7	E950.4	E962.0	E980.4
Lighter fluid	981	E862.1	—	E950.9	E962.1	E980.9
Lignocaine (infiltration) (topical)	968.5	E855.2	E938.5	E950.4	E962.0	E980.4
nerve block (peripheral) (plexus)	968.6	E855.2	E938.6	E950.4	E962.0	E980.4
Lignocaine — *continued*						
spinal	968.7	E855.2	E938.7	E950.4	E962.0	E980.4
Ligroin(e) (solvent)	981	E862.0	—	E950.9	E962.1	E980.9
vapor	987.1	E869.8	—	E952.8	E962.2	E982.8
Ligustrum vulgare	988.2	E865.3	—	E950.9	E962.1	E980.9
Lily of the valley	988.2	E865.4	—	E950.9	E962.1	E980.9
Lime (chloride)	983.2	E864.2	—	E950.7	E962.1	E980.6
solution, sulferated	976.4	E858.7	E946.4	E950.4	E962.0	E980.4
Limonene	982.8	E862.4	—	E950.9	E962.1	E980.9
Lincomycin	960.8	E856	E930.8	E950.4	E962.0	E980.4
Lindane (insecticide) (vapor)	989.2	E863.0	—	E950.6	E962.1	E980.7
anti-infective (topical)	976.0	E858.7	E946.0	E950.4	E962.0	E980.4
Liniments NEC	976.9	E858.7	E946.9	E950.4	E962.0	E980.4
Linoleic acid	972.2	E858.3	E942.2	E950.4	E962.0	E980.4
Liothyronine	962.7	E858.0	E932.7	E950.4	E962.0	E980.4
Liotrix	962.7	E858.0	E932.7	E950.4	E962.0	E980.4
Lipancreatin	973.4	E858.4	E943.4	E950.4	E962.0	E980.4
Lipo-Lutin	962.2	E858.0	E932.2	E950.4	E962.0	E980.4
Lipotropic agents	977.1	E858.8	E947.1	E950.4	E962.0	E980.4
Liquefied petroleum gases	987.0	E868.0	—	E951.1	E962.2	E981.1
piped (pure or mixed with air)	987.0	E867	—	E951.0	E962.2	E981.0
Liquid petrolatum	973.2	E858.4	E943.2	E950.4	E962.0	E980.4
substance	989.9	E866.9	—	E950.9	E962.1	E980.9
specified NEC	989.89	E866.8	—	E950.9	E962.1	E980.9
Lirugen	979.4	E858.8	E949.4	E950.4	E962.0	E980.4
Lithane	969.8	E855.8	E939.8	E950.3	E962.0	E980.3
Lithium	985.8	E866.4	—	E950.9	E962.1	E980.9
carbonate	969.8	E855.8	E939.8	E950.3	E962.0	E980.3
Lithonate	969.8	E855.8	E939.8	E950.3	E962.0	E980.3
Liver (extract) (injection) (preparations)	964.1	E858.2	E934.1	E950.4	E962.0	E980.4
Lizard (bite) (venom)	989.5	E905.0	—	E950.9	E962.1	E980.9
LMD	964.8	E858.2	E934.8	E950.4	E962.0	E980.4
Lobelia	988.2	E865.4	—	E950.9	E962.1	E980.9
Lobeline	970.0	E854.3	E940.0	E950.4	E962.0	E980.4
Locorten	976.0	E858.7	E946.0	E950.4	E962.0	E980.4
Lolium temulentum	988.2	E865.3	—	E950.9	E962.1	E980.9
Lomotil	973.5	E858.4	E943.5	E950.4	E962.0	E980.4
Lomustine	963.1	E858.1	E933.1	E950.4	E962.0	E980.4
Lophophora williamsii	969.6	E854.1	E939.6	E950.3	E962.0	E980.3
Lorazepam	969.4	E853.2	E939.4	E950.3	E962.0	E980.3
Lotions NEC	976.9	E858.7	E946.9	E950.4	E962.0	E980.4
Lotronex	973.8	E858.4	E943.8	E950.4	E962.0	E980.4
Lotusate	967.0	E851	E937.0	E950.1	E962.0	E980.1
Lowila	976.2	E858.7	E946.2	E950.4	E962.0	E980.4
Loxapine	969.3	E853.8	E939.3	E950.3	E962.0	E980.3
Lozenges (throat)	976.6	E858.7	E946.6	E950.4	E962.0	E980.4
LSD (25)	969.6	E854.1	E939.6	E950.3	E962.0	E980.3
L-Tryptophan — *see* amino acid						
Lubricating oil NEC	981	E862.2	—	E950.9	E962.1	E980.9
Lucanthone	961.6	E857	E931.6	E950.4	E962.0	E980.4
Luminal	967.0	E851	E937.0	E950.1	E962.0	E980.1
Lung irritant (gas) NEC	987.9	E869.9	—	E952.9	E962.2	E982.9
Lutocylol	962.2	E858.0	E932.2	E950.4	E962.0	E980.4
Lutromone	962.2	E858.0	E932.2	E950.4	E962.0	E980.4
Lututrin	975.0	E858.6	E945.0	E950.4	E962.0	E980.4
Lye (concentrated)	983.2	E864.2	—	E950.7	E962.1	E980.6
Lygranum (skin test)	977.8	E858.8	E947.8	E950.4	E962.0	E980.4
Lymecycline	960.4	E856	E930.4	E950.4	E962.0	E980.4
Lymphogranuloma venereum antigen	977.8	E858.8	E947.8	E950.4	E962.0	E980.4
Lynestrenol	962.2	E858.0	E932.2	E950.4	E962.0	E980.4
Lyovac Sodium Edecrin	974.4	E858.5	E944.4	E950.4	E962.0	E980.4
Lypressin	962.5	E858.0	E932.5	E950.4	E962.0	E980.4
Lysergic acid (amide) (diethylamide)	969.6	E854.1	E939.6	E950.3	E962.0	E980.3
Lysergide	969.6	E854.1	E939.6	E950.3	E962.0	E980.3
Lysine vasopressin	962.5	E858.0	E932.5	E950.4	E962.0	E980.4
Lysol	983.0	E864.0	—	E950.7	E962.1	E980.6
Lytta (vitatta)	976.8	E858.7	E946.8	E950.4	E962.0	E980.4
Mace	987.5	E869.3	—	E952.8	E962.2	E982.8
Macrolides (antibiotics)	960.3	E856	E930.3	E950.4	E962.0	E980.4
Mafenide	976.0	E858.7	E946.0	E950.4	E962.0	E980.4
Magaldrate	973.0	E858.4	E943.0	E950.4	E962.0	E980.4
Magic mushroom	969.6	E854.1	E939.6	E950.3	E962.0	E980.3
Magnamycin	960.8	E856	E930.8	E950.4	E962.0	E980.4
Magnesia magma	973.0	E858.4	E943.0	E950.4	E962.0	E980.4
Magnesium (compounds) (fumes) NEC	985.8	E866.4	—	E950.9	E962.1	E980.9

☑ Additional Digit Required — Refer to the Tabular List for Digit Selection

▽ Subterms under main terms may continue to next column or page

▶◀ Revised Text ● New Line ▲ Revised Code

		External Cause (E-Code)				
	Poisoning	Accident	Therapeutic Use	Suicide Attempt	Assault	Undetermined
Methaphenilene	963.0	E858.1	E933.0	E950.4	E962.0	E980.4
Methapyrilene	963.0	E858.1	E933.0	E950.4	E962.0	E980.4
Methaqualone (compounds)	967.4	E852.3	E937.4	E950.2	E962.0	E980.2
Metharbital, metharbitone	967.0	E851	E937.0	E950.1	E962.0	E980.1
Methazolamide	974.2	E858.5	E944.2	E950.4	E962.0	E980.4
Methdilazine	963.0	E858.1	E933.0	E950.4	E962.0	E980.4
Methedrine	969.7	E854.2	E939.7	E950.3	E962.0	E980.3
Methenamine (mandelate)	961.9	E857	E931.9	E950.4	E962.0	E980.4
Methenolone	962.1	E858.0	E932.1	E950.4	E962.0	E980.4
Methergine	975.0	E858.6	E945.0	E950.4	E962.0	E980.4
Methiacil	962.8	E858.0	E932.8	E950.4	E962.0	E980.4
Methicillin (sodium)	960.0	E856	E930.0	E950.4	E962.0	E980.4
Methimazole	962.8	E858.0	E932.8	E950.4	E962.0	E980.4
Methionine	977.1	E858.8	E947.1	E950.4	E962.0	E980.4
Methisazone	961.7	E857	E931.7	E950.4	E962.0	E980.4
Methitural	967.0	E851	E937.0	E950.1	E962.0	E980.1
Methixene	971.1	E855.4	E941.1	E950.4	E962.0	E980.4
Methobarbital, methobarbitone	967.0	E851	E937.0	E950.1	E962.0	E980.1
Methocarbamol	968.0	E855.1	E938.0	E950.4	E962.0	E980.4
Methohexital, methohexitone (sodium)	968.3	E855.1	E938.3	E950.4	E962.0	E980.4
Methoin	966.1	E855.0	E936.1	E950.4	E962.0	E980.4
Methopholine	965.7	E850.7	E935.7	E950.0	E962.0	E980.0
Methorate	975.4	E858.6	E945.4	E950.4	E962.0	E980.4
Methoserpidine	972.6	E858.3	E942.6	E950.4	E962.0	E980.4
Methotrexate	963.1	E858.1	E933.1	E950.4	E962.0	E980.4
Methotrimeprazine	967.8	E852.8	E937.8	E950.2	E962.0	E980.2
Methoxa-Dome	976.3	E858.7	E946.3	E950.4	E962.0	E980.4
Methoxamine	971.2	E855.5	E941.2	E950.4	E962.0	E980.4
Methoxsalen	976.3	E858.7	E946.3	E950.4	E962.0	E980.4
Methoxybenzyl penicillin	960.0	E856	E930.0	E950.4	E962.0	E980.4
Methoxychlor	989.2	E863.0	—	E950.6	E962.1	E980.7
Methoxyflurane	968.2	E855.1	E938.2	E950.4	E962.0	E980.4
Methoxyphenamine	971.2	E855.5	E941.2	E950.4	E962.0	E980.4
Methoxypromazine	969.1	E853.0	E939.1	E950.3	E962.0	E980.3
Methoxypsoralen	976.3	E858.7	E946.3	E950.4	E962.0	E980.4
Methscopolamine (bromide)	971.1	E855.4	E941.1	E950.4	E962.0	E980.4
Methsuximide	966.2	E855.0	E936.2	E950.4	E962.0	E980.4
Methyclothiazide	974.3	E858.5	E944.3	E950.4	E962.0	E980.4
Methyl						
acetate	982.8	E862.4	—	E950.9	E962.1	E980.9
acetone	982.8	E862.4	—	E950.9	E962.1	E980.9
alcohol	980.1	E860.2	—	E950.9	E962.1	E980.9
amphetamine	969.7	E854.2	E939.7	E950.3	E962.0	E980.3
androstanolone	962.1	E858.0	E932.1	E950.4	E962.0	E980.4
atropine	971.1	E855.4	E941.1	E950.4	E962.0	E980.4
benzene	982.0	E862.4	—	E950.9	E962.1	E980.9
bromide (gas)	987.8	E869.8	—	E952.8	E962.2	E982.8
fumigant	987.8	E863.8	—	E950.6	E962.2	E980.7
butanol	980.8	E860.8	—	E950.9	E962.1	E980.9
carbinol	980.1	E860.2	—	E950.9	E962.1	E980.9
cellosolve	982.8	E862.4	—	E950.9	E962.1	E980.9
cellulose	973.3	E858.4	E943.3	E950.4	E962.0	E980.4
chloride (gas)	987.8	E869.8	—	E952.8	E962.2	E982.8
cyclohexane	982.8	E862.4	—	E950.9	E962.1	E980.9
cyclohexanone	982.8	E862.4	—	E950.9	E962.1	E980.9
dihydromorphinone	965.09	E850.2	E935.2	E950.0	E962.0	E980.0
ergometrine	975.0	E858.6	E945.0	E950.4	E962.0	E980.4
ergonovine	975.0	E858.6	E945.0	E950.4	E962.0	E980.4
ethyl ketone	982.8	E862.4	—	E950.9	E962.1	E980.9
hydrazine	983.9	E864.3	—	E950.7	E962.1	E980.6
isobutyl ketone	982.8	E862.4	—	E950.9	E962.1	E980.9
morphine NEC	965.09	E850.2	E935.2	E950.0	E962.0	E980.0
parafynol	967.8	E852.8	E937.8	E950.2	E962.0	E980.2
parathion	989.3	E863.1	—	E950.6	E962.1	E980.7
pentynol NEC	967.8	E852.8	E937.8	E950.2	E962.0	E980.2
peridol	969.2	E853.1	E939.2	E950.3	E962.0	E980.3
phenidate	969.7	E854.2	E939.7	E950.3	E962.0	E980.3
prednisolone	962.0	E858.0	E932.0	E950.4	E962.0	E980.4
ENT agent	976.6	E858.7	E946.6	E950.4	E962.0	E980.4
ophthalmic preparation	976.5	E858.7	E946.5	E950.4	E962.0	E980.4
topical NEC	976.0	E858.7	E946.0	E950.4	E962.0	E980.4
propylcarbinol	980.8	E860.8	—	E950.9	E962.1	E980.9
rosaniline NEC	976.0	E858.7	E946.0	E950.4	E962.0	E980.4
salicylate NEC	976.3	E858.7	E946.3	E950.4	E962.0	E980.4
sulfate (fumes)	987.8	E869.8	—	E952.8	E962.2	E982.8
liquid	983.9	E864.3	—	E950.7	E962.1	E980.6
sulfonal	967.8	E852.8	E937.8	E950.2	E962.0	E980.2
testosterone	962.1	E858.0	E932.1	E950.4	E962.0	E980.4
Methyl — *continued*						
thiouracil	962.8	E858.0	E932.8	E950.4	E962.0	E980.4
Methylated spirit	980.0	E860.1	—	E950.9	E962.1	E980.9
Methyldopa	972.6	E858.3	E942.6	E950.4	E962.0	E980.4
Methylene						
blue	961.9	E857	E931.9	E950.4	E962.0	E980.4
chloride or dichloride (solvent) NEC	982.3	E862.4	—	E950.9	E962.1	E980.9
Methylhexabital	967.0	E851	E937.0	E950.1	E962.0	E980.1
Methylparaben (ophthalmic)	976.5	E858.7	E946.5	E950.4	E962.0	E980.4
Methyprylon	967.5	E852.4	E937.5	E950.2	E962.0	E980.2
Methysergide	971.3	E855.6	E941.3	E950.4	E962.0	E980.4
Metoclopramide	963.0	E858.1	E933.0	E950.4	E962.0	E980.4
Metofoline	965.7	E850.7	E935.7	E950.0	E962.0	E980.0
Metopon	965.09	E850.2	E935.2	E950.0	E962.0	E980.0
Metronidazole	961.5	E857	E931.5	E950.4	E962.0	E980.4
Metycaine	968.9	E855.2	E938.9	E950.4	E962.0	E980.4
infiltration (subcutaneous)	968.5	E855.2	E938.5	E950.4	E962.0	E980.4
nerve block (peripheral) (plexus)	968.6	E855.2	E938.6	E950.4	E962.0	E980.4
topical (surface)	968.5	E855.2	E938.5	E950.4	E962.0	E980.4
Metyrapone	977.8	E858.8	E947.8	E950.4	E962.0	E980.4
Mevinphos	989.3	E863.1	—	E950.6	E962.1	E980.7
Mezereon (berries)	988.2	E865.3	—	E950.9	E962.1	E980.9
Micatin	976.0	E858.7	E946.0	E950.4	E962.0	E980.4
Miconazole	976.0	E858.7	E946.0	E950.4	E962.0	E980.4
Midol	965.1	E850.3	E935.3	E950.0	E962.0	E980.0
Mifepristone	962.9	E858.0	E932.9	E950.4	E962.0	E980.4
Milk of magnesia	973.0	E858.4	E943.0	E950.4	E962.0	E980.4
Millipede (tropical) (venomous)	989.5	E905.4	—	E950.9	E962.1	E980.9
Miltown	969.5	E853.8	E939.5	E950.3	E962.0	E980.3
Mineral						
oil (medicinal)	973.2	E858.4	E943.2	E950.4	E962.0	E980.4
nonmedicinal	981	E862.1	—	E950.9	E962.1	E980.9
topical	976.3	E858.7	E946.3	E950.4	E962.0	E980.4
salts NEC	974.6	E858.5	E944.6	E950.4	E962.0	E980.4
spirits	981	E862.0	—	E950.9	E962.1	E980.9
Minocycline	960.4	E856	E930.4	E950.4	E962.0	E980.4
Mithramycin (antineoplastic)	960.7	E856	E930.7	E950.4	E962.0	E980.4
Mitobronitol	963.1	E858.1	E933.1	E950.4	E962.0	E980.4
Mitomycin (antineoplastic)	960.7	E856	E930.7	E950.4	E962.0	E980.4
Mitotane	963.1	E858.1	E933.1	E950.4	E962.0	E980.4
Moderil	972.6	E858.3	E942.6	E950.4	E962.0	E980.4
Mogadon — *see* Nitrazepam						
Molindone	969.3	E853.8	E939.3	E950.3	E962.0	E980.3
Monistat	976.0	E858.7	E946.0	E950.4	E962.0	E980.4
Monkshood	988.2	E865.4	—	E950.9	E962.1	E980.9
Monoamine oxidase inhibitors	969.0	E854.0	E939.0	E950.3	E962.0	E980.3
Monochlorobenzene	982.0	E862.4	—	E950.9	E962.1	E980.9
Monosodium glutamate	989.89	E866.8	—	E950.9	E962.1	E980.9
Monoxide, carbon — *see* Carbon, monoxide						
Moperone	969.2	E853.1	E939.2	E950.3	E962.0	E980.3
Morning glory seeds	969.6	E854.1	E939.6	E950.3	E962.0	E980.3
Moroxydine (hydrochloride)	961.7	E857	E931.7	E950.4	E962.0	E980.4
Morphazinamide	961.8	E857	E931.8	E950.4	E962.0	E980.4
Morphinans	965.09	E850.2	E935.2	E950.0	E962.0	E980.0
Morphine NEC	965.09	E850.2	E935.2	E950.0	E962.0	E980.0
antagonists	970.1	E854.3	E940.1	E950.4	E962.0	E980.4
Morpholinylethylmorphine	965.09	E850.2	E935.2	E950.0	E962.0	E980.0
Morrhuate sodium	972.7	E858.3	E942.7	E950.4	E962.0	E980.4
Moth balls — *see also* Pesticides	989.4	E863.4	—	E950.6	E962.1	E980.7
naphthalene	983.0	E863.4	—	E950.7	E962.1	E980.6
Motor exhaust gas — see Carbon, monoxide, exhaust gas						
Mouth wash	976.6	E858.7	E946.6	E950.4	E962.0	E980.4
Mucolytic agent	975.5	E858.6	E945.5	E950.4	E962.0	E980.4
Mucomyst	975.5	E858.6	E945.5	E950.4	E962.0	E980.4
Mucous membrane agents (external)	976.9	E858.7	E946.9	E950.4	E962.0	E980.4
specified NEC	976.8	E858.7	E946.8	E950.4	E962.0	E980.4
Mumps						
immune globulin (human)	964.6	E858.2	E934.6	E950.4	E962.0	E980.4
skin test antigen	977.8	E858.8	E947.8	E950.4	E962.0	E980.4
vaccine	979.6	E858.8	E949.6	E950.4	E962.0	E980.4

		External Cause (E-Code)				
	Poisoning	Accident	Therapeutic Use	Suicide Attempt	Assault	Undeter-mined
Mumpsvax	979.6	E858.8	E949.6	E950.4	E962.0	E980.4
Muriatic acid — *see* Hydrochloric acid						
Muscarine	971.0	E855.3	E941.0	E950.4	E962.0	E980.4
Muscle affecting agents NEC	975.3	E858.6	E945.3	E950.4	E962.0	E980.4
oxytocic	975.0	E858.6	E945.0	E950.4	E962.0	E980.4
relaxants	975.3	E858.6	E945.3	E950.4	E962.0	E980.4
central nervous system	968.0	E855.1	E938.0	E950.4	E962.0	E980.4
skeletal	975.2	E858.6	E945.2	E950.4	E962.0	E980.4
smooth	975.1	E858.6	E945.1	E950.4	E962.0	E980.4
Mushrooms, noxious	988.1	E865.5	—	E950.9	E962.1	E980.9
Mussel, noxious	988.0	E865.1	—	E950.9	E962.1	E980.9
Mustard (emetic)	973.6	E858.4	E943.6	E950.4	E962.0	E980.4
gas	987.8	E869.8	—	E952.8	E962.2	E982.8
nitrogen	963.1	E858.1	E933.1	E950.4	E962.0	E980.4
Mustine	963.1	E858.1	E933.1	E950.4	E962.0	E980.4
M-vac	979.4	E858.8	E949.4	E950.4	E962.0	E980.4
Mycifradin	960.8	E856	E930.8	E950.4	E962.0	E980.4
topical	976.0	E858.7	E946.0	E950.4	E962.0	E980.4
Mycitracin	960.8	E856	E930.8	E950.4	E962.0	E980.4
ophthalmic preparation	976.5	E858.7	E946.5	E950.4	E962.0	E980.4
Mycostatin	960.1	E856	E930.1	E950.4	E962.0	E980.4
topical	976.0	E858.7	E946.0	E950.4	E962.0	E980.4
Mydriacyl	971.1	E855.4	E941.1	E950.4	E962.0	E980.4
Myelobromal	963.1	E858.1	E933.1	E950.4	E962.0	E980.4
Myleran	963.1	E858.1	E933.1	E950.4	E962.0	E980.4
Myochrysin(e)	965.69	E850.6	E935.6	E950.0	E962.0	E980.0
Myoneural blocking agents	975.2	E858.6	E945.2	E950.4	E962.0	E980.4
Myristica fragrans	988.2	E865.3	—	E950.9	E962.1	E980.9
Myristicin	988.2	E865.3	—	E950.9	E962.1	E980.9
Mysoline	966.3	E855.0	E936.3	E950.4	E962.0	E980.4
Nafcillin (sodium)	960.0	E856	E930.0	E950.4	E962.0	E980.4
Nail polish remover	982.8	E862.4	—	E950.9	E962.1	E908.9
Nalidixic acid	961.9	E857	E931.9	E950.4	E962.0	E980.4
Nalorphine	970.1	E854.3	E940.1	E950.4	E962.0	E980.4
Naloxone	970.1	E854.3	E940.1	E950.4	E962.0	E980.4
Nandrolone (decanoate) (phenproprioate)	962.1	E858.0	E932.1	E950.4	E962.0	E980.4
Naphazoline	971.2	E855.5	E941.2	E950.4	E962.0	E980.4
Naphtha (painter's) (petroleum)	981	E862.0	—	E950.9	E962.1	E980.9
solvent	981	E862.0	—	E950.9	E962.1	E980.9
vapor	987.1	E869.8	—	E952.8	E962.2	E982.8
Naphthalene (chlorinated)	983.0	E864.0	—	E950.7	E962.1	E980.6
insecticide or moth repellent	983.0	E863.4	—	E950.7	E962.1	E980.6
vapor	987.8	E869.8	—	E952.8	E962.2	E982.8
Naphthol	983.0	E864.0	—	E950.7	E962.1	E980.6
Naphthylamine	983.0	E864.0	—	E950.7	E962.1	E980.6
Naprosyn — see Naproxen						
Naproxen	965.61	E850.6	E935.6	E950.0	E962.0	E980.0
Narcotic (drug)	967.9	E852.9	E937.9	E950.2	E962.0	E980.2
analgesic NEC	965.8	E850.8	E935.8	E950.0	E962.0	E980.0
antagonist	970.1	E854.3	E940.1	E950.4	E962.0	E980.4
specified NEC	967.8	E852.8	E937.8	E950.2	E962.0	E980.2
Narcotine	975.4	E858.6	E945.4	E950.4	E962.0	E980.4
Nardil	969.0	E854.0	E939.0	E950.3	E962.0	E980.3
Natrium cyanide — see Cyanide(s)						
Natural						
blood (product)	964.7	E858.2	E934.7	E950.4	E962.0	E980.4
gas (piped)	987.1	E867	—	E951.0	E962.2	E981.0
incomplete combustion	986	E867	—	E951.0	E962.2	E981.0
Nealbarbital, nealbarbitone	967.0	E851	E937.0	E950.1	E962.0	E980.1
Nectadon	975.4	E858.6	E945.4	E950.4	E962.0	E980.4
Nematocyst (sting)	989.5	E905.6	—	E950.9	E962.1	E980.9
Nembutal	967.0	E851	E937.0	E950.1	E962.0	E980.1
Neoarsphenamine	961.1	E857	E931.1	E950.4	E962.0	E980.4
Neocinchophen	974.7	E858.5	E944.7	E950.4	E962.0	E980.4
Neomycin	960.8	E856	E930.8	E950.4	E962.0	E980.4
ENT agent	976.6	E858.7	E946.6	E950.4	E962.0	E980.4
ophthalmic preparation	976.5	E858.7	E946.5	E950.4	E962.0	E980.4
topical NEC	976.0	E858.7	E946.0	E950.4	E962.0	E980.4
Neonal	967.0	E851	E937.0	E950.1	E962.0	E980.1
Neoprontosil	961.0	E857	E931.0	E950.4	E962.0	E980.4
Neosalvarsan	961.1	E857	E931.1	E950.4	E962.0	E980.4
Neosilversalvarsan	961.1	E857	E931.1	E950.4	E962.0	E980.4
Neosporin	960.8	E856	E930.8	E950.4	E962.0	E980.4
Neosporin — *continued*						
ENT agent	976.6	E858.7	E946.6	E950.4	E962.0	E980.4
opthalmic preparation	976.5	E858.7	E946.5	E950.4	E962.0	E980.4
topical NEC	976.0	E858.7	E946.0	E950.4	E962.0	E980.4
Neostigmine	971.0	E855.3	E941.0	E950.4	E962.0	E980.4
Neraval	967.0	E851	E937.0	E950.1	E962.0	E980.1
Neravan	967.0	E851	E937.0	E950.1	E962.0	E980.1
Nerium oleander	988.2	E865.4	—	E950.9	E962.1	E980.9
Nerve gases (war)	987.9	E869.9	—	E952.9	E962.2	E982.9
Nesacaine	968.9	E855.2	E938.9	E950.4	E962.0	E980.4
infiltration (subcutaneous)	968.5	E855.2	E938.5	E950.4	E962.0	E980.4
nerve block (peripheral) (plexus)	968.6	E855.2	E938.6	E950.4	E962.0	E980.4
Neurobarb	967.0	E851	E937.0	E950.1	E962.0	E980.1
Neuroleptics NEC	969.3	E853.8	E939.3	E950.3	E962.0	E980.3
Neuroprotective agent	977.8	E858.8	E947.8	E950.4	E962.0	E980.4
Neutral spirits	980.0	E860.1	—	E950.9	E962.1	E980.9
beverage	980.0	E860.0	—	E950.9	E962.1	E980.9
Niacin, niacinamide	972.2	E858.3	E942.2	E950.4	E962.0	E980.4
Nialamide	969.0	E854.0	E939.0	E950.3	E962.0	E980.3
Nickle (carbonyl) (compounds) (fumes) (tetracarbonyl) (vapor)	985.8	E866.4	—	E950.9	E962.1	E980.9
Niclosamide	961.6	E857	E931.6	E950.4	E962.0	E980.4
Nicomorphine	965.09	E850.2	E935.2	E950.0	E962.0	E980.0
Nicotinamide	972.2	E858.3	E942.2	E950.4	E962.0	E980.4
Nicotine (insecticide) (spray) (sulfate) NEC	989.4	E863.4	—	E950.6	E962.1	E980.7
not insecticide	989.89	E866.8	—	E950.9	E962.1	E980.9
Nicotinic acid (derivatives)	972.2	E858.3	E942.2	E950.4	E962.0	E980.4
Nicotinyl alcohol	972.2	E858.3	E942.2	E950.4	E962.0	E980.4
Nicoumalone	964.2	E858.2	E934.2	E950.4	E962.0	E980.4
Nifenazone	965.5	E850.5	E935.5	E950.0	E962.0	E980.0
Nifuraldezone	961.9	E857	E931.9	E950.4	E962.0	E980.4
Nightshade (deadly)	988.2	E865.4	—	E950.9	E962.1	E980.9
Nikethamide	970.0	E854.3	E940.0	E950.4	E962.0	E980.4
Nilstat	960.1	E856	E930.1	E950.4	E962.0	E980.4
topical	976.0	E858.7	E946.0	E950.4	E962.0	E980.4
Nimodipine	977.8	E858.8	E947.8	E950.4	E962.0	E980.4
Niridazole	961.6	E857	E931.6	E950.4	E962.0	E980.4
Nisentil	965.09	E850.2	E935.2	E950.0	E962.0	E980.0
Nitrates	972.4	E858.3	E942.4	E950.4	E962.0	E980.4
Nitrazepam	969.4	E853.2	E939.4	E950.3	E962.0	E980.3
Nitric						
acid (liquid)	983.1	E864.1	—	E950.7	E962.1	E980.6
vapor	987.8	E869.8	—	E952.8	E962.2	E982.8
oxide (gas)	987.2	E869.0	—	E952.8	E962.2	E982.8
Nitrite, amyl (medicinal) (vapor)	972.4	E858.3	E942.4	E950.4	E962.0	E980.4
Nitroaniline	983.0	E864.0	—	E950.7	E962.1	E980.6
vapor	987.8	E869.8	—	E952.8	E962.2	E982.8
Nitrobenzene, nitrobenzol	983.0	E864.0	—	E950.7	E962.1	E980.6
vapor	987.8	E869.8	—	E952.8	E962.2	E982.8
Nitrocellulose	976.3	E858.7	E946.3	E950.4	E962.0	E980.4
Nitrofuran derivatives	961.9	E857	E931.9	E950.4	E962.0	E980.4
Nitrofurantoin	961.9	E857	E931.9	E950.4	E962.0	E980.4
Nitrofurazone	976.0	E858.7	E946.0	E950.4	E962.0	E980.4
Nitrogen (dioxide) (gas) (oxide)	987.2	E869.0	—	E952.8	E962.2	E982.8
mustard (antineoplastic)	963.1	E858.1	E933.1	E950.4	E962.0	E980.4
nonmedicinal	989.89	E866.8	—	E950.9	E962.1	E980.9
fumes	987.8	E869.8	—	E952.8	E962.2	E982.8
Nitroglycerin, nitroglycerol (medicinal)	972.4	E858.3	E942.4	E950.4	E962.0	E980.4
Nitrohydrochloric acid	983.1	E864.1	—	E950.7	E962.1	E980.6
Nitromersol	976.0	E858.7	E946.0	E950.4	E962.0	E980.4
Nitronaphthalene	983.0	E864.0	—	E950.7	E962.2	E980.6
Nitrophenol	983.0	E864.0	—	E950.7	E962.2	E980.6
Nitrothiazol	961.6	E857	E931.6	E950.4	E962.0	E980.4
Nitrotoluene, nitrotoluol	983.0	E864.0	—	E950.7	E962.1	E980.6
vapor	987.8	E869.8	—	E952.8	E962.2	E982.8
Nitrous	968.2	E855.1	E938.2	E950.4	E962.0	E980.4
acid (liquid)	983.1	E864.1	—	E950.7	E962.1	E980.6
fumes	987.2	E869.0	—	E952.8	E962.2	E982.8
oxide (anesthetic) NEC	968.2	E855.1	E938.2	E950.4	E962.0	E980.4
Nitrozone	976.0	E858.7	E946.0	E950.4	E962.0	E980.4
Noctec	967.1	E852.0	E937.1	E950.2	E962.0	E980.2
Noludar	967.5	E852.4	E937.5	E950.2	E962.0	E980.2
Noptil	967.0	E851	E937.0	E950.1	E962.0	E980.1
Noradrenalin	971.2	E855.5	E941.2	E950.4	E962.0	E980.4
Noramidopyrine	965.5	E850.5	E935.5	E950.0	E962.0	E980.0

		External Cause (E-Code)				
	Poisoning	Accident	Therapeutic Use	Suicide Attempt	Assault	Undetermined
Norepinephrine	971.2	E855.5	E941.2	E950.4	E962.0	E980.4
Norethandrolone	962.1	E858.0	E932.1	E950.4	E962.0	E980.4
Norethindrone	962.2	E858.0	E932.2	E950.4	E962.0	E980.4
Norethisterone	962.2	E858.0	E932.2	E950.4	E962.0	E980.4
Norethynodrel	962.2	E858.0	E932.2	E950.4	E962.0	E980.4
Norlestrin	962.2	E858.0	E932.2	E950.4	E962.0	E980.4
Norlutin	962.2	E858.0	E932.2	E950.4	E962.0	E980.4
Normison — see Benzodiazepines						
Normorphine	965.09	E850.2	E935.2	E950.0	E962.0	E980.0
Nortriptyline	969.0	E854.0	E939.0	E950.3	E962.0	E980.3
Noscapine	975.4	E858.6	E945.4	E950.4	E962.0	E980.4
Nose preparations	976.6	E858.7	E946.6	E950.4	E962.0	E980.4
Novobiocin	960.8	E856	E930.8	E950.4	E962.0	E980.4
Novocain (infiltration) (topical)	968.5	E855.2	E938.5	E950.4	E962.0	E980.4
nerve block (peripheral) (plexus)	968.6	E855.2	E938.6	E950.4	E962.0	E980.4
spinal	968.7	E855.2	E938.7	E950.4	E962.0	E980.4
Noxythiolin	961.9	E857	E931.9	E950.4	E962.0	E980.4
NPH Iletin (insulin)	962.3	E858.0	E932.3	E950.4	E962.0	E980.4
Numorphan	965.09	E850.2	E935.2	E950.0	E962.0	E980.0
Nunol	967.0	E851	E937.0	E950.1	E962.0	E980.1
Nupercaine (spinal anesthetic)	968.7	E855.2	E938.7	E950.4	E962.0	E980.4
topical (surface)	968.5	E855.2	E938.5	E950.4	E962.0	E980.4
Nutmeg oil (liniment)	976.3	E858.7	E946.3	E950.4	E962.0	E980.4
Nux vomica	989.1	E863.7	—	E950.6	E962.1	E980.7
Nydrazid	961.8	E857	E931.8	E950.4	E962.0	E980.4
Nylidrin	971.2	E855.5	E941.2	E950.4	E962.0	E980.4
Nystatin	960.1	E856	E930.1	E950.4	E962.0	E980.4
topical	976.0	E858.7	E946.0	E950.4	E962.0	E980.4
Nytol	963.0	E858.1	E933.0	E950.4	E962.0	E980.4
Oblivion	967.8	E852.8	E937.8	E950.2	E962.0	E980.2
Octyl nitrite	972.4	E858.3	E942.4	E950.4	E962.0	E980.4
Oestradiol (cypionate) (dipropionate) (valerate)	962.2	E858.0	E932.2	E950.4	E962.0	E980.4
Oestriol	962.2	E858.0	E932.2	E950.4	E962.0	E980.4
Oestrone	962.2	E858.0	E932.2	E950.4	E962.0	E980.4
Oil (of) NEC	989.89	E866.8	—	E950.9	E962.1	E980.9
bitter almond	989.0	E866.8	—	E950.9	E962.1	E980.9
camphor	976.1	E858.7	E946.1	E950.4	E962.0	E980.4
colors	989.89	E861.6	—	E950.9	E962.1	E980.9
fumes	987.8	E869.8	—	E952.8	E962.2	E982.8
lubricating	981	E862.2	—	E950.9	E962.1	E980.9
specified source, other — see substance specified						
vitriol (liquid)	983.1	E864.1	—	E950.7	E962.1	E980.6
fumes	987.8	E869.8	—	E952.8	E962.2	E982.8
wintergreen (bitter) NEC	976.3	E858.7	E946.3	E950.4	E962.0	E980.4
Ointments NEC	976.9	E858.7	E946.9	E950.4	E962.0	E980.4
Oleander	988.2	E865.4	—	E950.9	E962.1	E980.9
Oleandomycin	960.3	E856	E930.3	E950.4	E962.0	E980.4
Oleovitamin A	963.5	E858.1	E933.5	E950.4	E962.0	E980.4
Oleum ricini	973.1	E858.4	E943.1	E950.4	E962.0	E980.4
Olive oil (medicinal) NEC	973.2	E858.4	E943.2	E950.4	E962.0	E980.4
OMPA	989.3	E863.1	—	E950.6	E962.1	E980.7
Oncovin	963.1	E858.1	E933.1	E950.4	E962.0	E980.4
Ophthaine	968.5	E855.2	E938.5	E950.4	E962.0	E980.4
Ophthetic	968.5	E855.2	E938.5	E950.4	E962.0	E980.4
Opiates, opioids, opium NEC	965.00	E850.2	E935.2	E950.0	E962.0	E980.0
antagonists	970.1	E854.3	E940.1	E950.4	E962.0	E980.4
Oracon	962.2	E858.0	E932.2	E950.4	E962.0	E980.4
Oragrafin	977.8	E858.8	E947.8	E950.4	E962.0	E980.4
Oral contraceptives	962.2	E858.0	E932.2	E950.4	E962.0	E980.4
Orciprenaline	975.1	E858.6	E945.1	E950.4	E962.0	E980.4
Organidin	975.5	E858.6	E945.5	E950.4	E962.0	E980.4
Organophosphates	989.3	E863.1	—	E950.6	E962.1	E980.7
Orimune	979.5	E858.8	E949.5	E950.4	E962.0	E980.4
Orinase	962.3	E858.0	E932.3	E950.4	E962.0	E980.4
Orphenadrine	966.4	E855.0	E936.4	E950.4	E962.0	E980.4
Ortal (sodium)	967.0	E851	E937.0	E950.1	E962.0	E980.1
Orthoboric acid	976.0	E858.7	E946.0	E950.4	E962.0	E980.4
ENT agent	976.6	E858.7	E946.6	E950.4	E962.0	E980.4
ophthalmic preparation	976.5	E858.7	E946.5	E950.4	E962.0	E980.4
Orthocaine	968.5	E855.2	E938.5	E950.4	E962.0	E980.4
Ortho-Novum	962.2	E858.0	E932.2	E950.4	E962.0	E980.4
Orthotolidine (reagent)	977.8	E858.8	E947.8	E950.4	E962.0	E980.4
Osmic acid (liquid)	983.1	E864.1	—	E950.7	E962.1	E980.6
fumes	987.8	E869.8	—	E952.8	E962.2	E982.8
Osmotic diuretics	974.4	E858.5	E944.4	E950.4	E962.0	E980.4
Ouabain	972.1	E858.3	E942.1	E950.4	E962.0	E980.4
Ovarian hormones (synthetic substitutes)	962.2	E858.0	E932.2	E950.4	E962.0	E980.4
Ovral	962.2	E858.0	E932.2	E950.4	E962.0	E980.4
Ovulation suppressants	962.2	E858.0	E932.2	E950.4	E962.0	E980.4
Ovulen	962.2	E858.0	E932.2	E950.4	E962.0	E980.4
Oxacillin (sodium)	960.0	E856	E930.0	E950.4	E962.0	E980.4
Oxalic acid	983.1	E864.1	—	E950.7	E962.1	E980.6
Oxanamide	969.5	E853.8	E939.5	E950.3	E962.0	E980.3
Oxandrolone	962.1	E858.0	E932.1	E950.4	E962.0	E980.4
Oxaprozin	965.61	E850.6	E935.6	E950.0	E962.0	E980.0
Oxazepam	969.4	E853.2	E939.4	E950.3	E962.0	E980.3
Oxazolidine derivatives	966.0	E855.0	E936.0	E950.4	E962.0	E980.4
Ox bile extract	973.4	E858.4	E943.4	E950.4	E962.0	E980.4
Oxedrine	971.2	E855.5	E941.2	E950.4	E962.0	E980.4
Oxeladin	975.4	E858.6	E945.4	E950.4	E962.0	E980.4
Oxethazaine NEC	968.5	E855.2	E938.5	E950.4	E962.0	E980.4
Oxidizing agents NEC	983.9	E864.3	—	E950.7	E962.1	E980.6
Oxolinic acid	961.3	E857	E931.3	E950.4	E962.0	E980.4
Oxophenarsine	961.1	E857	E931.1	E950.4	E962.0	E980.4
Oxsoralen	976.3	E858.7	E946.3	E950.4	E962.0	E980.4
Oxtriphylline	975.7	E858.6	E945.7	E950.4	E962.0	E980.4
Oxybuprocaine	968.5	E855.2	E938.5	E950.4	E962.0	E980.4
Oxybutynin	975.1	E858.6	E945.1	E950.4	E962.0	E980.4
Oxycodone	965.09	E850.2	E935.2	E950.0	E962.0	E980.0
Oxygen	987.8	E869.8	—	E952.8	E962.2	E982.8
Oxylone	976.0	E858.7	E946.0	E950.4	E962.0	E980.4
ophthalmic preparation	976.5	E858.7	E946.5	E950.4	E962.0	E980.4
Oxymesterone	962.1	E858.0	E932.1	E950.4	E962.0	E980.4
Oxymetazoline	971.2	E855.5	E941.2	E950.4	E962.0	E980.4
Oxymetholone	962.1	E858.0	E932.1	E950.4	E962.0	E980.4
Oxymorphone	965.09	E850.2	E935.2	E950.0	E962.0	E980.0
Oxypertine	969.0	E854.0	E939.0	E950.3	E962.0	E980.3
Oxyphenbutazone	965.5	E850.5	E935.5	E950.0	E962.0	E980.0
Oxyphencyclimine	971.1	E855.4	E941.1	E950.4	E962.0	E980.4
Oxyphenisatin	973.1	E858.4	E943.1	E950.4	E962.0	E980.4
Oxyphenonium	971.1	E855.4	E941.1	E950.4	E962.0	E980.4
Oxyquinoline	961.3	E857	E931.3	E950.4	E962.0	E980.4
Oxytetracycline	960.4	E856	E930.4	E950.4	E962.0	E980.4
Oxytocics	975.0	E858.6	E945.0	E950.4	E962.0	E980.4
Oxytocin	975.0	E858.6	E945.0	E950.4	E962.0	E980.4
Ozone	987.8	E869.8	—	E952.8	E962.2	E982.8
PABA	976.3	E858.7	E946.3	E950.4	E962.0	E980.4
Packed red cells	964.7	E858.2	E934.7	E950.4	E962.0	E980.4
Paint NEC	989.89	E861.6	—	E950.9	E962.1	E980.9
cleaner	982.8	E862.9	—	E950.9	E962.1	E980.9
fumes NEC	987.8	E869.8	—	E952.8	E962.1	E982.8
lead (fumes)	984.0	E861.5	—	E950.9	E962.1	E980.9
solvent NEC	982.8	E862.9	—	E950.9	E962.1	E980.9
stripper	982.8	E862.9	—	E950.9	E962.1	E980.9
Palfium	965.09	E850.2	E935.2	E950.0	E962.0	E980.0
Palivizumab	979.9	E858.8	E949.6	E950.4	E962.0	E980.4
Paludrine	961.4	E857	E931.4	E950.4	E962.0	E980.4
PAM	977.2	E855.8	E947.2	E950.4	E962.0	E980.4
Pamaquine (naphthoate)	961.4	E857	E931.4	E950.4	E962.0	E980.4
Pamprin	965.1	E850.3	E935.3	E950.0	E962.0	E980.0
Panadol	965.4	E850.4	E935.4	E950.0	E962.0	E980.0
Pancreatic dornase (mucolytic)	963.4	E858.1	E933.4	E950.4	E962.0	E980.4
Pancreatin	973.4	E858.4	E943.4	E950.4	E962.0	E980.4
Pancrelipase	973.4	E858.4	E943.4	E950.4	E962.0	E980.4
Pangamic acid	963.5	E858.1	E933.5	E950.4	E962.0	E980.4
Panthenol	963.5	E858.1	E933.5	E950.4	E962.0	E980.4
topical	976.8	E858.7	E946.8	E950.4	E962.0	E980.4
Pantopaque	977.8	E858.8	E947.8	E950.4	E962.0	E980.4
Pantopon	965.00	E850.2	E935.2	E950.0	E962.0	E980.0
Pantothenic acid	963.5	E858.1	E933.5	E950.4	E962.0	E980.4
Panwarfin	964.2	E858.2	E934.2	E950.4	E962.0	E980.4
Papain	973.4	E858.4	E943.4	E950.4	E962.0	E980.4
Papaverine	972.5	E858.3	E942.5	E950.4	E962.0	E980.4
Para-aminobenzoic acid	976.3	E858.7	E946.3	E950.4	E962.0	E980.4
Para-aminophenol derivatives	965.4	E850.4	E935.4	E950.0	E962.0	E980.0
Para-aminosalicylic acid (derivatives)	961.8	E857	E931.8	E950.4	E962.0	E980.4
Paracetaldehyde (medicinal)	967.2	E852.1	E937.2	E950.2	E962.0	E980.2
Paracetamol	965.4	E850.4	E935.4	E950.0	E962.0	E980.0
Paracodin	965.09	E850.2	E935.2	E950.0	E962.0	E980.0
Paradione	966.0	E855.0	E936.0	E950.4	E962.0	E980.4

	Poisoning	External Cause (E-Code)				
		Accident	Therapeutic Use	Suicide Attempt	Assault	Undetermined
Paraffin(s) (wax)	981	E862.3	—	E950.9	E962.1	E980.9
liquid (medicinal)	973.2	E858.4	E943.2	E950.4	E962.0	E980.4
nonmedicinal (oil)	981	E962.1	—	E950.9	E962.1	E980.9
Paraldehyde (medicinal)	967.2	E852.1	E937.2	E950.2	E962.0	E980.2
Paramethadione	966.0	E855.0	E936.0	E950.4	E962.0	E980.4
Paramethasone	962.0	E858.0	E932.0	E950.4	E962.0	E980.4
Paraquat	989.4	E863.5	—	E950.6	E962.1	E980.7
Parasympatholytics	971.1	E855.4	E941.1	E950.4	E962.0	E980.4
Parasympathomimetics	971.0	E855.3	E941.0	E950.4	E962.0	E980.4
Parathion	989.3	E863.1	—	E950.6	E962.1	E980.7
Parathormone	962.6	E858.0	E932.6	E950.4	E962.0	E980.4
Parathyroid (derivatives)	962.6	E858.0	E932.6	E950.4	E962.0	E980.4
Paratyphoid vaccine	978.1	E858.8	E948.1	E950.4	E962.0	E980.4
Paredrine	971.2	E855.5	E941.2	E950.4	E962.0	E980.4
Paregoric	965.00	E850.2	E935.2	E950.0	E962.0	E980.0
Pargyline	972.3	E858.3	E942.3	E950.4	E962.0	E980.4
Paris green	985.1	E866.3	—	E950.8	E962.1	E980.8
insecticide	985.1	E863.4	—	E950.8	E962.1	E980.8
Parnate	969.0	E854.0	E939.0	E950.3	E962.0	E980.3
Paromomycin	960.8	E856	E930.8	E950.4	E962.0	E980.4
Paroxypropione	963.1	E858.1	E933.1	E950.4	E962.0	E980.4
Parzone	965.09	E850.2	E935.2	E950.0	E962.0	E980.0
PAS	961.8	E857	E931.8	E950.4	E962.0	E980.4
PCBs	981	E862.3	—	E950.9	E962.1	E980.9
PCP (pentachlorophenol)	989.4	E863.6	—	E950.6	E962.1	E980.7
herbicide	989.4	E863.5	—	E950.6	E962.1	E980.7
insecticide	989.4	E863.4	—	E950.6	E962.1	E980.7
phencyclidine	968.3	E855.1	E938.3	E950.4	E962.0	E980.4
Peach kernel oil (emulsion)	973.2	E858.4	E943.2	E950.4	E962.0	E980.4
Peanut oil (emulsion) NEC	973.2	E858.4	E943.2	E950.4	E962.0	E980.4
topical	976.3	E858.7	E946.3	E950.4	E962.0	E980.4
Pearly Gates (morning glory seeds)	969.6	E854.1	E939.6	E950.3	E962.0	E980.3
Pecazine	969.1	E853.0	E939.1	E950.3	E962.0	E980.3
Pecilocin	960.1	E856	E930.1	E950.4	E962.0	E980.4
Pectin (with kaolin) NEC	973.5	E858.4	E943.5	E950.4	E962.0	E980.4
Pelletierine tannate	961.6	E857	E931.6	E950.4	E962.0	E980.4
Pemoline	969.7	E854.2	E939.7	E950.3	E962.0	E980.3
Pempidine	972.3	E858.3	E942.3	E950.4	E962.0	E980.4
Penamecillin	960.0	E856	E930.0	E950.4	E962.0	E980.4
Penethamate hydriodide	960.0	E856	E930.0	E950.4	E962.0	E980.4
Penicillamine	963.8	E858.1	E933.8	E950.4	E962.0	E980.4
Penicillin (any type)	960.0	E856	E930.0	E950.4	E962.0	E980.4
Penicillinase	963.4	E858.1	E933.4	E950.4	E962.0	E980.4
Pentachlorophenol (fungicide)	989.4	E863.6	—	E950.6	E962.1	E980.7
herbicide	989.4	E863.5	—	E950.6	E962.1	E980.7
insecticide	989.4	E863.4	—	E950.6	E962.1	E980.7
Pentaerythritol	972.4	E858.3	E942.4	E950.4	E962.0	E980.4
chloral	967.1	E852.0	E937.1	E950.2	E962.0	E980.2
tetranitrate NEC	972.4	E858.3	E942.4	E950.4	E962.0	E980.4
Pentagastrin	977.8	E858.8	E947.8	E950.4	E962.0	E980.4
Pentalin	982.3	E862.4	—	E950.9	E962.1	E980.9
Pentamethonium (bromide)	972.3	E858.3	E942.3	E950.4	E962.0	E980.4
Pentamidine	961.5	E857	E931.5	E950.4	E962.0	E980.4
Pentanol	980.8	E860.8	—	E950.9	E962.1	E980.9
Pentaquine	961.4	E857	E931.4	E950.4	E962.0	E980.4
Pentazocine	965.8	E850.8	E935.8	E950.0	E962.0	E980.0
Penthienate	971.1	E855.4	E941.1	E950.4	E962.0	E980.4
Pentobarbital, pentobarbitone (sodium)	967.0	E851	E937.0	E950.1	E962.0	E980.1
Pentolinium (tartrate)	972.3	E858.3	E942.3	E950.4	E962.0	E980.4
Pentothal	968.3	E855.1	E938.3	E950.4	E962.0	E980.4
Pentylenetetrazol	970.0	E854.3	E940.0	E950.4	E962.0	E980.4
Pentylsalicylamide	961.8	E857	E931.8	E950.4	E962.0	E980.4
Pepsin	973.4	E858.4	E943.4	E950.4	E962.0	E980.4
Peptavlon	977.8	E858.8	E947.8	E950.4	E962.0	E980.4
Percaine (spinal)	968.7	E855.2	E938.7	E950.4	E962.0	E980.4
topical (surface)	968.5	E855.2	E938.5	E950.4	E962.0	E980.4
Perchloroethylene (vapor)	982.3	E862.4	—	E950.9	E962.1	E980.9
medicinal	961.6	E857	E931.6	E950.4	E962.0	E980.4
Percodan	965.09	E850.2	E935.2	E950.0	E962.0	E980.0
Percogesic	965.09	E850.2	E935.2	E950.0	E962.0	E980.0
Percorten	962.0	E858.0	E932.0	E950.4	E962.0	E980.4
Pergonal	962.4	E858.0	E932.4	E950.4	E962.0	E980.4
Perhexiline	972.4	E858.3	E942.4	E950.4	E962.0	E980.4
Periactin	963.0	E858.1	E933.0	E950.4	E962.0	E980.4
Periclor	967.1	E852.0	E937.1	E950.2	E962.0	E980.2
Pericyazine	969.1	E853.0	E939.1	E950.3	E962.0	E980.3
Peritrate	972.4	E858.3	E942.4	E950.4	E962.0	E980.4
Permanganates NEC	983.9	E864.3	—	E950.7	E962.1	E980.6
Permanganates — *continued*						
potassium (topical)	976.0	E858.7	E946.0	E950.4	E962.0	E980.4
Pernocton	967.0	E851	E937.0	E950.1	E962.0	E980.1
Pernoston	967.0	E851	E937.0	E950.1	E962.0	E980.1
Peronin(e)	965.09	E850.2	E935.2	E950.0	E962.0	E980.0
Perphenazine	969.1	E853.0	E939.1	E950.3	E962.0	E980.3
Pertofrane	969.0	E854.0	E939.0	E950.3	E962.0	E980.3
Pertussis						
immune serum (human)	964.6	E858.2	E934.6	E950.4	E962.0	E980.4
vaccine (with diphtheria toxoid) (with tetanus toxoid)	978.6	E858.8	E948.6	E950.4	E962.0	E980.4
Peruvian balsam	976.8	E858.7	E946.8	E950.4	E962.0	E980.4
Pesticides (dust) (fumes) (vapor)	989.4	E863.4	—	E950.6	E962.1	E980.7
arsenic	985.1	E863.4	—	E950.8	E962.1	E980.8
chlorinated	989.2	E863.0	—	E950.6	E962.1	E980.7
cyanide	989.0	E863.4	—	E950.6	E962.1	E980.7
kerosene	981	E863.4	—	E950.6	E962.1	E980.7
mixture (of compounds)	989.4	E863.3	—	E950.6	E962.1	E980.7
naphthalene	983.0	E863.4	—	E950.7	E962.1	E980.6
organochlorine (compounds)	989.2	E863.0	—	E950.6	E962.1	E980.7
petroleum (distillate) (products) NEC	981	E863.4	—	E950.6	E962.1	E980.7
specified ingredient NEC	989.4	E863.4	—	E950.6	E962.1	E980.7
strychnine	989.1	E863.4	—	E950.6	E962.1	E980.7
thallium	985.8	E863.7	—	E950.6	E962.1	E980.7
Pethidine (hydrochloride)	965.09	E850.2	E935.2	E950.0	E962.0	E980.0
Petrichloral	967.1	E852.0	E937.1	E950.2	E962.0	E980.2
Petrol	981	E862.1	—	E950.9	E962.1	E980.9
vapor	987.1	E869.8	—	E952.8	E962.2	E982.8
Petrolatum (jelly) (ointment)	976.3	E858.7	E946.3	E950.4	E962.0	E980.4
hydrophilic	976.3	E858.7	E946.3	E950.4	E962.0	E980.4
liquid	973.2	E858.4	E943.2	E950.4	E962.0	E980.4
topical	976.3	E858.7	E946.3	E950.4	E962.0	E980.4
nonmedicinal	981	E862.1	—	E950.9	E962.1	E980.9
Petroleum (cleaners) (fuels) (products) NEC	981	E862.1	—	E950.9	E962.1	E980.9
benzin(e) — see Ligroin						
ether — see Ligroin						
jelly — see Petrolatum						
naphtha — see Ligroin						
pesticide	981	E863.4	—	E950.6	E962.1	E980.7
solids	981	E862.3	—	E950.9	E962.1	E980.9
solvents	981	E862.0	—	E950.9	E962.1	E980.9
vapor	987.1	E869.8	—	E952.8	E962.2	E982.8
Peyote	969.6	E854.1	E939.6	E950.3	E962.0	E980.3
Phanodorm, phanodorn	967.0	E851	E937.0	E950.1	E962.0	E980.1
Phanquinone, phanquone	961.5	E857	E931.5	E950.4	E962.0	E980.4
Pharmaceutical excipient or adjunct	977.4	E858.8	E947.4	E950.4	E962.0	E980.4
Phenacemide	966.3	E855.0	E936.3	E950.4	E962.0	E980.4
Phenacetin	965.4	E850.4	E935.4	E950.0	E962.0	E980.0
Phenadoxone	965.09	E850.2	E935.2	E950.0	E962.0	E980.0
Phenaglycodol	969.5	E853.8	E939.5	E950.3	E962.0	E980.3
Phenantoin	966.1	E855.0	E936.1	E950.4	E962.0	E980.4
Phenaphthazine reagent	977.8	E858.8	E947.8	E950.4	E962.0	E980.4
Phenazocine	965.09	E850.2	E935.2	E950.0	E962.0	E980.0
Phenazone	965.5	E850.5	E935.5	E950.0	E962.0	E980.0
Phenazopyridine	976.1	E858.7	E946.1	E950.4	E962.0	E980.4
Phenbenicillin	960.0	E856	E930.0	E950.4	E962.0	E980.4
Phenbutrazate	977.0	E858.8	E947.0	E950.4	E962.0	E980.4
Phencyclidine	968.3	E855.1	E938.3	E950.4	E962.0	E980.4
Phendimetrazine	977.0	E858.8	E947.0	E950.4	E962.0	E980.4
Phenelzine	969.0	E854.0	E939.0	E950.3	E962.0	E980.3
Phenergan	967.8	E852.8	E937.8	E950.2	E962.0	E980.2
Phenethicillin (potassium)	960.0	E856	E930.0	E950.4	E962.0	E980.4
Phenetsal	965.1	E850.3	E935.3	E950.0	E962.0	E980.0
Pheneturide	966.3	E855.0	E936.3	E950.4	E962.0	E980.4
Phenformin	962.3	E858.0	E932.3	E950.4	E962.0	E980.4
Phenglutarimide	971.1	E855.4	E941.1	E950.4	E962.0	E980.4
Phenicarbazide	965.8	E850.8	E935.8	E950.0	E962.0	E980.0
Phenindamine (tartrate)	963.0	E858.1	E933.0	E950.4	E962.0	E980.4
Phenindione	964.2	E858.2	E934.2	E950.4	E962.0	E980.4
Pheniprazine	969.0	E854.0	E939.0	E950.3	E962.0	E980.3
Pheniramine (maleate)	963.0	E858.1	E933.0	E950.4	E962.0	E980.4
Phenmetrazine	977.0	E858.8	E947.0	E950.4	E962.0	E980.4
Phenobal	967.0	E851	E937.0	E950.1	E962.0	E980.1
Phenobarbital	967.0	E851	E937.0	E950.1	E962.0	E980.1
Phenobarbitone	967.0	E851	E937.0	E950.1	E962.0	E980.1
Phenoctide	976.0	E858.7	E946.0	E950.4	E962.0	E980.4

		External Cause (E-Code)				
	Poisoning	Accident	Therapeutic Use	Suicide Attempt	Assault	Undetermined
Phenol (derivatives) NEC	983.0	E864.0	—	E950.7	E962.1	E980.6
disinfectant	983.0	E864.0	—	E950.7	E962.1	E980.6
pesticide	989.4	E863.4	—	E950.6	E962.1	E980.7
red	977.8	E858.8	E947.8	E950.4	E962.0	E980.4
Phenolphthalein	973.1	E858.4	E943.1	E950.4	E962.0	E980.4
Phenolsulfonphthalein	977.8	E858.8	E947.8	E950.4	E962.0	E980.4
Phenomorphan	965.09	E850.2	E935.2	E950.0	E962.0	E980.0
Phenonyl	967.0	E851	E937.0	E950.1	E962.0	E980.1
Phenoperidine	965.09	E850.2	E935.2	E950.0	E962.0	E980.0
Phenoquin	974.7	E858.5	E944.7	E950.4	E962.0	E980.4
Phenothiazines (tranquilizers) NEC	969.1	E853.0	E939.1	E950.3	E962.0	E980.3
insecticide	989.3	E863.4	—	E950.6	E962.1	E980.7
Phenoxybenzamine	971.3	E855.6	E941.3	E950.4	E962.0	E980.4
Phenoxymethyl penicillin	960.0	E856	E930.0	E950.4	E962.0	E980.4
Phenprocoumon	964.2	E858.2	E934.2	E950.4	E962.0	E980.4
Phensuximide	966.2	E855.0	E936.2	E950.4	E962.0	E980.4
Phentermine	977.0	E858.8	E947.0	E950.4	E962.0	E980.4
Phentolamine	971.3	E855.6	E941.3	E950.4	E962.0	E980.4
Phenyl						
butazone	965.5	E850.5	E935.5	E950.0	E962.0	E980.0
enediamine	983.0	E864.0	—	E950.7	E962.1	E980.6
hydrazine	983.0	E864.0	—	E950.7	E962.1	E980.6
antineoplastic	963.1	E858.1	E933.1	E950.4	E962.0	E980.4
mercuric compounds — see Mercury						
salicylate	976.3	E858.7	E946.3	E950.4	E962.0	E980.4
Phenylephrin	971.2	E855.5	E941.2	E950.4	E962.0	E980.4
Phenylethylbiguanide	962.3	E858.0	E932.3	E950.4	E962.0	E980.4
Phenylpropanolamine	971.2	E855.5	E941.2	E950.4	E962.0	E980.4
Phenylsulfthion	989.3	E863.1	—	E950.6	E962.1	E980.7
Phenyramidol, phenyramidon	965.7	E850.7	E935.7	E950.0	E962.0	E980.0
Phenytoin	966.1	E855.0	E936.1	E950.4	E962.0	E980.4
pHisoHex	976.2	E858.7	E946.2	E950.4	E962.0	E980.4
Pholcodine	965.09	E850.2	E935.2	E950.0	E962.0	E980.0
Phorate	989.3	E863.1	—	E950.6	E962.1	E980.7
Phosdrin	989.3	E863.1	—	E950.6	E962.1	E980.7
Phosgene (gas)	987.8	E869.8	—	E952.8	E962.2	E982.8
Phosphate (tricresyl)	989.89	E866.8	—	E950.9	E962.1	E980.9
organic	989.3	E863.1	—	E950.6	E962.1	E980.7
solvent	982.8	E862.4	—	E950.9	E926.1	E980.9
Phosphine	987.8	E869.8	—	E952.8	E962.2	E982.8
fumigant	987.8	E863.8	—	E950.6	E962.2	E980.7
Phospholine	971.0	E855.3	E941.0	E950.4	E962.0	E980.4
Phosphoric acid	983.1	E864.1	—	E950.7	E962.1	E980.6
Phosphorus (compounds) NEC	983.9	E864.3	—	E950.7	E962.1	E980.6
rodenticide	983.9	E863.7	—	E950.7	E962.1	E980.6
Phthalimidoglutarimide	967.8	E852.8	E937.8	E950.2	E962.0	E980.2
Phthalylsulfathiazole	961.0	E857	E931.0	E950.4	E962.0	E980.4
Phylloquinone	964.3	E858.2	E934.3	E950.4	E962.0	E980.4
Physeptone	965.02	E850.1	E935.1	E950.0	E962.0	E980.0
Physostigma venenosum	988.2	E865.4	—	E950.9	E962.1	E980.9
Physostigmine	971.0	E855.3	E941.0	E950.4	E962.0	E980.4
Phytolacca decandra	988.2	E865.4	—	E950.9	E962.1	E980.9
Phytomenadione	964.3	E858.2	E934.3	E950.4	E962.0	E980.4
Phytonadione	964.3	E858.2	E934.3	E950.4	E962.0	E980.4
Picric (acid)	983.0	E864.0	—	E950.7	E962.1	E980.6
Picrotoxin	970.0	E854.3	E940.0	E950.4	E962.0	E980.4
Pilocarpine	971.0	E855.3	E941.0	E950.4	E962.0	E980.4
Pilocarpus (jaborandi) extract	971.0	E855.3	E941.0	E950.4	E962.0	E980.4
Pimaricin	960.1	E856	E930.1	E950.4	E962.0	E980.4
Piminodine	965.09	E850.2	E935.2	E950.0	E962.0	E980.0
Pine oil, pinesol (disinfectant)	983.9	E861.4	—	E950.7	E962.1	E980.6
Pinkroot	961.6	E857	E931.6	E950.4	E962.0	E980.4
Pipadone	965.09	E850.2	E935.2	E950.0	E962.0	E980.0
Pipamazine	963.0	E858.1	E933.0	E950.4	E962.0	E980.4
Pipazethate	975.4	E858.6	E945.4	E950.4	E962.0	E980.4
Pipenzolate	971.1	E855.4	E941.1	E950.4	E962.0	E980.4
Piperacetazine	969.1	E853.0	E939.1	E950.3	E962.0	E980.3
Piperazine NEC	961.6	E857	E931.6	E950.4	E962.0	E980.4
estrone sulfate	962.2	E858.0	E932.2	E950.4	E962.0	E980.4
Piper cubeba	988.2	E865.4	—	E950.9	E962.1	E980.9
Piperidione	975.4	E858.6	E945.4	E950.4	E962.0	E980.4
Piperidolate	971.1	E855.4	E941.1	E950.4	E962.0	E980.4
Piperocaine	968.9	E855.2	E938.9	E950.4	E962.0	E980.4
infiltration (subcutaneous)	968.5	E855.2	E938.5	E950.4	E962.0	E980.4
Piperocaine — *continued*						
nerve block (peripheral) (plexus)	968.6	E855.2	E938.6	E950.4	E962.0	E980.4
topical (surface)	968.5	E855.2	E938.5	E950.4	E962.0	E980.4
Pipobroman	963.1	E858.1	E933.1	E950.4	E962.0	E980.4
Pipradrol	970.8	E854.3	E940.8	E950.4	E962.0	E980.4
Piscidia (bark) (erythrina)	965.7	E850.7	E935.7	E950.0	E962.0	E980.0
Pitch	983.0	E864.0	—	E950.7	E962.1	E980.6
Pitkin's solution	968.7	E855.2	E938.7	E950.4	E962.0	E980.4
Pitocin	975.0	E858.6	E945.0	E950.4	E962.0	E980.4
Pitressin (tannate)	962.5	E858.0	E932.5	E950.4	E962.0	E980.4
Pituitary extracts (posterior)	962.5	E858.0	E932.5	E950.4	E962.0	E980.4
anterior	962.4	E858.0	E932.4	E950.4	E962.0	E980.4
Pituitrin	962.5	E858.0	E932.5	E950.4	E962.0	E980.4
Placental extract	962.9	E858.0	E932.9	E950.4	E962.0	E980.4
Placidyl	967.8	E852.8	E937.8	E950.2	E962.0	E980.2
Plague vaccine	978.3	E858.8	E948.3	E950.4	E962.0	E980.4
Plant foods or fertilizers NEC	989.89	E866.5	—	E950.9	E962.1	E980.9
mixed with herbicides	989.4	E863.5	—	E950.6	E962.1	E980.7
Plants, noxious, used as food	988.2	E865.9	—	E950.9	E962.1	E980.9
berries and seeds	988.2	E865.3	—	E950.9	E962.1	E980.9
specified type NEC	988.2	E865.4	—	E950.9	E962.1	E980.9
Plasma (blood)	964.7	E858.2	E934.7	E950.4	E962.0	E980.4
expanders	964.8	E858.2	E934.8	E950.4	E962.0	E980.4
Plasmanate	964.7	E858.2	E934.7	E950.4	E962.0	E980.4
Plegicil	969.1	E853.0	E939.1	E950.3	E962.0	E980.3
Podophyllin	976.4	E858.7	E946.4	E950.4	E962.0	E980.4
Podophyllum resin	976.4	E858.7	E946.4	E950.4	E962.0	E980.4
Poison NEC	989.9	E866.9	—	E950.9	E962.1	E980.9
Poisonous berries	988.2	E865.3	—	E950.9	E962.1	E980.9
Pokeweed (any part)	988.2	E865.4	—	E950.9	E962.1	E980.9
Poldine	971.1	E855.4	E941.1	E950.4	E962.0	E980.4
Poliomyelitis vaccine	979.5	E858.8	E949.5	E950.4	E962.0	E980.4
Poliovirus vaccine	979.5	E858.8	E949.5	E950.4	E962.0	E980.4
Polish (car) (floor) (furniture) (metal) (silver)	989.89	E861.2	—	E950.9	E962.1	E980.9
abrasive	989.89	E861.3	—	E950.9	E962.1	E980.9
porcelain	989.89	E861.3	—	E950.9	E962.1	E980.9
Poloxalkol	973.2	E858.4	E943.2	E950.4	E962.0	E980.4
Polyaminostyrene resins	974.5	E858.5	E944.5	E950.4	E962.0	E980.4
Polychlorinated biphenyl — *see* PCBs						
Polycycline	960.4	E856	E930.4	E950.4	E962.0	E980.4
Polyester resin hardener	982.8	E862.4	—	E950.9	E962.1	E980.9
fumes	987.8	E869.8	—	E952.8	E962.2	E982.8
Polyestradiol (phosphate)	962.2	E858.0	E932.2	E950.4	E962.0	E980.4
Polyethanolamine alkyl sulfate	976.2	E858.7	E946.2	E950.4	E962.0	E980.4
Polyethylene glycol	976.3	E858.7	E946.3	E950.4	E962.0	E980.4
Polyferose	964.0	E858.2	E934.0	E950.4	E962.0	E980.4
Polymyxin B	960.8	E856	E930.8	E950.4	E962.0	E980.4
ENT agent	976.6	E858.7	E946.6	E950.4	E962.0	E980.4
ophthalmic preparation	976.5	E858.7	E946.5	E950.4	E962.0	E980.4
topical NEC	976.0	E858.7	E946.0	E950.4	E962.0	E980.4
Polynoxylin(e)	976.0	E858.7	E946.0	E950.4	E962.0	E980.4
Polyoxymethyleneurea	976.0	E858.7	E946.0	E950.4	E962.0	E980.4
Polytetrafluoroethylene (inhaled)	987.8	E869.8	—	E952.8	E962.2	E982.8
Polythiazide	974.3	E858.5	E944.3	E950.4	E962.0	E980.4
Polyvinylpyrrolidone	964.8	E858.2	E934.8	E950.4	E962.0	E980.4
Pontocaine (hydrochloride) (infiltration) (topical)	968.5	E855.2	E938.5	E950.4	E962.0	E980.4
nerve block (peripheral) (plexus)	968.6	E855.2	E938.6	E950.4	E962.0	E980.4
spinal	968.7	E855.2	E938.7	E950.4	E962.0	E980.4
Pot	969.6	E854.1	E939.6	E950.3	E962.0	E980.3
Potash (caustic)	983.2	E864.2	—	E950.7	E962.1	E980.6
Potassic saline injection (lactated)	974.5	E858.5	E944.5	E950.4	E962.0	E980.4
Potassium (salts) NEC	974.5	E858.5	E944.5	E950.4	E962.0	E980.4
aminosalicylate	961.8	E857	E931.8	E950.4	E962.0	E980.4
arsenite (solution)	985.1	E866.3	—	E950.8	E962.1	E980.8
bichromate	983.9	E864.3	—	E950.7	E962.1	E980.6
bisulfate	983.9	E864.3	—	E950.7	E962.1	E980.6
bromide (medicinal) NEC	967.3	E852.2	E937.3	E950.2	E962.0	E980.2
carbonate	983.2	E864.2	—	E950.7	E962.1	E980.6
chlorate NEC	983.9	E864.3	—	E950.7	E962.1	E980.6
cyanide — see Cyanide						

	Poisoning	External Cause (E-Code) Accident	Therapeutic Use	Suicide Attempt	Assault	Undetermined
Potassium (salts) — *continued*						
hydroxide	983.2	E864.2	—	E950.7	E962.1	E980.6
iodide (expectorant) NEC	975.5	E858.6	E945.5	E950.4	E962.0	E980.4
nitrate	989.89	E866.8	—	E950.9	E962.1	E980.9
oxalate	983.9	E864.3	—	E950.7	E962.1	E980.6
perchlorate NEC	977.8	E858.8	E947.8	E950.4	E962.0	E980.4
antithyroid	962.8	E858.0	E932.8	E950.4	E962.0	E980.4
permanganate	976.0	E858.7	E946.0	E950.4	E962.0	E980.4
nonmedicinal	983.9	E864.3	—	E950.7	E962.1	E980.6
Povidone-iodine (anti-infective) NEC	976.0	E858.7	E946.0	E950.4	E962.0	E980.4
Practolol	972.0	E858.3	E942.0	E950.4	E962.0	E980.4
Pralidoxime (chloride)	977.2	E858.8	E947.2	E950.4	E962.0	E980.4
Pramoxine	968.5	E855.2	E938.5	E950.4	E962.0	E980.4
Prazosin	972.6	E858.3	E942.6	E950.4	E962.0	E980.4
Prednisolone	962.0	E858.0	E932.0	E950.4	E962.0	E980.4
ENT agent	976.6	E858.7	E946.6	E950.4	E962.0	E980.4
ophthalmic preparation	976.5	E858.7	E946.5	E950.4	E962.0	E980.4
topical NEC	976.0	E858.7	E946.0	E950.4	E962.0	E980.4
Prednisone	962.0	E858.0	E932.0	E950.4	E962.0	E980.4
Pregnanediol	962.2	E858.0	E932.2	E950.4	E962.0	E980.4
Pregneninolone	962.2	E858.0	E932.2	E950.4	E962.0	E980.4
Preludin	977.0	E858.8	E947.0	E950.4	E962.0	E980.4
Premarin	962.2	E858.0	E932.2	E950.4	E962.0	E980.4
Prenylamine	972.4	E858.3	E942.4	E950.4	E962.0	E980.4
Preparation H	976.8	E858.7	E946.8	E950.4	E962.0	E980.4
Preservatives	989.89	E866.8	—	E950.9	E962.1	E980.9
Pride of China	988.2	E865.3	—	E950.9	E962.1	E980.9
Prilocaine	968.9	E855.2	E938.9	E950.4	E962.0	E980.4
infiltration (subcutaneous)	968.5	E855.2	E938.5	E950.4	E962.0	E980.4
nerve block (peripheral) (plexus)	968.6	E855.2	E938.6	E950.4	E962.0	E980.4
Primaquine	961.4	E857	E931.4	E950.4	E962.0	E980.4
Primidone	966.3	E855.0	E936.3	E950.4	E962.0	E980.4
Primula (veris)	988.2	E865.4	—	E950.9	E962.1	E980.9
Prinadol	965.09	E850.2	E935.2	E950.0	E962.0	E980.0
Priscol, Priscoline	971.3	E855.6	E941.3	E950.4	E962.0	E980.4
Privet	988.2	E865.4	—	E950.9	E962.1	E980.9
Privine	971.2	E855.5	E941.2	E950.4	E962.0	E980.4
Pro-Banthine	971.1	E855.4	E941.1	E950.4	E962.0	E980.4
Probarbital	967.0	E851	E937.0	E950.1	E962.0	E980.1
Probenecid	974.7	E858.5	E944.7	E950.4	E962.0	E980.4
Procainamide (hydrochloride)	972.0	E858.3	E942.0	E950.4	E962.0	E980.4
Procaine (hydrochloride) (infiltration) (topical)	968.5	E855.2	E938.5	E950.4	E962.0	E980.4
nerve block (peripheral) (plexus)	968.6	E855.2	E938.6	E950.4	E962.0	E980.4
penicillin G	960.0	E856	E930.0	E950.4	E962.0	E980.4
spinal	968.7	E855.2	E938.7	E950.4	E962.0	E980.4
Procalmidol	969.5	E853.8	E939.5	E950.3	E962.0	E980.3
Procarbazine	963.1	E858.1	E933.1	E950.4	E962.0	E980.4
Prochlorperazine	969.1	E853.0	E939.1	E950.3	E962.0	E980.3
Procyclidine	966.4	E855.0	E936.4	E950.4	E962.0	E980.4
Producer gas	986	E868.8	—	E952.1	E962.2	E982.1
Profenamine	966.4	E855.0	E936.4	E950.4	E962.0	E980.4
Profenil	975.1	E858.6	E945.1	E950.4	E962.0	E980.4
Progesterones	962.2	E858.0	E932.2	E950.4	E962.0	E980.4
Progestin	962.2	E858.0	E932.2	E950.4	E962.0	E980.4
Progestogens (with estrogens)	962.2	E858.0	E932.2	E950.4	E962.0	E980.4
Progestone	962.2	E858.0	E932.2	E950.4	E962.0	E980.4
Proguanil	961.4	E857	E931.4	E950.4	E962.0	E980.4
Prolactin	962.4	E858.0	E932.4	E950.4	E962.0	E980.4
Proloid	962.7	E858.0	E932.7	E950.4	E962.0	E980.4
Proluton	962.2	E858.0	E932.2	E950.4	E962.0	E980.4
Promacetin	961.8	E857	E931.8	E950.4	E962.0	E980.4
Promazine	969.1	E853.0	E939.1	E950.3	E962.0	E980.3
Promedol	965.09	E850.2	E935.2	E950.0	E962.0	E980.0
Promethazine	967.8	E852.8	E937.8	E950.2	E962.0	E980.2
Promin	961.8	E857	E931.8	E950.4	E962.0	E980.4
Pronestyl (hydrochloride)	972.0	E858.3	E942.0	E950.4	E962.0	E980.4
Pronetalol, pronethalol	972.0	E858.3	E942.0	E950.4	E962.0	E980.4
Prontosil	961.0	E857	E931.0	E950.4	E962.0	E980.4
Propamidine isethionate	961.5	E857	E931.5	E950.4	E962.0	E980.4
Propanal (medicinal)	967.8	E852.8	E937.8	E950.2	E962.0	E980.2
Propane (gas) (distributed in mobile container)	987.0	E868.0	—	E951.1	E962.2	E981.1
distributed through pipes	987.0	E867	—	E951.0	E962.2	E981.0
incomplete combustion of — see Carbon monoxide, Propane						
Propanidid	968.3	E855.1	E938.3	E950.4	E962.0	E980.4
Propanol	980.3	E860.4	—	E950.9	E962.1	E980.9
Propantheline	971.1	E855.4	E941.1	E950.4	E962.0	E980.4
Proparacaine	968.5	E855.2	E938.5	E950.4	E962.0	E980.4
Propatyl nitrate	972.4	E858.3	E942.4	E950.4	E962.0	E980.4
Propicillin	960.0	E856	E930.0	E950.4	E962.0	E980.4
Propiolactone (vapor)	987.8	E869.8	—	E952.8	E962.2	E982.8
Propiomazine	967.8	E852.8	E937.8	E950.2	E962.0	E980.2
Propionaldehyde (medicinal)	967.8	E852.8	E937.8	E950.2	E962.0	E980.2
Propionate compound	976.0	E858.7	E946.0	E950.4	E962.0	E980.4
Propion gel	976.0	E858.7	E946.0	E950.4	E962.0	E980.4
Propitocaine	968.9	E855.2	E938.9	E950.4	E962.0	E980.4
infiltration (subcutaneous)	968.5	E855.2	E938.5	E950.4	E962.0	E980.4
nerve block (peripheral) (plexus)	968.6	E855.2	E938.6	E950.4	E962.0	E980.4
Propoxur	989.3	E863.2	—	E950.6	E962.1	E980.7
Propoxycaine	968.9	E855.2	E938.9	E950.4	E962.0	E980.4
infiltration (subcutaneous)	968.5	E855.2	E938.5	E950.4	E962.0	E980.4
nerve block (peripheral) (plexus)	968.6	E855.2	E938.6	E950.4	E962.0	E980.4
topical (surface)	968.5	E855.2	E938.5	E950.4	E962.0	E980.4
Propoxyphene (hydrochloride)	965.8	E850.8	E935.8	E950.0	E962.0	E980.0
Propranolol	972.0	E858.3	E942.0	E950.4	E962.0	E980.4
Propyl						
alcohol	980.3	E860.4	—	E950.9	E962.1	E980.9
carbinol	980.3	E860.4	—	E950.9	E962.1	E980.9
hexadrine	971.2	E855.5	E941.2	E950.4	E962.0	E980.4
iodone	977.8	E858.8	E947.8	E950.4	E962.0	E980.4
thiouracil	962.8	E858.0	E932.8	E950.4	E962.0	E980.4
Propylene	987.1	E869.8	—	E952.8	E962.2	E982.8
Propylparaben (ophthalmic)	976.5	E858.7	E946.5	E950.4	E962.0	E980.4
Proscillaridin	972.1	E858.3	E942.1	E950.4	E962.0	E980.4
Prostaglandins	975.0	E858.6	E945.0	E950.4	E962.0	E980.4
Prostigmin	971.0	E855.3	E941.0	E950.4	E962.0	E980.4
Protamine (sulfate)	964.5	E858.2	E934.5	E950.4	E962.0	E980.4
zinc insulin	962.3	E858.0	E932.3	E950.4	E962.0	E980.4
Protectants (topical)	976.3	E858.7	E946.3	E950.4	E962.0	E980.4
Protein hydrolysate	974.5	E858.5	E944.5	E950.4	E962.0	E980.4
Prothiaden — *see* Dothiepin hydrochloride						
Prothionamide	961.8	E857	E931.8	E950.4	E962.0	E980.4
Prothipendyl	969.5	E853.8	E939.5	E950.3	E962.0	E980.3
Protokylol	971.2	E855.5	E941.2	E950.4	E962.0	E980.4
Protopam	977.2	E858.8	E947.2	E950.4	E962.0	E980.4
Protoveratrine(s) (A) (B)	972.6	E858.3	E942.6	E950.4	E962.0	E980.4
Protriptyline	969.0	E854.0	E939.0	E950.3	E962.0	E980.3
Provera	962.2	E858.0	E932.2	E950.4	E962.0	E980.4
Provitamin A	963.5	E858.1	E933.5	E950.4	E962.0	E980.4
Proxymetacaine	968.5	E855.2	E938.5	E950.4	E962.0	E980.4
Proxyphylline	975.1	E858.6	E945.1	E950.4	E962.0	E980.4
Prozac — *see* Fluoxetine hydrochloride						
Prunus						
laurocerasus	988.2	E865.4	—	E950.9	E962.1	E980.9
virginiana	988.2	E865.4	—	E950.9	E962.1	E980.9
Prussic acid	989.0	E866.8	—	E950.9	E962.1	E980.9
vapor	987.7	E869.8	—	E952.8	E962.2	E982.8
Pseudoephedrine	971.2	E855.5	E941.2	E950.4	E962.0	E980.4
Psilocin	969.6	E854.1	E939.6	E950.3	E962.0	E980.3
Psilocybin	969.6	E854.1	E939.6	E950.3	E962.0	E980.3
PSP	977.8	E858.8	E947.8	E950.4	E962.0	E980.4
Psychedelic agents	969.6	E854.1	E939.6	E950.3	E962.0	E980.3
Psychodysleptics	969.6	E854.1	E939.6	E950.3	E962.0	E980.3
Psychostimulants	969.7	E854.2	E939.7	E950.3	E962.0	E980.3
Psychotherapeutic agents	969.9	E855.9	E939.9	E950.3	E962.0	E980.3
antidepressants	969.0	E854.0	E939.0	E950.3	E962.0	E980.3
specified NEC	969.8	E855.8	E939.8	E950.3	E962.0	E980.3
tranquilizers NEC	969.5	E853.9	E939.5	E950.3	E962.0	E980.3
Psychotomimetic agents	969.6	E854.1	E939.6	E950.3	E962.0	E980.3
Psychotropic agents	969.9	E854.8	E939.9	E950.3	E962.0	E980.3
specified NEC	969.8	E854.8	E939.8	E950.3	E962.0	E980.3
Psyllium	973.3	E858.4	E943.3	E950.4	E962.0	E980.4
Pteroylglutamic acid	964.1	E858.2	E934.1	E950.4	E962.0	E980.4
Pteroyltriglutamate	963.1	E858.1	E933.1	E950.4	E962.0	E980.4
PTFE	987.8	E869.8	—	E952.8	E962.2	E982.8
Pulsatilla	988.2	E865.4	—	E950.9	E962.1	E980.9
Purex (bleach)	983.9	E864.3	—	E950.7	E962.1	E980.6
Purine diuretics	974.1	E858.5	E944.1	E950.4	E962.0	E980.4

	Poisoning	External Cause (E-Code)				
		Accident	Therapeutic Use	Suicide Attempt	Assault	Undetermined
Purinethol	963.1	E858.1	E933.1	E950.4	E962.0	E980.4
PVP	964.8	E858.2	E934.8	E950.4	E962.0	E980.4
Pyrabital	965.7	E850.7	E935.7	E950.0	E962.0	E980.0
Pyramidon	965.5	E850.5	E935.5	E950.0	E962.0	E980.0
Pyrantel (pamoate)	961.6	E857	E931.6	E950.4	E962.0	E980.4
Pyrathiazine	963.0	E858.1	E933.0	E950.4	E962.0	E980.4
Pyrazinamide	961.8	E857	E931.8	E950.4	E962.0	E980.4
Pyrazinoic acid (amide)	961.8	E857	E931.8	E950.4	E962.0	E980.4
Pyrazole (derivatives)	965.5	E850.5	E935.5	E950.0	E962.0	E980.0
Pyrazolone (analgesics)	965.5	E850.5	E935.5	E950.0	E962.0	E980.0
Pyrethrins, pyrethrum	989.4	E863.4	—	E950.6	E962.1	E980.7
Pyribenzamine	963.0	E858.1	E933.0	E950.4	E962.0	E980.4
Pyridine (liquid) (vapor)	982.0	E862.4	—	E950.9	E962.1	E980.9
aldoxime chloride	977.2	E858.8	E947.2	E950.4	E962.0	E980.4
Pyridium	976.1	E858.7	E946.1	E950.4	E962.0	E980.4
Pyridostigmine	971.0	E855.3	E941.0	E950.4	E962.0	E980.4
Pyridoxine	963.5	E858.1	E933.5	E950.4	E962.0	E980.4
Pyrilamine	963.0	E858.1	E933.0	E950.4	E962.0	E980.4
Pyrimethamine	961.4	E857	E931.4	E950.4	E962.0	E980.4
Pyrogallic acid	983.0	E864.0	—	E950.7	E962.1	E980.6
Pyroxylin	976.3	E858.7	E946.3	E950.4	E962.0	E980.4
Pyrrobutamine	963.0	E858.1	E933.0	E950.4	E962.0	E980.4
Pyrrocitine	968.5	E855.2	E938.5	E950.4	E962.0	E980.4
Pyrvinium (pamoate)	961.6	E857	E931.6	E950.4	E962.0	E980.4
PZI	962.3	E858.0	E932.3	E950.4	E962.0	E980.4
Quaalude	967.4	E852.3	E937.4	E950.2	E962.0	E980.2
Quaternary ammonium derivatives	971.1	E855.4	E941.1	E950.4	E962.0	E980.4
Quicklime	983.2	E864.2	—	E950.7	E962.1	E980.6
Quinacrine	961.3	E857	E931.3	E950.4	E962.0	E980.4
Quinaglute	972.0	E858.3	E942.0	E950.4	E962.0	E980.4
Quinalbarbitone	967.0	E851	E937.0	E950.1	E962.0	E980.1
Quinestradiol	962.2	E858.0	E932.2	E950.4	E962.0	E980.4
Quinethazone	974.3	E858.5	E944.3	E950.4	E962.0	E980.4
Quinidine (gluconate) (polygalacturonate) (salts) (sulfate)	972.0	E858.3	E942.0	E950.4	E962.0	E980.4
Quinine	961.4	E857	E931.4	E950.4	E962.0	E980.4
Quiniobine	961.3	E857	E931.3	E950.4	E962.0	E980.4
Quinolines	961.3	E857	E931.3	E950.4	E962.0	E980.4
Quotane	968.5	E855.2	E938.5	E950.4	E962.0	E980.4
Rabies						
immune globulin (human)	964.6	E858.2	E934.6	E950.4	E962.0	E980.4
vaccine	979.1	E858.8	E949.1	E950.4	E962.0	E980.4
Racemoramide	965.09	E850.2	E935.2	E950.0	E962.0	E980.0
Racemorphan	965.09	E850.2	E935.2	E950.0	E962.0	E980.0
Radiator alcohol	980.1	E860.2	—	E950.9	E962.1	E980.9
Radio-opaque (drugs) (materials)	977.8	E858.8	E947.8	E950.4	E962.0	E980.4
Ranunculus	988.2	E865.4	—	E950.9	E962.1	E980.9
Rat poison	989.4	E863.7	—	E950.6	E962.1	E980.7
Rattlesnake (venom)	989.5	E905.0	—	E950.9	E962.1	E980.9
Raudixin	972.6	E858.3	E942.6	E950.4	E962.0	E980.4
Rautensin	972.6	E858.3	E942.6	E950.4	E962.0	E980.4
Rautina	972.6	E858.3	E942.6	E950.4	E962.0	E980.4
Rautotal	972.6	E858.3	E942.6	E950.4	E962.0	E980.4
Rauwiloid	972.6	E858.3	E942.6	E950.4	E962.0	E980.4
Rauwoldin	972.6	E858.3	E942.6	E950.4	E962.0	E980.4
Rauwolfia (alkaloids)	972.6	E858.3	E942.6	E950.4	E962.0	E980.4
Realgar	985.1	E866.3	—	E950.8	E962.1	E980.8
Red cells, packed	964.7	E858.2	E934.7	E950.4	E962.0	E980.4
Reducing agents, industrial NEC	983.9	E864.3	—	E950.7	E962.1	E980.6
Refrigerant gas (freon)	987.4	E869.2	—	E952.8	E962.2	E982.8
central nervous system	968.0	E855.1	E938.0	E950.4	E962.0	E980.4
not freon	987.9	E869.9	—	E952.9	E962.2	E982.9
Regroton	974.4	E858.5	E944.4	E950.4	E962.0	E980.4
Rela	968.0	E855.1	E938.0	E950.4	E962.0	E980.4
Relaxants, skeletal muscle (autonomic)	975.2	E858.6	E945.2	E950.4	E962.0	E980.4
Renese	974.3	E858.5	E944.3	E950.4	E962.0	E980.4
Renografin	977.8	E858.8	E947.8	E950.4	E962.0	E980.4
Replacement solutions	974.5	E858.5	E944.5	E950.4	E962.0	E980.4
Rescinnamine	972.6	E858.3	E942.6	E950.4	E962.0	E980.4
Reserpine	972.6	E858.3	E942.6	E950.4	E962.0	E980.4
Resorcin, resorcinol	976.4	E858.7	E946.4	E950.4	E962.0	E980.4
Respaire	975.5	E858.6	E945.5	E950.4	E962.0	E980.4
Respiratory agents NEC	975.8	E858.6	E945.8	E950.4	E962.0	E980.4
Retinoic acid	976.8	E858.7	E946.8	E950.4	E962.0	E980.4
Retinol	963.5	E858.1	E933.5	E950.4	E962.0	E980.4
Rh (D) immune globulin (human)	964.6	E858.2	E934.6	E950.4	E962.0	E980.4
Rhodine	965.1	E850.3	E935.3	E950.0	E962.0	E980.0
RhoGAM	964.6	E858.2	E934.6	E950.4	E962.0	E980.4
Riboflavin	963.5	E858.1	E933.5	E950.4	E962.0	E980.4
Ricin	989.89	E866.8	—	E950.9	E962.1	E980.9
Ricinus communis	988.2	E865.3	—	E950.9	E962.1	E980.9
Rickettsial vaccine NEC	979.6	E858.8	E949.6	E950.4	E962.0	E980.4
with viral and bacterial vaccine	979.7	E858.8	E949.7	E950.4	E962.0	E980.4
Rifampin	960.6	E856	E930.6	E950.4	E962.0	E980.4
Rimifon	961.8	E857	E931.8	E950.4	E962.0	E980.4
Ringer's injection (lactated)	974.5	E858.5	E944.5	E950.4	E962.0	E980.4
Ristocetin	960.8	E856	E930.8	E950.4	E962.0	E980.4
Ritalin	969.7	E854.2	E939.7	E950.3	E962.0	E980.3
Roach killers — *see* Pesticides						
Rocky Mountain spotted fever vaccine	979.6	E858.8	E949.6	E950.4	E962.0	E980.4
Rodenticides	989.4	E863.7	—	E950.6	E962.1	E980.7
Rohypnol	969.4	E853.2	E939.4	E950.3	E962.0	E980.3
Rolaids	973.0	E858.4	E943.0	E950.4	E962.0	E980.4
Rolitetracycline	960.4	E856	E930.4	E950.4	E962.0	E980.4
Romilar	975.4	E858.6	E945.4	E950.4	E962.0	E980.4
Rose water ointment	976.3	E858.7	E946.3	E950.4	E962.0	E980.4
Rosuvastatin calcium	972.1	E858.3	E942.2	E950.4	E962.0	E980.4
Rotenone	989.4	E863.7	—	E950.6	E962.1	E980.7
Rotoxamine	963.0	E858.1	E933.0	E950.4	E962.0	E980.4
Rough-on-rats	989.4	E863.7	—	E950.6	E962.1	E980.7
RU486	962.9	E858.0	E932.9	E950.4	E962.0	E980.4
Rubbing alcohol	980.2	E860.3	—	E950.9	E962.1	E980.9
Rubella virus vaccine	979.4	E858.8	E949.4	E950.4	E962.0	E980.4
Rubelogen	979.4	E858.8	E949.4	E950.4	E962.0	E980.4
Rubeovax	979.4	E858.8	E949.4	E950.4	E962.0	E980.4
Rubidomycin	960.7	E856	E930.7	E950.4	E962.0	E980.4
Rue	988.2	E865.4	—	E950.9	E962.1	E980.9
Ruta	988.2	E865.4	—	E950.9	E962.1	E980.9
Sabadilla (medicinal)	976.0	E858.7	E946.0	E950.4	E962.0	E980.4
pesticide	989.4	E863.4	—	E950.6	E962.1	E980.7
Sabin oral vaccine	979.5	E858.8	E949.5	E950.4	E962.0	E980.4
Saccharated iron oxide	964.0	E858.2	E934.0	E950.4	E962.0	E980.4
Saccharin	974.5	E858.5	E944.5	E950.4	E962.0	E980.4
Safflower oil	972.2	E858.3	E942.2	E950.4	E962.0	E980.4
Salbutamol sulfate	975.7	E858.6	E945.7	E950.4	E962.0	E980.4
Salicylamide	965.1	E850.3	E935.3	E950.0	E962.0	E980.0
Salicylate(s)	965.1	E850.3	E935.3	E950.0	E962.0	E980.0
methyl	976.3	E858.7	E946.3	E950.4	E962.0	E980.4
theobromine calcium	974.1	E858.5	E944.1	E950.4	E962.0	E980.4
Salicylazosulfapyridine	961.0	E857	E931.0	E950.4	E962.0	E980.4
Salicylhydroxamic acid	976.0	E858.7	E946.0	E950.4	E962.0	E980.4
Salicylic acid (keratolytic) NEC	976.4	E858.7	E946.4	E950.4	E962.0	E980.4
congeners	965.1	E850.3	E935.3	E950.0	E962.0	E980.0
salts	965.1	E850.3	E935.3	E950.0	E962.0	E980.0
Saliniazid	961.8	E857	E931.8	E950.4	E962.0	E980.4
Salol	976.3	E858.7	E946.3	E950.4	E962.0	E980.4
Salt (substitute) NEC	974.5	E858.5	E944.5	E950.4	E962.0	E980.4
Saluretics	974.3	E858.5	E944.3	E950.4	E962.0	E980.4
Saluron	974.3	E858.5	E944.3	E950.4	E962.0	E980.4
Salvarsan 606 (neosilver) (silver)	961.1	E857	E931.1	E950.4	E962.0	E980.4
Sambucus canadensis	988.2	E865.4	—	E950.9	E962.1	E980.9
berry	988.2	E865.3	—	E950.9	E962.1	E980.9
Sandril	972.6	E858.3	E942.6	E950.4	E962.0	E980.4
Sanguinaria canadensis	988.2	E865.4	—	E950.9	E962.1	E980.9
Saniflush (cleaner)	983.9	E861.3	—	E950.7	E962.1	E980.6
Santonin	961.6	E857	E931.6	E950.4	E962.0	E980.4
Santyl	976.8	E858.7	E946.8	E950.4	E962.0	E980.4
Sarkomycin	960.7	E856	E930.7	E950.4	E962.0	E980.4
Saroten	969.0	E854.0	E939.0	E950.3	E962.0	E980.3
Saturnine — *see* Lead						
Savin (oil)	976.4	E858.7	E946.4	E950.4	E962.0	E980.4
Scammony	973.1	E858.4	E943.1	E950.4	E962.0	E980.4
Scarlet red	976.8	E858.7	E946.8	E950.4	E962.0	E980.4
Scheele's green	985.1	E866.3	—	E950.8	E962.1	E980.8
insecticide	985.1	E863.4	—	E950.8	E962.1	E980.8
Schradan	989.3	E863.1	—	E950.6	E962.1	E980.7
Schweinfurt(h) green	985.1	E866.3	—	E950.8	E962.1	E980.8
insecticide	985.1	E863.4	—	E950.8	E962.1	E980.8
Scilla — see Squill						
Sclerosing agents	972.7	E858.3	E942.7	E950.4	E962.0	E980.4

Substance	Poisoning	External Cause (E-Code) Accident	Therapeutic Use	Suicide Attempt	Assault	Undetermined
Scopolamine	971.1	E855.4	E941.1	E950.4	E962.0	E980.4
Scouring powder	989.89	E861.3	—	E950.9	E962.1	E980.9
Sea						
anemone (sting)	989.5	E905.6	—	E950.9	E962.1	E980.9
cucumber (sting)	989.5	E905.6	—	E950.9	E962.1	E980.9
snake (bite) (venom)	989.5	E905.0	—	E950.9	E962.1	E980.9
urchin spine (puncture)	989.5	E905.6	—	E950.9	E962.1	E980.9
Secbutabarbital	967.0	E851	E937.0	E950.1	E962.0	E980.1
Secbutabarbitone	967.0	E851	E937.0	E950.1	E962.0	E980.1
Secobarbital	967.0	E851	E937.0	E950.1	E962.0	E980.1
Seconal	967.0	E851	E937.0	E950.1	E962.0	E980.1
Secretin	977.8	E858.8	E947.8	E950.4	E962.0	E980.4
Sedatives, nonbarbiturate	967.9	E852.9	E937.9	E950.2	E962.0	E980.2
specified NEC	967.8	E852.8	E937.8	E950.2	E962.0	E980.2
Sedormid	967.8	E852.8	E937.8	E950.2	E962.0	E980.2
Seed (plant)	988.2	E865.3	—	E950.9	E962.1	E980.9
disinfectant or dressing	989.89	E866.5	—	E950.9	E962.1	E980.9
Selenium (fumes) NEC	985.8	E866.4	—	E950.9	E962.1	E980.9
disulfide or sulfide	976.4	E858.7	E946.4	E950.4	E962.0	E980.4
Selsun	976.4	E858.7	E946.4	E950.4	E962.0	E980.4
Senna	973.1	E858.4	E943.1	E950.4	E962.0	E980.4
Septisol	976.2	E858.7	E946.2	E950.4	E962.0	E980.4
Serax	969.4	E853.2	E939.4	E950.3	E962.0	E980.3
Serenesil	967.8	E852.8	E937.8	E950.2	E962.0	E980.2
Serenium (hydrochloride)	961.9	E857	E931.9	E950.4	E962.0	E980.4
Serepax — *see* Oxazepam						
Sernyl	968.3	E855.1	E938.3	E950.4	E962.0	E980.4
Serotonin	977.8	E858.8	E947.8	E950.4	E962.0	E980.4
Serpasil	972.6	E858.3	E942.6	E950.4	E962.0	E980.4
Sewer gas	987.8	E869.8	—	E952.8	E962.2	E982.8
Shampoo	989.6	E861.0	—	E950.9	E962.1	E980.9
Shellfish, nonbacterial or noxious	988.0	E865.1	—	E950.9	E962.1	E980.9
Silicones NEC	989.83	E866.8	E947.8	E950.9	E962.1	E980.9
Silvadene	976.0	E858.7	E946.0	E950.4	E962.0	E980.4
Silver (compound) (medicinal) NEC	976.0	E858.7	E946.0	E950.4	E962.0	E980.4
anti-infectives	976.0	E858.7	E946.0	E950.4	E962.0	E980.4
arsphenamine	961.1	E857	E931.1	E950.4	E962.0	E980.4
nitrate	976.0	E858.7	E946.0	E950.4	E962.0	E980.4
ophthalmic preparation	976.5	E858.7	E946.5	E950.4	E962.0	E980.4
toughened (keratolytic)	976.4	E858.7	E946.4	E950.4	E962.0	E980.4
nonmedicinal (dust)	985.8	E866.4	—	E950.9	E962.1	E980.9
protein (mild) (strong)	976.0	E858.7	E946.0	E950.4	E962.0	E980.4
salvarsan	961.1	E857	E931.1	E950.4	E962.0	E980.4
Simethicone	973.8	E858.4	E943.8	E950.4	E962.0	E980.4
Sinequan	969.0	E854.0	E939.0	E950.3	E962.0	E980.3
Singoserp	972.6	E858.3	E942.6	E950.4	E962.0	E980.4
Sintrom	964.2	E858.2	E934.2	E950.4	E962.0	E980.4
Sitosterols	972.2	E858.3	E942.2	E950.4	E962.0	E980.4
Skeletal muscle relaxants	975.2	E858.6	E945.2	E950.4	E962.0	E980.4
Skin						
agents (external)	976.9	E858.7	E946.9	E950.4	E962.0	E980.4
specified NEC	976.8	E858.7	E946.8	E950.4	E962.0	E980.4
test antigen	977.8	E858.8	E947.8	E950.4	E962.0	E980.4
Sleep-eze	963.0	E858.1	E933.0	E950.4	E962.0	E980.4
Sleeping draught (drug) (pill) (tablet)	967.9	E852.9	E937.9	E950.2	E962.0	E980.2
Smallpox vaccine	979.0	E858.8	E949.0	E950.4	E962.0	E980.4
Smelter fumes NEC	985.9	E866.4	—	E950.9	E962.1	E980.9
Smog	987.3	E869.1	—	E952.8	E962.2	E982.8
Smoke NEC	987.9	E869.9	—	E952.9	E962.2	E982.9
Smooth muscle relaxant	975.1	E858.6	E945.1	E950.4	E962.0	E980.4
Snail killer	989.4	E863.4	—	E950.6	E962.1	E980.7
Snake (bite) (venom)	989.5	E905.0	—	E950.9	E962.1	E980.9
Snuff	989.89	E866.8	—	E950.9	E962.1	E980.9
Soap (powder) (product)	989.6	E861.1	—	E950.9	E962.1	E980.9
bicarb	963.3	E858.1	E933.3	E950.4	E962.0	E980.4
chlorinated — see Sodium, hypochlorite						
medicinal, soft	976.2	E858.7	E946.2	E950.4	E962.0	E980.4
Soda (caustic)	983.2	E864.2	—	E950.7	E962.1	E980.6
Sodium						
acetosulfone	961.8	E857	E931.8	E950.4	E962.0	E980.4
acetrizoate	977.8	E858.8	E947.8	E950.4	E962.0	E980.4
amytal	967.0	E851	E937.0	E950.1	E962.0	E980.1
arsenate — see Arsenic						
bicarbonate	963.3	E858.1	E933.3	E950.4	E962.0	E980.4
bichromate	983.9	E864.3	—	E950.7	E962.1	E980.6
biphosphate	963.2	E858.1	E933.2	E950.4	E962.0	E980.4
bisulfate	983.9	E864.3	—	E950.7	E962.1	E980.6
Sodium — *continued*						
borate (cleanser)	989.6	E861.3	—	E950.9	E962.1	E980.9
bromide NEC	967.3	E852.2	E937.3	E950.2	E962.0	E980.2
cacodylate (nonmedicinal) NEC	978.8	E858.8	E948.8	E950.4	E962.0	E980.4
anti-infective	961.1	E857	E931.1	E950.4	E962.0	E980.4
herbicide	989.4	E863.5	—	E950.6	E962.1	E980.7
calcium edetate	963.8	E858.1	E933.8	E950.4	E962.0	E980.4
carbonate NEC	983.2	E864.2	—	E950.7	E962.1	E980.6
chlorate NEC	983.9	E864.3	—	E950.7	E962.1	E980.6
herbicide	983.9	E863.5	—	E950.7	E962.1	E980.6
chloride NEC	974.5	E858.5	E944.5	E950.4	E962.0	E980.4
chromate	983.9	E864.3	—	E950.7	E962.1	E980.6
citrate	963.3	E858.1	E933.3	E950.4	E962.0	E980.4
cyanide — see Cyanide(s)						
cyclamate	974.5	E858.5	E944.5	E950.4	E962.0	E980.4
diatrizoate	977.8	E858.8	E947.8	E950.4	E962.0	E980.4
dibunate	975.4	E858.6	E945.4	E950.4	E962.0	E980.4
dioctyl sulfosuccinate	973.2	E858.4	E943.2	E950.4	E962.0	E980.4
edetate	963.8	E858.1	E933.8	E950.4	E962.0	E980.4
ethacrynate	974.4	E858.5	E944.4	E950.4	E962.0	E980.4
fluoracetate (dust) (rodenticide)	989.4	E863.7	—	E950.6	E962.1	E980.7
fluoride — see Fluoride(s)						
free salt	974.5	E858.5	E944.5	E950.4	E962.0	E980.4
glucosulfone	961.8	E857	E931.8	E950.4	E962.0	E980.4
hydroxide	983.2	E864.2	—	E950.7	E962.1	E980.6
hypochlorite (bleach) NEC	983.9	E864.3	—	E950.7	E962.1	E980.6
disinfectant	983.9	E861.4	—	E950.7	E962.1	E980.6
medicinal (anti-infective) (external)	976.0	E858.7	E946.0	E950.4	E962.0	E980.4
vapor	987.8	E869.8	—	E952.8	E962.2	E982.8
hyposulfite	976.0	E858.7	E946.0	E950.4	E962.0	E980.4
indigotindisulfonate	977.8	E858.8	E947.8	E950.4	E962.0	E980.4
iodide	977.8	E858.8	E947.8	E950.4	E962.0	E980.4
iothalamate	977.8	E858.8	E947.8	E950.4	E962.0	E980.4
iron edetate	964.0	E858.2	E934.0	E950.4	E962.0	E980.4
lactate	963.3	E858.1	E933.3	E950.4	E962.0	E980.4
lauryl sulfate	976.2	E858.7	E946.2	E950.4	E962.0	E980.4
L-triiodothyronine	962.7	E858.0	E932.7	E950.4	E962.0	E980.4
metrizoate	977.8	E858.8	E947.8	E950.4	E962.0	E980.4
monofluoracetate (dust) (rodenticide)	989.4	E863.7	—	E950.6	E962.1	E980.7
morrhuate	972.7	E858.3	E942.7	E950.4	E962.0	E980.4
nafcillin	960.0	E856	E930.0	E950.4	E962.0	E980.4
nitrate (oxidizing agent)	983.9	E864.3	—	E950.7	E962.1	E980.6
nitrite (medicinal)	972.4	E858.3	E942.4	E950.4	E962.0	E980.4
nitroferricyanide	972.6	E858.3	E942.6	E950.4	E962.0	E980.4
nitroprusside	972.6	E858.3	E942.6	E950.4	E962.0	E980.4
para-aminohippurate	977.8	E858.8	E947.8	E950.4	E962.0	E980.4
perborate (nonmedicinal) NEC	989.89	E866.8	—	E950.9	E962.1	E980.9
medicinal	976.6	E858.7	E946.6	E950.4	E962.0	E980.4
soap	989.6	E861.1	—	E950.9	E962.1	E980.9
percarbonate — see Sodium, perborate						
phosphate	973.3	E858.4	E943.3	E950.4	E962.0	E980.4
polystyrene sulfonate	974.5	E858.5	E944.5	E950.4	E962.0	E980.4
propionate	976.0	E858.7	E946.0	E950.4	E962.0	E980.4
psylliate	972.7	E858.3	E942.7	E950.4	E962.0	E980.4
removing resins	974.5	E858.5	E944.5	E950.4	E962.0	E980.4
salicylate	965.1	E850.3	E935.3	E950.0	E962.0	E980.0
sulfate	973.3	E858.4	E943.3	E950.4	E962.0	E980.4
sulfoxone	961.8	E857	E931.8	E950.4	E962.0	E980.4
tetradecyl sulfate	972.7	E858.3	E942.7	E950.4	E962.0	E980.4
thiopental	968.3	E855.1	E938.3	E950.4	E962.0	E980.4
thiosalicylate	965.1	E850.3	E935.3	E950.0	E962.0	E980.0
thiosulfate	976.0	E858.7	E946.0	E950.4	E962.0	E980.4
tolbutamide	977.8	E858.8	E947.8	E950.4	E962.0	E980.4
tyropanoate	977.8	E858.8	E947.8	E950.4	E962.0	E980.4
valproate	966.3	E855.0	E936.3	E950.4	E962.0	E980.4
Solanine	977.8	E858.8	E947.8	E950.4	E962.0	E980.4
Solanum dulcamara	988.2	E865.4	—	E950.9	E962.1	E980.9
Solapsone	961.8	E857	E931.8	E950.4	E962.0	E980.4
Solasulfone	961.8	E857	E931.8	E950.4	E962.0	E980.4
Soldering fluid	983.1	E864.1	—	E950.7	E962.1	E980.6
Solid substance	989.9	E866.9	—	E950.9	E962.1	E980.9
specified NEC	989.9	E866.8	—	E950.9	E962.1	E980.9
Solvents, industrial	982.8	E862.9	—	E950.9	E962.1	E980.9
naphtha	981	E862.0	—	E950.9	E962.1	E980.9
petroleum	981	E862.0	—	E950.9	E962.1	E980.9
specified NEC	982.8	E862.4	—	E950.9	E962.1	E980.9

☑ Additional Digit Required — Refer to the Tabular List for Digit Selection

Subterms under main terms may continue to next column or page

	Poisoning	External Cause (E-Code)				
		Accident	Therapeutic Use	Suicide Attempt	Assault	Undetermined
Soma	968.0	E855.1	E938.0	E950.4	E962.0	E980.4
Somatotropin	962.4	E858.0	E932.4	E950.4	E962.0	E980.4
Sominex	963.0	E858.1	E933.0	E950.4	E962.0	E980.4
Somnos	967.1	E852.0	E937.1	E950.2	E962.0	E980.2
Somonal	967.0	E851	E937.0	E950.1	E962.0	E980.1
Soneryl	967.0	E851	E937.0	E950.1	E962.0	E980.1
Soothing syrup	977.9	E858.9	E947.9	E950.5	E962.0	E980.5
Sopor	967.4	E852.3	E937.4	E950.2	E962.0	E980.2
Soporific drug	967.9	E852.9	E937.9	E950.2	E962.0	E980.2
specified type NEC	967.8	E852.8	E937.8	E950.2	E962.0	E980.2
Sorbitol NEC	977.4	E858.8	E947.4	E950.4	E962.0	E980.4
Sotradecol	972.7	E858.3	E942.7	E950.4	E962.0	E980.4
Spacoline	975.1	E858.6	E945.1	E950.4	E962.0	E980.4
Spanish fly	976.8	E858.7	E946.8	E950.4	E962.0	E980.4
Sparine	969.1	E853.0	E939.1	E950.3	E962.0	E980.3
Sparteine	975.0	E858.6	E945.0	E950.4	E962.0	E980.4
Spasmolytics	975.1	E858.6	E945.1	E950.4	E962.0	E980.4
anticholinergics	971.1	E855.4	E941.1	E950.4	E962.0	E980.4
Spectinomycin	960.8	E856	E930.8	E950.4	E962.0	E980.4
Speed	969.7	E854.2	E939.7	E950.3	E962.0	E980.3
Spermicides	976.8	E858.7	E946.8	E950.4	E962.0	E980.4
Spider (bite) (venom)	989.5	E905.1	—	E950.9	E962.1	E980.9
antivenin	979.9	E858.8	E949.9	E950.4	E962.0	E980.4
Spigelia (root)	961.6	E857	E931.6	E950.4	E962.0	E980.4
Spiperone	969.2	E853.1	E939.2	E950.3	E962.0	E980.3
Spiramycin	960.3	E856	E930.3	E950.4	E962.0	E980.4
Spirilene	969.5	E853.8	E939.5	E950.3	E962.0	E980.3
Spirit(s) (neutral) NEC	980.0	E860.1	—	E950.9	E962.1	E980.9
beverage	980.0	E860.0	—	E950.9	E962.1	E980.9
industrial	980.9	E860.9	—	E950.9	E962.1	E980.9
mineral	981	E862.0	—	E950.9	E962.1	E980.9
of salt — see Hydrochloric acid						
surgical	980.9	E860.9	—	E950.9	E962.1	E980.9
Spironolactone	974.4	E858.5	E944.4	E950.4	E962.0	E980.4
Sponge, absorbable (gelatin)	964.5	E858.2	E934.5	E950.4	E962.0	E980.4
Sporostacin	976.0	E858.7	E946.0	E950.4	E962.0	E980.4
Sprays (aerosol)	989.89	E866.8	—	E950.9	E962.1	E980.9
cosmetic	989.89	E866.7	—	E950.9	E962.1	E980.9
medicinal NEC	977.9	E858.9	E947.9	E950.5	E962.0	E980.5
pesticides — see Pesticides						
specified content — see substance specified						
Spurge flax	988.2	E865.4	—	E950.9	E962.1	E980.9
Spurges	988.2	E865.4	—	E950.9	E962.1	E980.9
Squill (expectorant) NEC	975.5	E858.6	E945.5	E950.4	E962.0	E980.4
rat poison	989.4	E863.7	—	E950.6	E962.1	E980.7
Squirting cucumber (cathartic)	973.1	E858.4	E943.1	E950.4	E962.0	E980.4
Stains	989.89	E866.8	—	E950.9	E962.1	E980.9
Stannous — *see also* Tin						
fluoride	976.7	E858.7	E946.7	E950.4	E962.0	E980.4
Stanolone	962.1	E858.0	E932.1	E950.4	E962.0	E980.4
Stanozolol	962.1	E858.0	E932.1	E950.4	E962.0	E980.4
Staphisagria or stavesacre (pediculicide)	976.0	E858.7	E946.0	E950.4	E962.0	E980.4
Stelazine	969.1	E853.0	E939.1	E950.3	E962.0	E980.3
Stemetil	969.1	E853.0	E939.1	E950.3	E962.0	E980.3
Sterculia (cathartic) (gum)	973.3	E858.4	E943.3	E950.4	E962.0	E980.4
Sternutator gas	987.8	E869.8	—	E952.8	E962.2	E982.8
Steroids NEC	962.0	E858.0	E932.0	E950.4	E962.0	E980.4
ENT agent	976.6	E858.7	E946.6	E950.4	E962.0	E980.4
ophthalmic preparation	976.5	E858.7	E946.5	E950.4	E962.0	E980.4
topical NEC	976.0	E858.7	E946.0	E950.4	E962.0	E980.4
Stibine	985.8	E866.4	—	E950.9	E962.1	E980.9
Stibophen	961.2	E857	E931.2	E950.4	E962.0	E980.4
Stilbamide, stilbamidine	961.5	E857	E931.5	E950.4	E962.0	E980.4
Stilbestrol	962.2	E858.0	E932.2	E950.4	E962.0	E980.4
Stimulants (central nervous system)	970.9	E854.3	E940.9	E950.4	E962.0	E980.4
analeptics	970.0	E854.3	E940.0	E950.4	E962.0	E980.4
opiate antagonist	970.1	E854.3	E940.1	E950.4	E962.0	E980.4
psychotherapeutic NEC	969.0	E854.0	E939.0	E950.3	E962.0	E980.3
specified NEC	970.8	E854.3	E940.8	E950.4	E962.0	E980.4
Storage batteries (acid) (cells)	983.1	E864.1	—	E950.7	E962.1	E980.6
Stovaine	968.9	E855.2	E938.9	E950.4	E962.0	E980.4
infiltration (subcutaneous)	968.5	E855.2	E938.5	E950.4	E962.0	E980.4
nerve block (peripheral) (plexus)	968.6	E855.2	E938.6	E950.4	E962.0	E980.4
spinal	968.7	E855.2	E938.7	E950.4	E962.0	E980.4
Stovaine — *continued*						
topical (surface)	968.5	E855.2	E938.5	E950.4	E962.0	E980.4
Stovarsal	961.1	E857	E931.1	E950.4	E962.0	E980.4
Stove gas — *see* Gas, utility						
Stoxil	976.5	E858.7	E946.5	E950.4	E962.0	E980.4
STP	969.6	E854.1	E939.6	E950.3	E962.0	E980.3
Stramonium (medicinal) NEC	971.1	E855.4	E941.1	E950.4	E962.0	E980.4
natural state	988.2	E865.4	—	E950.9	E962.1	E980.9
Streptodornase	964.4	E858.2	E934.4	E950.4	E962.0	E980.4
Streptoduocin	960.6	E856	E930.6	E950.4	E962.0	E980.4
Streptokinase	964.4	E858.2	E934.4	E950.4	E962.0	E980.4
Streptomycin	960.6	E856	E930.6	E950.4	E962.0	E980.4
Streptozocin	960.7	E856	E930.7	E950.4	E962.0	E980.4
Stripper (paint) (solvent)	982.8	E862.9	—	E950.9	E962.1	E980.9
Strobane	989.2	E863.0	—	E950.6	E962.1	E980.7
Strophanthin	972.1	E858.3	E942.1	E950.4	E962.0	E980.4
Strophanthus hispidus or kombe	988.2	E865.4	—	E950.9	E962.1	E980.9
Strychnine (rodenticide) (salts)	989.1	E863.7	—	E950.6	E962.1	E980.7
medicinal NEC	970.8	E854.3	E940.8	E950.4	E962.0	E980.4
Strychnos (ignatii) — see Strychnine						
Styramate	968.0	E855.1	E938.0	E950.4	E962.0	E980.4
Styrene	983.0	E864.0	—	E950.7	E962.1	E980.6
Succinimide (anticonvulsant)	966.2	E855.0	E936.2	E950.4	E962.0	E980.4
mercuric — see Mercury						
Succinylcholine	975.2	E858.6	E945.2	E950.4	E962.0	E980.4
Succinylsulfathiazole	961.0	E857	E931.0	E950.4	E962.0	E980.4
Sucrose	974.5	E858.5	E944.5	E950.4	E962.0	E980.4
Sulfacetamide	961.0	E857	E931.0	E950.4	E962.0	E980.4
ophthalmic preparation	976.5	E858.7	E946.5	E950.4	E962.0	E980.4
Sulfachlorpyridazine	961.0	E857	E931.0	E950.4	E962.0	E980.4
Sulfacytine	961.0	E857	E931.0	E950.4	E962.0	E980.4
Sulfadiazine	961.0	E857	E931.0	E950.4	E962.0	E980.4
silver (topical)	976.0	E858.7	E946.0	E950.4	E962.0	E980.4
Sulfadimethoxine	961.0	E857	E931.0	E950.4	E962.0	E980.4
Sulfadimidine	961.0	E857	E931.0	E950.4	E962.0	E980.4
Sulfaethidole	961.0	E857	E931.0	E950.4	E962.0	E980.4
Sulfafurazole	961.0	E857	E931.0	E950.4	E962.0	E980.4
Sulfaguanidine	961.0	E857	E931.0	E950.4	E962.0	E980.4
Sulfamerazine	961.0	E857	E931.0	E950.4	E962.0	E980.4
Sulfameter	961.0	E857	E931.0	E950.4	E962.0	E980.4
Sulfamethizole	961.0	E857	E931.0	E950.4	E962.0	E980.4
Sulfamethoxazole	961.0	E857	E931.0	E950.4	E962.0	E980.4
Sulfamethoxydiazine	961.0	E857	E931.0	E950.4	E962.0	E980.4
Sulfamethoxypyridazine	961.0	E857	E931.0	E950.4	E962.0	E980.4
Sulfamethylthiazole	961.0	E857	E931.0	E950.4	E962.0	E980.4
Sulfamylon	976.0	E858.7	E946.0	E950.4	E962.0	E980.4
Sulfan blue (diagnostic dye)	977.8	E858.8	E947.8	E950.4	E962.0	E980.4
Sulfanilamide	961.0	E857	E931.0	E950.4	E962.0	E980.4
Sulfanilylguanidine	961.0	E857	E931.0	E950.4	E962.0	E980.4
Sulfaphenazole	961.0	E857	E931.0	E950.4	E962.0	E980.4
Sulfaphenylthiazole	961.0	E857	E931.0	E950.4	E962.0	E980.4
Sulfaproxyline	961.0	E857	E931.0	E950.4	E962.0	E980.4
Sulfapyridine	961.0	E857	E931.0	E950.4	E962.0	E980.4
Sulfapyrimidine	961.0	E857	E931.0	E950.4	E962.0	E980.4
Sulfarsphenamine	961.1	E857	E931.1	E950.4	E962.0	E980.4
Sulfasalazine	961.0	E857	E931.0	E950.4	E962.0	E980.4
Sulfasomizole	961.0	E857	E931.0	E950.4	E962.0	E980.4
Sulfasuxidine	961.0	E857	E931.0	E950.4	E962.0	E980.4
Sulfinpyrazone	974.7	E858.5	E944.7	E950.4	E962.0	E980.4
Sulfisoxazole	961.0	E857	E931.0	E950.4	E962.0	E980.4
ophthalmic preparation	976.5	E858.7	E946.5	E950.4	E962.0	E980.4
Sulfomyxin	960.8	E856	E930.8	E950.4	E962.0	E980.4
Sulfonal	967.8	E852.8	E937.8	E950.2	E962.0	E980.2
Sulfonamides (mixtures)	961.0	E857	E931.0	E950.4	E962.0	E980.4
Sulfones	961.8	E857	E931.8	E950.4	E962.0	E980.4
Sulfonethylmethane	967.8	E852.8	E937.8	E950.2	E962.0	E980.2
Sulfonmethane	967.8	E852.8	E937.8	E950.2	E962.0	E980.2
Sulfonphthal, sulfonphthol	977.8	E858.8	E947.8	E950.4	E962.0	E980.4
Sulfonylurea derivatives, oral	962.3	E858.0	E932.3	E950.4	E962.0	E980.4
Sulfoxone	961.8	E857	E931.8	E950.4	E962.0	E980.4
Sulfur, sulfureted, sulfuric, sulfurous, sulfuryl (compounds) NEC	989.89	E866.8	—	E950.9	E962.1	E980.9
acid	983.1	E864.1	—	E950.7	E962.1	E980.6
dioxide	987.3	E869.1	—	E952.8	E962.2	E982.8

☑ Additional Digit Required — Refer to the Tabular List for Digit Selection

Subterms under main terms may continue to next column or page

▶◀ Revised Text ● New Line ▲ Revised Code

		External Cause (E-Code)				
	Poisoning	Accident	Therapeutic Use	Suicide Attempt	Assault	Undetermined
Sulfur, sulfureted, sulfuric, sulfurous, sulfuryl (compounds) — *continued*						
ether — see Ether(s)						
hydrogen	987.8	E869.8	—	E952.8	E962.2	E982.8
medicinal (keratolytic) (ointment) NEC	976.4	E858.7	E946.4	E950.4	E962.0	E980.4
pesticide (vapor)	989.4	E863.4	—	E950.6	E962.1	E980.7
vapor NEC	987.8	E869.8	—	E952.8	E962.2	E982.8
Sulkowitch's reagent	977.8	E858.8	E947.8	E950.4	E962.0	E980.4
Sulphadione	961.8	E857	E931.8	E950.4	E962.0	E980.4
Sulph — *see also* Sulf-						
Sulthiame, sultiame	966.3	E855.0	E936.3	E950.4	E962.0	E980.4
Superinone	975.5	E858.6	E945.5	E950.4	E962.0	E980.4
Suramin	961.5	E857	E931.5	E950.4	E962.0	E980.4
Surfacaine	968.5	E855.2	E938.5	E950.4	E962.0	E980.4
Surital	968.3	E855.1	E938.3	E950.4	E962.0	E980.4
Sutilains	976.8	E858.7	E946.8	E950.4	E962.0	E980.4
Suxamethonium (bromide) (chloride) (iodide)	975.2	E858.6	E945.2	E950.4	E962.0	E980.4
Suxethonium (bromide)	975.2	E858.6	E945.2	E950.4	E962.0	E980.4
Sweet oil (birch)	976.3	E858.7	E946.3	E950.4	E962.0	E980.4
Sym-dichloroethyl ether	982.3	E862.4	—	E950.9	E962.1	E980.9
Sympatholytics	971.3	E855.6	E941.3	E950.4	E962.0	E980.4
Sympathomimetics	971.2	E855.5	E941.2	E950.4	E962.0	E980.4
Synagis	979.6	E858.8	E949.6	E950.4	E962.0	E980.4
Synalar	976.0	E858.7	E946.0	E950.4	E962.0	E980.4
Synthroid	962.7	E858.0	E932.7	E950.4	E962.0	E980.4
Syntocinon	975.0	E858.6	E945.0	E950.4	E962.0	E950.4
Syrosingopine	972.6	E858.3	E942.6	E950.4	E962.0	E980.4
Systemic agents (primarily)	963.9	E858.1	E933.9	E950.4	E962.0	E980.4
specified NEC	963.8	E858.1	E933.8	E950.4	E962.0	E980.4
Tablets — *see also* specified substance	977.9	E858.9	E947.9	E950.5	E962.0	E980.5
Tace	962.2	E858.0	E932.2	E950.4	E962.0	E980.4
Tacrine	971.0	E855.3	E941.0	E950.4	E962.0	E980.4
Talbutal	967.0	E851	E937.0	E950.1	E962.0	E980.1
Talc	976.3	E858.7	E946.3	E950.4	E962.0	E980.4
Talcum	976.3	E858.7	E946.3	E950.4	E962.0	E980.4
Tandearil, tanderil	965.5	E850.5	E935.5	E950.0	E962.0	E980.0
Tannic acid	983.1	E864.1	—	E950.7	E962.1	E980.6
medicinal (astringent)	976.2	E858.7	E946.2	E950.4	E962.0	E980.4
Tannin — see Tannic acid						
Tansy	988.2	E865.4	—	E950.9	E962.1	E980.9
TAO	960.3	E856	E930.3	E950.4	E962.0	E980.4
Tapazole	962.8	E858.0	E932.8	E950.4	E962.0	E980.4
Tar NEC	983.0	E864.0	—	E950.7	E962.1	E980.6
camphor — see Naphthalene						
fumes	987.8	E869.8	—	E952.8	E962.2	E982.8
Taractan	969.3	E853.8	E939.3	E950.3	E962.0	E980.3
Tarantula (venomous)	989.5	E905.1	—	E950.9	E962.1	E980.9
Tartar emetic (anti-infective)	961.2	E857	E931.2	E950.4	E962.0	E980.4
Tartaric acid	983.1	E864.1	—	E950.7	E962.1	E980.6
Tartrated antimony (anti-infective)	961.2	E857	E931.2	E950.4	E962.0	E980.4
TCA — *see* Trichloroacetic acid						
TDI	983.0	E864.0	—	E950.7	E962.1	E980.6
vapor	987.8	E869.8	—	E952.8	E962.2	E982.8
Tear gas	987.5	E869.3	—	E952.8	E962.2	E982.8
Teclothiazide	974.3	E858.5	E944.3	E950.4	E962.0	E980.4
Tegretol	966.3	E855.0	E936.3	E950.4	E962.0	E980.4
Telepaque	977.8	E858.8	E947.8	E950.4	E962.0	E980.4
Tellurium	985.8	E866.4	—	E950.9	E962.1	E980.9
fumes	985.8	E866.4	—	E950.9	E962.1	E980.9
TEM	963.1	E858.1	E933.1	E950.4	E962.0	E980.4
Temazepan — see Benzodiazepines						
TEPA	963.1	E858.1	E933.1	E950.4	E962.0	E980.4
TEPP	989.3	E863.1	—	E950.6	E962.1	E980.7
Terbutaline	971.2	E855.5	E941.2	E950.4	E962.0	E980.4
Teroxalene	961.6	E857	E931.6	E950.4	E962.0	E980.4
Terpin hydrate	975.5	E858.6	E945.5	E950.4	E962.0	E980.4
Terramycin	960.4	E856	E930.4	E950.4	E962.0	E980.4
Tessalon	975.4	E858.6	E945.4	E950.4	E962.0	E980.4
Testosterone	962.1	E858.0	E932.1	E950.4	E962.0	E980.4
Tetanus (vaccine)	978.4	E858.8	E948.4	E950.4	E962.0	E980.4
antitoxin	979.9	E858.8	E949.9	E950.4	E962.0	E980.4
immune globulin (human)	964.6	E858.2	E934.6	E950.4	E962.0	E980.4
toxoid	978.4	E858.8	E948.4	E950.4	E962.0	E980.4
with diphtheria toxoid	978.9	E858.8	E948.9	E950.4	E962.0	E980.4
Tetanus — *continued*						
toxoid — *continued*						
with diphtheria toxoid — *continued*						
with pertussis	978.6	E858.8	E948.6	E950.4	E962.0	E980.4
Tetrabenazine	969.5	E853.8	E939.5	E950.3	E962.0	E980.3
Tetracaine (infiltration) (topical)	968.5	E855.2	E938.5	E950.4	E962.0	E980.4
nerve block (peripheral) (plexus)	968.6	E855.2	E938.6	E950.4	E962.0	E980.4
spinal	968.7	E855.2	E938.7	E950.4	E962.0	E980.4
Tetrachlorethylene — see Tetrachloroethylene						
Tetrachlormethiazide	974.3	E858.5	E944.3	E950.4	E962.0	E980.4
Tetrachloroethane (liquid) (vapor)	982.3	E862.4	—	E950.9	E962.1	E980.9
paint or varnish	982.3	E861.6	—	E950.9	E962.1	E980.9
Tetrachloroethylene (liquid) (vapor)	982.3	E862.4	—	E950.9	E962.1	E980.9
medicinal	961.6	E857	E931.6	E950.4	E962.0	E980.4
Tetrachloromethane — see Carbon, tetrachloride						
Tetracycline	960.4	E856	E930.4	E950.4	E962.0	E980.4
ophthalmic preparation	976.5	E858.7	E946.5	E950.4	E962.0	E980.4
topical NEC	976.0	E858.7	E946.0	E950.4	E962.0	E980.4
Tetraethylammonium chloride	972.3	E858.3	E942.3	E950.4	E962.0	E980.4
Tetraethyl lead (antiknock compound)	984.1	E862.1	—	E950.9	E962.1	E980.9
Tetraethyl pyrophosphate	989.3	E863.1	—	E950.6	E962.1	E980.7
Tetraethylthiuram disulfide	977.3	E858.8	E947.3	E950.4	E962.0	E980.4
Tetrahydroaminoacridine	971.0	E855.3	E941.0	E950.4	E962.0	E980.4
Tetrahydrocannabinol	969.6	E854.1	E939.6	E950.3	E962.0	E980.3
Tetrahydronaphthalene	982.0	E862.4	—	E950.9	E962.1	E980.9
Tetrahydrozoline	971.2	E855.5	E941.2	E950.4	E962.0	E980.4
Tetralin	982.0	E862.4	—	E950.9	E962.1	E980.9
Tetramethylthiuram (disulfide) NEC	989.4	E863.6	—	E950.6	E962.1	E980.7
medicinal	976.2	E858.7	E946.2	E950.4	E962.0	E980.4
Tetronal	967.8	E852.8	E937.8	E950.2	E962.0	E980.2
Tetryl	983.0	E864.0	—	E950.7	E962.1	E980.6
Thalidomide	967.8	E852.8	E937.8	E950.2	E962.0	E980.2
Thallium (compounds) (dust) NEC	985.8	E866.4	—	E950.9	E962.1	E980.9
pesticide (rodenticide)	985.8	E863.7	—	E950.6	E962.1	E980.7
THC	969.6	E854.1	E939.6	E950.3	E962.0	E980.3
Thebacon	965.09	E850.2	E935.2	E950.0	E962.0	E980.0
Thebaine	965.09	E850.2	E935.2	E950.0	E962.0	E980.0
Theobromine (calcium salicylate)	974.1	E858.5	E944.1	E950.4	E962.0	E980.4
Theophylline (diuretic)	974.1	E858.5	E944.1	E950.4	E962.0	E980.4
ethylenediamine	975.7	E858.6	E945.7	E950.4	E962.0	E980.4
Thiabendazole	961.6	E857	E931.6	E950.4	E962.0	E980.4
Thialbarbital, thialbarbitone	968.3	E855.1	E938.3	E950.4	E962.0	E980.4
Thiamine	963.5	E858.1	E933.5	E950.4	E962.0	E980.4
Thiamylal (sodium)	968.3	E855.1	E938.3	E950.4	E962.0	E980.4
Thiazesim	969.0	E854.0	E939.0	E950.3	E962.0	E980.3
Thiazides (diuretics)	974.3	E858.5	E944.3	E950.4	E962.0	E980.4
Thiethylperazine	963.0	E858.1	E933.0	E950.4	E962.0	E980.4
Thimerosal (topical)	976.0	E858.7	E946.0	E950.4	E962.0	E980.4
ophthalmic preparation	976.5	E858.7	E946.5	E950.4	E962.0	E980.4
Thioacetazone	961.8	E857	E931.8	E950.4	E962.0	E980.4
Thiobarbiturates	968.3	E855.1	E938.3	E950.4	E962.0	E980.4
Thiobismol	961.2	E857	E931.2	E950.4	E962.0	E980.4
Thiocarbamide	962.8	E858.0	E932.8	E950.4	E962.0	E980.4
Thiocarbarsone	961.1	E857	E931.1	E950.4	E962.0	E980.4
Thiocarlide	961.8	E857	E931.8	E950.4	E962.0	E980.4
Thioguanine	963.1	E858.1	E933.1	E950.4	E962.0	E980.4
Thiomercaptomerin	974.0	E858.5	E944.0	E950.4	E962.0	E980.4
Thiomerin	974.0	E858.5	E944.0	E950.4	E962.0	E980.4
Thiopental, thiopentone (sodium)	968.3	E855.1	E938.3	E950.4	E962.0	E980.4
Thiopropazate	969.1	E853.0	E939.1	E950.3	E962.0	E980.3
Thioproperazine	969.1	E853.0	E939.1	E950.3	E962.0	E980.3
Thioridazine	969.1	E853.0	E939.1	E950.3	E962.0	E980.3
Thio-TEPA, thiotepa	963.1	E858.1	E933.1	E950.4	E962.0	E980.4
Thiothixene	969.3	E853.8	E939.3	E950.3	E962.0	E980.3
Thiouracil	962.8	E858.0	E932.8	E950.4	E962.0	E980.4
Thiourea	962.8	E858.0	E932.8	E950.4	E962.0	E980.4

Additional Digit Required — Refer to the Tabular List for Digit Selection

Subterms under main terms may continue to next column or page

▶◀ Revised Text ● New Line ▲ Revised Code

		External Cause (E-Code)				
	Poisoning	Accident	Therapeutic Use	Suicide Attempt	Assault	Undetermined
Thiphenamil	971.1	E855.4	E941.1	E950.4	E962.0	E980.4
Thiram NEC	989.4	E863.6	—	E950.6	E962.1	E980.7
medicinal	976.2	E858.7	E946.2	E950.4	E962.0	E980.4
Thonzylamine	963.0	E858.1	E933.0	E950.4	E962.0	E980.4
Thorazine	969.1	E853.0	E939.1	E950.3	E962.0	E980.3
Thornapple	988.2	E865.4	—	E950.9	E962.1	E980.9
Throat preparation (lozenges) NEC	976.6	E858.7	E946.6	E950.4	E962.0	E980.4
Thrombin	964.5	E858.2	E934.5	E950.4	E962.0	E980.4
Thrombolysin	964.4	E858.2	E934.4	E950.4	E962.0	E980.4
Thymol	983.0	E864.0	—	E950.7	E962.1	E980.6
Thymus extract	962.9	E858.0	E932.9	E950.4	E962.0	E980.4
Thyroglobulin	962.7	E858.0	E932.7	E950.4	E962.0	E980.4
Thyroid (derivatives) (extract)	962.7	E858.0	E932.7	E950.4	E962.0	E980.4
Thyrolar	962.7	E858.0	E932.7	E950.4	E962.0	E980.4
Thyrothrophin, thyrotropin	977.8	E858.8	E947.8	E950.4	E962.0	E980.4
Thyroxin(e)	962.7	E858.0	E932.7	E950.4	E962.0	E980.4
Tigan	963.0	E858.1	E933.0	E950.4	E962.0	E980.4
Tigloidine	968.0	E855.1	E938.0	E950.4	E962.0	E980.4
Tin (chloride) (dust) (oxide) NEC	985.8	E866.4	—	E950.9	E962.1	E980.9
anti-infectives	961.2	E857	E931.2	E950.4	E962.0	E980.4
Tinactin	976.0	E858.7	E946.0	E950.4	E962.0	E980.4
Tincture, iodine — *see* Iodine						
Tindal	969.1	E853.0	E939.1	E950.3	E962.0	E980.3
Titanium (compounds) (vapor)	985.8	E866.4	—	E950.9	E962.1	E980.9
ointment	976.3	E858.7	E946.3	E950.4	E962.0	E980.4
Titroid	962.7	E858.0	E932.7	E950.4	E962.0	E980.4
TMTD — *see* Tetramethylthiuram disulfide						
TNT	989.89	E866.8	—	E950.9	E962.1	E980.9
fumes	987.8	E869.8	—	E952.8	E962.2	E982.8
Toadstool	988.1	E865.5	—	E950.9	E962.1	E980.9
Tobacco NEC	989.84	E866.8	—	E950.9	E962.1	E980.9
Indian	988.2	E865.4	—	E950.9	E962.1	E980.9
smoke, second-hand	987.8	E869.4	—	—	—	—
Tocopherol	963.5	E858.1	E933.5	E950.4	E962.0	E980.4
Tocosamine	975.0	E858.6	E945.0	E950.4	E962.0	E980.4
Tofranil	969.0	E854.0	E939.0	E950.3	E962.0	E980.3
Toilet deodorizer	989.89	E866.8	—	E950.9	E962.1	E980.9
Tolazamide	962.3	E858.0	E932.3	E950.4	E962.0	E980.4
Tolazoline	971.3	E855.6	E941.3	E950.4	E962.0	E980.4
Tolbutamide	962.3	E858.0	E932.3	E950.4	E962.0	E980.4
sodium	977.8	E858.8	E947.8	E950.4	E962.0	E980.4
Tolmetin	965.69	E850.6	E935.6	E950.0	E962.0	E980.0
Tolnaftate	976.0	E858.7	E946.0	E950.4	E962.0	E980.4
Tolpropamine	976.1	E858.7	E946.1	E950.4	E962.0	E980.4
Tolserol	968.0	E855.1	E938.0	E950.4	E962.0	E980.4
Toluene (liquid) (vapor)	982.0	E862.4	—	E950.9	E962.1	E980.9
diisocyanate	983.0	E864.0	—	E950.7	E962.1	E980.6
Toluidine	983.0	E864.0	—	E950.7	E962.1	E980.6
vapor	987.8	E869.8	—	E952.8	E962.2	E982.8
Toluol (liquid) (vapor)	982.0	E862.4	—	E950.9	E962.1	E980.9
Tolylene-2, 4-diisocyanate	983.0	E864.0	—	E950.7	E962.1	E980.6
Tonics, cardiac	972.1	E858.3	E942.1	E950.4	E962.0	E980.4
Toxaphene (dust) (spray)	989.2	E863.0	—	E950.6	E962.1	E980.7
Toxoids NEC	978.8	E858.8	E948.8	E950.4	E962.0	E980.4
Tractor fuel NEC	981	E862.1	—	E950.9	E962.1	E980.9
Tragacanth	973.3	E858.4	E943.3	E950.4	E962.0	E980.4
Tramazoline	971.2	E855.5	E941.2	E950.4	E962.0	E980.4
Tranquilizers	969.5	E853.9	E939.5	E950.3	E962.0	E980.3
benzodiazepine-based	969.4	E853.2	E939.4	E950.3	E962.0	E980.3
butyrophenone-based	969.2	E853.1	E939.2	E950.3	E962.0	E980.3
major NEC	969.3	E853.8	E939.3	E950.3	E962.0	E980.3
phenothiazine-based	969.1	E853.0	E939.1	E950.3	E962.0	E980.3
specified NEC	969.5	E853.8	E939.5	E950.3	E962.0	E980.3
Trantoin	961.9	E857	E931.9	E950.4	E962.0	E980.4
Tranxene	969.4	E853.2	E939.4	E950.3	E962.0	E980.3
Tranylcypromine (sulfate)	969.0	E854.0	E939.0	E950.3	E962.0	E980.3
Trasentine	975.1	E858.6	E945.1	E950.4	E962.0	E980.4
Travert	974.5	E858.5	E944.5	E950.4	E962.0	E980.4
Trecator	961.8	E857	E931.8	E950.4	E962.0	E980.4
Tretinoin	976.8	E858.7	E946.8	E950.4	E962.0	E980.4
Triacetin	976.0	E858.7	E946.0	E950.4	E962.0	E980.4
Triacetyloleandomycin	960.3	E856	E930.3	E950.4	E962.0	E980.4
Triamcinolone	962.0	E858.0	E932.0	E950.4	E962.0	E980.4
ENT agent	976.6	E858.7	E946.6	E950.4	E962.0	E980.4
medicinal (keratolytic)	976.4	E858.7	E946.4	E950.4	E962.0	E980.4
Triamcinolone — *continued*						
ophthalmic preparation	976.5	E858.7	E946.5	E950.4	E962.0	E980.4
topical NEC	976.0	E858.7	E946.0	E950.4	E962.0	E980.4
Triamterene	974.4	E858.5	E944.4	E950.4	E962.0	E980.4
Triaziquone	963.1	E858.1	E933.1	E950.4	E962.0	E980.4
Tribromacetaldehyde	967.3	E852.2	E937.3	E950.2	E962.0	E980.2
Tribromoethanol	968.2	E855.1	E938.2	E950.4	E962.0	E980.4
Tribromomethane	967.3	E852.2	E937.3	E950.2	E962.0	E980.2
Trichlorethane	982.3	E862.4	—	E950.9	E962.1	E980.9
Trichlormethiazide	974.3	E858.5	E944.3	E950.4	E962.0	E980.4
Trichloroacetic acid	983.1	E864.1	—	E950.7	E962.1	E980.6
Trichloroethanol	967.1	E852.0	E937.1	E950.2	E962.0	E980.2
Trichloroethylene (liquid) (vapor)	982.3	E862.4	—	E950.9	E962.1	E980.9
anesthetic (gas)	968.2	E855.1	E938.2	E950.4	E962.0	E980.4
Trichloroethyl phosphate	967.1	E852.0	E937.1	E950.2	E962.0	E980.2
Trichlorofluoromethane NEC	987.4	E869.2	—	E952.8	E962.2	E982.8
Trichlorotriethylamine	963.1	E858.1	E933.1	E950.4	E962.0	E980.4
Trichomonacides NEC	961.5	E857	E931.5	E950.4	E962.0	E980.4
Trichomycin	960.1	E856	E930.1	E950.4	E962.0	E980.4
Triclofos	967.1	E852.0	E937.1	E950.2	E962.0	E980.2
Tricresyl phosphate	989.89	E866.8	—	E950.9	E962.1	E980.9
solvent	982.8	E862.4	—	E950.9	E962.1	E980.9
Tricyclamol	966.4	E855.0	E936.4	E950.4	E962.0	E980.4
Tridesilon	976.0	E858.7	E946.0	E950.4	E962.0	E980.4
Tridihexethyl	971.1	E855.4	E941.1	E950.4	E962.0	E980.4
Tridione	966.0	E855.0	E936.0	E950.4	E962.0	E980.4
Triethanolamine NEC	983.2	E864.2	—	E950.7	E962.1	E980.6
detergent	983.2	E861.0	—	E950.7	E962.1	E980.6
trinitrate	972.4	E858.3	E942.4	E950.4	E962.0	E980.4
Triethanomelamine	963.1	E858.1	E933.1	E950.4	E962.0	E980.4
Triethylene melamine	963.1	E858.1	E933.1	E950.4	E962.0	E980.4
Triethylenephosphoramide	963.1	E858.1	E933.1	E950.4	E962.0	E980.4
Triethylenethiophosphoramide	963.1	E858.1	E933.1	E950.4	E962.0	E980.4
Trifluoperazine	969.1	E853.0	E939.1	E950.3	E962.0	E980.3
Trifluperidol	969.2	E853.1	E939.2	E950.3	E962.0	E980.3
Triflupromazine	969.1	E853.0	E939.1	E950.3	E962.0	E980.3
Trihexyphenidyl	971.1	E855.4	E941.1	E950.4	E962.0	E980.4
Triiodothyronine	962.7	E858.0	E932.7	E950.4	E962.0	E980.4
Trilene	968.2	E855.1	E938.2	E950.4	E962.0	E980.4
Trimeprazine	963.0	E858.1	E933.0	E950.4	E962.0	E980.4
Trimetazidine	972.4	E858.3	E942.4	E950.4	E962.0	E980.4
Trimethadione	966.0	E855.0	E936.0	E950.4	E962.0	E980.4
Trimethaphan	972.3	E858.3	E942.3	E950.4	E962.0	E980.4
Trimethidinium	972.3	E858.3	E942.3	E950.4	E962.0	E980.4
Trimethobenzamide	963.0	E858.1	E933.0	E950.4	E962.0	E980.4
Trimethylcarbinol	980.8	E860.8	—	E950.9	E962.1	E980.9
Trimethylpsoralen	976.3	E858.7	E946.3	E950.4	E962.0	E980.4
Trimeton	963.0	E858.1	E933.0	E950.4	E962.0	E980.4
Trimipramine	969.0	E854.0	E939.0	E950.3	E962.0	E980.3
Trimustine	963.1	E858.1	E933.1	E950.4	E962.0	E980.4
Trinitrin	972.4	E858.3	E942.4	E950.4	E962.0	E980.4
Trinitrophenol	983.0	E864.0	—	E950.7	E962.1	E980.6
Trinitrotoluene	989.89	E866.8	—	E950.9	E962.1	E980.9
fumes	987.8	E869.8	—	E952.8	E962.2	E982.8
Trional	967.8	E852.8	E937.8	E950.2	E962.0	E980.2
Trioxide of arsenic — *see* Arsenic						
Trioxsalen	976.3	E858.7	E946.3	E950.4	E962.0	E980.4
Tripelennamine	963.0	E858.1	E933.0	E950.4	E962.0	E980.4
Triperidol	969.2	E853.1	E939.2	E950.3	E962.0	E980.3
Triprolidine	963.0	E858.1	E933.0	E950.4	E962.0	E980.4
Trisoralen	976.3	E858.7	E946.3	E950.4	E962.0	E980.4
Troleandomycin	960.3	E856	E930.3	E950.4	E962.0	E980.4
Trolnitrate (phosphate)	972.4	E858.3	E942.4	E950.4	E962.0	E980.4
Trometamol	963.3	E858.1	E933.3	E950.4	E962.0	E980.4
Tromethamine	963.3	E858.1	E933.3	E950.4	E962.0	E980.4
Tronothane	968.5	E855.2	E938.5	E950.4	E962.0	E980.4
Tropicamide	971.1	E855.4	E941.1	E950.4	E962.0	E980.4
Troxidone	966.0	E855.0	E936.0	E950.4	E962.0	E980.4
Tryparsamide	961.1	E857	E931.1	E950.4	E962.0	E980.4
Trypsin	963.4	E858.1	E933.4	E950.4	E962.0	E980.4
Tryptizol	969.0	E854.0	E939.0	E950.3	E962.0	E980.3
Tuaminoheptane	971.2	E855.5	E941.2	E950.4	E962.0	E980.4
Tuberculin (old)	977.8	E858.8	E947.8	E950.4	E962.0	E980.4
Tubocurare	975.2	E858.6	E945.2	E950.4	E962.0	E980.4
Tubocurarine	975.2	E858.6	E945.2	E950.4	E962.0	E980.4
Turkish green	969.6	E854.1	E939.6	E950.3	E962.0	E980.3
Turpentine (spirits of) (liquid) (vapor)	982.8	E862.4	—	E950.9	E962.1	E980.9

	Poisoning	External Cause (E-Code) Accident	Therapeutic Use	Suicide Attempt	Assault	Undetermined
Tybamate	969.5	E853.8	E939.5	E950.3	E962.0	E980.3
Tyloxapol	975.5	E858.6	E945.5	E950.4	E962.0	E980.4
Tymazoline	971.2	E855.5	E941.2	E950.4	E962.0	E980.4
Typhoid vaccine	978.1	E858.8	E948.1	E950.4	E962.0	E980.4
Typhus vaccine	979.2	E858.8	E949.2	E950.4	E962.0	E980.4
Tyrothricin	976.0	E858.7	E946.0	E950.4	E962.0	E980.4
ENT agent	976.6	E858.7	E946.6	E950.4	E962.0	E980.4
ophthalmic preparation	976.5	E858.7	E946.5	E950.4	E962.0	E980.4
Undecenoic acid	976.0	E858.7	E946.0	E950.4	E962.0	E980.4
Undecylenic acid	976.0	E858.7	E946.0	E950.4	E962.0	E980.4
Unna's boot	976.3	E858.7	E946.3	E950.4	E962.0	E980.4
Uracil mustard	963.1	E858.1	E933.1	E950.4	E962.0	E980.4
Uramustine	963.1	E858.1	E933.1	E950.4	E962.0	E980.4
Urari	975.2	E858.6	E945.2	E950.4	E962.0	E980.4
Urea	974.4	E858.5	E944.4	E950.4	E962.0	E980.4
topical	976.8	E858.7	E946.8	E950.4	E962.0	E980.4
Urethan(e) (antineoplastic)	963.1	E858.1	E933.1	E950.4	E962.0	E980.4
Urginea (maritima) (scilla) — *see* Squill						
Uric acid metabolism agents NEC	974.7	E858.5	E944.7	E950.4	E962.0	E980.4
Urokinase	964.4	E858.2	E934.4	E950.4	E962.0	E980.4
Urokon	977.8	E858.8	E947.8	E950.4	E962.0	E980.4
Urotropin	961.9	E857	E931.9	E950.4	E962.0	E980.4
Urtica	988.2	E865.4	—	E950.9	E962.1	E980.9
Utility gas — *see* Gas, utility						
Vaccine NEC	979.9	E858.8	E949.9	E950.4	E962.0	E980.4
bacterial NEC	978.8	E858.8	E948.8	E950.4	E962.0	E980.4
with						
other bacterial component	978.9	E858.8	E948.9	E950.4	E962.0	E980.4
pertussis component	978.6	E858.8	E948.6	E950.4	E962.0	E980.4
viral-rickettsial component	979.7	E858.8	E949.7	E950.4	E962.0	E980.4
mixed NEC	978.9	E858.8	E948.9	E950.4	E962.0	E980.4
BCG	978.0	E858.8	E948.0	E950.4	E962.0	E980.4
cholera	978.2	E858.8	E948.2	E950.4	E962.0	E980.4
diphtheria	978.5	E858.8	E948.5	E950.4	E962.0	E980.4
influenza	979.6	E858.8	E949.6	E950.4	E962.0	E980.4
measles	979.4	E858.8	E949.4	E950.4	E962.0	E980.4
meningococcal	978.8	E858.8	E948.8	E950.4	E962.0	E980.4
mumps	979.6	E858.8	E949.6	E950.4	E962.0	E980.4
paratyphoid	978.1	E858.8	E948.1	E950.4	E962.0	E980.4
pertussis (with diphtheria toxoid) (with tetanus toxoid)	978.6	E858.8	E948.6	E950.4	E962.0	E980.4
plague	978.3	E858.8	E948.3	E950.4	E962.0	E980.4
poliomyelitis	979.5	E858.8	E949.5	E950.4	E962.0	E980.4
poliovirus	979.5	E858.8	E949.5	E950.4	E962.0	E980.4
rabies	979.1	E858.8	E949.1	E950.4	E962.0	E980.4
respiratory syncytial virus	979.6	E858.8	E949.6	E950.4	E962.0	E980.4
rickettsial NEC	979.6	E858.8	E949.6	E950.4	E962.0	E980.4
with						
bacterial component	979.7	E858.8	E949.7	E950.4	E962.0	E980.4
pertussis component	978.6	E858.8	E948.6	E950.4	E962.0	E980.4
viral component	979.7	E858.8	E949.7	E950.4	E962.0	E980.4
Rocky mountain spotted fever	979.6	E858.8	E949.6	E950.4	E962.0	E980.4
rotavirus	979.6	E858.8	E949.6	E950.4	E962.0	E980.4
rubella virus	979.4	E858.8	E949.4	E950.4	E962.0	E980.4
sabin oral	979.5	E858.8	E949.5	E950.4	E962.0	E980.4
smallpox	979.0	E858.8	E949.0	E950.4	E962.0	E980.4
tetanus	978.4	E858.8	E948.4	E950.4	E962.0	E980.4
typhoid	978.1	E858.8	E948.1	E950.4	E962.0	E980.4
typhus	979.2	E858.8	E949.2	E950.4	E962.0	E980.4
viral NEC	979.6	E858.8	E949.6	E950.4	E962.0	E980.4
with						
bacterial component	979.7	E858.8	E949.7	E950.4	E962.0	E980.4
pertussis component	978.6	E858.8	E948.6	E950.4	E962.0	E980.4
rickettsial component	979.7	E858.8	E949.7	E950.4	E962.0	E980.4
yellow fever	979.3	E858.8	E949.3	E950.4	E962.0	E980.4
Vaccinia immune globulin (human)	964.6	E858.2	E934.6	E950.4	E962.0	E980.4
Vaginal contraceptives	976.8	E858.7	E946.8	E950.4	E962.0	E980.4
Valethamate	971.1	E855.4	E941.1	E950.4	E962.0	E980.4
Valisone	976.0	E858.7	E946.0	E950.4	E962.0	E980.4
Valium	969.4	E853.2	E939.4	E950.3	E962.0	E980.3
Valmid	967.8	E852.8	E937.8	E950.2	E962.0	E980.2
Vanadium	985.8	E866.4	—	E950.9	E962.1	E980.9
Vancomycin	960.8	E856	E930.8	E950.4	E962.0	E980.4
Vapor — *see also* Gas	987.9	E869.9	—	E952.9	E962.2	E982.9
kiln (carbon monoxide)	986	E868.8	—	E952.1	E962.2	E982.1
Vapor — *see also* Gas — *continued*						
lead — see Lead						
specified source NEC (see also specific substance)	987.8	E869.8	—	E952.8	E962.2	E982.8
Varidase	964.4	E858.2	E934.4	E950.4	E962.0	E980.4
Varnish	989.89	E861.6	—	E950.9	E962.1	E980.9
cleaner	982.8	E862.9	—	E950.9	E962.1	E980.9
Vaseline	976.3	E858.7	E946.3	E950.4	E962.0	E980.4
Vasodilan	972.5	E858.3	E942.5	E950.4	E962.0	E980.4
Vasodilators NEC	972.5	E858.3	E942.5	E950.4	E962.0	E980.4
coronary	972.4	E858.3	E942.4	E950.4	E962.0	E980.4
Vasopressin	962.5	E858.0	E932.5	E950.4	E962.0	E980.4
Vasopressor drugs	962.5	E858.0	E932.5	E950.4	E962.0	E980.4
Venom, venomous (bite) (sting)	989.5	E905.9	—	E950.9	E962.1	E980.9
arthropod NEC	989.5	E905.5	—	E950.9	E962.1	E980.9
bee	989.5	E905.3	—	E950.9	E962.1	E980.9
centipede	989.5	E905.4	—	E950.9	E962.1	E980.9
hornet	989.5	E905.3	—	E950.9	E962.1	E980.9
lizard	989.5	E905.0	—	E950.9	E962.1	E980.9
marine animals or plants	989.5	E905.6	—	E950.9	E962.1	E980.9
millipede (tropical)	989.5	E905.4	—	E950.9	E962.1	E980.9
plant NEC	989.5	E905.7	—	E950.9	E962.1	E980.9
marine	989.5	E905.6	—	E950.9	E962.1	E980.9
scorpion	989.5	E905.2	—	E950.9	E962.1	E980.9
snake	989.5	E905.0	—	E950.9	E962.1	E980.9
specified NEC	989.5	E905.8	—	E950.9	E962.1	E980.9
spider	989.5	E905.1	—	E950.9	E962.1	E980.9
wasp	989.5	E905.3	—	E950.9	E962.1	E980.9
Ventolin — *see* Salbutamol sulfate						
Veramon	967.0	E851	E937.0	E950.1	E962.0	E980.1
Veratrum						
album	988.2	E865.4	—	E950.9	E962.1	E980.9
alkaloids	972.6	E858.3	E942.6	E950.4	E962.0	E980.4
viride	988.2	E865.4	—	E950.9	E962.1	E980.9
Verdigris — *see also* Copper	985.8	E866.4	—	E950.9	E962.1	E980.9
Veronal	967.0	E851	E937.0	E950.1	E962.0	E980.1
Veroxil	961.6	E857	E931.6	E950.4	E962.0	E980.4
Versidyne	965.7	E850.7	E935.7	E950.0	E962.0	E980.0
Viagra	972.5	E858.3	E942.5	E950.4	E962.0	E980.4
Vienna						
green	985.1	E866.3	—	E950.8	E962.1	E980.8
insecticide	985.1	E863.4	—	E950.6	E962.1	E980.7
red	989.89	E866.8	—	E950.9	E962.1	E980.9
pharmaceutical dye	977.4	E858.8	E947.4	E950.4	E962.0	E980.4
Vinbarbital, vinbarbitone	967.0	E851	E937.0	E950.1	E962.0	E980.1
Vinblastine	963.1	E858.1	E933.1	E950.4	E962.0	E980.4
Vincristine	963.1	E858.1	E933.1	E950.4	E962.0	E980.4
Vinesthene, vinethene	968.2	E855.1	E938.2	E950.4	E962.0	E980.4
Vinyl						
bital	967.0	E851	E937.0	E950.1	E962.0	E980.1
ether	968.2	E855.1	E938.2	E950.4	E962.0	E980.4
Vioform	961.3	E857	E931.3	E950.4	E962.0	E980.4
topical	976.0	E858.7	E946.0	E930.4	E962.0	E980.4
Viomycin	960.6	E856	E930.6	E950.4	E962.0	E980.4
Viosterol	963.5	E858.1	E933.5	E950.4	E962.0	E980.4
Viper (venom)	989.5	E905.0	—	E950.9	E962.1	E980.9
Viprynium (embonate)	961.6	E857	E931.6	E950.4	E962.0	E980.4
Virugon	961.7	E857	E931.7	E950.4	E962.0	E980.4
Visine	976.5	E858.7	E946.5	E950.4	E962.0	E980.4
Vitamins NEC	963.5	E858.1	E933.5	E950.4	E962.0	E980.4
B_{12}	964.1	E858.2	E934.1	E950.4	E962.0	E980.4
hematopoietic	964.1	E858.2	E934.1	E950.4	E962.0	E980.4
K	964.3	E858.2	E934.3	E950.4	E962.0	E980.4
Vleminckx's solution	976.4	E858.7	E946.4	E950.4	E962.0	E980.4
Voltaren — *see* Diclofenac sodium						
Warfarin (potassium) (sodium)	964.2	E858.2	E934.2	E950.4	E962.0	E980.4
rodenticide	989.4	E863.7	—	E950.6	E962.1	E980.7
Wasp (sting)	989.5	E905.3	—	E950.9	E962.1	E980.9
Water						
balance agents NEC	974.5	E858.5	E944.5	E950.4	E962.0	E980.4
gas	987.1	E868.1	—	E951.8	E962.2	E981.8
incomplete combustion of — see Carbon, monoxide, fuel, utility						
hemlock	988.2	E865.4	—	E950.9	E962.1	E980.9

		External Cause (E-Code)				
	Poisoning	Accident	Therapeutic Use	Suicide Attempt	Assault	Undetermined
Water — *continued*						
moccasin (venom)	989.5	E905.0	—	E950.9	E962.1	E980.9
Wax (paraffin) (petroleum)	981	E862.3	—	E950.9	E962.1	E980.9
automobile	989.89	E861.2	—	E950.9	E962.1	E980.9
floor	981	E862.0	—	E950.9	E962.1	E980.9
Weed killers NEC	989.4	E863.5	—	E950.6	E962.1	E980.7
Welldorm	967.1	E852.0	E937.1	E950.2	E962.0	E980.2
White						
arsenic — see Arsenic						
hellebore	988.2	E865.4	—	E950.9	E962.1	E980.9
lotion (keratolytic)	976.4	E858.7	E946.4	E950.4	E962.0	E980.4
spirit	981	E862.0	—	E950.9	E962.1	E980.9
Whitewashes	989.89	E861.6	—	E950.9	E962.1	E980.9
Whole blood	964.7	E858.2	E934.7	E950.4	E962.0	E980.4
Wild						
black cherry	988.2	E865.4	—	E950.9	E962.1	E980.9
poisonous plants NEC	988.2	E865.4	—	E950.9	E962.1	E980.9
Window cleaning fluid	989.89	E861.3	—	E950.9	E962.1	E980.9
Wintergreen (oil)	976.3	E858.7	E946.3	E950.4	E962.0	E980.4
Witch hazel	976.2	E858.7	E946.2	E950.4	E962.0	E980.4
Wood						
alcohol	980.1	E860.2	—	E950.9	E962.1	E980.9
spirit	980.1	E860.2	—	E950.9	E962.1	E980.9
Woorali	975.2	E858.6	E945.2	E950.4	E962.0	E980.4
Wormseed, American	961.6	E857	E931.6	E950.4	E962.0	E980.4
Xanthine diuretics	974.1	E858.5	E944.1	E950.4	E962.0	E980.4
Xanthocillin	960.0	E856	E930.0	E950.4	E962.0	E980.4
Xanthotoxin	976.3	E858.7	E946.3	E950.4	E962.0	E980.4
Xigris	964.2	E858.2	E934.2	E950.4	E962.0	E980.4
Xylene (liquid) (vapor)	982.0	E862.4	—	E950.9	E962.1	E980.9
Xylocaine (infiltration) (topical)	968.5	E855.2	E938.5	E950.4	E962.0	E980.4
nerve block (peripheral) (plexus)	968.6	E855.2	E938.6	E950.4	E962.0	E980.4
spinal	968.7	E855.2	E938.7	E950.4	E962.0	E980.4
Xylol (liquid) (vapor)	982.0	E862.4	—	E950.9	E962.1	E980.9
Xylometazoline	971.2	E855.5	E941.2	E950.4	E962.0	E980.4
Yellow						
fever vaccine	979.3	E858.8	E949.3	E950.4	E962.0	E980.4
jasmine	988.2	E865.4	—	E950.9	E962.1	E980.9
Yew	988.2	E865.4	—	E950.9	E962.1	E980.9
Zactane	965.7	E850.7	E935.7	E950.0	E962.0	E980.0
Zaroxolyn	974.3	E858.5	E944.3	E950.4	E962.0	E980.4
Zephiran (topical)	976.0	E858.7	E946.0	E950.4	E962.0	E980.4
ophthalmic preparation	976.5	E858.7	E946.5	E950.4	E962.0	E980.4
Zerone	980.1	E860.2	—	E950.9	E962.1	E980.9
Zinc (compounds) (fumes) (salts) (vapor) NEC	985.8	E866.4	—	E950.9	E962.1	E980.9
anti-infectives	976.0	E858.7	E946.0	E950.4	E962.0	E980.4
antivaricose	972.7	E858.3	E942.7	E950.4	E962.0	E980.4
bacitracin	976.0	E858.7	E946.0	E950.4	E962.0	E980.4
chloride	976.2	E858.7	E946.2	E950.4	E962.0	E980.4
gelatin	976.3	E858.7	E946.3	E950.4	E962.0	E980.4
oxide	976.3	E858.7	E946.3	E950.4	E962.0	E980.4
peroxide	976.0	E858.7	E946.0	E950.4	E962.0	E980.4
pesticides	985.8	E863.4	—	E950.6	E962.1	E980.7
phosphide (rodenticide)	985.8	E863.7	—	E950.6	E962.1	E980.7
stearate	976.3	E858.7	E946.3	E950.4	E962.0	E980.4
sulfate (antivaricose)	972.7	E858.3	E942.7	E950.4	E962.0	E980.4
ENT agent	976.6	E858.7	E946.6	E950.4	E962.0	E980.4
ophthalmic solution	976.5	E858.7	E946.5	E950.4	E962.0	E980.4
topical NEC	976.0	E858.7	E946.0	E950.4	E962.0	E980.4
undecylenate	976.0	E858.7	E946.0	E950.4	E962.0	E980.4
Zovant	964.2	E858.2	E934.2	E950.4	E962.0	E980.4
Zoxazolamine	968.0	E855.1	E938.0	E950.4	E962.0	E980.4
Zygadenus (venenosus)	988.2	E865.4	—	E950.9	E962.1	E980.9

SECTION 3

Alphabetic Index to External Causes of Injury and Poisoning (E Code)

This section contains the index to the codes which classify environmental events, circumstances, and other conditions as the cause of injury and other adverse effects. Where a code from the section Supplementary Classification of External Causes of Injury and Poisoning (E800-E999) is applicable, it is intended that the E code shall be used in addition to a code from the main body of the classification, Chapters 1 to 17.

The alphabetic index to the E codes is organized by main terms which describe the accident, circumstance, event, or specific agent which caused the injury or other adverse effect.

Note — Transport accidents (E800-E848) include accidents involving:

aircraft and spacecraft (E840-E845)

watercraft (E830-E838)

motor vehicle (E810-E825)

railway (E800-E807)

other road vehicles (E826-E829)

For definitions and examples related to transport accidents — see Volume 1 code categories E800-E848.

The fourth-digit subdivisions for use with categories E800-E848 to identify the injured person are found at the end of this section.

For identifying the place in which an accident or poisoning occurred (circumstances classifiable to categories E850-E869 and E880-E928) — see the listing in this section under "Accident, occurring."

See the Table of Drugs and Chemicals (Section 2 of this volume) for identifying the specific agent involved in drug overdose or a wrong substance given or taken in error, and for intoxication or poisoning by a drug or other chemical substance.

The specific adverse effect, reaction, or localized toxic effect to a correct drug or substance properly administered in therapeutic or prophylactic dosage should be classified according to the nature of the adverse effect (e.g., allergy, dermatitis, tachycardia) listed in Section 1 of this volume.

A

Index

Assault — Catching fire —

☑ Additional Digit Required — Refer to the Tabular List for Digit Selection
Subterms under main terms may continue to next column or page

D

E

- **Fall, falling** — *continued*
  - in, on — *continued*
    - object
      - edged, pointed or sharp E888.0
      - other E888.1
    - pitchfork E888.0
    - railway rolling stock, train, vehicle (while alighting, boarding) E804 ☑
      - with
        - collision (*see also* Collision, railway) E800 ☑
        - derailment (*see also* Derailment, railway) E802 ☑
        - explosion (see also Explosion, railway engine) E803 ☑
    - scaffolding E881.1
    - scissors E888.0
    - staircase, stairs, steps (*see also* Fall, from, stairs) E880.9
    - street car E829 ☑
    - water transport (*see also* Fall, in, boat) E835 ☑
  - into
    - cavity E883.9
    - dock E883.9
      - from boat, ship, watercraft (*see also* Fall, from, boat) E832 ☑
    - hold (of ship) E834 ☑
      - due to accident to watercraft E831 ☑
    - hole E883.9
    - manhole E883.2
    - moving part of machinery — *see* Accident, machine
    - opening in surface NEC E883.9
    - pit E883.9
    - quarry E883.9
    - shaft E883.9
    - storm drain E883.2
    - tank E883.9
    - water (with drowning or submersion) E910.9
    - well E883.1
  - late effect of NEC E929.3
  - object (*see also* Hit by, object, falling) E916
  - other E888.8
  - over
    - animal E885.9
    - cliff E884.1
    - embankment E884.9
    - small object E885.9
  - overboard (*see also* Fall, from, boat) E832 ☑
  - resulting in striking against object E888.1
    - sharp E888.0
  - rock E916
  - same level NEC E888.9
    - aircraft (any kind) E843 ☑
      - resulting from accident to aircraft — *see* categories E840-E842 ☑
    - boat, ship, watercraft E835 ☑
      - due to accident to, collision, watercraft E831 ☑
    - from
      - collision, pushing, shoving, by or with other person(s) E886.9
        - as, or caused by, a crowd E917.6
        - in sports E886.0
      - in-line skates E885.1
      - roller skates E885.1
      - scooter (nonmotorized) E885.0
      - skateboard E885.2
      - slipping stumbling, tripping E885 ☑
      - snowboard E885.4
  - snowslide E916
    - as avalanche E909.2
  - stone E916
- **Fall, falling** — *continued*
  - through
    - hatch (on ship) E834 ☑
      - due to accident to watercraft E831 ☑
    - roof E882
    - window E882
  - timber E916
  - while alighting from, boarding, entering, leaving
    - aircraft (any kind) E843 ☑
    - motor bus, motor vehicle — *see* Fall, from, motor vehicle, while alighting, boarding
    - nonmotor road vehicle NEC E829 ☑
    - railway train E804 ☑
    - street car E829 ☑
- **Fell or jumped from high place, so stated** — *see* Jumping, from, high place
- **Felo-de-se** — *see also* Suicide E958.9
- **Fever**
  - heat — *see* Heat
  - thermic — *see* Heat
- **Fight** (hand) (fist) (foot) — *see also* Assault, fight E960.0
- **Fire** (accidental) (caused by great heat from appliance (electrical), hot object or hot substance) (secondary, resulting from explosion) E899
  - conflagration — *see* Conflagration
  - controlled, normal (in brazier, fireplace, furnace, or stove) (charcoal) (coal) (coke) (electric) (gas) (wood)
    - bonfire E897
    - brazier, not in building or structure E897
    - in building or structure, except private dwelling (barn) (church) (convalescent or residential home) (factory) (farm outbuilding) (hospital) (hotel) (institution (educational) (dormitory) (residential)) (private garage) (school) (shop) (store) (theatre) E896
    - in private dwelling (apartment) (boarding house) (camping place) (caravan) (farmhouse) (home (private)) (house) (lodging house) (rooming house) (tenement) E895
    - not in building or structure E897
    - trash E897
  - forest (uncontrolled) E892
  - grass (uncontrolled) E892
  - hay (uncontrolled) E892
  - homicide (attempt) E968.0
    - late effect of E969
  - in, of, on, starting in E892
    - aircraft (in transit) (powered) E841 ☑
      - at landing, take-off E840 ☑
      - stationary E892
      - unpowered (balloon) (glider) E842 ☑
    - balloon E842 ☑
    - boat, ship, watercraft — *see* categories E830 ☑, E831 ☑, E837 ☑
    - building or structure, except private dwelling (barn) (church) (convalescent or residential home) (factory) (farm outbuilding) (hospital) (hotel) (institution (educational) (dormitory) (residential)) (school) (shop) (store) (theatre) (*see also* Conflagration, building or structure, except private dwelling) E891.9
    - forest (uncontrolled) E892
    - glider E842 ☑
    - grass (uncontrolled) E892
- **Fire**, hot object or hot substance — *continued*
  - in, of, on, starting in — *continued*
    - hay (uncontrolled) E892
    - lumber (uncontrolled) E892
    - machinery — *see* Accident, machine
    - mine (uncontrolled) E892
    - motor vehicle (in motion) (on public highway) E818 ☑
      - not on public highway E825 ☑
      - stationary E892
    - prairie (uncontrolled) E892
    - private dwelling (apartment) (boarding house) (camping place) (caravan) (farmhouse) (home (private)) (house) (lodging house) (private garage) (rooming house) (tenement) (*see also* Conflagration, private dwelling) E890.9
    - railway rolling stock, train, vehicle (*see also* Explosion, railway engine) E803 ☑
      - stationary E892
    - room NEC E898.1
    - street car (in motion) E829 ☑
      - stationary E892
    - terrorism (by fire-producing device) E979.3
      - fittings or furniture (burning building) (uncontrolled fire) E979.3
      - from nuclear explosion E979.5
    - transport vehicle, stationary NEC E892
    - tunnel (uncontrolled) E892
    - war operations (by fire-producing device or conventional weapon) E990.9
      - from nuclear explosion E996
      - petrol bomb E990.0
  - late effect of NEC E929.4
  - lumber (uncontrolled) E892
  - mine (uncontrolled) E892
  - prairie (uncontrolled) E892
  - self-inflicted (unspecified whether accidental or intentional) E988.1
    - stated as intentional, purposeful E958.1
  - specified NEC E898.1
    - with
      - conflagration — *see* Conflagration
      - ignition (of)
        - clothing — *see* Ignition, clothes
        - highly inflammable material (benzine) (fat) (gasoline) (kerosene) (paraffin) (petrol) E894
  - started by other person
    - stated as
      - with intent to injure or kill E968.0
      - undetermined whether or not with intent to injure or kill E988.1
  - suicide (attempted) E958.1
    - late effect of E959
  - tunnel (uncontrolled) E892
- **Fireball effects from nuclear explosion**
  - in
    - terrorism E979.5
    - war operations E996
- **Fireworks** (explosion) E923.0
- **Flash burns from explosion** — *see also* Explosion E923.9
- **Flood** (any injury) (resulting from storm) E908.2
  - caused by collapse of dam or manmade structure E909.3
- **Forced landing** (aircraft) E840 ☑
- **Foreign body, object or material** (entrance into) (accidental)
  - air passage (causing injury) E915
    - with asphyxia, obstruction, suffocation E912
      - food or vomitus E911
    - nose (with asphyxia, obstruction, suffocation) E912
      - causing injury without asphyxia, obstruction, suffocation E915
  - alimentary canal (causing injury) (with obstruction) E915
    - with asphyxia, obstruction respiratory passage, suffocation E912
      - food E911
    - mouth E915
      - with asphyxia, obstruction, suffocation E912
        - food E911
    - pharynx E915
      - with asphyxia, obstruction, suffocation E912
        - food E911
  - aspiration (with asphyxia, obstruction respiratory passage, suffocation) E912
    - causing injury without asphyxia, obstruction respiratory passage, suffocation E915
    - food (regurgitated) (vomited) E911
      - causing injury without asphyxia, obstruction respiratory passage, suffocation E915
    - mucus (not of newborn) E912
    - phlegm E912
  - bladder (causing injury or obstruction) E915
  - bronchus, bronchi — *see* Foreign body, air passages
  - conjunctival sac E914
  - digestive system — *see* Foreign body, alimentary canal
  - ear (causing injury or obstruction) E915
  - esophagus (causing injury or obstruction) (*see also* Foreign body, alimentary canal) E915
  - eye (any part) E914
  - eyelid E914
  - hairball (stomach) (with obstruction) E915
  - ingestion — *see* Foreign body, alimentary canal
  - inhalation — *see* Foreign body, aspiration
  - intestine (causing injury or obstruction) E915
  - iris E914
  - lacrimal apparatus E914
  - larynx — *see* Foreign body, air passage
  - late effect of NEC E929.8
  - lung — *see* Foreign body, air passage
  - mouth — *see* Foreign body, alimentary canal, mouth
  - nasal passage — *see* Foreign body, air passage, nose
  - nose — *see* Foreign body, air passage, nose
  - ocular muscle E914
  - operation wound (left in) — *see* Misadventure, foreign object
  - orbit E914
  - pharynx — *see* Foreign body, alimentary canal, pharynx
  - rectum (causing injury or obstruction) E915
  - stomach (hairball) (causing injury or obstruction) E915
  - tear ducts or glands E914
  - trachea — *see* Foreign body, air passage
  - urethra (causing injury or obstruction) E915

J

K

Kicking against — *continued*
- object — *continued*
  - in sports E917.0
    - with subsequent fall E917.5
  - stationary E917.4
    - with subsequent fall E917.8
- person — *see* Striking against, person

Killed, killing (accidentally) NEC — *see also* Injury E928.9
- in
  - action — *see* War operations
  - brawl, fight (hand) (fists) (foot) E960.0
    - by weapon (*see also* Assault)
      - cutting, piercing E966
      - firearm — *see* Shooting, homicide
- self
  - stated as
    - accident E928.9
    - suicide — *see* Suicide
  - unspecified whether accidental or suicidal E988.9

Knocked down (accidentally) (by) NEC E928.9
- animal (not being ridden) E906.8
  - being ridden (in sport or transport) E828 ☑
- blast from explosion (*see also* Explosion) E923.9
- crowd, human stampede E917.6
- late effect of — *see* Late effect
- person (accidentally) E917.9
  - in brawl, fight E960.0
  - in sports E917.5
- transport vehicle — *see* vehicle involved under Hit by
- while boxing E917.5

L

Laceration NEC E928.9

Lack of
- air (refrigerator or closed place), suffocation by E913.2
- care (helpless person) (infant) (newborn) E904.0
  - homicidal intent E968.4
- food except as result of transport accident E904.1
  - helpless person, infant, newborn due to
    - abandonment or neglect E904.0
- water except as result of transport accident E904.2
  - helpless person, infant, newborn due to
    - abandonment or neglect E904.0

Landslide E909.2
- falling on, hitting
  - motor vehicle (any) (in motion) (on or off public highway) E909.2
  - railway rolling stock, train, vehicle E909.2

Late effect of
- accident NEC (accident classifiable to E928.9) E929.9
  - specified NEC (accident classifiable to E910–E928.8) E929.8
- assault E969
- fall, accidental (accident classifiable to E880–E888) E929.3
- fire, accident caused by (accident classifiable to E890–E899) E929.4
- homicide, attempt (any means) E969
- injury due to terrorism E999.1
- injury undetermined whether accidentally or purposely inflicted (injury classifiable to E980–E988) E989
- legal intervention (injury classifiable to E970–E976) E977
- medical or surgical procedure, test or therapy
  - as, or resulting in, or from
    - abnormal or delayed reaction or complication — *see* Reaction, abnormal
    - misadventure — *see* Misadventure
- motor vehicle accident (accident classifiable to E810–E825) E929.0
- natural or environmental factor, accident due to (accident classifiable to E900–E909) E929.5
- poisoning, accidental (accident classifiable to E850–E858, E860–E869) E929.2
- suicide, attempt (any means) E959
- transport accident NEC (accident classifiable to E800–E807, E826–E838, E840–E848) E929.1
- war operations, injury due to (injury classifiable to E990–E998) E999.0

Launching pad accident E845 ☑

Legal
- execution, any method E978
- intervention (by) (injury from) E976
  - baton E973
  - bayonet E974
  - blow E975
  - blunt object (baton) (nightstick) (stave) (truncheon) E973
  - cutting or piercing instrument E974
  - dynamite E971
  - execution, any method E973
  - explosive(s) (shell) E971
  - firearm(s) E970
  - gas (asphyxiation) (poisoning) (tear) E972
  - grenade E971
  - late effect of E977
  - machine gun E970
  - manhandling E975
  - mortar bomb E971
  - nightstick E973
  - revolver E970
  - rifle E970
  - specified means NEC E975
  - stabbing E974
  - stave E973
  - truncheon E973

Lifting, injury in E927

Lightning (shock) (stroke) (struck by) E907

Liquid (noncorrosive) in eye E914
- corrosive E924.1

Loss of control
- motor vehicle (on public highway) (without antecedent collision) E816 ☑
  - with
    - antecedent collision on public highway — *see* Collision, motor vehicle
      - involving any object, person or vehicle not on public highway E816 ☑
    - not on public highway, nontraffic accident E825 ☑
      - with antecedent collision — *see* Collision, motor vehicle, not on public highway
  - on public highway — *see* Collision, motor vehicle
- off-road type motor vehicle (not on public highway) E821 ☑
  - on public highway — *see* Loss of control, motor vehicle
- snow vehicle, motor-driven (not on public highway) E820 ☑
  - on public highway — *see* Loss of control, motor vehicle

Lost at sea E832 ☑
- with accident to watercraft E830 ☑
- in war operations E995

Low
- pressure, effects — *see* Effects of, air pressure
- temperature, effects — *see* Cold, exposure to

Lying before train, vehicle or other moving object (unspecified whether accidental or intentional) E988.0
- stated as intentional, purposeful, suicidal (attempt) E958.0

Lynching — *see also* Assault E968.9

M

Malfunction, atomic power plant in water transport E838 ☑

Mangled (accidentally) NEC E928.9

Manhandling (in brawl, fight) E960.0
- legal intervention E975

Manslaughter (nonaccidental) — *see* Assault

Marble in nose E912

Mauled by animal E906.8

Medical procedure, complication of
- delayed or as an abnormal reaction without mention of misadventure — *see* Reaction, abnormal
- due to or as a result of misadventure — *see* Misadventure

Melting of fittings and furniture in burning
- in terrorism E979.3

Minamata disease E865.2

Misadventure(s) to patient(s) during surgical or medical care E876.9
- contaminated blood, fluid, drug or biological substance (presence of agents and toxins as listed in E875) E875.9
  - administered (by) NEC E875.9
    - infusion E875.0
    - injection E875.1
    - specified means NEC E875.2
    - transfusion E875.0
    - vaccination E875.1
- cut, cutting, puncture, perforation or hemorrhage (accidental) (inadvertent) (inappropriate) (during) E870.9
  - aspiration of fluid or tissue (by puncture or catheterization, except heart) E870.5
  - biopsy E870.8
    - needle (aspirating) E870.5
  - blood sampling E870.5
  - catheterization E870.5
    - heart E870.6
  - dialysis (kidney) E870.2
  - endoscopic examination E870.4
  - enema E870.7
  - infusion E870.1
  - injection E870.3
  - lumbar puncture E870.5
  - needle biopsy E870.5
  - paracentesis, abdominal E870.5
  - perfusion E870.2
  - specified procedure NEC E870.8
  - surgical operation E870.0
  - thoracentesis E870.5
  - transfusion E870.1
  - vaccination E870.3
- excessive amount of blood or other fluid during transfusion or infusion E873.0
- failure
  - in dosage E873.9
    - electroshock therapy E873.4
    - inappropriate temperature (too hot or too cold) in local application and packing E873.5

Misadventure(s) to patient(s) during surgical or medical care — *continued*
- failure — *continued*
  - in dosage — *continued*
    - infusion
      - excessive amount of fluid E873.0
      - incorrect dilution of fluid E873.1
    - insulin-shock therapy E873.4
    - nonadministration of necessary drug or medicinal E873.6
    - overdose (*see also* Overdose)
      - radiation, in therapy E873.2
    - radiation
      - inadvertent exposure of patient (receiving radiation for test or therapy) E873.3
        - not receiving radiation for test or therapy — *see* Radiation
      - overdose E873.2
    - specified procedure NEC E873.8
    - transfusion
      - excessive amount of blood E873.0
  - mechanical, of instrument or apparatus (during procedure) E874.9
    - aspiration of fluid or tissue (by puncture or catheterization, except of heart) E874.4
    - biopsy E874.8
      - needle (aspirating) E874.4
    - blood sampling E874.4
    - catheterization E874.4
      - heart E874.5
    - dialysis (kidney) E874.2
    - endoscopic examination E874.3
    - enema E874.8
    - infusion E874.1
    - injection E874.8
    - lumbar puncture E874.4
    - needle biopsy E874.4
    - paracentesis, abdominal E874.4
    - perfusion E874.2
    - specified procedure NEC E874.8
    - surgical operation E874.0
    - thoracentesis E874.4
    - transfusion E874.1
    - vaccination E874.8
  - sterile precautions (during procedure) E872.9
    - aspiration of fluid or tissue (by puncture or catheterization, except heart) E872.5
    - biopsy E872.8
      - needle (aspirating) E872.5
    - blood sampling E872.5
    - catheterization E872.5
      - heart E872.6
    - dialysis (kidney) E872.2
    - endoscopic examination E872.4
    - enema E872.8
    - infusion E872.1
    - injection E872.3
    - lumbar puncture E872.5
    - needle biopsy E872.5
    - paracentesis, abdominal E872.5
    - perfusion E872.2
    - removal of catheter or packing E872.8
    - specified procedure NEC E872.8
    - surgical operation E872.0
    - thoracentesis E872.5
    - transfusion E872.1
    - vaccination E872.3
  - suture or ligature during surgical procedure E876.2
  - to introduce or to remove tube or instrument E876.4

Submersion (accidental) — *continued*
- due to — *continued*
  - hurricane E908.0
  - jumping into water E910.8
    - from boat, ship, watercraft
      - burning, crushed, sinking E830 ☑
      - involved in accident, collision E830 ☑
      - not involved in accident, for swim E910.2
    - in recreational activity (without diving equipment) E910.2
      - with or using diving equipment E910.1
    - to rescue another person E910.3
- homicide (attempt) E964
- in
  - bathtub E910.4
  - specified activity, not sport, transport or recreational E910.3
  - sport or recreational activity (without diving equipment) E910.2
    - with or using diving equipment E910.1
    - water skiing E910.0
  - swimming pool NEC E910.8
  - terrorism E979.8
  - war operations E995
  - water transport E832 ☑
    - due to accident to boat, ship, watercraft E830 ☑
- landslide E909.2
  - overturning boat, ship, watercraft E909.2
  - sinking boat, ship, watercraft E909.2
  - submersion boat, ship, watercraft E909.2
  - tidal wave E909.4
    - caused by storm E908.0
  - torrential rain E908.2
- late effect of NEC E929.8
- quenching tank E910.8
- self-inflicted (unspecified whether accidental or intentional) E984
  - in accidental circumstances — *see* category E910 ☑
  - stated as intentional, purposeful E954
- stated as undetermined whether accidental or intentional E984
- suicidal (attempted) E954
- while
  - attempting rescue of another person E910.3
  - engaged in
    - marine salvage E910.3
    - underwater construction or repairs E910.3
  - fishing, not from boat E910.2
  - hunting, not from boat E910.2
  - ice skating E910.2
  - pearl diving E910.3
  - placing fishing nets E910.3
  - playing in water E910.2
  - scuba diving E910.1
    - nonrecreational E910.3
  - skin diving E910.1
  - snorkel diving E910.2
  - spear fishing underwater E910.1
  - surfboarding E910.2
  - swimming (swimming pool) E910.2
  - wading (in water) E910.2
  - water skiing E910.0

Sucked
- into
  - jet (aircraft) E844 ☑

Suffocation (accidental) (by external means) (by pressure) (mechanical) E913.9

Suffocation — *continued*
- caused by other person
  - in accidental circumstances — *see* category E913 ☑
  - stated as
    - intentional, homicidal E963
    - undetermined whether accidental or intentional E983.9
      - by, in
        - hanging E983.0
        - plastic bag E983.1
        - specified means NEC E983.8
- due to, by
  - avalanche E909.2
  - bedclothes E913.0
  - bib E913.0
  - blanket E913.0
  - cave-in E913.3
    - caused by cataclysmic earth surface movement or eruption E909.9
  - conflagration — *see* Conflagration
  - explosion — *see* Explosion
  - falling earth, other substance E913.3
  - fire — *see* Fire
  - food, any type (ingestion) (inhalation) (regurgitated) (vomited) E911
  - foreign body, except food (ingestion) (inhalation) E912
  - ignition — *see* Ignition
  - landslide E909.2
  - machine(ry) — *see* Accident, machine
  - material, object except food entering by nose or mouth, ingested, inhaled E912
  - mucus (aspiration) (inhalation), not of newborn E912
  - phlegm (aspiration) (inhalation) E912
  - pillow E913.0
  - plastic bag — *see* Suffocation, in, plastic bag
  - sheet (plastic) E913.0
  - specified means NEC E913.8
  - vomitus (aspiration) (inhalation) E911
- homicidal (attempt) E963
- in
  - airtight enclosed place E913.2
  - baby carriage E913.0
  - bed E913.0
  - closed place E913.2
  - cot, cradle E913.0
  - perambulator E913.0
  - plastic bag (in accidental circumstances) E913.1
    - homicidal, purposely inflicted by other person E963
    - self-inflicted (unspecified whether accidental or intentional) E983.1
      - in accidental circumstances E913.1
    - intentional, suicidal E953.1
    - stated as undetermined whether accidentally or purposely inflicted E983.1
    - suicidal, purposely self-inflicted E953.1
  - refrigerator E913.2
- self-inflicted (*see also* Suffocation, stated as undetermined whether accidental or intentional) E953.9
  - in accidental circumstances — *see* category E913 ☑
  - stated as intentional, purposeful — *see* Suicide, suffocation
- stated as undetermined whether accidental or intentional E983.9
  - by, in
    - hanging E983.0

Suffocation — *continued*
- stated as undetermined whether accidental or intentional — *continued*
  - by, in — *continued*
    - plastic bag E983.1
    - specified means NEC E983.8
- suicidal — *see* Suicide, suffocation

Suicide, suicidal (attempted) (by) E958.9
- burning, burns E958.1
- caustic substance E958.7
  - poisoning E950.7
  - swallowed E950.7
- cold, extreme E958.3
- cut (any part of body) E956
- cutting or piercing instrument (classifiable to E920) E956
- drowning E954
- electrocution E958.4
- explosive(s) (classifiable to E923) E955.5
- fire E958.1
- firearm (classifiable to E922) — *see* Shooting, suicidal
- hanging E953.0
- jumping
  - before moving object, train, vehicle E958.0
  - from high place — *see* Jumping, from, high place, stated as, suicidal
- knife E956
- late effect of E959
- motor vehicle, crashing of E958.5
- poisoning — *see* Table of Drugs and Chemicals
- puncture (any part of body) E956
- scald E958.2
- shooting — *see* Shooting, suicidal
- specified means NEC E958.8
- stab (any part of body) E956
- strangulation — *see* Suicide, suffocation
- submersion E954
- suffocation E953.9
  - by, in
    - hanging E953.0
    - plastic bag E953.1
    - specified means NEC E953.8
- wound NEC E958.9

Sunburn E926.2

Sunstroke E900.0

Supersonic waves (causing injury) E928.1

Surgical procedure, complication of
- delayed or as an abnormal reaction without mention of misadventure — *see* Reaction, abnormal
- due to or as a result of misadventure — *see* Misadventure

Swallowed, swallowing
- foreign body — *see* Foreign body, alimentary canal
- poison — *see* Table of Drugs and Chemicals
- substance
  - caustic — *see* Table of Drugs and Chemicals
  - corrosive — *see* Table of Drugs and Chemicals
  - poisonous — *see* Table of Drugs and Chemicals

Swimmers cramp — *see also* category E910 E910.2
- not in recreation or sport E910.3

Syndrome, battered
- baby or child — *see* Abuse, child
- wife — *see* Assault

T

Tackle in sport E886.0

Terrorism (injury) (by) (in) E979.8
- air blast E979.2
- aircraft burned, destroyed, exploded, shot down E979.1
  - used as a weapon E979.1

Terrorism — *continued*
- anthrax E979.6
- asphyxia from
  - chemical (weapons) E979.7
  - fire, conflagration (caused by fire-producing device) E979.3
    - from nuclear explosion E979.5
  - gas or fumes E979.7
- bayonet E979.8
- biological agents E979.6
- blast (air) (effects) E979.2
  - from nuclear explosion E979.5
  - underwater E979.0
- bomb (antipersonnel) (mortar) (explosion) (fragments) E979.2
- bullet(s) (from carbine, machine gun, pistol, rifle, shotgun) E979.4
- burn from
  - chemical E979.7
  - fire, conflagration (caused by fire-producing device) E979.3
    - from nuclear explosion E979.5
  - gas E979.7
- burning aircraft E979.1
- chemical E979.7
- cholera E979.6
- conflagration E979.3
- crushed by falling aircraft E979.1
- depth-charge E979.0
- destruction of aircraft E979.1
- disability, as sequelae one year or more after injury E999.1
- drowning E979.8
- effect
  - of nuclear weapon (direct) (secondary) E979.5
  - secondary NEC E979.9
  - sequelae E999.1
- explosion (artillery shell) (breech-block) (cannon block) E979.2
  - aircraft E979.1
  - bomb (antipersonnel) (mortar) E979.2
    - nuclear (atom) (hydrogen) E979.5
  - depth-charge E979.0
  - grenade E979.2
  - injury by fragments from E979.2
  - land-mine E979.2
  - marine weapon E979.0
  - mine (land) E979.2
    - at sea or in harbor E979.0
    - marine E979.0
  - missile (explosive) NEC E979.2
  - munitions (dump) (factory) E979.2
  - nuclear (weapon) E979.5
    - other direct and secondary effects of E979.5
  - sea-based artillery shell E979.0
  - torpedo E979.0
- exposure to ionizing radiation from nuclear explosion E979.5
- falling aircraft E979.1
- firearms E979.4
- fireball effects from nuclear explosion E979.5
- fire or fire-producing device E979.3
- fragments from artillery shell, bomb NEC, grenade, guided missile, land-mine, rocket, shell, shrapnel E979.2
- gas or fumes E979.7
- grenade (explosion) (fragments) E979.2
- guided missile (explosion) (fragments) E979.2
  - nuclear E979.5
- heat from nuclear explosion E979.5
- hot substances E979.3
- hydrogen cyanide E979.7
- land-mine (explosion) (fragments) E979.2
- laser(s) E979.8
- late effect of E999.1
- lewisite E979.7

☑ Additional Digit Required — Refer to the Tabular List for Digit Selection

▼ Subterms under main terms may continue to next column or page

Railway Accidents (E800-E807)

The following fourth-digit subdivisions are for use with categories E800-E807 to identify the injured person:

.0 Railway employee
Any person who by virtue of his employment in connection with a railway, whether by the railway company or not, is at increased risk of involvement in a railway accident, such as:
catering staff on train
postal staff on train
driver
railway fireman
guard
shunter
porter
sleeping car attendant

.1 Passenger on railway
Any authorized person traveling on a train, except a railway employee
EXCLUDES intending passenger waiting at station (.8)
unauthorized rider on railway vehicle (.8)

.2 Pedestrian See definition (r), E-Codes-2

.3 Pedal cyclist See definition (p), E-Codes-2

.8 Other specified person Intending passenger waiting at station
Unauthorized rider on railway vehicle

.9 Unspecified person

Motor Vehicle Traffic and Nontraffic Accidents (E810-E825)

The following fourth-digit subdivisions are for use with categories E810-E819 and E820-E825 to identify the injured person:

.0 Driver of motor vehicle other than motorcycle See definition (1), E-Codes-2

.1 Passenger in motor vehicle other than motorcycle See definition (1), E-Codes-2

.2 Motorcyclist See definition (1), E-Codes-2

.3 Passenger on motorcycle See definition (1), E-Codes-2

.4 Occupant of streetcar

.5 Rider of animal; occupant of animal-drawn vehicle

.6 Pedal cyclist See definition (p), E-Codes-2

.7 Pedestrian See definition (r), E-Codes-2

.8 Other specified person
Occupant of vehicle other than above
Person in railway train involved in accident
Unauthorized rider of motor vehicle

.9 Unspecified person

Other Road Vehicle Accidents (E826-E829)

(animal-drawn vehicle, streetcar, pedal cycle, and other nonmotor road vehicle accidents)

The following fourth-digit subdivisions are for use with categories E826-E829 to identify the injured person:

.0 Pedestrian See definition (r), E-Codes-2

.1 Pedal cyclist (does not apply to codes E827, E828, E829) See definition (p), E-Codes-2

.2 Rider of animal (does not apply to code E829)

.3 Occupant of animal-drawn vehicle (does not apply to codes E828, E829)

.4 Occupant of streetcar

.8 Other specified person

.9 Unspecified person

Water Transport Accidents (E830-E838)

The following fourth-digit subdivisions are for use with categories E830-E838 to identify the injured person:

.0 Occupant of small boat, unpowered

.1 Occupant of small boat, powered See definition (t), E-Codes-2
EXCLUDES water skier (.4)

.2 Occupant of other watercraft — crew
Persons:
engaged in operation of watercraft
providing passenger services [cabin attendants, ship's physician, catering personnel]
working on ship during voyage in other capacity [musician in band, operators of shops and beauty parlors]

.3 Occupant of other watercraft — other than crew
Passenger
Occupant of lifeboat, other than crew, after abandoning ship

.4 Water skier

.5 Swimmer

.6 Dockers, stevedores
Longshoreman employed on the dock in loading and unloading ships

.8 Other specified person
Immigration and custom officials on board ship
Persons:
accompanying passenger or member of crew visiting boat
Pilot (guiding ship into port)

.9 Unspecified person

Air and Space Transport Accidents (E840-E845)

The following fourth-digit subdivisions are for use with categories E840-E845 to identify the injured person:

.0 Occupant of spacecraft
Crew
Passenger (civilian)
(military)
Troops
} in military aircraft [air force] [army] [national guard] [navy]

.1 Occupant of military aircraft, any
EXCLUDES occupants of aircraft operated under jurisdiction of police departments (.5) parachutist (.7)

.2 Crew of commercial aircraft (powered) in surface to surface transport

.3 Other occupant of commercial aircraft (powered) in surface to surface transport
Flight personnel:
not part of crew
on familiarization flight Passenger on aircraft

.4 Occupant of commercial aircraft (powered) in surface to air transport
Occupant [crew] [passenger] of aircraft (powered) engaged in activities, such as:
air drops of emergency supplies
air drops of parachutists, except from military craft
crop dusting
lowering of construction material [bridge or telephone pole]
sky writing

.5 Occupant of other powered aircraft
Occupant [crew] [passenger] of aircraft (powered) engaged in activities, such as:
aerial spraying (crops)(fire retardants)
aerobatic flying
aircraft racing
rescue operation
storm surveillance
traffic suveillance
Occupant of private plane NOS

.6 Occupant of unpowered aircraft, except parachutist
Occupant of aircraft classifiable to E842

.7 Parachutist (military)(other)
Person making voluntary descent
person making descent after accident to aircraft (.1-.6)

.8 Ground crew, airline employee
Persons employed at airfields (civil)(military) or launching pads, not occupants of aircraft

.9 Other person

1. INFECTIOUS AND PARASITIC DISEASES (001-139)

Note: Categories for "late effects" of infectious and parasitic diseases are to be found at 137-139.

INCLUDES diseases generally recognized as communicable or transmissible as well as a few diseases of unknown but possibly infectious origin

EXCLUDES *acute respiratory infections (460-466)*
carrier or suspected carrier of infectious organism (V02.0-V02.9)
certain localized infections
influenza (487.0-487.8)

INTESTINAL INFECTIOUS DISEASES (001-009)

EXCLUDES *helminthiases (120.0-129)*

✓4th **001 Cholera**

DEF: An acute infectious enteritis caused by a potent enterotoxin elaborated by *Vibrio cholerae*; the vibrio produces a toxin in the intestinal tract that changes the permeability of the mucosa leading to diarrhea and dehydration.

001.0 Due to Vibrio cholerae

001.1 Due to Vibrio cholerae el tor

001.9 Cholera, unspecified

✓4th **002 Typhoid and paratyphoid fevers**

DEF: Typhoid fever: an acute generalized illness caused by *Salmonella typhi*; notable clinical features are fever, headache, abdominal pain, cough, toxemia, leukopenia, abnormal pulse, rose spots on the skin, bacteremia, hyperplasia of intestinal lymph nodes, mesenteric lymphadenopathy, and Peyer's patches in the intestines.

DEF: Paratyphoid fever: a prolonged febrile illness, much like typhoid but usually less severe; caused by salmonella serotypes other than *S. typhi*, especially *S. enteritidis* serotypes paratyphi A and B and *S. choleraesuis*.

002.0 Typhoid fever
Typhoid (fever) (infection) [any site]

002.1 Paratyphoid fever A

002.2 Paratyphoid fever B

002.3 Paratyphoid fever C

002.9 Paratyphoid fever, unspecified

✓4th **003 Other salmonella infections**

INCLUDES infection or food poisoning by Salmonella [any serotype]

DEF: Infections caused by a genus of gram-negative, anaerobic bacteria of the family *Enterobacteriaceae*; affecting warm-blooded animals, like humans; major symptoms are enteric fevers, acute gastroenteritis and septicemia.

003.0 Salmonella gastroenteritis
Salmonellosis

003.1 Salmonella septicemia HIV

✓5th **003.2 Localized salmonella infections**

003.20 Localized salmonella infection, unspecified HIV

003.21 Salmonella meningitis HIV

003.22 Salmonella pneumonia HIV

003.23 Salmonella arthritis HIV

003.24 Salmonella osteomyelitis HIV

003.29 Other HIV

003.8 Other specified salmonella infections HIV

003.9 Salmonella infection, unspecified HIV

✓4th **004 Shigellosis**

INCLUDES bacillary dysentery

DEF: Acute infectious dysentery caused by the genus *Shigella*, of the family *Enterobacteriaceae*; affecting the colon causing the release of blood-stained stools with accompanying tenesmus, abdominal cramps and fever.

004.0 Shigella dysenteriae
Infection by group A Shigella (Schmitz) (Shiga)

004.1 Shigella flexneri
Infection by group B Shigella

004.2 Shigella boydii
Infection by group C Shigella

004.3 Shigella sonnei
Infection by group D Shigella

004.8 Other specified Shigella infections

004.9 Shigellosis, unspecified

✓4th **005 Other food poisoning (bacterial)**

EXCLUDES *salmonella infections (003.0-003.9)*
toxic effect of:
food contaminants (989.7)
noxious foodstuffs (988.0-988.9)

DEF: Enteritis caused by ingesting contaminated foods and characterized by diarrhea, abdominal pain, vomiting; symptoms may be mild or life threatening.

005.0 Staphylococcal food poisoning
Staphylococcal toxemia specified as due to food

005.1 Botulism
Food poisoning due to Clostridium botulinum

005.2 Food poisoning due to Clostridium perfringens [C. welchii]
Enteritis necroticans

005.3 Food poisoning due to other Clostridia

005.4 Food poisoning due to Vibrio parahaemolyticus

✓5th **005.8 Other bacterial food poisoning**

EXCLUDES *salmonella food poisoning (003.0-003.9)*

005.81 Food poisoning due to Vibrio vulnificus

005.89 Other bacterial food poisoning
Food poisoning due to Bacillus cereus

005.9 Food poisoning, unspecified

✓4th **006 Amebiasis**

INCLUDES infection due to Entamoeba histolytica

EXCLUDES *amebiasis due to organisms other than Entamoeba histolytica (007.8)*

DEF: Infection of the large intestine caused by *Entamoeba histolytica*; usually asymptomatic but symptoms may range from mild diarrhea to profound life-threatening dysentery. Extraintestinal complications include hepatic abscess, which may rupture into the lung, pericardium or abdomen, causing life-threatening infections.

006.0 Acute amebic dysentery without mention of abscess
Acute amebiasis

DEF: Sudden, severe *Entamoeba histolytica* infection causing bloody stools.

006.1 Chronic intestinal amebiasis without mention of abscess
Chronic:
amebiasis
amebic dysentery

006.2 Amebic nondysenteric colitis

DEF: *Entamoeba histolytica* infection with inflamed colon but no dysentery.

006.3 Amebic liver abscess
Hepatic amebiasis

006.4 Amebic lung abscess
Amebic abscess of lung (and liver)

006.5 Amebic brain abscess
Amebic abscess of brain (and liver) (and lung)

006.6 Amebic skin ulceration
Cutaneous amebiasis

006.8 Amebic infection of other sites
Amebic:
appendicitis
balanitis
Ameboma

EXCLUDES *specific infections by free-living amebae (136.2)*

006.9 Amebiasis, unspecified
Amebiasis NOS

4th **007 Other protozoal intestinal diseases**

INCLUDES protozoal:
colitis
diarrhea
dysentery

007.0 Balantidiasis
Infection by Balantidium coli

007.1 Giardiasis
Infection by Giardia lamblia
Lambliasis

007.2 Coccidiosis HIV
Infection by Isospora belli and Isospora hominis
Isosporiasis

007.3 Intestinal trichomoniasis
DEF: Colitis, diarrhea, or dysentery caused by the protozoa *Trichomonas.*

007.4 Cryptosporidiosis
AHA: 4Q, '97, 30
DEF: An intestinal infection by protozoan parasites causing intractable diarrhea in patients with AIDS and other immunosuppressed individuals.

007.5 Cyclosporiasis
AHA: 4Q, '00, 38
DEF: An infection of the small intestine by the protozoal organism, *Cyclospora caytenanesis*, spread to humans though ingestion of contaminated water or food. Symptoms include watery diarrhea with frequent explosive bowel movements, loss of appetite, loss of weight, bloating, increased gas, stomach cramps, nausea, vomiting, muscle aches, low grade fever, and fatigue.

007.8 Other specified protozoal intestinal diseases
Amebiasis due to organisms other than Entamoeba histolytica

007.9 Unspecified protozoal intestinal disease
Flagellate diarrhea
Protozoal dysentery NOS

4th **008 Intestinal infections due to other organisms**

INCLUDES any condition classifiable to 009.0-009.3 with mention of the responsible organisms

EXCLUDES *food poisoning by these organisms (005.0-005.9)*

5th **008.0 Escherichia coli [E. coli]**
AHA: 4Q, '92, 17

008.00 E. coli, unspecified
E. coli enteritis NOS

008.01 Enteropathogenic E. coli
DEF: *E. coli* causing inflammation of intestines.

008.02 Enterotoxigenic E. coli
DEF: A toxic reaction to *E. coli* of the intestinal mucosa, causing voluminous watery secretions.

008.03 Enteroinvasive E. coli
DEF: *E. coli* infection penetrating intestinal mucosa.

008.04 Enterohemorrhagic E. coli
DEF: *E. coli* infection penetrating the intestinal mucosa, producing microscopic ulceration and bleeding.

008.09 Other intestinal E. coli infections

008.1 Arizona group of paracolon bacilli

008.2 Aerobacter aerogenes
Enterobacter aeogenes

008.3 Proteus (mirabilis) (morganii)

5th **008.4 Other specified bacteria**
AHA: 4Q, '92, 18

008.41 Staphylococcus CC
Staphylococcal enterocolitis
CC Excl: 001.1, 002.0, 002.9-003.0, 004.9-005.2, 006.0-006.2, 006.9, 007.1-009.0, 014.80-014.86, 112.85, 129, 487.8, 536.3, 536.8, 555.0-557.9, 558.2-558.9, 564.1, 775.0-775.9, 777.5, 777.8

008.42 Pseudomonas CC
CC Excl: See code 008.41
AHA: 2Q, '89, 10

008.43 Campylobacter CC
CC Excl: See code 008.41

008.44 Yersinia enterocolitica CC
CC Excl: See code 008.41

008.45 Clostridium difficile CC
Pseudomembranous colitis
CC Excl: See code 008.41
DRG 182
DEF: An overgrowth of a species of bacterium that is a part of the normal colon flora in human infants and sometimes in adults; produces a toxin that causes pseudomembranous enterocolitis.; typically is seen in patients undergoing antibiotic therapy.

008.46 Other anaerobes CC
Anaerobic enteritis NOS
Bacteroides (fragilis)
Gram-negative anaerobes
CC Excl: See code 008.41

008.47 Other gram-negative bacteria CC
Gram-negative enteritis NOS
EXCLUDES *gram-negative anaerobes (008.46)*
CC Excl: See code 008.41

008.49 Other CC
CC Excl: See code 008.41
AHA: 2Q, '89, 10; 1Q, '88, 6

008.5 Bacterial enteritis, unspecified

5th **008.6 Enteritis due to specified virus**
AHA: 4Q, '92, 18

008.61 Rotavirus

008.62 Adenovirus

008.63 Norwalk virus
Norwalk-like agent

008.64 Other small round viruses [SRVs]
Small round virus NOS

008.65 Calicivirus
DEF: Enteritis due to a subgroup of *Picornaviruses.*

008.66 Astrovirus

008.67 Enterovirus NEC
Coxsackie virus
Echovirus
EXCLUDES *poliovirus (045.0-045.9)*

008.69 Other viral enteritis
Torovirus
AHA: 1Q, '03, 10

008.8 Other organism, not elsewhere classified
Viral:
enteritis NOS
Viral:
gastroenteritis
EXCLUDES *influenza with involvement of gastrointestinal tract (487.8)*
DRG 182

N Newborn Age: 0 | P Pediatric Age: 0-17 | M Maternity Age: 12-55 | A Adult Age: 15-124 | CC CC Condition | MC Major Complication | CD Complex Dx | HIV HIV Related Dx

✓4th 009 Ill-defined intestinal infections

EXCLUDES *diarrheal disease or intestinal infection due to specified organism (001.0-008.8)*
diarrhea following gastrointestinal surgery (564.4)
intestinal malabsorption (579.0-579.9)
ischemic enteritis (557.0-557.9)
other noninfectious gastroenteritis and colitis (558.1-558.9)
regional enteritis (555.0-555.9)
ulcerative colitis (556)

009.0 Infectious colitis, enteritis, and gastroenteritis

Colitis, Enteritis, Gastroenteritis } septic

Dysentery: NOS, catarrhal

Dysentery: hemorrhagic

AHA: 3Q, '99, 4

DEF: Colitis: An inflammation of mucous membranes of the colon.
DEF: Enteritis: An inflammation of mucous membranes of the small intestine.
DEF: Gastroenteritis: An inflammation of mucous membranes of stomach and intestines.

009.1 Colitis, enteritis, and gastroenteritis of presumed infectious origin

EXCLUDES *colitis NOS (558.9)*
enteritis NOS (558.9)
gastroenteritis NOS (558.9)

AHA: 3Q, '99, 6

009.2 Infectious diarrhea

Diarrhea:
dysenteric
epidemic
Infectious diarrheal disease NOS

009.3 Diarrhea of presumed infectious origin

EXCLUDES *diarrhea NOS (787.91)*

AHA: N-D, '87, 7

TUBERCULOSIS (010-018)

INCLUDES infection by Mycobacterium tuberculosis (human) (bovine)

EXCLUDES *congenital tuberculosis (771.2)*
late effects of tuberculosis (137.0-137.4)

The following fifth-digit subclassification is for use with categories 010-018:

0 unspecified
1 bacteriological or histological examination not done
2 bacteriological or histological examination unknown (at present)
3 tubercle bacilli found (in sputum) by microscopy
4 tubercle bacilli not found (in sputum) by microscopy, but found by bacterial culture
5 tubercle bacilli not found by bacteriological examination, but tuberculosis confirmed histologically
6 tubercle bacilli not found by bacteriological or histological examination but tuberculosis confirmed by other methods [inoculation of animals]

DEF: An infection by *Mycobacterium tuberculosis* causing the formation of small, rounded nodules, called tubercles, that can disseminate throughout the body via lymph and blood vessels. Localized tuberculosis is most often seen in the lungs.

✓4th 010 Primary tuberculous infection

DEF: Tuberculosis of the lungs occurring when the patient is first infected.

§ ✓5th **010.0 Primary tuberculous infection** HIV

EXCLUDES *nonspecific reaction to tuberculin skin test without active tuberculosis (795.5)*
positive PPD (795.5)
positive tuberculin skin test without active tuberculosis (795.5)

DEF: Hilar or paratracheal lymph node enlargement in pulmonary tuberculosis.

§ ✓5th **010.1 Tuberculous pleurisy in primary progressive tuberculosis** HIV

DEF: Inflammation and exudation in the lining of the tubercular lung.

§ ✓5th **010.8 Other primary progressive tuberculosis** HIV

EXCLUDES *tuberculous erythema nodosum (017.1)*

§ ✓5th **010.9 Primary tuberculous infection, unspecified** HIV

✓4th 011 Pulmonary tuberculosis HIV

Use additional code to identify any associated silicosis (502)

§ ✓5th **011.0 Tuberculosis of lung, infiltrative** CC HIV

CC Excl: 011.00-012.86, 017.90-018.96, 031.0, 031.2-031.9, 041.81-041.9, 137.0, 139.8, 480.0-480.2, 480.8-487.1, 494.0-508.9, 517.1, 518.89

§ ✓5th **011.1 Tuberculosis of lung, nodular** CC HIV

CC Excl: See code 011.0

§ ✓5th **011.2 Tuberculosis of lung with cavitation** CC HIV

CC Excl: See code 011.0

§ ✓5th **011.3 Tuberculosis of bronchus** CC HIV

EXCLUDES *isolated bronchial tuberculosis (012.2)*

CC Excl: See code 011.0

§ ✓5th **011.4 Tuberculous fibrosis of lung** CC HIV

CC Excl: See code 011.0

§ ✓5th **011.5 Tuberculous bronchiectasis** CC HIV

CC Excl: See code 011.0

§ ✓5th **011.6 Tuberculous pneumonia [any form]** CC HIV

CC Excl: For codes 011.60-011.65: See code 011.0

CC Excl: For code 011.66: 011.66, 139.8, 480.0-480.2, 480.8-487.1, 494.0-508.9, 517.1, 518.89

DEF: Inflammatory pulmonary reaction to tuberculous cells.

§ ✓5th **011.7 Tuberculous pneumothorax** CC HIV

CC Excl: See code 011.0

DEF: Spontaneous rupture of damaged tuberculous pulmonary tissue.

§ ✓5th **011.8 Other specified pulmonary tuberculosis** CC HIV

CC Excl: See code 011.0

§ ✓5th **011.9 Pulmonary tuberculosis, unspecified** CC HIV

Respiratory tuberculosis NOS
Tuberculosis of lung NOS

CC Excl: See code 011.0

§ Requires fifth-digit. See beginning of section 010-018 for codes and definitions.

✓4th **012 Other respiratory tuberculosis**
EXCLUDES *respiratory tuberculosis, unspecified (011.9)*

§ ✓5th **012.0 Tuberculous pleurisy** CC HIV
Tuberculosis of pleura
Tuberculous empyema
Tuberculous hydrothorax
EXCLUDES *pleurisy with effusion without mention of cause (511.9)*
tuberculous pleurisy in primary progressive tuberculosis (010.1)
CC Excl: See code 011.0
DEF: Inflammation and exudation in the lining of the tubercular lung.

§ ✓5th **012.1 Tuberculosis of intrathoracic lymph nodes** CC HIV
Tuberculosis of lymph nodes:
hilar
mediastinal
tracheobronchial
Tuberculous tracheobronchial adenopathy
EXCLUDES *that specified as primary (010.0-010.9)*
CC Excl: See code 011.0

§ ✓5th **012.2 Isolated tracheal or bronchial tuberculosis** HIV

§ ✓5th **012.3 Tuberculous laryngitis** HIV
Tuberculosis of glottis

§ ✓5th **012.8 Other specified respiratory tuberculosis** HIV
Tuberculosis of:
mediastinum
nasopharynx
Tuberculosis of:
nose (septum)
sinus [any nasal]

✓4th **013 Tuberculosis of meninges and central nervous system**

§ ✓5th **013.0 Tuberculous meningitis** CC HIV
Tuberculosis of meninges (cerebral) (spinal)
Tuberculous:
leptomeningitis
meningoencephalitis
EXCLUDES *tuberculoma of meninges (013.1)*
CC Excl: 003.21, 013.00-013.16, 013.40-013.56, 013.80-013.96, 017.90-017.96, 031.2, 031.8-031.9, 036.0, 041.81-041.89, 041.9, 047.0-047.9, 049.0-049.1, 053.0, 054.72, 072.1, 090.42, 091.81, 094.2, 098.89, 100.81, 112.83, 114.2, 115.01, 115.11, 115.91, 130.0, 137.1, 139.8, 320.0-320.9, 321.0-321.8, 322.0-322.9, 349.89, 349.9, 357.0

§ ✓5th **013.1 Tuberculoma of meninges** CC HIV
CC Excl: See code 013.0

§ ✓5th **013.2 Tuberculoma of brain** CC HIV
Tuberculosis of brain (current disease)
CC Excl: 013.20-013.36, 013.60-013.96, 017.90-017.96, 031.2-031.9, 041.81, 041.9, 137.1, 139.8

§ ✓5th **013.3 Tuberculous abscess of brain** CC HIV
CC Excl: See code 013.2

§ ✓5th **013.4 Tuberculoma of spinal cord** CC HIV
CC Excl: 013.00-013.16, 013.40-013.56, 013.80-013.96, 017.90-017.96, 031.2, 031.9, 041.81-041.89, 041.9, 137.1, 139.8

§ ✓5th **013.5 Tuberculous abscess of spinal cord** CC HIV
CC Excl: See code 013.4

§ ✓5th **013.6 Tuberculous encephalitis or myelitis** CC HIV
CC Excl: 013.20-013.36, 013.60-013.96, 017.90-017.96, 031.2-031.9, 041.81-041.89, 041.9, 137.1, 139.8

§ ✓5th **013.8 Other specified tuberculosis of central nervous system** CC HIV
CC Excl: 013.80-013.96, 017.90-017.96, 031.2-031.9, 041.81-041.89, 041.9, 137.1, 139.8

§ ✓5th **013.9 Unspecified tuberculosis of central nervous system** CC HIV
Tuberculosis of central nervous system NOS
CC Excl: See code 013.8

✓4th **014 Tuberculosis of intestines, peritoneum, and mesenteric glands**

§ ✓5th **014.0 Tuberculous peritonitis** CC HIV
Tuberculous ascites
CC Excl: 014.00-014.86, 017.90-017.96, 031.2-031.9, 041.81-041.9, 139.8
DEF: Tuberculous inflammation of the membrane lining the abdomen.

§ ✓5th **014.8 Other** CC HIV
Tuberculosis (of):
anus
intestine (large) (small)
mesenteric glands
rectum
retroperitoneal (lymph nodes)
Tuberculous enteritis
CC Excl: For code 014.80, 014.82-014.86: See code 014.0
CC Excl: For code 014.81: 014.81, 139.8

✓4th **015 Tuberculosis of bones and joints**
Use additional code to identify manifestation, as:
tuberculous:
arthropathy (711.4)
necrosis of bone (730.8)
osteitis (730.8)
osteomyelitis (730.8)
synovitis (727.01)
tenosynovitis (727.01)

§ ✓5th **015.0 Vertebral column** HIV
Pott's disease
Use additional code to identify manifestation, as:
curvature of spine [Pott's] (737.4)
kyphosis (737.4)
spondylitis (720.81)

§ ✓5th **015.1 Hip** HIV

§ ✓5th **015.2 Knee** HIV

§ ✓5th **015.5 Limb bones** HIV
Tuberculous dactylitis

§ ✓5th **015.6 Mastoid** HIV
Tuberculous mastoiditis

§ ✓5th **015.7 Other specified bone** HIV

§ ✓5th **015.8 Other specified joint** HIV

§ ✓5th **015.9 Tuberculosis of unspecified bones and joints** HIV

✓4th **016 Tuberculosis of genitourinary system**

§ ✓5th **016.0 Kidney** CC HIV
Renal tuberculosis
Use additional code to identify manifestation, as:
tuberculous:
nephropathy (583.81)
pyelitis (590.81)
pyelonephritis (590.81)
CC Excl: 016.00-016.36, 016.90-016.96, 017.90-017.96, 031.2-031.9, 041.81-041.89, 041.9, 137.2, 139.8

§ ✓5th **016.1 Bladder** CC HIV
CC Excl: See code 016.0

§ ✓5th **016.2 Ureter** CC HIV
CC Excl: See code 016.0

§ ✓5th **016.3 Other urinary organs** CC HIV
CC Excl: See code 016.0

§ Requires fifth-digit. See beginning of section 010-018 for codes and definitions.

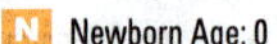 Newborn Age: 0  Pediatric Age: 0-17  Maternity Age: 12-55  Adult Age: 15-124 CC CC Condition MC Major Complication  Complex Dx HIV HIV Related Dx

§ ✓5th 016.4 **Epididymis** CC HIV ♂
CC Excl: 016.40-016.56, 016.90-016.96, 017.90-017.96, 031.2-031.9, 041.81-041.89, 041.9, 137.2, 139.8

§ ✓5th 016.5 **Other male genital organs** CC HIV ♂
Use additional code to identify manifestation, as:
tuberculosis of:
prostate (601.4)
seminal vesicle (608.81)
testis (608.81)
CC Excl: See code 016.4

§ ✓5th 016.6 **Tuberculous oophoritis and salpingitis** CC HIV ♀
CC Excl: 016.60-016.96, 017.90-017.96, 031.2-031.9, 041.81-041.9, 137.2, 139.8

§ ✓5th 016.7 **Other female genital organs** CC HIV ♀
Tuberculous:
cervicitis
endometritis
CC Excl: See code 016.6

§ ✓5th 016.9 **Genitourinary tuberculosis, unspecified** CC HIV
CC Excl: 016.90-016.96, 017.90-017.96, 031.2-031.9, 041.81-041.9, 137.2, 139.8

✓4th **017 Tuberculosis of other organs**

§ ✓5th 017.0 **Skin and subcutaneous cellular tissue** HIV
Lupus:
exedens
vulgaris
Scrofuloderma
Tuberculosis:
colliquativa
Tuberculosis:
cutis
lichenoides
papulonecrotica
verrucosa cutis
EXCLUDES *lupus erythematosus (695.4)*
disseminated (710.0)
lupus NOS (710.0)
nonspecific reaction to tuberculin skin test without active tuberculosis (795.5)
positive PPD (795.5)
positive tuberculin skin test without active tuberculosis (795.5)

§ ✓5th 017.1 **Erythema nodosum with hypersensitivity reaction in tuberculosis** HIV
Bazin's disease
Erythema:
induratum
Erythema:
nodosum, tuberculous
Tuberculosis indurativa
EXCLUDES *erythema nodosum NOS (695.2)*
DEF: Tender, inflammatory, bilateral nodules appearing on the shins and thought to be an allergic reaction to tuberculotoxin.

§ ✓5th 017.2 **Peripheral lymph nodes** CC HIV
Scrofula
Scrofulous abscess
Tuberculous adenitis
EXCLUDES *tuberculosis of lymph nodes:*
bronchial and mediastinal (012.1)
mesenteric and retroperitoneal (014.8)
tuberculous tracheobronchial adenopathy (012.1)
CC Excl: 017.20-017.26, 017.90-017.96, 031.2-031.9, 041.81-041.9, 139.8
DEF: Scrofula: Old name for tuberculous cervical lymphadenitis.

§ ✓5th 017.3 **Eye** CC HIV
Use additional code to identify manifestation, as:
tuberculous:
chorioretinitis, disseminated (363.13)
episcleritis (379.09)
interstitial keratitis (370.59)
iridocyclitis, chronic (364.11)
keratoconjunctivitis (phlyctenular) (370.31)
CC Excl: 017.30-017.36, 017.90-017.96, 031.2-031.9, 041.81-041.9, 139.8

§ ✓5th 017.4 **Ear** CC HIV
Tuberculosis of ear
Tuberculous otitis media
EXCLUDES *tuberculous mastoiditis (015.6)*
CC Excl: 017.40-017.46, 017.90-017.96, 031.2-031.9, 041.81-041.9, 139.8

§ ✓5th 017.5 **Thyroid gland** CC HIV
CC Excl: 017.50-017.56, 017.90-017.96, 031.2-031.9, 041.81-041.9, 139.8

§ ✓5th 017.6 **Adrenal glands** CC HIV
Addison's disease, tuberculous
CC Excl: 017.60-017.66, 017.90-017.96, 031.2-031.9, 041.81-041.9, 139.8

§ ✓5th 017.7 **Spleen** CC HIV
CC Excl: 017.70-017.76, 017.90-017.96, 031.2-031.9, 041.81-041.9, 139.8

§ ✓5th 017.8 **Esophagus** CC HIV
CC Excl: 017.80-017.96, 031.2-031.9, 041.81-041.9, 139.8

§ ✓5th 017.9 **Other specified organs** CC HIV
Use additional code to identify manifestation, as:
tuberculosis of:
endocardium [any valve] (424.91)
myocardium (422.0)
pericardium (420.0)
CC Excl: 017.90-017.96, 031.2-031.9, 041.81-041.9, 139.8

✓4th **018 Miliary tuberculosis**
INCLUDES tuberculosis:
disseminated
generalized
miliary, whether of a single specified site, multiple sites, or unspecified site
polyserositis
DEF: A form of tuberculosis caused by caseous material carried through the bloodstream planting seedlike tubercles in various body organs.

§ ✓5th 018.0 **Acute miliary tuberculosis** CC HIV
CC Excl: 017.90-018.96, 031.2-031.9, 041.81-041.9, 139.8

§ ✓5th 018.8 **Other specified miliary tuberculosis** CC HIV
CC Excl: See code 018.0

§ ✓5th 018.9 **Miliary tuberculosis, unspecified** CC HIV
CC Excl: See code 018.0

ZOONOTIC BACTERIAL DISEASES (020-027)

✓4th **020 Plague**
INCLUDES infection by Yersinia [Pasteurella] pestis

020.0 **Bubonic**
DEF: Most common acute and severe form of plague characterized by lymphadenopathy (buboes), chills, fever and headache.

020.1 **Cellulocutaneous**
DEF: Plague characterized by inflammation and necrosis of skin.

020.2 **Septicemic**
DEF: Plague characterized by massive infection in the bloodstream.

020.3 **Primary pneumonic**
DEF: Plague characterized by massive pulmonary infection.

020.4 **Secondary pneumonic**
DEF: Lung infection as a secondary complication of plague.

020.5 **Pneumonic, unspecified**

020.8 **Other specified types of plague**
Abortive plague
Ambulatory plague
Pestis minor

020.9 **Plague, unspecified**

§ Requires fifth-digit. See beginning of section 010-018 for codes and definitions.

 Additional Digit Required 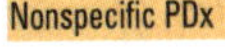 Nonspecific PDx Unacceptable PDx Manifestation Code MCV Major Cardiovascular Condition  Revised Text ● New Code ▲ Revised Code Title

✓4th 021 Tularemia

INCLUDES deerfly fever
infection by Francisella [Pasteurella] tularensis
rabbit fever

DEF: A febrile disease transmitted by the bites of deer flies, fleas and ticks, by inhalations of aerosolized *F. tularensis* or by ingestion of contaminated food or water; patients quickly develop fever, chills, weakness, headache, backache and malaise.

021.0 Ulceroglandular tularemia

DEF: Lesions occur at the site *Francisella tularensis* organism enters body, usually the fingers or hands.

021.1 Enteric tularemia

Tularemia:
cryptogenic
intestinal

Tularemia:
typhoidal

021.2 Pulmonary tularemia

Bronchopneumonic tularemia

021.3 Oculoglandular tularemia

DEF: Painful conjunctival infection by *Francisella tularensis* organism with possible corneal, preauricular lymph, or lacrimal involvement.

021.8 Other specified tularemia

Tularemia:
generalized or disseminated

Tularemia:
glandular

021.9 Unspecified tularemia

✓4th 022 Anthrax

AHA: 4Q '02, 70

DEF: An infectious bacterial disease usually transmitted by contact with infected animals or their discharges or products; it is classified by primary routes of inoculation as cutaneous, gastrointestinal and by inhalation.

022.0 Cutaneous anthrax

Malignant pustule

022.1 Pulmonary anthrax

Respiratory anthrax
Wool-sorters' disease

022.2 Gastrointestinal anthrax

022.3 Anthrax septicemia

022.8 Other specified manifestations of anthrax

022.9 Anthrax, unspecified

✓4th 023 Brucellosis

INCLUDES fever:
Malta
Mediterranean
undulant

DEF: An infectious disease caused by gram-negative, aerobic coccobacilli organisms; it is transmitted to humans through contact with infected tissue or dairy products; fever, sweating, weakness and aching are symptoms.

023.0 Brucella melitensis

DEF: Infection from direct or indirect contact with infected sheep or goats.

023.1 Brucella abortus

DEF: Infection from direct or indirect contact with infected cattle.

023.2 Brucella suis

DEF: Infection from direct or indirect contact with infected swine.

023.3 Brucella canis

DEF: Infection from direct or indirect contact with infected dogs.

023.8 Other brucellosis

Infection by more than one organism

023.9 Brucellosis, unspecified

024 Glanders

Infection by:
Actinobacillus mallei
Malleomyces mallei
Pseudomonas mallei

Farcy
Malleus

DEF: Equine infection causing mucosal inflammation and skin ulcers in humans.

025 Melioidosis

Infection by:
Malleomyces pseudomallei
Pseudomonas pseudomallei

Infection by:
Pseudoglanders
Whitmore's bacillus

DEF: Rare infection caused by *Pseudomonas pseudomallei*; clinical symptoms range from localized infection to fatal septicemia.

✓4th 026 Rat-bite fever

026.0 Spirillary fever

Rat-bite fever due to Spirillum minor [S. minus]
Sodoku

026.1 Streptobacillary fever

Epidemic arthritic erythema
Haverhill fever
Rat-bite fever due to Streptobacillus moniliformis

026.9 Unspecified rat-bite fever

✓4th 027 Other zoonotic bacterial diseases

027.0 Listeriosis

Infection } by Listeria monocytogenes
Septicemia }

Use additional code to identify manifestation, as meningitis (320.7)

EXCLUDES *congenital listeriosis (771.2)*

027.1 Erysipelothrix infection

Erysipeloid (of Rosenbach)
Infection } by Erysipelothrix insidiosa [E. rhusiopathiae]
Septicemia }

DEF: Usually associated with handling of fish, meat, or poultry; symptoms range from localized inflammation to septicemia.

027.2 Pasteurellosis

Pasteurella pseudotuberculosis infection
Mesenteric adenitis } by Pasteurella multocida [P. septica]
Septic infection (cat bite) (dog bite) }

EXCLUDES *infection by:*
Francisella [Pasteurella] tularensis (021.0-021.9)
Yersinia [Pasteurella] pestis (020.0-020.9)

DEF: Swelling, abscesses, or septicemia from *Pasteurella multocida*, commonly transmitted to humans by a dog or cat scratch.

027.8 Other specified zoonotic bacterial diseases

027.9 Unspecified zoonotic bacterial disease

OTHER BACTERIAL DISEASES (030-041)

EXCLUDES *bacterial venereal diseases (098.0-099.9)*
bartonellosis (088.0)

✓4th 030 Leprosy

INCLUDES Hansen's disease
infection by Mycobacterium leprae

030.0 Lepromatous [type L]

Lepromatous leprosy (macular) (diffuse) (infiltrated) (nodular) (neuritic)

DEF: Infectious, disseminated leprosy bacilli with lesions and deformities.

030.1 Tuberculoid [type T]

Tuberculoid leprosy (macular) (maculoanesthetic) (major) (minor) (neuritic)

DEF: Relatively benign, self-limiting leprosy with neuralgia and scales.

030.2 Indeterminate [group I]

Indeterminate [uncharacteristic] leprosy (macular) (neuritic)

DEF: Uncharacteristic leprosy, frequently an early manifestation.

030.3 Borderline [group B]

Borderline or dimorphous leprosy (infiltrated) (neuritic)

DEF: Transitional form of leprosy, neither lepromatous nor tuberculoid.

030.8 Other specified leprosy

030.9 Leprosy, unspecified

✓4th **031 Diseases due to other mycobacteria**

031.0 Pulmonary CC

Battey disease
Infection by Mycobacterium:
avium
intracellulare [Battey bacillus]
kansasii

CC Excl: 011.00-012.86, 017.90-017.96, 031.0, 031.2-031.9, 041.81-041.9, 137.0, 139.8, 480.0-480.2, 480.8-487.1, 494.0-508.9, 517.1, 518.89

031.1 Cutaneous

Buruli ulcer
Infection by Mycobacterium:
marinum [M. balnei]
ulcerans

031.2 Disseminated HIV

Disseminated mycobacterium avium-intracellulare complex (DMAC)
Mycobacterium avium-intracellulare complex (MAC) bacteremia

AHA: 4Q, '97, 31

DEF: Disseminated mycobacterium avium-intracellulare complex (DMAC): A serious systemic form of MAC commonly observed in patients in the late course of AIDS.

DEF: Mycobacterium avium-intracellulare complex (MAC) bacterium: Human pulmonary disease, lymphadenitis in children and systemic disease in immunocompromised individuals caused by a slow growing, gram-positive, aerobic organism.

031.8 Other specified mycobacterial diseases HIV

031.9 Unspecified diseases due to mycobacteria HIV

Atypical mycobacterium infection NOS

✓4th **032 Diphtheria**

INCLUDES infection by Corynebacterium diphtheriae

032.0 Faucial diphtheria

Membranous angina, diphtheritic

DEF: Diphtheria of the throat.

032.1 Nasopharyngeal diphtheria

032.2 Anterior nasal diphtheria

032.3 Laryngeal diphtheria

Laryngotracheitis, diphtheritic

✓5th **032.8 Other specified diphtheria**

032.81 Conjunctival diphtheria

Pseudomembranous diphtheritic conjunctivitis

032.82 Diphtheritic myocarditis

032.83 Diphtheritic peritonitis

032.84 Diphtheritic cystitis

032.85 Cutaneous diphtheria

032.89 Other

032.9 Diphtheria, unspecified

✓4th **033 Whooping cough**

INCLUDES pertussis

Use additional code to identify any associated pneumonia (484.3)

DEF: An acute, highly contagious respiratory tract infection caused by *Bordetella pertussis* and *B. bronchiseptica*; characteristic paroxysmal cough.

033.0 Bordetella pertussis [B. pertussis]

033.1 Bordetella parapertussis [B. parapertussis]

033.8 Whooping cough due to other specified organism

Bordetella bronchiseptica [B. bronchiseptica]

033.9 Whooping cough, unspecified organism

✓4th **034 Streptococcal sore throat and scarlet fever**

034.0 Streptococcal sore throat

Septic:
angina
sore throat
Streptococcal:
angina
Streptococcal:
laryngitis
pharyngitis
tonsillitis

034.1 Scarlet fever

Scarlatina

EXCLUDES *parascarlatina (057.8)*

DEF: Streptococcal infection and fever with red rash spreading from trunk.

035 Erysipelas

EXCLUDES *postpartum or puerperal erysipelas (670)*

DEF: An acute superficial cellulitis involving the dermal lymphatics; it is often caused by group A streptococci.

✓4th **036 Meningococcal infection**

036.0 Meningococcal meningitis CC

Cerebrospinal fever (meningococcal)
Meningitis:
cerebrospinal
epidemic

CC Excl: 003.21, 013.00-013.16, 036.0, 036.89-036.9, 041.81-041.9, 047.0-047.9, 049.0-049.1, 053.0, 054.72, 072.1, 090.42, 091.81, 094.2, 098.89, 100.81, 112.83, 114.2, 115.01, 115.11, 115.91, 130.0, 139.8, 320.0-322.9, 349.89-349.9, 357.0

036.1 Meningococcal encephalitis CC

CC Excl: 036.1, 036.89, 036.9, 041.81-041.89, 041.9, 139.8

036.2 Meningococcemia CC

Meningococcal septicemia

CC Excl: 003.1, 020.2, 036.2, 036.89-036.9, 038.0-038.9, 041.81-041.9, 054.5, 139.8, 995.90-995.94

036.3 Waterhouse-Friderichsen syndrome, meningococcal CC

Meningococcal hemorrhagic adrenalitis
Meningococcic adrenal syndrome
Waterhouse-Friderichsen syndrome NOS

CC Excl: 036.3, 036.89, 036.9, 041.81-041.89, 041.9, 139.8

✓5th **036.4 Meningococcal carditis**

036.40 Meningococcal carditis, unspecified CC

CC Excl: 036.40, 036.89-036.9, 041.81-041.9, 139.8

036.41 Meningococcal pericarditis CC

CC Excl: 036.41, 036.89-036.9, 041.81-041.9, 139.8

DEF: Meningococcal infection of the outer membrane of the heart.

036.42 Meningococcal endocarditis CC

CC Excl: 036.42, 036.89-036.9, 041.81-041.9, 139.8

DEF: Meningococcal infection of the membranes lining the cavities of the heart.

036.43 Meningococcal myocarditis CC

CC Excl: 036.43, 041.81-041.9, 139.8

DEF: Meningococcal infection of the muscle of the heart.

✓5th **036.8 Other specified meningococcal infections**

036.81 Meningococcal optic neuritis CC

CC Excl: 036.81, 036.89-036.9, 041.81-041.9, 139.8

036.82 Meningococcal arthropathy CC

CC Excl: 036.82-036.9, 041.81-041.9, 139.8

036.89 Other CC

CC Excl: 036.89-036.9, 041.81-041.9, 139.8

036.9 Meningococcal infection, unspecified CC

Meningococcal infection NOS

CC Excl: See code 036.89

037 Tetanus CC

EXCLUDES *tetanus:*
complicating:
abortion (634-638 with .0, 639.0)
ectopic or molar pregnancy (639.0)
neonatorum (771.3)
puerperal (670)

CC Excl: 037, 139.8

DEF: An acute, often fatal, infectious disease caused by the anaerobic, spore-forming bacillus *Clostridium tetani*; the bacillus most often enters the body through a contaminated wound, burns, surgical wounds, or cutaneous ulcers. Symptoms include lockjaw, spasms, seizures, and paralysis.

✓4th **038 Septicemia**

Use additional code for systemic inflammatory response syndrome (SIRS) (995.91-995.92)

EXCLUDES *bacteremia (790.7)*
during labor (659.3)
following ectopic or molar pregnancy (639.0)
following infusion, injection, transfusion, or vaccination (999.3)
postpartum, puerperal (670)
septicemia (sepsis) of newborn (771.81)
that complicating abortion (634-638 with .0, 639.0)

AHA: 2Q, '04, 16; 4Q, '88, 10; 3Q, '88, 12

DEF: A systemic disease associated with the presence and persistence of pathogenic microorganisms or their toxins in the blood.

038.0 Streptococcal septicemia CC HIV

CC Excl: 003.1, 020.2, 036.2, 038.0-038.9, 040.82-041.7, 041.81-041.9, 054.5, 139.8, 995.90-995.94, V09.0-V09.91

AHA: 4Q, '03, 79; 2Q, '96, 5

✓5th **038.1 Staphylococcal septicemia**

AHA: 4Q, '97, 32

038.10 Staphylococcal septicemia, unspecified CC HIV

CC Excl: See code 038.0

038.11 Staphylococcus aureus septicemia CC HIV

CC Excl: See code 038.0

AHA: 1Q, '05, 7; 2Q, '00, 5; 4Q, '98, 42

DRG 416

038.19 Other staphylococcal septicemia CC HIV

CC Excl: See code 038.0

AHA: 2Q, '00, 5

DRG 416

038.2 Pneumococcal septicemia [Streptococcus pneumoniae septicemia] CC HIV

CC Excl: See code 038.0

AHA: 2Q, '96, 5; 1Q, '91, 13

038.3 Septicemia due to anaerobes CC HIV

Septicemia due to bacteroides

EXCLUDES *gas gangrene (040.0)*
that due to anaerobic streptococci (038.0)

CC Excl: See code 038.0

✓5th **038.4 Septicemia due to other gram-negative organisms**

DEF: Infection of blood by microorganisms categorized as gram-negative by Gram's method of staining for identification of bacteria.

038.40 Gram-negative organism, unspecified CC HIV

Gram-negative septicemia NOS

CC Excl: See code 038.0

038.41 Hemophilus influenzae [H. influenzae] CC HIV

CC Excl: See code 038.0

038.42 Escherichia coli [E. coli] CC HIV

CC Excl: See code 038.0

AHA: 4Q, '03, 73

DRG 416

038.43 Pseudomonas CC HIV

CC Excl: See code 038.0

038.44 Serratia CC HIV

CC Excl: See code 038.0

038.49 Other CC HIV

CC Excl: See code 038.0

DRG 416

038.8 Other specified septicemias CC HIV

EXCLUDES *septicemia (due to):*
anthrax (022.3)
gonococcal (098.89)
herpetic (054.5)
meningococcal (036.2)
septicemic plague (020.2)

CC Excl: See code 038.0

038.9 Unspecified septicemia CC HIV

Septicemia NOS

EXCLUDES *bacteremia NOS (790.7)*

CC Excl: See code 038.0

AHA: ►2Q, '05, 18-19;◄ 2Q, '04, 16; 4Q, '03, 79; 2Q, '00, 3; 3Q, '99, 5, 9; 1Q, '98, 5; 3Q, '96, 16; 2Q, '96, 6

DRG 416

✓4th **039 Actinomycotic infections**

INCLUDES actinomycotic mycetoma
infection by Actinomycetales, such as species of Actinomyces, Actinomadura, Nocardia, Streptomyces
maduromycosis (actinomycotic)
schizomycetoma (actinomycotic)

DEF: Inflammatory lesions and abscesses at site of infection by *Actinomyces israelii.*

039.0 Cutaneous HIV

Erythrasma
Trichomycosis axillaris

039.1 Pulmonary HIV

Thoracic actinomycosis

039.2 Abdominal HIV

039.3 Cervicofacial

039.4 Madura foot HIV

EXCLUDES *madura foot due to mycotic infection (117.4)*

039.8 Of other specified sites HIV

039.9 Of unspecified site HIV

Actinomycosis NOS
Nocardiosis NOS
Maduromycosis NOS

✓4th **040 Other bacterial diseases**

EXCLUDES *bacteremia NOS (790.7)*
bacterial infection NOS (041.9)

040.0 Gas gangrene CC

Gas bacillus infection or gangrene
Infection by Clostridium:
histolyticum
oedematiens
perfringens [welchii]
septicum
sordellii
Malignant edema
Myonecrosis, clostridial
Myositis, clostridial

CC Excl: 040.0, 139.8

AHA: 1Q, '95, 11

040.1 Rhinoscleroma

DEF: Growths on the nose and nasopharynx caused by *Klebsiella rhinoscleromatis.*

N Newborn Age: 0  P Pediatric Age: 0-17 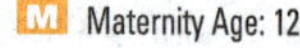 M Maternity Age: 12-55 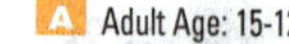 A Adult Age: 15-124  CC CC Condition MC Major Complication 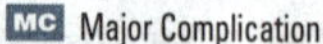 CD Complex Dx  HIV HIV Related Dx

040.2 Whipple's disease
Intestinal lipodystrophy

040.3 Necrobacillosis
DEF: Infection with *Fusobacterium necrophorum* causing abscess or necrosis.

✓5th **040.8 Other specified bacterial diseases**

040.81 Tropical pyomyositis

040.82 Toxic shock syndrome CC
Use additional code to identify the organism
CC Excl: 040.82, 338.0-338.4, 780.91-780.99, 785.50-785.59, 785.9, 799.81-799.89
AHA: 4Q, '02, 44
DEF: Syndrome caused by staphylococcal exotoxin that may rapidly progress to severe and intractable shock; symptoms include characteristic sunburn-like rash with peeling of skin on palms and soles, sudden onset high fever, vomiting, diarrhea, myalgia, and hypotension.

040.89 Other
AHA: N-D, '86, 7

✓4th **041 Bacterial infection in conditions classified elsewhere and of unspecified site**
Note: This category is provided to be used as an additional code to identify the bacterial agent in diseases classified elsewhere. This category will also be used to classify bacterial infections of unspecified nature or site.
EXCLUDES *bacteremia NOS (790.7)*
septicemia (038.0-038.9)
AHA: 2Q, '01, 12; J-A, '84, 19

✓5th **041.0 Streptococcus**

041.00 Streptococcus, unspecified

041.01 Group A
AHA: 1Q, '02, 3

041.02 Group B

041.03 Group C

041.04 Group D [Enterococcus]

041.05 Group G

041.09 Other Streptococcus

✓5th **041.1 Staphylococcus**

041.10 Staphylococcus, unspecified

041.11 Staphylococcus aureus
AHA: 4Q, '03, 104, 106; 2Q, '01, 11; 4Q, '98, 42, 54; 4Q, '97, 32

041.19 Other Staphylococcus

041.2 Pneumococcus

041.3 Friedländer's bacillus
Infection by Klebsiella pneumoniae

041.4 Escherichia coli [E. coli]

041.5 Hemophilus influenzae [H. influenzae]

041.6 Proteus (mirabilis) (morganii)

041.7 Pseudomonas
AHA: 4Q, '02, 45

✓5th **041.8 Other specified bacterial infections**

041.81 Mycoplasma
Eaton's agent
Pleuropneumonia-like organisms [PPLO]

041.82 Bacteroides fragilis
DEF: Anaerobic gram-negative bacilli of the gastrointestinal tract; frequently implicated in intra-abdominal infection; commonly resistant to antibiotics.

041.83 Clostridium perfringens

041.84 Other anaerobes
Gram-negative anaerobes
EXCLUDES *Helicobacter pylori (041.86)*

041.85 Other gram-negative organisms
Aerobacter aerogenes
Gram-negative bacteria NOS
Mima polymorpha
Serratia
EXCLUDES *gram-negative anaerobes (041.84)*
AHA: 1Q, '95, 18

041.86 Helicobacter pylori [H. pylori]
AHA: 4Q, '95, 60

041.89 Other specified bacteria
AHA: 2Q, '03, 7

041.9 Bacterial infection, unspecified
AHA: 2Q, '91, 9

HUMAN IMMUNODEFICIENCY VIRUS (HIV) INFECTION (042)

042 Human immunodeficiency virus [HIV] disease CC
Acquired immune deficiency syndrome
Acquired immunodeficiency syndrome
AIDS
AIDS-like syndrome
AIDS-related complex
ARC
HIV infection, symptomatic
Use additional code(s) to identify all manifestations of HIV
Use additional code to identify HIV-2 infection (079.53)
EXCLUDES *asymptomatic HIV infection status (V08)*
exposure to HIV virus (V01.79)
nonspecific serologic evidence of HIV (795.71)
CC Excl: 042, 139.8
AHA: 1Q, '05, 7; 2Q, '04, 11; 1Q, '04, 5; 1Q, '03, 15; 1Q, '99, 14; 4Q, '97, 30, 31; 1Q, '93, 21; 2Q, '92, 11; 3Q, '90, 17; J-A, '87, 8

POLIOMYELITIS AND OTHER NON-ARTHROPOD-BORNE VIRAL DISEASES OF CENTRAL NERVOUS SYSTEM (045-049)

✓4th **045 Acute poliomyelitis**
EXCLUDES *late effects of acute poliomyelitis (138)*

The following fifth-digit subclassification is for use with category 045:
0 poliovirus, unspecified type
1 poliovirus type I
2 poliovirus type II
3 poliovirus type III

✓5th **045.0 Acute paralytic poliomyelitis specified as bulbar**
Infantile paralysis (acute) } specified as bulbar
Poliomyelitis (acute) (anterior) } specified as bulbar
Polioencephalitis (acute) (bulbar)
Polioencephalomyelitis (acute) (anterior) (bulbar)
DEF: Acute paralytic infection occurring where the brain merges with the spinal cord; affecting breathing, swallowing, and heart rate.

✓5th **045.1 Acute poliomyelitis with other paralysis**
Paralysis:
acute atrophic, spinal
infantile, paralytic
Poliomyelitis (acute) } with paralysis except bulbar
anterior
epidemic
DEF: Paralytic infection affecting peripheral or spinal nerves.

✓5th **045.2 Acute nonparalytic poliomyelitis**
Poliomyelitis (acute) } specified as nonparalytic
anterior
epidemic
DEF: Nonparalytic infection causing pain, stiffness, and paresthesias.

✓5th **045.9 Acute poliomyelitis, unspecified**
Infantile paralysis } unspecified whether paralytic or nonparalytic
Poliomyelitis (acute)
anterior
epidemic

✓4th **046 Slow virus infection of central nervous system**

046.0 Kuru
DEF: A chronic, progressive, fatal nervous system disorder; clinical symptoms include cerebellar ataxia, trembling, spasticity and progressive dementia.

046.1 Jakob-Creutzfeldt disease
Subacute spongiform encephalopathy
DEF: Communicable, progressive spongiform encephalopathy thought to be caused by an infectious particle known as a "prion" (proteinaceous infection particle). This is a progressive, fatal disease manifested principally by mental deterioration.

046.2 Subacute sclerosing panencephalitis CC
Dawson's inclusion body encephalitis
Van Bogaert's sclerosing leukoencephalitis
CC Excl: 046.2, 139.8

DEF: Progressive viral infection causing cerebral dysfunction, blindness, dementia, and death (SSPE).

046.3 Progressive multifocal leukoencephalopathy HIV
Multifocal leukoencephalopathy NOS
DEF: Infection affecting cerebral cortex in patients with weakened immune systems.

046.8 Other specified slow virus infection of central nervous system HIV

046.9 Unspecified slow virus infection of central nervous system HIV

✓4th **047 Meningitis due to enterovirus**

INCLUDES meningitis:
abacterial
aseptic
viral

EXCLUDES *meningitis due to:*
adenovirus (049.1)
arthropod-borne virus (060.0-066.9)
leptospira (100.81)
virus of:
herpes simplex (054.72)
herpes zoster (053.0)
lymphocytic choriomeningitis (049.0)
mumps (072.1)
poliomyelitis (045.0-045.9)
any other infection specifically classified elsewhere

AHA: J-F, '87, 6

047.0 Coxsackie virus

047.1 ECHO virus
Meningo-eruptive syndrome

047.8 Other specified viral meningitis

047.9 Unspecified viral meningitis
Viral meningitis NOS

048 Other enterovirus diseases of central nervous system
Boston exanthem

✓4th **049 Other non-arthropod-borne viral diseases of central nervous system**

EXCLUDES *late effects of viral encephalitis (139.0)*

049.0 Lymphocytic choriomeningitis
Lymphocytic:
meningitis (serous) (benign)
meningoencephalitis (serous) (benign)

049.1 Meningitis due to adenovirus
DEF: Inflammation of lining of brain caused by Arenaviruses and usually occurring in adults in fall and winter months.

049.8 Other specified non-arthropod-borne viral diseases of central nervous system HIV
Encephalitis:
acute:
inclusion body
necrotizing
epidemic
lethargica
Rio Bravo
von Economo's disease

049.9 Unspecified non-arthropod-borne viral diseases of central nervous system HIV
Viral encephalitis NOS

VIRAL DISEASES ACCOMPANIED BY EXANTHEM (050-057)

EXCLUDES *arthropod-borne viral diseases (060.0-066.9)*
Boston exanthem (048)

✓4th **050 Smallpox**

050.0 Variola major
Hemorrhagic (pustular) smallpox
Malignant smallpox
Purpura variolosa
DEF: Form of smallpox known for its high mortality; exists only in laboratories.

050.1 Alastrim
Variola minor
DEF: Mild form of smallpox known for its low mortality rate.

050.2 Modified smallpox
Varioloid
DEF: Mild form occurring in patients with history of infection or vaccination.

050.9 Smallpox, unspecified

✓4th **051 Cowpox and paravaccinia**

051.0 Cowpox
Vaccinia not from vaccination
EXCLUDES *vaccinia (generalized) (from vaccination) (999.0)*
DEF: A disease contracted by milking infected cows; vesicles usually appear on the fingers, may spread to hands and adjacent areas and usually disappear without scarring; other associated features of the disease may include local edema, lymphangitis and regional lymphadenitis with or without fever.

051.1 Pseudocowpox
Milkers' node
DEF: Hand lesions and mild fever in dairy workers caused by exposure to paravaccinia.

051.2 Contagious pustular dermatitis
Ecthyma contagiosum
Orf
DEF: Skin eruptions caused by exposure to poxvirus-infected sheep or goats.

051.9 Paravaccinia, unspecified

✓4th **052 Chickenpox**
DEF: Contagious infection by *Varicella-zoster* virus causing rash with pustules and fever.

052.0 Postvaricella encephalitis CC
Postchickenpox encephalitis
CC Excl: 051.9-052.0, 052.7-052.9, 078.88-078.89, 079.81, 079.88-079.99, 139.8

052.1 Varicella (hemorrhagic) pneumonitis CC
CC Excl: 051.9-052.9, 078.88-078.89, 079.81, 079.88-079.99, 139.8

● **052.2 Postvaricella myelitis** CC
Postchickenpox myelitis
CC Excl: 051.9-052.9, 053.14, 054.74, 078.88-078.89, 079.81, 079.88-079.99, 139.8, 323.01-323.02, 323.41-323.82, 341.20-341.22

052.7 With other specified complications CC
CC Excl: 051.9, 052.7-052.9, 078.88-078.89, 079.81, 079.88-079.89, 079.98-079.99, 139.8
AHA: 1Q, '02, 3

052.8 With unspecified complication CC
CC Excl: See code 052.7

052.9 Varicella without mention of complication CC
Chickenpox NOS
Varicella NOS
CC Excl: See code 052.7

✓4th **053 Herpes zoster**

INCLUDES shingles
zona

DEF: Self-limiting infection by *varicella-zoster* virus causing unilateral eruptions and neuralgia along affected nerves.

053.0 With meningitis CC HIV
CC Excl: 003.21, 013.00-013.16, 036.0,047.0-047.9, 049.0-049.1, 053.0-053.19, 053.79-053.9, 054.72, 054.74-054.9, 072.1, 078.88-079.99, 090.42, 091.81, 094.2, 098.89, 100.81, 112.83, 114.2, 115.01, 115.11, 115.91, 130.0, 139.8, 320.0-322.9, 349.89-349.9, 357.0
DEF: *Varicella-zoster* virus infection causing inflammation of the lining of the brain and/or spinal cord.

✓5th **053.1 With other nervous system complications**

053.10 With unspecified nervous system complication CC HIV
CC Excl: 053.0-053.19, 053.79-053.9, 054.72, 054.74-054.9, 078.88-078.89, 079.81, 079.88-079.99, 139.8

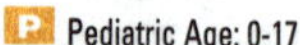 Newborn Age: 0  Pediatric Age: 0-17 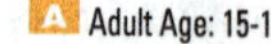 Maternity Age: 12-55  Adult Age: 15-124  CC Condition  Major Complication CD Complex Dx HIV HIV Related Dx

053.11 Geniculate herpes zoster CC HIV
Herpetic geniculate ganglionitis
CC Excl: See code 053.10
DEF: Unilateral eruptions and neuralgia along the facial nerve geniculum affecting face and outer and middle ear.

053.12 Postherpetic trigeminal neuralgia CC HIV
CC Excl: See code 053.10
DEF: Severe oral or nasal pain following a herpes zoster infection.

053.13 Postherpetic polyneuropathy CC HIV
CC Excl: See code 053.10
DEF: Multiple areas of pain following a herpes zoster infection.

● **053.14 Herpes zoster myelitis** CC HIV
CC Excl: 052.2, 053.0-053.19, 053.79-053.9, 054.72, 054.74-054.9, 078.88-078.89, 079.81, 079.88-079.99, 139.8, 323.01-323.02, 323.41-323.82, 341.20-341.22

053.19 Other CC HIV
CC Excl: See code 053.10

✓5th **053.2 With ophthalmic complications**

053.20 Herpes zoster dermatitis of eyelid HIV
Herpes zoster ophthalmicus

053.21 Herpes zoster keratoconjunctivitis HIV

053.22 Herpes zoster iridocyclitis HIV

053.29 Other HIV

✓5th **053.7 With other specified complications**

053.71 Otitis externa due to herpes zoster HIV

053.79 Other CC HIV
CC Excl: 053.0-054.71, 054.73-054.9, 078.88-078.89, 079.81, 079.88-079.99, 139.8

053.8 With unspecified complication CC HIV
CC Excl: See code 053.79

053.9 Herpes zoster without mention of complication HIV
Herpes zoster NOS

✓4th **054 Herpes simplex**
EXCLUDES *congenital herpes simplex (771.2)*

054.0 Eczema herpeticum HIV
Kaposi's varicelliform eruption
DEF: Herpes simplex virus invading site of preexisting skin inflammation.

✓5th **054.1 Genital herpes**
AHA: J-F, '87, 15, 16

054.10 Genital herpes, unspecified HIV
Herpes progenitalis

054.11 Herpetic vulvovaginitis HIV ♀

054.12 Herpetic ulceration of vulva HIV ♀

054.13 Herpetic infection of penis HIV ♂

054.19 Other HIV

054.2 Herpetic gingivostomatitis HIV

054.3 Herpetic meningoencephalitis CC HIV
Herpes encephalitis   Simian B disease
CC Excl: 054.3, 054.74-054.9, 139.8
DEF: Inflammation of the brain and its lining, caused by infection of herpes simplex 1 in adults and simplex 2 in newborns.

✓5th **054.4 With ophthalmic complications**

054.40 With unspecified ophthalmic complication HIV

054.41 Herpes simplex dermatitis of eyelid HIV

054.42 Dendritic keratitis HIV

054.43 Herpes simplex disciform keratitis HIV

054.44 Herpes simplex iridocyclitis HIV

054.49 Other HIV

054.5 Herpetic septicemia CC HIV
CC Excl: 003.1, 020.2, 036.2, 038.0, 038.10-038.9, 054.5, 054.74-054.9, 139.8, 995.90-995.94
AHA: 2Q, '00, 5

054.6 Herpetic whitlow HIV
Herpetic felon
DEF: A primary infection of the terminal segment of a finger by herpes simplex; intense itching and pain start the disease, vesicles form, and tissue ultimately is destroyed.

✓5th **054.7 With other specified complications**

054.71 Visceral herpes simplex CC HIV
CC Excl: 054.71-054.72, 054.74-054.9, 139.8

054.72 Herpes simplex meningitis CC HIV
CC Excl: 003.21, 013.00-013.16, 036.0,047.0-047.9, 049.0-049.1, 053.0, 054.72, 054.74-054.9, 072.1, 090.42, 091.81, 094.2, 098.89, 100.81, 112.83, 114.2, 115.01, 115.11, 115.91, 130.0, 139.8, 320.0-322.9, 349.89-349.9, 357.0

054.73 Herpes simplex otitis externa HIV

● **054.74 Herpes simplex myelitis** CC HIV
CC Excl: 052.2, 053.14, 054.74-054.9, 078.88-078.89, 079.81, 079.88-079.99, 139.8, 323.01-323.02, 323.41-323.82, 341.20-341.22

054.79 Other CC HIV
CC Excl: 054.74-054.9, 078.88-078.89, 079.81, 079.88-079.99, 139.8

054.8 With unspecified complication CC HIV
CC Excl: See code 054.79

054.9 Herpes simplex without mention of complication HIV

✓4th **055 Measles**
INCLUDES morbilli   rubeola

055.0 Postmeasles encephalitis CC
CC Excl: 055.0, 055.79-055.9, 078.88-078.89, 079.81, 079.88-079.99, 139.8

055.1 Postmeasles pneumonia CC
CC Excl: 055.1, 055.79-055.9, 078.88-078.89, 079.81, 079.88-079.99, 139.8

055.2 Postmeasles otitis media CC
CC Excl: 055.2, 055.79-055.9, 078.88-078.89, 079.81, 079.88-079.99, 139.8

✓5th **055.7 With other specified complications**

055.71 Measles keratoconjunctivitis CC
Measles keratitis
CC Excl: 055.71-055.9, 078.88-078.89, 079.81, 079.88-079.99, 139.8

055.79 Other CC
CC Excl: 055.79-055.9, 078.88-078.89, 079.81, 079.88--079.99, 139.8

055.8 With unspecified complication CC
CC Excl: 055.79, 055.8-055.9, 056.09, 078.88-078.89, 079.81, 079.88-079.89, 079.98-079.99, 139.8

055.9 Measles without mention of complication

✓4th **056 Rubella**
INCLUDES German measles
EXCLUDES *congenital rubella (771.0)*
DEF: Acute but usually benign togavirus infection causing fever, sore throat, and rash; associated with complications to fetus as a result of maternal infection.

✓5th **056.0 With neurological complications**

056.00 With unspecified neurological complication CC
CC Excl: 056.00-056.09, 056.79-056.9, 078.88-078.89, 079.81, 079.88-079.99, 139.8

056.01 Encephalomyelitis due to rubella CC
Encephalitis } due to rubella
Meningoencephalitis }
CC Excl: See code 056.00

056.09 Other CC
CC Excl: See code 056.00

✓5th **056.7 With other specified complications**

056.71 Arthritis due to rubella CC

CC Excl: 056.71-056.9, 078.88-078.89, 079.81, 079.88-079.99, 139.8

056.79 Other CC

CC Excl: See code 056.00

056.8 With unspecified complications CC

CC Excl: 056.00, 056.01, 056.79-056.9, 078.88-078.89, 079.81, 079.88-079.99, 139.8

056.9 Rubella without mention of complication

✓4th **057 Other viral exanthemata**

DEF: Skin eruptions or rashes and fever caused by viruses, including poxviruses.

057.0 Erythema infectiosum [fifth disease]

DEF: A moderately contagious, benign, epidemic disease, usually seen in children, and of probable viral etiology; a red macular rash appears on the face and may spread to the limbs and trunk.

057.8 Other specified viral exanthemata

Dukes (-Filatow) disease
Exanthema subitum [sixth disease]
Fourth disease
Parascarlatina
Pseudoscarlatina
Roseola infantum

057.9 Viral exanthem, unspecified

ARTHROPOD-BORNE VIRAL DISEASES (060-066)

Use additional code to identify any associated meningitis (321.2)

EXCLUDES *late effects of viral encephalitis (139.0)*

✓4th **060 Yellow fever**

DEF: Fever and jaundice from infection by mosquito-borne virus of genus *Flavivirus.*

060.0 Sylvatic

Yellow fever:
jungle

Yellow fever:
sylvan

DEF: Yellow fever transmitted from animal to man, via mosquito.

060.1 Urban

DEF: Yellow fever transmitted from man to man, via mosquito.

060.9 Yellow fever, unspecified

061 Dengue

Breakbone fever

EXCLUDES *hemorrhagic fever caused by dengue virus (065.4)*

DEF: Acute, self-limiting infection by mosquito-borne virus characterized by fever and generalized aches.

✓4th **062 Mosquito-borne viral encephalitis**

062.0 Japanese encephalitis

Japanese B encephalitis

DEF: Flavivirus causing inflammation of the brain, with a wide range of clinical manifestations.

062.1 Western equine encephalitis

DEF: Alphavirus WEE infection causing inflammation of the brain, found in areas west of the Mississippi; transmitted horse to mosquito to man.

062.2 Eastern equine encephalitis

EXCLUDES *Venezuelan equine encephalitis (066.2)*

DEF: Alphavirus EEE causing inflammation of the brain and spinal cord, found as far north as Canada and south into South America and Mexico; transmitted horse to mosquito to man.

062.3 St. Louis encephalitis

DEF: Epidemic form caused by Flavivirus and transmitted by mosquito, and characterized by fever, difficulty in speech, and headache.

062.4 Australian encephalitis

Australian arboencephalitis
Australian X disease
Murray Valley encephalitis

DEF: Flavivirus causing inflammation of the brain, occurring in Australia and New Guinea.

062.5 California virus encephalitis

Encephalitis:
California
La Crosse
Tahyna fever

DEF: Bunyamwere virus causing inflammation of the brain.

062.8 Other specified mosquito-borne viral encephalitis

Encephalitis by Ilheus virus

EXCLUDES *West Nile virus (066.40-066.49)*

062.9 Mosquito-borne viral encephalitis, unspecified

✓4th **063 Tick-borne viral encephalitis**

INCLUDES diphasic meningoencephalitis

063.0 Russian spring-summer [taiga] encephalitis

063.1 Louping ill

DEF: Inflammation of brain caused by virus transmitted sheep to tick to man; incidence usually limited to British Isles.

063.2 Central European encephalitis

DEF: Inflammation of brain caused by virus transmitted by tick; limited to central Europe and presenting with two distinct phases.

063.8 Other specified tick-borne viral encephalitis

Langat encephalitis
Powassan encephalitis

063.9 Tick-borne viral encephalitis, unspecified

064 Viral encephalitis transmitted by other and unspecified arthropods

Arthropod-borne viral encephalitis, vector unknown
Negishi virus encephalitis

EXCLUDES *viral encephalitis NOS (049.9)*

✓4th **065 Arthropod-borne hemorrhagic fever**

065.0 Crimean hemorrhagic fever [CHF Congo virus]

Central Asian hemorrhagic fever

065.1 Omsk hemorrhagic fever

065.2 Kyasanur Forest disease

065.3 Other tick-borne hemorrhagic fever

065.4 Mosquito-borne hemorrhagic fever

Chikungunya hemorrhagic fever
Dengue hemorrhagic fever

EXCLUDES *Chikungunya fever (066.3)*
dengue (061)
yellow fever (060.0-060.9)

065.8 Other specified arthropod-borne hemorrhagic fever

Mite-borne hemorrhagic fever

065.9 Arthropod-borne hemorrhagic fever, unspecified

Arbovirus hemorrhagic fever NOS

✓4th **066 Other arthropod-borne viral diseases**

066.0 Phlebotomus fever

Changuinola fever
Sandfly fever

DEF: Sandfly-borne viral infection occurring in Asia, Mideast and South America.

066.1 Tick-borne fever

Nairobi sheep disease
Tick fever:
American mountain
Colorado
Kemerovo
Quaranfil

066.2 Venezuelan equine fever

Venezuelan equine encephalitis

DEF: Alphavirus VEE infection causing inflammation of the brain, usually limited to South America, Mexico, and Florida; transmitted horse to mosquito to man

066.3 Other mosquito-borne fever
Fever (viral):
Bunyamwera
Bwamba
Chikungunya
Guama
Mayaro
Mucambo
O'Nyong-Nyong
Fever (viral):
Oropouche
Pixuna
Rift valley
Ross river
Wesselsbron
Zika
EXCLUDES *dengue (061)*
yellow fever (060.0-060.9)

✓5th **066.4 West Nile fever**
AHA: 4Q, '02, 44
DEF: Mosquito-borne fever causing fatal inflammation of the brain, the lining of the brain, or of the lining of the brain and spinal cord.

066.40 West Nile fever, unspecified
West Nile fever NOS
West Nile fever without complications
West Nile virus NOS

066.41 West Nile fever with encephalitis
West Nile encephalitis
West Nile encephalomyelitis
AHA: 4Q, '04, 51

066.42 West Nile fever with other neurologic manifestation
Use additional code to specify the neurologic manifestation
AHA: 4Q, '04, 51

066.49 West Nile fever with other complications
Use additional code to specify the other conditions

066.8 Other specified arthropod-borne viral diseases
Chandipura fever
Piry fever

066.9 Arthropod-borne viral disease, unspecified
Arbovirus infection NOS

OTHER DISEASES DUE TO VIRUSES AND CHLAMYDIAE (070-079)

✓4th **070 Viral hepatitis**
INCLUDES viral hepatitis (acute) (chronic)
EXCLUDES *cytomegalic inclusion virus hepatitis (078.5)*

The following fifth-digit subclassification is for use with categories 070.2 and 070.3:
- **0 acute or unspecified, without mention of hepatitis delta**
- **1 acute or unspecified, with hepatitis delta**
- **2 chronic, without mention of hepatitis delta**
- **3 chronic, with hepatitis delta**

DEF: Hepatitis A : HAV infection is self-limiting with flulike symptoms; transmission, fecal-oral.

DEF: Hepatitis B: HBV infection can be chronic and systemic; transmission, bodily fluids.

DEF: Hepatitis C: HCV infection can be chronic and systemic; transmission, blood transfusion and unidentified agents.

DEF: Hepatitis D (delta): HDV occurs only in the presence of hepatitis B virus.

DEF: Hepatitis E: HEV is epidemic form; transmission and nature under investigation.

070.0 Viral hepatitis A with hepatic coma

070.1 Viral hepatitis A without mention of hepatic coma
Infectious hepatitis

✓5th **070.2 Viral hepatitis B with hepatic coma** CC
CC Excl: 070.0-070.9, 078.88-078.89, 079.81, 079.88-079.99, 139.8
AHA: 4Q, '91, 28

✓5th **070.3 Viral hepatitis B without mention of hepatic coma** CC
Serum hepatitis
CC Excl: See code 070.2
AHA: 1Q, '93, 28; 4Q, '91, 28

✓5th **070.4 Other specified viral hepatitis with hepatic coma**
AHA: 4Q, '91, 28

070.41 Acute hepatitis C with hepatic coma CC
CC Excl: See code 070.2

070.42 Hepatitis delta without mention of active hepatitis B disease with hepatic coma CC
Hepatitis delta with hepatitis B carrier state
CC Excl: See code 070.2

070.43 Hepatitis E with hepatic coma CC
CC Excl: See code 070.2

070.44 Chronic hepatitis C with hepatic coma CC
CC Excl: See code 070.2

070.49 Other specified viral hepatitis with hepatic coma CC
CC Excl: See code 070.2

✓5th **070.5 Other specified viral hepatitis without mention of hepatic coma**
AHA: 4Q, '91, 28

070.51 Acute hepatitis C without mention of hepatic coma CC
CC Excl: See code 070.2

070.52 Hepatitis delta without mention of active hepatitis B disease or hepatic coma CC
CC Excl: See code 070.2

070.53 Hepatitis E without mention of hepatic coma CC
CC Excl: See code 070.2

070.54 Chronic hepatitis C without mention of hepatic coma CC
CC Excl: See code 070.2

070.59 Other specified viral hepatitis without mention of hepatic coma CC
CC Excl: See code 070.2

070.6 Unspecified viral hepatitis with hepatic coma CC
EXCLUDES *unspecified viral hepatitis C with hepatic coma (070.71)*
CC Excl: See code 070.2

✓5th **070.7 Unspecified viral hepatitis C**

070.70 Unspecified viral hepatitis C without hepatic coma CC
Unspecified viral hepatitis C NOS
CC Excl: See code 070.2
AHA: 4Q, '04, 52

070.71 Unspecified viral hepatitis C with hepatic coma CC
CC Excl: See code 070.2
AHA: 4Q, '04, 52

070.9 Unspecified viral hepatitis without mention of hepatic coma CC
Viral hepatitis NOS
EXCLUDES *unspecified viral hepatitis C without hepatic coma (070.70)*
CC Excl: See code 070.2

071 Rabies
Hydrophobia
Lyssa
DEF: Acute infectious disease of the CNS caused by a rhabdovirus; usually spread by virus-laden saliva from bites by infected animals; it progresses from fever, restlessness, and extreme excitability, to hydrophobia, seizures, confusion and death.

✓4th **072 Mumps**
DEF: Acute infectious disease caused by paramyxovirus; usually seen in children less than 15 years of age; salivary glands are typically enlarged, and other organs, such as testes, pancreas and meninges, are often involved.

072.0 Mumps orchitis CC ♂
CC Excl: 072.0, 072.79-072.9, 078.88-078.89, 079.81, 079.88-079.99, 139.8

072.1 Mumps meningitis CC
CC Excl: 003.21, 013.00-013.16, 036.0, 047.0-049.1, 053.0, 054.72, 072.1, 072.79-072.9, 078.88-078.89, 079.81, 079.88-079.99, 090.42, 091.81, 094.2, 098.89, 100.81, 112.83, 114.2, 115.01, 115.11, 115.91, 130.0, 139.8, 320.0-322.9, 349.89-349.9, 357.0

072.2 Mumps encephalitis CC
Mumps meningoencephalitis
CC Excl: 072.2, 072.79-072.9, 078.88-078.89, 079.81, 079.88-079.99, 139.8

072.3 Mumps pancreatitis CC
CC Excl: 072.3, 072.79-072.9, 078.88-078.89, 079.81, 079.88-079.99, 139.8

✓5th **072.7 Mumps with other specified complications**

072.71 Mumps hepatitis CC
CC Excl: 072.71, 072.79-072.9, 078.88-078.89, 079.81, 079.88-079.99, 139.8

072.72 Mumps polyneuropathy CC
CC Excl: 072.72-072.9, 078.88-078.89, 079.81, 079.88-079.99, 139.8

072.79 Other CC
CC Excl: 072.79-072.9, 078.88-078.89, 079.81, 079.88-079.99, 139.8

072.8 Mumps with unspecified complication CC
CC Excl: 072.79-072.9, 078.88-078.89, 079.81, 079.88-079.99

072.9 Mumps without mention of complication
Epidemic parotitis
Infectious parotitis

✓4th **073 Ornithosis**

INCLUDES parrot fever
psittacosis

DEF: *Chlamydia psittaci* infection often transmitted from birds to humans.

073.0 With pneumonia
Lobular pneumonitis due to ornithosis

073.7 With other specified complications

073.8 With unspecified complication

073.9 Ornithosis, unspecified

✓4th **074 Specific diseases due to Coxsackie virus**

EXCLUDES *Coxsackie virus:*
infection NOS (079.2)
meningitis (047.0)

074.0 Herpangina
Vesicular pharyngitis
DEF: Acute infectious coxsackie virus infection causing throat lesions, fever, and vomiting; generally affects children in summer.

074.1 Epidemic pleurodynia
Bornholm disease
Devil's grip
Epidemic:
myalgia
myositis
DEF: Paroxysmal pain in chest, accompanied by fever and usually limited to children and young adults; caused by coxsackie virus.

✓5th **074.2 Coxsackie carditis**

074.20 Coxsackie carditis, unspecified

074.21 Coxsackie pericarditis
DEF: Coxsackie infection of the outer lining of the heart.

074.22 Coxsackie endocarditis
DEF: Coxsackie infection within the heart's cavities.

074.23 Coxsackie myocarditis
Aseptic myocarditis of newborn
DEF: Coxsackie infection of the muscle of the heart.

074.3 Hand, foot, and mouth disease
Vesicular stomatitis and exanthem
DEF: Mild coxsackie infection causing lesions on hands, feet and oral mucosa, most commonly seen in preschool children.

074.8 Other specified diseases due to Coxsackie virus
Acute lymphonodular pharyngitis

075 Infectious mononucleosis
Glandular fever
Monocytic angina
Pfeiffer's disease
AHA: 3Q, '01, 13; M-A, '87, 8
DEF: Acute infection by Epstein-Barr virus causing fever, sore throat, enlarged lymph glands and spleen, and fatigue; usually seen in teens and young adults.

✓4th **076 Trachoma**

EXCLUDES *late effect of trachoma (139.1)*

DEF: A chronic infectious disease of the cornea and conjunctiva caused by a strain of the bacteria *Chlamydia trachomatis*; the infection can cause photophobia, pain, excessive tearing and sometimes blindness.

076.0 Initial stage
Trachoma dubium

076.1 Active stage
Granular conjunctivitis (trachomatous)
Trachomatous:
follicular conjunctivitis
pannus

076.9 Trachoma, unspecified
Trachoma NOS

✓4th **077 Other diseases of conjunctiva due to viruses and Chlamydiae**

EXCLUDES *ophthalmic complications of viral diseases classified elsewhere*

077.0 Inclusion conjunctivitis
Paratrachoma
Swimming pool conjunctivitis
EXCLUDES *inclusion blennorrhea (neonatal) (771.6)*
DEF: Pus in conjunctiva caused by *Chlamydiae trachomatis*.

077.1 Epidemic keratoconjunctivitis
Shipyard eye
DEF: Highly contagious corneal or conjunctival infection caused by adenovirus type 8; symptoms include inflammation and corneal infiltrates.

077.2 Pharyngoconjunctival fever
Viral pharyngoconjunctivitis

077.3 Other adenoviral conjunctivitis
Acute adenoviral follicular conjunctivitis

077.4 Epidemic hemorrhagic conjunctivitis
Apollo:
conjunctivitis
disease
Conjunctivitis due to enterovirus type 70
Hemorrhagic conjunctivitis (acute) (epidemic)

077.8 Other viral conjunctivitis
Newcastle conjunctivitis

✓5th **077.9 Unspecified diseases of conjunctiva due to viruses and Chlamydiae**

077.98 Due to Chlamydiae

077.99 Due to viruses
Viral conjunctivitis NOS

✓4th **078 Other diseases due to viruses and Chlamydiae**

EXCLUDES *viral infection NOS (079.0-079.9)*
viremia NOS (790.8)

078.0 Molluscum contagiosum
DEF: Benign poxvirus infection causing small bumps on the skin or conjunctiva; transmitted by close contact.

✓5th **078.1 Viral warts**
Viral warts due to human papilloma virus
AHA: 2Q, '97, 9; 4Q, '93, 22
DEF: A keratotic papilloma of the epidermis caused by the human papilloma virus; the superficial vegetative lesions last for varying durations and eventually regress spontaneously.

078.10 Viral warts, unspecified
Condyloma NOS
Verruca:
NOS
Verruca:
Vulgaris
Warts (infectious)

078.11 Condyloma acuminatum
DEF: Clusters of mucosa or epidermal lesions on external genitalia; viral infection is sexually transmitted.

078.19 Other specified viral warts
Genital warts NOS
Verruca:
plana
Verruca:
plantaris

078.2 Sweating fever
Miliary fever
Sweating disease
DEF: A viral infection characterized by profuse sweating; various papular, vesicular and other eruptions cause the blockage of sweat glands.

078.3 Cat-scratch disease
Benign lymphoreticulosis (of inoculation)
Cat-scratch fever

078.4 Foot and mouth disease
Aphthous fever
Epizootic: aphthae
Epizootic: stomatitis
DEF: Ulcers on oral mucosa, legs, and feet after exposure to infected animal.

078.5 Cytomegaloviral disease HIV
Cytomegalic inclusion disease
Salivary gland virus disease
Use additional code to identify manifestation, as:
cytomegalic inclusion virus:
hepatitis (573.1)
pneumonia (484.1)
EXCLUDES *congenital cytomegalovirus infection (771.1)*
AHA: 1Q, '03, 10; 3Q, '98, 4; 2Q, '93, 11; 1Q, '89, 9
DEF: A herpes virus inclusion associated with serious disease morbidity including fever, leukopenia, pneumonia, retinitis, hepatitis and organ transplant; often leads to syndromes such as hepatomegaly, splenomegaly and thrombocytopenia; a common post-transplant complication for organ transplant recipients.

078.6 Hemorrhagic nephrosonephritis
Hemorrhagic fever:
epidemic
Korean
Hemorrhagic fever:
Russian
with renal syndrome
DEF: Viral infection causing kidney dysfunction and bleeding disorders.

078.7 Arenaviral hemorrhagic fever
Hemorrhagic fever:
Argentine
Bolivian
Hemorrhagic fever:
Junin virus
Machupo virus

✓5th **078.8 Other specified diseases due to viruses and Chlamydiae**
EXCLUDES *epidemic diarrhea (009.2)*
lymphogranuloma venereum (099.1)

078.81 Epidemic vertigo

078.82 Epidemic vomiting syndrome
Winter vomiting disease

078.88 Other specified diseases due to Chlamydiae
AHA: 4Q, '96, 22

078.89 Other specified diseases due to viruses
Epidemic cervical myalgia
Marburg disease
Tanapox

✓4th **079 Viral and chlamydial infection in conditions classified elsewhere and of unspecified site**
Note: This category is provided to be used as an additional code to identify the viral agent in diseases classifiable elsewhere. This category will also be used to classify virus infection of unspecified nature or site.

079.0 Adenovirus

079.1 ECHO virus
DEF: An "orphan" enteric RNA virus, certain serotypes of which are associated with human disease, especially aseptic meningitis.

079.2 Coxsackie virus
DEF: A heterogenous group of viruses associated with aseptic meningitis, myocarditis, pericarditis, and acute onset juvenile diabetes.

079.3 Rhinovirus
DEF: Rhinoviruses affect primarily the upper respiratory tract. Over 100 distinct types infect humans.

079.4 Human papillomavirus
AHA: 2Q, '97, 9; 4Q, '93, 22
DEF: Viral infection caused by the genus *Papillomavirus* causing cutaneous and genital warts, including verruca vulgaris and condyloma acuminatum; certain types are associated with cervical dysplasia, cancer and other genital malignancies.

✓5th **079.5 Retrovirus**
EXCLUDES *human immunodeficiency virus, type 1 [HIV-1] (042)*
human T-cell lymphotrophic virus, type III [HTLV-III] (042)
lymphadenopathy-associated virus [LAV] (042)
AHA: 4Q, '93, 22, 23
DEF: A large group of RNA viruses that carry reverse transcriptase and include the leukoviruses and lentiviruses.

079.50 Retrovirus, unspecified

079.51 Human T-cell lymphotrophic virus, type I [HTLV-I]

079.52 Human T-cell lymphotrophic virus, type II [HTLV-II]

079.53 Human immunodeficiency virus, type 2 [HIV-2]

079.59 Other specified retrovirus

079.6 Respiratory syncytial virus (RSV)
AHA: 4Q, '96, 27, 28
DEF: The major respiratory pathogen of young children, causing severe bronchitis and bronchopneumonia, and minor infection in adults.

✓5th **079.8 Other specified viral and chlamydial infections**
AHA: 1Q, '88, 12

079.81 Hantavirus
AHA: 4Q, '95, 60
DEF: An infection caused by the Muerto Canyon virus whose primary rodent reservoir is the deer mouse Peromyscus maniculatus; commonly characterized by fever, myalgias, headache, cough and rapid decline.

079.82 SARS-associated coronavirus CC
CC Excl: 011.00-012.16, 012.80-012.86, 017.90-017.96, 021.2, 031.0, 039.1, 079.82, 079.89, 115.05, 115.15, 115.95, 122.1, 130.4, 136.3, 480.0-480.2, 480.8-487.1, 494.0-508.9, 517.1, 517.8, 518.89, 519.8-519.9, 748.61
AHA: 4Q, '03, 46
DEF: A life-threatening respiratory disease described as severe acute respiratory syndrome (SARS); etiology coronavirus; most common presenting symptoms may range from mild to more severe forms of flu-like conditions; fever, chills, cough, headache, myalgia; diagnosis of SARS is based upon clinical, laboratory, and epidemiological criteria.

079.88 Other specified chlamydial infection

079.89 Other specified viral infection

✓5th **079.9 Unspecified viral and chlamydial infections**
EXCLUDES *viremia NOS (790.8)*
AHA: 2Q, '91, 8

079.98 Unspecified chlamydial infection
Chlamydial infections NOS

079.99 Unspecified viral infection
Viral infections NOS

RICKETTSIOSES AND OTHER ARTHROPOD-BORNE DISEASES (080-088)

EXCLUDES *arthropod-borne viral diseases (060.0-066.9)*

080 Louse-borne [epidemic] typhus
Typhus (fever):
classical
epidemic
Typhus (fever):
exanthematic NOS
louse-borne
DEF: *Rickettsia prowazekii*; causes severe headache, rash, high fever.

✓4th 081 Other typhus

081.0 Murine [endemic] typhus

Typhus (fever): endemic

Typhus (fever): flea-borne

DEF: Milder typhus caused by *Rickettsia typhi (mooseri)*; transmitted by rat flea.

081.1 Brill's disease

Brill-Zinsser disease
Recrudescent typhus (fever)

081.2 Scrub typhus

Japanese river fever
Kedani fever
Mite-borne typhus
Tsutsugamushi

081.9 Typhus, unspecified

Typhus (fever) NOS

✓4th 082 Tick-borne rickettsioses

082.0 Spotted fevers

Rocky mountain spotted fever
Sao Paulo fever

082.1 Boutonneuse fever

African tick typhus
India tick typhus
Kenya tick typhus
Marseilles fever
Mediterranean tick fever

082.2 North Asian tick fever

Siberian tick typhus

082.3 Queensland tick typhus

✓5th 082.4 Ehrlichiosis

AHA: 4Q, '00, 38

082.40 Ehrlichiosis, unspecified

082.41 Ehrlichiosis chaffeensis [E. chaffeensis]

DEF: A febrile illness caused by bacterial infection, also called human monocytic ehrlichiosis (HME). Causal organism is *Ehrlichia chaffeensis*, transmitted by the Lone Star tick, *Amblyomma americanum*. Symptoms include fever, chills, myalgia, nausea, vomiting, diarrhea, confusion, and severe headache occurring one week after a tick bite. Clinical findings are lymphadenopathy, rash, thrombocytopenia, leukopenia, and abnormal liver function tests.

082.49 Other ehrlichiosis

082.8 Other specified tick-borne rickettsioses

Lone star fever

AHA: 4Q, '99, 19

082.9 Tick-borne rickettsiosis, unspecified

Tick-borne typhus NOS

✓4th 083 Other rickettsioses

083.0 Q fever

DEF: Infection of *Coxiella burnettii* usually acquired through airborne organisms.

083.1 Trench fever

Quintan fever
Wolhynian fever

083.2 Rickettsialpox

Vesicular rickettsiosis

DEF: Infection of *Rickettsia akari* usually acquired through a mite bite.

083.8 Other specified rickettsioses

083.9 Rickettsiosis, unspecified

✓4th 084 Malaria

Note: Subcategories 084.0-084.6 exclude the listed conditions with mention of pernicious complications (084.8-084.9).

EXCLUDES *congenital malaria (771.2)*

DEF: Mosquito-borne disease causing high fever and prostration and cataloged by species of *Plasmodium: P. falciparum, P. malariae, P. ovale,* and *P. vivax*.

084.0 Falciparum malaria [malignant tertian]

Malaria (fever):
by Plasmodium falciparum
subtertian

084.1 Vivax malaria [benign tertian]

Malaria (fever) by Plasmodium vivax

084.2 Quartan malaria

Malaria (fever) by Plasmodium malariae
Malariae malaria

084.3 Ovale malaria

Malaria (fever) by Plasmodium ovale

084.4 Other malaria

Monkey malaria

084.5 Mixed malaria

Malaria (fever) by more than one parasite

084.6 Malaria, unspecified

Malaria (fever) NOS

084.7 Induced malaria

Therapeutically induced malaria

EXCLUDES *accidental infection from syringe, blood transfusion, etc. (084.0-084.6, above, according to parasite species)*
transmission from mother to child during delivery (771.2)

084.8 Blackwater fever

Hemoglobinuric:
fever (bilious)
malaria

Malarial hemoglobinuria

DEF: Severe hemic and renal complication of *Plasmodium falciparum* infection.

084.9 Other pernicious complications of malaria

Algid malaria
Cerebral malaria
Use additional code to identify complication, as:
malarial:
hepatitis (573.2)
nephrosis (581.81)

✓4th 085 Leishmaniasis

085.0 Visceral [kala-azar]

Dumdum fever
Infection by Leishmania:
donovani
infantum

Leishmaniasis:
dermal, post-kala-azar
Mediterranean
visceral (Indian)

085.1 Cutaneous, urban

Aleppo boil
Baghdad boil
Delhi boil
Infection by Leishmania tropica (minor)

Leishmaniasis, cutaneous:
dry form
late
recurrent
ulcerating

Oriental sore

085.2 Cutaneous, Asian desert

Infection by Leishmania tropica major
Leishmaniasis, cutaneous:
acute necrotizing
rural
wet form
zoonotic form

085.3 Cutaneous, Ethiopian

Infection by Leishmania ethiopica
Leishmaniasis, cutaneous:
diffuse
lepromatous

085.4 Cutaneous, American

Chiclero ulcer
Infection by Leishmania mexicana
Leishmaniasis tegumentaria diffusa

085.5 Mucocutaneous (American)

Espundia
Infection by Leishmania braziliensis
Uta

085.9 Leishmaniasis, unspecified

✓4th 086 Trypanosomiasis

Use additional code to identify manifestations, as:
trypanosomiasis:
encephalitis (323.2)
meningitis (321.3)

086.0 Chagas' disease with heart involvement CC

American trypanosomiasis } with heart involvement
Infection by Trypanosoma cruzi } with heart involvement

Any condition classifiable to 086.2 with heart involvement

CC Excl: 086.0, 139.8

086.1 Chagas' disease with other organ involvement

American trypanosomiasis } with involvement of organ other than heart
Infection by Trypanosoma cruzi } with involvement of organ other than heart

Any condition classifiable to 086.2 with involvement of organ other than heart

086.2 Chagas' disease without mention of organ involvement

American trypanosomiasis
Infection by Trypanosoma cruzi

086.3 Gambian trypanosomiasis

Gambian sleeping sickness
Infection by Trypanosoma gambiense

086.4 Rhodesian trypanosomiasis

Infection by Trypanosoma rhodesiense
Rhodesian sleeping sickness

086.5 African trypanosomiasis, unspecified

Sleeping sickness NOS

086.9 Trypanosomiasis, unspecified

4th **087 Relapsing fever**

INCLUDES recurrent fever

DEF: Infection of *Borrelia;* symptoms are episodic and include fever and arthralgia.

087.0 Louse-borne

087.1 Tick-borne

087.9 Relapsing fever, unspecified

4th **088 Other arthropod-borne diseases**

088.0 Bartonellosis

Carrión's disease
Oroya fever
Verruga peruana

5th **088.8 Other specified arthropod-borne diseases**

088.81 Lyme disease

Erythema chronicum migrans

AHA: 4Q, '91, 15; 3Q, '90, 14; 2Q, '89, 10

DEF: A recurrent multisystem disorder caused by the spirochete *Borrelia burgdorferi* with the carrier being the tick *Ixodes dammini*; the disease begins with lesions of erythema chronicum migrans; it is followed by arthritis of the large joints, myalgia, malaise, and neurological and cardiac manifestations.

088.82 Babesiosis

Babesiasis

AHA: 4Q, '93, 23

DEF: A tick-borne disease caused by infection of *Babesia*, characterized by fever, malaise, listlessness, severe anemia and hemoglobinuria.

088.89 Other

088.9 Arthropod-borne disease, unspecified

SYPHILIS AND OTHER VENEREAL DISEASES (090-099)

EXCLUDES *nonvenereal endemic syphilis (104.0)*
urogenital trichomoniasis (131.0)

4th **090 Congenital syphilis**

DEF: Infection by spirochete *Treponema pallidum* acquired in utero from the infected mother.

090.0 Early congenital syphilis, symptomatic

Congenital syphilitic:
- choroiditis
- coryza (chronic)
- hepatomegaly
- mucous patches
- periostitis

Congenital syphilitic:
- splenomegaly

Syphilitic (congenital):
- epiphysitis
- osteochondritis
- pemphigus

Any congenital syphilitic condition specified as early or manifest less than two years after birth

090.1 Early congenital syphilis, latent

Congenital syphilis without clinical manifestations, with positive serological reaction and negative spinal fluid test, less than two years after birth

090.2 Early congenital syphilis, unspecified

Congenital syphilis NOS, less than two years after birth

090.3 Syphilitic interstitial keratitis

Syphilitic keratitis:
- parenchymatous

Syphilitic keratitis:
- punctata profunda

EXCLUDES *interstitial keratitis NOS (370.50)*

5th **090.4 Juvenile neurosyphilis**

Use additional code to identify any associated mental disorder

DEF: *Treponema pallidum* infection involving the nervous system.

090.40 Juvenile neurosyphilis, unspecified CC

Congenital neurosyphilis
Dementia paralytica juvenilis
Juvenile:
- general paresis
- tabes
- taboparesis

CC Excl: 090.0-097.9, 099.40-099.9, 139.8

090.41 Congenital syphilitic encephalitis CC

CC Excl: See code 090.40

DEF: Congenital *Treponema pallidum* infection involving the brain.

090.42 Congenital syphilitic meningitis CC

CC Excl: 003.21, 013.00-013.16, 036.0, 047.0-049.1, 053.0, 054.72, 072.1, 090.0-097.9, 098.89, 099.40-099.9, 100.81, 112.83, 114.2, 115.01, 115.11, 115.91, 130.0, 139.8, 320.0-322.9, 349.89-349.9, 357.0

DEF: Congenital *Treponema pallidum* infection involving the lining of the brain and/or spinal cord.

090.49 Other CC

CC Excl: See code 090.40

090.5 Other late congenital syphilis, symptomatic

Gumma due to congenital syphilis
Hutchinson's teeth
Syphilitic saddle nose
Any congenital syphilitic condition specified as late or manifest two years or more after birth

090.6 Late congenital syphilis, latent

Congenital syphilis without clinical manifestations, with positive serological reaction and negative spinal fluid test, two years or more after birth

090.7 Late congenital syphilis, unspecified

Congenital syphilis NOS, two years or more after birth

090.9 Congenital syphilis, unspecified

4th **091 Early syphilis, symptomatic**

EXCLUDES *early cardiovascular syphilis (093.0-093.9)*
early neurosyphilis (094.0-094.9)

091.0 Genital syphilis (primary)

Genital chancre

DEF: Genital lesion at the site of initial infection by *Treponema pallidum.*

091.1 Primary anal syphilis

DEF: Anal lesion at the site of initial infection by *Treponema pallidum.*

091.2 Other primary syphilis

Primary syphilis of:
- breast
- fingers

Primary syphilis of:
- lip
- tonsils

DEF: Lesion at the site of initial infection by *Treponema pallidum.*

091.3 Secondary syphilis of skin or mucous membranes
Condyloma latum
Secondary syphilis of:
anus
mouth
pharynx
Secondary syphilis of:
skin
tonsils
vulva
DEF: Transitory or chronic lesions following initial syphilis infection.

091.4 Adenopathy due to secondary syphilis
Syphilitic adenopathy (secondary)
Syphilitic lymphadenitis (secondary)

✓5th **091.5 Uveitis due to secondary syphilis**
091.50 Syphilitic uveitis, unspecified
091.51 Syphilitic chorioretinitis (secondary)
DEF: Inflammation of choroid and retina as a secondary infection.
091.52 Syphilitic iridocyclitis (secondary)
DEF: Inflammation of iris and ciliary body as a secondary infection.

✓5th **091.6 Secondary syphilis of viscera and bone**
091.61 Secondary syphilitic periostitis
DEF: Inflammation of outer layers of bone as a secondary infection.
091.62 Secondary syphilitic hepatitis
Secondary syphilis of liver
091.69 Other viscera

091.7 Secondary syphilis, relapse
Secondary syphilis, relapse (treated) (untreated)
DEF: Return of symptoms of syphilis following asymptomatic period.

✓5th **091.8 Other forms of secondary syphilis**
091.81 Acute syphilitic meningitis (secondary)
DEF: Sudden, severe inflammation of the lining of the brain and/or spinal cord as a secondary infection.
091.82 Syphilitic alopecia
DEF: Hair loss following initial syphillis infection.
091.89 Other

091.9 Unspecified secondary syphilis

✓4th **092 Early syphilis, latent**
INCLUDES syphilis (acquired) without clinical manifestations, with positive serological reaction and negative spinal fluid test, less than two years after infection
092.0 Early syphilis, latent, serological relapse after treatment
092.9 Early syphilis, latent, unspecified

✓4th **093 Cardiovascular syphilis**
093.0 Aneurysm of aorta, specified as syphilitic CC
Dilatation of aorta, specified as syphilitic
CC Excl: See code 090.40
093.1 Syphilitic aortitis CC
CC Excl: See code 090.40
DEF: Inflammation of the aorta – the main artery leading from the heart.

✓5th **093.2 Syphilitic endocarditis**
DEF: Inflammation of the tissues lining the cavities of the heart.
093.20 Valve, unspecified CC
Syphilitic ostial coronary disease
CC Excl: See code 090.40
093.21 Mitral valve CC
CC Excl: See code 090.40
093.22 Aortic valve CC
Syphilitic aortic incompetence or stenosis
CC Excl: See code 090.40
093.23 Tricuspid valve CC
CC Excl: See code 090.40
093.24 Pulmonary valve CC
CC Excl: See code 090.40

✓5th **093.8 Other specified cardiovascular syphilis**
093.81 Syphilitic pericarditis CC
CC Excl: See code 090.40
DEF: Inflammation of the outer lining of the heart.
093.82 Syphilitic myocarditis CC
CC Excl: See code 090.40
DEF: Inflammation of the muscle of the heart.
093.89 Other CC
CC Excl: See code 090.40

093.9 Cardiovascular syphilis, unspecified CC
CC Excl: See code 090.40

✓4th **094 Neurosyphilis**
Use additional code to identify any associated mental disorder
094.0 Tabes dorsalis CC
Locomotor ataxia (progressive)
Posterior spinal sclerosis (syphilitic)
Tabetic neurosyphilis
Use additional code to identify manifestation, as:
neurogenic arthropathy [Charcot's joint disease] (713.5)
CC Excl: See code 090.40
DEF: Progressive degeneration of nerves associated with long-term syphilis; causing pain, wasting away, incontinence, and ataxia.

094.1 General paresis CC
Dementia paralytica
General paralysis (of the insane) (progressive)
Paretic neurosyphilis
Taboparesis
CC Excl: See code 090.40
DEF: Degeneration of brain associated with long-term syphilis, causing loss of brain function, progressive dementia, and paralysis.

094.2 Syphilitic meningitis CC
Meningovascular syphilis
EXCLUDES *acute syphilitic meningitis (secondary) (091.81)*
CC Excl: See code 090.42
DEF: Inflammation of the lining of the brain and/or spinal cord.

094.3 Asymptomatic neurosyphilis CC
CC Excl: See code 090.40

✓5th **094.8 Other specified neurosyphilis**
094.81 Syphilitic encephalitis CC
CC Excl: See code 090.40
094.82 Syphilitic Parkinsonism
DEF: Decreased motor function, tremors, and muscular rigidity.
094.83 Syphilitic disseminated retinochoroiditis
DEF: Inflammation of retina and choroid due to neurosyphilis.
094.84 Syphilitic optic atrophy
DEF: Degeneration of the eye and its nerves due to neurosyphilis.

094.85 Syphilitic retrobulbar neuritis
DEF: Inflammation of the posterior optic nerve to neurosyphilis.

094.86 Syphilitic acoustic neuritis
DEF: Inflammation of acoustic nerve due to neurosyphilis.

094.87 Syphilitic ruptured cerebral aneurysm CC
CC Excl: See code 090.40

094.89 Other CC
CC Excl: See code 090.40

094.9 Neurosyphilis, unspecified CC
Gumma (syphilitic) | of central nervous system NOS
Syphilis (early) (late) | of central nervous system NOS
Syphiloma | of central nervous system NOS
CC Excl: See code 090.40

✓4th **095 Other forms of late syphilis, with symptoms**
INCLUDES gumma (syphilitic)
syphilis, late, tertiary, or unspecified stage

095.0 Syphilitic episcleritis
095.1 Syphilis of lung
095.2 Syphilitic peritonitis
095.3 Syphilis of liver
095.4 Syphilis of kidney
095.5 Syphilis of bone
095.6 Syphilis of muscle
Syphilitic myositis
095.7 Syphilis of synovium, tendon, and bursa
Syphilitic:
bursitis
synovitis
095.8 Other specified forms of late symptomatic syphilis
EXCLUDES *cardiovascular syphilis (093.0-093.9)*
neurosyphilis (094.0-094.9)
095.9 Late symptomatic syphilis, unspecified

096 Late syphilis, latent
Syphilis (acquired) without clinical manifestations, with positive serological reaction and negative spinal fluid test, two years or more after infection

✓4th **097 Other and unspecified syphilis**
097.0 Late syphilis, unspecified
097.1 Latent syphilis, unspecified
Positive serological reaction for syphilis
097.9 Syphilis, unspecified
Syphilis (acquired) NOS
EXCLUDES *syphilis NOS causing death under two years of age (090.9)*

✓4th **098 Gonococcal infections**
DEF: *Neisseria gonorrhoeae* infection generally acquired in utero or in sexual congress.

098.0 Acute, of lower genitourinary tract CC
Gonococcal:
Bartholinitis (acute)
urethritis (acute)
vulvovaginitis (acute)
Gonorrhea (acute):
NOS
genitourinary (tract) NOS
CC Excl: 098.0-098.39, 098.89, 099.40-099.9, 139.8

✓5th **098.1 Acute, of upper genitourinary tract**
098.10 Gonococcal infection (acute) of upper genitourinary tract, site unspecified CC
CC Excl: See code 098.0

098.11 Gonococcal cystitis (acute) CC
Gonorrhea (acute) of bladder
CC Excl: See code 098.0

098.12 Gonococcal prostatitis (acute) CC ♂
CC Excl: See code 098.0

098.13 Gonococcal epididymo-orchitis (acute) CC ♂
Gonococcal orchitis (acute)
CC Excl: See code 098.0
DEF: Acute inflammation of the testes.

098.14 Gonococcal seminal vesiculitis (acute) CC ♂
Gonorrhea (acute) of seminal vesicle
CC Excl: See code 098.0

098.15 Gonococcal cervicitis (acute) CC ♀
Gonorrhea (acute) of cervix
CC Excl: See code 098.0

098.16 Gonococcal endometritis (acute) CC ♀
Gonorrhea (acute) of uterus
CC Excl: See code 098.0

098.17 Gonococcal salpingitis, specified as acute CC ♀
CC Excl: See code 098.0
DEF: Acute inflammation of the fallopian tubes.

098.19 Other CC
CC Excl: See code 098.0

098.2 Chronic, of lower genitourinary tract
Gonococcal:
Bartholinitis
urethritis
vulvovaginitis
Gonorrhea:
NOS
genitourinary (tract)
} specified as chronic or with duration of two months or more
Any condition classifiable to 098.0 specified as chronic or with duration of two months or more

✓5th **098.3 Chronic, of upper genitourinary tract**
INCLUDES any condition classifiable to 098.1 stated as chronic or with a duration of two months or more

098.30 Chronic gonococcal infection of upper genitourinary tract, site unspecified

098.31 Gonococcal cystitis, chronic
Any condition classifiable to 098.11, specified as chronic
Gonorrhea of bladder, chronic

098.32 Gonococcal prostatitis, chronic ♂
Any condition classifiable to 098.12, specified as chronic

098.33 Gonococcal epididymo-orchitis, chronic ♂
Any condition classifiable to 098.13, specified as chronic
Chronic gonococcal orchitis
DEF: Chronic inflammation of the testes.

098.34 Gonococcal seminal vesiculitis, chronic ♂
Any condition classifiable to 098.14, specified as chronic
Gonorrhea of seminal vesicle, chronic

098.35 Gonococcal cervicitis, chronic ♀
Any condition classifiable to 098.15, specified as chronic
Gonorrhea of cervix, chronic

098.36 Gonococcal endometritis, chronic ♀
Any condition classifiable to 098.16, specified as chronic
DEF: Chronic inflammation of the uterus.

098.37 Gonococcal salpingitis (chronic) ♀
DEF: Chronic inflammation of the fallopian tubes.

098.39 Other

✓5th **098.4 Gonococcal infection of eye**

098.40 Gonococcal conjunctivitis (neonatorum)
Gonococcal ophthalmia (neonatorum)
DEF: Infection of conjunctiva present at birth.

098.41 Gonococcal iridocyclitis
DEF: Inflammation and infection of iris and ciliary body.

098.42 Gonococcal endophthalmia
DEF: Inflammation and infection of contents of eyeball.

098.43 Gonococcal keratitis
DEF: Inflammation and infection of the cornea.

098.49 Other

✓5th **098.5 Gonococcal infection of joint**

098.50 Gonococcal arthritis
Gonococcal infection of joint NOS

098.51 Gonococcal synovitis and tenosynovitis

098.52 Gonococcal bursitis
DEF: Inflammation of the sac-like cavities in a joint.

098.53 Gonococcal spondylitis

098.59 Other
Gonococcal rheumatism

098.6 Gonococcal infection of pharynx

098.7 Gonococcal infection of anus and rectum
Gonococcal proctitis

✓5th **098.8 Gonococcal infection of other specified sites**

098.81 Gonococcal keratosis (blennorrhagica)
DEF: Pustular skin lesions caused by *Neisseria gonorrhoeae.*

098.82 Gonococcal meningitis
DEF: Inflammation of lining of brain and/or spinal cord.

098.83 Gonococcal pericarditis
DEF: Inflammation of the outer lining of the heart.

098.84 Gonococcal endocarditis
DEF: Inflammation of tissues lining the cavities of heart.

098.85 Other gonococcal heart disease

098.86 Gonococcal peritonitis
DEF: Inflammation of the membrane lining the abdomen.

098.89 Other
Gonococcemia

✓4th **099 Other venereal diseases**

099.0 Chancroid

Bubo (inguinal):
- chancroidal
- due to Hemophilus ducreyi

Chancre:
- Ducrey's
- simple
- soft

Ulcus molle (cutis) (skin)

DEF: A sexually transmitted disease caused by *Haemophilus ducreyi;* it is identified by a painful primary ulcer at the site of inoculation (usually external genitalia) with related lymphadenitis.

099.1 Lymphogranuloma venereum
Climatic or tropical bubo
(Durand-) Nicolas-Favre disease
Esthiomene
Lymphogranuloma inguinale
DEF: Sexually transmitted infection of *Chlamydia trachomatis* causing skin lesions.

099.2 Granuloma inguinale
Donovanosis
Granuloma pudendi (ulcerating)
Granuloma venereum
Pudendal ulcer
DEF: Chronic, sexually transmitted infection of *Calymmatobacterium granulomatis* causing progressive, anogenital skin ulcers.

099.3 Reiter's disease
Reiter's syndrome
Use additional code for associated:
- arthropathy (711.1)
- conjunctivitis (372.33)

DEF: A symptom complex of unknown etiology consisting of urethritis, conjunctivitis, arthritis and myocutaneous lesions. It occurs most commonly in young men and patients with HIV and may precede or follow AIDS. Also a form of reactive arthritis.

✓5th **099.4 Other nongonococcal urethritis [NGU]**

099.40 Unspecified
Nonspecific urethritis

099.41 Chlamydia trachomatis

099.49 Other specified organism

✓5th **099.5 Other venereal diseases due to Chlamydia trachomatis**

EXCLUDES *Chlamydia trachomatis infection of conjunctiva (076.0-076.9, 077.0, 077.9)*
Lymphogranuloma venereum (099.1)

DEF: Venereal diseases caused by *Chlamydia trachomatis* at other sites besides the urethra (e.g., pharynx, anus and rectum, conjunctiva and peritoneum).

099.50 Unspecified site

099.51 Pharynx

099.52 Anus and rectum

099.53 Lower genitourinary sites
EXCLUDES *urethra (099.41)*
Use additional code to specify site of infection, such as:
- bladder (595.4)
- cervix (616.0)
- vagina and vulva (616.11)

099.54 Other genitourinary sites
Use additional code to specify site of infection, such as:
- pelvic inflammatory disease NOS (614.9)
- testis and epididymis (604.91)

099.55 Unspecified genitourinary site

099.56 Peritoneum
Perihepatitis

099.59 Other specified site

099.8 Other specified venereal diseases

099.9 Venereal disease, unspecified

OTHER SPIROCHETAL DISEASES (100-104)

✓4th **100 Leptospirosis**

DEF: An infection of any spirochete of the genus Leptospire in blood. This zoonosis is transmitted to humans most often by exposure with contaminated animal tissues or water and less often by contact with urine. Patients present with flulike symptoms, the most common being muscle aches involving the thighs and low back. Treatment is with hydration and antibiotics.

100.0 Leptospirosis icterohemorrhagica
Leptospiral or spirochetal jaundice (hemorrhagic)
Weil's disease

✓5th **100.8 Other specified leptospiral infections**

100.81 Leptospiral meningitis (aseptic)

100.89 Other

Fever:
- Fort Bragg
- pretibial
- swamp

Infection by Leptospira:
- australis
- bataviae
- pyrogenes

100.9 Leptospirosis, unspecified

101 Vincent's angina

Acute necrotizing ulcerative:
gingivitis
stomatitis
Fusospirochetal pharyngitis
Spirochetal stomatitis
Trench mouth
Vincent's:
gingivitis
infection [any site]

DEF: Painful ulceration with edema and hypermic patches of the oropharyngeal and throat membranes; it is caused by spreading of acute ulcerative gingivitis.

✓4th **102 Yaws**

INCLUDES frambesia
pian

DEF: An infectious, endemic, tropical disease caused by *Treponema pertenue*; it usually affects persons 15 years old or younger; a primary cutaneous lesion develops, then a granulomatous skin eruption, and occasionally lesions that destroy skin and bone.

102.0 Initial lesions

Chancre of yaws
Frambesia, initial or primary
Initial frambesial ulcer
Mother yaw

102.1 Multiple papillomata and wet crab yaws

Butter yaws
Frambesioma
Pianoma
Plantar or palmar papilloma of yaws

102.2 Other early skin lesions

Cutaneous yaws, less than five years after infection
Early yaws (cutaneous) (macular) (papular) (maculopapular) (micropapular)
Frambeside of early yaws

102.3 Hyperkeratosis

Ghoul hand
Hyperkeratosis, palmar or plantar (early) (late) due to yaws
Worm-eaten soles

DEF: Overgrowth of skin of palm of bottoms of feet, due to yaws.

102.4 Gummata and ulcers

Gummatous frambeside
Nodular late yaws (ulcerated)

DEF: Rubbery lesions and areas of dead skin caused by yaws.

102.5 Gangosa

Rhinopharyngitis mutilans

DEF: Massive, mutilating lesions of the nose and oral cavity caused by yaws.

102.6 Bone and joint lesions

Goundou
Gumma, bone
Gummatous osteitis or periostitis
} of yaws (late)

Hydrarthrosis
Osteitis
Periostitis (hypertrophic)
} of yaws (early) (late)

102.7 Other manifestations

Juxta-articular nodules of yaws
Mucosal yaws

102.8 Latent yaws

Yaws without clinical manifestations, with positive serology

102.9 Yaws, unspecified

✓4th **103 Pinta**

DEF: A chronic form of treponematosis, endemic in areas of tropical America; it is identified by the presence of red, violet, blue, coffee-colored or white spots on the skin.

103.0 Primary lesions

Chancre (primary)
Papule (primary)
Pintid
} of pinta [carate]

103.1 Intermediate lesions

Erythematous plaques
Hyperchromic lesions
Hyperkeratosis
} of pinta [carate]

103.2 Late lesions

Cardiovascular lesions
Skin lesions:
achromic
cicatricial
dyschromic
Vitiligo
} of pinta [carate]

103.3 Mixed lesions

Achromic and hyperchromic skin lesions of pinta [carate]

103.9 Pinta, unspecified

✓4th **104 Other spirochetal infection**

104.0 Nonvenereal endemic syphilis

Bejel
Njovera

DEF: *Treponema pallidum, T. pertenue*, or *T. carateum* infection transmitted non-sexually, causing lesions on mucosa and skin.

104.8 Other specified spirochetal infections

EXCLUDES *relapsing fever (087.0-087.9)*
syphilis (090.0-097.9)

104.9 Spirochetal infection, unspecified

MYCOSES (110-118)

Use additional code to identify manifestation as:
arthropathy (711.6)
meningitis (321.0-321.1)
otitis externa (380.15)

EXCLUDES *infection by Actinomycetales, such as species of Actinomyces, Actinomadura, Nocardia, Streptomyces (039.0-039.9)*

✓4th **110 Dermatophytosis**

INCLUDES infection by species of Epidermophyton, Microsporum, and Trichophyton
tinea, any type except those in 111

DEF: Superficial infection of the skin caused by a parasitic fungus.

110.0 Of scalp and beard

Kerion
Sycosis, mycotic
Trichophytic tinea [black dot tinea], scalp

110.1 Of nail

Dermatophytic onychia
Onychomycosis
Tinea unguium

110.2 Of hand

Tinea manuum

110.3 Of groin and perianal area

Dhobie itch
Eczema marginatum
Tinea cruris

110.4 Of foot

Athlete's foot
Tinea pedis

110.5 Of the body

Herpes circinatus
Tinea imbricata [Tokelau]

110.6 Deep seated dermatophytosis

Granuloma trichophyticum
Majocchi's granuloma

110.8 Of other specified sites

110.9 Of unspecified site

Favus NOS
Microsporic tinea NOS
Ringworm NOS

✓4th **111 Dermatomycosis, other and unspecified**

111.0 Pityriasis versicolor

Infection by Malassezia [Pityrosporum] furfur
Tinea flava
Tinea versicolor

111.1 Tinea nigra
Infection by Cladosporium species
Keratomycosis nigricans
Microsporosis nigra
Pityriasis nigra
Tinea palmaris nigra

111.2 Tinea blanca
Infection by Trichosporon (beigelii) cutaneum
White piedra

111.3 Black piedra
Infection by Piedraia hortai

111.8 Other specified dermatomycoses

111.9 Dermatomycosis, unspecified

✓4th **112 Candidiasis**

INCLUDES infection by Candida species
moniliasis

EXCLUDES *neonatal monilial infection (771.7)*

DEF: Fungal infection caused by Candida; usually seen in mucous membranes or skin.

112.0 Of mouth CC HIV
Thrush (oral)
CC Excl: 112.0-112.9, 117.9, 139.8

112.1 Of vulva and vagina ♀
Candidal vulvovaginitis Monilial vulvovaginitis

112.2 Of other urogenital sites
Candidal balanitis
AHA: 4Q, '03, 105; 4Q, '96, 33

112.3 Of skin and nails HIV
Candidal intertrigo
Candidal onychia
Candidal perionyxis [paronychia]

112.4 Of lung CC HIV
Candidal pneumonia
CC Excl: See code 112.0
AHA: 2Q, '98, 7

112.5 Disseminated CC HIV
Systemic candidiasis
CC Excl: See code 112.0
AHA: 2Q, '00, 5; 2Q, '89, 10

✓5th **112.8 Of other specified sites**

112.81 Candidal endocarditis CC HIV
CC Excl: See code 112.0

112.82 Candidal otitis externa CC HIV
Otomycosis in moniliasis
CC Excl: See code 112.0

112.83 Candidal meningitis CC HIV
CC Excl: 003.21, 013.00-013.16, 036.0, 047.0-047.9, 049.0-049.1, 053.0, 054.72, 072.1, 090.42, 091.81, 094.2, 098.89, 100.81, 112.0-112.9, 114.2, 115.01, 115.11, 115.91, 117.9, 130.0, 139.8, 320.0-322.9, 349.89-349.9, 357.0

112.84 Candidal esophagitis CC HIV
CC Excl: See code 112.0
AHA: 4Q, '92, 19

112.85 Candidal enteritis CC HIV
CC Excl: See code 112.0
AHA: 4Q, '92, 19

112.89 Other
AHA: 1Q, '92, 17; 3Q, '91, 20

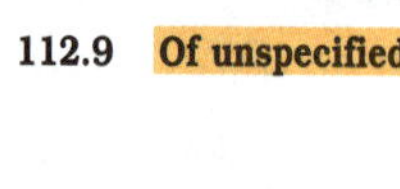

112.9 Of unspecified site HIV

✓4th **114 Coccidioidomycosis**

INCLUDES infection by Coccidioides (immitis)
Posada-Wernicke disease

AHA: 4Q, '93, 23

DEF: A fungal disease caused by inhalation of dust particles containing arthrospores of *Coccidiodes immitis*; a self-limited respiratory infection; the primary form is known as San Joaquin fever, desert fever or valley fever.

114.0 Primary coccidioidomycosis (pulmonary) CC HIV
Acute pulmonary coccidioidomycosis
Coccidioidomycotic pneumonitis
Desert rheumatism
Pulmonary coccidioidomycosis
San Joaquin Valley fever
CC Excl: 114.0, 114.3-114.9, 117.9, 139.8

DEF: Acute, self-limiting *Coccidioides immitis* infection of the lung.

114.1 Primary extrapulmonary coccidioidomycosis HIV
Chancriform syndrome
Primary cutaneous coccidioidomycosis

DEF: Acute, self-limiting *Coccidioides immitis* infection in nonpulmonary site.

114.2 Coccidioidal meningitis CC HIV
CC Excl: 003.21, 013.00-013.16, 036.0, 047.0-047.9, 049.0-049.1, 053.0, 054.72, 072.1, 090.42, 091.81, 094.2, 098.89, 100.81, 112.83, 114.2-114.9, 115.01, 115.11, 115.91, 117.9, 130.0, 139.8, 320.0-322.9, 349.89-349.9, 357.0

DEF: *Coccidioides immitis* infection of the lining of the brain and/or spinal cord.

114.3 Other forms of progressive coccidioidomycosis CC HIV
Coccidioidal granuloma
Disseminated coccidioidomycosis
CC Excl: 114.3, 114.9, 117.9, 139.8

114.4 Chronic pulmonary coccidioidomycosis HIV

114.5 Pulmonary coccidioidomycosis, unspecified HIV

114.9 Coccidioidomycosis, unspecified CC HIV
CC Excl: See code 114.3

✓4th **115 Histoplasmosis**

The following fifth-digit subclassification is for use with category 115:

0 without mention of manifestation
1 meningitis
2 retinitis
3 pericarditis
4 endocarditis
5 pneumonia
9 other

✓5th **115.0 Infection by Histoplasma capsulatum** CC 0-5 HIV
American histoplasmosis
Darling's disease
Reticuloendothelial cytomycosis
Small form histoplasmosis

CC Excl: For code 115.00: 115.00, 115.09, 115.90, 115.99, 117.9, 139.8; CC Excl: For code 115.01: 003.21, 013.00-013.16, 036.0, 047.0-049.1, 053.0, 054.72, 072.1, 090.42, 091.81, 094.2, 098.89, 100.81, 112.83, 114.2, 115.00-115.01, 115.09, 115.11, 115.90-115.91, 115.99, 117.9, 130.0, 139.8, 320.0-322.9, 349.89-349.9, 357.0; CC Excl: For code 115.02: 115.00, 115.02, 115.09, 115.90, 115.92, 115.99, 117.9, 139.8; CC Excl: For code 115.03: 115.00, 115.03, 115.09, 115.90, 115.93, 115.99, 117.9, 139.8; CC Excl: For code 115.04: 115.00, 115.04, 115.09, 115.90, 115.94, 115.99, 117.9, 139.8; CC Excl: For code 115.05: 115.00, 115.05-115.09, 115.90, 115.95-115.99, 117.9, 139.8, 480.0-480.2, 480.8-487.1, 494.0-508.9, 517.1, 518.89

N Newborn Age: 0 P Pediatric Age: 0-17 M Maternity Age: 12-55 A Adult Age: 15-124 CC CC Condition MC Major Complication CD Complex Dx HIV HIV Related Dx

✓5th **115.1 Infection by Histoplasma duboisii** CC HIV
African histoplasmosis
Large form histoplasmosis
CC Excl: For code 115.10: 115.10, 115.19, 115.90, 115.99, 117.9, 139.8; **CC Excl: For code 115.11:** 003.21, 013.00-013.16, 036.0, 047.0-047.9, 049.0-049.1, 053.0, 054.72, 072.1, 090.42, 091.81, 094.2, 098.89, 100.81, 112.83, 114.2, 115.01, 115.10-115.11, 115.19, 115.90-115.91, 115.99, 117.9, 130.0, 139.8, 320.0-322.9, 349.89-349.9, 357.0; **CC Excl: For code 115.12:** 115.10, 115.12, 115.19, 115.90, 115.92, 115.99, 117.9, 139.8; **CC Excl: For code 115.13:** 115.10, 115.13, 115.19, 115.90, 115.93, 115.99, 117.9, 139.8; **CC Excl: For code 115.14:** 115.10, 115.14, 115.19, 115.90, 115.94, 115.99, 117.9, 139.8; **CC Excl: For code 115.15:** 115.05, 115.10, 115.15-115.19, 115.90, 115.95-115.99, 117.9, 139.8, 480.0-480.2, 480.8-487.1, 494.0-508.9, 517.1, 518.89; **CC Excl: For code 115.19:** 115.10, 115.19, 115.90, 115.99, 117.9, 139.8

✓5th **115.9 Histoplasmosis, unspecified** CC HIV
Histoplasmosis NOS
CC Excl: For code 115.90: 115.90, 115.99, 117.9, 139.8; **CC Excl: For code 115.91:** 003.21, 013.00-013.16, 036.0, 047.0-047.9, 049.0-049.1, 053.0, 054.72, 072.1, 090.42, 091.81, 094.2, 098.89, 100.81, 112.83, 114.2, 115.01, 115.11, 115.91, 115.99, 117.9, 130.0, 139.8, 320.0-322.9, 349.89-349.9, 357.0; **CC Excl: For code 115.92:** 115.92, 115.99, 117.9, 139.8; **CC Excl: For code 115.93:** 115.93, 115.99, 117.9, 139.8; **CC Excl: For code 115.94:** 115.94, 115.99, 117.9, 139.8; **CC Excl: For code 115.95:** 115.05, 115.15, 115.95, 115.99, 117.9, 139.8; **CC Excl: For code 115.99:** 115.99, 117.9, 139.8

✓4th **116 Blastomycotic infection**

116.0 Blastomycosis CC
Blastomycotic dermatitis
Chicago disease
Cutaneous blastomycosis
Disseminated blastomycosis
Gilchrist's disease
Infection by Blastomyces [Ajellomyces] dermatitidis
North American blastomycosis
Primary pulmonary blastomycosis
CC Excl: 116.0, 117.9, 139.8

116.1 Paracoccidioidomycosis CC
Brazilian blastomycosis
Infection by Paracoccidioides [Blastomyces] brasiliensis
Lutz-Splendore-Almeida disease
Mucocutaneous-lymphangitic paracoccidioidomycosis
Pulmonary paracoccidioidomycosis
South American blastomycosis
Visceral paracoccidioidomycosis
CC Excl: 116.1, 117.9, 139.8

116.2 Lobomycosis
Infections by Loboa [Blastomyces] loboi
Keloidal blastomycosis
Lobo's disease

✓4th **117 Other mycoses**

117.0 Rhinosporidiosis
Infection by Rhinosporidium seeberi

117.1 Sporotrichosis
Cutaneous sporotrichosis
Disseminated sporotrichosis
Infection by Sporothrix [Sporotrichum] schenckii
Lymphocutaneous sporotrichosis
Pulmonary sporotrichosis
Sporotrichosis of the bones

117.2 Chromoblastomycosis
Chromomycosis
Infection by Cladosporidium carrionii, Fonsecaea compactum, Fonsecaea pedrosoi, Phialophora verrucosa

117.3 Aspergillosis CC
Infection by Aspergillus species, mainly A. fumigatus, A. flavus group, A. terreus group
CC Excl: 117.3, 117.9, 139.8
AHA: 4Q, '97, 40

117.4 Mycotic mycetomas CC
Infection by various genera and species of Ascomycetes and Deuteromycetes, such as Acremonium [Cephalosporium] falciforme, Neotestudina rosatii, Madurella grisea, Madurella mycetomii, Pyrenochaeta romeroi, Zopfia [Leptosphaeria] senegalensis
Madura foot, mycotic
Maduromycosis, mycotic
EXCLUDES *actinomycotic mycetomas (039.0-039.9)*
CC Excl: 117.4, 117.9, 139.8

117.5 Cryptococcosis CC HIV
Busse-Buschke's disease
European cryptococcosis
Infection by Cryptococcus neoformans
Pulmonary cryptococcosis
Systemic cryptococcosis
Torula
CC Excl: 117.5, 117.9, 139.8

117.6 Allescheriosis [Petriellidosis] CC
Infections by Allescheria [Petriellidium] boydii [Monosporium apiospermum]
EXCLUDES *mycotic mycetoma (117.4)*
CC Excl: 117.6, 117.9, 139.8

117.7 Zygomycosis [Phycomycosis or Mucormycosis] CC
Infection by species of Absidia, Basidiobolus, Conidiobolus, Cunninghamella, Entomophthora, Mucor, Rhizopus, Saksenaea
CC Excl: 117.7, 117.9, 139.8

117.8 Infection by dematiacious fungi, [Phaehyphomycosis]
Infection by dematiacious fungi, such as Cladosporium trichoides [bantianum], Dreschlera hawaiiensis, Phialophora gougerotii, Phialophora jeanselmi

117.9 Other and unspecified mycoses

118 Opportunistic mycoses CC HIV
Infection of skin, subcutaneous tissues, and/or organs by a wide variety of fungi generally considered to be pathogenic to compromised hosts only (e.g., infection by species of Alternaria, Dreschlera, Fusarium)
CC Excl: 117.9, 118, 139.8

HELMINTHIASES (120-129)

✓4th **120 Schistosomiasis [bilharziasis]**
DEF: Infection caused by *Schistosoma*, a genus of flukes or trematode parasites.

120.0 Schistosoma haematobium
Vesical schistosomiasis NOS

120.1 Schistosoma mansoni
Intestinal schistosomiasis NOS

120.2 Schistosoma japonicum
Asiatic schistosomiasis NOS
Katayama disease or fever

120.3 Cutaneous
Cercarial dermatitis
Infection by cercariae of Schistosoma
Schistosome dermatitis
Swimmers' itch

120.8 Other specified schistosomiasis
Infection by Schistosoma:
bovis
intercalatum
mattheii
spindale
Schistosomiasis chestermani

120.9 Schistosomiasis, unspecified
Blood flukes NOS
Hemic distomiasis

✓4th **121 Other trematode infections**

121.0 Opisthorchiasis
Infection by:
cat liver fluke
Opisthorchis (felineus) (tenuicollis) (viverrini)

121.1 Clonorchiasis
Biliary cirrhosis due to clonorchiasis
Chinese liver fluke disease
Hepatic distomiasis due to Clonorchis sinensis
Oriental liver fluke disease

121.2 Paragonimiasis
Infection by Paragonimus
Lung fluke disease (oriental)
Pulmonary distomiasis

121.3 Fascioliasis
Infection by Fasciola:
gigantica
hepatica
Liver flukes NOS
Sheep liver fluke infection

121.4 Fasciolopsiasis
Infection by Fasciolopsis (buski)
Intestinal distomiasis

121.5 Metagonimiasis
Infection by Metagonimus yokogawai

121.6 Heterophyiasis
Infection by:
Heterophyes heterophyes
Stellantchasmus falcatus

121.8 Other specified trematode infections
Infection by:
Dicrocoelium dendriticum
Echinostoma ilocanum
Gastrodiscoides hominis

121.9 Trematode infection, unspecified
Distomiasis NOS
Fluke disease NOS

✓4th **122 Echinococcosis**

INCLUDES echinococciasis
hydatid disease
hydatidosis

DEF: Infection caused by larval forms of tapeworms of the genus *Echinococcus.*

122.0 Echinococcus granulosus infection of liver
122.1 Echinococcus granulosus infection of lung
122.2 Echinococcus granulosus infection of thyroid
122.3 Echinococcus granulosus infection, other
122.4 Echinococcus granulosus infection, unspecified
122.5 Echinococcus multilocularis infection of liver
122.6 Echinococcus multilocularis infection, other
122.7 Echinococcus multilocularis infection, unspecified
122.8 Echinococcosis, unspecified, of liver
122.9 Echinococcosis, other and unspecified

✓4th **123 Other cestode infection**

123.0 Taenia solium infection, intestinal form
Pork tapeworm (adult) (infection)

123.1 Cysticercosis
Cysticerciasis
Infection by Cysticercus cellulosae [larval form of Taenia solium]
AHA: 2Q, '97, 8

123.2 Taenia saginata infection
Beef tapeworm (infection)
Infection by Taeniarhynchus saginatus

123.3 Taeniasis, unspecified

123.4 Diphyllobothriasis, intestinal
Diphyllobothrium (adult) (latum) (pacificum) infection
Fish tapeworm (infection)

123.5 Sparganosis [larval diphyllobothriasis]
Infection by:
Diphyllobothrium larvae
Sparganum (mansoni) (proliferum)
Spirometra larvae

123.6 Hymenolepiasis
Dwarf tapeworm (infection)
Hymenolepis (diminuta) (nana) infection
Rat tapeworm (infection)

123.8 Other specified cestode infection
Diplogonoporus (grandis) } infection
Dipylidium (caninum) } infection
Dog tapeworm (infection)

123.9 Cestode infection, unspecified
Tapeworm (infection) NOS

124 Trichinosis
Trichinella spiralis infection
Trichinellosis
Trichiniasis

DEF: Infection by *Trichinella spiralis*, the smallest of the parasitic nematodes.

✓4th **125 Filarial infection and dracontiasis**

125.0 Bancroftian filariasis
Chyluria
Elephantiasis
Infection
Lymphadenitis
Lymphangitis
} due to Wuchereria bancrofti
Wuchereriasis

125.1 Malayan filariasis
Brugia filariasis
Chyluria
Elephantiasis
Infection
Lymphadenitis
Lymphangitis
} due to Brugia [Wuchereria] malayi

125.2 Loiasis
Eyeworm disease of Africa
Loa loa infection

125.3 Onchocerciasis
Onchocerca volvulus infection
Onchocercosis

125.4 Dipetalonemiasis
Infection by:
Acanthocheilonema perstans
Dipetalonema perstans

125.5 Mansonella ozzardi infection
Filariasis ozzardi

125.6 Other specified filariasis
Dirofilaria infection
Infection by:
Acanthocheilonema streptocerca
Dipetalonema streptocerca

125.7 Dracontiasis
Guinea-worm infection
Infection by Dracunculus medinensis

125.9 Unspecified filariasis

✓4th **126 Ancylostomiasis and necatoriasis**

INCLUDES cutaneous larva migrans due to Ancylostoma
hookworm (disease) (infection)
uncinariasis

126.0 Ancylostoma duodenale
126.1 Necator americanus
126.2 Ancylostoma braziliense
126.3 Ancylostoma ceylanicum

126.8 Other specified Ancylostoma

126.9 Ancylostomiasis and necatoriasis, unspecified
Creeping eruption NOS
Cutaneous larva migrans NOS

✓4th **127 Other intestinal helminthiases**

127.0 Ascariasis
Ascaridiasis
Infection by Ascaris lumbricoides
Roundworm infection

127.1 Anisakiasis
Infection by Anisakis larva

127.2 Strongyloidiasis HIV
Infection by Strongyloides stercoralis
EXCLUDES *trichostrongyliasis (127.6)*

127.3 Trichuriasis
Infection by Trichuris trichiuria
Trichocephaliasis
Whipworm (disease) (infection)

127.4 Enterobiasis
Infection by Enterobius vermicularis
Oxyuriasis
Oxyuris vermicularis infection
Pinworm (disease) (infection)
Threadworm infection

127.5 Capillariasis
Infection by Capillaria philippinensis
EXCLUDES *infection by Capillaria hepatica (128.8)*

127.6 Trichostrongyliasis
Infection by Trichostrongylus species

127.7 Other specified intestinal helminthiasis
Infection by:
Oesophagostomum apiostomum and related species
Ternidens diminutus
other specified intestinal helminth
Physalopteriasis

127.8 Mixed intestinal helminthiasis
Infection by intestinal helminths classified to more than one of the categories 120.0-127.7
Mixed helminthiasis NOS

127.9 Intestinal helminthiasis, unspecified

✓4th **128 Other and unspecified helminthiases**

128.0 Toxocariasis
Larva migrans visceralis
Toxocara (canis) (cati) infection
Visceral larva migrans syndrome

128.1 Gnathostomiasis
Infection by Gnathostoma spinigerum and related species

128.8 Other specified helminthiasis
Infection by:
Angiostrongylus cantonensis
Capillaria hepatica
other specified helminth

128.9 Helminth infection, unspecified
Helminthiasis NOS Worms NOS

129 Intestinal parasitism, unspecified

OTHER INFECTIOUS AND PARASITIC DISEASES (130–136)

✓4th **130 Toxoplasmosis**
INCLUDES infection by toxoplasma gondii
toxoplasmosis (acquired)
EXCLUDES *congenital toxoplasmosis (771.2)*

130.0 Meningoencephalitis due to toxoplasmosis CC HIV
Encephalitis due to acquired toxoplasmosis
CC Excl: 130.0, 130.7-130.9, 139.8

130.1 Conjunctivitis due to toxoplasmosis CC HIV
CC Excl: 130.1, 130.7-130.9, 139.8

130.2 Chorioretinitis due to toxoplasmosis CC HIV
Focal retinochoroiditis due to acquired toxoplasmosis
CC Excl: 130.2, 130.7-130.9, 139.8

130.3 Myocarditis due to toxoplasmosis CC HIV
CC Excl: 130.3, 130.7-130.9, 139.8

130.4 Pneumonitis due to toxoplasmosis CC HIV
CC Excl: 130.4, 130.7-130.9, 139.8, 480.0-480.2, 480.8-487.1, 494.0-508.9, 517.1, 518.89

130.5 Hepatitis due to toxoplasmosis CC HIV
CC Excl: 130.5-130.9, 139.8

130.7 Toxoplasmosis of other specified sites CC HIV
CC Excl: 130.7-130.9, 139.8

130.8 Multisystemic disseminated toxoplasmosis CC HIV
Toxoplasmosis of multiple sites
CC Excl: See code 130.7

130.9 Toxoplasmosis, unspecified HIV

✓4th **131 Trichomoniasis**
INCLUDES infection due to Trichomonas (vaginalis)

✓5th **131.0 Urogenital trichomoniasis**

131.00 Urogenital trichomoniasis, unspecified
Fluor (vaginalis) } trichomonal or due to Trichomonas (vaginalis)
Leukorrhea (vaginalis) } trichomonal or due to Trichomonas (vaginalis)

DEF: ***Trichomonas vaginalis*** **infection of reproductive and urinary organs, transmitted through coitus.**

131.01 Trichomonal vulvovaginitis ♀
Vaginitis, trichomonal or due to Trichomonas (vaginalis)

DEF: ***Trichomonas vaginalis*** **infection of vulva and vagina; often asymptomatic, transmitted through coitus.**

131.02 Trichomonal urethritis

DEF: ***Trichomonas vaginalis*** **infection of the urethra.**

131.03 Trichomonal prostatitis ♂

DEF: ***Trichomonas vaginalis*** **infection of the prostate.**

131.09 Other

131.8 Other specified sites
EXCLUDES *intestinal (007.3)*

131.9 Trichomoniasis, unspecified

✓4th **132 Pediculosis and phthirus infestation**

132.0 Pediculus capitis [head louse]

132.1 Pediculus corporis [body louse]

132.2 Phthirus pubis [pubic louse]
Pediculus pubis

132.3 Mixed infestation
Infestation classifiable to more than one of the categories 132.0-132.2

132.9 Pediculosis, unspecified

✓4th **133 Acariasis**

133.0 Scabies
Infestation by Sarcoptes scabiei
Norwegian scabies
Sarcoptic itch

133.8 Other acariasis
Chiggers
Infestation by:
Demodex folliculorum
Infestation by:
Trombicula

133.9 Acariasis, unspecified
Infestation by mites NOS

✓4th 134 Other infestation

134.0 Myiasis

Infestation by:
- Dermatobia (hominis)
- fly larvae
- Gasterophilus (intestinalis)

Infestation by:
- maggots
- Oestrus ovis

134.1 Other arthropod infestation

Infestation by:
- chigoe
- sand flea
- Tunga penetrans

Jigger disease
Scarabiasis
Tungiasis

134.2 Hirudiniasis

Hirudiniasis (external) (internal)
Leeches (aquatic) (land)

134.8 Other specified infestations

134.9 Infestation, unspecified

Infestation (skin) NOS
Skin parasites NOS

135 Sarcoidosis CC

Besnier-Boeck-Schaumann disease
Lupoid (miliary) of Boeck
Lupus pernio (Besnier)
Lymphogranulomatosis, benign (Schaumann's)
Sarcoid (any site):
- NOS
- Boeck
- Darier-Roussy

Uveoparotid fever

CC Excl: 135, 139.8

DEF: A chronic, granulomatous reticulosis (abnormal increase in cells), affecting any organ or tissue; acute form has high rate of remission; chronic form is progressive.

✓4th 136 Other and unspecified infectious and parasitic diseases

136.0 Ainhum

Dactylolysis spontanea

DEF: A disease affecting the toes, especially the fifth digit, and sometimes the fingers, especially seen in black adult males; it is characterized by a linear constriction around the affected digit leading to spontaneous amputation of the distal part of the digit.

136.1 Behçet's syndrome

DEF: A chronic inflammatory disorder of unknown etiology involving the small blood vessels; it is characterized by recurrent aphthous ulceration of the oral and pharyngeal mucous membranes and the genitalia, skin lesions, severe uvetis, retinal vascularitis and optic atrophy.

136.2 Specific infections by free-living amebae

Meningoencephalitis due to Naegleria

136.3 Pneumocystosis CC HIV

Pneumonia due to Pneumocystis carinii
▶Pneumonia due to Pneumocystis jiroveci◀

CC Excl: 136.3, 139.8, 480.0- 480.2, 480.8-487.1, 494.0-508.9, 517.1, 518.89

AHA: 1Q, '05, 7; 1Q, '03, 15; N-D, '87, 5-6

DEF: *Pneumocystis carinii* fungus causing pneumonia in immunocompromised patients; a leading cause of death among AIDS patients.

136.4 Psorospermiasis

136.5 Sarcosporidiosis

Infection by Sarcocystis lindemanni

DEF: *Sarcocystis* infection causing muscle cysts of intestinal inflammation.

136.8 Other specified infectious and parasitic diseases HIV

Candiru infestation

136.9 Unspecified infectious and parasitic diseases

Infectious disease NOS
Parasitic disease NOS

AHA: 2Q, '91, 8

LATE EFFECTS OF INFECTIOUS AND PARASITIC DISEASES (137-139)

✓4th 137 Late effects of tuberculosis

Note: This category is to be used to indicate conditions classifiable to 010-018 as the cause of late effects, which are themselves classified elsewhere. The "late effects" include those specified as such, as sequelae, or as due to old or inactive tuberculosis, without evidence of active disease.

137.0 Late effects of respiratory or unspecified tuberculosis CC

CC Excl: 137.0, 139.8

137.1 Late effects of central nervous system tuberculosis CC

CC Excl: 137.1, 139.8

137.2 Late effects of genitourinary tuberculosis CC

CC Excl: 137.2, 139.8

137.3 Late effects of tuberculosis of bones and joints

137.4 Late effects of tuberculosis of other specified organs

138 Late effects of acute poliomyelitis CC

Note: This category is to be used to indicate conditions classifiable to 045 as the cause of late effects, which are themselves classified elsewhere. The "late effects" include conditions specified as such, or as sequelae, or as due to old or inactive poliomyelitis, without evidence of active disease.

CC Excl: 138, 139.8

✓4th 139 Late effects of other infectious and parasitic diseases

Note: This category is to be used to indicate conditions classifiable to categories 001-009, 020-041, 046-136 as the cause of late effects, which are themselves classified elsewhere. The "late effects" include conditions specified as such; they also include sequela of diseases classifiable to the above categories if there is evidence that the disease itself is no longer present.

139.0 Late effects of viral encephalitis

Late effects of conditions classifiable to 049.8-049.9, 062-064

139.1 Late effects of trachoma

Late effects of conditions classifiable to 076

139.8 Late effects of other and unspecified infectious and parasitic diseases

AHA: 4Q, '91, 15; 3Q, '90, 14; M-A, '87, 8

2. NEOPLASMS (140-239)

Notes:

1. Content

This chapter contains the following broad groups:

- 140-195 Malignant neoplasms, stated or presumed to be primary, of specified sites, except of lymphatic and hematopoietic tissue
- 196-198 Malignant neoplasms, stated or presumed to be secondary, of specified sites
- 199 Malignant neoplasms, without specification of site
- 200-208 Malignant neoplasms, stated or presumed to be primary, of lymphatic and hematopoietic tissue
- 210-229 Benign neoplasms
- 230-234 Carcinoma in situ
- 235-238 Neoplasms of uncertain behavior [see Note, above category 235]
- 239 Neoplasms of unspecified nature

2. Functional activity

All neoplasms are classified in this chapter, whether or not functionally active. An additional code from Chapter 3 may be used to identify such functional activity associated with any neoplasm, e.g.:

catecholamine-producing malignant pheochromocytoma of adrenal:

code 194.0, additional code 255.6

basophil adenoma of pituitary with Cushing's syndrome:

code 227.3, additional code 255.0

3. Morphology [Histology]

For those wishing to identify the histological type of neoplasms, a comprehensive coded nomenclature, which comprises the morphology rubrics of the ICD-Oncology, is given in Appendix A.

4. Malignant neoplasms overlapping site boundaries

Categories 140-195 are for the classification of primary malignant neoplasms according to their point of origin. A malignant neoplasm that overlaps two or more subcategories within a three-digit rubric and whose point of origin cannot be determined should be classified to the subcategory .8 "Other."

For example, "carcinoma involving tip and ventral surface of tongue" should be assigned to 141.8. On the other hand, "carcinoma of tip of tongue, extending to involve the ventral surface" should be coded to 141.2, as the point of origin, the tip, is known. Three subcategories (149.8, 159.8, 165.8) have been provided for malignant neoplasms that overlap the boundaries of three-digit rubrics within certain systems.

Overlapping malignant neoplasms that cannot be classified as indicated above should be assigned to the appropriate subdivision of category 195 (Malignant neoplasm of other and ill-defined sites).

AHA: 2Q, '90, 7

DEF: An abnormal growth, such as a tumor. Morphology determines behavior, i.e., whether it will remain intact (benign) or spread to adjacent tissue (malignant). The term mass is not synonymous with neoplasm, as it is often used to describe cysts and thickenings such as those occurring with hematoma or infection.

MALIGNANT NEOPLASM OF LIP, ORAL CAVITY, AND PHARYNX (140-149)

EXCLUDES *carcinoma in situ (230.0)*

✓4th **140 Malignant neoplasm of lip**

EXCLUDES *skin of lip (173.0)*

140.0 Upper lip, vermilion border

Upper lip: NOS; external
Upper lip: lipstick area

Lip

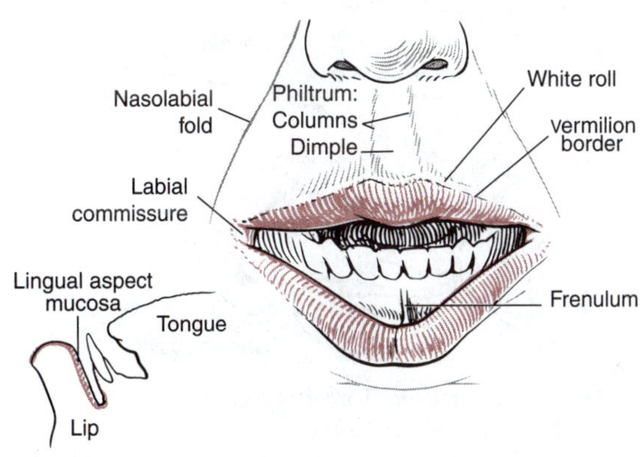

140.1 Lower lip, vermilion border

Lower lip: NOS; external
Lower lip: lipstick area

140.3 Upper lip, inner aspect

Upper lip: buccal aspect; frenulum
Upper lip: mucosa; oral aspect

140.4 Lower lip, inner aspect

Lower lip: buccal aspect; frenulum
Lower lip: mucosa; oral aspect

140.5 Lip, unspecified, inner aspect

Lip, not specified whether upper or lower:
- buccal aspect
- frenulum
- mucosa
- oral aspect

140.6 Commissure of lip

Labial commissure

140.8 Other sites of lip

Malignant neoplasm of contiguous or overlapping sites of lip whose point of origin cannot be determined

140.9 Lip, unspecified, vermilion border

Lip, not specified as upper or lower:
- NOS
- external
- lipstick area

✓4th **141 Malignant neoplasm of tongue**

141.0 Base of tongue

Dorsal surface of base of tongue
Fixed part of tongue NOS

141.1 Dorsal surface of tongue

Anterior two-thirds of tongue, dorsal surface
Dorsal tongue NOS
Midline of tongue

EXCLUDES *dorsal surface of base of tongue (141.0)*

Tongue

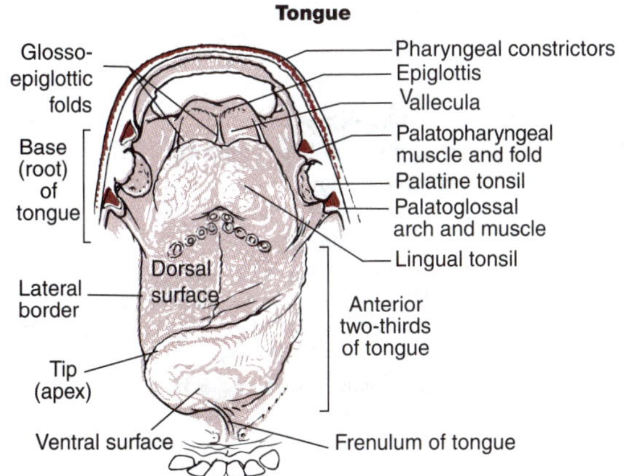

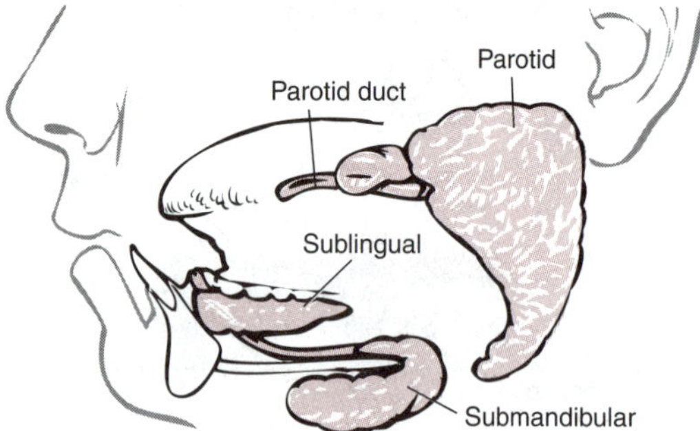

141.2 Tip and lateral border of tongue

141.3 Ventral surface of tongue
Anterior two-thirds of tongue, ventral surface
Frenulum linguae

141.4 Anterior two-thirds of tongue, part unspecified
Mobile part of tongue NOS

141.5 Junctional zone
Border of tongue at junction of fixed and mobile parts at insertion of anterior tonsillar pillar

141.6 Lingual tonsil

141.8 Other sites of tongue
Malignant neoplasm of contiguous or overlapping sites of tongue whose point of origin cannot be determined

141.9 Tongue, unspecified
Tongue NOS

✓4th 142 Malignant neoplasm of major salivary glands

INCLUDES salivary ducts

EXCLUDES *malignant neoplasm of minor salivary glands:*
NOS (145.9)
buccal mucosa (145.0)
soft palate (145.3)
tongue (141.0-141.9)
tonsil, palatine (146.0)

142.0 Parotid gland

142.1 Submandibular gland
Submaxillary gland

142.2 Sublingual gland

142.8 Other major salivary glands
Malignant neoplasm of contiguous or overlapping sites of salivary glands and ducts whose point of origin cannot be determined

142.9 Salivary gland, unspecified
Salivary gland (major) NOS

✓4th 143 Malignant neoplasm of gum

INCLUDES alveolar (ridge) mucosa
gingiva (alveolar) (marginal)
interdental papillae

EXCLUDES *malignant odontogenic neoplasms (170.0-170.1)*

143.0 Upper gum

143.1 Lower gum

143.8 Other sites of gum
Malignant neoplasm of contiguous or overlapping sites of gum whose point of origin cannot be determined

143.9 Gum, unspecified

✓4th 144 Malignant neoplasm of floor of mouth

144.0 Anterior portion
Anterior to the premolar-canine junction

144.1 Lateral portion

144.8 Other sites of floor of mouth
Malignant neoplasm of contiguous or overlapping sites of floor of mouth whose point of origin cannot be determined

144.9 Floor of mouth, part unspecified

✓4th 145 Malignant neoplasm of other and unspecified parts of mouth

EXCLUDES *mucosa of lips (140.0-140.9)*

145.0 Cheek mucosa
Buccal mucosa
Cheek, inner aspect

145.1 Vestibule of mouth
Buccal sulcus (upper) (lower)
Labial sulcus (upper) (lower)

145.2 Hard palate

145.3 Soft palate

EXCLUDES *nasopharyngeal [posterior] [superior] surface of soft palate (147.3)*

145.4 Uvula

145.5 Palate, unspecified
Junction of hard and soft palate
Roof of mouth

145.6 Retromolar area

145.8 Other specified parts of mouth
Malignant neoplasm of contiguous or overlapping sites of mouth whose point of origin cannot be determined

145.9 Mouth, unspecified
Buccal cavity NOS
Minor salivary gland, unspecified site
Oral cavity NOS

✓4th 146 Malignant neoplasm of oropharynx

146.0 Tonsil
Tonsil:
NOS
faucial
palatine

EXCLUDES *lingual tonsil (141.6)*
pharyngeal tonsil (147.1)

AHA: S-O, '87, 8

146.1 Tonsillar fossa

146.2 Tonsillar pillars (anterior) (posterior)
Faucial pillar
Glossopalatine fold
Palatoglossal arch
Palatopharyngeal arch

146.3 Vallecula
Anterior and medial surface of the pharyngoepiglottic fold

146.4 Anterior aspect of epiglottis
Epiglottis, free border [margin]
Glossoepiglottic fold(s)

EXCLUDES *epiglottis:*
NOS (161.1)
suprahyoid portion (161.1)

146.5 Junctional region
Junction of the free margin of the epiglottis, the aryepiglottic fold, and the pharyngoepiglottic fold

146.6 Lateral wall of oropharynx

146.7 Posterior wall of oropharynx

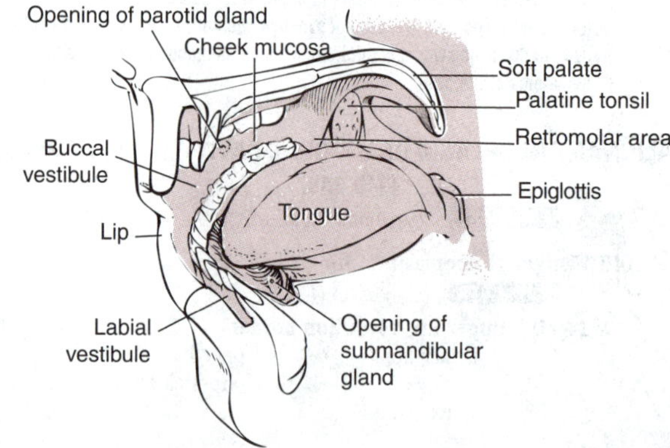

Oropharynx

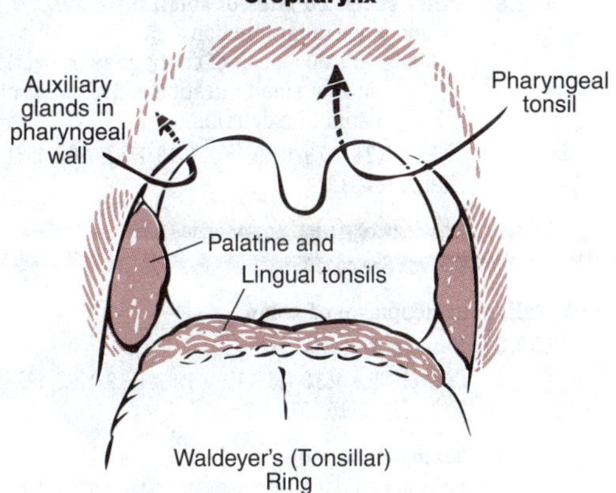

146.8 Other specified sites of oropharynx
Branchial cleft
Malignant neoplasm of contiguous or overlapping sites of oropharynx whose point of origin cannot be determined

146.9 Oropharynx, unspecified
AHA: 2Q, '02, 6

✓4th **147 Malignant neoplasm of nasopharynx**

147.0 Superior wall
Roof of nasopharynx

147.1 Posterior wall
Adenoid
Pharyngeal tonsil

147.2 Lateral wall
Fossa of Rosenmüller
Pharyngeal recess
Opening of auditory tube

147.3 Anterior wall
Floor of nasopharynx
Nasopharyngeal [posterior] [superior] surface of soft palate
Posterior margin of nasal septum and choanae

147.8 Other specified sites of nasopharynx
Malignant neoplasm of contiguous or overlapping sites of nasopharynx whose point of origin cannot be determined

147.9 Nasopharynx, unspecified
Nasopharyngeal wall NOS

✓4th **148 Malignant neoplasm of hypopharynx**

148.0 Postcricoid region

148.1 Pyriform sinus
Pyriform fossa

148.2 Aryepiglottic fold, hypopharyngeal aspect
Aryepiglottic fold or interarytenoid fold:
NOS
marginal zone
EXCLUDES *aryepiglottic fold or interarytenoid fold, laryngeal aspect (161.1)*

Nasopharynx

Nasal septum
Pharyngeal tonsil
Opening of auditory tube
Pharyngeal recess (of Rosenmüller)
Soft palate

Hypopharynx

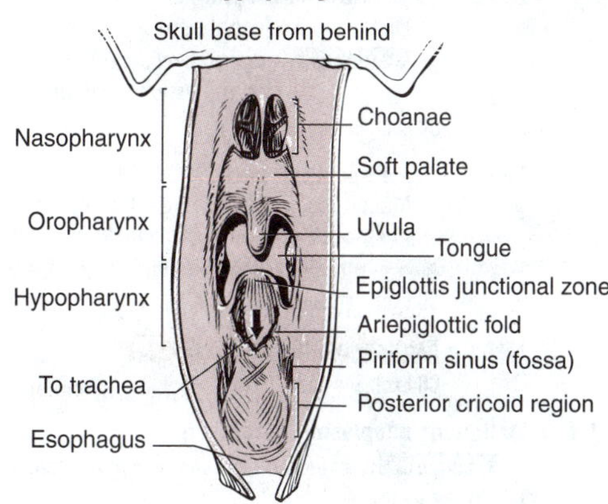

148.3 Posterior hypopharyngeal wall

148.8 Other specified sites of hypopharynx
Malignant neoplasm of contiguous or overlapping sites of hypopharynx whose point of origin cannot be determined

148.9 Hypopharynx, unspecified
Hypopharyngeal wall NOS
Hypopharynx NOS

✓4th **149 Malignant neoplasm of other and ill-defined sites within the lip, oral cavity, and pharynx**

149.0 Pharynx, unspecified

149.1 Waldeyer's ring

149.8 Other
Malignant neoplasms of lip, oral cavity, and pharynx whose point of origin cannot be assigned to any one of the categories 140-148
EXCLUDES *"book leaf" neoplasm [ventral surface of tongue and floor of mouth] (145.8)*

149.9 Ill-defined

MALIGNANT NEOPLASM OF DIGESTIVE ORGANS AND PERITONEUM (150-159)

EXCLUDES *carcinoma in situ (230.1-230.9)*

✓4th **150 Malignant neoplasm of esophagus**

150.0 Cervical esophagus CC
CC Excl: 150.0-150.9, 159.0, 159.8-159.9, 176.3, 195.8, 199.0-199.1, 239.0, 239.8-239.9

150.1 Thoracic esophagus CC
CC Excl: See code 150.0

150.2 Abdominal esophagus CC
EXCLUDES *adenocarcinoma (151.0)*
cardio-esophageal junction (151.0)
CC Excl: See code 150.0

150.3 Upper third of esophagus CC
CC Excl: See code 150.0
Proximal third of esophagus

150.4 Middle third of esophagus CC
CC Excl: See code 150.0

150.5 Lower third of esophagus CC
Distal third of esophagus
EXCLUDES *adenocarcinoma (151.0)*
cardio-esophageal junction (151.0)
CC Excl: See code 150.0

150.8 Other specified part CC
Malignant neoplasm of contiguous or overlapping sites of esophagus whose point of origin cannot be determined
CC Excl: See code 150.0

150.9 Esophagus, unspecified CC
CC Excl: See code 150.0

✓4th **151 Malignant neoplasm of stomach**
EXCLUDES ▶ *malignant stromal tumor of stomach (171.5)*◀

151.0 Cardia CC
Cardiac orifice
Cardio-esophageal junction
EXCLUDES *squamous cell carcinoma (150.2, 150.5)*
CC Excl: 151.0-151.9, 159.0, 159.8-159.9, 176.3, 195.8, 199.0-199.1, 239.0, 239.8-239.9

151.1 Pylorus CC
Prepylorus
Pyloric canal
CC Excl: See code 151.0

151.2 Pyloric antrum CC
Antrum of stomach NOS
CC Excl: See code 151.0

151.3 Fundus of stomach CC
CC Excl: See code 151.0

151.4 Body of stomach CC
CC Excl: See code 151.0

151.5 Lesser curvature, unspecified CC
Lesser curvature, not classifiable to 151.1-151.4
CC Excl: See code 151.0

151.6 Greater curvature, unspecified CC
Greater curvature, not classifiable to 151.0-151.4
CC Excl: See code 151.0

151.8 Other specified sites of stomach CC
Anterior wall, not classifiable to 151.0-151.4
Posterior wall, not classifiable to 151.0-151.4
Malignant neoplasm of contiguous or overlapping sites of stomach whose point of origin cannot be determined
CC Excl: See code 151.0

151.9 Stomach, unspecified CC
Carcinoma ventriculi
Gastric cancer
CC Excl: See code 151.0

AHA: 2Q, '01, 17

✓4th **152 Malignant neoplasm of small intestine, including duodenum**
EXCLUDES ▶ *malignant stromal tumor of small intestine (171.5)*◀

152.0 Duodenum CC
CC Excl: 152.0, 152.8-152.9, 159.0, 159.8-159.9, 176.3, 195.8, 199.0-199.1, 239.0, 239.8-239.9

152.1 Jejunum CC
CC Excl: 152.1, 152.8-152.9, 159.0, 159.8-159.9, 176.3, 195.8, 199.0-199.1, 239.0, 239.8-239.9

152.2 Ileum CC
EXCLUDES *ileocecal valve (153.4)*
CC Excl: 152.2, 152.8-152.9, 159.0, 159.8-159.9, 176.3, 195.8, 199.0-199.1, 239.0, 239.8-239.9

152.3 Meckel's diverticulum CC
CC Excl: 152.3-152.9, 159.0, 159.8-159.9, 176.3, 195.8, 199.0-199.1, 239.0, 239.8-239.9

152.8 Other specified sites of small intestine CC
Duodenojejunal junction
Malignant neoplasm of contiguous or overlapping sites of small intestine whose point of origin cannot be determined
CC Excl: 152.8-152.9, 159.0, 159.8-159.9, 176.3, 195.8, 199.0-199.1, 239.0, 239.8-239.9

152.9 Small intestine, unspecified CC
CC Excl: See code 152.8

✓4th **153 Malignant neoplasm of colon**

153.0 Hepatic flexure CC
CC Excl: 153.0, 153.8-153.9, 159.0, 159.8-159.9, 176.3, 195.8, 199.0-199.1, 239.0, 239.8-239.9

153.1 Transverse colon CC
CC Excl: 153.1, 153.8-153.9, 159.0, 159.8-159.9, 176.3, 195.8, 199.0-199.1, 239.0, 239.8-239.9

153.2 Descending colon CC
Left colon
CC Excl: 153.2, 153.8-153.9, 159.0, 159.8-159.9, 176.3, 195.8, 199.0-199.1, 239.0, 239.8-239.9

153.3 Sigmoid colon CC
Sigmoid (flexure)
EXCLUDES *rectosigmoid junction (154.0)*
CC Excl: 153.3, 153.8-153.9, 159.0, 159.8-159.9, 176.3, 195.8, 199.0-199.1, 239.0, 239.8-239.9

153.4 Cecum CC
Ileocecal valve
CC Excl: 153.4, 153.8-153.9, 159.0, 159.8-159.9, 176.3, 195.8, 199.0-199.1, 239.0, 239.8-239.9

153.5 Appendix CC
CC Excl: 153.5, 153.8-153.9, 159.0, 159.8-159.9, 176.3, 195.8, 199.0-199.1, 239.0, 239.8-239.9

153.6 Ascending colon CC
Right colon
CC Excl: 153.6, 153.8-153.9, 159.0, 159.8-159.9, 176.3, 195.8, 199.0-199.1, 239.0, 239.8-239.9

153.7 Splenic flexure CC
CC Excl: 153.7-153.9, 159.0, 159.8-159.9, 176.3, 195.8, 199.0-199.1, 239.0, 239.8-239.9

153.8 Other specified sites of large intestine CC
Malignant neoplasm of contiguous or overlapping sites of colon whose point of origin cannot be determined
EXCLUDES *ileocecal valve (153.4)*
rectosigmoid junction (154.0)
CC Excl: 153.8-153.9, 159.0, 159.8-159.9, 176.3, 195.8, 199.0-199.1, 239.0, 239.8-239.9

153.9 Colon, unspecified CC
Large intestine NOS
CC Excl: See code 153.8

✓4th **154 Malignant neoplasm of rectum, rectosigmoid junction, and anus**

154.0 Rectosigmoid junction CC
Colon with rectum
Rectosigmoid (colon)
CC Excl: 154.0, 154.8, 159.0, 159.8-159.9, 176.3, 195.8, 199.0-199.1, 239.0, 239.8-239.9

154.1 Rectum CC
Rectal ampulla
CC Excl: 154.1, 154.8, 159.0, 159.8-159.9, 176.3, 195.8, 199.0-199.1, 239.0, 239.8-239.9

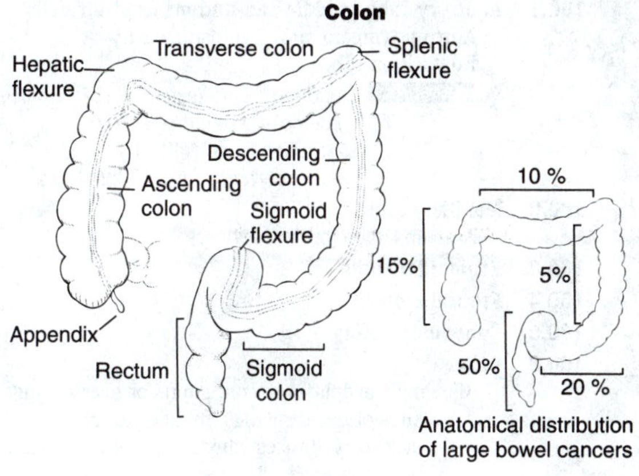

154.2 Anal canal CC
Anal sphincter
EXCLUDES *skin of anus (172.5, 173.5)*
CC Excl: 154.2-154.8, 159.0, 159.8-159.9, 176.3, 195.8, 199.0-199.1, 239.0, 239.8-239.9
AHA: 1Q, '01, 8

154.3 Anus, unspecified CC
EXCLUDES *anus:*
margin (172.5, 173.5)
skin (172.5, 173.5)
perianal skin (172.5, 173.5)
CC Excl: See code 154.2

154.8 Other CC
Anorectum
Cloacogenic zone
Malignant neoplasm of contiguous or overlapping sites of rectum, rectosigmoid junction, and anus whose point of origin cannot be determined
CC Excl: 154.8, 159.0, 159.8-159.9, 176.3, 195.8, 199.0-199.1, 239.0, 239.8-239.9

✓4th **155 Malignant neoplasm of liver and intrahepatic bile ducts**

155.0 Liver, primary CC
Carcinoma:
liver, specified as primary
hepatocellular
liver cell
Hepatoblastoma
CC Excl: 155.0-155.2, 159.0, 159.8-159.9, 176.3, 195.8, 199.0-199.1, 239.0, 239.8-239.9

155.1 Intrahepatic bile ducts CC
Canaliculi biliferi
Interlobular:
bile ducts
biliary canals
Intrahepatic:
biliary passages
canaliculi
gall duct
EXCLUDES *hepatic duct (156.1)*
CC Excl: See code 155.0

155.2 Liver, not specified as primary or secondary CC
CC Excl: See code 155.0

✓4th **156 Malignant neoplasm of gallbladder and extrahepatic bile ducts**

156.0 Gallbladder CC
CC Excl: 156.0, 156.8-156.9, 159.0, 159.8-159.9, 176.3, 195.8, 199.0-199.1, 239.0, 239.8-239.9

156.1 Extrahepatic bile ducts CC
Biliary duct or passage NOS
Common bile duct
Cystic duct
Hepatic duct
Sphincter of Oddi
CC Excl: 156.1, 156.8-156.9, 159.0, 159.8-159.9, 176.3, 195.8, 199.0-199.1, 239.0, 239.8-239.9

156.2 Ampulla of Vater CC
CC Excl: 156.2-156.9, 159.0, 159.8-159.9, 176.3, 195.8, 199.0-199.1, 239.0, 239.8-239.9

DEF: Malignant neoplasm in the area of dilation at the juncture of the common bile and pancreatic ducts near the opening into the lumen of the duodenum.

156.8 Other specified sites of gallbladder and extrahepatic bile ducts CC
Malignant neoplasm of contiguous or overlapping sites of gallbladder and extrahepatic bile ducts whose point of origin cannot be determined
CC Excl: 156.8-156.9, 159.0, 159.8-159.9, 176.3, 195.8, 199.0-199.1, 239.0, 239.8-239.9

156.9 Biliary tract, part unspecified CC
Malignant neoplasm involving both intrahepatic and extrahepatic bile ducts
CC Excl: See code 156.8

✓4th **157 Malignant neoplasm of pancreas**

157.0 Head of pancreas CC
CC Excl: 157.0-157.9, 159.0, 159.8-159.9, 176.3, 195.8, 199.0-199.1, 239.0, 239.8-239.9
AHA: ▶2Q, '05, 9;◀ 4Q, '00, 40

157.1 Body of pancreas CC
CC Excl: See code 157.0

157.2 Tail of pancreas CC
CC Excl: See code 157.0

157.3 Pancreatic duct CC
Duct of:
Santorini
Wirsung
CC Excl: See code 157.0

157.4 Islets of Langerhans CC
Islets of Langerhans, any part of pancreas
Use additional code to identify any functional activity
CC Excl: See code 157.0

DEF: Malignant neoplasm within the structures of the pancreas that produce insulin, somatostatin and glucagon.

157.8 Other specified sites of pancreas CC
Ectopic pancreatic tissue
Malignant neoplasm of contiguous or overlapping sites of pancreas whose point of origin cannot be determined
CC Excl: See code 157.0

157.9 Pancreas, part unspecified CC
CC Excl: See code 157.0
AHA: 4Q, '89, 11

✓4th **158 Malignant neoplasm of retroperitoneum and peritoneum**

158.0 Retroperitoneum
Periadrenal tissue
Perinephric tissue
Perirenal tissue
Retrocecal tissue

Neoplasms
154.2–158.0

Retroperitoneum and Peritoneum

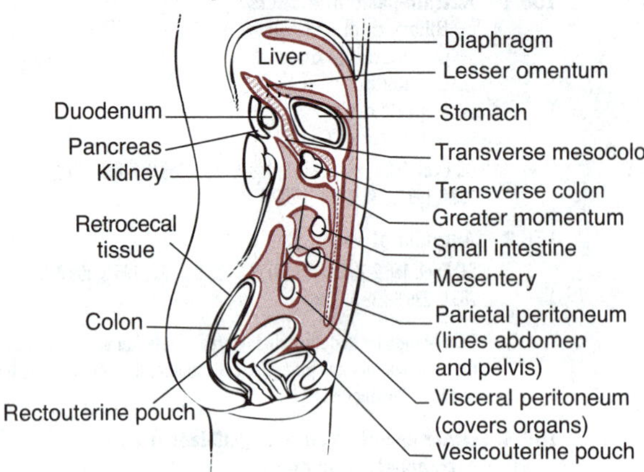

158.8 Specified parts of peritoneum
Cul-de-sac (of Douglas)
Mesentery
Mesocolon
Omentum
Peritoneum:
parietal
pelvic
Rectouterine pouch
Malignant neoplasm of contiguous or overlapping sites of retroperitoneum and peritoneum whose point of origin cannot be determined

158.9 Peritoneum, unspecified

✓4th **159 Malignant neoplasm of other and ill-defined sites within the digestive organs and peritoneum**

159.0 Intestinal tract, part unspecified
Intestine NOS

159.1 Spleen, not elsewhere classified
Angiosarcoma } of spleen
Fibrosarcoma }

EXCLUDES *Hodgkin's disease (201.0-201.9)*
lymphosarcoma (200.1)
reticulosarcoma (200.0)

159.8 Other sites of digestive system and intra-abdominal organs
Malignant neoplasm of digestive organs and peritoneum whose point of origin cannot be assigned to any one of the categories 150-158

EXCLUDES *anus and rectum (154.8)*
cardio-esophageal junction (151.0)
colon and rectum (154.0)

159.9 Ill-defined
Alimentary canal or tract NOS
Gastrointestinal tract NOS

EXCLUDES *abdominal NOS (195.2)*
intra-abdominal NOS (195.2)

MALIGNANT NEOPLASM OF RESPIRATORY AND INTRATHORACIC ORGANS (160-165)

EXCLUDES *carcinoma in situ (231.0-231.9)*

✓4th **160 Malignant neoplasm of nasal cavities, middle ear, and accessory sinuses**

160.0 Nasal cavities
Cartilage of nose
Conchae, nasal
Internal nose
Septum of nose
Vestibule of nose

EXCLUDES *nasal bone (170.0)*
nose NOS (195.0)
olfactory bulb (192.0)
posterior margin of septum and choanae (147.3)
skin of nose (172.3, 173.3)
turbinates (170.0)

160.1 Auditory tube, middle ear, and mastoid air cells
Antrum tympanicum
Tympanic cavity
Eustachian tube

EXCLUDES *auditory canal (external) (172.2, 173.2)*
bone of ear (meatus) (170.0)
cartilage of ear (171.0)
ear (external) (skin) (172.2, 173.2)

160.2 Maxillary sinus
Antrum (Highmore) (maxillary)

160.3 Ethmoidal sinus

160.4 Frontal sinus

160.5 Sphenoidal sinus

160.8 Other
Malignant neoplasm of contiguous or overlapping sites of nasal cavities, middle ear, and accessory sinuses whose point of origin cannot be determined

160.9 Accessory sinus, unspecified

✓4th **161 Malignant neoplasm of larynx**

161.0 Glottis
Intrinsic larynx
Laryngeal commissure (anterior) (posterior)
True vocal cord
Vocal cord NOS

161.1 Supraglottis
Aryepiglottic fold or interarytenoid fold, laryngeal aspect
Epiglottis (suprahyoid portion) NOS
Extrinsic larynx
False vocal cords
Posterior (laryngeal) surface of epiglottis
Ventricular bands

EXCLUDES *anterior aspect of epiglottis (146.4)*
aryepiglottic fold or interarytenoid fold:
NOS (148.2)
hypopharyngeal aspect (148.2)
marginal zone (148.2)

161.2 Subglottis

161.3 Laryngeal cartilages
Cartilage:
arytenoid
cricoid
Cartilage:
cuneiform
thyroid

161.8 Other specified sites of larynx
Malignant neoplasm of contiguous or overlapping sites of larynx whose point of origin cannot be determined

161.9 Larynx, unspecified

✓4th **162 Malignant neoplasm of trachea, bronchus, and lung**

162.0 Trachea
Cartilage } of trachea
Mucosa }

162.2 Main bronchus CC
Carina
Hilus of lung

CC Excl: 162.2, 162.8-162.9, 165.8-165.9, 176.4, 195.8, 199.0-199.1, 239.1, 239.8-239.9

162.3 Upper lobe, bronchus or lung CC

CC Excl: 162.3, 162.8-162.9, 165.8-165.9, 176.4, 195.8, 199.0-199.1, 239.1, 239.8-239.9

AHA: 1Q, '04, 4

162.4 Middle lobe, bronchus or lung CC

CC Excl: 162.4, 162.8-162.9, 165.8-165.9, 176.4, 195.8, 199.0-199.1, 239.1, 239.8-239.9

162.5 Lower lobe, bronchus or lung CC

CC Excl: 162.5-162.9, 165.8-165.9, 176.4, 195.8, 199.0-199.1, 239.1, 239.8-239.9

162.8 Other parts of bronchus or lung CC

Malignant neoplasm of contiguous or overlapping sites of bronchus or lung whose point of origin cannot be determined

CC Excl: 162.8-162.9, 165.8-165.9, 176.4, 195.8, 199.0-199.1, 239.1, 239.8-239.9

162.9 Bronchus and lung, unspecified CC

CC Excl: See code 162.8

AHA: 2Q, '97, 3; 4Q, '96, 48

✓4th **163 Malignant neoplasm of pleura**

163.0 Parietal pleura CC

CC Excl: 163.0-163.9, 165.8-165.9, 195.8, 199.0-199.1, 239.1, 239.8-239.9

163.1 Visceral pleura CC

CC Excl: See code 163.0

163.8 Other specified sites of pleura CC

Malignant neoplasm of contiguous or overlapping sites of pleura whose point of origin cannot be determined

CC Excl: See code 163.0

163.9 Pleura, unspecified CC

CC Excl: See code 163.0

✓4th **164 Malignant neoplasm of thymus, heart, and mediastinum**

164.0 Thymus CC

CC Excl: 164.0

164.1 Heart CC

Endocardium | Myocardium
Epicardium | Pericardium

EXCLUDES *great vessels (171.4)*

CC Excl: 164.1

164.2 Anterior mediastinum CC

CC Excl: 164.2-164.9, 165.8-165.9, 195.8, 199.0-199.1, 239.1, 239.8-239.9

164.3 Posterior mediastinum CC

CC Excl: See code 164.2

164.8 Other CC

Malignant neoplasm of contiguous or overlapping sites of thymus, heart, and mediastinum whose point of origin cannot be determined

CC Excl: See code 164.2

164.9 Mediastinum, part unspecified CC

CC Excl: See code 164.2

✓4th **165 Malignant neoplasm of other and ill-defined sites within the respiratory system and intrathoracic organs**

165.0 Upper respiratory tract, part unspecified

165.8 Other

Malignant neoplasm of respiratory and intrathoracic organs whose point of origin cannot be assigned to any one of the categories 160-164

165.9 Ill-defined sites within the respiratory system

Respiratory tract NOS

EXCLUDES *intrathoracic NOS (195.1)*
thoracic NOS (195.1)

MALIGNANT NEOPLASM OF BONE, CONNECTIVE TISSUE, SKIN, AND BREAST (170-176)

EXCLUDES *carcinoma in situ: breast (233.0)* | *carcinoma in situ: skin (232.0-232.9)*

✓4th **170 Malignant neoplasm of bone and articular cartilage**

INCLUDES cartilage (articular) (joint)
periosteum

EXCLUDES *bone marrow NOS (202.9)*
cartilage:
ear (171.0)
eyelid (171.0)
larynx (161.3)
nose (160.0)
synovia (171.0-171.9)

Skull

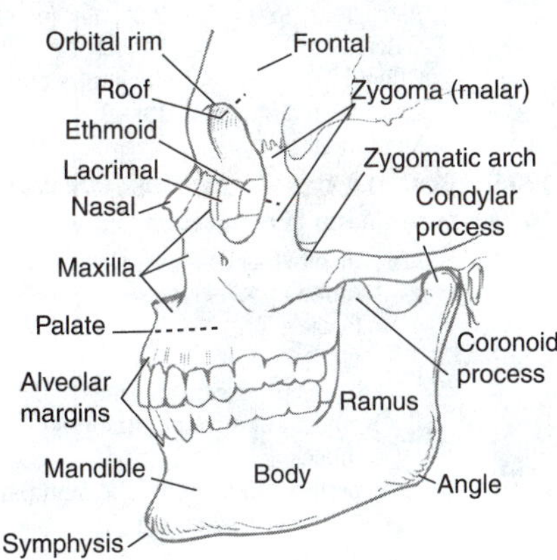

170.0 Bones of skull and face, except mandible

Bone: ethmoid, frontal, malar, nasal, occipital, orbital, parietal
Bone: sphenoid, temporal, zygomatic
Maxilla (superior)
Turbinate
Upper jaw bone
Vomer

EXCLUDES *carcinoma, any type except intraosseous or odontogenic:*
maxilla, maxillary (sinus) (160.2)
upper jaw bone (143.0)
jaw bone (lower) (170.1)

170.1 Mandible

Inferior maxilla
Jaw bone NOS
Lower jaw bone

EXCLUDES *carcinoma, any type except intraosseous or odontogenic:*
jaw bone NOS (143.9)
lower (143.1)
upper jaw bone (170.0)

170.2 Vertebral column, excluding sacrum and coccyx

Spinal column | Vertebra
Spine

EXCLUDES *sacrum and coccyx (170.6)*

170.3 Ribs, sternum, and clavicle

Costal cartilage
Costovertebral joint
Xiphoid process

170.4 Scapula and long bones of upper limb

Acromion | Radius
Bones NOS of upper limb | Ulna
Humerus

AHA: 2Q, '99, 9

170.5 Short bones of upper limb

Carpal | Scaphoid (of hand)
Cuneiform, wrist | Semilunar or lunate
Metacarpal | Trapezium
Navicular, of hand | Trapezoid
Phalanges of hand | Unciform
Pisiform

170.6 Pelvic bones, sacrum, and coccyx

Coccygeal vertebra | Pubic bone
Ilium | Sacral vertebra
Ischium

170.7 Long bones of lower limb

Bones NOS of lower limb
Femur
Fibula
Tibia

170.8 **Short bones of lower limb**
Astragalus [talus]
Calcaneus
Cuboid
Cuneiform, ankle
Metatarsal
Navicular (of ankle)
Patella
Phalanges of foot
Tarsal

170.9 **Bone and articular cartilage, site unspecified**

✓4th **171 Malignant neoplasm of connective and other soft tissue**

INCLUDES blood vessel
bursa
fascia
fat
ligament, except uterine
▶malignant stromal tumors◀
muscle
peripheral, sympathetic, and parasympathetic nerves and ganglia
synovia
tendon (sheath)

EXCLUDES *cartilage (of):*
articular (170.0-170.9)
larynx (161.3)
nose (160.0)
connective tissue:
breast (174.0-175.9)
internal organs ▶(except stromal tumors)◀— code to malignant neoplasm of the site [e.g., leiomyosarcoma of stomach, 151.9]
heart (164.1)
uterine ligament (183.4)

171.0 **Head, face, and neck**
Cartilage of:
ear
Cartilage of:
eyelid
AHA: 2Q, '99, 6

171.2 **Upper limb, including shoulder**
Arm
Finger
Forearm
Hand

171.3 **Lower limb, including hip**
Foot
Leg
Popliteal space
Thigh
Toe

171.4 **Thorax**
Axilla
Diaphragm
Great vessels
EXCLUDES *heart (164.1)*
mediastinum (164.2-164.9)
thymus (164.0)

171.5 **Abdomen**
Abdominal wall
Hypochondrium
EXCLUDES *peritoneum (158.8)*
retroperitoneum (158.0)

171.6 **Pelvis**
Buttock
Groin
Inguinal region
Perineum
EXCLUDES *pelvic peritoneum (158.8)*
retroperitoneum (158.0)
uterine ligament, any (183.3-183.5)

171.7 **Trunk, unspecified**
Back NOS
Flank NOS

171.8 **Other specified sites of connective and other soft tissue**
Malignant neoplasm of contiguous or overlapping sites of connective tissue whose point of origin cannot be determined

171.9 **Connective and other soft tissue, site unspecified**

✓4th **172 Malignant melanoma of skin**

INCLUDES melanocarcinoma
melanoma (skin) NOS

EXCLUDES *skin of genital organs (184.0-184.9, 187.1-187.9)*
sites other than skin—code to malignant neoplasm of the site

DEF: Malignant neoplasm of melanocytes; most common in skin, may involve oral cavity, esophagus, anal canal, vagina, leptomeninges, or conjunctiva.

172.0 **Lip**
EXCLUDES *vermilion border of lip (140.0-140.1, 140.9)*

172.1 **Eyelid, including canthus**

172.2 **Ear and external auditory canal**
Auricle (ear)
Auricular canal, external
External [acoustic] meatus
Pinna

172.3 **Other and unspecified parts of face**
Cheek (external)
Chin
Eyebrow
Forehead
Nose, external
Temple

172.4 **Scalp and neck**

172.5 **Trunk, except scrotum**
Axilla
Breast
Buttock
Groin
Perianal skin
Perineum
Umbilicus
EXCLUDES *anal canal (154.2)*
anus NOS (154.3)
scrotum (187.7)

172.6 **Upper limb, including shoulder**
Arm
Finger
Forearm
Hand

172.7 **Lower limb, including hip**
Ankle
Foot
Heel
Knee
Leg
Popliteal area
Thigh
Toe

172.8 **Other specified sites of skin**
Malignant melanoma of contiguous or overlapping sites of skin whose point of origin cannot be determined

172.9 **Melanoma of skin, site unspecified**

✓4th **173 Other malignant neoplasm of skin**

INCLUDES malignant neoplasm of:
sebaceous glands
sudoriferous, sudoriparous glands
sweat glands

EXCLUDES *Kaposi's sarcoma (176.0-176.9)*
malignant melanoma of skin (172.0-172.9)
skin of genital organs (184.0-184.9, 187.1-187.9)

AHA: 1Q, '00, 18; 2Q, '96, 12

173.0 **Skin of lip**
EXCLUDES *vermilion border of lip (140.0-140.1, 140.9)*

173.1 **Eyelid, including canthus**
EXCLUDES *cartilage of eyelid (171.0)*

173.2 **Skin of ear and external auditory canal**
Auricle (ear)
Auricular canal, external
External meatus
Pinna
EXCLUDES *cartilage of ear (171.0)*

173.3 **Skin of other and unspecified parts of face**
Cheek, external
Chin
Eyebrow
Forehead
Nose, external
Temple
AHA: 1Q, '00, 3

173.4 **Scalp and skin of neck**

173.5 **Skin of trunk, except scrotum**
Axillary fold
Perianal skin
Skin of:
abdominal wall
anus
back
breast
Skin of:
buttock
chest wall
groin
perineum
Umbilicus
EXCLUDES *anal canal (154.2)*
anus NOS (154.3)
skin of scrotum (187.7)
AHA: 1Q, '01, 8

Female Breast

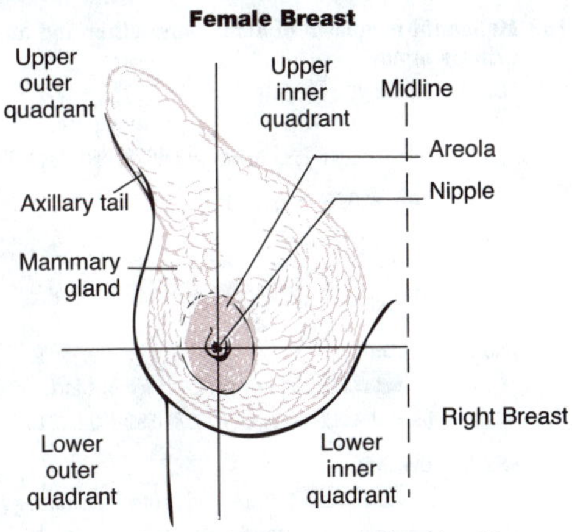

Upper outer quadrant
Upper inner quadrant
Midline
Areola
Nipple
Axillary tail
Mammary gland
Right Breast
Lower outer quadrant
Lower inner quadrant

173.6 Skin of upper limb, including shoulder
- Arm
- Forearm
- Finger
- Hand

173.7 Skin of lower limb, including hip
- Ankle
- Leg
- Foot
- Popliteal area
- Heel
- Thigh
- Knee
- Toe

173.8 Other specified sites of skin
Malignant neoplasm of contiguous or overlapping sites of skin whose point of origin cannot be determined

173.9 Skin, site unspecified

✓4th **174 Malignant neoplasm of female breast**
▶Use additional code to identify estrogen receptor status (V86.0, V86.1)◀

INCLUDES breast (female)
- connective tissue
- soft parts

Paget's disease of:
- breast
- nipple

EXCLUDES *skin of breast (172.5, 173.5)*

AHA: 3Q, '97, 8; 4Q, '89, 11

174.0 Nipple and areola ♀
174.1 Central portion ♀
174.2 Upper-inner quadrant ♀
174.3 Lower-inner quadrant ♀
174.4 Upper-outer quadrant ♀
AHA: 1Q, '04, 3

174.5 Lower-outer quadrant ♀
174.6 Axillary tail ♀
174.8 Other specified sites of female breast ♀
- Ectopic sites
- Midline of breast
- Inner breast
- Outer breast
- Lower breast
- Upper breast

Malignant neoplasm of contiguous or overlapping sites of breast whose point of origin cannot be determined

174.9 Breast (female), unspecified ♀
AHA: 3Q, '05, 11

✓4th **175 Malignant neoplasm of male breast**
▶Use additional code to identify estrogen receptor status (V86.0, V86.1)◀

EXCLUDES *skin of breast (172.5,173.5)*

175.0 Nipple and areola ♂
175.9 Other and unspecified sites of male breast ♂
Ectopic breast tissue, male

✓4th **176 Kaposi's sarcoma**
AHA: 4Q, '91, 24

176.0 Skin HIV
176.1 Soft tissue HIV
- Blood vessel
- Ligament
- Connective tissue
- Lymphatic(s) NEC
- Fascia
- Muscle

EXCLUDES *lymph glands and nodes (176.5)*

176.2 Palate HIV
176.3 Gastrointestinal sites HIV
176.4 Lung CC HIV
CC Excl: 162.8-162.9, 165.8-165.9, 176.4, 195.8, 199.0-199.1, 239.1, 239.8-239.9

176.5 Lymph nodes CC HIV
CC Excl: 176.5, 195.8, 196.0-196.9, 199.0-199.1, 239.8-239.9

176.8 Other specified sites HIV
Oral cavity NEC

176.9 Unspecified HIV
Viscera NOS

MALIGNANT NEOPLASM OF GENITOURINARY ORGANS (179-189)

EXCLUDES *carcinoma in situ (233.1-233.9)*

179 Malignant neoplasm of uterus, part unspecified ♀

✓4th **180 Malignant neoplasm of cervix uteri**
INCLUDES invasive malignancy [carcinoma]
EXCLUDES *carcinoma in situ (233.1)*

180.0 Endocervix ♀
- Cervical canal NOS
- Endocervical gland
- Endocervical canal

180.1 Exocervix ♀
180.8 Other specified sites of cervix ♀
Cervical stump
Squamocolumnar junction of cervix
Malignant neoplasm of contiguous or overlapping sites of cervix uteri whose point of origin cannot be determined

180.9 Cervix uteri, unspecified ♀

181 Malignant neoplasm of placenta ♀
Choriocarcinoma NOS
Chorioepithelioma NOS

EXCLUDES *chorioadenoma (destruens) (236.1)*
hydatidiform mole (630)
malignant (236.1)
invasive mole (236.1)
male choriocarcinoma NOS (186.0-186.9)

✓4th **182 Malignant neoplasm of body of uterus**
EXCLUDES *carcinoma in situ (233.2)*

182.0 Corpus uteri, except isthmus ♀
- Cornu
- Fundus
- Endometrium
- Myometrium

182.1 Isthmus ♀
Lower uterine segment

182.8 Other specified sites of body of uterus ♀
Malignant neoplasm of contiguous or overlapping sites of body of uterus whose point of origin cannot be determined

EXCLUDES *uterus NOS (179)*

✓4th **183 Malignant neoplasm of ovary and other uterine adnexa**
EXCLUDES *Douglas' cul-de-sac (158.8)*

183.0 Ovary ♀
Use additional code to identify any functional activity

183.2 Fallopian tube ♀
- Oviduct
- Uterine tube

183.3 Broad ligament ♀
- Mesovarium
- Parovarian region

183.4 Parametrium ♀
- Uterine ligament NOS
- Uterosacral ligament

183.5 Round ligament ♀
AHA: 3Q, '99, 5

183.8 Other specified sites of uterine adnexa ♀
Tubo-ovarian
Utero-ovarian
Malignant neoplasm of contiguous or overlapping sites of ovary and other uterine adnexa whose point of origin cannot be determined

183.9 Uterine adnexa, unspecified ♀

✓4th **184 Malignant neoplasm of other and unspecified female genital organs**

EXCLUDES *carcinoma in situ (233.3)*

184.0 Vagina ♀
Gartner's duct
Vaginal vault

184.1 Labia majora ♀
Greater vestibular [Bartholin's] gland

184.2 Labia minora ♀

184.3 Clitoris ♀

184.4 Vulva, unspecified ♀
External female genitalia NOS
Pudendum

184.8 Other specified sites of female genital organs ♀
Malignant neoplasm of contiguous or overlapping sites of female genital organs whose point of origin cannot be determined

184.9 Female genital organ, site unspecified ♀
Female genitourinary tract NOS

185 Malignant neoplasm of prostate ♂

EXCLUDES *seminal vesicles (187.8)*

AHA: 3Q, '03, 13; 3Q, '99, 5; 3Q, '92, 7

✓4th **186 Malignant neoplasm of testis**

Use additional code to identify any functional activity

186.0 Undescended testis ♂
Ectopic testis
Retained testis

186.9 Other and unspecified testis ♂
Testis:
NOS
descended
scrotal

✓4th **187 Malignant neoplasm of penis and other male genital organs**

187.1 Prepuce ♂
Foreskin

187.2 Glans penis ♂

187.3 Body of penis ♂
Corpus cavernosum

187.4 Penis, part unspecified ♂
Skin of penis NOS

187.5 Epididymis ♂

187.6 Spermatic cord ♂
Vas deferens

187.7 Scrotum ♂
Skin of scrotum

187.8 Other specified sites of male genital organs ♂
Seminal vesicle
Tunica vaginalis
Malignant neoplasm of contiguous or overlapping sites of penis and other male genital organs whose point of origin cannot be determined

187.9 Male genital organ, site unspecified ♂
Male genital organ or tract NOS

✓4th **188 Malignant neoplasm of bladder**

EXCLUDES *carcinoma in situ (233.7)*

188.0 Trigone of urinary bladder

188.1 Dome of urinary bladder

188.2 Lateral wall of urinary bladder

188.3 Anterior wall of urinary bladder

188.4 Posterior wall of urinary bladder

188.5 Bladder neck
Internal urethral orifice

188.6 Ureteric orifice

188.7 Urachus

188.8 Other specified sites of bladder
Malignant neoplasm of contiguous or overlapping sites of bladder whose point of origin cannot be determined

188.9 Bladder, part unspecified
Bladder wall NOS

AHA: 1Q, '00, 5

✓4th **189 Malignant neoplasm of kidney and other and unspecified urinary organs**

189.0 Kidney, except pelvis CC
Kidney NOS
Kidney parenchyma

CC Excl: 189.0-189.1, 189.8-189.9, 195.8, 199.0-199.1, 239.5, 239.8-239.9

AHA: ▶2Q, '05, 4;◀ 2Q, '04, 4

189.1 Renal pelvis CC
Renal calyces
Ureteropelvic junction

CC Excl: See code 189.0

189.2 Ureter CC

EXCLUDES *ureteric orifice of bladder (188.6)*

CC Excl: 189.2, 189.8-189.9, 195.8, 199.0-199.1, 239.5, 239.8-239.9

189.3 Urethra

EXCLUDES *urethral orifice of bladder (188.5)*

189.4 Paraurethral glands

189.8 Other specified sites of urinary organs
Malignant neoplasm of contiguous or overlapping sites of kidney and other urinary organs whose point of origin cannot be determined

189.9 Urinary organ, site unspecified
Urinary system NOS

MALIGNANT NEOPLASM OF OTHER AND UNSPECIFIED SITES (190-199)

EXCLUDES *carcinoma in situ (234.0-234.9)*

✓4th **190 Malignant neoplasm of eye**

EXCLUDES *carcinoma in situ (234.0)*
eyelid (skin) (172.1, 173.1)
cartilage (171.0)
optic nerve (192.0)
orbital bone (170.0)

190.0 Eyeball, except conjunctiva, cornea, retina, and choroid
Ciliary body
Crystalline lens
Iris
Sclera
Uveal tract

190.1 Orbit
Connective tissue of orbit
Extraocular muscle
Retrobulbar

EXCLUDES *bone of orbit (170.0)*

190.2 Lacrimal gland

190.3 Conjunctiva

190.4 Cornea

190.5 Retina

190.6 Choroid

190.7 Lacrimal duct
Lacrimal sac
Nasolacrimal duct

190.8 Other specified sites of eye
Malignant neoplasm of contiguous or overlapping sites of eye whose point of origin cannot be determined

190.9 Eye, part unspecified

✓4th **191 Malignant neoplasm of brain**

EXCLUDES *cranial nerves (192.0)*
retrobulbar area (190.1)

191.0 Cerebrum, except lobes and ventricles CC
Basal ganglia
Cerebral cortex
Corpus striatum
Globus pallidus
Hypothalamus
Thalamus

CC Excl: 191.0-191.9, 192.0-192.1, 192.8-192.9, 195.8, 199.0-199.1, 239.6-239.9

191.1 Frontal lobe CC

CC Excl: See code 191.0

AHA: ▶4Q, '05, 118◀

191.2 Temporal lobe CC
Hippocampus
Uncus

CC Excl: See code 191.0

N Newborn Age: 0 P Pediatric Age: 0-17 M Maternity Age: 12-55 A Adult Age: 15-124 CC CC Condition MC Major Complication CD Complex Dx HIV HIV Related Dx

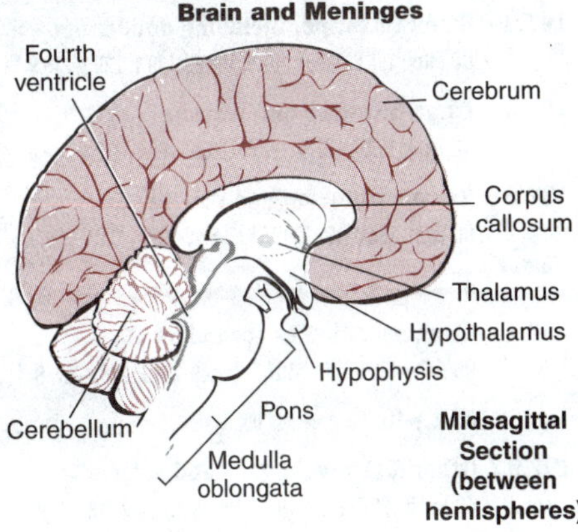

191.3 Parietal lobe CC
CC Excl: See code 191.0

191.4 Occipital lobe CC
CC Excl: See code 191.0

191.5 Ventricles CC
Choroid plexus
Floor of ventricle
CC Excl: See code 191.0

191.6 Cerebellum NOS CC
Cerebellopontine angle
CC Excl: See code 191.0

191.7 Brain stem CC
Cerebral peduncle
Medulla oblongata
Midbrain
Pons
CC Excl: See code 191.0

191.8 Other parts of brain CC
Corpus callosum
Tapetum
Malignant neoplasm of contiguous or overlapping sites of brain whose point of origin cannot be determined
CC Excl: See code 191.0

191.9 Brain, unspecified CC
Cranial fossa NOS
CC Excl: See code 191.0

4th **192 Malignant neoplasm of other and unspecified parts of nervous system**
EXCLUDES *peripheral, sympathetic, and parasympathetic nerves and ganglia (171.0-171.9)*

192.0 Cranial nerves CC
Olfactory bulb
CC Excl: 192.0, 192.8-192.9, 195.8, 199.0-199.1, 239.6-239.9

192.1 Cerebral meninges CC
Dura (mater)
Falx (cerebelli) (cerebri)
Meninges NOS
Tentorium
CC Excl: 192.1, 192.8-192.9, 195.8, 199.0-199.1, 239.6-239.9

192.2 Spinal cord CC
Cauda equina
CC Excl: 192.2, 192.8-192.9, 195.8, 199.0-199.1, 239.6-239.9

192.3 Spinal meninges CC
CC Excl: 192.3-192.9, 195.8, 199.0-199.1, 239.6-239.9

192.8 Other specified sites of nervous system CC
Malignant neoplasm of contiguous or overlapping sites of other parts of nervous system whose point of origin cannot be determined
CC Excl: 191.0-191.9, 192.0-192.9, 195.8, 199.0-199.1, 239.6-239.9

192.9 Nervous system, part unspecified
Nervous system (central) NOS
EXCLUDES *meninges NOS (192.1)*

193 Malignant neoplasm of thyroid gland
Sipple's syndrome
Thyroglossal duct
Use additional code to identify any functional activity

4th **194 Malignant neoplasm of other endocrine glands and related structures**
Use additional code to identify any functional activity
EXCLUDES *islets of Langerhans (157.4)*
ovary (183.0)
testis (186.0-186.9)
thymus (164.0)

194.0 Adrenal gland
Adrenal cortex
Adrenal medulla
Suprarenal gland

194.1 Parathyroid gland

194.3 Pituitary gland and craniopharyngeal duct
Craniobuccal pouch
Hypophysis
Rathke's pouch
Sella turcica
AHA: J-A, '85, 9

194.4 Pineal gland

194.5 Carotid body

194.6 Aortic body and other paraganglia
Coccygeal body
Glomus jugulare
Para-aortic body

194.8 Other
Pluriglandular involvement NOS
Note: If the sites of multiple involvements are known, they should be coded separately.

194.9 Endocrine gland, site unspecified

4th **195 Malignant neoplasm of other and ill-defined sites**
INCLUDES malignant neoplasms of contiguous sites, not elsewhere classified, whose point of origin cannot be determined
EXCLUDES *malignant neoplasm:*
lymphatic and hematopoietic tissue (200.0-208.9)
secondary sites (196.0-198.8)
unspecified site (199.0-199.1)

195.0 Head, face, and neck
Cheek NOS
Jaw NOS
Nose NOS
Supraclavicular region NOS
AHA: 4Q, '03, 107

195.1 Thorax
Axilla
Chest (wall) NOS
Intrathoracic NOS

195.2 Abdomen
Intra-abdominal NOS
AHA: 2Q, '97, 3

195.3 Pelvis
Groin
Inguinal region NOS
Presacral region
Sacrococcygeal region
Sites overlapping systems within pelvis, as:
rectovaginal (septum)
rectovesical (septum)

195.4 Upper limb

195.5 Lower limb

195.8 Other specified sites
Back NOS
Flank NOS
Trunk NOS

4th **196 Secondary and unspecified malignant neoplasm of lymph nodes**
EXCLUDES *any malignant neoplasm of lymph nodes, specified as primary (200.0-202.9)*
Hodgkin's disease (201.0-201.9)
lymphosarcoma (200.1)
other forms of lymphoma (202.0-202.9)
reticulosarcoma (200.0)
AHA: 2Q, '92, 3; M-J, '85, 3

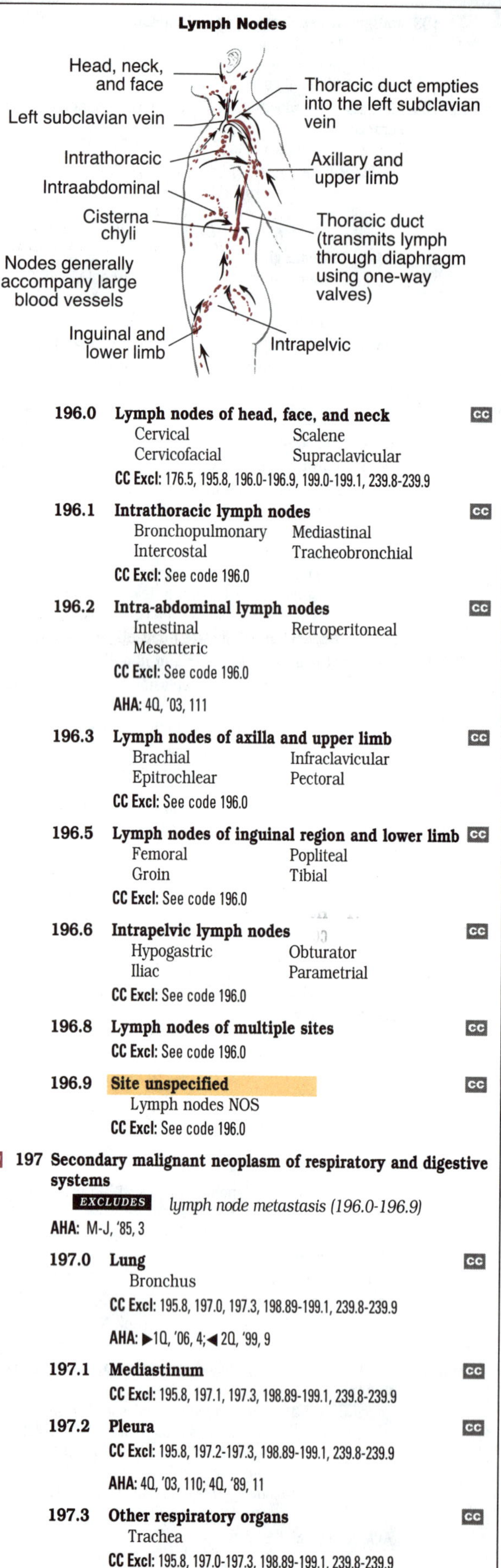

196.0 Lymph nodes of head, face, and neck CC

Cervical — Scalene
Cervicofacial — Supraclavicular

CC Excl: 176.5, 195.8, 196.0-196.9, 199.0-199.1, 239.8-239.9

196.1 Intrathoracic lymph nodes CC

Bronchopulmonary — Mediastinal
Intercostal — Tracheobronchial

CC Excl: See code 196.0

196.2 Intra-abdominal lymph nodes CC

Intestinal — Retroperitoneal
Mesenteric

CC Excl: See code 196.0

AHA: 4Q, '03, 111

196.3 Lymph nodes of axilla and upper limb CC

Brachial — Infraclavicular
Epitrochlear — Pectoral

CC Excl: See code 196.0

196.5 Lymph nodes of inguinal region and lower limb CC

Femoral — Popliteal
Groin — Tibial

CC Excl: See code 196.0

196.6 Intrapelvic lymph nodes CC

Hypogastric — Obturator
Iliac — Parametrial

CC Excl: See code 196.0

196.8 Lymph nodes of multiple sites CC

CC Excl: See code 196.0

196.9 Site unspecified CC

Lymph nodes NOS

CC Excl: See code 196.0

✓4th **197 Secondary malignant neoplasm of respiratory and digestive systems**

EXCLUDES *lymph node metastasis (196.0-196.9)*

AHA: M-J, '85, 3

197.0 Lung CC

Bronchus

CC Excl: 195.8, 197.0, 197.3, 198.89-199.1, 239.8-239.9

AHA: ►1Q, '06, 4;◄ 2Q, '99, 9

197.1 Mediastinum CC

CC Excl: 195.8, 197.1, 197.3, 198.89-199.1, 239.8-239.9

197.2 Pleura CC

CC Excl: 195.8, 197.2-197.3, 198.89-199.1, 239.8-239.9

AHA: 4Q, '03, 110; 4Q, '89, 11

197.3 Other respiratory organs CC

Trachea

CC Excl: 195.8, 197.0-197.3, 198.89-199.1, 239.8-239.9

197.4 Small intestine, including duodenum CC

CC Excl: 195.8, 197.4, 197.8, 198.89-199.1, 239.8-239.9

197.5 Large intestine and rectum CC

CC Excl: 195.8, 197.5, 197.8, 198.89-199.1, 239.8-239.9

197.6 Retroperitoneum and peritoneum CC

CC Excl: 195.8, 197.6, 197.8, 198.89-199.1, 239.8-239.9

AHA: 2Q, '04, 4; 4Q, '89, 11

197.7 Liver, specified as secondary CC

CC Excl: 195.8, 197.7-197.8, 198.89-199.1, 239.8-239.9

AHA: ►1Q, '06, 4;◄ 2Q, '05, 9

197.8 Other digestive organs and spleen CC

CC Excl: 195.8, 197.4-197.8, 198.89-199.1, 239.8-239.9

AHA: 2Q, '97, 3; 2Q, '92, 3

✓4th **198 Secondary malignant neoplasm of other specified sites**

EXCLUDES *lymph node metastasis (196.0-196.9)*

AHA: M-J, '85, 3

198.0 Kidney CC

CC Excl: 195.8, 198.0-198.1, 198.89-199.1, 239.8-239.9

198.1 Other urinary organs CC

CC Excl: See code 198.0

198.2 Skin CC

Skin of breast

CC Excl: 195.8, 198.2, 198.89-199.1, 239.8-239.9

198.3 Brain and spinal cord CC

CC Excl: 195.8, 198.3, 198.89-199.1, 239.8-239.9

AHA: 3Q, '99, 7

198.4 Other parts of nervous system CC

Meninges (cerebral) (spinal)

CC Excl: 195.8, 198.4, 198.89-199.1, 239.8-239.9

AHA: J-F, '87, 7

198.5 Bone and bone marrow CC

CC Excl: 195.8, 198.5, 198.89-199.1, 239.8-239.9

AHA: 4Q, '03, 110; 3Q, '99, 5; 2Q, '92, 3; 1Q, '91, 16; 4Q, '89, 10

DRG 239

198.6 Ovary CC ♀

CC Excl: 195.8, 198.6, 198.89-199.1, 239.8-239.9

198.7 Adrenal gland CC

Suprarenal gland

CC Excl: 195.8, 198.7, 198.89-199.1, 239.8-239.9

✓5th **198.8 Other specified sites**

198.81 Breast CC

EXCLUDES *skin of breast (198.2)*

CC Excl: 195.8, 198.81, 198.89-199.1, 239.8-239.9

198.82 Genital organs CC

CC Excl: 195.8, 198.82, 198.89-199.1, 239.8-239.9

198.89 Other CC

EXCLUDES *retroperitoneal lymph nodes (196.2)*

CC Excl: 195.8, 198.89-199.1, 239.8-239.9

AHA: 2Q, '05, 4; 2Q, '97, 4

✓4th **199 Malignant neoplasm without specification of site**

199.0 Disseminated CC

Carcinomatosis
Generalized:
  cancer
  malignancy
Multiple cancer
} unspecified site (primary) (secondary)

CC Excl: See code 198.89

AHA: 4Q, '89, 10

199.1 Other

Cancer } unspecified site (primary)
Carcinoma } (secondary)
Malignancy }

AHA: ▶1Q, '06, 4◀

MALIGNANT NEOPLASM OF LYMPHATIC AND HEMATOPOIETIC TISSUE (200-208)

EXCLUDES *secondary neoplasm of:*
bone marrow (198.5)
spleen (197.8)
secondary and unspecified neoplasm of lymph nodes (196.0-196.9)

The following fifth-digit subclassification is for use with categories 200-202:

- **0 unspecified site, extranodal and solid organ sites**
- **1 lymph nodes of head, face, and neck**
- **2 intrathoracic lymph nodes**
- **3 intra-abdominal lymph nodes**
- **4 lymph nodes of axilla and upper limb**
- **5 lymph nodes of inguinal region and lower limb**
- **6 intrapelvic lymph nodes**
- **7 spleen**
- **8 lymph nodes of multiple sites**

✓4th **200 Lymphosarcoma and reticulosarcoma**

AHA: 2Q, '92, 3; N-D, '86, 5

✓5th **200.0 Reticulosarcoma** CC HIV

Lymphoma (malignant):
histiocytic (diffuse):
nodular
pleomorphic cell type
reticulum cell type
Reticulum cell sarcoma:
NOS
pleomorphic cell type

CC Excl: For code 200.00: 200.00-200.08, 239.8-239.9: **For code 200.01:** 200.00, 200.01, 200.08, 239.8-239.9; **For code 200.02:** 200.00, 200.02, 200.08, 239.8-239.9; **For code 200.03:** 200.00, 200.03, 200.08, 239.8-239.9; **For code 200.04:** 200.00, 200.04, 200.08, 239.8-239.9; **For code 200.05:** 200.00, 200.05, 200.08, 239.8-239.9; **For code 200.06:** 200.00, 200.06, 200.08, 239.8-239.9; **For code 200.07:** 200.00, 200.07-200.08, 239.8-239.9; **For code 200.08:** 200.00-200.08, 239.8-239.9

AHA: For Code 200.03: 3Q, '01, 12

DEF: Malignant lymphoma of primarily histolytic cells; commonly originates in reticuloendothelium of lymph nodes.

✓5th **200.1 Lymphosarcoma** CC

Lymphoblastoma (diffuse)
Lymphoma (malignant):
lymphoblastic (diffuse)
lymphocytic (cell type) (diffuse)
lymphosarcoma type
Lymphosarcoma:
NOS
diffuse NOS
lymphoblastic (diffuse)
lymphocytic (diffuse)
prolymphocytic

EXCLUDES *lymphosarcoma:*
follicular or nodular (202.0)
mixed cell type (200.8)
lymphosarcoma cell leukemia (207.8)

CC Excl: For code 200.10: 200.10-200.18, 239.8-239.9; **For code 200.11:** 200.10, 200.11, 200.18, 239.8-239.9; **For code 200.12:** 200.10, 200.12, 200.18, 239.8-239.9; **For code 200.13:** 200.10, 200.13, 200.18, 239.8-239.9; **For code 200.14:** 200.10, 200.14, 200.18, 239.8-239.9; **For code 200.15:** 200.10, 200.15, 200.18, 239.8-239.9; **For code 200.16:** 200.10, 200.16, 200.18, 239.8-239.9; **For code 200.17:** 200.10, 200.17-200.18, 239.8-239.9; **For code 200.18:** 200.10-200.18, 239.8-239.9

DEF: Malignant lymphoma created from anaplastic lymphoid cells resembling lymphocytes or lymphoblasts.

✓5th **200.2 Burkitt's tumor or lymphoma** CC HIV

Malignant lymphoma, Burkitt's type

CC Excl: For code 200.20: 200.20-200.28, 239.8-239.9; **For code 200.21:** 200.20, 200.21, 200.28, 239.8-239.9; **For code 200.22:** 200.20, 200.22, 200.28, 239.8-239.9; **For code 200.23:** 200.20, 200.23, 200.28, 239.8-239.9; **For code 200.24:** 200.20, 200.24, 200.28, 239.8-239.9; **For code 200.25:** 200.20, 200.25, 200.28, 239.8-239.9; **For code 200.26:** 200.20, 200.26, 200.28, 239.8-239.9; **For code 200.27:** 200.20, 200.27-200.28, 239.8-239.9; **For code 200.28:** 200.20-200.28, 239.8-239.9

DEF: Large osteolytic lesion most common in jaw or as abdominal mass; usually found in central Africa but reported elsewhere.

✓5th **200.8 Other named variants** CC HIV

Lymphoma (malignant):
lymphoplasmacytoid type
mixed lymphocytic-histiocytic (diffuse)
Lymphosarcoma, mixed cell type (diffuse)
Reticulolymphosarcoma (diffuse)

CC Excl: For code 200.80: 200.80-200.88, 239.8-239.9; **For code 200.81:** 200.80, 200.81, 200.88, 239.8-239.9; **For code 200.82:** 200.80, 200.82, 200.88, 239.8-239.9; **For code 200.83:** 200.80, 200.83, 200.88, 239.8-239.9; **For code 200.84:** 200.80, 200.84, 200.88, 239.8-239.9; **For code 200.85:** 200.80, 200.85, 200.88, 239.8-239.9; **For code 200.86:** 200.80, 200.86, 200.88, 239.8-239.9; **For code 200.87:** 200.80, 200.87-200.88, 239.8-239.9; **For code 200.88:** 200.80-200.88, 239.8-239.9

✓4th **201 Hodgkin's disease**

AHA: 2Q, '92, 3; N-D, '86, 5

DEF: Painless, progressive enlargement of lymph nodes, spleen and general lymph tissue; symptoms include anorexia, lassitude, weight loss, fever, pruritis, night sweats, anemia.

✓5th **201.0 Hodgkin's paragranuloma** CC

CC Excl: For code 201.00: 201.00-201.08, 201.90, 239.8-239.9;
For code 201.01: 201.00, 201.01, 201.08, 201.90-201.91, 239.8-239.9;
For code 201.02: 201.00, 201.02, 201.08, 201.90, 201.92, 239.8-239.9;
For code 201.03: 201.00, 201.03, 201.08, 201.90, 201.93, 239.8-239.9;
For code 201.04: 201.00, 201.04, 201.08, 201.90, 201.94, 239.8-239.9;
For code 201.05: 201.00, 201.05, 201.08, 201.90, 201.95, 239.8-239.9;
For code 201.06: 201.00, 201.06, 201.08, 201.90, 201.96, 239.8-239.9;
For code 201.07: 201.00, 201.07-201.08, 201.90, 201.97, 239.8-239.9;
For code 201.08: 201.00-201.08, 201.90, 201.98, 239.8-239.9

✓5th **201.1 Hodgkin's granuloma** CC

CC Excl: For code 201.10: 201.10-201.18, 201.90, 201.98, 239.8-239.9; **For code 201.11:** 201.10, 201.11, 201.18, 201.90-201.91, 201.98, 239.8-239.9; **For code 201.12:** 201.10, 201.12, 201.18, 201.90, 201.92, 201.98, 239.8-239.9; **For code 201.13:** 201.10, 201.13, 201.18, 201.90, 201.93, 201.98, 239.8-239.9; **For code 201.14:** 201.10, 201.14, 201.18, 201.90, 201.94, 201.98, 239.8-239.9; **For code 201.15:** 201.10, 201.15, 201.18, 201.90, 201.95, 201.98, 239.8-239.9; **For code 201.16:** 201.10, 201.16, 201.18, 201.90, 201.96, 201.98, 239.8-239.9; **For code 201.17:** 201.10, 201.17-201.18, 201.90, 201.97-201.98, 239.8-239.9; **For code 201.18:** 201.10-201.18, 201.90, 201.98, 239.8-239.9

AHA: 2Q, '99, 7

✓5th **201.2 Hodgkin's sarcoma** CC

CC Excl: For code 201.20: 201.20-201.28, 201.90, 201.98, 239.8-239.9; **For code 201.21:** 201.20, 201.21, 201.28, 201.90-201.91, 201.98, 239.8-239.9; **For code 201.22:** 201.20, 201.22, 201.28, 201.90, 201.92, 201.98, 239.8-239.9; **For code 201.23:** 201.20, 201.23, 201.28, 201.90, 201.93, 201.98, 239.8-239.9; **For code 201.24:** 201.20, 201.24, 201.28, 201.90, 201.94, 201.98, 239.8-239.9; **For code 201.25:** 201.20, 201.25, 201.28, 201.90, 201.95, 201.98, 239.8-239.9; **For code 201.26:** 201.20, 201.26, 201.28, 201.90, 201.96, 201.98, 239.8-239.9; **For code 201.27:** 201.20, 201.27-201.28, 201.90, 201.97-201.98, 239.8-239.9; **For code 201.28:** 201.20-201.28, 201.90, 201.98, 239.8-239.9

Neoplasms

199.1–201.2

§ ✓5th 201.4 **Lymphocytic-histiocytic predominance** CC

CC Excl: For code 201.40: 201.40-201.48, 201.90, 201.98, 239.8-239.9; **For code 201.41:** 201.40, 201.41, 201.48, 201.90-201.91, 201.98, 239.8-239.9; **For code 201.42:** 201.40, 201.42, 201.48, 201.90, 201.92, 201.98, 239.8-239.9; **For code 201.43:** 201.40, 201.43, 201.48, 201.90, 201.93, 201.98, 239.8-239.9; **For code 201.44:** 201.40, 201.44, 201.48, 201.90, 201.94, 201.98, 239.8-239.9; **For code 201.45:** 201.40, 201.45, 201.48, 201.90, 201.95, 201.98, 239.8-239.9; **For code 201.46:** 201.40, 201.46, 201.48, 201.90, 201.96, 201.98, 239.8-239.9; **For code 201.47:** 201.40, 201.47-201.48, 201.90, 201.97-201.98, 239.8-239.9; **For code 201.48:** 201.40-201.48, 201.90, 201.98, 239.8-239.9

§ ✓5th 201.5 **Nodular sclerosis** CC

Hodgkin's disease, nodular sclerosis:
- NOS
- cellular phase

CC Excl: For code 201.50: 201.50-201.58, 201.90, 201.98, 239.8-239.9; **For code 201.51:** 201.50, 201.51, 201.58, 201.90-201.91, 201.98, 239.8-239.9; **For code 201.52:** 201.50, 201.52, 201.58, 201.90, 201.92, 201.98, 239.8-239.9; **For code 201.53:** 201.50, 201.53, 201.58, 201.90, 201.93, 201.98, 239.8-239.9; **For code 201.54:** 201.50, 201.54, 201.58, 201.90, 201.94, 201.98, 239.8-239.9; **For code 201.55:** 201.50, 201.55, 201.58, 201.90, 201.95, 201.98, 239.8-239.9; **For code 201.56:** 201.50, 201.56, 201.58, 201.90, 201.96, 201.98, 239.8-239.9; **For code 201.57:** 201.50, 201.57-201.58, 201.90, 201.97-201.98, 239.8-239.9; **For code 201.58:** 201.50-201.58, 201.90, 201.98, 239.8-239.9

§ ✓5th 201.6 **Mixed cellularity** CC

CC Excl: For code 201.60: 201.60-201.68, 201.90, 201.98, 239.8-239.9; **For code 201.61:** 201.60, 201.61, 201.68, 201.90-201.91, 201.98, 239.8-239.9; **For code 201.62:** 201.60, 201.62, 201.68, 201.90, 201.92, 201.98, 239.8-239.9; **For code 201.63:** 201.60, 201.63, 201.68, 201.90, 201.93, 201.98, 239.8-239.9; **For code 201.64:** 201.60, 201.64, 201.68, 201.90, 201.94, 201.98, 239.8-239.9; **For code 201.65:** 201.60, 201.65, 201.68, 201.90, 201.95, 201.98, 239.8-239.9; **For code 201.66:** 201.60, 201.66, 201.68, 201.90, 201.96, 201.98, 239.8-239.9; **For code 201.67:** 201.60, 201.67-201.68, 201.90, 201.97-201.98, 239.8-239.9; **For code 201.68:** 201.60-201.68, 201.90, 201.98, 239.8-239.9

§ ✓5th 201.7 **Lymphocytic depletion** CC

Hodgkin's disease, lymphocytic depletion:
- NOS
- diffuse fibrosis
- reticular type

CC Excl: For code 201.70: 201.70-201.78, 201.90, 201.98, 239.8-239.9;
For code 201.71: 201.70, 201.71, 201.78, 201.91, 201.98, 239.8-239.9;
For code 201.72: 201.70, 201.72, 201.78, 201.92, 201.98, 239.8-239.9;
For code 201.73: 201.70, 201.73, 201.78, 201.93, 201.98, 239.8-239.9;
For code 201.74: 201.70, 201.74, 201.78, 201.94, 201.98, 239.8-239.9;
For code 201.75: 201.70, 201.75, 201.78, 201.95, 201.98, 239.8-239.9;
For code 201.76: 201.70, 201.76, 201.78, 201.96, 201.98, 239.8-239.9;
For code 201.77: 201.70, 201.77-201.78, 201.97-201.98, 239.8-239.9;
For code 201.78: 201.70-201.78, 201.98, 239.8-239.9

§ ✓5th 201.9 **Hodgkin's disease, unspecified** CC

Hodgkin's:
- disease NOS
- lymphoma NOS

Malignant:
- lymphogranuloma
- lymphogranulomatosis

CC Excl: For code 201.90: 201.90-201.98, 239.8-239.9; **For code 201.91:** 201.90, 201.91, 201.98, 239.8-239.9; **For code 201.92:** 201.90, 201.92, 201.98, 239.8-239.9; **For code 201.93:** 201.90, 201.93, 201.98, 239.8-239.9; **For code 201.94:** 201.90, 201.94, 201.98, 239.8-239.9; **For code 201.95:** 201.90, 201.95, 201.98, 239.8-239.9; **For code 201.96:** 201.90, 201.96, 201.98, 239.8-239.9; **For code 201.97:** 201.90, 201.97-201.98, 239.8-239.9; **For code 201.98:** 201.90-201.98, 239.8-239.9

✓4th **202 Other malignant neoplasms of lymphoid and histiocytic tissue**

AHA: 2Q, '92, 3; N-D, '86, 5

§ ✓5th 202.0 **Nodular lymphoma** CC

Brill-Symmers disease
Lymphoma:
- follicular (giant)
- lymphocytic, nodular

Lymphosarcoma:
- follicular (giant)
- nodular

CC Excl: For code 202.00: 202.00-202.08, 202.80, 202.90, 239.8-239.9;
For code 202.01: 202.00, 202.01, 202.08, 202.81, 202.91, 239.8-239.9;
For code 202.02: 202.00, 202.02, 202.08, 202.82, 202.92, 239.8-239.9;
For code 202.03: 202.00, 202.03, 202.08, 202.83, 202.93, 239.8-239.9;
For code 202.04: 202.00, 202.04, 202.08, 202.84, 202.94, 239.8-239.9;
For code 202.05: 202.00, 202.05, 202.08, 202.85, 202.95, 239.8-239.9;
For code 202.06: 202.00, 202.06, 202.08, 202.86, 202.96, 239.8-239.9;
For code 202.07: 202.00, 202.07-202.08, 202.87, 202.97, 239.8-239.9;
For code 202.08: 202.00-202.08, 202.88, 202.98, 239.8-239.9

DEF: Lymphomatous cells clustered into nodules within the lymph node; usually occurs in older adults and may involve all nodes and possibly extranodal sites.

§ ✓5th 202.1 **Mycosis fungoides** CC

CC Excl: For code 202.10: 202.10-202.18, 202.80, 202.90, 239.8-239.9;
For code 202.11: 202.10, 202.11, 202.18, 202.81, 202.91, 239.8-239.9;
For code 202.12: 202.10, 202.12, 202.18, 202.82, 202.92, 239.8-239.9;
For code 202.13: 202.10, 202.13, 202.18, 202.83, 202.93, 239.8-239.9;
For code 202.14: 202.10, 202.14, 202.18, 202.84, 202.94, 239.8-239.9;
For code 202.15: 202.10, 202.15, 202.18, 202.85, 202.95, 239.8-239.9;
For code 202.16: 202.10, 202.16, 202.18, 202.86, 202.96, 239.8-239.9;
For code 202.17: 202.10, 202.17-202.18, 202.87, 202.97, 239.8-239.9;
For code 202.18: 202.10-202.18, 202.88, 202.98, 239.8-239.9

AHA: 2Q, '92, 4

DEF: Type of cutaneous T-cell lymphoma; may evolve into generalized lymphoma; formerly thought to be of fungoid origin.

§ ✓5th 202.2 **Sézary's disease** CC

CC Excl: For code 202.20: 202.20-202.28, 202.80, 202.90, 239.8-239.9;
For code 202.21: 202.20, 202.21, 202.28, 202.81, 202.91, 239.8-239.9;
For code 202.22: 202.20, 202.22, 202.28, 202.82, 202.92, 239.8-239.9;
For code 202.23: 202.20, 202.23, 202.28, 202.83, 202.93, 239.8-239.9;
For code 202.24: 202.20, 202.24, 202.28, 202.84, 202.94, 239.8-239.9;
For code 202.25: 202.20, 202.25, 202.28, 202.85, 202.95, 239.8-239.9;
For code 202.26: 202.20, 202.26, 202.28, 202.86, 202.96, 239.8-239.9;
For code 202.27: 202.20, 202.27-202.28, 202.87, 202.97, 239.8-239.9;
For code 202.28: 202.20-202.28, 202.88, 202.98, 239.8-239.9

AHA: 2Q, '99, 7

DEF: Type of cutaneous T-cell lymphoma with erythroderma, intense pruritus, peripheral lymphadenopathy, abnormal hyperchromatic mononuclear cells in skin, lymph nodes and peripheral blood.

§ ✓5th 202.3 **Malignant histiocytosis** CC

Histiocytic medullary reticulosis
Malignant:
- reticuloendotheliosis
- reticulosis

CC Excl: For code 202.30: 202.30-202.38, 202.80, 202.90, 239.8-239.9;
For code 202.31: 202.30, 202.31, 202.38, 202.81, 202.91, 239.8-239.9;
For code 202.32: 202.30, 202.32, 202.38, 202.82, 202.92, 239.8-239.9;
For code 202.33: 202.30, 202.33, 202.38, 202.83, 202.93, 239.8-239.9;
For code 202.34: 202.30, 202.34, 202.38, 202.84, 202.94, 239.8-239.9;
For code 202.35: 202.30, 202.35, 202.38, 202.85, 202.95, 239.8-239.9;
For code 202.36: 202.30, 202.36, 202.38, 202.86, 202.96, 239.8-239.9;
For code 202.37: 202.30, 202.37-202.38, 202.87, 202.97, 239.8-239.9;
For code 202.38: 202.30-202.38, 202.88, 202.98, 239.8-239.9

§ Requires fifth-digit. See beginning of section 200–208 for codes and definitions.

§ ✓5th **202.4 Leukemic reticuloendotheliosis** CC

Hairy-cell leukemia

CC Excl: For code 202.40: 202.40-202.48, 202.80, 202.90, 239.8-239.9; **For code 202.41:** 202.40, 202.41, 202.48, 202.81, 202.91, 239.8-239.9; **For code 202.42:** 202.40, 202.42, 202.48, 202.82, 202.92, 239.8-239.9; **For code 202.43:** 202.40, 202.43, 202.48, 202.83, 202.93, 239.8-239.9; **For code 202.44:** 202.40, 202.44, 202.48, 202.84, 202.94, 239.8-239.9; **For code 202.45:** 202.40, 202.45, 202.48, 202.85, 202.95, 239.8-239.9; **For code 202.46:** 202.40, 202.46, 202.48, 202.86, 202.96, 239.8-239.9; **For code 202.47:** 202.40, 202.47-202.48, 202.87, 202.97, 239.8-239.9: **For code 202.48:** 202.40-202.48, 202.88, 202.98, 239.8-239.9

DEF: Chronic leukemia with large, mononuclear cells with "hairy" appearance in marrow, spleen, liver, blood.

§ ✓5th **202.5 Letterer-Siwe disease** CC

Acute:
- differentiated progressive histiocytosis
- histiocytosis X (progressive)
- infantile reticuloendotheliosis
- reticulosis of infancy

EXCLUDES *Hand-Schüller-Christian disease (277.89)*
histiocytosis (acute) (chronic) (277.89)
histiocytosis X (chronic) (277.89)

CC Excl: For code 202.50: 202.50-202.58, 202.80, 202.90, 239.8-239.9; **For code 202.51:** 202.50, 202.51, 202.58, 202.81, 202.91, 239.8-239.9; **For code 202.52:** 202.50, 202.52, 202.58, 202.82, 202.92, 239.8-239.9; **For code 202.53:** 202.50, 202.53, 202.58, 202.83, 202.93, 239.8-239.9; **For code 202.54:** 202.50, 202.54, 202.58, 202.84, 202.94, 239.8-239.9; **For code 202.55:** 202.50, 202.55, 202.58, 202.85, 202.95, 239.8-239.9; **For code 202.56:** 202.50, 202.56, 202.58, 202.86, 202.96, 239.8-239.9; **For code 202.57:** 202.50, 202.57-202.58, 202.87, 202.97, 239.8-239.9; **For code 202.58:** 202.50-202.58, 202.88, 202.98, 239.8-239.9

DEF: A recessive reticuloendotheliosis of early childhood, with a hemorrhagic tendency, eczema-like skin eruption, hepatosplenomegaly, including lymph node enlargement, and progressive anemia; it is often a fatal disease with no established cause.

§ ✓5th **202.6 Malignant mast cell tumors** CC

Malignant:
- mastocytoma
- mastocytosis

Mast cell sarcoma
Systemic tissue mast cell disease

EXCLUDES *mast cell leukemia (207.8)*

CC Excl: For code 202.60: 202.60-202.68, 202.80, 202.90, 239.8-239.9; **For code 202.61:** 202.60, 202.61, 202.68, 202.81, 202.91, 239.8-239.9; **For code 202.62:** 202.60, 202.62, 202.68, 202.82, 202.92, 239.8-239.9; **For code 202.63:** 202.60, 202.63, 202.68, 202.83, 202.93, 239.8-239.9; **For code 202.64:** 202.60, 202.64, 202.68, 202.84, 202.94, 239.8-239.9; **For code 202.65:** 202.60, 202.65, 202.68, 202.85, 202.95, 239.8-239.9; **For code 202.66:** 202.60, 202.66, 202.68, 202.86, 202.96, 239.8-239.9; **For code 202.67:** 202.60, 202.67-202.68, 202.87, 202.97, 239.8-239.9; **For code 202.68:** 202.60-202.68, 202.88, 202.98, 239.8-239.9

§ ✓5th **202.8 Other lymphomas** CC HIV

Lymphoma (malignant):
- NOS
- diffuse

EXCLUDES *benign lymphoma (229.0)*

CC Excl: For code 202.80: 202.80-202.88, 202.90, 239.8-239.9; **For code 202.81:** 202.80, 202.81, 202.88, 202.91, 239.8-239.9; **For code 202.82:** 202.80, 202.82, 202.88, 202.92, 239.8-239.9; **For code 202.83:** 202.80, 202.83, 202.88, 202.93, 239.8-239.9; **For code 202.84:** 202.80, 202.84, 202.88, 202.94, 239.8-239.9; **For code 202.85:** 202.80, 202.85, 202.88, 202.95, 239.8-239.9; **For code 202.86:** 202.80, 202.86, 202.88, 202.96, 239.8-239.9; **For code 202.87:** 202.80, 202.87-202.88, 202.97, 239.8-239.9; **For code 202.88:** 202.80-202.88, 202.98, 239.8-239.9

AHA: 2Q, '92, 4

§ ✓5th **202.9 Other and unspecified malignant neoplasms of lymphoid and histiocytic tissue** CC

Follicular dendritic cell sarcoma
Interdigitating dendritic cell sarcoma
Langerhans cell sarcoma
Malignant neoplasm of bone marrow NOS

CC Excl: For code 202.90: 202.90-202.98, 239.8-239.9; **For code 202.91:** 202.90, 202.91, 202.98, 239.8-239.9; **For code 202.92:** 202.90, 202.92, 202.98, 239.8-239.9; **For code 202.93:** 202.90, 202.93, 202.98, 239.8-239.9; **For code 202.94:** 202.90, 202.94, 202.98, 239.8-239.9; **For code 202.95:** 202.90, 202.95, 202.98, 239.8-239.9; **For code 202.96:** 202.90, 202.96, 202.98, 239.8-239.9; **For code 202.97:** 202.90, 202.97-202.98, 239.8-239.9; **For code 202.98:** 202.90-202.98, 239.8-239.9

✓4th **203 Multiple myeloma and immunoproliferative neoplasms**

AHA: 4Q, '91, 26

The following fifth-digit subclassification is for use with category 203:
- **0 without mention of remission**
- **1 in remission**

✓5th **203.0 Multiple myeloma** CC

Kahler's disease
Myelomatosis

EXCLUDES *solitary myeloma (238.6)*

CC Excl: 203.00-208.91, 239.8-239.9

AHA: 1Q, '96, 16; 4Q, '89,10

✓5th **203.1 Plasma cell leukemia** CC

Plasmacytic leukemia

CC Excl: See code 203.0

AHA: 4Q, '90, 26; S-O, '86, 12

✓5th **203.8 Other immunoproliferative neoplasms** CC

CC Excl: See code 203.0

AHA: 4Q, '90, 26; S-O, '86, 12

✓4th **204 Lymphoid leukemia**

INCLUDES leukemia:
- lymphatic
- lymphoblastic
- lymphocytic
- lymphogenous

AHA: 3Q, '93, 4

The following fifth-digit subclassification is for use with category 204:
- **0 without mention of remission**
- **1 in remission**

✓5th **204.0 Acute** CC

EXCLUDES *acute exacerbation of chronic lymphoid leukemia (204.1)*

CC Excl: See code 203.0

AHA: 3Q, '99, 6

✓5th **204.1 Chronic** CC

CC Excl: See code 203.0

✓5th **204.2 Subacute** CC

CC Excl: See code 203.0

✓5th **204.8 Other lymphoid leukemia** CC

Aleukemic leukemia:
- lymphatic
- lymphocytic

Aleukemic leukemia:
- lymphoid

CC Excl: See code 203.0

✓5th **204.9 Unspecified lymphoid leukemia** CC

CC Excl: See code 203.0

§ Requires fifth-digit. See beginning of section 200–208 for codes and definitions.

✓4th 205 Myeloid leukemia

INCLUDES leukemia: granulocytic, myeloblastic, myelocytic, myelogenous; leukemia: myelomonocytic, myelosclerotic, myelosis

AHA: 3Q, '93, 3; 4Q, '91, 26; 4Q, '90, 3; M-J, '85, 18

The following fifth-digit subclassification is for use with category 205:
- **0 without mention of remission**
- **1 in remission**

✓5th 205.0 Acute CC

Acute promyelocytic leukemia

EXCLUDES *acute exacerbation of chronic myeloid leukemia (205.1)*

CC Excl: See code 203.0

✓5th 205.1 Chronic CC

Eosinophilic leukemia
Neutrophilic leukemia

CC Excl: See code 203.0

AHA: 1Q, '00, 6; J-A, '85, 13

✓5th 205.2 Subacute CC

CC Excl: See code 203.0

✓5th 205.3 Myeloid sarcoma CC

Chloroma
Granulocytic sarcoma

CC Excl: See code 203.0

✓5th 205.8 Other myeloid leukemia CC

Aleukemic leukemia: granulocytic, myelogenous
Aleukemic leukemia: myeloid
Aleukemic myelosis

CC Excl: See code 203.0

✓5th 205.9 Unspecified myeloid leukemia CC

CC Excl: See code 203.0

✓4th 206 Monocytic leukemia

INCLUDES leukemia: histiocytic, monoblastic, monocytoid

The following fifth-digit subclassification is for use with category 206:
- **0 without mention of remission**
- **1 in remission**

✓5th 206.0 Acute CC

EXCLUDES *acute exacerbation of chronic monocytic leukemia (206.1)*

CC Excl: See code 203.0

✓5th 206.1 Chronic CC

CC Excl: See code 203.0

✓5th 206.2 Subacute CC

CC Excl: See code 203.0

✓5th 206.8 Other monocytic leukemia CC

Aleukemic: monocytic leukemia, monocytoid leukemia

CC Excl: See code 203.0

✓5th 206.9 Unspecified monocytic leukemia CC

CC Excl: See code 203.0

✓4th 207 Other specified leukemia

EXCLUDES *leukemic reticuloendotheliosis (202.4)*
plasma cell leukemia (203.1)

The following fifth-digit subclassification is for use with category 207:
- **0 without mention of remission**
- **1 in remission**

✓5th 207.0 Acute erythremia and erythroleukemia CC

Acute erythremic myelosis
Di Guglielmo's disease
Erythremic myelosis

CC Excl: See code 203.0

DEF: Erythremia: polycythemia vera.

DEF: Erythroleukemia: a malignant blood dyscrasia (a myeloproliferative disorder).

✓5th 207.1 Chronic erythremia CC

Heilmeyer-Schöner disease

CC Excl: See code 203.0

✓5th 207.2 Megakaryocytic leukemia CC

Megakaryocytic myelosis
Thrombocytic leukemia

CC Excl: See code 203.0

✓5th 207.8 Other specified leukemia CC

Lymphosarcoma cell leukemia

CC Excl: See code 203.0

✓4th 208 Leukemia of unspecified cell type

The following fifth-digit subclassification is for use with category 208:
- **0 without mention of remission**
- **1 in remission**

✓5th 208.0 Acute CC

Acute leukemia NOS
Stem cell leukemia
Blast cell leukemia

EXCLUDES *acute exacerbation of chronic unspecified leukemia (208.1)*

CC Excl: See code 203.0

✓5th 208.1 Chronic CC

Chronic leukemia NOS

CC Excl: See code 203.0

✓5th 208.2 Subacute CC

Subacute leukemia NOS

CC Excl: See code 203.0

✓5th 208.8 Other leukemia of unspecified cell type CC

CC Excl: See code 203.0

✓5th 208.9 Unspecified leukemia CC

Leukemia NOS

CC Excl: See code 203.0

BENIGN NEOPLASMS (210-229)

✓4th 210 Benign neoplasm of lip, oral cavity, and pharynx

EXCLUDES *cyst (of):*
jaw (526.0-526.2,526.89)
oral soft tissue (528.4)
radicular (522.8)

210.0 Lip

Frenulum labii
Lip (inner aspect) (mucosa) (vermilion border)

EXCLUDES *labial commissure (210.4)*
skin of lip (216.0)

210.1 Tongue

Lingual tonsil

210.2 Major salivary glands
Gland: parotid, sublingual
Gland: submandibular
EXCLUDES *benign neoplasms of minor salivary glands:*
NOS (210.4)
buccal mucosa (210.4)
lips (210.0)
palate (hard) (soft) (210.4)
tongue (210.1)
tonsil, palatine (210.5)

210.3 Floor of mouth

210.4 Other and unspecified parts of mouth
Gingiva
Gum (upper) (lower)
Labial commissure
Oral cavity NOS
Oral mucosa
Palate (hard) (soft)
Uvula
EXCLUDES *benign odontogenic neoplasms of bone (213.0-213.1)*
developmental odontogenic cysts (526.0)
mucosa of lips (210.0)
nasopharyngeal [posterior] [superior] surface of soft palate (210.7)

210.5 Tonsil
Tonsil (faucial) (palatine)
EXCLUDES *lingual tonsil (210.1)*
pharyngeal tonsil (210.7)
tonsillar:
fossa (210.6)
pillars (210.6)

210.6 Other parts of oropharynx
Branchial cleft or vestiges
Epiglottis, anterior aspect
Fauces NOS
Mesopharynx NOS
Tonsillar: fossa, pillars
Vallecula
EXCLUDES *epiglottis:*
NOS (212.1)
suprahyoid portion (212.1)

210.7 Nasopharynx
Adenoid tissue
Lymphadenoid tissue
Pharyngeal tonsil
Posterior nasal septum

210.8 Hypopharynx
Arytenoid fold
Laryngopharynx
Postcricoidregion
Pyriform fossa

210.9 Pharynx, unspecified
Throat NOS

✓4th **211 Benign neoplasm of other parts of digestive system**
EXCLUDES ▶ *benign stromal tumors of digestive system (215.5)*◀

211.0 Esophagus

211.1 Stomach
Body, Cardia, Fundus } of stomach
Cardiac orifice
Pylorus

211.2 Duodenum, jejunum, and ileum
Small intestine NOS
EXCLUDES *ampulla of Vater (211.5)*
ileocecal valve (211.3)

211.3 Colon
Appendix
Cecum
Ileocecal valve
Large intestine NOS
EXCLUDES *rectosigmoid junction (211.4)*
AHA: 3Q, '05, 17; 2Q, '05, 16; 4Q, '01, 56
DRG 188

211.4 Rectum and anal canal
Anal canal or sphincter
Anus NOS
Rectosigmoid junction
EXCLUDES *anus:*
margin (216.5)
skin (216.5)
perianal skin (216.5)

211.5 Liver and biliary passages
Ampulla of Vater
Common bile duct
Cystic duct
Gallbladder
Hepatic duct
Sphincter of Oddi

211.6 Pancreas, except islets of Langerhans

211.7 Islets of Langerhans
Islet cell tumor
Use additional code to identify any functional activity

211.8 Retroperitoneum and peritoneum
Mesentery
Mesocolon
Omentum
Retroperitoneal tissue

211.9 Other and unspecified site
Alimentary tract NOS
Digestive system NOS
Gastrointestinal tract NOS
Intestinal tract NOS
Intestine NOS
Spleen, not elsewhere classified

✓4th **212 Benign neoplasm of respiratory and intrathoracic organs**

212.0 Nasal cavities, middle ear, and accessory sinuses
Cartilage of nose
Eustachian tube
Nares
Septum of nose
Sinus: ethmoidal, frontal, maxillary, sphenoidal
EXCLUDES *auditory canal (external) (216.2)*
bone of:
ear (213.0)
nose [turbinates] (213.0)
cartilage of ear (215.0)
ear (external) (skin) (216.2)
nose NOS (229.8)
skin (216.3)
olfactory bulb (225.1)
polyp of:
accessory sinus (471.8)
ear (385.30-385.35)
nasal cavity (471.0)
posterior margin of septum and choanae (210.7)

212.1 Larynx
Cartilage: arytenoid, cricoid, cuneiform, thyroid
Epiglottis (suprahyoid portion) NOS
Glottis
Vocal cords (false) (true)
EXCLUDES *epiglottis, anterior aspect (210.6)*
polyp of vocal cord or larynx (478.4)

212.2 Trachea

212.3 Bronchus and lung
Carina
Hilus of lung

212.4 Pleura

212.5 Mediastinum

212.6 Thymus

212.7 Heart
EXCLUDES *great vessels (215.4)*

212.8 Other specified sites

212.9 Site unspecified
Respiratory organ NOS
Upper respiratory tract NOS
EXCLUDES *intrathoracic NOS (229.8)*
thoracic NOS (229.8)

✓4th **213 Benign neoplasm of bone and articular cartilage**
INCLUDES cartilage (articular) (joint)
periosteum
EXCLUDES *cartilage of:*
ear (215.0)
eyelid (215.0)
larynx (212.1)
cartilage of:
nose (212.0)
exostosis NOS (726.91)
synovia (215.0-215.9)

213.0 Bones of skull and face
EXCLUDES *lower jaw bone (213.1)*

213.1 Lower jaw bone

213.2 **Vertebral column, excluding sacrum and coccyx**
213.3 **Ribs, sternum, and clavicle**
213.4 **Scapula and long bones of upper limb**
213.5 **Short bones of upper limb**
213.6 **Pelvic bones, sacrum, and coccyx**
213.7 **Long bones of lower limb**
213.8 **Short bones of lower limb**
213.9 **Bone and articular cartilage, site unspecified**

✓4th **214 Lipoma**

INCLUDES angiolipoma
fibrolipoma
hibernoma
lipoma (fetal) (infiltrating) (intramuscular)
myelolipoma
myxolipoma

DEF: Benign tumor frequently composed of mature fat cells; may occasionally be composed of fetal fat cells.

214.0 **Skin and subcutaneous tissue of face**
214.1 **Other skin and subcutaneous tissue**
214.2 **Intrathoracic organs**
214.3 **Intra-abdominal organs**
214.4 **Spermatic cord** ♂
214.8 **Other specified sites**
AHA: 3Q, '94, 7
214.9 **Lipoma, unspecified site**

✓4th **215 Other benign neoplasm of connective and other soft tissue**

INCLUDES blood vessel
bursa
fascia
ligament
muscle
peripheral, sympathetic, and parasympathetic nerves and ganglia
synovia
tendon (sheath)

EXCLUDES *cartilage:*
articular (213.0-213.9)
larynx (212.1)
nose (212.0)
connective tissue of:
breast (217)
internal organ, except lipoma and hemangioma—code to benign neoplasm of the site
lipoma (214.0-214.9)

215.0 **Head, face, and neck**
215.2 **Upper limb, including shoulder**
215.3 **Lower limb, including hip**
215.4 **Thorax**
EXCLUDES *heart (212.7)*
mediastinum (212.5)
thymus (212.6)
215.5 **Abdomen**
Abdominal wall
▶Benign stromal tumors of abdomen◀
Hypochondrium
215.6 **Pelvis**
Buttock
Groin
Inguinal region
Perineum
EXCLUDES *uterine:*
leiomyoma (218.0-218.9)
ligament, any (221.0)
215.7 **Trunk, unspecified**
Back NOS
Flank NOS
215.8 **Other specified sites**
215.9 **Site unspecified**

✓4th **216 Benign neoplasm of skin**

INCLUDES blue nevus
dermatofibroma
hydrocystoma
pigmented nevus
syringoadenoma
syringoma

EXCLUDES *skin of genital organs (221.0-222.9)*

AHA: 1Q, '00, 21

216.0 **Skin of lip**
EXCLUDES *vermilion border of lip (210.0)*
216.1 **Eyelid, including canthus**
EXCLUDES *cartilage of eyelid (215.0)*
216.2 **Ear and external auditory canal**
Auricle (ear)
Auricular canal, external
External meatus
Pinna
EXCLUDES *cartilage of ear (215.0)*
216.3 **Skin of other and unspecified parts of face**
Cheek, external
Eyebrow
Nose, external
Temple
216.4 **Scalp and skin of neck**
AHA: 3Q, '91, 12
216.5 **Skin of trunk, except scrotum**
Axillary fold
Perianal skin
Skin of:
abdominal wall
anus
back
breast
buttock
chest wall
groin
perineum
Umbilicus
EXCLUDES *anal canal (211.4)*
anus NOS (211.4)
skin of scrotum (222.4)
216.6 **Skin of upper limb, including shoulder**
216.7 **Skin of lower limb, including hip**
216.8 **Other specified sites of skin**
216.9 **Skin, site unspecified**

217 Benign neoplasm of breast

Breast (male) (female):
connective tissue
glandular tissue
soft parts

EXCLUDES *adenofibrosis (610.2)*
benign cyst of breast (610.0)
fibrocystic disease (610.1)
skin of breast (216.5)

AHA: 1Q, '00, 4

✓4th **218 Uterine leiomyoma**

INCLUDES fibroid (bleeding) (uterine)
uterine:
fibromyoma
myoma

DEF: Benign tumor primarily derived from uterine smooth muscle tissue; may contain fibrous, fatty, or epithelial tissue; also called uterine fibroid or myoma.

218.0 **Submucous leiomyoma of uterus** ♀
218.1 **Intramural leiomyoma of uterus** ♀
Interstitial leiomyoma of uterus
218.2 **Subserous leiomyoma of uterus** ♀
218.9 **Leiomyoma of uterus, unspecified** ♀
AHA: 1Q, '03, 4

✓4th **219 Other benign neoplasm of uterus**

219.0 **Cervix uteri** ♀
219.1 **Corpus uteri** ♀
Endometrium
Fundus
Myometrium
219.8 **Other specified parts of uterus** ♀
219.9 **Uterus, part unspecified** ♀

Types of Uterine Fibroids

Types of Uterine Fibroids

220 Benign neoplasm of ovary ♀

Use additional code to identify any functional activity (256.0-256.1)

EXCLUDES *cyst:*
corpus albicans (620.2)
corpus luteum (620.1)
endometrial (617.1)
follicular (atretic) (620.0)
graafian follicle (620.0)
ovarian NOS (620.2)
retention (620.2)

✓4th **221 Benign neoplasm of other female genital organs**

INCLUDES adenomatous polyp
benign teratoma

EXCLUDES *cyst:*
epoophoron (752.11)
fimbrial (752.11)
Gartner's duct (752.11)
parovarian (752.11)

221.0 Fallopian tube and uterine ligaments ♀
Oviduct
Parametruim
Uterine ligament (broad) (round) (uterosacral)
Uterine tube

221.1 Vagina ♀

221.2 Vulva ♀
Clitoris
External female genitalia NOS
Greater vestibular [Bartholin's] gland
Labia (majora) (minora)
Pudendum

EXCLUDES *Bartholin's (duct) (gland) cyst (616.2)*

221.8 Other specified sites of female genital organs ♀

221.9 Female genital organ, site unspecified ♀
Female genitourinary tract NOS

✓4th **222 Benign neoplasm of male genital organs**

222.0 Testis ♂
Use additional code to identify any functional activity

222.1 Penis ♂
Corpus cavernosum Prepuce
Glans penis

222.2 Prostate ♂

EXCLUDES *adenomatous hyperplasia of prostate (600.20-600.21)*
prostatic:
adenoma (600.20-600.21)
enlargement (600.00-600.01)
hypertrophy (600.00-600.01)

222.3 Epididymis ♂

222.4 Scrotum ♂
Skin of scrotum

222.8 Other specified sites of male genital organs ♂
Seminal vesicle
Spermatic cord

222.9 Male genital organ, site unspecified ♂
Male genitourinary tract NOS

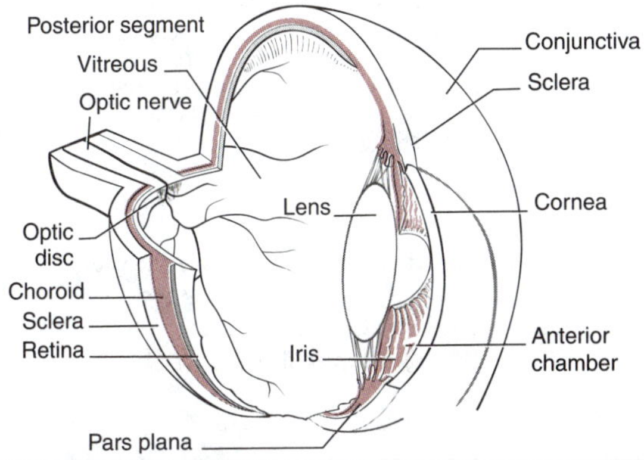

✓4th **223 Benign neoplasm of kidney and other urinary organs**

223.0 Kidney, except pelvis
Kidney NOS

EXCLUDES *renal:*
calyces (223.1)
pelvis (223.1)

223.1 Renal pelvis

223.2 Ureter

EXCLUDES *ureteric orifice of bladder (223.3)*

223.3 Bladder

✓5th **223.8 Other specified sites of urinary organs**

223.81 Urethra

EXCLUDES *urethral orifice of bladder (223.3)*

223.89 Other
Paraurethral glands

223.9 Urinary organ, site unspecified
Urinary system NOS

✓4th **224 Benign neoplasm of eye**

EXCLUDES *cartilage of eyelid (215.0)*
eyelid (skin) (216.1)
optic nerve (225.1)
orbital bone (213.0)

224.0 Eyeball, except conjunctiva, cornea, retina, and choroid
Ciliary body Sclera
Iris Uveal tract

224.1 Orbit

EXCLUDES *bone of orbit (213.0)*

224.2 Lacrimal gland

224.3 Conjunctiva

224.4 Cornea

224.5 Retina

EXCLUDES *hemangioma of retina (228.03)*

224.6 Choroid

224.7 Lacrimal duct
Lacrimal sac Nasolacrimal duct

224.8 Other specified parts of eye

224.9 Eye, part unspecified

✓4th **225 Benign neoplasm of brain and other parts of nervous system**

EXCLUDES *hemangioma (228.02)*
neurofibromatosis (237.7)
peripheral, sympathetic, and parasympathetic nerves and ganglia (215.0-215.9)
retrobulbar (224.1)

225.0 Brain

225.1 Cranial nerves
Acoustic neuroma
AHA: 4Q, '04, 113

225.2 Cerebral meninges
Meninges NOS Meningioma (cerebral)

225.3 Spinal cord
Cauda equina

225.4 Spinal meninges
Spinal meningioma

225.8 Other specified sites of nervous system

225.9 Nervous system, part unspecified
Nervous system (central) NOS

EXCLUDES *meninges NOS (225.2)*

226 Benign neoplasm of thyroid glands
Use additional code to identify any functional activity

✓4th **227 Benign neoplasm of other endocrine glands and related structures**
Use additional code to identify any functional activity

EXCLUDES *ovary (220)* *testis (222.0)*
pancreas (211.6)

227.0 Adrenal gland
Suprarenal gland

227.1 Parathyroid gland

227.3 Pituitary gland and craniopharyngeal duct (pouch)
Craniobuccal pouch
Hypophysis
Rathke's pouch
Sella turcica

227.4 Pineal gland
Pineal body

227.5 Carotid body

227.6 Aortic body and other paraganglia
Coccygeal body
Glomus jugulare
Para-aortic body
AHA: N-D, '84, 17

227.8 Other

227.9 Endocrine gland, site unspecified

✓4th **228 Hemangioma and lymphangioma, any site**

INCLUDES angioma (benign) (cavernous) (congenital) NOS
cavernous nevus
glomus tumor
hemangioma (benign) (congenital)

EXCLUDES *benign neoplasm of spleen, except hemangioma and lymphangioma (211.9)*
glomus jugulare (227.6)
nevus:
NOS (216.0-216.9)
blue or pigmented (216.0-216.9)
vascular (757.32)

AHA: 1Q, '00, 21

✓5th **228.0 Hemangioma, any site**
AHA: J-F, '85, 19
DEF: A common benign tumor usually occurring in infancy; composed of newly formed blood vessels due to malformation of angioblastic tissue.

228.00 Of unspecified site
228.01 Of skin and subcutaneous tissue
228.02 Of intracranial structures
228.03 Of retina
228.04 Of intra-abdominal structures
Peritoneum
Retroperitoneal tissue
228.09 Of other sites
Systemic angiomatosis
AHA: 3Q, '91, 20

228.1 Lymphangioma, any site
Congenital lymphangioma
Lymphatic nevus

✓4th **229 Benign neoplasm of other and unspecified sites**

229.0 Lymph nodes
EXCLUDES *lymphangioma (228.1)*

229.8 Other specified sites
Intrathoracic NOS
Thoracic NOS

229.9 Site unspecified

CARCINOMA IN SITU (230-234)

INCLUDES Bowen's disease
erythroplasia
Queyrat's erythroplasia

EXCLUDES *leukoplakia—see Alphabetic Index*

DEF: A neoplastic type; with tumor cells confined to epithelium of origin; without further invasion.

✓4th **230 Carcinoma in situ of digestive organs**

230.0 Lip, oral cavity, and pharynx
Gingiva
Hypopharynx
Mouth [any part]
Nasopharynx
Oropharynx
Salivary gland or duct
Tongue
EXCLUDES *aryepiglottic fold or interarytenoid fold, laryngeal aspect (231.0)*
epiglottis:
NOS (231.0)
suprahyoid portion (231.0)
skin of lip (232.0)

230.1 Esophagus

230.2 Stomach
Body, Cardia, Fundus } of stomach
Cardiac orifice
Pylorus

230.3 Colon
Appendix
Cecum
Ileocecal valve
Large intestine NOS
EXCLUDES *rectosigmoid junction (230.4)*

230.4 Rectum
Rectosigmoid junction

230.5 Anal canal
Anal sphincter

230.6 Anus, unspecified
EXCLUDES *anus:*
margin (232.5)
skin (232.5)
perianal skin (232.5)

230.7 Other and unspecified parts of intestine
Duodenum
Ileum
Jejunum
Small intestine NOS
EXCLUDES *ampulla of Vater (230.8)*

230.8 Liver and biliary system
Ampulla of Vater
Common bile duct
Cystic duct
Gallbladder
Hepatic duct
Sphincter of Oddi

230.9 Other and unspecified digestive organs
Digestive organ NOS
Gastrointestinal tract NOS
Pancreas
Spleen

✓4th **231 Carcinoma in situ of respiratory system**

231.0 Larynx
Cartilage:
arytenoid
cricoid
cuneiform
thyroid
Epiglottis:
NOS
posterior surface
suprahyoid portion
Vocal cords (false) (true)
EXCLUDES *aryepiglottic fold or interarytenoid fold:*
NOS (230.0)
hypopharyngeal aspect (230.0)
marginal zone (230.0)

231.1 Trachea

231.2 Bronchus and lung
Carina
Hilus of lung

231.8 Other specified parts of respiratory system
Accessory sinuses
Middle ear
Nasal cavities
Pleura
EXCLUDES *ear (external) (skin) (232.2)*
nose NOS (234.8)
skin (232.3)

231.9 Respiratory system, part unspecified
Respiratory organ NOS

✓4th **232 Carcinoma in situ of skin**

INCLUDES pigment cells

232.0 Skin of lip
EXCLUDES *vermilion border of lip (230.0)*

232.1 Eyelid, including canthus

232.2 Ear and external auditory canal

232.3 Skin of other and unspecified parts of face

232.4 Scalp and skin of neck

232.5 Skin of trunk, except scrotum
Anus, margin
Axillary fold
Perianal skin
Skin of:
abdominal wall
anus
back
breast
buttock
chest wall
groin
perineum
Umbilicus
EXCLUDES *anal canal (230.5)*
anus NOS (230.6)
skin of genital organs (233.3, 233.5-233.6)

232.6 Skin of upper limb, including shoulder

232.7 Skin of lower limb, including hip

232.8 Other specified sites of skin

232.9 Skin, site unspecified

✓4th 233 Carcinoma in situ of breast and genitourinary system

233.0 Breast

EXCLUDES *Paget's disease (174.0-174.9)*
skin of breast (232.5)

233.1 Cervix uteri ♀

▶Cervical intraepithelial glandular neoplasia◀
Cervical intraepithelial neoplasia III [CIN III]
Severe dysplasia of cervix

EXCLUDES *cervical intraepithelial neoplasia II [CIN II] (622.12)*
cytologic evidence of malignancy without histologic confirmation ▶(795.06)◀
high grade squamous intraepithelial lesion (HGSIL) (795.04)
moderate dysplasia of cervix (622.12)

AHA: 3Q, '92, 7; 3Q, '92, 8; 1Q, '91, 11

233.2 Other and unspecified parts of uterus ♀

233.3 Other and unspecified female genital organs ♀

233.4 Prostate ♂

233.5 Penis ♂

233.6 Other and unspecified male genital organs ♂

233.7 Bladder

233.9 Other and unspecified urinary organs

✓4th 234 Carcinoma in situ of other and unspecified sites

234.0 Eye

EXCLUDES *cartilage of eyelid (234.8)*
eyelid (skin) (232.1)
optic nerve (234.8)
orbital bone (234.8)

234.8 Other specified sites

Endocrine gland [any]

234.9 Site unspecified

Carcinoma in situ NOS

NEOPLASMS OF UNCERTAIN BEHAVIOR (235-238)

Note: Categories 235–238 classify by site certain histomorphologically well-defined neoplasms, the subsequent behavior of which cannot be predicted from the present appearance.

✓4th 235 Neoplasm of uncertain behavior of digestive and respiratory systems

EXCLUDES ▶ *stromal tumors of uncertain behavior of digestive system (238.1)*◀

235.0 Major salivary glands

Gland:
parotid
sublingual
submandibular

EXCLUDES *minor salivary glands (235.1)*

235.1 Lip, oral cavity, and pharynx

Gingiva
Hypopharynx
Minor salivary glands
Mouth
Nasopharynx
Oropharynx
Tongue

EXCLUDES *aryepiglottic fold or interarytenoid fold, laryngeal aspect (235.6)*
epiglottis:
NOS (235.6)
suprahyoid portion (235.6)
skin of lip (238.2)

235.2 Stomach, intestines, and rectum

235.3 Liver and biliary passages

Ampulla of Vater
Bile ducts [any]
Gallbladder
Liver

235.4 Retroperitoneum and peritoneum

235.5 Other and unspecified digestive organs

Anal:
canal
sphincter
Anus NOS
Esophagus
Pancreas
Spleen

EXCLUDES *anus:*
margin (238.2)
skin (238.2)
perianal skin (238.2)

235.6 Larynx

EXCLUDES *aryepiglottic fold or interarytenoid fold:*
NOS (235.1)
hypopharyngeal aspect (235.1)
marginal zone (235.1)

235.7 Trachea, bronchus, and lung

235.8 Pleura, thymus, and mediastinum

235.9 Other and unspecified respiratory organs

Accessory sinuses
Middle ear
Nasal cavities
Respiratory organ NOS

EXCLUDES *ear (external) (skin) (238.2)*
nose (238.8)
skin (238.2)

✓4th 236 Neoplasm of uncertain behavior of genitourinary organs

236.0 Uterus ♀

236.1 Placenta ♀

Chorioadenoma (destruens)
Invasive mole
Malignant hydatid(iform) mole

236.2 Ovary ♀

Use additional code to identify any functional activity

236.3 Other and unspecified female genital organs ♀

236.4 Testis ♂

Use additional code to identify any functional activity

236.5 Prostate ♂

236.6 Other and unspecified male genital organs ♂

236.7 Bladder

✓5th 236.9 Other and unspecified urinary organs

236.90 Urinary organ, unspecified

236.91 Kidney and ureter

236.99 Other

✓4th 237 Neoplasm of uncertain behavior of endocrine glands and nervous system

237.0 Pituitary gland and craniopharyngeal duct

Use additional code to identify any functional activity

237.1 Pineal gland

237.2 Adrenal gland

Suprarenal gland
Use additional code to identify any functional activity

237.3 Paraganglia

Aortic body
Carotid body
Coccygeal body
Glomus jugulare

AHA: N-D, '84, 17

237.4 Other and unspecified endocrine glands

Parathyroid gland
Thyroid gland

237.5 Brain and spinal cord

237.6 Meninges

Meninges:
NOS
cerebral
spinal

✓5th 237.7 Neurofibromatosis

von Recklinghausen's disease

DEF: An inherited condition with developmental changes in the nervous system, muscles, bones and skin; multiple soft tumors (neurofibromas) distributed over the entire body.

237.70 Neurofibromatosis, unspecified

237.71 Neurofibromatosis, type 1 [von Recklinghausen's disease]

237.72 Neurofibromatosis, type 2 [acoustic neurofibromatosis]

DEF: Inherited condition with cutaneous lesions, benign tumors of peripheral nerves and bilateral 8th nerve masses.

237.9 Other and unspecified parts of nervous system

Cranial nerves

EXCLUDES *peripheral, sympathetic, and parasympathetic nerves and ganglia (238.1)*

✓4th **238 Neoplasm of uncertain behavior of other and unspecified sites and tissues**

238.0 Bone and articular cartilage

EXCLUDES *cartilage:*
ear (238.1)
eyelid (238.1)
larynx (235.6)
nose (235.9)
synovia (238.1)

AHA: 4Q, '04, 128

238.1 Connective and other soft tissue

Peripheral, sympathetic, and parasympathetic nerves and ganglia
▶Stromal tumors of digestive system◀

EXCLUDES *cartilage (of):*
articular (238.0)
larynx (235.6)
nose (235.9)
connective tissue of breast (238.3)

238.2 Skin

EXCLUDES *anus NOS (235.5)*
skin of genital organs (236.3, 236.6)
vermilion border of lip (235.1)

238.3 Breast

EXCLUDES *skin of breast (238.2)*

238.4 Polycythemia vera

DEF: Abnormal proliferation of all bone marrow elements, increased red cell mass and total blood volume; unknown etiology, frequently associated with splenomegaly, leukocytosis, and thrombocythemia.

238.5 Histiocytic and mast cells

Mast cell tumor NOS Mastocytoma NOS

238.6 Plasma cells

Plasmacytoma NOS Solitary myeloma

✓5th **238.7 Other lymphatic and hematopoietic tissues**

EXCLUDES ▶ *acute myelogenous leukemia (205.0)*
chronic myelomonocytic leukemia (205.1)◀
myelofibrosis ▶*(289.83)*◀
myelosclerosis NOS (289.89)
myelosis:
NOS (205.9)
megakaryocytic (207.2)

AHA: 3Q, '01, 13; 1Q, '97, 5; 2Q, '89, 8

● **238.71 Essential thrombocythemia**

Essential hemorrhagic thrombocythemia
Essential thrombocytosis
Idiopathic (hemorrhagic) thrombocythemia
Primary thrombocytosis

● **238.72 Low grade myelodysplastic syndrome lesions**

Refractory anemia (RA)
Refractory anemia with ringed sideroblasts (RARS)
Refractory cytopenia with multilineage dysplasia (RCMD)
Refractory cytopenia with multilineage dysplasia and ringed sideroblasts (RCMD-RS)

DEF: Refractory anemia (RA): Form of bone marrow disorder (myelodysplastic syndrome) that interferes with red blood cell production in the bone marrow; malignancy unresponsive to hematinics; characteristic normal or hypercellular marrow with abnormal erythrocyte development and reticulocytopenia.

● **238.73 High grade myelodysplastic syndrome lesions**

Refractory anemia with excess blasts-1 (RAEB-1)
Refractory anemia with excess blasts-2 (RAEB-2)

● **238.74 Myelodysplastic syndrome with 5q deletion**

5q minus syndrome NOS

EXCLUDES *constitutional 5q deletion (758.39)*
high grade myelodysplastic syndrome with 5q deletion (238.73)

● **238.75 Myelodysplastic syndrome, unspecified**

● **238.76 Myelofibrosis with myeloid metaplasia**

Agnogenic myeloid metaplasia
Idiopathic myelofibrosis (chronic)
Myelosclerosis with myeloid metaplasia
Primary myelofibrosis

EXCLUDES *myelofibrosis NOS (289.83)*
myelophthisic anemia (284.2)
myelophthisis (284.2)
secondary myelofibrosis (289.83)

● **238.79 Other lymphatic and hematopoietic tissues**

Lymphoproliferative disease (chronic) NOS
Megakaryocytic myelosclerosis
Myeloproliferative disease (chronic) NOS
Panmyelosis (acute)

238.8 Other specified sites

Eye Heart

EXCLUDES *eyelid (skin) (238.2)*
cartilage (238.1)

238.9 Site unspecified

NEOPLASMS OF UNSPECIFIED NATURE (239)

✓4th **239 Neoplasms of unspecified nature**

Note: Category 239 classifies by site neoplasms of unspecified morphology and behavior. The term "mass,"unless otherwise stated, is not to be regarded as a neoplastic growth.

INCLUDES "growth" NOS new growth NOS
neoplasm NOS tumor NOS

239.0 Digestive system

EXCLUDES *anus:*
margin (239.2)
skin (239.2)
perianal skin (239.2)

239.1 Respiratory system

239.2 Bone, soft tissue, and skin

EXCLUDES *anal canal (239.0)*
anus NOS (239.0)
bone marrow (202.9)
cartilage:
larynx (239.1)
nose (239.1)
connective tissue of breast (239.3)
skin of genital organs (239.5)
vermilion border of lip (239.0)

239.3 Breast

EXCLUDES *skin of breast (239.2)*

239.4 Bladder

239.5 Other genitourinary organs

239.6 Brain

EXCLUDES *cerebral meninges (239.7)*
cranial nerves (239.7)

239.7 Endocrine glands and other parts of nervous system

EXCLUDES *peripheral, sympathetic, and parasympathetic nerves and ganglia (239.2)*

239.8 Other specified sites

EXCLUDES *eyelid (skin) (239.2)*
cartilage (239.2)
great vessels (239.2)
optic nerve (239.7)

239.9 Site unspecified

3. ENDOCRINE, NUTRITIONAL AND METABOLIC DISEASES, AND IMMUNITY DISORDERS (240-279)

EXCLUDES *endocrine and metabolic disturbances specific to the fetus and newborn (775.0-775.9)*

Note: All neoplasms, whether functionally active or not, are classified in Chapter 2. Codes in Chapter 3 (i.e., 242.8, 246.0, 251-253, 255-259) may be used to identify such functional activity associated with any neoplasm, or by ectopic endocrine tissue.

DISORDERS OF THYROID GLAND (240-246)

✓4th **240 Simple and unspecified goiter**

DEF: An enlarged thyroid gland often caused by an inadequate dietary intake of iodine.

240.0 Goiter, specified as simple

Any condition classifiable to 240.9, specified as simple

240.9 Goiter, unspecified

Enlargement of thyroid
Goiter or struma:
NOS
diffuse colloid
endemic
Goiter or struma:
hyperplastic
nontoxic (diffuse)
parenchymatous
sporadic

EXCLUDES *congenital (dyshormonogenic) goiter (246.1)*

✓4th **241 Nontoxic nodular goiter**

EXCLUDES *adenoma of thyroid (226)*
cystadenoma of thyroid (226)

241.0 Nontoxic uninodular goiter

Thyroid nodule
Uninodular goiter (nontoxic)

DEF: Enlarged thyroid, commonly due to decreased thyroid production, with single nodule; no clinical hypothyroidism.

241.1 Nontoxic multinodular goiter

Multinodular goiter (nontoxic)

DEF: Enlarged thyroid, commonly due to decreased thyroid production with multiple nodules; no clinical hypothyroidism.

241.9 Unspecified nontoxic nodular goiter

Adenomatous goiter
Nodular goiter (nontoxic) NOS
Struma nodosa (simplex)

✓4th **242 Thyrotoxicosis with or without goiter**

EXCLUDES *neonatal thyrotoxicosis (775.3)*

DEF: A condition caused by excess quantities of thyroid hormones being introduced into the tissues

The following fifth-digit subclassification is for use with category 242:
0 without mention of thyrotoxic crisis or storm
1 with mention of thyrotoxic crisis or storm

The Endocrine System

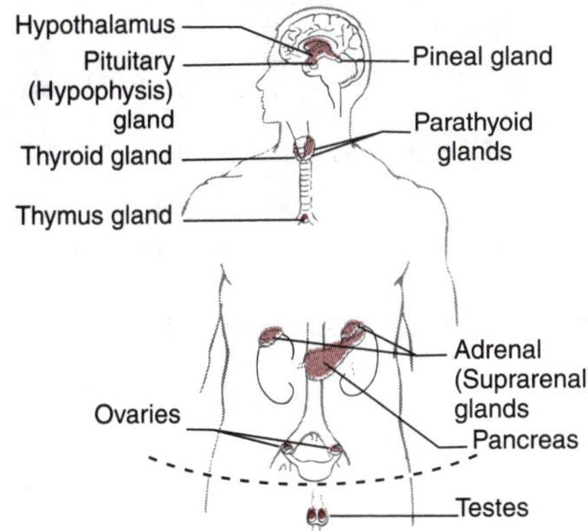

✓5th **242.0 Toxic diffuse goiter** CC

Basedow's disease
Exophthalmic or toxic goiter NOS
Graves' disease
Primary thyroid hyperplasia

CC Excl: 017.50-017.56, 017.90-017.96, 240.0-246.9, 259.8-259.9

DEF: Diffuse thyroid enlargement accompanied by hyperthyroidism, bulging eyes, and dermopathy.

✓5th **242.1 Toxic uninodular goiter** CC

Thyroid nodule } toxic or with hyperthyroidism
Uninodular goiter } toxic or with hyperthyroidism

CC Excl: See code 242.0

DEF: Symptomatic hyperthyroidism with a single nodule on the enlarged thyroid gland. Abrupt onset of symptoms; including extreme nervousness, insomnia, weight loss, tremors, and psychosis or coma.

✓5th **242.2 Toxic multinodular goiter** CC

Secondary thyroid hyperplasia

CC Excl: See code 242.0

DEF: Symptomatic hyperthyroidism with multiple nodules on the enlarged thyroid gland. Abrupt onset of symptoms; including extreme nervousness, insomnia, weight loss, tremors, and psychosis or coma

✓5th **242.3 Toxic nodular goiter, unspecified** CC

Adenomatous goiter } toxic or with hyperthyroidism
Nodular goiter } toxic or with hyperthyroidism
Struma nodosa } toxic or with hyperthyroidism

Any condition classifiable to 241.9 specified as toxic or with hyperthyroidism

CC Excl: See code 242.0

✓5th **242.4 Thyrotoxicosis from ectopic thyroid nodule** CC

CC Excl: See code 242.0

✓5th **242.8 Thyrotoxicosis of other specified origin** CC

Overproduction of thyroid-stimulating hormone [TSH]
Thyrotoxicosis:
factitia from ingestion of excessive thyroid material
Use additional E code to identify cause, if drug-induced

CC Excl: See code 242.0

✓5th **242.9 Thyrotoxicosis without mention of goiter or other cause** CC

Hyperthyroidism NOS
Thyrotoxicosis NOS

CC Excl: See code 242.0

243 Congenital hypothyroidism

Congenital thyroid insufficiency
Cretinism (athyrotic) (endemic)
Use additional code to identify associated mental retardation

EXCLUDES *congenital (dyshormonogenic) goiter (246.1)*

DEF: Underproduction of thyroid hormone present from birth.

✓4th **244 Acquired hypothyroidism**

INCLUDES athyroidism (acquired)
hypothyroidism (acquired)
myxedema (adult) (juvenile)
thyroid (gland) insufficiency (acquired)

244.0 Postsurgical hypothyroidism

DEF: Underproduction of thyroid hormone due to surgical removal of all or part of the thyroid gland.

244.1 Other postablative hypothyroidism

Hypothyroidism following therapy, such as irradiation

244.2 Iodine hypothyroidism
Hypothyroidism resulting from administration or ingestion of iodide
Use additional E code to identify drug

244.3 Other iatrogenic hypothyroidism
Hypothyroidism resulting from:
- P-aminosalicylic acid [PAS]
- Phenylbutazone
- Resorcinol

Iatrogenic hypothyroidism NOS
Use additional E code to identify drug

244.8 Other specified acquired hypothyroidism
Secondary hypothyroidism NEC
AHA: J-A, '85, 9

244.9 Unspecified hypothyroidism
Hypothyroidism } primary or NOS
Myxedema }
AHA: 3Q, '99, 19; 4Q, '96, 29

✓4th **245 Thyroiditis**

245.0 Acute thyroiditis
Abscess of thyroid
Thyroiditis:
- nonsuppurative, acute
- pyogenic
- suppurative

Use additional code to identify organism
DEF: Inflamed thyroid caused by infection, with abscess and liquid puris.

245.1 Subacute thyroiditis
Thyroiditis:
- de Quervain's
- giant cell
- granulomatous
- viral

DEF: Inflammation of the thyroid, characterized by fever and painful enlargement of the thyroid gland, with granulomas in the gland.

245.2 Chronic lymphocytic thyroiditis
Hashimoto's disease
Struma lymphomatosa
Thyroiditis:
- autoimmune
- lymphocytic (chronic)

DEF: Autoimmune disease of thyroid; lymphocytes infiltrate the gland and thyroid antibodies are produced; women more often affected.

245.3 Chronic fibrous thyroiditis
Struma fibrosa
Thyroiditis:
- invasive (fibrous)
- ligneous
- Riedel's

DEF: Persistent fibrosing inflammation of thyroid with adhesions to nearby structures; rare condition

245.4 Iatrogenic thyroiditis
Use additional code to identify cause
DEF: Thyroiditis resulting from treatment or intervention by physician or in a patient intervention setting.

245.8 Other and unspecified chronic thyroiditis
Chronic thyroiditis:
- NOS
- nonspecific

245.9 Thyroiditis, unspecified
Thyroiditis NOS

✓4th **246 Other disorders of thyroid**

246.0 Disorders of thyrocalcitonin secretion
Hypersecretion of calcitonin or thyrocalcitonin

246.1 Dyshormonogenic goiter
Congenital (dyshormonogenic) goiter
Goiter due to enzyme defect in synthesis of thyroid hormone
Goitrous cretinism (sporadic)

246.2 Cyst of thyroid
EXCLUDES *cystadenoma of thyroid (226)*

246.3 Hemorrhage and infarction of thyroid

246.8 Other specified disorders of thyroid
Abnormality of thyroid-binding globulin
Atrophy of thyroid
Hyper-TBG-nemia
Hypo-TBG-nemia

246.9 Unspecified disorder of thyroid

DISEASES OF OTHER ENDOCRINE GLANDS (250-259)

✓4th **250 Diabetes mellitus**
EXCLUDES *gestational diabetes (648.8)*
hyperglycemia NOS (790.6)
neonatal diabetes mellitus (775.1)
nonclinical diabetes (790.29)

The following fifth-digit subclassification is for use with category 250:

0 type II or unspecified type, not stated as uncontrolled
Fifth-digit 0 is for use for type II patients, even if the patient requires insulin
Use additional code, if applicable, for associated long-term (current) insulin use V58.67
1 type I [juvenile type], not stated as uncontrolled
2 type II or unspecified type, uncontrolled
Fifth-digit 2 is for use for type II patients, even if the patient requires insulin
Use additional code, if applicable, for associated long-term (current) insulin use V58.67
3 type I [juvenile type], uncontrolled

AHA: 4Q, '04, 56; 2Q, '04, 17; 2Q, '02, 13; 2Q,'01, 16; 2Q,'98, 15; 4Q, '97, 32; 2Q, '97, 14; 3Q, '96, 5; 4Q, '93, 19; 2Q, '92, 5; 3Q, '91, 3; 2Q, '90, 22; N-D, '85, 11

DEF: Diabetes mellitus: Inability to metabolize carbohydrates, proteins, and fats with insufficient secretion of insulin. Symptoms may be unremarkable, with long-term complications, involving kidneys, nerves, blood vessels, and eyes.

DEF: Uncontrolled diabetes: A nonspecific term indicating that the current treatment regimen does not keep the blood sugar level of a patient within acceptable levels.

8 ✓5th **250.0 Diabetes mellitus without mention of complication** CC 1-3
Diabetes mellitus without mention of complication or manifestation classifiable to 250.1-250.9
Diabetes (mellitus) NOS
CC Excl: For code 250.01-250.03: 250.00-251.3, 259.8-259.9

AHA:▶1Q, '06, 14;◀ 4Q, '97, 32; 3Q, '91, 3, 12; N-D, '85, 11; **For code 250.00:** 1Q, '05, 15; 4Q, '04, 55; 4Q, '03, 105, 108; 2Q, '03, 16; 1Q, '02, 7, 11; **For code 250.01:** 4Q, '04, 55; 4Q, '03, 110; 2Q, '03, 6; **For code 250.02:** 1Q, '03, 5

✓5th **250.1 Diabetes with ketoacidosis** CC 1-3
Diabetic:
acidosis } without mention of coma
ketosis }
CC Excl: For code 250.11-250.13: 250.00-251.3, 259.8-259.9
AHA: 3Q, '91, 6; **For code 250.11:** 4Q, '03, 82
DEF: Diabetic hyperglycemic crisis causing ketone presence in body fluids.

✓5th **250.2 Diabetes with hyperosmolarity** CC 1-3
Hyperosmolar (nonketotic) coma
CC Excl: For code 250.21-250.23: 250.00-251.3, 259.8-259.9
AHA: 4Q, '93, 19; 3Q, '91, 7

8 Questionable admission = 0

 Newborn Age: 0  Pediatric Age: 0-17  Maternity Age: 12-55 A Adult Age: 15-124 CC CC Condition MC Major Complication CD Complex Dx HIV HIV Related Dx

5th **250.3 Diabetes with other coma** CC 1-3
Diabetic coma (with ketoacidosis)
Diabetic hypoglycemic coma
Insulin coma NOS
EXCLUDES *diabetes with hyperosmolar coma (250.2)*
CC Excl: For code 250.31-250.33: See code 250.01
AHA: 3Q, '91, 7,12
DEF: Coma (not hyperosmolar) caused by hyperglycemia or hypoglycemia as complication of diabetes.

5th **250.4 Diabetes with renal manifestations** CC 1-3
Use additional code to identify manifestation, as:
chronic kidney disease (585.1-585.9)
diabetic:
nephropathy NOS (583.81)
nephrosis (581.81)
intercapillary glomerulosclerosis (581.81)
Kimmelstiel-Wilson syndrome (581.81)
CC Excl: For code 250.41-250.43: See code 250.01
AHA: 3Q, '91, 8,12; S-O, '87, 9; S-O, '84, 3; **For code 250.40:** 1Q, '03, 20
DRG 331 For code 250.40

5th **250.5 Diabetes with ophthalmic manifestations** CC 1-3
Use additional code to identify manifestation, as:
diabetic:
blindness (369.00-369.9)
cataract (366.41)
glaucoma (365.44)
macular edema (362.07)
retinal edema (362.07)
retinopathy (362.01-362.07)
CC Excl: For code 250.51-250.53: See code 250.01
AHA:▶4Q, '05, 65;◀ 3Q, '91, 8; S-O, '85, 11 ;
For code 250.50: ▶4Q, '05, 67◀

5th **250.6 Diabetes with neurological manifestations** CC 1-3
Use additional code to identify manifestation, as:
diabetic:
amyotrophy (358.1)
gastroparalysis (536.3)
gastroparesis (536.3)
mononeuropathy (354.0-355.9)
neurogenic arthropathy (713.5)
peripheral autonomic neuropathy (337.1)
polyneuropathy (357.2)
CC Excl: For code 250.61-250.63: See code 250.01
AHA: 2Q, '93, 6; 2Q, '92, 15; 3Q, '91, 9; N-D, '84, 9; **For code 250.60:** 4Q, '03, 105; **For code 250.61:** 2Q, '04, 7

5th **250.7 Diabetes with peripheral circulatory disorders** CC 1-3
Use additional code to identify manifestation, as:
diabetic:
gangrene (785.4)
peripheral angiopathy (443.81)
CC Excl: For code 250.71-250.73: See code 250.01
AHA: 1Q, '96, 10; 3Q, '94, 5; 2Q, '94, 17; 3Q, '91, 10, 12; 3Q, '90, 15; **For code 250.70:** 1Q, '04, 14
DRG 130 For code 250.70
DEF: Blood vessel damage or disease, usually in the feet, legs, or hands, as a complication of diabetes.

5th **250.8 Diabetes with other specified manifestations** CC 1-3
Diabetic hypoglycemia
Hypoglycemic shock
Use additional code to identify manifestation, as:
any associated ulceration (707.10-707.9)
diabetic bone changes (731.8)
Use additional E code to identify cause, if drug-induced
CC Excl: For code 250.81-250.83: See code 250.01
AHA: 4Q, '00, 44; 4Q, '97, 43; 2Q, '97, 16; 4Q, '93, 20; 3Q, '91, 10; **For code 250.80:** 1Q, '04, 14

5th **250.9 Diabetes with unspecified complication** CC 1-3
CC Excl: For code 250.91-250.93: See code 250.01
AHA: 2Q, '92, 15; 3Q, '91, 7, 12

4th **251 Other disorders of pancreatic internal secretion**

251.0 Hypoglycemic coma CC
Iatrogenic hyperinsulinism
Non-diabetic insulin coma
Use additional E code to identify cause, if drug-induced
EXCLUDES *hypoglycemic coma in diabetes mellitus (250.3)*
CC Excl: 250.00-251.3, 259.8-259.9
AHA: M-A, '85, 8
DEF: Coma induced by low blood sugar in non-diabetic patient.

251.1 Other specified hypoglycemia
Hyperinsulinism:
NOS
ectopic
functional
Hyperplasia of pancreatic islet beta cells NOS
EXCLUDES *hypoglycemia:*
in diabetes mellitus (250.8)
in infant of diabetic mother (775.0)
hypoglycemic coma (251.0)
neonatal hypoglycemia (775.6)
Use additional E code to identify cause, if drug-induced.
AHA: 1Q, '03, 10
DEF: Excessive production of insulin by the pancreas; associated with obesity and insulin-producing tumors.

251.2 Hypoglycemia, unspecified
Hypoglycemia:
NOS
reactive
Hypoglycemia:
spontaneous
EXCLUDES *hypoglycemia:*
with coma (251.0)
in diabetes mellitus (250.8)
leucine-induced (270.3)
AHA: M-A, '85, 8

251.3 Postsurgical hypoinsulinemia CC
Hypoinsulinemia following complete or partial pancreatectomy
Postpancreatectomy hyperglycemia
CC Excl: See code 251.0
AHA: 3Q, '91, 6

251.4 Abnormality of secretion of glucagon
Hyperplasia of pancreatic islet alpha cells with glucagon excess
DEF: Production malfunction of a pancreatic hormone secreted by cells of the islets of Langerhans.

251.5 Abnormality of secretion of gastrin
Hyperplasia of pancreatic alpha cells with gastrin excess
Zollinger-Ellison syndrome

251.8 Other specified disorders of pancreatic internal secretion
AHA: 2Q, '98, 15; 3Q, '91, 6

251.9 Unspecified disorder of pancreatic internal secretion
Islet cell hyperplasia NOS

Dorsal View of Parathyroid Glands

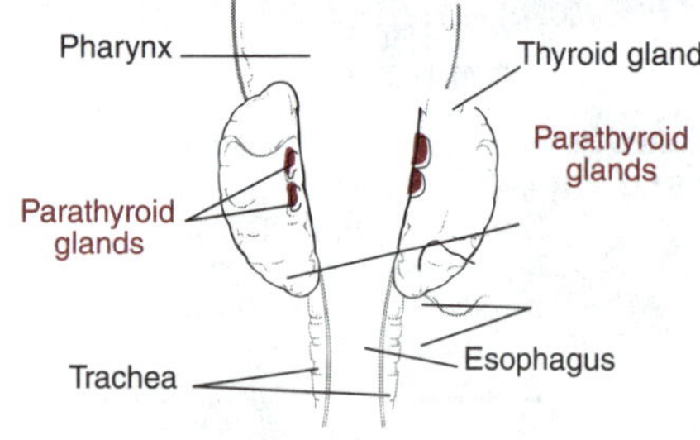

Parathyroid glands
↓
Parathyroid hormone (PTH)
↓
Calcium in bones ⟶ Calcium in blood

✓4th **252 Disorders of parathyroid gland**

✓5th **252.0 Hyperparathyroidism**

EXCLUDES *ectopic hyperparathyroidism (259.3)*

DEF: Abnormally high secretion of parathyroid hormones causing bone deterioration, reduced renal function, kidney stones.

252.00 Hyperparathyroidism, unspecified

252.01 Primary hyperparathyroidism

Hyperplasia of parathyroid

DEF: Parathyroid dysfunction commonly caused by hyperplasia of two or more glands; characteristic hypercalcemia and increased parathyroid hormone levels.

252.02 Secondary hyperparathyroidism, non-renal

EXCLUDES *secondary hyperparathyroidism (of renal origin) (588.81)*

AHA: 4Q, '04, 57-59

DEF: Underlying disease of nonrenal origin decreases blood levels of calcium causing the parathyroid to release increased levels of parathyroid hormone; parathyroid hormone levels return to normal once underlying condition is treated and blood calcium levels are normal.

252.08 Other hyperparathyroidism

Tertiary hyperparathyroidism

DEF: Tertiary hyperparathyroidism: chronic secondary hyperparathyroidism leads to adenomatous parathyroid causing irreversible abnormal production of parathyroid hormone (PTH); PTH remains high after the serum calcium levels are brought under control.

252.1 Hypoparathyroidism CC

Parathyroiditis (autoimmune)
Tetany:
  parathyroid
  parathyroprival

EXCLUDES *pseudohypoparathyroidism (275.4)*
pseudopseudohypoparathyroidism (275.4)
tetany NOS (781.7)
transitory neonatal hypoparathyroidism (775.4)

CC Excl: 252.00-252.9, 259.8-259.9

DEF: Abnormally low secretion of parathyroid hormones which causes decreased calcium and increased phosphorus in the blood. Resulting in muscle cramps, tetany, urinary frequency and cataracts.

252.8 Other specified disorders of parathyroid gland

Cyst } of parathyroid gland
Hemorrhage } of parathyroid gland

252.9 Unspecified disorder of parathyroid gland

✓4th **253 Disorders of the pituitary gland and its hypothalamic control**

INCLUDES the listed conditions whether the disorder is in the pituitary or the hypothalamus

EXCLUDES *Cushing's syndrome (255.0)*

253.0 Acromegaly and gigantism

Overproduction of growth hormone

DEF: Acromegaly: chronic, beginning in middle age; caused by hypersecretion of the pituitary growth hormone; produces enlarged parts of skeleton, especially the nose, ears, jaws, fingers and toes.

DEF: Gigantism: pituitary gigantism caused by excess growth of short flat bones; men may grow 78 to 80 inches tall.

253.1 Other and unspecified anterior pituitary hyperfunction

Forbes-Albright syndrome

EXCLUDES *overproduction of:*
ACTH (255.3)
thyroid-stimulating hormone [TSH] (242.8)

AHA: J-A, '85, 9

DEF: Spontaneous galactorrhea-amenorrhea syndrome unrelated to pregnancy; usually related to presence of pituitary tumor.

253.2 Panhypopituitarism CC

Cachexia, pituitary
Necrosis of pituitary (postpartum)
Pituitary insufficiency NOS
Sheehan's syndrome
Simmonds' disease

EXCLUDES *iatrogenic hypopituitarism (253.7)*

CC Excl: 253.0-253.9, 259.8-259.9

DEF: Damage to or absence of pituitary gland leading to impaired sexual function, weight loss, fatigue, bradycardia, hypotension, pallor, depression, and impaired growth in children; called Simmonds' disease if cachexia is prominent.

253.3 Pituitary dwarfism

Isolated deficiency of (human) growth hormone [HGH]
Lorain-Levi dwarfism

DEF: Dwarfism with infantile physical characteristics due to abnormally low secretion of growth hormone and gonadotropin deficiency.

253.4 Other anterior pituitary disorders

Isolated or partial deficiency of an anterior pituitary hormone, other than growth hormone
Prolactin deficiency

AHA: J-A, '85, 9

253.5 Diabetes insipidus CC

Vasopressin deficiency

EXCLUDES *nephrogenic diabetes insipidus (588.1)*

CC Excl: 253.1-253.2, 253.4-253.9, 259.8-259.9

DEF: Metabolic disorder causing insufficient antidiuretic hormone release; symptoms include frequent urination, thirst, ravenous hunger, loss of weight, fatigue.

253.6 Other disorders of neurohypophysis

Syndrome of inappropriate secretion of antidiuretic hormone [ADH]

EXCLUDES *ectopic antidiuretic hormone secretion (259.3)*

253.7 Iatrogenic pituitary disorders

Hypopituitarism:
  hormone-induced
  hypophysectomy-induced
Hypopituitarism:
  postablative
  radiotherapy-induced

Use additional E code to identify cause

DEF: Pituitary dysfunction that results from drug therapy, radiation therapy, or surgery, causing mild to severe symptoms.

253.8 Other disorders of the pituitary and other syndromes of diencephalohypophyseal origin

Abscess of pituitary
Adiposogenital dystrophy
Cyst of Rathke's pouch
Fröhlich's syndrome

EXCLUDES *craniopharyngioma (237.0)*

253.9 Unspecified

Dyspituitarism

✓4th **254 Diseases of thymus gland**

EXCLUDES *aplasia or dysplasia with immunodeficiency (279.2)*
hypoplasia with immunodeficiency (279.2)
myasthenia gravis (358.00-358.01)

254.0 Persistent hyperplasia of thymus
Hypertrophy of thymus
DEF: Continued abnormal growth of the twin lymphoid lobes that produce T lymphocytes.

254.1 Abscess of thymus CC
CC Excl: 254.0–254.9, 259.5–259.9

254.8 Other specified diseases of thymus gland
Atrophy } of thymus
Cyst }
EXCLUDES *thymoma (212.6)*

254.9 Unspecified disease of thymus gland

✓4th **255 Disorders of adrenal glands**

INCLUDES the listed conditions whether the basic disorder is in the adrenals or is pituitary-induced

255.0 Cushing's syndrome CC
Adrenal hyperplasia due to excess ACTH
Cushing's syndrome:
NOS
iatrogenic
idiopathic
pituitary-dependent
Ectopic ACTH syndrome
Iatrogenic syndrome of excess cortisol
Overproduction of cortisol
Use additional E code to identify cause, if drug-induced
EXCLUDES *congenital adrenal hyperplasia (255.2)*
CC Excl: 255.0-255.2, 259.8-259.9
DEF: Due to adrenal cortisol oversecretion or glucocorticoid medications; may cause fatty tissue of the face, neck and body; osteoporosis and curvature of spine, hypertension, diabetes mellitus, female genitourinary problems, male impotence, degeneration of muscle tissues, weakness.

✓5th **255.1 Hyperaldosteronism**
AHA: 4Q, '03, 48
DEF: Oversecretion of aldosterone causing fluid retention, hypertension.

▲ **255.10 Hyperaldosteronism, unspecified**
Aldosteronism NOS
▶Primary aldosteronism, unspecified◀
EXCLUDES *Conn's syndrome (255.12)*

255.11 Glucocorticoid-remediable aldosteronism
Familial aldosteronism type I
EXCLUDES *Conn's syndrome (255.12)*
DEF: A rare autosomal dominant familial form of primary aldosteronism in which the secretion of aldosterone is under the influence of adrenocortiotrophic hormone (ACTH) rather than the renin-angiotensin mechanism; characterized by moderate hypersecretion of aldosterone and suppressed plasma renin activity rapidly reversed by administration of glucosteroids; symptoms include hypertension and mild hypokalemia.

255.12 Conn's syndrome
DEF: A type of primary aldosteronism caused by an adenoma of the glomerulosa cells in the adrenal cortex; presence of hypertension.

255.13 Bartter's syndrome
DEF: A cluster of symptoms caused by a defect in the ability of the kidney to reabsorb potassium; signs include alkalosis (hypokalemic alkalosis), increased aldosterone, increased plasma renin, and normal blood pressure; symptoms include muscle cramping, weakness, constipation, frequency of urination, and failure to grow; also known as urinary potassium wasting or juxtaglomerular cell hyperplasia.

255.14 Other secondary aldosteronism

255.2 Adrenogenital disorders
Achard-Thiers syndrome
Adrenogenital syndromes, virilizing or feminizing, whether acquired or associated with congenital adrenal hyperplasia consequent on inborn enzyme defects in hormone synthesis
Congenital adrenal hyperplasia
Female adrenal pseudohermaphroditism
Male:
macrogenitosomia praecox
sexual precocity with adrenal hyperplasia
Virilization (female) (suprarenal)
EXCLUDES *adrenal hyperplasia due to excess ACTH (255.0)*
isosexual virilization (256.4)

255.3 Other corticoadrenal overactivity CC
Acquired benign adrenal androgenic overactivity
Overproduction of ACTH
CC Excl: 017.60-017.66, 017.90-017.96, 255.3-255.9, 259.5-259.9

255.4 Corticoadrenal insufficiency CC
Addisonian crisis
Addison's disease NOS
Adrenal:
atrophy (autoimmune)
calcification
Adrenal:
crisis
hemorrhage
infarction
insufficiency NOS
EXCLUDES *tuberculous Addison's disease (017.6)*
CC Excl: See code 255.3
DEF: Underproduction of adrenal hormones causing low blood pressure.

255.5 Other adrenal hypofunction CC
Adrenal medullary insufficiency
EXCLUDES *Waterhouse-Friderichsen syndrome (meningococcal) (036.3)*
CC Excl: See code 255.3

255.6 Medulloadrenal hyperfunction CC
Catecholamine secretion by pheochromocytoma
CC Excl: See code 255.3

255.8 Other specified disorders of adrenal glands
Abnormality of cortisol-binding globulin

255.9 Unspecified disorder of adrenal glands

✓4th **256 Ovarian dysfunction**
AHA: 4Q, '00, 51

256.0 Hyperestrogenism ♀
DEF: Excess secretion of estrogen by the ovaries; characterized by ovaries containing multiple follicular cysts filled with serous fluid.

256.1 Other ovarian hyperfunction ♀
Hypersecretion of ovarian androgens
AHA: 3Q, '95, 15

256.2 Postablative ovarian failure ♀
Ovarian failure:
iatrogenic
postirradiation
Ovarian failure:
postsurgical
Use additional code for states associated with artificial menopause (627.4)
EXCLUDES *acquired absence of ovary (V45.77)*
asymptomatic age-related (natural) postmenopausal status (V49.81)
AHA: 2Q, '02, 12
DEF: Failed ovarian function after medical or surgical intervention.

✓5th **256.3 Other ovarian failure**
Use additional code for states associated with natural menopause (627.2)
EXCLUDES *asymptomatic age-related (natural) postmenopausal status (V49.81)*
AHA: 4Q, '01, 41

256.31 Premature menopause A ♀
DEF: Permanent cessation of ovarian function before the age of 40 occuring naturally of unknown cause.

256.39 Other ovarian failure ♀
Delayed menarche
Ovarian hypofunction
Primary ovarian failure NOS

256.4 Polycystic ovaries ♀
Isosexual virilization
Stein-Leventhal syndrome

DEF: Multiple serous filled cysts of ovary; symptoms of infertility, hirsutism, oligomenorrhea or amenorrhea.

256.8 Other ovarian dysfunction ♀

256.9 Unspecified ovarian dysfunction ♀

✓4th **257 Testicular dysfunction**

257.0 Testicular hyperfunction ♂
Hypersecretion of testicular hormones

257.1 Postablative testicular hypofunction ♂
Testicular hypofunction:
iatrogenic
postirradiation
Testicular hypofunction:
postsurgical

257.2 Other testicular hypofunction
Defective biosynthesis of testicular androgen
Eunuchoidism:
NOS
hypogonadotropic
Failure:
Leydig's cell, adult
seminiferous tubule, adult
Testicular hypogonadism

EXCLUDES *azoospermia (606.0)*

257.8 Other testicular dysfunction

EXCLUDES *androgen insensitivity syndrome (259.5)*

257.9 Unspecified testicular dysfunction ♂

✓4th **258 Polyglandular dysfunction and related disorders**

258.0 Polyglandular activity in multiple endocrine adenomatosis CC
Wermer's syndrome

CC Excl: 240.0-259.9

DEF: Wermer's syndrome: A rare hereditary condition characterized by the presence of adenomas or hyperplasia in more than one endocrine gland causing premature aging.

258.1 Other combinations of endocrine dysfunction CC
Lloyd's syndrome
Schmidt's syndrome

CC Excl: See code 258.0

258.8 Other specified polyglandular dysfunction CC

CC Excl: See code 258.0

258.9 Polyglandular dysfunction, unspecified CC

CC Excl: See code 258.0

✓4th **259 Other endocrine disorders**

259.0 Delay in sexual development and puberty, not elsewhere classified
Delayed puberty

259.1 Precocious sexual development and puberty, not elsewhere classified P
Sexual precocity:
NOS
constitutional
Sexual precocity:
cryptogenic
idiopathic

259.2 Carcinoid syndrome CC
Hormone secretion by carcinoid tumors

CC Excl: 259.2-259.3, 259.5-259.9

DEF: Presence of carcinoid tumors that spread to liver; characterized by cyanotic flushing of skin, diarrhea, bronchospasm, acquired tricuspid and pulmonary stenosis, sudden drops in blood pressure, edema, ascites.

259.3 Ectopic hormone secretion, not elsewhere classified
Ectopic:
antidiuretic hormone secretion [ADH]
hyperparathyroidism

EXCLUDES *ectopic ACTH syndrome (255.0)*

AHA: N-D, '85, 4

259.4 Dwarfism, not elsewhere classified
Dwarfism:
NOS
constitutional

EXCLUDES *dwarfism:*
achondroplastic (756.4)
intrauterine (759.7)
nutritional (263.2)
pituitary (253.3)
renal (588.0)
progeria (259.8)

259.5 Androgen insensitivity syndrome
Partial androgen insensitivity
Reifenstein syndrome

AHA: ▶4Q, '05, 53◀

DEF: ▶X chromosome abnormality that prohibits the body from recognizing androgen; XY genotype with ambiguous genitalia; also called testicular feminization.◀

259.8 Other specified endocrine disorders
Pineal gland dysfunction
Progeria
Werner's syndrome

259.9 Unspecified endocrine disorder
Disturbance:
endocrine NOS
hormone NOS
Infantilism NOS

NUTRITIONAL DEFICIENCIES (260-269)

EXCLUDES *deficiency anemias (280.0-281.9)*

260 Kwashiorkor CC
Nutritional edema with dyspigmentation of skin and hair

CC Excl: 260-263.9

DEF: Syndrome, particularly of children; excessive carbohydrate with inadequate protein intake, inhibited growth potential, anomalies in skin and hair pigmentation, edema and liver disease.

261 Nutritional marasmus CC
Nutritional atrophy
Severe calorie deficiency
Severe malnutrition NOS

CC Excl: See code 260

DEF: Protein-calorie malabsorption or malnutrition of children; characterized by tissue wasting, dehydration, and subcutaneous fat depletion; may occur with infectious disease; also called infantile atrophy.

262 Other severe, protein-calorie malnutrition CC
Nutritional edema without mention of dyspigmentation of skin and hair

CC Excl: See code 260

AHA: 4Q, '92, 24; J-A, '85, 12

✓4th **263 Other and unspecified protein-calorie malnutrition**

AHA: 4Q, '92, 24

263.0 Malnutrition of moderate degree CC

CC Excl: See code 260

AHA: J-A, '85, 1

DEF: Malnutrition characterized by biochemical changes in electrolytes, lipids, blood plasma.

263.1 Malnutrition of mild degree CC

CC Excl: See code 260

AHA: J-A, '85, 1

263.2 Arrested development following protein-calorie malnutrition CC
Nutritional dwarfism
Physical retardation due to malnutrition

CC Excl: See code 260

263.8 Other protein-calorie malnutrition CC

CC Excl: See code 260

263.9 Unspecified protein-calorie malnutrition CC
Dystrophy due to malnutrition
Malnutrition (calorie) NOS
EXCLUDES *nutritional deficiency NOS (269.9)*
CC Excl: See code 260
AHA: 4Q, '03, 109; N-D, '84, 19

4th 264 Vitamin A deficiency

264.0 With conjunctival xerosis
DEF: Vitamin A deficiency with conjunctival dryness.

264.1 With conjunctival xerosis and Bitot's spot
Bitot's spot in the young child
DEF: Vitamin A deficiency with conjunctival dryness, superficial spots of keratinized epithelium.

264.2 With corneal xerosis
DEF: Vitamin A deficiency with corneal dryness.

264.3 With corneal ulceration and xerosis
DEF: Vitamin A deficiency with corneal dryness, epithelial ulceration.

264.4 With keratomalacia
DEF: Vitamin A deficiency creating corneal dryness; progresses to corneal insensitivity, softness, necrosis; usually bilateral.

264.5 With night blindness
DEF: Vitamin A deficiency causing vision failure in dim light.

264.6 With xerophthalmic scars of cornea
DEF: Vitamin A deficiency with corneal scars from dryness.

264.7 Other ocular manifestations of vitamin A deficiency
Xerophthalmia due to vitamin A deficiency

264.8 Other manifestations of vitamin A deficiency
Follicular keratosis } due to vitamin A
Xeroderma } deficiency

264.9 Unspecified vitamin A deficiency
Hypovitaminosis A NOS

4th 265 Thiamine and niacin deficiency states

265.0 Beriberi
DEF: Inadequate vitamin B_1 (thiamine) intake, affects heart and peripheral nerves; individual may become edematous and develop cardiac disease due to the excess fluid; alcoholics and people with a diet of excessive polished rice prone to the disease.

265.1 Other and unspecified manifestations of thiamine deficiency
Other vitamin B_1 deficiency states

265.2 Pellagra
Deficiency:
- niacin (-tryptophan)
- nicotinamide
- nicotinic acid

Deficiency:
- vitamin PP

Pellagra (alcoholic)

DEF: Niacin deficiency causing dermatitis, inflammation of mucous membranes, diarrhea, and psychic disturbances.

4th 266 Deficiency of B-complex components

266.0 Ariboflavinosis
Riboflavin [vitamin B_2] deficiency
AHA: S-O, '86, 10
DEF: Vitamin B_2 (riboflavin) deficiency marked by swollen lips and tongue fissures, corneal vascularization, scaling lesions, and anemia.

266.1 Vitamin B_6 deficiency
Deficiency:
- pyridoxal
- pyridoxamine

Deficiency:
- pyridoxine

Vitamin B_6 deficiency syndrome

EXCLUDES *vitamin B_6-responsive sideroblastic anemia (285.0)*
DEF: Vitamin B_6 deficiency causing skin, lip, and tongue disturbances, peripheral neuropathy; and convulsions in infants.

266.2 Other B-complex deficiencies
Deficiency:
- cyanocobalamin
- folic acid

Deficiency:
- vitamin B_{12}

EXCLUDES *combined system disease with anemia (281.0-281.1)*
deficiency anemias (281.0-281.9)
subacute degeneration of spinal cord with anemia (281.0-281.1)

266.9 Unspecified vitamin B deficiency

267 Ascorbic acid deficiency

Deficiency of vitamin C
Scurvy
EXCLUDES *scorbutic anemia (281.8)*
DEF: Vitamin C deficiency causing swollen gums, myalgia, weight loss, and weakness.

4th 268 Vitamin D deficiency

EXCLUDES *vitamin D-resistant:*
osteomalacia (275.3)
rickets (275.3)

268.0 Rickets, active
EXCLUDES *celiac rickets (579.0)*
renal rickets (588.0)
DEF: Inadequate vitamin D intake, usually in pediatrics, that affects bones most involved with muscular action; may cause nodules on ends and sides of bones; delayed closure of fontanels in infants; symptoms may include muscle soreness, and profuse sweating.

268.1 Rickets, late effect
Any condition specified as due to rickets and stated to be a late effect or sequela of rickets
Use additional code to identify the nature of late effect
DEF: Distorted or demineralized bones as a result of vitamin D deficiency.

268.2 Osteomalacia, unspecified
DEF: Softening of bones due to decrease in calcium; marked by pain, tenderness, muscular weakness, anorexia, and weight loss.

268.9 Unspecified vitamin D deficiency
Avitaminosis D

4th 269 Other nutritional deficiencies

269.0 Deficiency of vitamin K CC
EXCLUDES *deficiency of coagulation factor due to vitamin K deficiency (286.7)*
vitamin K deficiency of newborn (776.0)
CC Excl: 269.0

269.1 Deficiency of other vitamins
Deficiency:
- vitamin E

Deficiency:
- vitamin P

269.2 Unspecified vitamin deficiency
Multiple vitamin deficiency NOS

269.3 Mineral deficiency, not elsewhere classified
Deficiency:
- calcium, dietary

Deficiency:
- iodine

EXCLUDES *deficiency:*
calcium NOS (275.4)
potassium (276.8)
sodium (276.1)

269.8 Other nutritional deficiency
EXCLUDES *adult failure to thrive (783.7)*
failure to thrive in childhood (783.41)
feeding problems (783.3)
newborn (779.3)

269.9 Unspecified nutritional deficiency

OTHER METABOLIC AND IMMUNITY DISORDERS (270-279)

Use additional code to identify any associated mental retardation

4th 270 Disorders of amino-acid transport and metabolism

EXCLUDES *abnormal findings without manifest disease (790.0-796.9)*
disorders of purine and pyrimidine metabolism (277.1-277.2)
gout (274.0-274.9)

270.0 Disturbances of amino-acid transport

Cystinosis
Cystinuria
Fanconi (-de Toni) (-Debré) syndrome
Glycinuria (renal)
Hartnup disease

270.1 Phenylketonuria [PKU]

Hyperphenylalaninemia

DEF: Inherited metabolic condition causing excess phenylpyruvic and other acids in urine; results in mental retardation, neurological manifestations, including spasticity and tremors, light pigmentation, eczema, and mousy odor.

270.2 Other disturbances of aromatic amino-acid metabolism

Albinism
Alkaptonuria
Alkaptonuric ochronosis
Disturbances of metabolism of tyrosine and tryptophan
Homogentisic acid defects
Hydroxykynureninuria
Hypertyrosinemia
Indicanuria
Kynureninase defects
Oasthouse urine disease
Ochronosis
Tyrosinosis
Tyrosinuria
Waardenburg syndrome

EXCLUDES *vitamin B_6-deficiency syndrome (266.1)*

AHA: 3Q, '99, 20

270.3 Disturbances of branched-chain amino-acid metabolism

Disturbances of metabolism of leucine, isoleucine, and valine
Hypervalinemia
Intermittent branched-chain ketonuria
Leucine-induced hypoglycemia
Leucinosis
Maple syrup urine disease

AHA: 3Q, '00, 8

270.4 Disturbances of sulphur-bearing amino-acid metabolism

Cystathioninemia
Cystathioninuria
Disturbances of metabolism of methionine, homocystine, and cystathionine
Homocystinuria
Hypermethioninemia
Methioninemia

AHA: 1Q, '04, 6

270.5 Disturbances of histidine metabolism

Carnosinemia
Histidinemia
Hyperhistidinemia
Imidazole aminoaciduria

270.6 Disorders of urea cycle metabolism

Argininosuccinic aciduria
Citrullinemia
Disorders of metabolism of ornithine, citrulline, argininosuccinic acid, arginine, and ammonia
Hyperammonemia
Hyperornithinemia

270.7 Other disturbances of straight-chain amino-acid metabolism

Glucoglycinuria
Glycinemia (with methyl-malonic acidemia)
Hyperglycinemia
Hyperlysinemia
Other disturbances of metabolism of glycine, threonine, serine, glutamine, and lysine
Pipecolic acidemia
Saccharopinuria

AHA: 3Q, '00, 8

Lipid Metabolism

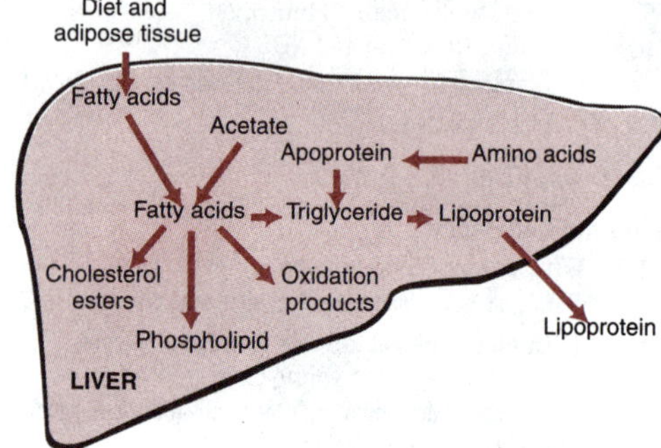

270.8 Other specified disorders of amino-acid metabolism

Alaninemia
Ethanolaminuria
Glycoprolinuria
Hydroxyprolinemia
Hyperprolinemia
Iminoacidopathy
Prolinemia
Prolinuria
Sarcosinemia

270.9 Unspecified disorder of amino-acid metabolism

4th 271 Disorders of carbohydrate transport and metabolism

EXCLUDES *abnormality of secretion of glucagon (251.4)*
diabetes mellitus (250.0-250.9)
hypoglycemia NOS (251.2)
mucopolysaccharidosis (277.5)

271.0 Glycogenosis

Amylopectinosis
Glucose-6-phosphatase deficiency
Glycogen storage disease
McArdle's disease
Pompe's disease
von Gierke's disease

AHA: 1Q, '98, 5

271.1 Galactosemia

Galactose-1-phosphate uridyl transferase deficiency
Galactosuria

DEF: Any of three genetic disorders due to defective galactose metabolism; symptoms include failure to thrive in infancy, jaundice, liver and spleen damage, cataracts, and mental retardation.

271.2 Hereditary fructose intolerance

Essential benign fructosuria
Fructosemia

DEF: Chromosome recessive disorder of carbohydrate metabolism; in infants, occurs after dietary sugar introduced; characterized by enlarged spleen, yellowish cast to skin, and progressive inability to thrive.

271.3 Intestinal disaccharidase deficiencies and disaccharide malabsorption

Intolerance or malabsorption (congenital) (of):
glucose-galactose
lactose
sucrose-isomaltose

271.4 Renal glycosuria

Renal diabetes

DEF: Persistent abnormal levels of glucose in urine, with normal blood glucose levels; caused by failure of the renal tubules to reabsorb glucose.

271.8 Other specified disorders of carbohydrate transport and metabolism

Essential benign pentosuria
Fucosidosis
Glycolic aciduria
Hyperoxaluria (primary)
Mannosidosis
Oxalosis
Xylosuria
Xylulosuria

271.9 Unspecified disorder of carbohydrate transport and metabolism

4th 272 Disorders of lipoid metabolism

EXCLUDES *localized cerebral lipidoses (330.1)*

272.0 Pure hypercholesterolemia

Familial hypercholesterolemia
Fredrickson Type IIa hyperlipoproteinemia
Hyperbetalipoproteinemia
Hyperlipidemia, Group A
Low-density-lipoid-type [LDL] hyperlipoproteinemia

AHA: ▶4Q, '05, 71◀

272.1 Pure hyperglyceridemia
Endogenous hyperglyceridemia
Fredrickson Type IV hyperlipoproteinemia
Hyperlipidemia, Group B
Hyperprebetalipoproteinemia
Hypertriglyceridemia, essential
Very-low-density-lipoid-type [VLDL] hyperlipoproteinemia

272.2 Mixed hyperlipidemia
Broad- or floating-betalipoproteinemia
Fredrickson Type IIb or III hyperlipoproteinemia
Hypercholesterolemia with endogenous hyperglyceridemia
Hyperbetalipoproteinemia with prebetalipoproteinemia
Tubo-eruptive xanthoma
Xanthoma tuberosum
DEF: Elevated levels of lipoprotein, a complex of fats and proteins, in blood due to inherited metabolic disorder.

272.3 Hyperchylomicronemia
Bürger-Grütz syndrome
Fredrickson type I or V hyperlipoproteinemia
Hyperlipidemia, Group D
Mixed hyperglyceridemia

272.4 Other and unspecified hyperlipidemia
Alpha-lipoproteinemia
Combined hyperlipidemia
Hyperlipidemia NOS
Hyperlipoproteinemia NOS
AHA: 1Q, '05, 17
DEF: Hyperlipoproteinemia: elevated levels of transient chylomicrons in the blood which are a form of lipoproteins which transport dietary cholesterol and triglycerides from the small intestine to the blood.

272.5 Lipoprotein deficiencies
Abetalipoproteinemia
Bassen-Kornzweig syndrome
High-density lipoid deficiency
Hypoalphalipoproteinemia
Hypobetalipoproteinemia (familial)
DEF: Abnormally low levels of lipoprotein, a complex of fats and protein, in the blood.

272.6 Lipodystrophy
Barraquer-Simons disease
Progressive lipodystrophy
Use additional E code to identify cause, if iatrogenic
EXCLUDES *intestinal lipodystrophy (040.2)*
DEF: Disturbance of fat metabolism resulting in loss of fatty tissue in some areas of the body.

272.7 Lipidoses
Chemically-induced lipidosis
Disease:
Anderson's
Fabry's
Gaucher's
I cell [mucolipidosis I]
lipoid storage NOS
Niemann-Pick
pseudo-Hurler's or mucolipdosis III
triglyceride storage, Type I or II
Wolman's or triglyceride storage, Type III
Mucolipidosis II
Primary familial xanthomatosis
EXCLUDES *cerebral lipidoses (330.1)*
Tay-Sachs disease (330.1)
DEF: Lysosomal storage diseases marked by an abnormal amount of lipids in reticuloendothelial cells.

272.8 Other disorders of lipoid metabolism
Hoffa's disease or liposynovitis prepatellaris
Launois-Bensaude's lipomatosis
Lipoid dermatoarthritis

272.9 Unspecified disorder of lipoid metabolism

✓4th **273 Disorders of plasma protein metabolism**
EXCLUDES *agammaglobulinemia and hypogammaglobulinemia (279.0-279.2)*
coagulation defects (286.0-286.9)
hereditary hemolytic anemias (282.0-282.9)

273.0 Polyclonal hypergammaglobulinemia
Hypergammaglobulinemic purpura:
benign primary
Waldenström's
DEF: Elevated blood levels of gamma globulins, frequently found in patients with chronic infectious diseases.

273.1 Monoclonal paraproteinemia
Benign monoclonal hypergammaglobulinemia [BMH]
Monoclonal gammopathy:
NOS
associated with lymphoplasmacytic dyscrasias
benign
Paraproteinemia:
benign (familial)
secondary to malignant or inflammatory disease

273.2 Other paraproteinemias
Cryoglobulinemic:
purpura
vasculitis
Mixed cryoglobulinemia

273.3 Macroglobulinemia CC
Macroglobulinemia (idiopathic) (primary)
Waldenström's macroglobulinemia
CC Excl: 273.0-273.3, 273.8-273.9
DEF: Elevated blood levels of macroglobulins (plasma globulins of high weight); characterized by malignant neoplasms of bone marrow, spleen, liver, or lymph nodes; symptoms include weakness, fatigue, bleeding disorders, and vision problems.

273.4 Alpha-1-antitrypsin deficiency
AAT deficiency
DEF: Disorder of plasma protein metabolism that results in a deficiency of Alpha-1-antitrypsin, an acute-phase reactive protein, released into the blood in response to infection or injury to protect tissue against the harmful effect of enzymes.

273.8 Other disorders of plasma protein metabolism
Abnormality of transport protein
Bisalbuminemia
AHA: 2Q, '98, 11

273.9 Unspecified disorder of plasma protein metabolism

✓4th **274 Gout**
EXCLUDES *lead gout (984.0-984.9)*
AHA: 2Q, '95, 4
DEF: Purine and pyrimidine metabolic disorders; manifested by hyperuricemia and recurrent acute inflammatory arthritis; monosodium urate or monohydrate crystals may be deposited in and around the joints, leading to joint destruction, and severe crippling.

274.0 Gouty arthropathy

✓5th **274.1 Gouty nephropathy**

274.10 Gouty nephropathy, unspecified
AHA: N-D, '85, 15

274.11 Uric acid nephrolithiasis
DEF: Sodium urate stones in the kidney.

274.19 Other

✓5th **274.8 Gout with other specified manifestations**

274.81 Gouty tophi of ear
DEF: Chalky sodium urate deposit in the ear due to gout; produces chronic inflammation of external ear.

274.82 Gouty tophi of other sites
Gouty tophi of heart

274.89 Other
Use additional code to identify manifestations, as:
gouty:
iritis (364.11)
neuritis (357.4)

274.9 Gout, unspecified

✓4th **275 Disorders of mineral metabolism**
EXCLUDES *abnormal findings without manifest disease (790.0-796.9)*

Endocrine, Nutritional and Metabolic, Immunity 272.1–275

275.0 Disorders of iron metabolism
Bronzed diabetes
Hemochromatosis
Pigmentary cirrhosis (of liver)
EXCLUDES *anemia:*
iron deficiency (280.0-280.9)
sideroblastic (285.0)
AHA: 2Q, '97, 11

275.1 Disorders of copper metabolism
Hepatolenticular degeneration
Wilson's disease

275.2 Disorders of magnesium metabolism
Hypermagnesemia
Hypomagnesemia

275.3 Disorders of phosphorus metabolism
Familial hypophosphatemia
Hypophosphatasia
Vitamin D-resistant:
osteomalacia
rickets

✓5th **275.4 Disorders of calcium metabolism**
EXCLUDES *parathyroid disorders (252.00-252.9)*
vitamin D deficiency (268.0-268.9)
AHA: 4Q, '97, 33

275.40 Unspecified disorder of calcium metabolism

275.41 Hypocalcemia
DEF: Abnormally decreased blood calcium level; symptoms include hyperactive deep tendon reflexes, muscle, abdominal cramps, and carpopedal spasm.

275.42 Hypercalcemia
AHA: 4Q, '03, 110
DEF: Abnormally increased blood calcium level; symptoms include muscle weakness, fatigue, nausea, depression, and constipation.

275.49 Other disorders of calcium metabolism
Nephrocalcinosis
Pseudohypoparathyroidism
Pseudopseudohypoparathyroidism
DEF: Nephrocalcinosis: calcium phosphate deposits in the tubules of the kidney with resultant renal insufficiency.
DEF: Pseudohypoparathyroidism: inherited disorder with signs and symptoms of hypoparathyroidism; caused by inadequate response to parathyroid hormone, not hormonal deficiency. Symptoms include muscle cramps, tetany, urinary frequency, blurred vision due to cataracts, and dry scaly skin.
DEF: Pseudopseudohypoparathyroidism: clinical manifestations of hypoparathyroidism without affecting blood calcium levels.

275.8 Other specified disorders of mineral metabolism

275.9 Unspecified disorder of mineral metabolism

✓4th **276 Disorders of fluid, electrolyte, and acid-base balance**
EXCLUDES *diabetes insipidus (253.5)*
familial periodic paralysis (359.3)

276.0 Hyperosmolality and/or hypernatremia CC
Sodium [Na] excess
Sodium [Na] overload
CC Excl: 276.0-276.9

276.1 Hyposmolality and/or hyponatremia CC
Sodium [Na] deficiency
CC Excl: See code 276.0
DRG 296

276.2 Acidosis CC
Acidosis:
NOS
lactic
metabolic
respiratory
EXCLUDES *diabetic acidosis (250.1)*
CC Excl: See code 276.0
AHA: J-F, '87, 15
DEF: Disorder involves decrease of pH (hydrogen ion) concentration in blood and cellular tissues; caused by increase in acid and decrease in bicarbonate.

276.3 Alkalosis CC
Alkalosis:
NOS
metabolic
respiratory
CC Excl: See code 276.0
DEF: Accumulation of base (non-acid part of salt), or loss of acid without relative loss of base in body fluids; caused by increased arterial plasma bicarbonate concentration or loss of carbon dioxide due to hyperventilation.

276.4 Mixed acid-base balance disorder CC
Hypercapnia with mixed acid-base disorder
CC Excl: See code 276.0

✓5th **276.5 Volume depletion**
EXCLUDES *hypovolemic shock:*
postoperative (998.0)
traumatic (958.4)
AHA: ▶4Q, '05, 54; 2Q, '05, 9;◀ 1Q, '03, 5, 22; 3Q, '02, 21; 4Q, '97, 30; 2Q, '88, 9

276.50 Volume depletion, unspecified CC
CC Excl: See code 276.0
DEF: ▶Depletion of total body water (dehydration) and/or contraction of total intravascular plasma (hypovolemia).◀

276.51 Dehydration CC
CC Excl: See code 276.0
DEF: ▶Depletion of total body water; blood volume may be normal while fluid is pulled from other tissues.◀

276.52 Hypovolemia CC
Depletion of volume of plasma
CC Excl: See code 276.0
DRG 296
DEF: ▶Depletion of volume plasma; depletion of total blood volume.◀

276.6 Fluid overload CC
Fluid retention
EXCLUDES *ascites (789.5)*
localized edema (782.3)
CC Excl: See code 276.0

276.7 Hyperpotassemia CC
Hyperkalemia
Potassium [K]:
excess
intoxication
overload
CC Excl: See code 276.0
AHA: 1Q, '05, 9; 2Q,'01, 12
DRG 296
DEF: Elevated blood levels of potassium; symptoms include abnormal EKG readings, weakness; related to defective renal excretion.

276.8 Hypopotassemia
Hypokalemia
Potassium [K] deficiency
DEF: Decreased blood levels of potassium; symptoms include neuromuscular disorders.

276.9 Electrolyte and fluid disorders not elsewhere classified CC
Electrolyte imbalance
Hyperchloremia
Hypochloremia
EXCLUDES *electrolyte imbalance:*
associated with hyperemesis gravidarum (643.1)
complicating labor and delivery (669.0)
following abortion and ectopic or molar pregnancy (634-638 with .4, 639.4)
CC Excl: See code 276.0
AHA: J-F, '87, 15

4th 277 Other and unspecified disorders of metabolism

5th 277.0 Cystic fibrosis
Fibrocystic disease of the pancreas
Mucoviscidosis
AHA: 4Q, '90, 16; 3Q, '90, 18
DEF: Generalized, genetic disorder of infants, children, and young adults marked by exocrine gland dysfunction; characterized by chronic pulmonary disease with excess mucus production, pancreatic deficiency, high levels of electrolytes in the sweat.

277.00 Without mention of meconium ileus CC
Cystic fibrosis NOS
CC Excl: 277.00-277.09
AHA: 2Q, '03, 12

277.01 With meconium ileus CC N
Meconium:
ileus (of newborn)
obstruction of intestine in mucoviscidosis
CC Excl: See code 277.00

277.02 With pulmonary manifestations CC
Cystic fibrosis with pulmonary exacerbation
Use additional code to identify any infectious organism present, such as:
pseudomonas (041.7)
CC Excl: See code 277.00

277.03 With gastrointestinal manifestations CC
EXCLUDES *with meconium ileus (277.01)*
CC Excl: See code 277.00
AHA: 4Q, '02, 45

277.09 With other manifestations CC
CC Excl: See code 277.00

277.1 Disorders of porphyrin metabolism
Hematoporphyria
Hematoporphyrinuria
Hereditary coproporphyria
Porphyria
Porphyrinuria
Protocoproporphyria
Protoporphyria
Pyrroloporphyria

277.2 Other disorders of purine and pyrimidine metabolism
Hypoxanthine-guanine-phosphoribosyltransferase deficiency [HG-PRT deficiency]
Lesch-Nyhan syndrome
Xanthinuria
EXCLUDES *gout (274.0-274.9)*
orotic aciduric anemia (281.4)

5th 277.3 Amyloidosis
AHA: 1Q, '96, 16
DEF: Conditions of diverse etiologies characterized by the accumulation of insoluble fibrillar proteins (amyloid) in various organs and tissues of the body, compromising vital functions.

● **277.30 Amyloidosis, unspecified**
Amyloidosis NOS

● **277.31 Familial Mediterranean fever**
Benign paroxysmal peritonitis
Hereditary amyloid nephropathy
Periodic familial polyserositis
Recurrent polyserositis

● **277.39 Other amyloidosis**
Hereditary cardiac amyloidosis
Inherited systemic amyloidosis
Neuropathic (Portuguese) (Swiss) amyloidosis
Secondary amyloidosis

277.4 Disorders of bilirubin excretion
Hyperbilirubinemia:
congenital
constitutional
Syndrome:
Crigler-Najjar
Syndrome:
Dubin-Johnson
Gilbert's
Rotor's
EXCLUDES *hyperbilirubinemias specific to the perinatal period (774.0-774.7)*

277.5 Mucopolysaccharidosis
Gargoylism
Hunter's syndrome
Hurler's syndrome
Lipochondrodystrophy
Maroteaux-Lamy syndrome
Morquio-Brailsford disease
Osteochondrodystrophy
Sanfilippo's syndrome
Scheie's syndrome
DEF: Metabolism disorders evidenced by excretion of various mucopolysaccharides in urine and infiltration of these substances into connective tissue, with resulting various defects of bone, cartilage and connective tissue.

277.6 Other deficiencies of circulating enzymes
Hereditary angioedema

277.7 Dysmetabolic syndrome X
Use additional code for associated manifestation, such as:
cardiovascular disease (414.00-414.07)
obesity (278.00-278.01)
AHA: 4Q, '01, 42
DEF: A specific group of metabolic disorders that are related to the state of insulin resistance (decreased cellular response to insulin) without elevated blood sugars; often related to elevated cholesterol and triglycerides, obesity, cardiovascular disease, and high blood pressure.

5th 277.8 Other specified disorders of metabolism
AHA: 4Q, '03, 50; 2Q, '01, 18; S-O, '87, 9

277.81 Primary carnitine deficiency

277.82 Carnitine deficiency due to inborn errors of metabolism

277.83 Iatrogenic carnitine deficiency
Carnitine deficiency due to:
hemodialysis
valproic acid therapy

277.84 Other secondary carnitine deficiency

277.85 Disorders of fatty acid oxidation
Carnitine palmitoyltransferase deficiencies (CPT1, CPT2)
Glutaric aciduria type II (type IIA, IIB, IIC)
Long chain 3-hydroxyacyl CoA dehydrogenase deficiency (LCHAD)
Long chain/very long chain acyl CoA dehydrogenase deficiency (LCAD, VLCAD)
Medium chain acyl CoA dehydrogenase deficiency (MCAD)
Short chain acyl CoA dehydrogenase deficiency (SCAD)
EXCLUDES *primary carnitine deficiency (277.81)*

277.86 Peroxisomal disorders
Adrenomyeloneuropathy
Neonatal adrenoleukodystrophy
Rhizomelic chrondrodysplasia punctata
X-linked adrenoleukodystrophy
Zellweger syndrome
EXCLUDES *infantile Refsum disease (356.3)*

277.87 Disorders of mitochondrial metabolism
Kearns-Sayre syndrome
Mitochondrial Encephalopathy, Lactic Acidosis and Stroke-like episodes (MELAS syndrome)
Mitochondrial Neurogastrointestinal Encephalopathy syndrome (MNGIE)
Myoclonus with Epilepsy and with Ragged Red Fibers (MERRF syndrome)
Neuropathy, Ataxia and Retinitis Pigmentosa (NARP syndrome)
Use additional code for associated conditions
EXCLUDES *disorders of pyruvate metabolism (271.8)*
Leber's optic atrophy (377.16)
Leigh's subacute necrotizing encephalopathy (330.8)
Reye's syndrome (331.81)
AHA: 4Q, '04, 62

Endocrine, Nutritional and Metabolic, Immunity 277–277.87

277.89 Other specified disorders of metabolism
Hand-Schüller-Christian disease
Histiocytosis (acute) (chronic)
Histiocytosis X (chronic)
EXCLUDES *histiocytosis:*
acute differentiated progressive (202.5)
X, acute (progressive) (202.5)

277.9 Unspecified disorder of metabolism
Enzymopathy NOS

4th 278 Overweight, obesity and other hyperalimentation
EXCLUDES *hyperalimentation NOS (783.6)*
poisoning by vitamins NOS (963.5)
polyphagia (783.6)

5th 278.0 Overweight and obesity
Use additional code to identify Body Mass Index (BMI), if known ▶(V85.0-V85.54)◀
EXCLUDES *adiposogenital dystrophy (253.8)*
obesity of endocrine origin NOS (259.9)
AHA: 4Q, '05, 97

278.00 Obesity, unspecified
Obesity NOS
AHA: 4Q, '01, 42; 1Q, '99, 5, 6

278.01 Morbid obesity
Severe obesity
AHA: 3Q, '03, 6-8
DEF: Increased weight beyond limits of skeletal and physical requirements (125 percent or more over ideal body weight), as a result of excess fat in subcutaneous connective tissues.
DEF: BMI (body mass index) between 30.0 and 39.9.

278.02 Overweight
AHA: 4Q, '05, 55
DEF: BMI (body mass index) between 25 and 29.9.

278.1 Localized adiposity
Fat pad

278.2 Hypervitaminosis A

278.3 Hypercarotinemia
DEF: Elevated blood carotene level due to ingesting excess carotenoids or the inability to convert carotenoids to vitamin A.

278.4 Hypervitaminosis D
DEF: Weakness, fatigue, loss of weight, and other symptoms resulting from ingesting excessive amounts of vitamin D.

278.8 Other hyperalimentation

4th 279 Disorders involving the immune mechanism

5th 279.0 Deficiency of humoral immunity
DEF: Inadequate immune response to bacterial infections with potential reinfection by viruses due to lack of circulating immunoglobulins (acquired antibodies).

279.00 Hypogammaglobulinemia, unspecified
Agammaglobulinemia NOS

279.01 Selective IgA immunodeficiency

279.02 Selective IgM immunodeficiency CC
CC Excl: 279.02-279.9

279.03 Other selective immunoglobulin deficiencies CC
Selective deficiency of IgG
CC Excl: See code 279.02

279.04 Congenital hypogammaglobulinemia CC
Agammaglobulinemia:
Bruton's type
X-linked
CC Excl: See code 279.02

279.05 Immunodeficiency with increased IgM CC
Immunodeficiency with hyper-IgM:
autosomal recessive
X-linked
CC Excl: See code 279.02

279.06 Common variable immunodeficiency CC
Dysgammaglobulinemia (acquired) (congenital) (primary)
Hypogammaglobulinemia:
acquired primary
congenital non-sex-linked
sporadic
CC Excl: See code 279.02

279.09 Other CC
Transient hypogammaglobulinemia of infancy
CC Excl: See code 279.02

5th 279.1 Deficiency of cell-mediated immunity

279.10 Immunodeficiency with predominant T-cell defect, unspecified CC
CC Excl: See code 279.02
AHA: S-O, '87, 10

279.11 DiGeorge's syndrome CC
Pharyngeal pouch syndrome
Thymic hypoplasia
CC Excl: See code 279.02
DEF: Congenital disorder due to defective development of the third and fourth pharyngeal pouches; results in hypoplasia or aplasia of the thymus, parathyroid glands; related to congenital heart defects, anomalies of the great vessels, esophageal atresia, and abnormalities of facial structures.

279.12 Wiskott-Aldrich syndrome CC
CC Excl: See code 279.02
DEF: A disease characterized by chronic conditions, such as eczema, suppurative otitis media and anemia; it results from an X-linked recessive gene and is classified as an immune deficiency syndrome.

279.13 Nezelof's syndrome CC
Cellular immunodeficiency with abnormal immunoglobulin deficiency
CC Excl: See code 279.02
DEF: Immune system disorder characterized by a pathological deficiency in cellular immunity and humoral antibodies resulting in inability to fight infectious diseases.

279.19 Other CC
EXCLUDES *ataxia-telangiectasia (334.8)*
CC Excl: See code 279.02

279.2 Combined immunity deficiency CC
Agammaglobulinemia:
autosomal recessive
Swiss-type
x-linked recessive
Severe combined immunodeficiency [SCID]
Thymic:
alymophoplasia
aplasia or dysplasia with immunodeficiency
EXCLUDES *thymic hypoplasia (279.11)*
CC Excl: See code 279.02
DEF: Agammaglobulinemia: No immunoglobulins in the blood.
DEF: Thymic alymphoplasia: Severe combined immunodeficiency; result of failed lymphoid tissue development.

279.3 Unspecified immunity deficiency CC
CC Excl: See code 279.02

279.4 Autoimmune disease, not elsewhere classified CC
Autoimmune disease NOS
EXCLUDES *transplant failure or rejection (996.80-996.89)*
CC Excl: See code 279.02

279.8 Other specified disorders involving the immune mechanism CC
Single complement [C_1-C_9] deficiency or dysfunction
CC Excl: See code 279.02

279.9 Unspecified disorder of immune mechanism CC
CC Excl: See code 279.02
AHA: 3Q, '92, 13

N Newborn Age: 0 P Pediatric Age: 0-17 M Maternity Age: 12-55 A Adult Age: 15-124 CC CC Condition MC Major Complication CD Complex Dx HIV HIV Related Dx

4. DISEASES OF THE BLOOD AND BLOOD-FORMING ORGANS (280-289)

EXCLUDES *anemia complicating pregnancy or the puerperium (648.2)*

✓4th **280 Iron deficiency anemias**

INCLUDES anemia:
- asiderotic
- hypochromic-microcytic
- sideropenic

EXCLUDES *familial microcytic anemia (282.49)*

280.0 Secondary to blood loss (chronic) CC

Normocytic anemia due to blood loss

EXCLUDES *acute posthemorrhagic anemia (285.1)*

CC Excl: 280.0-285.9, 289.81-289.9, 517.3

AHA: 4Q, '93, 34

280.1 Secondary to inadequate dietary iron intake

280.8 Other specified iron deficiency anemias

Paterson-Kelly syndrome
Plummer-Vinson syndrome
Sideropenic dysphagia

280.9 Iron deficiency anemia, unspecified

Anemia:
- achlorhydric
- chlorotic
- idiopathic hypochromic
- iron [Fe] deficiency NOS

✓4th **281 Other deficiency anemias**

281.0 Pernicious anemia

Anemia:
- Addison's
- Biermer's
- congenital pernicious

Congenital intrinsic factor [Castle's] deficiency

EXCLUDES *combined system disease without mention of anemia (266.2)*
subacute degeneration of spinal cord without mention of anemia (266.2)

AHA: N-D, '84, 1; S-O, '84, 16

DEF: Chronic progressive anemia due to Vitamin B12 malabsorption; caused by lack of a secretion known as intrinsic factor, which is produced by the gastric mucosa of the stomach.

281.1 Other vitamin B_{12} deficiency anemia

Anemia:
- vegan's
- vitamin B_{12} deficiency (dietary)
- due to selective vitamin B_{12} malabsorption with proteinuria

Syndrome:
- Imerslund's
- Imerslund-Gräsbeck

EXCLUDES *combined system disease without mention of anemia (266.2)*
subacute degeneration of spinal cord without mention of anemia (266.2)

281.2 Folate-deficiency anemia

Congenital folate malabsorption

Folate or folic acid deficiency anemia:
- NOS
- dietary
- drug-induced

Goat's milk anemia

Nutritional megaloblastic anemia (of infancy)

Use additional E code to identify drug

DEF: Macrocytic anemia resembles pernicious anemia but without absence of hydrochloric acid secretions; responsive to folic acid therapy.

281.3 Other specified megaloblastic anemias not elsewhere classified

Combined B_{12} and folate-deficiency anemia
Refractory megaloblastic anemia

DEF: Megaloblasts predominant in bone marrow with few normoblasts; rare familial type associated with proteinuria and genitourinary tract anomalies.

281.4 Protein-deficiency anemia CC

Amino-acid-deficiency anemia

CC Excl: See code 280.0

281.8 Anemia associated with other specified nutritional deficiency CC

Scorbutic anemia

CC Excl: See code 280.0

281.9 Unspecified deficiency anemia

Anemia:
- dimorphic
- macrocytic
- megaloblastic NOS

Anemia:
- nutritional NOS
- simple chronic

✓4th **282 Hereditary hemolytic anemias**

DEF: Escalated rate of erythrocyte destruction; similar to all anemias, occurs when imbalance exists between blood loss and blood production.

282.0 Hereditary spherocytosis

Acholuric (familial) jaundice
Congenital hemolytic anemia (spherocytic)
Congenital spherocytosis
Minkowski-Chauffard syndrome
Spherocytosis (familial)

EXCLUDES *hemolytic anemia of newborn (773.0-773.5)*

DEF: Hereditary, chronic illness marked by abnormal red blood cell membrane; symptoms include enlarged spleen, jaundice; and anemia in severe cases.

282.1 Hereditary elliptocytosis

Elliptocytosis (congenital)
Ovalocytosis (congenital) (hereditary)

DEF: Genetic hemolytic anemia characterized by malformed, elliptical erythrocytes; there is increased destruction of red cells with resulting anemia.

282.2 Anemias due to disorders of glutathione metabolism

Anemia:
- 6-phosphogluconic dehydrogenase deficiency
- enzyme deficiency, drug-induced
- erythrocytic glutathione deficiency
- glucose-6-phosphate dehydrogenase [G-6-PD] deficiency
- glutathione-reductase deficiency
- hemolytic nonspherocytic (hereditary), type I

Disorder of pentose phosphate pathway
Favism

282.3 Other hemolytic anemias due to enzyme deficiency

Anemia:
- hemolytic nonspherocytic (hereditary), type II
- hexokinase deficiency
- pyruvate kinase [PK] deficiency
- triosephosphate isomerase deficiency

✓5th **282.4 Thalassemias**

EXCLUDES *sickle-cell:*
disease (282.60-282.69)
trait (282.5)

AHA: 4Q, '03, 51

DEF: A group of inherited hemolytic disorders characterized by decreased production of at least one of the four polypeptide globin chains which results in defective hemoglobin synthesis; symptoms include severe anemia, expanded marrow spaces, transfusional and absorptive iron overload, impaired growth rate, thickened cranial bones, and pathologic fractures.

282.41 Sickle-cell thalassemia without crisis CC
Sickle-cell thalassemia NOS
Thalassemia Hb-S disease without crisis
CC Excl: See code 280.0

282.42 Sickle-cell thalassemia with crisis CC
Sickle-cell thalassemia with vaso-occlusive pain
Thalassemia Hb-S disease with crisis
Use additional code for type of crisis, such as:
acute chest syndrome (517.3)
splenic sequestration (289.52)
CC Excl: See code 280.0

282.49 Other thalassemia CC
Cooley's anemia
Hb-Bart's disease
Hereditary leptocytosis
Mediterranean anemia (with other hemoglobinopathy)
Microdrepanocytosis
Thalassemia (alpha) (beta) (intermedia) (major) (minima) (minor) (mixed) (trait) (with other hemoglobinopathy)
Thalassemia NOS
CC Excl: See code 280.0

282.5 Sickle-cell trait
Hb-AS genotype
Hemoglobin S [Hb-S] trait
Heterozygous:
hemoglobin S
Hb-S

EXCLUDES *that with other hemoglobinopathy (282.60-282.69)*
that with thalassemia (282.49)

DEF: Heterozygous genetic makeup characterized by one gene for normal hemoglobin and one for sickle-cell hemoglobin; clinical disease rarely present.

✓5th **282.6 Sickle-cell disease**
Sickle-cell anemia

EXCLUDES *sickle-cell thalassemia (282.41-282.42)*
sickle-cell trait (282.5)

DEF: Inherited blood disorder; sickle-shaped red blood cells are hard and pointed, clogging blood flow; anemia characterized by, periodic episodes of pain, acute abdominal discomfort, skin ulcerations of the legs, increased infections; occurs primarily in persons of African descent.

282.60 Sickle-cell disease, unspecified CC
Sickle-cell anemia NOS
CC Excl: See code 280.0
AHA: 2Q, '97, 11

282.61 Hb-SS disease without crisis CC
CC Excl: See code 280.0

282.62 Hb-SS disease with crisis CC
Hb-SS disease with vaso-occlusive pain
Sickle-cell crisis NOS
Use additional code for type of crisis, such as:
acute chest syndrome (517.3)
splenic sequestration (289.52)
CC Excl: See code 280.0
AHA: 4Q, '03, 56; 2Q, '98, 8; 2Q, '91, 15

282.63 Sickle-cell/Hb-C disease without crisis CC
Hb-S/Hb-C disease without crisis
CC Excl: See code 280.0

282.64 Sickle-cell/Hb-C disease with crisis CC
Hb-S/Hb-C disease with crisis
Sickle-cell/Hb-C disease with vaso-occlusive pain
Use additional code for type of crisis, such as:
acute chest syndrome (517.3)
splenic sequestration (289.52)
CC Excl: See code 280.0
AHA: 4Q, '03, 51

282.68 Other sickle-cell disease without crisis CC
Hb-S/Hb-D, Hb-S/Hb-E, Sickle-cell/Hb-D, Sickle-cell/Hb-E } disease without crisis
CC Excl: See code 280.0
AHA: 4Q, '03, 51

282.69 Other sickle-cell disease with crisis CC
Hb-S/Hb-D, Hb-S/Hb-E, Sickle-cell/Hb-D, Sickle-cell/Hb-E } disease with crisis
Other sickle-cell disease with vaso-occlusive pain
Use additional code for type of crisis, such as:
acute chest syndrome (517.3)
splenic sequestration (289.52)
CC Excl: See code 280.0

282.7 Other hemoglobinopathies
Abnormal hemoglobin NOS
Congenital Heinz-body anemia
Disease:
hemoglobin C [Hb-C]
hemoglobin D [Hb-D]
hemoglobin E [Hb-E]
hemoglobin Zurich [Hb-Zurich]
Hemoglobinopathy NOS
Hereditary persistence of fetal hemoglobin [HPFH]
Unstable hemoglobin hemolytic disease

EXCLUDES *familial polycythemia (289.6)*
hemoglobin M [Hb-M] disease (289.7)
high-oxygen-affinity hemoglobin (289.0)

DEF: Any disorder of hemoglobin due to alteration of molecular structure; may include overt anemia.

282.8 Other specified hereditary hemolytic anemias
Stomatocytosis

282.9 Hereditary hemolytic anemia, unspecified
Hereditary hemolytic anemia NOS

✓4th **283 Acquired hemolytic anemias**

DEF: Non-heriditary anemia characterized by premature destruction of red blood cells; caused by infectious organisms, poisons, and physical agents

AHA: N-D, '84, 1

283.0 Autoimmune hemolytic anemias CC

Autoimmune hemolytic disease (cold type) (warm type)
Chronic cold hemagglutinin disease
Cold agglutinin disease or hemoglobinuria
Hemolytic anemia:
cold type (secondary) (symptomatic)
drug-induced
warm type (secondary) (symptomatic)
Use additional E code to identify cause, if drug-induced

EXCLUDES *Evans' syndrome (287.32)*
hemolytic disease of newborn (773.0-773.5)

CC Excl: See code 280.0

✓5th **283.1 Non-autoimmune hemolytic anemias**

Use additional E code to identify cause

DEF: Hemolytic anemia and thrombocytopenia with acute renal failure; relatively rare condition; 50 percent of patients require renal dialysis.

AHA: 4Q, '93, 25

283.10 Non-autoimmune hemolytic anemia, unspecified CC

CC Excl: See code 280.0

283.11 Hemolytic-uremic syndrome CC

CC Excl: See code 280.0

283.19 Other non-autoimmune hemolytic anemias CC

Hemolytic anemia:
mechanical
microangiopathic
Hemolytic anemia:
toxic

CC Excl: See code 280.0

283.2 Hemoglobinuria due to hemolysis from external causes CC

Acute intravascular hemolysis
Hemoglobinuria:
from exertion
march
paroxysmal (cold) (nocturnal)
due to other hemolysis
Marchiafava-Micheli syndrome
Use additional E code to identify cause

CC Excl: See code 280.0

283.9 Acquired hemolytic anemia, unspecified CC

Acquired hemolytic anemia NOS
Chronic idiopathic hemolytic anemia

CC Excl: See code 280.0

▲ ✓4th **284 Aplastic anemia and other bone marrow failure syndromes**

AHA: 1Q, '91, 14; N-D, '84, 1; S-O, '84, 16

DEF: Bone marrow failure to produce the normal amount of blood components; generally non-responsive to usual therapy.

✓5th **284.0 Constitutional aplastic anemia**

AHA: 1Q, '91, 14

● **284.01 Constitutional red blood cell aplasia**

Aplasia, (pure) red cell:
congenital
of infants
primary
Blackfan-Diamond syndrome
Familial hypoplastic anemia

● **284.09 Other constitutional aplastic anemia**

Fanconi's anemia
Pancytopenia with malformations

● **284.1 Pancytopenia**

EXCLUDES *pancytopenia (due to) (with):*
aplastic anemia NOS (284.9)
bone marrow infiltration (284.2)
constitutional red blood cell aplasia (284.01)
drug induced (284.8)
hairy cell leukemia (202.4)
human immunodeficiency virus disease (042)
leukoerythroblastic anemia (284.2)
malformations (284.09)
myelodysplastic syndromes (238.72-238.75)
myeloproliferative disease (238.79)
other constitutional aplastic anemia (284.09)

● **284.2 Myelophthisis**

Leukoerythroblastic anemia
Myelophthisic anemia
Code first the underlying disorder, such as:
malignant neoplasm of breast (174.0-174.9, 175.0-175.9)
tuberculosis (015.0-015.9)

EXCLUDES *idiopathic myelofibrosis (238.76)*
myelofibrosis NOS (289.83)
myelofibrosis with myeloid metaplasia (238.76)
primary myelofibrosis (238.76)
secondary myelofibrosis (289.83)

284.8 Other specified aplastic anemias CC

Aplastic anemia (due to):
chronic systemic disease
drugs
infection
radiation
toxic (paralytic)
Red cell aplasia (acquired) (adult) (pure) (with thymoma)
Use additional E code to identify cause

CC Excl: See code 280.0

AHA: 3Q, '05, 11; 1Q, '97, 5; 1Q, '92, 15; 1Q, '91, 14

284.9 Aplastic anemia, unspecified CC

Anemia:
aplastic (idiopathic) NOS
aregenerative
hypoplastic NOS
nonregenerative
Medullary hypoplasia

EXCLUDES *refractory anemia ►(238.72)◄*

CC Excl: See code 280.0

✓4th **285 Other and unspecified anemias**

AHA: 1Q, '91, 14; N-D, '84, 1

285.0 Sideroblastic anemia CC

Anemia:
hypochromic with iron loading
sideroachrestic
sideroblastic:
acquired
congenital
hereditary
primary
sideroblastic:
secondary (drug-induced) (due to disease)
sex-linked hypochromic
vitamin B6-responsive
Pyridoxine-responsive (hypochromic) anemia
Use additional E code to identify cause, if drug induced

EXCLUDES *refractory sideroblastic anemia ►(238.72)◄*

CC Excl: See code 280.0

DEF: Characterized by a disruption of final heme synthesis; results in iron overload of reticuloendothelial tissues.

Blood and Blood-Forming Organs 283–285.0

285.1 Acute posthemorrhagic anemia CC
Anemia due to acute blood loss
EXCLUDES *anemia due to chronic blood loss (280.0)*
blood loss anemia NOS (280.0)
CC Excl: 280.0-285.9, 289.81-289.9, 958.2
AHA: 2Q, '92, 15

▲ ✓5th **285.2 Anemia of chronic disease**
▶Anemia in chronic illness◀
AHA: 4Q, '00, 39

285.21 Anemia in chronic kidney disease
Anemia in end stage renal disease
Erythropoietin-resistant anemia (EPO resistant anemia)

285.22 Anemia in neoplastic disease

▲ **285.29 Anemia of other chronic disease**
▶Anemia in other chronic illness◀

285.8 Other specified anemias
Anemia:
dyserythropoietic (congenital)
dyshematopoietic (congenital)
von Jaksch's
Infantile pseudoleukemia
AHA: 1Q, '91, 16

285.9 Anemia, unspecified
Anemia:
NOS
essential
normocytic, not due to blood loss
Anemia:
profound
progressive
secondary
Oligocythemia
EXCLUDES *anemia (due to):*
blood loss:
acute (285.1)
chronic or unspecified (280.0)
iron deficiency (280.0-280.9)
AHA: 1Q, '02, 14; 2Q, '92, 16; M-A, '85, 13; N-D, '84, 1

✓4th **286 Coagulation defects**

286.0 Congenital factor VIII disorder CC
Antihemophilic globulin [AHG] deficiency
Factor VIII (functional) deficiency
Hemophilia:
NOS
Hemophilia:
A
classical
familial
hereditary
Subhemophilia
EXCLUDES *factor VIII deficiency with vascular defect (286.4)*
CC Excl: 286.0-287.9, 289.81-289.9
DEF: Hereditary, sex-linked, results in missing antihemophilic globulin (AHG) (factor VIII); causes abnormal coagulation characterized by increased tendency to bleeding, large bruises of skin, soft tissue; may also be bleeding in mouth, nose, gastrointestinal tract; after childhood, hemorrhages in joints, resulting in swelling and impaired function.

286.1 Congenital factor IX disorder CC
Christmas disease
Deficiency:
factor IX (functional)
plasma thromboplastin component [PTC]
Hemophilia B
CC Excl: See code 286.0
DEF: Deficiency of plasma thromboplastin component (PTC) (factor IX) and plasma thromboplastin antecedent (PTA); PTC deficiency clinically indistinguishable from classical hemophilia; PTA deficiency found in both sexes.

286.2 Congenital factor XI deficiency CC
Hemophilia C
Plasma thromboplastin antecedent [PTA] deficiency
Rosenthal's disease
CC Excl: See code 286.0

286.3 Congenital deficiency of other clotting factors CC
Congenital afibrinogenemia
Deficiency:
AC globulin factor:
I [fibrinogen]
II [prothrombin]
V [labile]
VII [stable]
X [Stuart-Prower]
XII [Hageman]
XIII [fibrin stabilizing]
Laki-Lorand factor
proaccelerin
Disease
Owren's
Stuart-Prower
Dysfibrinogenemia (congenital)
Dysprothrombinemia (constitutional)
Hypoproconvertinemia
Hypoprothrmbinemia (hereditary)
Parahemophilia
CC Excl: See code 286.0

286.4 von Willebrand's disease CC
Angiohemophilia (A) (B)
Constitutional thrombopathy
Factor VIII deficiency with vascular defect
Pseudohemophilia type B
Vascular hemophilia
von Willebrand's (-Jürgens') disease
EXCLUDES *factor VIII deficiency:*
NOS (286.0)
with functional defect (286.0)
hereditary capillary fragility (287.8)
CC Excl: See code 286.0
DEF: Abnormal blood coagulation caused by deficient blood Factor VII; congenital; symptoms include excess or prolonged bleeding, such as hemorrhage during menstruation, following birthing, or after surgical procedure.

286.5 Hemorrhagic disorder due to intrinsic circulating anticoagulants CC
Antithrombinemia
Antithromboplastinemia
Antithromboplastino-genemia
Hyperheparinemia
Increase in:
anti-VIIIa
anti-IXa
anti-Xa
anti-XIa
antithrombin
Secondary hemophilia
Systemic lupus erythematosus [SLE] inhibitor
CC Excl: See code 286.0
AHA: 3Q, '92, 15; 3Q, '90, 14

286.6 Defibrination syndrome CC
Afibrinogenemia, acquired
Consumption coagulopathy
Diffuse or disseminated intravascular coagulation [DIC syndrome]
Fibrinolytic hemorrhage, acquired
Hemorrhagic fibrinogenolysis
Pathologic fibrinolysis
Purpura:
fibrinolytic
fulminans

EXCLUDES *that complicating:*
abortion (634-638 with .1, 639.1)
pregnancy or the puerperium (641.3, 666.3)
disseminated intravascular coagulation in newborn (776.2)

CC Excl: See code 286.0

AHA: 4Q, '93, 29

DEF: Characterized by destruction of circulating fibrinogen; often precipitated by other conditions, such as injury, causing release of thromboplastic particles in blood stream.

286.7 Acquired coagulation factor deficiency CC
Deficiency of coagulation factor due to:
liver disease
vitamin K deficiency
Hypoprothrombinemia, acquired
Use additional E code to identify cause, if drug induced

EXCLUDES *vitamin K deficiency of newborn (776.0)*

CC Excl: See code 286.0

AHA: 4Q, '93, 29

286.9 Other and unspecified coagulation defects CC
Defective coagulation NOS
Deficiency, coagulation factor NOS
Delay, coagulation
Disorder:
coagulation
hemostasis

EXCLUDES *abnormal coagulation profile (790.92)*
hemorrhagic disease of newborn (776.0)
that complicating:
abortion (634-638 with .1, 639.1)
pregnancy or the puerperium (641.3, 666.3)

CC Excl: See code 286.0

AHA: 4Q, '99, 22; 4Q, '93, 29

✓4th **287 Purpura and other hemorrhagic conditions**

EXCLUDES *hemorrhagic thrombocythemia ▶(238.79)◀*
purpura fulminans (286.6)

AHA: 1Q, '91, 14

287.0 Allergic purpura CC
Peliosis rheumatica
Purpura:
anaphylactoid
autoimmune
Henoch's
nonthrombocytopenic:
hemorrhagic
idiopathic
Purpura:
rheumatica
Schönlein-Henoch
vascular
Vasculitis, allergic

EXCLUDES *hemorrhagic purpura (287.39)*
purpura annularis telangiectodes (709.1)

CC Excl: See code 286.0

DEF: Any hemorrhagic condition, thrombocytic or nonthrombocytopenic in origin, caused by a presumed allergic reaction.

287.1 Qualitative platelet defects CC
Thrombasthenia (hemorrhagic) (hereditary)
Thrombocytasthenia
Thrombocytopathy (dystrophic)
Thrombopathy (Bernard-Soulier)

EXCLUDES *von Willebrand's disease (286.4)*

CC Excl: See code 286.0

287.2 Other nonthrombocytopenic purpuras CC
Purpura:
NOS
senile
simplex

CC Excl: See code 286.0

✓5th **287.3 Primary thrombocytopenia**

EXCLUDES *thrombotic thrombocytopenic purpura (446.6)*
transient thrombocytopenia of newborn (776.1)

AHA: 4Q, '05, 56

DEF: Decrease in number of blood platelets in circulating blood and purpural skin hemorrhages.

287.30 Primary thrombocytopenia, unspecified CC
Megakaryocytic hypoplasia

CC Excl: 286.0-287.9, 289.81-289.9

287.31 Immune thrombocytopenic purpura CC
Idiopathic thrombocytopenic purpura
Tidal platelet dysgenesis

CC Excl: See code 287.30

AHA: 4Q, '05, 57

DEF: Tidal platelet dysgenesis: Platelet counts fluctuate from normal to very low within periods of 20 to 40 days and may involve autoimmune platelet destruction.

287.32 Evans' syndrome CC

CC Excl: See code 287.30

DEF: Combination of immunohemolytic anemia and autoimmune hemolytic anemia, sometimes with neutropenia.

287.33 Congenital and hereditary thrombocytopenic purpura CC
Congenital and hereditary thrombocytopenia
Thrombocytopenia with absent radii (TAR) syndrome

EXCLUDES *Wiskott-Aldrich syndrome (279.12)*

CC Excl: See code 287.30

DEF: Thrombocytopenia with absent radii (TAR) syndrome: autosomal recessive syndrome characterized by thrombocytopenia and bilateral radial aplasia; manifestations include skeletal, gastrointestinal, hematologic, and cardiac system abnormalities.

287.39 Other primary thrombocytopenia CC

CC Excl: See code 287.30

287.4 Secondary thrombocytopenia CC
Posttransfusion purpura
Thrombocytopenia (due to):
dilutional
drugs
extracorporeal circulation of blood
massive blood transfusion
platelet alloimmunization
Use additional E code to identify cause

EXCLUDES *transient thrombocytopenia of newborn (776.1)*

CC Excl: See code 286.0

AHA: M-A, '85, 14

DEF: Reduced number of platelets in circulating blood as consequence of an underlying disease or condition.

Blood and Blood-Forming Organs

286.6–287.4

✓4th ✓5th Additional Digit Required | Nonspecific PDx | Unacceptable PDx | Manifestation Code | MCV Major Cardiovascular Condition | ▶◀ Revised Text | ● New Code | ▲ Revised Code Title

287.5 Thrombocytopenia, unspecified CC
CC Excl: See code 286.0

287.8 Other specified hemorrhagic conditions CC
Capillary fragility (hereditary)
Vascular pseudohemophilia
CC Excl: See code 286.0

287.9 Unspecified hemorrhagic conditions CC
Hemorrhagic diathesis (familial)
CC Excl: See code 286.0

✓4th **288 Diseases of white blood cells**
EXCLUDES *leukemia (204.0-208.9)*
AHA: 1Q, '91, 14

▲ ✓5th **288.0 Neutropenia**
▶Decreased absolute neutrophil count (ANC)
Use additional code for any associated fever (780.6)◀
EXCLUDES ▶ *neutropenic splenomegaly (289.53)*◀
transitory neonatal neutropenia (776.7)
AHA: 3Q, '05, 11; 3Q, '99, 6; 2Q, '99, 9; 3Q, '96, 16; 2Q, '96, 6

DEF: Sudden, severe condition characterized by reduced number of white blood cells; results in sores in the throat, stomach or skin; symptoms include chills, fever; some drugs can bring on condition.

● **288.00 Neutropenia, unspecified**

● **288.01 Congenital neutropenia**
Congenital agranulocytosis
Infantile genetic agranulocytosis
Kostmann's syndrome

● **288.02 Cyclic neutropenia**
Cyclic hematopoiesis
Periodic neutropenia

● **288.03 Drug induced neutropenia**
Use additional E code to identify drug

● **288.04 Neutropenia due to infection**

● **288.09 Other neutropenia**
Agranulocytosis
Neutropenia:
immune
toxic

288.1 Functional disorders of polymorphonuclear neutrophils CC
Chronic (childhood) granulomatous disease
Congenital dysphagocytosis
Job's syndrome
Lipochrome histiocytosis (familial)
Progressive septic granulomatosis
CC Excl: 288.00-288.9, 289.81-289.9

288.2 Genetic anomalies of leukocytes
Anomaly (granulation) (granulocyte) or syndrome:
Alder's (-Reilly)
Chédiak-Steinbrinck (-Higashi)
Jordan's
May-Hegglin
Pelger-Huet
Hereditary:
hypersegmentation
hyposegmentation
leukomelanopathy

288.3 Eosinophilia
Eosinophilia:
allergic
hereditary
idiopathic
Eosinophilia:
secondary
Eosinophilic leukocytosis
EXCLUDES *Löffler's syndrome (518.3)*
pulmonary eosinophilia (518.3)
AHA: 3Q, '00, 11

DEF: Elevated number of eosinophils in the blood; characteristic of allergic states and various parasitic infections.

● **288.4 Hemophagocytic syndromes**
Familial hemophagocytic lymphohistiocytosis
Familial hemophagocytic reticulosis
Hemophagocytic syndrome, infection-associated
Histiocytic syndromes
Macrophage activation syndrome

● ✓5th **288.5 Decreased white blood cell count**
EXCLUDES *neutropenia (288.01-288.09)*

● **288.50 Leukocytopenia, unspecified**
Decreased leukocytes, unspecified
Decreased white blood cell count, unspecified
Leukopenia NOS

● **288.51 Lymphocytopenia**
Decreased lymphocytes

● **288.59 Other decreased white blood cell count**
Basophilic leukopenia
Eosinophilic leukopenia
Monocytopenia
Plasmacytopenia

● ✓5th **288.6 Elevated white blood cell count**
EXCLUDES *eosinophilia (288.3)*

● **288.60 Leukocytosis, unspecified**
Elevated leukocytes, unspecified
Elevated white blood cell count, unspecified

● **288.61 Lymphocytosis (symptomatic)**
Elevated lymphocytes

● **288.62 Leukemoid reaction**
Basophilic leukemoid reaction
Lymphocytic leukemoid reaction
Monocytic leukemoid reaction
Myelocytic leukemoid reaction
Neutrophilic leukemoid reaction

● **288.63 Monocytosis (symptomatic)**
EXCLUDES *infectious mononucleosis (075)*

● **288.64 Plasmacytosis**

● **288.65 Basophilia**

● **288.69 Other elevated white blood cell count**

288.8 Other specified disease of white blood cells
EXCLUDES ▶ *decreased white blood cell counts (288.50-288.59)*
elevated white blood cell counts (288.60-288.69)◀
immunity disorders (279.0-279.9)
AHA: M-A, '87, 12

288.9 Unspecified disease of white blood cells

4th 289 Other diseases of blood and blood-forming organs

289.0 Polycythemia, secondary

High-oxygen-affinity hemoglobin
Polycythemia:
acquired
benign
due to:
fall in plasma volume
high altitude
Polycythemia:
emotional
erythropoietin
hypoxemic
nephrogenous
relative
spurious
stress

EXCLUDES *polycythemia:*
neonatal (776.4)
primary (238.4)
vera (238.4)

DEF: Elevated number of red blood cells in circulating blood as result of reduced oxygen supply to the tissues.

289.1 Chronic lymphadenitis

Chronic:
adenitis } any lymph node, except mesenteric
lymphadenitis }

EXCLUDES *acute lymphadenitis (683)*
mesenteric (289.2)
enlarged glands NOS (785.6)

DEF: Persistent inflammation of lymph node tissue; origin of infection is usually elsewhere.

289.2 Nonspecific mesenteric lymphadenitis

Mesenteric lymphadenitis (acute) (chronic)

DEF: Inflammation of the lymph nodes in peritoneal fold that encases abdominal organs; disease resembles acute appendicitis; unknown etiology.

289.3 Lymphadenitis, unspecified, except mesenteric

AHA: 2Q, '92, 8

289.4 Hypersplenism

"Big spleen" syndrome
Dyssplenism
Hypersplenia

EXCLUDES *primary splenic neutropenia ►(289.53)◄*

DEF: An overactive spleen; it causes a deficiency of the peripheral blood components, an increase in bone marrow cells and sometimes a notable increase in the size of the spleen.

5th 289.5 Other diseases of spleen

289.50 Disease of spleen, unspecified

289.51 Chronic congestive splenomegaly

289.52 Splenic sequestration

Code first sickle-cell disease in crisis (282.42, 282.62, 282.64, 282.69)

AHA: 4Q, '03, 51

DEF: Blood is entrapped in the spleen due to vessel occlusion; most often associated with sickle-cell disease; spleen becomes enlarged and there is a sharp drop in hemoglobin.

● **289.53 Neutropenic splenomegaly**

289.59 Other

Lien migrans
Perisplenitis
Splenic:
abscess
atrophy
cyst
Splenic:
fibrosis
infarction
rupture, nontraumatic
Splenitis
Wandering spleen

EXCLUDES *bilharzial splenic fibrosis (120.0-120.9)*
hepatolienal fibrosis (571.5)
splenomegaly NOS (789.2)

289.6 Familial polycythemia

Familial:
benign polycythemia
erythrocytosis

DEF: Elevated number of red blood cells.

289.7 Methemoglobinemia

Congenital NADH [DPNH]-methemoglobin-reductase deficiency
Hemoglobin M [Hb-M] disease
Methemoglobinemia:
NOS
acquired (with sulfhemoglobinemia)
hereditary
toxic
Stokvis' disease
Sulfhemoglobinemia
Use additional E code to identify cause

DEF: Presence in the blood of methemoglobin, a chemically altered form of hemoglobin; causes cyanosis, headache, dizziness, ataxia dyspnea, tachycardia, nausea, stupor, coma, and, rarely, death.

5th 289.8 Other specified diseases of blood and blood-forming organs

AHA: 4Q, '03, 56; 1Q, '02, 16; 2Q, '89, 8; M-A, '87, 12

DEF: Hypercoagulable states: a group of inherited or acquired abnormalities of specific proteins and anticoagulant factors; also called thromboembolic states or thrombotic disorders, these disorders result in the abnormal development of blood clots.

289.81 Primary hypercoagulable state CC

Activated protein C resistance
Antithrombin III deficiency
Factor V Leiden mutation
Lupus anticoagulant
Protein C deficiency
Protein S deficiency
Prothrombin gene mutation

CC Excl: 288.00-288.9, 289.81-289.9

DEF: Activated protein C resistance: decreased effectiveness of protein C to degrade factor V, necessary to inhibit clotting cascade; also called Factor V Leiden mutation.

DEF: Antithrombin III deficiency: deficiency in plasma antithrombin III one of six naturally occurring antithrombins that limit coagulation.

DEF: Factor V Leiden mutation: also called activated protein C resistance.

DEF: Lupus anticoagulant: deficiency in a circulating anticoagulant that inhibits the conversion of prothrombin into thrombin; autoimmune antibodies induce procoagulant surfaces in platelets; also called anti-phospholipid syndrome.

DEF: Protein C deficiency: deficiency of activated protein C which functions to bring the blood-clotting process into balance; same outcome as factor V Leiden mutation.

DEF: Protein S deficiency: similar to protein C deficiency; protein S is a vitamin K dependent cofactor in the activation of protein C.

DEF: Prothrombin gene mutation: increased levels of prothrombin, or factor II, a plasma protein that is converted to thrombin, which acts upon fibrinogen to form the fibrin.

289.82 Secondary hypercoagulable state CC

CC Excl: See code 289.81

● **289.83 Myelofibrosis**

Myelofibrosis NOS

Secondary myelofibrosis

Code first the underlying disorder, such as:

malignant neoplasm of breast (174.0-174.9, 175.0-175.9)

EXCLUDES *idiopathic myelofibrosis (238.76)*

leukoerythroblastic anemia (284.2)

myelofibrosis with myeloid metaplasia (238.76)

myelophthisic anemia (284.2)

myelophthisis (284.2)

primary myelofibrosis (238.76)

289.89 Other specified diseases of blood and blood-forming organs

Hypergammaglobulinemia

Pseudocholinesterase deficiency

289.9 Unspecified diseases of blood and blood-forming organs

Blood dyscrasia NOS

Erythroid hyperplasia

AHA: M-A, '85, 14

5. MENTAL DISORDERS (290-319)

PSYCHOSES (290-299)

EXCLUDES *mental retardation (317-319)*

ORGANIC PSYCHOTIC CONDITIONS (290-294)

INCLUDES psychotic organic brain syndrome

EXCLUDES *nonpsychotic syndromes of organic etiology (310.0-310.9)*
psychoses classifiable to 295-298 and without impairment of orientation, comprehension, calculation, learning capacity, and judgment, but associated with physical disease, injury, or condition affecting the brain [eg., following childbirth] (295.0-298.8)

✓4th **290 Dementias**

Code first the associated neurological condition

EXCLUDES *dementia due to alcohol (291.0-291.2)*
dementia due to drugs (292.82)
dementia not classified as senile, presenile, or arteriosclerotic (294.10-294.11)
psychoses classifiable to 295-298 occurring in the senium without dementia or delirium (295.0-298.8)
senility with mental changes of nonpsychotic severity (310.1)
transient organic psychotic conditions (293.0-293.9)

290.0 Senile dementia, uncomplicated A

Senile dementia:
NOS
simple type

EXCLUDES *mild memory disturbances, not amounting to dementia, associated with senile brain disease (310.1)*
senile dementia with:
delirium or confusion (290.3)
delusional [paranoid] features (290.20)
depressive features (290.21)

AHA: 4Q, '99, 4

✓5th **290.1 Presenile dementia**

Brain syndrome with presenile brain disease

EXCLUDES *arteriosclerotic dementia (290.40-290.43)*
dementia associated with other cerebral conditions (294.10-294.11)

AHA: N-D, '84, 20

290.10 Presenile dementia, uncomplicated A HIV

Presenile dementia: NOS
Presenile dementia: simple type

290.11 Presenile dementia with delirium A HIV

Presenile dementia with acute confusional state

AHA: 1Q, '88, 3

290.12 Presenile dementia with delusional features A HIV

Presenile dementia, paranoid type

290.13 Presenile dementia with depressive features A HIV

Presenile dementia, depressed type

✓5th **290.2 Senile dementia with delusional or depressive features**

EXCLUDES *senile dementia:*
NOS (290.0)
with delirium and/or confusion (290.3)

290.20 Senile dementia with delusional features A

Senile dementia, paranoid type
Senile psychosis NOS

290.21 Senile dementia with depressive features A

290.3 Senile dementia with delirium A

Senile dementia with acute confusional state

EXCLUDES *senile:*
dementia NOS (290.0)
psychosis NOS (290.20)

✓5th **290.4 Vascular dementia**

Multi-infarct dementia or psychosis
Use additional code to identify cerebral atherosclerosis (437.0)

EXCLUDES *suspected cases with no clear evidence of arteriosclerosis (290.9)*

AHA: 1Q, '88, 3

290.40 Vascular dementia, uncomplicated A

Arteriosclerotic dementia:
NOS
simple type

290.41 Vascular dementia with delirium A

Arteriosclerotic dementia with acute confusional state

290.42 Vascular dementia with delusions A

Arteriosclerotic dementia, paranoid type

290.43 Vascular dementia with depressed mood A

Arteriosclerotic dementia, depressed type

290.8 Other specified senile psychotic conditions

Presbyophrenic psychosis

290.9 Unspecified senile psychotic condition A

✓4th **291 Alcohol induced mental disorders**

EXCLUDES *alcoholism without psychosis (303.0-303.9)*

AHA: 1Q, '88, 3; S-O, '86, 3

291.0 Alcohol withdrawal delirium CC

Alcoholic delirium
Delirium tremens

EXCLUDES *alcohol withdrawal (291.81)*

CC Excl: 291.0-294.9, 303.00-305.03, 305.20-305.93, 790.3

AHA: 2Q, '91, 11

291.1 Alcohol induced persisting amnestic disorder CC

Alcoholic polyneuritic psychosis
Korsakoff's psychosis, alcoholic
Wernicke-Korsakoff syndrome (alcoholic)

CC Excl: See code 291.0

AHA: 1Q, '88, 3

DEF: Prominent and lasting reduced memory span, disordered time appreciation and confabulation, occurring in alcoholics, as sequel to acute alcoholic psychosis.

291.2 Alcohol induced persisting dementia CC

Alcoholic dementia NOS
Alcoholism associated with dementia NOS
Chronic alcoholic brain syndrome

CC Excl: See code 291.0

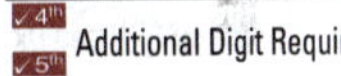

291.3 Alcohol induced psychotic disorder with hallucinations CC

Alcoholic:
- hallucinosis (acute)

Alcoholic:
- psychosis with hallucinosis

EXCLUDES *alcohol withdrawal with delirium (291.0)*
schizophrenia (295.0-295.9) and paranoid states (297.0-297.9) taking the form of chronic hallucinosis with clear consciousness in an alcoholic

CC Excl: See code 291.0

AHA: 2Q, '91, 11

DEF: Psychosis lasting less than six months with slight or no clouding of consciousness in which auditory hallucinations predominate.

291.4 Idiosyncratic alcohol intoxication CC

Pathologic:
- alcohol intoxication

Pathologic:
- drunkenness

EXCLUDES *acute alcohol intoxication (305.0)*
in alcoholism (303.0)
simple drunkenness (305.0)

CC Excl: See code 291.0

DEF: Unique behavioral patterns, like belligerence, after intake of relatively small amounts of alcohol; behavior not due to excess consumption.

291.5 Alcohol induced psychotic disorder with delusions CC

Alcoholic:
- paranoia

Alcoholic:
- psychosis, paranoid type

EXCLUDES *nonalcoholic paranoid states (297.0-297.9)*
schizophrenia, paranoid type (295.3)

✓5th **291.8 Other specified alcohol induced mental disorders**

AHA: 3Q, '94, 13; J-A, '85, 10

291.81 Alcohol withdrawal CC

Alcohol:
- abstinence syndrome or symptoms
- withdrawal syndrome or symptoms

EXCLUDES *alcohol withdrawal:*
delirium (291.0)
hallucinosis (291.3)
delirium tremens (291.0)

CC Excl: 291.0-294.9, 303.00-305.03, 305.20-305.93, 790.3

AHA: 4Q, '96, 28; 2Q, '91, 11

291.82 Alcohol induced sleep disorders

Alcohol induced circadian rhythm sleep disorders
Alcohol induced hypersomnia
Alcohol induced insomnia
Alcohol induced parasomnia

291.89 Other CC

Alcohol induced anxiety disorder
Alcohol induced mood disorder
Alcohol induced sexual dysfunction

CC Excl: See code 291.81

291.9 Unspecified alcohol induced mental disorders CC

Alcoholic:
- mania NOS
- psychosis NOS

Alcoholism (chronic) with psychosis
Alcohol related disorder NOS

CC Excl: See code 291.0

✓4th **292 Drug induced mental disorders**

INCLUDES organic brain syndrome associated with consumption of drugs

Use additional code for any associated drug dependence (304.0-304.9)

Use additional E code to identify drug

AHA: 3Q, '04, 8; 2Q, '91, 11; S-O, '86, 3

292.0 Drug withdrawal CC

Drug:
- abstinence syndrome or symptoms
- withdrawal syndrome or symptoms

CC Excl: See code 291.0

AHA: 1Q, '97, 12; 1Q, '88, 3

✓5th **292.1 Drug induced psychotic disorders**

292.11 Drug induced psychotic disorder with delusions CC

Paranoid state induced by drugs

CC Excl: See code 291.0

292.12 Drug induced psychotic disorder with hallucinations CC

Hallucinatory state induced by drugs

EXCLUDES *states following LSD or other hallucinogens, lasting only a few days or less ["bad trips"] (305.3)*

CC Excl: See code 291.0

292.2 Pathological drug intoxication CC

Drug reaction:
- NOS
- idiosyncratic
- pathologic

} resulting in brief psychotic states

EXCLUDES *expected brief psychotic reactions to hallucinogens ["bad trips"] (305.3)*
physiological side-effects of drugs (e.g., dystonias)

CC Excl: See code 291.0

✓5th **292.8 Other specified drug induced mental disorders**

292.81 Drug induced delirium CC

CC Excl: See code 291.0

AHA: 1Q, '88, 3

292.82 Drug induced persisting dementia CC

CC Excl: See code 291.0

292.83 Drug induced persisting amnestic disorder CC

CC Excl: See code 291.0

292.84 Drug induced mood disorder CC

Depressive state induced by drugs

CC Excl: See code 291.0

292.85 Drug induced sleep disorders

Drug induced circadian rhythm sleep disorder
Drug induced hypersomnia
Drug induced insomnia
Drug induced parasomnia

292.89 Other CC

Drug induced anxiety disorder
Drug induced organic personality syndrome
Drug induced sexual dysfunction
Drug intoxication

CC Excl: See code 291.0

292.9 Unspecified drug induced mental disorder CC

Drug related disorder NOS
Organic psychosis NOS due to or associated with drugs

CC Excl: See code 291.0

✓4th 293 Transient mental disorders due to conditions classified elsewhere

INCLUDES transient organic mental disorders not associated with alcohol or drugs

Code first the associated physical or neurological condition

EXCLUDES *confusional state or delirium superimposed on senile dementia (290.3)*
dementia due to:
alcohol (291.0-291.9)
arteriosclerosis (290.40-290.43)
drugs (292.82)
senility (290.0)

293.0 Delirium due to conditions classified elsewhere

Acute:
confusional state
infective psychosis
organic reaction
posttraumatic organic psychosis
psycho-organic syndrome

Acute psychosis associated with endocrine, metabolic, or cerebrovascular disorder

Epileptic:
confusional state
twilight state

AHA: 1Q, '88, 3

DRG 425

293.1 Subacute delirium

Subacute:
confusional state
infective psychosis
organic reaction
posttraumatic organic psychosis
psycho-organic syndrome
psychosis associated with endocrine or metabolic disorder

✓5th 293.8 Other specified transient mental disorders due to conditions classified elsewhere

293.81 Psychotic disorder with delusions in conditions classified elsewhere CC

Transient organic psychotic condition, paranoid type

CC Excl: 291.0-294.9, 303.00-305.03, 305.20-305.93, 790.3

293.82 Psychotic disorder with hallucinations in conditions classified elsewhere CC

Transient organic psychotic condition, hallucinatory type

CC Excl: See code 293.81

293.83 Mood disorder in conditions classified elsewhere CC

Transient organic psychotic condition, depressive type

CC Excl: See code 293.81

293.84 Anxiety disorder in conditions classified elsewhere CC

CC Excl: See code 293.81

AHA: 4Q, '96, 29

293.89 Other

Catatonic disorder in conditions classified elsewhere

293.9 Unspecified transient mental disorder in conditions classified elsewhere

Organic psychosis:
infective NOS
posttraumatic NOS

Organic psychosis:
transient NOS

Psycho-organic syndrome

✓4th 294 Persistent mental disorders due to conditions classified elsewhere

INCLUDES organic psychotic brain syndromes (chronic), not elsewhere classified

AHA: M-A, '85, 12

294.0 Amnestic disorder in conditions classified elsewhere

Korsakoff's psychosis or syndrome (nonalcoholic)

Code first underlying condition

EXCLUDES *alcoholic:*
amnestic syndrome (291.1)
Korsakoff's psychosis (291.1)

✓5th 294.1 Dementia in conditions classified elsewhere

Dementia of the Alzheimer's type

Code first any underlying physical condition, as:

dementia in:
Alzheimer's disease (331.0)
cerebral lipidoses (330.1)
dementia with Lewy bodies (331.82)
dementia with Parkinsonism (331.82)
epilepsy (345.0-345.9)
frontal dementia (331.19)
frontotemporal dementia (331.19)
general paresis [syphilis] (094.1)
hepatolenticular degeneration (275.1)
Huntington's chorea (333.4)
Jakob-Creutzfeldt disease (046.1)
multiple sclerosis (340)
Pick's disease of the brain (331.11)
polyarteritis nodosa (446.0)
syphilis (094.1)

EXCLUDES *dementia:*
arteriosclerotic (290.40-290.43)
presenile (290.10-290.13)
senile (290.0)
epileptic psychosis NOS (294.8)

AHA: 4Q, '00, 40; 1Q, '99, 14; N-D, '85, 5

294.10 Dementia in conditions classified elsewhere without behavioral disturbance

Dementia in conditions classified elsewhere NOS

294.11 Dementia in conditions classified elsewhere with behavioral disturbance

Aggressive behavior
Combative behavior
Violent behavior
Wandering off

AHA: 4Q, '00, 41

294.8 Other persistent mental disorders due to conditions classified elsewhere

Amnestic disorder NOS
Dementia NOS
Epileptic psychosis NOS
Mixed paranoid and affective organic psychotic states

Use additional code for associated epilepsy (345.0-345.9)

EXCLUDES *mild memory disturbances, not amounting to dementia (310.1)*

AHA: 3Q, '03, 14; 1Q, '88, 5

294.9 Unspecified persistent mental disorders due to conditions classified elsewhere HIV

Cognitive disorder NOS
Organic psychosis (chronic)

OTHER PSYCHOSES (295-299)

Use additional code to identify any associated physical disease, injury, or condition affecting the brain with psychoses classifiable to 295-298

✓4th 295 Schizophrenic disorders

INCLUDES schizophrenia of the types described in 295.0-295.9 occurring in children

EXCLUDES *childhood type schizophrenia (299.9)*
infantile autism (299.0)

The following fifth-digit subclassification is for use with category 295:

0 unspecified
1 subchronic
2 chronic
3 subchronic with acute exacerbation
4 chronic with acute exacerbation
5 in remission

DEF: Group of disorders with disturbances in thought (delusions, hallucinations), mood (blunted, flattened, inappropriate affect), sense of self, relationship to world; also bizarre, purposeless behavior, repetitious activity, or inactivity.

§ ✓5th 295.0 **Simple type** CC 0-4
Schizophrenia simplex
EXCLUDES *latent schizophrenia (295.5)*
CC Excl: For codes 295.00-295.04: 295.00-301.9, 306.0-319

§ ✓5th 295.1 **Disorganized type** CC 0-4
Hebephrenia
Hebephrenic type schizophrenia
CC Excl: For codes 295.10-295.14: See code 295.0

DEF: Inappropriate behavior; results in extreme incoherence and disorganization of time, place and sense of social appropriateness; withdrawal from routine social interaction may occur.

§ ✓5th 295.2 **Catatonic type** CC 1-4
Catatonic (schizophrenia):
- agitation
- excitation
- excited type
- stupor
- withdrawn type

Schizophrenic:
- catalepsy
- catatonia
- flexibilitas cerea

CC Excl: For codes 295.21-295.24: See code 295.0

DEF: Extreme changes in motor activity; one extreme is decreased response or reaction to the environment and the other is spontaneous activity.

§ ✓5th 295.3 **Paranoid type** CC 0-4
Paraphrenic schizophrenia
EXCLUDES *involutional paranoid state (297.2)*
paranoia (297.1)
paraphrenia (297.2)
CC Excl: For codes 295.30–295.34: See code 295.0

DRG 430 For code 295.34, 295.30

DEF: Preoccupied with delusional suspicions and auditory hallucinations related to single theme; usually hostile, grandiose, overly religious, occasionally hypochondriacal.

§ ✓5th 295.4 **Schizophreniform disorder** CC 0-4
Oneirophrenia
Schizophreniform:
- attack

Schizophreniform:
- psychosis, confusional type

EXCLUDES *acute forms of schizophrenia of:*
- *catatonic type (295.2)*
- *hebephrenic type (295.1)*
- *paranoid type (295.3)*
- *simple type (295.0)*
- *undifferentiated type (295.8)*

CC Excl: For codes 295.40-295.44: See code 295.0

§ ✓5th 295.5 **Latent schizophrenia**
Latent schizophrenic reaction
Schizophrenia:
- borderline
- incipient
- prepsychotic
- prodromal
- pseudoneurotic
- pseudopsychopathic

EXCLUDES *schizoid personality (301.20-301.22)*
AHA: For code 295.50; ▶1Q, '06, 10◀

§ ✓5th 295.6 **Residual type** CC 0-4
Chronic undifferentiated schizophrenia
Restzustand (schizophrenic)
Schizophrenic residual state
CC Excl: For codes 295.60-295.64: See code 295.0

§ ✓5th 295.7 **Schizoaffective disorder** CC 0-4
Cyclic schizophrenia
Mixed schizophrenic and affective psychosis
Schizo-affective psychosis
Schizophreniform psychosis, affective type
CC Excl: For codes 295.70-295.74: See code 295.0

DRG 430 For code 295.70

§ Requires fifth-digit. See category 295 for codes and definitions.

§ ✓5th 295.8 **Other specified types of schizophrenia** CC 0-4
Acute (undifferentiated) schizophrenia
Atypical schizophrenia
Cenesthopathic schizophrenia
EXCLUDES *infantile autism (299.0)*
CC Excl: For codes 295.80-295.84: See code 295.0

§ ✓5th 295.9 **Unspecified schizophrenia** CC 0-4
Schizophrenia:
- NOS
- mixed NOS
- undifferentiated NOS
- undifferentiated type

Schizophrenic reaction NOS
Schizophreniform psychosis NOS
CC Excl: For codes 295.90-295.94: See code 295.0

AHA: 3Q, '95, 6

✓4th **296 Episodic mood disorders**
INCLUDES episodic affective disorders
EXCLUDES *neurotic depression (300.4)*
reactive depressive psychosis (298.0)
reactive excitation (298.1)

The following fifth-digit subclassification is for use with categories 296.0-296.6:
- **0 unspecified**
- **1 mild**
- **2 moderate**
- **3 severe, without mention of psychotic behavior**
- **4 severe, specified as with psychotic behavior**
- **5 in partial or unspecified remission**
- **6 in full remission**

AHA: M-A, '85, 14

✓5th 296.0 **Bipolar I disorder, single manic episode** CC 4
Hypomania (mild) NOS
Hypomanic psychosis
Mania (monopolar) NOS
Manic-depressive psychosis or reaction:
- hypomanic
- manic

} single episode or unspecified

EXCLUDES *circular type, if there was a previous attack of depression (296.4)*
CC Excl: For code 296.04: See code 295.0

DEF: Mood disorder identified by hyperactivity; may show extreme agitation or exaggerated excitability; speech and thought processes may be accelerated.

✓5th 296.1 **Manic disorder, recurrent episode** CC 4
Any condition classifiable to 296.0, stated to be recurrent
EXCLUDES *circular type, if there was a previous attack of depression (296.4)*
CC Excl: For code 296.14: See code 295.0

✓5th 296.2 **Major depressive disorder, single episode**
Depressive psychosis
Endogenous depression
Involutional melancholia
Manic-depressive psychosis or reaction, depressed type
Monopolar depression
Psychotic depression

} single episode or unspecified

EXCLUDES *circular type, if previous attack was of manic type (296.5)*
depression NOS (311)
reactive depression (neurotic) (300.4)
psychotic (298.0)

DRG 430 For code 296.20

DEF: Mood disorder that produces depression; may exhibit as sadness, low self-esteem, or guilt feelings; other manifestations may be withdrawal from friends and family; interrupted sleep.

N Newborn Age: 0 P Pediatric Age: 0-17 M Maternity Age: 12-55 A Adult Age: 15-124 CC CC Condition MC Major Complication CD Complex Dx HIV HIV Related Dx

✓5th **296.3 Major depressive disorder, recurrent episode** CC 4
Any condition classifiable to 296.2, stated to be recurrent
EXCLUDES *circular type, if previous attack was of manic type (296.5)*
depression NOS (311)
reactive depression (neurotic) (300.4)
psychotic (298.0)
CC Excl: For code 296.34: See code 295.0
DRG 430 For code 296.30, 296.33 and 296.34

✓5th **296.4 Bipolar I disorder, most recent episode (or current) manic** CC 4
Bipolar disorder, now manic
Manic-depressive psychosis, circular type but currently manic
EXCLUDES *brief compensatory or rebound mood swings (296.99)*
CC Excl: For code 296.44: See code 295.0

✓5th **296.5 Bipolar I disorder, most recent episode (or current) depressed** CC 4
Bipolar disorder, now depressed
Manic-depressive psychosis, circular type but currently depressed
EXCLUDES *brief compensatory or rebound mood swings (296.99)*
CC Excl: For code 296.54: See code 295.0

✓5th **296.6 Bipolar I disorder, most recent episode (or current) mixed** CC 4
Manic-depressive psychosis, circular type, mixed
CC Excl: For code 296.64: See code 295.0

296.7 Bipolar I disorder, most recent episode (or current) unspecified
Atypical bipolar affective disorder NOS
Manic-depressive psychosis, circular type, current condition not specified as either manic or depressive
DEF: Manic-depressive disorder referred to as bipolar because of the mood range from manic to depressive.

✓5th **296.8 Other and unspecified bipolar disorders**
296.80 Bipolar disorder, unspecified
Bipolar disorder NOS
Manic-depressive:
reaction NOS
syndrome NOS
296.81 Atypical manic disorder
296.82 Atypical depressive disorder
296.89 Other
Bipolar II disorder
Manic-depressive psychosis, mixed type

✓5th **296.9 Other and unspecified episodic mood disorder**
EXCLUDES *psychogenic affective psychoses (298.0-298.8)*
296.90 Unspecified episodic mood disorder
Affective psychosis NOS
Melancholia NOS
Mood disorder NOS
AHA: M-A, '85, 14
296.99 Other specified episodic mood disorder
Mood swings: brief compensatory
Mood swings: rebound

✓4th **297 Delusional disorders**
INCLUDES paranoid disorders
EXCLUDES *acute paranoid reaction (298.3)*
alcoholic jealousy or paranoid state (291.5)
paranoid schizophrenia (295.3)
297.0 Paranoid state, simple
297.1 Delusional disorder
Chronic paranoid psychosis
Sander's disease
Systematized delusions
EXCLUDES *paranoid personality disorder (301.0)*

297.2 Paraphrenia
Involutional paranoid state
Late paraphrenia
Paraphrenia (involutional)
DEF: Paranoid schizophrenic disorder that persists over a prolonged period but does not distort personality despite persistent delusions.

297.3 Shared psychotic disorder
Folie à deux
Induced psychosis or paranoid disorder
DEF: Mental disorder two people share; first person with the delusional disorder convinces second person because of a close relationship and shared experiences to accept the delusions.

297.8 Other specified paranoid states
Paranoia querulans
Sensitiver Beziehungswahn
EXCLUDES *acute paranoid reaction or state (298.3)*
senile paranoid state (290.20)

297.9 Unspecified paranoid state
Paranoid: disorder NOS, psychosis NOS
Paranoid: reaction NOS, state NOS
AHA: J-A, '85, 9

✓4th **298 Other nonorganic psychoses**
INCLUDES psychotic conditions due to or provoked by:
emotional stress
environmental factors as major part of etiology

298.0 Depressive type psychosis CC
Psychogenic depressive psychosis
Psychotic reactive depression
Reactive depressive psychosis
EXCLUDES *manic-depressive psychosis, depressed type (296.2-296.3)*
neurotic depression (300.4)
reactive depression NOS (300.4)
CC Excl: See code 295.0

298.1 Excitative type psychosis
Acute hysterical psychosis
Reactive excitation
Psychogenic excitation
EXCLUDES *manic-depressive psychosis, manic type (296.0-296.1)*
DEF: Affective disorder similar to manic-depressive psychosis, in the manic phase, seemingly brought on by stress.

298.2 Reactive confusion
Psychogenic confusion
Psychogenic twilight state
EXCLUDES *acute confusional state (293.0)*
DEF: Confusion, disorientation, cloudiness in consciousness; brought on by severe emotional upheaval.

298.3 Acute paranoid reaction CC
Acute psychogenic paranoid psychosis
Bouffée délirante
EXCLUDES *paranoid states (297.0-297.9)*
CC Excl: See code 295.0

298.4 Psychogenic paranoid psychosis CC
Protracted reactive paranoid psychosis
CC Excl: See code 295.0

298.8 Other and unspecified reactive psychosis
Brief psychotic disorder
Brief reactive psychosis NOS
Hysterical psychosis
Psychogenic psychosis NOS
Psychogenic stupor
EXCLUDES *acute hysterical psychosis (298.1)*

298.9 Unspecified psychosis HIV
Atypical psychosis
Psychosis NOS
Psychotic disorder NOS
DRG 430

✓4th **299 Pervasive developmental disorders**

EXCLUDES *adult type psychoses occurring in childhood, as:*
affective disorders (296.0-296.9)
manic-depressive disorders (296.0-296.9)
schizophrenia (295.0-295.9)

The following fifth-digit subclassification is for use with category 299:
0 current or active state
1 residual state

✓5th **299.0 Autistic disorder** CC 0

Childhood autism
Infantile psychosis
Kanner's syndrome

EXCLUDES *disintegrative psychosis (299.1)*
Heller's syndrome (299.1)
schizophrenic syndrome of childhood (299.9)

CC Excl: For code 299.00: See code 295.0

DEF: Severe mental disorder of children, results in impaired social behavior; abnormal development of communicative skills, appears to be unaware of the need for emotional support and offers little emotional response to family members.

✓5th **299.1 Childhood disintegrative disorder** CC 0

Heller's syndrome
Use additional code to identify any associated neurological disorder

EXCLUDES *infantile autism (299.0)*
schizophrenic syndrome of childhood (299.9)

CC Excl: For code 299.10: See code 295.0

DEF: Mental disease of children identified by impaired development of reciprocal social skills, verbal and nonverbal communication skills, imaginative play.

✓5th **299.8 Other specified pervasive developmental disorders** CC 0

Asperger's disorder
Atypical childhood psychosis
Borderline psychosis of childhood

EXCLUDES *simple stereotypes without psychotic disturbance (307.3)*

CC Excl: For code 299.80: See code 295.0

✓5th **299.9 Unspecified pervasive developmental disorder** CC 0

Child psychosis NOS
Pervasive developmental disorder NOS
Schizophrenia, childhood type NOS
Schizophrenic syndrome of childhood NOS

EXCLUDES *schizophrenia of adult type occurring in childhood (295.0-295.9)*

CC Excl: For code 299.90: See code 295.0

NEUROTIC DISORDERS, PERSONALITY DISORDERS, AND OTHER NONPSYCHOTIC MENTAL DISORDERS (300-316)

✓4th **300 Anxiety, dissociative and somatoform disorders**

✓5th **300.0 Anxiety states**

EXCLUDES *anxiety in:*
acute stress reaction (308.0)
transient adjustment reaction (309.24)
neurasthenia (300.5)
psychophysiological disorders (306.0-306.9)
separation anxiety (309.21)

DEF: Mental disorder characterized by anxiety and avoidance behavior not particularly related to any specific situation or stimulus; symptoms include emotional instability, apprehension, fatigue.

300.00 Anxiety state, unspecified

Anxiety:
neurosis
reaction
Anxiety:
state (neurotic)
Atypical anxiety disorder

AHA: 1Q, '02, 6

DRG 425

300.01 Panic disorder without agoraphobia

Panic:
attack
Panic:
state

EXCLUDES *panic disorder with agoraphobia (300.21)*

DEF: Neurotic disorder characterized by recurrent panic or anxiety, apprehension, fear or terror; symptoms include shortness of breath, palpitations, dizziness, faintness or shakiness; fear of dying may persist or fear of other morbid consequences.

DRG 425

300.02 Generalized anxiety disorder

DRG 425

300.09 Other

✓5th **300.1 Dissociative, conversion and factitious disorders**

EXCLUDES *adjustment reaction (309.0-309.9)*
anorexia nervosa (307.1)
gross stress reaction (308.0-308.9)
hysterical personality (301.50-301.59)
psychophysiologic disorders (306.0-306.9)

300.10 Hysteria, unspecified

300.11 Conversion disorder

Astasia-abasia, hysterical
Conversion hysteria or reaction
Hysterical:
blindness
deafness
paralysis

AHA: N-D, '85, 15

DRG 425

DEF: Mental disorder that impairs physical functions with no physiological basis; sensory motor symptoms include seizures, paralysis, temporary blindness; increase in stress or avoidance of unpleasant responsibilities may precipitate.

300.12 Dissociative amnesia

Hysterical amnesia

300.13 Dissociative fugue

Hysterical fugue

DEF: Dissociative hysteria; identified by loss of memory, flight from familiar surroundings; conscious activity is not associated with perception of surroundings, no later memory of episode.

300.14 Dissociative identity disorder

300.15 Dissociative disorder or reaction, unspecified

DEF: Hysterical neurotic episode; sudden but temporary changes in perceived identity, memory, consciousness, segregated memory patterns exist separate from dominant personality.

300.16 Factitious disorder with predominantly psychological signs and symptoms

Compensation neurosis
Ganser's syndrome, hysterical

DEF: A disorder characterized by the purposeful assumption of mental illness symptoms; the symptoms are not real, possibly representing what the patient imagines mental illness to be like, and are acted out more often when another person is present.

300.19 Other and unspecified factitious illness

Factitious disorder (with combined psychological and physical signs and symptoms) (with predominantly physical signs and symptoms) NOS

EXCLUDES *multiple operations or hospital addiction syndrome (301.51)*

✓5th **300.2 Phobic disorders**

EXCLUDES *anxiety state not associated with a specific situation or object (300.00-300.09)*
obsessional phobias (300.3)

300.20 Phobia, unspecified

Anxiety-hysteria NOS
Phobia NOS

300.21 Agoraphobia with panic disorder
Fear of:
open spaces, streets, travel } with panic attacks
Panic disorder with agoraphobia
EXCLUDES *agoraphobia without panic disorder (300.22)*
panic disorder without agoraphobia (300.01)

300.22 Agoraphobia without mention of panic attacks
Any condition classifiable to 300.21 without mention of panic attacks

300.23 Social phobia
Fear of:
eating in public
public speaking
Fear of:
washing in public

300.29 Other isolated or specific phobias
Acrophobia
Animal phobias
Claustrophobia
Fear of crowds

300.3 Obsessive-compulsive disorders
Anancastic neurosis
Compulsive neurosis
Obsessional phobia [any]
EXCLUDES *obsessive-compulsive symptoms occurring in:*
endogenous depression (296.2-296.3)
organic states (eg., encephalitis)
schizophrenia (295.0-295.9)

300.4 Dysthymic disorder
Anxiety depression
Depression with anxiety
Depressive reaction
Neurotic depressive state
Reactive depression
EXCLUDES *adjustment reaction with depressive symptoms (309.0-309.1)*
depression NOS (311)
manic-depressive psychosis, depressed type (296.2-296.3)
reactive depressive psychosis (298.0)

DEF: Depression without psychosis; less severe depression related to personal change or unexpected circumstances; also referred to as "reactional depression."

300.5 Neurasthenia
Fatigue neurosis
Nervous debility
Psychogenic:
asthenia
general fatigue
Use additional code to identify any associated physical disorder
EXCLUDES *anxiety state (300.00-300.09)*
neurotic depression (300.4)
psychophysiological disorders (306.0-306.9)
specific nonpsychotic mental disorders following organic brain damage (310.0-310.9)

DEF: Physical and mental symptoms caused primarily by what is known as mental exhaustion; symptoms include chronic weakness, fatigue.

300.6 Depersonalization disorder
Derealization (neurotic)
Neurotic state with depersonalization episode
EXCLUDES *depersonalization associated with:*
anxiety (300.00-300.09)
depression (300.4)
manic-depressive disorder or psychosis (296.0-296.9)
schizophrenia (295.0-295.9)

DEF: Dissociative disorder characterized by feelings of strangeness about self or body image; symptoms include dizziness, anxiety, fear of insanity, loss of reality of surroundings.

300.7 Hypochondriasis
Body dysmorphic disorder
EXCLUDES *hypochondriasis in:*
hysteria (300.10-300.19)
manic-depressive psychosis, depressed type (296.2-296.3)
neurasthenia (300.5)
obsessional disorder (300.3)
schizophrenia (295.0-295.9)

✓5th **300.8 Somatoform disorders**

300.81 Somatization disorder
Briquet's disorder
Severe somatoform disorder

300.82 Undifferentiated somatoform disorder
Atypical somatoform disorder
Somatoform disorder NOS
AHA: 4Q, '96, 29

DEF: Disorders in which patients have symptoms that suggest an organic disease but no evidence of physical disorder after repeated testing.

300.89 Other somatoform disorders
Occupational neurosis, including writers' cramp
Psychasthenia
Psychasthenic neurosis

300.9 Unspecified nonpsychotic mental disorder
Psychoneurosis NOS
DRG 425

✓4th **301 Personality disorders**
INCLUDES character neurosis
Use additional code to identify any associated neurosis or psychosis, or physical condition
EXCLUDES *nonpsychotic personality disorder associated with organic brain syndromes (310.0-310.9)*

301.0 Paranoid personality disorder
Fanatic personality
Paranoid personality (disorder)
Paranoid traits
EXCLUDES *acute paranoid reaction (298.3)*
alcoholic paranoia (291.5)
paranoid schizophrenia (295.3)
paranoid states (297.0-297.9)
AHA: J-A, '85, 9

✓5th **301.1 Affective personality disorder**
EXCLUDES *affective psychotic disorders (296.0-296.9)*
neurasthenia (300.5)
neurotic depression (300.4)

301.10 Affective personality disorder, unspecified

301.11 Chronic hypomanic personality disorder
Chronic hypomanic disorder
Hypomanic personality

301.12 Chronic depressive personality disorder
Chronic depressive disorder
Depressive character or personality

301.13 Cyclothymic disorder
Cycloid personality
Cyclothymia
Cyclothymic personality

✓5th **301.2 Schizoid personality disorder**
EXCLUDES *schizophrenia (295.0-295.9)*

301.20 Schizoid personality disorder, unspecified

301.21 Introverted personality

301.22 Schizotypal personality disorder

301.3 Explosive personality disorder
Aggressive:
personality
reaction
Aggressiveness
Emotional instability (excessive)
Pathological emotionality
Quarrelsomeness
EXCLUDES *dyssocial personality (301.7)*
hysterical neurosis (300.10-300.19)

301.4 Obsessive-compulsive personality disorder
Anancastic personality
Obsessional personality
EXCLUDES *obsessive-compulsive disorder (300.3)*
phobic state (300.20-300.29)

✓5th **301.5 Histrionic personality disorder**
EXCLUDES *hysterical neurosis (300.10-300.19)*
DEF: Extreme emotional behavior, often theatrical; often concerned about own appeal; may demand attention, exhibit seductive behavior.

301.50 Histrionic personality disorder, unspecified
Hysterical personality NOS

301.51 Chronic factitious illness with physical symptoms
Hospital addiction syndrome
Multiple operations syndrome
Munchausen syndrome

301.59 Other histrionic personality disorder
Personality:
emotionally unstable
labile
psychoinfantile

301.6 Dependent personality disorder
Asthenic personality
Inadequate personality
Passive personality
EXCLUDES *neurasthenia (300.5)*
passive-aggressive personality (301.84)
DEF: Overwhelming feeling of helplessness; fears of abandonment may persist; difficulty in making personal decisions without confirmation by others; low self-esteem due to irrational sensitivity to criticism.

301.7 Antisocial personality disorder
Amoral personality
Asocial personality
Dyssocial personality
Personality disorder with predominantly sociopathic or asocial manifestation
EXCLUDES *disturbance of conduct without specifiable personality disorder (312.0-312.9)*
explosive personality (301.3)

AHA: S-0, '84, 16

DEF: Continuous antisocial behavior that violates rights of others; social traits include extreme aggression, total disregard for traditional social rules.

✓5th **301.8 Other personality disorders**

301.81 Narcissistic personality disorder
DEF: Grandiose fantasy or behavior, lack of social empathy, hypersensitive to the lack of others' judgment, exploits others; also sense of entitlement to have expectations met, need for continual admiration.

301.82 Avoidant personality disorder
DEF: Personality disorder marked by feelings of social inferiority; sensitivity to criticism, emotionally restrained due to fear of rejection.

301.83 Borderline personality disorder
DEF: Personality disorder characterized by unstable moods, self-image, and interpersonal relationships; uncontrolled anger, impulsive and self-destructive acts, fears of abandonment, feelings of emptiness and boredom, recurrent suicide threats or self-mutilation.

301.84 Passive-aggressive personality
DEF: Pattern of procrastination and refusal to meet standards; introduce own obstacles to success and exploit failure.

301.89 Other
Personality:
eccentric
"haltlose" type
immature
masochistic
psychoneurotic
EXCLUDES *psychoinfantile personality (301.59)*

301.9 Unspecified personality disorder
Pathological personality NOS
Personality disorder NOS
Psychopathic:
constitutional state
personality (disorder)

✓4th **302 Sexual and gender identity disorders**
EXCLUDES *sexual disorder manifest in:*
organic brain syndrome (290.0-294.9, 310.0-310.9)
psychosis (295.0-298.9)

302.0 Ego-dystonic sexual orientation
Ego-dystonic lesbianism
Sexual orientation conflict disorder
EXCLUDES *homosexual pedophilia (302.2)*

302.1 Zoophilia
Bestiality
DEF: A sociodeviant disorder marked by engaging in sexual intercourse with animals.

302.2 Pedophilia
DEF: A sociodeviant condition of adults characterized by sexual activity with children.

302.3 Transvestic fetishism
EXCLUDES *trans-sexualism (302.5)*
DEF: The desire to dress in clothing of opposite sex.

302.4 Exhibitionism
DEF: Sexual deviant behavior; exposure of genitals to strangers; behavior prompted by intense sexual urges and fantasies.

✓5th **302.5 Trans-sexualism**
EXCLUDES *transvestism (302.3)*
DEF: Gender identity disturbance; overwhelming desire to change anatomic sex, due to belief that individual is a member of the opposite sex.

302.50 With unspecified sexual history
302.51 With asexual history
302.52 With homosexual history
302.53 With heterosexual history

302.6 Gender identity disorder in children
Feminism in boys
Gender identity disorder NOS
EXCLUDES *gender identity disorder in adult (302.85)*
trans-sexualism (302.50-302.53)
transvestism (302.3)

✓5th **302.7 Psychosexual dysfunction**
EXCLUDES *impotence of organic origin (607.84)*
normal transient symptoms from ruptured hymen
transient or occasional failures of erection due to fatigue, anxiety, alcohol, or drugs

302.70 Psychosexual dysfunction, unspecified
Sexual dysfunction NOS

302.71 Hypoactive sexual desire disorder
EXCLUDES *decreased sexual desire NOS (799.81)*

302.72 With inhibited sexual excitement
Female sexual arousal disorder
Frigidity
Impotence
Male erectile disorder

302.73 Female orgasmic disorder ♀
302.74 Male orgasmic disorder ♂
302.75 Premature ejaculation ♂

N Newborn Age: 0 P Pediatric Age: 0-17 M Maternity Age: 12-55 A Adult Age: 15-124 CC CC Condition MC Major Complication CD Complex Dx HIV HIV Related Dx

302.76 Dyspareunia, psychogenic ♀

DEF: Difficult or painful sex due to psychosomatic state.

302.79 With other specified psychosexual dysfunctions

Sexual aversion disorder

✓5th **302.8 Other specified psychosexual disorders**

302.81 Fetishism

DEF: Psychosexual disorder noted for intense sexual urges and arousal precipitated by fantasies; use of inanimate objects, such as clothing, to stimulate sexual arousal, orgasm.

302.82 Voyeurism

DEF: Psychosexual disorder characterized by uncontrollable impulse to observe others, without their knowledge, who are nude or engaged in sexual activity.

302.83 Sexual masochism

DEF: Psychosexual disorder noted for need to achieve sexual gratification through humiliating or hurtful acts inflicted on self.

302.84 Sexual sadism

DEF: Psychosexual disorder noted for need to achieve sexual gratification through humiliating or hurtful acts inflicted on someone else.

302.85 Gender identity disorder in adolescents or adults

EXCLUDES *gender identity disorder NOS (302.6)*
gender identity disorder in children (302.6)

302.89 Other

Frotteurism
Nymphomania
Satyriasis

302.9 Unspecified psychosexual disorder

Paraphilia NOS
Pathologic sexuality NOS
Sexual deviation NOS
Sexual disorder NOS

✓4th **303 Alcohol dependence syndrome**

Use additional code to identify any associated condition, as:
- alcoholic psychoses (291.0-291.9)
- drug dependence (304.0-304.9)
- physical complications of alcohol, such as:
  - cerebral degeneration (331.7)
  - cirrhosis of liver (571.2)
  - epilepsy (345.0-345.9)
  - gastritis (535.3)
  - hepatitis (571.1)
  - liver damage NOS (571.3)

EXCLUDES *drunkenness NOS (305.0)*

The following fifth-digit subclassification is for use with category 303:

0 unspecified **2 episodic**
1 continuous **3 in remission**

AHA: 3Q, '95, 6; 2Q, '91, 9; 4Q, '88, 8; S-O, '86, 3

✓5th **303.0 Acute alcoholic intoxication** CC 0-2

Acute drunkenness in alcoholism

CC Excl: For codes 303.00-303.02: 291.0-292.9, 303.00-305.03, 305.20-305.93, 790.3

✓5th **303.9 Other and unspecified alcohol dependence** CC 0-2

Chronic alcoholism Dipsomania

CC Excl: For codes 303.90-303.92: See code 303.0

AHA: 2Q, '02, 4; 2Q, '89, 9

✓4th **304 Drug dependence**

EXCLUDES *nondependent abuse of drugs (305.1-305.9)*

The following fifth-digit subclassification is for use with category 304:

0 unspecified **2 episodic**
1 continuous **3 in remission**

AHA: 2Q, '91, 10; 4Q, '88, 8; S-O, '86, 3

✓5th **304.0 Opioid type dependence** CC 0-2

Heroin
Meperidine
Methadone
Morphine
Opium
Opium alkaloids and their derivatives
Synthetics with morphine-like effects

CC Excl: For codes 304.00-304.02: See code 303.0

✓5th **304.1 Sedative, hypnotic or anxiolytic dependence** CC 0-2

Barbiturates
Nonbarbiturate sedatives and tranquilizers with a similar effect:
- chlordiazepoxide
- diazepam
- glutethimide
- meprobamate
- methaqualone

CC Excl: For codes 304.10-304.12: See code 303.0

✓5th **304.2 Cocaine dependence** CC 0-2

Coca leaves and derivatives

CC Excl: For codes 304.20-304.22: See code 303.0

✓5th **304.3 Cannabis dependence**

Hashish
Hemp
Marihuana

✓5th **304.4 Amphetamine and other psychostimulant dependence** CC 0-2

Methylphenidate Phenmetrazine

CC Excl: For codes 304.40-304.42: See code 303.0

✓5th **304.5 Hallucinogen dependence** CC 0-2

Dimethyltryptamine [DMT]
Lysergic acid diethylamide [LSD] and derivatives
Mescaline
Psilocybin

CC Excl: For codes 304.50-304.52: See code 303.0

✓5th **304.6 Other specified drug dependence** CC 0-2

Absinthe addiction
Glue sniffing
Inhalant dependence
Phencyclidine dependence

EXCLUDES *tobacco dependence (305.1)*

CC Excl: For codes 304.60-304.62: See code 303.0

✓5th **304.7 Combinations of opioid type drug with any other** CC 0-2

CC Excl: For codes 304.70-304.72: See code 303.0

AHA: M-A, '86, 12

✓5th **304.8 Combinations of drug dependence excluding opioid type drug** CC 0-2

CC Excl: For codes 304.80-304.82: See code 303.0

AHA: M-A, '86, 12

✓5th **304.9 Unspecified drug dependence** CC 0-2

Drug addiction NOS Drug dependence NOS

CC Excl: For codes 304.90-304.92: See code 303.0

AHA: For code 304.90: 4Q, '03, 103

✓4th **305 Nondependent abuse of drugs**

Note: Includes cases where a person, for whom no other diagnosis is possible, has come under medical care because of the maladaptive effect of a drug on which he is not dependent and that he has taken on his own initiative to the detriment of his health or social functioning.

EXCLUDES *alcohol dependence syndrome (303.0-303.9)*
drug dependence (304.0-304.9)
drug withdrawal syndrome (292.0)
poisoning by drugs or medicinal substances (960.0-979.9)

The following fifth-digit subclassification is for use with codes 305.0, 305.2-305.9:

0 unspecified **2 episodic**
1 continuous **3 in remission**

AHA: 2Q, '91, 10; 4Q, '88, 8; S-O, '86, 3

§ ✓5th **305.0 Alcohol abuse** CC 0-2

Drunkenness NOS

Excessive drinking of alcohol NOS

"Hangover" (alcohol)

Inebriety NOS

EXCLUDES *acute alcohol intoxication in alcoholism (303.0)*

alcoholic psychoses (291.0-291.9)

CC Excl: For codes 305.00-305.02: See code 303.0

AHA: 3Q, '96, 16

305.1 Tobacco use disorder

Tobacco dependence

EXCLUDES *history of tobacco use (V15.82)*

▶*smoking complicating pregnancy (649.0)*

tobacco use disorder complicating pregnancy (649.0)◀

AHA: 2Q, '96, 10; N-D, '84, 12

§ ✓5th **305.2 Cannabis abuse**

§ ✓5th **305.3 Hallucinogen abuse** CC 0-2

Acute intoxication from hallucinogens ["bad trips"]

LSD reaction

CC Excl: For codes 305.30-305.32: See code 303.0

§ ✓5th **305.4 Sedative, hypnotic or anxiolytic abuse** CC 0-2

CC Excl: For codes 305.40-305.42: See code 303.0

§ ✓5th **305.5 Opioid abuse** CC 0-2

CC Excl: For codes 305.50-305.52: See code 303.0

§ ✓5th **305.6 Cocaine abuse** CC 0-2

CC Excl: For codes 305.60-305.62: See code 303.0

AHA: For code 305.60: 1Q, '05, 6; 1Q, '93, 25

§ ✓5th **305.7 Amphetamine or related acting sympathomimetic abuse** CC 0-2

CC Excl: For codes 305.70-305.72: See code 303.0

AHA: For code 305.70: 2Q, '03, 10–11

§ ✓5th **305.8 Antidepressant type abuse**

§ ✓5th **305.9 Other, mixed, or unspecified drug abuse** CC 0-2

Caffeine intoxication

Inhalant abuse

"Laxative habit"

Misuse of drugs NOS

Nonprescribed use of drugs or patent medicinals

Phencyclidine abuse

CC Excl: For codes 305.90-305.92: See code 303.0

AHA: 3Q, '99, 20

✓4th **306 Physiological malfunction arising from mental factors**

INCLUDES psychogenic:

physical symptoms / physiological manifestations } not involving tissue damage

EXCLUDES *hysteria (300.11-300.19)*

physical symptoms secondary to a psychiatric disorder classified elsewhere

psychic factors associated with physical conditions involving tissue damage classified elsewhere (316)

specific nonpsychotic mental disorders following organic brain damage (310.0-310.9)

DEF: Functional disturbances or interruptions due to mental or psychological causes; no tissue damage sustained in these conditions.

306.0 Musculoskeletal

Psychogenic paralysis

Psychogenic torticollis

EXCLUDES *Gilles de la Tourette's syndrome (307.23)*

paralysis as hysterical or conversion reaction (300.11)

tics (307.20-307.22)

§ Requires fifth-digit. See category 305 for codes and definitions.

306.1 Respiratory

Psychogenic:

air hunger

cough

hiccough

Psychogenic:

hyperventilation

yawning

EXCLUDES *psychogenic asthma (316 and 493.9)*

306.2 Cardiovascular

Cardiac neurosis

Cardiovascular neurosis

Neurocirculatory asthenia

Psychogenic cardiovascular disorder

EXCLUDES *psychogenic paroxysmal tachycardia (316 and 427.2)*

AHA: J-A, '85, 14

DEF: Neurocirculatory asthenia: functional nervous and circulatory irregularities with palpitations, dyspnea, fatigue, rapid pulse, precordial pain, fear of effort, discomfort during exercise, anxiety; also called DaCosta's syndrome, Effort syndrome, Irritable or Soldier's Heart.

306.3 Skin

Psychogenic pruritus

EXCLUDES *psychogenic:*

alopecia (316 and 704.00)

dermatitis (316 and 692.9)

eczema (316 and 691.8 or 692.9)

urticaria (316 and 708.0-708.9)

306.4 Gastrointestinal

Aerophagy

Cyclical vomiting, psychogenic

Diarrhea, psychogenic

Nervous gastritis

Psychogenic dyspepsia

EXCLUDES *cyclical vomiting NOS (536.2)*

globus hystericus (300.11)

mucous colitis (316 and 564.9)

psychogenic:

cardiospasm (316 and 530.0)

duodenal ulcer (316 and 532.0-532.9)

gastric ulcer (316 and 531.0-531.9)

peptic ulcer NOS (316 and 533.0-533.9)

vomiting NOS (307.54)

AHA: 2Q, '89, 11

DEF: Aerophagy: excess swallowing of air, usually unconscious; related to anxiety; results in distended abdomen or belching, often interpreted by the patient as a physical disorder.

✓5th **306.5 Genitourinary**

EXCLUDES *enuresis, psychogenic (307.6)*

frigidity (302.72)

impotence (302.72)

psychogenic dyspareunia (302.76)

306.50 Psychogenic genitourinary malfunction, unspecified

306.51 Psychogenic vaginismus ♀

Functional vaginismus

DEF: Psychogenic response resulting in painful contractions of vaginal canal muscles; can be severe enough to prevent sexual intercourse.

306.52 Psychogenic dysmenorrhea ♀

306.53 Psychogenic dysuria

306.59 Other

AHA: M-A, '87, 11

306.6 Endocrine

306.7 Organs of special sense

EXCLUDES *hysterical blindness or deafness (300.11)*

psychophysical visual disturbances (368.16)

306.8 Other specified psychophysiological malfunction

Bruxism

Teeth grinding

306.9 Unspecified psychophysiological malfunction

Psychophysiologic disorder NOS

Psychosomatic disorder NOS

✓4th 307 Special symptoms or syndromes, not elsewhere classified

Note: This category is intended for use if the psychopathology is manifested by a single specific symptom or group of symptoms which is not part of an organic illness or other mental disorder classifiable elsewhere.

EXCLUDES *those due to mental disorders classified elsewhere*
those of organic origin

307.0 Stuttering

EXCLUDES *dysphasia (784.5)*
lisping or lalling (307.9)
retarded development of speech (315.31-315.39)

307.1 Anorexia nervosa CC

EXCLUDES *eating disturbance NOS (307.50)*
feeding problem (783.3)
of nonorganic origin (307.59)
loss of appetite (783.0)
of nonorganic origin (307.59)

CC Excl: 306.4, 306.8-306.9, 307.1, 307.50-307.59, 309.22

AHA: 4Q, '89, 11

✓5th 307.2 Tics

EXCLUDES *nail-biting or thumb-sucking (307.9)*
stereotypes occurring in isolation (307.3)
tics of organic origin (333.3)

DEF: Involuntary muscle response usually confined to the face, shoulders.

307.20 Tic disorder, unspecified

Tic disorder NOS

307.21 Transient tic disorder

307.22 Chronic motor or vocal tic disorder

307.23 Tourette's disorder

Motor-verbal tic disorder

DEF: Syndrome of facial and vocal tics in childhood; progresses to spontaneous or involuntary jerking, obscene utterances, other uncontrollable actions considered inappropriate.

307.3 Stereotypic movement disorder

Body-rocking
Head banging
Spasmus nutans
Stereotypes NOS

EXCLUDES *tics (307.20-307.23)*
of organic origin (333.3)

✓5th 307.4 Specific disorders of sleep of nonorganic origin

EXCLUDES *narcolepsy (347.00-347.11)*
organic hypersomnia (327.10-327.19)
organic insomnia (327.00-327.09)
those of unspecified cause (780.50-780.59)

307.40 Nonorganic sleep disorder, unspecified

307.41 Transient disorder of initiating or maintaining sleep

Adjustment insomnia
Hyposomnia, Insomnia, Sleeplessness } associated with intermittent emotional reactions or conflicts

307.42 Persistent disorder of initiating or maintaining sleep

Hyposomnia, insomnia, or sleeplessness associated with:
- anxiety
- conditioned arousal
- depression (major) (minor)
- psychosis

Idiopathic insomnia
Paradoxical insomnia
Primary insomnia
Psychophysiological insomnia

307.43 Transient disorder of initiating or maintaining wakefulness

Hypersomnia associated with acute or intermittent emotional reactions or conflicts

307.44 Persistent disorder of initiating or maintaining wakefulness

Hypersomnia associated with depression (major) (minor)
Insufficient sleep syndrome
Primary hypersomnia

EXCLUDES *sleep deprivation (V69.4)*

307.45 Circadian rhythm sleep disorder of nonorganic origin

307.46 Sleep arousal disorder

Night terror disorder
Night terrors
Sleep terror disorder
Sleepwalking
Somnambulism

DEF: Sleepwalking marked by extreme terror, panic, screaming, confusion; no recall of event upon arousal; term may refer to simply the act of sleepwalking.

307.47 Other dysfunctions of sleep stages or arousal from sleep

Nightmare disorder
Nightmares:
- NOS
- REM-sleep type

Sleep drunkenness

307.48 Repetitive intrusions of sleep

Repetitive intrusion of sleep with:
- atypical polysomnographic features
- environmental disturbances
- repeated REM-sleep interruptions

307.49 Other

"Short-sleeper"
Subjective insomnia complaint

✓5th 307.5 Other and unspecified disorders of eating

EXCLUDES *anorexia:*
nervosa (307-1)
of unspecified cause (783.0)
overeating, of unspecified cause (783.6)
vomiting:
NOS (787.0)
cyclical (536.2)
psychogenic (306.4)

307.50 Eating disorder, unspecified

Eating disorder NOS

307.51 Bulimia nervosa

Overeating of nonorganic origin

DEF: Mental disorder commonly characterized by binge eating followed by self-induced vomiting; perceptions of being fat; and fear the inability to stop eating voluntarily.

307.52 Pica

Perverted appetite of nonorganic origin

DEF: Compulsive eating disorder characterized by craving for substances, other than food; such as paint chips or dirt.

307.53 Rumination disorder

Regurgitation, of nonorganic origin, of food with reswallowing

EXCLUDES *obsessional rumination (300.3)*

307.54 Psychogenic vomiting

307.59 Other

Feeding disorder of infancy or early childhood of nonorganic origin
Infantile feeding disturbances, Loss of appetite } of nonorganic origin

307.6 Enuresis

Enuresis (primary) (secondary) of nonorganic origin

EXCLUDES *enuresis of unspecified cause (788.3)*

DEF: Involuntary urination past age of normal control; also called bedwetting; no trace to biological problem; focus on psychological issues.

307.7 Encopresis

Encopresis (continuous) (discontinuous) of nonorganic origin

EXCLUDES *encopresis of unspecified cause (787.6)*

DEF: Inability to control bowel movements; cause traced to psychological, not biological, problems.

✓5th **307.8 Pain disorders related to psychological factors**

307.80 Psychogenic pain, site unspecified

307.81 Tension headache

EXCLUDES *headache:*
NOS (784.0)
migraine (346.0-346.9)

AHA: N-D, '85, 16

307.89 Other

Code first to ▶type or◀ site of pain

EXCLUDES *pain disorder exclusively attributed to psychological factors (307.80)*
psychogenic pain (307.80)

307.9 Other and unspecified special symptoms or syndromes, not elsewhere classified

Communication disorder NOS
Hair plucking
Lalling
Lisping
Masturbation
Nail-biting
Thumb-sucking

✓4th **308 Acute reaction to stress**

INCLUDES catastrophic stress
combat fatigue
gross stress reaction (acute)
transient disorders in response to exceptional physical or mental stress which usually subside within hours or days

EXCLUDES *adjustment reaction or disorder (309.0-309.9)*
chronic stress reaction (309.1-309.9)

308.0 Predominant disturbance of emotions

Anxiety } as acute reaction to exceptional [gross] stress
Emotional crisis
Panic state

308.1 Predominant disturbance of consciousness

Fugues as acute reaction to exceptional [gross] stress

308.2 Predominant psychomotor disturbance

Agitation states } as acute reaction to exceptional [gross] stress
Stupor

308.3 Other acute reactions to stress

Acute situational disturbance
Acute stress disorder

EXCLUDES *prolonged posttraumatic emotional disturbance (309.81)*

308.4 Mixed disorders as reaction to stress

308.9 Unspecified acute reaction to stress

✓4th **309 Adjustment reaction**

INCLUDES adjustment disorders
reaction (adjustment) to chronic stress

EXCLUDES *acute reaction to major stress (308.0-308.9)*
neurotic disorders (300.0-300.9)

309.0 Adjustment disorder with depressed mood

Grief reaction

EXCLUDES *affective psychoses (296.0-296.9)*
neurotic depression (300.4)
prolonged depressive reaction (309.1)
psychogenic depressive psychosis (298.0)

309.1 Prolonged depressive reaction

EXCLUDES *affective psychoses (296.0-296.9)*
brief depressive reaction (309.0)
neurotic depression (300.4)
psychogenic depressive psychosis (298.0)

✓5th **309.2 With predominant disturbance of other emotions**

309.21 Separation anxiety disorder

DEF: Abnormal apprehension by a child when physically separated from support environment; byproduct of abnormal symbiotic child-parent relationship.

309.22 Emancipation disorder of adolescence and early adult life

DEF: Adjustment reaction of late adolescence; conflict over independence from parental supervision; symptoms include difficulty in making decisions, increased reliance on parental advice, deliberate adoption of values in opposition of parents.

309.23 Specific academic or work inhibition

309.24 Adjustment disorder with anxiety

309.28 Adjustment disorder with mixed anxiety and depressed mood

Adjustment reaction with anxiety and depression

309.29 Other

Culture shock

309.3 Adjustment disorder with disturbance of conduct

Conduct disturbance } as adjustment reaction
Destructiveness

EXCLUDES *destructiveness in child (312.9)*
disturbance of conduct NOS (312.9)
dyssocial behavior without manifest psychiatric disorder (V71.01-V71.02)
personality disorder with predominantly sociopathic or asocial manifestations (301.7)

309.4 Adjustment disorder with mixed disturbance of emotions and conduct

✓5th **309.8 Other specified adjustment reactions**

309.81 Posttraumatic stress disorder

Chronic posttraumatic stress disorder
Concentration camp syndrome
Posttraumatic stress disorder NOS
▶Post-traumatic stress disorder (PTSD)◀

EXCLUDES *acute stress disorder (308.3)*
posttraumatic brain syndrome:
nonpsychotic (310.2)
psychotic (293.0-293.9)

DEF: Preoccupation with traumatic events beyond normal experience; events such as rape, personal assault, combat, natural disasters, accidents, torture precipitate disorder; also recurring flashbacks of trauma; symptoms include difficulty remembering, sleeping, or concentrating, and guilt feelings for surviving.

309.82 Adjustment reaction with physical symptoms

309.83 Adjustment reaction with withdrawal

Elective mutism as adjustment reaction
Hospitalism (in children) NOS

309.89 Other

309.9 Unspecified adjustment reaction

Adaptation reaction NOS
Adjustment reaction NOS

✓4th **310 Specific nonpsychotic mental disorders due to brain damage**

EXCLUDES *neuroses, personality disorders, or other nonpsychotic conditions occurring in a form similar to that seen with functional disorders but in association with a physical condition (300.0-300.9, 301.0-301.9)*

310.0 Frontal lobe syndrome

Lobotomy syndrome
Postleucotomy syndrome [state]

EXCLUDES *postcontusion syndrome (310.2)*

310.1 Personality change due to conditions classified elsewhere
Cognitive or personality change of other type, of nonpsychotic severity
Organic psychosyndrome of nonpsychotic severity
Presbyophrenia NOS
Senility with mental changes of nonpsychotic severity
EXCLUDES *memory loss of unknown cause (780.93)*

AHA: ▶2Q, '05, 6◀

DEF: Personality disorder caused by organic factors, such as brain lesions, head trauma, or cerebrovascular accident (CVA).

310.2 Postconcussion syndrome
Postcontusion syndrome or encephalopathy
Posttraumatic brain syndrome, nonpsychotic
Status postcommotio cerebri
EXCLUDES *frontal lobe syndrome (310.0)*
postencephalitic syndrome (310.8)
any organic psychotic conditions following head injury (293.0-294.0)

AHA: 4Q, '90, 24

DEF: Nonpsychotic disorder due to brain trauma, causes symptoms unrelated to any disease process; symptoms include amnesia, serial headaches, rapid heartbeat, fatigue, disrupted sleep patterns, inability to concentrate.

310.8 Other specified nonpsychotic mental disorders following organic brain damage
Mild memory disturbance
Postencephalitic syndrome
Other focal (partial) organic psychosyndromes

310.9 Unspecified nonpsychotic mental disorder following organic brain damage HIV
AHA: 4Q, '03, 103

311 Depressive disorder, not elsewhere classified
Depressive disorder NOS
Depression NOS
Depressive state NOS
EXCLUDES *acute reaction to major stress with depressive symptoms (308.0)*
affective personality disorder (301.10-301.13)
affective psychoses (296.0-296.9)
brief depressive reaction (309.0)
depressive states associated with stressful events (309.0-309.1)
disturbance of emotions specific to childhood and adolescence, with misery and unhappiness (313.1)
mixed adjustment reaction with depressive symptoms (309.4)
neurotic depression (300.4)
prolonged depressive adjustment reaction (309.1)
psychogenic depressive psychosis (298.0)

AHA: 4Q, '03, 75

✓4th **312 Disturbance of conduct, not elsewhere classified**
EXCLUDES *adjustment reaction with disturbance of conduct (309.3)*
drug dependence (304.0-304.9)
dyssocial behavior without manifest psychiatric disorder (V71.01-V71.02)
personality disorder with predominantly sociopathic or asocial manifestations (301.7)
sexual deviations (302.0-302.9)

The following fifth-digit subclassification is for use with categories 312.0-312.2:
0 unspecified
1 mild
2 moderate
3 severe

✓5th **312.0 Undersocialized conduct disorder, aggressive type**
Aggressive outburst
Anger reaction
Unsocialized aggressive disorder

DEF: Mental condition identified by behaviors disrespectful of others' rights and of age-appropriate social norms or rules; symptoms include bullying, vandalism, verbal and physical abusiveness, lying, stealing, defiance.

✓5th **312.1 Undersocialized conduct disorder, unaggressive type**
Childhood truancy, unsocialized
Solitary stealing
Tantrums

✓5th **312.2 Socialized conduct disorder**
Childhood truancy, socialized
Group delinquency
EXCLUDES *gang activity without manifest psychiatric disorder (V71.01)*

✓5th **312.3 Disorders of impulse control, not elsewhere classified**
312.30 Impulse control disorder, unspecified
312.31 Pathological gambling
312.32 Kleptomania
312.33 Pyromania
312.34 Intermittent explosive disorder
312.35 Isolated explosive disorder
312.39 Other
Trichotillomania

312.4 Mixed disturbance of conduct and emotions
Neurotic delinquency
EXCLUDES *compulsive conduct disorder (312.3)*

✓5th **312.8 Other specified disturbances of conduct, not elsewhere classified**
312.81 Conduct disorder, childhood onset type
312.82 Conduct disorder, adolescent onset type
312.89 Other conduct disorder
Conduct disorder of unspecified onset

312.9 Unspecified disturbance of conduct
Delinquency (juvenile)
Disruptive behavior disorder NOS

✓4th **313 Disturbance of emotions specific to childhood and adolescence**
EXCLUDES *adjustment reaction (309.0-309.9)*
emotional disorder of neurotic type (300.0-300.9)
masturbation, nail-biting, thumbsucking, and other isolated symptoms (307.0-307.9)

313.0 Overanxious disorder
Anxiety and fearfulness } of childhood and adolescence
Overanxious disorder } of childhood and adolescence
EXCLUDES *abnormal separation anxiety (309.21)*
anxiety states (300.00-300.09)
hospitalism in children (309.83)
phobic state (300.20-300.29)

313.1 Misery and unhappiness disorder
EXCLUDES *depressive neurosis (300.4)*

✓5th **313.2 Sensitivity, shyness, and social withdrawal disorder**
EXCLUDES *infantile autism (299.0)*
schizoid personality (301.20-301.22)
schizophrenia (295.0-295.9)

313.21 Shyness disorder of childhood
Sensitivity reaction of childhood or adolescence

313.22 Introverted disorder of childhood
Social withdrawal } of childhood or adolescence
Withdrawal reaction } of childhood or adolescence

313.23 Selective mutism
EXCLUDES *elective mutism as adjustment reaction (309.83)*

313.3 Relationship problems
Sibling jealousy
EXCLUDES *relationship problems associated with aggression, destruction, or other forms of conduct disturbance (312.0-312.9)*

✓5th **313.8 Other or mixed emotional disturbances of childhood or adolescence**

313.81 Oppositional defiant disorder
DEF: Mental disorder of children noted for pervasive opposition, defiance of authority.

313.82 Identity disorder
Identity problem
DEF: Distress of adolescents caused by inability to form acceptable self-identity; uncertainty about career choice, sexual orientation, moral values.

313.83 Academic underachievement disorder

313.89 Other P
Reactive attachment disorder of infancy or early childhood

313.9 Unspecified emotional disturbance of childhood or adolescence P
Mental disorder of infancy, childhood or adolescence NOS

✓4th **314 Hyperkinetic syndrome of childhood**
EXCLUDES *hyperkinesis as symptom of underlying disorder—code the underlying disorder*

✓5th **314.0 Attention deficit disorder**
Adult
Child
DEF: A behavioral disorder usually diagnosed at an early age; characterized by the inability to focus attention for a normal period of time.

314.00 Without mention of hyperactivity
Predominantly inattentive type
AHA: 1Q, '97, 8

314.01 With hyperactivity
Combined type
Overactivity NOS
Predominantly hyperactive/impulsive type
Simple disturbance of attention with overactivity
AHA: 1Q, '97, 8

314.1 Hyperkinesis with developmental delay
Developmental disorder of hyperkinesis
Use additional code to identify any associated neurological disorder

314.2 Hyperkinetic conduct disorder
Hyperkinetic conduct disorder without developmental delay
EXCLUDES *hyperkinesis with significant delays in specific skills (314.1)*

314.8 Other specified manifestations of hyperkinetic syndrome

314.9 Unspecified hyperkinetic syndrome
Hyperkinetic reaction of childhood or adolescence NOS
Hyperkinetic syndrome NOS

✓4th **315 Specific delays in development**
EXCLUDES *that due to a neurological disorder (320.0-389.9)*

✓5th **315.0 Specific reading disorder**

315.00 Reading disorder, unspecified

315.01 Alexia
DEF: Lack of ability to understand written language; manifestation of aphasia.

315.02 Developmental dyslexia
DEF: Serious impairment of reading skills unexplained in relation to general intelligence and teaching processes; it can be inherited or congenital.

315.09 Other
Specific spelling difficulty

315.1 Mathematics disorder
Dyscalculia

315.2 Other specific learning difficulties
Disorder of written expression
EXCLUDES *specific arithmetical disorder (315.1)*
specific reading disorder (315.00-315.09)

✓5th **315.3 Developmental speech or language disorder**

315.31 Expressive language disorder
Developmental aphasia
Word deafness
EXCLUDES *acquired aphasia (784.3)*
elective mutism (309.83, 313.0, 313.23)

315.32 Mixed receptive-expressive language disorder
AHA: ▶2Q, '05, 5;◀ 4Q, '96, 30

315.39 Other
Developmental articulation disorder
Dyslalia
Phonological disorder
EXCLUDES *lisping and lalling (307.9)*
stammering and stuttering (307.0)

315.4 Developmental coordination disorder
Clumsiness syndrome
Dyspraxia syndrome
Specific motor development disorder

315.5 Mixed development disorder
AHA: 2Q, '02, 11

315.8 Other specified delays in development

315.9 Unspecified delay in development
Developmental disorder NOS
Learning disorder NOS

316 Psychic factors associated with diseases classified elsewhere
Psychologic factors in physical conditions classified elsewhere
Use additional code to identify the associated physical condition, as:
psychogenic:
asthma (493.9)
dermatitis (692.9)
duodenal ulcer (532.0-532.9)
eczema (691.8, 692.9)
gastric ulcer (531.0-531.9)
mucous colitis (564.9)
paroxysmal tachycardia (427.2)
ulcerative colitis (556)
urticaria (708.0-708.9)
psychosocial dwarfism (259.4)
EXCLUDES *physical symptoms and physiological malfunctions, not involving tissue damage, of mental origin (306.0-306.9)*

MENTAL RETARDATION (317-319)

Use additional code(s) to identify any associated psychiatric or physical condition(s)

317 Mild mental retardation
High-grade defect
IQ 50-70
Mild mental subnormality

✓4th **318 Other specified mental retardation**

318.0 Moderate mental retardation
IQ 35-49
Moderate mental subnormality

318.1 Severe mental retardation
IQ 20-34
Severe mental subnormality

318.2 Profound mental retardation
IQ under 20
Profound mental subnormality

319 Unspecified mental retardation
Mental deficiency NOS
Mental subnormality NOS

N Newborn Age: 0 | P Pediatric Age: 0-17 | M Maternity Age: 12-55 | A Adult Age: 15-124 | CC CC Condition | MC Major Complication | CD Complex Dx | HIV HIV Related Dx

6. DISEASES OF THE NERVOUS SYSTEM AND SENSE ORGANS (320-389)

INFLAMMATORY DISEASES OF THE CENTRAL NERVOUS SYSTEM (320-326)

✓4th **320 Bacterial meningitis**

INCLUDES arachnoiditis, leptomeningitis, meningitis, meningoencephalitis, meningomyelitis, pachymeningitis } bacterial

AHA: J-F, '87, 6

DEF: Bacterial infection causing inflammation of the lining of the brain and/or spinal cord.

320.0 Hemophilus meningitis CC
Meningitis due to Hemophilus influenzae [H. influenzae]
CC Excl: 003.21, 013.00-013.16, 036.0, 047.0-047.9, 049.0-049.1, 053.0, 054.72, 072.1, 090.42, 091.81, 094.2, 098.89, 100.81, 112.83, 114.2, 115.01, 115.11, 115.91, 130.0, 250.60-250.63, 250.80-250.93, 320.0-322.9, 349.89, 349.9, 357.0

320.1 Pneumococcal meningitis CC
CC Excl: See code 320.0

320.2 Streptococcal meningitis CC
CC Excl: See code 320.0

320.3 Staphylococcal meningitis CC
CC Excl: See code 320.0

320.7 Meningitis in other bacterial diseases classified elsewhere CC
Code first underlying disease, as:
actinomycosis (039.8)
listeriosis (027.0)
typhoid fever (002.0)
whooping cough (033.0-033.9)

EXCLUDES *meningitis (in):*
epidemic (036.0)
gonococcal (098.82)
meningococcal (036.0)
salmonellosis (003.21)
syphilis:
NOS (094.2)
congenital (090.42)
meningovascular (094.2)
secondary (091.81)
tuberculous (013.0)

CC Excl: See code 320.0

✓5th **320.8 Meningitis due to other specified bacteria**

320.81 Anaerobic meningitis CC
Bacteroides (fragilis)
Gram-negative anaerobes
CC Excl: See code 320.0

320.82 Meningitis due to gram-negative bacteria, not elsewhere classified CC
Aerobacter aerogenes pneumoniae
Escherichia coli [E. coli]
Friedländer bacillus
Klebsiella
Proteus morganii
Pseudomonas

EXCLUDES *gram-negative anaerobes (320.81)*

CC Excl: See code 320.0

320.89 Meningitis due to other specified bacteria CC
Bacillus pyocyaneus
CC Excl: See code 320.0

320.9 Meningitis due to unspecified bacterium CC
Meningitis:
bacterial NOS
purulent NOS
pyogenic NOS
suppurative NOS
CC Excl: See code 320.0

✓4th **321 Meningitis due to other organisms**

AHA: J-F, '87, 6

DEF: Infection causing inflammation of the lining of the brain and/or spinal cord, due to organisms other than bacteria.

321.0 Cryptococcal meningitis CC
Code first underlying disease (117.5)
CC Excl: See code 320.0

321.1 Meningitis in other fungal diseases CC
Code first underlying disease (110.0-118)

EXCLUDES *meningitis in:*
candidiasis (112.83)
coccidioidomycosis (114.2)
histoplasmosis (115.01, 115.11, 115.91)

CC Excl: See code 320.0

321.2 Meningitis due to viruses not elsewhere classified CC
Code first underlying disease, as:
meningitis due to arbovirus (060.0-066.9)

EXCLUDES *meningitis (due to):*
abacterial (047.0-047.9)
adenovirus (049.1)
aseptic NOS (047.9)
Coxsackie (virus)(047.0)
ECHO virus (047.1)
enterovirus (047.0-047.9)
herpes simplex virus (054.72)
herpes zoster virus (053.0)
lymphocytic choriomeningitis virus (049.0)
mumps (072.1)
viral NOS (047.9)
meningo-eruptive syndrome (047.1)

CC Excl: 003.21, 013.00-013.16, 036.0, 047.0-047.9, 049.0-049.1, 053.0, 054.72, 072.1, 090.42, 091.81, 094.2, 098.89, 100.81, 112.83, 114.2, 115.01, 115.11, 115.91, 130.0, 320.0-322.9, 349.89, 349.9, 357.0

AHA: 4Q, '04, 51

321.3 Meningitis due to trypanosomiasis CC
Code first underlying disease (086.0-086.9)
CC Excl: 003.21, 013.00-013.16, 036.0, 047.0-047.9, 049.0-049.1, 053.0, 054.72, 072.1, 090.42, 091.81, 094.2, 098.89, 100.81, 112.83, 114.2, 115.01, 115.11, 115.91, 130.0, 250.60-250.63, 250.80-250.93, 320.0-320.9, 321.0-321.8, 322.0-322.9, 349.89, 349.9, 357.0

321.4 Meningitis in sarcoidosis CC
Code first underlying disease (135)
CC Excl: See code 321.3

321.8 Meningitis due to other nonbacterial organisms classified elsewhere CC
Code first underlying disease

EXCLUDES *leptospiral meningitis (100.81)*

CC Excl: See code 321.3

✓4th **322 Meningitis of unspecified cause**

INCLUDES arachnoiditis, leptomeningitis, meningitis, pachymeningitis } with no organism specified as cause

AHA: J-F, '87, 6

DEF: Infection causing inflammation of the lining of the brain and/or spinal cord, due to unspecified cause.

322.0 Nonpyogenic meningitis CC
Meningitis with clear cerebrospinal fluid
CC Excl: See code 321.3

322.1 Eosinophilic meningitis CC
CC Excl: See code 321.3

322.2 Chronic meningitis CC
CC Excl: See code 321.3

322.9 Meningitis, unspecified CC
CC Excl: See code 321.3

✓4th **323 Encephalitis, myelitis, and encephalomyelitis**

INCLUDES acute disseminated encephalomyelitis
meningoencephalitis, except bacterial
meningomyelitis, except bacterial
▶myelitis:◀
ascending
transverse

EXCLUDES ▶*acute transverse myelitis NOS (341.20)*
acute transverse myelitis in conditions classified elsewhere (341.21)◀
bacterial:
meningoencephalitis (320.0-320.9)
meningomyelitis (320.0-320.9)
▶*idiopathic transverse myelitis (341.22)*◀

DEF: Encephalitis: inflammation of brain tissues.
DEF: Myelitis: inflammation of the spinal cord.
DEF: Encephalomyelitis: inflammation of brain and spinal cord.

▲ ✓5th **323.0 Encephalitis, myelitis, and encephalomyelitis in viral diseases classified elsewhere**
Code first underlying disease, as:
cat-scratch disease (078.3)
infectious mononucleosis (075)
ornithosis (073.7)

● ***323.01 Encephalitis and encephalomyelitis in viral diseases classified elsewhere***
EXCLUDES *encephalitis (in):*
arthropod-borne viral (062.0-064)
herpes simplex (054.3)
mumps (072.2)
other viral diseases of central nervous system (049.8-049.9)
poliomyelitis (045.0-045.9)
rubella (056.01)
slow virus infections of central nervous system (046.0-046.9)
viral NOS (049.9)
West Nile (066.41)

● ***323.02 Myelitis in viral diseases classified elsewhere***
EXCLUDES *myelitis (in):*
herpes simplex (054.74)
herpes zoster (053.14)
poliomyelitis (045.0-045.9)
rubella (056.01)
other viral diseases of central nervous system (049.8-049.9)

▲ ***323.1 Encephalitis, myelitis, and encephalomyelitis in rickettsial diseases classified elsewhere***
Code first underlying disease (080-083.9)
DEF: Inflammation of the brain caused by rickettsial disease carried by louse, tick, or mite.

▲ ***323.2 Encephalitis, myelitis, and encephalomyelitis in protozoal diseases classified elsewhere***
Code first underlying disease, as:
malaria (084.0-084.9)
trypanosomiasis (086.0-086.9)
DEF: Inflammation of the brain caused by protozoal disease carried by mosquitoes and flies.

▲ ✓5th **323.4 Other encephalitis, myelitis, and encephalomyelitis due to infection classified elsewhere**
Code first underlying disease

● ***323.41 Other encephalitis and encephalomyelitis due to infection classified elsewhere***
EXCLUDES *encephalitis (in):*
meningococcal (036.1)
syphilis:
NOS (094.81)
congenital (090.41)
toxoplasmosis (130.0)
tuberculosis (013.6)
meningoencephalitis due to free-living ameba [Naegleria] (136.2)

● ***323.42 Other myelitis due to infection classified elsewhere***
EXCLUDES *myelitis (in):*
syphilis (094.89)
tuberculosis (013.6)

▲ ✓5th **323.5 Encephalitis, myelitis, and encephalomyelitis following immunization procedures**
Use additional E code to identify vaccine

● **323.51 Encephalitis and encephalomyelitis following immunization procedures**
Encephalitis postimmunization or postvaccinal
Encephalomyelitis postimmunization or postvaccinal

● **323.52 Myelitis following immunization procedures**
Myelitis postimmunization or postvaccinal

▲ ✓5th **323.6 Postinfectious encephalitis, myelitis, and encephalomyelitis**
Code first underlying disease
DEF: Infection, inflammation of brain several weeks following the outbreak of a systemic infection.

● ***323.61 Infectious acute disseminated encephalomyelitis [ADEM]***
Acute necrotizing hemorrhagic encephalopathy
EXCLUDES *noninfectious acute disseminated encephalomyelitis (ADEM) (323.81)*

● ***323.62 Other postinfectious encephalitis and encephalomyelitis***
EXCLUDES *encephalitis:*
postchickenpox (052.0)
postmeasles (055.0)

● ***323.63 Postinfectious myelitis***
EXCLUDES *postchickenpox myelitis (052.2)*
herpes simplex myelitis (054.74)
herpes zoster myelitis (053.14)

▲ ✓5th **323.7 Toxic encephalitis, myelitis, and encephalomyelitis**
Code first underlying cause, as:
carbon tetrachloride (982.1)
hydroxyquinoline derivatives (961.3)
lead (984.0-984.9)
mercury (985.0)
thallium (985.8)
AHA: 2Q, '97, 8

● ***323.71 Toxic encephalitis and encephalomyelitis***

● ***323.72 Toxic myelitis***

▲ ✓5th **323.8 Other causes of encephalitis, myelitis, and encephalomyelitis**

● **323.81 Other causes of encephalitis and encephalomyelitis** HIV
Noninfectious acute disseminated encephalomyelitis (ADEM)

● **323.82 Other causes of myelitis** HIV
Transverse myelitis NOS

▲ **323.9 Unspecified cause of encephalitis, myelitis, and encephalomyelitis** HIV
AHA: ▶1Q, '06, 8◀

✓4th **324 Intracranial and intraspinal abscess**

324.0 Intracranial abscess CC

Abscess (embolic):
- cerebellar
- cerebral

Abscess (embolic) of brain [any part]:
- epidural
- extradural
- otogenic
- subdural

EXCLUDES *tuberculous (013.3)*

CC Excl: 006.5, 013.20-013.36, 250.60-250.63, 250.80-250.93, 324.0-325, 348.8-348.9

324.1 Intraspinal abscess CC

Abscess (embolic) of spinal cord [any part]:
- epidural
- extradural
- subdural

EXCLUDES *tuberculous (013.5)*

CC Excl: 006.5, 013.20-013.36, 250.60-250.63, 250.80-250.93, 324.1

324.9 Of unspecified site CC

Extradural or subdural abscess NOS

CC Excl: 006.5, 013.20-013.36, 250.60-250.63, 250.80-250.93, 324.0-325

325 Phlebitis and thrombophlebitis of intracranial venous sinuses CC

Embolism, Endophlebitis, Phlebitis, septic or suppurative, Thrombophlebitis, Thrombosis } of cavernous, lateral, or other intracranial or unspecified intracranial venous sinus

EXCLUDES *that specified as:*
complicating pregnancy, childbirth, or the puerperium (671.5)
of nonpyogenic origin (437.6)

CC Excl: See code 324.9

DEF: Inflammation and formation of blood clot in a vein within the brain or its lining.

326 Late effects of intracranial abscess or pyogenic infection

Note: This category is to be used to indicate conditions whose primary classification is to 320-325 [excluding 320.7, 321.0-321.8, ▶323.01-323.42,◀ 323.6-323.7] as the cause of late effects, themselves classifiable elsewhere. The "late effects" include conditions specified as such, or as sequelae, which may occur at any time after the resolution of the causal condition.

Use additional code to identify condition, as:
- hydrocephalus (331.4)
- paralysis (342.0-342.9, 344.0-344.9)

▶ORGANIC SLEEP DISORDERS (327)◀

✓4th **327 Organic sleep disorders**

AHA: 4Q, '05, 59-64

✓5th **327.0 Organic disorders of initiating and maintaining sleep [Organic insomnia]**

EXCLUDES *insomnia NOS (780.52)*
insomnia not due to a substance or known physiological condition (307.41-307.42)
insomnia with sleep apnea NOS (780.51)

327.00 Organic insomnia, unspecified

327.01 Insomnia due to medical condition classified elsewhere

Code first underlying condition

EXCLUDES *insomnia due to mental disorder (327.02)*

327.02 Insomnia due to mental disorder

Code first mental disorder

EXCLUDES *alcohol induced insomnia (291.82)*
drug induced insomnia (292.85)

327.09 Other organic insomnia

✓5th **327.1 Organic disorder of excessive somnolence [Organic hypersomnia]**

EXCLUDES *hypersomnia NOS (780.54)*
hypersomnia not due to a substance or known physiological condition (307.43-307.44)
hypersomnia with sleep apnea NOS (780.53)

327.10 Organic hypersomnia, unspecified

327.11 Idiopathic hypersomnia with long sleep time

327.12 Idiopathic hypersomnia without long sleep time

327.13 Recurrent hypersomnia

Kleine-Levin syndrome
Menstrual related hypersomnia

327.14 Hypersomnia due to medical condition classified elsewhere

Code first underlying condition

EXCLUDES *hypersomnia due to mental disorder (327.15)*

327.15 Hypersomnia due to mental disorder

Code first mental disorder

EXCLUDES *alcohol induced hypersomnia (291.82)*
drug induced hypersomnia (292.85)

327.19 Other organic hypersomnia

✓5th **327.2 Organic sleep apnea**

EXCLUDES *Cheyne-Stokes breathing (786.04)*
hypersomnia with sleep apnea NOS (780.53)
insomnia with sleep apnea NOS (780.51)
sleep apnea in newborn (770.81-770.82)
sleep apnea NOS (780.57)

327.20 Organic sleep apnea, unspecified

327.21 Primary central sleep apnea

327.22 High altitude periodic breathing

327.23 Obstructive sleep apnea (adult) (pediatric)

327.24 Idiopathic sleep related nonobstructive alveolar hypoventilation

Sleep related hypoxia

327.25 Congenital central alveolar hypoventilation syndrome

327.26 Sleep related hypoventilation/hypoxemia in conditions classifiable elsewhere

Code first underlying condition

327.27 Central sleep apnea in conditions classified elsewhere

Code first underlying condition

327.29 Other organic sleep apnea

✓5th **327.3 Circadian rhythm sleep disorder**

Organic disorder of sleep wake cycle
Organic disorder of sleep wake schedule

EXCLUDES *alcohol induced circadian rhythm sleep disorder (291.82)*
circadian rhythm sleep disorder of nonorganic origin (307.45)
disruption of 24 hour sleep wake cycle NOS (780.55)
drug induced circadian rhythm sleep disorder (292.85)

327.30 Circadian rhythm sleep disorder, unspecified

327.31 Circadian rhythm sleep disorder, delayed sleep phase type

327.32 Circadian rhythm sleep disorder, advanced sleep phase type

327.33 Circadian rhythm sleep disorder, irregular sleep-wake type

327.34 Circadian rhythm sleep disorder, free-running type

327.35 Circadian rhythm sleep disorder, jet lag type

327.36 Circadian rhythm sleep disorder, shift work type

327.37 Circadian rhythm sleep disorder in conditions classified elsewhere

Code first underlying condition

327.39 Other circadian rhythm sleep disorder

✓5th **327.4 Organic parasomnia**

EXCLUDES *alcohol induced parasomnia (291.82)*
drug induced parasomnia (292.85)
parasomnia not due to a known physiological condition (307.47)

327.40 Organic parasomnia, unspecified

327.41 Confusional arousals

327.42 REM sleep behavior disorder

327.43 Recurrent isolated sleep paralysis

327.44 Parasomnia in conditions classified elsewhere

Code first underlying condition

327.49 Other organic parasomnia

✓5th **327.5 Organic sleep related movement disorders**

EXCLUDES ▶ *restless legs syndrome (333.94)*◀
sleep related movement disorder NOS (780.58)

327.51 Periodic limb movement disorder

Periodic limb movement sleep disorder

327.52 Sleep related leg cramps

327.53 Sleep related bruxism

327.59 Other organic sleep related movement disorders

327.8 Other organic sleep disorders

HEREDITARY AND DEGENERATIVE DISEASES OF THE CENTRAL NERVOUS SYSTEM (330-337)

EXCLUDES *hepatolenticular degeneration (275.1)*
multiple sclerosis (340)
other demyelinating diseases of central nervous system (341.0-341.9)

✓4th **330 Cerebral degenerations usually manifest in childhood**

Use additional code to identify associated mental retardation

330.0 Leukodystrophy

Krabbe's disease
Leukodystrophy:
NOS
globoid cell
metachromatic
sudanophilic
Pelizaeus-Merzbacher disease
Sulfatide lipidosis

DEF: Hereditary disease of arylsulfatase or cerebroside sulfatase; characterized by a diffuse loss of myelin in CNS; infantile form causes blindness, motor disturbances, rigidity, mental deterioration and, occasionally, convulsions.

330.1 Cerebral lipidoses

Amaurotic (familial) idiocy
Disease:
Batten
Jansky-Bielschowsky
Kufs'
Disease:
Spielmeyer-Vogt
Tay-Sachs
Gangliosidosis

DEF: Genetic disorder causing abnormal lipid accumulation in the reticuloendothelial cells of the brain.

330.2 Cerebral degeneration in generalized lipidoses

Code first underlying disease, as:
Fabry's disease (272.7)
Gaucher's disease (272.7)
Niemann-Pick disease (272.7)
sphingolipidosis (272.7)

330.3 Cerebral degeneration of childhood in other diseases classified elsewhere

Code first underlying disease, as:
Hunter's disease (277.5)
mucopolysaccharidosis (277.5)

330.8 Other specified cerebral degenerations in childhood

Alpers' disease or gray-matter degeneration
Infantile necrotizing encephalomyelopathy
Leigh's disease
Subacute necrotizing encephalopathy or encephalomyelopathy

AHA: N-D, '85, 5

330.9 Unspecified cerebral degeneration in childhood

✓4th **331 Other cerebral degenerations**

331.0 Alzheimer's disease

AHA: 4Q, '00, 41; 4Q, '99, 7; N-D, '84, 20

DEF: Diffuse atrophy of cerebral cortex; causing a progressive decline in intellectual and physical functions, including memory loss, personality changes and profound dementia.

✓5th **331.1 Frontotemporal dementia**

Use additional code for associated behavioral disturbance (294.10-294.11)

AHA: 4Q, '03, 57

DEF: Rare, progressive degenerative brain disease, similar to Alzheimer's; cortical atrophy affects the frontal and temporal lobes.

331.11 Pick's disease

DEF: A less common form of progressive frontotemporal dementia with asymmetrical atrophy of the frontal and temporal regions of the cerebral cortex including abnormal rounded brain cells called Pick cells together with the presence of abnormal staining of protein (called tau) within the cells, called Pick bodies; symptoms include prominent apathy, deterioration of social skills, behavioral changes such as disinhibition and restlessness, echolalia, impairment of language, memory, and intellect, increased carelessness, poor personal hygiene, and decreased attention span.

331.19 Other frontotemporal dementia

Frontal dementia

331.2 Senile degeneration of brain

EXCLUDES *senility NOS (797)*

331.3 Communicating hydrocephalus

EXCLUDES *congenital hydrocephalus (741.0, 742.3)*

AHA: S-O, '85, 12

DEF: Subarachnoid hemorrhage and meningitis causing excess buildup of cerebrospinal fluid in cavities due to nonabsorption of fluid back through fluid pathways.

331.4 Obstructive hydrocephalus CC

Acquired hydrocephalus NOS

EXCLUDES *congenital hydrocephalus (741.0, 742.3)*

CC Excl: 250.60-250.63, 250.80-250.93, 331.3-331.7, 331.82-331.9, 348.8-348.9, 741.00-741.03, 742.3-742.4, 742.59-742.9

AHA: 4Q, '03, 106; 1Q, '99, 9

DEF: Obstruction of cerebrospinal fluid passage from brain into spinal canal.

331.7 Cerebral degeneration in diseases classified elsewhere

Code first underlying disease, as:
alcoholism (303.0-303.9)
beriberi (265.0)
cerebrovascular disease (430-438)
congenital hydrocephalus (741.0, 742.3)
myxedema (244.0-244.9)
neoplastic disease (140.0-239.9)
vitamin B_{12} deficiency (266.2)

EXCLUDES *cerebral degeneration in:*
Jakob-Creutzfeldt disease (046.1)
progressive multifocal leukoencephalopathy (046.3)
subacute spongiform encephalopathy (046.1)

✓5th **331.8 Other cerebral degeneration**

331.81 Reye's syndrome P

DEF: Rare childhood illness, often developed after a bout of viral upper respiratory infection; characterized by vomiting, elevated serum transaminase, changes in liver and other viscera; symptoms may be followed by an encephalopathic phase with brain swelling, disturbances of consciousness and seizures; can be fatal.

331.82 Dementia with Lewy bodies
Dementia with Parkinsonism
Lewy body dementia
Lewy body disease
Use additional code for associated behavioral disturbance (294.10-294.11)
AHA: 4Q, '03, 57
DEF: A cerebral dementia with neurophysiologic changes including increased hippocampal volume, hypoperfusion in the occipital lobes, and beta amyloid deposits with neurofibrillarity tangles, atrophy of cortex and brainstem, hallmark neuropsychologic characteristics are fluctuating cognition with pronounced variation in attention and alertness; recurrent hallucinations; and parkinsonism.

● **331.83 Mild cognitive impairment, so stated**
EXCLUDES *altered mental status (780.97)*
cerebral degeneration (331.0-331.9)
change in mental status (780.97)
cognitive deficits following (late effects of) cerebral hemorrhage or infarction (438.0)
cognitive impairment due to intracranial or head injury (850-854, 959.01)
cognitive impairment due to late effect of intracranial injury (907.0)
dementia (290.0-290.43, 294.8)
mild memory disturbance (310.8)
neurologic neglect syndrome (781.8)
personality change, nonpsychotic (310.1)

331.89 Other
Cerebral ataxia

331.9 Cerebral degeneration, unspecified

✓4th **332 Parkinson's disease**
EXCLUDES *dementia with Parkinsonism (331.82)0*

332.0 Paralysis agitans
Parkinsonism or Parkinson's disease:
NOS
idiopathic
primary
AHA: M-A, '87, 7
DEF: Form of parkinsonism; progressive, occurs in senior years; characterized by masklike facial expression; condition affects ability to stand erect, walk smoothly; weakened muscles, also tremble and involuntarily movement.

332.1 Secondary Parkinsonism
Neuroleptic-induced Parkinsonism
Parkinsonism due to drugs
Use additional E code to identify drug, if drug-induced
EXCLUDES *Parkinsonism (in):*
Huntington's disease (333.4)
progressive supranuclear palsy (333.0)
Shy-Drager syndrome (333.0)
syphilitic (094.82)

✓4th **333 Other extrapyramidal disease and abnormal movement disorders**
INCLUDES other forms of extrapyramidal, basal ganglia, or striatopallidal disease
EXCLUDES *abnormal movements of head NOS (781.0)*
sleep related movement disorders (327.51-327.59)

333.0 Other degenerative diseases of the basal ganglia
Atrophy or degeneration:
olivopontocerebellar [Déjérine-Thomas syndrome]
pigmentary pallidal [Hallervorden-Spatz disease]
striatonigral
Parkinsonian syndrome associated with:
idiopathic orthostatic hypotension
symptomatic orthostatic hypotension
Progressive supranuclear ophthalmoplegia
Shy-Drager syndrome
AHA: 3Q, '96, 8

333.1 Essential and other specified forms of tremor
Benign essential tremor
Familial tremor
Medication-induced postural tremor
Use additional E code to identify drug, if drug-induced
EXCLUDES *tremor NOS (781.0)*

333.2 Myoclonus
Familial essential myoclonus
Progressive myoclonic epilepsy
Unverricht-Lundborg disease
Use additional E code to identify drug, if drug-induced
AHA: 3Q, '97, 4; M-A, '87, 12
DEF: Spontaneous movements or contractions of muscles.

333.3 Tics of organic origin
Use additional E code to identify drug, if drug-induced
EXCLUDES *Gilles de la Tourette's syndrome (307.23)*
habit spasm (307.22)
tic NOS (307.20)

333.4 Huntington's chorea
DEF: Genetic disease characterized by chronic progressive mental deterioration; dementia and death within 15 years of onset.

333.5 Other choreas
Hemiballism(us)
Paroxysmal choreo-athetosis
Use additional E code to identify drug, if drug-induced
EXCLUDES *Sydenham's or rheumatic chorea (392.0-392.9)*

▲ **333.6 Genetic torsion dystonia**
Dystonia:
deformans progressiva
musculorum deformans
(Schwalbe-) Ziehen-Oppenheim disease
DEF: Sustained muscular contractions, causing twisting and repetitive movements that result in abnormal postures of trunk and limbs; etiology unknown.

▲ ✓5th **333.7 Acquired torsion dystonia**

● **333.71 Athetoid cerebral palsy**
Double athetosis (syndrome)
Vogt's disease
EXCLUDES *infantile cerebral palsy (343.0-343.9)*

● **333.72 Acute dystonia due to drugs**
Acute dystonic reaction due to drugs
Neuroleptic induced acute dystonia
Use additional E code to identify drug
EXCLUDES *blepharospasm due to drugs (333.85)*
orofacial dyskinesia due to drugs (333.85)
secondary Parkinsonism (332.1)
subacute dyskinesia due to drugs (333.85)
tardive dyskinesia (333.85)

● **333.79 Other acquired torsion dystonia**

✓5th **333.8 Fragments of torsion dystonia**
Use additional E code to identify drug, if drug-induced

333.81 Blepharospasm
EXCLUDES ▶ *blepharospasm due to drugs (333.85)*◀
DEF: Uncontrolled winking or blinking due to orbicularis oculi muscle spasm.

333.82 Orofacial dyskinesia
EXCLUDES ▶ *orofacial dyskinesia due to drugs (333.85)*◀
DEF: Uncontrolled movement of mouth or facial muscles.

333.83 Spasmodic torticollis
EXCLUDES *torticollis:*
NOS (723.5)
hysterical (300.11)
psychogenic (306.0)
DEF: Uncontrolled movement of head due to spasms of neck muscle.

333.84 Organic writers' cramp
EXCLUDES *pychogenic (300.89)*

• **333.85 Subacute dyskinesia due to drugs**
Blepharospasm due to drugs
Orofacial dyskinesia due to drugs
Tardive dyskinesia
Use additional E code to identify drug
EXCLUDES *acute dystonia due to drugs (333.72)*
acute dystonic reaction due to drugs (333.72)
secondary Parkinsonism (332.1)

333.89 Other

✓5th **333.9 Other and unspecified extrapyramidal diseases and abnormal movement disorders**

333.90 Unspecified extrapyramidal disease and abnormal movement disorder
Medication-induced movement disorders NOS
Use additional E code to identify drug, if drug-induced

333.91 Stiff-man syndrome

333.92 Neuroleptic malignant syndrome
Use additional E code to identify drug
EXCLUDES ▶ *neuroleptic induced Parkinsonism (332.1)*◀
AHA: 4Q, '94, 37

333.93 Benign shuddering attacks
AHA: 4Q, '94, 37

• **333.94 Restless legs syndrome [RLS]**

333.99 Other
Neuroleptic-induced acute akathisia
Use additional E code to identify drug, if drug-induced
AHA: 4Q, '04, 95; 2Q, '04, 12; 4Q, '94, 37

✓4th **334 Spinocerebellar disease**
EXCLUDES *olivopontocerebellar degeneration (333.0)*
peroneal muscular atrophy (356.1)

334.0 Friedreich's ataxia
DEF: Genetic recessive disease of children; sclerosis of dorsal, lateral spinal cord columns; characterized by ataxia, speech impairment, swaying and irregular movements, with muscle paralysis, especially of lower limbs.

334.1 Hereditary spastic paraplegia

334.2 Primary cerebellar degeneration
Cerebellar ataxia:
Marie's
Sanger-Brown
Dyssynergia cerebellaris myoclonica
Primary cerebellar degeneration:
NOS
hereditary
sporadic
AHA: M-A, '87, 9

334.3 Other cerebellar ataxia
Cerebellar ataxia NOS
Use additional E code to identify drug, if drug-induced

334.4 *Cerebellar ataxia in diseases classified elsewhere*
Code first underlying disease, as:
alcoholism (303.0-303.9)
myxedema (244.0-244.9)
neoplastic disease (140.0-239.9)

334.8 Other spinocerebellar diseases
Ataxia-telangiectasia [Louis-Bar syndrome]
Corticostriatal-spinal degeneration

334.9 Spinocerebellar disease, unspecified

✓4th **335 Anterior horn cell disease**

335.0 Werdnig-Hoffmann disease CC
Infantile spinal muscular atrophy
Progressive muscular atrophy of infancy
CC Excl: 250.60-250.63, 250.80-250.93, 334.8-335.0, 335.10-337.9, 349.89-349.9
DEF: Spinal muscle atrophy manifested in prenatal period or shortly after birth; symptoms include hypotonia, atrophy of skeletal muscle; death occurs in infancy.

✓5th **335.1 Spinal muscular atrophy**

335.10 Spinal muscular atrophy, unspecified CC
CC Excl: See code 335.0

335.11 Kugelberg-Welander disease CC
Spinal muscular atrophy:
familial
juvenile
CC Excl: See code 335.0
DEF: Hereditary; juvenile muscle atrophy; appears during first two decades of life; due to lesions of anterior horns of spinal cord; includes wasting, diminution of lower body muscles and twitching.

335.19 Other CC
Adult spinal muscular atrophy
CC Excl: See code 335.0

✓5th **335.2 Motor neuron disease**

335.20 Amyotrophic lateral sclerosis CC A
Motor neuron disease (bulbar) (mixed type)
CC Excl: See code 335.0
AHA: 4Q, '95, 81

335.21 Progressive muscular atrophy CC
Duchenne-Aran muscular atrophy
Progressive muscular atrophy (pure)
CC Excl: See code 335.0

335.22 Progressive bulbar palsy CC
CC Excl: See code 335.0

335.23 Pseudobulbar palsy CC
CC Excl: See code 335.0

335.24 Primary lateral sclerosis CC
CC Excl: See code 335.0

335.29 Other CC
CC Excl: See code 335.0

335.8 Other anterior horn cell diseases CC
CC Excl: See code 335.0

335.9 Anterior horn cell disease, unspecified CC
CC Excl: See code 335.0

✓4th **336 Other diseases of spinal cord**

336.0 Syringomyelia and syringobulbia
AHA: 1Q, '89, 10

336.1 Vascular myelopathies
Acute infarction of spinal cord (embolic) (nonembolic)
Arterial thrombosis of spinal cord
Edema of spinal cord
Hematomyelia
Subacute necrotic myelopathy

336.2 *Subacute combined degeneration of spinalcord in diseases classified elsewhere*
Code first underlying disease, as:
pernicious anemia (281.0)
other vitamin B_{12} deficiency anemia (281.1)
vitamin B_{12} deficiency (266.2)

336.3 *Myelopathy in other diseases classified elsewhere*
Code first underlying disease, as:
myelopathy in neoplastic disease (140.0-239.9)
EXCLUDES *myelopathy in:*
intervertebral disc disorder (722.70-722.73)
spondylosis (721.1, 721.41-721.42, 721.91)
AHA: 3Q, '99, 5

336.8 Other myelopathy
Myelopathy: drug-induced
Myelopathy: radiation-induced
Use additonal E code to identify cause

336.9 Unspecified disease of spinal cord HIV
Cord compression NOS
Myelopathy NOS
EXCLUDES *myelitis ▶(323.02, 323.1, 323.2, 323.42, 323.52, 323.63, 323.72, 323.82, 323.9)◀*
spinal (canal) stenosis (723.0, 724.00-724.09)

✓4th **337 Disorders of the autonomic nervous system**
INCLUDES disorders of peripheral autonomic, sympathetic, parasympathetic, or vegetative system
EXCLUDES *familial dysautonomia [Riley-Day syndrome] (742.8)*

337.0 Idiopathic peripheral autonomic neuropathy
Carotid sinus syncope or syndrome
Cervical sympathetic dystrophy or paralysis

337.1 Peripheral autonomic neuropathy in disorders classified elsewhere
Code first underlying disease, as:
amyloidosis ▶(277.30-277.39)◀
diabetes (250.6)
AHA: 2Q, '93, 6; 3Q, '91, 9; N-D, '84, 9

✓5th **337.2 Reflex sympathetic dystrophy**
AHA: 4Q, '93, 24
DEF: Disturbance of the sympathetic nervous system evidenced by sweating, pain, pallor and edema following injury to nerves or blood vessels.
337.20 Reflex sympathetic dystrophy, unspecified
337.21 Reflex sympathetic dystrophy of the upper limb
337.22 Reflex sympathetic dystrophy of the lower limb
337.29 Reflex sympathetic dystrophy of other specified site

337.3 Autonomic dysreflexia
Use additional code to identify the cause, such as:
decubitus ulcer (707.00-707.09)
fecal impaction (560.39)
urinary tract infection (599.0)
AHA: 4Q, '98, 37
DEF: Noxious stimuli evokes paroxysmal hypertension, bradycardia, excess sweating, headache, pilomotor responses, facial flushing, and nasal congestion due to uncontrolled parasympathetic nerve response; usually occurs in patients with spinal cord injury above major sympathetic outflow tract (T_6).

337.9 Unspecified disorder of autonomic nervous system

▶PAIN (338)◀

● ✓4th **338 Pain, not elsewhere classified**
Use additional code to identify:
pain associated with psychological factors (307.89)
EXCLUDES *generalized pain (780.96)*
localized pain, unspecified type—code to pain by site
pain disorder exclusively attributed to psychological factors (307.80)

● **338.0 Central pain syndrome**
Déjérine-Roussy syndrome
Myelopathic pain syndrome
Thalamic pain syndrome (hyperesthetic)

● ✓5th **338.1 Acute pain**
● **338.11 Acute pain due to trauma**
● **338.12 Acute post-thoracotomy pain**
Post-thoracotomy pain NOS
● **338.18 Other acute postoperative pain**
Postoperative pain NOS
● **338.19 Other acute pain**
EXCLUDES *neoplasm related acute pain (338.3)*

● ✓5th **338.2 Chronic pain**
EXCLUDES *causalgia (355.9)*
lower limb (355.71)
upper limb (354.4)
chronic pain syndrome (338.4)
myofascial pain syndrome (729.1)
neoplasm related chronic pain (338.3)
reflex sympathetic dystrophy (337.20-337.29)
● **338.21 Chronic pain due to trauma**
● **338.22 Chronic post-thoracotomy pain**
● **338.28 Other chronic postoperative pain**
● **338.29 Other chronic pain**

● **338.3 Neoplasm related pain (acute) (chronic)**
Cancer associated pain
Pain due to malignancy (primary) (secondary)
Tumor associated pain

● **338.4 Chronic pain syndrome**
Chronic pain associated with significant psychosocial dysfunction

OTHER DISORDERS OF THE CENTRAL NERVOUS SYSTEM (340-349)

340 Multiple sclerosis CC
Disseminated or multiple sclerosis:
NOS
brain stem
cord
generalized
CC Excl: 250.60-250.63, 250.80-250.93, 340, 341.8-341.9

✓4th **341 Other demyelinating diseases of central nervous system**
341.0 Neuromyelitis optica
341.1 Schilder's disease
Baló's concentric sclerosis
Encephalitis periaxialis: concentrica [Baló's]
Encephalitis periaxialis: diffusa [Schilder's]
DEF: Chronic leukoencephalopathy of children and adolescents; symptoms include blindness, deafness, bilateral spasticity and progressive mental deterioration.

● ✓5th **341.2 Acute (transverse) myelitis**
EXCLUDES *acute (transverse) myelitis (in) (due to):*
following immunization procedures (323.52)
infection classified elsewhere (323.42)
postinfectious (323.63)
protozoal diseases classified elsewhere (323.2)
rickettsial diseases classified elsewhere (323.1)
toxic (323.72)
viral diseases classified elsewhere (323.02)
transverse myelitis NOS (323.82)
● **341.20 Acute (transverse) myelitis NOS**
● ***341.21 Acute (transverse) myelitis in conditions classified elsewhere***
Code first underlying condition
● **341.22 Idiopathic transverse myelitis**

341.8 Other demyelinating diseases of central nervous system
Central demyelination of corpus callosum
Central pontine myelinosis
Marchiafava (-Bignami) disease
AHA: N-D, '87, 6

341.9 Demyelinating disease of central nervous system, unspecified 

✓4th 342 Hemiplegia and hemiparesis

Note: This category is to be used when hemiplegia (complete) (incomplete) is reported without further specification, or is stated to be old or long-standing but of unspecified cause. The category is also for use in multiple coding to identify these types of hemiplegia resulting from any cause.

EXCLUDES *congenital (343.1)*
hemiplegia due to late effect of cerebrovascular accident (438.20-438.22)
infantile NOS (343.4)

The following fifth-digits are for use with codes 342.0-342.9:
0 affecting unspecified side
1 affecting dominant side
2 affecting nondominant side

AHA: 4Q, '94, 38

✓5th **342.0 Flaccid hemiplegia**
✓5th **342.1 Spastic hemiplegia**
✓5th **342.8 Other specified hemiplegia**
✓5th **342.9 Hemiplegia, unspecified**
AHA: 4Q, '98, 87

✓4th 343 Infantile cerebral palsy

INCLUDES cerebral:
palsy NOS
spastic infantile paralysis
congenital spastic paralysis (cerebral)
Little's disease
paralysis (spastic) due to birth injury:
intracranial
spinal

EXCLUDES ▶*athetoid cerebral palsy (333.71)*◀
hereditary cerebral paralysis, such as:
hereditary spastic paraplegia (334.1)
Vogt's disease ▶*(333.71)*◀
spastic paralysis specified as noncongenital or noninfantile (344.0-344.9)

343.0 Diplegic
Congenital diplegia
Congenital paraplegia
DEF: Paralysis affecting both sides of the body simultaneously.

343.1 Hemiplegic
Congenital hemiplegia
EXCLUDES *infantile hemiplegia NOS (343.4)*

343.2 Quadriplegic CC
Tetraplegic
CC Excl: 250.60-250.63, 250.80-250.93, 342.00-344.9, 348.8-348.9, 349.89-349.9, 742.59-742.9

343.3 Monoplegic

343.4 Infantile hemiplegia
Infantile hemiplegia (postnatal) NOS

343.8 Other specified infantile cerebral palsy

343.9 Infantile cerebral palsy, unspecified
Cerebral palsy NOS
AHA: 4Q, '05, 89

✓4th 344 Other paralytic syndromes

Note: This category is to be used when the listed conditions are reported without further specification or are stated to be old or long-standing but of unspecified cause. The category is also for use in multiple coding to identify these conditions resulting from any cause.

INCLUDES paralysis (complete) (incomplete), except as classifiable to 342 and 343

EXCLUDES *congenital or infantile cerebral palsy (343.0-343.9)*
hemiplegia (342.0-342.9)
congenital or infantile (343.1, 343.4)

✓5th **344.0 Quadriplegia and quadriparesis**

344.00 Quadriplegia unspecified CC
CC Excl: See code 343.2
AHA: 4Q, '03, 103; 4Q, '98, 38

344.01 C_1-C_4 complete CC
CC Excl: See code 343.2

344.02 C_1-C_4 incomplete CC
CC Excl: See code 343.2

344.03 C_5-C_7 complete CC
CC Excl: See code 343.2

344.04 C_5-C_7 incomplete CC
CC Excl: See code 343.2

344.09 Other CC
CC Excl: See code 343.2
AHA: 1Q, '01, 12; 4Q, '98, 39

344.1 Paraplegia
Paralysis of both lower limbs
Paraplegia (lower)
AHA: 4Q, '03, 110;M-A, '87, 10

344.2 Diplegia of upper limbs
Diplegia (upper)
Paralysis of both upper limbs

✓5th **344.3 Monoplegia of lower limb**
Paralysis of lower limb
EXCLUDES *monoplegia of lower limb due to late effect of cerebrovascular accident (438.40-438.42)*

344.30 Affecting unspecified side
344.31 Affecting dominant side
344.32 Affecting nondominant side

✓5th **344.4 Monoplegia of upper limb**
Paralysis of upper limb
EXCLUDES *monoplegia of upper limb due to late effect of cerebrovascular accident (438.30-438.32)*

344.40 Affecting unspecified side
344.41 Affecting dominant side
344.42 Affecting nondominant side

344.5 Unspecified monoplegia

✓5th **344.6 Cauda equina syndrome**
DEF: Dull pain and paresthesias in sacrum, perineum and bladder due to compression of spinal nerve roots; pain radiates down buttocks, back of thigh, calf of leg and into foot with prickling, burning sensations.

344.60 Without mention of neurogenic bladder
344.61 With neurogenic bladder
Acontractile bladder
Autonomic hyperreflexia of bladder
Cord bladder
Detrusor hyperreflexia
AHA: M-J, '87, 12; M-A, '87, 10

✓5th **344.8 Other specified paralytic syndromes**

344.81 Locked-in state
AHA: 4Q, '93, 24
DEF: State of consciousness where patients are paralyzed and unable to respond to environmental stimuli; patients have eye movements, and stimuli can enter the brain but patients cannot respond to stimuli.

344.89 Other specified paralytic syndrome
AHA: 2Q, '99, 4

344.9 Paralysis, unspecified

▲ **✓4th 345 Epilepsy and recurrent seizures**

The following fifth-digit subclassification is for use with categories 345.0, .1, .4-.9:
0 without mention of intractable epilepsy
1 with intractable epilepsy

EXCLUDES *progressive myoclonic epilepsy (333.2)*

AHA: 1Q, '93, 24; 2Q, '92, 8; 4Q, '92, 23

DEF: Brain disorder characterized by electrical-like disturbances; may include occasional impairment or loss of consciousness, abnormal motor phenomena and psychic or sensory disturbances.

✓5th **345.0 Generalized nonconvulsive epilepsy** CC 1

Absences:
- atonic
- typical

Minor epilepsy
Petit mal
Pykno-epilepsy
Seizures:
- akinetic
- atonic

CC Excl: For code 345.01: 250.60-250.63, 345.00-345.91, 348.8-348.9, 349.89, 349.9

AHA: For code 345.00: 1Q, '04, 18

✓5th **345.1 Generalized convulsive epilepsy** CC

Epileptic seizures:
- clonic
- myoclonic
- tonic

Epileptic seizures:
- tonic-clonic

Grand mal
Major epilepsy

EXCLUDES *convulsions:*
- *NOS ▶(780.39)◀*
- *infantile ▶(780.39)◀*
- *newborn (779.0)*

infantile spasms (345.6)

CC Excl: See code 345.01

AHA: 3Q, '97, 4

DEF: Convulsive seizures with tension of limbs (tonic) or rhythmic contractions (clonic).

345.2 Petit mal status CC

Epileptic absence status

CC Excl: 250.60-250.63, 250.80-250.93, 345.00-345.91, 348.8-348.9, 349.89, 349.9

DEF: Minor myoclonic spasms and sudden momentary loss of consciousness in epilepsy.

345.3 Grand mal status CC

Status epilepticus NOS

EXCLUDES *epilepsia partialis continua (345.7)*
status:
- *psychomotor (345.7)*
- *temporal lobe (345.7)*

CC Excl: See code 345.2

AHA: ▶3Q, '05, 12◀

DEF: Sudden loss of consciousness followed by generalized convulsions in epilepsy.

▲ ✓5th **345.4 Localization-related (focal) (partial) epilepsy and epileptic syndromes with complex partial seizures** CC 1

Epilepsy:
- limbic system
- partial:
  - secondarily generalized
  - ▶with impairment of consciousness◀
  - with memory and ideational disturbances
- psychomotor
- psychosensory
- temporal lobe

Epileptic automatism

CC Excl: For code 345.41: 250.60-250.63, 345.00-345.91, 348.8-348.9, 349.89, 349.9

▲ ✓5th **345.5 Localization-related (focal) (partial) epilepsy and epileptic syndromes with simple partial seizures** CC 1

Epilepsy:
- Bravais-Jacksonian NOS
- focal (motor) NOS
- Jacksonian NOS
- motor partial
- partial NOS:
  - ▶without impairment of consciousness◀
- sensory-induced
- somatomotor
- somatosensory
- visceral
- visual

CC Excl: For code 345.51: See code 345.4

✓5th **345.6 Infantile spasms** CC 1

Hypsarrhythmia
Lightning spasms
Salaam attacks

EXCLUDES *salaam tic (781.0)*

CC Excl: For code 345.61: See code 345.4

AHA: N-D, '84, 12

✓5th **345.7 Epilepsia partialis continua** CC 1

Kojevnikov's epilepsy

CC Excl: For code 345.71: See code 345.4

DEF: Continuous muscle contractions and relaxation; result of abnormal neural discharge.

▲ ✓5th **345.8 Other forms of epilepsy and recurrent seizures** CC 1

Epilepsy:
- cursive [running]

Epilepsy:
- gelastic

CC Excl: For code 345.81: See code 345.4

✓5th **345.9 Epilepsy, unspecified** CC 1

Epileptic convulsions, fits, or seizures NOS
▶Recurrent seizures NOS
Seizure disorder NOS◀

EXCLUDES ▶ *convulsion (convulsive) disorder (780.39)*◀
convulsive seizure or fit NOS ▶(780.39)◀
▶*recurrent convulsions (780.39)*◀

CC Excl: For code 345.91: See code 345.4

AHA: N-D, '87, 12

✓4th **346 Migraine**

DEF: Benign vascular headache of extreme pain; commonly associated with irritability, nausea, vomiting and often photophobia; premonitory visual hallucination of a crescent in the visual field (scotoma).

The following fifth-digit subclassification is for use with category 346:
- **0 without mention of intractable migraine**
- **1 with intractable migraine, so stated**

✓5th **346.0 Classical migraine**

Migraine preceded or accompanied by transient focal neurological phenomena
Migraine with aura

✓5th **346.1 Common migraine**

Atypical migraine
Sick headache

✓5th **346.2 Variants of migraine**

Cluster headache
Histamine cephalgia
Horton's neuralgia
Migraine:
- abdominal
- basilar

Migraine:
- lower half
- retinal

Neuralgia:
- ciliary
- migrainous

✓5th **346.8 Other forms of migraine**

Migraine:
- hemiplegic

Migraine:
- ophthalmoplegic

✓5th **346.9 Migraine, unspecified**

AHA: N-D, '85, 16

✓4th **347 Cataplexy and narcolepsy**

DEF: Cataplexy: Sudden onset of muscle weakness with loss of tone and strength; caused by aggressive or spontaneous emotions.

DEF: Narcolepsy: Brief, recurrent, uncontrollable episodes of sound sleep.

✓5th **347.0 Narcolepsy**

347.00 Without cataplexy

Narcolepsy NOS

347.01 With cataplexy

✓5th **347.1 Narcolepsy in conditions classified elsewhere**

Code first underlying condition

347.10 Without cataplexy

347.11 With cataplexy

✓4th **348 Other conditions of brain**

348.0 Cerebral cysts

Arachnoid cyst
Porencephalic cyst
Porencephaly, acquired
Pseudoporencephaly

EXCLUDES *porencephaly (congenital) (742.4)*

348.1 Anoxic brain damage CC

EXCLUDES *that occurring in:*
abortion (634-638 with .7, 639.8)
ectopic or molar pregnancy (639.8)
labor or delivery (668.2, 669.4)
that of newborn (767.0, 768.0-768.9, 772.1-772.2)

Use additional E code to identify cause

CC Excl: 250.60-250.63, 250.80-250.93, 348.1-348.2, 349.89, 349.9

DEF: Brain injury due to lack of oxygen, other than birth trauma.

348.2 Benign intracranial hypertension

Pseudotumor cerebri

EXCLUDES *hypertensive encephalopathy (437.2)*

DEF: Elevated pressure in brain due to fluid retention in brain cavities.

✓5th **348.3 Encephalopathy, not elsewhere classified**

AHA: 4Q, '03, 58; 3Q, '97, 4

348.30 Encephalopathy, unspecified HIV

348.31 Metabolic encephalopathy HIV

Septic encephalopathy

EXCLUDES ▶ *toxic metabolic encephalopathy (349.82)*◀

348.39 Other encephalopathy HIV

EXCLUDES *encephalopathy:*
alcoholic (291.2)
hepatic (572.2)
hypertensive (437.2)
toxic (349.82)

348.4 Compression of brain

Compression } brain (stem)
Herniation }

Posterior fossa compression syndrome

AHA: 4Q, '94, 37

DEF: Elevated pressure in brain due to blood clot, tumor, fracture, abscess, other condition.

348.5 Cerebral edema

DEF: Elevated pressure in the brain due to fluid retention in brain tissues.

348.8 Other conditions of brain

Cerebral:
calcification
Cerebral:
fungus

AHA: S-O, '87, 9

348.9 Unspecified condition of brain HIV

✓4th **349 Other and unspecified disorders of the nervous system**

349.0 Reaction to spinal or lumbar puncture

Headache following lumbar puncture

AHA: 2Q, '99, 9; 3Q, '90, 18

349.1 Nervous system complications from surgically implanted device CC

EXCLUDES *immediate postoperative complications (997.00-997.09)*
mechanical complications of nervous system device (996.2)

CC Excl: 250.60-250.63, 250.80-250.93, 349.1, 349.89, 349.9

Cranial Nerves

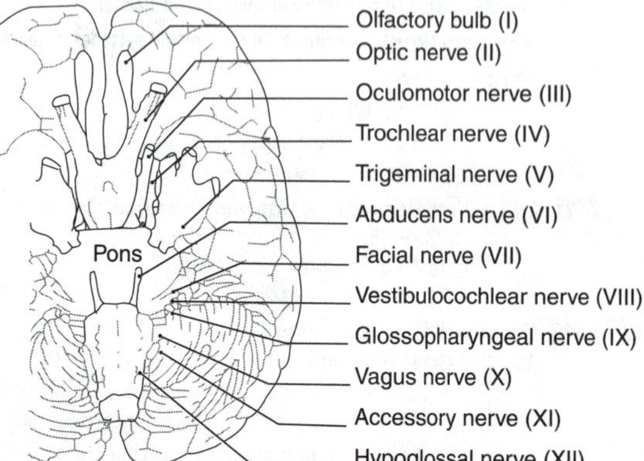

349.2 Disorders of meninges, not elsewhere classified

Adhesions, meningeal (cerebral) (spinal)
Cyst, spinal meninges
Meningocele, acquired
Pseudomeningocele, acquired

AHA: ▶1Q, '06, 15;◀ 2Q, '98, 18; 3Q, '94, 4

✓5th **349.8 Other specified disorders of nervous system**

349.81 Cerebrospinal fluid rhinorrhea CC

EXCLUDES *cerebrospinal fluid otorrhea (388.61)*

CC Excl: 250.60-250.63, 250.80-250.93, 349.81, 349.89, 349.9

DEF: Cerebrospinal fluid discharging from the nose; caused by fracture of frontal bone with tearing of dura mater and arachnoid.

349.82 Toxic encephalopathy CC

▶Toxic metabolic encephalopathy◀

Use additional E code to identify cause

AHA 4Q, '93, 29

CC Excl: 013.60-013.66, 017.90-017.96, 036.1, 049.8-049.9, 052.0, 054.3, 062.0-062.9, 063.0-063.9, 072.2, 090.41, 094.81, 130.0, 250.60-250.63, 250.80-250.93, 323.01-323.9, 341.20-341.22, 348.30-348.39, 348.8-348.9, 349.82-349.89, 349.9

DEF: Brain tissue degeneration due to toxic substance.

349.89 Other

349.9 Unspecified disorders of nervous system HIV

Disorder of nervous system (central) NOS

Peripheral Nervous System

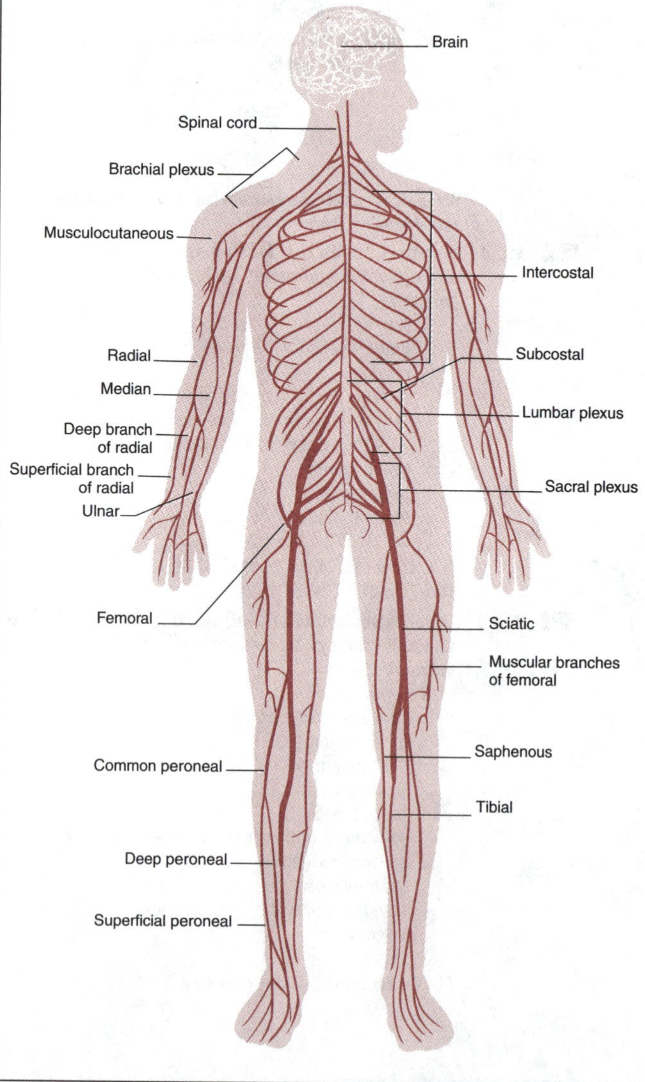

DISORDERS OF THE PERIPHERAL NERVOUS SYSTEM (350-359)

EXCLUDES *diseases of:*
acoustic [8th] nerve (388.5)
oculomotor [3rd, 4th, 6th] nerves (378.0-378.9)
optic [2nd] nerve (377.0-377.9)
peripheral autonomic nerves (337.0-337.9)
neuralgia / neuritis / radiculitis } NOS or "rheumatic" (729.2)
peripheral neuritis in pregnancy (646.4)

✓4th **350 Trigeminal nerve disorders**
INCLUDES disorders of 5th cranial nerve

350.1 Trigeminal neuralgia
Tic douloureux
Trigeminal neuralgia NOS
Trifacial neuralgia
EXCLUDES *postherpetic (053.12)*

350.2 Atypical face pain

350.8 Other specified trigeminal nerve disorders

350.9 Trigeminal nerve disorder, unspecified

✓4th **351 Facial nerve disorders**
INCLUDES disorders of 7th cranial nerve
EXCLUDES *that in newborn (767.5)*

351.0 Bell's palsy
Facial palsy
DEF: Unilateral paralysis of face due to lesion on facial nerve; produces facial distortion.

351.1 Geniculate ganglionitis
Geniculate ganglionitis NOS
EXCLUDES *herpetic (053.11)*
DEF: Inflammation of tissue at bend in facial nerve.

351.8 Other facial nerve disorders
Facial myokymia
Melkersson's syndrome
AHA: 3Q, '02, 13

351.9 Facial nerve disorder, unspecified

✓4th **352 Disorders of other cranial nerves**

352.0 Disorders of olfactory [lst] nerve

352.1 Glossopharyngeal neuralgia
AHA: 2Q, '02, 8
DEF: Pain between throat and ear along petrosal and jugular ganglia.

352.2 Other disorders of glossopharyngeal [9th] nerve

352.3 Disorders of pneumogastric [10th] nerve
Disorders of vagal nerve
EXCLUDES *paralysis of vocal cords or larynx (478.30-478.34)*
DEF: Nerve disorder affecting ear, tongue, pharynx, larynx, esophagus, viscera and thorax.

352.4 Disorders of accessory [11th] nerve
DEF: Nerve disorder affecting palate, pharynx, larynx, thoracic viscera, sternocleidomastoid and trapezius muscles.

352.5 Disorders of hypoglossal [12th] nerve
DEF: Nerve disorder affecting tongue muscles.

352.6 Multiple cranial nerve palsies
Collet-Sicard syndrome
Polyneuritis cranialis

352.9 Unspecified disorder of cranial nerves

✓4th **353 Nerve root and plexus disorders**
EXCLUDES *conditions due to:*
intervertebral disc disorders (722.0-722.9)
spondylosis (720.0-721.9)
vertebrogenic disorders (723.0-724.9)

353.0 Brachial plexus lesions
Cervical rib syndrome
Costoclavicular syndrome
Scalenus anticus syndrome
Thoracic outlet syndrome
EXCLUDES *brachial neuritis or radiculitis NOS (723.4)*
that in newborn (767.6)
DEF: Acquired disorder in tissue along nerves in shoulder; causes corresponding motor and sensory dysfunction.

Trigeminal and Facial Nerve Branches

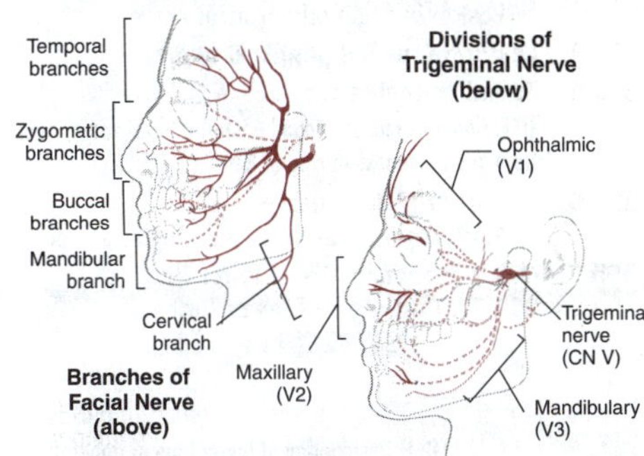

353.1 Lumbosacral plexus lesions
DEF: Acquired disorder in tissue along nerves in lower back; causes corresponding motor and sensory dysfunction.

353.2 Cervical root lesions, not elsewhere classified

353.3 Thoracic root lesions, not elsewhere classified

353.4 Lumbosacral root lesions, not elsewhere classified

353.5 Neuralgic amyotrophy
Parsonage-Aldren-Turner syndrome

353.6 Phantom limb (syndrome)
DEF: Abnormal tingling or a burning sensation, transient aches, and intermittent or continuous pain perceived as originating in the absent limb.

353.8 Other nerve root and plexus disorders

353.9 Unspecified nerve root and plexus disorder

✓4th **354 Mononeuritis of upper limb and mononeuritis multiplex**
DEF: Inflammation of a single nerve; known as mononeuritis multiplex when several nerves in unrelated body areas are affected.

354.0 Carpal tunnel syndrome
Median nerve entrapment
Partial thenar atrophy
DEF: Compression of median nerve by tendons; causes pain, tingling, numbness and burning sensation in hand.

354.1 Other lesion of median nerve
Median nerve neuritis

354.2 Lesion of ulnar nerve
Cubital tunnel syndrome
Tardy ulnar nerve palsy

354.3 Lesion of radial nerve
Acute radial nerve palsy
AHA: N-D, '87, 6

354.4 Causalgia of upper limb
EXCLUDES *causalgia:*
NOS (355.9)
lower limb (355.71)
DEF: Peripheral nerve damage, upper limb; usually due to injury; causes burning sensation and trophic skin changes.

354.5 Mononeuritis multiplex
Combinations of single conditions classifiable to 354 or 355

354.8 Other mononeuritis of upper limb

354.9 Mononeuritis of upper limb, unspecified

✓4th **355 Mononeuritis of lower limb**

355.0 Lesion of sciatic nerve
EXCLUDES *sciatica NOS (724.3)*
AHA: 2Q, '89, 12
DEF: Acquired disorder of sciatic nerve; causes motor and sensory dysfunction in back, buttock and leg.

355.1 Meralgia paresthetica
Lateral cutaneous femoral nerve of thigh compression or syndrome
DEF: Inguinal ligament entraps lateral femoral cutaneous nerve; causes tingling, pain and numbness along outer thigh.

355.2 Other lesion of femoral nerve

355.3 Lesion of lateral popliteal nerve
Lesion of common peroneal nerve

355.4 Lesion of medial popliteal nerve

355.5 Tarsal tunnel syndrome
DEF: Compressed, entrapped posterior tibial nerve; causes tingling, pain and numbness in sole of foot.

355.6 Lesion of plantar nerve
Morton's metatarsalgia, neuralgia, or neuroma

✓5th **355.7 Other mononeuritis of lower limb**

355.71 Causalgia of lower limb
EXCLUDES *causalgia:*
NOS (355.9)
upper limb (354.4)
DEF: Dysfunction of lower limb peripheral nerve, usually due to injury; causes burning pain and trophic skin changes.

355.79 Other mononeuritis of lower limb

355.8 Mononeuritis of lower limb, unspecified

355.9 Mononeuritis of unspecified site
Causalgia NOS
EXCLUDES *causalgia:*
lower limb (355.71)
upper limb (354.4)

✓4th **356 Hereditary and idiopathic peripheral neuropathy**

356.0 Hereditary peripheral neuropathy
Déjérine-Sottas disease

356.1 Peroneal muscular atrophy
Charcôt-Marie-Tooth disease
Neuropathic muscular atrophy
DEF: Genetic disorder, in muscles innervated by peroneal nerves; symptoms include muscle wasting in lower limbs and locomotor difficulties.

356.2 Hereditary sensory neuropathy
DEF: Inherited disorder in dorsal root ganglia, optic nerve, and cerebellum, causing sensory losses, shooting pains, and foot ulcers.

356.3 Refsum's disease
Heredopathia atactica polyneuritiformis
DEF: Genetic disorder of lipid metabolism; causes persistent, painful inflammation of nerves and retinitis pigmentosa.

356.4 Idiopathic progressive polyneuropathy

356.8 Other specified idiopathic peripheral neuropathy
Supranuclear paralysis

356.9 Unspecified

✓4th **357 Inflammatory and toxic neuropathy**

357.0 Acute infective polyneuritis CC
Guillain-Barré syndrome Postinfectious polyneuritis
CC Excl: 003.21, 013.00-013.16, 036.0, 036.89, 036.9, 041.81-041.89, 041.9, 047.0-047.9, 049.0-049.1, 053.0, 054.72, 072.1, 090.42, 091.81, 094.2, 098.89, 100.81, 112.83, 114.2, 115.01, 115.11, 115.91, 130.0, 139.8, 320.0-320.9, 321.0-321.8, 322.0-322.9, 349.89, 349.9, 357.0
AHA: 2Q, '98, 12
DEF: Guillain-Barré syndrome: acute demyelinatry polyneuropathy preceded by viral illness (i.e., herpes, cytomegalovirus [CMV], Epstein-Barr virus [EBV]) or a bacterial illness; areflexic motor paralysis with mild sensory disturbance and acellular rise in spinal fluid protein.

357.1 Polyneuropathy in collagen vasculardisease
Code first underlying disease, as:
disseminated lupus erythematosus (710.0)
polyarteritis nodosa (446.0)
rheumatoid arthritis (714.0)

357.2 Polyneuropathy in diabetes
Code first underlying disease (250.6)
AHA: 4Q, '03, 105; 2Q, '92, 15; 3Q, '91, 9

357.3 Polyneuropathy in malignant disease
Code first underlying disease (140.0-208.9)

357.4 Polyneuropathy in other diseases classified elsewhere
Code first underlying disease, as:
amyloidosis ▶(277.30-277.39)◀
beriberi (265.0)
▶chronic uremia (585.9)◀
deficiency of B vitamins (266.0-266.9)
diphtheria (032.0-032.9)
hypoglycemia (251.2)
pellagra (265.2)
porphyria (277.1)
sarcoidosis (135)
uremia ▶NOS (586)◀
EXCLUDES *polyneuropathy in:*
herpes zoster (053.13)
mumps (072.72)
AHA: 2Q, '98, 15

357.5 Alcoholic polyneuropathy

357.6 Polyneuropathy due to drugs
Use additional E code to identify drug

357.7 Polyneuropathy due to other toxic agents
Use additional E code to identify toxic agent

✓5th **357.8 Other**
AHA: 4Q, '02, 47; 2Q, '98, 12

357.81 Chronic inflammatory demyelinating polyneuritis
DEF: Inflammation of peripheral nerves resulting in destruction of myelin sheath; associated with diabetes mellitus, dys-proteinemias, renal failure and malnutrition; symptoms in-clude tingling, numbness, burning pain, diminished tendon reflexes, weakness, and atrophy in lower extremities.

357.82 Critical illness polyneuropathy
Acute motor neuropathy
AHA: 4Q, '03, 111
DEF: An acute axonal neuropathy, both sensory and motor, that is associated with Systemic Inflammatory Response Syndrome (SIRS).

357.89 Other inflammatory and toxic neuropathy

357.9 Unspecified

✓4th **358 Myoneural disorders**

✓5th **358.0 Myasthenia gravis**
AHA: 4Q, '03, 59
DEF: Autoimmune disorder of acetylcholine at neuromuscular junction; causing fatigue of voluntary muscles.

358.00 Myasthenia gravis without (acute) exacerbation CC
Myasthenia gravis NOS
CC Excl: 250.60-250.63, 250.80-250.93, 349.89, 349.9, 358.00-358.1

358.01 Myasthenia gravis with (acute) exacerbation CC
Myasthenia gravis in crisis
CC Excl: See code 358.00
AHA: 1Q, '05, 4; 4Q, '04, 139

358.1 Myasthenic syndromes in diseases classified elsewhere CC
Amyotrophy } from stated cause
Eaton-Lambert syndrome } classified elsewhere
Code first underlying disease, as:
botulism (005.1)
diabetes mellitus (250.6)
hypothyroidism (244.0-244.9)
malignant neoplasm (140.0-208.9)
pernicious anemia (281.0)
thyrotoxicosis (242.0-242.9)
CC Excl: See code 358.0

358.2 Toxic myoneural disorders
Use additional E code to identify toxic agent

358.8 Other specified myoneural disorders

358.9 Myoneural disorders, unspecified
AHA: 2Q, '02, 16

4th **359 Muscular dystrophies and other myopathies**

EXCLUDES *idiopathic polymyositis (710.4)*

359.0 Congenital hereditary muscular dystrophy CC

Benign congenital myopathy
Central core disease
Centronuclear myopathy
Myotubular myopathy
Nemaline body disease

EXCLUDES *arthrogryposis multiplex congenita (754.89)*

CC Excl: 250.60-250.63, 250.80-250.93, 349.89, 349.9, 359.0-359.1

DEF: Genetic disorder; causing progressive or nonprogressive muscle weakness.

359.1 Hereditary progressive muscular dystrophy CC

Muscular dystrophy:
- NOS
- distal
- Duchenne
- Erb's
- fascioscapulohumeral

Muscular dystrophy:
- Gower's
- Landouzy-Déjérine
- limb-girdle
- ocular
- oculopharyngeal

CC Excl: See code 359.0

DEF: Genetic degenerative, muscle disease; causes progressive weakness, wasting of muscle with no nerve involvement.

359.2 Myotonic disorders

Dystrophia myotonica
Eulenburg's disease
Myotonia congenita
Paramyotonia congenita
Steinert's disease
Thomsen's disease

DEF: Impaired movement due to spasmatic, rigid muscles.

359.3 Familial periodic paralysis

Hypokalemic familial periodic paralysis

DEF: Genetic disorder; characterized by rapidly progressive flaccid paralysis; attacks often occur after exercise or exposure to cold or dietary changes.

359.4 Toxic myopathy

Use additional E code to identify toxic agent

AHA: 1Q, '88, 5

DEF: Muscle disorder caused by toxic agent.

359.5 Myopathy in endocrine diseases classified elsewhere

Code first underlying disease, as:
- Addison's disease (255.4)
- Cushing's syndrome (255.0)
- hypopituitarism (253.2)
- myxedema (244.0-244.9)
- thyrotoxicosis (242.0-242.9)

DEF: Muscle disorder secondary to dysfunction in hormone secretion.

359.6 Symptomatic inflammatory myopathy in diseases classified elsewhere

Code first underlying disease, as:
- amyloidosis ▶(277.30-277.39)◀
- disseminated lupus erythematosus (710.0)
- malignant neoplasm (140.0-208.9)
- polyarteritis nodosa (446.0)
- rheumatoid arthritis (714.0)
- sarcoidosis (135)
- scleroderma (710.1)
- Sjögren's disease (710.2)

5th **359.8 Other myopathies**

AHA: 4Q, '02, 47; 3Q, '90, 17

359.81 Critical illness myopathy

Acute necrotizing myopathy
Acute quadriplegic myopathy
Intensive care (ICU) myopathy
Myopathy of critical illness

359.89 Other myopathies

359.9 Myopathy, unspecified

DISORDERS OF THE EYE AND ADNEXA (360-379)

4th **360 Disorders of the globe**

INCLUDES disorders affecting multiple structures of eye

5th **360.0 Purulent endophthalmitis**

EXCLUDES ▶ *bleb associated endophthalmitis (379.63)*◀

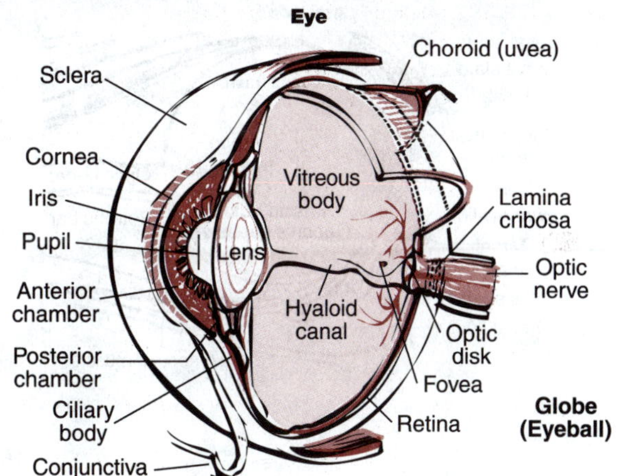

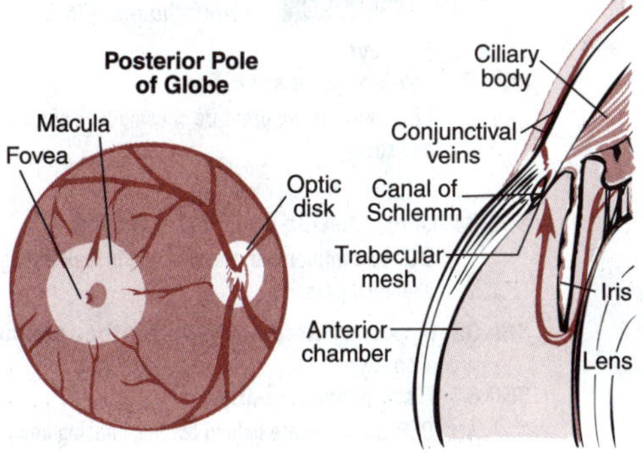

360.00 Purulent endophthalmitis, unspecified
360.01 Acute endophthalmitis
360.02 Panophthalmitis
360.03 Chronic endophthalmitis
360.04 Vitreous abscess

5th **360.1 Other endophthalmitis**

EXCLUDES ▶ *bleb associated endophthalmitis (379.63)*◀

360.11 Sympathetic uveitis

DEF: Inflammation of vascular layer of uninjured eye; follows injury to other eye.

360.12 Panuveitis

DEF: Inflammation of entire vascular layer of eye, including choroid, iris and ciliary body.

360.13 Parasitic endophthalmitis NOS

DEF: Parasitic infection causing inflammation of the entire eye.

360.14 Ophthalmia nodosa

DEF: Conjunctival inflammation caused by embedded hairs.

360.19 Other

Phacoanaphylactic endophthalmitis

5th **360.2 Degenerative disorders of globe**

AHA: 3Q, '91, 3

360.20 Degenerative disorder of globe, unspecified
360.21 Progressive high (degenerative) myopia

Malignant myopia

DEF: Severe, progressive nearsightedness in adults, complicated by serious disease of the choroid; leads to retinal detachment and blindness.

360.23 Siderosis

DEF: Iron pigment deposits within tissue of eyeball; caused by high iron content of blood.

360.24 Other metallosis

Chalcosis

DEF: Metal deposits, other than iron, within eyeball tissues.

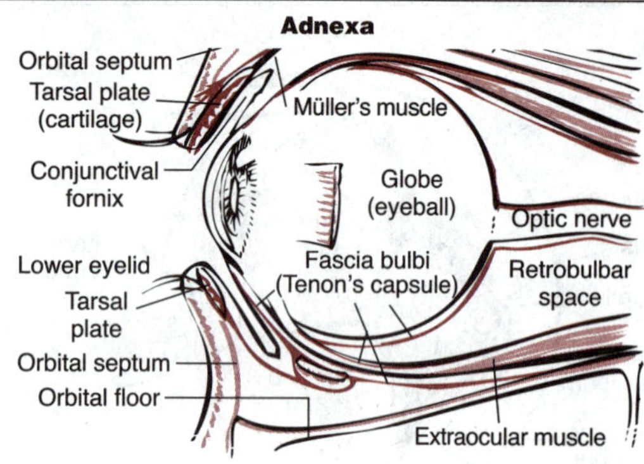

360.29 Other
EXCLUDES *xerophthalmia (264.7)*

✓5th **360.3 Hypotony of eye**
360.30 Hypotony, unspecified
DEF: Low osmotic pressure causing lack of tone, tension and strength.
360.31 Primary hypotony
360.32 Ocular fistula causing hypotony
DEF: Low intraocular pressure due to leak through abnormal passage.
360.33 Hypotony associated with other ocular disorders
360.34 Flat anterior chamber
DEF: Low pressure behind cornea, causing compression.

✓5th **360.4 Degenerated conditions of globe**
360.40 Degenerated globe or eye, unspecified
360.41 Blind hypotensive eye
Atrophy of globe
Phthisis bulbi
DEF: Vision loss due to extremely low intraocular pressure.
360.42 Blind hypertensive eye
Absolute glaucoma
DEF: Vision loss due to painful, high intraocular pressure.
360.43 Hemophthalmos, except current injury
EXCLUDES *traumatic (871.0-871.9, 921.0-921.9)*
DEF: Pool of blood within eyeball, not from current injury.
360.44 Leucocoria
DEF: Whitish mass or reflex in the pupil behind lens; also called cat's eye reflex; often indicative of retinoblastoma.

✓5th **360.5 Retained (old) intraocular foreign body, magnetic**
EXCLUDES *current penetrating injury with magnetic foreign body (871.5)*
retained (old) foreign body of orbit (376.6)
360.50 Foreign body, magnetic, intraocular, unspecified
360.51 Foreign body, magnetic, in anterior chamber
360.52 Foreign body, magnetic, in iris or ciliary body
360.53 Foreign body, magnetic, in lens
360.54 Foreign body, magnetic, in vitreous
360.55 Foreign body, magnetic, in posterior wall
360.59 Foreign body, magnetic, in other or multiple sites

✓5th **360.6 Retained (old) intraocular foreign body, nonmagnetic**
Retained (old) foreign body:
NOS
nonmagnetic
EXCLUDES *current penetrating injury with (nonmagnetic) foreign body (871.6)*
retained (old) foreign body in orbit (376.6)
360.60 Foreign body, intraocular, unspecified
360.61 Foreign body in anterior chamber
360.62 Foreign body in iris or ciliary body
360.63 Foreign body in lens
360.64 Foreign body in vitreous
360.65 Foreign body in posterior wall
360.69 Foreign body in other or multiple sites

✓5th **360.8 Other disorders of globe**
360.81 Luxation of globe
DEF: Displacement of eyeball.
360.89 Other

360.9 Unspecified disorder of globe

✓4th **361 Retinal detachments and defects**
DEF: Light-sensitive layer at back of eye, separates from blood supply; disrupting vision.

✓5th **361.0 Retinal detachment with retinal defect**
Rhegmatogenous retinal detachment
EXCLUDES *detachment of retinal pigment epithelium (362.42-362.43)*
retinal detachment (serous) (without defect) (361.2)
361.00 Retinal detachment with retinal defect, unspecified
361.01 Recent detachment, partial, with single defect
361.02 Recent detachment, partial, with multiple defects
361.03 Recent detachment, partial, with giant tear
361.04 Recent detachment, partial, with retinal dialysis
Dialysis (juvenile) of retina (with detachment)
361.05 Recent detachment, total or subtotal
361.06 Old detachment, partial
Delimited old retinal detachment
361.07 Old detachment, total or subtotal

✓5th **361.1 Retinoschisis and retinal cysts**
EXCLUDES *juvenile retinoschisis (362.73)*
microcystoid degeneration of retina (362.62)
parasitic cyst of retina (360.13)
361.10 Retinoschisis, unspecified
DEF: Separation of retina due to degenerative process of aging; should not be confused with acute retinal detachment.
361.11 Flat retinoschisis
DEF: Slow, progressive split of retinal sensory layers
361.12 Bullous retinoschisis
DEF: Fluid retention between split retinal sensory layers.
361.13 Primary retinal cysts
361.14 Secondary retinal cysts
361.19 Other
Pseudocyst of retina

361.2 Serous retinal detachment
Retinal detachment without retinal defect
EXCLUDES *central serous retinopathy (362.41)*
retinal pigment epithelium detachment (362.42-362.43)

N Newborn Age: 0 P Pediatric Age: 0-17 M Maternity Age: 12-55 A Adult Age: 15-124 CC CC Condition MC Major Complication CD Complex Dx HIV HIV Related Dx

✓5th **361.3 Retinal defects without detachment**

EXCLUDES *chorioretinal scars after surgery for detachment (363.30-363.35)*
peripheral retinal degeneration without defect (362.60-362.66)

361.30 Retinal defect, unspecified
Retinal break(s) NOS

361.31 Round hole of retina without detachment

361.32 Horseshoe tear of retina without detachment
Operculum of retina without mention of detachment

361.33 Multiple defects of retina without detachment

✓5th **361.8 Other forms of retinal detachment**

361.81 Traction detachment of retina
Traction detachment with vitreoretinal organization

361.89 Other
AHA: 3Q, '99, 12

361.9 Unspecified retinal detachment
AHA: N-D, '87, 10

✓4th **362 Other retinal disorders**

EXCLUDES *chorioretinal scars (363.30-363.35)*
chorioretinitis (363.0-363.2)

✓5th **362.0 Diabetic retinopathy**
Code first diabetes (250.5)
DEF: Retinal changes in diabetes of long duration; causes hemorrhages, microaneurysms, waxy deposits and proliferative noninflammatory degenerative disease of retina.
AHA: 4Q, '05, 65; 3Q, '91, 8

362.01 Background diabetic retinopathy
Diabetic retinal microaneurysms
Diabetic retinopathy NOS

362.02 Proliferative diabetic retinopathy
AHA: 3Q, '96, 5
DEF: Occurrence of the ischemic effects of vessel blockages result in neovascularization; new blood vessels begin to form to compensate for restricted blood flow; multiple areas of the retina and inner vitreous may be affected.

362.03 Nonproliferative diabetic retinopathy NOS

362.04 Mild nonproliferative diabetic retinopathy
DEF: Early stages of degenerative condition of the retina due to diabetes; microaneurysm formation; small balloon-like swelling of the retinal vessels.

362.05 Moderate nonproliferative diabetic retinopathy
DEF: Stage of degenerative condition of the retina due to diabetes with pronounced microaneurysms; vessel blockages can occur.

362.06 Severe nonproliferative diabetic retinopathy
AHA: 4Q, '05, 67
DEF: Stage of degenerative condition of the retina due to diabetes in which vascular breakdown in the retina results in multiple vascular blockages, or "beadings," intraretinal hemorrhages can be numerous.

362.07 Diabetic macular edema
Note: Code 362.07 must be used with a code for diabetic retinopathy (362.01-362.06)
Diabetic retinal edema
DEF: Leakage from retinal blood vessels causes swelling of the macula and impaired vision; exudates or plaques may develop in the posterior pole of the retina due to the breakdown of retinal vasculature.

✓5th **362.1 Other background retinopathy and retinal vascular changes**

362.10 Background retinopathy, unspecified
AHA: ▶1Q, '06, 12◀

362.11 Hypertensive retinopathy
AHA: 3Q, '90, 3
DEF: Retinal irregularities caused by systemic hypertension.

362.12 Exudative retinopathy
Coats' syndrome
AHA: 3Q, '99, 12

362.13 Changes in vascular appearance
Vascular sheathing of retina
Use additional code for any associated atherosclerosis (440.8)

362.14 Retinal microaneurysms NOS
DEF: Microscopic dilation of retinal vessels in nondiabetic.

362.15 Retinal telangiectasia
DEF:Dilation of blood vessels of the retina.

362.16 Retinal neovascularization NOS
Neovascularization:
choroidal
subretinal
DEF: New and abnormal vascular growth in the retina.

362.17 Other intraretinal microvascular abnormalities
Retinal sclerosis
Retinal varices

362.18 Retinal vasculitis
Eales' disease
Retinal:
arteritis
endarteritis
Retinal:
perivasculitis
phlebitis
DEF: Inflammation of retinal blood vessels.

✓5th **362.2 Other proliferative retinopathy**

362.21 Retrolental fibroplasia
DEF: Fibrous tissue in vitreous, from retina to lens, causing blindness; associated with premature infants requiring high amounts of oxygen.

362.29 Other nondiabetic proliferative retinopathy
AHA: 3Q, '96, 5

✓5th **362.3 Retinal vascular occlusion**
DEF: Obstructed blood flow to and from retina.

362.30 Retinal vascular occlusion, unspecified

362.31 Central retinal artery occlusion

362.32 Arterial branch occlusion

362.33 Partial arterial occlusion
Hollenhorst plaque
Retinal microembolism

362.34 Transient arterial occlusion
Amaurosis fugax
AHA: 1Q, '00, 16

362.35 Central retinal vein occlusion
AHA: 2Q, '93, 6

362.36 Venous tributary (branch) occlusion

362.37 Venous engorgement
Occlusion:
incipient } of retinal vein
partial } of retinal vein

✓5th **362.4 Separation of retinal layers**

EXCLUDES *retinal detachment (serous) (361.2)*
rhegmatogenous (361.00-361.07)

362.40 Retinal layer separation, unspecified

362.41 Central serous retinopathy
DEF: Serous-filled blister causing detachment of retina from pigment epithelium.

362.42 Serous detachment of retinal pigment epithelium
Exudative detachment of retinal pigment epithelium
DEF: Blister of fatty fluid causing detachment of retina from pigment epithelium.

362.43 Hemorrhagic detachment of retinal pigment epithelium
DEF: Blood-filled blister causing detachment of retina from pigment epithelium.

✓5th **362.5 Degeneration of macula and posterior pole**

EXCLUDES *degeneration of optic disc (377.21-377.24)*
hereditary retinal degeneration [dystrophy] (362.70-362.77)

362.50 Macular degeneration (senile), unspecified

362.51 Nonexudative senile macular degeneration
Senile macular degeneration:
atrophic
dry

362.52 Exudative senile macular degeneration
Kuhnt-Junius degeneration
Senile macular degeneration:
disciform
wet
DEF: Leakage in macular blood vessels with loss of visual acuity.

362.53 Cystoid macular degeneration
Cystoid macular edema
DEF: Retinal swelling and cyst formation in macula.

362.54 Macular cyst, hole, or pseudohole

362.55 Toxic maculopathy
Use additional E code to identify drug, if drug induced

362.56 Macular puckering
Preretinal fibrosis

362.57 Drusen (degenerative)
DEF: White, hyaline deposits on Bruch's membrane (lamina basalis choroideae).

✓5th **362.6 Peripheral retinal degenerations**

EXCLUDES *hereditary retinal degeneration [dystrophy] (362.70-362.77)*
retinal degeneration with retinal defect (361.00-361.07)

362.60 Peripheral retinal degeneration, unspecified

362.61 Paving stone degeneration
DEF: Degeneration of peripheral retina; causes thinning through which choroid is visible.

362.62 Microcystoid degeneration
Blessig's cysts Iwanoff's cysts

362.63 Lattice degeneration
Palisade degeneration of retina
DEF: Degeneration of retina; often bilateral, usually benign; characterized by lines intersecting at irregular intervals in peripheral retina; retinal thinning and retinal holes may occur.

362.64 Senile reticular degeneration
DEF: Net-like appearance of retina; sign of degeneration.

362.65 Secondary pigmentary degeneration
Pseudoretinitis pigmentosa

362.66 Secondary vitreoretinal degenerations

✓5th **362.7 Hereditary retinal dystrophies**
DEF: Genetically induced progressive changes in retina.

362.70 Hereditary retinal dystrophy, unspecified

362.71 Retinal dystrophy in systemic or cerebroretinal lipidoses
Code first underlying disease, as:
cerebroretinal lipidoses (330.1)
systemic lipidoses (272.7)

362.72 Retinal dystrophy in other systemic disorders and syndromes
Code first underlying disease, as:
Bassen-Kornzweig syndrome (272.5)
Refsum's disease (356.3)

362.73 Vitreoretinal dystrophies
Juvenile retinoschisis

362.74 Pigmentary retinal dystrophy
Retinal dystrophy, albipunctate
Retinitis pigmentosa

362.75 Other dystrophies primarily involving the sensory retina
Progressive cone(-rod) dystrophy
Stargardt's disease

362.76 Dystrophies primarily involving the retinal pigment epithelium
Fundus flavimaculatus
Vitelliform dystrophy

362.77 Dystrophies primarily involving Bruch's membrane
Dystrophy:
hyaline
pseudoinflammatory foveal
Hereditary drusen

✓5th **362.8 Other retinal disorders**

EXCLUDES *chorioretinal inflammations (363.0-363.2)*
chorioretinal scars (363.30-363.35)

362.81 Retinal hemorrhage
Hemorrhage:
preretinal
retinal (deep) (superficial)
subretinal
AHA: 4Q, '96, 43

362.82 Retinal exudates and deposits

362.83 Retinal edema
Retinal:
cotton wool spots
edema (localized) (macular) (peripheral)
DEF: Retinal swelling due to fluid accumulation.

362.84 Retinal ischemia
DEF: Reduced retinal blood supply.

362.85 Retinal nerve fiber bundle defects

362.89 Other retinal disorders

362.9 Unspecified retinal disorder

✓4th **363 Chorioretinal inflammations, scars, and other disorders of choroid**

✓5th **363.0 Focal chorioretinitis and focal retinochoroiditis**

EXCLUDES *focal chorioretinitis or retinochoroiditis in:*
histoplasmosis (115.02, 115.12, 115.92)
toxoplasmosis (130.2)
congenital infection (771.2)

363.00 Focal chorioretinitis, unspecified
Focal:
choroiditis or chorioretinitis NOS
retinitis or retinochoroiditis NOS

363.01 Focal choroiditis and chorioretinitis, juxtapapillary

363.03 Focal choroiditis and chorioretinitis of other posterior pole

363.04 Focal choroiditis and chorioretinitis, peripheral

363.05 Focal retinitis and retinochoroiditis, juxtapapillary
Neuroretinitis

363.06 Focal retinitis and retinochoroiditis, macular or paramacular

363.07 Focal retinitis and retinochoroiditis of other posterior pole

363.08 Focal retinitis and retinochoroiditis, peripheral

✓5th **363.1 Disseminated chorioretinitis and disseminated retinochoroiditis**

EXCLUDES *disseminated choroiditis or chorioretinitis in secondary syphilis (091.51)*
neurosyphilitic disseminated retinitis or retinochoroiditis (094.83)
retinal (peri)vasculitis (362.18)

363.10 Disseminated chorioretinitis, unspecified
Disseminated:
choroiditis or chorioretinitis NOS
retinitis or retinochoroiditis NOS

363.11 Disseminated choroiditis and chorioretinitis, posterior pole

363.12 Disseminated choroiditis and chorioretinitis, peripheral

363.13 Disseminated choroiditis and chorioretinitis, generalized
Code first any underlying disease, as:
tuberculosis (017.3)

363.14 Disseminated retinitis and retinochoroiditis, metastatic

363.15 Disseminated retinitis and retinochoroiditis, pigment epitheliopathy
Acute posterior multifocal placoid pigment epitheliopathy
DEF: Widespread inflammation of retina and choroid; characterized by pigmented epithelium involvement.

✓5th **363.2 Other and unspecified forms of chorioretinitis and retinochoroiditis**
EXCLUDES *panophthalmitis (360.02)*
sympathetic uveitis (360.11)
uveitis NOS (364.3)

363.20 Chorioretinitis, unspecified
Choroiditis NOS
Retinitis NOS
Uveitis, posterior NOS

363.21 Pars planitis
Posterior cyclitis
DEF: Inflammation of peripheral retina and ciliary body; characterized by bands of white cells.

363.22 Harada's disease
DEF: Retinal detachment and bilateral widespread exudative choroiditis; symptoms include headache, vomiting, increased lymphocytes in cerebrospinal fluid; and temporary or permanent deafness may occur.

✓5th **363.3 Chorioretinal scars**
Scar (postinflammatory) (postsurgical) (posttraumatic):
choroid
retina

363.30 Chorioretinal scar, unspecified

363.31 Solar retinopathy
DEF: Retinal scarring caused by solar radiation.

363.32 Other macular scars

363.33 Other scars of posterior pole

363.34 Peripheral scars

363.35 Disseminated scars

✓5th **363.4 Choroidal degenerations**

363.40 Choroidal degeneration, unspecified
Choroidal sclerosis NOS

363.41 Senile atrophy of choroid
DEF: Wasting away of choroid; due to aging.

363.42 Diffuse secondary atrophy of choroid
DEF: Wasting away of choroid in systemic disease.

363.43 Angioid streaks of choroid
DEF: Degeneration of choroid; characterized by dark brown steaks radiating from optic disk; occurs with pseudoxanthoma, elasticum or Paget's disease.

✓5th **363.5 Hereditary choroidal dystrophies**
Hereditary choroidal atrophy:
partial [choriocapillaris]
total [all vessels]

363.50 Hereditary choroidal dystrophy or atrophy, unspecified

363.51 Circumpapillary dystrophy of choroid, partial

363.52 Circumpapillary dystrophy of choroid, total
Helicoid dystrophy of choroid

363.53 Central dystrophy of choroid, partial
Dystrophy, choroidal:
central areolar
circinate

363.54 Central choroidal atrophy, total
Dystrophy, choroidal:
central gyrate
serpiginous

363.55 Choroideremia
DEF: Hereditary choroid degeneration, occurs in first decade; characterized by constricted visual field and ultimately blindness in males; less debilitating in females.

363.56 Other diffuse or generalized dystrophy, partial
Diffuse choroidal sclerosis

363.57 Other diffuse or generalized dystrophy, total
Generalized gyrate atrophy, choroid

✓5th **363.6 Choroidal hemorrhage and rupture**

363.61 Choroidal hemorrhage, unspecified

363.62 Expulsive choroidal hemorrhage

363.63 Choroidal rupture

✓5th **363.7 Choroidal detachment**

363.70 Choroidal detachment, unspecified

363.71 Serous choroidal detachment
DEF: Detachment of choroid from sclera; due to blister of serous fluid.

363.72 Hemorrhagic choroidal detachment
DEF: Detachment of choroid from sclera; due to blood-filled blister.

363.8 Other disorders of choroid
AHA: ▶1Q, '06, 12◀

363.9 Unspecified disorder of choroid

✓4th **364 Disorders of iris and ciliary body**

✓5th **364.0 Acute and subacute iridocyclitis**
Anterior uveitis, Cyclitis, Iridocyclitis, Iritis } acute, subacute
EXCLUDES *gonococcal (098.41)*
herpes simplex (054.44)
herpes zoster (053.22)

364.00 Acute and subacute iridocyclitis, unspecified

364.01 Primary iridocyclitis

364.02 Recurrent iridocyclitis

364.03 Secondary iridocyclitis, infectious

364.04 Secondary iridocyclitis, noninfectious
Aqueous:
cells
fibrin
Aqueous:
flare

364.05 Hypopyon
DEF: Accumulation of white blood cells between cornea and lens.

✓5th **364.1 Chronic iridocyclitis**
EXCLUDES *posterior cyclitis (363.21)*

364.10 Chronic iridocyclitis, unspecified

364.11 Chronic iridocyclitis in diseases classified elsewhere
Code first underlying disease, as:
sarcoidosis (135)
tuberculosis (017.3)
EXCLUDES *syphilitic iridocyclitis (091.52)*
DEF: Persistent inflammation of iris and ciliary body; due to underlying disease or condition.

✓5th **364.2 Certain types of iridocyclitis**
EXCLUDES *posterior cyclitis (363.21)*
sympathetic uveitis (360.11)

364.21 Fuchs' heterochromic cyclitis
DEF: Chronic cyclitis characterized by differences in the color of the two irises; the lighter iris appears in the inflamed eye.

364.22 Glaucomatocyclitic crises
DEF: One-sided form of secondary open angle glaucoma; recurrent, uncommon and of short duration; causes high intraocular pressure, rarely damage.

364.23 Lens-induced iridocyclitis
DEF: Inflammation of iris; due to immune reaction to proteins in lens following trauma or other lens abnormality.

364.24 Vogt-Koyanagi syndrome
DEF: Uveomeningitis with exudative iridocyclitis and choroiditis; causes depigmentation of hair and skin, detached retina; tinnitus and loss of hearing may occur.

364.3 Unspecified iridocyclitis
Uveitis NOS

✓5th **364.4 Vascular disorders of iris and ciliary body**

364.41 Hyphema
Hemorrhage of iris or ciliary body
DEF: Hemorrhage in anterior chamber; also called hyphemia or "blood shot" eyes.

364.42 Rubeosis iridis
Neovascularization of iris or ciliary body
DEF: Blood vessel and connective tissue formation on surface of iris; symptomatic of diabetic retinopathy, central retinal vein occlusion and retinal detachment.

✓5th **364.5 Degenerations of iris and ciliary body**

364.51 Essential or progressive iris atrophy

364.52 Iridoschisis
DEF: Splitting of the iris into two layers.

364.53 Pigmentary iris degeneration
Acquired heterochromia } of iris
Pigment dispersion syndrome } of iris
Translucency } of iris

364.54 Degeneration of pupillary margin
Atrophy of sphincter } of iris
Ectropion of pigment epithelium } of iris

364.55 Miotic cysts of pupillary margin
DEF: Serous-filled sacs in pupillary margin of iris.

364.56 Degenerative changes of chamber angle

364.57 Degenerative changes of ciliary body

364.59 Other iris atrophy
Iris atrophy (generalized) (sector shaped)

✓5th **364.6 Cysts of iris, ciliary body, and anterior chamber**
EXCLUDES *miotic pupillary cyst (364.55)*
parasitic cyst (360.13)

364.60 Idiopathic cysts
DEF: Fluid-filled sacs in iris or ciliary body; unknown etiology.

364.61 Implantation cysts
Epithelial down-growth, anterior chamber
Implantation cysts (surgical) (traumatic)

364.62 Exudative cysts of iris or anterior chamber

364.63 Primary cyst of pars plana
DEF: Fluid-filled sacs of outermost ciliary ring.

364.64 Exudative cyst of pars plana
DEF: Protein, fatty-filled sacs of outermost ciliary ring; due to fluid lead from blood vessels.

✓5th **364.7 Adhesions and disruptions of iris and ciliary body**
EXCLUDES *flat anterior chamber (360.34)*

364.70 Adhesions of iris, unspecified
Synechiae (iris) NOS

364.71 Posterior synechiae
DEF: Adhesion binding iris to lens.

364.72 Anterior synechiae
DEF: Adhesion binding the iris to cornea.

364.73 Goniosynechiae
Peripheral anterior synechiae
DEF: Adhesion binding the iris to cornea at the angle of the anterior chamber.

364.74 Pupillary membranes
Iris bombé
Pupillary:
occlusion
seclusion
DEF: Membrane traversing the pupil and blocking vision.

364.75 Pupillary abnormalities
Deformed pupil
Ectopic pupil
Rupture of sphincter, pupil

364.76 Iridodialysis
DEF: Separation of the iris from the ciliary body base; due to trauma or surgical accident.

364.77 Recession of chamber angle
DEF: Receding of anterior chamber angle of the eye; restricts vision.

364.8 Other disorders of iris and ciliary body
Prolapse of iris NOS
EXCLUDES *prolapse of iris in recent wound (871.1)*

364.9 Unspecified disorder of iris and ciliary body

✓4th **365 Glaucoma**
EXCLUDES *blind hypertensive eye [absolute glaucoma] (360.42)*
congenital glaucoma (743.20-743.22)
DEF: Rise in intraocular pressure which restricts blood flow; multiple causes.

✓5th **365.0 Borderline glaucoma [glaucoma suspect]**
AHA: 1Q, '90, 8

365.00 Preglaucoma, unspecified

365.01 Open angle with borderline findings
Open angle with:
borderline intraocular pressure
cupping of optic discs
DEF: Minor block of aqueous outflow from eye.

365.02 Anatomical narrow angle

365.03 Steroid responders

365.04 Ocular hypertension
DEF: High fluid pressure within eye; no apparent cause.

✓5th **365.1 Open-angle glaucoma**

365.10 Open-angle glaucoma, unspecified
Wide-angle glaucoma NOS

365.11 Primary open angle glaucoma
Chronic simple glaucoma
DEF: High intraocular pressure, despite free flow of aqueous.

365.12 Low tension glaucoma

365.13 Pigmentary glaucoma
DEF: High intraocular pressure; due to iris pigment granules blocking aqueous flow.

365.14 Glaucoma of childhood
Infantile or juvenile glaucoma

365.15 Residual stage of open angle glaucoma

✓5th **365.2 Primary angle-closure glaucoma**

365.20 Primary angle-closure glaucoma, unspecified

365.21 Intermittent angle-closure glaucoma
Angle-closure glaucoma:
interval
subacute
DEF: Recurring attacks of high intraocular pressure; due to blocked aqueous flow.

365.22 Acute angle-closure glaucoma
DEF: Sudden, severe rise in intraocular pressure due to blockage in aqueous drainage.

365.23 Chronic angle-closure glaucoma
AHA: 2Q, '98, 16

365.24 Residual stage of angle-closure glaucoma

✓5th **365.3 Corticosteroid-induced glaucoma**
DEF: Elevated intraocular pressure; due to long-term corticosteroid therapy.

365.31 Glaucomatous stage

365.32 Residual stage

✓5th **365.4 Glaucoma associated with congenital anomalies, dystrophies, and systemic syndromes**

365.41 Glaucoma associated with chamber angle anomalies
Code first associated disorder, as:
Axenfeld's anomaly (743.44)
Rieger's anomaly or syndrome (743.44)

365.42 ***Glaucoma associated with anomalies of iris***
Code first associated disorder, as:
aniridia (743.45)
essential iris atrophy (364.51)

365.43 ***Glaucoma associated with other anterior segment anomalies***
Code first associated disorder, as:
microcornea (743.41)

365.44 ***Glaucoma associated with systemic syndromes***
Code first associated disease, as
neurofibromatosis (237.7)
Sturge-Weber (-Dimitri) syndrome (759.6)

✓5th **365.5 Glaucoma associated with disorders of the lens**

365.51 Phacolytic glaucoma
Use additional code for associated hypermature cataract (366.18)
DEF: Elevated intraocular pressure; due to lens protein blocking aqueous flow.

365.52 Pseudoexfoliation glaucoma
Use additional code for associated pseudoexfoliation of capsule (366.11)
DEF: Glaucoma characterized by small grayish particles deposited on the lens.

365.59 Glaucoma associated with other lens disorders
Use additional code for associated disorder, as:
dislocation of lens (379.33-379.34)
spherophakia (743.36)

✓5th **365.6 Glaucoma associated with other ocular disorders**

365.60 Glaucoma associated with unspecified ocular disorder

365.61 Glaucoma associated with pupillary block
Use additional code for associated disorder, as:
seclusion of pupil [iris bombé] (364.74)
DEF: Acute, open-angle glaucoma caused by mature cataract; aqueous flow is blocked by lens material and macrophages.

365.62 Glaucoma associated with ocular inflammations
Use additional code for associated disorder, as:
glaucomatocyclitic crises (364.22)
iridocyclitis (364.0-364.3)

365.63 Glaucoma associated with vascular disorders
Use additional code for associated disorder, as:
central retinal vein occlusion (362.35)
hyphema (364.41)

Aqueous Misdirection Syndrome

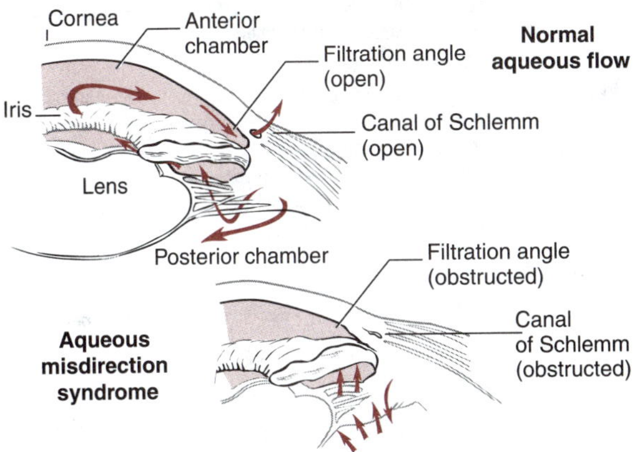

365.64 Glaucoma associated with tumors or cysts
Use additional code for associated disorder, as:
benign neoplasm (224.0-224.9)
epithelial down-growth (364.61)
malignant neoplasm (190.0-190.9)

365.65 Glaucoma associated with ocular trauma
Use additional code for associated condition, as:
contusion of globe (921.3)
recession of chamber angle (364.77)

✓5th **365.8 Other specified forms of glaucoma**

365.81 Hypersecretion glaucoma

365.82 Glaucoma with increased episcleral venous pressure

365.83 Aqueous misdirection
Malignant glaucoma
AHA: 4Q, '02, 48
DEF: A form of glaucoma that occurs when aqueous humor flows into the posterior chamber of the eye (vitreous) rather than through the normal recycling channels into the anterior chamber.

365.89 Other specified glaucoma
AHA: 2Q, '98, 16

365.9 Unspecified glaucoma
AHA: 3Q, '03, 14; 2Q, '01, 16

✓4th **366 Cataract**
DEF: A variety of conditions that create a cloudy, or calcified lens that obstructs vision.
EXCLUDES *congenital cataract (743.30-743.34)*

✓5th **366.0 Infantile, juvenile, and presenile cataract**

366.00 Nonsenile cataract, unspecified

366.01 Anterior subcapsular polar cataract
DEF: Defect within the front, center lens surface.

366.02 Posterior subcapsular polar cataract
DEF: Defect within the rear, center lens surface.

366.03 Cortical, lamellar, or zonular cataract
DEF: Opacities radiating from center to edge of lens; appear as thin, concentric layers of lens.

366.04 Nuclear cataract

366.09 Other and combined forms of nonsenile cataract

✓5th **366.1 Senile cataract**
AHA: 3Q, '91, 9; S-O, '85, 10

366.10 Senile cataract, unspecified A
AHA: 1Q, '03, 5

366.11 Pseudoexfoliation of lens capsule A

366.12 Incipient cataract A

Cataract:	Cataract:
coronary	punctate
immature NOS	Water clefts

DEF: Minor disorders of lens not affecting vision; due to aging.

366.13 Anterior subcapsular polar senile cataract A

366.14 Posterior subcapsular polar senile cataract A

366.15 Cortical senile cataract A

366.16 Nuclear sclerosis A
Cataracta brunescens
Nuclear cataract

366.17 Total or mature cataract A

366.18 Hypermature cataract A
Morgagni cataract

366.19 Other and combined forms of senile cataract A

Cataract

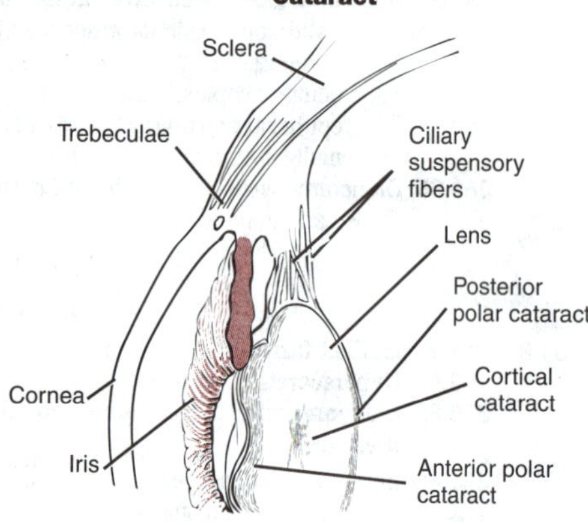

✓5th **366.2 Traumatic cataract**
- **366.20 Traumatic cataract, unspecified**
- **366.21 Localized traumatic opacities**
  - Vossius' ring
- **366.22 Total traumatic cataract**
- **366.23 Partially resolved traumatic cataract**

✓5th **366.3 Cataract secondary to ocular disorders**
- **366.30 Cataracta complicata, unspecified**
- **366.31 Glaucomatous flecks (subcapsular)**
  - Code first underlying glaucoma (365.0-365.9)
- **366.32 Cataract in inflammatory disorders**
  - Code first underlying condition, as:
    - chronic choroiditis (363.0-363.2)
- **366.33 Cataract with neovascularization**
  - Code first underlying condition, as:
    - chronic iridocyclitis (364.10)
- **366.34 Cataract in degenerative disorders**
  - Sunflower cataract
  - Code first underlying condition, as:
    - chalcosis (360.24)
    - degenerative myopia (360.21)
    - pigmentary retinal dystrophy (362.74)

✓5th **366.4 Cataract associated with other disorders**
- ***366.41 Diabetic cataract***
  - *Code first diabetes (250.5)*
  - AHA: 3Q, '91, 9; S-O, '85, 11
- ***366.42 Tetanic cataract***
  - *Code first underlying disease, as:*
    - calcinosis (275.4)
    - hypoparathyroidism (252.1)
- ***366.43 Myotonic cataract***
  - *Code first underlying disorder (359.2)*
- ***366.44 Cataract associated with other syndromes***
  - *Code first underlying condition, as:*
    - craniofacial dysostosis (756.0)
    - galactosemia (271.1)
- **366.45 Toxic cataract**
  - Drug-induced cataract
  - Use additional E code to identify drug or other toxic substance
- **366.46 Cataract associated with radiation and other physical influences**
  - Use additional E code to identify cause

✓5th **366.5 After-cataract**
- **366.50 After-cataract, unspecified**
  - Secondary cataract NOS
- **366.51 Soemmering's ring**
  - DEF: A donut-shaped lens remnant and a capsule behind the pupil as a result of cataract surgery or trauma.
- **366.52 Other after-cataract, not obscuring vision**
- **366.53 After-cataract, obscuring vision**

366.8 Other cataract
- Calcification of lens

366.9 Unspecified cataract

✓4th **367 Disorders of refraction and accommodation**

367.0 Hypermetropia
- Far-sightedness Hyperopia
- DEF: Refraction error, called also hyperopia, focal point is posterior to retina; abnormally short anteroposterior diameter or subnormal refractive power; causes farsightedness.

367.1 Myopia
- Near-sightedness
- DEF: Refraction error, focal point is anterior to retina; causes near-sightedness.

✓5th **367.2 Astigmatism**
- **367.20 Astigmatism, unspecified**
- **367.21 Regular astigmatism**
- **367.22 Irregular astigmatism**

✓5th **367.3 Anisometropia and aniseikonia**
- **367.31 Anisometropia**
  - DEF: Eyes with refractive powers that differ by at least one diopter.
- **367.32 Aniseikonia**
  - DEF: Eyes with unequal retinal imaging; usually due to refractive error.

367.4 Presbyopia
- DEF: Loss of crystalline lens elasticity; causes errors of accommodation; due to aging.

✓5th **367.5 Disorders of accommodation**
- **367.51 Paresis of accommodation**
  - Cycloplegia
  - DEF: Partial paralysis of ciliary muscle; causing focus problems.
- **367.52 Total or complete internal ophthalmoplegia**
  - DEF: Total paralysis of ciliary muscle; large pupil incapable of focus.
- **367.53 Spasm of accommodation**
  - DEF: Abnormal contraction of ciliary muscle; causes focus problems.

✓5th **367.8 Other disorders of refraction and accommodation**
- **367.81 Transient refractive change**
- **367.89 Other**
  - Drug-induced } disorders of refraction and accommodation
  - Toxic }

367.9 Unspecified disorder of refraction and accommodation

✓4th **368 Visual disturbances**

EXCLUDES *electrophysiological disturbances (794.11-794.14)*

✓5th **368.0 Amblyopia ex anopsia**
- DEF: Vision impaired due to disuse; esotropia often cause.
- **368.00 Amblyopia, unspecified**
- **368.01 Strabismic amblyopia**
  - Suppression amblyopia
- **368.02 Deprivation amblyopia**
  - DEF: Decreased vision associated with suppressed retinal image of one eye.
- **368.03 Refractive amblyopia**

✓5th **368.1 Subjective visual disturbances**
- **368.10 Subjective visual disturbance, unspecified**
- **368.11 Sudden visual loss**
- **368.12 Transient visual loss**
  - Concentric fading Scintillating scotoma
- **368.13 Visual discomfort**
  - Asthenopia Photophobia
  - Eye strain
- **368.14 Visual distortions of shape and size**
  - Macropsia Micropsia
  - Metamorphopsia

368.15 Other visual distortions and entoptic phenomena
Photopsia
Refractive:
diplopia
Refractive:
polyopia
Visual halos

368.16 Psychophysical visual disturbances
Visual:
agnosia
disorientation syndrome
Visual:
hallucinations

368.2 Diplopia
Double vision

✓5th **368.3 Other disorders of binocular vision**

368.30 Binocular vision disorder, unspecified

368.31 Suppression of binocular vision

368.32 Simultaneous visual perception without fusion

368.33 Fusion with defective stereopsis
DEF: Faulty depth perception though normal ability to focus.

368.34 Abnormal retinal correspondence

✓5th **368.4 Visual field defects**

368.40 Visual field defect, unspecified

368.41 Scotoma involving central area
Scotoma:
central
centrocecal
Scotoma:
paracentral
DEF: Vision loss (blind spot) in central five degrees of visual field.

368.42 Scotoma of blind spot area
Enlarged:
angioscotoma
blind spot
Paracecal scotoma

368.43 Sector or arcuate defects
Scotoma:
arcuate
Bjerrum
Scotoma:
Seidel
DEF: Arc-shaped blind spot caused by retinal nerve damage.

368.44 Other localized visual field defect
Scotoma:
NOS
ring
Visual field defect:
nasal step
peripheral

368.45 Generalized contraction or constriction

368.46 Homonymous bilateral field defects
Hemianopsia (altitudinal) (homonymous)
Quadrant anopia
DEF: Disorders found in the corresponding vertical halves of the visual fields of both eyes.

368.47 Heteronymous bilateral field defects
Hemianopsia:
binasal
Hemianopsia:
bitemporal
DEF: Disorders in the opposite halves of the visual fields of both eyes.

✓5th **368.5 Color vision deficiencies**
Color blindness

368.51 Protan defect
Protanomaly
Protanopia
DEF: Mild difficulty distinguishing green and red hues with shortened spectrum; sex-linked affecting one percent of males.

368.52 Deutan defect
Deuteranomaly
Deuteranopia
DEF: Male-only disorder; difficulty in distinguishing green and red, no shortened spectrum.

368.53 Tritan defect
Tritanomaly
Tritanopia
DEF: Difficulty in distinguishing blue and yellow; occurs often due to drugs, retinal detachment and central nervous system diseases.

368.54 Achromatopsia
Monochromatism (cone) (rod)
DEF: Complete color blindness; caused by disease, injury to retina, optic nerve or pathway.

368.55 Acquired color vision deficiencies

368.59 Other color vision deficiencies

✓5th **368.6 Night blindness**
Nyctalopia
DEF: Nyctalopia: disorder of vision in dim light or night blindness.

368.60 Night blindness, unspecified

368.61 Congenital night blindness
Hereditary night blindness
Oguchi's disease

368.62 Acquired night blindness
EXCLUDES *that due to vitamin A deficiency (264.5)*

368.63 Abnormal dark adaptation curve
Abnormal threshold } of cones or rods
Delayed adaptation }

368.69 Other night blindness

368.8 Other specified visual disturbances
Blurred vision NOS
AHA: 4Q, '02, 56

368.9 Unspecified visual disturbance
AHA: 1Q, '04, 15

✓4th **369 Blindness and low vision**

Note: Visual impairment refers to a functional limitation of the eye (e.g., limited visual acuity or visual field). It should be distinguished from visual disability, indicating a limitation of the abilities of the individual (e.g., limited reading skills, vocational skills), and from visual handicap, indicating a limitation of personal and socioeconomic independence (e.g., limited mobility, limited employability).

The levels of impairment defined in the table on the next page are based on the recommendations of the WHO Study Group on Prevention of Blindness (Geneva, November 6–10, 1972; WHO Technical Report Series 518), and of the International Council of Ophthalmology (1976).

Note that definitions of blindness vary in different settings.

For international reporting WHO defines blindness as profound impairment. This definition can be applied to blindness of one eye (369.1, 369.6) and to blindness of the individual (369.0).

For determination of benefits in the U.S.A., the definition of legal blindness as severe impairment is often used. This definition applies to blindness of the individual only.

EXCLUDES *correctable impaired vision due to refractive errors (367.0-367.9)*

✓5th **369.0 Profound impairment, both eyes**

369.00 Impairment level not further specified
Blindness:
NOS according to WHO definition
both eyes

369.01 Better eye: total impairment; lesser eye: total impairment

369.02 Better eye: near-total impairment; lesser eye: not further specified

369.03 Better eye: near-total impairment; lesser eye: total impairment

369.04 Better eye: near-total impairment; lesser eye: near-total impairment

369.05 Better eye: profound impairment; lesser eye: not further specified

369.06 Better eye: profound impairment; lesser eye: total impairment

369.07 Better eye: profound impairment; lesser eye: near-total impairment

369.08 Better eye: profound impairment; lesser eye: profound impairment

✓4th **369.1 Moderate or severe impairment, better eye, profound impairment lesser eye**

369.10 Impairment level not further specified
Blindness, one eye, low vision other eye

369.11 Better eye: severe impairment; lesser eye: blind, not further specified

369.12 Better eye: severe impairment; lesser eye: total impairment

369.13 Better eye: severe impairment; lesser eye: near-total impairment

369.14 Better eye: severe impairment; lesser eye: profound impairment

369.15 Better eye: moderate impairment; lesser eye: blind, not further specified

369.16 Better eye: moderate impairment; lesser eye: total impairment

369.17 Better eye: moderate impairment; lesser eye: near-total impairment

369.18 Better eye: moderate impairment; lesser eye: profound impairment

✓5th **369.2 Moderate or severe impairment, both eyes**

369.20 Impairment level not further specified
Low vision, both eyes NOS

369.21 Better eye: severe impairment; lesser eye: not further specified

369.22 Better eye: severe impairment; lesser eye: severe impairment

369.23 Better eye: moderate impairment; lesser eye: not further specified

369.24 Better eye: moderate impairment; lesser eye: severe impairment

369.25 Better eye: moderate impairment; lesser eye: moderate impairment

369.3 Unqualified visual loss, both eyes

EXCLUDES *blindness NOS:*
legal [U.S.A. definition] (369.4)
WHO definition (369.00)

369.4 Legal blindness, as defined in U.S.A.
Blindness NOS according to U.S.A. definition

EXCLUDES *legal blindness with specification of impairment level (369.01-369.08, 369.11-369.14, 369.21-369.22)*

✓5th **369.6 Profound impairment, one eye**

369.60 Impairment level not further specified
Blindness, one eye

369.61 One eye: total impairment; other eye: not specified

369.62 One eye: total impairment; other eye: near-normal vision

369.63 One eye: total impairment; other eye: normal vision

369.64 One eye: near-total impairment; other eye: not specified

369.65 One eye: near-total impairment; other eye: near-normal vision

369.66 One eye: near-total impairment; other eye: normal vision

369.67 One eye: profound impairment; other eye: not specified

369.68 One eye: profound impairment; other eye: near-normal vision

369.69 One eye: profound impairment; other eye: normal vision

✓5th **369.7 Moderate or severe impairment, one eye**

369.70 Impairment level not further specified
Low vision, one eye

369.71 One eye: severe impairment; other eye: not specified

Classification "legal"	Classification WHO	LEVELS OF VISUAL IMPAIRMENT — Visual acuity and/or visual field limitation (whichever is worse)	Additional descriptors which may be encountered
	(NEAR-) NORMAL VISION	RANGE OF NORMAL VISION 20/10 20/13 20/16 20/20 20/25 2.0 1.6 1.25 1.0 0.8	
	(NEAR-) NORMAL VISION	NEAR-NORMAL VISION 20/30 20/40 20/50 20/60 0.7 0.6 0.5 0.4 0.3	
	LOW VISION	MODERATE VISUAL IMPAIRMENT 20/70 20/80 20/100 20/125 20/160 0.25 0.20 0.16 0.12	Moderate low vision
LEGAL BLINDNESS (U.S.A.) both eyes	LOW VISION	SEVERE VISUAL IMPAIRMENT 20/200 20/250 20/320 20/400 0.10 0.08 0.06 0.05 Visual field: 20 degrees or less	Severe low vision, "Legal" blindness
LEGAL BLINDNESS (U.S.A.) both eyes	BLINDNESS (WHO) one or both eyes	PROFOUND VISUAL IMPAIRMENT 20/500 20/630 20/800 20/1000 0.04 0.03 0.025 0.02 Count fingers at: less than 3m (10 ft.) Visual field: 10 degrees or less	Profound low vision, Moderate blindness
LEGAL BLINDNESS (U.S.A.) both eyes	BLINDNESS (WHO) one or both eyes	NEAR-TOTAL VISUAL IMPAIRMENT Visual acuity: less than 0.02 (20/1000) Count fingers at: 1m (3 ft.) or less Hand movements: 5m (15 ft.) or less Light projection, light perception Visual field: 5 degrees or less	Severe blindness, Near-total blindness
LEGAL BLINDNESS (U.S.A.) both eyes	BLINDNESS (WHO) one or both eyes	TOTAL VISUAL IMPAIRMENT No light perception (NLP)	Total blindness

Visual acuity refers to best achievable acuity with correction.
Non-listed Snellen fractions may be classified by converting to the nearest decimal equivalent, e.g. 10/200 = 0.05, 6/30 = 0.20.
CF (count fingers) without designation of distance, may be classified to profound impairment.
HM (hand motion) without designation of distance, may be classified to near-total impairment.
Visual field measurements refer to the largest field diameter for a 1/100 white test object.

369.72 One eye: severe impairment; other eye: near-normal vision

369.73 One eye: severe impairment; other eye: normal vision

369.74 One eye: moderate impairment; other eye: not specified

369.75 One eye: moderate impairment; other eye: near-normal vision

369.76 One eye: moderate impairment; other eye: normal vision

369.8 Unqualified visual loss, one eye

369.9 Unspecified visual loss
AHA: 4Q, '02, 114; 3Q, '02, 20

✓4th **370 Keratitis**

✓5th **370.0 Corneal ulcer**

EXCLUDES *that due to vitamin A deficiency (264.3)*

370.00 Corneal ulcer, unspecified

370.01 Marginal corneal ulcer

370.02 Ring corneal ulcer

370.03 Central corneal ulcer

370.04 Hypopyon ulcer
Serpiginous ulcer
DEF: Corneal ulcer with an accumulation of pus in the eye's anterior chamber..

370.05 Mycotic corneal ulcer
DEF: Fungal infection causing corneal tissue loss.

370.06 Perforated corneal ulcer
DEF: Tissue loss through all layers of cornea.

370.07 Mooren's ulcer
DEF: Tissue loss, with chronic inflammation, at junction of cornea and sclera; seen in elderly.

✓5th **370.2 Superficial keratitis without conjunctivitis**
EXCLUDES *dendritic [herpes simplex] keratitis (054.42)*

370.20 Superficial keratitis, unspecified

370.21 Punctate keratitis
Thygeson's superficial punctate keratitis
DEF: Formation of cellular and fibrinous deposits (keratic precipitates) on posterior surface; deposits develop after injury or iridocyclitis.

370.22 Macular keratitis
Keratitis:
areolar
nummular
stellate
striate

370.23 Filamentary keratitis
DEF: Keratitis characterized by twisted filaments of mucoid material on the cornea's surface.

370.24 Photokeratitis
Snow blindness
Welders' keratitis
AHA: 3Q, '96, 6
DEF: Painful, inflamed cornea; due to extended exposure to ultraviolet light.

✓5th **370.3 Certain types of keratoconjunctivitis**

370.31 Phlyctenular keratoconjunctivitis
Phlyctenulosis
Use additional code for any associated tuberculosis (017.3)
DEF: Miniature blister on conjunctiva or cornea; associated with tuberculosis and malnutrition disorders.

370.32 Limbar and corneal involvement in vernal conjunctivitis
Use additional code for vernal conjunctivitis (372.13)
DEF: Corneal itching and inflammation in conjunctivitis; often limited to lining of eyelids.

370.33 Keratoconjunctivitis sicca, not specified as Sjögren's
EXCLUDES *Sjögren's syndrome (710.2)*
DEF: Inflammation of conjunctiva and cornea; characterized by "horny" looking tissue and excess blood in these areas; decreased flow of lacrimal (tear) is a contributing factor.

370.34 Exposure keratoconjunctivitis
AHA: 3Q, '96, 6
DEF: Incomplete closure of eyelid causing dry, inflamed eye.

370.35 Neurotrophic keratoconjunctivitis

✓5th **370.4 Other and unspecified keratoconjunctivitis**

370.40 Keratoconjunctivitis, unspecified
Superficial keratitis with conjunctivitis NOS

370.44 Keratitis or keratoconjunctivitis in exanthema
Code first underlying condition (050.0-052.9)
EXCLUDES *herpes simplex (054.43)*
herpes zoster (053.21)
measles (055.71)

370.49 Other
EXCLUDES *epidemic keratoconjunctivitis (077.1)*

✓5th **370.5 Interstitial and deep keratitis**

370.50 Interstitial keratitis, unspecified

370.52 Diffuse interstitial keratitis
Cogan's syndrome
DEF: Inflammation of cornea; with deposits in middle corneal layers; may obscure vision.

370.54 Sclerosing keratitis
DEF: Chronic corneal inflammation leading to opaque scarring.

370.55 Corneal abscess
DEF: Pocket of pus and inflammation on the cornea.

370.59 Other
EXCLUDES *disciform herpes simplex keratitis (054.43)*
syphilitic keratitis (090.3)

✓5th **370.6 Corneal neovascularization**

370.60 Corneal neovascularization, unspecified

370.61 Localized vascularization of cornea
DEF: Limited infiltration of cornea by new blood vessels.

370.62 Pannus (corneal)
AHA: 3Q, '02, 20
DEF: Buildup of superficial vascularization and granulated tissue under epithelium of cornea.

370.63 Deep vascularization of cornea
DEF: Deep infiltration of cornea by new blood vessels.

370.64 Ghost vessels (corneal)

370.8 Other forms of keratitis
AHA: 3Q, '94, 5

370.9 Unspecified keratitis

✓4th **371 Corneal opacity and other disorders of cornea**

✓5th **371.0 Corneal scars and opacities**
EXCLUDES *that due to vitamin A deficiency (264.6)*

371.00 Corneal opacity, unspecified
Corneal scar NOS

371.01 Minor opacity of cornea
Corneal nebula

371.02 Peripheral opacity of cornea
Corneal macula not interfering with central vision

371.03 Central opacity of cornea
Corneal:
leucoma } interfering with central vision
macula }

371.04 Adherent leucoma
DEF: Dense, opaque corneal growth adhering to the iris; also spelled as leukoma.

371.05 Phthisical cornea
Code first underlying tuberculosis (017.3)

✓5th **371.1 Corneal pigmentations and deposits**

371.10 Corneal deposit, unspecified

371.11 Anterior pigmentations
Stähli's lines

371.12 Stromal pigmentations
Hematocornea

371.13 Posterior pigmentations
Krukenberg spindle

371.14 Kayser-Fleischer ring
DEF: Copper deposits forming ring at outer edge of cornea; seen in Wilson's disease and other liver disorders.

371.15 Other deposits associated with metabolic disorders

371.16 Argentous deposits
DEF: Silver deposits in cornea.

✓5th **371.2 Corneal edema**

371.20 Corneal edema, unspecified

371.21 Idiopathic corneal edema
DEF: Corneal swelling and fluid retention of unknown cause.

371.22 Secondary corneal edema
DEF: Corneal swelling and fluid retention caused by an underlying disease, injury, or condition.

371.23 Bullous keratopathy
DEF: Corneal degeneration; characterized by recurring, rupturing epithelial "blisters;" ruptured blebs expose corneal nerves, cause great pain; occurs in glaucoma, iridocyclitis and Fuchs' epithelial dystrophy.

371.24 Corneal edema due to wearing of contact lenses

✓5th **371.3 Changes of corneal membranes**
371.30 Corneal membrane change, unspecified
371.31 Folds and rupture of Bowman's membrane
371.32 Folds in Descemet's membrane
371.33 Rupture in Descemet's membrane

✓5th **371.4 Corneal degenerations**
371.40 Corneal degeneration, unspecified
371.41 Senile corneal changes
Arcus senilis
Hassall-Henle bodies

371.42 Recurrent erosion of cornea
EXCLUDES *Mooren's ulcer (370.07)*

371.43 Band-shaped keratopathy
DEF: Horizontal bands of superficial corneal calcium deposits.

371.44 Other calcerous degenerations of cornea
371.45 Keratomalacia NOS
EXCLUDES *that due to vitamin A deficiency (264.4)*
DEF: Destruction of the cornea by keratinization of the epithelium with ulceration and perforation of the cornea; seen in cases of vitamin A deficiency.

371.46 Nodular degeneration of cornea
Salzmann's nodular dystrophy

371.48 Peripheral degenerations of cornea
Marginal degeneration of cornea [Terrien's]

371.49 Other
Discrete colliquative keratopathy

✓5th **371.5 Hereditary corneal dystrophies**
DEF: Genetic disorder; leads to opacities, edema or lesions of cornea.

371.50 Corneal dystrophy, unspecified
371.51 Juvenile epithelial corneal dystrophy
371.52 Other anterior corneal dystrophies
Corneal dystrophy:
microscopic cystic
Corneal dystrophy:
ring-like

371.53 Granular corneal dystrophy
371.54 Lattice corneal dystrophy
371.55 Macular corneal dystrophy
371.56 Other stromal corneal dystrophies
Crystalline corneal dystrophy

371.57 Endothelial corneal dystrophy
Combined corneal dystrophy
Cornea guttata
Fuchs' endothelial dystrophy

371.58 Other posterior corneal dystrophies
Polymorphous corneal dystrophy

✓5th **371.6 Keratoconus**
DEF: Bilateral bulging protrusion of anterior cornea; often due to noninflammatory thinning.

371.60 Keratoconus, unspecified
371.61 Keratoconus, stable condition
371.62 Keratoconus, acute hydrops

✓5th **371.7 Other corneal deformities**
371.70 Corneal deformity, unspecified

371.71 Corneal ectasia
DEF: Bulging protrusion of thinned, scarred cornea.

371.72 Descemetocele
DEF: Protrusion of Descemet's membrane into cornea.

371.73 Corneal staphyloma
DEF: Protrusion of cornea into adjacent tissue.

✓5th **371.8 Other corneal disorders**
371.81 Corneal anesthesia and hypoesthesia
DEF: Decreased or absent sensitivity of cornea.

371.82 Corneal disorder due to contact lens
EXCLUDES *corneal edema due to contact lens (371.24)*
DEF: Contact lens wear causing cornea disorder, excluding swelling.

371.89 Other
AHA: 3Q, '99, 12

371.9 Unspecified corneal disorder

✓4th **372 Disorders of conjunctiva**
EXCLUDES *keratoconjunctivitis (370.3-370.4)*

✓5th **372.0 Acute conjunctivitis**
372.00 Acute conjunctivitis, unspecified
372.01 Serous conjunctivitis, except viral
EXCLUDES *viral conjunctivitis NOS (077.9)*

372.02 Acute follicular conjunctivitis
Conjunctival folliculosis NOS
EXCLUDES *conjunctivitis:*
adenoviral (acute follicular) (077.3)
epidemic hemorrhagic (077.4)
inclusion (077.0)
Newcastle (077.8)
epidemic keratoconjunctivitis (077.1)
pharyngoconjunctival fever (077.2)
DEF: Severe conjunctival inflammation with dense infiltrations of lymphoid tissues of inner eyelids; may be traced to a viral or chlamydial etiology.

372.03 Other mucopurulent conjunctivitis
Catarrhal conjunctivitis
EXCLUDES *blennorrhea neonatorum (gonococcal) (098.40)*
neonatal conjunctivitis(771.6)
ophthalmia neonatorum NOS (771.6)

372.04 Pseudomembranous conjunctivitis
Membranous conjunctivitis
EXCLUDES *diphtheritic conjunctivitis (032.81)*
DEF: Severe inflammation of conjunctiva; false membrane develops on inner surface of eyelid; membrane can be removed without harming epithelium, due to bacterial infections, toxic and allergic factors, and viral infections.

372.05 Acute atopic conjunctivitis
DEF: Sudden, severe conjunctivitis due to allergens.

✓5th **372.1 Chronic conjunctivitis**
372.10 Chronic conjunctivitis, unspecified
372.11 Simple chronic conjunctivitis
372.12 Chronic follicular conjunctivitis
DEF: Persistent conjunctival inflammation with dense, localized infiltrations of lymphoid tissues of inner eyelids.

372.13 Vernal conjunctivitis
AHA: 3Q, '96, 8

372.14 Other chronic allergic conjunctivitis
AHA: 3Q, '96, 8

372.15 Parasitic conjunctivitis
Code first underlying disease, as:
filariasis (125.0-125.9)
mucocutaneous leishmaniasis (085.5)

✓5th **372.2 Blepharoconjunctivitis**
372.20 Blepharoconjunctivitis, unspecified
372.21 Angular blepharoconjunctivitis
DEF: Inflammation at junction of upper and lower eyelids; may block lacrimal secretions.
372.22 Contact blepharoconjunctivitis

✓5th **372.3 Other and unspecified conjunctivitis**
372.30 Conjunctivitis, unspecified
372.31 Rosacea conjunctivitis
Code first underlying rosacea dermatitis (695.3)
372.33 Conjunctivitis in mucocutaneous disease
Code first underlying disease, as:
erythema multiforme (695.1)
Reiter's disease (099.3)
EXCLUDES *ocular pemphigoid (694.61)*
372.39 Other

✓5th **372.4 Pterygium**
EXCLUDES *pseudopterygium (372.52)*
DEF: Wedge-shaped, conjunctival thickening that advances from the inner corner of the eye toward the cornea.
372.40 Pterygium, unspecified
372.41 Peripheral pterygium, stationary
372.42 Peripheral pterygium, progressive
372.43 Central pterygium
372.44 Double pterygium
372.45 Recurrent pterygium

✓5th **372.5 Conjunctival degenerations and deposits**
372.50 Conjunctival degeneration, unspecified
372.51 Pinguecula
DEF: Proliferative spot on the bulbar conjunctiva located near the sclerocorneal junction, usually on the nasal side; it is seen in elderly people.
372.52 Pseudopterygium
DEF: Conjunctival scar joined to the cornea; it looks like a pterygium but is not attached to the tissue.
372.53 Conjunctival xerosis
EXCLUDES *conjunctival xerosis due to vitamin A deficiency (264.0, 264.1, 264.7)*
DEF: Dry conjunctiva due to vitamin A deficiency; related to Bitot's spots; may develop into xerophthalmia and keratomalacia.
372.54 Conjunctival concretions
DEF: Calculus or deposit on conjunctiva.
372.55 Conjunctival pigmentations
Conjunctival argyrosis
DEF: Color deposits in conjunctiva.
372.56 Conjunctival deposits

✓5th **372.6 Conjunctival scars**
372.61 Granuloma of conjunctiva
372.62 Localized adhesions and strands of conjunctiva
DEF: Abnormal fibrous connections in conjunctiva.
372.63 Symblepharon
Extensive adhesions of conjunctiva
DEF: Adhesion of the eyelids to the eyeball.
372.64 Scarring of conjunctiva
Contraction of eye socket (after enucleation)

✓5th **372.7 Conjunctival vascular disorders and cysts**
372.71 Hyperemia of conjunctiva
DEF: Conjunctival blood vessel congestion causing eye redness.
372.72 Conjunctival hemorrhage
Hyposphagma
Subconjunctival hemorrhage
372.73 Conjunctival edema
Chemosis of conjunctiva
Subconjunctival edema
DEF: Fluid retention and swelling in conjunctival tissue.
372.74 Vascular abnormalities of conjunctiva
Aneurysm(ata) of conjunctiva
372.75 Conjunctival cysts
DEF: Abnormal sacs of fluid in conjunctiva.

✓5th **372.8 Other disorders of conjunctiva**
372.81 Conjunctivochalasis
AHA: 4Q, '00, 41
DEF: Bilateral condition of redundant conjunctival tissue between globe and lower eyelid margin; may cover lower punctum, interferring with normal tearing.
372.89 Other disorders of conjunctiva

372.9 Unspecified disorder of conjunctiva

✓4th **373 Inflammation of eyelids**

✓5th **373.0 Blepharitis**
EXCLUDES *blepharoconjunctivitis (372.20-372.22)*
373.00 Blepharitis, unspecified
373.01 Ulcerative blepharitis
373.02 Squamous blepharitis

✓5th **373.1 Hordeolum and other deep inflammation of eyelid**
DEF: Purulent, localized, staphylococcal infection in sebaceous glands of eyelids.
373.11 Hordeolum externum
Hordeolum NOS Stye
DEF: Infection of the oil glands in the eyelash follicles.
373.12 Hordeolum internum
Infection of meibomian gland
DEF: Infection of the oil gland of the eyelid margin.
373.13 Abscess of eyelid
Furuncle of eyelid
DEF: Inflamed pocket of pus on the eyelid.

373.2 Chalazion
Meibomian (gland) cyst
EXCLUDES *infected meibomian gland (373.12)*
DEF: Chronic inflammation of the meibomian gland, causing an eyelid mass.

✓5th **373.3 Noninfectious dermatoses of eyelid**
373.31 Eczematous dermatitis of eyelid
373.32 Contact and allergic dermatitis of eyelid
373.33 Xeroderma of eyelid
373.34 Discoid lupus erythematosus of eyelid

373.4 Infective dermatitis of eyelid of types resulting in deformity
Code first underlying disease, as:
leprosy (030.0-030.9)
lupus vulgaris (tuberculous) (017.0)
yaws (102.0-102.9)

373.5 Other infective dermatitis of eyelid
Code first underlying disease, as:
actinomycosis (039.3)
impetigo (684)
mycotic dermatitis (110.0-111.9)
vaccinia (051.0)
postvaccination (999.0)
EXCLUDES *herpes:*
simplex (054.41)
zoster (053.20)

Entropion and Ectropion

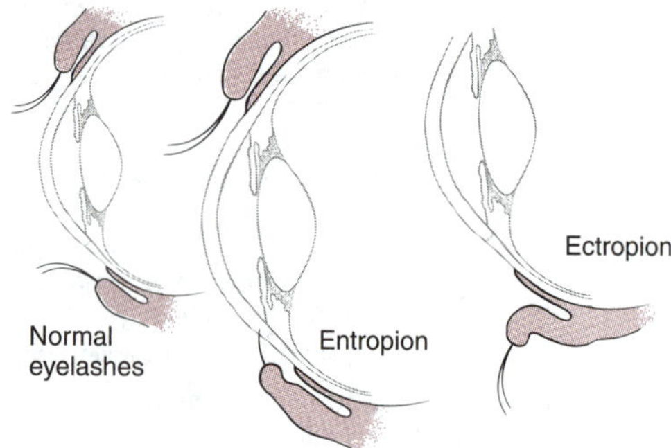

373.6 *Parasitic infestation of eyelid*

Code first underlying disease, as:
leishmaniasis (085.0-085.9)
loiasis (125.2)
onchocerciasis (125.3)
pediculosis (132.0)

373.8 Other inflammations of eyelids

373.9 Unspecified inflammation of eyelid

✓4th **374 Other disorders of eyelids**

✓5th **374.0 Entropion and trichiasis of eyelid**

DEF: Entropion: turning inward of eyelid edge toward eyeball.

DEF: Trichiasis: ingrowing eyelashes marked by irritation with possible distortion of sight.

374.00 Entropion, unspecified
374.01 Senile entropion A
374.02 Mechanical entropion
374.03 Spastic entropion
374.04 Cicatricial entropion
374.05 Trichiasis without entropion

✓5th **374.1 Ectropion**

DEF: Turning outward (eversion) of eyelid edge; exposes palpebral conjunctiva; dryness irritation result.

374.10 Ectropion, unspecified
374.11 Senile ectropion A
374.12 Mechanical ectropion
374.13 Spastic ectropion
374.14 Cicatricial ectropion

✓5th **374.2 Lagophthalmos**

DEF: Incomplete closure of eyes; causes dry eye and other complications.

374.20 Lagophthalmos, unspecified
374.21 Paralytic lagophthalmos
374.22 Mechanical lagophthalmos
374.23 Cicatricial lagophthalmos

✓5th **374.3 Ptosis of eyelid**

374.30 Ptosis of eyelid, unspecified

AHA: 2Q, '96, 11

374.31 Paralytic ptosis

DEF: Drooping of upper eyelid due to nerve disorder.

374.32 Myogenic ptosis

DEF: Drooping of upper eyelid due to muscle disorder.

374.33 Mechanical ptosis

DEF: Outside force causes drooping of upper eyelid.

374.34 Blepharochalasis

Pseudoptosis

DEF: Loss of elasticity, thickened or indurated skin of eyelids associated with recurrent episodes of idiopathic edema causing intracellular tissue atrophy.

✓5th **374.4 Other disorders affecting eyelid function**

EXCLUDES *blepharoclonus (333.81)*
blepharospasm (333.81)
facial nerve palsy (351.0)
third nerve palsy or paralysis (378.51-378.52)
tic (psychogenic) (307.20-307.23)
organic (333.3)

374.41 Lid retraction or lag
374.43 Abnormal innervation syndrome

Jaw-blinking
Paradoxical facial movements

374.44 Sensory disorders
374.45 Other sensorimotor disorders

Deficient blink reflex

374.46 Blepharophimosis

Ankyloblepharon

DEF: Narrowing of palpebral fissure horizontally; caused by laterally displaced inner canthi; either acquired or congenital.

✓5th **374.5 Degenerative disorders of eyelid and periocular area**

374.50 Degenerative disorder of eyelid, unspecified

374.51 ***Xanthelasma***

Xanthoma (planum) (tuberosum) of eyelid
Code first underlying condition (272.0-272.9)

DEF: Fatty tumors of the eyelid linked to high fat content of blood.

374.52 Hyperpigmentation of eyelid

Chloasma Dyspigmentation

DEF: Excess pigment of eyelid.

374.53 Hypopigmentation of eyelid

Vitiligo of eyelid

DEF: Lack of color pigment of the eyelid.

374.54 Hypertrichosis of eyelid

DEF: Excessive eyelash growth.

374.55 Hypotrichosis of eyelid

Madarosis of eyelid

DEF: Less than normal, or absent, eyelashes.

374.56 Other degenerative disorders of skin affecting eyelid

✓5th **374.8 Other disorders of eyelid**

374.81 Hemorrhage of eyelid

EXCLUDES *black eye (921.0)*

374.82 Edema of eyelid

Hyperemia of eyelid

DEF: Swelling and fluid retention in eyelid.

374.83 Elephantiasis of eyelid

DEF: Filarial disease causing dermatitis and enlargement of eyelid.

374.84 Cysts of eyelids

Sebaceous cyst of eyelid

374.85 Vascular anomalies of eyelid
374.86 Retained foreign body of eyelid
374.87 Dermatochalasis

DEF: Acquired form of connective tissue disorder associated with decreased elastic tissue and abnormal elastin formation resulting in loss of elasticity of the skin of the eyelid, generally associated with aging.

374.89 Other disorders of eyelid

374.9 Unspecified disorder of eyelid

✓4th **375 Disorders of lacrimal system**

✓5th **375.0 Dacryoadenitis**

375.00 Dacryoadenitis, unspecified
375.01 Acute dacryoadenitis

DEF: Severe, sudden inflammation of the lacrimal gland.

375.02 Chronic dacryoadenitis

DEF: Persistent inflammation of the lacrimal gland.

375.03 Chronic enlargement of lacrimal gland

✓5th **375.1 Other disorders of lacrimal gland**

375.11 Dacryops

DEF: Overproduction and constant flow of tears; may cause distended lacrimal duct.

375.12 Other lacrimal cysts and cystic degeneration

375.13 Primary lacrimal atrophy

375.14 Secondary lacrimal atrophy

DEF: Wasting away of the lacrimal gland due to another disease.

375.15 Tear film insufficiency, unspecified

Dry eye syndrome

AHA: 3Q, '96, 6

DEF: Eye dryness and irritation from insufficient tear production.

375.16 Dislocation of lacrimal gland

✓5th **375.2 Epiphora**

DEF: Abnormal development of tears due to stricture of lacrimal passages.

375.20 Epiphora, unspecified as to cause

375.21 Epiphora due to excess lacrimation

DEF: Tear overflow due to overproduction.

375.22 Epiphora due to insufficient drainage

DEF: Tear overflow due to blocked drainage.

✓5th **375.3 Acute and unspecified inflammation of lacrimal passages**

EXCLUDES *neonatal dacryocystitis (771.6)*

375.30 Dacryocystitis, unspecified

375.31 Acute canaliculitis, lacrimal

375.32 Acute dacryocystitis

Acute peridacryocystitis

375.33 Phlegmonous dacryocystitis

DEF: Infection of the tear sac with pockets of pus.

✓5th **375.4 Chronic inflammation of lacrimal passages**

375.41 Chronic canaliculitis

375.42 Chronic dacryocystitis

375.43 Lacrimal mucocele

✓5th **375.5 Stenosis and insufficiency of lacrimal passages**

375.51 Eversion of lacrimal punctum

DEF: Abnormal turning outward of the tear duct.

375.52 Stenosis of lacrimal punctum

DEF: Abnormal narrowing of the tear duct.

375.53 Stenosis of lacrimal canaliculi

375.54 Stenosis of lacrimal sac

DEF: Abnormal narrowing of the tear sac.

375.55 Obstruction of nasolacrimal duct, neonatal

EXCLUDES *congenital anomaly of nasolacrimal duct (743.65)*

DEF: Acquired, abnormal obstruction of tear drainage system from the eye to the nose; in an infant.

375.56 Stenosis of nasolacrimal duct, acquired

375.57 Dacryolith

DEF: Concretion or stone anywhere in lacrimal system.

✓5th **375.6 Other changes of lacrimal passages**

375.61 Lacrimal fistula

DEF: Abnormal communication from the lacrimal system.

375.69 Other

✓5th **375.8 Other disorders of lacrimal system**

375.81 Granuloma of lacrimal passages

DEF: Abnormal nodules within lacrimal system.

375.89 Other

375.9 Unspecified disorder of lacrimal system

Lacrimal System

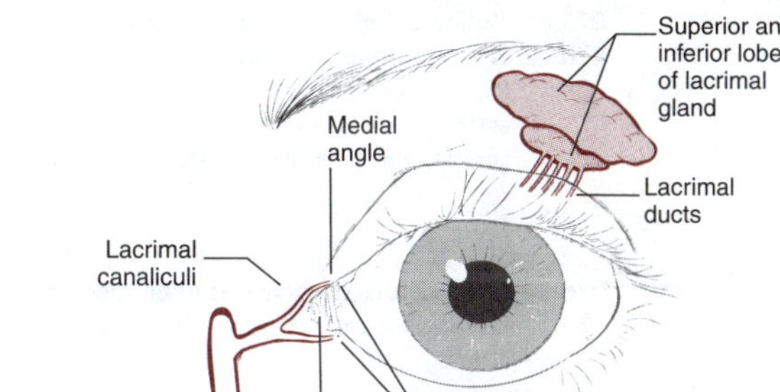

✓4th **376 Disorders of the orbit**

✓5th **376.0 Acute inflammation of orbit**

376.00 Acute inflammation of orbit, unspecified

376.01 Orbital cellulitis

Abscess of orbit

DEF: Infection of tissue between the orbital bone and eyeball.

376.02 Orbital periostitis

DEF: Inflammation of connective tissue covering the orbital bone.

376.03 Orbital osteomyelitis

DEF: Inflammation of the orbital bone.

376.04 Tenonitis

✓5th **376.1 Chronic inflammatory disorders of orbit**

376.10 Chronic inflammation of orbit, unspecified

376.11 Orbital granuloma

Pseudotumor (inflammatory) of orbit

DEF: Abnormal nodule between orbital bone and eyeball.

376.12 Orbital myositis

DEF: Painful inflammation of the muscles of the eye.

376.13 Parasitic infestation of orbit

Code first underlying disease, as:

hydatid infestation of orbit (122.3, 122.6, 122.9)

myiasis of orbit (134.0)

✓5th **376.2 Endocrine exophthalmos**

Code first underlying thyroid disorder (242.0-242.9)

376.21 Thyrotoxic exophthalmos

DEF: Painful inflammation of eye muscles.

376.22 Exophthalmic ophthalmoplegia

DEF: Inability to rotate eye as a result of bulging eyes.

✓5th **376.3 Other exophthalmic conditions**

376.30 Exophthalmos, unspecified

DEF: Abnormal protrusion of eyeball.

376.31 Constant exophthalmos

DEF: Continuous, abnormal protrusion or bulging of eyeball.

376.32 Orbital hemorrhage

DEF: Bleeding behind the eyeball, causing it to bulge forward.

376.33 Orbital edema or congestion

DEF: Fluid retention behind eyeball, causing forward bulge.

376.34 Intermittent exophthalmos

376.35 Pulsating exophthalmos

DEF: Bulge or protrusion; associated with a carotid-cavernous fistula.

376.36 Lateral displacement of globe

DEF: Abnormal displacement of the eyeball away from nose, toward temple.

✓5th **376.4 Deformity of orbit**

376.40 Deformity of orbit, unspecified

376.41 Hypertelorism of orbit

DEF: Abnormal increase in interorbital distance; associated with congenital facial deformities; may be accompanied by mental deficiency.

376.42 Exostosis of orbit

DEF: Abnormal bony growth of orbit.

376.43 Local deformities due to bone disease

DEF: Acquired abnormalities of orbit; due to bone disease.

376.44 Orbital deformities associated with craniofacial deformities

376.45 Atrophy of orbit

DEF: Wasting away of bone tissue of orbit.

376.46 Enlargement of orbit

376.47 Deformity due to trauma or surgery

✓5th **376.5 Enophthalmos**

DEF: Recession of eyeball deep into eye socket.

376.50 Enophthalmos, unspecified as to cause

376.51 Enophthalmos due to atrophy of orbital tissue

376.52 Enophthalmos due to trauma or surgery

376.6 Retained (old) foreign body following penetrating wound of orbit

Retrobulbar foreign body

✓5th **376.8 Other orbital disorders**

376.81 Orbital cysts

Encephalocele of orbit

AHA: 3Q, '99, 13

376.82 Myopathy of extraocular muscles

DEF: Disease in the muscles that control eyeball movement.

376.89 Other

376.9 Unspecified disorder of orbit

✓4th **377 Disorders of optic nerve and visual pathways**

✓5th **377.0 Papilledema**

377.00 Papilledema, unspecified CC

CC Excl: 017.30-017.36, 017.90-017.96, 036.81, 250.50-250.53, 250.80-250.93, 377.00-377.03, 377.14, 377.24, 379.60-379.90, 379.99, 743.8-743.9

377.01 Papilledema associated with increased intracranial pressure CC

CC Excl: See code 377.00

377.02 Papilledema associated with decreased ocular pressure CC

CC Excl: See code 377.00

377.03 Papilledema associated with retinal disorder

377.04 Foster-Kennedy syndrome

DEF: Retrobulbar optic neuritis, central scotoma and optic atrophy; caused by tumors in frontal lobe of brain that press downward.

✓5th **377.1 Optic atrophy**

377.10 Optic atrophy, unspecified

377.11 Primary optic atrophy

EXCLUDES *neurosyphilitic optic atrophy (094.84)*

377.12 Postinflammatory optic atrophy

DEF: : Adverse effect of inflammation causing wasting away of eye.

377.13 Optic atrophy associated with retinal dystrophies

DEF: Progressive changes in retinal tissue due to metabolic disorder causing wasting away of eye.

377.14 Glaucomatous atrophy [cupping] of optic disc

377.15 Partial optic atrophy

Temporal pallor of optic disc

377.16 Hereditary optic atrophy

Optic atrophy:
dominant hereditary

Optic atrophy:
Leber's

✓5th **377.2 Other disorders of optic disc**

377.21 Drusen of optic disc

377.22 Crater-like holes of optic disc

377.23 Coloboma of optic disc

DEF: Ocular malformation caused by the failure of fetal fissure of optic stalk to close.

377.24 Pseudopapilledema

✓5th **377.3 Optic neuritis**

EXCLUDES *meningococcal optic neuritis (036.81)*

377.30 Optic neuritis, unspecified

377.31 Optic papillitis

DEF: Swelling and inflammation of the optic disc.

377.32 Retrobulbar neuritis (acute)

EXCLUDES *syphilitic retrobulbar neuritis (094.85)*

DEF: Inflammation of optic nerve immediately behind the eyeball.

377.33 Nutritional optic neuropathy

DEF: Malnutrition causing optic nerve disorder.

377.34 Toxic optic neuropathy

Toxic amblyopia

DEF: Toxic substance causing optic nerve disorder.

377.39 Other

EXCLUDES *ischemic optic neuropathy (377.41)*

✓5th **377.4 Other disorders of optic nerve**

377.41 Ischemic optic neuropathy

DEF: Decreased blood flow affecting optic nerve.

377.42 Hemorrhage in optic nerve sheaths

DEF: Bleeding in meningeal lining of optic nerve.

● **377.43 Optic nerve hypoplasia**

377.49 Other

Compression of optic nerve

✓5th **377.5 Disorders of optic chiasm**

377.51 Associated with pituitary neoplasms and disorders

DEF: Abnormal pituitary growth causing disruption in nerve chain from retina to brain.

377.52 Associated with other neoplasms

DEF: Abnormal growth, other than pituitary, causing disruption in nerve chain from retina to brain.

377.53 Associated with vascular disorders

DEF: Vascular disorder causing disruption in nerve chain from retina to brain.

377.54 Associated with inflammatory disorders

DEF: Inflammatory disease causing disruption in nerve chain from retina to brain.

✓5th **377.6 Disorders of other visual pathways**

377.61 Associated with neoplasms

377.62 Associated with vascular disorders

377.63 Associated with inflammatory disorders

✓5th **377.7 Disorders of visual cortex**

EXCLUDES *visual:*
agnosia (368.16)
hallucinations (368.16)
halos (368.15)

377.71 Associated with neoplasms

377.72 Associated with vascular disorders

377.73 Associated with inflammatory disorders

377.75 Cortical blindness

DEF: Blindness due to brain disorder, rather than eye disorder.

377.9 Unspecified disorder of optic nerve and visual pathways

✓4th **378 Strabismus and other disorders of binocular eye movements**

EXCLUDES *nystagmus and other irregular eye movements (379.50-379.59)*

DEF: Misalignment of the eyes due to imbalance in extraocular muscles.

✓5th **378.0 Esotropia**

Convergent concomitant strabismus

EXCLUDES *intermittent esotropia (378.20-378.22)*

DEF: Visual axis deviation created by one eye fixing upon an image and the other eye deviating inward.

378.00 Esotropia, unspecified

378.01 Monocular esotropia

378.02 Monocular esotropia with A pattern

378.03 Monocular esotropia with V pattern

378.04 Monocular esotropia with other noncomitancies

Monocular esotropia with X or Y pattern

378.05 Alternating esotropia

378.06 Alternating esotropia with A pattern

378.07 Alternating esotropia with V pattern

378.08 Alternating esotropia with other noncomitancies

Alternating esotropia with X or Y pattern

✓5th **378.1 Exotropia**

Divergent concomitant strabismus

EXCLUDES *intermittent exotropia (378.20, 378.23-378.24)*

DEF: Visual axis deviation created by one eye fixing upon an image and the other eye deviating outward.

378.10 Exotropia, unspecified

378.11 Monocular exotropia

378.12 Monocular exotropia with A pattern

378.13 Monocular exotropia with V pattern

378.14 Monocular exotropia with other noncomitancies

Monocular exotropia with X or Y pattern

378.15 Alternating exotropia

378.16 Alternating exotropia with A pattern

378.17 Alternating exotropia with V pattern

378.18 Alternating exotropia with other noncomitancies

Alternating exotropia with X or Y pattern

✓5th **378.2 Intermittent heterotropia**

EXCLUDES *vertical heterotropia (intermittent) (378.31)*

DEF: Deviation of eyes seen only at intervals; it is also called strabismus.

Eye Musculature

Muscles and actions (right eye)

Monocular (one eye only) esotropia (inward)

Monocular exotropia (outward)

Monocular hypertropia (upward)

378.20 Intermittent heterotropia, unspecified

Intermittent: esotropia NOS

Intermittent: exotropia NOS

378.21 Intermittent esotropia, monocular

378.22 Intermittent esotropia, alternating

378.23 Intermittent exotropia, monocular

378.24 Intermittent exotropia, alternating

✓5th **378.3 Other and unspecified heterotropia**

378.30 Heterotropia, unspecified

378.31 Hypertropia

Vertical heterotropia (constant) (intermittent)

378.32 Hypotropia

378.33 Cyclotropia

378.34 Monofixation syndrome

Microtropia

378.35 Accommodative component in esotropia

✓5th **378.4 Heterophoria**

DEF: Deviation occurring only when the other eye is covered.

378.40 Heterophoria, unspecified

378.41 Esophoria

378.42 Exophoria

378.43 Vertical heterophoria

378.44 Cyclophoria

378.45 Alternating hyperphoria

✓5th **378.5 Paralytic strabismus**

DEF: Deviation of the eye due to nerve paralysis affecting muscle.

378.50 Paralytic strabismus, unspecified

378.51 Third or oculomotor nerve palsy, partial

AHA: 3Q, '91, 9

378.52 Third or oculomotor nerve palsy, total

AHA: 2Q, '89, 12

378.53 Fourth or trochlear nerve palsy

AHA: 2Q, '01, 21

378.54 Sixth or abducens nerve palsy

AHA: 2Q, '89, 12

378.55 External ophthalmoplegia

378.56 Total ophthalmoplegia

✓5th **378.6 Mechanical strabismus**

DEF: Deviation of the eye due to an outside force upon the extraocular muscles.

378.60 Mechanical strabismus, unspecified

378.61 Brown's (tendon) sheath syndrome

DEF: Congenital or acquired shortening of the anterior sheath of the superior oblique muscle; the eye is unable to move upward and inward; it is usually unilateral.

378.62 Mechanical strabismus from other musculofascial disorders

378.63 Limited duction associated with other conditions

✓5th **378.7 Other specified strabismus**

378.71 Duane's syndrome

DEF: Congenital, affects one eye; due to abnormal fibrous bands attached to rectus muscle; inability to abduct affected eye with retraction of globe.

378.72 Progressive external ophthalmoplegia

DEF: Paralysis progressing from one eye muscle to another.

378.73 Strabismus in other neuromuscular disorders

✓5th **378.8 Other disorders of binocular eye movements**

EXCLUDES *nystagmus (379.50-379.56)*

378.81 Palsy of conjugate gaze

DEF: Paralysis progressing from one eye muscle to another.

378.82 Spasm of conjugate gaze
DEF: Muscle contractions impairing parallel movement of eye.

378.83 Convergence insufficiency or palsy

378.84 Convergence excess or spasm

378.85 Anomalies of divergence

378.86 Internuclear ophthalmoplegia
DEF: Eye movement anomaly due to brainstem lesion.

378.87 Other dissociated deviation of eye movements
Skew deviation

378.9 Unspecified disorder of eye movements
Ophthalmoplegia NOS Strabismus NOS
AHA: 2Q, '01, 21

✓4th **379 Other disorders of eye**

✓5th **379.0 Scleritis and episcleritis**
EXCLUDES *syphilitic episcleritis (095.0)*

379.00 Scleritis, unspecified
Episcleritis NOS

379.01 Episcleritis periodica fugax
DEF: Hyperemia (engorgement) of the sclera and overlying conjunctiva characterized by a sudden onset and short duration.

379.02 Nodular episcleritis
DEF: Inflammation of the outermost layer of the sclera, with formation of nodules.

379.03 Anterior scleritis

379.04 Scleromalacia perforans
DEF: Scleral thinning, softening and degeneration; seen with rheumatoid arthritis.

379.05 Scleritis with corneal involvement
Scleroperikeratitis

379.06 Brawny scleritis
DEF: Severe scleral inflammation with thickening corneal margins.

379.07 Posterior scleritis
Sclerotenonitis

379.09 Other
Scleral abscess

✓5th **379.1 Other disorders of sclera**
EXCLUDES *blue sclera (743.47)*

379.11 Scleral ectasia
Scleral staphyloma NOS
DEF: Protrusion of the contents of the eyeball where the sclera has thinned.

379.12 Staphyloma posticum
DEF: Ring-shaped protrusion or bulging of sclera and uveal tissue at posterior pole of eye.

379.13 Equatorial staphyloma
DEF: Ring-shaped protrusion or bulging of sclera and uveal tissue midway between front and back of eye.

379.14 Anterior staphyloma, localized

379.15 Ring staphyloma

379.16 Other degenerative disorders of sclera

379.19 Other

✓5th **379.2 Disorders of vitreous body**
DEF: Disorder of clear gel that fills space between retina and lens.

379.21 Vitreous degeneration
Vitreous: cavitation, detachment
Vitreous: liquefaction

379.22 Crystalline deposits in vitreous
Asteroid hyalitis Synchysis scintillans

379.23 Vitreous hemorrhage
AHA: 3Q, '91, 15

379.24 Other vitreous opacities
Vitreous floaters

379.25 Vitreous membranes and strands

379.26 Vitreous prolapse
DEF: Slipping of vitreous from normal position.

379.29 Other disorders of vitreous
EXCLUDES *vitreous abscess (360.04)*
AHA: 1Q, '99, 11

✓5th **379.3 Aphakia and other disorders of lens**
EXCLUDES *after-cataract (366.50-366.53)*

379.31 Aphakia
EXCLUDES *cataract extraction status (V45.61)*
DEF: Absence of eye's crystalline lens.

379.32 Subluxation of lens

379.33 Anterior dislocation of lens
DEF: Lens displaced toward iris.

379.34 Posterior dislocation of lens
DEF: Lens displaced backward toward vitreous.

379.39 Other disorders of lens

✓5th **379.4 Anomalies of pupillary function**

379.40 Abnormal pupillary function, unspecified

379.41 Anisocoria
DEF: Unequal pupil diameter.

379.42 Miosis (persistent), not due to miotics
DEF: Abnormal contraction of pupil less than 2 millimeters.

379.43 Mydriasis (persistent), not due to mydriatics
DEF: Morbid dilation of pupil.

379.45 Argyll Robertson pupil, atypical
Argyll Robertson phenomenon or pupil, nonsyphilitic
EXCLUDES *Argyll Robertson pupil (syphilitic) (094.89)*
DEF: Failure of pupil to respond to light; affects both eyes; may be caused by diseases such as syphilis of the central nervous system or miosis.

379.46 Tonic pupillary reaction
Adie's pupil or syndrome

379.49 Other
Hippus Pupillary paralysis

✓5th **379.5 Nystagmus and other irregular eye movements**

379.50 Nystagmus, unspecified
AHA: 4Q, '02, 68; 2Q, '01, 21
DEF: Involuntary, rapid, rhythmic movement of eyeball; vertical, horizontal, rotatory or mixed; cause may be congenital, acquired, physiological, neurological, myopathic, or due to ocular diseases.

379.51 Congenital nystagmus

379.52 Latent nystagmus

379.53 Visual deprivation nystagmus

379.54 Nystagmus associated with disorders of the vestibular system

379.55 Dissociated nystagmus

Ear and Mastoid Process

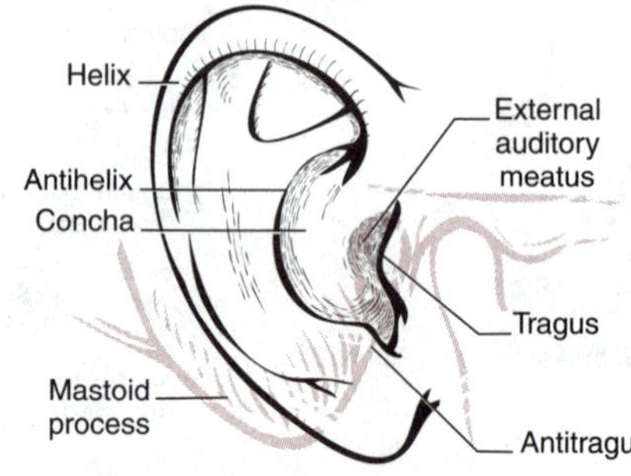

N Newborn Age: 0 P Pediatric Age: 0-17 M Maternity Age: 12-55 A Adult Age: 15-124 CC CC Condition MC Major Complication CD Complex Dx HIV HIV Related Dx

379.56 Other forms of nystagmus

379.57 Deficiencies of saccadic eye movements
Abnormal optokinetic response
DEF: Saccadic eye movements; small, rapid, involuntary movements by both eyes simultaneously, due to changing point of fixation on visualized object.

379.58 Deficiencies of smooth pursuit movements

379.59 Other irregularities of eye movements
Opsoclonus

● ✓5th **379.6 Inflammation (infection) of postprocedural bleb**
Postprocedural blebitis

● **379.60 Inflammation (infection) of postprocedural bleb, unspecified**

● **379.61 Inflammation (infection) of postprocedural bleb, stage 1**

● **379.62 Inflammation (infection) of postprocedural bleb, stage 2**

● **379.63 Inflammation (infection) of postprocedural bleb, stage 3**
Bleb associated endophthalmitis

379.8 Other specified disorders of eye and adnexa

✓5th **379.9 Unspecified disorder of eye and adnexa**

379.90 Disorder of eye, unspecified

379.91 Pain in or around eye

379.92 Swelling or mass of eye

379.93 Redness or discharge of eye

379.99 Other ill-defined disorders of eye
EXCLUDES *blurred vision NOS (368.8)*

DISEASES OF THE EAR AND MASTOID PROCESS (380-389)

✓4th **380 Disorders of external ear**

✓5th **380.0 Perichondritis and chondritis of pinna**
Chondritis of auricle
Perichondritis of auricle

380.00 Perichondritis of pinna, unspecified

380.01 Acute perichondritis of pinna

380.02 Chronic perichondritis of pinna

380.03 Chondritis of pinna
AHA: 4Q, '04, 76
DEF: Infection that has progressed into the cartilage; presents as indurated and edematous skin over the pinna; vascular compromise occurs with tissue necrosis and deformity.

✓5th **380.1 Infective otitis externa**

380.10 Infective otitis externa, unspecified
Otitis externa (acute):
NOS
circumscribed
diffuse
Otitis externa (acute):
hemorrhagica
infective NOS

380.11 Acute infection of pinna
EXCLUDES *furuncular otitis externa (680.0)*

380.12 Acute swimmers' ear
Beach ear
Tank ear
DEF: Otitis externa due to swimming.

380.13 Other acute infections of external ear
Code first underlying disease, as:
erysipelas (035)
impetigo (684)
seborrheic dermatitis (690.10-690.18)
EXCLUDES *herpes simplex (054.73)*
herpes zoster (053.71)

380.14 Malignant otitis externa
DEF: Severe necrotic otitis externa; due to bacteria.

380.15 Chronic mycotic otitis externa
Code first underlying disease, as:
aspergillosis (117.3)
otomycosis NOS (111.9)
EXCLUDES *candidal otitis externa (112.82)*

380.16 Other chronic infective otitis externa
Chronic infective otitis externa NOS

✓5th **380.2 Other otitis externa**

380.21 Cholesteatoma of external ear
Keratosis obturans of external ear (canal)
EXCLUDES *cholesteatoma NOS (385.30-385.35)*
postmastoidectomy (383.32)
DEF: Cystlike mass filled with debris, including cholesterol; rare, congenital condition.

380.22 Other acute otitis externa
Acute otitis externa:
actinic
chemical
contact
Acute otitis externa:
eczematoid
reactive

380.23 Other chronic otitis externa
Chronic otitis externa NOS

✓5th **380.3 Noninfectious disorders of pinna**

380.30 Disorder of pinna, unspecified

380.31 Hematoma of auricle or pinna

380.32 Acquired deformities of auricle or pinna
EXCLUDES *cauliflower ear (738.7)*
AHA: 3Q, '03, 12

380.39 Other
EXCLUDES *gouty tophi of ear (274.81)*

380.4 Impacted cerumen
Wax in ear

✓5th **380.5 Acquired stenosis of external ear canal**
Collapse of external ear canal

380.50 Acquired stenosis of external ear canal, unspecified as to cause

380.51 Secondary to trauma
DEF: Narrowing of the external ear canal; due to trauma.

380.52 Secondary to surgery
DEF: Postsurgical narrowing of the external ear canal.

380.53 Secondary to inflammation
DEF: Narrowing of the external ear canal; due to chronic inflammation.

✓5th **380.8 Other disorders of external ear**

380.81 Exostosis of external ear canal

380.89 Other

380.9 Unspecified disorder of external ear

✓4th **381 Nonsuppurative otitis media and Eustachian tube disorders**

✓5th **381.0 Acute nonsuppurative otitis media**
Acute tubotympanic catarrh
Otitis media, acute or subacute:
catarrhal
exudative
transudative
with effusion
EXCLUDES *otitic barotrauma (993.0)*

381.00 Acute nonsuppurative otitis media, unspecified

381.01 Acute serous otitis media
Acute or subacute secretory otitis media
DEF: Sudden, severe infection of the middle ear.

381.02 Acute mucoid otitis media
Acute or subacute seromucinous otitis media
Blue drum syndrome
DEF: Sudden, severe infection of the middle ear, with mucous.

381.03 Acute sanguinous otitis media
DEF: Sudden, severe infection of the middle ear, with blood.

381.04 Acute allergic serous otitis media

381.05 Acute allergic mucoid otitis media

381.06 Acute allergic sanguinous otitis media

✓5th **381.1 Chronic serous otitis media**
Chronic tubotympanic catarrh
381.10 Chronic serous otitis media, simple or unspecified
DEF: Persistent infection of the middle ear, without pus.
381.19 Other
Serosanguinous chronic otitis media

✓5th **381.2 Chronic mucoid otitis media**
Glue ear
EXCLUDES *adhesive middle ear disease (385.10-385.19)*
DEF: Chronic condition; characterized by viscous fluid in middle ear; due to obstructed Eustachian tube.
381.20 Chronic mucoid otitis media, simple or unspecified
381.29 Other
Mucosanguinous chronic otitis media

381.3 Other and unspecified chronic nonsuppurative otitis media
Otitis media, chronic:
allergic
exudative
secretory
Otitis media, chronic:
seromucinous
transudative
with effusion

381.4 Nonsuppurative otitis media, not specified as acute or chronic
Otitis media:
allergic
catarrhal
exudative
mucoid
secretory
Otitis media:
seromucinous
serous
transudative
with effusion

✓5th **381.5 Eustachian salpingitis**
381.50 Eustachian salpingitis, unspecified
381.51 Acute Eustachian salpingitis
DEF: Sudden, severe inflammation of the Eustachian tube.
381.52 Chronic Eustachian salpingitis
DEF: Persistent inflammation of the Eustachian tube.

✓5th **381.6 Obstruction of Eustachian tube**
Stenosis } of Eustachian tube
Stricture }
381.60 Obstruction of Eustachian tube, unspecified
381.61 Osseous obstruction of Eustachian tube
Obstruction of Eustachian tube from cholesteatoma, polyp, or other osseous lesion
381.62 Intrinsic cartilagenous obstruction of Eustachian tube
DEF: Blockage of Eustachian tube; due to cartilage overgrowth.
381.63 Extrinsic cartilagenous obstruction of Eustachian tube
Compression of Eustachian tube

381.7 Patulous Eustachian tube
DEF: Distended, oversized Eustachian tube.

✓5th **381.8 Other disorders of Eustachian tube**
381.81 Dysfunction of Eustachian tube
381.89 Other

381.9 Unspecified Eustachian tube disorder

✓4th **382 Suppurative and unspecified otitis media**

✓5th **382.0 Acute suppurative otitis media**
Otitis media, acute:
necrotizing NOS
Otitis media, acute:
purulent
382.00 Acute suppurative otitis media without spontaneous rupture of ear drum
DEF: Sudden, severe inflammation of middle ear, with pus.
382.01 Acute suppurative otitis media with spontaneous rupture of ear drum
DEF: Sudden, severe inflammation of middle ear, with pressure tearing ear drum tissue.
382.02 Acute suppurative otitis media in diseases classified elsewhere
Code first underlying disease, as:
influenza (487.8)
scarlet fever (034.1)
EXCLUDES *postmeasles otitis (055.2)*

382.1 Chronic tubotympanic suppurative otitis media
Benign chronic suppurative otitis media } (with anterior perforation of ear drum)
Chronic tubotympanic disease }
DEF: Inflammation of tympanic cavity and auditory tube; with pus formation.

382.2 Chronic atticoantral suppurative otitis media
Chronic atticoantral disease } (with posterior or superior marginal perforation of ear drum)
Persistent mucosal disease }
DEF: Inflammation of upper tympanic membrane and mastoid antrum with pus formation.

382.3 Unspecified chronic suppurative otitis media
Chronic purulent otitis media
EXCLUDES *tuberculous otitis media (017.4)*

382.4 Unspecified suppurative otitis media
Purulent otitis media NOS

382.9 Unspecified otitis media
Otitis media:
NOS
acute NOS
Otitis media:
chronic NOS
AHA: N-D, '84, 16

✓4th **383 Mastoiditis and related conditions**

✓5th **383.0 Acute mastoiditis**
Abscess of mastoid
Empyema of mastoid
383.00 Acute mastoiditis without complications
DEF: Sudden, severe inflammation of mastoid air cells.
383.01 Subperiosteal abscess of mastoid CC
CC Excl: 015.60-015.66, 017.40-017.46, 017.90-017.96, 383.00-388.9, 744.00, 744.02, 744.09, 744.29, 744.3
DEF: Pocket of pus within the mastoid bone.
383.02 Acute mastoiditis with other complications
Gradenigo's syndrome

383.1 Chronic mastoiditis
Caries of mastoid
Fistula of mastoid
EXCLUDES *tuberculous mastoiditis (015.6)*
DEF: Persistent inflammation of the mastoid air cells.

Middle and Inner Ear

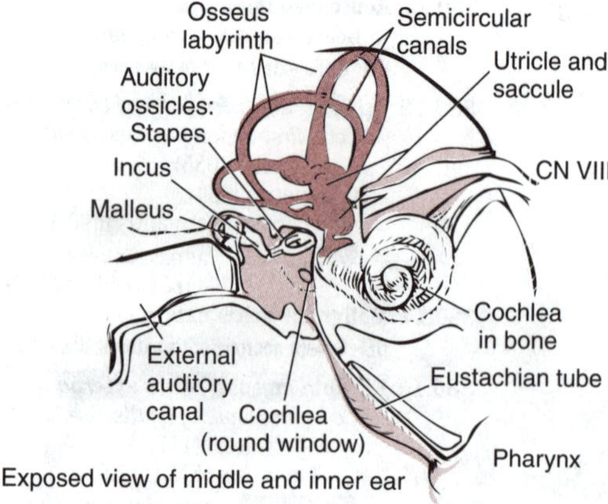

Exposed view of middle and inner ear

✓5th 383.2 **Petrositis**

Coalescing osteitis, Inflammation, Osteomyelitis } of petrous bone

383.20 **Petrositis, unspecified**

383.21 **Acute petrositis**

DEF: Sudden, severe inflammation of dense bone behind the ear.

383.22 **Chronic petrositis**

DEF: Persistent inflammation of dense bone behind the ear.

✓5th 383.3 **Complications following mastoidectomy**

383.30 **Postmastoidectomy complication, unspecified** CC

CC Excl: See code 383.01

383.31 **Mucosal cyst of postmastoidectomy cavity**

DEF: Mucous-lined cyst cavity following removal of mastoid bone.

383.32 **Recurrent cholesteatoma of postmastoidectomy cavity**

DEF: Cystlike mass of cell debris in cavity following removal of mastoid bone.

383.33 **Granulations of postmastoidectomy cavity**

Chronic inflammation of postmastoidectomy cavity

DEF: Granular tissue in cavity following removal of mastoid bone.

✓5th 383.8 **Other disorders of mastoid**

383.81 **Postauricular fistula** CC

CC Excl: See code 383.01

DEF: Abnormal passage behind mastoid cavity.

383.89 **Other**

383.9 **Unspecified mastoiditis**

✓4th 384 **Other disorders of tympanic membrane**

✓5th 384.0 **Acute myringitis without mention of otitis media**

384.00 **Acute myringitis, unspecified**

Acute tympanitis NOS

DEF: Sudden, severe inflammation of ear drum.

384.01 **Bullous myringitis**

Myringitis bullosa hemorrhagica

DEF: Type of viral otitis media characterized by the appearance of serous or hemorrhagic blebs on the tympanic membrane.

384.09 **Other**

384.1 **Chronic myringitis without mention of otitis media**

Chronic tympanitis

DEF: Persistent inflammation of ear drum; with no evidence of middle ear infection.

✓5th 384.2 **Perforation of tympanic membrane**

Perforation of ear drum: NOS, persistent posttraumatic

Perforation of ear drum: postinflammatory

EXCLUDES *otitis media with perforation of tympanic membrane (382.00-382.9)*

traumatic perforation [current injury] (872.61)

384.20 **Perforation of tympanic membrane, unspecified**

384.21 **Central perforation of tympanic membrane**

384.22 **Attic perforation of tympanic membrane**

Pars flaccida

384.23 **Other marginal perforation of tympanic membrane**

384.24 **Multiple perforations of tympanic membrane**

384.25 **Total perforation of tympanic membrane**

✓5th 384.8 **Other specified disorders of tympanic membrane**

384.81 **Atrophic flaccid tympanic membrane**

Healed perforation of ear drum

384.82 **Atrophic nonflaccid tympanic membrane**

384.9 **Unspecified disorder of tympanic membrane**

✓4th 385 **Other disorders of middle ear and mastoid**

EXCLUDES *mastoiditis (383.0-383.9)*

✓5th 385.0 **Tympanosclerosis**

385.00 **Tympanosclerosis, unspecified as to involvement**

385.01 **Tympanosclerosis involving tympanic membrane only**

DEF: Tough, fibrous tissue impeding functions of ear drum.

385.02 **Tympanosclerosis involving tympanic membrane and ear ossicles**

DEF: Tough, fibrous tissue impeding functions of middle ear bones (stapes, malleus, incus).

385.03 **Tympanosclerosis involving tympanic membrane, ear ossicles, and middle ear**

DEF: Tough, fibrous tissue impeding functions of ear drum, middle ear bones and middle ear canal.

385.09 **Tympanosclerosis involving other combination of structures**

✓5th 385.1 **Adhesive middle ear disease**

Adhesive otitis

Otitis media: chronic adhesive

Otitis media: fibrotic

EXCLUDES *glue ear (381.20-381.29)*

DEF: Adhesions of middle ear structures.

385.10 **Adhesive middle ear disease, unspecified as to involvement**

385.11 **Adhesions of drum head to incus**

385.12 **Adhesions of drum head to stapes**

385.13 **Adhesions of drum head to promontorium**

385.19 **Other adhesions and combinations**

✓5th 385.2 **Other acquired abnormality of ear ossicles**

385.21 **Impaired mobility of malleus**

Ankylosis of malleus

385.22 **Impaired mobility of other ear ossicles**

Ankylosis of ear ossicles, except malleus

385.23 **Discontinuity or dislocation of ear ossicles**

DEF: Disruption in auditory chain; created by malleus, incus and stapes.

385.24 **Partial loss or necrosis of ear ossicles**

DEF: Tissue loss in malleus, incus and stapes.

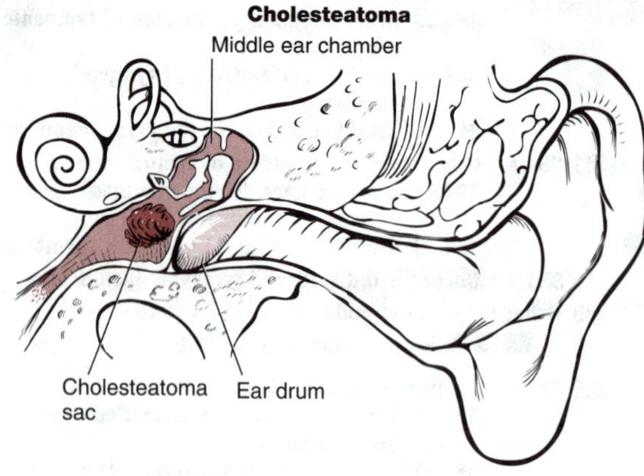

✓5th **385.3 Cholesteatoma of middle ear and mastoid**

Cholesterosis, Epidermosis, Keratosis, Polyp } of (middle) ear

EXCLUDES *cholesteatoma:*
external ear canal (380.21)
recurrent of postmastoidectomy cavity (383.32)

DEF: Cystlike mass of middle ear and mastoid antrum filled with debris, including cholesterol.

385.30 Cholesteatoma, unspecified
385.31 Cholesteatoma of attic
385.32 Cholesteatoma of middle ear
385.33 Cholesteatoma of middle ear and mastoid
AHA: 3Q, '00, 10
DEF: Cystlike mass of cell debris in middle ear and mastoid air cells behind ear.
385.35 Diffuse cholesteatosis

✓5th **385.8 Other disorders of middle ear and mastoid**

385.82 Cholesterin granuloma
DEF: Granuloma formed of fibrotic tissue; contains cholesterol crystals surrounded by foreign-body cells; found in the middle ear and mastoid area.
385.83 Retained foreign body of middle ear
AHA: 3Q, '94, 7; N-D, '87, 9
385.89 Other

385.9 Unspecified disorder of middle ear and mastoid

✓4th **386 Vertiginous syndromes and other disorders of vestibular system**

EXCLUDES *vertigo NOS (780.4)*

AHA: M-A, '85, 12

✓5th **386.0 Ménière's disease**

Endolymphatic hydrops
Lermoyez's syndrome
Ménière's syndrome or vertigo

DEF: Distended membranous labyrinth of middle ear from endolymphatic hydrops; causes ischemia, failure of nerve function; hearing and balance dysfunction; symptoms include fluctuating deafness, ringing in ears and dizziness.

386.00 Ménière's disease, unspecified
Ménière's disease (active)
386.01 Active Ménière's disease, cochleovestibular
386.02 Active Ménière's disease, cochlear
386.03 Active Ménière's disease, vestibular
386.04 Inactive Ménière's disease
Ménière's disease in remission

✓5th **386.1 Other and unspecified peripheral vertigo**

EXCLUDES *epidemic vertigo (078.81)*

386.10 Peripheral vertigo, unspecified
386.11 Benign paroxysmal positional vertigo
Benign paroxysmal positional nystagmus
386.12 Vestibular neuronitis
Acute (and recurrent) peripheral vestibulopathy
DEF: Transient benign vertigo, unknown cause; characterized by response to caloric stimulation on one side, nystagmus with rhythmic movement of eyes; normal auditory function present; occurs in young adults.
386.19 Other
Aural vertigo
Otogenic vertigo

386.2 Vertigo of central origin

Central positional nystagmus
Malignant positional vertigo

✓5th **386.3 Labyrinthitis**

386.30 Labyrinthitis, unspecified
386.31 Serous labyrinthitis
Diffuse labyrinthitis
DEF: Inflammation of labyrinth; with fluid buildup.
386.32 Circumscribed labyrinthitis
Focal labyrinthitis
386.33 Suppurative labyrinthitis
Purulent labyrinthitis
DEF: Inflammation of labyrinth; with pus.
386.34 Toxic labyrinthitis
DEF: Inflammation of labyrinth; due to toxic reaction.
386.35 Viral labyrinthitis

✓5th **386.4 Labyrinthine fistula**

386.40 Labyrinthine fistula, unspecified
386.41 Round window fistula
386.42 Oval window fistula
386.43 Semicircular canal fistula
386.48 Labyrinthine fistula of combined sites

✓5th **386.5 Labyrinthine dysfunction**

386.50 Labyrinthine dysfunction, unspecified
386.51 Hyperactive labyrinth, unilateral
DEF: Abnormal increased sensitivity of labyrinth to stimuli such as sound, pressure or gravitational change, affecting one ear.
386.52 Hyperactive labyrinth, bilateral
DEF: Abnormal increased sensitivity of labyrinth to stimuli such as sound, pressure or gravitational change, affecting both ears.
386.53 Hypoactive labyrinth, unilateral
DEF: Abnormal decreased sensitivity of labyrinth to stimuli such as sound, pressure or gravitational change, affecting one ear.
386.54 Hypoactive labyrinth, bilateral
DEF: Abnormal decreased sensitivity of labyrinth to stimuli such as sound, pressure or gravitational change, affecting both ears.
386.55 Loss of labyrinthine reactivity, unilateral
DEF: Decreased function of the labyrinth sensors, affecting one ear
386.56 Loss of labyrinthine reactivity, bilateral
DEF: Decreased function of the labyrinth sensors, affecting both ears
386.58 Other forms and combinations

386.8 Other disorders of labyrinth

386.9 Unspecified vertiginous syndromes and labyrinthine disorders

✓4th **387 Otosclerosis**

INCLUDES otospongiosis

DEF: Synonym for otospongiosis, spongy bone formation in the labyrinth bones of the ear; it causes progressive hearing impairment.

387.0 Otosclerosis involving oval window, nonobliterative
DEF: Tough, fibrous tissue impeding functions of oval window.

387.1 **Otosclerosis involving oval window, obliterative**
DEF: Tough, fibrous tissue blocking oval window.

387.2 **Cochlear otosclerosis**
Otosclerosis involving: otic capsule
Otosclerosis involving: round window
DEF: Tough, fibrous tissue impeding functions of cochlea.

387.8 **Other otosclerosis**

387.9 **Otosclerosis, unspecified**

✓4th **388 Other disorders of ear**

✓5th 388.0 **Degenerative and vascular disorders of ear**
388.00 **Degenerative and vascular disorders, unspecified**
388.01 **Presbyacusis**
DEF: Progressive, bilateral perceptive hearing loss caused by advancing age; it is also known as presbycusis.
388.02 **Transient ischemic deafness**
DEF: Restricted blood flow to auditory organs causing temporary hearing loss.

✓5th 388.1 **Noise effects on inner ear**
388.10 **Noise effects on inner ear, unspecified**
388.11 **Acoustic trauma (explosive) to ear**
Otitic blast injury
388.12 **Noise-induced hearing loss**

388.2 **Sudden hearing loss, unspecified**

✓5th 388.3 **Tinnitus**
DEF: Abnormal noises in ear; may be heard by others beside the affected individual; noises include ringing, clicking, roaring and buzzing.
388.30 **Tinnitus, unspecified**
388.31 **Subjective tinnitus**
388.32 **Objective tinnitus**

✓5th 388.4 **Other abnormal auditory perception**
388.40 **Abnormal auditory perception, unspecified**
388.41 **Diplacusis**
DEF: Perception of a single auditory sound as two sounds at two different levels of intensity.
388.42 **Hyperacusis**
DEF: Exceptionally acute sense of hearing caused by such conditions as Bell's palsy; this term may also refer to painful sensitivity to sounds.
388.43 **Impairment of auditory discrimination**
DEF: Impaired ability to distinguish tone of sound.
388.44 **Recruitment**
DEF: Perception of abnormally increased loudness caused by a slight increase in sound intensity; it is a term used in audiology.

388.5 **Disorders of acoustic nerve**
Acoustic neuritis
Degeneration } of acoustic or eighth nerve
Disorder } of acoustic or eighth nerve
EXCLUDES *acoustic neuroma (225.1)*
syphilitic acoustic neuritis (094.86)
AHA: M-A, '87, 8

✓5th 388.6 **Otorrhea**
388.60 **Otorrhea, unspecified**
Discharging ear NOS
388.61 **Cerebrospinal fluid otorrhea**
EXCLUDES *cerebrospinal fluid rhinorrhea (349.81)*
DEF: Spinal fluid leakage from ear.
388.69 **Other**
Otorrhagia

✓5th 388.7 **Otalgia**
388.70 **Otalgia, unspecified**
Earache NOS
388.71 **Otogenic pain**
388.72 **Referred pain**

388.8 **Other disorders of ear**

388.9 **Unspecified disorder of ear**

✓4th **389 Hearing loss**

✓5th 389.0 **Conductive hearing loss**
Conductive deafness
AHA: 4Q, '89, 5
DEF: Dysfunction in sound-conducting structures of external or middle ear causing hearing loss.
389.00 **Conductive hearing loss, unspecified**
389.01 **Conductive hearing loss, external ear**
389.02 **Conductive hearing loss, tympanic membrane**
389.03 **Conductive hearing loss, middle ear**
389.04 **Conductive hearing loss, inner ear**
389.08 **Conductive hearing loss of combined types**

✓5th 389.1 **Sensorineural hearing loss**
Perceptive hearing loss or deafness
EXCLUDES *abnormal auditory perception (388.40-388.44)*
psychogenic deafness (306.7)
AHA: 4Q, '89, 5
DEF: Nerve conduction causing hearing loss.
389.10 **Sensorineural hearing loss, unspecified**
AHA: 1Q, '93, 29
▲ 389.11 **Sensory hearing loss, bilateral**
▲ 389.12 **Neural hearing loss, bilateral**
▲ 389.14 **Central hearing loss, bilateral**
● 389.15 **Sensorineural hearing loss, unilateral**
● 389.16 **Sensorineural hearing loss, asymmetrical**
▲ 389.18 **Sensorineural hearing loss of combined types, bilateral**

389.2 **Mixed conductive and sensorineural hearing loss**
Deafness or hearing loss of type classifiable to 389.0 with type classifiable to 389.1

389.7 **Deaf mutism, not elsewhere classifiable**
Deaf, nonspeaking

389.8 **Other specified forms of hearing loss**

389.9 **Unspecified hearing loss**
Deafness NOS
AHA: 1Q, '04, 15

7. DISEASES OF THE CIRCULATORY SYSTEM (390-459)

ACUTE RHEUMATIC FEVER (390-392)

DEF: Febrile disease occurs mainly in children or young adults following throat infection by group A *streptococci*; symptoms include fever, joint pain, lesions of heart, blood vessels and joint connective tissue, abdominal pain, skin changes, and chorea.

390 Rheumatic fever without mention of heart involvement

Arthritis, rheumatic, acute or subacute
Rheumatic fever (active) (acute)
Rheumatism, articular, acute or subacute

EXCLUDES *that with heart involvement (391.0-391.9)*

✓4th **391 Rheumatic fever with heart involvement**

EXCLUDES *chronic heart diseases of rheumatic origin (398.0-398.9) unless rheumatic fever is also present or there is evidence of recrudescence or activity of the rheumatic process*

391.0 Acute rheumatic pericarditis

Rheumatic:
fever (active) (acute) with pericarditis
pericarditis (acute)
Any condition classifiable to 390 with pericarditis

EXCLUDES *that not specified as rheumatic (420.0-420.9)*

DEF: Sudden, severe inflammation of heart lining due to rheumatic fever.

391.1 Acute rheumatic endocarditis

Rheumatic:
endocarditis, acute
fever (active) (acute) with endocarditis or valvulitis
valvulitis acute
Any condition classifiable to 390 with endocarditis or valvulitis

DEF: Sudden, severe inflammation of heart cavities due to rheumatic fever.

391.2 Acute rheumatic myocarditis

Rheumatic fever (active) (acute) with myocarditis
Any condition classifiable to 390 with myocarditis

DEF: Sudden, severe inflammation of heart muscles due to rheumatic fever.

391.8 Other acute rheumatic heart disease

Rheumatic:
fever (active) (acute) with other or multiple types of heart involvement
pancarditis, acute
Any condition classifiable to 390 with other or multiple types of heart involvement

391.9 Acute rheumatic heart disease, unspecified

Rheumatic:
carditis, acute
fever (active) (acute) with unspecified type of heart involvement
heart disease, active or acute
Any condition classifiable to 390 with unspecified type of heart involvement

✓4th **392 Rheumatic chorea**

INCLUDES Sydenham's chorea

EXCLUDES *chorea:*
NOS (333.5)
Huntington's (333.4)

DEF: Childhood disease linked with rheumatic fever and streptococcal infections; symptoms include spasmodic, involuntary movements of limbs or facial muscles, psychic symptoms, and irritability.

392.0 With heart involvement

Rheumatic chorea with heart involvement of any type classifiable to 391

392.9 Without mention of heart involvement

CHRONIC RHEUMATIC HEART DISEASE (393-398)

393 Chronic rheumatic pericarditis

Adherent pericardium, rheumatic
Chronic rheumatic:
mediastinopericarditis
myopericarditis

EXCLUDES *pericarditis NOS or not specified as rheumatic (423.0-423.9)*

DEF: Persistent inflammation of heart lining due to rheumatic heart disease.

✓4th **394 Diseases of mitral valve**

EXCLUDES *that with aortic valve involvement (396.0-396.9)*

394.0 Mitral stenosis CC

Mitral (valve):
obstruction (rheumatic)
stenosis NOS

CC Excl: 390, 391.8-391.9, 394.0-394.9, 396.0-396.9, 397.9, 398.90, 398.99, 424.0, 459.89, 459.9

DEF: Narrowing, of mitral valve between left atrium and left ventricle; due to rheumatic heart disease.

394.1 Rheumatic mitral insufficiency CC

Rheumatic mitral:
incompetence
regurgitation

EXCLUDES *that not specified as rheumatic (424.0)*

CC Excl: See code 394.0

AHA: ▶2Q, '05, 14◀

DEF: Malfunction of mitral valve between left atrium and left ventricle; due to rheumatic heart disease.

394.2 Mitral stenosis with insufficiency CC

Mitral stenosis with incompetence or regurgitation

CC Excl: See code 394.0

DEF: A narrowing or stricture of the mitral valve situated between the left atrium and left ventricle. The stenosis interferes with blood flow from the atrium into the ventricle. If the valve does not completely close, it becomes insufficient (inadequate) and cannot prevent regurgitation (abnormal backward flow) into the atrium when the left ventricle contracts. This abnormal function is also called incompetence.

394.9 Other and unspecified mitral valve diseases CC

Mitral (valve):
disease (chronic)
failure

CC Excl: See code 394.0

✓4th **395 Diseases of aortic valve**

EXCLUDES *that not specified as rheumatic (424.1)*
that with mitral valve involvement (396.0-396.9)

395.0 Rheumatic aortic stenosis CC

Rheumatic aortic (valve) obstruction

CC Excl: 390, 391.8-391.9, 395.0-395.9, 396.0-396.9, 397.9, 398.90, 398.99, 424.1, 459.89, 459.9

AHA: 4Q, '88, 8

DEF: Narrowing of the aortic valve; results in backflow into ventricle; due to rheumatic heart disease.

395.1 Rheumatic aortic insufficiency CC

Rheumatic aortic:
incompetence
regurgitation

CC Excl: See code 395.0

DEF: Malfunction of the aortic valve; results in backflow into left ventricle; due to rheumatic heart disease.

395.2 Rheumatic aortic stenosis with insufficiency CC

Rheumatic aortic stenosis with incompetence or regurgitation

CC Excl: See code 395.0

DEF: Malfunction and narrowing, of the aortic valve; results in backflow into left ventricle; due to rheumatic heart disease.

395.9 Other and unspecified rheumatic aortic diseases CC

Rheumatic aortic (valve) disease

CC Excl: See code 395.0

✓4th **396 Diseases of mitral and aortic valves**

INCLUDES involvement of both mitral and aortic valves, whether specified as rheumatic or not

AHA: N-D, '87, 8

396.0 Mitral valve stenosis and aortic valve stenosis CC

Atypical aortic (valve) stenosis
Mitral and aortic (valve) obstruction (rheumatic)

CC Excl: 390, 391.8-391.9, 394.0-394.9, 395.0-395.9, 396.0-396.9, 397.9, 398.90, 398.99, 424.0-424.1, 459.89, 459.9

396.1 Mitral valve stenosis and aortic valve insufficiency CC

CC Excl: See code 396.0

396.2 Mitral valve insufficiency and aortic valve stenosis CC

CC Excl: See code 396.0

AHA: 2Q, '00, 16

396.3 Mitral valve insufficiency and aortic valve insufficiency CC

Mitral and aortic (valve): incompetence
Mitral and aortic (valve): regurgitation

CC Excl: See code 396.0

396.8 Multiple involvement of mitral and aortic valves CC

Stenosis and insufficiency of mitral or aortic valve with stenosis or insufficiency, or both, of the other valve

CC Excl: See code 396.0

396.9 Mitral and aortic valve diseases, unspecified CC

CC Excl: See code 396.0

✓4th **397 Diseases of other endocardial structures**

397.0 Diseases of tricuspid valve CC

Tricuspid (valve) (rheumatic):
- disease
- insufficiency
- obstruction
- regurgitation
- stenosis

CC Excl: 397.0, 398.90, 398.99, 424.2, 459.89, 459.9

AHA: 2Q, '00, 16

DEF: Malfunction of the valve between right atrium and right ventricle; due to rheumatic heart disease.

397.1 Rheumatic diseases of pulmonary valve CC

EXCLUDES *that not specified as rheumatic (424.3)*

CC Excl: 397.1, 398.90, 398.99, 424.3, 459.89, 459.9

397.9 Rheumatic diseases of endocardium, valve unspecified CC

Rheumatic:
- endocarditis (chronic)
- valvulitis (chronic)

EXCLUDES *that not specified as rheumatic (424.90-424.99)*

CC Excl: 390, 391.1, 391.8-391.9, 394.0-394.9, 395.0-395.9, 397.1, 397.9, 398.90, 398.99, 421.0-421.9, 424.0-424.99, 459.89, 459.9

✓4th **398 Other rheumatic heart disease**

398.0 Rheumatic myocarditis CC

Rheumatic degeneration of myocardium

EXCLUDES *myocarditis not specified as rheumatic (429.0)*

CC Excl: 390, 391.2-391.9, 398.0, 398.90, 398.99, 422.0, 422.90-422.99, 429.0, 429.71-429.79, 459.89, 459.9

DEF: Chronic inflammation of heart muscle; due to rheumatic heart disease.

✓5th **398.9 Other and unspecified rheumatic heart diseases**

398.90 Rheumatic heart disease, unspecified

Rheumatic:
- carditis
- heart disease NOS

EXCLUDES *carditis not specified as rheumatic (429.89)*
heart disease NOS not specified as rheumatic (429.9)

398.91 Rheumatic heart failure (congestive) CC MC CD MCV

Rheumatic left ventricular failure

CC Excl: 398.90-398.99, 402.01, 402.11, 402.91, 428.0-428.9, 459.89, 459.9

AHA: 2Q, '05, 14; 1Q, '95, 6; 3Q, '88, 3

DEF: Decreased cardiac output, edema and hypertension; due to rheumatic heart disease.

398.99 Other

HYPERTENSIVE DISEASE (401-405)

EXCLUDES *that complicating pregnancy, childbirth, or the puerperium (642.0-642.9)*
that involving coronary vessels (410.00-414.9)

AHA: 3Q, '90, 3; 2Q, '89, 12; S-O, '87, 9; J-A, '84, 11

✓4th **401 Essential hypertension**

INCLUDES high blood pressure
hyperpiesia
hyperpiesis
hypertension (arterial) (essential) (primary) (systemic)
hypertensive vascular:
- degeneration
- disease

EXCLUDES *elevated blood pressure without diagnosis of hypertension (796.2)*
pulmonary hypertension (416.0-416.9)
that involving vessels of:
- *brain (430-438)*
- *eye (362.11)*

AHA: 2Q, '92, 5

DEF: Hypertension that occurs without apparent organic cause; idiopathic.

401.0 Malignant CC

CC Excl: 401.0-405.99, 459.89, 459.9

AHA: M-J, '85, 19

DEF: Severe high arterial blood pressure; results in necrosis in kidney, retina, etc.; hemorrhages occur and death commonly due to uremia or rupture of cerebral vessel.

401.1 Benign

DEF: Mildly elevated arterial blood pressure.

401.9 Unspecified

AHA: 4Q, '05, 71; 3Q, '05, 8; 4Q, '04, 78; 4Q, '03, 105, 108, 111; 3Q, '03, 14; 2Q, '03, 16; 4Q, '97, 37

✓4th **402 Hypertensive heart disease**

INCLUDES hypertensive:
- cardiomegaly
- cardiopathy
- cardiovascular disease
- heart (disease) (failure)

any condition classifiable to 429.0-429.3, 429.8, 429.9 due to hypertension

Use additional code to specify type of heart failure (428.0-428.43), if known

AHA: 4Q, '02, 49; 2Q, '93, 9; N-D, '84, 18

✓5th **402.0 Malignant**

402.00 Without heart failure CC

CC Excl: See code 401.0

402.01 With heart failure CC MC CD MCV

CC Excl: 398.91, 401.0-405.99, 428.0-428.9, 459.89, 459.9

✓5th **402.1 Benign**

402.10 Without heart failure

402.11 With heart failure CC MC CD MCV

CC Excl: See code 402.01

✓5th **402.9 Unspecified**

402.90 Without heart failure

402.91 With heart failure CC MC CD MCV

CC Excl: See code 402.01

AHA: 4Q, '02, 52; 1Q, '93, 19; 2Q, '89, 12

DRG 127

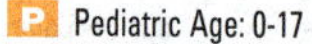 Newborn Age: 0  Pediatric Age: 0-17 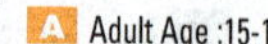 Maternity Age: 12-55 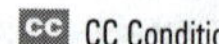 Adult Age :15-124 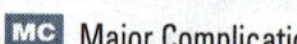 CC Condition MC Major Complication CD Complex Dx  HIV Related Dx

▲ ✓4th **403 Hypertensive chronic kidney disease**

INCLUDES arteriolar nephritis
arteriosclerosis of:
kidney
renal arterioles
arteriosclerotic nephritis (chronic) (interstitial)
hypertensive:
nephropathy
renal failure
uremia (chronic)
nephrosclerosis
renal sclerosis with hypertension
any condition classifiable to 585, 586, or 587 with any condition classifiable to 401

EXCLUDES *acute renal failure (584.5-584.9)*
renal disease stated as not due to hypertension
renovascular hypertension (405.0-405.9 with fifth-digit 1)

The following fifth-digit subclassification is for use with category 403:

▲ **0 with chronic kidney disease stage I through stage IV, or unspecified**
▶Use additional code to identify the stage of chronic kidney disease (585.1-585.4, 585.9)◀

▲ **1 with chronic kidney disease stage V or end stage renal disease**
▶Use additional code to identify the stage of chronic kidney disease (585.5, 585.6)◀

AHA: 4Q, '05, 68; 4Q, '92, 22; 2Q, '92, 5

✓5th **403.0 Malignant** CC
CC Excl: 401.0-405.99, 459.89, 459.9

✓5th **403.1 Benign** CC 1
CC Excl: For code 403.11: See code 403.0

✓5th **403.9 Unspecified** CC 1
CC Excl: For code 403.91: See code 403.0

AHA: For code 403.91: 4Q, '05, 69; 1Q, '04, 14; 1Q, '03, 20; 2Q, '01, 11; 3Q, '91, 8

DRG 316 For code 403.91

▲ ✓4th **404 Hypertensive heart and chronic kidney disease**

INCLUDES disease:
cardiorenal
cardiovascular renal
any condition classifiable to 402 with any condition classifiable to 403

Use additional code to specify type of heart failure (428.0-428.43), if known

The following fifth-digit subclassification is for use with category 404:

▲ **0 without heart failure and with chronic kidney disease stage I through stage IV, or unspecified**
▶Use additional code to identify the stage of chronic kidney disease (585.1-585.4, 585.9)◀

▲ **1 with heart failure and with chronic kidney disease stage I through stage IV, or unspecified** MC CD MCV
▶Use additional code to identify the stage of chronic kidney disease (585.1-585.4, 585.9)◀

▲ **2 without heart failure and with chronic kidney disease stage V or end stage renal disease**
▶Use additional code to identify the stage of chronic kidney disease (585.5, 585.6)◀

▲ **3 with heart failure and chronic kidney disease stage V or end stage renal disease** MC CD MCV
▶Use additional code to identify the stage of chronic kidney disease (585.5-585.6)◀

AHA: 4Q, '05, 68; 4Q, '02, 49; 3Q, '90, 3; J-A, '84, 14

✓5th **404.0 Malignant** CC
CC Excl: See code 403.0

✓5th **404.1 Benign** CC 1-3
CC Excl: For codes 404.11-404.13: See code 403.0

✓5th **404.9 Unspecified** CC 1-3
CC Excl: For codes 404.91-404.93: See code 403.0

✓4th **405 Secondary hypertension**

AHA: 3Q, '90, 3; S-O, '87, 9, 11; J-A, '84, 14

DEF: High arterial blood pressure due to or with a variety of primary diseases, such as renal disorders, CNS disorders, endocrine, and vascular diseases.

✓5th **405.0 Malignant**

405.01 Renovascular CC
CC Excl: 401.0-405.99, 459.89, 459.9

405.09 Other CC
CC Excl: See code 405.01

✓5th **405.1 Benign**

405.11 Renovascular

405.19 Other

✓5th **405.9 Unspecified**

405.91 Renovascular

405.99 Other
AHA: 3Q, '00, 4

ISCHEMIC HEART DISEASE (410-414)

INCLUDES that with mention of hypertension

Use additional code to identify presence of hypertension (401.0-405.9)

AHA: 3Q, '91, 10; J-A, '84, 5

✓4th **410 Acute myocardial infarction**

INCLUDES cardiac infarction
coronary (artery):
embolism
occlusion
rupture
thrombosis
infarction of heart, myocardium, or ventricle
rupture of heart, myocardium, or ventricle
ST elevation (STEMI) and non-ST elevation (NSTEMI) myocardial infarction
any condition classifiable to 414.1-414.9 specified as acute or with a stated duration of 8 weeks or less

The following fifth-digit subclassification is for use with category 410:

0 episode of care unspecified
Use when the source document does not contain sufficient information for the assignment of fifth digit 1 or 2.

1 initial episode of care MCV
Use fifth-digit 1 to designate the first episode of care (regardless of facility site) for a newly diagnosed myocardial infarction. The fifth-digit 1 is assigned regardless of the number of times a patient may be transferred during the initial episode of care.

2 subsequent episode of care
Use fifth-digit 2 to designate an episode of care following the initial episode when the patient is admitted for further observation, evaluation or treatment for a myocardial infarction that has received initial treatment, but is still less than 8 weeks old.

AHA: 4Q, '05, 69; 3Q, '01, 21; 3Q, '98, 15; 4Q, '97, 37; 3Q, '95, 9; 4Q, '92, 24; 1Q, '92,10; 3Q, '91, 18; 1Q, '91, 14; 3Q, '89, 3

DEF: A sudden insufficiency of blood supply to an area of the heart muscle; usually due to a coronary artery occlusion.

✓5th **410.0 Of anterolateral wall** CC 1
ST elevation myocardial infarction (STEMI) of anterolateral wall
CC Excl: For code 410.01: 410.00-410.92, 459.89, 459.9

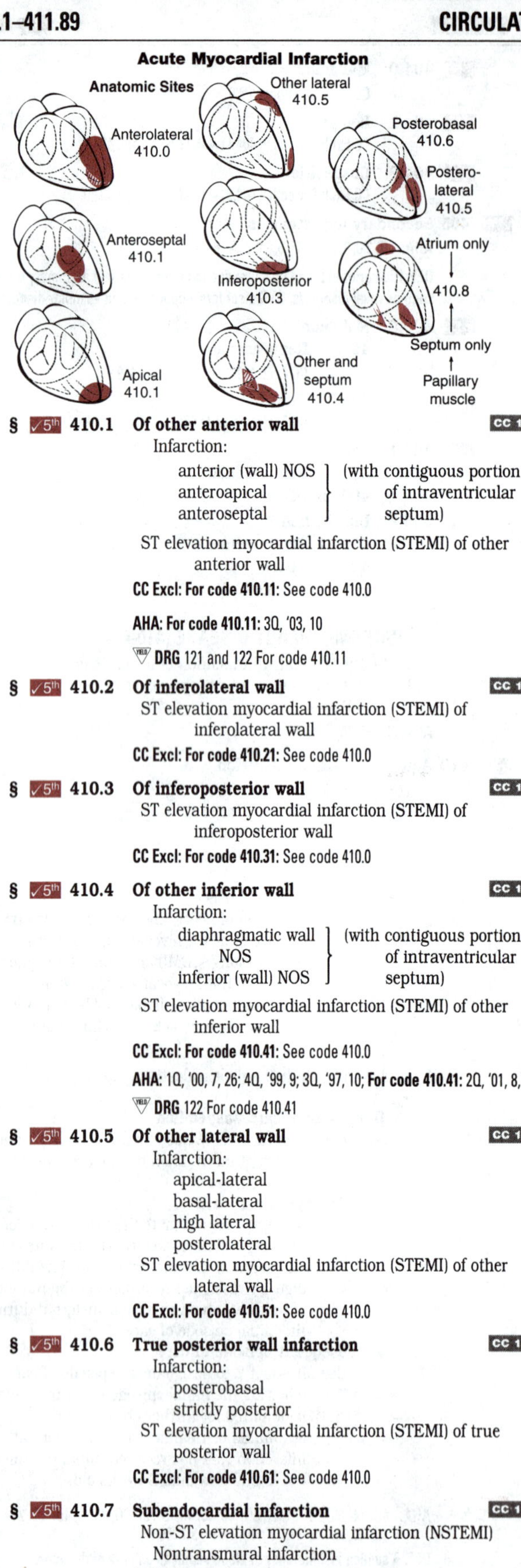

§ ✓5th 410.1 Of other anterior wall CC 1

Infarction:

anterior (wall) NOS / anteroapical / anteroseptal } (with contiguous portion of intraventricular septum)

ST elevation myocardial infarction (STEMI) of other anterior wall

CC Excl: For code 410.11: See code 410.0

AHA: For code 410.11: 3Q, '03, 10

DRG 121 and 122 For code 410.11

§ ✓5th 410.2 Of inferolateral wall CC 1

ST elevation myocardial infarction (STEMI) of inferolateral wall

CC Excl: For code 410.21: See code 410.0

§ ✓5th 410.3 Of inferoposterior wall CC 1

ST elevation myocardial infarction (STEMI) of inferoposterior wall

CC Excl: For code 410.31: See code 410.0

§ ✓5th 410.4 Of other inferior wall CC 1

Infarction:

diaphragmatic wall NOS / inferior (wall) NOS } (with contiguous portion of intraventricular septum)

ST elevation myocardial infarction (STEMI) of other inferior wall

CC Excl: For code 410.41: See code 410.0

AHA: 1Q, '00, 7, 26; 4Q, '99, 9; 3Q, '97, 10; **For code 410.41:** 2Q, '01, 8, 9

DRG 122 For code 410.41

§ ✓5th 410.5 Of other lateral wall CC 1

Infarction:

apical-lateral
basal-lateral
high lateral
posterolateral

ST elevation myocardial infarction (STEMI) of other lateral wall

CC Excl: For code 410.51: See code 410.0

§ ✓5th 410.6 True posterior wall infarction CC 1

Infarction:

posterobasal
strictly posterior

ST elevation myocardial infarction (STEMI) of true posterior wall

CC Excl: For code 410.61: See code 410.0

§ ✓5th 410.7 Subendocardial infarction CC 1

Non-ST elevation myocardial infarction (NSTEMI)
Nontransmural infarction

CC Excl: For code 410.71: See code 410.0

AHA: 1Q, '00, 7; **For code 410.71:** 4Q, '05, 71; 2Q, '05, 19

DRG 121 and 122 For code 410.71

§ ✓5th 410.8 Of other specified sites CC 1

Infarction of:

atrium
papillary muscle
septum alone

ST elevation myocardial infarction (STEMI) of other specified sites

CC Excl: For code 410.81: See code 410.0

§ ✓5th 410.9 Unspecified site CC 1

Acute myocardial infarction NOS
Coronary occlusion NOS
Myocardial infarction NOS

CC Excl: For code 410.91: See code 410.0

AHA: 1Q, '96, 17; 1Q, '92, 9; **For code 410.91:** 2Q, '05, 18; 3Q, '02, 5

DRG 121 and 122 For code 410.91

✓4th 411 Other acute and subacute forms of ischemic heart disease

AHA: 4Q, '94, 55; 3Q, '91, 24

411.0 Postmyocardial infarction syndrome CC MC CD MCV

Dressler's syndrome

CC Excl: 411.0, 411.81, 411.89, 459.89, 459.9

DEF: Complication developing several days/weeks after myocardial infarction; symptoms include fever, leukocytosis, chest pain, evidence of pericarditis, pleurisy, and pneumonitis; tendency to recur.

9 **411.1 Intermediate coronary syndrome** CC CD MCV

Impending infarction
Preinfarction angina
Preinfarction syndrome
Unstable angina

EXCLUDES *angina (pectoris) (413.9)*
decubitus (413.0)

CC Excl: 410.00-410.92, 411.1-411.89, 413.0-413.9, 414.8-414.9, 459.89, 459.9

AHA: 4Q, '05, 105; 2Q, '04, 3; 1Q, '03, 12; 3Q, '01, 15; 2Q, '01, 7, 9; 4Q, '98, 86; 2Q, '96, 10; 3Q, '91, 24; 1Q, '91, 14; 3Q, '90, 6; 4Q, '89, 10

DRG 140

DEF: A condition representing an intermediate stage between angina of effort and acute myocardial infarction. It is often documented by the physician as "unstable angina."

✓5th 411.8 Other

AHA: 3Q, '91, 18; 3Q, '89, 4

9 **411.81 Acute coronary occlusion without myocardial infarction** CC CD MCV

Acute coronary (artery):

embolism / obstruction / occlusion / thrombosis } without or not resulting in myocardial infarction

EXCLUDES *obstruction without infarction due to atherosclerosis (414.00-414.07)*
occlusion without infarction due to atherosclerosis (414.00-414.07)

CC Excl: 410.00-410.92, 411.0-411.89, 413.0-413.9, 414.8-414.9, 459.89, 459.9

AHA: 3Q, '91, 24; 1Q, '91, 14

DEF: Interrupted blood flow to a portion of the heart; without tissue death.

411.89 Other CC CD

Coronary insufficiency (acute)
Subendocardial ischemia

CC Excl: See code 411.81

AHA: 3Q, '01, 14; 1Q, '92, 9

DRG 140

9 MCV for DRGs 551 and 553 only.
§ Requires fifth-digit. See category 410 for codes and definitions.

412 Old myocardial infarction
Healed myocardial infarction
Past myocardial infarction diagnosed on ECG [EKG] or other special investigation, but currently presenting no symptoms
AHA: 2Q, '03, 10; 2Q, '01, 9; 3Q, '98, 15; 2Q, '91, 22; 3Q, '90, 7

✓4th **413 Angina pectoris**
DEF: Severe constricting pain in the chest, often radiating from the precordium to the left shoulder and down the arm, due to ischemia of the heart muscle; usually caused by coronary disease; pain is often precipitated by effort or excitement.

413.0 Angina decubitus CC
Nocturnal angina
CC Excl: 410.00-410.92, 411.1-411.89, 413.0-413.9, 414.8-414.9, 459.89, 459.9
DEF: Angina occurring only in the recumbent position.

413.1 Prinzmetal angina CC
Variant angina pectoris
CC Excl: See code 413.0
DEF Angina occurring when patient is recumbent; associated with ST-segment elevations.

413.9 Other and unspecified angina pectoris CC
Angina:
- NOS
- cardiac
- of effort

Anginal syndrome
Status anginosus
Stenocardia
Syncope anginosa

EXCLUDES *preinfarction angina (411.1)*
CC Excl: See code 413.0
AHA: 3Q, '02, 4; 3Q, '91, 16; 3Q, '90, 6
DRG 140

✓4th **414 Other forms of chronic ischemic heart disease**
EXCLUDES *arteriosclerotic cardiovascular disease [ASCVD] (429.2)*
cardiovascular:
arteriosclerosis or sclerosis (429.2)
degeneration or disease (429.2)

✓5th **414.0 Coronary atherosclerosis**
Arteriosclerotic heart disease [ASHD]
Atherosclerotic heart disease
Coronary (artery):
- arteriosclerosis
- arteritis or endarteritis
- atheroma
- sclerosis
- stricture

EXCLUDES *embolism of graft (996.72)*
occlusion NOS of graft (996.72)
thrombus of graft (996.72)
AHA: 2Q, '97, 13; 2Q, '95, 17; 4Q, '94, 49; 2Q, '94, 13; 1Q, '94, 6; 3Q, '90, 7
DEF: A chronic condition marked by thickening and loss of elasticity of the coronary artery; caused by deposits of plaque containing cholesterol, lipoid material and lipophages.

414.00 Of unspecified type of vessel, native or graft A
AHA: 1Q, '04, 24; 2Q, '03, 16; 3Q, '01, 15; 4Q, '99, 4; 3Q, '97, 15; 4Q, '96, 31
DRG 124, 125 and 132

414.01 Of native coronary artery A
AHA: 4Q, '05, 71; 2Q, '04, 3; 4Q, '03, 108; 3Q, '03, 9, 14; 3Q, '02, 4-9; 3Q, '01, 15; 2Q, '01, 8, 9; 3Q, '97, 15; 2Q, '96, 10; 4Q, '96, 31
DRG 132, 124, and 125
DEF: Plaque deposits in natural heart vessels.

414.02 Of autologous vein bypass graft A
DEF: Plaque deposit in grafted vein originating within patient.

414.03 Of nonautologous biological bypass graft A
DEF: Plaque deposits in grafted vessel originating outside patient.

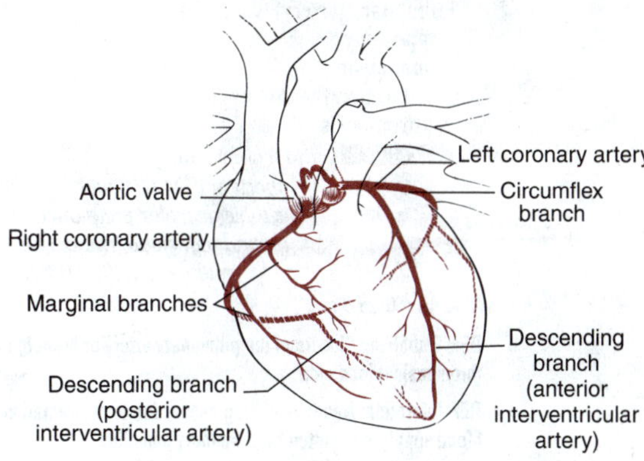

414.04 Of artery bypass graft A
Internal mammary artery
AHA: 4Q, '96, 31
DEF: Plaque deposits in grafted artery originating within patient.

414.05 Of unspecified type of bypass graft A
Bypass graft NOS
AHA: 3Q, '97, 15; 4Q, '96, 31

414.06 Of native coronary artery of transplanted heart
AHA: 4Q, '03, 60; 4Q, '02, 53

414.07 Of bypass graft (artery) (vein) of transplanted heart A

✓5th **414.1 Aneurysm and dissection of heart**
AHA: 4Q, '02, 54

414.10 Aneurysm of heart (wall) MC MCV
Aneurysm (arteriovenous):
- mural
- ventricular

414.11 Aneurysm of coronary vessels MC MCV
Aneurysm (arteriovenous) of coronary vessels
AHA: 3Q, '03, 10; 1Q, '99, 17
DEF: Dilatation of all three-vessel wall layers forming a sac filled with blood.

414.12 Dissection of coronary artery MC MCV
DEF: A tear in the intimal arterial wall of a coronary artery resulting in the sudden intrusion of blood within the layers of the wall.

414.19 Other aneurysm of heart MC MCV
Arteriovenous fistula, acquired, of heart

414.8 Other specified forms of chronic ischemic heart disease
Chronic coronary insufficiency
Ischemia, myocardial (chronic)
Any condition classifiable to 410 specified as chronic, or presenting with symptoms after 8 weeks from date of infarction
EXCLUDES *coronary insufficiency (acute) (411.89)*
AHA: 3Q, '01, 15; 1Q, '92, 10; 3Q, '90, 7, 15; 2Q, '90, 19

414.9 Chronic ischemic heart disease, unspecified
Ischemic heart disease NOS

DISEASES OF PULMONARY CIRCULATION (415-417)

✓4th **415 Acute pulmonary heart disease**

415.0 Acute cor pulmonale CC CD MCV
EXCLUDES *cor pulmonale NOS (416.9)*
CC Excl: 415.0, 416.8-416.9, 459.89, 459.9
DEF: A heart-lung disease marked by dilation and failure of the right side of heart; due to pulmonary embolism; ventilatory function is impaired and pulmonary hypertension results within hours.

✓5th **415.1 Pulmonary embolism and infarction**
Pulmonary (artery) (vein):
apoplexy
embolism
infarction (hemorrhagic)
thrombosis
EXCLUDES *that complicating:*
abortion (634-638 with .6, 639.6)
ectopic or molar pregnancy (639.6)
pregnancy, childbirth, or the puerperium (673.0-673.8)

AHA: 4Q, '90, 25

DEF: Embolism: Closure of the pulmonary artery or branch; due to thrombosis (blood clot).

DEF: Infarction: Necrosis of lung tissue; due to obstructed arterial blood supply, most often by pulmonary embolism.

10 **415.11 Iatrogenic pulmonary embolism and infarction** CC MC CD MCV
CC Excl: 415.11, 415.19, 459.89, 459.9
AHA: 4Q, '95, 58

10 **415.19 Other** CC MC CD MCV
CC Excl: 415.11, 415.19, 459.89, 459.9

✓4th **416 Chronic pulmonary heart disease**

416.0 Primary pulmonary hypertension CC MC
Idiopathic pulmonary arteriosclerosis
Pulmonary hypertension (essential) (idiopathic) (primary)
CC Excl: 416.0, 416.8-416.9, 417.8-417.9, 459.89, 459.9

DEF: A rare increase in pulmonary circulation, often resulting in right ventricular failure or fatal syncope.

416.1 Kyphoscoliotic heart disease
DEF: High blood pressure within the lungs as a result of curvature of the spine.

416.8 Other chronic pulmonary heart diseases
Pulmonary hypertension, secondary

416.9 Chronic pulmonary heart disease, unspecified
Chronic cardiopulmonary disease
Cor pulmonale (chronic) NOS

✓4th **417 Other diseases of pulmonary circulation**

417.0 Arteriovenous fistula of pulmonary vessels
EXCLUDES *congenital arteriovenous fistula (747.3)*
DEF: Abnormal communication between blood vessels within lung.

417.1 Aneurysm of pulmonary artery
EXCLUDES *congenital aneurysm (747.3)*

417.8 Other specified diseases of pulmonary circulation
Pulmonary:
arteritis
Pulmonary:
endarteritis
Rupture } of pulmonary vessel
Stricture } of pulmonary vessel

417.9 Unspecified disease of pulmonary circulation

OTHER FORMS OF HEART DISEASE (420-429)

✓4th **420 Acute pericarditis**
INCLUDES acute:
mediastinopericarditis
myopericarditis
pericardial effusion
pleuropericarditis
pneumopericarditis
EXCLUDES *acute rheumatic pericarditis (391.0)*
postmyocardial infarction syndrome [Dressler's] (411.0)

DEF: Inflammation of the pericardium (heart sac); pericardial friction rub results from this inflammation and is heard as a scratchy or leathery sound.

Anatomy

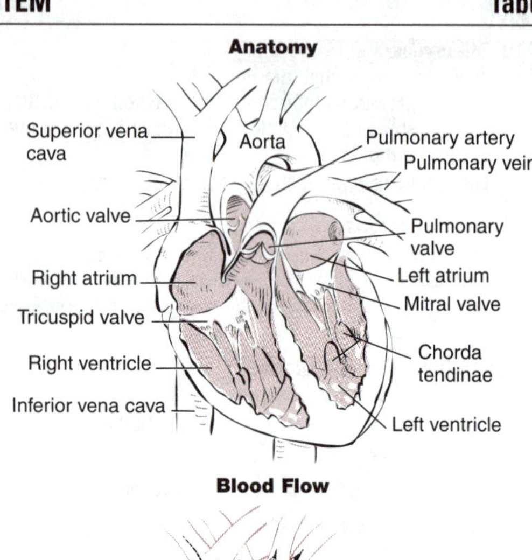

Blood Flow

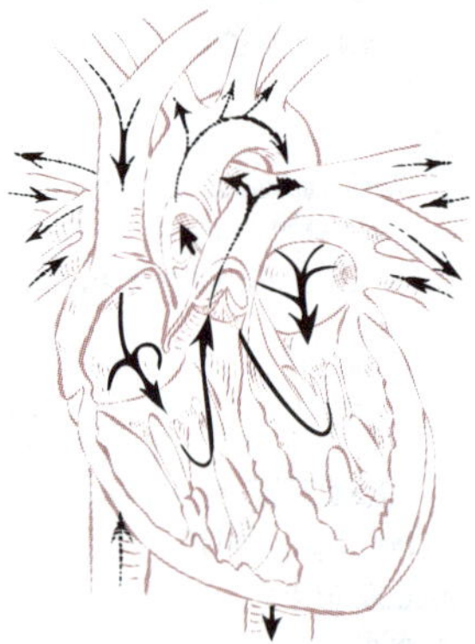

420.0 Acute pericarditis in diseases classified elsewhere CC CD MCV
Code first underlying disease, as:
actinomycosis (039.8)
amebiasis (006.8)
▶chronic uremia (585.9)◀
nocardiosis (039.8)
tuberculosis (017.9)
uremia ▶NOS (586)◀
EXCLUDES *pericarditis (acute) (in):*
Coxsackie (virus) (074.21)
gonococcal (098.83)
histoplasmosis (115.0-115.9 with fifth-digit 3)
meningococcal infection (036.41)
syphilitic (093.81)
CC Excl: 391.0, 393, 420.0-420.99, 423.8-423.9, 459.89, 459.9

✓5th **420.9 Other and unspecified acute pericarditis**

420.90 Acute pericarditis, unspecified CC CD MCV
Pericarditis (acute):
NOS
infective NOS
Pericarditis (acute):
sicca
CC Excl: See code 420.0
AHA: 2Q, '89, 12

420.91 Acute idiopathic pericarditis CC CD MCV
Pericarditis, acute:
benign
nonspecific
Pericarditis, acute:
viral
CC Excl: See code 420.0

420.99 Other CC CD MCV
Pericarditis (acute):
pneumococcal
purulent
staphylococcal
streptococcal
Pericarditis (acute):
suppurative
Pneumopyopericardium
Pyopericardium
EXCLUDES *pericarditis in diseases classified elsewhere (420.0)*
CC Excl: See code 420.0

10 MCV as SDx only.

N Newborn Age: 0 P Pediatric Age: 0-17 M Maternity Age: 12-55 A Adult Age :15-124 CC CC Condition MC Major Complication CD Complex Dx HIV HIV Related Dx

421 Acute and subacute endocarditis

DEF: Bacterial inflammation of the endocardium (intracardiac area); major symptoms include fever, fatigue, heart murmurs, splenomegaly, embolic episodes and areas of infarction.

421.0 Acute and subacute bacterial endocarditis CC CD HIV MCV

Endocarditis (acute) (chronic) (subacute):
- bacterial
- infective NOS
- lenta
- malignant
- purulent
- septic

Endocarditis (acute) (chronic) (subacute):
- ulcerative
- vegetative

Infective aneurysm

Subacute bacterial endocarditis [SBE]

Use additional code to identify infectious organism [e.g., Streptococcus 041.0, Staphylococcus 041.1]

CC Excl: 391.1, 397.9, 421.0-421.9, 424.90-424.99, 459.89, 459.9

AHA: 1Q, '99, 12; 1Q, '91, 15

421.1 Acute and subacute infective endocarditis in diseases classified elsewhere CC CD MCV

Code first underlying disease, as:
- blastomycosis (116.0)
- Q fever (083.0)
- typhoid (fever) (002.0)

EXCLUDES *endocarditis (in):*
- *Coxsackie (virus) (074.22)*
- *gonococcal (098.84)*
- *histoplasmosis (115.0-115.9 with fifth-digit 4)*
- *meningococcal infection (036.42)*
- *monilial (112.81)*

CC Excl: See code 421.0

421.9 Acute endocarditis, unspecified CC CD HIV MCV

Endocarditis, Myoendocarditis, Periendocarditis } acute or subacute

EXCLUDES *acute rheumatic endocarditis (391.1)*

CC Excl: See code 421.0

422 Acute myocarditis

EXCLUDES *acute rheumatic myocarditis (391.2)*

DEF: Acute inflammation of the muscular walls of the heart (myocardium).

422.0 Acute myocarditis in diseases classified elsewhere CC CD

Code first underlying disease, as:
- myocarditis (acute):
  - influenzal (487.8)
  - tuberculous (017.9)

EXCLUDES *myocarditis (acute) (due to):*
- *aseptic, of newborn (074.23)*
- *Coxsackie (virus) (074.23)*
- *diphtheritic (032.82)*
- *meningococcal infection (036.43)*
- *syphilitic (093.82)*
- *toxoplasmosis (130.3)*

CC Excl: 391.2, 398.0, 422.0-422.99, 429.0, 429.71, 429.79, 459.89, 459.9

422.9 Other and unspecified acute myocarditis

422.90 Acute myocarditis, unspecified CC CD HIV

Acute or subacute (interstitial) myocarditis

CC Excl: See code 422.0

422.91 Idiopathic myocarditis CC CD HIV

Myocarditis (acute or subacute):
- Fiedler's
- giant cell
- isolated (diffuse) (granulomatous)
- nonspecific granulomatous

CC Excl: See code 422.0

422.92 Septic myocarditis CC CD HIV MCV

Myocarditis, acute or subacute:
- pneumococcal
- staphylococcal

Use additional code to identify infectious organism [e.g., Staphylococcus 041.1]

EXCLUDES *myocarditis, acute or subacute:*
- *in bacterial diseases classified elsewhere (422.0)*
- *streptococcal (391.2)*

CC Excl: See code 422.0

422.93 Toxic myocarditis CC CD HIV

CC Excl: See code 422.0

DEF: Inflammation of the heart muscle due to an adverse reaction to certain drugs or chemicals reaching the heart through the bloodstream.

422.99 Other CC CD HIV

CC Excl: See code 422.0

423 Other diseases of pericardium

EXCLUDES *that specified as rheumatic (393)*

423.0 Hemopericardium CC CD MCV

CC Excl: 423.0-423.9, 459.89, 459.9

DEF: Blood in the pericardial sac (pericardium).

423.1 Adhesive pericarditis CC

Adherent pericardium

Fibrosis of pericardium

Milk spots

Pericarditis:
- adhesive
- obliterative

Soldiers' patches

CC Excl: See code 423.0

DEF: Two layers of serous pericardium adhere to each other by fibrous adhesions.

423.2 Constrictive pericarditis CC

Concato's disease

Pick's disease of heart (and liver)

CC Excl: See code 423.0

DEF: Inflammation identified by a rigid, thickened and sometimes calcified pericardium; ventricles of the heart cannot be adequately filled and congestive heart failure may result.

423.8 Other specified diseases of pericardium

Calcification, Fistula } of pericardium

AHA: 2Q, '89, 12

423.9 Unspecified disease of pericardium

424 Other diseases of endocardium

EXCLUDES *bacterial endocarditis (421.0-421.9)*
rheumatic endocarditis (391.1, 394.0-397.9)
syphilitic endocarditis (093.20-093.24)

424.0 Mitral valve disorders CC

Mitral (valve):
- incompetence, insufficiency, regurgitation } NOS of specified cause, except rheumatic

EXCLUDES *mitral (valve):*
- *disease (394.9)*
- *failure (394.9)*
- *stenosis (394.0)*

the listed conditions:
- *specified as rheumatic (394.1)*
- *unspecified as to cause but with mention of:*
  - *diseases of aortic valve (396.0-396.9)*
  - *mitral stenosis or obstruction (394.2)*

CC Excl: 394.0-394.9, 396.0-396.9, 424.0, 459.89, 459.9

AHA: 2Q, '00, 16; 3Q, '98, 11; N-D, '87, 8; N-D, '84, 8

Circulatory System

421–424.0

424.1 Aortic valve disorders CC

Aortic (valve):

incompetence insufficiency regurgitation stenosis	NOS of specified cause, except rheumatic

EXCLUDES *hypertrophic subaortic stenosis (425.1)*
that specified as rheumatic (395.0-395.9)
that of unspecified cause but with mention of diseases of mitral valve (396.0-396.9)

CC Excl: 395.0-395.9, 396.0-396.9, 424.1, 459.89, 459.9

AHA: 4Q, '88, 8; N-D, '87, 8

424.2 Tricuspid valve disorders, specified as nonrheumatic CC

Tricuspid valve:

incompetence insufficiency regurgitation stenosis	of specified cause, except rheumatic

EXCLUDES *rheumatic or of unspecified cause (397.0)*

CC Excl: 397.0, 424.2, 459.89, 459.9

424.3 Pulmonary valve disorders CC

Pulmonic: incompetence NOS insufficiency NOS	Pulmonic: regurgitation NOS stenosis NOS

EXCLUDES *that specified as rheumatic (397.1)*

CC Excl: 397.1, 424.3, 459.89, 459.9

✓5th **424.9 Endocarditis, valve unspecified**

424.90 Endocarditis, valve unspecified, unspecified cause CC CD MCV

Endocarditis (chronic):
NOS
nonbacterial thrombotic

Valvular:

incompetence insufficiency regurgitation stenosis	of unspecified valve, unspecified cause

Valvulitis (chronic)

CC Excl: 424.90-424.99, 459.89, 459.9

424.91 Endocarditis in diseases classified elsewhere CC CD

Code first underlying disease as:
atypical verrucous endocarditis [Libman-Sacks] (710.0)
disseminated lupus erythematosus (710.0)
tuberculosis (017.9)

EXCLUDES *syphilitic (093.20-093.24)*

CC Excl: See code 424.90

424.99 Other CC

Any condition classifiable to 424.90 with specified cause, except rheumatic

EXCLUDES *endocardial fibroelastosis (425.3)*
that specified as rheumatic (397.9)

CC Excl: See code 424.90

✓4th **425 Cardiomyopathy**

INCLUDES myocardiopathy

AHA: J-A, '85, 15

425.0 Endomyocardial fibrosis CC

CC Excl: 425.0-425.9, 459.89, 459.9

425.1 Hypertrophic obstructive cardiomyopathy CC

Hypertrophic subaortic stenosis (idiopathic)

CC Excl: See code 425.0

DEF: Cardiomyopathy marked by left ventricle hypertrophy, enlarged septum; results in obstructed blood flow.

Heart Valve Disorders

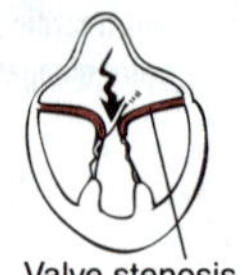

Normal Heart Valve Function

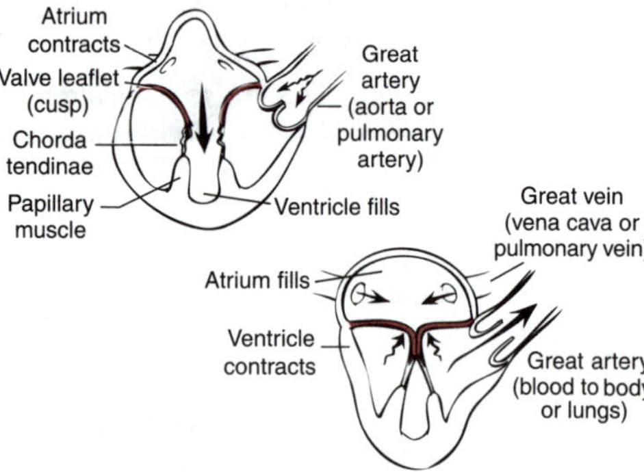

425.2 Obscure cardiomyopathy of Africa CC CD

Becker's disease
Idiopathic mural endomyocardial disease

CC Excl: See code 425.0

425.3 Endocardial fibroelastosis CC CD

Elastomyofibrosis

CC Excl: See code 425.0

DEF: A condition marked by left ventricle hypertrophy and conversion of the endocardium into a thick fibroelastic coat; capacity of the ventricle may be reduced, but is often increased.

425.4 Other primary cardiomyopathies CC CD

Cardiomyopathy: NOS congestive constrictive familial hypertrophic	Cardiomyopathy: idiopathic nonobstructive obstructive restrictive Cardiovascular collagenosis

CC Excl: See code 425.0

AHA: 2Q, '05, 14; 1Q, '00, 22; 4Q, '97, 55; 2Q, '90, 19

425.5 Alcoholic cardiomyopathy CC CD

CC Excl: See code 425.0

AHA: S-O, '85, 15

DEF: Heart disease as result of excess alcohol consumption.

425.7 Nutritional and metabolic cardiomyopathy CC CD

Code first underlying disease, as:
amyloidosis ►(277.30-277.39)◄
beriberi (265.0)
cardiac glycogenosis (271.0)
mucopolysaccharidosis (277.5)
thyrotoxicosis (242.0-242.9)

EXCLUDES *gouty tophi of heart (274.82)*

CC Excl: See code 425.0

Nerve Conduction of the Heart

Sinoatrial node (pacemaker)
Internodal tracts:
Anterior
Middle
Posterior
Atrioventricular node
Common bundle (of His)
Atrioventricular block
Accessory bundle (of Kent)
Right bundle branch
Right bundle branch block
Moderator band
Purkinje fibers
Bachmann's bundle
Left bundle branch block
Left bundle branch:
Anterior fascicle
Posterior fascicle
Left bundle branch hemiblock

425.8 *Cardiomyopathy in other diseases classified elsewhere* CC CD

Code first underlying disease, as:

Friedreich's ataxia (334.0)
myotonia atrophica (359.2)
progressive muscular dystrophy (359.1)
sarcoidosis (135)

EXCLUDES *cardiomyopathy in Chagas' disease (086.0)*

CC Excl: See code 425.0

AHA: 2Q, '93, 9

425.9 Secondary cardiomyopathy, unspecified CC CD

CC Excl: See code 425.0

✓4th **426 Conduction disorders**

DEF: Disruption or disturbance in the electrical impulses that regulate heartbeats.

[11] **426.0 Atrioventricular block, complete** CC MC MCV

Third degree atrioventricular block

CC Excl: 426.0-427.5, 427.89, 459.89, 459.9

✓5th **426.1 Atrioventricular block, other and unspecified**

426.10 Atrioventricular block, unspecified MC

Atrioventricular [AV] block (incomplete) (partial)

426.11 First degree atrioventricular block

Incomplete atrioventricular block, first degree
Prolonged P-R interval NOS

426.12 Mobitz (type) II atrioventricular block CC MC

Incomplete atrioventricular block:
Mobitz (type) II
second degree, Mobitz (type) II

CC Excl: See code 426.0

DEF: Impaired conduction of excitatory impulse from cardiac atrium to ventricle through AV node.

426.13 Other second degree atrioventricular block CC MC

Incomplete atrioventricular block:
Mobitz (type) I [Wenckebach's]
second degree:
NOS
Mobitz (type) I
with 2:1 atrioventricular response [block]
Wenckebach's phenomenon

CC Excl: See code 426.0

DEF: Wenckebach's phenomenon: impulses generated at constant rate to sinus node, P-R interval lengthens; results in cycle of ventricular inadequacy and shortened P-R interval; second-degree A-V block commonly called "Mobitz type 1."

426.2 Left bundle branch hemiblock

Block:
left anterior fascicular
left posterior fascicular

Normal and Long QT Electrocardiogram

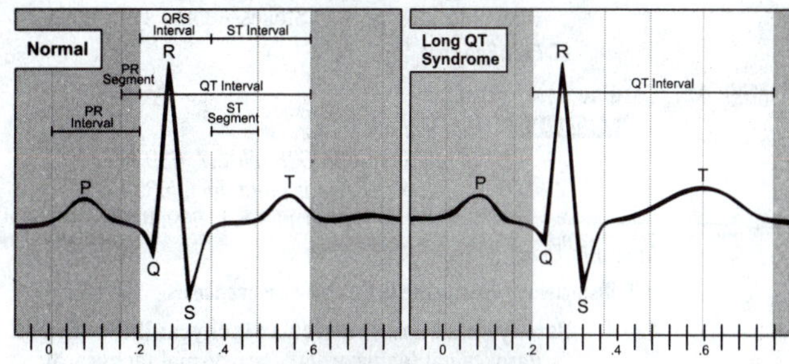

426.3 Other left bundle branch block MC

Left bundle branch block:
NOS
anterior fascicular with posterior fascicular
complete
main stem

426.4 Right bundle branch block

AHA: 3Q, '00, 3

✓5th **426.5 Bundle branch block, other and unspecified**

426.50 Bundle branch block, unspecified

426.51 Right bundle branch block and left posterior fascicular block MC

426.52 Right bundle branch block and left anterior fascicular block MC

[11] **426.53 Other bilateral bundle branch block** CC MC MCV

Bifascicular block NOS
Bilateral bundle branch block NOS
Right bundle branch with left bundle branch block (incomplete) (main stem)

CC Excl: See code 426.0

[11] **426.54 Trifascicular block** CC MC MCV

CC Excl: See code 426.0

426.6 Other heart block CC

Intraventricular block:
NOS
diffuse
myofibrillar
Sinoatrial block
Sinoauricular block

CC Excl: See code 426.0

426.7 Anomalous atrioventricular excitation CC

Atrioventricular conduction:
accelerated
accessory
pre-excitation
Ventricular pre-excitation
Wolff-Parkinson-White syndrome

CC Excl: See code 426.0

DEF: Wolff-Parkinson-White: normal conduction pathway is bypassed; results in short P-R interval on EKG; tendency to supraventricular tachycardia.

✓5th **426.8 Other specified conduction disorders**

426.81 Lown-Ganong-Levine syndrome CC

Syndrome of short P-R interval, normal QRS complexes, and supraventricular tachycardias

CC Excl: See code 426.0

426.82 Long QT syndrome

AHA: 4Q, '05, 72

DEF: Condition characterized by recurrent syncope, malignant arrhythmias, and sudden death; characteristic prolonged Q-T interval on electrocardiogram.

426.89 Other CC

Dissociation:
atrioventricular [AV]
interference
isorhythmic
Nonparoxysmal AV nodal tachycardia

CC Excl: See code 426.0

[11] MCV for DRGs 547, 549, 553, 555, and 557 only.

✓4th ✓5th Additional Digit Required | Nonspecific PDx | Unacceptable PDx | Manifestation Code | MCV Major Cardiovascular Condition | ▶◀ Revised Text | ● New Code | ▲ Revised Code Title

426.9 Conduction disorder, unspecified CC
Heart block NOS Stokes-Adams syndrome
CC Excl: See code 426.0

✓4th **427 Cardiac dysrhythmias**
EXCLUDES *that complicating:*
abortion (634-638 with .7, 639.8)
ectopic or molar pregnancy (639.8)
labor or delivery (668.1, 669.4)
AHA: J-A, '85, 15
DEF: Disruption or disturbance in the rhythm of heartbeats.

427.0 Paroxysmal supraventricular tachycardia CC MC
Paroxysmal tachycardia:
atrial [PAT]
atrioventricular [AV]
Paroxysmal tachycardia:
junctional
nodal
CC Excl: See code 426.0
DEF: Rapid atrial rhythm.

427.1 Paroxysmal ventricular tachycardia CC MC CD MCV
Ventricular tachycardia (paroxysmal)
CC Excl: See code 426.0
AHA: 3Q, '95, 9; M-A, '86, 11
▽ **DRG** 138
DEF: Rapid ventricular rhythm.

427.2 Paroxysmal tachycardia, unspecified CC MC
Bouveret-Hoffmann syndrome
Paroxysmal tachycardia:
essential
NOS
CC Excl: See code 426.0

✓5th **427.3 Atrial fibrillation and flutter**

427.31 Atrial fibrillation CC MC
CC Excl: See code 426.0
AHA: 3Q, '05, 8; 4Q, '04, 78, 121; 3Q, '04, 7; 4Q, '03, 95, 105; 1Q, '03, 8; 2Q, '99, 17; 3Q, '95, 8
▽ **DRG** 138
DEF: Irregular, rapid atrial contractions.

427.32 Atrial flutter CC MC
CC Excl: See code 426.0
AHA: 4Q, '03, 94
▽ **DRG** 138
DEF: Regular, rapid atrial contractions.

✓5th **427.4 Ventricular fibrillation and flutter**

427.41 Ventricular fibrillation CC MC MCV
CC Excl: See code 426.0
AHA: 3Q, '02, 5
DEF: Irregular, rapid ventricular contractions.

427.42 Ventricular flutter CC MC
CC Excl: See code 426.0
DEF: Regular, rapid, ventricular contractions.

427.5 Cardiac arrest CC MC CD MCV
Cardiorespiratory arrest
CC Excl: 427.0-427.5, 459.89, 459.9
AHA: 3Q,'02, 5; 2Q, '00, 12; 3Q, '95, 8; 2Q, '88, 8

✓5th **427.6 Premature beats**

427.60 Premature beats, unspecified
Ectopic beats
Extrasystoles
Extrasystolic arrhythmia
Premature contractions or systoles NOS

427.61 Supraventricular premature beats
Atrial premature beats, contractions, or systoles

427.69 Other
Ventricular premature beats, contractions, or systoles
AHA: 4Q, '93, 42

✓5th **427.8 Other specified cardiac dysrhythmias**

427.81 Sinoatrial node dysfunction
Sinus bradycardia:
persistent
severe
Syndrome:
sick sinus
tachycardia-bradycardia
EXCLUDES *sinus bradycardia NOS (427.89)*
AHA: 3Q, '00, 8
DEF: Complex cardiac arrhythmia; appears as severe sinus bradycardia, sinus bradycardia with tachycardia, or sinus bradycardia with atrioventricular block.

427.89 Other
Rhythm disorder:
coronary sinus
ectopic
Rhythm disorder:
nodal
Wandering (atrial) pacemaker
EXCLUDES *carotid sinus syncope (337.0)*
neonatal bradycardia (779.81)
neonatal tachycardia (779.82)
reflex bradycardia (337.0)
tachycardia NOS (785.0)
▽ **DRG** 138

427.9 Cardiac dysrhythmia, unspecified
Arrhythmia (cardiac) NOS
AHA: 2Q, '89, 10

✓4th **428 Heart failure**
Code, if applicable, heart failure due to hypertension first (402.0-402.9, with fifth-digit 1 or 404.0-404.9 with fifth-digit 1 or 3)
EXCLUDES *following cardiac surgery (429.4)*
rheumatic (398.91)
that complicating:
abortion (634-638 with .7, 639.8)
ectopic or molar pregnancy (639.8)
labor or delivery (668.1, 669.4)
AHA: 4Q, '02, 49; 3Q, '98, 5; 2Q, '90, 16; 2Q, '90, 19; 2Q, '89, 10; 3Q, '88, 3

428.0 Congestive heart failure, unspecified CC MC CD MCV
Congestive heart disease
Right heart failure (secondary to left heart failure)
EXCLUDES *fluid overload NOS (276.6)*
CC Excl: 398.91, 402.01, 402.11, 402.91, 428.0-428.9, 459.89, 459.9, 518.4
AHA: 4Q, '05, 120; 3Q, '05, 8; 1Q, '05, 5, 9; 1Q, '05, 5, 9; 4Q, '04, 140; 3Q, '04, 7;4Q, '03, 109; 1Q, '03, 9; 4Q, '02, 52; 2Q, '01, 13; 4Q, '00, 48; 2Q, '00, 16; 1Q, '00, 22; 4Q, '99, 4; 1Q, '99, 11; 4Q, '97, 55; 3Q, '97, 10; 3Q, '96, 9; 3Q, '91, 18; 3Q, '91, 19; 2Q, '89, 12
▽ **DRG** 121, 124 and 127
DEF: Mechanical inadequacy; caused by inability of heart to pump and circulate blood; results in fluid collection in lungs, hypertension, congestion and edema of tissue.

428.1 Left heart failure CC MC CD MCV
Acute edema of lung } with heart disease NOS
Acute pulmonary edema } or heart failure
Cardiac asthma
Left ventricular failure
CC Excl: See code 428.0
DEF: Mechanical inadequacy of left ventricle; causing fluid in lungs.

Echocardiography of Heart Failure

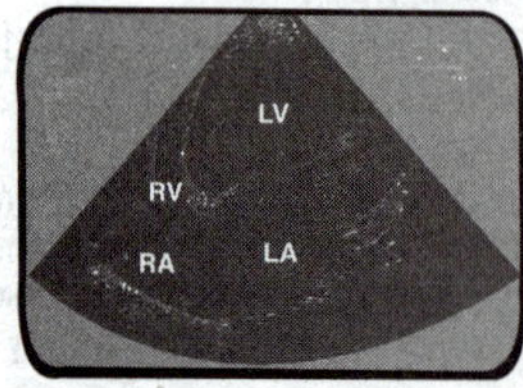

Systolic dysfunction with dilated LV

Four-chamber echocardiograms, two-dimensional views.
LV: Left ventricle
RV: Right ventricle
RA: Right atrium
LA: Left atrium

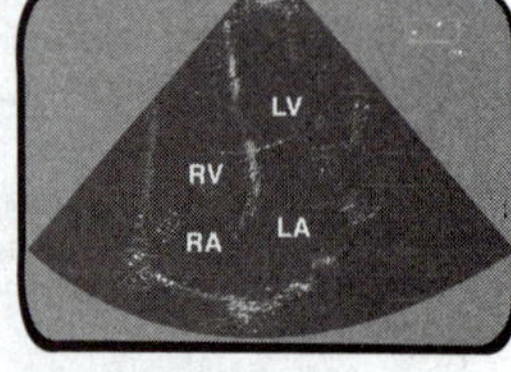

Diastolic dysfunction with LV hypertrophy

✓5th **428.2 Systolic heart failure**

EXCLUDES *combined systolic and diastolic heart failure (428.40-428.43)*

DEF: Heart failure due to a defect in expulsion of blood caused by an abnormality in systolic function, or ventricular contractile dysfunction.

428.20 Unspecified CC MC CD MCV
CC Excl: See code 428.0

428.21 Acute CC MC CD MCV
CC Excl: See code 428.0

428.22 Chronic CC MC CD MCV
CC Excl: See code 428.0
AHA: 4Q, '05, 120

428.23 Acute on chronic CC MC CD MCV
CC Excl: See code 428.0
AHA: 1Q, '03, 9

✓5th **428.3 Diastolic heart failure**

EXCLUDES *combined systolic and diastolic heart failure (428.40-428.43)*

DEF: Heart failure due to resistance to ventricular filling caused by an abnormality in the diastolic function.

428.30 Unspecified CC MC CD MCV
CC Excl: See code 428.0
AHA: 4Q, '02, 52

428.31 Acute CC MC CD MCV
CC Excl: See code 428.0

428.32 Chronic CC MC CD MCV
CC Excl: See code 428.0

428.33 Acute on chronic CC MC CD MCV
CC Excl: See code 428.0

✓5th **428.4 Combined systolic and diastolic heart failure**

428.40 Unspecified CC MC CD MCV
CC Excl: See code 428.0

428.41 Acute CC MC CD MCV
CC Excl: See code 428.0
AHA: 4Q, '04, 140

428.42 Chronic CC MC CD MCV
CC Excl: See code 428.0

428.43 Acute on chronic CC MC CD MCV
CC Excl: See code 428.0
AHA: 4Q, '02, 52

428.9 Heart failure, unspecified CC MC CD MCV

Cardiac failure NOS
Heart failure NOS
Myocardial failure NOS
Weak heart

CC Excl: See code 428.0
AHA: 2Q, '89, 10; N-D, '85, 14

✓4th **429 Ill-defined descriptions and complications of heart disease**

429.0 Myocarditis, unspecified

Myocarditis:
- NOS
- chronic (interstitial)
- fibroid
- senile

} (with mention of arteriosclerosis)

Use additional code to identify presence of arteriosclerosis

EXCLUDES *acute or subacute (422.0-422.9)*
rheumatic (398.0)
acute (391.2)
that due to hypertension (402.0-402.9)

429.1 Myocardial degeneration

Degeneration of heart or myocardium:
- fatty
- mural
- muscular

Myocardial:
- degeneration
- disease

} (with mention of arteriosclerosis)

Use additional code to identify presence of arteriosclerosis

EXCLUDES *that due to hypertension (402.0-402.9)*

429.2 Cardiovascular disease, unspecified

Arteriosclerotic cardiovascular disease [ASCVD]
Cardiovascular arteriosclerosis
Cardiovascular:
- degeneration
- disease
- sclerosis

} (with mention of arteriosclerosis)

Use additional code to identify presence of arteriosclerosis

EXCLUDES *that due to hypertension (402.0-402.9)*

429.3 Cardiomegaly

Cardiac:
- dilatation
- hypertrophy

Ventricular dilatation

EXCLUDES *that due to hypertension (402.0-402.9)*

429.4 Functional disturbances following cardiac surgery CC CD

Cardiac insufficiency } following cardiac surgery or due to prosthesis
Heart failure }

Postcardiotomy syndrome
Postvalvulotomy syndrome

EXCLUDES *cardiac failure in the immediate postoperative period (997.1)*

CC Excl: 429.4, 429.71-429.79, 459.89, 459.9
AHA: 2Q, '02, 12; N-D, '85, 6

429.5 Rupture of chordae tendineae CC MC CD MCV
CC Excl: 429.5, 429.71, 429.79, 459.89, 459.9

DEF: Torn tissue, between heart valves and papillary muscles.

429.6 Rupture of papillary muscle CC MC CD MCV
CC Excl: 429.6-429.81, 459.89, 459.9

DEF: Torn muscle, between chordae tendineae and heart wall.

✓5th **429.7 Certain sequelae of myocardial infarction, not elsewhere classified**

Use additional code to identify the associated myocardial infarction:
- with onset of 8 weeks or less (410.00-410.92)
- with onset of more than 8 weeks (414.8)

EXCLUDES *congenital defects of heart (745, 746)*
coronary aneurysm (414.11)
disorders of papillary muscle (429.6, 429.81)
postmyocardial infarction syndrome (411.0)
rupture of chordae tendineae (429.5)

AHA: 3Q, '89, 5

429.71 Acquired cardiac septal defect CC CD MCV A

EXCLUDES *acute septal infarction (410.00-410.92)*

CC Excl: 422.0-422.99, 429.0, 429.4-429.82, 459.89-459.9, 745.0-745.9, 746.89, 746.9, 747.83-747.9, 759.7-759.89

DEF: Abnormal communication, between opposite heart chambers; due to defect of septum; not present at birth.

429.79 Other CC CD MCV A

Mural thrombus (atrial) (ventricular), acquired, following myocardial infarction

CC Excl: See code 429.71
AHA: 1Q, '92, 10

✓5th **429.8 Other ill-defined heart diseases**

429.81 Other disorders of papillary muscle CC MC CD MCV

Papillary muscle:
- atrophy
- degeneration
- dysfunction

Papillary muscle:
- incompetence
- incoordination
- scarring

CC Excl: 429.6, 429.71-429.79, 429.81, 459.89, 459.9

429.82 Hyperkinetic heart disease CC CD
CC Excl: 429.71-429.79, 429.82, 459.89, 459.9

DEF: Condition of unknown origin in young adults; marked by increased cardiac output at rest, increased rate of ventricular ejection; may lead to heart failure.

✓4th ✓5th Additional Digit Required | Nonspecific PDx | Unacceptable PDx | Manifestation Code | MCV Major Cardiovascular Condition | ▶◀ Revised Text | ● New Code | ▲ Revised Code Title

● **429.83 Takotsubo syndrome**
Broken heart syndrome
Reversible left ventricular dysfunction following sudden emotional stress
Stress induced cardiomyopathy
Transient left ventricular apical ballooning syndrome

429.89 Other
Carditis
EXCLUDES *that due to hypertension (402.0-402.9)*
AHA: 3Q, '05, 14; 1Q, '92, 10

429.9 Heart disease, unspecified
Heart disease (organic) NOS
Morbus cordis NOS
EXCLUDES *that due to hypertension (402.0-402.9)*
AHA: 1Q, '93, 19

CEREBROVASCULAR DISEASE (430-438)

INCLUDES with mention of hypertension (conditions classifiable to 401-405)

Use additional code to identify presence of hypertension

EXCLUDES *any condition classifiable to 430-434, 436, 437 occurring during pregnancy, childbirth, or the puerperium, or specified as puerperal (674.0)*
iatrogenic cerebrovascular infarction or hemorrhage (997.02)

AHA: 1Q, '93, 27; 3Q, '91, 10; 3Q, '90, 3; 2Q, '89, 8; M-A, '85, 6

[10] **430 Subarachnoid hemorrhage** CC MC MCV
Meningeal hemorrhage
Ruptured:
berry aneurysm
(congenital) cerebral aneurysm NOS
EXCLUDES *syphilitic ruptured cerebral aneurysm (094.87)*
CC Excl: 430, 432.9, 459.89, 459.9, 780.01-780.09, 800.00-801.99, 803.00-804.96, 850.0-852.19, 852.21-854.19
AHA: 4Q, '04, 77
DEF: Bleeding in space between brain and lining.

[10] **431 Intracerebral hemorrhage** CC MC MCV
Hemorrhage (of):
basilar
bulbar
cerebellar
cerebral
cerebromeningeal
cortical
internal capsule
intrapontine
pontine
subcortical
ventricular
Rupture of blood vessel in brain
CC Excl: See code 430
AHA: 4Q, '04, 77
DRG 014
DEF: Bleeding within the brain.

✓4th **432 Other and unspecified intracranial hemorrhage**
AHA: 4Q, '04, 7

[10] **432.0 Nontraumatic extradural hemorrhage** CC MC MCV
Nontraumatic epidural hemorrhage
CC Excl: See code 430
DEF: Bleeding, nontraumatic, between skull and brain lining.

Berry Aneurysms

Anterior communicating artery
40 %
34%
Berry aneurysm
Internal carotid
20 %
4%
Posterior cerebral arteries
Basilar artery
Vertebral arteries
Arrows depict blood flow

Cerebrovascular Arteries

Posterior parietal
Parietal-occipital
Calcarine
Posterior cerebral
Anterior inferior cerebellar
Posterior inferior cerebellar
Basilar
Vertebral
Callosal-marginal
Pericallosal
Anterior cerebral
Anterior communicating
Middle cerebral
Ophthalmic
Posterior communicating
External carotid
Internal carotid
Aorta

[10] **432.1 Subdural hemorrhage** CC MC MCV
Subdural hematoma, nontraumatic
CC Excl: See code 430
DEF: Bleeding, between outermost and other layers of brain lining.

[10] **432.9 Unspecified intracranial hemorrhage** MC MCV
Intracranial hemorrhage NOS

✓4th **433 Occlusion and stenosis of precerebral arteries**

INCLUDES embolism, narrowing, obstruction, thrombosis } of basilar, carotid, and vertebral arteries

EXCLUDES *insufficiency NOS of precerebral arteries (435.0-435.9)*

The following fifth-digit subclassification is for use with category 433:
0 without mention of cerebral infarction
1 with cerebral infarction MC MCV

AHA: 2Q, '95, 14; 3Q, '90, 16
DEF: Blockage, stricture, arteries branching into brain.

[10] ✓5th **433.0 Basilar artery** CC 1
CC Excl: For code 433.01: 250.70-250.93, 433.00-433.91, 435.0, 459.89, 459.9

[10] ✓5th **433.1 Carotid artery** CC 1
CC Excl: For code 433.11: 250.70-250.93, 433.00-433.91, 459.89, 459.9
AHA: 1Q, '00, 16; **For code 433.10:** ▶1Q, '06, 17;◀ 1Q, '02, 7, 10
DRG 015 For code 433.10

[10] ✓5th **433.2 Vertebral artery** CC 1
CC Excl: For code 433.21: 250.70-250.93, 433.00-433.91, 435.1, 459.89, 459.9

[10] ✓5th **433.3 Multiple and bilateral** CC 1
CC Excl: For code 443.30: ▶1Q, '06, 17;◀ **For code 433.31:** See code 433.11
AHA: 2Q, '02, 19
DRG 015 For code 433.30

[10] ✓5th **433.8 Other specified precerebral artery** CC 1
CC Excl: For code 433.81: See code 433.01

[1,10] ✓5th **433.9 Unspecified precerebral artery**
Precerebral artery NOS
CC Excl: For code 433.91: See code 433.01

✓4th **434 Occlusion of cerebral arteries**

The following fifth-digit subclassification is for use with category 434:
0 without mention of cerebral infarction
1 with cerebral infarction

AHA: 2Q, '95, 14

[10] ✓5th **434.0 Cerebral thrombosis** CC 1 MC MCV
Thrombosis of cerebral arteries
CC Excl: For code 434.01: 250.70-250.93, 434.00-434.91, 436, 459.89, 459.9
AHA: For code 434.01: 4Q, '04, 77

[1] Nonspecific PDx=0
[10] MCV as SDx only.

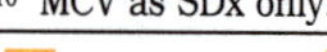 Newborn Age: 0  Pediatric Age: 0-17 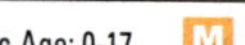 Maternity Age: 12-55  Adult Age :15-124  CC Condition  Major Complication 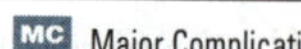 Complex Dx  HIV Related Dx

10 ✓5th **434.1 Cerebral embolism** CC 1 MC MCV

CC Excl: For code 434.11: See code 434.01

AHA: For code 434.11: 4Q, '04, 77; 3Q, '97, 11

DRG 014 For code 434.11

1,10 ✓5th **434.9 Cerebral artery occlusion, unspecified** CC 1 MC MCV

CC Excl: For code 434.91: See code 434.01

AHA: For code 434.91: 4Q, '04, 77-78; 4Q, '98, 87

DRG 014 For code 434.91

✓4th **435 Transient cerebral ischemia**

INCLUDES cerebrovascular insufficiency (acute) with transient focal neurological signs and symptoms
insufficiency of basilar, carotid, and vertebral arteries
spasm of cerebral arteries

EXCLUDES *acute cerebrovascular insufficiency NOS (437.1)*
that due to any condition classifiable to 433 (433.0-433.9)

435.0 Basilar artery syndrome

435.1 Vertebral artery syndrome

435.2 Subclavian steal syndrome

DEF: Cerebrovascular insufficiency, due to occluded subclavian artery; symptoms include pain in mastoid and posterior head regions, flaccid paralysis of arm and diminished or absent radial pulse on affected side.

435.3 Vertebrobasilar artery syndrome

AHA: 4Q, '95, 60

DEF: Transient ischemic attack; due to brainstem dysfunction; symptoms include confusion, vertigo, binocular blindness, diplopia, unilateral or bilateral weakness and paresthesis of extremities.

435.8 Other specified transient cerebral ischemias

DRG 524

435.9 Unspecified transient cerebral ischemia

Impending cerebrovascular accident
Intermittent cerebral ischemia
Transient ischemic attack [TIA]

AHA: N-D, '85, 12

DRG 524

10 **436 Acute, but ill-defined, cerebrovascular disease** CC MC MCV

Apoplexy, apoplectic:
- NOS
- attack
- cerebral
- seizure

Cerebral seizure

EXCLUDES *any condition classifiable to categories 430-435*
cerebrovascular accident (434.91)
CVA (ischemic) (434.91)
embolic (434.11)
hemorrhagic (430, 431, 432.0-432.9)
thrombotic (434.01)
postoperative cerebrovascular accident (997.02)
stroke (ischemic) (434.91)
embolic (434.11)
hemorrhagic (430, 431, 432.0-432.9)
thrombotic (434.01)

CC Excl: 250.70-250.93, 430-432.9, 434.00-434.91, 436, 459.89-459.9, 780.01-780.09, 800.00-801.99, 803.00-804.96, 850.0-852.19, 852.21-854.19

AHA: 4Q, '04, 77; 4Q, '99, 3

DRG 015

✓4th **437 Other and ill-defined cerebrovascular disease**

437.0 Cerebral atherosclerosis A

Atheroma of cerebral arteries
Cerebral arteriosclerosis

437.1 Other generalized ischemic cerebrovascular disease

Acute cerebrovascular insufficiency NOS
Cerebral ischemia (chronic)

437.2 Hypertensive encephalopathy CC

CC Excl: 250.70-250.93, 437.2, 459.89, 459.9

AHA: J-A, '84, 14

DEF: Cerebral manifestations (such as visual disturbances and headache) due to high blood pressure.

437.3 Cerebral aneurysm, nonruptured

Internal carotid artery, intracranial portion
Internal carotid artery NOS

EXCLUDES *congenital cerebral aneurysm, nonruptured (747.81)*
internal carotid artery, extracranial portion (442.81)

437.4 Cerebral arteritis CC

CC Excl: 250.70-250.93, 437.4, 459.89, 459.9

AHA: 4Q, '99, 21

DEF: Inflammation of a cerebral artery or arteries.

437.5 Moyamoya disease CC

CC Excl: 250.70-250.93, 437.5, 459.89, 459.9

DEF: Cerebrovascular ischemia; vessels occlude and rupture causing tiny hemorrhages at base of brain; predominantly affects Japanese.

437.6 Nonpyogenic thrombosis of intracranial venous sinus CC

EXCLUDES *pyogenic (325)*

CC Excl: 250.70-250.93, 437.6, 459.89, 459.9

437.7 Transient global amnesia

AHA: 4Q, '92, 20

DEF: Episode of short-term memory loss, not often recurrent; pathogenesis unknown; with no signs or symptoms of neurological disorder.

437.8 Other

437.9 Unspecified

Cerebrovascular disease or lesion NOS

✓4th **438 Late effects of cerebrovascular disease**

Note: This category is to be used to indicate conditions in 430-437 as the cause of late effects. The "late effects" include conditions specified as such, as sequelae, which may occur at any time after the onset of the causal condition.

AHA: 4Q, '99, 4, 6, 7; 4Q, '98, 39, 88; 4Q, '97, 35, 37; 4Q, '92, 21;N-D,'86, 12; M-A, '86, 7

438.0 Cognitive deficits

✓5th **438.1 Speech and language deficits**

438.10 Speech and language deficit, unspecified

438.11 Aphasia

AHA: 4Q, '03, 105; 4Q, '97, 36

DEF: Impairment or absence of the ability to communicate by speech, writing or signs or to comprehend the spoken or written language due to disease or injury to the brain. Total aphasia is the loss of function of both sensory and motor areas of the brain.

438.12 Dysphasia

AHA: 4Q, '99, 3, 9

DEF: Impaired speech; marked by inability to sequence language.

438.19 Other speech and language deficits

✓5th **438.2 Hemiplegia/hemiparesis**

DEF: Paralysis of one side of the body.

438.20 Hemiplegia affecting unspecified side

AHA: 4Q, '03, 105; 4Q, '99, 3, 9

438.21 Hemiplegia affecting dominant side

438.22 Hemiplegia affecting nondominant side

AHA: 4Q, '03, 105; 1Q, '02, 16

✓5th **438.3 Monoplegia of upper limb**

DEF: Paralysis of one limb or one muscle group.

438.30 Monoplegia of upper limb affecting unspecified side

438.31 Monoplegia of upper limb affecting dominant side

1 Nonspecific PDx=0
10 MCV as SDx only.

Map of Major Arteries

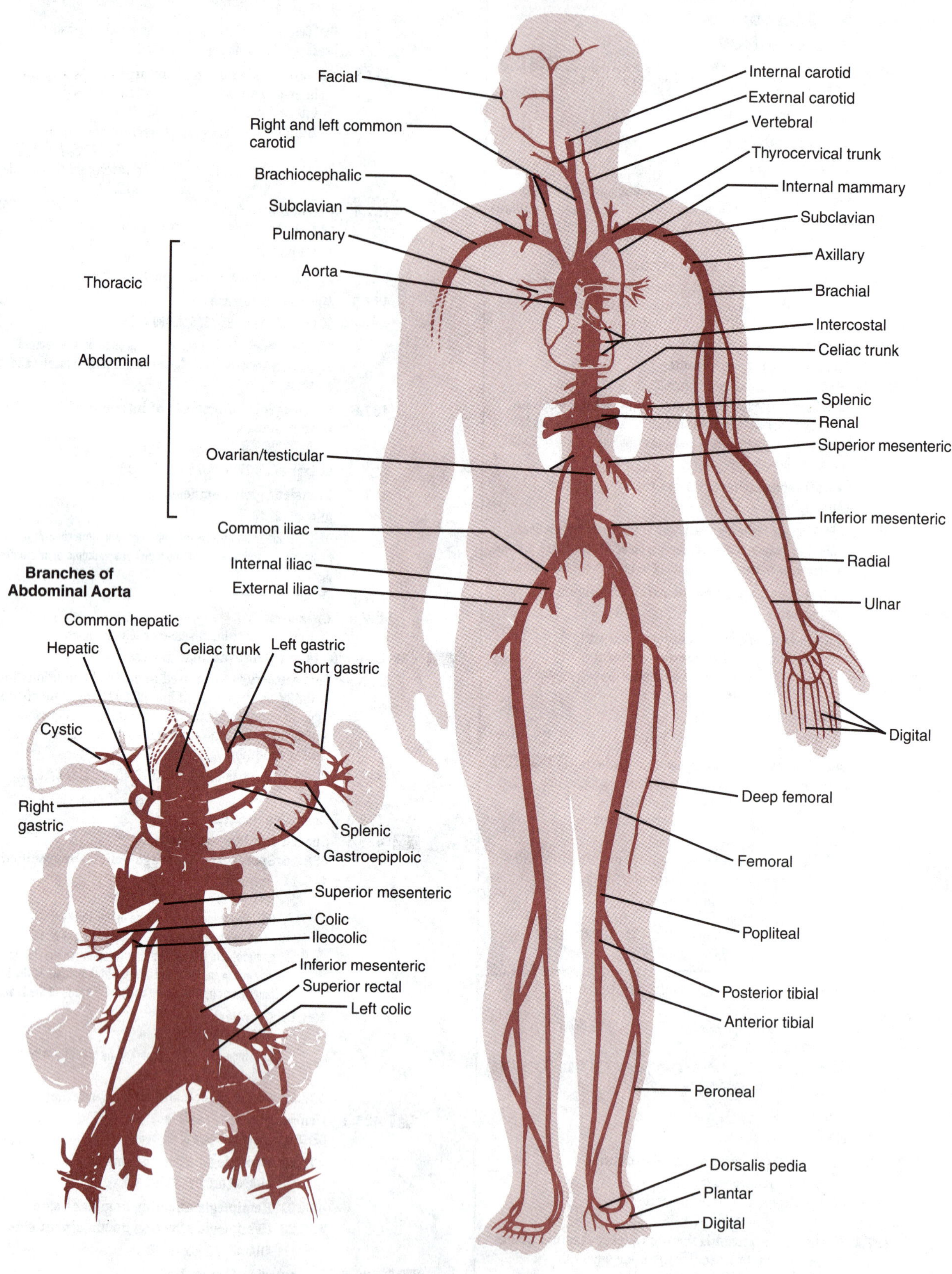

438.32 **Monoplegia of upper limb affecting nondominant side**

✓5th 438.4 **Monoplegia of lower limb**

438.40 **Monoplegia of lower limb affecting unspecified side**

438.41 **Monoplegia of lower limb affecting dominant side**

438.42 **Monoplegia of lower limb affecting nondominant side**

✓5th 438.5 **Other paralytic syndrome**

Use additional code to identify type of paralytic syndrome, such as:
locked-in state (344.81)
quadriplegia (344.00-344.09)

EXCLUDES *late effects of cerebrovascular accident with:*
hemiplegia/hemiparesis (438.20-438.22)
monoplegia of lower limb (438.40-438.42)
monoplegia of upper limb (438.30-438.32)

438.50 **Other paralytic syndrome affecting unspecified side**

438.51 **Other paralytic syndrome affecting dominant side**

438.52 **Other paralytic syndrome affecting nondominant side**

438.53 **Other paralytic syndrome, bilateral**

AHA: 4Q, '98, 39

438.6 **Alterations of sensations**

Use additional code to identify the altered sensation

438.7 **Disturbances of vision**

Use additional code to identify the visual disturbance

AHA: 4Q, '02, 56

✓5th 438.8 **Other late effects of cerebrovascular disease**

438.81 **Apraxia**

DEF: Inability to activate learned movements; no known sensory or motor impairment.

438.82 **Dysphagia**

DEF: Inability or difficulty in swallowing.

438.83 **Facial weakness**

Facial droop

438.84 **Ataxia**

AHA: 4Q, '02, 56

438.85 **Vertigo**

438.89 **Other late effects of cerebrovascular disease**

Use additional code to identify the late effect

AHA: 1Q, '05, 13; 4Q, '98, 39

438.9 **Unspecified late effects of cerebrovascular disease**

DISEASES OF ARTERIES, ARTERIOLES, AND CAPILLARIES (440-448)

✓4th 440 **Atherosclerosis**

INCLUDES arteriolosclerosis
arteriosclerosis (obliterans) (senile)
arteriosclerotic vascular disease
atheroma
degeneration:
arterial
arteriovascular
vascular
endarteritis deformans or obliterans
senile:
arteritis
endarteritis

EXCLUDES *atheroembolism (445.01-445.89)*
atherosclerosis of bypass graft of the extremities (440.30-440.32)

DEF: Stricture and reduced elasticity of an artery; due to plaque deposits.

440.0 **Of aorta** A

AHA: 2Q, '93, 7; 2Q, '93, 8; 4Q, '88, 8

440.1 **Of renal artery** A

EXCLUDES *atherosclerosis of renal arterioles (403.00-403.91)*

✓5th 440.2 **Of native arteries of the extremities**

EXCLUDES *atherosclerosis of bypass graft of the extremities (440.30-440.32)*

AHA: 4Q, '94, 49; 4Q, '93, 27; 4Q, '92, 25; 3Q, '90, 15; M-A, '87, 6

440.20 **Atherosclerosis of the extremities, unspecified** A

440.21 **Atherosclerosis of the extremities with intermittent claudication** A

DEF: Atherosclerosis; marked by pain, tension and weakness after walking; no symptoms while at rest.

440.22 **Atherosclerosis of the extremities with rest pain** A

INCLUDES any condition classifiable to 440.21

DEF: Atherosclerosis, marked by pain, tension and weakness while at rest.

440.23 **Atherosclerosis of the extremities with ulceration** A

INCLUDES any condition classifiable to 440.21 and 440.22

Use additional code for any associated ulceration (707.10-707.9)

AHA: 4Q, '00, 44

440.24 **Atherosclerosis of the extremities with gangrene** CC

INCLUDES any condition classifiable to 440.21, 440.22, and 440.23 with ischemic gangrene 785.4

▶Use additional code for any associated ulceration (707.10-707.9)◀

EXCLUDES *gas gangrene (040.0)*

CC Excl: 338.0-338.4, 440.24, 780.91-780.99, 785.4, 799.81-799.89

AHA: 4Q, '03, 109; 3Q, '03, 14; 4Q, '95, 54; 1Q, '95, 11

440.29 **Other** A

✓5th 440.3 **Of bypass graft of extremities**

EXCLUDES *atherosclerosis of native arteries of the extremities (440.21-440.24)*
embolism [occlusion NOS] [thrombus] of graft (996.74)

AHA: 4Q, '94, 49

440.30 **Of unspecified graft** A

440.31 **Of autologous vein bypass graft** A

440.32 **Of nonautologous biological bypass graft** A

440.8 **Of other specified arteries** A

EXCLUDES *basilar (433.0)*
carotid (433.1)
cerebral (437.0)
coronary (414.00-414.07)
mesenteric (557.1)
precerebral (433.0-433.9)
pulmonary (416.0)
vertebral (433.2)

440.9 **Generalized and unspecified atherosclerosis** A

Arteriosclerotic vascular disease NOS

EXCLUDES *arteriosclerotic cardiovascular disease [ASCVD] (429.2)*

✓4th 441 **Aortic aneurysm and dissection**

EXCLUDES *syphilitic aortic aneurysm (093.0)*
traumatic aortic aneurysm (901.0, 902.0)

✓5th 441.0 **Dissection of aorta**

AHA: 4Q, '89, 10

DEF: Dissection or splitting of wall of the aorta; due to blood entering through intimal tear or interstitial hemorrhage.

441.00 **Unspecified site** CC MC MCV

CC Excl: 250.70-250.93, 441.00-441.9, 459.89, 459.9

441.01 **Thoracic** CC MC MCV

CC Excl: See code 441.00

Thoracic and Abdominal Aortic Aneurysm

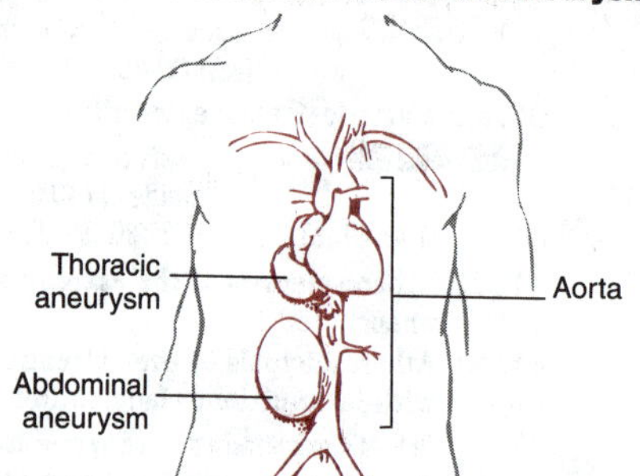

441.02 **Abdominal** CC MC MCV
CC Excl: See code 441.00

441.03 **Thoracoabdominal** CC MC MCV
CC Excl: See code 441.00

441.1 **Thoracic aneurysm, ruptured** CC MCV
CC Excl: See code 441.00

441.2 **Thoracic aneurysm without mention of rupture**
AHA: 3Q, '92, 10

441.3 **Abdominal aneurysm, ruptured** CC MCV
CC Excl: See code 441.00

441.4 **Abdominal aneurysm without mention of rupture**
AHA: 4Q, '00, 64; 1Q, '99, 15, 16, 17; 3Q, '92, 10

441.5 **Aortic aneurysm of unspecified site, ruptured** CC MCV
Rupture of aorta NOS
CC Excl: See code 441.00

441.6 **Thoracoabdominal aneurysm, ruptured** CC MCV
CC Excl: See code 441.00

441.7 **Thoracoabdominal aneurysm, without mention of rupture**

441.9 **Aortic aneurysm of unspecified site without mention of rupture**
Aneurysm } of aorta
Dilatation } of aorta
Hyaline necrosis } of aorta

✓4th **442 Other aneurysm**

INCLUDES aneurysm (ruptured) (cirsoid) (false) (varicose)
aneurysmal varix

EXCLUDES *arteriovenous aneurysm or fistula:*
acquired (447.0)
congenital (747.60-747.69)
traumatic (900.0-904.9)

DEF: Dissection or splitting of arterial wall; due to blood entering through intimal tear or interstitial hemorrhage.

442.0 **Of artery of upper extremity**

442.1 **Of renal artery**

442.2 **Of iliac artery**
AHA: 1Q, '99, 16, 17

442.3 **Of artery of lower extremity**
Aneurysm:
femoral } artery
popliteal } artery
AHA: 3Q, '02, 24-26; 1Q, '99, 16

✓5th 442.8 **Of other specified artery**

442.81 **Artery of neck**
Aneurysm of carotid artery (common) (external) (internal, extracranial portion)
EXCLUDES *internal carotid artery, intracranial portion (437.3)*

442.82 **Subclavian artery**

442.83 **Splenic artery**

442.84 **Other visceral artery**
Aneurysm:
celiac } artery
gastroduodenal } artery
gastroepiploic } artery
hepatic } artery
pancreaticoduodenal } artery
superior mesenteric } artery

442.89 **Other**
Aneurysm:
mediastinal } artery
spinal } artery
EXCLUDES *cerebral (nonruptured) (437.3)*
congenital (747.81)
ruptured (430)
coronary (414.11)
heart (414.10)
pulmonary (417.1)

442.9 **Of unspecified site**

✓4th **443 Other peripheral vascular disease**

443.0 **Raynaud's syndrome**
Raynaud's:
disease
phenomenon (secondary)
Use additional code to identify gangrene (785.4)

DEF: Constriction of the arteries, due to cold or stress; bilateral ischemic attacks of fingers, toes, nose or ears; symptoms include pallor, paresthesia and pain; more common in females.

443.1 **Thromboangiitis obliterans [Buerger's disease]**
Presenile gangrene

DEF: Inflammatory disease of extremity blood vessels, mainly the lower; occurs primarily in young men and leads to tissue ischemia and gangrene.

✓5th 443.2 **Other arterial dissection**
EXCLUDES *dissection of aorta (441.00-441.03)*
dissection of coronary arteries (414.12)
AHA: 4Q, '02, 54

443.21 **Dissection of carotid artery**

443.22 **Dissection of iliac artery** MCV

443.23 **Dissection of renal artery**

443.24 **Dissection of vertebral artery**

443.29 **Dissection of other artery** MCV

✓5th 443.8 **Other specified peripheral vascular diseases**

443.81 ***Peripheral angiopathy in diseases classified elsewhere***
Code first underlying disease, as:
diabetes mellitus (250.7)
AHA: 1Q, '04, 14; 3Q, '91, 10

443.82 **Erythromelalgia**
AHA: 4Q, '05, 73

DEF: Rare syndrome of paroxysmal vasodilation; maldistribution of blood flow causes redness, pain, increased skin temperature, and burning sensations in various parts of the body.

Arterial Diseases and Disorders

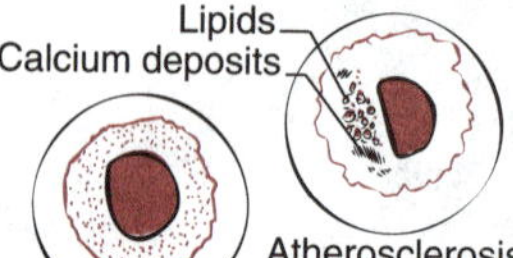

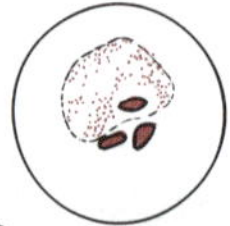

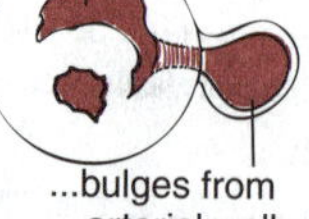

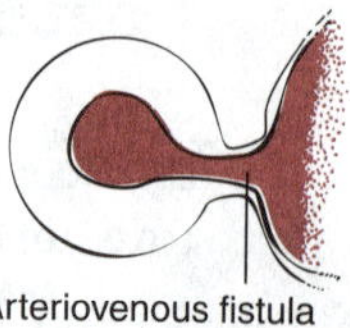
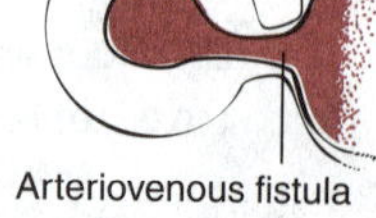

443.89 Other
Acrocyanosis
Erythrocyanosis
Acroparesthesia:
simple [Schultze's type]
vasomotor [Nothnagel's type]
EXCLUDES *chilblains (991.5)*
frostbite (991.0-991.3)
immersion foot (991.4)

443.9 Peripheral vascular disease, unspecified
Intermittent claudication NOS
Peripheral:
angiopathy NOS
vascular disease NOS
Spasm of artery
EXCLUDES *atherosclerosis of the arteries of the extremities (440.20-440.22)*
spasm of cerebral artery (435.0-435.9)
AHA: 4Q, '92, 25; 3Q, '91, 10
DRG 130

✓4th **444 Arterial embolism and thrombosis**
INCLUDES infarction:
embolic
thrombotic
occlusion
EXCLUDES *that complicating:*
abortion (634-638 with .6, 639.6)
atheroembolism (445.01-445.89)
ectopic or molar pregnancy (639.6)
pregnancy, childbirth, or the puerperium (673.0-673.8)
AHA: 2Q, '92, 11; 4Q, '90, 27

444.0 Of abdominal aorta CC MCV
Aortic bifurcation syndrome
Aortoiliac obstruction
Leriche's syndrome
Saddle embolus
CC Excl: 250.70-250.93, 444.0, 444.89, 444.9, 459.89, 459.9
AHA: 2Q, '93, 7; 4Q, '90, 27

444.1 Of thoracic aorta CC MCV
Embolism or thrombosis of aorta (thoracic)
CC Excl: 250.70-250.93, 444.1, 444.89, 444.9, 459.89, 459.9

✓5th **444.2 Of arteries of the extremities**
AHA: M-A, '87, 6

444.21 Upper extremity CC
CC Excl: 250.70-250.93, 444.21, 444.89, 444.9, 459.89, 459.9

444.22 Lower extremity CC
Arterial embolism or thrombosis:
femoral
peripheral NOS
popliteal
EXCLUDES *iliofemoral (444.81)*
CC Excl: 250.70-250.93, 444.22, 444.89, 444.9, 459.89, 459.9
AHA: 3Q, '03, 10; 1Q, '03, 17; 3Q, '90, 16

✓5th **444.8 Of other specified artery**

444.81 Iliac artery CC
CC Excl: 250.70-250.93, 444.81-444.9, 459.89, 459.9
AHA: 1Q, '03, 16

444.89 Other CC
EXCLUDES *basilar (433.0)*
carotid (433.1)
cerebral (434.0-434.9)
coronary (410.00-410.92)
mesenteric (557.0)
ophthalmic (362.30-362.34)
precerebral (433.0-433.9)
pulmonary (415.19)
renal (593.81)
retinal (362.30-362.34)
vertebral (433.2)
CC Excl: 250.70-250.93, 444.89, 444.9, 459.89, 459.9

444.9 Of unspecified artery CC
CC Excl: See code 444.89

✓4th **445 Atheroembolism**
INCLUDES atherothrombotic microembolism
cholesterol embolism
AHA: 4Q, '02, 57

✓5th **445.0 Of extremities**

445.01 Upper extremity CC
CC Excl: 250.70-250.73, 250.80-250.83, 250.90-250.93, 444.89, 444.9, 445.01, 459.89, 459.9

445.02 Lower extremity CC
CC Excl: 250.70-250.73, 250.80-250.83, 250.90-250.93, 444.89, 444.9, 445.02, 459.89, 459.9

✓5th **445.8 Of other sites**

10 **445.81 Kidney** CC MCV
▶Use additional code for any associated acute renal failure or chronic kidney disease (584, 585)◀
CC Excl: 250.70-250.73, 250.80-250.83, 250.90-250.93, 444.89, 444.9, 445.81, 459.89, 459.9

445.89 Other site CC
CC Excl: 250.70-250.73, 250.80-250.83, 250.90-250.93, 444.89, 444.9, 445.89, 459.9

✓4th **446 Polyarteritis nodosa and allied conditions**

446.0 Polyarteritis nodosa CC
Disseminated necrotizing periarteritis
Necrotizing angiitis
Panarteritis (nodosa)
Periarteritis (nodosa)
CC Excl: 250.70-250.93, 446.0-446.7, 459.89, 459.9
DEF: Inflammation of small and mid-size arteries; symptoms related to involved arteries in kidneys, muscles, gastrointestinal tract and heart; results in tissue death.

446.1 Acute febrile mucocutaneous lymph node syndrome [MCLS]
Kawasaki disease
DEF: Acute febrile disease of children; marked by erythema of conjunctiva and mucous membranes of upper respiratory tract, skin eruptions and edema.

✓5th **446.2 Hypersensitivity angiitis**
EXCLUDES *antiglomerular basement membrane disease without pulmonary hemorrhage (583.89)*

446.20 Hypersensitivity angiitis, unspecified CC
CC Excl: See code 446.0

446.21 Goodpasture's syndrome CC
Antiglomerular basement membrane antibody-mediated nephritis with pulmonary hemorrhage
Use additional code to identify renal disease (583.81)
CC Excl: See code 446.0
DEF: Glomerulonephritis associated with hematuria, progresses rapidly; results in death from renal failure.

446.29 Other specified hypersensitivity angiitis CC
CC Excl: See code 446.0
AHA: 1Q, '95, 3

446.3 Lethal midline granuloma CC
Malignant granuloma of face
CC Excl: See code 446.0
DEF: Granulomatous lesion; in nose or paranasal sinuses; often fatal; occurs chiefly in males.

10 MCV as SDx only.

✓4th ✓5th Additional Digit Required | Nonspecific PDx | Unacceptable PDx | Manifestation Code | MCV Major Cardiovascular Condition | ▶◀ Revised Text | ● New Code | ▲ Revised Code Title

Map of Major Veins

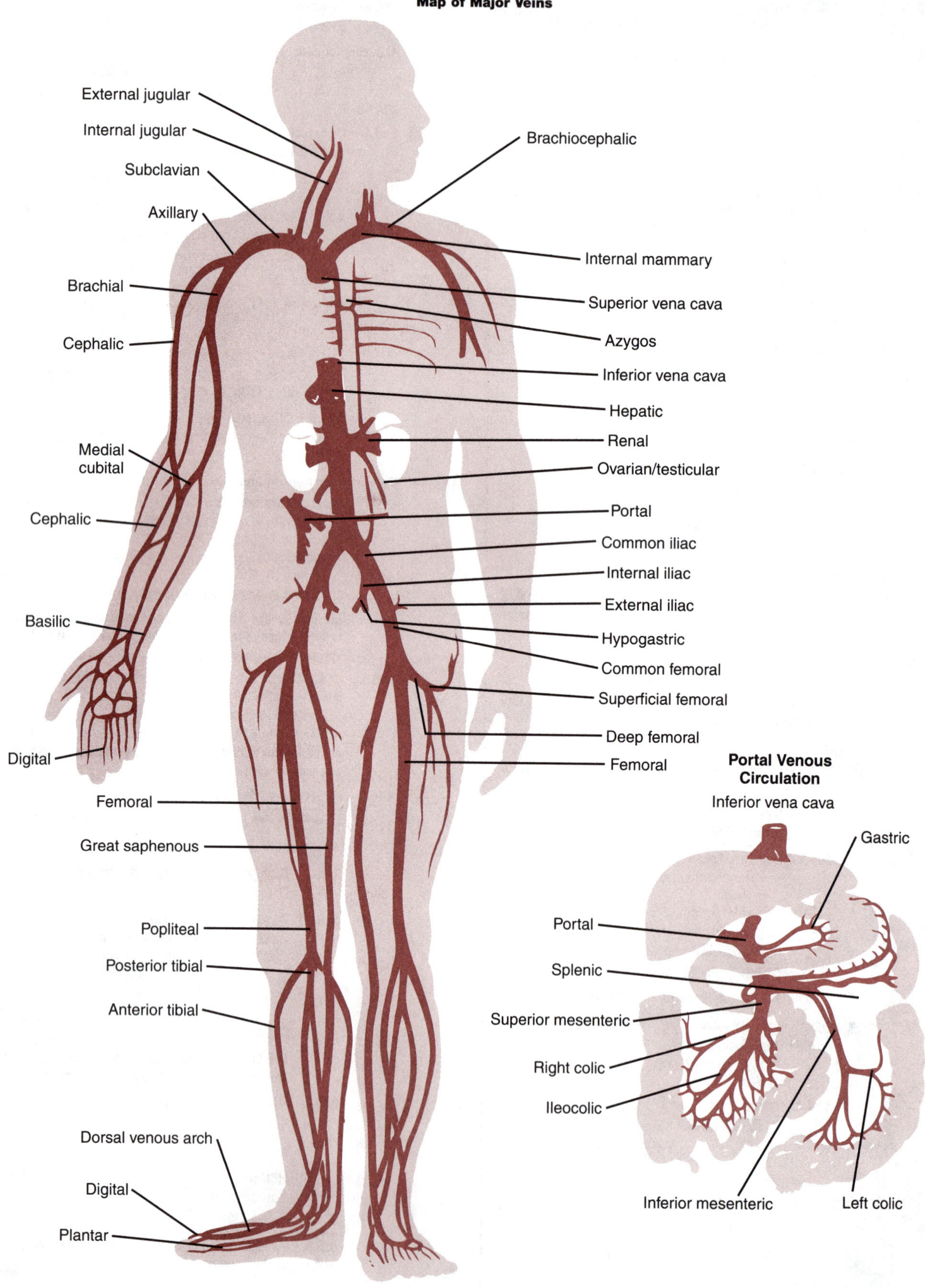

446.4 **Wegener's granulomatosis** CC
Necrotizing respiratory granulomatosis
Wegener's syndrome
CC Excl: See code 446.0
AHA: 3Q, '00, 11
DEF: A disease occurring mainly in men; marked by necrotizing granulomas and ulceration of the upper respiratory tract; underlying condition is a vasculitis affecting small vessels and is possibly due to an immune disorder.

446.5 **Giant cell arteritis** CC
Bagratuni's syndrome
Cranial arteritis
Horton's disease
Temporal arteritis
CC Excl: See code 446.0
DEF: Inflammation of arteries; due to giant cells affecting carotid artery branches, resulting in occlusion; symptoms include fever, headache and neurological problems; occurs in elderly.

446.6 **Thrombotic microangiopathy** CC
Moschcowitz's syndrome
Thrombotic thrombocytopenic purpura
CC Excl: See code 446.0
DEF: Blockage of small blood vessels; due to hyaline deposits; symptoms include purpura, CNS disorders; results in protracted disease or rapid death.

446.7 **Takayasu's disease** CC
Aortic arch arteritis
Pulseless disease
CC Excl: See code 446.0
DEF: Progressive obliterative arteritis of brachiocephalic trunk, left subclavian, and left common carotid arteries above aortic arch; results in ischemia in brain, heart and arm; pulses impalpable in head, neck and arms; more common in young adult females.

✓4th **447 Other disorders of arteries and arterioles**

447.0 **Arteriovenous fistula, acquired**
Arteriovenous aneurysm, acquired
EXCLUDES *cerebrovascular (437.3)*
coronary (414.19)
pulmonary (417.0)
surgically created arteriovenous shunt or fistula:
complication (996.1, 996.61-996.62)
status or presence (V45.1)
traumatic (900.0-904.9)
DEF: Communication between an artery and vein caused by error in healing.

447.1 **Stricture of artery**
AHA: 2Q, '93, 8; M-A, '87, 6

447.2 **Rupture of artery**
Erosion } of artery
Fistula, except arteriovenous } of artery
Ulcer } of artery
EXCLUDES *traumatic rupture of artery (900.0-904.9)*

447.3 **Hyperplasia of renal artery**
Fibromuscular hyperplasia of renal artery
DEF: Overgrowth of cells in muscular lining of renal artery.

447.4 **Celiac artery compression syndrome**
Celiac axis syndrome
Marable's syndrome

447.5 **Necrosis of artery**

447.6 **Arteritis, unspecified**
Aortitis NOS
Endarteritis NOS
EXCLUDES *arteritis, endarteritis:*
aortic arch (446.7)
cerebral (437.4)
coronary (414.00-414.07)
deformans (440.0-440.9)
obliterans (440.0-440.9)
pulmonary (417.8)
senile (440.0-440.9)
polyarteritis NOS (446.0)
syphilitic aortitis (093.1)
AHA: 1Q, '95, 3

447.8 **Other specified disorders of arteries and arterioles**
Fibromuscular hyperplasia of arteries, except renal

447.9 **Unspecified disorders of arteries and arterioles**

✓4th **448 Disease of capillaries**

448.0 **Hereditary hemorrhagic telangiectasia**
Rendu-Osler-Weber disease
DEF: Genetic disease with onset after puberty; results in multiple telangiectases, dilated venules on skin and mucous membranes; recurrent bleeding may occur.

448.1 **Nevus, non-neoplastic**
Nevus:
araneus
senile
spider
stellar
EXCLUDES *neoplastic (216.0-216.9)*
port wine (757.32)
strawberry (757.32)
DEF: Enlarged or malformed blood vessels of skin; results in reddish swelling, skin patch, or birthmark.

448.9 **Other and unspecified capillary diseases**
Capillary:
hemorrhage
hyperpermeability
thrombosis
EXCLUDES *capillary fragility (hereditary) (287.8)*

DISEASES OF VEINS AND LYMPHATICS, AND OTHER DISEASES OF CIRCULATORY SYSTEM (451-459)

✓4th **451 Phlebitis and thrombophlebitis**
INCLUDES endophlebitis
inflammation, vein
periphlebitis
suppurative phlebitis
Use additional E code to identify drug, if drug-induced
EXCLUDES *that complicating:*
abortion (634-638 with .7, 639.8)
ectopic or molar pregnancy (639.8)
pregnancy, childbirth, or the puerperium (671.0-671.9)
that due to or following:
implant or catheter device (996.61-996.62)
infusion, perfusion, or transfusion (999.2)
AHA: 1Q, '92, 16
DEF: Inflammation of a vein (phlebitis) with formation of a thrombus (thrombophlebitis).

451.0 **Of superficial vessels of lower extremities** CC
Saphenous vein (greater) (lesser)
CC Excl: 250.70-250.93, 451.0-451.9, 459.89, 459.9
AHA: 3Q, '91, 16

✓5th 451.1 **Of deep vessels of lower extremities**
AHA: 3Q, '91, 16

451.11 **Femoral vein (deep) (superficial)** CC
CC Excl: See code 451.0
DRG 128

451.19 **Other** CC
Femoropopliteal vein
Tibial vein
Popliteal vein
CC Excl: See code 451.0
DRG 128

451.2 **Of lower extremities, unspecified** CC
CC Excl: See code 451.0
AHA: 4Q, '04, 80
DRG 128

✓5th 451.8 **Of other sites**
EXCLUDES *intracranial venous sinus (325)*
nonpyogenic (437.6)
portal (vein) (572.1)

451.81 **Iliac vein** CC
CC Excl: See code 451.0

451.82 **Of superficial veins of upper extremities**
Antecubital vein
Basilic vein
Cephalic vein

451.83 **Of deep veins of upper extremities**
Brachial vein
Radial vein
Ulnar vein

451.84 **Of upper extremities, unspecified**

451.89 **Other**
Axillary vein
Jugular vein
Subclavian vein
Thrombophlebitis of breast (Mondor's disease)

451.9 **Of unspecified site**

452 **Portal vein thrombosis** CC
Portal (vein) obstruction
EXCLUDES *hepatic vein thrombosis (453.0)*
phlebitis of portal vein (572.1)
CC Excl: 250.70-250.93, 452, 453.40-453.9, 459.89, 459.9
DEF: Formation of a blood clot in main vein of liver.

✓4th 453 **Other venous embolism and thrombosis**
EXCLUDES *that complicating:*
abortion (634-638 with .7, 639.8)
ectopic or molar pregnancy (639.8)
pregnancy, childbirth, or the puerperium (671.0-671.9)
that with inflammation, phlebitis, and thrombophlebitis (451.0-451.9)
AHA: 1Q, '92, 16

453.0 **Budd-Chiari syndrome** CC
Hepatic vein thrombosis
CC Excl: 250.70-250.93, 453.0, 453.40-453.9, 459.89, 459.9
DEF: Thrombosis or other obstruction of hepatic vein; symptoms include enlarged liver, extensive collateral vessels, intractable ascites and severe portal hypertension.

453.1 **Thrombophlebitis migrans** CC
CC Excl: 250.70-250.93, 453.1, 453.40-453.9, 459.89, 459.9
DEF: Slow, advancing thrombophlebitis; appearing first in one vein then another.

453.2 **Of vena cava** CC MCV
CC Excl: 250.70-250.93, 453.2, 453.40-453.9, 459.89, 459.9
DRG 128

453.3 **Of renal vein** CC
CC Excl: 250.70-250.93, 453.3-453.9, 459.89, 459.9

✓5th 453.4 **Venous embolism and thrombosis of deep vessels of lower extremity**

453.40 **Venous embolism and thrombosis of unspecified deep vessels of lower extremity** CC
Deep vein thrombosis NOS
DVT NOS
CC Excl: 250.70-250.93, 453.40-453.9, 453.40-453.9, 459.89-459.9

453.41 **Venous embolism and thrombosis of deep vessels of proximal lower extremity** CC
Femoral
Iliac
Popliteal
Thigh
Upper leg NOS
CC Excl: See code 453.40
AHA: 4Q, '04, 79

453.42 **Venous embolism and thrombosis of deep vessels of distal lower extremity** CC
Calf
Lower leg NOS
Peroneal
Tibial
CC Excl: See code 453.40

453.8 **Of other specified veins** CC
EXCLUDES *cerebral (434.0-434.9)*
coronary (410.00-410.92)
intracranial venous sinus (325)
nonpyogenic (437.6)
mesenteric (557.0)
portal (452)
precerebral (433.0-433.9)
pulmonary (415.19)
CC Excl: 250.70-250.93, 453.8-453.9, 459.89, 459.9
AHA: 3Q, '91, 16; M-A, '87, 6
DRG 130

453.9 **Of unspecified site** CC
Embolism of vein
Thrombosis (vein)
CC Excl: See code 453.8

✓4th 454 **Varicose veins of lower extremities**
EXCLUDES *that complicating pregnancy, childbirth, or the puerperium (671.0)*
AHA: 2Q, '91, 20
DEF: Dilated leg veins; due to incompetent vein valves that allow reversed blood flow and cause tissue erosion or weakness of wall; may be painful.

454.0 **With ulcer** A
Varicose ulcer (lower extremity, any part)
Varicose veins with ulcer of lower extremity [any part] or of unspecified site
Any condition classifiable to 454.9 with ulcer or specified as ulcerated
AHA: 4Q, '99, 18

454.1 **With inflammation** A
Stasis dermatitis
Varicose veins with inflammation of lower extremity [any part] or of unspecified site
Any condition classifiable to 454.9 with inflammation or specified as inflamed

454.2 **With ulcer and inflammation** A
Varicose veins with ulcer and inflammation of lower extremity [any part] or of unspecified site
Any condition classifiable to 454.9 with ulcer and inflammation
DRG 188

454.8 **With other complications**
Edema
Pain
Swelling
AHA: 4Q, '02, 58

454.9 **Asymptomatic varicose veins** A
Phlebectasia, Varicose veins, Varix } of lower extremity [any part] or of unspecified site
Varicose veins NOS
AHA: 4Q, '02, 58

✓4th 455 **Hemorrhoids**
INCLUDES hemorrhoids (anus) (rectum)
piles
varicose veins, anus or rectum
EXCLUDES *that complicating pregnancy, childbirth, or the puerperium (671.8)*
DEF: Varicose condition of external hemorrhoidal veins causing painful swellings at the anus.

455.0 **Internal hemorrhoids without mention of complication**
AHA: 3Q, '05, 17

455.1 **Internal thrombosed hemorrhoids**

455.2 Internal hemorrhoids with other complication
Internal hemorrhoids: bleeding, prolapsed
Internal hemorrhoids: strangulated, ulcerated
AHA: ▶3Q, '05, 17;◀ 1Q, '03, 8
DRG 188

455.3 External hemorrhoids without mention of complication
AHA: ▶3Q, '05, 17◀

455.4 External thrombosed hemorrhoids

455.5 External hemorrhoids with other complication
External hemorrhoids: bleeding, prolapsed
External hemorrhoids: strangulated, ulcerated
AHA:▶ 3Q, '05, 17;◀ 1Q, '03, 8

455.6 Unspecified hemorrhoids without mention of complication
Hemorrhoids NOS

455.7 Unspecified thrombosed hemorrhoids
Thrombosed hemorrhoids, unspecified whether internal or external

455.8 Unspecified hemorrhoids with other complication
Hemorrhoids, unspecified whether internal or external:
bleeding
prolapsed
strangulated
ulcerated

455.9 Residual hemorrhoidal skin tags
Skin tags, anus or rectum

✓4th 456 Varicose veins of other sites

456.0 Esophageal varices with bleeding CC
CC Excl: 251.5, 456.0, 456.20, 459.89, 459.9, 530.20-530.21, 530.7, 530.82, 530.85, 531.00-534.91, 535.01, 535.11, 535.21, 535.31, 535.41, 535.51, 535.61, 537.83, 562.02-562.03, 562.12-562.13, 569.3, 569.85, 578.0-578.9
DEF: Distended, tortuous, veins of lower esophagus, usually due to portal hypertension.

456.1 Esophageal varices without mention of bleeding

✓5th 456.2 Esophageal varices in diseases classified elsewhere
Code first underlying cause, as:
cirrhosis of liver (571.0-571.9)
portal hypertension (572.3)

456.20 With bleeding CC
CC Excl: 456.0, 456.20, 459.89, 459.9, 530.82
AHA: N-D, '85, 14

456.21 Without mention of bleeding
AHA: ▶3Q, '05, 15;◀ 2Q, '02, 4

456.3 Sublingual varices
DEF: Distended, tortuous veins beneath tongue.

456.4 Scrotal varices ♂
Varicocele

456.5 Pelvic varices
Varices of broad ligament

456.6 Vulval varices ♀
Varices of perineum
EXCLUDES *that complicating pregnancy, childbirth, or the puerperium (671.1)*

456.8 Varices of other sites
Varicose veins of nasal septum (with ulcer)
EXCLUDES *placental varices (656.7)*
retinal varices (362.17)
varicose ulcer of unspecified site (454.0)
varicose veins of unspecified site (454.9)
AHA: 2Q, '02, 4

✓4th 457 Noninfectious disorders of lymphatic channels

457.0 Postmastectomy lymphedema syndrome A
Elephantiasis } due to mastectomy
Obliteration of lymphatic vessel } due to mastectomy
AHA: 2Q, '02, 12
DEF: Reduced lymphatic circulation following mastectomy; symptoms include swelling of the arm on the operative side.

457.1 Other lymphedema
Elephantiasis (nonfilarial) NOS
Lymphangiectasis
Lymphedema: acquired (chronic)
Lymphedema: praecox, secondary
Obliteration, lymphatic vessel
EXCLUDES *elephantiasis (nonfilarial):*
congenital (757.0)
eyelid (374.83)
vulva (624.8)
AHA: 3Q, '04, 5
DEF: Fluid retention due to reduced lymphatic circulation; due to other than mastectomy.

457.2 Lymphangitis
Lymphangitis: NOS, chronic
Lymphangitis: subacute
EXCLUDES *acute lymphangitis (682.0-682.9)*

457.8 Other noninfectious disorders of lymphatic channels
Chylocele (nonfilarial)
Chylous: ascites, cyst
Lymph node or vessel: fistula, infarction, rupture
EXCLUDES *chylocele:*
filarial (125.0-125.9)
tunica vaginalis (nonfilarial) (608.84)
AHA: 1Q, '04, 5; 3Q, '03, 17

457.9 Unspecified noninfectious disorder of lymphatic channels

✓4th 458 Hypotension
INCLUDES hypopiesis
EXCLUDES *cardiovascular collapse (785.50)*
maternal hypotension syndrome (669.2)
shock (785.50-785.59)
Shy-Drager syndrome (333.0)

458.0 Orthostatic hypotension
Hypotension: orthostatic (chronic)
Hypotension: postural
AHA: 3Q, '00, 8; 3Q, '91, 9
DEF: Low blood pressure; occurs when standing.

458.1 Chronic hypotension
Permanent idiopathic hypotension
DEF: Persistent low blood pressure.

✓5th 458.2 Iatrogenic hypotension
AHA: 4Q, '03, 60; 3Q, '02, 12; 4Q, '95, 57
DEF: Abnormally low blood pressure; due to medical treatment.

458.21 Hypotension of hemodialysis
Intra-dialytic hypotension
AHA: 4Q, '03, 61

458.29 Other iatrogenic hypotension
Postoperative hypotension

458.8 Other specified hypotension MC
AHA: 4Q, '97, 37

458.9 Hypotension, unspecified MC
Hypotension (arterial) NOS

✓4th **459 Other disorders of circulatory system**

459.0 Hemorrhage, unspecified CC

Rupture of blood vessel NOS
Spontaneous hemorrhage NEC

EXCLUDES *hemorrhage:*
gastrointestinal NOS (578.9)
in newborn NOS (772.9)
secondary or recurrent following trauma (958.2)
traumatic rupture of blood vessel (900.0-904.9)

CC Excl: 459.0, 459.89, 459.9

AHA: 4Q, '90, 26

✓5th **459.1 Postphlebitic syndrome**

Chronic venous hypertension due to deep vein thrombosis

EXCLUDES *chronic venous hypertension without deep vein thrombosis (459.30-459.39)*

AHA: 4Q, '02, 58; 2Q, '91, 20

DEF: Various conditions following deep vein thrombosis; including edema, pain, stasis dermatitis, cellulitis, varicose veins and ulceration of the lower leg.

459.10 Postphlebitic syndrome without complications

Asymptomatic postphlebitic syndrome
Postphlebitic syndrome NOS

459.11 Postphlebitic syndrome with ulcer

459.12 Postphlebitic syndrome with inflammation

459.13 Postphlebitic syndrome with ulcer and inflammation

459.19 Postphlebitic syndrome with other complication

459.2 Compression of vein

Stricture of vein
Vena cava syndrome (inferior) (superior)

✓5th **459.3 Chronic venous hypertension (idiopathic)**

Stasis edema

EXCLUDES *chronic venous hypertension due to deep vein thrombosis (459.10-459.9)*
varicose veins (454.0-454.9)

AHA: 4Q, '02, 59

459.30 Chronic venous hypertension without complications

Asymptomatic chronic venous hypertension
Chronic venous hypertension NOS

459.31 Chronic venous hypertension with ulcer

AHA: 4Q, '02, 43

459.32 Chronic venous hypertension with inflammation

459.33 Chronic venous hypertension with ulcer and inflammation

459.39 Chronic venous hypertension with other complication

✓5th **459.8 Other specified disorders of circulatory system**

459.81 Venous (peripheral) insufficiency, unspecified

Chronic venous insufficiency NOS
Use additional code for any associated ulceration (707.10-707.9)

AHA: 3Q, '04, 5; 2Q, '91, 20; M-A, '87, 6

DEF: Insufficient drainage, venous blood, any part of body, results in edema or dermatosis.

DRG 130

459.89 Other

Collateral circulation (venous), any site
Phlebosclerosis
Venofibrosis

459.9 Unspecified circulatory system disorder

8. DISEASES OF THE RESPIRATORY SYSTEM (460-519)

Use additional code to identify infectious organism

ACUTE RESPIRATORY INFECTIONS (460-466)

EXCLUDES *pneumonia and influenza (480.0-487.8)*

460 Acute nasopharyngitis [common cold]

Coryza (acute)
Nasal catarrh, acute
Nasopharyngitis:
NOS
acute
Nasopharyngitis:
infective NOS
Rhinitis:
acute
infective

EXCLUDES *nasopharyngitis, chronic (472.2)*
pharyngitis:
acute or unspecified (462)
chronic (472.1)
rhinitis:
allergic (477.0-477.9)
chronic or unspecified (472.0)
sore throat:
acute or unspecified (462)
chronic (472.1)

AHA: 1Q, '88, 12

DEF: Acute inflammation of mucous membranes; extends from nares to pharynx.

✓4th **461 Acute sinusitis**

INCLUDES abscess, empyema, infection, inflammation, suppuration } acute, of sinus (accessory) (nasal)

EXCLUDES *chronic or unspecified sinusitis (473.0-473.9)*

461.0 Maxillary
Acute antritis

461.1 Frontal

461.2 Ethmoidal

461.3 Sphenoidal

461.8 Other acute sinusitis
Acute pansinusitis

461.9 Acute sinusitis, unspecified
Acute sinusitis NOS

462 Acute pharyngitis

Acute sore throat NOS
Pharyngitis (acute):
NOS
gangrenous
infective
phlegmonous
pneumococcal
Pharyngitis (acute):
staphylococcal
suppurative
ulcerative
Sore throat (viral) NOS
Viral pharyngitis

EXCLUDES *abscess:*
peritonsillar [quinsy] (475)
pharyngeal NOS (478.29)
retropharyngeal (478.24)
chronic pharyngitis (472.1)
infectious mononucleosis (075)
that specified as (due to):
Coxsackie (virus) (074.0)
gonococcus (098.6)
herpes simplex (054.79)
influenza (487.1)
septic (034.0)
streptococcal (034.0)

AHA: 4Q, '99, 26; S-O, '85, 8

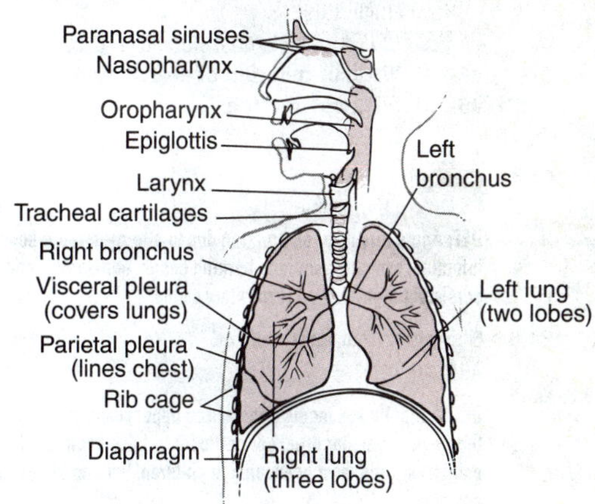

463 Acute tonsillitis

Tonsillitis (acute):
NOS
follicular
gangrenous
infective
pneumococcal
Tonsillitis (acute):
septic
staphylococcal
suppurative
ulcerative
viral

EXCLUDES *chronic tonsillitis (474.0)*
hypertrophy of tonsils (474.1)
peritonsillar abscess [quinsy] (475)
sore throat:
acute or NOS (462)
septic (034.0)
streptococcal tonsillitis (034.0)

AHA: N-D, '84, 16

✓4th **464 Acute laryngitis and tracheitis**

EXCLUDES *that associated with influenza (487.1)*
that due to Streptococcus (034.0)

✓5th **464.0 Acute laryngitis**

Laryngitis (acute):
NOS
edematous
Hemophilus influenzae [H. influenzae]
pneumococcal
septic
suppurative
ulcerative

EXCLUDES *chronic laryngitis (476.0-476.1)*
influenzal laryngitis (487.1)

464.00 Without mention of obstruction

464.01 With obstruction

✓5th **464.1 Acute tracheitis**

Tracheitis (acute):
NOS
catarrhal
Tracheitis (acute):
viral

EXCLUDES *chronic tracheitis (491.8)*

464.10 Without mention of obstruction

464.11 With obstruction CC

CC Excl: 012.20-012.86, 017.90-017.96, 464.10-464.31, 519.8-519.9

✓5th **464.2 Acute laryngotracheitis**

Laryngotracheitis (acute)
Tracheitis (acute) with laryngitis (acute)

EXCLUDES *chronic laryngotracheitis (476.1)*

464.20 Without mention of obstruction

464.21 With obstruction CC

CC Excl: See code 464.11

Respiratory System

460–464.21

✓4th ✓5th Additional Digit Required | Nonspecific PDx | Unacceptable PDx | Manifestation Code | MCV Major Cardiovascular Condition | ►◄ Revised Text | ● New Code | ▲ Revised Code Title

✓5th **464.3 Acute epiglottitis**
Viral epiglottitis
EXCLUDES *epiglottitis, chronic (476.1)*

464.30 Without mention of obstruction

464.31 With obstruction CC
CC Excl: See code 464.11

464.4 Croup
Croup syndrome
DEF: Acute laryngeal obstruction due to allergy, foreign body or infection; symptoms include barking cough, hoarseness and harsh, persistent high-pitched respiratory sound.

✓5th **464.5 Supraglottitis, unspecified**
AHA: 4Q, '01, 42

DEF: A rapidly advancing generalized upper respiratory infection of the lingual tonsillar area, epiglottic folds, false vocal cords, and the epiglottis; seen most commonly in children, but can affect people of any age.

464.50 Without mention of obstruction
AHA: 4Q, '01, 43

464.51 With obstruction

✓4th **465 Acute upper respiratory infections of multiple or unspecified sites**
EXCLUDES *upper respiratory infection due to:*
influenza (487.1)
Streptococcus (034.0)

465.0 Acute laryngopharyngitis
DEF: Acute infection of the vocal cords and pharynx.

465.8 Other multiple sites
Multiple URI

465.9 Unspecified site
Acute URI NOS
Upper respiratory infection (acute)

✓4th **466 Acute bronchitis and bronchiolitis**
INCLUDES that with:
bronchospasm
obstruction

466.0 Acute bronchitis
Bronchitis, acute or subacute:
fibrinous
membranous
pneumococcal
purulent
septic
Bronchitis, acute or subacute:
viral
with tracheitis
Croupous bronchitis
Tracheobronchitis, acute
EXCLUDES *acute bronchitis with chronic obstructive pulmonary disease (491.22)*
AHA: 4Q, '04, 137; 1Q, '04, 3; 4Q, '02, 46; 4Q, '96, 28; 4Q, '91, 24; 1Q, '88, 12

DRG 096

DEF: Acute inflammation of main branches of bronchial tree due to infectious or irritant agents; symptoms include cough with a varied production of sputum, fever, substernal soreness, and lung rales.

✓5th **466.1 Acute bronchiolitis**
Bronchiolitis (acute) Capillary pneumonia
DEF: Acute inflammation of finer subdivisions of bronchial tree due to infectious or irritant agents; symptoms include cough with a varied production of sputum, fever, substernal soreness, and lung rales.

466.11 Acute bronchiolitis due to respiratory syncytial virus (RSV)
AHA: 1Q, '05, 10; 4Q, '96, 27

466.19 Acute bronchiolitis due to other infectious organisms
Use additional code to identify organism

OTHER DISEASES OF THE UPPER RESPIRATORY TRACT (470-478)

470 Deviated nasal septum
Deflected septum (nasal) (acquired)
EXCLUDES *congenital (754.0)*

✓4th **471 Nasal polyps**
EXCLUDES *adenomatous polyps (212.0)*

471.0 Polyp of nasal cavity
Polyp:
choanal
Polyp:
nasopharyngeal

471.1 Polypoid sinus degeneration
Woakes' syndrome or ethmoiditis

471.8 Other polyp of sinus
Polyp of sinus:
accessory
ethmoidal
maxillary
sphenoidal

471.9 Unspecified nasal polyp
Nasal polyp NOS

✓4th **472 Chronic pharyngitis and nasopharyngitis**

472.0 Chronic rhinitis
Ozena
Rhinitis:
NOS
atrophic
granulomatous
Rhinitis:
hypertrophic
obstructive
purulent
ulcerative
EXCLUDES *allergic rhinitis (477.0-477.9)*
DEF: Persistent inflammation of mucous membranes of nose.

472.1 Chronic pharyngitis
Chronic sore throat
Pharyngitis:
atrophic
Pharyngitis:
granular (chronic)
hypertrophic

472.2 Chronic nasopharyngitis
EXCLUDES *acute or unspecified nasopharyngitis (460)*
DEF: Persistent inflammation of mucous membranes extending from nares to pharynx.

Upper Respiratory System

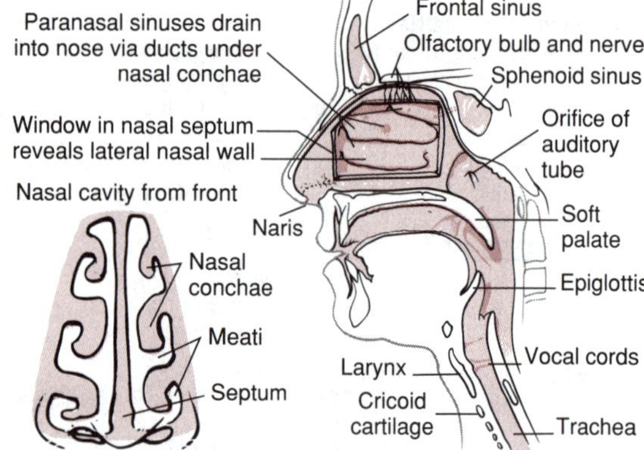

Paranasal Sinuses

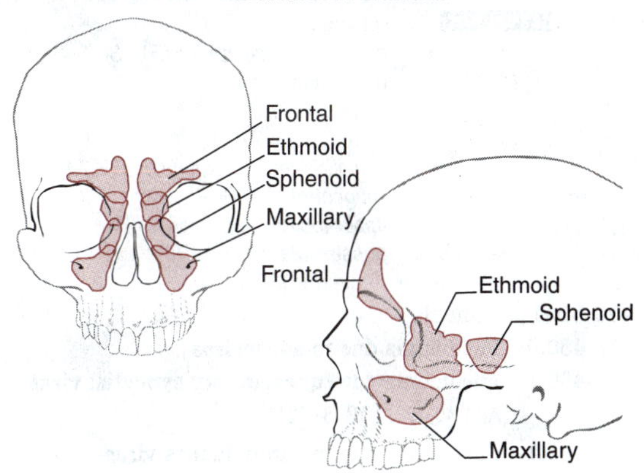

473 Chronic sinusitis

INCLUDES abscess, empyema, infection, suppuration (chronic) of sinus (accessory) (nasal)

EXCLUDES *acute sinusitis (461.0-461.9)*

473.0 Maxillary
Antritis (chronic)

473.1 Frontal

473.2 Ethmoidal
EXCLUDES *Woakes' ethmoiditis (471.1)*

473.3 Sphenoidal

473.8 Other chronic sinusitis
Pansinusitis (chronic)

473.9 Unspecified sinusitis (chronic)
Sinusitis (chronic) NOS

474 Chronic disease of tonsils and adenoids

474.0 Chronic tonsillitis and adenoiditis
EXCLUDES *acute or unspecified tonsillitis (463)*
AHA: 4Q, '97, 38

474.00 Chronic tonsillitis

474.01 Chronic adenoiditis

474.02 Chronic tonsillitis and adenoiditis

474.1 Hypertrophy of tonsils and adenoids
Enlargement, Hyperplasia, Hypertrophy of tonsils or adenoids
EXCLUDES *that with:*
adenoiditis (474.01)
adenoiditis and tonsillitis (474.02)
tonsillitis (474.00)

474.10 Tonsils with adenoids
AHA: 2Q, '05, 16

474.11 Tonsils alone

474.12 Adenoids alone

474.2 Adenoid vegetations
DEF: Fungus-like growth of lymph tissue between the nares and pharynx.

474.8 Other chronic disease of tonsils and adenoids
Amygdalolith
Calculus, tonsil
Cicatrix of tonsil (and adenoid)
Tonsillar tag
Ulcer, tonsil

474.9 Unspecified chronic disease of tonsils and adenoids
Disease (chronic) of tonsils (and adenoids)

475 Peritonsillar abscess CC
Abscess of tonsil
Peritonsillar cellulitis
Quinsy
EXCLUDES *tonsillitis:*
acute or NOS (463)
chronic (474.0)
CC Excl: 475, 519.8-519.9

476 Chronic laryngitis and laryngotracheitis

476.0 Chronic laryngitis
Laryngitis:
catarrhal
hypertrophic
sicca

476.1 Chronic laryngotracheitis
Laryngitis, chronic, with tracheitis (chronic)
Tracheitis, chronic, with laryngitis
EXCLUDES *chronic tracheitis (491.8)*
laryngitis and tracheitis, acute or unspecified (464.00-464.51)

477 Allergic rhinitis

INCLUDES allergic rhinitis (nonseasonal) (seasonal)
hay fever
spasmodic rhinorrhea

EXCLUDES *allergic rhinitis with asthma (bronchial) (493.0)*

DEF: True immunoglobulin E (IgE)-mediated allergic reaction of nasal mucosa; seasonal (typical hay fever) or perennial (year-round allergens: dust, food, dander).

477.0 Due to pollen
Pollinosis

477.1 Due to food
AHA: 4Q, '00, 42

477.2 Due to animal (cat) (dog) hair and dander

477.8 Due to other allergen

477.9 Cause unspecified
AHA: 2Q, '97, 9

478 Other diseases of upper respiratory tract

478.0 Hypertrophy of nasal turbinates
DEF: Overgrowth, enlargement of shell-shaped bones, in nasal cavity.

478.1 Other diseases of nasal cavity and sinuses
EXCLUDES *varicose ulcer of nasal septum (456.8)*

● **478.11 Nasal mucositis (ulcerative)**
Use additional E code to identify adverse effects of therapy, such as:
antineoplastic and immunosuppressive drugs (E930.7, E933.1)
radiation therapy (E879.2)

● **478.19 Other diseases of nasal cavity and sinuses**
Abscess, Necrosis, Ulcer of nose (septum)
Cyst or mucocele of sinus (nasal)
Rhinolith

478.2 Other diseases of pharynx, not elsewhere classified

478.20 Unspecified disease of pharynx

478.21 Cellulitis of pharynx or nasopharynx CC
CC Excl: 478.20-478.24, 519.8-519.9

478.22 Parapharyngeal abscess CC
CC Excl: See code 478.21

478.24 Retropharyngeal abscess CC
CC Excl: See code 478.21
DEF: Purulent infection, behind pharynx and front of precerebral fascia.

478.25 Edema of pharynx or nasopharynx

478.26 Cyst of pharynx or nasopharynx

478.29 Other
Abscess of pharynx or nasopharynx
EXCLUDES *ulcerative pharyngitis (462)*

478.3 Paralysis of vocal cords or larynx
DEF: Loss of motor ability of vocal cords or larynx; due to nerve or muscle damage.

478.30 Paralysis, unspecified CC
Laryngoplegia
Paralysis of glottis
CC Excl: 478.30-478.34, 478.5, 478.70, 519.8-519.9

478.31 **Unilateral, partial** CC
CC Excl: See code 478.30

478.32 **Unilateral, complete** CC
CC Excl: See code 478.30

478.33 **Bilateral, partial** CC
CC Excl: See code 478.30

478.34 **Bilateral, complete** CC
CC Excl: See code 478.30

478.4 Polyp of vocal cord or larynx
EXCLUDES *adenomatous polyps (212.1)*

478.5 Other diseases of vocal cords
Abscess / Cellulitis / Granuloma / Leukoplakia } of vocal cords
Chorditis (fibrinous) (nodosa) (tuberosa)
Singers' nodes

478.6 Edema of larynx
Edema (of):
glottis
subglottic
Edema (of):
supraglottic

✓5th **478.7 Other diseases of larynx, not elsewhere classified**

478.70 Unspecified disease of larynx

478.71 Cellulitis and perichondritis of larynx
DEF: Inflammation of deep soft tissues or lining of bone of the larynx.

478.74 Stenosis of larynx

478.75 Laryngeal spasm
Laryngismus (stridulus)
DEF: Involuntary muscle contraction of the larynx.

478.79 Other
Abscess / Necrosis / Obstruction / Pachyderma / Ulcer } of larynx
EXCLUDES *ulcerative laryngitis (464.00-464.01)*
AHA: 3Q, '91, 20

478.8 Upper respiratory tract hypersensitivity reaction, site unspecified
EXCLUDES *hypersensitivity reaction of lower respiratory tract, as:*
extrinsic allergic alveolitis (495.0-495.9)
pneumoconiosis (500-505)

478.9 Other and unspecified diseases of upper respiratory tract
Abscess / Cicatrix } of trachea

Lungs

Right Lung (Three Lobes)
Bronchopulmonary segments:
Upper lobe
Middle lobe
Lower lobe
Diaphragm
S1 S3 S2 S5 S4 S8 S9 S10 S7
Trachea
Primary bronchus
Left Lung (Two Lobes)
Secondary bronchus
S1,2
S3 S4 S5 Upper lobe
S6
S7,8
Lower lobe
S9
S10

PNEUMONIA AND INFLUENZA (480-487)

EXCLUDES *pneumonia:*
allergic or eosinophilic (518.3)
aspiration:
NOS (507.0)
newborn (770.18)
solids and liquids (507.0-507.8)
congenital (770.0)
lipoid (507.1)
passive (514)
rheumatic (390)

✓4th **480 Viral pneumonia**

480.0 Pneumonia due to adenovirus

480.1 Pneumonia due to respiratory syncytial virus
AHA: 4Q, '96, 28; 1Q, '88, 12

480.2 Pneumonia due to parainfluenza virus

480.3 Pneumonia due to SARS-associated coronavirus CC
CC Excl: 011.00-012.16, 012.80-012.86, 017.90-017.96, 021.2, 031.0, 039.1, 115.05, 115.15, 115.95, 122.1, 130.4, 136.3, 480.0-487.1, 494.0-508.9, 517.1, 517.8, 518.89, 519.8-519.9, 748.61
AHA: 4Q, '03, 46-47
DEF: A severe adult respiratory syndrome caused by the coronavirus, specified as inflammation of the lungs with consolidation.

480.8 Pneumonia due to other virus not elsewhere classified HIV
EXCLUDES *congenital rubella pneumonitis (771.0)*
influenza with pneumonia, any form (487.0)
pneumonia complicating viral diseases classified elsewhere (484.1-484.8)

480.9 Viral pneumonia, unspecified HIV
AHA: 3Q, '98, 5

481 Pneumococcal pneumonia [Streptococcus pneumoniae pneumonia] CC MC HIV
Lobar pneumonia, organism unspecified
CC Excl: 011.00-012.16, 012.80-012.86, 017.90-017.96, 021.2, 031.0, 039.1, 115.05, 115.15, 115.95, 122.1, 130.4, 136.3, 480.0-480.2, 480.8-487.1, 494.0-508.9, 517.1, 517.8, 518.89, 519.8-519.9, 748.61
AHA: 2Q, '98, 7; 4Q, '92, 19; 1Q, '92, 18; 1Q, '91, 13; 1Q, '88, 13; M-A, '85, 6

✓4th **482 Other bacterial pneumonia**
AHA: 4Q, '93, 39

482.0 Pneumonia due to Klebsiella pneumoniae CC MC HIV
CC Excl: See code 481

482.1 Pneumonia due to Pseudomonas CC MC HIV
CC Excl: See code 481
DRG 079

482.2 Pneumonia due to Hemophilus influenzae [H. influenzae] CC MC HIV
CC Excl: See code 481
AHA: ▶2Q, '05, 19◀

✓5th **482.3 Pneumonia due to Streptococcus**
EXCLUDES *Streptococcus pneumoniae (481)*
AHA: 1Q, '88, 13

482.30 Streptococcus, unspecified CC MC HIV
CC Excl: See code 481

482.31 Group A CC MC HIV
CC Excl: See code 481

482.32 Group B CC MC HIV
CC Excl: See code 481

482.39 Other Streptococcus CC MC HIV
CC Excl: See code 481

N Newborn Age: 0  Pediatric Age: 0-17 M Maternity Age: 12-55 A Adult Age: 15-124 CC CC Condition MC Major Complication CD Complex Dx HIV HIV Related Dx

✓5th **482.4 Pneumonia due to Staphylococcus**
AHA: 3Q, '91, 16

482.40 Pneumonia due to Staphylococcus, unspecified CC MC HIV
CC Excl: See code 481

482.41 Pneumonia due to Staphylococcus aureus CC MC HIV
CC Excl: See code 481
DRG 079

482.49 Other Staphylococcus pneumonia CC MC HIV
CC Excl: See code 481

✓5th **482.8 Pneumonia due to other specified bacteria**
EXCLUDES *pneumonia, complicating infectious disease classified elsewhere (484.1-484.8)*
AHA: 3Q, '88, 11

482.81 Anaerobes CC MC HIV
Bacteroides (melaninogenicus)
Gram-negative anaerobes
CC Excl: See code 481

482.82 Escherichia coli [E. coli] CC MC HIV
CC Excl: See code 481

482.83 Other gram-negative bacteria CC MC HIV
Gram-negative pneumonia NOS
Proteus
Serratia marcescens
EXCLUDES *gram-negative anaerobes (482.81)*
Legionnaires' disease (482.84)
CC Excl: See code 481
AHA: 2Q, '98, 5; 3Q, '94, 9
DRG 079

482.84 Legionnaires' disease CC HIV
CC Excl: See code 481
AHA: 4Q, '97, 38
DEF: Severe and often fatal infection by Legionella pneumophilia; symptoms include high fever, gastrointestinal pain, headache, myalgia, dry cough, and pneumonia; transmitted airborne via air conditioning systems, humidifiers, water faucets, shower heads; not person-to-person contact.

482.89 Other specified bacteria CC MC HIV
CC Excl: See code 481
AHA: 2Q, '97, 6

482.9 Bacterial pneumonia unspecified CC MC HIV
CC Excl: See code 481
AHA: 2Q, '98, 6; 2Q, '97, 6; 1Q, '94, 17

✓4th **483 Pneumonia due to other specified organism**
AHA: N-D, '87, 5

483.0 Mycoplasma pneumoniae CC MC
Eaton's agent
Pleuropneumonia-like organism [PPLO]
CC Excl: See code 481

483.1 Chlamydia CC MC
CC Excl: See code 481
AHA: 4Q, '96, 31

483.8 Other specified organism CC MC
CC Excl: See code 481

✓4th **484 Pneumonia in infectious diseases classified elsewhere**
EXCLUDES *influenza with pneumonia, any form (487.0)*

484.1 *Pneumonia in cytomegalic inclusion disease* CC MC
Code first underlying disease (078.5)
CC Excl: See code 481

484.3 *Pneumonia in whooping cough* CC MC
Code first underlying disease (033.0-033.9)
CC Excl: See code 481

484.5 *Pneumonia in anthrax* CC MC
Code first underlying disease (022.1)
CC Excl: See code 481

484.6 *Pneumonia in aspergillosis* CC MC
Code first underlying disease (117.3)
CC Excl: See code 481
AHA: 4Q, '97, 40

484.7 *Pneumonia in other systemic mycoses* CC MC
Code first underlying disease
EXCLUDES *pneumonia in:*
candidiasis (112.4)
coccidioidomycosis (114.0)
histoplasmosis (115.0-115.9 with fifth-digit 5)
CC Excl: See code 481

484.8 *Pneumonia in other infectious diseases classified elsewhere* CC MC
Code first underlying disease, as:
Q fever (083.0)
typhoid fever (002.0)
EXCLUDES *pneumonia in:*
actinomycosis (039.1)
measles (055.1)
nocardiosis (039.1)
ornithosis (073.0)
Pneumocystis carinii (136.3)
salmonellosis (003.22)
toxoplasmosis (130.4)
tuberculosis (011.6)
tularemia (021.2)
varicella (052.1)
CC Excl: See code 481

485 Bronchopneumonia, organism unspecified CC MC
Bronchopneumonia:
hemorrhagic
terminal
Pneumonia:
lobular
segmental
Pleurobronchopneumonia
EXCLUDES *bronchiolitis (acute) (466.11-466.19)*
chronic (491.8)
lipoid pneumonia (507.1)
CC Excl: See code 481

486 Pneumonia, organism unspecified CC MC HIV

EXCLUDES *hypostatic or passive pneumonia (514)*
influenza with pneumonia, any form (487.0)
inhalation or aspiration pneumonia due to foreign materials (507.0-507.8)
pneumonitis due to fumes and vapors (506.0)

CC Excl: See code 481

AHA: 4Q, '99, 6; 3Q, '99, 9; 3Q, '98, 7; 2Q, '98, 4, 5; 1Q, '98, 8; 3Q, '97, 9; 3Q, '94, 10; 3Q, '88, 11

DRG 089 and 475

✓4th **487 Influenza**

EXCLUDES *Hemophilus influenzae [H. influenzae]:*
infection NOS (041.5)
laryngitis (464.00-464.01)
meningitis (320.0)

487.0 With pneumonia CC MC

Influenza with pneumonia, any form
Influenzal:
bronchopneumonia
pneumonia
Use additional code to identify the type of pneumonia (480.0-480.9, 481, 482.0-482.9, 483.0-483.8, 485)

CC Excl: See code 481

AHA: ▶1Q, '06, 18; 2Q, '05, 18◀

487.1 With other respiratory manifestations

Influenza NOS
Influenzal:
laryngitis
pharyngitis
respiratory infection (upper) (acute)

AHA: ▶1Q, '06, 18;◀ 2Q, '05, 18; 4Q, '99, 26

487.8 With other manifestations

Encephalopathy due to influenza
Influenza with involvement of gastrointestinal tract

EXCLUDES *"intestinal flu" [viral gastroenteritis] (008.8)*

CHRONIC OBSTRUCTIVE PULMONARY DISEASE AND ALLIED CONDITIONS (490-496)

AHA: 3Q, '88, 5

490 Bronchitis, not specified as acute or chronic

Bronchitis NOS:
catarrhal
with tracheitis NOS
Tracheobronchitis NOS

EXCLUDES *bronchitis:*
allergic NOS (493.9)
asthmatic NOS (493.9)
due to fumes and vapors (506.0)

DRG 096

✓4th **491 Chronic bronchitis**

EXCLUDES *chronic obstructive asthma (493.2)*

491.0 Simple chronic bronchitis

Catarrhal bronchitis, chronic
Smokers' cough

Bronchioli and Alveoli

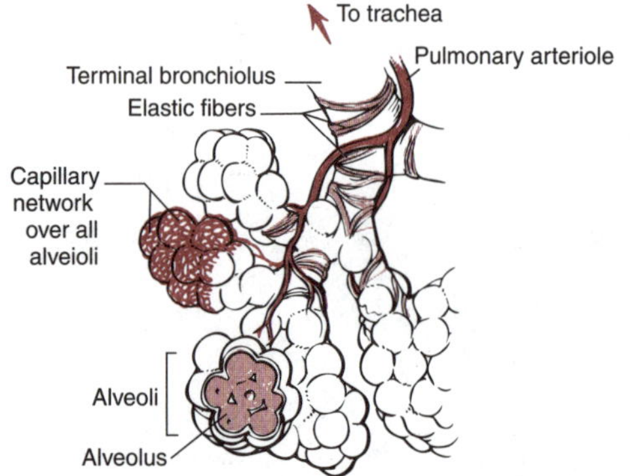

Interrelationship Between Chronic Airway Obstruction, Chronic Bronchitis, and Emphysema

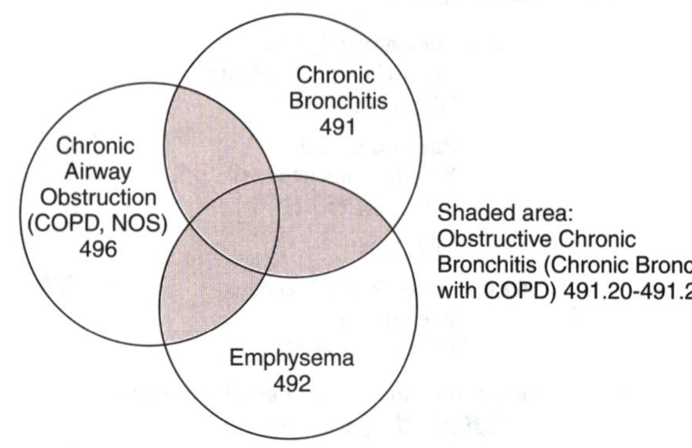

491.1 Mucopurulent chronic bronchitis CC

Bronchitis (chronic) (recurrent):
fetid
mucopurulent
purulent

CC Excl: 491.1-491.9, 493.20-493.21

AHA: 3Q, '88, 12

DEF: Chronic bronchial infection characterized by both mucus and pus secretions in the bronchial tree; recurs after asymptomatic periods; signs are coughing, expectoration and secondary changes in the lung.

✓5th **491.2 Obstructive chronic bronchitis**

Bronchitis:
emphysematous
obstructive (chronic) (diffuse)
Bronchitis with:
chronic airway obstruction
emphysema

EXCLUDES *asthmatic bronchitis (acute) NOS (493.9)*
chronic obstructive asthma (493.2)

AHA: 3Q, '97, 9; 4Q, '91, 25; 2Q, '91, 21

491.20 Without exacerbation CC

Emphysema with chronic bronchitis

CC Excl: See code 491.1

AHA: 3Q, '97, 9

491.21 With (acute) exacerbation CC

Acute exacerbation of chronic obstructive pulmonary disease [COPD]
Decompensated chronic obstructive pulmonary disease [COPD]
Decompensated chronic obstructive pulmonary disease [COPD] with exacerbation

EXCLUDES *chronic obstructive asthma with acute exacerbation (493.22)*

CC Excl: See code 491.1

AHA: 1Q, '04, 3; 3Q, '02, 18, 19; 4Q, '01, 43; 2Q, '96, 10

DRG 088 and 475

491.22 With acute bronchitis CC

CC Excl: See code 491.1

AHA: 4Q, '04, 82

DRG 088

491.8 Other chronic bronchitis CC

Chronic:
tracheitis
tracheobronchitis

CC Excl: See code 491.1

491.9 Unspecified chronic bronchitis CC

CC Excl: See code 491.1

✓4th **492 Emphysema**
AHA: 2Q, '91, 21

492.0 Emphysematous bleb
Giant bullous emphysema
Ruptured emphysematous bleb
Tension pneumatocele
Vanishing lung
AHA: 2Q, '93, 3

DEF: Formation of vesicle or bulla in emphysematous lung, more than one millimeter; contains serum or blood.

492.8 Other emphysema CC
Emphysema (lung or pulmonary):
NOS
centriacinar
centrilobular
obstructive
panacinar
panlobular

Emphysema (lung or pulmonary):
unilateral
vesicular
MacLeod's syndrome
Swyer-James syndrome
Unilateral hyperlucent lung

EXCLUDES *emphysema:*
with chronic bronchitis (491.20-491.22)
compensatory (518.2)
due to fumes and vapors (506.4)
interstitial (518.1)
newborn (770.2)
mediastinal (518.1)
surgical (subcutaneous) (998.81)
traumatic (958.7)

CC Excl: 492.0, 492.8, 493.20-493.21

AHA: 1Q, '05, 4; 4Q, '93, 41; J-A, '84, 17

✓4th **493 Asthma**
EXCLUDES *wheezing NOS (786.07)*

The following fifth-digit subclassification is for use with codes 493.0-493.2, 493.9:
0 unspecified
1 with status asthmaticus
2 with (acute) exacerbation

AHA: 4Q, '04, 137; 4Q, '03, 62; 4Q, '01, 43; 4Q, '00, 42; 1Q, '91, 13; 3Q, '88, 9; J-A, '85, 8; N-D, '84, 17

DEF: Status asthmaticus: severe, intractable episode of asthma unresponsive to normal therapeutic measures.

✓5th **493.0 Extrinsic asthma** CC 1-2
Asthma:
allergic with stated cause
atopic
childhood

Asthma:
hay
platinum
Hay fever with asthma

EXCLUDES *asthma:*
allergic NOS (493.9)
detergent (507.8)
miners' (500)
wood (495.8)

CC Excl: For code 493.01 and 493.02: 493.00-493.92, 517.8, 518.89, 519.8-519.9

DEF: Transient stricture of airway diameters of bronchi; due to environmental factor; also called allergic (bronchial) asthma.

✓5th **493.1 Intrinsic asthma** CC 1-2
Late-onset asthma
CC Excl: For code 493.11 and 493.12: See code 493.0

AHA: 3Q, '88, 9; M-A, '85, 7

DEF: Transient stricture, of airway diameters of bronchi; due to pathophysiological disturbances.

✓5th **493.2 Chronic obstructive asthma** CC
Asthma with chronic obstructive pulmonary disease [COPD]
Chronic asthmatic bronchitis
EXCLUDES *acute bronchitis (466.0)*
chronic obstructive bronchitis (491.20-491.22)

CC Excl: For code 493.20 and 493.21: 491.1-493.92, 517.8, 518.89, 519.8-519.9; For code 493.22: 493.00-493.92, 517.8, 518.89, 519.8-519.9

AHA: 2Q, '91, 21; 2Q, '90, 20; For code 493.20: 4Q, '03, 108

DRG 088 For code 493.22

DEF: Persistent narrowing of airway diameters in the bronchial tree, restricting airflow and causing constant labored breathing.

✓5th **493.8 Other forms of asthma**
AHA: 4Q, '03, 62

493.81 Exercise induced bronchospasm

493.82 Cough variant asthma

✓5th **493.9 Asthma, unspecified** CC 1-2
Asthma (bronchial) (allergic NOS)
Bronchitis:
allergic
asthmatic

CC Excl: For code 493.91 and 493.92: 493.00-493.92, 517.8, 518.89, 519.8-519.9

AHA: 4Q, '97, 40, For code 493.90: 4Q, '04, 137; 4Q, '03, 108; 4Q, '99, 25; 1Q, '97, 7; For code 493.91: 1Q, '05, 5; For code 493.92: 1Q, '03, 9

DRG 096 For code 493.90 and 493.92

✓4th **494 Bronchiectasis**
Bronchiectasis (fusiform) (postinfectious) (recurrent)
Bronchiolectasis
EXCLUDES *congenital (748.61)*
tuberculous bronchiectasis (current disease) (011.5)

AHA: 4Q, '00, 42

DEF: Dilation of bronchi; due to infection or chronic conditions; causes decreased lung capacity and recurrent infections of lungs.

494.0 Bronchiectasis without acute exacerbation

494.1 Bronchiectasis with acute exacerbation CC
CC Excl: 017.90-017.96, 487.1, 494.1, 496, 506.1, 506.4, 506.9, 748.61

✓4th **495 Extrinsic allergic alveolitis**
INCLUDES allergic alveolitis and pneumonitis due to inhaled organic dust particles of fungal, thermophilic actinomycete, or other origin

DEF: Pneumonitis due to particles inhaled into lung, often at workplace; symptoms include cough, chills, fever, increased heart and respiratory rates; develops within hours of exposure.

495.0 Farmers' lung CC
CC Excl: 011.00-012.16, 012.80-012.86, 017.90-017.96, 021.2, 031.0, 039.1, 115.05, 115.15, 115.95, 122.1, 130.4, 136.3, 480.0-487.1, 494.0-508.9, 517.1, 517.8, 518.89, 519.8-519.9, 748.61

495.1 Bagassosis CC
CC Excl: See code 495.0

495.2 Bird-fanciers' lung CC
Budgerigar-fanciers' disease or lung
Pigeon-fanciers' disease or lung
CC Excl: See code 495.0

495.3 Suberosis CC
Cork-handlers' disease or lung
CC Excl: See code 495.0

495.4 Malt workers' lung CC
Alveolitis due to Aspergillus clavatus
CC Excl: See code 495.0

495.5 Mushroom workers' lung CC
CC Excl: See code 495.0

495.6 Maple bark-strippers' lung CC
Alveolitis due to Cryptostroma corticale
CC Excl: See code 495.0

Respiratory System 492–495.6

✓4th ✓5th Additional Digit Required | Nonspecific PDx | Unacceptable PDx | Manifestation Code | MCV Major Cardiovascular Condition | ▶◀ Revised Text | ● New Code | ▲ Revised Code Title

495.7 "Ventilation" pneumonitis CC
Allergic alveolitis due to fungal, thermophilic actinomycete, and other organisms growing in ventilation [air conditioning] systems
CC Excl: See code 495.0

495.8 Other specified allergic alveolitis and pneumonitis CC
Cheese-washers' lung
Coffee workers' lung
Fish-meal workers' lung
Furriers' lung
Grain-handlers' disease or lung
Pituitary snuff-takers' disease
Sequoiosis or red-cedar asthma
Wood asthma
CC Excl: See code 495.0

495.9 Unspecified allergic alveolitis and pneumonitis CC
Alveolitis, allergic (extrinsic)
Hypersensitivity pneumonitis
CC Excl: See code 495.0

496 Chronic airway obstruction, not elsewhere classified CC
Note: This code is not to be used with any code from categories 491-493
Chronic:
nonspecific lung disease
obstructive lung disease
obstructive pulmonary disease [COPD] NOS
EXCLUDES *chronic obstructive lung disease [COPD] specified (as) (with):*
allergic alveolitis (495.0-495.9)
asthma (493.20-493.22)
bronchiectasis (494.0-494.1)
bronchitis (491.20-491.22)
with emphysema (491.20-491.22)
▶*decompensated (491.21)*◀
emphysema (492.0-492.8)
CC Excl: 017.90-017.96, 487.1, 494.0-494.1, 496, 506.1, 506.4, 506.9, 748.61
AHA: 4Q, '03, 109; 2Q, '00, 15; 2Q, '92, 16; 2Q, '91, 21; 3Q, '88, 56

PNEUMOCONIOSES AND OTHER LUNG DISEASES DUE TO EXTERNAL AGENTS (500-508)

DEF: Permanent deposits of particulate matter, within lungs; due to occupational or environmental exposure; results in chronic induration and fibrosis. (See specific listings in 500-508 code range)

500 Coal workers' pneumoconiosis A
Anthracosilicosis
Anthracosis
Black lung disease
Coal workers' lung
Miner's asthma

501 Asbestosis A

502 Pneumoconiosis due to other silica or silicates
Pneumoconiosis due to talc
Silicotic fibrosis (massive) of lung
Silicosis (simple) (complicated)

503 Pneumoconiosis due to other inorganic dust
Aluminosis (of lung)
Baritosis
Bauxite fibrosis (of lung)
Berylliosis
Graphite fibrosis (of lung)
Siderosis
Stannosis

504 Pneumonopathy due to inhalation of other dust
Byssinosis
Cannabinosis
Flax-dressers' disease
EXCLUDES *allergic alveolitis (495.0-495.9)*
asbestosis (501)
bagassosis (495.1)
farmers' lung (495.0)

505 Pneumoconiosis, unspecified

✓4th **506 Respiratory conditions due to chemical fumes and vapors**
Use additional E code to identify cause

506.0 Bronchitis and pneumonitis due to fumes and vapors CC
Chemical bronchitis (acute)
CC Excl: 011.00-011.96, 012.10-012.16, 012.80-012.86, 017.90-017.96, 021.2, 031.0, 039.1, 115.05, 115.15, 115.95, 122.1, 130.4, 136.3, 480.0-408.2, 480.8-487.1, 494.0-508.9, 517.1, 517.8, 518.89, 519.8-519.9, 748.61

506.1 Acute pulmonary edema due to fumes and vapors CC
Chemical pulmonary edema (acute)
EXCLUDES *acute pulmonary edema NOS (518.4)*
chronic or unspecified pulmonary edema (514)
CC Excl: See code 506.0
AHA: 3Q, '88, 4

506.2 Upper respiratory inflammation due to fumes and vapors
AHA: 3Q, '05, 10

506.3 Other acute and subacute respiratory conditions due to fumes and vapors

506.4 Chronic respiratory conditions due to fumes and vapors
Emphysema (diffuse) (chronic)
Obliterative bronchiolitis (chronic) (subacute)
Pulmonary fibrosis (chronic)
} due to inhalation of chemical fumes and vapors

506.9 Unspecified respiratory conditions due to fumes and vapors
Silo-fillers' disease

✓4th **507 Pneumonitis due to solids and liquids**
EXCLUDES *fetal aspiration pneumonitis (770.18)*
AHA: 3Q, '91, 16

507.0 Due to inhalation of food or vomitus CC MC
Aspiration pneumonia (due to):
NOS
food (regurgitated)
gastric secretions
milk
saliva
vomitus
CC Excl: See code 506.0
AHA: 1Q, '89, 10
DRG 079 and 475

507.1 Due to inhalation of oils and essences CC MC
Lipoid pneumonia (exogenous)
EXCLUDES *endogenous lipoid pneumonia (516.8)*
CC Excl: See code 506.0

507.8 Due to other solids and liquids CC MC
Detergent asthma
CC Excl: See code 506.0

✓4th **508 Respiratory conditions due to other and unspecified external agents**
Use additional E code to identify cause

508.0 Acute pulmonary manifestations due to radiation CC
Radiation pneumonitis
CC Excl: See code 506.0
AHA: 2Q, '88, 4

508.1 Chronic and other pulmonary manifestations due to radiation CC
Fibrosis of lung following radiation
CC Excl: See code 506.0

508.8 Respiratory conditions due to other specified external agents

508.9 Respiratory conditions due to unspecified external agent

OTHER DISEASES OF RESPIRATORY SYSTEM (510-519)

✓4th **510 Empyema**

Use additional code to identify infectious organism (041.0-041.9)

EXCLUDES *abscess of lung (513.0)*

DEF: Purulent infection; within pleural space.

510.0 With fistula CC

Fistula:
- bronchocutaneous
- bronchopleural
- hepatopleural
- mediastinal
- pleural
- thoracic

Any condition classifiable to 510.9 with fistula

CC Excl: 510.0-510.9, 517.8, 518.89, 519.8-519.9

DEF: Purulent infection of respiratory cavity; with communication from cavity to another structure.

510.9 Without mention of fistula CC

Abscess:
- pleura
- thorax

Empyema (chest) (lung) (pleura)

Fibrinopurulent pleurisy

Pleurisy:
- purulent
- septic
- seropurulent
- suppurative

Pyopneumothorax

Pyothorax

CC Excl: See code 510.0

AHA: 3Q, '94, 6

✓4th **511 Pleurisy**

EXCLUDES *malignant pleural effusion (197.2)*
pleurisy with mention of tuberculosis, current disease (012.0)

DEF: Inflammation of serous membrane of lungs and lining of thoracic cavity; causes exudation in cavity or membrane surface.

511.0 Without mention of effusion or current tuberculosis

Adhesion, lung or pleura

Calcification of pleura

Pleurisy (acute) (sterile):
- diaphragmatic
- fibrinous
- interlobar

Pleurisy:
- NOS
- pneumococcal
- staphylococcal
- streptococcal

Thickening of pleura

AHA: 3Q, '94, 5

511.1 With effusion, with mention of a bacterial cause other than tuberculosis CC

Pleurisy with effusion (exudative) (serous):
- pneumococcal
- staphylococcal
- streptococcal
- other specified nontuberculous bacterial cause

CC Excl: 011.00-012.16, 012.80-012.86, 017.90-017.96, 511.0-511.9, 517.8, 518.89, 519.8-519.9

511.8 Other specified forms of effusion, except tuberculous CC

Encysted pleurisy

Hemopneumothorax

Hemothorax

Hydropneumothorax

Hydrothorax

EXCLUDES *traumatic (860.2-860.5, 862.29, 862.39)*

CC Excl: See code 511.1

AHA: 1Q, '97, 10

511.9 Unspecified pleural effusion CC

Pleural effusion NOS

Pleurisy:
- exudative
- serofibrinous
- serous
- with effusion NOS

CC Excl: See code 511.1

AHA: 2Q, '03, 7; 3Q, '91, 19; 4Q, '89, 11

✓4th **512 Pneumothorax**

DEF: Collapsed lung; due to gas or air in pleural space.

512.0 Spontaneous tension pneumothorax CC

CC Excl: 512.0-512.1, 512.8, 517.8, 518.89, 519.8-519.9

AHA: 3Q, '94, 5

DEF: Leaking air from lung into lining causing collapse.

512.1 Iatrogenic pneumothorax CC

Postoperative pneumothorax

CC Excl: See code 512.0

AHA: 4Q, '94, 40

DEF: Air trapped in the lining of the lung following surgery.

512.8 Other spontaneous pneumothorax CC

Pneumothorax:
- NOS
- acute
- chronic

EXCLUDES *pneumothorax:*
congenital (770.2)
traumatic (860.0-860.1, 860.4-860.5)
tuberculous, current disease (011.7)

CC Excl: See code 512.0

AHA: 2Q, '93, 3

✓4th **513 Abscess of lung and mediastinum**

513.0 Abscess of lung CC

Abscess (multiple) of lung

Gangrenous or necrotic pneumonia

Pulmonary gangrene or necrosis

CC Excl: 006.4, 011.00-012.16, 012.80-012.86, 017.90-017.96, 513.0, 519.8-519.9

AHA: 2Q, '98, 7

513.1 Abscess of mediastinum CC

CC Excl: 513.1, 519.8-519.9

514 Pulmonary congestion and hypostasis

Hypostatic:
- bronchopneumonia
- pneumonia

Passive pneumonia

Pulmonary congestion (chronic) (passive)

Pulmonary edema:
- NOS
- chronic

EXCLUDES *acute pulmonary edema:*
NOS (518.4)
with mention of heart disease or failure (428.1)
▶*hypostatic pneumonia due to or specified as a specific type of pneumonia—code to the type of pneumonia (480.0-480.9, 481, 482.0-482.49, 483.0-483.8, 485, 486, 487.0)*◀

AHA: 2Q, '98, 6; 3Q, '88, 5

DEF: Excessive retention of interstitial fluid in the lungs and pulmonary vessels; due to poor circulation.

515 Postinflammatory pulmonary fibrosis CC

Cirrhosis of lung
Fibrosis of lung (atrophic) (confluent) (massive) (perialveolar) (peribronchial)
Induration of lung
} chronic or unspecified

CC Excl: 011.00-012.16, 012.80-012.86, 017.90-017.96, 494.0-508.9, 515-517, 517.2, 517.8, 518.89, 519.8-519.9, 748.61

DEF: Fibrosis and scarring of the lungs due to inflammatory reaction.

✓4th **516 Other alveolar and parietoalveolar pneumonopathy**

516.0 Pulmonary alveolar proteinosis CC

CC Excl: See code 515

DEF: Reduced ventilation; due to proteinaceous deposits on alveoli; symptoms include dyspnea, cough, chest pain, weakness, weight loss, and hemoptysis.

516.1 Idiopathic pulmonary hemosiderosis CC

Code first underlying disease (275.0)
Essential brown induration of lung

CC Excl: See code 515

DEF: Fibrosis of alveolar walls; marked by abnormal amounts hemosiderin in lungs; primarily affects children; symptoms include anemia, fluid in lungs, and blood in sputum; etiology unknown.

516.2 Pulmonary alveolar microlithiasis CC

CC Excl: See code 515

DEF: Small calculi in pulmonary alveoli resembling sand-like particles on x-ray.

516.3 Idiopathic fibrosing alveolitis CC

Alveolar capillary block
Diffuse (idiopathic) (interstitial) pulmonary fibrosis
Hamman-Rich syndrome

CC Excl: See code 515

516.8 Other specified alveolar and parietoalveolar pneumonopathies CC

Endogenous lipoid pneumonia
Interstitial pneumonia (desquamative) (lymphoid)

EXCLUDES *lipoid pneumonia, exogenous or unspecified (507.1)*

CC Excl: See code 515

AHA: 1Q, '92, 12

516.9 Unspecified alveolar and parietoalveolar pneumonopathy CC

CC Excl: See code 515

✓4th **517 Lung involvement in conditions classified elsewhere**

EXCLUDES *rheumatoid lung (714.81)*

517.1 Rheumatic pneumonia CC

Code first underlying disease (390)

CC Excl: 011.00-012.16, 012.80-012.86, 017.90-017.96, 480.0-480.2, 480.8-487.1, 494.0-508.9, 515-517.8, 518.89, 519.8-519.9, 748.61

517.2 Lung involvement in systemic sclerosis CC

Code first underlying disease (710.1)

CC Excl: 011.00-012.16, 012.80-012.86, 017.90-017.96, 494.0-508.9, 515-517, 517.2, 517.8, 518.89, 519.8-519.9, 748.61

517.3 Acute chest syndrome

Code first sickle-cell disease in crisis (282.42, 282.62, 282.64, 282.69)

AHA: 4Q, '03, 51, 56

517.8 Lung involvement in other diseases classified elsewhere CC

Code first underlying disease, as:
amyloidosis ▶(277.30-277.39)◀
polymyositis (710.4)
sarcoidosis (135)
Sjögren's disease (710.2)
systemic lupus erythematosus (710.0)

EXCLUDES *syphilis (095.1)*

CC Excl: See code 517.2

AHA: 2Q, '03, 7

✓4th **518 Other diseases of lung**

518.0 Pulmonary collapse CC MC

Atelectasis
Collapse of lung
Middle lobe syndrome

EXCLUDES *atelectasis:*
congenital (partial) (770.5)
primary (770.4)
tuberculous, current disease (011.8)

CC Excl: 518.0, 519.8-519.9

AHA: 4Q, '90, 25

518.1 Interstitial emphysema CC

Mediastinal emphysema

EXCLUDES *surgical (subcutaneous) emphysema (998.81)*
that in fetus or newborn (770.2)
traumatic emphysema (958.7)

CC Excl: 518.1, 519.8-519.9

DEF: Escaped air from the alveoli trapped in the interstices of the lung; trauma or cough may cause the disease.

518.2 Compensatory emphysema

DEF: Distention of all or part of the lung caused by disease processes or surgical intervention that decreased volume in another part of the lung; overcompensation reaction to the loss of capacity in another part of the lung.

518.3 Pulmonary eosinophilia

Eosinophilic asthma
Löffler's syndrome
Pneumonia:
allergic
eosinophilic
Tropical eosinophilia

DEF: Infiltration, into pulmonary parenchyma of eosinophilia; results in cough, fever, and dyspnea.

518.4 Acute edema of lung, unspecified CC

Acute pulmonary edema NOS
Pulmonary edema, postoperative

EXCLUDES *pulmonary edema:*
acute, with mention of heart disease or failure (428.1)
chronic or unspecified (514)
due to external agents (506.0-508.9)

CC Excl: 398.91, 428.0-428.9, 518.4, 519.8-519.9

DEF: Severe, sudden fluid retention within lung tissues.

518.5 Pulmonary insufficiency following trauma and surgery CC MC
Adult respiratory distress syndrome
Pulmonary insufficiency following:
shock
surgery
trauma
Shock lung
EXCLUDES *adult respiratory distress syndrome associated with other conditions (518.82)*
pneumonia:
aspiration (507.0)
hypostatic (514)
respiratory failure in other conditions (518.81, 518.83-518.84)
CC Excl: 518.5, 519.8-519.9
AHA: 4Q, '04, 139; 3Q, '88, 3; 3Q, '88, 7; S-O, '87, 1

518.6 Allergic bronchopulmonary aspergillosis CC
CC Excl: 518.6, 519.8-519.9
AHA: 4Q, '97, 39
DEF: Noninvasive hypersensitive reaction; due to allergic reaction to *Aspergillus fumigatus* (mold).

● **518.7 Transfusion related acute lung injury [TRALI]** CC
CC Excl: 518.7, 997.3, 997.91-997.99, 998.81, 998.83-998.9

✓5th **518.8 Other diseases of lung**

518.81 Acute respiratory failure CC MC
Respiratory failure NOS
EXCLUDES *acute and chronic respiratory failure (518.84)*
acute respiratory distress (518.82)
chronic respiratory failure (518.83)
respiratory arrest (799.1)
respiratory failure, newborn (770.84)
CC Excl: 518.81-518.89, 519.8-519.9, 799.1
AHA: 4Q, '05, 96; 2Q, '05, 19; 1Q, '05, 3-8; 1Q, '05, 3–8; 4Q, '04, 139; 1Q, '03, 15; 4Q, '98, 41; 3Q, '91, 14; 2Q, '91, 3; 4Q, '90, 25; 2Q, '90, 20; 3Q, '88, 7; 3Q, '88, 10; S-O, '87, 1
DRG 087 and 475

518.82 Other pulmonary insufficiency, not elsewhere classified CC
Acute respiratory distress
Acute respiratory insufficiency
Adult respiratory distress syndrome NEC
EXCLUDES *adult respiratory distress syndrome associated with trauma and surgery (518.5)*
pulmonary insufficiency following trauma and surgery (518.5)
respiratory distress:
NOS (786.09)
newborn (770.89)
syndrome, newborn (769)
shock lung (518.5)
CC Excl: See code 518.81
AHA: 4Q, '03, 105; 2Q, '91, 21; 3Q, '88, 7

518.83 Chronic respiratory failure CC MC
CC Excl: See code 518.81
AHA: 4Q, '05, 96; 4Q, '03, 103, 111

518.84 Acute and chronic respiratory failure CC MC
Acute on chronic respiratory failure
CC Excl: See code 518.81
DRG 087 and 475

518.89 Other diseases of lung, not elsewhere classified
Broncholithiasis
Calcification of lung
Lung disease NOS
Pulmolithiasis
AHA: 3Q, '90, 18; 4Q, '88, 6
DEF: Broncholithiasis: calculi in lumen of transbronchial tree.
DEF: Pulmolithiasis: calculi in lung.

✓4th **519 Other diseases of respiratory system**

✓5th **519.0 Tracheostomy complications**

519.00 Tracheostomy complication, unspecified CC
CC Excl: 519.00-519.19, 519.8-519.9

519.01 Infection of tracheostomy CC
Use additional code to identify type of infection, such as:
abscess or cellulitis of neck (682.1)
septicemia (038.0-038.9)
Use additional code to identify organism (041.00-041.9)
CC Excl: See code 519.00
AHA: 4Q, '98, 41

519.02 Mechanical complication of tracheostomy CC
Tracheal stenosis due to tracheostomy
CC Excl: See code 519.00

519.09 Other tracheostomy complications CC
Hemorrhage due to tracheostomy
Tracheoesophageal fistula due to tracheostomy
CC Excl: See code 519.00

✓5th **519.1 Other diseases of trachea and bronchus, not elsewhere classified**
AHA: 3Q, '02, 18; 3Q, '88, 6

● **519.11 Acute bronchospasm**
Bronchospasm NOS
EXCLUDES *acute bronchitis with bronchospasm (466.0)*
asthma (493.00-493.92)
exercise induced bronchospasm (493.81)

● **519.19 Other diseases of trachea and bronchus**
Calcification, Stenosis, Ulcer } of bronchus or trachea

519.2 Mediastinitis CC
CC Excl: 519.2-519.3, 519.8-519.9
DEF: Inflammation of tissue between organs behind sternum.

519.3 Other diseases of mediastinum, not elsewhere classified
Fibrosis, Hernia, Retraction } of mediastinum

519.4 Disorders of diaphragm
Diaphragmitis
Paralysis of diaphragm
Relaxation of diaphragm
EXCLUDES *congenital defect of diaphragm (756.6)*
diaphragmatic hernia (551-553 with .3)
congenital (756.6)

519.8 Other diseases of respiratory system, not elsewhere classified
AHA: 4Q, '89, 12

519.9 Unspecified disease of respiratory system
Respiratory disease (chronic) NOS

9. DISEASES OF THE DIGESTIVE SYSTEM (520-579)

DISEASES OF ORAL CAVITY, SALIVARY GLANDS, AND JAWS (520-529)

✓4th **520 Disorders of tooth development and eruption**

520.0 Anodontia
Absence of teeth (complete) (congenital) (partial)
Hypodontia
Oligodontia
EXCLUDES *acquired absence of teeth (525.10-525.19)*

520.1 Supernumerary teeth
Distomolar
Fourth molar
Mesiodens
Paramolar
Supplemental teeth
EXCLUDES *supernumerary roots (520.2)*

520.2 Abnormalities of size and form
Concrescence } of teeth
Fusion } of teeth
Gemination } of teeth

Dens evaginatus
Dens in dente
Dens invaginatus
Enamel pearls
Macrodontia
Microdontia
Peg-shaped [conical] teeth
Supernumerary roots
Taurodontism
Tuberculum paramolare
EXCLUDES *that due to congenital syphilis (090.5)*
tuberculum Carabelli, which is regarded as a normal variation

520.3 Mottled teeth
Mottling of enamel
Dental fluorosis
Nonfluoride enamel opacities

Digestive System

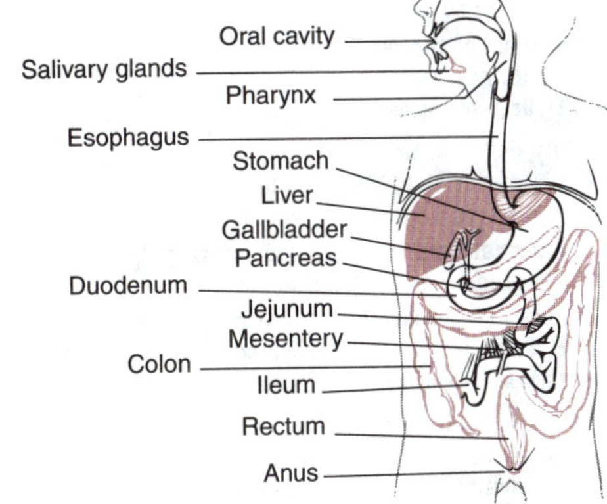

The Oral Cavity

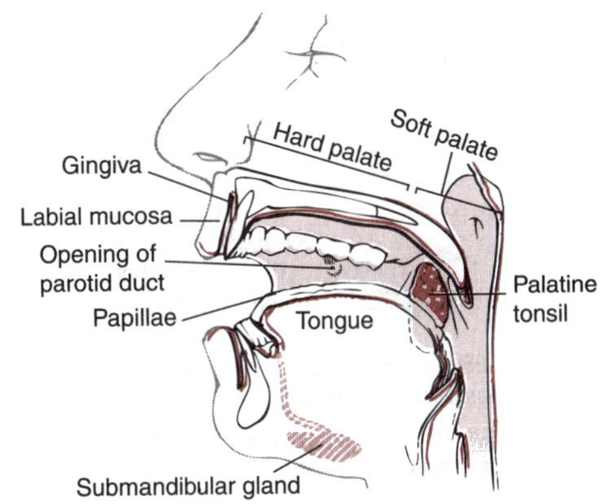

Teeth

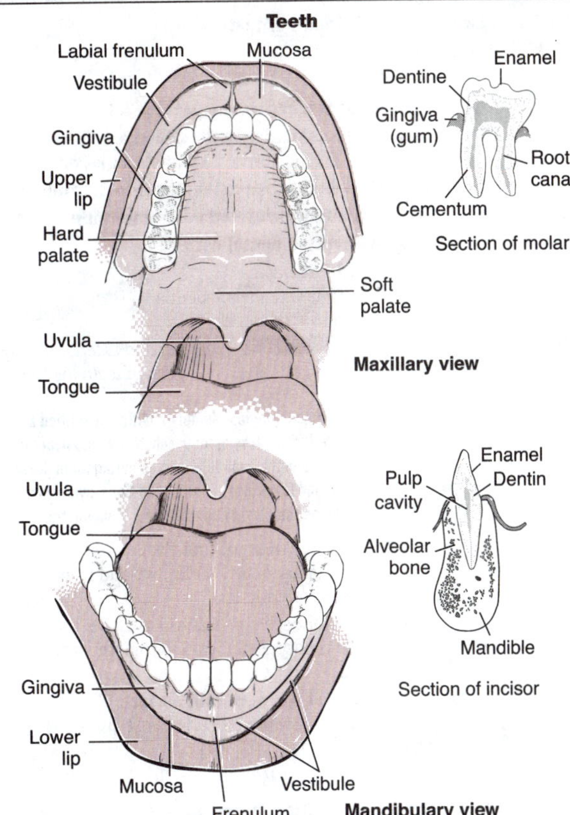

520.4 Disturbances of tooth formation
Aplasia and hypoplasia of cementum
Dilaceration of tooth
Enamel hypoplasia (neonatal) (postnatal) (prenatal)
Horner's teeth
Hypocalcification of teeth
Regional odontodysplasia
Turner's tooth
EXCLUDES *Hutchinson's teeth and mulberry molars in congenital syphilis (090.5)*
mottled teeth (520.3)

520.5 Hereditary disturbances in tooth structure, not elsewhere classified
Amelogenesis } imperfecta
Dentinogenesis } imperfecta
Odontogenesis } imperfecta

Dentinal dysplasia
Shell teeth

520.6 Disturbances in tooth eruption
Teeth:
- embedded
- impacted
- natal
- neonatal
- ▶prenatal◀
- primary [deciduous]:
  - persistent
  - shedding, premature

Tooth eruption:
- late
- obstructed
- premature

EXCLUDES *exfoliation of teeth (attributable to disease of surrounding tissues) (525.0-525.19)*

AHA: ▶1Q, '06, 18;◀ 2Q, '05, 15

520.7 Teething syndrome

520.8 Other specified disorders of tooth development and eruption
Color changes during tooth formation
Pre-eruptive color changes
EXCLUDES *posteruptive color changes (521.7)*

520.9 Unspecified disorder of tooth development and eruption

✓4th **521 Diseases of hard tissues of teeth**

✓5th **521.0 Dental caries**
AHA: 4Q, '01, 44

521.00 Dental caries, unspecified

521.01 Dental caries limited to enamel
Initial caries
White spot lesion

521.02 Dental caries extending into dentine

521.03 Dental caries extending into pulp

521.04 Arrested dental caries

521.05 Odontoclasia
Infantile melanodontia
Melanodontoclasia
EXCLUDES *internal and external resorption of teeth (521.40-521.49)*
DEF: A pathological dental condition described as stained areas, loss of tooth substance, and hypoplasia linked to nutritional deficiencies during tooth development and to cariogenic oral conditions; synonyms are melanodontoclasia and infantile melanodontia.

521.06 Dental caries pit and fissure
▶Primary dental caries, pit and fissure origin◀

521.07 Dental caries of smooth surface
▶Primary dental caries, smooth surface origin◀

521.08 Dental caries of root surface
▶Primary dental caries, root surface◀

521.09 Other dental caries
AHA: 3Q, '02, 14

✓5th **521.1 Excessive attrition (approximal wear) (occlusal wear)**

521.10 Excessive attrition, unspecified

521.11 Excessive attrition, limited to enamel

521.12 Excessive attrition, extending into dentine

521.13 Excessive attrition, extending into pulp

521.14 Excessive attrition, localized

521.15 Excessive attrition, generalized

✓5th **521.2 Abrasion**
Abrasion:
dentifrice
habitual
occupational
ritual
traditional
Wedge defect NOS
} of teeth

521.20 Abrasion, unspecified

521.21 Abrasion, limited to enamel

521.22 Abrasion, extending into dentine

521.23 Abrasion, extending into pulp

521.24 Abrasion, localized

521.25 Abrasion, generalized

✓5th **521.3 Erosion**
Erosion of teeth:
NOS
due to:
medicine
persistent vomiting
Erosion of teeth:
idiopathic
occupational

521.30 Erosion, unspecified

521.31 Erosion, limited to enamel

521.32 Erosion, extending into dentine

521.33 Erosion, extending into pulp

521.34 Erosion, localized

521.35 Erosion, generalized

✓5th **521.4 Pathological resorption**
DEF: Loss of dentin and cementum due to disease process.

521.40 Pathological resorption, unspecified

521.41 Pathological resorption, internal

521.42 Pathological resorption, external

521.49 Other pathological resorption
Internal granuloma of pulp

521.5 Hypercementosis
Cementation hyperplasia
DEF: Excess deposits of cementum, on tooth root.Primary dental caries, root surface

521.6 Ankylosis of teeth
DEF: Adhesion of tooth to surrounding bone.

521.7 Intrinsic posteruptive color changes
Staining [discoloration] of teeth:
NOS
due to:
drugs
metals
pulpal bleeding
EXCLUDES *accretions [deposits] on teeth (523.6)*
extrinsic color changes (523.6)
pre-eruptive color changes (520.8)

✓5th **521.8 Other specified diseases of hard tissues of teeth**

● **521.81 Cracked tooth**
EXCLUDES *asymptomatic craze lines in enamel—omit code*
broken tooth due to trauma (873.63, 873.73)
fractured tooth due to trauma (873.63, 873.73)

● **521.89 Other specified diseases of hard tissues of teeth**
Irradiated enamel
Sensitive dentin

521.9 Unspecified disease of hard tissues of teeth

✓4th **522 Diseases of pulp and periapical tissues**

522.0 Pulpitis
Pulpal:
abscess
polyp
Pulpitis:
acute
Pulpitis:
chronic (hyperplastic) (ulcerative)
suppurative

522.1 Necrosis of the pulp
Pulp gangrene
DEF: Death of pulp tissue.

522.2 Pulp degeneration
Denticles
Pulp calcifications
Pulp stones

522.3 Abnormal hard tissue formation in pulp
Secondary or irregular dentin

522.4 Acute apical periodontitis of pulpal origin
DEF: Severe inflammation of periodontal ligament due to pulpal inflammation or necrosis.

522.5 Periapical abscess without sinus
Abscess:
dental
Abscess:
dentoalveolar
EXCLUDES *periapical abscess with sinus (522.7)*

522.6 Chronic apical periodontitis
Apical or periapical granuloma
Apical periodontitis NOS

522.7 Periapical abscess with sinus
Fistula:
alveolar process
Fistula:
dental

522.8 Radicular cyst
Cyst:
apical (periodontal)
periapical
Cyst:
radiculodental
residual radicular
EXCLUDES *lateral developmental or lateral periodontal cyst (526.0)*
DEF: Cyst in tissue around tooth apex due to chronic infection of granuloma around root.

522.9 Other and unspecified diseases of pulp and periapical tissues

4th **523 Gingival and periodontal diseases**

5th **523.0 Acute gingivitis**

EXCLUDES *acute necrotizing ulcerative gingivitis (101)*
herpetic gingivostomatitis (054.2)

● **523.00 Acute gingivitis, plaque induced**
Acute gingivitis NOS

● **523.01 Acute gingivitis, non-plaque induced**

5th **523.1 Chronic gingivitis**

Gingivitis (chronic):
desquamative
hyperplastic
simple marginal
ulcerative

EXCLUDES *herpetic gingivostomatitis (054.2)*

● **523.10 Chronic gingivitis, plaque induced**
Chronic gingivitis NOS
Gingivitis NOS

● **523.11 Chronic gingivitis, non-plaque induced**

5th **523.2 Gingival recession**

Gingival recession (postinfective) (postoperative)

523.20 Gingival recession, unspecified
523.21 Gingival recession, minimal
523.22 Gingival recession, moderate
523.23 Gingival recession, severe
523.24 Gingival recession, localized
523.25 Gingival recession, generalized

▲ 5th **523.3 Aggressive and acute periodontitis**

Acute:
pericementitis
pericoronitis

EXCLUDES *acute apical periodontitis (522.4)*
periapical abscess (522.5, 522.7)

DEF: Severe inflammation, of tissues supporting teeth.

● **523.30 Aggressive periodontitis, unspecified**
● **523.31 Aggressive periodontitis, localized**
Periodontal abscess
● **523.32 Aggressive periodontitis, generalized**
● **523.33 Acute periodontitis**

5th **523.4 Chronic periodontitis**

Chronic pericoronitis
Pericementitis (chronic)
Periodontitis:
complex
simplex
NOS

EXCLUDES *chronic apical periodontitis (522.6)*

● **523.40 Chronic periodontitis, unspecified**
● **523.41 Chronic periodontitis, localized**
● **523.42 Chronic periodontitis, generalized**

523.5 Periodontosis

523.6 Accretions on teeth

Dental calculus:
subgingival
supragingival
Deposits on teeth:
betel
materia alba
soft
tartar
tobacco
Extrinsic discoloration of teeth

EXCLUDES *intrinsic discoloration of teeth (521.7)*

DEF: Foreign material on tooth surface, usually plaque or calculus.

523.8 Other specified periodontal diseases

Giant cell:
epulis
peripheral granuloma
Gingival:
cysts
enlargement NOS
fibromatosis
Gingival polyp
Periodontal lesions due to traumatic occlusion
Peripheral giant cell granuloma

EXCLUDES *leukoplakia of gingiva (528.6)*

523.9 Unspecified gingival and periodontal disease

AHA: 3Q,'02, 14

4th **524 Dentofacial anomalies, including malocclusion**

5th **524.0 Major anomalies of jaw size**

EXCLUDES *hemifacial atrophy or hypertrophy (754.0)*
unilateral condylar hyperplasia or hypoplasia of mandible (526.89)

524.00 Unspecified anomaly
DEF: Unspecified deformity of jaw size.

524.01 Maxillary hyperplasia
DEF: Overgrowth or over development of upper jaw bone.

524.02 Mandibular hyperplasia
DEF: Overgrowth or over development of lower jaw bone.

524.03 Maxillary hypoplasia
DEF: Incomplete or underdeveloped, upper jaw bone.

524.04 Mandibular hypoplasia
DEF: Incomplete or underdeveloped, lower jaw bone.

524.05 Macrogenia
DEF: Enlarged, jaw, especially chin; affects bone, soft tissue, or both.

524.06 Microgenia
DEF: Underdeveloped mandible, characterized by an extremely small chin.

524.07 Excessive tuberosity of jaw
▶Entire maxillary tuberosity◀

524.09 Other specified anomaly

5th **524.1 Anomalies of relationship of jaw to cranial base**

524.10 Unspecified anomaly
Prognathism
Retrognathism
DEF: Prognathism: protrusion of lower jaw.
DEF: Retrognathism: jaw is located posteriorly to a normally positioned jaw; backward position of mandible.

524.11 Maxillary asymmetry
DEF: Absence of symmetry of maxilla.

524.12 Other jaw asymmetry

524.19 Other specified anomaly

5th **524.2 Anomalies of dental arch relationship**

▶Anomaly of dental arch◀

EXCLUDES *hemifacial atrophy or hypertrophy (754.0)*
soft tissue impingement (524.81-524.82)
unilateral condylar hyperplasia or hypoplasia of mandible (526.89)

524.20 Unspecified anomaly of dental arch relationship

▲ **524.21 Malocclusion, Angle's class I**
Neutro-occlusion

▲ **524.22 Malocclusion, Angle's class II**
Disto-occlusion Division I
Disto-occlusion Division II

▲ **524.23 Malocclusion, Angle's class III**
Mesio-occlusion

524.24 Open anterior occlusal relationship
▶Anterior open bite◀

524.25 Open posterior occlusal relationship
▶Posterior open bite◀

524.26 Excessive horizontal overlap
▶Excessive horizontal overjet◀

524.27 Reverse articulation
Anterior articulation
▶Crossbite◀
Posterior articulation

524.28 Anomalies of interarch distance
Excessive interarch distance
Inadequate interarch distance

524.29 Other anomalies of dental arch relationship
▶Other anomalies of dental arch◀

Digestive System

523–524.29

Angle's Classification of Malocclusion

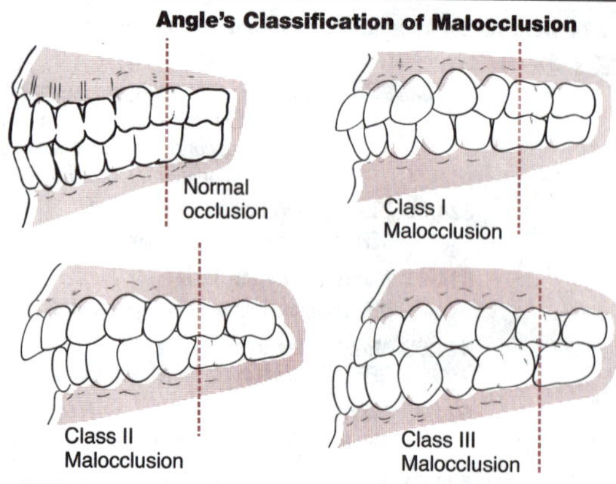

✓5th **524.3 Anomalies of tooth position of fully erupted teeth**
EXCLUDES *impacted or embedded teeth with abnormal position of such teeth or adjacent teeth (520.6)*

524.30 Unspecified anomaly of tooth position
Diastema of teeth NOS
Displacement of teeth NOS
Transposition of teeth NOS

524.31 Crowding of teeth

524.32 Excessive spacing of teeth

524.33 Horizontal displacement of teeth
▶Tipped teeth◀
Tipping of teeth

524.34 Vertical displacement of teeth
▶Extruded tooth◀
Infraeruption of teeth
▶Intruded tooth◀
Supraeruption of teeth

▲ **524.35 Rotation of tooth/teeth**

524.36 Insufficient interocclusal distance of teeth (ridge)
▶Lack of adequate intermaxillary vertical dimension◀

524.37 Excessive interocclusal distance of teeth
▶Excessive intermaxillary vertical dimension◀
Loss of occlusal vertical dimension

524.39 Other anomalies of tooth position

524.4 Malocclusion, unspecified
DEF: Malposition of top and bottom teeth; interferes with chewing.

✓5th **524.5 Dentofacial functional abnormalities**

524.50 Dentofacial functional abnormality, unspecified

524.51 Abnormal jaw closure

524.52 Limited mandibular range of motion

524.53 Deviation in opening and closing of the mandible

524.54 Insufficient anterior guidance
▶Insufficient anterior occlusal guidance◀

524.55 Centric occlusion maximum intercuspation discrepancy
▶Centric occlusion of teeth discrepancy◀

524.56 Non-working side interference
▶Balancing side interference◀

524.57 Lack of posterior occlusal support

524.59 Other dentofacial functional abnormalities
Abnormal swallowing
Mouth breathing
Sleep postures
Tongue, lip, or finger habits

✓5th **524.6 Temporomandibular joint disorders**
EXCLUDES *current temporomandibular joint: dislocation (830.0-830.1) strain (848.1)*

524.60 Temporomandibular joint disorders, unspecified
Temporomandibular joint-pain-dysfunction syndrome [TMJ]

524.61 Adhesions and ankylosis (bony or fibrous)
DEF: Stiffening or union of temporomandibular joint due to bony or fibrous union across joint.

524.62 Arthralgia of temporomandibular joint
DEF: Pain in temporomandibular joint; not inflammatory in nature.

524.63 Articular disc disorder (reducing or non-reducing)

524.64 Temporomandibular joint sounds on opening and/or closing the jaw

524.69 Other specified temporomandibular joint disorders

✓5th **524.7 Dental alveolar anomalies**

524.70 Unspecified alveolar anomaly

524.71 Alveolar maxillary hyperplasia
DEF: Excessive tissue formation in the dental alveoli of upper jaw.

524.72 Alveolar mandibular hyperplasia
DEF: Excessive tissue formation in the dental alveoli of lower jaw.

524.73 Alveolar maxillary hypoplasia
DEF: Incomplete or underdeveloped, alveolar tissue of upper jaw.

524.74 Alveolar mandibular hypoplasia
DEF: Incomplete or underdeveloped, alveolar tissue of lower jaw.

524.75 Vertical displacement of alveolus and teeth
Extrusion of alveolus and teeth

524.76 Occlusal plane deviation

524.79 Other specified alveolar anomaly

✓5th **524.8 Other specified dentofacial anomalies**

524.81 Anterior soft tissue impingement

524.82 Posterior soft tissue impingement

524.89 Other specified dentofacial anomalies

524.9 Unspecified dentofacial anomalies

✓4th **525 Other diseases and conditions of the teeth and supporting structures**

525.0 Exfoliation of teeth due to systemic causes
DEF: Deterioration of teeth and surrounding structures due to systemic disease.

✓5th **525.1 Loss of teeth due to trauma, extraction, or periodontal disease**
Code first class of edentulism (525.40-525.44, 525.50-525.54)
AHA: 4Q, '05, 74; 4Q, '01, 44

525.10 Acquired absence of teeth, unspecified
Tooth extraction status, NOS

525.11 Loss of teeth due to trauma

525.12 Loss of teeth due to periodontal disease

525.13 Loss of teeth due to caries

525.19 Other loss of teeth

✓5th **525.2 Atrophy of edentulous alveolar ridge**

525.20 Unspecified atrophy of edentulous alveolar ridge
Atrophy of the mandible NOS
Atrophy of the maxilla NOS

525.21 Minimal atrophy of the mandible

525.22 Moderate atrophy of the mandible

525.23 Severe atrophy of the mandible

525.24 Minimal atrophy of the maxilla

525.25 Moderate atrophy of the maxilla

525.26 Severe atrophy of the maxilla

525.3 Retained dental root

✓5th **525.4 Complete edentulism**
Use additional code to identify cause of edentulism (525.10-525.19)
AHA: 4Q, '05, 74

525.40 Complete edentulism, unspecified
Edentulism NOS

525.41 Complete edentulism, class I

N Newborn Age: 0 | P Pediatric Age: 0-17 | M Maternity Age: 12-55 | A Adult Age: 15-124 | CC CC Condition | MC Major Complication | CD Complex Dx | HIV HIV Related Dx

525.42 **Complete edentulism, class II**

525.43 **Complete edentulism, class III**

525.44 **Complete edentulism, class IV**

✓5th 525.5 **Partial edentulism**

Use additional code to identify cause of edentulism (525.10-525.19)

AHA: 4Q, '05, 74

525.50 **Partial edentulism, unspecified**

525.51 **Partial edentulism, class I**

525.52 **Partial edentulism, class II**

525.53 **Partial edentulism, class III**

525.54 **Partial edentulism, class IV**

● ✓5th 525.6 **Unsatisfactory restoration of tooth**

Defective bridge, crown, fillings
Defective dental restoration

EXCLUDES *dental restoration status (V45.84)*
unsatisfactory endodontic treatment (526.61-526.69)

● 525.60 **Unspecified unsatisfactory restoration of tooth**

Unspecified defective dental restoration

● 525.61 **Open restoration margins**

Dental restoration failure of marginal integrity
Open margin on tooth restoration

● 525.62 **Unrepairable overhanging of dental restorative materials**

Overhanging of tooth restoration

● 525.63 **Fractured dental restorative material without loss of material**

EXCLUDES *cracked tooth (521.81)*
fractured tooth (873.63, 873.73)

● 525.64 **Fractured dental restorative material with loss of material**

EXCLUDES *cracked tooth (521.81)*
fractured tooth (873.63, 873.73)

● 525.65 **Contour of existing restoration of tooth biologically incompatible with oral health**

Dental restoration failure of periodontal anatomical integrity
Unacceptable contours of existing restoration
Unacceptable morphology of existing restoration

● 525.66 **Allergy to existing dental restorative material**

Use additional code to identify the specific type of allergy

● 525.67 **Poor aesthetics of existing restoration**

Dental restoration aesthetically inadequate or displeasing

● 525.69 **Other unsatisfactory restoration of existing tooth**

525.8 **Other specified disorders of the teeth and supporting structures**

Enlargement of alveolar ridge NOS
Irregular alveolar process

525.9 **Unspecified disorder of the teeth and supporting structures**

✓4th **526 Diseases of the jaws**

526.0 **Developmental odontogenic cysts**

Cyst:	Cyst:
dentigerous	lateral periodontal
eruption	primordial
follicular	Keratocyst
lateral developmental	

EXCLUDES *radicular cyst (522.8)*

526.1 **Fissural cysts of jaw**

Cyst:	Cyst:
globulomaxillary	median palatal
incisor canal	nasopalatine
median anterior maxillary	palatine of papilla

EXCLUDES *cysts of oral soft tissues (528.4)*

526.2 **Other cysts of jaws**

Cyst of jaw:	Cyst of jaw:
NOS	hemorrhagic
aneurysmal	traumatic

526.3 **Central giant cell (reparative) granuloma**

EXCLUDES *peripheral giant cell granuloma (523.8)*

526.4 **Inflammatory conditions**

Abscess, Osteitis, Osteomyelitis (neonatal), Periostitis } of jaw (acute) (chronic) (suppurative)

Sequestrum of jaw bone

EXCLUDES *alveolar osteitis (526.5)*

526.5 **Alveolitis of jaw**

Alveolar osteitis
Dry socket

DEF: Inflammation, of alveoli or tooth socket.

● ✓5th 526.6 **Periradicular pathology associated with previous endodontic treatment**

● 526.61 **Perforation of root canal space**

● 526.62 **Endodontic overfill**

● 526.63 **Endodontic underfill**

● 526.69 **Other periradicular pathology associated with previous endodontic treatment**

✓5th 526.8 **Other specified diseases of the jaws**

526.81 **Exostosis of jaw**

Torus mandibularis
Torus palatinus

DEF: Spur or bony outgrowth on the jaw.

526.89 **Other**

Cherubism, Fibrous dysplasia, Latent bone cyst, Osteoradionecrosis } of jaw(s)

Unilateral condylar hyperplasia or hypoplasia of mandible

526.9 **Unspecified disease of the jaws**

✓4th **527 Diseases of the salivary glands**

527.0 **Atrophy**

DEF: Wasting away, necrosis of salivary gland tissue.

527.1 **Hypertrophy**

DEF: Overgrowth or overdeveloped salivary gland tissue.

527.2 **Sialoadenitis**

Parotitis:	Sialoangitis
NOS	Sialodochitis
allergic	
toxic	

EXCLUDES *epidemic or infectious parotitis (072.0-072.9)*
uveoparotid fever (135)

DEF: Inflammation of salivary gland.

527.3 **Abscess** CC

CC Excl: 527.0-527.9, 537.89, 537.9

527.4 **Fistula** CC

EXCLUDES *congenital fistula of salivary gland (750.24)*

CC Excl: See code 527.3

527.5 **Sialolithiasis**

Calculus, Stone } of salivary gland or duct

Sialodocholithiasis

527.6 **Mucocele**

Mucous:
extravasation cyst of salivary gland
retention cyst of salivary gland
Ranula

DEF: Dilated salivary gland cavity filled with mucous.

527.7 Disturbance of salivary secretion
Hyposecretion
Ptyalism
Sialorrhea
Xerostomia

527.8 Other specified diseases of the salivary glands
Benign lymphoepithelial lesion of salivary gland
Sialectasia
Sialosis
Stenosis } of salivary duct
Stricture } of salivary duct

527.9 Unspecified disease of the salivary glands

✓4th **528 Diseases of the oral soft tissues, excluding lesions specific for gingiva and tongue**

▲ ✓5th **528.0 Stomatitis and mucositis (ulcerative)**
EXCLUDES ▶*cellulitis and abscess of mouth (528.3)*
diphtheritic stomatitis (032.0)
epizootic stomatitis (078.4)
gingivitis (523.0-523.1)
oral thrush (112.0)
Stevens-Johnson syndrome (695.1)◀
stomatitis:
acute necrotizing ulcerative (101)
aphthous (528.2)
gangrenous (528.1)
herpetic (054.2)
Vincent's (101)

AHA: 2Q, '99, 9

DEF: Stomatitis: Inflammation of oral mucosa; labial and buccal mucosa, tongue, palate, floor of the mouth, and gingivae.

● **528.00 Stomatitis and mucositis, unspecified**
Mucositis NOS
Ulcerative mucositis NOS
Ulcerative stomatitis NOS
Vesicular stomatitis NOS

● **528.01 Mucositis (ulcerative) due to antineoplastic therapy**
Use additional E code to identify adverse effects of therapy, such as:
antineoplastic and immunosuppressive drugs (E930.7, E933.1)
radiation therapy (E879.2)

● **528.02 Mucositis (ulcerative) due to other drugs**
Use additional E code to identify drug

● **528.09 Other stomatitis and mucositis (ulcerative)**

528.1 Cancrum oris
Gangrenous stomatitis
Noma

DEF: A severely gangrenous lesion of mouth due to fusospirochetal infection; destroys buccal, labial and facial tissues; can be fatal; found primarily in debilitated and malnourished children.

528.2 Oral aphthae
Aphthous stomatitis
Canker sore
Periadenitis mucosa necrotica recurrens
Recurrent aphthous ulcer
Stomatitis herpetiformis

EXCLUDES *herpetic stomatitis (054.2)*

DEF: Small oval or round ulcers of the mouth marked by a grayish exudate and a red halo effect.

528.3 Cellulitis and abscess CC
Cellulitis of mouth (floor)
Ludwig's angina
Oral fistula

EXCLUDES *abscess of tongue (529.0)*
cellulitis or abscess of lip (528.5)
fistula (of):
dental (522.7)
lip (528.5)
gingivitis ▶*(523.00-523.11)*◀

CC Excl: 528.00-528.09, 528.3, 529.0, 529.2

528.4 Cysts
Dermoid cyst } of mouth
Epidermoid cyst } of mouth
Epstein's pearl } of mouth
Lymphoepithelial cyst } of mouth
Nasoalveolar cyst } of mouth
Nasolabial cyst } of mouth

EXCLUDES *cyst:*
gingiva (523.8)
cyst:
tongue (529.8)

528.5 Diseases of lips
Abscess } of lip(s)
Cellulitis } of lip(s)
Fistula } of lip(s)
Hypertrophy } of lip(s)
Cheilitis:
NOS
angular
Cheilodynia
Cheilosis

EXCLUDES *actinic cheilitis (692.79)*
congenital fistula of lip (750.25)
leukoplakia of lips (528.6)

AHA: S-O, '86, 10

528.6 Leukoplakia of oral mucosa, including tongue
Leukokeratosis of oral mucosa
Leukoplakia of:
gingiva
lips
tongue

EXCLUDES *carcinoma in situ (230.0, 232.0)*
leukokeratosis nicotina palati (528.79)

DEF: Thickened white patches of epithelium on mucous membranes of mouth.

✓5th **528.7 Other disturbances of oral epithelium, including tongue**
EXCLUDES *carcinoma in situ (230.0, 232.0)*
leukokeratosis NOS (702)

528.71 Minimal keratinized residual ridge mucosa
▶Minimal keratinization of alveolar ridge mucosa◀

528.72 Excessive keratinized residual ridge mucosa
▶Excessive keratinization of alveolar ridge mucosa◀

528.79 Other disturbances of oral epithelium, including tongue
Erythroplakia of mouth or tongue
Focal epithelial hyperplasia of mouth or tongue
Leukoedema of mouth or tongue
Leukokeratosis nicotina palate
▶Other oral epithelium disturbances◀

528.8 Oral submucosal fibrosis, including of tongue

528.9 Other and unspecified diseases of the oral soft tissues
Cheek and lip biting
Denture sore mouth
Denture stomatitis
Melanoplakia
Papillary hyperplasia of palate
Eosinophilic granuloma } of oral mucosa
Irritative hyperplasia } of oral mucosa
Pyogenic granuloma } of oral mucosa
Ulcer (traumatic) } of oral mucosa

✓4th **529 Diseases and other conditions of the tongue**

529.0 Glossitis
Abscess } of tongue
Ulceration (traumatic) } of tongue

EXCLUDES *glossitis:*
benign migratory (529.1)
Hunter's (529.4)
median rhomboid (529.2)
Moeller's (529.4)

529.1 Geographic tongue
Benign migratory glossitis
Glossitis areata exfoliativa

DEF: Chronic glossitis; marked by filiform papillae atrophy and inflammation; no known etiology.

529.2 Median rhomboid glossitis

DEF: A noninflammatory, congenital disease characterized by rhomboid-like lesions at the middle third of the tongue's dorsal surface.

529.3 Hypertrophy of tongue papillae
Black hairy tongue
Coated tongue
Hypertrophy of foliate papillae
Lingua villosa nigra

529.4 Atrophy of tongue papillae
Bald tongue
Glazed tongue
Glossitis:
Hunter's
Glossitis:
Moeller's
Glossodynia exfoliativa
Smooth atrophic tongue

529.5 Plicated tongue
Fissured } tongue
Furrowed } tongue
Scrotal } tongue
EXCLUDES *fissure of tongue, congenital (750.13)*
DEF: Cracks, fissures or furrows, on dorsal surface of tongue.

529.6 Glossodynia
Glossopyrosis
Painful tongue
EXCLUDES *glossodynia exfoliativa (529.4)*

529.8 Other specified conditions of the tongue
Atrophy } (of) tongue
Crenated } (of) tongue
Enlargement } (of) tongue
Hypertrophy } (of) tongue
Glossocele
Glossoptosis
EXCLUDES *erythroplasia of tongue (528.79)*
leukoplakia of tongue (528.6)
macroglossia (congenital) (750.15)
microglossia (congenital) (750.16)
oral submucosal fibrosis (528.8)

529.9 Unspecified condition of the tongue

DISEASES OF ESOPHAGUS, STOMACH, AND DUODENUM ▶(530-538)◀

4th **530 Diseases of esophagus**
EXCLUDES *esophageal varices (456.0-456.2)*

530.0 Achalasia and cardiospasm
Achalasia (of cardia)
Aperistalsis of esophagus
Megaesophagus
EXCLUDES *congenital cardiospasm (750.7)*
DEF: Failure of smooth muscle fibers to relax, at gastrointestinal junctures; such as esophagogastric sphincter when swallowing.

5th **530.1 Esophagitis**
Abscess of esophagus
Esophagitis:
NOS
chemical
Esophagitis:
peptic
postoperative
regurgitant
Use additional E code to identify cause, if induced by chemical
EXCLUDES *tuberculous esophagitis (017.8)*
AHA: 4Q, '93, 27; 1Q, '92, 17; 3Q, '91, 20

530.10 Esophagitis, unspecified
AHA: 3Q, '05, 17

530.11 Reflux esophagitis
AHA: 4Q, '95, 82
DEF: Inflammation of lower esophagus; due to regurgitated gastric acid.

530.12 Acute esophagitis
AHA: 4Q, '01, 45
DEF: An acute inflammation of the mucous lining or submucosal coat of the esophagus.

530.19 Other esophagitis
AHA: 3Q, '01, 10

5th **530.2 Ulcer of esophagus**
Ulcer of esophagus:
fungal
Ulcer of esophagus:
peptic
Ulcer of esophagus due to ingestion of:
aspirin
chemicals
medicines
Use additional E code to identify cause, if induced by chemical or drug
AHA: 4Q, '03, 63

530.20 Ulcer of esophagus without bleeding
Ulcer of esophagus NOS

530.21 Ulcer of esophagus with bleeding CC
EXCLUDES *bleeding esophageal varices (456.0, 456.20)*
CC Excl: 251.5, 456.0, 530.20-530.21, 530.7, 530.82, 530.85, 531.00-534.91, 535.01, 535.11, 535.21, 535.31, 535.41, 535.51, 535.61, 537.89-537.9, 562.02-562.03, 562.12-562.13, 569.3, 569.85, 578.0-578.9

530.3 Stricture and stenosis of esophagus
Compression of esophagus
Obstruction of esophagus
EXCLUDES *congenital stricture of esophagus (750.3)*
AHA: 2Q, '01, 4; 2Q, '97, 3; 1Q, '88, 13

530.4 Perforation of esophagus CC
Rupture of esophagus
EXCLUDES *traumatic perforation of esophagus (862.22, 862.32, 874.4-874.5)*
CC Excl: 530.4, 530.7-530.81, 530.83-530.9

530.5 Dyskinesia of esophagus
Corkscrew esophagus
Curling esophagus
Esophagospasm
Spasm of esophagus
EXCLUDES *cardiospasm (530.0)*
AHA: 1Q, '88, 13; N-D, '84, 19
DEF: Difficulty performing voluntary esophageal movements.

530.6 Diverticulum of esophagus, acquired
Diverticulum, acquired:
epiphrenic
pharyngoesophageal
pulsion
subdiaphragmatic
Diverticulum, acquired:
traction
Zenker's (hypopharyngeal)
Esophageal pouch, acquired
Esophagocele, acquired
EXCLUDES *congenital diverticulum of esophagus (750.4)*
AHA: J-F, '85, 3

530.7 Gastroesophageal laceration-hemorrhage syndrome CC
Mallory-Weiss syndrome
CC Excl: 251.5, 456.0, 530.20-530.21, 530.4, 530.7-530.85, 530.89-534.91, 535.01, 535.11, 535.21, 535.31, 535.41, 535.51, 535.61, 537.83, 562.02-562.03, 562.12-562.13, 569.3, 569.85, 578.0-578.9
DEF: Laceration of distal esophagus and proximal stomach due to vomiting, hiccups or other sustained activity.

5th **530.8 Other specified disorders of esophagus**

530.81 Esophageal reflux
Gastroesophageal reflux
EXCLUDES *reflux esophagitis (530.11)*
AHA: 2Q, '01, 4; 1Q, '95, 7; 4Q, '92, 27
DEF: Regurgitation of the gastric contents into esophagus and possibly pharynx; where aspiration may occur between the vocal cords and down into the trachea.
DRG 182

530.82 Esophageal hemorrhage CC
EXCLUDES *hemorrhage due to esophageal varices (456.0-456.2)*
CC Excl: 251.5, 456.0, 456.20, 459.89-459.9, 530.20-530.21, 530.7, 530.82, 530.85, 531.00-534.91, 535.01, 535.11, 535.21, 535.31, 535.41, 535.51, 535.61, 537.83, 562.02-562.03, 562.12-562.13, 569.3, 569.85, 578.0-578.9
AHA: 1Q, '05, 17

Esophagus

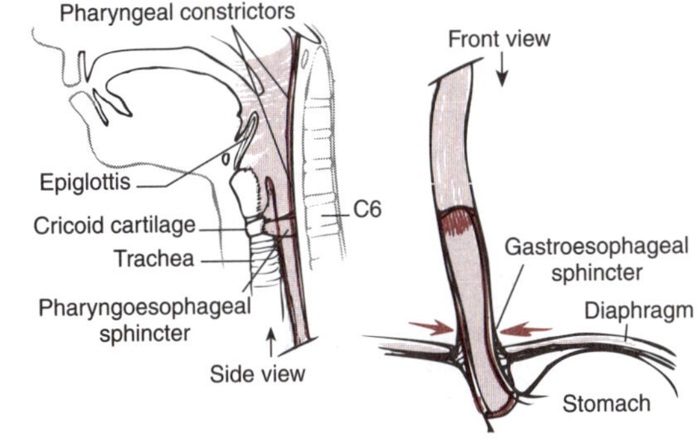

530.83 **Esophageal leukoplakia**

530.84 **Tracheoesophageal fistula** CC
EXCLUDES *congenital tracheoesophageal fistula (750.3)*
CC Excl: 530.4, 530.7, 530.81, 530.83-530.9

530.85 **Barrett's esophagus**
AHA: 4Q, '03, 63
DEF: A metaplastic disorder in which specialized columnar epithelial cells replace the normal squamous epithelial cells; an acquired condition secondary to chronic gastroesophageal reflux damage to the mucosa; associated with increased risk of developing adenocarcinoma.

530.86 **Infection of esophagostomy** CC
Use additional code to specify infection
CC Excl: 530.86-530.87, 536.40-536.49, 997.4, 997.91-997.99, 998.81, 998.83-998.9

530.87 **Mechanical complication of esophagostomy** CC
Malfunction of esophagostomy
CC Excl: See code 530.8

530.89 **Other**
EXCLUDES *Paterson-Kelly syndrome (280.8)*

530.9 **Unspecified disorder of esophagus**

4th **531 Gastric ulcer**
INCLUDES ulcer (peptic):
prepyloric
pylorus
stomach
Use additional E code to identify drug, if drug-induced
EXCLUDES *peptic ulcer NOS (533.0-533.9)*

The following fifth-digit subclassification is for use with category 531:
0 without mention of obstruction
1 with obstruction

AHA: 1Q, '91, 15; 4Q, '90, 27
DEF: Destruction of tissue in lumen of stomach due to action of gastric acid and pepsin on gastric mucosa decreasing resistance to ulcers.

5th 531.0 **Acute with hemorrhage** CC
CC Excl: 251.5, 456.0, 530.20-530.21, 530.7, 530.82, 530.85, 531.00-534.91, 535.01, 535.11, 535.21, 535.31, 535.41, 535.51, 535.61, 537.83, 537.89, 537.9, 562.02-562.03, 562.12-562.13, 569.3, 569.85, 578.0-578.9
AHA: N-D, '84, 15

5th 531.1 **Acute with perforation** CC
CC Excl: See code 531.0

5th 531.2 **Acute with hemorrhage and perforation** CC
CC Excl: See code 531.0

5th 531.3 **Acute without mention of hemorrhage or perforation** CC 1
CC Excl: For code 531.31: see code 531.0

5th 531.4 **Chronic or unspecified with hemorrhage** CC
CC Excl: See code 531.0
AHA: 4Q, '90, 22
DRG 174 For code 531.40

5th 531.5 **Chronic or unspecified with perforation** CC
CC Excl: See code 531.0

Stomach

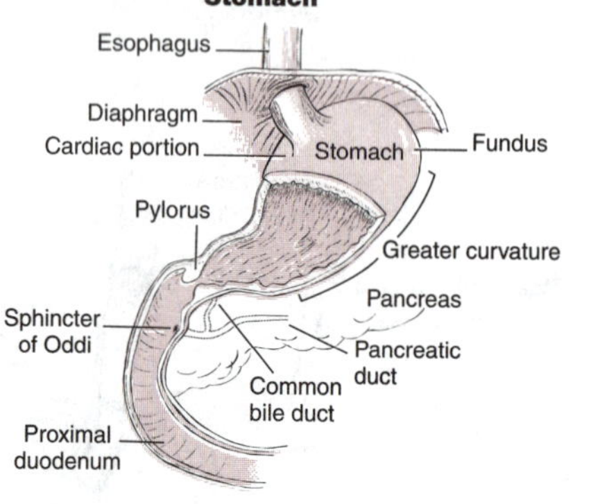

5th 531.6 **Chronic or unspecified with hemorrhage and perforation** CC
CC Excl: See code 531.0

5th 531.7 **Chronic without mention of hemorrhage or perforation** CC 1
CC Excl: For code 531.71: see code 531.0

5th 531.9 **Unspecified as acute or chronic, without mention of hemorrhage or perforation** CC 1
CC Excl: For code 531.91: see code 531.0

4th **532 Duodenal ulcer**
INCLUDES erosion (acute) of duodenum
ulcer (peptic):
duodenum
postpyloric
Use additional E code to identify drug, if drug-induced
EXCLUDES *peptic ulcer NOS (533.0-533.9)*

The following fifth-digit subclassification is for use with category 532:
0 without mention of obstruction
1 with obstruction

AHA: 4Q, '90, 27; 1Q, '91, 15
DEF: Ulcers in duodenum due to action of gastric acid and pepsin on mucosa decreasing resistance to ulcers.

5th 532.0 **Acute with hemorrhage** CC
CC Excl: 251.5, 456.0, 530.20-530-21, 530.7, 530.82, 530.85, 531.00-534.91, 535.01, 535.11, 535.21, 535.31, 535.41, 535.51, 535.61, 537.3, 537.83, 537.89, 537.9, 562.02-562.03, 562.12-562.13, 569.3, 569.85, 578.0-578.9
AHA: 4Q, '90, 22

5th 532.1 **Acute with perforation** CC
CC Excl: See code 532.0

5th 532.2 **Acute with hemorrhage and perforation** CC
CC Excl: See code 532.0

5th 532.3 **Acute without mention of hemorrhage or perforation** CC 1
CC Excl: For code 532.31: See code 532.0

5th 532.4 **Chronic or unspecified with hemorrhage** CC
CC Excl: See code 532.0
DRG 174 For code 532.40

5th 532.5 **Chronic or unspecified with perforation** CC
CC Excl: See code 532.0

5th 532.6 **Chronic or unspecified with hemorrhage and perforation** CC
CC Excl: See code 532.0

5th 532.7 **Chronic without mention of hemorrhage or perforation** CC 1
CC Excl: For code 532.71: See code 532.0

5th 532.9 **Unspecified as acute or chronic, without mention of hemorrhage or perforation** CC 1
CC Excl: For code 532.91: See code 532.0

4th **533 Peptic ulcer, site unspecified**
INCLUDES gastroduodenal ulcer NOS
peptic ulcer NOS
stress ulcer NOS
Use additional E code to identify drug, if drug-induced
EXCLUDES *peptic ulcer:*
duodenal (532.0-532.9)
gastric (531.0-531.9)

The following fifth-digit subclassification is for use with category 533:
0 without mention of obstruction
1 with obstruction

AHA: 1Q, '91, 15; 4Q, '90, 27
DEF: Ulcer of mucous membrane of esophagus, stomach or duodenum due to gastric acid secretion.

5th 533.0 **Acute with hemorrhage** CC
CC Excl: See code 532.0

5th 533.1 **Acute with perforation** CC
CC Excl: See code 532.0

§ ✓5th 533.2 **Acute with hemorrhage and perforation** CC
CC Excl: See code 532.0

§ ✓5th 533.3 **Acute without mention of hemorrhage and perforation** CC 1
CC Excl: For code 533.31: See code 532.0

§ ✓5th 533.4 **Chronic or unspecified with hemorrhage** CC
CC Excl: See code 532.0

§ ✓5th 533.5 **Chronic or unspecified with perforation** CC
CC Excl: See code 532.0

§ ✓5th 533.6 **Chronic or unspecified with hemorrhage and perforation** CC
CC Excl: See code 532.0

§ ✓5th 533.7 **Chronic without mention of hemorrhage or perforation** CC 1
CC Excl: For code 533.71: See code 532.0
AHA: 2Q, '89, 16

§ ✓5th 533.9 **Unspecified as acute or chronic, without mention of hemorrhage or perforation** CC 1
CC Excl: For code 533.91: See code 532.0

✓4th **534 Gastrojejunal ulcer**

INCLUDES ulcer (peptic) or erosion:
anastomotic
gastrocolic
gastrointestinal
gastrojejunal

ulcer (peptic) or erosion:
jejunal
marginal
stomal

EXCLUDES *primary ulcer of small intestine (569.82)*

The following fifth-digit subclassification is for use with category 534:
0 without mention of obstruction
1 with obstruction

AHA: 1Q, '91, 15; 4Q, '90, 27

✓5th 534.0 **Acute with hemorrhage** CC
CC Excl: 251.5, 456.0, 530.20-530.21, 530.7, 530.82, 530.85, 531.00-534.91, 535.01, 535.11, 535.21, 535.31, 535.41, 535.51, 535.61, 537.83, 537.89, 537.9, 562.02-562.03, 562.12-562.13, 569.3, 569.85, 578.0-578.9

✓5th 534.1 **Acute with perforation** CC
CC Excl: See code 534.0

✓5th 534.2 **Acute with hemorrhage and perforation** CC
CC Excl: See code 534.0

✓5th 534.3 **Acute without mention of hemorrhage or perforation** CC 1
CC Excl: For code 534.31: See code 534.0

✓5th 534.4 **Chronic or unspecified with hemorrhage** CC
CC Excl: See code 534.0

✓5th 534.5 **Chronic or unspecified with perforation** CC
CC Excl: See code 534.0

✓5th 534.6 **Chronic or unspecified with hemorrhage and perforation** CC
CC Excl: See code 534.0

✓5th 534.7 **Chronic without mention of hemorrhage or perforation** CC 1
CC Excl: For code 534.71: See code 534.0

✓5th 534.9 **Unspecified as acute or chronic, without mention of hemorrhage or perforation** CC 1
CC Excl: For code 534.91: See code 534.0

✓4th **535 Gastritis and duodenitis**

The following fifth-digit subclassification is for use with category 535:
0 without mention of hemorrhage
1 with hemorrhage

AHA: 2Q, '92, 9; 4Q, '91, 25

✓5th 535.0 **Acute gastritis** CC 1
CC Excl: For code 535.01: 251.5, 456.0, 530.20-530.21, 530.7, 530.82, 530.85, 531.00-534.91, 535.01, 535.11, 535.21, 535.31, 535.41, 535.51, 535.61, 537.83, 562.02-562.03, 562.12-562.13, 569.3, 569.85, 578.0-578.9
AHA: 2Q, '92, 8; N-D, '86, 9

✓5th 535.1 **Atrophic gastritis** CC 1
Gastritis:
atrophic-hyperplastic
Gastritis:
chronic (atrophic)
CC Excl: For code 535.11: See code 535.01
AHA: 1Q, '94, 18
DEF: Inflammation of stomach, with mucous membrane atrophy and peptic gland destruction.

✓5th 535.2 **Gastric mucosal hypertrophy** CC 1
Hypertrophic gastritis
CC Excl: For code 535.21: See code 535.01

✓5th 535.3 **Alcoholic gastritis** CC 1
CC Excl: For code 535.31: See code 535.01

✓5th 535.4 **Other specified gastritis** CC 1
Gastritis:
allergic
bile induced
irritant
Gastritis:
superficial
toxic
CC Excl: For code 535.41: See code 535.01
AHA: 4Q, '90, 27

✓5th 535.5 **Unspecified gastritis and gastroduodenitis** CC 1
CC Excl: For code 535.51: See code 535.01
AHA: For code 535.50: ▶3Q, '05, 17;◀ 4Q, '99, 25

✓5th 535.6 **Duodenitis** CC 1
CC Excl: For code 535.61: See code 535.01
AHA: For code 535.60: ▶3Q, '05, 17◀
DEF: Inflammation of intestine, between pylorus and jejunum.

✓4th **536 Disorders of function of stomach**

EXCLUDES *functional disorders of stomach specified as psychogenic (306.4)*

536.0 **Achlorhydria**
DEF: Absence of gastric acid due to gastric mucosa atrophy; unresponsive to histamines; also known as gastric anacidity.

536.1 **Acute dilatation of stomach** CC
Acute distention of stomach
CC Excl: 536.1

536.2 **Persistent vomiting**
Habit vomiting
Persistent vomiting [not of pregnancy]
Uncontrollable vomiting
EXCLUDES *excessive vomiting in pregnancy (643.0-643.9)*
vomiting NOS (787.0)

536.3 **Gastroparesis**
Gastroparalysis
AHA: 2Q, '04, 7; 2Q, '01, 4; 4Q, '94, 42
DEF: Slight degree of paralysis within muscular coat of stomach.

✓5th 536.4 **Gastrostomy complications**
AHA: 4Q, '98, 42

536.40 **Gastrostomy complication,unspecified** CC
CC Excl: 530.86-530.87, 536.40-536.49, 997.4, 997.71, 997.91, 997.99, 998.81, 998.83-998.9

536.41 **Infection of gastrostomy** CC
Use additional code to specify type of infection, such as:
abscess or cellulitis of abdomen (682.2)
septicemia (038.0-038.9)
Use additional code to identify organism (041.00-041.9)
CC Excl: See code 536.40
AHA: 4Q, '98, 42

536.42 **Mechanical complication of gastrostomy** CC
CC Excl: See code 536.40

536.49 **Other gastrostomy complications** CC
CC Excl: See code 536.40
AHA: 4Q, '98, 42

§ Requires fifth digit. See category 533 for codes and definitions.

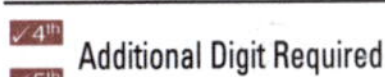
Additional Digit Required | Nonspecific PDx | Unacceptable PDx | Manifestation Code | MCV Major Cardiovascular Condition | ▶◀ Revised Text | ● New Code | ▲ Revised Code Title

536.8 Dyspepsia and other specified disorders of function of stomach

Achylia gastrica
Hourglass contraction of stomach
Hyperacidity
Hyperchlorhydria
Hypochlorhydria
Indigestion
▶ Tachygastria ◀

EXCLUDES *achlorhydria (536.0)*
heartburn (787.1)

AHA: 2Q, '93, 6; 2Q, '89, 16; N-D, '84, 9

536.9 Unspecified functional disorder of stomach

Functional gastrointestinal:
- disorder
- disturbance
- irritation

✓4th 537 Other disorders of stomach and duodenum

537.0 Acquired hypertrophic pyloric stenosis CC

Constriction, Obstruction, Stricture } of pylorus, acquired or adult

EXCLUDES *congenital or infantile pyloric stenosis (750.5)*

CC Excl: 536.3, 536.8-536.9, 537.0, 537.3, 750.5, 750.8-750.9, 751.1, 751.5

AHA: 2Q, '01, 4; J-F, '85, 14

537.1 Gastric diverticulum

EXCLUDES *congenital diverticulum of stomach (750.7)*

AHA: J-F, '85, 4

DEF: Herniated sac or pouch, within stomach or duodenum.

537.2 Chronic duodenal ileus

DEF: Persistent obstruction between pylorus and jejunum.

537.3 Other obstruction of duodenum CC

Cicatrix, Stenosis, Stricture, Volvulus } of duodenum

EXCLUDES *congenital obstruction of duodenum (751.1)*

CC Excl: 537.3, 750.8-750.9, 751.1, 751.5

537.4 Fistula of stomach or duodenum CC

Gastrocolic fistula
Gastrojejunocolic fistula

CC Excl: 537.4, 750.8-750.9, 751.5

537.5 Gastroptosis

DEF: Downward displacement of stomach.

537.6 Hourglass stricture or stenosis of stomach

Cascade stomach

EXCLUDES *congenital hourglass stomach (750.7)*
hourglass contraction of stomach (536.8)

✓5th 537.8 Other specified disorders of stomach and duodenum

AHA: 4Q, '91, 25

537.81 Pylorospasm

EXCLUDES *congenital pylorospasm (750.5)*

DEF: Spasm of the pyloric sphincter.

Duodenum

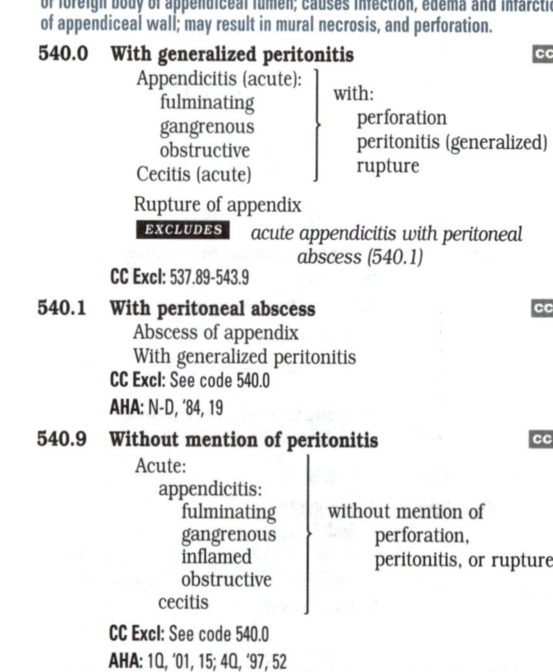

537.82 Angiodysplasia of stomach and duodenum (without mention of hemorrhage)

AHA: 3Q, '96, 10; 4Q, '90, 4

537.83 Angiodysplasia of stomach and duodenum with hemorrhage CC

CC Excl: 251.5, 456.0, 530.20-530.21, 530.7, 530.82, 530.85, 531.00-534.91, 535.01, 535.11, 535.21, 535.31, 535.41, 535.51, 535.61, 537.83, 562.02-562.03, 562.12-562.13, 569.3, 569.85, 578.0-578.9

DEF: Bleeding of stomach and duodenum due to vascular abnormalities.

537.84 Dieulafoy lesion (hemorrhagic) of stomach and duodenum CC

CC Excl: 251.5, 456.0, 530.20-530.21, 530.7, 530.82, 530.85, 531.00-534.91, 535.01, 535.11, 535.21, 535.31, 535.41, 535.51, 535.61, 537.83-537.84, 562.02-562.03, 562.12-562.13, 569.3, 569.85, 578.0-578.9

AHA: 4Q, '02, 60

DEF: An abnormally large and convoluted submucosal artery protruding through a defect in the mucosa in the stomach or intestines that can erode the epithelium causing hemorrhaging; also called Dieulafoy's vascular malformation.

537.89 Other

Gastric or duodenal:
- prolapse
- rupture

Intestinal metaplasia of gastric mucosa
Passive congestion of stomach

EXCLUDES *diverticula of duodenum (562.00-562.01)*
gastrointestinal hemorrhage (578.0-578.9)

AHA: 3Q, '05, 15; N-D, '84, 7

537.9 Unspecified disorder of stomach and duodenum

● **538 Gastrointestinal mucositis (ulcerative)**

Use additional E code to identify adverse effects of therapy, such as:
- antineoplastic and immunosuppressive drugs (E930.7, E933.1)
- radiation therapy (E879.2)

EXCLUDES *mucositis (ulcerative) of mouth and oral soft tissue (528.00- 528.09)*

APPENDICITIS (540-543)

✓4th 540 Acute appendicitis

AHA: N-D, '84, 19

DEF: Inflammation of vermiform appendix due to fecal obstruction, neoplasm or foreign body of appendiceal lumen; causes infection, edema and infarction of appendiceal wall; may result in mural necrosis, and perforation.

540.0 With generalized peritonitis CC

Appendicitis (acute): fulminating, gangrenous, obstructive; Cecitis (acute) } with: perforation, peritonitis (generalized), rupture

Rupture of appendix

EXCLUDES *acute appendicitis with peritoneal abscess (540.1)*

CC Excl: 537.89-543.9

540.1 With peritoneal abscess CC

Abscess of appendix
With generalized peritonitis

CC Excl: See code 540.0

AHA: N-D, '84, 19

540.9 Without mention of peritonitis CC

Acute: appendicitis: fulminating, gangrenous, inflamed, obstructive; cecitis } without mention of perforation, peritonitis, or rupture

CC Excl: See code 540.0

AHA: 1Q, '01, 15; 4Q, '97, 52

Appendix

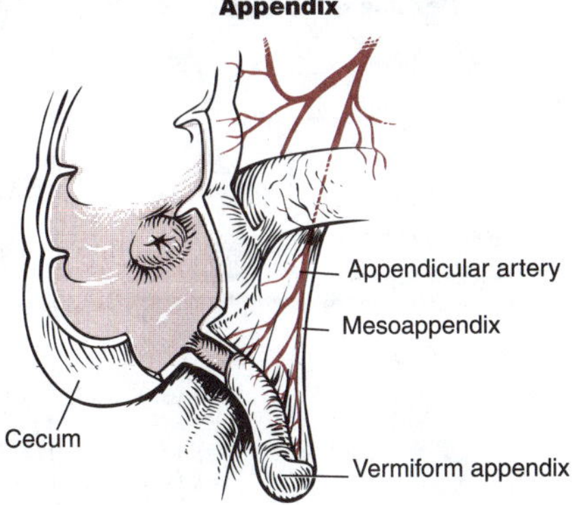

541 Appendicitis, unqualified
AHA: 2Q, '90, 26

542 Other appendicitis
Appendicitis:
chronic
recurrent
relapsing
subacute
EXCLUDES *hyperplasia (lymphoid) of appendix (543.0)*
AHA: 1Q, '01, 15

✓4th **543 Other diseases of appendix**

543.0 Hyperplasia of appendix (lymphoid)
DEF: Proliferation of cells in appendix tissue.

543.9 Other and unspecified diseases of appendix
Appendicular or appendiceal:
colic
concretion
fistula
Diverticulum, Fecalith, Intussusception, Mucocele, Stercolith } of appendix

HERNIA OF ABDOMINAL CAVITY (550-553)

INCLUDES hernia:
acquired
congenital, except diaphragmatic or hiatal

✓4th **550 Inguinal hernia**
INCLUDES bubonocele
inguinal hernia (direct) (double) (indirect) (oblique) (sliding)
scrotal hernia

The following fifth-digit subclassification is for use with category 550:
0 unilateral or unspecified (not specified as recurrent)
Unilateral NOS
1 unilateral or unspecified, recurrent
2 bilateral (not specified as recurrent)
Bilateral NOS
3 bilateral, recurrent

AHA: N-D, '85, 12

DEF: Hernia protrusion of an abdominal organ or tissue through inguinal canal.

DEF: Indirect inguinal hernia: (external or oblique) leaves abdomen through deep inguinal ring, passes through inguinal canal lateral to the inferior epigastric artery.

DEF: Direct inguinal hernia: (internal) emerges between inferior epigastric artery and rectus muscle edge.

✓5th **550.0 Inguinal hernia, with gangrene** CC
Inguinal hernia with gangrene (and obstruction)
CC Excl: 537.89-537.9, 550.00-550.93, 552.8-552.9, 553.8-553.9

✓5th **550.1 Inguinal hernia, with obstruction, without mention of gangrene** CC
Inguinal hernia with mention of incarceration, irreducibility, or strangulation
CC Excl: See code 550.0

✓5th **550.9 Inguinal hernia, without mention of obstruction or gangrene**
Inguinal hernia NOS
AHA: For code 550.91: 3Q, '03, 10; 1Q, '03, 4

✓4th **551 Other hernia of abdominal cavity, with gangrene**
INCLUDES that with gangrene (and obstruction)

✓5th **551.0 Femoral hernia with gangrene**

551.00 Unilateral or unspecified (not specified as recurrent) CC
Femoral hernia NOS with gangrene
CC Excl: 537.89-537.9, 551.00-551.03, 552.8-553.03, 553.8-553.9

551.01 Unilateral or unspecified, recurrent CC
CC Excl: See code 551.00

551.02 Bilateral (not specified as recurrent) CC
CC Excl: See code 551.00

551.03 Bilateral, recurrent CC
CC Excl: See code 551.00

551.1 Umbilical hernia with gangrene CC
Parumbilical hernia specified as gangrenous
CC Excl: 537.89-537.9, 551.1-551.29, 552.1-552.29, 552.8-552.9, 553.1-553.29, 553.8-553.9

✓5th **551.2 Ventral hernia with gangrene**

551.20 Ventral, unspecified, with gangrene CC
CC Excl: See code 551.1

551.21 Incisional, with gangrene CC
Hernia:
postoperative, recurrent, ventral } specified as gangrenous
CC Excl: See code 551.1

551.29 Other CC
Epigastric hernia specified as gangrenous
CC Excl: See code 551.1

551.3 Diaphragmatic hernia with gangrene CC
Hernia:
hiatal (esophageal) (sliding), paraesophageal } specified as gangrenous
Thoracic stomach } specified as gangrenous
EXCLUDES *congenital diaphragmatic hernia (756.6)*
CC Excl: 551.3, 552.3-552.9, 553.3, 553.8-553.9

Inguinal Hernias

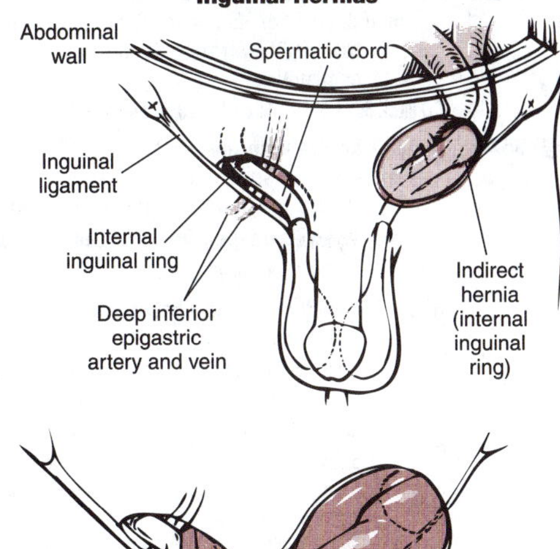

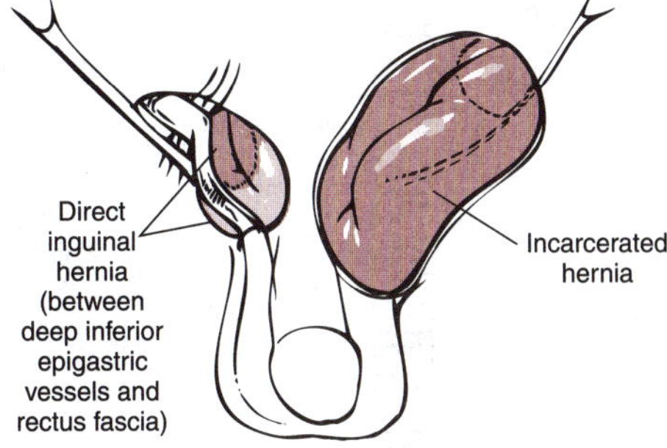

Femoral Hernia

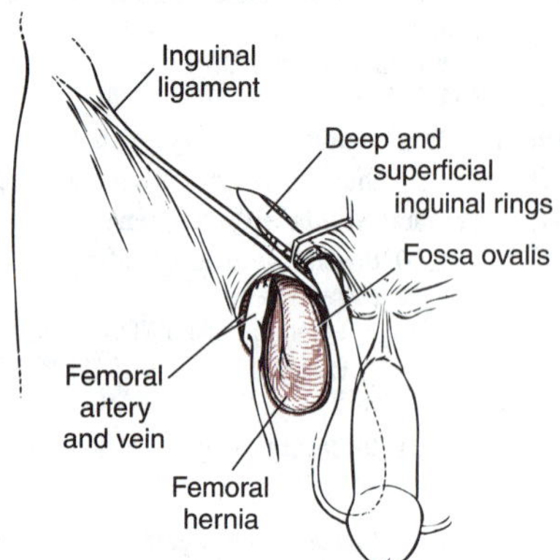

551.8 Hernia of other specified sites, with gangrene CC
Any condition classifiable to 553.8 if specified as gangrenous
CC Excl: 537.89, 537.9, 550.00-553.9

551.9 Hernia of unspecified site, with gangrene CC
Any condition classifiable to 553.9 if specified as gangrenous
CC Excl: See code 551.8

✓4th **552 Other hernia of abdominal cavity, with obstruction, but without mention of gangrene**
EXCLUDES *that with mention of gangrene (551.0-551.9)*

✓5th **552.0 Femoral hernia with obstruction**
Femoral hernia specified as incarcerated, irreducible, strangulated, or causing obstruction

552.00 Unilateral or unspecified (not specified as recurrent) CC
CC Excl: 537.89-537.9, 551.00-551.03, 552.00-552.03, 552.8-552.9, 553.00-553.03, 553.8-553.9

552.01 Unilateral or unspecified, recurrent CC
CC Excl: See code 552.00

552.02 Bilateral (not specified as recurrent) CC
CC Excl: See code 552.00

552.03 Bilateral, recurrent CC
CC Excl: See code 552.00

552.1 Umbilical hernia with obstruction CC
Parumbilical hernia specified as incarcerated, irreducible, strangulated, or causing obstruction
CC Excl: 551.1-551.29, 552.1-552.29, 552.8-552.9, 553.8-553.9

✓5th **552.2 Ventral hernia with obstruction**
Ventral hernia specified as incarcerated, irreducible, strangulated, or causing obstruction

552.20 Ventral, unspecified, with obstruction CC
CC Excl: See code 552.1

552.21 Incisional, with obstruction CC
Hernia:
postoperative, recurrent, ventral } specified as incarcerated, irreducible, strangulated, or causing obstruction
CC Excl: See code 552.1
AHA: 3Q, '03, 11

552.29 Other CC
Epigastric hernia specified as incarcerated, irreducible, strangulated, or causing obstruction
CC Excl: See code 552.1

Hernias of Abdominal Cavity

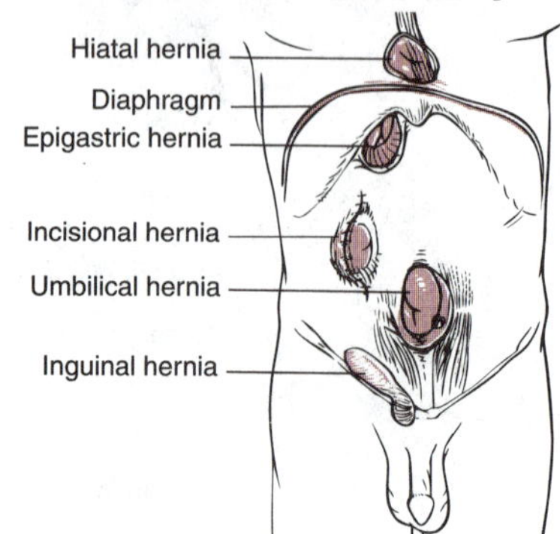

552.3 Diaphragmatic hernia with obstruction CC
Hernia:
hiatal (esophageal) (sliding), paraesophageal, Thoracic stomach } specified as incarcerated, irreducible, strangulated, or causing obstruction
EXCLUDES *congenital diaphragmatic hernia (756.6)*
CC Excl: 551.3, 552.3-552.9, 553.3-553.9

552.8 Hernia of other specified sites, with obstruction CC
Any condition classifiable to 553.8 if specified as incarcerated, irreducible, strangulated, or causing obstruction
EXCLUDES *hernia due to adhesion with obstruction (560.81)*
CC Excl: 550.00-553.9
AHA: 1Q, '04, 10

552.9 Hernia of unspecified site, with obstruction CC
Any condition classifiable to 553.9 if specified as incarcerated, irreducible, strangulated, or causing obstruction
CC Excl: See code 552.8

✓4th **553 Other hernia of abdominal cavity without mention of obstruction or gangrene**
EXCLUDES *the listed conditions with mention of:*
gangrene (and obstruction) (551.0-551.9)
obstruction (552.0-552.9)

✓5th **553.0 Femoral hernia**

553.00 Unilateral or unspecified (not specified as recurrent)
Femoral hernia NOS

553.01 Unilateral or unspecified, recurrent

553.02 Bilateral (not specified as recurrent)

553.03 Bilateral, recurrent

553.1 Umbilical hernia
Parumbilical hernia

✓5th **553.2 Ventral hernia**

553.20 Ventral, unspecified
AHA: 3Q, '03, 6

553.21 Incisional
Hernia: postoperative
Hernia: recurrent, ventral
AHA: 3Q, '03, 6

553.29 Other
Hernia: epigastric
Hernia: spigelian

553.3 Diaphragmatic hernia
Hernia:
hiatal (esophageal) (sliding)
paraesophageal
Thoracic stomach
EXCLUDES *congenital:*
diaphragmatic hernia (756.6)
hiatal hernia (750.6)
esophagocele (530.6)
AHA: 2Q, '01, 6; 1Q, '00, 6

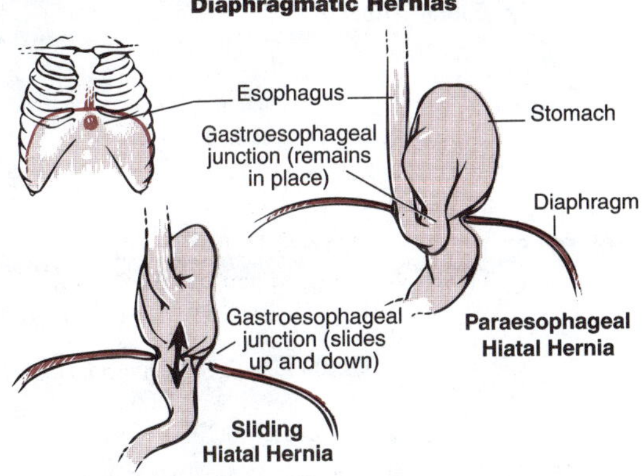

553.8 Hernia of other specified sites

Hernia:
- ischiatic
- ischiorectal
- lumbar
- obturator

Hernia:
- pudendal
- retroperitoneal
- sciatic

Other abdominal hernia of specified site

EXCLUDES *vaginal enterocele (618.6)*

553.9 Hernia of unspecified site

Enterocele
Epiplocele
Hernia:
- NOS
- interstitial

Hernia:
- intestinal
- intra-abdominal

Rupture (nontraumatic)
Sarcoepiplocele

NONINFECTIOUS ENTERITIS AND COLITIS (555-558)

✓4th **555 Regional enteritis**

INCLUDES Crohn's disease
Granulomatous enteritis

EXCLUDES *ulcerative colitis (556)*

DEF: Inflammation of intestine; classified to site.

555.0 Small intestine

Ileitis:
- regional
- segmental
- terminal

Regional enteritis or Crohn's disease of:
- duodenum
- ileum
- jejunum

555.1 Large intestine

Colitis:
- granulmatous
- regional
- transmural

Regional enteritis or Crohn's disease of:
- colon
- large bowel
- rectum

AHA: 3Q, '99, 8

555.2 Small intestine with large intestine

Regional ileocolitis

AHA: 1Q, '03, 18

555.9 Unspecified site

Crohn's disease NOS
Regional enteritis NOS

AHA: ▶2Q, '05, 11;◀ 3Q, '99, 8; 4Q, '97, 42; 2Q, '97, 3

✓4th **556 Ulcerative colitis**

AHA: 3Q, '99, 8

DEF: Chronic inflammation of mucosal lining of intestinal tract; may be single area or entire colon.

556.0 Ulcerative (chronic) enterocolitis

556.1 Ulcerative (chronic) ileocolitis

556.2 Ulcerative (chronic) proctitis

556.3 Ulcerative (chronic) proctosigmoiditis

556.4 Pseudopolyposis of colon

556.5 Left-sided ulcerative (chronic) colitis

556.6 Universal ulcerative (chronic) colitis

Pancolitis

556.8 Other ulcerative colitis

556.9 Ulcerative colitis, unspecified

Ulcerative enteritis NOS

AHA: 1Q, '03, 10

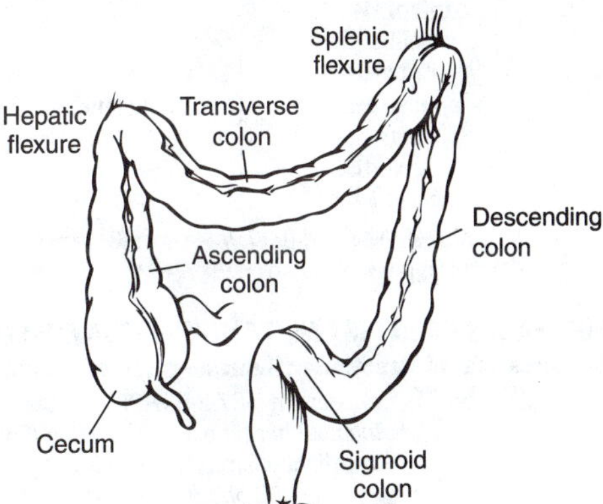

✓4th **557 Vascular insufficiency of intestine**

EXCLUDES *necrotizing enterocolitis of the newborn (777.5)*

DEF: Inadequacy of intestinal vessels.

557.0 Acute vascular insufficiency of intestine CC

Acute:
- hemorrhagic enterocolitis
- ischemic colitis, enteritis, or enterocolitis
- massive necrosis of intestine

Bowel infarction
Embolism of mesenteric artery
Fulminant enterocolitis
Hemorrhagic necrosis of intestine
Infarction of appendices epiploicae
Intestinal gangrene
Intestinal infarction (acute) (agnogenic) (hemorrhagic) (nonocclusive)
Mesenteric infarction (embolic) (thrombotic)
Necrosis of intestine
Terminal hemorrhagic enteropathy
Thrombosis of mesenteric artery

CC Excl: 557.0-557.1

DRG 188

AHA: 4Q, '01, 53

557.1 Chronic vascular insufficiency of intestine

Angina, abdominal
Chronic ischemic colitis, enteritis, or enterocolitis
Ischemic stricture of intestine
Mesenteric:
- angina
- artery syndrome (superior)
- vascular insufficiency

AHA: 3Q, '96, 9; 4Q, '90, 4; N-D, '86, 11; N-D, '84, 7

557.9 Unspecified vascular insufficiency of intestine

Alimentary pain due to vascular insufficiency
Ischemic colitis, enteritis, or enterocolitis NOS

DRG 188

✓4th **558 Other and unspecified noninfectious gastroenteritis and colitis**

EXCLUDES *infectious:*
- *colitis, enteritis, or gastroenteritis (009.0-009.1)*
- *diarrhea (009.2-009.3)*

558.1 Gastroenteritis and colitis due to radiation CC

Radiation enterocolitis

CC Excl: 558.1

558.2 Toxic gastroenteritis and colitis CC

Use additional E code to identify cause

CC Excl: 558.2

558.3 Allergic gastroenteritis and colitis

Use additional code to identify type of food allergy (V15.01-V15.05)

AHA: 1Q, '03, 12; 4Q, '00, 42

DEF: True immunoglobulin E (IgE)-mediated allergic reaction of the lining of the stomach, intestines, or colon to food proteins; causes nausea, vomiting, diarrhea, and abdominal cramping.

558.9 Other and unspecified noninfectious gastroenteritis and colitis

Colitis, Enteritis, Gastroenteritis, Ileitis, Jejunitis, Sigmoiditis } NOS, dietetic, or noninfectious

AHA: 3Q, '99, 4, 6; N-D, '87, 7

DRG 182

OTHER DISEASES OF INTESTINES AND PERITONEUM (560-569)

✓4th **560 Intestinal obstruction without mention of hernia**

EXCLUDES *duodenum (537.2-537.3)*
inguinal hernia with obstruction (550.1)
intestinal obstruction complicating hernia (552.0-552.9)
mesenteric:
embolism (557.0)
infarction (557.0)
thrombosis (557.0)
neonatal intestinal obstruction (277.01, 777.1-777.2, 777.4)

560.0 Intussusception CC

Intussusception (colon) (intestine) (rectum)
Invagination of intestine or colon

EXCLUDES *intussusception of appendix (543.9)*

CC Excl: 560.0-560.9, 569.89, 569.9

AHA: 4Q, '98, 82

DEF: Prolapse of a bowel section into adjacent section; occurs primarily in children; symptoms include paroxysmal pain, vomiting, presence of lower abdominal tumor and blood, and mucous passage from rectum.

560.1 Paralytic ileus CC

Adynamic ileus
Ileus (of intestine) (of bowel) (of colon)
Paralysis of intestine or colon

EXCLUDES *gallstone ileus (560.31)*

CC Excl: See code 560.0

AHA: J-F, '87, 13

DEF: Obstruction of ileus due to inhibited bowel motility.

DRG 180

560.2 Volvulus CC

Knotting, Strangulation, Torsion, Twist } of intestine, bowel, or colon

CC Excl: See code 560.0

DEF: Entanglement of bowel; causes obstruction; may compromise bowel circulation.

✓5th **560.3 Impaction of intestine**

560.30 Impaction of intestine, unspecified CC

Impaction of colon

CC Excl: See code 560.0

560.31 Gallstone ileus CC

Obstruction of intestine by gallstone

CC Excl: See code 560.0

Volvulus and Diverticulitis

Knotted intestine (volvulus)
Diverticulum

560.39 Other CC

Concretion of intestine
Enterolith
Fecal impaction

CC Excl: See code 560.0

AHA: 4Q, '98, 38

DRG 180

✓5th **560.8 Other specified intestinal obstruction**

560.81 Intestinal or peritoneal adhesions with obstruction (postoperative) (postinfection) CC

EXCLUDES *adhesions without obstruction (568.0)*

CC Excl: See code 560.0

AHA: 4Q, '95, 55; 3Q, '95, 6; N-D, '87, 9

DEF: Obstruction of peritoneum or intestine due to abnormal union of tissues.

DRG 180

560.89 Other CC

Acute pseudo-obstruction of intestine
Mural thickening causing obstruction

EXCLUDES *ischemic stricture of intestine (557.1)*

CC Excl: See code 560.0

AHA: 2Q, '97, 3; 1Q, '88, 6

DRG 180

560.9 Unspecified intestinal obstruction CC

Enterostenosis

Obstruction, Occlusion, Stenosis, Stricture } of intestine or colon

EXCLUDES *congenital stricture or stenosis of intestine (751.1-751.2)*

CC Excl: See code 560.0

DRG 180

✓4th **562 Diverticula of intestine**

Use additional code to identify any associated:
peritonitis (567.0-567.9)

EXCLUDES *congenital diverticulum of colon (751.5)*
diverticulum of appendix (543.9)
Meckel's diverticulum (751.0)

AHA: 4Q, '91, 25; J-F, '85, 1

✓5th **562.0 Small intestine**

562.00 Diverticulosis of small intestine (without mention of hemorrhage)

Diverticulosis:
duodenum, ileum, jejunum } without mention of diverticulitis

DEF: Saclike herniations of mucous lining of small intestine.

562.01 Diverticulitis of small intestine (without mention of hemorrhage)

Diverticulitis (with diverticulosis):
duodenum
ileum
jejunum
small intestine

DEF: Inflamed saclike herniations of mucous lining of small intestine.

562.02 Diverticulosis of small intestine with hemorrhage CC

CC Excl: 251.5, 456.0, 530.20-530.21, 530.7, 530.82, 530.85, 531.00-534.91, 535.01, 535.11, 535.21, 535.31, 535.41, 535.51, 535.61, 537.83, 562.02-562.03, 562.12-562.13, 569.3, 569.85, 578.0-578.9

562.03 Diverticulitis of small intestine with hemorrhage CC

CC Excl: See code 562.02

✓5th **562.1 Colon**

562.10 Diverticulosis of colon (without mention of hemorrhage)

Diverticulosis: NOS, intestine (large); Diverticular disease (colon) } without mention of diverticulitis

AHA: ▶3Q, '05, 17;◀ 3Q, '02, 15; 4Q, '90, 21; J-F, '85, 5

DEF: Saclike herniations of mucous lining of large intestine.

562.11 Diverticulitis of colon (without mention of hemorrhage)

Diverticulitis (with diverticulosis):
NOS
colon
intestine (large)

AHA: 1Q, '96, 14; J-F, '85, 5

DEF: Inflamed saclike herniations of mucosal lining of large intestine.

562.12 Diverticulosis of colon with hemorrhage CC

CC Excl: See code 562.02

DRG 174 and 182

562.13 Diverticulitis of colon with hemorrhage CC

CC Excl: See code 562.02

✓4th **564 Functional digestive disorders, not elsewhere classified**

EXCLUDES *functional disorders of stomach (536.0-536.9)*
those specified as psychogenic (306.4)

✓5th **564.0 Constipation**

AHA: 4Q, '01, 45

564.00 Constipation, unspecified

564.01 Slow transit constipation

DEF: Delay in the transit of fecal material through the colon secondary to smooth muscle dysfunction or decreased peristaltic contractions along the colon: also called colonic inertia or delayed transit.

564.02 Outlet dysfunction constipation

DEF: Failure to relax the paradoxical contractions of the striated pelvic floor muscles during the attempted defecation.

564.09 Other constipation

564.1 Irritable bowel syndrome

Irritable colon
Spastic colon

AHA: 1Q, '88, 6

DEF: Functional gastrointestinal disorder (FGID); symptoms following meals include diarrhea, constipation, abdominal pain; other symptoms include bloating, gas, distended abdomen, nausea, vomiting, appetite loss, emotional distress, and depression.

564.2 Postgastric surgery syndromes

Dumping syndrome
Jejunal syndrome
Postgastrectomy syndrome
Postvagotomy syndrome

EXCLUDES *malnutrition following gastrointestinal surgery (579.3)*
postgastrojejunostomy ulcer (534.0-534.9)

AHA: 1Q, '95, 11

564.3 Vomiting following gastrointestinal surgery

Vomiting (bilious) following gastrointestinal surgery

564.4 Other postoperative functional disorders

Diarrhea following gastrointestinal surgery

EXCLUDES *colostomy and enterostomy complications (569.60-569.69)*

564.5 Functional diarrhea

EXCLUDES *diarrhea:*
NOS (787.91)
psychogenic (306.4)

DEF: Diarrhea with no detectable organic cause.

564.6 Anal spasm

Proctalgia fugax

Anal Fistula and Abscess

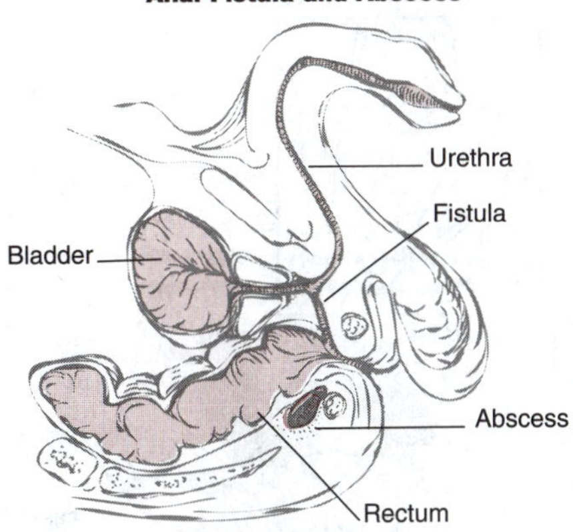

564.7 Megacolon, other than Hirschsprung's

Dilatation of colon

EXCLUDES *megacolon:*
congenital [Hirschsprung's] (751.3)
toxic (556)

DEF: Enlarged colon; congenital or acquired; can occur acutely or become chronic.

✓5th **564.8 Other specified functional disorders of intestine**

EXCLUDES *malabsorption (579.0-579.9)*

AHA: 1Q, '88, 6

564.81 Neurogenic bowel

AHA: 1Q, '01, 12; 4Q, '98, 45

DEF: Disorder of bowel due to spinal cord lesion above conus medullaris; symptoms include precipitous micturition, nocturia, catheter intolerance, headache, sweating, nasal obstruction and spastic contractions.

564.89 Other functional disorders of intestine

Atony of colon

564.9 Unspecified functional disorder of intestine

✓4th **565 Anal fissure and fistula**

565.0 Anal fissure

Tear of anus, nontraumatic

EXCLUDES *traumatic (863.89, 863.99)*

DEF: Ulceration of cleft at anal mucosa; causes pain, itching, bleeding, infection, and sphincter spasm; may occur with hemorrhoids.

565.1 Anal fistula

Fistula:
anorectal
rectal
rectum to skin

EXCLUDES *fistula of rectum to internal organs—see Alphabetic Index*
ischiorectal fistula (566)
rectovaginal fistula (619.1)

DEF: Abnormal opening on cutaneous surface near anus; may lack connection with rectum.

566 Abscess of anal and rectal regions CC

Abscess:
ischiorectal
perianal
perirectal

Cellulitis:
anal
perirectal
rectal

Ischiorectal fistula

CC Excl: 566

Psoas Muscle Abscess

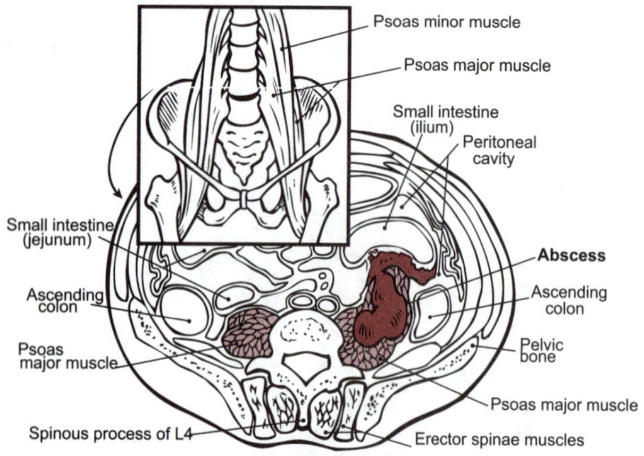

✓4th **567 Peritonitis and retroperitoneal infections**

EXCLUDES *peritonitis:*
benign paroxysmal ▶(277.31)◀
pelvic, female (614.5, 614.7)
periodic familial ▶(277.31)◀
puerperal (670)
with or following:
abortion (634-638 with .0, 639.0)
appendicitis (540.0-540.1)
ectopic or molar pregnancy (639.0)

DEF: Inflammation of the peritoneal cavity.

567.0 *Peritonitis in infectious diseases classified elsewhere* CC

Code first underlying disease

EXCLUDES *peritonitis:*
gonococcal (098.86)
syphilitic (095.2)
tuberculous (014.0)

CC Excl: 567.0-567.29, 567.38-567.9, 569.89, 569.9

567.1 Pneumococcal peritonitis CC

CC Excl: See code 567.0

✓5th **567.2 Other suppurative peritonitis**

AHA: 4Q, '05, 74; 2Q, '01, 11, 12; 3Q, '99, 9; 2Q, '98, 19

567.21 Peritonitis (acute) generalized CC

Pelvic peritonitis, male

CC Excl: See code 567.0

567.22 Peritoneal abscess CC

Abscess (of):
abdominopelvic
mesenteric
omentum
peritoneum
retrocecal
subdiaphragmatic
subhepatic
subphrenic

CC Excl: See code 567.0

567.23 Spontaneous bacterial peritonitis CC

EXCLUDES ▶ *bacterial peritonitis NOS (567.29)*◀

CC Excl: See code 567.0

567.29 Other suppurative peritonitis CC

Subphrenic peritonitis

CC Excl: See code 567.0

✓5th **567.3 Retroperitoneal infections**

AHA: 4Q, '05, 74

567.31 Psoas muscle abscess CC

CC Excl: 567.31, 728.0, 728.11-728.3, 728.81, 728.86

DEF: Infection that extends into or around the psoas muscle that connects the lumbar vertebrae to the femur.

567.38 Other retroperitoneal abscess CC

AHA: 4Q, '05, 77

CC Excl: See code 567.0

567.39 Other retroperitoneal infections CC

CC Excl: See code 567.0

✓5th **567.8 Other specified peritonitis**

AHA: 4Q, '05, 74

567.81 Choleperitonitis CC

Peritonitis due to bile

CC Excl: See code 567.0

DEF: Inflammation or infection due to presence of bile in the peritoneum resulting from rupture of the bile passages or gallbladder.

567.82 Sclerosing mesenteritis CC

Fat necrosis of peritoneum
(Idiopathic) sclerosing mesenteric fibrosis
Mesenteric lipodystrophy
Mesenteric panniculitis
Retractile mesenteritis

CC Excl: See code 567.0

AHA: 4Q, '05, 77

DEF: Inflammatory processes involving the mesenteric fat; progresses to fibrosis and necrosis of tissue.

567.89 Other specified peritonitis CC

Chronic proliferative peritonitis
Mesenteric saponification
Peritonitis due to urine

CC Excl: See code 567.0

567.9 Unspecified peritonitis CC

Peritonitis NOS
Peritonitis of unspecified cause

CC Excl: See code 567.0

AHA: 1Q, '04, 10

✓4th **568 Other disorders of peritoneum**

568.0 Peritoneal adhesions (postoperative) (postinfection)

Adhesions (of):
abdominal (wall)
diaphragm
intestine
male pelvis
Adhesions (of):
mesenteric
omentum
stomach
Adhesive bands

EXCLUDES *adhesions:*
pelvic, female (614.6)
with obstruction:
duodenum (537.3)
intestine (560.81)

AHA: 3Q, '03, 7, 11; 4Q, '95, 55; 3Q, '95, 7; S-O, '85, 11

DEF: Abnormal union of tissues in peritoneum.

✓5th **568.8 Other specified disorders of peritoneum**

568.81 Hemoperitoneum (nontraumatic) CC

CC Excl: 568.81

568.82 Peritoneal effusion (chronic)

EXCLUDES *ascites NOS (789.5)*

DEF: Persistent leakage of fluid within peritoneal cavity.

568.89 Other

Peritoneal:
cyst
Peritoneal:
granuloma

568.9 Unspecified disorder of peritoneum

✓4th **569 Other disorders of intestine**

569.0 Anal and rectal polyp

Anal and rectal polyp NOS

EXCLUDES *adenomatous anal and rectal polyp (211.4)*

Rectum and Anus

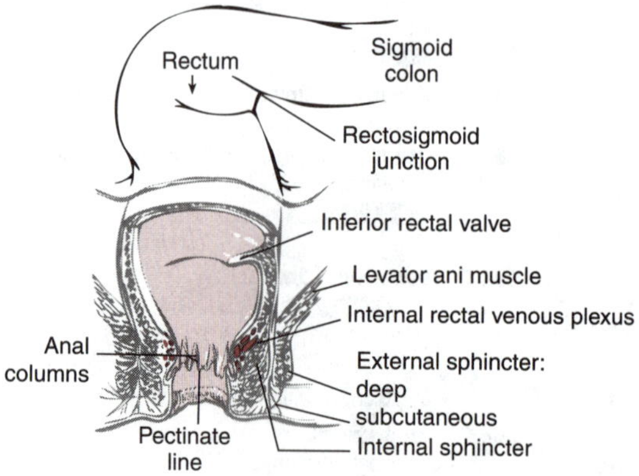

569.1 Rectal prolapse
Procidentia:
anus (sphincter)
rectum (sphincter)
Prolapse:
anal canal
rectal mucosa
Proctoptosis
EXCLUDES *prolapsed hemorrhoids (455.2, 455.5)*

569.2 Stenosis of rectum and anus
Stricture of anus (sphincter)

569.3 Hemorrhage of rectum and anus CC
EXCLUDES *gastrointestinal bleeding NOS (578.9)*
melena (578.1)
CC Excl: 251.5, 456.0, 530.20-530.21, 530.7, 530.82, 530.85, 531.00-534.91, 535.01, 535.11, 535.21, 535.31, 535.41, 535.51, 535.61, 537.83, 562.02-562.03, 562.12-562.13, 569.3, 569.85, 578.0-578.9
AHA: ▶3Q, '05, 17◀

✓5th **569.4 Other specified disorders of rectum and anus**

569.41 Ulcer of anus and rectum
Solitary ulcer } of anus (sphincter) or rectum (sphincter)
Stercoral ulcer

569.42 Anal or rectal pain
AHA: 1Q, '03, 8; 1Q, '96, 13

569.49 Other
Granuloma } of rectum (sphincter)
Rupture
Hypertrophy of anal papillae
Proctitis NOS
EXCLUDES *fistula of rectum to:*
internal organs—see Alphabetic Index
skin (565.1)
hemorrhoids (455.0-455.9)
incontinence of sphincter ani (787.6)

569.5 Abscess of intestine CC
EXCLUDES *appendiceal abscess (540.1)*
CC Excl: 569.5

✓5th **569.6 Colostomy and enterostomy complications**
AHA: 4Q, '95, 58
DEF: Complication in a surgically created opening, from intestine to surface skin.

569.60 Colostomy and enterostomy complication, unspecified CC
CC Excl: 569.60-569.69

569.61 Infection of colostomy or enterostomy CC
Use additional code to identify organism (041.00-041.9)
Use additional code to specify type of infection, such as:
abscess or cellulitis of abdomen (682.2)
septicemia (038.0-038.9)
CC Excl: see code 569.60

569.62 Mechanical complication of colostomy and enterostomy CC
Malfunction of colostomy and enterostomy
CC Excl: 530.86-530.87, 536.40-536.49, 569.60-569.69, 997.4, 997.71, 997.91-997.99, 998.81, 998.83-998.9
AHA: ▶2Q, '05, 11◀; 1Q, '03, 10; 4Q, '98, 44

569.69 Other complication CC
Fistula
Hernia
Prolapse
CC Excl: see code 569.60
AHA: 3Q, '98, 16

✓5th **569.8 Other specified disorders of intestine**
AHA: 4Q, '91, 25

569.81 Fistula of intestine, excluding rectum and anus
Fistula:
abdominal wall
enterocolic
Fistula:
enteroenteric
ileorectal
EXCLUDES *fistula of intestine to internal organs—see Alphabetic Index*
persistent postoperative fistula (998.6)
AHA: 3Q, '99, 8

569.82 Ulceration of intestine
Primary ulcer of intestine
Ulceration of colon
EXCLUDES *that with perforation (569.83)*

569.83 Perforation of intestine CC
CC Excl: 569.83

569.84 Angiodysplasia of intestine (without mention of hemorrhage)
AHA: 3Q, '96, 10; 4Q, '90, 4; 4Q, '90, 21
DEF: Small vascular abnormalities of the intestinal tract without bleeding problems.

569.85 Angiodysplasia of intestine with hemorrhage CC
CC Excl: 251.5, 456.0, 530.20-530.21, 530.7, 530.82, 530.85, 531.00-534.91, 535.01, 535.11, 535.21, 535.31, 535.41, 535.51, 535.61, 537.83, 562.02-562.03, 562.12-562.13, 569.3, 569.85, 578.0-578.9
AHA: 3Q, '96, 9
DEF: Small vascular abnormalities of the intestinal tract with bleeding problems.

569.86 Dieulafoy lesion (hemorrhagic) of intestine CC
CC Excl: See 569.85
AHA: 4Q, '02, 60-61

569.89 Other
Enteroptosis
Granuloma } of intestine
Prolapse
Pericolitis
Perisigmoiditis
Visceroptosis
EXCLUDES *gangrene of intestine, mesentery, or omentum (557.0)*
hemorrhage of intestine NOS (578.9)
obstruction of intestine (560.0-560.9)
AHA: 3Q, '96, 9

569.9 Unspecified disorder of intestine

OTHER DISEASES OF DIGESTIVE SYSTEM (570-579)

570 Acute and subacute necrosis of liver CC
Acute hepatic failure
Acute or subacute hepatitis, not specified as infective
Necrosis of liver (acute) (diffuse) (massive) (subacute)
Parenchymatous degeneration of liver
Yellow atrophy (liver) (acute) (subacute)
EXCLUDES *icterus gravis of newborn (773.0-773.2)*
serum hepatitis (070.2-070.3)
that with:
abortion (634-638 with .7, 639.8)
ectopic or molar pregnancy (639.8)
pregnancy, childbirth, or the puerperium (646.7)
viral hepatitis (070.0-070.9)
CC Excl: 570, 573.4-573.9
AHA: ▶2Q, '05, 9;◀ 1Q, '00, 22

✓4th ✓5th Additional Digit Required | Nonspecific PDx | Unacceptable PDx | Manifestation Code | MCV Major Cardiovascular Condition | ▶◀ Revised Text | ● New Code | ▲ Revised Code Title

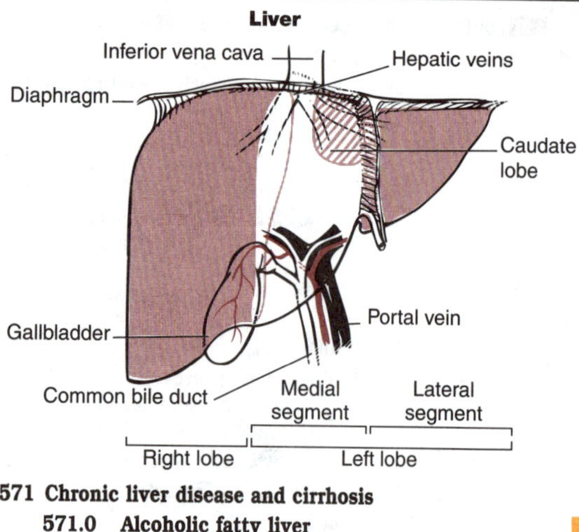

✓4th 571 Chronic liver disease and cirrhosis

571.0 Alcoholic fatty liver A

571.1 Acute alcoholic hepatitis A
Acute alcoholic liver disease
AHA: 2Q, '02, 4

571.2 Alcoholic cirrhosis of liver CC A
Florid cirrhosis
Laennec's cirrhosis (alcoholic)
CC Excl: 571.2, 573.8-573.9
AHA: 2Q, '02, 4; 1Q, '02, 3; N-D, '85, 14
DEF: Fibrosis and dysfunction, of liver; due to alcoholic liver disease.

571.3 Alcoholic liver damage, unspecified A

✓5th 571.4 Chronic hepatitis
EXCLUDES *viral hepatitis (acute) (chronic) (070.0-070.9)*

571.40 Chronic hepatitis, unspecified

571.41 Chronic persistent hepatitis

571.49 Other CC
Chronic hepatitis:
active
aggressive
Recurrent hepatitis
CC Excl: 571.49-571.9, 573.8-573.9
AHA: 3Q, '99, 19; N-D, '85, 14

571.5 Cirrhosis of liver without mention of alcohol CC
Cirrhosis of liver:
NOS
cryptogenic
macronodular
micronodular
posthepatitic
Cirrhosis of liver:
postnecrotic
Healed yellow atrophy (liver)
Portal cirrhosis
CC Excl: See code 571.49
DEF: Fibrosis and dysfunction of liver; not alcohol related.

571.6 Biliary cirrhosis CC
Chronic nonsuppurative destructive cholangitis
Cirrhosis:
cholangitic
cholestatic
CC Excl: See code 571.49

571.8 Other chronic nonalcoholic liver disease
Chronic yellow atrophy (liver)
Fatty liver, without mention of alcohol
AHA: 2Q, '96, 12

571.9 Unspecified chronic liver disease without mention of alcohol

✓4th 572 Liver abscess and sequelae of chronic liver disease

572.0 Abscess of liver CC
EXCLUDES *amebic liver abscess (006.3)*
CC Excl: 006.3, 572.0-572.1, 573.8-573.9

572.1 Portal pyemia CC
Phlebitis of portal vein
Portal thrombophlebitis
Pylephlebitis
Pylethrombophlebitis
CC Excl: See code 572.0
DEF: Inflammation of portal vein or branches; may be due to intestinal disease; symptoms include fever, chills, jaundice, sweating, and abscess in various body parts.

572.2 Hepatic coma CC
Hepatic encephalopathy
Hepatocerebral intoxication
Portal-systemic encephalopathy
CC Excl: 572.2, 573.8-573.9
AHA: 2Q, '05, 9; 1Q, '02, 3; 3Q, '95, 14

572.3 Portal hypertension
AHA: 3Q, '05, 15
DEF: Abnormally high blood pressure in the portal vein.

572.4 Hepatorenal syndrome CC
EXCLUDES *that following delivery (674.8)*
CC Excl: 572.4, 573.8-573.9
AHA: 3Q, '93, 15
DEF: Hepatic and renal failure characterized by cirrhosis with ascites or obstructive jaundice, oliguria, and low sodium concentration.

572.8 Other sequelae of chronic liver disease

✓4th 573 Other disorders of liver
EXCLUDES *amyloid or lardaceous degeneration of liver ▶(277.39)◀*
congenital cystic disease of liver (751.62)
glycogen infiltration of liver (271.0)
hepatomegaly NOS (789.1)
portal vein obstruction (452)

573.0 Chronic passive congestion of liver
DEF: Blood accumulation in liver tissue.

573.1 Hepatitis in viral diseases classified elsewhere CC
Code first underlying disease as:
Coxsackie virus disease (074.8)
cytomegalic inclusion virus disease (078.5)
infectious mononucleosis (075)
EXCLUDES *hepatitis (in):*
mumps (072.71)
viral (070.0-070.9)
yellow fever (060.0-060.9)
CC Excl: 573.1-573.3, 573.8-573.9

573.2 Hepatitis in other infectious diseases classified elsewhere CC
Code first underlying disease, as:
malaria (084.9)
EXCLUDES *hepatitis in:*
late syphilis (095.3)
secondary syphilis (091.62)
toxoplasmosis (130.5)
CC Excl: See code 573.1

573.3 Hepatitis, unspecified CC
Toxic (noninfectious) hepatitis
Use additional E code to identify cause
CC Excl: See code 573.1
AHA: 3Q, '98, 3, 4; 4Q, '90, 26

573.4 Hepatic infarction CC
CC Excl: 570, 573.4-573.9

573.8 Other specified disorders of liver
Hepatoptosis

573.9 Unspecified disorder of liver

N Newborn Age: 0 P Pediatric Age: 0-17 M Maternity Age: 12-55 A Adult Age: 15-124 CC CC Condition MC Major Complication CD Complex Dx HIV HIV Related Dx

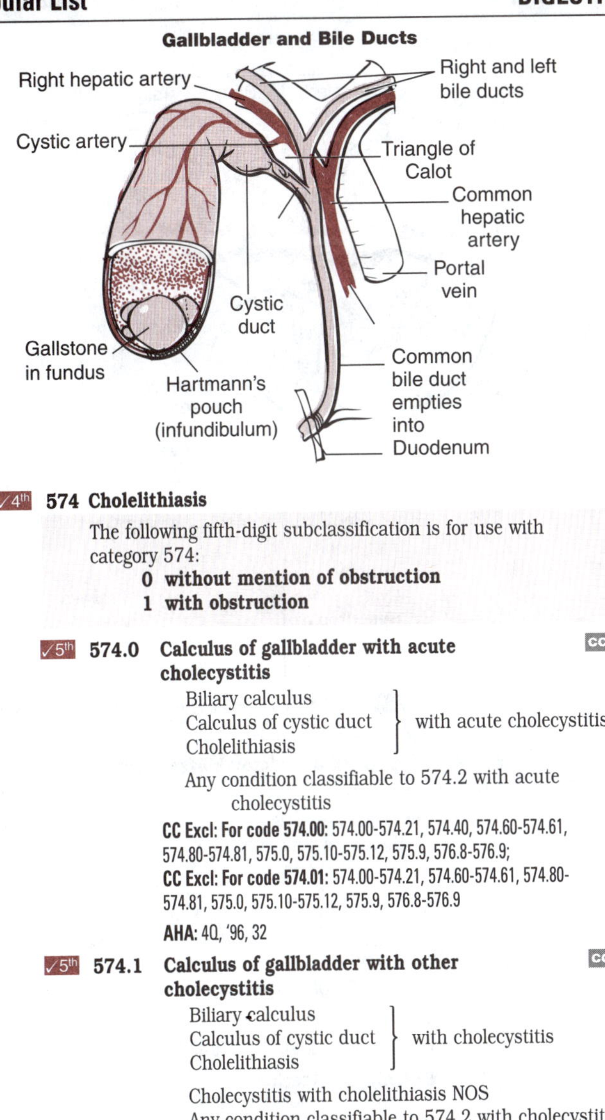

4th 574 Cholelithiasis

The following fifth-digit subclassification is for use with category 574:

- **0 without mention of obstruction**
- **1 with obstruction**

5th 574.0 Calculus of gallbladder with acute cholecystitis CC

Biliary calculus / Calculus of cystic duct / Cholelithiasis } with acute cholecystitis

Any condition classifiable to 574.2 with acute cholecystitis

CC Excl: For code 574.00: 574.00-574.21, 574.40, 574.60-574.61, 574.80-574.81, 575.0, 575.10-575.12, 575.9, 576.8-576.9;
CC Excl: For code 574.01: 574.00-574.21, 574.60-574.61, 574.80-574.81, 575.0, 575.10-575.12, 575.9, 576.8-576.9

AHA: 4Q, '96, 32

5th 574.1 Calculus of gallbladder with other cholecystitis CC

Biliary calculus / Calculus of cystic duct / Cholelithiasis } with cholecystitis

Cholecystitis with cholelithiasis NOS
Any condition classifiable to 574.2 with cholecystitis (chronic)

CC Excl: See code 574.01

AHA: 3Q, '99, 9; 4Q, '96, 32, 69; 2Q, '96, 13; **For code 574.10:** 1Q, '03, 5

5th 574.2 Calculus of gallbladder without mention of cholecystitis CC 1

Biliary:
calculus NOS
colic NOS
Calculus of cystic duct
Cholelithiasis NOS
Colic (recurrent) of gallbladder
Gallstone (impacted)

CC Excl: For code 574.21: See code 574.01

AHA: For code 574.20: 1Q, '88, 14

5th 574.3 Calculus of bile duct with acute cholecystitis CC

Calculus of bile duct [any] / Choledocholithiasis } with acute cholecystitis

Any condition classifiable to 574.5 with acute cholecystitis

CC Excl: 574.30-575.12, 576.8-576.9

5th 574.4 Calculus of bile duct with other cholecystitis CC

Calculus of bile duct [any] / Choledocholithiasis } with cholecystitis (chronic)

Any condition classifiable to 574.5 with cholecystitis (chronic)

CC Excl: See code 574.3

5th 574.5 Calculus of bile duct without mention of cholecystitis CC

Calculus of:
bile duct [any]
common duct
hepatic duct
Choledocholithiasis
Hepatic:
colic (recurrent)
lithiasis

CC Excl: See code 574.3

AHA: 3Q, '94, 11

5th 574.6 Calculus of gallbladder and bile duct with acute cholecystitis CC

Any condition classifiable to 574.0 and 574.3

CC Excl: 574.60-574.61, 575.0-575.12, 575.9, 576.8-576.9

AHA: 4Q, '96, 32

5th 574.7 Calculus of gallbladder and bile duct with other cholecystitis CC

Any condition classifiable to 574.1 and 574.4

CC Excl: 574.30-575.12, 576.8-576.9

AHA: 4Q, '96, 32

5th 574.8 Calculus of gallbladder and bile duct with acute and chronic cholecystitis CC

Any condition classifiable to 574.6 and 574.7

CC Excl: 574.80-574.81, 575.0-575.12, 575.9, 576.8-576.9

AHA: 4Q, '96, 32

5th 574.9 Calculus of gallbladder and bile duct without cholecystitis CC

Any condition classifiable to 574.2 and 574.5

CC Excl: See code 574.7

AHA: 4Q, '96, 32

4th 575 Other disorders of gallbladder

575.0 Acute cholecystitis CC

Abscess of gallbladder / Angiocholecystitis / Cholecystitis: emphysematous (acute), gangrenous, suppurative / Empyema of gallbladder / Gangrene of gallbladder } without mention of calculus

EXCLUDES *that with:*
acute and chronic cholecystitis (575.12)
choledocholithiasis (574.3)
choledocholithiasis and cholelithiasis (574.6)
cholelithiasis (574.0)

CC Excl: 574.60-574.61, 574.80-574.81, 575.0-575.12, 575.9, 576.8-576.9

AHA: 3Q, '91, 17

5th 575.1 Other cholecystitis

Cholecystitis: NOS, chronic } without mention of calculus

EXCLUDES *that with:*
choledocholithiasis (574.4)
choledocholithiasis and cholelithiasis (574.8)
cholelithiasis (574.1)

AHA: 4Q, '96, 32

575.10 Cholecystitis, unspecified
Cholecystitis NOS

575.11 Chronic cholecystitis

575.12 Acute and chronic cholecystitis CC

CC Excl: 575.0, 575.10-575.12, 575.9, 576.8-576.9

AHA: 4Q, '97, 52; 4Q, '96, 32

Digestive System

574–575.12

4th 5th Additional Digit Required | Nonspecific PDx | Unacceptable PDx | Manifestation Code | MCV Major Cardiovascular Condition | ▶◀ Revised Text | ● New Code | ▲ Revised Code Title

575.2 Obstruction of gallbladder CC

Occlusion / Stenosis / Stricture } of cystic duct or gallbladder without mention of calculus

EXCLUDES *that with calculus (574.0-574.2 with fifth-digit 1)*

CC Excl: 575.2-575.9, 576.8-576.9

575.3 Hydrops of gallbladder CC

Mucocele of gallbladder

CC Excl: See code 575.2

AHA: 2Q, '89, 13

DEF: Serous fluid accumulation in bladder.

575.4 Perforation of gallbladder CC

Rupture of cystic duct or gallbladder

CC Excl: See code 575.2

575.5 Fistula of gallbladder CC

Fistula:
- cholecystoduodenal

Fistula:
- cholecystoenteric

CC Excl: See code 575.2

575.6 Cholesterolosis of gallbladder

Strawberry gallbladder

AHA: 4Q, '90, 17

DEF: Cholesterol deposits in gallbladder tissue.

575.8 Other specified disorders of gallbladder

Adhesions / Atrophy / Cyst / Hypertrophy / Nonfunctioning / Ulcer } (of) cystic duct or gallbladder

Biliary dyskinesia

EXCLUDES *Hartmann's pouch of intestine (V44.3)*
nonvisualization of gallbladder (793.3)

AHA: 4Q, '90, 26; 2Q, '89, 13

575.9 Unspecified disorder of gallbladder

✓4th **576 Other disorders of biliary tract**

EXCLUDES *that involving the:*
cystic duct (575.0-575.9)
gallbladder (575.0-575.9)

576.0 Postcholecystectomy syndrome

AHA: 1Q, '88, 10

DEF: Jaundice or abdominal pain following cholecystectomy.

576.1 Cholangitis CC

Cholangitis:
- NOS
- acute
- ascending
- chronic
- primary

Cholangitis:
- recurrent
- sclerosing
- secondary
- stenosing
- suppurative

CC Excl: 576.1, 576.8-576.9

AHA: 2Q, '99, 13

576.2 Obstruction of bile duct

Occlusion / Stenosis / Stricture } of bile duct, except cystic duct, without mention of calculus

EXCLUDES *congenital (751.61)*
that with calculus (574.3-574.5 with fifth-digit 1)

AHA: 3Q, '03, 17-18; 1Q, '01, 8; 2Q, '99, 13

576.3 Perforation of bile duct CC

Rupture of bile duct, except cystic duct

CC Excl: 576.3-576.4, 576.8-576.9

576.4 Fistula of bile duct CC

Choledochoduodenal fistula

CC Excl: See code 576.3

576.5 Spasm of sphincter of Oddi

Pancreas

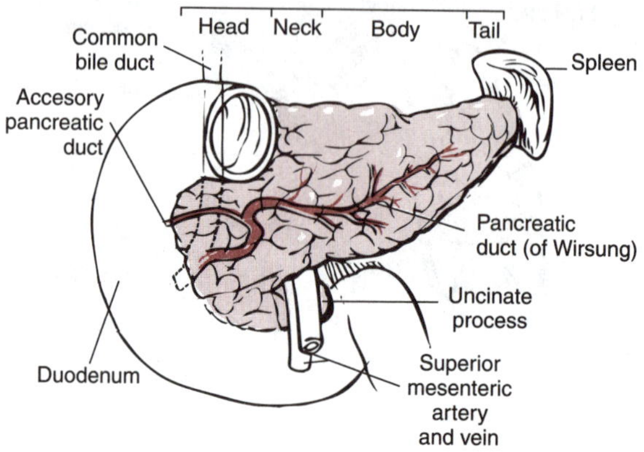

576.8 Other specified disorders of biliary tract

Adhesions / Atrophy / Cyst / Hypertrophy / Stasis / Ulcer } of bile duct [any]

EXCLUDES *congenital choledochal cyst (751.69)*

AHA: 3Q, '03, 17; 2Q, '99, 14

576.9 Unspecified disorder of biliary tract

✓4th **577 Diseases of pancreas**

577.0 Acute pancreatitis CC

Abscess of pancreas

Necrosis of pancreas:
- acute
- infective

Pancreatitis:
- NOS

Pancreatitis:
- acute (recurrent)
- apoplectic
- hemorrhagic
- subacute
- suppurative

EXCLUDES *mumps pancreatitis (072.3)*

CC Excl: 577.0-577.1, 577.8-577.9

AHA: 3Q, '99, 9; 2Q, '98, 19; 2Q, '96, 13; 2Q, '89, 9

577.1 Chronic pancreatitis

Chronic pancreatitis:
- NOS
- infectious
- interstitial

Pancreatitis:
- painless
- recurrent
- relapsing

AHA: 1Q, '01, 8; 2Q, '96, 13; 3Q, '94, 11

577.2 Cyst and pseudocyst of pancreas CC

CC Excl: 577.2, 577.8-577.9

577.8 Other specified diseases of pancreas

Atrophy / Calculus / Cirrhosis / Fibrosis } of pancreas

Pancreatic:
- infantilism
- necrosis:
  - NOS
  - aseptic
  - fat

Pancreatolithiasis

EXCLUDES *fibrocystic disease of pancreas (277.00-277.09)*
islet cell tumor of pancreas (211.7)
pancreatic steatorrhea (579.4)

AHA: 1Q, '01, 8

577.9 Unspecified disease of pancreas

✓4th 578 Gastrointestinal hemorrhage

EXCLUDES *that with mention of:*
angiodysplasia of stomach and duodenum (537.83)
angiodysplasia of intestine (569.85)
diverticulitis, intestine:
large (562.13)
small (562.03)
diverticulosis, intestine:
large (562.12)
small (562.02)
gastritis and duodenitis (535.0-535.6)
ulcer:
duodenal, gastric, gastrojejuunal or peptic (531.00-534.91)

AHA: 2Q, '92, 9; 4Q, '90, 20

578.0 Hematemesis CC

Vomiting of blood

CC Excl: 251.5, 456.0, 530.20-530.21, 530.7, 530.82, 530.85, 531.00-534.91, 535.01, 535.11, 535.21, 535.31, 535.41, 535.51, 535.61, 537.83, 562.02-562.03, 562.12-562.13, 569.3, 569.85, 578.0-578.9

AHA: 2Q, '02, 4

578.1 Blood in stool CC

Melena

EXCLUDES *melena of the newborn (772.4, 777.3)*
occult blood (792.1)

CC Excl: See code 578.0

AHA: 2Q, '92, 8

DRG 174

578.9 Hemorrhage of gastrointestinal tract, unspecified CC

Gastric hemorrhage
Intestinal hemorrhage

CC Excl: See code 578.0

AHA: ▶3Q, '05, 17;◀ N-D, '86, 9

DRG 174

✓4th 579 Intestinal malabsorption

579.0 Celiac disease

Celiac:
crisis
infantilism
rickets
Gee (-Herter) disease
Gluten enteropathy
Idiopathic steatorrhea
Nontropical sprue

DEF: Malabsorption syndrome due to gluten consumption; symptoms include fetid, bulky, frothy, oily stools; distended abdomen, gas, weight loss, asthenia, electrolyte depletion and vitamin B, D and K deficiency.

579.1 Tropical sprue

Sprue:
NOS
tropical
Tropical steatorrhea

DEF: Diarrhea, occurs in tropics; may be due to enteric infection and malnutrition.

579.2 Blind loop syndrome

Postoperative blind loop syndrome

DEF: Obstruction or impaired passage in small intestine due to alterations, from strictures or surgery; causes stasis, abnormal bacterial flora, diarrhea, weight loss, multiple vitamin deficiency, and megaloblastic anemia.

579.3 Other and unspecified postsurgical nonabsorption CC

Hypoglycemia } following gastrointestinal surgery
Malnutrition }

CC Excl: 579.3-579.9

AHA: 4Q, '03, 104

579.4 Pancreatic steatorrhea

DEF: Excess fat in feces due to absence of pancreatic juice in intestine.

579.8 Other specified intestinal malabsorption

Enteropathy:
exudative
protein-losing
Steatorrhea (chronic)

AHA: 1Q, '88, 6

579.9 Unspecified intestinal malabsorption

Malabsorption syndrome NOS

AHA: 4Q, '04, 59

10. DISEASES OF THE GENITOURINARY SYSTEM (580-629)

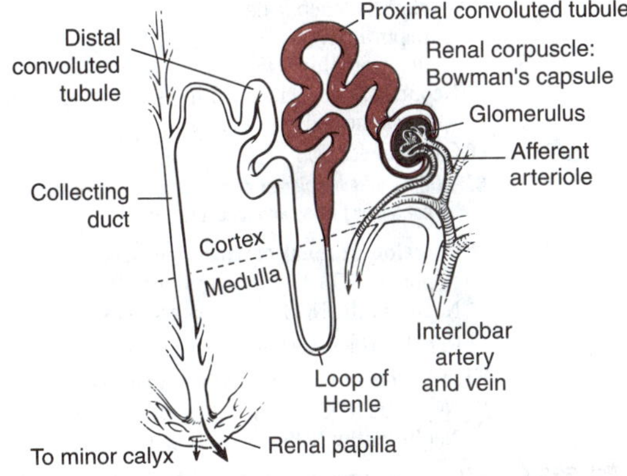

NEPHRITIS, NEPHROTIC SYNDROME, AND NEPHROSIS (580-589)

EXCLUDES ▶ *hypertensive chronic kidney disease (403.00-403.91, 404.00-404.93)*◀

✓4th **580 Acute glomerulonephritis**

INCLUDES acute nephritis

DEF: Acute, severe inflammation in tuft of capillaries that filter the kidneys.

580.0 With lesion of proliferative glomerulonephritis CC
- Acute (diffuse) proliferative glomerulonephritis
- Acute poststreptococcal glomerulonephritis

CC Excl: 016.00-016.06, 016.30-016.36, 016.90-016.96, 017.90-017.96, 098.10, 098.19, 098.30-098.31, 098.89, 112.2, 131.00, 131.8-131.9, 250.40-250.43, 250.80-250.93, 274.10, 274.19, 580.0-591, 593.0-593.2, 593.89, 593.9, 599.7-599.9

580.4 With lesion of rapidly progressive glomerulonephritis CC
- Acute nephritis with lesion of necrotizing glomerulitis

CC Excl: See code 580.0

DEF: Acute glomerulonephritis; progresses to ESRD with diffuse epithelial proliferation.

✓5th **580.8 With other specified pathological lesion in kidney**

580.81 ***Acute glomerulonephritis in diseases classified elsewhere*** CC

Code first underlying disease, as:
- infectious hepatitis (070.0-070.9)
- mumps (072.79)
- subacute bacterial endocarditis (421.0)
- typhoid fever (002.0)

CC Excl: See code 580.0

580.89 Other CC

Glomerulonephritis, acute, with lesion of:
- exudative nephritis
- interstitial (diffuse) (focal) nephritis

CC Excl: 016.00-016.06, 016.30-016.36, 016.90-016.96, 017.90-017.96, 098.10, 098.19, 098.30-098.31, 098.89, 112.2, 131.00, 131.8-131.9, 274.10, 274.19, 580.0-591, 593.0-593.2, 593.89, 593.9, 599.7-599.9

580.9 Acute glomerulonephritis with unspecified pathological lesion in kidney CC

Glomerulonephritis: NOS, hemorrhagic; Nephritis; Nephropathy — specified as acute

CC Excl: 016.00-016.06, 016.30-016.36, 016.90-016.96, 017.90-017.96, 098.10, 098.19, 098.30-098.31, 098.89, 112.2, 131.00, 131.8-131.9, 250.40-250.43, 250.80-250.93, 274.10, 274.19, 580.0-591, 593.0-593.2, 593.89, 593.9, 599.7-599.9

✓4th **581 Nephrotic syndrome**

DEF: Disease process marked by symptoms such as; extensive edema, notable proteinuria, hypoalbuminemia, and susceptibility to intercurrent infections.

581.0 With lesion of proliferative glomerulonephritis CC

CC Excl: See code 580.9

581.1 With lesion of membranous glomerulonephritis CC
- Epimembranous nephritis
- Idiopathic membranous glomerular disease
- Nephrotic syndrome with lesion of:
  - focal glomerulosclerosis
  - sclerosing membranous glomerulonephritis
  - segmental hyalinosis

CC Excl: See code 580.9

581.2 With lesion of membranoproliferative glomerulonephritis CC

Nephrotic syndrome with lesion (of): endothelial, hypocomplementemic persistent, lobular, mesangiocapillary, mixed membranous and proliferative — glomerulonephritis

CC Excl: See code 580.9

DEF: Glomerulonephritis combined with clinical features of nephrotic syndrome; characterized by uneven thickening of glomerular capillary walls and mesangial cell increase; slowly progresses to ESRD.

581.3 With lesion of minimal change glomerulonephritis CC
- Foot process disease
- Lipoid nephrosis
- Minimal change:
  - glomerular disease
  - glomerulitis
  - nephrotic syndrome

CC Excl: See code 580.9

✓4th **581.8 With other specified pathological lesion in kidney**

581.81 ***Nephrotic syndrome in diseases classified elsewhere*** CC

Code first underlying disease, as:
- amyloidosis ▶(277.30-277.39)◀
- diabetes mellitus (250.4)
- malaria (084.9)
- polyarteritis (446.0)
- systemic lupus erythematosus (710.0)

EXCLUDES *nephrosis in epidemic hemorrhagic fever (078.6)*

CC Excl: See code 580.9

AHA: 3Q, '91, 8,12; S-O, '85, 3

581.89 Other CC

Glomerulonephritis with edema and lesion of:
- exudative nephritis
- interstitial (diffuse) (focal) nephritis

CC Excl: See code 580.9

581.9 Nephrotic syndrome with unspecified pathological lesion in kidney CC
Glomerulonephritis with edema NOS
Nephritis:
nephrotic NOS
with edema NOS
Nephrosis NOS
Renal disease with edema NOS
CC Excl: See code 580.9

✓4th **582 Chronic glomerulonephritis**
INCLUDES chronic nephritis
DEF: Slow progressive type of nephritis characterized by inflammation of the capillary loops in the glomeruli of the kidney, which leads to renal failure.

582.0 With lesion of proliferative glomerulonephritis
Chronic (diffuse) proliferative glomerulonephritis

582.1 With lesion of membranous glomerulonephritis
Chronic glomerulonephritis:
membranous
sclerosing
Focal glomerulosclerosis
Segmental hyalinosis
AHA: S-O, '84, 16

582.2 With lesion of membranoproliferative glomerulonephritis
Chronic glomerulonephritis:
endothelial
hypocomplementemic persistent
lobular
membranoproliferative
mesangiocapillary
mixed membranous and proliferative
DEF: Chronic glomerulonephritis with mesangial cell proliferation.

582.4 With lesion of rapidly progressive glomerulonephritis
Chronic nephritis with lesion of necrotizing glomerulitis
DEF: Chronic glomerulonephritisrapidly progresses to ESRD; marked by diffuse epithelial proliferation.

✓5th **582.8 With other specified pathological lesion in kidney**

582.81 Chronic glomerulonephritis in diseases classified elsewhere
Code first underlying disease, as:
amyloidosis ▶(277.30-277.39)◀
systemic lupus erythematosus (710.0)

582.89 Other
Chronic glomerulonephritis with lesion of:
exudative nephritis
interstitial (diffuse) (focal) nephritis

582.9 Chronic glomerulonephritis with unspecified pathological lesion in kidney
Glomerulonephritis: NOS, hemorrhagic; Nephritis; Nephropathy — specified as chronic
AHA: 2Q, '01, 12

✓4th **583 Nephritis and nephropathy, not specified as acute or chronic**
INCLUDES "renal disease" so stated, not specified as acute or chronic but with stated pathology or cause

583.0 With lesion of proliferative glomerulonephritis
Proliferative:
glomerulonephritis (diffuse) NOS
Proliferative:
nephritis NOS
nephropathy NOS

583.1 With lesion of membranous glomerulonephritis
Membranous:
glomerulonephritis NOS
nephritis NOS
Membranous nephropathy NOS
DEF: Kidney inflammation or dysfunction with deposits on glomerular capillary basement membranes.

583.2 With lesion of membranoproliferative glomerulonephritis
Membranoproliferative:
glomerulonephritis NOS
nephritis NOS
nephropathy NOS
Nephritis NOS, with lesion of: hypocomplementemic persistent, lobular, mesangiocapillary, mixed membranous and proliferative — glomerulonephritis
DEF: Kidney inflammation or dysfunction with mesangial cell proliferation.

583.4 With lesion of rapidly progressive glomerulonephritis CC
Necrotizing or rapidly progressive:
glomerulitis NOS
glomerulonephritis NOS
nephritis NOS
nephropathy NOS
Nephritis, unspecified, with lesion of necrotizing glomerulitis
CC Excl: See code 580.9
DEF: Kidney inflammation or dysfunction; rapidly progresses to ESRD marked by diffuse epithelial proliferation.

583.6 With lesion of renal cortical necrosis
Nephritis NOS; Nephropathy NOS — with (renal) cortical necrosis
Renal cortical necrosis NOS

583.7 With lesion of renal medullary necrosis
Nephritis NOS; Nephropathy NOS — with (renal) medullary [papillary] necrosis

✓5th **583.8 With other specified pathological lesion in kidney**

583.81 Nephritis and nephropathy, not specified as acute or chronic, in diseases classified elsewhere
Code first underlying disease, as:
amyloidosis ▶(277.30-277.39)◀
diabetes mellitus (250.4)
gonococcal infection (098.19)
Goodpasture's syndrome (446.21)
systemic lupus erythematosus (710.0)
tuberculosis (016.0)
EXCLUDES *gouty nephropathy (274.10)*
syphilitic nephritis (095.4)
AHA: 2Q, '03, 7; 3Q, '91, 8; S-O, '85, 3

583.89 Other
Glomerulitis; Glomerulonephritis; Nephritis; Nephropathy; Renal disease — with lesion of: exudative nephritis, interstitial nephritis

583.9 With unspecified pathological lesion in kidney
Glomerulitis; Glomerulonephritis; Nephritis; Nephropathy — NOS
EXCLUDES *nephropathy complicating pregnancy, labor, or the puerperium (642.0-642.9, 646.2)*
renal disease NOS with no stated cause (593.9)

584 Acute renal failure

EXCLUDES *following labor and delivery (669.3)*
posttraumatic (958.5)
that complicating:
abortion (634-638 with .3, 639.3)
ectopic or molar pregnancy (639.3)

AHA: 1Q, '93, 18; 2Q, '92, 5; 4Q, '92, 22

DEF: State resulting from increasing urea and related substances from the blood (azotemia), often with urine output of less than 500 ml per day.

584.5 With lesion of tubular necrosis CC MC
Lower nephron nephrosis
Renal failure with (acute) tubular necrosis
Tubular necrosis:
NOS
acute
CC Excl: 250.40-250.43, 250.80-250.93, 274.10, 274.19, 580.0-591, 593.0-593.2, 593.89, 593.9, 599.7-599.9, 753.0-753.3, 753.9

DEF: Acute decline in kidney efficiency with destruction of tubules.

584.6 With lesion of renal cortical necrosis CC MC
CC Excl: See code 584.5

DEF: Acute decline in kidney efficiency with destruction of renal tissues that filter blood.

584.7 With lesion of renal medullary [papillary] necrosis CC MC
Necrotizing renal papillitis
CC Excl: See code 584.5

DEF: Acute decline in kidney efficiency with destruction of renal tissues that collect urine.

584.8 With other specified pathological lesion in kidney CC MC
CC Excl: 250.40-250.43, 250.80-250.93, 274.10, 274.19, 580.0-591, 593.0-593.2, 593.89, 593.9, 599.7-599.9
AHA: N-D, '85, 1

584.9 Acute renal failure, unspecified CC MC
CC Excl: 250.40-250.43, 250.80-250.93, 274.10, 274.19, 580.0-591, 593.0-593.2, 593.89-593.9, 599.7-599.9, 753.0-753.3, 753.9
AHA: 2Q, '05, 18; 2Q, '03, 7; 1Q, '03, 22; 3Q, '02, 21, 28; 2Q, '01, 14; 1Q, '00, 22; 3Q, '96, 9; 4Q, '88, 1
DRG 316

585 Chronic kidney disease [CKD]
Chronic uremia
▶Code first hypertensive chronic kidney disease, if applicable, (403.00-403.91, 404.00-404.94)◀
Use additional code to identify kidney transplant status, if applicable (V42.0)
Use additional code to identify manifestation as:
uremic:
neuropathy (357.4)
pericarditis (420.0)

AHA: 4Q, '05, 68, 77; 1Q, '04, 5; 4Q, '03, 61, 111; 2Q, '03, 7; 2Q, '01, 12, 13; 1Q, '01, 3; 4Q, '98, 55; 3Q, '98, 6, 7; 2Q, '98, 20; 3Q, '96, 9; 1Q, '93, 18; 3Q, '91, 8; 4Q, '89, 1; N-D, '85, 15; S-O, '84, 3

585.1 Chronic kidney disease, Stage I CC
CC Excl: 250.40-250.43, 250.80-250.83, 250.90-250.93, 274.10, 274.19, 580.0-591, 593.0-593.2, 593.89-593.9, 599.7-599.9, 753.0-753.3, 753.9

DEF: Some kidney damage; normal or slightly increased GFR (> 90).

585.2 Chronic kidney disease, Stage II (mild) CC
CC Excl: See code 585.1

DEF: Kidney damage with mild decrease in GFR (60–89).

585.3 Chronic kidney disease, Stage III (moderate) CC
CC Excl: See code 585.1
AHA: 4Q, '05, 69

DEF: Kidney damage with moderate decrease in GFR (30–59).

585.4 Chronic kidney disease, Stage IV (severe) CC
CC Excl: See code 585.1

DEF: Kidney damage with severe decrease in GFR (15–29).

585.5 Chronic kidney disease, Stage V CC
EXCLUDES ▶ *chronic kidney disease, stage V requiring chronic dialysis (585.6)*◀
CC Excl: See code 585.1

DEF: Kidney failure with GFR value of less than 15.

585.6 End stage renal disease CC
▶Chronic kidney disease requiring chronic dialysis◀
CC Excl: See code 585.1
AHA: 4Q, '05, 79

DEF: Federal government indicator of a stage V CKD patient undergoing treatment by dialysis or transplantation.

585.9 Chronic kidney disease, unspecified CC
Chronic renal disease
Chronic renal failure NOS
Chronic renal insufficiency
CC Excl: See code 585.1
AHA: 4Q, '05, 79

586 Renal failure, unspecified
Uremia NOS

EXCLUDES *following labor and delivery (669.3)*
posttraumatic renal failure (958.5)
that complicating:
abortion (634-638 with .3, 639.3)
ectopic or molar pregnancy (639.3)
uremia:
extrarenal (788.9)
prerenal (788.9)
with any condition classifiable to 401 (403.0-403.9 with fifth-digit 1)

AHA: 3Q, '98, 6; 1Q, '93, 18; 1Q, '88, 3

DEF: Renal failure: kidney functions cease; malfunction may be due to inability to excrete metabolized substances or retain level of electrolytes.

DEF: Uremia: excess urea, creatinine and other nitrogenous products of protein and amino acid metabolism in blood due to reduced excretory function in bilateral kidney disease; also called azotemia.

587 Renal sclerosis, unspecified
Atrophy of kidney
Contracted kidney
Renal:
cirrhosis
fibrosis

EXCLUDES *nephrosclerosis (arteriolar) (arteriosclerotic) (403.00-403.91)*
with hypertension (403.00-403.91)

588 Disorders resulting from impaired renal function

588.0 Renal osteodystrophy
Azotemic osteodystrophy
Phosphate-losing tubular disorders
Renal:
dwarfism
infantilism
rickets

DEF: Bone disorder that results in various bone diseases such as osteomalacia, osteoporosis or osteosclerosis; caused by impaired renal function, an abnormal level of phosphorus in the blood and impaired stimulation of the parathyroid.

588.1 Nephrogenic diabetes insipidus
EXCLUDES *diabetes insipidus NOS (253.5)*

DEF: Type of diabetes due to renal tubules inability to reabsorb water; not responsive to vasopressin; may develop into chronic renal insufficiency.

588.8 Other specified disorders resulting from impaired renal function
EXCLUDES *secondary hypertension (405.0-405.9)*

588.81 Secondary hyperparathyroidism (of renal origin)
Secondary hyperparathyroidism NOS
AHA: 4Q, '04, 58-59

DEF: Parathyroid dysfunction caused by chronic renal failure; phosphate clearance is impaired, phosphate is released from bone, vitamin D is not produced, intestinal calcium absorption is low, and blood levels of calcium are lowered causing excessive production of parathyroid hormone.

Genitourinary System 584–588.81

588.89 Other specified disorders resulting from impaired renal function
Hypokalemic nephropathy

588.9 Unspecified disorder resulting from impaired renal function

✓4th **589 Small kidney of unknown cause**

589.0 Unilateral small kidney

589.1 Bilateral small kidneys

589.9 Small kidney, unspecified

OTHER DISEASES OF URINARY SYSTEM (590-599)

✓4th **590 Infections of kidney**
Use additional code to identify organism, such as Escherichia coli [E. coli] (041.4)

✓5th **590.0 Chronic pyelonephritis**
Chronic pyelitis
Chronic pyonephrosis
Code if applicable, any casual condition first

590.00 Without lesion of renal medullary necrosis

590.01 With lesion of renal medullary necrosis

✓5th **590.1 Acute pyelonephritis**
Acute pyelitis
Acute pyonephrosis

590.10 Without lesion of renal medullary necrosis CC
CC Excl: 016.00-016.06, 016.30-016.36, 016.90-016.96, 017.90-017.96, 098.10, 098.19, 098.30-098.31, 098.89, 112.2, 131.00, 131.8-131.9, 250.40-250.43, 250.80-250.93, 274.10, 274.19, 580.0-591, 593.0-593.2, 593.89, 593.9, 599.0, 599.7-599.9

DRG 320

590.11 With lesion of renal medullary necrosis CC
CC Excl: See code 590.10

590.2 Renal and perinephric abscess CC
Abscess:
kidney
nephritic
Abscess:
perirenal
Carbuncle of kidney
CC Excl: See code 590.10

590.3 Pyeloureteritis cystica CC
Infection of renal pelvis and ureter
Ureteritis cystica
CC Excl: 016.00-016.06, 016.30-016.36, 016.90-016.96, 017.90-017.96, 098.10, 098.19, 098.30-098.31, 098.89, 112.2, 131.00, 131.8-131.9, 274.10, 274.19, 580.0-591, 593.0-593.2, 593.89, 593.9, 599.0, 599.7-599.9

DEF: Inflammation and formation of submucosal cysts in the kidney, pelvis, and ureter.

✓5th **590.8 Other pyelonephritis or pyonephrosis, not specified as acute or chronic**

590.80 Pyelonephritis, unspecified CC
Pyelitis NOS
Pyelonephritis NOS
CC Excl: See code 590.3
AHA: 1Q, '98, 10; 4Q, '97, 40

DRG 320

590.81 Pyelitis or pyelonephritis in diseases classified elsewhere CC
Code first underlying disease, as:
tuberculosis (016.0)
CC Excl: See code 590.3

590.9 Infection of kidney, unspecified CC
EXCLUDES *urinary tract infection NOS (599.0)*
CC Excl: See code 590.3

Genitourinary System

Inferior vena cava
Aorta
Left kidney
Right kidney
Ureter
Anterior division of internal iliac artery
Ovarian or testicular artery and vein
Superior and Inferior vesicular arteries
Urinary bladder
Ureteral orifice
Urogenital diaphragm
Urethra

591 Hydronephrosis CC
Hydrocalycosis
Hydronephrosis
Hydroureteronephrosis
EXCLUDES *congenital hydronephrosis (753.29)*
hydroureter (593.5)
CC Excl: See code 590.3
AHA: 2Q, '98, 9
DEF: Distention of kidney and pelvis, with urine build-up due to ureteral obstruction; pyonephrosis may result.

✓4th **592 Calculus of kidney and ureter**
EXCLUDES *nephrocalcinosis (275.4)*

592.0 Calculus of kidney
Nephrolithiasis NOS
Renal calculus or stone
Staghorn calculus
Stone in kidney
EXCLUDES *uric acid nephrolithiasis (274.11)*
AHA: 1Q, '00, 4

592.1 Calculus of ureter CC
Ureteric stone
Ureterolithiasis
CC Excl: 592.0-592.9, 593.3-593.5, 593.89-594.9, 599.60-599.9
AHA: 2Q, '98, 9; 1Q, '98, 10; 1Q, '91, 11

592.9 Urinary calculus, unspecified
AHA: 1Q, '98, 10; 4Q, '97, 40

✓4th **593 Other disorders of kidney and ureter**

593.0 Nephroptosis
Floating kidney
Mobile kidney

593.1 Hypertrophy of kidney

593.2 Cyst of kidney, acquired
Cyst (multiple) (solitary) of kidney, not congenital
Peripelvic (lymphatic) cyst
EXCLUDES *calyceal or pyelogenic cyst of kidney (591)*
congenital cyst of kidney (753.1)
polycystic (disease of) kidney (753.1)
AHA: 4Q, '90, 3
DEF: Abnormal, fluid-filled sac in the kidney, not present at birth.

593.3 Stricture or kinking of ureter
Angulation } of ureter (post-operative)
Constriction }
Stricture of pelviureteric junction
AHA: 2Q, '98, 9
DEF: Stricture or knot in tube connecting kidney to bladder.

593.4 Other ureteric obstruction
Idiopathic retroperitoneal fibrosis
Occlusion NOS of ureter
EXCLUDES *that due to calculus (592.1)*
AHA: 2Q, '97, 4

593.5 Hydroureter CC

EXCLUDES *congenital hydroureter (753.22)*
hydrouretеronephrosis (591)

CC Excl: 593.3-593.5, 593.89, 593.9, 595.0-595.9, 596.8-596.9, 599.0, 599.60-599.9, 753.4-753.5, 753.9

593.6 Postural proteinuria

Benign postural proteinuria
Orthostatic proteinuria

EXCLUDES *proteinuria NOS (791.0)*

DEF: Excessive amounts of serum protein in the urine caused by the body position, e.g., orthostatic and lordotic.

✓5th **593.7 Vesicoureteral reflux**

AHA: 4Q, '94, 42

DEF: Backflow of urine, from bladder into ureter due to obstructed bladder neck.

593.70 Unspecified or without reflux nephropathy
593.71 With reflux nephropathy, unilateral
593.72 With reflux nephropathy, bilateral
593.73 With reflux nephropathy NOS

✓5th **593.8 Other specified disorders of kidney and ureter**

593.81 Vascular disorders of kidney

Renal (artery):
embolism
hemorrhage
Renal (artery):
thrombosis
Renal infarction

593.82 Ureteral fistula

Intestinoureteral fistula

EXCLUDES *fistula between ureter and female genital tract (619.0)*

DEF: Abnormal communication, between tube connecting kidney to bladder and another structure.

593.89 Other

Adhesions, kidney or ureter
Periureteritis
Polyp of ureter
Pyelectasia
Ureterocele

EXCLUDES *tuberculosis of ureter (016.2)*
ureteritis cystica (590.3)

593.9 Unspecified disorder of kidney and ureter

Acute renal disease
Acute renal insufficiency
Renal disease NOS
Salt-losing nephritis or syndrome

EXCLUDES *chronic renal insufficiency (585.9)*
cystic kidney disease (753.1)
nephropathy, so stated (583.0-583.9)
renal disease:
arising in pregnancy or the puerperium (642.1-642.2, 642.4-642.7, 646.2)
not specified as acute or chronic, but with stated pathology or cause (583.0-583.9)

AHA: ▶4Q, '05, 79;◀ 1Q, '93, 17

DRG 331

✓4th **594 Calculus of lower urinary tract**

594.0 Calculus in diverticulum of bladder

DEF: Stone or mineral deposit in abnormal sac on the bladder wall.

594.1 Other calculus in bladder

Urinary bladder stone

EXCLUDES *staghorn calculus (592.0)*

DEF: Stone or mineral deposit in bladder.

594.2 Calculus in urethra

DEF: Stone or mineral deposit in tube that empties urine from bladder.

594.8 Other lower urinary tract calculus

AHA: J-F, '85, 16

594.9 Calculus of lower urinary tract, unspecified

EXCLUDES *calculus of urinary tract NOS (592.9)*

✓4th **595 Cystitis**

EXCLUDES *prostatocystitis (601.3)*

Use additional code to identify organism, such as Escherichia coli [E. coli] (041.4)

595.0 Acute cystitis CC

EXCLUDES *trigonitis (595.3)*

CC Excl: 016.10-016.16, 016.30-016.36, 016.90-016.96, 017.90-017.96, 098.0, 098.11, 098.2, 098.39, 098.89, 112.2, 131.00, 131.8-131.9, 593.3-593.5, 593.89, 593.9, 595.0-595.9, 596.8-596.9, 599.0, 599.60-599.9

AHA: 2Q, '99, 15

DEF: Acute inflammation of bladder.

595.1 Chronic interstitial cystitis CC

Hunner's ulcer
Panmural fibrosis of bladder
Submucous cystitis

CC Excl: See code 595.0

DEF: Inflamed lesion affecting bladder wall; symptoms include urinary frequency, pain on bladder filling, nocturia, and distended bladder.

595.2 Other chronic cystitis CC

Chronic cystitis NOS
Subacute cystitis

EXCLUDES *trigonitis (595.3)*

CC Excl: See code 595.0

DEF: Persistent inflammation of bladder.

595.3 Trigonitis

Follicular cystitis
Trigonitis (acute) (chronic)
Urethrotrigonitis

DEF: Inflammation of the triangular area of the bladder called the trigonum vesicae.

595.4 ***Cystitis in diseases classified elsewhere*** CC

Code first underlying disease, as:
actinomycosis (039.8)
amebiasis (006.8)
bilharziasis (120.0-120.9)
Echinococcus infestation (122.3, 122.6)

EXCLUDES *cystitis:*
diphtheritic (032.84)
gonococcal (098.11, 098.31)
monilial (112.2)
trichomonal (131.09)
tuberculous (016.1)

CC Excl: See code 595.0

✓5th **595.8 Other specified types of cystitis**

595.81 Cystitis cystica CC

CC Excl: See code 595.0

DEF: Inflammation of the bladder characterized by formation of multiple cysts.

595.82 Irradiation cystitis CC

Use additional E code to identify cause

CC Excl: See code 595.0

DEF: Inflammation of the bladder due to effects of radiation.

595.89 Other CC

Abscess of bladder
Cystitis:
bullous
Cystitis:
emphysematous
glandularis

CC Excl: See code 595.0

595.9 Cystitis, unspecified CC

CC Excl: See code 595.0

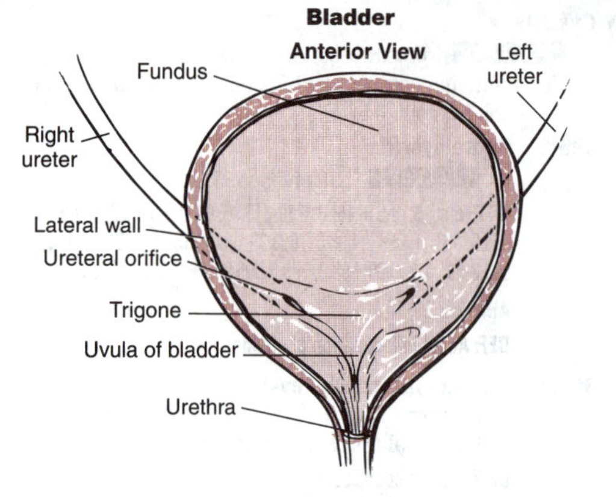

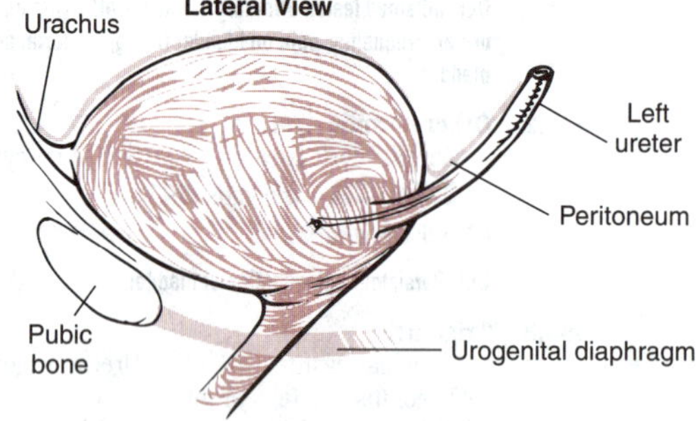

✓4th 596 Other disorders of bladder

Use additional code to identify urinary incontinence (625.6, 788.30-788.39)

AHA: M-A, '87, 10

596.0 Bladder neck obstruction CC

Contracture (acquired) / Obstruction (acquired) / Stenosis (acquired) } of bladder neck or vesicourethral orifice

EXCLUDES *congenital (753.6)*

CC Excl: 185, 188.0-188.9, 189.3-189.9, 596.0, 596.4, 596.51-596.59, 596.8-596.9, 600.00-600.9, 601.0-602.9

AHA: 3Q, '02, 28; 2Q, '01, 14; N-D, '86, 10

DEF: Bladder outlet and vesicourethral obstruction; occurs more often in males as a consequence of benign prostatic hypertrophy or prostatic cancer; may also occur in either sex due to strictures, following radiation, cystoscopy, catheterization, injury, infection, blood clots, bladder cancer, impaction or disease compressing bladder neck.

596.1 Intestinovesical fistula CC

Fistula:
- enterovesical
- vesicocolic

Fistula:
- vesicoenteric
- vesicorectal

CC Excl: 098.0, 098.2, 098.39, 098.89, 596.1-596.2, 596.8-596.9, 599.7-599.9, 788.1

DEF: Abnormal communication, between intestine and bladder.

596.2 Vesical fistula, not elsewhere classified CC

Fistula:
- bladder NOS
- urethrovesical

Fistula:
- vesicocutaneous
- vesicoperineal

EXCLUDES *fistula between bladder and female genital tract (619.0)*

CC Excl: See code 596.1

DEF: Abnormal communication between bladder and another structure.

596.3 Diverticulum of bladder

Diverticulitis / Diverticulum (acquired) (false) } of bladder

EXCLUDES *that with calculus in diverticulum of bladder (594.0)*

DEF: Abnormal pouch in bladder wall.

596.4 Atony of bladder CC

High compliance bladder

Hypotonicity / Inertia } of bladder

EXCLUDES *neurogenic bladder (596.54)*

CC Excl: 596.4, 596.51-596.59, 596.8-596.9, 599.7-599.9, 788.1

DEF: Distended, bladder with loss of expulsive force; linked to CNS disease.

✓5th 596.5 Other functional disorders of bladder

EXCLUDES *cauda equina syndrome with neurogenic bladder (344.61)*

596.51 Hypertonicity of bladder

Hyperactivity
Overactive bladder

DEF: Abnormal tension of muscular wall of bladder; may appear after surgery of voluntary nerve.

596.52 Low bladder compliance

DEF: Low bladder capacity; causes increased pressure and frequent urination.

596.53 Paralysis of bladder

DEF: Impaired bladder motor function due to nerve or muscle damage.

596.54 Neurogenic bladder NOS

AHA: 1Q, '01, 12

DEF: Unspecified dysfunctional bladder due to lesion of central, peripheral nervous system; may result in incontinence, residual urine retention, urinary infection, stones and renal failure.

596.55 Detrusor sphincter dyssynergia

DEF: Instability of the urinary bladder sphincter muscle associated with urinary incontinence..

596.59 Other functional disorder of bladder

Detrusor instability

DEF: Detrusor instability: instability of bladder; marked by uninhibited contractions often leading to incontinence.

596.6 Rupture of bladder, nontraumatic CC

CC Excl: 596.6-596.9, 599.7-599.9, 788.1

596.7 Hemorrhage into bladder wall CC

Hyperemia of bladder

EXCLUDES *acute hemorrhagic cystitis (595.0)*

CC Excl: See code 596.6

596.8 Other specified disorders of bladder

Bladder:
- calcified
- contracted

Bladder:
- hemorrhage
- hypertrophy

EXCLUDES *cystocele, female (618.01-618.02, 618.09, 618.2-618.4)*
hernia or prolapse of bladder, female (618.01-618.02, 618.09, 618.2-618.4)

AHA: J-F, '85, 8

596.9 Unspecified disorder of bladder

AHA: J-F, '85, 8

✓4th 597 Urethritis, not sexually transmitted, and urethral syndrome

EXCLUDES *nonspecific urethritis, so stated (099.4)*

597.0 Urethral abscess CC

Abscess:
- periurethral
- urethral (gland)

Abscess of:
- bulbourethral gland

Abscess of:
- Cowper's gland
- Littré's gland

Periurethral cellulitis

EXCLUDES *urethral caruncle (599.3)*

CC Excl: 098.0, 098.2, 098.39, 098.89, 099.40-099.49, 112.2, 131.00, 131.02, 131.8-131.9, 597.0-598.01, 598.8-599.0, 599.60-599.9, 607.1-607.83, 607.85-607.9, 608.4-608.81, 608.85, 608.87-608.89, 752.61-752.69, 752.81-752.9, 753.6-753.9, 788.1

DEF: Pocket of pus in tube that empties urine from the bladder.

✓5th **597.8 Other urethritis**

597.80 Urethritis, unspecified

597.81 Urethral syndrome NOS

597.89 Other

Adenitis, Skene's glands
Cowperitis
Meatitis, urethral
Ulcer, urethra (meatus)
Verumontanitis

EXCLUDES *trichomonal (131.02)*

✓4th **598 Urethral stricture**

Use additional code to identify urinary incontinence (625.6, 788.30-788.39)

INCLUDES pinhole meatus
stricture of urinary meatus

EXCLUDES *congenital stricture of urethra and urinary meatus (753.6)*

DEF: Narrowing of tube that empties urine from bladder.

✓5th **598.0 Urethral stricture due to infection**

598.00 Due to unspecified infection

598.01 Due to infective diseases classified elsewhere

Code first underlying disease, as:
gonococcal infection (098.2)
schistosomiasis (120.0-120.9)
syphilis (095.8)

598.1 Traumatic urethral stricture CC

Stricture of urethra: late effect of injury
Stricture of urethra: postobstetric

EXCLUDES *postoperative following surgery on genitourinary tract (598.2)*

CC Excl: 098.0, 098.2, 098.39, 098.89, 131.02, 598.1-598.9, 599.60-599.9, 752.61-752.65, 752.69, 753.6-753.9, 788.1

598.2 Postoperative urethral stricture CC

Postcatheterization stricture of urethra

CC Excl: See code 598.1

AHA: 3Q, '97, 6

598.8 Other specified causes of urethral stricture

AHA: N-D, '84, 9

598.9 Urethral stricture, unspecified

✓4th **599 Other disorders of urethra and urinary tract**

599.0 Urinary tract infection, site not specified CC

EXCLUDES *candidiasis of urinary tract (112.2)*
urinary tract infection of newborn (771.82)

Use additional code to identify organism, such as Escherichia coli [E. coli] (041.4)

CC Excl: 098.2, 098.39, 098.89, 099.40-099.49, 112.2, 131.00, 131.8-131.9, 590.10-590.9, 591, 593.89, 593.9, 595.0-595.9, 599.0, 599.6-599.9, 788.1, 996.64

AHA: 3Q, '05, 12; 2Q, '04, 13; 4Q, '03, 79; 4Q, '99, 6; 2Q, '99, 15;1Q, '98, 5; 2Q, '96, 7; 4Q, '96, 33; 2Q, '95, 7; 1Q, '92, 13

▽ **DRG** 320

599.1 Urethral fistula

Fistula:
urethroperineal
urethrorectal
Urinary fistula NOS

EXCLUDES *fistula:*
urethroscrotal (608.89)
urethrovaginal (619.0)
urethrovesicovaginal (619.0)

AHA: 3Q, '97, 6

599.2 Urethral diverticulum

DEF: Abnormal pouch in urethral wall.

599.3 Urethral caruncle

Polyp of urethra

599.4 Urethral false passage CC

CC Excl: 597.0-598.9, 599.1-599.9, 607.1-607.83, 607.85-607.9, 608.4-608.81, 608.85, 608.87-608.89, 752.61-752.69, 752.81-752.9, 753.9, 788.1

DEF: Abnormal opening in urethra due to surgery; trauma or disease.

599.5 Prolapsed urethral mucosa

Prolapse of urethra
Urethrocele

EXCLUDES *urethrocele, female (618.03, 618.09, 618.2-618.4)*

✓5th **599.6 Urinary obstruction**

Use additional code to identify urinary incontinence (625.6, 788.30-788.39)

EXCLUDES *obstructive nephropathy NOS (593.89)*

AHA: 4Q, '05, 80

599.60 Urinary obstruction, unspecified CC

Obstructive uropathy NOS
Urinary (tract) obstruction NOS

CC Excl: 185, 188.0-188.9, 189.2-189.9, 274.11, 344.61, 592.1-592.9, 593.3-593.5, 593.89-596.0, 596.51-596.59, 596.8-602.9, 753.0-753.9, 788.1

599.69 Urinary obstruction, not elsewhere classified CC

▶Code, if applicable, any causal condition first, such as:
hyperplasia of prostate (600.0-600.9 with fifth-digit 1)◀

CC Excl: See code 599.60

599.7 Hematuria CC

Hematuria (benign) (essential)

EXCLUDES *hemoglobinuria (791.2)*

CC Excl: 592.0-592.9, 593.89, 593.9, 594.0-594.9, 596.6-596.7, 599.7-599.9

AHA: 1Q, '00, 5; 3Q, '95, 8

DEF: Blood in urine.

✓5th **599.8 Other specified disorders of urethra and urinary tract**

Use additional code to identify urinary incontinence (625.6, 788.30-788.39), if present

EXCLUDES *symptoms and other conditions classifiable to 788.0-788.2, 788.4-788.9, 791.0-791.9*

599.81 Urethral hypermobility

DEF: Hyperactive urethra.

599.82 Intrinsic (urethral) spincter deficiency [ISD]

AHA: 2Q, '96, 15

DEF: Malfunctioning urethral sphincter.

599.83 Urethral instability

DEF: Inconsistent functioning of urethra.

599.84 Other specified disorders of urethra

Rupture of urethra (nontraumatic)
Urethral:
cyst
granuloma

DEF: Rupture of urethra due to herniation or breaking down of tissue; not due to trauma.

DEF: Urethral cyst: abnormal sac in urethra; usually fluid filled.

DEF: Granuloma: inflammatory cells forming small nodules in urethra.

599.89 Other specified disorders of urinary tract

599.9 Unspecified disorder of urethra and urinary tract

DISEASES OF MALE GENITAL ORGANS (600-608)

✓4th **600 Hyperplasia of prostate**

INCLUDES ▶ enlarged prostate◀

AHA: 3Q, '05, 20; 4Q, '00, 43; 3Q, '94, 12; 3Q, '92, 7; N-D, '86, 10

DEF: Fibrostromal proliferation in periurethral glands, causes blood in urine; etiology unknown.

✓5th **600.0 Hypertrophy (benign) of prostate**

Benign prostatic hypertrophy
Enlargement of prostate
Smooth enlarged prostate
Soft enlarged prostate

AHA: 3Q, '05, 20; 4Q, '03, 63; 1Q, '03, 6; 3Q, '02, 28; 2Q, '01, 14

▲ **600.00 Hypertrophy (benign) of prostate without urinary obstruction and other lower urinary tract symptoms [LUTS]** A ♂

Hypertrophy (benign) of prostate NOS

▲ **600.01 Hypertrophy (benign) of prostate with urinary obstruction and other lower urinary tract symptoms [LUTS]** A ♂

Hypertrophy (benign) of prostate with urinary retention

▶Use additional code to identify symptoms:
incomplete bladder emptying (788.21)
nocturia (788.43)
straining on urination (788.65)
urinary frequency (788.41)
urinary hesitancy (788.64)
urinary incontinence (788.30-788.39)
urinary obstruction (599.69)
urinary retention (788.20)
urinary urgency (788.63)
weak urinary stream (788.62)◀

AHA: 4Q, '03, 64

✓5th **600.1 Nodular prostate**

Hard, firm prostate
Multinodular prostate

EXCLUDES *malignant neoplasm of prostate (185)*

AHA: 4Q, '03, 63

DEF: Hard, firm nodule in prostate.

600.10 Nodular prostate without urinary obstruction A ♂

Nodular prostate NOS

600.11 Nodular prostate with urinary obstruction A ♂

Nodular prostate with urinary retention

✓5th **600.2 Benign localized hyperplasia of prostate**

Adenofibromatous hypertrophy of prostate
Adenoma of prostate
Fibroadenoma of prostate
Fibroma of prostate
Myoma of prostate
Polyp of prostate

EXCLUDES *benign neoplasms of prostate (222.2)*
hypertrophy of prostate (600.00-600.01)
malignant neoplasm of prostate (185)

AHA: 4Q, '03, 63

DEF: Benign localized hyperplasia is a clearly defined epithelial tumor. Other terms used for this condition are adenofibromatous hypertrophy of prostate, adenoma of prostate, fibroadenoma of prostate, fibroma of prostate, myoma of prostate, and polyp of prostate.

▲ **600.20 Benign localized hyperplasia of prostate without urinary obstruction and other lower urinary tract symptoms [LUTS]** A ♂

Benign localized hyperplasia of prostate NOS

Male Pelvic Organs

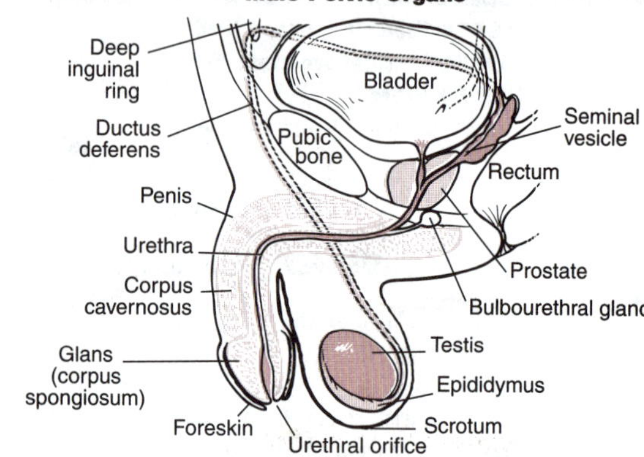

▲ **600.21 Benign localized hyperplasia of prostate with urinary obstruction and other lower urinary tract symptoms [LUTS]** A ♂

Benign localized hyperplasia of prostate with urinary retention

▶Use additional code to identify symptoms:
incomplete bladder emptying (788.21)
nocturia (788.43)
straining on urination (788.65)
urinary frequency (788.41)
urinary hesitancy (788.64)
urinary incontinence (788.30-788.39)
urinary obstruction (599.69)
urinary retention (788.20)
urinary urgency (788.63)
weak urinary stream (788.62)◀

600.3 Cyst of prostate A ♂

DEF: Sacs of fluid, which differentiate this from either nodular or adenomatous tumors.

✓5th **600.9 Hyperplasia of prostate, unspecified**

Median bar
Prostatic obstruction NOS

AHA: 4Q, '03, 63

▲ **600.90 Hyperplasia of prostate, unspecified, without urinary obstruction and other lower urinary tract symptoms [LUTS]** A ♂

Hyperplasia of prostate NOS

▲ **600.91 Hyperplasia of prostate, unspecified with urinary obstruction and other lower urinary tract symptoms [LUTS]** A ♂

Hyperplasia of prostate, unspecified, with urinary retention

▶Use additional code to identify symptoms:
incomplete bladder emptying (788.21)
nocturia (788.43)
straining on urination (788.65)
urinary frequency (788.41)
urinary hesitancy (788.64)
urinary incontinence (788.30-788.39)
urinary obstruction (599.69)
urinary retention (788.20)
urinary urgency (788.63)
weak urinary stream (788.62)◀

✓4th **601 Inflammatory diseases of prostate**

Use additional code to identify organism, such as Staphylococcus (041.1), or Streptococcus (041.0)

601.0 Acute prostatitis CC A ♂

CC Excl: 098.12, 098.32, 098.89, 112.2, 131.00, 131.03, 131.8-131.9, 600.00-602.9

601.1 Chronic prostatitis A ♂

601.2 Abscess of prostate CC A ♂

CC Excl: See code 601.0

601.3 Prostatocystitis CC A ♂

CC Excl: See code 601.0

N Newborn Age: 0  P Pediatric Age: 0-17 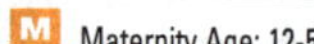 M Maternity Age: 12-55  A Adult Age: 15-124  CC CC Condition  MC Major Complication  CD Complex Dx HIV HIV Related Dx

601.4 Prostatitis in diseases classified elsewhere A ♂

Code first underlying disease, as:

actinomycosis (039.8)
blastomycosis (116.0)
syphilis (095.8)
tuberculosis (016.5)

EXCLUDES *prostatitis:*
gonococcal (098.12, 098.32)
monilial (112.2)
trichomonal (131.03)

601.8 Other specified inflammatory diseases of prostate A ♂

Prostatitis:
cavitary
diverticular

Prostatitis:
granulomatous

601.9 Prostatitis, unspecified A ♂

Prostatitis NOS

✓4th **602 Other disorders of prostate**

602.0 Calculus of prostate A ♂

Prostatic stone

DEF: Stone or mineral deposit in prostate.

602.1 Congestion or hemorrhage of prostate CC A ♂

CC Excl: See code 601.0

DEF: Bleeding or fluid collection in prostate.

602.2 Atrophy of prostate A ♂

602.3 Dysplasia of prostate ♂

Prostatic intraepithelial neoplasia I (PIN I)
Prostatic intraepithelial neoplasia II (PIN II)

EXCLUDES *prostatic intraepithelial neoplasia III (PIN III) (233.4)*

AHA: 4Q, '01, 46

DEF: Abnormality of shape and size of the intraepithelial tissues of the prostate; pre-malignant condition characterized by stalks and absence of a basilar cell layer; synonyms are intraductal dysplasia, large acinar atypical hyperplasia, atypical primary hyperplasia, hyperplasia with malignant changes, marked atypia, or duct-acinar dysplasia.

602.8 Other specified disorders of prostate A ♂

Fistula }
Infarction } of prostate
Stricture }

Periprostatic adhesions

602.9 Unspecified disorder of prostate A ♂

✓4th **603 Hydrocele**

INCLUDES hydrocele of spermatic cord, testis, or tunica vaginalis

EXCLUDES *congenital (778.6)*

DEF: Circumscribed collection of fluid in tunica vaginalis, spermatic cord or testis.

603.0 Encysted hydrocele

603.1 Infected hydrocele CC

Use additional code to identify organism

CC Excl: 112.2, 131.00, 131.8-131.9, 603.0-603.9

603.8 Other specified types of hydrocele

603.9 Hydrocele, unspecified

✓4th **604 Orchitis and epididymitis**

Use additional code to identify organism, such as Escherichia coli [E. coli] (041.4), Staphylococcus (041.1), or Streptococcus (041.0)

604.0 Orchitis, epididymitis, and epididymo-orchitis, with abscess CC ♂

Abscess of epididymis or testis

CC Excl: 072.0, 098.13-098.14, 098.33-098.34, 098.89, 112.2, 131.00, 131.8-131.9, 604.0-604.99

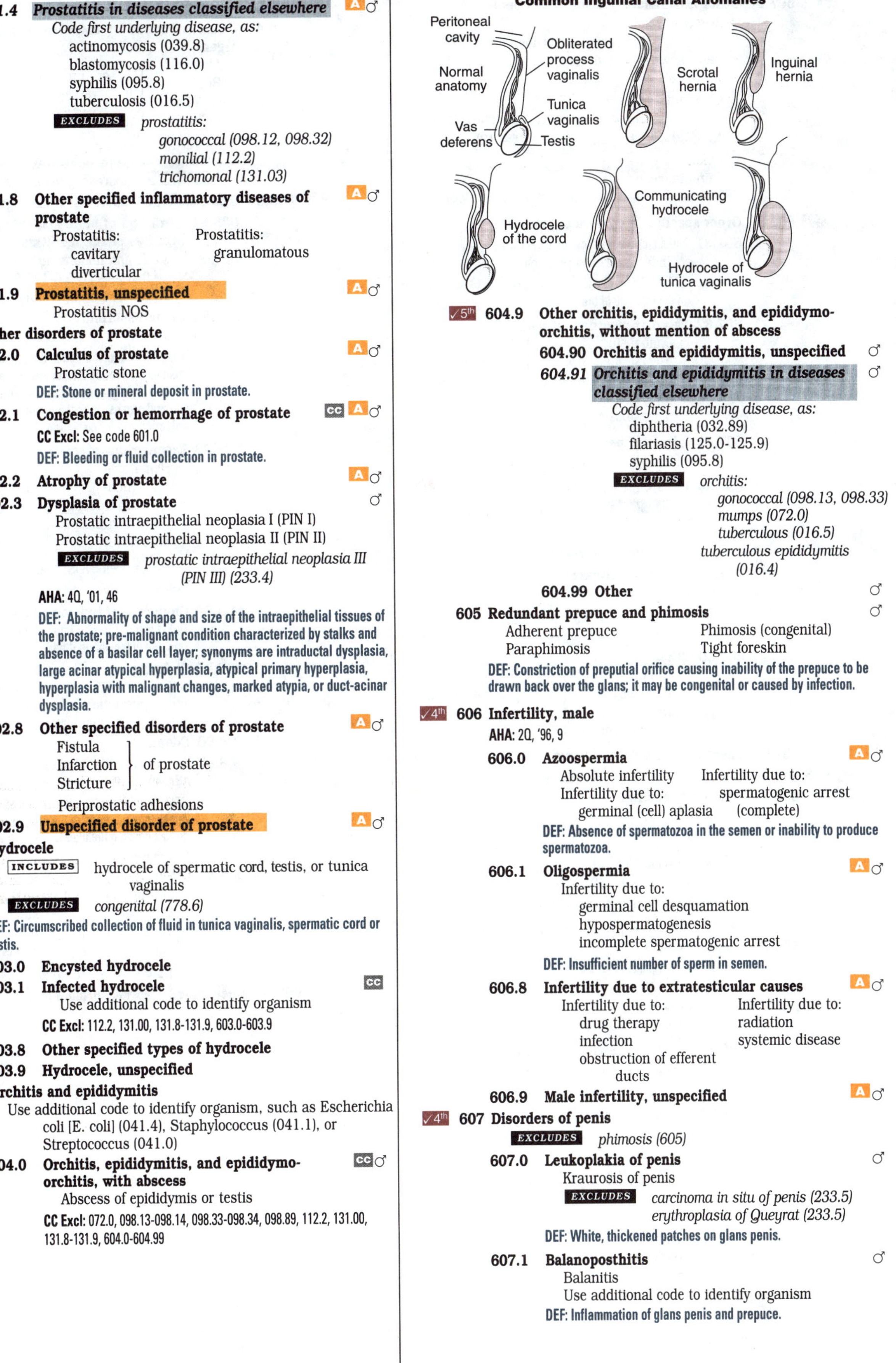

✓5th **604.9 Other orchitis, epididymitis, and epididymo-orchitis, without mention of abscess**

604.90 Orchitis and epididymitis, unspecified ♂

604.91 Orchitis and epididymitis in diseases classified elsewhere ♂

Code first underlying disease, as:

diphtheria (032.89)
filariasis (125.0-125.9)
syphilis (095.8)

EXCLUDES *orchitis:*
gonococcal (098.13, 098.33)
mumps (072.0)
tuberculous (016.5)
tuberculous epididymitis (016.4)

604.99 Other ♂

605 Redundant prepuce and phimosis ♂

Adherent prepuce
Paraphimosis
Phimosis (congenital)
Tight foreskin

DEF: Constriction of preputial orifice causing inability of the prepuce to be drawn back over the glans; it may be congenital or caused by infection.

✓4th **606 Infertility, male**

AHA: 2Q, '96, 9

606.0 Azoospermia A ♂

Absolute infertility
Infertility due to:
germinal (cell) aplasia
spermatogenic arrest (complete)

DEF: Absence of spermatozoa in the semen or inability to produce spermatozoa.

606.1 Oligospermia A ♂

Infertility due to:
germinal cell desquamation
hypospermatogenesis
incomplete spermatogenic arrest

DEF: Insufficient number of sperm in semen.

606.8 Infertility due to extratesticular causes A ♂

Infertility due to:
drug therapy
infection
obstruction of efferent ducts
radiation
systemic disease

606.9 Male infertility, unspecified A ♂

✓4th **607 Disorders of penis**

EXCLUDES *phimosis (605)*

607.0 Leukoplakia of penis ♂

Kraurosis of penis

EXCLUDES *carcinoma in situ of penis (233.5)*
erythroplasia of Queyrat (233.5)

DEF: White, thickened patches on glans penis.

607.1 Balanoposthitis ♂

Balanitis
Use additional code to identify organism

DEF: Inflammation of glans penis and prepuce.

607.2 Other inflammatory disorders of penis ♂

Abscess, Boil, Carbuncle, Cellulitis } of corpus cavernosum or penis

Cavernitis (penis)

Use additional code to identify organism

EXCLUDES *herpetic infection (054.13)*

607.3 Priapism ♂

Painful erection

DEF: Prolonged penile erection without sexual stimulation.

✓5th **607.8 Other specified disorders of penis**

607.81 Balanitis xerotica obliterans ♂

Induratio penis plastica

DEF: Inflammation of the glans penis, caused by stricture of the opening of the prepuce.

607.82 Vascular disorders of penis ♂

Embolism, Hematoma (nontraumatic), Hemorrhage, Thrombosis } of corpus cavernosum or penis

607.83 Edema of penis ♂

DEF: Fluid retention within penile tissues.

607.84 Impotence of organic origin A ♂

EXCLUDES *nonorganic (302.72)*

AHA: 3Q, '91, 11

DEF: Physiological cause interfering with erection.

607.85 Peyronie's disease ♂

AHA: 4Q, '03, 64

DEF: A severe curvature of the erect penis due to fibrosis of the cavernous sheaths.

607.89 Other ♂

Atrophy, Fibrosis, Hypertrophy, Ulcer (chronic) } of corpus cavernosum or penis

607.9 Unspecified disorder of penis ♂

✓4th **608 Other disorders of male genital organs**

608.0 Seminal vesiculitis ♂

Abscess, Cellulitis } of seminal vesicle

Vesiculitis (seminal)

Use additional code to identify organism

EXCLUDES *gonococcal infection (098.14, 098.34)*

DEF: Inflammation of seminal vesicle.

608.1 Spermatocele ♂

DEF: Cystic enlargement of the epididymis or the testis; the cysts contain spermatozoa.

✓5th **608.2 Torsion of testis**

DEF: Twisted or rotated testis; may compromise blood flow.

● **608.20 Torsion of testis, unspecified** ♂

● **608.21 Extravaginal torsion of spermatic cord** ♂

● **608.22 Intravaginal torsion of spermatic cord** ♂

● **608.23 Torsion of appendix testis** ♂

● **608.24 Torsion of appendix epididymis** ♂

Torsion of Testes

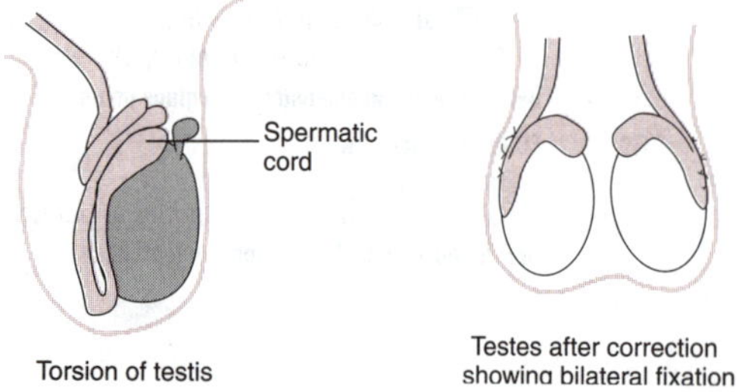

Torsion of testis

Testes after correction showing bilateral fixation

608.3 Atrophy of testis ♂

608.4 Other inflammatory disorders of male genital organs ♂

Abscess, Boil, Carbuncle, Cellulitis } of scrotum, spermatic cord, testis [except abscess], tunica vaginalis, or vas deferens

Vasitis

Use additional code to identify organism

EXCLUDES *abscess of testis (604.0)*

✓5th **608.8 Other specified disorders of male genital organs**

608.81 Disorders of male genital organs in diseases classified elsewhere ♂

Code first underlying disease, as:

filariasis (125.0-125.9)

tuberculosis (016.5)

608.82 Hematospermia ♂

AHA: 4Q, '01, 46

DEF: Presence of blood in the ejaculate; relatively common, affecting men of any age after puberty; cause is often difficult to determine since the semen originates in several organs, often the result of a viral or bacterial infection and inflammation.

608.83 Vascular disorders ♂

Hematoma (non-traumatic), Hemorrhage, Thrombosis } of seminal vesicle, spermatic cord, testis, scrotum, tunica vaginalis, or vas deferens

Hematocele NOS, male

AHA: 4Q, '03, 110

608.84 Chylocele of tunica vaginalis ♂

DEF: Chylous effusion into tunica vaginalis; due to infusion of lymphatic fluids.

608.85 Stricture ♂

Stricture of: spermatic cord, tunica vaginalis

Stricture of: vas deferens

608.86 Edema ♂

608.87 Retrograde ejaculation ♂

AHA: 4Q, '01, 46

DEF: Condition where the semen travels to the bladder rather than out through the urethra due to damaged nerves causing the bladder neck to remain open during ejaculation.

608.89 Other ♂

Atrophy, Fibrosis, Hypertrophy, Ulcer } of seminal vesicle, spermatic cord, testis, scrotum, tunica vaginalis, or vas deferens

EXCLUDES *atrophy of testis (608.3)*

608.9 Unspecified disorder of male genital organs ♂

DISORDERS OF BREAST (610-611)

✓4th 610 Benign mammary dysplasias

610.0 Solitary cyst of breast
Cyst (solitary) of breast

610.1 Diffuse cystic mastopathy A
Chronic cystic mastitis
Cystic breast
Fibrocystic disease of breast
DEF: Extensive formation of nodular cysts in breast tissue; symptoms include tenderness, change in size and hyperplasia of ductal epithelium.

610.2 Fibroadenosis of breast
Fibroadenosis of breast:
NOS
chronic
cystic
Fibroadenosis of breast:
diffuse
periodic
segmental
DEF: Non-neoplastic nodular condition of breast.

610.3 Fibrosclerosis of breast
DEF: Fibrous tissue in breast.

610.4 Mammary duct ectasia
Comedomastitis
Duct ectasia
Mastitis:
periductal
plasma cell
DEF: Atrophy of duct epithelium; causes distended collecting ducts of mammary gland; drying up of breast secretion, intraductal inflammation and periductal and interstitial chronic inflammatory reaction.

610.8 Other specified benign mammary dysplasias
Mazoplasia
Sebaceous cyst of breast

610.9 Benign mammary dysplasia, unspecified

✓4th 611 Other disorders of breast
EXCLUDES *that associated with lactation or the puerperium (675.0-676.9)*

611.0 Inflammatory disease of breast
Abscess (acute) (chronic) (nonpuerperal) of:
areola
breast
Mammillary fistula
Mastitis (acute) (subacute) (nonpuerperal):
NOS
infective
retromammary
submammary
EXCLUDES *carbuncle of breast (680.2)*
chronic cystic mastitis (610.1)
neonatal infective mastitis (771.5)
thrombophlebitis of breast [Mondor's disease] (451.89)

611.1 Hypertrophy of breast
Gynecomastia
Hypertrophy of breast:
NOS
Hypertrophy of breast:
massive pubertal

611.2 Fissure of nipple

611.3 Fat necrosis of breast
Fat necrosis (segmental) of breast
DEF: Splitting of neutral fats in adipose tissue cells as a result of trauma; a firm circumscribed mass is then formed in the breast.

611.4 Atrophy of breast

611.5 Galactocele

611.6 Galactorrhea not associated with childbirth

✓5th 611.7 Signs and symptoms in breast

611.71 Mastodynia
Pain in breast

611.72 Lump or mass in breast CC
CC Excl: 610.0-610.9, 611.0-611.9
AHA: 2Q, '03, 4-5

611.79 Other
Induration of breast
Inversion of nipple
Nipple discharge
Retraction of nipple

611.8 Other specified disorders of breast
Hematoma (nontraumatic) } of breast
Infarction } of breast
Occlusion of breast duct
Subinvolution of breast (postlactational) (postpartum)

611.9 Unspecified breast disorder

INFLAMMATORY DISEASE OF FEMALE PELVIC ORGANS (614-616)

Use additional code to identify organism, such as Staphylococcus (041.1), or Streptococcus (041.0)

EXCLUDES *that associated with pregnancy, abortion, childbirth, or the puerperium (630-676.9)*

✓4th 614 Inflammatory disease of ovary, fallopian tube, pelvic cellular tissue, and peritoneum
EXCLUDES *endometritis (615.0-615.9)*
major infection following delivery (670)
that complicating:
abortion (634-638 with .0, 639.0)
ectopic or molar pregnancy (639.0)
pregnancy or labor (646.6)

614.0 Acute salpingitis and oophoritis CC ♀
Any condition classifiable to 614.2, specified as acute or subacute
CC Excl: 016.60-016.96, 017.90-017.96, 098.15-098.17, 098.35-098.37, 098.89, 112.2, 131.00, 131.8-131.9, 614.0-615.9, 616.8-616.9, 625.8-625.9, 629.20-629.9, 752.81-752.9
DEF: Acute inflammation, of ovary and fallopian tube.

614.1 Chronic salpingitis and oophoritis ♀
Hydrosalpinx
Salpingitis:
follicularis
isthmica nodosa
Any condition classifiable to 614.2, specified as chronic
DEF: Persistent inflammation of ovary and fallopian tube.

614.2 Salpingitis and oophoritis not specified as acute, subacute, or chronic ♀
Abscess (of):
fallopian tube
ovary
tubo-ovarian
Oophoritis
Perioophoritis
Pyosalpinx
Perisalpingitis
Salpingitis
Salpingo-oophoritis
Tubo-ovarian inflammatory disease
EXCLUDES *gonococcal infection (chronic) (098.37)*
acute (098.17)
tuberculous (016.6)
AHA: 2Q, '91, 5

614.3 Acute parametritis and pelvic cellulitis CC ♀
Acute inflammatory pelvic disease
Any condition classifiable to 614.4, specified as acute
CC Excl: See code 614.0
DEF: Parametritis: inflammation of the parametrium; pelvic cellulitis is a synonym for parametritis.

614.4 Chronic or unspecified parametritis and pelvic cellulitis ♀
Abscess (of):
broad ligament } chronic or NOS
parametrium } chronic or NOS
pelvis, female } chronic or NOS
pouch of Douglas } chronic or NOS
Chronic inflammatory pelvic disease
Pelvic cellulitis, female
EXCLUDES *tuberculous (016.7)*

614.5 Acute or unspecified pelvic peritonitis, female CC ♀
CC Excl: See code 614.0
AHA: ►4Q, '05, 74◄

Female Genitourinary System

Uterine (fallopian) tube
Ovary
Rectouterine pouch (of Douglas)
Uterus (fundus)
Cervix
Bladder
Rectum
Pubic bone
Clitoris
Urogenital diaphragm
Anus
Urethral orifice (meatus)
Labia minora
Labia majora
Vaginal canal

614.6 Pelvic peritoneal adhesions, female (postoperative) (postinfection) ♀

Adhesions: peritubal

Adhesions: tubo-ovarian

Use additional code to identify any associated infertility (628.2)

AHA: 3Q, '03, 6; 1Q, '03, 4; 3Q, '95, 7; 3Q, '94, 12

DEF: Fibrous scarring abnormally joining structures within abdomen.

614.7 Other chronic pelvic peritonitis, female ♀

EXCLUDES *tuberculous(016.7)*

614.8 Other specified inflammatory disease of female pelvic organs and tissues ♀

614.9 Unspecified inflammatory disease of female pelvic organs and tissues ♀

Pelvic infection or inflammation, female NOS

Pelvic inflammatory disease [PID]

✓4th **615 Inflammatory diseases of uterus, except cervix**

EXCLUDES *following delivery (670)*
hyperplastic endometritis (621.30-621.33)
that complicating:
abortion (634-638 with .0, 639.0)
ectopic or molar pregnancy (639.0)
pregnancy or labor (646.6)

615.0 Acute CC ♀

Any condition classifiable to 615.9, specified as acute or subacute

CC Excl: 016.60-016.96, 017.90-017.96, 098.15-098.17, 098.35-098.37, 098.89, 112.2, 131.00, 131.8-131.9, 614.0-616.0, 616.8-616.9, 621.8-621.9, 625.8-625.9, 629.20-629.9, 752.81-752.9

615.1 Chronic ♀

Any condition classifiable to 615.9, specified as chronic

615.9 Unspecified inflammatory disease of uterus ♀

Endometritis
Endomyometritis
Intrauterine infection
Metritis
Myometritis
Perimetritis
Pyometra
Uterine abscess

✓4th **616 Inflammatory disease of cervix, vagina, and vulva**

EXCLUDES *that complicating:*
abortion (634-638 with .0, 639.0)
ectopic or molar pregnancy (639.0)
pregnancy, childbirth, or the puerperium (646.6)

616.0 Cervicitis and endocervicitis ♀

Cervicitis } with or without mention of
Endocervicitis } erosion or ectropion

Nabothian (gland) cyst or follicle

EXCLUDES *erosion or ectropion without mention of cervicitis (622.0)*

✓5th **616.1 Vaginitis and vulvovaginitis**

DEF: Inflammation or infection of vagina or external female genitalia.

616.10 Vaginitis and vulvovaginitis, unspecified ♀

Vaginitis:
NOS
postirradiation
Vulvitis NOS
Vulvovaginitis NOS

Use additional code to identify organism, such as Escherichia coli [E. coli] (041.4), Staphylococcus (041.1), or Streptococcus (041.0)

EXCLUDES *noninfective leukorrhea (623.5)*
postmenopausal or senile vaginitis (627.3)

616.11 Vaginitis and vulvovaginitis in diseases classified elsewhere ♀

Code first underlying disease, as:
pinworm vaginitis (127.4)

EXCLUDES *herpetic vulvovaginitis (054.11)*
monilial vulvovaginitis (112.1)
trichomonal vaginitis or vulvovaginitis (131.01)

616.2 Cyst of Bartholin's gland ♀

Bartholin's duct cyst

DEF: Fluid-filled sac within gland of vaginal orifice.

616.3 Abscess of Bartholin's gland CC ♀

Vulvovaginal gland abscess

CC Excl: 016.70-016.96, 017.90-017.96, 112.1-112.2, 131.00-131.01, 131.8-131.9, 616.10-616.9, 624.3-624.9, 625.8-625.9, 629.20-629.9, 752.81-752.9

616.4 Other abscess of vulva CC ♀

Abscess }
Carbuncle } of vulva
Furuncle }

CC Excl: See code 616.3

✓5th **616.5 Ulceration of vulva**

616.50 Ulceration of vulva, unspecified ♀

Ulcer NOS of vulva

616.51 Ulceration of vulva in diseases classified elsewhere ♀

Code first underlying disease, as:
Behçet's syndrome (136.1)
tuberculosis (016.7)

EXCLUDES *vulvar ulcer (in):*
gonococcal (098.0)
herpes simplex (054.12)
syphilitic (091.0)

✓5th **616.8 Other specified inflammatory diseases of cervix, vagina, and vulva**

EXCLUDES *noninflammatory disorders of:*
cervix (622.0-622.9)
vagina (623.0-623.9)
vulva (624.0-624.9)

● **616.81 Mucositis (ulcerative) of cervix, vagina, and vulva** ♀

Use additional E code to identify adverse effects of therapy, such as:
antineoplastic and immunosuppressive drugs (E930.7, E933.1)
radiation therapy (E879.2)

● **616.89 Other inflammatory disease of cervix, vagina and vulva** ♀

Caruncle, vagina or labium
Ulcer, vagina

616.9 Unspecified inflammatory disease of cervix, vagina, and vulva ♀

OTHER DISORDERS OF FEMALE GENITAL TRACT (617-629)

✓4th 617 Endometriosis

617.0 Endometriosis of uterus ♀

Adenomyosis
Endometriosis:
cervix
internal
myometrium

EXCLUDES *stromal endometriosis (236.0)*

AHA: 3Q, '92, 7

DEF: Aberrant uterine mucosal tissue; creating products of menses and inflamed uterine tissues.

617.1 Endometriosis of ovary ♀

Chocolate cyst of ovary
Endometrial cystoma of ovary

DEF: Aberrant uterine tissue; creating products of menses and inflamed ovarian tissues.

617.2 Endometriosis of fallopian tube ♀

DEF: Aberrant uterine tissue; creating products of menses and inflamed tissues of fallopian tubes.

617.3 Endometriosis of pelvic peritoneum ♀

Endometriosis:
broad ligament
cul-de-sac (Douglas')
parametrium
round ligament

DEF: Aberrant uterine tissue; creating products of menses and inflamed peritoneum tissues.

617.4 Endometriosis of rectovaginal septum and vagina ♀

DEF: Aberrant uterine tissue; creating products of menses and inflamed tissues in and behind vagina.

617.5 Endometriosis of intestine ♀

Endometriosis:
appendix
colon
rectum

DEF: Aberrant uterine tissue; creating products of menses and inflamed intestinal tissues.

617.6 Endometriosis in scar of skin ♀

617.8 Endometriosis of other specified sites ♀

Endometriosis:
bladder
lung
umbilicus
vulva

617.9 Endometriosis, site unspecified ♀

✓4th 618 Genital prolapse

Use additional code to identify urinary incontinence (625.6, 788.31, 788.33-788.39)

EXCLUDES *that complicating pregnancy, labor, or delivery (654.4)*

✓5th 618.0 Prolapse of vaginal walls without mention of uterine prolapse

EXCLUDES *that with uterine prolapse (618.2-618.4)*
enterocele (618.6)
vaginal vault prolapse following hysterectomy (618.5)

618.00 Unspecified prolapse of vaginal walls ♀

Vaginal prolapse NOS

618.01 Cystocele, midline ♀

Cystocele NOS

DEF: Defect in the pubocervical fascia, the supportive layer of the bladder, causing bladder drop and herniated into the vagina along the midline.

Common Sites of Endometriosis

Common sites of endometriosis, in descending order of frequency:
(1) ovary
(2) cul de sac
(3) utersacral ligaments
(4) broad ligaments
(5) fallopian tube
(6) uterovesical fold
(7) round ligament
(8) vermiform appedix
(9) vagina
(10) rectovaginal septum

Vaginal Midline Cystocele

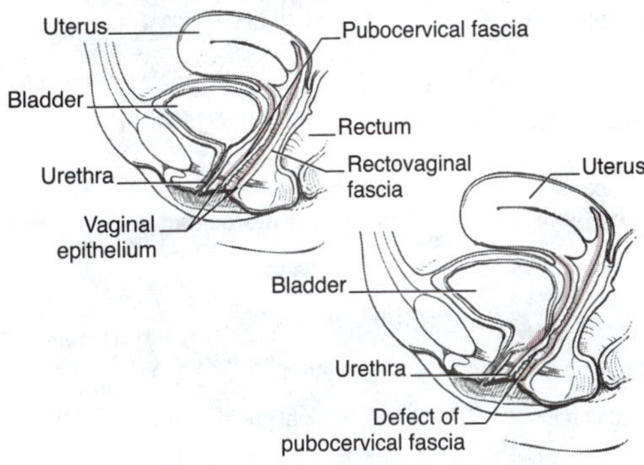

618.02 Cystocele, lateral ♀

Paravaginal

DEF: Loss of support of the lateral attachment of the vagina at the arcus tendinous results in bladder drop; bladder herniates into the vagina laterally; also called paravaginal defect.

618.03 Urethrocele ♀

618.04 Rectocele ♀

Proctocele

618.05 Perineocele ♀

618.09 Other prolapse of vaginal walls without mention of uterine prolapse ♀

Cystourethrocele

618.1 Uterine prolapse without mention of vaginal wall prolapse ♀

Descensus uteri
Uterine prolapse:
NOS
complete
Uterine prolapse:
first degree
second degree
third degree

EXCLUDES *that with mention of cystocele, urethrocele, or rectocele (618.2-618.4)*

618.2 Uterovaginal prolapse, incomplete ♀

DEF: Downward displacement of uterus downward into vagina.

618.3 Uterovaginal prolapse, complete ♀

DEF: Downward displacement of uterus exposed within external genitalia.

618.4 Uterovaginal prolapse, unspecified ♀

618.5 Prolapse of vaginal vault after hysterectomy ♀

618.6 Vaginal enterocele, congenital or acquired ♀

Pelvic enterocele, congenital or acquired

DEF: Vaginal vault hernia formed by the loop of the small intestine protruding into the rectal vaginal pouch; can also accompany uterine prolapse or follow hysterectomy.

618.7 Old laceration of muscles of pelvic floor ♀

Vaginal Lateral Cystocele

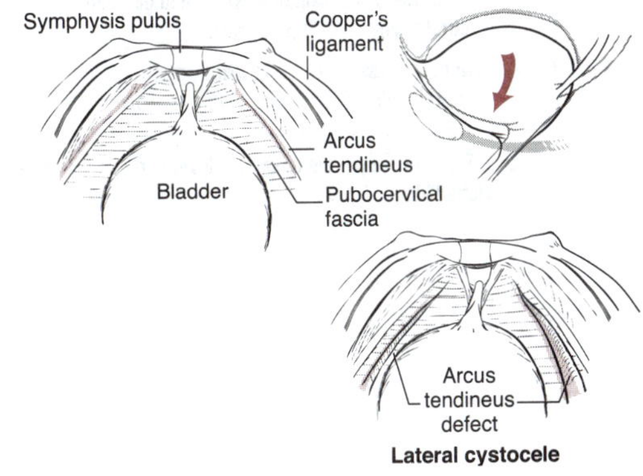

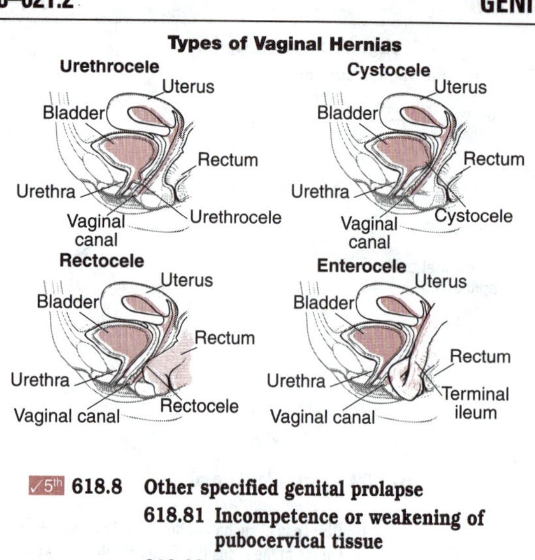

✓5th **618.8 Other specified genital prolapse**

618.81 Incompetence or weakening of pubocervical tissue ♀

618.82 Incompetence or weakening of rectovaginal tissue ♀

618.83 Pelvic muscle wasting ♀
Disuse atrophy of pelvic muscles and anal sphincter

● **618.84 Cervical stump prolapse** ♀

618.89 Other specified genital prolapse ♀

618.9 Unspecified genital prolapse ♀

✓4th **619 Fistula involving female genital tract**

EXCLUDES *vesicorectal and intestinovesical fistula (596.1)*

619.0 Urinary-genital tract fistula, female ♀
Fistula:
cervicovesical
ureterovaginal
urethrovaginal
urethrovesicovaginal
Fistula:
uteroureteric
uterovesical
vesicocervicovaginal
vesicovaginal

619.1 Digestive-genital tract fistula, female ♀
Fistula:
intestinouterine
intestinovaginal
rectovaginal
Fistula:
rectovulval
sigmoidovaginal
uterorectal

619.2 Genital tract-skin fistula, female ♀
Fistula:
uterus to abdominal wall
Fistula:
vaginoperineal

619.8 Other specified fistulas involving female genital tract ♀
Fistula:
cervix
cul-de-sac (Douglas')
Fistula:
uterus
vagina

619.9 Unspecified fistula involving female genital tract ♀

✓4th **620 Noninflammatory disorders of ovary, fallopian tube, and broad ligament**

EXCLUDES *hydrosalpinx (614.1)*

620.0 Follicular cyst of ovary ♀
Cyst of graafian follicle
DEF: Fluid-filled, encapsulated cyst due to occluded follicle duct that secretes hormones into ovaries.

620.1 Corpus luteum cyst or hematoma ♀
Corpus luteum hemorrhage or rupture
Lutein cyst
DEF: Fluid-filled cyst due to serous developing from corpus luteum or clotted blood.

Uterus and Ovaries

Fundus of uterus
Mesosalpinx
Mesovarium
Suspensory ligaments
Uterine (fallopian tube)
Ligament of ovary
Body
Ovary
Uterosacral ligament
Cervix
Vagina
Fimbria
Ovary
Broad ligament

620.2 Other and unspecified ovarian cyst ♀
Cyst:
NOS
corpus albicans
retention NOS
serous
theca-lutein
} of ovary
Simple cystoma of ovary

EXCLUDES *cystadenoma (benign) (serous) (220)*
developmental cysts (752.0)
neoplastic cysts (220)
polycystic ovaries (256.4)
Stein-Leventhal syndrome (256.4)

620.3 Acquired atrophy of ovary and fallopian tube ♀
Senile involution of ovary

620.4 Prolapse or hernia of ovary and fallopian tube ♀
Displacement of ovary and fallopian tube
Salpingocele

620.5 Torsion of ovary, ovarian pedicle, or fallopian tube ♀
Torsion:
accessory tube
Torsion:
hydatid of Morgagni

620.6 Broad ligament laceration syndrome ♀
Masters-Allen syndrome

620.7 Hematoma of broad ligament CC ♀
Hematocele, broad ligament
CC Excl: 620.6-620.9, 625.8-625.9, 629.20-629.9, 752.81-752.9
DEF: Blood within peritoneal fold that supports uterus.

620.8 Other noninflammatory disorders of ovary, fallopian tube, and broad ligament ♀
Cyst
Polyp
} of broad ligament or fallopian tube

Infarction
Rupture
} of ovary or fallopian tube

Hematosalpinx

EXCLUDES *hematosalpinx in ectopic pregnancy (639.2)*
peritubal adhesions (614.6)
torsion of ovary, ovarian pedicle, or fallopian tube (620.5)

620.9 Unspecified noninflammatory disorder of ovary, fallopian tube, and broad ligament ♀

✓4th **621 Disorders of uterus, not elsewhere classified**

621.0 Polyp of corpus uteri ♀
Polyp:
endometrium
Polyp:
uterus NOS

EXCLUDES *cervical polyp NOS (622.7)*

621.1 Chronic subinvolution of uterus ♀

EXCLUDES *puerperal (674.8)*

AHA: 1Q, '91, 11
DEF: Abnormal size of uterus after delivery; the uterus does not return to its normal size after the birth of a child.

621.2 Hypertrophy of uterus ♀
Bulky or enlarged uterus

EXCLUDES *puerperal (674.8)*

✓5th **621.3 Endometrial hyperplasia**
Hyperplasia (adenomatous) (cystic) (glandular) of endometrium
DEF: Abnormal cystic overgrowth of endometrial tissue.

621.30 Endometrial hyperplasia, unspecified ♀
Endometrial hyperplasia NOS

621.31 Simple endometrial hyperplasia without atypia ♀

621.32 Complex endometrial hyperplasia without atypia ♀

621.33 Endometrial hyperplasia with atypia ♀

621.4 Hematometra ♀
Hemometra
EXCLUDES *that in congenital anomaly (752.2-752.3)*
DEF: Accumulated blood in uterus.

621.5 Intrauterine synechiae ♀
Adhesions of uterus Band(s) of uterus

621.6 Malposition of uterus ♀
Anteversion, Retroflexion, Retroversion } of uterus
EXCLUDES *malposition complicating pregnancy, labor, or delivery (654.3-654.4)*

621.7 Chronic inversion of uterus ♀
EXCLUDES *current obstetrical trauma (665.2)*
prolapse of uterus (618.1-618.4)

621.8 Other specified disorders of uterus, not elsewhere classified ♀
Atrophy, acquired, Cyst, Fibrosis NOS, Old laceration (postpartum), Ulcer } of uterus
EXCLUDES *bilharzial fibrosis (120.0-120.9)*
endometriosis (617.0)
fistulas (619.0-619.8)
inflammatory diseases (615.0-615.9)

621.9 Unspecified disorder of uterus ♀

✓4th **622 Noninflammatory disorders of cervix**
EXCLUDES *abnormality of cervix complicating pregnancy, labor, or delivery (654.5-654.6)*
fistula (619.0-619.8)

622.0 Erosion and ectropion of cervix ♀
Eversion, Ulcer } of cervix
EXCLUDES *that in chronic cervicitis (616.0)*
DEF: Ulceration or turning outward of uterine cervix.

✓5th **622.1 Dysplasia of cervix (uteri)**
EXCLUDES *abnormal results from cervical cytologic examination without histologic confirmation (795.00-795.09)*
carcinoma in situ of cervix (233.1)
cervical intraepithelial neoplasia III [CIN III] (233.1)
AHA: 1Q, '91, 11
DEF: Abnormal cell structures in portal between uterus and vagina.

622.10 Dysplasia of cervix, unspecified ♀
Anaplasia of cervix; Cervical atypism; Cervical dysplasia NOS

622.11 Mild dysplasia of cervix ♀
Cervical intraepithelial neoplasia I [CIN I]

622.12 Moderate dysplasia of cervix ♀
Cervical intraepithelial neoplasia II [CIN II]
EXCLUDES *carcinoma in situ of cervix (233.1)*
cervical intraepithelial neoplasia III [CIN III] (233.1)
severe dysplasia (233.1)

622.2 Leukoplakia of cervix (uteri) ♀
EXCLUDES *carcinoma in situ of cervix (233.1)*
DEF: Thickened, white patches on portal between uterus and vagina.

622.3 Old laceration of cervix ♀
Adhesions, Band(s), Cicatrix (postpartum) } of cervix
EXCLUDES *current obstetrical trauma (665.3)*
DEF: Scarring or other evidence of old wound on cervix.

622.4 Stricture and stenosis of cervix ♀
Atresia (acquired), Contracture, Occlusion } of cervix
Pinpoint os uteri
EXCLUDES *congenital (752.49)*
that complicating labor (654.6)

622.5 Incompetence of cervix ♀
EXCLUDES *complicating pregnancy (654.5)*
that affecting fetus or newborn (761.0)
DEF: Inadequate functioning of cervix; marked by abnormal widening during pregnancy; causing miscarriage.

622.6 Hypertrophic elongation of cervix ♀
DEF: Overgrowth of cervix tissues extending down into vagina.

622.7 Mucous polyp of cervix ♀
Polyp NOS of cervix
EXCLUDES *adenomatous polyp of cervix (219.0)*

622.8 Other specified noninflammatory disorders of cervix ♀
Atrophy (senile), Cyst, Fibrosis, Hemorrhage } of cervix
EXCLUDES *endometriosis (617.0)*
fistula (619.0-619.8)
inflammatory diseases (616.0)

622.9 Unspecified noninflammatory disorder of cervix ♀

✓4th **623 Noninflammatory disorders of vagina**
EXCLUDES *abnormality of vagina complicating pregnancy, labor, or delivery (654.7)*
congenital absence of vagina (752.49)
congenital diaphragm or bands (752.49)
fistulas involving vagina (619.0-619.8)

623.0 Dysplasia of vagina ♀
EXCLUDES *carcinoma in situ of vagina (233.3)*

623.1 Leukoplakia of vagina ♀
DEF: Thickened white patches on vaginal canal.

623.2 Stricture or atresia of vagina ♀
Adhesions (postoperative) (postradiation) of vagina
Occlusion of vagina
Stenosis, vagina
Use additional E code to identify any external cause
EXCLUDES *congenital atresia or stricture (752.49)*

623.3 Tight hymenal ring ♀
Rigid hymen, Tight hymenal ring, Tight introitus } acquired or congenital
EXCLUDES *imperforate hymen (752.42)*

623.4 Old vaginal laceration ♀
EXCLUDES *old laceration involving muscles of pelvic floor (618.7)*
DEF: Scarring or other evidence of old wound on vagina.

623.5 Leukorrhea, not specified as infective ♀
Leukorrhea NOS of vagina
Vaginal discharge NOS
EXCLUDES *trichomonal (131.00)*
DEF: Viscid whitish discharge, from vagina.

623.6 Vaginal hematoma ♀
EXCLUDES *current obstetrical trauma (665.7)*

623.7 Polyp of vagina ♀

623.8 Other specified noninflammatory disorders of vagina ♀
Cyst } of vagina
Hemorrhage } of vagina

623.9 Unspecified noninflammatory disorder of vagina ♀

✓4th 624 Noninflammatory disorders of vulva and perineum
EXCLUDES *abnormality of vulva and perineum complicating pregnancy, labor, or delivery (654.8)*
condyloma acuminatum (078.1)
fistulas involving:
perineum — see Alphabetic Index
vulva (619.0-619.8)
vulval varices (456.6)
vulvar involvement in skin conditions (690-709.9)

624.0 Dystrophy of vulva ♀
Kraurosis } of vulva
Leukoplakia } of vulva
EXCLUDES *carcinoma in situ of vulva (233.3)*

624.1 Atrophy of vulva ♀

624.2 Hypertrophy of clitoris ♀
EXCLUDES *that in endocrine disorders (255.2, 256.1)*

624.3 Hypertrophy of labia ♀
Hypertrophy of vulva NOS
DEF: Overgrowth of fleshy folds on either side of vagina.

624.4 Old laceration or scarring of vulva ♀
DEF: Scarring or other evidence of old wound on external female genitalia.

624.5 Hematoma of vulva ♀
EXCLUDES *that complicating delivery (664.5)*
DEF: Blood in tissue of external genitalia.

624.6 Polyp of labia and vulva ♀

624.8 Other specified noninflammatory disorders of vulva and perineum ♀
Cyst } of vulva
Edema } of vulva
Stricture } of vulva
AHA: 1Q, '03, 13; 1Q, '95, 8

624.9 Unspecified noninflammatory disorder of vulva and perineum ♀

✓4th 625 Pain and other symptoms associated with female genital organs

625.0 Dyspareunia ♀
EXCLUDES *psychogenic dyspareunia (302.76)*
DEF: Difficult or painful sexual intercourse.

625.1 Vaginismus ♀
Colpospasm Vulvismus
EXCLUDES *psychogenic vaginismus (306.51)*
DEF: Vaginal spasms; due to involuntary contraction of musculature; prevents intercourse.

625.2 Mittelschmerz ♀
Intermenstrual pain Ovulation pain
DEF: Pain occurring between menstrual periods.

625.3 Dysmenorrhea ♀
Painful menstruation
EXCLUDES *psychogenic dysmenorrhea (306.52)*
AHA: 2Q, '94, 12

625.4 Premenstrual tension syndromes ♀
Menstrual:
migraine
molimen
Premenstrual dysphoric disorder
Premenstrual syndrome
Premenstrual tension NOS
AHA: 4Q, '03, 116

625.5 Pelvic congestion syndrome ♀
Congestion-fibrosis syndrome Taylor's syndrome
DEF: Excessive accumulation of blood in vessels of pelvis; may occur after orgasm; causes abnormal menstruation, lower back pain and vaginal discharge.

625.6 Stress incontinence, female ♀
EXCLUDES *mixed incontinence (788.33)*
stress incontinence, male (788.32)
DEF: Involuntary leakage of urine due to insufficient sphincter control; occurs upon sneezing, laughing, coughing, sudden movement or lifting.

625.8 Other specified symptoms associated with female genital organs ♀
AHA: N-D, '85, 16

625.9 Unspecified symptom associated with female genital organs ♀

✓4th 626 Disorders of menstruation and other abnormal bleeding from female genital tract
EXCLUDES *menopausal and premenopausal bleeding (627.0)*
pain and other symptoms associated with menstrual cycle (625.2-625.4)
postmenopausal bleeding (627.1)

626.0 Absence of menstruation ♀
Amenorrhea (primary) (secondary)

626.1 Scanty or infrequent menstruation ♀
Hypomenorrhea Oligomenorrhea

626.2 Excessive or frequent menstruation ♀
Heavy periods Menorrhagia
Menometrorrhagia Plymenorrhea
EXCLUDES *premenopausal(627.0)*
that in puberty (626.3)

626.3 Puberty bleeding ♀
Excessive bleeding associated with onset of menstrual periods
Pubertal menorrhagia

626.4 Irregular menstrual cycle ♀
Irregular:
bleeding NOS
menstruation
Irregular:
periods

626.5 Ovulation bleeding ♀
Regular intermenstrual bleeding

626.6 Metrorrhagia ♀
Bleeding unrelated to menstrual cycle
Irregular intermenstrual bleeding

626.7 Postcoital bleeding ♀
DEF: Bleeding from vagina after sexual intercourse.

626.8 Other ♀
Dysfunctional or functional uterine hemorrhage NOS
Menstruation:
retained
suppression of

626.9 Unspecified ♀

✓4th 627 Menopausal and postmenopausal disorders
EXCLUDES *asymptomatic age-related (natural) postmenopausal status (V49.81)*

627.0 Premenopausal menorrhagia ♀
Excessive bleeding associated with onset of menopause
Menorrhagia:
climacteric
menopausal
preclimacteric

627.1 Postmenopausal bleeding ♀

627.2 Symptomatic menopausal or female climacteric states ♀
Symptoms, such as flushing, sleeplessness, headache, lack of concentration, associated with the menopause

627.3 Postmenopausal atrophic vaginitis ♀
Senile (atrophic) vaginitis

627.4 Symptomatic states associated with artificial menopause ♀
Postartificial menopause syndromes
Any condition classifiable to 627.1, 627.2, or 627.3 which follows induced menopause

DEF: Conditions arising after hysterectomy.

627.8 Other specified menopausal and postmenopausal disorders ♀
EXCLUDES *premature menopause NOS (256.31)*

627.9 Unspecified menopausal and postmenopausal disorder ♀

✓4th **628 Infertility, female**
INCLUDES primary and secondary sterility

AHA: 2Q, '96, 9; 1Q, '95, 7

DEF: Infertility: inability to conceive for at least one year with regular intercourse.

DEF: Primary infertility: occurring in patients who have never conceived.

DEF: Secondary infertility: occurring in patients who have previously conceived.

628.0 Associated with anovulation ♀
Anovulatory cycle
Use additional code for any associated Stein-Leventhal syndrome (256.4)

628.1 Of pituitary-hypothalamic origin ♀
Code first underlying cause, as:
adiposogenital dystrophy (253.8)
anterior pituitary disorder (253.0-253.4)

628.2 Of tubal origin ♀
Infertility associated with congenital anomaly of tube
Tubal:
block
occlusion
stenosis
Use additional code for any associated peritubal adhesions (614.6)

628.3 Of uterine origin ♀
Infertility associated with congenital anomaly of uterus
Nonimplantation
Use additional code for any associated tuberculous endometritis (016.7)

628.4 Of cervical or vaginal origin ♀
Infertility associated with:
anomaly of cervical mucus
congenital structural anomaly
dysmucorrhea

628.8 Of other specified origin ♀

628.9 Of unspecified origin ♀

✓4th **629 Other disorders of female genital organs**

629.0 Hematocele, female, not elsewhere classified ♀
EXCLUDES *hematocele or hematoma:*
broad ligament (620.7)
fallopian tube (620.8)
that associated with ectopic pregnancy (633.00-633.91)
uterus (621.4)
vagina (623.6)
vulva (624.5)

629.1 Hydrocele, canal of Nuck ♀
Cyst of canal of Nuck (acquired)
EXCLUDES *congenital (752.41)*

✓5th **629.2 Female genital mutilation status**
Female circumcision status
▶Female genital cutting◀

AHA: 4Q, '04, 88

629.20 Female genital mutilation status, unspecified ♀
▶Female genital cutting status, unspecified◀
Female genital mutilation status NOS

629.21 Female genital mutilation Type I status ♀
Clitorectomy status
▶Female genital cutting Type I status◀

DEF: Female genital mutilation involving clitorectomy, with part or all of the clitoris removed.

629.22 Female genital mutilation Type II status ♀
Clitorectomy with excision of labia minora status
▶Female genital cutting Type II status◀

AHA: 4Q, '04, 90

DEF: Female genital mutilation involving clitoris and the labia minora amputation.

629.23 Female genital mutilation Type III status ♀
▶Female genital cutting Type III status◀
Infibulation status

AHA: 4Q, '04, 90

DEF: Female genital mutilation involving removal, most or all of the labia minora excised, labia majora incised which is then made into a hood of skin over the urethral and vaginal opening.

● **629.29 Other female genital mutilation status** ♀
Female genital cutting Type IV status
Female genital mutilation Type IV status
Other female genital cutting status

✓5th **629.8 Other specified disorders of female genital organs**

● **629.81 Habitual aborter without current pregnancy** ♀
EXCLUDES *habitual aborter with current pregnancy (646.3)*

● **629.89 Other specified disorders of female genital organs** ♀

629.9 Unspecified disorder of female genital organs ♀

Genitourinary System 627.3–629.9

11. COMPLICATIONS OF PREGNANCY, CHILDBIRTH, AND THE PUERPERIUM (630-677)

ECTOPIC AND MOLAR PREGNANCY (630-633)

Use additional code from category 639 to identify any complications

630 Hydatidiform mole M ♀

Trophoblastic disease NOS Vesicularmole

EXCLUDES *chorioadenoma (destruens) (236.1)*
chorionepithelioma (181)
malignant hydatidiform mole (236.1)

DEF: Abnormal product of pregnancy; marked by mass of cysts resembling bunch of grapes due to chorionic villi proliferation, and dissolution; must be surgically removed.

631 Other abnormal product of conception M ♀

Blighted ovum
Mole:
NOS
carneous
fleshy
stone

632 Missed abortion M ♀

Early fetal death before completion of 22 weeks' gestation with retention of dead fetus

Retained products of conception, not following spontaneous or induced abortion or delivery

EXCLUDES *failed induced abortion (638.0-638.9)*
fetal death (intrauterine) (late) (656.4)
missed delivery (656.4)
that with abnormal product of conception (630, 631)

AHA: 1Q, '01, 5

✓4th **633 Ectopic pregnancy**

INCLUDES ruptured ectopic pregnancy

AHA: 4Q, '02, 61

DEF: Fertilized egg develops outside uterus.

✓5th **633.0 Abdominal pregnancy**

Intraperitoneal pregnancy

633.00 Abdominal pregnancy without intrauterine pregnancy M ♀

633.01 Abdominal pregnancy with intrauterine pregnancy M ♀

✓5th **633.1 Tubal pregnancy**

Fallopian pregnancy
Rupture of (fallopian) tube due to pregnancy
Tubal abortion

AHA: 2Q, '90, 27

633.10 Tubal pregnancy without intrauterine pregnancy M ♀

633.11 Tubal pregnancy with intrauterine pregnancy M ♀

✓5th **633.2 Ovarian pregnancy**

633.20 Ovarian pregnancy without intrauterine pregnancy M ♀

633.21 Ovarian pregnancy with intrauterine pregnancy M ♀

✓5th **633.8 Other ectopic pregnancy**

Pregnancy:
cervical
combined
cornual

Pregnancy:
intraligamentous
mesometric
mural

633.80 Other ectopic pregnancy without intrauterine pregnancy M ♀

633.81 Other ectopic pregnancy with intrauterine pregnancy M ♀

✓5th **633.9 Unspecified ectopic pregnancy**

633.90 Unspecified ectopic pregnancy without intrauterine pregnancy M ♀

633.91 Unspecified ectopic pregnancy with intrauterine pregnancy M ♀

Ectopic Pregnancy Sites

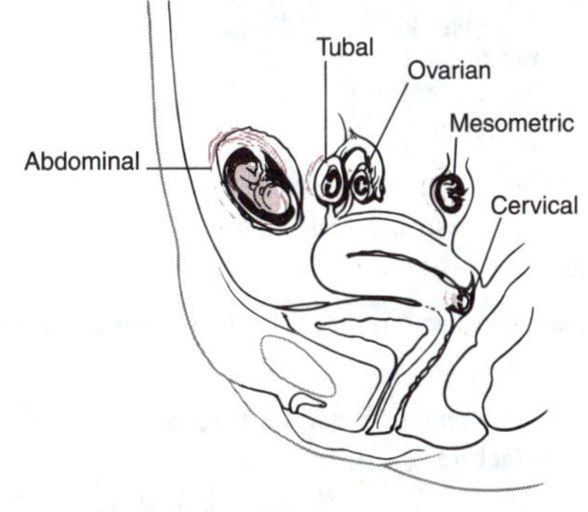

OTHER PREGNANCY WITH ABORTIVE OUTCOME (634-639)

The following fourth-digit subdivisions are for use with categories 634-638:

.0 Complicated by genital tract and pelvic infection

Endometritis
Salpingo-oophoritis
Sepsis NOS
Septicemia NOS
Any condition classifiable to 639.0, with condition classifiable to 634-638

EXCLUDES *urinary tract infection (634-638 with .7)*

.1 Complicated by delayed or excessive hemorrhage

Afibrinogenemia
Defibrination syndrome
Intravascular hemolysis
Any condition classifiable to 639.1, with condition classifiable to 634-638

.2 Complicated by damage to pelvic organs and tissues

Laceration, perforation, or tear of:
bladder
uterus
Any condition classifiable to 639.2, with condition classifiable to 634-638

.3 Complicated by renal failure

Oliguria
Uremia
Any condition classifiable to 639.3, with condition classifiable to 634-638

.4 Complicated by metabolic disorder

Electrolyte imbalance with conditions classifiable to 634-638

.5 Complicated by shock

Circulatory collapse
Shock (postoperative) (septic)
Any condition classifiable to 639.5, with condition classifiable to 634-638

.6 Complicated by embolism

Embolism:
NOS
amniotic fluid
pulmonary
Any condition classifiable to 639.6, with condition classifiable to 634-638

.7 With other specified complications

Cardiac arrest or failure
Urinary tract infection
Any condition classifiable to 639.8, with condition classifiable to 634-638

.8 With unspecified complication

.9 Without mention of complication

§ ✓4th **634 Spontaneous abortion**

Requires fifth-digit to identify stage:
0 unspecified
1 incomplete
2 complete

INCLUDES miscarriage
spontaneous abortion

AHA: 2Q, '91, 16

DEF: Spontaneous premature expulsion of the products of conception from the uterus.

✓5th **634.0 Complicated by genital tract and pelvic infection** CC M ♀
CC Excl: 634.00-638.9, 640.00-641.23, 646.80-646.93, 648.90-650, 669.40-669.44, 669.80-669.94

✓5th **634.1 Complicated by delayed or excessive hemorrhage** CC M ♀
CC Excl: See code 634.0
AHA: For Code 634.11: 1Q, '03, 6

✓5th **634.2 Complicated by damage to pelvic organs or tissues** CC M ♀
CC Excl: See code 634.0

✓5th **634.3 Complicated by renal failure** CC M ♀
CC Excl: See code 634.0

✓5th **634.4 Complicated by metabolic disorder** CC M ♀
CC Excl: See code 634.0

✓5th **634.5 Complicated by shock** CC M ♀
CC Excl: See code 634.0

✓5th **634.6 Complicated by embolism** CC M ♀
CC Excl: See code 634.0

✓5th **634.7 With other specified complications** CC M ♀
CC Excl: See code 634.0

✓5th **634.8 With unspecified complication** CC M ♀
CC Excl: See code 634.0

✓5th **634.9 Without mention of complication** CC M ♀
CC Excl: See code 634.0

§ ✓4th **635 Legally induced abortion**

Requires fifth-digit to identify stage:
0 unspecified
1 incomplete
2 complete

INCLUDES abortion or termination of pregnancy:
elective
legal
therapeutic

EXCLUDES *menstrual extraction or regulation (V25.3)*

AHA: 2Q, '94, 14

DEF: Intentional expulsion of products of conception from uterus performed by medical professionals inside boundaries of law.

✓5th **635.0 Complicated by genital tract and pelvic infection** M ♀
✓5th **635.1 Complicated by delayed or excessive hemorrhage** M ♀
✓5th **635.2 Complicated by damage to pelvic organs or tissues** M ♀
✓5th **635.3 Complicated by renal failure** M ♀
✓5th **635.4 Complicated by metabolic disorder** M ♀
✓5th **635.5 Complicated by shock** M ♀
✓5th **635.6 Complicated by embolism** M ♀
✓5th **635.7 With other specified complications** M ♀
✓5th **635.8 With unspecified complication** M ♀
✓5th **635.9 Without mention of complication** M ♀
AHA: For code 635.92; 2Q, '94, 14

§ ✓4th **636 Illegally induced abortion**

Requires fifth-digit to identify stage:
0 unspecified
1 incomplete
2 complete

INCLUDES abortion:
criminal
illegal
self-induced

DEF: Intentional expulsion of products of conception from uterus; outside boundaries of law.

✓5th **636.0 Complicated by genital tract and pelvic infection** M ♀
✓5th **636.1 Complicated by delayed or excessive hemorrhage** M ♀
✓5th **636.2 Complicated by damage to pelvic organs or tissues** M ♀
✓5th **636.3 Complicated by renal failure** M ♀
✓5th **636.4 Complicated by metabolic disorder** M ♀
✓5th **636.5 Complicated by shock** M ♀
✓5th **636.6 Complicated by embolism** M ♀
✓5th **636.7 With other specified complications** M ♀
✓5th **636.8 With unspecified complication** M ♀
✓5th **636.9 Without mention of complication** M ♀

§ ✓4th **637 Unspecified abortion**

Requires fifth-digit to identify stage:
0 unspecified
1 incomplete
2 complete

INCLUDES abortion NOS
retained products of conception following abortion, not classifiable elsewhere

✓5th **637.0 Complicated by genital tract and pelvic infection** M ♀
✓5th **637.1 Complicated by delayed or excessive hemorrhage** M ♀
✓5th **637.2 Complicated by damage to pelvic organs or tissues** M ♀
✓5th **637.3 Complicated by renal failure** M ♀
✓5th **637.4 Complicated by metabolic disorder** M ♀
✓5th **637.5 Complicated by shock** M ♀
✓5th **637.6 Complicated by embolism** M ♀
✓5th **637.7 With other specified complications** M ♀
✓5th **637.8 With unspecified complication** M ♀
✓5th **637.9 Without mention of complication** M ♀

§ ✓4th **638 Failed attempted abortion**

INCLUDES failure of attempted induction of (legal) abortion

EXCLUDES *incomplete abortion (634.0-637.9)*

DEF: Continued pregnancy despite an attempted legal abortion.

638.0 Complicated by genital tract and pelvic infection M ♀
638.1 Complicated by delayed or excessive hemorrhage M ♀
638.2 Complicated by damage to pelvic organs or tissues M ♀
638.3 Complicated by renal failure M ♀
638.4 Complicated by metabolic disorder M ♀
638.5 Complicated by shock M ♀
638.6 Complicated by embolism M ♀
638.7 With other specified complications M ♀
638.8 With unspecified complication M ♀
638.9 Without mention of complication M ♀

§ See beginning of section 634-639 for fourth-digit definitions.

N Newborn Age: 0 P Pediatric Age: 0-17 M Maternity Age: 12-55 A Adult Age: 15-124 CC CC Condition MC Major Complication CD Complex Dx HIV HIV Related Dx

639 Complications following abortion and ectopic and molar pregnancies

Note: This category is provided for use when it is required to classify separately the complications classifiable to the fourth-digit level in categories 634-638; for example:

a) when the complication itself was responsible for an episode of medical care, the abortion, ectopic or molar pregnancy itself having been dealt with at a previous episode

b) when these conditions are immediate complications of ectopic or molar pregnancies classifiable to 630-633 where they cannot be identified at fourth-digit level.

639.0 Genital tract and pelvic infection CC M ♀

Endometritis
Parametritis
Pelvic peritonitis
Salpingitis
Salpingo-oophoritis
Sepsis NOS
Septicemia NOS
} following conditions classifiable to 630-638

EXCLUDES *urinary tract infection (639.8)*

CC Excl: 639.0, 639.2-641.23, 646.80-646.93, 648.90-650, 669.40-669.44, 669.80-669.94

639.1 Delayed or excessive hemorrhage CC M ♀

Afibrinogenemia
Defibrination syndrome
Intravascular hemolysis
} following conditions classifiable to 630-638

CC Excl: 639.1-639.9, 640.00-640.93, 641.00-641.23, 646.80-646.93, 648.90-648.94, 650, 669.40-669.44, 669.80-669.94

639.2 Damage to pelvic organs and tissues CC M ♀

Laceration, perforation, or tear of:
bladder
bowel
broad ligament
cervix
periurethral tissue
uterus
vagina
} following conditions classifiable to 630-638

CC Excl: 639.2-639.9, 640.00-640.93, 641.00-641.23, 646.80-646.93, 648.90-648.94, 650, 669.40-669.44, 669.80-669.94

639.3 Renal failure CC M ♀

Oliguria
Renal:
failure (acute)
shutdown
tubular necrosis
Uremia
} following conditions classifiable to 630-638

CC Excl: See code 639.2

639.4 Metabolic disorders CC M ♀

Electrolyte imbalance following conditions classifiable to 630-638

CC Excl: See code 639.2

639.5 Shock CC M ♀

Circulatory collapse
Shock (postoperative) (septic)
} following conditions classifiable to 630-638

CC Excl: See code 639.2

639.6 Embolism CC M ♀

Embolism:
NOS
air
amniotic fluid
blood-clot
fat
pulmonary
pyemic
septic
soap
} following conditions classifiable to 630-638

CC Excl: See code 639.2

639.8 Other specified complications following abortionor ectopic and molar pregnancy CC M ♀

Acute yellow atrophy or necrosis of liver
Cardiac arrest or failure
Cerebral anoxia
Urinary tract infection
} following conditions classifiable to 630-638

CC Excl: See code 639.2

639.9 Unspecified complication following abortion orectopic and molar pregnancy CC M ♀

Complication(s) not further specified following conditions classifiable to 630-638

CC Excl: See code 639.2

COMPLICATIONS MAINLY RELATED TO PREGNANCY ▶(640-649)◀

INCLUDES the listed conditions even if they arose or were present during labor, delivery, or the puerperium

AHA: 2Q, '90, 11

The following fifth-digit subclassification is for use with categories ▶640-649◀ to denote the current episode of care. Valid fifth-digits are in [brackets] under each code.

0 unspecified as to episode of care or not applicable

1 delivered, with or without mention of antepartum condition
Antepartum condition with delivery
Delivery NOS (with mention of antepartum complication during current episode of care)
Intrapartum obstetric condition (with mention of antepartum complication during current episode of care)
Pregnancy, delivered (with mention of antepartum complication during current episode of care)

2 delivered, with mention of postpartum complication
Delivery with mention of puerperal complication during current episode of care

3 antepartum condition or complication
Antepartum obstetric condition, not delivered during the current episode of care

4 postpartum condition or complication
Postpartum or puerperal obstetric condition or complication following delivery that occurred:
during previous episode of care
outside hospital, with subsequent admission for observation or care

640 Hemorrhage in early pregnancy

INCLUDES hemorrhage before completion of 22 weeks' gestation

640.0 Threatened abortion [0,1,3] CC M ♀

CC Excl: 640.00-640.93, 641.00-641.13, 646.80-646.93, 648.90-648.94, 650, 669.40-669.44, 669.80-669.94

DEF: Bloody discharge during pregnancy; cervix may be dilated and pregnancy is threatened, but the pregnancy is not terminated.

640.8 Other specified hemorrhage in early pregnancy [0,1,3] CC M ♀

CC Excl: See code 640.0

Placenta Previa

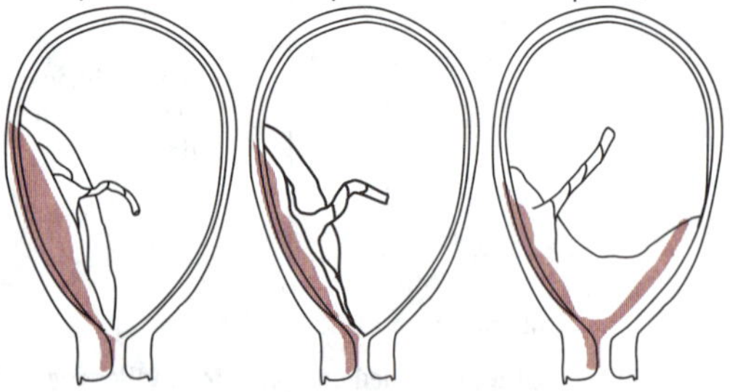

Low (marginal) implantation | Partial placenta previa | Total placenta previa

§ ✓5th **640.9** **Unspecified hemorrhage in early pregnancy** CC M ♀
[0,1,3] **CC Excl:** See code 640.0

✓4th **641 Antepartum hemorrhage, abruptio placentae, and placenta previa**

1 § ✓5th **641.0** **Placenta previa without hemorrhage** CC M ♀
[0,1,3]

Low impantation of placenta } without hemorrhage
Placenta previa noted:
  during pregnancy
  before labor (and delivered by caesarean delivery.)

CC Excl: See code 640.0

DEF: Placenta implanted in lower segment of uterus; commonly causes hemorrhage in the last trimester of pregnancy.

1 § ✓5th **641.1** **Hemorrhage from placenta previa** CC M ♀
[0,1,3]

Low-lying placenta } NOS or with hemorrhage (intrapartum)
Placenta previa
  incomplete
  marginal
  partial
  total

EXCLUDES *hemorrhage from vasa previa (663.5)*

CC Excl: See code 640.0

1 § ✓5th **641.2** **Premature separation of placenta** M ♀
[0,1,3]

Ablatio placentae
Abruptio placentae
Accidental antepartum hemorrhage
Couvelaire uterus
Detachment of placenta (premature)
Premature separation of normally implanted placenta

DEF: Abruptio placentae: premature detachment of the placenta, characterized by shock, oliguria and decreased fibrinogen.

1 § ✓5th **641.3** **Antepartum hemorrhage associated with coagulation defects** CC M ♀
[0,1,3]

Antepartum or intrapartum hemorrhage associated with:
  afibrinogenemia
  hyperfibrinolysis
  hypofibrinogenemia

EXCLUDES ▶*coagulation defects not associated with antepartum hemorrhage (649.3)*◀

CC Excl: 641.30-641.93, 646.80-646.93, 648.90-650, 669.40-669.44, 669.80-669.94

DEF: Uterine hemorrhage prior to delivery.

1 § ✓5th **641.8** **Other antepartum hemorrhage** CC M ♀
[0,1,3]

Antepartum or intrapartum hemorrhage associated with:
  trauma
  uterine leiomyoma

CC Excl: See code 641.3

§ ✓5th **641.9** **Unspecified antepartum hemorrhage** CC M ♀
[0,1,3]

Hemorrhage:
  antepartum NOS
  intrapartum NOS
Hemorrhage:
  of pregnancy NOS

CC Excl: See code 641.3

Abruptio Placentae

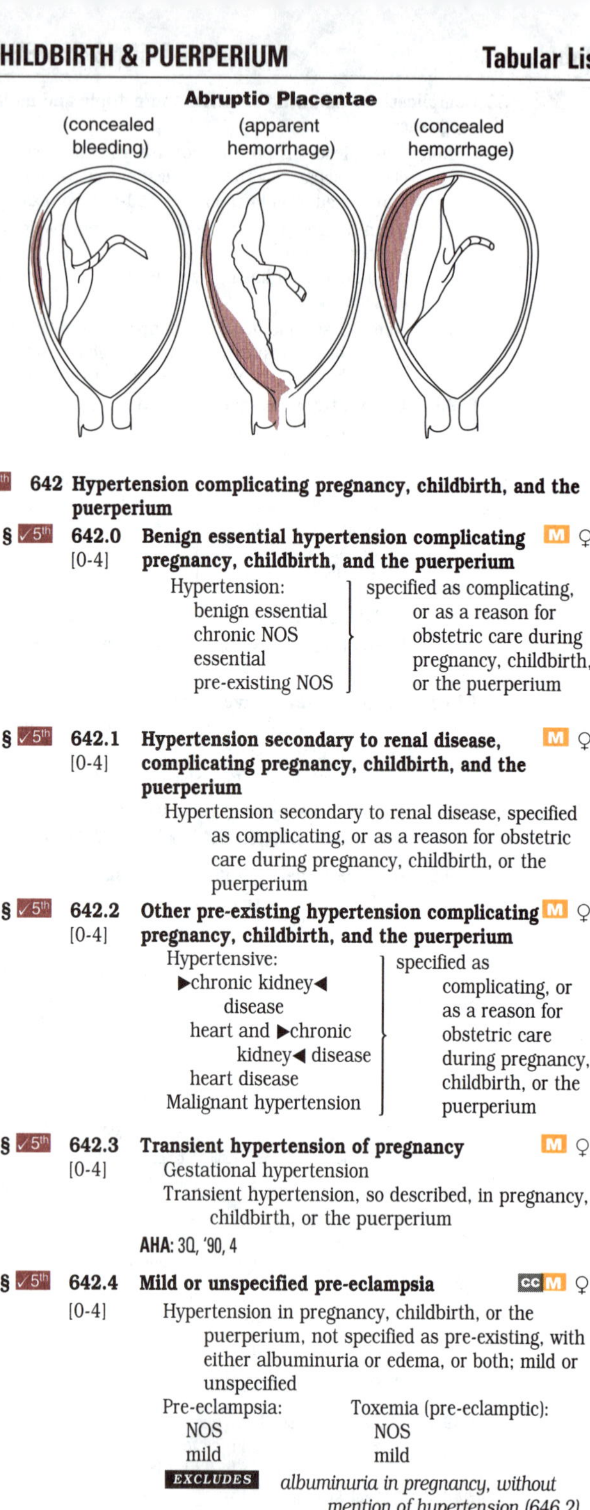

✓4th **642 Hypertension complicating pregnancy, childbirth, and the puerperium**

1 § ✓5th **642.0** **Benign essential hypertension complicating pregnancy, childbirth, and the puerperium** M ♀
[0-4]

Hypertension: } specified as complicating, or as a reason for obstetric care during pregnancy, childbirth, or the puerperium
  benign essential
  chronic NOS
  essential
  pre-existing NOS

1 § ✓5th **642.1** **Hypertension secondary to renal disease, complicating pregnancy, childbirth, and the puerperium** M ♀
[0-4]

Hypertension secondary to renal disease, specified as complicating, or as a reason for obstetric care during pregnancy, childbirth, or the puerperium

1 § ✓5th **642.2** **Other pre-existing hypertension complicating pregnancy, childbirth, and the puerperium** M ♀
[0-4]

Hypertensive: } specified as complicating, or as a reason for obstetric care during pregnancy, childbirth, or the puerperium
  ▶chronic kidney◀ disease
  heart and ▶chronic kidney◀ disease
  heart disease
Malignant hypertension

1 § ✓5th **642.3** **Transient hypertension of pregnancy** M ♀
[0-4]

Gestational hypertension
Transient hypertension, so described, in pregnancy, childbirth, or the puerperium

AHA: 3Q, '90, 4

1 § ✓5th **642.4** **Mild or unspecified pre-eclampsia** CC M ♀
[0-4]

Hypertension in pregnancy, childbirth, or the puerperium, not specified as pre-existing, with either albuminuria or edema, or both; mild or unspecified

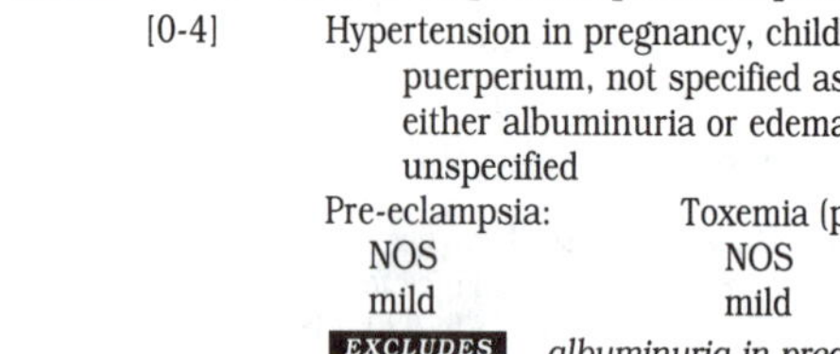

Pre-eclampsia:
  NOS
  mild
Toxemia (pre-eclamptic):
  NOS
  mild

EXCLUDES *albuminuria in pregnancy, without mention of hypertension (646.2)*
edema in pregnancy, without mention of hypertension (646.1)

CC Excl: 642.00-642.94, 646.10-646.14, 646.80-646.93, 648.90-650, 669.40-669.44, 669.80-669.94

1 § ✓5th **642.5** **Severe pre-eclampsia** CC M ♀
[0-4]

Hypertension in pregnancy, childbirth, or the puerperium, not specified as pre-existing, with either albuminuria or edema, or both; specified as severe
Pre-eclampsia, severe
Toxemia (pre-eclamptic), severe

CC Excl: See code 642.4

AHA: N-D, '85, 3

1 Nonspecific PDx=0
§ Requires fifth-digit. Valid digits are in [brackets] under each code. See beginning of section 640-649 for codes and definitions.

N Newborn Age: 0 P Pediatric Age: 0-17 M Maternity Age: 12-55 A Adult Age: 15-124 CC CC Condition MC Major Complication CD Complex Dx HIV HIV Related Dx

1 § ✓5th **642.6 Eclampsia** CC M♀
[0-4]
Toxemia:
eclamptic
with convulsions
CC Excl: See code 642.4

1 § ✓5th **642.7 Pre-eclampsia or eclampsia superimposed on pre-existing hypertension** CC M♀
[0-4]
Conditions classifiable to 642.4-642.6, with conditions classifiable to 642.0-642.2
CC Excl: See code 642.4

1 § ✓5th **642.9 Unspecified hypertension complicating pregnancy, childbirth, or the puerperium** M♀
[0-4]
Hypertension NOS, without mention of albuminuria or edema, complicating pregnancy, childbirth, or the puerperium

✓4th **643 Excessive vomiting in pregnancy**

INCLUDES hyperemesis } arising during pregnancy
vomiting:
persistent
vicious
hyperemesis gravidarum

1 § ✓5th **643.0 Mild hyperemesis gravidarum** M♀
[0,1,3]
Hyperemesis gravidarum, mild or unspecified, starting before the end of the 22nd week of gestation
DEF: Detrimental vomiting and nausea.

1 § ✓5th **643.1 Hyperemesis gravidarum with metabolic disturbance** M♀
[0,1,3]
Hyperemesis gravidarum, starting before the end of the 22nd week of gestation, with metabolic disturbance, such as:
carbohydrate depletion
dehydration
electrolyte imbalance

1 § ✓5th **643.2 Late vomiting of pregnancy** M♀
[0,1,3]
Excessive vomiting starting after 22 completed weeks of gestation

1 § ✓5th **643.8 Other vomiting complicating pregnancy** M♀
[0,1,3]
Vomiting due to organic disease or other cause, specified as complicating pregnancy, or as a reason for obstetric care during pregnancy
Use additional code to specify cause

1 § ✓5th **643.9 Unspecified vomiting of pregnancy** M♀
[0,1,3]
Vomiting as a reason for care during pregnancy, length of gestation unspecified

✓4th **644 Early or threatened labor**

1 § ✓5th **644.0 Threatened premature labor** CC M♀
[0,3]
Premature labor after 22 weeks, but before 37 completed weeks of gestation without delivery
EXCLUDES *that occurring before 22 completed weeks of gestation (640.0)*
CC Excl: 644.00-644.21, 646.80-646.93, 648.90-650, 669.40-669.44, 669.80-669.94

1 § ✓5th **644.1 Other threatened labor** CC M♀
[0,3]
False labor:
NOS } without delivery
after 37 completed weeks of gestation } without delivery
Threatened labor NOS } without delivery
CC Excl: See code 644.0

1 § ✓5th **644.2 Early onset of delivery** M♀
[0,1]
Onset (spontaneous) of delivery } before 37 completed weeks of gestation
Premature labor with onset of delivery } before 37 completed weeks of gestation
AHA: 2Q, '91, 16

✓4th **645 Late pregnancy**
AHA: 4Q, '00, 43; 4Q, '91, 26

§ ✓5th **645.1 Post term pregnancy** M♀
[0,1,3]
Pregnancy over 40 completed weeks to 42 completed weeks gestation

§ ✓5th **645.2 Prolonged pregnancy** M♀
[0,1,3]
Pregnancy which has advanced beyond 42 completed weeks gestation

✓4th **646 Other complications of pregnancy, not elsewhere classified**
Use additional code(s) to further specify complication
AHA: 4Q, '95, 59

1 § ✓5th **646.0 Papyraceous fetus** M♀
[0,1,3]
DEF: Fetus that dies in the second trimester of pregnancy and is retained in the uterus, with subsequent atrophy and mummification; commonly occurs in twin pregnancy, nonviable fetus becomes compressed by growth of living twin and exhibits parchment-like skin.

1 § ✓5th **646.1 Edema or excessive weight gain in pregnancy, without mention of hypertension** M♀
[0-4]
Gestational edema
Maternal obesity syndrome
EXCLUDES *that with mention of hypertension (642.0-642.9)*

1 § ✓5th **646.2 Unspecified renal disease in pregnancy, without mention of hypertension** M♀
[0-4]
Albuminuria } in pregnancy or the puerperium, without mention of hypertension
Nephropathy NOS } in pregnancy or the puerperium, without mention of hypertension
Renal disease NOS } in pregnancy or the puerperium, without mention of hypertension
Uremia } in pregnancy or the puerperium, without mention of hypertension
Gestational proteinuria
EXCLUDES *that with mention of hypertension (642.0-642.9)*

1 § ✓5th **646.3 Habitual aborter** M♀
[0,1,3]
EXCLUDES *with current abortion (634.0-634.9)*
without current pregnancy (629.9)
DEF: Three or more consecutive spontaneous abortions.

1 § ✓5th **646.4 Peripheral neuritis in pregnancy** M♀
[0-4]

1 § ✓5th **646.5 Asymptomatic bacteriuria in pregnancy** M♀
[0-4]

1 § ✓5th **646.6 Infections of genitourinary tract in pregnancy** CC M♀
[0-4]
Conditions classifiable to 590, 595, 597, 599.0, 616 complicating pregnancy, childbirth, or the puerperium
Conditions classifiable to 614.0-614.5, 614.7-614.9, 615 complicating pregnancy or labor
EXCLUDES *major puerperal infection (670)*
CC Excl: 646.60-646.64, 646.80-646.93, 648.90-648.94, 650, 669.40-669.44, 669.80-669.94
AHA: For code **646.63:** 4Q, '04, 90

1 § ✓5th **646.7 Liver disorders in pregnancy** CC M♀
[0,1,3]
Acute yellow atrophy of liver (obstetric) (true) } of pregnancy
Icterus gravis } of pregnancy
Necrosis of liver } of pregnancy
EXCLUDES *hepatorenal syndrome following delivery (674.8)*
viral hepatitis (647.6)
CC Excl: 646.70-646.93, 648.90-650, 669.40-669.44, 669.80-669.94

1 § ✓5th **646.8 Other specified complications of pregnancy** M♀
[0-4]
Fatigue during pregnancy
Herpes gestationis
Insufficient weight gain of pregnancy
AHA: 3Q, '98, 16; J-F, '85, 15

1 § ✓5th **646.9 Unspecified complication of pregnancy** M♀
[0,1,3]

1 Nonspecific PDx=0
§ Requires fifth-digit. Valid digits are in [brackets] under each code. See beginning of section 640-649 for codes and definitions.

Additional Digit Required Nonspecific PDx Unacceptable PDx Manifestation Code MCV Major Cardiovascular Condition ▶◀ Revised Text ● New Code ▲ Revised Code Title

✓4th 647 Infectious and parasitic conditions in the mother classifiable elsewhere, but complicating pregnancy, childbirth, or the puerperium

INCLUDES the listed conditions when complicating the pregnant state, aggravated by the pregnancy, or when a main reason for obstetric care

EXCLUDES *those conditions in the mother known or suspected to have affected the fetus (655.0-655.9)*

Use additional code(s) to further specify complication

[1] § ✓5th **647.0 Syphilis** M♀
[0-4] Conditions classifiable to 090-097

[1] § ✓5th **647.1 Gonorrhea** M♀
[0-4] Conditions classifiable to 098

[1] § ✓5th **647.2 Other venereal diseases** M♀
[0-4] Conditions classifiable to 099

[1] § ✓5th **647.3 Tuberculosis** CC M♀
[0-4] Conditions classifiable to 010-018
CC Excl: 646.80-646.93, 647.30-647.34, 648.90-650, 669.40-669.44, 669.80-669.94

[1] § ✓5th **647.4 Malaria** CC M♀
[0-4] Conditions classifiable to 084
CC Excl: 646.80-646.93, 647.30-647.34, 648.90-650, 669.40-669.44, 669.80-669.94

[1] § ✓5th **647.5 Rubella** M♀
[0-4] Conditions classifiable to 056

[1] § ✓5th **647.6 Other viral diseases** M♀
[0-4] Conditions classifiable to 042 and 050-079, except 056
AHA: J-F, '85, 15

[1] § ✓5th **647.8 Other specified infectious and parasitic diseases** M♀
[0-4]

§ ✓5th **647.9 Unspecified infection or infestation** M♀
[0-4]

✓4th 648 Other current conditions in the mother classifiable elsewhere, but complicating pregnancy, childbirth, or the puerperium

INCLUDES the listed conditions when complicating the pregnant state, aggravated by the pregnancy, or when a main reason for obstetric care

EXCLUDES *those conditions in the mother known or suspected to have affected the fetus (655.0-665.9)*

Use additional code(s) to identify the condition

[1] § ✓5th **648.0 Diabetes mellitus** CC M♀
[0-4] Conditions classifiable to 250
EXCLUDES *gestational diabetes (648.8)*
CC Excl: 646.80-646.93, 648.00-648.04, 648.90-650, 669.40-669.44, 669.80-669.94
AHA: 3Q, '91, 5, 11

[1] § ✓5th **648.1 Thyroid dysfunction** M♀
[0-4] Conditions classifiable to 240-246

[1] § ✓5th **648.2 Anemia** CC M♀
[0-4] Conditions classifiable to 280-285
CC Excl: 646.80-646.93, 648.20-648.24, 648.90-650,669.40-669.44, 669.80-669.94
AHA: For Code 648.22: 1Q, '02, 14

[1] § ✓5th **648.3 Drug dependence** CC M♀
[0-4] Conditions classifiable to 304
CC Excl: 646.80-646.93, 648.30-648.34, 648.90-650, 669.40-669.44, 669.80-669.94
AHA: 2Q, '98, 13; 4Q, '88, 8

[1] § ✓5th **648.4 Mental disorders** M♀
[0-4] Conditions classifiable to 290-303, ▶305.0, 305.2-305.9, 306-316, 317-319◀
AHA: 2Q, '98, 13; 4Q, '95, 63

[1] § ✓5th **648.5 Congenital cardiovascular disorders** CC M♀
[0-4] Conditions classifiable to 745-747
CC Excl: 646.80-646.93, 648.50-648.64, 648.90-648.94, 650, 669.40-669.44, 669.80-669.94

[1] § ✓5th **648.6 Other cardiovascular diseases** CC M♀
[0-4] Conditions classifiable to 390-398, 410-429
EXCLUDES *cerebrovascular disorders in the puerperium (674.0)*
peripartum cardiomyopathy (674.5)
venous complications (671.0-671.9)
CC Excl: See code 648.5
AHA: 3Q, '98, 11

[1] § ✓5th **648.7 Bone and joint disorders of back, pelvis, and lower limbs** M♀
[0-4] Conditions classifiable to 720-724, and those classifiable to 711-719 or 725-738, specified as affecting the lower limbs

[1] § ✓5th **648.8 Abnormal glucose tolerance** M♀
[0-4] Conditions classifiable to 790.21-790.29
Gestational diabetes
Use additional code, if applicable, for associated long-term (current) insulin use (V58.67)
AHA: 3Q, '91, 5; **For code 648.83:** 4Q, '04, 56
DEF: Glucose intolerance arising in pregnancy, resolving at end of pregnancy.

[1] § ✓5th **648.9 Other current conditions classifiable elsewhere** M♀
[0-4] Conditions classifiable to 440-459
Nutritional deficiencies [conditions classifiable to 260-269]
AHA: 4Q, '04, 88; N-D, '87, 10; **For code 648.91:** 1Q, '02, 14; **For code 648.93:** 4Q, '04, 90

● **✓4th 649 Other conditions or status of the mother complicating pregnancy, childbirth, or the puerperium**

● § ✓5th **649.0 Tobacco use disorder complicating pregnancy, childbirth, or the puerperium** M♀
[0-4] Smoking complicating pregnancy, childbirth, or the puerperium

● § ✓5th **649.1 Obesity complicating pregnancy, childbirth, or the puerperium** M♀
[0-4] Use additional code to identify the obesity (278.00, 278.01)

● § ✓5th **649.2 Bariatric surgery status complicating pregnancy, childbirth, or the puerperium** M♀
[0-4] Gastric banding status complicating pregnancy, childbirth, or the puerperium
Gastric bypass status for obesity complicating pregnancy, childbirth, or the puerperium
Obesity surgery status complicating pregnancy, childbirth, or the puerperium

● § ✓5th **649.3 Coagulation defects complicating pregnancy, childbirth, or the puerperium** M♀
[0-4] Conditions classifiable to 286
Use additional code to identify the specific coagulation defect (286.0-286.9)
EXCLUDES *coagulation defects causing antepartum hemorrhage (641.3)*
postpartum coagulation defects (666.3)

● § ✓5th **649.4 Epilepsy complicating pregnancy, childbirth, or the puerperium** M♀
[0-4] Conditions classifiable to 345
Use additional code to identify the specific type of epilepsy (345.00-345.91)
EXCLUDES *eclampsia (642.6)*

● § ✓5th **649.5 Spotting complicating pregnancy** M♀
[0,1,3] EXCLUDES *antepartum hemorrhage (641.0-641.9)*
hemorrhage in early pregnancy (640.0-640.9)

● § ✓5th **649.6 Uterine size date discrepancy** M♀
[0-4]

[1] Nonspecific PDx=0
§ Requires fifth-digit. Valid digits are in [brackets] under each code. See beginning of section 640-649 for codes and definitions.

N Newborn Age: 0 P Pediatric Age: 0-17 M Maternity Age: 12-55 A Adult Age: 15-124 CC CC Condition MC Major Complication CD Complex Dx HIV HIV Related Dx

NORMAL DELIVERY, AND OTHER INDICATIONS FOR CARE IN PREGNANCY, LABOR, AND DELIVERY (650-659)

The following fifth-digit subclassification is for use with categories 651-659 to denote the current episode of care. Valid fifth-digits are in [brackets] under each code.

0 unspecified as to episode of care or not applicable
1 delivered, with or without mention of antepartum condition
2 delivered, with mention of postpartum complication
3 antepartum condition or complication
4 postpartum condition or complication

650 Normal delivery M♀

Delivery requiring minimal or no assistance, with or without episiotomy, without fetal manipulation [e.g., rotation version] or instrumentation [forceps] of spontaneous, cephalic, vaginal, full-term, single, live-born infant. This code is for use as a single diagnosis code and is not to be used with any other code in the range 630-676.

EXCLUDES *breech delivery (assisted) (spontaneous) NOS (652.2)*
delivery by vacuum extractor, forceps, cesarean section, or breech extraction, without specified complication (669.5-669.7)

Use additional code to indicate outcome of delivery (V27.0)

AHA: 2Q, '02, 10; 3Q, '01, 12; 3Q, '00, 5; 4Q, '95, 28, 59

✓4th **651 Multiple gestation**

1 § ✓5th **651.0 Twin pregnancy** M♀
[0,1,3]

1 § ✓5th **651.1 Triplet pregnancy** M♀
[0,1,3]

1 § ✓5th **651.2 Quadruplet pregnancy** M♀
[0,1,3]

1 § ✓5th **651.3 Twin pregnancy with fetal loss and retention of one fetus** M♀
[0,1,3]

1 § ✓5th **651.4 Triplet pregnancy with fetal loss and retention of one or more fetus(es)** M♀
[0,1,3]

1 § ✓5th **651.5 Quadruplet pregnancy with fetal loss and retention of one or more fetus(es)** M♀
[0,1,3]

1 § ✓5th **651.6 Other multiple pregnancy with fetal loss and retention of one or more fetus(es)** M♀
[0,1,3]

§ ✓5th **651.7 Multiple gestation following (elective) fetal reduction** M♀
[0,1,3]
Fetal reduction of multiple fetuses reduced to single fetus

AHA: For code 651.71: ▶4Q, '05, 81◀

1 § ✓5th **651.8 Other specified multiple gestation** M♀
[0,1,3]

§ ✓5th **651.9 Unspecified multiple gestation** M♀
[0,1,3]

✓4th **652 Malposition and malpresentation of fetus**

Code first any associated obstructed labor (660.0)

1 § ✓5th **652.0 Unstable lie** M♀
[0,1,3] DEF: Changing fetal position.

Malposition and Malpresentation

Breech
Shoulder (arm prolapse)
Mother's pelvis
Face (mentum)
Compound (extremity together with head)
Oblique

Cephalopelvic Disproportion

Pubic symphysis
Ischial tuberosity
Contraction of pelvic outlet (from below)
Cephalopelvic disproportion due to: Contraction of pelvic inlet, or large fetus, or hydrocephalus
Pubic symphysis
Pelvic inlet from above

1 § ✓5th **652.1 Breech or other malpresentation successfully converted to cephalic presentation** M♀
[0,1,3]
Cephalic version NOS

1 § ✓5th **652.2 Breech presentation without mention of version** M♀
[0,1,3]
Breech delivery (assisted) (spontaneous) NOS
Buttocks presentation
Complete breech
Frank breech

EXCLUDES *footling presentation (652.8)*
incomplete breech (652.8)

DEF: Fetal presentation of buttocks or feet at birth canal.

1 § ✓5th **652.3 Transverse or oblique presentation** M♀
[0,1,3]
Oblique lie
Transverse lie

EXCLUDES *transverse arrest of fetal head (660.3)*

1 § ✓5th **652.4 Face or brow presentation** M♀
[0,1,3]
Mentum presentation

1 § ✓5th **652.5 High head at term** M♀
[0,1,3]
Failure of head to enter pelvic brim

1 § ✓5th **652.6 Multiple gestation with malpresentation of one fetus or more** M♀
[0,1,3]

1 § ✓5th **652.7 Prolapsed arm** M♀
[0,1,3]

1 § ✓5th **652.8 Other specified malposition or malpresentation** M♀
[0,1,3]
Compound presentation

§ ✓5th **652.9 Unspecified malposition or malpresentation** M♀
[0,1,3]

✓4th **653 Disproportion**

Code first any associated obstructed labor (660.1)

1 § ✓5th **653.0 Major abnormality of bony pelvis, not further specified** M♀
[0,1,3]
Pelvic deformity NOS

1 § ✓5th **653.1 Generally contracted pelvis** M♀
[0,1,3]
Contracted pelvis NOS

1 § ✓5th **653.2 Inlet contraction of pelvis** M♀
[0,1,3]
Inlet contraction (pelvis)

1 § ✓5th **653.3 Outlet contraction of pelvis** M♀
[0,1,3]
Outlet contraction (pelvis)

1 § ✓5th **653.4 Fetopelvic disproportion** M♀
[0,1,3]
Cephalopelvic disproportion NOS
Disproportion of mixed maternal and fetal origin, with normally formed fetus

1 § ✓5th **653.5 Unusually large fetus causing disproportion** M♀
[0,1,3]
Disproportion of fetal origin with normally formed fetus
Fetal disproportion NOS

EXCLUDES *that when the reason for medical care was concern for the fetus (656.6)*

1 § ✓5th **653.6 Hydrocephalic fetus causing disproportion** M♀
[0,1,3]

EXCLUDES *that when the reason for medical care was concern for the fetus (655.0)*

1 § ✓5th **653.7 Other fetal abnormality causing disproportion** M♀
[0,1,3]
Conjoined twins
Fetal:
ascites
hydrops
Fetal:
myelomeningocele
sacral teratoma
tumor

1 Nonspecific PDx=0
§ Requires fifth-digit. Valid digits are in [brackets] under each code. See beginning of section 640-649 for codes and definitions.

1 § ✓5th **653.8 Disproportion of other origin** M♀
[0,1,3] EXCLUDES *shoulder (girdle) dystocia (660.4)*

§ ✓5th **653.9 Unspecified disproportion** M♀
[0,1,3]

✓4th **654 Abnormality of organs and soft tissues of pelvis**
INCLUDES the listed conditions during pregnancy, childbirth, or the puerperium
Code first any associated obstructed labor (660.2)

1 § ✓5th **654.0 Congenital abnormalities of uterus** M♀
[0-4] Double uterus; Uterus bicornis

1 § ✓5th **654.1 Tumors of body of uterus** M♀
[0-4] Uterine fibroids

1 § ✓5th **654.2 Previous cesarean delivery** M♀
[0,1,3] Uterine scar from previous cesarean delivery
AHA: 1Q, '92, 8

1 § ✓5th **654.3 Retroverted and incarcerated gravid uterus** M♀
[0-4]
DEF: Retroverted: tilted back uterus; no change in angle of longitudinal axis.
DEF: Incarcerated: immobile, fixed uterus.

1 § ✓5th **654.4 Other abnormalities in shape or position of gravid uterus and of neighboring structures** M♀
[0-4] Cystocele; Prolapse of gravid uterus; Pelvic floor repair; Rectocele; Pendulous abdomen; Rigid pelvic floor

1 § ✓5th **654.5 Cervical incompetence** M♀
[0-4] Presence of Shirodkar suture with or without mention of cervical incompetence
DEF: Abnormal cervix; tendency to dilate in second trimester; causes premature fetal expulsion.
DEF: Shirodkar suture: purse-string suture used to artificially close incompetent cervix.

1 § ✓5th **654.6 Other congenital or acquired abnormality of cervix** M♀
[0-4] Cicatricial cervix; Rigid cervix (uteri); Polyp of cervix; Stenosis or stricture of cervix; Previous surgery to cervix; Tumor of cervix

1 § ✓5th **654.7 Congenital or acquired abnormality of vagina** M♀
[0-4] Previous surgery to vagina; Stricture of vagina; Septate vagina; Tumor of vagina
Stenosis of vagina (acquired) (congenital)

1 § ✓5th **654.8 Congenital or acquired abnormality of vulva** M♀
[0-4] Fibrosis of perineum; Rigid perineum; Persistent hymen; Tumor of vulva; Previous surgery to perineum or vulva
EXCLUDES *varicose veins of vulva (671.1)*
AHA: 1Q, '03, 14

§ ✓5th **654.9 Other and unspecified** M♀
[0-4] Uterine scar NEC

✓4th **655 Known or suspected fetal abnormality affecting management of mother**
INCLUDES the listed conditions in the fetus as a reason for observation or obstetrical care of the mother, or for termination of pregnancy
AHA: 3Q, '90, 4

1 § ✓5th **655.0 Central nervous system malformation in fetus** M♀
[0,1,3] Fetal or suspected fetal:
anencephaly
hydrocephalus
spina bifida (with myelomeningocele)

1 § ✓5th **655.1 Chromosomal abnormality in fetus** M♀
[0,1,3]

1 § ✓5th **655.2 Hereditary disease in family possibly affecting fetus** M♀
[0,1,3]

1 § ✓5th **655.3 Suspected damage to fetus from viral disease in the mother** M♀
[0,1,3] Suspected damage to fetus from maternal rubella

1 § ✓5th **655.4 Suspected damage to fetus from other disease in the mother** M♀
[0,1,3] Suspected damage to fetus from maternal:
alcohol addiction
listeriosis
toxoplasmosis

1 § ✓5th **655.5 Suspected damage to fetus from drugs** M♀
[0,1,3]

1 § ✓5th **655.6 Suspected damage to fetus from radiation** M♀
[0,1,3]

1 § ✓5th **655.7 Decreased fetal movements** M♀
[0,1,3] **AHA:** 4Q, '97, 41

1 § ✓5th **655.8 Other known or suspected fetal abnormality, not elsewhere classified** M♀
[0,1,3] Suspected damage to fetus from:
environmental toxins
intrauterine contraceptive device

§ ✓5th **655.9 Unspecified** M♀
[0,1,3]

✓4th **656 Other fetal and placental problems affecting management of mother**

1 § ✓5th **656.0 Fetal-maternal hemorrhage** M♀
[0,1,3] Leakage (microscopic) of fetal blood into maternal circulation

1 § ✓5th **656.1 Rhesus isoimmunization** M♀
[0,1,3] Anti-D [Rh] antibodies
Rh incompatibility
DEF: Antibodies developing against Rh factor; mother with Rh negative develops antibodies against Rh positive fetus.

1 § ✓5th **656.2 Isoimmunization from other and unspecified blood-group incompatibility** M♀
[0,1,3] ABO isoimmunization.

1 § ✓5th **656.3 Fetal distress** M♀
[0,1,3] Fetal metabolic acidemia
EXCLUDES *abnormal fetal acid-base balance (656.8)*
abnormality in fetal heart rate or rhythm (659.7)
fetal bradycardia (659.7)
fetal tachycardia (659.7)
meconium in liquor (656.8)
AHA: N-D, '86, 4
DEF: Life-threatening disorder; fetal anoxia, hemolytic disease and other miscellaneous diseases cause fetal distress.

1 § ✓5th **656.4 Intrauterine death** M♀
[0,1,3] Fetal death:
NOS
after completion of 22 weeks' gestation
late
Missed delivery
EXCLUDES *missed abortion (632)*

1 § ✓5th **656.5 Poor fetal growth** M♀
[0,1,3] "Light-for-dates"
"Placental insufficiency"
"Small-for-dates"

1 § ✓5th **656.6 Excessive fetal growth** M♀
[0,1,3] "Large-for-dates"

1 § ✓5th **656.7 Other placental conditions** M♀
[0,1,3] Abnormal placenta
Placental infarct
EXCLUDES *placental polyp (674.4)*
placentitis (658.4)

1 § ✓5th **656.8 Other specified fetal and placental problems** M♀
[0,1,3] Abnormal acid-base balance
Intrauterine acidosis
Lithopedian
Meconium in liquor
DEF: Lithopedion: Calcified fetus; not expelled by mother.

1 § ✓5th **656.9 Unspecified fetal and placental problem** M♀
[0,1,3]

1 Nonspecific PDx=0
§ Requires fifth-digit. Valid digits are in [brackets] under each code. See beginning of section 640-649 for codes and definitions.

N Newborn Age: 0 | P Pediatric Age: 0-17 | M Maternity Age: 12-55 | A Adult Age: 15-124 | CC CC Condition | MC Major Complication | CD Complex Dx | HIV HIV Related Dx

1 ✓4th **657 Polyhydramnios** M♀
[0,1,3]
§ ✓5th Use 0 as fourth-digit for this category
Hydramnios
AHA: 4Q, '91, 26
DEF: Excess amniotic fluid.

✓4th **658 Other problems associated with amniotic cavity and membranes**
EXCLUDES *amniotic fluid embolism (673.1)*

1 § ✓5th **658.0 Oligohydramnios** M♀
[0,1,3]
Oligohydramnios without mention of rupture of membranes
DEF: Deficient amount of amniotic fluid.

1 § ✓5th **658.1 Premature rupture of membranes** M♀
[0,1,3]
Rupture of amniotic sac less than 24 hours prior to the onset of labor
AHA: For code 658.13: 1Q, '01, 5; 4Q, '98, 77

1 § ✓5th **658.2 Delayed delivery after spontaneous or unspecified rupture of membranes** M♀
[0,1,3]
Prolonged rupture of membranes NOS
Rupture of amniotic sac 24 hours or more prior to the onset of labor

1 § ✓5th **658.3 Delayed delivery after artificial rupture of membranes** M♀
[0,1,3]

1 § ✓5th **658.4 Infection of amniotic cavity** M♀
[0,1,3]
Amnionitis
Chorioamnionitis
Membranitis
Placentitis

1 § ✓5th **658.8 Other** M♀
[0,1,3]
Amnion nodosum
Amniotic cyst

§ ✓5th **658.9 Unspecified** M♀
[0,1,3]

✓4th **659 Other indications for care or intervention related to labor and delivery, not elsewhere classified**

1 § ✓5th **659.0 Failed mechanical induction** M♀
[0,1,3]
Failure of induction of labor by surgical or other instrumental methods

1 § ✓5th **659.1 Failed medical or unspecified induction** M♀
[0,1,3]
Failed induction NOS
Failure of induction of labor by medical methods, such as oxytocic drugs

1 § ✓5th **659.2 Maternal pyrexia during labor, unspecified** M♀
[0,1,3]
DEF: Fever during labor.

1 § ✓5th **659.3 Generalized infection during labor** CC M♀
[0,1,3]
Septicemia during labor
CC Excl: 646.80-646.93, 648.90-650, 659.30-659.33, 669.40-669.44, 669.80-669.94

1 § ✓5th **659.4 Grand multiparity** M♀
[0,1,3]
EXCLUDES *supervision only, in pregnancy (V23.3)*
without current pregnancy (V61.5)
DEF: Having borne six or more children previously.

1 § ✓5th **659.5 Elderly primigravida** M♀
[0,1,3]
First pregnancy in a woman who will be 35 years of age or older at expected date of delivery
EXCLUDES *supervision only, in pregnancy (V23.81)*
AHA: 3Q, '01, 12

1 § ✓5th **659.6 Elderly multigravida** M♀
[0,1,3]
Second or more pregnancy in a woman who will be 35 years of age or older at expected date of delivery
EXCLUDES *elderly primigravida 659.5*
supervision only, in pregnancy (V23.82)
AHA: 3Q, '01, 12

1 § ✓5th **659.7 Abnormality in fetal heart rate or rhythm** M♀
[0,1,3]
Depressed fetal heart tones
Fetal:
bradycardia
tachycardia
Fetal heart rate decelerations
Non-reassuring fetal heart rate or rhythm
AHA: 4Q, '98, 48

1 § ✓5th **659.8 Other specified indications for care or intervention related to labor and delivery** M♀
[0,1,3]
Pregnancy in a female less than 16 years old at expected date of delivery
Very young maternal age
AHA: 3Q, '01, 12

§ ✓5th **659.9 Unspecified indication for care or intervention related to labor and delivery** M♀
[0,1,3]

COMPLICATIONS OCCURRING MAINLY IN THE COURSE OF LABOR AND DELIVERY (660-669)

The following fifth-digit subclassification is for use with categories 660-669 to denote the current episode of care. Valid fifth-digits are in [brackets] under each code.

0 unspecified as to episode of care or not applicable
1 delivered, with or without mention of antepartum condition
2 delivered, with mention of postpartum complication
3 antepartum condition or complication
4 postpartum condition or complication

✓4th **660 Obstructed labor**
AHA: 3Q, '95, 10

1 § ✓5th **660.0 Obstruction caused by malposition of fetus at onset of labor** M♀
[0,1,3]
Any condition classifiable to 652, causing obstruction during labor
Use additional code from 652.0-652.9 to identify condition

1 § ✓5th **660.1 Obstruction by bony pelvis** M♀
[0,1,3]
Any condition classifiable to 653, causing obstruction during labor
Use additional code from 653.0-653.9 to identify condition

1 § ✓5th **660.2 Obstruction by abnormal pelvic soft tissues** M♀
[0,1,3]
Prolapse of anterior lip of cervix
Any condition classifiable to 654, causing obstruction during labor
Use additional code from 654.0-654.9 to identify condition

1 § ✓5th **660.3 Deep transverse arrest and persistent occipitoposterior position** M♀
[0,1,3]

1 § ✓5th **660.4 Shoulder (girdle) dystocia** M♀
[0,1,3]
Impacted shoulders
DEF: Obstructed labor due to impacted fetal shoulders.

1 § ✓5th **660.5 Locked twins** M♀
[0,1,3]

1 § ✓5th **660.6 Failed trial of labor, unspecified** M♀
[0,1,3]
Failed trial of labor, without mention of condition or suspected condition

1 § ✓5th **660.7 Failed forceps or vacuum extractor, unspecified** M♀
[0,1,3]
Application of ventouse or forceps, without mention of condition

1 § ✓5th **660.8 Other causes of obstructed labor** M♀
[0,1,3]
Use additional code to identify condition
AHA: 4Q, '04, 88

1 § ✓5th **660.9 Unspecified obstructed labor** M♀
[0,1,3]
Dystocia:
NOS
fetal NOS
Dystocia:
maternal NOS

1 Nonspecific PDx=0
§ Requires fifth-digit. Valid digits are in [brackets] under each code. See beginning of section 640-649 for codes and definitions.

✓4th ✓5th Additional Digit Required 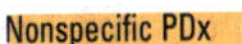 Nonspecific PDx Unacceptable PDx 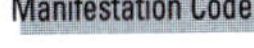 Manifestation Code  MCV Major Cardiovascular Condition  ▶◀ Revised Text ● New Code ▲ Revised Code Title

✓4th **661 Abnormality of forces of labor**

1 § ✓5th **661.0 Primary uterine inertia** M♀
[0,1,3]
Failure of cervical dilation
Hypotonic uterine dysfunction, primary
Prolonged latent phase of labor
DEF: Lack of efficient contractions during labor causing prolonged labor.

1 § ✓5th **661.1 Secondary uterine inertia** M♀
[0,1,3]
Arrested active phase of labor
Hypotonic uterine dysfunction, secondary

1 § ✓5th **661.2 Other and unspecified uterine inertia** M♀
[0,1,3]
Desultory labor
Irregular labor
Poor contractions
Slow slope active phase of labor

1 § ✓5th **661.3 Precipitate labor** M♀
[0,1,3]
DEF: Rapid labor and delivery.

1 § ✓5th **661.4 Hypertonic, incoordinate, or prolonged uterine contractions** M♀
[0,1,3]
Cervical spasm
Contraction ring (dystocia)
Dyscoordinate labor
Hourglass contraction of uterus
Hypertonic uterine dysfunction
Incoordinate uterine action
Retraction ring (Bandl's) (pathological)
Tetanic contractions
Uterine dystocia NOS
Uterine spasm

§ ✓5th **661.9 Unspecified abnormality of labor** M♀
[0,1,3]

✓4th **662 Long labor**

1 § ✓5th **662.0 Prolonged first stage** M♀
[0,1,3]

1 § ✓5th **662.1 Prolonged labor, unspecified** M♀
[0,1,3]

1 § ✓5th **662.2 Prolonged second stage** M♀
[0,1,3]

1 § ✓5th **662.3 Delayed delivery of second twin, triplet, etc.** M♀
[0,1,3]

✓4th **663 Umbilical cord complications**

1 § ✓5th **663.0 Prolapse of cord** M♀
[0,1,3]
Presentation of cord
DEF: Abnormal presentation of fetus; marked by protruding umbilical cord during labor; can cause fetal death.

1 § ✓5th **663.1 Cord around neck, with compression** M♀
[0,1,3]
Cord tightly around neck

1 § ✓5th **663.2 Other and unspecified cord entanglement, with compression** M♀
[0,1,3]
Entanglement of cords of twins in mono-amniotic sac
Knot in cord (with compression)

1 § ✓5th **663.3 Other and unspecified cord entanglement, without mention of compression** M♀
[0,1,3]
AHA: For code 663.31: 2Q, '03, 9

1 § ✓5th **663.4 Short cord** M♀
[0,1,3]

1 § ✓5th **663.5 Vasa previa** M♀
[0,1,3]
DEF: Abnormal presentation of fetus marked by blood vessels of umbilical cord in front of fetal head.

1 § ✓5th **663.6 Vascular lesions of cord** M♀
[0,1,3]
Bruising of cord
Hematoma of cord
Thrombosis of vessels of cord

1 § ✓5th **663.8 Other umbilical cord complications** M♀
[0,1,3]
Velamentous insertion of umbilical cord

§ ✓5th **663.9 Unspecified umbilical cord complication** M♀
[0,1,3]

Perineal Lacerations

✓4th **664 Trauma to perineum and vulva during delivery**
INCLUDES damage from instruments
that from extension of episiotomy
AHA: 1Q, '92, 11; N-D, '84, 10

1 § ✓5th **664.0 First-degree perineal laceration** M♀
[0,1,4]
Perineal laceration, rupture, or tear involving:
fourchette
hymen
labia
skin
vagina
vulva

1 § ✓5th **664.1 Second-degree perineal laceration** M♀
[0,1,4]
Perineal laceration, rupture, or tear (following episiotomy) involving:
pelvic floor
perineal muscles
vaginal muscles
EXCLUDES *that involving anal sphincter (664.2)*

1 § ✓5th **664.2 Third-degree perineal laceration** M♀
[0,1,4]
Perineal laceration, rupture, or tear (following episiotomy) involving:
anal sphincter
rectovaginal septum
sphincter NOS
EXCLUDES *that with anal or rectal mucosal laceration (664.3)*

1 § ✓5th **664.3 Fourth-degree perineal laceration** M♀
[0,1,4]
Perineal laceration, rupture, or tear as classifiable to 664.2 and involving also:
anal mucosa
rectal mucosa

§ ✓5th **664.4 Unspecified perineal laceration** M♀
[0,1,4]
Central laceration
AHA: 1Q, '92, 8

1 § ✓5th **664.5 Vulval and perineal hematoma** M♀
[0,1,4]
AHA: N-D, '84, 10

1 § ✓5th **664.8 Other specified trauma to perineum and vulva** M♀
[0,1,4]

§ ✓5th **664.9 Unspecified trauma to perineum and vulva** M♀
[0,1,4]

✓4th **665 Other obstetrical trauma**
INCLUDES damage from instruments

1 § ✓5th **665.0 Rupture of uterus before onset of labor** CC M♀
[0,1,3]
CC Excl: 646.80-646.93, 648.90-650, 655.70-655.73, 665.00-665.11, 665.50-665.54, 665.80-665.94, 669.40-669.44, 669.80-669.94

1 § ✓5th **665.1 Rupture of uterus during labor** CC M♀
[0,1]
Rupture of uterus NOS
CC Excl: See code 665.0

1 § ✓5th **665.2 Inversion of uterus** M♀
[0,2,4]

1 Nonspecific PDx=0
§ Requires fifth-digit. Valid digits are in [brackets] under each code. See beginning of section 640-649 for codes and definitions.

N Newborn Age: 0 P Pediatric Age: 0-17 M Maternity Age: 12-55 A Adult Age: 15-124 CC CC Condition MC Major Complication CD Complex Dx HIV HIV Related Dx

1 § 5th **665.3 Laceration of cervix** M ♀
[0,1,4]

1 § 5th **665.4 High vaginal laceration** M ♀
[0,1,4]
Laceration of vaginal wall or sulcus without mention of perineal laceration

1 § 5th **665.5 Other injury to pelvic organs** M ♀
[0,1,4]
Injury to:
bladder
Injury to:
urethra
AHA: M-A, '87, 10

1 § 5th **665.6 Damage to pelvic joints and ligaments** M ♀
[0,1,4]
Avulsion of inner symphyseal cartilage
Damage to coccyx
Separation of symphysis (pubis)
AHA: N-D, '84, 12

1 § 5th **665.7 Pelvic hematoma** M ♀
[0,1,2,4]
Hematoma of vagina

1 § 5th **665.8 Other specified obstetrical trauma** M ♀
[0-4]

§ 5th **665.9 Unspecified obstetrical trauma** M ♀
[0-4]

4th **666 Postpartum hemorrhage**
AHA: 1Q, '88, 14

1 § 5th **666.0 Third-stage hemorrhage** M ♀
[0,2,4]
Hemorrhage associated with retained, trapped, or adherent placenta
Retained placenta NOS

1 § 5th **666.1 Other immediate postpartum hemorrhage** M ♀
[0,2,4]
Atony of uterus ▶with hemorrhage◀
Hemorrhage within the first 24 hours following delivery of placenta
Postpartum hemorrhage (atonic) NOS
EXCLUDES ▶ *atony of uterus without hemorrhage (669.8)*◀

1 § 5th **666.2 Delayed and secondary postpartum hemorrhage** M ♀
[0,2,4]
Hemorrhage:
after the first 24 hours following delivery
associated with retained portions of placenta or membranes
Postpartum hemorrhage specified as delayed or secondary
Retained products of conception NOS, following delivery

1 § 5th **666.3 Postpartum coagulation defects** CC 2,4 M ♀
[0,2,4]
Postpartum:
afibrinogenemia
Postpartum:
fibrinolysis
CC Excl: For codes 666.32-666.34: 646.80-646.93, 648.90-650, 666.00-666.34, 669.40-669.44, 669.80-669.94

4th **667 Retained placenta or membranes, without hemorrhage**
AHA: 1Q, '88, 14
DEF: Postpartum condition resulting from failure to expel placental membrane tissues due to failed contractions of uterine wall.

1 § 5th **667.0 Retained placenta without hemorrhage** M ♀
[0,2,4]
Placenta accreta
Retained placenta:
NOS
total
} without hemorrhage

1 § 5th **667.1 Retained portions of placenta or membranes, without hemorrhage** M ♀
[0,2,4]
Retained products of conception following delivery, without hemorrhage

4th **668 Complications of the administration of anesthetic or other sedation in labor and delivery**
INCLUDES complications arising from the administration of a general or local anesthetic, analgesic, or other sedation in labor and delivery
EXCLUDES *reaction to spinal or lumbar puncture (349.0)*
spinal headache (349.0)
Use additional code(s) to further specify complication

1 § 5th **668.0 Pulmonary complications** CC M ♀
[0-4]
Inhalation [aspiration] of stomach contents or secretions
Mendelson's syndrome
Pressure collapse of lung
} following anesthesia or other sedation in labor or delivery
CC Excl: 646.80-646.93, 648.90-650, 668.00-668.04, 669.40-669.44, 669.80-669.94

1 § 5th **668.1 Cardiac complications** CC M ♀
[0-4]
Cardiac arrest or failure following anesthesia or other sedation in labor and delivery
CC Excl: 646.80-646.93, 648.90-650, 668.10-668.14, 669.40-669.44, 669.80-669.94

1 § 5th **668.2 Central nervous system complications** CC M ♀
[0-4]
Cerebral anoxia following anesthesia or other sedation in labor and delivery
CC Excl: 646.80-646.93, 648.90-650, 668.20-668.24, 669.40-669.44, 669.80-669.94

1 § 5th **668.8 Other complications of anesthesia or other sedation in labor and delivery** CC M ♀
[0-4]
CC Excl: 646.80-646.93, 648.90-650, 668.80-94, 668,669.40-669.44, 669.80-669.94
AHA: 2Q, '99, 9

§ 5th **668.9 Unspecified complication of anesthesia and other sedation** CC M ♀
[0-4]
CC Excl: See code 668.8

4th **669 Other complications of labor and delivery, not elsewhere classified**

1 § 5th **669.0 Maternal distress** M ♀
[0-4]
Metabolic disturbance in labor and delivery

1 § 5th **669.1 Shock during or following labor and delivery** CC M ♀
[0-4]
Obstetric shock
CC Excl: 646.80-646.93, 648.90-650, 669.10-669.14, 669.40-669.44, 669.80-669.94

1 § 5th **669.2 Maternal hypotension syndrome** M ♀
[0-4]
DEF: Low arterial blood pressure, in mother, during labor and delivery.

1 § 5th **669.3 Acute renal failure following labor and delivery** CC M ♀
[0,2,4]
CC Excl: 646.80-646.93, 648.90-650, 669.30-669.44, 669.80-669.94

1 § 5th **669.4 Other complications of obstetrical surgery and procedures** M ♀
[0-4]
Cardiac:
arrest
failure
Cerebral anoxia
} following cesarean or other obstetrical surgery or procedure, including delivery NOS
EXCLUDES *complications of obstetrical surgical wounds (674.1-674.3)*

1 § 5th **669.5 Forceps or vacuum extractor delivery without mention of indication** M ♀
[0,1]
Delivery by ventouse, without mention of indication

1 § 5th **669.6 Breech extraction, without mention of indication** M ♀
[0,1]
EXCLUDES *breech delivery NOS (652.2)*

1 § 5th **669.7 Cesarean delivery, without mention of indication** M ♀
[0,1]
AHA: For code 669.71: 1Q, '01, 11

1 § 5th **669.8 Other complications of labor and delivery** M ♀
[0-4]

§ 5th **669.9 Unspecified complication of labor and delivery** M ♀
[0-4]

1 Nonspecific PDx=0
§ Requires fifth-digit. Valid digits are in [brackets] under each code. See beginning of section 640-649 for codes and definitions.

 Additional Digit Required 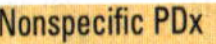 Nonspecific PDx 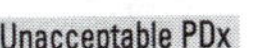 Unacceptable PDx   Manifestation Code   MCV Major Cardiovascular Condition   ▶◀ Revised Text   ● New Code   ▲ Revised Code Title

COMPLICATIONS OF THE PUERPERIUM (670-677)

Note: Categories 671 and 673-676 include the listed conditions even if they occur during pregnancy or childbirth.

The following fifth-digit subclassification is for use with categories 670-676 to denote the current episode of care. Valid fifth-digits are in [brackets] under each code.

- **0 unspecified as to episode of care or not applicable**
- **1 delivered, with or without mention of antepartum condition**
- **2 delivered, with mention of postpartum complication**
- **3 antepartum condition or complication**
- **4 postpartum condition or complication**

1 ✓4th **670 Major puerperal infection** CC M♀
[0,2,4]

§ ✓5th Use 0 as fourth-digit for this category

Puerperal:
- endometritis
- fever (septic)
- pelvic:
  - cellulitis
  - sepsis

Puerperal:
- peritonitis
- pyemia
- salpingitis
- septicemia

EXCLUDES *infection following abortion (639.0)*
minor genital tract infection following delivery (646.6)
puerperal pyrexia NOS (672)
puerperal fever NOS (672)
puerperal pyrexia of unknown origin (672)
urinary tract infection following delivery (646.6)

CC Excl: 646.80-646.93, 648.90-650, 669.40-669.44, 669.80-669.94, 670.00-670.04

AHA: 4Q, '91, 26; 2Q, '91, 7

DEF: Infection and inflammation, following childbirth.

✓4th **671 Venous complications in pregnancy and the puerperium**

1 § ✓5th **671.0 Varicose veins of legs** M♀
[0-4]
Varicose veins NOS

DEF: Distended, tortuous veins on legs associated with pregnancy.

1 § ✓5th **671.1 Varicose veins of vulva and perineum** M♀
[0-4]

DEF: Distended, tortuous veins on external female genitalia associated with pregnancy.

1 § ✓5th **671.2 Superficial thrombophlebitis** CC M♀
[0-4]
Thrombophlebitis (superficial)

CC Excl: 646.80-646.93, 648.90-650, 669.40-669.44, 669.80-669.94, 671.20-671.94

1 § ✓5th **671.3 Deep phlebothrombosis, antepartum** CC M♀
[0,1,3]
Deep-vein thrombosis, antepartum

CC Excl: See code 671.2

1 § ✓5th **671.4 Deep phlebothrombosis, postpartum** CC M♀
[0,2,4]
Deep-vein thrombosis, postpartum
Pelvic thrombophlebitis, postpartum
Phlegmasia alba dolens (puerperal)

CC Excl: See code 671.2

1 § ✓5th **671.5 Other phlebitis and thrombosis** M♀
[0-4]
Cerebral venous thrombosis
Thrombosis of intracranial venous sinus

1 § ✓5th **671.8 Other venous complications** M♀
[0-4]
Hemorrhoids

§ ✓5th **671.9 Unspecified venous complication** M♀
[0-4]
Phlebitis NOS
Thrombosis NOS

1 ✓4th **672 Pyrexia of unknown origin during the puerperium** M♀
[0,2,4]

§ ✓5th Use 0 as fourth-digit for this category

Postpartum fever NOS
Puerperal fever NOS
Puerperal pyrexia NOS

AHA: 4Q, '91, 26

DEF: Fever of unknown origin experienced by the mother after childbirth.

✓4th **673 Obstetrical pulmonary embolism**

INCLUDES pulmonary emboli in pregnancy, childbirth, or the puerperium, or specified as puerperal

EXCLUDES *embolism following abortion (639.6)*

1 § ✓5th **673.0 Obstetrical air embolism** CC M♀
[0-4]

CC Excl: 646.80-646.93, 648.90-648.94, 650, 669.40-669.44, 669.80-669.94, 673.00-673.84

DEF: Sudden blocking of pulmonary artery with air or nitrogen bubbles during puerperium.

1 § ✓5th **673.1 Amniotic fluid embolism** CC M♀
[0-4]

CC Excl: See code 673.0

DEF: Sudden onset of pulmonary artery blockage from amniotic fluid entering the mother's circulation near the end of pregnancy due to strong uterine contractions.

1 § ✓5th **673.2 Obstetrical blood-clot embolism** CC M♀
[0-4]
Puerperal pulmonary embolism NOS

CC Excl: See code 673.0

AHA: For code 673.24: 1Q, '05, 6

DEF: Blood clot blocking artery in the lung; associated with pregnancy.

1 § ✓5th **673.3 Obstetrical pyemic and septic embolism** CC M♀
[0-4]

CC Excl: See code 673.0

1 § ✓5th **673.8 Other pulmonary embolism** CC M♀
[0-4]
Fat embolism

CC Excl: See code 673.0

✓4th **674 Other and unspecified complications of the puerperium, not elsewhere classified**

1 § ✓5th **674.0 Cerebrovascular disorders in the puerperium** CC M♀
[0-4]
Any condition classifiable to 430-434, 436-437 occurring during pregnancy, childbirth, or the puerperium, or specified as puerperal

EXCLUDES *intracranial venous sinus thrombosis (671.5)*

CC Excl: 646.80-646.93, 648.90-650, 669.40-669.44, 669.80-669.94, 674.00-674.04, 674.50-674.54

1 § ✓5th **674.1 Disruption of cesarean wound** CC 0,2 M♀
[0,2,4]
Dehiscence or disruption of uterine wound

EXCLUDES *uterine rupture before onset of labor (665.0)*
uterine rupture during labor (665.1)

CC Excl: For Codes 674.10 and 674.12: 646.80-646.93, 648.90-650, 669.40-669.44, 669.80-669.94, 674.10, 674.34

1 § ✓5th **674.2 Disruption of perineal wound** CC M♀
[0,2,4]
Breakdown of perineum
Disruption of wound of:
- episiotomy
- perineal laceration

Secondary perineal tear

CC Excl: 646.80-646.93, 648.90-650, 669.40-669.44, 669.80-669.94, 674.10, 674.34

AHA: For code 674.24: 1Q, '97, 9

1 Nonspecific PDx=0
§ Requires fifth-digit. Valid digits are in [brackets] under each code. See beginning of section 640-649 for codes and definitions.

N Newborn Age: 0 | P Pediatric Age: 0-17 | M Maternity Age: 12-55 | A Adult Age: 15-124 | CC CC Condition | MC Major Complication | CD Complex Dx | HIV HIV Related Dx

1 § 5th **674.3 Other complications of obstetrical surgical wounds** M ♀
[0,2,4]
Hematoma, Hemorrhage, Infection } of cesarean section or perineal wound

EXCLUDES damage from instruments in delivery (664.0-665.9)

AHA: 2Q, '91, 7

1 § 5th **674.4 Placental polyp** M ♀
[0,2,4]

1 § 5th **674.5 Peripartum cardiomyopathy** CC M ♀
[0-4]
Postpartum cardiomyopathy
CC Excl: 646.80-646.93, 648.90-650, 669.40-669.44, 669.80-669.94, 674.00-674.04, 674.50-674.54

AHA: 4Q, '03, 65

DEF: Any structural or functional abnormality of the ventricular myocardium, non-inflammatory disease of obscure or unknown etiology with onset during the postpartum period.

1 § 5th **674.8 Other** M ♀
[0,2,4]
Hepatorenal syndrome, following delivery
Postpartum:
  subinvolution of uterus
  uterine hypertrophy

AHA: 3Q, '98, 16

§ 5th **674.9 Unspecified** M ♀
[0,2,4]
Sudden death of unknown cause during the puerperium

4th **675 Infections of the breast and nipple associated with childbirth**

INCLUDES the listed conditions during pregnancy, childbirth, or the puerperium

1 § 5th **675.0 Infections of nipple** M ♀
[0-4]
Abscess of nipple

1 § 5th **675.1 Abscess of breast** CC 0-2 M ♀
[0-4]
Abscess:
  mammary
  subareolar
  submammary
  purulent
  retromammary
  submammary

CC Excl: For codes 675.10-675.12: 646.80-646.93, 648.90-650, 669.40-669.44, 669.80-669.94, 675.00-675.94

1 § 5th **675.2 Nonpurulent mastitis** M ♀
[0-4]
Lymphangitis of breast
Mastitis:
  NOS
  interstitial
  parenchymatous

1 § 5th **675.8 Other specified infections of the breast and nipple** M ♀
[0-4]

1 § 5th **675.9 Unspecified infection of the breast and nipple** M ♀
[0-4]

4th **676 Other disorders of the breast associated with childbirth and disorders of lactation**

INCLUDES the listed conditions during pregnancy, the puerperium, or lactation

1 § 5th **676.0 Retracted nipple** M ♀
[0-4]

Lactation Process: Ejection Reflex Arc

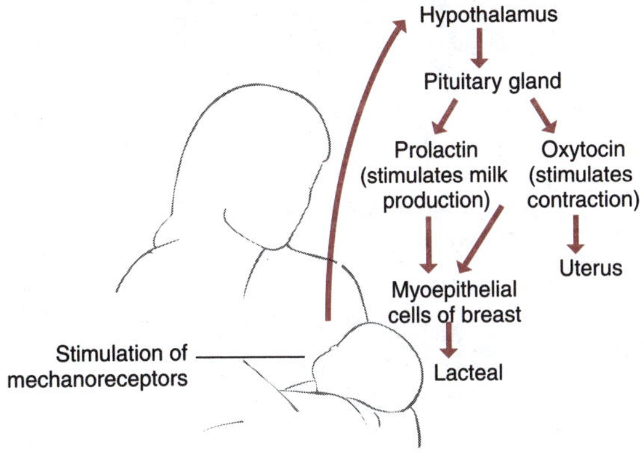

Hypothalamus
Pituitary gland
Prolactin (stimulates milk production)
Oxytocin (stimulates contraction)
Uterus
Myoepithelial cells of breast
Stimulation of mechanoreceptors
Lacteal

1 § 5th **676.1 Cracked nipple** M ♀
[0-4]
Fissure of nipple

1 § 5th **676.2 Engorgement of breasts** M ♀
[0-4]

DEF: Abnormal accumulation of milk in ducts of breast.

1 § 5th **676.3 Other and unspecified disorder of breast** M ♀
[0-4]

1 § 5th **676.4 Failure of lactation** M ♀
[0-4]
Agalactia

DEF: Abrupt ceasing of milk secretion by breast.

1 § 5th **676.5 Suppressed lactation** M ♀
[0-4]

1 § 5th **676.6 Galactorrhea** M ♀
[0-4]
EXCLUDES *galactorrhea not associated with childbirth (611.6)*

DEF: Excessive or persistent milk secretion by breast; may be in absence of nursing.

1 § 5th **676.8 Other disorders of lactation** M ♀
[0-4]
Galactocele

DEF: Galactocele: Obstructed mammary gland, creating retention cyst, results in milk-filled cysts enlarging mammary gland.

§ 5th **676.9 Unspecified disorder of lactation** M ♀
[0-4]

677 Late effect of complication of pregnancy, childbirth, and the puerperium ♀

Note: This category is to be used to indicate conditions in 632-648.9 and 651-676.9 as the cause of the late effect, themselves classifiable elsewhere. The "late effects" include conditions specified as such, or as sequelae, which may occur at any time after puerperium.

Code first any sequelae

AHA: 1Q, '97, 9; 4Q, '94, 42

1 Nonspecific PDx=0
§ Requires fifth-digit. Valid digits are in [brackets] under each code. See beginning of section 640-649 for codes and definitions.

12. DISEASES OF THE SKIN AND SUBCUTANEOUS TISSUE (680-709)

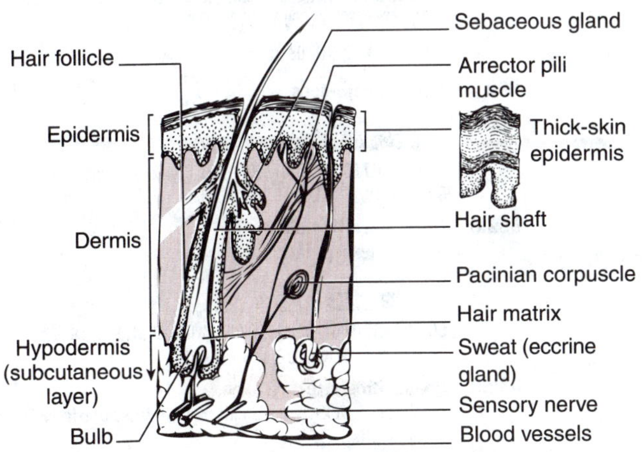

INFECTIONS OF SKIN AND SUBCUTANEOUS TISSUE (680-686)

EXCLUDES *certain infections of skin classified under "Infectious and Parasitic Diseases," such as:*
erysipelas (035)
erysipeloid of Rosenbach (027.1)
herpes:
simplex (054.0-054.9)
zoster (053.0-053.9)
molluscum contagiosum (078.0)
viral warts (078.1)

✓4th **680 Carbuncle and furuncle**

INCLUDES boil
furunculosis

DEF: Carbuncle: necrotic boils in skin and subcutaneous tissue of neck or back mainly due to staphylococcal infection.

DEF: Furuncle: circumscribed inflammation of corium and subcutaneous tissue due to staphylococcal infection.

680.0 Face CC
Ear [any part]
Face [any part, except eye]
Nose (septum)
Temple (region)
EXCLUDES *eyelid (373.13)*
lacrimal apparatus (375.31)
orbit (376.01)
CC Excl: 017.00-017.06, 017.90-017.96, 040.82-041.9, 680.0, 680.8-680.9, 686.00-686.9, 705.83, 709.8, V09.0-V09.91

680.1 Neck CC
CC Excl: 017.00-017.06, 017.90-017.96, 040.82-041.9, 680.1, 680.8-680.9, 686.00-686.9, 705.83, 709.8, V09.0-V09.91

680.2 Trunk CC
Abdominal wall
Back [any part, except buttocks]
Breast
Chest wall
Flank
Groin
Pectoral region
Perineum
Umbilicus
EXCLUDES *buttocks (680.5)*
external genital organs:
female (616.4)
male (607.2, 608.4)
CC Excl: 017.00-017.06, 017.90-017.96, 040.82-041.9, 680.2, 680.8-680.9, 686.00-686.9, 705.83, 709.8, V09.0-V09.91

680.3 Upper arm and forearm CC
Arm [any part, except hand]
Axilla
Shoulder
CC Excl: 017.00-017.06, 017.90-017.96, 040.82-041.9, 680.3, 680.8-680.9, 686.00-686.9, 705.83, 709.8, V09.0-V09.91

680.4 Hand CC
Finger [any]
Thumb
Wrist
CC Excl: 017.00-017.06, 017.90-017.96, 040.82-041.9, 680.4, 680.8-680.9, 686.00-686.9, 705.83, 709.8, V09.0-V09.91

680.5 Buttock CC
Anus
Gluteal region
CC Excl: 017.00-017.06, 017.90-017.96, 040.82-041.9, 680.5, 680.8-680.9, 686.00-686.9, 705.83, 709.8, V09.0-V09.91

680.6 Leg, except foot CC
Ankle
Hip
Knee
Thigh
CC Excl: 017.00-017.06, 017.90-017.96, 040.82-041.9, 680.6, 680.8-680.9, 686.00-686.9, 705.83, 709.8, V09.0-V09.91

680.7 Foot CC
Heel
Toe
CC Excl: 017.00-017.06, 017.90-017.96, 040.82-041.9, 680.7-680.9, 686.00-686.9, 705.83, 709.8, V09.0-V09.91

680.8 Other specified sites CC
Head [any part, except face]
Scalp
EXCLUDES *external genital organs:*
female (616.4)
male (607.2, 608.4)
CC Excl: 017.00-017.06, 017.90-017.96, 040.82-041.9, 680.8-680.9, 686.00-686.9, 705.83, 709.8, V09.0-V09.91

680.9 Unspecified site CC
Boil NOS
Carbuncle NOS
Furuncle NOS
CC Excl: See code 680.8

✓4th **681 Cellulitis and abscess of finger and toe**

INCLUDES that with lymphangitis

Use additional code to identify organism, such as Staphylococcus (041.1)

AHA: 2Q, '91, 5; J-F, '87, 12

DEF: Acute suppurative inflammation and edema in subcutaneous tissue or muscle of finger or toe.

✓5th **681.0 Finger**

681.00 Cellulitis and abscess, unspecified

681.01 Felon
Pulp abscess
Whitlow
EXCLUDES *herpetic whitlow (054.6)*
DEF: Painful abscess of fingertips caused by infection in the closed space of terminal phalanx.

681.02 Onychia and paronychia of finger
Panaritium } of finger
Perionychia } of finger
DEF: Onychia: inflammation of nail matrix; causes nail loss.
DEF: Paronychia: inflammation of tissue folds around nail.

✓5th **681.1 Toe**

681.10 Cellulitis and abscess, unspecified
AHA: 1Q, '05, 14

681.11 Onychia and paronychia of toe
Panaritium } of toe
Perionychia } of toe

681.9 Cellulitis and abscess of unspecified digit
Infection of nail NOS

✓4th **682 Other cellulitis and abscess**

INCLUDES abscess (acute) / cellulitis (diffuse) / lymphangitis, acute } (with lymphangitis) except of finger or toe

Use additional code to identify organism, such as Staphylococcus (041.1)

EXCLUDES *lymphangitis (chronic) (subacute) (457.2)*

AHA: 2Q, '91, 5; J-F, '87, 12; S-O, '85, 10

DEF: Cellulitis: Acute suppurative inflammation of deep subcutaneous tissue and sometimes muscle due to infection of wound, burn or other lesion.

682.0 Face CC
Cheek, external
Chin
Forehead
Nose, external
Submandibular
Temple (region)

EXCLUDES *ear [any part] (380.10-380.16)*
eyelid (373.13)
lacrimal apparatus (375.31)
lip (528.5)
mouth (528.3)
nose (internal) (478.1)
orbit (376.01)

CC Excl: 017.00-017.06, 017.90-017.96, 040.82-041.9, 682.0, 682.8-682.9, 686.00-686.9, 705.83, 709.8, V09.0-V09.91

682.1 Neck CC
CC Excl: 017.00-017.06, 017.90-017.96, 040.89, 041.00-041.89, 041.9, 682.1, 682.8-682.9, 686.00-686.01, 686.09, 686.1-686.9, 705.83, 709.8, V09.0-V09.91

682.2 Trunk CC
Abdominal wall
Back [any part, except buttock]
Chest wall
Flank
Groin
Pectoral region
Perineum
Umbilicus, except newborn

EXCLUDES *anal and rectal regions (566)*
breast:
NOS (611.0)
puerperal (675.1)
external genital organs:
female (616.3-616.4)
male (604.0, 607.2, 608.4)
umbilicus, newborn (771.4)

CC Excl: 017.00-017.06, 017.90-017.96, 040.82-041.9, 682.2, 682.8-682.9, 686.00-686.9, 705.83, 709.8, V09.0-V09.91

AHA: 4Q, '98, 42

682.3 Upper arm and forearm CC
Arm [any part, except hand]
Axilla
Shoulder

EXCLUDES *hand (682.4)*

CC Excl: 017.00-017.06, 017.90-017.96, 040.82-041.9, 682.3, 682.8-682.9, 686.00-686.9, 705.83, 709.8, V09.0-V09.91

AHA: 2Q, '03, 7

682.4 Hand, except fingers and thumb
Wrist

EXCLUDES *finger and thumb (681.00-681.02)*

682.5 Buttock CC
Gluteal region

EXCLUDES *anal and rectal regions (566)*

CC Excl: 017.00-017.06, 017.90-017.96, 040.82-041.9, 682.5, 682.8-682.9, 686.00-686.9, 705.83, 709.8, V09.0-V09.91

682.6 Leg, except foot CC
Ankle
Hip
Knee
Thigh

CC Excl: 017.00-017.06, 017.90-017.96, 040.82-041.9, 682.6, 682.8-682.9, 686.00-686.9, 705.83, 709.8, V09.0-V09.91

AHA: 3Q, '04, 5; 4Q, '03, 108

682.7 Foot, except toes CC
Heel

EXCLUDES *toe (681.10-681.11)*

CC Excl: 017.00-017.06, 017.90-017.96, 040.82-041.9, 682.7-682.9, 686.00-686.9, 705.83, 709.8, V09.0-V09.91

682.8 Other specified sites CC
Head [except face]
Scalp

EXCLUDES *face (682.0)*

CC Excl: 017.00-017.06, 017.90-017.96, 040.82-041.9, 682.8-682.9, 686.00-686.9, 705.83, 709.8, V09.0-V09.91

682.9 Unspecified site CC
Abscess NOS
Cellulitis NOS
Lymphangitis, acute NOS

EXCLUDES *lymphangitis NOS (457.2)*

CC Excl: See code 682.8

683 Acute lymphadenitis

Abscess (acute) / Adenitis, acute / Lymphadenitis, acute } lymph gland or node, except mesenteric

Use additional code to identify organism, such as Staphylococcus (041.1)

EXCLUDES *enlarged glands NOS (785.6)*
lymphadenitis:
chronic or subacute, except mesenteric (289.1)
mesenteric (acute) (chronic) (subacute) (289.2)
unspecified (289.3)

DEF: Acute inflammation of lymph nodes due to primary infection located elsewhere in the body.

684 Impetigo CC
Impetiginization of other dermatoses
Impetigo (contagiosa) [any site] [any organism]:
bullous
circinate
neonatorum
simplex
Pemphigus neonatorum

EXCLUDES *impetigo herpetiformis (694.3)*

CC Excl: 684, 686.00-686.9, 709.8

DEF: Infectious skin disease commonly occurring in children; caused by group A streptococci or *Staphylococcus aureus*; skin lesions usually appear on the face and consist of subcorneal vesicles and bullae that burst and form yellow crusts.

Lymphatic System of Head and Neck

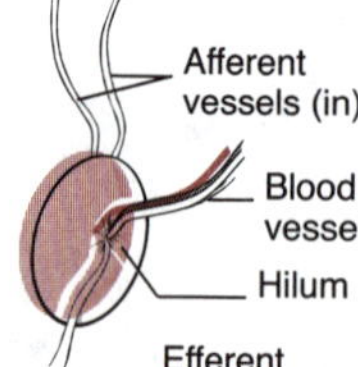

Schematic of lymph node

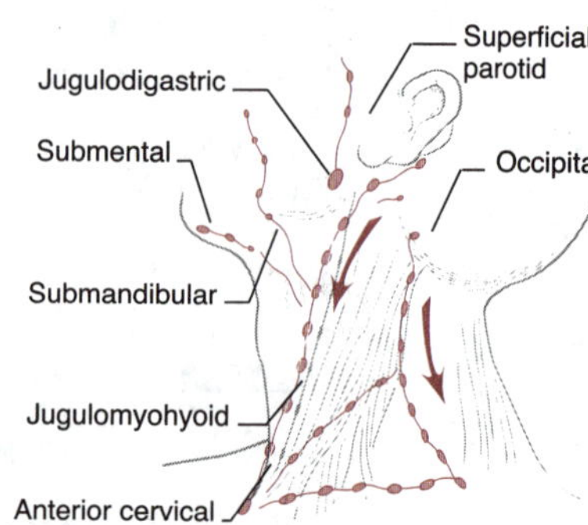

Lymphatic drainage of the head, neck, and face

Stages of Pilonidal Disease

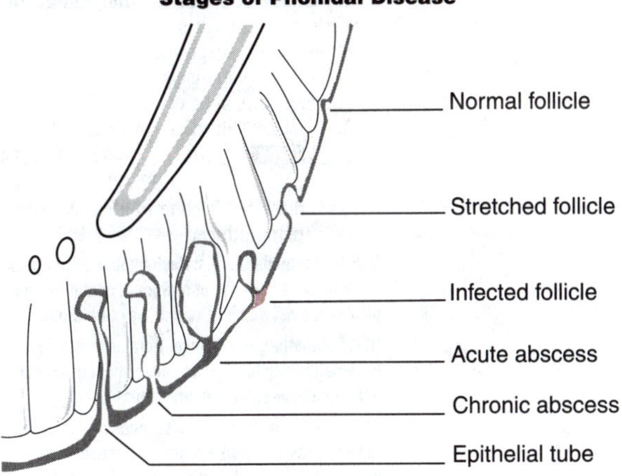

✓4th **685 Pilonidal cyst**

INCLUDES fistula } coccygeal or pilonidal
sinus }

DEF: Hair-containing cyst or sinus in the tissues of the sacrococcygeal area; often drains through opening at the postanal dimple.

685.0 With abscess CC
CC Excl: 685.0-685.1, 709.8

685.1 Without mention of abscess

✓4th **686 Other local infections of skin and subcutaneous tissue**
Use additional code to identify any infectious organism (041.0-041.8)

✓5th **686.0 Pyoderma**
Dermatitis:
purulent
septic
suppurative

DEF: Nonspecific purulent skin disease related most to furuncles, pustules, or possibly carbuncles.

686.00 Pyoderma, unspecified

686.01 Pyoderma gangrenosum
AHA: 4Q, '97, 42

DEF: Persistent debilitating skin disease, characterized by irregular, boggy, blue-red ulcerations, with central healing and undermined edges.

686.09 Other pyoderma

686.1 Pyogenic granuloma
Granuloma:
septic
suppurative
telangiectaticum

EXCLUDES *pyogenic granuloma of oral mucosa (528.9)*

DEF: Solitary polypoid capillary hemangioma often asociated with local irritation, trauma, and superimposed inflammation; located on the skin and gingival or oral mucosa.

686.8 Other specified local infections of skin and subcutaneous tissue
Bacterid (pustular)
Dermatitis vegetans
Ecthyma
Perlèche

EXCLUDES *dermatitis infectiosa eczematoides (690.8)*
panniculitis (729.30-729.39)

686.9 Unspecified local infection of skin and subcutaneous tissue
Fistula of skin NOS
Skin infection NOS

EXCLUDES *fistula to skin from internal organs — see Alphabetic Index*

OTHER INFLAMMATORY CONDITIONS OF SKIN AND SUBCUTANEOUS TISSUE (690-698)

EXCLUDES *panniculitis (729.30-729.39)*

✓4th **690 Erythematosquamous dermatosis**

EXCLUDES *eczematous dermatitis of eyelid (373.31)*
parakeratosis variegata (696.2)
psoriasis (696.0-696.1)
seborrheic keratosis (702.11-702.19)

✓5th **690.1 Seborrheic dermatitis**
AHA: 4Q, '95, 58

690.10 Seborrheic dermatitis, unspecified
Seborrheic dermatitis NOS

690.11 Seborrhea capitis P
Cradle cap

690.12 Seborrheic infantile dermatitis P

690.18 Other seborrheic dermatitis

690.8 Other erythematosquamous dermatosis

✓4th **691 Atopic dermatitis and related conditions**

DEF: Atopic dermatitis: chronic, pruritic, inflammatory skin disorder found on the face and antecubital and popliteal fossae; noted in persons with a hereditary predisposition to pruritus, and often accompanied by allergic rhinitis, hay fever, asthma, and extreme itching; also called allergic dermatitis, allergic or atopic eczema, or disseminated neurodermatitis.

691.0 Diaper or napkin rash
Ammonia dermatitis
Diaper or napkin:
dermatitis
erythema
rash
Psoriasiform napkin eruption

691.8 Other atopic dermatitis and related conditions
Atopic dermatitis
Besnier's prurigo
Eczema:
atopic
flexural
intrinsic (allergic)
Neurodermatitis:
atopic
diffuse (of Brocq)

✓4th **692 Contact dermatitis and other eczema**

INCLUDES dermatitis:
NOS
contact
occupational
venenata
eczema (acute) (chronic):
NOS
allergic
erythematous
occupational

EXCLUDES *allergy NOS (995.3)*
contact dermatitis of eyelids (373.32)
dermatitis due to substances taken internally (693.0-693.9)
eczema of external ear (380.22)
perioral dermatitis (695.3)
urticarial reactions (708.0-708.9, 995.1)

DEF: Contact dermatitis: acute or chronic dermatitis caused by initial irritant effect of a substance, or by prior sensitization to a substance coming once again in contact with skin.

692.0 Due to detergents

692.1 Due to oils and greases

692.2 Due to solvents
Dermatitis due to solvents of:
chlorocompound }
cyclohexane }
ester } group
glycol }
hydrocarbon }
ketone }

692.3 Due to drugs and medicines in contact with skin

Dermatitis (allergic) (contact) due to:
- arnica
- fungicides
- iodine
- keratolytics
- mercurials
- neomycin
- pediculocides
- phenols
- scabicides
- any drug applied to skin

Dermatitis medicamentosa due to drug applied to skin

Use additional E code to identify drug

EXCLUDES *allergy NOS due to drugs ▶(995.27)◀*
dermatitis due to ingested drugs (693.0)
dermatitis medicamentosa NOS (693.0)

692.4 Due to other chemical products

Dermatitis due to:
- acids
- adhesive plaster
- alkalis
- caustics
- dichromate
- insecticide
- nylon
- plastic
- rubber

AHA: 2Q, '89, 16

692.5 Due to food in contact with skin

Dermatitis, contact, due to:
- cereals
- fish
- flour
- fruit
- meat
- milk

EXCLUDES *dermatitis due to:*
dyes (692.89)
ingested foods (693.1)
preservatives (692.89)

692.6 Due to plants [except food]

Dermatitis due to:
- lacquer tree [Rhus verniciflua]
- poison:
  - ivy [Rhus toxicodendron]
  - oak [Rhus diversiloba]
  - sumac [Rhus venenata]
  - vine [Rhus radicans]
- primrose [Primula]
- ragweed [Senecio jacobae]
- other plants in contact with the skin

EXCLUDES *allergy NOS due to pollen (477.0)*
nettle rash (708.8)

✓5th **692.7 Due to solar radiation**

EXCLUDES *sunburn due to other ultraviolet radiation exposure (692.82)*

692.70 Unspecified dermatitis due to sun

692.71 Sunburn

First degree sunburn
Sunburn NOS

AHA: 4Q, '01, 47

692.72 Acute dermatitis due to solar radiation

Berlogue dermatitis
Photoallergic response
Phototoxic response
Polymorphus light eruption
Acute solar skin damage NOS

EXCLUDES *sunburn (692.71, 692.76-692.77)*

Use additional E code to identify drug, if drug induced

DEF: Berloque dermatitis: Phytophotodermatitis due to sun exposure after use of a product containing bergamot oil; causes red patches, which may turn brown.

DEF: Photoallergic response: Dermatitis due to hypersensitivity to the sun; causes papulovesicular, eczematous or exudative eruptions.

DEF: Phototoxic response: Chemically induced sensitivity to sun causes burn-like reaction, occasionally vesiculation and subsequent hyperpigmentation.

DEF: Polymorphous light eruption: Inflammatory skin eruptions due to sunlight exposure; eruptions differ in size and shape.

DEF: Acute solar skin damage (NOS): Rapid, unspecified injury to skin from sun.

692.73 Actinic reticuloid and actinic granuloma

DEF: Actinic reticuloid: Dermatosis aggravated by light, causes chronic eczema-like eruption on exposed skin which extends to other unexposed surfaces; occurs in the eldery.

DEF: Actinic granuloma: Inflammatory response of skin to sun causing small nodule of microphages.

692.74 Other chronic dermatitis due to solar radiation

Chronic solar skin damage NOS
Solar elastosis

EXCLUDES *actinic [solar] keratosis (702.0)*

DEF: Solar elastosis: Premature aging of skin of light-skinned people; causes inelasticity, thinning or thickening, wrinkling, dryness, scaling and hyperpigmentation.

DEF: Chronic solar skin damage (NOS): Chronic skin impairment due to exposure to the sun, not otherwise specified.

692.75 Disseminated superficial actinic porokeratosis [DSAP]

DEF: Autosomal dominant skin condition occurring in skin that has been overexposed to the sun. Primarily affects women over the age of 16; characterized by numerous superficial annular, keratotic, brownish-red spots or thickenings with depressed centers and sharp, ridged borders. High risk that condition will evolve into squamous cell carcinoma.

AHA: 4Q, '00, 43

692.76 Sunburn of second degree

AHA: 4Q, '01, 47

692.77 Sunburn of third degree

AHA: 4Q, '01, 47

692.79 Other dermatitis due to solar radiation

Hydroa aestivale
Photodermatitis } (due to sun)
Photosensitiveness } (due to sun)
Solar skin damage NOS

✓5th **692.8 Due to other specified agents**

692.81 Dermatitis due to cosmetics

692.82 Dermatitis due to other radiation

Infrared rays
Light, except from sun
Radiation NOS
Tanning bed
Ultraviolet rays, except from sun
X-rays

EXCLUDES *solar radiation (692.70-692.79)*

AHA: 4Q, '01, 47; 3Q, '00, 5

692.83 Dermatitis due to metals

Jewelry

692.84 Due to animal (cat) (dog) dander
Due to animal (cat) (dog) hair

692.89 Other
Dermatitis due to: cold weather, dyes
Dermatitis due to: hot weather, preservatives
EXCLUDES *allergy (NOS) (rhinitis) due to animal hair or dander (477.2)*
allergy to dust (477.8)
sunburn (692.71, 692.76-692.77)

692.9 Unspecified cause
Dermatitis:
NOS
contact NOS
venenata NOS
Eczema NOS

✓4th **693 Dermatitis due to substances taken internally**
EXCLUDES *adverse effect NOS of drugs and medicines ▶(995.20)◀*
allergy NOS (995.3)
contact dermatitis (692.0-692.9)
urticarial reactions (708.0-708.9, 995.1)

DEF: Inflammation of skin due to ingested substance.

693.0 Due to drugs and medicines
Dermatitis medicamentosa NOS
Use additional E code to identify drug
EXCLUDES *that due to drugs in contact with skin (692.3)*

693.1 Due to food

693.8 Due to other specified substances taken internally

693.9 Due to unspecified substance taken internally
EXCLUDES *dermatitis NOS (692.9)*

✓4th **694 Bullous dermatoses**

694.0 Dermatitis herpetiformis
Dermatosis herpetiformis
Duhring's disease
Hydroa herpetiformis
EXCLUDES *herpes gestationis (646.8)*
dermatitis herpetiformis:
juvenile (694.2)
senile (694.5)

DEF: Chronic, relapsing multisystem disease manifested most in the cutaneous system; seen as an extremely pruritic eruption of various combinations of lesions that frequently heal leaving hyperpigmentation or hypopigmentation and occasionally scarring; usually associated with an asymptomatic gluten-sensitive enteropathy, and immunogenic factors are believed to play a role in its origin.

694.1 Subcorneal pustular dermatosis
Sneddon-Wilkinson disease or syndrome

DEF: Chronic relapses of sterile pustular blebs beneath the horny skin layer of the trunk and skin folds; resembles dermatitis herpetiformis.

694.2 Juvenile dermatitis herpetiformis
Juvenile pemphigoid

694.3 Impetigo herpetiformis

DEF: Rare dermatosis associated with pregnancy; marked by itching pustules in third trimester, hypocalcemia, tetany, fever and lethargy; may result in maternal or fetal death.

694.4 Pemphigus CC
Pemphigus: NOS, erythematosus, foliaceus
Pemphigus: malignant, vegetans, vulgaris
EXCLUDES *pemphigus neonatorum (684)*
CC Excl: 694.4-694.9, 709.8

DEF: Chronic, relapsing, sometimes fatal skin diseases; causes vesicles, bullae; autoantibodies against intracellular connections cause acantholysis.

694.5 Pemphigoid CC
Benign pemphigus NOS
Bullous pemphigoid
Herpes circinatus bullosus
Senile dermatitis herpetiformis
CC Excl: See code 694.4

✓5th **694.6 Benign mucous membrane pemphigoid**
Cicatricial pemphigoid
Mucosynechial atrophic bullous dermatitis

694.60 Without mention of ocular involvement

694.61 With ocular involvement
Ocular pemphigus

DEF: Mild self-limiting, subepidermal blistering of mucosa including the conjunctiva, seen predominantly in the elderly. It produces adhesions and scarring.

694.8 Other specified bullous dermatoses
EXCLUDES *herpes gestationis (646.8)*

694.9 Unspecified bullous dermatoses

✓4th **695 Erythematous conditions**

695.0 Toxic erythema CC
Erythema venenatum
CC Excl: 695.0-695.4, 709.8

695.1 Erythema multiforme
Erythema iris
Herpes iris
Lyell's syndrome
Scalded skin syndrome
Stevens-Johnson syndrome
Toxic epidermal necrolysis

DEF: Symptom complex with a varied skin eruption pattern of macular, bullous, papular, nodose, or vesicular lesions on the neck, face, and legs; gastritis and rheumatic pains are also noticeable, first-seen symptoms; complex is secondary to a number of factors, including infections, ingestants, physical agents, malignancy and pregnancy.

695.2 Erythema nodosum
EXCLUDES *tuberculous erythema nodosum (017.1)*

DEF: Panniculitis (an inflammatory reaction of the subcutaneous fat) of women, usually seen as a hypersensitivity reaction to various infections, drugs, sarcoidosis, and specific enteropathies; the acute stage is often associated with other symptoms, including fever, malaise, and arthralgia; the lesions are pink to blue in color, appear in crops as tender nodules and are found on the front of the legs below the knees.

695.3 Rosacea
Acne:
erythematosa
rosacea
Perioral dermatitis
Rhinophyma

DEF: Chronic skin disease, usually of the face, characterized by persistent erythema and sometimes by telangiectasis with acute episodes of edema, engorgement papules, and pustules.

695.4 Lupus erythematosus
Lupus:
erythematodes (discoid)
erythematosus (discoid), not disseminated
EXCLUDES *lupus (vulgaris) NOS (017.0)*
systemic [disseminated] lupus erythematosus (710.0)

DEF: Group of connective tissue disorders occurring as various cutaneous diseases of unknown origin; it primarily affects women between the ages of 20 and 40.

✓5th **695.8 Other specified erythematous conditions**

695.81 Ritter's disease
Dermatitis exfoliativa neonatorum

DEF: Infectious skin disease of infants and young children marked by eruptions ranging from a localized bullous type to widespread development of easily ruptured fine vesicles and bullae; results in exfoliation of large planes of skin and leaves raw areas; also called staphylococcal scalded skin syndrome.

Skin and Subcutaneous Tissue

692.84–695.81

✓4th ✓5th Additional Digit Required | Nonspecific PDx | Unacceptable PDx | Manifestation Code | MCV Major Cardiovascular Condition | ▶◀ Revised Text | ● New Code | ▲ Revised Code Title

695.89 Other
Erythema intertrigo
Intertrigo
Pityriasis rubra (Hebra)
EXCLUDES *mycotic intertrigo (111.0-111.9)*
AHA:: S-0, '86, 10

695.9 Unspecified erythematous condition
Erythema NOS
Erythroderma (secondary)

✓4th **696 Psoriasis and similar disorders**

696.0 Psoriatic arthropathy CC
CC Excl: 015.80-015.96, 017.90-017.96, 036.82, 056.71, 098.50-098.51, 098.59, 098.89, 696.0, 711.00-714.0, 715.00, 715.09-715.10, 715.18-716.99, 718.00-718.08, 719.00-719.09, 719.10, 719.18-719.99
DEF: Psoriasis associated with inflammatory arthritis; often involves interphalangeal joints.

696.1 Other psoriasis
Acrodermatitis continua
Dermatitis repens
Psoriasis:
NOS
any type, except arthropathic
EXCLUDES *psoriatic arthropathy (696.0)*

696.2 Parapsoriasis
Parakeratosis variegata
Parapsoriasis lichenoides chronica
Pityriasis lichenoides et varioliformis
DEF: Erythrodermas similar to lichen, planus and psoriasis; symptoms include redness and itching; resistant to treatment.

696.3 Pityriasis rosea
Pityriasis circinata (et maculata)
DEF: Common, self-limited rash of unknown etiology marked by a solitary erythematous, salmon or fawn-colored herald plaque on the trunk, arms or thighs; followed by development of papular or macular lesions that tend to peel and form a scaly collarette.

696.4 Pityriasis rubra pilaris
Devergie's disease
Lichen ruber acuminatus
EXCLUDES *pityriasis rubra (Hebra) (695.89)*
DEF: Inflammatory disease of hair follicles; marked by firm, red lesions topped by horny plugs; may form patches; occurs on fingers elbows, knees.

696.5 Other and unspecified pityriasis
Pityriasis:
NOS
alba
streptogenes
EXCLUDES *pityriasis:*
simplex (690.18)
versicolor (111.0)

696.8 Other

✓4th **697 Lichen**
EXCLUDES *lichen:*
obtusus corneus (698.3)
pilaris (congenital) (757.39)
ruber acuminatus (696.4)
sclerosus et atrophicus (701.0)
scrofulosus (017.0)
simplex chronicus (698.3)
spinulosus (congenital) (757.39)
urticatus (698.2)

697.0 Lichen planus
Lichen:
planopilaris
ruber planus
DEF: Inflammatory, pruritic skin disease; marked by angular, flat-top, violet-colored papules; may be acute and widespread or chronic and localized.

697.1 Lichen nitidus
Pinkus' disease
DEF: Chronic, inflammatory, usually asymptomatic skin disorder, characterized by numerous glistening, flat-topped, discrete, smooth, skin-colored micropapules most often on penis, lower abdomen, inner thighs, wrists, forearms, breasts and buttocks.

697.8 Other lichen, not elsewhere classified
Lichen:
ruber moniliforme
striata

697.9 Lichen, unspecified

✓4th **698 Pruritus and related conditions**
EXCLUDES *pruritus specified as psychogenic (306.3)*
DEF: Pruritus: Intense, persistent itching due to irritation of sensory nerve endings from organic or psychogenic causes.

698.0 Pruritus ani
Perianal itch

698.1 Pruritus of genital organs

698.2 Prurigo
Lichen urticatus
Prurigo:
NOS
Hebra's
mitis
simplex
Urticaria papulosa (Hebra)
EXCLUDES *prurigo nodularis (698.3)*

698.3 Lichenification and lichen simplex chronicus
Hyde's disease
Neurodermatitis (circumscripta) (local)
Prurigo nodularis
EXCLUDES *neurodermatitis, diffuse (of Brocq) (691.8)*
DEF: Lichenification: thickening of skin due to prolonged rubbing or scratching.
DEF: Lichen simplex chronicus: eczematous dermatitis, of face, neck, extremities, scrotum, vulva, and perianal region due to repeated itching, rubbing and scratching; spontaneous or evolves with other dermatoses.

698.4 Dermatitis factitia [artefacta]
Dermatitis ficta
Neurotic excoriation
Use additional code to identify any associated mental disorder
DEF: Various types of self-inflicted skin lesions characterized in appearance as an erythema to a gangrene.

698.8 Other specified pruritic conditions
Pruritus:
hiemalis
senilis
Winter itch

698.9 Unspecified pruritic disorder
Itch NOS
Pruritus NOS

OTHER DISEASES OF SKIN AND SUBCUTANEOUS TISSUE (700-709)

EXCLUDES *conditions confined to eyelids (373.0-374.9)*
congenital conditions of skin, hair, and nails (757.0-757.9)

700 Corns and callosities
Callus
Clavus
DEF: Corns: Conical or horny thickening of skin on toes, due to friction, pressure from shoes and hosiery; pain and inflammation may develop.
DEF: Callosities: Localized overgrowth (hyperplasia) of the horny epidermal layer due to pressure or friction.

✓4th **701 Other hypertrophic and atrophic conditions of skin**
EXCLUDES *dermatomyositis (710.3)*
hereditary edema of legs (757.0)
scleroderma (generalized) (710.1)

701.0 Circumscribed scleroderma
Addison's keloid
Dermatosclerosis, localized
Lichen sclerosus et atrophicus
Morphea
Scleroderma, circumscribed or localized
DEF: Thickened, hardened, skin and subcutaneous tissue; may involve musculoskeletal system.

701.1 Keratoderma, acquired
Acquired:
ichthyosis
keratoderma palmaris et plantaris
Elastosis perforans serpiginosa
Hyperkeratosis:
NOS
follicularis in cutem penetrans
palmoplantaris climacterica
Keratoderma:
climactericum
tylodes, progressive
Keratosis (blennorrhagica)
EXCLUDES *Darier's disease [keratosis follicularis] (congenital) (757.39)*
keratosis:
arsenical (692.4)
gonococcal (098.81)
AHA: 4Q, '94, 48

701.2 Acquired acanthosis nigricans
Keratosis nigricans
DEF: Diffuse velvety hyperplasia of the spinous skin layer of the axilla and other body folds marked by gray, brown, or black pigmentation; in adult form it is often associated with an internal carcinoma (malignant acanthosis nigricans) in a benign, nevoid form it is relatively generalized; benign juvenile form with obesity is sometimes caused by an endocrine disturbance.

701.3 Striae atrophicae
Atrophic spots of skin
Atrophoderma maculatum
Atrophy blanche (of Milian)
Degenerative colloid atrophy
Senile degenerative atrophy
Striae distensae
DEF: Bands of atrophic, depressed, wrinkled skin associated with stretching of skin from pregnancy, obesity, or rapid growth during puberty.

701.4 Keloid scar
Cheloid
Hypertrophic scar
Keloid
DEF: Overgrowth of scar tissue due to excess amounts of collagen during connective tissue repair; occurs mainly on upper trunk, face.

701.5 Other abnormal granulation tissue
Excessive granulation

701.8 Other specified hypertrophic and atrophic conditions of skin
Acrodermatitis atrophicans chronica
Atrophia cutis senilis
Atrophoderma neuriticum
Confluent and reticulate papillomatosis
Cutis laxa senilis
Elastosis senilis
Folliculitis ulerythematosa reticulata
Gougerot-Carteaud syndrome or disease

701.9 Unspecified hypertrophic and atrophic conditions of skin
Skin tag
Atrophoderma

✓4th **702 Other dermatoses**
EXCLUDES *carcinoma in situ (232.0-232.9)*

702.0 Actinic keratosis
AHA: 1Q, '92, 18
DEF: Wart-like growth, red or skin-colored; may form a cutaneous horn.

✓5th **702.1 Seborrheic keratosis**
DEF: Common, benign, lightly pigmented, warty growth composed of basaloid cells.

702.11 Inflamed seborrheic keratosis
AHA: 4Q, '94, 48

702.19 Other seborrheic keratosis
Seborrheic keratosis NOS

702.8 Other specified dermatoses

✓4th **703 Diseases of nail**
EXCLUDES *congenital anomalies (757.5)*
onychia and paronychia (681.02, 681.11)

703.0 Ingrowing nail
Ingrowing nail with infection
Unguis incarnatus
EXCLUDES *infection, nail NOS (681.9)*

703.8 Other specified diseases of nail
Dystrophia unguium
Hypertrophy of nail
Koilonychia
Leukonychia (punctata) (striata)
Onychauxis
Onychogryposis
Onycholysis

703.9 Unspecified disease of nail

✓4th **704 Diseases of hair and hair follicles**
EXCLUDES *congenital anomalies (757.4)*

✓5th **704.0 Alopecia**
EXCLUDES *madarosis (374.55)*
syphilitic alopecia (091.82)
DEF: Lack of hair, especially on scalp; often called baldness; may be partial or total; occurs at any age.

704.00 Alopecia, unspecified
Baldness
Loss of hair

704.01 Alopecia areata
Ophiasis
DEF: Alopecia areata: usually reversible, inflammatory, patchy hair loss found in beard or scalp.
DEF: Ophiasis: alopecia areata of children; marked by band around temporal and occipital scalp margins.

704.02 Telogen effluvium
DEF: Shedding of hair from premature telogen development in follicles due to stress, including shock, childbirth, surgery, drugs or weight loss.

704.09 Other
Folliculitis decalvans
Hypotrichosis:
NOS
postinfectional NOS
Pseudopelade

704.1 Hirsutism
Hypertrichosis:
NOS
lanuginosa, acquired
Polytrichia
EXCLUDES *hypertrichosis of eyelid (374.54)*
DEF: Excess hair growth; often in unexpected places and amounts.

704.2 Abnormalities of the hair
Atrophic hair
Clastothrix
Fragilitas crinium
Trichiasis:
NOS
cicatrical
Trichorrhexis (nodosa)
EXCLUDES *trichiasis of eyelid (374.05)*

704.3 Variations in hair color
Canities (premature)
Grayness, hair (premature)
Heterochromia of hair
Poliosis:
NOS
circumscripta, acquired

704.8 Other specified diseases of hair and hair follicles
Folliculitis:
NOS
abscedens et suffodiens
pustular
Perifolliculitis:
NOS
capitis abscedens et suffodiens
scalp
Sycosis:
NOS
barbae [not parasitic]
lupoid
vulgaris

704.9 Unspecified disease of hair and hair follicles

✓4th **705 Disorders of sweat glands**

705.0 Anhidrosis
Hypohidrosis
Oligohidrosis
DEF: Lack or deficiency of ability to sweat.

705.1 Prickly heat
Heat rash
Sudamina
Miliaria rubra (tropicalis)

✓5th **705.2 Focal hyperhidrosis**
EXCLUDES *generalized (secondary) hyperhidrosis (780.8)*

705.21 Primary focal hyperhidrosis
Focal hyperhidrosis NOS
Hyperhidrosis NOS
Hyperhidrosis of:
axilla
face
palms
soles

AHA: 4Q, '04, 91

DEF: A rare condition that is a disorder of the sweat glands resulting in excessive production of sweat; occurs in the absence of any underlying or causative condition and is almost always focal, confined to one or more specific areas of the body.

705.22 Secondary focal hyperhidrosis
Frey's syndrome

AHA: 4Q, '04, 91

DEF: Secondary focal hyperhidrosis: a symptom of an underlying disease process resulting in excessive sweating beyond what the body requires to maintain thermal control, confined to one or more specific areas of the body.

DEF: Frey's syndrome: an auriculotemporal syndrome due to lesion on the parotid gland; characteristic redness and excessive sweating on the cheek in connection with eating.

✓5th **705.8 Other specified disorders of sweat glands**

705.81 Dyshidrosis
Cheiropompholyx
Pompholyx

DEF: Vesicular eruption, on hands, feet causing itching and burning.

705.82 Fox-Fordyce disease

DEF: Chronic, usually pruritic disease chiefly of women evidenced by small follicular papular eruptions, especially in the axillary and pubic areas; develops from the closure and rupture of the affected apocrine glands' intraepidermal portion of the ducts.

705.83 Hidradenitis
Hidradenitis suppurativa

DEF: Inflamed sweat glands.

705.89 Other
Bromhidrosis
Chromhidrosis
Granulosis rubra nasi
Urhidrosis

EXCLUDES *generalized hyperhidrosis (780.8)*
hidrocystoma (216.0-216.9)

DEF: Bromhidrosis: foul-smelling axillary sweat due to decomposed bacteria.

DEF: Chromhidrosis: secretion of colored sweat.

DEF: Granulosis rubra nasi: ideopathic condition of children; causes redness, sweating around nose, face and chin; tends to end by puberty.

DEF: Urhidrosis: urinous substance, such as uric acid, in sweat; occurs in uremia.

705.9 Unspecified disorder of sweat glands
Disorder of sweat glands NOS

✓4th **706 Diseases of sebaceous glands**

706.0 Acne varioliformis
Acne:
frontalis
necrotica

DEF: Rare form of acne characterized by persistent brown papulo-pustules usually on the brow and temporoparietal part of the scalp.

706.1 Other acne
Acne:
NOS
conglobata
cystic
pustular
vulgaris
Blackhead
Comedo

EXCLUDES *acne rosacea (695.3)*

Four Stages of Decubitus Ulcers

First Stage
Nonblanchable erythema

Subcutaneous tissue

Second Stage
Partial thickness skin loss involving epidermis, dermis, or both

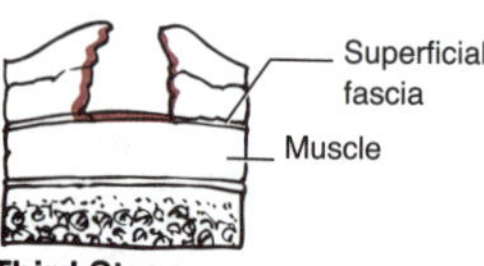

Third Stage
Full thickness skin loss extending through subcutaneous tissue

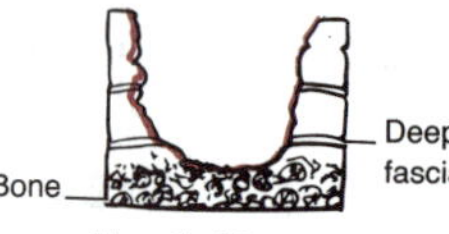

Fourth Stage
Full thickness skin loss extending to muscle and bone

706.2 Sebaceous cyst
Atheroma, skin
Keratin cyst
Wen

DEF: Benign epidermal cyst, contains sebum and keratin; presents as firm, circumscribed nodule.

706.3 Seborrhea
EXCLUDES *seborrhea:*
capitis (690.11)
sicca (690.18)
seborrheic
dermatitis (690.10)
keratosis (702.11-702.19)

DEF: Seborrheic dermatitis marked by excessive secretion of sebum; the sebum forms an oily coating, crusts, or scales on the skin; it is also called hypersteatosis.

706.8 Other specified diseases of sebaceous glands
Asteatosis (cutis)
Xerosis cutis

706.9 Unspecified disease of sebaceous glands

✓4th **707 Chronic ulcer of skin**
INCLUDES non-infected sinus of skin
non-healing ulcer

EXCLUDES *specific infections classified under "Infectious and Parasitic Diseases" (001.0-136.9)*
varicose ulcer (454.0, 454.2)

AHA: 4Q, '04, 92

✓5th **707.0 Decubitus ulcer**
Bed sore
Decubitus ulcer [any site]
Plaster ulcer
Pressure ulcer

AHA: 1Q, '04, 14; 4Q, '03, 110; 4Q, '99, 20; 1Q, '96, 15; 3Q, '90, 15; N-D, '87, 9

707.00 Unspecified site CC MC
CC Excl: 707.0, 707.8-707.9, 709.8

707.01 Elbow CC MC
CC Excl: See code 707.00

707.02 Upper back CC MC
Shoulder blades
CC Excl: See code 707.00

707.03 Lower back CC MC
Sacrum
CC Excl: See code 707.00

AHA: 1Q, '05, 16

707.04 Hip CC MC
CC Excl: See code 707.00

707.05 Buttock CC MC
CC Excl: See code 707.00

707.06 Ankle CC MC
CC Excl: See code 707.00

707.07 Heel CC MC
CC Excl: See code 707.00

AHA: 1Q, '05, 16

707.09 Other site CC MC
Head
CC Excl: See code 707.00

✓5th 707.1 Ulcer of lower limbs, except decubitus

Ulcer, chronic: neurogenic, trophic } of lower limb

Code, if applicable, any causal condition first:
- atherosclerosis of the extremities with ulceration (440.23)
- chronic venous hypertension with ulcer (459.31)
- chronic venous hypertension with ulcer and inflammation (459.33)
- diabetes mellitus (250.80-250.83)
- postphlebitic syndrome with ulcer (459.11)
- postphlebitic syndrome with ulcer and inflammation (459.13)

AHA: 4Q, '00, 44; 4Q, '99, 15

707.10 Ulcer of lower limb, unspecified CC
CC Excl: 440.23, 707.10-707.9, 709.8
AHA: 3Q, '04, 5; 4Q, '02, 43

707.11 Ulcer of thigh CC
CC Excl: See code 707.10

707.12 Ulcer of calf CC
CC Excl: See code 707.10

707.13 Ulcer of ankle CC
CC Excl: See code 707.10

707.14 Ulcer of heel and midfoot CC
Plantar surface of midfoot
CC Excl: See code 707.10

707.15 Ulcer of other part of foot CC
Toes
CC Excl: See code 707.10

707.19 Ulcer of other part of lower limb CC
CC Excl: See code 707.10

707.8 Chronic ulcer of other specified sites

Ulcer, chronic: neurogenic, trophic } of other specified sites

707.9 Chronic ulcer of unspecified site

Chronic ulcer NOS
Trophic ulcer NOS
Tropical ulcer NOS
Ulcer of skin NOS

✓4th 708 Urticaria

EXCLUDES *edema:*
angioneurotic (995.1)
Quincke's (995.1)
hereditary angioedema (277.6)
urticaria:
giant (995.1)
papulosa (Hebra) (698.2)
pigmentosa (juvenile) (congenital) (757.33)

DEF: Skin disorder marked by raised edematous patches of skin or mucous membrane with intense itching; also called hives.

708.0 Allergic urticaria

708.1 Idiopathic urticaria

708.2 Urticaria due to cold and heat
Thermal urticaria

708.3 Dermatographic urticaria
Dermatographia
Factitial urticaria

708.4 Vibratory urticaria

708.5 Cholinergic urticaria

708.8 Other specified urticaria
Nettle rash
Urticaria: chronic
Urticaria: recurrent periodic

708.9 Urticaria, unspecified
Hives NOS

Cutaneous Lesions

Surface Lesions

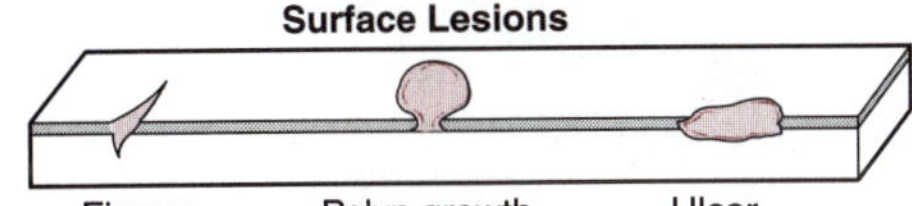

Solid Lesions

Flat macule
Slightly elevated wheal
Solid papule

Sac Lesions

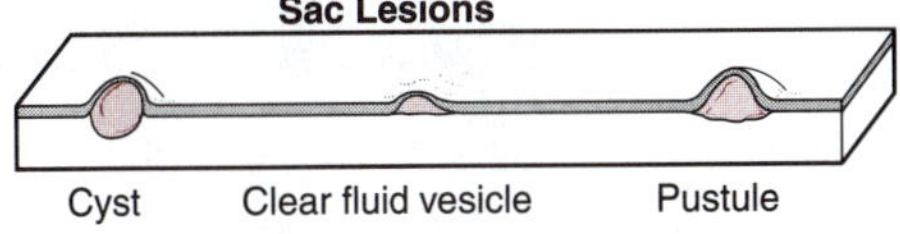

✓4th 709 Other disorders of skin and subcutaneous tissue

✓5th 709.0 Dyschromia

EXCLUDES *albinism (270.2)*
pigmented nevus (216.0-216.9)
that of eyelid (374.52-374.53)

DEF: Pigment disorder of skin or hair.

709.00 Dyschromia, unspecified

709.01 Vitiligo
DEF: Persistent, progressive development of nonpigmented white patches on otherwise normal skin.

709.09 Other

709.1 Vascular disorders of skin
Angioma serpiginosum
Purpura (primary)annularis telangiectodes

709.2 Scar conditions and fibrosis of skin
Adherent scar (skin)
Cicatrix
Disfigurement (due to scar)
Fibrosis, skin NOS
Scar NOS

EXCLUDES *keloid scar (701.4)*

AHA: N-D, '84, 19

709.3 Degenerative skin disorders
Calcinosis: circumscripta, cutis
Colloid milium
Degeneration, skin
Deposits, skin
Senile dermatosis NOS
Subcutaneous calcification

709.4 Foreign body granuloma of skin and subcutaneous tissue

EXCLUDES *residual foreign body without granuloma of skin and subcutaneous tissue (729.6)*
that of muscle (728.82)

709.8 Other specified disorders of skin
Epithelial hyperplasia
Menstrual dermatosis
Vesicular eruption

AHA: N-D, '87, 6

DEF: Epithelial hyperplasia: increased number of epitheleal cells.

DEF: Vesicular eruption: liquid-filled structures appearing through skin.

709.9 Unspecified disorder of skin and subcutaneous tissue
Dermatosis NOS

13. DISEASES OF THE MUSCULOSKELETAL SYSTEM AND CONNECTIVE TISSUE (710-739)

Joint Structures

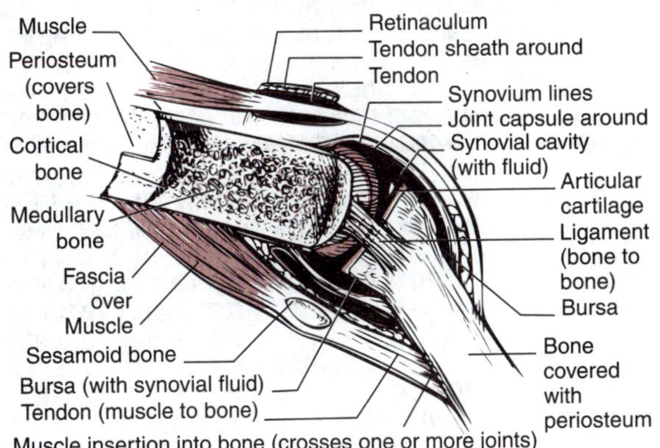

The following fifth-digit subclassification is for use with categories 711-712, 715-716, 718-719, and 730:

0 site unspecified

1 shoulder region
Acromioclavicular joint(s)
Clavicle
Glenohumeral joint(s)
Scapula
Sternoclavicular joint(s)

2 upper arm
Elbow joint
Humerus

3 forearm
Radius
Ulna
Wrist joint

4 hand
Carpus
Metacarpus
Phalanges [fingers]

5 pelvic region and thigh
Buttock
Femur
Hip (joint)

6 lower leg
Fibula
Knee joint
Patella
Tibia

7 ankle and foot
Ankle joint
Digits [toes]
Metatarsus
Phalanges, foot
Tarsus
Other joints in foot

8 other specified sites
Head
Neck
Ribs
Skull
Trunk
Vertebral column

9 multiple sites

ARTHROPATHIES AND RELATED DISORDERS (710-719)

EXCLUDES *disorders of spine (720.0-724.9)*

✓4th **710 Diffuse diseases of connective tissue**

INCLUDES all collagen diseases whose effects are not mainly confined to a single system

EXCLUDES *those affecting mainly the cardiovascular system, i.e., polyarteritis nodosa and allied conditions (446.0-446.7)*

710.0 Systemic lupus erythematosus CC
Disseminated lupus erythematosus
Libman-Sacks disease
Use additional code to identify manifestation, as:
endocarditis (424.91)
nephritis (583.81)
chronic (582.81)
nephrotic syndrome (581.81)

EXCLUDES *lupus erythematosus (discoid) NOS (695.4)*

CC Excl: 710.0

AHA: 2Q, '03, 7-8; 2Q, '97, 8

DEF: A chronic multisystemic inflammatory disease affecting connective tissue; marked by anemia, leukopenia, muscle and joint pains, fever, rash of a butterfly pattern around cheeks and forehead area; of unknown etiology.

710.1 Systemic sclerosis CC
Acrosclerosis
CRST syndrome
Progressive systemic sclerosis
Scleroderma

EXCLUDES *circumscribed scleroderma (701.0)*

Use additional code to identify manifestation, as:
lung involvement (517.2)
myopathy (359.6)

CC Excl: 710.1

AHA: 1Q, '88, 6

DEF: Systemic disease, involving excess fibrotic collagen build-up; symptoms include thickened skin; fibrotic degenerative changes in various organs; and vascular abnomalities; condition occurs more often in females.

710.2 Sicca syndrome
Keratoconjunctivitis sicca
Sjögren's disease

DEF: Autoimmune disease; associated with keratoconjunctivitis, laryngopharyngitis, rhinitis, dry mouth, enlarged parotid gland, and chronic polyarthritis.

710.3 Dermatomyositis CC
Poikilodermatomyositis
Polymyositis with skin involvement

CC Excl: 710.3

DEF: Polymyositis associated with flat-top purple papules on knuckles; marked by upper eyelid rash, edema of eyelids and orbit area, red rash on forehead, neck, shoulders, trunk and arms; symptoms include fever, weight loss aching muscles; visceral cancer (in individuals older than 40).

710.4 Polymyositis CC

CC Excl: 710.4

DEF: Chronic, progressive, inflammatory skeletal muscle disease; causes weakness of limb girdles, neck, pharynx; may precede or follow scleroderma, Sjogren's disease, systemic lupus erythematosus, arthritis, or malignancy.

710.5 Eosinophilia myalgia syndrome CC
Toxic oil syndrome
Use additional E code to identify drug, if drug induced

CC Excl: 292.0-293.9, 710.5

AHA: 4Q, '92, 21

DEF: Eosinophilia myalgia syndrome (EMS): inflammatory, multisystem fibrosis; associated with ingesting elementary L-tryptophan; symptoms include myalgia, weak limbs and bulbar muscles, distal sensory loss, areflexia, arthralgia, cough, fever, fatigue, skin rashes, myopathy, and eosinophil counts greater than 1000/microliter.

DEF: Toxic oil syndrome: syndrome similar to EMS due to ingesting contaminated cooking oil.

710.8 Other specified diffuse diseases of connective tissue CC

Multifocal fibrosclerosis (idiopathic) NEC
Systemic fibrosclerosing syndrome

CC Excl: 710.8

AHA: M-A, '87, 12

710.9 Unspecified diffuse connective tissue disease

Collagen disease NOS

✓4th 711 Arthropathy associated with infections

INCLUDES arthritis, arthropathy, polyarthritis, polyarthropathy } associated with conditions classifiable below

EXCLUDES *rheumatic fever (390)*

The following fifth-digit subclassification is for use with category 711; valid digits are in [brackets] under each code. See list at beginning of chapter for definitions.

0 site unspecified
1 shoulder region
2 upper arm
3 forearm
4 hand
5 pelvic region and thigh
6 lower leg
7 ankle and foot
8 other specified sites
9 multiple sites

AHA: 1Q, '92, 17

§ ✓5th **711.0 Pyogenic arthritis** CC

[0-9]

Arthritis or polyarthritis (due to):
coliform [Escherichia coli]
Hemophilus influenzae [H. influenzae]
pneumococcal
Pseudomonas
staphylococcal
streptococcal

Pyarthrosis

Use additional code to identify infectious organism (041.0-041.8)

CC Excl: For code 711.00: 015.80-015.96, 017.90-017.96, 036.82, 056.71, 098.50-098.51, 098.59, 098.89, 711.00-714.0, 715.00, 715.09-715.10, 715.18-716.99, 718.00-718.08, 719.00-719.10, 719.18-719.99 **For code 711.01**: 015.80-015.96, 017.90-017.96, 036.82, 056.71, 098.50-098.51, 098.59, 098.89, 711.00-711.01, 711.08-711.11, 711.18-711.21, 711.28-711.31, 711.38-711.41, 711.48-711.51, 711.58-711.61, 711.68-711.71, 711.78-711.81, 711.88-711.91, 711.98-711.99, 712.10-712.11, 712.18-712.21, 712.28-712.31, 712.38-712.81, 712.88-712.91, 712.98-712.99, 713.0-713.8, 714.0, 715.00, 715.09-715.11, 715.18-715.21, 715.28-715.31, 715.38-715.91, 715.98, 716.00-716.01, 716.08-716.11, 716.18-716.21, 716.28-716.31, 716.38-716.41, 716.48-716.51, 716.58-716.61, 716.68-716.81, 716.88-716.91, 716.98-716.99, 718.00-718.01, 718.08, 719.00-719.01, 719.08-719.11, 719.18-719.21, 719.28-719.31, 719.38-719.41, 719.48-719.51, 719.58-719.61, 719.68-719.7, 719.80-719.81, 719.88-719.91, 719.98-719.99
For code 711.02: 015.80-015.96, 017.90-017.96, 036.82, 056.71, 098.50-098.51, 098.59, 098.89, 711.00, 711.02, 711.08-711.10, 711.12, 711.18-711.20, 711.22, 711.28-711.30, 711.32, 711.38-711.40, 711.42, 711.48-711.50, 711.52, 711.58-711.60, 711.62, 711.68-711.70, 711.72, 711.78-711.80, 711.82, 711.88-711.90, 711.92, 711.98-711.99, 712.10, 712.12, 712.18-712.20, 712.22, 712.28-712.30, 712.32, 712.38-712.80, 712.82, 712.88-712.90, 712.92, 712.98-712.99, 713.0-713.8, 714.0, 715.00, 715.09-715.10, 715.12, 715.18, 715.20, 715.22, 715.28, 715.30, 715.32, 715.38-715.90, 715.92, 715.98, 716.00, 716.02, 716.08-716.10, 716.12, 716.18-716.20, 716.22, 716.28-716.30, 716.32, 716.38-716.40, 716.42, 716.48-716.50, 716.52, 716.58-716.60, 716.62, 716.68, 716.80, 716.82, 716.88-716.90, 716.92, 716.98-716.99, 718.00, 718.02, 718.08, 719.00, 719.02, 719.08-719.10, 719.12, 719.18-719.20, 719.22, 719.28-719.30, 719.32, 719.38-719.40, 719.42, 719.48-719.50, 719.52, 719.58-719.60, 719.62, 719.68-719.7, 719.80, 719.82, 719.88-719.90, 719.92, 719.98-719.99 **For code 711.03**: 015.80-015.96, 017.90-017.96, 036.82, 056.71, 098.50-098.51, 098.59, 098.89, 711.00, 711.03, 711.08-711.10, 711.13, 711.18-711.20, 711.23, 711.28-711.30, 711.33, 711.38-711.40, 711.43, 711.48-711.50, 711.53, 711.58-711.60, 711.63, 711.68-711.70, 711.73, 711.78-711.80, 711.83, 711.88-711.90, 711.93, 711.98-711.99, 712.10, 712.13, 712.18-712.20, 712.23, 712.28-712.30, 712.33, 712.38-712.80, 712.83, 712.88-712.90, 712.93, 712.98-712.99, 713.0-713.8, 714.0, 715.00, 715.09-715.10, 715.13, 715.18, 715.20, 715.23, 715.28, 715.30, 715.33, 715.38-715.90, 715.93, 715.98, 716.00, 716.03, 716.08-716.10, 716.13, 716.18-716.20, 716.23, 716.28-716.30, 716.33, 716.38-716.40, 716.43, 716.48-716.50, 716.53, 716.58-716.60, 716.63, 716.68, 716.80, 716.83, 716.88-716.90, 716.93, 716.98-716.99, 718.00, 718.03, 718.08, 719.00, 719.03, 719.08-719.10, 719.13, 719.18-719.20, 719.23, 719.28-719.30, 719.33, 719.38-719.40, 719.43, 719.48-719.50, 719.53, 719.58-719.60, 719.63, 719.68-719.7, 719.80, 719.83, 719.88-719.90, 719.93, 719.98-719.99 **For code 711.04**: 015.80-015.96, 017.90-017.96, 036.82, 056.71, 098.50-098.51, 098.59, 098.89, 711.00, 711.04, 711.08-711.10, 711.14, 711.18-711.20, 711.24, 711.28-711.30, 711.34, 711.38-711.40, 711.44, 711.48-711.50, 711.54, 711.58-711.60, 711.64, 711.68-711.70, 711.74, 711.78-711.80, 711.84, 711.88-711.90, 711.94, 711.98-711.99, 712.10, 712.14, 712.18-712.20, 712.24, 712.28-712.30, 712.34, 712.38-712.80, 712.84, 712.88-712.90, 712.94, 712.98-712.99, 713.0-713.8, 714.0, 715.00-715.10, 715.14, 715.18, 715.20, 715.24, 715.28, 715.30, 715.34, 715.38-715.90, 715.94, 715.98, 716.00, 716.04, 716.08-716.10, 716.14, 716.18-716.20, 716.24, 716.28-716.30, 716.34, 716.38-716.40, 716.44, 716.48-716.50, 716.54, 716.58-716.60, 716.64, 716.68, 716.80, 716.84, 716.88-716.90, 716.94, 716.98-716.99, 718.00, 718.04, 718.08, 719.00, 719.04, 719.08-719.10, 719.14, 719.18-719.20, 719.24, 719.28-719.30, 719.34, 719.38-719.40, 719.44, 719.48-719.50, 719.54, 719.58-719.60, 719.64, 719.68-719.7, 719.80, 719.84, 719.88-719.90, 719.94, 719.98-719.99: **For code 711.05**: 015.80-015.96, 017.90-017.96, 036.82, 056.71, 098.50-098.51, 098.59, 098.89, 711.00, 711.05, 711.08-711.10, 711.15, 711.18-711.20, 711.25, 711.28-711.30, 711.35, 711.38-711.40, 711.45, 711.48-711.50, 711.55, 711.58-711.60, 711.65, 711.68-711.70, 711.75, 711.78-711.80, 711.85, 711.88-711.90, 711.95, 711.98-711.99, 712.10, 712.15, 712.18-712.20, 712.25, 712.28-712.30, 712.35, 712.38-712.80, 712.85, 712.88-712.90, 712.95, 712.98-712.99, 713.0-713.8, 714.0, 715.00, 715.09-715.10, 715.15, 715.18, 715.20, 715.25, 715.28, 715.30, 715.35, 715.38-715.90, 715.95, 715.98, 716.00, 716.05, 716.08-716.10, 716.15, 716.18-716.20, 716.25, 716.28-716.30, 716.35, 716.38-716.40, 716.45, 716.48-716.50, 716.55, 716.58-716.60, 716.65, 716.68, 716.80, 716.85, 716.88-716.90, 716.95, 716.98-716.99, 718.00, 718.05, 718.08, 719.00, 719.05, 719.08-719.10, 719.15, 719.18-719.20, 719.25, 719.28-719.30, 719.35, 719.38-719.40, 719.45, 719.48-719.50, 719.55, 719.58-719.60, 719.65, 719.68-719.7, 719.80, 719.85, 719.88-719.90, 719.95, 719.98-719.99 **For code 711.06**: 015.80-015.96, 017.90-017.96, 036.82, 056.71, 098.50-098.51, 098.59, 098.89, 711.00, 711.06, 711.08-711.10, 711.16, 711.18-711.20, 711.26, 711.28-711.30, 711.36, 711.38-711.40, 711.46, 711.48-711.50, 711.56, 711.58-711.60, 711.66, 711.68-711.70, 711.76, 711.78-711.80, 711.86, 711.88-711.90, 711.96, 711.98-711.99, 712.10, 712.16, 712.18-712.20, 712.26, 712.28-712.30, 712.36, 712.38-712.80, 712.86, 712.88-712.90, 712.96, 712.98-712.99, 713.0-713.8, 714.0, 715.00, 715.09-715.10, 715.16, 715.18, 715.20, 715.26, 715.28, 715.30, 715.36, 715.38-715.90, 715.96, 715.98, 716.00, 716.06, 716.08-716.10, 716.16, 716.18-716.20, 716.26, 716.28-716.30, 716.36, 716.38-716.40, 716.46, 716.48-716.50, 716.56, 716.58-716.60, 716.66, 716.68, 716.80, 716.86, 716.88-716.90, 716.96, 716.98-716.99, 718.00, 718.08, 719.00, 719.06, 719.08-719.10, 719.16, 719.18-719.20, 719.26, 719.28-719.30, 719.36, 719.38-719.40, 719.46, 719.48-719.50, 719.56, 719.58-719.60, 719.66, 719.68-719.7, 719.80, 719.86, 719.88-719.90, 719.96, 719.98-719.99 **For code 711.07**: 015.80-015.96, 017.90-017.96, 036.82, 056.71, 098.50-098.51, 098.59, 098.89, 711.00, 711.07-711.10, 711.17-711.20, 711.27-711.30, 711.37-711.40, 711.47-711.50, 711.57-711.60, 711.67-711.70, 711.77-711.80, 711.87-711.90, 711.97-711.99, 712.10, 712.17-712.20, 712.27-712.30, 712.37-712.80, 712.87-712.90, 712.97-712.99, 713.0-713.8, 714.0, 715.00, 715.09-715.10, 715.17-715.18, 715.20, 715.27-715.28, 715.30, 715.37-715.90, 715.97-715.98, 716.00, 716.07-716.10, 716.17-716.20, 716.27-716.30, 716.37-716.40, 716.47-716.50, 716.57-716.60, 716.67-716.68, 716.80, 716.87-716.90, 716.97-716.99, 718.00, 718.07-718.08, 719.00, 719.07-719.10, 719.17-719.20, 719.27-719.30, 719.37-719.40, 719.47-719.50, 719.57-719.60, 719.67-719.7, 719.80, 719.87-719.90, 719.97-719.99 **For code 711.08**: 015.80-015.96, 017.90-017.96, 036.82, 056.71, 098.50-098.51, 098.59, 098.89, 711.00-714.0, 715.00, 715.09-715.10, 715.18-716.99, 718.00-718.08, 719.00-719.10, 719.18-719.99 **For code 711.09**: See code 711.08

AHA: 1Q, '92, 16; 1Q, '91, 15

DEF: Infectious arthritis caused by various bacteria; marked by inflamed synovial membranes, and purulent effusion in joints.

§ Requires fifth-digit. Valid digits are in [brackets] under each code. See beginning of section 710-739 for codes and definitions.

§ ✓5th **711.1** [0-9] ***Arthropathy associated with Reiter's disease and nonspecific urethritis***

Code first underlying disease as:
- nonspecific urethritis (099.4)
- Reiter's disease (099.3)

DEF: Reiter's disease: joint disease marked by diarrhea, urethritis, conjunctivitis, keratosis and arthritis; of unknown etiology; affects young males.

DEF: Urethritis: inflamed urethra.

§ ✓5th **711.2** [0-9] ***Arthropathy in Behçet's syndrome***

Code first underlying disease (136.1)

DEF: Behçet's syndrome: Chronic inflammatory disorder, of unknown etiology; affects small blood vessels; causes ulcers of oral and pharyngeal mucous membranes and genitalia, skin lesions, retinal vasculitis, optic atrophy and severe uveitis.

§ ✓5th **711.3** [0-9] ***Postdysenteric arthropathy***

Code first underlying disease as:
- dysentery (009.0)
- enteritis, infectious (008.0-009.3)
- paratyphoid fever (002.1-002.9)
- typhoid fever (002.0)

EXCLUDES *salmonella arthritis (003.23)*

§ ✓5th **711.4** [0-9] ***Arthropathy associated with other bacterial diseases***

Code first underlying disease as:
- diseases classifiable to 010-040, 090-099, except as in 711.1, 711.3, and 713.5
- leprosy (030.0-030.9)
- tuberculosis (015.0-015.9)

EXCLUDES *gonococcal arthritis (098.50)*
meningococcal arthritis (036.82)

§ ✓5th **711.5** [0-9] ***Arthropathy associated with other viral diseases***

Code first underlying disease as:
- diseases classifiable to 045-049, 050-079, 480, 487
- O'nyong nyong (066.3)

EXCLUDES *that due to rubella (056.71)*

§ ✓5th **711.6** [0-9] ***Arthropathy associated with mycoses*** CC

Code first underlying disease (110.0-118)

CC Excl: For code 711.60: See code 711.08: **For code 711.61:** 015.80-015.96, 017.90-017.96, 036.82, 056.71, 098.50-098.51, 098.59, 098.89, 711.00-711.01, 711.08-711.11, 711.18-711.21, 711.28-711.31, 711.38-711.41, 711.48-711.51, 711.58-711.61, 711.68-711.71, 711.78-711.81, 711.88-711.91, 711.98-711.99, 712.10-712.11, 712.18-712.21, 712.28-712.31, 712.38-712.81, 712.88-712.91, 712.98-712.99, 713.0-713.8, 714.0, 715.00, 715.09-715.11, 715.18-715.21, 715.28, 715.30-715.31, 715.38-715.91, 715.98, 716.00-716.01, 716.08-716.11, 716.18-716.21, 716.28-716.31, 716.38-716.41, 716.48-716.51, 716.58-716.61, 716.68, 716.80-716.81, 716.88-716.91, 716.98-716.99, 718.00-718.01, 718.08, 719.00-719.01, 719.08-719.11, 719.18-719.21, 719.28-719.31, 719.38-719.41, 719.48-719.51, 719.58-719.61, 719.68-719.7, 719.80-719.81, 719.88-719.91, 719.98-719.99: **For code 711.62:** 015.80-015.96, 017.90-017.96, 036.82, 056.71, 098.50-098.51, 098.59, 098.89, 711.00, 711.02, 711.08-711.10, 711.12, 711.18-711.20, 711.22, 711.28-711.30, 711.32, 711.38-711.40, 711.42, 711.48-711.50, 711.52, 711.58-711.60, 711.62, 711.68-711.70, 711.72, 711.78-711.80, 711.82, 711.88-711.90, 711.92, 711.98-711.99, 712.10, 712.12, 712.18-712.20, 712.22, 712.28-712.30, 712.32, 712.38-712.80, 712.82, 712.88-712.90, 712.92, 712.98-712.99, 713.0-713.8, 714.0, 715.00, 715.09-715.10, 715.12, 715.18, 715.20, 715.22, 715.28, 715.30, 715.32, 715.38-715.90, 715.92, 715.98, 716.00, 716.02, 716.08-716.10, 716.12, 716.18-716.20, 716.22, 716.28-716.30, 716.32, 716.38-716.40, 716.42, 716.48-716.50, 716.52, 716.58-716.60, 716.62, 716.68, 716.80, 716.82, 716.88-716.90, 716.92, 716.98-716.99, 718.00, 718.02, 718.08, 719.00, 719.02, 719.08-719.10, 719.12, 719.18-719.20, 719.22, 719.28-719.30, 719.32, 719.38-719.40, 719.42, 719.48-719.50, 719.52, 719.58-719.60, 719.62, 719.68-719.7, 719.80, 719.82, 719.88-719.90, 719.92, 719.98-719.99: **For code 711.63:** 015.80-015.96, 017.90-017.96, 036.82, 056.71, 098.50-098.51, 098.59, 098.89, 711.00, 711.03, 711.08-711.10, 711.13, 711.18-711.20, 711.23, 711.28-711.30, 711.33, 711.38-711.40, 711.43, 711.48-711.50, 711.53, 711.58-711.60, 711.63, 711.68-711.70, 711.73, 711.78-711.80, 711.83, 711.88-711.90, 711.93, 711.98-711.99, 712.10, 712.13, 712.18-712.20, 712.23, 712.28-712.30, 712.33, 712.38-712.80, 712.83, 712.88-712.90, 712.93, 712.98-712.99, 713.0-713.8, 714.0, 715.00, 715.09-715.10, 715.13, 715.18, 715.20, 715.23, 715.28, 715.30, 715.33, 715.38-715.90, 715.93, 715.98, 716.00, 716.03, 716.08-716.10, 716.13, 716.18-716.20, 716.23, 716.28-716.30, 716.33, 716.38-716.40, 716.43, 716.48-716.50, 716.53, 716.58-716.60, 716.63, 716.68, 716.80, 716.83, 716.88-716.90, 716.93, 716.98-716.99, 718.00, 718.03, 718.08, 719.00, 719.03, 719.08-719.10, 719.13, 719.18-719.20, 719.23, 719.28-719.30, 719.33, 719.38-719.40, 719.43, 719.48-719.50, 719.53, 719.58-719.60, 719.63, 719.68-719.7, 719.80, 719.83, 719.88-719.90, 719.93, 719.98-719.99 **For code 711.64:** 015.80-015.96, 017.90-017.96, 036.82, 056.71, 098.50-098.51, 098.59, 098.89, 711.00, 711.04, 711.08-711.10, 711.14, 711.18-711.20, 711.24, 711.28-711.30, 711.34, 711.38-711.40, 711.44, 711.48-711.50, 711.58-711.60, 711.64, 711.68-711.70, 711.74, 711.78-711.80, 711.84, 711.88-711.90, 711.94, 711.98-711.99, 712.10, 712.14, 712.18-712.20, 712.24, 712.28-712.30, 712.34, 712.38-712.80, 712.84, 712.88-712.90, 712.94, 712.98-712.99, 713.0-713.8, 714.0, 715.00-715.10, 715.14, 715.18, 715.20, 715.24, 715.28, 715.30, 715.34, 715.38-715.90, 715.94, 715.98, 716.00, 716.04, 716.08-716.10, 716.14, 716.18-716.20, 716.24, 716.28-716.30, 716.34, 716.38-716.40, 716.44, 716.48-716.50, 716.54, 716.58-716.60, 716.64, 716.68, 716.80, 716.84, 716.88-716.90, 716.94, 716.98-716.99, 718.00, 718.04, 718.08, 719.00, 719.04, 719.08-719.10, 719.14, 719.18-719.20, 719.24, 719.28-719.30, 719.34, 719.38-719.40, 719.44, 719.48-719.50, 719.54, 719.58-719.60, 719.64, 719.68-719.7, 719.80, 719.84, 719.88-719.90, 719.94, 719.98-719.99 **For code 711.65:** 015.80-015.96, 017.90-017.96, 036.82, 056.71, 098.50-098.51, 098.59, 098.89, 711.00, 711.05, 711.08-711.10, 711.15, 711.18-711.20, 711.25, 711.28-711.30, 711.35, 711.38-711.40, 711.45, 711.48-711.50, 711.55, 711.58-711.60, 711.65, 711.68-711.70, 711.75, 711.78-711.80, 711.85, 711.88-711.90, 711.95, 711.98-711.99, 712.10, 712.15, 712.18-712.20, 712.25, 712.28-712.30, 712.35, 712.38-712.80, 712.85, 712.88-712.90, 712.95, 712.98-712.99, 713.0-713.8, 714.0, 715.00, 715.09-715.10, 715.15, 715.18, 715.20, 715.25, 715.28, 715.30, 715.35, 715.38-715.90, 715.95, 715.98, 716.00, 716.05, 716.08-716.10, 716.15, 716.18-716.20, 716.25, 716.28-716.30, 716.35, 716.38-716.40, 716.45, 716.48-716.50, 716.55, 716.58-716.60, 716.65, 716.68, 716.80, 716.85, 716.88-716.90, 716.95, 716.98-716.99, 718.00, 718.05, 718.08, 719.00, 719.05, 719.08-719.10, 719.15, 719.18-719.20, 719.25, 719.28-719.30, 719.35, 719.38-719.40, 719.45, 719.48-719.50, 719.55, 719.58-719.60, 719.65, 719.68-719.7, 719.80, 719.85, 719.88-719.90, 719.95, 719.98-719.99
For code 711.66: 015.80-015.96, 017.90-017.96, 036.82, 056.71, 098.50-098.51, 098.59, 098.89, 711.00, 711.06, 711.08-711.10, 711.16, 711.18-711.20, 711.26, 711.28-711.30, 711.36, 711.38-711.40, 711.46, 711.48-711.50, 711.56, 711.58-711.60, 711.66, 711.68-711.70, 711.76, 711.78-711.80, 711.86, 711.88-711.90, 711.96, 711.98-711.99, 712.10, 712.16, 712.18-712.20, 712.26, 712.28-712.30, 712.36, 712.38-712.80, 712.86, 712.88-712.90, 712.96, 712.98-712.99, 713.0-713.8, 714.0, 715.00, 715.09-715.10, 715.16, 715.18, 715.20, 715.26, 715.28, 715.30, 715.36, 715.38-715.90, 715.96, 715.98, 716.00, 716.06, 716.08-716.10, 716.16, 716.18-716.20, 716.26, 716.28-716.30, 716.36, 716.38-716.40, 716.46, 716.48-716.50, 716.56, 716.58-716.60, 716.66, 716.68, 716.80, 716.86, 716.88-716.90, 716.96, 716.98-716.99, 718.00, 718.08, 719.00, 719.06, 719.08-719.10, 719.16, 719.18-719.20, 719.26, 719.28-719.30, 719.36, 719.38-719.40, 719.46, 719.48-719.50, 719.56, 719.58-719.60, 719.66, 719.68-719.7, 719.80, 719.86, 719.88-719.90, 719.96, 719.98-719.99 **For code 711.67:** 015.80-015.96, 017.90-017.96, 036.82, 056.71, 098.50-098.51, 098.59, 098.89, 711.00, 711.07-711.10, 711.17-711.20, 711.27-711.30, 711.37-711.40, 711.47-711.50, 711.57-711.60, 711.67-711.70, 711.77-711.80, 711.87-711.90, 711.97-711.99, 712.10, 712.17-712.20, 712.27-712.30, 712.37-712.80, 712.87-712.90, 712.97-712.99, 713.0-713.8, 714.0, 715.00, 715.09-715.10, 715.17-715.18, 715.20, 715.27-715.28, 715.30, 715.37-715.90, 715.97-715.98, 716.00, 716.07-716.10, 716.17-716.20, 716.27-716.30, 716.37-716.40, 716.47-716.50, 716.57-716.60, 716.67-716.80, 716.87-716.90, 716.97-716.99, 718.00, 718.07-718.08, 719.00, 719.07-719.10, 719.17-719.20, 719.27-719.30, 719.37-719.40, 719.47-719.50, 719.57-719.60, 719.67-719.7, 719.80, 719.87-719.90, 719.97-719.99 **For code 711.68:** 015.80-015.96, 017.90-017.96, 036.82, 056.71, 098.50-098.51, 098.59, 098.89, 711.00-711.99, 712.10-712.99, 713.0-713.8, 714.0, 715.00, 715.09-715.10, 715.18-715.98, 716.00-716.99, 718.00-718.08, 719.00-719.10, 719.18-719.99 **For code 711.69:** See code 711.68

§ Requires fifth-digit. Valid digits are in [brackets] under each code. See beginning of section 710-739 for codes and definitions.

§ 5th **711.7** ***Arthropathy associated with helminthiasis***
[0-9]
Code first underlying disease as:
filariasis (125.0-125.9)

§ 5th **711.8** ***Arthropathy associated with other infectious and parasitic diseases***
[0-9]
Code first underlying disease as:
diseases classifiable to 080-088, 100-104, 130-136
EXCLUDES *arthropathy associated with sarcoidosis (713.7)*
AHA: 4Q, '91, 15; 3Q, '90, 14

§ 5th **711.9** **Unspecified infective arthritis**
[0-9]
Infective arthritis or polyarthritis (acute) (chronic) (subacute) NOS

4th **712 Crystal arthropathies**
INCLUDES crystal-induced arthritis and synovitis
EXCLUDES *gouty arthropathy (274.0)*
DEF: Joint disease due to urate crystal deposit in joints or synovial membranes.

The following fifth-digit subclassification is for use with category 712; valid digits are in [brackets] under each code. See list at beginning of chapter for definitions.

0 site unspecified
1 shoulder region
2 upper arm
3 forearm
4 hand
5 pelvic region and thigh
6 lower leg
7 ankle and foot
8 other specified sites
9 multiple sites

§ 5th **712.1** ***Chondrocalcinosis due to dicalcium phosphate crystals***
[0-9]
Chondrocalcinosis due to dicalcium phosphate crystals (with other crystals)
Code first underlying disease (275.4)

§ 5th **712.2** ***Chondrocalcinosis due to pyrophosphate crystals***
[0-9]
Code first underlying disease (275.4)

§ 5th **712.3** ***Chondrocalcinosis, unspecified***
[0-9]
Code first underlying disease (275.4)

§ 5th **712.8** **Other specified crystal arthropathies**
[0-9]

§ 5th **712.9** **Unspecified crystal arthropathy**
[0-9]

4th **713 Arthropathy associated with other disorders classified elsewhere**
INCLUDES arthritis, arthropathy, polyarthritis, polyarthropathy } associated with conditions classifiable below

713.0 ***Arthropathy associated with other endocrine and metabolic disorders***
Code first underlying disease as:
acromegaly (253.0)
hemochromatosis (275.0)
hyperparathyroidism (252.00-252.08)
hypogammaglobulinemia (279.00-279.09)
hypothyroidism (243-244.9)
lipoid metabolism disorder (272.0-272.9)
ochronosis (270.2)
EXCLUDES *arthropathy associated with:*
amyloidosis (713.7)
crystal deposition disorders, except gout (712.1-712.9)
diabetic neuropathy (713.5)
gouty arthropathy (274.0)

713.1 ***Arthropathy associated with gastrointestinal conditions other than infections***
Code first underlying disease as:
regional enteritis (555.0-555.9)
ulcerative colitis (556)

713.2 ***Arthropathy associated with hematological disorders***
Code first underlying disease as:
hemoglobinopathy (282.4-282.7)
hemophilia (286.0-286.2)
leukemia (204.0-208.9)
malignant reticulosis (202.3)
multiple myelomatosis (203.0)
EXCLUDES *arthropathy associated with Henoch-Schönlein purpura (713.6)*

713.3 ***Arthropathy associated with dermatological disorders***
Code first underlying disease as:
erythema multiforme (695.1)
erythema nodosum (695.2)
EXCLUDES *psoriatic arthropathy (696.0)*

713.4 ***Arthropathy associated with respiratory disorders***
Code first underlying disease as:
diseases classifiable to 490-519
EXCLUDES *arthropathy associated with respiratory infections (711.0, 711.4-711.8)*

713.5 ***Arthropathy associated with neurological disorders***
Charcôt's arthropathy, Neuropathic arthritis } associated with diseases classifiable elsewhere
Code first underlying disease as:
neuropathic joint disease [Charcôt's joints]:
NOS (094.0)
diabetic (250.6)
syringomyelic (336.0)
tabetic [syphilitic] (094.0)

713.6 ***Arthropathy associated with hypersensitivity reaction***
Code first underlying disease as:
Henoch (-Schönlein) purpura (287.0)
serum sickness (999.5)
EXCLUDES *allergic arthritis NOS (716.2)*

713.7 ***Other general diseases with articular involvement***
Code first underlying disease as:
amyloidosis ▶(277.30-277.39)◀
familial Mediterranean fever ▶(277.31)◀
sarcoidosis (135)
AHA: 2Q, '97, 12

713.8 ***Arthropathy associated with other condition classifiable elsewhere***
Code first underlying disease as:
conditions classifiable elsewhere except as in 711.1-711.8, 712, and 713.0-713.7

4th **714 Rheumatoid arthritis and other inflammatory polyarthropathies**
EXCLUDES *rheumatic fever (390)*
rheumatoid arthritis of spine NOS (720.0)
AHA: 2Q, '95, 3

714.0 **Rheumatoid arthritis**
Arthritis or polyarthritis:
atrophic
rheumatic (chronic)
Use additional code to identify manifestation, as:
myopathy (359.6)
polyneuropathy (357.1)
EXCLUDES *juvenile rheumatoid arthritis NOS (714.30)*
AHA: 1Q, '90, 5
DEF: Chronic systemic disease principally of joints, manifested by inflammatory changes in articular structures and synovial membranes, atrophy, and loss in bone density.

§ Requires fifth-digit. Valid digits are in [brackets] under each code. See beginning of section 710-739 for codes and definitions.

N Newborn Age: 0 P Pediatric Age: 0-17 M Maternity Age: 12-55 A Adult Age: 15-124 CC CC Condition MC Major Complication CD Complex Dx HIV HIV Related Dx

714.1 Felty's syndrome CC
Rheumatoid arthritis with splenoadenomegaly and leukopenia
CC Excl: 036.82, 056.71, 711.00-714.4, 715.00, 715.09-715.10, 715.18-716.99, 718.00-718.08, 719.00-719.10, 719.18-719.99
DEF: Syndrome marked by rheumatoid arthritis, splenomegaly, leukopenia, pigmented spots on lower extremity skin, anemia, and thrombocytopenia.

714.2 Other rheumatoid arthritis with visceral or systemic involvement CC
Rheumatoid carditis
CC Excl: See code 714.1

✓5th **714.3 Juvenile chronic polyarthritis**
DEF: Rheumatoid arthritis of more than one joint; lasts longer than six weeks in age 17 or younger; symptoms include fever, erythematous rash, weight loss, lymphadenopathy, hepatosplenomegaly and pericarditis.

714.30 Polyarticular juvenile rheumatoid arthritis, chronic or unspecified CC
Juvenile rheumatoid arthritis NOS
Still's disease
CC Excl: See code 714.1

714.31 Polyarticular juvenile rheumatoid arthritis, acute CC
CC Excl: See code 714.1

714.32 Pauciarticular juvenile rheumatoid arthritis CC
CC Excl: See code 714.1

714.33 Monoarticular juvenile rheumatoid arthritis CC
CC Excl: See code 714.1

714.4 Chronic postrheumatic arthropathy
Chronic rheumatoid nodular fibrositis
Jaccoud's syndrome
DEF: Persistent joint disorder; follows previous rheumatic infection.

✓5th **714.8 Other specified inflammatory polyarthropathies**

714.81 Rheumatoid lung
Caplan's syndrome
Diffuse interstitial rheumatoid disease of lung
Fibrosing alveolitis, rheumatoid
DEF: Lung disorders associated with rheumatoid arthritis.

714.89 Other

714.9 Unspecified inflammatory polyarthropathy
Inflammatory polyarthropathy or polyarthritis NOS
EXCLUDES *polyarthropathy NOS (716.5)*

✓4th **715 Osteoarthrosis and allied disorders**
Note: Localized, in the subcategories below, includes bilateral involvement of the same site.
INCLUDES arthritis or polyarthritis:
degenerative
hypertrophic
degenerative joint disease
osteoarthritis
EXCLUDES *Marie-Strümpell spondylitis (720.0)*
osteoarthrosis [osteoarthritis] of spine (721.0-721.9)

The following fifth-digit subclassification is for use with category 715; valid digits are in [brackets] under each code. See list at beginning of chapter for definitions.

0 site unspecified
1 shoulder region
2 upper arm
3 forearm
4 hand
5 pelvic region and thigh
6 lower leg
7 ankle and foot
8 other specified sites
9 multiple sites

§ ✓5th **715.0 Osteoarthrosis, generalized**
[0,4,9]
Degenerative joint disease, involving multiple joints
Primary generalized hypertrophic osteoarthrosis
DEF: Chronic noninflammatory arthritis; marked by degenerated articular cartilage and enlarged bone; symptoms include pain and stiffness with activity; occurs among elderly.

§ ✓5th **715.1 Osteoarthrosis, localized, primary**
[0-8]
Localized osteoarthropathy, idiopathic

§ ✓5th **715.2 Osteoarthrosis, localized, secondary**
[0-8]
Coxae malum senilis

§ ✓5th **715.3 Osteoarthrosis, localized, not specified whether primary or secondary**
[0-8]
Otto's pelvis
AHA: For code 715.35: 3Q, '04, 12; 2Q, '04, 15; For code 715.36: 4Q, '03, 118; 2Q, '95, 5

§ ✓5th **715.8 Osteoarthrosis involving, or with mention of more than one site, but not specified as generalized**
[0,9]

1 § ✓5th **715.9 Osteoarthrosis, unspecified whether generalized or localized**
[0-8]
AHA: For code 715.90: 2Q, '97, 12

✓4th **716 Other and unspecified arthropathies**
EXCLUDES *cricoarytenoid arthropathy (478.79)*

The following fifth-digit subclassification is for use with category 716; valid digits are in [brackets] under each code. See list at beginning of chapter for definitions.

0 site unspecified
1 shoulder region
2 upper arm
3 forearm
4 hand
5 pelvic region and thigh
6 lower leg
7 ankle and foot
8 other specified sites
9 multiple sites

AHA: 2Q, '95, 3

§ ✓5th **716.0 Kaschin-Beck disease**
[0-9]
Endemic polyarthritis
DEF: Chronic degenerative disease of spine and peripheral joints; occurs in eastern Siberian, northern Chinese, and Korean youth; may be a mycotoxicosis caused by eating cereals infected with fungus.

§ ✓5th **716.1 Traumatic arthropathy**
[0-9]
AHA: For Code 716.11: 1Q, '02, 9

1 Nonspecific PDx=0
§ Requires fifth-digit. Valid digits are in [brackets] under each code. See beginning of section 710-739 for codes and definitions.

§ ✓5th **716.2 Allergic arthritis**
[0-9]
EXCLUDES *arthritis associated with Henoch-Schönlein purpura or serum sickness (713.6)*

§ ✓5th **716.3 Climacteric arthritis** ♀
[0-9]
Menopausal arthritis

DEF: Ovarian hormone deficiency; causes pain in small joints, shoulders, elbows or knees; affects females at menopause; also called arthropathia ovaripriva.

§ ✓5th **716.4 Transient arthropathy**
[0-9]
EXCLUDES *palindromic rheumatism (719.3)*

§ ✓5th **716.5 Unspecified polyarthropathy or polyarthritis**
[0-9]

§ ✓5th **716.6 Unspecified monoarthritis**
[0-8]
Coxitis

§ ✓5th **716.8 Other specified arthropathy**
[0-9]

§ ✓5th **716.9 Arthropathy, unspecified**
[0-9]
Arthritis } (acute) (chronic) (subacute)
Arthropathy }
Articular rheumatism (chronic)
Inflammation of joint NOS

✓4th **717 Internal derangement of knee**

INCLUDES degeneration, rupture, old, tear, old } of articular cartilage or meniscus of knee

EXCLUDES *acute derangement of knee (836.0-836.6)*
ankylosis (718.5)
contracture (718.4)
current injury (836.0-836.6)
deformity (736.4-736.6)
recurrent dislocation (718.3)

717.0 Old bucket handle tear of medial meniscus
Old bucket handle tear of unspecified cartilage

717.1 Derangement of anterior horn of medial meniscus

717.2 Derangement of posterior horn of medial meniscus

717.3 Other and unspecified derangement of medial meniscus
Degeneration of internal semilunar cartilage

✓5th **717.4 Derangement of lateral meniscus**

717.40 Derangement of lateral meniscus, unspecified

717.41 Bucket handle tear of lateral meniscus

717.42 Derangement of anterior horn of lateral meniscus

717.43 Derangement of posterior horn of lateral meniscus

717.49 Other

717.5 Derangement of meniscus, not elsewhere classified
Congenital discoid meniscus
Cyst of semilunar cartilage
Derangement of semilunar cartilage NOS

Disruption and Tears of Meniscus

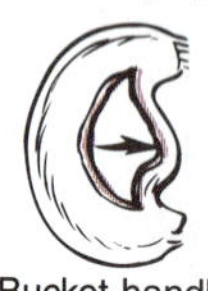
Bucket-handle

Flap-type

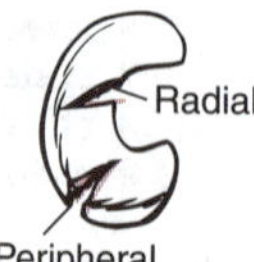

Peripheral

Horizontal cleavage

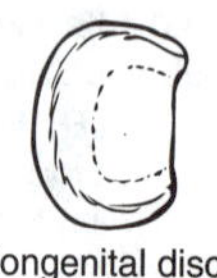
Vertical

Congenital discoid meniscus

Internal Derangements of Knee

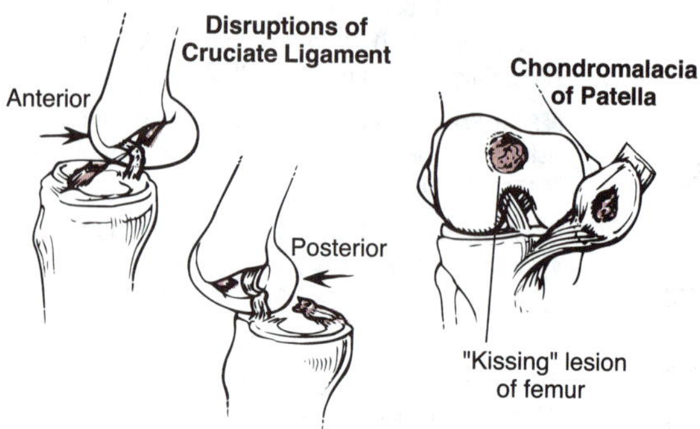

717.6 Loose body in knee
Joint mice, knee
Rice bodies, knee (joint)

DEF: The presence in the joint synovial area of a small, frequently calcified, loose body created from synovial membrane, organized fibrin fragments of articular cartilage or arthritis osteophytes.

717.7 Chondromalacia of patella
Chondromalacia patellae
Degeneration [softening] of articular cartilage of patella

AHA: M-A, '85, 14; N-D, '84, 9

DEF: Softened patella cartilage.

✓5th **717.8 Other internal derangement of knee**

717.81 Old disruption of lateral collateral ligament

717.82 Old disruption of medial collateral ligament

717.83 Old disruption of anterior cruciate ligament

717.84 Old disruption of posterior cruciate ligament

717.85 Old disruption of other ligaments of knee
Capsular ligament of knee

717.89 Other
Old disruption of ligaments NOS

717.9 Unspecified internal derangement of knee
Derangement NOS of knee

✓4th **718 Other derangement of joint**

EXCLUDES *current injury (830.0-848.9)*
jaw (524.60-524.69)

The following fifth-digit subclassification is for use with category 718; valid digits are in [brackets] under each code. See list at beginning of chapter for definitions.

0 site unspecified
1 shoulder region
2 upper arm
3 forearm
4 hand
5 pelvic region and thigh
6 lower leg
7 ankle and foot
8 other specified sites
9 multiple sites

§ ✓5th **718.0 Articular cartilage disorder**
[0-5,7-9]
Meniscus:
disorder
rupture, old
Meniscus:
tear, old
Old rupture of ligament(s) of joint NOS

EXCLUDES *articular cartilage disorder:*
in ochronosis (270.2)
knee (717.0-717.9)
chondrocalcinosis (275.4)
metastatic calcification (275.4)

§ Requires fifth-digit. Valid digits are in [brackets] under each code. See beginning of section 710-739 for codes and definitions.

§ ✓5th **718.1 Loose body in joint**
[0-5,7-9] Joint mice
EXCLUDES *knee (717.6)*
AHA: For code 718.17: 2Q, '01, 15
DEF: Calcified loose bodies in synovial fluid; due to arthritic osteophytes.

§ ✓5th **718.2 Pathological dislocation**
[0-9] Dislocation or displacement of joint, not recurrent and not current injury
Spontaneous dislocation (joint)

§ ✓5th **718.3 Recurrent dislocation of joint**
[0-9] **AHA:** N-D, '87, 7

2 § ✓5th **718.4 Contracture of joint**
[0-9] **AHA:** 4Q, '98, 40

1 § ✓5th **718.5 Ankylosis of joint**
[0-9] Ankylosis of joint (fibrous) (osseous)
EXCLUDES *spine (724.9)*
stiffness of joint without mention of ankylosis (719.5)
DEF: Immobility and solidification, of joint; due to disease, injury or surgical procedure.

§ ✓5th **718.6 Unspecified intrapelvic protrusion of acetabulum**
[0,5] Protrusio acetabuli, unspecified
DEF: Sinking of the floor of acetabulum; causing femoral head to protrude, limits hip movement; of unknown etiology.

1 § ✓5th **718.7 Developmental dislocation of joint**
[0-9] **EXCLUDES** *congenital dislocation of joint (754.0-755.8)*
traumatic dislocation of joint (830-839)
AHA: 4Q, '01, 48

§ ✓5th **718.8 Other joint derangement, not elsewhere classified**
[0-9] Flail joint (paralytic) Instability of joint
EXCLUDES *deformities classifiable to 736 (736.0-736.9)*
AHA: For code 718.81: 2Q, '00, 14

§ ✓5th **718.9 Unspecified derangement of joint**
[0-5,7-9] **EXCLUDES** *knee (717.9)*

✓4th **719 Other and unspecified disorders of joint**
EXCLUDES *jaw (524.60-524.69)*

The following fifth-digit subclassification is for use with codes 719.0-719.6, 719.8-719.9; valid digits are in [brackets] under each code. See list at beginning of chapter for definitions.

0 site unspecified
1 shoulder region
2 upper arm
3 forearm
4 hand
5 pelvic region and thigh
6 lower leg
7 ankle and foot
8 other specified sites
9 multiple sites

§ ✓5th **719.0 Effusion of joint**
[0-9] Hydrarthrosis
Swelling of joint, with or without pain
EXCLUDES *intermittent hydrarthrosis (719.3)*

§ ✓5th **719.1 Hemarthrosis**
[0-9] **EXCLUDES** *current injury (840.0-848.9)*

§ ✓5th **719.2 Villonodular synovitis**
[0-9]
DEF: Overgrowth of synovial tissue, especially at knee joint; due to macrophage infiltration of giant cells in synovial villi and fibrous nodules.

Joint Derangements and Disorders

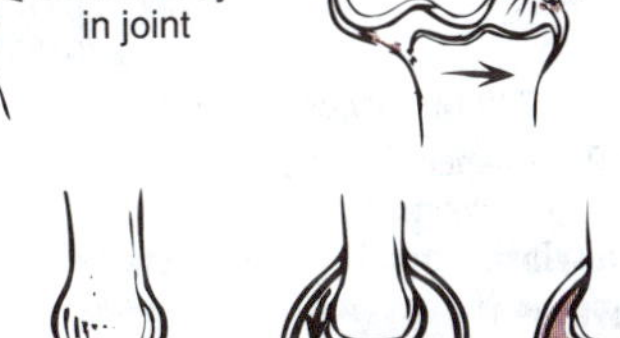

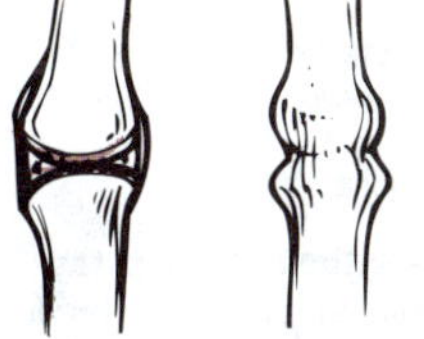

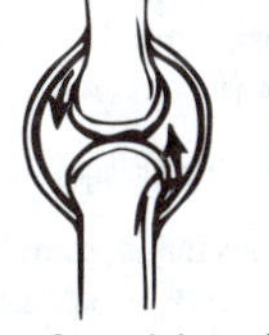

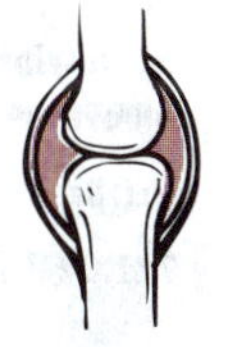

§ ✓5th **719.3 Palindromic rheumatism**
[0-9] Hench-Rosenberg syndrome
Intermittent hydrarthrosis
DEF: Recurrent episodes of afebrile arthritis and periarthritis marked by their complete disappearance after a few days or hours; causes swelling, redness, and disability usually affecting only one joint; no known cause; affects adults of either sex.

§ ✓5th **719.4 Pain in joint**
[0-9] Arthralgia
AHA: For code 719.46: 1Q, '01, 3

§ ✓5th **719.5 Stiffness of joint, not elsewhere classified**
[0-9]

§ ✓5th **719.6 Other symptoms referable to joint**
[0-9] Joint crepitus Snapping hip
AHA: 1Q, '94, 15

719.7 Difficulty in walking
EXCLUDES *abnormality of gait (781.2)*
AHA: 2Q, '04, 15; 4Q, '03, 66

§ ✓5th **719.8 Other specified disorders of joint**
[0-9] Calcification of joint Fistula of joint
EXCLUDES *temporomandibular joint-pain-dysfunction syndrome [Costen's syndrome] (524.60)*

§ ✓5th **719.9 Unspecified disorder of joint**
[0-9]

DORSOPATHIES (720-724)

EXCLUDES *curvature of spine (737.0-737.9)*
osteochondrosis of spine (juvenile) (732.0)
adult (732.8)

✓4th **720 Ankylosing spondylitis and other inflammatory spondylopathies**

720.0 Ankylosing spondylitis
Rheumatoid arthritis of spine NOS
Spondylitis:
Marie-Strümpell
rheumatoid
DEF: Rheumatoid arthritis of spine and sacroiliac joints; fusion and deformity in spine follows; affects mainly males; cause unknown.

720.1 Spinal enthesopathy
Disorder of peripheral ligamentous or muscular attachments of spine
Romanus lesion
DEF: Tendinous or muscular vertebral bone attachment abnormality.

720.2 Sacroiliitis, not elsewhere classified
Inflammation of sacroiliac joint NOS
DEF: Pain due to inflammation in joint, at juncture of sacrum and hip.

1 Nonspecific PDx=0
2 Nonspecific PDx=9
§ Requires fifth-digit. Valid digits are in [brackets] under each code. See beginning of section 710-739 for codes and definitions.

✓5th **720.8 Other inflammatory spondylopathies**

720.81 *Inflammatory spondylopathies in diseases classified elsewhere*

Code first underlying disease as:
tuberculosis (015.0)

720.89 Other

720.9 Unspecified inflammatory spondylopathy
Spondylitis NOS

✓4th **721 Spondylosis and allied disorders**
AHA: 2Q, '89, 14

DEF: Degenerative changes in spinal joint.

721.0 Cervical spondylosis without myelopathy
Cervical or cervicodorsal:
arthritis
osteoarthritis
spondylarthritis

721.1 Cervical spondylosis with myelopathy
Anterior spinal artery compression syndrome
Spondylogenic compression of cervical spinal cord
Vertebral artery compression syndrome

721.2 Thoracic spondylosis without myelopathy
Thoracic:
arthritis
osteoarthritis
spondylarthritis

721.3 Lumbosacral spondylosis without myelopathy
Lumbar or lumbosacral:
arthritis
osteoarthritis
spondylarthritis
AHA: 4Q, '02, 107

DRG 243

✓5th **721.4 Thoracic or lumbar spondylosis with myelopathy**

721.41 Thoracic region
Spondylogenic compression of thoracic spinal cord

721.42 Lumbar region
Spondylogenic compression of lumbar spinal cord

721.5 Kissing spine
Baastrup's syndrome

DEF: Compression of spinous processes of adjacent vertebrae; due to mutual contact.

721.6 Ankylosing vertebral hyperostosis

721.7 Traumatic spondylopathy
Kümmell's disease or spondylitis

721.8 Other allied disorders of spine

✓5th **721.9 Spondylosis of unspecified site**

721.90 Without mention of myelopathy
Spinal:
arthritis (deformans) (degenerative) (hypertrophic)
osteoarthritis NOS
Spondylarthrosis NOS

721.91 With myelopathy
Spondylogenic compression of spinal cord NOS

Normal Anatomy of Vertebral Disc

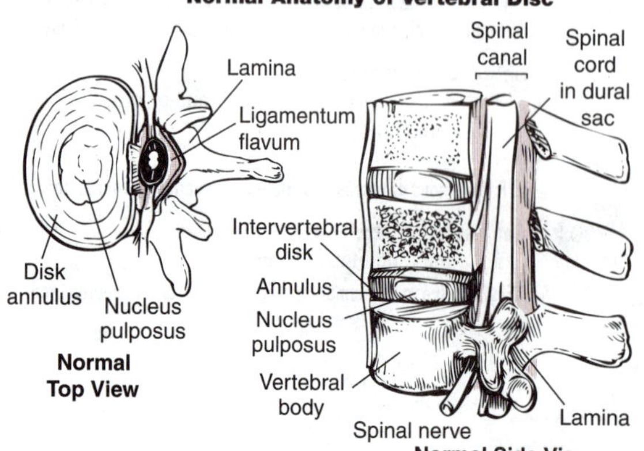

Derangement of Vertebral Disc

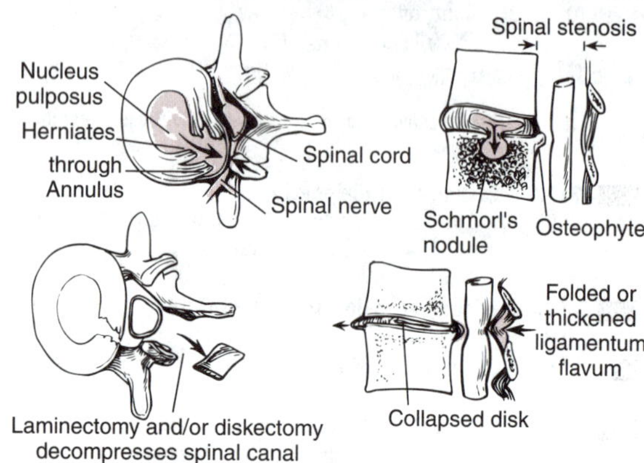

✓4th **722 Intervertebral disc disorders**
AHA: 1Q, '88, 10

722.0 Displacement of cervical intervertebral disc without myelopathy
Neuritis (brachial) or radiculitis due to displacement or rupture of cervical intervertebral disc
Any condition classifiable to 722.2 of the cervical or cervicothoracic intervertebral disc

✓5th **722.1 Displacement of thoracic or lumbar intervertebral disc without myelopathy**

722.10 Lumbar intervertebral disc without myelopathy
Lumbago or sciatica due to displacement of intervertebral disc
Neuritis or radiculitis due to displacement or rupture of lumbar intervertebral disc
Any condition classifiable to 722.2 of the lumbar or lumbosacral intervertebral disc
AHA: 3Q, '03, 12; 1Q, '03, 7; 4Q, '02, 107

DRG 243

722.11 Thoracic intervertebral disc without myelopathy
Any condition classifiable to 722.2 of thoracic intervertebral disc

722.2 Displacement of intervertebral disc, site unspecified, without myelopathy
Discogenic syndrome NOS
Herniation of nucleus pulposus NOS
Intervertebral disc NOS:
extrusion
prolapse
protrusion
rupture
Neuritis or radiculitis due to displacement or rupture of intervertebral disc

✓5th **722.3 Schmorl's nodes**

DEF: Irregular bone defect in the margin of the vertebral body; causes herniation into end plate of vertebral body.

722.30 Unspecified region
722.31 Thoracic region
722.32 Lumbar region
722.39 Other

722.4 Degeneration of cervical intervertebral disc
Degeneration of cervicothoracic intervertebral disc

✓5th **722.5 Degeneration of thoracic or lumbar intervertebral disc**

722.51 Thoracic or thoracolumbar intervertebral disc

722.52 Lumbar or lumbosacral intervertebral disc
AHA: 4Q, '04, 133

DRG 243

722.6 Degeneration of intervertebral disc, site unspecified
Degenerative disc disease NOS
Narrowing of intervertebral disc or space NOS

✓5th **722.7 Intervertebral disc disorder with myelopathy**
722.70 Unspecified region
722.71 Cervical region
722.72 Thoracic region
722.73 Lumbar region

✓5th **722.8 Postlaminectomy syndrome**
AHA: J-F, '87, 7
DEF: Spinal disorder due to spinal laminectomy surgery.
722.80 Unspecified region CC
CC Excl: 722.51-722.93
722.81 Cervical region CC
CC Excl: See code 722.80
722.82 Thoracic region CC
CC Excl: See code 722.80
722.83 Lumbar region CC
CC Excl: See code 722.80
AHA: 2Q, '97, 15

✓5th **722.9 Other and unspecified disc disorder**
Calcification of intervertebral cartilage or disc
Discitis
722.90 Unspecified region
AHA: N-D, '84, 19
722.91 Cervical region
722.92 Thoracic region
722.93 Lumbar region

✓4th **723 Other disorders of cervical region**
EXCLUDES *conditions due to:*
intervertebral disc disorders (722.0-722.9)
spondylosis (721.0-721.9)
AHA: 3Q, '94, 14; 2Q, '89, 14

723.0 Spinal stenosis in cervical region
AHA: 4Q, '03, 101

723.1 Cervicalgia
Pain in neck
DEF: Pain in cervical spine or neck region.

723.2 Cervicocranial syndrome
Barré-Liéou syndrome
Posterior cervical sympathetic syndrome
DEF: Neurologic disorder of upper cervical spine and nerve roots.

Spinal Stenosis in Cervical Region

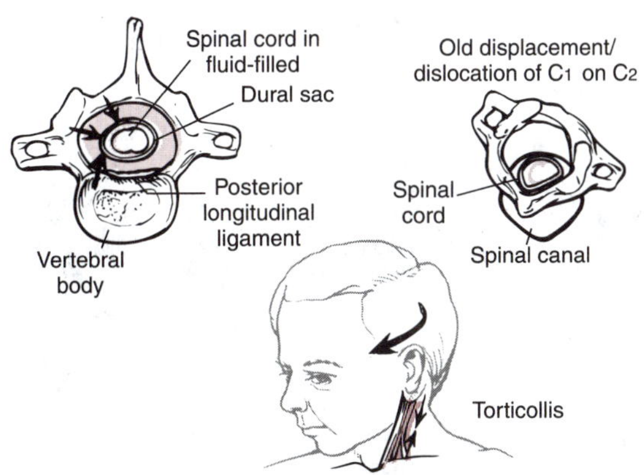

723.3 Cervicobrachial syndrome (diffuse)
AHA: N-D, '85, 12
DEF: Complex of symptoms due to scalenus anterior muscle compressing the brachial plexus; pain radiates from shoulder to arm or back of neck.

723.4 Brachial neuritis or radiculitis NOS CC
Cervical radiculitis
Radicular syndrome of upper limbs
CC Excl: 722.6-722.71, 722.80-722.81, 722.90-722.91, 723.0-723.9

723.5 Torticollis, unspecified CC
Contracture of neck
EXCLUDES *congenital (754.1)*
due to birth injury (767.8)
hysterical (300.11)
ocular torticollis (781.93)
psychogenic (306.0)
spasmodic (333.83)
traumatic, current (847.0)
CC Excl: 053.71, 722.6-722.71, 722.80-722.81, 722.90-722.91, 723.0-723.9
AHA: 2Q, '01, 21; 1Q, '95, 7
DEF: Abnormally positioned neck relative to head; due to cervical muscle or fascia contractions; also called wryneck.

723.6 Panniculitis specified as affecting neck
DEF: Inflammation of the panniculus adiposus (subcutaneous fat) in the neck.

723.7 Ossification of posterior longitudinal ligament in cervical region

723.8 Other syndromes affecting cervical region
Cervical syndrome NEC
Klippel's disease
Occipital neuralgia
AHA: 1Q, '00, 7

723.9 Unspecified musculoskeletal disorders and symptoms referable to neck
Cervical (region) disorder NOS

✓4th **724 Other and unspecified disorders of back**
EXCLUDES *collapsed vertebra (code to cause, e.g., osteoporosis, 733.00-733.09)*
conditions due to:
intervertebral disc disorders (722.0-722.9)
spondylosis (721.0-721.9)
AHA: 2Q, '89, 14

✓5th **724.0 Spinal stenosis, other than cervical**
724.00 Spinal stenosis, unspecified region
724.01 Thoracic region
724.02 Lumbar region
AHA: 4Q, '99, 13
DRG 243
724.09 Other

724.1 Pain in thoracic spine

724.2 Lumbago
Low back pain
Lumbalgia
Low back syndrome
AHA: N-D, '85, 12
DRG 243

724.3 Sciatica
Neuralgia or neuritis of sciatic nerve
EXCLUDES *specified lesion of sciatic nerve (355.0)*
AHA: 2Q, '89, 12

724.4 Thoracic or lumbosacral neuritis or radiculitis, unspecified
Radicular syndrome of lower limbs
AHA: 2Q, '99, 3

724.5 Backache, unspecified
Vertebrogenic (pain) syndrome NOS
DRG 243

724.6 Disorders of sacrum
Ankylosis } lumbosacral or sacroiliac (joint)
Instability }

✓5th **724.7 Disorders of coccyx**

724.70 Unspecified disorder of coccyx

724.71 Hypermobility of coccyx

724.79 Other

Coccygodynia

724.8 Other symptoms referable to back

Ossification of posterior longitudinal ligament NOS
Panniculitis specified as sacral or affecting back

724.9 Other unspecified back disorders

Ankylosis of spine NOS
Compression of spinal nerve root NEC
Spinal disorder NOS

EXCLUDES *sacroiliitis (720.2)*

RHEUMATISM, EXCLUDING THE BACK (725-729)

INCLUDES disorders of muscles and tendons and their attachments, and of other soft tissues

725 Polymyalgia rheumatica

DEF: Joint and muscle pain, pelvis, and shoulder girdle stiffness, high sedimentation rate and temporal arteritis; occurs in elderly.

✓4th **726 Peripheral enthesopathies and allied syndromes**

Note: Enthesopathies are disorders of peripheral ligamentous or muscular attachments.

EXCLUDES *spinal enthesopathy (720.1)*

726.0 Adhesive capsulitis of shoulder

✓5th **726.1 Rotator cuff syndrome of shoulder and allied disorders**

726.10 Disorders of bursae and tendons in shoulder region, unspecified

Rotator cuff syndrome NOS
Supraspinatus syndrome NOS

AHA: 2Q, '01, 11

726.11 Calcifying tendinitis of shoulder

726.12 Bicipital tenosynovitis

726.19 Other specified disorders

EXCLUDES *complete rupture of rotator cuff, nontraumatic (727.61)*

726.2 Other affections of shoulder region, not elsewhere classified

Periarthritis of shoulder
Scapulohumeral fibrositis

✓5th **726.3 Enthesopathy of elbow region**

726.30 Enthesopathy of elbow, unspecified

726.31 Medial epicondylitis

726.32 Lateral epicondylitis

Epicondylitis NOS
Golfers' elbow
Tennis elbow

726.33 Olecranon bursitis

Bursitis of elbow

726.39 Other

726.4 Enthesopathy of wrist and carpus

Bursitis of hand or wrist
Periarthritis of wrist

726.5 Enthesopathy of hip region

Bursitis of hip
Gluteal tendinitis
Iliac crest spur
Psoas tendinitis
Trochanteric tendinitis

✓5th **726.6 Enthesopathy of knee**

726.60 Enthesopathy of knee, unspecified

Bursitis of knee NOS

726.61 Pes anserinus tendinitis or bursitis

DEF: Inflamed tendons of sartorius, gracilis and semitendinosus muscles of medial aspect of knee.

726.62 Tibial collateral ligament bursitis

Pellegrini-Stieda syndrome

726.63 Fibular collateral ligament bursitis

726.64 Patellar tendinitis

726.65 Prepatellar bursitis

726.69 Other

Bursitis:
infrapatellar
subpatellar

✓5th **726.7 Enthesopathy of ankle and tarsus**

726.70 Enthesopathy of ankle and tarsus, unspecified

Metatarsalgia NOS

EXCLUDES *Morton's metatarsalgia (355.6)*

726.71 Achilles bursitis or tendinitis

726.72 Tibialis tendinitis

Tibialis (anterior) (posterior) tendinitis

726.73 Calcaneal spur

DEF: Overgrowth of calcaneous bone; causes pain on walking; due to chronic avulsion injury of plantar fascia from calcaneus.

726.79 Other

Peroneal tendinitis

726.8 Other peripheral enthesopathies

✓5th **726.9 Unspecified enthesopathy**

726.90 Enthesopathy of unspecified site

Capsulitis NOS
Periarthritis NOS
Tendinitis NOS

726.91 Exostosis of unspecified site

Bone spur NOS

AHA: 2Q, '01, 15

✓4th **727 Other disorders of synovium, tendon, and bursa**

✓5th **727.0 Synovitis and tenosynovitis**

727.00 Synovitis and tenosynovitis, unspecified

Synovitis NOS
Tenosynovitis NOS

Bunion

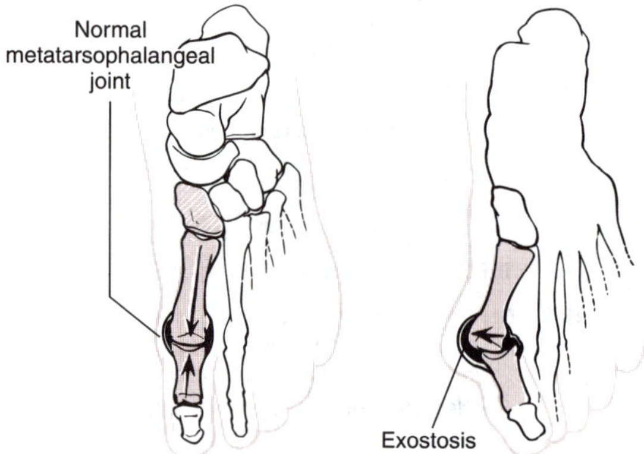

Ganglia

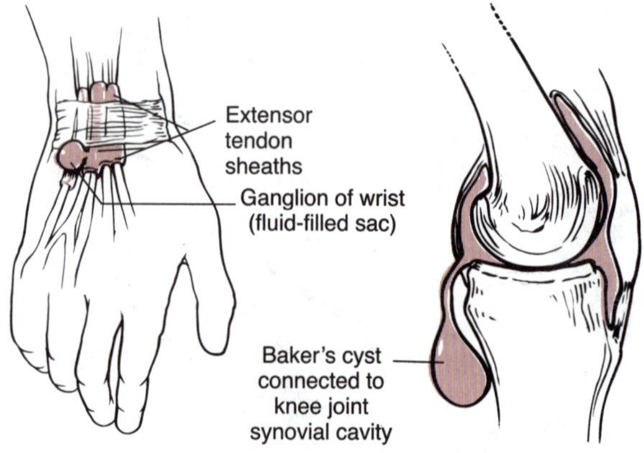

727.01 ***Synovitis and tenosynovitis in diseases classified elsewhere***
Code first underlying disease as:
tuberculosis (015.0-015.9)
EXCLUDES *crystal-induced (275.4)*
gonococcal (098.51)
gouty (274.0)
syphilitic (095.7)

727.02 Giant cell tumor of tendon sheath

727.03 Trigger finger (acquired)
DEF: Stenosing tenosynovitis or nodule in flexor tendon; cessation of flexion or extension movement in finger, followed by snapping into place.

727.04 Radial styloid tenosynovitis
de Quervain's disease

727.05 Other tenosynovitis of hand and wrist

727.06 Tenosynovitis of foot and ankle

727.09 Other

727.1 Bunion
DEF: Enlarged first metatarsal head due to inflamed bursa; results in laterally displaced great toe.

727.2 Specific bursitides often of occupational origin
Beat:
elbow
hand
knee
Miners':
elbow
knee
Chronic crepitant synovitis of wrist

727.3 Other bursitis
Bursitis NOS
EXCLUDES *bursitis:*
gonococcal (098.52)
subacromial (726.19)
subcoracoid (726.19)
subdeltoid (726.19)
syphilitic (095.7)
"frozen shoulder" (726.0)

✓5th **727.4 Ganglion and cyst of synovium, tendon, and bursa**

727.40 Synovial cyst, unspecified
EXCLUDES *that of popliteal space (727.51)*
AHA: 2Q, '97, 6

727.41 Ganglion of joint

727.42 Ganglion of tendon sheath

727.43 Ganglion, unspecified

727.49 Other
Cyst of bursa

✓5th **727.5 Rupture of synovium**

727.50 Rupture of synovium, unspecified

727.51 Synovial cyst of popliteal space
Baker's cyst (knee)

727.59 Other

✓5th **727.6 Rupture of tendon, nontraumatic**

727.60 Nontraumatic rupture of unspecified tendon

727.61 Complete rupture of rotator cuff

727.62 Tendons of biceps (long head)

727.63 Extensor tendons of hand and wrist

727.64 Flexor tendons of hand and wrist

727.65 Quadriceps tendon

727.66 Patellar tendon

727.67 Achilles tendon

727.68 Other tendons of foot and ankle

727.69 Other

✓5th **727.8 Other disorders of synovium, tendon, and bursa**

727.81 Contracture of tendon (sheath)
Short Achilles tendon (acquired)

727.82 Calcium deposits in tendon and bursa
Calcification of tendon NOS
Calcific tendinitis NOS
EXCLUDES *peripheral ligamentous or muscular attachments (726.0-726.9)*

727.83 Plica syndrome
Plica knee
AHA: 4Q, '00, 44
DEF: A fold in the synovial tissue that begins to form before birth, creating a septum between two pockets of synovial tissue; two most common plicae are the medial patellar plica and the suprapatellar plica. Plica syndrome, or plica knee, refers to symptomatic plica. Experienced by females more commonly than males.

727.89 Other
Abscess of bursa or tendon
EXCLUDES *xanthomatosis localized to tendons (272.7)*
AHA: 2Q, '89, 15

727.9 Unspecified disorder of synovium, tendon, and bursa

✓4th **728 Disorders of muscle, ligament, and fascia**
EXCLUDES *enthesopathies (726.0-726.9)*
muscular dystrophies (359.0-359.1)
myoneural disorders (358.00-358.9)
myopathies (359.2-359.9)
old disruption of ligaments of knee (717.81-717.89)

728.0 Infective myositis CC
Myositis:
purulent
suppurative
EXCLUDES *myositis:*
epidemic (074.1)
interstitial (728.81)
syphilitic (095.6)
tropical (040.81)
CC Excl: 567.31, 728.0, 728.11-728.3, 728.81, 728.86
DEF: Inflamed connective septal tissue of muscle.

✓5th **728.1 Muscular calcification and ossification**

728.10 Calcification and ossification, unspecified
Massive calcification (paraplegic)

728.11 Progressive myositis ossificans
DEF: Progressive myositic disease; marked by bony tissue formed by voluntary muscle; occurs among very young.

728.12 Traumatic myositis ossificans
Myositis ossificans (circumscripta)

728.13 Postoperative heterotopic calcification
DEF: Abnormal formation of calcium deposits in muscular tissue after surgery, marked by a corresponding loss of muscle tone and tension.

728.19 Other
Polymyositis ossificans

728.2 Muscular wasting and disuse atrophy, not elsewhere classified
Amyotrophia NOS
Myofibrosis
EXCLUDES *neuralgic amyotrophy (353.5)*
pelvic muscle wasting and disuse atrophy (618.83)
progressive muscular atrophy (335.0-335.9)

728.3 Other specific muscle disorders
Arthrogryposis
Immobility syndrome (paraplegic)
EXCLUDES *arthrogryposis multiplex congenita (754.89)*
stiff-man syndrome (333.91)

728.4 Laxity of ligament

728.5 Hypermobility syndrome

728.6 Contracture of palmar fascia A

Dupuytren's contracture

DEF: Dupuytren's contracture: flexion deformity of finger, due to shortened, thickened fibrosing of palmar fascia; cause unknown; associated with long-standing epilepsy; occurs more often in males.

✓5th **728.7 Other fibromatoses**

728.71 Plantar fascial fibromatosis

Contracture of plantar fascia
Plantar fasciitis (traumatic)

DEF: Plantar fascia fibromatosis; causes nodular swelling and pain; not associated with contractures.

728.79 Other

Garrod's or knuckle pads
Nodular fasciitis
Pseudosarcomatous fibromatosis (proliferative) (subcutaneous)

DEF: Knuckle pads: Pea-size nodules on dorsal surface of interphalangeal joints; new growth of fibrous tissue with thickened dermis and epidermis.

✓5th **728.8 Other disorders of muscle, ligament, and fascia**

728.81 Interstitial myositis

DEF: Inflammation of septal connective parts of muscle tissue.

728.82 Foreign body granuloma of muscle

Talc granuloma of muscle

728.83 Rupture of muscle, nontraumatic

728.84 Diastasis of muscle

Diastasis recti (abdomen)

EXCLUDES *diastasis recti complicating pregnancy, labor, and delivery (665.8)*

DEF: Muscle separation, such as recti abdominis after repeated pregnancies.

728.85 Spasm of muscle

728.86 Necrotizing fasciitis CC

Use additional code to identify:
infectious organism (041.00-041.89)
gangrene (785.4), if applicable

CC Excl: 567.31, 728.0, 728.11-728.3, 728.81, 728.86, 728.88

AHA: 4Q, '95, 54

DEF: Fulminating infection begins with extensive cellulitis, spreads to superficial and deep fascia; causes thrombosis of subcutaneous vessels, and gangrene of underlying tissue.

728.87 Muscle weakness (generalized)

EXCLUDES *generalized weakness (780.79)*

AHA: 1Q, '05, 13; 4Q, '03, 66

728.88 Rhabdomyolysis CC

CC Excl: 567.31, 728.0, 728.11-728.3, 728.81, 728.86, 728.88

AHA: 4Q, '03, 66

DEF: A disintegration or destruction of muscle; an acute disease characterized by the excretion of myoglobin into the urine.

728.89 Other

Eosinophilic fasciitis
Use additional E code to identify drug, if drug induced

AHA: 3Q, '02, 28; 2Q, '01, 14, 15

DEF: Eosinophilic fasciitis: inflammation of fascia of extremities associated with eosinophilia, edema, and swelling; occurs alone or as part of myalgia syndrome.

728.9 Unspecified disorder of muscle, ligament, and fascia

AHA: 4Q, '88, 11

✓4th **729 Other disorders of soft tissues**

EXCLUDES *acroparesthesia (443.89)*
carpal tunnel syndrome (354.0)
disorders of the back (720.0-724.9)
entrapment syndromes (354.0-355.9)
palindromic rheumatism (719.3)
periarthritis (726.0-726.9)
psychogenic rheumatism (306.0)

729.0 Rheumatism, unspecified and fibrositis

DEF: General term describes diseases of muscle, tendon, nerve, joint, or bone; symptoms include pain and stiffness.

729.1 Myalgia and myositis, unspecified

Fibromyositis NOS

DEF: Myalgia: muscle pain.

DEF: Myositis: inflamed voluntary muscle.

DEF: Fibromyositis: inflamed fibromuscular tissue.

729.2 Neuralgia, neuritis, and radiculitis, unspecified

EXCLUDES *brachial radiculitis (723.4)*
cervical radiculitis (723.4)
lumbosacral radiculitis (724.4)
mononeuritis (354.0-355.9)
radiculitis due to intervertebral disc involvement (722.0-722.2, 722.7)
sciatica (724.3)

DEF: Neuralgia: paroxysmal pain along nerve; symptoms include brief pain and tenderness at point nerve exits.

DEF: Neuritis: inflamed nerve, symptoms include paresthesia, paralysis and loss of reflexes at nerve site.

DEF: Radiculitis: inflamed nerve root.

✓5th **729.3 Panniculitis, unspecified**

DEF: Inflammatory reaction of subcutaneous fat; causes nodules; often develops in abdominal region.

729.30 Panniculitis, unspecified site

Weber-Christian disease

DEF: Febrile, nodular, nonsuppurative, relapsing inflammation of subcutaneous fat.

729.31 Hypertrophy of fat pad, knee

Hypertrophy of infrapatellar fat pad

729.39 Other site

EXCLUDES *panniculitis specified as (affecting):*
back (724.8)
neck (723.6)
sacral (724.8)

729.4 Fasciitis, unspecified

EXCLUDES *necrotizing fasciitis (728.86)*
nodular fasciitis (728.79)

AHA: 2Q, '94, 13

729.5 Pain in limb

729.6 Residual foreign body in soft tissue

EXCLUDES *foreign body granuloma:*
muscle (728.82)
skin and subcutaneous tissue (709.4)

● ✓5th **729.7 Nontraumatic compartment syndrome**

EXCLUDES *compartment syndrome NOS (958.90)*
traumatic compartment syndrome (958.90-958.99)

● **729.71 Nontraumatic compartment syndrome of upper extremity**

Nontraumatic compartment syndrome of shoulder, arm, forearm, wrist, hand, and fingers

● **729.72 Nontraumatic compartment syndrome of lower extremity**

Nontraumatic compartment syndrome of hip, buttock, thigh, leg, foot, and toes

● **729.73 Nontraumatic compartment syndrome of abdomen**

● **729.79 Nontraumatic compartment syndrome of other sites**

✓5th **729.8 Other musculoskeletal symptoms referable to limbs**

729.81 Swelling of limb

AHA: 4Q, '88, 6

729.82 Cramp

729.89 Other

EXCLUDES *abnormality of gait (781.2)*
tetany (781.7)
transient paralysis of limb (781.4)

AHA: 4Q, '88, 12

729.9 Other and unspecified disorders of soft tissue

Polyalgia

OSTEOPATHIES, CHONDROPATHIES, AND ACQUIRED MUSCULOSKELETAL DEFORMITIES (730-739)

✓4th **730 Osteomyelitis, periostitis, and other infections involving bone**

EXCLUDES *jaw (526.4-526.5)*
petrous bone (383.2)

Use additional code to identify organism, such as Staphylococcus (041.1)

The following fifth-digit subclassification is for use with category 730; valid digits are in [brackets] under each code. See list at beginning of chapter for definitions.

0 site unspecified
1 shoulder region
2 upper arm
3 forearm
4 hand
5 pelvic region and thigh
6 lower leg
7 ankle and foot
8 other specified sites
9 multiple sites

AHA: 4Q, '97, 43

DEF: Osteomyelitis: bacterial inflammation of bone tissue and marrow.

DEF: Periostitis: inflammation of specialized connective tissue; causes swelling of bone and aching pain.

1 ✓5th **730.0 Acute osteomyelitis** CC
[0-9]

Abscess of any bone except accessory sinus, jaw, or mastoid

Acute or subacute osteomyelitis, with or without mention of periostitis

▶Use additional code to identify major osseous defect, if applicable (731.3)◀

CC Excl: For code 730.00: 015.50-015.56, 015.70-015.76, 015.90-015.96, 017.90-017.96, 730.00-730.39, 730.80-730.99 **For code 730.01:** 015.50-015.56, 015.70-015.76, 015.90-015.96, 017.90-017.96, 730.00, 730.08-730.11, 730.18-730.21, 730.28-730.31, 730.38-730.39, 730.80-730.81, 730.88-730.91, 730.98-730.99 **For code 730.02:** 015.50-015.56, 015.70-015.76, 015.90-015.96, 017.90-017.96, 730.00, 730.08-730.10, 730.12, 730.18-730.20, 730.22, 730.28-730.30, 730.32, 730.38-730.39, 730.80, 730.82, 730.88-730.90, 730.92, 730.98-730.99 **For code 730.03:** 015.50-015.56, 015.70-015.76, 015.90-015.96, 017.90-017.96, 730.00, 730.08-730.10, 730.13, 730.18-730.20, 730.23, 730.28-730.30, 730.33, 730.38-730.39, 730.80, 730.83, 730.88-730.90, 730.93, 730.98-730.99: **For code 730.04:** 015.50-015.56, 015.70-015.76, 015.90-015.96, 017.90-017.96, 730.00, 730.08-730.10, 730.14, 730.18-730.20, 730.24, 730.28-730.30, 730.34, 730.38-730.39, 730.80, 730.84, 730.88-730.90, 730.94, 730.98-730.99 **For code 730.05:** 015.10-015.16, 015.50-015.56, 015.70-015.76, 015.90-015.96, 017.90-017.96, 730.00, 730.08-730.10, 730.15, 730.18-730.20, 730.25, 730.28-730.30, 730.35, 730.38-730.39, 730.80, 730.85, 730.88-730.90, 730.95, 730.98-730.99: **For code 730.06:** 015.20-015.26, 015.70-015.76, 015.90-015.96, 017.90-017.96, 730.00, 730.08-730.10, 730.16, 730.18-730.20, 730.26, 730.28-730.30, 730.36, 730.38-730.39, 730.80, 730.86, 730.88-730.90, 730.96, 730.98-730.99 **For code 730.07:** 015.50-015.56, 015.70-015.76, 015.90-015.96, 017.90-017.96, 730.00, 730.08-730.10, 730.17-730.20, 730.27-730.30, 730.37-730.39, 730.80, 730.87-730.90, 730.97-730.99 **For code 730.08:** 015.00-015.06, 015.50-015.56, 015.70-015.76, 015.90-015.96, 017.90-017.96, 730.00-730.39, 730.80-730.99 **For code 730.09:** 015.50-015.56, 015.70-015.76, 015.90-015.96, 017.90-017.96, 730.00-730.39, 730.80-730.99

AHA: For code 730.06: 1Q, '02, 4; **For code 730.07:** 1Q, '04, 14

1 Nonspecific PDx=0

1 ✓5th **730.1 Chronic osteomyelitis**
[0-9]

Brodie's abscess

Chronic or old osteomyelitis, with or without mention of periostitis

Sequestrum of bone

Sclerosing osteomyelitis of Garré

▶Use additional code to identify major osseous defect, if applicable (731.3)◀

EXCLUDES *aseptic necrosis of bone (733.40-733.49)*

AHA: For code 730.17: 3Q, '00, 4

1 ✓5th **730.2 Unspecified osteomyelitis**
[0-9]

Osteitis or osteomyelitis NOS, with or without mention of periostitis

▶Use additional code to identify major osseous defect, if applicable (731.3)◀

1 ✓5th **730.3 Periostitis without mention of osteomyelitis**
[0-9]

Abscess of periosteum } without mention of osteomyelitis
Periostosis }

EXCLUDES *that in secondary syphilis (091.61)*

✓5th ***730.7 Osteopathy resulting from poliomyelitis***
[0-9]

Code first underlying disease (045.0-045.9)

✓5th ***730.8 Other infections involving bone in diseases classified elsewhere*** CC
[0-9]

Code first underlying disease as:
tuberculosis (015.0-015.9)
typhoid fever (002.0)

EXCLUDES *syphilis of bone NOS (095.5)*

CC Excl: For code 730.80: See code 730.09 **CC Excl: For code 730.81:** 015.50-015.56, 015.70-015.76, 015.90-015.96, 017.90-017.96, 730.00-730.01, 730.08-730.11, 730.18-730.21, 730.28-730.31, 730.38-730.39, 730.80, 730.88-730.91, 730.98-730.99 **For code 730.82:** 015.50-015.56, 015.70-015.76, 015.90-015.96, 017.90-017.96, 730.00, 730.02, 730.08-730.10, 730.12, 730.18-730.20, 730.22, 730.28-730.30, 730.32, 730.38-730.39, 730.80, 730.88-730.90, 730.92, 730.98-730.99l: **For code 730.83:** 015.50-015.56, 015.70-015.76, 015.90-015.96, 017.90-017.96, 730.00, 730.03, 730.08-730.10, 730.13, 730.18-730.20, 730.23, 730.28-730.30, 730.33, 730.38-730.39, 730.80, 730.88-730.90, 730.93, 730.98-730.99: **For code 730.84:** 015.50-015.56, 015.70-015.76, 015.90-015.96, 017.90-017.96, 730.00, 730.04, 730.08-730.10, 730.14, 730.18-730.20, 730.24, 730.28-730.30, 730.34, 730.38-730.39, 730.80, 730.88-730.90, 730.94, 730.98-730.99 **For code 730.85:** 015.10-015.16, 015.50-015.56, 015.70-015.76, 015.90-015.96, 017.90-017.96, 730.00, 730.05, 730.08-730.10, 730.15, 730.18-730.20, 730.25, 730.28-730.30, 730.35, 730.38-730.39, 730.80, 730.88-730.90, 730.95, 730.98-730.99 **For code 730.86:** 015.20-015.26, 015.50-015.56, 015.70-015.76, 015.90-015.96, 017.90-017.96, 730.00, 730.06, 730.08-730.10, 730.16, 730.18-730.20, 730.26, 730.28-730.30, 730.36, 730.38-730.39, 730.80, 730.88-730.90, 730.96, 730.98-730.99 **For code 730.87:** 015.50-015.56, 015.70-015.76, 015.90-015.96, 017.90-017.96, 730.00, 730.07-730.10, 730.17-730.20, 730.27-730.30, 730.37-730.39, 730.80, 730.88-730.90, 730.97-730.99 **For code 730.88:** 015.00-015.06, 015.50-015.56, 015.70-015.76, 015.90-015.96, 017.90-017.96, 730.00-730.39, 730.80-730.99: **For code 730.89:** 015.50-015.56, 015.70-015.76, 015.90-015.96, 017.90-017.96, 730.00-730.39, 730.80-730.99

AHA: 2Q, '97, 16; 3Q, '91, 10

✓5th **730.9 Unspecified infection of bone** CC
[0-9]

CC Excl: For code 730.90: See code 730.89 **For code 730.91:** 015.50-015.56, 015.70-015.76, 015.90-015.96, 017.90-017.96, 730.00-730.01, 730.08-730.11, 730.18-730.21, 730.28-730.31, 730.38-730.39, 730.80-730.81, 730.88-730.90, 730.98-730.99 **For code 730.92:** 015.50-015.56, 015.70-015.76, 015.90-015.96, 017.90-017.96, 730.00, 730.02, 730.08-730.10, 730.12, 730.18-730.20, 730.22, 730.28-730.30, 730.32, 730.38-730.39, 730.80, 730.82, 730.88-730.90, 730.98-730.99: **For code 730.93:** 015.50-015.56, 015.70-015.76, 015.90-015.96, 017.90-017.96, 730.00, 730.03, 730.08-730.10, 730.13, 730.18-730.20, 730.23, 730.28-730.30, 730.33, 730.38-730.39, 730.80, 730.83, 730.88-730.90, 730.98-730.99**For code 730.94:** 015.50-015.56, 015.70-015.76, 015.90-015.96, 017.90-017.96, 730.00, 730.04, 730.08-730.10, 730.14, 730.18-730.20, 730.24, 730.28-730.30, 730.34, 730.38-730.39, 730.80, 730.84, 730.88-730.90, 730.98-730.99: **For code 730.95:** 015.10-015.16, 015.50-015.56, 015.70-015.76, 015.90-015.96, 017.90-017.96, 730.00, 730.05, 730.08-730.10, 730.15, 730.18-730.20, 730.25, 730.28-730.30, 730.35, 730.38-730.39, 730.80, 730.85, 730.88-730.90, 730.98-730.99 **For code 730.96:** 015.20-015.26, 015.50-015.56, 015.70-015.76, 015.90-015.96, 017.90-017.96, 730.00, 730.06, 730.08-730.10, 730.16, 730.18-730.20, 730.26, 730.28-730.30, 730.36, 730.38-730.39, 730.80, 730.86, 730.88-730.90, 730.98-730.99: **For code 730.97:** 015.50-015.56, 015.70-015.76, 015.90-015.96, 017.90-017.96, 730.00, 730.07-730.10, 730.17-730.20, 730.27-730.30, 730.37-730.39, 730.80, 730.87-730.90, 730.98-730.99: **For code 730.98:** 015.00-015.06, 015.50-015.56, 015.70-015.76, 015.90-015.96, 017.90-017.96, 730.00-730.39, 730.80-730.99 **For code 730.99:** 015.50-015.56, 015.70-015.76, 015.90-015.96, 017.90-017.96, 730.00-730.39, 730.80-730.99

Slipped Femoral Epiphysis

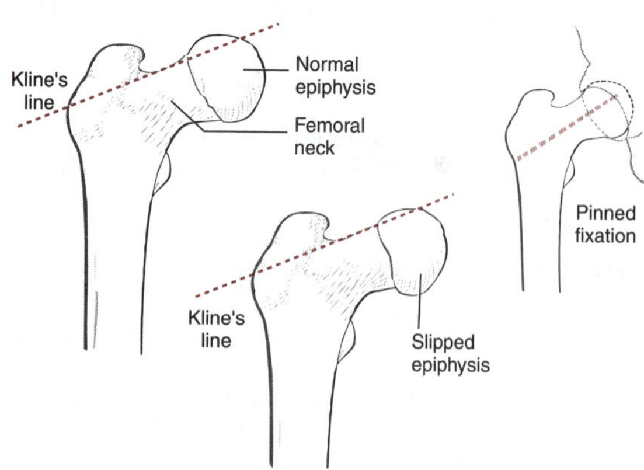

4th 731 Osteitis deformans and osteopathies associated with other disorders classified elsewhere

DEF: Osteitis deformans: Bone disease marked by episodes of increased bone loss, excessive repair attempts follow; causes weakened, deformed bones with increased mass, bowed long bones, deformed flat bones, pain and pathological fractures; may be fatal if associated with congestive heart failure, giant cell tumors or bone sarcoma; also called Paget's disease.

731.0 Osteitis deformans without mention of bone tumor
Paget's disease of bone

731.1 Osteitis deformans in diseases classified elsewhere
Code first underlying disease as:
malignant neoplasm of bone (170.0-170.9)

731.2 Hypertrophic pulmonary osteoarthropathy
Bamberger-Marie disease
DEF: Clubbing, of fingers and toes; related to enlarged ends of long bones; due to chronic lung and heart disease.

● **731.3 Major osseous defects**
Code first underlying disease, if known, such as:
aseptic necrosis (733.40-733.49)
malignant neoplasm of bone (170.0-170.9)
osteomyelitis (730.00-730.29)
osteoporosis (733.00-733.09)
peri-prosthetic osteolysis (996.45)

731.8 Other bone involvement in diseases classified elsewhere
Code first underlying disease as:
diabetes mellitus (250.8)
Use additional code to specify bone condition, such as:
acute osteomyelitis (730.00-730.09)
AHA: 1Q, '04, 14; 4Q, '97, 43; 2Q, '97, 16

4th 732 Osteochondropathies

DEF: Conditions related to both bone and cartilage, or conditions in which cartilage is converted to bone (enchondral ossification).

732.0 Juvenile osteochondrosis of spine
Juvenile osteochondrosis (of):
marginal or vertebral epiphysis (of Scheuermann)
spine NOS
Vertebral epiphysitis
EXCLUDES *adolescent postural kyphosis (737.0)*

732.1 Juvenile osteochondrosis of hip and pelvis
Coxa plana
Ischiopubic synchondrosis (of van Neck)
Osteochondrosis (juvenile) of:
acetabulum
head of femur (of Legg-Calvé-Perthes)
iliac crest (of Buchanan)
symphysis pubis (of Pierson)
Pseudocoxalgia

732.2 Nontraumatic slipped upper femoral epiphysis
Slipped upper femoral epiphysis NOS

732.3 Juvenile osteochondrosis of upper extremity
Osteochondrosis (juvenile) of:
capitulum of humerus (of Panner)
carpal lunate (of Kienbock)
hand NOS
head of humerus (of Haas)
heads of metacarpals (of Mauclaire)
lower ulna (of Burns)
radial head (of Brailsford)
upper extremity NOS

732.4 Juvenile osteochondrosis of lower extremity, excluding foot
Osteochondrosis (juvenile) of:
lower extremity NOS
primary patellar center (of Köhler)
proximal tibia (of Blount)
secondary patellar center (of Sinding-Larsen)
tibial tubercle (of Osgood-Schlatter)
Tibia vara

732.5 Juvenile osteochondrosis of foot
Calcaneal apophysitis
Epiphysitis, os calcis
Osteochondrosis (juvenile) of:
astragalus (of Diaz)
calcaneum (of Sever)
foot NOS
metatarsal
second (of Freiberg)
fifth (of Iselin)
os tibiale externum (of Haglund)
tarsal navicular (of Köhler)

732.6 Other juvenile osteochondrosis
Apophysitis, Epiphysitis, Osteochondritis, Osteochondrosis } specified as juvenile, of other site, or site NOS

732.7 Osteochondritis dissecans

732.8 Other specified forms of osteochondropathy
Adult osteochondrosis of spine

732.9 Unspecified osteochondropathy
Apophysitis, Epiphysitis, Osteochondritis, Osteochondrosis } NOS not specified as adult or juvenile, of unspecified site

4th 733 Other disorders of bone and cartilage

EXCLUDES *bone spur (726.91)*
cartilage of, or loose body in, joint (717.0-717.9, 718.0-718.9)
giant cell granuloma of jaw (526.3)
osteitis fibrosa cystica generalisata (252.01)
osteomalacia (268.2)
polyostotic fibrous dysplasia of bone (756.54)
prognathism, retrognathism (524.1)
xanthomatosis localized to bone (272.7)

5th 733.0 Osteoporosis
▶Use additional code to identify major osseous defect, if applicable (731.3)◀
DEF: Bone mass reduction that ultimately results in fractures after minimal trauma; dorsal kyphosis or loss of height often occur.

733.00 Osteoporosis, unspecified
Wedging of vertebra NOS
AHA: 3Q, '01, 19; 2Q, '98, 12

733.01 Senile osteoporosis
Postmenopausal osteoporosis

733.02 Idiopathic osteoporosis

733.03 Disuse osteoporosis

733.09 Other
Drug-induced osteoporosis
Use additional E code to identify drug
AHA: 4Q, '03, 108

✓5th **733.1 Pathologic fracture**
Spontaneous fracture
EXCLUDES *stress fracture (733.93-733.95)*
traumatic fracture (800-829)
AHA: 4Q, '93, 25; N-D, '86, 10; N-D, '85, 16
DEF: Fracture due to bone structure weakening by pathological processes (e.g., osteoporosis, neoplasms and osteomalacia).

733.10 Pathologic fracture, unspecified site CC
CC Excl: 733.10-733.19, 733.93-733.95

733.11 Pathologic fracture of humerus CC
CC Excl: See code 733.10

733.12 Pathologic fracture of distal radius and ulna CC
Wrist NOS
CC Excl: See code 733.10

733.13 Pathologic fracture of vertebrae CC
Collapse of vertebra NOS
CC Excl: See code 733.10
AHA: 3Q, '99, 5
DRG 239

733.14 Pathologic fracture of neck of femur CC
Femur NOS Hip NOS
CC Excl: See code 733.10
AHA: 1Q, '01, 1; 1Q, '96, 16

733.15 Pathologic fracture of other specified part of femur CC
CC Excl: See code 733.10
AHA: 2Q, '98, 12

733.16 Pathologic fracture of tibia or fibula CC
Ankle NOS
CC Excl: See code 733.10

733.19 Pathologic fracture of other specified site CC
CC Excl: See code 733.10

✓4th **733.2 Cyst of bone**
733.20 Cyst of bone (localized), unspecified
733.21 Solitary bone cyst
Unicameral bone cyst
733.22 Aneurysmal bone cyst
DEF: Solitary bone lesion, bulges into periosteum; marked by calcified rim.

733.29 Other
Fibrous dysplasia (monostotic)
EXCLUDES *cyst of jaw (526.0-526.2, 526.89)*
osteitis fibrosa cystica (252.01)
polyostotic fibrousdyplasia of bone (756.54)

733.3 Hyperostosis of skull
Hyperostosis interna frontalis
Leontiasis ossium
DEF: Abnormal bone growth on inner aspect of cranial bones.

✓5th **733.4 Aseptic necrosis of bone**
EXCLUDES *osteochondropathies (732.0-732.9)*
▶Use additional code to identify major osseous defect, if applicable (731.3)◀
DEF: Infarction of bone tissue due to a nonfectious etiology, such as a fracture, ischemic disorder or administration of immunosuppressive drugs; leads to degenerative joint disease or nonunion of fractures.

733.40 Aseptic necrosis of bone, site unspecified
733.41 Head of humerus
733.42 Head and neck of femur
Femur NOS
EXCLUDES *Legg-Calvé-Perthes disease (732.1)*
733.43 Medial femoral condyle
733.44 Talus
733.49 Other

733.5 Osteitis condensans
Piriform sclerosis of ilium
DEF: Idiopathic condition marked by low back pain; associated with oval or triangular sclerotic, opaque bone next to sacroiliac joints in the ileum.

733.6 Tietze's disease
Costochondral junction syndrome
Costochondritis
DEF: Painful, idiopathic, nonsuppurative, swollen costal cartilage sometimes confused with cardiac symptoms because the anterior chest pain resembles that of coronary artery disease.

733.7 Algoneurodystrophy
Disuse atrophy of bone Sudeck's atrophy
DEF: Painful, idiopathic.

✓5th **733.8 Malunion and nonunion of fracture**
AHA: 2Q, '94, 5

733.81 Malunion of fracture CC
CC Excl: 733.81-733.82

733.82 Nonunion of fracture CC
Pseudoarthrosis (bone)
CC Excl: See code 733.81

✓5th **733.9 Other and unspecified disorders of bone and cartilage**
733.90 Disorder of bone and cartilage, unspecified
733.91 Arrest of bone development or growth
Epiphyseal arrest
733.92 Chondromalacia
Chondromalacia:
NOS
localized, except patella
systemic
tibial plateau
EXCLUDES *chondromalacia of patella (717.7)*
DEF: Articular cartilage softening.

733.93 Stress fracture of tibia or fibula CC
Stress reaction of tibia or fibula
CC Excl: 733.10-733.19, 733.93-733.95
AHA: 4Q, '01, 48

733.94 Stress fracture of the metatarsals CC
Stress reaction of metatarsals
CC Excl: See code 733.93
AHA: 4Q, '01, 48

733.95 Stress fracture of other bone CC
Stress reaction of other bone
CC Excl: See code 733.93
AHA: 4Q, '01, 48

733.99 Other
Diaphysitis
Hypertrophy of bone
Relapsing polychondritis
AHA: J-F, '87, 14

734 Flat foot
Pes planus (acquired)
Talipes planus (acquired)
EXCLUDES *congenital (754.61)*
rigid flat foot (754.61)
spastic (everted) flat foot (754.61)

✓4th **735 Acquired deformities of toe**
EXCLUDES *congenital (754.60-754.69, 755.65-755.66)*

735.0 Hallux valgus (acquired)
DEF: Angled displacement of the great toe, causing it to ride over or under other toes.

Acquired Deformities of Toe

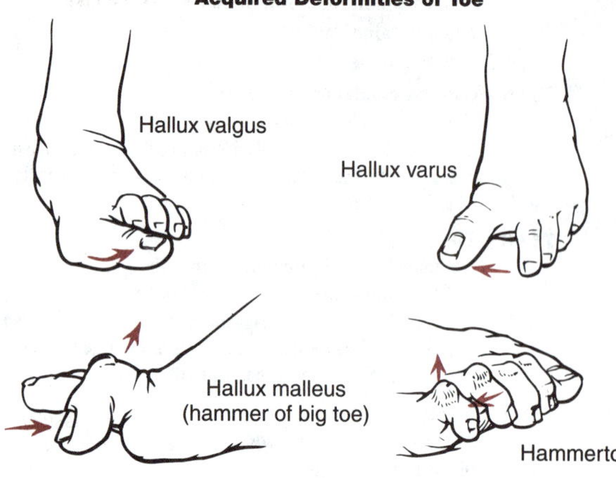

735.1 Hallux varus (acquired)

DEF: Angled displacement of the great toe toward the body midline, away from the other toes.

735.2 Hallux rigidus

DEF: Limited flexion movement at metatarsophalangeal joint of great toe; due to degenerative joint disease.

735.3 Hallux malleus

DEF: Extended proximal phalanx, flexed distal phalanges, of great toe; foot resembles claw or hammer.

735.4 Other hammer toe (acquired)

735.5 Claw toe (acquired)

DEF: Hyperextended proximal phalanges, flexed middle and distal phalanges.

735.8 Other acquired deformities of toe

735.9 Unspecified acquired deformity of toe

✓4th **736 Other acquired deformities of limbs**

EXCLUDES *congenital (754.3-755.9)*

✓5th **736.0 Acquired deformities of forearm, excluding fingers**

736.00 Unspecified deformity

Deformity of elbow, forearm, hand, or wrist (acquired) NOS

736.01 Cubitus valgus (acquired)

DEF: Deviation of the elbow away from the body midline upon extension; it occurs when the palm is turning outward.

736.02 Cubitus varus (acquired)

DEF: Elbow joint displacement angled laterally; when the forearm is extended, it is deviated toward the midline of the body; also called "gun stock" deformity.

736.03 Valgus deformity of wrist (acquired)

DEF: Abnormal angulation away from the body midline.

736.04 Varus deformity of wrist (acquired)

DEF: Abnormal angulation toward the body midline.

736.05 Wrist drop (acquired)

DEF: Inability to extend the hand at the wrist due to extensor muscle paralysis

736.06 Claw hand (acquired)

DEF: Flexion and atrophy of the hand and fingers; found in ulnar nerve lesions, syringomyelia, and leprosy.

736.07 Club hand, acquired

DEF: Twisting of the hand out of shape or position; caused by the congenital absence of the ulna or radius.

736.09 Other

736.1 Mallet finger

DEF: Permanently flexed distal phalanx.

✓5th **736.2 Other acquired deformities of finger**

736.20 Unspecified deformity

Deformity of finger (acquired) NOS

736.21 Boutonniere deformity

DEF: A deformity of the finger caused by flexion of the proximal interphalangeal joint and hyperextension of the distal joint; also called buttonhole deformity.

736.22 Swan-neck deformity

DEF: Flexed distal and hyperextended proximal interphalangeal joint.

736.29 Other

EXCLUDES *trigger finger (727.03)*

AHA: ▶2Q, '05, 7;◀ 2Q, '89, 13

✓5th **736.3 Acquired deformities of hip**

736.30 Unspecified deformity

Deformity of hip (acquired) NOS

736.31 Coxa valga (acquired)

DEF: Increase of at least 140 degrees in the angle formed by the axis of the head and the neck of the femur, and the axis of its shaft.

736.32 Coxa vara (acquired)

DEF: The bending downward of the neck of the femur: causing difficulty in movement; a right angle or less may be formed by the axis of the head and neck of the femur, and the axis of its shaft.

736.39 Other

AHA: 2Q, '91, 18

✓5th **736.4 Genu valgum or varum (acquired)**

736.41 Genu valgum (acquired)

DEF: Abnormally close together and an abnormally large space between the ankles; also called "knock-knees."

736.42 Genu varum (acquired)

DEF: Abnormally separated knees and the inward bowing of the legs; it is also called "bowlegs."

736.5 Genu recurvatum (acquired)

DEF: Hyperextended knees; also called "backknee."

736.6 Other acquired deformities of knee

Deformity of knee (acquired) NOS

Acquired Deformities of Forearm

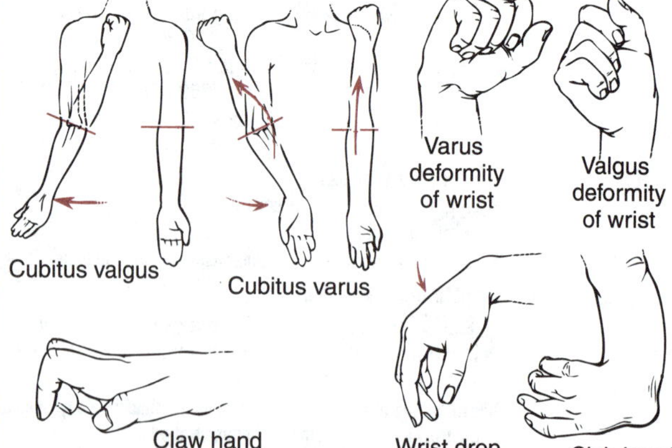

Acquired Deformities of Hip

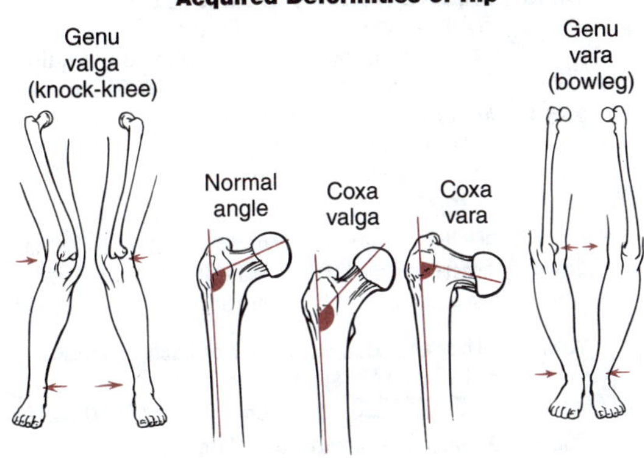

Acquired Deformities of Lower Limb

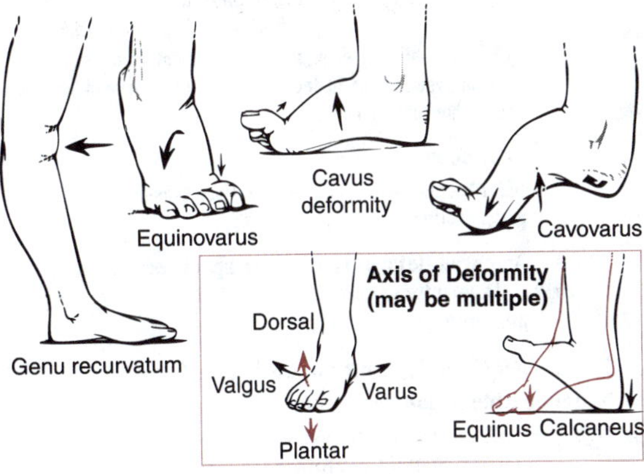

✓5th **736.7 Other acquired deformities of ankle and foot**

EXCLUDES *deformities of toe (acquired) (735.0-735.9)*
pes planus (acquired) (734)

736.70 Unspecified deformity of ankle and foot, acquired

736.71 Acquired equinovarus deformity
Clubfoot, acquired
EXCLUDES *clubfoot not specified as acquired (754.5-754.7)*

736.72 Equinus deformity of foot, acquired
DEF: A plantar flexion deformity that forces people to walk on their toes.

736.73 Cavus deformity of foot
EXCLUDES *that with claw foot (736.74)*
DEF: Abnormally high longitudinal arch of the foot.

736.74 Claw foot, acquired
DEF: High foot arch with hyperextended toes at metatarsophalangeal joint and flexed toes at distal joints; also called "main en griffe."

736.75 Cavovarus deformity of foot, acquired
DEF: Inward turning of the heel from the midline of the leg and an abnormally high longitudinal arch.

736.76 Other calcaneus deformity

736.79 Other
Acquired:
pes } not elsewhere classified
talipes } not elsewhere classified

✓5th **736.8 Acquired deformities of other parts of limbs**

736.81 Unequal leg length (acquired)

736.89 Other
Deformity (acquired):
arm or leg, not elsewhere classified
shoulder

736.9 Acquired deformity of limb, site unspecified

✓4th **737 Curvature of spine**

EXCLUDES *congenital (754.2)*

737.0 Adolescent postural kyphosis
EXCLUDES *osteochondrosis of spine (juvenile) (732.0)*
adult (732.8)

✓5th **737.1 Kyphosis (acquired)**

737.10 Kyphosis (acquired) (postural)

737.11 Kyphosis due to radiation

737.12 Kyphosis, postlaminectomy
AHA: J-F, '87, 7

737.19 Other
EXCLUDES *that associated with conditions classifiable elsewhere (737.41)*

✓5th **737.2 Lordosis (acquired)**

DEF: Swayback appearance created by an abnormally increased spinal curvature; it is also referred to as "hollow back" or "saddle back."

737.20 Lordosis (acquired) (postural)

737.21 Lordosis, postlaminectomy

737.22 Other postsurgical lordosis

737.29 Other
EXCLUDES *that associated with conditions classifiable elsewhere (737.42)*

✓5th **737.3 Kyphoscoliosis and scoliosis**

DEF: Kyphoscoliosis: backward and lateral curvature of the spinal column; it is found in vertebral osteochondrosis.

DEF: Scoliosis: an abnormal deviation of the spine to the left or right of the midline

737.30 Scoliosis [and kyphoscoliosis], idiopathic
AHA: 3Q, '03, 19

737.31 Resolving infantile idiopathic scoliosis

737.32 Progressive infantile idiopathic scoliosis
AHA: 3Q, '02, 12

737.33 Scoliosis due to radiation

737.34 Thoracogenic scoliosis

737.39 Other
EXCLUDES *that associated with conditions classifiable elsewhere (737.43)*
that in kyphoscoliotic heart disease (416.1)

AHA: 2Q, '02, 16

Kyphosis and Lordosis

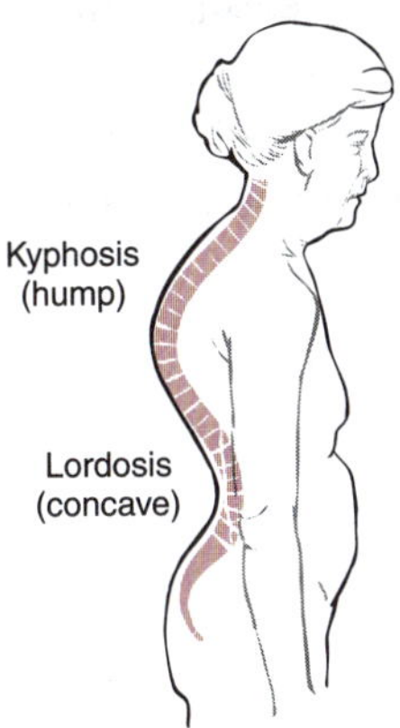

Scoliosis and Kyphoscoliosis

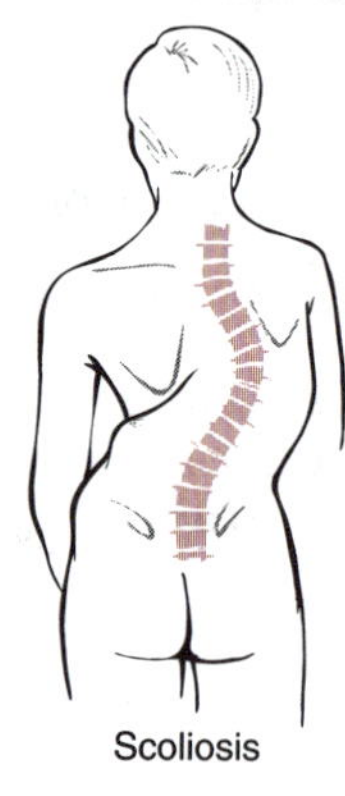

Scoliosis

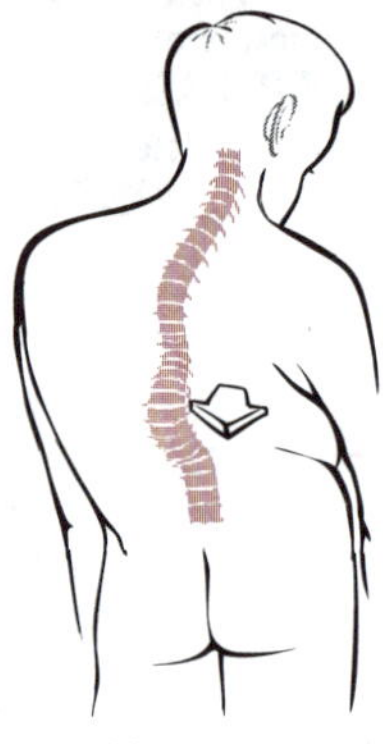

Kyphoscoliosis

✓5th **737.4 Curvature of spine associated with other conditions**

Code first associated condition as:

- Charcôt-Marie-Tooth disease (356.1)
- mucopolysaccharidosis (277.5)
- neurofibromatosis (237.7)
- osteitis deformans (731.0)
- osteitis fibrosa cystica (252.01)
- osteoporosis (733.00-733.09)
- poliomyelitis (138)
- tuberculosis [Pott's curvature] (015.0)

737.40 *Curvature of spine, unspecified*

737.41 *Kyphosis*

737.42 *Lordosis*

737.43 *Scoliosis*

737.8 Other curvatures of spine

737.9 Unspecified curvature of spine

Curvature of spine (acquired) (idiopathic) NOS
Hunchback, acquired

EXCLUDES *deformity of spine NOS (738.5)*

✓4th **738 Other acquired deformity**

EXCLUDES *congenital (754.0-756.9, 758.0-759.9)*
dentofacial anomalies (524.0-524.9)

738.0 Acquired deformity of nose

Deformity of nose (acquired)
Overdevelopment of nasal bones

EXCLUDES *deflected or deviated nasal septum (470)*

✓5th **738.1 Other acquired deformity of head**

738.10 Unspecified deformity

738.11 Zygomatic hyperplasia

DEF: Abnormal enlargement of the zygoma (processus zygomaticus temporalis).

738.12 Zygomatic hypoplasia

DEF: Underdevelopment of the zygoma (processus zygomaticus temporalis).

738.19 Other specified deformity

AHA: ►1Q, '06, 6;◄ 2Q, '03, 13

738.2 Acquired deformity of neck

738.3 Acquired deformity of chest and rib

Deformity:
- chest (acquired)
- rib (acquired)

Pectus:
- carinatum, acquired
- excavatum, acquired

738.4 Acquired spondylolisthesis

Degenerative spondylolisthesis
Spondylolysis, acquired

EXCLUDES *congenital (756.12)*

DEF: Vertebra displaced forward over another; due to bilateral defect in vertebral arch, eroded articular surface of posterior facts and elongated pedicle between fifth lumbar vertebra and sacrum.

738.5 Other acquired deformity of back or spine

Deformity of spine NOS

EXCLUDES *curvature of spine (737.0-737.9)*

738.6 Acquired deformity of pelvis

Pelvic obliquity

EXCLUDES *intrapelvic protrusion of acetabulum (718.6)*
that in relation to labor and delivery (653.0-653.4, 653.8-653.9)

DEF: Pelvic obliquity: slanting or inclination of the pelvis at an angle between 55 and 60 degrees between the plane of the pelvis and the horizontal plane.

738.7 Cauliflower ear

DEF: Abnormal external ear; due to injury, subsequent perichondritis.

738.8 Acquired deformity of other specified site

Deformity of clavicle

AHA: 2Q, '01, 15

738.9 Acquired deformity of unspecified site

✓4th **739 Nonallopathic lesions, not elsewhere classified**

INCLUDES segmental dysfunction
somatic dysfunction

DEF: Disability, loss of function or abnormality of a body part that is neither classifiable to a particular system nor brought about therapeutically to counteract another disease.

739.0 Head region

Occipitocervical region

739.1 Cervical region

Cervicothoracic region

739.2 Thoracic region

Thoracolumbar region

739.3 Lumbar region

Lumbosacral region

739.4 Sacral region

Sacrococcygeal region Sacroiliac region

739.5 Pelvic region

Hip region Pubic region

739.6 Lower extremities

739.7 Upper extremities

Acromioclavicular region
Sternoclavicular region

739.8 Rib cage

Costochondral region Sternochondral region
Costovertebral region

739.9 Abdomen and other

AHA: 2Q, '89, 14

14. CONGENITAL ANOMALIES (740-759)

740 Anencephalus and similar anomalies

740.0 Anencephalus

Acrania
Amyelencephalus
Hemicephaly
Hemianencephaly

DEF: Fetus without cerebrum, cerebellum and flat bones of skull.

740.1 Craniorachischisis

DEF: Congenital slit in cranium and vertebral column

740.2 Iniencephaly

DEF: Spinal cord passes through enlarged occipital bone (foramen magnum); absent vertebral bone layer and spinal processes; resulting in both reduction in number and proper fusion of the vertebrae.

741 Spina bifida

EXCLUDES *spina bifida occulta (756.17)*

The following fifth-digit subclassification is for use with category 741:

- **0 unspecified region**
- **1 cervical region**
- **2 dorsal [thoracic] region**
- **3 lumbar region**

AHA: 3Q, '94, 7

DEF: Lack of closure of spinal cord's bony encasement; marked by cord protrusion into lumbosacral area; evident by elevated alpha-fetoprotein of amniotic fluid

741.0 With hydrocephalus CC

Arnold-Chiari syndrome, type II
Any condition classifiable to 741.9 with any condition classifiable to 742.3
Chiari malformation, type II

CC Excl: 741.00-741.93, 742.59-742.9, 759.7-759.89

AHA: 4Q, '97, 51; 4Q, '94, 37; S-O, '87, 10

741.9 Without mention of hydrocephalus CC

Hydromeningocele (spinal)
Hydromyelocele
Meningocele (spinal)
Meningomyelocele
Myelocele
Myelocystocele
Rachischisis
Spina bifida (aperta)
Syringomyelocele

CC Excl: See code 741.0

742 Other congenital anomalies of nervous system

EXCLUDES *congenital central alveolar hypoventilation syndrome (327.25)*

742.0 Encephalocele

Encephalocystocele
Encephalomyelocele
Hydroencephalocele
Hydromeningocele, cranial
Meningocele, cerebral
Meningoencephalocele

AHA: 4Q, '94, 37

DEF: Brain tissue protrudes through skull defect.

Spina Bifida

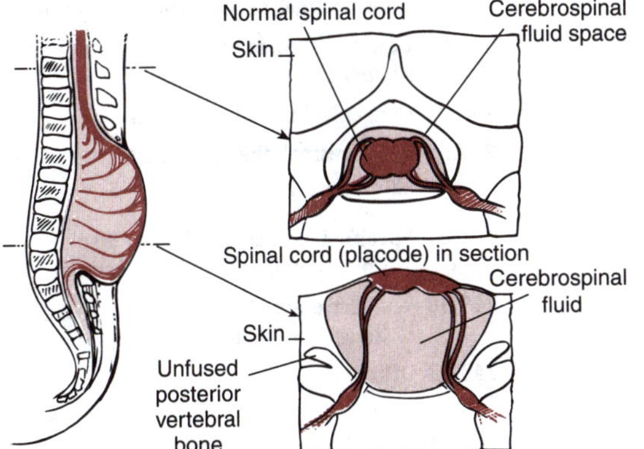

Normal Ventricles and Hydrocephalus

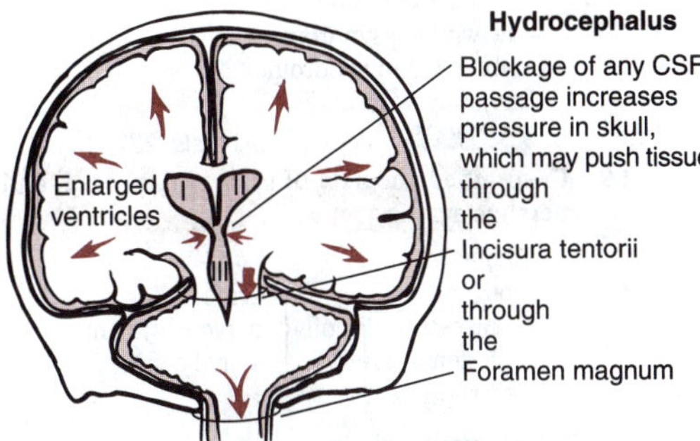

742.1 Microcephalus

Hydromicrocephaly
Micrencephaly

DEF: Extremely small head or brain.

742.2 Reduction deformities of brain

Absence, Agenesis, Aplasia, Hypoplasia } of part of brain

Agyria
Arhinencephaly
Holoprosencephaly
Microgyria

AHA: 3Q, '03, 15; 4Q, '94, 37

742.3 Congenital hydrocephalus

Aqueduct of Sylvius:
- anomaly
- obstruction, congenital
- stenosis

Atresia of foramina of Magendie and Luschka
Hydrocephalus in newborn

EXCLUDES *hydrocephalus:*
- *acquired (331.3-331.4)*
- *due to congenital toxoplasmosis (771.2)*
- *with any condition classifiable to 741.9 (741.0)*

AHA: ►4Q, '05, 83◄

DEF: Fluid accumulation within the skull; involves subarachnoid (external) or ventricular (internal) brain spaces.

742.4 Other specified anomalies of brain

Congenital cerebral cyst
Macroencephaly
Macrogyria
Megalencephaly
Multiple anomalies of brain NOS
Porencephaly
Ulegyria

AHA: 1Q, '99, 9; 3Q, '92, 12

742.5 Other specified anomalies of spinal cord

742.51 Diastematomyelia

DEF: Congenital anomaly often associated with spina bifida; the spinal cord is separated into halves by a bony tissue resembling a "spike" (a spicule), each half surrounded by a dural sac.

742.53 Hydromyelia
Hydrorhachis
DEF: Dilated central spinal cord canal; characterized by increased fluid accumulation.

742.59 Other
Amyelia
Atelomyelia
Congenital anomaly of spinal meninges
Defective development of cauda equina
Hypoplasia of spinal cord
Myelatelia
Myelodysplasia
AHA: 2Q, '91, 14; 1Q, '89, 10

742.8 Other specified anomalies of nervous system
Agenesis of nerve
Displacement of brachial plexus
Familial dysautonomia
Jaw-winking syndrome
Marcus-Gunn syndrome
Riley-Day syndrome
EXCLUDES *neurofibromatosis (237.7)*

742.9 Unspecified anomaly of brain, spinal cord, and nervous system
Anomaly, Congenital: disease, lesion, Deformity of: brain, nervous system, spinal cord

✓4th **743 Congenital anomalies of eye**

✓5th **743.0 Anophthalmos**
DEF: Complete absence of the eyes or the presence of vestigial eyes.

743.00 Clinical anophthalmos, unspecified
Agenesis / Congenital absence } of eye
Anophthalmos NOS

743.03 Cystic eyeball, congenital

743.06 Cryptophthalmos
DEF: Eyelids continue over eyeball, results in apparent absence of eyelids.

✓5th **743.1 Microphthalmos**
Dysplasia / Hypoplasia } of eye
Rudimentary eye
DEF: Abnormally small eyeballs, may be opacities of cornea and lens, scarring of choroid and retina.

743.10 Microphthalmos, unspecified

743.11 Simple microphthalmos

743.12 Microphthalmos associated with other anomalies of eye and adnexa

✓5th **743.2 Buphthalmos**
Glaucoma: congenital, newborn
Hydrophthalmos
EXCLUDES *glaucoma of childhood (365.14)*
traumatic glaucoma due to birth injury (767.8)
DEF: Distended, enlarged fibrous coats of eye; due to intraocular pressure of congenital glaucoma.

743.20 Buphthalmos, unspecified

743.21 Simple buphthalmos

743.22 Buphthalmos associated with other ocular anomalies
Keratoglobus, congenital / Megalocornea } associated with buphthalmos

✓5th **743.3 Congenital cataract and lens anomalies**
EXCLUDES *infantile cataract (366.00-366.09)*
DEF: Opaque eye lens.

743.30 Congenital cataract, unspecified

743.31 Capsular and subcapsular cataract

743.32 Cortical and zonular cataract

743.33 Nuclear cataract

743.34 Total and subtotal cataract, congenital

743.35 Congenital aphakia
Congenital absence of lens

743.36 Anomalies of lens shape
Microphakia
Spherophakia

743.37 Congenital ectopic lens

743.39 Other

✓5th **743.4 Coloboma and other anomalies of anterior segment**
DEF: Coloboma: ocular tissue defect associated with defect of ocular fetal intraocular fissure; may cause small pit on optic disk, major defects of iris, ciliary body, choroid, and retina.

743.41 Anomalies of corneal size and shape
Microcornea
EXCLUDES *that associated with buphthalmos (743.22)*

743.42 Corneal opacities, interfering with vision, congenital

743.43 Other corneal opacities, congenital

743.44 Specified anomalies of anterior chamber, chamber angle, and related structures
Anomaly: Axenfeld's, Peters'
Anomaly: Rieger's

743.45 Aniridia
AHA: 3Q, '02, 20
DEF: Incompletely formed or absent iris; affects both eyes; dominant trait; also called congenital hyperplasia of iris.

743.46 Other specified anomalies of iris and ciliary body
Anisocoria, congenital
Atresia of pupil
Coloboma of iris
Corectopia

743.47 Specified anomalies of sclera

743.48 Multiple and combined anomalies of anterior segment

743.49 Other

✓5th **743.5 Congenital anomalies of posterior segment**

743.51 Vitreous anomalies
Congenital vitreous opacity

743.52 Fundus coloboma
DEF: Absent retinal and choroidal tissue; occurs in lower fundus; a bright white ectatic zone of exposed sclera extends into and changes the optic disk.

743.53 Chorioretinal degeneration, congenital

743.54 Congenital folds and cysts of posterior segment

743.55 Congenital macular changes

743.56 Other retinal changes, congenital
AHA: 3Q, '99, 12

743.57 Specified anomalies of optic disc
Coloboma of optic disc (congenital)

743.58 Vascular anomalies
Congenital retinal aneurysm

743.59 Other

✓5th **743.6 Congenital anomalies of eyelids, lacrimal system, and orbit**

743.61 Congenital ptosis
DEF: Drooping of eyelid.

743.62 Congenital deformities of eyelids
Ablepharon
Absence of eyelid
Accessory eyelid
Congenital:
ectropion
entropion
AHA: 1Q, '00, 22

743.63 Other specified congenital anomalies of eyelid
Absence, agenesis, of cilia

743.64 Specified congenital anomalies of lacrimal gland

743.65 Specified congenital anomalies of lacrimal passages
Absence, agenesis of:
lacrimal apparatus
punctum lacrimale
Accessory lacrimal canal

743.66 Specified congenital anomalies of orbit

743.69 Other
Accessory eye muscles

743.8 Other specified anomalies of eye
EXCLUDES *congenital nystagmus (379.51)*
ocular albinism (270.2)
▶*optic nerve hypoplasia (377.43)*◀
retinitis pigmentosa (362.74)

743.9 Unspecified anomaly of eye
Congenital:
anomaly NOS } of eye [any part]
deformity NOS }

✓4th **744 Congenital anomalies of ear, face, and neck**
EXCLUDES *anomaly of:*
cervical spine (754.2, 756.10-756.19)
larynx (748.2-748.3)
nose (748.0-748.1)
parathyroid gland (759.2)
thyroid gland (759.2)
cleft lip (749.10-749.25)

✓5th **744.0 Anomalies of ear causing impairment of hearing**
EXCLUDES *congenital deafness without mention of cause (389.0-389.9)*

744.00 Unspecified anomaly of ear with impairment of hearing

744.01 Absence of external ear
Absence of:
auditory canal (external)
auricle (ear) (with stenosis or atresia of auditory canal)

744.02 Other anomalies of external ear with impairment of hearing
Atresia or stricture of auditory canal (external)

744.03 Anomaly of middle ear, except ossicles
Atresia or stricture of osseous meatus (ear)

744.04 Anomalies of ear ossicles
Fusion of ear ossicles

744.05 Anomalies of inner ear
Congenital anomaly of:
membranous labyrinth
organ of Corti

744.09 Other
Absence of ear, congenital

744.1 Accessory auricle
Accessory tragus
Polyotia
Preauricular appendage
Supernumerary:
ear
lobule
DEF: Redundant tissue or structures of ear.

✓5th **744.2 Other specified anomalies of ear**
EXCLUDES *that with impairment of hearing (744.00-744.09)*

744.21 Absence of ear lobe, congenital

744.22 Macrotia
DEF: Abnormally large pinna of ear.

744.23 Microtia
DEF: Hypoplasia of pinna; associated with absent or closed auditory canal.

744.24 Specified anomalies of Eustachian tube
Absence of Eustachian tube

744.29 Other
Bat ear
Darwin's tubercle
Pointed ear
Prominence of auricle
Ridge ear
EXCLUDES *preauricular sinus (744.46)*

744.3 Unspecified anomaly of ear
Congenital:
anomaly NOS } of ear, not elsewhere classified
deformity NOS }

✓5th **744.4 Branchial cleft cyst or fistula; preauricular sinus**

744.41 Branchial cleft sinus or fistula
Branchial:
sinus (external) (internal)
vestige
DEF: Cyst due to failed closure of embryonic branchial cleft.

744.42 Branchial cleft cyst

744.43 Cervical auricle

744.46 Preauricular sinus or fistula

744.47 Preauricular cyst

744.49 Other
Fistula (of):
auricle, congenital
cervicoaural

744.5 Webbing of neck
Pterygium colli
DEF: Thick, triangular skinfold, stretches from lateral side of neck across shoulder; associated with Turner's and Noonan's syndromes.

✓5th **744.8 Other specified anomalies of face and neck**

744.81 Macrocheilia
Hypertrophy of lip, congenital
DEF: Abnormally large lips.

744.82 Microcheilia
DEF: Abnormally small lips.

744.83 Macrostomia
DEF: Bilateral or unilateral anomaly, of mouth due to malformed maxillary and mandibular processes; results in mouth extending toward ear.

744.84 Microstomia
DEF: Abnormally small mouth.

744.89 Other
EXCLUDES *congenital fistula of lip (750.25)*
musculoskeletal anomalies (754.0-754.1, 756.0)

744.9 Unspecified anomalies of face and neck
Congenital:
anomaly NOS } of face [any part] or neck [any part]
deformity NOS }

Congenital Anomalies

743.6–744.9

✓4th ✓5th Additional Digit Required   Nonspecific PDx   Unacceptable PDx   Manifestation Code   MSP Medicare Secondary Payer   ▶◀ Revised Text   ● New Code   ▲ Revised Code Title

Heart Defects

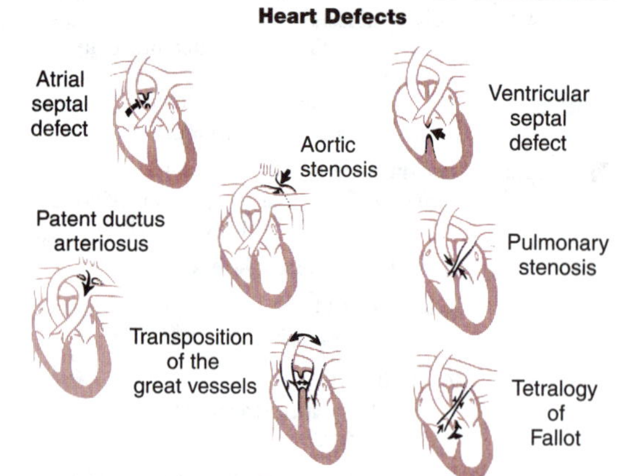

745 Bulbus cordis anomalies and anomalies of cardiac septal closure

745.0 Common truncus CC

Absent septum } between aorta and
Communication (abnormal) } pulmonary artery

Aortic septal defect
Common aortopulmonary trunk
Persistent truncus arteriosus

CC Excl: 429.71, 429.79, 745.0-745.9, 746.89, 746.9, 747.83-747.9, 759.7-759.89

745.1 Transposition of great vessels

745.10 Complete transposition of great vessels CC

Transposition of great vessels:
NOS
classical

CC Excl: See code 745.0

745.11 Double outlet right ventricle CC

Dextratransposition of aorta
Incomplete transposition of great vessels
Origin of both great vessels from right ventricle
Taussig-Bing syndrome or defect

CC Excl: See code 745.0

745.12 Corrected transposition of great vessels CC

CC Excl: See code 745.0

745.19 Other CC

CC Excl: See code 745.0

745.2 Tetralogy of Fallot CC

Fallot's pentalogy
Ventricular septal defect with pulmonary stenosis or atresia, dextraposition of aorta, and hypertrophy of right ventricle

EXCLUDES *Fallot's triad (746.09)*

CC Excl: See code 745.0

DEF: Obstructed cardiac outflow causes pulmonary stenosis, interventricular septal defect and right ventricular hypertrophy.

745.3 Common ventricle CC

Cor triloculare biatriatum
Single ventricle

CC Excl: See code 745.0

745.4 Ventricular septal defect CC

Eisenmenger's defect or complex
Gerbo dedefect
Interventricular septal defect
Left ventricular-right atrial communication
Roger's disease

EXCLUDES *common atrioventricular canal type (745.69)*
single ventricle (745.3)

CC Excl: See code 745.0

745.5 Ostium secundum type atrial septal defect

Defect:
atrium secundum
fossa ovalis

Patent or persistent:
foramen ovale
ostium secundum

Lutembacher's syndrome

DEF: Opening in atrial septum due to failure of the septum secondum and the endocardial cushions to fuse; there is a rim of septum surrounding the defect.

745.6 Endocardial cushion defects

DEF: Atrial and/or ventricular septal defects causing abnormal fusion of cushions in atrioventricular canal.

745.60 Endocardial cushion defect, unspecified type CC

CC Excl: See code 745.0

DEF: Septal defect due to imperfect fusion of endocardial cushions.

745.61 Ostium primum defect

Persistent ostium primum

DEF: Opening in low, posterior septum primum; causes cleft in basal portion of atrial septum; associated with cleft mitral valve.

745.69 Other CC

Absence of atrial septum
Atrioventricular canal type ventricular septal defect
Common atrioventricular canal
Common atrium

CC Excl: See code 745.0

745.7 Cor biloculare CC

Absence of atrial and ventricular septa

CC Excl: See code 745.0

DEF: Atrial and ventricular septal defect; marked by heart with two cardiac chambers (one atrium, one ventricle), and one atrioventricular valve.

745.8 Other

745.9 Unspecified defect of septal closure

Septal defect NOS

746 Other congenital anomalies of heart

EXCLUDES *endocardial fibroelastosis (425.3)*

746.0 Anomalies of pulmonary valve

EXCLUDES *infundibular or subvalvular pulmonic stenosis (746.83)*
tetralogy of Fallot (745.2)

746.00 Pulmonary valve anomaly, unspecified

746.01 Atresia, congenital CC

Congenital absence of pulmonary valve

CC Excl: 746.00-746.09, 746.89, 746.9, 747.83-747.9, 759.7-759.89

746.02 Stenosis, congenital CC

CC Excl: See code 746.01

AHA: 1Q, '04, 16

DEF: Stenosis of opening between pulmonary artery and right ventricle; causes obstructed blood outflow from right ventricle.

746.09 Other

Congenital insufficiency of pulmonary valve
Fallot's triad or trilogy

746.1 Tricuspid atresia and stenosis, congenital CC

Absence of tricuspid valve

CC Excl: 746.1-746.7, 746.89, 746.9, 747.83-747.9, 759.7-759.89

746.2 Ebstein's anomaly CC

CC Excl: See code 746.1

DEF: Malformation of the tricuspid valve characterized by septal and posterior leaflets attaching to the wall of the right ventricle; causing the right ventricle to fuse with the atrium producing a large right atrium and a small ventricle; causes a malfunction of the right ventricle with accompanying complications such as heart failure and abnormal cardiac rhythm.

746.3 Congenital stenosis of aortic valve CC

Congenital aortic stenosis

EXCLUDES *congenital:*
subaortic stenosis (746.81)
supravalvular aortic stenosis (747.22)

CC Excl: See code 746.1

AHA: 4Q, '88, 8

DEF: Stenosis of orifice of aortic valve; obstructs blood outflow from left ventricle.

746.4 Congenital insufficiency of aortic valve CC

Bicuspid aortic valve
Congenital aortic insufficiency

CC Excl: See code 746.1

DEF: Impaired functioning of aortic valve due to incomplete closure; causes backflow (regurgitation) of blood from aorta to left ventricle.

746.5 Congenital mitral stenosis CC

Fused commissure } of mitral valve
Parachute deformity } of mitral valve
Supernumerary cusps } of mitral valve

CC Excl: See code 746.1

DEF: Stenosis of left atrioventricular orifice.

746.6 Congenital mitral insufficiency CC

CC Excl: See code 746.1

DEF: Impaired functioning of mitral valve due to incomplete closure; causes backflow of blood from left ventricle to left atrium.

746.7 Hypoplastic left heart syndrome CC

Atresia, or marked hypoplasia, of aortic orifice or valve, with hypoplasia of ascending aorta and defective development of left ventricle (with mitral valve atresia)

CC Excl: See code 746.1

✓5th **746.8 Other specified anomalies of heart**

746.81 Subaortic stenosis CC

CC Excl: 746.81-746.84, 746.89, 746.9, 747.83-747.9, 759.7-759.89

DEF: Stenosis, of left ventricular outflow tract due to fibrous tissue ring or septal hypertrophy below aortic valve.

746.82 Cor triatriatum CC

CC Excl: See code 746.81

DEF: Transverse septum divides left atrium due to failed resorption of embryonic common pulmonary vein; results in three atrial chambers.

746.83 Infundibular pulmonic stenosis CC

Subvalvular pulmonic stenosis

CC Excl: See code 746.81

DEF: Stenosis of right ventricle outflow tract within infundibulum due to fibrous diaphragm below valve or long, narrow fibromuscular channel.

746.84 Obstructive anomalies of heart, not elsewhere classified CC

Uhl's disease

CC Excl: See code 746.81

746.85 Coronary artery anomaly

Anomalous origin or communication of coronary artery
Arteriovenous malformation of coronary artery
Coronary artery:
absence
arising from aorta or pulmonary trunk
single

AHA: N-D, '85, 3

746.86 Congenital heart block CC

Complete or incomplete atrioventricular [AV] block

CC Excl: 746.86, 746.89, 746.9, 747.83, 747.89, 747.9, 759.7-759.89

DEF: Impaired conduction of electrical impulses; due to maldeveloped junctional tissue.

746.87 Malposition of heart and cardiac apex

Abdominal heart
Dextrocardia
Ectopia cordis
Levocardia (isolated)
Mesocardia

EXCLUDES *dextrocardia with complete transposition of viscera (759.3)*

746.89 Other

Atresia } of cardiac vein
Hypoplasia } of cardiac vein

Congenital:
cardiomegaly
diverticulum, left ventricle

Congenital:
pericardial defect

AHA: 3Q, '00, 3; 1Q, '99, 11; J-F, '85, 3

746.9 Unspecified anomaly of heart

Congenital:
anomaly of heart NOS
heart disease NOS

✓4th **747 Other congenital anomalies of circulatory system**

747.0 Patent ductus arteriosus

Patent ductus Botalli
Persistent ductus arteriosus

DEF: Open lumen in ductus arteriosus causes arterial blood recirculation in lungs; inhibits blood supply to aorta; symptoms such as shortness of breath more noticeable upon activity.

✓5th **747.1 Coarctation of aorta**

DEF: Localized deformity of aortic media seen as a severe constriction of the vessel lumen; major symptom is high blood pressure in the arms and low pressure in the legs; a CVA, rupture of the aorta, bacterial endocarditis or congestive heart failure can follow if left untreated.

747.10 Coarctation of aorta (preductal) (postductal) CC

Hypoplasia of aortic arch

CC Excl: No Exclusions

AHA: 1Q, '99, 11; 4Q, '88, 8

747.11 Interruption of aortic arch CC

CC Excl: 747.10-747.22, 747.83-747.9, 759.7-759.89

✓5th **747.2 Other anomalies of aorta**

747.20 Anomaly of aorta, unspecified

747.21 Anomalies of aortic arch

Anomalous origin, right subclavian artery
Dextraposition of aorta
Double aortic arch
Kommerell's diverticulum
Overriding aorta
Persistent:
  convolutions, aortic arch
  right aortic arch
Vascular ring

EXCLUDES *hypoplasia of aortic arch (747.10)*

AHA: 1Q, '03, 15

747.22 Atresia and stenosis of aorta CC

Absence, Aplasia, Hypoplasia, Stricture } of aorta

Supra (valvular)-aortic stenosis

EXCLUDES *congenital aortic (valvular) stenosis or stricture, so stated (746.3)*
hypoplasia of aorta in hypoplastic left heart syndrome (746.7)

CC Excl: See code 747.11

747.29 Other

Aneurysm of sinus of Valsalva
Congenital:
  aneurysm, dilation } of aorta

747.3 Anomalies of pulmonary artery

Agenesis, Anomaly, Atresia, Coarctation, Hypoplasia, Stenosis } of pulmonary artery

Pulmonary arteriovenous aneurysm

AHA: 1Q, '04, 16; 1Q, '94, 15; 4Q, '88, 8

✓5th **747.4 Anomalies of great veins**

747.40 Anomaly of great veins, unspecified

Anomaly NOS of:
  pulmonary veins
Anomaly NOS of:
  vena cava

747.41 Total anomalous pulmonary venous connection

Total anomalous pulmonary venous return [TAPVR]:
  subdiaphragmatic
  supradiaphragmatic

747.42 Partial anomalous pulmonary venous connection

Partial anomalous pulmonary venous return

747.49 Other anomalies of great veins

Absence, Congenital stenosis } of vena cava (inferior) (superior)

Persistent:
  left posterior cardinal vein
  left superior vena cava
Scimitar syndrome
Transposition of pulmonary veins NOS

747.5 Absence or hypoplasia of umbilical artery

Single umbilical artery

✓5th **747.6 Other anomalies of peripheral vascular system**

Absence, Anomaly, Atresia } of artery or vein, NEC

Arteriovenous aneurysm (peripheral)
Arteriovenous malformation of the peripheral vascular system
Congenital:
  aneurysm (peripheral)
  phlebectasia
  stricture, artery
  varix
Multiple renal arteries

EXCLUDES *anomalies of:*
  cerebral vessels (747.81)
  pulmonary artery (747.3)
congenital retinal aneurysm (743.58)
hemangioma (228.00-228.09)
lymphangioma (228.1)

747.60 Anomaly of the peripheral vascular system, unspecified site

747.61 Gastrointestinal vessel anomaly

AHA: 3Q, '96, 10

747.62 Renal vessel anomaly

747.63 Upper limb vessel anomaly

747.64 Lower limb vessel anomaly

747.69 Anomalies of other specified sites of peripheral vascular system

✓5th **747.8 Other specified anomalies of circulatory system**

747.81 Anomalies of cerebrovascular system

Arteriovenous malformation of brain
Cerebral arteriovenous aneurysm, congenital
Congenital anomalies of cerebral vessels

EXCLUDES *ruptured cerebral (arteriovenous) aneurysm (430)*

747.82 Spinal vessel anomaly

Arteriovenous malformation of spinal vessel

AHA: 3Q, '95, 5

747.83 Persistent fetal circulation N

Persistent pulmonary hypertension
Primary pulmonary hypertension of newborn

AHA: 4Q, '02, 62

DEF: A return to fetal-type circulation due to constriction of pulmonary arterioles and opening of the ductus arteriosus and foramen ovale, right-to-left shunting occurs, oxygenation of the blood does not occur, and the lungs remain constricted after birth; PFC is seen in term or post-term infants causes include asphyxiation, meconium aspiration syndrome, acidosis, sepsis, and developmental immaturity.

Persistent Fetal Circulation

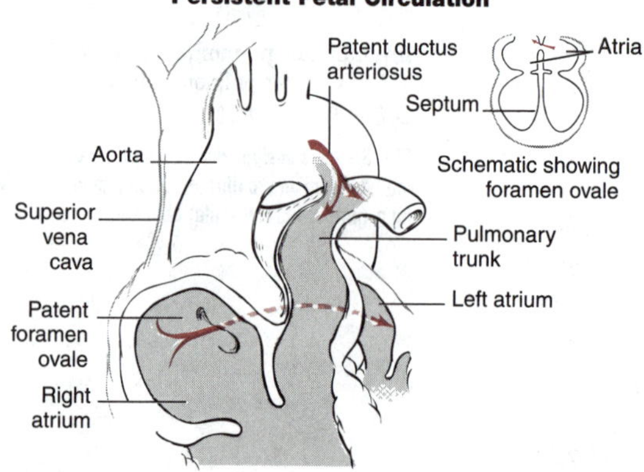

747.89 Other
Aneurysm, congenital, specified site not elsewhere classified
EXCLUDES *congenital aneurysm:*
coronary (746.85)
peripheral (747.6)
pulmonary (747.3)
retinal (743.58)
AHA: 4Q, '02, 63

747.9 Unspecified anomaly of circulatory system

4th **748 Congenital anomalies of respiratory system**
EXCLUDES *congenital central alveolar hypoventilation syndrome (327.25)*
congenital defect of diaphragm (756.6)

748.0 Choanal atresia
Atresia } of nares (anterior)
Congenital stenosis } (posterior)
DEF: Occluded posterior nares (choana), bony or membranous due to failure of embryonic bucconasal membrane to rupture.

748.1 Other anomalies of nose
Absent nose
Accessory nose
Cleft nose
Congenital:
deformity of nose
Congenital:
notching of tip of nose
perforation of wall of nasal sinus
Deformity of wall of nasal sinus
EXCLUDES *congenital deviation of nasal septum (754.0)*

748.2 Web of larynx
Web of larynx:
NOS
glottic
Web of larynx:
subglottic
DEF: Malformed larynx; marked by thin, translucent, or thick, fibrotic spread between vocal folds; affects speech.

748.3 Other anomalies of larynx, trachea, and bronchus
Absence or agenesis of:
bronchus
larynx
trachea
Anomaly(of):
cricoid cartilage
epiglottis
thyroid cartilage
tracheal cartilage
Atresia (of):
epiglottis
glottis
larynx
trachea
Cleft thyroid, cartilage, congenital
Congenital:
dilation, trachea
stenosis:
larynx
trachea
tracheocele
Diverticulum:
bronchus
trachea
Fissure of epiglottis
Laryngocele
Posterior cleft of cricoid cartilage (congenital)
Rudimentary tracheal bronchus
Stridor, laryngeal, congenital
AHA: 1Q, '99, 14

748.4 Congenital cystic lung CC
Disease, lung:
cystic, congenital
polycystic, congenital
Honeycomb lung, congenital
EXCLUDES *acquired or unspecified cystic lung (518.89)*
CC Excl: 748.4-748.9
DEF: Enlarged air spaces of lung parenchyma.

748.5 Agenesis, hypoplasia, and dysplasia of lung CC
Absence of lung (fissures) (lobe)
Aplasia of lung
Hypoplasia of lung
Sequestration of lung
CC Excl: See code 748.4

5th **748.6 Other anomalies of lung**

748.60 Anomaly of lung, unspecified

748.61 Congenital bronchiectasis CC
CC Excl: 494.0-494.1, 496, 506.1, 506.4, 506.9, 748.61

748.69 Other
Accessory lung (lobe)
Azygos lobe (fissure), lung

748.8 Other specified anomalies of respiratory system
Abnormal communication between pericardial and pleural sacs
Anomaly, pleural folds
Atresia of nasopharynx
Congenital cyst of mediastinum

748.9 Unspecified anomaly of respiratory system
Anomaly of respiratory system NOS

4th **749 Cleft palate and cleft lip**

5th **749.0 Cleft palate**

749.00 Cleft palate, unspecified

749.01 Unilateral, complete

749.02 Unilateral, incomplete
Cleft uvula

749.03 Bilateral, complete

749.04 Bilateral, incomplete

5th **749.1 Cleft lip**
Cheiloschisis
Congenital fissure of lip
Harelip
Labium leporinum

749.10 Cleft lip, unspecified

749.11 Unilateral, complete

749.12 Unilateral, incomplete

749.13 Bilateral, complete

749.14 Bilateral, incomplete

5th **749.2 Cleft palate with cleft lip**
Cheilopalatoschisis

749.20 Cleft palate with cleft lip, unspecified

749.21 Unilateral, complete

749.22 Unilateral, incomplete

749.23 Bilateral, complete
AHA: 1Q, '96, 14

749.24 Bilateral, incomplete

749.25 Other combinations

4th **750 Other congenital anomalies of upper alimentary tract**
EXCLUDES *dentofacial anomalies (524.0-524.9)*

750.0 Tongue tie
Ankyloglossia
DEF: Restricted tongue movement due to lingual frenum extending toward tip of tongue. Tongue may be fused to mouth floor affecting speech.

Cleft Lip and Palate

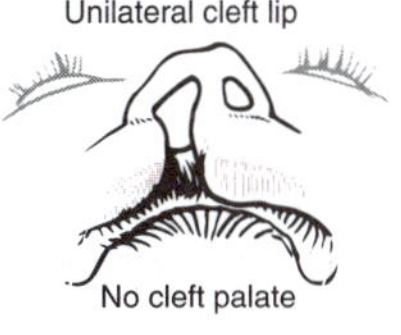

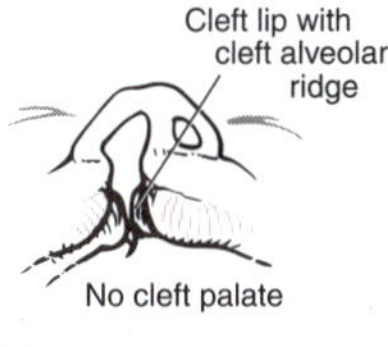

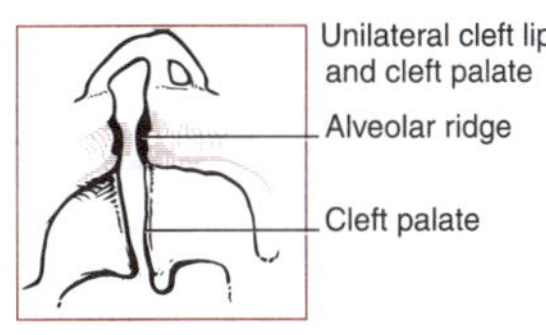

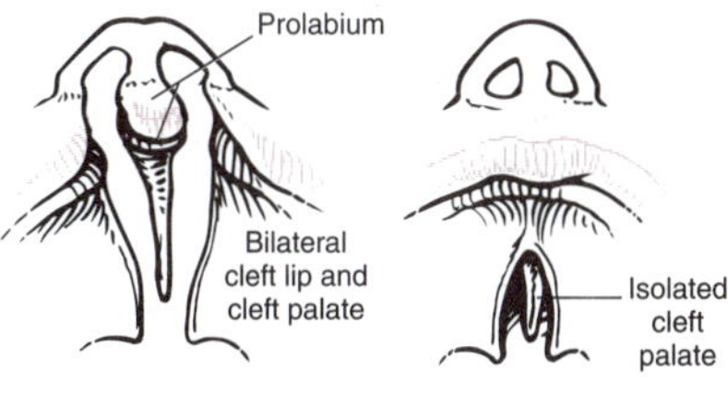

✓5th **750.1 Other anomalies of tongue**

750.10 Anomaly of tongue, unspecified

750.11 Aglossia

DEF: Absence of tongue.

750.12 Congenital adhesions of tongue

750.13 Fissure of tongue

Bifid tongue Double tongue

750.15 Macroglossia

Congenital hypertrophy of tongue

750.16 Microglossia

Hypoplasia of tongue

750.19 Other

✓5th **750.2 Other specified anomalies of mouth and pharynx**

750.21 Absence of salivary gland

750.22 Accessory salivary gland

750.23 Atresia, salivary duct

Imperforate salivary duct

750.24 Congenital fistula of salivary gland

750.25 Congenital fistula of lip

Congenital (mucus) lip pits

750.26 Other specified anomalies of mouth

Absence of uvula

750.27 Diverticulum of pharynx

Pharyngeal pouch

750.29 Other specified anomalies of pharynx

Imperforate pharynx

750.3 Tracheoesophageal fistula, esophageal atresia and stenosis

Absent esophagus
Atresia of esophagus
Congenital:
esophageal ring
stenosis of esophagus
stricture of esophagus
Congenital fistula:
esophagobronchial
esophagotracheal
Imperforate esophagus
Webbed esophagus

750.4 Other specified anomalies of esophagus

Dilatation, congenital
Displacement, congenital
Diverticulum
Duplication
Giant
} (of) esophagus

Esophageal pouch

EXCLUDES *congenital hiatus hernia (750.6)*

AHA: J-F, '85, 3

750.5 Congenital hypertrophic pyloric stenosis

Congenital or infantile:
constriction
hypertrophy
spasm
stenosis
stricture
} of pylorus

DEF: Obstructed pylorus due to overgrowth of pyloric muscle.

750.6 Congenital hiatus hernia

Displacement of cardia through esophageal hiatus

EXCLUDES *congenital diaphragmatic hernia (756.6)*

750.7 Other specified anomalies of stomach

Congenital:
cardiospasm
hourglass stomach
Displacement of stomach
Diverticulum of stomach, congenital
Duplication of stomach
Megalogastria
Microgastria
Transposition of stomach

750.8 Other specified anomalies of upper alimentary tract

750.9 Unspecified anomaly of upper alimentary tract

Congenital:
anomaly NOS
deformity NOS
} of upper alimentary tract [any part, except tongue]

✓4th **751 Other congenital anomalies of digestive system**

751.0 Meckel's diverticulum

Meckel's diverticulum (displaced) (hypertrophic)
Persistent:
omphalomesenteric duct
vitelline duct

AHA: 1Q, '04, 10

DEF: Malformed sacs or appendages of ileum of small intestine; can cause strangulation, volvulus and intussusception.

751.1 Atresia and stenosis of small intestine P

Atresia of:
duodenum
ileum
intestine NOS
Congenital:
absence
obstruction
stenosis
stricture
} of small intestine or intestine NOS
Imperforate jejunum

751.2 Atresia and stenosis of large intestine, rectum, and anal canal P

Absence:
anus (congenital)
appendix, congenital
large intestine, congenital
rectum
Atresia of:
anus
colon
rectum
Congenital or infantile:
obstruction of large intestine
occlusion of anus
stricture of anus
Imperforate:
anus
rectum
Stricture of rectum, congenital

AHA: 2Q, '98, 16

751.3 Hirschsprung's disease and other congenital functional disorders of colon

Aganglionosis
Congenital dilation of colon
Congenital megacolon
Macrocolon

DEF: Hirschsprung's disease: enlarged or dilated colon (megacolon), with absence of ganglion cells in the narrowed wall distally; causes inability to defecate.

751.4 Anomalies of intestinal fixation

Congenital adhesions:
omental, anomalous
peritoneal
Jackson's membrane
Malrotation of colon
Rotation of cecum or colon:
failure of
incomplete
insufficient
Universal mesentery

751.5 Other anomalies of intestine

Congenital diverticulum, colon
Dolichocolon
Duplication of:
anus
appendix
cecum
intestine
Ectopic anus
Megaloappendix
Megaloduodenum
Microcolon
Persistent cloaca
Transposition of:
appendix
colon
intestine

AHA: 3Q, '02, 11; 3Q, '01, 8

✓5th **751.6 Anomalies of gallbladder, bile ducts, and liver**

751.60 Unspecified anomaly of gallbladder, bile ducts, and liver

751.61 Biliary atresia P

Congenital:
absence
hypoplasia
obstruction
stricture
} of bile duct (common) or passage

AHA: S-O, '87, 8

751.62 Congenital cystic disease of liver
Congenital polycystic disease of liver
Fibrocystic disease of liver

751.69 Other anomalies of gallbladder, bile ducts, and liver
Absence of:
gallbladder, congenital
liver (lobe)
Accessory:
hepatic ducts
liver
Congenital:
choledochal cyst
hepatomegaly
Duplication of:
biliary duct
cystic duct
gallbladder
liver
Floating:
gallbladder
liver
Intrahepatic gallbladder

AHA: S-O, '87, 8

751.7 Anomalies of pancreas
Absence
Accessory
Agenesis
Annular
Hypoplasia
} (of) pancreas
Ectopic pancreatic tissue
Pancreatic heterotopia
EXCLUDES *diabetes mellitus:*
congenital (250.0-250.9)
neonatal (775.1)
fibrocystic disease of pancreas (277.00-277.09)

751.8 Other specified anomalies of digestive system
Absence (complete) (partial) of alimentary tract NOS
Duplication
Malposition, congenital
} of digestive organs NOS
EXCLUDES *congenital diaphragmatic hernia (756.6)*
congenital hiatus hernia (750.6)

751.9 Unspecified anomaly of digestive system
Congenital:
anomaly NOS
deformity NOS
} of digestive system NOS

✓4th **752 Congenital anomalies of genital organs**
EXCLUDES *syndromes associated with anomalies in the number and form of chromosomes (758.0-758.9)*
testicular feminization syndrome (259.5)

752.0 Anomalies of ovaries ♀
Absence, congenital
Accessory
Ectopic
Streak
} (of) ovary

✓5th **752.1 Anomalies of fallopian tubes and broad ligaments**

752.10 Unspecified anomaly of fallopian tubes and broad ligaments ♀

752.11 Embryonic cyst of fallopian tubes and broad ligaments ♀
Cyst:
epoophoron
fimbrial
parovarian

AHA: S-O, '85, 13

752.19 Other ♀
Absence
Accessory
Atresia
} (of) fallopian tube or broad ligament

752.2 Doubling of uterus ♀
Didelphic uterus
Doubling of uterus [any degree] (associated with doubling of cervix and vagina)

752.3 Other anomalies of uterus ♀
Absence, congenital
Agenesis
Aplasia
Bicornuate
} (of) uterus
Uterus unicornis
Uterus with only one functioning horn

✓5th **752.4 Anomalies of cervix, vagina, and external female genitalia**

752.40 Unspecified anomaly of cervix, vagina, and external female genitalia ♀

752.41 Embryonic cyst of cervix, vagina, and external female genitalia ♀
Cyst of:
canal of Nuck, congenital
Gartner's duct
vagina, embryonal
vulva, congenital

DEF: Embryonic fluid-filled cysts, of cervix, vagina or external female genitalia.

752.42 Imperforate hymen ♀
DEF: Complete closure of membranous fold around external opening of vagina.

752.49 Other anomalies of cervix, vagina, and external female genitalia ♀
Absence
Agenesis
} of cervix, clitoris, vagina, or vulva
Congenital stenosis or stricture of:
cervical canal
vagina
EXCLUDES *double vagina associated with total duplication (752.2)*

✓5th **752.5 Undescended and retractile testicle**
AHA: 4Q, '96, 33

752.51 Undescended testis ♂
Cryptorchism
Ectopic testis

752.52 Retractile testis ♂

✓5th **752.6 Hypospadias and epispadias and other penile anomalies**
AHA: 4Q, '96, 34, 35

752.61 Hypospadias ♂
AHA: 4Q, '03, 67-68; 3Q, '97, 6
DEF: Abnormal opening of urethra on the ventral surface of the penis or perineum; also a rare defect of vagina.

752.62 Epispadias ♂
Anaspadias
DEF: Urethra opening on dorsal surface of penis; in females appears as a slit in the upper wall of urethra.

752.63 Congenital chordee ♂
DEF: Ventral bowing of penis due to fibrous band along corpus spongiosum; occurs with hypospadias.

Hypospadias and Epispadias

752.64 Micropenis ♂

752.65 Hidden penis ♂

752.69 Other penile anomalies ♂

752.7 Indeterminate sex and pseudohermaphroditism

Gynandrism
Hermaphroditism
Ovotestis
Pseudohermaphroditism (male) (female)
Pure gonadal dysgenesis

EXCLUDES *pseudohermaphroditism:*
female, with adrenocortical disorder (255.2)
male, with gonadal disorder (257.8)
with specified chromosomal anomaly (758.0-758.9)
testicular feminization syndrome (259.5)

DEF: Pseudohermaphroditism: presence of gonads of one sex and external genitalia of other sex.

✓5th **752.8 Other specified anomalies of genital organs**

EXCLUDES *congenital hydrocele (778.6)*
penile anomalies (752.61-752.69)
phimosis or paraphimosis (605)

752.81 Scrotal transposition ♂

AHA: 4Q, '03, 67-68

752.89 Other specified anomalies of genital organs

Absence of:
prostate
spermatic cord
vas deferens
Anorchism
Aplasia (congenital) of:
prostate
round ligament
testicle
Atresia of:
ejaculatory duct
vas deferens
Fusion of testes
Hypoplasia of testis
Monorchism
Polyorchism

752.9 Unspecified anomaly of genital organs

Congenital:
anomaly NOS } of genital organ,
deformity NOS } not elsewhere classified

✓4th **753 Congenital anomalies of urinary system**

753.0 Renal agenesis and dysgenesis

Atrophy of kidney:
congenital
infantile
Congenital absence of kidney(s)
Hypoplasia of kidney(s)

✓5th **753.1 Cystic kidney disease**

EXCLUDES *acquired cyst of kidney (593.2)*

AHA: 4Q, '90, 3

753.10 Cystic kidney disease, unspecified

753.11 Congenital single renal cyst

753.12 Polycystic kidney, unspecified type

753.13 Polycystic kidney, autosomal dominant

DEF: Slow progressive disease characterized by bilateral cysts causing increased kidney size and impaired function.

753.14 Polycystic kidney, autosomal recessive

DEF: Rare disease characterized by multiple cysts involving kidneys and liver, producing renal and hepatic failure in childhood or adolescence.

753.15 Renal dysplasia

753.16 Medullary cystic kidney

Nephronopthisis

DEF: Diffuse kidney disease results in uremia onset prior to age 20.

753.17 Medullary sponge kidney

DEF: Dilated collecting tubules; usually asymptomatic but calcinosis in tubules may cause renal insufficiency.

753.19 Other specified cystic kidney disease

Multicystic kidney

✓5th **753.2 Obstructive defects of renal pelvis and ureter**

AHA: 4Q, '96, 35

753.20 Unspecified obstructive defect of renal pelvis and ureter

753.21 Congenital obstruction of ureteropelvic junction

DEF: Stricture at junction of ureter and renal pelvis.

753.22 Congenital obstruction of ureterovesical junction

Adynamic ureter
Congenital hydroureter

DEF: Stricture at junction of ureter and bladder.

753.23 Congenital ureterocele

753.29 Other

753.3 Other specified anomalies of kidney

Accessory kidney
Congenital:
calculus of kidney
displaced kidney
Discoid kidney
Double kidney with double pelvis
Ectopic kidney
Fusion of kidneys
Giant kidney
Horseshoe kidney
Hyperplasia of kidney
Lobulation of kidney
Malrotation of kidney
Trifid kidney (pelvis)

753.4 Other specified anomalies of ureter

Absent ureter
Accessory ureter
Deviation of ureter
Displaced ureteric orifice
Double ureter
Ectopic ureter
Implantation, anomalous of ureter

753.5 Exstrophy of urinary bladder

Ectopia vesicae
Extroversion of bladder

DEF: Absence of lower abdominal and anterior bladder walls with posterior bladder wall protrusion.

753.6 Atresia and stenosis of urethra and bladder neck

Congenital obstruction:
bladder neck
urethra
Congenital stricture of:
urethra (valvular)
urinary meatus
vesicourethral orifice
Imperforate urinary meatus
Impervious urethra
Urethral valve formation

753.7 Anomalies of urachus

Cyst }
Fistula } (of) urachussinus
Patent }
Persistent umbilical sinus

753.8 Other specified anomalies of bladder and urethra

Absence, congenital of:
bladder
urethra
Accessory:
bladder
urethra
Congenital:
diverticulum of bladder
hernia of bladder
Congenital urethrorectal fistula
Congenital prolapse of:
bladder (mucosa)
urethra
Double:
urethra
urinary meatus

753.9 Unspecified anomaly of urinary system

Congenital:
anomaly NOS } of urinary system [any part,
deformity NOS } except urachus]

✓4th **754 Certain congenital musculoskeletal deformities**

INCLUDES nonteratogenic deformities which are considered to be due to intrauterine malposition and pressure

754.0 Of skull, face, and jaw

Asymmetry of face
Compression facies
Depressions in skull
Deviation of nasal septum, congenital
Dolichocephaly
Plagiocephaly
Potter's facies
Squashed or bent nose, congenital

EXCLUDES *dentofacial anomalies (524.0-524.9)*
syphilitic saddle nose (090.5)

754.1 Of sternocleidomastoid muscle

Congenital sternomastoid torticollis
Congenital wryneck
Contracture of sternocleidomastoid (muscle)
Sternomastoid tumor

754.2 Of spine

Congenital postural:
lordosis
scoliosis

✓5th **754.3 Congenital dislocation of hip**

754.30 Congenital dislocation of hip, unilateral
Congenital dislocation of hip NOS

754.31 Congenital dislocation of hip, bilateral

754.32 Congenital subluxation of hip, unilateral
Congenital flexion deformity, hip or thigh
Predislocation status of hip at birth
Preluxation of hip, congenital

754.33 Congenital subluxation of hip, bilateral

754.35 Congenital dislocation of one hip with subluxation of other hip

✓5th **754.4 Congenital genu recurvatum and bowing of long bones of leg**

754.40 Genu recurvatum
DEF: Backward curving of knee joint.

754.41 Congenital dislocation of knee (with genu recurvatum)

754.42 Congenital bowing of femur

754.43 Congenital bowing of tibia and fibula

754.44 Congenital bowing of unspecified long bones of leg

✓5th **754.5 Varus deformities of feet**

EXCLUDES *acquired (736.71, 736.75, 736.79)*

754.50 Talipes varus
Congenital varus deformity of foot, unspecified
Pes varus
DEF: Inverted foot marked by outer sole resting on ground.

754.51 Talipes equinovarus
Equinovarus (congenital)
DEF: Elevated, outward rotation of heel; also called clubfoot.

754.52 Metatarsus primus varus
DEF: Malformed first metatarsal bone, with bone angled toward body.

754.53 Metatarsus varus

754.59 Other
Talipes calcaneovarus

✓5th **754.6 Valgus deformities of feet**

EXCLUDES *valgus deformity of foot (acquired) (736.79)*

754.60 Talipes valgus
Congenital valgus deformity of foot, unspecified

754.61 Congenital pes planus
Congenital rocker bottom flat foot
Flat foot, congenital
EXCLUDES *pes planus (acquired) (734)*

754.62 Talipes calcaneovalgus

754.69 Other
Talipes:
equinovalgus
Talipes:
planovalgus

✓5th **754.7 Other deformities of feet**

EXCLUDES *acquired (736.70-736.79)*

754.70 Talipes, unspecified
Congenital deformity of foot NOS

754.71 Talipes cavus
Cavus foot (congenital)

754.79 Other
Asymmetric talipes
Talipes:
calcaneus
equinus

✓5th **754.8 Other specified nonteratogenic anomalies**

754.81 Pectus excavatum
Congenital funnel chest

754.82 Pectus carinatum
Congenital pigeon chest [breast]

754.89 Other
Club hand (congenital)
Congenital:
deformity of chest wall
dislocation of elbow
Generalized flexion contractures of lower limb joints, congenital
Spade-like hand (congenital)

✓4th **755 Other congenital anomalies of limbs**

EXCLUDES *those deformities classifiable to 754.0-754.8*

✓5th **755.0 Polydactyly**

755.00 Polydactyly, unspecified digits
Supernumerary digits

755.01 Of fingers
Accessory fingers

755.02 Of toes
Accessory toes

✓5th **755.1 Syndactyly**

Symphalangy
Webbing of digits

755.10 Of multiple and unspecified sites

755.11 Of fingers without fusion of bone

755.12 Of fingers with fusion of bone

755.13 Of toes without fusion of bone

755.14 Of toes with fusion of bone

✓5th **755.2 Reduction deformities of upper limb**

755.20 Unspecified reduction deformity of upper limb
Ectromelia NOS } of upper limb
Hemimelia NOS } of upper limb
Shortening of arm, congenital

755.21 Transverse deficiency of upper limb
Amelia of upper limb
Congenital absence of:
fingers, all (complete or partial)
forearm, including hand and fingers
upper limb, complete
Congenital amputation of upper limb
Transverse hemimelia of upper limb

755.22 Longitudinal deficiency of upper limb, not elsewhere classified
Phocomelia NOS of upper limb
Rudimentary arm

755.23 Longitudinal deficiency, combined, involving humerus, radius, and ulna (complete or incomplete)
Congenital absence of arm and forearm (complete or incomplete) with or without metacarpal deficiency and/or phalangeal deficiency, incomplete
Phocomelia, complete, of upper limb

755.24 Longitudinal deficiency, humeral, complete or partial (with or without distal deficiencies, incomplete)
Congenital absence of humerus (with or without absence of some [but not all] distal elements)
Proximal phocomelia of upper limb

755.25 Longitudinal deficiency, radioulnar, complete or partial (with or without distal deficiencies, incomplete)
Congenital absence of radius and ulna (with or without absence of some [but not all] distal elements)
Distal phocomelia of upper limb

755.26 Longitudinal deficiency, radial, complete or partial (with or without distal deficiencies, incomplete)
Agenesis of radius
Congenital absence of radius (with or without absence of some [but not all] distal elements)

755.27 Longitudinal deficiency, ulnar, complete or partial (with or without distal deficiencies, incomplete)
Agenesis of ulna
Congenital absence of ulna (with or without absence of some [but not all] distal elements)

755.28 Longitudinal deficiency, carpals or metacarpals, complete or partial (with or without incomplete phalangeal deficiency)

755.29 Longitudinal deficiency, phalanges, complete or partial
Absence of finger, congenital
Aphalangia of upper limb, terminal, complete or partial
EXCLUDES *terminal deficiency of all five digits (755.21)*
transverse deficiency of phalanges (755.21)

✓5th **755.3 Reduction deformities of lower limb**

755.30 Unspecified reduction deformity of lower limb
Ectromelia NOS } of lower limb
Hemimelia NOS } of lower limb
Shortening of leg, congenital

755.31 Transverse deficiency of lower limb
Amelia of lower limb
Congenital absence of:
- foot
- leg, including foot and toes
- lower limb, complete
- toes, all, complete

Transverse hemimelia of lower limb

755.32 Longitudinal deficiency of lower limb, not elsewhere classified
Phocomelia NOS of lower limb

755.33 Longitudinal deficiency, combined, involving femur, tibia, and fibula (complete or incomplete)
Congenital absence of thigh and (lower) leg (complete or incomplete) with or without metacarpal deficiency and/or phalangeal deficiency, incomplete
Phocomelia, complete, of lower limb

755.34 Longitudinal deficiency, femoral, complete or partial (with or without distal deficiencies, incomplete)
Congenital absence of femur (with or without absence of some [but not all] distal elements)
Proximal phocomelia of lower limb

755.35 Longitudinal deficiency, tibiofibular, complete or partial (with or without distal deficiencies, incomplete)
Congenital absence of tibia and fibula (with or without absence of some [but not all] distal elements)
Distal phocomelia of lower limb

755.36 Longitudinal deficiency, tibia, complete or partial (with or without distal deficiencies, incomplete)
Agenesis of tibia
Congenital absence of tibia (with or without absence of some [but not all] distal elements)

755.37 Longitudinal deficiency, fibular, complete or partial (with or without distal deficiencies, incomplete)
Agenesis of fibula
Congenital absence of fibula (with or without absence of some [but not all] distal elements)

755.38 Longitudinal deficiency, tarsals or metatarsals, complete or partial (with or without incomplete phalangeal deficiency)

755.39 Longitudinal deficiency, phalanges, complete or partial
Absence of toe, congenital
Aphalangia of lower limb, terminal, complete or partial
EXCLUDES *terminal deficiency of all five digits (755.31)*
transverse deficiency of phalanges (755.31)

755.4 Reduction deformities, unspecified limb
Absence, congenital (complete or partial) of limb NOS
Amelia } of unspecified limb
Ectromelia } of unspecified limb
Hemimelia } of unspecified limb
Phocomelia } of unspecified limb

✓5th **755.5 Other anomalies of upper limb, including shoulder girdle**

755.50 Unspecified anomaly of upper limb

755.51 Congenital deformity of clavicle

755.52 Congenital elevation of scapula
Sprengel's deformity

755.53 Radioulnar synostosis
DEF: Osseous adhesion of radius and ulna.

755.54 Madelung's deformity
DEF: Distal ulnar overgrowth or radial shortening; also called carpus curvus.

755.55 Acrocephalosyndactyly
Apert's syndrome
DEF: Premature cranial suture fusion (craniostenosis); marked by cone-shaped or pointed (acrocephaly) head and webbing of the fingers (syndactyly); it is very similar to craniofacial dysostosis.

755.56 Accessory carpal bones

755.57 Macrodactylia (fingers)

DEF: Abnormally large fingers, toes.

755.58 Cleft hand, congenital

Lobster-claw hand

DEF: Extended separation between fingers into metacarpus; also may refer to large fingers and absent middle fingers of hand.

755.59 Other

Cleidocranial dysostosis

Cubitus:
- valgus, congenital
- varus, congenital

EXCLUDES *club hand (congenital) (754.89)*
congenital dislocation of elbow (754.89)

✓5th **755.6 Other anomalies of lower limb, including pelvic girdle**

755.60 Unspecified anomaly of lower limb

755.61 Coxa valga, congenital

DEF: Abnormally wide angle between the neck and shaft of the femur.

755.62 Coxa vara, congenital

DEF: Diminished angle between neck and shaft of femur.

755.63 Other congenital deformity of hip (joint)

Congenital anteversion of femur (neck)

EXCLUDES *congenital dislocation of hip (754.30-754.35)*

AHA: 1Q, '94, 15; S-O, '84, 15

755.64 Congenital deformity of knee (joint)

Congenital:
- absence of patella
- genu valgum [knock-knee]
- genu varum [bowleg]

Rudimentary patella

755.65 Macrodactylia of toes

DEF: Abnormally large toes.

755.66 Other anomalies of toes

Congenital:
- hallux valgus
- hallux varus

Congenital:
- hammer toe

755.67 Anomalies of foot, not elsewhere classified

Astragaloscaphoid synostosis
Calcaneonavicular bar
Coalition of calcaneus
Talonavicular synostosis
Tarsal coalitions

755.69 Other

Congenital:
- angulation of tibia
- deformity (of):
  - ankle (joint)
  - sacroiliac (joint)
- fusion of sacroiliac joint

755.8 Other specified anomalies of unspecified limb

755.9 Unspecified anomaly of unspecified limb

Congenital:
- anomaly NOS } of unspecified limb
- deformity NOS } of unspecified limb

EXCLUDES *reduction deformity of unspecified limb (755.4)*

✓4th **756 Other congenital musculoskeletal anomalies**

EXCLUDES *those deformities classifiable to 754.0-754.8*

756.0 Anomalies of skull and face bones

Absence of skull bones
Acrocephaly
Congenital deformity of forehead
Craniosynostosis
Crouzon's disease
Hypertelorism
Imperfect fusion of skull
Oxycephaly
Platybasia
Premature closure of cranial sutures
Tower skull
Trigonocephaly

EXCLUDES *acrocephalosyndactyly [Apert's syndrome] (755.55)*
dentofacial anomalies (524.0-524.9)
skull defects associated with brain anomalies, such as:
- *anencephalus (740.0)*
- *encephalocele (742.0)*
- *hydrocephalus (742.3)*
- *microcephalus (742.1)*

AHA: 3Q, '98, 9; 3Q, '96, 15

✓5th **756.1 Anomalies of spine**

756.10 Anomaly of spine, unspecified

756.11 Spondylolysis, lumbosacral region

Prespondylolisthesis (lumbosacral)

DEF: Bilateral or unilateral defect through the pars interarticularis of a vertebra causes spondylolisthesis.

756.12 Spondylolisthesis

DEF: Downward slipping of lumbar vertebra over next vertebra; usually related to pelvic deformity.

756.13 Absence of vertebra, congenital

756.14 Hemivertebra

DEF: Incomplete development of one side of a vertebra.

756.15 Fusion of spine [vertebra], congenital

756.16 Klippel-Feil syndrome

DEF: Short, wide neck; limits range of motion due to abnormal number of cervical vertebra or fused hemivertebrae.

756.17 Spina bifida occulta

EXCLUDES *spina bifida (aperta) (741.0-741.9)*

DEF: Spina bifida marked by a bony spinal canal defect without a protrusion of the cord or meninges; it is diagnosed by radiography and has no symptoms.

756.19 Other

Platyspondylia
Supernumerary vertebra

756.2 Cervical rib

Supernumerary rib in the cervical region

DEF: Costa cervicalis: extra rib attached to cervical vertebra.

756.3 Other anomalies of ribs and sternum

Congenital absence of:
- rib
- sternum

Congenital:
- fissure of sternum
- fusion of ribs

Sternum bifidum

EXCLUDES *nonteratogenic deformity of chest wall (754.81-754.89)*

756.4 Chondrodystrophy

Achondroplasia
Chondrodystrophia (fetalis)
Dyschondroplasia
Enchondromatosis
Ollier's disease

EXCLUDES *lipochondrodystrophy [Hurler's syndrome] (277.5)*
Morquio's disease (277.5)

AHA: 2Q, '02, 16; S-O, '87, 10

DEF: Abnormal development of cartilage.

✓5th **756.5 Osteodystrophies**

756.50 Osteodystrophy, unspecified

756.51 Osteogenesis imperfecta

Fragilitas ossium Osteopsathyrosis

DEF: A collagen disorder commonly characterized by brittle, osteoporotic, easily fractured bones, hypermobility of joints, blue sclerae, and a tendency to hemorrhage.

756.52 Osteopetrosis

DEF: Abnormally dense bone, optic atrophy, hepatosplenomegaly, deafness; sclerosing depletes bone marrow and nerve foramina of skull; often fatal.

756.53 Osteopoikilosis

DEF: Multiple sclerotic foci on ends of long bones, stippling in round, flat bones; identified by x-ray.

756.54 Polyostotic fibrous dysplasia of bone

DEF: Fibrous tissue displaces bone results in segmented ragged-edge café-au-lait spots; occurs in girls of early puberty.

756.55 Chondroectodermal dysplasia

Ellis-van Creveld syndrome

DEF: Inadequate enchondral bone formation; impaired development of hair and teeth, polydactyly, and cardiac septum defects.

756.56 Multiple epiphyseal dysplasia

756.59 Other

Albright (-McCune)-Sternberg syndrome

756.6 Anomalies of diaphragm

Absence of diaphragm Eventration of diaphragm
Congenital hernia:
diaphragmatic
foramen of Morgagni

EXCLUDES *congenital hiatus hernia (750.6)*

✓5th **756.7 Anomalies of abdominal wall**

756.70 Anomaly of abdominal wall, unspecified

756.71 Prune belly syndrome

Eagle-Barrett syndrome
Prolapse of bladder mucosa

AHA: 4Q, '97, 44

DEF: Prune belly syndrome: absence of lower rectus abdominis muscle and lower and medial oblique muscles; results in dilated bladder and ureters, dysplastic kidneys and hydronephrosis; more common in male infants with undescended testicles.

756.79 Other congenital anomalies of abdominal wall

Exomphalos Omphalocele
Gastroschisis

EXCLUDES *umbilical hernia (551-553 with .1)*

DEF: Exomphalos: umbilical hernia prominent navel.

DEF: Gastroschisis: fissure of abdominal wall, results in protruding small or large intestine.

DEF: Omphalocele: hernia of umbilicus due to impaired abdominal wall; results in membrane-covered intestine protruding through peritoneum and amnion.

✓5th **756.8 Other specified anomalies of muscle, tendon, fascia, and connective tissue**

756.81 Absence of muscle and tendon

Absence of muscle (pectoral)

756.82 Accessory muscle

756.83 Ehlers-Danlos syndrome

DEF: Danlos syndrome: connective tissue disorder causes hyperextended skin and joints; results in fragile blood vessels with bleeding, poor wound healing and subcutaneous pseudotumors.

756.89 Other

Amyotrophia congenita
Congenital shortening of tendon

AHA: 3Q, '99, 16

756.9 Other and unspecified anomalies of musculoskeletal system

Congenital:
anomaly NOS } of musculoskeletal system,
deformity NOS } not elsewhere classified

✓4th **757 Congenital anomalies of the integument**

INCLUDES anomalies of skin, subcutaneous tissue, hair, nails, and breast

EXCLUDES *hemangioma (228.00-228.09)*
pigmented nevus (216.0-216.9)

757.0 Hereditary edema of legs

Congenital lymphedema
Hereditary trophedema
Milroy's disease

757.1 Ichthyosis congenita

Congenital ichthyosis
Harlequin fetus
Ichthyosiform erythroderma

DEF: Overproduction of skin cells causes scaling of skin; may result in stillborn fetus or death soon after birth.

757.2 Dermatoglyphic anomalies

Abnormal palmar creases

DEF: Abnormal skin-line patterns of fingers, palms, toes and soles; initial finding of possible chromosomal abnormalities.

✓5th **757.3 Other specified anomalies of skin**

757.31 Congenital ectodermal dysplasia

DEF: Tissues and structures originate in embryonic ectoderm; includes anhidrotic and hidrotic ectodermal dysplasia and EEC syndrome.

757.32 Vascular hamartomas

Birthmarks Strawberry nevus
Port-wine stain

DEF: Benign tumor of blood vessels; due to malformed angioblastic tissues.

757.33 Congenital pigmentary anomalies of skin

Congenital poikiloderma
Urticaria pigmentosa
Xeroderma pigmentosum

EXCLUDES *albinism (270.2)*

757.39 Other

Accessory skin tags, congenital
Congenital scar
Epidermolysis bullosa
Keratoderma (congenital)

EXCLUDES *pilonidal cyst (685.0-685.1)*

757.4 Specified anomalies of hair

Congenital:
alopecia
atrichosis
beaded hair

Congenital:
hypertrichosis
monilethrix
Persistent lanugo

757.5 Specified anomalies of nails

Anonychia
Congenital:
clubnail
koilonychia

Congenital:
leukonychia
onychauxis
pachyonychia

757.6 Specified anomalies of breast

Absent
Accessory } breast or nipple
Supernumerary

Hypoplasia of breast

EXCLUDES *absence of pectoral muscle (756.81)*

757.8 Other specified anomalies of the integument

757.9 Unspecified anomaly of the integument

Congenital:
- anomaly NOS } of integument
- deformity NOS } of integument

✓4th 758 Chromosomal anomalies

INCLUDES syndromes associated with anomalies in the number and form of chromosomes

Use additional codes for conditions associated with the chromosomal anomalies

758.0 Down's syndrome

Mongolism
Translocation Down's syndrome
Trisomy:
- 21 or 22
- G

758.1 Patau's syndrome

Trisomy:
- 13
- D_1

DEF: Trisomy of 13th chromosome; characteristic failure to thrive, severe mental impairment, seizures, abnormal eyes, low-set ears and sloped forehead.

758.2 Edwards' syndrome

Trisomy:
- 18
- E_3

DEF: Trisomy of 18th chromosome; characteristic mental and physical impairments; mainly affects females.

✓5th **758.3 Autosomal deletion syndromes**

758.31 Cri-du-chat syndrome

Deletion 5p

DEF: Hereditary congenital syndrome caused by a microdeletion of short arm of chromosome 5; characterized by catlike cry in newborn, microencephaly, severe mental deficiency, and hypertelorism.

758.32 Velo-cardio-facial syndrome

Deletion 22q11.2

DEF: Microdeletion syndrome affecting multiple organs; characteristic cleft palate, heart defects, elongated face with almond-shaped eyes, wide nose, small ears, weak immune systems, weak musculature, hypothyroidism, short stature, and scoliosis; deletion at q11.2 on the long arm of the chromosome 22.

758.33 Other microdeletions

Miller-Dieker syndrome
Smith-Magenis syndrome

DEF: Miller-Dieker syndrome: deletion from the short arm of chromosome 17; characteristic mental retardation, speech and motor development delays, neurological complications, and multiple abnormalities affecting the kidneys, heart, gastrointestinal tract, and other organ; death in infancy or early childhood.

DEF: Smith-Magenis syndrome: deletion in a certain area of chromosome 17 that results in craniofacial changes, speech delay, hoarse voice, hearing loss in many, and behavioral problems, such as self-destructive head banging, wrist biting, and tearing at nails.

758.39 Other autosomal deletions

758.4 Balanced autosomal translocation in normal individual

758.5 Other conditions due to autosomal anomalies

Accessory autosomes NEC

758.6 Gonadal dysgenesis

Ovarian dysgenesis
XO syndrome
Turner's syndrome

EXCLUDES *pure gonadal dysgenesis (752.7)*

758.7 Klinefelter's syndrome ♂

XXY syndrome

DEF: Impaired embryonic development of seminiferous tubes; results in small testes, azoospermia, infertility and enlarged mammary glands.

✓5th **758.8 Other conditions due to chromosome anomalies**

758.81 Other conditions due to sex chromosome anomalies

758.89 Other

758.9 Conditions due to anomaly of unspecified chromosome

✓4th 759 Other and unspecified congenital anomalies

759.0 Anomalies of spleen

- Aberrant } spleen
- Absent } spleen
- Accessory } spleen

Congenital splenomegaly
Ectopic spleen
Lobulation of spleen

759.1 Anomalies of adrenal gland

- Aberrant } adrenal gland
- Absent } adrenal gland
- Accessory } adrenal gland

EXCLUDES *adrenogenital disorders (255.2)*
congenital disorders of steroid metabolism (255.2)

759.2 Anomalies of other endocrine glands

Absent parathyroid gland
Accessory thyroid gland
Persistent thyroglossal or thyrolingual duct
Thyroglossal (duct) cyst

EXCLUDES *congenital:*
- *goiter (246.1)*
- *hypothyroidism (243)*

759.3 Situs inversus

Situs inversus or transversus:
- abdominalis
- thoracis

Transposition of viscera:
- abdominal
- thoracic

EXCLUDES *dextrocardia without mention of complete transposition (746.87)*

DEF: Laterally transposed thoracic and abdominal viscera.

759.4 Conjoined twins

Craniopagus
Dicephalus
Pygopagus
Thoracopagus
Xiphopagus

759.5 Tuberous sclerosis

Bourneville's disease
Epiloia

DEF: Hamartomas of brain, retina and viscera, impaired mental ability, seizures and adenoma sebaceum.

759.6 Other hamartoses, not elsewhere classified

Syndrome:
- Peutz-Jeghers
- Sturge-Weber (-Dimitri)

Syndrome:
- von Hippel-Lindau

EXCLUDES *neurofibromatosis (237.7)*

AHA: 3Q, '92, 12

DEF: Peutz-Jeghers: hereditary syndrome characterized by hamartomas of small intestine.

DEF: Sturge-Weber: congenital syndrome characterized by unilateral port-wine stain over trigeminal nerve, underlying meninges and cerebral cortex.

DEF: von Hipple-Lindau: hereditary syndrome of congenital angiomatosis of the retina and cerebellum.

759.7 Multiple congenital anomalies, so described

Congenital:
anomaly, multiple NOS
deformity, multiple NOS

✓5th **759.8 Other specified anomalies**

AHA: S-O, '87, 9; S-O, '85, 11

759.81 Prader-Willi syndrome

759.82 Marfan syndrome

AHA: 3Q, '93, 11

759.83 Fragile X syndrome

AHA: 4Q, '94, 41

759.89 Other

Congenital malformation syndromes affecting multiple systems, not elsewhere classified

Laurence-Moon-Biedl syndrome

AHA: ►2Q, '05, 17;◄ 2Q, '04, 12; 1Q, '01, 3; 3Q, '99, 17, 18; 3Q, '98, 8

759.9 Congenital anomaly, unspecified

15. CERTAIN CONDITIONS ORIGINATING IN THE PERINATAL PERIOD (760-779)

INCLUDES conditions which have their origin in the perinatal period, before birth through the first 28 days after birth, even though death or morbidity occurs later

Use additional code(s) to further specify condition

MATERNAL CAUSES OF PERINATAL MORBIDITY AND MORTALITY (760-763)

AHA: 2Q, '89, 14; 3Q, '90, 5

✓4th **760 Fetus or newborn affected by maternal conditions which may be unrelated to present pregnancy**

INCLUDES the listed maternal conditions only when specified as a cause of mortality or morbidity of the fetus or newborn

EXCLUDES *maternal endocrine and metabolic disorders affecting fetus or newborn (775.0-775.9)*

AHA: 1Q, '94, 8; 2Q, '92, 12; N-D, '84, 11

760.0 Maternal hypertensive disorders
Fetus or newborn affected by maternal conditions classifiable to 642

760.1 Maternal renal and urinary tract diseases
Fetus or newborn affected by maternal conditions classifiable to 580-599

760.2 Maternal infections
Fetus or newborn affected by maternal infectious disease classifiable to 001-136 and 487, but fetus or newborn not manifesting that disease

EXCLUDES *congenital infectious diseases (771.0-771.8)*
maternal genital tract and other localized infections (760.8)

760.3 Other chronic maternal circulatory and respiratory diseases
Fetus or newborn affected by chronic maternal conditions classifiable to 390-459, 490-519, 745-748

760.4 Maternal nutritional disorders
Fetus or newborn affected by:
maternal disorders classifiable to 260-269
maternal malnutrition NOS

EXCLUDES *fetal malnutrition (764.10-764.29)*

760.5 Maternal injury
Fetus or newborn affected by maternal conditions classifiable to 800-995

760.6 Surgical operation on mother

EXCLUDES *cesarean section for present delivery (763.4)*
damage to placenta from amniocentesis, cesarean section, or surgical induction (762.1)
previous surgery to uterus or pelvic organs (763.89)

✓5th **760.7 Noxious influences affecting fetus or newborn via placenta or breast milk**
Fetus or newborn affected by noxious substance transmitted via placenta or breast milk

EXCLUDES *anesthetic and analgesic drugs administered during labor and delivery (763.5)*
drug withdrawal syndrome in newborn (779.5)

AHA: 3Q, '91, 21

760.70 Unspecified noxious substance
Fetus or newborn affected by:
Drug NEC

760.71 Alcohol
Fetal alcohol syndrome

760.72 Narcotics

760.73 Hallucinogenic agents

760.74 Anti-infectives
Antibiotics
Antifungals

760.75 Cocaine
AHA: 3Q, '94, 6; 2Q, '92, 12; 4Q, '91, 26

760.76 Diethylstilbestrol [DES]
AHA: 4Q, '94, 45

760.77 Anticonvulsants N
Carbamazepine
Phenobarbital
Phenytoin
Valproic acid

AHA: ▶4Q, '05, 82◀

760.78 Antimetabolic agents N
Methotrexate
Retinoic acid
Statins

AHA: ▶4Q, '05, 82-83◀

760.79 Other
Fetus or newborn affected by:
immune sera } transmitted via placenta or breast
medicinal agents NEC } transmitted via placenta or breast
toxic substance NEC } transmitted via placenta or breast

760.8 Other specified maternal conditions affecting fetus or newborn
Maternal genital tract and other localized infection affecting fetus or newborn, but fetus or newborn not manifesting that disease

EXCLUDES *maternal urinary tract infection affecting fetus or newborn (760.1)*

760.9 Unspecified maternal condition affecting fetus or newborn

✓4th **761 Fetus or newborn affected by maternal complications of pregnancy**

INCLUDES the listed maternal conditions only when specified as a cause of mortality or morbidity of the fetus or newborn

761.0 Incompetent cervix
DEF: Inadequate functioning of uterine cervix.

761.1 Premature rupture of membranes

761.2 Oligohydramnios

EXCLUDES *that due to premature rupture of membranes (761.1)*

DEF: Deficient amniotic fluid.

761.3 Polyhydramnios
Hydramnios (acute) (chronic)
DEF: Excess amniotic fluid.

761.4 Ectopic pregnancy
Pregnancy:
abdominal
intraperitoneal
tubal

761.5 Multiple pregnancy
Triplet (pregnancy)
Twin (pregnancy)

761.6 Maternal death

761.7 Malpresentation before labor
Breech presentation } before labor
External version } before labor
Oblique lie } before labor
Transverse lie } before labor
Unstable lie } before labor

761.8 Other specified maternal complications of pregnancy affecting fetus or newborn
Spontaneous abortion, fetus

761.9 Unspecified maternal complication of pregnancy affecting fetus or newborn

4th **762 Fetus or newborn affected by complications of placenta, cord, and membranes**

INCLUDES the listed maternal conditions only when specified as a cause of mortality or morbidity in the fetus or newborn

AHA: 1Q, '94, 8

762.0 Placenta previa N

DEF: Placenta developed in lower segment of uterus; causes hemorrhaging in last trimester.

762.1 Other forms of placental separation and hemorrhage N

Abruptio placentae
Antepartum hemorrhage
Damage to placenta from amniocentesis, cesarean section, or surgical induction
Maternal blood loss
Premature separation of placenta
Rupture of marginal sinus

762.2 Other and unspecified morphological and functional abnormalities of placenta N

Placental:
dysfunction
infarction
insufficiency

762.3 Placental transfusion syndromes N

Placental and cord abnormality resulting in twin-to-twin or other transplacental transfusion
Use additional code to indicate resultant condition in fetus or newborn:
fetal blood loss (772.0)
polycythemia neonatorum (776.4)

762.4 Prolapsed cord N

Cord presentation

762.5 Other compression of umbilical cord N

Cord around neck
Entanglement of cord
Knot in cord
Torsion of cord

AHA: 2Q, '03, 9

762.6 Other and unspecified conditions of umbilical cord N

Short cord
Thrombosis, Varices, Velamentous insertion, Vasa previa } of umbilical cord

EXCLUDES *infection of umbilical cord (771.4)*
single umbilical artery (747.5)

762.7 Chorioamnionitis N

Amnionitis
Membranitis
Placentitis

DEF: Inflamed fetal membrane.

762.8 Other specified abnormalities of chorion and amnion N

762.9 Unspecified abnormality of chorion and amnion N

4th **763 Fetus or newborn affected by other complications of labor and delivery**

INCLUDES the listed conditions only when specified as a cause of mortality or morbidity in the fetus or newborn

AHA: 1Q, '94, 8

763.0 Breech delivery and extraction N

763.1 Other malpresentation, malposition, and disproportion during labor and delivery N

Fetus or newborn affected by:
abnormality of bony pelvis
contracted pelvis
persistent occipitoposterior position
shoulder presentation
transverse lie
conditions classifiable to 652, 653, and 660

763.2 Forceps delivery N

Fetus or newborn affected by forceps extraction

763.3 Delivery by vacuum extractor N

763.4 Cesarean delivery N

EXCLUDES *placental separation or hemorrhage from cesarean section (762.1)*

763.5 Maternal anesthesia and analgesia N

Reactions and intoxications from maternal opiates and tranquilizers during labor and delivery

EXCLUDES *drug withdrawal syndrome in newborn (779.5)*

763.6 Precipitate delivery N

Rapid second stage

763.7 Abnormal uterine contractions N

Fetus or newborn affected by:
contraction ring
hypertonic labor
hypotonic uterine dysfunction
uterine inertia or dysfunction
conditions classifiable to 661, except 661.3

5th **763.8 Other specified complications of labor and delivery affecting fetus or newborn**

AHA: 4Q, '98, 46

763.81 Abnormality in fetal heart rate or rhythm before the onset of labor N

763.82 Abnormality in fetal heart rate or rhythm during labor N

AHA: 4Q, '98, 46

763.83 Abnormality in fetal heart rate or rhythm, unspecified as to time of onset N

763.84 Meconium passage during delivery N

EXCLUDES *meconium aspiration (770.11, 770.12)*
meconium staining (779.84)

AHA: ▶4Q, '05, 83◀

DEF: ▶Fetal intestinal activity that increases in response to a distressed state during delivery; anal sphincter relaxes, and meconium is passed into the amniotic fluid.◀

763.89 Other specified complications of labor and delivery affecting fetus or newborn N

Fetus or newborn affected by:
abnormality of maternal soft tissues
destructive operation on live fetus to facilitate delivery
induction of labor (medical)
previous surgery to uterus or pelvic organs
other conditions classifiable to 650-669
other procedures used in labor and delivery

763.9 Unspecified complication of labor and delivery affecting fetus or newborn N

OTHER CONDITIONS ORIGINATING IN THE PERINATAL PERIOD (764-779)

The following fifth-digit subclassification is for use with category 764 and codes 765.0-765.1 to denote birthweight:

0 unspecified [weight]
1 less than 500 grams
2 500-749 grams
3 750-999 grams
4 1,000-1,249 grams
5 1,250-1,499 grams
6 1,500-1,749 grams
7 1,750-1,999 grams
8 2,000-2,499 grams
9 2,500 grams and over

4th **764 Slow fetal growth and fetal malnutrition**
AHA: 3Q, '04, 4; 4Q, '02, 63; 1Q,"94, 8; 2Q, '91, 19; 2Q, '89, 15

5th **764.0 "Light-for-dates" without mention of fetal malnutrition** N
Infants underweight for gestational age
"Small-for-dates"

5th **764.1 "Light-for-dates" with signs of fetal malnutrition** N
Infants "light-for-dates" classifiable to 764.0, who in addition show signs of fetal malnutrition, such as dry peeling skin and loss of subcutaneous tissue

5th **764.2 Fetal malnutrition without mention of "light-for-dates"** N
Infants, not underweight for gestational age, showing signs of fetal malnutrition, such as dry peeling skin and loss of subcutaneous tissue
Intrauterine malnutrition

5th **764.9 Fetal growth retardation, unspecified** N
Intrauterine growth retardation
AHA: For code 764.97: 1Q, '97, 6

4th **765 Disorders relating to short gestation and low birthweight**
INCLUDES the listed conditions, without further specification, as causes of mortality, morbidity, or additional care, in fetus or newborn
AHA: 1Q, '97, 6; 1Q, '94, 8; 2Q, '91, 19; 2Q, '89, 15

5th **765.0 Extreme immaturity** CC 1-8 N
Note: Usually implies a birthweight of less than 1000 grams.
Use additional code for weeks of gestation (765.20-765.29)
CC Excl: For codes 765.01-765.08: 764.00-765.29, 767.8-767.9, 779.8, 779.81-779.89
AHA: 3Q, '04, 4; 4Q, '02, 63; For code 765.03: 4Q, '01, 51

5th **765.1 Other preterm infants** N
Note: Usually implies a birthweight of 1000-2499 grams.
Prematurity NOS
Prematurity or small size, not classifiable to 765.0 or as "light-for-dates" in 764
Use additional code for weeks of gestation (765.20-765.29)
AHA: 3Q, '04, 4; 4Q, '02, 63; For code 765.10: 1Q, '94, 14; For code 765.17: 1Q, '97, 6; For code 765.18: 4Q, '02, 64

5th **765.2 Weeks of gestation**
AHA: 3Q, '04, 4; 4Q, '02, 63

765.20 Unspecified weeks of gestation N
765.21 Less than 24 completed weeks of gestation N
765.22 24 completed weeks of gestation N
765.23 25-26 completed weeks of gestation N
765.24 27-28 completed weeks of gestation N
765.25 29-30 completed weeks of gestation N
765.26 31-32 completed weeks of gestation N
765.27 33-34 completed weeks of gestation N
765.28 35-36 completed weeks of gestation N
AHA: 4Q, '02, 64
765.29 37 or more completed weeks of gestation N

4th **766 Disorders relating to long gestation and high birthweight**
INCLUDES the listed conditions, without further specification, as causes of mortality, morbidity, or additional care, in fetus or newborn

766.0 Exceptionally large baby N
Note: Usually implies a birthweight of 4500 grams or more.

766.1 Other "heavy-for-dates" infants N
Other fetus or infant "heavy-" or "large-for-dates" regardless of period of gestation

5th **766.2 Late infant, not "heavy-for-dates"**

766.21 Post-term infant N
Infant with gestation period over 40 completed weeks to 42 completed weeks
AHA: 4Q, '03, 69

766.22 Prolonged gestation of infant N
Infant with gestation period over 42 completed weeks
Postmaturity NOS

4th **767 Birth trauma**

767.0 Subdural and cerebral hemorrhage CC N
Subdural and cerebral hemorrhage, whether described as due to birth trauma or to intrapartum anoxia or hypoxia
Subdural hematoma (localized)
Tentorial tear
Use additional code to identify cause
EXCLUDES *intraventricular hemorrhage (772.10-772.14)*
subarachnoid hemorrhage (772.2)
CC Excl: 767.0, 767.8-767.9, 779.81-779.89

5th **767.1 Injuries to scalp**
AHA: 4Q, '03, 69

767.11 Epicranial subaponeurotic hemorrhage (massive) CC N
Subgaleal hemorrhage
CC Excl: 767.0-767.11, 767.8-767.9, 779.81-779.89
DEF: A hemorrhage that occurs within the space between the galea aponeurotica, or epicranial aponeurosis, a thin tendinous structure that is attached to the skull laterally and provides an insertion site for the occipitalis posteriorly and the frontalis muscle anteriorly, and the periosteum of the skull.

767.19 Other injuries to scalp N
Caput succedaneum
Cephalhematoma
Chignon (from vacuum extraction)

767.2 Fracture of clavicle N

Epicranial Subaponeurosis

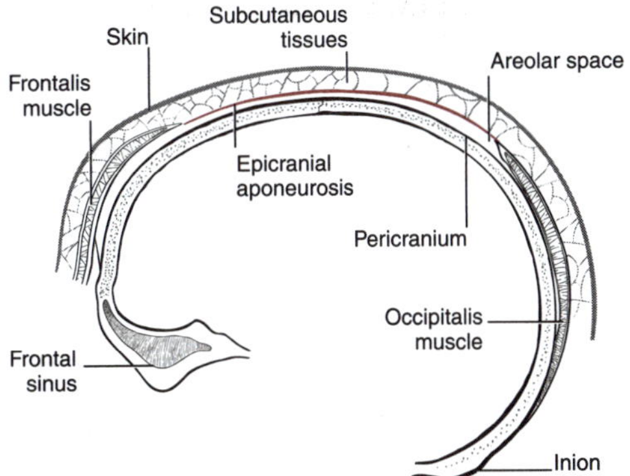

767.3 Other injuries to skeleton N
Fracture of:
long bones
skull
EXCLUDES *congenital dislocation of hip (754.30-754.35)*
fracture of spine, congenital (767.4)

767.4 Injury to spine and spinal cord N
Dislocation, Fracture, Laceration, Rupture } of spine or spinal cord due to birth trauma

767.5 Facial nerve injury N
Facial palsy

767.6 Injury to brachial plexus N
Palsy or paralysis:
brachial
Erb (-Duchenne)
Klumpke (-Déjérine)

767.7 Other cranial and peripheral nerve injuries N
Phrenic nerve paralysis

767.8 Other specified birth trauma N
Eye damage
Hematoma of:
liver (subcapsular)
testes
vulva
Rupture of:
liver
spleen
Scalpel wound
Traumatic glaucoma
EXCLUDES *hemorrhage classifiable to 772.0-772.9*

767.9 Birth trauma, unspecified N
Birth injury NOS

✓4th **768 Intrauterine hypoxia and birth asphyxia**
Use only when associated with newborn morbidity classifiable elsewhere
EXCLUDES ▶ *acidemia NOS of newborn (775.81)*
acidosis NOS of newborn (775.81)
cerebral ischemia NOS (779.2)
hypoxia NOS of newborn (770.88)
mixed metabolic and respiratory acidosis of newborn (775.81)
respiratory arrest of newborn (770.87)◀
AHA: 4Q, '92, 20

DEF: Oxygen intake insufficiency due to interrupted placental circulation or premature separation of placenta.

768.0 Fetal death from asphyxia or anoxia before onset of labor or at unspecified time N

768.1 Fetal death from asphyxia or anoxia during labor N

768.2 Fetal distress before onset of labor, in liveborn infant N
Fetal metabolic acidemia before onset of labor, in liveborn infant

▲ **768.3 Fetal distress first noted during labor and delivery, in liveborn infant** N
Fetal metabolic acidemia first noted during labor ▶and delivery,◀ in liveborn infant

768.4 Fetal distress, unspecified as to time of onset, in liveborn infant N
Fetal metabolic acidemia unspecified as to time of onset, in liveborn infant
AHA: N-D, '86, 10

768.5 Severe birth asphyxia CC N
Birth asphyxia with neurologic involvement
EXCLUDES ▶ *hypoxic-ischemic encephalopathy [HIE] (768.7)*◀
CC Excl: 768.5-770.9, 779.81-779.89
AHA: N-D, '86, 3

768.6 Mild or moderate birth asphyxia N
Birth asphyxia (without mention of neurologic involvement)
EXCLUDES ▶ *hypoxic-ischemic encephalopathy [HIE] (768.7)*◀
AHA: N-D, '86, 3

● **768.7 Hypoxic-ischemic encephalopathy [HIE]** N

768.9 Unspecified birth asphyxia in liveborn infant N
Anoxia, Asphyxia } NOS, in liveborn infant

769 Respiratory distress syndrome CC N
Cardiorespiratory distress syndrome of newborn
Hyaline membrane disease (pulmonary)
Idiopathic respiratory distress syndrome [IRDS or RDS] of newborn
Pulmonary hypoperfusion syndrome
EXCLUDES *transient tachypnea of newborn (770.6)*
CC Excl: See code 768.5
AHA: 1Q, '89, 10; N-D, '86, 6

DEF: Severe chest contractions upon air intake and expiratory grunting; infant appears blue due to oxygen deficiency and has rapid respiratory rate; formerly called hyaline membrane disease.

✓4th **770 Other respiratory conditions of fetus and newborn**

770.0 Congenital pneumonia CC N
Infective pneumonia acquired prenatally
EXCLUDES *pneumonia from infection acquired after birth (480.0-486)*
CC Excl: See code 768.5
AHA: 1Q, '05, 10

✓5th **770.1 Fetal and newborn aspiration**
EXCLUDES *aspiration of postnatal stomach contents (770.85, 770.86)*
meconium passage during delivery (763.84)
meconium staining (779.84)
AHA: 4Q, '05, 83

770.10 Fetal and newborn aspiration, unspecified N

770.11 Meconium aspiration without respiratory symptoms N
Meconium aspiration NOS

770.12 Meconium aspiration with respiratory symptoms CC N
Meconium aspiration pneumonia
Meconium aspiration pneumonitis
Meconium aspiration syndrome NOS
Use additional code to identify any secondary pulmonary hypertension (416.8), if applicable
CC Excl: See code 768.5

DEF: Meconium aspiration syndrome: aspiration of fetal intestinal material during or prior to delivery, usually a complication of placental insufficiency, causing pneumonitis and bronchial obstruction (inflammatory reaction of lungs).

770.13 Aspiration of clear amniotic fluid without respiratory symptoms N
Aspiration of clear amniotic fluid NOS

770.14 Aspiration of clear amniotic fluid with respiratory symptoms CC N
Aspiration of clear amniotic fluid with pneumonia
Aspiration of clear amniotic fluid with pneumonitis
Use additional code to identify any secondary pulmonary hypertension (416.8), if applicable
CC Excl: See code 768.5

770.15 Aspiration of blood without respiratory symptoms N
Aspiration of blood NOS

N Newborn Age: 0  Pediatric Age: 0-17  Maternity Age: 12-55  Adult Age: 15-124  CC Condition  Major Complication 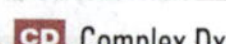 Complex Dx  HIV Related Dx

770.16 Aspiration of blood with respiratory symptoms CC N
Aspiration of blood with pneumonia
Aspiration of blood with pneumonitis
Use additional code to identify any secondary pulmonary hypertension (416.8), if applicable
CC Excl: See code 768.5

770.17 Other fetal and newborn aspiration without respiratory symptoms N

770.18 Other fetal and newborn aspiration with respiratory symptoms CC N
Other aspiration pneumonia
Other aspiration pneumonitis
Use additional code to identify any secondary pulmonary hypertension (416.8), if applicable
CC Excl: See code 768.5

770.2 Interstitial emphysema and related conditions CC N
Pneumomediastinum, Pneumopericardium, Pneumothorax } originating in the perinatal period
CC Excl: See code 768.5

770.3 Pulmonary hemorrhage CC N
Hemorrhage:
alveolar (lung), intra-alveolar (lung), massive pulmonary } originating in the perinatal period
CC Excl: See code 768.5

770.4 Primary atelectasis CC N
Pulmonary immaturity NOS
CC Excl: See code 768.5

DEF: Alveoli fail to expand causing insufficient air intake by newborn.

770.5 Other and unspecified atelectasis CC N
Atelectasis:
NOS, partial, secondary; Pulmonary collapse } originating in the perinatal period
CC Excl: See code 768.5

770.6 Transitory tachypnea of newborn N
Idiopathic tachypnea of newborn
Wet lung syndrome
EXCLUDES *respiratory distress syndrome (769)*
AHA: 4Q, '95, 4; 1Q, '94, 12; 3Q, '93, 7; 1Q, '89, 10; N-D, '86, 6
DEF: Quick, shallow breathing of newborn; short-term problem.

770.7 Chronic respiratory disease arising in the perinatal period CC
Bronchopulmonary dysplasia
Interstitial pulmonary fibrosis of prematurity
Wilson-Mikity syndrome
CC Excl: See code 768.5
AHA: 2Q, '91, 19; N-D, '86, 11

✓5th **770.8 Other respiratory problems after birth**
EXCLUDES ▶ *mixed metabolic and respiratory acidosis of newborn (775.81)*◀
AHA: 4Q, '02, 65; 2Q, '98, 10; 2Q, '96, 10

770.81 Primary apnea of newborn N
Apneic spells of newborn NOS
Essential apnea of newborn
Sleep apnea of newborn
DEF: Cessation of breathing when a neonate makes no respiratory effort for 15 seconds, resulting in cyanosis and bradycardia.

770.82 Other apnea of newborn N
Obstructive apnea of newborn

770.83 Cyanotic attacks of newborn N

770.84 Respiratory failure of newborn CC N
EXCLUDES *respiratory distress syndrome (769)*
CC Excl: See code 768.5

770.85 Aspiration of postnatal stomach contents without respiratory symptoms N
Aspiration of postnatal stomach contents NOS
AHA: 4Q, '05, 83

770.86 Aspiration of postnatal stomach contents with respiratory symptoms CC N
Aspiration of postnatal stomach contents with pneumonia
Aspiration of postnatal stomach contents with pneumonitis
Use additional code to identify any secondary pulmonary hypertension (416.8), if applicable
CC Excl: See code 768.5
AHA: 4Q, '05, 83

● **770.87 Respiratory arrest of newborn** N

● **770.88 Hypoxemia of newborn** N
Hypoxia NOS of newborn

770.89 Other respiratory problems after birth N

770.9 Unspecified respiratory condition of fetus and newborn N

✓4th **771 Infections specific to the perinatal period**
INCLUDES infections acquired before or during birth or via the umbilicus or during the first 28 days after birth
EXCLUDES *congenital pneumonia (770.0)*
congenital syphilis (090.0-090.9)
maternal infectious disease as a cause of mortality or morbidity in fetus or newborn, but fetus or newborn not manifesting the disease (760.2)
ophthalmia neonatorum due to gonococcus (098.40)
other infections not specifically classified to this category
AHA: N-D, '85, 4

771.0 Congenital rubella CC N
Congenital rubella pneumonitis
CC Excl: 771.0-771.2, 779.81-779.89

771.1 Congenital cytomegalovirus infection CC N
Congenital cytomegalic inclusion disease
CC Excl: See code 771.0

771.2 Other congenital infections N
Congenital:
herpes simplex
listeriosis
malaria
toxoplasmosis
tuberculosis

771.3 Tetanus neonatorum CC N
Tetanus omphalitis
EXCLUDES *hypocalcemic tetany (775.4)*
CC Excl: 771.3, 779.81-779.89

DEF: Severe infection of central nervous system; due to exotoxin of tetanus bacillus from navel infection prompted by nonsterile technique during umbilical ligation.

771.4 Omphalitis of the newborn N
Infection:
navel cord
umbilical stump
EXCLUDES *tetanus omphalitis (771.3)*
DEF: Inflamed umbilicus.

771.5 Neonatal infective mastitis N
EXCLUDES *noninfective neonatal mastitis (778.7)*

771.6 Neonatal conjunctivitis and dacryocystitis N
Ophthalmia neonatorum NOS
EXCLUDES *ophthalmia neonatorum due to gonococcus (098.40)*

771.7 Neonatal Candida infection N
Neonatal moniliasis
Thrush in newborn

✓5th **771.8 Other infection specific to the perinatal period**
Use additional code to identify organism (041.00-041.9)
AHA: 4Q, '02, 66

771.81 Septicemia [sepsis] of newborn CC N
CC Excl: 771.4-771.89, 776.0-776.9, 779.81-779.89

771.82 Urinary tract infection of newborn N

771.83 Bacteremia of newborn CC N
CC Excl: See code 771.81

771.89 Other infections specific to the perinatal period N
Intra-amniotic infection of fetus NOS
Infection of newborn NOS

✓4th **772 Fetal and neonatal hemorrhage**
EXCLUDES *hematological disorders of fetus and newborn (776.0-776.9)*

772.0 Fetal blood loss N
Fetal blood loss from:
cut end of co-twin's cord
placenta
ruptured cord
vasa previa
Fetal exsanguination
Fetal hemorrhage into:
co-twin
mother's circulation

✓5th **772.1 Intraventricular hemorrhage**
Intraventricular hemorrhage from any perinatal cause
AHA: 4Q, '01, 49; 3Q, '92, 8; 4Q, '88, 8

772.10 Unspecified grade CC N
CC Excl: 772.0-772.2, 772.8-772.9, 776.0-776.9, 779.81-779.89

772.11 Grade I CC N
Bleeding into germinal matrix
CC Excl: See code 772.10

772.12 Grade II CC N
Bleeding into ventricle
CC Excl: See code 772.10

772.13 Grade III CC N
Bleeding with enlargement of ventricle
CC Excl: See code 772.10
AHA: 4Q, '01, 51

772.14 Grade IV CC N
Bleeding into cerebral cortex
CC Excl: See code 772.10

772.2 Subarachnoid hemorrhage CC N
Subarachnoid hemorrhage from any perinatal cause
EXCLUDES *subdural and cerebral hemorrhage (767.0)*
CC Excl: 772.0-772.2, 772.8-772.9, 776.0-776.9, 779.7-779.89

772.3 Umbilical hemorrhage after birth N
Slipped umbilical ligature

772.4 Gastrointestinal hemorrhage CC N
EXCLUDES *swallowed maternal blood (777.3)*
CC Excl: 772.0, 772.4-772.5, 772.8-772.9, 776.0-776.9, 779.81-779.89

772.5 Adrenal hemorrhage CC N
CC Excl: See code 772.4

772.6 Cutaneous hemorrhage N
Bruising, Ecchymoses, Petechiae, Superficial hematoma — in fetus or newborn

772.8 Other specified hemorrhage of fetus or newborn N
EXCLUDES *hemorrhagic disease of newborn (776.0)*
pulmonary hemorrhage (770.3)

772.9 Unspecified hemorrhage of newborn N

✓4th **773 Hemolytic disease of fetus or newborn, due to isoimmunization**
DEF: Hemolytic anemia of fetus or newborn due to maternal antibody formation against fetal erythrocytes; infant blood contains nonmaternal antigen.

773.0 Hemolytic disease due to Rh isoimmunization CC N
Anemia, Erythroblastosis (fetalis), Hemolytic disease (fetus) (newborn) — due to RH: antibodies, isoimmunization, maternal/fetal incompatibility
Rh hemolytic disease
Rh isoimmunization
CC Excl: 773.0-773.5, 779.81-779.89

773.1 Hemolytic disease due to ABO isoimmunization CC N
ABO hemolytic disease
ABO isoimmunization
Anemia, Erythroblastosis (fetalis), Hemolytic disease (fetus) (newborn), Jaundice — due to ABO: antibodies, isoimmunization, maternal/fetal incompatibility
CC Excl: See code 773.0
AHA: 3Q, '92, 8
DEF: Incompatible Rh fetal-maternal blood grouping; prematurely destroys red blood cells; detected by Coombs test.

773.2 Hemolytic disease due to other and unspecified isoimmunization CC N
Eythroblastosis (fetalis) (neonatorum) NOS
Hemolytic disease (fetus) (newborn) NOS
Jaundice or anemia due to other and unspecified blood-group incompatibility
CC Excl: See code 773.0
AHA: 1Q, '94, 13

773.3 Hydrops fetalis due to isoimmunization CC N
Use additional code to identify type of isoimmunization (773.0-773.2)
CC Excl: See code 773.0
DEF: Massive edema of entire body and severe anemia; may result in fetal death or stillbirth.

773.4 Kernicterus due to isoimmunization CC N
Use additional code to identify type of isoimmunization (773.0-773.2)
CC Excl: See code 773.0
DEF: Complication of erythroblastosis fetalis associated with severe neural symptoms, high blood bilirubin levels and nerve cell destruction; results in bilirubin-pigmented gray matter of central nervous system.

773.5 Late anemia due to isoimmunization N

✓4th **774 Other perinatal jaundice**

774.0 Perinatal jaundice from hereditary hemolyticanemias CC N
Code first underlying disease (282.0-282.9)
CC Excl: 774.0-774.7, 779.81-779.89

774.1 Perinatal jaundice from other excessive hemolysis CC N
Fetal or neonatal jaundice from:
bruising
drugs or toxins transmitted from mother
infection
polycythemia
swallowed maternal blood
Use additional code to identify cause
EXCLUDES *jaundice due to isoimmunization (773.0-773.2)*
CC Excl: See code 774.0

774.2 Neonatal jaundice associated with preterm delivery CC N
Hyperbilirubinemia of prematurity
Jaundice due to delayed conjugation associated with preterm delivery
CC Excl: See code 774.0
AHA: 3Q, '91, 21

✓5th **774.3 Neonatal jaundice due to delayed conjugation from other causes**

774.30 Neonatal jaundice due to delayed conjugation, cause unspecified CC N
CC Excl: See code 774.0
DEF: Jaundice of newborn with abnormal bilirubin metabolism; causes excess accumulated unconjugated bilirubin in blood.

774.31 *Neonatal jaundice due to delayed conjugation in diseases classified elsewhere* CC N
Code first underlying diseases as:
congenital hypothyroidism (243)
Crigler-Najjar syndrome (277.4)
Gilbert's syndrome (277.4)
CC Excl: See code 774.0

774.39 Other CC N
Jaundice due to delayed conjugation from causes, such as:
breast milk inhibitors
delayed development of conjugating system
CC Excl: See code 774.0

774.4 Perinatal jaundice due to hepatocellular damage CC N
Fetal or neonatal hepatitis
Giant cell hepatitis
Inspissated bile syndrome
CC Excl: See code 774.0

774.5 *Perinatal jaundice from other causes* CC N
Code first underlying cause as:
congenital obstruction of bile duct (751.61)
galactosemia (271.1)
mucoviscidosis (277.00-277.09)
CC Excl: See code 774.0

774.6 Unspecified fetal and neonatal jaundice N
Icterus neonatorum
Neonatal hyperbilirubinemia (transient)
Physiologic jaundice NOS in newborn
EXCLUDES *that in preterm infants (774.2)*
AHA: 1Q, '94, 13; 2Q, '89, 15

774.7 Kernicterus not due to isoimmunization CC N
Bilirubin encephalopathy
Kernicterus of newborn NOS
EXCLUDES *kernicterus due to isoimmunization (773.4)*
CC Excl: See code 774.0

✓4th **775 Endocrine and metabolic disturbances specific to the fetus and newborn**
INCLUDES transitory endocrine and metabolic disturbances caused by the infant's response to maternal endocrine and metabolic factors, its removal from them, or its adjustment to extrauterine existence

775.0 Syndrome of "infant of a diabetic mother" N
Maternal diabetes mellitus affecting fetus or newborn (with hypoglycemia)
AHA: 1Q, '04, 7-8; 3Q, '91, 5

775.1 Neonatal diabetes mellitus CC N
Diabetes mellitus syndrome in newborn infant
CC Excl: 775.0-775.9, 779.81-779.89
AHA: 3Q, '91, 6

775.2 Neonatal myasthenia gravis CC N
CC Excl: See code 775.1

775.3 Neonatal thyrotoxicosis CC N
Neonatal hyperthydroidism (transient)
CC Excl: See code 775.1

775.4 Hypocalcemia and hypomagnesemia of newborn CC N
Cow's milk hypocalcemia
Hypocalcemic tetany, neonatal
Neonatal hypoparathyroidism
Phosphate-loading hypocalcemia
CC Excl: See code 775.1

775.5 Other transitory neonatal electrolyte disturbances CC N
Dehydration, neonatal
CC Excl: See code 775.1
AHA: 1Q, '05, 9

775.6 Neonatal hypoglycemia CC N
EXCLUDES *infant of mother with diabetes mellitus (775.0)*
CC Excl: See code 775.1
AHA: 1Q, '94, 8

775.7 Late metabolic acidosis of newborn CC N
CC Excl: See code 775.1

▲ **775.8 Other neonatal endocrine and metabolic disturbances**

● **775.81 Other acidosis of newborn** N
Acidemia NOS of newborn
Acidosis of newborn NOS
Mixed metabolic and respiratory acidosis of newborn

● **775.89 Other neonatal endocrine and metabolic disturbances** N
Amino-acid metabolic disorders described as transitory

775.9 Unspecified endocrine and metabolic disturbances specific to the fetus and newborn N

✓4th **776 Hematological disorders of fetus and newborn**
INCLUDES disorders specific to the fetus or newborn

776.0 Hemorrhagic disease of newborn CC N
Hemorrhagic diathesis of newborn
Vitamin K deficiency of newborn
EXCLUDES *fetal or neonatal hemorrhage (772.0-772.9)*
CC Excl: 776.0-776.9, 779.81-779.89

776.1 Transient neonatal thrombocytopenia CC N
Neonatal thrombocytopenia due to:
exchange transfusion
idiopathic maternal thrombocytopenia
isoimmunization
CC Excl: See code 776.0
DEF: Temporary decrease in blood platelets of newborn.

776.2 Disseminated intravascular coagulation in newborn CC N

CC Excl: See code 776.0

DEF: Disseminated intravascular coagulation of newborn: clotting disorder due to excess thromboplastic agents in blood as a result of disease or trauma; causes blood clotting within vessels and reduces available elements necessary for blood coagulation.

776.3 Other transient neonatal disorders of coagulation CC N

Transient coagulation defect, newborn

CC Excl: See code 776.0

776.4 Polycythemia neonatorum N

Plethora of newborn
Polycythemia due to:
donor twin transfusion
Polycythemia due to:
maternal-fetal transfusion

DEF: Abnormal increase of total red blood cells of newborn.

776.5 Congenital anemia N

Anemia following fetal blood loss

EXCLUDES *anemia due to isoimmunization (773.0-773.2, 773.5)*
hereditary hemolytic anemias (282.0-282.9)

776.6 Anemia of prematurity N

776.7 Transient neonatal neutropenia N

Isoimmune neutropenia
Maternal transfer neutropenia

EXCLUDES *congenital neutropenia (nontransient)* ►*(288.01)*◄

DEF: Decreased neutrophilic leukocytes in blood of newborn.

776.8 Other specified transient hematological disorders N

776.9 Unspecified hematological disorder specific to fetus or newborn N

✓4th **777 Perinatal disorders of digestive system**

INCLUDES disorders specific to the fetus and newborn

EXCLUDES *intestinal obstruction classifiable to 560.0-560.9*

777.1 Meconium obstruction CC N

Congenital fecaliths
Delayed passage of meconium
Meconium ileus NOS
Meconium plug syndrome

EXCLUDES *meconium ileus in cystic fibrosis (277.01)*

CC Excl: 777.1-777.9, 779.81-779.89

DEF: Meconium blocked digestive tract of newborn.

777.2 Intestinal obstruction due to inspissated milk CC N

CC Excl: See code 777.1

777.3 Hematemesis and melena due to swallowed maternal blood N

Swallowed blood syndrome in newborn

EXCLUDES *that not due to swallowed maternal blood (772.4)*

777.4 Transitory ileus of newborn N

EXCLUDES *Hirschsprung's disease (751.3)*

777.5 Necrotizing enterocolitis in fetus or newborn CC N

Pseudomembranous enterocolitis in newborn

CC Excl: See code 777.1

DEF: Acute inflammation of small intestine due to pseudomembranous plaque over ulceration; may be due to aggressive antibiotic therapy.

777.6 Perinatal intestinal perforation CC N

Meconium peritonitis

CC Excl: See code 777.1

777.8 Other specified perinatal disorders of digestive system N

777.9 Unspecified perinatal disorder of digestive system N

✓4th **778 Conditions involving the integument and temperature regulation of fetus and newborn**

778.0 Hydrops fetalis not due to isoimmunization CC N

Idiopathic hydrops

EXCLUDES *hydrops fetalis due to isoimmunization (773.3)*

CC Excl: 778.0, 779.81-779.89

DEF: Edema of entire body, unrelated to immune response.

778.1 Sclerema neonatorum N

Subcutaneous fat necrosis

DEF: Diffuse, rapidly progressing white, waxy, nonpitting hardening of tissue, usually of legs and feet, life-threatening; found in preterm or debilitated infants; unknown etiology.

778.2 Cold injury syndrome of newborn N

778.3 Other hypothermia of newborn N

778.4 Other disturbances of temperature regulation of newborn N

Dehydration fever in newborn
Environmentally-induced pyrexia
Hyperthermia in newborn
Transitory fever of newborn

778.5 Other and unspecified edema of newborn N

Edema neonatorum

778.6 Congenital hydrocele

Congenital hydrocele of tunica vaginalis

778.7 Breast engorgement in newborn N

Noninfective mastitis of newborn

EXCLUDES *infective mastitis of newborn (771.5)*

778.8 Other specified conditions involving the integument of fetus and newborn N

Urticaria neonatorum

EXCLUDES *impetigo neonatorum (684)*
pemphigus neonatorum (684)

778.9 Unspecified condition involving the integument and temperature regulation of fetus and newborn N

✓4th **779 Other and ill-defined conditions originating in the perinatal period**

779.0 Convulsions in newborn CC N

Fits } in newborn
Seizures } in newborn

CC Excl: 779.0-779.1, 779.81-779.89

AHA: N-D, '94, 11

779.1 Other and unspecified cerebral irritability in newborn CC N

CC Excl: See code 779.0

779.2 Cerebral depression, coma, and other abnormal cerebral signs N

►Cerebral ischemia NOS of newborn◄
CNS dysfunction in newborn NOS

EXCLUDES ► *cerebral ischemia due to birth trauma (767.0)*
intrauterine cerebral ischemia (768.2-768.9)
intraventricular hemorrhage (772.10-772.14)◄

779.3 Feeding problems in newborn CC N

Regurgitation of food } in newborn
Slow feeding } in newborn
Vomiting } in newborn

CC Excl: 779.3

AHA: 2Q, '89, 15

779.4 Drug reactions and intoxications specific to newborn CC N

Gray syndrome from chloramphenicol administration in newborn

EXCLUDES *fetal alcohol syndrome (760.71)*
reactions and intoxications from maternal opiates and tranquilizers (763.5)

CC Excl: 779.4-779.5

779.5 Drug withdrawal syndrome in newborn N

Drug withdrawal syndrome in infant of dependent mother

EXCLUDES *fetal alcohol syndrome (760.71)*

AHA: 3Q, '94, 6

779.6 Termination of pregnancy (fetus) N

Fetal death due to:
induced abortion
termination of pregnancy

EXCLUDES *spontaneous abortion (fetus) (761.8)*

779.7 Periventricular leukomalacia CC

CC Excl: 772.0-772.2, 772.8, 772.9, 776.0-776.9, 779.7-779.89

AHA: 4Q, '01, 50, 51

DEF: Necrosis of white matter adjacent to lateral ventricles with the formation of cysts; cause of PVL has not been firmly established, but thought to be related to inadequate blood flow in certain areas of the brain.

✓5th **779.8 Other specified conditions originating in the perinatal period**

AHA: 4Q, '02, 67; 1Q, '94, 15

779.81 Neonatal bradycardia N

EXCLUDES *abnormality in fetal heart rate or rhythm complicating labor and delivery (763.81-763.83)*
bradycardia due to birth asphyxia (768.5-768.9)

779.82 Neonatal tachycardia N

EXCLUDES *abnormality in fetal heart rate or rhythm complicating labor and delivery (763.81-763.83)*

779.83 Delayed separation of umbilical cord N

AHA: 4Q, '03, 71

779.84 Meconium staining N

EXCLUDES *meconium aspiration (770.11, 770.12)*
meconium passage during delivery (763.84)

AHA: 4Q, '05, 83, 88

● **779.85 Cardiac arrest of newborn** N

779.89 Other specified conditions originating in the perinatal period N

Use additional code to specify condition

AHA: ▶1Q, '06, 18; 2Q, '05, 15;◀ 1Q, '05, 9

779.9 Unspecified condition originating in the perinatal period N

Congenital debility NOS
Stillbirth NEC

16. SYMPTOMS, SIGNS, AND ILL-DEFINED CONDITIONS (780-799)

This section includes symptoms, signs, abnormal results of laboratory or other investigative procedures, and ill-defined conditions regarding which no diagnosis classifiable elsewhere is recorded.

Signs and symptoms that point rather definitely to a given diagnosis are assigned to some category in the preceding part of the classification. In general, categories 780-796 include the more ill-defined conditions and symptoms that point with perhaps equal suspicion to two or more diseases or to two or more systems of the body, and without the necessary study of the case to make a final diagnosis. Practically all categories in this group could be designated as "not otherwise specified," or as "unknown etiology," or as "transient." The Alphabetic Index should be consulted to determine which symptoms and signs are to be allocated here and which to more specific sections of the classification; the residual subcategories numbered .9 are provided for other relevant symptoms which cannot be allocated elsewhere in the classification.

The conditions and signs or symptoms included in categories 780-796 consist of: (a) cases for which no more specific diagnosis can be made even after all facts bearing on the case have been investigated; (b) signs or symptoms existing at the time of initial encounter that proved to be transient and whose causes could not be determined; (c) provisional diagnoses in a patient who failed to return for further investigation or care; (d) cases referred elsewhere for investigation or treatment before the diagnosis was made; (e) cases in which a more precise diagnosis was not available for any other reason; (f) certain symptoms which represent important problems in medical care and which it might be desired to classify in addition to a known cause.

SYMPTOMS (780-789)

AHA: 1Q, '91, 12; 2Q, '90, 3; 2Q, '90, 5; 2Q, '90, 15; M-A, '85, 3

✓4th **780 General symptoms**

✓5th **780.0 Alteration of consciousness**

EXCLUDES *coma:*
diabetic (250.2-250.3)
hepatic (572.2)
originating in the perinatal period (779.2)

AHA: 4Q, '92, 20

780.01 Coma CC

CC Excl: 070.0-070.9, 250.00-251.3, 338.0-338.4, 348.8-348.9, 349.89, 349.9, 430-432.9, 572.2, 780.01-780.09, 780.2, 780.4, 780.91-780.99, 799.81-799.89, 800.00-801.99, 803.00-804.96, 850.0-852.19, 852.21-854.19

AHA: 3Q, '96, 16

DEF: State of unconsciousness from which the patient cannot be awakened.

780.02 Transient alteration of awareness

DEF: Temporary, recurring spells of reduced consciousness.

780.03 Persistent vegetative state CC

CC Excl: See code 780.01

DEF: Persistent wakefulness without consciousness due to nonfunctioning cerebral cortex.

780.09 Other

Drowsiness
Semicoma
Somnolence
Stupor
Unconsciousness

780.1 Hallucinations CC

Hallucinations:
NOS
auditory
gustatory
olfactory
tactile

EXCLUDES *those associated with mental disorders, as functional psychoses (295.0-298.9)*
organic brain syndromes (290.0-294.9, 310.0-310.9)
visual hallucinations (368.16)

CC Excl: 338.0-338.4, 780.1, 780.4, 780.91-780.99, 799.81-799.89

DEF: Perception of external stimulus in absence of stimulus; inability to distinguish between real and imagined.

780.2 Syncope and collapse

Blackout
Fainting
(Near) (Pre) syncope
Vasovagal attack

EXCLUDES *carotid sinus syncope (337.0)*
heat syncope (992.1)
neurocirculatory asthenia (306.2)
orthostatic hypotension (458.0)
shock NOS (785.50)

AHA: 1Q, '02, 6; 3Q, '00, 12; 3Q, '95, 14; N-D, '85, 12

DEF: Sudden unconsciousness due to reduced blood flow to brain.

✓5th **780.3 Convulsions**

EXCLUDES *convulsions:*
epileptic (345.10-345.91)
in newborn (779.0)

AHA: 2Q, '97, 8; 1Q, '97, 12; 3Q, '94, 9; 1Q, '93, 24; 4Q, '92, 23; N-D, '87, 12

DEF: Sudden, involuntary contractions of the muscles.

▲ **780.31 Febrile convulsions (simple), unspecified** CC

Febrile seizure ▶NOS◀

CC Excl: 338.0-338.4, 345.00-345.91, 348.81-348.9, 349.89, 349.9, 779.0-779.1, 780.31, 780.39, 780.91-780.99, 799.81-799.89

AHA: 4Q, '97, 45

● **780.32 Complex febrile convulsions** CC

Febrile seizure:
atypical
complex
complicated

EXCLUDES *status epilepticus (345.3)*

CC Excl: See code 780.31

780.39 Other convulsions CC

Convulsive disorder NOS
Fit NOS
▶Recurrent convulsions NOS◀
Seizure NOS

CC Excl: See code 780.31

AHA: 4Q, '04, 51; 1Q, '03, 7; 2Q, '99, 17; 4Q, '98, 39

780.4 Dizziness and giddiness

Light-headedness
Vertigo NOS

EXCLUDES *Ménière's disease and other specified vertiginous syndromes (386.0-386.9)*

AHA: 2Q, '03, 11; 3Q, '00, 12; 2Q, '97, 9; 2Q, '91, 17

DEF: Whirling sensations in head with feeling of falling.

✓5th **780.5 Sleep disturbances**

EXCLUDES *circadian rhythm sleep disorders (327.30-327.39)*
organic hypersomnia (327.10-327.19)
organic insomnia (327.00-327.09)
organic sleep apnea (327.20-327.29)
organic sleep related movement disorders (327.51-327.59)
parasomnias (327.40-327.49)
that of nonorganic origin (307.40-307.49)

AHA: 4Q, '05, 59

780.50 Sleep disturbance, unspecified

780.51 Insomnia with sleep apnea, unspecified

DEF: Transient cessation of breathing disturbing sleep.

780.52 Insomnia, unspecified

DEF: Inability to maintain adequate sleep cycle.

780.53 Hypersomnia with sleep apnea, unspecified

AHA: 1Q, '93, 28; N-D, '85, 4

DEF: Autonomic response inhibited during sleep; causes insufficient oxygen intake, acidosis and pulmonary hypertension.

780.54 Hypersomnia, unspecified

DEF: Prolonged sleep cycle.

780.55 Disruptions of 24 hour sleep wake cycle, unspecified

780.56 Dysfunctions associated with sleep stages or arousal from sleep

780.57 Unspecified sleep apnea

AHA: 1Q, '01, 6 ; 1Q, '97, 5; 1Q, '93, 28

780.58 Sleep related movement disorder, unspecified

EXCLUDES ▶ *restless legs syndrome (333.94)*◀

AHA: 4Q, '04, 95

780.59 Other

780.6 Fever

Chills with fever
Fever NOS
Fever of unknown origin (FUO)
Hyperpyrexia NOS
Pyrexia
Pyrexia of unknown origin

▶Code first underlying condition when associated fever is present, such as with:
leukemia (codes from categories 204-208)
neutropenia (288.00-288.09)
sickle-cell disease (282.60-282.69)◀

EXCLUDES *pyrexia of unknown origin (during):*
in newborn (778.4)
labor (659.2)
the puerperium (672)

AHA: 3Q, '05, 16; 3Q, '00,13; 4Q, '99, 26; 2Q, '91, 8

DEF: Elevated body temperature; no known cause.

✓5th **780.7 Malaise and fatigue**

EXCLUDES *debility, unspecified (799.3)*
fatigue (during):
combat (308.0-308.9)
heat (992.6)
pregnancy (646.8)
neurasthenia (300.5)
senile asthenia (797)

AHA: 4Q, '88, 12; M-A, '87, 8

780.71 Chronic fatigue syndrome

AHA: 4Q, '98, 48

DEF: Persistent fatigue, symptoms include weak muscles, sore throat, lymphadenitis, headache, depression and mild fever; no known cause; also called chronic mononucleosis, benign myalgic encephalomyelitis, Iceland disease and neurosthenia.

780.79 Other malaise and fatigue

Asthenia NOS
Lethargy
Postviral (asthenic) syndrome
Tiredness

AHA: 4Q, '04, 78; 1Q, '00, 6; 4Q, '99, 26

DEF: Asthenia: Any weakness, lack of strength or loss of energy, especially neuromuscular.

DEF: Lethargy: Listlessness, drowsiness, stupor and apathy.

DEF: Malaise: Vague feeling of debility or lack of good health.

DEF: Postviral (asthenic) syndrome: Listlessness, drowsiness, stupor and apathy; follows acute viral infection.

DEF: Tiredness: General exhaustion or fatigue.

780.8 Generalized hyperhidrosis

Diaphoresis
Excessive sweating
Secondary hyperhidrosis

EXCLUDES *focal (localized) (primary) (secondary) hyperhidrosis (705.21-705.22)*
Frey's syndrome (705.22)

DEF: Excessive sweating, appears as droplets on skin; general or localized.

✓5th **780.9 Other general symptoms**

EXCLUDES *hypothermia:*
NOS (accidental) (991.6)
due to anesthesia (995.89)
of newborn (778.2-778.3)
memory disturbance as part of a pattern of mental disorder

AHA: 4Q, '02, 67; 4Q, '99, 10; 3Q, '93, 11; N-D, '85, 12

780.91 Fussy infant (baby) P

780.92 Excessive crying of infant (baby) N

EXCLUDES *excessive crying of child, adolescent or adult (780.95)*

780.93 Memory loss

Amnesia (retrograde)
Memory loss NOS

EXCLUDES *mild memory disturbance due to organic brain damage (310.1)*
transient global amnesia (437.7)

AHA: 4Q, '03, 71

780.94 Early satiety

AHA: 4Q, '03, 72

DEF: The premature feeling of being full; mechanism of satiety is mutlifactorial.

▲ **780.95 Excessive crying of child, adolescent, or adult**

EXCLUDES *excessive crying of infant (baby) (780.92)*

AHA: 4Q, '05, 89

● **780.96 Generalized pain**

Pain NOS

● **780.97 Altered mental status**

Change in mental status

EXCLUDES *altered level of consciousness (780.01-780.09)*
altered mental status due to known condition—code to condition
delirium NOS (780.09)

780.99 Other general symptoms

Chill(s) NOS
Hypothermia, not associated with low environmental temperature

AHA: 4Q, '03, 103

✓4th **781 Symptoms involving nervous and musculoskeletal systems**

EXCLUDES *depression NOS (311)*
disorders specifically relating to:
back (724.0-724.9)
hearing (388.0-389.9)
joint (718.0-719.9)
limb (729.0-729.9)
neck (723.0-723.9)
vision (368.0-369.9)
pain in limb (729.5)

781.0 Abnormal involuntary movements

Abnormal head movements
Fasciculation
Spasms NOS
Tremor NOS

EXCLUDES *abnormal reflex (796.1)*
chorea NOS (333.5)
infantile spasms (345.60-345.61)
spastic paralysis (342.1, 343.0-344.9)
specified movement disorders classifiable to 333 (333.0-333.9)
that of nonorganic origin (307.2-307.3)

781.1 Disturbances of sensation of smell and taste
Anosmia
Parosmia
Parageusia
DEF: Anosmia: loss of sense of smell due to organic factors, including loss of olfactory nerve conductivity, cerebral disease, nasal fossae formation and peripheral olfactory nerve diseases; can also be psychological disorder.
DEF: Parageusia: distorted sense of taste, or bad taste in mouth.
DEF: Parosmia: distorted sense of smell.

781.2 Abnormality of gait
Gait:
ataxic
paralytic
spastic
staggering
EXCLUDES *ataxia:*
NOS (781.3)
locomotor (progressive) (094.0)
difficulty in walking (719.7)
AHA: 2Q, '05, 6; 2Q, '04, 15
DEF: Abnormal, asymmetric gait.

781.3 Lack of coordination
Ataxia NOS
Muscular incoordination
EXCLUDES *ataxic gait (781.2)*
cerebellar ataxia (334.0-334.9)
difficulty in walking (719.7)
vertigo NOS (780.4)
AHA: 4Q, '04, 51; 3Q, '97, 12

781.4 Transient paralysis of limb
Monoplegia, transient NOS
EXCLUDES *paralysis (342.0-344.9)*

781.5 Clubbing of fingers
DEF: Enlarged soft tissue of distal fingers.

781.6 Meningismus
Dupré's syndrome
Meningism
AHA: 3Q, '00,13; J-F, '87, 7
DEF: Condition with signs and symptoms that resemble meningeal irritation; it is associated with febrile illness and dehydration with no evidence of infection.

781.7 Tetany CC
Carpopedal spasm
EXCLUDES *tetanus neonatorum (771.3)*
tetany:
hysterical (300.11)
newborn (hypocalcemic) (775.4)
parathyroid (252.1)
psychogenic (306.0)
CC Excl: 037, 332.0-334.4, 338.0-338.4, 342.10-342.12, 771.3, 780.91-780.99, 781.7, 799.81-799.89
DEF: Nerve and muscle hyperexcitability; symptoms include muscle spasms, twitching, cramps, laryngospasm with inspiratory stridor, hyperreflexia and choreiform movements.

781.8 Neurologic neglect syndrome
Asomatognosia
Hemi-akinesia
Hemi-inattention
Hemispatial neglect
Left-sided neglect
Sensory extinction
Sensory neglect
Visuospatial neglect
AHA: 4Q, '94, 37

✓5th **781.9 Other symptoms involving nervous and musculoskeletal systems**
AHA: 4Q, '00, 45

781.91 Loss of height
EXCLUDES *osteoporosis (733.00-733.09)*

781.92 Abnormal posture

781.93 Ocular torticollis
AHA: 4Q, '02, 68
DEF: Abnormal head posture as a result of a contracted state of cervical muscles to correct a visual disturbance; either double vision or a visual field defect.

781.94 Facial weakness
Facial droop
EXCLUDES *facial weakness due to late effect of cerebrovascular accident (438.83)*
AHA: 4Q, '03, 72

781.99 Other symptoms involving nervous and musculoskeletal systems

✓4th **782 Symptoms involving skin and other integumentary tissue**
EXCLUDES *symptoms relating to breast (611.71-611.79)*

782.0 Disturbance of skin sensation
Anesthesia of skin
Burning or prickling sensation
Hyperesthesia
Hypoesthesia
Numbness
Paresthesia
Tingling

782.1 Rash and other nonspecific skin eruption
Exanthem
EXCLUDES *vesicular eruption (709.8)*

782.2 Localized superficial swelling, mass, or lump
Subcutaneous nodules
EXCLUDES *localized adiposity (278.1)*

782.3 Edema
Anasarca
Dropsy
Localized edema NOS
EXCLUDES *ascites (789.5)*
edema of:
newborn NOS (778.5)
pregnancy (642.0-642.9, 646.1)
fluid retention (276.6)
hydrops fetalis (773.3, 778.0)
hydrothorax (511.8)
nutritional edema (260, 262)
AHA: 2Q, '00, 18
DEF: Edema: excess fluid in intercellular body tissue.
DEF: Anasarca: massive edema in all body tissues.
DEF: Dropsy: serous fluid accumulated in body cavity or cellular tissue.
DEF: Localized edema: edema in specific body areas.

782.4 Jaundice, unspecified, not of newborn
Cholemia NOS
Icterus NOS
EXCLUDES *jaundice in newborn (774.0-774.7)*
due to isoimmunization (773.0-773.2, 773.4)
DEF: Bilirubin deposits of skin, causing yellow cast.

782.5 Cyanosis
EXCLUDES *newborn (770.83)*
DEF: Deficient oxygen of blood; causes blue cast to skin.

✓5th **782.6 Pallor and flushing**

782.61 Pallor

782.62 Flushing
Excessive blushing

782.7 Spontaneous ecchymoses
Petechiae
EXCLUDES *ecchymosis in fetus or newborn (772.6)*
purpura (287.0-287.9)
DEF: Hemorrhagic spots of skin; resemble freckles.

782.8 Changes in skin texture
Induration } of skin
Thickening }

782.9 Other symptoms involving skin and integumentary tissues

✓4th **783 Symptoms concerning nutrition, metabolism, and development**

783.0 Anorexia
Loss of appetite
EXCLUDES *anorexia nervosa (307.1)*
loss of appetite of nonorganic origin (307.59)

783.1 Abnormal weight gain
EXCLUDES *excessive weight gain in pregnancy (646.1)*
obesity (278.00)
morbid (278.01)

✓5th **783.2 Abnormal loss of weight and underweight**
Use additional code to identify Body Mass Index (BMI), if known ►(V85.0-V85.54)◄
AHA: 4Q, '00, 45

783.21 Loss of weight
AHA: 4Q, '05, 96

783.22 Underweight
AHA: 4Q, '05, 96

783.3 Feeding difficulties and mismanagement
Feeding problem (elderly) (infant)
EXCLUDES *feeding disturbance or problems:*
in newborn (779.3)
of nonorganic origin (307.50-307.59)
AHA: 3Q, '97, 12

✓5th **783.4 Lack of expected normal physiological development in childhood**
EXCLUDES *delay in sexual development and puberty (259.0)*
gonadal dysgenesis (758.6)
pituitary dwarfism (253.3)
slow fetal growth and fetal malnutrition (764.00-764.99)
specific delays in mental development (315.0-315.9)
AHA: 4Q, '00, 45; 3Q, '97, 4

783.40 Lack of normal physiological development, unspecified
Inadequate development
Lack of development

783.41 Failure to thrive P
Failure to gain weight
AHA: 1Q, '03, 12
DEF: Organic failure to thrive: acute or chronic illness that interferes with nutritional intake, absorption, metabolism excretion and energy requirements. Nonorganic FTT is symptom of neglect or abuse.

783.42 Delayed milestones P
Late talker
Late walker

783.43 Short stature
Growth failure
Growth retardation
Lack of growth
Physical retardation
DEF: Constitutional short stature: stature inconsistent with chronological age. Genetic short stature is when skeletal maturation matches chronological age.

783.5 Polydipsia
Excessive thirst

783.6 Polyphagia
Excessive eating
Hyperalimentation NOS
EXCLUDES *disorders of eating of nonorganic origin (307.50-307.59)*

783.7 Adult failure to thrive A

783.9 Other symptoms concerning nutrition, metabolism, and development
Hypometabolism
EXCLUDES *abnormal basal metabolic rate (794.7)*
dehydration (276.51)
other disorders of fluid, electrolyte, and acid-base balance (276.0-276.9)
AHA: 2Q, '04, 3

✓4th **784 Symptoms involving head and neck**
EXCLUDES *encephalopathy NOS (348.30)*
specific symptoms involving neck classifiable to 723 (723.0-723.9)

784.0 Headache
Facial pain
Pain in head NOS
EXCLUDES *atypical face pain (350.2)*
migraine (346.0-346.9)
tension headache (307.81)
AHA: 3Q, '00, 13; 1Q, '90, 4; 3Q, '92, 14

784.1 Throat pain
EXCLUDES *dysphagia (787.2)*
neck pain (723.1)
sore throat (462)
chronic (472.1)

784.2 Swelling, mass, or lump in head and neck
Space-occupying lesion, intracranial NOS
AHA: 1Q, '03, 8

784.3 Aphasia
EXCLUDES ► *aphasia due to late effects of cerebrovascular disease (438.11)*◄
developmental aphasia (315.31)
AHA: 4Q, '04, 78; 4Q, '98, 87; 3Q, '97, 12
DEF: Inability to communicate through speech, written word, or sign language.

✓5th **784.4 Voice disturbance**

784.40 Voice disturbance, unspecified

784.41 Aphonia
Loss of voice

784.49 Other
Change in voice
Dysphonia
Hoarseness
Hypernasality
Hyponasality

784.5 Other speech disturbance
Dysarthria
Dysphasia
Slurred speech
EXCLUDES *stammering and stuttering (307.0)*
that of nonorganic origin (307.0, 307.9)

✓5th **784.6 Other symbolic dysfunction**
EXCLUDES *developmental learning delays (315.0-315.9)*

784.60 Symbolic dysfunction, unspecified

784.61 Alexia and dyslexia
Alexia (with agraphia)
DEF: Alexia: Inability to understand written word due to central brain lesion.
DEF: Dyslexia: Ability to recognize letters but inability to read, spell, and write words; genetic.

784.69 Other
Acalculia
Agnosia
Agraphia NOS
Apraxia

784.7 Epistaxis
Hemorrhage from nose
Nosebleed
AHA: 3Q, '04, 7

784.8 Hemorrhage from throat
EXCLUDES *hemoptysis (786.3)*

✓5th **784.9 Other symptoms involving head and neck**

● **784.91 Postnasal drip**

● **784.99 Other symptoms involving head and neck**
Choking sensation
Halitosis
Mouth breathing
Sneezing

✓4th **785 Symptoms involving cardiovascular system**
EXCLUDES *heart failure NOS (428.9)*

785.0 Tachycardia, unspecified
Rapid heart beat
EXCLUDES *neonatal tachycardia (779.82)*
paroxysmal tachycardia (427.0-427.2)
AHA: 2Q, '03, 11
DEF: Excessively rapid heart rate.

785.1 Palpitations
Awareness of heart beat
EXCLUDES *specified dysrhythmias (427.0-427.9)*

785.2 Undiagnosed cardiac murmurs
Heart murmurs NOS
AHA: 4Q, '92, 16

785.3 Other abnormal heart sounds
Cardiac dullness, increased or decreased
Friction fremitus, cardiac
Precordial friction

N Newborn Age: 0 P Pediatric Age: 0-17 M Maternity Age: 12-55 A Adult Age: 15-124 CC CC Condition MC Major Complication CD Complex Dx HIV HIV Related Dx

785.4 Gangrene CC

Gangrene:
NOS
spreading cutaneous
Gangrenous cellulitis
Phagedena
Code first any associated underlying condition

EXCLUDES *gangrene of certain sites — see Alphabetic Index*
gangrene with atherosclerosis of the extremities (440.24)
gas gangrene (040.0

CC Excl: 338.0-338.4, 440.24, 780.91-780.99, 785.4, 799.81-799.89
AHA: 1Q, '04, 14; 3Q, '91, 12; 3Q, '90, 15; M-A, '86, 12
DEF: Gangrene: necrosis of skin tissue due to bacterial infection, diabetes, embolus and vascular supply loss.
DEF: Gangrenous cellulitis: group A streptococcal infection; begins with severe cellulitis, spreads to superficial and deep fascia; produces gangrene of underlying tissues.

✓5th **785.5 Shock without mention of trauma**

785.50 Shock, unspecified CC MC CD MCV

Failure of peripheral circulation
CC Excl: 338.0-338.4, 780.91-780.99, 785.50-785.59, 785.9, 799.81-799.89
AHA: 2Q, '96, 10
DEF: Peripheral circulatory failure due to heart insufficiencies.

785.51 Cardiogenic shock CC MC CD MCV

CC Excl: See code 785.50
AHA: 3Q, '05, 14
DEF: Shock syndrome: associated with myocardial infarction, cardiac tamponade and massive pulmonary embolism; symptoms include mental confusion, reduced blood pressure, tachycardia, pallor and cold, clammy skin.

785.52 Septic shock CC

Shock:
endotoxic
gram-negative
Code first:
systemic inflammatory response syndrome due to infectious process with organ dysfunction (995.92)
CC Excl: See code 785.50
AHA: 2Q, '05, 18-19; 4Q, '03, 73, 79

785.59 Other CC

Shock:
hypovolemic

EXCLUDES *shock (due to):*
anesthetic (995.4)
anaphylactic (995.0)
due to serum (999.4)
electric (994.8)
following abortion (639.5)
lightning (994.0)
obstetrical (669.1)
postoperative (998.0)
traumatic (958.4)

CC Excl: see code 785.50
AHA: 2Q, '00, 3

785.6 Enlargement of lymph nodes

Lymphadenopathy
"Swollen glands"

EXCLUDES *lymphadenitis (chronic) (289.1-289.3)*
acute (683)

785.9 Other symptoms involving cardiovascular system

Bruit (arterial)
Weak pulse

✓4th **786 Symptoms involving respiratory system and other chest symptoms**

✓5th **786.0 Dyspnea and respiratory abnormalities**

786.00 Respiratory abnormality, unspecified

786.01 Hyperventilation

EXCLUDES *hyperventilation, psychogenic (306.1)*

DEF: Rapid breathing causes carbon dioxide loss from blood.

786.02 Orthopnea

DEF: Difficulty breathing except in upright position.

786.03 Apnea CC

EXCLUDES *apnea of newborn (770.81, 770.82)*
sleep apnea (780.51, 780.53, 780.57)

CC Excl: 518.81-518.84, 519.8, 519.9, 786.03, 786.04, 799.1
AHA: 4Q, '98, 50
DEF: Cessation of breathing.

786.04 Cheyne-Stokes respiration CC

CC Excl: 518.81-518.84, 519.8, 519.9, 786.03, 786.04, 799.1
AHA: 4Q, '98, 50
DEF: Rhythmic increase of depth and frequency of breathing with apnea; occurs in frontal lobe and diencephalic dysfunction.

786.05 Shortness of breath

AHA: 4Q, '99, 25; 1Q, '99, 6; 4Q, '98, 50
DEF: Inability to take in sufficient oxygen.

786.06 Tachypnea

EXCLUDES *transitory tachypnea of newborn (770.6)*

AHA: 4Q, '98, 50
DEF: Abnormal rapid respiratory rate; called hyperventilation.

786.07 Wheezing

EXCLUDES *asthma (493.00-493.92)*

AHA: 4Q, '98, 50
DEF: Stenosis of respiratory passageway; causes whistling sound; due to asthma, coryza, croup, emphysema, hay fever, edema, and pleural effusion.

786.09 Other

Respiratory:
distress
Respiratory:
insufficiency

EXCLUDES *respiratory distress:*
following trauma and surgery (518.5)
newborn (770.89)
syndrome (newborn) (769)
adult (518.5)
respiratory failure (518.81, 518.83-518.84)
newborn (770.84)

AHA: 4Q, '05, 90; 2Q, '98, 10; 1Q, '97, 7; 1Q, '90, 9

786.1 Stridor

EXCLUDES *congenital laryngeal stridor (748.3)*

DEF: Obstructed airway causes harsh sound.

786.2 Cough

EXCLUDES *cough:*
psychogenic (306.1)
smokers' (491.0)
with hemorrhage (786.3)

AHA: 4Q, '99, 26

786.3 Hemoptysis CC

Cough with hemorrhage
Pulmonary hemorrhage NOS

EXCLUDES *pulmonary hemorrhage of newborn (770.3)*

CC Excl: 338.0-338.4, 780.91-780.99, 786.3-786.4, 786.9, 799.81-799.89
AHA: 4Q, '90, 26
DEF: Coughing up blood or blood-stained sputum.

786.4 Abnormal sputum

Abnormal:
amount
color
odor
Excessive
} (of) sputum

✓5th **786.5 Chest pain**

786.50 Chest pain, unspecified

AHA: 1Q, '03, 6; 1Q, '02, 4; 4Q, '99, 25
DRG 125

786.51 Precordial pain

DEF: Chest pain over heart and lower thorax.

786.52 Painful respiration
Pain:
anterior chest wall
pleuritic
Pleurodynia
EXCLUDES *epidemic pleurodynia (074.1)*
AHA: N-D, '84, 17

786.59 Other
Discomfort } in chest
Pressure } in chest
Tightness } in chest
EXCLUDES *pain in breast (611.71)*
AHA: 1Q, '02, 6
DRG 125

786.6 Swelling, mass, or lump in chest
EXCLUDES *lump in breast (611.72)*

786.7 Abnormal chest sounds
Abnormal percussion, chest
Friction sounds, chest
Rales
Tympany, chest
EXCLUDES *wheezing (786.07)*

786.8 Hiccough
EXCLUDES *psychogenic hiccough (306.1)*

786.9 Other symptoms involving respiratory system and chest
Breath-holding spell

✓4th **787 Symptoms involving digestive system**
EXCLUDES *constipation (564.00-564.09)*
pylorospasm (537.81)
congenital (750.5)

✓5th **787.0 Nausea and vomiting**
Emesis
EXCLUDES *hematemesis NOS (578.0)*
vomiting:
bilious, following gastrointestinal surgery (564.3)
cyclical (536.2)
psychogenic (306.4)
excessive, in pregnancy (643.0-643.9)
habit (536.2)
of newborn (779.3)
psychogenic NOS (307.54)
AHA: M-A, '85, 11

787.01 Nausea with vomiting
AHA: 1Q, '03, 5
DRG 182

787.02 Nausea alone
AHA: 3Q, '00, 12; 2Q, '97, 9

787.03 Vomiting alone

787.1 Heartburn
Pyrosis
Waterbrash
EXCLUDES *dyspepsia or indigestion (536.8)*
AHA: 2Q, '01, 6

787.2 Dysphagia
Difficulty in swallowing
AHA: 4Q, '03, 103, 109; 2Q, '01, 4

787.3 Flatulence, eructation, and gas pain
Abdominal distention (gaseous)
Bloating
Tympanites (abdominal) (intestinal)
EXCLUDES *aerophagy (306.4)*
DEF: Flatulence: excess air or gas in intestine or stomach.
DEF: Eructation: belching, expelling gas through mouth.
DEF: Gas pain: gaseous pressure affecting gastrointestinal system.

787.4 Visible peristalsis
Hyperperistalsis
DEF: Increase in involuntary movements of intestines.

787.5 Abnormal bowel sounds
Absent bowel sounds
Hyperactive bowel sounds

787.6 Incontinence of feces
Encopresis NOS
Incontinence of sphincter ani
EXCLUDES *that of nonorganic origin (307.7)*
AHA: 1Q, '97, 9

787.7 Abnormal feces
Bulky stools
EXCLUDES *abnormal stool content (792.1)*
melena:
NOS (578.1)
newborn (772.4, 777.3)

✓5th **787.9 Other symptoms involving digestive system**
EXCLUDES *gastrointestinal hemorrhage (578.0-578.9)*
intestinal obstruction (560.0-560.9)
specific functional digestive disorders:
esophagus (530.0-530.9)
stomach and duodenum (536.0-536.9)
those not elsewhere classified (564.00-564.9)

787.91 Diarrhea
Diarrhea NOS
AHA: 4Q, '95, 54

787.99 Other
Change in bowel habits
Tenesmus (rectal)
DEF: Tenesmus: Painful, ineffective straining at the rectum with limited passage of fecal matter.

✓4th **788 Symptoms involving urinary system**
EXCLUDES *hematuria (599.7)*
nonspecific findings on examination of the urine (791.0-791.9)
small kidney of unknown cause (589.0-589.9)
uremia NOS (586)
▶*urinary obstruction (599.60, 599.69)*◀

788.0 Renal colic
Colic (recurrent) of:
kidney
Colic (recurrent) of:
ureter
AHA: 3Q, '04, 8
DEF: Kidney pain.

788.1 Dysuria
Painful urination
Strangury

✓5th **788.2 Retention of urine**
▶Code, if applicable, any causal condition first, such as:
hyperplasia of prostate (600.0-600.9 with fifth-digit 1)◀
DEF: Accumulation of urine in the bladder due to inability to void

788.20 Retention of urine, unspecified CC
CC Excl: 274.11, 338.0-338.4, 344.61, 593.3-593.5, 596.0, 596.4- 596.59, 596.8-596.9, 599.60-599.69, 600.00-602.9, 753.0-753.9,-780.91-780.99, 788.20-788.29, 788.61-788.69, 788.9, 799.81-799.89
AHA: 2Q, '04, 18; 3Q, '03, 12-13; 1Q, '03, 6; 3Q, '96, 10

788.21 Incomplete bladder emptying

788.29 Other specified retention of urine CC
CC Excl: See code 788.20

✓5th **788.3 Urinary incontinence**
Code, if applicable, any causal condition first, such as:
congenital ureterocele (753.23)
genital prolapse (618.00-618.9)
▶hyperplasia of prostate (600.0-600.9 with fifth-digit 1)◀
EXCLUDES *that of nonorganic origin (307.6)*
AHA: 4Q, '92, 22

788.30 Urinary incontinence, unspecified
Enuresis NOS

788.31 Urge incontinence
AHA: 1Q, '00, 19
DEF: Inability to control urination, upon urge to urinate.

788.32 Stress incontinence, male ♂
EXCLUDES *stress incontinence, female (625.6)*
DEF: Inability to control urination associated with weak sphincter in males.

788.33 Mixed incontinence, (male) (female)
Urge and stress
DEF: Urge, stress incontinence: involuntary discharge of urine due to anatomic displacement.

788.34 Incontinence without sensory awareness
DEF: Involuntary discharge of urine without sensory warning.

788.35 Post-void dribbling
DEF: Involuntary discharge of residual urine after voiding.

788.36 Nocturnal enuresis
DEF: Involuntary discharge of urine during the night.

788.37 Continuous leakage
DEF: Continuous, involuntary urine seepage.

788.38 Overflow incontinence
DEF: Leakage caused by pressure of retained urine in the bladder after the bladder has fully contracted due to weakened bladder muscles or an obstruction of the urethra.

788.39 Other urinary incontinence

✓5th **788.4 Frequency of urination and polyuria**
▶Code, if applicable, any causal condition first, such as:
hyperplasia of prostate (600.0-600.9 with fifth-digit 1)◀

788.41 Urinary frequency
Frequency of micturition

788.42 Polyuria
DEF: Excessive urination.

788.43 Nocturia
DEF: Urination affecting sleep patterns.

788.5 Oliguria and anuria
Deficient secretion of urine
Suppression of urinary secretion
EXCLUDES *that complicating:*
abortion (634-638 with .3, 639.3)
ectopic or molar pregnancy (639.3)
pregnancy, childbirth, or the puerperium (642.0-642.9, 646.2)
DEF: Oliguria: diminished urinary secretion related to fluid intake.
DEF: Anuria: lack of urinary secretion due to renal failure or obstructed urinary tract.

✓5th **788.6 Other abnormality of urination**
▶Code, if applicable, any causal condition first, such as:
hyperplasia of prostate (600.0-600.9 with fifth-digit 1)◀

788.61 Splitting of urinary stream
Intermittent urinary stream

788.62 Slowing of urinary stream
Weak stream

788.63 Urgency of urination
EXCLUDES *urge incontinence (788.31, 788.33)*
AHA: 4Q, '03, 74
DEF: Feeling of intense need to urinate; abrupt sensation of imminent urination.

● **788.64 Urinary hesitancy**

● **788.65 Straining on urination**

788.69 Other

788.7 Urethral discharge
Penile discharge
Urethrorrhea

788.8 Extravasation of urine
DEF: Leaking or infiltration of urine into tissues.

788.9 Other symptoms involving urinary system
Extrarenal uremia
Vesical:
pain
Vesical:
tenesmus
AHA: 1Q, '05, 12; 4Q, '88, 1

✓4th **789 Other symptoms involving abdomen and pelvis**
EXCLUDES *symptoms referable to genital organs:*
female (625.0-625.9)
male (607.0-608.9)
psychogenic (302.70-302.79)

The following fifth-digit subclassification is to be used for codes 789.0, 789.3, 789.4, 789.6:
- **0 unspecified site**
- **1 right upper quadrant**
- **2 left upper quadrant**
- **3 right lower quadrant**
- **4 left lower quadrant**
- **5 periumbilic**
- **6 epigastric**
- **7 generalized**
- **9 other specified site**
  Multiple sites

✓5th **789.0 Abdominal pain**
Colic:
NOS
Colic:
infantile
Cramps, abdominal
EXCLUDES *renal colic (788.0)*
AHA: 1Q, '95, 3; For code 789.06: 1Q, '02, 5

789.1 Hepatomegaly
Enlargement of liver

789.2 Splenomegaly
Enlargement of spleen

✓5th **789.3 Abdominal or pelvic swelling, mass, or lump**
Diffuse or generalized swelling or mass:
abdominal NOS
umbilical
EXCLUDES *abdominal distention (gaseous) (787.3)*
ascites (789.5)

✓5th **789.4 Abdominal rigidity**

789.5 Ascites CC
Fluid in peritoneal cavity
CC Excl: 338.0-338.4, 780.91-780.99, 789.30-789.5, 789.9, 799.81-799.89
AHA: 2Q, '05, 8; 4Q, '89, 11
DEF: Serous fluid effusion and accumulation in abdominal cavity.

✓5th **789.6 Abdominal tenderness**
Rebound tenderness

789.9 Other symptoms involving abdomen and pelvis
Umbilical:
bleeding
Umbilical:
discharge

NONSPECIFIC ABNORMAL FINDINGS (790-796)

AHA: 2Q, '90, 16

✓4th **790 Nonspecific findings on examination of blood**
EXCLUDES *abnormality of:*
platelets (287.0-287.9)
thrombocytes (287.0-287.9)
white blood cells ▶(288.00-288.9)◀

✓5th **790.0 Abnormality of red blood cells**
EXCLUDES *anemia:*
congenital (776.5)
newborn, due to isoimmunization (773.0-773.2, 773.5)
of premature infant (776.6)
other specified types (280.0-285.9)
hemoglobin disorders (282.5-282.7)
polycythemia:
familial (289.6)
neonatorum (776.4)
secondary (289.0)
vera (238.4)
AHA: 4Q, '00, 46

790.01 Precipitous drop in hematocrit
Drop in hematocrit

Symptoms, Signs, and Ill-Defined Conditions 788.32–790.01

✓4th ✓5th Additional Digit Required | Nonspecific PDx | Unacceptable PDx | Manifestation Code | MCV Major Cardiovascular Condition | ▶◀ Revised Text | ● New Code | ▲ Revised Code Title

790.09 Other abnormality of red blood cells
Abnormal red cell morphology NOS
Abnormal red cell volume NOS
Anisocytosis
Poikilocytosis

790.1 Elevated sedimentation rate

✓5th **790.2 Abnormal glucose**
EXCLUDES *diabetes mellitus (250.00-250.93)*
dysmetabolic syndrome X (277.7)
gestational diabetes (648.8)
glycosuria (791.5)
hypoglycemia (251.2)
that complicating pregnancy, childbirth, or puerperium (648.8)
AHA: 4Q, '03, 74; 3Q, '91, 5

790.21 Impaired fasting glucose
Elevated fasting glucose

790.22 Impaired glucose tolerance test (oral)
Elevated glucose tolerance test

790.29 Other abnormal glucose
Abnormal glucose NOS
Abnormal non-fasting glucose
▶Hyperglycemia NOS◀
Pre-diabetes NOS
AHA: 2Q, '05, 21

790.3 Excessive blood level of alcohol
Elevated blood-alcohol
AHA: S-O, '86, 3

790.4 Nonspecific elevation of levels of transaminase or lactic acid dehydrogenase [LDH]

790.5 Other nonspecific abnormal serum enzyme levels
Abnormal serum level of:
acid phosphatase
alkaline phosphatase
amylase
lipase
EXCLUDES *deficiency of circulating enzymes (277.6)*

790.6 Other abnormal blood chemistry
Abnormal blood level of:
cobalt
copper
iron
▶lead◀
Abnormal blood level of:
lithium
magnesium
mineral
zinc
EXCLUDES *abnormality of electrolyte or acid-base balance (276.0-276.9)*
hypoglycemia NOS (251.2)
▶*lead poisoning (984.0-984.9)*◀
specific finding indicating abnormality of:
amino-acid transport and metabolism (270.0-270.9)
carbohydrate transport and metabolism (271.0-271.9)
lipid metabolism (272.0-272.9)
uremia NOS (586)
AHA: 4Q, '88, 1

790.7 Bacteremia CC
EXCLUDES *bacteremia of newborn (771.83)*
septicemia (038)
Use additional code to identify organism (041)
CC Excl: 338.0-338.4, 780.91-780.99, 790.7-790.99, 799.81-799.89
AHA: 2Q, '03, 7; 4Q, '93, 29; 3Q, '88, 12
DEF: Laboratory finding of bacteria in the blood in the absence of two or more signs of sepsis; transient in nature, progresses to septicemia with severe infectious process.
DRG 416

790.8 Viremia, unspecified
AHA: 4Q, '88, 10
DEF: Presence of a virus in the blood stream.

✓5th **790.9 Other nonspecific findings on examination of blood**
AHA: 4Q, '93, 29

790.91 Abnormal arterial blood gases

790.92 Abnormal coagulation profile
Abnormal or prolonged:
bleeding time
coagulation time
partial thromboplastin time [PTT]
prothrombintime [PT]
EXCLUDES *coagulation (hemorrhagic) disorders (286.0-286.9)*

790.93 Elevated prostate specific antigen, [PSA] A ♂

790.94 Euthyroid sick syndrome
AHA: 4Q, '97, 45
DEF: Transient alteration of thyroid hormone metabolism due to nonthyroid illness or stress.

790.95 Elevated C-reactive protein [CRP]
DEF: Inflammation in an arterial wall results in elevated C-reactive protein (CRP) in the blood; CRP is a recognized risk factor in cardiovascular disease.

790.99 Other
AHA: 2Q, '03, 14

✓4th **791 Nonspecific findings on examination of urine**
EXCLUDES *hematuria NOS (599.7)*
specific findings indicating abnormality of:
amino-acid transport and metabolism (270.0-270.9)
carbohydrate transport and metabolism (271.0-271.9)

791.0 Proteinuria
Albuminuria
Bence-Jones proteinuria
EXCLUDES *postural proteinuria (593.6)*
that arising during pregnancy or the puerperium (642.0-642.9, 646.2)
AHA: 3Q, '91, 8
DEF: Excess protein in urine.

791.1 Chyluria CC
EXCLUDES *filarial (125.0-125.9)*
CC Excl: 338.0-338.4, 780.91-780.99, 791.1, 791.9, 799.81-799.89
DEF: Excess chyle in urine.

791.2 Hemoglobinuria
DEF: Free hemoglobin in blood due to rapid hemolysis of red blood cells.

791.3 Myoglobinuria CC
CC Excl: 338.0-338.4, 780.91-780.99, 791.2-791.3, 791.9, 799.81-799.89
DEF: Myoglobin (oxygen-transporting pigment) in urine.

791.4 Biliuria
DEF: Bile pigments in urine.

791.5 Glycosuria
EXCLUDES *renal glycosuria (271.4)*
DEF: Sugar in urine.

791.6 Acetonuria
Ketonuria
DEF: Excess acetone in urine.

791.7 Other cells and casts in urine

791.9 Other nonspecific findings on examination of urine
Crystalluria
Elevated urine levels of:
17-ketosteroids
catecholamines
Elevated urine levels of:
indolacetic acid
vanillylmandelic acid [VMA]
Melanuria
AHA: 1Q, '05, 12

✓4th 792 Nonspecific abnormal findings in other body substances

EXCLUDES *that in chromosomal analysis (795.2)*

792.0 Cerebrospinal fluid

792.1 Stool contents

Abnormal stool color	Occult stool
Fat in stool	Pus in stool
Mucus in stool	

EXCLUDES *blood in stool [melena] (578.1)*
newborn (772.4, 777.3)

AHA: 2Q, '92, 9

792.2 Semen ♂

Abnormal spermatozoa

EXCLUDES *azoospermia (606.0)*
oligospermia (606.1)

792.3 Amniotic fluid M ♀

AHA: N-D, '86, 4

DEF: Nonspecific abnormal findings in amniotic fluid.

792.4 Saliva

EXCLUDES *that in chromosomal analysis (795.2)*

792.5 Cloudy (hemodialysis) (peritoneal) dialysis effluent

AHA: 4Q, '00, 46

792.9 Other nonspecific abnormal findings in body substances

Peritoneal fluid	Synovial fluid
Pleural fluid	Vaginal fluids

✓4th 793 Nonspecific abnormal findings on radiological and other examination of body structure

INCLUDES nonspecific abnormal findings of:
thermography
ultrasound examination [echogram]
x-ray examination

EXCLUDES *abnormal results of function studies and radioisotope scans (794.0-794.9)*

793.0 Skull and head

EXCLUDES *nonspecific abnormal echoencephalogram (794.01)*

793.1 Lung field

Coin lesion } (of) lung
Shadow }

DEF: Coin lesion of lung: coin-shaped, solitary pulmonary nodule.

793.2 Other intrathoracic organ

Abnormal:	Abnormal:
echocardiogram	ultrasound cardiogram
heart shadow	Mediastinal shift

793.3 Biliary tract

Nonvisualization of gallbladder

793.4 Gastrointestinal tract

793.5 Genitourinary organs

Filling defect:	Filling defect:
bladder	ureter
kidney	

793.6 Abdominal area, including retroperitoneum

793.7 Musculoskeletal system

✓5th 793.8 Breast

AHA: 4Q, '01, 51

793.80 Abnormal mammogram, unspecified

793.81 Mammographic microcalcification

EXCLUDES ▶ *mammographic calcification (793.89)*
mammographic calculus (793.89)◀

DEF: Calcium and cellular debris deposits in the breast that cannot be felt but can be detected on a mammogram; can be a sign of cancer, benign conditions, or changes in the breast tissue as a result of inflammation, injury, or obstructed duct.

793.89 Other abnormal findings on radiological examination of breast

▶Mammographic calcification
Mammographic calculus◀

✓5th 793.9 Other

EXCLUDES *abnormal finding by radioisotope localization of placenta (794.9)*

● **793.91 Image test inconclusive due to excess body fat**

Use additional code to identify Body Mass Index (BMI), if known (V85.0-V85.54)

● **793.99 Other nonspecific abnormal findings on radiological and other examinations of body structure**

Abnormal:
placental finding by x-ray or ultrasound method
radiological findings in skin and subcutaneous tissue

✓4th 794 Nonspecific abnormal results of function studies

INCLUDES radioisotope:
scans
uptake studies
scintiphotography

✓5th 794.0 Brain and central nervous system

794.00 Abnormal function study, unspecified

794.01 Abnormal echoencephalogram

794.02 Abnormal electroencephalogram [EEG]

794.09 Other

Abnormal brain scan

✓5th 794.1 Peripheral nervous system and special senses

794.10 Abnormal response to nerve stimulation, unspecified

794.11 Abnormal retinal function studies

Abnormal electroretinogram [ERG]

794.12 Abnormal electro-oculogram [EOG]

794.13 Abnormal visually evoked potential

794.14 Abnormal oculomotor studies

794.15 Abnormal auditory function studies

AHA: 1Q, '04, 15-16

794.16 Abnormal vestibular function studies

794.17 Abnormal electromyogram [EMG]

EXCLUDES *that of eye (794.14)*

794.19 Other

794.2 Pulmonary

Abnormal lung scan	Reduced:
Reduced:	vital capacity
ventilatory capacity	

✓5th 794.3 Cardiovascular

794.30 Abnormal function study, unspecified

794.31 Abnormal electrocardiogram [ECG] [EKG]

EXCLUDES *long QT syndrome (426.82)*

794.39 Other

Abnormal:	Abnormal:
ballistocardiogram	vectorcardiogram
phonocardiogram	

794.4 Kidney

Abnormal renal function test

794.5 Thyroid

Abnormal thyroid:	Abnormal thyroid:
scan	uptake

794.6 Other endocrine function study

794.7 Basal metabolism

Abnormal basal metabolic rate [BMR]

794.8 Liver

Abnormal liver scan

794.9 Other

Bladder	Placenta
Pancreas	Spleen

✓4th **795 Other and nonspecific abnormal cytological, histological, immunological and DNA test findings**

EXCLUDES *nonspecific abnormalities of red blood cells (790.01-790.09)*

✓5th **795.0 Abnormal Papanicolaou smear of cervix and cervical HPV**

Abnormal thin preparation smear of cervix
Abnormal cervical cytology

EXCLUDES *carcinoma in-situ of cervix (233.1)*
cervical intraepithelial neoplasia I (CIN I) (622.11)
cervical intraepithelial neoplasia II (CIN II) (622.12)
cervical intraepithelial neoplasia III (CIN III) (233.1)
dysplasia (histologically confirmed) of cervix (uteri) NOS (622.10)
mild dysplasia (histologically confirmed) (622.11)
moderate dysplasia (histologically confirmed) (622.12)
severe dysplasia (histologically confirmed) (233.1)

AHA: 4Q, '02, 69

795.00 Abnormal glandular Papanicolaou smear of cervix ♀

Atypical endocervical cells NOS
Atypical endometrial cells NOS
Atypical glandular cells NOS

795.01 Papanicolaou smear of cervix with atypical squamous cells of undetermined significance [ASC-US] ♀

795.02 Papanicolaou smear of cervix with atypical squamous cells cannot exclude high grade squamous intraepithelial lesion [ASC-H] ♀

795.03 Papanicolaou smear of cervix with low grade squamous intraepithelial lesion [LGSIL] ♀

795.04 Papanicolaou smear of cervix with high grade squamous intraepithelial lesion [HGSIL] ♀

795.05 Cervical high risk human papillomavirus [HPV] DNA test positive ♀

● **795.06 Papanicolaou smear of cervix with cytologic evidence of malignancy** ♀

795.08 Unsatisfactory smear ♀

Inadequate sample

795.09 Other abnormal Papanicolaou smear of cervix and cervical HPV ♀

Cervical low risk human papillomavirus (HPV) DNA test positive
Use additional code for associated human papillomavirus (079.4)

EXCLUDES *encounter for Papanicolaou cervical smear to confirm findings of recent normal smear following initial abnormal smear (V72.32)*

795.1 Nonspecific abnormal Papanicolaou smear of other site

795.2 Nonspecific abnormal findings on chromosomal analysis

Abnormal karyotype

✓5th **795.3 Nonspecific positive culture findings**

Positive culture findings in:
nose
sputum
throat
wound

EXCLUDES *that of:*
blood (790.7-790.8)
urine (791.9)

795.31 Nonspecific positive findings for anthrax

Positive findings by nasal swab

AHA: 4Q, '02, 70

795.39 Other nonspecific positive culture findings

795.4 Other nonspecific abnormal histological findings

795.5 Nonspecific reaction to tuberculin skin test without active tuberculosis

Abnormal result of Mantoux test
PPD positive
Tuberculin (skin test):
positive
reactor

795.6 False positive serological test for syphilis

False positive Wassermann reaction

✓5th **795.7 Other nonspecific immunological findings**

EXCLUDES ▶ *abnormal tumor markers (795.81-795.89)*
elevated prostate specific antigen [PSA] (790.93)
elevated tumor associated antigens (795.81-795.89)◀
isoimmunization, in pregnancy (656.1-656.2)
affecting fetus or newborn (773.0-773.2)

AHA: 2Q, '93, 6

795.71 Nonspecific serologic evidence of human immunodeficiency virus [HIV]

Inclusive human immunodeficiency [HIV] test (adult) (infant)

Note: This code is **only** to be used when a test finding is reported as nonspecific. Asymptomatic positive findings are coded to V08. If any HIV infection symptom or condition is present, see code 042. Negative findings are not coded.

EXCLUDES *acquired immunodeficiency syndrome [AIDS] (042)*
asymptomatic human immunodeficiency virus, [HIV] infection status (V08)
HIV infection, symptomatic (042)
human immunodeficiency virus [HIV] disease (042)
positive (status) NOS (V08)

AHA: 2Q, '04, 11; 1Q, '93, 21; 1Q, '93, 22; 2Q, '92, 11; J-A, '87, 24

795.79 Other and unspecified nonspecific immunological findings

Raised antibody titer
Raised level of immunoglobulins

● ✓5th **795.8 Abnormal tumor markers**

Elevated tumor associated antigens [TAA]
Elevated tumor specific antigens [TSA]

EXCLUDES *elevated prostate specific antigen [PSA] (790.93)*

● **795.81 Elevated carcinoembryonic antigen [CEA]**

● **795.82 Elevated cancer antigen 125 [CA 125]**

● **795.89 Other abnormal tumor markers**

N Newborn Age: 0 P Pediatric Age: 0-17 M Maternity Age: 12-55 A Adult Age: 15-124 CC CC Condition MC Major Complication CD Complex Dx HIV HIV Related Dx

✓4th **796 Other nonspecific abnormal findings**

796.0 Nonspecific abnormal toxicological findings
Abnormal levels of heavy metals or drugs in blood, urine, or other tissue
EXCLUDES *excessive blood level of alcohol (790.3)*
AHA: 1Q, '97, 16

796.1 Abnormal reflex

796.2 Elevated blood pressure reading without diagnosis of hypertension
Note: This category is to be used to record an episode of elevated blood pressure in a patient in whom no formal diagnosis of hypertension has been made, or as an incidental finding.
AHA: 2Q, '03, 11; 3Q, '90, 4; J-A, '84, 12

796.3 Nonspecific low blood pressure reading

796.4 Other abnormal clinical findings
AHA: 1Q, '97, 16

796.5 Abnormal finding on antenatal screening ♀ M
AHA: 4Q, '97, 46

796.6 Abnormal findings on neonatal screening N
EXCLUDES *nonspecific serologic evidence of human immunodeficiency virus [HIV] (795.71)*
AHA: 4Q, '04, 99

796.9 Other

ILL-DEFINED AND UNKNOWN CAUSES OF MORBIDITY AND MORTALITY (797-799)

797 Senility without mention of psychosis
Old age
Senescence
Senile asthenia
Senile:
debility
exhaustion
EXCLUDES *senile psychoses (290.0-290.9)*

✓4th **798 Sudden death, cause unknown**

798.0 Sudden infant death syndrome P
Cot death
Crib death
Sudden death of nonspecific cause in infancy
DEF: Death of infant under age one due to nonspecific cause.

798.1 Instantaneous death

798.2 Death occurring in less than 24 hours from onset of symptoms, not otherwise explained
Death known not to be violent or instantaneous, for which no cause could be discovered
Died without sign of disease

798.9 Unattended death
Death in circumstances where the body of the deceased was found and no cause could be discovered
Found dead

✓4th **799 Other ill-defined and unknown causes of morbidity and mortality**

✓5th **799.0 Asphyxia and hypoxemia**
EXCLUDES *asphyxia and hypoxemia (due to):*
carbon monoxide (986)
hypercapnia (786.09)
inhalation of food or foreign body (932-934.9)
newborn (768.0-768.9)
traumatic (994.7)

799.01 Asphyxia CC
CC Excl: 338.0-338.4, 518.81-518.84, 780.91-780.99, 798.0, 799.01-799.1, 799.81-799.89
AHA: 4Q, '05, 90
DEF: Lack of oxygen in inspired air, causing a deficiency of oxygen in tissues (hypoxia) and elevated levels of arterial carbon dioxide (hypercapnia).

799.02 Hypoxemia CC
CC Excl: See code 799.01
AHA: 4Q, '05, 90
DEF: Deficient oxygenation of the blood.

799.1 Respiratory arrest CC
Cardiorespiratory failure
EXCLUDES *cardiac arrest (427.5)*
failure of peripheral circulation (785.50)
respiratory distress:
NOS (786.09)
acute (518.82)
following trauma and surgery (518.5)
newborn (770.89)
syndrome (newborn) (769)
adult (following trauma and surgery) (518.5)
other (518.82)
respiratory failure (518.81, 518.83-518.84)
newborn (770.84)
respiratory insufficiency (786.09)
acute (518.82)
CC Excl: 338.0-338.4, 518.81-518.84, 780.91-780.99, 798.0, 799.01-799.1, 799.81-799.89

799.2 Nervousness
"Nerves"

799.3 Debility, unspecified
EXCLUDES *asthenia (780.79)*
nervous debility (300.5)
neurasthenia (300.5)
senile asthenia (797)

799.4 Cachexia CC
Wasting disease
▶Code first underlying condition, if known◀
CC Excl: 780.91-780.99, 799.3-799.4, 799.81-799.89
AHA: 3Q, '90, 17
DEF: General ill health and poor nutrition.

✓5th **799.8 Other ill-defined conditions**

799.81 Decreased libido A
Decreased sexual desire
EXCLUDES *psychosexual dysfunction with inhibited sexual desire (302.71)*
AHA: 4Q, '03, 75

799.89 Other ill-defined conditions

799.9 Other unknown and unspecified cause
Undiagnosed disease, not specified as to site or system involved
Unknown cause of morbidity or mortality
AHA: 1Q, '98,.4; 1Q, '90, 20

17. INJURY AND POISONING (800-999)

Use E code(s) to identify the cause and intent of the injury or poisoning (E800-E999)

Note:

1. The principle of multiple coding of injuries should be followed wherever possible. Combination categories for multiple injuries are provided for use when there is insufficient detail as to the nature of the individual conditions, or for primary tabulation purposes when it is more convenient to record a single code; otherwise, the component injuries should be coded separately.

   Where multiple sites of injury are specified in the titles, the word "with" indicates involvement of both sites, and the word "and" indicates involvement of either or both sites. The word "finger" includes thumb.

2. Categories for "late effect" of injuries are to be found at 905-909.

FRACTURES (800-829)

EXCLUDES *malunion (733.81)*
nonunion (733.82)
pathological or spontaneous fracture (733.10-733.19)
stress fractures (733.93-733.95)

The terms "condyle," "coronoid process," "ramus," and "symphysis" indicate the portion of the bone fractured, not the name of the bone involved.

The descriptions "closed" and "open" used in the fourth-digit subdivisions include the following terms:

closed (with or without delayed healing):

comminuted	impacted
depressed	linear
elevated	simple
fissured	slipped epiphysis
fracture NOS	spiral
greenstick	

open (with or without delayed healing):

compound	puncture
infected	with foreign body
missile	

A fracture not indicated as closed or open should be classified as closed.

AHA: 4Q, '90, 26; 3Q, '90, 5; 3Q, '90, 13; 2Q, '90, 7; 2Q, '89, 15, S-O, '85, 3

FRACTURE OF SKULL (800-804)

The following fifth-digit subclassification is for use with the appropriate codes in categories 800, 801, 803, and 804:

0 unspecified state of consciousness
1 with no loss of consciousness
2 with brief [less than one hour] loss of consciousness
3 with moderate [1-24 hours] loss of consciousness
4 with prolonged [more than 24 hours] loss of consciousness and return to pre-existing conscious level
5 with prolonged [more than 24 hours] loss of consciousness, without return to pre-existing conscious level
Use fifth-digit 5 to designate when a patient is unconscious and dies before regaining consciousness, regardless of the duration of the loss of consciousness
6 with loss of consciousness of unspecified duration
9 with concussion, unspecified

✓4th **800 Fracture of vault of skull**

INCLUDES frontal bone
parietal bone

AHA: 4Q,'96, 36

DEF: Fracture of bone that forms skull dome and protects brain.

Fractures

Fracture-dislocation
Impacted
Avulsion
Linear (fissured)
Greenstick
Open (skin broken)
Oblique
Closed
spiral
Epiphyseal
Depressed
March
Comminuted

✓5th **800.0 Closed without mention of intracranial injury** CC
CC Excl: 800.00-801.99, 803.00-804.99, 829.0-829.1, 850.0-852.19, 852.21-854.19, 873.8-873.9, 879.8-879.9, 905.0, 925.1-925.2, 929.0-929.9, 958.8, 959.01, 959.09, 959.8-959.9

✓5th **800.1 Closed with cerebral laceration and contusion** CC
CC Excl: See code 800.0

✓5th **800.2 Closed with subarachnoid, subdural, and extradural hemorrhage** CC
CC Excl: See code 800.0

✓5th **800.3 Closed with other and unspecified intracranial hemorrhage** CC
CC Excl: See code 800.0

✓5th **800.4 Closed with intracranial injury of other and unspecified nature** CC
CC Excl: See code 800.0

✓5th **800.5 Open without mention of intracranial injury** CC
CC Excl: See code 800.0

✓5th **800.6 Open with cerebral laceration and contusion** CC
CC Excl: See code 800.0

✓5th **800.7 Open with subarachnoid, subdural, and extradural hemorrhage** CC
CC Excl: See code 800.0

✓5th **800.8 Open with other and unspecified intracranial hemorrhage** CC
CC Excl: See code 800.0

✓5th **800.9 Open with intracranial injury of other and unspecified nature** CC
CC Excl: See code 800.0

Skull

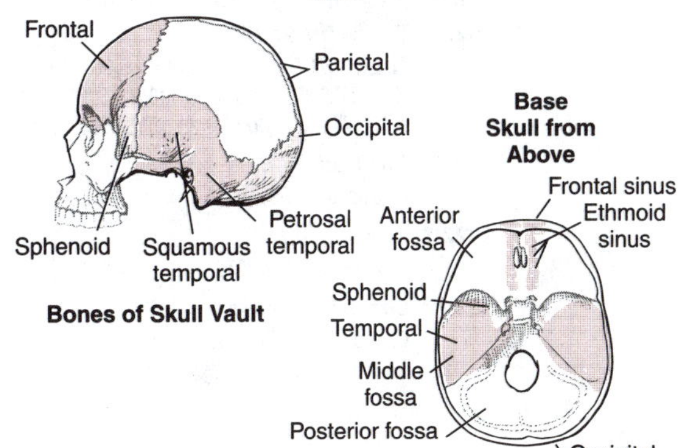

✓4th 801 Fracture of base of skull

INCLUDES fossa:
- anterior
- middle
- posterior

occiput bone
orbital roof
sinus:
- ethmoid
- frontal

sphenoid bone
temporal bone

AHA: 4Q, '96, 36

DEF: Fracture of bone that forms skull floor.

§ ✓5th **801.0 Closed without mention of intracranial injury** CC
CC Excl: See code 800.0

§ ✓5th **801.1 Closed with cerebral laceration and contusion** CC
CC Excl: See code 800.0
AHA: 4Q, '96, 36

§ ✓5th **801.2 Closed with subarachnoid, subdural, and extradural hemorrhage** CC
CC Excl: See code 800.0

§ ✓5th **801.3 Closed with other and unspecified intracranial hemorrhage** CC
CC Excl: See code 800.0

§ ✓5th **801.4 Closed with intracranial injury of other and unspecified nature** CC
CC Excl: See code 800.0

§ ✓5th **801.5 Open without mention of intracranial injury** CC
CC Excl: See code 800.0

§ ✓5th **801.6 Open with cerebral laceration and contusion** CC
CC Excl: See code 800.0

§ ✓5th **801.7 Open with subarachnoid, subdural, and extradural hemorrhage** CC
CC Excl: See code 800.0

§ ✓5th **801.8 Open with other and unspecified intracranial hemorrhage** CC
CC Excl: See code 800.0

§ ✓5th **801.9 Open with intracranial injury of other and unspecified nature** CC
CC Excl: See code 800.0

✓4th 802 Fracture of face bones

AHA: 4Q, '96, 36

802.0 Nasal bones, closed

802.1 Nasal bones, open CC
CC Excl: 800.00-802.1, 803.00-804.99, 829.0-829.1, 850.0-852.19, 852.21-854.19, 873.8-873.9, 879.8-879.9, 905.0, 925.1-925.2, 929.0-929.9, 958.8-959.09, 959.8-959.9

✓5th **802.2 Mandible, closed**
Inferior maxilla
Lower jaw (bone)

802.20 Unspecified site CC
CC Excl: 800.00-801.99, 802.20-802.5, 803.00-804.99, 829.0-830.1, 850.0-852.19, 852.21-854.19, 873.8-873.9, 879.8-879.9, 905.0, 925.1-925.2, 929.0-929.9, 958.8-959.09, 959.8-959.9

802.21 Condylar process CC
CC Excl: See code 802.20

802.22 Subcondylar CC
CC Excl: See code 802.20

802.23 Coronoid process CC
CC Excl: See code 802.20

Facial Fractures

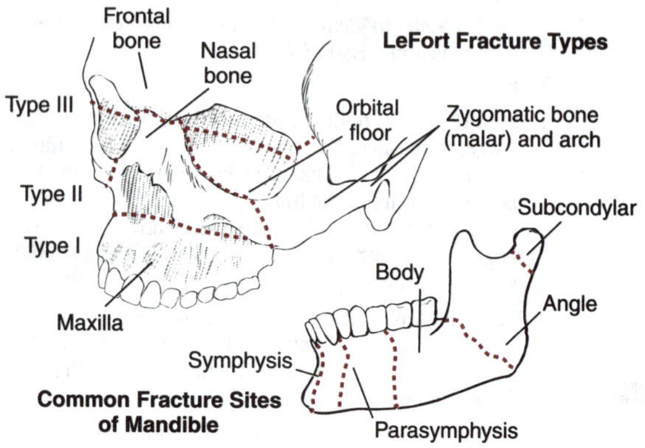

LeFort Fracture Types

Frontal bone
Nasal bone
Type III
Orbital floor
Zygomatic bone (malar) and arch
Type II
Type I
Maxilla
Subcondylar
Body
Angle
Symphysis
Parasymphysis

Common Fracture Sites of Mandible

802.24 Ramus, unspecified CC
CC Excl: See code 802.20

802.25 Angle of jaw CC
CC Excl: See code 802.20

802.26 Symphysis of body CC
CC Excl: See code 802.20

802.27 Alveolar border of body CC
CC Excl: See code 802.20

802.28 Body, other and unspecified CC
CC Excl: See code 802.20

802.29 Multiple sites CC
CC Excl: See code 802.20

✓5th **802.3 Mandible, open**

802.30 Unspecified site CC
CC Excl: See code 802.20

802.31 Condylar process CC
CC Excl: See code 802.20

802.32 Subcondylar CC
CC Excl: See code 802.20

802.33 Coronoid process CC
CC Excl: See code 802.20

802.34 Ramus, unspecified CC
CC Excl: See code 802.20

802.35 Angle of jaw CC
CC Excl: See code 802.20

802.36 Symphysis of body CC
CC Excl: See code 802.20

802.37 Alveolar border of body CC
CC Excl: See code 802.20

802.38 Body, other and unspecified CC
CC Excl: See code 802.20

802.39 Multiple sites CC
CC Excl: See code 802.20

802.4 Malar and maxillary bones, closed CC
Superior maxilla
Upper jaw (bone)
Zygoma
Zygomatic arch
CC Excl: See code 802.20

802.5 Malar and maxillary bones, open CC
CC Excl: See code 802.20

802.6 Orbital floor (blow-out), closed CC
CC Excl: 800.00-801.99, 802.6-804.99, 829.0-829.1, 850.0-852.19, 852.21-854.19, 873.8-873.9, 879.8-879.9, 905.0, 925.1-925.2, 929.0-929.9, 958.8-959.09, 959.8-959.9

§ Requires fifth-digit. See beginning of section 800-804 for codes and definitions.

802.7 Orbital floor (blow-out), open CC
CC Excl: See code 802.6

802.8 Other facial bones, closed CC
Alveolus
Palate
Orbit:
NOS
part other than roof or floor
EXCLUDES *orbital:*
floor (802.6)
roof (801.0-801.9)
CC Excl: See code 802.6

802.9 Other facial bones, open CC
CC Excl: See code 802.6

✓4th **803 Other and unqualified skull fractures**
INCLUDES skull NOS
skull multiple NOS
AHA: 4Q, '96, 36

§ ✓5th **803.0 Closed without mention of intracranial injury** CC
CC Excl: 800.00-801.99, 803.00-804.99, 829.0-829.1, 850.0-852.19, 852.21-854.19, 873.8-873.9, 879.8-879.9, 905.0, 925.1-925.2, 929.0-929.9, 958.8-959.09, 959.8-959.9

§ ✓5th **803.1 Closed with cerebral laceration and contusion** CC
CC Excl: See code 803.0

§ ✓5th **803.2 Closed with subarachnoid, subdural, and extradural hemorrhage** CC
CC Excl: See code 803.0

§ ✓5th **803.3 Closed with other and unspecified intracranial hemorrhage** CC
CC Excl: See code 803.0

§ ✓5th **803.4 Closed with intracranial injury of other and unspecified nature** CC
CC Excl: See code 803.0

§ ✓5th **803.5 Open without mention of intracranial injury** CC
CC Excl: See code 803.0

§ ✓5th **803.6 Open with cerebral laceration and contusion** CC
CC Excl: See code 803.0

§ ✓5th **803.7 Open with subarachnoid, subdural, and extradural hemorrhage** CC
CC Excl: See code 803.0

§ ✓5th **803.8 Open with other and unspecified intracranial hemorrhage** CC
CC Excl: See code 803.0

§ ✓5th **803.9 Open with intracranial injury of other and unspecified nature** CC
CC Excl: See code 803.0

✓4th **804 Multiple fractures involving skull or face with other bones**
AHA: 4Q, '96, 36

§ ✓5th **804.0 Closed without mention of intracranial injury** CC
CC Excl: See code 803.0

§ ✓5th **804.1 Closed with cerebral laceration and contusion** CC
CC Excl: See code 803.0
AHA: For code 804.10: ▶1Q, '06, 6◀

§ ✓5th **804.2 Closed with subarachnoid, subdural, and extradural hemorrhage** CC
CC Excl: See code 803.0

§ ✓5th **804.3 Closed with other and unspecified intracranial hemorrhage** CC
CC Excl: See code 803.0

§ ✓5th **804.4 Closed with intracranial injury of other and unspecified nature** CC
CC Excl: See code 803.0

§ ✓5th **804.5 Open without mention of intracranial injury** CC
CC Excl: See code 803.0

§ ✓5th **804.6 Open with cerebral laceration and contusion** CC
CC Excl: See code 803.0

§ ✓5th **804.7 Open with subarachnoid, subdural, and extradural hemorrhage** CC
CC Excl: See code 803.0

§ ✓5th **804.8 Open with other and unspecified intracranial hemorrhage** CC
CC Excl: See code 803.0

§ ✓5th **804.9 Open with intracranial injury of other and unspecified nature** CC
CC Excl: See code 803.0

FRACTURE OF NECK AND TRUNK (805-809)

✓4th **805 Fracture of vertebral column without mention of spinal cord injury**
INCLUDES neural arch
spine
spinous process
transverse process
vertebra

The following fifth-digit subclassification is for use with codes 805.0-805.1:

0 cervical vertebra, unspecified level
1 first cervical vertebra
2 second cervical vertebra
3 third cervical vertebra
4 fourth cervical vertebra
5 fifth cervical vertebra
6 sixth cervical vertebra
7 seventh cervical vertebra
8 multiple cervical vertebrae

✓5th **805.0 Cervical, closed** CC
Atlas
Axis
CC Excl: 805.00-805.18, 805.8-806.19, 806.8-806.9, 829.0-829.1, 839.00-839.18, 839.40, 839.49-839.50, 839.59, 839.69, 839.79-839.9, 847.0, 847.9, 848.8-848.9, 879.8-879.9, 905.1, 926.11, 929.0-929.9, 952.00-952.09, 952.8-952.9, 958.8-958.99, 959.11-959.19, 959.8-959.9
DRG 243

✓5th **805.1 Cervical, open** CC
CC Excl: See code 805.0

805.2 Dorsal [thoracic], closed CC
CC Excl: 805.2-805.3, 805.8-805.9, 806.20-806.39, 806.8-806.9, 829.0-829.1, 839.21, 839.31, 839.40, 839.49-839.50, 839.59, 839.69, 839.79-839.9, 847.1, 847.9, 848.8-848.9, 879.8-879.9, 905.1, 926.11, 929.0-929.9, 952.10-952.19, 952.8-952.9, 958.8-958.99, 959.11-959.19, 959.8-959.9

805.3 Dorsal [thoracic], open CC
CC Excl: See code 805.2

805.4 Lumbar, closed CC
CC Excl: 805.4-805.5, 805.8-805.9, 806.4-806.5, 806.8-806.9, 829.0-829.1, 839.20, 839.30, 839.40, 839.49-839.50, 839.59, 839.69, 839.79-839.9, 847.2, 847.9, 848.8-848.9, 879.8-879.9, 905.1, 926.11, 929.0-929.9, 952.2, 952.8-952.9, 958.8-958.99, 959.11-959.19, 959.8-959.9
AHA: 4Q, '99, 12
DRG 243

805.5 Lumbar, open CC
CC Excl: See code 805.4

805.6 Sacrum and coccyx, closed CC
CC Excl: 805.6-805.9, 806.60-806.9, 829.0-829.1, 839.40-839.59, 839.69, 839.79-839.9, 846.0-846.9, 847.3-847.9, 848.5-848.9, 879.8-879.9, 905.1, 926.11, 929.0-929.9, 952.3-952.9, 958.8-958.99, 959.11-959.19, 959.8-959.9

§ Requires fifth-digit. See beginning of section 800-804 for codes and definitions.

Additional Digit Required   Nonspecific PDx   Unacceptable PDx   Manifestation Code   MCV Major Cardiovascular Condition   ▶◀ Revised Text   ● New Code   ▲ Revised Code Title

Vertebral Column

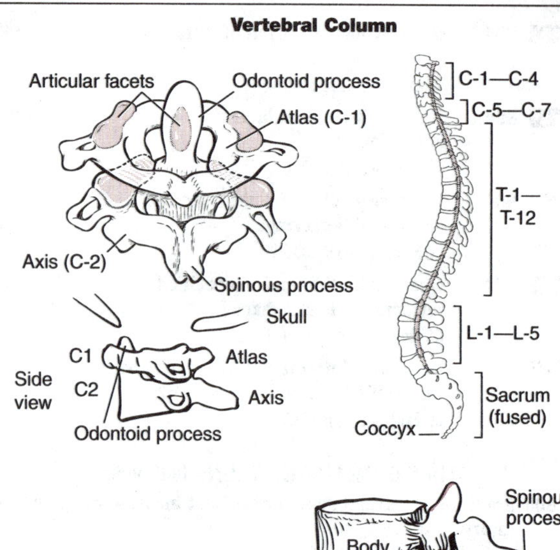

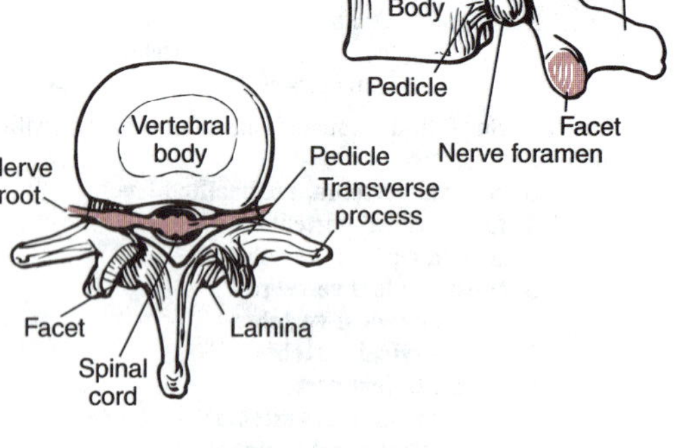

805.7 Sacrum and coccyx, open CC
CC Excl: See code 805.6

805.8 Unspecified, closed CC
CC Excl: 733.10-733.19, 733.93-733.95, 805.00-805.9, 806.00-806.9, 829.0-829.1, 839.00-839.59, 839.69, 839.79, 839.8-839.9, 846.0-846.9, 847.0-847.9, 848.5-848.9, 879.8-879.9, 905.1, 926.11, 929.0, 929.9, 952.00-952.9, 958.8-958.99, 959.11-959.19, 959.8-959.9

805.9 Unspecified, open CC
CC Excl: See code 805.8

✓4th **806 Fracture of vertebral column with spinal cord injury**

INCLUDES any condition classifiable to 805 with:
- complete or incomplete transverse lesion (of cord)
- hematomyelia
- injury to:
  - cauda equina
  - nerve
- paralysis
- paraplegia
- quadriplegia
- spinal concussion

✓5th **806.0 Cervical, closed**

806.00 C_1-C_4 level with unspecified spinal cord injury CC
Cervical region NOS with spinal cord injury NOS
CC Excl: 733.10-733.19, 733.93-733.95, 805.00-805.18, 805.8-806.19, 806.8-806.9, 829.0-829.1, 839.00-839.18, 839.40, 839.49-839.50, 839.59, 839.69, 839.79-839.9, 847.9, 848.8-848.9, 879.8-879.9, 905.1, 926.11, 929.0-929.9, 952.00-952.09, 952.8-952.9, 958.8-958.99, 959.11-959.19, 959.8-959.9

806.01 C_1-C_4 level with complete lesion of cord CC
CC Excl: See code 806.00

806.02 C_1-C_4 level with anterior cord syndrome CC
CC Excl: See code 806.00

806.03 C_1-C_4 level with central cord Syndrome CC
CC Excl: See code 806.00

806.04 C_1-C_4 level with other specified spinal cord injury CC
C_1-C_4 level with:
- incomplete spinal cord lesion NOS
- posterior cord syndrome

CC Excl: See code 806.00

806.05 C_5-C_7 level with unspecified spinal cord injury CC
CC Excl: See code 806.00

806.06 C_5-C_7 level with complete lesion of cord CC
CC Excl: See code 806.00

806.07 C_5-C_7 level with anterior cord syndrome CC
CC Excl: See code 806.00

806.08 C_5-C_7 level with central cord syndrome CC
CC Excl: See code 806.00

806.09 C_5-C_7 level with other specified spinal cord injury CC
C_5-C_7 level with:
- incomplete spinal cord lesion NOS
- posterior cord syndrome

CC Excl: See code 806.00

✓5th **806.1 Cervical, open**

806.10 C_1-C_4 level with unspecified spinal cord injury CC
CC Excl: See code 806.00

806.11 C_1-C_4 level with complete lesion of cord CC
CC Excl: See code 806.00

806.12 C_1-C_4 level with anterior cord syndrome CC
CC Excl: See code 806.00

806.13 C_1-C_4 level with central cord syndrome CC
CC Excl: See code 806.00

806.14 C_1-C_4 level with other specified spinal cord injury CC
C_1-C_4 level with:
- incomplete spinal cord lesion NOS
- posterior cord syndrome

CC Excl: See code 806.00

806.15 C_5-C_7 level with unspecified spinal cord injury CC
CC Excl: See code 806.00

806.16 C_5-C_7 level with complete lesion of cord CC
CC Excl: See code 806.00

806.17 C_5-C_7 level with anterior cord syndrome CC
CC Excl: See code 806.00

806.18 C_5-C_7 level with central cord syndrome CC
CC Excl: See code 806.00

806.19 C_5-C_7 level with other specified spinal cord injury CC
C_5-C_7 level with:
- incomplete spinal cord lesion NOS
- posterior cord syndrome

CC Excl: See code 806.00

✓5th **806.2 Dorsal [thoracic], closed**

806.20 T_1-T_6 level with unspecified spinal cord injury CC

Thoracic region NOS with spinal cord injury NOS

CC Excl: 733.10-733.19, 733.93-733.95, 805.2-805.3, 805.8-805.9, 806.20-806.39, 806.8-806.9, 829.0-829.1, 839.21, 839.31-839.40, 839.49-839.50, 839.59, 839.69, 839.79, 839.8-839.9, 847.1, 847.9, 848.8-848.9, 879.8-879.9, 905.1, 926.11, 929.0, 929.9, 952.10-952.19, 952.8-952.9, 958.8-958.99, 959.11-959.19, 959.8-959.9

806.21 T_1-T_6 level with complete lesion of cord CC

CC Excl: See code 806.20

806.22 T_1-T_6 level with anterior cord syndrome CC

CC Excl: See code 806.20

806.23 T_1-T_6 level with central cord syndrome CC

CC Excl: See code 806.20

806.24 T_1-T_6 level with other specified spinal cord injury CC

T_1-T_6 level with:

incomplete spinal cord lesion NOS

posterior cord syndrome

CC Excl: See code 806.20

806.25 T_7-T_{12} level with unspecified spinal cord injury CC

CC Excl: See code 806.20

806.26 T_7-T_{12} level with complete lesion of cord CC

CC Excl: See code 806.20

806.27 T_7-T_{12} level with anterior cord syndrome CC

CC Excl: See code 806.20

806.28 T_7-T_{12} level with central cord syndrome CC

CC Excl: See code 806.20

806.29 T_7-T_{12} level with other specified spinal cord injury CC

T_7-T_{12} level with:

incomplete spinal cord lesion NOS

posterior cord syndrome

CC Excl: See code 806.20

✓5th **806.3 Dorsal [thoracic], open**

806.30 T_1-T_6 level with unspecified spinal cord injury CC

CC Excl: See code 806.20

806.31 T_1-T_6 level with complete lesion of cord CC

CC Excl: See code 806.20

806.32 T_1-T_6 level with anteriorr cord syndrome CC

CC Excl: See code 806.20

806.33 T_1-T_6 level with centralr cord syndrome CC

CC Excl: See code 806.20

806.34 T_1-T_6 level with other specified spinal cord injury CC

T_1-T_6 level with:

incomplete spinal cord lesion NOS

posterior cord syndrome

CC Excl: See code 806.20

806.35 T_7-T_{12} level with unspecified spinal cord injury CC

CC Excl: See code 806.20

806.36 T_7-T_{12} level with complete lesion of cord CC

CC Excl: See code 806.20

806.37 T_7-T_{12} level with anterior cord syndrome CC

CC Excl: See code 806.20

806.38 T_7-T_{12} level with central cord syndrome CC

CC Excl: See code 806.20

806.39 T_7-T_{12} level with other specified spinal cord injury CC

T_7-T_{12} level with:

incomplete spinal cord lesion NOS

posterior cord syndrome

CC Excl: See code 806.20

806.4 Lumbar, closed CC

CC Excl: 733.10-733.19, 733.93-733.95, 805.4-805.5, 805.8-805.9, 806.4-806.5, 806.8-806.9, 829.0-829.1, 839.20, 839.30, 839.40, 839.49-839.50, 839.59, 839.69, 839.79, 839.8-839.9, 847.2, 847.9, 848.8-848.9, 879.8-879.9, 905.1, 926.11, 929.0, 929.9, 952.2, 952.8-952.9, 958.8-958.99, 959.11-959.19, 959.8-959.9

AHA: 4Q, '99, 11, 13

806.5 Lumbar, open CC

CC Excl: See code 806.4

✓5th **806.6 Sacrum and coccyx, closed**

806.60 With unspecified spinal cord injury CC

CC Excl: 733.10-733.19, 733.93-733.95, 805.6-805.9, 806.60-806.9, 829.0-829.1, 839.40-839.59, 839.69, 839.79, 839.8-839.9, 846.0-846.9, 847.0, 847.3-847.9, 848.5-848.9, 879.8-879.9, 905.1, 926.11, 929.0, 929.9, 952.3-952.9, 958.8-958.99, 959.11-959.19, 959.8-959.9

806.61 With complete cauda equina lesion CC

CC Excl: See code 806.60

806.62 With other cauda equina injury CC

CC Excl: See code 806.60

806.69 With other spinal cord injury CC

CC Excl: See code 806.60

✓5th **806.7 Sacrum and coccyx, open**

806.70 With unspecified spinal cord injury CC

CC Excl: See code 806.60

806.71 With complete cauda equina lesion CC

CC Excl: See code 806.60

806.72 With other cauda equina injury CC

CC Excl: See code 806.60

806.79 With other spinal cord injury CC

CC Excl: See code 806.60

806.8 Unspecified, closed CC

CC Excl: 733.10-733.19, 733.93-733.95, 805.00-805.09, 806.00-806.9, 829.0-829.1, 839.00-839.59, 839.69, 839.79, 839.8-839.9, 846.0-846.9, 847.0-847.9, 848.5-848.9, 879.8-879.9, 905.1, 926.11, 929.0, 929.9, 952.00-952.9, 958.8-958.99, 959.11-959.19, 959.8-959.9

806.9 Unspecified, open CC

CC Excl: See code 806.8

✓4th **807 Fracture of rib(s), sternum, larynx, and trachea**

The following fifth-digit subclassification is for use with codes 807.0-807.1:

- **0 rib(s), unspecified**
- **1 one rib**
- **2 two ribs**
- **3 three ribs**
- **4 four ribs**
- **5 five ribs**
- **6 six ribs**
- **7 seven ribs**
- **8 eight or more ribs**
- **9 multiple ribs, unspecified**

✓5th **807.0 Rib(s), closed** CC 4-9

CC Excl: For codes 807.04-807.09: 807.00-807.19, 807.4, 819.0-819.1, 828.0-829.1, 848.8-848.9, 879.8-879.9, 929.0-929.9, 958.8-958.99, 959.8-959.9

✓5th **807.1 Rib(s), open** CC

CC Excl: 807.00-807.19, 807.4, 819.0-819.1, 828.0-829.1, 848.8-848.9, 879.8-879.9, 929.0-929.9, 958.8-958.99, 959.8-959.9

807.2 Sternum, closed CC

CC Excl: 807.2-807.4, 829.0-829.1, 848.8-848.9, 879.8-879.9, 929.0, 929.9, 958.8-958.99, 959.8-959.9

DEF: Break in flat bone (breast bone) in anterior thorax.

807.3 Sternum, open CC

CC Excl: See code 807.2

DEF: Break, with open wound, in flat bone in mid anterior thorax.

807.4 Flail chest CC

CC Excl: 807.00-807.4, 829.0-829.1, 848.8-848.9, 879.8-879.9, 929.0, 929.9, 958.8-958.99, 959.8-959.9

807.5 Larynx and trachea, closed CC

Hyoid bone
Thyroid cartilage
Trachea

CC Excl: 807.5-807.6, 829.0-829.1, 848.8-848.9, 879.8-879.9, 929.0, 929.9, 958.8-958.99, 959.8-959.9

807.6 Larynx and trachea, open CC

CC Excl: See code 807.5

✓4th **808 Fracture of pelvis**

808.0 Acetabulum, closed CC

CC Excl: 733.10-733.19, 733.93-733.95, 808.0-808.1, 808.43-808.49, 808.53-809.1, 829.0-829.1, 835.00-835.13, 843.0-843.9, 846.0-846.9, 879.8-879.9, 929.0-929.9, 958.8-958.99, 959.6, 959.8-959.9

808.1 Acetabulum, open CC

CC Excl: 808.0-808.1, 808.43-808.49, 808.53-809.1, 829.0-829.1, 835.00-835.13, 843.0-843.9, 846.0-846.9, 848.5-848.9, 879.8-879.9, 929.0-929.9, 958.8-958.99, 959.6, 959.8-959.9

808.2 Pubis, closed CC

CC Excl: 733.10-733.19, 733.93-733.95, 808.2-808.3, 808.43-808.49, 808.53-809.1, 829.0-829.1, 835.00-835.13, 843.0-843.9, 846.0-846.9, 848.5-848.9, 879.8-879.9, 929.0-929.9, 958.8-958.99, 959.6, 959.8-959.9

808.3 Pubis, open CC

CC Excl: See code 808.2

Ribs, Sternum, Larynx, and Trachea

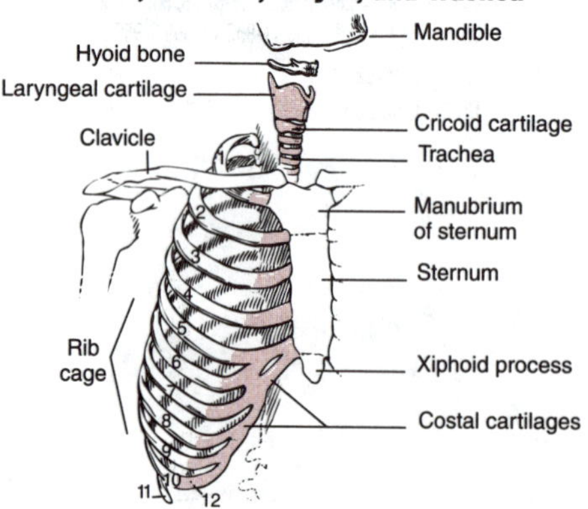

Pelvis and Pelvic Fractures

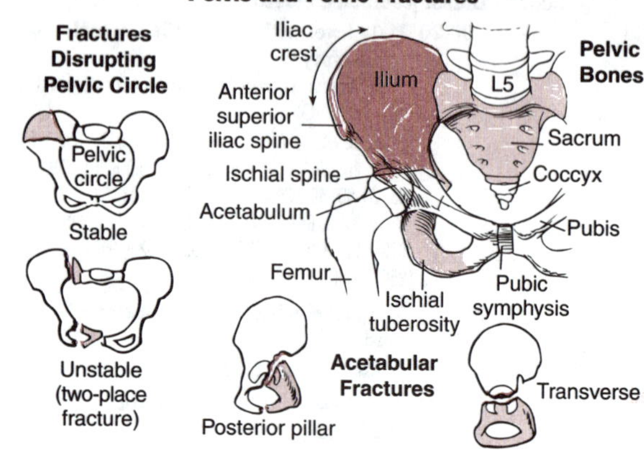

✓5th **808.4 Other specified part, closed**

808.41 Ilium

808.42 Ischium

808.43 Multiple pelvic fractures with disruption of pelvic circle CC

CC Excl: 733.10-733.19, 733.93-733.95, 808.0-809.1, 829.0-829.1, 835.00-835.13, 843.0-843.9, 846.0-846.9, 848.5-848.9, 879.8-879.9, 929.0-929.9, 958.8-958.99, 959.6, 959.8-959.9

808.49 Other CC

Innominate bone
Pelvic rim

CC Excl: See code 808.43

✓5th **808.5 Other specified part, open**

808.51 Ilium CC

CC Excl: 733.10-733.19, 733.93-733.95, 808.41, 808.43-808.49, 808.51, 808.53-809.1, 829.0-829.1, 835.00-835.13, 843.0-843.9, 846.0-846.9, 848.5-848.9, 879.8-879.9, 929.0-929.9, 958.8-958.99, 959.6, 959.8-959.9

808.52 Ischium CC

CC Excl: 733.10-733.19, 733.93-733.95, 808.42-808.49, 808.52-809.1, 829.0-829.1, 835.00-835.13, 843.0-843.9, 846.0-846.9, 848.5-848.9, 879.8-879.9, 929.0-929.9, 958.8-958.99, 959.6, 959.8-959.9

808.53 Multiple pelvic fractures with disruption of pelvic circle CC

CC Excl: 733.10-733.19, 733.93-733.95, 808.0-809.1, 829.0-829.1, 835.00-835.13, 843.0-843.9, 846.0-846.9, 848.5-848.9, 879.8-879.9, 929.0-929.9, 958.8-958.99, 959.6, 959.8-959.9

808.59 Other CC

CC Excl: See code 808.53

808.8 Unspecified, closed CC

CC Excl: See code 808.53

808.9 Unspecified, open CC

CC Excl: See code 808.53

✓4th **809 Ill-defined fractures of bones of trunk**

INCLUDES bones of trunk with other bones except those of skull and face
multiple bones of trunk

EXCLUDES *multiple fractures of:*
pelvic bones alone (808.0-808.9)
ribs alone (807.0-807.1, 807.4)
ribs or sternum with limb bones (819.0-819.1, 828.0-828.1)
skull or face with other bones (804.0-804.9)

809.0 Fracture of bones of trunk, closed

809.1 Fracture of bones of trunk, open

FRACTURE OF UPPER LIMB (810-819)

✓4th **810 Fracture of clavicle**

INCLUDES collar bone
interligamentous part of clavicle

The following fifth-digit subclassification is for use with category 810:

0 unspecified part
Clavicle NOS
1 sternal end of clavicle
2 shaft of clavicle
3 acromial end of clavicle

✓5th **810.0 Closed**

✓5th **810.1 Open**

✓4th **811 Fracture of scapula**

INCLUDES shoulder blade

The following fifth-digit subclassification is for use with category 811:

0 unspecified part
1 acromial process
Acromion (process)
2 coracoid process
3 glenoid cavity and neck of scapula
9 other

✓5th **811.0 Closed**

✓5th **811.1 Open**

✓4th **812 Fracture of humerus**

✓5th **812.0 Upper end, closed**

812.00 Upper end, unspecified part
Proximal end Shoulder

812.01 Surgical neck
Neck of humerus NOS

812.02 Anatomical neck

812.03 Greater tuberosity

812.09 Other
Head Upper epiphysis
Lesser tuberosity

✓5th **812.1 Upper end, open**

812.10 Upper end, unspecified part
812.11 Surgical neck
812.12 Anatomical neck
812.13 Greater tuberosity
812.19 Other

✓5th **812.2 Shaft or unspecified part, closed**

812.20 Unspecified part of humerus
Humerus NOS Upper arm NOS
Lesser tuberosity

812.21 Shaft of humerus
AHA: ▶4Q, '05, 129;◀ 3Q, '99, 14

✓5th **812.3 Shaft or unspecified part, open**

812.30 Unspecified part of humerus
812.31 Shaft of humerus

Right Clavicle and Scapula, Anterior View

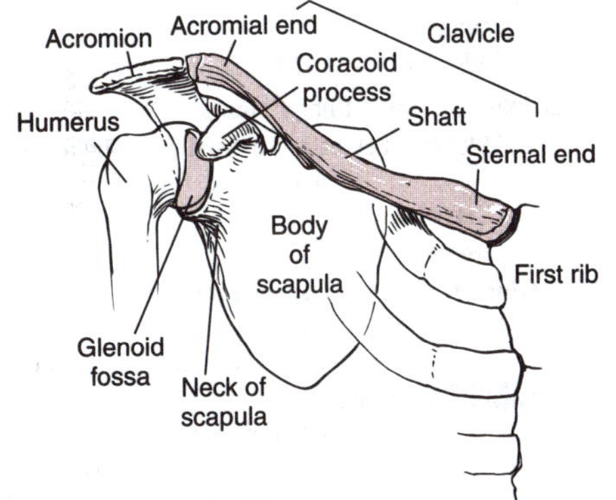

Right Humerus, Anterior View

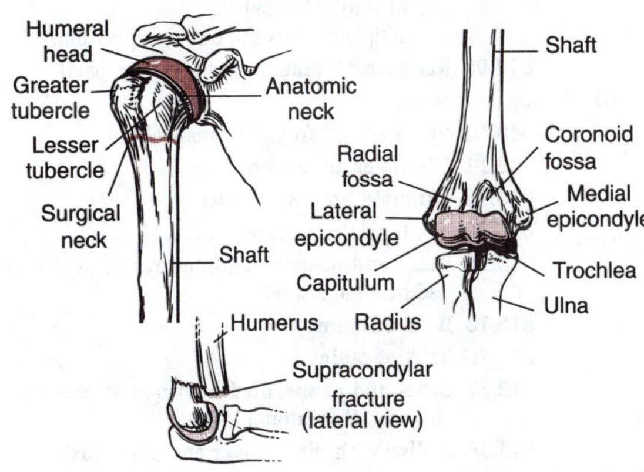

✓5th **812.4 Lower end, closed**
Distal end of humerus Elbow

812.40 Lower end, unspecified part

812.41 Supracondylar fracture of humerus

812.42 Lateral condyle
External condyle

812.43 Medial condyle
Internal epicondyle

812.44 Condyle(s), unspecified
Articular process NOS
Lower epiphysis NOS

812.49 Other
Multiple fractures of lower end
Trochlea

✓5th **812.5 Lower end, open**

812.50 Lower end, unspecified part
812.51 Supracondylar fracture of humerus
812.52 Lateral condyle
812.53 Medial condyle
812.54 Condyle(s), unspecified
812.59 Other

✓4th **813 Fracture of radius and ulna**

✓5th **813.0 Upper end, closed**
Proximal end

813.00 Upper end of forearm, unspecified

813.01 Olecranon process of ulna

813.02 Coronoid process of ulna

813.03 Monteggia's fracture
DEF: Fracture near the head of the ulnar shaft, causing dislocation of the radial head.

813.04 Other and unspecified fractures of proximal end of ulna (alone)
Multiple fractures of ulna, upper end

813.05 Head of radius

813.06 Neck of radius

Right Radius and Ulna, Anterior View

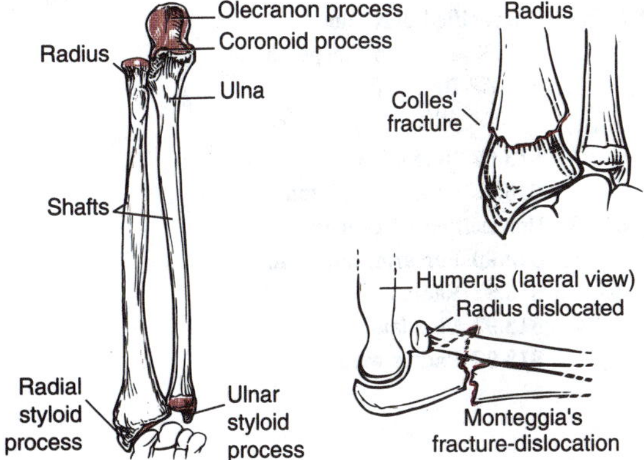

813.07 Other and unspecified fractures of proximal end of radius (alone)
Multiple fractures of radius, upper end
813.08 Radius with ulna, upper end [any part]

✓5th **813.1 Upper end, open**
813.10 Upper end of forearm, unspecified
813.11 Olecranon process of ulna
813.12 Coronoid process of ulna
813.13 Monteggia's fracture
813.14 Other and unspecified fractures of proximal end of ulna (alone)
813.15 Head of radius
813.16 Neck of radius
813.17 Other and unspecified fractures of proximal end of radius (alone)
813.18 Radius with ulna, upper end [any part]

✓5th **813.2 Shaft, closed**
813.20 Shaft, unspecified
813.21 Radius (alone)
813.22 Ulna (alone)
813.23 Radius with ulna

✓5th **813.3 Shaft, open**
813.30 Shaft, unspecified
813.31 Radius (alone)
813.32 Ulna (alone)
813.33 Radius with ulna

✓5th **813.4 Lower end, closed**
Distal end
813.40 Lower end of forearm, unspecified
813.41 Colles' fracture
Smith's fracture
DEF: Break of lower end of radius; associated with backward movement of the radius lower section.
813.42 Other fractures of distal end of radius (alone)
Dupuytren's fracture, radius
Radius, lower end
DEF: Dupuytren's fracture: fracture and dislocation of the forearm; the fracture is of the radius above the wrist, and the dislocation is of the ulna at the lower end.
813.43 Distal end of ulna (alone)
Ulna:
head
lower end
lower epiphysis
styloid process
813.44 Radius with ulna, lower end
813.45 Torus fracture of radius
AHA: 4Q, '02, 70

✓5th **813.5 Lower end, open**
813.50 Lower end of forearm, unspecified
813.51 Colles' fracture
813.52 Other fractures of distal end of radius (alone)
813.53 Distal end of ulna (alone)
813.54 Radius with ulna, lower end

✓5th **813.8 Unspecified part, closed**
813.80 Forearm, unspecified
813.81 Radius (alone)
AHA: 2Q, '98, 19
813.82 Ulna (alone)
813.83 Radius with ulna

✓5th **813.9 Unspecified part, open**
813.90 Forearm, unspecified
813.91 Radius (alone)
813.92 Ulna (alone)
813.93 Radius with ulna

Hand Fractures

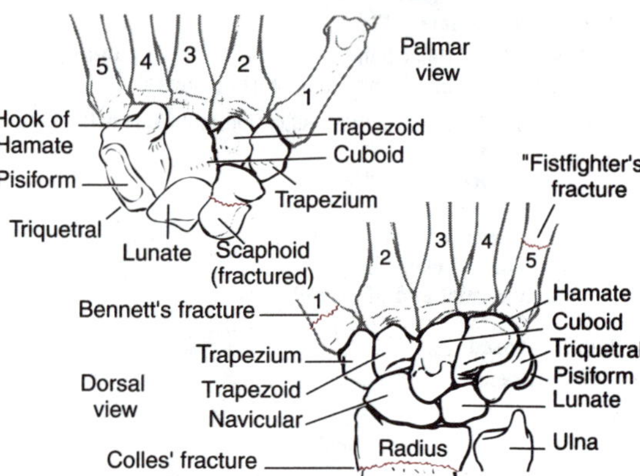

✓4th **814 Fracture of carpal bone(s)**

The following fifth-digit subclassification is for use with category 814:
0 carpal bone, unspecified
Wrist NOS
1 navicular [scaphoid] of wrist
2 lunate [semilunar] bone of wrist
3 triquetral [cuneiform] bone of wrist
4 pisiform
5 trapezium bone [larger multangular]
6 trapezoid bone [smaller multangular]
7 capitate bone [os magnum]
8 hamate [unciform] bone
9 other

✓5th **814.0 Closed**
✓5th **814.1 Open**

✓4th **815 Fracture of metacarpal bone(s)**

INCLUDES hand [except finger]
metacarpus

The following fifth-digit subclassification is for use with category 815:
0 metacarpal bone(s), site unspecified
1 base of thumb [first] metacarpal
Bennett's fracture
2 base of other metacarpal bone(s)
3 shaft of metacarpal bone(s)
4 neck of metacarpal bone(s)
9 multiple sites of metacarpus

✓5th **815.0 Closed**
✓5th **815.1 Open**

✓4th **816 Fracture of one or more phalanges of hand**

INCLUDES finger(s) thumb

The following fifth-digit subclassification is for use with category 816:
0 phalanx or phalanges, unspecified
1 middle or proximal phalanx or phalanges
2 distal phalanx or phalanges
3 multiple sites

✓5th **816.0 Closed**
✓5th **816.1 Open**
AHA: For code 816.12: 4Q, '03, 77

✓4th **817 Multiple fractures of hand bones**

INCLUDES metacarpal bone(s) with phalanx or phalanges of same hand

817.0 Closed
817.1 Open

✓4th **818 Ill-defined fractures of upper limb**

INCLUDES arm NOS
multiple bones of same upper limb

EXCLUDES *multiple fractures of:*
metacarpal bone(s) with phalanx or phalanges (817.0-817.1)
phalanges of hand alone (816.0-816.1)
radius with ulna (813.0-813.9)

818.0 **Closed**

818.1 **Open**

✓4th **819 Multiple fractures involving both upper limbs, and upper limb with rib(s) and sternum**

INCLUDES arm(s) with rib(s) or sternum
both arms [any bones]

819.0 **Closed**

819.1 **Open**

FRACTURE OF LOWER LIMB (820-829)

✓4th **820 Fracture of neck of femur**

✓5th **820.0 Transcervical fracture, closed**

820.00 Intracapsular section, unspecified CC
CC Excl: 733.10-733.19, 733.93-733.95, 820.00-821.39, 827.0-829.1, 843.0-843.9, 848.8-848.9, 879.8-879.9, 929.0-929.9, 958.8, 959.6, 959.8-959.9

820.01 Epiphysis (separation) (upper) CC
Transepiphyseal
CC Excl: See code 820.00

820.02 Midcervical section CC
Transcervical NOS
CC Excl: See code 820.00
AHA: 3Q, '03, 12

820.03 Base of neck CC
Cervicotrochanteric section
CC Excl: See code 820.00

820.09 Other CC
Head of femur
Subcapital
CC Excl: See code 820.00

✓5th **820.1 Transcervical fracture, open**

820.10 Intracapsular section, unspecified CC
CC Excl: See code 820.00

820.11 Epiphysis (separation) (upper) CC
CC Excl: See code 820.00

820.12 Midcervical section CC
CC Excl: See code 820.00

820.13 Base of neck CC
CC Excl: See code 820.00

820.19 Other CC
CC Excl: See code 820.00

✓5th **820.2 Pertrochanteric fracture, closed**

820.20 Trochanteric section, unspecified CC
Trochanter: NOS, greater
Trochanter: lesser
CC Excl: See code 820.00

820.21 Intertrochanteric section CC
CC Excl: See code 820.00

820.22 Subtrochanteric section CC
CC Excl: See code 820.00

✓5th **820.3 Pertrochanteric fracture, open**

820.30 Trochanteric section, unspecified CC
CC Excl: See code 820.00

820.31 Intertrochanteric section CC
CC Excl: See code 820.00

820.32 Subtrochanteric section CC
CC Excl: See code 820.00

820.8 Unspecified part of neck of femur, closed CC
Hip NOS
Neck of femur NOS
CC Excl: See code 820.00

Right Femur, Anterior View

Head
Greater trochanter
Intertrochanteric line
Lesser trochanter
Neck
Shaft
Medial epicondyle
Lateral epicondyle
Articular cartilage

820.9 Unspecified part of neck of femur, open CC
CC Excl: See code 820.00

✓4th **821 Fracture of other and unspecified parts of femur**

✓5th **821.0 Shaft or unspecified part, closed**

821.00 Unspecified part of femur CC
Thigh
Upper leg
EXCLUDES *hip NOS (820.8)*
CC Excl: See code 820.00

821.01 Shaft CC
CC Excl: See code 820.00
AHA: 1Q, '99, 5

✓5th **821.1 Shaft or unspecified part, open**

821.10 Unspecified part of femur CC
CC Excl: See code 820.00

821.11 Shaft CC
CC Excl: See code 820.00

✓5th **821.2 Lower end, closed**
Distal end

821.20 Lower end, unspecified part
821.21 Condyle, femoral
821.22 Epiphysis, lower (separation)
821.23 Supracondylar fracture of femur
821.29 Other
Multiple fractures of lower end

✓5th **821.3 Lower end, open**

821.30 Lower end, unspecified part
821.31 Condyle, femoral
821.32 Epiphysis, lower (separation)
821.33 Supracondylar fracture of femur
821.39 Other

✓4th **822 Fracture of patella**

822.0 **Closed**

822.1 **Open**

Right Tibia and Fibula, Anterior View

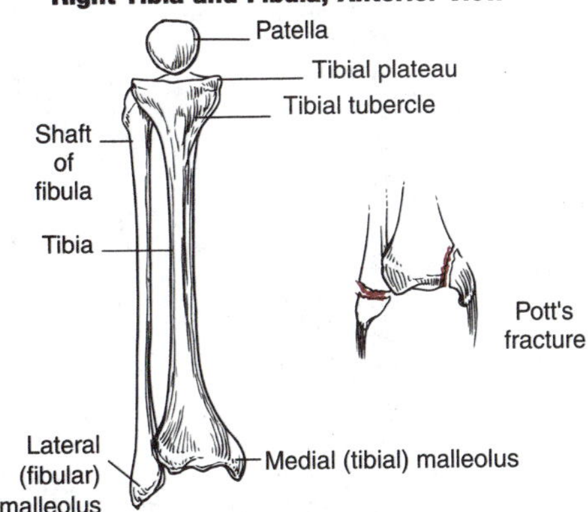

✓4th 823 **Fracture of tibia and fibula**

EXCLUDES *Dupuytren's fracture (824.4-824.5)*
ankle (824.4-824.5)
radius (813.42, 813.52)
Pott's fracture (824.4-824.5)
that involving ankle (824.0-824.9)

The following fifth-digit subclassification is for use with category 823:

0 tibia alone
1 fibula alone
2 fibula with tibia

✓5th 823.0 **Upper end, closed**
Head
Proximal end
Tibia:
condyles
tuberosity

✓5th 823.1 **Upper end, open**

✓5th 823.2 **Shaft, closed**

✓5th 823.3 **Shaft, open**

✓5th 823.4 **Torus fracture**
AHA: 4Q, '02, 70
DEF: A bone deformity in children, occurring commonly in the tibia and fibula, in which the bone bends and buckles but does not fracture.

✓5th 823.8 **Unspecified part, closed**
Lower leg NOS
AHA: For code 823.82: 1Q, '97, 8

✓5th 823.9 **Unspecified part, open**

✓4th 824 **Fracture of ankle**

824.0 **Medial malleolus, closed**
Tibia involving:
ankle
Tibia involving:
malleolus
AHA: 1Q, '04, 9

824.1 **Medial malleolus, open**

824.2 **Lateral malleolus, closed**
Fibula involving:
ankle
malleolus
AHA: 2Q, '02, 3

824.3 **Lateral malleolus, open**

824.4 **Bimalleolar, closed**
Dupuytren's fracture, fibula
Pott's fracture
DEF: Bimalleolar, closed: Breaking of both nodules (malleoli) on either side of ankle joint, without an open wound.
DEF: Dupuytren's fracture (Pott's fracture): The breaking of the farthest end of the lower leg bone (fibula), with injury to the farthest end joint of the other lower leg bone (tibia).

824.5 **Bimalleolar, open**

824.6 **Trimalleolar, closed**
Lateral and medial malleolus with anterior or posterior lip of tibia

824.7 **Trimalleolar, open**

Torus Fracture

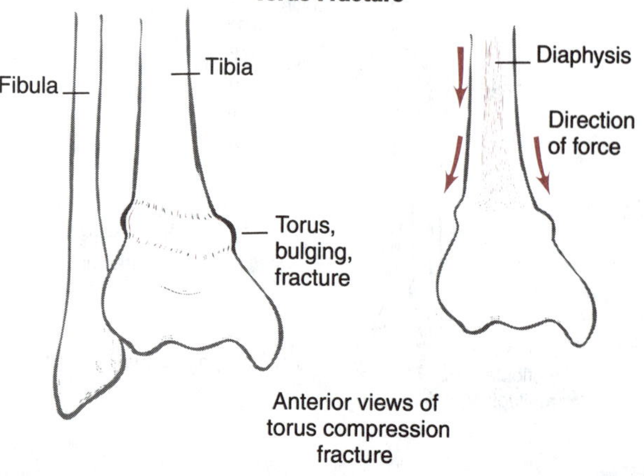

Right Foot, Dorsal

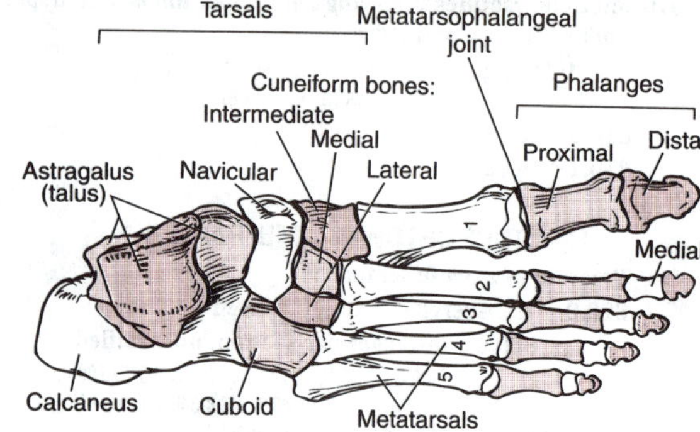

824.8 **Unspecified, closed**
Ankle NOS
AHA: 3Q, '00, 12

824.9 **Unspecified, open**

✓4th 825 **Fracture of one or more tarsal and metatarsal bones**

825.0 **Fracture of calcaneus, closed**
Heel bone
Os calcis

825.1 **Fracture of calcaneus, open**

✓5th 825.2 **Fracture of other tarsal and metatarsal bones, closed**

825.20 **Unspecified bone(s) of foot [except toes]**
Instep

825.21 **Astragalus**
Talus

825.22 **Navicular [scaphoid], foot**

825.23 **Cuboid**

825.24 **Cuneiform, foot**

825.25 **Metatarsal bone(s)**

825.29 **Other**
Tarsal with metatarsal bone(s) only
EXCLUDES *calcaneus (825.0)*

✓5th 825.3 **Fracture of other tarsal and metatarsal bones, open**

825.30 **Unspecified bone(s) of foot [except toes]**

825.31 **Astragalus**

825.32 **Navicular [scaphoid], foot**

825.33 **Cuboid**

825.34 **Cuneiform, foot**

825.35 **Metatarsal bone(s)**

825.39 **Other**

✓4th 826 **Fracture of one or more phalanges of foot**

INCLUDES toe(s)

826.0 **Closed**

826.1 **Open**

✓4th 827 **Other, multiple, and ill-defined fractures of lower limb**

INCLUDES leg NOS
multiple bones of same lower limb

EXCLUDES *multiple fractures of:*
ankle bones alone (824.4-824.9)
phalanges of foot alone (826.0-826.1)
tarsal with metatarsal bones (825.29, 825.39)
tibia with fibula (823.0-823.9 with fifth-digit 2)

827.0 **Closed**

827.1 **Open**

✓4th 828 **Multiple fractures involving both lower limbs, lower with upper limb, and lower limb(s) with rib(s) and sternum**

INCLUDES arm(s) with leg(s) [any bones]
both legs [any bones]
leg(s) with rib(s) or sternum

828.0 **Closed**

828.1 **Open**

✓4th 829 Fracture of unspecified bones

829.0 Unspecified bone, closed

829.1 Unspecified bone, open

DISLOCATION (830-839)

INCLUDES displacement
subluxation

EXCLUDES *congenital dislocation (754.0-755.8)*
pathological dislocation (718.2)
recurrent dislocation (718.3)

The descriptions "closed" and "open," used in the fourth-digit subdivisions, include the following terms:

closed:	open:
complete	compound
dislocation NOS	infected
partial	with foreign body
simple	
uncomplicated	

A dislocation not indicated as closed or open should be classified as closed.

AHA: 3Q, '90, 12

✓4th 830 Dislocation of jaw

INCLUDES jaw (cartilage) (meniscus)
mandible
maxilla (inferior)
temporomandibular (joint)

830.0 Closed dislocation

830.1 Open dislocation

✓4th 831 Dislocation of shoulder

EXCLUDES *sternoclavicular joint (839.61, 839.71)*
sternum (839.61, 839.71)

The following fifth-digit subclassification is for use with category 831:

0 shoulder, unspecified
Humerus NOS
1 anterior dislocation of humerus
2 posterior dislocation of humerus
3 inferior dislocation of humerus
4 acromioclavicular (joint)
Clavicle
9 other
Scapula

✓5th 831.0 Closed dislocation

✓5th 831.1 Open dislocation

✓4th 832 Dislocation of elbow

The following fifth-digit subclassification is for use with category 832:

0 elbow unspecified
1 anterior dislocation of elbow
2 posterior dislocation of elbow
3 medial dislocation of elbow
4 lateral dislocation of elbow
9 other

✓5th 832.0 Closed dislocation

✓5th 832.1 Open dislocation

✓4th 833 Dislocation of wrist

The following fifth-digit subclassification is for use with category 833:

0 wrist, unspecified part
Carpal (bone)
Radius, distal end
1 radioulnar (joint), distal
2 radiocarpal (joint)
3 midcarpal (joint)
4 carpometacarpal (joint)
5 metacarpal (bone), proximal end
9 other
Ulna, distal end

✓5th 833.0 Closed dislocation

✓5th 833.1 Open dislocation

✓4th 834 Dislocation of finger

INCLUDES finger(s)
phalanx of hand
thumb

The following fifth-digit subclassification is for use with category 834:

0 finger, unspecified part
1 metacarpophalangeal (joint)
Metacarpal (bone), distal end
2 interphalangeal (joint), hand

✓5th 834.0 Closed dislocation

✓5th 834.1 Open dislocation

✓4th 835 Dislocation of hip

The following fifth-digit subclassification is for use with category 835:

0 dislocation of hip, unspecified
1 posterior dislocation
2 obturator dislocation
3 other anterior dislocation

✓5th 835.0 Closed dislocation

✓5th 835.1 Open dislocation

✓4th 836 Dislocation of knee

EXCLUDES *dislocation of knee:*
old or pathological (718.2)
recurrent (718.3)
internal derangement of knee joint (717.0-717.5, 717.8-717.9)
old tear of cartilage or meniscus of knee (717.0-717.5, 717.8-717.9)

836.0 Tear of medial cartilage or meniscus of knee, current

Bucket handle tear: } current injury
NOS
medial meniscus

836.1 Tear of lateral cartilage or meniscus of knee, current

836.2 Other tear of cartilage or meniscus of knee, current

Tear of:
cartilage (semilunar) } current injury, not specified as medial or lateral
meniscus

836.3 Dislocation of patella, closed

836.4 Dislocation of patella, open

✓5th 836.5 Other dislocation of knee, closed

836.50 Dislocation of knee, unspecified

836.51 Anterior dislocation of tibia, proximal end
Posterior dislocation of femur, distal end

836.52 Posterior dislocation of tibia, proximal end
Anterior dislocation of femur, distal end

836.53 Medial dislocation of tibia, proximal end

836.54 Lateral dislocation of tibia, proximal end

836.59 Other

✓5th 836.6 Other dislocation of knee, open

836.60 Dislocation of knee, unspecified

836.61 Anterior dislocation of tibia, proximal end

836.62 Posterior dislocation of tibia, proximal end

836.63 Medial dislocation of tibia, proximal end

836.64 Lateral dislocation of tibia, proximal end

836.69 Other

✓4th 837 Dislocation of ankle

INCLUDES astragalus
fibula, distal end
navicular, foot
scaphoid, foot
tibia, distal end

837.0 Closed dislocation

837.1 Open dislocation

✓4th **838 Dislocation of foot**

The following fifth-digit subclassification is for use with category 838:

- **0 foot, unspecified**
- **1 tarsal (bone), joint unspecified**
- **2 midtarsal (joint)**
- **3 tarsometatarsal (joint)**
- **4 metatarsal (bone), joint unspecified**
- **5 metatarsophalangeal (joint)**
- **6 interphalangeal (joint), foot**
- **9 other**
  - Phalanx of foot
  - Toe(s)

✓5th **838.0 Closed dislocation**

✓5th **838.1 Open dislocation** CC 9

CC Excl: No Exclusions

✓4th **839 Other, multiple, and ill-defined dislocations**

✓5th **839.0 Cervical vertebra, closed**

Cervical spine Neck

839.00 Cervical vertebra, unspecified CC

CC Excl: 805.00-805.18, 806.00-806.19, 806.8-806.9, 839.00-839.18, 847.0, 848.8-848.9, 879.8-879.9, 929.0, 929.9, 952.00-952.09, 958.8-958.99, 959.8-959.9

839.01 First cervical vertebra CC

CC Excl: See code 839.00

839.02 Second cervical vertebra CC

CC Excl: See code 839.00

839.03 Third cervical vertebra CC

CC Excl: See code 839.00

839.04 Fourth cervical vertebra CC

CC Excl: See code 839.00

839.05 Fifth cervical vertebra CC

CC Excl: See code 839.00

839.06 Sixth cervical vertebra CC

CC Excl: See code 839.00

839.07 Seventh cervical vertebra CC

CC Excl: See code 839.00

839.08 Multiple cervical vertebrae CC

CC Excl: See code 839.00

✓5th **839.1 Cervical vertebra, open**

839.10 Cervical vertebra, unspecified CC

CC Excl: See code 839.00

839.11 First cervical vertebra CC

CC Excl: See code 839.00

839.12 Second cervical vertebra CC

CC Excl: See code 839.00

839.13 Third cervical vertebra CC

CC Excl: See code 839.00

839.14 Fourth cervical vertebra CC

CC Excl: See code 839.00

839.15 Fifth cervical vertebra CC

CC Excl: See code 839.00

839.16 Sixth cervical vertebra CC

CC Excl: See code 839.00

839.17 Seventh cervical vertebra CC

CC Excl: See code 839.00

839.18 Multiple cervical vertebrae CC

CC Excl: See code 839.00

✓5th **839.2 Thoracic and lumbar vertebra, closed**

839.20 Lumbar vertebra

839.21 Thoracic vertebra

Dorsal [thoracic] vertebra

✓5th **839.3 Thoracic and lumbar vertebra, open**

839.30 Lumbar vertebra

839.31 Thoracic vertebra

✓5th **839.4 Other vertebra, closed**

839.40 Vertebra, unspecified site

Spine NOS

839.41 Coccyx

839.42 Sacrum

Sacroiliac (joint)

839.49 Other

✓5th **839.5 Other vertebra, open**

839.50 Vertebra, unspecified site

839.51 Coccyx

839.52 Sacrum

839.59 Other

✓5th **839.6 Other location, closed**

839.61 Sternum

Sternoclavicular joint

839.69 Other

Pelvis

✓5th **839.7 Other location, open**

839.71 Sternum

839.79 Other

839.8 Multiple and ill-defined, closed

Arm
Back
Hand
Multiple locations, except fingers or toes alone
Other ill-defined locations
Unspecified location

839.9 Multiple and ill-defined, open

SPRAINS AND STRAINS OF JOINTS AND ADJACENT MUSCLES (840-848)

INCLUDES avulsion, hemarthrosis, laceration, rupture, sprain, strain, tear of: joint capsule, ligament, muscle, tendon

EXCLUDES *laceration of tendon in open wounds (880-884 and 890-894 with .2)*

✓4th **840 Sprains and strains of shoulder and upper arm**

840.0 Acromioclavicular (joint) (ligament)

840.1 Coracoclavicular (ligament)

840.2 Coracohumeral (ligament)

840.3 Infraspinatus (muscle) (tendon)

840.4 Rotator cuff (capsule)

EXCLUDES *complete rupture of rotator cuff, nontraumatic (727.61)*

840.5 Subscapularis (muscle)

840.6 Supraspinatus (muscle) (tendon)

840.7 Superior glenoid labrum lesion

SLAP lesion

AHA: 4Q,'01, 52

DEF: Detachment injury of the superior aspect of the glenoid labrum which is the ring of fibrocartilage attached to the rim of the glenoid cavity of the scapula.

840.8 Other specified sites of shoulder and upper arm

840.9 Unspecified site of shoulder and upper arm

Arm NOS Shoulder NOS

✓4th **841 Sprains and strains of elbow and forearm**

841.0 Radial collateral ligament

841.1 Ulnar collateral ligament

841.2 Radiohumeral (joint)

841.3 Ulnohumeral (joint)

841.8 Other specified sites of elbow and forearm

841.9 Unspecified site of elbow and forearm

Elbow NOS

N Newborn Age: 0  Pediatric Age: 0-17 M Maternity Age: 12-55 A Adult Age: 15-124 CC CC Condition  Major Complication  Complex Dx  HIV Related Dx

✓4th **842 Sprains and strains of wrist and hand**

✓5th **842.0 Wrist**

842.00 Unspecified site

842.01 Carpal (joint)

842.02 Radiocarpal (joint) (ligament)

842.09 Other

Radioulnar joint, distal

✓5th **842.1 Hand**

842.10 Unspecified site

842.11 Carpometacarpal (joint)

842.12 Metacarpophalangeal (joint)

842.13 Interphalangeal (joint)

842.19 Other

Midcarpal (joint)

✓4th **843 Sprains and strains of hip and thigh**

843.0 Iliofemoral (ligament)

843.1 Ischiocapsular (ligament)

843.8 Other specified sites of hip and thigh

843.9 Unspecified site of hip and thigh

Hip NOS Thigh NOS

✓4th **844 Sprains and strains of knee and leg**

844.0 Lateral collateral ligament of knee

844.1 Medial collateral ligament of knee

844.2 Cruciate ligament of knee

844.3 Tibiofibular (joint) (ligament), superior

844.8 Other specified sites of knee and leg

844.9 Unspecified site of knee and leg

Knee NOS Leg NOS

✓4th **845 Sprains and strains of ankle and foot**

✓5th **845.0 Ankle**

845.00 Unspecified site

AHA: 2Q, '02, 3

845.01 Deltoid (ligament), ankle

Internal collateral (ligament), ankle

845.02 Calcaneofibular (ligament)

845.03 Tibiofibular (ligament), distal

AHA: 1Q, '04, 9

845.09 Other

Achilles tendon

✓5th **845.1 Foot**

845.10 Unspecified site

845.11 Tarsometatarsal (joint) (ligament)

845.12 Metatarsophalangeal (joint)

845.13 Interphalangeal (joint), toe

845.19 Other

✓4th **846 Sprains and strains of sacroiliac region**

846.0 Lumbosacral (joint) (ligament)

846.1 Sacroiliac ligament

846.2 Sacrospinatus (ligament)

846.3 Sacrotuberous (ligament)

846.8 Other specified sites of sacroiliac region

846.9 Unspecified site of sacroiliac region

✓4th **847 Sprains and strains of other and unspecified parts of back**

EXCLUDES *lumbosacral (846.0)*

847.0 Neck

Anterior longitudinal (ligament), cervical
Atlanto-axial (joints)
Atlanto-occipital (joints)
Whiplash injury

EXCLUDES *neck injury NOS (959.0)*
thyroid region (848.2)

847.1 Thoracic

847.2 Lumbar

847.3 Sacrum

Sacrococcygeal (ligament)

847.4 Coccyx

847.9 Unspecified site of back

Back NOS

✓4th **848 Other and ill-defined sprains and strains**

848.0 Septal cartilage of nose

848.1 Jaw

Temporomandibular (joint) (ligament)

848.2 Thyroid region

Cricoarytenoid (joint) (ligament)
Cricothyroid (joint) (ligament)
Thyroid cartilage

848.3 Ribs

Chondrocostal (joint) } without mention of injury to sternum
Costal cartilage }

✓5th **848.4 Sternum**

848.40 Unspecified site

848.41 Sternoclavicular (joint) (ligament)

848.42 Chondrosternal (joint)

848.49 Other

Xiphoid cartilage

848.5 Pelvis

Symphysis pubis

EXCLUDES *that in childbirth (665.6)*

848.8 Other specified sites of sprains and strains

848.9 Unspecified site of sprain and strain

INTRACRANIAL INJURY, EXCLUDING THOSE WITH SKULL FRACTURE (850-854)

EXCLUDES *intracranial injury with skull fracture (800-801 and 803-804, except .0 and .5)*
open wound of head without intracranial injury (870.0-873.9)
skull fracture alone (800-801 and 803-804 with .0, .5)

The description "with open intracranial wound," used in the fourth-digit subdivisions, includes those specified as open or with mention of infection or foreign body.

The following fifth-digit subclassification is for use with categories 851-854:

0 unspecified state of consciousness
1 with no loss of consciousness
2 with brief [less than one hour] loss of consciousness
3 with moderate [1-24 hours] loss of consciousness
4 with prolonged [more than 24 hours] loss of consciousness and return to pre-existing conscious level
5 with prolonged [more than 24 hours] loss of consciousness,without return to pre-existing conscious level

Use fifth-digit 5 to designate when a patient is unconscious and dies before regaining consciousness, regardless of the duration of the loss of consciousness

6 with loss of consciousness of unspecified duration
9 with concussion, unspecified

AHA: 1Q, '93, 22

✓4th **850 Concussion**

INCLUDES commotio cerebri

EXCLUDES *concussion with:*
cerebral laceration or contusion (851.0-851.9)
cerebral hemorrhage (852-853)
head injury NOS (959.01)

AHA: 2Q, '96, 6; 4Q, '90, 24

850.0 With no loss of consciousness CC

Concussion with mental confusion or disorientation, without loss of consciousness

CC Excl: 800.00-800.99, 801.00-801.99, 803.00-803.99, 804.00-804.99, 850.0-850.9, 851.00-851.99, 852.00-852.19, 852.21-852.59, 853.00-853.19, 854.00-854.19, 873.8-873.9, 879.8-879.9, 905.0, 925.1-925.2, 929.0, 929.9, 958.8, 959.01, 959.09, 959.8-959.9

✓5th **850.1 With brief loss of consciousness**

Loss of consciousness for less than one hour

AHA: 4Q, '03, 76; 1Q, '99, 10; 2Q, '92, 5

850.11 With loss of consciousness of 30 minutes or less CC

CC Excl: See code 850.0

850.12 With loss of consciousness from 31 to 59 minutes CC

CC Excl: See code 850.0

850.2 With moderate loss of consciousness CC

Loss of consciousness for 1-24 hours

CC Excl: See code 850.0

850.3 With prolonged loss of consciousness and return to pre-existing conscious level CC

Loss of consciousness for more than 24 hours with complete recovery

CC Excl: See code 850.0

850.4 With prolonged loss of consciousness, without return to pre-existing conscious level CC

CC Excl: See code 850.0

850.5 With loss of consciousness of unspecified duration CC

CC Excl: See code 850.0

850.9 Concussion, unspecified CC

CC Excl: See code 850.0

Brain

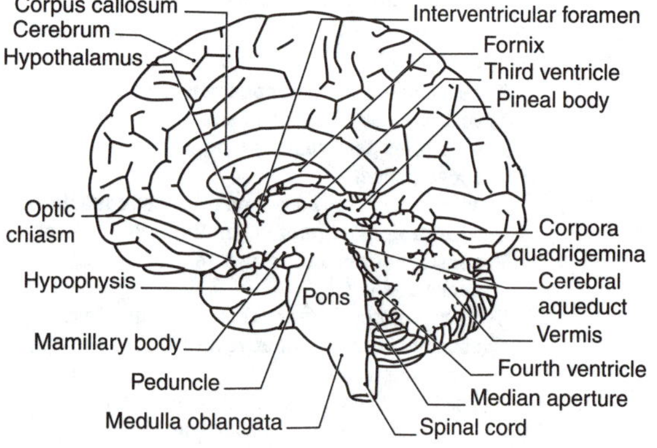

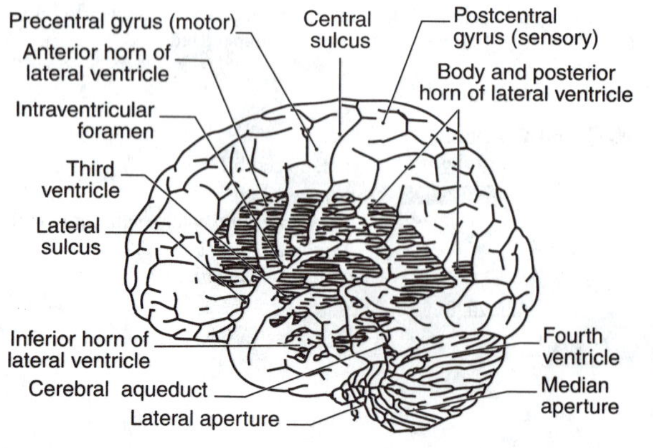

✓4th **851 Cerebral laceration and contusion**

AHA: 4Q, '96, 36; 1Q, '93, 22; 4Q, '90, 24

§ ✓5th **851.0 Cortex (cerebral) contusion without mention of open intracranial wound** CC

CC Excl: See code 850.0

§ ✓5th **851.1 Cortex (cerebral) contusion with open intracranial wound** CC

CC Excl: See code 850.0

AHA: 1Q, '92, 9

§ ✓5th **851.2 Cortex (cerebral) laceration without mention of open intracranial wound** CC

CC Excl: See code 850.0

§ ✓5th **851.3 Cortex (cerebral) laceration with open intracranial wound** CC

CC Excl: See code 850.0

§ ✓5th **851.4 Cerebellar or brain stem contusion without mention of open intracranial wound** CC

CC Excl: See code 850.0

§ ✓5th **851.5 Cerebellar or brain stem contusion with open intracranial wound** CC

CC Excl: See code 850.0

§ ✓5th **851.6 Cerebellar or brain stem laceration without mention of open intracranial wound** CC

CC Excl: See code 850.0

§ ✓5th **851.7 Cerebellar or brain stem laceration with open intracranial wound** CC

CC Excl: See code 850.0

§ ✓5th **851.8 Other and unspecified cerebral laceration and contusion, without mention of open intracranial wound** CC

Brain (membrane) NOS

CC Excl: See code 850.0

AHA: 4Q, '96, 37

§ ✓5th **851.9 Other and unspecified cerebral laceration and contusion, with open intracranial wound** CC

CC Excl: See code 850.0

✓4th **852 Subarachnoid, subdural, and extradural hemorrhage, following injury**

EXCLUDES *Cerebral contusion or laceration (with hemorrhage) (851.0-851.9)*

DEF: Bleeding from lining of brain; due to injury.

§ ✓5th **852.0 Subarachnoid hemorrhage following injury without mention of open intracranial wound** CC

Middle meningeal hemorrhage following injury

CC Excl: See code 850.0

§ ✓5th **852.1 Subarachnoid hemorrhage following injury with open intracranial wound** CC

CC Excl: See code 850.0

§ ✓5th **852.2 Subdural hemorrhage following injury without mention of open intracranial wound** CC

CC Excl: For code 852.20: 800.00-801.99, 803.00-804.99, 850.0-854.19, 873.8-873.9, 879.8-879.9, 905.0, 925.1-925.2, 929.0-929.9, 958.8-959.09, 959.8-959.9 **For code 852.21-852.29:** 800.00-801.99, 803.00-804.99, 850.0-852.19, 852.21-854.19, 873.8-873.9, 879.8-879.9, 905.0, 925.1-925.2, 929.0-929.9, 958.8-959.09, 959.8-959.9

AHA: 4Q, '96, 43

§ ✓5th **852.3 Subdural hemorrhage following injury with open intracranial wound** CC

CC Excl: See code 852.21

§ Requires fifth-digit. See beginning of section 850-854 for codes and definitions.

§ ✓5th **852.4 Extradural hemorrhage following injury without mention of open intracranial wound** CC
Epidural hematoma following injury
CC Excl: See code 852.21

§ ✓5th **852.5 Extradural hemorrhage following injury with open intracranial wound** CC
CC Excl: See code 852.21

✓4th **853 Other and unspecified intracranial hemorrhage following injury**

§ ✓5th **853.0 Without mention of open intracranial wound** CC
Cerebral compression due to injury
Intracranial hematoma following injury
Traumatic cerebral hemorrhage
CC Excl: See code 852.21
AHA: 3Q, '90, 14

§ ✓5th **853.1 With open intracranial wound** CC
CC Excl: See code 852.21

✓4th **854 Intracranial injury of other and unspecified nature**
INCLUDES brain injury NOS
cavernous sinus
intracranial injury
EXCLUDES *any condition classifiable to 850-853*
head injury NOS (959.01)
AHA: 1Q, '99, 10; 2Q, '92, 6

§ ✓5th **854.0 Without mention of open intracranial wound** CC
CC Excl: See code 852.21
AHA: For code 854.00: 2Q, '05, 6

§ ✓5th **854.1 With open intracranial wound** CC
CC Excl: See code 852.21

INTERNAL INJURY OF THORAX, ABDOMEN, AND PELVIS (860-869)

INCLUDES blast injuries, blunt trauma, bruise, concussion injuries (except cerebral), crushing, hematoma, laceration, puncture, tear, traumatic rupture } of internal organs

EXCLUDES *concussion NOS (850.0-850.9)*
flail chest (807.4)
foreign body entering through orifice (930.0-939.9)
injury to blood vessels (901.0-902.9)

The description "with open wound," used in the fourth-digit subdivisions, includes those with mention of infection or foreign body.

✓4th **860 Traumatic pneumothorax and hemothorax**
AHA: 2Q, '93, 4
DEF: Traumatic pneumothorax: air or gas leaking into pleural space of lung due to trauma.
DEF: Traumatic hemothorax: blood buildup in pleural space of lung due to trauma.

860.0 Pneumothorax without mention of open wound into thorax CC
CC Excl: 860.0-860.5, 861.20-861.32, 862.29, 862.39, 862.8-862.9, 875.0-875.1, 879.8-879.9, 929.0, 929.9, 958.7-958.99, 959.8-959.9

860.1 Pneumothorax with open wound into thorax CC
CC Excl: See code 860.0

860.2 Hemothorax without mention of open wound into thorax CC
CC Excl: See code 860.0

860.3 Hemothorax with open wound into thorax CC
CC Excl: See code 860.0

860.4 Pneumohemothorax without mention of open wound into thorax CC
CC Excl: See code 860.0

860.5 Pneumohemothorax with open wound into thorax CC
CC Excl: See code 860.0

✓4th **861 Injury to heart and lung**
EXCLUDES *injury to blood vessels of thorax (901.0-901.9)*

✓5th **861.0 Heart, without mention of open wound into thorax**
AHA: 1Q, '92, 9

861.00 Unspecified injury

861.01 Contusion CC
Cardiac contusion Myocardial contusion
CC Excl: 861.00-861.13, 862.29, 862.39, 862.8-862.9, 875.0-875.1, 879.8-879.9, 929.0, 929.9, 958.7-958.99, 959.8-959.9
DEF: Bruising within the pericardium with no mention of open wound.

861.02 Laceration without penetration of heart chambers CC MCV
CC Excl: See code 861.01
DEF: Tearing injury of heart tissue, without penetration of chambers; no open wound.

861.03 Laceration with penetration of heart chambers CC MCV
CC Excl: See code 861.01

✓5th **861.1 Heart, with open wound into thorax**

861.10 Unspecified injury CC MCV
CC Excl: See code 861.01

861.11 Contusion CC MCV
CC Excl: See code 861.01

861.12 Laceration without penetration of heart chambers CC MCV
CC Excl: See code 861.01

861.13 Laceration with penetration of heart chambers CC MCV
CC Excl: See code 861.01

✓5th **861.2 Lung, without mention of open wound into thorax**

861.20 Unspecified injury

861.21 Contusion
DEF: Bruising of lung without mention of open wound.

861.22 Laceration CC
CC Excl: 861.20-861.32, 862.29, 862.39, 862.8-862.9, 875.0-875.1, 879.8-879.9, 929.0, 929.9, 958.7-958.99, 959.8-959.9

✓5th **861.3 Lung, with open wound into thorax**

861.30 Unspecified injury CC
CC Excl: See code 861.22

861.31 Contusion CC
CC Excl: See code 861.22

861.32 Laceration CC
CC Excl: See code 861.22

✓4th **862 Injury to other and unspecified intrathoracic organs**
EXCLUDES *injury to blood vessels of thorax (901.0-901.9)*

862.0 Diaphragm, without mention of open wound into cavity

862.1 Diaphragm, with open wound into cavity CC
CC Excl: 862.0-862.1, 862.29, 862.39-862.9, 875.0-875.1, 879.8-879.9, 929.0-929.9, 958.7-958.99, 959.8-959.9

§ Requires fifth-digit. See beginning of section 850-854 for codes and definitions.

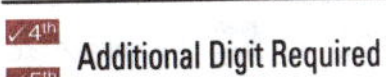

✓5th **862.2 Other specified intrathoracic organs, without mention of open wound into cavity**

862.21 Bronchus CC
CC Excl: 862.21, 862.29, 862.31, 862.39-862.9, 875.0-875.1, 879.8-879.9, 929.0-929.9, 958.7-958.99, 959.8-959.9

862.22 Esophagus CC
CC Excl: 862.22-862.29, 862.32-862.9, 875.0-875.1, 879.8-879.9, 929.0-929.9, 958.7-958.99, 959.8-959.9

862.29 Other CC
Pleura
Thymus gland
CC Excl: 862.29, 862.39-862.9, 875.0-875.1, 879.8-879.9, 929.0-929.9, 958.7-958.99, 959.8-959.9

✓5th **862.3 Other specified intrathoracic organs, with open wound into cavity**

862.31 Bronchus CC
CC Excl: 862.21, 862.29, 862.31, 862.39-862.9, 875.0-875.1, 879.8-879.9, 929.0-929.9, 958.7-958.99, 959.8-959.9

862.32 Esophagus CC
CC Excl: 862.22-862.29, 862.32-862.9, 875.0-875.1, 879.8-879.9, 929.0-929.9, 958.7-958.99, 959.8-959.9

862.39 Other CC
CC Excl: 862.29, 862.39-862.9, 875.0-875.1, 879.8-879.9, 929.0-929.9, 958.7-958.99, 959.8-959.9

862.8 Multiple and unspecified intrathoracic organs, without mention of open wound into cavity
Crushed chest
Multiple intrathoracic organs

[10] **862.9 Multiple and unspecified intrathoracic organs, with open wound into cavity** CC MCV
CC Excl: See code 862.39

✓4th **863 Injury to gastrointestinal tract**

EXCLUDES *anal sphincter laceration during delivery (664.2)*
bile duct (868.0-868.1 with fifth-digit 2)
gallbladder (868.0-868.1 with fifth-digit 2)

863.0 Stomach, without mention of open wound into cavity

863.1 Stomach, with open wound into cavity CC
CC Excl: 863.0-863.1, 863.80, 863.89-863.90, 863.99, 868.00, 868.03-868.10, 868.13-868.19, 869.0-869.1, 879.2-879.9, 929.0, 929.9, 958.8-958.99, 959.8-959.9

✓5th **863.2 Small intestine, without mention of open wound into cavity**

863.20 Small intestine, unspecified site
863.21 Duodenum
863.29 Other

✓5th **863.3 Small intestine, with open wound into cavity**

863.30 Small intestine, unspecified site CC
CC Excl: 863.20-863.39, 863.80, 863.89-863.90, 863.99, 868.00, 868.03-868.10, 868.13-868.19, 869.0-869.1, 879.2-879.9, 929.0, 929.9, 958.8-958.99, 959.8-959.9

863.31 Duodenum CC
CC Excl: 863.21, 863.31, 863.39, 863.80, 863.89-863.90, 863.99, 868.00, 868.03-868.10, 868.13-868.19, 869.0-869.1, 879.2-879.9, 929.0, 929.9, 958.8-958.99, 959.8-959.9

863.39 Other CC
CC Excl: See Code 863.30

✓5th **863.4 Colon or rectum, without mention of open wound into cavity**

863.40 Colon, unspecified site
863.41 Ascending [right] colon
863.42 Transverse colon
863.43 Descending [left] colon
863.44 Sigmoid colon
863.45 Rectum
863.46 Multiple sites in colon and rectum
863.49 Other

✓5th **863.5 Colon or rectum, with open wound into cavity**

863.50 Colon, unspecified site CC
CC Excl: 863.40-863.80, 863.89-863.90, 863.99, 868.00, 868.03-868.10, 868.13-869.1, 879.2-879.9, 929.0-929.9, 958.8-958.99, 959.8-959.9

863.51 Ascending [right] colon CC
CC Excl: See code 863.50

863.52 Transverse colon CC
CC Excl: See code 863.50

863.53 Descending [left] colon CC
CC Excl: See code 863.50

863.54 Sigmoid colon CC
CC Excl: See code 863.50

863.55 Rectum CC
CC Excl: See code 863.50

863.56 Multiple sites in colon and rectum CC
CC Excl: See code 863.50

863.59 Other CC
CC Excl: See code 863.50

✓5th **863.8 Other and unspecified gastrointestinal sites, without mention of open wound into cavity**

863.80 Gastrointestinal tract, unspecified site
863.81 Pancreas, head
863.82 Pancreas, body
863.83 Pancreas, tail
863.84 Pancreas, multiple and unspecified sites
863.85 Appendix
863.89 Other
Intestine NOS

✓5th **863.9 Other and unspecified gastrointestinal sites, with open wound into cavity**

863.90 Gastrointestinal tract, unspecified site CC
CC Excl: 863.80-863.84, 863.89-863.94, 863.99, 868.00, 868.03-868.10, 868.13-868.19, 869.0-869.1, 879.2-879.9, 929.0, 929.9, 958.8-958.99, 959.8-959.9

863.91 Pancreas, head CC
CC Excl: 863.80-863.84, 863.91-863.94, 863.99, 868.00, 868.03-868.10, 868.13-868.19, 869.0-869.1, 879.2-879.9, 929.0, 929.9, 958.8-958.99, 959.8-959.9

863.92 Pancreas, body CC
CC Excl: See code 863.91

863.93 Pancreas, tail CC
CC Excl: See code 863.91

863.94 Pancreas, multiple and unspecified sites CC
CC Excl: See code 863.91

863.95 Appendix CC
CC Excl: 863.80, 863.85, 863.95, 863.99, 868.00, 868.03-868.10, 868.13-868.19, 869.0-869.1, 879.2-879.9, 929.0, 929.9, 958.99, 959.8-959.9

863.99 Other CC
CC Excl: 863.80, 863.99, 868.00, 868.03-868.10, 868.13-868.19, 869.0-869.1, 879.2-879.9, 929.0, 929.9, 958.8-958.99, 959.8-959.9

[10] MCV as SDx only

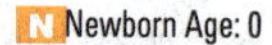 Newborn Age: 0  Pediatric Age: 0-17  Maternity Age: 12-55  Adult Age: 15-124 CC CC Condition MC Major Complication CD Complex Dx HIV HIV Related Dx

√4th 864 Injury to liver

The following fifth-digit subclassification is for use with category 864:

- **0 unspecified injury**
- **1 hematoma and contusion**
- **2 laceration, minor**
  Laceration involving capsule only, or without significant involvement of hepatic parenchyma [i.e., less than 1 cm deep]
- **3 laceration, moderate**
  Laceration involving parenchyma but without major disruption of parenchyma [i.e., less than 10 cm long and less than 3 cm deep]
- **4 laceration, major**
  Laceration with significant disruption of hepatic parenchyma [i.e., 10 cm long and 3 cm deep]
  Multiple moderate lacerations, with or without hematoma
  Stellate lacerations of liver
- **5 laceration, unspecified**
- **9 other**

√5th 864.0 Without mention of open wound into cavity CC
CC Excl: 863.80, 863.99-864.19, 868.00, 868.03-868.10, 868.13-869.1, 879.2-879.9, 929.0-929.9, 958.8-958.99, 959.8-959.9

√5th 864.1 With open wound into cavity CC
CC Excl: See code 864.0

√4th 865 Injury to spleen

The following fifth-digit subclassification is for use with category 865:

- **0 unspecified injury**
- **1 hematoma without rupture of capsule**
- **2 capsular tears, without major disruption of parenchyma**
- **3 laceration extending into parenchyma**
- **4 massive parenchymal disruption**
- **9 other**

√5th 865.0 Without mention of open wound into cavity CC
CC Excl: 865.00-865.19, 868.00, 868.03-868.10, 868.13-869.1, 879.2-879.9, 929.0-929.9, 958.8-958.99, 959.8-959.9

√5th 865.1 With open wound into cavity CC
CC Excl: See code 865.0

√4th 866 Injury to kidney

The following fifth-digit subclassification is for use with category 866:

- **0 unspecified injury**
- **1 hematoma without rupture of capsule**
- **2 laceration**
- **3 complete disruption of kidney parenchyma**

√5th 866.0 Without mention of open wound into cavity CC
CC Excl: 866.00-866.13, 868.00, 868.03-868.10, 868.13-868.19, 869.0-869.1, 879.2-879.9, 929.0, 929.9, 958.8-958.99, 959.8-959.9

√5th 866.1 With open wound into cavity CC
CC Excl: See code 866.0

√4th 867 Injury to pelvic organs

EXCLUDES *injury during delivery (664.0-665.9)*

867.0 Bladder and urethra, without mention of open wound into cavity CC
CC Excl: 867.0-867.1, 867.6-868.00, 868.03-868.10, 868.13-869.1, 879.2-879.9, 929.0-929.9, 958.8-958.99, 959.8-959.9
AHA: N-D, '85, 15

867.1 Bladder and urethra, with open wound into cavity CC
CC Excl: See code 867.0

867.2 Ureter, without mention of open wound into cavity CC
CC Excl: 867.2-867.3, 867.6-868.00, 868.03-868.10, 868.13-869.1, 879.2-879.9, 929.0-929.9, 958.8-958.99, 959.8-959.9

867.3 Ureter, with open wound into cavity CC
CC Excl: See code 867.2

867.4 Uterus, without mention of open wound intocavity CC ♀
CC Excl: 867.4-868.00, 868.03-868.10, 868.13-869.1, 879.2-879.9, 929.0-929.9, 958.8-958.99, 959.8-959.9

867.5 Uterus, with open wound into cavity CC ♀
CC Excl: See code 867.4

867.6 Other specified pelvic organs, without mention of open wound into cavity CC
Fallopian tube
Ovary
Prostate
Seminal vesicle
Vas deferens
CC Excl: 867.6-868.00, 868.03-868.10, 868.13-869.1, 879.2-879.9, 929.0-929.9, 958.8-958.99, 959.8-959.9

867.7 Other specified pelvic organs, with open wound into cavity CC
CC Excl: See code 867.6

867.8 Unspecified pelvic organ, without mention of open wound into cavity CC
CC Excl: See code 867.6

867.9 Unspecified pelvic organ, with open wound into cavity CC
CC Excl: See code 867.6

√4th 868 Injury to other intra-abdominal organs

The following fifth-digit subclassification is for use with category 868:

- **0 unspecified intra-abdominal organ**
- **1 adrenal gland**
- **2 bile duct and gallbladder**
- **3 peritoneum**
- **4 retroperitoneum**
- **9 other and multiple intra-abdominal organs**

√5th 868.0 Without mention of open wound into cavity CC
CC Excl: **For code 868.00:** 868.00, 868.03-868.10, 868.13-869.1, 879.2-879.9, 929.0-929.9, 958.8-958.99, 959.8-959.9 **For code 868.01:** 868.00-868.01, 868.03-868.11, 868.13-869.1, 879.2-879.9, 929.0-929.9, 958.8-958.99, 959.8-959.9 **For code 868.02:** 868.00, 868.02-868.10, 868.13-869.1, 879.2-879.9, 929.0-929.9, 958.8-958.99, 959.8-959.9 **For codes 868.03-868.09:** See Code 868.00

√5th 868.1 With open wound into cavity CC
CC Excl: **For code 868.10:** See code 868.03 **For code 868.11:** 868.00, 868.01, 868.03-868.11, 868.13-868.19, 869.0-869.1, 879.2-879.9, 929.0, 929.9, 958.8-958.99, 959.8-959.9 **For code 868.12:** 868.00, 868.03-868.10, 868.12-868.19, 869.0-869.1, 879.2-879.9, 929.0, 929.9, 958.8-958.99, 959.8-959.9 **For codes 868.13-868.19:** See Code 868.10

√4th 869 Internal injury to unspecified or ill-defined organs

INCLUDES internal injury NOS
multiple internal injury NOS

869.0 Without mention of open wound into cavity CC
CC Excl: See code 868.10

869.1 With open wound into cavity CC
CC Excl: See code 868.10
AHA: 2Q, '89, 15

Injury and Poisoning

864–869.1

OPEN WOUND (870-897)

INCLUDES animal bite
avulsion
cut
laceration
puncture wound
traumatic amputation

EXCLUDES *burn (940.0-949.5)*
crushing (925-929.9)
puncture of internal organs (860.0-869.1)
superficial injury (910.0-919.9)
that incidental to:
dislocation (830.0-839.9)
fracture (800.0-829.1)
internal injury (860.0-869.1)
intracranial injury (851.0-854.1)

Note: The description "complicated" used in the fourth-digit subdivisions includes those with mention of delayed healing, delayed treatment, foreign body, or infection. Use additional code to identify infection

AHA: 4Q, '01, 52

OPEN WOUND OF HEAD, NECK, AND TRUNK (870-879)

✓4th **870 Open wound of ocular adnexa**

870.0 Laceration of skin of eyelid and periocular area

870.1 Laceration of eyelid, full-thickness, not involving lacrimal passages

870.2 Laceration of eyelid involving lacrimal passages

870.3 Penetrating wound of orbit, without mention of foreign body CC
CC Excl: 870.0-871.9, 879.8-879.9, 929.0-929.9, 958.8-958.99, 959.8-959.9

870.4 Penetrating wound of orbit with foreign body CC
EXCLUDES *retained (old) foreign body in orbit (376.6)*
CC Excl: See code 870.3

870.8 Other specified open wounds of ocular adnexa CC
CC Excl: See code 870.3

870.9 Unspecified open wound of ocular adnexa CC
CC Excl: See code 870.3

✓4th **871 Open wound of eyeball**

EXCLUDES *2nd cranial nerve [optic] injury (950.0-950.9)*
3rd cranial nerve [oculomotor] injury (951.0)

871.0 Ocular laceration without prolapse of intraocular tissue CC
CC Excl: See code 870.3
AHA: 3Q, '96, 7
DEF: Tear in ocular tissue without displacing structures.

871.1 Ocular laceration with prolapse or exposure of intraocular tissue CC
CC Excl: See code 870.3

871.2 Rupture of eye with partial loss of intraocular tissue CC
CC Excl: See code 870.3
DEF: Forcible tearing of eyeball, with tissue loss.

871.3 Avulsion of eye CC
Traumatic enucleation
CC Excl: See code 870.3
DEF: Traumatic extraction of eyeball from socket.

871.4 Unspecified laceration of eye CC
CC Excl: See code 870.3

871.5 Penetration of eyeball with magnetic foreign body
EXCLUDES *retained (old) magnetic foreign body in globe (360.50-360.59)*

871.6 Penetration of eyeball with (nonmagnetic) foreign body
EXCLUDES *retained (old) (nonmagnetic) foreign body in globe (360.60-360.69)*

871.7 Unspecified ocular penetration

871.9 Unspecified open wound of eyeball CC
CC Excl: See code 870.3

✓4th **872 Open wound of ear**

✓5th **872.0 External ear, without mention of complication**
872.00 External ear, unspecified site
872.01 Auricle, ear
Pinna
DEF: Open wound of fleshy, outer ear.
872.02 Auditory canal
DEF: Open wound of passage from external ear to eardrum.

✓5th **872.1 External ear, complicated**
872.10 External ear, unspecified site
872.11 Auricle, ear
872.12 Auditory canal

✓5th **872.6 Other specified parts of ear, without mention of complication**
872.61 Ear drum
Drumhead Tympanic membrane
872.62 Ossicles
872.63 Eustachian tube
DEF: Open wound of channel between nasopharynx and tympanic cavity.
872.64 Cochlea
DEF: Open wound of snail shell shaped tube of inner ear.
872.69 Other and multiple sites

✓5th **872.7 Other specified parts of ear, complicated**
872.71 Ear drum
872.72 Ossicles CC
CC Excl: 872.00-872.9, 879.8-879.9, 929.0, 929.9, 958.8-958.99, 959.8-959.9
872.73 Eustachian tube CC
CC Excl: See code 872.72
872.74 Cochlea CC
CC Excl: See code 872.72
872.79 Other and multiple sites

872.8 Ear, part unspecified, without mention of complication
Ear NOS

872.9 Ear, part unspecified, complicated

✓4th **873 Other open wound of head**

873.0 Scalp, without mention of complication

873.1 Scalp, complicated

✓5th **873.2 Nose, without mention of complication**
873.20 Nose, unspecified site
873.21 Nasal septum
DEF: Open wound between nasal passages.
873.22 Nasal cavity
DEF: Open wound of nostrils.
873.23 Nasal sinus
DEF: Open wound of mucous-lined respiratory cavities.
873.29 Multiple sites

✓5th **873.3 Nose, complicated**
873.30 Nose, unspecified site
873.31 Nasal septum
873.32 Nasal cavity
873.33 Nasal sinus CC
CC Excl: 873.20-873.39, 879.8-879.9, 929.0, 929.9, 958.8-958.99, 959.8-959.9
873.39 Multiple sites

✓5th **873.4 Face, without mention of complication**
873.40 Face, unspecified site
873.41 Cheek
873.42 Forehead
Eyebrow
AHA: 4Q, '96, 43
873.43 Lip
873.44 Jaw
873.49 Other and multiple sites

✓5th **873.5 Face, complicated**
873.50 Face, unspecified site
873.51 Cheek
873.52 Forehead
873.53 Lip
873.54 Jaw
873.59 Other and multiple sites

✓5th **873.6 Internal structures of mouth, without mention of complication**
873.60 Mouth, unspecified site
873.61 Buccal mucosa
DEF: Open wound of inside of cheek.
873.62 Gum (alveolar process)
▲ **873.63 Tooth (broken) (fractured) (due to trauma)**
EXCLUDES ▶ *cracked tooth (521.81)*◀
AHA: 1Q, '04, 17
873.64 Tongue and floor of mouth
873.65 Palate
DEF: Open wound of roof of mouth.
873.69 Other and multiple sites

✓5th **873.7 Internal structures of mouth, complicated**
873.70 Mouth, unspecified site
873.71 Buccal mucosa
873.72 Gum (alveolar process)
▲ **873.73 Tooth (broken) (fractured) (due to trauma)**
EXCLUDES ▶ *cracked tooth (521.81)*◀
AHA: 1Q, '04, 17
873.74 Tongue and floor of mouth
873.75 Palate
873.79 Other and multiple sites

873.8 Other and unspecified open wound of head without mention of complication
Head NOS

873.9 Other and unspecified open wound of head, complicated CC
CC Excl: 847.0, 873.40-873.79, 873.9, 874.8-874.9, 879.8-879.9, 929.0, 929.9, 958.8-958.99, 959.8-959.9

✓4th **874 Open wound of neck**

✓5th **874.0 Larynx and trachea, without mention of complication**
874.00 Larynx with trachea CC
CC Excl: 847.0, 874.00-874.12, 874.8-874.9, 879.8-879.9, 929.0, 929.9, 958.8-958.99, 959.8-959.9
874.01 Larynx CC
CC Excl: See code 874.00
874.02 Trachea CC
CC Excl: See code 874.00

✓5th **874.1 Larynx and trachea, complicated**
874.10 Larynx with trachea CC
CC Excl: See code 874.00
874.11 Larynx CC
CC Excl: See code 874.00
874.12 Trachea CC
CC Excl: See code 874.00

874.2 Thyroid gland, without mention of complication

874.3 Thyroid gland, complicated CC
CC Excl: 847.0, 874.2-874.3, 874.8-874.9, 879.8-879.9, 929.0, 929.9, 958.8-958.99, 959.8-959.9

874.4 Pharynx, without mention of complication
Cervical esophagus

874.5 Pharynx, complicated CC
CC Excl: 847.0, 874.4-874.9, 879.8-879.9, 929.0, 929.9, 958.8-958.99, 959.8-959.9

874.8 Other and unspecified parts, without mention of complication
Nape of neck
Throat NOS
Supraclavicular region

874.9 Other and unspecified parts, complicated

✓4th **875 Open wound of chest (wall)**
EXCLUDES *open wound into thoracic cavity (860.0-862.9)*
traumatic pneumothorax and hemothorax (860.1, 860.3, 860.5)
AHA: 3Q, '93, 17

875.0 Without mention of complication CC
CC Excl: 847.1, 862.29, 862.39, 862.8-862.9, 875.0-875.1, 879.8-879.9, 929.0, 929.9, 958.7-958.99, 959.8-959.9

875.1 Complicated CC
CC Excl: See code 875.0

✓4th **876 Open wound of back**
INCLUDES loin
lumbar region
EXCLUDES *open wound into thoracic cavity (860.0-862.9)*
traumatic pneumothorax and hemothorax (860.1, 860.3, 860.5)

876.0 Without mention of complication
876.1 Complicated

✓4th **877 Open wound of buttock**
INCLUDES sacroiliac region

877.0 Without mention of complication
877.1 Complicated

✓4th **878 Open wound of genital organs (external), including traumatic amputation**
EXCLUDES *injury during delivery (664.0-665.9)*
internal genital organs (867.0-867.9)

878.0 Penis, without mention of complication ♂
878.1 Penis, complicated ♂
878.2 Scrotum and testes, without mention of complication ♂
878.3 Scrotum and testes, complicated ♂
878.4 Vulva, without mention of complication ♀
Labium (majus) (minus)
878.5 Vulva, complicated ♀
878.6 Vagina, without mention of complication ♀
878.7 Vagina, complicated ♀
878.8 Other and unspecified parts, without mention of complication
878.9 Other and unspecified parts, complicated

✓4th **879 Open wound of other and unspecified sites, except limbs**

879.0 Breast, without mention of complication
879.1 Breast, complicated
879.2 Abdominal wall, anterior, without mention of complication
Abdominal wall NOS
Pubic region
Epigastric region
Umbilical region
Hypogastric region
AHA: 2Q, '91, 22
879.3 Abdominal wall, anterior, complicated
879.4 Abdominal wall, lateral, without mention of complication
Flank
Iliac (region)
Groin
Inguinal region
Hypochondrium
879.5 Abdominal wall, lateral, complicated

879.6 **Other and unspecified parts of trunk, without mention of complication**
Pelvic region
Perineum
Trunk NOS

879.7 **Other and unspecified parts of trunk, complicated**

879.8 **Open wound(s) (multiple) of unspecified site(s) without mention of complication**
Multiple open wounds NOS
Open wound NOS

879.9 **Open wound(s) (multiple) of unspecified site(s), complicated**

OPEN WOUND OF UPPER LIMB (880-887)

AHA: N-D, '85, 5

✓4th **880 Open wound of shoulder and upper arm**

The following fifth-digit subclassification is for use with category 880:
- **0 shoulder region**
- **1 scapular region**
- **2 axillary region**
- **3 upper arm**
- **9 multiple sites**

✓5th 880.0 **Without mention of complication**

✓5th 880.1 **Complicated**

✓5th 880.2 **With tendon involvement**

✓4th **881 Open wound of elbow, forearm, and wrist**

The following fifth-digit subclassification is for use with category 881:
- **0 forearm**
- **1 elbow**
- **2 wrist**

✓5th 881.0 **Without mention of complication**

✓5th 881.1 **Complicated**

✓5th 881.2 **With tendon involvement**

✓4th **882 Open wound of hand except finger(s) alone**

882.0 **Without mention of complication**

882.1 **Complicated**

882.2 **With tendon involvement**

✓4th **883 Open wound of finger(s)**

INCLUDES fingernail
thumb (nail)

883.0 **Without mention of complication**

883.1 **Complicated**

883.2 **With tendon involvement**

✓4th **884 Multiple and unspecified open wound of upper limb**

INCLUDES arm NOS
multiple sites of one upper limb
upper limb NOS

884.0 **Without mention of complication**

884.1 **Complicated**

884.2 **With tendon involvement**

✓4th **885 Traumatic amputation of thumb (complete) (partial)**

INCLUDES thumb(s) (with finger(s) of either hand)

885.0 **Without mention of complication**
AHA: 1Q, '03, 7

885.1 **Complicated**

✓4th **886 Traumatic amputation of other finger(s) (complete) (partial)**

INCLUDES finger(s) of one or both hands, without mention of thumb(s)

886.0 **Without mention of complication**

886.1 **Complicated**

✓4th **887 Traumatic amputation of arm and hand (complete) (partial)**

887.0 **Unilateral, below elbow, without mention of complication** CC
CC Excl: 880.00-887.7, 929.0-929.9, 958.8-958.99, 959.8-959.9

887.1 **Unilateral, below elbow, complicated** CC
CC Excl: See code 887.0

887.2 **Unilateral, at or above elbow, without mention of complication** CC
CC Excl: See code 887.0

887.3 **Unilateral, at or above elbow, complicated** CC
CC Excl: See code 887.0

887.4 **Unilateral, level not specified, without mention of complication** CC
CC Excl: See code 887.0

887.5 **Unilateral, level not specified, complicated** CC
CC Excl: See code 887.0

887.6 **Bilateral [any level], without mention of complication** CC
One hand and other arm
CC Excl: See code 887.0

887.7 **Bilateral [any level], complicated** CC
CC Excl: See code 887.0

OPEN WOUND OF LOWER LIMB (890-897)

AHA: N-D, '85, 5

✓4th **890 Open wound of hip and thigh**

890.0 **Without mention of complication**

890.1 **Complicated**

890.2 **With tendon involvement**

✓4th **891 Open wound of knee, leg [except thigh], and ankle**

INCLUDES leg NOS
multiple sites of leg, except thigh

EXCLUDES *that of thigh (890.0-890.2)*
with multiple sites of lower limb (894.0-894.2)

891.0 **Without mention of complication**

891.1 **Complicated**

891.2 **With tendon involvement**

✓4th **892 Open wound of foot except toe(s) alone**

INCLUDES heel

892.0 **Without mention of complication**

892.1 **Complicated**

892.2 **With tendon involvement**

✓4th **893 Open wound of toe(s)**

INCLUDES toenail

893.0 **Without mention of complication**

893.1 **Complicated**

893.2 **With tendon involvement**

✓4th **894 Multiple and unspecified open wound of lower limb**

INCLUDES lower limb NOS
multiple sites of one lower limb, with thigh

894.0 **Without mention of complication**

894.1 **Complicated**

894.2 **With tendon involvement**

✓4th **895 Traumatic amputation of toe(s) (complete) (partial)**

INCLUDES toe(s) of one or both feet

895.0 **Without mention of complication**

895.1 **Complicated**

✓4th **896 Traumatic amputation of foot (complete) (partial)**

896.0 **Unilateral, without mention of complication** CC
CC Excl: 890.0-897.7, 929.0-929.9, 958.8-958.99, 959.8-959.9

896.1 **Unilateral, complicated** CC
CC Excl: See code 896.0

896.2 **Bilateral, without mention of complication** CC
EXCLUDES *one foot and other leg (897.6-897.7)*
CC Excl: See code 896.0

896.3 **Bilateral, complicated** CC
CC Excl: See code 896.0

✓4th **897 Traumatic amputation of leg(s) (complete) (partial)**

897.0 **Unilateral, below knee, without mention of complication** CC
CC Excl: See code 896.0

897.1 Unilateral, below knee, complicated CC
CC Excl: See code 896.0

897.2 Unilateral, at or above knee, without mention of complication CC
CC Excl: See code 896.0

897.3 Unilateral, at or above knee, complicated CC
CC Excl: See code 896.0

897.4 Unilateral, level not specified, without mention of complication CC
CC Excl: See code 896.0

897.5 Unilateral, level not specified, complicated CC
CC Excl: See code 896.0

897.6 Bilateral [any level], without mention of complication CC
One foot and other leg
CC Excl: See code 896.0

897.7 Bilateral [any level], complicated CC
CC Excl: See code 896.0
AHA: 3Q, '90, 5

INJURY TO BLOOD VESSELS (900-904)

INCLUDES arterial hematoma, avulsion, cut, laceration, rupture, traumatic aneurysm or fistula (arteriovenous) } of blood vessel, secondary to other injuries e.g., fracture or open wound

EXCLUDES *accidental puncture or laceration during medical procedure (998.2)*
intracranial hemorrhage following injury (851.0-854.1)

AHA: 3Q, '90, 5

✓4th **900 Injury to blood vessels of head and neck**

✓5th **900.0 Carotid artery**

900.00 Carotid artery, unspecified CC
CC Excl: 900.00, 900.82-900.9, 904.9, 929.0-929.9, 958.8-958.99, 959.8-959.9

900.01 Common carotid artery CC
CC Excl: See code 900.00

900.02 External carotid artery CC
CC Excl: See code 900.00

900.03 Internal carotid artery CC
CC Excl: See code 900.00

900.1 Internal jugular vein CC
CC Excl: 900.82-900.9, 904.9, 929.0-929.9, 958.8-958.99, 959.8-959.9

✓5th **900.8 Other specified blood vessels of head and neck**

900.81 External jugular vein
Jugular vein NOS
CC Excl: See code 900.1

900.82 Multiple blood vessels of head and neck CC
CC Excl: See code 900.1

900.89 Other CC
CC Excl: See code 900.1

900.9 Unspecified blood vessel of head and neck CC
CC Excl: See code 900.1

✓4th **901 Injury to blood vessels of thorax**

EXCLUDES *traumatic hemothorax (860.2-860.5)*

901.0 Thoracic aorta CC
CC Excl: 901.0, 904.9, 929.0, 929.9, 958.8-958.99, 959.8-959.9

901.1 Innominate and subclavian arteries CC
CC Excl: 901.1, 904.9, 929.0, 929.9, 958.8-958.99, 959.8-959.9

901.2 Superior vena cava CC
CC Excl: 901.2, 904.9, 929.0, 929.9, 958.8-958.99, 959.8-959.9

901.3 Innominate and subclavian veins CC
CC Excl: 901.3, 904.9, 929.0, 929.9, 958.8-958.99, 959.8-959.9

✓5th **901.4 Pulmonary blood vessels**

901.40 Pulmonary vessel(s), unspecified

901.41 Pulmonary artery CC
CC Excl: 901.40, 901.41, 904.9, 929.0, 929.9, 958.8-958.99, 959.8-959.9

901.42 Pulmonary vein CC
CC Excl: 901.40, 901.42, 904.9, 929.0, 929.9, 958.8-958.99, 959.8-959.9

✓5th **901.8 Other specified blood vessels of thorax**

901.81 Intercostal artery or vein

901.82 Internal mammary artery or vein

901.83 Multiple blood vessels of thorax CC
CC Excl: 904.9, 929.0, 929.9, 958.8-958.99, 959.8-959.9

901.89 Other
Azygos vein
Hemiazygos vein

901.9 Unspecified blood vessel of thorax

✓4th **902 Injury to blood vessels of abdomen and pelvis**

902.0 Abdominal aorta CC
CC Excl: 902.0, 902.87, 902.89, 902.9, 904.9, 929.0, 929.9, 958.8-958.99, 959.8-959.9

✓5th **902.1 Inferior vena cava**

902.10 Inferior vena cava, unspecified CC
CC Excl: 902.10, 902.87-902.9, 904.9, 929.0, 929.9, 958.8-958.99, 959.8-959.9

902.11 Hepatic veins CC
CC Excl: 902.11, 902.87-902.9, 904.9, 929.0, 929.9, 958.8-958.99, 959.8-959.9

902.19 Other CC
CC Excl: 902.19, 902.87-902.9, 904.9, 929.0, 929.9, 958.8-958.99, 959.8-959.9

✓5th **902.2 Celiac and mesenteric arteries**

902.20 Celiac and mesenteric arteries, unspecified CC
CC Excl: 902.20, 902.87-902.9, 904.9, 929.0, 929.9, 958.8-958.99, 959.8-959.9

902.21 Gastric artery

902.22 Hepatic artery CC
CC Excl: 902.22, 902.87, 902.89, 902.9, 904.9, 929.0, 929.9, 958.8-958.99, 959.8-959.9

902.23 Splenic artery CC
CC Excl: 902.23, 902.87-902.9, 904.9, 929.0, 929.9, 958.8-958.99, 959.8-959.9

902.24 Other specified branches of celiac axis CC
CC Excl: 902.24, 902.87-902.9, 904.9, 929.0, 929.9, 958.8-958.99, 959.8-959.9

902.25 Superior mesenteric artery (trunk) CC
CC Excl: 902.25, 902.87-902.9, 904.9, 929.0, 929.9, 958.8-958.99, 959.8-959.9

902.26 Primary branches of superior mesenteric artery CC
Ileocolic artery
CC Excl: 902.26, 902.87-902.9, 904.9, 929.0, 929.9, 958.8-958.99, 959.8-959.9

902.27 Inferior mesenteric artery CC
CC Excl: 902.27, 902.87-902.9, 904.9, 929.0, 929.9, 958.8-958.99, 959.8-959.9

902.29 Other CC
CC Excl: 902.29, 902.87-902.9, 904.9, 929.0, 929.9, 958.8-958.99, 959.8-959.9

✓5th 902.3 Portal and splenic veins

902.31 Superior mesenteric vein and primary subdivisions CC
Ileocolic vein
CC Excl: 902.31, 902.87-902.9, 904.9, 929.0, 929.9, 958.8-958.99, 959.8-959.9

902.32 Inferior mesenteric vein CC
CC Excl: 902.32, 902.87-902.9, 904.9, 929.0, 929.9, 958.8-958.99, 959.8-959.9

902.33 Portal vein CC
CC Excl: 902.33, 902.87-902.9, 904.9, 929.0, 929.9, 958.8-958.99, 959.8-959.9

902.34 Splenic vein CC
CC Excl: 902.34, 902.87-902.9, 904.9, 929.0, 929.9, 958.8-958.99, 959.8-959.9

902.39 Other CC
Cystic vein
Gastric vein
CC Excl: 902.39, 902.87, 902.9, 904.9, 929.0, 929.9, 958.8-958.99, 959.8-959.9

✓5th 902.4 Renal blood vessels

902.40 Renal vessel(s), unspecified CC
CC Excl: 902.40, 902.87-902.9, 904.9, 929.0, 929.9, 958.8-958.99, 959.8-959.9

902.41 Renal artery CC
CC Excl: 902.41, 902.87-902.9, 904.9, 929.0, 929.9, 958.8-958.99, 959.8-959.9

902.42 Renal vein CC
CC Excl: 902.42, 902.87-902.9, 904.9, 929.0, 929.9, 958.8-958.99, 959.8-959.9

902.49 Other CC
Suprarenal arteries
CC Excl: 902.49, 902.87-902.9, 904.9, 929.0, 929.9, 958.8-958.99, 959.8-959.9

✓5th 902.5 Iliac blood vessels

902.50 Iliac vessel(s), unspecified CC
CC Excl: 902.50, 902.53-902.54, 902.59, 902.87-902.9, 904.9, 929.0, 929.9, 958.8-958.99, 959.8-959.9

902.51 Hypogastric artery CC
CC Excl: 902.51, 902.87-902.9, 904.9, 929.0, 929.9, 958.8-958.99, 959.8-959.9

902.52 Hypogastric vein CC
CC Excl: 902.52, 902.87, 902.9, 904.9, 929.0, 929.9, 958.8-958.99, 959.8-959.9

902.53 Iliac artery CC
CC Excl: 902.50, 902.53, 902.59, 902.87-902.9, 904.9, 929.0, 929.9, 958.8-958.99, 959.8-959.9

902.54 Iliac vein CC
CC Excl: 902.50, 902.54, 902.59, 902.87-902.9, 904.9, 929.0, 929.9, 958.8-958.99, 959.8-959.9

902.55 Uterine artery ♀

902.56 Uterine vein ♀

902.59 Other CC
CC Excl: 902.50, 902.53-902.54, 902.59, 902.87-902.9, 904.9, 929.0, 929.9, 958.8-958.99, 959.8-959.9

✓5th 902.8 Other specified blood vessels of abdomen and pelvis

902.81 Ovarian artery ♀

902.82 Ovarian vein ♀

902.87 Multiple blood vessels of abdomen and pelvis CC
CC Excl: 902.87-902.9, 904.9, 929.0, 929.9, 958.8-958.99, 959.8-959.9

902.89 Other

902.9 Unspecified blood vessel of abdomen and pelvis

✓4th 903 Injury to blood vessels of upper extremity

✓5th 903.0 Axillary blood vessels

903.00 Axillary vessel(s), unspecified

903.01 Axillary artery

903.02 Axillary vein

903.1 Brachial blood vessels

903.2 Radial blood vessels

903.3 Ulnar blood vessels

903.4 Palmar artery

903.5 Digital blood vessels

903.8 Other specified blood vessels of upper extremity
Multiple blood vessels of upper extremity

903.9 Unspecified blood vessel of upper extremity

✓4th 904 Injury to blood vessels of lower extremity and unspecified sites

904.0 Common femoral artery CC
Femoral artery above profunda origin
CC Excl: No exclusions

904.1 Superficial femoral artery

904.2 Femoral veins

904.3 Saphenous veins
Saphenous vein (greater) (lesser)

✓5th 904.4 Popliteal blood vessels

904.40 Popliteal vessel(s), unspecified

904.41 Popliteal artery

904.42 Popliteal vein

✓5th 904.5 Tibial blood vessels

904.50 Tibial vessel(s), unspecified

904.51 Anterior tibial artery

904.52 Anterior tibial vein

904.53 Posterior tibial artery

904.54 Posterior tibial vein

904.6 Deep plantar blood vessels

904.7 Other specified blood vessels of lower extremity
Multiple blood vessels of lower extremity

904.8 Unspecified blood vessel of lower extremity

904.9 Unspecified site
Injury to blood vessel NOS

LATE EFFECTS OF INJURIES, POISONINGS, TOXIC EFFECTS, AND OTHER EXTERNAL CAUSES (905-909)

Note: These categories are to be used to indicate conditions classifiable to 800-999 as the cause of late effects, which are themselves classified elsewhere. The "late effects" include those specified as such, or as sequelae, which may occur at any time after the acute injury.

✓4th 905 Late effects of musculoskeletal and connective tissue injuries
AHA: 1Q, '95, 10; 2Q, '94, 3

905.0 Late effect of fracture of skull and face bones
Late effect of injury classifiable to 800-804
AHA: 3Q, '97, 12

905.1 Late effect of fracture of spine and trunk without mention of spinal cord lesion
Late effect of injury classifiable to 805, 807-809

905.2 Late effect of fracture of upper extremities
Late effect of injury classifiable to 810-819

905.3 Late effect of fracture of neck of femur
Late effect of injury classifiable to 820

905.4 Late effect of fracture of lower extremities
Late effect of injury classifiable to 821-827

905.5 Late effect of fracture of multiple and unspecified bones
Late effect of injury classifiable to 828-829

905.6 Late effect of dislocation
Late effect of injury classifiable to 830-839

 Newborn Age: 0  Pediatric Age: 0-17  Maternity Age: 12-55  Adult Age: 15-124  CC Condition  Major Complication  Complex Dx HIV Related Dx

905.7 Late effect of sprain and strain without mention of tendon injury
Late effect of injury classifiable to 840-848, except tendon injury

905.8 Late effect of tendon injury
Late effect of tendon injury due to:
open wound [injury classifiable to 880-884 with .2, 890-894 with .2]
sprain and strain [injury classifiable to 840-848]
AHA: 2Q, '89, 13; 2Q, '89, 15

905.9 Late effect of traumatic amputation
Late effect of injury classifiable to 885-887, 895-897
EXCLUDES *late amputation stump complication (997.60-997.69)*

4th **906 Late effects of injuries to skin and subcutaneous tissues**

906.0 Late effect of open wound of head, neck, and trunk
Late effect of injury classifiable to 870-879

906.1 Late effect of open wound of extremities without mention of tendon injury
Late effect of injury classifiable to 880-884, 890-894 except .2

906.2 Late effect of superficial injury
Late effect of injury classifiable to 910-919

906.3 Late effect of contusion
Late effect of injury classifiable to 920-924

906.4 Late effect of crushing
Late effect of injury classifiable to 925-929

906.5 Late effect of burn of eye, face, head, and neck
Late effect of injury classifiable to 940-941
AHA: 4Q, '04, 76

906.6 Late effect of burn of wrist and hand
Late effect of injury classifiable to 944
AHA: 4Q, '94, 22

906.7 Late effect of burn of other extremities
Late effect of injury classifiable to 943 or 945
AHA: 4Q, '94, 22

906.8 Late effect of burns of other specified sites
Late effect of injury classifiable to 942, 946-947
AHA: 4Q, '94, 22

906.9 Late effect of burn of unspecified site
Late effect of injury classifiable to 948-949
AHA: 4Q, '94, 22

4th **907 Late effects of injuries to the nervous system**

907.0 Late effect of intracranial injury without mention of skull fracture
Late effect of injury classifiable to 850-854
AHA: 4Q, '03, 103; 3Q, '90, 14

907.1 Late effect of injury to cranial nerve
Late effect of injury classifiable to 950-951

907.2 Late effect of spinal cord injury
Late effect of injury classifiable to 806, 952
AHA: 4Q, '03, 103; 4Q, '98, 38

907.3 Late effect of injury to nerve root(s), spinal plexus(es), and other nerves of trunk
Late effect of injury classifiable to 953-954

907.4 Late effect of injury to peripheral nerve of shoulder girdle and upper limb
Late effect of injury classifiable to 955

907.5 Late effect of injury to peripheral nerve of pelvic girdle and lower limb
Late effect of injury classifiable to 956

907.9 Late effect of injury to other and unspecified nerve
Late effect of injury classifiable to 957

4th **908 Late effects of other and unspecified injuries**

908.0 Late effect of internal injury to chest
Late effect of injury classifiable to 860-862

908.1 Late effect of internal injury to intra-abdominal organs
Late effect of injury classifiable to 863-866, 868

908.2 Late effect of internal injury to other internal organs
Late effect of injury classifiable to 867 or 869

908.3 Late effect of injury to blood vessel of head, neck, and extremities
Late effect of injury classifiable to 900, 903-904

908.4 Late effect of injury to blood vessel of thorax, abdomen, and pelvis
Late effect of injury classifiable to 901-902

908.5 Late effect of foreign body in orifice
Late effect of injury classifiable to 930-939

908.6 Late effect of certain complications of trauma
Late effect of complications classifiable to 958

908.9 Late effect of unspecified injury
Late effect of injury classifiable to 959
AHA: 3Q, '00, 4

4th **909 Late effects of other and unspecified external causes**

909.0 Late effect of poisoning due to drug, medicinal or biological substance
Late effect of conditions classifiable to 960-979
EXCLUDES *late effect of adverse effect of drug, medicinal or biological substance (909.5)*
AHA: 4Q, '03, 103

909.1 Late effect of toxic effects of nonmedical substances
Late effect of conditions classifiable to 980-989

909.2 Late effect of radiation
Late effect of conditions classifiable to 990

909.3 Late effect of complications of surgical and medical care
Late effect of conditions classifiable to 996-999
AHA: 1Q, '93, 29

909.4 Late effect of certain other external causes
Late effect of conditions classifiable to 991-994

909.5 Late effect of adverse effect of drug, medical or biological substance
EXCLUDES *late effect of poisoning due to drug, medicinal or biological substance (909.0)*
AHA: 4Q, '94, 48

909.9 Late effect of other and unspecified external causes

SUPERFICIAL INJURY (910-919)

EXCLUDES
burn (blisters) (940.0-949.5)
contusion (920-924.9)
foreign body:
granuloma (728.82)
inadvertently left in operative wound (998.4)
residual in soft tissue (729.6)
insect bite, venomous (989.5)
open wound with incidental foreign body (870.0-897.7)

AHA: 2Q, '89, 15

4th **910 Superficial injury of face, neck, and scalp except eye**

INCLUDES
cheek, ear, gum, lip, nose, throat

EXCLUDES *eye and adnexa (918.0-918.9)*

910.0 Abrasion or friction burn without mention of infection
910.1 Abrasion or friction burn, infected
910.2 Blister without mention of infection
910.3 Blister, infected
910.4 Insect bite, nonvenomous, without mention of infection
910.5 Insect bite, nonvenomous, infected
910.6 Superficial foreign body (splinter) without major open wound and without mention of infection
910.7 Superficial foreign body (splinter) without major open wound, infected

910.8 **Other and unspecified superficial injury of face, neck, and scalp without mention of infection**

910.9 **Other and unspecified superficial injury of face, neck, and scalp, infected**

✓4th 911 Superficial injury of trunk

INCLUDES abdominal wall, anus, back, breast, buttock, chest wall, flank, groin, interscapular region, labium (majus) (minus), penis, perineum, scrotum, testis, vagina, vulva

EXCLUDES *hip (916.0-916.9)*
scapular region (912.0-912.9)

911.0 **Abrasion or friction burn without mention of infection**
AHA: 3Q, '01, 10

911.1 **Abrasion or friction burn, infected**

911.2 **Blister without mention of infection**

911.3 **Blister, infected**

911.4 **Insect bite, nonvenomous, without mention of infection**

911.5 **Insect bite, nonvenomous, infected**

911.6 **Superficial foreign body (splinter) without major open wound and without mention of infection**

911.7 **Superficial foreign body (splinter) without major open wound, infected**

911.8 **Other and unspecified superficial injury of trunk without mention of infection**

911.9 **Other and unspecified superficial injury of trunk, infected**

✓4th 912 Superficial injury of shoulder and upper arm

INCLUDES axilla, scapular region

912.0 **Abrasion or friction burn without mention of infection**

912.1 **Abrasion or friction burn, infected**

912.2 **Blister without mention of infection**

912.3 **Blister, infected**

912.4 **Insect bite, nonvenomous, without mention of infection**

912.5 **Insect bite, nonvenomous, infected**

912.6 **Superficial foreign body (splinter) without major open wound and without mention of infection**

912.7 **Superficial foreign body (splinter) without major open wound, infected**

912.8 **Other and unspecified superficial injury of shoulder and upper arm without mention of infection**

912.9 **Other and unspecified superficial injury of shoulder and upper arm, infected**

✓4th 913 Superficial injury of elbow, forearm, and wrist

913.0 **Abrasion or friction burn without mention of infection**

913.1 **Abrasion or friction burn, infected**

913.2 **Blister without mention of infection**

913.3 **Blister, infected**

913.4 **Insect bite, nonvenomous, without mention of infection**

913.5 **Insect bite, nonvenomous, infected**

913.6 **Superficial foreign body (splinter) without major open wound and without mention of infection**

913.7 **Superficial foreign body (splinter) without major open wound, infected**

913.8 **Other and unspecified superficial injury of elbow, forearm, and wrist without mention of infection**

913.9 **Other and unspecified superficial injury of elbow, forearm, and wrist, infected**

✓4th 914 Superficial injury of hand(s) except finger(s) alone

914.0 **Abrasion or friction burn without mention of infection**

914.1 **Abrasion or friction burn, infected**

914.2 **Blister without mention of infection**

914.3 **Blister, infected**

914.4 **Insect bite, nonvenomous, without mention of infection**

914.5 **Insect bite, nonvenomous, infected**

914.6 **Superficial foreign body (splinter) without major open wound and without mention of infection**

914.7 **Superficial foreign body (splinter) without major open wound, infected**

914.8 **Other and unspecified superficial injury of hand without mention of infection**

914.9 **Other and unspecified superficial injury of hand, infected**

✓4th 915 Superficial injury of finger(s)

INCLUDES fingernail, thumb (nail)

915.0 **Abrasion or friction burn without mention of infection**

915.1 **Abrasion or friction burn, infected**

915.2 **Blister without mention of infection**

915.3 **Blister, infected**

915.4 **Insect bite, nonvenomous, without mention of infection**

915.5 **Insect bite, nonvenomous, infected**

915.6 **Superficial foreign body (splinter) without major open wound and without mention of infection**

915.7 **Superficial foreign body (splinter) without major open wound, infected**

915.8 **Other and unspecified superficial injury of fingers without mention of infection**
AHA: 3Q, '01, 10

915.9 **Other and unspecified superficial injury of fingers, infected**

✓4th 916 Superficial injury of hip, thigh, leg, and ankle

916.0 **Abrasion or friction burn without mention of infection**

916.1 **Abrasion or friction burn, infected**

916.2 **Blister without mention of infection**

916.3 **Blister, infected**

916.4 **Insect bite, nonvenomous, without mention of infection**

916.5 **Insect bite, nonvenomous, infected**

916.6 **Superficial foreign body (splinter) without major open wound and without mention of infection**

916.7 **Superficial foreign body (splinter) without major open wound, infected**

916.8 **Other and unspecified superficial injury of hip, thigh, leg, and ankle without mention of infection**

916.9 **Other and unspecified superficial injury of hip, thigh, leg, and ankle, infected**

✓4th 917 Superficial injury of foot and toe(s)

INCLUDES heel, toenail

917.0 **Abrasion or friction burn without mention of infection**

917.1 **Abrasion or friction burn, infected**

917.2 **Blister without mention of infection**

917.3 **Blister, infected**

917.4 **Insect bite, nonvenomous, without mention of infection**

917.5 **Insect bite, nonvenomous, infected**

917.6 **Superficial foreign body (splinter) without major open wound and without mention of infection**

917.7 **Superficial foreign body (splinter) without major open wound, infected**

917.8 **Other and unspecified superficial injury of foot and toes without mention of infection**
AHA: 1Q, '03, 13

917.9 **Other and unspecified superficial injury of foot and toes, infected**
AHA: 1Q, '03, 13

✓4th **918 Superficial injury of eye and adnexa**

EXCLUDES *burn (940.0-940.9)*
foreign body on external eye (930.0-930.9)

918.0 Eyelids and periocular area
Abrasion
Insect bite
Superficial foreign body (splinter)

918.1 Cornea
Corneal abrasion
Superficial laceration
EXCLUDES *corneal injury due to contact lens (371.82)*

918.2 Conjunctiva

918.9 Other and unspecified superficial injuries of eye
Eye (ball) NOS

✓4th **919 Superficial injury of other, multiple, and unspecified sites**

EXCLUDES *multiple sites classifiable to the same three-digit category (910.0-918.9)*

919.0 Abrasion or friction burn without mention of infection

919.1 Abrasion or friction burn, infected

919.2 Blister without mention of infection

919.3 Blister, infected

919.4 Insect bite, nonvenomous, without mention of infection

919.5 Insect bite, nonvenomous, infected

919.6 Superficial foreign body (splinter) without major open wound and without mention of infection

919.7 Superficial foreign body (splinter) without major open wound, infected

919.8 Other and unspecified superficial injury without mention of infection

919.9 Other and unspecified superficial injury, infected

CONTUSION WITH INTACT SKIN SURFACE (920-924)

INCLUDES bruise } without fracture or open wound
hematoma }

EXCLUDES *concussion (850.0-850.9)*
hemarthrosis (840.0-848.9)
internal organs (860.0-869.1)
that incidental to:
crushing injury (925-929.9)
dislocation (830.0-839.9)
fracture (800.0-829.1)
internal injury (860.0-869.1)
intracranial injury (850.0-854.1)
nerve injury (950.0-957.9)
open wound (870.0-897.7)

920 Contusion of face, scalp, and neck except eye(s)
Cheek
Ear (auricle)
Gum
Lip
Mandibular joint area
Nose
Throat

✓4th **921 Contusion of eye and adnexa**

921.0 Black eye, not otherwise specified

921.1 Contusion of eyelids and periocular area

921.2 Contusion of orbital tissues

921.3 Contusion of eyeball
AHA: J-A, '85, 16

921.9 Unspecified contusion of eye
Injury of eye NOS

✓4th **922 Contusion of trunk**

922.0 Breast

922.1 Chest wall

922.2 Abdominal wall
Flank
Groin

✓5th **922.3 Back**
AHA: 4Q, '96, 39

922.31 Back
EXCLUDES *interscapular region (922.33)*
AHA: 3Q, '99, 14

922.32 Buttock

922.33 Interscapular region

922.4 Genital organs
Labium (majus) (minus)
Penis
Perineum
Scrotum
Vulva
Vagina
Testis

922.8 Multiple sites of trunk

922.9 Unspecified part
Trunk NOS

✓4th **923 Contusion of upper limb**

✓5th **923.0 Shoulder and upper arm**

923.00 Shoulder region

923.01 Scapular region

923.02 Axillary region

923.03 Upper arm

923.09 Multiple sites

✓5th **923.1 Elbow and forearm**

923.10 Forearm

923.11 Elbow

✓5th **923.2 Wrist and hand(s), except finger(s) alone**

923.20 Hand(s)

923.21 Wrist

923.3 Finger
Fingernail
Thumb (nail)

923.8 Multiple sites of upper limb

923.9 Unspecified part of upper limb
Arm NOS

✓4th **924 Contusion of lower limb and of other and unspecified sites**

✓5th **924.0 Hip and thigh**

924.00 Thigh

924.01 Hip

✓5th **924.1 Knee and lower leg**

924.10 Lower leg

924.11 Knee

✓5th **924.2 Ankle and foot, excluding toe(s)**

924.20 Foot
Heel

924.21 Ankle

924.3 Toe
Toenail

924.4 Multiple sites of lower limb

924.5 Unspecified part of lower limb
Leg NOS

924.8 Multiple sites, not elsewhere classified
AHA: 1Q, '03, 7

924.9 Unspecified site

CRUSHING INJURY (925-929)

Use additional code to identify any associated injuries, such as:
fractures (800-829)
internal injuries (860.0-869.1)
intracranial injuries (850.0-854.1)

AHA: 4Q, '03, 77; 2Q, '93, 7

✓4th **925 Crushing injury of face, scalp, and neck**
Cheek
Ear
Larynx
Pharynx
Throat

925.1 Crushing injury of face and scalp CC
Cheek
Ear
CC Excl: 873.8-873.9, 905.0, 925.1-925.2, 929.0, 929.9, 958.8-959.09, 959.8-959.9

925.2 Crushing injury of neck CC
Larynx
Pharynx
Throat
CC Excl: 873.8-873.9, 905.0, 925.1-925.2, 929.0, 929.9, 958.8-959.09, 959.8-959.9

✓4th 926 Crushing injury of trunk

926.0 External genitalia
Labium (majus) (minus)
Penis
Scrotum
Testis
Vulva

✓5th 926.1 Other specified sites
926.11 Back
926.12 Buttock
926.19 Other
Breast

926.8 Multiple sites of trunk
926.9 Unspecified site
Trunk NOS

✓4th 927 Crushing injury of upper limb

✓5th 927.0 Shoulder and upper arm
927.00 Shoulder region
927.01 Scapular region
927.02 Axillary region
927.03 Upper arm
927.09 Multiple sites

✓5th 927.1 Elbow and forearm
927.10 Forearm
927.11 Elbow

✓5th 927.2 Wrist and hand(s), except finger(s) alone
927.20 Hand(s)
927.21 Wrist

927.3 Finger(s)
AHA: 4Q, '03, 77

927.8 Multiple sites of upper limb
927.9 Unspecified site
Arm NOS

✓4th 928 Crushing injury of lower limb

✓5th 928.0 Hip and thigh
928.00 Thigh
928.01 Hip

✓5th 928.1 Knee and lower leg
928.10 Lower leg
928.11 Knee

✓5th 928.2 Ankle and foot, excluding toe(s) alone
928.20 Foot
Heel
928.21 Ankle

928.3 Toe(s)
928.8 Multiple sites of lower limb
928.9 Unspecified site
Leg NOS

✓4th 929 Crushing injury of multiple and unspecified sites

929.0 Multiple sites, not elsewhere classified CC
CC Excl: 929.0, 929.9, 958.8-958.99, 959.8-959.9

929.9 Unspecified site

EFFECTS OF FOREIGN BODY ENTERING THROUGH ORIFICE (930-939)

EXCLUDES *foreign body:*
granuloma (728.82)
inadvertently left in operative wound (998.4, 998.7)
in open wound (800-839, 851-897)
residual in soft tissues (729.6)
superficial without major open wound (910-919 with .6 or .7)

✓4th 930 Foreign body on external eye

EXCLUDES *foreign body in penetrating wound of:*
eyeball (871.5-871.6)
retained (old) (360.5-360.6)
ocular adnexa (870.4)
retained (old) (376.6)

930.0 Corneal foreign body
930.1 Foreign body in conjunctival sac
930.2 Foreign body in lacrimal punctum
930.8 Other and combined sites
930.9 Unspecified site
External eye NOS

931 Foreign body in ear
Auditory canal
Auricle

932 Foreign body in nose
Nasal sinus
Nostril

✓4th 933 Foreign body in pharynx and larynx

933.0 Pharynx
Nasopharynx
Throat NOS

933.1 Larynx
Asphyxia due to foreign body
Choking due to:
food (regurgitated)
phlegm

✓4th 934 Foreign body in trachea, bronchus, and lung

934.0 Trachea
934.1 Main bronchus
AHA: 3Q, '02, 18

934.8 Other specified parts
Bronchioles
Lung

934.9 Respiratory tree, unspecified
Inhalation of liquid or vomitus, lower respiratory tract NOS

✓4th 935 Foreign body in mouth, esophagus, and stomach

935.0 Mouth
935.1 Esophagus
AHA: 1Q, '88, 13

935.2 Stomach

936 Foreign body in intestine and colon

937 Foreign body in anus and rectum
Rectosigmoid (junction)

938 Foreign body in digestive system, unspecified
Alimentary tract NOS
Swallowed foreign body

✓4th 939 Foreign body in genitourinary tract

939.0 Bladder and urethra
939.1 Uterus, any part ♀
EXCLUDES *intrauterine contraceptive device:*
complications from (996.32, 996.65)
presence of (V45.51)

939.2 Vulva and vagina ♀
939.3 Penis ♂
939.9 Unspecified site

BURNS (940-949)

INCLUDES burns from:
electrical heating appliance
electricity
flame
hot object
lightning
radiation
chemical burns (external) (internal)
scalds

EXCLUDES *friction burns (910-919 with .0, .1)*
sunburn (692.71, 692.76-692.77)

AHA: 4Q, 94, 22; 2Q, '90, 7; 4Q, '88, 3; M-A, '86, 9

✓4th 940 Burn confined to eye and adnexa

940.0 Chemical burn of eyelids and periocular area
940.1 Other burns of eyelids and periocular area
940.2 Alkaline chemical burn of cornea and conjunctival sac
940.3 Acid chemical burn of cornea and conjunctival sac
940.4 Other burn of cornea and conjunctival sac
940.5 Burn with resulting rupture and destruction of eyeball
940.9 Unspecified burn of eye and adnexa

✓4th **941 Burn of face, head, and neck**

EXCLUDES *mouth (947.0)*

The following fifth-digit subclassification is for use with category 941:

0 face and head, unspecified site
1 ear [any part]
2 eye (with other parts of face, head, and neck)
3 lip(s)
4 chin
5 nose (septum)
6 scalp [any part]
Temple (region)
7 forehead and cheek
8 neck
9 multiple sites [except with eye] of face, head, and neck

AHA: 4Q, '94, 22; M-A, '86, 9

✓5th **941.0 Unspecified degree**

✓5th **941.1 Erythema [first degree]**

AHA: For code 941.19: ▶3Q, '05, 10◀

✓5th **941.2 Blisters, epidermal loss [second degree]**

✓5th **941.3 Full-thickness skin loss [third degree NOS]**

✓5th **941.4 Deep necrosis of underlying tissues [deep third degree] without mention of loss of a body part**

✓5th **941.5 Deep necrosis of underlying tissues [deep third degree] with loss of a body part**

✓4th **942 Burn of trunk**

EXCLUDES *scapular region (943.0-943.5 with fifth-digit 6)*

The following fifth-digit subclassification is for use with category 942:

0 trunk, unspecified site
1 breast
2 chest wall, excluding breast and nipple
3 abdominal wall
Flank
Groin
4 back [any part]
Buttock
Interscapular region
5 genitalia
Labium (majus) (minus)
Penis
Perineum
Scrotum
Testis
Vulva
9 other and multiple sites of trunk

AHA: 4Q, '94, 22; M-A, '86, 9

✓5th **942.0 Unspecified degree**

✓5th **942.1 Erythema [first degree]**

✓5th **942.2 Blisters, epidermal loss [second degree]**

✓5th **942.3 Full-thickness skin loss [third degree NOS]**

✓5th **942.4 Deep necrosis of underlying tissues [deep third degree] without mention of loss of a body part**

✓5th **942.5 Deep necrosis of underlying tissues [deep third degree] with loss of a body part**

✓4th **943 Burn of upper limb, except wrist and hand**

The following fifth-digit subclassification is for use with category 943:

0 upper limb, unspecified site
1 forearm
2 elbow
3 upper arm
4 axilla
5 shoulder
6 scapular region
9 multiple sites of upper limb, except wrist and hand

AHA: 4Q, '94, 22; M-A, '86, 9

✓5th **943.0 Unspecified degree**

✓5th **943.1 Erythema [first degree]**

✓5th **943.2 Blisters, epidermal loss [second degree]**

✓5th **943.3 Full-thickness skin loss [third degree NOS]**

✓5th **943.4 Deep necrosis of underlying tissues [deep third degree] without mention of loss of a body part**

✓5th **943.5 Deep necrosis of underlying tissues [deep third degree] with loss of a body part**

✓4th **944 Burn of wrist(s) and hand(s)**

The following fifth-digit subclassification is for use with category 944:

0 hand, unspecified site
1 single digit [finger (nail)] other than thumb
2 thumb (nail)
3 two or more digits, not including thumb
4 two or more digits including thumb
5 palm
6 back of hand
7 wrist
8 multiple sites of wrist(s) and hand(s)

✓5th **944.0 Unspecified degree**

✓5th **944.1 Erythema [first degree]**

✓5th **944.2 Blisters, epidermal loss [second degree]**

✓5th **944.3 Full-thickness skin loss [third degree NOS]**

✓5th **944.4 Deep necrosis of underlying tissues [deep third degree] without mention of loss of a body part**

✓5th **944.5 Deep necrosis of underlying tissues [deep third degree] with loss of a body part**

✓4th **945 Burn of lower limb(s)**

The following fifth-digit subclassification is for use with category 945:

0 lower limb [leg], unspecified site
1 toe(s) (nail)
2 foot
3 ankle
4 lower leg
5 knee
6 thigh [any part]
9 multiple sites of lower limb(s)

AHA: 4Q, '94, 22; M-A, '86, 9

✓5th **945.0 Unspecified degree**

✓5th **945.1 Erythema [first degree]**

✓5th **945.2 Blisters, epidermal loss [second degree]**

✓5th **945.3 Full-thickness skin loss [third degree NOS]**

✓5th **945.4 Deep necrosis of underlying tissues [deep third degree] without mention of loss of a body part**

✓5th **945.5 Deep necrosis of underlying tissues [deep third degree] with loss of a body part**

✓4th **946 Burns of multiple specified sites**

INCLUDES burns of sites classifiable to more than one three-digit category in 940-945

EXCLUDES *multiple burns NOS (949.0-949.5)*

AHA: 4Q, '94, 22; M-A, '86, 9

946.0 Unspecified degree

946.1 Erythema [first degree]

946.2 Blisters, epidermal loss [second degree]

946.3 Full-thickness skin loss [third degree NOS]

946.4 Deep necrosis of underlying tissues [deep third degree] without mention of loss of a body part

946.5 Deep necrosis of underlying tissues [deep third degree] with loss of a body part

✓4th **947 Burn of internal organs**

INCLUDES burns from chemical agents (ingested)

AHA: 4Q, '94, 22; M-A, '86, 9

947.0 Mouth and pharynx
Gum
Tongue

947.1 Larynx, trachea, and lung

947.2 Esophagus

947.3 Gastrointestinal tract
Colon
Rectum
Small intestine
Stomach

947.4 Vagina and uterus ♀

947.8 Other specified sites

947.9 Unspecified site

✓4th **948 Burns classified according to extent of body surface involved**

Note: This category is to be used when the site of the burn is unspecified, or with categories 940-947 when the site is specified.

EXCLUDES *sunburn (692.71, 692.76-692.77)*

The following fifth-digit subclassification is for use with category 948 to indicate the percent of body surface with third degree burn; valid digits are in [brackets] under each code:

0 less than 10 percent or unspecified
1 10-19%
2 20-29%
3 30-39%
4 40-49%
5 50-59%
6 60-69%
7 70-79%
8 80-89%
9 90% or more of body surface

AHA: 4Q, '94, 22; 4Q, '88, 3; M-A, '86, 9; N-D, '84, 13

✓5th 948.0 [0] **Burn [any degree] involving less than 10 percent of body surface**

✓5th 948.1 [0-1] **10-19 percent of body surface**

✓5th 948.2 [0-2] **20-29 percent of body surface**

✓5th 948.3 [0-3] **30-39 percent of body surface**

✓5th 948.4 [0-4] **40-49 percent of body surface**

✓5th 948.5 [0-5] **50-59 percent of body surface**

✓5th 948.6 [0-6] **60-69 percent of body surface**

✓5th 948.7 [0-7] **70-79 percent of body surface**

✓5th 948.8 [0-8] **80-89 percent of body surface**

✓5th 948.9 [0-9] **90 percent or more of body surface**

Burns

Degrees of Burns

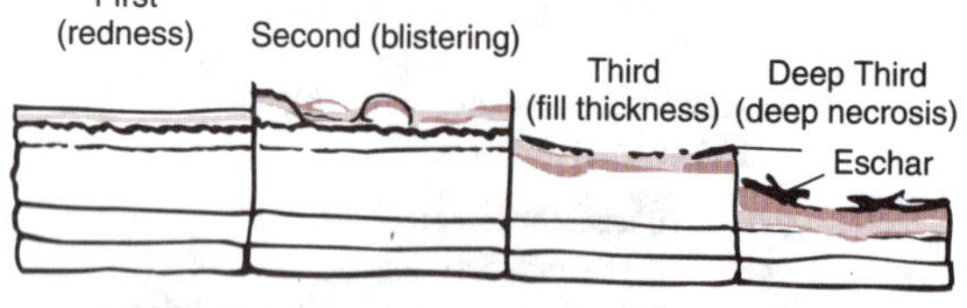

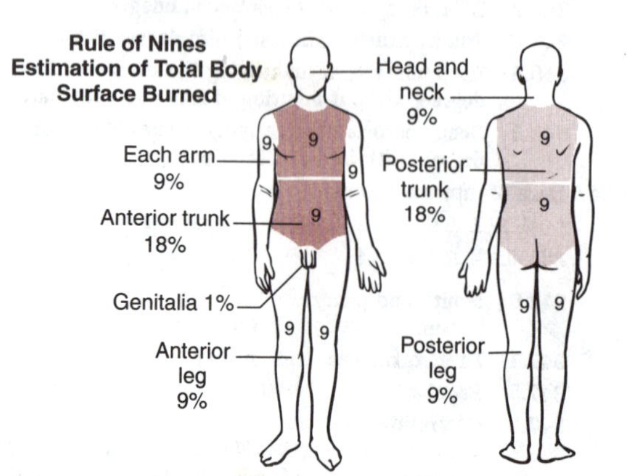

✓4th **949 Burn, unspecified**

INCLUDES burn NOS multiple burns NOS

EXCLUDES *burn of unspecified site but with statement of the extent of body surface involved (948.0-948.9)*

AHA: 4Q, '94, 22; M-A, '86, 9

949.0 **Unspecified degree**

949.1 **Erythema [first degree]**

949.2 **Blisters, epidermal loss [second degree]**

949.3 **Full-thickness skin loss [third degree NOS]**

949.4 **Deep necrosis of underlying tissues [deep third degree] without mention of loss of a body part**

949.5 **Deep necrosis of underlying tissues [deep third degree] with loss of a body part**

INJURY TO NERVES AND SPINAL CORD (950-957)

INCLUDES division of nerve, lesion in continuity, traumatic neuroma, traumatic transient paralysis (with open wound)

EXCLUDES *accidental puncture or laceration during medical procedure (998.2)*

✓4th **950 Injury to optic nerve and pathways**

950.0 **Optic nerve injury**
Second cranial nerve

950.1 **Injury to optic chiasm**

950.2 **Injury to optic pathways**

950.3 **Injury to visual cortex**

950.9 **Unspecified**
Traumatic blindness NOS

✓4th **951 Injury to other cranial nerve(s)**

951.0 **Injury to oculomotor nerve**
Third cranial nerve

951.1 **Injury to trochlear nerve**
Fourth cranial nerve

951.2 **Injury to trigeminal nerve**
Fifth cranial nerve

951.3 **Injury to abducens nerve**
Sixth cranial nerve

951.4 **Injury to facial nerve**
Seventh cranial nerve

951.5 **Injury to acoustic nerve**
Auditory nerve
Eighth cranial nerve
Traumatic deafness NOS

951.6 **Injury to accessory nerve**
Eleventh cranial nerve

951.7 **Injury to hypoglossal nerve**
Twelfth cranial nerve

951.8 **Injury to other specified cranial nerves**
Glossopharyngeal [9th cranial] nerve
Olfactory [1st cranial] nerve
Pneumogastric [10th cranial] nerve
Traumatic anosmia NOS
Vagus [10th cranial] nerve

951.9 **Injury to unspecified cranial nerve**

✓4th **952 Spinal cord injury without evidence of spinal bone injury**

✓5th 952.0 **Cervical**

952.00 **C_1-C_4 level with unspecified spinal cord injury** CC
Spinal cord injury, cervical region NOS
CC Excl: 805.00-805.18, 805.8-806.19, 806.8-806.9, 839.00-839.18, 839.40, 839.49-839.50, 839.59, 839.69, 839.79-839.9, 847.9, 905.1, 926.11, 952.00-952.09, 952.8-952.9, 958.8-958.99, 959.11-959.19, 959.8-959.9

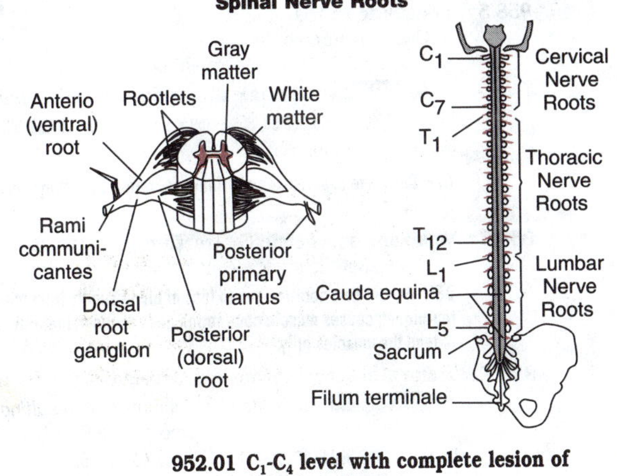

952.01 C_1-C_4 level with complete lesion of spinal cord CC
CC Excl: See code 952.00

952.02 C_1-C_4 level with anterior cord syndrome CC
CC Excl: See code 952.00

952.03 C_1-C_4 level with central cord syndrome CC
CC Excl: See code 952.00

952.04 C_1-C_4 level with other specified spinal cord injury CC
Incomplete spinal cord lesion at C_1-C_4 level:
NOS
with posterior cord syndrome
CC Excl: See code 952.00

952.05 C_5-C_7 level with unspecified spinal cord injury CC
CC Excl: See code 952.00

952.06 C_5-C_7 level with complete lesion of spinal cord CC
CC Excl: See code 952.00

952.07 C_5-C_7 level with anterior cord syndrome CC
CC Excl: See code 952.00

952.08 C_5-C_7 level with central cord syndrome CC
CC Excl: See code 952.00

952.09 C_5-C_7 level with other specified spinal cord injury CC
Incomplete spinal cord lesion at C_5-C_7 level:
NOS
with posterior cord syndrome
CC Excl: See code 952.00

✓5th **952.1 Dorsal [thoracic]**

952.10 T_1-T_6 level with unspecified spinal cord injury CC
Spinal cord injury, thoracic region NOS
CC Excl: 805.8-805.9, 806.20-806.39, 839.40, 839.49-839.50, 839.59, 839.69, 839.79, 839.8-839.9, 847.9, 905.1, 926.11, 952.10-952.19, 952.8-952.9, 958.8-958.99, 959.11-959.19, 959.8-959.9

952.11 T_1-T_6 level with complete lesion of spinal cord CC
CC Excl: See code 952.10

952.12 T_1-T_6 level with anterior cord syndrome CC
CC Excl: See code 952.10

952.13 T_1-T_6 level with central cord syndrome CC
CC Excl: See code 952.10

952.14 T_1-T_6 level with other specified spinal cord injury CC
Incomplete spinal cord lesion at T_1-T_6 level:
NOS
with posterior cord syndrome
CC Excl: See code 952.10

952.15 T_7-T_{12} level with unspecified spinal cord injury CC
CC Excl: See code 952.10

952.16 T_7-T_{12} level with complete lesion of spinal cord CC
CC Excl: See code 952.10

952.17 T_7-T_{12} level with anterior cord syndrome CC
CC Excl: See code 952.10

952.18 T_7-T_{12} level with central cord syndrome CC
CC Excl: See code 952.10

952.19 T_7-T_{12} level with other specified spinal cord injury CC
Incomplete spinal cord lesion at T_7-T_{12} level:
NOS
with posterior cord syndrome
CC Excl: See code 952.10

952.2 Lumbar CC
CC Excl: 805.8-805.9, 806.4-806.5, 839.40, 839.49-839.50, 839.59, 839.69, 839.79-839.9, 847.9, 905.1, 926.11, 952.2, 952.8-952.9, 958.8-958.99, 959.11-959.19, 959.8-959.9

952.3 Sacral CC
CC Excl: 805.8-805.9, 806.60-806.79, 839.40, 839.49-839.50, 839.59, 839.69, 839.79-839.9, 847.9, 905.1, 926.11, 952.3-952.4, 952.8-952.9, 958.8-958.99, 959.11-959.19, 959.8-959.9

952.4 Cauda equina CC
CC Excl: See code 952.3

952.8 Multiple sites of spinal cord CC
CC Excl: 805.8-805.9, 839.40, 839.49-839.50, 839.59, 839.69, 839.79-839.9, 847.9, 905.1, 926.11, 952.8-952.9, 958.8-958.99, 959.11-959.19, 959.8-959.9

952.9 Unspecified site of spinal cord CC
CC Excl: See Code 952.8

✓4th **953 Injury to nerve roots and spinal plexus**

953.0 Cervical root CC
CC Excl: 953.8-953.9, 958.8, 959.8-959.9

953.1 Dorsal root CC
CC Excl: See code 953.0

953.2 Lumbar root CC
CC Excl: See code 953.0

953.3 Sacral root CC
CC Excl: See code 953.0

953.4 Brachial plexus CC
CC Excl: See code 953.0

953.5 Lumbosacral plexus CC
CC Excl: See code 953.0

953.8 Multiple sites CC
CC Excl: See code 953.0

953.9 Unspecified site CC
CC Excl: See code 953.0

✓4th **954 Injury to other nerve(s) of trunk, excluding shoulder and pelvic girdles**

954.0 Cervical sympathetic

954.1 Other sympathetic
Celiac ganglion or plexus
Inferior mesenteric plexus
Splanchnic nerve(s)
Stellate ganglion

954.8 Other specified nerve(s) of trunk

954.9 Unspecified nerve of trunk

✓4th **955 Injury to peripheral nerve(s) of shoulder girdle and upper limb**

955.0 Axillary nerve

955.1 Median nerve

955.2 Ulnar nerve

955.3 Radial nerve

955.4 Musculocutaneous nerve

955.5 Cutaneous sensory nerve, upper limb

955.6 Digital nerve

955.7 Other specified nerve(s) of shoulder girdle and upper limb

955.8 Multiple nerves of shoulder girdle and upper limb

955.9 Unspecified nerve of shoulder girdle and upper limb

956 Injury to peripheral nerve(s) of pelvic girdle and lower limb

956.0 Sciatic nerve

956.1 Femoral nerve

956.2 Posterior tibial nerve

956.3 Peroneal nerve

956.4 Cutaneous sensory nerve, lower limb

956.5 Other specified nerve(s) of pelvic girdle and lower limb

956.8 Multiple nerves of pelvic girdle and lower limb

956.9 Unspecified nerve of pelvic girdle and lower limb

957 Injury to other and unspecified nerves

957.0 Superficial nerves of head and neck

957.1 Other specified nerve(s)

957.8 Multiple nerves in several parts

Multiple nerve injury NOS

957.9 Unspecified site

Nerve injury NOS

CERTAIN TRAUMATIC COMPLICATIONS AND UNSPECIFIED INJURIES (958-959)

958 Certain early complications of trauma

EXCLUDES *adult respiratory distress syndrome (518.5)*
flail chest (807.4)
shock lung (518.5)
that occurring during or following medical procedures (996.0-999.9)

958.0 Air embolism CC

Pneumathemia

EXCLUDES *that complicating:*
abortion (634-638 with .6, 639.6)
ectopic or molar pregnancy (639.6)
pregnancy, childbirth, or the puerperium (673.0)

CC Excl: 958.0, 958.8-958.99, 959.8-959.9, 997.91, 997.99, 998.81, 998.83-999.1

DEF: Arterial obstruction due to introduction of air bubbles into the veins following surgery or trauma.

958.1 Fat embolism CC

EXCLUDES *that complicating:*
abortion (634-638 with .6, 639.6)
pregnancy, childbirth, or the puerperium (673.8)

CC Excl: 958.1, 958.8-958.99, 959.8-959.9, 997.91, 997.99, 998.81, 998.83-998.9

DEF: Arterial blockage due to the entrance of fat in circulatory system, after fracture of large bones or administration of corticosteroids.

958.2 Secondary and recurrent hemorrhage CC

CC Excl: 958.2, 958.8-958.99, 959.8-959.9, 997.91, 997.99, 998.81, 998.83-998.9

958.3 Posttraumatic wound infection, not elsewhere classified CC

EXCLUDES *infected open wounds–code to complicated open wound of site*

CC Excl: 958.3, 958.8-958.99, 959.8-959.9, 997.91, 997.99, 998.81, 998.83-998.9

AHA: 4Q, '01, 53; S-O, '85, 10

958.4 Traumatic shock CC

Shock (immediate) (delayed) following injury

EXCLUDES *shock:*
anaphylactic (995.0)
due to serum (999.4)
anesthetic (995.4)
electric (994.8)
following abortion (639.5)
lightning (994.0)
nontraumatic NOS (785.50)
obstetric (669.1)
postoperative (998.0)

CC Excl: 958.4, 958.8-958.99, 959.8-959.9, 997.91, 997.99, 998.81, 998.83-998.9

DEF: Shock, immediate or delayed following injury.

958.5 Traumatic anuria CC

Crush syndrome
Renal failure following crushing

EXCLUDES *that due to a medical procedure (997.5)*

CC Excl: 958.5, 958.8-958.99, 959.8-959.9, 995.4, 997.91, 997.99, 998.0, 998.11-998.13, 998.81, 998.83-998.9

DEF: Complete suppression of urinary secretion by kidneys due to trauma.

958.6 Volkmann's ischemic contracture

Posttraumatic muscle contracture

DEF: Muscle deterioration due to loss of blood supply from injury or tourniquet; causes muscle contraction and results in inability to extend the muscles fully.

958.7 Traumatic subcutaneous emphysema CC

EXCLUDES *subcutaneous emphysema resulting from a procedure (998.81)*

CC Excl: 860.0-860.5, 861.20-861.32, 862.0-862.1, 862.29, 862.31-862.9, 875.0-875.1, 958.7-958.99, 959.8-959.9, 997.91, 997.99, 998.81, 998.83-998.9

958.8 Other early complications of trauma

AHA: 2Q, '92, 13

DEF: Compartmental syndrome is abnormal pressure in confined anatomical space, as in swollen muscle restricted by fascia.

● **958.9 Traumatic compartment syndrome**

EXCLUDES *nontraumatic compartment syndrome (729.71-729.79)*

● **958.90 Compartment syndrome, unspecified**

● **958.91 Traumatic compartment syndrome of upper extremity**

Traumatic compartment syndrome of shoulder, arm, forearm, wrist, hand, and fingers

● **958.92 Traumatic compartment syndrome of lower extremity**

Traumatic compartment syndrome of hip, buttock, thigh, leg, foot, and toes

● **958.93 Traumatic compartment syndrome of abdomen**

● **958.99 Traumatic compartment syndrome of other sites**

959 Injury, other and unspecified

INCLUDES injury NOS

EXCLUDES *injury NOS of:*
blood vessels (900.0-904.9)
eye (921.0-921.9)
internal organs (860.0-869.1)
intracranial sites (854.0-854.1)
nerves (950.0-951.9, 953.0-957.9)
spinal cord (952.0-952.9)

959.0 Head, face and neck

959.01 Head injury, unspecified

EXCLUDES *concussion (850.1-850.9)*
with head injury NOS (850.1-850.9)
head injury NOS with loss of consciousness (850.1-850.5)
specified intracranial injuries (850.0-854.1)

AHA: 4Q, '97, 46

959.09 Injury of face and neck

Cheek	Mouth
Ear	Nose
Eyebrow	Throat
Lip	

AHA: 4Q, '97, 46

959.1 Trunk

EXCLUDES *scapular region (959.2)*

AHA: 4Q, '03, 78; 1Q, '99, 10

959.11 Other injury of chest wall

959.12 Other injury of abdomen

959.13 **Fracture of corpus cavernosum penis** ♂

959.14 **Other injury of external genitals**

959.19 **Other injury of other sites of trunk**
Injury of trunk NOS

959.2 **Shoulder and upper arm**
Axilla
Scapular region

959.3 **Elbow, forearm, and wrist**
AHA: 1Q, '97, 8

959.4 **Hand, except finger**

959.5 **Finger**
Fingernail
Thumb (nail)

959.6 **Hip and thigh**
Upper leg

959.7 **Knee, leg, ankle, and foot**

959.8 **Other specified sites, including multiple**
EXCLUDES *multiple sites classifiable to the same four-digit category (959.0-959.7)*

959.9 **Unspecified site**

POISONING BY DRUGS, MEDICINAL AND BIOLOGICAL SUBSTANCES (960-979)

INCLUDES overdose of these substances
wrong substance given or taken in error

EXCLUDES *adverse effects ["hypersensitivity," "reaction," etc.] of correct substance properly administered. Such cases are to be classified according to the nature of the adverse effect, such as:*
adverse effect NOS ▶(995.20)◀
allergic lymphadenitis (289.3)
aspirin gastritis (535.4)
blood disorders (280.0-289.9)
dermatitis:
contact (692.0-692.9)
due to ingestion (693.0-693.9)
nephropathy (583.9)
[The drug giving rise to the adverse effect may be identified by use of categories E930-E949.]
drug dependence (304.0-304.9)
drug reaction and poisoning affecting the newborn (760.0-779.9)
nondependent abuse of drugs (305.0-305.9)
pathological drug intoxication (292.2)

Use additional code to specify the effects of the poisoning

AHA: 2Q, '90, 11

✓4th **960 Poisoning by antibiotics**
EXCLUDES *antibiotics:*
ear, nose, and throat (976.6)
eye (976.5)
local (976.0)

960.0 **Penicillins**
Ampicillin
Carbenicillin
Cloxacillin
Penicillin G

960.1 **Antifungal antibiotics**
Amphotericin B
Griseofulvin
Nystatin
Trichomycin
EXCLUDES *preparations intended for topical use (976.0-976.9)*

960.2 **Chloramphenicol group**
Chloramphenicol
Thiamphenicol

960.3 **Erythromycin and other macrolides**
Oleandomycin
Spiramycin

960.4 **Tetracycline group**
Doxycycline
Minocycline
Oxytetracycline

960.5 **Cephalosporin group**
Cephalexin
Cephaloglycin
Cephaloridine
Cephalothin

960.6 **Antimycobacterial antibiotics**
Cycloserine
Kanamycin
Rifampin
Streptomycin

960.7 **Antineoplastic antibiotics**
Actinomycin such as:
Bleomycin
Cactinomycin
Dactinomycin
Daunorubicin
Mitomycin

960.8 **Other specified antibiotics**

960.9 **Unspecified antibiotic**

✓4th **961 Poisoning by other anti-infectives**
EXCLUDES *anti-infectives:*
ear, nose, and throat (976.6)
eye (976.5)
local (976.0)

961.0 **Sulfonamides**
Sulfadiazine
Sulfafurazole
Sulfamethoxazole

961.1 **Arsenical anti-infectives**

961.2 **Heavy metal anti-infectives**
Compounds of:
antimony
bismuth
Compounds of:
lead
mercury
EXCLUDES *mercurial diuretics (974.0)*

961.3 **Quinoline and hydroxyquinoline derivatives**
Chiniofon
Diiodohydroxyquin
EXCLUDES *antimalarial drugs (961.4)*

961.4 **Antimalarials and drugs acting on other blood protozoa**
Chloroquine
Cycloguanil
Primaquine
Proguanil [chloroguanide]
Pyrimethamine
Quinine

961.5 **Other antiprotozoal drugs**
Emetine

961.6 **Anthelmintics**
Hexylresorcinol
Piperazine
Thiabendazole

961.7 **Antiviral drugs**
Methisazone
EXCLUDES *amantadine (966.4)*
cytarabine (963.1)
idoxuridine (976.5)

961.8 **Other antimycobacterial drugs**
Ethambutol
Ethionamide
Isoniazid
Para-aminosalicylic acid derivatives
Sulfones

961.9 **Other and unspecified anti-infectives**
Flucytosine
Nitrofuran derivatives

✓4th **962 Poisoning by hormones and synthetic substitutes**
EXCLUDES *oxytocic hormones (975.0)*

962.0 **Adrenal cortical steroids**
Cortisone derivatives
Desoxycorticosterone derivatives
Fluorinated corticosteroids

962.1 **Androgens and anabolic congeners**
Methandriol
Nandrolone
Oxymetholone
Testosterone

962.2 **Ovarian hormones and synthetic substitutes**
Contraceptives, oral
Estrogens
Estrogens and progestogens, combined
Progestogens

962.3 **Insulins and antidiabetic agents**
Acetohexamide
Biguanide derivatives, oral
Chlorpropamide
Glucagon
Insulin
Phenformin
Sulfonylurea derivatives, oral
Tolbutamide
AHA: M-A, '85, 8

962.4 **Anterior pituitary hormones**
Corticotropin
Gonadotropin
Somatotropin [growth hormone]

962.5 **Posterior pituitary hormones**
Vasopressin
EXCLUDES *oxytocic hormones (975.0)*

962.6 **Parathyroid and parathyroid derivatives**

962.7 Thyroid and thyroid derivatives
Dextrothyroxin
Levothyroxine sodium
Liothyronine
Thyroglobulin

962.8 Antithyroid agents
Iodides
Thiouracil
Thiourea

962.9 Other and unspecified hormones and synthetic substitutes

✓4th **963 Poisoning by primarily systemic agents**

963.0 Antiallergic and antiemetic drugs
Antihistamines
Chlorpheniramine
Diphenhydramine
Diphenylpyraline
Thonzylamine
Tripelennamine
EXCLUDES *phenothiazine-based tranquilizers (969.1)*

963.1 Antineoplastic and immunosuppressive drugs
Azathioprine
Busulfan
Chlorambucil
Cyclophosphamide
Cytarabine
Fluorouracil
Mercaptopurine
thio-TEPA
EXCLUDES *antineoplastic antibiotics (960.7)*

963.2 Acidifying agents

963.3 Alkalizing agents

963.4 Enzymes, not elsewhere classified
Penicillinase

963.5 Vitamins, not elsewhere classified
Vitamin A
Vitamin D
EXCLUDES *nicotinic acid (972.2)*
vitamin K (964.3)

963.8 Other specified systemic agents
Heavy metal antagonists

963.9 Unspecified systemic agent

✓4th **964 Poisoning by agents primarily affecting blood constituents**

964.0 Iron and its compounds
Ferric salts
Ferrous sulfate and other ferrous salts

964.1 Liver preparations and other antianemic agents
Folic acid

964.2 Anticoagulants
Coumarin
Heparin
Phenindione
Warfarin sodium
AHA: 1Q, '94, 22

964.3 Vitamin K [phytonadione]

964.4 Fibrinolysis-affecting drugs
Aminocaproic acid
Streptodornase
Streptokinase
Urokinase

964.5 Anticoagulant antagonists and other coagulants
Hexadimethrine
Protamine sulfate

964.6 Gamma globulin

964.7 Natural blood and blood products
Blood plasma
Human fibrinogen
Packed red cells
Whole blood
EXCLUDES *transfusion reactions (999.4-999.8)*

964.8 Other specified agents affecting blood constituents
Macromolecular blood substitutes
Plasma expanders

964.9 Unspecified agent affecting blood constituents

✓4th **965 Poisoning by analgesics, antipyretics, and antirheumatics**
EXCLUDES *drug dependence (304.0-304.9)*
nondependent abuse (305.0-305.9)

✓5th **965.0 Opiates and related narcotics**

965.00 Opium (alkaloids), unspecified

965.01 Heroin
Diacetylmorphine

965.02 Methadone

965.09 Other
Codeine [methylmorphine]
Meperidine [pethidine]
Morphine

965.1 Salicylates
Acetylsalicylic acid [aspirin]
Salicylic acid salts
AHA: N-D, '94, 15

965.4 Aromatic analgesics, not elsewhere classified
Acetanilid
Paracetamol [acetaminophen]
Phenacetin [acetophenetidin]

965.5 Pyrazole derivatives
Aminophenazone [aminopyrine]
Phenylbutazone

✓5th **965.6 Antirheumatics [antiphlogistics]**
EXCLUDES *salicylates (965.1)*
steroids (962.0-962.9)
AHA: 4Q, '98, 50

965.61 Propionic acid derivatives
Fenoprofen
Flurbiprofen
Ibuprofen
Ketoprofen
Naproxen
Oxaprozin
AHA: 4Q, '98, 50

965.69 Other antirheumatics
Gold salts
Indomethacin

965.7 Other non-narcotic analgesics
Pyrabital

965.8 Other specified analgesics and antipyretics
Pentazocine

965.9 Unspecified analgesic and antipyretic

✓4th **966 Poisoning by anticonvulsants and anti-Parkinsonism drugs**

966.0 Oxazolidine derivatives
Paramethadione
Trimethadione

966.1 Hydantoin derivatives
Phenytoin

966.2 Succinimides
Ethosuximide
Phensuximide

966.3 Other and unspecified anticonvulsants
Primidone
EXCLUDES *barbiturates (967.0)*
sulfonamides (961.0)

966.4 Anti-Parkinsonism drugs
Amantadine
Ethopropazine [profenamine]
Levodopa [L-dopa]

✓4th **967 Poisoning by sedatives and hypnotics**
EXCLUDES *drug dependence (304.0-304.9)*
nondependent abuse (305.0-305.9)

967.0 Barbiturates
Amobarbital [amylobarbitone]
Barbital [barbitone]
Butabarbital [butabarbitone]
Pentobarbital [pentobarbitone]
Phenobarbital [phenobarbitone]
Secobarbital [quinalbarbitone]
EXCLUDES *thiobarbiturate anesthetics (968.3)*

967.1 Chloral hydrate group

967.2 Paraldehyde

967.3 Bromine compounds
Bromide
Carbromal (derivatives)

967.4 Methaqualone compounds

967.5 Glutethimide group

967.6 Mixed sedatives, not elsewhere classified

967.8 Other sedatives and hypnotics

967.9 Unspecified sedative or hypnotic
Sleeping:
drug } NOS
pill } NOS
tablet } NOS

✓4th 968 Poisoning by other central nervous system depressants and anesthetics

EXCLUDES *drug dependence (304.0-304.9)*
nondependent abuse (305.0-305.9)

968.0 Central nervous system muscle-tone depressants
Chlorphenesin (carbamate)
Mephenesin
Methocarbamol

968.1 Halothane

968.2 Other gaseous anesthetics
Ether
Halogenated hydrocarbon derivatives, except halothane
Nitrous oxide

968.3 Intravenous anesthetics
Ketamine
Methohexital [methohexitone]
Thiobarbiturates, such as thiopental sodium

968.4 Other and unspecified general anesthetics

968.5 Surface [topical] and infiltration anesthetics
Cocaine
Lidocaine [lignocaine]
Procaine
Tetracaine

AHA: 1Q, '93, 25

968.6 Peripheral nerve- and plexus-blocking anesthetics

968.7 Spinal anesthetics

968.9 Other and unspecified local anesthetics

✓4th 969 Poisoning by psychotropic agents

EXCLUDES *drug dependence (304.0-304.9)*
nondependent abuse (305.0-305.9)

969.0 Antidepressants
Amitriptyline
Imipramine
Monoamine oxidase [MAO] inhibitors

969.1 Phenothiazine-based tranquilizers
Chlorpromazine
Fluphenazine
Prochlorperazine
Promazine

969.2 Butyrophenone-based tranquilizers
Haloperidol
Spiperone
Trifluperidol

969.3 Other antipsychotics, neuroleptics, and major tranquilizers

969.4 Benzodiazepine-based tranquilizers
Chlordiazepoxide
Diazepam
Flurazepam
Lorazepam
Medazepam
Nitrazepam

969.5 Other tranquilizers
Hydroxyzine
Meprobamate

969.6 Psychodysleptics [hallucinogens]
Cannabis (derivatives)
Lysergide [LSD]
Marihuana (derivatives)
Mescaline
Psilocin
Psilocybin

969.7 Psychostimulants
Amphetamine
Caffeine

EXCLUDES *central appetite depressants (977.0)*

AHA: 2Q, '03, 11

969.8 Other specified psychotropic agents

969.9 Unspecified psychotropic agent

✓4th 970 Poisoning by central nervous system stimulants

970.0 Analeptics
Lobeline
Nikethamide

970.1 Opiate antagonists
Levallorphan
Nalorphine
Naloxone

970.8 Other specified central nervous system stimulants

AHA: 1Q, '05, 6

970.9 Unspecified central nervous system stimulant

✓4th 971 Poisoning by drugs primarily affecting the autonomic nervous system

971.0 Parasympathomimetics [cholinergics]
Acetylcholine
Anticholinesterase:
organophosphorus
reversible
Pilocarpine

971.1 Parasympatholytics [anticholinergics and antimuscarinics] and spasmolytics
Atropine
Homatropine
Hyoscine [scopolamine]
Quaternary ammonium derivatives

EXCLUDES *papaverine (972.5)*

971.2 Sympathomimetics [adrenergics]
Epinephrine [adrenalin]
Levarterenol [noradrenalin]

971.3 Sympatholytics [antiadrenergics]
Phenoxybenzamine
Tolazolinehydrochloride

971.9 Unspecified drug primarily affecting autonomic nervous system

✓4th 972 Poisoning by agents primarily affecting the cardiovascular system

972.0 Cardiac rhythm regulators
Practolol
Procainamide
Propranolol
Quinidine

EXCLUDES *lidocaine (968.5)*

972.1 Cardiotonic glycosides and drugs of similar action
Digitalis glycosides
Digoxin
Strophanthins

972.2 Antilipemic and antiarteriosclerotic drugs
Clofibrate
Nicotinic acid derivatives

972.3 Ganglion-blocking agents
Pentamethonium bromide

972.4 Coronary vasodilators
Dipyridamole
Nitrates [nitroglycerin]
Nitrites

972.5 Other vasodilators
Cyclandelate
Diazoxide
Papaverine

EXCLUDES *nicotinic acid (972.2)*

972.6 Other antihypertensive agents
Clonidine
Guanethidine
Rauwolfia alkaloids
Reserpine

972.7 Antivaricose drugs, including sclerosing agents
Sodium morrhuate
Zinc salts

972.8 Capillary-active drugs
Adrenochrome derivatives
Metaraminol

972.9 Other and unspecified agents primarily affecting the cardiovascular system

✓4th 973 Poisoning by agents primarily affecting the gastrointestinal system

973.0 Antacids and antigastric secretion drugs
Aluminum hydroxide
Magnesium trisilicate

AHA: 1Q, '03, 19

973.1 Irritant cathartics
Bisacodyl
Castor oil
Phenolphthalein

973.2 Emollient cathartics
Dioctyl sulfosuccinates

973.3 Other cathartics, including intestinal atonia drugs
Magnesium sulfate

973.4 Digestants
Pancreatin
Papain
Pepsin

973.5 Antidiarrheal drugs
Kaolin
Pectin

EXCLUDES *anti-infectives (960.0-961.9)*

973.6 Emetics

973.8 Other specified agents primarily affecting the gastrointestinal system

973.9 Unspecified agent primarily affecting the gastrointestinal system

✓4th 974 Poisoning by water, mineral, and uric acid metabolism drugs

974.0 Mercurial diuretics
Chlormerodrin
Mercaptomerin
Mersalyl

974.1 Purine derivative diuretics
Theobromine
Theophylline

EXCLUDES *aminophylline [theophylline ethylenediamine] (975.7)*
caffeine (969.7)

974.2 Carbonic acid anhydrase inhibitors
Acetazolamide

974.3 Saluretics
Benzothiadiazides
Chlorothiazide group

974.4 Other diuretics
Ethacrynic acid
Furosemide

974.5 Electrolytic, caloric, and water-balance agents

974.6 Other mineral salts, not elsewhere classified

974.7 Uric acid metabolism drugs
Allopurinol
Probenecid
Colchicine

✓4th **975 Poisoning by agents primarily acting on the smooth and skeletal muscles and respiratory system**

975.0 Oxytocic agents
Ergot alkaloids
Prostaglandins
Oxytocin

975.1 Smooth muscle relaxants
Adiphenine
Metaproterenol [orciprenaline]
EXCLUDES *papaverine (972.5)*

975.2 Skeletal muscle relaxants

975.3 Other and unspecified drugs acting on muscles

975.4 Antitussives
Dextromethorphan
Pipazethate

975.5 Expectorants
Acetylcysteine
Terpin hydrate
Guaifenesin

975.6 Anti-common cold drugs

975.7 Antiasthmatics
Aminophylline [theophylline ethylenediamine]

975.8 Other and unspecified respiratory drugs

✓4th **976 Poisoning by agents primarily affecting skin and mucous membrane, ophthalmological, otorhinolaryngological, and dental drugs**

976.0 Local anti-infectives and anti-inflammatory drugs

976.1 Antipruritics

976.2 Local astringents and local detergents

976.3 Emollients, demulcents, and protectants

976.4 Keratolytics, keratoplastics, other hair treatment drugs and preparations

976.5 Eye anti-infectives and other eye drugs
Idoxuridine

976.6 Anti-infectives and other drugs and preparations for ear, nose, and throat

976.7 Dental drugs topically applied
EXCLUDES *anti-infectives (976.0)*
local anesthetics (968.5)

976.8 Other agents primarily affecting skin and mucous membrane
Spermicides [vaginal contraceptives]

976.9 Unspecified agent primarily affecting skin and mucous membrane

✓4th **977 Poisoning by other and unspecified drugs and medicinal substances**

977.0 Dietetics
Central appetite depressants

977.1 Lipotropic drugs

977.2 Antidotes and chelating agents, not elsewhere classified

977.3 Alcohol deterrents

977.4 Pharmaceutical excipients
Pharmaceutical adjuncts

977.8 Other specified drugs and medicinal substances
Contrast media used for diagnostic x-ray procedures
Diagnostic agents and kits

977.9 Unspecified drug or medicinal substance

✓4th **978 Poisoning by bacterial vaccines**

978.0 BCG

978.1 Typhoid and paratyphoid

978.2 Cholera

978.3 Plague

978.4 Tetanus

978.5 Diphtheria

978.6 Pertussis vaccine, including combinations with a pertussis component

978.8 Other and unspecified bacterial vaccines

978.9 Mixed bacterial vaccines, except combinations with a pertussis component

✓4th **979 Poisoning by other vaccines and biological substances**
EXCLUDES *gamma globulin (964.6)*

979.0 Smallpox vaccine

979.1 Rabies vaccine

979.2 Typhus vaccine

979.3 Yellow fever vaccine

979.4 Measles vaccine

979.5 Poliomyelitis vaccine

979.6 Other and unspecified viral and rickettsial vaccines
Mumps vaccine

979.7 Mixed viral-rickettsial and bacterial vaccines, except combinations with a pertussis component
EXCLUDES *combinations with a pertussis component (978.6)*

979.9 Other and unspecified vaccines and biological substances

TOXIC EFFECTS OF SUBSTANCES CHIEFLY NONMEDICINAL AS TO SOURCE (980-989)

EXCLUDES *burns from chemical agents (ingested) (947.0-947.9)*
localized toxic effects indexed elsewhere (001.0-799.9)
respiratory conditions due to external agents (506.0-508.9)

Use additional code to specify the nature of the toxic effect

✓4th **980 Toxic effect of alcohol**

980.0 Ethyl alcohol
Denatured alcohol
Grain alcohol
Ethanol
Use additional code to identify any associated:
acute alcohol intoxication (305.0)
in alcoholism (303.0)
drunkenness (simple) (305.0)
pathological (291.4)
AHA: 3Q, '96, 16

980.1 Methyl alcohol
Methanol
Wood alcohol

980.2 Isopropyl alcohol
Dimethyl carbinol
Rubbing alcohol
Isopropanol

980.3 Fusel oil
Alcohol:
amyl
butyl
Alcohol:
propyl

980.8 Other specified alcohols

980.9 Unspecified alcohol

981 Toxic effect of petroleum products
Benzine
Gasoline
Kerosene
Paraffin wax
Petroleum:
ether
naphtha
spirit

✓4th **982 Toxic effect of solvents other than petroleum-based**

982.0 Benzene and homologues

982.1 Carbon tetrachloride

982.2 Carbon disulfide
Carbon bisulfide

982.3 Other chlorinated hydrocarbon solvents
Tetrachloroethylene
Trichloroethylene
EXCLUDES *chlorinated hydrocarbon preparations other than solvents (989.2)*

982.4 Nitroglycol

982.8 Other nonpetroleum-based solvents
Acetone

✓4th **983 Toxic effect of corrosive aromatics, acids, and caustic alkalis**

983.0 Corrosive aromatics
Carbolic acid or phenol
Cresol

983.1 Acids
Acid:
hydrochloric
nitric
Acid:
sulfuric

983.2 Caustic alkalis
Lye
Potassium hydroxide
Sodium hydroxide

983.9 Caustic, unspecified

✓4th **984 Toxic effect of lead and its compounds (including fumes)**

INCLUDES that from all sources except medicinal substances

984.0 Inorganic lead compounds
Lead dioxide
Lead salts

984.1 Organic lead compounds
Lead acetate
Tetraethyl lead

984.8 Other lead compounds

984.9 Unspecified lead compound

✓4th **985 Toxic effect of other metals**

INCLUDES that from all sources except medicinal substances

985.0 Mercury and its compounds
Minamata disease

985.1 Arsenic and its compounds

985.2 Manganese and its compounds

985.3 Beryllium and its compounds

985.4 Antimony and its compounds

985.5 Cadmium and its compounds

985.6 Chromium

985.8 Other specified metals
Brass fumes
Copper salts
Iron compounds
Nickel compounds
AHA: 1Q, '88, 5

985.9 Unspecified metal

986 Toxic effect of carbon monoxide
Carbon monoxide from any source

✓4th **987 Toxic effect of other gases, fumes, or vapors**

987.0 Liquefied petroleum gases
Butane
Propane

987.1 Other hydrocarbon gas

987.2 Nitrogen oxides
Nitrogen dioxide
Nitrous fumes

987.3 Sulfur dioxide

987.4 Freon
Dichloromonofluoromethane

987.5 Lacrimogenic gas
Bromobenzyl cyanide
Chloroacetophenone
Ethyliodoacetate

987.6 Chlorine gas

987.7 Hydrocyanic acid gas

987.8 Other specified gases, fumes, or vapors
Phosgene
Polyester fumes

987.9 Unspecified gas, fume, or vapor
AHA: ▶3Q, '05, 10◀

✓4th **988 Toxic effect of noxious substances eaten as food**

EXCLUDES *allergic reaction to food, such as:*
gastroenteritis (558.3)
rash (692.5, 693.1)
food poisoning (bacterial) (005.0-005.9)
toxic effects of food contaminants, such as:
aflatoxin and other mycotoxin (989.7)
mercury (985.0)

988.0 Fish and shellfish

988.1 Mushrooms

988.2 Berries and other plants

988.8 Other specified noxious substances eaten as food

988.9 Unspecified noxious substance eaten as food

✓4th **989 Toxic effect of other substances, chiefly nonmedicinal as to source**

989.0 Hydrocyanic acid and cyanides
Potassium cyanide
Sodium cyanide

EXCLUDES *gas and fumes (987.7)*

989.1 Strychnine and salts

989.2 Chlorinated hydrocarbons
Aldrin
Chlordane
DDT
Dieldrin

EXCLUDES *chlorinated hydrocarbon solvents (982.0-982.3)*

989.3 Organophosphate and carbamate
Carbaryl
Dichlorvos
Malathion
Parathion
Phorate
Phosdrin

989.4 Other pesticides, not elsewhere classified
Mixtures of insecticides

989.5 Venom
Bites of venomous snakes, lizards, and spiders
Tick paralysis

989.6 Soaps and detergents

989.7 Aflatoxin and other mycotoxin [food contaminants]

✓5th **989.8 Other substances, chiefly nonmedicinal as to source**
AHA: 4Q, '95, 60

989.81 Asbestos

EXCLUDES *asbestosis (501)*
exposure to asbestos (V15.84)

989.82 Latex

989.83 Silicone

EXCLUDES *silicone used in medical devices, implants and grafts (996.00-996.79)*

989.84 Tobacco

989.89 Other

989.9 Unspecified substance, chiefly nonmedicinal as to source

OTHER AND UNSPECIFIED EFFECTS OF EXTERNAL CAUSES (990-995)

990 Effects of radiation, unspecified
Complication of:
phototherapy
radiation therapy
Radiation sickness

EXCLUDES *specified adverse effects of radiation. Such conditions are to be classified according to the nature of the adverse effect, as:*
burns (940.0-949.5)
dermatitis (692.7-692.8)
leukemia (204.0-208.9)
pneumonia (508.0)
sunburn (692.71, 692.76-692.77)
[The type of radiation giving rise to the adverse effect may be identified by use of the E codes.]

✓4th **991 Effects of reduced temperature**

991.0 Frostbite of face

991.1 Frostbite of hand

991.2 Frostbite of foot

991.3 Frostbite of other and unspecified sites

991.4 Immersion foot
Trench foot

DEF: Paresthesia, edema, blotchy cyanosis of foot, the skin is soft (macerated), pale and wrinkled, and the sole is swollen with surface ridging and following sustained immersion in water.

991.5 Chilblains
Erythema pernio
Perniosis

DEF: Red, swollen, itchy skin; follows damp cold exposure; also associated with pruritus and a burning feeling, in hands, feet, ears, and face in children, legs and toes in women, and hands and fingers in men.

991.6 **Hypothermia**
Hypothermia (accidental)
EXCLUDES *hypothermia following anesthesia (995.89)*
hypothermia not associated with low environmental temperature (780.99)
DEF: Reduced body temperature due to low environmental temperatures.

991.8 **Other specified effects of reduced temperature**

991.9 **Unspecified effect of reduced temperature**
Effects of freezing or excessive cold NOS

✓4th **992 Effects of heat and light**
EXCLUDES *burns (940.0-949.5)*
diseases of sweat glands due to heat (705.0-705.9)
malignant hyperpyrexia following anesthesia (995.86)
sunburn (692.71, 692.76-692.77)

992.0 **Heat stroke and sunstroke**
Heat apoplexy
Heat pyrexia
Ictus solaris
Siriasis
Thermoplegia
DEF: Headache, vertigo, cramps and elevated body temperature due to high environmental temperatures.

992.1 **Heat syncope**
Heat collapse

992.2 **Heat cramps**

992.3 **Heat exhaustion, anhydrotic**
Heat prostration due to water depletion
EXCLUDES *that associated with salt depletion (992.4)*

992.4 **Heat exhaustion due to salt depletion**
Heat prostration due to salt (and water) depletion

992.5 **Heat exhaustion, unspecified**
Heat prostration NOS

992.6 **Heat fatigue, transient**

992.7 **Heat edema**
DEF: Fluid retention due to high environmental temperatures.

992.8 **Other specified heat effects**

992.9 **Unspecified**

✓4th **993 Effects of air pressure**

993.0 **Barotrauma, otitic**
Aero-otitis media
Effects of high altitude on ears
DEF: Ringing ears, deafness, pain and vertigo due to air pressure changes.

993.1 **Barotrauma, sinus**
Aerosinusitis
Effects of high altitude on sinuses

993.2 **Other and unspecified effects of high altitude**
Alpine sickness
Andes disease
Anoxia due to high altitude
Hypobaropathy
Mountain sickness
AHA: 3Q, '88, 4

993.3 **Caisson disease**
Bends
Compressed-air disease
Decompression sickness
Divers' palsy or paralysis
DEF: Rapid reduction in air pressure while breathing compressed air; symptoms include skin lesions, joint pains, respiratory and neurological problems.

993.4 **Effects of air pressure caused by explosion**

993.8 **Other specified effects of air pressure**

993.9 **Unspecified effect of air pressure**

✓4th **994 Effects of other external causes**
EXCLUDES *certain adverse effects not elsewhere classified (995.0-995.8)*

994.0 **Effects of lightning**
Shock from lightning
Struck by lightning NOS
EXCLUDES *burns (940.0-949.5)*

994.1 **Drowning and nonfatal submersion**
Bathing cramp
Immersion
AHA: 3Q, '88, 4

994.2 **Effects of hunger**
Deprivation of food
Starvation

994.3 **Effects of thirst**
Deprivation of water

994.4 **Exhaustion due to exposure**

994.5 **Exhaustion due to excessive exertion**
Overexertion

994.6 **Motion sickness**
Air sickness
Seasickness
Travel sickness

994.7 **Asphyxiation and strangulation**
Suffocation (by):
- bedclothes
- cave-in
- constriction
- mechanical
- plastic bag
- pressure
- strangulation

EXCLUDES *asphyxia from:*
carbon monoxide (986)
inhalation of food or foreign body (932-934.9)
other gases, fumes, and vapors (987.0-987.9)

994.8 **Electrocution and nonfatal effects of electric current**
Shock from electric current
EXCLUDES *electric burns (940.0-949.5)*

994.9 **Other effects of external causes**
Effects of:
- abnormal gravitational [G] forces or states
- weightlessness

✓4th **995 Certain adverse effects not elsewhere classified**
EXCLUDES *complications of surgical and medical care (996.0-999.9)*

995.0 **Other anaphylactic shock**
Allergic shock
Anaphylactic reaction
Anaphylaxis
} NOS or due to adverse effect of correct medicinal substance properly administered

Use additional E code to identify external cause, such as:
adverse effects of correct medicinal substance properly administered [E930-E949]
EXCLUDES *anaphylactic reaction to serum (999.4)*
anaphylactic shock due to adverse food reaction (995.60-995.69)
AHA: 4Q, '93, 30
DEF: Immediate sensitivity response after exposure to specific antigen; results in life-threatening respiratory distress; usually followed by vascular collapse, shock , urticaria, angioedema and pruritus.

995.1 **Angioneurotic edema**
Giant urticaria
EXCLUDES *urticaria:*
due to serum (999.5)
other specified (698.2, 708.0-708.9, 757.33)
DEF: Circulatory response of deep dermis, subcutaneous or submucosal tissues; causes localized edema and wheals.

▲ ✓5th **995.2 Other and unspecified adverse effect of drug, medicinal and biological substance**

Adverse effect, Allergic reaction, Hypersensitivity, Idiosyncrasy } (due) to correct medicinal substance properly administered

Drug: hypersensitivity NOS
Drug: reaction NOS

EXCLUDES *pathological drug intoxication (292.2)*

AHA: 2Q, '97, 12; 3Q, '95, 13; 3Q, '92, 16

● **995.20 Unspecified adverse effect of unspecified drug, medicinal and biological substance**

● **995.21 Arthus phenomenon**
Arthus reaction

● **995.22 Unspecified adverse effect of anesthesia**

● **995.23 Unspecified adverse effect of insulin**

● **995.27 Other drug allergy**
Drug allergy NOS
Drug hypersensitivity NOS

● **995.29 Unspecified adverse effect of other drug, medicinal and biological substance**

995.3 Allergy, unspecified
Allergic reaction NOS
Hypersensitivity NOS
Idiosyncrasy NOS

EXCLUDES *allergic reaction NOS to correct medicinal substance properly administered ▶(995.27)◀*
▶allergy to existing dental restorative materials (525.66)◀
specific types of allergic reaction, such as:
allergic diarrhea (558.3)
dermatitis (691.0-693.9)
hayfever (477.0-477.9)

995.4 Shock due to anesthesia CC
Shock due to anesthesia in which the correct substance was properly administered

EXCLUDES *complications of anesthesia in labor or delivery (668.0-668.9)*
overdose or wrong substance given (968.0-969.9)
postoperative shock NOS (998.0)
specified adverse effects of anesthesia classified elsewhere, such as:
anoxic brain damage (348.1)
hepatitis (070.0-070.9), etc.
unspecified adverse effect of anesthesia ▶(995.22)◀

CC Excl: 958.4, 995.4, 997.91-998.13, 998.81, 998.83-998.9

✓5th **995.5 Child maltreatment syndrome**
Use additional code(s), if applicable, to identify any associated injuries
Use additional E code to identify:
nature of abuse (E960-E968)
perpetrator (E967.0-E967.9)

AHA: 1Q, '98, 11

995.50 Child abuse, unspecified P

995.51 Child emotional/psychological abuse P
AHA: 4Q, '96, 38, 40

995.52 Child neglect (nutritional) P
AHA: 4Q, '96, 38, 40

995.53 Child sexual abuse P
AHA: 4Q, '96, 39, 40

995.54 Child physical abuse P
Battered baby or child syndrome
EXCLUDES *shaken infant syndrome (995.55)*
AHA: 3Q, '99, 14; 4Q, '96, 39, 40

995.55 Shaken infant syndrome P
Use additional code(s) to identify any associated injuries
AHA: 4Q, '96, 40, 43

995.59 Other child abuse and neglect P
Multiple forms of abuse

✓5th **995.6 Anaphylactic shock due to adverse food reaction**
Anaphylactic shock due to nonpoisonous foods
AHA: 4Q, '93, 30

995.60 Due to unspecified food
995.61 Due to peanuts
995.62 Due to crustaceans
995.63 Due to fruits and vegetables
995.64 Due to tree nuts and seeds
995.65 Due to fish
995.66 Due to food additives
995.67 Due to milk products
995.68 Due to eggs
995.69 Due to other specified food

995.7 Other adverse food reactions, not elsewhere classified
Use additional code to identify the type of reaction, such as:
hives (708.0)
wheezing (786.07)

EXCLUDES *anaphylactic shock due to adverse food reaction (995.60-995.69)*
asthma (493.0, 493.9)
dermatitis due to food (693.1)
in contact with skin (692.5)
gastroenteritis and colitis due to food (558.3)
rhinitis due to food (477.1)

✓5th **995.8 Other specified adverse effects, not elsewhere classified**

995.80 Adult maltreatment, unspecified A
Abused person NOS
Use additional code to identify:
any associated injury
perpetrator (E967.0-E967.9)
AHA: 4Q, '96, 41, 43

995.81 Adult physical abuse A
Battered: person syndrome NEC, man
Battered: spouse, woman
Use additional code to identify:
any association injury
nature of abuse (E960-E968)
perpetrator (E967.0-E967.9)
AHA: 4Q, '96, 42, 43

995.82 Adult emotional/psychological abuse A
Use additional E code to identify perpetrator (E967.0-E967.9)

995.83 Adult sexual abuse A
Use additional code(s) to identify:
any associated injury
perpetrator (E967.0-E967.9)

995.84 Adult neglect (nutritional) A
Use addition code(s) to identify:
intent of neglect (E904.0, E968.4)
perpetrator (E967.0-E967.9)

995.85 Other adult abuse and neglect A
Multiple forms of abuse and neglect
Use additional code(s) to identify
any associated injury
intent of neglect (E904.0, E968.4)
nature of abuse (E960-E968)
perpetrator (E967.0-E967.9)

995.86 Malignant hyperthermia CC
Malignant hyperpyrexia due to anesthesia
CC Excl: 958.4, 995.4, 995.86, 997.91-998.13, 998.81, 998.83-998.9
AHA: 4Q, '98, 51

995.89 Other
Hypothermia due to anesthesia
AHA: 2Q, '04, 18; 3Q, '03, 12

Injury and Poisoning 995.2–995.89

✓4th ✓5th Additional Digit Required | Nonspecific PDx | Unacceptable PDx | Manifestation Code | MCV Major Cardiovascular Condition | ▶◀ Revised Text | ● New Code | ▲ Revised Code Title

Continuum of Illness Due to Infection

Bacteremia → Septicemia → Sepsis → Severe Sepsis → Severe Sepsis with Septic Shock → MODS (Multiple Organ Dysfunction Syndrome) → Death

✓5th **995.9 Systemic inflammatory response syndrome (SIRS)**

AHA: 2Q, '04, 16; 4Q, '02, 71

DEF: Clinical response to infection or trauma that can trigger an acute inflammatory reaction and progresses to coagulation, impaired fibrinolysis, and organ failure; manifested by two or more of the following symptoms: fever, tachycardia, tachypnea, leukocytosis or leukopenia.

995.90 Systemic inflammatory response syndrome, unspecified CC

SIRS NOS

CC Excl: 003.1, 020.2, 036.2, 038.0-038.9, 040.82-041.9, 054.5, 139.8, 995.90-995.94, V09.0-V09.91

▲ **995.91 Sepsis** CC

▶Systemic inflammatory response syndrome due to infectious process without acute organ dysfunction◀

▶Code first underlying infection◀

EXCLUDES ▶ *sepsis with acute organ dysfunction (995.92)*
sepsis with multiple organ dysfunction (995.92)
severe sepsis (995.92)◀

CC Excl: See code 995.90

AHA: 2Q, '04, 16; 4Q, '03, 79

▲ **995.92 Severe sepsis** CC

▶Sepsis with acute organ dysfunction
Sepsis with multiple organ dysfunction (MOD)
Systemic inflammatory response syndrome due to infectious process with acute organ dysfunction
Code first underlying infection◀
Use additional code to specify ▶acute◀ organ dysfunction, such as:
acute renal failure (584.5-584.9)
acute respiratory failure (518.81)
critical illness myopathy (359.81)
critical illness polyneuropathy (357.82)
▶disseminated intravascular coagulopathy [DIC] (286.6)◀
encephalopathy (348.31)
hepatic failure (570)
septic shock (785.52)

CC Excl: See code 995.90

AHA: 2Q, '05, 18-19; 1Q, '05, 7; 1Q, '05, 7; 2Q, '04, 16; 4Q, '03, 73, 79

▲ **995.93 Systemic inflammatory response syndrome due to noninfectious process without acute organ dysfunction** CC

▶Code first underlying conditions, such as:
acute pancreatitis (577.0)
trauma◀

EXCLUDES ▶ *systemic inflammatory response syndrome due to noninfectious process with acute organ dysfunction (995.94)*◀

CC Excl: See code 995.90

▲ **995.94 Systemic inflammatory response syndrome due to noninfectious process with acute organ dysfunction** CC

▶Code first underlying conditions, such as:
acute pancreatitis (577.0)
trauma◀
Use additional code to specify ▶acute◀ organ dysfunction, such as:
acute renal failure (584.5-584.9)
acute respiratory failure (518.81)
critical illness myopathy (359.81)
critical illness polyneuropathy (357.82)
▶disseminated intravascular coagulopathy [DIC] syndrome (286.6)◀
encephalopathy (348.31)
hepatic failure (570)

EXCLUDES ▶ *severe sepsis (995.92)*◀

CC Excl: See code 995.90

AHA: 4Q, '03, 79

COMPLICATIONS OF SURGICAL AND MEDICAL CARE, NOT ELSEWHERE CLASSIFIED (996-999)

EXCLUDES *adverse effects of medicinal agents (001.0-799.9, 995.0-995.8)*
burns from local applications and irradiation (940.0-949.5)
complications of:
conditions for which the procedure was performed
surgical procedures during abortion, labor, and delivery (630-676.9)
poisoning and toxic effects of drugs and chemicals (960.0-989.9)
postoperative conditions in which no complications are present, such as:
artificial opening status (V44.0-V44.9)
closure of external stoma (V55.0-V55.9)
fitting of prosthetic device (V52.0-V52.9)
specified complications classified elsewhere
anesthetic shock (995.4)
electrolyte imbalance (276.0-276.9)
postlaminectomy syndrome (722.80-722.83)
postmastectomy lymphedema syndrome (457.0)
postoperative psychosis (293.0-293.9)
any other condition classified elsewhere in the Alphabetic Index when described as due to a procedure

✓4th **996 Complications peculiar to certain specified procedures**

INCLUDES complications, not elsewhere classified, in the use of artificial substitutes [e.g., Dacron, metal, Silastic, Teflon] or natural sources [e.g., bone] involving:
anastomosis (internal)
graft (bypass) (patch)
implant
internal device:
catheter
electronic
fixation
prosthetic
reimplant
transplant

EXCLUDES *accidental puncture or laceration during procedure (998.2)*
complications of internal anastomosis of:
gastrointestinal tract (997.4)
urinary tract (997.5)
mechanical complication of respirator (V46.14)
other specified complications classified elsewhere, such as:
hemolytic anemia (283.1)
functional cardiac disturbances (429.4)
serum hepatitis (070.2-070.3)

AHA: 1Q, '94, 3

✓5th **996.0 Mechanical complication of cardiac device, implant, and graft**

Breakdown (mechanical)
Displacement
Leakage
Obstruction, mechanical
Perforation
Protrusion

AHA: 2Q, '93, 9

996.00 Unspecified device, implant, and graft CC
CC Excl: 996.00, 996.04, 996.61-996.62, 996.70-996.74, 997.91, 997.99, 998.81, 998.83-998.9

996.01 Due to cardiac pacemaker (electrode) CC
CC Excl: 996.01, 997.91, 997.99, 998.81, 998.83-998.9
AHA: 2Q, '99, 11

996.02 Due to heart valve prosthesis CC
CC Excl: 996.02, 997.91, 997.99, 998.81, 998.83-998.9

996.03 Due to coronary bypass graft CC
EXCLUDES *atherosclerosis of graft (414.02, 414.03)*
embolism [occlusion NOS] [thrombus] of graft (996.72)
CC Excl: 996.03, 997.91, 997.99, 998.81, 998.83-998.9
AHA: 2Q, '95, 17; N-D, '86, 5

996.04 Due to automatic implantable cardiac defibrillator CC
CC Excl: 996.04, 997.91, 997.99, 998.81, 998.83-998.9
AHA: 2Q, '05, 3

996.09 Other CC
CC Excl: 996.09, 997.91, 997.99, 998.81, 998.83-998.9
AHA: 2Q, '93, 9

996.1 Mechanical complication of other vascular device, implant, and graft CC
Mechanical complications involving:
aortic (bifurcation) graft (replacement)
arteriovenous:
dialysis catheter, fistula, shunt } surgically created
balloon (counterpulsation) device, intra-aortic
carotid artery bypass graft
femoral-popliteal bypass graft
umbrella device, vena cava
EXCLUDES *atherosclerosis of biological graft (440.30-440.32)*
embolism [occlusion NOS] [thrombus] of (biological) (synthetic) graft (996.74)
peritoneal dialysis catheter (996.56)
CC Excl: 996.1, 997.91, 997.99, 998.81, 998.83-998.9
AHA: ▶1Q, '06, 10;◀ 2Q, '05, 8; 1Q, '02, 13; 1Q, '95, 3

996.2 Mechanical complication of nervous system device, implant, and graft CC
Mechanical complications involving:
dorsal column stimulator
electrodes implanted in brain [brain "pacemaker"]
peripheral nerve graft
ventricular (communicating) shunt
CC Excl: 996.2, 996.63, 996.75, 997.91, 997.99, 998.81, 998.83-998.9
AHA: 2Q, '99, 4; S-O, '87, 10

✓5th **996.3 Mechanical complication of genitourinary device, implant, and graft**
AHA: 3Q, '01, 13; S-O, '85, 3

996.30 Unspecified device, implant, and graft CC
CC Excl: 996.30, 996.64-996.65, 996.76, 997.91, 997.99, 998.81, 998.83-998.9

996.31 Due to urethral [indwelling] catheter

996.32 Due to intrauterine contraceptive device ♀

996.39 Other CC
Cystostomy catheter
Prosthetic reconstruction of vas deferens
Repair (graft) of ureter without mention of resection
EXCLUDES *complications due to:*
external stoma of urinary tract (997.5)
internal anastomosis of urinary tract (997.5)
CC Excl: 996.39, 996.64-996.65, 996.76, 997.91, 997.99, 998.81, 998.83-998.9

✓5th **996.4 Mechanical complication of internal orthopedic device, implant, and graft**
Mechanical complications involving:
external (fixation) device utilizing internal screw(s), pin(s) or other methods of fixation
grafts of bone, cartilage, muscle, or tendon
internal (fixation) device such as nail, plate, rod, etc.
Use additional code to identify prosthetic joint with mechanical complication (V43.60-V43.69)
EXCLUDES *complications of external orthopedic device, such as:*
pressure ulcer due to cast (707.00-707.09)
AHA: 4Q, '05, 91; 2Q, '99, 10; 2Q, '98, 19; 2Q, '96, 11; 3Q, '95, 16; N-D, '85, 11

996.40 Unspecified mechanical complication of internal orthopedic device, implant, and graft CC
CC Excl: 996.40-996.49, 996.66-996.67, 996.77-996.78, 997.91-997.99, 998.81, 991.83-998.9

996.41 Mechanical loosening of prosthetic joint CC
Aseptic loosening
CC Excl: See code 996.40
AHA: 4Q, '05, 112

996.42 Dislocation of prosthetic joint CC
Instability of prosthetic joint
Subluxation of prosthetic joint
CC Excl: See code 996.40

996.43 Prosthetic joint implant failure CC
Breakage (fracture) of prosthetic joint
CC Excl: See code 996.40

996.44 Peri-prosthetic fracture around prosthetic joint CC
CC Excl: See code 996.40
AHA: 4Q, '05, 93

996.45 Peri-prosthetic osteolysis CC
▶Use additional code to identify major osseous defect, if applicable (731.3)◀
CC Excl: See code 996.40

996.46 Articular bearing surface wear of prosthetic joint CC
CC Excl: See code 996.40

996.47 Other mechanical complication of prosthetic joint implant CC
Mechanical complication of prosthetic joint NOS
CC Excl: See code 996.40

996.49 Other mechanical complication of other internal orthopedic device, implant, and graft CC
EXCLUDES *mechanical complication of prosthetic joint implant (996.41-996.47)*
CC Excl: See code 996.40

✓5th **996.5 Mechanical complication of other specified prosthetic device, implant, and graft**
Mechanical complications involving:
prosthetic implant in:
bile duct, breast, chin, orbit of eye
nonabsorbable surgical material NOS
other graft, implant, and internal device, not elsewhere classified
AHA: 1Q, '98, 11

996.51 Due to corneal graft CC
CC Excl: 996.51, 997.91, 997.99

Injury and Poisoning — 996.00–996.51

✓4th ✓5th Additional Digit Required | Nonspecific PDx | Unacceptable PDx | Manifestation Code | MCV Major Cardiovascular Condition | ▶◀ Revised Text | ● New Code | ▲ Revised Code Title

996.52 Due to graft of other tissue, not elsewhere classified CC
Skin graft failure or rejection
EXCLUDES *failure of artificial skin graft (996.55)*
failure of decellularized allodermis (996.55)
sloughing of temporary skin allografts or xenografts (pigskin)—omit code
CC Excl: 996.52, 996.55, 997.91, 997.99
AHA: 1Q, '96, 10

996.53 Due to ocular lens prosthesis CC
EXCLUDES *contact lenses—code to condition*
CC Excl: 996.53, 997.91, 997.99
AHA: 1Q, '00, 9

996.54 Due to breast prosthesis CC
Breast capsule (prosthesis)
Mammary implant
CC Excl: 996.54, 997.91, 997.99
AHA: 2Q, '98, 14; 3Q, '92, 4

996.55 Due to artificial skin graft and decellularized allodermis CC
Dislodgement
Displacement
Failure
Non-adherence
Poor incorporation
Shearing
CC Excl: 996.52, 996.55-996.60, 996.68-996.69, 996.70, 996.79, 997.91, 997.99
AHA: 4Q, '98, 52

996.56 Due to peritoneal dialysis catheter CC
EXCLUDES *mechanical complication of arteriovenous dialysis catheter (996.1)*
CC Excl: 996.56-996.60, 996.68-996.70, 996.79, 997.91, 997.99
AHA: 4Q, '98, 54

996.57 Due to insulin pump CC
CC Excl: 996.00-996.30, 996.39-996.79, 997.91-997.99, 998.81, 998.83-998.9
AHA: 4Q, '03, 81-82

996.59 Due to other implant and internal device, not elsewhere classified CC
Nonabsorbable surgical material NOS
Prosthetic implant in:
bile duct
chin
orbit of eye
CC Excl: 996.59-996.60, 996.68-996.70, 996.79, 997.91-997.99
AHA: 2Q, '99, 13; 3Q, '94, 7

✓5th **996.6 Infection and inflammatory reaction due to internal prosthetic device, implant, and graft**
Infection (causing obstruction) } due to (presence of) any device, implant, and graft classifiable to 996.0-996.5
Inflammation }
Use additional code to identify specified infections
AHA: 2Q, '89, 16; J-F, '87, 14

996.60 Due to unspecified device, implant, and graft CC
CC Excl: 996.00-996.30, 996.39, 996.4-996.79, 997.91-997.99, 998.81, 998.83-998.9

996.61 Due to cardiac device, implant, and graft CC MCV
Cardiac pacemaker or defibrillator:
electrode(s), lead(s)
pulse generator
subcutaneous pocket
Coronary artery bypass graft
Heart valve prosthesis
CC Excl: 996.00-996.1, 996.52, 996.55-996.62, 996.68-996.74, 996.79, 997.91, 997.99, 998.81, 998.83-998.9

996.62 Due to other vascular device, implant, and graft CC MC MCV
Arterial graft
Arteriovenous fistula or shunt
Infusion pump
Vascular catheter (arterial) (dialysis) (venous)
CC Excl: See code 996.61
AHA: 2Q, '04, 16; 1Q, '04, 5; 4Q, '03, 107, 111; 2Q, '03, 7; 2Q, '94, 13

996.63 Due to nervous system device, implant, and graft CC
Electrodes implanted in brain
Peripheral nerve graft
Spinal canal catheter
Ventricular (communicating) shunt (catheter)
CC Excl: 996.2, 996.52, 996.55-996.60, 996.63, 996.68-996.70, 996.75, 996.79, 997.91, 997.99, 998.81, 998.83-998.9

996.64 Due to indwelling urinary catheter CC
Use additional code to identify specified infections, such as:
Cystitis (595.0-595.9)
Sepsis (038.0-038.9)
CC Excl: 599.0, 996.30, 996.39, 996.56-996.60, 996.64-996.65, 996.68-996.70, 996.76, 996.79, 997.91, 997.99, 998.81, 998.83-998.9
AHA: 3Q, '93, 6
DRG 331

996.65 Due to other genitourinary device, implant, and graft CC
Intrauterine contraceptive device
CC Excl: 996.30, 996.39, 996.52, 996.55-996.60, 996.64-996.65, 996.68-996.70, 996.76, 996.79, 997.91, 997.99, 998.81, 998.83-998.9
AHA: 1Q, '00, 15

996.66 Due to internal joint prosthesis CC
Use additional code to identify infected prosthetic joint (V43.60-V43.69)
CC Excl: 996.40-996.49, 996.52, 996.55-996.60, 996.66-996.70, 996.77-996.79, 997.91-997.99, 998.81, 998.83-998.9
AHA: 4Q, '05, 91, 113; 2Q, '91, 18

996.67 Due to other internal orthopedic device, implant, and graft CC
Bone growth stimulator (electrode)
Internal fixation device (pin) (rod) (screw)
CC Excl: See code 996.66

996.68 Due to peritoneal dialysis catheter CC
Exit-site infection or inflammation
CC Excl: 996.56-996.60, 996.68-996.70, 996.79, 997.91, 997.99
AHA: 4Q, '98, 54

996.69 Due to other internal prosthetic device, implant, and graft CC
Breast prosthesis
Ocular lens prosthesis
Prosthetic orbital implant
CC Excl: 996.00-996.30, 996.39-996.79, 997.91-997.99, 998.81, 998.83-998.9
AHA: 4Q, '03, 108; 4Q, '98, 52

✓5th **996.7 Other complications of internal (biological) (synthetic) prosthetic device, implant, and graft**
Complication NOS
occlusion NOS
Embolism
Fibrosis
Hemorrhage
Pain
Stenosis
Thrombus
} due to (presence of) any device, implant, and graft classifiable to 996.0-996.5
▶Use additional code to identify complication, such as:
pain due to presence of device, implant or graft (338.18-338.19, 338.28-338.29)◀
EXCLUDES *transplant rejection (996.8)*
AHA: 4Q, '05, 94; 1Q, '89, 9; N-D, '86, 5

996.70 Due to unspecified device, implant, and graft CC
CC Excl: See code 996.69

996.71 Due to heart valve prosthesis CC
CC Excl: 996.00, 996.02, 996.09, 996.1, 996.52, 996.55-996.62, 996.68-996.74, 996.79, 997.91-997.99, 998.81, 998.83-998.9

996.72 Due to other cardiac device, implant, and graft CC MC MCV
Cardiac pacemaker or defibrillator:
electrode(s), lead(s)
subcutaneous pocket
Coronary artery bypass (graft)
EXCLUDES *occlusion due to atherosclerosis (414.02-414.06)*
CC Excl: 996.00-996.02, 996.04, 996.09, 996.1, 996.52, 996.55-996.62, 996.68-996.74, 996.79, 997.91-997.99, 998.81, 998.83-998.9
AHA: 3Q, '01, 20

996.73 Due to renal dialysis device, implant, and graft CC
CC Excl: 996.1, 996.52, 996.55-996.60, 996.68-996.70, 996.73, 996.79, 997.91, 997.99, 998.81, 998.83-998.9
AHA: 2Q, '91, 18

996.74 Due to other vascular device, implant, and graft CC
EXCLUDES *occlusion of biological graft due to atherosclerosis (440.30-440.32)*
CC Excl: See code 996.71
AHA: 1Q, '03, 16, 17

996.75 Due to nervous system device, implant, and graft CC
CC Excl: 996.2, 996.52, 996.55-996.60, 996.63, 996.68-996.70, 996.75, 996.79, 997.91, 997.99, 998.81, 998.83-998.9

996.76 Due to genitourinary device, implant, and graft CC
CC Excl: 996.30, 996.39, 996.52, 996.55-996.60, 996.64-996.65, 996.68-996.70, 996.76, 996.79, 997.91, 997.99, 998.81, 998.83-998.9
AHA: 1Q, '00, 15

996.77 Due to internal joint prosthesis CC
CC Excl: 996.40-996.49, 996.52, 996.55-996.60, 996.66-996.67, 996.69-996.70, 996.77-996.79, 997.91-997.99, 998.81, 998.83-998.9
AHA: 4Q, '05, 91

996.78 Due to other internal orthopedic device, implant, and graft CC
CC Excl: See code 996.77
AHA: 2Q, '03, 14

996.79 Due to other internal prosthetic device, implant, and graft CC
CC Excl: 996.00-996.30, 996.39, 996.4-996.79, 997.91, 997.99, 998.81, 998.83-998.9
AHA: 2Q, '04, 7; 1Q,'01, 8; 3Q, '95, 14; 3Q, '92, 4

5th **996.8 Complications of transplanted organ**
Transplant failure or rejection
Use additional code to identify nature of complication, such as:
Cytomegalovirus (CMV) infection (078.5)
AHA: 3Q, '01, 12; 3Q, '93, 3, 4; 2Q, '93, 11; 1Q, '93, 24

996.80 Transplanted organ, unspecified CC
CC Excl: 996.80, 996.87, 997.91, 997.99

996.81 Kidney CC
CC Excl: 996.81, 997.91, 997.99
AHA: 3Q, '03, 16; 3Q, '98, 6, 7; 3Q, '94, 8; 2Q, '94, 9; 1Q, '93, 24
DRG 331

996.82 Liver CC
CC Excl: 996.82, 997.91, 997.99
AHA: 3Q, '03, 17; 3Q, '98, 3, 4

996.83 Heart CC MCV
CC Excl: 996.83, 997.91, 997.99
AHA: 3Q, '03, 16; 4Q, '02, 53; 3Q, '98, 5

996.84 Lung CC
CC Excl: 996.84, 997.91, 997.99
AHA: 2Q, '03, 12; 3Q, '98, 5

996.85 Bone marrow CC
Graft-versus-host disease (acute) (chronic)
CC Excl: 996.85, 997.91, 997.99
AHA: 4Q, '90, 4

996.86 Pancreas CC
CC Excl: 996.86, 997.91, 997.99

996.87 Intestine CC
CC Excl: 996.80, 996.87, 997.91, 997.99

996.89 Other specified transplanted organ CC
CC Excl: 996.89, 997.91, 997.99
AHA: 3Q, '94, 5

5th **996.9 Complications of reattached extremity or body part**

996.90 Unspecified extremity CC
CC Excl: 996.90, 997.91, 997.99, 998.81, 998.83-998.9

996.91 Forearm CC
CC Excl: 996.91, 997.91, 997.99, 998.81, 998.83-998.9

996.92 Hand CC
CC Excl: 996.92, 997.91, 997.99, 998.81, 998.83-998.9

996.93 Finger(s) CC
CC Excl: 996.93, 997.91, 997.99, 998.81, 998.83-998.9

996.94 Upper extremity, other and unspecified CC
CC Excl: 996.94, 997.91, 997.99, 998.81, 998.83-998.9

996.95 Foot and toe(s) CC
CC Excl: 996.95, 997.91, 997.99, 998.81, 998.83-998.9

996.96 Lower extremity, other and unspecified CC
CC Excl: 996.96, 997.91, 997.99, 998.81, 998.83-998.9

996.99 Other specified body part CC
CC Excl: 996.99, 997.91, 997.99, 998.81, 998.83-998.9

4th **997 Complications affecting specified body systems, not elsewhere classified**
Use additional code to identify complications
EXCLUDES *the listed conditions when specified as:*
causing shock (998.0)
complications of:
anesthesia:
adverse effect (001.0-799.9, 995.0-995.8)
in labor or delivery (668.0-668.9)
poisoning (968.0-969.9)
implanted device or graft (996.0-996.9)
obstetrical procedures (669.0-669.4)
reattached extremity (996.90-996.96)
transplanted organ (996.80-996.89)
AHA: 1Q, '94, 4; 1Q, '93, 26

5th **997.0 Nervous system complications**
CC Excl: For codes 997.00-997.09: 997.00-997.09, 997.91, 997.99, 998.81, 998.83, 998.89, 998.9

997.00 Nervous system complication, unspecified CC

997.01 Central nervous system complication CC
Anoxic brain damage
Cerebral hypoxia
EXCLUDES *cerebrovascular hemorrhage or infarction (997.02)*
AHA: ▶1Q, '06, 15◀

997.02 Iatrogenic cerebrovascular infarction or hemorrhage CC
Postoperative stroke
AHA: 2Q, '04, 8; 4Q, '95, 57

997.09 Other nervous system complications CC

4th 5th Additional Digit Required · Nonspecific PDx · Unacceptable PDx · Manifestation Code · MCV Major Cardiovascular Condition · ▶◀ Revised Text · ● New Code · ▲ Revised Code Title

997.1 Cardiac complications CC

Cardiac:
  arrest
  insufficiency
Cardiorespiratory failure
Heart failure
} during or resulting from a procedure

EXCLUDES *the listed conditions as long-term effects of cardiac surgery or due to the presence of cardiac prosthetic device (429.4)*

CC Excl: 997.1, 997.91, 997.99, 998.81, 998.83-998.9

AHA: 2Q, '02, 12

997.2 Peripheral vascular complications CC

Phlebitis or thrombophlebitis during or resulting from a procedure

EXCLUDES *the listed conditions due to:*
implant or catheter device (996.62)
infusion, perfusion, or transfusion (999.2)
complications affecting blood vessels (997.71-997.79)

CC Excl: 997.2, 997.79, 997.91, 997.99, 998.81, 998.83-998.9

AHA: 1Q, '03, 6; 3Q, '02, 24-26

997.3 Respiratory complications CC

Mendelson's syndrome
Pneumonia (aspiration)
} resulting from a procedure

EXCLUDES *iatrogenic [postoperative] pneumothorax (512.1)*
iatrogenic pulmonary embolism (415.11)
Mendelson's syndrome in labor and delivery (668.0)
specified complications classified elsewhere, such as:
adult respiratory distress syndrome (518.5)
pulmonary edema, postoperative (518.4)
respiratory insufficiency, acute, postoperative (518.5)
shock lung (518.5)
tracheostomy complications (519.00-519.09)
▶*transfusion related acute lung injury [TRALI] (518.7)*◀

CC Excl: 518.7, 997.3, 997.91, 997.99, 998.81, 998.83, 998.83-998.9

AHA: 1Q, '97, 10; 2Q, '93, 3; 2Q, '93, 9; 4Q, '90, 25

DEF: Mendelson's syndrome: acid pneumonitis due to aspiration of gastric acids, may occur after anesthesia or sedation.

997.4 Digestive system complications CC

Complications of:
  intestinal (internal) anastomosis and bypass, not elsewhere classified, except that involving urinary tract
Hepatic failure
Hepatorenal syndrome
Intestinal obstruction NOS
} specified as due to a procedure

EXCLUDES *gastrostomy complications (536.40-536.49)*
specified gastrointestinal complications classified elsewhere, such as:
blind loop syndrome (579.2)
colostomy and enterostomy complications (569.60-569.69)
gastrojejunal ulcer (534.0-534.9)
infection of esophagostomy (530.86)
infection of external stoma (569.61)
mechanical complication of esophagostomy (530.87)
pelvic peritoneal adhesions, female (614.6)
peritoneal adhesions (568.0)
peritoneal adhesions with obstruction (560.81)
postcholecystectomy syndrome (576.0)
postgastric surgery syndromes (564.2)
vomiting following gastrointestinal surgery (564.3)

CC Excl: 530.86-530.87, 536.40-536.49, 997.4, 997.71, 997.91-997.99, 998.81, 998.83-998.9

AHA: 2Q, '01, 4-6; 3Q, '99, 4; 2Q, '99, 14; 3Q, '97, 7; 1Q, '97, 11; 2Q, '95, 7; 1Q, '93, 26; 3Q, '92, 15; 2Q, '89, 15; 1Q, '88, 14

DRG 188

997.5 Urinary complications CC

Complications of:
  external stoma of urinary tract
  internal anastomosis and bypass of urinary tract, including that involving intestinal tract
Oliguria or anuria
Renal:
  failure (acute)
  insufficiency (acute)
Tubular necrosis (acute)
} specified as due to procedure

EXCLUDES *specified complications classified elsewhere, such as:*
postoperative stricture of:
ureter (593.3)
urethra (598.2)

CC Excl: 997.5, 997.72, 997.91, 997.99, 998.81, 998.83-998.9

AHA: 3Q, '03, 13; 3Q, '96, 10, 15; 4Q, '95, 73; 1Q, '92, 13; 2Q, '89, 16; M-A, '87, 10; S-O, '85, 3

DRG 331

✓5th **997.6 Amputation stump complication**

EXCLUDES *admission for treatment for a current traumatic amputation — code to complicated traumatic amputation*
phantom limb (syndrome) (353.6)

AHA: 4Q, '95, 82

997.60 Unspecified complication

997.61 Neuroma of amputation stump

DEF: Hyperplasia generated nerve cell mass following amputation.

997.62 Infection (chronic) CC

Use additional code to identify the organism

CC Excl: 997.60, 997.62, 997.69, 997.91, 997.99, 998.81, 998.83-998.9

AHA: 1Q, '05, 15 4Q, '96, 46

997.69 Other

AHA: 1Q, '05, 15

✓5th **997.7 Vascular complications of other vessels**

EXCLUDES *peripheral vascular complications (997.2)*

997.71 Vascular complications of mesenteric artery CC

CC Excl: 997.2, 997.71-997.79, 997.91, 997.99, 998.81 998.83-998.9

AHA: 4Q, '01, 53

997.72 Vascular complications of renal artery CC

CC Excl: See code 997.71

997.79 Vascular complications of other vessels CC

CC Excl: See code 997.71

✓5th **997.9 Complications affecting other specified body systems, not elsewhere classified** CC

EXCLUDES *specified complications classified elsewhere, such as:*
broad ligament laceration syndrome (620.6)
postartificial menopause syndrome (627.4)
postoperative stricture of vagina (623.2)

997.91 Hypertension

EXCLUDES *essential hypertension (401.0-401.9)*

AHA: 4Q, '95, 57

997.99 Other CC

Vitreous touch syndrome

CC Excl: 997.91, 997.99, 998.81, 998.83-998.9

AHA: 2Q, '94, 12; 1Q, '94, 17

DEF: Vitreous touch syndrome: vitreous protruding through pupil and attaches to corneal epithelium; causes aqueous fluid in vitreous body; marked by corneal edema, loss of lucidity; complication of cataract surgery.

✓4th **998 Other complications of procedures, not elsewhere classified**

AHA: 1Q, '94, 4

998.0 Postoperative shock CC

Collapse NOS; Shock (endotoxic) (hypovolemic) (septic) } during or resulting from a surgical procedure

EXCLUDES *shock:*
anaphylactic due to serum (999.4)
anesthetic (995.4)
electric (994.8)
following abortion (639.5)
obstetric (669.1)
traumatic (958.4)

CC Excl: 958.4, 995.4, 997.91-998.13, 998.81, 998.83-998.9

✓5th **998.1 Hemorrhage or hematoma or seroma complicating a procedure**

EXCLUDES *hemorrhage, hematoma, or seroma:*
complicating cesarean section or puerperal perineal wound (674.3)

998.11 Hemorrhage complicating a procedure CC

CC Excl: 456.0, 456.20, 530.81-530.83, 530.89, 531.00-531.01, 531.20-531.21, 531.40-531.41, 531.60-531.61, 532.00-532.01, 532.20-532.21, 532.40-532.41, 532.60-532.61, 533.00-533.01, 533.20-533.21, 533.40-533.41, 533.60-533.61, 534.00-534.01, 534.20-534.21, 534.40-534.41, 534.60-534.61, 535.01, 535.11, 535.21, 535.31, 535.41, 535.51, 535.61, 537.83, 562.02-562.03, 562.12-562.13, 569.3, 569.85, 578.0-578.1, 578.9, 772.4, 997.91-998.13, 998.81, 998.89, 998.9

AHA: 3Q, '03, 13; 1Q, '03, 4; 4Q, '97, 52; 1Q, '97, 10

998.12 Hematoma complicating a procedure CC

CC Excl: see code 998.11

AHA: 1Q, '03, 6; 3Q, '02, 24, 26

998.13 Seroma complicating a procedure CC

CC Excl: See code 998.11

AHA: 4Q, '96, 46; 1Q, '93, 26; 2Q, '92, 15; S-O, '87, 8

998.2 Accidental puncture or laceration during a procedure CC

Accidental perforation by catheter or other instrument during a procedure on:
blood vessel
nerve
organ

EXCLUDES *iatrogenic [postoperative] pneumothorax (512.1)*
puncture or laceration caused by implanted device intentionally left in operation wound (996.0-996.5)
specified complications classified elsewhere, such as:
broad ligament laceration syndrome (620.6)
trauma from instruments during delivery (664.0-665.9)

CC Excl: 997.91, 997.99, 998.2, 998.81, 998.83-998.9

AHA: ▶1Q, '06, 15;◀ 3Q, '02, 24, 26; 3Q, '94, 6; 3Q, '90, 17; 3Q, '90, 18

✓5th **998.3 Disruption of operation wound**

Dehiscence; Rupture } of operation wound

EXCLUDES *disruption of:*
cesarean wound (674.1)
perineal wound, puerperal (674.2)

AHA: 4Q, '02, 73; 1Q, '93, 19

998.31 Disruption of internal operation wound CC

CC Excl: 997.91-997.99, 998.31, 998.32, 998.81-998.89, 998.9

998.32 Disruption of external operation wound CC

Disruption of operation wound NOS

CC Excl: See code 998.31

AHA: ▶1Q, '06, 8;◀ 1Q, '05, 11; 4Q, '03, 104, 106

998.4 Foreign body accidentally left during a procedure CC

Adhesions; Obstruction; Perforation } due to foreign body accidentally left in operative wound or body cavity during a procedure

EXCLUDES *obstruction or perforation caused by implanted device intentionally left in body (996.0-996.5)*

CC Excl: 997.91, 997.99, 998.4, 998.81, 998.83-998.9

AHA: 1Q, '89, 9

✓5th **998.5 Postoperative infection**

EXCLUDES ▶ *bleb associated endophthalmitis (379.63)*◀
infection due to:
implanted device (996.60-996.69)
infusion, perfusion, or transfusion (999.3)
postoperative obstetrical wound infection (674.3)

998.51 Infected postoperative seroma CC

Use additional code to identify organism

CC Excl: 997.91, 997.99, 998.51-998.59, 998.81, 998.83-998.9

AHA: 4Q, '96, 46

998.59 Other postoperative infection CC

Abscess: intra-abdominal; stitch; subphrenic; wound; Septicemia } postoperative

Use additional code to identify infection

CC Excl: See code 998.51

AHA: 4Q, '04, 76; 4Q, '03, 104, 106-107; 3Q, '98, 3; 3Q, '95, 5; 2Q, '95, 7; 3Q, '94, 6; 1Q, '93, 19; J-F, '87, 14

998.6 Persistent postoperative fistula CC

CC Excl: 997.91, 997.99, 998.6, 998.81, 998.83-998.9

AHA: J-F, '87, 14

998.7 Acute reaction to foreign substance accidentally left during a procedure CC
Peritonitis:
aseptic
Peritonitis:
chemical
CC Excl: 997.91, 997.99, 998.7, 998.81, 998.83-998.9

✓5th **998.8 Other specified complications of procedures, not elsewhere classified**
AHA: 4Q, '94, 46; 1Q, '89, 9

998.81 Emphysema (subcutaneous) (surgical) resulting from a procedure

998.82 Cataract fragments in eye following cataract surgery

998.83 Non-healing surgical wound CC
CC Excl: 997.91, 997.99, 998.81, 998.83, 998.89, 998.9
AHA 4Q, '96, 47

998.89 Other specified complications CC
CC Excl: See code 998.83
AHA: 3Q, '05, 16; 3Q, '99, 13; 2Q, '98, 16

998.9 Unspecified complication of procedure, not elsewhere classified CC
Postoperative complication NOS
EXCLUDES *complication NOS of obstetrical, surgery or procedure (669.4)*
CC Excl: See code 998.83
AHA: 4Q, '93, 37

✓4th **999 Complications of medical care, not elsewhere classified**
INCLUDES complications, not elsewhere classified, of:
dialysis (hemodialysis) (peritoneal) (renal)
extracorporeal circulation
hyperalimentation therapy
immunization
infusion
inhalation therapy
injection
inoculation
perfusion
transfusion
vaccination
ventilation therapy
EXCLUDES *specified complications classified elsewhere such as:*
complications of implanted device (996.0-996.9)
contact dermatitis due to drugs (692.3)
dementia dialysis (294.8)
transient (293.9)
dialysis disequilibrium syndrome (276.0-276.9)
poisoning and toxic effects of drugs and chemicals (960.0-989.9)
postvaccinal encephalitis ▶(323.51)◀
water and electrolyte imbalance (276.0-276.9)

999.0 Generalized vaccinia
DEF: Skin eruption, self-limiting; follows vaccination; due to transient viremia with virus localized in skin.

999.1 Air embolism CC
Air embolism to any site following infusion, perfusion, or transfusion
EXCLUDES *embolism specified as:*
complicating:
abortion (634-638 with .6, 639.6)
ectopic or molar pregnancy (639.6)
pregnancy, childbirth, or the puerperium (673.0)
due to implanted device (996.7)
traumatic (958.0)
CC Excl: 958.0, 999.1

999.2 Other vascular complications CC
Phlebitis / Thromboembolism / Thrombophlebitis } following infusion, perfusion, or transfusion
EXCLUDES *the listed conditions when specified as:*
due to implanted device (996.61-996.62. 996.72-996.74)
postoperative NOS (997.2, 997.71-997.79)
CC Excl: 999.2
AHA: 2Q, '97, 5

999.3 Other infection CC
Infection / Sepsis / Septicemia } following infusion, injection, transfusion, or vaccination
EXCLUDES *the listed conditions when specified as:*
due to implanted device (996.60-996.69)
postoperative NOS (998.51-998.59)
CC Excl: 999.3
AHA: 2Q, '01, 11, 12; 2Q, '97, 5; J-F, '87, 14

999.4 Anaphylactic shock due to serum CC
EXCLUDES *shock:*
allergic NOS (995.0)
anaphylactic:
NOS (995.0)
due to drugs and chemicals (995.0)
CC Excl: 999.4
DEF: Life-threatening hypersensitivity to foreign serum; causes respiratory distress, vascular collapse, and shock.

999.5 Other serum reaction CC
Intoxication by serum
Protein sickness
Serum rash
Serum sickness
Urticaria due to serum
EXCLUDES *serum hepatitis (070.2-070.3)*
CC Excl: 999.5
DEF: Serum sickness: Hypersensitivity to foreign serum; causes fever, hives, swelling, and lymphadenopathy.

999.6 ABO incompatibility reaction CC
Incompatible blood transfusion
Reaction to blood group incompatibility in infusion or transfusion
CC Excl: 999.6

999.7 Rh incompatibility reaction CC
Elevation of Rh titer
Reactions due to Rh factor in infusion or transfusion
CC Excl: 999.7

999.8 Other transfusion reaction CC
Septic shock due to transfusion
Transfusion reaction NOS
EXCLUDES *postoperative shock (998.0)*
▶transfusion related acute lung injury [TRALI] (518.7)◀
CC Excl: 999.8
AHA: 3Q, '00, 9

999.9 Other and unspecified complications of medical care, not elsewhere classified
Complications, not elsewhere classified, of:
electroshock / inhalation / ultrasound / ventilation } therapy
Unspecified misadventure of medical care
EXCLUDES *unspecified complication of:*
phototherapy (990)
radiation therapy (999)
AHA: 1Q, '03, 19; 2Q, '97, 5

SUPPLEMENTARY CLASSIFICATION OF FACTORS INFLUENCING HEALTH STATUS AND CONTACT WITH HEALTH SERVICES ▶(V01-V86)◀

This classification is provided to deal with occasions when circumstances other than a disease or injury classifiable to categories 001-999 (the main part of ICD) are recorded as "diagnoses" or "problems." This can arise mainly in three ways:

a) When a person who is not currently sick encounters the health services for some specific purpose, such as to act as a donor of an organ or tissue, to receive prophylactic vaccination, or to discuss a problem which is in itself not a disease or injury. This will be a fairly rare occurrence among hospital inpatients, but will be relatively more common among hospital outpatients and patients of family practitioners, health clinics, etc.

b) When a person with a known disease or injury, whether it is current or resolving, encounters the health care system for a specific treatment of that disease or injury (e.g., dialysis for renal disease; chemotherapy for malignancy; cast change).

c) When some circumstance or problem is present which influences the person's health status but is not in itself a current illness or injury. Such factors may be elicited during population surveys, when the person may or may not be currently sick, or be recorded as an additional factor to be borne in mind when the person is receiving care for some current illness or injury classifiable to categories 001-999.

In the latter circumstances the V code should be used only as a supplementary code and should not be the one selected for use in primary, single cause tabulations. Examples of these circumstances are a personal history of certain diseases, or a person with an artificial heart valve in situ.

AHA: J-F, '87, 8

PERSONS WITH POTENTIAL HEALTH HAZARDS RELATED TO COMMUNICABLE DISEASES (V01-V06)

EXCLUDES *family history of infectious and parasitic diseases (V18.8)*
personal history of infectious and parasitic diseases (V12.0)

✓4th **V01 Contact with or exposure to communicable diseases**

V01.0 Cholera
Conditions classifiable to 001

V01.1 Tuberculosis
Conditions classifiable to 010-018

V01.2 Poliomyelitis
Conditions classifiable to 045

V01.3 Smallpox
Conditions classifiable to 050

V01.4 Rubella
Conditions classifiable to 056

V01.5 Rabies
Conditions classifiable to 071

V01.6 Venereal diseases
Conditions classifiable to 090-099

✓5th **V01.7 Other viral diseases**
Conditions classifiable to 042-078 and V08, except as above
AHA: 2Q, '92, 11

[3] **V01.71 Varicella**
[3] **V01.79 Other viral diseases**

✓5th **V01.8 Other communicable diseases**
Conditions classifiable to 001-136, except as above
AHA: J-A, '87, 24

V01.81 Anthrax
AHA: 4Q, '02, 70, 78

[3] **V01.82 Exposure to SARS-associated coronavirus**
AHA: 4Q, '03, 46-47

[3] **V01.83 Escherichia coli (E. coli)**
[3] **V01.84 Meningococcus**
V01.89 Other communicable diseases

V01.9 Unspecified communicable disease

✓4th **V02 Carrier or suspected carrier of infectious diseases**
AHA: 3Q, '95, 18; 3Q, '94, 4

V02.0 Cholera
V02.1 Typhoid
V02.2 Amebiasis
V02.3 Other gastrointestinal pathogens
V02.4 Diphtheria

✓5th **V02.5 Other specified bacterial diseases**

V02.51 Group B streptococcus
AHA: 1Q, '02, 14; 4Q, '98, 56

V02.52 Other streptococcus
V02.59 Other specified bacterial diseases
Meningococcal Staphylococcal

✓5th **V02.6 Viral hepatitis**
Hepatitis Australian-antigen [HAA] [SH] carrier
Serum hepatitis carrier

V02.60 Viral hepatitis carrier, unspecified
AHA: 4Q, '97, 47

V02.61 Hepatitis B carrier
AHA: 4Q, '97, 47

V02.62 Hepatitis C carrier
AHA: 4Q, '97, 47

V02.69 Other viral hepatitis carrier
AHA: 4Q, '97, 47

V02.7 Gonorrhea
V02.8 Other venereal diseases
V02.9 Other specified infectious organism
AHA: 3Q, '95, 18; 1Q, '93, 22; J-A, '87, 24

✓4th **V03 Need for prophylactic vaccination and inoculation against bacterial diseases**

EXCLUDES *vaccination not carried out (V64.00-V64.09)*
vaccines against combinations of diseases (V06.0-V06.9)

V03.0 Cholera alone
V03.1 Typhoid-paratyphoid alone [TAB]
V03.2 Tuberculosis [BCG]
V03.3 Plague
V03.4 Tularemia
V03.5 Diphtheria alone
V03.6 Pertussis alone
V03.7 Tetanus toxoid alone

✓5th **V03.8 Other specified vaccinations against single bacterial diseases**

V03.81 Hemophilus influenza, type B [Hib]
V03.82 Streptococcus pneumoniae [pneumococcus]
V03.89 Other specified vaccination
AHA: 2Q, '00, 9

V03.9 Unspecified single bacterial disease

✓4th **V04 Need for prophylactic vaccination and inoculation against certain viral diseases**

EXCLUDES *vaccines against combinations of diseases (V06.0-V06.9)*

V04.0 Poliomyelitis
V04.1 Smallpox
V04.2 Measles alone
V04.3 Rubella alone
V04.4 Yellow fever
V04.5 Rabies
V04.6 Mumps alone
V04.7 Common cold

✓5th **V04.8 Other viral diseases**
AHA: 4Q, '03, 83

V04.81 Influenza
V04.82 Respiratory syncytial virus (RSV)
V04.89 Other viral diseases

[3] These V codes may be used as principal diagnosis on Medicare patients.

✓4th **V05 Need for other prophylactic vaccination and inoculation against single diseases**

EXCLUDES *vaccines against combinations of diseases (V06.0-V06.9)*

V05.0 Athropod-borne viral encephalitis

V05.1 Other arthropod-borne viral diseases

V05.2 Leishmaniasis

V05.3 Viral hepatitis

V05.4 Varicella

Chickenpox

V05.8 Other specified disease

AHA: 1Q, '01, 4; 3Q, '91, 20

V05.9 Unspecified single disease

✓4th **V06 Need for prophylactic vaccination and inoculation against combinations of diseases**

Note: Use additional single vaccination codes from categories V03-V05 to identify any vaccinations not included in a combination code.

V06.0 Cholera with typhoid-paratyphoid [cholera+TAB]

V06.1 Diphtheria-tetanus-pertussis, combined [DTP] [DTaP]

AHA: 4Q, '03, 83; 3Q, '98, 13

V06.2 Diphtheria-tetanus-pertussis with typhoid-paratyphoid [DTP+TAB]

V06.3 Diphtheria-tetanus-pertussis with poliomyelitis [DTP+polio]

V06.4 Measles-mumps-rubella [MMR]

V06.5 Tetanus-diphtheria [Td] [DT]

AHA: 4Q, '03, 83

V06.6 Streptococcus pneumoniae [pneumococcus] and influenza

V06.8 Other combinations

EXCLUDES *multiple single vaccination codes (V03.0-V05.9)*

AHA: 1Q, '94, 19

V06.9 Unspecified combined vaccine

PERSONS WITH NEED FOR ISOLATION, OTHER POTENTIAL HEALTH HAZARDS AND PROPHYLACTIC MEASURES (V07-V09)

✓4th **V07 Need for isolation and other prophylactic measures**

EXCLUDES *prophylactic organ removal (V50.41-V50.49)*

[3] **V07.0 Isolation**

Admission to protect the individual from his surroundings or for isolation of individual after contact with infectious diseases

V07.1 Desensitization to allergens

V07.2 Prophylactic immunotherapy

Administration of:
- antivenin
- immune sera [gamma globulin]
- RhoGAM
- tetanus antitoxin

✓5th **V07.3 Other prophylactic chemotherapy**

V07.31 Prophylactic fluoride administration

[3] **V07.39 Other prophylactic chemotherapy**

EXCLUDES *maintenance chemotherapy following disease ▶(V58.11)◀*

V07.4 Hormone replacement therapy (postmenopausal) ♀

[3] **V07.8 Other specified prophylactic measure**

AHA: 1Q, '92, 11

V07.9 Unspecified prophylactic measure

V08 Asymptomatic human immunodeficiency virus [HIV] infection status

HIV positive NOS

Note: This code is *only* to be used when no HIV infection symptoms or conditions are present. If any HIV infection symptoms or conditions are present, see code 042.

EXCLUDES
AIDS (042)
human immunodeficiency virus [HIV] disease (042)
exposure to HIV (V01.79)
nonspecific serologic evidence of HIV (795.71)
symptomatic human immunodeficiency virus [HIV] infection (042)

AHA: 2Q, '04, 11; 2Q, '99, 8; 3Q, '95, 18

✓4th **V09 Infection with drug-resistant microorganisms**

Note: This category is intended for use as an additional code for infectious conditions classified elsewhere to indicate the presence of drug-resistance of the infectious organism.

AHA: 3Q, '94, 4; 4Q, '93, 22

V09.0 Infection with microorganisms resistant to penicillins

Methicillin-resistant staphylococcus aureus (MRSA)

AHA: 4Q, '03, 104, 106

V09.1 Infection with microorganisms resistant to cephalosporins and other B-lactam antibiotics

V09.2 Infection with microorganisms resistant to macrolides

V09.3 Infection with microorganisms resistant to tetracyclines

V09.4 Infection with microorganisms resistant to aminoglycosides

✓5th **V09.5 Infection with microorganisms resistant to quinolones and fluoroquinolones**

V09.50 Without mention of resistance to multiple quinolones and fluoroquinoles

V09.51 With resistance to multiple quinolones and fluoroquinoles

V09.6 Infection with microorganisms resistant to sulfonamides

✓5th **V09.7 Infection with microorganisms resistant to other specified antimycobacterial agents**

EXCLUDES
Amikacin (V09.4)
Kanamycin (V09.4)
Streptomycin [SM] (V09.4)

V09.70 Without mention of resistance to multiple antimycobacterial agents

V09.71 With resistance to multiple antimycobacterial agents

✓5th **V09.8 Infection with microorganisms resistant to other specified drugs**

Vancomycin (glycopeptide) intermediate staphylococcus aureus (VISA/GISA)

Vancomycin (glycopeptide) resistant enterococcus (VRE)

Vancomycin (glycopeptide) resistant staphylococcus aureus (VRSA/GRSA)

V09.80 Without mention of resistance to multiple drugs

V09.81 With resistance to multiple drugs

✓5th **V09.9 Infection with drug-resistant microorganisms, unspecified**

Drug resistance, NOS

V09.90 Without mention of multiple drug resistance

V09.91 With multiple drug resistance

Multiple drug resistance NOS

[3] These V codes may be used as principal diagnosis on Medicare patients.

N Newborn Age: 0 | P Pediatric Age: 0-17 | M Maternity Age: 12-55 | A Adult Age: 15-124 | CC CC Condition | MC Major Complication | CD Complex Dx | HIV HIV Related Dx

PERSONS WITH POTENTIAL HEALTH HAZARDS RELATED TO PERSONAL AND FAMILY HISTORY (V10-V19)

EXCLUDES *obstetric patients where the possibility that the fetus might be affected is the reason for observation or management during pregnancy (655.0-655.9)*

AHA: J-F, '87, 1

4th **V10 Personal history of malignant neoplasm**
AHA: 4Q, '02, 80; 4Q, '98, 69; 1Q, '95, 4; 3Q, '92, 5; M-J, '85, 10; 2Q, '90, 9

5th **V10.0 Gastrointestinal tract**
History of conditions classifiable to 140-159
V10.00 Gastrointestinal tract, unspecified
V10.01 Tongue
V10.02 Other and unspecified oral cavity and pharynx
V10.03 Esophagus
V10.04 Stomach
V10.05 Large intestine
AHA: 3Q, '99, 7; 1Q, '95, 4
V10.06 Rectum, rectosigmoid junction, and anus
V10.07 Liver
V10.09 Other
AHA: 4Q, '03, 111

5th **V10.1 Trachea, bronchus, and lung**
History of conditions classifiable to 162
V10.11 Bronchus and lung
V10.12 Trachea

5th **V10.2 Other respiratory and intrathoracic organs**
History of conditions classifiable to 160, 161, 163-165
V10.20 Respiratory organ, unspecified
V10.21 Larynx
AHA: 4Q, '03, 108, 110
V10.22 Nasal cavities, middle ear, and accessory sinuses
V10.29 Other

V10.3 Breast
History of conditions classifiable to 174 and 175
AHA: 2Q, '03, 5; 4Q, '01, 66; 4Q, '98, 65; 4Q, '97, 50; 1Q, '91, 16; 1Q, '90, 21

5th **V10.4 Genital organs**
History of conditions classifiable to 179-187
V10.40 Female genital organ, unspecified ♀
V10.41 Cervix uteri ♀
V10.42 Other parts of uterus ♀
V10.43 Ovary ♀
V10.44 Other female genital organs ♀
V10.45 Male genital organ, unspecified ♂
V10.46 Prostate ♂
V10.47 Testis ♂
V10.48 Epididymis ♂
V10.49 Other male genital organs ♂

5th **V10.5 Urinary organs**
History of conditions classifiable to 188 and 189
V10.50 Urinary organ, unspecified
V10.51 Bladder
V10.52 Kidney
AHA: 2Q, '04, 4
EXCLUDES *renal pelvis (V10.53)*
V10.53 Renal pelvis
AHA: 4Q, '01, 55
V10.59 Other

5th **V10.6 Leukemia**
Conditions classifiable to 204-208
EXCLUDES *leukemia in remission (204-208)*
AHA: 2Q, '92, 13; 4Q, '91, 26; 4Q, '90, 3
V10.60 Leukemia, unspecified
V10.61 Lymphoid leukemia
V10.62 Myeloid leukemia
V10.63 Monocytic leukemia
V10.69 Other

5th **V10.7 Other lymphatic and hematopoietic neoplasms**
Conditions classifiable to 200-203
EXCLUDES *listed conditions in 200-203 in remission*
AHA: M-J, '85, 18
V10.71 Lymphosarcoma and reticulosarcoma
V10.72 Hodgkin's disease
V10.79 Other

5th **V10.8 Personal history of malignant neoplasm of other sites**
History of conditions classifiable to 170-173, 190-195
V10.81 Bone
AHA: 2Q, '03, 13
V10.82 Malignant melanoma of skin
V10.83 Other malignant neoplasm of skin
V10.84 Eye
V10.85 Brain
AHA: 1Q, '01, 6
V10.86 Other parts of nervous system
EXCLUDES *peripheral sympathetic, and parasympathetic nerves (V10.89)*
V10.87 Thyroid
V10.88 Other endocrine glands and related structures
V10.89 Other

V10.9 Unspecified personal history of malignant neoplasm

4th **V11 Personal history of mental disorder**

V11.0 Schizophrenia
EXCLUDES *that in remission (295.0-295.9 with fifth-digit 5)*

V11.1 Affective disorders
Personal history of manic-depressive psychosis
EXCLUDES *that in remission (296.0-296.6 with fifth-digit 5, 6)*

V11.2 Neurosis
V11.3 Alcoholism
V11.8 Other mental disorders
V11.9 Unspecified mental disorder

4th **V12 Personal history of certain other diseases**
AHA: 3Q, '92, 11

5th **V12.0 Infectious and parasitic diseases**
EXCLUDES *personal history of infectious diseases specific to a body system*
V12.00 Unspecified infectious and parasitic disease
V12.01 Tuberculosis
V12.02 Poliomyelitis
V12.03 Malaria
V12.09 Other

V12.1 Nutritional deficiency
V12.2 Endocrine, metabolic, and immunity disorders
EXCLUDES *history of allergy (V14.0-V14.9, V15.01-V15.09)*
V12.3 Diseases of blood and blood-forming organs

5th **V12.4 Disorders of nervous system and sense organs**
V12.40 Unspecified disorder of nervous system and sense organs
V12.41 Benign neoplasm of the brain
AHA: 4Q, '97, 48
V12.42 Infections of the central nervous system
Encephalitis Meningitis
AHA: ▶4Q, '05, 95◀
V12.49 Other disorders of nervous system and sense organs
AHA: 4Q, '98, 59

5th **V12.5 Diseases of circulatory system**
AHA: 4Q, '95, 61
EXCLUDES *old myocardial infarction (412)*
postmyocardial infarction syndrome (411.0)
V12.50 Unspecified circulatory disease

V12.51 **Venous thrombosis and embolism**
Pulmonary embolism
AHA: 4Q, '03, 108; 1Q, '02, 15

V12.52 **Thrombophlebitis**

V12.59 **Other**
AHA: 4Q, '99, 4; 4Q, '98, 88; 4Q, '97, 37

✓5th V12.6 **Diseases of respiratory system**
EXCLUDES *tuberculosis (V12.01)*

V12.60 **Unspecified disease of respiratory system**

V12.61 **Pneumonia (recurrent)**
AHA: ▶4Q, '05, 95◀

V12.69 **Other diseases of respiratory system**

✓5th V12.7 **Diseases of digestive system**
AHA: 1Q, '95, 3; 2Q, '89, 16

V12.70 **Unspecified digestive disease**

V12.71 **Peptic ulcer disease**

V12.72 **Colonic polyps**
AHA: 3Q, '02, 15

V12.79 **Other**

✓4th **V13 Personal history of other diseases**

✓5th V13.0 **Disorders of urinary system**

V13.00 **Unspecified urinary disorder**

V13.01 **Urinary calculi**

V13.02 **Urinary (tract) infection**
AHA: ▶4Q, '05, 95◀

V13.03 **Nephrotic syndrome**
AHA: ▶4Q, '05, 95◀

V13.09 **Other**

V13.1 **Trophoblastic disease** ♀
EXCLUDES *supervision during a current pregnancy (V23.1)*

✓5th V13.2 **Other genital system and obstetric disorders**
EXCLUDES *supervision during a current pregnancy of a woman with poor obstetric history (V23.0-V23.9)*
habitual aborter (646.3)
without current pregnancy (629.9)

V13.21 **Personal history of pre-term labor** ♀
EXCLUDES *current pregnancy with history of pre-term labor (V23.41)*
AHA: 4Q, '02, 78

V13.29 **Other genital system and obstetric disorders** ♀

V13.3 **Diseases of skin and subcutaneous tissue**

V13.4 **Arthritis**

V13.5 **Other musculoskeletal disorders**

✓5th V13.6 **Congenital malformations**
AHA: 4Q, '98, 63

V13.61 **Hypospadias** ♂

V13.69 **Other congenital malformations**
AHA: 1Q, '04, 16

V13.7 **Perinatal problems**
EXCLUDES *low birth weight status (V21.30-V21.35)*

V13.8 **Other specified diseases**

V13.9 **Unspecified disease**

✓4th **V14 Personal history of allergy to medicinal agents**

V14.0 **Penicillin**

V14.1 **Other antibiotic agent**

V14.2 **Sulfonamides**

V14.3 **Other anti-infective agent**

V14.4 **Anesthetic agent**

V14.5 **Narcotic agent**

V14.6 **Analgesic agent**

V14.7 **Serum or vaccine**

V14.8 **Other specified medicinal agents**

V14.9 **Unspecified medicinal agent**

✓4th **V15 Other personal history presenting hazards to health**

✓5th V15.0 **Allergy, other than to medicinal agents**
EXCLUDES *allergy to food substance used as base for medicinal agent (V14.0-V14.9)*
AHA: 4Q, '00, 42, 49

V15.01 **Allergy to peanuts**

V15.02 **Allergy to milk products**
EXCLUDES *lactose intolerance (271.3)*
AHA: 1Q, '03, 12

V15.03 **Allergy to eggs**

V15.04 **Allergy to seafood**
Seafood (octopus) (squid) ink
Shellfish

V15.05 **Allergy to other foods**
Food additives Nuts other than peanuts

V15.06 **Allergy to insects**
Bugs
Insect bites and stings
Spiders

V15.07 **Allergy to latex**
Latex sensitivity

V15.08 **Allergy to radiographic dye**
Contrast media used for diagnostic x-ray procedures

V15.09 **Other allergy, other than to medicinal agents**

V15.1 **Surgery to heart and great vessels**
EXCLUDES *replacement by transplant or other means (V42.1-V42.2, V43.2-V43.4)*
AHA: 1Q, '04, 16

V15.2 **Surgery to other major organs**
EXCLUDES *replacement by transplant or other means (V42.0-V43.8)*

V15.3 **Irradiation**
Previous exposure to therapeutic or other ionizing radiation

✓5th V15.4 **Psychological trauma**
EXCLUDES *history of condition classifiable to 290-316 (V11.0-V11.9)*

V15.41 **History of physical abuse**
Rape
AHA: 3Q, '99, 15

V15.42 **History of emotional abuse**
Neglect
AHA: 3Q, '99, 15

V15.49 **Other**
AHA: 3Q, '99, 15

V15.5 **Injury**

V15.6 **Poisoning**

V15.7 **Contraception**
EXCLUDES *current contraceptive management (V25.0-V25.4)*
presence of intrauterine contraceptive device as incidental finding (V45.5)

✓5th V15.8 **Other specified personal history presenting hazards to health**
AHA: 4Q, '95, 62

V15.81 **Noncompliance with medical treatment**
AHA: 2Q, '03, 7; 2Q, '01, 11, 12, 13; 2Q, '99, 17; 2Q, '97, 11; 1Q, '97, 12; 3Q, '96, 9

V15.82 **History of tobacco use**
EXCLUDES *tobacco dependence (305.1)*

V15.84 **Exposure to asbestos**

V15.85 **Exposure to potentially hazardous body fluids**

V15.86 **Exposure to lead**

V15.87 **History of extracorporeal membrane oxygenation [ECMO]**
AHA: 4Q, '03, 84

V15.88 **History of fall**
At risk for falling
AHA: ▶4Q, '05, 95◀

V15.89 **Other**
AHA: 1Q, '90, 21; N-D, '84, 12

V15.9 **Unspecified personal history presenting hazards to health**

N Newborn Age: 0 P Pediatric Age: 0-17 M Maternity Age: 12-55 A Adult Age: 15-124 CC CC Condition MC Major Complication CD Complex Dx HIV HIV Related Dx

✓4th **V16 Family history of malignant neoplasm**
V16.0 Gastrointestinal tract
Family history of condition classifiable to 140-159
AHA: 1Q, '99, 4
V16.1 Trachea, bronchus, and lung
Family history of condition classifiable to 162
V16.2 Other respiratory and intrathoracic organs
Family history of condition classifiable to 160-161, 163-165
V16.3 Breast
Family history of condition classifiable to 174
AHA: 4Q, '04, 107; 2Q, '03, 4; 2Q, '00, 8; 1Q, '92, 11
✓5th **V16.4 Genital organs**
Family history of condition classifiable to 179-187
AHA: 4Q, '97, 48
V16.40 Genital organ, unspecified
V16.41 Ovary
V16.42 Prostate
V16.43 Testis
V16.49 Other
✓5th **V16.5 Urinary organs**
Family history of condition classifiable to 189
V16.51 Kidney
V16.59 Other
V16.6 Leukemia
Family history of condition classifiable to 204-208
V16.7 Other lymphatic and hematopoietic neoplasms
Family history of condition classifiable to 200-203
V16.8 Other specified malignant neoplasm
Family history of other condition classifiable to 140-199
V16.9 Unspecified malignant neoplasm

✓4th **V17 Family history of certain chronic disabling diseases**
V17.0 Psychiatric condition
EXCLUDES *family history of mental retardation (V18.4)*
V17.1 Stroke (cerebrovascular)
V17.2 Other neurological diseases
Epilepsy Huntington's chorea
V17.3 Ischemic heart disease
V17.4 Other cardiovascular diseases
AHA: 1Q, '04, 6
V17.5 Asthma
V17.6 Other chronic respiratory conditions
V17.7 Arthritis
✓5th **V17.8 Other musculoskeletal diseases**
V17.81 Osteoporosis
AHA: 4Q, '05, 95
V17.89 Other musculoskeletal diseases

✓4th **V18 Family history of certain other specific conditions**
V18.0 Diabetes mellitus
AHA: 1Q, '04, 8
V18.1 Other endocrine and metabolic diseases
V18.2 Anemia
V18.3 Other blood disorders
V18.4 Mental retardation
✓5th **V18.5 Digestive disorders**
● **V18.51 Colonic polyps**
EXCLUDES *family history of malignant neoplasm of gastrointestinal tract (V16.0)*
● **V18.59 Other digestive disorders**
✓5th **V18.6 Kidney diseases**
V18.61 Polycystic kidney
V18.69 Other kidney diseases
V18.7 Other genitourinary diseases
V18.8 Infectious and parasitic diseases
V18.9 Genetic disease carrier
AHA: 4Q, '05, 95

[3] These V codes may be used as principal diagnosis on Medicare patients.

✓4th **V19 Family history of other conditions**
V19.0 Blindness or visual loss
V19.1 Other eye disorders
V19.2 Deafness or hearing loss
V19.3 Other ear disorders
V19.4 Skin conditions
V19.5 Congenital anomalies
V19.6 Allergic disorders
V19.7 Consanguinity
V19.8 Other condition

PERSONS ENCOUNTERING HEALTH SERVICES IN CIRCUMSTANCES RELATED TO REPRODUCTION AND DEVELOPMENT (V20-V29)

✓4th **V20 Health supervision of infant or child**
[3] **V20.0 Foundling** P
V20.1 Other healthy infant or child receiving care P
Medical or nursing care supervision of healthy infant in cases of:
maternal illness, physical or psychiatric
socioeconomic adverse condition at home
too many children at home preventing or interfering with normal care
AHA: 1Q, '00, 25; 3Q, '89, 14
V20.2 Routine infant or child health check P
Developmental testing of infant or child
Immunizations appropriate for age
▶Initial and subsequent routine newborn check◀
Routine vision and hearing testing
Use additional code(s) to identify:
special screening examination(s) performed (V73.0-V82.9)
EXCLUDES *special screening for developmental handicaps (V79.3)*
AHA: 1Q, '04, 15

✓4th **V21 Constitutional states in development**
V21.0 Period of rapid growth in childhood
V21.1 Puberty
V21.2 Other adolescence
✓5th **V21.3 Low birth weight status**
EXCLUDES *history of perinatal problems*
AHA: 4Q, '00, 51
V21.30 Low birth weight status, unspecified
V21.31 Low birth weight status, less than 500 grams
V21.32 Low birth weight status, 500-999 grams
V21.33 Low birth weight status, 1000-1499 grams
V21.34 Low birth weight status, 1500-1999 grams
V21.35 Low birth weight status, 2000-2500 grams
V21.8 Other specified constitutional states in development
V21.9 Unspecified constitutional state in development

✓4th **V22 Normal pregnancy**
EXCLUDES *pregnancy examination or test, pregnancy unconfirmed (V72.40)*
V22.0 Supervision of normal first pregnancy ♀
AHA: 3Q, '99, 16
V22.1 Supervision of other normal pregnancy ♀
AHA: 3Q, '99, 16
V22.2 Pregnant state, incidental ♀
Pregnant state NOS

✓4th **V23 Supervision of high-risk pregnancy**
AHA: 1Q, '90, 10
V23.0 Pregnancy with history of infertility M♀
V23.1 Pregnancy with history of trophoblastic disease M♀
Pregnancy with history of:
hydatidiform mole vesicular mole
EXCLUDES *that without current pregnancy (V13.1)*

✓4th ✓5th Additional Digit Required | Nonspecific PDx | Unacceptable PDx | Manifestation Code | MCV Major Cardiovascular Condition | ▶◀ Revised Text | ● New Code | ▲ Revised Code Title

V23.2 Pregnancy with history of abortion M♀
Pregnancy with history of conditions classifiable to 634-638
EXCLUDES *habitual aborter:*
care during pregnancy (646.3)
that without current pregnancy (629.9)

V23.3 Grand multiparity M♀
EXCLUDES *care in relation to labor and delivery (659.4)*
that without current pregnancy (V61.5)

✓5th **V23.4 Pregnancy with other poor obstetric history**
Pregnancy with history of other conditions classifiable to 630-676

V23.41 Pregnancy with history of pre-term labor M♀
AHA: 4Q, '02, 79

V23.49 Pregnancy with other poor obstetric history M♀

V23.5 Pregnancy with other poor reproductive history M♀
Pregnancy with history of stillbirth or neonatal death

V23.7 Insufficient prenatal care CC M♀
History of little or no prenatal care
CC Excl: V22.0-V23.9

✓5th **V23.8 Other high-risk pregnancy**
AHA: 4Q, '98, 56, 63

V23.81 Elderly primigravida CC M♀
First pregnancy in a woman who will be 35 years of age or older at expected date of delivery
EXCLUDES *elderly primigravida complicating pregnancy (659.5)*
CC Excl: See code V23.7

V23.82 Elderly multigravida CC M♀
Second or more pregnancy in a woman who will be 35 years of age or older at expected date of delivery
EXCLUDES *elderly multigravida complicating pregnancy (659.6)*
CC Excl: See code V23.7

V23.83 Young primigravida CC M♀
First pregnancy in a female less than 16 years old at expected date of delivery
EXCLUDES *young primigravida complicating pregnancy (659.8)*
CC Excl: See code V23.7

V23.84 Young multigravida CC M♀
Second or more pregnancy in a female less than 16 years old at expected date of delivery
EXCLUDES *young multigravida complicating pregnancy (659.8)*

V23.89 Other high-risk pregnancy CC M♀
CC Excl: See code V23.7

V23.9 Unspecified high-risk pregnancy CC M♀
CC Excl: See code V23.7

✓4th **V24 Postpartum care and examination**

3 **V24.0 Immediately after delivery** M♀
Care and observation in uncomplicated cases

V24.1 Lactating mother ♀
Supervision of lactation

V24.2 Routine postpartum follow-up ♀

✓4th **V25 Encounter for contraceptive management**
AHA: 4Q, '92, 24

✓5th **V25.0 General counseling and advice**

V25.01 Prescription of oral contraceptives ♀

V25.02 Initiation of other contraceptive measures
Fitting of diaphragm
Prescription of foams, creams, or other agents
AHA: 3Q, '97, 7

V25.03 Encounter for emergency contraceptive counseling and prescription
Encounter for postcoital contraceptive counseling and prescription
AHA: 4Q, '03, 84

V25.09 Other
Family planning advice

V25.1 Insertion of intrauterine contraceptive device ♀

3 **V25.2 Sterilization**
Admission for interruption of fallopian tubes or vas deferens

3 **V25.3 Menstrual extraction** ♀
Menstrual regulation

✓5th **V25.4 Surveillance of previously prescribed contraceptive methods**
Checking, reinsertion, or removal of contraceptive device
Repeat prescription for contraceptive method
Routine examination in connection with contraceptive maintenance
EXCLUDES *presence of intrauterine contraceptive device as incidental finding (V45.5)*

V25.40 Contraceptive surveillance, unspecified

V25.41 Contraceptive pill ♀

V25.42 Intrauterine contraceptive device ♀
Checking, reinsertion, or removal of intrauterine device

V25.43 Implantable subdermal contraceptive ♀

V25.49 Other contraceptive method
AHA: 3Q, '97, 7

V25.5 Insertion of implantable subdermal contraceptive ♀
AHA: 3Q, '92, 9

V25.8 Other specified contraceptive management
Postvasectomy sperm count
EXCLUDES *sperm count following sterilization reversal (V26.22)*
sperm count for fertility testing (V26.21)
AHA: 3Q, '96, 9

V25.9 Unspecified contraceptive management

✓4th **V26 Procreative management**

3 **V26.0 Tuboplasty or vasoplasty after previous sterilization**
AHA: 2Q, '95, 10

V26.1 Artificial insemination ♀

✓5th **V26.2 Investigation and testing**
EXCLUDES *postvasectomy sperm count (V25.8)*
AHA: 4Q, '00, 56

V26.21 Fertility testing
Fallopian insufflation
Sperm count for fertility testing
EXCLUDES *genetic counseling and testing ▶(V26.31-V26.39)◀*

V26.22 Aftercare following sterilization reversal
Fallopian insufflation following sterilization reversal
Sperm count following sterilization reversal

V26.29 Other investigation and testing
AHA: 2Q, '96, 9; N-D, '85, 15

✓5th **V26.3 Genetic counseling and testing**
EXCLUDES *fertility testing (V26.21)*
▶nonprocreative genetic screening (V82.71, V82.79)◀
AHA: 4Q, '05, 96

3 These V codes may be used as principal diagnosis on Medicare patients.

▲ V26.31 **Testing of female for genetic disease carrier status** ♀

▲ V26.32 **Other genetic testing of female** ♀

▶Use additional code to identify habitual aborter (629.81, 646.3)◀

V26.33 **Genetic counseling**

● V26.34 **Testing of male for genetic disease carrier status** ♂

● V26.35 **Encounter for testing of male partner of habitual aborter** ♂

● V26.39 **Other genetic testing of male** ♂

V26.4 **General counseling and advice**

✓5th V26.5 **Sterilization status**

V26.51 **Tubal ligation status** ♀

EXCLUDES *infertility not due to previous tubal ligation (628.0-628.9)*

V26.52 **Vasectomy status** ♂

V26.8 **Other specified procreative management**

V26.9 **Unspecified procreative management**

✓4th **V27 Outcome of delivery**

Note: This category is intended for the coding of the outcome of delivery on the mother's record.

AHA: 2Q, '91, 16

V27.0 **Single liveborn** M♀

AHA: 4Q, '05, 81; 2Q, '03, 9; 2Q, '02, 10; 1Q, '01, 10; 3Q, '00, 5; 4Q, '98, 77; 4Q, '95, 59; 1Q, '92, 9

V27.1 **Single stillborn** M♀

V27.2 **Twins, both liveborn** M♀

V27.3 **Twins, one liveborn and one stillborn** M♀

V27.4 **Twins, both stillborn** M♀

V27.5 **Other multiple birth, all liveborn** M♀

V27.6 **Other multiple birth, some liveborn** M♀

V27.7 **Other multiple birth, all stillborn** M♀

V27.9 **Unspecified outcome of delivery** M♀

Single birth }
Multiple birth } outcome to infant unspecified

▲ ✓4th **V28 Encounter for antenatal screening of mother**

EXCLUDES *abnormal findings on screening — code to findings*
routine prenatal care (V22.0-V23.9)

AHA: 1Q, '04, 11

V28.0 **Screening for chromosomal anomalies by amniocentesis** M♀

V28.1 **Screening for raised alpha-fetoprotein levels in amniotic fluid** M♀

V28.2 **Other screening based on amniocentesis** M♀

V28.3 **Screening for malformation using ultrasonics** ♀

V28.4 **Screening for fetal growth retardation using ultrasonics** ♀

V28.5 **Screening for isoimmunization** ♀

V28.6 **Screening for Streptococcus B** M♀

AHA: 4Q, '97, 46

V28.8 **Other specified antenatal screening** ♀

AHA: 3Q, '99, 16

V28.9 **Unspecified antenatal screening** ♀

✓4th **V29 Observation and evaluation of newborns and infants for suspected condition not found**

Note: This category is to be used for newborns, within the neonatal period, (the first 28 days of life) who are suspected of having an abnormal condition resulting from exposure from the mother or the birth process, but without signs or symptoms, and, which after examination and observation, is found not to exist.

AHA: 1Q, '00, 25; 4Q, '94, 47; 1Q, '94, 9; 4Q, '92, 21

3 V29.0 **Observation for suspected infectious condition** N

AHA: 1Q, '01, 10

3 V29.1 **Observation for suspected neurological condition** N

3 V29.2 **Observation for suspected respiratory condition** N

V29.3 **Observation for suspected genetic or metabolic condition** N

AHA: 2Q, '05, 21; 4Q, '98, 59, 68

3 V29.8 **Observation for other specified suspected condition** N

AHA: 2Q, '03, 15

V29.9 **Observation for unspecified suspected condition** N

AHA: 1Q, '02, 6

LIVEBORN INFANTS ACCORDING TO TYPE OF BIRTH (V30-V39)

Note: These categories are intended for the coding of liveborn infants who are consuming health care [e.g., crib or bassinet occupancy].

The following fourth-digit subdivisions are for use with categories V30-V39:

✓5th **0 Born in hospital** N
1 Born before admission to hospital N
2 Born outside hospital and not hospitalized

The following two fifth-digits are for use with the fourth-digit .0, Born in hospital:

0 delivered without mention of cesarean delivery
1 delivered by cesarean delivery

AHA: 1Q, '01, 10

4 ✓4th **V30 Single liveborn**

AHA: 2Q, '03, 9; 4Q, '98, 46, 59; 1Q, '94, 9; For code V30.00: 1Q, '04, 8, 16; 4Q, '03, 68; For code V30.01: 4Q, '05, 88

4 ✓4th **V31 Twin, mate liveborn**

AHA: 3Q, '92, 10

4 ✓4th **V32 Twin, mate stillborn**

4 ✓4th **V33 Twin, unspecified**

4 ✓4th **V34 Other multiple, mates all liveborn**

4 ✓4th **V35 Other multiple, mates all stillborn**

4 ✓4th **V36 Other multiple, mates live and stillborn**

4 ✓4th **V37 Other multiple, unspecified**

5 ✓4th **V39 Unspecified**

PERSONS WITH A CONDITION INFLUENCING THEIR HEALTH STATUS (V40-V49)

Note: These categories are intended for use when these conditions are recorded as "diagnoses" or "problems."

✓4th **V40 Mental and behavioral problems**

V40.0 **Problems with learning**

V40.1 **Problems with communication [including speech]**

V40.2 **Other mental problems**

V40.3 **Other behavioral problems**

V40.9 **Unspecified mental or behavioral problem**

✓4th **V41 Problems with special senses and other special functions**

V41.0 **Problems with sight**

V41.1 **Other eye problems**

V41.2 **Problems with hearing**

V41.3 **Other ear problems**

V41.4 **Problems with voice production**

V41.5 **Problems with smell and taste**

V41.6 **Problems with swallowing and mastication**

V41.7 **Problems with sexual function**

EXCLUDES *marital problems (V61.10)*
psychosexual disorders (302.0-302.9)

3 These V codes may be used as principal diagnosis on Medicare patients.
4 These codes with the fourth digit of 0 or 1, may be used as a principal diagnosis for Medicare patients.
5 These V codes are acceptable as principal diagnosis with the fourth digit of 0.

✓4th ✓5th Additional Digit Required | Nonspecific PDx | Unacceptable PDx | Manifestation Code | MCV Major Cardiovascular Condition | ▶◀ Revised Text | ● New Code | ▲ Revised Code Title

V41.8 **Other problems with special functions**

V41.9 **Unspecified problem with special functions**

✓4th **V42 Organ or tissue replaced by transplant**

INCLUDES homologous or heterologous (animal) (human) transplant organ status

AHA: 3Q, '98, 3, 4

V42.0 **Kidney** CC
CC Excl: 996.80-996.81, 996.87, V42.0, V42.89-V42.9
AHA: 1Q, '03, 10; 3Q, '01, 12

V42.1 **Heart** CC
CC Excl: 996.80, 996.83, 996.87, V42.1, V42.89-V42.9
AHA: 3Q, '03, 16; 3Q, '01, 13

V42.2 **Heart valve** CC
CC Excl: 996.71, V42.2, V42.89-V42.9

V42.3 **Skin**

V42.4 **Bone**

V42.5 **Cornea**

V42.6 **Lung** CC
CC Excl: 996.80, 996.84, 996.87, V42.6, V42.89-V42.9

V42.7 **Liver** CC
CC Excl: 996.80, 996.82, 996.87, 996.87, V42.7, V42.89-V42.9

✓5th V42.8 **Other specified organ or tissue**
AHA: 4Q, '98, 64; 4Q, '97, 49

V42.81 **Bone marrow** CC
CC Excl: 996.80, 996.85, 996.87, V42.9

V42.82 **Peripheral stem cells** CC
CC Excl: 996.80, 996.87, V42.9

V42.83 **Pancreas** CC
CC Excl: 996.80, 996.86-996.87, V42.83, V42.9
AHA: 1Q, '03, 10; 2Q, '01, 16

V42.84 **Intestines** CC
CC Excl: 996.80, 996.89, V42.84-V42.9
AHA: 4Q, '00, 48, 50

V42.89 **Other** CC
CC Excl: 996.80, 996.87-996.89, V42.89-V42.9

V42.9 **Unspecified organ or tissue**

✓4th **V43 Organ or tissue replaced by other means**

INCLUDES organ or tissue assisted by other means
replacement of organ by:
artificial device
mechanical device
prosthesis

EXCLUDES *cardiac pacemaker in situ (V45.01)*
fitting and adjustment of prosthetic device (V52.0-V52.9)
renal dialysis status (V45.1)

V43.0 **Eye globe**

V43.1 **Lens**
Pseudophakos
AHA: 4Q, '98, 65

✓5th V43.2 **Heart**
AHA: 4Q, '03, 85

V43.21 **Heart assist device** CC
CC Excl: 996.80, 996.83, 996.87, V42.1, V43.21-V43.22

V43.22 **Fully implantable artificial heart** CC
CC Excl: See code V43.21

V43.3 **Heart valve**
AHA: 3Q, '02, 13, 14

V43.4 **Blood vessel**

V43.5 **Bladder**

✓5th V43.6 **Joint**
AHA: 4Q, '05, 91

V43.60 **Unspecified joint**

V43.61 **Shoulder**

V43.62 **Elbow**

V43.63 **Wrist**

V43.64 **Hip**
AHA: 4Q, '05, 93, 112; 2Q, '04, 15

V43.65 **Knee**

V43.66 **Ankle**

V43.69 **Other**

V43.7 **Limb**

✓5th V43.8 **Other organ or tissue**

V43.81 **Larynx**
AHA: 4Q, '95, 55

V43.82 **Breast**
AHA: 4Q, '95, 55

V43.83 **Artificial skin**

V43.89 **Other**

✓4th **V44 Artificial opening status**

EXCLUDES *artificial openings requiring attention or management (V55.0-V55.9)*

V44.0 **Tracheostomy**
AHA: 4Q, '03, 103, 107, 111; 1Q, '01, 6

V44.1 **Gastrostomy**
AHA: 4Q, '03, 103, 107-108, 110; 1Q, '01, 12; 3Q, '97, 12; 1Q, '93, 26

V44.2 **Ileostomy**

V44.3 **Colostomy**
AHA: 4Q, '03, 110

V44.4 **Other artificial opening of gastrointestinal tract**

✓5th V44.5 **Cystostomy**

V44.50 **Cystostomy, unspecified**

V44.51 **Cutaneous-vesicostomy**

V44.52 **Appendico-vesicostomy**

V44.59 **Other cystostomy**

V44.6 **Other artificial opening of urinary tract**
Nephrostomy
Urethrostomy
Ureterostomy

V44.7 **Artificial vagina**

V44.8 **Other artificial opening status**

V44.9 **Unspecified artificial opening status**

✓4th **V45 Other postprocedural states**

EXCLUDES *aftercare management (V51-V58.9)*
malfunction or other complication — code to condition

AHA: 4Q, '03, 85

✓5th V45.0 **Cardiac device in situ**

EXCLUDES *artificial heart (V43.22)*
heart assist device (V43.21)

V45.00 **Unspecified cardiac device**

V45.01 **Cardiac pacemaker**

V45.02 **Automatic implantable cardiac defibrillator**

V45.09 **Other specified cardiac device**
Carotid sinus pacemaker in situ

V45.1 **Renal dialysis status** CC
Hemodialysis status
Patient requiring intermittent renal dialysis
Peritoneal dialysis status
Presence of arterial-venous shunt (for dialysis)

EXCLUDES *admission for dialysis treatment or session (V56.0)*

CC Excl: 996.73, V45.1
AHA: 4Q, '05, 96; 2Q, '03, 7; 2Q, '01, 12, 13

V45.2 **Presence of cerebrospinal fluid drainage device**
Cerebral ventricle (communicating) shunt, valve, or device in situ

EXCLUDES *malfunction (996.2)*

AHA: 4Q, '03, 106

V45.3 **Intestinal bypass or anastomosis status**

EXCLUDES ▶ *bariatric surgery status (V45.86)*
gastric bypass status (V45.86)
obesity surgery status (V45.86)◀

V45.4 **Arthrodesis status**
AHA: N-D, '84, 18

√5th **V45.5 Presence of contraceptive device**

EXCLUDES *checking, reinsertion, or removal of device (V25.42)*
complication from device (996.32)
insertion of device (V25.1)

V45.51 Intrauterine contraceptive device ♀

V45.52 Subdermal contraceptive implant

V45.59 Other

√5th **V45.6 States following surgery of eye and adnexa**

Cataract extraction
Filtering bleb
Surgical eyelid adhesion
} state following eye surgery

EXCLUDES *aphakia (379.31)*
artificial eye globe (V43.0)

AHA: 4Q, '98, 65; 4Q, '97, 49

V45.61 Cataract extraction status
Use additional code for associated artificial lens status (V43.1)

V45.69 Other states following surgery of eye and adnexa
AHA: 2Q, '01, 16; 1Q, '98, 10; 4Q, '97, 19

√5th **V45.7 Acquired absence of organ**
AHA: 4Q, '98, 65; 4Q, '97, 50

3 **V45.71 Acquired absence of breast**
AHA: 4Q, '01, 66; 4Q, '97, 50

V45.72 Acquired absence of intestine (large) (small)

V45.73 Acquired absence of kidney

V45.74 Other parts of urinary tract
Bladder
AHA: 4Q, '00, 51

V45.75 Stomach
AHA: 4Q, '00, 51

V45.76 Lung
AHA: 4Q, '00, 51

V45.77 Genital organs
EXCLUDES *female genital mutilation status ▶(629.20-629.29)◀*
AHA: 1Q, '03, 13, 14; 4Q, '00, 51

V45.78 Eye
AHA: 4Q, '00, 51

V45.79 Other acquired absence of organ
AHA: 4Q, '00, 51

√5th **V45.8 Other postprocedural status**

V45.81 Aortocoronary bypass status
AHA: 4Q, '03, 105; 3Q, '01, 15; 3Q, '97, 16

V45.82 Percutaneous transluminal coronary angioplasty status

V45.83 Breast implant removal status
AHA: 4Q, '95, 55

V45.84 Dental restoration status
Dental crowns status
Dental fillings status
AHA: 4Q, '01, 54

V45.85 Insulin pump status

● **V45.86 Bariatric surgery status**
Gastric banding status
Gastric bypass status for obesity
Obesity surgery status
EXCLUDES *bariatric surgery status complicating pregnancy, childbirth or the puerperium (649.2)*
intestinal bypass or anastomosis status (V45.3)

V45.89 Other
Presence of neuropacemaker or other electronic device
EXCLUDES *artificial heart valve in situ (V43.3)*
vascular prosthesis in situ (V43.4)
AHA: 1Q, '95, 11

√4th **V46 Other dependence on machines**

V46.0 Aspirator

√5th **V46.1 Respirator [Ventilator]**
Iron lung
AHA: 4Q, '05, 96; 4Q, '03, 103; 1Q, '01, 12; J-F, '87, 7 3

3 **V46.11 Dependence on respirator, status** CC
CC Excl: V46.0-V46.9
AHA: 4Q, '04, 100

3 **V46.12 Encounter for respirator dependence during power failure** CC
CC Excl: See code V46.11
AHA: 4Q, '04, 100

3 **V46.13 Encounter for weaning from respirator [ventilator]** CC
CC Excl: See code V46.11

3 **V46.14 Mechanical complication of respirator [ventilator]** CC
Mechanical failure of respirator [ventilator]
CC Excl: See code V46.11

V46.2 Supplemental oxygen
Long-term oxygen therapy
AHA: 4Q, '03, 108; 4Q, '02, 79

V46.8 Other enabling machines
Hyperbaric chamber
Possum [Patient-Operated-Selector-Mechanism]
EXCLUDES *cardiac pacemaker (V45.0)*
kidney dialysis machine (V45.1)

V46.9 Unspecified machine dependence

√4th **V47 Other problems with internal organs**

V47.0 Deficiencies of internal organs

V47.1 Mechanical and motor problems with internal organs

V47.2 Other cardiorespiratory problems
Cardiovascular exercise intolerance with pain (with):
at rest
less than ordinary activity
ordinary activity

V47.3 Other digestive problems

V47.4 Other urinary problems

V47.5 Other genital problems

V47.9 Unspecified

√4th **V48 Problems with head, neck, and trunk**

V48.0 Deficiencies of head
EXCLUDES *deficiencies of ears, eyelids, and nose (V48.8)*

V48.1 Deficiencies of neck and trunk

V48.2 Mechanical and motor problems with head

V48.3 Mechanical and motor problems with neck and trunk

V48.4 Sensory problem with head

V48.5 Sensory problem with neck and trunk

V48.6 Disfigurements of head

V48.7 Disfigurements of neck and trunk

V48.8 Other problems with head, neck, and trunk

V48.9 Unspecified problem with head, neck, or trunk

√4th **V49 Other conditions influencing health status**

V49.0 Deficiencies of limbs

V49.1 Mechanical problems with limbs

V49.2 Motor problems with limbs

V49.3 Sensory problems with limbs

V49.4 Disfigurements of limbs

V49.5 Other problems of limbs

3 These V codes may be used as principal diagnosis on Medicare patients.

✓5th **V49.6 Upper limb amputation status**
AHA: 4Q, '05, 94; 4Q, '98, 42; 4Q, '94, 39

V49.60 Unspecified level
V49.61 Thumb
V49.62 Other finger(s)
AHA: ▶2Q, '05, 7◀
V49.63 Hand
V49.64 Wrist
Disarticulation of wrist
V49.65 Below elbow
V49.66 Above elbow
Disarticulation of elbow
V49.67 Shoulder
Disarticulation of shoulder

✓5th **V49.7 Lower limb amputation status**
AHA: ▶4Q, '05, 94;◀ 4Q, '98, 42; 4Q, '94, 39

V49.70 Unspecified level
V49.71 Great toe
V49.72 Other toe(s)
V49.73 Foot
V49.74 Ankle
Disarticulation of ankle
V49.75 Below knee
V49.76 Above knee
Disarticulation of knee
AHA: ▶2Q, '05, 14◀
V49.77 Hip
Disarticulation of hip

✓5th **V49.8 Other specified conditions influencing health status**
AHA: 4Q, '00, 51

V49.81 Asymptomatic postmenopausal status (age-related) (natural) A ♀
EXCLUDES *menopausal and premenopausal disorder (627.0-627.9)*
postsurgical menopause (256.2)
premature menopause (256.31)
symptomatic menopause (627.0-627.9)
AHA: 4Q, '02, 79; 4Q, '00, 54
V49.82 Dental sealant status
AHA: 4Q, '01, 54
V49.83 Awaiting organ transplant status CC
CC Excl: V49.83
V49.84 Bed confinement status
AHA:▶ 4Q, '05, 96◀
V49.89 Other specified conditions influencing health status
AHA:▶ 4Q, '05, 94◀

V49.9 Unspecified

PERSONS ENCOUNTERING HEALTH SERVICES FOR SPECIFIC PROCEDURES AND AFTERCARE (V50-V59)

Note: Categories V51-V58 are intended for use to indicate a reason for care in patients who may have already been treated for some disease or injury not now present, or who are receiving care to consolidate the treatment, to deal with residual states, or to prevent recurrence.

EXCLUDES *follow-up examination for medical surveillance following treatment (V67.0-V67.9)*

✓4th **V50 Elective surgery for purposes other than remedying health states**

[3] **V50.0 Hair transplant**
[3] **V50.1 Other plastic surgery for unacceptable cosmetic appearance**
Breast augmentation or reduction
Face-lift
EXCLUDES *plastic surgery following healed injury or operation (V51)*
[3] **V50.2 Routine or ritual circumcision** ♂
Circumcision in the absence of significant medical indication
V50.3 Ear piercing

✓5th **V50.4 Prophylactic organ removal**
EXCLUDES *organ donations (V59.0-V59.9)*
therapeutic organ removal — code to condition
AHA: 4Q, '94, 44

[3] **V50.41 Breast**
AHA: 4Q, '04, 107
[3] **V50.42 Ovary** ♀
[3] **V50.49 Other**

V50.8 Other
V50.9 Unspecified

[3] **V51 Aftercare involving the use of plastic surgery**
Plastic surgery following healed injury or operation
EXCLUDES *cosmetic plastic surgery (V50.1)*
plastic surgery as treatment for current injury — code to condition
repair of scarred tissue — code to scar

✓4th **V52 Fitting and adjustment of prosthetic device and implant**
INCLUDES removal of device
EXCLUDES *malfunction or complication of prosthetic device (996.0-996.7)*
status only, without need for care (V43.0-V43.8)
AHA: ▶4Q, '05, 94;◀ 4Q, '95, 55 ; 1Q, '90, 7

[3] **V52.0 Artificial arm (complete) (partial)**
[3] **V52.1 Artificial leg (complete) (partial)**
[3] **V52.2 Artificial eye**
[3] **V52.3 Dental prosthetic device**
[3] **V52.4 Breast prosthesis and implant** ♀
EXCLUDES *admission for implant insertion (V50.1)*
AHA: 4Q, '95, 80, 81
[3] **V52.8 Other specified prosthetic device**
AHA: 2Q, '02, 12, 16
V52.9 Unspecified prosthetic device

✓4th **V53 Fitting and adjustment of other device**
INCLUDES removal of device
replacement of device
EXCLUDES *status only, without need for care (V45.0-V45.8)*

✓5th **V53.0 Devices related to nervous system and special senses**
AHA: 4Q, '98, 66; 4Q, '97, 51

[3] **V53.01 Fitting and adjustment of cerebral ventricular (communicating) shunt**
AHA: 4Q, '97, 51
[3] **V53.02 Neuropacemaker (brain) (peripheral nerve) (spinal cord)**
[3] **V53.09 Fitting and adjustment of other devices related to nervous system and special senses**
Auditory substitution device
Visual substitution device
AHA: 2Q, '99, 4

V53.1 Spectacles and contact lenses
V53.2 Hearing aid

✓5th **V53.3 Cardiac device**
Reprogramming
AHA: 3Q, '92, 3; 1Q, '90, 7; M-J, '87, 8 ; N-D, '84, 18

V53.31 Cardiac pacemaker
EXCLUDES *mechanical complication of cardiac pacemaker (996.01)*
AHA: 1Q, '02, 3
V53.32 Automatic implantable cardiac defibrillator
AHA: ▶3Q, '05, 8◀
V53.39 Other cardiac device

V53.4 Orthodontic devices

[3] These V codes may be used as principal diagnosis on Medicare patients.

N Newborn Age: 0 P Pediatric Age: 0-17 M Maternity Age: 12-55 A Adult Age: 15-124 CC CC Condition MC Major Complication CD Complex Dx HIV HIV Related Dx

V53.5 **Other intestinal appliance**
EXCLUDES *colostomy (V55.3)*
ileostomy (V55.2)
other artificial opening of digestive tract (V55.4)

V53.6 **Urinary devices**
Urinary catheter
EXCLUDES *cystostomy (V55.5)*
nephrostomy (V55.6)
ureterostomy (V55.6)
urethrostomy (V55.6)

V53.7 **Orthopedic devices**
Orthopedic:
brace
cast
Orthopedic:
corset
shoes
EXCLUDES *other orthopedic aftercare (V54)*

V53.8 **Wheelchair**

✓5th V53.9 **Other and unspecified device**
AHA: 2Q, '03, 6

V53.90 **Unspecified device**

V53.91 **Fitting and adjustment of insulin pump**
Insulin pump titration

V53.99 **Other device**

✓4th **V54 Other orthopedic aftercare**
EXCLUDES *fitting and adjustment of orthopedic devices (V53.7)*
malfunction of internal orthopedic device (996.40-996.49)
other complication of nonmechanical nature (996.60-996.79)
AHA: 3Q, '95, 3

✓5th V54.0 **Aftercare involving internal fixation device**
EXCLUDES *malfunction of internal orthopedic device (996.40-996.49)*
other complication of nonmechanical nature (996.60-996.79)
removal of external fixation device (V54.89)
AHA: 4Q, '03, 87

3 V54.01 **Encounter for removal of internal fixation device**

3 V54.02 **Encounter for lengthening/adjustment of growth rod**

3 V54.09 **Other aftercare involving internal fixation device**

✓5th V54.1 **Aftercare for healing traumatic fracture**
EXCLUDES ▶ *aftercare for amputation stump (V54.89)*◀
AHA: 4Q, '02, 80

3 V54.10 **Aftercare for healing traumatic fracture of arm, unspecified**

3 V54.11 **Aftercare for healing traumatic fracture of upper arm**

3 V54.12 **Aftercare for healing traumatic fracture of lower arm**

3 V54.13 **Aftercare for healing traumatic fracture of hip**
AHA: 4Q, '03, 103, 105; 2Q, '03, 16

3 V54.14 **Aftercare for healing traumatic fracture of leg, unspecified**

3 V54.15 **Aftercare for healing traumatic fracture of upper leg**
EXCLUDES *aftercare for healing traumatic fracture of hip (V54.13)*

3 V54.16 **Aftercare for healing traumatic fracture of lower leg**

3 V54.17 **Aftercare for healing traumatic fracture of vertebrae**

3 V54.19 **Aftercare for healing traumatic fracture of other bone**
AHA: 1Q, '05, 13; 4Q, '02, 80

✓5th V54.2 **Aftercare for healing pathologic fracture**
AHA: 4Q, '02, 80

3 V54.20 **Aftercare for healing pathologic fracture of arm, unspecified**

3 V54.21 **Aftercare for healing pathologic fracture of upper arm**

3 V54.22 **Aftercare for healing pathologic fracture of lower arm**

3 V54.23 **Aftercare for healing pathologic fracture of hip**

3 V54.24 **Aftercare for healing pathologic fracture of leg, unspecified**

3 V54.25 **Aftercare for healing pathologic fracture of upper leg**
EXCLUDES *aftercare for healing pathologic fracture of hip (V54.23)*

3 V54.26 **Aftercare for healing pathologic fracture of lower leg**

3 V54.27 **Aftercare for healing pathologic fracture of vertebrae**
AHA: 4Q, '03, 108

3 V54.29 **Aftercare for healing pathologic fracture of other bone**
AHA: 4Q, '02, 80

✓5th V54.8 **Other orthopedic aftercare**
AHA: 3Q, '01, 19; 4Q, '99, 5

3 V54.81 **Aftercare following joint replacement**
Use additional code to identify joint replacement site (V43.60-V43.69)
AHA: 2Q, '04, 15; 4Q, '02, 80

3 V54.89 **Other orthopedic aftercare**
Aftercare for healing fracture NOS

V54.9 **Unspecified orthopedic aftercare**

✓4th **V55 Attention to artificial openings**
INCLUDES adjustment or repositioning of catheter
closure
passage of sounds or bougies
reforming
removal or replacement of catheter
toilet or cleansing
EXCLUDES *complications of external stoma (519.00-519.09, 569.60-569.69, 997.4, 997.5)*
status only, without need for care (V44.0-V44.9)

3 V55.0 **Tracheostomy**

3 V55.1 **Gastrostomy**
AHA: 4Q, '99, 9; 3Q, '97, 7, 8; 1Q, '96, 14; 3Q, '95, 13

3 V55.2 **Ileostomy**

3 V55.3 **Colostomy**
AHA: 2Q, '05, 4; 3Q, '97, 9

3 V55.4 **Other artificial opening of digestive tract**
AHA: 2Q, '05, 14; 1Q, '03, 10

3 V55.5 **Cystostomy**

3 V55.6 **Other artificial opening of urinary tract**
Nephrostomy
Ureterostomy
Urethrostomy

3 V55.7 **Artificial vagina**

3 V55.8 **Other specified artificial opening**

V55.9 **Unspecified artificial opening**

✓4th **V56 Encounter for dialysis and dialysis catheter care**
Use additional code to identify the associated condition
EXCLUDES *dialysis preparation — code to condition*
AHA: 4Q, '98, 66; 1Q, '93, 29

3 V56.0 **Extracorporeal dialysis**
Dialysis (renal) NOS
EXCLUDES *dialysis status (V45.1)*
AHA: 4Q, '05, 79; 1Q, '04, 23; 4Q, '00, 40; 3Q, '98, 6; 2Q, '98, 20

3 These V codes may be used as principal diagnosis on Medicare patients.

[6] **V56.1 Fitting and adjustment of extracorporeal dialysis catheter**
Removal or replacement of catheter
Toilet or cleansing
Use additional code for any concurrent extracorporeal dialysis (V56.0)
AHA: 2Q, '98, 20

V56.2 Fitting and adjustment of peritoneal dialysis catheter
Use additional code for any concurrent peritoneal dialysis (V56.8)
AHA: 4Q, '98, 55

✓5th **V56.3 Encounter for adequacy testing for dialysis**
AHA: 4Q, '00, 55

V56.31 Encounter for adequacy testing for hemodialysis

V56.32 Encounter for adequacy testing for peritoneal dialysis
Peritoneal equilibration test

[3] **V56.8 Other dialysis**
Peritoneal dialysis
AHA: 4Q, '98, 55

✓4th **V57 Care involving use of rehabilitation procedures**
Use additional code to identify underlying condition
AHA: 1Q, '02, 19; 3Q, '97, 12; 1Q, '90, 6; S-O, '86, 3

V57.0 Breathing exercises

[6] **V57.1 Other physical therapy**
Therapeutic and remedial exercises, except breathing
AHA: 2Q, '04, 15; 4Q, '02, 56; 4Q, '99, 5

✓5th **V57.2 Occupational therapy and vocational rehabilitation**

[6] **V57.21 Encounter for occupational therapy**
AHA: 4Q, '99, 7

[6] **V57.22 Encounter for vocational therapy**

[6] **V57.3 Speech therapy**
AHA: 4Q, '97, 36

V57.4 Orthoptic training

✓5th **V57.8 Other specified rehabilitation procedure**

V57.81 Orthotic training
Gait training in the use of artificial limbs

[6] **V57.89 Other**
Multiple training or therapy
AHA: 4Q, '03, 105-106, 108; 2Q, '03, 16; 1Q, '02, 16; 3Q, '01, 21; 3Q, '97, 11, 12; S-O, '86, 4

[6] **V57.9 Unspecified rehabilitation procedure**

✓4th **V58 Encounter for other and unspecified procedures and aftercare**
EXCLUDES *convalescence and palliative care (V66)*

[3] **V58.0 Radiotherapy**
Encounter or admission for radiotherapy
EXCLUDES *encounter for radioactive implant — code to condition*
radioactive iodine therapy — code to condition
AHA: 3Q, '92, 5; 2Q, '90, 7; J-F, '87, 13

✓5th **V58.1 Encounter for antineoplastic chemotherapy and immunotherapy**
Encounter or admission for chemotherapy
EXCLUDES *chemotherapy and immunotherapy for nonneoplastic conditions — code to condition*
prophylactic chemotherapy against disease which has never been present (V03.0-V07.9)
AHA: 1Q, '04, 13; 2Q, '03, 16; 3Q, '93, 4; 2Q, '92, 6; 2Q, '91, 17; 2Q, '90, 7; S-O, '84, 5

[3] **V58.11 Encounter for antineoplastic chemotherapy**
AHA: 4Q, '05, 98

[3] **V58.12 Encounter for antineoplastic immunotherapy**
AHA: 4Q, '05, 98

V58.2 Blood transfusion, without reported diagnosis

▲ ✓5th **V58.3 Attention to dressings and sutures**
▶Change or removal of wound packing◀
EXCLUDES ▶ *attention to drains (V58.49)*
planned postoperative wound closure (V58.41)◀
AHA: 2Q, '05, 14

● **V58.30 Encounter for change or removal of nonsurgical wound dressing**
Encounter for change or removal of wound dressing NOS

● **V58.31 Encounter for change or removal of surgical wound dressing**

● **V58.32 Encounter for removal of sutures**
Encounter for removal of staples

✓5th **V58.4 Other aftercare following surgery**
Note: Codes from this subcategory should be used in conjunction with other aftercare codes to fully identify the reason for the aftercare encounter
EXCLUDES *aftercare following sterilization reversal surgery (V26.22)*
attention to artificial openings (V55.0-V55.9)
orthopedic aftercare (V54.0-V54.9)
AHA: 4Q, '99, 9; N-D, '87, 9

[7] **V58.41 Encounter for planned postoperative wound closure**
EXCLUDES *disruption of operative wound (998.3)*
▶*encounter for dressings and suture aftercare (V58.30-V58.32)*◀
AHA: 4Q, '99, 15

[7] **V58.42 Aftercare following surgery for neoplasm**
Conditions classifiable to 140-239
AHA: 4Q, '02, 80

[7] **V58.43 Aftercare following surgery for injury and trauma**
Conditions classifiable to 800-999
EXCLUDES *aftercare for healing traumatic fracture (V54.10-V54.19)*
AHA: 4Q, '02, 80

[7] **V58.44 Aftercare following organ transplant**
Use additional code to identify the organ transplanted (V42.0-V42.9)
AHA: 4Q, '04, 101

[7] **V58.49 Other specified aftercare following surgery**
▶Change or removal of drains◀
AHA: 1Q, '96, 8, 9

[7] **V58.5 Orthodontics**
EXCLUDES *fitting and adjustment of orthodontic device (V53.4)*

✓5th **V58.6 Long-term (current) drug use**
EXCLUDES *drug abuse (305.00-305.93)*
drug dependence (304.00-304.93)
hormone replacement therapy (postmenopausal) (V07.4)
AHA: 4Q, '03, 85; 4Q, '02, 84; 3Q, '02, 15; 4Q, '95, 61

[7] **V58.61 Long-term (current) use of anticoagulants**
EXCLUDES *long-term (current) use of aspirin (V58.66)*
AHA 3Q, '04, 7; 4Q, '03, 108; 3Q, '02, 13-16; 1Q, '02, 15, 16

V58.62 Long-term (current) use of antibiotics
AHA: 4Q, '98, 59

V58.63 Long-term (current) use of antiplatelets/antithrombotics
EXCLUDES *long-term (current) use of aspirin (V58.66)*

[3] These V codes may be used as principal diagnosis on Medicare patients.
[6] Rehabilitation codes acceptable as a principal diagnosis when accompanied by a secondary diagnosis reflecting the condition treated.
[7] These V codes are acceptable as principal diagnosis and group to DRGs 465-466.

V58.64 Long-term (current) use of non-steroidal anti-inflammatories (NSAID)
EXCLUDES *long-term (current) use of aspirin (V58.66)*

V58.65 Long-term (current) use of steroids

V58.66 Long-term (current) use of aspirin
AHA: 4Q, '04, 102

V58.67 Long-term (current) use of insulin
AHA: 4Q, '04, 55-56, 103

7 **V58.69 Long-term (current) use of other medications**
High-risk medications
AHA: 2Q, '04, 10; 1Q, '04, 13; 1Q, '03, 11; 2Q, '00, 8; 3Q, '99, 13; 2Q, '99, 17; 1Q, '97, 12; 2Q, '96, 7

✓5th **V58.7 Aftercare following surgery to specified body systems, not elsewhere classified**
Note: Codes from this subcategory should be used in conjunction with other aftercare codes to fully identify the reason for the aftercare encounter
EXCLUDES *aftercare following organ transplant (V58.44)*
aftercare following surgery for neoplasm (V58.42)
AHA: 4Q, '03, 104; 4Q, '02, 80

7 **V58.71 Aftercare following surgery of the sense organs, NEC**
Conditions classifiable to 360-379, 380-389

7 **V58.72 Aftercare following surgery of the nervous system, NEC**
Conditions classifiable to 320-359
EXCLUDES *aftercare following surgery of the sense organs, NEC (V58.71)*

7 **V58.73 Aftercare following surgery of the circulatory system, NEC**
Conditions classifiable to 390-459
AHA: 4Q, '03, 105

7 **V58.74 Aftercare following surgery of the respiratory system, NEC**
Conditions classifiable to 460-519

7 **V58.75 Aftercare following surgery of the teeth, oral cavity and digestive system, NEC**
Conditions classifiable to 520-579
AHA: ▶2Q, '05, 14◀

7 **V58.76 Aftercare following surgery of the genitourinary system, NEC**
Conditions classifiable to 580-629
EXCLUDES *aftercare following sterilization reversal (V26.22)*
AHA: 1Q, '05, 11-12

7 **V58.77 Aftercare following surgery of the skin and subcutaneous tissue, NEC**
Conditions classifiable to 680-709

7 **V58.78 Aftercare following surgery of the musculoskeletal system, NEC**
Conditions classifiable to 710-739

✓5th **V58.8 Other specified procedures and aftercare**
AHA: 4Q, '94, 45; 2Q, '94, 8

7 **V58.81 Fitting and adjustment of vascular catheter**
Removal or replacement of catheter
Toilet or cleansing
EXCLUDES *complication of renal dialysis (996.73)*
complication of vascular catheter (996.74)
dialysis preparation — code to condition
encounter for dialysis (V56.0-V56.8)
fitting and adjustment of dialysis catheter (V56.1)

7 **V58.82 Fitting and adjustment of nonvascular catheter, NEC**
Removal or replacement of catheter
Toilet or cleansing
EXCLUDES *fitting and adjustment of peritoneal dialysis catheter (V56.2)*
fitting and adjustment of urinary catheter (V53.6)

7 **V58.83 Encounter for therapeutic drug monitoring**
Use additional code for any associated long-term (current) drug use (V58.61-V58.69)
EXCLUDES *blood-drug testing for medicolegal reasons (V70.4)*
AHA: 2Q, '04, 10; 1Q, '04, 13;4Q, '03, 85; 4Q, '02, 84; 3Q, '02, 13-16
DEF: Drug monitoring: Measurement of the level of a specific drug in the body or measurement of a specific function to assess effectiveness of a drug.

V58.89 Other specified aftercare
AHA: 4Q, '98, 59

7 **V58.9 Unspecified aftercare**

✓4th **V59 Donors**
EXCLUDES *examination of potential donor (V70.8)*
self-donation of organ or tissue — code to condition
AHA: 4Q, '95, 62; 1Q, '90, 10; N-D, '84, 8

✓5th **V59.0 Blood**
V59.01 Whole blood
V59.02 Stem cells
V59.09 Other

3 **V59.1 Skin**
3 **V59.2 Bone**
3 **V59.3 Bone marrow**
3 **V59.4 Kidney**
3 **V59.5 Cornea**
3 **V59.6 Liver**

✓5th **V59.7 Egg (oocyte) (ovum)**
AHA: ▶4Q, '05, 99◀

V59.70 Egg (oocyte) (ovum) donor, unspecified ♀

V59.71 Egg (oocyte) (ovum) donor, under age 35, anonymous recipient ♀
Egg donor, under age 35 NOS

V59.72 Egg (oocyte) (ovum) donor, under age 35, designated recipient ♀

V59.73 Egg (oocyte) (ovum) donor, age 35 and over, anonymous recipient ♀
Egg donor, age 35 and over NOS

V59.74 Egg (oocyte) (ovum) donor, age 35 and over, designated recipient ♀

3 **V59.8 Other specified organ or tissue**
AHA: 3Q, '02, 20

3 **V59.9 Unspecified organ or tissue**

PERSONS ENCOUNTERING HEALTH SERVICES IN OTHER CIRCUMSTANCES (V60-V69)

✓4th **V60 Housing, household, and economic circumstances**

V60.0 Lack of housing
Hobos
Social migrants
Tramps
Transients
Vagabonds

V60.1 Inadequate housing
Lack of heating
Restriction of space
Technical defects in home preventing adequate care

V60.2 Inadequate material resources
Economic problem
Poverty NOS

V60.3 Person living alone

3 These V codes may be used as principal diagnosis on Medicare patients.
7 These V codes are acceptable as principal diagnosis and group to DRGs 465-466.

V60.4 No other household member able to render care
Person requiring care (has) (is):
family member too handicapped, ill, or otherwise unsuited to render care
partner temporarily away from home
temporarily away from usual place of abode
EXCLUDES *holiday relief care (V60.5)*

V60.5 Holiday relief care
Provision of health care facilities to a person normally cared for at home, to enable relatives to take a vacation

V60.6 Person living in residential institution
Boarding school resident

V60.8 Other specified housing or economic circumstances

V60.9 Unspecified housing or economic circumstance

✓4th **V61 Other family circumstances**
INCLUDES when these circumstances or fear of them, affecting the person directly involved or others, are mentioned as the reason, justified or not, for seeking or receiving medical advice or care
AHA: 1Q, '90, 9

V61.0 Family disruption
Divorce
Estrangement

✓5th **V61.1 Counseling for marital and partner problems**
EXCLUDES *problems related to:*
psychosexual disorders (302.0-302.9)
sexual function (V41.7)

V61.10 Counseling for marital and partner problems,unspecified
Marital conflict
Marital relationship problem
Partner conflict
Partner relationship problem

V61.11 Counseling for victim of spousal and partner abuse
EXCLUDES *encounter for treatment of current injuries due to abuse (995.80-995.85)*

V61.12 Counseling for perpetrator of spousal and partner abuse

✓5th **V61.2 Parent-child problems**

V61.20 Counseling for parent-child problem, unspecified
Concern about behavior of child
Parent-child conflict
Parent-child relationship problem

[3] **V61.21 Counseling for victim of child abuse**
Child battering
Child neglect
EXCLUDES *current injuries due to abuse (995.50-995.59)*

V61.22 Counseling for perpetrator of parental child abuse
EXCLUDES *counseling for non-parental abuser (V62.83)*

V61.29 Other
Problem concerning adopted or foster child
AHA: 3Q, '99, 16

V61.3 Problems with aged parents or in-laws

✓5th **V61.4 Health problems within family**

V61.41 Alcoholism in family

V61.49 Other
Care of } sick or handicapped person
Presence of } in family or household

V61.5 Multiparity

V61.6 Illegitimacy or illegitimate pregnancy M ♀

V61.7 Other unwanted pregnancy M ♀

V61.8 Other specified family circumstances
Problems with family members NEC
Sibling relationship problem

V61.9 Unspecified family circumstance

✓4th **V62 Other psychosocial circumstances**
INCLUDES those circumstances or fear of them, affecting the person directly involved or others, mentioned as the reason, justified or not, for seeking or receiving medical advice or care
EXCLUDES *previous psychological trauma (V15.41-V15.49)*

V62.0 Unemployment
EXCLUDES *circumstances when main problem is economic inadequacy or poverty (V60.2)*

V62.1 Adverse effects of work environment

V62.2 Other occupational circumstances or maladjustment
Career choice problem
Dissatisfaction with employment
Occupational problem

V62.3 Educational circumstances
Academic problem
Dissatisfaction with school environment
Educational handicap

V62.4 Social maladjustment
Acculturation problem
Cultural deprivation
Political, religious, or sex discrimination
Social:
isolation
persecution

V62.5 Legal circumstances
Imprisonment
Legal investigation
Litigation
Prosecution

V62.6 Refusal of treatment for reasons of religion or conscience

✓5th **V62.8 Other psychological or physical stress, not elsewhere classified**

V62.81 Interpersonal problems, not elsewhere classified
Relational problem NOS

V62.82 Bereavement, uncomplicated
EXCLUDES *bereavement as adjustment reaction (309.0)*

V62.83 Counseling for perpetrator of physical/sexual abuse
EXCLUDES *counseling for perpetrator of parental child abuse (V61.22)*
counseling for perpetrator of spousal and partner abuse (V61.12)

V62.84 Suicidal ideation
EXCLUDES *suicidal tendencies (300.9)*
AHA: ▶4Q, '05, 96◀
DEF:▶ Thoughts of committing suicide; no actual attempt of suicide has been made.◀

V62.89 Other
Borderline intellectual functioning
Life circumstance problems
Phase of life problems
Religious or spiritual problem

V62.9 Unspecified psychosocial circumstance

✓5th **V63 Unavailability of other medical facilities for care**
AHA: 1Q, '91, 21

V63.0 Residence remote from hospital or other health care facility

V63.1 Medical services in home not available
EXCLUDES *no other household member able to render care (V60.4)*
AHA: 4Q, '01, 67; 1Q, '01, 12

V63.2 Person awaiting admission to adequate facility elsewhere

V63.8 Other specified reasons for unavailability of medical facilities
Person on waiting list undergoing social agency investigation

V63.9 Unspecified reason for unavailability of medical facilities

[3] These V codes may be used as principal diagnosis on Medicare patients.

N Newborn Age: 0 P Pediatric Age: 0-17 M Maternity Age: 12-55 A Adult Age: 15-124 CC CC Condition MC Major Complication CD Complex Dx HIV HIV Related Dx

✓4th **V64 Persons encountering health services for specific procedures, not carried out**

✓5th **V64.0 Vaccination not carried out**
AHA: 4Q, '05, 99

V64.00 Vaccination not carried out, unspecified reason

V64.01 Vaccination not carried out because of acute illness

V64.02 Vaccination not carried out because of chronic illness or condition

V64.03 Vaccination not carried out because of immune compromised state

V64.04 Vaccination not carried out because of allergy to vaccine or component

V64.05 Vaccination not carried out because of caregiver refusal

V64.06 Vaccination not carried out because of patient refusal

V64.07 Vaccination not carried out for religious reasons

V64.08 Vaccination not carried out because patient had disease being vaccinated against

V64.09 Vaccination not carried out for other reason

V64.1 Surgical or other procedure not carried out because of contraindication

V64.2 Surgical or other procedure not carried out because of patient's decision
AHA: 2Q, '01, 8

V64.3 Procedure not carried out for other reasons

✓5th **V64.4 Closed surgical procedure converted to open procedure**
AHA: 4Q, '03, 87; 4Q, '98, 68; 4Q, '97, 52

V64.41 Laparoscopic surgical procedure converted to open procedure

V64.42 Thoracoscopic surgical procedure converted to open procedure

V64.43 Arthroscopic surgical procedure converted to open procedure

✓4th **V65 Other persons seeking consultation**

3 **V65.0 Healthy person accompanying sick person**
Boarder

✓5th **V65.1 Person consulting on behalf of another person**
Advice or treatment for nonattending third party
EXCLUDES *concern (normal) about sick person in family (V61.41-V61.49)*
AHA: 4Q, '03, 84

V65.11 Pediatric pre-birth visit for expectant mother M ♀

V65.19 Other person consulting on behalf of another person

3 **V65.2 Person feigning illness**
Malingerer
Peregrinating patient
AHA: 3Q, '99, 20

V65.3 Dietary surveillance and counseling
Dietary surveillance and counseling (in):
NOS
colitis
diabetes mellitus
food allergies or intolerance
gastritis
hypercholesterolemia
hypoglycemia
obesity
▶Use additional code to identify Body Mass Index (BMI), if known (V85.0-V85.54)◀
AHA: 4Q, '05, 96

✓5th **V65.4 Other counseling, not elsewhere classified**
Health:
advice
education
instruction
EXCLUDES *counseling (for):*
contraception (V25.40-V25.49)
genetic ▶(V26.31-V26.39)◀
on behalf of third party (V65.11-V65.19)
procreative management (V26.4)

V65.40 Counseling NOS

V65.41 Exercise counseling

V65.42 Counseling on substance use and abuse

V65.43 Counseling on injury prevention

V65.44 Human immunodeficiency virus [HIV] counseling

V65.45 Counseling on other sexually transmitted diseases

V65.46 Encounter for insulin pump training

V65.49 Other specified counseling
AHA: 2Q, '00, 8

V65.5 Person with feared complaint in whom no diagnosis was made
Feared condition not demonstrated
Problem was normal state
"Worried well"

V65.8 Other reasons for seeking consultation
EXCLUDES *specified symptoms*
AHA: 3Q, '92, 4

V65.9 Unspecified reason for consultation

✓4th **V66 Convalescence and palliative care**

3 **V66.0 Following surgery**

3 **V66.1 Following radiotherapy**

3 **V66.2 Following chemotherapy**

3 **V66.3 Following psychotherapy and other treatment for mental disorder**

3 **V66.4 Following treatment of fracture**

V66.5 Following other treatment

3 **V66.6 Following combined treatment**

V66.7 Encounter for palliative care
End of life care
Hospice care
Terminal care
Code first underlying disease
AHA: 2Q, '05, 9; 4Q, '03, 107; 1Q, '98, 11; 4Q, '96, 47, 48

V66.9 Unspecified convalescence
AHA: 4Q, '99, 8

✓4th **V67 Follow-up examination**
INCLUDES surveillance only following completed treatment
EXCLUDES *surveillance of contraception (V25.40-V25.49)*
AHA: 2Q, '03, 5

✓5th **V67.0 Following surgery**
AHA: 4Q, '00, 56; 4Q, '98, 69; 4Q, '97, 50; 2Q, '95, 8;1Q, '95, 4; 3Q, '92, 11

7 **V67.00 Following surgery, unspecified**

7 **V67.01 Follow-up vaginal pap smear** ♀
Vaginal pap-smear, status-post hysterectomy for malignant condition
Use additional code to identify:
acquired absence of uterus (V45.77)
personal history of malignant neoplasm (V10.40-V10.44)
EXCLUDES *vaginal pap smear status-post hysterectomy for non-malignant condition (V76.47)*

7 **V67.09 Following other surgery**
EXCLUDES *sperm count following sterilization reversal (V26.22)*
sperm count for fertility testing (V26.21)
AHA: 3Q, '03, 16; 3Q, '02, 15

3 **V67.1 Following radiotherapy**

3 **V67.2 Following chemotherapy**
Cancer chemotherapy follow-up

3 **V67.3 Following psychotherapy and other treatment for mental disorder**

3 These V codes may be used as principal diagnosis on Medicare patients.
7 These V codes are acceptable as principal diagnosis and group to DRGs 465-466.

7 **V67.4 Following treatment of healed fracture**
EXCLUDES *current (healing) fracture aftercare (V54.0-V54.9)*
AHA: 1Q, '90, 7

✓5th **V67.5 Following other treatment**
3 **V67.51 Following completed treatment with high-risk medications, not elsewhere classified**
EXCLUDES *long-term (current) drug use (V58.61-V58.69)*
AHA: 1Q, '99, 5, 6;4Q, '95, 61 ; 1Q, '90, 18
3 **V67.59 Other**

3 **V67.6 Following combined treatment**

V67.9 Unspecified follow-up examination

✓4th **V68 Encounters for administrative purposes**

V68.0 Issue of medical certificates
Issue of medical certificate of:
cause of death
fitness
incapacity
EXCLUDES *encounter for general medical examination (V70.0-V70.9)*

V68.1 Issue of repeat prescriptions
Issue of repeat prescription for:
appliance
glasses
medications
EXCLUDES *repeat prescription for contraceptives (V25.41-V25.49)*

V68.2 Request for expert evidence

✓5th **V68.8 Other specified administrative purpose**
V68.81 Referral of patient without examination or treatment
V68.89 Other

V68.9 Unspecified administrative purpose

✓4th **V69 Problems related to lifestyle**
AHA: 4Q, '94, 48

V69.0 Lack of physical exercise

V69.1 Inappropriate diet and eating habits
EXCLUDES *anorexia nervosa (307.1)*
bulimia (783.6)
malnutrition and other nutritional deficiencies (260-269.9)
other and unspecified eating disorders (307.50-307.59)

V69.2 High-risk sexual behavior

V69.3 Gambling and betting
EXCLUDES *pathological gambling (312.31)*

V69.4 Lack of adequate sleep
Sleep deprivation
EXCLUDES *insomnia (780.52)*

V69.5 Behavioral insomnia of childhood P
AHA: ▶4Q, '05, 99◀
DEF: ▶Behaviors on the part of the child or caregivers that cause negative compliance with a child's sleep schedule; results in lack of adequate sleep.◀

V69.8 Other problems related to lifestyle
Self-damaging behavior

V69.9 Problem related to lifestyle, unspecified

PERSONS WITHOUT REPORTED DIAGNOSIS ENCOUNTERED DURING EXAMINATION AND INVESTIGATION OF INDIVIDUALS AND POPULATIONS ▶(V70-V82)◀

Note: Nonspecific abnormal findings disclosed at the time of these examinations are classifiable to categories 790-796.

✓4th **V70 General medical examination**
Use additional code(s) to identify any special screening examination(s) performed (V73.0-V82.9)

V70.0 Routine general medical examination at a health care facility
Health checkup
EXCLUDES *health checkup of infant or child (V20.2)*
pre-procedural general physical examination (V72.83)

3 **V70.1 General psychiatric examination, requested by the authority**

V70.2 General psychiatric examination, other and unspecified

V70.3 Other medical examination for administrative purposes
General medical examination for:
admission to old age home
adoption
camp
driving license
immigration and naturalization
insurance certification
marriage
prison
school admission
sports competition
EXCLUDES *attendance for issue of medical certificates (V68.0)*
pre-employment screening (V70.5)
AHA: 1Q, '90, 6

3 **V70.4 Examination for medicolegal reasons**
Blood-alcohol tests
Blood-drug tests
Paternity testing
EXCLUDES *examination and observation following:*
accidents (V71.3, V71.4)
assault (V71.6)
rape (V71.5)

3 **V70.5 Health examination of defined subpopulations**
Armed forces personnel
Inhabitants of institutions
Occupational health examinations
Pre-employment screening
Preschool children
Prisoners
Prostitutes
Refugees
School children
Students

V70.6 Health examination in population surveys
EXCLUDES *special screening (V73.0-V82.9)*

3 **V70.7 Examination of participant in clinical trial**
Examination of participant or control in clinical research
AHA: 4Q, '01, 55

V70.8 Other specified general medical examinations
Examination of potential donor of organ or tissue

V70.9 Unspecified general medical examination

✓4th **V71 Observation and evaluation for suspected conditions not found**
INCLUDES This category is to be used when persons without a diagnosis are suspected of having an abnormal condition, without signs or symptoms, which requires study, but after examination and observation, is found not to exist. This category is also for use for administrative and legal observation status.
AHA: 4Q, '94, 47; 2Q, '90, 5; M-A, '87, 1

✓5th **V71.0 Observation for suspected mental condition**
3 **V71.01 Adult antisocial behavior** A
Dyssocial behavior or gang activity in adult without manifest psychiatric disorder
3 **V71.02 Childhood or adolescent antisocial behavior**
Dyssocial behavior or gang activity in child or adolescent without manifest psychiatric disorder
3 **V71.09 Other suspected mental condition**

3 **V71.1 Observation for suspected malignant neoplasm**

3 **V71.2 Observation for suspected tuberculosis**

3 **V71.3 Observation following accident at work**

3 **V71.4 Observation following other accident**
Examination of individual involved in motor vehicle traffic accident
AHA: ▶1Q, '06, 9◀

3 These V codes may be used as principal diagnosis on Medicare patients.
7 These V codes are acceptable as principal diagnosis and group to DRGs 465-466.

[3] **V71.5 Observation following alleged rape or seduction**
Examination of victim or culprit

[3] **V71.6 Observation following other inflicted injury**
Examination of victim or culprit

[3] **V71.7 Observation for suspected cardiovascular disease**
AHA: 1Q, '04, 6; 3Q, '90, 10; S-O, '87, 10

✓5th **V71.8 Observation and evaluation for other specified suspected conditions**
AHA: 4Q, '00, 54 ; 1Q, '90, 19

[3] **V71.81 Abuse and neglect**
EXCLUDES *adult abuse and neglect (995.80-995.85)*
child abuse and neglect (995.50-995.59)
AHA: 4Q, '00, 55

[3] **V71.82 Observation and evaluation for suspected exposure to anthrax**
AHA: 4Q, '02, 70, 85

[3] **V71.83 Observation and evaluation for suspected exposure to other biological agent**
AHA: 4Q, '03, 47

[3] **V71.89 Other specified suspected conditions**
AHA: 2Q, '03, 15

V71.9 Observation for unspecified suspected condition
AHA: 1Q, '02, 6

✓4th **V72 Special investigations and examinations**
INCLUDES routine examination of specific system
EXCLUDES *general medical examination (V70.0-V70.4)*
general screening examination of defined population groups (V70.5, V70.6, V70.7)
routine examination of infant or child (V20.2)
Use additional code(s) to identify any special screening examination(s) performed (V73.0-V82.9)

[3] **V72.0 Examination of eyes and vision**
AHA: 1Q, '04, 15

✓5th **V72.1 Examination of ears and hearing**
AHA: 1Q, '04, 15

● **V72.11 Encounter for hearing examination following failed hearing screening**

● **V72.19 Other examination of ears and hearing**

V72.2 Dental examination

✓5th **V72.3 Gynecological examination**
EXCLUDES *cervical Papanicolaou smear without general gynecological examination (V76.2)*
routine examination in contraceptive management (V25.40-V25.49)

[3] **V72.31 Routine gynecological examination** ♀
General gynecological examination with or without Papanicolaou cervical smear
Pelvic examination (annual) (periodic)
Use additional code to identify routine vaginal Papanicolaou smear (V76.47)
AHA: 4Q, '05, 9

[3] **V72.32 Encounter for Papanicolaou cervical smear to confirm findings of recent normal smear following initial abnormal smear** ♀

✓5th **V72.4 Pregnancy examination or test**
AHA: 4Q, '05, 98

[3] **V72.40 Pregnancy examination or test, pregnancy unconfirmed** ♀
Possible pregnancy, not (yet) confirmed

[3] **V72.41 Pregnancy examination or test, negative result** ♀

[3] **V72.42 Pregnancy examination or test, positive result** ♀ M

V72.5 Radiological examination, not elsewhere classified
Routine chest x-ray
EXCLUDES *examination for suspected tuberculosis (V71.2)*
AHA: 1Q, '90, 19

V72.6 Laboratory examination
EXCLUDES *that for suspected disorder (V71.0-V71.9)*
AHA: 1Q, '90, 22

V72.7 Diagnostic skin and sensitization tests
Allergy tests
Skin tests for hypersensitivity
EXCLUDES *diagnostic skin tests for bacterial diseases (V74.0-V74.9)*

✓5th **V72.8 Other specified examinations**

[3] **V72.81 Pre-operative cardiovascular examination**
Pre-procedural cardiovascular examination

[3] **V72.82 Pre-operative respiratory examination**
Pre-procedural respiratory examination
AHA: 3Q, '96, 14

[3] **V72.83 Other specified pre-operative examination**
Other pre-procedural examination
Pre-procedural general physical examination
EXCLUDES *routine general medical examination (V70.0)*
AHA: 3Q, '96, 14

V72.84 Pre-operative examination, unspecified
Pre-procedural examination, unspecified

V72.85 Other specified examination
AHA: 4Q, '05, 96; 1Q, '04, 12

V72.86 Encounter for blood typing

V72.9 Unspecified examination

✓4th **V73 Special screening examination for viral and chlamydial diseases**
AHA: 1Q, '04, 11

V73.0 Poliomyelitis

V73.1 Smallpox

V73.2 Measles

V73.3 Rubella

V73.4 Yellow fever

V73.5 Other arthropod-borne viral diseases
Dengue fever
Hemorrhagic fever
Viral encephalitis:
mosquito-borne
tick-borne

V73.6 Trachoma

✓5th **V73.8 Other specified viral and chlamydial diseases**

V73.88 Other specified chlamydial diseases

V73.89 Other specified viral diseases

✓5th **V73.9 Unspecified viral and chlamydial disease**

V73.98 Unspecified chlamydial disease

V73.99 Unspecified viral disease

✓4th **V74 Special screening examination for bacterial and spirochetal diseases**
INCLUDES diagnostic skin tests for these diseases
AHA: 1Q, '04, 11

V74.0 Cholera

V74.1 Pulmonary tuberculosis

V74.2 Leprosy [Hansen's disease]

V74.3 Diphtheria

V74.4 Bacterial conjunctivitis

V74.5 Venereal disease

V74.6 Yaws

V74.8 Other specified bacterial and spirochetal diseases
Brucellosis
Leptospirosis
Plague
Tetanus
Whooping cough

V74.9 Unspecified bacterial and spirochetal disease

[3] These V codes may be used as principal diagnosis on Medicare patients.

✓4th **V75 Special screening examination for other infectious diseases**
AHA: 1Q, '04, 11

V75.0 Rickettsial diseases

V75.1 Malaria

V75.2 Leishmaniasis

V75.3 Trypanosomiasis
Chagas' disease
Sleeping sickness

V75.4 Mycotic infections

V75.5 Schistosomiasis

V75.6 Filariasis

V75.7 Intestinal helminthiasis

V75.8 Other specified parasitic infections

V75.9 Unspecified infectious disease

✓4th **V76 Special screening for malignant neoplasms**
AHA: 1Q, '04, 11

V76.0 Respiratory organs

✓5th **V76.1 Breast**
AHA: 4Q, '98, 67

V76.10 Breast screening, unspecified

V76.11 Screening mammogram for high-risk patient ♀
AHA: 2Q, '03, 4

V76.12 Other screening mammogram
AHA: 2Q, '03, 3-4

V76.19 Other screening breast examination

V76.2 Cervix ♀
Routine cervical Papanicolaou smear
EXCLUDES *that as part of a general gynecological examination (V72.31)*

V76.3 Bladder

✓5th **V76.4 Other sites**

V76.41 Rectum

V76.42 Oral cavity

V76.43 Skin

V76.44 Prostate ♂

V76.45 Testis ♂

V76.46 Ovary ♀
AHA: 4Q, '00, 52

V76.47 Vagina ♀
Vaginal pap smear status-post hysterectomy for non-malignant condition
Use additional code to identify acquired absence of uterus (V45.77)
EXCLUDES *vaginal pap smear status-post hysterectomy for malignant condition (V67.01)*
AHA: 4Q, '00, 52

V76.49 Other sites
AHA: 1Q, '99, 4

✓5th **V76.5 Intestine**
AHA: 4Q, '00, 52

V76.50 Intestine, unspecified

V76.51 Colon
EXCLUDES *rectum (V76.41)*
AHA: 4Q, '01, 56

V76.52 Small intestine

✓5th **V76.8 Other neoplasm**
AHA: 4Q, '00, 52

V76.81 Nervous system

V76.89 Other neoplasm

V76.9 Unspecified

✓4th **V77 Special screening for endocrine, nutritional, metabolic, and immunity disorders**
AHA: 1Q, '04, 11

V77.0 Thyroid disorders

V77.1 Diabetes mellitus

V77.2 Malnutrition

V77.3 Phenylketonuria [PKU]

V77.4 Galactosemia

V77.5 Gout

V77.6 Cystic fibrosis
Screening for mucoviscidosis

V77.7 Other inborn errors of metabolism

V77.8 Obesity

✓5th **V77.9 Other and unspecified endocrine, nutritional, metabolic, and immunity disorders**
AHA: 4Q, '00, 53

V77.91 Screening for lipoid disorders
Screening for cholesterol level
Screening for hypercholesterolemia
Screening for hyperlipidemia

V77.99 Other and unspecified endocrine, nutritional, metabolic, and immunity disorders

✓4th **V78 Special screening for disorders of blood and blood-forming organs**
AHA: 1Q, '04, 11

V78.0 Iron deficiency anemia

V78.1 Other and unspecified deficiency anemia

V78.2 Sickle cell disease or trait

V78.3 Other hemoglobinopathies

V78.8 Other disorders of blood and blood-forming organs

V78.9 Unspecified disorder of blood and blood-forming organs

✓4th **V79 Special screening for mental disorders and developmental handicaps**
AHA: 1Q, '04, 11

V79.0 Depression

V79.1 Alcoholism

V79.2 Mental retardation

V79.3 Developmental handicaps in early childhood

V79.8 Other specified mental disorders and developmental handicaps

V79.9 Unspecified mental disorder and developmental handicap

✓4th **V80 Special screening for neurological, eye, and ear diseases**
AHA: 1Q, '04, 11

V80.0 Neurological conditions

V80.1 Glaucoma

V80.2 Other eye conditions
Screening for:
cataract
congenital anomaly of eye
Screening for:
senile macular lesions
EXCLUDES *general vision examination (V72.0)*

V80.3 Ear diseases
EXCLUDES *general hearing examination (V72.1)*

✓4th **V81 Special screening for cardiovascular, respiratory, and genitourinary diseases**
AHA: 1Q, '04, 11

V81.0 Ischemic heart disease

V81.1 Hypertension

V81.2 Other and unspecified cardiovascular conditions

V81.3 Chronic bronchitis and emphysema

V81.4 Other and unspecified respiratory conditions
EXCLUDES *screening for:*
lung neoplasm (V76.0)
pulmonary tuberculosis (V74.1)

V81.5 Nephropathy
Screening for asymptomatic bacteriuria

V81.6 Other and unspecified genitourinary conditions

✓4th **V82 Special screening for other conditions**
AHA: 1Q, '04, 11

V82.0 Skin conditions

V82.1 Rheumatoid arthritis

V82.2 Other rheumatic disorders

V82.3 Congenital dislocation of hip

V82.4 Maternal postnatal screening for chromosomal anomalies ♀

EXCLUDES *antenatal screening by amniocentesis (V28.0)*

V82.5 Chemical poisoning and other contamination

Screening for:
- heavy metal poisoning
- ingestion of radioactive substance
- poisoning from contaminated water supply
- radiation exposure

V82.6 Multiphasic screening

● ✓5th **V82.7 Genetic screening**

EXCLUDES *genetic testing for procreative management (V26.31-V26.32)*

● **V82.71 Screening for genetic disease carrier status**

● **V82.79 Other genetic screening**

✓5th **V82.8 Other specified conditions**

AHA: 4Q, '00, 53

V82.81 Osteoporosis

Use additional code to identify:
- hormone replacement therapy (postmenopausal) status (V07.4)
- postmenopausal (age-related) (natural) status (V49.81)

AHA: 4Q, '00, 54

V82.89 Other specified conditions

V82.9 Unspecified condition

▶GENETICS (V83-V84)◀

✓4th **V83 Genetic carrier status**

AHA: 4Q, '02, 79; 4Q, '01, 54

✓5th **V83.0 Hemophilia A carrier**

V83.01 Asymptomatic hemophilia A carrier

V83.02 Symptomatic hemophilia A carrier

✓5th **V83.8 Other genetic carrier status**

V83.81 Cystic fibrosis gene carrier

V83.89 Other genetic carrier status

✓4th **V84 Genetic susceptibility to disease**

INCLUDES confirmed abnormal gene

Use additional code, if applicable, for any associated family history of the disease (V16-V19)

AHA: 4Q, '04, 106

✓5th **V84.0 Genetic susceptibility to malignant neoplasm**

Code first, if applicable, any current malignant neoplasms (140.0-195.8, 200.0-208.9, 230.0-234.9)

Use additional code, if applicable, for any personal history of malignant neoplasm (V10.0-V10.9)

V84.01 Genetic susceptibility to malignant neoplasm of breast

AHA: 4Q, '04, 107

V84.02 Genetic susceptibility to malignant neoplasm of ovary ♀

V84.03 Genetic susceptibility to malignant neoplasm of prostate ♂

V84.04 Genetic susceptibility to malignant neoplasm of endometrium ♀

V84.09 Genetic susceptibility to other malignant neoplasm

V84.8 Genetic susceptibility to other disease

▶BODY MASS INDEX (V85)◀

▲ ✓4th **V85 Body Mass Index [BMI]**

Kilograms per meters squared

Note: BMI adult codes are for use for persons over 20 years old

AHA: 4Q, '05, 97

V85.0 Body Mass Index less than 19, adult A

V85.1 Body Mass Index between 19-24, adult A

✓5th **V85.2 Body Mass Index between 25-29, adult**

V85.21 Body Mass Index 25.0-25.9, adult A

V85.22 Body Mass Index 26.0-26.9, adult A

V85.23 Body Mass Index 27.0-27.9, adult A

V85.24 Body Mass Index 28.0-28.9, adult A

V85.25 Body Mass Index 29.0-29.9, adult A

✓5th **V85.3 Body Mass Index between 30-39, adult**

V85.30 Body Mass Index 30.0-30.9, adult A

V85.31 Body Mass Index 31.0-31.9, adult A

V85.32 Body Mass Index 32.0-32.9, adult A

V85.33 Body Mass Index 33.0-33.9, adult A

V85.34 Body Mass Index 34.0-34.9, adult A

V85.35 Body Mass Index 35.0-35.9, adult A

V85.36 Body Mass Index 36.0-36.9, adult A

V85.37 Body Mass Index 37.0-37.9, adult A

V85.38 Body Mass Index 38.0-38.9, adult A

V85.39 Body Mass Index 39.0-39.9, adult A

V85.4 Body Mass Index 40 and over, adult A

● ✓5th **V85.5 Body Mass Index, pediatric**

Note: BMI pediatric codes are for use for persons age 2-20 years old. These percentiles are based on the growth charts published by the Centers for Disease Control and Prevention (CDC)

● **V85.51 Body Mass Index, pediatric, less than 5th percentile for age** P

● **V85.52 Body Mass Index, pediatric, 5th percentile to less than 85th percentile for age** P

● **V85.53 Body Mass Index, pediatric, 85th percentile to less than 95th percentile for age** P

● **V85.54 Body Mass Index, pediatric, greater than or equal to 95th percentile for age** P

▶ESTROGEN RECEPTOR STATUS (V86)◀

● ✓4th **V86 Estrogen receptor status**

Code first malignant neoplasm of breast (174.0-174.9, 175.0-175.9)

● **V86.0 Estrogen receptor positive status [ER+]**

● **V86.1 Estrogen receptor negative status [ER-]**

SUPPLEMENTARY CLASSIFICATION OF EXTERNAL CAUSES OF INJURY AND POISONING (E800-E999)

This section is provided to permit the classification of environmental events, circumstances, and conditions as the cause of injury, poisoning, and other adverse effects. Where a code from this section is applicable, it is intended that it shall be used in addition to a code from one of the main chapters of ICD-9-CM, indicating the nature of the condition. Certain other conditions which may be stated to be due to external causes are classified in Chapters 1 to 16 of ICD-9-CM. For these, the "E" code classification should be used as an additional code for more detailed analysis.

Machinery accidents [other than those connected with transport] are classifiable to category E919, in which the fourth-digit allows a broad classification of the type of machinery involved. If a more detailed classification of type of machinery is required, it is suggested that the "Classification of Industrial Accidents according to Agency," prepared by the International Labor Office, be used in addition. This is reproduced in Appendix D for optional use.

Categories for "late effects" of accidents and other external causes are to be found at E929, E959, E969, E977, E989, and E999.

DEFINITIONS AND EXAMPLES RELATED TO TRANSPORT ACCIDENTS

(a) A **transport accident** (E800-E848) is any accident involving a device designed primarily for, or being used at the time primarily for, conveying persons or goods from one place to another.

INCLUDES accidents involving:
- aircraft and spacecraft (E840-E845)
- watercraft (E830-E838)
- motor vehicle (E810-E825)
- railway (E800-E807)
- other road vehicles (E826-E829)

In classifying accidents which involve more than one kind of transport, the above order of precedence of transport accidents should be used.

Accidents involving agricultural and construction machines, such as tractors, cranes, and bulldozers, are regarded as transport accidents only when these vehicles are under their own power on a highway [otherwise the vehicles are regarded as machinery]. Vehicles which can travel on land or water, such as hovercraft and other amphibious vehicles, are regarded as watercraft when on the water, as motor vehicles when on the highway, and as off-road motor vehicles when on land, but off the highway.

EXCLUDES *accidents:*
- *in sports which involve the use of transport but where the transport vehicle itself was not involved in the accident*
- *involving vehicles which are part of industrial equipment used entirely on industrial premises*
- *occurring during transportation but unrelated to the hazards associated with the means of transportation [e.g., injuries received in a fight on board ship; transport vehicle involved in a cataclysm such as an earthquake]*
- *to persons engaged in the maintenance or repair of transport equipment or vehicle not in motion, unlesss injured by another vehicle in motion*

(b) A **railway accident** is a transport accident involving a railway train or other railway vehicle operated on rails, whether in motion or not.

EXCLUDES *accidents:*
- *in repair shops*
- *in roundhouse or on turntable*
- *on railway premises but not involving a train or other railway vehicle*

(c) A **railway train** or **railway vehicle** is any device with or without cars coupled to it, desiged for traffic on a railway.

INCLUDES interurban:
- electric car, streetcar (operated chiefly on its own right-of-way, not open to other traffic)
- railway train, any power [diesel] [electric] [steam]
  - funicular
  - monorail or two-rail
  - subterranean or elevated
- other vehicle designed to run on a railway track

EXCLUDES *interurban electric cars [streetcars] specified to be operating on a right-of-way that forms part of the public street or highway [definition (n)]*

(d) A **railway** or **railroad** is a right-of-way designed for traffic on rails, which is used by carriages or wagons transporting passengers or freight, and by other rolling stock, and which is not open to other public vehicular traffic.

(e) A **motor vehicle accident** is a transport accident involving a motor vehicle. It is defined as a motor vehicle traffic accident or as a motor vehicle nontraffic accident according to whether the accident occurs on a public highway or elsewhere.

EXCLUDES
- *injury or damage due to cataclysm*
- *injury or damage while a motor vehicle, not under its own power, is being loaded on, or unloaded from, another conveyance*

(f) A **motor vehicle traffic accident** is any motor vehicle accident occurring on a public highway [i.e., originating, terminating, or involving a vehicle partially on the highway]. A motor vehicle accident is assumed to have occurred on the highway unless another place is specified, except in the case of accidents involving only off-road motor vehicles which are classified as nontraffic accidents unless the contrary is stated.

(g) A **motor vehicle nontraffic accident** is any motor vehicle accident which occurs entirely in any place other than a public highway.

(h) A **public highway [trafficway]** or **street** is the entire width between property lines [or other boundary lines] of every way or place, of which any part is open to the use of the public for purposes of vehicular traffic as a matter of right or custom. A **roadway** is that part of the public highway designed, improved, and ordinarily used, for vehicular travel.

INCLUDES approaches (public) to:
- docks
- public building
- station

EXCLUDES
- *driveway (private)*
- *parking lot*
- *ramp*
- *roads in:*
  - *airfield*
  - *farm*
  - *industrial premises*
  - *mine*
  - *private grounds*
  - *quarry*

(i) A **motor vehicle** is any mechanically or electrically powered device, not operated on rails, upon which any person or property may be transported or drawn upon a highway. Any object such as a trailer, coaster, sled, or wagon being towed by a motor vehicle is considerd a part of the motor vehicle.

INCLUDES
- automobile [any type]
- bus
- construction machinery, farm and industrial machinery, steam roller, tractor, army tank, highway grader, or similar vehicle on wheels or treads, while in transport under own power
- fire engine (motorized)
- motorcycle
- motorized bicycle [moped] or scooter
- trolley bus not operating on rails
- truck
- van

EXCLUDES
- *devices used solely to move persons or materials within the confines of a building and its premises, such as:*
  - *building elevator*
  - *coal car in mine*
  - *electric baggage or mail truck used solely within a railroad station*
  - *electric truck used solely within an industrial plant*
  - *moving overhead crane*

(j) A **motorcycle** is a two-wheeled motor vehicle having one or two riding saddles and sometimes having a third wheel for the support of a sidecar. The sidecar is considered part of the motorcycle.

INCLUDES
- motorized:
  - bicycle [moped]
  - scooter
  - tricycle

(k) An **off-road motor vehicle** is a motor vehicle of special design, to enable it to negotiate rough or soft terrain or snow. Examples of special design are high construction, special wheels and tires, driven by treads, or support on a cushion of air.

INCLUDES
- all terrain vehicle [ATV]
- army tank
- hovercraft, on land or swamp
- snowmobile

(l) A **driver** of a motor vehicle is the occupant of the motor vehicle operating it or intending to operate it. A **motorcyclist** is the driver of a motorcycle. Other authorized occupants of a motor vehicle are **passengers**.

(m) An **other road vehicle** is any device, except a motor vehicle, in, on, or by which any person or property may be transported on a highway.

INCLUDES
- animal carrying a person or goods
- animal-drawn vehicles
- animal harnessed to conveyance
- bicycle [pedal cycle]
- streetcar
- tricycle (pedal)

EXCLUDES
- *pedestrian conveyance [definition (q)]*

(n) A **streetcar** is a device designed and used primarily for transporting persons within a municipality, running on rails, usually subject to normal traffic control signals, and operated principally on a right-of-way that forms part of the traffic way. A trailer being towed by a streetcar is considered a part of the streetcar.

INCLUDES
- interurban or intraurban electric or streetcar, when specified to be operating on a street or public highway
- tram (car)
- trolley (car)

(o) A **pedal cycle** is any road transport vehicle operated solely by pedals.

INCLUDES
- bicycle
- pedal cycle
- tricycle

EXCLUDES
- *motorized bicycle [definition (i)]*

(p) A **pedal cyclist** is any person riding on a pedal cycle or in a sidecar attached to such a vehicle.

(q) A **pedestrian conveyance** is any human powered device by which a pedestrian may move other than by walking or by which a walking person may move another pedestrian.

INCLUDES
- baby carriage
- coaster wagon
- ice skates
- perambulator
- pushcart
- pushchair
- roller skates
- scooter
- skateboard
- skis
- sled
- wheelchair

(r) A **pedestrian** is any person involved in an accident who was not at the time of the accident riding in or on a motor vehicle, railroad train, streetcar, animal-drawn or other vehicle, or on a bicycle or animal.

INCLUDES
- person:
  - changing tire of vehicle
  - in or operating a pedestrian conveyance
  - making adjustment to motor of vehicle
  - on foot

(s) A **watercraft** is any device for transporting passengers or goods on the water.

(t) A **small boat** is any watercraft propelled by paddle, oars, or small motor, with a passenger capacity of less than ten.

INCLUDES
- boat NOS
- canoe
- coble
- dinghy
- punt
- raft
- rowboat
- rowing shell
- scull
- skiff
- small motorboat

EXCLUDES
- *barge*
- *lifeboat (used after abandoning ship)*
- *raft (anchored) being used as a diving platform*
- *yacht*

(u) An **aircraft** is any device for transporting passengers or goods in the air.

INCLUDES
- airplane [any type]
- balloon
- bomber
- dirigible
- glider (hang)
- military aircraft
- parachute

(v) A **commercial transport aircraft** is any device for collective passenger or freight transportation by air, whether run on commercial lines for profit or by government authorities, with the exception of military craft.

RAILWAY ACCIDENTS (E800-E807)

Note: For definitions of railway accident and related terms see definitions (a) to (d).

EXCLUDES *accidents involving railway train and:*
aircraft (E840.0-E845.9)
motor vehicle (E810.0-E825.9)
watercraft (E830.0-E838.9)

The following fourth-digit subdivisions are for use with categories E800-E807 to identify the injured person:

.0 Railway employee
Any person who by virtue of his employment in connection with a railway, whether by the railway company or not, is at increased risk of involvement in a railway accident, such as:
catering staff of train
driver
guard
porter
postal staff on train
railway fireman
shunter
sleeping car attendant

.1 Passenger on railway
Any authorized person traveling on a train, except a railway employee.
EXCLUDES *intending passenger waiting at station (.8)*
unauthorized rider on railway vehicle (.8)

.2 Pedestrian
See definition (r)

.3 Pedal cyclist
See definition (p)

.8 Other specified person
Intending passenger or bystander waiting at station
Unauthorized rider on railway vehicle

.9 Unspecified person

✓4th E800 Railway accident involving collision with rolling stock
INCLUDES collision between railway trains or railway vehicles, any kind
collision NOS on railway
derailment with antecedent collision with rolling stock or NOS

✓4th E801 Railway accident involving collision with other object
INCLUDES collision of railway train with:
buffers
fallen tree on railway
gates
platform
rock on railway
streetcar
other nonmotor vehicle
other object
EXCLUDES *collision with:*
aircraft (E840.0-E842.9)
motor vehicle (E810.0-E810.9, E820.0-E822.9)

✓4th E802 Railway accident involving derailment without antecedent collision

✓4th E803 Railway accident involving explosion, fire, or burning
EXCLUDES *explosion or fire, with antecedent derailment (E802.0-E802.9)*
explosion or fire, with mention of antecedent collision (E800.0-E801.9)

✓4th E804 Fall in, on, or from railway train
INCLUDES fall while alighting from or boarding railway train
EXCLUDES *fall related to collision, derailment, or explosion of railway train (E800.0-E803.9)*

✓4th E805 Hit by rolling stock
INCLUDES crushed / injured / killed / knocked down / run over } by railway train or part
EXCLUDES *pedestrian hit by object set in motion by railway train (E806.0-E806.9)*

✓4th E806 Other specified railway accident
INCLUDES hit by object falling in railway train
injured by door or window on railway train
nonmotor road vehicle or pedestrian hit by object set in motion by railway train
railway train hit by falling:
earth NOS
rock
tree
other object
EXCLUDES *railway accident due to cataclysm (E908-E909)*

✓4th E807 Railway accident of unspecified nature
INCLUDES found dead / injured } on railway right-of-way NOS
railway accident NOS

MOTOR VEHICLE TRAFFIC ACCIDENTS (E810-E819)

Note: For definitions of motor vehicle traffic accident, and related terms, see definitions (e) to (k).

EXCLUDES *accidents involving motor vehicle and aircraft (E840.0-E845.9)*

The following fourth-digit subdivisions are for use with categories E810-E819 to identify the injured person:

.0 Driver of motor vehicle other than motorcycle
See definition (l)

.1 Passenger in motor vehicle other than motorcycle
See definition (l)

.2 Motorcyclist
See definition (l)

.3 Passenger on motorcycle
See definition (l)

.4 Occupant of streetcar

.5 Rider of animal; occupant of animal-drawn vehicle

.6 Pedal cyclist
See definition (p)

.7 Pedestrian
See definition (r)

.8 Other specified person
Occupant of vehicle other than above
Person in railway train involved in accident
Unauthorized rider of motor vehicle

.9 Unspecified person

✓4th E810 Motor vehicle traffic accident involving collision with train
EXCLUDES *motor vehicle collision with object set in motion by railway train (E815.0-E815.9)*
railway train hit by object set in motion by motor vehicle (E818.0-E818.9)

✓4th E811 Motor vehicle traffic accident involving re-entrant collision with another motor vehicle
INCLUDES collision between motor vehicle which accidentally leaves the roadway then re-enters the same roadway, or the opposite roadway on a divided highway, and another motor vehicle
EXCLUDES *collision on the same roadway when none of the motor vehicles involved have left and re-entered the highway (E812.0-E812.9)*

✓4th Fourth-digit Required ▶◀ Revised Text ● New Code ▲ Revised Code Title

§ ✓4th **E812 Other motor vehicle traffic accident involving collision with motor vehicle**

INCLUDES collision with another motor vehicle parked, stopped, stalled, disabled, or abandoned on the highway
motor vehicle collision NOS

EXCLUDES *collision with object set in motion by another motor vehicle (E815.0-E815.9)*
re-entrant collision with another motor vehicle (E811.0-E811.9)

§ ✓4th **E813 Motor vehicle traffic accident involving collision with other vehicle**

INCLUDES collision between motor vehicle, any kind, and:
other road (nonmotor transport) vehicle, such as:
animal carrying a person
animal-drawn vehicle
pedal cycle
streetcar

EXCLUDES *collision with:*
object set in motion by nonmotor road vehicle (E815.0-E815.9)
pedestrian (E814.0-E814.9)
nonmotor road vehicle hit by object set in motion by motor vehicle (E818.0-E818.9)

§ ✓4th **E814 Motor vehicle traffic accident involving collision with pedestrian**

INCLUDES collision between motor vehicle, any kind, and pedestrian
pedestrian dragged, hit, or run over by motor vehicle, any kind

EXCLUDES *pedestrian hit by object set in motion by motor vehicle (E818.0-E818.9)*

§ ✓4th **E815 Other motor vehicle traffic accident involving collision on the highway**

INCLUDES collision (due to loss of control) (on highway) between motor vehicle, any kind, and:
abutment (bridge) (overpass)
animal (herded) (unattended)
fallen stone, traffic sign, tree, utility pole
guard rail or boundary fence
interhighway divider
landslide (not moving)
object set in motion by railway train or road vehicle (motor) (nonmotor)
object thrown in front of motor vehicle
other object, fixed, movable, or moving
safety island
temporary traffic sign or marker
wall of cut made for road

EXCLUDES *collision with:*
any object off the highway (resulting from loss of control) (E816.0-E816.9)
any object which normally would have been off the highway and is not stated to have been on it (E816.0-E816.9)
motor vehicle parked, stopped, stalled, disabled, or abandoned on highway (E812.0-E812.9)
moving landslide (E909)
motor vehicle hit by object:
set in motion by railway train or road vehicle (motor) (nonmotor) (E818.0-E818.9)
thrown into or on vehicle (E818.0-E818.9)

§ ✓4th **E816 Motor vehicle traffic accident due to loss of control, without collision on the highway**

INCLUDES motor vehicle:
failing to make curve
going out of control (due to):
blowout
burst tire
driver falling asleep
driver inattention
excessive speed
failure of mechanical part
} and:
coliding with object off the highway
overturning
stopping abruptly off the highway

EXCLUDES *collision on highway following loss of control (E810.0-E815.9)*
loss of control of motor vehicle following collision on the highway (E810.0-E815.9)

§ ✓4th **E817 Noncollision motor vehicle traffic accident while boarding or alighting**

INCLUDES fall down stairs of motor bus
fall from car in street
injured by moving part of the vehicle
trapped by door of motor bus
} while boarding or alighting

§ ✓4th **E818 Other noncollision motor vehicle traffic accident**

INCLUDES accidental poisoning from exhaust gas generated by
breakage of any part of
explosion of any part of
fall, jump, or being accidentally pushed from
fire starting in
hit by object thrown into or on
injured by being thrown against some part of, or object in
injury from moving part of
object falling in or on
object thrown on
} motor vehicle while in motion

collision of railway train or road vehicle except motor vehicle, with object set in motion by motor vehicle
motor vehicle hit by object set in motion by railway train or road vehicle (motor) (nonmotor)
pedestrian, railway train, or road vehicle (motor) (nonmotor) hit by object set in motion by motor vehicle

EXCLUDES *collision between motor vehicle and:*
object set in motion by railway train or road vehicle (motor) (nonmotor) (E815.0-E815.9)
object thrown towards the motor vehicle (E815.0-E815.9)
person overcome by carbon monoxide generated by stationary motor vehicle off the roadway with motor running (E868.2)

§ ✓4th **E819 Motor vehicle traffic accident of unspecified nature**

INCLUDES motor vehicle traffic accident NOS
traffic accident NOS

§ Requires fourth-digit. See beginning of section E810-E819 for codes and definitions.

MOTOR VEHICLE NONTRAFFIC ACCIDENTS (E820-E825)

Note: For definitions of motor vehicle nontraffic accident and related terms see definition (a) to (k).

INCLUDES accidents involving motor vehicles being used in recreational or sporting activities off the highway
collision and noncollision motor vehicle accidents occurring entirely off the highway

EXCLUDES *accidents involving motor vehicle and:*
aircraft (E840.0-E845.9)
watercraft (E830.0-E838.9)
accidents, not on the public highway, involving agricultural and construction machinery but not involving another motor vehicle (E919.0, E919.2, E919.7)

The following fourth-digit subdivisions are for use with categories E820-E825 to identify the injured person:

.0 Driver of motor vehicle other than motorcycle
See definition (l)

.1 Passenger in motor vehicle other than motorcycle
See definition (l)

.2 Motorcyclist
See definition (l)

.3 Passenger on motorcycle
See definition (l)

.4 Occupant of streetcar

.5 Rider of animal; occupant of animal-drawn vehicle

.6 Pedal cyclist
See definition (p)

.7 Pedestrian
See definition (r)

.8 Other specified person
Occupant of vehicle other than above
Person on railway train involved in accident
Unauthorized rider of motor vehicle

.9 Unspecified person

✓4th E820 Nontraffic accident involving motor-driven snow vehicle

INCLUDES breakage of part of / fall from / hit by / overturning of / run over or dragged by } motor-driven snow vehicle (not on public highway)

collision of motor-driven snow vehicle with:
animal (being ridden) (-drawn vehicle)
another off-road motor vehicle
other motor vehicle, not on public highway
railway train
other object, fixed or movable
injury caused by rough landing of motor-driven snow vehicle (after leaving ground on rough terrain)

EXCLUDES *accident on the public highway involving motor driven snow vehicle (E810.0-E819.9)*

✓4th E821 Nontraffic accident involving other off-road motor vehicle

INCLUDES breakage of part of / fall from / hit by / overturning of / run over or dragged by / thrown against some part of or object in } off-road motor vehicle, except snow vehicle (not on public highway)

collision with:
animal (being ridden) (-drawn vehicle)
another off-road motor vehicle, except snow vehicle
other motor vehicle, not on public highway
other object, fixed or movable

EXCLUDES *accident on public highway involving off-road motor vehicle (E810.0-E819.9)*
collision between motor driven snow vehicle and other off-road motor vehicle (E820.0-E820.9)
hovercraft accident on water (E830.0-E838.9)

✓4th E822 Other motor vehicle nontraffic accident involving collision with moving object

INCLUDES collision, not on public highway, between motor vehicle, except off-road motor vehicle and:
animal
nonmotor vehicle
other motor vehicle, except off-road motor vehicle
pedestrian
railway train
other moving object

EXCLUDES *collision with:*
motor-driven snow vehicle (E820.0-E820.9)
other off-road motor vehicle (E821.0-E821.9)

✓4th E823 Other motor vehicle nontraffic accident involving collision with stationary object

INCLUDES collision, not on public highway, between motor vehicle, except off-road motor vehicle, and any object, fixed or movable, but not in motion

✓4th E824 Other motor vehicle nontraffic accident while boarding and alighting

INCLUDES fall / injury from moving part of motor vehicle / trapped by door of motor vehicle } while boarding or alighting from motor vehicle, except off-road motor vehicle, not on public highway

§ ✓4th **E825 Other motor vehicle nontraffic accident of other and unspecified nature**

INCLUDES accidental poisoning from carbon monoxide generated by
breakage of any part of
explosion of any part of
fall, jump, or being accidentally pushed from
fire starting in
hit by object thrown into, towards, or on
injured by being thrown against some part of, or object in
injury from moving part of
object falling in or on
} motor vehicle while in motion, not on public highway

motor vehicle nontraffic accident NOS

EXCLUDES *fall from or in stationary motor vehicle (E884.9, E885.9)*
overcome by carbon monoxide or exhaust gas generated by stationary motor vehicle off the roadway with motor running (E868.2)
struck by falling object from or in stationary motor vehicle (E916)

OTHER ROAD VEHICLE ACCIDENTS (E826-E829)

Note: Other road vehicle accidents are transport accidents involving road vehicles other than motor vehicles. For definitions of other road vehicle and related terms see definitions (m) to (o).

INCLUDES accidents involving other road vehicles being used in recreational or sporting activities

EXCLUDES *collision of other road vehicle [any] with:*
aircraft (E840.0-E845.9)
motor vehicle (E813.0-E813.9, E820.0-E822.9)
railway train (E801.0-E801.9)

The following fourth-digit subdivisions are for use with categories E826-E829 to identify the injured person.

.0 Pedestrian
See definition (r)
.1 Pedal cyclist
See definition (p)
.2 Rider of animal
.3 Occupant of animal-drawn vehicle
.4 Occupant of streetcar
.8 Other specified person
.9 Unspecified person

✓4th **E826 Pedal cycle accident**

[0-9] INCLUDES breakage of any part of pedal cycle
collision between pedal cycle and:
animal (being ridden) (herded) (unattended)
another pedal cycle
any pedestrian
nonmotor road vehicle
other object, fixed, movable, or moving, not set in motion by motor vehicle, railway train, or aircraft
entanglement in wheel of pedal cycle
fall from pedal cycle
hit by object falling or thrown on the pedal cycle
pedal cycle accident NOS
pedal cycle overturned

✓4th **E827 Animal-drawn vehicle accident**

[0,2-4,8,9] INCLUDES breakage of any part of vehicle
collision between animal-drawn vehicle and:
animal (being ridden) (herded) (unattended)
nonmotor road vehicle, except pedal cycle
pedestrian, pedestrian conveyance, or pedestrian vehicle
other object, fixed, movable, or moving, not set in motion by motor vehicle, railway train, or aircraft
fall from
knocked down by
overturning of
run over by
thrown from
} animal-drawn vehicle

EXCLUDES *collision of animal-drawn vehicle with pedal cycle (E826.0-E826.9)*

✓4th **E828 Accident involving animal being ridden**

[0,2,4,8,9] INCLUDES collision between animal being ridden and:
another animal
nonmotor road vehicle, except pedal cycle, and animal-drawn vehicle
pedestrian, pedestrian conveyance, or pedestrian vehicle
other object, fixed, movable, or moving, not set in motion by motor vehicle, railway train, or aircraft
fall from
knocked down by
thrown from
trampled by
} animal being ridden
ridden animal stumbled and fell

EXCLUDES *collision of animal being ridden with:*
animal-drawn vehicle (E827.0-E827.9)
pedal cycle (E826.0-E826.9)

✓4th **E829 Other road vehicle accidents**

[0,4,8,9] INCLUDES accident while boarding or alighting from
blow from object in
breakage of any part of
caught in door of-
derailment of
fall in, on, or from
fire in
} streetcar nonmotor road vehicle not classifiable to E826-E828

collision between streetcar or nonmotor road vehicle, except as in E826-E828, and:
animal (not being ridden)
another nonmotor road vehicle not classifiable to E826-E828
pedestrian
other object, fixed, movable, or moving, not set in motion by motor vehicle, railway train, or aircraft
nonmotor road vehicle accident NOS
streetcar accident NOS

EXCLUDES *collision with:*
animal being ridden (E828.0-E828.9)
animal-drawn vehicle (E827.0-E827.9)
pedal cycle (E826.0-E826.9)

§ Requires fourth-digit. Valid digits are in [brackets] under each code. See beginning of section E820-E825 for codes and definitions.

WATER TRANSPORT ACCIDENTS (E830-E838)

Note: For definitions of water transport accident and related terms see definitions (a), (s), and (t).

INCLUDES watercraft accidents in the course of recreational activities

EXCLUDES *accidents involving both aircraft, including objects set in motion by aircraft, and watercraft (E840.0-E845.9)*

The following fourth-digit subdivisions are for use with categories E830-E838 to identify the injured person:

.0 Occupant of small boat, unpowered

.1 Occupant of small boat, powered
See definition (t)
EXCLUDES *water skier (.4)*

.2 Occupant of other watercraft — crew
Persons:
engaged in operation of watercraft
providing passenger services [cabin attendants, ship's physician, catering personnel]
working on ship during voyage in other capacity [musician in band, operators of shops and beauty parlors]

.3 Occupant of other watercraft — other than crew
Passenger
Occupant of lifeboat, other than crew, after abandoning ship

.4 Water skier

.5 Swimmer

.6 Dockers, stevedores
Longshoreman employed on the dock in loading and unloading ships

.8 Other specified person
Immigration and custom officials on board ship
Person:
accompanying passenger or member of crew visiting boat
Pilot (guiding ship into port)

.9 Unspecified person

✓4th E830 Accident to watercraft causing submersion

INCLUDES submersion and drowning due to:
boat overturning
boat submerging
falling or jumping from burning ship
falling or jumping from crushed watercraft
ship sinking
other accident to watercraft

✓4th E831 Accident to watercraft causing other injury

INCLUDES any injury, except submersion and drowning, as a result of an accident to watercraft
burned while ship on fire
crushed between ships in collision
crushed by lifeboat after abandoning ship
fall due to collision or other accident to watercraft
hit by falling object due to accident to watercraft
injured in watercraft accident involving collision
struck by boat or part thereof after fall or jump from damaged boat

EXCLUDES *burns from localized fire or explosion on board ship (E837.0-E837.9)*

✓4th E832 Other accidental submersion or drowning in water transport accident

INCLUDES submersion or drowning as a result of an accident other than accident to the watercraft, such as:
fall:
from gangplank
from ship
overboard
thrown overboard by motion of ship
washed overboard

EXCLUDES *submersion or drowning of swimmer or diver who voluntarily jumps from boat not involved in an accident (E910.0-E910.9)*

✓4th E833 Fall on stairs or ladders in water transport

EXCLUDES *fall due to accident to watercraft (E831.0-E831.9)*

✓4th E834 Other fall from one level to another in water transport

EXCLUDES *fall due to accident to watercraft (E831.0-E831.9)*

✓4th E835 Other and unspecified fall in water transport

EXCLUDES *fall due to accident to watercraft (E831.0-E831.9)*

✓4th E836 Machinery accident in water transport

INCLUDES injuries in water transport caused by:
deck, engine room, galley, laundry, loading } machinery

✓4th E837 Explosion, fire, or burning in watercraft

INCLUDES explosion of boiler on steamship
localized fire on ship

EXCLUDES *burning ship (due to collision or explosion) resulting in:*
submersion or drowning (E830.0-E830.9)
other injury (E831.0-E831.9)

✓4th E838 Other and unspecified water transport accident

INCLUDES accidental poisoning by gases or fumes on ship
atomic power plant malfunction in watercraft
crushed between ship and stationary object [wharf]
crushed between ships without accident to watercraft
crushed by falling object on ship or while loading or unloading
hit by boat while water skiing
struck by boat or part thereof (after fall from boat)
watercraft accident NOS

AIR AND SPACE TRANSPORT ACCIDENTS (E840-E845)

Note: For definition of aircraft and related terms see definitions (u) and (v).

The following fourth-digit subdivisions are for use with categories E840-E845 to identify the injured person. Valid fourth digits are in [brackets] under codes E842-E845.

.0 Occupant of spacecraft

.1 Occupant of military aircraft, any
- Crew in military aircraft [air force] [army] [national guard] [navy]
- Passenger (civilian) (military) in military aircraft [air force] [army] [national guard] [navy]
- Troops in military aircraft [air force] [army] [national guard] [navy]

EXCLUDES *occupants of aircraft operated under jurisdiction of police departments (.5)*
parachutist (.7)

.2 Crew of commercial aircraft (powered) in surface to surface transport

.3 Other occupant of commercial aircraft (powered) in surface to surface transport
- Flight personnel:
  - not part of crew
  - on familiarization flight
- Passenger on aircraft (powered) NOS

.4 Occupant of commercial aircraft (powered) in surface to air transport
- Occupant [crew] [passenger] of aircraft (powered) engaged in activities, such as:
  - aerial spraying (crops) (fire retardants)
  - air drops of emergency supplies
  - air drops of parachutists, except from military craft
  - crop dusting
  - lowering of construction material [bridge or telephone pole]
  - sky writing

.5 Occupant of other powered aircraft
- Occupant [crew][passenger] of aircraft [powered] engaged in activities, such as:
  - aerobatic flying
  - aircraft racing
  - rescue operation
  - storm surveillance
  - traffic surveillance
- Occupant of private plane NOS

.6 Occupant of unpowered aircraft, except parachutist
- Occupant of aircraft classifiable to E842

.7 Parachutist (military) (other)
- Person making voluntary descent

EXCLUDES *person making descent after accident to aircraft (.1-.6)*

.8 Ground crew, airline employee
- Persons employed at airfields (civil) (military) or launching pads, not occupants of aircraft

.9 Other person

✓4th E840 Accident to powered aircraft at takeoff or landing

INCLUDES
- collision of aircraft with any object, fixed, movable, or moving } while taking off or landing
- crash } while taking off or landing
- explosion on aircraft } while taking off or landing
- fire on aircraft } while taking off or landing
- forced landing } while taking off or landing

✓4th E841 Accident to powered aircraft, other and unspecified

INCLUDES
- aircraft accident NOS
- aircraft crash or wreck NOS
- any accident to powered aircraft while in transit or when not specified whether in transit, taking off, or landing
- collision of aircraft with another aircraft, bird, or any object, while in transit
- explosion on aircraft while in transit
- fire on aircraft while in transit

✓4th E842 Accident to unpowered aircraft

[6-9]

INCLUDES
- any accident, except collision with powered aircraft, to:
  - balloon
  - glider
  - hang glider
  - kite carrying a person
- hit by object falling from unpowered aircraft

✓4th E843 Fall in, on, or from aircraft

[0-9]

INCLUDES
- accident in boarding or alighting from aircraft, any kind
- fall in, on, or from aircraft [any kind], while in transit, taking off, or landing, except when as a result of an accident to aircraft

✓4th E844 Other specified air transport accidents

[0-9]

INCLUDES
- hit by:
  - aircraft
  - object falling from aircraft } without accident to aircraft
- injury by or from:
  - machinery on aircraft } without accident to aircraft
  - rotating propeller } without accident to aircraft
  - voluntary parachute descent } without accident to aircraft
- poisoning by carbon monoxide from aircraft while in transit } without accident to aircraft
- sucked into jet
- any accident involving other transport vehicle (motor) (nonmotor) due to being hit by object set in motion by aircraft (powered)

EXCLUDES
- *air sickness (E903)*
- *effects of:*
  - *high altitude (E902.0-E902.1)*
  - *pressure change (E902.0-E902.1)*
- *injury in parachute descent due to accident to aircraft (E840.0-E842-9)*

✓4th E845 Accident involving spacecraft

[0,8,9]

INCLUDES launching pad accident

EXCLUDES *effects of weightlessness in spacecraft (E928.0)*

VEHICLE ACCIDENTS NOT ELSEWHERE CLASSIFIABLE (E846-E848)

E846 Accidents involving powered vehicles used solely within the buildings and premises of industrial or commercial establishment

Accident to, on, or involving:
- battery powered airport passenger vehicle
- battery powered trucks (baggage) (mail)
- coal car in mine
- logging car
- self propelled truck, industrial
- station baggage truck (powered)
- tram, truck, or tub (powered) in mine or quarry

Collision with:
- pedestrian
- other vehicle or object within premises

Explosion of / Fall from / Overturning of / Struck by } powered vehicle, industrial or commercial

EXCLUDES *accidental poisoning by exhaust gas from vehicle not elsewhere classifiable (E868.2)*
injury by crane, lift (fork), or elevator (E919.2)

E847 Accidents involving cable cars not running on rails

Accident to, on, or involving:
- cable car, not on rails
- ski chair-lift
- ski-lift with gondola
- téléférique

Breakage of cable

Caught or dragged by / Fall or jump from / Object thrown from or in } cable car, not on rails

E848 Accidents involving other vehicles, not elsewhere classifiable

Accident to, on, or involving:
- ice yacht
- land yacht
- nonmotor, nonroad vehicle NOS

✓4th ***E849 Place of occurrence***

The following category is for use to denote the place where the injury or poisoning occurred.

E849.0 Home

Apartment
Boarding house
Farm house
Home premises
House (residential)
Noninstitutional place of residence
Private:
driveway
Private:
garage
garden
home
walk
Swimming pool in private house or garden
Yard of home

EXCLUDES *home under construction but not yet occupied (E849.3)*
institutional place of residence (E849.7)

E849.1 Farm

Farm:
buildings
land under cultivation

EXCLUDES *farm house and home premises of farm (E849.0)*

E849.2 Mine and quarry

Gravel pit
Sand pit
Tunnel under construction

E849.3 Industrial place and premises

Building under construction
Dockyard
Dry dock
Factory
building
premises
Garage (place of work)
Industrial yard
Loading platform (factory) (store)
Plant, industrial
Railway yard
Shop (place of work)
Warehouse
Workhouse

E849.4 Place for recreation and sport

Amusement park
Baseball field
Basketball court
Beach resort
Cricket ground
Fives court
Football field
Golf course
Gymnasium
Hockey field
Holiday camp
Ice palace
Lake resort
Mountain resort
Playground, including school playground
Public park
Racecourse
Resort NOS
Riding school
Rifle range
Seashore resort
Skating rink
Sports palace
Stadium
Swimming pool, public
Tennis court
Vacation resort

EXCLUDES *that in private house or garden (E849.0)*

E849.5 Street and highway

E849.6 Public building

Building (including adjacent grounds) used by the general public or by a particular group of the public, such as:

airport
bank
café
casino
church
cinema
clubhouse
courthouse
dance hall
garage building (for car storage)
hotel
market (grocery or other commodity)
movie house
music hall
nightclub
office
office building
opera house
post office
public hall
radio broadcasting station
restaurant
school (state) (public) (private)
shop, commercial
station (bus) (railway)
store
theater

EXCLUDES *home garage (E849.0)*
industrial building or workplace (E849.3)

E849.7 Residential institution

Children's home
Dormitory
Hospital
Jail
Old people's home
Orphanage
Prison
Reform school

E849.8 Other specified places

Beach NOS
Canal
Caravan site NOS
Derelict house
Desert
Dock
Forest
Harbor
Hill
Lake NOS
Mountain
Parking lot
Parking place
Pond or pool (natural)
Prairie
Public place NOS
Railway line
Reservoir
River
Sea
Seashore NOS
Stream
Swamp
Trailer court
Woods

E849.9 Unspecified place

ACCIDENTAL POISONING BY DRUGS, MEDICINAL SUBSTANCES, AND BIOLOGICALS (E850-E858)

INCLUDES accidental overdose of drug, wrong drug given or taken in error, and drug taken inadvertently
accidents in the use of drugs and biologicals in medical and surgical procedures

EXCLUDES *administration with suicidal or homicidal intent or intent to harm, or in circumstances classifiable to E980-E989 (E950.0-E950.5, E962.0, E980.0-E980.5)*
correct drug properly administered in therapeutic or prophylactic dosage, as the cause of adverse effect (E930.0-E949.9)

See Alphabetic Index for more complete list of specific drugs to be classified under the fourth-digit subdivisions. The American Hospital Formulary numbers can be used to classify new drugs listed by the American Hospital Formulary Service (AHFS). See Appendix C.

✓4th **E850 Accidental poisoning by analgesics, antipyretics, and antirheumatics**

E850.0 Heroin
Diacetylmorphine

E850.1 Methadone

E850.2 Other opiates and related narcotics
Codeine [methylmorphine] Morphine
Meperidine [pethidine] Opium (alkaloids)

E850.3 Salicylates
Acetylsalicylic acid [aspirin]
Amino derivatives of salicylic acid
Salicylic acid salts

E850.4 Aromatic analgesics, not elsewhere classified
Acetanilid
Paracetamol [acetaminophen]
Phenacetin [acetophenetidin]

E850.5 Pyrazole derivatives
Aminophenazone [amidopyrine]
Phenylbutazone

E850.6 Antirheumatics [antiphlogistics]
Gold salts Indomethacin
EXCLUDES *salicylates (E850.3)*
steroids (E858.0)

E850.7 Other non-narcotic analgesics
Pyrabital

E850.8 Other specified analgesics and antipyretics
Pentazocine

E850.9 Unspecified analgesic or antipyretic

E851 Accidental poisoning by barbiturates
Amobarbital [amylobarbitone] Pentobarbital [pentobarbitone]
Barbital [barbitone] Phenobarbital [phenobarbitone]
Butabarbital [butabarbitone] Secobarbital [quinalbarbitone]
EXCLUDES *thiobarbiturates (E855.1)*

✓4th **E852 Accidental poisoning by other sedatives and hypnotics**

E852.0 Chloral hydrate group

E852.1 Paraldehyde

E852.2 Bromine compounds
Bromides Carbromal (derivatives)

E852.3 Methaqualone compounds

E852.4 Glutethimide group

E852.5 Mixed sedatives, not elsewhere classified

E852.8 Other specified sedatives and hypnotics

E852.9 Unspecified sedative or hypnotic
Sleeping:
drug } NOS
pill } NOS
tablet } NOS

✓4th **E853 Accidental poisoning by tranquilizers**

E853.0 Phenothiazine-based tranquilizers
Chlorpromazine Prochlorperazine
Fluphenazine Promazine

E853.1 Butyrophenone-based tranquilizers
Haloperidol Trifluperidol
Spiperone

E853.2 Benzodiazepine-based tranquilizers
Chlordiazepoxide Lorazepam
Diazepam Medazepam
Flurazepam Nitrazepam

E853.8 Other specified tranquilizers
Hydroxyzine Meprobamate

E853.9 Unspecified tranquilizer

✓4th **E854 Accidental poisoning by other psychotropic agents**

E854.0 Antidepressants
Amitriptyline
Imipramine
Monoamine oxidase [MAO] inhibitors

E854.1 Psychodysleptics [hallucinogens]
Cannabis derivatives Mescaline
Lysergide [LSD] Psilocin
Marihuana (derivatives) Psilocybin

E854.2 Psychostimulants
Amphetamine Caffeine
EXCLUDES *central appetite depressants (E858.8)*

E854.3 Central nervous system stimulants
Analeptics Opiate antagonists

E854.8 Other psychotropic agents

✓4th **E855 Accidental poisoning by other drugs acting on central and autonomic nervous system**

E855.0 Anticonvulsant and anti-Parkinsonism drugs
Amantadine
Hydantoin derivatives
Levodopa [L-dopa]
Oxazolidine derivatives [paramethadione] [trimethadione]
Succinimides

E855.1 Other central nervous system depressants
Ether
Gaseous anesthetics
Halogenated hydrocarbon derivatives
Intravenous anesthetics
Thiobarbiturates, such as thiopental sodium

E855.2 Local anesthetics
Cocaine Procaine
Lidocaine [lignocaine] Tetracaine

E855.3 Parasympathomimetics [cholinergics]
Acetylcholine Pilocarpine
Anticholinesterase:
organophosphorus
reversible

E855.4 Parasympatholytics [anticholinergics and antimuscarinics] and spasmolytics
Atropine
Homatropine
Hyoscine [scopolamine]
Quaternary ammonium derivatives

E855.5 Sympathomimetics [adrenergics]
Epinephrine [adrenalin]
Levarterenol [noradrenalin]

E855.6 Sympatholytics [antiadrenergics]
Phenoxybenzamine
Tolazoline hydrochloride

E855.8 Other specified drugs acting on central and autonomic nervous systems

E855.9 Unspecified drug acting on central and autonomic nervous systems

E856 Accidental poisoning by antibiotics

E857 Accidental poisoning by other anti-infectives

✓4th **E858 Accidental poisoning by other drugs**

E858.0 Hormones and synthetic substitutes

E858.1 Primarily systemic agents

E858.2 Agents primarily affecting blood constituents

E858.3 Agents primarily affecting cardiovascular system

E858.4 Agents primarily affecting gastrointestinal system

E858.5 Water, mineral, and uric acid metabolism drugs

E858.6 Agents primarily acting on the smooth and skeletal muscles and respiratory system

E858.7 Agents primarily affecting skin and mucous membrane, ophthalmological, otorhinolaryngological, and dental drugs

E858.8 Other specified drugs

Central appetite depressants

E858.9 Unspecified drug

ACCIDENTAL POISONING BY OTHER SOLID AND LIQUID SUBSTANCES, GASES, AND VAPORS (E860-E869)

Note: Categories in this section are intended primarily to indicate the external cause of poisoning states classifiable to 980-989. They may also be used to indicate external causes of localized effects classifiable to 001-799.

✓4th E860 Accidental poisoning by alcohol, not elsewhere classified

E860.0 Alcoholic beverages

Alcohol in preparations intended for consumption

E860.1 Other and unspecified ethyl alcohol and its products

Denatured alcohol; Ethanol NOS; Grain alcohol NOS; Methylated spirit

E860.2 Methyl alcohol

Methanol; Wood alcohol

E860.3 Isopropyl alcohol

Dimethyl carbinol; Isopropanol; Rubbing alcohol subsitute; Secondary propyl alcohol

E860.4 Fusel oil

Alcohol:
- amyl
- butyl
- propyl

E860.8 Other specified alcohols

E860.9 Unspecified alcohol

✓4th E861 Accidental poisoning by cleansing and polishing agents, disinfectants, paints, and varnishes

E861.0 Synthetic detergents and shampoos

E861.1 Soap products

E861.2 Polishes

E861.3 Other cleansing and polishing agents

Scouring powders

E861.4 Disinfectants

Household and other disinfectants not ordinarily used on the person

EXCLUDES *carbolic acid or phenol (E864.0)*

E861.5 Lead paints

E861.6 Other paints and varnishes

Lacquers; Oil colors; Paints, other than lead; White washes

E861.9 Unspecified

✓4th E862 Accidental poisoning by petroleum products, other solvents and their vapors, not elsewhere classified

E862.0 Petroleum solvents

Petroleum:
- ether
- benzine
- naphtha

E862.1 Petroleum fuels and cleaners

Antiknock additives to petroleum fuels
Gas oils
Gasoline or petrol
Kerosene

EXCLUDES *kerosene insecticides (E863.4)*

E862.2 Lubricating oils

E862.3 Petroleum solids

Paraffin wax

E862.4 Other specified solvents

Benzene

E862.9 Unspecified solvent

✓4th E863 Accidental poisoning by agricultural and horticultural chemical and pharmaceutical preparations other than plant foods and fertilizers

EXCLUDES *plant foods and fertilizers (E866.5)*

E863.0 Insecticides of organochlorine compounds

Benzene hexachloride; Chlordane; DDT; Dieldrin; Endrine; Toxaphene

E863.1 Insecticides of organophosphorus compounds

Demeton; Diazinon; Dichlorvos; Malathion; Methyl parathion; Parathion; Phenylsulphthion; Phorate; Phosdrin

E863.2 Carbamates

Aldicarb; Carbaryl; Propoxur

E863.3 Mixtures of insecticides

E863.4 Other and unspecified insecticides

Kerosene insecticides

E863.5 Herbicides

2, 4-Dichlorophenoxyacetic acid [2, 4-D]
2, 4, 5-Trichlorophenoxyacetic acid [2, 4, 5-T]
Chlorates
Diquat
Mixtures of plant foods and fertilizers with herbicides
Paraquat

E863.6 Fungicides

Organic mercurials (used in seed dressing)
Pentachlorophenols

E863.7 Rodenticides

Fluoroacetates; Squill and derivatives; Thallium; Warfarin; Zinc phosphide

E863.8 Fumigants

Cyanides; Methyl bromide; Phosphine

E863.9 Other and unspecified

✓4th E864 Accidental poisoning by corrosives and caustics, not elsewhere classified

EXCLUDES *those as components of disinfectants (E861.4)*

E864.0 Corrosive aromatics

Carbolic acid or phenol

E864.1 Acids

Acid:
- hydrochloric
- nitric
- sulfuric

E864.2 Caustic alkalis

Lye

E864.3 Other specified corrosives and caustics

E864.4 Unspecified corrosives and caustics

✓4th E865 Accidental poisoning from poisonous foodstuffs and poisonous plants

INCLUDES any meat, fish, or shellfish
plants, berries, and fungi eaten as, or in mistake for, food, or by a child

EXCLUDES *anaphylactic shock due to adverse food reaction (995.60-995.69)*
food poisoning (bacterial) (005.0-005.9)
poisoning and toxic reactions to venomous plants (E905.6-E905.7)

E865.0 Meat

E865.1 Shellfish

E865.2 Other fish

E865.3 Berries and seeds

E865.4 Other specified plants

E865.5 Mushrooms and other fungi

E865.8 Other specified foods

E865.9 Unspecified foodstuff or poisonous plant

✓4th E866 Accidental poisoning by other and unspecified solid and liquid substances

EXCLUDES *these substances as a component of:*
medicines (E850.0-E858.9)
paints (E861.5-E861.6)
pesticides (E863.0-E863.9)
petroleum fuels (E862.1)

E866.0 Lead and its compounds and fumes

E866.1 Mercury and its compounds and fumes

E866.2 Antimony and its compounds and fumes

E866.3 Arsenic and its compounds and fumes

E866.4 Other metals and their compounds and fumes

Beryllium (compounds)
Brass fumes
Cadmium (compounds)
Copper salts
Iron (compounds)
Manganese (compounds)
Nickel (compounds)
Thallium (compounds)

E866.5 Plant foods and fertilizers

EXCLUDES *mixtures with herbicides (E863.5)*

E866.6 Glues and adhesives

E866.7 Cosmetics

E866.8 Other specified solid or liquid substances

E866.9 Unspecified solid or liquid substance

E867 Accidental poisoning by gas distributed by pipeline

Carbon monoxide from incomplete combustion of piped gas
Coal gas NOS
Liquefied petroleum gas distributed through pipes (pure or mixed with air)
Piped gas (natural) (manufactured)

✓4th E868 Accidental poisoning by other utility gas and other carbon monoxide

E868.0 Liquefied petroleum gas distributed in mobile containers

Butane
Liquefied hydrocarbon gas NOS
Propane
} or carbon monoxide from incomplete conbustion of these gases

E868.1 Other and unspecified utility gas

Acetylene
Gas NOS used for lighting, heating, or cooking
Water gas
} or carbon monoxide from incomplete conbustion of these gases

E868.2 Motor vehicle exhaust gas

Exhaust gas from:
farm tractor, not in transit
gas engine
motor pump
motor vehicle, not in transit
any type of combustion engine not in watercraft

EXCLUDES *poisoning by carbon monoxide from:*
aircraft while in transit (E844.0-E844.9)
motor vehicle while in transit (E818.0-E818.9)
watercraft whether or not in transit (E838.0-E838.9)

E868.3 Carbon monoxide from incomplete combustion of other domestic fuels

Carbon monoxide from incomplete combustion of:
coal
coke
kerosene
wood
} in domestic stove or fireplace

EXCLUDES *carbon monoxide from smoke and fumes due to conflagration (E890.0-E893.9)*

E868.8 Carbon monoxide from other sources

Carbon monoxide from:
blast furnace gas
incomplete combustion of fuels in industrial use
kiln vapor

E868.9 Unspecified carbon monoxide

✓4th E869 Accidental poisoning by other gases and vapors

EXCLUDES *effects of gases used as anesthetics (E855.1, E938.2)*
fumes from heavy metals (E866.0-E866.4)
smoke and fumes due to conflagration or explosion (E890.0-E899)

E869.0 Nitrogen oxides

E869.1 Sulfur dioxide

E869.2 Freon

E869.3 Lacrimogenic gas [tear gas]

Bromobenzyl cyanide
Chloroacetophenone
Ethyliodoacetate

E869.4 Second-hand tobacco smoke

E869.8 Other specified gases and vapors

Chlorine
Hydrocyanic acid gas

E869.9 Unspecified gases and vapors

MISADVENTURES TO PATIENTS DURING SURGICAL AND MEDICAL CARE (E870-E876)

EXCLUDES *accidental overdose of drug and wrong drug given in error (E850.0-E858.9)*
surgical and medical procedures as the cause of abnormal reaction by the patient, without mention of misadventure at the time of procedure (E878.0-E879.9)

✓4th E870 Accidental cut, puncture, perforation, or hemorrhage during medical care

E870.0 Surgical operation

E870.1 Infusion or transfusion

E870.2 Kidney dialysis or other perfusion

E870.3 Injection or vaccination

E870.4 Endoscopic examination

E870.5 Aspiration of fluid or tissue, puncture, and catheterization

Abdominal paracentesis
Aspirating needle biopsy
Blood sampling
Lumbar puncture
Thoracentesis

EXCLUDES *heart catheterization (E870.6)*

E870.6 Heart catheterization

E870.7 Administration of enema

E870.8 Other specified medical care

E870.9 Unspecified medical care

✓4th E871 Foreign object left in body during procedure

E871.0 Surgical operation

E871.1 Infusion or transfusion

E871.2 Kidney dialysis or other perfusion

E871.3 Injection or vaccination

E871.4 Endoscopic examination

E871.5 Aspiration of fluid or tissue, puncture, and catheterization

Abdominal paracentesis
Aspiration needle biopsy
Blood sampling
Lumbar puncture
Thoracentesis

EXCLUDES *heart catheterization (E871.6)*

E871.6 Heart catheterization

E871.7 Removal of catheter or packing

E871.8 Other specified procedures

E871.9 Unspecified procedure

✓4th E872 Failure of sterile precautions during procedure

E872.0 Surgical operation

E872.1 Infusion or transfusion

E872.2 Kidney dialysis and other perfusion

E872.3 Injection or vaccination

E872.4 Endoscopic examination

E872.5 Aspiration of fluid or tissue, puncture, and catheterization

Abdominal paracentesis
Aspiration needle biopsy
Blood sampling
Lumbar puncture
Thoracentesis

EXCLUDES *heart catheterization (E872.6)*

E872.6 Heart catheterization

E872.8 Other specified procedures

E872.9 Unspecified procedure

✓4th **E873 Failure in dosage**

EXCLUDES *accidental overdose of drug, medicinal or biological substance (E850.0-E858.9)*

E873.0 Excessive amount of blood or other fluid during transfusion or infusion

E873.1 Incorrect dilution of fluid during infusion

E873.2 Overdose of radiation in therapy

E873.3 Inadvertent exposure of patient to radiation during medical care

E873.4 Failure in dosage in electroshock or insulin-shock therapy

E873.5 Inappropriate [too hot or too cold] temperature in local application and packing

E873.6 Nonadministration of necessary drug or medicinal substance

E873.8 Other specified failure in dosage

E873.9 Unspecified failure in dosage

✓4th **E874 Mechanical failure of instrument or apparatus during procedure**

E874.0 Surgical operation

E874.1 Infusion and transfusion

Air in system

E874.2 Kidney dialysis and other perfusion

E874.3 Endoscopic examination

E874.4 Aspiration of fluid or tissue, puncture, and catheterization

Abdominal paracentesis
Aspiration needle biopsy
Blood sampling
Lumbar puncture
Thoracentesis

EXCLUDES *heart catheterization (E874.5)*

E874.5 Heart catheterization

E874.8 Other specified procedures

E874.9 Unspecified procedure

✓4th **E875 Contaminated or infected blood, other fluid, drug, or biological substance**

INCLUDES presence of:
bacterial pyrogens
endotoxin-producing bacteria
serum hepatitis-producing agent

E875.0 Contaminated substance transfused or infused

E875.1 Contaminated substance injected or used for vaccination

E875.2 Contaminated drug or biological substance administered by other means

E875.8 Other

E875.9 Unspecified

✓4th **E876 Other and unspecified misadventures during medical care**

E876.0 Mismatched blood in transfusion

E876.1 Wrong fluid in infusion

E876.2 Failure in suture and ligature during surgical operation

E876.3 Endotracheal tube wrongly placed during anesthetic procedure

E876.4 Failure to introduce or to remove other tube or instrument

EXCLUDES *foreign object left in body during procedure (E871.0-E871.9)*

E876.5 Performance of inappropriate operation

E876.8 Other specified misadventures during medical care

Performance of inappropriate treatment NEC

E876.9 Unspecified misadventure during medical care

SURGICAL AND MEDICAL PROCEDURES AS THE CAUSE OF ABNORMAL REACTION OF PATIENT OR LATER COMPLICATION, WITHOUT MENTION OF MISADVENTURE AT THE TIME OF PROCEDURE (E878-E879)

INCLUDES procedures as the cause of abnormal reaction, such as:
displacement or malfunction of prosthetic device
hepatorenal failure, postoperative
malfunction of external stoma
postoperative intestinal obstruction
rejection of transplanted organ

EXCLUDES *anesthetic management properly carried out as the cause of adverse effect (E937.0-E938.9)*
infusion and transfusion, without mention of misadventure in the technique of procedure (E930.0-E949.9)

✓4th **E878 Surgical operation and other surgical procedures as the cause of abnormal reaction of patient, or of later complication, without mention of misadventure at the time of operation**

E878.0 Surgical operation with transplant of whole organ

Transplantation of:
heart
kidney
Transplantation of:
liver

E878.1 Surgical operation with implant of artificial internal device

Cardiac pacemaker
Electrodes implanted in brain
Heart valve prosthesis
Internal orthopedic device

E878.2 Surgical operation with anastomosis, bypass, or graft, with natural or artificial tissues used as implant

Anastomosis:
arteriovenous
gastrojejunal
Graft of blood vessel, tendon, or skin

EXCLUDES *external stoma (E878.3)*

E878.3 Surgical operation with formation of external stoma

Colostomy
Cystostomy
Duodenostomy
Gastrostomy
Ureterostomy

E878.4 Other restorative surgery

E878.5 Amputation of limb(s)

E878.6 Removal of other organ (partial) (total)

E878.8 Other specified surgical operations and procedures

E878.9 Unspecified surgical operations and procedures

✓4th **E879 Other procedures, without mention of misadventure at the time of procedure, as the cause of abnormal reaction of patient, or of later complication**

E879.0 Cardiac catheterization

E879.1 Kidney dialysis

E879.2 Radiological procedure and radiotherapy

EXCLUDES *radio-opaque dyes for diagnostic x-ray procedures (E947.8)*

E879.3 Shock therapy

Electroshock therapy
Insulin-shock therapy

E879.4 Aspiration of fluid

Lumbar puncture
Thoracentesis

E879.5 Insertion of gastric or duodenal sound

E879.6 Urinary catheterization

E879.7 Blood sampling

E879.8 Other specified procedures

Blood transfusion

E879.9 Unspecified procedure

ACCIDENTAL FALLS (E880-E888)

EXCLUDES *falls (in or from):*
burning building (E890.8, E891.8)
into fire (E890.0-E899)
into water (with submersion or drowning) (E910.0-E910.9)
machinery (in operation) (E919.0-E919.9)
on edged, pointed, or sharp object (E920.0-E920.9)
transport vehicle (E800.0-E845.9)
vehicle not elsewhere classifiable (E846-E848)

✓4th **E880 Fall on or from stairs or steps**

E880.0 Escalator

E880.1 Fall on or from sidewalk curb

EXCLUDES *fall from moving sidewalk (E885.9)*

E880.9 Other stairs or steps

✓4th **E881 Fall on or from ladders or scaffolding**

E881.0 Fall from ladder

E881.1 Fall from scaffolding

E882 Fall from or out of building or other structure

Fall from:
balcony
bridge
building
flagpole
tower

Fall from:
turret
viaduct
wall
window

Fall through roof

EXCLUDES *collapse of a building or structure (E916)*
fall or jump from burning building (E890.8, E891.8)

✓4th **E883 Fall into hole or other opening in surface**

INCLUDES fall into:
cavity
dock
hole
pit
quarry

fall into:
shaft
swimming pool
tank
well

EXCLUDES *fall into water NOS (E910.9)*
that resulting in drowning or submersion without mention of injury (E910.0-E910.9)

E883.0 Accident from diving or jumping into water [swimming pool]

Strike or hit:
against bottom when jumping or diving into water
wall or board of swimming pool
water surface

EXCLUDES *diving with insufficient air supply (E913.2)*
effects of air pressure from diving (E902.2)

E883.1 Accidental fall into well

E883.2 Accidental fall into storm drain or manhole

E883.9 Fall into other hole or other opening in surface

✓4th **E884 Other fall from one level to another**

E884.0 Fall from playground equipment

EXCLUDES *recreational machinery (E919.8)*

E884.1 Fall from cliff

E884.2 Fall from chair

E884.3 Fall from wheelchair

E884.4 Fall from bed

E884.5 Fall from other furniture

E884.6 Fall from commode

Toilet

E884.9 Other fall from one level to another

Fall from:
embankment
haystack

Fall from:
stationary vehicle
tree

✓4th **E885 Fall on same level from slipping, tripping, or stumbling**

E885.0 Fall from (nonmotorized) scooter

E885.1 Fall from roller skates

In-line skates

E885.2 Fall from skateboard

E885.3 Fall from skis

E885.4 Fall from snowboard

E885.9 Fall from other slipping, tripping, or stumbling

Fall on moving sidewalk

✓4th **E886 Fall on same level from collision, pushing, or shoving, by or with other person**

EXCLUDES *crushed or pushed by a crowd or human stampede (E917.1, E917.6)*

E886.0 In sports

Tackles in sports

EXCLUDES *kicked, stepped on, struck by object, in sports (E917.0, E917.5)*

E886.9 Other and unspecified

Fall from collision of pedestrian (conveyance) with another pedestrian (conveyance)

E887 Fracture, cause unspecified

✓4th **E888 Other and unspecified fall**

Accidental fall NOS
Fall on same level NOS

E888.0 Fall resulting in striking against sharp object

Use additional external cause code to identify object (E920)

E888.1 Fall resulting in striking against other object

E888.8 Other fall

E888.9 Unspecified fall

Fall NOS

ACCIDENTS CAUSED BY FIRE AND FLAMES (E890-E899)

INCLUDES asphyxia or poisoning due to conflagration or ignition
burning by fire
secondary fires resulting from explosion

EXCLUDES *arson (E968.0)*
fire in or on:
machinery (in operation) (E919.0-E919.9)
transport vehicle other than stationary vehicle (E800.0-E845.9)
vehicle not elsewhere classifiable (E846-E848)

✓4th **E890 Conflagration in private dwelling**

INCLUDES conflagration in:
apartment
boarding house
camping place
caravan
farmhouse
house

conflagration in:
lodging house
mobile home
private garage
rooming house
tenement

conflagration originating from sources classifiable to E893-E898 in the above buildings

E890.0 Explosion caused by conflagration

E890.1 Fumes from combustion of polyvinylchloride [PVC] and similar material in conflagration

E890.2 Other smoke and fumes from conflagration

Carbon monoxide, Fumes NOS, Smoke NOS } from conflagration in private building

E890.3 Burning caused by conflagration

E890.8 Other accident resulting from conflagration

Collapse of, Fall from, Hit by object falling from, Jump from } burning private building

E890.9 Unspecified accident resulting from conflagration in private dwelling

✓4th E891 Conflagration in other and unspecified building or structure

Conflagration in:
- barn
- church
- convalescent and other residential home
- dormitory of educational institution
- factory
- farm outbuildings
- hospital
- hotel
- school
- store
- theater

Conflagration originating from sources classifiable to E893-E898, in the above buildings

E891.0 Explosion caused by conflagration

E891.1 Fumes from combustion of polyvinylchloride [PVC] and similar material in conflagration

E891.2 Other smoke and fumes from conflagration

Carbon monoxide, Fumes NOS, Smoke NOS } from conflagration in building or structure

E891.3 Burning caused by conflagration

E891.8 Other accident resulting from conflagration

Collapse of, Fall from, Hit by object falling from, Jump from } burning building or structure

E891.9 Unspecified accident resulting from conflagration of other and unspecified building or structure

E892 Conflagration not in building or structure

Fire (uncontrolled) (in) (of):
- forest
- grass
- hay
- lumber
- mine
- prairie
- transport vehicle [any], except while in transit
- tunnel

✓4th E893 Accident caused by ignition of clothing

EXCLUDES *ignition of clothing:*
from highly inflammable material (E894)
with conflagration (E890.0-E892)

E893.0 From controlled fire in private dwelling

Ignition of clothing from:
normal fire (charcoal) (coal) (electric) (gas) (wood) in:
- brazier
- fireplace
- furnace
- stove

} in private dwelling (as listed in E890)

E893.1 From controlled fire in other building or structure

Ignition of clothing from:
normal fire (charcoal) (coal) (electric) (gas) (wood) in:
- brazier
- fireplace
- furnace
- stove

} in other building or structure (as listed in E81)

E893.2 From controlled fire not in building or structure

Ignition of clothing from:
- bonfire (controlled)
- brazier fire (controlled), not in building or structure
- trash fire (controlled)

EXCLUDES *conflagration not in building (E892)*
trash fire out of control (E892)

E893.8 From other specified sources

Ignition of clothing from:
- blowlamp
- blowtorch
- burning bedspread
- candle
- cigar
- cigarette
- lighter
- matches
- pipe
- welding torch

E893.9 Unspecified source

Ignition of clothing (from controlled fire NOS) (in building NOS) NOS

E894 Ignition of highly inflammable material

Ignition of:
benzine, gasoline, fat, kerosene, paraffin, petrol } (with ignition of clothing)

EXCLUDES *ignition of highly inflammable material with:*
conflagration (E890.0-E892)
explosion (E923.0-E923.9)

E895 Accident caused by controlled fire in private dwelling

Burning by (flame of) normal fire (charcoal) (coal) (electric) (gas) (wood) in:
- brazier
- fireplace
- furnace
- stove

} in private dwelling (as listed in E890)

EXCLUDES *burning by hot objects not producing fire or flames (E924.0-E924.9)*
ignition of clothing from these sources (E893.0)
poisoning by carbon monoxide from incomplete combustion of fuel (E867-E868.9)
that with conflagration (E890.0-E890.9)

E896 Accident caused by controlled fire in other and unspecified building or structure

Burning by (flame of) normal fire (charcoal) (coal) (electric) (gas) (wood) in:
brazier, fireplace, furnace, stove } in other building or structure (as listed in E891)

EXCLUDES *burning by hot objects not producing fire or flames (E924.0-E924.9)*
ignition of clothing from these sources (E893.1)
poisoning by carbon monoxide from incomplete combustion of fuel (E867-E868.9)
that with conflagration (E891.0-E891.9)

E897 Accident caused by controlled fire not in building or structure

Burns from flame of:
bonfire, brazier fire, not in building or structure, trash fire } controlled

EXCLUDES *ignition of clothing from these sources (E893.2)*
trash fire out of control (E892)
that with conflagration (E892)

✓4th E898 Accident caused by other specified fire and flames

EXCLUDES *conflagration (E890.0-E892)*
that with ignition of:
clothing (E893.0-E893.9)
highly inflammable material (E894)

E898.0 Burning bedclothes

Bed set on fire NOS

E898.1 Other

Burning by:
- blowlamp
- blowtorch
- candle
- cigar
- cigarette
- fire in room NOS
- lamp
- lighter
- matches
- pipe
- welding torch

E899 Accident caused by unspecified fire

Burning NOS

ACCIDENTS DUE TO NATURAL AND ENVIRONMENTAL FACTORS (E900-E909)

✓4th E900 Excessive heat

E900.0 Due to weather conditions

Excessive heat as the external cause of:
- ictus solaris
- siriasis
- sunstroke

E900.1 Of man-made origin

Heat (in):
- boiler room
- drying room
- factory
- furnace room

Heat (in):
- generated in transport vehicle
- kitchen

E900.9 Of unspecified origin

✓4th **E901 Excessive cold**

E901.0 Due to weather conditions

Excessive cold as the cause of:
- chilblains NOS
- immersion foot

E901.1 Of man-made origin

Contact with or inhalation of:
- dry ice
- liquid air
- liquid hydrogen
- liquid nitrogen

Prolonged exposure in:
- deep freeze unit
- refrigerator

E901.8 Other specified origin

E901.9 Of unspecified origin

✓4th **E902 High and low air pressure and changes in air pressure**

E902.0 Residence or prolonged visit at high altitude

Residence or prolonged visit at high altitude as the cause of:
- Acosta syndrome
- Alpine sickness
- altitude sickness
- Andes disease
- anoxia, hypoxia
- barotitis, barodontalgia, barosinusitis, otitic barotrauma
- hypobarism, hypobaropathy
- mountain sickness
- range disease

E902.1 In aircraft

Sudden change in air pressure in aircraft during ascent or descent as the cause of:
- aeroneurosis
- aviators' disease

E902.2 Due to diving

High air pressure from rapid descent in water
Reduction in atmospheric pressure while surfacing from deep water diving
} as the cause of:
- caisson disease
- divers' disease
- divers' palsy or paralysis

E902.8 Due to other specified causes

Reduction in atmospheric pressure whilesurfacing from underground

E902.9 Unspecified cause

E903 Travel and motion

✓4th **E904 Hunger, thirst, exposure, and neglect**

EXCLUDES *any condition resulting from homicidal intent (E968.0-E968.9)*
hunger, thirst, and exposure resulting from accidents connected with transport (E800.0-E848)

E904.0 Abandonment or neglect of infants and helpless persons

Exposure to weather conditions
Hunger or thirst
} resulting from abandonment or neglect

Desertion of newborn
Inattention at or after birth
Lack of care (helpless person) (infant)

EXCLUDES *criminal [purposeful] neglect (E968.4)*

E904.1 Lack of food

Lack of food as the cause of:
- inanition
- insufficient nourishment
- starvation

EXCLUDES *hunger resulting from abandonment or neglect (E904.0)*

E904.2 Lack of water

Lack of water as the cause of:
- dehydration
- inanition

EXCLUDES *dehydration due to acute fluid loss (276.51)*

E904.3 Exposure (to weather conditions), not elsewhere classifiable

Exposure NOS
Humidity
Struck by hailstones

EXCLUDES *struck by lightning (E907)*

E904.9 Privation, unqualified

Destitution

✓4th **E905 Venomous animals and plants as the cause of poisoning and toxic reactions**

INCLUDES chemical released by animal
insects
release of venom through fangs, hairs, spines, tentacles, and other venom apparatus

EXCLUDES *eating of poisonous animals or plants (E865.0-E865.9)*

E905.0 Venomous snakes and lizards

Cobra
Copperhead snake
Coral snake
Fer de lance
Gila monster
Krait
Mamba
Rattlesnake
Sea snake
Snake (venomous)
Viper
Water moccasin

EXCLUDES *bites of snakes and lizards known to be nonvenomous (E906.2)*

E905.1 Venomous spiders

Black widow spider
Brown spider
Tarantula (venomous)

E905.2 Scorpion

E905.3 Hornets, wasps, and bees

Yellow jacket

E905.4 Centipede and venomous millipede (tropical)

E905.5 Other venomous arthropods

Sting of:
- ant

Sting of:
- caterpillar

E905.6 Venomous marine animals and plants

Puncture by sea urchin spine

Sting of:
- coral
- jelly fish
- nematocysts

Sting of:
- sea anemone
- sea cucumber
- other marine animal or plant

EXCLUDES *bites and other injuries caused by nonvenomous marine animal (E906.2-E906.8)*
bite of sea snake (venomous) (E905.0)

E905.7 Poisoning and toxic reactions caused by other plants

Injection of poisons or toxins into or through skin by plant thorns, spines, or other mechanisms

EXCLUDES *puncture wound NOS by plant thorns or spines (E920.8)*

E905.8 Other specified

E905.9 Unspecified

Sting NOS
Venomous bite NOS

✓4th **E906 Other injury caused by animals**

EXCLUDES *poisoning and toxic reactions caused by venomous animals and insects (E905.0-E905.9)*
road vehicle accident involving animals (E827.0-E828.9)
tripping or falling over an animal (E885.9)

E906.0 Dog bite

E906.1 Rat bite

E906.2 Bite of nonvenomous snakes and lizards

E906.3 Bite of other animal except arthropod

Cats
Moray eel
Rodents, except rats
Shark

E906.4 Bite of nonvenomous arthropod

Insect bite NOS

E906.5 Bite by unspecified animal

Animal bite NOS

E906.8 Other specified injury caused by animal

Butted by animal
Fallen on by horse or other animal, not being ridden
Gored by animal
Implantation of quills of porcupine
Pecked by bird
Run over by animal, not being ridden
Stepped on by animal, not being ridden

EXCLUDES *injury by animal being ridden (E828.0-E828.9)*

E906.9 Unspecified injury caused by animal

E907 Lightning

EXCLUDES *injury from:*
fall of tree or other object caused by lightning (E916)
fire caused by lightning (E890.0-E892)

✓4th **E908 Cataclysmic storms, and floods resulting from storms**

EXCLUDES *collapse of dam or man-made structure causing flood (E909.3)*

E908.0 Hurricane

Storm surge
"Tidal wave" caused by storm action
Typhoon

E908.1 Tornado

Cyclone
Twisters

E908.2 Floods

Torrential rainfall
Flash flood

EXCLUDES *collapse of dam or man-made structure causing flood (E909.3)*

E908.3 Blizzard (snow) (ice)

E908.4 Dust storm

E908.8 Other cataclysmic storms

Cloudburst

E908.9 Unspecified cataclysmic storms, and floods resulting from storms

Storm NOS

✓4th **E909 Cataclysmic earth surface movements and eruptions**

E909.0 Earthquakes

E909.1 Volcanic eruptions

Burns from lava
Ash inhalation

E909.2 Avalanche, landslide, or mudslide

E909.3 Collapse of dam or man-made structure

E909.4 Tidalwave caused by earthquake

Tidalwave NOS
Tsunami

EXCLUDES *tidalwave caused by tropical storm (E908.0)*

E909.8 Other cataclysmic earth surface movements and eruptions

E909.9 Unspecified cataclysmic earth surface movements and eruptions

ACCIDENTS CAUSED BY SUBMERSION, SUFFOCATION, AND FOREIGN BODIES (E910-E915)

✓4th **E910 Accidental drowning and submersion**

INCLUDES immersion
swimmers' cramp

EXCLUDES *diving accident (NOS) (resulting in injury except drowning) (E883.0)*
diving with insufficient air supply (E913.2)
drowning and submersion due to:
cataclysm (E908-E909)
machinery accident (E919.0-E919.9)
transport accident (E800.0-E845.9)
effect of high and low air pressure (E902.2)
injury from striking against objects while in running water (E917.2)

E910.0 While water-skiing

Fall from water skis with submersion or drowning

EXCLUDES *accident to water-skier involving a watercraft and resulting in submersion or other injury (E830.4, E831.4)*

E910.1 While engaged in other sport or recreational activity with diving equipment

Scuba diving NOS
Skin diving NOS
Underwater spear fishing NOS

E910.2 While engaged in other sport or recreational activity without diving equipment

Fishing or hunting, except from boat or with diving equipment
Ice skating
Playing in water
Surfboarding
Swimming NOS
Voluntarily jumping from boat, not involved in accident, for swim NOS
Wading in water

EXCLUDES *jumping into water to rescue another person (E910.3)*

E910.3 While swimming or diving for purposes other than recreation or sport

Marine salvage
Pearl diving
Placement of fishing nets
Rescue (attempt) of another person
Underwater construction or repairs
} (with diving equipment)

E910.4 In bathtub

E910.8 Other accidental drowning or submersion

Drowning in:
quenching tank
swimming pool

E910.9 Unspecified accidental drowning or submersion

Accidental fall into water NOS
Drowning NOS

E911 Inhalation and ingestion of food causing obstruction of respiratory tract or suffocation

Aspiration and inhalation of food [any] (into respiratory tract) NOS

Asphyxia by
Choked on
Suffocation by
} food [including bone, seed in food, regurgitated food]

Compression of trachea
Interruption of respiration
Obstruction of respiration
} by food lodged in esophagus

Obstruction of pharynx by food (bolus)

EXCLUDES *injury, except asphyxia and obstruction of respiratory passage, caused by food (E915)*
obstruction of esophagus by food without mention of asphyxia or obstruction of respiratory passage (E915)

✓4th Fourth-digit Required ▶◀ Revised Text ● New Code ▲ Revised Code Title

E912 Inhalation and ingestion of other object causing obstruction of respiratory tract or suffocation

Aspiration and inhalation of foreign body except food (into respiratory tract) NOS
Foreign object [bean] [marble] in nose
Obstruction of pharynx by foreign body
Compression, Interruption of respiration, Obstruction of respiration } by foreign body in esophagus

EXCLUDES *injury, except asphyxia and obstruction of respiratory passage, caused by foreign body (E915)*
obstruction of esophagus by foreign body without mention of asphyxia or obstruction in respiratory passage (E915)

✓4th **E913 Accidental mechanical suffocation**

EXCLUDES *mechanical suffocation from or by:*
accidental inhalation or ingestion of:
food (E911)
foreign object (E912)
cataclysm (E908-E909)
explosion (E921.0-E921.9, E923.0-E923.9)
machinery accident (E919.0-E919.9)

E913.0 In bed or cradle
EXCLUDES *suffocation by plastic bag (E913.1)*

E913.1 By plastic bag

E913.2 Due to lack of air (in closed place)
Accidentally closed up in refrigerator or other airtight enclosed space
Diving with insufficient air supply
EXCLUDES *suffocation by plastic bag (E913.1)*

E913.3 By falling earth or other substance
Cave-in NOS
EXCLUDES *cave-in caused by cataclysmic earth surface movements and eruptions (E909)*
struck by cave-in without asphyxiation or suffocation (E916)

E913.8 Other specified means
Accidental hanging, except in bed or cradle

E913.9 Unspecified means
Asphyxia, mechanical NOS Suffocation NOS
Strangulation NOS

E914 Foreign body accidentally entering eye and adnexa
EXCLUDES *corrosive liquid (E924.1)*

E915 Foreign body accidentally entering other orifice
EXCLUDES *aspiration and inhalation of foreign body, any, (into respiratory tract) NOS (E911-E912)*

OTHER ACCIDENTS (E916-E928)

E916 Struck accidentally by falling object

Collapse of building, except on fire
Falling:
- rock
- snowslide NOS
- stone
- tree

Object falling from:
- machine, not in operation
- stationary vehicle

Code first:
- collapse of building on fire (E890.0-E891.9)
- falling object in:
  - cataclysm (E908-E909)
  - machinery accidents (E919.0-E919.9)
  - transport accidents (E800.0-E845.9)
  - vehicle accidents not elsewhere classifiable (E846-E848)
- object set in motion by:
  - explosion (E921.0-E921.9, E923.0-E923.9)
  - firearm (E922.0-E922.9)
  - projected object (E917.0-E917.9)

✓4th **E917 Striking against or struck accidentally by objects or persons**

INCLUDES bumping into or against, colliding with, kicking against, stepping on, struck by } object (moving) (projected) (stationary), pedestrian conveyance, person

EXCLUDES *fall from:*
collision with another person, except when caused by a crowd (E886.0-E886.9)
stumbling over object (E885.9)
fall resulting in striking against object (E888.0, E888.1)
injury caused by:
assault (E960.0-E960.1, E967.0-E967.9)
cutting or piercing instrument (E920.0-E920.9)
explosion (E921.0-E921.9, E923.0-E923.9)
firearm (E922.0-E922.9)
machinery (E919.0-E919.9)
transport vehicle (E800.0-E845.9)
vehicle not elsewhere classifiable (E846-E848)

E917.0 In sports without subsequent fall
Kicked or stepped on during game (football) (rugby)
Struck by hit or thrown ball
Struck by hockey stick or puck

E917.1 Caused by a crowd, by collective fear or panic without subsequent fall
Crushed, Pushed, Stepped on } by crowd or human stampede

E917.2 In running water without subsequent fall
EXCLUDES *drowning or submersion (E910.0-E910.9)*
that in sports (E917.0, E917.5)

E917.3 Furniture without subsequent fall
EXCLUDES *fall from furniture (E884.2, E884.4-E884.5)*

E917.4 Other stationary object without subsequent fall
Bath tub
Fence
Lamp-post

E917.5 Object in sports with subsequent fall
Knocked down while boxing

E917.6 Caused by a crowd, by collective fear or panic with subsequent fall

E917.7 Furniture with subsequent fall
EXCLUDES *fall from furniture (E884.2, E884.4-E884.5)*

E917.8 Other stationary object with subsequent fall
Bath tub
Fence
Lamp-post

E917.9 Other striking against with or without subsequent fall

E918 Caught accidentally in or between objects

Caught, crushed, jammed, or pinched in or between moving or stationary objects, such as:
- escalator
- folding object
- hand tools, appliances, or implements
- sliding door and door frame
- under packing crate
- washing machine wringer

EXCLUDES *injury caused by:*
cutting or piercing instrument (E920.0-E920.9)
machinery (E919.0-E919.9)
transport vehicle (E800.0-E845.9)
vehicle not elsewhere classifiable (E846-E848)
struck accidentally by:
falling object (E916)
object (moving) (projected) (E917.0-E917.9)

✓4th E919 Accidents caused by machinery

INCLUDES burned by / caught in (moving parts of) / collapse of / crushed by / cut or pierced by / drowning or submersion caused by / explosion of, on, in / fall from or into moving part of / fire starting in or on / mechanical suffocation caused by / object falling from, on, in motion by / overturning of / pinned under / run over by / struck by / thrown from } machinery (accident)

caught between machinery and other object
machinery accident NOS

EXCLUDES *accidents involving machinery, not in operation (E884.9, E916-E918)*
injury caused by:
electric current in connection with machinery (E925.0-E925.9)
escalator (E880.0, E918)
explosion of pressure vessel in connection with machinery (E921.0-E921.9)
moving sidewalk (E885.9)
powered hand tools, appliances, and implements (E916-E918, E920.0-E921.9, E923.0-E926.9)
transport vehicle accidents involving machinery (E800.0-E848)
poisoning by carbon monoxide generated by machine (E868.8)

E919.0 Agricultural machines

Animal-powered agricultural machine
Combine
Derrick, hay
Farm machinery NOS
Farm tractor
Harvester
Hay mower or rake
Reaper
Thresher

EXCLUDES *that in transport under own power on the highway (E810.0-E819.9)*
that being towed by another vehicle on the highway (E810.0-E819.9, E827.0-E827.9, E829.0-E829.9)
that involved in accident classifiable to E820-E829 (E820.0-E829.9)

E919.1 Mining and earth-drilling machinery

Bore or drill (land) (seabed)
Shaft hoist
Shaft lift
Under-cutter

EXCLUDES *coal car, tram, truck, and tub in mine (E846)*

E919.2 Lifting machines and appliances

Chain hoist / Crane / Derrick / Elevator (building) (grain) / Forklift truck / Lift / Pulley block / Winch } except in agricultural or mining operations

EXCLUDES *that being towed by another vehicle on the highway (E810.0-E819.9, E827.0-E827.9, E829.0-829.9)*
that in transport under own power on the highway (E810.0-E819.9)
that involved in accident classifiable to E820-E829 (E820.0-E829.9)

E919.3 Metalworking machines

Abrasive wheel
Forging machine
Lathe
Mechanical shears
Metal:
drilling machine
milling machine
power press
rolling-mill
sawing machine

E919.4 Woodworking and forming machines

Band saw
Bench saw
Circular saw
Molding machine
Overhead plane
Powered saw
Radial saw
Sander

EXCLUDES *hand saw (E920.1)*

E919.5 Prime movers, except electrical motors

Gas turbine
Internal combustion engine
Steam engine
Water driven turbine

EXCLUDES *that being towed by other vehicle on the highway (E810.0-E819.9, E827.0-E827.9, E829.0-E829.9)*
that in transport under own power on the highway (E810.0-E819.9)

E919.6 Transmission machinery

Transmission:
belt
cable
chain
gear
Transmission:
pinion
pulley
shaft

E919.7 Earth moving, scraping, and other excavating machines

Bulldozer
Road scraper
Steam shovel

EXCLUDES *that being towed by other vehicle on the highway (E810.0-E819.9, E827.0-E827.9, E829.0-E829.9)*
that in transport under own power on the highway (E810.0-E819.9)

E919.8 Other specified machinery

Machines for manufacture of:
clothing
foodstuffs and beverages
paper
Printing machine
Recreational machinery
Spinning, weaving, and textile machines

E919.9 Unspecified machinery

✓4th E920 Accidents caused by cutting and piercing instruments or objects

INCLUDES accidental injury (by) } object: edged / pointed / sharp

E920.0 Powered lawn mower

E920.1 Other powered hand tools

Any powered hand tool [compressed air] [electric] [explosive cartridge] [hydraulic power], such as:
drill
hand saw
hedge clipper
rivet gun
snow blower
staple gun

EXCLUDES *band saw (E919.4)*
bench saw (E919.4)

E920.2 Powered household appliances and implements

Blender
Electric:
beater or mixer
can opener
Electric:
fan
knife
sewing machine
Garbage disposal appliance

E920.3 Knives, swords, and daggers

E920.4 Other hand tools and implements
- Axe
- Can opener NOS
- Chisel
- Fork
- Hand saw
- Hoe
- Ice pick
- Needle (sewing)
- Paper cutter
- Pitchfork
- Rake
- Scissors
- Screwdriver
- Sewing machine, not powered
- Shovel

E920.5 Hypodermic needle
- Contaminated needle
- Needle stick

E920.8 Other specified cutting and piercing instruments or objects
- Arrow
- Broken glass
- Dart
- Edge of stiff paper
- Lathe turnings
- Nail
- Plant thorn
- Splinter
- Tin can lid

EXCLUDES *animal spines or quills (E906.8)*
flying glass due to explosion (E921.0-E923.9)

E920.9 Unspecified cutting and piercing instrument or object

✓4th **E921 Accident caused by explosion of pressure vessel**

INCLUDES accidental explosion of pressure vessels, whether or not part of machinery

EXCLUDES *explosion of pressure vessel on transport vehicle (E800.0-E845.9)*

E921.0 Boilers

E921.1 Gas cylinders
- Air tank
- Pressure gas tank

E921.8 Other specified pressure vessels
- Aerosol can
- Automobile tire
- Pressure cooker

E921.9 Unspecified pressure vessel

✓4th **E922 Accident caused by firearm, and air gun missile**

E922.0 Handgun
- Pistol
- Revolver

EXCLUDES *Verey pistol (E922.8)*

E922.1 Shotgun (automatic)

E922.2 Hunting rifle

E922.3 Military firearms
- Army rifle
- Machine gun

E922.4 Air gun
- BB gun
- Pellet gun

E922.5 Paintball gun

E922.8 Other specified firearm missile
- Verey pistol [flare]

E922.9 Unspecified firearm missile
- Gunshot wound NOS
- Shot NOS

✓4th **E923 Accident caused by explosive material**

INCLUDES flash burns and other injuries resulting from explosion of explosive material
ignition of highly explosive material with explosion

EXCLUDES *explosion:*
in or on machinery (E919.0-E919.9)
on any transport vehicle, except stationary motor vehicle (E800.0-E848)
with conflagration (E890.0, E891.0,E892)
secondary fires resulting from explosion (E890.0-E899)

E923.0 Fireworks

E923.1 Blasting materials
- Blasting cap
- Detonator
- Dynamite
- Explosive [any] used in blasting operations

E923.2 Explosive gases
- Acetylene
- Butane
- Coal gas
- Explosion in mine NOS
- Fire damp
- Gasoline fumes
- Methane
- Propane

E923.8 Other explosive materials
- Bomb
- Explosive missile
- Grenade
- Mine
- Shell
- Torpedo
- Explosion in munitions:
  - dump
  - factory

E923.9 Unspecified explosive material
- Explosion NOS

✓4th **E924 Accident caused by hot substance or object, caustic or corrosive material, and steam**

EXCLUDES *burning NOS (E899)*
chemical burn resulting from swallowing a corrosive substance (E860.0-E864.4)
fire caused by these substances and objects (E890.0-E894)
radiation burns (E926.0-E926.9)
therapeutic misadventures (E870.0-E876.9)

E924.0 Hot liquids and vapors, including steam

Burning or scalding by:
- boiling water
- hot or boiling liquids not primarily caustic or corrosive
- liquid metal
- steam
- other hot vapor

EXCLUDES *hot (boiling) tap water (E924.2)*

E924.1 Caustic and corrosive substances

Burning by:
- acid [any kind]
- ammonia
- caustic oven cleaner or other substance

Burning by:
- corrosive substance
- lye
- vitriol

E924.2 Hot (boiling) tap water

E924.8 Other

Burning by:
- heat from electric heating appliance
- hot object NOS
- light bulb
- steam pipe

E924.9 Unspecified

✓4th **E925 Accident caused by electric current**

INCLUDES electric current from exposed wire, faulty appliance, high voltage cable, live rail, or open electric socket as the cause of:
- burn
- cardiac fibrillation
- convulsion
- electric shock
- electrocution
- puncture wound
- respiratory paralysis

EXCLUDES *burn by heat from electrical appliance (E924.8)*
lightning (E907)

E925.0 Domestic wiring and appliances

E925.1 Electric power generating plants, distribution stations, transmission lines
- Broken power line

E925.2 Industrial wiring, appliances, and electrical machinery
- Conductors
- Control apparatus
- Electrical equipment and machinery
- Transformers

E925.8 Other electric current

Wiring and appliances in or on:
- farm [not farmhouse]
- outdoors
- public building
- residential institutions
- schools

E925.9 Unspecified electric current
Burns or other injury from electric current NOS
Electric shock NOS
Electrocution NOS

✓4th **E926 Exposure to radiation**

EXCLUDES *abnormal reaction to or complication of treatment without mention of misadventure (E879.2)*
atomic power plant malfunction in water transport (E838.0-E838.9)
misadventure to patient in surgical and medical procedures (E873.2-E873.3)
use of radiation in war operations (E996-E997.9)

E926.0 Radiofrequency radiation

Overexposure to:	from:
microwave radiation	high-powered radio and television transmitters
radar radiation	industrial radiofrequency induction heaters
radiofrequency	radar installations
radiofrequency radiation [any]	

E926.1 Infrared heaters and lamps
Exposure to infrared radiation from heaters and lamps as the cause of:
blistering
burning
charring
inflammatory change

EXCLUDES *physical contact with heater or lamp (E924.8)*

E926.2 Visible and ultraviolet light sources
Arc lamps
Black light sources
Electrical welding arc
Oxygas welding torch
Sun rays
Tanning bed

EXCLUDES *excessive heat from these sources (E900.1-E900.9)*

E926.3 X-rays and other electromagnetic ionizing radiation
Gamma rays
X-rays (hard) (soft)

E926.4 Lasers

E926.5 Radioactive isotopes
Radiobiologicals
Radiopharmaceuticals

E926.8 Other specified radiation
Artificially accelerated beams of ionized particles generated by:
betatrons
synchrotrons

E926.9 Unspecified radiation
Radiation NOS

E927 Overexertion and strenuous movements
Excessive physical exercise
Overexertion (from):
lifting
pulling
pushing
Strenuous movements in:
recreational activities
other activities

✓4th **E928 Other and unspecified environmental and accidental causes**

E928.0 Prolonged stay in weightless environment
Weightlessness in spacecraft (simulator)

E928.1 Exposure to noise
Noise (pollution)
Sound waves
Supersonic waves

E928.2 Vibration

E928.3 Human bite

E928.4 External constriction caused by hair

E928.5 External constriction caused by other object

E928.8 Other

E928.9 Unspecified accident

Accident NOS Blow NOS Casualty (not due to war) Decapitation	stated as accidentally inflicted
Knocked down Killed Injury [any part of body, or unspecified] Mangled Wound	stated as accidentally inflicted, but not otherwise specified

EXCLUDES *fracture, cause unspecified (E887)*
injuries undetermined whether accidentally or purposely inflicted (E980.0-E989)

LATE EFFECTS OF ACCIDENTAL INJURY (E929)

Note: This category is to be used to indicate accidental injury as the cause of death or disability from late effects, which are themselves classifiable elsewhere. The "late effects" include conditions reported as such, or as sequelae which may occur at any time after the attempted suicide or self-inflicted injury.

✓4th **E929 Late effects of accidental injury**

EXCLUDES *late effects of:*
surgical and medical procedures (E870.0-E879.9)
therapeutic use of drugs and medicines (E930.0-E949.9)

E929.0 Late effects of motor vehicle accident
Late effects of accidents classifiable to E810-E825

E929.1 Late effects of other transport accident
Late effects of accidents classifiable to E800-E807, E826-E838, E840-E848

E929.2 Late effects of accidental poisoning
Late effects of accidents classifiable to E850-E858, E860-E869

E929.3 Late effects of accidental fall
Late effects of accidents classifiable to E880-E888

E929.4 Late effects of accident caused by fire
Late effects of accidents classifiable to E890-E899

E929.5 Late effects of accident due to natural and environmental factors
Late effects of accidents classifiable to E900-E909

E929.8 Late effects of other accidents
Late effects of accidents classifiable to E910-E928.8

E929.9 Late effects of unspecified accident
Late effects of accidents classifiable to E928.9

DRUGS, MEDICINAL AND BIOLOGICAL SUBSTANCES CAUSING ADVERSE EFFECTS IN THERAPEUTIC USE (E930-E949)

INCLUDES correct drug properly administered in therapeutic or prophylactic dosage, as the cause of any adverse effect including allergic or hypersensitivity reactions

EXCLUDES *accidental overdose of drug and wrong drug given or taken in error (E850.0-E858.9)*
accidents in the technique of administration of drug or biological substance, such as accidental puncture during injection, or contamination of drug (E870.0-E876.9)
administration with suicidal or homicidal intent or intent to harm, or in circumstances classifiable to E980-E989 (E950.0-E950.5, E962.0, E980.0-E980.5)

See Alphabetic Index for more complete list of specific drugs to be classified under the fourth-digit subdivisions. The American Hospital Formulary numbers can be used to classify new drugs listed by the American Hospital Formulary Service (AHFS). See Appendix C.

✓4th **E930 Antibiotics**

EXCLUDES *that used as eye, ear, nose, and throat [ENT], and local anti-infectives (E946.0-E946.9)*

E930.0 Penicillins

Natural
Synthetic
Semisynthetic, such as:
ampicillin
cloxacillin
nafcillin
oxacillin

E930.1 Antifungal antibiotics

Amphotericin B
Griseofulvin
Hachimycin [trichomycin]
Nystatin

E930.2 Chloramphenicol group

Chloramphenicol
Thiamphenicol

E930.3 Erythromycin and other macrolides

Oleandomycin
Spiramycin

E930.4 Tetracycline group

Doxycycline
Minocycline
Oxytetracycline

E930.5 Cephalosporin group

Cephalexin
Cephaloglycin
Cephaloridine
Cephalothin

E930.6 Antimycobacterial antibiotics

Cycloserine
Kanamycin
Rifampin
Streptomycin

E930.7 Antineoplastic antibiotics

Actinomycins, such as:
Bleomycin
Cactinomycin
Dactinomycin
Daunorubicin
Mitomycin

EXCLUDES *other antineoplastic drugs (E933.1)*

E930.8 Other specified antibiotics

E930.9 Unspecified antibiotic

✓4th E931 Other anti-infectives

EXCLUDES *ENT, and local anti-infectives (E946.0-E946.9)*

E931.0 Sulfonamides

Sulfadiazine
Sulfafurazole
Sulfamethoxazole

E931.1 Arsenical anti-infectives

E931.2 Heavy metal anti-infectives

Compounds of:
antimony
bismuth
lead
mercury

EXCLUDES *mercurial diuretics (E944.0)*

E931.3 Quinoline and hydroxyquinoline derivatives

Chiniofon
Diiodohydroxyquin

EXCLUDES *antimalarial drugs (E931.4)*

E931.4 Antimalarials and drugs acting on other blood protozoa

Chloroquine phosphate
Cycloguanil
Primaquine
Proguanil [chloroguanide]
Pyrimethamine
Quinine (sulphate)

E931.5 Other antiprotozoal drugs

Emetine

E931.6 Anthelmintics

Hexylresorcinol
Male fern oleoresin
Piperazine
Thiabendazole

E931.7 Antiviral drugs

Methisazone

EXCLUDES *amantadine (E936.4)*
cytarabine (E933.1)
idoxuridine (E946.5)

E931.8 Other antimycobacterial drugs

Ethambutol
Ethionamide
Isoniazid
Para-aminosalicylic acid derivatives
Sulfones

E931.9 Other and unspecified anti-infectives

Flucytosine
Nitrofuranderivatives

✓4th E932 Hormones and synthetic substitutes

E932.0 Adrenal cortical steroids

Cortisone derivatives
Desoxycorticosterone derivatives
Fluorinated corticosteroid

E932.1 Androgens and anabolic congeners

Nandrolone phenpropionate
Oxymetholone
Testosterone and preparations

E932.2 Ovarian hormones and synthetic substitutes

Contraceptives, oral
Estrogens
Estrogens and progestogens combined
Progestogens

E932.3 Insulins and antidiabetic agents

Acetohexamide
Biguanide derivatives, oral
Chlorpropamide
Glucagon
Insulin
Phenformin
Sulfonylurea derivatives, oral
Tolbutamide

EXCLUDES *adverse effect of insulin administered for shock therapy (E879.3)*

E932.4 Anterior pituitary hormones

Corticotropin
Gonadotropin
Somatotropin [growth hormone]

E932.5 Posterior pituitary hormones

Vasopressin

EXCLUDES *oxytocic agents (E945.0)*

E932.6 Parathyroid and parathyroid derivatives

E932.7 Thyroid and thyroid derivatives

Dextrothyroxine
Levothyroxine sodium
Liothyronine
Thyroglobulin

E932.8 Antithyroid agents

Iodides
Thiouracil
Thiourea

E932.9 Other and unspecified hormones and synthetic substitutes

✓4th E933 Primarily systemic agents

E933.0 Antiallergic and antiemetic drugs

Antihistamines
Chlorpheniramine
Diphenhydramine
Diphenylpyraline
Thonzylamine
Tripelennamine

EXCLUDES *phenothiazine-based tranquilizers (E939.1)*

E933.1 Antineoplastic and immunosuppressive drugs

Azathioprine
Busulfan
Chlorambucil
Cyclophosphamide
Cytarabine
Fluorouracil
Mechlorethamine hydrochloride
Mercaptopurine
Triethylenethiophosphoramide [thio-TEPA]

EXCLUDES *antineoplastic antibiotics (E930.7)*

E933.2 Acidifying agents

E933.3 Alkalizing agents

E933.4 Enzymes, not elsewhere classified

Penicillinase

E933.5 Vitamins, not elsewhere classified

Vitamin A
Vitamin D

EXCLUDES *nicotinic acid (E942.2)*
vitamin K (E934.3)

E933.8 Other systemic agents, not elsewhere classified

Heavy metal antagonists

E933.9 Unspecified systemic agent

✓4th E934 Agents primarily affecting blood constituents

E934.0 Iron and its compounds

Ferric salts
Ferrous sulphate and other ferrous salts

E934.1 Liver preparations and other antianemic agents

Folic acid

E934.2 Anticoagulants

Coumarin
Heparin
Phenindione
Prothrombin synthesis inhibitor
Warfarin sodium

E934.3 Vitamin K [phytonadione]

E934.4 Fibrinolysis-affecting drugs

Aminocaproic acid
Streptodornase
Streptokinase
Urokinase

E934.5 Anticoagulant antagonists and other coagulants
Hexadimethrine bromide
Protamine sulfate

E934.6 Gamma globulin

E934.7 Natural blood and blood products
Blood plasma
Human fibrinogen
Packed red cells
Whole blood

E934.8 Other agents affecting blood constituents
Macromolecular blood substitutes

E934.9 Unspecified agent affecting blood constituents

✓4th **E935 Analgesics, antipyretics, and antirheumatics**

E935.0 Heroin
Diacetylmorphine

E935.1 Methadone

E935.2 Other opiates and related narcotics
Codeine [methylmorphine]
Meperidine [pethidine]
Morphine
Opium (alkaloids)

E935.3 Salicylates
Acetylsalicylic acid [aspirin]
Amino derivatives of salicylic acid
Salicylic acid salts

E935.4 Aromatic analgesics, not elsewhere classified
Acetanilid
Paracetamol [acetaminophen]
Phenacetin [acetophenetidin]

E935.5 Pyrazole derivatives
Aminophenazone [aminopyrine]
Phenylbutazone

E935.6 Antirheumatics [antiphlogistics]
Gold salts
Indomethacin

EXCLUDES *salicylates (E935.3)*
steroids (E932.0)

E935.7 Other non-narcotic analgesics
Pyrabital

E935.8 Other specified analgesics and antipyretics
Pentazocine

E935.9 Unspecified analgesic and antipyretic

✓4th **E936 Anticonvulsants and anti-Parkinsonism drugs**

E936.0 Oxazolidine derivatives
Paramethadione
Trimethadione

E936.1 Hydantoin derivatives
Phenytoin

E936.2 Succinimides
Ethosuximide
Phensuximide

E936.3 Other and unspecified anticonvulsants
Beclamide
Primidone

E936.4 Anti-Parkinsonism drugs
Amantadine
Ethopropazine [profenamine]
Levodopa [L-dopa]

✓4th **E937 Sedatives and hypnotics**

E937.0 Barbiturates
Amobarbital [amylobarbitone]
Barbital [barbitone]
Butabarbital [butabarbitone]
Pentobarbital [pentobarbitone]
Phenobarbital [phenobarbitone]
Secobarbital [quinalbarbitone]

EXCLUDES *thiobarbiturates (E938.3)*

E937.1 Chloral hydrate group

E937.2 Paraldehyde

E937.3 Bromine compounds
Bromide
Carbromal (derivatives)

E937.4 Methaqualone compounds

E937.5 Glutethimide group

E937.6 Mixed sedatives, not elsewhere classified

E937.8 Other sedatives and hypnotics

E937.9 Unspecified
Sleeping:
drug } NOS
pill } NOS
tablet } NOS

✓4th **E938 Other central nervous system depressants and anesthetics**

E938.0 Central nervous system muscle-tone depressants
Chlorphenesin (carbamate)
Mephenesin
Methocarbamol

E938.1 Halothane

E938.2 Other gaseous anesthetics
Ether
Halogenated hydrocarbon derivatives, except halothane
Nitrous oxide

E938.3 Intravenous anesthetics
Ketamine
Methohexital [methohexitone]
Thiobarbiturates, such as thiopental sodium

E938.4 Other and unspecified general anesthetics

E938.5 Surface and infiltration anesthetics
Cocaine
Lidocaine [lignocaine]
Procaine
Tetracaine

E938.6 Peripheral nerve- and plexus-blocking anesthetics

E938.7 Spinal anesthetics

E938.9 Other and unspecified local anesthetics

✓4th **E939 Psychotropic agents**

E939.0 Antidepressants
Amitriptyline
Imipramine
Monoamine oxidase [MAO] inhibitors

E939.1 Phenothiazine-based tranquilizers
Chlorpromazine
Fluphenazine
Phenothiazine
Prochlorperazine
Promazine

E939.2 Butyrophenone-based tranquilizers
Haloperidol
Spiperone
Trifluperidol

E939.3 Other antipsychotics, neuroleptics, and major tranquilizers

E939.4 Benzodiazepine-based tranquilizers
Chlordiazepoxide
Diazepam
Flurazepam
Lorazepam
Medazepam
Nitrazepam

E939.5 Other tranquilizers
Hydroxyzine
Meprobamate

E939.6 Psychodysleptics [hallucinogens]
Cannabis (derivatives)
Lysergide [LSD]
Marihuana (derivatives)
Mescaline
Psilocin
Psilocybin

E939.7 Psychostimulants
Amphetamine
Caffeine

EXCLUDES *central appetite depressants (E947.0)*

E939.8 Other psychotropic agents

E939.9 Unspecified psychotropic agent

✓4th **E940 Central nervous system stimulants**

E940.0 Analeptics
Lobeline
Nikethamide

E940.1 Opiate antagonists
Levallorphan
Nalorphine
Naloxone

E940.8 Other specified central nervous system stimulants

E940.9 Unspecified central nervous system stimulant

✓4th **E941 Drugs primarily affecting the autonomic nervous system**

E941.0 Parasympathomimetics [cholinergics]
Acetylcholine
Anticholinesterase:
organophosphorus
reversible
Pilocarpine

✓4th Fourth-digit Required ▶◀ Revised Text ● New Code ▲ Revised Code Title

E941.1 Parasympatholytics [anticholinergics and antimuscarinics] and spasmolytics
Atropine
Homatropine
Hyoscine [scopolamine]
Quaternary ammonium derivatives
EXCLUDES *papaverine (E942.5)*

E941.2 Sympathomimetics [adrenergics]
Epinephrine [adrenalin]
Levarterenol [noradrenalin]

E941.3 Sympatholytics [antiadrenergics]
Phenoxybenzamine
Tolazolinehydrochloride

E941.9 Unspecified drug primarily affecting the autonomic nervous system

✓4th E942 Agents primarily affecting the cardiovascular system

E942.0 Cardiac rhythm regulators
Practolol
Procainamide
Propranolol
Quinidine

E942.1 Cardiotonic glycosides and drugs of similar action
Digitalis glycosides
Digoxin
Strophanthins

E942.2 Antilipemic and antiarteriosclerotic drugs
Cholestyramine
Clofibrate
Nicotinic acid derivatives
Sitosterols
EXCLUDES *dextrothyroxine (E932.7)*

E942.3 Ganglion-blocking agents
Pentamethonium bromide

E942.4 Coronary vasodilators
Dipyridamole
Nitrates [nitroglycerin]
Nitrites
Prenylamine

E942.5 Other vasodilators
Cyclandelate
Diazoxide
Hydralazine
Papaverine

E942.6 Other antihypertensive agents
Clonidine
Guanethidine
Rauwolfia alkaloids
Reserpine

E942.7 Antivaricose drugs, including sclerosing agents
Monoethanolamine
Zinc salts

E942.8 Capillary-active drugs
Adrenochrome derivatives
Bioflavonoids
Metaraminol

E942.9 Other and unspecified agents primarily affecting the cardiovascular system

✓4th E943 Agents primarily affecting gastrointestinal system

E943.0 Antacids and antigastric secretion drugs
Aluminum hydroxide
Magnesium trisilicate

E943.1 Irritant cathartics
Bisacodyl
Castor oil
Phenolphthalein

E943.2 Emollient cathartics
Sodium dioctyl sulfosuccinate

E943.3 Other cathartics, including intestinal atonia drugs
Magnesium sulfate

E943.4 Digestants
Pancreatin
Papain
Pepsin

E943.5 Antidiarrheal drugs
Bismuth subcarbonate
Pectin or Kaolin
EXCLUDES *anti-infectives (E930.0-E931.9)*

E943.6 Emetics

E943.8 Other specified agents primarily affecting the gastrointestinal system

E943.9 Unspecified agent primarily affecting the gastrointestinal system

✓4th E944 Water, mineral, and uric acid metabolism drugs

E944.0 Mercurial diuretics
Chlormerodrin
Mercaptomerin
Mercurophylline
Mersalyl

E944.1 Purine derivative diuretics
Theobromine
Theophylline
EXCLUDES *aminophylline [theophylline ethylenediamine] (E945.7)*

E944.2 Carbonic acid anhydrase inhibitors
Acetazolamide

E944.3 Saluretics
Benzothiadiazides
Chlorothiazide group

E944.4 Other diuretics
Ethacrynic acid
Furosemide

E944.5 Electrolytic, caloric, and water-balance agents

E944.6 Other mineral salts, not elsewhere classified

E944.7 Uric acid metabolism drugs
Cinchophen and congeners
Colchicine
Phenoquin
Probenecid

✓4th E945 Agents primarily acting on the smooth and skeletal muscles and respiratory system

E945.0 Oxytocic agents
Ergot alkaloids
Prostaglandins

E945.1 Smooth muscle relaxants
Adiphenine
Metaproterenol [orciprenaline]
EXCLUDES *papaverine (E942.5)*

E945.2 Skeletal muscle relaxants
Alcuronium chloride
Suxamethonium chloride

E945.3 Other and unspecified drugs acting on muscles

E945.4 Antitussives
Dextromethorphan
Pipazethate hydrochloride

E945.5 Expectorants
Acetylcysteine
Cocillana
Guaifenesin [glyceryl guaiacolate]
Ipecacuanha
Terpin hydrate

E945.6 Anti-common cold drugs

E945.7 Antiasthmatics
Aminophylline [theophylline ethylenediamine]

E945.8 Other and unspecified respiratory drugs

✓4th E946 Agents primarily affecting skin and mucous membrane, ophthalmological, otorhinolaryngological, and dental drugs

E946.0 Local anti-infectives and anti-inflammatory drugs

E946.1 Antipruritics

E946.2 Local astringents and local detergents

E946.3 Emollients, demulcents, and protectants

E946.4 Keratolytics, kerstoplastics, other hair treatment drugs and preparations

E946.5 Eye anti-infectives and other eye drugs
Idoxuridine

E946.6 Anti-infectives and other drugs and preparations for ear, nose, and throat

E946.7 Dental drugs topically applied

E946.8 Other agents primarily affecting skin and mucous membrane
Spermicides

E946.9 Unspecified agent primarily affecting skin and mucous membrane

✓4th E947 Other and unspecified drugs and medicinal substances

E947.0 Dietetics

E947.1 Lipotropic drugs

E947.2 Antidotes and chelating agents, not elsewhere classified

E947.3 Alcohol deterrents

E947.4 Pharmaceutical excipients

E947.8 Other drugs and medicinal substances
Contrast media used for diagnostic x-ray procedures
Diagnostic agents and kits

E947.9 Unspecified drug or medicinal substance

✓4th E948 Bacterial vaccines

E948.0 BCG vaccine

E948.1 Typhoid and paratyphoid
E948.2 Cholera
E948.3 Plague
E948.4 Tetanus
E948.5 Diphtheria
E948.6 Pertussis vaccine, including combinations with a pertussis component
E948.8 Other and unspecified bacterial vaccines
E948.9 Mixed bacterial vaccines, except combinations with a pertussis component

✓4th **E949 Other vaccines and biological substances**
EXCLUDES *gamma globulin (E934.6)*
E949.0 Smallpox vaccine
E949.1 Rabies vaccine
E949.2 Typhus vaccine
E949.3 Yellow fever vaccine
E949.4 Measles vaccine
E949.5 Poliomyelitis vaccine
E949.6 Other and unspecified viral and rickettsial vaccines
Mumps vaccine
E949.7 Mixed viral-rickettsial and bacterial vaccines, except combinations with a pertussis component
EXCLUDES *combinations with a pertussis component (E948.6)*
E949.9 Other and unspecified vaccines and biological substances

SUICIDE AND SELF-INFLICTED INJURY (E950-E959)

INCLUDES injuries in suicide and attempted suicide
self-inflicted injuries specified as intentional

✓4th **E950 Suicide and self-inflicted poisoning by solid or liquid substances**
E950.0 Analgesics, antipyretics, and antirheumatics
E950.1 Barbiturates
E950.2 Other sedatives and hypnotics
E950.3 Tranquilizers and other psychotropic agents
E950.4 Other specified drugs and medicinal substances
E950.5 Unspecified drug or medicinal substance
E950.6 Agricultural and horticultural chemical and pharmaceutical preparations other than plant foods and fertilizers
E950.7 Corrosive and caustic substances
Suicide and self-inflicted poisoning by substances classifiable to E864
E950.8 Arsenic and its compounds
E950.9 Other and unspecified solid and liquid substances

✓4th **E951 Suicide and self-inflicted poisoning by gases in domestic use**
E951.0 Gas distributed by pipeline
E951.1 Liquefied petroleum gas distributed in mobile containers
E951.8 Other utility gas

✓4th **E952 Suicide and self-inflicted poisoning by other gases and vapors**
E952.0 Motor vehicle exhaust gas
E952.1 Other carbon monoxide
E952.8 Other specified gases and vapors
E952.9 Unspecified gases and vapors

✓4th **E953 Suicide and self-inflicted injury by hanging, strangulation, and suffocation**
E953.0 Hanging
E953.1 Suffocation by plastic bag
E953.8 Other specified means
E953.9 Unspecified means

E954 Suicide and self-inflicted injury by submersion [drowning]

✓4th **E955 Suicide and self-inflicted injury by firearms, air guns and explosives**
E955.0 Handgun
E955.1 Shotgun
E955.2 Hunting rifle
E955.3 Military firearms
E955.4 Other and unspecified firearm
Gunshot NOS
Shot NOS
E955.5 Explosives
E955.6 Air gun
BB gun
Pellet gun
E955.7 Paintball gun
E955.9 Unspecified

E956 Suicide and self-inflicted injury by cutting and piercing instrument

✓4th **E957 Suicide and self-inflicted injuries by jumping from high place**
E957.0 Residential premises
E957.1 Other man-made structures
E957.2 Natural sites
E957.9 Unspecified

✓4th **E958 Suicide and self-inflicted injury by other and unspecified means**
E958.0 Jumping or lying before moving object
E958.1 Burns, fire
E958.2 Scald
E958.3 Extremes of cold
E958.4 Electrocution
E958.5 Crashing of motor vehicle
E958.6 Crashing of aircraft
E958.7 Caustic substances, except poisoning
EXCLUDES *poisoning by caustic substance (E950.7)*
E958.8 Other specified means
E958.9 Unspecified means

E959 Late effects of self-inflicted injury
Note: This category is to be used to indicate circumstances classifiable to E950-E958 as the cause of death or disability from late effects, which are themselves classifiable elsewhere. The "late effects" include conditions reported as such, or as sequelae which may occur at any time after the attempted suicide or self-inflicted injury.

HOMICIDE AND INJURY PURPOSELY INFLICTED BY OTHER PERSONS (E960-E969)

INCLUDES injuries inflicted by another person with intent to injure or kill, by any means

EXCLUDES *injuries due to:*
legal intervention (E970-E978)
operations of war (E990-E999)
terrorism (E979)

✓4th **E960 Fight, brawl, rape**
E960.0 Unarmed fight or brawl
Beatings NOS
Brawl or fight with hands, fists, feet
Injured or killed in fight NOS
EXCLUDES *homicidal:*
injury by weapons (E965.0-E966, E969)
strangulation (E963)
submersion (E964)
E960.1 Rape

E961 Assault by corrosive or caustic substance, except poisoning
Injury or death purposely caused by corrosive or caustic substance, such as:
acid [any]
corrosive substance
vitriol
EXCLUDES *burns from hot liquid (E968.3)*
chemical burns from swallowing a corrosive substance (E962.0-E962.9)

✓4th Fourth-digit Required ▶◀ Revised Text ● New Code ▲ Revised Code Title

✓4th E962 Assault by poisoning

E962.0 Drugs and medicinal substances
Homicidal poisoning by any drug or medicinal substance

E962.1 Other solid and liquid substances

E962.2 Other gases and vapors

E962.9 Unspecified poisoning

E963 Assault by hanging and strangulation
Homicidal (attempt):
garrotting or ligature
hanging
Homicidal (attempt):
strangulation
suffocation

E964 Assault by submersion [drowning]

✓4th E965 Assault by firearms and explosives

E965.0 Handgun
Pistol
Revolver

E965.1 Shotgun

E965.2 Hunting rifle

E965.3 Military firearms

E965.4 Other and unspecified firearm

E965.5 Antipersonnel bomb

E965.6 Gasoline bomb

E965.7 Letter bomb

E965.8 Other specified explosive
Bomb NOS (placed in):
car
house
Dynamite

E965.9 Unspecified explosive

E966 Assault by cutting and piercing instrument
Assassination (attempt), homicide (attempt) by any instrument classifiable under E920
Homicidal:
cut
puncture
stab
Stabbed
} any part of body

✓4th E967 Perpetrator of child and adult abuse
Note: Selection of the correct perpetrator code is based on the relationship between the perpetrator and the victim

E967.0 By father, stepfather, or boyfriend
Male partner of child's parent or guardian

E967.1 By other specified person

E967.2 By mother, stepmother, or girlfriend
Female partner of child's parent or guardian

E967.3 By spouse or partner
Abuse of spouse or partner by ex-spouse or ex-partner

E967.4 By child

E967.5 By sibling

E967.6 By grandparent

E967.7 By other relative

E967.8 By non-related caregiver

E967.9 By unspecified person

✓4th E968 Assault by other and unspecified means

E968.0 Fire
Arson
Homicidal burns NOS
EXCLUDES *burns from hot liquid (E968.3)*

E968.1 Pushing from a high place

E968.2 Striking by blunt or thrown object

E968.3 Hot liquid
Homicidal burns by scalding

E968.4 Criminal neglect
Abandonment of child, infant, or other helpless person with intent to injure or kill

E968.5 Transport vehicle
Being struck by other vehicle or run down with intent to injure
Pushed in front of, thrown from, or dragged by moving vehicle with intent to injure

E968.6 Air gun
BB gun
Pellet gun

E968.7 Human bite

E968.8 Other specified means

E968.9 Unspecified means
Assassination (attempt) NOS
Homicidal (attempt):
injury NOS
wound NOS
Manslaughter (nonaccidental)
Murder (attempt) NOS
Violence, non-accidental

E969 Late effects of injury purposely inflicted by other person
Note: This category is to be used to indicate circumstances classifiable to E960-E968 as the cause of death or disability from late effects, which are themselves classifiable elsewhere. The "late effects" include conditions reported as such, or as sequelae which may occur at any time after injury purposely inflicted by another person.

LEGAL INTERVENTION (E970-E978)

INCLUDES injuries inflicted by the police or other law-enforcing agents, including military on duty, in the course of arresting or attempting to arrest lawbreakers, suppressing disturbances, maintaining order, and other legal action
legal execution

EXCLUDES *injuries caused by civil insurrections (E990.0-E999)*

E970 Injury due to legal intervention by firearms
Gunshot wound
Injury by:
machine gun
revolver
Injury by:
rifle pellet or rubber bullet
shot NOS

E971 Injury due to legal intervention by explosives
Injury by:
dynamite
explosive shell
Injury by:
grenade
mortar bomb

E972 Injury due to legal intervention by gas
Asphyxiation by gas
Injury by tear gas
Poisoning by gas

E973 Injury due to legal intervention by blunt object
Hit, struck by:
baton (nightstick)
blunt object
Hit, struck by:
stave

E974 Injury due to legal intervention by cutting and piercing instrument
Cut
Incised wound
Injured by bayonet
Stab wound

E975 Injury due to legal intervention by other specified means
Blow
Manhandling

E976 Injury due to legal intervention by unspecified means

E977 Late effects of injuries due to legal intervention
Note: This category is to be used to indicate circumstances classifiable to E970-E976 as the cause of death or disability from late effects, which are themselves classifiable elsewhere. The "late effects" include conditions reported as such, or as sequelae, which may occur at any time after the injury due to legal intervention.

E978 Legal execution
All executions performed at the behest of the judiciary or ruling authority [whether permanent or temporary] as:
asphyxiation by gas
beheading, decapitation (by guillotine)
capital punishment
electrocution
hanging
poisoning
shooting
other specified means

TERRORISM (E979)

✓4th E979 Terrorism

Injuries resulting from the unlawful use of force or violence against persons or property to intimidate or coerce a Government, the civilian population, or any segment thereof, in furtherance of political or social objective

E979.0 Terrorism involving explosion of marine weapons
- Depth-charge
- Marine mine
- Mine NOS, at sea or in harbour
- Sea-based artillery shell
- Torpedo
- Underwater blast

E979.1 Terrorism involving destruction of aircraft
- Aircraft used as a weapon
- Aircraft:
  - burned
  - exploded
  - shot down
- Crushed by falling aircraft

E979.2 Terrorism involving other explosions and fragments
- Antipersonnel bomb (fragments)
- Blast NOS
- Explosion (of):
  - artillery shell
  - breech-block
  - cannon block
  - mortar bomb
  - munitions being used in terrorism
  - NOS
- Fragments from:
  - artillery shell
  - bomb
  - grenade
  - guided missile
  - land-mine
  - rocket
  - shell
  - shrapnel
- Mine NOS

E979.3 Terrorism involving fires, conflagration and hot substances
- Burning building or structure:
  - collapse of
  - fall from
  - hit by falling object in
  - jump from
- Conflagration NOS
- Fire (causing):
  - Asphyxia
  - Burns
  - NOS
  - Other injury
- Melting of fittings and furniture in burning
- Petrol bomb
- Smouldering building or structure

E979.4 Terrorism involving firearms
- Bullet:
  - carbine
  - machine gun
  - pistol
  - rifle
  - rubber (rifle)
- Pellets (shotgun)

E979.5 Terrorism involving nuclear weapons
- Blast effects
- Exposure to ionizing radiation from nuclear weapon
- Fireball effects
- Heat from nuclear weapon
- Other direct and secondary effects of nuclear weapons

E979.6 Terrorism involving biological weapons
- Anthrax
- Cholera
- Smallpox

E979.7 Terrorism involving chemical weapons
- Gases, fumes, chemicals
- Hydrogen cyanide
- Phosgene
- Sarin

E979.8 Terrorism involving other means
- Drowning and submersion
- Lasers
- Piercing or stabbing instruments
- Terrorism NOS

E979.9 Terrorism, secondary effects

Note: This code is for use to identify conditions occurring subsequent to a terrorist attack not those that are due to the initial terrorist act

EXCLUDES *late effect of terrorist attack (E999.1)*

INJURY UNDETERMINED WHETHER ACCIDENTALLY OR PURPOSELY INFLICTED (E980-E989)

Note: Categories E980-E989 are for use when it is unspecified or it cannot be determined whether the injuries are accidental (unintentional), suicide (attempted), or assault.

✓4th E980 Poisoning by solid or liquid substances, undetermined whether accidentally or purposely inflicted

E980.0 Analgesics, antipyretics, and antirheumatics

E980.1 Barbiturates

E980.2 Other sedatives and hypnotics

E980.3 Tranquilizers and other psychotropic agents

E980.4 Other specified drugs and medicinal substances

E980.5 Unspecified drug or medicinal substance

E980.6 Corrosive and caustic substances

Poisoning, undetermined whether accidental or purposeful, by substances classifiable to E864

E980.7 Agricultural and horticultural chemical and pharmaceutical preparations other than plant foods and fertilizers

E980.8 Arsenic and its compounds

E980.9 Other and unspecified solid and liquid substances

✓4th E981 Poisoning by gases in domestic use, undetermined whether accidentally or purposely inflicted

E981.0 Gas distributed by pipeline

E981.1 Liquefied petroleum gas distributed in mobile containers

E981.8 Other utility gas

✓4th E982 Poisoning by other gases, undetermined whether accidentally or purposely inflicted

E982.0 Motor vehicle exhaust gas

E982.1 Other carbon monoxide

E982.8 Other specified gases and vapors

E982.9 Unspecified gases and vapors

✓4th E983 Hanging, strangulation, or suffocation, undetermined whether accidentally or purposely inflicted

E983.0 Hanging

E983.1 Suffocation by plastic bag

E983.8 Other specified means

E983.9 Unspecified means

E984 Submersion [drowning], undetermined whether accidentally or purposely inflicted

✓4th E985 Injury by firearms, air guns and explosives, undetermined whether accidentally or purposely inflicted

E985.0 Handgun

E985.1 Shotgun

E985.2 Hunting rifle

E985.3 Military firearms

E985.4 Other and unspecified firearm

E985.5 Explosives

E985.6 Air gun

BB gun Pellet gun

E985.7 Paintball gun

E986 Injury by cutting and piercing instruments, undetermined whether accidentally or purposely inflicted

✓4th **E987 Falling from high place, undetermined whether accidentally or purposely inflicted**

E987.0 Residential premises

E987.1 Other man-made structures

E987.2 Natural sites

E987.9 Unspecified site

✓4th **E988 Injury by other and unspecified means, undetermined whether accidentally or purposely inflicted**

E988.0 Jumping or lying before moving object

E988.1 Burns, fire

E988.2 Scald

E988.3 Extremes of cold

E988.4 Electrocution

E988.5 Crashing of motor vehicle

E988.6 Crashing of aircraft

E988.7 Caustic substances, except poisoning

E988.8 Other specified means

E988.9 Unspecified means

E989 Late effects of injury, undetermined whether accidentally or purposely inflicted

Note: This category is to be used to indicate circumstances classifiable to E980-E988 as the cause of death or disability from late effects, which are themselves classifiable elsewhere. The "late effects" include conditions reported as such, or as sequelae, which may occur at any time after injury, undetermined whether accidentally or purposely inflicted.

INJURY RESULTING FROM OPERATIONS OF WAR (E990-E999)

INCLUDES injuries to military personnel and civilians caused by war and civil insurrections and occurring during the time of war and insurrection

EXCLUDES *accidents during training of military personnel*
manufacture of war material and transport, unless attributable to enemy action

✓4th **E990 Injury due to war operations by fires and conflagrations**

INCLUDES asphyxia, burns, or other injury originating from fire caused by a fire-producing device or indirectly by any conventional weapon

E990.0 From gasoline bomb

E990.9 From other and unspecified source

✓4th **E991 Injury due to war operations by bullets and fragments**

E991.0 Rubber bullets (rifle)

E991.1 Pellets (rifle)

E991.2 Other bullets

Bullet [any, except rubber bullets and pellets]
- carbine
- machine gun
- pistol
- rifle
- shotgun

E991.3 Antipersonnel bomb (fragments)

E991.9 Other and unspecified fragments

Fragments from:
- artillery shell
- bombs, except anti-personnel
- grenade
- guided missile

Fragments from:
- land mine
- rockets
- shell

Shrapnel

E992 Injury due to war operations by explosion of marine weapons

Depth charge
Marine mines
Mine NOS, at sea or in harbor
Sea-based artillery shell
Torpedo
Underwater blast

E993 Injury due to war operations by other explosion

Accidental explosion of munitions being used in war
Accidental explosion of own weapons
Air blast NOS
Blast NOS
Explosion NOS

Explosion of:
- artillery shell
- breech block
- cannon block
- mortar bomb

Injury by weapon burst

E994 Injury due to war operations by destruction of aircraft

Airplane:
- burned
- exploded

Airplane:
- shot down

Crushed by falling airplane

E995 Injury due to war operations by other and unspecified forms of conventional warfare

Battle wounds
Bayonet injury
Drowned in war operations

E996 Injury due to war operations by nuclear weapons

Blast effects
Exposure to ionizing radiation from nuclear weapons
Fireball effects
Heat
Other direct and secondary effects of nuclear weapons

✓4th **E997 Injury due to war operations by other forms of unconventional warfare**

E997.0 Lasers

E997.1 Biological warfare

E997.2 Gases, fumes, and chemicals

E997.8 Other specified forms of unconventional warfare

E997.9 Unspecified form of unconventional warfare

E998 Injury due to war operations but occurring after cessation of hostilities

Injuries due to operations of war but occurring after cessation of hostilities by any means classifiable under E990-E997

Injuries by explosion of bombs or mines placed in the course of operations of war, if the explosion occurred after cessation of hostilities

✓4th **E999 Late effect of injury due to war operations and terrorism**

Note: This category is to be used to indicate circumstances classifiable to E979, E990-E998 as the cause of death or disability from late effects, which are themselves classifiable elsewhere. The "late effects" include conditions reported as such, or as sequelae, which may occur at any time after the injury, resulting from operations of war or terrorism

E999.0 Late effect of injury due to war operations

E999.1 Late effect of injury due to terrorism

Official ICD-9-CM Government Appendixes

MORPHOLOGY OF NEOPLASMS

The World Health Organization has published an adaptation of the International Classification of Diseases for oncology (ICD-O). It contains a coded nomenclature for the morphology of neoplasms, which is reproduced here for those who wish to use it in conjunction with Chapter 2 of the International Classification of Diseases, 9th Revision, Clinical Modification.

The morphology code numbers consist of five digits; the first four identify the histological type of the neoplasm and the fifth indicates its behavior. The one-digit behavior code is as follows:

- /0 Benign
- /1 Uncertain whether benign or malignant
Borderline malignancy
- /2 Carcinoma in situ
Intraepithelial
Noninfiltrating
Noninvasive
- /3 Malignant, primary site
- /6 Malignant, metastatic site
Secondary site
- /9 Malignant, uncertain whether primary or metastatic site

In the nomenclature below, the morphology code numbers include the behavior code appropriate to the histological type of neoplasm, but this behavior code should be changed if other reported information makes this necessary. For example, "chordoma (M9370/3)" is assumed to be malignant; the term "benign chordoma" should be coded M9370/0. Similarly, "superficial spreading adenocarcinoma (M8143/3)" described as "noninvasive" should be coded M8143/2 and "melanoma (M8720/3)" described as "secondary" should be coded M8720/6.

The following table shows the correspondence between the morphology code and the different sections of Chapter 2:

Morphology Code Histology/Behavior		ICD-9-CM Chapter 2	
Any	0	210-229	Benign neoplasms
M8000-M8004	1	239	Neoplasms of unspecified nature
M8010+	1	235-238	Neoplasms of uncertain behavior
Any	2	230-234	Carcinoma in situ
Any	3	140-195 200-208	Malignant neoplasms, stated or presumed to be primary
Any	6	196-198	Malignant neoplasms, stated or presumed to be secondary

The ICD-O behavior digit /9 is inapplicable in an ICD context, since all malignant neoplasms are presumed to be primary (/3) or secondary (/6) according to other information on the medical record.

Only the first-listed term of the full ICD-O morphology nomenclature appears against each code number in the list below. The ICD-9-CM Alphabetical Index (Volume 2), however, includes all the ICD-O synonyms as well as a number of other morphological names still likely to be encountered on medical records but omitted from ICD-O as outdated or otherwise undesirable.

A coding difficulty sometimes arises where a morphological diagnosis contains two qualifying adjectives that have different code numbers. An example is "transitional cell epidermoid carcinoma." "Transitional cell carcinoma NOS" is M8120/3 and "epidermoid carcinoma NOS" is M8070/3. In such circumstances, the higher number (M8120/3 in this example) should be used, as it is usually more specific.

CODED NOMENCLATURE FOR MORPHOLOGY OF NEOPLASMS

M800 Neoplasms NOS

M8000/0 *Neoplasm, benign*
M8000/1 *Neoplasm, uncertain whether benign or malignant*
M8000/3 *Neoplasm, malignant*
M8000/6 *Neoplasm, metastatic*
M8000/9 *Neoplasm, malignant, uncertain whether primary or metastatic*
M8001/0 *Tumor cells, benign*
M8001/1 *Tumor cells, uncertain whether benign or malignant*
M8001/3 *Tumor cells, malignant*
M8002/3 *Malignant tumor, small cell type*
M8003/3 *Malignant tumor, giant cell type*
M8004/3 *Malignant tumor, fusiform cell type*

M801-M804 Epithelial neoplasms NOS

M8010/0 *Epithelial tumor, benign*
M8010/2 *Carcinoma in situ NOS*
M8010/3 *Carcinoma NOS*
M8010/6 *Carcinoma, metastatic NOS*
M8010/9 *Carcinomatosis*
M8011/0 *Epithelioma, benign*
M8011/3 *Epithelioma, malignant*
M8012/3 *Large cell carcinoma NOS*
M8020/3 *Carcinoma, undifferentiated type NOS*
M8021/3 *Carcinoma, anaplastic type NOS*
M8022/3 *Pleomorphic carcinoma*
M8030/3 *Giant cell and spindle cell carcinoma*
M8031/3 *Giant cell carcinoma*
M8032/3 *Spindle cell carcinoma*
M8033/3 *Pseudosarcomatous carcinoma*
M8034/3 *Polygonal cell carcinoma*
M8035/3 *Spheroidal cell carcinoma*
M8040/1 *Tumorlet*
M8041/3 *Small cell carcinoma NOS*
M8042/3 *Oat cell carcinoma*
M8043/3 *Small cell carcinoma, fusiform cell type*

M805-M808 Papillary and squamous cell neoplasms

M8050/0 *Papilloma NOS (except Papilloma of urinary bladder M8120/1)*
M8050/2 *Papillary carcinoma in situ*
M8050/3 *Papillary carcinoma NOS*
M8051/0 *Verrucous papilloma*
M8051/3 *Verrucous carcinoma NOS*
M8052/0 *Squamous cell papilloma*
M8052/3 *Papillary squamous cell carcinoma*
M8053/0 *Inverted papilloma*
M8060/0 *Papillomatosis NOS*
M8070/2 *Squamous cell carcinoma in situ NOS*
M8070/3 *Squamous cell carcinoma NOS*
M8070/6 *Squamous cell carcinoma, metastatic NOS*
M8071/3 *Squamous cell carcinoma, keratinizing type NOS*
M8072/3 *Squamous cell carcinoma, large cell, nonkeratinizing type*
M8073/3 *Squamous cell carcinoma, small cell, nonkeratinizing type*
M8074/3 *Squamous cell carcinoma, spindle cell type*
M8075/3 *Adenoid squamous cell carcinoma*
M8076/2 *Squamous cell carcinoma in situ with questionable stromal invasion*
M8076/3 *Squamous cell carcinoma, microinvasive*
M8080/2 *Queyrat's erythroplasia*
M8081/2 *Bowen's disease*
M8082/3 *Lymphoepithelial carcinoma*

M809-M811 Basal cell neoplasms

M8090/1 *Basal cell tumor*
M8090/3 *Basal cell carcinoma NOS*
M8091/3 *Multicentric basal cell carcinoma*
M8092/3 *Basal cell carcinoma, morphea type*
M8093/3 *Basal cell carcinoma, fibroepithelial type*
M8094/3 *Basosquamous carcinoma*
M8095/3 *Metatypical carcinoma*
M8096/0 *Intraepidermal epithelioma of Jadassohn*
M8100/0 *Trichoepithelioma*
M8101/0 *Trichofolliculoma*
M8102/0 *Tricholemmoma*
M8110/0 *Pilomatrixoma*

M812-M813 Transitional cell papillomas and carcinomas

M8120/0 *Transitional cell papilloma NOS*
M8120/1 *Urothelial papilloma*
M8120/2 *Transitional cell carcinoma in situ*
M8120/3 *Transitional cell carcinoma NOS*
M8121/0 *Schneiderian papilloma*
M8121/1 *Transitional cell papilloma, inverted type*
M8121/3 *Schneiderian carcinoma*
M8122/3 *Transitional cell carcinoma, spindle cell type*
M8123/3 *Basaloid carcinoma*
M8124/3 *Cloacogenic carcinoma*
M8130/3 *Papillary transitional cell carcinoma*

M814-M838 Adenomas and adenocarcinomas

M8140/0 *Adenoma NOS*
M8140/1 *Bronchial adenoma NOS*
M8140/2 *Adenocarcinoma in situ*
M8140/3 *Adenocarcinoma NOS*
M8140/6 *Adenocarcinoma, metastatic NOS*
M8141/3 *Scirrhous adenocarcinoma*
M8142/3 *Linitis plastica*
M8143/3 *Superficial spreading adenocarcinoma*
M8144/3 *Adenocarcinoma, intestinal type*
M8145/3 *Carcinoma, diffuse type*
M8146/0 *Monomorphic adenoma*
M8147/0 *Basal cell adenoma*
M8150/0 *Islet cell adenoma*
M8150/3 *Islet cell carcinoma*
M8151/0 *Insulinoma NOS*
M8151/3 *Insulinoma, malignant*
M8152/0 *Glucagonoma NOS*
M8152/3 *Glucagonoma, malignant*
M8153/1 *Gastrinoma NOS*

M8153/3 *Gastrinoma, malignant*
M8154/3 *Mixed islet cell and exocrine adenocarcinoma*
M8160/0 *Bile duct adenoma*
M8160/3 *Cholangiocarcinoma*
M8161/0 *Bile duct cystadenoma*
M8161/3 *Bile duct cystadenocarcinoma*
M8170/0 *Liver cell adenoma*
M8170/3 *Hepatocellular carcinoma NOS*
M8180/0 *Hepatocholangioma, benign*
M8180/3 *Combined hepatocellular carcinoma and cholangiocarcinoma*
M8190/0 *Trabecular adenoma*
M8190/3 *Trabecular adenocarcinoma*
M8191/0 *Embryonal adenoma*
M8200/0 *Eccrine dermal cylindroma*
M8200/3 *Adenoid cystic carcinoma*
M8201/3 *Cribriform carcinoma*
M8210/0 *Adenomatous polyp NOS*
M8210/3 *Adenocarcinoma in adenomatous polyp*
M8211/0 *Tubular adenoma NOS*
M8211/3 *Tubular adenocarcinoma*
M8220/0 *Adenomatous polyposis coli*
M8220/3 *Adenocarcinoma in adenomatous polyposis coli*
M8221/0 *Multiple adenomatous polyps*
M8230/3 *Solid carcinoma NOS*
M8231/3 *Carcinoma simplex*
M8240/1 *Carcinoid tumor NOS*
M8240/3 *Carcinoid tumor, malignant*
M8241/1 *Carcinoid tumor, argentaffin NOS*
M8241/3 *Carcinoid tumor, argentaffin, malignant*
M8242/1 *Carcinoid tumor, nonargentaffin NOS*
M8242/3 *Carcinoid tumor, nonargentaffin, malignant*
M8243/3 *Mucocarcinoid tumor, malignant*
M8244/3 *Composite carcinoid*
M8250/1 *Pulmonary adenomatosis*
M8250/3 *Bronchiolo-alveolar adenocarcinoma*
M8251/0 *Alveolar adenoma*
M8251/3 *Alveolar adenocarcinoma*
M8260/0 *Papillary adenoma NOS*
M8260/3 *Papillary adenocarcinoma NOS*
M8261/1 *Villous adenoma NOS*
M8261/3 *Adenocarcinoma in villous adenoma*
M8262/3 *Villous adenocarcinoma*
M8263/0 *Tubulovillous adenoma*
M8270/0 *Chromophobe adenoma*
M8270/3 *Chromophobe carcinoma*
M8280/0 *Acidophil adenoma*
M8280/3 *Acidophil carcinoma*
M8281/0 *Mixed acidophil-basophil adenoma*
M8281/3 *Mixed acidophil-basophil carcinoma*
M8290/0 *Oxyphilic adenoma*
M8290/3 *Oxyphilic adenocarcinoma*
M8300/0 *Basophil adenoma*
M8300/3 *Basophil carcinoma*
M8310/0 *Clear cell adenoma*
M8310/3 *Clear cell adenocarcinoma NOS*
M8311/1 *Hypernephroid tumor*
M8312/3 *Renal cell carcinoma*
M8313/0 *Clear cell adenofibroma*
M8320/3 *Granular cell carcinoma*
M8321/0 *Chief cell adenoma*
M8322/0 *Water-clear cell adenoma*
M8322/3 *Water-clear cell adenocarcinoma*
M8323/0 *Mixed cell adenoma*
M8323/3 *Mixed cell adenocarcinoma*
M8324/0 *Lipoadenoma*
M8330/0 *Follicular adenoma*
M8330/3 *Follicular adenocarcinoma NOS*
M8331/3 *Follicular adenocarcinoma, well differentiated type*
M8332/3 *Follicular adenocarcinoma, trabecular type*
M8333/0 *Microfollicular adenoma*
M8334/0 *Macrofollicular adenoma*
M8340/3 *Papillary and follicular adenocarcinoma*
M8350/3 *Nonencapsulated sclerosing carcinoma*
M8360/1 *Multiple endocrine adenomas*
M8361/1 *Juxtaglomerular tumor*
M8370/0 *Adrenal cortical adenoma NOS*
M8370/3 *Adrenal cortical carcinoma*
M8371/0 *Adrenal cortical adenoma, compact cell type*
M8372/0 *Adrenal cortical adenoma, heavily pigmented variant*
M8373/0 *Adrenal cortical adenoma, clear cell type*
M8374/0 *Adrenal cortical adenoma, glomerulosa cell type*
M8375/0 *Adrenal cortical adenoma, mixed cell type*
M8380/0 *Endometrioid adenoma NOS*
M8380/1 *Endometrioid adenoma, borderline malignancy*
M8380/3 *Endometrioid carcinoma*
M8381/0 *Endometrioid adenofibroma NOS*
M8381/1 *Endometrioid adenofibroma, borderline malignancy*
M8381/3 *Endometrioid adenofibroma, malignant*

M839-M842 Adnexal and skin appendage neoplasms

M8390/0 *Skin appendage adenoma*
M8390/3 *Skin appendage carcinoma*
M8400/0 *Sweat gland adenoma*
M8400/1 *Sweat gland tumor NOS*
M8400/3 *Sweat gland adenocarcinoma*
M8401/0 *Apocrine adenoma*
M8401/3 *Apocrine adenocarcinoma*
M8402/0 *Eccrine acrospiroma*
M8403/0 *Eccrine spiradenoma*
M8404/0 *Hidrocystoma*
M8405/0 *Papillary hydradenoma*
M8406/0 *Papillary syringadenoma*
M8407/0 *Syringoma NOS*
M8410/0 *Sebaceous adenoma*
M8410/3 *Sebaceous adenocarcinoma*
M8420/0 *Ceruminous adenoma*
M8420/3 *Ceruminous adenocarcinoma*

M843 Mucoepidermoid neoplasms

M8430/1 *Mucoepidermoid tumor*
M8430/3 *Mucoepidermoid carcinoma*

M844-M849 Cystic, mucinous, and serous neoplasms

M8440/0 *Cystadenoma NOS*
M8440/3 *Cystadenocarcinoma NOS*
M8441/0 *Serous cystadenoma NOS*
M8441/1 *Serous cystadenoma, borderline malignancy*
M8441/3 *Serous cystadenocarcinoma NOS*
M8450/0 *Papillary cystadenoma NOS*
M8450/1 *Papillary cystadenoma, borderline malignancy*
M8450/3 *Papillary cystadenocarcinoma NOS*
M8460/0 *Papillary serous cystadenoma NOS*
M8460/1 *Papillary serous cystadenoma, borderline malignancy*
M8460/3 *Papillary serous cystadenocarcinoma*
M8461/0 *Serous surface papilloma NOS*
M8461/1 *Serous surface papilloma, borderline malignancy*
M8461/3 *Serous surface papillary carcinoma*
M8470/0 *Mucinous cystadenoma NOS*
M8470/1 *Mucinous cystadenoma, borderline malignancy*
M8470/3 *Mucinous cystadenocarcinoma NOS*
M8471/0 *Papillary mucinous cystadenoma NOS*
M8471/1 *Papillary mucinous cystadenoma, borderline malignancy*
M8471/3 *Papillary mucinous cystadenocarcinoma*
M8480/0 *Mucinous adenoma*
M8480/3 *Mucinous adenocarcinoma*
M8480/6 *Pseudomyxoma peritonei*
M8481/3 *Mucin-producing adenocarcinoma*
M8490/3 *Signet ring cell carcinoma*
M8490/6 *Metastatic signet ring cell carcinoma*

M850-M854 Ductal, lobular, and medullary neoplasms

M8500/2 *Intraductal carcinoma, noninfiltrating NOS*
M8500/3 *Infiltrating duct carcinoma*
M8501/2 *Comedocarcinoma, noninfiltrating*
M8501/3 *Comedocarcinoma NOS*
M8502/3 *Juvenile carcinoma of the breast*
M8503/0 *Intraductal papilloma*
M8503/2 *Noninfiltrating intraductal papillary adenocarcinoma*
M8504/0 *Intracystic papillary adenoma*
M8504/2 *Noninfiltrating intracystic carcinoma*
M8505/0 *Intraductal papillomatosis NOS*
M8506/0 *Subareolar duct papillomatosis*
M8510/3 *Medullary carcinoma NOS*
M8511/3 *Medullary carcinoma with amyloid stroma*
M8512/3 *Medullary carcinoma with lymphoid stroma*
M8520/2 *Lobular carcinoma in situ*
M8520/3 *Lobular carcinoma NOS*
M8521/3 *Infiltrating ductular carcinoma*
M8530/3 *Inflammatory carcinoma*
M8540/3 *Paget's disease, mammary*
M8541/3 *Paget's disease and infiltrating duct carcinoma of breast*
M8542/3 *Paget's disease, extramammary (except Paget's disease of bone)*

M855 Acinar cell neoplasms

M8550/0 *Acinar cell adenoma*
M8550/1 *Acinar cell tumor*
M8550/3 *Acinar cell carcinoma*

M856-M858 Complex epithelial neoplasms

M8560/3 *Adenosquamous carcinoma*
M8561/0 *Adenolymphoma*
M8570/3 *Adenocarcinoma with squamous metaplasia*
M8571/3 *Adenocarcinoma with cartilaginous and osseous metaplasia*
M8572/3 *Adenocarcinoma with spindle cell metaplasia*
M8573/3 *Adenocarcinoma with apocrine metaplasia*
M8580/0 *Thymoma, benign*
M8580/3 *Thymoma, malignant*

M859-M867 Specialized gonadal neoplasms

M8590/1 *Sex cord-stromal tumor*
M8600/0 *Thecoma NOS*
M8600/3 *Theca cell carcinoma*
M8610/0 *Luteoma NOS*
M8620/1 *Granulosa cell tumor NOS*
M8620/3 *Granulosa cell tumor, malignant*
M8621/1 *Granulosa cell-theca cell tumor*
M8630/0 *Androblastoma, benign*
M8630/1 *Androblastoma NOS*
M8630/3 *Androblastoma, malignant*
M8631/0 *Sertoli-Leydig cell tumor*
M8632/1 *Gynandroblastoma*
M8640/0 *Tubular androblastoma NOS*
M8640/3 *Sertoli cell carcinoma*
M8641/0 *Tubular androblastoma with lipid storage*

M8650/0 *Leydig cell tumor, benign*
M8650/1 *Leydig cell tumor NOS*
M8650/3 *Leydig cell tumor, malignant*
M8660/0 *Hilar cell tumor*
M8670/0 *Lipid cell tumor of ovary*
M8671/0 *Adrenal rest tumor*

M868-M871 Paragangliomas and glomus tumors

M8680/1 *Paraganglioma NOS*
M8680/3 *Paraganglioma, malignant*
M8681/1 *Sympathetic paraganglioma*
M8682/1 *Parasympathetic paraganglioma*
M8690/1 *Glomus jugulare tumor*
M8691/1 *Aortic body tumor*
M8692/1 *Carotid body tumor*
M8693/1 *Extra-adrenal paraganglioma NOS*
M8693/3 *Extra-adrenal paraganglioma, malignant*
M8700/0 *Pheochromocytoma NOS*
M8700/3 *Pheochromocytoma, malignant*
M8710/3 *Glomangiosarcoma*
M8711/0 *Glomus tumor*
M8712/0 *Glomangioma*

M872-M879 Nevi and melanomas

M8720/0 *Pigmented nevus NOS*
M8720/3 *Malignant melanoma NOS*
M8721/3 *Nodular melanoma*
M8722/0 *Balloon cell nevus*
M8722/3 *Balloon cell melanoma*
M8723/0 *Halo nevus*
M8724/0 *Fibrous papule of the nose*
M8725/0 *Neuronevus*
M8726/0 *Magnocellular nevus*
M8730/0 *Nonpigmented nevus*
M8730/3 *Amelanotic melanoma*
M8740/0 *Junctional nevus*
M8740/3 *Malignant melanoma in junctional nevus*
M8741/2 *Precancerous melanosis NOS*
M8741/3 *Malignant melanoma in precancerous melanosis*
M8742/2 *Hutchinson's melanotic freckle*
M8742/3 *Malignant melanoma in Hutchinson's melanotic freckle*
M8743/3 *Superficial spreading melanoma*
M8750/0 *Intradermal nevus*
M8760/0 *Compound nevus*
M8761/1 *Giant pigmented nevus*
M8761/3 *Malignant melanoma in giant pigmented nevus*
M8770/0 *Epithelioid and spindle cell nevus*
M8771/3 *Epithelioid cell melanoma*
M8772/3 *Spindle cell melanoma NOS*
M8773/3 *Spindle cell melanoma, type A*
M8774/3 *Spindle cell melanoma, type B*
M8775/3 *Mixed epithelioid and spindle cell melanoma*
M8780/0 *Blue nevus NOS*
M8780/3 *Blue nevus, malignant*
M8790/0 *Cellular blue nevus*

M880 Soft tissue tumors and sarcomas NOS

M8800/0 *Soft tissue tumor, benign*
M8800/3 *Sarcoma NOS*
M8800/9 *Sarcomatosis NOS*
M8801/3 *Spindle cell sarcoma*
M8802/3 *Giant cell sarcoma (except of bone M9250/3)*
M8803/3 *Small cell sarcoma*
M8804/3 *Epithelioid cell sarcoma*

M881-M883 Fibromatous neoplasms

M8810/0 *Fibroma NOS*
M8810/3 *Fibrosarcoma NOS*
M8811/0 *Fibromyxoma*
M8811/3 *Fibromyxosarcoma*
M8812/0 *Periosteal fibroma*
M8812/3 *Periosteal fibrosarcoma*
M8813/0 *Fascial fibroma*
M8813/3 *Fascial fibrosarcoma*
M8814/3 *Infantile fibrosarcoma*
M8820/0 *Elastofibroma*
M8821/1 *Aggressive fibromatosis*
M8822/1 *Abdominal fibromatosis*
M8823/1 *Desmoplastic fibroma*
M8830/0 *Fibrous histiocytoma NOS*
M8830/1 *Atypical fibrous histiocytoma*
M8830/3 *Fibrous histiocytoma, malignant*
M8831/0 *Fibroxanthoma NOS*
M8831/1 *Atypical fibroxanthoma*
M8831/3 *Fibroxanthoma, malignant*
M8832/0 *Dermatofibroma NOS*
M8832/1 *Dermatofibroma protuberans*
M8832/3 *Dermatofibrosarcoma NOS*

M884 Myxomatous neoplasms

M8840/0 *Myxoma NOS*
M8840/3 *Myxosarcoma*

M885-M888 Lipomatous neoplasms

M8850/0 *Lipoma NOS*
M8850/3 *Liposarcoma NOS*
M8851/0 *Fibrolipoma*
M8851/3 *Liposarcoma, well differentiated type*
M8852/0 *Fibromyxolipoma*
M8852/3 *Myxoid liposarcoma*
M8853/3 *Round cell liposarcoma*
M8854/3 *Pleomorphic liposarcoma*
M8855/3 *Mixed type liposarcoma*
M8856/0 *Intramuscular lipoma*
M8857/0 *Spindle cell lipoma*
M8860/0 *Angiomyolipoma*
M8860/3 *Angiomyoliposarcoma*
M8861/0 *Angiolipoma NOS*
M8861/1 *Angiolipoma, infiltrating*
M8870/0 *Myelolipoma*
M8880/0 *Hibernoma*
M8881/0 *Lipoblastomatosis*

M889-M892 Myomatous neoplasms

M8890/0 *Leiomyoma NOS*
M8890/1 *Intravascular leiomyomatosis*
M8890/3 *Leiomyosarcoma NOS*
M8891/1 *Epithelioid leiomyoma*
M8891/3 *Epithelioid leiomyosarcoma*
M8892/1 *Cellular leiomyoma*
M8893/0 *Bizarre leiomyoma*
M8894/0 *Angiomyoma*
M8894/3 *Angiomyosarcoma*
M8895/0 *Myoma*
M8895/3 *Myosarcoma*
M8900/0 *Rhabdomyoma NOS*
M8900/3 *Rhabdomyosarcoma NOS*
M8901/3 *Pleomorphic rhabdomyosarcoma*
M8902/3 *Mixed type rhabdomyosarcoma*
M8903/0 *Fetal rhabdomyoma*
M8904/0 *Adult rhabdomyoma*
M8910/3 *Embryonal rhabdomyosarcoma*
M8920/3 *Alveolar rhabdomyosarcoma*

M893-M899 Complex mixed and stromal neoplasms

M8930/3 *Endometrial stromal sarcoma*
M8931/1 *Endolymphatic stromal myosis*
M8932/0 *Adenomyoma*
M8940/0 *Pleomorphic adenoma*
M8940/3 *Mixed tumor, malignant NOS*
M8950/3 *Mullerian mixed tumor*
M8951/3 *Mesodermal mixed tumor*
M8960/1 *Mesoblastic nephroma*
M8960/3 *Nephroblastoma NOS*
M8961/3 *Epithelial nephroblastoma*
M8962/3 *Mesenchymal nephroblastoma*
M8970/3 *Hepatoblastoma*
M8980/3 *Carcinosarcoma NOS*
M8981/3 *Carcinosarcoma, embryonal type*
M8982/0 *Myoepithelioma*
M8990/0 *Mesenchymoma, benign*
M8990/1 *Mesenchymoma NOS*
M8990/3 *Mesenchymoma, malignant*
M8991/3 *Embryonal sarcoma*

M900-M903 Fibroepithelial neoplasms

M9000/0 *Brenner tumor NOS*
M9000/1 *Brenner tumor, borderline malignancy*
M9000/3 *Brenner tumor, malignant*
M9010/0 *Fibroadenoma NOS*
M9011/0 *Intracanalicular fibroadenoma NOS*
M9012/0 *Pericanalicular fibroadenoma*
M9013/0 *Adenofibroma NOS*
M9014/0 *Serous adenofibroma*
M9015/0 *Mucinous adenofibroma*
M9020/0 *Cellular intracanalicular fibroadenoma*
M9020/1 *Cystosarcoma phyllodes NOS*
M9020/3 *Cystosarcoma phyllodes, malignant*
M9030/0 *Juvenile fibroadenoma*

M904 Synovial neoplasms

M9040/0 *Synovioma, benign*
M9040/3 *Synovial sarcoma NOS*
M9041/3 *Synovial sarcoma, spindle cell type*
M9042/3 *Synovial sarcoma, epithelioid cell type*
M9043/3 *Synovial sarcoma, biphasic type*
M9044/3 *Clear cell sarcoma of tendons and aponeuroses*

M905 Mesothelial neoplasms

M9050/0 *Mesothelioma, benign*
M9050/3 *Mesothelioma, malignant*
M9051/0 *Fibrous mesothelioma, benign*
M9051/3 *Fibrous mesothelioma, malignant*
M9052/0 *Epithelioid mesothelioma, benign*
M9052/3 *Epithelioid mesothelioma, malignant*
M9053/0 *Mesothelioma, biphasic type, benign*
M9053/3 *Mesothelioma, biphasic type, malignant*
M9054/0 *Adenomatoid tumor NOS*

M906-M909 Germ cell neoplasms

M9060/3 *Dysgerminoma*
M9061/3 *Seminoma NOS*
M9062/3 *Seminoma, anaplastic type*
M9063/3 *Spermatocytic seminoma*
M9064/3 *Germinoma*
M9070/3 *Embryonal carcinoma NOS*
M9071/3 *Endodermal sinus tumor*
M9072/3 *Polyembryoma*
M9073/1 *Gonadoblastoma*
M9080/0 *Teratoma, benign*
M9080/1 *Teratoma NOS*
M9080/3 *Teratoma, malignant NOS*
M9081/3 *Teratocarcinoma*
M9082/3 *Malignant teratoma, undifferentiated type*
M9083/3 *Malignant teratoma, intermediate type*
M9084/0 *Dermoid cyst*
M9084/3 *Dermoid cyst with malignant transformation*
M9090/0 *Struma ovarii NOS*
M9090/3 *Struma ovarii, malignant*
M9091/1 *Strumal carcinoid*

M910 Trophoblastic neoplasms

M9100/0 *Hydatidiform mole NOS*
M9100/1 *Invasive hydatidiform mole*
M9100/3 *Choriocarcinoma*
M9101/3 *Choriocarcinoma combined with teratoma*
M9102/3 *Malignant teratoma, trophoblastic*

M911 Mesonephromas

M9110/0 *Mesonephroma, benign*
M9110/1 *Mesonephric tumor*
M9110/3 *Mesonephroma, malignant*
M9111/1 *Endosalpingioma*

M912-M916 Blood vessel tumors
M9120/0 *Hemangioma NOS*
M9120/3 *Hemangiosarcoma*
M9121/0 *Cavernous hemangioma*
M9122/0 *Venous hemangioma*
M9123/0 *Racemose hemangioma*
M9124/3 *Kupffer cell sarcoma*
M9130/0 *Hemangioendothelioma, benign*
M9130/1 *Hemangioendothelioma NOS*
M9130/3 *Hemangioendothelioma, malignant*
M9131/0 *Capillary hemangioma*
M9132/0 *Intramuscular hemangioma*
M9140/3 *Kaposi's sarcoma*
M9141/0 *Angiokeratoma*
M9142/0 *Verrucous keratotic hemangioma*
M9150/0 *Hemangiopericytoma, benign*
M9150/1 *Hemangiopericytoma NOS*
M9150/3 *Hemangiopericytoma, malignant*
M9160/0 *Angiofibroma NOS*
M9161/1 *Hemangioblastoma*

M917 Lymphatic vessel tumors
M9170/0 *Lymphangioma NOS*
M9170/3 *Lymphangiosarcoma*
M9171/0 *Capillary lymphangioma*
M9172/0 *Cavernous lymphangioma*
M9173/0 *Cystic lymphangioma*
M9174/0 *Lymphangiomyoma*
M9174/1 *Lymphangiomyomatosis*
M9175/0 *Hemolymphangioma*

M918-M920 Osteomas and osteosarcomas
M9180/0 *Osteoma NOS*
M9180/3 *Osteosarcoma NOS*
M9181/3 *Chondroblastic osteosarcoma*
M9182/3 *Fibroblastic osteosarcoma*
M9183/3 *Telangiectatic osteosarcoma*
M9184/3 *Osteosarcoma in Paget's disease of bone*
M9190/3 *Juxtacortical osteosarcoma*
M9191/0 *Osteoid osteoma NOS*
M9200/0 *Osteoblastoma*

M921-M924 Chondromatous neoplasms
M9210/0 *Osteochondroma*
M9210/1 *Osteochondromatosis NOS*
M9220/0 *Chondroma NOS*
M9220/1 *Chondromatosis NOS*
M9220/3 *Chondrosarcoma NOS*
M9221/0 *Juxtacortical chondroma*
M9221/3 *Juxtacortical chondrosarcoma*
M9230/0 *Chondroblastoma NOS*
M9230/3 *Chondroblastoma, malignant*
M9240/3 *Mesenchymal chondrosarcoma*
M9241/0 *Chondromyxoid fibroma*

M925 Giant cell tumors
M9250/1 *Giant cell tumor of bone NOS*
M9250/3 *Giant cell tumor of bone, malignant*
M9251/1 *Giant cell tumor of soft parts NOS*
M9251/3 *Malignant giant cell tumor of soft parts*

M926 Miscellaneous bone tumors
M9260/3 *Ewing's sarcoma*
M9261/3 *Adamantinoma of long bones*
M9262/0 *Ossifying fibroma*

M927-M934 Odontogenic tumors
M9270/0 *Odontogenic tumor, benign*
M9270/1 *Odontogenic tumor NOS*
M9270/3 *Odontogenic tumor, malignant*
M9271/0 *Dentinoma*
M9272/0 *Cementoma NOS*
M9273/0 *Cementoblastoma, benign*
M9274/0 *Cementifying fibroma*
M9275/0 *Gigantiform cementoma*
M9280/0 *Odontoma NOS*
M9281/0 *Compound odontoma*
M9282/0 *Complex odontoma*
M9290/0 *Ameloblastic fibro-odontoma*
M9290/3 *Ameloblastic odontosarcoma*
M9300/0 *Adenomatoid odontogenic tumor*
M9301/0 *Calcifying odontogenic cyst*
M9310/0 *Ameloblastoma NOS*
M9310/3 *Ameloblastoma, malignant*
M9311/0 *Odontoameloblastoma*
M9312/0 *Squamous odontogenic tumor*
M9320/0 *Odontogenic myxoma*
M9321/0 *Odontogenic fibroma NOS*
M9330/0 *Ameloblastic fibroma*
M9330/3 *Ameloblastic fibrosarcoma*
M9340/0 *Calcifying epithelial odontogenic tumor*

M935-M937 Miscellaneous tumors
M9350/1 *Craniopharyngioma*
M9360/1 *Pinealoma*
M9361/1 *Pineocytoma*
M9362/3 *Pineoblastoma*
M9363/0 *Melanotic neuroectodermal tumor*
M9370/3 *Chordoma*

M938-M948 Gliomas
M9380/3 *Glioma, malignant*
M9381/3 *Gliomatosis cerebri*
M9382/3 *Mixed glioma*
M9383/1 *Subependymal glioma*
M9384/1 *Subependymal giant cell astrocytoma*
M9390/0 *Choroid plexus papilloma NOS*
M9390/3 *Choroid plexus papilloma, malignant*
M9391/3 *Ependymoma NOS*
M9392/3 *Ependymoma, anaplastic type*
M9393/1 *Papillary ependymoma*
M9394/1 *Myxopapillary ependymoma*
M9400/3 *Astrocytoma NOS*
M9401/3 *Astrocytoma, anaplastic type*
M9410/3 *Protoplasmic astrocytoma*
M9411/3 *Gemistocytic astrocytoma*
M9420/3 *Fibrillary astrocytoma*
M9421/3 *Pilocytic astrocytoma*
M9422/3 *Spongioblastoma NOS*
M9423/3 *Spongioblastoma polare*
M9430/3 *Astroblastoma*
M9440/3 *Glioblastoma NOS*
M9441/3 *Giant cell glioblastoma*
M9442/3 *Glioblastoma with sarcomatous component*
M9443/3 *Primitive polar spongioblastoma*
M9450/3 *Oligodendroglioma NOS*
M9451/3 *Oligodendroglioma, anaplastic type*
M9460/3 *Oligodendroblastoma*
M9470/3 *Medulloblastoma NOS*
M9471/3 *Desmoplastic medulloblastoma*
M9472/3 *Medullomyoblastoma*
M9480/3 *Cerebellar sarcoma NOS*
M9481/3 *Monstrocellular sarcoma*

M949-M952 Neuroepitheliomatous neoplasms
M9490/0 *Ganglioneuroma*
M9490/3 *Ganglioneuroblastoma*
M9491/0 *Ganglioneuromatosis*
M9500/3 *Neuroblastoma NOS*
M9501/3 *Medulloepithelioma NOS*
M9502/3 *Teratoid medulloepithelioma*
M9503/3 *Neuroepithelioma NOS*
M9504/3 *Spongioneuroblastoma*
M9505/1 *Ganglioglioma*
M9506/0 *Neurocytoma*
M9507/0 *Pacinian tumor*
M9510/3 *Retinoblastoma NOS*
M9511/3 *Retinoblastoma, differentiated type*
M9512/3 *Retinoblastoma, undifferentiated type*
M9520/3 *Olfactory neurogenic tumor*
M9521/3 *Esthesioneurocytoma*
M9522/3 *Esthesioneuroblastoma*
M9523/3 *Esthesioneuroepithelioma*

M953 Meningiomas
M9530/0 *Meningioma NOS*
M9530/1 *Meningiomatosis NOS*
M9530/3 *Meningioma, malignant*
M9531/0 *Meningotheliomatous meningioma*
M9532/0 *Fibrous meningioma*
M9533/0 *Psammomatous meningioma*
M9534/0 *Angiomatous meningioma*
M9535/0 *Hemangioblastic meningioma*
M9536/0 *Hemangiopericytic meningioma*
M9537/0 *Transitional meningioma*
M9538/1 *Papillary meningioma*
M9539/3 *Meningeal sarcomatosis*

M954-M957 Nerve sheath tumor
M9540/0 *Neurofibroma NOS*
M9540/1 *Neurofibromatosis NOS*
M9540/3 *Neurofibrosarcoma*
M9541/0 *Melanotic neurofibroma*
M9550/0 *Plexiform neurofibroma*
M9560/0 *Neurilemmoma NOS*
M9560/1 *Neurinomatosis*
M9560/3 *Neurilemmoma, malignant*
M9570/0 *Neuroma NOS*

M958 Granular cell tumors and alveolar soft part sarcoma
M9580/0 *Granular cell tumor NOS*
M9580/3 *Granular cell tumor, malignant*
M9581/3 *Alveolar soft part sarcoma*

M959-M963 Lymphomas, NOS or diffuse
M9590/0 *Lymphomatous tumor, benign*
M9590/3 *Malignant lymphoma NOS*
M9591/3 *Malignant lymphoma, non Hodgkin's type*
M9600/3 *Malignant lymphoma, undifferentiated cell type NOS*
M9601/3 *Malignant lymphoma, stem cell type*
M9602/3 *Malignant lymphoma, convoluted cell type NOS*
M9610/3 *Lymphosarcoma NOS*
M9611/3 *Malignant lymphoma, lymphoplasmacytoid type*
M9612/3 *Malignant lymphoma, immunoblastic type*
M9613/3 *Malignant lymphoma, mixed lymphocytic-histiocytic NOS*
M9614/3 *Malignant lymphoma, centroblastic-centrocytic, diffuse*
M9615/3 *Malignant lymphoma, follicular center cell NOS*
M9620/3 *Malignant lymphoma, lymphocytic, well differentiated NOS*
M9621/3 *Malignant lymphoma, lymphocytic, intermediate differentiation NOS*
M9622/3 *Malignant lymphoma, centrocytic*
M9623/3 *Malignant lymphoma, follicular center cell, cleaved NOS*
M9630/3 *Malignant lymphoma, lymphocytic, poorly differentiated NOS*
M9631/3 *Prolymphocytic lymphosarcoma*
M9632/3 *Malignant lymphoma, centroblastic type NOS*
M9633/3 *Malignant lymphoma, follicular center cell, noncleaved NOS*

M964 *Reticulosarcomas*
M9640/3 *Reticulosarcoma NOS*
M9641/3 *Reticulosarcoma, pleomorphic cell type*
M9642/3 *Reticulosarcoma, nodular*

M965-M966 *Hodgkin's disease*
M9650/3 *Hodgkin's disease NOS*
M9651/3 *Hodgkin's disease, lymphocytic predominance*
M9652/3 *Hodgkin's disease, mixed cellularity*
M9653/3 *Hodgkin's disease, lymphocytic depletion NOS*
M9654/3 *Hodgkin's disease, lymphocytic depletion, diffuse fibrosis*
M9655/3 *Hodgkin's disease, lymphocytic depletion, reticular type*

M9656/3 *Hodgkin's disease, nodular sclerosis NOS*
M9657/3 *Hodgkin's disease, nodular sclerosis, cellular phase*
M9660/3 *Hodgkin's paragranuloma*
M9661/3 *Hodgkin's granuloma*
M9662/3 *Hodgkin's sarcoma*

M969 Lymphomas, nodular or follicular
M9690/3 *Malignant lymphoma, nodular NOS*
M9691/3 *Malignant lymphoma, mixed lymphocytic-histiocytic, nodular*
M9692/3 *Malignant lymphoma, centroblastic-centrocytic, follicular*
M9693/3 *Malignant lymphoma, lymphocytic, well differentiated, nodular*
M9694/3 *Malignant lymphoma, lymphocytic, intermediate differentiation, nodular*
M9695/3 *Malignant lymphoma, follicular center cell, cleaved, follicular*
M9696/3 *Malignant lymphoma, lymphocytic, poorly differentiated, nodular*
M9697/3 *Malignant lymphoma, centroblastic type, follicular*
M9698/3 *Malignant lymphoma, follicular center cell, noncleaved, follicular*

M970 Mycosis fungoides
M9700/3 *Mycosis fungoides*
M9701/3 *Sezary's disease*

M971-M972 Miscellaneous reticuloendothelial neoplasms
M9710/3 *Microglioma*
M9720/3 *Malignant histiocytosis*
M9721/3 *Histiocytic medullary reticulosis*
M9722/3 *Letterer-Siwe's disease*

M973 Plasma cell tumors
M9730/3 *Plasma cell myeloma*
M9731/0 *Plasma cell tumor, benign*
M9731/1 *Plasmacytoma NOS*
M9731/3 *Plasma cell tumor, malignant*

M974 Mast cell tumors
M9740/1 *Mastocytoma NOS*
M9740/3 *Mast cell sarcoma*
M9741/3 *Malignant mastocytosis*

M975 Burkitt's tumor
M9750/3 *Burkitt's tumor*

M980-M994 Leukemias

M980 Leukemias NOS
M9800/3 *Leukemia NOS*
M9801/3 *Acute leukemia NOS*
M9802/3 *Subacute leukemia NOS*
M9803/3 *Chronic leukemia NOS*
M9804/3 *Aleukemic leukemia NOS*

M981 Compound leukemias
M9810/3 *Compound leukemia*

M982 Lymphoid leukemias
M9820/3 *Lymphoid leukemia NOS*
M9821/3 *Acute lymphoid leukemia*
M9822/3 *Subacute lymphoid leukemia*
M9823/3 *Chronic lymphoid leukemia*
M9824/3 *Aleukemic lymphoid leukemia*
M9825/3 *Prolymphocytic leukemia*

M983 Plasma cell leukemias
M9830/3 *Plasma cell leukemia*

M984 Erythroleukemias
M9840/3 *Erythroleukemia*
M9841/3 *Acute erythremia*
M9842/3 *Chronic erythremia*

M985 Lymphosarcoma cell leukemias
M9850/3 *Lymphosarcoma cell leukemia*

M986 Myeloid leukemias
M9860/3 *Myeloid leukemia NOS*
M9861/3 *Acute myeloid leukemia*
M9862/3 *Subacute myeloid leukemia*
M9863/3 *Chronic myeloid leukemia*
M9864/3 *Aleukemic myeloid leukemia*
M9865/3 *Neutrophilic leukemia*
M9866/3 *Acute promyelocytic leukemia*

M987 Basophilic leukemias
M9870/3 *Basophilic leukemia*

M988 Eosinophilic leukemias
M9880/3 *Eosinophilic leukemia*

M989 Monocytic leukemias
M9890/3 *Monocytic leukemia NOS*
M9891/3 *Acute monocytic leukemia*
M9892/3 *Subacute monocytic leukemia*
M9893/3 *Chronic monocytic leukemia*
M9894/3 *Aleukemic monocytic leukemia*

M990-M994 Miscellaneous leukemias
M9900/3 *Mast cell leukemia*
M9910/3 *Megakaryocytic leukemia*
M9920/3 *Megakaryocytic myelosis*
M9930/3 *Myeloid sarcoma*
M9940/3 *Hairy cell leukemia*

M995-M997 Miscellaneous myeloproliferative and lymphoproliferative disorders
M9950/1 *Polycythemia vera*
M9951/1 *Acute panmyelosis*
M9960/1 *Chronic myeloproliferative disease*
M9961/1 *Myelosclerosis with myeloid metaplasia*
M9962/1 *Idiopathic thrombocythemia*
M9970/1 *Chronic lymphoproliferative disease*

Appendix B
was officially deleted
October 1, 2004

CLASSIFICATION OF DRUGS BY AMERICAN HOSPITAL FORMULARY SERVICE LIST NUMBER AND THEIR ICD-9-CM EQUIVALENTS

The coding of adverse effects of drugs is keyed to the continually revised Hospital Formulary of the American Hospital Formulary Service (AHFS) published under the direction of the American Society of Hospital Pharmacists.

The following section gives the ICD-9-CM diagnosis code for each AHFS list.

	AHFS* List	ICD-9-CM Diagnosis Code
4:00	ANTIHISTAMINE DRUGS	963.0
8:00	ANTI-INFECTIVE AGENTS	
8:04	Amebacides	961.5
	hydroxyquinoline derivatives	961.3
	arsenical anti-infectives	961.1
8:08	Anthelmintics	961.6
	quinoline derivatives	961.3
8:12.04	Antifungal Antibiotics	960.1
	nonantibiotics	961.9
8:12.06	Cephalosporins	960.5
8:12.08	Chloramphenicol	960.2
8:12.12	The Erythromycins	960.3
8:12.16	The Penicillins	960.0
8:12.20	The Streptomycins	960.6
8:12.24	The Tetracyclines	960.4
8:12.28	Other Antibiotics	960.8
	antimycobacterial antibiotics	960.6
	macrolides	960.3
8:16	Antituberculars	961.8
	antibiotics	960.6
8:18	Antivirals	961.7
8:20	Plasmodicides (antimalarials)	961.4
8:24	Sulfonamides	961.0
8:26	The Sulfones	961.8
8:28	Treponemicides	961.2
8:32	Trichomonacides	961.5
	hydroxyquinoline derivatives	961.3
	nitrofuran derivatives	961.9
8:36	Urinary Germicides	961.9
	quinoline derivatives	961.3
8:40	Other Anti-Infectives	961.9
10:00	ANTINEOPLASTIC AGENTS	963.1
	antibiotics	960.7
	progestogens	962.2
12:00	AUTONOMIC DRUGS	
12:04	Parasympathomimetic (Cholinergic) Agents	971.0
12:08	Parasympatholytic (Cholinergic Blocking) Agents	971.1
12:12	Sympathomimetic (Adrenergic) Agents	971.2
12:16	Sympatholytic (Adrenergic Blocking) Agents	971.3
12:20	Skeletal Muscle Relaxants	975.2
	central nervous system muscle-tone depressants	968.0
16:00	BLOOD DERIVATIVES	964.7
20:00	BLOOD FORMATION AND COAGULATION	
20:04	Antianemia Drugs	964.1
20:04.04	Iron Preparations	964.0
20:04.08	Liver and Stomach Preparations	964.1
20:12.04	Anticoagulants	964.2
20:12.08	Antiheparin Agents	964.5
20:12.12	Coagulants	964.5
20.12.16	Hemostatics	964.5
	capillary-active drugs	972.8
	fibrinolysis-affecting agents	964.4
	natural products	964.7
24:00	CARDIOVASCULAR DRUGS	
24:04	Cardiac Drugs	972.9
	cardiotonic agents	972.1
	rhythm regulators	972.0
24:06	Antilipemic Agents	972.2
	thyroid derivatives	962.7
24:08	Hypotensive Agents	972.6
	adrenergic blocking agents	971.3
	ganglion-blocking agents	972.3
	vasodilators	972.5
24:12	Vasodilating Agents	972.5
	coronary	972.4
	nicotinic acid derivatives	972.2
24:16	Sclerosing Agents	972.7
28:00	CENTRAL NERVOUS SYSTEM DRUGS	
28:04	General Anesthetics	968.4
	gaseous anesthetics	968.2
	halothane	968.1
	intravenous anesthetics	968.3
28:08	Analgesics and Antipyretics	965.9
	antirheumatics	965.61-965.69
	aromatic analgesics	965.4
	non-narcotics NEC	965.7
	opium alkaloids	965.00
	heroin	965.01
	methadone	965.02
	specified type NEC	965.09
	pyrazole derivatives	965.5
	salicylates	965.1
	specified type NEC	965.8
28:10	Narcotic Antagonists	970.1
28:12	Anticonvulsants	966.3
	barbiturates	967.0
	benzodiazepine-based tranquilizers	969.4
	bromides	967.3
	hydantoin derivatives	966.1
	oxazolidine derivative	966.0
	succinimides	966.2
28:16.04	Antidepressants	969.0
28:16.08	Tranquilizers	969.5
	benzodiazepine-based	969.4
	butyrophenone-based	969.2
	major NEC	969.3
	phenothiazine-based	969.1
28:16.12	Other Psychotherapeutic Agents	969.8
28:20	Respiratory and Cerebral Stimulants	970.9
	analeptics	970.0
	anorexigenic agents	977.0
	psychostimulants	969.7
	specified type NEC	970.8
28:24	Sedatives and Hypnotics	967.9
	barbiturates	967.0
	benzodiazepine-based tranquilizers	969.4
	chloral hydrate group	967.1
	glutethamide group	967.5
	intravenous anesthetics	968.3
	methaqualone	967.4
	paraldehyde	967.2
	phenothiazine-based tranquilizers	969.1
	specified type NEC	967.8
	thiobarbiturates	968.3
	tranquilizer NEC	969.5
36:00	DIAGNOSTIC AGENTS	977.8
40:00	ELECTROLYTE, CALORIC, AND WATER BALANCE AGENTS NEC	974.5
40:04	Acidifying Agents	963.2
40:08	Alkalinizing Agents	963.3
40:10	Ammonia Detoxicants	974.5
40:12	Replacement Solutions NEC	974.5
	plasma volume expanders	964.8
40:16	Sodium-Removing Resins	974.5
40:18	Potassium-Removing Resins	974.5
40:20	Caloric Agents	974.5
40:24	Salt and Sugar Substitutes	974.5
40:28	Diuretics NEC	974.4
	carbonic acid anhydrase inhibitors	974.2
	mercurials	974.0
	purine derivatives	974.1
	saluretics	974.3
40:36	Irrigating Solutions	974.5
40:40	Uricosuric Agents	974.7
44:00	ENZYMES NEC	963.4
	fibrinolysis-affecting agents	964.4
	gastric agents	973.4

	AHFS* List	ICD-9-CM Diagnosis Code
48:00	EXPECTORANTS AND COUGH PREPARATIONS	
	antihistamine agents	963.0
	antitussives	975.4
	codeine derivatives	965.09
	expectorants	975.5
	narcotic agents NEC	965.09
52:00	EYE, EAR, NOSE, AND THROAT PREPARATIONS	
52:04	Anti-Infectives	
	ENT	976.6
	ophthalmic	976.5
52:04.04	Antibiotics	
	ENT	976.6
	ophthalmic	976.5
52:04.06	Antivirals	
	ENT	976.6
	ophthalmic	976.5
52:04.08	Sulfonamides	
	ENT	976.6
	ophthalmic	976.5
52:04.12	Miscellaneous Anti-Infectives	
	ENT	976.6
	ophthalmic	976.5
52:08	Anti-Inflammatory Agents	
	ENT	976.6
	ophthalmic	976.5
52:10	Carbonic Anhydrase Inhibitors	974.2
52:12	Contact Lens Solutions	976.5
52:16	Local Anesthetics	968.5
52:20	Miotics	971.0
52:24	Mydriatics	
	adrenergics	971.2
	anticholinergics	971.1
	antimuscarinics	971.1
	parasympatholytics	971.1
	spasmolytics	971.1
	sympathomimetics	971.2
52:28	Mouth Washes and Gargles	976.6
52:32	Vasoconstrictors	971.2
52:36	Unclassified Agents	
	ENT	976.6
	ophthalmic	976.5
56:00	GASTROINTESTINAL DRUGS	
56:04	Antacids and Absorbents	973.0
56:08	Anti-Diarrhea Agents	973.5
56:10	Antiflatulents	973.8
56:12	Cathartics NEC	973.3
	emollients	973.2
	irritants	973.1
56:16	Digestants	973.4
56:20	Emetics and Antiemetics	
	antiemetics	963.0
	emetics	973.6
56:24	Lipotropic Agents	977.1
60:00	GOLD COMPOUNDS	965.69
64:00	HEAVY METAL ANTAGONISTS	963.8
68:00	HORMONES AND SYNTHETIC SUBSTITUTES	
68:04	Adrenals	962.0
68:08	Androgens	962.1
68:12	Contraceptives	962.2
68:16	Estrogens	962.2
68:18	Gonadotropins	962.4
68:20	Insulins and Antidiabetic Agents	962.3
68:20.08	Insulins	962.3
68:24	Parathyroid	962.6
68:28	Pituitary	
	anterior	962.4
	posterior	962.5
68:32	Progestogens	962.2
68:34	Other Corpus Luteum Hormones	962.2
68:36	Thyroid and Antithyroid	
	antithyroid	962.8
	thyroid	962.7

	AHFS* List	ICD-9-CM Diagnosis Code
72:00	LOCAL ANESTHETICS NEC	968.9
	topical (surface) agents	968.5
	infiltrating agents (intradermal) (subcutaneous) (submucosal)	968.5
	nerve blocking agents (peripheral) (plexus) (regional)	968.6
	spinal	968.7
76:00	OXYTOCICS	975.0
78:00	RADIOACTIVE AGENTS	990
80:00	SERUMS, TOXOIDS, AND VACCINES	
80:04	Serums	979.9
	immune globulin (gamma) (human)	964.6
80:08	Toxoids NEC	978.8
	diphtheria	978.5
	and tetanus	978.9
	with pertussis component	978.6
	tetanus	978.4
	and diphtheria	978.9
	with pertussis component	978.6
80:12	Vaccines NEC	979.9
	bacterial NEC	978.8
	with	
	other bacterial component	978.9
	pertussis component	978.6
	viral and rickettsial component	979.7
	rickettsial NEC	979.6
	with	
	bacterial component	979.7
	pertussis component	978.6
	viral component	979.7
	viral NEC	979.6
	with	
	bacterial component	979.7
	pertussis component	978.6
	rickettsial component	979.7
84:00	SKIN AND MUCOUS MEMBRANE PREPARATIONS	
84:04	Anti-Infectives	976.0
84:04.04	Antibiotics	976.0
84:04.08	Fungicides	976.0
84:04.12	Scabicides and Pediculicides	976.0
84:04.16	Miscellaneous Local Anti-Infectives	976.0
84:06	Anti-Inflammatory Agents	976.0
84:08	Antipruritics and Local Anesthetics	
	antipruritics	976.1
	local anesthetics	968.5
84:12	Astringents	976.2
84:16	Cell Stimulants and Proliferants	976.8
84:20	Detergents	976.2
84:24	Emollients, Demulcents, and Protectants	976.3
84:28	Keratolytic Agents	976.4
84:32	Keratoplastic Agents	976.4
84:36	Miscellaneous Agents	976.8
86:00	SPASMOLYTIC AGENTS	975.1
	antiasthmatics	975.7
	papaverine	972.5
	theophyllin	974.1
88:00	VITAMINS	
88:04	Vitamin A	963.5
88:08	Vitamin B Complex	963.5
	hematopoietic vitamin	964.1
	nicotinic acid derivatives	972.2
88:12	Vitamin C	963.5
88:16	Vitamin D	963.5
88:20	Vitamin E	963.5
88:24	Vitamin K Activity	964.3
88:28	Multivitamin Preparations	963.5
92:00	UNCLASSIFIED THERAPEUTIC AGENTS	977.8

* American Hospital Formulary Service

CLASSIFICATION OF INDUSTRIAL ACCIDENTS ACCORDING TO AGENCY

Annex B to the Resolution concerning Statistics of Employment Injuries adopted by the Tenth International Conference of Labor Statisticians on 12 October 1962

1 MACHINES

11 Prime-Movers, except Electrical Motors
111 *Steam engines*
112 *Internal combustion engines*
119 *Others*
12 Transmission Machinery
121 *Transmission shafts*
122 *Transmission belts, cables, pulleys, pinions, chains, gears*
129 *Others*
13 Metalworking Machines
131 *Power presses*
132 *Lathes*
133 *Milling machines*
134 *Abrasive wheels*
135 *Mechanical shears*
136 *Forging machines*
137 *Rolling-mills*
139 *Others*
14 Wood and Assimilated Machines
141 *Circular saws*
142 *Other saws*
143 *Molding machines*
144 *Overhand planes*
149 *Others*
15 Agricultural Machines
151 *Reapers (including combine reapers)*
152 *Threshers*
159 *Others*
16 Mining Machinery
161 *Under-cutters*
169 *Others*
19 Other Machines Not Elsewhere Classified
191 *Earth-moving machines, excavating and scraping machines, except means of transport*
192 *Spinning, weaving and other textile machines*
193 *Machines for the manufacture of foodstuffs and beverages*
194 *Machines for the manufacture of paper*
195 *Printing machines*
199 *Others*

2 MEANS OF TRANSPORT AND LIFTING EQUIPMENT

21 Lifting Machines and Appliances
211 *Cranes*
212 *Lifts and elevators*
213 *Winches*
214 *Pulley blocks*
219 *Others*
22 Means of Rail Transport
221 *Inter-urban railways*
222 *Rail transport in mines, tunnels, quarries, industrial establishments, docks, etc.*
229 *Others*
23 Other Wheeled Means of Transport, Excluding Rail Transport
231 *Tractors*
232 *Lorries*
233 *Trucks*
234 *Motor vehicles, not elsewhere classified*
235 *Animal-drawn vehicles*
236 *Hand-drawn vehicles*
239 *Others*
24 Means of Air Transport
25 Means of Water Transport
251 *Motorized means of water transport*
252 *Non-motorized means of water transport*
26 Other Means of Transport
261 *Cable-cars*
262 *Mechanical conveyors, except cable-cars*
269 *Others*

3 OTHER EQUIPMENT

31 Pressure Vessels
311 *Boilers*
312 *Pressurized containers*
313 *Pressurized piping and accessories*
314 *Gas cylinders*
315 *Caissons, diving equipment*
319 *Others*
32 Furnaces, Ovens, Kilns
321 *Blast furnaces*
322 *Refining furnaces*
323 *Other furnaces*
324 *Kilns*
325 *Ovens*
33 Refrigerating Plants
34 Electrical Installations, Including Electric Motors, but Excluding Electric Hand Tools
341 *Rotating machines*
342 *Conductors*
343 *Transformers*
344 *Control apparatus*
349 *Others*
35 Electric Hand Tools
36 Tools, Implements, and Appliances, Except Electric Hand Tools
361 *Power-driven hand tools, except electric hand tools*
362 *Hand tools, not power-driven*
369 *Others*
37 Ladders, Mobile Ramps
38 Scaffolding
39 Other Equipment, Not Elsewhere Classified

4 MATERIALS, SUBSTANCES AND RADIATIONS

41 Explosives
42 Dusts, Gases, Liquids and Chemicals, Excluding Explosives
421 *Dusts*
422 *Gases, vapors, fumes*
423 *Liquids, not elsewhere classified*
424 *Chemicals, not elsewhere classified*
43 Flying Fragments
44 Radiations
441 *Ionizing radiations*
449 *Others*
49 Other Materials and Substances Not Elsewhere Classified

5 WORKING ENVIRONMENT

51 Outdoor
511 *Weather*
512 *Traffic and working surfaces*
513 *Water*
519 *Others*
52 Indoor
521 *Floors*
522 *Confined quarters*
523 *Stairs*
524 *Other traffic and working surfaces*
525 *Floor openings and wall openings*
526 *Environmental factors (lighting, ventilation, temperature, noise, etc.)*
529 *Others*
53 Underground
531 *Roofs and faces of mine roads and tunnels, etc.*
532 *Floors of mine roads and tunnels, etc.*
533 *Working-faces of mines, tunnels, etc.*
534 *Mine shafts*
535 *Fire*
536 *Water*
539 *Others*

6 OTHER AGENCIES, NOT ELSEWHERE CLASSIFIED

61 Animals
611 *Live animals*
612 *Animal products*
69 Other Agencies, Not Elsewhere Classified

7 AGENCIES NOT CLASSIFIED FOR LACK OF SUFFICIENT DATA

LIST OF THREE-DIGIT CATEGORIES

1. INFECTIOUS AND PARASITIC DISEASES

Intestinal infectious diseases (001-009)
001 Cholera
002 Typhoid and paratyphoid fevers
003 Other salmonella infections
004 Shigellosis
005 Other food poisoning (bacterial)
006 Amebiasis
007 Other protozoal intestinal diseases
008 Intestinal infections due to other organisms
009 Ill-defined intestinal infections

Tuberculosis (010-018)
010 Primary tuberculous infection
011 Pulmonary tuberculosis
012 Other respiratory tuberculosis
013 Tuberculosis of meninges and central nervous system
014 Tuberculosis of intestines, peritoneum, and mesenteric glands
015 Tuberculosis of bones and joints
016 Tuberculosis of genitourinary system
017 Tuberculosis of other organs
018 Miliary tuberculosis

Zoonotic bacterial diseases (020-027)
020 Plague
021 Tularemia
022 Anthrax
023 Brucellosis
024 Glanders
025 Melioidosis
026 Rat-bite fever
027 Other zoonotic bacterial diseases

Other bacterial diseases (030-042)
030 Leprosy
031 Diseases due to other mycobacteria
032 Diphtheria
033 Whooping cough
034 Streptococcal sore throat and scarlatina
035 Erysipelas
036 Meningococcal infection
037 Tetanus
038 Septicemia
039 Actinomycotic infections
040 Other bacterial diseases
041 Bacterial infection in conditions classified elsewhere and of unspecified site

Human immunodeficiency virus (042)
042 Human immunodeficiency virus [HIV] disease

Poliomyelitis and other non-arthropod-borne viral diseases of central nervous system (045-049)
045 Acute poliomyelitis
046 Slow virus infection of central nervous system
047 Meningitis due to enterovirus
048 Other enterovirus diseases of central nervous system
049 Other non-arthropod-borne viral diseases of central nervous system

Viral diseases accompanied by exanthem (050-057)
050 Smallpox
051 Cowpox and paravaccinia
052 Chickenpox
053 Herpes zoster
054 Herpes simplex
055 Measles
056 Rubella
057 Other viral exanthemata

Arthropod-borne viral diseases (060-066)
060 Yellow fever
061 Dengue
062 Mosquito-borne viral encephalitis
063 Tick-borne viral encephalitis
064 Viral encephalitis transmitted by other and unspecified arthropods
065 Arthropod-borne hemorrhagic fever
066 Other arthropod-borne viral diseases

Other diseases due to viruses and Chlamydiae (070-079)
070 Viral hepatitis
071 Rabies
072 Mumps
073 Ornithosis
074 Specific diseases due to Coxsackievirus
075 Infectious mononucleosis
076 Trachoma
077 Other diseases of conjunctiva due to viruses and Chlamydiae
078 Other diseases due to viruses and Chlamydiae
079 Viral infection in conditions classified elsewhere and of unspecified site

Rickettsioses and other arthropod-borne diseases (080-088)
080 Louse-borne [epidemic] typhus
081 Other typhus
082 Tick-borne rickettsioses
083 Other rickettsioses
084 Malaria
085 Leishmaniasis
086 Trypanosomiasis
087 Relapsing fever
088 Other arthropod-borne diseases

Syphilis and other venereal diseases (090-099)
090 Congenital syphilis
091 Early syphilis, symptomatic
092 Early syphilis, latent
093 Cardiovascular syphilis
094 Neurosyphilis
095 Other forms of late syphilis, with symptoms
096 Late syphilis, latent
097 Other and unspecified syphilis
098 Gonococcal infections
099 Other venereal diseases

Other spirochetal diseases (100-104)
100 Leptospirosis
101 Vincent's angina
102 Yaws
103 Pinta
104 Other spirochetal infection

Mycoses (110-118)
110 Dermatophytosis
111 Dermatomycosis, other and unspecified
112 Candidiasis
114 Coccidioidomycosis
115 Histoplasmosis
116 Blastomycotic infection
117 Other mycoses
118 Opportunistic mycoses

Helminthiases (120-129)
120 Schistosomiasis [bilharziasis]
121 Other trematode infections
122 Echinococcosis
123 Other cestode infection
124 Trichinosis
125 Filarial infection and dracontiasis
126 Ancylostomiasis and necatoriasis
127 Other intestinal helminthiases
128 Other and unspecified helminthiases
129 Intestinal parasitism, unspecified

Other infectious and parasitic diseases (130-136)
130 Toxoplasmosis
131 Trichomoniasis
132 Pediculosis and phthirus infestation
133 Acariasis
134 Other infestation
135 Sarcoidosis
136 Other and unspecified infectious and parasitic diseases

Late effects of infectious and parasitic diseases (137-139)
137 Late effects of tuberculosis
138 Late effects of acute poliomyelitis
139 Late effects of other infectious and parasitic diseases

2. NEOPLASMS

Malignant neoplasm of lip, oral cavity, and pharynx (140-149)
140 Malignant neoplasm of lip
141 Malignant neoplasm of tongue
142 Malignant neoplasm of major salivary glands
143 Malignant neoplasm of gum
144 Malignant neoplasm of floor of mouth
145 Malignant neoplasm of other and unspecified parts of mouth
146 Malignant neoplasm of oropharynx
147 Malignant neoplasm of nasopharynx
148 Malignant neoplasm of hypopharynx
149 Malignant neoplasm of other and ill-defined sites within the lip, oral cavity, and pharynx

Malignant neoplasm of digestive organs and peritoneum (150-159)
150 Malignant neoplasm of esophagus
151 Malignant neoplasm of stomach
152 Malignant neoplasm of small intestine, including duodenum
153 Malignant neoplasm of colon
154 Malignant neoplasm of rectum, rectosigmoid junction, and anus
155 Malignant neoplasm of liver and intrahepatic bile ducts
156 Malignant neoplasm of gallbladder and extrahepatic bile ducts
157 Malignant neoplasm of pancreas
158 Malignant neoplasm of retroperitoneum and peritoneum
159 Malignant neoplasm of other and ill-defined sites within the digestive organs and peritoneum

Malignant neoplasm of respiratory and intrathoracic organs (160-165)
160 Malignant neoplasm of nasal cavities, middle ear, and accessory sinuses
161 Malignant neoplasm of larynx
162 Malignant neoplasm of trachea, bronchus, and lung
163 Malignant neoplasm of pleura
164 Malignant neoplasm of thymus, heart, and mediastinum
165 Malignant neoplasm of other and ill-defined sites within the respiratory system and intrathoracic organs

Malignant neoplasm of bone, connective tissue, skin, and breast (170-176)
170 Malignant neoplasm of bone and articular cartilage
171 Malignant neoplasm of connective and other soft tissue
172 Malignant melanoma of skin
173 Other malignant neoplasm of skin
174 Malignant neoplasm of female breast
175 Malignant neoplasm of male breast
176 Kaposi's sarcoma

Malignant neoplasm of genitourinary organs (179-189)
179 Malignant neoplasm of uterus, part unspecified
180 Malignant neoplasm of cervix uteri
181 Malignant neoplasm of placenta
182 Malignant neoplasm of body of uterus
183 Malignant neoplasm of ovary and other uterine adnexa
184 Malignant neoplasm of other and unspecified female genital organs
185 Malignant neoplasm of prostate

186 Malignant neoplasm of testis
187 Malignant neoplasm of penis and other male genital organs
188 Malignant neoplasm of bladder
189 Malignant neoplasm of kidney and other unspecified urinary organs

Malignant neoplasm of other and unspecified sites (190-199)
190 Malignant neoplasm of eye
191 Malignant neoplasm of brain
192 Malignant neoplasm of other and unspecified parts of nervous system
193 Malignant neoplasm of thyroid gland
194 Malignant neoplasm of other endocrine glands and related structures
195 Malignant neoplasm of other and ill-defined sites
196 Secondary and unspecified malignant neoplasm of lymph nodes
197 Secondary malignant neoplasm of respiratory and digestive systems
198 Secondary malignant neoplasm of other specified sites
199 Malignant neoplasm without specification of site

Malignant neoplasm of lymphatic and hematopoietic tissue (200-208)
200 Lymphosarcoma and reticulosarcoma
201 Hodgkin's disease
202 Other malignant neoplasm of lymphoid and histiocytic tissue
203 Multiple myeloma and immunoproliferative neoplasms
204 Lymphoid leukemia
205 Myeloid leukemia
206 Monocytic leukemia
207 Other specified leukemia
208 Leukemia of unspecified cell type

Benign neoplasms (210-229)
210 Benign neoplasm of lip, oral cavity, and pharynx
211 Benign neoplasm of other parts of digestive system
212 Benign neoplasm of respiratory and intrathoracic organs
213 Benign neoplasm of bone and articular cartilage
214 Lipoma
215 Other benign neoplasm of connective and other soft tissue
216 Benign neoplasm of skin
217 Benign neoplasm of breast
218 Uterine leiomyoma
219 Other benign neoplasm of uterus
220 Benign neoplasm of ovary
221 Benign neoplasm of other female genital organs
222 Benign neoplasm of male genital organs
223 Benign neoplasm of kidney and other urinary organs
224 Benign neoplasm of eye
225 Benign neoplasm of brain and other parts of nervous system
226 Benign neoplasm of thyroid gland
227 Benign neoplasm of other endocrine glands and related structures
228 Hemangioma and lymphangioma, any site
229 Benign neoplasm of other and unspecified sites

Carcinoma in situ (230-234)
230 Carcinoma in situ of digestive organs
231 Carcinoma in situ of respiratory system
232 Carcinoma in situ of skin
233 Carcinoma in situ of breast and genitourinary system
234 Carcinoma in situ of other and unspecified sites

Neoplasms of uncertain behavior (235-238)
235 Neoplasm of uncertain behavior of digestive and respiratory systems
236 Neoplasm of uncertain behavior of genitourinary organs
237 Neoplasm of uncertain behavior of endocrine glands and nervous system
238 Neoplasm of uncertain behavior of other and unspecified sites and tissues

Neoplasms of unspecified nature (239)
239 Neoplasm of unspecified nature

3. ENDOCRINE, NUTRITIONAL AND METABOLIC DISEASES, AND IMMUNITY DISORDERS

Disorders of thyroid gland (240-246)
240 Simple and unspecified goiter
241 Nontoxic nodular goiter
242 Thyrotoxicosis with or without goiter
243 Congenital hypothyroidism
244 Acquired hypothyroidism
245 Thyroiditis
246 Other disorders of thyroid

Diseases of other endocrine glands (250-259)
250 Diabetes mellitus
251 Other disorders of pancreatic internal secretion
252 Disorders of parathyroid gland
253 Disorders of the pituitary gland and its hypothalamic control
254 Diseases of thymus gland
255 Disorders of adrenal glands
256 Ovarian dysfunction
257 Testicular dysfunction
258 Polyglandular dysfunction and related disorders
259 Other endocrine disorders

Nutritional deficiencies (260-269)
260 Kwashiorkor
261 Nutritional marasmus
262 Other severe protein-calorie malnutrition
263 Other and unspecified protein-calorie malnutrition
264 Vitamin A deficiency
265 Thiamine and niacin deficiency states
266 Deficiency of B-complex components
267 Ascorbic acid deficiency
268 Vitamin D deficiency
269 Other nutritional deficiencies

Other metabolic disorders and immunity disorders (270-279)
270 Disorders of amino-acid transport and metabolism
271 Disorders of carbohydrate transport and metabolism
272 Disorders of lipoid metabolism
273 Disorders of plasma protein metabolism
274 Gout
275 Disorders of mineral metabolism
276 Disorders of fluid, electrolyte, and acid-base balance
277 Other and unspecified disorders of metabolism
278 Overweight, obesity and other hyperalimentation
279 Disorders involving the immune mechanism

4. DISEASES OF BLOOD AND BLOOD-FORMING ORGANS (280-289)

280 Iron deficiency anemias
281 Other deficiency anemias
282 Hereditary hemolytic anemias
283 Acquired hemolytic anemias
284 Aplastic anemia
285 Other and unspecified anemias
286 Coagulation defects
287 Purpura and other hemorrhagic conditions
288 Diseases of white blood cells
289 Other diseases of blood and blood-forming organs

5. MENTAL DISORDERS

Organic psychotic conditions (290-294)
290 Senile and presenile organic psychotic conditions
291 Alcoholic psychoses
292 Drug psychoses
293 Transient organic psychotic conditions
294 Other organic psychotic conditions (chronic)

Other psychoses (295-299)
295 Schizophrenic psychoses
296 Affective psychoses
297 Paranoid states
298 Other nonorganic psychoses
299 Psychoses with origin specific to childhood

Neurotic disorders, personality disorders, and other nonpsychotic mental disorders (300-316)
300 Neurotic disorders
301 Personality disorders
302 Sexual deviations and disorders
303 Alcohol dependence syndrome
304 Drug dependence
305 Nondependent abuse of drugs
306 Physiological malfunction arising from mental factors
307 Special symptoms or syndromes, not elsewhere classified
308 Acute reaction to stress
309 Adjustment reaction
310 Specific nonpsychotic mental disorders following organic brain damage
311 Depressive disorder, not elsewhere classified
312 Disturbance of conduct, not elsewhere classified
313 Disturbance of emotions specific to childhood and adolescence
314 Hyperkinetic syndrome of childhood
315 Specific delays in development
316 Psychic factors associated with diseases classified elsewhere

Mental retardation (317-319)
317 Mild mental retardation
318 Other specified mental retardation
319 Unspecified mental retardation

6. DISEASES OF THE NERVOUS SYSTEM AND SENSE ORGANS

Inflammatory diseases of the central nervous system (320-326)
320 Bacterial meningitis
321 Meningitis due to other organisms
322 Meningitis of unspecified cause
323 Encephalitis, myelitis, and encephalomyelitis
324 Intracranial and intraspinal abscess
325 Phlebitis and thrombophlebitis of intracranial venous sinuses
326 Late effects of intracranial abscess or pyogenic infection

Organic Sleep Disorders (327)
327 Organic sleep disorders

Hereditary and degenerative diseases of the central nervous system (330-337)
330 Cerebral degenerations usually manifest in childhood
331 Other cerebral degenerations
332 Parkinson's disease
333 Other extrapyramidal diseases and abnormal movement disorders
334 Spinocerebellar disease
335 Anterior horn cell disease
336 Other diseases of spinal cord
337 Disorders of the autonomic nervous system

Pain (338)
338 Pain, not elsewhere classified

Other disorders of the central nervous system (340-349)
340 Multiple sclerosis
341 Other demyelinating diseases of central nervous system
342 Hemiplegia and hemiparesis
343 Infantile cerebral palsy
344 Other paralytic syndromes
345 Epilepsy and recurrent seizures
346 Migraine
347 Cataplexy and narcolepsy
348 Other conditions of brain
349 Other and unspecified disorders of the nervous system

Disorders of the peripheral nervous system (350-359)
350 Trigeminal nerve disorders
351 Facial nerve disorders
352 Disorders of other cranial nerves
353 Nerve root and plexus disorders
354 Mononeuritis of upper limb and mononeuritis multiplex
355 Mononeuritis of lower limb
356 Hereditary and idiopathic peripheral neuropathy
357 Inflammatory and toxic neuropathy
358 Myoneural disorders
359 Muscular dystrophies and other myopathies

Disorders of the eye and adnexa (360-379)
360 Disorders of the globe
361 Retinal detachments and defects
362 Other retinal disorders
363 Chorioretinal inflammations and scars and other disorders of choroid
364 Disorders of iris and ciliary body
365 Glaucoma
366 Cataract
367 Disorders of refraction and accommodation
368 Visual disturbances
369 Blindness and low vision
370 Keratitis
371 Corneal opacity and other disorders of cornea
372 Disorders of conjunctiva
373 Inflammation of eyelids
374 Other disorders of eyelids
375 Disorders of lacrimal system
376 Disorders of the orbit
377 Disorders of optic nerve and visual pathways
378 Strabismus and other disorders of binocular eye movements
379 Other disorders of eye

Diseases of the ear and mastoid process (380-389)
380 Disorders of external ear
381 Nonsuppurative otitis media and Eustachian tube disorders
382 Suppurative and unspecified otitis media
383 Mastoiditis and related conditions
384 Other disorders of tympanic membrane
385 Other disorders of middle ear and mastoid
386 Vertiginous syndromes and other disorders of vestibular system
387 Otosclerosis
388 Other disorders of ear
389 Hearing loss

7. DISEASES OF THE CIRCULATORY SYSTEM

Acute rheumatic fever (390-392)
390 Rheumatic fever without mention of heart involvement
391 Rheumatic fever with heart involvement
392 Rheumatic chorea

Chronic rheumatic heart disease (393-398)
393 Chronic rheumatic pericarditis
394 Diseases of mitral valve
395 Diseases of aortic valve
396 Diseases of mitral and aortic valves
397 Diseases of other endocardial structures
398 Other rheumatic heart disease

Hypertensive disease (401-405)
401 Essential hypertension
402 Hypertensive heart disease
403 Hypertensive kidney disease
404 Hypertensive heart and kidney disease
405 Secondary hypertension

Ischemic heart disease (410-414)
410 Acute myocardial infarction
411 Other acute and subacute form of ischemic heart disease
412 Old myocardial infarction
413 Angina pectoris
414 Other forms of chronic ischemic heart disease

Diseases of pulmonary circulation (415-417)
415 Acute pulmonary heart disease
416 Chronic pulmonary heart disease
417 Other diseases of pulmonary circulation

Other forms of heart disease (420-429)
420 Acute pericarditis
421 Acute and subacute endocarditis
422 Acute myocarditis
423 Other diseases of pericardium
424 Other diseases of endocardium
425 Cardiomyopathy
426 Conduction disorders
427 Cardiac dysrhythmias
428 Heart failure
429 Ill-defined descriptions and complications of heart disease

Cerebrovascular disease (430-438)
430 Subarachnoid hemorrhage
431 Intracerebral hemorrhage
432 Other and unspecified intracranial hemorrhage
433 Occlusion and stenosis of precerebral arteries
434 Occlusion of cerebral arteries
435 Transient cerebral ischemia
436 Acute but ill-defined cerebrovascular disease
437 Other and ill-defined cerebrovascular disease
438 Late effects of cerebrovascular disease

Diseases of arteries, arterioles, and capillaries (440-448)
440 Atherosclerosis
441 Aortic aneurysm and dissection
442 Other aneurysm
443 Other peripheral vascular disease
444 Arterial embolism and thrombosis
445 Atheroembolism
446 Polyarteritis nodosa and allied conditions
447 Other disorders of arteries and arterioles
448 Diseases of capillaries

Diseases of veins and lymphatics, and other diseases of circulatory system (451-459)
451 Phlebitis and thrombophlebitis
452 Portal vein thrombosis
453 Other venous embolism and thrombosis
454 Varicose veins of lower extremities
455 Hemorrhoids
456 Varicose veins of other sites
457 Noninfective disorders of lymphatic channels
458 Hypotension
459 Other disorders of circulatory system

8. DISEASES OF THE RESPIRATORY SYSTEM

Acute respiratory infections (460-466)
460 Acute nasopharyngitis [common cold]
461 Acute sinusitis
462 Acute pharyngitis
463 Acute tonsillitis
464 Acute laryngitis and tracheitis
465 Acute upper respiratory infections of multiple or unspecified sites
466 Acute bronchitis and bronchiolitis

Other diseases of upper respiratory tract (470-478)
470 Deviated nasal septum
471 Nasal polyps
472 Chronic pharyngitis and nasopharyngitis
473 Chronic sinusitis
474 Chronic disease of tonsils and adenoids
475 Peritonsillar abscess
476 Chronic laryngitis and laryngotracheitis
477 Allergic rhinitis
478 Other diseases of upper respiratory tract

Pneumonia and influenza (480-487)
480 Viral pneumonia
481 Pneumococcal pneumonia [Streptococcus pneumoniae pneumonia]
482 Other bacterial pneumonia
483 Pneumonia due to other specified organism
484 Pneumonia in infectious diseases classified elsewhere
485 Bronchopneumonia, organism unspecified
486 Pneumonia, organism unspecified
487 Influenza

Chronic obstructive pulmonary disease and allied conditions (490-496)
490 Bronchitis, not specified as acute or chronic
491 Chronic bronchitis
492 Emphysema
493 Asthma
494 Bronchiectasis
495 Extrinsic allergic alveolitis
496 Chronic airways obstruction, not elsewhere classified

Pneumoconioses and other lung diseases due to external agents (500-508)
500 Coal workers' pneumoconiosis
501 Asbestosis
502 Pneumoconiosis due to other silica or silicates
503 Pneumoconiosis due to other inorganic dust
504 Pneumopathy due to inhalation of other dust
505 Pneumoconiosis, unspecified
506 Respiratory conditions due to chemical fumes and vapors
507 Pneumonitis due to solids and liquids
508 Respiratory conditions due to other and unspecified external agents

Other diseases of respiratory system (510-519)
510 Empyema
511 Pleurisy
512 Pneumothorax
513 Abscess of lung and mediastinum
514 Pulmonary congestion and hypostasis
515 Postinflammatory pulmonary fibrosis
516 Other alveolar and parietoalveolar pneumopathy
517 Lung involvement in conditions classified elsewhere
518 Other diseases of lung
519 Other diseases of respiratory system

9. DISEASES OF THE DIGESTIVE SYSTEM

Diseases of oral cavity, salivary glands, and jaws (520-529)
520 Disorders of tooth development and eruption
521 Diseases of hard tissues of teeth
522 Diseases of pulp and periapical tissues
523 Gingival and periodontal diseases
524 Dentofacial anomalies, including malocclusion
525 Other diseases and conditions of the teeth and supporting structures
526 Diseases of the jaws
527 Diseases of the salivary glands

528 Diseases of the oral soft tissues, excluding lesions specific for gingiva and tongue
529 Diseases and other conditions of the tongue

Diseases of esophagus, stomach, and duodenum (530-538)

530 Diseases of esophagus
531 Gastric ulcer
532 Duodenal ulcer
533 Peptic ulcer, site unspecified
534 Gastrojejunal ulcer
535 Gastritis and duodenitis
536 Disorders of function of stomach
537 Other disorders of stomach and duodenum
538 Gastrointestinal mucositis (ulcerative)

Appendicitis (540-543)

540 Acute appendicitis
541 Appendicitis, unqualified
542 Other appendicitis
543 Other diseases of appendix

Hernia of abdominal cavity (550-553)

550 Inguinal hernia
551 Other hernia of abdominal cavity, with gangrene
552 Other hernia of abdominal cavity, with obstruction, but without mention of gangrene
553 Other hernia of abdominal cavity without mention of obstruction or gangrene

Noninfective enteritis and colitis (555-558)

555 Regional enteritis
556 Ulcerative colitis
557 Vascular insufficiency of intestine
558 Other noninfective gastroenteritis and colitis

Other diseases of intestines and peritoneum (560-569)

560 Intestinal obstruction without mention of hernia
562 Diverticula of intestine
564 Functional digestive disorders, not elsewhere classified
565 Anal fissure and fistula
566 Abscess of anal and rectal regions
567 Peritonitis and retroperitoneal infections
568 Other disorders of peritoneum
569 Other disorders of intestine

Other diseases of digestive system (570-579)

570 Acute and subacute necrosis of liver
571 Chronic liver disease and cirrhosis
572 Liver abscess and sequelae of chronic liver disease
573 Other disorders of liver
574 Cholelithiasis
575 Other disorders of gallbladder
576 Other disorders of biliary tract
577 Diseases of pancreas
578 Gastrointestinal hemorrhage
579 Intestinal malabsorption

10. DISEASES OF THE GENITOURINARY SYSTEM

Nephritis, nephrotic syndrome, and nephrosis (580-589)

580 Acute glomerulonephritis
581 Nephrotic syndrome
582 Chronic glomerulonephritis
583 Nephritis and nephropathy, not specified as acute or chronic
584 Acute renal failure
585 Chronic kidney disease (CKD)
586 Renal failure, unspecified
587 Renal sclerosis, unspecified
588 Disorders resulting from impaired renal function
589 Small kidney of unknown cause

Other diseases of urinary system (590-599)

590 Infections of kidney
591 Hydronephrosis
592 Calculus of kidney and ureter
593 Other disorders of kidney and ureter
594 Calculus of lower urinary tract
595 Cystitis
596 Other disorders of bladder
597 Urethritis, not sexually transmitted, and urethral syndrome
598 Urethral stricture
599 Other disorders of urethra and urinary tract

Diseases of male genital organs (600-608)

600 Hyperplasia of prostate
601 Inflammatory diseases of prostate
602 Other disorders of prostate
603 Hydrocele
604 Orchitis and epididymitis
605 Redundant prepuce and phimosis
606 Infertility, male
607 Disorders of penis
608 Other disorders of male genital organs

Disorders of breast (610-611)

610 Benign mammary dysplasias
611 Other disorders of breast

Inflammatory disease of female pelvic organs (614-616)

614 Inflammatory disease of ovary, fallopian tube, pelvic cellular tissue, and peritoneum
615 Inflammatory diseases of uterus, except cervix
616 Inflammatory disease of cervix, vagina, and vulva

Other disorders of female genital tract (617-629)

617 Endometriosis
618 Genital prolapse
619 Fistula involving female genital tract
620 Noninflammatory disorders of ovary, fallopian tube, and broad ligament
621 Disorders of uterus, not elsewhere classified
622 Noninflammatory disorders of cervix
623 Noninflammatory disorders of vagina
624 Noninflammatory disorders of vulva and perineum
625 Pain and other symptoms associated with female genital organs
626 Disorders of menstruation and other abnormal bleeding from female genital tract
627 Menopausal and postmenopausal disorders
628 Infertility, female
629 Other disorders of female genital organs

11. COMPLICATIONS OF PREGNANCY, CHILDBIRTH AND THE PUERPERIUM

Ectopic and molar pregnancy and other pregnancy with abortive outcome (630-639)

630 Hydatidiform mole
631 Other abnormal product of conception
632 Missed abortion
633 Ectopic pregnancy
634 Spontaneous abortion
635 Legally induced abortion
636 Illegally induced abortion
637 Unspecified abortion
638 Failed attempted abortion
639 Complications following abortion and ectopic and molar pregnancies

Complications mainly related to pregnancy (640-649)

640 Hemorrhage in early pregnancy
641 Antepartum hemorrhage, abruptio placentae, and placenta previa
642 Hypertension complicating pregnancy, childbirth, and the puerperium
643 Excessive vomiting in pregnancy
644 Early or threatened labor
645 Prolonged pregnancy
646 Other complications of pregnancy, not elsewhere classified
647 Infective and parasitic conditions in the mother classifiable elsewhere but complicating pregnancy, childbirth, and the puerperium
648 Other current conditions in the mother classifiable elsewhere but complicating pregnancy, childbirth, and the puerperium
649 Other conditions or status of the mother complicating pregnancy, childbirth, or puerperium

Normal delivery, and other indications for care in pregnancy, labor, and delivery (650-659)

650 Normal delivery
651 Multiple gestation
652 Malposition and malpresentation of fetus
653 Disproportion
654 Abnormality of organs and soft tissues of pelvis
655 Known or suspected fetal abnormality affecting management of mother
656 Other fetal and placental problems affecting management of mother
657 Polyhydramnios
658 Other problems associated with amniotic cavity and membranes
659 Other indications for care or intervention related to labor and delivery and not elsewhere classified

Complications occurring mainly in the course of labor and delivery (660-669)

660 Obstructed labor
661 Abnormality of forces of labor
662 Long labor
663 Umbilical cord complications
664 Trauma to perineum and vulva during delivery
665 Other obstetrical trauma
666 Postpartum hemorrhage
667 Retained placenta or membranes, without hemorrhage
668 Complications of the administration of anesthetic or other sedation in labor and delivery
669 Other complications of labor and delivery, not elsewhere classified

Complications of the puerperium (670-677)

670 Major puerperal infection
671 Venous complications in pregnancy and the puerperium
672 Pyrexia of unknown origin during the puerperium
673 Obstetrical pulmonary embolism
674 Other and unspecified complications of the puerperium, not elsewhere classified
675 Infections of the breast and nipple associated with childbirth
676 Other disorders of the breast associated with childbirth, and disorders of lactation
677 Late effect of complication of pregnancy, childbirth, and the puerperium

12. DISEASES OF THE SKIN AND SUBCUTANEOUS TISSUE

Infections of skin and subcutaneous tissue (680-686)

680 Carbuncle and furuncle
681 Cellulitis and abscess of finger and toe
682 Other cellulitis and abscess
683 Acute lymphadenitis
684 Impetigo
685 Pilonidal cyst
686 Other local infections of skin and subcutaneous tissue

Other inflammatory conditions of skin and subcutaneous tissue (690-698)

690 Erythematosquamous dermatosis
691 Atopic dermatitis and related conditions
692 Contact dermatitis and other eczema
693 Dermatitis due to substances taken internally
694 Bullous dermatoses
695 Erythematous conditions
696 Psoriasis and similar disorders

697 Lichen
698 Pruritus and related conditions

Other diseases of skin and subcutaneous tissue (700-709)

700 Corns and callosities
701 Other hypertrophic and atrophic conditions of skin
702 Other dermatoses
703 Diseases of nail
704 Diseases of hair and hair follicles
705 Disorders of sweat glands
706 Diseases of sebaceous glands
707 Chronic ulcer of skin
708 Urticaria
709 Other disorders of skin and subcutaneous tissue

13. DISEASES OF THE MUSCULOSKELETAL SYSTEM AND CONNECTIVE TISSUE

Arthropathies and related disorders (710-719)

710 Diffuse diseases of connective tissue
711 Arthropathy associated with infections
712 Crystal arthropathies
713 Arthropathy associated with other disorders classified elsewhere
714 Rheumatoid arthritis and other inflammatory polyarthropathies
715 Osteoarthrosis and allied disorders
716 Other and unspecified arthropathies
717 Internal derangement of knee
718 Other derangement of joint
719 Other and unspecified disorder of joint

Dorsopathies (720-724)

720 Ankylosing spondylitis and other inflammatory spondylopathies
721 Spondylosis and allied disorders
722 Intervertebral disc disorders
723 Other disorders of cervical region
724 Other and unspecified disorders of back

Rheumatism, excluding the back (725-729)

725 Polymyalgia rheumatica
726 Peripheral enthesopathies and allied syndromes
727 Other disorders of synovium, tendon, and bursa
728 Disorders of muscle, ligament, and fascia
729 Other disorders of soft tissues

Osteopathies, chondropathies, and acquired musculoskeletal deformities (730-739)

730 Osteomyelitis, periostitis, and other infections involving bone
731 Osteitis deformans and osteopathies associated with other disorders classified elsewhere
732 Osteochondropathies
733 Other disorders of bone and cartilage
734 Flat foot
735 Acquired deformities of toe
736 Other acquired deformities of limbs
737 Curvature of spine
738 Other acquired deformity
739 Nonallopathic lesions, not elsewhere classified

14. CONGENITAL ANOMALIES

740 Anencephalus and similar anomalies
741 Spina bifida
742 Other congenital anomalies of nervous system
743 Congenital anomalies of eye
744 Congenital anomalies of ear, face, and neck
745 Bulbus cordis anomalies and anomalies of cardiac septal closure
746 Other congenital anomalies of heart
747 Other congenital anomalies of circulatory system
748 Congenital anomalies of respiratory system
749 Cleft palate and cleft lip
750 Other congenital anomalies of upper alimentary tract
751 Other congenital anomalies of digestive system
752 Congenital anomalies of genital organs
753 Congenital anomalies of urinary system
754 Certain congenital musculoskeletal deformities
755 Other congenital anomalies of limbs
756 Other congenital musculoskeletal anomalies
757 Congenital anomalies of the integument
758 Chromosomal anomalies
759 Other and unspecified congenital anomalies

15. CERTAIN CONDITIONS ORIGINATING IN THE PERINATAL PERIOD

Maternal causes of perinatal morbidity and mortality (760-763)

760 Fetus or newborn affected by maternal conditions which may be unrelated to present pregnancy
761 Fetus or newborn affected by maternal complications of pregnancy
762 Fetus or newborn affected by complications of placenta, cord, and membranes
763 Fetus or newborn affected by other complications of labor and delivery

Other conditions originating in the perinatal period (764-779)

764 Slow fetal growth and fetal malnutrition
765 Disorders relating to short gestation and unspecified low birthweight
766 Disorders relating to long gestation and high birthweight
767 Birth trauma
768 Intrauterine hypoxia and birth asphyxia
769 Respiratory distress syndrome
770 Other respiratory conditions of fetus and newborn
771 Infections specific to the perinatal period
772 Fetal and neonatal hemorrhage
773 Hemolytic disease of fetus or newborn, due to isoimmunization
774 Other perinatal jaundice
775 Endocrine and metabolic disturbances specific to the fetus and newborn
776 Hematological disorders of fetus and newborn
777 Perinatal disorders of digestive system
778 Conditions involving the integument and temperature regulation of fetus and newborn
779 Other and ill-defined conditions originating in the perinatal period

16. SYMPTOMS, SIGNS, AND ILL-DEFINED CONDITIONS

Symptoms (780-789)

780 General symptoms
781 Symptoms involving nervous and musculoskeletal systems
782 Symptoms involving skin and other integumentary tissue
783 Symptoms concerning nutrition, metabolism, and development
784 Symptoms involving head and neck
785 Symptoms involving cardiovascular system
786 Symptoms involving respiratory system and other chest symptoms
787 Symptoms involving digestive system
788 Symptoms involving urinary system
789 Other symptoms involving abdomen and pelvis

Nonspecific abnormal findings (790-796)

790 Nonspecific findings on examination of blood
791 Nonspecific findings on examination of urine
792 Nonspecific abnormal findings in other body substances
793 Nonspecific abnormal findings on radiological and other examination of body structure
794 Nonspecific abnormal results of function studies
795 Nonspecific abnormal histological and immunological findings
796 Other nonspecific abnormal findings

Ill-defined and unknown causes of morbidity and mortality (797-799)

797 Senility without mention of psychosis
798 Sudden death, cause unknown
799 Other ill-defined and unknown causes of morbidity and mortality

17. INJURY AND POISONING

Fracture of skull (800-804)

800 Fracture of vault of skull
801 Fracture of base of skull
802 Fracture of face bones
803 Other and unqualified skull fractures
804 Multiple fractures involving skull or face with other bones

Fracture of spine and trunk (805-809)

805 Fracture of vertebral column without mention of spinal cord lesion
806 Fracture of vertebral column with spinal cord lesion
807 Fracture of rib(s), sternum, larynx, and trachea
808 Fracture of pelvis
809 Ill-defined fractures of bones of trunk

Fracture of upper limb (810-819)

810 Fracture of clavicle
811 Fracture of scapula
812 Fracture of humerus
813 Fracture of radius and ulna
814 Fracture of carpal bone(s)
815 Fracture of metacarpal bone(s)
816 Fracture of one or more phalanges of hand
817 Multiple fractures of hand bones
818 Ill-defined fractures of upper limb
819 Multiple fractures involving both upper limbs, and upper limb with rib(s) and sternum

Fracture of lower limb (820-829)

820 Fracture of neck of femur
821 Fracture of other and unspecified parts of femur
822 Fracture of patella
823 Fracture of tibia and fibula
824 Fracture of ankle
825 Fracture of one or more tarsal and metatarsal bones
826 Fracture of one or more phalanges of foot
827 Other, multiple, and ill-defined fractures of lower limb
828 Multiple fractures involving both lower limbs, lower with upper limb, and lower limb(s) with rib(s) and sternum
829 Fracture of unspecified bones

Dislocation (830-839)

830 Dislocation of jaw
831 Dislocation of shoulder
832 Dislocation of elbow
833 Dislocation of wrist
834 Dislocation of finger
835 Dislocation of hip
836 Dislocation of knee
837 Dislocation of ankle
838 Dislocation of foot
839 Other, multiple, and ill-defined dislocations

Sprains and strains of joints and adjacent muscles (840-848)

840 Sprains and strains of shoulder and upper arm
841 Sprains and strains of elbow and forearm
842 Sprains and strains of wrist and hand
843 Sprains and strains of hip and thigh

844 Sprains and strains of knee and leg
845 Sprains and strains of ankle and foot
846 Sprains and strains of sacroiliac region
847 Sprains and strains of other and unspecified parts of back
848 Other and ill-defined sprains and strains

Intracranial injury, excluding those with skull fracture (850-854)

850 Concussion
851 Cerebral laceration and contusion
852 Subarachnoid, subdural, and extradural hemorrhage, following injury
853 Other and unspecified intracranial hemorrhage following injury
854 Intracranial injury of other and unspecified nature

Internal injury of chest, abdomen, and pelvis (860-869)

860 Traumatic pneumothorax and hemothorax
861 Injury to heart and lung
862 Injury to other and unspecified intrathoracic organs
863 Injury to gastrointestinal tract
864 Injury to liver
865 Injury to spleen
866 Injury to kidney
867 Injury to pelvic organs
868 Injury to other intra-abdominal organs
869 Internal injury to unspecified or ill-defined organs

Open wound of head, neck, and trunk (870-879)

870 Open wound of ocular adnexa
871 Open wound of eyeball
872 Open wound of ear
873 Other open wound of head
874 Open wound of neck
875 Open wound of chest (wall)
876 Open wound of back
877 Open wound of buttock
878 Open wound of genital organs (external), including traumatic amputation
879 Open wound of other and unspecified sites, except limbs

Open wound of upper limb (880-887)

880 Open wound of shoulder and upper arm
881 Open wound of elbow, forearm, and wrist
882 Open wound of hand except finger(s) alone
883 Open wound of finger(s)
884 Multiple and unspecified open wound of upper limb
885 Traumatic amputation of thumb (complete) (partial)
886 Traumatic amputation of other finger(s) (complete) (partial)
887 Traumatic amputation of arm and hand (complete) (partial)

Open wound of lower limb (890-897)

890 Open wound of hip and thigh
891 Open wound of knee, leg [except thigh], and ankle
892 Open wound of foot except toe(s) alone
893 Open wound of toe(s)
894 Multiple and unspecified open wound of lower limb
895 Traumatic amputation of toe(s) (complete) (partial)
896 Traumatic amputation of foot (complete) (partial)
897 Traumatic amputation of leg(s) (complete) (partial)

Injury to blood vessels (900-904)

900 Injury to blood vessels of head and neck
901 Injury to blood vessels of thorax
902 Injury to blood vessels of abdomen and pelvis
903 Injury to blood vessels of upper extremity
904 Injury to blood vessels of lower extremity and unspecified sites

Late effects of injuries, poisonings, toxic effects, and other external causes (905-909)

905 Late effects of musculoskeletal and connective tissue injuries
906 Late effects of injuries to skin and subcutaneous tissues
907 Late effects of injuries to the nervous system
908 Late effects of other and unspecified injuries
909 Late effects of other and unspecified external causes

Superficial injury (910-919)

910 Superficial injury of face, neck, and scalp except eye
911 Superficial injury of trunk
912 Superficial injury of shoulder and upper arm
913 Superficial injury of elbow, forearm, and wrist
914 Superficial injury of hand(s) except finger(s) alone
915 Superficial injury of finger(s)
916 Superficial injury of hip, thigh, leg, and ankle
917 Superficial injury of foot and toe(s)
918 Superficial injury of eye and adnexa
919 Superficial injury of other, multiple, and unspecified sites

Contusion with intact skin surface (920-924)

920 Contusion of face, scalp, and neck except eye(s)
921 Contusion of eye and adnexa
922 Contusion of trunk
923 Contusion of upper limb
924 Contusion of lower limb and of other and unspecified sites

Crushing injury (925-929)

925 Crushing injury of face, scalp, and neck
926 Crushing injury of trunk
927 Crushing injury of upper limb
928 Crushing injury of lower limb
929 Crushing injury of multiple and unspecified sites

Effects of foreign body entering through orifice (930-939)

930 Foreign body on external eye
931 Foreign body in ear
932 Foreign body in nose
933 Foreign body in pharynx and larynx
934 Foreign body in trachea, bronchus, and lung
935 Foreign body in mouth, esophagus, and stomach
936 Foreign body in intestine and colon
937 Foreign body in anus and rectum
938 Foreign body in digestive system, unspecified
939 Foreign body in genitourinary tract

Burns (940-949)

940 Burn confined to eye and adnexa
941 Burn of face, head, and neck
942 Burn of trunk
943 Burn of upper limb, except wrist and hand
944 Burn of wrist(s) and hand(s)
945 Burn of lower limb(s)
946 Burns of multiple specified sites
947 Burn of internal organs
948 Burns classified according to extent of body surface involved
949 Burn, unspecified

Injury to nerves and spinal cord (950-957)

950 Injury to optic nerve and pathways
951 Injury to other cranial nerve(s)
952 Spinal cord injury without evidence of spinal bone injury
953 Injury to nerve roots and spinal plexus
954 Injury to other nerve(s) of trunk excluding shoulder and pelvic girdles
955 Injury to peripheral nerve(s) of shoulder girdle and upper limb
956 Injury to peripheral nerve(s) of pelvic girdle and lower limb
957 Injury to other and unspecified nerves

Certain traumatic complications and unspecified injuries (958-959)

958 Certain early complications of trauma
959 Injury, other and unspecified

Poisoning by drugs, medicinals and biological substances (960-979)

960 Poisoning by antibiotics
961 Poisoning by other anti-infectives
962 Poisoning by hormones and synthetic substitutes
963 Poisoning by primarily systemic agents
964 Poisoning by agents primarily affecting blood constituents
965 Poisoning by analgesics, antipyretics, and antirheumatics
966 Poisoning by anticonvulsants and anti-Parkinsonism drugs
967 Poisoning by sedatives and hypnotics
968 Poisoning by other central nervous system depressants and anesthetics
969 Poisoning by psychotropic agents
970 Poisoning by central nervous system stimulants
971 Poisoning by drugs primarily affecting the autonomic nervous system
972 Poisoning by agents primarily affecting the cardiovascular system
973 Poisoning by agents primarily affecting the gastrointestinal system
974 Poisoning by water, mineral, and uric acid metabolism drugs
975 Poisoning by agents primarily acting on the smooth and skeletal muscles and respiratory system
976 Poisoning by agents primarily affecting skin and mucous membrane, ophthalmological, otorhinolaryngological, and dental drugs
977 Poisoning by other and unspecified drugs and medicinals
978 Poisoning by bacterial vaccines
979 Poisoning by other vaccines and biological substances

Toxic effects of substances chiefly nonmedicinal as to source (980-989)

980 Toxic effect of alcohol
981 Toxic effect of petroleum products
982 Toxic effect of solvents other than petroleum-based
983 Toxic effect of corrosive aromatics, acids, and caustic alkalis
984 Toxic effect of lead and its compounds (including fumes)
985 Toxic effect of other metals
986 Toxic effect of carbon monoxide
987 Toxic effect of other gases, fumes, or vapors
988 Toxic effect of noxious substances eaten as food
989 Toxic effect of other substances, chiefly nonmedicinal as to source

Other and unspecified effects of external causes (990-995)

990 Effects of radiation, unspecified
991 Effects of reduced temperature
992 Effects of heat and light
993 Effects of air pressure
994 Effects of other external causes
995 Certain adverse effects, not elsewhere classified

Complications of surgical and medical care, not elsewhere classified (996-999)

996 Complications peculiar to certain specified procedures
997 Complications affecting specified body systems, not elsewhere classified
998 Other complications of procedures, not elsewhere classified

999 Complications of medical care, not elsewhere classified

SUPPLEMENTARY CLASSIFICATION OF FACTORS INFLUENCING HEALTH STATUS AND CONTACT WITH HEALTH SERVICES

Persons with potential health hazards related to communicable diseases (V01-V09)

V01 Contact with or exposure to communicable diseases
V02 Carrier or suspected carrier of infectious diseases
V03 Need for prophylactic vaccination and inoculation against bacterial diseases
V04 Need for prophylactic vaccination and inoculation against certain viral diseases
V05 Need for other prophylactic vaccination and inoculation against single diseases
V06 Need for prophylactic vaccination and inoculation against combinations of diseases
V07 Need for isolation and other prophylactic measures
V08 Asymptomatic human immunodeficiency virus [HIV] infection status
V09 Infection with drug-resistant microorganisms

Persons with potential health hazards related to personal and family history (V10-V19)

V10 Personal history of malignant neoplasm
V11 Personal history of mental disorder
V12 Personal history of certain other diseases
V13 Personal history of other diseases
V14 Personal history of allergy to medicinal agents
V15 Other personal history presenting hazards to health
V16 Family history of malignant neoplasm
V17 Family history of certain chronic disabling diseases
V18 Family history of certain other specific conditions
V19 Family history of other conditions

Persons encountering health services in circumstances related to reproduction and development (V20-V29)

V20 Health supervision of infant or child
V21 Constitutional states in development
V22 Normal pregnancy
V23 Supervision of high-risk pregnancy
V24 Postpartum care and examination
V25 Encounter for contraceptive management
V26 Procreative management
V27 Outcome of delivery
V28 Antenatal screening
V29 Observation and evaluation of newborns and infants for suspected condition not found

Liveborn infants according to type of birth (V30-V39)

V30 Single liveborn
V31 Twin, mate liveborn
V32 Twin, mate stillborn
V33 Twin, unspecified
V34 Other multiple, mates all liveborn
V35 Other multiple, mates all stillborn
V36 Other multiple, mates live- and stillborn
V37 Other multiple, unspecified
V39 Unspecified

Persons with a condition influencing their health status (V40-V49)

V40 Mental and behavioral problems
V41 Problems with special senses and other special functions
V42 Organ or tissue replaced by transplant
V43 Organ or tissue replaced by other means
V44 Artificial opening status
V45 Other postprocedural states
V46 Other dependence on machines
V47 Other problems with internal organs
V48 Problems with head, neck, and trunk
V49 Problems with limbs and other problems

Persons encountering health services for specific procedures and aftercare (V50-V59)

V50 Elective surgery for purposes other than remedying health states
V51 Aftercare involving the use of plastic surgery
V52 Fitting and adjustment of prosthetic device
V53 Fitting and adjustment of other device
V54 Other orthopedic aftercare
V55 Attention to artificial openings
V56 Encounter for dialysis and dialysis catheter care
V57 Care involving use of rehabilitation procedures
V58 Encounter for other and unspecified procedures and aftercare
V59 Donors

Persons encountering health services in other circumstances (V60-V69)

V60 Housing, household, and economic circumstances
V61 Other family circumstances
V62 Other psychosocial circumstances
V63 Unavailability of other medical facilities for care
V64 Persons encountering health services for specific procedures, not carried out
V65 Other persons seeking consultation
V66 Convalescence and palliative care
V67 Follow-up examination
V68 Encounters for administrative purposes
V69 Problems related to lifestyle

Persons without reported diagnosis encountered during examination and investigation of individuals and populations (V70-V82)

V70 General medical examination
V71 Observation and evaluation for suspected conditions not found
V72 Special investigations and examinations
V73 Special screening examination for viral and chlamydial diseases
V74 Special screening examination for bacterial and spirochetal diseases
V75 Special screening examination for other infectious diseases
V76 Special screening for malignant neoplasms
V77 Special screening for endocrine, nutritional, metabolic, and immunity disorders
V78 Special screening for disorders of blood and blood-forming organs
V79 Special screening for mental disorders and developmental handicaps
V80 Special screening for neurological, eye, and ear diseases
V81 Special screening for cardiovascular, respiratory, and genitourinary diseases
V82 Special screening for other conditions

Genetics (V83-V84)

V83 Genetic carrier status
V84 Genetic susceptibility to disease

Body mass index (V85)

V85 Body Mass Index

Estrogen receptor status (V86)

V86 Estrogen receptor status

SUPPLEMENTARY CLASSIFICATION OF EXTERNAL CAUSES OF INJURY AND POISONING

Railway accidents (E800-E807)

E800 Railway accident involving collision with rolling stock
E801 Railway accident involving collision with other object
E802 Railway accident involving derailment without antecedent collision
E803 Railway accident involving explosion, fire, or burning
E804 Fall in, on, or from railway train
E805 Hit by rolling stock
E806 Other specified railway accident
E807 Railway accident of unspecified nature

Motor vehicle traffic accidents (E810-E819)

E810 Motor vehicle traffic accident involving collision with train
E811 Motor vehicle traffic accident involving re-entrant collision with another motor vehicle
E812 Other motor vehicle traffic accident involving collision with another motor vehicle
E813 Motor vehicle traffic accident involving collision with other vehicle
E814 Motor vehicle traffic accident involving collision with pedestrian
E815 Other motor vehicle traffic accident involving collision on the highway
E816 Motor vehicle traffic accident due to loss of control, without collision on the highway
E817 Noncollision motor vehicle traffic accident while boarding or alighting
E818 Other noncollision motor vehicle traffic accident
E819 Motor vehicle traffic accident of unspecified nature

Motor vehicle nontraffic accidents (E820-E825)

E820 Nontraffic accident involving motor-driven snow vehicle
E821 Nontraffic accident involving other off-road motor vehicle
E822 Other motor vehicle nontraffic accident involving collision with moving object
E823 Other motor vehicle nontraffic accident involving collision with stationary object
E824 Other motor vehicle nontraffic accident while boarding and alighting
E825 Other motor vehicle nontraffic accident of other and unspecified nature

Other road vehicle accidents (E826-E829)

E826 Pedal cycle accident
E827 Animal-drawn vehicle accident
E828 Accident involving animal being ridden
E829 Other road vehicle accidents

Water transport accidents (E830-E838)

E830 Accident to watercraft causing submersion
E831 Accident to watercraft causing other injury
E832 Other accidental submersion or drowning in water transport accident
E833 Fall on stairs or ladders in water transport
E834 Other fall from one level to another in water transport
E835 Other and unspecified fall in water transport
E836 Machinery accident in water transport
E837 Explosion, fire, or burning in watercraft
E838 Other and unspecified water transport accident

Air and space transport accidents (E840-E845)

E840 Accident to powered aircraft at takeoff or landing
E841 Accident to powered aircraft, other and unspecified
E842 Accident to unpowered aircraft
E843 Fall in, on, or from aircraft
E844 Other specified air transport accidents
E845 Accident involving spacecraft

Vehicle accidents, not elsewhere classifiable (E846-E849)

E846 Accidents involving powered vehicles used solely within the buildings and premises of an industrial or commercial establishment
E847 Accidents involving cable cars not running on rails
E848 Accidents involving other vehicles, not elsewhere classifiable
E849 Place of occurrence

Accidental poisoning by drugs, medicinal substances, and biologicals (E850-E858)

E850 Accidental poisoning by analgesics, antipyretics, and antirheumatics
E851 Accidental poisoning by barbiturates
E852 Accidental poisoning by other sedatives and hypnotics
E853 Accidental poisoning by tranquilizers
E854 Accidental poisoning by other psychotropic agents
E855 Accidental poisoning by other drugs acting on central and autonomic nervous systems
E856 Accidental poisoning by antibiotics
E857 Accidental poisoning by anti-infectives
E858 Accidental poisoning by other drugs

Accidental poisoning by other solid and liquid substances, gases, and vapors (E860-E869)

E860 Accidental poisoning by alcohol, not elsewhere classified
E861 Accidental poisoning by cleansing and polishing agents, disinfectants, paints, and varnishes
E862 Accidental poisoning by petroleum products, other solvents and their vapors, not elsewhere classified
E863 Accidental poisoning by agricultural and horticultural chemical and pharmaceutical preparations other than plant foods and fertilizers
E864 Accidental poisoning by corrosives and caustics, not elsewhere classified
E865 Accidental poisoning from poisonous foodstuffs and poisonous plants
E866 Accidental poisoning by other and unspecified solid and liquid substances
E867 Accidental poisoning by gas distributed by pipeline
E868 Accidental poisoning by other utility gas and other carbon monoxide
E869 Accidental poisoning by other gases and vapors

Misadventures to patients during surgical and medical care (E870-E876)

E870 Accidental cut, puncture, perforation, or hemorrhage during medical care
E871 Foreign object left in body during procedure
E872 Failure of sterile precautions during procedure
E873 Failure in dosage
E874 Mechanical failure of instrument or apparatus during procedure
E875 Contaminated or infected blood, other fluid, drug, or biological substance
E876 Other and unspecified misadventures during medical care

Surgical and medical procedures as the cause of abnormal reaction of patient or later complication, without mention of misadventure at the time of procedure (E878-E879)

E878 Surgical operation and other surgical procedures as the cause of abnormal reaction of patient, or of later complication, without mention of misadventure at the time of operation
E879 Other procedures, without mention of misadventure at the time of procedure, as the cause of abnormal reaction of patient, or of later complication

Accidental falls (E880-E888)

E880 Fall on or from stairs or steps
E881 Fall on or from ladders or scaffolding
E882 Fall from or out of building or other structure
E883 Fall into hole or other opening in surface
E884 Other fall from one level to another
E885 Fall on same level from slipping, tripping, or stumbling
E886 Fall on same level from collision, pushing or shoving, by or with other person
E887 Fracture, cause unspecified
E888 Other and unspecified fall

Accidents caused by fire and flames (E890-E899)

E890 Conflagration in private dwelling
E891 Conflagration in other and unspecified building or structure
E892 Conflagration not in building or structure
E893 Accident caused by ignition of clothing
E894 Ignition of highly inflammable material
E895 Accident caused by controlled fire in private dwelling
E896 Accident caused by controlled fire in other and unspecified building or structure
E897 Accident caused by controlled fire not in building or structure
E898 Accident caused by other specified fire and flames
E899 Accident caused by unspecified fire

Accidents due to natural and environmental factors (E900-E909)

E900 Excessive heat
E901 Excessive cold
E902 High and low air pressure and changes in air pressure
E903 Travel and motion
E904 Hunger, thirst, exposure, and neglect
E905 Venomous animals and plants as the cause of poisoning and toxic reactions
E906 Other injury caused by animals
E907 Lightning
E908 Cataclysmic storms, and floods resulting from storms
E909 Cataclysmic earth surface movements and eruptions

Accidents caused by submersion, suffocation, and foreign bodies (E910-E915)

E910 Accidental drowning and submersion
E911 Inhalation and ingestion of food causing obstruction of respiratory tract or suffocation
E912 Inhalation and ingestion of other object causing obstruction of respiratory tract or suffocation
E913 Accidental mechanical suffocation
E914 Foreign body accidentally entering eye and adnexa
E915 Foreign body accidentally entering other orifice

Other accidents (E916-E928)

E916 Struck accidentally by falling object
E917 Striking against or struck accidentally by objects or persons
E918 Caught accidentally in or between objects
E919 Accidents caused by machinery
E920 Accidents caused by cutting and piercing instruments or objects
E921 Accident caused by explosion of pressure vessel
E922 Accident caused by firearm missile
E923 Accident caused by explosive material
E924 Accident caused by hot substance or object, caustic or corrosive material, and steam
E925 Accident caused by electric current
E926 Exposure to radiation
E927 Overexertion and strenuous movements
E928 Other and unspecified environmental and accidental causes

Late effects of accidental injury (E929)

E929 Late effects of accidental injury

Drugs, medicinal and biological substances causing adverse effects in therapeutic use (E930-E949)

E930 Antibiotics
E931 Other anti-infectives
E932 Hormones and synthetic substitutes
E933 Primarily systemic agents
E934 Agents primarily affecting blood constituents
E935 Analgesics, antipyretics, and antirheumatics
E936 Anticonvulsants and anti-Parkinsonism drugs
E937 Sedatives and hypnotics
E938 Other central nervous system depressants and anesthetics
E939 Psychotropic agents
E940 Central nervous system stimulants
E941 Drugs primarily affecting the autonomic nervous system
E942 Agents primarily affecting the cardiovascular system
E943 Agents primarily affecting gastrointestinal system
E944 Water, mineral, and uric acid metabolism drugs
E945 Agents primarily acting on the smooth and skeletal muscles and respiratory system
E946 Agents primarily affecting skin and mucous membrane, ophthalmological, otorhinolaryngological, and dental drugs
E947 Other and unspecified drugs and medicinal substances
E948 Bacterial vaccines
E949 Other vaccines and biological substances

Suicide and self-inflicted injury (E950-E959)

E950 Suicide and self-inflicted poisoning by solid or liquid substances
E951 Suicide and self-inflicted poisoning by gases in domestic use
E952 Suicide and self-inflicted poisoning by other gases and vapors
E953 Suicide and self-inflicted injury by hanging, strangulation, and suffocation
E954 Suicide and self-inflicted injury by submersion [drowning]
E955 Suicide and self-inflicted injury by firearms and explosives
E956 Suicide and self-inflicted injury by cutting and piercing instruments
E957 Suicide and self-inflicted injuries by jumping from high place
E958 Suicide and self-inflicted injury by other and unspecified means
E959 Late effects of self-inflicted injury

Homicide and injury purposely inflicted by other persons (E960-E969)

E960 Fight, brawl, and rape
E961 Assault by corrosive or caustic substance, except poisoning
E962 Assault by poisoning
E963 Assault by hanging and strangulation
E964 Assault by submersion [drowning]
E965 Assault by firearms and explosives
E966 Assault by cutting and piercing instrument
E967 Child and adult battering and other maltreatment
E968 Assault by other and unspecified means
E969 Late effects of injury purposely inflicted by other person

Legal intervention (E970-E978)

E970 Injury due to legal intervention by firearms
E971 Injury due to legal intervention by explosives
E972 Injury due to legal intervention by gas
E973 Injury due to legal intervention by blunt object
E974 Injury due to legal intervention by cutting and piercing instruments
E975 Injury due to legal intervention by other specified means
E976 Injury due to legal intervention by unspecified means
E977 Late effects of injuries due to legal intervention
E978 Legal execution

Terrorism (E979)

E979 Terrorism

Injury undetermined whether accidentally or purposely inflicted (E980-E989)

E980 Poisoning by solid or liquid substances, undetermined whether accidentally or purposely inflicted

E981 Poisoning by gases in domestic use, undetermined whether accidentally or purposely inflicted

E982 Poisoning by other gases, undetermined whether accidentally or purposely inflicted

E983 Hanging, strangulation, or suffocation, undetermined whether accidentally or purposely inflicted

E984 Submersion [drowning], undetermined whether accidentally or purposely inflicted

E985 Injury by firearms and explosives, undetermined whether accidentally or purposely inflicted

E986 Injury by cutting and piercing instruments, undetermined whether accidentally or purposely inflicted

E987 Falling from high place, undetermined whether accidentally or purposely inflicted

E988 Injury by other and unspecified means, undetermined whether accidentally or purposely inflicted

E989 Late effects of injury, undetermined whether accidentally or purposely inflicted

Injury resulting from operations of war (E990-E999)

E990 Injury due to war operations by fires and conflagrations

E991 Injury due to war operations by bullets and fragments

E992 Injury due to war operations by explosion of marine weapons

E993 Injury due to war operations by other explosion

E994 Injury due to war operations by destruction of aircraft

E995 Injury due to war operations by other and unspecified forms of conventional warfare

E996 Injury due to war operations by nuclear weapons

E997 Injury due to war operations by other forms of unconventional warfare

E998 Injury due to war operations but occurring after cessation of hostilities

E999 Late effects of injury due to war operations

A

Note — Also use 00.40, 00.41, 00.42, or 00.43 to show the total number of vessels treated. ▶Use code 00.44 once to show procedure on a bifurcated vessel.◀ In addition, use 00.45, 00.46, 00.47, or 00.48 to show the number of vascular stents inserted.

☑ Additional Digit Required — Refer to the Tabular List for Digit Selection

Subterms under main terms may continue to next column or page

▶◀ Revised Text ● New Line ▲ Revised Code

☑ Additional Digit Required — Refer to the Tabular List for Digit Selection
▶◀ Revised Text ● New Line ▲ Revised Code
Subterms under main terms may continue to next column or page

Evacuation — *continued*
- anterior chamber (eye) (aqueous) (hyphema) 12.91
- cyst (*see also* Excision, lesion, by site)
  - breast 85.91
  - kidney 55.01
  - liver 50.29
- hematoma (*see also* Incision, hematoma)
  - obstetrical 75.92
    - incisional 75.91
- hemorrhoids (thrombosed) 49.47
- pelvic blood clot (by incision) 54.19
  - by
    - culdocentesis 70.0
    - culdoscopy 70.22
- retained placenta
  - with curettage 69.02
  - manual 75.4
- streptothrix from lacrimal duct 09.42

Evaluation (of)
- audiological 95.43
- cardiac rhythm device (CRT-D) (CRT-P) (AICD) (pacemaker) — *see* Interrogation
- criminal responsibility, psychiatric 94.11
- functional (physical therapy) 93.01
- hearing NEC 95.49
- orthotic (for brace fitting) 93.02
- prosthetic (for artificial limb fitting) 93.03
- psychiatric NEC 94.19
  - commitment 94.13
- psychologic NEC 94.08
- testimentary capacity, psychiatric 94.11

Evans operation (release of clubfoot) 83.84

Evisceration
- eyeball 16.39
  - with implant (into scleral shell) 16.31
- ocular contents 16.39
  - with implant (into scleral shell) 16.31
- orbit (*see also* Exenteration, orbit) 16.59
- pelvic (anterior) (posterior) (partial) (total) (female) 68.8
  - male 57.71

Evulsion
- nail (bed) (fold) 86.23
- skin 86.3
- subcutaneous tissue 86.3

Examination (for)
- breast
  - manual 89.36
  - radiographic NEC 87.37
  - thermographic 88.85
  - ultrasonic 88.73
- cervical rib (by x-ray) 87.43
- colostomy stoma (digital) 89.33
- dental (oral mucosa) (peridontal) 89.31
  - radiographic NEC 87.12
- enterostomy stoma (digital) 89.33
- eye 95.09
  - color vision 95.06
  - comprehensive 95.02
  - dark adaptation 95.07
  - limited (with prescription of spectacles) 95.01
  - under anesthesia 95.04
- fetus, intrauterine 75.35
- general physical 89.7
- glaucoma 95.03
- gynecological 89.26
- hearing 95.47

Examination — *continued*
- microscopic (specimen) (of) 91.9 ☑

> *Note — Use the following fourth-digit subclassification with categories 90–91 to identify type of examination:*
>
> 1 *bacterial smear*
>
> 2 *culture*
>
> 3 *culture and sensitivity*
>
> 4 *parasitology*
>
> 5 *toxicology*
>
> 6 *cell block and Papanicolaou smear*
>
> 9 *other microsopic examination*

  - adenoid 90.3 ☑
  - adrenal gland 90.1 ☑
  - amnion 91.4 ☑
  - anus 90.9 ☑
  - appendix 90.9 ☑
  - bile ducts 91.0 ☑
  - bladder 91.3 ☑
  - blood 90.5 ☑
  - bone 91.5 ☑
    - marrow 90.6 ☑
  - brain 90.0 ☑
  - breast 91.6 ☑
  - bronchus 90.4 ☑
  - bursa 91.5 ☑
  - cartilage 91.5 ☑
  - cervix 91.4 ☑
  - chest wall 90.4 ☑
  - chorion 91.4 ☑
  - colon 90.9 ☑
  - cul-de-sac 91.1 ☑
  - dental 90.8 ☑
  - diaphragm 90.4 ☑
  - duodenum 90.8 ☑
  - ear 90.3 ☑
  - endocrine gland NEC 90.1 ☑
  - esophagus 90.8 ☑
  - eye 90.2 ☑
  - fallopian tube 91.4 ☑
  - fascia 91.5 ☑
  - female genital tract 91.4 ☑
  - fetus 91.4 ☑
  - gallbladder 91.0 ☑
  - hair 91.6 ☑
  - ileum 90.9 ☑
  - jejunum 90.9 ☑
  - joint fluid 91.5 ☑
  - kidney 91.2 ☑
  - large intestine 90.9 ☑
  - larynx 90.3 ☑
  - ligament 91.5 ☑
  - liver 91.0 ☑
  - lung 90.4 ☑
  - lymph (node) 90.7 ☑
  - meninges 90.0 ☑
  - mesentery 91.1 ☑
  - mouth 90.8 ☑
  - muscle 91.5 ☑
  - musculoskeletal system 91.5 ☑
  - nails 91.6 ☑
  - nerve 90.0 ☑
  - nervous system 90.0 ☑
  - nose 90.3 ☑
  - omentum 91.1 ☑
  - operative wound 91.7 ☑
  - ovary 91.4 ☑
  - pancreas 91.0 ☑
  - parathyroid gland 90.1 ☑
  - penis 91.3 ☑
  - perirenal tissue 91.2 ☑
  - peritoneum (fluid) 91.1 ☑
  - periureteral tissue 91.2 ☑
  - perivesical (tissue) 91.3 ☑
  - pharynx 90.3 ☑
  - pineal gland 90.1 ☑
  - pituitary gland 90.1 ☑
  - placenta 91.4 ☑
  - pleura (fluid) 90.4 ☑

Examination — *continued*
- microscopic — *continued*
  - prostate 91.3 ☑
  - rectum 90.9 ☑
  - retroperitoneum 91.1 ☑
  - semen 91.3 ☑
  - seminal vesicle 91.3 ☑
  - sigmoid 90.9 ☑
  - skin 91.6 ☑
  - small intestine 90.9 ☑
  - specified site NEC 91.8 ☑
  - spinal fluid 90.0 ☑
  - spleen 90.6 ☑
  - sputum 90.4 ☑
  - stomach 90.8 ☑
  - stool 90.9 ☑
  - synovial membrane 91.5 ☑
  - tendon 91.5 ☑
  - thorax NEC 90.4 ☑
  - throat 90.3 ☑
  - thymus 90.1 ☑
  - thyroid gland 90.1 ☑
  - tonsil 90.3 ☑
  - trachea 90.4 ☑
  - ureter 91.2 ☑
  - urethra 91.3 ☑
  - urine 91.3 ☑
  - uterus 91.4 ☑
  - vagina 91.4 ☑
  - vas deferens 91.3 ☑
  - vomitus 90.8 ☑
  - vulva 91.4 ☑
- neurologic 89.13
- neuro-ophthalmology 95.03
- ophthalmoscopic 16.21
- panorex, mandible 87.12
- pelvic (manual) 89.26
  - instrumental (by pelvimeter) 88.25
  - pelvimetric 88.25
- physical, general 89.7
- postmortem 89.8
- rectum (digital) 89.34
  - endoscopic 48.23
    - through stoma (artificial) 48.22
    - transabdominal 48.21
- retinal disease 95.03
- specified type (manual) NEC 89.39
- thyroid field, postoperative 06.02
- uterus (digital) 68.11
  - endoscopic 68.12
- vagina 89.26
  - endoscopic 70.21
- visual field 95.05

Exchange transfusion 99.01
- intrauterine 75.2

Excision
- aberrant tissue — *see* Excision, lesion, by site of tissue origin
- abscess — *see* Excision, lesion, by site
- accessory tissue (*see also* Excision, lesion, by site of tissue origin)
  - lung 32.29
    - endoscopic 32.28
  - spleen 41.93
- adenoids (tag) 28.6
  - with tonsillectomy 28.3
- adenoma — *see* Excision, lesion, by site
- adrenal gland (*see also* Adrenalectomy) 07.22
- ampulla of Vater (with reimplantation of common duct) 51.62
- anal papilla 49.39
  - endoscopic 49.31
- aneurysm (arteriovenous) (*see also* Aneurysmectomy) 38.60
  - coronary artery 36.91
  - heart 37.32
  - myocardium 37.32
  - sinus of Valsalva 35.39
  - ventricle (heart) 37.32
- anus (complete) (partial) 49.6
- aortic subvalvular ring 35.35
- apocrine gland 86.3
- aponeurosis 83.42

Excision — *continued*
- aponeurosis — *continued*
  - hand 82.33
- appendiceal stump 47.09
  - laparoscopic 47.01
- appendices epiploicae 54.4
- appendix (*see also* Appendectomy) 47.01, 47.09
  - epididymis 63.3
  - testis 62.2
- arcuate ligament (spine) — omit code
- arteriovenous fistula (*see also* Aneurysmectomy) 38.60
- artery (*see also* Arteriectomy) 38.60
- Baker's cyst, knee 83.39
- Bartholin's gland 71.24
- basal ganglion 01.59
- bile duct 51.69
  - endoscopic 51.64
- bladder (*see also* Cystectomy)
- bleb (emphysematous), lung 32.29
  - endoscopic 32.28
- blood vessel (*see also* Angiectomy) 38.60
- bone (ends) (partial), except facial — *see* category 77.8 ☑
  - for graft (autograft) (homograft) — *see* category 77.7 ☑
  - facial NEC 76.39
    - total 76.45
      - with reconstruction 76.44
  - fragments (chips) (*see also* Incision, bone) 77.10
    - joint (*see also* Arthrotomy) 80.10
    - necrotic (*see also* Sequestrectomy, bone) 77.00
  - heterotopic, from
    - muscle 83.32
      - hand 82.22
    - skin 86.3
    - tendon 83.31
      - hand 82.21
  - mandible 76.31
    - with arthrodesis — *see* Arthrodesis
    - total 76.42
      - with reconstruction 76.41
  - spur — *see* Excision, lesion, bone
  - total, except facial — *see* category 77.9 ☑
    - facial NEC 76.45
      - with reconstruction 76.44
    - mandible 76.42
      - with reconstruction 76.41
- brain 01.59
  - hemisphere 01.52
  - lobe 01.53
- branchial cleft cyst or vestige 29.2
- breast (*see also* Mastectomy) 85.41
  - aberrant tissue 85.24
  - accessory 85.24
  - ectopic 85.24
  - nipple 85.25
    - accessory 85.24
  - segmental 85.23
  - supernumerary 85.24
  - wedge 85.21
- broad ligament 69.19
- bronchogenic cyst 32.09
  - endoscopic 32.01
- bronchus (wide sleeve) NEC 32.1
- buccal mucosa 27.49
- bulbourethral gland 58.92
- bulbous tuberosities (mandible) (maxilla) (fibrous) (osseous) 24.31
- bunion (*see also* Bunionectomy) 77.59
- bunionette (with osteotomy) 77.54
- bursa 83.5
  - hand 82.31
- canal of Nuck 69.19
- cardioma 37.33
- carotid body (lesion) (partial) (total) 39.8

☑ Additional Digit Required — Refer to the Tabular List for Digit Selection

Subterms under main terms may continue to next column or page

▶◀ Revised Text ● New Line ▲ Revised Code

Index

Extraction — Fixation

H

☑ Additional Digit Required — Refer to the Tabular List for Digit Selection

Subterms under main terms may continue to next column or page

▶◀ Revised Text ● New Line ▲ Revised Code

☑ Additional Digit Required — Refer to the Tabular List for Digit Selection
Subterms under main terms may continue to next column or page
▶◀ Revised Text ● New Line ▲ Revised Code

Injection — Insertion

☑ Additional Digit Required — Refer to the Tabular List for Digit Selection
Subterms under main terms may continue to next column or page
▶◀ Revised Text ● New Line ▲ Revised Code

☑ Additional Digit Required — Refer to the Tabular List for Digit Selection

Subterms under main terms may continue to next column or page

▶◀ Revised Text ● New Line ▲ Revised Code

☑ Additional Digit Required — Refer to the Tabular List for Digit Selection
Subterms under main terms may continue to next column or page

▶◀ Revised Text ● New Line ▲ Revised Code

N

O

☑ Additional Digit Required — Refer to the Tabular List for Digit Selection
▽ Subterms under main terms may continue to next column or page
▶◀ Revised Text ● New Line ▲ Revised Code

☑ Additional Digit Required — Refer to the Tabular List for Digit Selection

▶◀ Revised Text ● New Line ▲ Revised Code

Subterms under main terms may continue to next column or page

☑ Additional Digit Required — Refer to the Tabular List for Digit Selection
Subterms under main terms may continue to next column or page

V

00. PROCEDURES AND INTERVENTIONS, NOT ELSEWHERE CLASSIFIED (00)

✓3rd **00 Procedures and interventions, not elsewhere classified**

✓4th **00.0 Therapeutic ultrasound**

EXCLUDES *diagnostic ultrasound (non-invasive) (88.71-88.79)*
intracardiac echocardiography [ICE] (heart chamber(s)) (37.28)
intravascular imaging (adjunctive) (00.21-00.29)

AHA: 4Q, '02, 90

DEF: Interventional treatment modality using lower frequency and higher intensity levels of ultrasound energy than used in diagnostic ultrasound modality for the purpose of limiting intimal hyperpalsia, or restenosis, associated with atherosclerotic vascular disease.

00.01 Therapeutic ultrasound of vessels of head and neck
Anti-restenotic ultrasound
Intravascular non-ablative ultrasound
EXCLUDES *diagnostic ultrasound of:*
eye (95.13)
head and neck (88.71)
that of inner ear (20.79)
ultrasonic:
angioplasty of non-coronary vessel (39.50)
embolectomy (38.01, 38.02)
endarterectomy (38.11, 38.12)
thrombectomy (38.01, 38.02)

00.02 Therapeutic ultrasound of heart
Anti-restenotic ultrasound
Intravascular non-ablative ultrasound
EXCLUDES *diagnostic ultrasound of heart (88.72)*
ultrasonic ablation of heart lesion (37.34)
ultrasonic angioplasty of coronary vessels (00.66, 36.09)

00.03 Therapeutic ultrasound of peripheral vascular vessels
Anti-restenotic ultrasound
Intravascular non-ablative ultrasound
EXCLUDES *diagnostic ultrasound of peripheral vascular system (88.77)*
ultrasonic angioplasty of:
non-coronary vessel (39.50)

00.09 Other therapeutic ultrasound
EXCLUDES *ultrasonic:*
fragmentation of urinary stones (59.95)
percutaneous nephrostomy with fragmentation (55.04)
physical therapy (93.35)
transurethral guided laser induced prostatectomy (TULIP) (60.21)

✓4th **00.1 Pharmaceuticals**

00.10 Implantation of chemotherapeutic agent
Brain wafer chemotherapy
Interstitial/intracavitary
EXCLUDES *injection or infusion of cancer chemotherapeutic substance (99.25)*
AHA: 4Q, '02, 93
DEF: Brain wafer chemotherapy: Placement of wafers containing antineoplastic agent against the wall of the resection cavity subsequent to the surgeon completing a tumor excision to deliver chemotherapy directly to the tumor site; used to treat glioblastoma multiforme (GBM).

00.11 Infusion of drotrecogin alfa (activated)
Infusion of recombinant protein
AHA: 4Q, '02, 93

00.12 Administration of inhaled nitric oxide
Nitric oxide therapy
AHA: 4Q, '02, 94

00.13 Injection or infusion of nesiritide
Human B-type natriuretic peptide (hBNP)
AHA: 4Q, '02, 94

00.14 Injection or infusion of oxazolidinone class of antibiotics
Linezolid injection
AHA: 4Q, '02, 95

00.15 High-dose infusion interleukin-2 [IL-2]
Infusion (IV bolus, CIV) interleukin
Injection of aldesleukin
EXCLUDES *low-dose infusion interleukin-2 (99.28)*
AHA: 4Q, '03, 92
DEF: A high-dose anti-neoplastic therapy using a biological response modifier (BRM); the body naturally produces substances called interleukins, which are multi-function cytokines in the generation of an immune response.

00.16 Pressurized treatment of venous bypass graft [conduit] with pharmaceutical substance
Ex-vivo treatment of vessel
Hyperbaric pressurized graft [conduit]
DEF: Ex-vivo process of delivering small nucleic acid molecules that block protein transcription factors essential for the expression of genes controlling cell proliferation into graft tissue under nondistending pressure; reduces intimal hyperplasia and vein graft failure.

00.17 Infusion of vasopressor agent

00.18 Infusion of immunosuppressive antibody therapy during induction phase of solid organ transplantation
Monoclonal antibody therapy
Polyclonal antibody therapy
AHA: ▶4Q, '05, 101◀

✓4th **00.2 Intravascular imaging of blood vessels**

Note: Real-time imaging of lumen of blood vessel(s) using sound waves
Endovascular ultrasonography
Intravascular [ultrasound] imaging of blood vessels
Intravascular ultrasound (IVUS)
Code also any synchronous diagnostic or therapeutic procedures
EXCLUDES *adjunct vascular system procedures, number of vessels treated (00.40-00.43)*
diagnostic procedures on blood vessels (38.21-38.29)
diagnostic ultrasound of peripheral vascular system (88.77)
magnetic resonance imaging (MRI) (88.91-88.97)
therapeutic ultrasound (00.01-00.09)

00.21 Intravascular imaging of extracranial cerebral vessels
Common carotid vessels and branches
Intravascular ultrasound (IVUS), extracranial cerebral vessels
EXCLUDES *diagnostic ultrasound (non-invasive) of head and neck (88.71)*

00.22 Intravascular imaging of intrathoracic vessels
Aorta and aortic arch
Intravascular ultrasound (IVUS), intrathoracic vessels
Vena cava (superior) (inferior)
EXCLUDES *diagnostic ultrasound (non-invasive) of other sites of thorax (88.73)*

✓3rd ✓4th Additional Digit Required | Nonspecific OR Procedure | Valid OR Procedure | Non-OR Procedure | Adjunct Code

00.23 Intravascular imaging of peripheral vessels
Imaging of:
vessels of arm(s)
vessels of leg(s)
Intravascular ultrasound (IVUS), peripheral vessels
EXCLUDES *diagnostic ultrasound (non-invasive) of peripheral vascular system (88.77)*

00.24 Intravascular imaging of coronary vessels
Intravascular ultrasound (IVUS), coronary vessels
EXCLUDES *diagnostic ultrasound (non-invasive) of heart (88.72)*
intracardiac echocardiography [ICE] (ultrasound of heart chamber(s)) (37.28)

00.25 Intravascular imaging of renal vessels
Intravascular ultrasound (IVUS), renal vessels
Renal artery
EXCLUDES *diagnostic ultrasound (non-invasive) of urinary system (88.75)*

00.28 Intravascular imaging, other specified vessel(s)

00.29 Intravascular imagining unspecified vessel(s)

✓4th **00.3 Computer assisted surgery [CAS]**
CT-free navigation
Image guided navigation (IGN)
Image guided surgery (IGS)
Imageless navigation
Code also diagnostic or therapeutic procedure
EXCLUDES *stereotactic frame application only (93.59)*

00.31 Computer assisted surgery with CT/CTA
AHA: 4Q, '04, 113

00.32 Computer assisted surgery with MR/MRA
AHA: 4Q, '04, 113

00.33 Computer assisted surgery with fluoroscopy

00.34 Imageless computer assisted surgery

00.35 Computer assisted surgery with multiple datasets

00.39 Other computer assisted surgery
Computer assisted surgery NOS

✓4th **00.4 Adjunct vascular system procedures**
Note: These codes can apply to both coronary and peripheral vessels. These codes are to be used in conjunction with other therapeutic procedure codes to provide additional information on the number of vessels upon which a procedure was performed and/or the number of stents inserted. As appropriate, code both the number of vessels operated on (00.40-00.43), and the number of stents inserted (00.45-00.48).
Code also any:
angioplasty or atherectomy (00.61-00.62, 00.66, 39.50)
endarterectomy (38.10-38.18)
insertion of vascular stent(s) (00.55, 00.63-00.65, 36.06-36.07, 39.90)
other removal of coronary artery obstruction (36.09)
AHA: 4Q, '05, 101

00.40 Procedure on single vessel
Number of vessels, unspecified
EXCLUDES *(aorto)coronary bypass (36.10-36.19)*
intravascular imaging of blood vessels (00.21-00.29)
AHA: 4Q, '05, 71, 106

00.41 Procedure on two vessels
EXCLUDES *(aorto)coronary bypass (36.10-36.19)*
intravascular imaging of blood vessels (00.21-00.29)
AHA: 4Q, '05, 105

00.42 Procedure on three vessels
EXCLUDES *(aorto)coronary bypass (36.10-36.19)*
intravascular imaging of blood vessels (00.21-00.29)

00.43 Procedure on four or more vessels
EXCLUDES *(aorto)coronary bypass (36.10-36.19)*
intravascular imaging of blood vessels (00.21-00.29)

● **00.44 Procedure on vessel bifurcation**
Note: This code is to be used to identify the presence of a vessel bifurcation; it does not describe a specific bifurcation stent. Use this code only once per operative episode, irrespective of the number of bifurcations in vessels.

00.45 Insertion of one vascular stent
Number of stents, unspecified
AHA: 4Q, '05, 71

00.46 Insertion of two vascular stents
AHA: 4Q, '05, 105-106

00.47 Insertion of three vascular stents

00.48 Insertion of four or more vascular stents

✓4th **00.5 Other cardiovascular procedures**
AHA: 4Q, '02, 95

00.50 Implantation of cardiac resynchronization pacemaker without mention of defibrillation, total system [CRT-P]
▶Note: Device testing during procedure—*omit code*◀
▶Biventricular pacemaker◀
Biventricular pacing without internal cardiac defibrillator
▶BiV pacemaker◀
Implantation of cardiac resynchronization (biventricular) pulse generator pacing device, formation of pocket, transvenous leads including placement of lead into left ventricular coronary venous system, and intraoperative procedures for evaluation of lead signals
That with CRT-P generator and one or more leads
EXCLUDES *implantation of cardiac resynchronization defibrillator, total system [CRT-D] (00.51)*
insertion or replacement of any type pacemaker device (37.80-37.87)
replacement of cardiac resynchronization:
defibrillator, pulse generator only [CRT-D] (00.54)
pacemaker, pulse generator only [CRT-P] (00.53)
AHA: 3Q, '05, 3-9; 4Q, '02, 100

DEF: Cardiac resynchronization pacemaker: CRT-P, or biventricular pacing, adds a third lead to traditional pacemaker designs that connects to the left ventricle. The device provides electrical stimulation to the right atrium, right ventricle, and left ventricle, and coordinates ventricular contractions to improve cardiac output.

00.51 Implantation of cardiac resynchronization defibrillator, total system [CRT-D]

▶Note: Device testing during procedure—*omit code*◀

▶BiV defibrillator

Biventricular defibrillator◀

Biventricular pacing with internal cardiac defibrillator

▶BiV ICD

BiV pacemaker with defibrillator

BiV pacing with defibrillator◀

Implantation of cardiac resynchronization (biventricular) pulse generator with defibrillator [AICD], formation of pocket, transvenous leads, including placement of lead into left ventricular coronary venous system, intraoperative procedures for evaluation of lead signals, and obtaining defibrillator threshold measurements

That with CRT-D generator and one or more leads

EXCLUDES *implantation of cardiac resynchronization pacemaker, total system [CRT-P] (00.50)*

implantation or replacement of automatic cardioverter/defibrillator, total system [AICD] (37.94)

replacement of cardiac resynchronization defibrillator, pulse generator only [CRT-D] (00.54)

AHA: 3Q, '05, 3-9; 4Q, '02, 99, 100

00.52 Implantation or replacement of transvenous lead [electrode] into left ventricular coronary venous system

EXCLUDES *implantation of cardiac resynchronization:*

defibrillator, total system [CRT-D] (00.51)

pacemaker, total system [CRT-P] (00.50)

initial insertion of transvenous lead [electrode] (37.70-37.72)

replacement of transvenous atrial and/or ventricular lead(s) [electrodes] (37.76)

● **00.53 Implantation or replacement of cardiac resynchronization pacemaker, pulse generator only [CRT-P]**

▶Note: Device testing during procedure—*omit code*◀

Implantation of CRT-P device with removal of any existing CRT-P or other pacemaker device

EXCLUDES *implantation of cardiac resynchronization pacemaker, total system [CRT-P] (00.50)*

implantation or replacement of cardiac resynchronization defibrillator, pulse generator only [CRT-D] (00.54)

insertion or replacement of any type pacemaker device (37.80-37.87)

AHA: 3Q, '05, 3-9

● **00.54 Implantation or replacement of cardiac resynchronization defibrillator, pulse generator device only [CRT-D]**

▶Note: Device testing during procedure—*omit code*◀

Implantation of CRT-D device with removal of any existing CRT-D, CRT-P, pacemaker, or defibrillator device

EXCLUDES *implantation of automatic cardioverter/defibrillator pulse generator only (37.96)*

implantation of cardiac resynchronization defibrillator, total system [CRT-D] (00.51)

implantation or replacement of cardiac resynchronization pacemaker, pulse generator only [CRT-P] (00.53)

AHA: 3Q, '05, 3-9; 4Q, '02, 100

00.55 Insertion of drug-eluting peripheral vessel stent(s)

Endograft(s)

Endovascular graft(s)

Stent graft(s)

Code also any:

angioplasty or atherectomy of other non-coronary vessel(s) (39.50)

number of vascular stents inserted (00.45-00.48)

number of vessels treated (00.40-00.43)

▶procedure on vessel bifurcation (00.44)◀

EXCLUDES *drug-coated peripheral stents, e.g., heparin coated (39.90)*

insertion of cerebrovascular stent(s) (00.63-00.65)

insertion of drug-eluting coronary artery stent (36.07)

insertion of non-drug-eluting stent(s):

coronary artery (36.06)

peripheral vessel (39.90)

that for aneurysm repair (39.71-39.79)

AHA: 4Q, '02, 101

00.56 Insertion or replacement of implantable pressure sensor (lead) for intracardiac hemodynamic monitoring

Code also any associated implantation or replacement of monitor (00.57)

EXCLUDES *circulatory monitoring (blood gas, arterial or venous pressure, cardiac output and coronary blood flow) (89.60-89.69)*

00.57 Implantation or replacement of subcutaneous device for intracardiac hemodynamic monitoring

Implantation of monitoring device with formation of subcutaneous pocket and connection to intracardiac pressure sensor (lead)

Code also any associated insertion or replacement of implanted pressure sensor (lead) (00.56)

4th 00.6 Procedures on blood vessels

00.61 Percutaneous angioplasty or atherectomy of precerebral (extracranial) vessel(s)

Basilar
Carotid
Vertebral
Code also any:
- injection or infusion of thrombolytic agent (99.10)
- number of vascular stents inserted (00.45-00.48)
- number of vessels treated (00.40-00.43)
- percutaneous insertion of carotid artery stent(s) (00.63)
- percutaneous insertion of other precerebral artery stent(s) (00.64)
- ▶procedure on vessel bifurcation (00.44)◀

EXCLUDES *angioplasty or atherectomy of other non-coronary vessel(s) (39.50)*
removal of cerebrovascular obstruction of vessel(s) by open approach (38.01-38.02, 38.11-38.12, 38.31-38.32, 38.41-38.42)

00.62 Percutaneous angioplasty or atherectomy intracranial vessel(s) NC

Code also any:
- injection or infusion of thrombolytic agent (99.10)
- number of vascular stents inserted (00.45-00.48)
- number of vessels treated (00.40-00.43)
- percutaneous insertion of intracranial stent(s) (00.65)
- ▶procedure on vessel bifurcation (00.44)◀

EXCLUDES *angioplasty or atherectomy of other non-coronary vessel(s) (39.50)*
removal of cerebrovascular obstruction of vessel(s) by open approach (38.01-38.02, 38.11-38.12, 38.31-38.32, 38.41-38.42)

00.63 Percutaneous insertion of carotid artery stent(s)

Includes the use of any embolic protection device, distal protection device, filter device, or stent delivery system
Non-drug-eluting stent
Code also any:
- number of vascular stents inserted (00.45-00.48)
- number of vessels treated (00.40-00.43)
- percutaneous angioplasty or atherectomy of precerebral vessel(s) (00.61)
- ▶procedure on vessel bifurcation (00.44)◀

EXCLUDES *angioplasty or atherectomy of other non-coronary vessel(s) (39.50)*
insertion of drug-eluting peripheral vessel stent(s) (00.55)

00.64 Percutaneous insertion of other precerebral (extracranial) artery stent(s)

Includes the use of any embolic protection device, distal protection device, filter device, or stent delivery system
Basilar stent
Vertebral stent
Code also any:
- number of vascular stents inserted (00.45-00.48)
- number of vessels treated (00.40-00.43)
- percutaneous angioplasty or atherectomy of precerebral vessel(s) (00.61)
- ▶procedure on vessel bifurcation (00.44)◀

EXCLUDES *angioplasty or atherectomy of other non-coronary vessel(s) (39.50)*
insertion of drug-eluting peripheral vessel stent(s) (00.55)

00.65 Percutaneous insertion of intracranial vascular stent(s)

Includes the use of any embolic protection device, distal protection device, filter device, or stent delivery system
Code also any:
- number of vascular stents inserted (00.45-00.48)
- number of vessels treated (00.40-00.43)
- percutaneous angioplasty or atherectomy of intracranial vessel(s) (00.62)
- ▶procedure on vessel bifurcation (00.44)◀

EXCLUDES *angioplasty or atherectomy of other non-coronary vessel(s) (39.50)*
insertion of drug-eluting peripheral vessel stent(s) (00.55)

00.66 Percutaneous transluminal coronary angioplasty [PTCA] or coronary atherectomy

Balloon angioplasty of coronary artery
Coronary atherectomy
Percutaneous coronary angioplasty NOS
PTCA NOS
Code also any:
- injection or infusion of thrombolytic agent (99.10)
- insertion of coronary artery stent(s) (36.06-36.07)
- intracoronary artery thrombolytic infusion (36.04)
- number of vascular stents inserted (00.45-00.48)
- number of vessels treated (00.40-00.43)
- ▶procedure on vessel bifurcation (00.44)◀

AHA: 4Q, '05, 71, 101; **The following references pertain to deleted PTCA codes (36.01, 36.02, 36.05):** 1Q, '04, 10; 3Q, '03, 9; 4Q, '02, 114; 3Q, '02, 19; 1Q, '01, 9; 2Q, '01, 24; 1Q, '00, 11; 1Q, '99, 17; 4Q, '98, 74, 85; 1Q, '97, 3; 1Q, '94, 3; 3Q, '91, 24

DEF: Balloon angioplasty: Insertion of catheter with inflation of balloon to flatten plaque and widen vessels.

PTCA (Balloon Angioplasty)

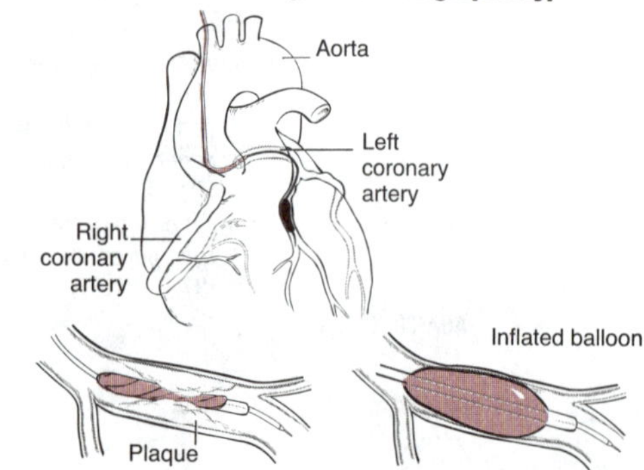

✓4th 00.7 Other hip procedures

AHA: 4Q, '05, 106

00.70 Revision of hip replacement, both acetabular and femoral components BI

Total hip revision

Code also any:

removal of (cement) (joint) spacer (84.57)

type of bearing surface, if known ▶(00.74-00.77)◀

EXCLUDES *revision of hip replacement, acetabular component only (00.71)*

revision of hip replacement, femoral component only (00.72)

revision of hip replacement, not otherwise specified (81.53)

revision with replacement of acetabular liner and/or femoral head only (00.73)

AHA: 4Q, '05, 113

00.71 Revision of hip replacement, acetabular component BI

Partial, acetabular component only

That with:

exchange of acetabular cup and liner

exchange of femoral head

Code also any type of bearing surface, if known ▶(00.74-00.77)◀

EXCLUDES *revision of hip replacement, both acetabular and femoral components (00.70)*

revision of hip replacement, femoral component (00.72)

revision of hip replacement, not otherwise specified (81.53)

revision with replacement of acetabular liner and/or femoral head only (00.73)

AHA: 4Q, '05, 112

00.72 Revision of hip replacement, femoral component BI

Partial, femoral component only

That with:

exchange of acetabular liner

exchange of femoral stem and head

Code also any type of bearing surface, if known ▶(00.74-00.77)◀

EXCLUDES *revision of hip replacement, acetabular component (00.71)*

revision of hip replacement, both acetabular and femoral components (00.70)

revision of hip replacement, not otherwise specified (81.53)

revision with replacement of acetabular liner and/or femoral head only (00.73)

00.73 Revision of hip replacement, acetabular liner and/or femoral head only BI

Code also any type of bearing surface, if known ▶(00.74-00.77)◀

00.74 Hip replacement bearing surface, metal on polyethylene

00.75 Hip replacement bearing surface, metal-on-metal

00.76 Hip replacement bearing surface, ceramic-on-ceramic

AHA: 4Q, '05, 112

● **00.77 Hip replacement bearing surface, ceramic-on-polyethylene**

▲ **✓4th 00.8 Other knee and hip procedures**

Note: Report up to two components using 00.81-00.83 to describe revision of knee replacements. If all three components are revised, report 00.80.

AHA: 4Q, '05, 113

00.80 Revision of knee replacement, total (all components) BI

Replacement of femoral, tibial, and patellar components (all components)

Code also any removal of (cement) (joint) spacer (84.57)

EXCLUDES *revision of only one or two components (tibial, femoral or patellar component) (00.81-00.84)*

00.81 Revision of knee replacement, tibial component BI

Replacement of tibial baseplate and tibial insert (liner)

EXCLUDES *revision of knee replacement, total (all components) (00.80)*

AHA: 4Q, '05, 117

00.82 Revision of knee replacement, femoral component BI

That with replacement of tibial insert (liner)

EXCLUDES *revision of knee replacement, total (all components) (00.80)*

AHA: 4Q, '05, 117

00.83 Revision of knee replacement, patellar component BI

EXCLUDES *revision of knee replacement, total (all components) (00.80)*

00.84 Revision of total knee replacement, tibial insert (liner) BI

Replacement of tibial insert (liner)

EXCLUDES *that with replacement of tibial component (tibial baseplate and liner) (00.81)*

● **00.85 Resurfacing hip, total, acetabulum and femoral head** BI

Hip resurfacing arthroplasty, total

● **00.86 Resurfacing hip, partial, femoral head** BI

Hip resurfacing arthroplasty, NOS

Hip resurfacing arthroplasty, partial, femoral head

EXCLUDES *that with resurfacing of acetabulum (00.85)*

● **00.87 Resurfacing hip, partial, acetabulum** BI

Hip resurfacing arthroplasty, partial, acetabulum

EXCLUDES *that with resurfacing of femoral head (00.85)*

✓4th 00.9 Other procedures and interventions

00.91 Transplant from live related donor

Code also organ transplant procedure

00.92 Transplant from live non-related donor

Code also organ transplant procedure

AHA: 4Q, '04, 117

00.93 Transplant from cadaver

Code also organ transplant procedure

1. OPERATIONS ON THE NERVOUS SYSTEM (01-05)

✓3rd **01 Incision and excision of skull, brain, and cerebral meninges**

✓4th **01.0 Cranial puncture**

01.01 Cisternal puncture
Cisternal aspiration
Cisternal tap
EXCLUDES *pneumocisternogram (87.02)*
DEF: Needle insertion through subarachnoid space to withdraw cerebrospinal fluid.

01.02 Ventriculopuncture through previously implanted catheter
Puncture of ventricular shunt tubing
DEF: Piercing of artificial, fluid-diverting tubing in the brain for withdrawal of cerebrospinal fluid.

01.09 Other cranial puncture
Aspiration of:
subarachnoid space
subdural space
Cranial aspiration NOS
Puncture of anterior fontanel
Subdural tap (through fontanel)

✓4th **01.1 Diagnostic procedures on skull, brain, and cerebral meninges**

01.11 Closed [percutaneous] [needle] biopsy of cerebral meninges
Burr hole approach
DEF: Needle excision of tissue sample through skin into cerebral membranes; no other procedure performed.

01.12 Open biopsy of cerebral meninges
DEF: Open surgical excision of tissue sample from cerebral membrane.

01.13 Closed [percutaneous] [needle] biopsy of brain
Burr hole approach
Stereotactic method
AHA: M-A, '87, 9
DEF: Removal by needle of brain tissue sample through skin.

01.14 Open biopsy of brain
DEF: Open surgical excision of brain tissue sample.

01.15 Biopsy of skull

01.18 Other diagnostic procedures on brain and cerebral meninges
EXCLUDES *cerebral:*
arteriography (88.41)
thermography (88.81)
contrast radiogram of brain (87.01-87.02)
echoencephalogram (88.71)
electroencephalogram (89.14)
microscopic examination of specimen from nervous system and of spinal fluid (90.01-90.09)
neurologic examination (89.13)
phlebography of head and neck (88.61)
pneumoencephalogram (87.01)
radioisotope scan:
cerebral (92.11)
head NEC (92.12)
tomography of head:
C.A.T. scan (87.03)
other (87.04)
AHA: 3Q, '98, 12

01.19 Other diagnostic procedures on skull
EXCLUDES *transillumination of skull (89.16)*
x-ray of skull (87.17)

✓4th **01.2 Craniotomy and craniectomy**
EXCLUDES *decompression of skull fracture (02.02)*
exploration of orbit (16.01-16.09)
that as operative approach — omit code
AHA: 1Q, '91, 1
DEF: Craniotomy: Incision into skull.
DEF: Craniectomy: Excision of part of skull.

01.21 Incision and drainage of cranial sinus
DEF: Incision for drainage, including drainage of air cavities in skull bones.

01.22 Removal of intracranial neurostimulator lead(s)
Code also any removal of neurostimulator pulse generator (86.05)
EXCLUDES *removal with synchronous replacement (02.93)*

01.23 Reopening of craniotomy site
DEF: Reopening of skull incision.

01.24 Other craniotomy
Cranial:
decompression
exploration
trephination
Craniotomy NOS
Craniotomy with removal of:
epidural abscess
extradural hematoma
foreign body of skull
EXCLUDES *removal of foreign body with incision into brain (01.39)*
AHA: 2Q, '91, 14

01.25 Other craniectomy
Debridement of skull NOS
Sequestrectomy of skull
EXCLUDES *debridement of compound fracture of skull (02.02)*
strip craniectomy (02.01)
AHA: ▶1Q, '06, 6◀

▲ **01.26 Insertion of catheter(s) into cranial cavity or tissue**
Code also any concomitant procedure (e.g. resection (01.59))
EXCLUDES ▶ *placement of intracerebral catheter(s) via burr hole(s) (01.28)*◀
AHA: 4Q, '05, 117-118

▲ **01.27 Removal of catheter(s) from cranial cavity or tissue**
AHA: 4Q, '05, 117-118

● **01.28 Placement of intracerebral catheter(s) via burr hole(s)**
Convection enhanced delivery
Stereotactic placement of intracerebral catheter(s)
Code also infusion of medication
EXCLUDES *insertion of catheter(s) into cranial cavity or tissue(s) (01.26)*

✓4th **01.3 Incision of brain and cerebral meninges**

01.31 Incision of cerebral meninges
Drainage of:
intracranial hygroma
subarachnoid abscess (cerebral)
subdural empyema

01.32 Lobotomy and tractotomy
Division of:
brain tissue
cerebral tracts
Percutaneous (radiofrequency) cingulotomy
DEF: Lobotomy: Incision of nerve fibers of brain lobe, usually frontal.
DEF: Tractotomy: Severing of a nerve fiber group to relieve pain.

01.39 Other incision of brain
Amygdalohippocampotomy
Drainage of intracerebral hematoma
Incision of brain NOS
EXCLUDES *division of cortical adhesions (02.91)*

✓4th **01.4 Operations on thalamus and globus pallidus**

01.41 Operations on thalamus

Chemothalamectomy Thalamotomy

EXCLUDES *that by stereotactic radiosurgery (92.30-92.39)*

01.42 Operations on globus pallidus

Pallidoansectomy Pallidotomy

EXCLUDES *that by stereotactic radiosurgery (92.30-92.39)*

✓4th **01.5 Other excision or destruction of brain and meninges**

AHA: 4Q, '93, 33

01.51 Excision of lesion or tissue of cerebral meninges

Decortication, Resection, Stripping of subdural membrane } of (cerebral) meninges

EXCLUDES *biopsy of cerebral meninges (01.11-01.12)*

01.52 Hemispherectomy

DEF: Removal of one half of the brain. Most often performed for malignant brain tumors or intractable epilepsy.

01.53 Lobectomy of brain

DEF: Excision of a brain lobe.

01.59 Other excision or destruction of lesion or tissue of brain

Curettage of brain
Debridement of brain
Marsupialization of brain cyst
Transtemporal (mastoid) excision of brain tumor

EXCLUDES *biopsy of brain (01.13-01.14)*
that by stereotactic radiosurgery (92.30-92.39)

AHA: 4Q, '05, 118; 3Q, '99, 7; 1Q, '99, 9; 3Q, '98, 12; 1Q, '98, 6

01.6 Excision of lesion of skull

Removal of granulation tissue of cranium

EXCLUDES *biopsy of skull (01.15)*
sequestrectomy (01.25)

✓3rd **02 Other operations on skull, brain, and cerebral meninges**

✓4th **02.0 Cranioplasty**

EXCLUDES *that with synchronous repair of encephalocele (02.12)*

02.01 Opening of cranial suture

Linear craniectomy
Strip craniectomy

DEF: Opening of the lines of junction between the bones of the skull for removal of strips of skull bone.

02.02 Elevation of skull fracture fragments

Debridement of compound fracture of skull
Decompression of skull fracture
Reduction of skull fracture
Code also any synchronous debridement of brain (01.59)

EXCLUDES *debridement of skull NOS (01.25)*
removal of granulation tissue of cranium (01.6)

02.03 Formation of cranial bone flap

Repair of skull with flap

02.04 Bone graft to skull

Pericranial graft (autogenous) (heterogenous)

02.05 Insertion of skull plate

Replacement of skull plate

02.06 Other cranial osteoplasty

Repair of skull NOS
Revision of bone flap of skull

AHA: ▶1Q, '06, 6◀ 1Q, '05, 11; 3Q, '98, 9

DEF: Plastic surgery repair of skull bones.

02.07 Removal of skull plate

EXCLUDES *removal with synchronous replacement (02.05)*

✓4th **02.1 Repair of cerebral meninges**

EXCLUDES *marsupialization of cerebral lesion (01.59)*

02.11 Simple suture of dura mater of brain

02.12 Other repair of cerebral meninges

Closure of fistula of cerebrospinal fluid
Dural graft
Repair of encephalocele including synchronous cranioplasty
Repair of meninges NOS
Subdural patch

02.13 Ligation of meningeal vessel

Ligation of:
longitudinal sinus
middle meningeal artery

02.14 Choroid plexectomy

Cauterization of choroid plexus

DEF: Excision or destruction of the ependymal cells that form the membrane lining in the third, fourth, and lateral ventricles of the brain and secrete cerebrospinal fluid.

02.2 Ventriculostomy

Anastomosis of ventricle to:
cervical subarachnoid space
cisterna magna
Insertion of Holter valve
Ventriculocisternal intubation

DEF: Surgical creation of an opening of ventricle; often performed to drain cerebrospinal fluid in treating hydrocephalus.

✓4th **02.3 Extracranial ventricular shunt**

INCLUDES that with insertion of valve

DEF: Placement of shunt or creation of artificial passage leading from skull cavities to site outside skull to relieve excess cerebrospinal fluid created in the chorioid plexuses of the third and fourth ventricles of the brain.

02.31 Ventricular shunt to structure in head and neck

Ventricle to nasopharynx shunt
Ventriculomastoid anastomosis

02.32 Ventricular shunt to circulatory system

Ventriculoatrial anastomosis
Ventriculocaval shunt

02.33 Ventricular shunt to thoracic cavity

Ventriculopleural anastomosis

02.34 Ventricular shunt to abdominal cavity and organs

Ventriculocholecystostomy
Ventriculoperitoneostomy

02.35 Ventricular shunt to urinary system

Ventricle to ureter shunt

02.39 Other operations to establish drainage of ventricle

Ventricle to bone marrow shunt
Ventricular shunt to extracranial site NEC

✓4th **02.4 Revision, removal, and irrigation of ventricular shunt**

EXCLUDES *revision of distal catheter of ventricular shunt (54.95)*

02.41 Irrigation and exploration of ventricular shunt

Exploration of ventriculoperitoneal shunt at ventricular site
Re-programming of ventriculoperitoneal shunt

02.42 Replacement of ventricular shunt
Reinsertion of Holter valve
Replacement of ventricular catheter
Revision of ventriculoperitoneal shunt at ventricular site
AHA: N-D, '86, 8

02.43 Removal of ventricular shunt
AHA: N-D, '86, 8

✓4th **02.9 Other operations on skull, brain, and cerebral meninges**
EXCLUDES *operations on:*
pineal gland (07.17, 07.51-07.59)
pituitary gland [hypophysis] (07.13-07.15, 07.61-07.79)

02.91 Lysis of cortical adhesions
DEF: Breaking up of fibrous structures in brain outer layer.

02.92 Repair of brain

02.93 Implantation or replacement of intracranial neurostimulator lead(s)
Implantation, insertion, placement, or replacement of intracranial:
brain pacemaker [neuropacemaker]
depth electrodes
epidural pegs
electroencephalographic receiver
foramen ovale electrodes
intracranial electrostimulator
subdural grids
subdural strips
Code also any insertion of neurostimulator pulse generator ▶(86.94-86.98)◀
AHA: 4Q, '97, 57; 4Q, '92, 28

02.94 Insertion or replacement of skull tongs or halo traction device
AHA: 3Q, '01, 8; 3Q, '96, 14
DEF: Halo traction device: Metal or plastic band encircles the head or neck secured to the skull with four pins and attached to a metal chest plate by rods; provides support and stability for the head and neck.
DEF: Skull tongs: Device inserted into each side of the skull used to apply parallel traction to the long axis of the cervical spine.

02.95 Removal of skull tongs or halo traction device

02.96 Insertion of sphenoidal electrodes
AHA: 4Q, '92, 28

02.99 Other
EXCLUDES *chemical shock therapy (94.24)*
electroshock therapy:
subconvulsive (94.26)
other (94.27)

Laminotomy with Decompression

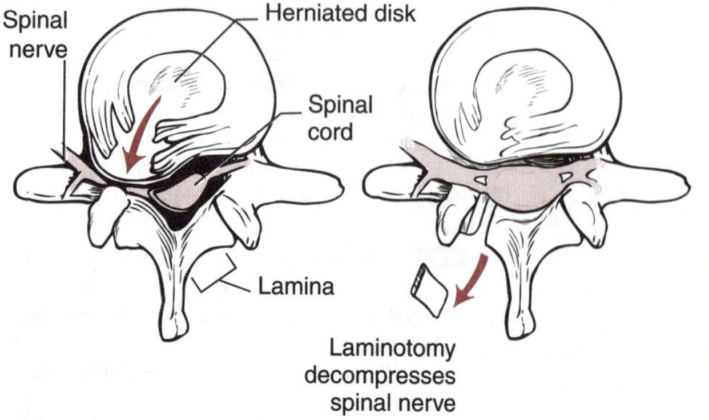

✓3rd **03 Operations on spinal cord and spinal canal structures**
Code also any application or administration of an adhesion barrier substance (99.77)

✓4th **03.0 Exploration and decompression of spinal canal structures**

03.01 Removal of foreign body from spinal canal

03.02 Reopening of laminectomy site

03.09 Other exploration and decompression of spinal canal
Decompression:
laminectomy laminotomy
Expansile laminoplasty
Exploration of spinal nerve root
Foraminotomy
EXCLUDES *drainage of spinal fluid by anastomosis (03.71-03.79)*
laminectomy with excision of intervertebral disc (80.51)
spinal tap (03.31)
that as operative approach — omit code
AHA: 3Q, '04, 6; 4Q, '02, 109; 2Q, '02, 15; 4Q, '99, 14; 2Q, '97, 6; 2Q, '95, 9; 2Q, '95, 10; 2Q, '90, 22; S-Q, '86, 12
DEF: Decompression of spinal canal: Excision of bone pieces, hematoma or other lesion to relieve spinal cord pressure.
DEF: Expansile laminoplasty: Lamina is incised at the level of the pedicle to relieve pressure; no tissue is excised.
DEF: Foraminotomy: Removal of root opening between vertebrae to relieve nerve root pressure.

03.1 Division of intraspinal nerve root
Rhizotomy
DEF: Rhizotomy: Surgical severing of spinal nerve roots within spinal canal for pain relief.

✓4th **03.2 Chordotomy**
DEF: Chordotomy: Surgical cutting of lateral spinothalamic tract of spinal cord to relieve pain.

03.21 Percutaneous chordotomy
Stereotactic chordotomy
DEF: Percutaneous chordotomy: Insertion of hollow needle through skin to interrupt spinal nerve root.
DEF: Stereotactic chordotomy: Use of three-dimensional imaging to locate spinal nerve root for surgical interruption.

03.29 Other chordotomy
Chordotomy NOS
Tractotomy (one-stage) (two-stage) of spinal cord
Transection of spinal cord tracts
DEF: Tractotomy (one stage) (two stages) of the spinal cord: Surgical incision or severing of a nerve tract of spinal cord.
DEF: Transection of spinal cord tracts: Use of transverse incision to divide spinal nerve root.

✓4th **03.3 Diagnostic procedures on spinal cord and spinal canal structures**

03.31 Spinal tap
Lumbar puncture for removal of dye
EXCLUDES *lumbar puncture for injection of dye [myelogram] (87.21)*
AHA: 2Q, '90, 22
DEF: Puncture into lumbar subarachnoid space to tap cerebrospinal fluid.

03.32 Biopsy of spinal cord or spinal meninges

03.39 Other diagnostic procedures on spinal cord and spinal canal structures

EXCLUDES *microscopic examination of specimen from nervous system or of spinal fluid (90.01-90.09)*
x-ray of spine (87.21-87.29)

03.4 Excision or destruction of lesion of spinal cord or spinal meninges

Curettage, Debridement, Marsupialization of cyst, Resection } of spinal cord or spinal meninges

EXCLUDES *biopsy of spinal cord or meninges (03.32)*

AHA: 3Q, '95, 5

✓4th **03.5 Plastic operations on spinal cord structures**

03.51 Repair of spinal meningocele

Repair of meningocele NOS

DEF: Restoration of hernial protrusion of spinal meninges through defect in vertebral column.

03.52 Repair of spinal myelomeningocele

DEF: Restoration of hernial protrusion of spinal cord and meninges through defect in vertebral column.

03.53 Repair of vertebral fracture

Elevation of spinal bone fragments
Reduction of fracture of vertebrae
Removal of bony spicules from spinal canal

EXCLUDES *kyphoplasty (81.66)*
vertebroplasty (81.65)

AHA: 4Q, '04, 126; 2Q, '02, 14; 4Q, '99, 11, 12, 13; 3Q, '96, 14

03.59 Other repair and plastic operations on spinal cord structures

Repair of:
- diastematomyelia
- spina bifida NOS
- spinal cord NOS
- spinal meninges NOS
- vertebral arch defect

03.6 Lysis of adhesions of spinal cord and nerve roots

AHA: 2Q, '98, 18

✓4th **03.7 Shunt of spinal theca**

INCLUDES that with valve

DEF: Surgical passage created from spinal cord dura mater to another channel.

03.71 Spinal subarachnoid-peritoneal shunt

03.72 Spinal subarachnoid-ureteral shunt

03.79 Other shunt of spinal theca

Lumbar-subarachnoid shunt NOS
Pleurothecal anastomosis
Salpingothecal anastomosis

AHA: 1Q, '97, 7

03.8 Injection of destructive agent into spinal canal

✓4th **03.9 Other operations on spinal cord and spinal canal structures**

03.90 Insertion of catheter into spinal canal for infusion of therapeutic or palliative substances

Insertion of catheter into epidural, subarachnoid, or subdural space of spine with intermittent or continuous infusion of drug (with creation of any reservoir)

Code also any implantation of infusion pump (86.06)

03.91 Injection of anesthetic into spinal canal for analgesia

EXCLUDES *that for operative anesthesia — omit code*

AHA: 3Q, '00, 15; 1Q, '99, 8; 2Q, '98, 18

Lumbar Spinal Puncture

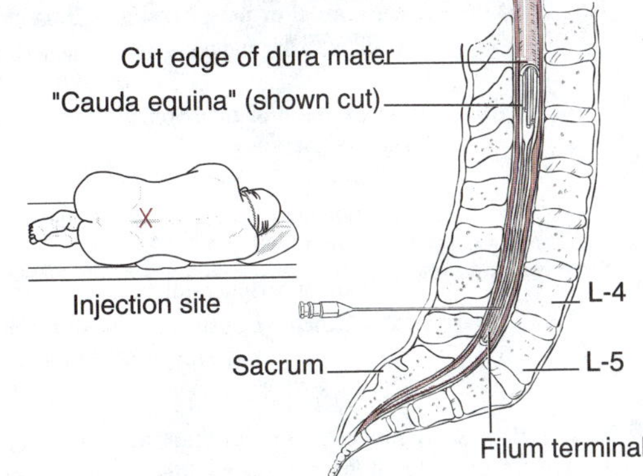

03.92 Injection of other agent into spinal canal

Intrathecal injection of steroid
Subarachnoid perfusion of refrigerated saline

EXCLUDES *injection of:*
contrast material for myelogram (87.21)
destructive agent into spinal canal (03.8)

AHA: 2Q, '03, 6; 3Q, '00, 15; 2Q, '98, 18

03.93 Implantation or replacement of spinal neurostimulator lead(s)

Code also any insertion of neurostimulator pulse generator ▶(86.94-86.98)◀

AHA: 1Q, '00, 19

03.94 Removal of spinal neurostimulator lead(s)

Code also any removal of neurostimulator pulse generator (86.05)

03.95 Spinal blood patch

DEF: Injection of blood into epidural space to patch hole in outer spinal membrane when blood clots.

03.96 Percutaneous denervation of facet

03.97 Revision of spinal thecal shunt

AHA: 2Q, '99, 4

03.98 Removal of spinal thecal shunt

03.99 Other

✓3rd **04 Operations on cranial and peripheral nerves**

✓4th **04.0 Incision, division, and excision of cranial and peripheral nerves**

EXCLUDES *opticociliary neurectomy (12.79)*
sympathetic ganglionectomy (05.21-05.29)

04.01 Excision of acoustic neuroma

That by craniotomy

EXCLUDES *that by stereotactic radiosurgery (92.3)*

AHA: 2Q, '98, 20; 2Q, '95, 8; 4Q, '92, 26

04.02 Division of trigeminal nerve

Retrogasserian neurotomy

DEF: Transection of sensory root fibers of trigeminal nerve for relief of trigeminal neuralgia.

04.03 Division or crushing of other cranial and peripheral nerves

EXCLUDES *that of:*
glossopharyngeal nerve (29.92)
laryngeal nerve (31.91)
nerves to adrenal glands (07.42)
phrenic nerve for collapse of lung (33.31)
vagus nerve (44.00-44.03)

AHA: 2Q, '98, 20

04.04 Other incision of cranial and peripheral nerves

04.05 Gasserian ganglionectomy

04.06 Other cranial or peripheral ganglionectomy

EXCLUDES *sympathetic ganglionectomy (05.21-05.29)*

04.07 Other excision or avulsion of cranial and peripheral nerves

Curettage / Debridement / Resection } of peripheral nerve

Excision of peripheral neuroma [Morton's]

EXCLUDES *biopsy of cranial or peripheral nerve (04.11-04.12)*

AHA: 2Q, '95, 8; 4Q, '92, 26

✓4th **04.1 Diagnostic procedures on peripheral nervous system**

04.11 Closed [percutaneous] [needle] biopsy of cranial or peripheral nerve or ganglion

04.12 Open biopsy of cranial or peripheral nerve or ganglion

04.19 Other diagnostic procedures on cranial and peripheral nerves and ganglia

EXCLUDES *microscopic examination of specimen from nervous system (90.01-90.09)*
neurologic examination (89.13)

04.2 Destruction of cranial and peripheral nerves

Destruction of cranial or peripheral nerves by:
cryoanalgesia
injection of neurolytic agent
radiofrequency
Radiofrequency ablation

AHA: 3Q, '02, 10, 11; 4Q, '95, 74

DEF: Radiofrequency ablation: High frequency radio waves are applied to injure the nerve resulting in interruption of the pain signal.

04.3 Suture of cranial and peripheral nerves

✓4th **04.4 Lysis of adhesions and decompression of cranial and peripheral nerves**

04.41 Decompression of trigeminal nerve root

04.42 Other cranial nerve decompression

AHA: 3Q, '02, 13

04.43 Release of carpal tunnel

04.44 Release of tarsal tunnel

04.49 Other peripheral nerve or ganglion decompression or lysis of adhesions

Peripheral nerve neurolysis NOS

04.5 Cranial or peripheral nerve graft

Release of Carpal Tunnel

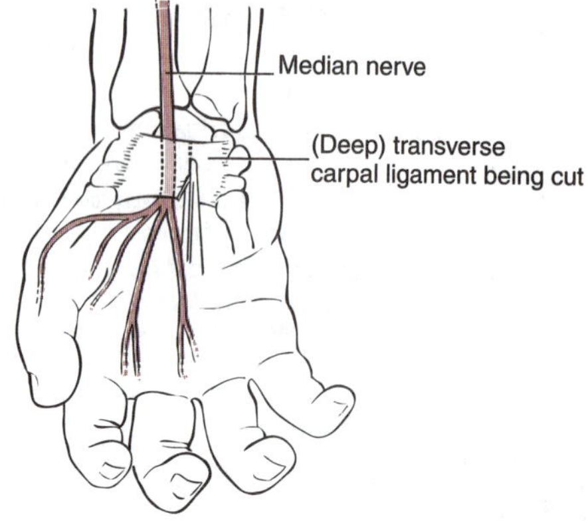

04.6 Transposition of cranial and peripheral nerves

Nerve transplantation

DEF: Relocation of cranial or peripheral nerves without detaching or severing them.

✓4th **04.7 Other cranial or peripheral neuroplasty**

04.71 Hypoglossal-facial anastomosis

DEF: Surgical connection of hypoglossal nerve to facial nerve.

04.72 Accessory-facial anastomosis

DEF: Surgical connection of accessory nerve to facial nerve.

04.73 Accessory-hypoglossal anastomosis

DEF: Surgical connection of accessory nerve to hypoglossal nerve.

04.74 Other anastomosis of cranial or peripheral nerve

04.75 Revision of previous repair of cranial and peripheral nerves

04.76 Repair of old traumatic injury of cranial and peripheral nerves

04.79 Other neuroplasty

AHA: ▶1Q, '06, 11◀

✓4th **04.8 Injection into peripheral nerve**

EXCLUDES *destruction of nerve (by injection of neurolytic agent) (04.2)*

04.80 Peripheral nerve injection, not otherwise specified

04.81 Injection of anesthetic into peripheral nerve for analgesia

EXCLUDES *that for operative anesthesia — omit code*

AHA: 1Q, '00, 7

04.89 Injection of other agent, except neurolytic

EXCLUDES *injection of neurolytic agent (04.2)*

✓4th **04.9 Other operations on cranial and peripheral nerves**

04.91 Neurectasis

DEF: Surgical stretching of peripheral or cranial nerve.

04.92 Implantation or replacement of peripheral neurostimulator lead(s)

Code also any insertion of neurostimulator pulse generator ▶(86.94-86.98)◀

AHA: 2Q, '04, 7; 3Q, '01, 16; 2Q, '00, 22; 3Q, '96, 12

DEF: Placement of or removal and replacement of neurostimulator lead(s) during the same episode.

04.93 Removal of peripheral neurostimulator lead(s)

Code also any removal of neurostimulator pulse generator (86.05)

AHA: 3Q, '01, 16

04.99 Other

✓3rd **05 Operations on sympathetic nerves or ganglia**

EXCLUDES *paracervical uterine denervation (69.3)*

05.0 Division of sympathetic nerve or ganglion

EXCLUDES *that of nerves to adrenal glands (07.42)*

✓4th **05.1 Diagnostic procedures on sympathetic nerves or ganglia**

05.11 Biopsy of sympathetic nerve or ganglion

05.19 Other diagnostic procedures on sympathetic nerves or ganglia

✓4th **05.2 Sympathectomy**

DEF: Sympathectomy: Division of nerve pathway at a specific site of a sympathetic nerve.

05.21 Sphenopalatine ganglionectomy

05.22 Cervical sympathectomy

05.23 Lumbar sympathectomy
DEF: Excision, resection of lumber chain nerve group to relieve causalgia, Raynaud's disease, or lower extremity thromboangiitis.

05.24 Presacral sympathectomy
DEF: Excision or resection of hypogastric nerve network.

05.25 Periarterial sympathectomy
DEF: Removal of arterial sheath containing sympathetic nerve fibers.

05.29 Other sympathectomy and ganglionectomy
Excision or avulsion of sympathetic nerve NOS
Sympathetic ganglionectomy NOS
EXCLUDES *biopsy of sympathetic nerve or ganglion (05.11)*
opticociliary neurectomy (12.79)
periarterial sympathectomy (05.25)
tympanosympathectomy (20.91)

✓4th **05.3 Injection into sympathetic nerve or ganglion**
EXCLUDES *injection of ciliary sympathetic ganglion (12.79)*

05.31 Injection of anesthetic into sympathetic nerve for analgesia

05.32 Injection of neurolytic agent into sympathetic nerve

05.39 Other injection into sympathetic nerve or ganglion

✓4th **05.8 Other operations on sympathetic nerves or ganglia**

05.81 Repair of sympathetic nerve or ganglion

05.89 Other

05.9 Other operations on nervous system

2. OPERATIONS ON THE ENDOCRINE SYSTEM (06-07)

✓3rd **06 Operations on thyroid and parathyroid glands**

INCLUDES incidental resection of hyoid bone

✓4th **06.0 Incision of thyroid field**

EXCLUDES *division of isthmus (06.91)*

06.01 Aspiration of thyroid field

Percutaneous or needle drainage of thyroid field

EXCLUDES *aspiration biopsy of thyroid (06.11)*
drainage by incision (06.09)
postoperative aspiration of field (06.02)

06.02 Reopening of wound of thyroid field

Reopening of wound of thyroid field for:
- control of (postoperative) hemorrhage
- examination
- exploration
- removal of hematoma

06.09 Other incision of thyroid field

Drainage of hematoma
Drainage of thyroglossal tract
Exploration:
- neck
- thyroid (field)

Removal of foreign body
Thyroidotomy NOS
} by incision

EXCLUDES *postoperative exploration (06.02)*
removal of hematoma by aspiration (06.01)

✓4th **06.1 Diagnostic procedures on thyroid and parathyroid glands**

06.11 Closed [percutaneous] [needle] biopsy of thyroid gland

Aspiration biopsy of thyroid

DEF: Insertion of needle-type device for removal of thyroid tissue sample.

06.12 Open biopsy of thyroid gland

06.13 Biopsy of parathyroid gland

06.19 Other diagnostic procedures on thyroid and parathyroid glands

EXCLUDES *radioisotope scan of:*
parathyroid (92.13)
thyroid (92.01)
soft tissue x-ray of thyroid field (87.09)

Thyroidectomy

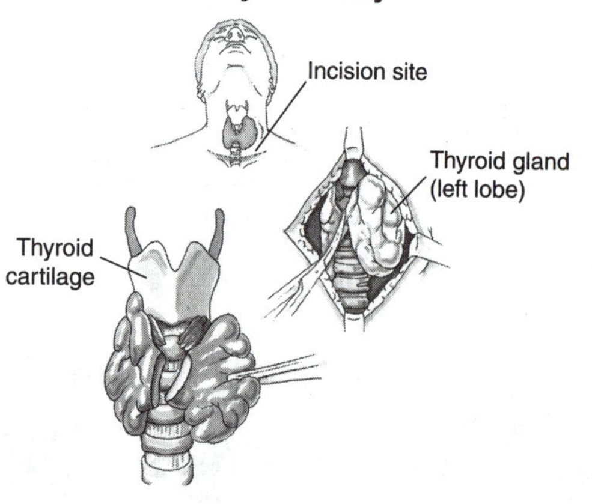

06.2 Unilateral thyroid lobectomy

Complete removal of one lobe of thyroid (with removal of isthmus or portion of other lobe)
Hemithyroidectomy

EXCLUDES *partial substernal thyroidectomy (06.51)*

DEF: Excision of thyroid lobe.

✓4th **06.3 Other partial thyroidectomy**

06.31 Excision of lesion of thyroid

EXCLUDES *biopsy of thyroid (06.11-06.12)*

DEF: Removal of growth on thyroid.

06.39 Other

Isthmectomy
Partial thyroidectomy NOS

EXCLUDES *partial substernal thyroidectomy (06.51)*

06.4 Complete thyroidectomy

EXCLUDES *complete substernal thyroidectomy (06.52)*
that with laryngectomy (30.3-30.4)

✓4th **06.5 Substernal thyroidectomy**

DEF: Removal of thyroid tissue below breastbone.

06.50 Substernal thyroidectomy, not otherwise specified

06.51 Partial substernal thyroidectomy

06.52 Complete substernal thyroidectomy

06.6 Excision of lingual thyroid

Excision of thyroid by:
- submental route
- transoral route

DEF: Excision of thyroid tissue at base of tongue.

06.7 Excision of thyroglossal duct or tract

✓4th **06.8 Parathyroidectomy**

DEF: Removal of parathyroid glands.

06.81 Complete parathyroidectomy

06.89 Other parathyroidectomy

Parathyroidectomy NOS
Partial parathyroidectomy

EXCLUDES *biopsy of parathyroid (06.13)*

✓4th **06.9 Other operations on thyroid (region) and parathyroid**

06.91 Division of thyroid isthmus

Transection of thyroid isthmus

DEF: Cutting or division of tissue at narrowest point of thyroid.

06.92 Ligation of thyroid vessels

06.93 Suture of thyroid gland

06.94 Thyroid tissue reimplantation

Autotransplantation of thyroid tissue

DEF: Placement of thyroid tissue graft into functional site.

DEF: Autotransplantation of thyroid tissue: Tissue graft from patient thyroid tissue to another site on thyroid.

06.95 Parathyroid tissue reimplantation

Autotransplantation of parathyroid tissue

DEF: Placement of parathyroid tissue graft into functional site.

DEF: Autotransplantation of parathyroid tissue: Use of patient parathyroid tissue for graft.

06.98 Other operations on thyroid glands

06.99 Other operations on parathyroid glands

✓3rd 07 Operations on other endocrine glands

INCLUDES operations on:
adrenal glands
pineal gland
pituitary gland
thymus

EXCLUDES *operations on:*
aortic and carotid bodies (39.8)
ovaries (65.0-65.99)
pancreas (52.01-52.99)
testes (62.0-62.99)

✓4th 07.0 Exploration of adrenal field

EXCLUDES *incision of adrenal (gland) (07.41)*

07.00 Exploration of adrenal field, not otherwise specified

07.01 Unilateral exploration of adrenal field

DEF: Investigation of one adrenal gland for diagnostic reasons.

07.02 Bilateral exploration of adrenal field

DEF: Investigation of both adrenal glands for diagnostic reasons.

✓4th 07.1 Diagnostic procedures on adrenal glands, pituitary gland, pineal gland, and thymus

07.11 Closed [percutaneous] [needle] biopsy of adrenal gland

07.12 Open biopsy of adrenal gland

07.13 Biopsy of pituitary gland, transfrontal approach

DEF: Excision of pituitary gland tissue for exam through frontal bone.

07.14 Biopsy of pituitary gland, transsphenoidal approach

DEF: Excision of pituitary gland tissue for exam through sphenoid bone.

07.15 Biopsy of pituitary gland, unspecified approach

07.16 Biopsy of thymus

07.17 Biopsy of pineal gland

07.19 Other diagnostic procedures on adrenal glands, pituitary gland, pineal gland, and thymus

EXCLUDES *microscopic examination of specimen from endocrine gland (90.11-90.19)*
radioisotope scan of pituitary gland (92.11)

✓4th 07.2 Partial adrenalectomy

07.21 Excision of lesion of adrenal gland

EXCLUDES *biopsy of adrenal gland (07.11-07.12)*

07.22 Unilateral adrenalectomy

Adrenalectomy NOS

EXCLUDES *excision of remaining adrenal gland (07.3)*

DEF: Excision of one adrenal gland.

07.29 Other partial adrenalectomy

Partial adrenalectomy NOS

AHA: ▶2Q, '05, 4◀

07.3 Bilateral adrenalectomy

Excision of remaining adrenal gland

EXCLUDES *bilateral partial adrenalectomy (07.29)*

✓4th 07.4 Other operations on adrenal glands, nerves, and vessels

07.41 Incision of adrenal gland

Adrenalotomy (with drainage)

07.42 Division of nerves to adrenal glands

07.43 Ligation of adrenal vessels

07.44 Repair of adrenal gland

07.45 Reimplantation of adrenal tissue

Autotransplantation of adrenal tissue

DEF: Autotransplantation of adrenal tissue: Use of tissue graft from the patient's own body.

07.49 Other

✓4th 07.5 Operations on pineal gland

07.51 Exploration of pineal field

EXCLUDES *that with incision of pineal gland (07.52)*

07.52 Incision of pineal gland

07.53 Partial excision of pineal gland

EXCLUDES *biopsy of pineal gland (07.17)*

07.54 Total excision of pineal gland

Pinealectomy (complete) (total)

07.59 Other operations on pineal gland

✓4th 07.6 Hypophysectomy

DEF: Excision, destruction of pituitary gland.

07.61 Partial excision of pituitary gland, transfrontal approach

Cryohypophysectomy, partial
Division of hypophyseal stalk
Excision of lesion of pituitary [hypophysis]
Hypophysectomy, subtotal
Infundibulectomy, hypophyseal
} transfrontal approach

EXCLUDES *biopsy of pituitary gland, transfrontal approach (07.13)*

DEF: Removal of pituitary gland, partial, through frontal bone.

07.62 Partial excision of pituitary gland, transsphenoidal approach

EXCLUDES *biopsy of pituitary gland, transsphenoidal approach (07.14)*

DEF: Removal of pituitary gland, partial, through sphenoid bone.

07.63 Partial excision of pituitary gland, unspecified approach

EXCLUDES *biopsy of pituitary gland NOS (07.15)*

07.64 Total excision of pituitary gland, transfrontal approach

Ablation of pituitary by implantation (strontiumyttrium)
Cryohypophysectomy, complete
} transfrontal approach

DEF: Removal of pituitary gland, total, through frontal bone.

07.65 Total excision of pituitary gland, transsphenoidal approach

DEF: Removal of pituitary gland, total, through sphenoid bone.

07.68 Total excision of pituitary gland, other specified approach

DEF: Destroy or remove pituitary gland by a specified approach, other than those listed.

Operations on the Endocrine System

07–07.68

07.69 Total excision of pituitary gland, unspecified approach
Hypophysectomy NOS
Pituitectomy NOS

✓4th **07.7 Other operations on hypophysis**

07.71 Exploration of pituitary fossa
EXCLUDES *exploration with incision of pituitary gland (07.72)*
DEF: Exploration of region of pituitary gland.

07.72 Incision of pituitary gland
Aspiration of:
craniobuccal pouch
craniopharyngioma
hypophysis
Aspiration of:
pituitary gland
Rathke's pouch

07.79 Other
Insertion of pack into sella turcica

✓4th **07.8 Thymectomy**

07.80 Thymectomy, not otherwise specified

07.81 Partial excision of thymus
EXCLUDES *biopsy of thymus (07.16)*

07.82 Total excision of thymus

✓4th **07.9 Other operations on thymus**

07.91 Exploration of thymus field
EXCLUDES *exploration with incision of thymus (07.92)*

07.92 Incision of thymus

07.93 Repair of thymus

07.94 Transplantation of thymus
DEF: Placement of thymus tissue grafts into functional area of gland.

07.99 Other
Thymopexy

3. OPERATIONS ON THE EYE (08-16)

✓3rd **08 Operations on eyelids**

INCLUDES operations on the eyebrow

✓4th **08.0 Incision of eyelid**

08.01 Incision of lid margin

DEF: Cutting into eyelid edge.

08.02 Severing of blepharorrhaphy

DEF: Freeing of eyelids previously sutured shut.

08.09 Other incision of eyelid

✓4th **08.1 Diagnostic procedures on eyelid**

08.11 Biopsy of eyelid

08.19 Other diagnostic procedures on eyelid

✓4th **08.2 Excision or destruction of lesion or tissue of eyelid**

Code also any synchronous reconstruction (08.61-08.74)

EXCLUDES *biopsy of eyelid (08.11)*

08.20 Removal of lesion of eyelid, not otherwise specified

Removal of meibomian gland NOS

08.21 Excision of chalazion

08.22 Excision of other minor lesion of eyelid

Excision of: verruca
Excision of: wart

08.23 Excision of major lesion of eyelid, partial-thickness

Excision involving one-fourth or more of lid margin, partial-thickness

DEF: Excision of lesion not in all eyelid layers.

08.24 Excision of major lesion of eyelid, full-thickness

Excision involving one-fourth or more of lid margin, full-thickness
Wedge resection of eyelid

DEF: Excision of growth in all eyelid layers, full thickness.

08.25 Destruction of lesion of eyelid

✓4th **08.3 Repair of blepharoptosis and lid retraction**

08.31 Repair of blepharoptosis by frontalis muscle technique with suture

DEF: Correction of drooping upper eyelid with suture of frontalis muscle.

08.32 Repair of blepharoptosis by frontalis muscle technique with fascial sling

DEF: Correction of drooping upper eyelid with fascial tissue sling of frontalis muscle.

08.33 Repair of blepharoptosis by resection or advancement of levator muscle or aponeurosis

DEF: Correction of drooping upper eyelid with levator muscle, extended, cut, or by expanded tendon.

08.34 Repair of blepharoptosis by other levator muscle techniques

08.35 Repair of blepharoptosis by tarsal technique

DEF: Correction of drooping upper eyelid with tarsal muscle.

08.36 Repair of blepharoptosis by other techniques

Correction of eyelid ptosis NOS
Orbicularis oculi muscle sling for correction of blepharoptosis

08.37 Reduction of overcorrection of ptosis

DEF: Correction, release of previous plastic repair of drooping eyelid.

08.38 Correction of lid retraction

DEF: Fixing of withdrawn eyelid into normal position.

✓4th **08.4 Repair of entropion or ectropion**

08.41 Repair of entropion or ectropion by thermocauterization

DEF: Restoration of eyelid margin to normal position with heat cautery.

08.42 Repair of entropion or ectropion by suture technique

DEF: Restoration of eyelid margin to normal position by suture.

08.43 Repair of entropion or ectropion with wedge resection

DEF: Restoration of eyelid margin to normal position by removing tissue.

08.44 Repair of entropion or ectropion with lid reconstruction

DEF: Reconstruction of eyelid margin.

08.49 Other repair of entropion or ectropion

✓4th **08.5 Other adjustment of lid position**

08.51 Canthotomy

DEF: Incision into outer canthus of eye.

08.52 Blepharorrhaphy

Canthorrhaphy Tarsorrhaphy

DEF: Suture together of eyelids, partial or repair; done to shorten palpebral fissure or protect cornea.

08.59 Other

Canthoplasty NOS
Repair of epicanthal fold

✓4th **08.6 Reconstruction of eyelid with flaps or grafts**

EXCLUDES *that associated with repair of entropion and ectropion (08.44)*

08.61 Reconstruction of eyelid with skin flap or graft

DEF: Rebuild of eyelid by graft or flap method.

08.62 Reconstruction of eyelid with mucous membrane flap or graft

DEF: Rebuild of eyelid with mucous membrane by graft or flap method.

08.63 Reconstruction of eyelid with hair follicle graft

DEF: Rebuild of eyelid with hair follicle graft.

08.64 Reconstruction of eyelid with tarsoconjunctival flap

Transfer of tarsoconjunctival flap from opposing lid

DEF: Recreation of eyelid with tarsoconjunctival tissue.

08.69 Other reconstruction of eyelid with flaps or grafts

✓4th **08.7 Other reconstruction of eyelid**

EXCLUDES *that associated with repair of entropion and ectropion (08.44)*

08.70 Reconstruction of eyelid, not otherwise specified

AHA: 2Q, '96, 11

08.71 Reconstruction of eyelid involving lid margin, partial-thickness

DEF: Repair of eyelid margin not using all lid layers.

08.72 Other reconstruction of eyelid, partial-thickness

DEF: Reshape of eyelid not using all lid layers.

08.73 **Reconstruction of eyelid involving lid margin, full-thickness**
DEF: Repair of eyelid and margin using all tissue layers.

08.74 **Other reconstruction of eyelid, full-thickness**
DEF: Other repair of eyelid using all tissue layers.

4th 08.8 **Other repair of eyelid**

08.81 **Linear repair of laceration of eyelid or eyebrow**

08.82 **Repair of laceration involving lid margin, partial-thickness**
DEF: Repair of laceration not involving all layers of eyelid margin.

08.83 **Other repair of laceration of eyelid, partial thickness**
DEF: Repair of eyelid tear not involving all eyelid layers.

08.84 **Repair of laceration involving lid margin, full-thickness**
DEF: Repair of eyelid margin tear involving all margin layers.

08.85 **Other repair of laceration of eyelid, full-thickness**
DEF: Repair of eyelid tear involving all layers.

08.86 **Lower eyelid rhytidectomy**
DEF: Removal of wrinkles from lower eyelid.

08.87 **Upper eyelid rhytidectomy**
AHA: 2Q, '96, 11
DEF: Removal of wrinkles from upper eyelid.

08.89 **Other eyelid repair**
AHA: 1Q, '00, 22

4th 08.9 **Other operations on eyelids**

08.91 **Electrosurgical epilation of eyelid**
DEF: Electrical removal of eyelid hair roots.

08.92 **Cryosurgical epilation of eyelid**
DEF: Removal of eyelid hair roots by freezing.

08.93 **Other epilation of eyelid**

08.99 **Other**

3rd 09 **Operations on lacrimal system**

4th 09.0 **Incision of lacrimal gland**
Incision of lacrimal cyst (with drainage)

4th 09.1 **Diagnostic procedures on lacrimal system**

09.11 **Biopsy of lacrimal gland**

09.12 **Biopsy of lacrimal sac**

09.19 **Other diagnostic procedures on lacrimal system**
EXCLUDES *contrast dacryocystogram (87.05)*
soft tissue x-ray of nasolacrimal duct (87.09)

4th 09.2 **Excision of lesion or tissue of lacrimal gland**

09.20 **Excision of lacrimal gland, not otherwise specified**

09.21 **Excision of lesion of lacrimal gland**
EXCLUDES *biopsy of lacrimal gland (09.11)*

09.22 **Other partial dacryoadenectomy**
EXCLUDES *biopsy of lacrimal gland (09.11)*
DEF: Excision, partial, of tear gland.

09.23 **Total dacryoadenectomy**
DEF: Excision, total, of tear gland.

09.3 **Other operations on lacrimal gland**

4th 09.4 **Manipulation of lacrimal passage**
INCLUDES removal of calculus
that with dilation
EXCLUDES *contrast dacryocystogram (87.05)*

09.41 **Probing of lacrimal punctum**
DEF: Exploration of tear duct entrance with flexible rod.

09.42 **Probing of lacrimal canaliculi**
DEF: Exploration of tear duct with flexible rod.

09.43 **Probing of nasolacrimal duct**
EXCLUDES *that with insertion of tube or stent (09.44)*
DEF: Exploration of passage between tear sac and nose with flexible rod.

09.44 **Intubation of nasolacrimal duct**
Insertion of stent into nasolacrimal duct
AHA: 2Q, '94, 11

09.49 **Other manipulation of lacrimal passage**

4th 09.5 **Incision of lacrimal sac and passages**

09.51 **Incision of lacrimal punctum**

09.52 **Incision of lacrimal canaliculi**

09.53 **Incision of lacrimal sac**
DEF: Cutting into lacrimal pouch of tear gland.

09.59 **Other incision of lacrimal passages**
Incision (and drainage) of nasolacrimal duct NOS

09.6 **Excision of lacrimal sac and passage**
EXCLUDES *biopsy of lacrimal sac (09.12)*
DEF: Removal of pouch and passage of tear gland.

09.7 **Repair of canaliculus and punctum**
EXCLUDES *repair of eyelid (08.81-08.89)*

09.71 **Correction of everted punctum**
DEF: Repair of an outwardly turned tear duct entrance.

09.72 **Other repair of punctum**

09.73 **Repair of canaliculus**

4th 09.8 **Fistulization of lacrimal tract to nasal cavity**

09.81 **Dacryocystorhinostomy [DCR]**
DEF: Creation of entrance between tear gland and nasal passage for tear flow.

09.82 **Conjunctivocystorhinostomy**
Conjunctivodacryocystorhinostomy [CDCR]
EXCLUDES *that with insertion of tube or stent (09.83)*
DEF: Creation of tear drainage path from lacrimal sac to nasal cavity through conjunctiva.

09.83 **Conjunctivorhinostomy with insertion of tube or stent**
DEF: Creation of passage between eye sac membrane and nasal cavity with tube or stent.

4th 09.9 **Other operations on lacrimal system**

09.91 **Obliteration of lacrimal punctum**
DEF: Destruction, total of tear gland opening in eyelid.

09.99 **Other**
AHA: 2Q, '94, 11

3rd 10 **Operations on conjunctiva**

10.0 **Removal of embedded foreign body from conjunctiva by incision**
EXCLUDES *removal of:*
embedded foreign body without incision (98.22)
superficial foreign body (98.21)

10.1 **Other incision of conjunctiva**

✓4th **10.2 Diagnostic procedures on conjunctiva**

10.21 Biopsy of conjunctiva

10.29 Other diagnostic procedures on conjunctiva

✓4th **10.3 Excision or destruction of lesion or tissue of conjunctiva**

10.31 Excision of lesion or tissue of conjunctiva

Excision of ring of conjunctiva around cornea

EXCLUDES *biopsy of conjunctiva (10.21)*

AHA: 4Q, '00, 41; 3Q, '96, 7

DEF: Removal of growth or tissue from eye membrane.

10.32 Destruction of lesion of conjunctiva

EXCLUDES *excision of lesion (10.31)*
thermocauterization for entropion (08.41)

DEF: Destruction of eye membrane growth; not done by excision.

10.33 Other destructive procedures on conjunctiva

Removal of trachoma follicles

✓4th **10.4 Conjunctivoplasty**

DEF: Correction of conjunctiva by plastic surgery.

10.41 Repair of symblepharon with free graft

AHA: 3Q, '96, 7

10.42 Reconstruction of conjunctival cul-de-sac with free graft

EXCLUDES *revision of enucleation socket with graft (16.63)*

DEF: Rebuilding of eye membrane fold with graft of unattached tissue.

10.43 Other reconstruction of conjunctival cul-de-sac

EXCLUDES *revision of enucleation socket (16.64)*

10.44 Other free graft to conjunctiva

10.49 Other conjunctivoplasty

EXCLUDES *repair of cornea with conjunctival flap (11.53)*

10.5 Lysis of adhesions of conjunctiva and eyelid

Division of symblepharon (with insertion of conformer)

10.6 Repair of laceration of conjunctiva

EXCLUDES *that with repair of sclera (12.81)*

✓4th **10.9 Other operations on conjunctiva**

10.91 Subconjunctival injection

AHA: 3Q, '96, 7

10.99 Other

✓3rd **11 Operations on cornea**

11.0 Magnetic removal of embedded foreign body from cornea

EXCLUDES *that with incision (11.1)*

11.1 Incision of cornea

Incision of cornea for removal of foreign body

✓4th **11.2 Diagnostic procedures on cornea**

11.21 Scraping of cornea for smear or culture

11.22 Biopsy of cornea

11.29 Other diagnostic procedures on cornea

✓4th **11.3 Excision of pterygium**

11.31 Transposition of pterygium

DEF: Cutting into membranous structure extending from eye membrane to cornea and suturing it in a downward position.

11.32 Excision of pterygium with corneal graft

DEF: Surgical removal and repair of membranous structure extending from eye membrane to cornea using corneal tissue transplant.

11.39 Other excision of pterygium

✓4th **11.4 Excision or destruction of tissue or other lesion of cornea**

11.41 Mechanical removal of corneal epithelium

That by chemocauterization

EXCLUDES *that for smear or culture (11.21)*

AHA: 3Q, '02, 20

DEF: Removal of outer layer of cornea by mechanical means.

11.42 Thermocauterization of corneal lesion

DEF: Destruction of corneal lesion by electrical cautery.

11.43 Cryotherapy of corneal lesion

DEF: Destruction of corneal lesion with cold therapy.

11.49 Other removal or destruction of corneal lesion

Excision of cornea NOS

EXCLUDES *biopsy of cornea (11.22)*

✓4th **11.5 Repair of cornea**

11.51 Suture of corneal laceration

AHA: 3Q, '96, 7

11.52 Repair of postoperative wound dehiscence of cornea

DEF: Repair of ruptured postoperative corneal wound.

11.53 Repair of corneal laceration or wound with conjunctival flap

DEF: Correction corneal wound or tear with conjunctival tissue.

11.59 Other repair of cornea

✓4th **11.6 Corneal transplant**

EXCLUDES *excision of pterygium with corneal graft (11.32)*

11.60 Corneal transplant, not otherwise specified

Note: To report donor sources — see codes 00.91-00.93

Keratoplasty NOS

11.61 Lamellar keratoplasty with autograft

DEF: Restoration of sight using patient's own corneal tissue, partial thickness.

11.62 Other lamellar keratoplasty

AHA: S-O, '85, 6

DEF: Restoration of sight using donor corneal tissue, partial thickness.

11.63 Penetrating keratoplasty with autograft

Perforating keratoplasty with autograft

11.64 Other penetrating keratoplasty

Perforating keratoplasty (with homograft)

11.69 Other corneal transplant

✓4th **11.7 Other reconstructive and refractive surgery on cornea**

11.71 Keratomileusis NC

DEF: Restoration of corneal shape by removing portion of cornea, freezing, reshaping curve and reattaching it.

11.72 Keratophakia NC

DEF: Correction of eye lens loss by dissecting the central zone of the cornea and replacing it with a thickened graft of the cornea.

11.73 Keratoprosthesis

DEF: Placement of corneal artificial implant.

11.74 Thermokeratoplasty

DEF: Reshaping and reforming cornea by heat application.

11.75 **Radial keratotomy** NC

DEF: Incisions around cornea radius to correct nearsightedness.

11.76 **Epikeratophakia** NC

DEF: Repair lens loss by cornea graft sutured to central corneal zone.

11.79 **Other**

✓4th 11.9 **Other operations on cornea**

11.91 **Tattooing of cornea**

11.92 **Removal of artificial implant from cornea**

11.99 **Other**

AHA: 3Q, '02, 20

✓3rd 12 **Operations on iris, ciliary body, sclera, and anterior chamber**

EXCLUDES *operations on cornea (11.0-11.99)*

✓4th 12.0 **Removal of intraocular foreign body from anterior segment of eye**

12.00 **Removal of intraocular foreign body from anterior segment of eye, not otherwise specified**

12.01 **Removal of intraocular foreign body from anterior segment of eye with use of magnet**

12.02 **Removal of intraocular foreign body from anterior segment of eye without use of magnet**

✓4th 12.1 **Iridotomy and simple iridectomy**

EXCLUDES *iridectomy associated with:*
cataract extraction (13.11-13.69)
removal of lesion (12.41-12.42)
scleral fistulization (12.61-12.69)

12.11 **Iridotomy with transfixion**

12.12 **Other iridotomy**

Corectomy
Discission of iris
Iridotomy NOS

DEF: Corectomy: Incision into iris (also called iridectomy).

12.13 **Excision of prolapsed iris**

DEF: Removal of downwardly placed portion of iris.

12.14 **Other iridectomy**

Iridectomy (basal) (peripheral) (total)

DEF: Removal, partial or total of iris.

✓4th 12.2 **Diagnostic procedures on iris, ciliary body, sclera, and anterior chamber**

12.21 **Diagnostic aspiration of anterior chamber of eye**

DEF: Suction withdrawal of fluid from anterior eye chamber for diagnostic reasons.

12.22 **Biopsy of iris**

12.29 **Other diagnostic procedures on iris, ciliary body, sclera, and anterior chamber**

✓4th 12.3 **Iridoplasty and coreoplasty**

DEF: Correction or abnormal iris or pupil by plastic surgery.

12.31 **Lysis of goniosynechiae**

Lysis of goniosynechiae by injection of air or liquid

DEF: Freeing of fibrous structures between cornea and iris by injecting air or liquid.

12.32 **Lysis of other anterior synechiae**

Lysis of anterior synechiae:
NOS
by injection of air or liquid

12.33 **Lysis of posterior synechiae**

Lysis of iris adhesions NOS

12.34 **Lysis of corneovitreal adhesions**

DEF: Release of adhesions of cornea and vitreous body.

12.35 **Coreoplasty**

Needling of pupillary membrane

DEF: Correction of an iris defect.

12.39 **Other iridoplasty**

✓4th 12.4 **Excision or destruction of lesion of iris and ciliary body**

12.40 **Removal of lesion of anterior segment of eye, not otherwise specified**

12.41 **Destruction of lesion of iris, nonexcisional**

Destruction of lesion of iris by:
cauterization
cryotherapy
photocoagulation

12.42 **Excision of lesion of iris**

EXCLUDES *biopsy of iris (12.22)*

12.43 **Destruction of lesion of ciliary body, nonexcisional**

12.44 **Excision of lesion of ciliary body**

✓4th 12.5 **Facilitation of intraocular circulation**

12.51 **Goniopuncture without goniotomy**

DEF: Stab incision into anterior chamber of eye to relieve optic pressure.

12.52 **Goniotomy without goniopuncture**

DEF: Incision into Schlemm's canal to drain aqueous and relieve pressure.

12.53 **Goniotomy with goniopuncture**

12.54 **Trabeculotomy ab externo**

DEF: Incision into supporting connective tissue strands of eye capsule, via exterior approach.

12.55 **Cyclodialysis**

DEF: Creation of passage between anterior chamber and suprachoroidal space.

12.59 **Other facilitation of intraocular circulation**

✓4th 12.6 **Scleral fistulization**

EXCLUDES *exploratory sclerotomy (12.89)*

12.61 **Trephination of sclera with iridectomy**

DEF: Cut around sclerocornea to remove part of the iris.

12.62 **Thermocauterization of sclera with iridectomy**

DEF: Destruction of outer eyeball layer with partial excision of iris using heat.

12.63 **Iridencleisis and iridotasis**

DEF: Creation of permanent drain in iris by transposing or stretching iris tissue.

12.64 **Trabeculectomy ab externo**

DEF: Excision of supporting connective tissue strands of eye capsule, via exterior approach.

Trabeculectomy Ab Externo

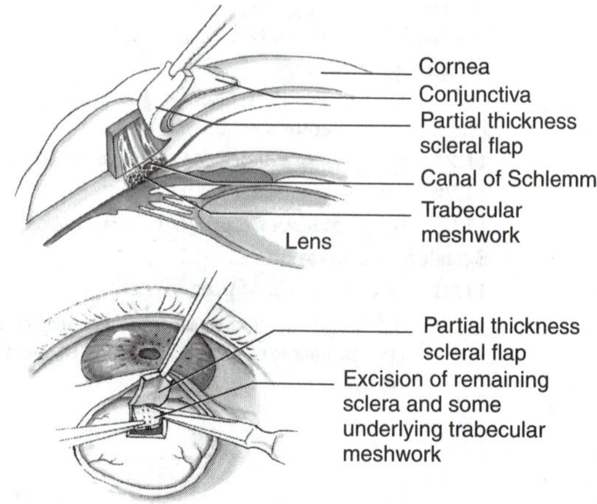

12.65 **Other scleral fistulization with iridectomy**
Holth's sclerectomy
DEF: Creation of outer eyeball layer passage with partial excision of iris.

12.66 **Postoperative revision of scleral fistulization procedure**
Revision of filtering bleb
EXCLUDES *repair of fistula (12.82)*
AHA: 2Q, '01, 16

12.69 **Other fistulizing procedure**

✓4th 12.7 **Other procedures for relief of elevated intraocular pressure**

12.71 **Cyclodiathermy**
DEF: Destruction of ciliary body tissue with heat.

12.72 **Cyclocryotherapy**
DEF: Destruction of ciliary body tissue by freezing.

12.73 **Cyclophotocoagulation**
DEF: Destruction of ciliary body tissue by high energy light source.

12.74 **Diminution of ciliary body, not otherwise specified**

12.79 **Other glaucoma procedures**
AHA: 2Q, '98, 16

✓4th 12.8 **Operations on sclera**
EXCLUDES *those associated with:*
retinal reattachment (14.41-14.59)
scleral fistulization (12.61-12.69)

12.81 **Suture of laceration of sclera**
Suture of sclera with synchronous repair of conjunctiva

12.82 **Repair of scleral fistula**
EXCLUDES *postoperative revision of scleral fistulization procedure (12.66)*

12.83 **Revision of operative wound of anterior segment, not elsewhere classified**
EXCLUDES *postoperative revision of scleral fistulization procedure (12.66)*

12.84 **Excision or destruction of lesion of sclera**

12.85 **Repair of scleral staphyloma with graft**
DEF: Repair of protruding outer eyeball layer with a graft.

12.86 **Other repair of scleral staphyloma**

12.87 **Scleral reinforcement with graft**
DEF: Restoration of outer eyeball shape with tissue graft.

12.88 **Other scleral reinforcement**

12.89 **Other operations on sclera**
Exploratory sclerotomy

✓4th 12.9 **Other operations on iris, ciliary body, and anterior chamber**

12.91 **Therapeutic evacuation of anterior chamber**
Paracentesis of anterior chamber
EXCLUDES *diagnostic aspiration (12.21)*

12.92 **Injection into anterior chamber**
Injection of:
air
liquid
medication
} into anterior chamber
AHA: J-A, '84, 1

12.93 **Removal or destruction of epithelial downgrowth from anterior chamber**
EXCLUDES *that with iridectomy (12.41-12.42)*
DEF: Excision or destruction of epithelial overgrowth in anterior eye chamber.

12.97 **Other operations on iris**

12.98 **Other operations on ciliary body**

12.99 **Other operations on anterior chamber**

✓3rd 13 **Operations on lens**

✓4th 13.0 **Removal of foreign body from lens**
EXCLUDES *removal of pseudophakos (13.8)*

13.00 **Removal of foreign body from lens, not otherwise specified**

13.01 **Removal of foreign body from lens with use of magnet**

13.02 **Removal of foreign body from lens without use of magnet**

✓4th 13.1 **Intracapsular extraction of lens**
Code also any synchronous insertion of pseudophakos (13.71)
AHA: S-O, '85, 6

13.11 **Intracapsular extraction of lens by temporal inferior route**
DEF: Extraction of lens and capsule via anterior approach through outer side of eyeball.

13.19 **Other intracapsular extraction of lens**
Cataract extraction NOS
Cryoextraction of lens
Erysiphake extraction of cataract
Extraction of lens NOS

13.2 **Extracapsular extraction of lens by linear extraction technique**
AHA: S-O, '85, 6
DEF: Excision of lens without the posterior capsule at junction between the cornea and outer eyeball layer by means of a linear incision.

13.3 **Extracapsular extraction of lens by simple aspiration (and irrigation) technique**
Irrigation of traumatic cataract
AHA: S-O, '85, 6
DEF: Removal of lens without the posterior capsule by suctioning and flushing out the area.

✓4th 13.4 **Extracapsular extraction of lens by fragmentation and aspiration technique**
AHA: S-O, '85, 6
DEF: Removal of lens after division into smaller pieces with posterior capsule left intact.

13.41 **Phacoemulsification and aspiration of cataract**
AHA: 3Q, '96, 4; 1Q, '94, 16

13.42 **Mechanical phacofragmentation and aspiration of cataract by posterior route**
Code also any synchronous vitrectomy (14.74)

Extraction of Lens (with insertion of intraocular lens prosthesis)

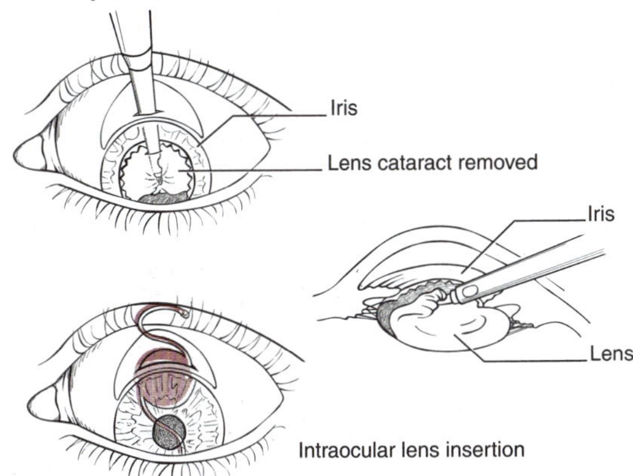

Laser Surgery (YAG)

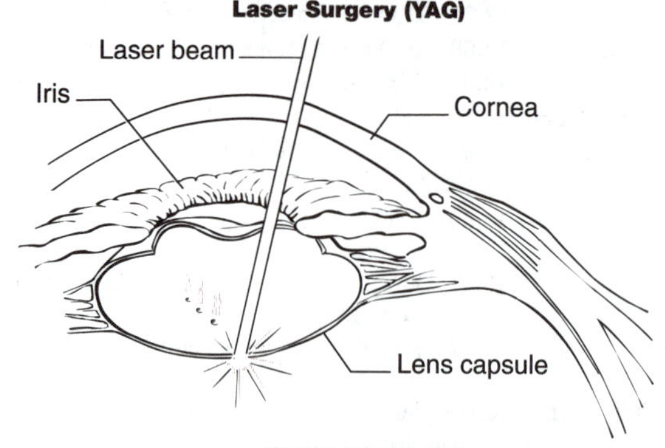

13.43 **Mechanical phacofragmentation and other aspiration of cataract**

✓4th 13.5 **Other extracapsular extraction of lens**

Code also any synchronous insertion of pseudophakos (13.71)

AHA: S-O, '85, 6

13.51 **Extracapsular extraction of lens by temporal inferior route**

DEF: Removal of lens through outer eyeball with posterior capsule left intact.

13.59 **Other extracapsular extraction of lens**

✓4th 13.6 **Other cataract extraction**

Code also any synchronous insertion of pseudophakos (13.71)

AHA: S-O, '85, 6

13.64 **Discission of secondary membrane [after cataract]**

DEF: Breaking up of fibrotic lens capsule developed after previous lens extraction.

13.65 **Excision of secondary membrane [after cataract]**

Capsulectomy

DEF: Capsulectomy: Excision of lens capsule membrane after previous lens extraction.

13.66 **Mechanical fragmentation of secondary membrane [after cataract]**

DEF: Breaking up and removal of fibrotic lens capsule developed after previous lens extraction.

13.69 **Other cataract extraction**

✓4th 13.7 **Insertion of prosthetic lens [pseudophakos]**

EXCLUDES ▶ *implantation of intraocular telescope prosthesis (13.91)*◀

AHA: J-A, '84, 1

DEF: Insertion of ocular implant, following lens extraction.

13.70 **Insertion of pseudophakos, not otherwise specified**

13.71 **Insertion of intraocular lens prosthesis at time of cataract extraction, one-stage**

Code also synchronous extraction of cataract (13.11-13.69)

AHA: 3Q, '96, 4

13.72 **Secondary insertion of intraocular lens prosthesis**

13.8 **Removal of implanted lens**

Removal of pseudophakos

✓4th 13.9 **Other operations on lens**

AHA: 1Q, '00, 9

● 13.90 **Operation on lens, not elsewhere classified**

● 13.91 **Implantation of intraocular telescope prosthesis**

Implantable miniature telescope

INCLUDES removal of lens, any method

EXCLUDES *secondary insertion of ocular implant (16.61)*

✓3rd 14 **Operations on retina, choroid, vitreous, and posterior chamber**

✓4th 14.0 **Removal of foreign body from posterior segment of eye**

EXCLUDES *removal of surgically implanted material (14.6)*

14.00 **Removal of foreign body from posterior segment of eye, not otherwise specified**

14.01 **Removal of foreign body from posterior segment of eye with use of magnet**

14.02 **Removal of foreign body from posterior segment of eye without use of magnet**

✓4th 14.1 **Diagnostic procedures on retina, choroid, vitreous, and posterior chamber**

14.11 **Diagnostic aspiration of vitreous**

14.19 **Other diagnostic procedures on retina, choroid, vitreous, and posterior chamber**

✓4th 14.2 **Destruction of lesion of retina and choroid**

INCLUDES destruction of chorioretinopathy or isolated chorioretinal lesion

EXCLUDES *that for repair of retina (14.31-14.59)*

DEF: Destruction of damaged retina and choroid tissue.

14.21 **Destruction of chorioretinal lesion by diathermy**

14.22 **Destruction of chorioretinal lesion by cryotherapy**

14.23 **Destruction of chorioretinal lesion by xenon arc photocoagulation**

14.24 **Destruction of chorioretinal lesion by laser photocoagulation**

14.25 **Destruction of chorioretinal lesion by photocoagulation of unspecified type**

14.26 **Destruction of chorioretinal lesion by radiation therapy**

14.27 **Destruction of chorioretinal lesion by implantation of radiation source**

14.29 **Other destruction of chorioretinal lesion**

Destruction of lesion of retina and choroid NOS

✓4th 14.3 **Repair of retinal tear**

INCLUDES repair of retinal defect

EXCLUDES *repair of retinal detachment (14.41-14.59)*

14.31 **Repair of retinal tear by diathermy**

14.32 **Repair of retinal tear by cryotherapy**

14.33 **Repair of retinal tear by xenon arc photocoagulation**

14.34 **Repair of retinal tear by laser photocoagulation**

AHA: 1Q, '94, 17

14.35 **Repair of retinal tear by photocoagulation of unspecified type**

14.39 **Other repair of retinal tear**

✓4th 14.4 **Repair of retinal detachment with scleral buckling and implant**

DEF: Placement of material around eye to indent sclera and close a hole or tear or to reduce vitreous traction.

14.41 **Scleral buckling with implant**

AHA: 3Q, '96, 6

14.49 **Other scleral buckling**

Scleral buckling with:
- air tamponade
- resection of sclera
- vitrectomy

AHA: 1Q, '94, 16

✓4th 14.5 **Other repair of retinal detachment**

INCLUDES that with drainage

14.51 **Repair of retinal detachment with diathermy**

14.52 **Repair of retinal detachment with cryotherapy**

14.53 **Repair of retinal detachment with xenon arc photocoagulation**

14.54 **Repair of retinal detachment with laser photocoagulation**

AHA: N-D, '87, 10

14.55 **Repair of retinal detachment with photocoagulation of unspecified type**

14.59 **Other**

14.6 **Removal of surgically implanted material from posterior segment of eye**

✓4th 14.7 **Operations on vitreous**

14.71 **Removal of vitreous, anterior approach**

Open sky technique
Removal of vitreous, anterior approach (with replacement)

DEF: Removal of all or part of the eyeball fluid via the anterior segment of the eyeball.

14.72 **Other removal of vitreous**

Aspiration of vitreous by posterior sclerotomy

14.73 **Mechanical vitrectomy by anterior approach**

AHA: 3Q, '96, 4, 5

DEF: Removal of abnormal tissue in eyeball fluid to control fibrotic overgrowth in severe intraocular injury.

14.74 **Other mechanical vitrectomy**

▶Posterior approach◀

AHA: 3Q, '96, 4, 5

14.75 **Injection of vitreous substitute**

EXCLUDES *that associated with removal (14.71-14.72)*

AHA: 1Q, '98, 6; 3Q, '96, 4, 5; 1Q, '94, 17

14.79 **Other operations on vitreous**

AHA: 3Q, '99, 12; 1Q, '99, 11; 1Q, '98, 6

14.9 **Other operations on retina, choroid, and posterior chamber**

AHA: 3Q, '96, 5

✓3rd 15 **Operations on extraocular muscles**

✓4th 15.0 **Diagnostic procedures on extraocular muscles or tendons**

15.01 **Biopsy of extraocular muscle or tendon**

15.09 **Other diagnostic procedures on extraocular muscles and tendons**

✓4th 15.1 **Operations on one extraocular muscle involving temporary detachment from globe**

15.11 **Recession of one extraocular muscle**

AHA: 3Q, '96, 3

DEF: Detachment of exterior eye muscle with posterior reattachment to correct strabismus.

15.12 **Advancement of one extraocular muscle**

DEF: Detachment of exterior eye muscle with forward reattachment to correct strabismus.

15.13 **Resection of one extraocular muscle**

15.19 **Other operations on one extraocular muscle involving temporary detachment from globe**

EXCLUDES *transposition of muscle (15.5)*

✓4th 15.2 **Other operations on one extraocular muscle**

15.21 **Lengthening procedure on one extraocular muscle**

DEF: Extension of exterior eye muscle length.

Lengthening Procedure on One Extraocular Muscle

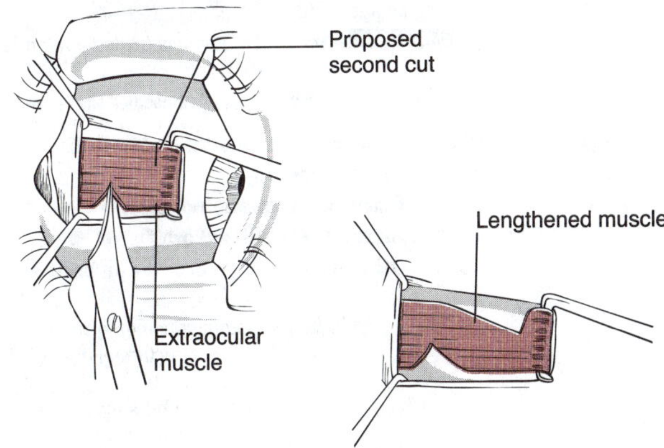

Shortening Procedure on One Extraocular Muscle

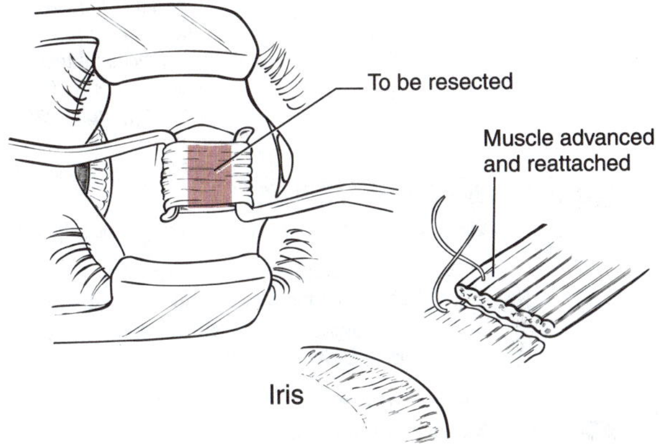

15.22 **Shortening procedure on one extraocular muscle**

DEF: Shortening of exterior eye muscle.

15.29 **Other**

15.3 **Operations on two or more extraocular muscles involving temporary detachment from globe, one or both eyes**

AHA: 3Q, '96, 3

15.4 **Other operations on two or more extraocular muscles, one or both eyes**

15.5 **Transposition of extraocular muscles**

EXCLUDES *that for correction of ptosis (08.31-08.36)*

DEF: Relocation of exterior eye muscle to a more functional site.

15.6 **Revision of extraocular muscle surgery**

DEF: Repair of previous exterior eye muscle surgery.

15.7 **Repair of injury of extraocular muscle**

Freeing of entrapped extraocular muscle
Lysis of adhesions of extraocular muscle
Repair of laceration of extraocular muscle, tendon, or Tenon's capsule

15.9 **Other operations on extraocular muscles and tendons**

✓3rd 16 **Operations on orbit and eyeball**

EXCLUDES *reduction of fracture of orbit (76.78-76.79)*

✓4th 16.0 **Orbitotomy**

16.01 **Orbitotomy with bone flap**

Orbitotomy with lateral approach

DEF: Incision into orbital bone with insertion of small bone piece.

16.02 **Orbitotomy with insertion of orbital implant**

EXCLUDES *that with bone flap (16.01)*

16.09 **Other orbitotomy**

16.1 Removal of penetrating foreign body from eye, not otherwise specified
EXCLUDES *removal of nonpenetrating foreign body (98.21)*
DEF: Removal of foreign body from an unspecified site in eye.

✓4th **16.2 Diagnostic procedures on orbit and eyeball**
16.21 Ophthalmoscopy
16.22 Diagnostic aspiration of orbit
16.23 Biopsy of eyeball and orbit
16.29 Other diagnostic procedures on orbit and eyeball
EXCLUDES *examination of form and structure of eye (95.11-95.16)*
general and subjective eye examination (95.01-95.09)
microscopic examination of specimen from eye (90.21-90.29)
objective functional tests of eye (95.21-95.26)
ocular thermography (88.82)
tonometry (89.11)
x-ray of orbit (87.14, 87.16)

✓4th **16.3 Evisceration of eyeball**
DEF: Removal of eyeball, leaving sclera and occasionally cornea.
16.31 Removal of ocular contents with synchronous implant into scleral shell
DEF: Removal of eyeball leaving outer eyeball layer with ocular implant into shell.
16.39 Other evisceration of eyeball

✓4th **16.4 Enucleation of eyeball**
DEF: Removal of entire eyeball after severing eye muscles and optic nerves.
16.41 Enucleation of eyeball with synchronous implant into Tenon's capsule with attachment of muscles
Integrated implant of eyeball
DEF: Removal of eyeball with insertion of ocular implant and muscle attachment.
16.42 Enucleation of eyeball with other synchronous implant
16.49 Other enucleation of eyeball
Removal of eyeball NOS

✓4th **16.5 Exenteration of orbital contents**
16.51 Exenteration of orbit with removal of adjacent structures
Radical orbitomaxillectomy
DEF: Removal of contents of bony cavity of eye as well as related tissues and structures.
DEF: Radical orbitomaxillectomy: Removal of contents of bony cavity of eye, related tissues and structures, and a portion of maxillary bone.
16.52 Exenteration of orbit with therapeutic removal of orbital bone
16.59 Other exenteration of orbit
Evisceration of orbit NOS
Exenteration of orbit with temporalis muscle transplant

✓4th **16.6 Secondary procedures after removal of eyeball**
EXCLUDES *that with synchronous:*
enucleation of eyeball (16.41-16.42)
evisceration of eyeball (16.31)
16.61 Secondary insertion of ocular implant
DEF: Insertion of ocular implant after previous eye removal.
16.62 Revision and reinsertion of ocular implant
DEF: Reimplant or correction of ocular implant.
16.63 Revision of enucleation socket with graft
DEF: Implant of tissue to correct socket after eye removal.
16.64 Other revision of enucleation socket
16.65 Secondary graft to exenteration cavity
DEF: Implant of tissue in place of eye after removal.
16.66 Other revision of exenteration cavity
16.69 Other secondary procedures after removal of eyeball

✓4th **16.7 Removal of ocular or orbital implant**
16.71 Removal of ocular implant
16.72 Removal of orbital implant

✓4th **16.8 Repair of injury of eyeball and orbit**
16.81 Repair of wound of orbit
EXCLUDES *reduction of orbital fracture (76.78-76.79)*
repair of extraocular muscles (15.7)
16.82 Repair of rupture of eyeball
Repair of multiple structures of eye
EXCLUDES *repair of laceration of:*
cornea (11.51-11.59)
sclera (12.81)
16.89 Other repair of injury of eyeball or orbit

✓4th **16.9 Other operations on orbit and eyeball**
EXCLUDES *irrigation of eye (96.51)*
prescription and fitting of low vision aids (95.31-95.33)
removal of:
eye prosthesis NEC (97.31)
nonpenetrating foreign body from eye without incision (98.21)
16.91 Retrobulbar injection of therapeutic agent
EXCLUDES *injection of radiographic contrast material (87.14)*
opticociliary injection (12.79)
16.92 Excision of lesion of orbit
EXCLUDES *biopsy of orbit (16.23)*
16.93 Excision of lesion of eye, unspecified structure
EXCLUDES *biopsy of eye NOS (16.23)*
16.98 Other operations on orbit
16.99 Other operations on eyeball

4. OPERATIONS ON THE EAR (18-20)

✓3rd **18 Operations on external ear**

INCLUDES operations on:
external auditory canal
skin and cartilage of:
auricle
meatus

✓4th **18.0 Incision of external ear**

EXCLUDES *removal of intraluminal foreign body (98.11)*

18.01 Piercing of ear lobe
Piercing of pinna

18.02 Incision of external auditory canal

18.09 Other incision of external ear

✓4th **18.1 Diagnostic procedures on external ear**

18.11 Otoscopy
DEF: Exam of the ear with instrument designed for visualization.

18.12 Biopsy of external ear

18.19 Other diagnostic procedures on external ear

EXCLUDES *microscopic examination of specimen from ear (90.31-90.39)*

✓4th **18.2 Excision or destruction of lesion of external ear**

18.21 Excision of preauricular sinus
Radical excision of preauricular sinus or cyst

EXCLUDES *excision of preauricular remnant [appendage] (18.29)*

DEF: Excision of preauricular sinus or cyst with adjacent tissues.

18.29 Excision or destruction of other lesion of external ear

Cauterization, Coagulation, Cryosurgery, Curettage, Electrocoagulation, Enucleation } of external ear

Excision of:
exostosis of external auditory canal
preauricular remnant [appendage]
Partial excision of ear

EXCLUDES *biopsy of external ear (18.12)*
radical excision of lesion (18.31)
removal of cerumen (96.52)

✓4th **18.3 Other excision of external ear**

EXCLUDES *biopsy of external ear (18.12)*

18.31 Radical excision of lesion of external ear

EXCLUDES *radical excision of preauricular sinus (18.21)*

DEF: Removal of damaged, diseased ear and adjacent tissue.

18.39 Other
Amputation of external ear

EXCLUDES *excision of lesion (18.21-18.29, 18.31)*

18.4 Suture of laceration of external ear

18.5 Surgical correction of prominent ear
Ear:
pinning
setback

DEF: Reformation of protruding outer ear.

18.6 Reconstruction of external auditory canal
Canaloplasty of external auditory meatus
Construction [reconstruction] of external meatus of ear:
osseous portion
skin-lined portion (with skin graft)

DEF: Repair of outer ear canal.

✓4th **18.7 Other plastic repair of external ear**

18.71 Construction of auricle of ear
Prosthetic appliance for absent ear
Reconstruction:
auricle
ear

DEF: Reformation or repair of external ear flap.

18.72 Reattachment of amputated ear

18.79 Other plastic repair of external ear
Otoplasty NOS
Postauricular skin graft
Repair of lop ear

AHA: 3Q, '03, 12

DEF: Postauricular skin graft: Graft repair behind ear.

DEF: Repair of lop ear: Reconstruction of ear that is at right angle to head.

18.9 Other operations on external ear

EXCLUDES *irrigation of ear (96.52)*
packing of external auditory canal (96.11)
removal of:
cerumen (96.52)
foreign body (without incision) (98.11)

✓3rd **19 Reconstructive operations on middle ear**

19.0 Stapes mobilization
Division, otosclerotic:
material
process
Remobilization of stapes
Stapediolysis
Transcrural stapes mobilization

EXCLUDES *that with synchronous stapedectomy (19.11-19.19)*

DEF: Repair of innermost bone of middle ear to enable movement and response to sound.

✓4th **19.1 Stapedectomy**

EXCLUDES *revision of previous stapedectomy (19.21-19.29)*
stapes mobilization only (19.0)

DEF: Removal of innermost bone of middle ear.

19.11 Stapedectomy with incus replacement
Stapedectomy with incus:
homograft
prosthesis

DEF: Removal of innermost bone of middle ear with autograft or prosthesis replacement.

19.19 Other stapedectomy

Stapedectomy with Incus Replacement

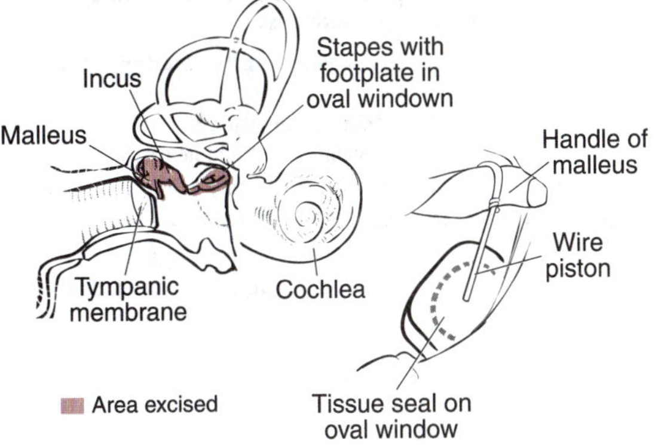

✓4th **19.2 Revision of stapedectomy**

19.21 Revision of stapedectomy with incus replacement

19.29 Other revision of stapedectomy

19.3 Other operations on ossicular chain

Incudectomy NOS
Ossiculectomy NOS
Reconstruction of ossicles, second stage

DEF: Incudectomy: Excision of middle bone of middle ear, not otherwise specified.

DEF: Ossiculectomy: Excision of middle ear bones, not otherwise specified.

DEF: Reconstruction of ossicles, second stage: Repair of middle ear bones following previous surgery.

19.4 Myringoplasty

Epitympanic, type I
Myringoplasty by:
cauterization
graft
Tympanoplasty (type I)

DEF: Epitympanic, type I: Repair over or upon eardrum.

DEF: Myringoplasty by cauterization: Plastic repair of tympanic membrane of eardrum by heat.

DEF: Graft: Plastic repair using implanted tissue.

DEF: Tympanoplasty (type I): Reconstruction of eardrum to restore hearing.

✓4th **19.5 Other tympanoplasty**

19.52 Type II tympanoplasty

Closure of perforation with graft against incus or malleus

19.53 Type III tympanoplasty

Graft placed in contact with mobile and intact stapes

AHA: M-A, '85, 15

19.54 Type IV tympanoplasty

Mobile footplate left exposed with air pocket between round window and graft

19.55 Type V tympanoplasty

Fenestra in horizontal semicircular canal covered by graft

19.6 Revision of tympanoplasty

DEF: Repair or correction of previous plastic surgery on eardrum.

19.9 Other repair of middle ear

Closure of mastoid fistula
Mastoid myoplasty
Obliteration of tympanomastoid cavity

DEF: Closure of mastoid fistula: Closing of abnormal channel in mastoid.

DEF: Mastoid myoplasty: Restoration or repair of mastoid muscle.

DEF: Obliteration of tympanomastoid cavity: Removal, total, of functional elements of middle ear.

✓3rd **20 Other operations on middle and inner ear**

✓4th **20.0 Myringotomy**

DEF: Myringotomy: Puncture of tympanic membrane or eardrum, also called tympanocentesis

20.01 Myringotomy with insertion of tube

Myringostomy

20.09 Other myringotomy

Aspiration of middle ear NOS

20.1 Removal of tympanostomy tube

✓4th **20.2 Incision of mastoid and middle ear**

20.21 Incision of mastoid

20.22 Incision of petrous pyramid air cells

20.23 Incision of middle ear

Atticotomy
Division of tympanum
Lysis of adhesions of middle ear

EXCLUDES *division of otosclerotic process (19.0)*
stapediolysis (19.0)
that with stapedectomy (19.11-19.19)

✓4th **20.3 Diagnostic procedures on middle and inner ear**

20.31 Electrocochleography

DEF: Measure of electric potential of eighth cranial nerve by electrode applied sound.

20.32 Biopsy of middle and inner ear

20.39 Other diagnostic procedures on middle and inner ear

EXCLUDES *auditory and vestibular function tests (89.13, 95.41-95.49)*
microscopic examination of specimen from ear (90.31-90.39)

✓4th **20.4 Mastoidectomy**

Code also any:
skin graft (18.79)
tympanoplasty (19.4-19.55)

EXCLUDES *that with implantation of cochlear prosthetic device (20.96-20.98)*

DEF: Mastoidectomy: Excision of bony protrusion behind ear.

20.41 Simple mastoidectomy

20.42 Radical mastoidectomy

20.49 Other mastoidectomy

Atticoantrostomy
Mastoidectomy:
NOS
modified radical

DEF: Atticoantrotomy: Opening of cavity of mastoid bone and middle ear.

✓4th **20.5 Other excision of middle ear**

EXCLUDES *that with synchronous mastoidectomy (20.41-20.49)*

20.51 Excision of lesion of middle ear

EXCLUDES *biopsy of middle ear (20.32)*

20.59 Other

Apicectomy of petrous pyramid
Tympanectomy

✓4th **20.6 Fenestration of inner ear**

20.61 Fenestration of inner ear (initial)

Fenestration of:
labyrinth
semicircular canals
vestibule
} with graft (skin) (vein)

EXCLUDES *that with tympanoplasty, type V (19.55)*

DEF: Creation of inner ear opening.

20.62 Revision of fenestration of inner ear

✓4th **20.7 Incision, excision, and destruction of inner ear**

20.71 Endolymphatic shunt

DEF: Insertion of tube to drain fluid in inner ear cavities.

20.72 Injection into inner ear

Destruction by injection (alcohol):
inner ear
semicircular canals
vestibule

20.79 Other incision, excision, and destruction of inner ear

Decompression of labyrinth
Drainage of inner ear
Fistulization:
endolymphatic sac
labyrinth
Incision of endolymphatic sac
Labyrinthectomy (transtympanic)
Opening of bony labyrinth
Perilymphatic tap

EXCLUDES *biopsy of inner ear (20.32)*

DEF: Decompression of labyrinth: Controlled relief of pressure in cavities of inner ear.

DEF: Drainage of inner ear: Removal of fluid from inner ear.

DEF: Fistulization of endolymphatic sac: Creation of passage to fluid sac in inner ear cavities.

DEF: Fistulization of labyrinth: Creation of passage to inner ear cavities.

DEF: Incision of endolymphatic sac: Cutting into fluid sac in inner ear cavities.

DEF: Labyrinthectomy (transtympanic): Excision of cavities across eardrum.

DEF: Opening of bony labyrinth: Cutting into inner ear bony cavities.

DEF: Perilymphatic tap: Puncture or incision into fluid sac of inner ear cavities.

20.8 Operations on Eustachian tube

Catheterization
Inflation
Injection (Teflon paste)
Insufflation (boric acid-salicylic acid)
Intubation
Politzerization
} of Eustachian tube

DEF: Catheterization: Passing catheter into passage between pharynx and middle ear.

DEF: Inflation: Blowing air, gas or liquid into passage between pharynx and middle ear to inflate.

DEF: Injection (Teflon paste): Forcing fluid (Teflon paste) into passage between pharynx and middle ear.

DEF: Insufflation (boric acid-salicylic acid): Blowing gas or liquid into passage between pharynx and middle ear.

DEF: Intubation: Placing tube into passage between pharynx and middle ear.

DEF: Politzerization: Inflating passage between pharynx and middle ear with Politzer bag.

✓4th **20.9 Other operations on inner and middle ear**

20.91 Tympanosympathectomy

DEF: Excision or chemical suppression of impulses of middle ear nerves.

20.92 Revision of mastoidectomy

AHA: 2Q, '98, 20

DEF: Correction of previous removal of mastoid cells from temporal or mastoid bone.

20.93 Repair of oval and round windows

Closure of fistula:
oval window
perilymph

Closure of fistula:
round window

DEF: Restoration of middle ear openings.

20.94 Injection of tympanum

20.95 Implantation of electromagnetic hearing device

Bone conduction hearing device

EXCLUDES *cochlear prosthetic device (20.96-20.98)*

AHA: 4Q, '89, 5

20.96 Implantation or replacement of cochlear prosthetic device, not otherwise specified

Implantation of receiver (within skull) and insertion of electrode(s) in the cochlea

INCLUDES mastoidectomy

EXCLUDES *electromagnetic hearing device (20.95)*

AHA: 4Q, '89, 5

20.97 Implantation or replacement of cochlear prosthetic device, single channel

Implantation of receiver (within skull) and insertion of electrode in the cochlea

INCLUDES mastoidectomy

EXCLUDES *electromagnetic hearing device (20.95)*

AHA: 4Q, '89, 5

20.98 Implantation or replacement of cochlear prosthetic device, multiple channel

Implantation of receiver (within skull) and insertion of electrodes in the cochlea

INCLUDES mastoidectomy

EXCLUDES *electromagnetic hearing device (20.95)*

AHA: 4Q, '89, 5

20.99 Other operations on middle and inner ear

Repair or removal of cochlear prosthetic device (receiver) (electrode)

EXCLUDES *adjustment (external components) of cochlear prosthetic device (95.49)*
fitting of hearing aid (95.48)

AHA: 4Q, '89, 7

5. OPERATIONS ON THE NOSE, MOUTH, AND PHARYNX (21-29)

✓3rd **21 Operations on nose**

INCLUDES operations on:
bone } of nose
skin

AHA: 1Q, '94, 5

✓4th **21.0 Control of epistaxis**

21.00 Control of epistaxis, not otherwise specified

21.01 Control of epistaxis by anterior nasal packing

21.02 Control of epistaxis by posterior (and anterior) packing

21.03 Control of epistaxis by cauterization (and packing)

21.04 Control of epistaxis by ligation of ethmoidal arteries

21.05 Control of epistaxis by (transantral) ligation of the maxillary artery

21.06 Control of epistaxis by ligation of the external carotid artery

21.07 Control of epistaxis by excision of nasal mucosa and skin grafting of septum and lateral nasal wall

21.09 Control of epistaxis by other means

21.1 Incision of nose

Chondrotomy
Nasal septotomy
Incision of skin of nose

DEF: Chondrotomy: Incision or division of nasal cartilage.

DEF: Nasal septotomy: Incision into bone dividing nose into two chambers.

✓4th **21.2 Diagnostic procedures on nose**

21.21 Rhinoscopy

DEF: Visualization of nasal passage with nasal speculum.

21.22 Biopsy of nose

21.29 Other diagnostic procedures on nose

EXCLUDES *microscopic examination of specimen from nose (90.31-90.39)*
nasal:
function study (89.12)
x-ray (87.16)
rhinomanometry (89.12)

✓4th **21.3 Local excision or destruction of lesion of nose**

EXCLUDES *biopsy of nose (21.22)*
nasal fistulectomy (21.82)

21.30 Excision or destruction of lesion of nose, not otherwise specified

21.31 Local excision or destruction of intranasal lesion

Nasal polypectomy

21.32 Local excision or destruction of other lesion of nose

AHA: 2Q, '89, 16

21.4 Resection of nose

Amputation of nose

21.5 Submucous resection of nasal septum

DEF: Resection, partial, of nasal septum with mucosa reimplanted after excision.

✓4th **21.6 Turbinectomy**

DEF: Removal, partial, or total of turbinate bones; inferior turbinate is most often excised.

21.61 Turbinectomy by diathermy or cryosurgery

DEF: Destruction of turbinate bone by heat or freezing.

Excision of Turbinate

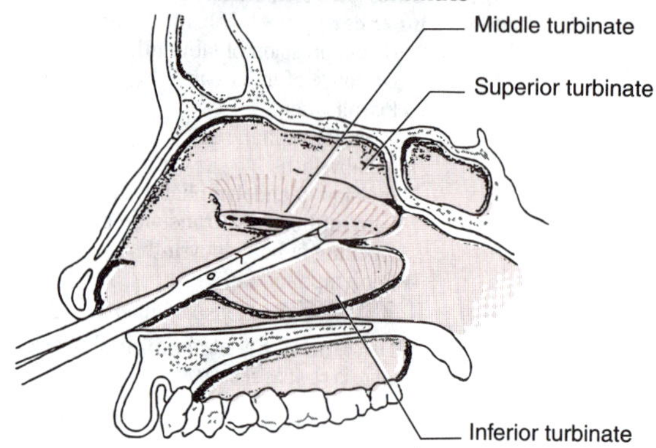

21.62 Fracture of the turbinates

DEF: Surgical breaking of turbinate bones.

21.69 Other turbinectomy

EXCLUDES *turbinectomy associated with sinusectomy (22.31-22.39, 22.42, 22.60-22.64)*

✓4th **21.7 Reduction of nasal fracture**

21.71 Closed reduction of nasal fracture

21.72 Open reduction of nasal fracture

✓4th **21.8 Repair and plastic operations on the nose**

21.81 Suture of laceration of nose

21.82 Closure of nasal fistula

Nasolabial
Nasopharyngeal } fistulectomy
Oronasal

DEF: Sealing off crack or hole between nose and lip, nose and pharynx, or nose and mouth.

21.83 Total nasal reconstruction

Reconstruction of nose with:
arm flap
forehead flap

DEF: Reformation, plastic, of nasal structure with tissue flap from arm or forehead.

21.84 Revision rhinoplasty

Rhinoseptoplasty
Twisted nose rhinoplasty

DEF: Rhinoseptoplasty: Repair of nose and the bone dividing the nose into two chambers.

DEF: Twisted nose rhinoplasty: Repair of nose alignment following reconstructive surgery.

21.85 Augmentation rhinoplasty

Augmentation rhinoplasty with:
graft
synthetic implant

DEF: Implant of tissue or synthetic graft to enlarge nose.

21.86 Limited rhinoplasty

Plastic repair of nasolabial flaps
Tip rhinoplasty

DEF: Plastic repair of nasolabial flaps: Reconstruction of nasal area above lips.

DEF: Tip rhinoplasty: Reconstruction or restoration of nasal tip.

21.87 Other rhinoplasty

Rhinoplasty NOS

21.88 **Other septoplasty**
Crushing of nasal septum
Repair of septal perforation
EXCLUDES *septoplasty associated with submucous resection of septum (21.5)*

DEF: Crushing of nasal septum: Division and reconstruction of defects in bone dividing nasal chambers.

DEF: Repair of septal perforation: Repair of hole in bone dividing nasal chambers with adjacent tissue.

21.89 **Other repair and plastic operations on nose**
Reattachment of amputated nose

✓4th 21.9 **Other operations on nose**

21.91 **Lysis of adhesions of nose**
Posterior nasal scrub

DEF: Posterior nasal scrub: Clearing out of abnormal adhesions in posterior nasal area.

21.99 **Other**
EXCLUDES *dilation of frontonasal duct (96.21)*
irrigation of nasal passages (96.53)
removal of:
intraluminal foreign body without incision (98.12)
nasal packing (97.32)
replacement of nasal packing (97.21)

✓3rd 22 **Operations on nasal sinuses**

✓4th 22.0 **Aspiration and lavage of nasal sinus**

22.00 **Aspiration and lavage of nasal sinus, not otherwise specified**

22.01 **Puncture of nasal sinus for aspiration or lavage**

22.02 **Aspiration or lavage of nasal sinus through natural ostium**

DEF: Withdrawal of fluid and washing of nasal cavity through natural opening.

✓4th 22.1 **Diagnostic procedures on nasal sinus**

22.11 **Closed [endoscopic] [needle] biopsy of nasal sinus**

22.12 **Open biopsy of nasal sinus**

22.19 **Other diagnostic procedures on nasal sinuses**
Endoscopy without biopsy
EXCLUDES *transillumination of sinus (89.35)*
x-ray of sinus (87.15-87.16)

22.2 **Intranasal antrotomy**
EXCLUDES *antrotomy with external approach (22.31-22.39)*

DEF: Incision of intranasal sinus.

✓4th 22.3 **External maxillary antrotomy**

22.31 **Radical maxillary antrotomy**
Removal of lining membrane of maxillary sinus using Caldwell-Luc approach

DEF: Caldwell-Luc approach: Removal of membrane lining the maxillary cavity through incision above canine teeth.

22.39 **Other external maxillary antrotomy**
Exploration of maxillary antrum with Caldwell-Luc approach

✓4th 22.4 **Frontal sinusotomy and sinusectomy**

22.41 **Frontal sinusotomy**

22.42 **Frontal sinusectomy**
Excision of lesion of frontal sinus
Obliteration of frontal sinus (with fat)
EXCLUDES *biopsy of nasal sinus (22.11-22.12)*

✓4th 22.5 **Other nasal sinusotomy**

22.50 **Sinusotomy, not otherwise specified**

22.51 **Ethmoidotomy**

22.52 **Sphenoidotomy**

22.53 **Incision of multiple nasal sinuses**

✓4th 22.6 **Other nasal sinusectomy**
INCLUDES that with incidental turbinectomy
EXCLUDES *biopsy of nasal sinus (22.11-22.12)*

22.60 **Sinusectomy, not otherwise specified**

22.61 **Excision of lesion of maxillary sinus with Caldwell-Luc approach**

22.62 **Excision of lesion of maxillary sinus with other approach**

22.63 **Ethmoidectomy**

DEF: Removal of ethmoid cells and bone, partial or total includes excising mucosal lining, partial or total.

22.64 **Sphenoidectomy**

DEF: Removal of wedge shaped sphenoid bone at base of brain.

✓4th 22.7 **Repair of nasal sinus**

22.71 **Closure of nasal sinus fistula**
Repair of oro-antral fistula

22.79 **Other repair of nasal sinus**
Reconstruction of frontonasal duct
Repair of bone of accessory sinus

22.9 **Other operations on nasal sinuses**
Exteriorization of maxillary sinus
Fistulization of sinus
EXCLUDES *dilation of frontonasal duct (96.21)*

DEF: Exteriorization of maxillary sinus: Creation of external maxillary cavity opening.

DEF: Fistulization of sinus: Creation of fistula canal in nasal cavity.

✓3rd 23 **Removal and restoration of teeth**

✓4th 23.0 **Forceps extraction of tooth**

23.01 **Extraction of deciduous tooth**

23.09 **Extraction of other tooth**
Extraction of tooth NOS

✓4th 23.1 **Surgical removal of tooth**

23.11 **Removal of residual root**

23.19 **Other surgical extraction of tooth**
Odontectomy NOS
Removal of impacted tooth
Tooth extraction with elevation of mucoperiosteal flap

23.2 **Restoration of tooth by filling**

23.3 **Restoration of tooth by inlay**

DEF: Restoration of tooth by cementing in a molded filling.

✓4th 23.4 **Other dental restoration**

23.41 **Application of crown**

23.42 **Insertion of fixed bridge**

23.43 **Insertion of removable bridge**

23.49 **Other**

23.5 **Implantation of tooth**

DEF: Insertion of a sound tooth to replace extracted tooth.

23.6 **Prosthetic dental implant**
Endosseous dental implant

DEF: Implant of artificial denture within bone covering tooth socket.

✓4th 23.7 **Apicoectomy and root canal therapy**

23.70 **Root canal, not otherwise specified**

23.71 **Root canal therapy with irrigation**

Operations on the Nose, Mouth, and Pharynx 21.88–23.71

✓3rd ✓4th Additional Digit Required | Nonspecific OR Procedure | Valid OR Procedure | Non-OR Procedure | Adjunct Code

23.72 Root canal therapy with apicoectomy
DEF: Removal of tooth root to treat damaged root canal tissue.

23.73 Apicoectomy

✓3rd **24 Other operations on teeth, gums, and alveoli**

24.0 Incision of gum or alveolar bone
Apical alveolotomy

✓4th **24.1 Diagnostic procedures on teeth, gums, and alveoli**

24.11 Biopsy of gum

24.12 Biopsy of alveolus

24.19 Other diagnostic procedures on teeth, gums, and alveoli
EXCLUDES *dental:*
examination (89.31)
x-ray:
full-mouth (87.11)
other (87.12)
microscopic examination of dental specimen (90.81-90.89)

24.2 Gingivoplasty
Gingivoplasty with bone or soft tissue graft
DEF: Repair of gum tissue.

✓4th **24.3 Other operations on gum**

24.31 Excision of lesion or tissue of gum
EXCLUDES *biopsy of gum (24.11)*
excision of odontogenic lesion (24.4)

24.32 Suture of laceration of gum

24.39 Other

24.4 Excision of dental lesion of jaw
Excision of odontogenic lesion

24.5 Alveoloplasty
Alveolectomy (interradicular) (intraseptal) (radical) (simple) (with graft or implant)
EXCLUDES *biopsy of alveolus (24.12)*
en bloc resection of alveolar process and palate (27.32)
DEF: Repair or correction of bony tooth socket.

24.6 Exposure of tooth

24.7 Application of orthodontic appliance
Application, insertion, or fitting of:
arch bars
orthodontic obturator
orthodontic wiring
periodontal splint
EXCLUDES *nonorthodontic dental wiring (93.55)*

24.8 Other orthodontic operation
Closure of diastema (alveolar) (dental)
Occlusal adjustment
Removal of arch bars
Repair of dental arch
EXCLUDES *removal of nonorthodontic wiring (97.33)*

✓4th **24.9 Other dental operations**

24.91 Extension or deepening of buccolabial or lingual sulcus

24.99 Other
EXCLUDES *dental:*
debridement (96.54)
examination (89.31)
prophylaxis (96.54)
scaling and polishing (96.54)
wiring (93.55)
fitting of dental appliance [denture] (99.97)
microscopic examination of dental specimen (90.81-90.89)
removal of dental:
packing (97.34)
prosthesis (97.35)
wiring (97.33)
replacement of dental packing (97.22)

✓3rd **25 Operations on tongue**

✓4th **25.0 Diagnostic procedures on tongue**

25.01 Closed [needle] biopsy of tongue

25.02 Open biopsy of tongue
Wedge biopsy

25.09 Other diagnostic procedures on tongue

25.1 Excision or destruction of lesion or tissue of tongue
EXCLUDES *biopsy of tongue (25.01-25.02)*
frenumectomy:
labial (27.41)
lingual (25.92)
AHA: 2Q, '02, 5

25.2 Partial glossectomy

25.3 Complete glossectomy
Glossectomy NOS
Code also any neck dissection (40.40-40.42)

25.4 Radical glossectomy
Code also any:
neck dissection (40.40-40.42)
tracheostomy (31.1-31.29)

✓4th **25.5 Repair of tongue and glossoplasty**

25.51 Suture of laceration of tongue

25.59 Other repair and plastic operations on tongue
Fascial sling of tongue
Fusion of tongue (to lip)
Graft of mucosa or skin to tongue
EXCLUDES *lysis of adhesions of tongue (25.93)*
AHA: 1Q, '97, 5

✓4th **25.9 Other operations on tongue**

25.91 Lingual frenotomy
EXCLUDES *labial frenotomy (27.91)*
DEF: Extension of groove between cheek and lips or cheek and tongue.

25.92 Lingual frenectomy
EXCLUDES *labial frenectomy (27.41)*
DEF: Frenectomy: Removal of vertical membrane attaching tongue to floor of mouth.

25.93 Lysis of adhesions of tongue

25.94 Other glossotomy

25.99 Other

✓3rd **26 Operations on salivary glands and ducts**
INCLUDES operations on:
lesser salivary, parotid, sublingual, submaxillary } gland and duct
Code also any neck dissection (40.40-40.42)

26.0 Incision of salivary gland or duct

26.1 Diagnostic procedures on salivary glands and ducts
- **26.11 Closed [needle] biopsy of salivary gland or duct**
- **26.12 Open biopsy of salivary gland or duct**
- **26.19 Other diagnostic procedures on salivary glands and ducts**
  EXCLUDES *x-ray of salivary gland (87.09)*

26.2 Excision of lesion of salivary gland
- **26.21 Marsupialization of salivary gland cyst**
  DEF: Creation of pouch of salivary gland cyst to drain and promote healing.
- **26.29 Other excision of salivary gland lesion**
  EXCLUDES *biopsy of salivary gland (26.11-26.12)*
  salivary fistulectomy (26.42)

26.3 Sialoadenectomy
DEF: Removal of salivary gland.
- **26.30 Sialoadenectomy, not otherwise specified**
- **26.31 Partial sialoadenectomy**
- **26.32 Complete sialoadenectomy**
  En bloc excision of salivary gland lesion
  Radical sialoadenectomy

26.4 Repair of salivary gland or duct
- **26.41 Suture of laceration of salivary gland**
- **26.42 Closure of salivary fistula**
  DEF: Closing of abnormal opening in salivary gland.
- **26.49 Other repair and plastic operations on salivary gland or duct**
  Fistulization of salivary gland
  Plastic repair of salivary gland or duct NOS
  Transplantation of salivary duct opening

26.9 Other operations on salivary gland or duct
- **26.91 Probing of salivary duct**
- **26.99 Other**

27 Other operations on mouth and face
INCLUDES operations on:
lips
palate
soft tissue of face and mouth, except tongue and gingiva
EXCLUDES *operations on:*
gingiva (24.0-24.99)
tongue (25.01-25.99)

27.0 Drainage of face and floor of mouth
Drainage of:
facial region (abscess)
fascial compartment of face
Ludwig's angina
EXCLUDES *drainage of thyroglossal tract (06.09)*

27.1 Incision of palate

27.2 Diagnostic procedures on oral cavity
- **27.21 Biopsy of bony palate**
- **27.22 Biopsy of uvula and soft palate**
- **27.23 Biopsy of lip**
- **27.24 Biopsy of mouth, unspecified structure**
- **27.29 Other diagnostic procedures on oral cavity**
  EXCLUDES *soft tissue x-ray (87.09)*

27.3 Excision of lesion or tissue of bony palate
- **27.31 Local excision or destruction of lesion or tissue of bony palate**
  Local excision or destruction of palate by:
  cautery
  chemotherapy
  cryotherapy
  EXCLUDES *biopsy of bony palate (27.21)*
- **27.32 Wide excision or destruction of lesion or tissue of bony palate**
  En bloc resection of alveolar process and palate

27.4 Excision of other parts of mouth
- **27.41 Labial frenectomy**
  EXCLUDES *division of labial frenum (27.91)*
  DEF: Removal of mucous membrane fold of lip.
- **27.42 Wide excision of lesion of lip**
- **27.43 Other excision of lesion or tissue of lip**
- **27.49 Other excision of mouth**
  EXCLUDES *biopsy of mouth NOS (27.24)*
  excision of lesion of:
  palate (27.31-27.32)
  tongue (25.1)
  uvula (27.72)
  fistulectomy of mouth (27.53)
  frenectomy of:
  lip (27.41)
  tongue (25.92)
  AHA: ►2Q, '05, 8◄

27.5 Plastic repair of mouth
EXCLUDES *palatoplasty (27.61-27.69)*
- **27.51 Suture of laceration of lip**
- **27.52 Suture of laceration of other part of mouth**
- **27.53 Closure of fistula of mouth**
  EXCLUDES *fistulectomy:*
  nasolabial (21.82)
  oro-antral (22.71)
  oronasal (21.82)
- **27.54 Repair of cleft lip**
- **27.55 Full-thickness skin graft to lip and mouth**
- **27.56 Other skin graft to lip and mouth**
- **27.57 Attachment of pedicle or flap graft to lip and mouth**
  AHA: 1Q, '96, 14
  DEF: Repair of lip or mouth with tissue pedicle or flap still connected to original vascular base.
- **27.59 Other plastic repair of mouth**

27.6 Palatoplasty
- **27.61 Suture of laceration of palate**
- **27.62 Correction of cleft palate**
  Correction of cleft palate by push-back operation
  EXCLUDES *revision of cleft palate repair (27.63)*
- **27.63 Revision of cleft palate repair**
  Secondary:
  attachment of pharyngeal flap
  lengthening of palate
  AHA: 1Q, '96, 14
- **27.64 Insertion of palatal implant**
  DEF: Nonabsorbable polyester implants into the soft palate at the back of the roof of the mouth; one implant placed at the soft palate midline and two are positioned on either side; to support and stiffen the palate reducing vibration (snoring).
- **27.69 Other plastic repair of palate**
  Code also any insertion of palatal implant (27.64)
  EXCLUDES *fistulectomy of mouth (27.53)*
  AHA: 3Q, '99, 22; 1Q, '97, 14; 3Q, '92, 18

27.7 Operations on uvula
- **27.71 Incision of uvula**
- **27.72 Excision of uvula**
  EXCLUDES *biopsy of uvula (27.22)*
- **27.73 Repair of uvula**
  EXCLUDES *that with synchronous cleft palate repair (27.62)*
  uranostaphylorrhaphy (27.62)

27.79 Other operations on uvula
AHA: 3Q, '92, 18

✓4th **27.9 Other operations on mouth and face**

27.91 Labial frenotomy
Division of labial frenum
EXCLUDES *lingual frenotomy (25.91)*
DEF: Division of labial frenum: Cutting and separating mucous membrane fold of lip.

27.92 Incision of mouth, unspecified structure
EXCLUDES *incision of:*
gum (24.0)
palate (27.1)
salivary gland or duct (26.0)
tongue (25.94)
uvula (27.71)

27.99 Other operations on oral cavity
Graft of buccal sulcus
EXCLUDES *removal of:*
intraluminal foreign body (98.01)
penetrating foreign body from mouth without incision (98.22)
DEF: Graft of buccal sulcus: Implant of tissue into groove of interior cheek lining.

✓3rd **28 Operations on tonsils and adenoids**

28.0 Incision and drainage of tonsil and peritonsillar structures
Drainage (oral) (transcervical) of:
parapharyngeal, peritonsillar, retropharyngeal, tonsillar } abscess

✓4th **28.1 Diagnostic procedures on tonsils and adenoids**

28.11 Biopsy of tonsils and adenoids

28.19 Other diagnostic procedures on tonsils and adenoids
EXCLUDES *soft tissue x-ray (87.09)*

28.2 Tonsillectomy without adenoidectomy
AHA: 1Q, '97, 5; 2Q, '90, 23

28.3 Tonsillectomy with adenoidectomy
AHA: ▶2Q, '05, 16◀

28.4 Excision of tonsil tag

28.5 Excision of lingual tonsil

28.6 Adenoidectomy without tonsillectomy
Excision of adenoid tag

28.7 Control of hemorrhage after tonsillectomy and adenoidectomy
AHA: ▶2Q, '05, 16◀

✓4th **28.9 Other operations on tonsils and adenoids**

28.91 Removal of foreign body from tonsil and adenoid by incision
EXCLUDES *that without incision (98.13)*

28.92 Excision of lesion of tonsil and adenoid
EXCLUDES *biopsy of tonsil and adenoid (28.11)*

28.99 Other

✓3rd **29 Operations on pharynx**
INCLUDES operations on:
hypopharynx
nasopharynx
oropharynx
operations on:
pharyngeal pouch
pyriform sinus

29.0 Pharyngotomy
Drainage of pharyngeal bursa
EXCLUDES *incision and drainage of retropharyngeal abscess (28.0)*
removal of foreign body (without incision) (98.13)

✓4th **29.1 Diagnostic procedures on pharynx**

29.11 Pharyngoscopy

29.12 Pharyngeal biopsy
Biopsy of supraglottic mass

29.19 Other diagnostic procedures on pharynx
EXCLUDES *x-ray of nasopharynx:*
contrast (87.06)
other (87.09)

29.2 Excision of branchial cleft cyst or vestige
EXCLUDES *branchial cleft fistulectomy (29.52)*

✓4th **29.3 Excision or destruction of lesion or tissue of pharynx**
AHA: 2Q, '89, 18

29.31 Cricopharyngeal myotomy
EXCLUDES *that with pharyngeal diverticulectomy (29.32)*
DEF: Removal of outward pouching of throat.

29.32 Pharyngeal diverticulectomy

29.33 Pharyngectomy (partial)
EXCLUDES *laryngopharyngectomy (30.3)*

29.39 Other excision or destruction of lesion or tissue of pharynx

29.4 Plastic operation on pharynx
Correction of nasopharyngeal atresia
EXCLUDES *pharyngoplasty associated with cleft palate repair (27.62-27.63)*
AHA: 3Q, '99, 22; 1Q, '97, 5; 3Q, '92, 18
DEF: Correction of nasopharyngeal atresia: Construction of normal opening for throat stricture behind nose.

✓4th **29.5 Other repair of pharynx**

29.51 Suture of laceration of pharynx

29.52 Closure of branchial cleft fistula
DEF: Sealing off an abnormal opening of the branchial fissure in throat.

29.53 Closure of other fistula of pharynx
Pharyngoesophageal fistulectomy

29.54 Lysis of pharyngeal adhesions

29.59 Other
AHA: 2Q, '89, 18

✓4th **29.9 Other operations on pharynx**

29.91 Dilation of pharynx
Dilation of nasopharynx

29.92 Division of glossopharyngeal nerve

29.99 Other
EXCLUDES *insertion of radium into pharynx and nasopharynx (92.27)*
removal of intraluminal foreign body (98.13)

6. OPERATIONS ON THE RESPIRATORY SYSTEM (30-34)

✓3rd **30 Excision of larynx**

✓4th **30.0 Excision or destruction of lesion or tissue of larynx**

30.01 Marsupialization of laryngeal cyst

DEF: Incision of cyst of larynx with the edges sutured open to create pouch.

30.09 Other excision or destruction of lesion or tissue of larynx

Stripping of vocal cords

EXCLUDES *biopsy of larynx (31.43)*
laryngeal fistulectomy (31.62)
laryngotracheal fistulectomy (31.62)

30.1 Hemilaryngectomy

DEF: Excision of one side (half) of larynx.

✓4th **30.2 Other partial laryngectomy**

30.21 Epiglottidectomy

30.22 Vocal cordectomy

Excision of vocal cords

30.29 Other partial laryngectomy

Excision of laryngeal cartilage

30.3 Complete laryngectomy

Block dissection of larynx (with thyroidectomy) (with synchronous tracheostomy)
Laryngopharyngectomy

EXCLUDES *that with radical neck dissection (30.4)*

30.4 Radical laryngectomy

Complete [total] laryngectomy with radical neck dissection (with thyroidectomy) (with synchronous tracheostomy)

✓3rd **31 Other operations on larynx and trachea**

31.0 Injection of larynx

Injection of inert material into larynx or vocal cords

31.1 Temporary tracheostomy

Tracheotomy for assistance in breathing

AHA: 1Q, '97, 6

✓4th **31.2 Permanent tracheostomy**

31.21 Mediastinal tracheostomy

DEF: Placement of artificial breathing tube in windpipe through mediastinum, for long-term use.

31.29 Other permanent tracheostomy

EXCLUDES *that with laryngectomy (30.3-30.4)*

AHA: ▶2Q, '05, 8;◀ 2Q, '02, 6

31.3 Other incision of larynx or trachea

EXCLUDES *that for assistance in breathing (31.1-31.29)*

✓4th **31.4 Diagnostic procedures on larynx and trachea**

31.41 Tracheoscopy through artificial stoma

EXCLUDES *that with biopsy (31.43-31.44)*

DEF: Exam by scope of trachea through an artificial opening.

Temporary Tracheostomy

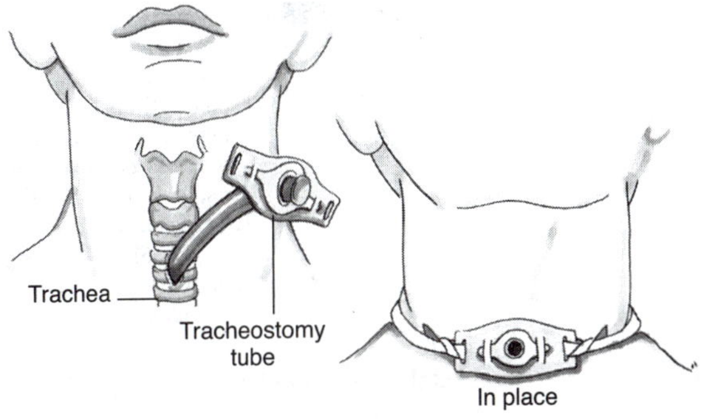

Closed Endoscopic Biopsy of Larynx

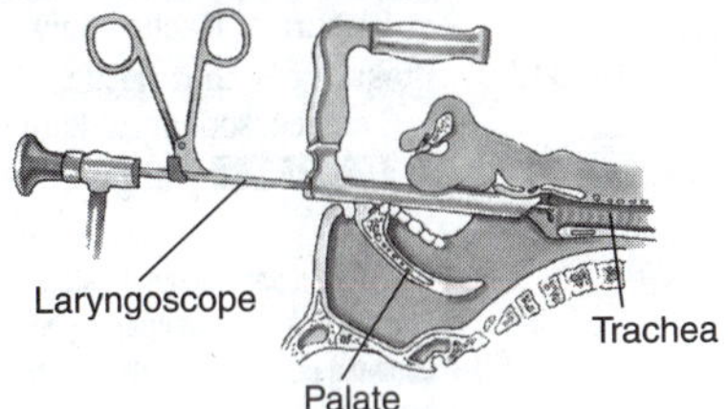

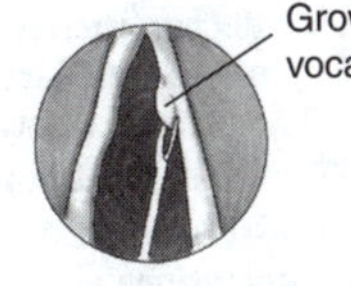

31.42 Laryngoscopy and other tracheoscopy

EXCLUDES *that with biopsy (31.43-31.44)*

31.43 Closed [endoscopic] biopsy of larynx

31.44 Closed [endoscopic] biopsy of trachea

31.45 Open biopsy of larynx or trachea

31.48 Other diagnostic procedures on larynx

EXCLUDES *contrast laryngogram (87.07)*
microscopic examination of specimen from larynx (90.31-90.39)
soft tissue x-ray of larynx NEC (87.09)

31.49 Other diagnostic procedures on trachea

EXCLUDES *microscopic examination of specimen from trachea (90.41-90.49)*
x-ray of trachea (87.49)

31.5 Local excision or destruction of lesion or tissue of trachea

EXCLUDES *biopsy of trachea (31.44-31.45)*
laryngotracheal fistulectomy (31.62)
tracheoesophageal fistulectomy (31.73)

✓4th **31.6 Repair of larynx**

31.61 Suture of laceration of larynx

31.62 Closure of fistula of larynx

Laryngotracheal fistulectomy
Take-down of laryngostomy

DEF: Laryngotracheal fistulectomy: Excision and closing of passage between voice box and trachea.

DEF: Take-down of laryngostomy: Removal of laryngostomy tube and restoration of voice box.

31.63 Revision of laryngostomy

31.64 Repair of laryngeal fracture

DEF: Alignment and positioning of harder structures of larynx such as hyoid bone; following fracture.

31.69 Other repair of larynx

Arytenoidopexy
Cordopexy
Graft of larynx
Transposition of vocal cords

EXCLUDES *construction of artificial larynx (31.75)*

DEF: Arytenoidopexy: Fixation of pitcher-shaped cartilage in voice box.

DEF: Graft of larynx: Implant of graft tissue into voice box.

DEF: Transposition of the vocal cords: Placement of vocal cords into more functional positions.

✓4th **31.7 Repair and plastic operations on trachea**

31.71 Suture of laceration of trachea

31.72 **Closure of external fistula of trachea**
Closure of tracheotomy

31.73 **Closure of other fistula of trachea**
Tracheoesophageal fistulectomy
EXCLUDES *laryngotracheal fistulectomy (31.62)*
DEF: Tracheoesophageal fistulectomy: Excision and closure of abnormal opening between windpipe and esophagus.

31.74 **Revision of tracheostomy**

31.75 **Reconstruction of trachea and construction of artificial larynx**
Tracheoplasty with artificial larynx

31.79 **Other repair and plastic operations on trachea**

✓4th 31.9 **Other operations on larynx and trachea**

31.91 **Division of laryngeal nerve**

31.92 **Lysis of adhesions of trachea or larynx**

31.93 **Replacement of laryngeal or tracheal stent**
DEF: Removal and substitution of tubed molding into larynx or trachea.

31.94 **Injection of locally-acting therapeutic substance into trachea**

31.95 **Tracheoesophageal fistulization**
DEF: Creation of passage between trachea and esophagus.

31.98 **Other operations on larynx**
Dilation, Division of congenital web, Removal of keel or stent } of larynx
EXCLUDES *removal of intraluminal foreign body from larynx without incision (98.14)*
DEF: Dilation: Increasing larynx size by stretching.
DEF: Division of congenital web: Cutting and separating congenital membranes around larynx.
DEF: Removal of keel or stent: Removal of prosthetic device from larynx.

31.99 **Other operations on trachea**
EXCLUDES *removal of:*
intraluminal foreign body from trachea without incision (98.15)
tracheostomy tube (97.37)
replacement of tracheostomy tube (97.23)
tracheostomy toilette (96.55)
AHA: 1Q, '97, 14

✓3rd 32 **Excision of lung and bronchus**
INCLUDES rib resection
sternotomy
sternum-splitting incision
thoracotomy } as operative approach
Code also any synchronous bronchoplasty (33.48)
DEF: Rib resection: Cutting of ribs to access operative field.
DEF: Sternotomy: Cut through breastbone as an operative approach.
DEF: Sternum-splitting incision: Breaking through breastbone to access operative field.

✓4th 32.0 **Local excision or destruction of lesion or tissue of bronchus**
EXCLUDES *biopsy of bronchus (33.24-33.25)*
bronchial fistulectomy (33.42)
AHA: 4Q, '88, 11

Lung Volume Reduction

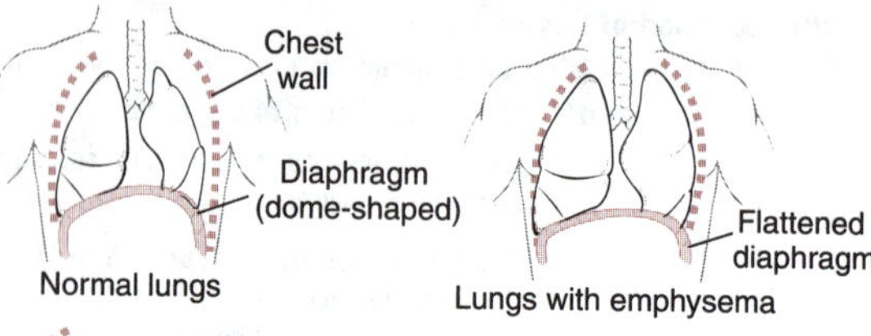

32.01 **Endoscopic excision or destruction of lesion or tissue of bronchus**

32.09 **Other local excision or destruction of lesion or tissue of bronchus**
EXCLUDES *that by endoscopic approach (32.01)*

32.1 **Other excision of bronchus**
Resection (wide sleeve) of bronchus
EXCLUDES *radical dissection [excision] of bronchus (32.6)*
DEF: Resection (wide sleeve) of bronchus: Excision and partial, lengthwise removal of a lung branch.

✓4th 32.2 **Local excision or destruction of lesion or tissue of lung**

32.21 **Plication of emphysematous bleb**
DEF: Stitching of a swollen vesicle into folds or tuck.

32.22 **Lung volume reduction surgery** LC
AHA: 1Q, '97, 6; 3Q, '96, 20; 4Q, '95, 64
DEF: Excision of portion of lung(s) to reduce respiratory effort in moderate to severe emphysema.

● 32.23 **Open ablation of lung lesion or tissue**

● 32.24 **Percutaneous ablation of lung lesion or tissue**

● 32.25 **Thoracoscopic ablation of lung lesion or tissue**

● 32.26 **Other and unspecified ablation of lung lesion or tissue**

32.28 **Endoscopic excision or destruction of lesion or tissue of lung**
EXCLUDES ▶ *ablation of lung lesion or tissue:*
open (32.23)
other (32.26)
percutaneous (32.24)
thoracoscopic (32.25)◀
biopsy of lung (33.26-33.27)

32.29 **Other local excision or destruction of lesion or tissue of lung**
Resection of lung: NOS
Resection of lung: wedge
EXCLUDES ▶ *ablation of lung lesion or tissue:*
open (32.23)
other (32.26)
percutaneous (32.24)
thoracoscopic (32.25)◀
biopsy of lung (33.26-33.27)
that by endoscopic approach (32.28)
wide excision of lesion of lung (32.3)
AHA: 3Q, '99, 3

32.3 **Segmental resection of lung**
Partial lobectomy

32.4 Lobectomy of lung
Lobectomy with segmental resection of adjacent lobes of lung
EXCLUDES *that with radical dissection [excision] of thoracic structures (32.6)*

32.5 Complete pneumonectomy
Excision of lung NOS
Pneumonectomy (with mediastinal dissection)
AHA: 1Q, '99, 6

32.6 Radical dissection of thoracic structures
Block [en bloc] dissection of bronchus, lobe of lung, brachial plexus, intercostal structure, ribs (transverse process), and sympathetic nerves

32.9 Other excision of lung
EXCLUDES *biopsy of lung and bronchus (33.24-33.27)*
pulmonary decortication (34.51)

✓3rd **33 Other operations on lung and bronchus**
INCLUDES rib resection, sternotomy, sternum-splitting incision, thoracotomy } as operative approach

33.0 Incision of bronchus

33.1 Incision of lung
EXCLUDES *puncture of lung (33.93)*

✓4th **33.2 Diagnostic procedures on lung and bronchus**

33.21 Bronchoscopy through artificial stoma
EXCLUDES *that with biopsy (33.24, 33.27)*
DEF: Visual exam of lung and its branches via tube through artificial opening.

33.22 Fiber-optic bronchoscopy
EXCLUDES *that with biopsy (33.24, 33.27)*
AHA: 1Q, '04, 4
DEF: Exam of lung and bronchus via flexible optical instrument for visualization.

33.23 Other bronchoscopy
EXCLUDES *that for:*
aspiration (96.05)
biopsy (33.24, 33.27)
AHA: 3Q, '02, 18; 1Q, '99, 6

33.24 Closed [endoscopic] biopsy of bronchus
Bronchoscopy (fiberoptic) (rigid) with:
brush biopsy of "lung"
brushing or washing for specimen collection
excision (bite) biopsy
Diagnostic bronchoalveolar lavage (BAL)
EXCLUDES *closed biopsy of lung, other than brush biopsy of "lung" (33.26, 33.27)*
whole lung lavage (33.99)
AHA: 3Q, '04, 9; 3Q, '02, 16; 4Q, '92, 27; 3Q, '91, 15
DEF: Bronchoalveolar lavage (BAL): Saline is introduced into the subsegment of a lobe and retrieved using gentle suction; also called 'liquid biopsy'.
DEF: Brush biopsy: Obtaining cell or tissue samples via bristled instrument without incision.

Bronchoscopy with Bite Biopsy

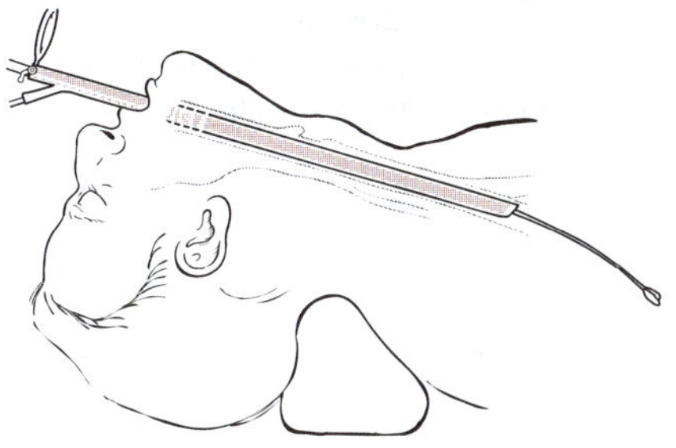

33.25 Open biopsy of bronchus
EXCLUDES *open biopsy of lung (33.28)*

33.26 Closed [percutaneous] [needle] biopsy of lung
EXCLUDES *endoscopic biopsy of lung (33.27)*
AHA: 3Q, '92, 12

33.27 Closed endoscopic biopsy of lung
Fiber-optic (flexible) bronchoscopy with fluoroscopic guidance with biopsy
Transbronchial lung biopsy
EXCLUDES *brush biopsy of "lung" (33.24)*
percutaneous biopsy of lung (33.26)
AHA: 3Q, '04, 9; 3Q, '02, 16; 4Q, '92, 27; 3Q, '91, 15; S-O, '86, 11

33.28 Open biopsy of lung
AHA: 3Q, '99, 3; 3Q, '92, 12

33.29 Other diagnostic procedures on lung and bronchus
EXCLUDES *contrast bronchogram:*
endotracheal (87.31)
other (87.32)
lung scan (92.15)
magnetic resonance imaging (88.92)
microscopic examination of specimen from bronchus or lung (90.41-90.49)
routine chest x-ray (87.44)
ultrasonography of lung (88.73)
vital capacity determination (89.37)
x-ray of bronchus or lung NOS (87.49)

✓4th **33.3 Surgical collapse of lung**

33.31 Destruction of phrenic nerve for collapse of lung
DEF: Therapeutic deadening or destruction of diaphragmatic nerve to collapse the lung.

33.32 Artificial pneumothorax for collapse of lung
Thoracotomy for collapse of lung
DEF: Forcing air or gas into diaphragmatic space to achieve therapeutic collapse of lung.
DEF: Thoracotomy for collapse of lung: Incision into chest for therapeutic collapse of lung.

33.33 Pneumoperitoneum for collapse of lung
DEF: Forcing air or gas into abdominal serous membrane to achieve therapeutic collapse of lung.

33.34 Thoracoplasty
DEF: Removal of ribs for therapeutic collapse of lungs.

33.39 Other surgical collapse of lung
Collapse of lung NOS

✓4th **33.4 Repair and plastic operation on lung and bronchus**

33.41 Suture of laceration of bronchus

33.42 Closure of bronchial fistula
Closure of bronchostomy
Fistulectomy:
bronchocutaneous
bronchoesophageal
bronchovisceral
EXCLUDES *closure of fistula:*
bronchomediastinal (34.73)
bronchopleural (34.73)
bronchopleuromediastinal (34.73)
DEF: Closure of bronchostomy: Removal of bronchostomy tube and repair of surgical wound.
DEF: Fistulectomy: Closure of abnormal passage.
Bronchocutaneous: Between skin and lung branch.
Bronchoesophagus: Between esophagus and lung branch.
Bronchovisceral: Between an internal organ and lung branch.

33.43 Closure of laceration of lung

33.48 Other repair and plastic operations on bronchus

33.49 Other repair and plastic operations on lung

EXCLUDES *closure of pleural fistula (34.73)*

✓4th **33.5 Lung transplant**

Note: To report donor source — *see* codes 00.91-00.93

Code also cardiopulmonary bypass [extracorporeal circulation] [heart-lung machine] [39.61]

EXCLUDES *combined heart-lung transplantation (33.6)*

AHA: 4Q, '95, 75

33.50 Lung transplantation, not otherwise specified LC

33.51 Unilateral lung transplantation LC

33.52 Bilateral lung transplantation LC

Double-lung transplantation

En bloc transplantation

DEF: Sequential excision and implant of both lungs.

33.6 Combined heart-lung transplantation LC

Note: To report donor source — *see* codes 00.91-00.93

Code also cardiopulmonary bypass [extracorporeal circulation] [heart-lung machine] (39.61)

● ✓4th **33.7 Endoscopic insertion, replacement, and removal of therapeutic device or substances in bronchus or lung**

Biologic lung volume reduction (BLVR)

EXCLUDES *insertion of tracheobronchial stent (96.05)*

● **33.71 Endoscopic insertion or replacement of bronchial valve(s)**

Endobronchial airflow redirection valve

Intrabronchial airflow redirection valve

● **33.78 Endoscopic removal of bronchial device(s) or substances**

● **33.79 Endoscopic insertion of other bronchial device or substances**

Biologic lung volume reduction NOS (BLVR)

✓4th **33.9 Other operations on lung and bronchus**

33.91 Bronchial dilation

AHA: 1Q, '97, 14

33.92 Ligation of bronchus

DEF: Tying off of a lung branch.

33.93 Puncture of lung

EXCLUDES *needle biopsy (33.26)*

DEF: Piercing of lung with surgical instrument.

33.98 Other operations on bronchus

EXCLUDES *bronchial lavage (96.56)*
removal of intraluminal foreign body from bronchus without incision (98.15)

33.99 Other operations on lung

Whole lung lavage

EXCLUDES *other continuous mechanical ventilation (96.70-96.72)*
respiratory therapy (93.90-93.99)

AHA: 3Q, '02, 17

✓3rd **34 Operations on chest wall, pleura, mediastinum, and diaphragm**

EXCLUDES *operations on breast (85.0-85.99)*

✓4th **34.0 Incision of chest wall and pleura**

EXCLUDES *that as operative approach — omit code*

34.01 Incision of chest wall

Extrapleural drainage

EXCLUDES *incision of pleura (34.09)*

AHA: 3Q, '00, 12; 1Q, '92, 13

DEF: Extrapleural drainage: Incision to drain fluid from external pleura.

34.02 Exploratory thoracotomy

34.03 Reopening of recent thoracotomy site

34.04 Insertion of intercostal catheter for drainage

Chest tube

Closed chest drainage

Revision of intercostal catheter (chest tube) (with lysis of adhesions)

AHA: 2Q, '03, 7; 1Q, '99, 10; 2Q, '99, 12; 1Q, '95, 5; 1Q, '92, 12

DEF: Insertion of catheter between ribs for drainage.

34.05 Creation of pleuroperitoneal shunt

AHA: 4Q, '94, 50

34.09 Other incision of pleura

Creation of pleural window for drainage

Intercostal stab

Open chest drainage

EXCLUDES *thoracoscopy (34.21)*
thoracotomy for collapse of lung (33.32)

AHA: 3Q, '02, 22; 1Q, '94, 7; 4Q, '94, 50

DEF: Creation of pleural window: Creation of circumscribed drainage hole in serous membrane of chest.

DEF: Intercostal stab: Creation of penetrating stab wound between ribs.

DEF: Open chest drainage: Insertion of tube through ribs and serous membrane of chest for drainage.

34.1 Incision of mediastinum

EXCLUDES *mediastinoscopy (34.22)*
mediastinotomy associated with pneumonectomy (32.5)

✓4th **34.2 Diagnostic procedures on chest wall, pleura, mediastinum, and diaphragm**

34.21 Transpleural thoracoscopy

AHA: 3Q, '02, 27

DEF: Exam of chest through serous membrane using scope.

34.22 Mediastinoscopy

Code also any lymph node biopsy (40.11)

DEF: Exam of lung cavity and heart using scope.

34.23 Biopsy of chest wall

34.24 Pleural biopsy

AHA: 3Q, '02, 22, 27; 1Q, '92, 14

34.25 Closed [percutaneous] [needle] biopsy of mediastinum

34.26 Open biopsy of mediastinum

34.27 Biopsy of diaphragm

34.28 Other diagnostic procedures on chest wall, pleura, and diaphragm

EXCLUDES *angiocardiography (88.50-88.58)*
aortography (88.42)
arteriography of:
intrathoracic vessels NEC (88.44)
pulmonary arteries (88.43)
microscopic examination of specimen from chest wall, pleura, and diaphragm (90.41-90.49)
phlebography of:
intrathoracic vessels NEC (88.63)
pulmonary veins (88.62)
radiological examinations of thorax:
C.A.T. scan (87.41)
diaphragmatic x-ray (87.49)
intrathoracic lymphangiogram (87.34)
routine chest x-ray (87.44)
sinogram of chest wall (87.38)
soft tissue x-ray of chest wall NEC (87.39)
tomogram of thorax NEC (87.42)
ultrasonography of thorax (88.73)

34.29 Other diagnostic procedures on mediastinum

EXCLUDES *mediastinal:*
pneumogram (87.33)
x-ray NEC (87.49)

34.3 Excision or destruction of lesion or tissue of mediastinum

EXCLUDES *biopsy of mediastinum (34.25-34.26)*
mediastinal fistulectomy (34.73)

34.4 Excision or destruction of lesion of chest wall

Excision of lesion of chest wall NOS (with excision of ribs)

EXCLUDES *biopsy of chest wall (34.23)*
costectomy not incidental to thoracic procedure (77.91)
excision of lesion of:
breast (85.20-85.25)
cartilage (80.89)
skin (86.2-86.3)
fistulectomy (34.73)

✓4th **34.5 Pleurectomy**

34.51 Decortication of lung

DEF: Removal of thickened serous membrane for lung expansion.

34.59 Other excision of pleura

Excision of pleural lesion

EXCLUDES *biopsy of pleura (34.24)*
pleural fistulectomy (34.73)

34.6 Scarification of pleura

Pleurosclerosis

EXCLUDES *injection of sclerosing agent (34.92)*

AHA: 1Q, '92, 12

DEF: Destruction of fluid-secreting serous membrane cells of chest.

✓4th **34.7 Repair of chest wall**

34.71 Suture of laceration of chest wall

EXCLUDES *suture of skin and subcutaneous tissue alone (86.59)*

34.72 Closure of thoracostomy

34.73 Closure of other fistula of thorax

Closure of:
bronchopleural, bronchopleurocutaneous, bronchopleuromediastinal } fistula

34.74 Repair of pectus deformity

Repair of:
pectus carinatum, pectus excavatum } (with implant)

AHA: 2Q, '04, 6

DEF: Pectus carinatum repair: Restoration of prominent chest bone defect with implant.

DEF: Pectus excavatum: Restoration of depressed chest bone defect with implant.

34.79 Other repair of chest wall

Repair of chest wall NOS

AHA: 2Q, '04, 6; J-F, '87, 13

✓4th **34.8 Operations on diaphragm**

34.81 Excision of lesion or tissue of diaphragm

EXCLUDES *biopsy of diaphragm (34.27)*

34.82 Suture of laceration of diaphragm

34.83 Closure of fistula of diaphragm

Thoracicoabdominal, Thoracicogastric, Thoracicointestinal } fistulectomy

DEF: Fistulectomy: Closure of abnormal passage.

34.84 Other repair of diaphragm

EXCLUDES *repair of diaphragmatic hernia (53.7-53.82)*

34.85 Implantation of diaphragmatic pacemaker

34.89 Other operations on diaphragm

✓4th **34.9 Other operations on thorax**

34.91 Thoracentesis

AHA: S-O, '85, 6

DEF: Puncture of pleural cavity for fluid aspiration, also called pleurocentesis.

34.92 Injection into thoracic cavity

Chemical pleurodesis
Injection of cytotoxic agent or tetracycline
▶Instillation into thoracic cavity◀
Requires additional code for any cancer chemotherapeutic substance (99.25)

EXCLUDES *that for collapse of lung (33.32)*

AHA: 1Q, '92, 12; 2Q, '89, 17

DEF: Chemical pleurodesis: Tetracycline hydrochloride injections to create adhesions between parietal and visceral pleura for treatment of pleural effusion.

34.93 Repair of pleura

34.99 Other

EXCLUDES *removal of:*
mediastinal drain (97.42)
sutures (97.43)
thoracotomy tube (97.41)

AHA: 1Q, '00, 17; 1Q, '88, 9

DEF: Pleural tent: Extrapleural mobilization of parietal pleura that allows draping of membrane over visceral pleura to eliminate intrapleural dead space and seal visceral pleura.

Operations on the Respiratory System 34.28–34.99

✓3rd ✓4th Additional Digit Required | Nonspecific OR Procedure | Valid OR Procedure | Non-OR Procedure | Adjunct Code

7. OPERATIONS ON THE CARDIOVASCULAR SYSTEM (35-39)

✓3rd **35 Operations on valves and septa of heart**

INCLUDES sternotomy (median) (transverse) thoracotomy } as operative approach

Code also cardiopulmonary bypass [extracorporeal circulation] [heart-lung machine] (39.61)

✓4th **35.0 Closed heart valvotomy**

EXCLUDES *percutaneous (balloon) valvuloplasty (35.96)*

DEF: Incision into valve to restore function.

35.00 Closed heart valvotomy, unspecified valve

35.01 Closed heart valvotomy, aortic valve

35.02 Closed heart valvotomy, mitral valve

35.03 Closed heart valvotomy, pulmonary valve

35.04 Closed heart valvotomy, tricuspid valve

✓4th **35.1 Open heart valvuloplasty without replacement**

INCLUDES open heart valvotomy

Code also cardiopulmonary bypass, if performed [extracorporeal circulation] [heart-lung machine] (39.61)

EXCLUDES *that associated with repair of:*
endocardial cushion defect (35.54,35.63,35.73)
percutaneous (balloon) valvuloplasty (35.96)
valvular defect associated with atrial and ventricular septal defects (35.54, 35.63, 35.73)

DEF: Incision into heart for plastic repair of valve without replacing valve.

35.10 Open heart valvuloplasty without replacement, unspecified valve

35.11 Open heart valvuloplasty of aortic valve without replacement

35.12 Open heart valvuloplasty of mitral valve without replacement

AHA: 1Q, '97, 13

35.13 Open heart valvuloplasty of pulmonary valve without replacement

35.14 Open heart valvuloplasty of tricuspid valve without replacement

✓4th **35.2 Replacement of heart valve**

INCLUDES excision of heart valve with replacement

Code also cardiopulmonary bypass [extracorporeal circulation] [heart-lung machine] (39.61)

EXCLUDES *that associated with repair of:*
endocardial cushion defect (35.54,35.63, 35.73)
valvular defect associated with atrial and ventricular septal defects (35.54, 35.63, 35.73)

DEF: Removal and replacement of valve with tissue from patient, animal, other human, or prosthetic (synthetic) valve.

35.20 Replacement of unspecified heart valve

Repair of unspecified heart valve with tissue graft or prosthetic implant

35.21 Replacement of aortic valve with tissue graft

Repair of aortic valve with tissue graft (autograft) (heterograft) (homograft)

AHA: 2Q, '97, 8

35.22 Other replacement of aortic valve

Repair of aortic valve with replacement:
NOS
prosthetic (partial) (synthetic) (total)

AHA: 1Q, '96, 11

35.23 Replacement of mitral valve with tissue graft

Repair of mitral valve with tissue graft (autograft) (heterograft) (homograft)

35.24 Other replacement of mitral valve

Repair of mitral valve with replacement:
NOS
prosthetic (partial) (synthetic) (total)

AHA: 4Q, '97, 55

35.25 Replacement of pulmonary valve with tissue graft

Repair of pulmonary valve with tissue graft (autograft) (heterograft) (homograft)

AHA: 1Q, '04, 16; 2Q, '97, 8

35.26 Other replacement of pulmonary valve

Repair of pulmonary valve with replacement:
NOS
prosthetic (partial) (synthetic) (total)

35.27 Replacement of tricuspid valve with tissue graft

Repair of tricuspid valve with tissue graft (autograft) (heterograft) (homograft)

35.28 Other replacement of tricuspid valve

Repair of tricuspid valve with replacement:
NOS
prosthetic (partial) (synthetic) (total)

✓4th **35.3 Operations on structures adjacent to heart valves**

Code also cardiopulmonary bypass [extracorporeal circulation] [heart-lung machine] (39.61)

35.31 Operations on papillary muscle

Division
Reattachment } of papillary muscle
Repair

35.32 Operations on chordae tendineae

Division
Repair } chordae tendineae

35.33 Annuloplasty

Plication of annulus

AHA: 1Q, '97, 13; 1Q, '88, 10

DEF: Plication of annulus: Tuck stitched in valvular ring for tightening.

35.34 Infundibulectomy

Right ventricular infundibulectomy

DEF: Infundibulectomy: Excision of funnel-shaped heart passage.

DEF: Right ventricular infundibulectomy: Excision of funnel-shaped passage in right upper heart chamber.

35.35 Operations on trabeculae carneae cordis

Division
Excision } of trabeculae carneae cordis

Excision of aortic subvalvular ring

35.39 Operations on other structures adjacent to valves of heart

Repair of sinus of Valsalva (aneurysm)

✓4th **35.4 Production of septal defect in heart**

35.41 Enlargement of existing atrial septal defect

Rashkind procedure
Septostomy (atrial) (balloon)

DEF: Enlargement of partition wall defect in lower heart chamber to improve function.

DEF: Rashkind procedure: Enlargement of partition wall defect between the two lower heart chambers by balloon catheter.

35.42 Creation of septal defect in heart

Blalock-Hanlon operation

DEF: Blalock-Hanlon operation: Removal of partition wall defect in lower heart chamber.

✓4th 35.5 Repair of atrial and ventricular septa with prosthesis

INCLUDES repair of septa with synthetic implant or patch

Code also cardiopulmonary bypass [extracorporeal circulation] [heart-lung machine] (39.61)

35.50 Repair of unspecified septal defect of heart with prosthesis

EXCLUDES *that associated with repair of:*
endocardial cushion defect (35.54)
septal defect associated with valvular defect (35.54)

35.51 Repair of atrial septal defect with prosthesis, open technique

Atrioseptoplasty; Correction of atrial septal defect; Repair: foramen ovale (patent), ostium secundum defect — with prosthesis

EXCLUDES *that associated with repair of:*
atrial septal defect associated with valvular and ventricular septal defects (35.54)
endocardial cushion defect (35.54)

DEF: Repair of opening or weakening in septum separating the atria; prosthesis implanted through heart incision.

35.52 Repair of atrial septal defect with prosthesis, closed technique

Insertion of atrial septal umbrella [King-Mills]

AHA: 2Q, '05, 17; 3Q, '98, 11

DEF: Correction of partition wall defect in lower heart chamber with artificial material; without incision into heart.

DEF: Insertion of atrial septal umbrella (King-Mills): Correction of partition wall defect in lower heart chamber with atrial septal umbrella.

▲ **35.53 Repair of ventricular septal defect with prosthesis, open technique**

Correction of ventricular septal defect; Repair of supracristal defect — with prosthesis

EXCLUDES *that associated with repair of:*
endocardial cushion defect (35.54)
ventricular defect associated with valvular and atrial septal defects (35.54)

35.54 Repair of endocardial cushion defect with prosthesis

Repair: atrioventricular canal, ostium primum defect, valvular defect associated with atrial and ventricular — with prosthesis (grafted to septa)

EXCLUDES *repair of isolated:*
atrial septal defect (35.51-35.52)
valvular defect (35.20, 35.22, 35.24, 35.26, 35.28)
ventricular septal defect (35.53)

● **35.55 Repair of ventricular septal defect with prosthesis, closed technique**

✓4th 35.6 Repair of atrial and ventricular septa with tissue graft

Code also cardiopulmonary bypass [extracorporeal circulation] [heart-lung machine] (39.61)

35.60 Repair of unspecified septal defect of heart with tissue graft

EXCLUDES *that associated with repair of:*
endocardial cushion defect (35.63)
septal defect associated with valvular defect (35.63)

35.61 Repair of atrial septal defect with tissue graft

Atrioseptoplasty; Correction of atrial septal defect; Repair: foramen ovale (patent), ostium secundum defect — with tissue graft

EXCLUDES *that associated with repair of:*
atrial septal defect associated with valvular and ventricular septal defects (35.63)
endocardial cushion defect (35.63)

35.62 Repair of ventricular septal defect with tissue graft

Correction of ventricular septal defect; Repair of supracristal defect — with tissue graft

EXCLUDES *that associated with repair of:*
endocardial cushion defect (35.63)
ventricular defect associated with valvular and atrial septal defects (35.63)

35.63 Repair of endocardial cushion defect with tissue graft

Repair of: atrioventricular canal, ostium primum defect, valvular defect associated with atrial and ventricular septal defects — with tissue graft

EXCLUDES *repair of isolated:*
atrial septal defect (35.61)
valvular defect (35.20-35.21, 35.23, 35.25, 35.27)
ventricular septal defect (35.62)

✓4th 35.7 Other and unspecified repair of atrial and ventricular septa

Code also cardiopulmonary bypass [extracorporeal circulation] [heart-lung machine] (39.61)

35.70 Other and unspecified repair of unspecified septal defect of heart

Repair of septal defect NOS

EXCLUDES *that associated with repair of:*
endocardial cushion defect (35.73)
septal defect associated with valvular defect (35.73)

✓3rd ✓4th Additional Digit Required | Nonspecific OR Procedure | Valid OR Procedure | Non-OR Procedure | Adjunct Code

35.71 Other and unspecified repair of atrial septal defect
Repair NOS:
atrial septum
foramen ovale (patent)
ostium secundum defect
EXCLUDES *that associated with repair of:*
atrial septal defect associated with valvular and ventricular septal defects (35.73)
endocardial cushion defect (35.73)

35.72 Other and unspecified repair of ventricular septal defect
Repair NOS:
supracristal defect
ventricular septum
EXCLUDES *that associated with repair of:*
endocardial cushion defect (35.73)
ventricular septal defect associated with valvular and atrial septal defects (35.73)

35.73 Other and unspecified repair of endocardial cushion defect
Repair NOS:
atrioventricular canal
ostium primum defect
valvular defect associated with atrial and ventricular septal defects
EXCLUDES *repair of isolated:*
atrial septal defect (35.71)
valvular defect (35.20, 35.22, 35.24, 35.26, 35.28)
ventricular septal defect (35.72)

✓4th **35.8 Total repair of certain congenital cardiac anomalies**
Note: For partial repair of defect [e.g. repair of atrial septal defect in tetralogy of Fallot] — code to specific procedure

35.81 Total repair of tetralogy of Fallot
One-stage total correction of tetralogy of Fallot with or without:
commissurotomy of pulmonary valve
infundibulectomy
outflow tract prosthesis
patch graft of outflow tract
prosthetic tube for pulmonary artery
repair of ventricular septal defect (with prosthesis)
take-down of previous systemic-pulmonary artery anastomosis

35.82 Total repair of total anomalous pulmonary venous connection
One-stage total correction of total anomalous pulmonary venous connection with or without:
anastomosis between (horizontal) common pulmonary trunk and posterior wall of left atrium (side-to-side)
enlargement of foramen ovale
incision [excision] of common wall between posterior left atrium and coronary sinus and roofing of resultant defect with patch graft (synthetic)
ligation of venous connection (descending anomalous vein) (to left innominate vein) (to superior vena cava)
repair of atrial septal defect (with prosthesis)

35.83 Total repair of truncus arteriosus
One-stage total correction of truncus arteriosus with or without:
construction (with aortic homograft) (with prosthesis) of a pulmonary artery placed from right ventricle to arteries supplying the lung
ligation of connections between aorta and pulmonary artery
repair of ventricular septal defect (with prosthesis)

35.84 Total correction of transposition of great vessels, not elsewhere classified
Arterial switch operation [Jatene]
Total correction of transposition of great arteries at the arterial level by switching the great arteries, including the left or both coronary arteries, implanted in the wall of the pulmonary artery
EXCLUDES *baffle operation [Mustard] [Senning] (35.91)*
creation of shunt between right ventricle and pulmonary artery [Rastelli] (35.92)

✓4th **35.9 Other operations on valves and septa of heart**
Code also cardiopulmonary bypass, if performed [extracorporeal circulation] [heart-lung machine] (39.61)

35.91 Interatrial transposition of venous return
Baffle:
atrial
interatrial
Mustard's operation
Resection of atrial septum and insertion of patch to direct systemic venous return to tricuspid valve and pulmonary venous return to mitral valve
DEF: Atrial baffle: Correction of venous flow of abnormal or deviated lower heart chamber.
DEF: Interatrial baffle: Correction of venous flow between abnormal lower heart chambers.
DEF: Mustard's operation: Creates intra-atrial baffle using pericardial tissue to correct transposition of the great vessels.

35.92 Creation of conduit between right ventricle and pulmonary artery
Creation of shunt between right ventricle and (distal) pulmonary artery
EXCLUDES *that associated with total repair of truncus arteriosus (35.83)*

35.93 Creation of conduit between left ventricle and aorta
Creation of apicoaortic shunt
Shunt between apex of left ventricle and aorta

35.94 Creation of conduit between atrium and pulmonary artery
Fontan procedure

35.95 Revision of corrective procedure on heart
Replacement of prosthetic heart valve poppet
Resuture of prosthesis of:
septum
valve
EXCLUDES *complete revision — code to specific procedure*
replacement of prosthesis or graft of:
septum (35.50-35.63)
valve (35.20-35.28)
DEF: Replacement of prosthetic heart valve poppet: Removal and replacement of valve-supporting prosthesis.
DEF: Resuture of prosthesis of septum: Restitching of prosthesis in partition wall.
DEF: Resuture of prosthesis of valve: Restitching of prosthetic valve.

35.96 Percutaneous valvuloplasty
Percutaneous balloon valvuloplasty
AHA: 3Q, '04, 10; M-J, '86, 6; N-D, '85, 10
DEF: Repair of valve with catheter.
DEF: Percutaneous balloon valvuloplasty: Repair of valve with inflatable catheter.

35.98 Other operations on septa of heart

35.99 Other operations on valves of heart

✓3rd **36 Operations on vessels of heart**

INCLUDES sternotomy (median) (transverse) } as operative approach
thoracotomy } as operative approach

Code also any:
injection or infusion of platelet inhibitor (99.20)
injection or infusion of thrombolytic agent (99.10)
Code also cardiopulmonary bypass, if performed [extracorporeal circulation] [heart-lung machine] (39.61)

✓4th **36.0 Removal of coronary artery obstruction and insertion of stent(s)**
AHA: 4Q, '95, 66; 2Q, '94, 13; 1Q, '94, 3; 2Q, '90, 23; N-D, '86, 8

36.03 Open chest coronary artery angioplasty
Coronary (artery):
endarterectomy (with patch graft)
thromboendarterectomy (with patch graft)
Open surgery for direct relief of coronary artery obstruction
Code also any:
insertion of drug-eluting coronary stent(s) (36.07)
insertion of non-drug-eluting coronary stent(s) (36.06)
number of vascular stents inserted (00.45-00.48)
number of vessels treated (00.40-00.43)
▶procedure on vessel bifurcation (00.44)◀
EXCLUDES *that with coronary artery bypass graft (36.10-36.19)*
AHA: 2Q, '01, 24; 3Q, '93, 7
DEF: Endarterectomy (with patch graft): Excision of thickened material within coronary artery; repair with patch graft.
DEF: Thromboendarterectomy (with patch graft): Excision of blood clot and thickened material within coronary artery; repair with patch graft.
DEF: Open surgery for direct relief of coronary artery obstruction: Removal of coronary artery obstruction through opening in chest.

36.04 Intracoronary artery thrombolytic infusion
That by direct coronary artery injection, infusion, or catheterization
enzyme infusion
platelet inhibitor
EXCLUDES *infusion of platelet inhibitor (99.20)*
infusion of thrombolytic agent (99.10)
that associated with any procedure in 36.03
AHA: 4Q, '05, 102; 4Q, '02, 114; 3Q, '02, 20; 2Q, '01, 24; 4Q, '98, 85; 1Q, '97, 3; 4Q, '95, 67
DEF: Infusion of clot breaking solution into intracoronary artery.

Coronary Bypass

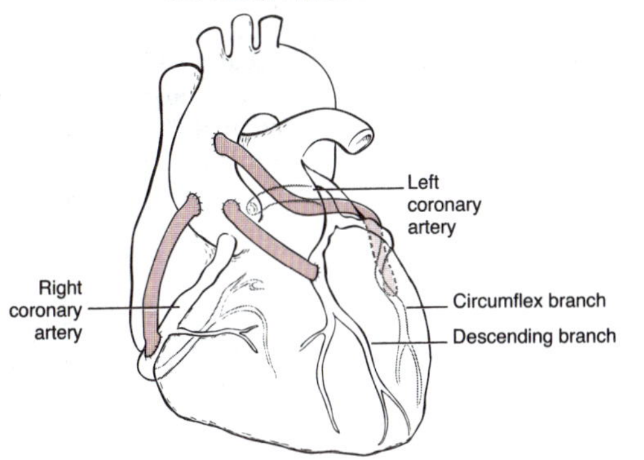

Transmyocardial Revascularization

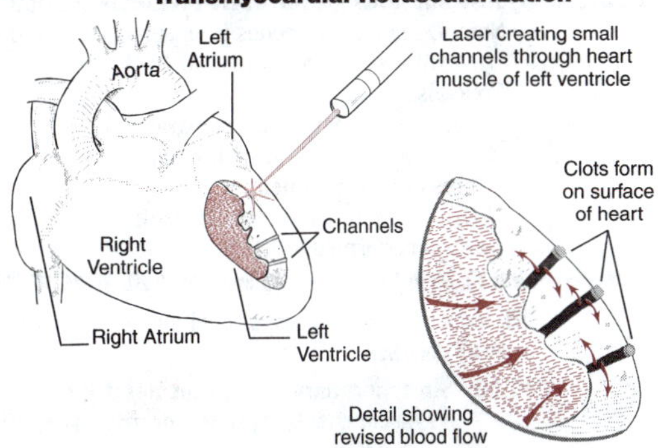

36.06 Insertion of non-drug-eluting coronary artery stent(s)
Bare stent(s)
Bonded stent(s)
Drug-coated stent(s), e.g., heparin coated
Endograft(s)
Endovascular graft(s)
Stent graft(s)
Code also any:
number of vascular stents inserted (00.45-00.48)
number of vessels treated (00.40-00.43)
open chest coronary artery angioplasty (36.03)
percutaneous transluminal coronary angioplasty [PTCA] or coronary atherectomy (00.66)
▶procedure on vessel bifurcation (00.44)◀
EXCLUDES *insertion of drug-eluting coronary artery stent(s) (36.07)*
AHA: 4Q, '05, 71; 2Q, '04, 3; 4Q, '02, 101; 1Q,'01, 9; 2Q, '01, 24; 1Q, '00, 11; 1Q, '99, 17
DEF: Percutaneous implant via catheter of metal stent, to enlarge, maintain lumen size of coronary artery.

36.07 Insertion of drug-eluting coronary artery stent(s)
Endograft(s)
Endovascular graft(s)
Stent graft(s)
Code also any:
number of vascular stents inserted (00.45-00.48)
number of vessels treated (00.40-00.43)
open chest coronary artery angioplasty (36.03)
percutaneous transluminal coronary angioplasty [PTCA] or coronary atherectomy (00.66)
▶procedure on vessel bifurcation (00.44)◀
EXCLUDES *drug-coated stents, e.g., heparin coated (36.06)*
insertion of non-drug-eluting coronary artery stent(s) (36.06)
AHA: 4Q, '05, 105-106; 4Q, '02, 101
DEF: Drug-eluting stent technology developed to prevent the accumulation of scar tissue that can narrow reopened coronary arteries. A special polymer is used to coat the drug onto the stent, which slowly releases into the coronary artery wall tissue.

36.09 Other removal of coronary artery obstruction
Coronary angioplasty NOS
Code also any:
number of vascular stents inserted (00.45-00.48)
number of vessels treated (00.40-00.43)
▶procedure on vessel bifurcation (00.44)◀
EXCLUDES *that by open angioplasty (36.03)*
that by percutaneous transluminal coronary angioplasty [PTCA] or coronary atherectomy (00.66)

Additional Digit Required | Nonspecific OR Procedure | Valid OR Procedure | Non-OR Procedure | Adjunct Code

✓4th **36.1 Bypass anastomosis for heart revascularization**

Note: Do not assign codes from series 00.40-00.43 with codes from series 36.10-36.19

Code also:
- cardiopulmonary bypass [extracorporeal circulation] [heart-lung machine] (39.61)
- pressurized treatment of venous bypass graft [conduit] with pharmaceutical substance, if performed (00.16)

AHA: 2Q, '96, 7; 3Q, '95, 7; 3Q, '93, 8; 1Q, '91, 7; 2Q, '90, 24; 4Q, '89, 3

DEF: Insertion of tube to bypass blocked coronary artery, correct coronary blood flow.

36.10 Aortocoronary bypass for heart revascularization, not otherwise specified

Direct revascularization:
- cardiac, coronary, heart muscle, myocardial } with catheter stent, prosthesis, or vein graft

Heart revascularization NOS

AHA: 2Q, '96, 7

36.11 (Aorto)coronary bypass of one coronary artery

AHA: 3Q, '02, 4, 9; 4Q, '89, 3

36.12 (Aorto)coronary bypass of two coronary arteries

AHA: 3Q, '02, 8; 4Q, '99, 15; 2Q, '96, 7; 3Q, '97, 14; 4Q, '89, 3

36.13 (Aorto)coronary bypass of three coronary arteries

AHA: 3Q, '02, 6, 7, 9; 2Q, '96, 7; 4Q, '89, 3

36.14 (Aorto)coronary bypass of four or more coronary arteries

AHA: 3Q, '02, 5; 2Q, '96, 7; 4Q, '89, 3

36.15 Single internal mammary-coronary artery bypass

Anastomosis (single):
- mammary artery to coronary artery
- thoracic artery to coronary artery

AHA: 3Q, '02, 4-9; 4Q, '99, 15; 3Q, '97, 14; 2Q, '96, 7

36.16 Double internal mammary-coronary artery bypass

Anastomosis, double:
- mammary artery to coronary artery
- thoracic artery to coronary artery

AHA: 3Q, '02, 6, 8, 9; 2Q, '96, 7

36.17 Abdominal-coronary artery bypass

Anastomosis:
- gastroepiploic artery to coronary artery

AHA: 3Q, '97, 14; 4Q, '96, 64

36.19 Other bypass anastomosis for heart revascularization

AHA: 2Q, '96, 7

36.2 Heart revascularization by arterial implant

Implantation of:
- aortic branches [ascending aortic branches] into heart muscle
- blood vessels into myocardium
- internal mammary artery [internal thoracic artery] into:
  - heart muscle
  - myocardium
  - ventricle
  - ventricular wall

Indirect heart revascularization NOS

✓4th **36.3 Other heart revascularization**

36.31 Open chest transmyocardial revascularization

DEF: Transmyocardial revascularization (TMR): Laser creation of channels through myocardium allows oxygenated blood flow from sinusoids to myocardial tissue.

36.32 Other transmyocardial revascularization

AHA: 4Q, '98, 74

● **36.33 Endoscopic transmyocardial revascularization**

Robot-assisted transmyocardial revascularization

Thoracoscopic transmyocardial revascularization

● **36.34 Percutaneous transmyocardial revascularization**

Endovascular transmyocardial revascularization

36.39 Other heart revascularization

Abrasion of epicardium

Cardio-omentopexy

Intrapericardial poudrage

Myocardial graft:
- mediastinal fat
- omentum

Myocardial graft:
- pectoral muscles

DEF: Cardio-omentopexy: Suture of omentum segment to heart after drawing segment through incision in diaphragm to improve blood supply.

DEF: Intrapericardial poudrage: Application of powder to heart lining to promote fusion.

✓4th **36.9 Other operations on vessels of heart**

Code also cardiopulmonary bypass [extracorporeal circulation] [heart-lung machine] (39.61)

36.91 Repair of aneurysm of coronary vessel

36.99 Other operations on vessels of heart

- Exploration, Incision, Ligation } of coronary artery

Repair of arteriovenous fistula

AHA: 3Q, '03, 18; 1Q, '94, 3

✓3rd **37 Other operations on heart and pericardium**

Code also any injection or infusion of platelet inhibitor (99.20)

37.0 Pericardiocentesis

DEF: Puncture of the heart lining to withdraw fluid.

✓4th **37.1 Cardiotomy and pericardiotomy**

Code also cardiopulmonary bypass [extracorporeal circulation] [heart-lung machine] (39.61)

37.10 Incision of heart, not otherwise specified

Cardiolysis NOS

37.11 Cardiotomy

Incision of:
- atrium
- endocardium

Incision of:
- myocardium
- ventricle

37.12 Pericardiotomy

Pericardial window operation

Pericardiolysis

Pericardiotomy

DEF: Pericardial window operation: Incision into heart lining for drainage.

DEF: Pericardiolysis: Destruction of heart tissue lining.

✓4th **37.2 Diagnostic procedures on heart and pericardium**

● **37.20 Non-invasive programmed electrical stimulation [NIPS]**

EXCLUDES *catheter based invasive electrophysiologic testing (37.26)*

device interrogation only without arrhythmia induction (bedside check) (89.45-89.49)

that as part of intraoperative testing—omit code

Intracardiac Echocardiography

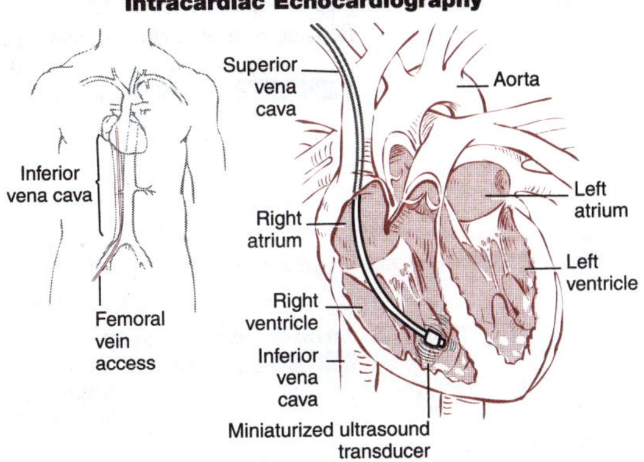

37.21 Right heart cardiac catheterization
Cardiac catheterization NOS
EXCLUDES *that with catheterization of left heart (37.23)*
AHA: 3Q, '04, 10; 3Q, '03, 9; 2Q, '90, 23; M-J, '87, 11

37.22 Left heart cardiac catheterization
EXCLUDES *that with catheterization of right heart (37.23)*
AHA: 4Q, '05, 71; 3Q, '05, 14; 3Q, '04, 10; 2Q, '04, 3; 1Q, '00, 21; 2Q, '90, 23; 4Q, '88, 4; M-J, '87, 11

37.23 Combined right and left heart cardiac catheterization
AHA: 2Q, '05, 17; 3Q, '04, 10; 2Q, '01, 8; 1Q, '00, 20; 3Q, '98, 11; 2Q, '90, 23; M-J, '87, 11

37.24 Biopsy of pericardium

37.25 Biopsy of heart
AHA: 3Q, '03, 16; 3Q, '94, 8

▲ **37.26 Catheter based invasive electrophysiologic testing**
Electrophysiologic studies [EPS]
Code also any concomitant procedure
EXCLUDES *device interrogation only without arrhythmia induction (bedside check) (89.45-89.49)*
His bundle recording (37.29)
▶*non-invasive programmed electrical stimulation (NIPS) (37.20)*
that as part of intraoperative testing—omit code◀
AHA: 3Q, '03, 23; 2Q, '03, 19; 1Q, '02, 8, 9; 1Q, '99, 3; 2Q, '97, 10; 3Q, '90, 11
DEF: Diagnostic mapping and measurement of intracardiac electrical activity; requires inserting three to six catheters into heart blood vessels and positioning catheters under fluoroscopic guidance to determine site of the tachycardia or abnormal impulse pathway; may also be used to terminate arrhythmias.

37.27 Cardiac mapping
Code also any concomitant procedure
EXCLUDES *electrocardiogram (89.52)*
His bundle recording (37.29)

37.28 Intracardiac echocardiography
Echocardiography of heart chambers
ICE
Code also any synchronous Doppler flow mapping (88.72)
EXCLUDES *intravascular imaging of coronary vessels (intravascular ultrasound) (IVUS) (00.24)*
AHA: 4Q, '01, 62
DEF: Creation of a two-dimensional graphic of heart using endoscopic echocardiographic equipment.

37.29 Other diagnostic procedures on heart and pericardium
EXCLUDES *angiocardiography (88.50-88.58)*
cardiac function tests (89.41-89.69)
cardiovascular radioisotopic scan and function study (92.05)
coronary arteriography (88.55-88.57)
diagnostic pericardiocentesis (37.0)
diagnostic ultrasound of heart (88.72)
x-ray of heart (87.49)
AHA: S-O, '87, 3

✓4th **37.3 Pericardiectomy and excision of lesion of heart**
Code also cardiopulmonary bypass [extracorporeal circulation] [heart-lung machine] (39.61)

37.31 Pericardiectomy
Excision of:
adhesions of pericardium
constricting scar of:
epicardium
pericardium
DEF: Excision of a portion of heart lining.

37.32 Excision of aneurysm of heart
Repair of aneurysm of heart

37.33 Excision or destruction of other lesion or tissue of heart, open approach
Ablation of heart tissue (cryoablation) (electrocurrent) (laser) (microwave) (radiofrequency) (resection), open chest approach
Cox-maze procedure
Maze procedure
Modified maze procedure, trans-thoracic approach
EXCLUDES *ablation, excision or destruction of lesion or tissue of heart, endovascular approach (37.34)*
AHA: 4Q, '03, 93-94; 2Q, '94, 12

37.34 Excision or destruction of other lesion or tissue of heart, other approach
Ablation of heart tissue (cryoablation) (electrocurrent) (laser) (microwave) (radiofrequency) (resection), via peripherally inserted catheter
Modified maze procedure, endovascular approach
AHA: 4Q, '03, 93-95; 1Q, '00, 20
DEF: Destruction of heart tissue or lesion by freezing, electric current or resection.

37.35 Partial ventriculectomy NC
Ventricular reduction surgery
Ventricular remodeling
Code also any synchronous:
mitral valve repair (35.02, 35.12)
mitral valve replacement (35.23-35.24)
AHA: 4Q, '97, 54, 55
DEF: Removal of elliptical slice of ventricle between anterior and posterior papillary muscle; also called Batiste operation.

Ventricular Reduction Surgery

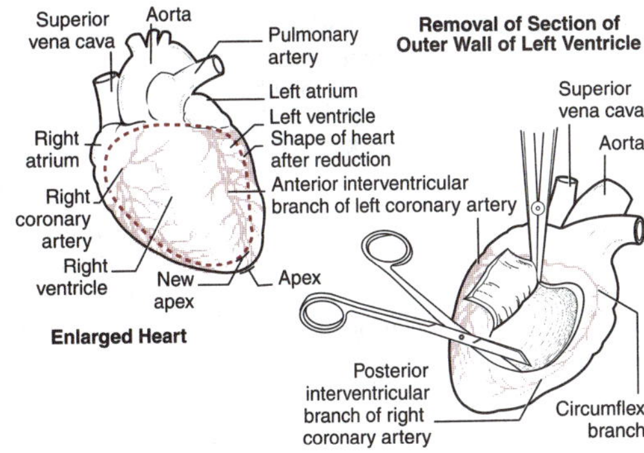

4th **37.4 Repair of heart and pericardium**
AHA: 2Q, '90, 24

37.41 Implantation of prosthetic cardiac support device around the heart
Cardiac support device (CSD)
Epicardial support device
Fabric (textile) (mesh) device
Ventricular support device on surface of heart
Code also any:
cardiopulmonary bypass [extracorporeal circulation] [heart-lung machine] if performed (39.61)
mitral valve repair (35.02, 35.12)
mitral valve replacement (35.23-35.24)
transesophageal echocardiography (88.72)
EXCLUDES *circulatory assist systems (37.61-37.68)*
AHA: 4Q, '05, 119-120
DEF: Cardiac support device: any device implanted around the ventricles of the heart for cardiac support
DEF: Fabric (textile) (mesh) device: textile mesh net sutured around the heart for support.

37.49 Other repair of heart and pericardium

4th **37.5 Heart replacement procedures**
AHA: 4Q, '03, 96

37.51 Heart transplantation LC
EXCLUDES *combined heart-lung transplantation (33.6)*
AHA: 2Q, '05, 14

37.52 Implantation of total replacement heart system NC
Artificial heart
Implantation of fully implantable total replacement heart system, including ventriculectomy
EXCLUDES *implantation of heart assist system [VAD] (37.62, 37.65, 37.66)*

37.53 Replacement or repair of thoracic unit of total replacement heart system NC
EXCLUDES *replacement and repair of heart assist system [VAD] (37.63)*

37.54 Replacement or repair of other implantable component of total replacement heart system NC
Implantable battery
Implantable controller
Transcutaneous energy transfer [TET] device
EXCLUDES *replacement and repair of heart assist system [VAD] (37.63)*
replacement or repair of thoracic unit of total replacement heart system (37.53)

4th **37.6 Implantation of heart and circulatory assist system**
EXCLUDES *implantation of prosthetic cardiac support system (37.41)*
AHA: 4Q, '95, 68
DEF: Implant of device for assisting heart in circulating blood.

37.61 Implant of pulsation balloon
AHA: 3Q, '05, 14

37.62 Insertion of non-implantable heart assist system
Insertion of heart assist system, NOS
Insertion of heart pump
EXCLUDES *implantation of total replacement heart system (37.52)*
insertion of percutaneous external heart assist device (37.68)
AHA: 4Q, '03, 116; 2Q, '90, 25

37.63 Repair of heart assist system
Replacement of parts of an existing ventricular assist device (VAD)
EXCLUDES *replacement or repair of other implantable component of total replacement heart system [artificial heart] (37.54)*
replacement or repair of thoracic unit of total replacement heart system [artificial heart] (37.53)

37.64 Removal of heart assist system
EXCLUDES *explantation [removal] of percutaneous external heart assist device (97.44)*
that with replacement of implant (37.63)
nonoperative removal of heart assist system (97.44)

37.65 Implant of external heart assist system
Note: Device (outside the body but connected to heart) with external circulation and pump
INCLUDES open chest (sternotomy) procedure for cannulae attachments
EXCLUDES *implantation of total replacement heart system (37.52)*
implant of pulsation balloon (37.61)
insertion of percutaneous external heart assist device (37.68)
DEF: Insertion of short-term circulatory support device with pump outside body.

37.66 Insertion of implantable heart assist system LC
Note: Device directly connected to the heart and implanted in the upper left quadrant of peritoneal cavity.
▶ This device can be used for either destination therapy (DT) or bridge-to-transplant (BTT).◀
Axial flow heart assist system
Diagonal pump heart assist system
Left ventricular assist device (LVAD)
Pulsatile heart assist system
Right ventricular assist device (RVAD)
Rotary pump heart assist system
Transportable, implantable heart assist system
Ventricular assist device (VAD) not otherwise specified
EXCLUDES *implantation of total replacement heart system [artificial heart] (37.52)*
implant of pulsation balloon (37.61)
insertion of percutaneous external heart assist device (37.68)
AHA: 4Q, '03, 116; 1Q, '98, 8
DEF: Insertion of long-term circulatory support device with pump in body.

37.67 Implantation of cardiomyostimulation system
Note: Two-step open procedure consisting of tranfer of one end of the latissimus dorsi muscle; wrapping it around the heart; rib resection; implantation of epicardial cardiac pacing leads into the right ventricle; tunneling and pocket creation for the cardiomyostimulator.
AHA: 4Q, '98, 75; 1Q, '98, 8

37.68 Insertion of percutaneous external heart assist device
Circulatory assist device
Extrinsic heart assist device
pVAD
Percutaneous heart assist device
INCLUDES percutaneous [femoral] insertion of cannulae attachments

▲ ✓4th **37.7 Insertion, revision, replacement, and removal of leads; insertion of temporary pacemaker system; or revision of cardiac device pocket**
Code also any insertion and replacement of pacemaker device (37.80-37.87)
EXCLUDES *implantation or replacement of transvenous lead [electrode] into left ventricular cardiac venous system (00.52)*
AHA: 1Q, '94, 16; 3Q, '92, 3; M-J, '87, 1

12 **37.70 Initial insertion of lead [electrode], not otherwise specified**
EXCLUDES *insertion of temporary transvenous pacemaker system (37.78)*
replacement of atrial and/or ventricular lead(s) (37.76)

12 **37.71 Initial insertion of transvenous lead [electrode] into ventricle**
EXCLUDES *insertion of temporary transvenous pacemaker system (37.78)*
replacement of atrial and/or ventricular lead(s) (37.76)

13 **37.72 Initial insertion of transvenous leads [electrodes] into atrium and ventricle**
EXCLUDES *insertion of temporary transvenous pacemaker system (37.78)*
replacement of atrial and/or ventricular lead(s) (37.76)
AHA: 2Q, '97, 4

12 **37.73 Initial insertion of transvenous lead [electrode] into atrium**
EXCLUDES *insertion of temporary transvenous pacemaker system (37.78)*
replacement of atrial and/or ventricular lead(s) (37.76)

15 **37.74 Insertion or replacement of epicardial lead [electrode] into epicardium**
Insertion or replacement of epicardial lead by:
sternotomy
thoracotomy
EXCLUDES *replacement of atrial and/or ventricular lead(s) (37.76)*
AHA: 3Q, '05, 3-9

37.75 Revision of lead [electrode]
Repair of electrode [removal with re-insertion]
Repositioning of ▶lead(s) (AICD) (cardiac device) (CRT-D) (CRT-P) (defibrillator) (pacemaker) (pacing) (sensing) [electrode]◀
Revision of lead NOS
EXCLUDES *repositioning of temporary transvenous pacemaker system — omit code*
AHA: 3Q, '05, 8; 2Q, '99, 11

14 **37.76 Replacement of transvenous atrial and/or ventricular lead(s) [electrode]**
Removal or abandonment of existing transvenous or epicardial lead(s) with transvenous lead(s) replacement
EXCLUDES *replacement of epicardial lead [electrode] (37.74)*
AHA: 3Q, '05, 3-92

37.77 Removal of lead(s) [electrode] without replacement
Removal:
epicardial lead (transthoracic approach)
transvenous lead(s)
EXCLUDES *removal of temporary transvenous pacemaker system — omit code*
that with replacement of:
atrial and/or ventricular lead(s) [electrode] (37.76)
epicardial lead [electrode] (37.74)

37.78 Insertion of temporary transvenous pacemaker system
EXCLUDES *intraoperative cardiac pacemaker (39.64)*
AHA: 3Q, '05, 7; 3Q, '93, 12; 1Q, '89, 2

37.79 Revision or relocation of cardiac device pocket
Debridement and reforming pocket (skin and subcutaneous tissue)
▶Insertion of loop recorder◀
Relocation of pocket [creation of new pocket] pacemaker or CRT-P
▶Removal of cardiac device/pulse generator without replacement
Removal of the implantable hemodynamic pressure sensor [lead] and monitor device
Removal without replacement of cardiac resynchronization defibrillator device
Repositioning of implantable hemodynamic pressure sensor [lead] and monitor device
Repositioning of pulse generator
Revision of cardioverter/defibrillator (automatic) pocket
Revision of pocket for intracardiac hemodynamic monitoring
Revision or relocation of CRT-D pocket◀
Revision or relocation of pacemaker, defibrillator, or other implanted cardiac device pocket
EXCLUDES ▶ *removal of loop recorder (86.05)*◀
AHA: 3Q, '05, 3-9

✓4th **37.8 Insertion, replacement, removal, and revision of pacemaker device**
▶Note: Device testing during procedure—*omit code*◀
Code also any lead insertion, lead replacement, lead removal and/or lead revision (37.70-37.77)
EXCLUDES *implantation of cardiac resynchronization pacemaker, total system [CRT-P] (00.50)*
implantation or replacement of cardiac resynchronization pacemaker pulse generator only [CRT-P] (00.53)
AHA: M-J, '87, 1

37.80 Insertion of permanent pacemaker, initial or replacement, type of device not specified

16 **37.81 Initial insertion of single-chamber device, not specified as rate responsive**
EXCLUDES *replacement of existing pacemaker device (37.85-37.87)*

16 **37.82 Initial insertion of single-chamber device, rate responsive**
Rate responsive to physiologic stimuli other than atrial rate
EXCLUDES *replacement of existing pacemaker device (37.85-37.87)*

12 Valid OR procedure code if accompanied by one of the following codes: 37.80, 37.81, 37.82, 37.85, 37.86, 37.87
13 Valid OR procedure code if accompanied by one of the following codes: 37.80, 37.83
14 Valid OR procedure code if accompanied by one of the following codes: 37.80, 37.85, 37.86, 37.87
15 Valid OR procedure code if accompanied by one of the following codes: 37.80, 37.81, 37.82, 37.83, 37.85, 37.86, 37.87
16 Valid OR procedure code if accompanied by one of the following codes: 37.72, 37.76

✓3rd ✓4th Additional Digit Required | Nonspecific OR Procedure | Valid OR Procedure | Non-OR Procedure | Adjunct Code

Insertion of Pacemaker

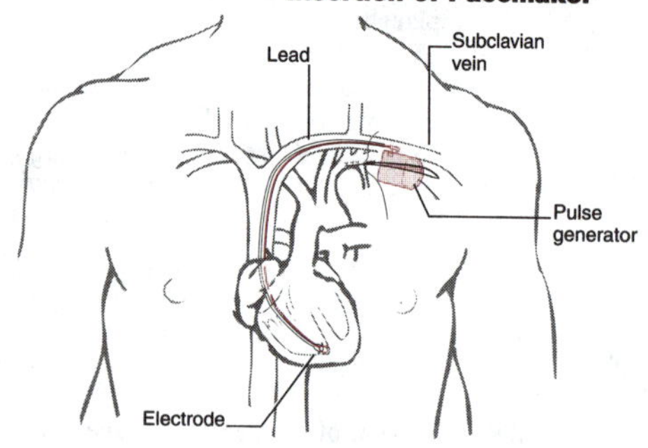

[17] **37.83 Initial insertion of dual-chamber device**
Atrial ventricular sequential device
EXCLUDES *replacement of existing pacemaker device (37.85-37.87)*
AHA: 2Q, '97, 4

37.85 Replacement of any type pacemaker device with single-chamber device, not specified as rate responsive

37.86 Replacement of any type pacemaker device with single-chamber device, rate responsive
Rate responsive to physiologic stimuli other than atrial rate

37.87 Replacement of any type pacemaker device with dual-chamber device
Atrial ventricular sequential device

37.89 Revision or removal of pacemaker device
Removal without replacement of cardiac resynchronization pacemaker device [CRT-P]
Repair of pacemaker device
EXCLUDES *removal of temporary transvenous pacemaker system — omit code*
replacement of existing pacemaker device (37.85-37.87)
replacement of existing pacemaker device with CRT-P pacemaker device (00.53)
AHA: N-D, '86, 1

4th **37.9 Other operations on heart and pericardium**
AHA: 3Q, '90, 11

37.90 Insertion of left atrial appendage device
Left atrial filter
Left atrial occluder
Transseptal catheter technique
AHA: 4Q, '04, 121
DEF: Implantation of a filtering device within the left atrial appendage (LAA) to block emboli from exiting the LAA causing stroke or systemic thromboembolism.

37.91 Open chest cardiac massage
EXCLUDES *closed chest cardiac massage (99.63)*
AHA: 4Q, '88, 12
DEF: Massage of heart through opening in chest wall to reinstate or maintain circulation.

Left Atrial Appendage Device Insertion

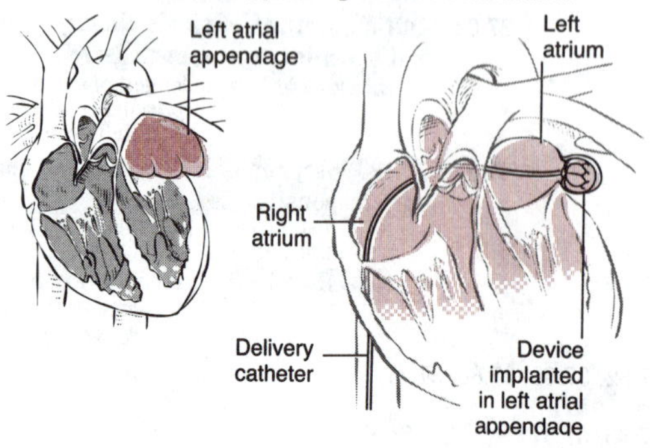

Automatic Implantable Cardioverter/Defibrillator

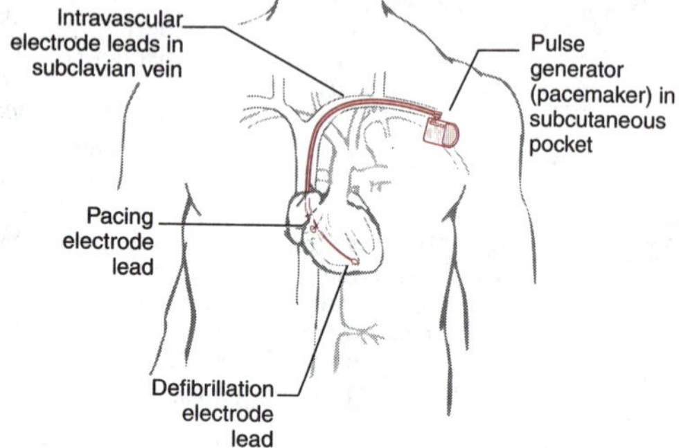

37.92 Injection of therapeutic substance into heart

37.93 Injection of therapeutic substance into pericardium

37.94 Implantation or replacement of automatic cardioverter/defibrillator, total system [AICD]
▶Note: Device testing during procedure—*omit code*◀
Implantation of defibrillator with leads (epicardial patches), formation of pocket (abdominal fascia) (subcutaneous), any transvenous leads, intraoperative procedures for evaluation of lead signals, and obtaining defibrillator threshold measurements
Techniques:
lateral thoracotomy
medial sternotomy
subxiphoid procedure
Code also extracorporeal circulation, if performed (39.61)
Code also any concomitant procedure [e.g., coronary bypass] (36.01-36.19)
EXCLUDES *implantation of cardiac resynchronization defibrillator, total system [CRT-D] (00.51)*
AHA: 2Q, '03, 19; 3Q, '01, 5-7; 3Q, '99, 12; 1Q, '99, 3; 3Q, '90, 11; S-O, '87, 5
DEF: Direct insertion, of defibrillator/cardioverter system to deliver shock and restore heart rhythm.

37.95 Implantation of automatic cardioverter/defibrillator lead(s) only
AHA: 3Q, '90, 11

37.96 Implantation of automatic cardioverter/defibrillator pulse generator only
▶Note: Device testing during procedure—*omit code*◀
EXCLUDES *implantation or replacement of cardiac resynchronization defibrillator, pulse generator device only [CRT-D] (00.54)*
AHA: 3Q, '90, 11

37.97 Replacement of automatic cardioverter/defibrillator lead(s) only
EXCLUDES ▶ *replacement of epicardial lead [electrode] into epicardium (37.74)*
replacement of transvenous lead [electrode] into left ventricular coronary venous system (00.52)◀
AHA: 3Q, '05, 3-9; 3Q, '90, 11

37.98 Replacement of automatic cardioverter defibrillator pulse generator only
▶Note: Device testing during procedure—*omit code*◀
EXCLUDES *replacement of cardiac resynchronization defibrillator, pulse generator device only [CRT-D] (00.54)*
AHA: 1Q, '99, 3; 3Q, '90, 11

[17] Valid OR procedure code if accompanied by one of the following codes: 37.70, 37.71, 37.73, 37.76

37.99 **Other**

EXCLUDES *cardiac retraining (93.36)*
conversion of cardiac rhythm (99.60-99.69)
implantation of prosthetic cardiac support device (37.41)
insertion of left atrial appendage device (37.90)
maze procedure (Cox-maze), open (37.33)
maze procedure, endovascular approach (37.34)
▶*repositioning of pulse generator (37.79)*
revision of lead(s) (37.75)
revision or relocation of pacemaker, defibrillator or other implanted cardiac device pocket (37.79)◀

AHA: 3Q, '05, 5; 2Q, '05, 14; 1Q, '97, 12; 1Q, '94, 19; 3Q, '90, 11; 1Q, '89, 11

✓3rd **38 Incision, excision, and occlusion of vessels**

Code also any application or administration of an adhesion barrier substance (99.77)

Code also cardiopulmonary bypass [extracorporeal circulation] [heart-lung machine] (39.61)

EXCLUDES *that of coronary vessels* ▶*(00.66, 36.03, 36.04, 36.09, 36.10-36.99)*◀

The following fourth-digit subclassification is for use with appropriate categories in section 38.0, 38.1, 38.3, 38.5, 38.6, and 38.8 according to site. Valid fourth-digits are in [brackets] under each code.

0 unspecified

1 intracranial vessels
Cerebral (anterior) (middle)
Circle of Willis
Posterior communicating artery

2 other vessels of head and neck
Carotid artery (common) (external) (internal)
Jugular vein (external) (internal)

3 upper limb vessels
Axillary
Brachial
Radial
Ulnar

4 aorta

5 other thoracic vessels
Innominate
Pulmonary (artery) (vein)
Subclavian
Vena cava, superior

6 abdominal arteries
Celiac
Gastric
Hepatic
Iliac
Mesenteric
Renal
Splenic
Umbilical
EXCLUDES *abdominal aorta (4)*

7 abdominal veins
Iliac
Portal
Renal
Splenic
Vena cava (inferior)

8 lower limb arteries
Femoral (common) (superficial)
Popliteal
Tibial

9 lower limb veins
Femoral
Popliteal
Saphenous
Tibial

Endarterectomy of Aortic Bifurcation

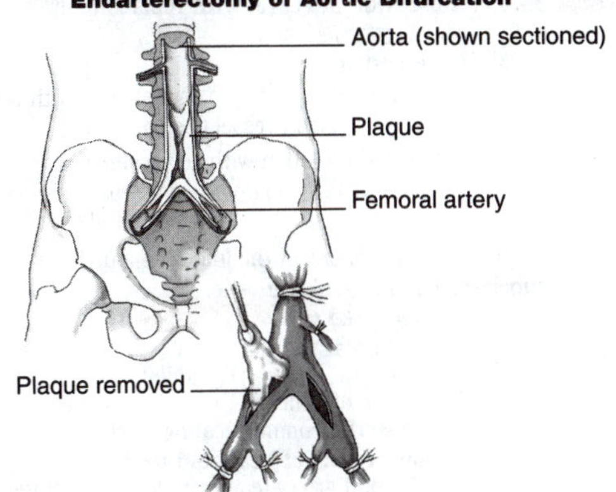

18 § ✓4th **38.0 Incision of vessel**
[0-9]
Embolectomy
Thrombectomy
EXCLUDES ▶ *endovascular removal of obstruction from head and neck vessel(s) (39.74)*◀
puncture or catheterization of any:
artery (38.91, 38.98)
vein (38.92-38.95, 38.99)

AHA: 2Q, '98, 23; **For code 38.08 and 38.09:** 1Q, '03, 17

18 § ✓4th **38.1 Endarterectomy**
[0-6,8]
Endarterectomy with:
embolectomy
patch graft
temporary bypass during procedure
thrombectomy
Code also any:
number of vascular stents inserted (00.45-00.48)
number of vessels treated (00.40-00.43)
▶procedure on vessel bifurcation (00.44)◀

AHA: 1Q, '00, 16; 2Q, '99, 5; 2Q, '95, 16; **For code 38.12:** 1Q, '02, 10

DEF: Excision of tunica intima of artery to relieve arterial walls thickened by plaque or chronic inflammation.

✓4th **38.2 Diagnostic procedures on blood vessels**

EXCLUDES *adjunct vascular system procedures (00.40-00.43)*

38.21 **Biopsy of blood vessel**

38.22 **Percutaneous angioscopy**

EXCLUDES *angioscopy of eye (95.12)*

DEF: Exam, with fiberoptic catheter inserted through peripheral artery to visualize inner lining of blood vessels.

38.29 **Other diagnostic procedures on blood vessels**

EXCLUDES *blood vessel thermography (88.86)*
circulatory monitoring (89.61-89.69)
contrast:
angiocardiography (88.50-88.58)
arteriography (88.40-88.49)
phlebography (88.60-88.67)
impedance phlebography (88.68)
peripheral vascular ultrasonography (88.77)
plethysmogram (89.58)

AHA: 3Q, '00, 16; 1Q, '99, 7

18 § ✓4th **38.3 Resection of vessel with anastomosis**
[0-9]
Angiectomy
Excision of:
aneurysm (arteriovenous) } with anastomosis
blood vessel (lesion) } with anastomosis

DEF: Reconstruction and reconnection of vessel after partial excision.

§ Requires fourth-digit. Valid digits are in [brackets] under each code. See category 38 for definitions.
18 Nonspecific OR procedure = 0

[18] §§ ✓4th **38.4 Resection of vessel with replacement**
[0-9]
Angiectomy
Excision of:
aneurysm (arteriovenous) or } with replacement
blood vessel (lesion) }
▶Partial resection with replacement◀
EXCLUDES *endovascular repair of aneurysm (39.71-39.79)*

Requires the use of one of the following fourth-digit subclassifications to identify site:

0 unspecified site

1 intracranial vessels
Cerebral (anterior) (middle)
Circle of Willis
Posterior communicating artery

2 other vessels of head and neck
Carotid artery (common) (external) (internal)
Jugular vein (external) (internal)

3 upper limb vessels
Axillary
Brachial
Radial
Ulnar

4 aorta, abdominal
Code also any thoracic vessel involvement (thoracoabdominal procedure) (38.45)

5 thoracic vessel
Aorta (thoracic)
Innominate
Pulmonary (artery) (vein)
Subclavian
Vena cava, superior
Code also any abdominal aorta involvement (thoracoabdominal procedure) (38.44)

6 abdominal arteries
Celiac
Gastric
Hepatic
Iliac
Mesenteric
Renal
Splenic
Umbilical
EXCLUDES *abdominal aorta (4)*

7 abdominal veins
Iliac
Portal
Renal
Splenic
Vena cava (inferior)

8 lower limb arteries
Femoral (common) (superficial)
Tibial

9 lower limb veins
Femoral
Popliteal
Saphenous
Tibial

AHA: 2Q, '99, 5, 6

DEF: Excision of aneurysm (arteriovenous): Excision and replacement of segment of stretched or bulging blood vessel.

DEF: Excision of blood vessel (lesion): Excision and replacement of segment of vessel containing lesion.

[18] § ✓4th **38.5 Ligation and stripping of varicose veins**
[0-3,5,7,9] **EXCLUDES** *ligation of varices:*
esophageal (42.91)
gastric (44.91)

AHA: For code 38.59: 2Q, '97, 7

DEF: Ligation of varicose veins: Typing off vein with thread or wire to eliminate blood flow; stripping involves excising length of vein.

[18] § ✓4th **38.6 Other excision of vessels**
[0-9]
Excision of blood vessel (lesion) NOS
EXCLUDES *excision of vessel for aortocoronary bypass (36.10-36.14)*
excision with:
anastomosis (38.30-38.39)
graft replacement (38.40-38.49)
implant (38.40-38.49)

AHA: 3Q, '90, 17

38.7 Interruption of the vena cava
Insertion of implant or sieve in vena cava
Ligation of vena cava (inferior) (superior)
Plication of vena cava

AHA: 2Q, '94, 9; S-O, '85, 5

DEF: Interruption of the blood flow through the venous heart vessels to prevent clots from reaching the chambers of the heart by means of implanting a sieve or implant, separating off a portion or by narrowing the venous blood vessels.

Methods of Vessel Anastomoses

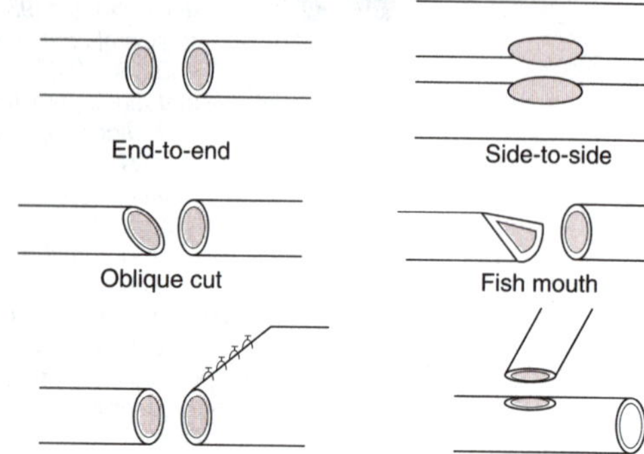

[18] § ✓4th **38.8 Other surgical occlusion of vessels**
[0-9]
Clamping }
Division } of blood vessel
Ligation }
Occlusion }
EXCLUDES *adrenal vessels (07.43)*
esophageal varices (42.91)
gastric or duodenal vessel for ulcer (44.40-44.49)
gastric varices (44.91)
meningeal vessel (02.13)
percutaneous transcatheter infusion embolization (99.29)
spermatic vein for varicocele (63.1)
surgical occlusion of vena cava (38.7)
that for chemoembolization (99.25)
that for control of (postoperative) hemorrhage:
anus (49.95)
bladder (57.93)
following vascular procedure (39.41)
nose (21.00-21.09)
prostate (60.94)
tonsil (28.7)
thyroid vessel (06.92)

AHA: 2Q, '90, 23; M-A, '87, 9; **For code 38.85:** 1Q, '03, 15; **For code 38.86:** 1Q, '05, 14; N-D, '87, 4

✓4th **38.9 Puncture of vessel**
EXCLUDES *that for circulatory monitoring (89.60-89.69)*

38.91 Arterial catheterization
AHA: 1Q, '05, 14; 1Q, '97, 3; 1Q, '95, 3; 2Q, '91, 15; 2Q, '90, 23

38.92 Umbilical vein catheterization

38.93 Venous catheterization, not elsewhere classified
EXCLUDES *that for cardiac catheterization (37.21-37.23)*
that for renal dialysis (38.95)
AHA: 3Q, '00, 9; 2Q, '98, 24; 1Q, '96, 3; 2Q, '96, 15; 3Q, '91, 13; 4Q, '90, 14; 2Q, '90, 24; 3Q, '88, 13

38.94 Venous cutdown
DEF: Incision of vein to place needle or catheter.

38.95 Venous catheterization for renal dialysis
EXCLUDES *insertion of totally implantable vascular access device [VAD] (86.07)*
AHA: 3Q, '98, 13; 2Q, '94, 11

38.98 Other puncture of artery
EXCLUDES *that for:*
arteriography (88.40-88.49)
coronary arteriography (88.55-88.57)

§ Requires fourth-digit. Valid digits are in [brackets] under each code. See category 38 for definitions.
§§ Requires fourth-digit. Valid digits are in [brackets] under each code. See subcategory 38.4 for definitions.
[18] Nonspecific OR procedure = 0

Typical Venous Cutdown

38.99 Other puncture of vein
Phlebotomy
EXCLUDES *that for:*
angiography (88.60-88.68)
extracorporeal circulation (39.61, 50.92)
injection or infusion of:
sclerosing solution (39.92)
therapeutic or prophylactic substance (99.11-99.29)
perfusion (39.96, 39.97)
phlebography (88.60-88.68)
transfusion (99.01-99.09)
AHA: 4Q, '94, 50; 1Q, '88, 11

✓3rd **39 Other operations on vessels**
EXCLUDES *those on coronary vessels (36.0-36.99)*

39.0 Systemic to pulmonary artery shunt
Descending aorta-pulmonary artery } anastomosis (graft)
Left to right } anastomosis (graft)
Subclavian-pulmonary } anastomosis (graft)
Code also cardiopulmonary bypass [extracorporeal circulation] [heart-lung machine] (39.61)
DEF: Descending aorta-pulmonary artery anastomosis (graft): Connection of descending main heart artery to pulmonary artery.
DEF: Left to right anastomosis (graft): Connection of systemic arterial blood vessel to venous pulmonary system.
DEF: Subclavian-pulmonary anastomosis (graft): Connection of subclavian artery to pulmonary artery

39.1 Intra-abdominal venous shunt
Anastomosis:
mesocaval
portacaval
portal vein to inferior vena cava
splenic and renal veins
transjugular intrahepatic portosystemic shunt [TIPS]
EXCLUDES *peritoneovenous shunt (54.94)*
AHA: 2Q, '02, 4; 4Q, '94, 50; 4Q, '93, 31; 2Q, '93, 8
DEF: Connection of two venous blood vessels within abdominal cavity.

✓4th **39.2 Other shunt or vascular bypass**
Code also pressurized treatment of venous bypass graft [conduit] with pharmaceutical substance, if performed (00.16)
DEF: Creation of supplemental blood flow to area with inadequate blood supply due to disease or injury of vessels.

39.21 Caval-pulmonary artery anastomosis
Code also cardiopulmonary bypass (39.61)

39.22 Aorta-subclavian-carotid bypass
Bypass (arterial):
aorta to carotid and brachial
aorta to subclavian and carotid
carotid to subclavian

39.23 Other intrathoracic vascular shunt or bypass
Intrathoracic (arterial) bypass graft NOS
EXCLUDES *coronary artery bypass (36.10-36.19)*

39.24 Aorta-renal bypass

39.25 Aorta-iliac-femoral bypass
Bypass:
aortofemoral
aortoiliac
aortoiliac to popliteal
Bypass:
aortopopliteal
iliofemoral [iliac-femoral]
AHA: 1Q, '03, 16; 4Q, '90, 27; 1Q, '88, 10

39.26 Other intra-abdominal vascular shunt or bypass
Bypass:
aortoceliac
aortic-superior mesenteric
common hepatic-common iliac-renal
Intra-abdominal arterial bypass graft NOS
EXCLUDES *peritoneovenous shunt (54.94)*

39.27 Arteriovenostomy for renal dialysis
Anastomosis for renal dialysis
Formation of (peripheral) arteriovenous fistula for renal [kidney] dialysis
Code also any renal dialysis (39.95)
AHA: ▶1Q, '06, 10◀

39.28 Extracranial-intracranial (EC-IC) vascular bypass NC
AHA: 2Q, '92, 7; 4Q, '91, 22

39.29 Other (peripheral) vascular shunt or bypass
Bypass (graft):
axillary-brachial
axillary-femoral [axillofemora] (superficial)
brachial
femoral-femoral
femoroperoneal
femoropopliteal (arteries)
femorotibial (anterior) (posterior)
popliteal
vascular NOS
EXCLUDES *peritoneovenous shunt (54.94)*
AHA: 1Q, '03, 17; 2Q, '02, 8; 1Q, '02, 13; S-O, '85, 13

✓4th **39.3 Suture of vessel**
Repair of laceration of blood vessel
EXCLUDES *any other vascular puncture closure device — omit code*
suture of aneurysm (39.52)
that for control of hemorrhage (postoperative):
anus (49.95)
bladder (57.93)
following vascular procedure (39.41)
nose (21.00-21.09)
prostate (60.94)
tonsil (28.7)

39.30 Suture of unspecified blood vessel
39.31 Suture of artery
39.32 Suture of vein

✓4th **39.4 Revision of vascular procedure**

39.41 Control of hemorrhage following vascular surgery
EXCLUDES *that for control of hemorrhage (postoperative):*
anus (49.95)
bladder (57.93)
nose (21.00-21.09)
prostate (60.94)
tonsil (28.7)

39.42 Revision of arteriovenous shunt for renal dialysis
Conversion of renal dialysis:
end-to-end anastomosis to end-to-side
end-to-side anastomosis to end-to-end
vessel-to-vessel cannula to arteriovenous shunt
Removal of old arteriovenous shunt and creation of new shunt
EXCLUDES *replacement of vessel-to-vessel cannula (39.94)*
AHA: 2Q, '94, 15; 4Q, '93, 33

39.43 Removal of arteriovenous shunt for renal dialysis
EXCLUDES *that with replacement [revision] of shunt (39.42)*

39.49 Other revision of vascular procedure
Declotting (graft)
Revision of:
anastomosis of blood vessel
vascular procedure (previous)
AHA: 2Q, '98, 17; 1Q, '97, 3; 2Q, '94, 15
DEF: Declotting (graft): Removal of clot from graft.

4th 39.5 Other repair of vessels

39.50 Angioplasty or atherectomy of other non-coronary vessel(s)
Percutaneous transluminal angioplasty (PTA) of non-coronary vessels:
lower extremity vessels
mesenteric artery
renal artery
upper extremity vessels
Code also any:
injection or infusion of thrombolytic agent (99.10)
insertion of non-coronary stent(s) or stent grafts(s) (39.90)
number of vascular stents inserted (00.45-00.48)
number of vessels treated (00.40-00.43)
▶procedure on vessel bifurcation (00.44)◀
EXCLUDES *percutaneous angioplasty or atherectomy of precerebral or cerebral vessel(s) (00.61-00.62)*
AHA: 3Q, '03, 10; 1Q, '02, 13; 2Q, '01, 23; 2Q, '00, 10; 1Q, '00, 12; 2Q, '98, 17; 1Q, '97, 3; 4Q, '96, 63; 4Q, '95, 66

39.51 Clipping of aneurysm
EXCLUDES *clipping of arteriovenous fistula (39.53)*

39.52 Other repair of aneurysm
Repair of aneurysm by:
coagulation
electrocoagulation
filipuncture
methyl methacrylate
suture
wiring
wrapping
EXCLUDES *endovascular repair of aneurysm (39.71-39.79)*
re-entry operation (aorta) (39.54)
that with:
graft replacement (38.40-38.49)
resection (38.30-38.49, 38.60-38.69)
AHA: 3Q, '02, 25, 26; 1Q, '99, 15, 16, 17; 1Q, '88, 10
DEF: Application of device in abnormally stretched blood vessel to prevent movement of material collected in vessel.
DEF: Repair of aneurysm by: Coagulation: Clotting or solidifying. Electrocoagulation: Electrically produced clotting. Filipuncture: Insertion of wire or thread. Methyl methacrylate: Injection or insertion of plastic material. Suture: Stitching. Wiring: Insertion of wire. Wrapping: Compression.

39.53 Repair of arteriovenous fistula
Embolization of carotid cavernous fistula
Repair of arteriovenous fistula by:
clipping
coagulation
ligation and division
EXCLUDES *repair of:*
arteriovenous shunt for renal dialysis (39.42)
head and neck vessels, endovascular approach (39.72)
that with:
graft replacement (38.40-38.49)
resection (38.30-38.49, 38.60-38.69)
AHA: 1Q, '00, 8
DEF: Correction of arteriovenous fistula by application of clamps, causing coagulation or by tying off and dividing the connection.

39.54 Re-entry operation (aorta)
Fenestration of dissecting aneurysm of thoracic aorta
Code also cardiopulmonary bypass [extracorporeal circulation] [heart-lung machine] (39.61)
DEF: Re-entry operation: Creation of passage between stretched wall of the vessel and major arterial channel to heart.
DEF: Fenestration of dissecting aneurysm of thoracic aorta: Creation of passage between stretched arterial heart vessel and functional part of vessel.

39.55 Reimplantation of aberrant renal vessel
DEF: Reimplant of renal vessel into normal position.

39.56 Repair of blood vessel with tissue patch graft
EXCLUDES *that with resection (38.40-38.49)*
AHA: 1Q, '04, 16

39.57 Repair of blood vessel with synthetic patch graft
EXCLUDES *that with resection (38.40-38.49)*

39.58 Repair of blood vessel with unspecified type of patch graft
EXCLUDES *that with resection (38.40-38.49)*

39.59 Other repair of vessel
Aorticopulmonary window operation
Arterioplasty NOS
Construction of venous valves (peripheral)
Plication of vein (peripheral)
Reimplantation of artery
Code also cardiopulmonary bypass [extracorporeal circulation] [heart-lung machine] (39.61)
EXCLUDES *interruption of the vena cava (38.7)*
reimplantation of renal artery (39.55)
that with:
graft (39.56-39.58)
resection (38.30-38.49, 38.60-38.69)
AHA: 4Q, '93, 31; 2Q, '89, 17; N-D, '86, 8; S-O, '85, 5; M-A, '85, 15
DEF: Aorticopulmonary window operation: Repair of abnormal opening between major heart arterial vessel above valves and pulmonary artery.
DEF: Construction of venous valves (peripheral): Reconstruction of valves within peripheral veins.
DEF: Plication of vein (peripheral): Shortening of peripheral vein.
DEF: Reimplantation of artery: Reinsertion of artery into its normal position.

4th 39.6 Extracorporeal circulation and procedures auxiliary to heart surgery
AHA: 1Q, '95, 5

39.61 Extracorporeal circulation auxiliary to open heart surgery
Artificial heart and lung
Cardiopulmonary bypass
Pump oxygenator
EXCLUDES *extracorporeal hepatic assistance (50.92)*
extracorporeal membrane oxygenation [ECMO] (39.65)
hemodialysis (39.95)
percutaneous cardiopulmonary bypass (39.66)
AHA: 1Q, '04, 16; 3Q, '02, 5; 4Q, '97, 55; 3Q, '97, 14; 2Q, '97, 8; 2Q, '90, 24

39.62 Hypothermia (systemic) incidental to open heart surgery

39.63 Cardioplegia

Arrest:
- anoxic

Arrest:
- circulatory

DEF: Purposely inducing electromechanical cardiac arrest.

39.64 Intraoperative cardiac pacemaker

Temporary pacemaker used during and immediately following cardiac surgery

AHA: 1Q, '89, 2; M-J, '87, 3

39.65 Extracorporeal membrane oxygenation [ECMO]

EXCLUDES *extracorporeal circulation auxiliary to open heart surgery (39.61)*
percutaneous cardiopulmonary bypass (39.66)

AHA: 2Q, '90, 23; 2Q, '89, 17; 4Q, '88, 5

DEF: Creation of closed-chest, heart-lung bypass or Bard cardiopulmonary assist system with tube insertion.

39.66 Percutaneous cardiopulmonary bypass

Closed chest

EXCLUDES *extracorporeal circulation auxiliary to open heart surgery (39.61)*
extracorporeal hepatic assistance (50.92)
extracorporeal membrane oxygenation [ECMO] (39.65)
hemodialysis (39.95)

AHA: 3Q, '96, 11

DEF: Use of mechanical pump system to oxygenate and pump blood throughout the body via catheter in the femoral artery and vein.

✓4th **39.7 Endovascular repair of vessel**

Endoluminal repair

EXCLUDES *angioplasty or atherectomy of other non-coronary vessel(s) (39.50)*
insertion of non-drug-eluting peripheral vessel stent(s) (39.90)
other repair of aneurysm (39.52)
percutaneous insertion of carotid artery stent(s) (00.63)
percutaneous insertion of intracranial stent(s) (00.65)
percutaneous insertion of other precerebral artery stent(s) (00.64)
resection of abdominal aorta with replacement (38.44)
resection of lower limb arteries with replacement (38.48)
resection of thoracic aorta with replacement (38.45)
resection of upper limb vessels with replacement (38.43)

39.71 Endovascular implantation of graft in abdominal aorta

Endovascular repair of abdominal aortic aneurysm with graft
Stent graft(s)

AHA: 1Q, '02, 13; 4Q, '00, 63, 64

DEF: Replacement of a section of abdominal aorta with mesh graft; via catheters inserted through femoral arteries.

Endovascular Repair of Abdominal Aortic Aneurysm

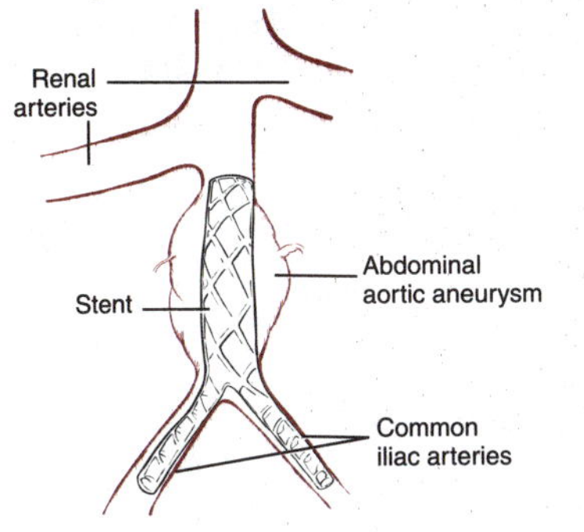

39.72 Endovascular repair or occlusion of head and neck vessels

Coil embolization or occlusion
Endograft(s)
Endovascular graft(s)
Liquid tissue adhesive (glue) embolization or occlusion
Other implant or substance for repair, embolization or occlusion
That for repair of aneurysm, arteriovenous malformation [AVM] or fistula

EXCLUDES ▶ *mechanical thrombectomy of pre-cerebral and cerebral vessels (39.74)*◀

AHA: 4Q, '02, 103

DEF: Coil embolization or occlusion: Utilizing x-ray guidance a neuro-microcatheter is guided from entry in the femoral artery in the groin to the site of the aneurysm of the head and neck vessels for delivery of micro-coils that stop blood flow to the arteriovenous malfomation (AVM).

39.73 Endovascular implantation of graft in thoracic aorta

Endograft(s)
Endovascular graft(s)
Endovascular repair of defect of thoracic aorta with graft(s) or device(s)
Stent graft(s) or device(s)
That for repair of aneurysm, dissection, or injury

EXCLUDES *fenestration of dissecting aneurysm of thoracic aorta (39.54)*

AHA: 4Q, '05, 120

DEF: Intravascular transcatheter deployment of an expanding stent-graft for repair of thoracic aortic aneurysm, performed without opening the chest.

● **39.74 Endovascular removal of obstruction from head and neck vessel(s)**

Endovascular embolectomy
Endovascular thrombectomy of pre-cerebral and cerebral vessels
Mechanical embolectomy or thrombectomy
Code also:
- any injection or infusion of thrombolytic agent (99.10)
- number of vessels treated (00.40-00.43)
- procedure on vessel bifurcation (00.44)

EXCLUDES *endarterectomy of intracranial vessels and other vessels of head and neck (38.11-38.12)*
occlusive endovascular repair of head or neck vessels (39.72)
open embolectomy or thrombectomy (38.01-38.02)

External Arteriovenous Shunt

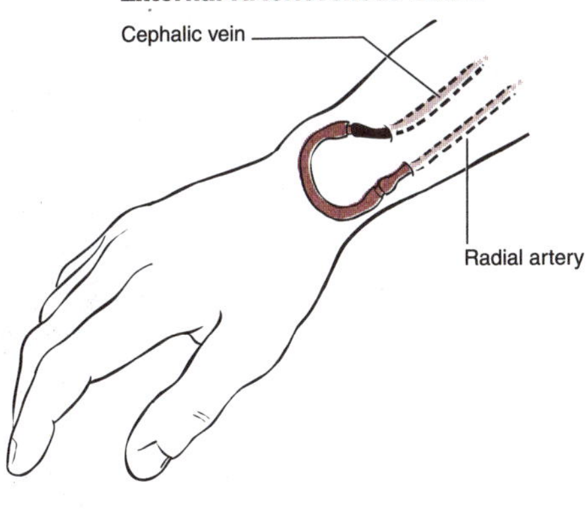

✓3rd ✓4th Additional Digit Required | Nonspecific OR Procedure | Valid OR Procedure | Non-OR Procedure | Adjunct Code

39.79 Other endovascular repair (of aneurysm) of other vessels
Coil embolization or occlusion
Endograft(s)
Endovascular graft(s)
Liquid tissue adhesive (glue) embolization or occlusion
Other implant or substance for repair, embolization or occlusion
EXCLUDES *endovascular implantation of graft in thoracic aorta (39.73)*
endovascular repair or occlusion of head and neck vessels (39.72)
insertion of drug-eluting peripheral vessel stent(s) (00.55)
insertion of non-drug-eluting peripheral vessel stent(s) (for other than aneurysm repair) (39.90)
non-endovascular repair of arteriovenous fistula (39.53)
other surgical occlusion of vessels–see category 38.8
percutaneous transcatheter infusion (99.29)
transcatheter embolization for gastric or duodenal bleeding (44.44)
AHA: 4Q, '02, 103; 3Q, '01, 17,18; 4Q, '00, 64

39.8 Operations on carotid body and other vascular bodies
Chemodectomy
Denervation of:
aortic body
carotid body
Glomectomy, carotid
Implantation into carotid body:
electronic stimulator
pacemaker
EXCLUDES *excision of glomus jugulare (20.51)*
DEF: Chemodectomy: Removal of a chemoreceptor vascular body.
DEF: Denervation of aortic body: Destruction of nerves attending the major heart blood vessels.
DEF: Destruction of carotid body: Destruction of nerves of carotid artery.
DEF: Glomectomy, carotid: Removal of the carotid artery framework.

✓4th **39.9 Other operations on vessels**

39.90 Insertion of non-drug-eluting peripheral vessel stent(s)
Bare stent(s)
Bonded stent(s)
Drug-coated stent(s), i.e., heparin coated
Endograft(s)
Endovascular graft(s)
Endovascular recanalization techniques
Stent graft(s)
Code also any:
non-coronary angioplasty or atherectomy (39.50)
number of vascular stents inserted (00.45-00.48)
number of vessels treated (00.40-00.43)
▶procedure on vessel bifurcation (00.44)◀
EXCLUDES *insertion of drug-eluting, peripheral vessel stent(s) (00.55)*
percutaneous insertion of carotid artery stent(s) (00.63)
percutaneous insertion of intracranial stent(s) (00.65)
percutaneous insertion of other precerebral artery stent(s) (00.64)
that for aneurysm repair (39.71-39.79)
AHA: 4Q, '02, 101; 1Q, '00, 12; 4Q, '96, 63

39.91 Freeing of vessel
Dissection and freeing of adherent tissue:
artery-vein-nerve bundle
vascular bundle
AHA: 3Q, '02, 12

39.92 Injection of sclerosing agent into vein
EXCLUDES *injection:*
esophageal varices (42.33)
hemorrhoids (49.42)
AHA: 2Q, '92, 17

39.93 Insertion of vessel-to-vessel cannula
Formation of:
arteriovenous:
fistula } by external cannula
shunt } by external cannula
Code also any renal dialysis (39.95)
AHA: 3Q, '88, 13; S-O, '85, 5 & 12

39.94 Replacement of vessel-to-vessel cannula
Revision of vessel-to-vessel cannula

39.95 Hemodialysis
Artificial kidney
Hemofiltration
Hemodiafiltration
Renal dialysis
EXCLUDES *peritoneal dialysis (54.98)*
AHA: 1Q, '04, 22; 4Q, '03, 111; 2Q, '01, 2-14; 4Q, '00, 40; 2Q, '98, 20; S-O, '86, 11
DEF: Filtration process to treat acute and chronic renal failure by eliminating toxic end products of nitrogen metabolism from blood.

39.96 Total body perfusion
Code also substance perfused (99.21-99.29)

39.97 Other perfusion
Perfusion NOS
Perfusion, local [regional] of:
carotid artery
coronary artery
head
lower limb
neck
upper limb
Code also substance perfused (99.21-99.29)
EXCLUDES *perfusion of:*
kidney (55.95)
large intestine (46.96)
liver (50.93)
small intestine (46.95)
AHA: 3Q, '96, 11

39.98 Control of hemorrhage, not otherwise specified
Angiotripsy
Control of postoperative hemorrhage NOS
Venotripsy
EXCLUDES *control of hemorrhage (postoperative):*
anus (49.95)
bladder (57.93)
following vascular procedure (39.41)
nose (21.00-21.09)
prostate (60.94)
tonsil (28.7)
that by:
ligation (38.80-38.89)
suture (39.30-39.32)
DEF: Angiotripsy: Clamping of tissue to stop arterial blood flow.
DEF: Venotripsy: Clamping of tissue to stop venous blood flow.

39.99 Other operations on vessels
EXCLUDES *injection or infusion of therapeutic or prophylactic substance (99.11-99.29)*
transfusion of blood and blood components (99.01-99.09)
AHA: 1Q, '89, 11

8. OPERATIONS ON THE HEMIC AND LYMPHATIC SYSTEMS (40-41)

✓3rd **40 Operations on lymphatic system**

40.0 Incision of lymphatic structures

✓4th **40.1 Diagnostic procedures on lymphatic structures**

40.11 Biopsy of lymphatic structure

40.19 Other diagnostic procedures on lymphatic structures

EXCLUDES *lymphangiogram:*
abdominal (88.04)
cervical (87.08)
intrathoracic (87.34)
lower limb (88.36)
upper limb (88.34)
microscopic examination of specimen (90.71-90.79)
radioisotope scan (92.16)
thermography (88.89)

✓4th **40.2 Simple excision of lymphatic structure**

EXCLUDES *biopsy of lymphatic structure (40.11)*

DEF: Removal of lymphatic structure only.

40.21 Excision of deep cervical lymph node

AHA: 4Q, '99, 16

40.22 Excision of internal mammary lymph node

40.23 Excision of axillary lymph node

AHA: 2Q, '02, 7

40.24 Excision of inguinal lymph node

40.29 Simple excision of other lymphatic structure

Excision of:
cystic hygroma
lymphangioma
Simple lymphadenectomy

AHA: 1Q, '99, 6

DEF: Lymphangioma: Removal of benign congenital lymphatic malformation.

DEF: Simple lymphadenectomy: Removal of lymph node.

40.3 Regional lymph node excision

Extended regional lymph node excision
Regional lymph node excision with excision of lymphatic drainage area including skin, subcutaneous tissue, and fat

AHA: 2Q, '92, 7

DEF: Extended regional lymph node excision: Removal of lymph node group, including area around nodes.

✓4th **40.4 Radical excision of cervical lymph nodes**

Resection of cervical lymph nodes down to muscle and deep fascia

EXCLUDES *that associated with radical laryngectomy (30.4)*

40.40 Radical neck dissection, not otherwise specified

40.41 Radical neck dissection, unilateral

AHA: ▶2Q, '05, 8;◀ 2Q, '99, 6

DEF: Dissection, total, of cervical lymph nodes on one side of neck.

40.42 Radical neck dissection, bilateral

DEF: Dissection, total, of cervical lymph nodes on both sides of neck.

✓4th **40.5 Radical excision of other lymph nodes**

EXCLUDES *that associated with radical mastectomy (85.45-85.48)*

40.50 Radical excision of lymph nodes, not otherwise specified

Radical (lymph) node dissection NOS

40.51 Radical excision of axillary lymph nodes

40.52 Radical excision of periaortic lymph nodes

40.53 Radical excision of iliac lymph nodes

40.54 Radical groin dissection

40.59 Radical excision of other lymph nodes

EXCLUDES *radical neck dissection (40.40-40.42)*

✓4th **40.6 Operations on thoracic duct**

40.61 Cannulation of thoracic duct

DEF: Placement of cannula in main lymphatic duct of chest.

40.62 Fistulization of thoracic duct

DEF: Creation of passage in main lymphatic duct of chest.

40.63 Closure of fistula of thoracic duct

DEF: Closure of fistula in main lymphatic duct of chest.

40.64 Ligation of thoracic duct

DEF: Tying off main lymphatic duct of chest.

40.69 Other operations on thoracic duct

40.9 Other operations on lymphatic structures

Anastomosis, Dilation, Ligation, Obliteration, Reconstruction, Repair, Transplantation } of peripheral lymphatics

Correction of lymphedema of limb, NOS

EXCLUDES *reduction of elephantiasis of scrotum (61.3)*

✓3rd **41 Operations on bone marrow and spleen**

✓4th **41.0 Bone marrow or hematopoietic stem cell transplant**

Note: To report donor source — see codes 00.91-00.93

EXCLUDES *aspiration of bone marrow from donor (41.91)*

AHA: 4Q, '00, 64; 1Q, '91, 3; 4Q, '91, 26

41.00 Bone marrow transplant, not otherwise specified

19 **41.01 Autologous bone marrow transplant without purging** NC

EXCLUDES *that with purging (41.09)*

DEF: Transplant of patient's own bone marrow.

20 **41.02 Allogeneic bone marrow transplant with purging** NC

Allograft of bone marrow with in vitro removal (purging) of T-cells

DEF: Transplant of bone marrow from donor to patient after donor marrow purged of undesirable cells.

20 **41.03 Allogeneic bone marrow transplant without purging** NC

Allograft of bone marrow NOS

19 **41.04 Autologous hematopoietic stem cell transplant without purging** NC

EXCLUDES *that with purging (41.07)*

AHA: 4Q, '94, 52

20 **41.05 Allogeneic hematopoietic stem cell transplant without purging** NC

EXCLUDES *that with purging (41.08)*

AHA: 4Q, '97, 55

19 Non-covered procedure only when the following diagnoses are present as either principal or secondary diagnosis: 204.00, 205.00, 205.10, 205.11, 206.00, 207.00, 208.00

20 Non-covered procedure only when the following diagnoses are present as either principal or secondary diagnosis: 203.00, 203.01

Additional Digit Required | Nonspecific OR Procedure | Valid OR Procedure | Non-OR Procedure | Adjunct Code

Partial Splenectomy

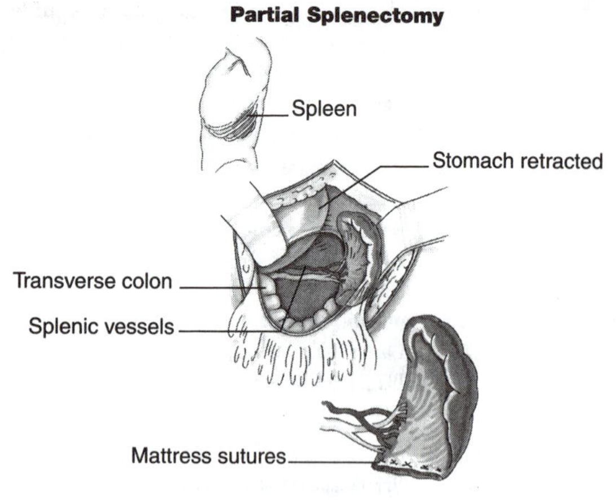

41.06 Cord blood stem cell transplant
AHA: 4Q, '97, 56

19 **41.07 Autologous hematopoietic stem cell transplant with purging** NC
Cell depletion

20 **41.08 Allogeneic hematopoietic stem cell transplant with purging** NC
Cell depletion

19 **41.09 Autologous bone marrow transplant with purging** NC
With extracorporeal purging of malignant cells from marrow
Cell depletion

41.1 Puncture of spleen
EXCLUDES *aspiration biopsy of spleen (41.32)*

41.2 Splenotomy

✓4th **41.3 Diagnostic procedures on bone marrow and spleen**

41.31 Biopsy of bone marrow

41.32 Closed [aspiration] [percutaneous] biopsy of spleen
Needle biopsy of spleen

41.33 Open biopsy of spleen

41.38 Other diagnostic procedures on bone marrow
EXCLUDES *microscopic examination of specimen from bone marrow (90.61-90.69)*
radioisotope scan (92.05)

41.39 Other diagnostic procedures on spleen
EXCLUDES *microscopic examination of specimen from spleen (90.61-90.69)*
radioisotope scan (92.05)

Total Splenectomy

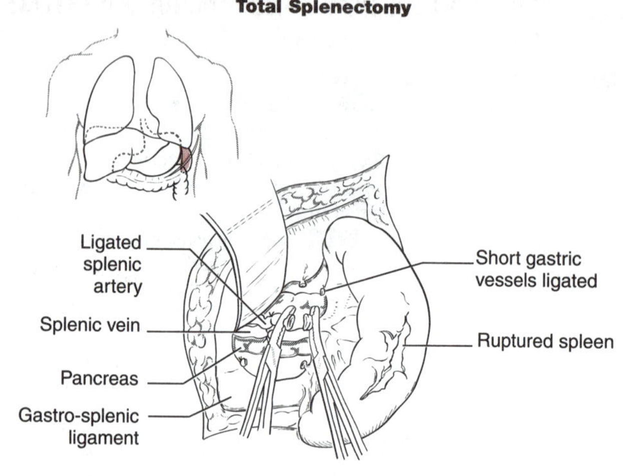

✓4th **41.4 Excision or destruction of lesion or tissue of spleen**
Code also any application or administration of an adhesion barrier substance (99.77)
EXCLUDES *excision of accessory spleen (41.93)*

41.41 Marsupialization of splenic cyst
DEF: Incision of cyst of spleen with edges sutured open to create pouch.

41.42 Excision of lesion or tissue of spleen
EXCLUDES *biopsy of spleen (41.32-41.33)*

41.43 Partial splenectomy
DEF: Removal of spleen, partial.

41.5 Total splenectomy
Splenectomy NOS
Code also any application or administration of an adhesion barrier substance (99.77)

✓4th **41.9 Other operations on spleen and bone marrow**
Code also any application or administration of an adhesion barrier substance (99.77)

41.91 Aspiration of bone marrow from donor for transplant
EXCLUDES *biopsy of bone marrow (41.31)*
AHA: 1Q, '91, 3

41.92 Injection into bone marrow
EXCLUDES *bone marrow transplant (41.00-41.03)*
AHA: 3Q, '96, 17

41.93 Excision of accessory spleen

41.94 Transplantation of spleen

41.95 Repair and plastic operations on spleen

41.98 Other operations on bone marrow

41.99 Other operations on spleen

19 Non-covered procedure only when the following diagnoses are present as either principal or secondary diagnosis: 204.00, 205.00, 205.10, 205.11, 206.00, 207.00, 208.00

20 Non-covered procedure only when the following diagnoses are present as either principal or secondary diagnosis: 203.00, 203.01

9. OPERATIONS ON THE DIGESTIVE SYSTEM (42-54)

✓3rd **42 Operations on esophagus**

✓4th **42.0 Esophagotomy**

42.01 Incision of esophageal web

DEF: Cutting into congenital esophageal membrane.

42.09 Other incision of esophagus

Esophagotomy NOS

EXCLUDES *esophagomyotomy (42.7)*
esophagostomy (42.10-42.19)

✓4th **42.1 Esophagostomy**

42.10 Esophagostomy, not otherwise specified

42.11 Cervical esophagostomy

DEF: Creation of opening into upper region of esophagus.

42.12 Exteriorization of esophageal pouch

DEF: Transfer of section of esophageal pouch to exterior of the body.

42.19 Other external fistulization of esophagus

Thoracic esophagostomy
Code also any resection (42.40-42.42)

✓4th **42.2 Diagnostic procedures on esophagus**

42.21 Operative esophagoscopy by incision

DEF: Esophageal examination with an endoscope through incision.

42.22 Esophagoscopy through artificial stoma

EXCLUDES *that with biopsy (42.24)*

42.23 Other esophagoscopy

EXCLUDES *that with biopsy (42.24)*

AHA: 1Q, '00, 20; 3Q, '98, 11

42.24 Closed [endoscopic] biopsy of esophagus

Brushing or washing for specimen collection
Esophagoscopy with biopsy
Suction biopsy of the esophagus

EXCLUDES *esophagogastroduodenoscopy [EGD] with closed biopsy (45.16)*

DEF: Scope passed through mouth and throat to obtain biopsy specimen, usually by brushing and swabbing.

42.25 Open biopsy of esophagus

42.29 Other diagnostic procedures on esophagus

EXCLUDES *barium swallow (87.61)*
esophageal manometry (89.32)
microscopic examination of specimen from esophagus (90.81-90.89)

AHA: 3Q, '96, 12

✓4th **42.3 Local excision or destruction of lesion or tissue of esophagus**

42.31 Local excision of esophageal diverticulum

42.32 Local excision of other lesion or tissue of esophagus

EXCLUDES *biopsy of esophagus (42.24-42.25)*
esophageal fistulectomy (42.84)

42.33 Endoscopic excision or destruction of lesion or tissue of esophagus

Ablation of esophageal neoplasm } by endoscopic approach
Control of esophageal bleeding
Esophageal polypectomy
Esophageal varices
Injection of esophageal varices

EXCLUDES *biopsy of esophagus (42.24-42.25)*
fistulectomy (42.84)
open ligation of esophageal varices (42.91)

42.39 Other destruction of lesion or tissue of esophagus

EXCLUDES *that by endoscopic approach (42.33)*

✓4th **42.4 Excision of esophagus**

EXCLUDES *esophagogastrectomy NOS (43.99)*

42.40 Esophagectomy, not otherwise specified

42.41 Partial esophagectomy

Code also any synchronous:
anastomosis other than end-to-end (42.51-42.69)
esophagostomy (42.10-42.19)
gastrostomy (43.11-43.19)

DEF: Surgical removal of any part of esophagus.

42.42 Total esophagectomy

Code also any synchronous:
gastrostomy (43.11-43.19)
interposition or anastomosis other than end-to-end (42.51-42.69)

EXCLUDES *esophagogastrectomy (43.99)*

AHA: 4Q, '88, 11

DEF: Surgical removal of entire esophagus.

✓4th **42.5 Intrathoracic anastomosis of esophagus**

Code also any synchronous:
esophagectomy (42.40-42.42)
gastrostomy (43.1)

DEF: Connection of esophagus to conduit within chest.

42.51 Intrathoracic esophagoesophagostomy

DEF: Connection of both ends of esophagus within chest cavity.

42.52 Intrathoracic esophagogastrostomy

DEF: Connection of esophagus to stomach within chest; follows esophagogastrectomy.

42.53 Intrathoracic esophageal anastomosis with interposition of small bowel

42.54 Other intrathoracic esophagoenterostomy

Anastomosis of esophagus to intestinal segment NOS

42.55 Intrathoracic esophageal anastomosis with interposition of colon

42.56 Other intrathoracic esophagocolostomy

Esophagocolostomy NOS

42.58 Intrathoracic esophageal anastomosis with other interposition

Construction of artificial esophagus
Retrosternal formation of reversed gastric tube

DEF: Construction of artificial esophagus: Creation of artificial esophagus.

DEF: Retrosternal anastomosis of reversed gastric tube: Formation of gastric tube behind breastbone.

Operations on the Digestive System

42.59 Other intrathoracic anastomosis of esophagus
AHA: 4Q, '88, 11

✓4th **42.6 Antesternal anastomosis of esophagus**
Code also any synchronous:
esophagectomy (42.40-42.42)
gastrostomy (43.1)

42.61 Antesternal esophagoesophagostomy
42.62 Antesternal esophagogastrostomy
42.63 Antesternal esophageal anastomosis with interposition of small bowel
42.64 Other antesternal esophagoenterostomy
Antethoracic:
esophagoenterostomy
esophagoileostomy
esophagojejunostomy

42.65 Antesternal esophageal anastomosis with interposition of colon
DEF: Connection of esophagus with colon segment.

42.66 Other antesternal esophagocolostomy
Antethoracic esophagocolostomy

42.68 Other antesternal esophageal anastomosis with interposition
42.69 Other antesternal anastomosis of esophagus

42.7 Esophagomyotomy
DEF: Division of esophageal muscle, usually distal.

✓4th **42.8 Other repair of esophagus**

42.81 Insertion of permanent tube into esophagus
AHA: 1Q, '97, 15

42.82 Suture of laceration of esophagus
42.83 Closure of esophagostomy
42.84 Repair of esophageal fistula, not elsewhere classified
EXCLUDES *repair of fistula:*
bronchoesophageal (33.42)
esophagopleurocutaneous (34.73)
pharyngoesophageal (29.53)
tracheoesophageal (31.73)

42.85 Repair of esophageal stricture
42.86 Production of subcutaneous tunnel without esophageal anastomosis
DEF: Surgical formation of esophageal passage, without cutting, and reconnection.

42.87 Other graft of esophagus
EXCLUDES *antesternal esophageal anastomosis with interposition of:*
colon (42.65)
small bowel (42.63)
antesternal esophageal anastomosis with other interposition (42.68)
intrathoracic esophageal anastomosis with interposition of:
colon (42.55)
small bowel (42.53)
intrathoracic esophageal anastomosis with other interposition (42.58)

42.89 Other repair of esophagus

✓4th **42.9 Other operations on esophagus**

42.91 Ligation of esophageal varices
EXCLUDES *that by endoscopic approach (42.33)*
DEF: Destruction of dilated veins by suture strangulation.

42.92 Dilation of esophagus
Dilation of cardiac sphincter
EXCLUDES *intubation of esophagus (96.03, 96.06-96.08)*
DEF: Passing of balloon or hydrostatic dilators through esophagus to enlarge esophagus and relieve obstruction.

42.99 Other
EXCLUDES *insertion of Sengstaken tube (96.06)*
intubation of esophagus (96.03, 96.06-96.08)
removal of intraluminal foreign body from esophagus without incision (98.02)
tamponade of esophagus (96.06)

✓3rd **43 Incision and excision of stomach**
Code also any application or administration of an adhesion barrier substance (99.77)

43.0 Gastrotomy
EXCLUDES *gastrostomy (43.11-43.19)*
that for control of hemorrhage (44.49)
AHA: 3Q, '89, 14

✓4th **43.1 Gastrostomy**
AHA: S-O, '85, 5

43.11 Percutaneous [endoscopic] gastrostomy [PEG]
Percutaneous transabdominal gastrostomy
DEF: Endoscopic positioning of tube through abdominal wall into stomach.

43.19 Other gastrostomy
EXCLUDES *percutaneous [endoscopic] gastrostomy [PEG] (43.11)*
AHA: 1Q, '92, 14; 3Q, '89, 14

43.3 Pyloromyotomy
DEF: Cutting into longitudinal and circular muscular membrane between stomach and small intestine.

✓4th **43.4 Local excision or destruction of lesion or tissue of stomach**

43.41 Endoscopic excision or destruction of lesion or tissue of stomach
Gastric polypectomy by endoscopic approach
Gastric varices by endoscopic approach
EXCLUDES *biopsy of stomach (44.14-44.15)*
control of hemorrhage (44.43)
open ligation of gastric varices (44.91)
AHA: 3Q, '96, 10

43.42 Local excision of other lesion or tissue of stomach
EXCLUDES *biopsy of stomach (44.14-44.15)*
gastric fistulectomy (44.62-44.63)
partial gastrectomy (43.5-43.89)

43.49 Other destruction of lesion or tissue of stomach
EXCLUDES *that by endoscopic approach (43.41)*
AHA: N-D, '87, 5; S-O, '85, 6

43.5 Partial gastrectomy with anastomosis to esophagus
Proximal gastrectomy

Biliopancreatic Diversion Without Duodenal Switch

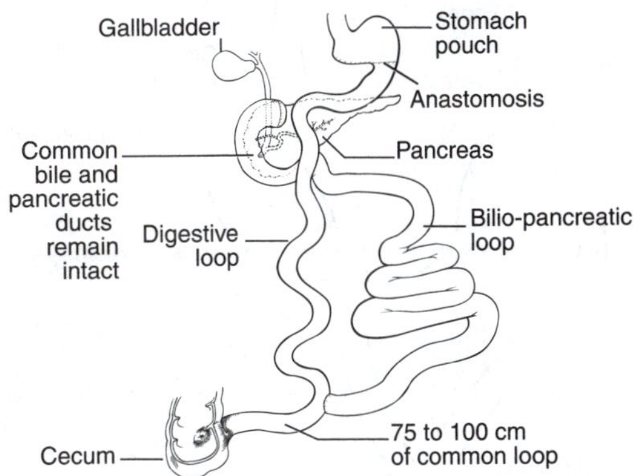

43.6 Partial gastrectomy with anastomosis to duodenum
Billroth I operation
Gastropylorectomy
Distal gastrectomy

43.7 Partial gastrectomy with anastomosis to jejunum
Billroth II operation
AHA: 3Q, '03, 7

✓4th **43.8 Other partial gastrectomy**

43.81 Partial gastrectomy with jejunal transposition
Henley jejunal transposition operation
Code also any synchronous intestinal resection (45.51)

43.89 Other
Partial gastrectomy with bypass gastrogastrostomy
Sleeve resection of stomach
AHA: 3Q, '03, 6-8

✓4th **43.9 Total gastrectomy**

43.91 Total gastrectomy with intestinal interposition

43.99 Other total gastrectomy
Complete gastroduodenectomy
Esophagoduodenostomy with complete gastrectomy
Esophagogastrectomy NOS
Esophagojejunostomy with complete gastrectomy
Radical gastrectomy

✓3rd **44 Other operations on stomach**
Code also any application or administration of an adhesion barrier substance (99.77)

✓4th **44.0 Vagotomy**

44.00 Vagotomy, not otherwise specified
Division of vagus nerve NOS
DEF: Cutting of vagus nerve to reduce acid production.

44.01 Truncal vagotomy
DEF: Surgical removal of vagus nerve segment near stomach branches.

Biliopancreatic Diversion with Duodenal Switch

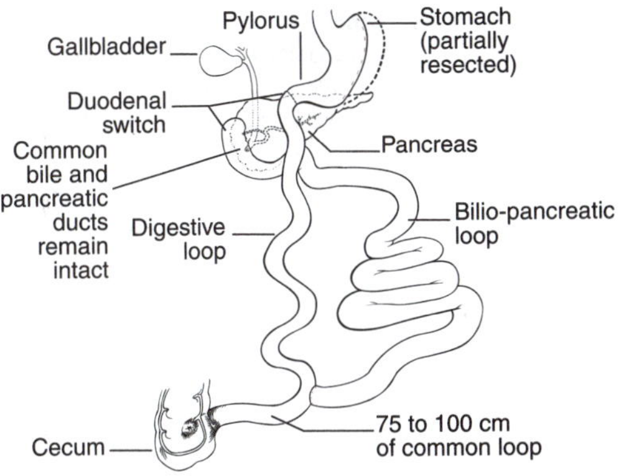

Partial Gastrectomy with Anastomosis to Duodenum

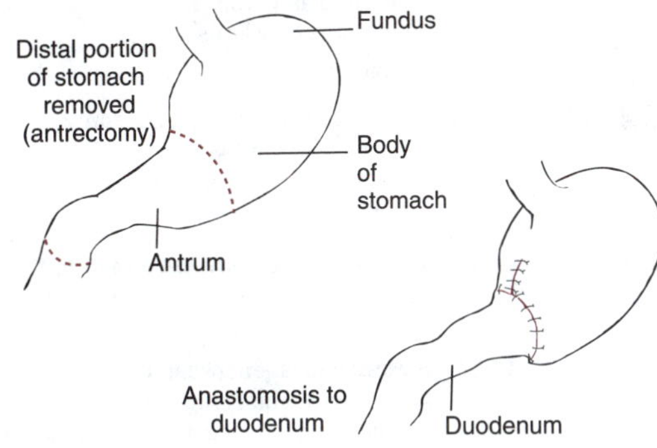

44.02 Highly selective vagotomy
Parietal cell vagotomy
Selective proximal vagotomy
DEF: Cutting select gastric branches of vagus nerve to reduce acid production and preserve other nerve functions.

44.03 Other selective vagotomy

✓4th **44.1 Diagnostic procedures on stomach**

44.11 Transabdominal gastroscopy
Intraoperative gastroscopy
EXCLUDES *that with biopsy (44.14)*

44.12 Gastroscopy through artificial stoma
EXCLUDES *that with biopsy (44.14)*

44.13 Other gastroscopy
EXCLUDES *that with biopsy (44.14)*
AHA: 1Q, '88, 15; N-D, '87, 5

44.14 Closed [endoscopic] biopsy of stomach
Brushing or washing for specimen collection
EXCLUDES *esophagogastroduodenoscopy [EGD] with closed biopsy (45.16)*
AHA: 1Q, '88, 15; N-D, '87, 5

44.15 Open biopsy of stomach

44.19 Other diagnostic procedures on stomach
EXCLUDES *gastric lavage (96.33)*
microscopic examination of specimen from stomach (90.81-90.89)
upper GI series (87.62)

✓4th **44.2 Pyloroplasty**

44.21 Dilation of pylorus by incision
DEF: Cutting and suturing pylorus to relieve obstruction.

44.22 Endoscopic dilation of pylorus
Dilation with balloon endoscope
Endoscopic dilation of gastrojejunostomy site
AHA: 2Q, '01, 17

Types of Vagotomy Procedures

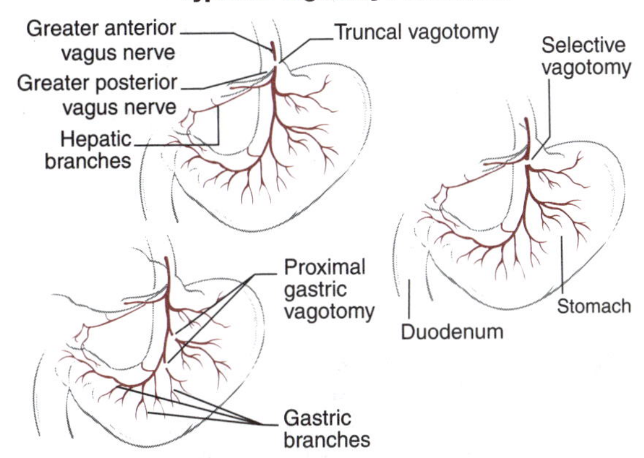

Operations on the Digestive System

43.6–44.22

44.29 Other pyloroplasty
Pyloroplasty NOS
Revision of pylorus
AHA: 3Q, '99, 3

✓4th **44.3 Gastroenterostomy without gastrectomy**

44.31 High gastric bypass
Printen and Mason gastric bypass
AHA: M-J, '85, 17

DEF: Connection of middle part of small intestine to upper stomach to divert food passage from upper intestine.

44.32 Percutaneous [endoscopic] gastrojejunostomy
Endoscopic conversion of gastrostomy to jejunostomy

DEF: Percutaneous placement of a thin feeding tube through a gastrostomy tube and then pulling the tube into the proximal end of the jejunum.

44.38 Laparoscopic gastroenterostomy
Bypass:
gastroduodenostomy
gastroenterostomy
gastrogastrostomy
Laparoscopic gastrojejunostomy without gastrectomy NEC
EXCLUDES *gastroenterostomy, open approach (44.39)*

44.39 Other gastroenterostomy
Bypass:
gastroduodenostomy
gastroenterostomy
gastrogastrostomy
Gastrojejunostomy without gastrectomy NOS
AHA: 3Q, '03, 6; 1Q, '01, 16, 17

✓4th **44.4 Control of hemorrhage and suture of ulcer of stomach or duodenum**

44.40 Suture of peptic ulcer, not otherwise specified

44.41 Suture of gastric ulcer site
EXCLUDES *ligation of gastric varices (44.91)*

44.42 Suture of duodenal ulcer site
AHA: J-F, '87, 11

44.43 Endoscopic control of gastric or duodenal bleeding
AHA: 2Q, '04, 12; 2Q, '92, 17; N-D, '87, 4

44.44 Transcatheter embolization for gastric or duodenal bleeding
EXCLUDES *surgical occlusion of abdominal vessels (38.86-38.87)*
AHA: 1Q, '88, 15; N-D, '87, 4

DEF: Therapeutic blocking of stomach or upper small intestine blood vessel to stop hemorrhaging; accomplished by introducing various substances using a catheter.

44.49 Other control of hemorrhage of stomach or duodenum
That with gastrotomy

44.5 Revision of gastric anastomosis
Closure of:
gastric anastomosis
gastroduodenostomy
gastrojejunostomy
Pantaloon operation

✓4th **44.6 Other repair of stomach**

44.61 Suture of laceration of stomach
EXCLUDES *that of ulcer site (44.41)*

44.62 Closure of gastrostomy

Roux-en-Y Operation (Gastrojejunostomy without gastrectomy)

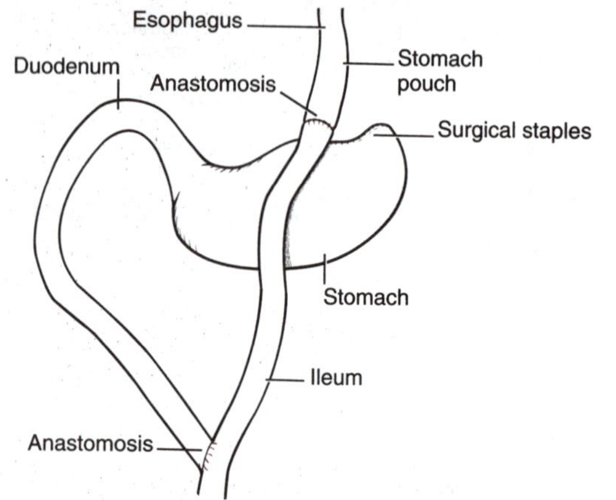

44.63 Closure of other gastric fistula
Closure of:
gastrocolic fistula
gastrojejunocolic fistula

44.64 Gastropexy
AHA: M-J, '85, 17

DEF: Suturing of stomach into position.

44.65 Esophagogastroplasty
Belsey operation
Esophagus and stomach cardioplasty
AHA: M-J, '85, 17

44.66 Other procedures for creation of esophagogastric sphincteric competence
Fundoplication
Gastric cardioplasty
Nissen's fundoplication
Restoration of cardio-esophageal angle
EXCLUDES *that by laparoscopy (44.67)*
AHA: 2Q, '03, 12; 2Q, '01, 3, 5, 6; 3Q, '98, 10; M-J, '85, 17

44.67 Laparoscopic procedures for creation of esophagogastric sphincteric competence
Fundoplication
Gastric cardioplasty
Nissen's fundoplication
Restoration of cardio-esophageal angle

44.68 Laparoscopic gastroplasty
Banding
Silastic vertical banding
Vertical banded gastroplasty (VBG)
Code also any synchronous laparoscopic gastroenterostomy (44.38)
EXCLUDES *insertion, laparoscopic adjustable gastric band (restrictive procedure) (44.95)*
other repair of stomach, open approach (44.61-44.65, 44.69)

44.69 Other
Inversion of gastric diverticulum
Repair of stomach NOS
AHA: 3Q, '03, 8; 2Q, '01, 3; 3Q, '99, 3; M-J, '85, 17; N-D, '84, 13

DEF: Inversion of gastric diverticulum: Turning stomach inward to repair outpouch of wall.

✓4th **44.9 Other operations on stomach**

44.91 Ligation of gastric varices

EXCLUDES *that by endoscopic approach (43.41)*

DEF: Destruction of dilated veins by suture or strangulation.

44.92 Intraoperative manipulation of stomach

Reduction of gastric volvulus

44.93 Insertion of gastric bubble (balloon) NC

44.94 Removal of gastric bubble (balloon)

44.95 Laparoscopic gastric restrictive procedure

Adjustable gastric band and port insertion

EXCLUDES *laparoscopic gastroplasty (44.68)*
other repair of stomach (44.69)

44.96 Laparoscopic revision of gastric restrictive procedure

Revision or replacement of:
adjustable gastric band
subcutaneous gastric port device

44.97 Laparoscopic removal of gastric restrictive device(s)

Removal of either or both:
adjustable gastric band
subcutaneous port device

EXCLUDES *nonoperative removal of gastric restrictive device(s) (97.86)*
open removal of gastric restrictive device(s) (44.99)

44.98 (Laparoscopic) adjustment of size of adjustable gastric restrictive device

Infusion of saline for device tightening
Withdrawal of saline for device loosening
Code also any:
abdominal ultrasound (88.76)
abdominal wall fluoroscopy (88.09)
barium swallow (87.61)

44.99 Other

EXCLUDES *change of gastrostomy tube (97.02)*
dilation of cardiac sphincter (42.92)
gastric:
cooling (96.31)
freezing (96.32)
gavage (96.35)
hypothermia (96.31)
lavage (96.33)
insertion of nasogastric tube (96.07)
irrigation of gastrostomy (96.36)
irrigation of nasogastric tube (96.34)
removal of:
gastrostomy tube (97.51)
intraluminal foreign body from stomach without incision (98.03)
replacement of:
gastrostomy tube (97.02)
(naso-)gastric tube (97.01)

AHA: 3Q, '04, 5

✓3rd **45 Incision, excision, and anastomosis of intestine**

Code also any application or administration of an adhesion barrier substance (99.77)

✓4th **45.0 Enterotomy**

EXCLUDES *duodenocholedochotomy (51.41-51.42, 51.51)*
that for destruction of lesion (45.30-45.34)
that of exteriorized intestine (46.14, 46.24, 46.31)

45.00 Incision of intestine not otherwise specified

45.01 Incision of duodenum

45.02 Other incision of small intestine

45.03 Incision of large intestine

EXCLUDES *proctotomy (48.0)*

✓4th **45.1 Diagnostic procedures on small intestine**

Code also any laparotomy (54.11-54.19)

45.11 Transabdominal endoscopy of small intestine

Intraoperative endoscopy of small intestine

EXCLUDES *that with biopsy (45.14)*

DEF: Endoscopic exam of small intestine through abdominal wall.

DEF: Intraoperative endoscope of small intestine: Endoscopic exam of small intestine during surgery.

45.12 Endoscopy of small intestine through artificial stoma

EXCLUDES *that with biopsy (45.14)*

AHA: M-J, '85, 17

45.13 Other endoscopy of small intestine

Esophagogastroduodenoscopy [EGD]

EXCLUDES *that with biopsy (45.14, 45.16)*

AHA: 3Q, '04, 5; N-D, '87, 5

45.14 Closed [endoscopic] biopsy of small intestine

Brushing or washing for specimen collection

EXCLUDES *esophagogastroduodenoscopy [EGD] with closed biopsy (45.16)*

45.15 Open biopsy of small intestine

AHA: ►2Q, '05, 12◄

45.16 Esophagogastroduodenoscopy [EGD] with closed biopsy

Biopsy of one or more sites involving esophagus, stomach, and/or duodenum

AHA: ►3Q, '05, 17;◄ 2Q, '01, 9

45.19 Other diagnostic procedures on small intestine

EXCLUDES *microscopic examination of specimen from small intestine (90.91-90.99)*
radioisotope scan (92.04)
ultrasonography (88.74)
x-ray (87.61-87.69)

✓4th **45.2 Diagnostic procedures on large intestine**

Code also any laparotomy (54.11-54.19)

45.21 Transabdominal endoscopy of large intestine

Intraoperative endoscopy of large intestine

EXCLUDES *that with biopsy (45.25)*

DEF: Endoscopic exam of large intestine through abdominal wall.

DEF: Intraoperative endoscopy of large intestine: Endoscopic exam of large intestine during surgery.

Esophagogastroduodenoscopy

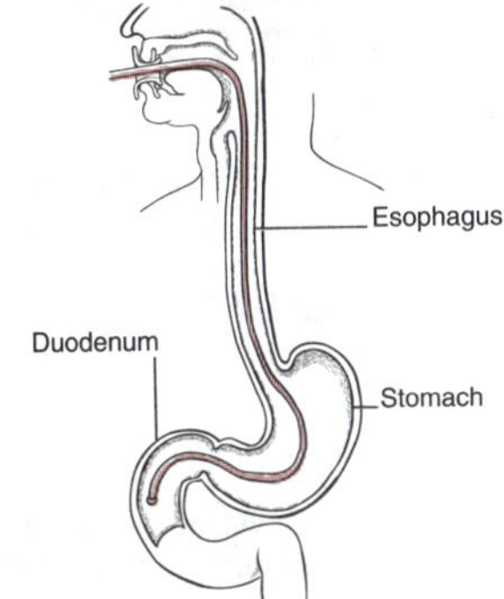

45.22 **Endoscopy of large intestine through artificial stoma**

EXCLUDES *that with biopsy (45.25)*

DEF: Endoscopic exam of large intestine lining from rectum to cecum via colostomy stoma.

45.23 **Colonoscopy**

Flexible fiberoptic colonoscopy

EXCLUDES *endoscopy of large intestine through artificial stoma (45.22)*
flexible sigmoidoscopy (45.24)
rigid proctosigmoidoscopy (48.23)
transabdominal endoscopy of large intestine (45.21)

AHA: ▶3Q, '05, 17;◀ S-O, '85, 5

DEF: Endoscopic exam of descending colon, splenic flexure, transverse colon, hepatic flexure and cecum.

45.24 **Flexible sigmoidoscopy**

Endoscopy of descending colon

EXCLUDES *rigid proctosigmoidoscopy (48.23)*

DEF: Endoscopic exam of anus, rectum and sigmoid colon.

45.25 **Closed [endoscopic] biopsy of large intestine**

Biopsy, closed, of unspecified intestinal site
Brushing or washing for specimen collection
Colonoscopy with biopsy

EXCLUDES *proctosigmoidoscopy with biopsy (48.24)*

AHA: 1Q, '03, 10

45.26 **Open biopsy of large intestine**

45.27 **Intestinal biopsy, site unspecified**

45.28 **Other diagnostic procedures on large intestine**

45.29 **Other diagnostic procedures on intestine, site unspecified**

EXCLUDES *microscopic examination of specimen (90.91-90.99)*
scan and radioisotope function study (92.04)
ultrasonography (88.74)
x-ray (87.61-87.69)

✓4th 45.3 **Local excision or destruction of lesion or tissue of small intestine**

45.30 **Endoscopic excision or destruction of lesion of duodenum**

EXCLUDES *biopsy of duodenum (45.14-45.15)*
control of hemorrhage (44.43)
fistulectomy (46.72)

45.31 **Other local excision of lesion of duodenum**

EXCLUDES *biopsy of duodenum (45.14-45.15)*
fistulectomy (46.72)
multiple segmental resection (45.61)
that by endoscopic approach (45.30)

45.32 **Other destruction of lesion of duodenum**

EXCLUDES *that by endoscopic approach (45.30)*

AHA: N-D, '87, 5; S-O, '85, 6

45.33 **Local excision of lesion or tissue of small intestine, except duodenum**

Excision of redundant mucosa of ileostomy

EXCLUDES *biopsy of small intestine (45.14-45.15)*
fistulectomy (46.74)
multiple segmental resection (45.61)

45.34 **Other destruction of lesion of small intestine, except duodenum**

✓4th 45.4 **Local excision or destruction of lesion or tissue of large intestine**

AHA: N-D, '87, 11

45.41 **Excision of lesion or tissue of large intestine**

Excision of redundant mucosa of colostomy

EXCLUDES *biopsy of large intestine (45.25-45.27)*
endoscopic polypectomy of large intestine (45.42)
fistulectomy (46.76)
multiple segmental resection (45.71)
that by endoscopic approach (45.42-45.43)

45.42 **Endoscopic polypectomy of large intestine**

EXCLUDES *that by open approach (45.41)*

AHA: ▶2Q, '05, 16;◀ 2Q, '90, 25

DEF: Endoscopic removal of polyp from large intestine.

45.43 **Endoscopic destruction of other lesion or tissue of large intestine**

Endoscopic ablation of tumor of large intestine
Endoscopic control of colonic bleeding

EXCLUDES *endoscopic polypectomy of large intestine (45.42)*

AHA: 4Q, '02, 61

45.49 **Other destruction of lesion of large intestine**

EXCLUDES *that by endoscopic approach (45.43)*

✓4th 45.5 **Isolation of intestinal segment**

Code also any synchronous:
anastomosis other than end-to-end (45.90-45.94)
enterostomy (46.10-46.39)

45.50 **Isolation of intestinal segment, not otherwise specified**

Isolation of intestinal pedicle flap
Reversal of intestinal segment

DEF: Isolation of small intestinal pedicle flap: Separation of intestinal pedicle flap.

DEF: Reversal of intestinal segment: Separation of intestinal segment.

45.51 **Isolation of segment of small intestine**

Isolation of ileal loop
Resection of small intestine for interposition

AHA: ▶2Q, '05, 12;◀ 3Q, '03, 6-8; 2Q, '03, 11; 3Q, '00, 7

45.52 **Isolation of segment of large intestine**

Resection of colon for interposition

Colectomy

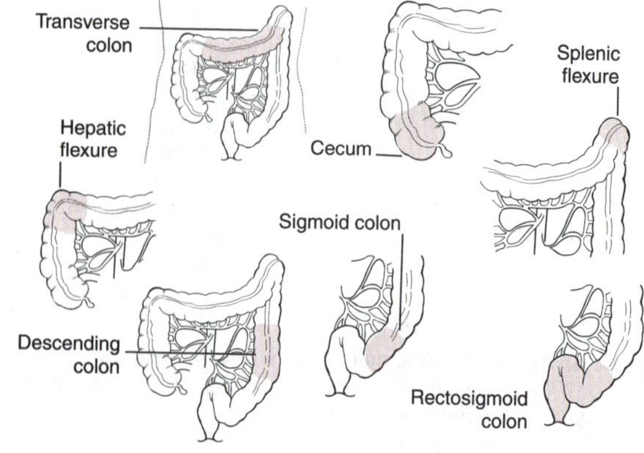

✓4th **45.6 Other excision of small intestine**
Code also any synchronous:
anastomosis other than end-to-end (45.90-45.93, 45.95)
colostomy (46.10-46.13)
enterostomy (46.10-46.39)
EXCLUDES *cecectomy (45.72)*
enterocolectomy (45.79)
gastroduodenectomy (43.6-43.99)
ileocolectomy (45.73)
pancreatoduodenectomy (52.51-52.7)

45.61 Multiple segmental resection of small intestine
Segmental resection for multiple traumatic lesions of small intestine

45.62 Other partial resection of small intestine
Duodenectomy Jejunectomy
Ileectomy
EXCLUDES *duodenectomy with synchronous pancreatectomy (52.51-52.7)*
resection of cecum and terminal ileum (45.72)
AHA: 1Q, '04, 10; 1Q, '03, 18

45.63 Total removal of small intestine

✓4th **45.7 Partial excision of large intestine**
Code also any synchronous:
anastomosis other than end-to-end (45.92-45.94)
enterostomy (46.10-46.39)
AHA: 4Q, '92, 27

45.71 Multiple segmental resection of large intestine
Segmental resection for multiple traumatic lesions of large intestine

45.72 Cecectomy
Resection of cecum and terminal ileum

45.73 Right hemicolectomy
Ileocolectomy
Right radical colectomy
AHA: 3Q, '99, 10

45.74 Resection of transverse colon

45.75 Left hemicolectomy
EXCLUDES *proctosigmoidectomy (48.41-48.69)*
second stage Mikulicz operation (46.04)
DEF: Excision of left descending large intestine.

45.76 Sigmoidectomy
AHA: 1Q, '96, 9; 3Q, '89, 15

45.79 Other partial excision of large intestine
Enterocolectomy NEC
AHA: 1Q, '03, 18; 3Q, '97, 9; 2Q, '91, 16

45.8 Total intra-abdominal colectomy
Excision of cecum, colon, and sigmoid
EXCLUDES *coloproctectomy (48.41-48.69)*

Intestinal Anastomosis

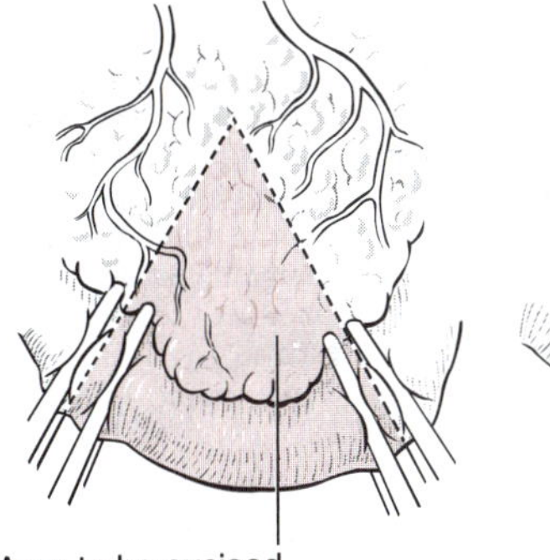

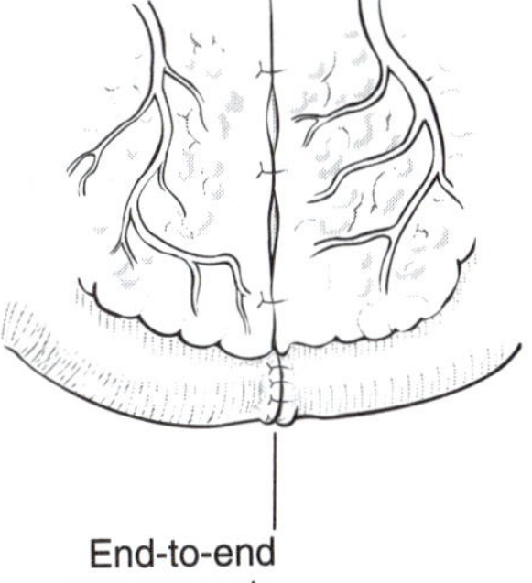

✓4th **45.9 Intestinal anastomosis**
Code also any synchronous resection (45.31-45.8, 48.41-48.69)
EXCLUDES *end-to-end anastomosis — omit code*

45.90 Intestinal anastomosis, not otherwise specified

45.91 Small-to-small intestinal anastomosis
AHA: 3Q, '03, 6-8; M-J, '85, 17

45.92 Anastomosis of small intestine to rectal stump
Hampton procedure

45.93 Other small-to-large intestinal anastomosis
AHA: 1Q, '03, 18; N-D, '86, 11

45.94 Large-to-large intestinal anastomosis
EXCLUDES *rectorectostomy (48.74)*
AHA: 3Q, '89, 15

45.95 Anastomosis to anus
Formation of endorectal ileal pouch (J-pouch) (H-pouch) (S-pouch) with anastomosis of small intestine to anus
AHA: ►2Q, '05, 13◄

✓3rd **46 Other operations on intestine**
Code also any application or administration of an adhesion barrier substance (99.77)

✓4th **46.0 Exteriorization of intestine**
INCLUDES loop enterostomy
multiple stage resection of intestine
DEF: Bringing intestinal segment to body surface.

46.01 Exteriorization of small intestine
Loop ileostomy

46.02 Resection of exteriorized segment of small intestine

46.03 Exteriorization of large intestine
Exteriorization of intestine NOS
First stage Mikulicz exteriorization of intestine
Loop colostomy

46.04 Resection of exteriorized segment of large intestine
Resection of exteriorized segment of intestine NOS
Second stage Mikulicz operation

✓4th **46.1 Colostomy**
Code also any synchronous resection (45.49, 45.71-45.79, 45.8)
EXCLUDES *loop colostomy (46.03)*
that with abdominoperineal resection of rectum (48.5)
that with synchronous anterior rectal resection (48.62)
DEF: Creation of opening from large intestine through abdominal wall to body surface.

46.10 Colostomy, not otherwise specified
46.11 Temporary colostomy
46.13 Permanent colostomy
46.14 Delayed opening of colostomy

✓4th **46.2 Ileostomy**
Code also any synchronous resection (45.34, 45.61-45.63)
EXCLUDES *loop ileostomy (46.01)*
DEF: Creation of artificial anus by bringing ileum through abdominal wall to body surface.

46.20 Ileostomy, not otherwise specified
46.21 Temporary ileostomy
46.22 Continent ileostomy
AHA: M-J, '85, 17
DEF: Creation of opening from third part of small intestine through abdominal wall, with pouch outside abdomen.

46.23 Other permanent ileostomy
46.24 Delayed opening of ileostomy

✓4th **46.3 Other enterostomy**

Code also any synchronous resection (45.61-45.8)

46.31 Delayed opening of other enterostomy

46.32 Percutaneous (endoscopic) jejunostomy [PEJ]

DEF: Endoscopic placement of tube in midsection of small intestine through abdominal wall.

46.39 Other

Duodenostomy Feeding enterostomy

AHA: 3Q, '89, 15

✓4th **46.4 Revision of intestinal stoma**

DEF: Revision of opening surgically created from intestine through abdominal wall, to skin surface.

46.40 Revision of intestinal stoma, not otherwise specified

Plastic enlargement of intestinal stoma
Reconstruction of stoma of intestine
Release of scar tissue of intestinal stoma

EXCLUDES *excision of redundant mucosa (45.41)*

46.41 Revision of stoma of small intestine

EXCLUDES *excision of redundant mucosa (45.33)*

AHA: ▶2Q, '05, 11◀

46.42 Repair of pericolostomy hernia

46.43 Other revision of stoma of large intestine

EXCLUDES *excision of redundant mucosa (45.41)*

AHA: 2Q, '02, 9

✓4th **46.5 Closure of intestinal stoma**

Code also any synchronous resection (45.34, 45.49, 45.61-45.8)

46.50 Closure of intestinal stoma, not otherwise specified

46.51 Closure of stoma of small intestine

46.52 Closure of stoma of large intestine

Closure or take-down of cecostomy
Closure or take-down of colostomy
Closure or take-down of sigmoidostomy

AHA: ▶2Q, '05, 4;◀ 3Q, '97, 9; 2Q, '91, 16; N-D, '87, 8

✓4th **46.6 Fixation of intestine**

46.60 Fixation of intestine not otherwise specified

Fixation of intestine to abdominal wall

46.61 Fixation of small intestine to abdominal wall

Ileopexy

46.62 Other fixation of small intestine

Noble plication of small intestine
Plication of jejunum

DEF: Noble plication of small intestine: Fixing small intestine into place with tuck in small intestine.
DEF: Plication of jejunum: Fixing small intestine into place with tuck in midsection.

46.63 Fixation of large intestine to abdominal wall

Cecocoloplicopexy
Sigmoidopexy (Moschowitz)

46.64 Other fixation of large intestine

Cecofixation Colofixation

✓4th **46.7 Other repair of intestine**

EXCLUDES *closure of:*
ulcer of duodenum (44.42)
vesicoenteric fistula (57.83)

46.71 Suture of laceration of duodenum

46.72 Closure of fistula of duodenum

46.73 Suture of laceration of small intestine, except duodenum

46.74 Closure of fistula of small intestine, except duodenum

EXCLUDES *closure of:*
artificial stoma (46.51)
vaginal fistula (70.74)
repair of gastrojejunocolic fistula (44.63)

46.75 Suture of laceration of large intestine

46.76 Closure of fistula of large intestine

EXCLUDES *closure of:*
gastrocolic fistula (44.63)
rectal fistula (48.73)
sigmoidovesical fistula (57.83)
stoma (46.52)
vaginal fistula (70.72-70.73)
vesicocolic fistula (57.83)
vesicosigmoidovaginal fistula (57.83)

AHA: 3Q, '99, 8

46.79 Other repair of intestine

Duodenoplasty

AHA: 3Q, '02, 11

✓4th **46.8 Dilation and manipulation of intestine**

AHA: 1Q, '03, 14

46.80 Intra-abdominal manipulation of intestine, not otherwise specified

Correction of intestinal malrotation
Reduction of:
intestinal torsion
intestinal volvulus
intussusception

EXCLUDES *reduction of intussusception with:*
fluoroscopy (96.29)
ionizing radiation enema (96.29)
ultrasonography guidance (96.29)

AHA: 4Q, '98, 82

DEF: Correction of intestinal malrotation: Repair of abnormal rotation.

DEF: Reduction of:
Intestinal torsion: Repair of twisted segment.
Intestinal volvulus: Repair of a knotted segment.
Intussusception: Repair of prolapsed segment.

46.81 Intra-abdominal manipulation of small intestine

46.82 Intra-abdominal manipulation of large intestine

46.85 Dilation of intestine

Dilation (balloon) of duodenum
Dilation (balloon) of jejunum
Endoscopic dilation (balloon) of large intestine
That through rectum or colostomy

AHA: 3Q, '89, 15

✓4th **46.9 Other operations on intestines**

46.91 Myotomy of sigmoid colon

46.92 Myotomy of other parts of colon

46.93 Revision of anastomosis of small intestine

46.94 Revision of anastomosis of large intestine

46.95 Local perfusion of small intestine

Code also substance perfused (99.21-99.29)

46.96 Local perfusion of large intestine

Code also substance perfused (99.21-99.29)

46.97 Transplant of intestine LC

Note: To report donor source — see codes 00.91-00.93

AHA: 4Q, '00, 66

46.99 Other
Ileoentectropy
EXCLUDES *diagnostic procedures on intestine (45.11-45.29)*
dilation of enterostomy stoma (96.24)
intestinal intubation (96.08)
removal of:
intraluminal foreign body from large intestine without incision (98.04)
intraluminal foreign body from small intestine without incision (98.03)
tube from large intestine (97.53)
tube from small intestine (97.52)
replacement of:
large intestine tube or enterostomy device (97.04)
small intestine tube or enterostomy device (97.03)

AHA: 3Q, '99, 11; 1Q, '89, 11

✓3rd **47 Operations on appendix**
INCLUDES appendiceal stump
Code also any application or administration of an adhesion barrier substance (99.77)

✓4th **47.0 Appendectomy**
EXCLUDES *incidental appendectomy, so described (47.11, 47.19)*
AHA: 4Q, '96, 64; 3Q, '92, 12

47.01 Laparoscopic appendectomy
AHA: 1Q, '01, 15; 4Q, '96, 64

47.09 Other appendectomy
AHA: 4Q, '97, 52

✓4th **47.1 Incidental appendectomy**
DEF: Removal of appendix during abdominal surgery as prophylactic measure, without significant appendiceal pathology.

47.11 Laparoscopic incidental appendectomy
47.19 Other incidental appendectomy
AHA: 4Q, '96, 65

47.2 Drainage of appendiceal abscess
EXCLUDES *that with appendectomy (47.0)*

✓4th **47.9 Other operations on appendix**
47.91 Appendicostomy
47.92 Closure of appendiceal fistula
47.99 Other
Anastomosis of appendix
EXCLUDES *diagnostic procedures on appendix (45.21-45.29)*
AHA: 3Q, '01, 16

✓3rd **48 Operations on rectum, rectosigmoid, and perirectal tissue**
Code also any application or administration of an adhesion barrier substance (99.77)

48.0 Proctotomy
Decompression of imperforate anus
Panas' operation [linear proctotomy]
EXCLUDES *incision of perirectal tissue (48.81)*
AHA: 3Q, '99, 8
DEF: Incision into rectal portion of large intestine.
DEF: Decompression of imperforate anus: opening a closed anus by means of an incision.
DEF: Panas' operation (linear proctotomy): Linear incision into rectal portion of large intestine

48.1 Proctostomy

✓4th **48.2 Diagnostic procedures on rectum, rectosigmoid, and perirectal tissue**
48.21 Transabdominal proctosigmoidoscopy
Intraoperative proctosigmoidoscopy
EXCLUDES *that with biopsy (48.24)*
48.22 Proctosigmoidoscopy through artificial stoma
EXCLUDES *that with biopsy (48.24)*
48.23 Rigid proctosigmoidoscopy
EXCLUDES *flexible sigmoidoscopy (45.24)*
AHA: 1Q, '01, 8
DEF: Endoscopic exam of anus, rectum and lower sigmoid colon.
48.24 Closed [endoscopic] biopsy of rectum
Brushing or washing for specimen collection
Proctosigmoidoscopy with biopsy
AHA: 1Q, '03, 14
48.25 Open biopsy of rectum
48.26 Biopsy of perirectal tissue
48.29 Other diagnostic procedures on rectum, rectosigmoid, and perirectal tissue
EXCLUDES *digital examination of rectum (89.34)*
lower GI series (87.64)
microscopic examination of specimen from rectum (90.91-90.99)

✓4th **48.3 Local excision or destruction of lesion or tissue of rectum**
48.31 Radical electrocoagulation of rectal lesion or tissue
DEF: Destruction of lesion or tissue of large intestine, rectal part.
48.32 Other electrocoagulation of rectal lesion or tissue
AHA: 2Q, '98, 18
48.33 Destruction of rectal lesion or tissue by laser
48.34 Destruction of rectal lesion or tissue by cryosurgery
48.35 Local excision of rectal lesion or tissue
EXCLUDES *biopsy of rectum (48.24-48.25)*
[endoscopic] polypectomy of rectum (48.36)
excision of perirectal tissue (48.82)
hemorrhoidectomy (49.46)
rectal fistulectomy (48.73)
48.36 [Endoscopic] polypectomy of rectum
AHA: 4Q, '95, 65

✓4th **48.4 Pull-through resection of rectum**
Code also any synchronous anastomosis other than end-to-end (45.90, 45.92-45.95)
48.41 Soave submucosal resection of rectum
Endorectal pull-through operation
DEF: Soave submucosal resection: Resection of submucosal rectal part of large intestine by pull-through technique.
DEF: Endorectal pull-through operation: Resection of interior large intestine by pull-through technique.
48.49 Other pull-through resection of rectum
Abdominoperineal pull-through
Altemeier operation
Swenson proctectomy
EXCLUDES *Duhamel abdominoperineal pull-through (48.65)*
AHA: 3Q, '01, 8; 2Q, '99, 13
DEF: Abdominoperineal pull-through: Resection of large intestine, latter part, by pull-through of abdomen, scrotum or vulva and anus.
DEF: Swenson proctatectomy: Excision of large intestine, rectal by pull-through and preserving muscles that close the anus.

48.5 Abdominoperineal resection of rectum

INCLUDES with synchronous colostomy

Combined abdominoendorectal resection

Complete proctectomy

Code also any synchronous anastomosis other than end-to-end (45.90, 45.92-45.95)

EXCLUDES *Duhamel abdominoperineal pull-through (48.65)*
that as part of pelvic exenteration (68.8)

AHA: 2Q, '97, 5

DEF: Rectal excision through cavities formed by abdomen, anus, vulva or scrotum.

✓4th **48.6 Other resection of rectum**

Code also any synchronous anastomosis other than end-to-end (45.90, 45.92-45.95)

48.61 Transsacral rectosigmoidectomy

DEF: Excision through sacral bone area of sigmoid and last parts of large intestine.

48.62 Anterior resection of rectum with synchronous colostomy

DEF: Resection of front terminal end of large intestine and creation of colostomy.

48.63 Other anterior resection of rectum

EXCLUDES *that with synchronous colostomy (48.62)*

AHA: 1Q, '96, 9

48.64 Posterior resection of rectum

48.65 Duhamel resection of rectum

Duhamel abdominoperineal pull-through

48.69 Other

Partial proctectomy
Rectal resection NOS

AHA: ►2Q, '05, 13;◄ J-F, '87, 11; N-D, '86, 11

✓4th **48.7 Repair of rectum**

EXCLUDES *repair of:*
current obstetric laceration (75.62)
vaginal rectocele (70.50, 70.52)

48.71 Suture of laceration of rectum

48.72 Closure of proctostomy

48.73 Closure of other rectal fistula

EXCLUDES *fistulectomy:*
perirectal (48.93)
rectourethral (58.43)
rectovaginal (70.73)
rectovesical (57.83)
rectovesicovaginal (57.83)

48.74 Rectorectostomy

Rectal anastomosis NOS

DEF: Connection of two cut portions of large intestine, rectal end.

48.75 Abdominal proctopexy

Frickman procedure
Ripstein repair of rectal prolapse

DEF: Fixation of rectum to adjacent abdominal structures.

48.76 Other proctopexy

Delorme repair of prolapsed rectum
Proctosigmoidopexy
Puborectalis sling operation

EXCLUDES *manual reduction of rectal prolapse (96.26)*

DEF: Delorme repair of prolapsed rectum: Fixation of collapsed large intestine, rectal part.

DEF: Proctosigmoidopexy: Suturing of twisted large intestine, rectal part.

DEF: Puborectalis sling operation: Fixation of large intestine, rectal part by forming puborectalis muscle into sling.

48.79 Other repair of rectum

Repair of old obstetric laceration of rectum

EXCLUDES *anastomosis to:*
large intestine (45.94)
small intestine (45.92-45.93)
repair of:
current obstetrical laceration (75.62)
vaginal rectocele (70.50, 70.52)

✓4th **48.8 Incision or excision of perirectal tissue or lesion**

INCLUDES pelvirectal tissue
rectovaginal septum

48.81 Incision of perirectal tissue

Incision of rectovaginal septum

48.82 Excision of perirectal tissue

EXCLUDES *perirectal biopsy (48.26)*
perirectofistulectomy (48.93)
rectal fistulectomy (48.73)

✓4th **48.9 Other operations on rectum and perirectal tissue**

48.91 Incision of rectal stricture

48.92 Anorectal myectomy

DEF: Excision of anorectal muscle.

48.93 Repair of perirectal fistula

EXCLUDES *that opening into rectum (48.73)*

DEF: Closure of abdominal passage in tissue around large intestine, rectal part.

48.99 Other

EXCLUDES *digital examination of rectum (89.34)*
dilation of rectum (96.22)
insertion of rectal tube (96.09)
irrigation of rectum (96.38-96.39)
manual reduction of rectal prolapse (96.26)
proctoclysis (96.37)
rectal massage (99.93)
rectal packing (96.19)
removal of:
impacted feces (96.38)
intraluminal foreign body from rectum without incision (98.05)
rectal packing (97.59)
transanal enema (96.39)

✓3rd **49 Operations on anus**

Code also any application or administration of an adhesion barrier substance (99.77)

✓4th **49.0 Incision or excision of perianal tissue**

49.01 Incision of perianal abscess

AHA: ►2Q, '05, 10◄

49.02 Other incision of perianal tissue

Undercutting of perianal tissue

EXCLUDES *anal fistulotomy (49.11)*

49.03 Excision of perianal skin tags

49.04 Other excision of perianal tissue

EXCLUDES *anal fistulectomy (49.12)*
biopsy of perianal tissue (49.22)

AHA: 1Q, '01, 8

✓4th **49.1 Incision or excision of anal fistula**

EXCLUDES *closure of anal fistula (49.73)*

49.11 Anal fistulotomy

49.12 Anal fistulectomy

✓4th **49.2 Diagnostic procedures on anus and perianal tissue**

49.21 Anoscopy

49.22 Biopsy of perianal tissue

49.23 Biopsy of anus

49.29 **Other diagnostic procedures on anus and perianal tissue**
EXCLUDES *microscopic examination of specimen from anus (90.91-90.99)*

✓4th 49.3 **Local excision or destruction of other lesion or tissue of anus**
Anal cryptotomy
Cauterization of lesion of anus
EXCLUDES *biopsy of anus (49.23)*
control of (postoperative) hemorrhage of anus (49.95)
hemorrhoidectomy (49.46)

49.31 **Endoscopic excision or destruction of lesion or tissue of anus**

49.39 **Other local excision or destruction of lesion or tissue of anus**
EXCLUDES *that by endoscopic approach (49.31)*
AHA: 1Q, '01, 8

✓4th 49.4 **Procedures on hemorrhoids**

49.41 **Reduction of hemorrhoids**
DEF: Manual manipulation to reduce hemorrhoids.

49.42 **Injection of hemorrhoids**

49.43 **Cauterization of hemorrhoids**
Clamp and cautery of hemorrhoids

49.44 **Destruction of hemorrhoids by cryotherapy**

49.45 **Ligation of hemorrhoids**

49.46 **Excision of hemorrhoids**
Hemorrhoidectomy NOS

49.47 **Evacuation of thrombosed hemorrhoids**
DEF: Removal of clotted material from hemorrhoid.

49.49 **Other procedures on hemorrhoids**
Lord procedure

✓4th 49.5 **Division of anal sphincter**

49.51 **Left lateral anal sphincterotomy**

49.52 **Posterior anal sphincterotomy**

49.59 **Other anal sphincterotomy**
Division of sphincter NOS

49.6 **Excision of anus**

✓4th 49.7 **Repair of anus**
EXCLUDES *repair of current obstetric laceration (75.62)*

49.71 **Suture of laceration of anus**

49.72 **Anal cerclage**
DEF: Encircling anus with ring or sutures.

49.73 **Closure of anal fistula**
EXCLUDES *excision of anal fistula (49.12)*

49.74 **Gracilis muscle transplant for anal incontinence**
DEF: Moving pubic attachment of gracilis muscle to restore anal control.

Dynamic Graciloplasty

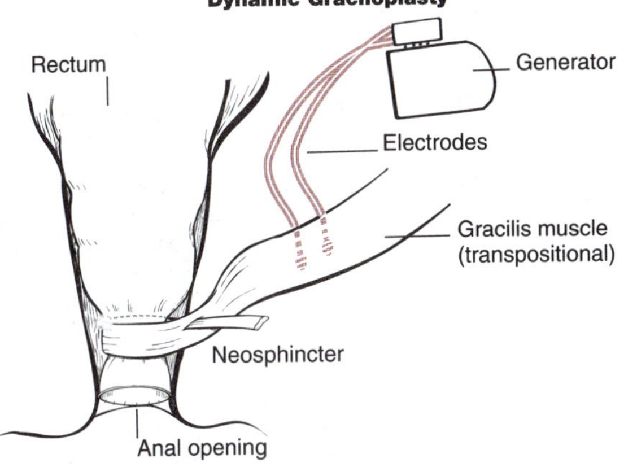

49.75 **Implantation or revision of artificial anal sphincter**
Removal with subsequent replacement
Replacement during same or subsequent operative episode
AHA: 4Q, '02, 105

49.76 **Removal of artificial anal sphincter**
Explantation or removal without replacement
EXCLUDES *revision with implantation during same operative episode (49.75)*
AHA: 4Q, '02, 105

49.79 **Other repair of anal sphincter**
Repair of old obstetric laceration of anus
EXCLUDES *anoplasty with synchronous hemorrhoidectomy (49.46)*
repair of current obstetric laceration (75.62)
AHA: 2Q, '98, 16; 1Q, '97, 9

✓4th 49.9 **Other operations on anus**
EXCLUDES *dilation of anus (sphincter) (96.23)*

49.91 **Incision of anal septum**

49.92 **Insertion of subcutaneous electrical anal stimulator**

49.93 **Other incision of anus**
Removal of:
foreign body from anus with incision
seton from anus
EXCLUDES *anal fistulotomy (49.11)*
removal of intraluminal foreign body without incision (98.05)

49.94 **Reduction of anal prolapse**
EXCLUDES *manual reduction of rectal prolapse (96.26)*
DEF: Manipulation of displaced anal tissue to normal position.

49.95 **Control of (postoperative) hemorrhage of anus**

49.99 **Other**

✓3rd 50 **Operations on liver**
Code also any application or administration of an adhesion barrier substance (99.77)

50.0 **Hepatotomy**
Incision of abscess of liver
Removal of gallstones from liver
Stromeyer-Little operation

✓4th 50.1 **Diagnostic procedures on liver**

50.11 **Closed (percutaneous) (needle) biopsy of liver**
Diagnostic aspiration of liver
AHA: ▶3Q, '05, 24◀; 4Q, '88, 12

50.12 **Open biopsy of liver**
Wedge biopsy
AHA: ▶3Q, '05, 24; 2Q, '05, 13◀

Closed Liver Biopsy

8
9
Inserted along midaxillary line
10
11
(12 behind)

Liver Biopsy (Open, Wedge)

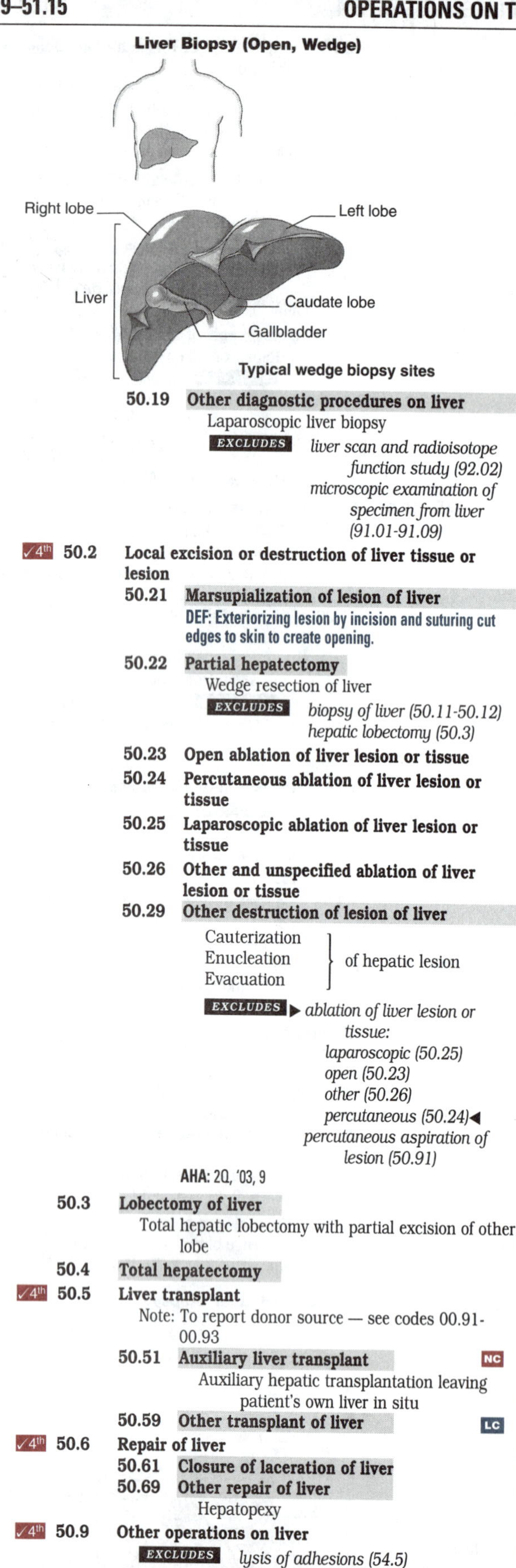

50.19 Other diagnostic procedures on liver
Laparoscopic liver biopsy
EXCLUDES *liver scan and radioisotope function study (92.02)*
microscopic examination of specimen from liver (91.01-91.09)

✓4th **50.2 Local excision or destruction of liver tissue or lesion**

50.21 Marsupialization of lesion of liver
DEF: Exteriorizing lesion by incision and suturing cut edges to skin to create opening.

50.22 Partial hepatectomy
Wedge resection of liver
EXCLUDES *biopsy of liver (50.11-50.12)*
hepatic lobectomy (50.3)

● **50.23 Open ablation of liver lesion or tissue**

● **50.24 Percutaneous ablation of liver lesion or tissue**

● **50.25 Laparoscopic ablation of liver lesion or tissue**

● **50.26 Other and unspecified ablation of liver lesion or tissue**

50.29 Other destruction of lesion of liver
Cauterization
Enucleation } of hepatic lesion
Evacuation
EXCLUDES ▶ *ablation of liver lesion or tissue:*
laparoscopic (50.25)
open (50.23)
other (50.26)
percutaneous (50.24)◀
percutaneous aspiration of lesion (50.91)
AHA: 2Q, '03, 9

50.3 Lobectomy of liver
Total hepatic lobectomy with partial excision of other lobe

50.4 Total hepatectomy

✓4th **50.5 Liver transplant**
Note: To report donor source — see codes 00.91-00.93

50.51 Auxiliary liver transplant NC
Auxiliary hepatic transplantation leaving patient's own liver in situ

50.59 Other transplant of liver LC

✓4th **50.6 Repair of liver**

50.61 Closure of laceration of liver

50.69 Other repair of liver
Hepatopexy

✓4th **50.9 Other operations on liver**
EXCLUDES *lysis of adhesions (54.5)*

50.91 Percutaneous aspiration of liver
EXCLUDES *percutaneous biopsy (50.11)*
DEF: Incision into liver through body wall to withdraw fluid.

50.92 Extracorporeal hepatic assistance
Liver dialysis
AHA: 2Q, '01, 21
DEF: Devices used outside body to assist liver function.

50.93 Localized perfusion of liver

50.94 Other injection of therapeutic substance into liver

50.99 Other

✓3rd **51 Operations on gallbladder and biliary tract**
INCLUDES operations on:
ampulla of Vater
common bile duct
cystic duct
hepatic duct
intrahepatic bile duct
sphincter of Oddi
Code also any application or administration of an adhesion barrier substance (99.77)

✓4th **51.0 Cholecystotomy and cholecystostomy**

51.01 Percutaneous aspiration of gallbladder
Percutaneous cholecystotomy for drainage
That by: needle or catheter
EXCLUDES *needle biopsy (51.12)*

51.02 Trocar cholecystostomy
AHA: 3Q, '89, 18
DEF: Creating opening in gallbladder with catheter.

51.03 Other cholecystostomy

51.04 Other cholecystotomy
Cholelithotomy NOS

✓4th **51.1 Diagnostic procedures on biliary tract**
EXCLUDES *that for endoscopic procedures classifiable to 51.64, 51.84-51.88, 52.14, 52.21, 52.93 - 52.94, 52.97-52.98*
AHA: 2Q, '97, 7

51.10 Endoscopic retrograde cholangiopancreatography [ERCP]
EXCLUDES *endoscopic retrograde:*
cholangiography [ERC] (51.11)
pancreatography [ERP] (52.13)
AHA: 4Q, '03, 118; 3Q, '03, 17; 1Q, '01, 8; 2Q, '99, 13
DEF: Endoscopic and radioscopic exam of pancreatic and common bile ducts with contrast material injected in opposite direction of normal flow through catheter.

51.11 Endoscopic retrograde cholangiography [ERC]
Laparoscopic exploration of common bile duct
EXCLUDES *endoscopic retrograde:*
cholangiopancreatography [ERCP] (51.10)
pancreatography [ERP] (52.13)
AHA: 1Q, '96, 12; 3Q, '89, 18; 4Q, '88, 7
DEF: Endoscopic and radioscopic exam of common bile ducts with contrast material injected in opposite direction of normal flow through catheter.

51.12 Percutaneous biopsy of gallbladder or bile ducts
Needle biopsy of gallbladder

51.13 Open biopsy of gallbladder or bile ducts

51.14 Other closed [endoscopic] biopsy of biliary duct or sphincter of Oddi
Brushing or washing for specimen collection
Closed biopsy of biliary duct or sphincter of Oddi by procedures classifiable to 51.10-51.11, 52.13
DEF: Endoscopic biopsy of muscle tissue around pancreatic and common bile ducts.

51.15 Pressure measurement of sphincter of Oddi
Pressure measurement of sphincter by procedures classifiable to 51.10-51.11, 52.13
DEF: Pressure measurement tests of muscle tissue surrounding pancreatic and common bile ducts.

Laparoscopic Cholecystectomy by Laser

Gallbladder
Liver
Laser beam
Cystic duct
Liver
Hepatic duct
Common bile duct
Trocar for passing coagulating devices and dissecting tools
Laparoscope
Trocar sheaths for introducing instruments to retract gallbladder

51.19 Other diagnostic procedures on biliary tract
EXCLUDES *biliary tract x-ray (87.51-87.59)*
microscopic examination of specimen from biliary tract (91.01-91.09)

✓4th **51.2 Cholecystectomy**
AHA: 1Q, '93, 17; 4Q, '91, 26; 3Q, '89, 18

51.21 Other partial cholecystectomy
Revision of prior cholecystectomy
EXCLUDES *that by laparoscope (51.24)*
AHA: 4Q, '96, 69

51.22 Cholecystectomy
EXCLUDES *laparoscopic cholecystectomy (51.23)*
AHA: 4Q, '97, 52; 2Q, '91, 16

51.23 Laparoscopic cholecystectomy
That by laser
AHA: 3Q, '98, 10; 4Q, '97, 52; 1Q, '96, 12; 2Q, '95, 11; 4Q, '91, 26
DEF: Endoscopic removal of gallbladder.

51.24 Laparoscopic partial cholecystectomy
AHA: 4Q, '96, 69

✓4th **51.3 Anastomosis of gallbladder or bile duct**
EXCLUDES *resection with end-to-end anastomosis (51.61-51.69)*

51.31 Anastomosis of gallbladder to hepatic ducts
51.32 Anastomosis of gallbladder to intestine
51.33 Anastomosis of gallbladder to pancreas
51.34 Anastomosis of gallbladder to stomach
51.35 Other gallbladder anastomosis
Gallbladder anastomosis NOS

51.36 Choledochoenterostomy
DEF: Connection of common bile duct to intestine.

51.37 Anastomosis of hepatic duct to gastrointestinal tract
Kasai portoenterostomy
AHA: 2Q, '02, 12
DEF: Kaisi portoenterostomy: A duct to drain bile from the liver is formed by anastomosing the porta hepatis to a loop of bowel.

51.39 Other bile duct anastomosis
Anastomosis of bile duct NOS
Anastomosis of unspecified bile duct to:
intestine
liver
pancreas
stomach

✓4th **51.4 Incision of bile duct for relief of obstruction**

51.41 Common duct exploration for removal of calculus
EXCLUDES *percutaneous extraction (51.96)*
AHA: 1Q, '96, 12; 3Q, '89, 18; 4Q, '88, 7

51.42 Common duct exploration for relief of other obstruction
AHA: 3Q, '89, 18

51.43 Insertion of choledochohepatic tube for decompression
Hepatocholedochostomy
AHA: 3Q, '89, 18; 4Q, '88, 7

51.49 Incision of other bile ducts for relief of obstruction
AHA: 3Q, '89, 18

✓4th **51.5 Other incision of bile duct**
EXCLUDES *that for relief of obstruction (51.41-51.49)*

51.51 Exploration of common duct
Incision of common bile duct
AHA: 2Q, '97, 16; 1Q, '96, 12

51.59 Incision of other bile duct
AHA: 2Q, '97, 16; 3Q, '89, 18

✓4th **51.6 Local excision or destruction of lesion or tissue of biliary ducts and sphincter of Oddi**
Code also anastomosis other than end-to-end (51.31, 51.36-51.39)
EXCLUDES *biopsy of bile duct (51.12-51.13)*

51.61 Excision of cystic duct remnant
AHA: 3Q, '89, 18

51.62 Excision of ampulla of Vater (with reimplantation of common duct)
51.63 Other excision of common duct
Choledochectomy
EXCLUDES *fistulectomy (51.72)*

51.64 Endoscopic excision or destruction of lesion of biliary ducts or sphincter of Oddi
Excision or destruction of lesion of biliary duct by procedures classifiable to 51.10-51.11, 52.13

51.69 Excision of other bile duct
Excision of lesion of bile duct NOS
EXCLUDES *fistulectomy (51.79)*

✓4th **51.7 Repair of bile ducts**

51.71 Simple suture of common bile duct
51.72 Choledochoplasty
Repair of fistula of common bile duct

51.79 Repair of other bile ducts
Closure of artificial opening of bile duct NOS
Suture of bile duct NOS
EXCLUDES *operative removal of prosthetic device (51.95)*

✓4th **51.8 Other operations on biliary ducts and sphincter of Oddi**

51.81 Dilation of sphincter of Oddi
Dilation of ampulla of Vater
EXCLUDES *that by endoscopic approach (51.84)*
DEF: Dilation of muscle around common bile and pancreatic ducts; to mitigate constriction obstructing bile flow.

51.82 Pancreatic sphincterotomy
Incision of pancreatic sphincter
Transduodenal ampullary sphincterotomy
EXCLUDES *that by endoscopic approach (51.85)*
DEF: Pancreatic sphincterotomy: Division of muscle around common bile and pancreatic ducts.
DEF: Transduodenal ampullary sphincterotomy: Incision into muscle around common bile and pancreatic ducts; closing approach through first section of small intestine.

51.83 Pancreatic sphincteroplasty
51.84 Endoscopic dilation of ampulla and biliary duct
Dilation of ampulla and biliary duct by procedures classifiable to 51.10-51.11, 52.13

51.85 Endoscopic sphincterotomy and papillotomy
Sphincterotomy and papillotomy by procedures classifiable to 51.10-51.11, 52.13
AHA: 4Q, '03, 118; 3Q, '03, 17; 2Q, '97, 7
DEF: Incision of muscle around common bile and pancreatic ducts and closing the duodenal papilla.

51.86 Endoscopic insertion of nasobiliary drainage tube
Insertion of nasobiliary tube by procedures classifiable to 51.10-51.11, 52.13

51.87 Endoscopic insertion of stent (tube) into bile duct
Endoprosthesis of bile duct
Insertion of stent into bile duct by procedures classifiable to 51.10-51.11, 52.13
EXCLUDES *nasobiliary drainage tube (51.86)*
replacement of stent (tube) (97.05)
AHA: 3Q, '03, 17

51.88 Endoscopic removal of stone(s) from biliary tract
Laparoscopic removal of stone(s) from biliary tract
Removal of biliary tract stone(s) by procedures classifiable to 51.10-51.11, 52.13
EXCLUDES *percutaneous extraction of common duct stones (51.96)*
AHA: 2Q, '00, 11; 2Q, '97, 7

51.89 Other operations on sphincter of Oddi

✓4th **51.9 Other operations on biliary tract**

51.91 Repair of laceration of gallbladder

51.92 Closure of cholecystostomy

51.93 Closure of other biliary fistula
Cholecystogastroenteric fistulectomy

51.94 Revision of anastomosis of biliary tract

51.95 Removal of prosthetic device from bile duct
EXCLUDES *nonoperative removal (97.55)*

51.96 Percutaneous extraction of common duct stones
AHA: 4Q, '88, 7

51.98 Other percutaneous procedures on biliary tract
Percutaneous biliary endoscopy via existing T-tube or other tract for:
dilation of biliary duct stricture
removal of stone(s) except common duct stone
exploration (postoperative)
Percutaneous transhepatic biliary drainage
EXCLUDES *percutaneous aspiration of gallbladder (51.01)*
percutaneous biopsy and/or collection of specimen by brushing or washing (51.12)
percutaneous removal of common duct stone(s) (51.96)
AHA: 1Q, '97, 14; 3Q, '89, 18; N-D, '87, 1

51.99 Other
Insertion or replacement of biliary tract prosthesis
EXCLUDES *biopsy of gallbladder (51.12-51.13)*
irrigation of cholecystostomy and other biliary tube (96.41)
lysis of peritoneal adhesions (54.5)
nonoperative removal of:
cholecystostomy tube (97.54)
tube from biliary tract or liver (97.55)

✓3rd **52 Operations on pancreas**
INCLUDES operations on pancreatic duct
Code also any application or administration of an adhesion barrier substance (99.77)

✓4th **52.0 Pancreatotomy**

52.01 Drainage of pancreatic cyst by catheter

52.09 Other pancreatotomy
Pancreatolithotomy
EXCLUDES *drainage by anastomosis (52.4, 52.96)*
incision of pancreatic sphincter (51.82)
marsupialization of cyst (52.3)
DEF: Pancreatolithotomy: Incision into pancreas to remove stones.

✓4th **52.1 Diagnostic procedures on pancreas**

52.11 Closed [aspiration] [needle] [percutaneous] biopsy of pancreas

52.12 Open biopsy of pancreas

52.13 Endoscopic retrograde pancreatography [ERP]
EXCLUDES *endoscopic retrograde:*
cholangiography [ERC] (51.11)
cholangiopancreatography [ERCP] (51.10)
that for procedures classifiable to 51.14-51.15, 51.64, 51.84-51.88, 52.14, 52.21, 52.92-52.94, 52.97-52.98

52.14 Closed [endoscopic] biopsy of pancreatic duct
Closed biopsy of pancreatic duct by procedures classifiable to 51.10-51.11, 52.13

52.19 Other diagnostic procedures on pancreas
EXCLUDES *contrast pancreatogram (87.66)*
endoscopic retrograde pancreatography [ERP] (52.13)
microscopic examination of specimen from pancreas (91.01-91.09)

✓4th **52.2 Local excision or destruction of pancreas and pancreatic duct**
EXCLUDES *biopsy of pancreas (52.11-52.12, 52.14)*
pancreatic fistulectomy (52.95)

52.21 Endoscopic excision or destruction of lesion or tissue of pancreatic duct
Excision or destruction of lesion or tissue of pancreatic duct by procedures classifiable to 51.10-51.11, 52.13

52.22 Other excision or destruction of lesion or tissue of pancreas or pancreatic duct

52.3 Marsupialization of pancreatic cyst
EXCLUDES *drainage of cyst by catheter (52.01)*
DEF: Incision into pancreas and suturing edges to form pocket; promotes drainage and healing.

52.4 Internal drainage of pancreatic cyst
Pancreaticocystoduodenostomy
Pancreaticocystogastrostomy
Pancreaticocystojejunostomy
DEF: Withdrawing fluid from pancreatic cyst by draining it through a created passage to another organ.
DEF: Pancreaticocystoduodenostomy: Creation of passage from pancreatic cyst to first portion of small intestine.
DEF: Pancreaticocystogastrostomy: Creation of passage from pancreatic cyst to stomach.
DEF: Pancreaticocystojejunostomy: Creation of passage from pancreatic cyst to midsection of small intestine.

✓4th **52.5 Partial pancreatectomy**

EXCLUDES *pancreatic fistulectomy (52.95)*

52.51 Proximal pancreatectomy

Excision of head of pancreas (with part of body)

Proximal pancreatectomy with synchronous duodenectomy

52.52 Distal pancreatectomy

Excision of tail of pancreas (with part of body)

52.53 Radical subtotal pancreatectomy

52.59 Other partial pancreatectomy

52.6 Total pancreatectomy

Pancreatectomy with synchronous duodenectomy

AHA: 4Q, '96, 71

52.7 Radical pancreaticoduodenectomy

One-stage pancreaticoduodenal resection with choledochojejunal anastomosis, pancreaticojejunal anastomosis, and gastrojejunostomy

Two-stage pancreaticoduodenal resection (first stage) (second stage)

Radical resection of the pancreas

Whipple procedure

EXCLUDES *radical subtotal pancreatectomy (52.53)*

AHA: 1Q, '01, 13

DEF: Whipple procedure: pancreaticoduodenectomy involving the removal of the head of the pancreas and part of the small intestines; pancreaticojejunostomy, choledochojejunal anastomosis, and gastrojejunostomy included in the procedure.

✓4th **52.8 Transplant of pancreas**

Note: To report donor source—*see* codes 00.91-00.93

[21] **52.80 Pancreatic transplant, not otherwise specified** NC

52.81 Reimplantation of pancreatic tissue

[21] **52.82 Homotransplant of pancreas** NC

52.83 Heterotransplant of pancreas NC

52.84 Autotransplantation of cells of islets of Langerhans

Homotransplantation of islet cells of pancreas

AHA: 4Q, '96, 70, 71

DEF: Transplantation of Islet cells from pancreas to another location of same patient.

52.85 Allotransplantation of cells of islets of Langerhans

Heterotransplantation of islet cells of pancreas

AHA: 4Q, '96, 70, 71

DEF: Transplantation of Islet cells from one individual to another.

52.86 Transplantation of cells of islets of Langerhans, not otherwise specified

AHA: 4Q, '96, 70

✓4th **52.9 Other operations on pancreas**

DEF: Placement of tube into pancreatic duct, without an endoscope.

52.92 Cannulation of pancreatic duct

EXCLUDES *that by endoscopic approach (52.93)*

52.93 Endoscopic insertion of stent (tube) into pancreatic duct

Insertion of cannula or stent into pancreatic duct by procedures classifiable to 51.10-51.11, 52.13

EXCLUDES *endoscopic insertion of nasopancreatic drainage tube (52.97)*
replacement of stent (tube) (97.05)

AHA: 2Q, '97, 7

52.94 Endoscopic removal of stone(s) from pancreatic duct

Removal of stone(s) from pancreatic duct by procedures classifiable to 51.10-51.11, 52.13

52.95 Other repair of pancreas

Fistulectomy } of pancreas
Simple suture }

52.96 Anastomosis of pancreas

Anastomosis of pancreas (duct) to:
intestine
jejunum
stomach

EXCLUDES *anastomosis to:*
bile duct (51.39)
gallbladder (51.33)

52.97 Endoscopic insertion of nasopancreatic drainage tube

Insertion of nasopancreatic drainage tube by procedures classifiable to 51.10-51.11, 52.13

EXCLUDES *drainage of pancreatic cyst by catheter (52.01)*
replacement of stent (tube) (97.05)

52.98 Endoscopic dilation of pancreatic duct

Dilation of Wirsung's duct by procedures classifiable to 51.10-51.11, 52.13

52.99 Other

Dilation of pancreatic [Wirsung's] duct } by open approach
Repair of pancreatic [Wirsung's] duct }

EXCLUDES *irrigation of pancreatic tube (96.42)*
removal of pancreatic tube (97.56)

✓3rd **53 Repair of hernia**

INCLUDES hernioplasty
herniorrhaphy
herniotomy

Code also any application or administration of an adhesion barrier substance (99.77)

EXCLUDES *manual reduction of hernia (96.27)*

AHA: 3Q, '94, 8

DEF: Repair of hernia: Restoration of abnormally protruding organ or tissue.
DEF: Herniorrhaphy: Repair of hernia.
DEF: Herniotomy: Division of constricted, strangulated, irreducible hernia.

✓4th **53.0 Unilateral repair of inguinal hernia**

53.00 Unilateral repair of inguinal hernia, not otherwise specified

Inguinal herniorrhaphy NOS

AHA: 3Q, '03, 10

53.01 Repair of direct inguinal hernia

AHA: 4Q, '96, 66

Indirect Repair of Hernia

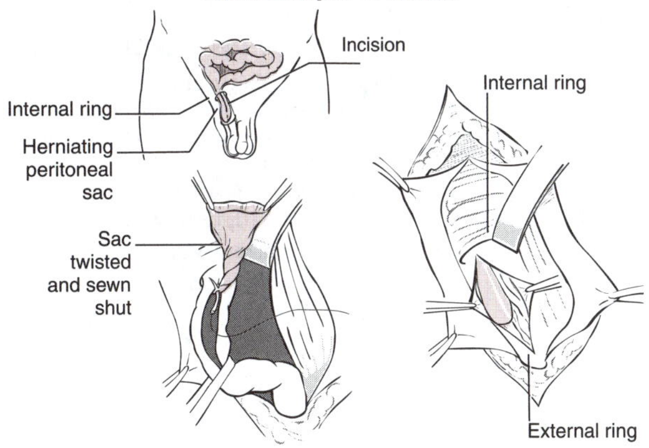

[21] Noncovered procedure unless a diagnosis code is present from 250.00-250.93.

53.02 Repair of indirect inguinal hernia

53.03 Repair of direct inguinal hernia with graft or prosthesis

53.04 Repair of indirect inguinal hernia with graft or prosthesis

53.05 Repair of inguinal hernia with graft or prosthesis, not otherwise specified

✓4th **53.1 Bilateral repair of inguinal hernia**

53.10 Bilateral repair of inguinal hernia, not otherwise specified

53.11 Bilateral repair of direct inguinal hernia

53.12 Bilateral repair of indirect inguinal hernia

53.13 Bilateral repair of inguinal hernia, one direct and one indirect

53.14 Bilateral repair of direct inguinal hernia with graft or prosthesis

53.15 Bilateral repair of indirect inguinal hernia with graft or prosthesis

53.16 Bilateral repair of inguinal hernia, one direct and one indirect, with graft or prosthesis

53.17 Bilateral inguinal hernia repair with graft or prosthesis, not otherwise specified

✓4th **53.2 Unilateral repair of femoral hernia**

53.21 Unilateral repair of femoral hernia with graft or prosthesis

53.29 Other unilateral femoral herniorrhaphy

✓4th **53.3 Bilateral repair of femoral hernia**

53.31 Bilateral repair of femoral hernia with graft or prosthesis

53.39 Other bilateral femoral herniorrhaphy

✓4th **53.4 Repair of umbilical hernia**

EXCLUDES *repair of gastroschisis (54.71)*

53.41 Repair of umbilical hernia with prosthesis

53.49 Other umbilical herniorrhaphy

✓4th **53.5 Repair of other hernia of anterior abdominal wall (without graft or prosthesis)**

53.51 Incisional hernia repair

AHA: 3Q, '03, 6

53.59 Repair of other hernia of anterior abdominal wall

Repair of hernia:
- epigastric
- hypogastric

Repair of hernia:
- spigelian
- ventral

AHA: 3Q, '03, 6; 3Q, '96, 15

✓4th **53.6 Repair of other hernia of anterior abdominal wall with graft or prosthesis**

53.61 Incisional hernia repair with prosthesis

AHA: 3Q, '03, 11

53.69 Repair of other hernia of anterior abdominal wall with prosthesis

53.7 Repair of diaphragmatic hernia, abdominal approach

✓4th **53.8 Repair of diaphragmatic hernia, thoracic approach**

DEF: Repair of diaphragmatic hernia though abdomen and thorax.

53.80 Repair of diaphragmatic hernia with thoracic approach, not otherwise specified

Thoracoabdominal repair of diaphragmatic hernia

53.81 Plication of the diaphragm

DEF: Tuck repair of diaphragmatic hernia.

53.82 Repair of parasternal hernia

DEF: Repair of hernia protruding into breastbone area.

53.9 Other hernia repair

Repair of hernia:
- ischiatic
- ischiorectal
- lumbar
- obturator

Repair of hernia:
- omental
- retroperitoneal
- sciatic

EXCLUDES *relief of strangulated hernia with exteriorization of intestine (46.01, 46.03)*
repair of pericolostomy hernia (46.42)
repair of vaginal enterocele (70.92)

✓3rd **54 Other operations on abdominal region**

INCLUDES operations on:
- epigastric region
- flank
- groin region
- hypochondrium
- inguinal region
- loin region

operations on:
- male pelvic cavity
- mesentery
- omentum
- peritoneum
- retroperitoneal tissue space

Code also any application or administration of an adhesion barrier substance (99.77)

EXCLUDES *female pelvic cavity (69.01-70.92)*
hernia repair (53.00-53.9)
obliteration of cul-de-sac (70.92)
retroperitoneal tissue dissection (59.00-59.09)
skin and subcutaneous tissue of abdominal wall (86.01-86.99)

54.0 Incision of abdominal wall

Drainage of:
- abdominal wall
- extraperitoneal abscess
- retroperitoneal abscess

EXCLUDES *incision of peritoneum (54.95)*
laparotomy (54.11-54.19)

AHA: ▶4Q, '05, 77;◀ 1Q, '97, 11; N-D, '87, 12

✓4th **54.1 Laparotomy**

AHA: 1Q, '92, 13

DEF: Incision into abdomen.

54.11 Exploratory laparotomy

EXCLUDES *exploration incidental to intra-abdominal surgery — omit code*

AHA: 3Q, '89, 14; 4Q, '88, 12

DEF: Exam of peritoneal cavity through incision into abdomen.

54.12 Reopening of recent laparotomy site

Reopening of recent laparotomy site for:
- control of hemorrhage
- exploration
- incision of hematoma

54.19 Other laparotomy

Drainage of intraperitoneal abscess or hematoma

EXCLUDES *culdocentesis (70.0)*
drainage of appendiceal abscess (47.2)
exploration incidental to intra-abdominal surgery — omit code
Ladd operation (54.95)
percutaneous drainage of abdomen (54.91)
removal of foreign body (54.92)

AHA: 3Q, '03, 17

✓4th **54.2 Diagnostic procedures of abdominal region**

54.21 Laparoscopy

Peritoneoscopy

EXCLUDES *laparoscopic cholecystectomy (51.23)*
that incidental to destruction of fallopian tubes (66.21-66.29)

DEF: Endoscopic exam of peritoneal cavity through abdominal incision.

54.22 Biopsy of abdominal wall or umbilicus

54.23 Biopsy of peritoneum

Biopsy of:
mesentery
omentum
peritoneal implant

EXCLUDES *closed biopsy of:*
omentum (54.24)
peritoneum (54.24)

54.24 Closed [percutaneous] [needle] biopsy of intra-abdominal mass

Closed biopsy of:
omentum
peritoneal implant
peritoneum

EXCLUDES *that of:*
fallopian tube (66.11)
ovary (65.11)
uterine ligaments (68.15)
uterus (68.16)

AHA: 4Q, '97, 57

54.25 Peritoneal lavage

Diagnostic peritoneal lavage

EXCLUDES *peritoneal dialysis (54.98)*

AHA: 2Q, '98, 19; 4Q, '93, 28

DEF: Irrigation of peritoneal cavity with siphoning of liquid contents for analysis.

54.29 Other diagnostic procedures on abdominal region

EXCLUDES *abdominal lymphangiogram (88.04)*
abdominal x-ray NEC (88.19)
angiocardiography of venae cavae (88.51)
C.A.T. scan of abdomen (88.01)
contrast x-ray of abdominal cavity (88.11-88.15)
intra-abdominal arteriography NEC (88.47)
microscopic examination of peritoneal and retroperitoneal specimen (91.11-91.19)
phlebography of:
intra-abdominal vessels NEC (88.65)
portal venous system (88.64)
sinogram of abdominal wall (88.03)
soft tissue x-ray of abdominal wall NEC (88.09)
tomography of abdomen NEC (88.02)
ultrasonography of abdomen and retroperitoneum (88.76)

54.3 Excision or destruction of lesion or tissue of abdominal wall or umbilicus

Debridement of abdominal wall
Omphalectomy

EXCLUDES *biopsy of abdominal wall or umbilicus (54.22)*
size reduction operation (86.83)
that of skin of abdominal wall (86.22, 86.26, 86.3)

AHA: 1Q, '89, 11

54.4 Excision or destruction of peritoneal tissue

Excision of:
appendices epiploicae
falciform ligament
gastrocolic ligament
lesion of:
mesentery
omentum
peritoneum
presacral lesion NOS
retroperitoneal lesion NOS

EXCLUDES *biopsy of peritoneum (54.23)*
endometrectomy of cul-de-sac (70.32)

✓4th **54.5 Lysis of peritoneal adhesions**

Freeing of adhesions of:
biliary tract
intestines
liver
pelvic peritoneum
peritoneum
spleen
uterus

EXCLUDES *lysis of adhesions of:*
bladder (59.11)
fallopian tube and ovary (65.81, 65.89)
kidney (59.02)
ureter (59.02-59.03)

AHA: 3Q, '94, 8; 4Q, '90, 18

54.51 Laparoscopic lysis of peritoneal adhesions

AHA: 3Q, '03, 6-7; 4Q, '96, 65

54.59 Other lysis of peritoneal adhesions

AHA: 3Q, '03, 11; 1Q, '03, 14; 4Q, '96, 66

✓4th **54.6 Suture of abdominal wall and peritoneum**

54.61 Reclosure of postoperative disruption of abdominal wall

54.62 Delayed closure of granulating abdominal wound

Tertiary subcutaneous wound closure

DEF: Closure of outer layers of abdominal wound; follows procedure to close initial layers of wound.

54.63 Other suture of abdominal wall

Suture of laceration of abdominal wall

EXCLUDES *closure of operative wound — omit code*

54.64 Suture of peritoneum

Secondary suture of peritoneum

EXCLUDES *closure of operative wound — omit code*

✓4th **54.7 Other repair of abdominal wall and peritoneum**

54.71 Repair of gastroschisis

AHA: 2Q, '02, 9

DEF: Repair of congenital fistula of abdominal wall.

54.72 Other repair of abdominal wall

54.73 Other repair of peritoneum

Suture of gastrocolic ligament

54.74 Other repair of omentum
Epiplorrhaphy
Graft of omentum
Omentopexy
Reduction of torsion of omentum
EXCLUDES *cardio-omentopexy (36.39)*
AHA: J-F, '87, 11
DEF: Epiplorrhaphy: Suture of abdominal serous membrane.
DEF: Graft of omentum: Implantation of tissue into abdominal serous membrane.
DEF: Omentopexy: Anchoring of abdominal serous membrane.
DEF: Reduction of torsion of omentum: Reduction of twisted abdominal serous membrane.

54.75 Other repair of mesentery
Mesenteric plication
Mesenteropexy
DEF: Creation of folds in mesentery for shortening.
DEF: Mesenteriopexy: Fixation of torn, incised mesentery.

✓4th **54.9 Other operations of abdominal region**
EXCLUDES *removal of ectopic pregnancy (74.3)*

54.91 Percutaneous abdominal drainage
Paracentesis
EXCLUDES *creation of cutaneoperitoneal fistula (54.93)*
AHA: 3Q, '99, 9; 2Q, '99, 14; 3Q, '98, 12; 1Q, '92, 14; 2Q, '90, 25
DEF: Puncture for removal of fluid.

54.92 Removal of foreign body from peritoneal cavity
AHA: 1Q, '89, 11

54.93 Creation of cutaneoperitoneal fistula
AHA: 2Q, '95, 10; N-D, '84, 6
DEF: Creation of opening between skin and peritoneal cavity.

54.94 Creation of peritoneovascular shunt
Peritoneovenous shunt
AHA: 1Q, '94, 7; 1Q, '88, 9; S-O, '85, 6
DEF: Peritoneal vascular shunt: Construction of shunt to connect peritoneal cavity with vascular system.
DEF: Peritoneovenous shunt: Construction of shunt to connect peritoneal cavity with vein.

54.95 Incision of peritoneum
Exploration of ventriculoperitoneal shunt at peritoneal site
Ladd operation
Revision of distal catheter of ventricular shunt
Revision of ventriculoperitoneal shunt at peritoneal site
EXCLUDES *that incidental to laparotomy (54.11-54.19)*
AHA: 4Q, '95, 65
DEF: Ladd operation: Peritoneal attachment of incompletely rotated cecum, obstructing duodenum.

54.96 Injection of air into peritoneal cavity
Pneumoperitoneum
EXCLUDES *that for:*
collapse of lung (33.33)
radiography (88.12-88.13, 88.15)

54.97 Injection of locally-acting therapeutic substance into peritoneal cavity
EXCLUDES *peritoneal dialysis (54.98)*

54.98 Peritoneal dialysis
EXCLUDES *peritoneal lavage (diagnostic) (54.25)*
AHA: 4Q, '93, 28; N-D, '84, 6
DEF: Separation of blood elements by diffusion through membrane.

54.99 Other
EXCLUDES *removal of:*
abdominal wall sutures (97.83)
peritoneal drainage device (97.82)
retroperitoneal drainage device (97.81)
AHA: 1Q, '99, 4

10. OPERATIONS ON THE URINARY SYSTEM (55-59)

✓3rd **55 Operations on kidney**

INCLUDES operations on renal pelvis

Code also any application or administration of an adhesion barrier substance (99.77)

EXCLUDES *perirenal tissue (59.00-59.09, 59.21-59.29, 59.91-59.92)*

✓4th **55.0 Nephrotomy and nephrostomy**

EXCLUDES *drainage by:*
anastomosis (55.86)
aspiration (55.92)

55.01 Nephrotomy

Evacuation of renal cyst
Exploration of kidney
Nephrolithotomy

DEF: Nephrotomy: Incision into kidney.

DEF: Evacuation of renal cyst: Draining contents of cyst.

DEF: Exploration of kidney: Exploration through incision.

DEF: Nephrolithotomy: Removal of kidney stone through incision.

55.02 Nephrostomy

AHA: 2Q, '97, 4

55.03 Percutaneous nephrostomy without fragmentation

Nephrostolithotomy, percutaneous (nephroscopic)
Percutaneous removal of kidney stone(s) by:
forceps extraction (nephroscopic)
basket extraction
Pyelostolithotomy, percutaneous (nephroscopic)
With placement of catheter down ureter

EXCLUDES *percutaneous removal by fragmentation (55.04)*
repeat nephroscopic removal during current episode (55.92)

AHA: 2Q, '96, 5

DEF: Insertion of tube through abdominal wall without breaking up stones.

DEF: Nephrostolithotomy: Insertion of tube through the abdominal wall to remove stones.

DEF: Basket extraction: Removal, percutaneous of stone with grasping forceps.

DEF: Pyelostolithotomy: Removal, percutaneous of stones from funnel-shaped portion of kidney.

55.04 Percutaneous nephrostomy with fragmentation

Percutaneous nephrostomy with disruption of kidney stone by ultrasonic energy and extraction (suction) through endoscope
With placement of catheter down ureter
With fluoroscopic guidance

EXCLUDES *repeat fragmentation during current episode (59.95)*

AHA: 1Q, '89, 1; S-O, '86, 11

DEF: Insertion of tube through abdominal wall into kidney to break up stones.

✓4th **55.1 Pyelotomy and pyelostomy**

EXCLUDES *drainage by anastomosis (55.86)*
percutaneous pyelostolithotomy (55.03)
removal of calculus without incision (56.0)

55.11 Pyelotomy

Exploration of renal pelvis
Pyelolithotomy

55.12 Pyelostomy

Insertion of drainage tube into renal pelvis

✓4th **55.2 Diagnostic procedures on kidney**

55.21 Nephroscopy

DEF: Endoscopic exam of renal pelvis; retrograde through ureter, percutaneous or open exposure.

55.22 Pyeloscopy

DEF: Fluoroscopic exam of kidney pelvis, calyces and ureters; follows IV or retrograde injection of contrast.

55.23 Closed [percutaneous] [needle] biopsy of kidney

Endoscopic biopsy via existing nephrostomy, nephrotomy, pyelostomy, or pyelotomy

55.24 Open biopsy of kidney

55.29 Other diagnostic procedures on kidney

EXCLUDES *microscopic examination of specimen from kidney (91.21-91.29)*
pyelogram:
intravenous (87.73)
percutaneous (87.75)
retrograde (87.74)
radioisotope scan (92.03)
renal arteriography (88.45)
tomography:
C.A.T scan (87.71)
other (87.72)

✓4th **55.3 Local excision or destruction of lesion or tissue of kidney**

55.31 Marsupialization of kidney lesion

DEF: Exteriorization of lesion by incising anterior wall and suturing cut edges to create open pouch.

● **55.32 Open ablation of renal lesion or tissue**

● **55.33 Percutaneous ablation of renal lesion or tissue**

● **55.34 Laparoscopic ablation of renal lesion or tissue**

● **55.35 Other and unspecified ablation of renal lesion or tissue**

55.39 Other local destruction or excision of renal lesion or tissue

Obliteration of calyceal diverticulum

EXCLUDES ▶ *ablation of renal lesion or tissue:*
laparoscopic (55.34)
open (55.32)
other (55.35)
percutaneous (55.33)◀
biopsy of kidney (55.23-55.24)
partial nephrectomy (55.4)
percutaneous aspiration of kidney (55.92)
wedge resection of kidney (55.4)

55.4 Partial nephrectomy

Calycectomy
Wedge resection of kidney
Code also any synchronous resection of ureter (56.40-56.42)

DEF: Surgical removal of a part of the kidney.

DEF: Calycectomy: Removal of indentations in kidney.

✓4th **55.5 Complete nephrectomy**
Code also any synchronous excision of:
adrenal gland (07.21-07.3)
bladder segment (57.6)
lymph nodes (40.3, 40.52-40.59)

55.51 Nephroureterectomy
Nephroureterectomy with bladder cuff
Total nephrectomy (unilateral)
EXCLUDES *removal of transplanted kidney (55.53)*
AHA: ▶2Q, '05, 4◀
DEF: Complete removal of the kidney and all or portion of the ureter.
DEF: Nephroureterectomy with bladder cuff: Removal of kidney, ureter, and portion of bladder attached to ureter.
DEF: Total nephrectomy (unilateral): Complete excision of one kidney.

55.52 Nephrectomy of remaining kidney
Removal of solitary kidney
EXCLUDES *removal of transplanted kidney (55.53)*

55.53 Removal of transplanted or rejected kidney

55.54 Bilateral nephrectomy
EXCLUDES *complete nephrectomy NOS (55.51)*
DEF: Removal of both kidneys same operative session.

✓4th **55.6 Transplant of kidney**
Note: To report donor source — see codes 00.91-00.93

55.61 Renal autotransplantation

55.69 Other kidney transplantation
AHA: ▶4Q, '04, 117;◀ 4Q, '96, 71

55.7 Nephropexy
Fixation or suspension of movable [floating] kidney

✓4th **55.8 Other repair of kidney**

55.81 Suture of laceration of kidney

55.82 Closure of nephrostomy and pyelostomy
DEF: Removal of tube from kidney and closure of site of tube insertion.

55.83 Closure of other fistula of kidney

55.84 Reduction of torsion of renal pedicle
DEF: Restoration of twisted renal pedicle into normal position.

55.85 Symphysiotomy for horseshoe kidney
DEF: Division of congenitally malformed kidney into two parts.

55.86 Anastomosis of kidney
Nephropyeloureterostomy
Pyeloureterovesical anastomosis
Ureterocalyceal anastomosis
EXCLUDES *nephrocystanastomosis NOS (56.73)*
DEF: Nephropyeloureterostomy: Creation of passage between kidney and ureter.
DEF: Pyeloureterovesical anastomosis: Creation of passage between kidney and bladder.
DEF: Ureterocalyceal anastomosis: Creation of passage between ureter and kidney indentations.

55.87 Correction of ureteropelvic junction

55.89 Other

✓4th **55.9 Other operations on kidney**
EXCLUDES *lysis of perirenal adhesions (59.02)*

55.91 Decapsulation of kidney
Capsulectomy } of kidney
Decortication }

Symphysiostomy for Horseshoe Kidney

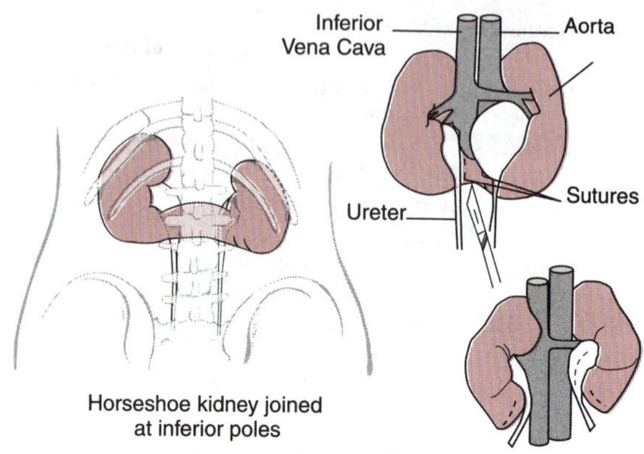

Horseshoe kidney joined at inferior poles

55.92 Percutaneous aspiration of kidney (pelvis)
Aspiration of renal cyst
Renipuncture
EXCLUDES *percutaneous biopsy of kidney (55.23)*
AHA: N-D, '84, 20
DEF: Insertion of needle into kidney to withdraw fluid.

55.93 Replacement of nephrostomy tube

55.94 Replacement of pyelostomy tube

55.95 Local perfusion of kidney
DEF: Fluid passage through kidney.

55.96 Other injection of therapeutic substance into kidney
Injection into renal cyst

55.97 Implantation or replacement of mechanical kidney

55.98 Removal of mechanical kidney

55.99 Other
EXCLUDES *removal of pyelostomy or nephrostomy tube (97.61)*

✓3rd **56 Operations on ureter**
Code also any application or administration of an adhesion barrier substance (99.77)

56.0 Transurethral removal of obstruction from ureter and renal pelvis
Removal of:
blood clot }
calculus } from ureter or renal pelvis without incision
foreign body }
EXCLUDES *manipulation without removal of obstruction (59.8)*
that by incision (55.11,56.2)
transurethral insertion of ureteral stent for passage of calculus (59.8)
AHA: 1Q, '89, 1; S-O, '86, 12
DEF: Removal of obstruction by tube inserted through urethra to ureter.

56.1 Ureteral meatotomy
DEF: Incision into ureteral meatus to enlarge passage.

56.2 Ureterotomy
Incision of ureter for:
drainage
exploration
Incision of ureter for:
removal of calculus
EXCLUDES *cutting of ureterovesical orifice (56.1)*
removal of calculus without incision (56.0)
transurethral insertion of ureteral stent for passage of calculus (59.8)
urinary diversion (56.51-56.79)
AHA: S-O, '86, 10

56.3 Diagnostic procedures on ureter

56.31 Ureteroscopy

56.32 Closed percutaneous biopsy of ureter

EXCLUDES *endoscopic biopsy of ureter (56.33)*

56.33 Closed endoscopic biopsy of ureter

Cystourethroscopy with ureteral biopsy
Transurethral biopsy of ureter
Ureteral endoscopy with biopsy through ureterotomy
Ureteroscopy with biopsy

EXCLUDES *percutaneous biopsy of ureter (56.32)*

56.34 Open biopsy of ureter

56.35 Endoscopy (cystoscopy) (looposcopy) of ileal conduit

DEF: Endoscopic exam of created opening between ureters and one end of small intestine; other end used to form artificial opening.

56.39 Other diagnostic procedures on ureter

EXCLUDES *microscopic examination of specimen from ureter (91.21-91.29)*

56.4 Ureterectomy

Code also anastomosis other than end-to-end (56.51-56.79)

EXCLUDES *fistulectomy (56.84)*
nephroureterectomy (55.51-55.54)

56.40 Ureterectomy, not otherwise specified

56.41 Partial ureterectomy

Excision of lesion of ureter
Shortening of ureter with reimplantation

EXCLUDES *biopsy of ureter (56.32-56.34)*

56.42 Total ureterectomy

56.5 Cutaneous uretero-ileostomy

56.51 Formation of cutaneous uretero-ileostomy

Construction of ileal conduit
External ureteral ileostomy
Formation of open ileal bladder
Ileal loop operation
Ileoureterostomy (Bricker's) (ileal bladder)
Transplantation of ureter into ileum with external diversion

EXCLUDES *closed ileal bladder (57.87)*
replacement of ureteral defect by ileal segment (56.89)

DEF: Creation of urinary passage by connecting the terminal end of small intestine to ureter then connected to opening through abdominal wall.

DEF: Construction of ileal conduit: Formation of conduit from terminal end of small intestine.

56.52 Revision of cutaneous uretero-ileostomy

AHA: 3Q, '96, 15; 4Q, '88, 7

56.6 Other external urinary diversion

56.61 Formation of other cutaneous ureterostomy

Anastomosis of ureter to skin
Ureterostomy NOS

56.62 Revision of other cutaneous ureterostomy

Revision of ureterostomy stoma

EXCLUDES *nonoperative removal of ureterostomy tube (97.62)*

56.7 Other anastomosis or bypass of ureter

EXCLUDES *ureteropyelostomy (55.86)*

56.71 Urinary diversion to intestine

Anastomosis of ureter to intestine
Internal urinary diversion NOS
Code also any synchronous colostomy (46.10-46.13)

EXCLUDES *external ureteral ileostomy (56.51)*

56.72 Revision of ureterointestinal anastomosis

EXCLUDES *revision of external ureteral ileostomy (56.52)*

56.73 Nephrocystanastomosis, not otherwise specified

DEF: Connection of kidney to bladder.

56.74 Ureteroneocystostomy

Replacement of ureter with bladder flap
Ureterovesical anastomosis

DEF: Transfer of ureter to another site in bladder.
DEF: Ureterovesical anastomosis: Implantation of ureter into bladder.

56.75 Transureteroureterostomy

EXCLUDES *ureteroureterostomy associated with partial resection (56.41)*

DEF: Separating one ureter and joining the ends to the opposite ureter.

56.79 Other

56.8 Repair of ureter

56.81 Lysis of intraluminal adhesions of ureter

EXCLUDES *lysis of periureteral adhesions (59.01-59.02)*
ureterolysis (59.02-59.03)

DEF: Destruction of adhesions within urethral cavity.

56.82 Suture of laceration of ureter

56.83 Closure of ureterostomy

56.84 Closure of other fistula of ureter

56.85 Ureteropexy

56.86 Removal of ligature from ureter

56.89 Other repair of ureter

Graft of ureter
Replacement of ureter with ileal segment implanted into bladder
Ureteroplication

DEF: Graft of ureter: Tissue from another site for graft replacement or repair of ureter.
DEF: Replacement of ureter with ileal segment implanted into bladder and ureter replacement with terminal end of small intestine.
DEF: Ureteroplication: Creation of tucks in ureter.

56.9 Other operations on ureter

56.91 Dilation of ureteral meatus

56.92 Implantation of electronic ureteral stimulator

56.93 Replacement of electronic ureteral stimulator

56.94 Removal of electronic ureteral stimulator

EXCLUDES *that with synchronous replacement (56.93)*

56.95 Ligation of ureter

56.99 Other

EXCLUDES *removal of ureterostomy tube and ureteral catheter (97.62)*
ureteral catheterization (59.8)

57 Operations on urinary bladder

Code also any application or administration of an adhesion barrier substance (99.77)

EXCLUDES *perivesical tissue (59.11-59.29, 59.91-59.92)*
ureterovesical orifice (56.0-56.99)

57.0 Transurethral clearance of bladder

Drainage of bladder without incision
Removal of:
blood clot, calculus, foreign body } from bladder without incision

EXCLUDES *that by incision (57.19)*

AHA: S-O, '86, 11

DEF: Insertion of device through urethra to cleanse bladder.

✓4th 57.1 Cystotomy and cystostomy

EXCLUDES *cystotomy and cystostomy as operative approach — omit code*

DEF: Cystotomy: Incision of bladder.

DEF: Cystostomy: Creation of opening into bladder.

57.11 Percutaneous aspiration of bladder

57.12 Lysis of intraluminal adhesions with incision into bladder

EXCLUDES *transurethral lysis of intraluminal adhesions (57.41)*

DEF: Incision into bladder to destroy lesions.

57.17 Percutaneous cystostomy

Closed cystostomy

Percutaneous suprapubic cystostomy

EXCLUDES *removal of cystostomy tube (97.63)*
replacement of cystostomy tube (59.94)

DEF: Incision through body wall into bladder to insert tube.

DEF: Percutaneous (closed) suprapubic cystostomy: Incision above pubic arch, through body wall, into the bladder to insert tube.

57.18 Other suprapubic cystostomy

EXCLUDES *percutaneous cystostomy (57.17)*
removal of cystostomy tube (97.63)
replacement of cystostomy tube (59.94)

57.19 Other cystotomy

Cystolithotomy

EXCLUDES *percutaneous cystostomy (57.17)*
suprapubic cystostomy (57.18)

AHA: 4Q, '95, 73; S-O, '86, 11

✓4th 57.2 Vesicostomy

EXCLUDES *percutaneous cystostomy (57.17)*
suprapubic cystostomy (57.18)

57.21 Vesicostomy

Creation of permanent opening from bladder to skin using a bladder flap

DEF: Creation of permanent opening from the bladder to the skin.

57.22 Revision or closure of vesicostomy

EXCLUDES *closure of cystostomy (57.82)*

✓4th 57.3 Diagnostic procedures on bladder

57.31 Cystoscopy through artificial stoma

57.32 Other cystoscopy

Transurethral cystoscopy

EXCLUDES *cystourethroscopy with ureteral biopsy (56.33)*
retrograde pyelogram (87.74)
that for control of hemorrhage (postoperative):
bladder (57.93)
prostate (60.94)

AHA: 1Q, '01, 14

57.33 Closed [transurethral] biopsy of bladder

57.34 Open biopsy of bladder

AHA: ▶2Q, '05, 12◀

Transurethral Cystourethroscopy

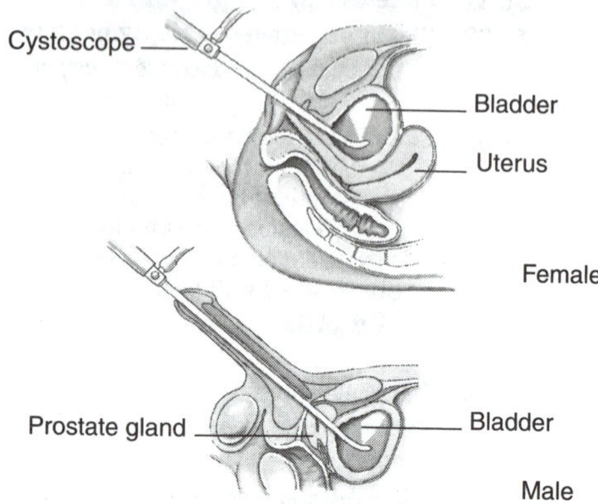

57.39 Other diagnostic procedures on bladder

EXCLUDES *cystogram NEC (87.77)*
microscopic examination of specimen from bladder (91.31-91.39)
retrograde cystourethrogram (87.76)
therapeutic distention of bladder (96.25)

✓4th 57.4 Transurethral excision or destruction of bladder tissue

DEF: Destruction of bladder tissue with instrument inserted into urethra.

57.41 Transurethral lysis of intraluminal adhesions

57.49 Other transurethral excision or destruction of lesion or tissue of bladder

Endoscopic resection of bladder lesion

EXCLUDES *transurethral biopsy of bladder (57.33)*
transurethral fistulectomy (57.83-57.84)

✓4th 57.5 Other excision or destruction of bladder tissue

EXCLUDES *that with transurethral approach (57.41-57.49)*

57.51 Excision of urachus

Excision of urachal sinus of bladder

EXCLUDES *excision of urachal cyst of abdominal wall (54.3)*

57.59 Open excision or destruction of other lesion or tissue of bladder

Endometrectomy of bladder

Suprapubic excision of bladder lesion

EXCLUDES *biopsy of bladder (57.33-57.34)*
fistulectomy of bladder (57.83-57.84)

DEF: Endometrectomy of bladder: Removal of inner lining.

DEF: Suprapubic excision of bladder lesion: Removal of lesion by excision above suprapubic bone arch.

57.6 Partial cystectomy

Excision of bladder dome

Trigonectomy

Wedge resection of bladder

✓4th **57.7 Total cystectomy**

INCLUDES total cystectomy with urethrectomy

57.71 Radical cystectomy

Pelvic exenteration in male
Removal of bladder, prostate, seminal vesicles and fat
Removal of bladder, urethra, and fat in a female
Code also any:
lymph node dissection (40.3, 40.5)
urinary diversion (56.51-56.79)

EXCLUDES *that as part of pelvic exenteration in female (68.8)*

DEF: Radical cystectomy: Removal of bladder and surrounding tissue.

DEF: Pelvic exenteration in male: Excision of bladder, prostate, seminal vessels and fat.

57.79 Other total cystectomy

✓4th **57.8 Other repair of urinary bladder**

EXCLUDES *repair of:*
current obstetric laceration (75.61)
cystocele (70.50-70.51)
that for stress incontinence (59.3-59.79)

57.81 Suture of laceration of bladder

57.82 Closure of cystostomy

57.83 Repair of fistula involving bladder and intestine

Rectovesicovaginal } fistulectomy
Vesicosigmoidovaginal }

57.84 Repair of other fistula of bladder

Cervicovesical } fistulectomy
Urethroperineovesical }
Uterovesical }
Vaginovesical }

EXCLUDES *vesicoureterovaginal fistulectomy (56.84)*

57.85 Cystourethroplasty and plastic repair of bladder neck

Plication of sphincter of urinary bladder
V-Y plasty of bladder neck

DEF: Cystourethroplasty: Reconstruction of narrowed portion of bladder.

DEF: Plication of sphincter or urinary bladder: Creation of tuck in bladder sphincter.

DEF: V-Y plasty of bladder neck: Surgical reconstruction of the narrowed portion of bladder by V-Y technique.

57.86 Repair of bladder exstrophy

DEF: Surgical correction of a congenital bladder wall defect.

57.87 Reconstruction of urinary bladder

Anastomosis of bladder with isolated segment of ileum
Augmentation of bladder
Replacement of bladder with ileum or sigmoid [closed ileal bladder]
Code also resection of intestine (45.50-45.52)

AHA: ►2Q, '05, 12;◄ 2Q, '03, 11; 3Q, '00, 7

DEF: Anastomosis of bladder with isolated segment of ileum: Creation of connection between bladder and separated terminal end of small intestine.

57.88 Other anastomosis of bladder

Anastomosis of bladder to intestine NOS
Cystocolic anastomosis

EXCLUDES *formation of closed ileal bladder (57.87)*

57.89 Other repair of bladder

Bladder suspension, not elsewhere classified
Cystopexy NOS
Repair of old obstetric laceration of bladder

EXCLUDES *repair of current obstetric laceration (75.61)*

✓4th **57.9 Other operations on bladder**

57.91 Sphincterotomy of bladder

Division of bladder neck

AHA: 2Q, '90, 26

57.92 Dilation of bladder neck

57.93 Control of (postoperative) hemorrhage of bladder

57.94 Insertion of indwelling urinary catheter

57.95 Replacement of indwelling urinary catheter

57.96 Implantation of electronic bladder stimulator NC

57.97 Replacement of electronic bladder stimulator NC

57.98 Removal of electronic bladder stimulator

EXCLUDES *that with synchronous replacement (57.97)*

57.99 Other

EXCLUDES *irrigation of:*
cystostomy (96.47)
other indwelling urinary catheter (96.48)
lysis of external adhesions (59.11)
removal of:
cystostomy tube (97.63)
other urinary drainage device (97.64)
therapeutic distention of bladder (96.25)

✓3rd **58 Operations on urethra**

INCLUDES operations on:
bulbourethral gland [Cowper's gland]
periurethral tissue

Code also any application or administration of an adhesion barrier substance (99.77)

58.0 Urethrotomy

Excision of urethral septum
Formation of urethrovaginal fistula
Perineal urethrostomy
Removal of calculus from urethra by incision

EXCLUDES *drainage of bulbourethral gland or periurethral tissue (58.91)*
internal urethral meatotomy (58.5)
removal of urethral calculus without incision (58.6)

58.1 Urethral meatotomy

EXCLUDES *internal urethral meatotomy (58.5)*

DEF: Incision of urethra to enlarge passage.

✓4th **58.2 Diagnostic procedures on urethra**

58.21 Perineal urethroscopy

58.22 Other urethroscopy

58.23 Biopsy of urethra

58.24 Biopsy of periurethral tissue

DEF: Removal for biopsy of tissue around urethra.

58.29 Other diagnostic procedures on urethra and periurethral tissue

EXCLUDES *microscopic examination of specimen from urethra (91.31-91.39)*
retrograde cystourethrogram (87.76)
urethral pressure profile (89.25)
urethral sphincter electromyogram (89.23)

✓4th **58.3 Excision or destruction of lesion or tissue of urethra**

EXCLUDES *biopsy of urethra (58.23)*
excision of bulbourethral gland (58.92)
fistulectomy (58.43)
urethrectomy as part of:
complete cystectomy (57.79)
pelvic evisceration (68.8)
radical cystectomy (57.71)

58.31 Endoscopic excision or destruction of lesion or tissue of urethra

Fulguration of urethral lesion

58.39 Other local excision or destruction of lesion or tissue of urethra

Excision of:
congenital valve, lesion, stricture } of urethra

Urethrectomy

EXCLUDES *that by endoscopic appoach (58.31)*

✓4th **58.4 Repair of urethra**

EXCLUDES *repair of current obstetric laceration (75.61)*

58.41 Suture of laceration of urethra

58.42 Closure of urethrostomy

58.43 Closure of other fistula of urethra

EXCLUDES *repair of urethroperineovesical fistula (57.84)*

58.44 Reanastomosis of urethra

Anastomosis of urethra

DEF: Repair of severed urethra.

58.45 Repair of hypospadias or epispadias

AHA: 3Q, '97, 6; 4Q, '96, 35

DEF: Repair of abnormal urethral opening.

58.46 Other reconstruction of urethra

Urethral construction

58.47 Urethral meatoplasty

DEF: Reconstruction of urethral opening.

58.49 Other repair of urethra

Benenenti rotation of bulbous urethra
Repair of old obstetric laceration of urethra
Urethral plication

EXCLUDES *repair of:*
current obstetric laceration (75.61)
urethrocele (70.50-70.51)

58.5 Release of urethral stricture

Cutting of urethral sphincter
Internal urethral meatotomy
Urethrolysis

AHA: 1Q, '97, 13

58.6 Dilation of urethra

Dilation of urethrovesical junction
Passage of sounds through urethra
Removal of calculus from urethra without incision

EXCLUDES *urethral calibration (89.29)*

AHA: 1Q, '01, 14; 1Q, '97, 13

✓4th **58.9 Other operations on urethra and periurethral tissue**

58.91 Incision of periurethral tissue

Drainage of bulbourethral gland

DEF: Incision of tissue around urethra.

58.92 Excision of periurethral tissue

EXCLUDES *biopsy of periurethral tissue (58.24)*
lysis of periurethral adhesions (59.11-59.12)

58.93 Implantation of artificial urinary sphincter [AUS]

Placement of inflatable:
urethral sphincter
bladder sphincter
Removal with replacement of sphincter device [AUS]
With pump and/or reservoir

58.99 Other

Repair of inflatable sphincter pump and/or reservoir
Surgical correction of hydraulic pressure of inflatable sphincter device
Removal of inflatable urinary sphincter without replacement

EXCLUDES *removal of:*
intraluminal foreign body from urethra without incision (98.19)
urethral stent (97.65)

✓3rd **59 Other operations on urinary tract**

Code also any application or administration of an adhesion barrier substance (99.77)

✓4th **59.0 Dissection of retroperitoneal tissue**

59.00 Retroperitoneal dissection, not otherwise specified

59.02 Other lysis of perirenal or periureteral adhesions

EXCLUDES *that by laparoscope (59.03)*

59.03 Laparoscopic lysis of perirenal or periureteral adhesions

59.09 Other incision of perirenal or periureteral tissue

Exploration of perinephric area
Incision of perirenal abscess

DEF: Exploration of the perinephric area: Exam of tissue around the kidney by incision.

DEF: Incision of perirenal abscess: Incising abscess in tissue around kidney.

✓4th **59.1 Incision of perivesical tissue**

DEF: Incising tissue around bladder.

59.11 Other lysis of perivesical adhesions

59.12 Laparoscopic lysis of perivesical adhesions

59.19 Other incision of perivesical tissue

Exploration of perivesical tissue
Incision of hematoma of space of Retzius
Retropubic exploration

✓4th **59.2 Diagnostic procedures on perirenal and perivesical tissue**

59.21 Biopsy of perirenal or perivesical tissue

59.29 Other diagnostic procedures on perirenal tissue, perivesical tissue, and retroperitoneum

EXCLUDES *microscopic examination of specimen from:*
perirenal tissue (91.21-91.29)
perivesical tissue (91.31-91.39)
retroperitoneum NEC (91.11-91.19)
retroperitoneal x-ray (88.14-88.16)

59.3 Plication of urethrovesical junction

Kelly-Kennedy operation on urethra
Kelly-Stoeckel urethral plication

DEF: Suturing a tuck in tissues around urethra at junction with bladder; changes angle of junction and provides support.

59.4 Suprapubic sling operation
Goebel-Frangenheim-Stoeckel urethrovesical suspension
Millin-Read urethrovesical suspension
Oxford operation for urinary incontinence
Urethrocystopexy by suprapubic suspension
DEF: Suspension of urethra from suprapubic periosteum to restore support to bladder and urethra.

59.5 Retropubic urethral suspension
Burch procedure
Marshall-Marchetti-Krantz operation
Suture of periurethral tissue to symphysis pubis
Urethral suspension NOS
AHA: 1Q, '97, 11

DEF: Suspension of urethra from pubic bone with suture placed from symphysis pubis to paraurethral tissues; elevates urethrovesical angle, restores urinary continence.

59.6 Paraurethral suspension
Pereyra paraurethral suspension
Periurethral suspension
DEF: Suspension of bladder neck from fibrous membranes of anterior abdominal wall; upward traction applied; changes angle of urethra, improves urinary control.

✓4th **59.7 Other repair of urinary stress incontinence**

59.71 Levator muscle operation for urethrovesical suspension
Cystourethropexy with levator muscle sling
Gracilis muscle transplant for urethrovesical suspension
Pubococcygeal sling

59.72 Injection of implant into urethra and/or bladder neck
Collagen implant
Endoscopic injection of implant
Fat implant
Polytef implant
AHA: 4Q, '95, 72, 73

DEF: Injection of collagen into submucosal tissues to increase tissue bulk and improve urinary control.

59.79 Other
Anterior urethropexy
Repair of stress incontinence NOS
Tudor "rabbit ear" urethropexy
AHA: 2Q, '01, 20; 1Q, '00, 14, 15, 19

DEF: Pubovaginal sling for treatment of stress incontinence: A strip of fascia is harvested and the vaginal epithelium is mobilized and then sutured to the midline at the urethral level to the rectus muscle to create a sling supporting the bladder.

DEF: Vaginal wall sling with bone anchors for treatment of stress incontinence: A sling for the bladder is formed by a suture attachment of vaginal wall to the abdominal wall. In addition, a suture is run from the vagina to a bone anchor placed in the pubic bone.

DEF: Transvaginal endoscopic bladder neck suspension for treatment of stress incontinence: Endoscopic surgical suturing of the vaginal epithelium and the pubocervical fascia at the bladder neck level on both sides of the urethra. Two supporting sutures are run from the vagina to an anchor placed in the pubic bone on each side.

59.8 Ureteral catheterization
Drainage of kidney by catheter
Insertion of ureteral stent
Ureterovesical orifice dilation
Code also any ureterotomy (56.2)
EXCLUDES *that for:*
transurethral removal of calculus or clot from ureter and renal pelvis (56.0)
retrograde pyelogram (87.74)
AHA: ▶2Q, '05, 12;◀ 2Q, '03, 11; 3Q, '00, 7; 1Q, '89, 1; S-O, '86, 10

✓4th **59.9 Other operations on urinary system**
EXCLUDES *nonoperative removal of therapeutic device (97.61-97.69)*

59.91 Excision of perirenal or perivesical tissue
EXCLUDES *biopsy of perirenal or perivesical tissue (59.21)*

59.92 Other operations on perirenal or perivesical tissue

59.93 Replacement of ureterostomy tube
Change of ureterostomy tube
Reinsertion of ureterostomy tube
EXCLUDES *nonoperative removal of ureterostomy tube (97.62)*

59.94 Replacement of cystostomy tube
EXCLUDES *nonoperative removal of cystostomy tube (97.63)*

59.95 Ultrasonic fragmentation of urinary stones
Shattered urinary stones
EXCLUDES *percutaneous nephrostomy with fragmentation (55.04)*
shockwave disintegration (98.51)
AHA: 1Q, '89, 1; S-O, '86, 11

59.99 Other
EXCLUDES *instillation of medication into urinary tract (96.49)*
irrigation of urinary tract (96.45-96.48)

11. OPERATIONS ON THE MALE GENITAL ORGANS (60-64)

✓3rd **60 Operations on prostate and seminal vesicles**

Code also any application or administration of an adhesion barrier substance (99.77)

INCLUDES operations on periprostatic tissue

EXCLUDES *that associated with radical cystectomy (57.71)*

60.0 Incision of prostate ♂

Drainage of prostatic abscess
Prostatolithotomy

EXCLUDES *drainage of periprostatic tissue only (60.81)*

✓4th **60.1 Diagnostic procedures on prostate and seminal vesicles**

60.11 Closed [percutaneous] [needle] biopsy of prostate ♂

Approach:
transrectal
transurethral
Punch biopsy

DEF: Excision of prostate tissue by closed technique for biopsy.

60.12 Open biopsy of prostate ♂

60.13 Closed [percutaneous] biopsy of seminal vesicles ♂

Needle biopsy of seminal vesicles

60.14 Open biopsy of seminal vesicles ♂

60.15 Biopsy of periprostatic tissue ♂

60.18 Other diagnostic procedures on prostate and periprostatic tissue ♂

EXCLUDES *microscopic examination of specimen from prostate (91.31-91.39)*
x-ray of prostate (87.92)

60.19 Other diagnostic procedures on seminal vesicles ♂

EXCLUDES *microscopic examination of specimen from seminal vesicles (91.31-91.39)*
x-ray:
contrast seminal vesiculogram (87.91)
other (87.92)

✓4th **60.2 Transurethral prostatectomy**

EXCLUDES *local excision of lesion of prostate (60.61)*

AHA: 2Q, '94, 9; 3Q, '92, 13

60.21 Transurethral (ultrasound) guided laser induced prostatectomy (TULIP) ♂

Ablation (contact) (noncontact) by laser

AHA: 4Q, '95, 7

60.29 Other transurethral prostatectomy ♂

Excision of median bar by transurethral approach
Transurethral electrovaporization of prostate (TEVAP)
Transurethral enucleative procedure
Transurethral prostatectomy NOS
Transurethral resection of prostate (TURP)

DEF: Excision of median bar by transurethral approach: Removal of fibrous structure of prostate.

DEF: Transurethral enucleative procedure: Transurethral prostatectomy.

AHA: 3Q, '97, 3

Transurethral Prostatectomy

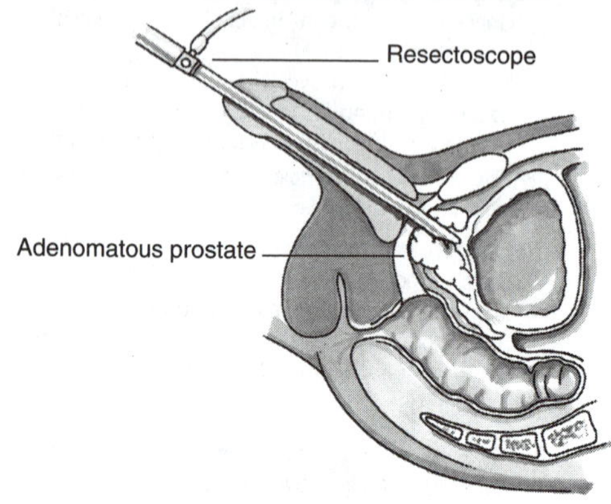

60.3 Suprapubic prostatectomy ♂

Transvesical prostatectomy

EXCLUDES *local excision of lesion of prostate (60.61)*
radical prostatectomy (60.5)

DEF: Resection of prostate through incision in abdomen above pubic arch.

60.4 Retropubic prostatectomy ♂

EXCLUDES *local excision of lesion of prostate (60.61)*
radical prostatectomy (60.5)

DEF: Removal of the prostate using an abdominal approach with direct cutting into prostatic capsule.

60.5 Radical prostatectomy ♂

Prostatovesiculectomy
Radical prostatectomy by any approach

EXCLUDES *cystoprostatectomy (57.71)*

AHA: 3Q, '93, 12

DEF: Removal of prostate, epididymis and vas ampullae.

DEF: Prostatovesiculectomy: Removal of prostate and epididymis.

✓4th **60.6 Other prostatectomy**

60.61 Local excision of lesion of prostate ♂

Excision of prostatic lesion by any approach

EXCLUDES *biopsy of prostate (60.11-60.12)*

60.62 Perineal prostatectomy ♂

Cryoablation of prostate
Cryoprostatectomy
Cryosurgery of prostate
Radical cryosurcial ablation of prostate (RCSA)

EXCLUDES *local excision of lesion of prostate (60.61)*

AHA: 4Q, '95, 71

DEF: Excision of prostate tissue through incision between scrotum and anus.

60.69 Other ♂

✓4th **60.7 Operations on seminal vesicles**

60.71 Percutaneous aspiration of seminal vesicle ♂

EXCLUDES *needle biopsy of seminal vesicle (60.13)*

60.72 Incision of seminal vesicle ♂

60.73 Excision of seminal vesicle ♂

Excision of Müllerian duct cyst
Spermatocystectomy

EXCLUDES *biopsy of seminal vesicle (60.13-60.14)*
prostatovesiculectomy (60.5)

60.79 Other operations on seminal vesicles ♂

✓4th **60.8 Incision or excision of periprostatic tissue**

60.81 Incision of periprostatic tissue ♂

Drainage of periprostatic abscess

60.82 Excision of periprostatic tissue ♂

Excision of lesion of periprostatic tissue

EXCLUDES *biopsy of periprostatic tissue (60.15)*

✓4th **60.9 Other operations on prostate**

60.91 Percutaneous aspiration of prostate ♂

EXCLUDES *needle biopsy of prostate (60.11)*

60.92 Injection into prostate ♂

60.93 Repair of prostate ♂

60.94 Control of (postoperative) hemorrhage of prostate ♂

Coagulation of prostatic bed

Cystoscopy for control of prostatic hemorrhage

60.95 Transurethral balloon dilation of the prostatic urethra ♂

AHA: 4Q, '91, 23

DEF: Insertion and inflation of balloon to stretch prostate passage.

60.96 Transurethral destruction of prostate tissue by microwave thermotherapy ♂

Transurethral microwave thermotherapy (TUMT) of prostate

EXCLUDES *Prostatectomy:*
other (60.61-60.69)
radical (60.5)
retropubic (60.4)
suprapubic (60.3)
transurethral (60.21-60.29)

AHA: 4Q, '00, 67

60.97 Other transurethral destruction of prostate tissue by other thermotherapy ♂

Radiofrequency thermotherapy

Transurethral needle ablation (TUNA) of prostate

EXCLUDES *Prostatectomy:*
other (60.61-60.69)
radical (60.5)
retropubic (60.4)
suprapubic (60.3)
transurethral (60.21-60.29)

AHA: 4Q, '00, 67

60.99 Other ♂

EXCLUDES *prostatic massage (99.94)*

AHA: 3Q, '90, 12

✓3rd **61 Operations on scrotum and tunica vaginalis**

61.0 Incision and drainage of scrotum and tunica vaginalis ♂

EXCLUDES *percutaneous aspiration of hydrocele (61.91)*

✓4th **61.1 Diagnostic procedures on scrotum and tunica vaginalis**

61.11 Biopsy of scrotum or tunica vaginalis ♂

61.19 Other diagnostic procedures on scrotum and tunica vaginalis ♂

61.2 Excision of hydrocele (of tunica vaginalis) ♂

Bottle repair of hydrocele of tunica vaginalis

EXCLUDES *percutaneous aspiration of hydrocele (61.91)*

DEF: Removal of fluid collected in serous membrane of testes.

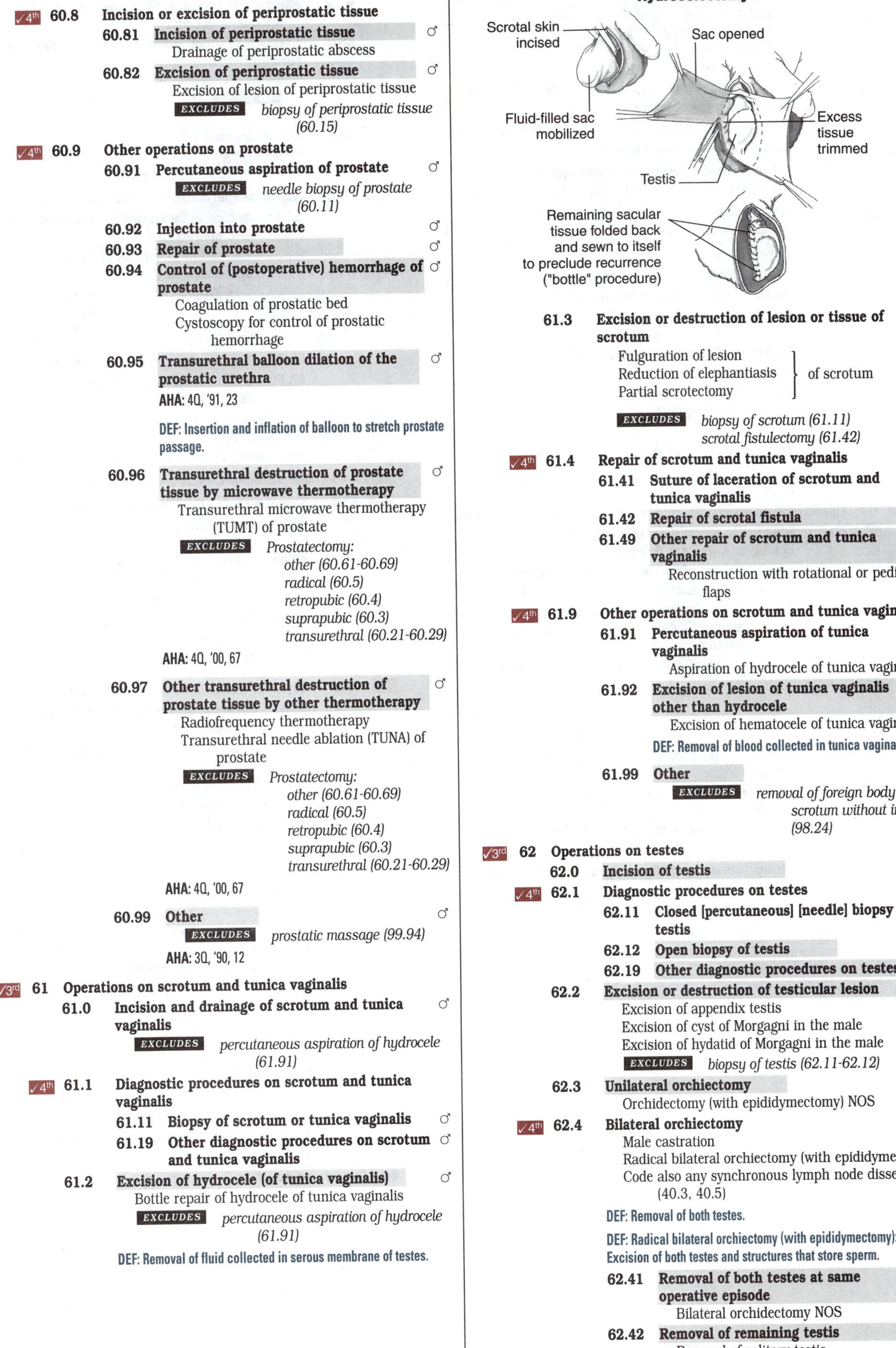

61.3 Excision or destruction of lesion or tissue of scrotum ♂

Fulguration of lesion } of scrotum
Reduction of elephantiasis } of scrotum
Partial scrotectomy } of scrotum

EXCLUDES *biopsy of scrotum (61.11)*
scrotal fistulectomy (61.42)

✓4th **61.4 Repair of scrotum and tunica vaginalis**

61.41 Suture of laceration of scrotum and tunica vaginalis ♂

61.42 Repair of scrotal fistula ♂

61.49 Other repair of scrotum and tunica vaginalis ♂

Reconstruction with rotational or pedicle flaps

✓4th **61.9 Other operations on scrotum and tunica vaginalis**

61.91 Percutaneous aspiration of tunica vaginalis ♂

Aspiration of hydrocele of tunica vaginalis

61.92 Excision of lesion of tunica vaginalis other than hydrocele ♂

Excision of hematocele of tunica vaginalis

DEF: Removal of blood collected in tunica vaginalis.

61.99 Other ♂

EXCLUDES *removal of foreign body from scrotum without incision (98.24)*

✓3rd **62 Operations on testes**

62.0 Incision of testis ♂

✓4th **62.1 Diagnostic procedures on testes**

62.11 Closed [percutaneous] [needle] biopsy of testis ♂

62.12 Open biopsy of testis ♂

62.19 Other diagnostic procedures on testes ♂

62.2 Excision or destruction of testicular lesion ♂

Excision of appendix testis

Excision of cyst of Morgagni in the male

Excision of hydatid of Morgagni in the male

EXCLUDES *biopsy of testis (62.11-62.12)*

62.3 Unilateral orchiectomy ♂

Orchidectomy (with epididymectomy) NOS

✓4th **62.4 Bilateral orchiectomy**

Male castration

Radical bilateral orchiectomy (with epididymectomy)

Code also any synchronous lymph node dissection (40.3, 40.5)

DEF: Removal of both testes.

DEF: Radical bilateral orchiectomy (with epididymectomy): Excision of both testes and structures that store sperm.

62.41 Removal of both testes at same operative episode ♂

Bilateral orchidectomy NOS

62.42 Removal of remaining testis ♂

Removal of solitary testis

62.5 Orchiopexy ♂
Mobilization and replacement of testis in scrotum
Orchiopexy with detorsion of testis
Torek (-Bevan) operation (orchidopexy) (first stage) (second stage)
Transplantation to and fixation of testis in scrotum

DEF: Fixation of testis in scrotum.

DEF: Orchiopexy with detorsion of testis: Fixation and placement of testis in scrotum after correcting angle.

DEF: Torek operation (first stage) (second stage): Transfer of congenitally undescended testis from inguinal canal to scrotum.

DEF: Transplantation to and fixation of testis in scrotum: Transfer of displaced testis to scrotum.

✓4th **62.6 Repair of testes**
EXCLUDES *reduction of torsion (63.52)*

62.61 Suture of laceration of testis ♂

62.69 Other repair of testis ♂
Testicular graft

62.7 Insertion of testicular prosthesis ♂

✓4th **62.9 Other operations on testes**

62.91 Aspiration of testis ♂
EXCLUDES *percutaneous biopsy of testis (62.11)*

62.92 Injection of therapeutic substance into testis ♂

62.99 Other ♂

✓3rd **63 Operations on spermatic cord, epididymis, and vas deferens**

✓4th **63.0 Diagnostic procedures on spermatic cord, epididymis, and vas deferens**

63.01 Biopsy of spermatic cord, epididymis, or vas deferens ♂

63.09 Other diagnostic procedures on spermatic cord, epididymis, and vas deferens ♂
EXCLUDES *contrast epididymogram (87.93)*
contrast vasogram (87.94)
other x-ray of epididymis and vas deferens (87.95)

63.1 Excision of varicocele and hydrocele of spermatic cord ♂
High ligation of spermatic vein
Hydrocelectomy of canal of Nuck

DEF: Removal of a swollen vein and collected fluid from spermatic cord.

DEF: High ligation of spermatic vein: Tying off of spermatic vein.

DEF: Hydrocelectomy of canal of Nuck: Removal of fluid collected from serous membrane of inguinal canal.

Varicocelectomy

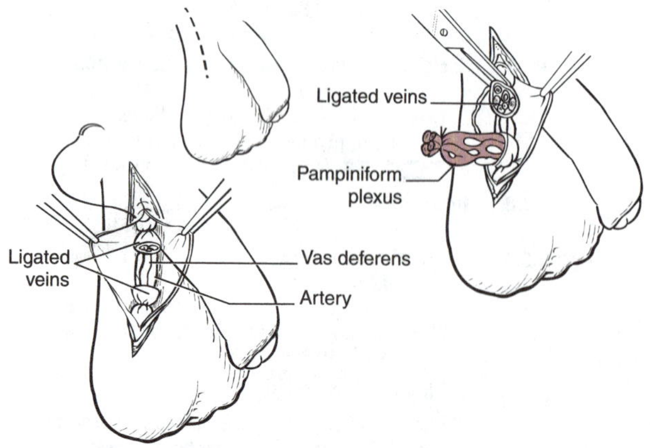

63.2 Excision of cyst of epididymis ♂
Spermatocelectomy

63.3 Excision of other lesion or tissue of spermatic cord and epididymis ♂
Excision of appendix epididymis
EXCLUDES *biopsy of spermatic cord or epididymis (63.01)*

63.4 Epididymectomy ♂
EXCLUDES *that synchronous with orchiectomy (62.3-62.42)*

✓4th **63.5 Repair of spermatic cord and epididymis**

63.51 Suture of laceration of spermatic cord and epididymis ♂

63.52 Reduction of torsion of testis or spermatic cord ♂
EXCLUDES *that associated with orchiopexy (62.5)*

DEF: Correction of twisted testicle or spermatic cord.

63.53 Transplantation of spermatic cord ♂

63.59 Other repair of spermatic cord and epididymis ♂

63.6 Vasotomy ♂
Vasostomy

DEF: Vasotomy: Incision of ducts carrying sperm from testicles.

DEF: Vasostomy: Creation of an opening into duct.

✓4th **63.7 Vasectomy and ligation of vas deferens**

63.70 Male sterilization procedure, not otherwise specified NC ♂

63.71 Ligation of vas deferens NC ♂
Crushing of vas deferens
Division of vas deferens

63.72 Ligation of spermatic cord NC ♂

63.73 Vasectomy NC ♂
AHA: 2Q, '98, 13

✓4th **63.8 Repair of vas deferens and epididymis**

63.81 Suture of laceration of vas deferens and epididymis ♂

63.82 Reconstruction of surgically divided vas deferens ♂

63.83 Epididymovasostomy ♂

DEF: Creation of new connection between vas deferens and epididymis.

63.84 Removal of ligature from vas deferens ♂

63.85 Removal of valve from vas deferens ♂

63.89 Other repair of vas deferens and epididymis ♂

✓4th **63.9 Other operations on spermatic cord, epididymis, and vas deferens**

63.91 Aspiration of spermatocele ♂

DEF: Puncture of cystic distention of epididymis.

63.92 Epididymotomy ♂

DEF: Incision of epididymis.

63.93 Incision of spermatic cord ♂

DEF: Incision into sperm storage structure.

63.94 Lysis of adhesions of spermatic cord ♂

63.95 Insertion of valve in vas deferens ♂

63.99 Other ♂

✓3rd **64 Operations on penis**
INCLUDES operations on:
corpora cavernosa
glans penis
prepuce

64.0 Circumcision ♂

DEF: Removal of penis foreskin.

✓4th **64.1 Diagnostic procedures on the penis**

64.11 Biopsy of penis ♂

64.19 Other diagnostic procedures on penis ♂

64.2 Local excision or destruction of lesion of penis ♂

EXCLUDES *biopsy of penis (64.11)*

64.3 Amputation of penis ♂

✓4th **64.4 Repair and plastic operation on penis**

64.41 Suture of laceration of penis ♂

64.42 Release of chordee ♂

AHA: 4Q, '96, 34

DEF: Correction of downward displacement of penis.

64.43 Construction of penis ♂

64.44 Reconstruction of penis ♂

64.45 Replantation of penis ♂

Reattachment of amputated penis

64.49 Other repair of penis ♂

EXCLUDES *repair of epispadias and hypospadias (58.45)*

64.5 Operations for sex transformation, not elsewhere classified NC ♂

✓4th **64.9 Other operations on male genital organs**

64.91 Dorsal or lateral slit of prepuce ♂

64.92 Incision of penis ♂

64.93 Division of penile adhesions ♂

64.94 Fitting of external prosthesis of penis ♂

Penile prosthesis NOS

64.95 Insertion or replacement of non-inflatable penile prosthesis ♂

Insertion of semi-rigid rod prosthesis into shaft of penis

EXCLUDES *external penile prosthesis (64.94)*
inflatable penile prosthesis (64.97)
plastic repair, penis (64.43-64.49)
that associated with:
construction (64.43)
reconstruction (64.44)

64.96 Removal of internal prosthesis of penis ♂

Removal without replacement of non-inflatable or inflatable penile prosthesis

64.97 Insertion or replacement of inflatable penile prosthesis ♂

Insertion of cylinders into shaft of penis and placement of pump and reservoir

EXCLUDES *external penile prosthesis (64.94)*
non-inflatable penile prosthesis (64.95)
plastic repair, penis (64.43-64.49)

64.98 Other operations on penis ♂

Corpora cavernosa-corpus spongiosum shunt

Corpora-saphenous shunt

Irrigation of corpus cavernosum

EXCLUDES *removal of foreign body:*
intraluminal (98.19)
without incision (98.24)
stretching of foreskin (99.95)

AHA: 3Q, '92, 9

DEF: Corpora cavernosa-corpus spongiosum shunt: Insertion of shunt between erectile tissues of penis.

DEF: Corpora-saphenous shunt: Insertion of shunt between erectile tissue and vein of penis.

DEF: Irrigation of corpus cavernosum: Washing of erectile tissue forming dorsum and side of penis.

64.99 Other ♂

EXCLUDES *collection of sperm for artificial insemination (99.96)*

12. OPERATIONS ON THE FEMALE GENITAL ORGANS (65-71)

✓3rd **65 Operations on ovary**
Code also any application or administration of an adhesion barrier substance (99.77)

✓4th **65.0 Oophorotomy**
Salpingo-oophorotomy
DEF: Incision into ovary.
DEF: Salpingo-oophorotomy: Incision into ovary and the fallopian tube.

65.01 Laparoscopic oophorotomy ♀
65.09 Other oophorotomy ♀

✓4th **65.1 Diagnostic procedures on ovaries**

65.11 Aspiration biopsy of ovary ♀
65.12 Other biopsy of ovary ♀
65.13 Laparoscopic biopsy of ovary ♀
AHA: 4Q, '96, 67
65.14 Other laparoscopic diagnostic procedures on ovaries ♀
65.19 Other diagnostic procedures on ovaries ♀
EXCLUDES *microscopic examination of specimen from ovary (91.41-91.49)*

✓4th **65.2 Local excision or destruction of ovarian lesion or tissue**

65.21 Marsupialization of ovarian cyst ♀
EXCLUDES *that by laparoscope (65.23)*
DEF: Exteriorized cyst to outside by incising anterior wall and suturing cut edges to create open pouch.
65.22 Wedge resection of ovary ♀
EXCLUDES *that by laparoscope (65.24)*
65.23 Laparoscopic marsupialization of ovarian cyst ♀
65.24 Laparoscopic wedge resection of ovary ♀
65.25 Other laparoscopic local excision or destruction of ovary ♀
65.29 Other local excision or destruction of ovary ♀
Bisection, Cauterization, Partial excision } of ovary
EXCLUDES *biopsy of ovary (65.11-65.13)*
that by laparoscope (65.25)

✓4th **65.3 Unilateral oophorectomy**

65.31 Laparoscopic unilateral oophorectomy ♀
65.39 Other unilateral oophorectomy ♀
EXCLUDES *that by laparoscope (65.31)*
AHA: 4Q, '96, 66

✓4th **65.4 Unilateral salpingo-oophorectomy**

65.41 Laparoscopic unilateral salpingo-oophorectomy ♀
AHA: 4Q, '96, 67
65.49 Other unilateral salpingo-oophorectomy ♀

Oophorectomy

✓4th **65.5 Bilateral oophorectomy**

65.51 Other removal of both ovaries at same operative episode ♀
Female castration
EXCLUDES *that by laparoscope (65.53)*
65.52 Other removal of remaining ovary ♀
Removal of solitary ovary
EXCLUDES *that by laparoscope (65.54)*
65.53 Laparoscopic removal of both ovaries at same operative eisode ♀
65.54 Laparoscopic removal of remaining ovary ♀

✓4th **65.6 Bilateral salpingo-oophorectomy**

65.61 Other removal of both ovaries and tubes at same operative episode ♀
EXCLUDES *that by laparoscope (65.53)*
AHA: 4Q, '96, 65
65.62 Other removal of remaining ovary and tube ♀
Removal of solitary ovary and tube
EXCLUDES *that by laparoscope (65.54)*
65.63 Laparoscopic removal of both ovaries and tubes at the same operative episode ♀
AHA: 4Q, '96, 68
65.64 Laparoscopic removal of remaining ovary and tube ♀

✓4th **65.7 Repair of ovary**
EXCLUDES *salpingo-oophorostomy (66.72)*

65.71 Other simple suture of ovary ♀
EXCLUDES *that by laparoscope (65.74)*
65.72 Other reimplantation of ovary ♀
EXCLUDES *that by laparoscope (65.75)*
DEF: Grafting and repositioning of ovary at same site.
65.73 Other salpingo-oophoroplasty ♀
EXCLUDES *that by laparoscope (65.76)*
65.74 Laparoscopic simple suture of ovary ♀
65.75 Laparoscopic reimplantation of ovary ♀
65.76 Laparoscopic salpingo-oophoroplasty ♀
65.79 Other repair of ovary ♀
Oophoropexy

✓4th **65.8 Lysis of adhesions of ovary and fallopian tube**

65.81 Laparoscopic lysis of adhesions of ovary and fallopian tube ♀
AHA: 4Q, '96, 67
65.89 Other lysis of adhesions of ovary and fallopian tube ♀
EXCLUDES *that by laparoscope (65.81)*

✓4th **65.9 Other operations on ovary**

65.91 Aspiration of ovary ♀
EXCLUDES *aspiration biopsy of ovary (65.11)*
65.92 Transplantation of ovary ♀
EXCLUDES *reimplantation of ovary (65.72, 65.75)*
65.93 Manual rupture of ovarian cyst ♀
DEF: Breaking up an ovarian cyst using manual technique or blunt instruments.
65.94 Ovarian denervation ♀
DEF: Destruction of nerve tracts to ovary.
65.95 Release of torsion of ovary ♀
65.99 Other ♀
Ovarian drilling
AHA: N-D, '86, 9

Endoscopic Ligation of Fallopian Tubes

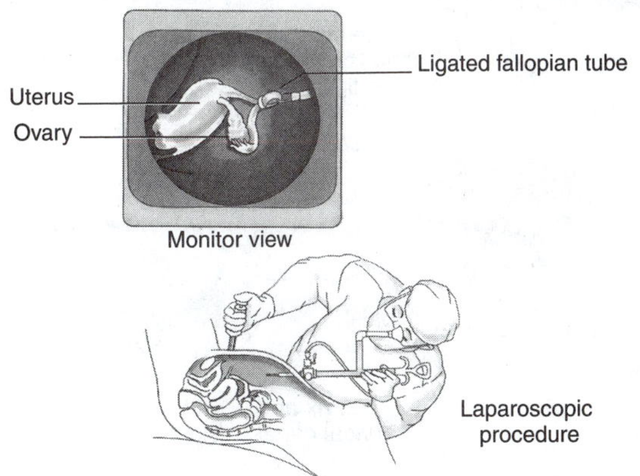

✓3rd **66 Operations on fallopian tubes**

Code also any application or administration of an adhesion barrier substance (99.77)

✓4th **66.0 Salpingotomy and salpingostomy**

66.01 Salpingotomy ♀

66.02 Salpingostomy ♀

✓4th **66.1 Diagnostic procedures on fallopian tubes**

66.11 Biopsy of fallopian tube ♀

66.19 Other diagnostic procedures on fallopian tubes ♀

EXCLUDES *microscopic examination of specimen from fallopian tubes (91.41-91.49)*
radiography of fallopian tubes (87.82-87.83, 87.85)
Rubin's test (66.8)

✓4th **66.2 Bilateral endoscopic destruction or occlusion of fallopian tubes**

INCLUDES bilateral endoscopic destruction or occlusion of fallopian tubes by:
culdoscopy
endoscopy
hysteroscopy
laparoscopy
peritoneoscopy
endoscopic destruction of solitary fallopian tube

DEF: Endoscopic blockage or destruction of both fallopian tubes.

DEF: Bilateral endoscopic destruction or occlusion of fallopian tubes by:

Culdoscopy: Endoscopic insertion through posterior structure of vagina.

Hysteroscopy: Endoscopic insertion through uterus.

Laparoscopy: Endoscopic insertion through abdomen.

Peritoneoscopy: Endoscopic insertion through abdominal serous membrane cavity.

Endoscopic destruction of solitary fallopian tube: Endoscopic destruction of one fallopian tube.

66.21 Bilateral endoscopic ligation and crushing of fallopian tubes NC ♀

66.22 Bilateral endoscopic ligation and division of fallopian tubes NC ♀

66.29 Other bilateral endoscopic destruction or occlusion of fallopian tubes NC ♀

✓4th **66.3 Other bilateral destruction or occlusion of fallopian tubes**

INCLUDES destruction of solitary fallopian tube

EXCLUDES *endoscopic destruction or occlusion of fallopian tubes (66.21-66.29)*

66.31 Other bilateral ligation and crushing of fallopian tubes NC ♀

66.32 Other bilateral ligation and division of fallopian tubes NC ♀

Pomeroy operation

66.39 Other bilateral destruction or occlusion of fallopian tubes NC ♀

Female sterilization operation NOS

66.4 Total unilateral salpingectomy ♀

✓4th **66.5 Total bilateral salpingectomy**

EXCLUDES *bilateral partial salpingectomy for sterilization (66.39)*
that with oophorectomy (65.61-65.64)

66.51 Removal of both fallopian tubes at same operative episode ♀

66.52 Removal of remaining fallopian tube ♀

Removal of solitary fallopian tube

✓4th **66.6 Other salpingectomy**

INCLUDES salpingectomy by:
cauterization
coagulation
electrocoagulation
excision

EXCLUDES *fistulectomy (66.73)*

66.61 Excision or destruction of lesion of fallopian tube ♀

EXCLUDES *biopsy of fallopian tube (66.11)*

66.62 Salpingectomy with removal of tubal pregnancy ♀

Code also any synchronous oophorectomy (65.31, 65.39)

AHA: 3Q, '95, 15; S-O, '85, 14

66.63 Bilateral partial salpingectomy, not otherwise specified ♀

66.69 Other partial salpingectomy ♀

✓4th **66.7 Repair of fallopian tube**

66.71 Simple suture of fallopian tube ♀

66.72 Salpingo-oophorostomy ♀

66.73 Salpingo-salpingostomy ♀

66.74 Salpingo-uterostomy ♀

66.79 Other repair of fallopian tube ♀

Graft of fallopian tube
Reopening of divided fallopian tube
Salpingoplasty

AHA: 2Q, '95, 10

DEF: Graft of fallopian: Repair of fallopian tube with implanted graft.

DEF: Reopening of divided fallopian tube: Reconnection of severed fallopian tube to restore patency.

DEF: Salpingoplasty: Plastic reconstruction of fallopian tube defect.

66.8 Insufflation of fallopian tube ♀

Insufflation of fallopian tube with:
air
dye
gas
saline
Rubin's test

EXCLUDES *insufflation of therapeutic agent (66.95)*
that for hysterosalpingography (87.82-87.83)

DEF: Forceful blowing of gas or liquid into fallopian tubes.

DEF: Rubin's test: Introduction of carbon dioxide gas into fallopian tubes.

✓3rd ✓4th Additional Digit Required | Nonspecific OR Procedure | Valid OR Procedure | Non-OR Procedure | Adjunct Code

✓4th **66.9 Other operations on fallopian tubes**

66.91 Aspiration of fallopian tube ♀

66.92 Unilateral destruction or occlusion of fallopian tube ♀

EXCLUDES *that of solitary tube (66.21-66.39)*

66.93 Implantation or replacement of prosthesis of fallopian tube ♀

66.94 Removal of prosthesis of fallopian tube ♀

66.95 Insufflation of therapeutic agent into fallopian tubes ♀

66.96 Dilation of fallopian tube ♀

66.97 Burying of fimbriae in uterine wall ♀

DEF: Implantation of fallopian tube, fringed edges into uterine wall.

66.99 Other ♀

EXCLUDES *lysis of adhesions of ovary and tube (65.81, 65.89)*

AHA: 2Q, '94, 11

✓3rd **67 Operations on cervix**

Code also any application or administration of an adhesion barrier substance (99.77)

67.0 Dilation of cervical canal ♀

EXCLUDES *dilation and curettage (69.01-69.09)*
that for induction of labor (73.1)

✓4th **67.1 Diagnostic procedures on cervix**

67.11 Endocervical biopsy ♀

EXCLUDES *conization of cervix (67.2)*

67.12 Other cervical biopsy ♀

Punch biopsy of cervix NOS

EXCLUDES *conization of cervix (67.2)*

67.19 Other diagnostic procedures on cervix ♀

EXCLUDES *microscopic examination of specimen from cervix (91.41-91.49)*

67.2 Conization of cervix ♀

EXCLUDES *that by:*
cryosurgery (67.33)
electrosurgery (67.32)

DEF: Removal of cone-shaped section from distal cervix; cervical function preserved.

✓4th **67.3 Other excision or destruction of lesion or tissue of cervix**

67.31 Marsupialization of cervical cyst ♀

DEF: Incision and then suturing open of a cyst in the neck of the uterus.

67.32 Destruction of lesion of cervix by cauterization ♀

Electroconization of cervix
LEEP (loop electrosurgical excision procedure)
LLETZ (large loop excision of the transformation zone)

AHA: 1Q, '98, 3

DEF: Destruction of lesion of uterine neck by applying intense heat.

DEF: Electroconization of cervix: Electrocautery excision of multilayer cone-shaped section from uterine neck.

67.33 Destruction of lesion of cervix by cryosurgery ♀

Cryoconization of cervix

DEF: Destruction of lesion of uterine neck by freezing.

DEF: Cryoconization of cervix: Excision by freezing of multilayer cone-shaped section of abnormal tissue in uterine neck.

67.39 Other excision or destruction of lesion or tissue of cervix ♀

EXCLUDES *biopsy of cervix (67.11-67.12)*
cervical fistulectomy (67.62)
conization of cervix (67.2)

Cerclage of Cervix

Suture material is inserted around cervix and tightened
Cervix and cervical canal
Uterus
Cervix and cervical canal

67.4 Amputation of cervix ♀

Cervicectomy with synchronous colporrhaphy

DEF: Excision of lower uterine neck.

DEF: Cervicectomy with synchronous colporrhaphy: Excision of lower uterine neck with suture of vaginal stump.

✓4th **67.5 Repair of internal cervical os**

AHA: 4Q, '01, 63; 3Q, '00, 11

DEF: Repair of cervical opening defect.

67.51 Transabdominal cerclage of cervix ♀

67.59 Other repair of internal cervical os ♀

Cerclage of isthmus uteri
McDonald operation
Shirodkar operation
Transvaginal cerclage

EXCLUDES *laparoscopically assisted supracervical hysterectomy [LASH] (68.31)*
transabdominal cerclage of cervix (67.51)

DEF: Cerclage of isthmus uteri: Placement of encircling suture between neck and body of uterus.

DEF: Shirodkar operation: Placement of purse-string suture in internal cervical opening.

✓4th **67.6 Other repair of cervix**

EXCLUDES *repair of current obstetric laceration (75.51)*

67.61 Suture of laceration of cervix ♀

67.62 Repair of fistula of cervix ♀

Cervicosigmoidal fistulectomy

EXCLUDES *fistulectomy:*
cervicovesical (57.84)
ureterocervical (56.84)
vesicocervicovaginal (57.84)

DEF: Closure of fistula in lower uterus.

DEF: Cervicosigmoidal fistulectomy: Excision of abnormal passage between uterine neck and torsion of large intestine.

67.69 Other repair of cervix ♀

Repair of old obstetric laceration of cervix

✓3rd **68 Other incision and excision of uterus**

Code also any application or administration of an adhesion barrier substance (99.77)

68.0 Hysterotomy ♀

Hysterotomy with removal of hydatidiform mole

EXCLUDES *hysterotomy for termination of pregnancy (74.91)*

DEF: Incision into the uterus.

4th 68.1 Diagnostic procedures on uterus and supporting structures

68.11 Digital examination of uterus ♀
EXCLUDES *pelvic examination, so described (89.26)*
postpartal manual exploration of uterine cavity (75.7)

68.12 Hysteroscopy ♀
EXCLUDES *that with biopsy (68.16)*

68.13 Open biopsy of uterus ♀
EXCLUDES *closed biopsy of uterus (68.16)*

68.14 Open biopsy of uterine ligaments ♀
EXCLUDES *closed biopsy of uterine ligaments (68.15)*

68.15 Closed biopsy of uterine ligaments ♀
Endoscopic (laparoscopy) biopsy of uterine adnexa, except ovary and fallopian tube

68.16 Closed biopsy of uterus ♀
Endoscopic (laparoscopy) (hysteroscopy) biopsy of uterus
EXCLUDES *open biopsy of uterus (68.13)*

68.19 Other diagnostic procedures on uterus and supporting structures ♀
EXCLUDES *diagnostic:*
aspiration curettage (69.59)
dilation and curettage (69.09)
microscopic examination of specimen from uterus (91.41-91.49)
pelvic examination (89.26)
radioisotope scan of:
placenta (92.17)
uterus (92.19)
ultrasonography of uterus (88.78-88.79)
x-ray of uterus (87.81-87.89)

4th 68.2 Excision or destruction of lesion or tissue of uterus

68.21 Division of endometrial synechiae ♀
Lysis of intraluminal uterine adhesions
DEF: Separation of uterine adhesions.
DEF: Lysis of intraluminal uterine adhesion: Surgical destruction of adhesive, fibrous structures inside uterine cavity.

68.22 Incision or excision of congenital septum of uterus ♀

68.23 Endometrial ablation ♀
Dilation and curettage
Hysteroscopic endometrial ablation
AHA: 4Q, '96, 68
DEF: Removal or destruction of uterine lining; usually by electrocautery or loop electrosurgical excision procedure (LEEP).

68.29 Other excision or destruction of lesion of uterus ♀
Uterine myomectomy
EXCLUDES *biopsy of uterus (68.13)*
uterine fistulectomy (69.42)
AHA: 1Q, '96, 14

Vaginal Hysterectomy

Total hysterectomy (uterus only removed)

Total hysterectomy with bilateral salpingectomy (uterus and tubes removed)

Total hysterectomy with bilateral salpingo-oophorectomy (uterus, tubes, and ovaries removed)

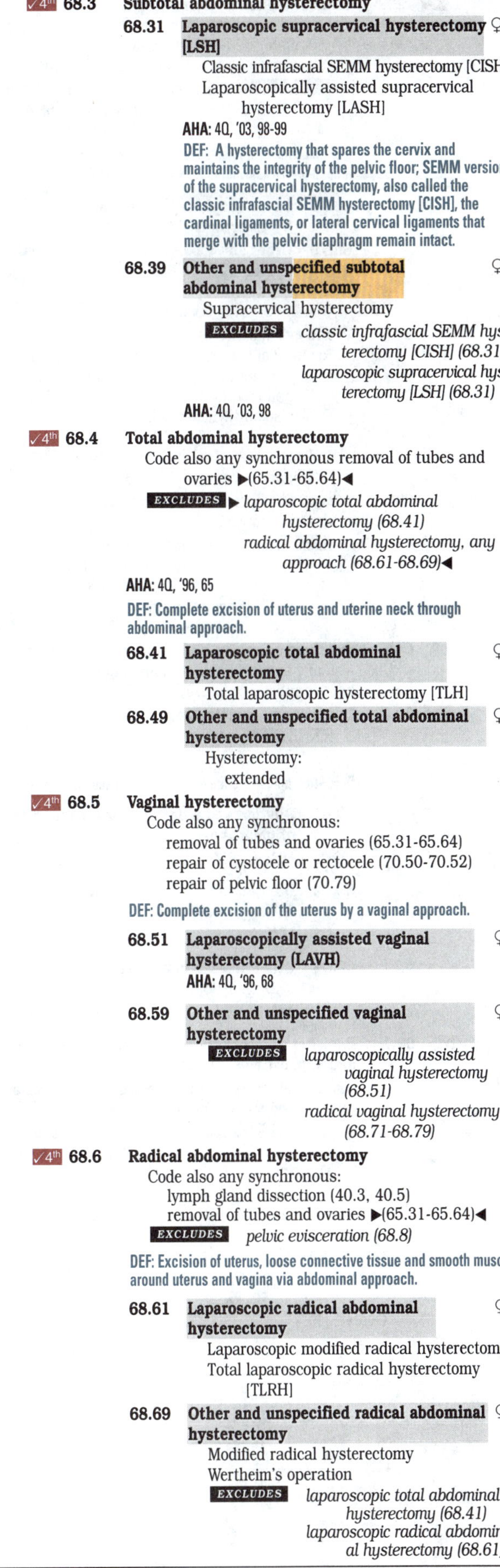

4th 68.3 Subtotal abdominal hysterectomy

68.31 Laparoscopic supracervical hysterectomy [LSH] ♀
Classic infrafascial SEMM hysterectomy [CISH]
Laparoscopically assisted supracervical hysterectomy [LASH]
AHA: 4Q, '03, 98-99
DEF: A hysterectomy that spares the cervix and maintains the integrity of the pelvic floor; SEMM version of the supracervical hysterectomy, also called the classic infrafascial SEMM hysterectomy [CISH], the cardinal ligaments, or lateral cervical ligaments that merge with the pelvic diaphragm remain intact.

68.39 Other and unspecified subtotal abdominal hysterectomy ♀
Supracervical hysterectomy
EXCLUDES *classic infrafascial SEMM hysterectomy [CISH] (68.31)*
laparoscopic supracervical hysterectomy [LSH] (68.31)
AHA: 4Q, '03, 98

4th 68.4 Total abdominal hysterectomy
Code also any synchronous removal of tubes and ovaries ▶(65.31-65.64)◀
EXCLUDES ▶ *laparoscopic total abdominal hysterectomy (68.41)*
radical abdominal hysterectomy, any approach (68.61-68.69)◀
AHA: 4Q, '96, 65
DEF: Complete excision of uterus and uterine neck through abdominal approach.

68.41 Laparoscopic total abdominal hysterectomy ♀
Total laparoscopic hysterectomy [TLH]

68.49 Other and unspecified total abdominal hysterectomy ♀
Hysterectomy:
extended

4th 68.5 Vaginal hysterectomy
Code also any synchronous:
removal of tubes and ovaries (65.31-65.64)
repair of cystocele or rectocele (70.50-70.52)
repair of pelvic floor (70.79)
DEF: Complete excision of the uterus by a vaginal approach.

68.51 Laparoscopically assisted vaginal hysterectomy (LAVH) ♀
AHA: 4Q, '96, 68

68.59 Other and unspecified vaginal hysterectomy ♀
EXCLUDES *laparoscopically assisted vaginal hysterectomy (68.51)*
radical vaginal hysterectomy (68.71-68.79)

4th 68.6 Radical abdominal hysterectomy
Code also any synchronous:
lymph gland dissection (40.3, 40.5)
removal of tubes and ovaries ▶(65.31-65.64)◀
EXCLUDES *pelvic evisceration (68.8)*
DEF: Excision of uterus, loose connective tissue and smooth muscle around uterus and vagina via abdominal approach.

68.61 Laparoscopic radical abdominal hysterectomy ♀
Laparoscopic modified radical hysterectomy
Total laparoscopic radical hysterectomy [TLRH]

68.69 Other and unspecified radical abdominal hysterectomy ♀
Modified radical hysterectomy
Wertheim's operation
EXCLUDES *laparoscopic total abdominal hysterectomy (68.41)*
laparoscopic radical abdominal hysterectomy (68.61)

Operations on the Female Genital Organs 68.1–68.69

3rd 4th Additional Digit Required | Nonspecific OR Procedure | Valid OR Procedure | Non-OR Procedure | Adjunct Code

✓4th **68.7 Radical vaginal hysterectomy**
Code also any synchronous:
lymph gland dissection (40.3, 40.5)
removal of tubes and ovaries ▶(65.31-65.64)◀
EXCLUDES ▶ *abdominal hysterectomy, any approach (68.31-68.39, 68.41-68.49, 68.61-68.69, 68.9)*◀
DEF: Excision of uterus, loose connective tissue and smooth muscle around uterus and vagina via vaginal approach.

● **68.71 Laparoscopic radical vaginal hysterectomy [LRVH]** ♀

● **68.79 Other and unspecified radical vaginal hysterectomy** ♀
Hysterocolpectomy
Schauta operation

68.8 Pelvic evisceration ♀
Removal of ovaries, tubes, uterus, vagina, bladder, and urethra (with removal of sigmoid colon and rectum)
Code also any synchronous:
colostomy (46.10-46.13)
lymph gland dissection (40.3, 40.5)
urinary diversion (56.51-56.79)

68.9 Other and unspecified hysterectomy ♀
Hysterectomy NOS
EXCLUDES *abdominal hysterectomy, any approach* ▶*(68.31-68.39, 68.41-68.49, 68.61-68.69)*◀
vaginal hysterectomy, any approach ▶*(68.51-68.59, 68.71-68.79)*◀

✓3rd **69 Other operations on uterus and supporting structures**
Code also any application or administration of an adhesion barrier substance (99.77)

✓4th **69.0 Dilation and curettage of uterus**
EXCLUDES *aspiration curettage of uterus (69.51-69.59)*
DEF: Stretching of uterine neck to scrape tissue from walls.

69.01 Dilation and curettage for termination of pregnancy ♀
AHA: 1Q, '98, 4

69.02 Dilation and curettage following delivery or abortion ♀
AHA: 3Q, '93, 6

69.09 Other dilation and curettage ♀
Diagnostic D and C
AHA: 1Q, '98, 4

✓4th **69.1 Excision or destruction of lesion or tissue of uterus and supporting structures**

69.19 Other excision or destruction of uterus and supporting structures ♀
EXCLUDES *biopsy of uterine ligament (68.14)*

Dilation and Curettage

✓4th **69.2 Repair of uterine supporting structures**

69.21 Interposition operation ♀
Watkins procedure
DEF: Repositioning or realignment of bladder and uterus.

69.22 Other uterine suspension ♀
Hysteropexy
Manchester operation
Plication of uterine ligament
DEF: Hysteropexy: Fixation or anchoring of uterus.
DEF: Manchester operation: Fixation or anchoring of uterus with supportive banding tissue of uterine neck and vagina.
DEF: Plication of uterine ligament: Creation of tucks in suppurative uterine banding tissue.

69.23 Vaginal repair of chronic inversion of uterus ♀
DEF: Repositioning of inverted uterus via vaginal approach.

69.29 Other repair of uterus and supporting structures ♀

69.3 Paracervical uterine denervation ♀

✓4th **69.4 Uterine repair**
EXCLUDES *repair of current obstetric laceration (75.50-75.52)*

69.41 Suture of laceration of uterus ♀

69.42 Closure of fistula of uterus ♀
EXCLUDES *uterovesical fistulectomy (57.84)*

69.49 Other repair of uterus ♀
Repair of old obstetric laceration of uterus

✓4th **69.5 Aspiration curettage of uterus**
EXCLUDES *menstrual extraction (69.6)*

69.51 Aspiration curettage of uterus for termination of pregnancy ♀
Therapeutic abortion NOS

69.52 Aspiration curettage following delivery or abortion ♀

69.59 Other aspiration curettage of uterus ♀
AHA: 1Q, '98, 7

69.6 Menstrual extraction or regulation ♀
DEF: Induction of menstruation by low pressure suction.

69.7 Insertion of intrauterine contraceptive device ♀

✓4th **69.9 Other operations on uterus, cervix, and supporting structures** ♀
EXCLUDES *obstetric dilation or incision of cervix (73.1, 73.93)*

69.91 Insertion of therapeutic device into uterus ♀
EXCLUDES *insertion of:*
intrauterine contraceptive device (69.7)
laminaria (69.93)
obstetric insertion of bag, bougie, or pack (73.1)

69.92 Artificial insemination ♀

69.93 Insertion of laminaria ♀
DEF: Placement of laminaria, a sea kelp, in cervical os to induce labor; applied for six to 12 hours.

69.94 Manual replacement of inverted uterus ♀
EXCLUDES *that in immediate postpartal period (75.94)*

69.95 Incision of cervix ♀
EXCLUDES *that to assist delivery (73.93)*

69.96 Removal of cerclage material from cervix
DEF: Removal of ring inserted to restore uterine neck competency.

BI Bilateral Procedure NC Non-covered Procedure LC Limited Coverage Procedure ▶◀ Revised Text ● New Code ▲ Revised Code Title

69.97 Removal of other penetrating foreign body from cervix ♀
EXCLUDES *removal of intraluminal foreign body from cervix (98.16)*

69.98 Other operations on supporting structures of uterus ♀
EXCLUDES *biopsy of uterine ligament (68.14)*

69.99 Other operations on cervix and uterus ♀
EXCLUDES *removal of:*
foreign body (98.16)
intrauterine contraceptive device (97.71)
obstetric bag, bougie, or pack (97.72)
packing (97.72)

✓3rd **70 Operations on vagina and cul-de-sac**
Code also any application or administration of an adhesion barrier substance (99.77)

70.0 Culdocentesis ♀
AHA: 2Q, '90, 26
DEF: Insertion of needle into upper vaginal vault encircling cervix to withdraw fluid.

✓4th **70.1 Incision of vagina and cul-de-sac**
70.11 Hymenotomy ♀
70.12 Culdotomy ♀
DEF: Incision into pocket between terminal end of large intestine and posterior uterus.
70.13 Lysis of intraluminal adhesions of vagina ♀
70.14 Other vaginotomy ♀
Division of vaginal septum
Drainage of hematoma of vaginal cuff
DEF: Division of vaginal septum: Incision into partition of vaginal walls.
DEF: Drainage of hematoma of vaginal cuff: Incision into vaginal tissue to drain collected blood.

✓4th **70.2 Diagnostic procedures on vagina and cul-de-sac**
70.21 Vaginoscopy ♀
70.22 Culdoscopy ♀
DEF: Endoscopic exam of pelvic viscera through incision in posterior vaginal wall.
70.23 Biopsy of cul-de-sac ♀
70.24 Vaginal biopsy ♀
70.29 Other diagnostic procedures on vagina and cul-de-sac ♀

✓4th **70.3 Local excision or destruction of vagina and cul-de-sac**
70.31 Hymenectomy ♀
70.32 Excision or destruction of lesion of cul-de-sac ♀
Endometrectomy of cul-de-sac
EXCLUDES *biopsy of cul-de-sac (70.23)*
70.33 Excision or destruction of lesion of vagina ♀
EXCLUDES *biopsy of vagina (70.24)*
vaginal fistulectomy (70.72-70.75)

70.4 Obliteration and total excision of vagina ♀
Vaginectomy
EXCLUDES *obliteration of vaginal vault (70.8)*
DEF: Vaginectomy: Removal of vagina.

✓4th **70.5 Repair of cystocele and rectocele**
70.50 Repair of cystocele and rectocele ♀
DEF: Repair of anterior and posterior vaginal wall bulges.
70.51 Repair of cystocele ♀
Anterior colporrhaphy (with urethrocele repair)
AHA: N-D, '84, 20
70.52 Repair of rectocele ♀
Posterior colporrhaphy
AHA: ▶1Q, '06, 12◀

✓4th **70.6 Vaginal construction and reconstruction**
70.61 Vaginal construction ♀
70.62 Vaginal reconstruction ♀
AHA: N-D, '84, 20

✓4th **70.7 Other repair of vagina**
EXCLUDES *lysis of intraluminal adhesions (70.13)*
repair of current obstetric laceration (75.69)
that associated with cervical amputation (67.4)
70.71 Suture of laceration of vagina ♀
AHA: N-D, '84, 20
70.72 Repair of colovaginal fistula ♀
DEF: Correction of abnormal opening between midsection of large intestine and vagina.
70.73 Repair of rectovaginal fistula ♀
DEF: Correction of abnormal opening between last section of large intestine and vagina.
70.74 Repair of other vaginoenteric fistula ♀
DEF: Correction of abnormal opening between vagina and intestine; other than mid or last sections.
70.75 Repair of other fistula of vagina ♀
EXCLUDES *repair of fistula:*
rectovesicovaginal (57.83)
ureterovaginal (56.84)
urethrovaginal (58.43)
uterovaginal (69.42)
vesicocervicovaginal (57.84)
vesicosigmoidovaginal (57.83)
vesicoureterovaginal (56.84)
vesicovaginal (57.84)
70.76 Hymenorrhaphy ♀
DEF: Closure of vagina with suture of hymenal ring or hymenal remnant flaps.
70.77 Vaginal suspension and fixation ♀
DEF: Repair of vaginal protrusion, sinking or laxity by suturing vagina into position.
70.79 Other repair of vagina ♀
Colpoperineoplasty
Repair of old obstetric laceration of vagina

70.8 Obliteration of vaginal vault ♀
LeFort operation
DEF: LeFort operation: Uniting or sewing together vaginal walls.

✓4th **70.9 Other operations on vagina and cul-de-sac**
70.91 Other operations on vagina ♀
EXCLUDES *insertion of:*
diaphragm (96.17)
mold (96.15)
pack (96.14)
pessary (96.18)
suppository (96.49)
removal of:
diaphragm (97.73)
foreign body (98.17)
pack (97.75)
pessary (97.74)
replacement of:
diaphragm (97.24)
pack (97.26)
pessary (97.25)
vaginal dilation (96.16)
vaginal douche (96.44)
70.92 Other operations on cul-de-sac ♀
Obliteration of cul-de-sac
Repair of vaginal enterocele
AHA: 4Q, '94, 54
DEF: Repair of vaginal enterocele: Elimination of herniated cavity within pouch between last part of large intestine and posterior uterus.

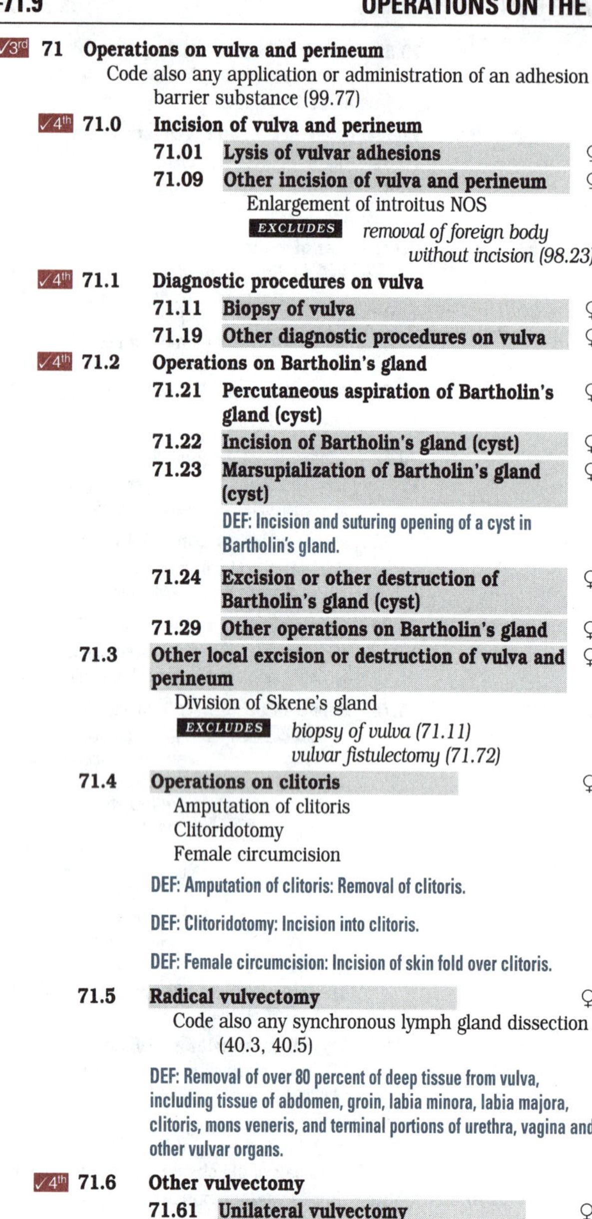

✓3rd **71 Operations on vulva and perineum**

Code also any application or administration of an adhesion barrier substance (99.77)

✓4th **71.0 Incision of vulva and perineum**

71.01 Lysis of vulvar adhesions ♀

71.09 Other incision of vulva and perineum ♀

Enlargement of introitus NOS

EXCLUDES *removal of foreign body without incision (98.23)*

✓4th **71.1 Diagnostic procedures on vulva**

71.11 Biopsy of vulva ♀

71.19 Other diagnostic procedures on vulva ♀

✓4th **71.2 Operations on Bartholin's gland**

71.21 Percutaneous aspiration of Bartholin's gland (cyst) ♀

71.22 Incision of Bartholin's gland (cyst) ♀

71.23 Marsupialization of Bartholin's gland (cyst) ♀

DEF: Incision and suturing opening of a cyst in Bartholin's gland.

71.24 Excision or other destruction of Bartholin's gland (cyst) ♀

71.29 Other operations on Bartholin's gland ♀

71.3 Other local excision or destruction of vulva and perineum ♀

Division of Skene's gland

EXCLUDES *biopsy of vulva (71.11)*
vulvar fistulectomy (71.72)

71.4 Operations on clitoris ♀

Amputation of clitoris
Clitoridotomy
Female circumcision

DEF: Amputation of clitoris: Removal of clitoris.

DEF: Clitoridotomy: Incision into clitoris.

DEF: Female circumcision: Incision of skin fold over clitoris.

71.5 Radical vulvectomy ♀

Code also any synchronous lymph gland dissection (40.3, 40.5)

DEF: Removal of over 80 percent of deep tissue from vulva, including tissue of abdomen, groin, labia minora, labia majora, clitoris, mons veneris, and terminal portions of urethra, vagina and other vulvar organs.

✓4th **71.6 Other vulvectomy**

71.61 Unilateral vulvectomy ♀

71.62 Bilateral vulvectomy ♀

Vulvectomy NOS

Marsupialization

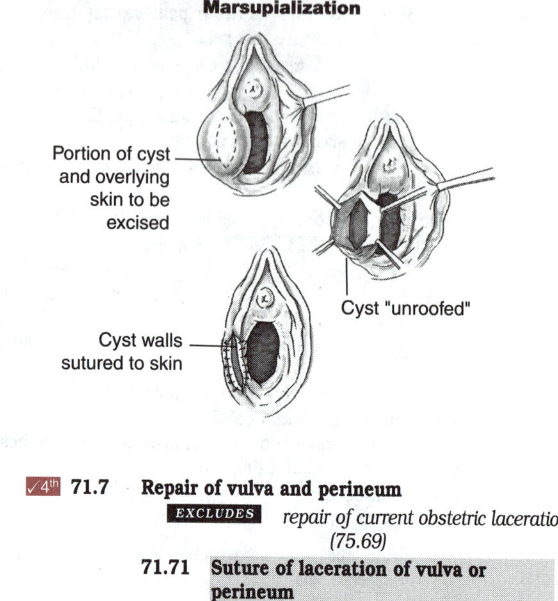

✓4th **71.7 Repair of vulva and perineum**

EXCLUDES *repair of current obstetric laceration (75.69)*

71.71 Suture of laceration of vulva or perineum ♀

71.72 Repair of fistula of vulva or perineum ♀

EXCLUDES *repair of fistula:*
urethroperineal (58.43)
urethroperineovesical (57.84)
vaginoperineal (70.75)

71.79 Other repair of vulva and perineum ♀

Repair of old obstetric laceration of vulva or perineum

AHA: 1Q, '97, 9

71.8 Other operations on vulva ♀

EXCLUDES *removal of:*
foreign body without incision (98.23)
packing (97.75)
replacement of packing (97.26)

71.9 Other operations on female genital organs ♀

AHA: 4Q, '04, 90; 1Q, '03, 13

13. OBSTETRICAL PROCEDURES (72-75)

✓3rd **72 Forceps, vacuum, and breech delivery**

72.0 Low forceps operation ♀
Outlet forceps operation

72.1 Low forceps operation with episiotomy ♀
Outlet forceps operation with episiotomy

✓4th **72.2 Mid forceps operation**

72.21 Mid forceps operation with episiotomy ♀

72.29 Other mid forceps operation ♀

✓4th **72.3 High forceps operation**

72.31 High forceps operation with episiotomy ♀

72.39 Other high forceps operation ♀

72.4 Forceps rotation of fetal head ♀
DeLee maneuver
Key-in-lock rotation
Kielland rotation
Scanzoni's maneuver
Code also any associated forceps extraction (72.0-72.39)

✓4th **72.5 Breech extraction**

72.51 Partial breech extraction with forceps to aftercoming head ♀

72.52 Other partial breech extraction ♀

72.53 Total breech extraction with forceps to aftercoming head ♀

72.54 Other total breech extraction ♀

72.6 Forceps application to aftercoming head ♀
Piper forceps operation
EXCLUDES *partial breech extraction with forceps to aftercoming head (72.51)*
total breech extraction with forceps to aftercoming head (72.53)

✓4th **72.7 Vacuum extraction**
INCLUDES Malstöm's extraction

72.71 Vacuum extraction with episiotomy ♀

72.79 Other vacuum extraction ♀

72.8 Other specified instrumental delivery ♀

72.9 Unspecified instrumental delivery ♀

✓3rd **73 Other procedures inducing or assisting delivery**

✓4th **73.0 Artificial rupture of membranes**

73.01 Induction of labor by artificial rupture of membranes ♀
Surgical induction NOS
EXCLUDES *artificial rupture of membranes after onset of labor (73.09)*
AHA: 3Q, '00, 5

73.09 Other artificial rupture of membranes ♀
Artificial rupture of membranes at time of delivery

Breech Extraction

73.1 Other surgical induction of labor ♀
Induction by cervical dilation
EXCLUDES *injection for abortion (75.0)*
insertion of suppository for abortion (96.49)

✓4th **73.2 Internal and combined version and extraction**

73.21 Internal and combined version without extraction ♀
Version NOS

73.22 Internal and combined version with extraction ♀

73.3 Failed forceps ♀
Application of forceps without delivery
Trial forceps

73.4 Medical induction of labor ♀
EXCLUDES *medication to augment active labor — omit code*

✓4th **73.5 Manually assisted delivery** ♀

73.51 Manual rotation of fetal head ♀

73.59 Other manually assisted delivery ♀
Assisted spontaneous delivery
Credé maneuver
AHA: 4Q, '98, 76

73.6 Episiotomy ♀
Episioproctotomy
Episiotomy with subsequent episiorrhaphy
EXCLUDES *that with:*
high forceps (72.31)
low forceps (72.1)
mid forceps (72.21)
outlet forceps (72.1)
vacuum extraction (72.71)
AHA: 1Q, '92, 10

73.8 Operations on fetus to facilitate delivery ♀
Clavicotomy on fetus
Destruction of fetus
Needling of hydrocephalic head

✓4th **73.9 Other operations assisting delivery**

73.91 External version ♀

73.92 Replacement of prolapsed umbilical cord ♀

73.93 Incision of cervix to assist delivery ♀
Dührssen's incisions

73.94 Pubiotomy to assist delivery ♀
Obstetrical symphysiotomy

73.99 Other ♀
EXCLUDES *dilation of cervix, obstetrical, to induce labor (73.1)*
insertion of bag or bougie to induce labor (73.1)
removal of cerclage material (69.96)

✓3rd **74 Cesarean section and removal of fetus**
Code also any synchronous:
hysterectomy (68.3-68.4, 68.6, 68.8)
myomectomy (68.29)
sterilization (66.31-66.39, 66.63)

74.0 Classical cesarean section ♀
Transperitoneal classical cesarean section

74.1 Low cervical cesarean section ♀
Lower uterine segment cesarean section
AHA: 1Q, '01, 11

74.2 Extraperitoneal cesarean section ♀
Supravesical cesarean section

74.3 Removal of extratubal ectopic pregnancy ♀
Removal of:
ectopic abdominal pregnancy
fetus from peritoneal or extraperitoneal cavity following uterine or tubal rupture
EXCLUDES *that by salpingostomy (66.02)*
that by salpingotomy (66.01)
that with synchronous salpingectomy (66.62)
AHA: 4Q, '92, 25; 2Q, '90, 25; 2Q, '90, 27; 1Q, '89, 11

74.4 Cesarean section of other specified type ♀
Peritoneal exclusion cesareansection
Transperitoneal cesarean section NOS
Vaginal cesarean section

✓4th **74.9 Cesarean section of unspecified type**

74.91 Hysterotomy to terminate pregnancy ♀
Therapeutic abortion by hysterotomy

74.99 Other cesarean section of unspecified type ♀
Cesarean section NOS
Obstetrical abdominouterotomy
Obstetrical hysterotomy

✓3rd **75 Other obstetric operations**

75.0 Intra-amniotic injection for abortion ♀
Injection of:
prostaglandin } for induction of abortion
saline }
Termination of pregnancy by intrauterine injection
EXCLUDES *insertion of prostaglandin suppository for abortion (96.49)*

75.1 Diagnostic amniocentesis ♀

75.2 Intrauterine transfusion ♀
Exchange transfusion in utero
Insertion of catheter into abdomen of fetus for transfusion
Code also any hysterotomy approach (68.0)

✓4th **75.3 Other intrauterine operations on fetus and amnion**
Code also any hysterotomy approach (68.0)

75.31 Amnioscopy ♀
Fetoscopy
Laparoamnioscopy

75.32 Fetal EKG (scalp) ♀

75.33 Fetal blood sampling and biopsy ♀

75.34 Other fetal monitoring ♀
Antepartum fetal nonstress test
Fetal monitoring, not otherwise specified
EXCLUDES *fetal pulse oximetry (75.38)*

Amniocentesis

Amniotic sac

Aspiration of amniotic fluid

75.35 Other diagnostic procedures on fetus and amnion ♀
Intrauterine pressure determination
EXCLUDES *amniocentesis (75.1)*
diagnostic procedures on gravid uterus and placenta (87.81, 88.46, 88.78, 92.17)

75.36 Correction of fetal defect ♀

75.37 Amnioinfusion
Code also injection of antibiotic (99.21)
AHA: 4Q, '98, 76

75.38 Fetal pulse oximetry
Transcervical fetal oxygen saturation monitoring
Transcervical fetal SpO_2 monitoring
DEF: Single-use sensor inserted through the birth canal and positioned to rest against the fetal cheek, forehead, or temple; infrared beam of light aimed at the fetal skin is reflected back through the sensor for analysis.
AHA: 4Q, '01, 64

75.4 Manual removal of retained placenta ♀
EXCLUDES *aspiration curettage (69.52)*
dilation and curettage (69.02)

✓4th **75.5 Repair of current obstetric laceration of uterus**

75.50 Repair of current obstetric laceration of uterus, not otherwise specified ♀

75.51 Repair of current obstetric laceration of cervix ♀

75.52 Repair of current obstetric laceration of corpus uteri ♀

✓4th **75.6 Repair of other current obstetric laceration**
AHA: 1Q, '92, 11

75.61 Repair of current obstetric laceration of bladder and urethra ♀

75.62 Repair of current obstetric laceration of rectum and sphincter ani ♀

75.69 Repair of other current obstetric laceration ♀
Episioperineorrhaphy
Repair of:
pelvic floor
perineum
vagina
vulva
Secondary repair of episiotomy
EXCLUDES *repair of routine episiotomy (73.6)*

75.7 Manual exploration of uterine cavity, postpartum ♀

75.8 Obstetric tamponade of uterus or vagina ♀
EXCLUDES *antepartum tamponade (73.1)*

✓4th **75.9 Other obstetric operations**

75.91 Evacuation of obstetrical incisional hematoma of perineum ♀
Evacuation of hematoma of:
episiotomy
perineorrhaphy

75.92 Evacuation of other hematoma of vulva or vagina ♀

75.93 Surgical correction of inverted uterus ♀
Spintelli operation
EXCLUDES *vaginal repair of chronic inversion of uterus (69.23)*

75.94 Manual replacement of inverted uterus ♀

75.99 Other ♀

14. OPERATIONS ON THE MUSCULOSKELETAL SYSTEM (76-84)

✓3rd **76 Operations on facial bones and joints**

EXCLUDES *accessory sinuses (22.00-22.9)*
nasal bones (21.00-21.99)
skull (01.01-02.99)

✓4th **76.0 Incision of facial bone without division**

76.01 Sequestrectomy of facial bone

Removal of necrotic bone chip from facial bone

76.09 Other incision of facial bone

Reopening of osteotomy site of facial bone

EXCLUDES *osteotomy associated with orthognathic surgery (76.61-76.69)*
removal of internal fixation device (76.97)

✓4th **76.1 Diagnostic procedures on facial bones and joints**

76.11 Biopsy of facial bone

76.19 Other diagnostic procedures on facial bones and joints

EXCLUDES *contrast arthrogram of temporomandibular joint (87.13)*
other x-ray (87.11-87.12, 87.14-87.16)

AHA: N-D, '87, 12

76.2 Local excision or destruction of lesion of facial bone

EXCLUDES *biopsy of facial bone (76.11)*
excision of odontogenic lesion (24.4)

✓4th **76.3 Partial ostectomy of facial bone**

76.31 Partial mandibulectomy

Hemimandibulectomy

EXCLUDES *that associated with temporomandibular arthroplasty (76.5)*

AHA: ►2Q, '05, 8◄

DEF: Excision, partial of lower jawbone.

DEF: Hemimandibulectomy: Excision of one-half of lower jawbone.

76.39 Partial ostectomy of other facial bone

Hemimaxillectomy (with bonegraft or prosthesis)

AHA: J-F, '87, 14

DEF: Excision, partial of facial bone; other than lower jawbone.

DEF: Hemimaxillectomy (with bone graft or prosthesis): Excision of one side of upper jawbone and restoration with bone graft or prosthesis.

✓4th **76.4 Excision and reconstruction of facial bones**

76.41 Total mandibulectomy with synchronous reconstruction

76.42 Other total mandibulectomy

76.43 Other reconstruction of mandible

EXCLUDES *genioplasty (76.67-76.68)*
that with synchronous total mandibulectomy (76.41)

AHA: 2Q, '03, 13

76.44 Total ostectomy of other facial bone with synchronous reconstruction

AHA: 3Q, '93, 6

DEF: Excision, facial bone, total with reconstruction during same operative session.

76.45 Other total ostectomy of other facial bone

76.46 Other reconstruction of other facial bone

EXCLUDES *that with synchronous total ostectomy (76.44)*

76.5 Temporomandibular arthroplasty

AHA: 4Q, '99, 20

✓4th **76.6 Other facial bone repair and orthognathic surgery**

Code also any synchronous:
bone graft (76.91)
synthetic implant (76.92)

EXCLUDES *reconstruction of facial bones (76.41-76.46)*

76.61 Closed osteoplasty [osteotomy] of mandibular ramus

Gigli saw osteotomy

DEF: Reshaping and restoration of lower jawbone projection; closed surgical field.

DEF: Gigli saw osteotomy: Plastic repair using a flexible wire with saw teeth.

76.62 Open osteoplasty [osteotomy] of mandibular ramus

76.63 Osteoplasty [osteotomy] of body of mandible

76.64 Other orthognathic surgery on mandible

Mandibular osteoplasty NOS
Segmental or subapical osteotomy

AHA: 2Q, '04, 9, 10

76.65 Segmental osteoplasty [osteotomy] of maxilla

Maxillary osteoplasty NOS

76.66 Total osteoplasty [osteotomy] of maxilla

76.67 Reduction genioplasty

Reduction mentoplasty

DEF: Reduction of protruding chin or lower jawbone.

76.68 Augmentation genioplasty

Mentoplasty:
NOS
with graft or implant

DEF: Extension of the lower jawbone to a functional position by means of plastic surgery.

76.69 Other facial bone repair

Osteoplasty of facial bone NOS

✓4th **76.7 Reduction of facial fracture**

INCLUDES internal fixation

Code also any synchronous:
bone graft (76.91)
synthetic implant (76.92)

EXCLUDES *that of nasal bones (21.71-21.72)*

76.70 Reduction of facial fracture, not otherwise specified

76.71 Closed reduction of malar and zygomatic fracture

76.72 Open reduction of malar and zygomatic fracture

76.73 Closed reduction of maxillary fracture

76.74 Open reduction of maxillary fracture

76.75 Closed reduction of mandibular fracture

76.76 Open reduction of mandibular fracture

76.77 Open reduction of alveolar fracture

Reduction of alveolar fracture with stabilization of teeth

76.78 Other closed reduction of facial fracture

Closed reduction of orbital fracture

EXCLUDES *nasal bone (21.71)*

76.79 Other open reduction of facial fracture

Open reduction of orbit rim or wall

EXCLUDES *nasal bone (21.72)*

✓4th **76.9 Other operations on facial bones and joints**

76.91 Bone graft to facial bone

Autogenous, Bone bank, Heterogenous } graft to facial bone

76.92 Insertion of synthetic implant in facial bone

Alloplastic implant to facial bone

76.93 Closed reduction of temporomandibular dislocation

76.94 Open reduction of temporomandibular dislocation

76.95 Other manipulation of temporomandibular joint

76.96 Injection of therapeutic substance into temporomandibular joint

76.97 Removal of internal fixation device from facial bone

EXCLUDES *removal of:*
dental wiring (97.33)
external mandibular fixation device NEC (97.36)

76.99 Other

✓3rd **77 Incision, excision, and division of other bones**

EXCLUDES *laminectomy for decompression (03.09)*
operations on:
accessory sinuses (22.00-22.9)
ear ossicles (19.0-19.55)
facial bones (76.01-76.99)
joint structures (80.00-81.99)
mastoid (19.9-20.99)
nasal bones (21.00-21.99)
skull (01.01-02.99)

The following fourth-digit subclassification is for use with appropriate categories in section 77 to identify the site. Valid fourth-digit categories are in [brackets] under each code.

0 unspecified site
1 scapula, clavicle, and thorax [ribs and sternum]
2 humerus
3 radius and ulna
4 carpals and metacarpals
5 femur
6 patella
7 tibia and fibula
8 tarsals and metatarsals
9 other
Pelvic bones
Phalanges (of foot) (of hand)
Vertebrae

18 § ✓4th **77.0 Sequestrectomy**
[0-9]
DEF: Excision and removal of dead bone.

§ ✓4th **77.1 Other incision of bone without division**
[0-9]
Reopening of osteotomy site

EXCLUDES *aspiration of bone marrow, (41.31, 41.91)*
removal of internal fixation device (78.60-78.69)

AHA: For code 77.17: 1Q, '02, 3

DEF: Incision into bone without division of site.

18 § ✓4th **77.2 Wedge osteotomy**
[0-9]
EXCLUDES *that for hallux valgus (77.51)*

DEF: Removal of wedge-shaped piece of bone.

§ ✓4th **77.3 Other division of bone**
[0-9]
Osteoarthrotomy

EXCLUDES *clavicotomy of fetus (73.8)*
laminotomy or incision of vertebra (03.01-03.09)
pubiotomy to assist delivery (73.94)
sternotomy incidental to thoracic operation — omit code

§ ✓4th **77.4 Biopsy of bone**
[0-9]
AHA: 2Q, '98, 12

✓4th **77.5 Excision and repair of bunion and other toe deformities**

Repair of Hammer Toe

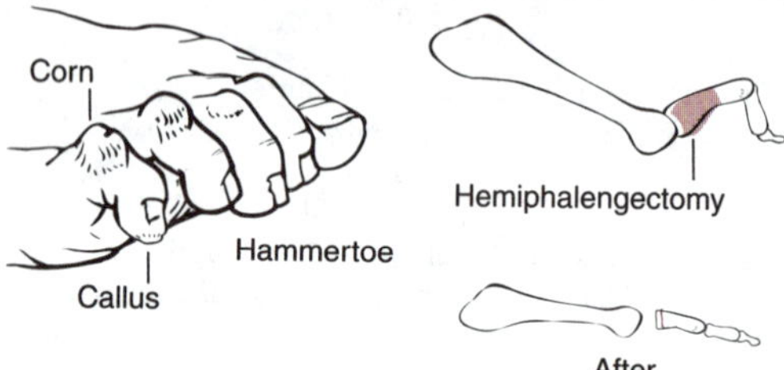

77.51 Bunionectomy with soft tissue correction and osteotomy of the first metatarsal

DEF: Incision and removal of big toe bony prominence and reconstruction with soft tissue.

77.52 Bunionectomy with soft tissue correction and arthrodesis

DEF: Removal of big toe bony prominence and reconstruction with soft tissue and joint fixation.

77.53 Other bunionectomy with soft tissue correction

77.54 Excision or correction of bunionette
That with osteotomy

DEF: Resection of fifth metatarsal head via exposure of joint; includes imbrication of capsule.

77.56 Repair of hammer toe
Fusion } of hammer toe
Phalangectomy (partial) } of hammer toe
Filleting } of hammer toe

DEF: Repair of clawlike toe defect by joint fusion, or partial removal of toe via traction technique.

77.57 Repair of claw toe
Fusion } of claw toe
Phalangectomy (partial) } of claw toe
Capsulotomy } of claw toe
Tendon lengthening } of claw toe

DEF: Repair of clawlike toe defect by joint fusion, partial removal of toe, joint capsule incision or lengthening of fibrous muscle attachment.

77.58 Other excision, fusion, and repair of toes
Cockup toe repair
Overlapping toe repair
That with use of prosthetic materials

77.59 Other bunionectomy
Resection of hallux valgus joint with insertion of prosthesis

DEF: Resection of hallux valgus joint with insertion of prosthesis: Cutting away part of big toe with prosthesis insertion to correct bony prominence.

18 § ✓4th **77.6 Local excision of lesion or tissue of bone**
[0-9]
EXCLUDES *biopsy of bone (77.40-77.49)*
debridement of compound fracture (79.60-79.69)

AHA: For code 77.61: 3Q, '01, 9; For code 77.65: 4Q, '04, 128; S-O, '85, 4; For code 77.67: 1Q, '02, 3; 1Q, '99, 8; For code 77.69: 2Q, '00, 18

18 § ✓4th **77.7 Excision of bone for graft**
[0-9]
AHA: 4Q, '99, 11, 13; For code 77.71: 3Q, '03, 19; For code 77.79: 2Q, '03, 13; 4Q, '02, 107, 109-110; 2Q, '02, 16; 2Q, '00 12, 13; 4Q, '99, 11, 13

§ Requires fourth-digit. Valid digits are in [brackets] under each code. See category 77 for definitions.
18 Nonspecific OR procedure=0

BI Bilateral Procedure NC Non-covered Procedure LC Limited Coverage Procedure ▶◀ Revised Text ● New Code ▲ Revised Code Title

18 § ✓4th **77.8 Other partial ostectomy**
[0-9]
Condylectomy
EXCLUDES *amputation (84.00-84.19, 84.91)*
arthrectomy (80.90-80.99)
excision of bone ends associated with:
arthrodesis (81.00-81.29)
arthroplasty (81.51-81.59, 81.71-81.81, 81.84)
excision of cartilage (80.5-80.6, 80.80-80.99)
excision of head of femur with synchronous replacement (00.70-00.73, 81.51-81.53)
hemilaminectomy (03.01-03.09)
laminectomy (03.01-03.09)
ostectomy for hallux valgus (77.51-77.59)
partial amputation:
finger (84.01)
thumb (84.02)
toe (84.11)
resection of ribs incidental to thoracic operation — omit code
that incidental to other operation — omit code
AHA: For code 77.89: 2Q, '02, 8

18 § ✓4th **77.9 Total ostectomy**
[0-9]
EXCLUDES *amputation of limb (84.00-84.19, 84.91)*
that incidental to other operation — omit code

✓3rd **78 Other operations on bones, except facial bones**
EXCLUDES *operations on:*
accessory sinuses (22.00-22.9)
facial bones (76.01-76.99)
joint structures (80.00-81.99)
nasal bones (21.00-21.99)
skull (01.01-02.99)

The following fourth-digit subclassification is for use with categories in section 78 to identify the site. Valid fourth-digit categories are in [brackets] under each code.
0 unspecified site
1 scapula, clavicle, and thorax [ribs and sternum]
2 humerus
3 radius and ulna
4 carpals and metacarpals
5 femur
6 patella
7 tibia and fibula
8 tarsals and metatarsals
9 other
Pelvic bones
Phalanges (of foot) (of hand)
Vertebrae

18 ✓4th **78.0 Bone graft**
[0-9]
Bone:
bank graft
graft (autogenous) (heterogenous)
That with debridement of bone graft site (removal of sclerosed, fibrous, or necrotic bone or tissue)
Transplantation of bone
Code also any excision of bone for graft (77.70-77.79)
EXCLUDES *that for bone lengthening (78.30-78.39)*
AHA: 2Q, '02, 11; 2Q, '98, 12; 3Q, '94, 10; 1Q, '91, 3

18 ✓4th **78.1 Application of external fixator device**
[0-9]
Fixator with insertion of pins/wires/screws into bone
Code also any type of fixator device, if known (84.71-84.73)
EXCLUDES *other immobilization, pressure, and attention to wound (93.51-93.59)*
AHA: 2Q, '94, 4; **For code 78.12:** ▶4Q, '05, 129◀

18 ✓4th **78.2 Limb shortening procedures**
[0,2-5,7-9]
Epiphyseal stapling
Open epiphysiodesis
Percutaneous epiphysiodesis
Resection/osteotomy

18 ✓4th **78.3 Limb lengthening procedures**
[0,2-5,7-9]
Bone graft with or without internal fixation devices or osteotomy
Distraction technique with or without corticotomy/osteotomy
Code also any application of an external fixation device (78.10-78.19)

18 ✓4th **78.4 Other repair or plastic operations on bone**
[0-9]
Other operation on bone NEC
Repair of malunion or nonunion fracture NEC
EXCLUDES *application of external fixation device (78.10-78.19)*
limb lengthening procedures (78.30-78.39)
limb shortening procedures (78.20-78.29)
osteotomy (77.3)
reconstruction of thumb (82.61-82.69)
repair of pectus deformity (34.74)
repair with bone graft (78.00-78.09)
AHA: 3Q, '91, 20; 4Q, '88, 11; **For code 78.41:** 2Q, '02, 16; **For code 78.47:** 3Q, '91, 20; **For code 78.49:** 3Q, '04, 9; 2Q, '03, 22; 3Q, '02, 12; 2Q, '02, 14, 15; 4Q, '99, 22; 1Q, '97, 5

18 ✓4th **78.5 Internal fixation of bone without fracture reduction**
[0-9]
Internal fixation of bone (prophylactic)
Reinsertion of internal fixation device
Revision of displaced or broken fixation device
EXCLUDES *arthroplasty and arthrodesis (81.00-81.85)*
bone graft (78.00-78.09)
limb shortening procedures (78.20-78.29)
that for fracture reduction (79.10-79.19, 79.30-79.59)
AHA: 2Q, '99, 11; 2Q, '94, 4; **For Code 78.59:** 3Q, '04, 6; 2Q, '03, 15; 4Q, '99, 13

✓4th **78.6 Removal of implanted devices from bone**
[0-9]
External fixator device (invasive)
Internal fixation device
Removal of bone growth stimulator (invasive)
Removal of internal limb lengthening device
EXCLUDES *removal of cast, splint, and traction device (Kirschner wire) (Steinmann pin) (97.88)*
removal of skull tongs or halo traction device (02.95)
AHA: 1Q, '00, 15; **For Code 78.67** 2Q, '03, 14; **For Code 78.69:** 4Q, '02, 110; 2Q, '00, 18

18 ✓4th **78.7 Osteoclasis**
[0-9]
DEF: Surgical breaking or rebreaking of bone.

18 ✓4th **78.8 Diagnostic procedures on bone, not elsewhere classified**
[0-9]
EXCLUDES *biopsy of bone (77.40-77.49)*
magnetic resonance imaging (88.94)
microscopic examination of specimen from bone (91.51-91.59)
radioisotope scan (92.14)
skeletal x-ray (87.21-87.29, 87.43, 88.21-88.33)
thermography (88.83)

18 ✓4th **78.9 Insertion of bone growth stimulator**
[0-9]
Insertion of:
bone stimulator (electrical) to aid bone healing
osteogenic electrodes for bone growth stimulation
totally implanted device (invasive)
EXCLUDES *non-invasive (transcutaneous) (surface) stimulator (99.86)*

§ Requires fourth-digit. Valid digits are in [brackets] under each code. See category 77 for definitions.
18 Nonspecific OR procedure=0

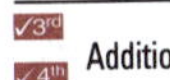
Additional Digit Required | Nonspecific OR Procedure | Valid OR Procedure | Non-OR Procedure | Adjunct Code

✓3rd **79 Reduction of fracture and dislocation**

INCLUDES application of cast or splint
reduction with insertion of traction device (Kirschner wire) (Steinmann pin)

Code also any:
application of external fixator device (78.10-78.19)
type of fixator device, if known (84.71-84.73)

EXCLUDES *external fixation alone for immobilization of fracture (93.51-93.56, 93.59)*
internal fixation without reduction of fracture (78.50-78.59)
operations on:
facial bones(76.70-76.79)
nasal bones (21.71-21.72)
orbit (76.78-76.79)
skull (02.02)
vertebrae (03.53)
removal of cast or splint (97.88)
replacement of cast or splint (97.11-97.14)
traction alone for reduction of fracture (93.41-93.46)

The following fourth-digit subclassification is for use with appropriate categories in section 79 to identify the site. Valid fourth-digit categories are in [brackets] under each code.

0 unspecified site
1 humerus
2 radius and ulna
Arm NOS
3 carpals and metacarpals
Hand NOS
4 phalanges of hand
5 femur
6 tibia and fibula
Leg NOS
7 tarsals and metatarsals
Foot NOS
8 phalanges of foot
9 other specified bone

✓4th **79.0 Closed reduction of fracture without internal fixation**
[0-9]
EXCLUDES *that for separation of epiphysis (79.40-79.49)*
AHA: 2Q, '94, 3; 3Q, '89, 17; 4Q, '88, 11;
For code 79.01: ▶4Q, '05, 129;◀ For code 79.05: 3Q, '89, 16
DEF: Manipulative realignment of fracture; without incision or internal fixation.

18 ✓4th **79.1 Closed reduction of fracture with internal fixation**
[0-9]
EXCLUDES *that for separation of epiphysis (79.40-79.49)*
AHA: 2Q, '94, 4; 4Q, '93, 35; 1Q, '93, 27
DEF: Manipulative realignment of fracture; with internal fixation but without incision.

18 ✓4th **79.2 Open reduction of fracture without internal fixation**
[0-9]
EXCLUDES *that for separation of epiphysis (79.50-79.59)*
AHA: 2Q, '94, 3

18 ✓4th **79.3 Open reduction of fracture with internal fixation**
[0-9]
EXCLUDES *that for separation of epiphysis (79.50-79.59)*
AHA: 2Q, '98, 12; 3Q, '94, 10; 2Q, '94, 3; 4Q, '93, 35
DEF: Realignment of fracture with incision and internal fixation.

18 ✓4th **79.4 Closed reduction of separated epiphysis**
[0-2,5,6,9] Reduction with or without internal fixation
DEF: Manipulative reduction of expanded joint end of long bone to normal position without incision.

18 ✓4th **79.5 Open reduction of separated epiphysis**
[0-2,5,6,9] Reduction with or without internal fixation
DEF: Reduction of expanded joint end of long bone with incision.

18 Nonspecific OR procedure=0

18 ✓4th **79.6 Debridement of open fracture site**
[0-9] Debridement of compound fracture
AHA: 3Q, '95, 12; 3Q, '89, 16
DEF: Removal of damaged tissue at fracture site.

✓4th **79.7 Closed reduction of dislocation**
INCLUDES closed reduction (with external traction device)
EXCLUDES *closed reduction of dislocation of temporomandibular joint (76.93)*
DEF: Manipulative reduction of displaced joint without incision; with or without external traction.

79.70 Closed reduction of dislocation of unspecified site
79.71 Closed reduction of dislocation of shoulder
79.72 Closed reduction of dislocation of elbow
79.73 Closed reduction of dislocation of wrist
79.74 Closed reduction of dislocation of hand and finger
79.75 Closed reduction of dislocation of hip
79.76 Closed reduction of dislocation of knee
AHA: N-D, '86, 7
79.77 Closed reduction of dislocation of ankle
79.78 Closed reduction of dislocation of foot and toe
79.79 Closed reduction of dislocation of other specified sites

18 ✓4th **79.8 Open reduction of dislocation**
INCLUDES open reduction (with internal and external fixation devices)
EXCLUDES *open reduction of dislocation of temporomandibular joint (76.94)*
DEF: Reduction of displaced joint via incision; with or without internal and external fixation.

79.80 Open reduction of dislocation of unspecified site
79.81 Open reduction of dislocation of shoulder
79.82 Open reduction of dislocation of elbow
79.83 Open reduction of dislocation of wrist
79.84 Open reduction of dislocation of hand and finger
79.85 Open reduction of dislocation of hip
79.86 Open reduction of dislocation of knee
79.87 Open reduction of dislocation of ankle
79.88 Open reduction of dislocation of foot and toe
79.89 Open reduction of dislocation of other specified sites

18 ✓4th **79.9 Unspecified operation on bone injury**
[0-9]

✓3rd **80 Incision and excision of joint structures**

INCLUDES operations on:
capsule of joint
cartilage
condyle
ligament
meniscus
synovial membrane

EXCLUDES *cartilage of:*
ear (18.01-18.9)
nose (21.00-21.99)
temporomandibular joint (76.01-76.99)

The following fourth-digit subclassification is for use with appropriate categories in section 80 to identify the site:

0 unspecified site
1 shoulder
2 elbow
3 wrist
4 hand and finger
5 hip
6 knee
7 ankle
8 foot and toe
9 other specified sites
Spine

18 § ✓4th **80.0 Arthrotomy for removal of prosthesis**
Code also any:
insertion of (cement) (joint) spacer (84.56)
removal of (cement) (joint) spacer (84.57)
AHA: For code 80.06: 2Q, '97, 10
DEF: Incision into joint to remove prosthesis.

18 § ✓4th **80.1 Other arthrotomy**
Arthrostomy
EXCLUDES *that for:*
arthrography (88.32)
arthroscopy (80.20-80.29)
injection of drug (81.92)
operative approach — omit code
DEF: Incision into joint; other than to remove prosthesis.
DEF: Arthrostomy: Creation of opening into joint.

18 § ✓4th **80.2 Arthroscopy**
AHA: 3Q, '93, 5

§ ✓4th **80.3 Biopsy of joint structure**
Aspiration biopsy
AHA: For code 80.39: 3Q, '05, 13-14

18 § ✓4th **80.4 Division of joint capsule, ligament, or cartilage**
Goldner clubfoot release
Heyman-Herndon(-Strong) correction of metatarsus varus
Release of:
adherent or constrictive joint capsule
joint
ligament
EXCLUDES *symphysiotomy to assist delivery (73.94)*
that for:
carpal tunnel syndrome (04.43)
tarsal tunnel syndrome (04.44)
AHA: For code 80.49: 2Q, '02, 16
DEF: Incision and separation of joint tissues, including capsule, fibrous bone attachment or cartilage.

✓4th **80.5 Excision or destruction of intervertebral disc**

80.50 Excision or destruction of intervertebral disc, unspecified
Unspecified as to excision or destruction

80.51 Excision of intervertebral disc
Code also any concurrent spinal fusion (81.00-81.08)
Diskectomy
Level:
cervical
thoracic
lumbar (lumbosacral)
Removal of herniated nucleus pulposus
That by laminotomy or hemilaminectomy
That with decompression of spinal nerve root at same level
Requires additional code for any concomitant decompression of spinal nerve root at different level from excision site
EXCLUDES *intervertebral chemonucleolysis (80.52)*
laminectomyfor exploration of intraspinal canal (03.09)
laminotomy for decompression of spinal nerve root only (03.09)
that for insertion of (non-fusion) spinal disc replacement device (84.60-84.69)
▶*that with corpectomy, (vertebral) (80.99)*◀
AHA:▶ 1Q, '06, 12;◀ 4Q, '04, 133; 3Q, '03, 12; 1Q, '96, 7; 2Q, '95, 9; 2Q, '90, 27; S-O, '86, 12
DEF: Diskectomy: Removal of intervertebral disc.
DEF: Removal of a herniated nucleus pulposus: Removal of displaced intervertebral disc, central part.

80.52 Intervertebral chemonucleolysis
With aspiration of disc fragments
With diskography
Injection of proteolytic enzyme into intervertebral space (chymopapain)
EXCLUDES *injection of anesthetic substance (03.91)*
injection of other substances (03.92)
DEF: Destruction of intervertebral disc via injection of enzyme.

80.59 Other destruction of intervertebral disc
Destruction NEC
That by laser
AHA: 3Q, '02, 10

80.6 Excision of semilunar cartilage of knee
Excision of meniscus of knee
AHA: 2Q, '03, 18; 3Q, '00, 4; 2Q, '96, 3; 1Q, '93, 23

18 § ✓4th **80.7 Synovectomy**
Complete or partial resection of synovial membrane
EXCLUDES *excision of Baker's cyst (83.39)*
DEF: Excision of inner membrane of joint capsule.

18 § ✓4th **80.8 Other local excision or destruction of lesion of joint**

18 § ✓4th **80.9 Other excision of joint**
EXCLUDES *cheilectomy of joint (77.80-77.89)*
excision of bone ends (77.80-77.89)

✓3rd **81 Repair and plastic operations on joint structures**

✓4th **81.0 Spinal fusion**
INCLUDES arthrodesis of spine with:
bone graft
internal fixation
Code also any:
insertion of interbody spinal fusion device (84.51)
insertion of recombinant bone morphogenetic protein (84.52)
Code also the total number of vertebrae fused (81.62-81.64)
EXCLUDES *corrections of pseudarthrosis of spine (81.30-81.39)*
refusion of spine (81.30-81.39)
AHA: 4Q, '03, 99
DEF: Spinal fusion: Immobilization of spinal column.
DEF: Anterior interbody fusion: Arthrodesis by excising disc and cartilage end plates with bone graft insertion between two vertebrae.
DEF: Lateral fusion: Arthrodesis by decorticating and bone grafting lateral surface of zygapophysial joint, pars interarticularis and transverse process.
DEF: Posterior fusion: Arthrodesis by decorticating and bone grafting of neural arches between right and left zygapophysial joints.
DEF: Posterolateral fusion: Arthrodesis by decorticating and bone grafting zygapophysial joint, pars interarticularis and transverse processes

81.00 Spinal fusion, not otherwise specified

81.01 Atlas-axis spinal fusion
Craniocervical fusion, C1-C2 fusion, Occiput C2 fusion } by anterior transoral or posterior technique

81.02 Other cervical fusion, anterior technique
Arthrodesis of C2 level or below:
anterior (interbody) technique
anterolateral technique
AHA: 4Q, '03, 101; 1Q, '01, 6; 1Q, '96, 7

81.03 Other cervical fusion, posterior technique
Arthrodesis of C2 level or below:
posterior (interbody) technique
posterolateral technique

§ Requires fourth-digit. Valid digits are in [brackets] under each code. See category 80 for definitions.
18 Nonspecific OR procedure=0

Types of Grafts for Anterior Arthrodesis

Anteroposterior Anteroposterior Anteroposterior

Lateral Lateral Lateral

81.04 Dorsal and dorsolumbar fusion, anterior technique

Arthrodesis of thoracic or thoracolumbar region:
- anterior (interbody) technique
- anterolateral technique

AHA: 3Q, '03, 19

81.05 Dorsal and dorsolumbar fusion, posterior technique

Arthrodesis of thoracic or thoracolumbar region:
- posterior (interbody) technique
- posterolateral technique

AHA: 2Q, '02, 16; 4Q, '99, 11

81.06 Lumbar and lumbosacral fusion, anterior technique

Anterior lumbar interbody fusion (ALIF)
Arthrodesis of lumbar or lumbosacral region:
- anterior (interbody) technique
- anterolateral technique

AHA: 4Q, '05, 122; 4Q, '02, 107; 4Q, '99, 11

81.07 Lumbar and lumbosacral fusion, lateral transverse process technique

AHA: 4Q, '02, 108

81.08 Lumbar and lumbosacral fusion, posterior technique

Arthrodesis of lumbar or lumbosacral region:
- posterior (interbody) technique
- posterolateral technique

Posterior lumbar interbody fusion (PLIF)
Transforaminal lumbar interbody fusion (TLIF)

AHA: ▶ 1Q, '06, 12, 13; ◀ 4Q, '05, 122-123; 4Q, '02, 107, 109; 2Q, '00, 12, 13; 4Q, '99, 13; 2Q, '95, 9

✓4th **81.1 Arthrodesis and arthroereisis of foot and ankle**

INCLUDES arthrodesis of foot and ankle with:
- bone graft
- external fixation device

DEF: Fixation of foot or ankle joints.

81.11 Ankle fusion

Tibiotalar fusion

81.12 Triple arthrodesis

Talus to calcaneus and calcaneus to cuboid and navicular

81.13 Subtalar fusion

EXCLUDES *arthroereisis (81.18)*

81.14 Midtarsal fusion

81.15 Tarsometatarsal fusion

81.16 Metatarsophalangeal fusion

81.17 Other fusion of foot

81.18 Subtalar joint arthroereisis

AHA: 4Q, '05, 124

DEF: Insertion of an endoprostheses to limit excessive valgus motion of the subtalar joint; nonfusion procedure to prevent pronation.

Subtalar Joint Arthroereisis

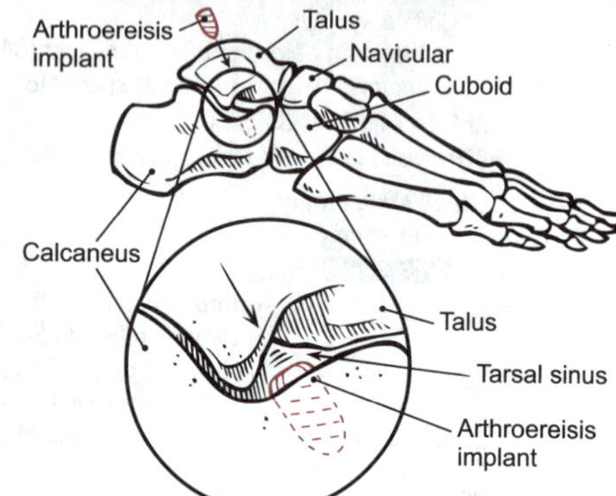

✓4th **81.2 Arthrodesis of other joint**

INCLUDES arthrodesis with:
- bone graft
- external fixation device

excision of bone ends and compression

81.20 Arthrodesis of unspecified joint

81.21 Arthrodesis of hip

81.22 Arthrodesis of knee

81.23 Arthrodesis of shoulder

81.24 Arthrodesis of elbow

81.25 Carporadial fusion

81.26 Metacarpocarpal fusion

81.27 Metacarpophalangeal fusion

81.28 Interphalangeal fusion

81.29 Arthrodesis of other specified joints

✓4th **81.3 Refusion of spine**

INCLUDES arthrodesis of spine with:
- bone graft
- internal fixation

correction of pseudarthrosis of spine

Code also any:
- insertion of interbody spinal fusion device (84.51)
- insertion of recombinant bone morphogenetic protein (84.52)

Code also the total number of vertebrae fused (81.62-81.64)

AHA: 4Q, '03, 99; 4Q, '01, 64

81.30 Refusion of spine, not otherwise specified

81.31 Refusion of atlas-axis spine

Craniocervical fusion, C1-C2 fusion, Occiput C2 fusion — by anterior transoral or posterior technique

81.32 Refusion of other cervical spine, anterior technique

Arthrodesis of C2 level or below:
- anterior (interbody) technique
- anterolateral technique

81.33 Refusion of other cervical spine, posterior technique

Arthrodesis of C2 level or below:
- posterior (interbody) technique
- posterolateral technique

81.34 Refusion of dorsal and dorsolumbar spine, anterior technique

Arthrodesis of thoracic or thoracolumbar region:
- anterior (interbody) technique
- anterolateral technique

81.35 Refusion of dorsal and dorsolumbar spine, posterior technique

Arthrodesis of thoracic or thoracolumbar region:
- posterior (interbody) technique
- posterolateral technique

Partial Hip Replacement

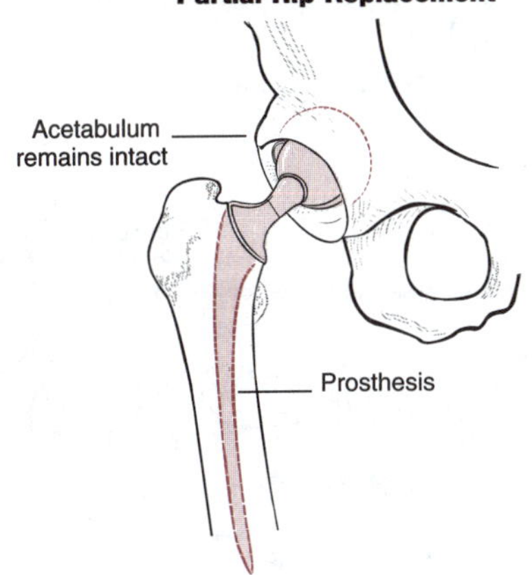

Total Hip Replacement

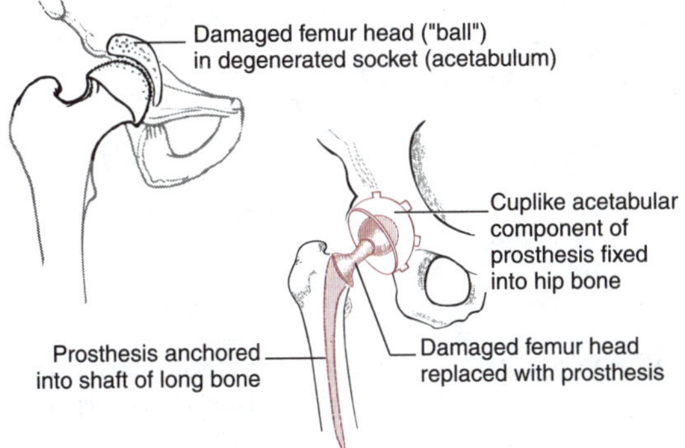

81.36 Refusion of lumbar and lumbosacral spine, anterior technique

Anterior lumbar interbody fusion (ALIF)
Arthrodesis of lumbar or lumbosacral region:
anterior (interbody) technique
anterolateral technique

AHA: 4Q, '05, 122-123

81.37 Refusion of lumbar and lumbosacral spine, lateral transverse process technique

81.38 Refusion of lumbar and lumbosacral spine, posterior technique

Arthrodesis of lumbar or lumbosacral region:
posterior (interbody) technique
posterolateral technique
Posterior lumbar interbody fusion (PLIF)
Transforaminal lumbar interbody fusion (TLIF)

AHA: 4Q, '05, 122-123; 4Q, '02, 110

81.39 Refusion of spine, not elsewhere classified

✓4th **81.4 Other repair of joint of lower extremity**

INCLUDES arthroplasty of lower extremity with:
external traction or fixation
graft of bone (chips) or cartilage
internal fixation device

AHA: S-O, '85, 4

81.40 Repair of hip, not elsewhere classified

81.42 Five-in-one repair of knee

Medial meniscectomy, medial collateral ligament repair, vastus medialis advancement, semitendinosus advancement, and pes anserinus transfer

81.43 Triad knee repair

Medial meniscectomy with repair of the anterior cruciate ligament and the medial collateral ligament
O'Donoghue procedure

81.44 Patellar stabilization

Roux-Goldthwait operation for recurrent dislocation of patella

DEF: Roux-Goldthwait operation: Stabilization of patella via lateral ligament transposed at insertion beneath undisturbed medial insertion; excision of capsule ellipse and medial patella retinaculum; capsule reefed for lateral patella hold.

81.45 Other repair of the cruciate ligaments

AHA: M-A, '87, 12

81.46 Other repair of the collateral ligaments

81.47 Other repair of knee

AHA: 2Q, '03, 18; 1Q, '00, 12, 13; 1Q, '96, 3; 3Q, '93, 5

81.49 Other repair of ankle

AHA: 2Q, '01, 15; 3Q, '00, 4

✓4th **81.5 Joint replacement of lower extremity**

INCLUDES arthroplasty of lower extremity with:
external traction or fixation
graft of bone (chips) or cartilage
internal fixation device or prosthesis
removal of cement spacer

AHA: S-O, '85, 4

81.51 Total hip replacement BI

Replacement of both femoral head and acetabulum by prosthesis
Total reconstruction of hip
Code also any type of bearing surface, if known ▶(00.74-00.77)◀

AHA: 4Q, '04, 113; 2Q, '91, 18

DEF: Repair of both surfaces of hip joint with prosthesis.

81.52 Partial hip replacement BI

Bipolar endoprosthesis
Code also any type of bearing surface, if known ▶(00.74-00.77)◀

AHA: 2Q, '91, 18

DEF: Repair of single surface of hip joint with prosthesis.

81.53 Revision of hip replacement, not otherwise specified BI

Revision of hip replacement, not specified as to component(s) replaced, (acetabular, femoral or both)
Code also any:
removal of (cement) (joint) spacer (84.57)
type of bearing surface, if known ▶(00.74-00.77)◀

EXCLUDES *revision of hip replacement, components specified (00.70-00.73)*

AHA: 4Q, '05, 125; 3Q, '97, 12

81.54 Total knee replacement BI

Bicompartmental
Tricompartmental
Unicompartmental (hemijoint)

DEF: Repair of a knee joint with prosthetic implant in one, two, or three compartments.

Total Knee Replacement

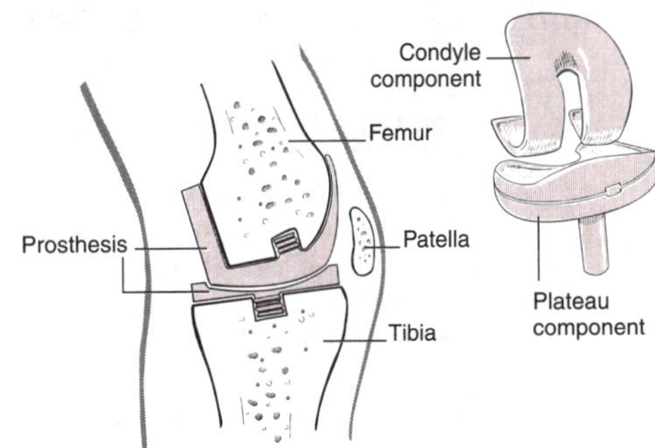

81.55 Revision of knee replacement, not otherwise specified BI
Code also any removal of (cement) (joint) spacer (84.57)
EXCLUDES *arthrodesis of knee (81.22)*
revision of knee replacement, components specified (00.80-00.84)
AHA: 4Q, '05, 113; 2Q, '97, 10

81.56 Total ankle replacement BI

81.57 Replacement of joint of foot and toe

81.59 Revision of joint replacement of lower extremity, not elsewhere classified

✓4th **81.6 Other procedures on spine**

Note: Number of vertebrae
The vertebral spine consists of 25 vertebrae in the following order and number:
Cervical: C1 (atlas), C2 (axis), C3, C4, C5, C6, C7
Thoracic or Dorsal: T1, T2, T3, T4, T5, T6, T7, T8, T9, T10, T11, T12
Lumbar and Sacral: L1, L2, L3, L4, L5, S1
Coders should report only one code from the series 81.62-81.64 to show the total number of vertebrae fused on the patient.
Code also the level and approach of the fusion or refusion (81.00-81.08, 81.30-81.39)
AHA: 4Q, '03, 99
DEF: A combined posterior and anterior fusion performed by a surgeon through one incision: lateral transverse, posterior, or anterior.

81.62 Fusion or refusion of 2-3 vertebrae
AHA: ▶1Q, '06, 12, 13;◀ 4Q, '05, 123; 4Q, '03, 99

81.63 Fusion or refusion of 4-8 vertebrae
AHA: 4Q, '03, 99-101

81.64 Fusion or refusion of 9 or more vertebrae
AHA: 4Q, '03, 99

81.65 Vertebroplasty
Injection of bone void filler (cement) (polymethylmethacrylate) (PMMA) into the diseased or fractured vertebral body
EXCLUDES *kyphoplasty (81.66)*

81.66 Kyphoplasty
Insertion of inflatable balloon, bone tamp, or other device to create a cavity for partial restoration of height of diseased or fractured vertebral body prior to injection of bone void filler (cement) (polymethylmethacrylate) (PMMA)
EXCLUDES *vertebroplasty (81.65)*
AHA: 4Q, '04, 126

✓4th **81.7 Arthroplasty and repair of hand, fingers, and wrist**
INCLUDES arthroplasty of hand and finger with:
external traction or fixation
graft of bone (chips) or cartilage
internal fixation device or prosthesis
EXCLUDES *operations on muscle, tendon, and fascia of hand (82.01-82.99)*
DEF: Plastic surgery of hand, fingers and wrist joints.

81.71 Arthroplasty of metacarpophalangeal and interphalangeal joint with implant

81.72 Arthroplasty of metacarpophalangeal and interphalangeal joint without implant
AHA: 1Q, '93, 28

81.73 Total wrist replacement

81.74 Arthroplasty of carpocarpal or carpometacarpal joint with implant

81.75 Arthroplasty of carpocarpal or carpometacarpal joint without implant
AHA: 3Q, '93, 8

81.79 Other repair of hand, fingers, and wrist

Vertebroplasty

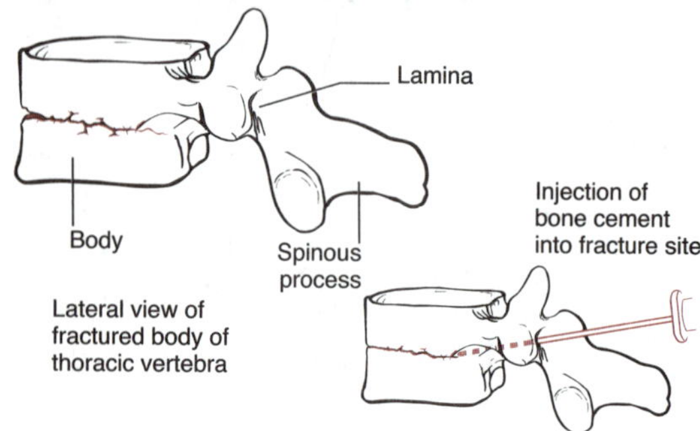

Kyphoplasty

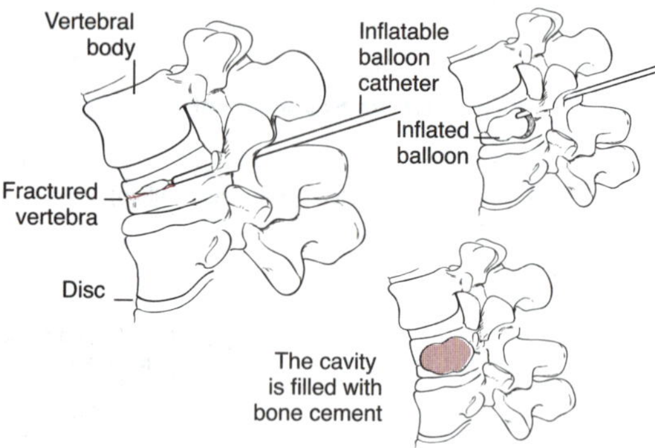

✓4th **81.8 Arthroplasty and repair of shoulder and elbow**
INCLUDES arthroplasty of upper limb NEC with:
external traction or fixation
graft of bone (chips) or cartilage
internal fixation device or prosthesis

81.80 Total shoulder replacement

81.81 Partial shoulder replacement

81.82 Repair of recurrent dislocation of shoulder
AHA: 3Q, '95, 15

81.83 Other repair of shoulder
Revision of arthroplasty of shoulder
AHA: 1Q, '02, 9; 4Q, '01, 51; 2Q, '00, 14; 3Q, '93, 5

81.84 Total elbow replacement

81.85 Other repair of elbow

✓4th **81.9 Other operations on joint structures**

81.91 Arthrocentesis
Joint aspiration
EXCLUDES *that for:*
arthrography (88.32)
biopsy of joint structure (80.30-80.39)
injection of drug (81.92)
DEF: Insertion of needle to withdraw fluid from joint.

81.92 Injection of therapeutic substance into joint or ligament
AHA: 2Q, '00, 14; 3Q, '89, 16

Arthrocentesis

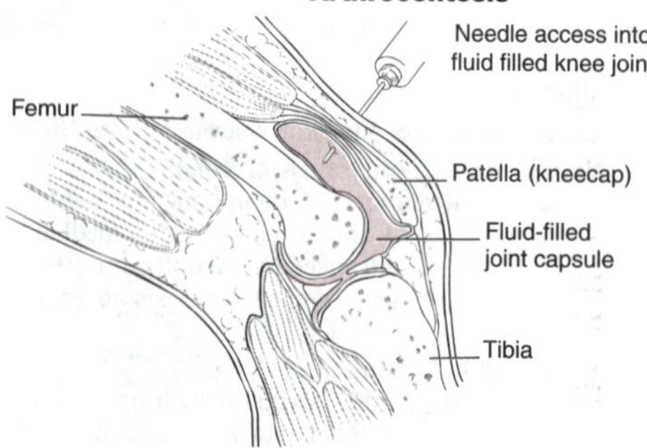

81.93 Suture of capsule or ligament of upper extremity
EXCLUDES *that associated with arthroplasty (81.71-81.75, 81.80-81.81, 81.84)*

81.94 Suture of capsule or ligament of ankle and foot
EXCLUDES *that associated with arthroplasty (81.56-81.59)*

81.95 Suture of capsule or ligament of other lower extremity
EXCLUDES *that associated with arthroplasty (81.51-81.55, 81.59)*

81.96 Other repair of joint

81.97 Revision of joint replacement of upper extremity
Partial
Total
Removal of cement spacer
AHA: 1Q, '04, 12

81.98 Other diagnostic procedures on joint structures
EXCLUDES *arthroscopy (80.20-80.29)*
biopsy of joint structure (80.30-80.39)
microscopic examination of specimen from joint (91.51-91.59)
thermography (88.83)
x-ray (87.21-87.29, 88.21-88.33)

81.99 Other
AHA: ▶4Q, '05, 124◀

✓3rd **82 Operations on muscle, tendon, and fascia of hand**
INCLUDES operations on:
aponeurosis
synovial membrane (tendon sheath)
tendon sheath

✓4th **82.0 Incision of muscle, tendon, fascia, and bursa of hand**

82.01 Exploration of tendon sheath of hand
Incision of } tendon sheath of hand
Removal of rice bodies in } tendon sheath of hand
EXCLUDES *division of tendon (82.11)*
DEF: Incision into and exploring the hand's muscle and its accompanying supportive, connective tissue, bands, and sacs.

82.02 Myotomy of hand
EXCLUDES *myotomy for division (82.19)*
DEF: Incision into hand muscle.

82.03 Bursotomy of hand

82.04 Incision and drainage of palmar or thenar space

82.09 Other incision of soft tissue of hand
EXCLUDES *incision of skin and subcutaneous tissue alone (86.01-86.09)*
AHA: N-D, '87, 10

✓4th **82.1 Division of muscle, tendon, and fascia of hand**

82.11 Tenotomy of hand
Division of tendon of hand

82.12 Fasciotomy of hand
Division of fascia of hand

82.19 Other division of soft tissue of hand
Division of muscle of hand

✓4th **82.2 Excision of lesion of muscle, tendon, and fascia of hand**

82.21 Excision or lesion of tendon sheath of hand
Ganglionectomy of tendon sheath (wrist)

82.22 Excision of lesion of muscle of hand

82.29 Excision of other lesion of soft tissue of hand
EXCLUDES *excision of lesion of skin and subcutaneous tissue (86.21-86.3)*

✓4th **82.3 Other excision of soft tissue of hand**
Code also any skin graft (86.61-86.62, 86.73)
EXCLUDES *excision of skin and subcutaneous tissue (86.21-86.3)*

82.31 Bursectomy of hand

82.32 Excision of tendon of hand for graft
DEF: Resection and excision of fibrous tissue connecting bone to hand muscle for grafting.

82.33 Other tenonectomy of hand
Tenosynovectomy of hand
EXCLUDES *excision of lesion of:*
tendon (82.29)
sheath (82.21)
DEF: Removal of fibrous bands connecting muscle to bone of hand.
DEF: Tenosynovectomy of hand: Excision of fibrous band connecting muscle and bone of hand and removal of coverings.

82.34 Excision of muscle or fascia of hand for graft

82.35 Other fasciectomy of hand
Release of Dupuytren's contracture
EXCLUDES *excision of lesion of fascia (82.29)*
DEF: Excision of fibrous connective tissue; other than for grafting or removing lesion.
DEF: Release of Dupuytren's contracture: Excision of fibrous connective tissue to correct flexion of fingers.

82.36 Other myectomy of hand
EXCLUDES *excision of lesion of muscle (82.22)*

82.39 Other excision of soft tissue of hand
EXCLUDES *excision of skin (86.21-86.3)*
excision of soft tissue lesion (82.29)

✓4th **82.4 Suture of muscle, tendon, and fascia of hand**

82.41 Suture of tendon sheath of hand

82.42 Delayed suture of flexor tendon of hand
DEF: Suture of fibrous band between flexor muscle and bone; following initial repair.

82.43 Delayed suture of other tendon of hand

82.44 Other suture of flexor tendon of hand
EXCLUDES *delayed suture of flexor tendon of hand (82.42)*

82.45 Other suture of other tendon of hand
EXCLUDES *delayed suture of other tendon of hand (82.43)*

82.46 Suture of muscle or fascia of hand

✓4th **82.5 Transplantation of muscle and tendon of hand**
AHA: 1Q, '93, 28

82.51 Advancement of tendon of hand
DEF: Detachment of fibrous connective muscle band and bone with reattachment at advanced point of hand.

82.52 Recession of tendon of hand
DEF: Detachment of fibrous band of muscle and bone with reattachment at drawn-back point of hand.

82.53 Reattachment of tendon of hand

82.54 Reattachment of muscle of hand

82.55 Other change in hand muscle or tendon length

82.56 Other hand tendon transfer or transplantation
EXCLUDES *pollicization of thumb (82.61)*
transfer of finger, except thumb (82.81)
AHA: 2Q, '99, 10; 4Q, '98, 40

82.57 **Other hand tendon transposition**
AHA: 1Q, '93, 28; 3Q, '93, 8

82.58 **Other hand muscle transfer or transplantation**

82.59 **Other hand muscle transposition**

✓4th **82.6 Reconstruction of thumb**
INCLUDES digital transfer to act as thumb
Code also any amputation for digital transfer (84.01, 84.11)

82.61 **Pollicization operation carrying over nerves and blood supply**
DEF: Creation or reconstruction of a thumb with another digit, commonly the index finger.

82.69 **Other reconstruction of thumb**
"Cocked-hat" procedure [skin flap and bone]
Grafts:
bone } to thumb
skin (pedicle) } to thumb

✓4th **82.7 Plastic operation on hand with graft or implant**

82.71 **Tendon pulley reconstruction**
Reconstruction for opponensplasty
DEF: Reconstruction of fibrous band between muscle and bone of hand.

82.72 **Plastic operation on hand with graft of muscle or fascia**

82.79 **Plastic operation on hand with other graft or implant**
Tendon graft to hand
AHA: J-F, '87, 6

✓4th **82.8 Other plastic operations on hand**

82.81 **Transfer of finger, except thumb**
EXCLUDES *pollicization of thumb (82.61)*
AHA: ▶2Q, '05, 7◀

82.82 **Repair of cleft hand**
DEF: Correction of fissure defect of hand.

82.83 **Repair of macrodactyly**
DEF: Reduction in size of abnormally large fingers.

82.84 **Repair of mallet finger**
DEF: Repair of flexed little finger.

82.85 **Other tenodesis of hand**
Tendon fixation of hand NOS
DEF: Fixation of fibrous connective band between muscle and bone of hand.

82.86 **Other tenoplasty of hand**
Myotenoplasty of hand
DEF: Myotenoplasty of hand: Plastic repair of muscle and fibrous band connecting muscle to bone.

82.89 **Other plastic operations on hand**
Plication of fascia
Repair of fascial hernia
EXCLUDES *that with graft or implant (82.71-82.79)*

✓4th **82.9 Other operations on muscle, tendon, and fascia of hand**
EXCLUDES *diagnostic procedures on soft tissue of hand (83.21-83.29)*

82.91 **Lysis of adhesions of hand**
Freeing of adhesions of fascia, muscle, and tendon of hand
EXCLUDES *decompression of carpal tunnel (04.43)*
that by stretching or manipulation only (93.26)

82.92 **Aspiration of bursa of hand**

82.93 **Aspiration of other soft tissue of hand**
EXCLUDES *skin and subcutaneous tissue (86.01)*

82.94 **Injection of therapeutic substance into bursa of hand**

82.95 **Injection of therapeutic substance into tendon of hand**

82.96 **Other injection of locally-acting therapeutic substance into soft tissue of hand**
EXCLUDES *subcutaneous or intramuscular injection (99.11-99.29)*

82.99 **Other operations on muscle, tendon, and fascia of hand**

✓3rd **83 Operations on muscle, tendon, fascia, and bursa, except hand**
INCLUDES operations on:
aponeurosis
synovial membrane of bursa and tendon sheaths
tendon sheaths
EXCLUDES *diaphragm (34.81-34.89)*
hand (82.01-82.99)
muscles of eye (15.01-15.9)

✓4th **83.0 Incision of muscle, tendon, fascia, and bursa**

83.01 **Exploration of tendon sheath**
Incision of tendon sheath
Removal of rice bodies from tendon sheath
DEF: Incision of external covering of fibrous cord for exam.
DEF: Removal of rice bodies from tendon sheath: Incision and removal of small bodies resembling grains of rice.

83.02 **Myotomy**
EXCLUDES *cricopharyngeal myotomy (29.31)*
AHA: 2Q, '89, 18

83.03 **Bursotomy**
Removal of calcareous deposit of bursa
EXCLUDES *aspiration of bursa (percutaneous) (83.94)*

83.09 **Other incision of soft tissue**
Incision of fascia
EXCLUDES *incision of skin and subcutaneous tissue alone (86.01-86.09)*

✓4th **83.1 Division of muscle, tendon, and fascia**

83.11 **Achillotenotomy**

83.12 **Adductor tenotomy of hip**
DEF: Incision into fibrous attachment between adductor muscle and hip bone.

83.13 **Other tenotomy**
Aponeurotomy
Division of tendon
Tendon release
Tendon transection
Tenotomy for thoracic outlet decompression
DEF: Aponeurotomy: Incision and separation of fibrous cords attaching a muscle to bone to aid movement.
DEF: Division of tendon: Separation of fibrous band connecting muscle to bone.
DEF: Tendon release: Surgical detachment of fibrous band from muscle and/or bone.
DEF: Tendon transection: Incision across width of fibrous bands between muscle and bone.
DEF: Tenotomy for thoracic outlet decompression: Incision of fibrous muscle with separation from bone to relieve compressed thoracic outlet.

83.14 **Fasciotomy**
Division of fascia
Division of iliotibial band
Fascia stripping
Release of Volkmann's contracture by fasciotomy
AHA: 3Q, '98, 8
DEF: Division of fascia: Incision to separate fibrous connective tissue.
DEF: Division of iliotibial band: Incision to separate fibrous band connecting tibial bone to muscle in flank.
DEF: Fascia stripping: Incision and lengthwise separation of fibrous connective tissue.
DEF: Release of Volkmann's contracture by fasciotomy: Divisional incision of connective tissue to correct defect in flexion of finger(s).

BI Bilateral Procedure NC Non-covered Procedure LC Limited Coverage Procedure ▶◀ Revised Text ● New Code ▲ Revised Code Title

83.19 Other division of soft tissue
Division of muscle
Muscle release
Myotomy for thoracic outlet decompression
Myotomy with division
Scalenotomy
Transection of muscle

✓4th **83.2 Diagnostic procedures on muscle, tendon, fascia, and bursa, including that of hand**

83.21 Biopsy of soft tissue
EXCLUDES *biopsy of chest wall (34.23)*
biopsy of skin and subcutaneous tissue (86.11)

83.29 Other diagnostic procedures on muscle, tendon, fascia, and bursa, including that of hand
EXCLUDES *microscopic examination of specimen (91.51-91.-59)*
soft tissue x-ray (87.09, 87.38-87.39, 88.09, 88.35, 88.37)
thermography of muscle (88.84)

✓4th **83.3 Excision of lesion of muscle, tendon, fascia, and bursa**
EXCLUDES *biopsy of soft tissue (83.21)*

83.31 Excision of lesion of tendon sheath
Excision of ganglion of tendon sheath, except of hand

83.32 Excision of lesion of muscle
Excision of:
heterotopic bone
muscle scar for release of Volkmann's contracture
myositis ossificans
DEF: Heterotopic bone: Bone lesion in muscle.
DEF: Muscle scar for release of Volkmann's contracture: Scarred muscle tissue interfering with finger flexion.
DEF: Myositis ossificans: Bony deposits in muscle.

83.39 Excision of lesion of other soft tissue
Excision of Baker's cyst
EXCLUDES *bursectomy (83.5)*
excision of lesion of skin and subcutaneous tissue (86.3)
synovectomy (80.70-80.79)
AHA: 2Q, '05, 3; 2Q, '97, 6

✓4th **83.4 Other excision of muscle, tendon, and fascia**

83.41 Excision of tendon for graft

83.42 Other tenonectomy
Excision of:
aponeurosis
tendon sheath
Tenosynovectomy

83.43 Excision of muscle or fascia for graft

83.44 Other fasciectomy
DEF: Excision of fascia; other than for graft.

83.45 Other myectomy
Debridement of muscle NOS
Scalenectomy
AHA: 1Q, '99, 8
DEF: Scalenectomy: Removal of thoracic scaleni muscle tissue.

83.49 Other excision of soft tissue

83.5 Bursectomy
AHA: 2Q, '99, 11

✓4th **83.6 Suture of muscle, tendon, and fascia**

83.61 Suture of tendon sheath

83.62 Delayed suture of tendon

83.63 Rotator cuff repair
AHA: ►1Q, '06, 6;◄ 2Q, '93, 8
DEF: Repair of musculomembranous structure around shoulder joint capsule.

83.64 Other suture of tendon
Achillorrhaphy
Aponeurorrhaphy
EXCLUDES *delayed suture of tendon (83.62)*
DEF: Achillorrhaphy: Suture of fibrous band connecting Achilles tendon to heel bone.
DEF: Aponeurorrhaphy: Suture of fibrous cords connecting muscle to bone.

83.65 Other suture of muscle or fascia
Repair of diastasis recti

✓4th **83.7 Reconstruction of muscle and tendon**
EXCLUDES *reconstruction of muscle and tendon associated with arthroplasty*

83.71 Advancement of tendon
DEF: Detaching fibrous cord between muscle and bone with reattachment at advanced point.

83.72 Recession of tendon
DEF: Detaching fibrous cord between muscle and bone with reattachment at drawn-back point.

83.73 Reattachment of tendon

83.74 Reattachment of muscle

83.75 Tendon transfer or transplantation

83.76 Other tendon transposition

83.77 Muscle transfer or transplantation
Release of Volkmann's contracture by muscle transplantation

83.79 Other muscle transposition

✓4th **83.8 Other plastic operations on muscle, tendon, and fascia**
EXCLUDES *plastic operations on muscle, tendon, and fascia associated with arthroplasty*

83.81 Tendon graft

83.82 Graft of muscle or fascia
AHA: 3Q, '01, 9

83.83 Tendon pulley reconstruction
DEF: Reconstruction of fibrous cord between muscle and bone; at any site other than hand.

83.84 Release of clubfoot, not elsewhere classified
Evans operation on clubfoot

83.85 Other change in muscle or tendon length
Hamstring lengthening
Heel cord shortening
Plastic achillotenotomy
Tendon plication
DEF: Plastic achillotenotomy: Increase in heel cord length.
DEF: Tendon plication: Surgical tuck of tendon.

83.86 Quadricepsplasty
DEF: Correction of quadriceps femoris muscle.

83.87 Other plastic operations on muscle
Musculoplasty
Myoplasty
AHA: 1Q, '97, 9

83.88 Other plastic operations on tendon
Myotenoplasty
Tendon fixation
Tenodesis
Tenoplasty

83.89 Other plastic operations on fascia
Fascia lengthening
Fascioplasty
Plication of fascia

✓4th **83.9 Other operations on muscle, tendon, fascia, and bursa**
EXCLUDES *nonoperative:*
manipulation (93.25-93.29)
stretching (93.27-93.29)

83.91 Lysis of adhesions of muscle, tendon, fascia, and bursa
EXCLUDES *that for tarsal tunnel syndrome (04.44)*
DEF: Separation of created fibrous structures from muscle, connective tissues, bands and sacs.

83.92 Insertion or replacement of skeletal muscle stimulator

Implantation, insertion, placement, or replacement of skeletal muscle:
- electrodes
- stimulator

AHA: 2Q, '99, 10

83.93 Removal of skeletal muscle stimulator

83.94 Aspiration of bursa

83.95 Aspiration of other soft tissue

EXCLUDES *that of skin and subcutaneous tissue (86.01)*

83.96 Injection of therapeutic substance into bursa

83.97 Injection of therapeutic substance into tendon

83.98 Injection of locally-acting therapeutic substance into other soft tissue

EXCLUDES *subcutaneous or intramuscular injection (99.11-99.29)*

83.99 Other operations on muscle, tendon, fascia, and bursa

Suture of bursa

✓3rd 84 Other procedures on musculoskeletal system

✓4th 84.0 Amputation of upper limb

EXCLUDES *revision of amputation stump (84.3)*

84.00 Upper limb amputation, not otherwise specified

Closed flap amputation, Kineplastic amputation, Open or guillotine amputation, Revision of current traumatic amputation } of upper limb NOS

DEF: Closed flap amputation: Sewing a created skin flap over stump end of upper limb.

DEF: Kineplastic amputation: Amputation and preparation of stump of upper limb to permit movement.

DEF: Open or guillotine amputation: Straight incision across upper limb; used when primary closure is contraindicated.

DEF: Revision of current traumatic amputation: Reconstruction of traumatic amputation of upper limb to enable closure.

84.01 Amputation and disarticulation of finger

EXCLUDES *ligation of supernumerary finger (86.26)*

84.02 Amputation and disarticulation of thumb

84.03 Amputation through hand

Amputation through carpals

84.04 Disarticulation of wrist

84.05 Amputation through forearm

Forearm amputation

84.06 Disarticulation of elbow

DEF: Amputation of forearm through elbow joint.

84.07 Amputation through humerus

Upper arm amputation

84.08 Disarticulation of shoulder

DEF: Amputation of arm through shoulder joint.

84.09 Interthoracoscapular amputation

Forequarter amputation

DEF: Removal of upper arm, shoulder bone and collarbone.

✓4th 84.1 Amputation of lower limb

EXCLUDES *revision of amputation stump (84.3)*

84.10 Lower limb amputation, not otherwise specified

Closed flap amputation, Kineplastic amputation, Open or guillotine amputation, Revision of current traumatic amputation } of lower limb NOS

DEF: Closed flap amputation: Sewing a created skin flap over stump of lower limb.

DEF: Kineplastic amputation: Amputation and preparation of stump of lower limb to permit movement.

DEF: Open or guillotine amputation: Straight incision across lower limb; used when primary closure is contraindicated.

DEF: Revision of current traumatic amputation: Reconstruction of traumatic amputation of lower limb to enable closure.

84.11 Amputation of toe

Amputation through metatarsophalangeal joint
Disarticulation of toe
Metatarsal head amputation
Ray amputation of foot (disarticulation of the metatarsal head of the toe extending across the forefoot, just proximal to the metatarsophalangeal crease)

EXCLUDES *ligation of supernumerary toe (86.26)*

AHA: ▶2Q, '05, 7;◀ 4Q, '99, 19

84.12 Amputation through foot

Amputation of forefoot
Amputation through middle of foot
Chopart's amputation
Midtarsal amputation
Transmetatarsal amputation (amputation of the forefoot, including the toes)

EXCLUDES *Ray amputation of foot (84.11)*

AHA: 4Q, '99, 19

DEF: Amputation of forefoot: Removal of foot in front of joint between toes and body of foot.

DEF: Chopart's amputation: Removal of foot with retention of heel, ankle and other associated ankle bones.

DEF: Midtarsal amputation: Amputation of foot through tarsals.

DEF: Transmetatarsal amputation: Amputation of foot through metatarsals.

84.13 Disarticulation of ankle

DEF: Removal of foot through ankle bone.

84.14 Amputation of ankle through malleoli of tibia and fibula

84.15 Other amputation below knee

Amputation of leg through tibia and fibula NOS

84.16 Disarticulation of knee

Batch, Spitler, and McFaddin amputation
Mazet amputation
S.P. Roger's amputation

DEF: Removal of lower leg through knee joint.

84.17 Amputation above knee

Amputation of leg through femur
Amputation of thigh
Conversion of below-knee amputation into above-knee amputation
Supracondylar above-knee amputation

AHA: 1Q, '05, 16; 1Q, '05, 16; 3Q, '03, 14

84.18 Disarticulation of hip

DEF: Removal of leg through hip joint.

84.19 Abdominopelvic amputation

Hemipelvectomy
Hindquarter amputation

DEF: Removal of leg and portion of pelvic bone.

DEF: Hemipelvectomy: Removal of leg and lateral pelvis.

✓4th **84.2 Reattachment of extremity**

AHA: 1Q, '95, 8

84.21 Thumb reattachment

84.22 Finger reattachment

84.23 Forearm, wrist, or hand reattachment

84.24 Upper arm reattachment

Reattachment of arm NOS

84.25 Toe reattachment

84.26 Foot reattachment

84.27 Lower leg or ankle reattachment

Reattachment of leg NOS

84.28 Thigh reattachment

84.29 Other reattachment

84.3 Revision of amputation stump

Reamputation } of stump
Secondary closure } of stump
Trimming } of stump

EXCLUDES *revision of current traumatic amputation [revision by further amputation of current injury] (84.00-84.19, 84.91)*

AHA: 4Q, '99, 15; 2Q, '98, 15; 4Q, '88, 12

✓4th **84.4 Implantation or fitting of prosthetic limb device**

84.40 Implantation or fitting of prosthetic limb device, not otherwise specified

84.41 Fitting of prosthesis of upper arm and shoulder

84.42 Fitting of prosthesis of lower arm and hand

84.43 Fitting of prosthesis of arm, not otherwise specified

84.44 Implantation of prosthetic device of arm

84.45 Fitting of prosthesis above knee

84.46 Fitting of prosthesis below knee

84.47 Fitting of prosthesis of leg, not otherwise specified

84.48 Implantation of prosthetic device of leg

✓4th **84.5 Implantation of other musculoskeletal devices and substances**

EXCLUDES *insertion of (non-fusion) spinal disc replacement device (84.60-84.69)*

84.51 Insertion of interbody spinal fusion device

Insertion of:
- cages (carbn, ceramic, metal, plastic or titanium)
- interbody fusion cage
- synthetic cages or spacers
- threaded bone dowels

Code also refusion of spine (81.30-81.39)
Code also spinal fusion (81.00-81.08)

AHA: 4Q, '05, 123; 1Q, '04, 21; 4Q, '02, 108-110

84.52 Insertion of recombinant bone morphogenetic protein

rhBMP
That via collagen sponge, coral, ceramic and other carriers
Code also primary procedure performed:
- fracture repair (79.00-79.99)
- spinal fusion (81.00-81.08)
- spinal refusion (81.30-81.39)

AHA: 4Q, '02, 110

DEF: Surgical implantation of bone morphogenetic proteins (BMP) and recombinant BMP (rhBMP) to induce new bone growth formation; clinical applications include delayed unions and nonunions, fractures, and spinal fusions.

Spinal Fusion with Metal Cage

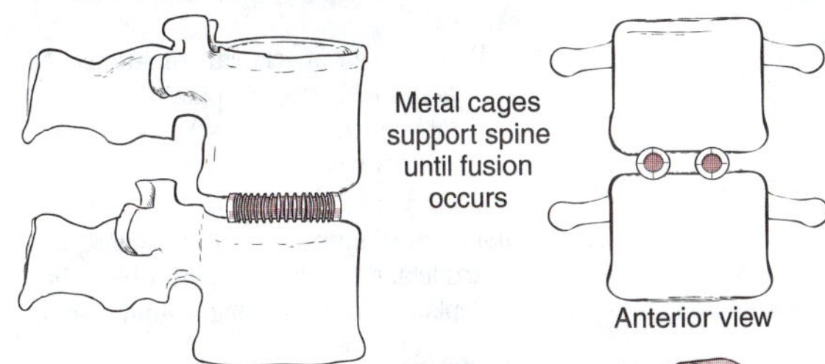

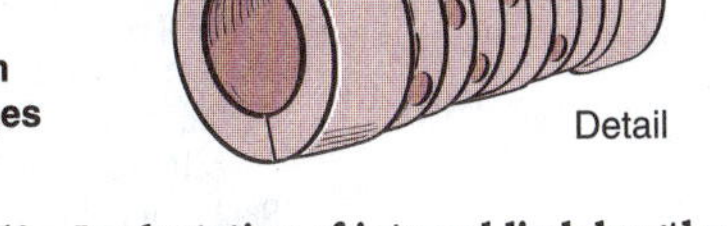

84.53 Implantation of internal limb lengthening device with kinetic distraction

Code also limb lengthening procedure (78.30-78.39)

84.54 Implantation of other internal limb lengthening device

Implantation of internal limb lengthening device, not otherwise specified (NOS)
Code also limb lengthening procedure (78.30-78.39)

84.55 Insertion of bone void filler

Insertion of:
- acrylic cement (PMMA)
- bone void cement
- calcium based bone void filler
- polymethylmethacrylate (PMMA)

EXCLUDES *that with kyphoplasty (81.66)*
that with vertebroplasty (81.65)

AHA: 4Q, '04, 128

84.56 Insertion of (cement) spacer

Insertion of joint spacer

AHA: 4Q, '05, 124

DEF: Implantation of an interspinous process decompressive (IPD) device between the spinous processes to limit extension; nonfusion, posterior approach procedure.

84.57 Removal of (cement) spacer

Removal of joint spacer

AHA: 4Q, '05, 113, 124-125

84.58 Implantation of interspinous process decompression device

EXCLUDES *fusion of spine (81.00-81.08, 81.30-81.39)*

AHA: 4Q, '05, 126

84.59 Insertion of other spinal devices

▶Insertion of non-fusion spinal stabilization device◀

✓4th **84.6 Replacement of spinal disc**

INCLUDES non-fusion arthroplasty of the spine with insertion of artificial disc prosthesis

84.60 Insertion of spinal disc prosthesis, not otherwise specified

Replacement of spinal disc, NOS

INCLUDES diskectomy (discectomy)

84.61 Insertion of partial spinal disc prosthesis, cervical

Nuclear replacement device, cervical
Partial artificial disc prosthesis (flexible), cervical
Replacement of nuclear disc (nucleus pulposus), cervical

INCLUDES diskectomy (discectomy)

✓3rd ✓4th Additional Digit Required | Nonspecific OR Procedure | Valid OR Procedure | Non-OR Procedure | Adjunct Code

84.62 Insertion of total spinal disc prosthesis, cervical

Replacement of cervical spinal disc, NOS
Replacement of total spinal disc, cervical
Total artificial disc prosthesis (flexible), cervical

INCLUDES diskectomy (discectomy)

84.63 Insertion of spinal disc prosthesis, thoracic

Artificial disc prosthesis (flexible), thoracic
Replacement of thoracic spinal disc, partial or total

INCLUDES diskectomy (discectomy)

84.64 Insertion of partial spinal disc prosthesis, lumbosacral

Nuclear replacement device, lumbar
Partial artificial disc prosthesis (flexible), lumbar
Replacement of nuclear disc (nucleus pulposus), lumbar

INCLUDES diskectomy (discectomy)

84.65 Insertion of total spinal disc prosthesis, lumbosacral

Replacement of lumbar spinal disc, NOS
Replacement of total spinal disc, lumbar
Total artificial disc prosthesis (flexible), lumbar

INCLUDES diskectomy (discectomy)

AHA: 4Q, '04, 133

84.66 Revision or replacement of artificial spinal disc prosthesis, cervical

Removal of (partial) (total) spinal disc prosthesis with synchronous insertion of new (partial) (total) spinal disc prosthesis, cervical
Repair of previously inserted spinal disc prosthesis, cervical

84.67 Revision or replacement of artificial spinal disc prosthesis, thoracic

Removal of (partial) (total) spinal disc prosthesis with synchronous insertion of new (partial) (total) spinal disc prosthesis, thoracic
Repair of previously inserted spinal disc prosthesis, thoracic

84.68 Revision or replacement of artificial spinal disc prosthesis, lumbosacral

Removal of (partial) (total) spinal disc prosthesis with synchronous insertion of new (partial) (total) spinal disc prosthesis, lumbosacral
Repair of previously inserted spinal disc prosthesis, lumbosacral

84.69 Revision or replacement of artificial spinal disc prosthesis, not otherwise specified

Removal of (partial) (total) spinal disc prosthesis with synchronous insertion of new (partial) (total) spinal disc prosthesis
Repair of previously inserted spinal disc prosthesis

✓4th **84.7 Adjunct codes for external fixator devices**

Code also any primary procedure performed:
application of external fixator device (78.10, 78.12-78.13, 78.15, 78.17-78.19)
reduction of fracture and dislocation (79.00-79.89)

AHA: 4Q, '05, 127-129

84.71 Application of external fixator device, monoplanar system

EXCLUDES *other hybrid device or system (84.73)*
ring device or system (84.72)

AHA: 4Q, '05, 129

DEF: Instrumentation that provides percutaneous neutralization, compression, and /or distraction of bone in a single plane by applying force within that plane.

84.72 Application of external fixator device, ring system

Ilizarov type
Sheffield type

EXCLUDES *monoplanar device or system (84.71)*
other hybrid device or system (84.73)

DEF: Instrumentation that provides percutaneous neutralization, compression, and/or distraction of bone through 360 degrees of force application.

84.73 Application of hybrid external fixator device

▶Computer (assisted) (dependent) external fixator device◀
Hybrid system using both ring and monoplanar devices

EXCLUDES *monoplanar device or system, when used alone (84.71)*
ring device or system, when used alone (84.72)

DEF: Instrumentation that provides percutaneous neutralization, compression, and /or distraction of bone by applying multiple external forces using monoplanar and ring device combinations.

✓4th **84.9 Other operations on musculoskeletal system**

EXCLUDES *nonoperative manipulation (93.25-93.29)*

84.91 Amputation, not otherwise specified

84.92 Separation of equal conjoined twins

84.93 Separation of unequal conjoined twins

Separation of conjoined twins NOS

84.99 Other

External Fixator Devices

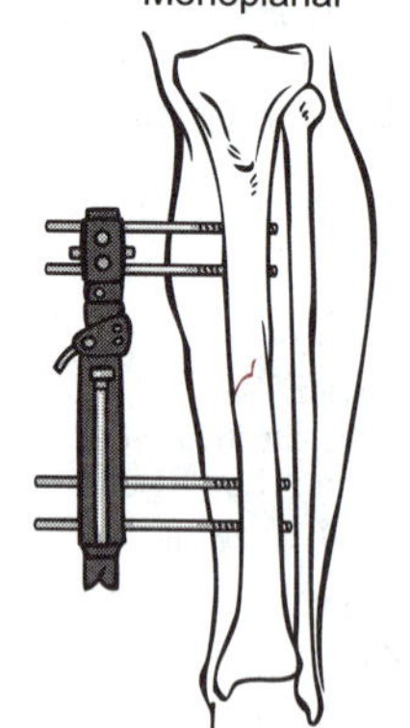

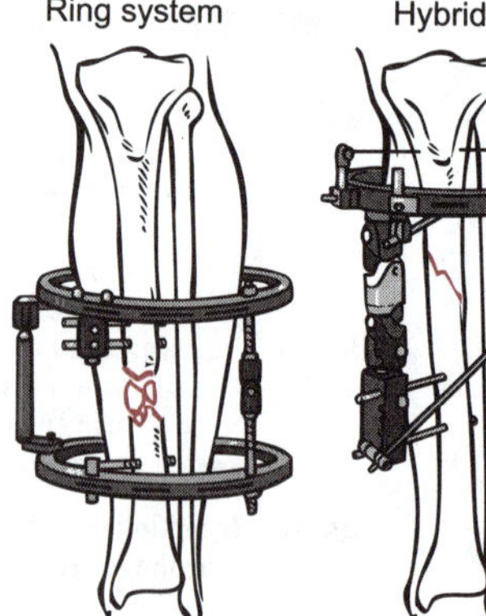

15. OPERATIONS ON THE INTEGUMENTARY SYSTEM (85-86)

✓3rd **85 Operations on the breast**

INCLUDES operations on the skin and subcutaneous tissue of:
breast } female or
previous mastectomy site } male
revision of previous mastectomy site

85.0 Mastotomy
Incision of breast (skin)
Mammotomy
EXCLUDES *aspiration of breast (85.91)*
removal of implant (85.94)
AHA: 1Q, '04, 3; 2Q, '90, 27

✓4th **85.1 Diagnostic procedures on breast**

85.11 Closed [percutaneous] [needle] biopsy of breast
AHA: 2Q, '00, 10; 3Q, '89, 17
DEF: Mammatome biopsy: Excision of breast tissue using a needle inserted through a small incision; followed by a full cut circle of tissue surrounding the core biopsy to obtain; multiple contiguous directional sampling for definitive diagnosis and staging of cancer.

85.12 Open biopsy of breast
AHA: 3Q, '89, 17; M-A, '86, 11
DEF: Excision of breast tissue for examination.

85.19 Other diagnostic procedures on breast
EXCLUDES *mammary ductogram (87.35)*
mammography NEC (87.37)
manual examination (89.36)
microscopic examination of specimen (91.61-91.69)
thermography (88.85)
ultrasonography (88.73)
xerography (87.36)

✓4th **85.2 Excision or destruction of breast tissue**
EXCLUDES *mastectomy (85.41-85.48)*
reduction mammoplasty (85.31-85.32)

85.20 Excision or destruction of breast tissue, not otherwise specified

85.21 Local excision of lesion of breast
Lumpectomy
Removal of area of fibrosis from breast
EXCLUDES *biopsy of breast (85.11-85.12)*
AHA: 2Q, '90, 27; 3Q, '89, 17; M-A, '86, 11

85.22 Resection of quadrant of breast

85.23 Subtotal mastectomy
EXCLUDES *quadrant resection (85.22)*
AHA: 2Q, '92, 7
DEF: Excision of a large portion of breast tissue.

85.24 Excision of ectopic breast tissue
Excision of accessory nipple
DEF: Excision of breast tissue outside normal breast region.

85.25 Excision of nipple
EXCLUDES *excision of accessory nipple (85.24)*

✓4th **85.3 Reduction mammoplasty and subcutaneous mammectomy**
AHA: 4Q, '95, 79, 80

85.31 Unilateral reduction mammoplasty
Unilateral:
amputative mammoplasty
size reduction mammoplasty

85.32 Bilateral reduction mammoplasty
Amputative mammoplasty
Biesenberger operation
Reduction mammoplasty (for gynecomastia)

85.33 Unilateral subcutaneous mammectomy with synchronous implant
EXCLUDES *that without synchronous implant (85.34)*
DEF: Removal of mammary tissue, leaving skin and nipple intact with implant of prosthesis.

85.34 Other unilateral subcutaneous mammectomy
Removal of breast tissue with preservation of skin and nipple
Subcutaneous mammectomy NOS
DEF: Excision of mammary tissue, leaving skin and nipple intact.

85.35 Bilateral subcutaneous mammectomy with synchronous implant
EXCLUDES *that without synchronous implant (85.36)*
DEF: Excision of mammary tissue, both breasts, leaving skin and nipples intact; with prosthesis.

85.36 Other bilateral subcutaneous mammectomy

✓4th **85.4 Mastectomy**

85.41 Unilateral simple mastectomy
Mastectomy: NOS
Mastectomy: complete
DEF: Removal of one breast.

85.42 Bilateral simple mastectomy
Bilateral complete mastectomy
DEF: Removal of both breasts.

85.43 Unilateral extended simple mastectomy
Extended simple mastectomy NOS
Modified radical mastectomy
Simple mastectomy with excision of regional lymph nodes
AHA: 2Q, '92, 7; 3Q, '91, 24; 2Q, '91, 21
DEF: Removal of one breast and lymph nodes under arm.

85.44 Bilateral extended simple mastectomy
AHA: 2Q, '92, 7; 3Q, '91, 24; 2Q, '91, 21

85.45 Unilateral radical mastectomy
Excision of breast, pectoral muscles, and regional lymph nodes [axillary, clavicular, supraclavicular]
Radical mastectomy NOS
AHA: 2Q, '91, 21
DEF: Removal of one breast and regional lymph nodes, pectoral muscle and adjacent tissue.

Mastectomy

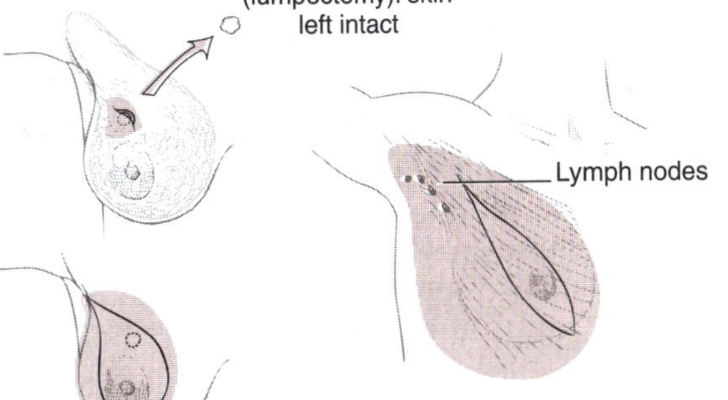

Operations on the Integumentary System 85–85.45

85.46 **Bilateral radical mastectomy**
AHA: 2Q, '91, 21

85.47 **Unilateral extended radical mastectomy**
Excision of breast, muscles, and lymph nodes [axillary, clavicular, supraclavicular, internal mammary, and mediastinal]
Extended radical mastectomy NOS
DEF: Removal of one breast, regional and middle chest lymph nodes, chest muscle and adjacent tissue.

85.48 **Bilateral extended radical mastectomy**
DEF: Removal of both breasts, regional and middle chest lymph nodes, chest muscle and adjacent tissue.

✓4th 85.5 **Augmentation mammoplasty**
EXCLUDES *that associated with subcutaneous mammectomy (85.33, 85.35)*
AHA: 3Q, '97, 12; 4Q, '95, 76, 80
DEF: Plastic surgery to increase breast size.

85.50 **Augmentation mammoplasty, not otherwise specified**

85.51 **Unilateral injection into breast for augmentation**

85.52 **Bilateral injection into breast for augmentation**
Injection into breast for augmentation NOS

85.53 **Unilateral breast implant**
AHA: 2Q, '00 18; 2Q, '98, 14

85.54 **Bilateral breast implant**
Breast implant NOS

85.6 **Mastopexy**
DEF: Anchoring of pendulous breast.

85.7 **Total reconstruction of breast**
AHA: 4Q, '95, 77; 1Q, '93, 27

✓4th 85.8 **Other repair and plastic operations on breast**
EXCLUDES *that for:*
augmentation (85.50-85.54)
reconstruction (85.7)
reduction (85.31-85.32)
AHA: 4Q, '95, 77

85.81 **Suture of laceration of breast**

85.82 **Split-thickness graft to breast**

85.83 **Full-thickness graft to breast**
AHA: 4Q, '95, 77

85.84 **Pedicle graft to breast**
AHA: 4Q, '95, 77
DEF: Implantation of transferred muscle tissue still connected to vascular source.

85.85 **Muscle flap graft to breast**
AHA: 4Q, '95, 77
DEF: Relocation of nipple.

85.86 **Transposition of nipple**
AHA: 4Q, '95, 78

85.87 **Other repair or reconstruction of nipple**
AHA: 4Q, '95, 78

85.89 **Other mammoplasty**

✓4th 85.9 **Other operations on the breast**

85.91 **Aspiration of breast**
EXCLUDES *percutaneous biopsy of breast (85.11)*

85.92 **Injection of therapeutic agent into breast**
EXCLUDES *that for augmentation of breast (85.51-85.52)*

85.93 **Revision of implant of breast**
AHA: 2Q, '98, 14; 4Q, '95, 76

85.94 **Removal of implant of breast**
AHA: 2Q, '98, 14; 3Q, '92, 4

85.95 **Insertion of breast tissue expander**
Insertion (soft tissue) of tissue expander (one or more) under muscle or platysma to develop skin flaps for donor use

85.96 **Removal of breast tissue expander(s)**
AHA: 2Q, '00, 18; 4Q, '95, 77

85.99 **Other**

✓3rd 86 **Operations on skin and subcutaneous tissue**
INCLUDES operations on:
hair follicles
male perineum
nails
sebaceous glands
operations on:
subcutaneous fat pads
sudoriferous glands
superficial fossae

EXCLUDES *those on skin of:*
anus (49.01-49.99)
breast (mastectomy site) (85.0-85.99)
ear (18.01-18.9)
eyebrow (08.01-08.99)
eyelid (08.01-08.99)
female perineum (71.01-71.9)
lips (27.0-27.99)
nose (21.00-21.99)
penis (64.0-64.99)
scrotum (61.0-61.99)
vulva (71.01-71.9)

✓4th 86.0 **Incision of skin and subcutaneous tissue**

86.01 **Aspiration of skin and subcutaneous tissue**
Aspiration of:
abscess, hematoma, seroma } of nail, skin, or subcutaneous tissue
AHA: 3Q, '89, 16

86.02 **Injection or tattooing of skin lesion or defect**
Insertion, Injection } of filling material
Pigmenting of skin
DEF: Pigmenting of skin: Adding color to skin.

86.03 **Incision of pilonidal sinus or cyst**
EXCLUDES *marsupialization (86.21)*

86.04 **Other incision with drainage of skin and subcutaneous tissue**
EXCLUDES *drainage of:*
fascial compartments of face and mouth (27.0)
palmar or thenar space (82.04)
pilonidal sinus or cyst (86.03)
AHA: 4Q, '04, 76

86.05 **Incision with removal of foreign body or device from skin and subcutaneous tissue**
Removal of loop recorder
Removal of neurostimulator pulse generator (single array, dual array)
Removal of tissue expander(s) from skin or soft tissue other than breast tissue
EXCLUDES *removal of foreign body without incision (98.20-98.29)*
AHA: 2Q, '96, 15; N-D, '87, 10; N-D, '86, 9

86.06 Insertion of totally implantable infusion pump
Code also any associated catheterization
EXCLUDES *insertion of totally implantable vascular access device (86.07)*
AHA: 2Q, '99, 4; 4Q, '90, 14

86.07 Insertion of totally implantable vascular access device [VAD]
Totally implanted port
EXCLUDES *insertion of totally implantable infusion pump (86.06)*
AHA: 1Q, '01, 13; 1Q, '96, 3; 2Q, '94, 11; 3Q, '91, 13; 4Q, '90, 15

DEF: Placement of vascular access infusion catheter system under skin to allow for frequent manual infusions into blood vessel.

86.09 Other incision of skin and subcutaneous tissue
Creation of thalamic stimulator pulse generator pocket, new site
Escharotomy
Exploration:
sinus tract, skin
superficial fossa
Relocation of subcutaneous device pocket NEC
Reopening subcutaneous pocket for device revision without replacement
Undercutting of hair follicle
EXCLUDES *that of:*
cardiac pacemaker pocket, new site (37.79)
creation of loop recorder pocket, new site and insertion/relocation of device (37.79)
creation of pocket for implantable, patient-activated cardiac event recorder and insertion/relocation of device (37.79)
fascial compartments of face and mouth (27.0)
removal of catheter from cranial cavity (01.27)
AHA: 1Q, '05, 17; 2Q, '04, 7, 8; 4Q, '00, 68; 4Q, '99, 21; 4Q, '97, 57; 3Q, '89, 17; N-D, '86, 1; N-D, '84, 6

✓4th **86.1 Diagnostic procedures on skin and subcutaneous tissue**

86.11 Biopsy of skin and subcutaneous tissue

86.19 Other diagnostic procedures on skin and subcutaneous tissue
EXCLUDES *microscopic examination of specimen from skin and subcutaneous tissue (91.61-91.79)*

✓4th **86.2 Excision or destruction of lesion or tissue of skin and subcutaneous tissue**

86.21 Excision of pilonidal cyst or sinus
Marsupialization of cyst
EXCLUDES *incision of pilonidal cyst or sinus (86.03)*

DEF: Marsupialization of cyst: Incision of cyst and suturing edges to skin to open site.

86.22 Excisional debridement of wound, infection, or burn
Removal by excision of:
devitalized tissue
necrosis
slough
EXCLUDES *debridement of:*
abdominal wall (wound) (54.3)
bone (77.60-77.69)
muscle (83.45)
of hand (82.36)
nail (bed) (fold) (86.27)
nonexcisional debridement of wound, infection, or burn (86.28)
open fracture site (79.60-79.69)
pedicle or flap graft (86.75)
AHA: 1Q, '05, 14; 4Q, '04, 138; 3Q,'02, 23; 2Q, '00, 9; 1Q, '99, 8; 2Q, '92, 17; 3Q, '91, 18; 3Q, '89, 16; 4Q, '88, 5; N-D, '86, 1

86.23 Removal of nail, nailbed, or nail fold

86.24 Chemosurgery of skin
Chemical peel of skin

DEF: Chemicals applied to destroy skin tissue.

DEF: Chemical peel of skin: Chemicals used to peel skin layers.

86.25 Dermabrasion
That with laser
EXCLUDES *dermabrasion of wound to remove embedded debris (86.28)*

DEF: Removal of wrinkled or scarred skin; with fine sandpaper, wire, brushes or laser.

86.26 Ligation of dermal appendage
EXCLUDES *excision of preauricular appendage (18.29)*

DEF: Tying off extra skin.

86.27 Debridement of nail, nail bed, or nail fold
Removal of:
necrosis
slough
EXCLUDES *removal of nail, nail bed, or nail fold (86.23)*

86.28 Nonexcisional debridement of wound, infection, or burn
Debridement NOS
Maggot therapy
Removal of devitalized tissue, necrosis, and slough by such methods as:
brushing
irrigation (under pressure)
scrubbing
washing
▶Water scalpel (jet)◀
AHA: 1Q, '05, 14; 2Q, '04, 5, 6; 4Q, '03, 110; 2Q, '03, 15; 3Q, '02, 23; 2Q, '01, 18; 3Q, '91, 18; 4Q, '88, 5

DEF: Removal of damaged skin; by methods other than excision.

86.3 Other local excision or destruction of lesion or tissue of skin and subcutaneous tissue
Destruction of skin by:
cauterization
cryosurgery
fulguration
laser beam
That with Z-plasty
EXCLUDES *adipectomy (86.83)*
biopsy of skin (86.11)
wide or radical excision of skin (86.4)
Z-plasty without excision (86.84)
AHA: 1Q, '96, 15; 2Q, '90, 27; 1Q, '89, 12; 3Q, '89, 18; 4Q, '88, 7

Operations on the Integumentary System 86.06–86.3

86.4 Radical excision of skin lesion
Wide excision of skin lesion involving underlying or adjacent structure
Code also any lymph node dissection (40.3-40.5)

✓4th **86.5 Suture or other closure of skin and subcutaneous tissue**

86.51 Replantation of scalp

86.59 Closure of skin and subcutaneous tissue of other sites
Adhesives (surgical) (tissue)
Staples
Sutures
EXCLUDES *application of adhesive strips (butterfly) — omit code*
AHA: 4Q, '99, 23

✓4th **86.6 Free skin graft**
INCLUDES excision of skin for autogenous graft
EXCLUDES *construction or reconstruction of:*
penis (64.43-64.44)
trachea (31.75)
vagina (70.61-70.62)
DEF: Transplantation of skin to another site.

86.60 Free skin graft, not otherwise specified

86.61 Full-thickness skin graft to hand
EXCLUDES *heterograft (86.65)*
homograft (86.66)

86.62 Other skin graft to hand
EXCLUDES *heterograft (86.65)*
homograft (86.66)

86.63 Full-thickness skin graft to other sites
EXCLUDES *heterograft (86.65)*
homograft (86.66)

86.64 Hair transplant
EXCLUDES *hair follicle transplant to eyebrow or eyelash (08.63)*

86.65 Heterograft to skin
Pigskin graft
Porcine graft
EXCLUDES *application of dressing only (93.57)*
AHA: 3Q,'02, 23
DEF: Implantation of nonhuman tissue.

86.66 Homograft to skin
Graft to skin of:
amnionic membrane } from donor
skin } from donor
DEF: Implantation of tissue from human donor.

86.67 Dermal regenerative graft
Artificial skin, NOS
Creation of "neodermis"
Decellularized allodermis
Integumentary matrix implants
Prosthetic implant of dermal layer of skin
Regenerate dermal layer of skin
EXCLUDES *heterograft to skin (86.65)*
homograft to skin (86.66)
AHA: 4Q, '98, 76, 79
DEF: Replacement of dermis and epidermal layer of skin by cultured or regenerated autologous tissue; used to treat full-thickness or deep partial-thickness burns; also called cultured epidermal autograft (CEA).

86.69 Other skin graft to other sites
EXCLUDES *heterograft (86.65)*
homograft (86.66)
AHA: 4Q, '99, 15

✓4th **86.7 Pedicle grafts or flaps**
EXCLUDES *construction or reconstruction of:*
penis (64.43-64.44)
trachea (31.75)
vagina (70.61-70.62)
DEF: Full thickness skin and subcutaneous tissue partially attached to the body by a narrow strip of tissue so that it retains its blood supply. The unattached portion is sutured to the defect.

86.70 Pedicle or flap graft, not otherwise specified

86.71 Cutting and preparation of pedicle grafts or flaps
Elevation of pedicle from its bed
Flap design and raising
Partial cutting of pedicle or tube
Pedicle delay
EXCLUDES *pollicization or digital transfer (82.61,82.81)*
revision of pedicle (86.75)
AHA: 4Q, '01, 66
DEF: Elevation of pedicle from its bed: Separation of tissue implanted from its bed.
DEF: Flap design and raising: Planing and elevation of tissue to be implanted.
DEF: Pedicle delay: Elevation and preparation of tissue still attached to vascular bed; delayed implant.

86.72 Advancement of pedicle graft
AHA: 3Q, '99, 9, 10

86.73 Attachment of pedicle or flap graft to hand
EXCLUDES *pollicization or digital transfer (82.61, 82.81)*

86.74 Attachment of pedicle or flap graft to other sites
Attachment by:
advanced flap
double pedicled flap
pedicle graft
Attachment by:
rotating flap
sliding flap
tube graft
AHA: 3Q, '99, 9; 1Q, '96, 15
DEF: Attachment by:
Advanced flap: Sliding tissue implant into new position.
Double pedicle flap: Implant connected to two vascular beds.
Pedicle graft: Implant connected to vascular bed.
Rotating flap: Implant rotated along curved incision.
Sliding flap: Sliding implant to site.
Tube graft: Double tissue implant to form tube with base connected to original site.

86.75 Revision of pedicle or flap graft
Debridement } of pedicle or flap graft
Defatting } of pedicle or flap graft
DEF: Connection of implant still attached to its vascular tissue.

✓4th **86.8 Other repair and reconstruction of skin and subcutaneous tissue**
DEF: Revision and tightening of excess, wrinkled facial skin.

86.81 Repair for facial weakness

86.82 Facial rhytidectomy
Face lift
EXCLUDES *rhytidectomy of eyelid (08.86-08.87)*

86.83 Size reduction plastic operation
Liposuction
Reduction of adipose tissue of:
abdominal wall (pendulous)
arms (batwing)
buttock
thighs (trochanteric lipomatosis)
EXCLUDES *breast (85.31-85.32)*
DEF: Excision and plastic repair of excess skin and underlying tissue.

86.84 Relaxation of scar or web contracture of skin
Z-plasty of skin
EXCLUDES *Z-plasty with excision of lesion (86.3)*

86.85 Correction of syndactyly
DEF: Plastic repair of webbed fingers or toes.

86.86 Onychoplasty
DEF: Plastic repair of nail or nail bed.

86.89 Other repair and reconstruction of skin and subcutaneous tissue
EXCLUDES *mentoplasty (76.67-76.68)*
AHA: 4Q, '02, 107; 1Q, '00, 26; 2Q, '98, 20; 2Q, '93, 11; 2Q, '92, 17

✓4th **86.9 Other operations on skin and subcutaneous tissue**

86.91 Excision of skin for graft
Excision of skin with closure of donor site
EXCLUDES *that with graft at same operative episode (86.60-86.69)*

86.92 Electrolysis and other epilation of skin
EXCLUDES *epilation of eyelid (08.91-08.93)*

86.93 Insertion of tissue expander
Insertion (subcutaneous) (soft tissue) of expander (one or more) in scalp (subgaleal space), face, neck, trunk except breast, and upper and lower extremities for development of skin flaps for donor use
EXCLUDES *flap graft preparation (86.71)*
tissue expander, breast (85.95)

86.94 Insertion or replacement of single array neurostimulator pulse generator, not specified as rechargeable
Pulse generator (single array, single channel) for intracranial, spinal, and peripheral neurostimulator
Code also any associated lead implantation (02.93, 03.93, 04.92)
EXCLUDES *insertion or replacement of single array rechargeable neurostimulator pulse generator (86.97)*
AHA: 4Q, '04, 135

86.95 Insertion or replacement of dual array neurostimulator pulse generator, not specified as rechargeable
Pulse generator (dual array, dual channel) for intracranial, spinal, and peripheral neurostimulator
Code also any associated lead implantation (02.93, 03.93, 04.92)
EXCLUDES *insertion or replacement of dual array rechargeable neurostimulator pulse generator (86.98)*

86.96 Insertion or replacement of other neurostimulator pulse generator
Code also any associated lead implantation (02.93, 03.93, 04.92)
EXCLUDES *insertion of dual array neurostimulator pulse generator (86.95, 86.98)*
insertion of single array neurostimulator pulse generator (86.94, 86.97)

86.97 Insertion or replacement of single array rechargeable neurostimulator pulse generator
Rechargeable pulse generator (single array, single channel) for intracranial, spinal, and peripheral neurostimulator
Code also any associated lead implantation (02.93, 03.93, 04.92)
AHA: ▶4Q, '05, 130◀

86.98 Insertion or replacement of dual array rechargeable neurostimulator pulse generator
Rechargeable pulse generator (dual array, dual channel) for intracranial, spinal, and peripheral neurostimulator
Code also any associated lead implantation (02.93, 03.93, 04.92)
AHA: ▶4Q, '05, 130◀

86.99 Other
EXCLUDES *removal of sutures from:*
abdomen (97.83)
head and neck (97.38)
thorax (97.43)
trunk NEC (97.84)
wound catheter:
irrigation (96.58)
replacement (97.15)
AHA: 4Q, '97, 57; N-D, '86, 1

16. MISCELLANEOUS DIAGNOSTIC AND THERAPEUTIC PROCEDURES (87-99)

✓3rd **87 Diagnostic radiology**

✓4th **87.0 Soft tissue x-ray of face, head, and neck**

EXCLUDES *angiography (88.40-88.68)*

87.01 Pneumoencephalogram

DEF: Radiographic exam of cerebral ventricles and subarachnoid spaces; with injection of air or gas for contrast.

87.02 Other contrast radiogram of brain and skull

Pneumocisternogram
Pneumoventriculogram
Posterior fossa myelogram

DEF: Pneumocisternogram: radiographic exam of subarachnoid spaces after injection of gas or contrast.

DEF: Pneumoventriculography: radiographic exam of cerebral ventricles after injection of gas or contrast.

DEF: Posterior fossa myelogram: radiographic exam of posterior channel of spinal cord after injection of gas or contrast.

87.03 Computerized axial tomography of head

C.A.T. scan of head

AHA: ▶3Q, '05, 12;◀ 3Q, '99, 7

87.04 Other tomography of head

87.05 Contrast dacryocystogram

DEF: Radiographic exam of tear sac after injection of contrast.

87.06 Contrast radiogram of nasopharynx

87.07 Contrast laryngogram

87.08 Cervical lymphangiogram

DEF: Radiographic exam of lymph vessels of neck; with or without contrast.

87.09 Other soft tissue x-ray of face, head, and neck

Noncontrast x-ray of:
- adenoid
- larynx
- nasolacrimal duct
- nasopharynx

Noncontrast x-ray of:
- salivary gland
- thyroid region
- uvula

EXCLUDES *x-ray study of eye (95.14)*

✓4th **87.1 Other x-ray of face, head, and neck**

EXCLUDES *angiography (88.40-88.68)*

87.11 Full-mouth x-ray of teeth

87.12 Other dental x-ray

Orthodontic cephalogram or cephalometrics
Panorex examination of mandible
Root canal x-ray

87.13 Temporomandibular contrast arthrogram

87.14 Contrast radiogram of orbit

87.15 Contrast radiogram of sinus

87.16 Other x-ray of facial bones

X-ray of:
- frontal area
- mandible
- maxilla
- nasal sinuses
- nose

X-ray of:
- orbit
- supraorbital area
- symphysis menti
- zygomaticomaxillary complex

87.17 Other x-ray of skull

Lateral projection } of skull
Sagittal projection } of skull
Tangential projection } of skull

DEF: Lateral projection: Side to side view of head.

DEF: Sagittal projection: View of body in plane running midline from front to back.

DEF: Tangential projection: Views from adjacent skull surfaces.

✓4th **87.2 X-ray of spine**

87.21 Contrast myelogram

DEF: Radiographic exam of space between middle and outer spinal cord coverings after injection of contrast.

87.22 Other x-ray of cervical spine

87.23 Other x-ray of thoracic spine

87.24 Other x-ray of lumbosacral spine

Sacrococcygeal x-ray

87.29 Other x-ray of spine

Spinal x-ray NOS

✓4th **87.3 Soft tissue x-ray of thorax**

EXCLUDES *angiocardiography (88.50-88.58)*
angiography (88.40-88.68)

87.31 Endotracheal bronchogram

DEF: Radiographic exam of lung, main branch, with contrast introduced through windpipe.

87.32 Other contrast bronchogram

Transcricoid bronchogram

DEF: Transcricoid bronchogram: Radiographic exam of lung, main branch, with contrast introduced through cartilage of neck.

87.33 Mediastinal pneumogram

DEF: Radiographic exam of cavity containing heart, esophagus and adjacent structures.

87.34 Intrathoracic lymphangiogram

DEF: Radiographic exam of lymphatic vessels within chest; with or without contrast.

87.35 Contrast radiogram of mammary ducts

DEF: Radiographic exam of mammary ducts; with contrast.

87.36 Xerography of breast

DEF: Radiographic exam of breast via selenium-coated plates.

87.37 Other mammography

AHA: 3Q, '89, 17; 2Q, '90, 28; N-D, '87, 1

87.38 Sinogram of chest wall

Fistulogram of chest wall

DEF: Fistulogram of chest wall: Radiographic exam of abnormal opening in chest.

87.39 Other soft tissue x-ray of chest wall

✓4th **87.4 Other x-ray of thorax**

EXCLUDES *angiocardiography (88.50-88.58)*
angiography (88.40-88.68)

87.41 Computerized axial tomography of thorax

C.A.T. scan } of thorax
Crystal linea scan of x-ray beam } of thorax
Electronic subtraction } of thorax
Photoelectric response } of thorax
Tomography with use of computer, x-rays, and camera } of thorax

87.42 Other tomography of thorax

Cardiac tomogram

DEF: Radiographic exam of chest plane.

87.43 X-ray of ribs, sternum, and clavicle

Examination for:
- cervical rib
- fracture

87.44 Routine chest x-ray, so described

X-ray of chest NOS

87.49 Other chest x-ray

X-ray of:
- bronchus NOS
- diaphragm NOS
- heart NOS

X-ray of:
- lung NOS
- mediastinum NOS
- trachea NOS

✓4th **87.5 Biliary tract x-ray**

87.51 Percutaneous hepatic cholangiogram

AHA: 2Q, '90, 28; N-D, '87, 1

DEF: Radiographic exam of bile tract of gallbladder; with needle injection of contrast into bile duct of liver.

87.52 Intravenous cholangiogram

DEF: Radiographic exam of bile ducts; with intravenous contrast injection.

87.53 Intraoperative cholangiogram

AHA: 1Q, '96, 12; 2Q, '90, 28; 3Q, '89, 18; 4Q, '88, 7

DEF: Radiographic exam of bile ducts; with contrast; following gallbladder removal.

87.54 Other cholangiogram

87.59 Other biliary tract x-ray

Cholecystogram

✓4th **87.6 Other x-ray of digestive system**

87.61 Barium swallow

87.62 Upper GI series

87.63 Small bowel series

87.64 Lower GI series

87.65 Other x-ray of intestine

87.66 Contrast pancreatogram

87.69 Other digestive tract x-ray

✓4th **87.7 X-ray of urinary system**

EXCLUDES *angiography of renal vessels (88.45, 88.65)*

87.71 Computerized axial tomography of kidney

C.A.T. scan of kidney

87.72 Other nephrotomogram

DEF: Radiographic exam of kidney plane.

87.73 Intravenous pyelogram

Diuretic infusion pyelogram

DEF: Radiographic exam of lower kidney, with intravenous contrast injection.

DEF: Diuretic infusion pyelogram: Radiographic exam of lower kidney with diuretic contrast.

87.74 Retrograde pyelogram

87.75 Percutaneous pyelogram

87.76 Retrograde cystourethrogram

DEF: Radiographic exam of bladder and urethra with contrast injected through catheter into bladder.

87.77 Other cystogram

87.78 Ileal conduitogram

AHA: M-J, '87, 11

DEF: Radiographic exam of passage created between ureter and artificial opening into abdomen.

87.79 Other x-ray of the urinary system

KUB x-ray

Ureteropyelography

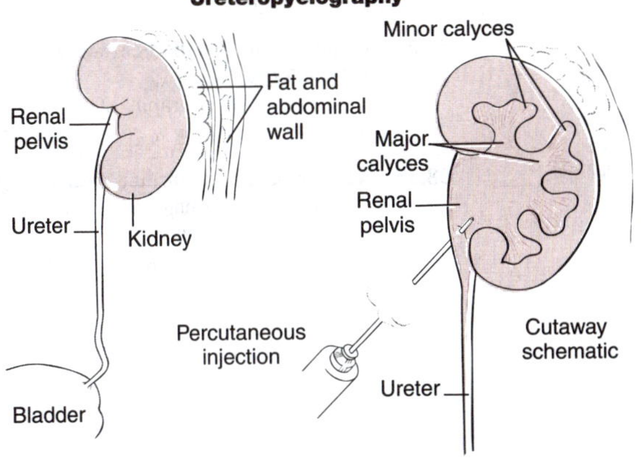

✓4th **87.8 X-ray of female genital organs**

87.81 X-ray of gravid uterus ♀

Intrauterine cephalometry by x-ray

87.82 Gas contrast hysterosalpingogram ♀

DEF: Radiographic exam of uterus and fallopian tubes; with gas contrast.

87.83 Opaque dye contrast hysterosalpingogram ♀

87.84 Percutaneous hysterogram ♀

DEF: Radiographic exam of uterus with contrast injected through body wall.

87.85 Other x-ray of fallopian tubes and uterus ♀

87.89 Other x-ray of female genital organs ♀

✓4th **87.9 X-ray of male genital organs**

87.91 Contrast seminal vesiculogram ♂

87.92 Other x-ray of prostate and seminal vesicles ♂

87.93 Contrast epididymogram ♂

87.94 Contrast vasogram ♂

87.95 Other x-ray of epididymis and vas deferens ♂

87.99 Other x-ray of male genital organs ♂

✓3rd **88 Other diagnostic radiology and related techniques**

✓4th **88.0 Soft tissue x-ray of abdomen**

EXCLUDES *angiography (88.40-88.68)*

88.01 Computerized axial tomography of abdomen

C.A.T. scan of abdomen

EXCLUDES *C.A.T. scan of kidney (87.71)*

AHA: 2Q, '98, 13

88.02 Other abdomen tomography

EXCLUDES *nephrotomogram (87.72)*

88.03 Sinogram of abdominal wall

Fistulogram of abdominal wall

DEF: Radiographic exam of abnormal abdominal passage.

88.04 Abdominal lymphangiogram

DEF: Radiographic exam of abdominal lymphatic vessels; with contrast.

88.09 Other soft tissue x-ray of abdominal wall

✓4th **88.1 Other x-ray of abdomen**

88.11 Pelvic opaque dye contrast radiography

88.12 Pelvic gas contrast radiography

Pelvic pneumoperitoneum

88.13 Other peritoneal pneumogram

88.14 Retroperitoneal fistulogram

88.15 Retroperitoneal pneumogram

88.16 Other retroperitoneal x-ray

88.19 Other x-ray of abdomen

Flat plate of abdomen

AHA: 3Q, '99, 9

✓4th **88.2 Skeletal x-ray of extremities and pelvis**

EXCLUDES *contrast radiogram of joint (88.32)*

88.21 Skeletal x-ray of shoulder and upper arm

88.22 Skeletal x-ray of elbow and forearm

88.23 Skeletal x-ray of wrist and hand

88.24 Skeletal x-ray of upper limb, not otherwise specified

88.25 Pelvimetry

DEF: Imaging of pelvic bones to measure pelvic capacity.

88.26 Other skeletal x-ray of pelvis and hip

88.27 Skeletal x-ray of thigh, knee, and lower leg

88.28 Skeletal x-ray of ankle and foot

88.29 Skeletal x-ray of lower limb, not otherwise specified

✓4th **88.3 Other x-ray**

88.31 Skeletal series

X-ray of whole skeleton

88.32 Contrast arthrogram

EXCLUDES *that of temporomandibular joint (87.13)*

88.33 Other skeletal x-ray

EXCLUDES *skeletal x-ray of:*
extremities and pelvis (88.21-88.29)
face, head, and neck (87.11-87.17)
spine (87.21-87.29)
thorax (87.43)

88.34 Lymphangiogram of upper limb

88.35 Other soft tissue x-ray of upper limb

88.36 Lymphangiogram of lower limb

88.37 Other soft tissue x-ray of lower limb

EXCLUDES *femoral angiography (88.48, 88.66)*

88.38 Other computerized axial tomography

C.A.T. scan NOS

EXCLUDES *C.A.T. scan of:*
abdomen (88.01)
head (87.03)
kidney (87.71)
thorax (87.41)

AHA: ▶3Q, '05, 13-14◀

88.39 X-ray, other and unspecified

✓4th **88.4 Arteriography using contrast material**

Note: The fourth-digit subclassification identifies the site to be viewed, not the site of injection.

INCLUDES angiography of arteries
arterial puncture for injection of contrast material
radiography of arteries (by fluoroscopy)
retrograde arteriography

EXCLUDES *arteriography using:*
radioisotopes or radionuclides (92.01-92.19)
ultrasound (88.71-88.79)
fluorescein angiography of eye (95.12)

AHA: N-D, '85, 14

DEF: Electromagnetic wave photography of arteries; with contrast.

88.40 Arteriography using contrast material, unspecified site

88.41 Arteriography of cerebral arteries

Angiography of:
basilar artery
carotid (internal)
posterior cerebral circulation
vertebral artery

AHA: 1Q, '00, 16; 1Q, '99, 7; 1Q, '97, 3

88.42 Aortography

Arteriography of aorta and aortic arch

AHA: 1Q, '99, 17

88.43 Arteriography of pulmonary arteries

88.44 Arteriography of other intrathoracic vessels

EXCLUDES *angiocardiography (88.50-88.58)*
arteriography of coronary arteries (88.55-88.57)

88.45 Arteriography of renal arteries

88.46 Arteriography of placenta ♀

Placentogram using contrast material

88.47 Arteriography of other intra-abdominal arteries

AHA: 1Q, '00, 18; N-D, '87, 4

88.48 Arteriography of femoral and other lower extremity arteries

AHA: 3Q, '03, 10; 1Q, '03, 17; 2Q, '96, 6; 2Q, '89, 17

88.49 Arteriography of other specified sites

✓4th **88.5 Angiocardiography using contrast material**

INCLUDES arterial puncture and insertion of arterial catheter for injection of contrast material
cineangiocardiography
selective angiocardiography

Code also synchronous cardiac catheterization (37.21-37.23)

EXCLUDES *angiography of pulmonary vessels (88.43, 88.62)*

AHA: 3Q, '92, 10; M-J, '87, 11

DEF: Electromagnetic wave photography of heart and great vessels; with contrast.

88.50 Angiocardiography, not otherwise specified

88.51 Angiocardiography of venae cavae

Inferior vena cavography
Phlebography of vena cava (inferior) (superior)

88.52 Angiocardiography of right heart structures

Angiocardiography of:
pulmonary valve
right atrium
right ventricle (outflow tract)

EXCLUDES *that combined with left heart angiocardiography (88.54)*

88.53 Angiocardiography of left heart structures

Angiocardiography of:
aortic valve
left atrium
left ventricle (outflow tract)

EXCLUDES *that combined with right heart angiocardiography (88.54)*

AHA: ▶4Q, '05, 71; 3Q, '05, 14;◀ 1Q, '00, 20; 4Q, '88, 4

88.54 Combined right and left heart angiocardiography

88.55 Coronary arteriography using a single catheter

Coronary arteriography by Sones technique
Direct selective coronary arteriography using a single catheter

AHA: 3Q, '02, 20

88.56 Coronary arteriography using two catheters

Coronary arteriography by:
Judkins technique
Ricketts and Abrams technique
Direct selective coronary arteriography using two catheters

AHA: 1Q, '00, 20; 4Q, '88, 4

88.57 Other and unspecified coronary arteriography

Coronary arteriography NOS

AHA: ▶4Q, '05, 71; 3Q, '05, 14; 2Q, '05, 17;◀ 1Q, '00, 21

88.58 Negative-contrast cardiac roentgenography

Cardiac roentgenography with injection of carbon dioxide

✓4th **88.6 Phlebography**

Note: The fourth-digit subclassification (88.60-88.67) identifies the site to be viewed, not the site of injection.

INCLUDES angiography of veins
radiography of veins (by fluoroscopy)
retrograde phlebography
venipuncture for injection of contrast material
venography using contrast material

EXCLUDES *angiography using:*
radioisotopes or radionuclides (92.01-92.19)
ultrasound (88.71-88.79)
fluorescein angiography of eye (95.12)

DEF: Electromagnetic wave photography of veins; with contrast.

88.60 Phlebography using contrast material, unspecified site

88.61 Phlebography of veins of head and neck using contrast material

88.62 Phlebography of pulmonary veins using contrast material

88.63 Phlebography of other intrathoracic veins using contrast material

88.64 Phlebography of the portal venous system using contrast material
Splenoportogram (by splenic arteriography)

88.65 Phlebography of other intra-abdominal veins using contrast material

88.66 Phlebography of femoral and other lower extremity veins using contrast material

88.67 Phlebography of other specified sites using contrast material

88.68 Impedance phlebography

✓4th **88.7 Diagnostic ultrasound**

INCLUDES echography
non-invasive ultrasound
ultrasonic angiography
ultrasonography

EXCLUDES *intravascular imaging (adjunctive) (IVUS) (00.21-00.29)*
therapeutic ultrasound (00.01-00.09)

DEF: Graphic recording of anatomical structures via high frequency, sound-wave imaging and computer graphics.

88.71 Diagnostic ultrasound of head and neck
Determination of midline shift of brain
Echoencephalography
EXCLUDES *eye (95.13)*
AHA: 1Q, '02, 10; 1Q, '92, 11

88.72 Diagnostic ultrasound of heart
Echocardiography
Transesophageal echocardiography
EXCLUDES *echocardiography of heart chambers (37.28)*
intracardiac echocardiography (ICE) (37.28)
intravascular (IVUS) imaging of coronary vessels (00.24)
AHA: ▶3Q, '05, 14; 2Q, '05, 17;◀ 4Q, '04, 121; 1Q, '04, 16; 1Q, '00, 20, 21; 1Q, '99, 6; 3Q, '98, 11

88.73 Diagnostic ultrasound of other sites of thorax
Aortic arch, Breast, Lung } ultrasonography

88.74 Diagnostic ultrasound of digestive system

88.75 Diagnostic ultrasound of urinary system

88.76 Diagnostic ultrasound of abdomen and retroperitoneum
AHA: 2Q, '99, 14

88.77 Diagnostic ultrasound of peripheral vascular system
Deep vein thrombosis ultrasonic scanning
EXCLUDES *adjunct vascular system procedures (00.40-00.43)*
AHA: 4Q, '99, 17; 1Q, '99, 12; 1Q, '92, 11

88.78 Diagnostic ultrasound of gravid uterus ♀
Intrauterine cephalometry:
echo
ultrasonic
Placental localization by ultrasound

88.79 Other diagnostic ultrasound
Ultrasonography of:
multiple sites
nongravid uterus
total body

✓4th **88.8 Thermography**

DEF: Infrared photography to determine various body temperatures.

88.81 Cerebral thermography

88.82 Ocular thermography

88.83 Bone thermography
Osteoarticular thermography

88.84 Muscle thermography

88.85 Breast thermography

88.86 Blood vessel thermography
Deep vein thermography

88.89 Thermographay of other sites
Lymph gland thermography
Thermography NOS

✓4th **88.9 Other diagnostic imaging**

88.90 Diagnostic imaging, not elsewhere classified

88.91 Magnetic resonance imaging of brain and brain stem
EXCLUDES *intraoperative magnetic resonance imaging (88.96)*
real-time magnetic resonance imaging (88.96)

88.92 Magnetic resonance imaging of chest and myocardium
For evaluation of hilar and mediastinal lymphadenopathy

88.93 Magnetic resonance imaging of spinal canal
Spinal cord levels:
cervical
thoracic
lumbar (lumbosacral)
Spinal cord
Spine

88.94 Magnetic resonance imaging of musculoskeletal
Bone marrow blood supply
Extremities (upper) (lower)

88.95 Magnetic resonance imaging of pelvis, prostate, and bladder

88.96 Other intraoperative magnetic resonance imaging
iMRI
Real-time magnetic resonance imaging
AHA: 4Q, '02, 111

88.97 Magnetic resonance imaging of other and unspecified sites
Abdomen
Eye orbit
Face
Neck

88.98 Bone mineral density studies
Dual photon absorptiometry
Quantitative computed tomography (CT) studies
Radiographic densitometry
Single photon absorptiometry
DEF: Dual photon absorptiometry: Measurement of bone mineral density by comparing dissipation of emission from two separate photoelectric energy peaks.
DEF: Quantitative computed tomography (CT) studies: Computer assisted analysis of x-ray absorption through bone to determine density.
DEF: Radiographic densiometry: Measurement of bone mineral density by degree of bone radiopacity.
DEF: Single photon absorptiometry: Measurement of bone mineral density by degree of dissipation of emission from one photoelectric energy peaks emitted by gadolinium 153.

✓3rd **89 Interview, evaluation, consultation, and examination**

✓4th **89.0 Diagnostic interview, consultation, and evaluation**
EXCLUDES *psychiatric diagnostic interview (94.11-94.19)*

89.01 Interview and evaluation, described as brief
Abbreviated history and evaluation

89.02 Interview and evaluation, described as limited
Interval history and evaluation

89.03 Interview and evaluation, described as comprehensive
History and evaluation of new problem

89.04 Other interview and evaluation

89.05 Diagnostic interview and evaluation, not otherwise specified

89.06 Consultation, described as limited
Consultation on a single organ system

89.07 Consultation, described as comprehensive

89.08 Other consultation

89.09 Consulation, not otherwise specified

✓4th **89.1 Anatomic and physiologic measurements and manual examinations — nervous system and sense organs**
EXCLUDES *ear examination (95.41-95.49)*
eye examination (95.01-95.26)
the listed procedures when done as part of a general physical examination (89.7)

89.10 Intracarotid amobarbital test
Wada test
DEF: Amobarbital injections into internal carotid artery to induce hemiparalysis to determine the hemisphere that controls speech and language.

89.11 Tonometry
DEF: Pressure measurements inside eye.

89.12 Nasal function study
Rhinomanometry
DEF: Rhinomanometry: Measure of degree of nasal cavity obstruction.

89.13 Neurologic examination

89.14 Electroencephalogram
EXCLUDES *that with polysomnogram (89.17)*
AHA: ▶3Q, '05, 12◀
DEF: Recording of electrical currents in brain via electrodes to detect epilepsy, lesions and other encephalopathies.

89.15 Other nonoperative neurologic function tests
AHA: 3Q, '95, 5; 2Q, '91, 14; J-F, '87, 16; N-D, '84, 6

89.16 Transillumination of newborn skull
DEF: Light passed through newborn skull for diagnostic purposes.

89.17 Polysomnogram
Sleep recording
DEF: Graphic studies of sleep patterns.

89.18 Other sleep disorder function tests
Multiple sleep latency test [MSLT]

89.19 Video and radio-telemetered electroencephalographic monitoring
Radiographic } EEG Monitoring
Video }
AHA: 1Q, '92, 17; 2Q, '90, 27

✓4th **89.2 Anatomic and physiologic measurements and manual examinations — genitourinary system**
EXCLUDES *the listed procedures when done as part of a general physical examination (89.7)*
AHA: 1Q, '90, 27

89.21 Urinary manometry
Manometry through:
indwelling ureteral catheter
nephrostomy
pyelostomy
ureterostomy
DEF: Measurement of urinary pressure.
DEF: Manometry through:
Indwelling urinary catheter: Semipermanent urinary catheter.
Nephrostomy: Opening into pelvis of kidney.
Pyelostomy: Opening in lower kidney.
Ureterostomy: Opening into ureter.

89.22 Cystometrogram
DEF: Pressure recordings at various stages of bladder filling.

89.23 Urethral sphincter electromyogram

89.24 Uroflowmetry [UFR]
DEF: Continuous recording of urine flow.

89.25 Urethral pressure profile [UPP]

89.26 Gynecological examination ♀
Pelvic examination

89.29 Other nonoperative genitourinary system measurements
Bioassay of urine
Urine chemistry
Renal clearance
AHA: N-D, '84, 6

✓4th **89.3 Other anatomic and physiologic measurements and manual examinations**
EXCLUDES *the listed procedures when done as part of a general physical examination (89.7)*

89.31 Dental examination
Oral mucosal survey
Periodontal survey

89.32 Esophageal manometry
AHA: 3Q, '96, 13
DEF: Measurement of esophageal fluid and gas pressures.

89.33 Digital examination of enterostomy stoma
Digital examination of colostomy stoma

89.34 Digital examination of rectum

89.35 Transillumination of nasal sinuses

89.36 Manual examination of breast

89.37 Vital capacity determination
DEF: Measurement of expelled gas volume after full inhalation.

89.38 Other nonoperative respiratory measurements
Plethysmography for measurement of respiratory function
Thoracic impedance plethysmography
AHA: S-O, '87, 6
DEF: Plethysmography for measurement of respiratory function: Registering changes in respiratory function as noted in blood circulation.

89.39 Other nonoperative measurements and examinations
14 C-Urea breath test
Basal metabolic rate [BMR]
Gastric:
analysis
function NEC
EXCLUDES *body measurement (93.07)*
cardiac tests (89.41-89.69)
fundus photography (95.11)
limb length measurement (93.06)
AHA: 2Q, '01, 9; 3Q, '00, 9; 3Q, '96, 12; 1Q, '94, 18; N-D, '84, 6

✓4th **89.4 Cardiac stress tests, pacemaker and defibrillator checks**

89.41 Cardiovascular stress test using treadmill
AHA: 1Q, '88, 11

89.42 Masters' two-step stress test
AHA: 1Q, '88, 11

89.43 Cardiovascular stress test using bicycle ergometer
AHA: 1Q, '88, 11
DEF: Electrocardiogram during exercise on bicycle with device capable of measuring muscular, metabolic and respiratory effects of exercise.

89.44 Other cardiovascular stress test
Thallium stress test with or without transesophageal pacing

89.45 Artificial pacemaker rate check
Artificial pacemaker function check NOS
Bedside device check of pacemaker or cardiac resynchronization pacemaker [CRT-P]
Interrogation only without arrhythmia induction
EXCLUDES ▶ *catheter based invasive electrophysiologic testing (37.26)*◀
non-invasive programmed electrical stimulation [NIPS] (arrhythmia induction) ▶*(37.20)*◀
AHA: 1Q, '02, 3

89.46 Artificial pacemaker artifact wave form check

89.47 Artificial pacemaker electrode impedance check

89.48 Artificial pacemaker voltage or amperage threshold check

89.49 Automatic implantable cardioverter/defibrillator (AICD) check
Bedside check of an AICD or cardiac resynchronization defibrillator [CRT-D]
Checking pacing thresholds of device
Interrogation only without arrhythmia induction
EXCLUDES ▶ *catheter based invasive electrophysiologic testing (37.26)*◀
non-invasive programmed electrical stimulation [NIPS] (arrhythmia induction) ▶*(37.20)*◀
AHA: 4Q, '04, 136

✓4th **89.5 Other nonoperative cardiac and vascular diagnostic procedures**
EXCLUDES *fetal EKG (75.32)*

89.50 Ambulatory cardiac monitoring
Analog devices [Holter-type]
AHA: 4Q, '99, 21; 4Q, '91, 23

89.51 Rhythm electrocardiogram
Rhythm EKG (with one to three leads)

89.52 Electrocardiogram
ECG NOS
EKG (with 12 or more leads)
AHA: 1Q, '88, 11; S-O, '87, 6

89.53 Vectorcardiogram (with ECG)

89.54 Electrographic monitoring
Telemetry
EXCLUDES *ambulatory cardiac monitoring (89.50)*
electrographic monitoring during surgery — omit code
AHA: 4Q, '91, 23; 1Q, '88, 11
DEF: Evaluation of heart electrical activity by continuous screen monitoring.
DEF: Telemetry: Evaluation of heart electrical activity; with radio signals at distance from patient.

89.55 Phonocardiogram with ECG lead

89.56 Carotid pulse tracing with ECG lead
EXCLUDES *oculoplethysmography (89.58)*

89.57 Apexcardiogram (with ECG lead)
AHA: J-F, '87, 16

89.58 Plethysmogram
Penile plethysmography with nerve stimulation
EXCLUDES *plethysmography (for):*
measurement of respiratory function (89.38)
thoracic impedance (89.38)
AHA: S-O, '87, 7
DEF: Determination and recording of blood pressure variations present or passing through an organ.

89.59 Other nonoperative cardiac and vascular measurements
AHA: 3Q, '05, 21; 3Q, '03, 23; 2Q, '92, 12

✓4th **89.6 Circulatory monitoring**
EXCLUDES *electrocardiographic monitoring during surgery — omit code*
▶*implantation or replacement of subcutaneous device for intracardiac hemodynamic monitoring (00.57)*
insertion or replacement of implantable pressure sensor (lead) for intracardiac hemodynamic monitoring (00.56)◀
AHA: M-J, '87, 11

89.60 Continuous intra-arterial blood gas monitoring
Insertion of blood gas monitoring system and continuous monitoring of blood gases through an intra-arterial sensor
AHA: 4Q, '02, 111

89.61 Systemic arterial pressure monitoring

89.62 Central venous pressure monitoring

89.63 Pulmonary artery pressure monitoring
EXCLUDES *pulmonary artery wedge monitoring (89.64)*

89.64 Pulmonary artery wedge monitoring
Pulmonary capillary wedge [PCW] monitoring
Swan-Ganz catheterization
DEF: Monitoring pulmonary artery pressure via catheter inserted through right lower and upper heart chambers into pulmonary artery and advancing the balloon-tip to wedge it in the distal pulmonary artery branch.

Central Venous Pressure Monitoring

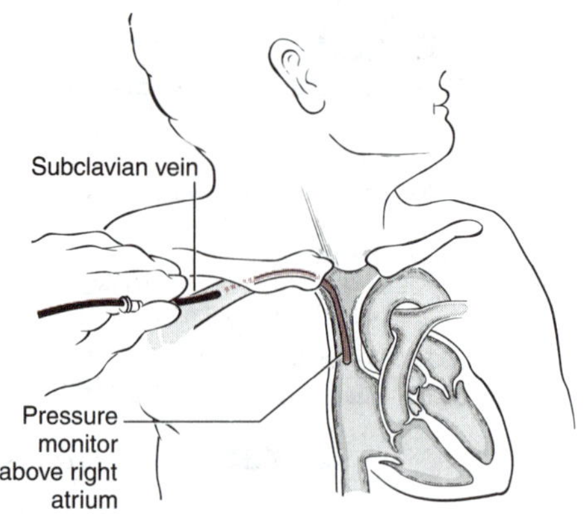

89.65 **Measurement of systemic arterial blood gases**
EXCLUDES *continuous intra-arterial blood gas monitoring (89.60)*

89.66 **Measurement of mixed venous blood gases**

89.67 **Monitoring of cardiac output by oxygen consumption technique**
Fick method
DEF: Fick method: Indirect measure of cardiac output through blood volume flow over pulmonary capillaries; determines oxygen absorption by measurement of arterial oxygen content versus venous oxygen content.

89.68 **Monitoring of cardiac output by other technique**
Cardiac output monitor by thermodilution indicator
DEF: Cardiac output monitor by thermodilution indicator: Injection of ice cold dextrose solution into right lower heart chamber; temperature sensitive catheter monitors disappearance from beat to beat to measure expelled blood volume.

89.69 **Monitoring of coronary blood flow**
Coronary blood flow monitoring by coincidence counting technique

89.7 **General physical examination**

89.8 **Autopsy**

✓3rd 90 **Microscopic examination - I**

The following fourth-digit subclassification is for use with categories in section 90 to identify type of examination:

1 **bacterial smear**
2 **culture**
3 **culture and sensitivity**
4 **parasitology**
5 **toxicology**
6 **cell block and Papanicolaou smear**
9 **other microscopic examination**

✓4th 90.0 **Microscopic examination of specimen from nervous system and of spinal fluid**

✓4th 90.1 **Microscopic examination of specimen from endocrine gland, not elsewhere classified**

✓4th 90.2 **Microscopic examination of specimen from eye**

✓4th 90.3 **Microscopic examination of specimen from ear, nose, throat, and larynx**

✓4th 90.4 **Microscopic examination of specimen from trachea, bronchus, pleura, lung, and other thoracic specimen, and of sputum**

✓4th 90.5 **Microscopic examination of blood**

✓4th 90.6 **Microscopic examination of specimen from spleen and of bone marrow**

✓4th 90.7 **Microscopic examination of specimen from lymph node and of lymph**

✓4th 90.8 **Microscopic examination of specimen from upper gastrointestinal tract and of vomitus**

✓4th 90.9 **Microscopic examination of specimen from lower gastrointestinal tract and of stool**

✓3rd 91 **Microscopic examination - II**

The following fourth-digit subclassification is for use with categories in section 91 to identify type of examination:

1 **bacterial smear**
2 **culture**
3 **culture and sensitivity**
4 **parasitology**
5 **toxicology**
6 **cell block and Papanicolaou smear**
9 **other microscopic examination**

✓4th 91.0 **Microscopic examination of specimen from liver, biliary tract, and pancreas**

✓4th 91.1 **Microscopic examination of peritoneal and retroperitoneal specimen**

✓4th 91.2 **Microscopic examination of specimen from kidney, ureter, perirenal and periureteral tissue**

✓4th 91.3 **Microscopic examination of specimen from bladder, urethra, prostate, seminal vesicle, perivesical tissue, and of urine and semen**

✓4th 91.4 **Microscopic examination of specimen from female genital tract** ♀
Amnionic sac
Fetus

✓4th 91.5 **Microscopic examination of specimen from musculoskeletal system and of joint fluid**
Microscopic examination of:
bone
bursa
cartilage
fascia
ligament
muscle
synovial membrane
tendon

✓4th 91.6 **Microscopic examination of specimen from skin and other integument**
Microscopic examination of:
hair
nails
skin
EXCLUDES *mucous membrane — code to organ site that of operative wound (91.71-91.79)*

✓4th 91.7 **Microscopic examination of specimen from operative wound**

✓4th 91.8 **Microscopic examination of specimen from other site**

✓4th 91.9 **Microscopic examination of specimen from unspecified site**

✓3rd 92 **Nuclear medicine**

✓4th 92.0 **Radioisotope scan and function study**

92.01 **Thyroid scan and radioisotope function studies**
Iodine-131 uptake
Protein-bound iodine
Radio-iodine uptake

92.02 **Liver scan and radioisotope function study**

92.03 **Renal scan and radioisotope function study**
Renal clearance study

92.04 **Gastrointestinal scan and radioisotope function study**
Radio-cobalt B_{12} Schilling test
Radio-iodinated triolein study

92.05 **Cardiovascular and hematopoietic scan and radioisotope function study**
Bone marrow, Cardiac output, Circulation time, Radionuclide cardiac ventriculogram, Spleen } scan or function study
AHA: 2Q, '92, 7; 1Q, '88, 11

92.09 **Other radioisotope function studies**

BI Bilateral Procedure · NC Non-covered Procedure · LC Limited Coverage Procedure · ▶◀ Revised Text · ● New Code · ▲ Revised Code Title

✓4th **92.1 Other radioisotope scan**

92.11 Cerebral scan
Pituitary

92.12 Scan of other sites of head
EXCLUDES *eye (95.16)*

92.13 Parathyroid scan

92.14 Bone scan

92.15 Pulmonary scan

92.16 Scan of lymphatic system

92.17 Placental scan ♀

92.18 Total body scan

92.19 Scan of other sites

✓4th **92.2 Therapeutic radiology and nuclear medicine**
EXCLUDES *that for:*
ablation of pituitary gland (07.64-07.69)
destruction of chorioretinal lesion (14.26-14.27)

AHA: 3Q, '92, 5

DEF: Radiation and nuclear isotope treatment of diseased tissue.

92.20 Infusion of liquid brachytherapy radioisotope
I-125 radioisotope
Intracavitary brachytherapy
INCLUDES removal of radioisotope
AHA: ▶4Q, '05, 117-118◀

92.21 Superficial radiation
Contact radiation [up to 150 KVP]

92.22 Orthovoltage radiation
Deep radiation [200-300 KVP]

92.23 Radioisotopic teleradiotherapy
Teleradiotherapy using:
cobalt-60
iodine-125
radioactive cesium

92.24 Teleradiotherapy using photons
Megavoltage NOS
Supervoltage NOS
Use of:
Betatron
linear accelerator

92.25 Teleradiotherapy using electrons
Beta particles

92.26 Teleradiotherapy of other particulate radiation
Neutrons
Protons NOS

92.27 Implantation or insertion of radioactive elements
Intravascular brachytherapy
Code also incision of site
EXCLUDES *infusion of liquid brachytherapy radioisotope (92.20)*
AHA: 1Q, '04, 3-4; 1Q, '00, 11, 12; 3Q, '94, 11; 1Q, '88, 4

92.28 Injection or instillation of radioisotopes
Injection or infusion of radioimmunoconjugate
Intracavitary injection or instillation
Intravenous injection or instillation
Iodine-131 [I-131] tositumomab
Radioimmunotherapy
Ytrium-90 [Y-90] ibritumomab tiuxetan
EXCLUDES *infusion of liquid brachytherapy radioisotope (92.20)*

92.29 Other radiotherapeutic procedure

✓4th **92.3 Stereotactic radiosurgery**
Code also stereotactic head frame application (93.59)
EXCLUDES *stereotactic biopsy*
AHA: 4Q, '98, 79; 4Q, '95, 70

DEF: Ablation of deep intracranial lesions; single procedure; placement of head frame for 3-D analysis of lesion, followed by radiation treatment from helmet attached to frame.

92.30 Stereotactic radiosurgery, not otherwise specified

92.31 Single source photon radiosurgery
High energy x-rays
Linear accelerator (LINAC)

92.32 Multi-source photon radiosurgery
Cobalt 60 radiation
Gamma irradiation
AHA: 4Q, '04, 113

92.33 Particulate radiosurgery
Particle beam radiation (cyclotron)
Proton accelerator

92.39 Stereotactic radiosurgery, not elsewhere classified

✓3rd **93 Physical therapy, respiratory therapy, rehabilitation, and related procedures**

✓4th **93.0 Diagnostic physical therapy**
AHA: N-D, '86, 7

93.01 Functional evaluation

93.02 Orthotic evaluation

93.03 Prosthetic evaluation

93.04 Manual testing of muscle function
AHA: J-F, '87, 16

93.05 Range of motion testing
AHA: J-F, '87, 16

93.06 Measurement of limb length

93.07 Body measurement
Girth measurement
Measurement of skull circumference

93.08 Electromyography
EXCLUDES *eye EMG (95.25)*
that with polysomnogram (89.17)
urethral sphincter EMG (89.23)
AHA: J-F, '87, 16

DEF: Graphic recording of electrical activity of muscle.

93.09 Other diagnostic physical therapy procedure

✓4th **93.1 Physical therapy exercises**
AHA: J-F, '87, 16; N-D, '86, 7

93.11 Assisting exercise
EXCLUDES *assisted exercise in pool (93.31)*

93.12 Other active musculoskeletal exercise

93.13 Resistive exercise

93.14 Training in joint movements

93.15 Mobilization of spine

93.16 Mobilization of other joints
EXCLUDES *manipulation of temporomandibular joint (76.95)*

93.17 Other passive musculoskeletal exercise

93.18 Breathing exercise

93.19 Exercise, not elsewhere classified

✓4th **93.2 Other physical therapy musculoskeletal manipulation**
AHA: N-D, '86, 7

93.21 Manual and mechanical traction
EXCLUDES *skeletal traction (93.43-93.44)*
skin traction (93.45-93.46)
spinal traction (93.41-93.42)

93.22 Ambulation and gait training

93.23 Fitting of orthotic device

93.24 Training in use of prosthetic or orthotic device
Training in crutch walking

93.25 Forced extension of limb

93.26 Manual rupture of joint adhesions

DEF: Therapeutic application of force to rupture adhesions restricting movement.

93.27 Stretching of muscle or tendon

93.28 Stretching of fascia

93.29 Other forcible correction of deformity

AHA: N-D, '85, 11

✓4th **93.3 Other physical therapy therapeutic procedures**

93.31 Assisted exercise in pool

93.32 Whirlpool treatment

93.33 Other hydrotherapy

93.34 Diathermy

93.35 Other heat therapy

Acupuncture with smouldering moxa
Hot packs
Hyperthermia NEC
Infrared irradiation
Moxibustion
Paraffin bath

EXCLUDES *hyperthermia for treatment of cancer (99.85)*

DEF: Moxibustion: Igniting moxa, a Chinese plant, for counterirritation of skin.

DEF: Paraffin bath: Hot wax treatment.

93.36 Cardiac retraining

DEF: Cardiac rehabilitation regimen following myocardial infarction or coronary bypass graft procedure.

93.37 Prenatal training

Training for natural childbirth

93.38 Combined physical therapy without mention of the components

93.39 Other physical therapy

AHA: 2Q, '05, 6; 4Q, '03, 105-106, 108-110; 3Q, '97, 12; 3Q, '91, 15

✓4th **93.4 Skeletal traction and other traction**

93.41 Spinal traction using skull device

Traction using:	Traction using:
caliper tongs	halo device
Crutchfield tongs	Vinke tongs

EXCLUDES *insertion of tongs or halo traction device (02.94)*

AHA: 3Q, '01, 8; 3Q, '96, 14; 2Q, '94, 3

DEF: Applying device to head to exert pulling force on spine.

93.42 Other spinal traction

Cotrel's traction

EXCLUDES *cervical collar (93.52)*

DEF: Pulling force exerted on spine without skull device.

93.43 Intermittent skeletal traction

93.44 Other skeletal traction

Bryant's
Dunlop's
Lyman Smith
Russell's
} traction

93.45 Thomas' splint traction

DEF: Thomas splint: Placement of ring around thigh, attached to rods running length of leg for therapeutic purposes.

93.46 Other skin traction of limbs

Adhesive tape traction	Buck's traction
Boot traction	Gallows traction

✓4th **93.5 Other immobilization, pressure, and attention to wound**

EXCLUDES *external fixator device (84.71-84.73)*
wound cleansing (96.58-96.59)

93.51 Application of plaster jacket

EXCLUDES *Minerva jacket (93.52)*

93.52 Application of neck support

Application of:
cervical collar
Minerva jacket
molded neck support

93.53 Application of other cast

93.54 Application of splint

Plaster splint   Tray splint

EXCLUDES *periodontal splint (24.7)*

93.55 Dental wiring

EXCLUDES *that for orthodontia (24.7)*

93.56 Application of pressure dressing

Application of:
Gibney bandage
Robert Jones' bandage
Shanz dressing

93.57 Application of other wound dressing

Porcine wound dressing

AHA: 3Q, '02, 23

93.58 Application of pressure trousers

Application of:
anti-shock trousers
MAST trousers
vasopneumatic device

AHA: 3Q, '96, 13

93.59 Other immobilization, pressure, and attention to wound

Elastic stockings
Electronic gaiter
Intermittent pressure device
Oxygenation of wound (hyperbaric)
Stereotactic head frame application
▶Strapping (non-traction)◀
Velpeau dressing

AHA: 3Q, '99, 7; 1Q, '99, 12, 13; 1Q, '91, 11; 1Q, '89, 12

✓4th **93.6 Osteopathic manipulative treatment**

93.61 Osteopathic manipulative treatment for general mobilization

General articulatory treatment

93.62 Osteopathic manipulative treatment using high-velocity, low-amplitude forces

Thrusting forces

93.63 Osteopathic manipulative treatment using low-velocity, high-amplitude forces

Springing forces

93.64 Osteopathic manipulative treatment using isotonic, isometric forces

93.65 Osteopathic manipulative treatment using indirect forces

93.66 Osteopathic manipulative treatment to move tissue fluids

Lymphatic pump

93.67 Other specified osteopathic manipulative treatment

✓4th **93.7 Speech and reading rehabilitation and rehabilitation of the blind**

93.71 Dyslexia training

93.72 Dysphasia training

DEF: Speech training to coordinate and arrange words in proper sequence.

93.73 Esophageal speech training

DEF: Speech training after voice box removal; sound is produced by vibration of air column in esophagus against the cricopharangeal sphincter.

93.74 Speech defect training

93.75 Other speech training and therapy

AHA: 4Q, '03, 105, 109; 4Q, '97, 36; 3Q, '97, 12

93.76 Training in use of lead dog for the blind

93.77 Training in braille or Moon

93.78 Other rehabilitation for the blind

✓4th **93.8 Other rehabilitation therapy**

93.81 Recreational therapy

Diversional therapy   Play therapy

EXCLUDES *play psychotherapy (94.36)*

93.82 Educational therapy
Education of bed-bound children
Special schooling for the handicapped

93.83 Occupational therapy
Daily living activities therapy
EXCLUDES *training in activities of daily living for the blind (93.78)*
AHA: ▶2Q, '05, 6;◀ 4Q, '03, 105-106, 108, 110; 3Q, '97, 12

93.84 Music therapy

93.85 Vocational rehabilitation
Sheltered employment
Vocational:
assessment
retraining
training

93.89 Rehabilitation, not elsewhere classified
AHA: ▶2Q, '05, 6◀

✓4th **93.9 Respiratory therapy**
EXCLUDES *insertion of airway (96.01-96.05)*
other continuous mechanical ventilation (96.70-96.72)

93.90 Continuous positive airway pressure [CPAP]
Bi-level airway pressure
Non-invasive positive pressure (NIPPV)
AHA: 3Q, '04, 3; 1Q, '02, 12, 13; 3Q, '98, 14; 4Q, '91, 21
DEF: Noninvasive ventilation support system that augments the ability to breathe spontaneously without the insertion of an endotracheal tube or tracheostomy.

93.91 Intermittent positive pressure breathing [IPPB]
AHA: 4Q, '91, 21

93.93 Nonmechanical methods of resuscitation
Artificial respiration
Manual resuscitation
Mouth-to-mouth resuscitition
AHA: 2Q, '03, 17

93.94 Respiratory medication administered by nebulizer
Mist therapy

93.95 Hyperbaric oxygenation
EXCLUDES *oxygenation of wound (93.59)*

93.96 Other oxygen enrichment
Catalytic oxygen therapy
Cytoreductive effect
Oxygenators
Oxygen therapy
EXCLUDES *oxygenation of wound (93.59)*

93.97 Decompression chamber

93.98 Other control of atmospheric pressure and composition
Antigen-free air conditioning
Helium therapy
EXCLUDES *inhaled nitric oxide therapy (INO) (00.12)*
AHA: 1Q, '02, 14

93.99 Other respiratory procedures
Continuous negative pressure ventilation [CNP]
Postural drainage
AHA: 4Q, '03, 108; 3Q, '99, 11; 4Q, '91, 22

✓3rd **94 Procedures related to the psyche**

✓4th **94.0 Psychologic evaluation and testing**

94.01 Administration of intelligence test
Administration of:
Stanford-Binet
Wechsler Adult Intelligence Scale
Wechsler Intelligence Scale for Children

94.02 Administration of psychologic test
Administration of:
Bender Visual-Motor Gestalt Test
Benton Visual Retention Test
Minnesota Multiphasic Personality Inventory
Wechsler Memory Scale

94.03 Character analysis

94.08 Other psychologic evaluation and testing

94.09 Psychologic mental status determination, not otherwise specified

✓4th **94.1 Psychiatric interviews, consultations, and evaluations**

94.11 Psychiatric mental status determination
Clinical psychiatric mental status determination
Evaluation for criminal responsibility
Evaluation for testimentary capacity
Medicolegal mental status determination
Mental status determination NOS

94.12 Routine psychiatric visit, not otherwise specified

94.13 Psychiatric commitment evaluation
Pre-commitment interview

94.19 Other psychiatric interview and evaluation
Follow-up psychiatric interview NOS

✓4th **94.2 Psychiatric somatotherapy**
DEF: Biological treatment of mental disorders.

94.21 Narcoanalysis
Narcosynthesis

94.22 Lithium therapy

94.23 Neuroleptic therapy

94.24 Chemical shock therapy

94.25 Other psychiatric drug therapy
AHA: S-O, '86, 4

94.26 Subconvulsive electroshock therapy

94.27 Other electroshock therapy
Electroconvulsive therapy (ECT)
EST

94.29 Other psychiatric somatotherapy

✓4th **94.3 Individual psychotherapy**

94.31 Psychoanalysis

94.32 Hypnotherapy
Hypnodrome
Hypnosis

94.33 Behavior therapy
Aversion therapy
Behavior modification
Desensitization therapy
Extinction therapy
Relaxation training
Token economy

94.34 Individual therapy for psychosexual dysfunction
EXCLUDES *that performed in group setting (94.41)*

94.35 Crisis intervention

94.36 Play psychotherapy

94.37 Exploratory verbal psychotherapy

94.38 Supportive verbal psychotherapy

94.39 Other individual psychotherapy
Biofeedback

✓4th **94.4 Other psychotherapy and counselling**

94.41 Group therapy for psychosexual dysfunction

94.42 Family therapy

94.43 Psychodrama

94.44 Other group therapy

94.45 Drug addiction counselling

94.46 Alcoholism counselling

94.49 Other counselling

✓3rd ✓4th Additional Digit Required | Nonspecific OR Procedure | Valid OR Procedure | Non-OR Procedure | Adjunct Code

✓4th **94.5 Referral for psychologic rehabilitation**

94.51 Referral for psychotherapy

94.52 Referral for psychiatric aftercare

That in:
halfway house
outpatient (clinic) facility

94.53 Referral for alcoholism rehabilitation

94.54 Referral for drug addiction rehabilitation

94.55 Referral for vocational rehabilitation

94.59 Referral for other psychologic rehabilitation

✓4th **94.6 Alcohol and drug rehabilitation and detoxification**

AHA: 2Q, '91, 12

94.61 Alcohol rehabilitation

DEF: Program designed to restore social and physical functioning, free of the dependence of alcohol.

94.62 Alcohol detoxification

DEF: Treatment of physical symptoms during withdrawal from alcohol dependence.

94.63 Alcohol rehabilitation and detoxification

94.64 Drug rehabilitation

DEF: Program designed to restore social and physical functioning, free of the dependence of drugs.

94.65 Drug detoxification

DEF: Treatment of physical symptoms during withdrawal from drug dependence.

94.66 Drug rehabilitation and detoxification

94.67 Combined alcohol and drug rehabilitation

94.68 Combined alcohol and drug detoxification

94.69 Combined alcohol and drug rehabilitation and detoxification

✓3rd **95 Ophthalmologic and otologic diagnosis and treatment**

✓4th **95.0 General and subjective eye examination**

95.01 Limited eye examination

Eye examination with prescription of spectacles

95.02 Comprehensive eye examination

Eye examination covering all aspects of the visual system

95.03 Extended ophthalmologic work-up

Examination (for):
glaucoma
neuro-ophthalmology
retinal disease

95.04 Eye examination under anesthesia

Code also type of examination

95.05 Visual field study

95.06 Color vision study

95.07 Dark adaptation study

DEF: Exam of eye's adaption to dark.

95.09 Eye examination, not otherwise specified

Vision check NOS

✓4th **95.1 Examinations of form and structure of eye**

95.11 Fundus photography

95.12 Fluorescein angiography or angioscopy of eye

95.13 Ultrasound study of eye

95.14 X-ray study of eye

95.15 Ocular motility study

95.16 P_{32} and other tracer studies of eye

✓4th **95.2 Objective functional tests of eye**

EXCLUDES *that with polysomnogram (89.17)*

95.21 Electroretinogram [ERG]

95.22 Electro-oculogram [EOG]

95.23 Visual evoked potential [VEP]

DEF: Measuring and recording evoked visual responses of body and senses.

95.24 Electronystagmogram [ENG]

DEF: Monitoring of brain waves to record induced and spontaneous eye movements.

95.25 Electromyogram of eye [EMG]

95.26 Tonography, provocative tests, and other glaucoma testing

✓4th **95.3 Special vision services**

95.31 Fitting and dispensing of spectacles

95.32 Prescription, fitting, and dispensing of contact lens

95.33 Dispensing of other low vision aids

95.34 Ocular prosthetics

95.35 Orthoptic training

95.36 Ophthalmologic counselling and instruction

Counselling in:
adaptation to visual loss
use of low vision aids

✓4th **95.4 Nonoperative procedures related to hearing**

95.41 Audiometry

Békésy 5-tone audiometry
Impedance audiometry
Stapedial reflex response
Subjective audiometry
Tympanogram

95.42 Clinical test of hearing

Tuning fork test
Whispered speech test

95.43 Audiological evaluation

Audiological evaluation by:
Bárány noise machine
blindfold test
delayed feedback
masking
Weber lateralization

95.44 Clinical vestibular function tests

Thermal test of vestibular function

95.45 Rotation tests

Bárány chair

DEF: Irrigation of ear canal with warm or cold water to evaluate vestibular function.

95.46 Other auditory and vestibular function tests

95.47 Hearing examination, not otherwise specified

95.48 Fitting of hearing aid

EXCLUDES *implantation of electromagnetic hearing device (20.95)*

AHA: 4Q, '89, 5

95.49 Other nonoperative procedures related to hearing

Adjustment (external components) of cochlear prosthetic device

✓3rd **96 Nonoperative intubation and irrigation**

✓4th **96.0 Nonoperative intubation of gastrointestinal and respiratory tracts**

96.01 Insertion of nasopharyngeal airway

96.02 Insertion of oropharyngeal airway

96.03 Insertion of esophageal obturator airway

Endotracheal Intubation

Laryngoscope
Larynx
Trachea
Balloon inflated above carina

96.04 Insertion of endotracheal tube
AHA: 4Q, '05, 88; 3Q, '05, 10; 2Q, '05, 19

96.05 Other intubation of respiratory tract
EXCLUDES ▶ *endoscopic insertion or replacement of bronchial device or substance (33.71, 33.79)*◀
AHA: 1Q, '97, 14

96.06 Insertion of Sengstaken tube
Esophageal tamponade
DEF: Insertion of Sengstaken tube: Nonsurgical emergency measure to stop esophageal bleeding using compression exerted by inflated balloons; additional tube ports to aspirate blood and clots.

96.07 Insertion of other (naso-) gastric tube
Intubation for decompression
EXCLUDES *that for enteral infusion of nutritional substance (96.6)*

96.08 Insertion of (naso-) intestinal tube
Miller-Abbott tube (for decompression)

96.09 Insertion of rectal tube
Replacement of rectal tube

✓4th **96.1 Other nonoperative insertion**
EXCLUDES *nasolacrimal intubation (09.44)*

96.11 Packing of external auditory canal
96.14 Vaginal packing ♀
96.15 Insertion of vaginal mold ♀
96.16 Other vaginal dilation ♀
96.17 Insertion of vaginal diaphragm ♀
96.18 Insertion of other vaginal pessary ♀
96.19 Rectal packing

✓4th **96.2 Nonoperative dilation and manipulation**

96.21 Dilation of frontonasal duct
96.22 Dilation of rectum
96.23 Dilation of anal sphincter
96.24 Dilation and manipulation of enterostomy stoma
96.25 Therapeutic distention of bladder
Intermittent distention of bladder
96.26 Manual reduction of rectal prolapse
96.27 Manual reduction of hernia
96.28 Manual reduction of enterostomy prolapse
AHA: N-D, '87, 11
96.29 Reduction of intussusception of alimentary tract
With:
fluoroscopy
ionizing radiation enema
ultrasonography guidance
Hydrostatic reduction
Pneumatic reduction
EXCLUDES *intra-abdominal manipulation of intestine, not otherwise specified (46.80)*
AHA: 4Q, '98, 82

✓4th **96.3 Nonoperative alimentary tract irrigation, cleaning, and local instillation**

96.31 Gastric cooling
Gastric hypothermia
DEF: Reduction of internal stomach temperature.
96.32 Gastric freezing
96.33 Gastric lavage
96.34 Other irrigation of (naso-)gastric tube
96.35 Gastric gavage
DEF: Food forced into stomach.
96.36 Irrigation of gastrostomy or enterostomy
96.37 Proctoclysis
DEF: Slow introduction of large amounts of fluids into lower large intestine.7
96.38 Removal of impacted feces
Removal of impaction:
by flushing manually
96.39 Other transanal enema
Rectal irrigation
EXCLUDES *reduction of intussusception of alimentary tract by ionizing radiation enema (96.29)*

✓4th **96.4 Nonoperative irrigation, cleaning, and local instillation of other digestive and genitourinary organs**

96.41 Irrigation of cholecystostomy and other biliary tube
96.42 Irrigation of pancreatic tube
96.43 Digestive tract instillation, except gastric gavage
96.44 Vaginal douche ♀
96.45 Irrigation of nephrostomy and pyelostomy
96.46 Irrigation of ureterostomy and ureteral catheter
96.47 Irrigation of cystostomy
96.48 Irrigation of other indwelling urinary catheter
96.49 Other genitourinary instillation
Insertion of prostaglandin suppository
AHA: 1Q, '01, 5

✓4th **96.5 Other nonoperative irrigation and cleaning**

96.51 Irrigation of eye
Irrigation of cornea
EXCLUDES *irrigation with removal of foreign body (98.21)*
96.52 Irrigation of ear
Irrigation with removal of cerumen
96.53 Irrigation of nasal passages
96.54 Dental scaling, polishing, and debridement
Dental prophylaxis Plaque removal
96.55 Tracheostomy toilette
96.56 Other lavage of bronchus and trachea
EXCLUDES *diagnostic bronchoalveolar lavage (BAL) (33.24)*
whole lung lavage (33.99)
AHA: 3Q, '02, 18
96.57 Irrigation of vascular catheter
AHA: 3Q, '93, 5
96.58 Irrigation of wound catheter
96.59 Other irrigation of wound
Wound cleaning NOS
EXCLUDES *debridement (86.22, 86.27-86.28)*
AHA: S-O, '85, 7

96.6 Enteral infusion of concentrated-nutritional substances

✓4th **96.7 Other continuous mechanical ventilation**

INCLUDES Endotracheal respiratory assistance
Intermittent mandatory ventilation [IMV]
Positive end expiratory pressure [PEEP]
Pressure support ventilation [PSV]
That by tracheostomy
Weaning of an intubated (endotracheal tube) patient

EXCLUDES *bi-level airway pressure (93.90)*
continuous negative pressure ventilation [CNP] (iron lung) (cuirass) (93.99)
continuous positive airway pressure [CPAP] (93.90)
intermittent positive pressure breathing [IPPB] (93.91)
non-invasive positive pressure (NIPPV) (93.90)
that by face mask (93.90-93.99)
that by nasal cannula (93.90-93.99)
that by nasal catheter (93.90-93.99)

Code also any associated:
endotracheal tube insertion (96.04)
tracheostomy (31.1-31.29)

Note: Endotracheal intubation

To calculate the number of hours (duration) of continuous mechanical ventilation during a hospitalization, begin the count from the start of the (endotracheal) intubation. The duration ends with (endotracheal) extubation.

If a patient is intubated prior to admission, begin counting the duration from the time of the admission. If a patient is transferred (discharged) while intubated, the duration would end at the time of transfer (discharge).

For patients who begin on (endotracheal) intubation and subsequently have a tracheostomy performed for mechanical ventilation, the duration begins with the (endotracheal) intubation and ends when the mechanical ventilation is turned off (after the weaning period).

Tracheostomy

To calculate the number of hours of continuous mechanical ventilation during a hospitalization, begin counting the duration when mechanical ventilation is started. The duration ends when the mechanical ventilator is turned off (after the weaning period).

If a patient has received a tracheostomy prior to admission and is on mechanical ventilation at the time of admission, begin counting the duration from the time of admission. If a patient is transferred (discharged) while still on mechanical ventilation via tracheostomy, the duration would end at the time of the transfer (discharge).

AHA: 3Q, '04, 3; 2Q, '92, 13; 4Q, '91, 16; 4Q, '91, 18; 4Q, '91, 21

96.70 Continuous mechanical ventilation of unspecified duration
Mechanical ventilation NOS

96.71 Continuous mechanical ventilation for less than 96 consecutive hours
AHA: ▶3Q, '05, 10;◀ 3Q, '04, 11; 2Q, '02, 19; 1Q, '02, 12; 1Q, '01, 6

96.72 Continuous mechanical ventilation for 96 consecutive hours or more
AHA: ▶2Q, '05, 19;◀ 1Q, '04, 23

✓3rd **97 Replacement and removal of therapeutic appliances**

✓4th **97.0 Nonoperative replacement of gastrointestinal appliance**

97.01 Replacement of (naso-)gastric or esophagostomy tube

97.02 Replacement of gastrostomy tube
AHA: 1Q, '97, 11

97.03 Replacement of tube or enterostomy device of small intestine
AHA: 1Q, '03, 10

97.04 Replacement of tube or enterostomy device of large intestine

97.05 Replacement of stent (tube) in biliary or pancreatic duct
AHA: 2Q, '99, 13

✓4th **97.1 Nonoperative replacement of musculoskeletal and integumentary system appliance**

97.11 Replacement of cast on upper limb

97.12 Replacement of cast on lower limb

97.13 Replacement of other cast

97.14 Replacement of other device for musculoskeletal immobilization

97.15 Replacement of wound catheter

97.16 Replacement of wound packing or drain
EXCLUDES *repacking of:*
dental wound (97.22)
vulvar wound (97.26)

✓4th **97.2 Other nonoperative replacement**

97.21 Replacement of nasal packing

97.22 Replacement of dental packing

97.23 Replacement of tracheostomy tube
AHA: N-D, '87, 11

97.24 Replacement and refitting of vagina diaphragm ♀

97.25 Replacement of other vaginal pessary ♀

97.26 Replacement of vaginal or vulvar packing or drain ♀

97.29 Other nonoperative replacements
AHA: 3Q, '99, 9; 3Q, '98, 12

✓4th **97.3 Nonoperative removal of therapeutic device from head and neck**

97.31 Removal of eye prosthesis
EXCLUDES *removal of ocular implant (16.71)*
removal of orbital implant (16.72)

97.32 Removal of nasal packing

97.33 Removal of dental wiring

97.34 Removal of dental packing

97.35 Removal of dental prosthesis

97.36 Removal of other external mandibular fixation device

97.37 Removal of tracheostomy tube

97.38 Removal of sutures from head and neck

97.39 Removal of other therapeutic device from head and neck
EXCLUDES *removal of skull tongs (02.94)*

✓4th **97.4 Nonoperative removal of therapeutic device from thorax**

97.41 Removal of thoracotomy tube or pleural cavity drain
AHA: 1Q, '99, 10

97.42 Removal of mediastinal drain

Intraaortic Balloon Pump

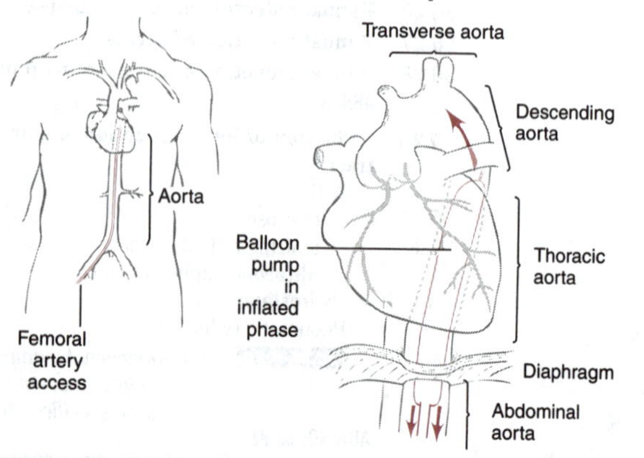

97.43 Removal of sutures from thorax

97.44 Nonoperative removal of heart assist system
Explantation [removal] of circulatory assist device
Explantation [removal] of percutaneous external heart assist device
Removal of extrinsic heart assist device
Removal of pVAD
Removal of percutaneous heart assist device
AHA: 4Q, '01, 65

DEF: Non-invasive removal of ventricular assist systems, or intraaortic balloon pump, which is a balloon catheter placed into the descending thoracic aorta and timed to inflate and deflate with the patient's own heart rhythm to aid in blood circulation.

97.49 Removal of other device from thorax
AHA: N-D, '86, 9

✓4th **97.5 Nonoperative removal of therapeutic device from digestive system**

97.51 Removal of gastrostomy tube

97.52 Removal of tube from small intestine

97.53 Removal of tube from large intestine or appendix

97.54 Removal of cholecystostomy tube

97.55 Removal of T-tube, other bile duct tube, or liver tube
Removal of bile duct stent
AHA: 1Q, '01, 8

97.56 Removal of pancreatic tube or drain

97.59 Removal of other device from digestive system
Removal of rectal packing

✓4th **97.6 Nonoperative removal of therapeutic device from urinary system**

97.61 Removal of pyelostomy and nephrostomy tube
DEF: Nonsurgical removal of tubes from lower part of kidney.

97.62 Removal of ureterostomy tube and ureteral catheter

97.63 Removal of cystostomy tube

97.64 Removal of other urinary drainage device
Removal of indwelling urinary catheter

97.65 Removal of urethral stent

97.69 Removal of other device from urinary system

✓4th **97.7 Nonoperative removal of therapeutic device from genital system**

97.71 Removal of intrauterine contraceptive device ♀

97.72 Removal of intrauterine pack ♀

97.73 Removal of vaginal diaphragm ♀

97.74 Removal of other vaginal pessary ♀

97.75 Removal of vaginal or vulvar packing ♀

97.79 Removal of other device from genital tract
Removal of sutures

✓4th **97.8 Other nonoperative removal of therapeutic device**

97.81 Removal of retroperitoneal drainage device

97.82 Removal of peritoneal drainage device
AHA: 2Q, '90, 28; S-O, '86, 12

97.83 Removal of abdominal wall sutures

97.84 Removal of sutures from trunk, not elsewhere classified

97.85 Removal of packing from trunk, not elsewhere classified

97.86 Removal of other device from abdomen

97.87 Removal of other device from trunk

97.88 Removal of external immobilization device
Removal of:
brace
cast
Removal of:
splint

97.89 Removal of other therapeutic device

✓3rd **98 Nonoperative removal of foreign body or calculus**

✓4th **98.0 Removal of intraluminal foreign body from digestive system without incision**
EXCLUDES *removal of therapeutic device (97.51-97.59)*

DEF: Retrieval of foreign body from digestive system lining without incision.

98.01 Removal of intraluminal foreign body from mouth without incision

98.02 Removal of intraluminal foreign body from esophagus without incision

98.03 Removal of intraluminal foreign body from stomach and small intestine without incision

98.04 Removal of intraluminal foreign body from large intestine without incision

98.05 Removal of intraluminal foreign body from rectum and anus without incision

✓4th **98.1 Removal of intraluminal foreign body from other sites without incision**
EXCLUDES *removal of therapeutic device (97.31-97.49, 97.61-97.89)*

98.11 Removal of intraluminal foreign body from ear without incision

98.12 Removal of intraluminal foreign body from nose without incision

98.13 Removal of intraluminal foreign body from pharynx without incision

98.14 Removal of intraluminal foreign body from larynx without incision

98.15 Removal of intraluminal foreign body from trachea and bronchus without incision

98.16 Removal of intraluminal foreign body from uterus without incision ♀
EXCLUDES *removal of intrauterine contraceptive device (97.71)*

98.17 Removal of intraluminal foreign body from vagina without incision ♀

98.18 Removal of intraluminal foreign body from artificial stoma without incision

98.19 Removal of intraluminal foreign body from urethra without incision

✓4th **98.2 Removal of other foreign body without incision**
EXCLUDES *removal of intraluminal foreign body (98.01-98.19)*

98.20 Removal of foreign body, not otherwise specified

98.21 Removal of superficial foreign body from eye without incision

98.22 Removal of other foreign body without incision from head and neck
Removal of embedded foreign body from eyelid or conjunctiva without incision

98.23 Removal of foreign body from vulva without incision ♀

98.24 Removal of foreign body from scrotum or penis without incision ♂

Extracorporeal Shock Wave Lithotripsy

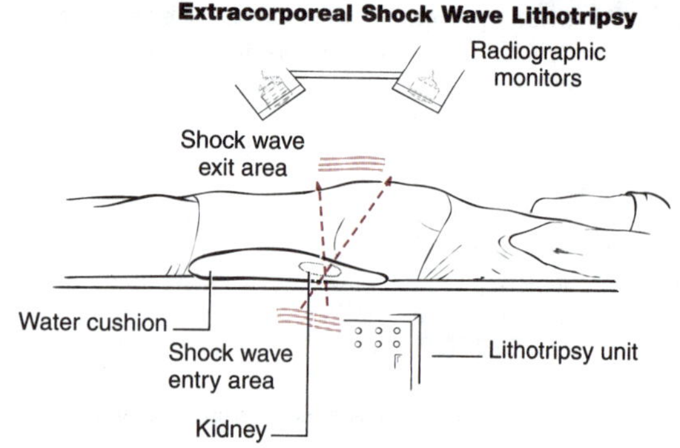

98.25 Removal of other foreign body without incision from trunk except scrotum, penis, or vulva

98.26 Removal of foreign body from hand without incision

AHA: N-D, '87, 10

98.27 Removal of foreign body without incision from upper limb, except hand

98.28 Removal of foreign body from foot without incision

98.29 Removal of foreign body without incision from lower limb, except foot

✓4th **98.5 Extracorporeal shockwave lithotripsy [ESWL]**

Lithotriptor tank procedure
Disintegration of stones by extracorporeal induced shockwaves
That with insertion of stent

DEF: Breaking of stones with high voltage condenser device synchronized with patient R waves.

98.51 Extracorporeal shockwave lithotripsy [ESWL] of the kidney, ureter and/or bladder

AHA: 4Q, '95, 73; 1Q, '89, 2

98.52 Extracorporeal shockwave lithotripsy [ESWL] of the gallbladder and/or bile duct NC

98.59 Extracorporeal shockwave lithotripsy of other sites NC

✓3rd **99 Other nonoperative procedures**

✓4th **99.0 Transfusion of blood and blood components**

Use additional code for that done via catheter or cutdown (38.92-38.94)

99.00 Perioperative autologous transfusion of whole blood or blood components

Intraoperative blood collection
Postoperative blood collection
Salvage

AHA: 4Q, '95, 69

DEF: Salvaging patient blood with reinfusion during perioperative period.

99.01 Exchange transfusion

Transfusion:
exsanguination

Transfusion:
replacement

AHA: 2Q, '89, 15

DEF: Repetitive withdrawal of blood, replaced by donor blood.

99.02 Transfusion of previously collected autologous blood

Blood component

AHA: 4Q, '95, 69; 1Q, '90, 10; J-A, '85, 16

DEF: Transfusion with patient's own previously withdrawn and stored blood.

99.03 Other transfusion of whole blood

Transfusion:
blood NOS
hemodilution

Transfusion:
NOS

99.04 Transfusion of packed cells

99.05 Transfusion of platelets

Transfusion of thrombocytes

99.06 Transfusion of coagulation factors

Transfusion of antihemophilic factor

99.07 Transfusion of other serum

Transfusion of plasma

EXCLUDES *injection [transfusion] of:*
antivenin (99.16)
gamma globulin (99.14)

99.08 Transfusion of blood expander

Transfusion of Dextran

99.09 Transfusion of other substance

Transfusion of:
blood surrogate
granulocytes

EXCLUDES *transplantation [transfusion] of bone marrow (41.0)*

✓4th **99.1 Injection or infusion of therapeutic or prophylactic substance**

INCLUDES injection or infusion given:
hypodermically
intramuscularly
intravenously
} acting locally or systemically

99.10 Injection or infusion of thrombolytic agent

▶Alteplase
Anistreplase
Reteplase◀
Streptokinase
▶Tenecteplase◀
Tissue plasminogen activator (TPA)
Urokinase

EXCLUDES *aspirin — omit code*
GP IIb/IIIa platelet inhibitors (99.20)
heparin (99.19)
warfarin — omit code

AHA: 4Q, '05, 101-103; 2Q, '01, 7-9, 23; 4Q, '98, 83

99.11 Injection of Rh immune globulin

Injection of:
Anti-D (Rhesus) globulin
RhoGAM

99.12 Immunization for allergy

Desensitization

99.13 Immunization for autoimmune disease

99.14 Injection of gamma globulin

Injection of immune sera

99.15 Parenteral infusion of concentrated nutritional substances

Hyperalimentation
Total parenteral nutrition [TPN]
Peripheral parenteral nutrition [PPN]

AHA: 4Q, '03, 104

DEF: Administration of greater than necessary amount of nutrients via other than the alimentary canal (e.g., infusion).

99.16 Injection of antidote

Injection of:
antivenin

Injection of:
heavy metal antagonist

99.17 Injection of insulin

99.18 Injection or infusion of electrolytes

99.19 Injection of anticoagulant

EXCLUDES *infusion of drotrecogin alfa (activated) (00.11)*

✓4th **99.2 Injection or infusion of other therapeutic or prophylactic substance**

INCLUDES injection or infusion given:
hypodermically, intramuscularly, intravenously } acting locally or systemically

Use additional code for:
injection (into):
breast (85.92)
bursa (82.94, 83.96)
intraperitoneal (cavity) (54.97)
intrathecal (03.92)
joint (76.96, 81.92)
injection (into):
kidney (55.96)
liver (50.94)
orbit (16.91)
other sites — see Alphabetic Index
perfusion:
NOS (39.97)
intestine (46.95, 46.96)
kidney (55.95)
perfusion:
liver (50.93)
total body (39.96)

99.20 Injection or infusion of platelet inhibitor
Glycoprotein IIb/IIIa inhibitor
GP IIb-IIIa inhibitor
GP IIb/IIIa inhibitor
EXCLUDES *infusion of heparin (99.19)*
injection or infusion of thrombolytic agent (99.10)
AHA: 2Q, '04, 3; 4Q, '02, 114; 4Q, '98, 85

99.21 Injection of antibiotic
EXCLUDES *injection or infusion of oxazolidinone class of antibiotics (00.14)*
AHA: 4Q, '98, 76; 2Q, '90, 24; M-A, '87, 9

99.22 Injection of other anti-infective
EXCLUDES *injection or infusion of oxazolidinone class of antibiotics (00.14)*

99.23 Injection of steroid
Injection of cortisone
Subdermal implantation of progesterone
AHA: 3Q, '00, 15; 1Q, '99, 8; 3Q, '96, 7; 3Q, '92, 9; S-O, '85, 7

99.24 Injection of other hormone
AHA: ▶1Q, '06, 9◀

99.25 Injection or infusion of cancer chemotherapeutic substance
Chemoembolization
Injection or infusion of antineoplastic agent
EXCLUDES *immunotherapy, antineoplastic (00.15, 99.28)*
implantation of chemotherapeutic agent (00.10)
injection of radioisotope (92.28)
injection or infusion of biological response modifier [BRM] as an antineoplastic agent (99.28)
AHA: 2Q, '03, 6, 16; 4Q, '02, 93; 1Q, '99, 4; 1Q, '98, 6; 3Q, '96, 11; 4Q, '95, 67; 2Q, '92, 7; 1Q, '92, 12; 1Q, '88, 8; N-D, '86, 11

99.26 Injection of tranquilizer

99.27 Iontophoresis
DEF: Iontophoresis: Introduction of soluble salts into tissues via electric current.

99.28 Injection or infusion of biological response modifier [BRM] as an antineoplastic agent
Immunotherapy, antineoplastic
▶Infusion of cintredekin besudotox◀
Interleukin therapy
Low-dose interleukin-2 [IL-2] therapy
Tumor vaccine
EXCLUDES *high-dose infusion interleukin-2 [IL-2] (00.15)*
AHA: 4Q, '03, 92; 2Q, '99, 8; 2Q, '98, 10; 4Q, '94, 51

99.29 Injection or infusion of other therapeutic or prophylactic substance
EXCLUDES *administration of neuroprotective agent (99.75)*
immunization (99.31-99.59)
injection of sclerosing agent into:
esophageal varices (42.33)
hemorrhoids (49.42)
veins (39.92)
injection or infusion of:
human B-type natriuretic peptide (hBNP) (00.13)
nesiritide (00.13)
platelet inhibitor (99.20)
thrombolytic agent (99.10)
AHA: 2Q, '03, 10; 3Q, '02, 19, 24; 1Q, '01, 15; 2Q, '00, 14; 1Q, '00, 8, 18, 23; 4Q, '99, 17; 3Q, '99, 21; 4Q, '98, 83; 2Q, '98, 17, 18, 23, 24; 1Q, '98, 6; 2Q, '97, 11; 1Q, '97, 3; 4Q, '95, 67; 2Q, '95, 12; 4Q, '90, 14; 2Q, '90, 23; 2Q, '89, 17; 1Q, '88, 9; N-D, '87, 4; S-O, '87, 11

✓4th **99.3 Prophylactic vaccination and inoculation against certain bacterial diseases**
DEF: Administration of a killed bacteria suspension to produce immunity.

99.31 Vaccination against cholera

99.32 Vaccination against typhoid and paratyphoid fever
Administration of TAB vaccine

99.33 Vaccination against tuberculosis
Administration of BCG vaccine

99.34 Vaccination against plague

99.35 Vaccination against tularemia

99.36 Administration of diphtheria toxoid
EXCLUDES *administration of:*
diphtheria antitoxin (99.58)
diphtheria-tetanus-pertussis, combined (99.39)

99.37 Vaccination against pertussis
EXCLUDES *administration of diphtheria-tetanus-pertussis, combined (99.39)*

99.38 Administration of tetanus toxoid
EXCLUDES *administration of:*
diphtheria-tetanus-pertussis, combined (99.39)
tetanus antitoxin (99.56)

99.39 Administration of diphtheria-tetanus-pertussis, combined

✓4th **99.4 Prophylactic vaccination and inoculation against certain viral diseases**

DEF: Administration of a killed virus suspension to produce immunity.

99.41 Administration of poliomyelitis vaccine

99.42 Vaccination against smallpox

99.43 Vaccination against yellow fever

99.44 Vaccination against rabies

99.45 Vaccination against measles

EXCLUDES *administration of measles-mumps-rubella vaccine (99.48)*

99.46 Vaccination against mumps

EXCLUDES *administration of measles-mumps-rubella vaccine (99.48)*

99.47 Vaccination against rubella

EXCLUDES *administration of measles-mumps-rubella vaccine (99.48)*

99.48 Administration of measles-mumps-rubella vaccine

✓4th **99.5 Other vaccination and inoculation**

99.51 Prophylactic vaccination against the common cold

99.52 Prophylactic vaccination against influenza

99.53 Prophylactic vaccination against arthropod-borne viral encephalitis

99.54 Prophylactic vaccination against other arthropod-borne viral diseases

99.55 Prophylactic administration of vaccine against other diseases

Vaccination against:
- anthrax
- brucellosis
- Rocky Mountain spotted fever

Vaccination against:
- Staphylococcus
- Streptococcus
- typhus

AHA: 2Q, '00, 9; 1Q, '94, 10

99.56 Administration of tetanus antitoxin

99.57 Administration of botulism antitoxin

99.58 Administration of other antitoxins

Administration of:
- diphtheria antitoxin
- gas gangrene antitoxin
- scarlet fever antitoxin

99.59 Other vaccination and inoculation

Vaccination NOS

EXCLUDES *injection of:*
- *gamma globulin (99.14)*
- *Rh immune globulin (99.11)*

immunization for:
- *allergy (99.12)*
- *autoimmune disease (99.13)*

✓4th **99.6 Conversion of cardiac rhythm**

EXCLUDES *open chest cardiac:*
- *electric stimulation (37.91)*
- *massage (37.91)*

DEF: Correction of cardiac rhythm.

99.60 Cardiopulmonary resuscitation, not otherwise specified

AHA: 1Q, '94, 16

99.61 Atrial cardioversion

DEF: Application of electric shock to upper heart chamber to restore normal heart rhythm.

99.62 Other electric countershock of heart

Cardioversion:
- NOS
- external

Conversion to sinus rhythm

Defibrillation

External electrode stimulation

99.63 Closed chest cardiac massage

Cardiac massage NOS

Manual external cardiac massage

DEF: Application of alternating manual pressure over breastbone to restore normal heart rhythm.

99.64 Carotid sinus stimulation

99.69 Other conversion of cardiac rhythm

AHA: 4Q, '88, 11

✓4th **99.7 Therapeutic apheresis or other injection, administration, or infusion of other therapeutic or prophylactic substance**

99.71 Therapeutic plasmapheresis

EXCLUDES *extracorporeal immunoadsorption [ECI] (99.76)*

99.72 Therapeutic leukopheresis

Therapeutic leukocytapheresis

99.73 Therapeutic erythrocytapheresis

Therapeutic erythropheresis

AHA: 1Q, '94, 20

99.74 Therapeutic plateletpheresis

99.75 Administration of neuroprotective agent

AHA: 4Q, '00, 68

DEF: Direct application of neuroprotective agent (e.g., nimodipine) to miinimize ischemic injury by inhibiting toxic neurotransmitters, blocking free ions, removing free radicals, and causing vasodilation.

99.76 Extracorporeal immunoadsorption

Removal of antibodies from plasma with protein A columns

AHA: 4Q, '02, 112

99.77 Application or administration of adhesion barrier substance

AHA: 4Q, '02, 113

99.78 Aquapheresis

Plasma water removal

Ultrafiltration [for water removal]

EXCLUDES *hemodiafiltration (39.95)*
hemodialysis (39.95)
therapeutic plasmapheresis (99.71)

99.79 Other

Apheresis (harvest) of stem cells

AHA: ▶1Q, '06, 12, 13;◀ 1Q, '05, 16; 4Q, '97, 55

✓4th **99.8 Miscellaneous physical procedures**

99.81 Hypothermia (central) (local)

EXCLUDES *gastric cooling (96.31)*
gastric freezing (96.32)
that incidental to open heart surgery (39.62)

99.82 Ultraviolet light therapy

Actinotherapy

99.83 Other phototherapy

Phototherapy of the newborn

EXCLUDES *extracorporeal photochemotherapy (99.88)*
photocoagulation of retinal lesion (14.23-14.25, 14.33-14.35, 14.53-14.55)

AHA: 2Q, '89, 15

DEF: Treating disease with light rays of various concentrations.

99.84 Isolation
Isolation after contact with infectious disease
Protection of individual from his surroundings
Protection of surroundings from individual

99.85 Hyperthermia for treatment of cancer
Hyperthermia (adjunct therapy) induced by microwave, ultrasound, low energy radio frequency, probes (interstitial), or other means in the treatment of cancer
Code also any concurrent chemotherapy or radiation therapy
AHA: 3Q, '96, 11; 3Q, '89, 17

99.86 Non-invasive placement of bone growth stimulator
Transcutaneous (surface) placement of pads or patches for stimulation to aid bone healing
EXCLUDES *insertion of invasive or semi-invasive bone growth stimulators (device) (percutaneous electrodes) (78.90-78.99)*

99.88 Therapeutic photopheresis
Extracorporeal photochemotherapy
Extracorporeal photopheresis
EXCLUDES *other phototherapy (99.83)*
ultraviolet light therapy (99.82)
AHA: 2Q, '99, 7
DEF: Extracorporeal photochemotherapy: Treating disease with drugs that react to ultraviolet radiation or sunlight.

✓4th **99.9 Other miscellaneous procedures**

99.91 Acupuncture for anesthesia

99.92 Other acupuncture
EXCLUDES *that with smouldering moxa (93.35)*

99.93 Rectal massage (for levator spasm)

99.94 Prostatic massage ♂

99.95 Stretching of foreskin ♂

99.96 Collection of sperm for artificial insemination ♂

99.97 Fitting of denture

99.98 Extraction of milk from lactating breast ♀

99.99 Other
Leech therapy

Diagnostic and Therapeutic Procedures 99.84–99.99

✓3rd ✓4th Additional Digit Required | Nonspecific OR Procedure | Valid OR Procedure | Non-OR Procedure | Adjunct Code